The Rough Guide to

Britain

written and researched by

**Robert Andrews, Jules Brown, Rob Humphreys, Phil Lee,
Donald Reid and Paul Whitfield**

ROUGH GUIDES

NEW YORK · LONDON · DELHI

www.roughguides.com

Contents

Festivals and events
insert following p.312

Coastal Britain insert
following p.600

Literary Britain insert
following p.936

A

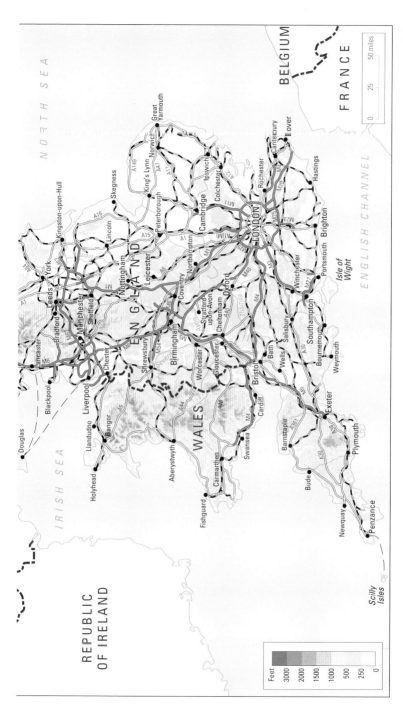

Introduction to
Britain

If you were planning a country from scratch, you would never try to force England, Scotland and Wales together into a single United Kingdom. Britain is not one country but three, with three capitals (London, Cardiff and Edinburgh), three national identities and myriad accent shifts as you travel around. The three countries have had centuries to get used to each other, but it often feels there's little love lost: Wales has long been resentful of English dominance; Scotland is happiest as far away from both as possible; northern England is contemptuous of the south; and Londoners are convinced they're in a league of their own.

All this regional diversity means there's enough in Britain for months of travels if you have the time: start in dynamic, cosmopolitan London and head up to the remotest Scottish fishing villages; leave England's postindustrial heartland and explore the former mining regions of the Welsh valleys; or even walk or cycle from Land's End to John O'Groats, the longest journey in the country, as charity-fundraisers often do. Travelling around Britain is not without its idiosyncrasies. Public transport, especially the railways, is in disarray, and commuters and long-distance travellers are in an almost permanent state of delay and revolt. Drivers will find the motorways and ring roads aren't much better, and are often gridlocked around major cities. And those who have just arrived clutching euros from a tour of "The Continent" will be swiftly disabused of the notion that Britain is an integral part of Europe.

Britain has dithered for decades about its role in the world: having ruled the roost for several hundred years, Brits are still uncertain about their place in the new world order. Paradoxically, it's the Welsh and the Scots, for so long under the English thumb, who have emerged with their national identities intact and tangible political power embodied in their own parliamentary assemblies. The English, still without a regional voice, are left unsure of how to modernize their institutions, ever-fearful of conflict erupting between town and country, north and south, rich and poor, blacks, Asians and whites, and increasingly lagging behind the social and political change that is being wrought as effectively in Edinburgh as in Brussels. England remains the dominant and most urbanized member of the British partnership, but crossing the border into predominantly rural Wales brings you into an unmistakeably Celtic land, while in Scotland (a nation whose absorption into the state was rather more recent) the presence of a profoundly non-English world-view is striking.

Fact file

• **Britain** (or Great Britain) is a geographical term referring to the largest of the British Isles. "United Kingdom" is a political term, referring to the state comprising England, Scotland, Wales and Northern Ireland.

• The **population** of Britain – which, at 93,000 square miles, is slightly smaller than the US state of Oregon – is about 58 million: 50 million in England, 5 million in Scotland and 3 million in Wales. The biggest city is London, with some 7.4 million inhabitants. **Ethnic minorities** represent about six percent of the total population, the largest groups being those of Caribbean or African descent (875,000 people), Indians (840,000), and Pakistanis and Bangladeshis (640,000). The official **language** is English, though Welsh also has official status in Wales. Scottish Gaelic is used in parts of Scotland.

• The **lowest point** is in the Fens of eastern England, at 13ft below sea level; the **highest point** is the summit of Ben Nevis at 4406ft. From the south coast of England to the extreme north of Scotland is about 600 miles; the **longest journey**, from Land's End to John O'Groats, is nearer 850 miles.

• The UK, comprising Britain and Northern Ireland, is a **constitutional monarchy**, whose head of state is Queen Elizabeth II. The bicameral parliament is composed of the directly elected **House of Commons** and the unelected **House of Lords**. There is no written constitution, and real power is concentrated in the hands of the **Prime Minister**, head of the largest party in the House of Commons.

▲ London's Gherkin

Who do the British think they are?

As a glance at the popular papers will confirm, Britain is a nation of overweight, football-mad, beer-swilling, sex- and celebrity-obsessed TV addicts. Yet it's also a nation of animal-loving, tea-drinking charity donors, thriving on irony and Radio 4. It's a place where accent and vocabulary can stamp a person's identity like a brand, where a tiny aristocracy still owns most of the land, and where multiple homes are the rule for some, and squalid destitution and homelessness the norm for others. But multicultural Britain, despite pockets of racism and xenophobia, is also a genuine haven for refugees, and is home to immigrants from more than a hundred ethnic backgrounds; commitment and passion in the fields of social and environmental responsibility flourish in Britain like nowhere else. Britain has perhaps the most dynamic media in the world and journalists are brazenly provocative – to the point where cynicism has become the entry price for intelligent conversation. Yet millions of Britons will stand in silence to honour the dead of the country's great wars, and the duties of public office are still accorded immense respect – the merest whiff of corrupt practice draws down immediate scandal and legal action.

Ask any Briton to comment on all this and – assuming you're not trying to talk to a stranger in a public place, which in London at least, can be seen as tantamount to physical assault – you will get an entertaining range of views. There is no national identity, no national day and no national dress – and nobody can agree on what it means to be British. Or whether it even matters.

If ever a nation were both hostage to and beneficiary of its history, it's Britain. Across the country, virtually every town bears a mark of former wealth and power, whether it be a Gothic cathedral financed from a monarch's treasury, a parish church funded by the tycoons of medieval trade, or a triumphalist Victorian civic building, raised on the income of the British Empire. Elsewhere, you'll find old dockyards from which the Royal Navy patrolled the oceans, and mills that employed the populations of entire towns. Meanwhile, Britain's museums and galleries – several ranking among the world's finest and most of the major ones with free admission – are full of treasures trawled from its imperial conquests. Heritage is big business in Britain, with everyone from the Queen in Buckingham Palace to the seedy tourist shops in John O'Groats cashing in on whatever

▼ Deckchairs, Brighton Pier

assets are available. At times, the wheels of the heritage industry grind a bit too hard for comfort.

Where Britain seems to feel most at ease with itself is in the urbane world of arts and city life. Although the hearts of many towns – and increasingly their outskirts – consist of identikit retail zones, pockmarked with car parks and full of the same stores, the vibrant music scenes of London, Bristol, Cardiff and a dozen other cities, the fashionable restaurants and bars of Manchester and Glasgow, and the outstanding contemporary architecture of Liverpool and Newcastle all provide a palpable buzz and confidence. Indeed, there's always been an innovative flair to British popular culture, which contrasts sharply with the bucolic image of Britain favoured by many tourist boards. The countryside may yield all manner of delights, from walkers' trails around the hills and lakes, through prehistoric stone circles, to traditional village pubs, but Britain's urban culture is fast becoming as popular a draw as its countryside and history.

Where to go

England

London is the place to start. Nowhere in the country can match the scope and innovation of the metropolis, a colossal, frenetic city, perhaps not as immediately attractive as its European counterparts, but with so much variety that the only obstacle to a great time is the shockingly high cost of everything. It's here that you'll find Britain's

best spread of nightlife, cultural events, museums, galleries, pubs and restaurants. The other large cities, such as **Birmingham**, **Newcastle**, **Leeds**, **Manchester** and **Liverpool**, each have their strengths too. Birmingham has a resurgent arts scene, for example, while people travel for miles to sample Newcastle's nightlife. Manchester these days can match the capital for glamour in cafés and clubs, and also boasts the inimitable draw of the world's best-known football team, while its near-neighbour Liverpool will be European Capital of Culture in 2008.

> **Britain's urban culture is becoming as popular a draw as its countryside and history**

England's ancient cathedral cities, such as **Lincoln**, **York**, **Salisbury**, **Durham** and **Winchester**, cannot be equalled for sheer physical beauty, and wherever you're based, you're never more than a few miles from a ruined castle, a majestic country house, a secluded chapel or a monastery. In the southwest there are remnants of a Celtic culture that was all but eradicated elsewhere by the Romans, and everywhere you can find traces of prehistoric settlers – most famously the megalithic circles of **Stonehenge** and **Avebury**.

Most beguiling of all are the long-established villages of England, hundreds of which amount to nothing more than a pub, a shop, a gaggle of cottages and a farmhouse offering bed and breakfast. **Devon**, **Cornwall**, the **Cotswolds** and the **Yorkshire Dales** harbour some especially picturesque specimens, but every county can boast a decent showing. Then, of course, there's the English countryside, an extraordinarily diverse terrain from which Constable, Turner, Wordsworth, Emily Brontë and a host of other writers and artists took inspiration. **Exmoor**, **Dartmoor**, **Bodmin Moor**, the **North York Moors** and the **Lake District** are the most dramatic and best known of the national parks, each offering an array of landscapes crisscrossed with walking routes.

Wales

Although **Cardiff** boasts most of Wales's national institutions, including the National Museum, the

Standing stones

Why the prehistoric peoples of Britain built circles of standing stones may never be fully known. The theories are as diverse as the sites themselves: perhaps they were places of sacrifice and celebration, or erected for an astronomical function. But two things remain obvious, even at a distance of five thousand years. Firstly, each series of standing stones represents a highly organized effort by ancient peoples once thought of as unsophisticated. And secondly, whatever their function, the circles retain a powerful presence even today, recognized by the disparate bands of druids and New Age travellers who still seek solace in the stones. Mass tourism has dragged famous sites like Stonehenge into the embrace of the heritage industry, but there are other sites which retain their sense of mystery and isolation. At Castlerigg in the Lake District, Calanais in western Scotland (see picture above), or Holy Island in North Wales, you can still wander alone, forming your own theories as the early morning mist rises above the stones.

◄ Sheep near the Abergwesyn Pass, Wales

appeal of a visit lies outside the towns, where there's ample evidence of the warmongering which shaped the country's development. Castles are everywhere, from the little stone keeps of the early Welsh princes and the mighty **Carreg Cennan** to Edward I's doughty fortresses such as Beaumaris, **Conwy** and Harlech. Passage graves and stone circles (such as on **Holy Island**) offer a link to the pre-Roman era when the priestly order of druids ruled over early Celtic peoples, and great medieval monastic houses, like ruined **Tintern Abbey**, are easily accessible.

All these attractions are enhanced by the beauty of the wild Welsh countryside. The backbone of the Cambrian Mountains terminates in the soaring peaks of **Snowdonia National Park** and the angular ridges of the **Brecon Beacons**; both are superb walking country, as is the **Pembrokeshire Coast** in the southwest. Much of the rest of the coast remains unspoilt, though long sweeps of sand are often backed by traditional British seaside resorts, such as **Llandudno** in the north or **Tenby** in the south.

Scotland

The Scottish capital, **Edinburgh**, is a handsome and ancient city, famous for its magnificent **castle** and **Palace of Holyroodhouse** as well as for an acclaimed international arts festival and some excellent museums – not least the outstanding **National Museum of Scotland**. A short journey west

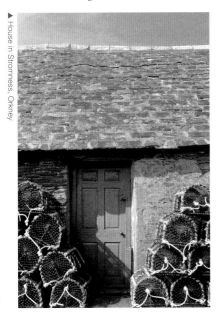

▶ House in Stromness, Orkney

is **Glasgow**, a sprawling industrial metropolis that has done much to improve its image in recent years and can now boast a range of fine museums and galleries and dynamic nightlife to complement the impressive architectural legacy of its eighteenth- and nineteenth-century heyday.

Southern Scotland, often underrated, features some gorgeous scenery, but nothing quite to compare with the shadowy glens and well-walked hills of the **Trossachs**, or with the **Highlands**, whose multitude of mountains, sea cliffs, glens and lochs cover the northern two-thirds of the country. **Inverness** is an obvious base here, although **Fort William**, near **Ben Nevis**, Britain's highest mountain, is an alternative.

Some of Britain's most thrilling wilderness experiences are to be had on the Scottish islands, the most accessible of which extend in a long rocky chain off the Atlantic coast, from **Arran** through **Skye** (the most visited of the Hebrides) to the **Western Isles**, where the remarkably hostile terrain harbours some of the last bastions of the Gaelic language. At Britain's northern extreme lie the sea- and wind-buffeted **Orkney** and

Shetland islands, whose rich Norse heritage makes them distinct in dialect and culture from mainland Scotland, while their wild scenery offers some of Britain's finest birdwatching and some stunning archeological remains.

When to go

onsidering the temperate nature of the British **climate**, it's amazing how much mileage the locals get out of the subject: a two-day cold snap is discussed as if it were the onset of a new Ice Age, and a week in the upper 70s starts rumours of a heatwave. The fact is that summers rarely get hot and the winters don't get very cold, except in the north of Scotland and on the highest points of the Welsh and Scottish uplands. Rainfall is fairly even, though again mountainous areas get higher quantities throughout the year (the west coast of Scotland is especially damp, and Llanberis, at the foot of Snowdon, gets more than twice as much rainfall as Caernarfon, seven miles away).

▶ Otters in Derbyshire

In general, the south is warmer and sunnier than the north, but the bottom line is that it's impossible to say with any degree of certainty what the weather will

13

be like. May might be wet and grey one year and gloriously sunny the next; November stands an equal chance of being crisp and clear or foggy and grim. If you're planning to lie on a beach, or camp in the dry, you'll want to visit between June and September – a period when you shouldn't go anywhere without booking your accommodation in advance. Otherwise, if you're balancing the clemency of the weather against the density of the crowds, the best months to explore are April, May, September and October.

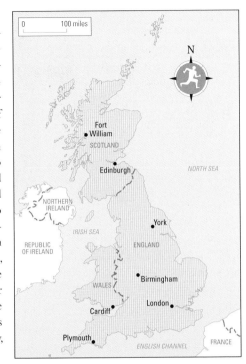

Average daily maximum temperatures

	Jan	Feb	Mar	Apr	May	Jun	Jul	Aug	Sep	Oct	Nov	Dec
Birmingham												
°F	42	43	48	54	61	66	68	68	63	55	48	44
°C	5	6	9	12	16	19	20	20	17	13	9	7
Cardiff												
°F	45	45	50	56	60	68	69	69	64	58	51	46
°C	7	7	10	13	16	20	21	21	18	14	11	8
Edinburgh												
°F	42	43	46	51	56	64	65	64	61	54	48	44
°C	5	6	8	11	13	18	18	18	16	12	9	7
Fort William												
°F	43	44	48	52	58	61	62	63	61	54	49	45
°C	6	7	9	11	14	16	17	17	16	12	9	7
London												
°F	43	44	50	56	62	69	71	71	65	58	50	45
°C	6	7	10	13	17	21	22	22	19	14	10	7
Plymouth												
°F	47	47	50	54	59	64	66	67	64	58	52	49
°C	8	8	10	12	15	18	19	19	18	14	11	9
York												
°F	43	44	49	55	61	67	70	69	64	57	49	45
°C	6	7	10	13	16	19	21	21	18	14	9	7

35

things not to miss

It's not possible to see everything that Britain has to offer in one trip – and we don't suggest you try. What follows is a selective taste of the highlights of England, Wales and Scotland: outstanding buildings, spectacular scenery, great festivals and unforgettable journeys. They're arranged in five colour-coded categories, which you can browse through to find the very best things to see and experience. All entries have a page reference to take you straight into the Guide, where you can find out more.

01 **A night on the town, Newcastle upon Tyne** Page **655** •
Northeastern England's premier arts and nightlife destination has a scintillating quayside of bridges, bars, galleries and concert halls.

02 Surfing, Newquay
Page **376** • The beaches strung along the north coast of Devon and Cornwall offer some great breaks, and Newquay is still the place to see and be seen.

04 London's markets Page **163** • From Borough's foodie treats to Columbia Road's flowers and the arty, boho clothes of Greenwich, London's markets have something for everyone.

03 Oxford Page **266** • One of the world's finest academic cities glories in its dreaming spires, honey-coloured stone and manicured quadrangles.

05 Whale- and dolphin-watching Page **1100** • Take a boat trip in the Cromarty Firth to see these beautiful marine creatures.

06 Stately homes and castles
Page **40** • For tangible proof of Britain's history, the country's many castles and stately homes – like Castle Howard in Yorkshire – can't be bettered.

07 Kinloch Castle, Rùm
Page **1006** • Stay in the servants' quarters of this Edwardian Scottish-island hideaway or in a four-poster bed.

08 Snowdonia Page **775** • One of Britain's finest national parks, a wedge of mountainous Welsh territory focused on the Snowdon massif.

09 Edinburgh Castle Page **821** • Dominating Scotland's capital, this fortress-cum-royal palace is intimately linked to the country's history.

11 Whisky Page **1050** • Sup a dram in northeast Scotland's "whisky triangle", whose Malt Whisky Trail showcases the best distilleries.

12 British Museum Page **103** • In parts controversial and generally not British, the collections of the BM are still the greatest in the world.

10 Coasteering Page **723** • An exhilarating combination of rock-scrambling, cliff-jumping and swimming, at its best on the Pembrokeshire coast of Wales.

13 Iona Page **976** • The home of Celtic Christian spirituality, an island of pilgrimage today as in antiquity.

14 West Highland Railway Page **1060** • Take a trip on one of the great railway journeys of the world.

15 A pint down the pub Page **53** • Drink a pint of beer in the local pub - the centre of British social life for hundreds of years.

16 Glasgow School of Art Page **903** • The finest example of the unique style of Glasgow architect and designer Charles Rennie Mackintosh.

17 Punting on the Cam Page **420** • Pack a picnic and take a trip down the river by punt in the handsome university town of Cambridge.

19 **Bath** Page **309** • Whether you're visiting the Roman baths, England's most elegant Georgian terrace, or the new high-tech spa, Bath has it all.

18 **Portmeirion** Page **788** • Decidedly un-Welsh architecture makes this Italianate village a unique attraction.

21 **Shopping in Leeds** Page **592** • Glorious Victorian arcades packed with designer labels, plus indoor markets and Harvey Nick's – there's no better place to blow your budget.

20 **Whitby music festivals** Page **630** • Yorkshire's most charming resort hosts some terrific annual music festivals, from traditional folk to eclectic world.

22 **Harlech** Page **750** • An evocative castle and twisting narrow streets make this town a highlight of the Cambrian coast.

23 **Cairngorms National Park** Page **1068** • The most extensive mountain range in Britain offers unmatched walking and water-sports opportunities.

24 **Hill-walking** Page **63** • There's no better way to explore Britain than on foot, at your own pace; whether it's hill-walking or a Sunday stroll, there's a route to suit.

25 **National Museum of Wales** Page **697** • Find out everything you ever wanted to know about Wales in Cardiff's National Museum and Gallery.

26 **Hadrian's Wall** Page **658** • Once the frontier against Britain's northern tribes, the Roman wall today is remarkably well preserved – and you can walk its length along the 84-mile Hadrian's Wall Path.

27 **Ullswater** Page **573** • Serene Ullswater is many people's favourite Lake District lake, overlooked by the heights of Helvellyn and by Wordsworth's dancing daffodils.

28 **York Minster** Page **615** • See the world's largest medieval stained-glass window at Britain's biggest and most dramatic Gothic church.

29 Eden Project, Cornwall
Page **363** • Spectacular and refreshingly ungimmicky display of the planet's plant life, mainly housed in vast geodesic "biomes".

30 Melrose Abbey Page **864**
• Melrose and its fine abbey ruins are reason enough for visiting the Scottish Borders region.

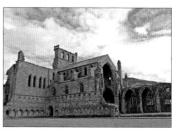

31 Loch Shiel Page **1082** • Among Scotland's myriad lochs, Shiel stands out for its serene beauty and compelling history.

32 Tobermory Page **973** • Scotland's most picturesque fishing port, bar none.

33 Avebury Page **255** • Avebury's stone circle rivals Stonehenge in aspect and grandeur, and its function is as hotly debated.

34 St David's Cathedral Page **722** • Serene cathedral set in a quiet village that has drawn pilgrims to this westernmost tip of Wales for well over a thousand years.

35 Tate St Ives, Cornwall
Page **374** • Southwest England's best art collection occupies a superb site overlooking Porthmeor Beach.

Basics

Basics

Getting there

For most travellers to Britain, the range of options will be greatest – and the fares usually the lowest – flying into London, one of the world's busiest transport hubs. However, if you're planning to tour the north of England or Scotland, you should consider a nonstop flight into one of the country's regional airports instead, such as Manchester, Birmingham or Glasgow. It's also possible to connect in London to many other regional airports around England, Wales or Scotland on a domestic carrier.

London's biggest airports – **Heathrow** and **Gatwick** – take the bulk of transatlantic and long-haul flights into the UK, and are about equal in terms of convenient access to the capital. London's three smaller airports – **Stansted**, **Luton** and **City** – are well served by low-cost flights from mainland Europe, as are other regional airports, including **Manchester** in the Northwest, **Birmingham** in the West Midlands, **Bristol** in the West Country, **Leeds/Bradford** in Yorkshire, **Newcastle** in northeast England, **Nottingham East Midlands**, in the East Midlands, and **Edinburgh**, **Glasgow** and **Aberdeen** in Scotland and **Cardiff** in Wales.

Airfares to Britain are highest from early June to mid-September, at Easter, and at Christmas and New Year; fares drop during the "shoulder" seasons – mid-September to early November and mid-April to early June – and it's usually cheapest during the low season, November through to April. Note that flying at **weekends** is generally more expensive, and that quoted prices are nearly always exclusive of **taxes and fees**, which can add significantly to the cost.

Tickets are available either direct from the airlines or from a **discount travel agent**, which sometimes offers student and youth fares as well as a range of other travel-related services. Many airline and **travel websites** can now also book package holidays, accommodation and car rental. You can turn up some great online deals, but always check the small print as many tickets are nonchangeable and nonrefundable. **Package tours** of Britain, where all flights, accommodation and ground transport are arranged for you, take the hassle

out of travel and can sometimes be cheaper than organizing things yourself (see p.31 for details).

Travelling from mainland **Europe**, drivers and foot and rail passengers can either cross the Channel by **ferry** or go under it, by **Eurotunnel** (the drive-on drive-off shuttle train for vehicles) or **Eurostar** (the high-speed passenger train from Paris and Brussels to London). If you're on a very tight budget, you might consider picking up a **bus** from any of the major European cities. **From Ireland**, it's quickest to fly, but there are also plenty of ferry crossings – especially useful if you're planning to tour around Scotland, Wales or the west of England.

Booking flights and services online

Ⓦ **www.cheapflights.com**, Ⓦ **www .cheapflights.com.au**, Ⓦ **www.cheapflights.ca** Price comparison on flights, short breaks, packages and other deals, with links to agents and other travel sites.

Ⓦ **www.cheaptickets.com** Discount flight specialists, plus hotel and car bookings (US only).

Ⓦ **www.ebookers.com** Efficient, easy-to-use flight finder with competitive fares.

Ⓦ **www.expedia.com**, Ⓦ **www.expedia.ca** Discount airfares, all-airline search engine, and daily deals on hotels, cars and packages.

Ⓦ **www.hotwire.com** Cheap flights and accommodation from the US only.

Ⓦ **www.lastminute.com**, Ⓦ **www .us.lastminute.com**, Ⓦ **www.au.lastminute .com** Good last-minute flights, holiday packages, hotel bookings and car rental deals.

Ⓦ **www.travelocity.com**, Ⓦ **www.travelocity .co.uk**, Ⓦ **www.travelocity.ca** Destination guides, hot fares from North America on major airlines and good deals on car rental, rail passes and accommodation.

ⓦ**www.travelshop.com.au** Australian website offering discount flights, packages, accommodation and insurance.

ⓦ**www.travel.yahoo.com** Flights, accommodation and other deals, plus Rough Guide material in its destination coverage.

From the US and Canada

Many airlines fly direct **from the US** to England – mainly London – but there are also some flights to Manchester and Birmingham. New York has the most nonstop services to England, though there are also nonstop flights from Washington, DC, Boston, Chicago, Miami, Orlando, Las Vegas, San Francisco and Los Angeles. There's only a limited range of nonstop flights from the US to Scotland, including Continental Airlines flights from New York to Glasgow or Edinburgh. Depending on the airline, low-season midweek fares to London from New York cost under $300, from Los Angeles more like $400–500, but bear in mind that the very cheapest deals tend to have little or no flexibility. Be aware that taxes and fees can also add up to $100 to any quoted price.

From **Canada**, airlines like Air Canada or bmi/British Midland fly nonstop from the gateway cities of Toronto, Montréal and Vancouver to London or Manchester. Low-season fares from Toronto start at around CDN$400 return, from Vancouver more like CDN$600–700. The charter operator Air Transat has good-value flights to London, Manchester, Newcastle, Birmingham and Exeter, mainly from Toronto, but also from Vancouver. Last-minute deals can be as low as CDN$200 return.

Flying time from New York or Toronto to any British airport is six to seven hours (it's an hour extra going back, due to head-winds). Most eastbound flights cross the Atlantic overnight, arriving in the UK early the next morning. From LA or Vancouver, flight time to the UK is more like ten hours, with most late-afternoon/early-evening flights arriving in Britain around noon.

The airlines listed below all have nonstop flights to Britain. You might find alternative or cheaper deals on other European airlines, though they tend to route through their respective European hubs, adding (some-times significantly) to your journey time.

Airlines

Air Canada ☎1-888/247-2262, ⓦwww .aircanada.ca.
Air Transat ☎1-866/847-1112, ⓦwww .airtransat.com.
American Airlines ☎1-800/433-7300, ⓦwww .aa.com.
bmi/British Midland Airways ☎1-800/788-0555, ⓦwww.flybmi.com.
British Airways ☎1-800/AIRWAYS, ⓦwww .ba.com.
Continental Airlines ☎1-800/231-0856, ⓦwww.continental.com.
Delta Air Lines ☎1-800/241-4141, ⓦwww .delta.com.
United Airlines ☎1-800/538-2929, ⓦwww .united.com.
Virgin Atlantic Airways ☎1-800/821-5438, ⓦwww.virgin-atlantic.com.

Discount flight agents

Air Brokers International ☎1-800/883-3273, ⓦwww.airbrokers.com.
Flightcentre US ☎1-866/WORLD-51, ⓦwww .flightcentre.us, Canada ☎1-877/GR8-TRIP, ⓦwww.flightcentre.ca.
STA Travel US ☎1-800/329-9537, Canada ☎1-888/427-5639, ⓦwww.statravel.com.
TFI Tours ☎1-800/745-8000, ⓦwww .lowestairprice.com.
Travel Cuts Canada ☎1-800/592-CUTS, US ☎1-866/246-9762, ⓦwww.travelcuts.com.
Worldtek Travel ☎1-800/243-1723, ⓦwww .worldtek.com.

From Australia and New Zealand

The route from Australasia to London is highly competitive, with the lowest return **fares** usually in the range of A$1600–2000/NZ$1600–2000. The very cheapest tickets rarely have much, if any, flexibility and you might want to pay more to be able to change your dates or to travel with one of the major airlines like Qantas, British Airways, Air New Zealand or Singapore Airlines. These airlines also tend to be able to arrange things like fly-drive and accommodation packages or onward travel to other British destinations

– flights to Manchester, for example, are sometimes available at no extra cost. To reach Scotland, you'll have to change planes either in London – the most popular choice – or in another European gateway such as Paris or Amsterdam.

The cheapest and most direct flights **from Australia** are usually via Asia and Europe. From **New Zealand**, however, the most direct route is via North America, stopping in Los Angeles. That said, it's usually cheaper to fly from New Zealand to London via Asia. **Travel time** from Australia or New Zealand to the UK is over twenty hours, even with the best connections, so you might want to consider a stopover – most airlines will let you do this for no extra charge.

Airlines

Air New Zealand Australia ☎13 24 76, ⒲www .airnewzealand.com.au; New Zealand ☎0800/737 000, ⒲www.airnewzealand.co.nz.
British Airways Australia ☎1300/767 7177, New Zealand ☎0800/274 847, ⒲www.ba.com.
Cathay Pacific Australia ☎13 17 47, New Zealand ☎0800/800 454, ⒲www.cathaypacific.com.
Emirates Australia ☎1300/303 777 or 02/9290 9700, New Zealand ☎09/377 6004, ⒲www .emirates.com
Malaysia Airlines Australia ☎13 26 27, New Zealand ☎0800/777 747, ⒲www.malaysia -airlines.com.
Qantas Australia ☎13 13 13, New Zealand ☎0800/808 767, ⒲www.qantas.com.
Singapore Airlines Australia ☎13 10 11, New Zealand ☎0800/808 909, ⒲www.singaporeair .com.
Thai Airways Australia ☎1300/651 960, New Zealand ☎09/377 3886, ⒲www.thaiair.com.
United Airlines Australia ☎13 17 77, ⒲www .united.com.
Virgin Atlantic Australia ☎1300/727 340, ⒲www.virgin-atlantic.com.

Discount flight agents

Flight Centre Australia ☎13 31 33, ⒲www .flightcentre.com.au; New Zealand ☎0800/243 544, ⒲www.flightcentre.co.nz.
Holiday Shoppe New Zealand ☎0800/808 480, ⒲www.holidayshoppe.co.nz.
STA Travel Australia ☎1300/733 035, New Zealand ☎0508/782 872, ⒲www.statravel.com.
Trailfinders Australia ☎02/9247 7666, ⒲www .trailfinders.com.au.

From Ireland

Stiff competition on routes between Ireland and Britain keeps the cost of **flights** low, though characteristically the earlier you book, the cheaper your ticket will be. **From the Republic**, Ryanair (☎0818/303030, ⒲www.ryanair.com) often has the cheapest tickets – special deals sometimes even offer free flights, with passengers paying just the taxes (around €20). If there are no special offers, you can usually expect to pay from €50 return. Ryanair flies to around fourteen airports in Britain from Dublin, Cork, Kerry, Knock and Shannon, while fellow budget airline bmibaby (☎1890/340 122, ⒲www.bmibaby.com) flies from Cork to Durham Tees Valley, Leeds/Bradford, Manchester, Nottingham and Birmingham, and from Knock to Durham Tees Valley, Manchester and Birmingham as well as from Dublin to London Heathrow. Aer Lingus (☎0818/365000, ⒲www.aerlingus.ie) offers good deals on its flights from Shannon and Cork to London Heathrow and from Dublin to Birmingham, Bristol, Edinburgh, Glasgow, Liverpool, London Heathrow and Manchester. British Airways (☎1890/626 747, ⒲www.ba.com) flies from Shannon to London Heathrow and from Dublin to Glasgow and London Heathrow. Finally, Air Wales (UK ☎0870/777 3131, ⒲www .airwales.com) flies from Cork to Plymouth, Cardiff and Durham Tees Valley as well as from Dublin to Cardiff, Norwich, Plymouth.

The cheapest options **from Belfast** are easyJet (☎1890/923922, ⒲www.easyjet .com; one-way flights from £7.99) to Bristol, Edinburgh, Glasgow, Inverness, Liverpool, London Gatwick, London Stansted, Luton and Newcastle; flybe (☎0871/700 0535, ⒲www.flybe.com; flights from £15.99) which serves nine British airports; and bmibaby (☎0870/264 2229, ⒲www.bmibaby.com) to Birmingham, Cardiff, London Heathrow, Manchester and Nottingham. Air Wales (UK ☎0870/777 3131, ⒲www.airwales.com) flies from Belfast to Cardiff.

Unless you're bringing your own vehicle to tour the UK, there's little point in coming **by ferry** from either the Republic or Northern Ireland, as crossings take longer and are usually pricier than flying. The main **direct services to England** are from

Dublin or Belfast to Liverpool with P&O Irish Sea (www.poirishsea.com) and Norse Merchant (www.norsemerchant.com), or the faster route from Larne to Fleetwood in northwest England (Stena Line; www.stenaline.co.uk), which takes around two hours. There are also direct services from Belfast and Dublin to Douglas on the Isle of Man (Isle of Man Steam Packet; www.steam-packet.com). As for **ferries to Wales** from Ireland, there are car ferries from Dun Laoghaire to Holyhead (Stena Line; www.stenaline.co.uk), from Dublin to Holyhead (Irish ferries; www.irishferries.com & Stena Line), from Cork to Swansea (Swansea Cork ferries; www.swanseacorkferries.com), and from Rosslare to Fishguard (Stena Line) and Pembroke (Irish Ferries). **To Scotland by ferry**, there are services from Belfast to Stranraer (Stena Line), Larne to Troon and Cairnryan (both P&O Irish Sea; www.poirishsea.co.uk) Fares on all routes vary according to the time of year, time and type of crossing, and number travelling – Direct Ferries (☎1800/932 151, www.directferries.ie) has a very useful website that compares all the options.

More convenient for many are the integrated **train and ferry** services that you can book from almost any station in Ireland to any British station. The quickest Dublin–London route – via the Dun Laoghaire–Holyhead high-speed ferry – takes seven hours with fares from €50 return; information on any route can be had from **Iarnród Éireann** (Irish Rail; ☎01/703 1884, www.irishrail.ie).

Alternatively, there's the Eurolines (www.eurolines.com) **bus and ferry** option, with regular coach services from Belfast to London (from £29 return), and from Dublin to Birmingham, Oxford, London, Liverpool, Manchester, Leeds, Blackpool and Glasgow (all from €39 return). You can also arrange connections from any major town in Ireland. Tickets are sold at any Bus Éireann travel centre and, while fares are pretty good value, the downside is that these trips often involve an overnight ferry crossing, arriving in Britain at the crack of dawn, and are very time-consuming.

From continental Europe

Low-cost airlines have not only reduced the cost of flying to Britain considerably, but have opened up many regional airports, so you don't necessarily have to start your trip in London. Depending on your location, and the airline you choose, airports at Manchester, Liverpool, Newcastle, Durham Tees Valley and Leeds/Bradford open up the north of England; Bournemouth and Southampton do the same for England's south coast; Nottingham is handy for the East Midlands; Birmingham for the West Midlands; Stansted and Norwich for East Anglia; Bristol and Exeter for the Southwest; Cardiff and Swansea for Wales; and Aberdeen, Edinburgh and Glasgow for Scotland. The main budget airlines that fly to British airports from all over the continent include Ryanair (www.ryanair.com), easyJet (www.easyjet.com), bmibaby (www.bmibaby.com), flybe (www.flybe.com), VLM (www.vlm-airlines.com), Virgin Express (www.virgin-express.com), Hapag-Lloyd Express (www.hlx.com) and others.

Direct **Eurostar trains** (France ☎08.92.35.35.39, Belgium ☎02 528 2828; www.eurostar.com) run roughly hourly through the Channel Tunnel to London Waterloo International from Lille (1hr 40min), Paris (2hr 35min) and Brussels (2hr 20min). Return fares start from €70–90 return from Paris or Lille and €85 from Brussels, though these rates come with many restrictions. More flexible tickets cost at least €150 return, though discounted flexible youth (for under-26s) and senior (over-60s) fares are available. Eurail, InterRail and Britrail pass holders qualify for a Carte Internationale (Passholder) return which allows unrestricted cross-Channel journeys for e120–150.

Drivers use **Eurotunnel** (France ☎08 10 63 03 04, Belgium ☎07 022 3210, www.eurotunnel.com) instead, which operates drive-on-drive-off shuttle trains through the Channel Tunnel from Calais/Coquelles to Folkestone. The 24-hour service runs every twenty minutes throughout the day and, though you can just turn up, booking is advised, especially at weekends, or if you want the best deals. Off-peak return fares for a car and passengers start at around €140 (book at least 14 days in advance), though fully flexible fares allowing changes cost much more than this.

Ferries cross from several European countries to ports in Britain. The quickest and cheapest services are on the traditional cross-Channel routes **from France** (Calais, Boulogne and Dieppe) to Dover and Newhaven in the southeast. However, other services might be more convenient, depending on your departure point and destination: you can reach Portsmouth and Poole in the south and Plymouth in the southwest from Brittany and **Spain** (Bilbao, Santander); Harwich in East Anglia from **Denmark** (Esbjerg) and **Holland** (Hook of Holland); Hull in East Yorkshire from **Belgium** (Zeebrugge) and Holland (Rotterdam); Newcastle in the Northeast from Holland (Amsterdam Ijmuiden) and **Norway** (Stavanger, Bergen, Kristiansand); or Lerwick in the Shetlands from Bergen in Norway. Ticket prices vary according to route, departure date, size of car etc, while sleeping accommodation is often obligatory on night crossings. Any travel agent can supply up-to-date schedules and ticket information, or consult the encyclopedic Ⓦwww .directferries.com, which has details about, and links to, every ferry service to Britain.

Finally, Eurolines (Ⓦwww.eurolines.com) is Europe's largest international **bus** network, comprising independent coach companies operating services to London from dozens of European cities, including Amsterdam, Brussels, Frankfurt, Hamburg, Madrid, Paris and Rome. Prices start at €39 return from Paris – though, once you've factored in the travel time, a flight to the UK booked well in advance with a low-cost airline might be just as economical.

Packages, activity holidays and organized tours

Many outfits in the UK and overseas offer standard **coach-tour** itineraries of Britain's historic highlights, while **special-interest operators** can help you explore the country's unique pleasures: countryside walking or cycling, canal trips, activity holidays, or themed tours based on Britain's literary heritage, art and architecture, gardens and stately homes, culture or sports. The **UK-based operators** listed below organize itineraries, transport, guides and accommodation, though usually not flights or other transport into Britain.

Most operators offering **activity holidays** – walking and cycling are the mainstays – tend to have two types of trip, escorted (or guide-led) and self-guided, the latter usually slightly cheaper. Both are designed to be hassle-free, so you can expect your luggage to be transported to each night's lodging, pre-booked accommodation, detailed route instructions, a packed lunch and back-up support. Some companies offer budget versions of their holidays, staying in hostels or B&Bs, as well as hotel packages.

All-inclusive **city breaks** from North America can provide a good introduction to Britain, though in most cases this means London. Airlines with tour operator arms, like British Airways and Virgin Atlantic, or major travel agencies can all oblige. From New York (with add-ons available from most US or Canadian cities), a three-night midweek stay in a three-star London hotel (flights, transfers and breakfast included) usually costs under $600 (plus taxes).

Tour operators in the UK

General

Thomas Cook ℡0870/750 5711, Ⓦwww .thomascook.co.uk. Wide range of UK breaks, plus hotel and theatre-ticket bookings.

Backpacker travel

Carry On Tours ℡0800/187 9433 or 0845/070 2797; from outside the UK 01273/597974; Ⓦwww.carryontours.com. One-day (£37–47) and two-day (£89–99) minibus activity tours out of London to a variety of destinations (Stonehenge, Cheddar Gorge, Stratford-upon-Avon), or a 6-day London–Edinburgh tour (£185 plus kitty) of Britain's highlights.
Contiki Holidays ℡020/8290 6777, Ⓦwww .contiki.com. Lively adventure tours for 18–35s, in particular 3- and 5-day London trips or an 8-day all-Britain tour.
Road Trip ℡0845/200 6791, Ⓦwww.roadtrip .co.uk. Inclusive, activity-filled budget bus tours around England, departing from London. Three-day weekend tours (from £75) to Cornwall, Liverpool and the Lakes, or Cambridge and the Norfolk Broads; plus five-day tours of the north or south (from £139). An extra kitty paid on all tours covers accommodation, meals and entrance fees. Day-trips from London (£55–65) also available.

Boating and water sports

Blakes Holiday Boating ℡01282/844284, ⓦwww.blakes.co.uk. Cruisers, yachts and narrow-boats on the Norfolk Broads, rivers Thames and Ouse, and various English canals.

Classic Sailing ℡01872/580022, ⓦwww.classic-sailing.co.uk. Hands-on sailing holidays on traditional wooden boats and tall ships, from short breaks on the Solent to Scilly Isles voyages.

Hoseasons Holidays ℡01502/502588, ⓦwww.hoseasons.co.uk. Self-drive cruisers on the Norfolk Broads and River Thames, as well as traditional narrowboats on inland waterways.

Outdoor activities

Above The Line ℡01946/726229, ⓦwww.wasdale.com. Mountain courses (hill walking for softies, guided ascents, navigation etc), with accommodation in the Wasdale Head Inn, the Lake District birthplace of British mountaineering.

Explore Britain ℡01388/650900, ⓦwww.xplorebritain.com. Horse-riding holidays, including beach trail weekends (from £350) or 8-night tours in the North York Moors or Lake District (from £1000), plus guided/independent walking and cycling holidays.

Outward Bound ℡0870/513 4227, ⓦwww.outwardbound-uk.org. Residential courses and activity holidays in the Lake District geared towards young people and families, including climbing, caving, sailing and canoeing.

White Tor Stables ℡01822/810760, ⓦwww.whitetor.co.uk. Riding holidays on some of Dartmoor's wilder tracts, on "Western-style" riding excursions, mainly for experienced riders. From £155/day for a weekend or from £105 (from 6 days), all-inclusive.

Wildlife Encounters ℡01737/214214, ⓦwww.wildlife-encounters.co.uk. Top-rated wildlife-watching tours, including whale-watching in Scotland.

YHA ℡0870/770 6113, ⓦwww.yha.org.uk. Huge range of good-value hostel-based activity weekends and holidays, from walking, climbing and biking to surfing, kayaking and caving.

Cycling

Capital Sport ℡01296/631671, ⓦwww.capital-sport.co.uk. Gentle self-guided cycling tours to Windsor, Oxford and the Cotswolds, in either B&B (from £99 for 1-night/2-day trips) or "fine" accommodation (from £195).

Country Lanes ℡01425/655022, ⓦwww.countrylanes.co.uk. Ranging from day-trips to week-long outings in the Cotswolds, Lake District and New Forest.

Holiday Lakeland ℡01697/371871, ⓦwww.holiday-lakeland.co.uk. Offers 2- to 5-day tours in the Lake District, Northumberland and the Pennines, including coast-to-coast, Pennine Cycle Way and Hadrian's Wall Cycle Way routes – from £95 to £375 B&B.

Rough Tracks ℡0700/0560 749, ⓦwww.roughtracks.co.uk. Mountain-bike and road weekend tours (from £125) in the North Downs, Wiltshire and Somerset, or a 4-day coast-to-coast journey (£345).

Saddle Skedaddle ℡0191/265 1110, ⓦwww.skedaddle.co.uk. Cycling holidays, biking adventures and classic road rides – includes on- and off-road tours in the Cotswolds, Northumberland and from coast to coast, from one day to a week.

Walking

Cloudberry Holidays ℡01539/733522, ⓦwww.cloudberry.co.uk. Budget walking holidays based in YHA hostels in the Lake District. Small groups, guide-led, from £105 for 2 nights, £260 for 5 nights, meals included.

Contours Walking Holidays ℡01768/480451, ⓦwww.contours.co.uk. Walking holidays and self-guided hikes in every region, north and south, from famous trails to little-known local routes. Short breaks from £200, 7-night holidays from £400-500.

Countrywide ℡01707/386800, ⓦwww.countrywidewalking.com. Sociable guided walking tours (scenic, themed or special interest) all over England, including the Isle of Man, starting at under £200 for 3 nights.

Footpath Holidays ℡01985/840049, ⓦwww.footpath-holidays.com. Guided and self-guided packages to various hill and coastal districts, with 5 nights B&B and walking in the Lakes or Devon and Cornwall, from around £350.

Sherpa Expeditions ℡020/8577 2717, ⓦwww.sherpa-walking-holidays.co.uk. At-your-own-pace, self-guided walks (and cycle tours) between country pubs, mainly in Yorkshire, the Lakes and the Southwest. Most trips are 8 days, from around £450.

Walkabout Scotland ℡0131/661 7168, ⓦwww.walkaboutscotland.com. A great way to get a taste of hiking in Scotland, with guided hill-walking holidays, tours and day-trips with all transport included.

Walking Women ℡0845/644 5335, ⓦwww.walkingwomen.co.uk. Women-only walking holidays and short breaks (Feb–Nov), mainly in the Lake District – 2 nights all-in from £150, but also long-distance trails like the Dales Way or South Downs Way (£360–460).

Art, history and culture

Martin Randall Travel ☏ 020/8742 3355, ⓦ www.martinrandall.com. Highly regarded historical and cultural tours led by experts – 5-day all-inclusive tours of West Country churches, or medieval East Anglia, for example, from around £700.

Tour operators in North America

General

Abercrombie & Kent ☏ 1-800/554-7016, ⓦ www.abercrombiekent.com. Classy travel specialist, with no-expense-spared escorted and independent trips, and River Thames cruises.

British Airways Holidays ☏ 1-877/4-A-VACATION, ⓦ www.british-airways.com. Flight-inclusive vacations and customized itineraries, including London city breaks.

British Travel International ☏ 1-800/327-6097, ⓦ www.britishtravel.com. Agent for all independent arrangements: rail and bus passes, car rental, hotels and a comprehensive accommodation reservation service.

CIE Tours International US ☏ 1-800/CIE-TOUR, ⓦ www.cietours.com. Long-established operator offering escorted Britain coach tours (from $1700), or self-drive B&B holidays (from $700).

Delta Vacations ☏ 1-800/654-6559, ⓦ www.deltavacations.com. General tour operator with London and Manchester city breaks.

Maupintour ☏ 1-800/255-4266, ⓦ www.maupintour.com. Quality, all-inclusive, themed escorted tours – London at Christmas, Lakes and Literature, Grand Rail Tour, or a visit based around the Chelsea Flower Show, for example.

Virgin Vacations ☏ 1-800/862-8621, ⓦ www.virgin-atlantic.com. Custom-made packages for independent travellers, including flights, hotels, car rental and tours.

Outdoor activities

Adventures Abroad ☏ 1-800/665-3998, ⓦ www.adventures-abroad.com. Walking and sightseeing tours of Scotland and England.

Backroads ☏ 1-800/462-2848, ⓦ www.backroads.com. World hiking specialists offering a Cotswolds rambling trip – 5 nights in elegant country-house hotels for $3100.

BCT Scenic Walking ☏ 1-800/473-1210, ⓦ www.bctwalk.com. Tempting line-up of walking trips in the Cotswolds, Skye and the Highlands.

Classic Journeys ☏ 1-800/200-3887, ⓦ www.classicjourneys.com. Upmarket guided (walking) tours of classic English and Scottish destinations, including the Cotswolds, the Cornish coast, Edinburgh and the Highlands.

English Lakeland Ramblers ☏ 1-800/724-8801, ⓦ www.ramblers.com. Guided walking tours (May to October), either inn-to-inn in the Lake District or based in a country hotel in the Cotswolds, from $2360.

Le Boat ☏ 1-800/992-0291, ⓦ www.leboat.com. Take a hotel-barge trip in Gloucestershire or on the River Thames, or a self-drive cruiser on the Norfolk Broads, Leeds–Liverpool Canal or Severn and Avon rivers.

REI Adventures ☏ 1-800/622-2236, ⓦ www.rei.com. Hiking tours in the Highlands.

Wilderness Travel ☏ 1-800/368-2794 or 510/558-2488, ⓦ www.wildernesstravel.com. Inn-to-inn hiking packages, either coast-to-coast or along Hadrian's Wall. 14-day trips from $3895.

Art, history and culture

Adventures Abroad ☏ 1-800/665-3998, ⓦ www.adventures-abroad.com. Visit a major museum and gallery a day on the London "culture crawl" – 8 days from $1480.

Cross-Culture ☏ 1-800/491-1148, ⓦ www.crosscultureinc.com. Small-group cultural tours, including all across Wales, Devon and Cornwall, and the Scottish Highlands.

English Experience ☏ 1-800/892-9317, ⓦ www.english-experience.com. Small-group guided tours in B&Bs or hotels, covering the historic sights in Sussex, Kent, the Cotswolds, Lake District, Yorkshire Dales, Devon and Cornwall, or East Anglia.

Tour operators in Australia and New Zealand

Adventure World Australia ☏ 02/8913 0755, ⓦ www.adventureworld.com.au; New Zealand ☏ 09/524 5118, ⓦ www.adventureworld.co.nz. Wide variety of independent, customized or escorted tours – Lake District trips, self-drive holidays, coach trips, walking/cycling holidays etc.

Adventures Abroad Australia ☏ 1800/147 827, New Zealand ☏ 0800/800 434, ⓦ www.adventures-abroad.com. English tours include a London "culture crawl" or a 13-day coastal walking trip in Devon and Cornwall.

Explore Holidays Australia ☏ 02/9857 6200 or 1300/731 000, ⓦ www.exploreholidays.com.au. Organizes customized holidays that include accommodation, passes to sights and tours all over the UK, plus London packages, car rental and the like.

Red tape and visas

EU citizens have the right of entry into and are permitted free movement within the UK, with just a passport or national identity card. US, Canadian, Australian and New Zealand citizens can stay in Britain for up to six months without a visa, provided they have a valid passport. Most other nationalities – but not citizens of EEA countries like Norway – require a visa, obtainable from the British consular office in the country of application. Incidentally, the Channel Islands and the Isle of Man have their own immigration laws and policies, but UK visa offices can issue visas for these islands if required. For current details about entry and visa requirements, consult the UK's Foreign and Commonwealth Office's visa website Ⓦ www.ukvisas.gov.uk.

Extending your stay

Citizens of EU countries who want to stay in the UK long-term can apply for a residence permit. Non-EU citizens can apply to extend their visas, though this must be done before the current visa expires. In both cases, you should first contact the **Immigration and Nationality Directorate**, Lunar House, 40 Wellesley Rd, Croydon CR9 2BY (Ⓣ0870/606 7766, Ⓦwww.ind.homeoffice.gov.uk). US, Canadian, Australian and New Zealand citizens who want to stay longer than six months will need an **entry clearance certificate**, available from the British consular office at the embassy or High Commission in their own country.

British embassies and high commissions abroad

Australia British High Commission, Commonwealth Ave, Yarralumla, Canberra, ACT 2600 Ⓣ02/6270 6666, Ⓦwww.britaus.net.
Canada British High Commission, 80 Elgin St, Ottawa, ON K1P 5K7 Ⓣ613/237-1530, Ⓦwww.britainincanada.org.
Ireland British Embassy, 29 Merrion Rd, Ballsbridge, Dublin 4 Ⓣ01/205 3700, Ⓦwww.britishembassy.ie.
New Zealand British High Commission, 44 Hill St, Thorndon, Wellington Ⓣ04/924 2888, Ⓦwww.britain.org.nz.
USA British Embassy, 3100 Massachusetts Ave NW, Washington, DC 20008 Ⓣ202/588-6500, Ⓦwww.britainusa.com.

Customs

Travellers coming into Britain directly **from another EU country** can bring almost as many cigarettes and as much wine or beer into the country as they can carry. The guidance levels are 10 litres of spirits, 90 litres of wine and 110 litres of beer – any more than this and you'll have to provide proof that it's for personal use only. The general guidelines for tobacco are 3200 cigarettes, 400 cigarillos, 200 cigars or 3kg of loose tobacco – but note that the limits from some new EU member countries are lower than this.

If you're travelling from (or to) a non-EU country, you can still buy **duty-free goods**, but within the EU, this perk no longer exists. The duty-free allowances are:

Tobacco: 200 cigarettes; or 100 cigarillos; or 50 cigars; or 250 grammes of loose tobacco.

Alcohol: 2 litres of still wine plus 1 litre of drink over 22 percent alcohol; or 2 litres of alcoholic drinks not over 22 percent.

Perfumes: 60ml of perfume plus 250ml of toilet water.

Other goods to the value of £145.

If you need any clarification on British import regulations, contact **HM Revenue and Customs** (Ⓣ0845/010 9000 or +4420/8929 0152 for international callers; Ⓦwww.hmrv.gov.uk).

Tax-free shopping

Most goods in Britain, with the chief exceptions of books and food, are subject to

17.5-percent **Value Added Tax** (VAT), which is included in the marked price of goods. Visitors from non-EU countries can save a lot of money through the **Retail Export Scheme** (tax-free shopping), which allows a refund of VAT on goods to be taken out of the country. (Savings will usually be minimal for EU nationals because of the rates at which the goods will be taxed upon import to the home country.) Note that not all shops participate in this scheme (those doing so will display a sign to this effect), and you cannot reclaim VAT charged on hotel bills or other services.

Information, websites and maps

Britain's tourism authority, VisitBritain, has offices worldwide, while regional tourism boards within the UK concentrate on particular areas. The official national websites, ⓦ www.visitbritain.com, ⓦ www.visitengland.com, ⓦ www.visitscotland .com, and ⓦ www.visitwales.com are all very useful, covering everything from local accommodation to festival dates, but there is also a large number of regional and other specialist websites devoted to the UK.

Tourist information

Tourist offices (also called Tourist Information Centres, or "TICs" for short) exist in virtually every British town. They tend to follow standard shop hours (Mon–Sat 9am–5.30/6pm), though they also often open on Sundays, with hours extended during the spring and summer **season** (usually Easter until the end of October) and curtailed in **winter** (November to Easter).

Staff at tourist offices will nearly always be able to **book accommodation**, reserve space on guided tours, and sell guides, maps and hiking leaflets. They can also provide lists of local cafés, restaurants and pubs, and though the staff aren't supposed to recommend particular places you'll often be able to get a feel for the best local places to eat. A few of the larger TICs provide free Internet access.

Areas designated as **national parks** (such as the Lake District, Yorkshire Dales, North York Moors and Dartmoor) tend to have their own dedicated information centres, which offer similar services to TICs but can also provide expert guidance on local walks and outdoor pursuits.

Visit Britain offices overseas

Australia ☎ 02/9021 4400 or 1300/858589, ⓦ www.visitbritain.com/au.
Canada ☎ 1-888/847-4885, ⓦ www.visitbritain .com/ca.
Ireland ☎ 01/670 8000, ⓦ www.visitbritain .com/ie.
New Zealand ☎ 0800/700 741, ⓦ www .visitbritain.com/nz.
USA ☎ 1-800/462-2748, ⓦ www.visitbritain .com/us.

English regional tourist boards

East of England Tourist Board ☎ 0870/225 4800, ⓦ www.visiteastofengland.com. Bedfordshire, Cambridgeshire, Hertfordshire, Essex, Norfolk and Suffolk.
East Midlands Tourism ⓦ www.enjoyeastmidlands .com. Derbyshire and the Peaks, Lincolnshire, Nottinghamshire, Leicestershire, Rutland and Northamptonshire.
England's Northwest ⓦ www .visitenglandsnorthwest.com. Cumbria and the Lake District, Cheshire, Lancashire, Manchester, Liverpool and Merseyside.
Heart of England Tourism ☎ 01905/761100, ⓦ www.visitheartofengland.com. Herefordshire,

Shropshire, Worcestershire, Staffordshire, West
Midlands and Warwickshire.

South West Tourism ☏0870/442 0880, ⓦwww
.visitsouthwest.co.uk. Bath, Bristol, Devon, Cornwall,
Isles of Scilly, Dorset, Gloucestershire and the
Cotswolds, Somerset and Wiltshire.

Tourism South East ☏02380/625400, ⓦwww
.visitsoutheastengland.com. Sussex, Kent, Surrey,
Berkshire, Hampshire, Oxfordshire, Buckinghamshire
and Isle of Wight.

Visit London ⓦwww.visitlondon.com.
Greater London.

Tourism Northeast ☏08701/601781,
ⓦwww.visitnorthumbria.com. County Durham,
Northumberland, Tees Valley, and Tyne and Wear.

Yorkshire Tourist Board ☏0870/609 0000,
ⓦwww.yorkshirevisitor.com

Scottish regional tourism boards

Aberdeen and Grampian ☏ 01224/288828,
ⓦwww.agtb.org

Angus and Dundee ☏01382/527527, ⓦwww
.angusanddundee.co.uk

**Argyll, the Isles, Loch Lomond, Stirling and
Trossachs** ⓦwww.visitscottishheartlands.com

Ayrshire and Arran ☏0845/225 5121, ⓦwww
.ayrshire-arran.com

Dumfries and Galloway ☏ 01387/253862,
ⓦwww.visitdumfriesandgalloway.co.uk

Edinburgh and the Lothians ⓦwww.edinburgh
.org

Fife ⓦwww.standrews.co.uk

Greater Glasgow and Clyde Valley ⓦwww
.seeglasgow.com

Hebrides ⓦwww.witb.co.uk

Highlands of Scotland ⓦwww.visithighlands
.com

Orkney ☏01856/872856, ⓦwww.visitorkney.com

Perthshire ⓦwww.perthshire.co.uk

Scottish Borders ⓦwww.scot-borders.co.uk

Shetland ☏08701/999 440, ⓦwww.visitshetland
.com

Welsh regional tourism boards

Mid & South Wales Tourism ☏0870/080 3436,
ⓦwww.visitmidwales.co.uk

North Wales Tourism ☏01492/531731, ⓦwww
.nwt.co.uk

Websites

Throughout the Guide, we've included
websites for specific accommodation,
museums, galleries, transport, entertainment venues and other attractions. If you're

looking for more general information about
Britain, or just a different take on things, then
the list below is a useful starting point.

Guides and destinations

ⓦ**www.goodguides.com** A cocktail of information
from the very useful *Good Britain Guide* and *Good
Pub Guide*.

ⓦ**www.information-britain.co.uk**
Comprehensive site with a county-by-county guide, as
well as listings on every conceivable subject.

ⓦ**www.londontheatre.co.uk** What's on in the
West End, and how to get theatre tickets.

ⓦ**www.which.net** Britain's biggest consumer
organization provides reviews from its respected *Good
Food* and *Hotels* guides, alongside online access to its
consumer reports on everything from electric toasters
to holidays.

News, views and current affairs

ⓦ**www.bbc.co.uk** The website of one of the
world's most respected news organizations, good for
news, current affairs, sport and weather.

ⓦ**www.guardian.co.uk** Official website of *The
Guardian*, the UK's main left-leaning broadsheet,
particularly good for news and reviews.

Idiosyncratically British

ⓦ**www.ceolas.org** A very informative Celtic music
site, both historical and contemporary, with lots of
music to listen to.

ⓦ**www.knowhere.co.uk** A self-styled user's guide
to Britain incorporating scurrilous readers' comments,
including best-of and worst-of sections.

ⓦ**www.loo.co.uk** Find Britain's Loo of the Year,
if you want to know the best place to go away from
home.

ⓦ**www.met-office.gov.uk** England's favourite
topic, the weather, discussed in detail with full
regional forecasts.

ⓦ**www.ngs.org.uk** The National Gardens
Scheme details gardens, many of them private, open
throughout the year for charity. Britain at its green-
fingered best.

ⓦ**www.piers.co.uk** A monthly round-up of news
celebrating Britain's glorious Victorian piers (longest
one, Southend-on-Sea).

ⓦ**www.sealedknot.org** Famous English Civil
War re-enactment society, dedicated to fighting
seventeenth-century battles (or at least polishing their
muskets) at events across England.

ⓦ**www.tea.co.uk** In search of the perfect cuppa?
The tea council website sponsors the annual Top Tea
Awards.

ⓦ**www.theheraldrysociety.com** How to get a coat of arms, and other thorny contemporary social issues.

ⓦ**www.themorrisring.org** Six hundred years of bells, clogs, sticks and swords – everything you ever wanted to know about morris men, maypoles and sword dancing but never dared ask.

ⓦ**www.tylwythteg.com** Welsh witchcraft homepage, with links to druidry, benign witchcraft and festival listings.

Maps

Road maps of Britain come in many different scales and sizes, but the clearest are produced by the Geographers' A–Z Map Company Limited (ⓦwww.a–zmaps.co.uk), whose excellent *Great Britain Road Atlas* (2.5 miles to the inch; 1:158400) is widely available and includes over forty city-centre maps. For anything in more detail, it has to be the maps produced by the **Ordnance Survey** (OS; ⓦwww.ordsvy.gov.uk), which are renowned for their accuracy and clarity. The maps in their 1:50,000 (pink) Landranger series cover the whole of Britain and show enough detail to be useful for most walkers and cyclists, and there's more detail still in the full-colour 1:25,000 (orange) Explorer series, which also covers the whole of

Britain. As for **London**, the Geographers' A–Z Map Company publishes several versions of the benchmark *London A–Z* street guide, while the **Rough Guides' London maps** (1:5000/25,000), which are on waterproof, tearproof paper, are also recommended and come complete with full city listings. Finally, the **National Cycle Network** of cross-country routes along country lanes and traffic-free paths is covered by a series of excellent waterproof maps (1:100,000) published by Sustrans (ⓦwww.sustrans.org.uk).

All the maps mentioned above are available from large bookshops in the UK or **specialist map and travel stores** in North America and Australasia. Alternatively, try mail order from ⓦwww.amazon.co.uk/com or a world map specialist like ⓦwww.randmcnally.com, while visitors to London, Bristol or Manchester should call in at **Stanfords** (ⓦwww.stanfords.co.uk), England's premier map and travel specialist.

Useful map websites

ⓦ**www.multimap.com** Town plans and area maps with scales up to 1:10,000, plus address search, traffic info and more.

ⓦ**www.visitmap.com** The Britain Visitor Atlas has a clickable A–Z of town and city maps.

Health

No vaccinations are required for entry into Britain. Citizens of all EU and EEA countries are entitled to free medical treatment within the UK's National Health Service (NHS), which includes the vast majority of hospitals and doctors, on production of their European Health Insurance Card (EHIC) or, in extremis, their passport or national identity card. The same applies to those Commonwealth countries which have reciprocal healthcare arrangements with the UK – for example Australia and New Zealand. If you don't fall into either of these categories, you will be charged for all medical services, so health insurance is strongly advised.

Pharmacies and medical treatment

Pharmacists (known as **chemists** in Britain) can dispense only a limited range of drugs

without a doctor's prescription. Most chemists are open standard shop hours, though in large towns some stay open until 9pm – local newspapers often carry lists of late-opening "duty" pharmacies, and the information may also be posted on pharmacy doors. For generic, off-the-shelf pain-relief tablets, cold cures and the like, the local supermarket is usually the cheapest option.

Minor complaints and injuries can be dealt with at a **doctor's (GP's) surgery** – any tourist office or hotel should be able to point you in the right direction. For complaints that require immediate attention, you can turn up at the 24-hour casualty (A&E) department of the local **hospital** (detailed in our main city and town accounts). In an **emergency**, call the paramedics/ambulance service on ☎999.

NHS Direct (☎0845/4647, ⓦwww .nhsdirect.nhs.uk) provides 24-hour medical advice by phone, and also runs an increasing number of **walk-in centres** (usually daily 7.30am–9pm) in the bigger towns and cities.

Insurance

Visitors are advised to take out an insurance policy before travelling to the UK to cover against theft, loss and illness or injury. A typical policy will provide cover for loss of baggage, tickets and – up to a certain limit – cash or travellers' cheques, as well as enforced cancellation or curtailment of your journey. Most exclude so-called dangerous sports unless an extra premium is paid: in Britain this can mean most water sports, rock climbing and mountaineering, though probably not hiking or kayaking.

Medical coverage is strongly advised, especially for non–EU/EEA nationals, though before you pay up you should always ascertain whether benefits will be paid as treatment proceeds or only after you return home, and whether there is a 24-hour medical emergency number. When securing **baggage cover**, make sure that the per-article limit will cover your most valuable possession. If you need to make a claim, you should keep receipts for medicines and medical treatment, and in the event you have anything stolen you must obtain an official statement from the police – we've noted the contact details for police stations in most major towns and cities.

Rough Guides travel insurance

In conjunction with Columbus Direct, Rough Guides provides tailor-made travel insurance. Readers can choose from policies that include a low-cost **backpacker** option for long stays; a **short-break** option for city getaways; a typical **holiday package** option; and many others. There are also annual **multi-trip** policies for those who travel regularly, with variable levels of cover available. Different **sports and activities** (trekking, skiing etc) can be included on most policies, if required. Rough Guides travel insurance can be purchased by residents of 36 countries on our website, ⓦwww.roughguidesinsurance.com, which also has various language options. Alternatively, UK residents can call ☎0800/083 9507, US citizens ☎1-800/749-4922, and Australians ☎1-300/669 999. All other nationalities should call ☎+44 870/890 2843.

Costs, money and banks

Britain is an expensive place to visit by North American and Australasian standards, and about on a par with much of western Europe and Scandinavia. Even if you're camping or hostelling, using public transport, buying picnic lunches and eating in pubs and cafés your minimum expenditure will be around £30 per person per day. Couples staying in B&Bs, eating at unpretentious restaurants and visiting a fair number of tourist attractions, will spend around £50–60 per person, while if you're renting a car, staying in hotels and eating well, budget for at least £100 each. This last figure, of course, won't even cover your accommodation if you're staying in stylish city or grand country-house hotels, while on any visit to London you'll need an extra £25 per day to get the best out of the city.

Currency

Britain's currency is the **pound sterling** (£), divided into 100 pence (p). Coins come in denominations of 1p, 2p, 5p, 10p, 20p, 50p and £1 and £2. Notes are in denominations of £5, £10, £20 and £50. Occasionally you may receive Scottish banknotes: they're legal tender throughout Britain, though some traders may be unwilling to accept them.

Banks, ATMs, cheques and cards

Every sizeable town and village has a branch of at least one of the main high-street **banks**: Barclays, Halifax, HSBC, Lloyds-TSB and NatWest. **Opening hours** are generally Monday to Friday 9.30am to 4.30pm, though some branches in larger towns open at 9am, close at 5.30pm and also open on Saturdays.

The easiest way to get hold of cash is to use your **debit card** in an ATM. You'll find **ATMs** outside banks, at all major points of arrival and motorway service areas, at most large supermarkets, some petrol stations and even in some pubs, rural post offices and village shops (though a charge may be levied on cash withdrawals at small, stand-alone ATMs).

Some overseas travellers still prefer sterling **travellers' cheques**, at least as a back-up. The most commonly accepted are issued by American Express, followed by Visa and Thomas Cook. If the cheques are lost or stolen, the issuing company will expect you to report the loss immediately; most companies claim to replace lost or stolen cheques within 24 hours. Neither American Express nor Thomas Cook charge commission if you exchange cheques at their own

Taxes and tipping

Most goods (except books and food) are subject to a 17.5 percent tax called **Value Added Tax** (VAT). It's nearly always included in the price, though hotel bills and bills for other services are sometimes calculated with the tax added on separately.

Some restaurants levy a "discretionary" or "optional" **service charge** of a further 10 or 12.5 percent. If they've done this, it should be clearly stated on the menu and on the bill. However, you are not obliged to pay the charge, and certainly not if the food or service wasn't what you expected. Otherwise, although there are no fixed rules for **tipping**, a ten to fifteen percent tip is anticipated by restaurant waiters and expected by taxi drivers. It is not normal to leave tips in pubs, but the bar staff are sometimes offered drinks, which they may accept in the form of money. The only other occasions when you'll be expected to tip are in hairdressers, and in upmarket hotels where porters, bellboys and table waiters expect and usually get a pound or two.

offices, but banks will charge around 1.5 percent commission. Note that in the UK you are unlikely to be able to use your travellers' cheques as cash – you'll always have to cash them first, making them an unreliable source of funds in more remote areas.

Outside banking hours, you can change cheques or cash at **post offices** (locations are detailed in the Guide) and **bureaux de change**, which tend to be open longer hours and are found in many city centres, and at major airports and train stations. However, try to avoid changing cash or cheques in hotels, where the rates are normally poor.

Finally, **credit cards** can be used widely either in ATMs or over the counter. Master-Card and Visa are accepted in most hotels, shops and restaurants in the UK, American Express and Diners Club less so. Plastic is less useful in rural areas, and smaller establishments all over the country, such as B&Bs, will often accept cash only. Remember that cash advances from ATMs using your credit card are treated as loans, with interest accruing daily from the date of withdrawal.

Admission charges

Many of Britain's historic attractions – from castles to stately homes – are owned and/or operated by either the **National Trust** (℡0870/458 4000, ⓦwww.nationaltrust .org.uk), covering England and Wales, or the **National Trust for Scotland** (℡0131/243 9300, ⓦwww.nts.org.uk) – whose properties are denoted in the Guide with "NT" or "NTS". Both organizations charge entry fees for most of their sites (usually £4–8), though the less significant ones are free. If you plan to visit more than half a dozen places owned by either, it's worth considering an **annual membership** (£38/£35 per adult, less for families and couples), which allows unlimited entry to each organization's respective properties, and you can join on your first visit. Many of England's other historic sites are operated by **English Heritage** (℡0870/333 1181, ⓦwww.english-heritage.org.uk; "EH"), whose admission and membership fees are similar, though they also offer an **Overseas Visitors Pass** (7 days £17, 14 days £21), again for unlimited free entry to their properties. There are equivalent organizations in Scotland and Wales – **Historic Scotland** (HS;

℡0131/668 8600, ⓦwww.historic-scotland .gov.uk) and **CADW Welsh Historic Monuments** (CADW; ℡01443/336000, ⓦwww .cadw.wales.gov.uk). For further details concerning membership fees and special deals, consult the respective websites.

Many **stately homes** remain firmly in the hands of the landed gentry, who tend to charge £7–10 for admission to edited highlights of their domain. Other old buildings are owned by local authorities, who are generally more lenient with their admission charges, and often allow free access. **Municipal art galleries and museums** across the UK mostly have free admission, as do the great **state museums**, such as the British Museum and National Gallery in London, Cardiff's National Museum of Wales, and the National Museum of Scotland and National Gallery of Scotland in Edinburgh. Private museums and other collections usually charge for entrance, but rarely more than £5. Several of the country's **cathedrals** charge admission – of around £4 – but most ask for voluntary donations, as do many churches.

The **admission charges given in the Guide** are the full adult rate, unless otherwise stated.

Concessions and discounts

Concessionary rates for senior citizens (over 60) and children (from 5 to 16) apply almost everywhere, from fee-paying attractions to public transport, and typically give around fifty percent discount; you'll need official identification as proof of age. The unemployed and full-time students are often entitled to discounts too, and the under-5s are rarely charged anything at all.

Full-time students are eligible for the **International Student ID Card** (ISIC; ⓦwww .isiccard.com), which entitles them to special air, rail and bus fares and discounts at museums, theatres and other attractions. The **International Youth Travel Card** provides similar benefits for under-26s, while teachers qualify for the **International Teacher Card**. Several other travel organizations and accommodation groups (including the youth hostel organization, IYHF) have their own cards providing various discounts. Specialist travel agencies in your home country (including STA world-wide) can provide more information and application forms.

Non-UK residents can buy a **Great British Heritage Pass** (4 days £28; 7 days £39; 15 days £52; 1 month £70), which gives free entry to 600 cultural and historic properties. You can buy it (at equivalent local rates) from travel agents in your own country before you come, or at major tourist offices in the UK on arrival: see Ⓦwww.visitbritain.com for more details.

Getting around

Almost every town and village across the UK can be reached by train and/or bus, but costs are among the highest in Europe and travelling around can eat up a large wedge of money. It pays to investigate all the train and bus passes and special deals on offer, though note that some are only available outside the UK and must be purchased before you arrive. It's often cheaper to drive yourself around the country (certainly if you're sharing costs), though fuel and car rental tariffs are again among the highest in Europe. Congestion around the main cities can be bad, and even the motorways (notoriously the M25, London's orbital road) are liable to sporadic gridlock, especially on public holidays.

Given these transport weaknesses, **domestic flights** can seem an attractive option, especially as the budget airlines have both forced prices right down and provided many different routings. Given the congested state of the roads, **cycling** might not seem the most obvious (or safest) way to get around, but many people do bring bikes or rent once they arrive, and the country has a growing network of cycleways and traffic-free routes.

Principal train and bus (but not plane) routes and schedules are indicated at the end of every chapter in "Travel details".

Domestic flights

UK airlines provide a complex web of domestic routings with four of the main players being **easyJet** (which flies from Bristol to Edinburgh, Glasgow, Inverness and Newcastle; London Gatwick to Edinburgh and Inverness; London Stansted to Edinburgh, Glasgow, Inverness and Newcastle; Luton to Aberdeen, Edinburgh, Glasgow and Inverness; and Nottingham East Midlands to Edinburgh); **British Airways** (who link Birmingham with Aberdeen, Edinburgh and Glasgow; Bristol and Southampton with Edinburgh and Glasgow; London City with Edinburgh; London Gatwick with Aberdeen, Edinburgh, Glasgow, Inverness, the Isle of Man and Newcastle; London Heathrow with Aberdeen, Edinburgh, Glasgow, Manchester and Newcastle; Luton with the Isle of Man; Manchester with Aberdeen, Edinburgh, Glasgow, Inverness and the Isle of Man); **Ryanair** (who operate flights from Bournemouth and London Stansted to Glasgow Prestwick; Stansted to Blackpool for the Lake District, and Newquay in Cornwall); and **bmibaby** (London Heathrow and Norwich to Aberdeen; London Heathrow to Inverness; Birmingham to Edinburgh; Cardiff, London Heathrow, Manchester, Leeds/Bradford and Nottingham East Midlands to Edinburgh and Glasgow; Newquay to Durham Tees Valley). Fares on these domestic routes can drop as low as £25 return, depending on when you book, although a more realistic average is around £50 return.

However, flying really comes into its own in the **Scottish Highlands and Islands**, where a flight can save a day of travel by local bus and ferry. The remoter parts of Scotland have numerous minor airports – though some are little more than gravel strips – and fares are pretty reasonable: a one-way BA fare from Glasgow to Barra can set you back as little as £40. Most flights within Scotland are operated by British Airways or Loganair (a BA subsidiary), who combine to offer a number of discount air passes, but competition is beginning to emerge with **Highland Airways**, for example, flying a few routes from Inverness.

Airlines within Britain

Air Wales ☎ 0870/777 3131, ⊛ www.airwales.co.uk

bmibaby ☎ 0870/264 2229, ⊛ www.bmibaby.com

British Airways ☎ 0870/850 9850, ⊛ www.ba.com

easyJet ☎ 0905/821 0905 (premium line), ⊛ www.easyjet.com

flyBE ☎ 0871/700 0535, ⊛ www.flybe.com

Highland Airways ☎ 0845/450 2245, ⊛ www.highlandairways.co.uk

Loganair ☎ 0870/850 9850, ⊛ www.loganair.co.uk

Ryanair ☎ 0871/246 0000, ⊛ www.ryanair.com

Scot Airways ☎ 0870/606 0707, ⊛ www.scotairways.com

Trains

The **British rail network** does not compare favourably with other European systems either in terms of efficiency or cost, at least in part because the national network was privatized and broken up into a number of different companies several years ago – still a real sore point for many Brits. That said, few major towns in **England** lack rail links and mainline routes out of London are fast and frequent – York or Exeter, for instance, can be reached in two hours – though travelling cross-country, east–west, can be a real pain, often involving a couple of train changes. **Scotland**, on the other hand, has a more modest rail network, at its densest in the central belt between Edinburgh and Glasgow, at its most skeletal in the Highlands, and all-but-nonexistent in the Islands. The West Highland Line, from Glasgow to Fort William, deserves a mention as probably the most scenic train ride in Britain. In **Wales**, there are only two main lines, one

in the north from Chester to Holyhead, the other in the south running from Newport to Fishguard. In all instances, an essential first call for timetable and route information is the **National Rail Enquiries** information line or website (see listing below).

Given the huge variety of available options, it's almost impossible to give any useful advice about the **cost of tickets**, except to say that the earlier you book, the cheaper your ticket will be. Travelling on a Friday, or just turning up at the station and buying a ticket, are the most expensive ways to go. The various train-operating companies have different names for different tickets, all with byzantine restrictions and arcane rules (for instance, it's often cheaper to travel return from the north to London, rather than from London to the north). Basically, the **cheapest tickets** need to be booked 7, 14 or even more days in advance and, as only limited numbers are issued, they sell out quickly. To give an idea of the differing fares, an open, fully flexible London–Manchester return ticket can cost £175-plus, while booking at least two weeks in advance (no refund, no changes), travelling off-peak and accepting certain restrictions can bring the return fare as low as £25.

You can buy through tickets at any station, though advance credit-card **reservations** can also be made through the rail companies themselves (National Rail Enquiries can supply the necessary contact name and number). Or use an **online booking** service – there are links from the National Rail Enquiries website, or see the listing below.

A seat **reservation** is usually included with the ticket – vital if you want to ensure a seat and not a perch in the corridor next to the toilets. At weekends and on public holidays, many long-distance services let you upgrade your ticket by buying a **first-class supplement** (£5–15), well worth paying if you're facing a five-hour journey on a popular route. If the station's ticket office is closed or does not have a vending machine, you may buy your ticket on the train. Otherwise, **boarding without a ticket** will render you liable to paying the full fare to your destination (ouch!).

Useful rail contacts

National Rail Enquiries ☎ 08457/484950, ⊛ www.nationalrail.co.uk. Advice on timetables,

routes, tickets and services throughout the country.
ⓦ www.seat61.com The world's finest train travel website. It's almost nerdishly comprehensive, with more detail than you ever wanted to know about train travel in the UK (and worldwide), but full of incredibly useful tips and links.

ⓦ www.thetrainline.com Ticket sales and seat reservations for any UK journey.

Rail passes

For overseas visitors planning to travel widely by train, a **Britrail pass** might be a wise investment. It gives unlimited travel in England, Scotland and Wales and is valid for varied periods of up to 1 month (consecutive days travel) or 2 months (flexi-travel). The pass is available in a wide variety of types, with first- and second-class versions, discounted Youth Passes (second-class only) and Senior Passes (first-class only). Other BritRail combo passes are tailored to families or small groups. Note that BritRail passes have to be bought **before you enter the UK**. Any good travel agent or tour operator can supply up-to-date information, or consult ⓦwww.raileurope.com (North America), ⓦwww.railplus.com.au (Australia) or ⓦwww.railplus.co.nz (New Zealand). **Eurail** passes (ⓦwww.eurail.com) are not valid in the UK, though they do provide discounts on the Eurostar service (see p.30) to England.

European residents (proof of residency required) can buy an **InterRail pass** (ⓦwww.raileurope.co.uk/inter-rail), which provides free, unlimited travel in the UK, as well as discounts on Eurostar and certain cross-Channel ferries.

In addition, some **UK discount passes** are available only in Britain itself, to locals and to visitors. These include the **Young Person's Railcard** (£20), available to full-time students and those aged between 16 and 25, and **Senior Railcard** for people over 60 (£20), both of which give a third off most fares. Families can buy a **Family Railcard** (£20), which entitles up to four adults to a 33 percent discount, and up to four children to a sixty percent reduction of the child's full fare. You can buy the passes at most UK stations – take along two passport photographs and proof of age or status.

Buses

Long-distance bus services duplicate many rail routes, very often at half the price of the train or less. Services between major towns and cities are frequent and the buses – often referred to as coaches – are modern and comfortable. However, journey times are often much slower than the equivalent train ride, partly due to traffic congestion.

By far the biggest operator is **National Express** (☎0870/5808080, ⓦwww.national express.com), whose network extends to every corner of England as well as parts of Wales; its sister company **Scottish Citylink** (☎0870/550 5050, ⓦwww.citylink .co.uk) takes over north of the border. On busy routes, and on any route at weekends and during holidays, it's advisable to book ahead, rather than just turn up. Fares are very reasonable, with big discounts for under-26s, over-60s and families, while advance-purchase fares and special deals are common – fares from £1 from London to major cities, for example. Overseas-passport-holders can buy a **BritXplorer** pass (in 7-, 14- or 28-day versions) in the UK, from National Express travel shops, or at major ports and airports, though you'd have to do a lot of bus travelling to make it pay.

Local bus services are run by a bewildering array of companies. In many cases, timetables and routes are well integrated, but it's increasingly the case that private companies duplicate the busiest routes in an attempt to undercut the opposition, leaving the more remote spots neglected. As a rule, the further away from urban areas you get, the less frequent and more expensive bus services become, but there are very few rural areas which aren't served by at least an occasional minibus.

In the summer, many national park areas support a network of **weekend and bank holiday buses**, taking visitors to beauty spots, villages and hiking trailheads. In addition, many rural areas not covered by other forms of public transport are served by inexpensive weekday **Postbus** minibuses (☎0845/774 0740, ⓦwww.royalmail.com /postbus), that carry mail and fare-paying passengers.

For up-to-date **information**, the website and phone service **Traveline** (☎0870/608 2608, ⓦwww.traveline.org.uk) has details of all national and local bus routes and schedules.

Driving

In order **to drive** in the UK you need a current full driving licence. If you're bringing your own vehicle into the country you should also carry your vehicle registration, ownership and insurance documents at all times.

In Britain you **drive on the left**. Motorways – "M" roads – and main "A" roads have four or six lanes, but you should still expect crowded roads and delays at peak travel times and on public holidays. In the country, on "B" roads and minor roads, there might only be one lane (single track), so you need to drive carefully – especially as locals (who know the roads) tend to assume there's nothing else coming. Also, don't underestimate the British weather – snow, ice, fog and wind cause havoc every year, and driving conditions on motorways as much as in rural areas can deteriorate quickly. Local radio stations and national Radio Five Live feature constantly updated traffic bulletins.

Speed limits are 20–40mph in built-up areas, 70mph on motorways and dual carriageways (freeways) and 60mph on most other roads. As a rule, assume that in any area with street lighting the speed limit is 30mph unless otherwise stated. The UK has so far resisted toll roads (apart from one or two minor examples), but the principle has been broached by the success of **congestion charging** in London – if you intend to drive a car into central London, there is a charge – see p.82 for more.

Fuel is expensive – unleaded petrol (gasoline) and diesel cost in the region of £1 per litre, a little more for leaded 4-star. The lowest prices of all are charged at out-of-town supermarkets; suburban service stations are usually fairly reasonable; and the highest prices are charged by motorway stations.

The AA (Automobile Association; ⓦwww .theaa.com), RAC (Royal Automobile Club; ⓦwww.rac.co.uk) and Green Flag (ⓦwww .greenflag.co.uk) all operate **24-hour emergency breakdown** services, as well as other motoring and leisure facilities (including useful online route plans). You may be able to arrange breakdown cover with the AA or RAC during your stay in Britain through a motoring organization in your home country – check with your own association before setting out. Alternatively, you can make use of these emergency services if you are not a member of the organization, but you will need to join at the roadside and will incur a hefty surcharge for doing so.

Parking

Car parking in towns, cities and popular tourist spots can be a nightmare and will cost you a small fortune. If you're in a tourist city for a day, look out for **park-and-ride schemes** where you can park on the outskirts and take a cheap or free bus to the centre. Parking in long- or short-stay **car parks** will be cheaper than using on-street meters, which restrict parking time to two or three hours at the most. As a rule, the smaller the town, the cheaper the parking. Some towns operate free **disc-zone parking**, which allows limited-hours town-centre parking in designated areas: if that's what roadside signs indicate, you need to pick up a cardboard disc from any local shop and display it in your windscreen. A yellow line along the edge of the road indicates **parking restrictions**; check the nearest sign to see exactly what they are. A double-yellow line means no parking at any time, though you can stop briefly to unload or pick up people or goods, while a red line means absolutely no stopping at all.

Vehicle rental

Car rental is usually cheaper arranged in advance from home through one of the large multinational chains (Avis, Budget, Hertz, Holiday Autos, National or Thrifty, for example), or through your tour operator as part of a fly-drive package.

If you rent a car from a company in the UK (see below), expect to pay around £20 per day, £50 for a weekend or from £140 per week. You can sometimes find last-minute or Web fares of under £15 per day, through companies such as easyCar, though you'll need to book well in advance for the cheapest rates and be prepared for extra charges (like cleaning fees). Otherwise, small **local agencies** often undercut the major chains – we've highlighted some in the "Listings" sections of certain towns and cities. **Automatics** are rare at the lower end of the price scale – if you want one, you should book well ahead. Few companies will rent to drivers with less than one year's experience and most will only rent to people between 21 and 75 years of age.

For **camper van** rental, Just Go (☎0870/240 1918, ⊛www.justgo.uk.com) can supply quality vehicles sleeping four to six people, equipped with CD/DVD, full bathrooms, kitchen and bike racks. Rates range from £350 to £950 per week, depending on the vehicle and season; minimum hire is five days (winter) or seven days (summer).

Car rental companies in the UK

Avis ☎0870/010 0287, ⊛www.avis.co.uk
Budget ☎08701/539 170, ⊛www.budget.co.uk
easyCar ☎0906/333 3333, ⊛www.easycar.com
Europcar ☎0845/607 5000, ⊛www.europcar
.co.uk
Hertz ☎0870/844 8844, ⊛www.hertz.co.uk
Holiday Autos ☎0870/400 0099, ⊛www
.holidayautos.co.uk
National ☎0870/536 5365, ⊛www.nationalcar
.co.uk
Suncars ☎0870/500 5566, ⊛www.suncars
.com
Thrifty ☎01494/751600, ⊛www.thrifty.co.uk

Cycling

No one would choose to get around Britain by **cycling** on the main "A" roads – there's simply too much traffic and cyclists are given scant regard by many motorists – and bicycles are not permitted on motorways at all. If you have to use the roads, it's far better to stick to the quieter "B" roads, and country lanes, which generally have enough pubs and B&Bs to make the experience pleasant. Best of all, however, is to follow one of the **traffic-free trails** of the extensive National Cycle Network – for more on which see the section on "Sports and outdoor activities" (p.61).

Surprisingly, **cycle helmets** are not compulsory in the UK – but if you're hell-bent on tackling the congestion, pollution and aggression of city traffic, you're well advised to wear one. You do have to have a **rear reflector** and front and back **lights** when riding at night, and you are not allowed to carry children without a special **child seat**. It is also illegal to cycle on pavements (sidewalks), and in most public parks, while **off-road** cyclists must stick to bridleways and byways designated for their use.

Bike rental is available at cycle shops in most large towns, and at villages within national parks and other scenic areas; contact details are given in the Guide. Expect to pay around £15–20 per day, with discounts for longer periods; you may have to provide credit card details, or leave a passport as a deposit.

Accommodation

Britain has hundreds of hotels, ranging from plain, chain motorway motels to lavish country retreats, as well as budget accommodation in bed-and-breakfasts (B&Bs), guest houses and hostels. You'll want to stay in at least one nicely refurbished old building – the historic towns of Britain are full of former coaching inns and similarly ancient hostelries – while out in the countryside there are numerous converted mansions and manor houses, often with brilliant restaurants attached. That said, the standard of many middle-market hotels, more especially in England than Scotland and Wales, can be very disappointing, though we have, as you would expect, omitted them from this guide.

Nearly all tourist offices will **reserve rooms** for you. In some areas you pay a deposit that's deducted from your first night's bill (usually ten percent), in others the office will take a percentage or flat-rate commission – usually around £3. Another useful service is the "Book-a-bed-ahead" service, which locates accommodation in your next port of call – again for a charge of about £3, though the service is sometimes free.

A nationwide **grading system** awards stars to hotels (five stars is the top rank), guest houses and B&Bs. There's not a hard and fast correlation between rank and price, but the grading system does lay down minimum levels of standards and service albeit in objectively observable areas – the number of en-suite rooms, range of facilities and so forth – and as a result, a five-star hotel is not necessarily going to be a better place to stay than a simple B&B. On the whole, British people don't tend to insist on seeing a room before taking it (unlike,

say, in France or Spain), but you shouldn't be afraid to ask – any place worth its salt, be it designer hotel or humble B&B, should have no objection.

Hotels

Hotels vary wildly in size, style and comfort, but the starting price for one-star accommodation is around £60 per night for a double/twin room, breakfast usually included. Three-star hotels can easily cost £100 a night, while four- and five-star properties charge up to £200 a night, often considerably more in London or in resort or country-house hotels. It's worth noting that many upper-end town and city hotels charge a room-rate only – breakfast can be another £10 or £15 on top.

However, many larger urban hotels offer cut-price **weekend rates** to fill the rooms vacated by the weekday business trade. Also, an increasing number of budget hotel chains – *Premier Travel Inn*

Accommodation price codes

Throughout this guide, accommodation is graded on a scale of ❶ to ❾, the number indicating the lowest price you could expect to pay per night in that establishment for a **double room in high season**. Breakfast is included unless otherwise stated. We've given the exact cost for **dorm accommodation** in youth and backpackers' hostels, and student halls of residence, as well as price codes for those hostels that have private double rooms.

❶ under £40	❹ £61–70	❼ £111–150
❷ £41–50	❺ £71–90	❽ £151–200
❸ £51–60	❻ £91–110	❾ over £201

don't expect a great deal of space (or indeed a bath) in these "bathrooms".

In some traditional resorts, like Blackpool, Largs and Skegness, competition is such that you'll be able to get a room for as little as £12–15 per person, though around £40 per night for a double or twin room is more normal. At this price, however, expect to share bathroom facilities with other guests.

Above these prices – say from £60–70 per room – you can expect a range of services and facilities such as fresh flowers, gourmet breakfasts, king-sized beds and quality bathrooms. Many B&Bs and small guest houses have raised their game in recent years and some are truly excellent. Note that many B&Bs don't have single rooms, so **solo travellers** should expect to pay 60–80 percent of the going rate to occupy a double.

Finally, don't assume that a B&B is no good if it's ungraded. There are so many B&Bs in the UK that the inspectors can't possibly keep track of them all, and in the rural backwaters some of the most enjoyable accommodation is to be found in **farmhouses** and other properties whose facilities may technically fall short of official standards.

In towns and villages, many **pubs** also offer B&B, again often not graded. Standards vary wildly – some are great, others truly awful – but at best you'll be staying in a friendly spot with a sociable bar on hand, and you'll rarely pay more than £60 a room.

(Ⓦwww.premiertravelinn.co.uk), *Holiday Inn Express* (Ⓦwww.hiexpress.com), *Jury's Doyle* (Ⓦwww.jurys.hotel-and-inn.com), *Comfort Inn* and *Quality Inn* (both Ⓦwww.choice hotelseurope.com), and others – have properties usefully located in city centres across the country. The style at these tends towards the no-frills (with breakfast charged extra), but at £50–60 for an en-suite room (often sleeping up to four), they're a good deal for families and people travelling in small groups.

B&Bs and guest houses

At its most basic, the typical British **bed-and-breakfast (B&B)** is an ordinary private house with a couple of bedrooms set aside for paying guests. Larger establishments with more rooms, particularly in resorts, style themselves **guest houses**, but they are basically the same thing.

Even in the most basic of places, you should get a sink, a TV and a kettle in the room, and the use of a guest lounge. These days, many B&Bs and guest houses have en-suite shower and toilet facilities – you'll pay a few pounds more for the privilege, but

Useful contacts

B&B My Guest ☎0870/444 3840, Ⓦwww.beduk .co.uk. Online bookings at 300 traditional or historic B&B properties.
Distinctly Different ☎01225/866842, Ⓦwww .distinctlydifferent.co.uk. Stay the night in converted buildings across the country, from old brothel to Baptist chapel, windmill to lighthouse.
Farm Stay UK ☎0247/669 6909, free brochure on ☎01271/336141, Ⓦwww.farmstay.co.uk. The largest network of farm-based accommodation in the UK.
Wolsey Lodges ☎01473/822058, Ⓦwww .wolseylodges.com. Superior B&B in inspected properties across England, from Elizabethan manor houses to Victorian rectories.

Hostels, camping barns and student halls

The **Youth Hostels Association** (YHA; ☎0870/770 8868, ⓦwww.yha.org.uk) has over 200 properties in England and Wales and the **Scottish Youth Hostels Association** (SYHA; ☎0870/155 3255, ⓦwww.syha.org.uk) has around 70 properties in Scotland. Both are affiliated to Hostelling International (HI) and both are responsible for a wide range of premises, from big old houses to thatched cottages, offering bunk-bed accommodation in single-sex dormitories or smaller rooms of four to six beds. Many hostels now also have private double and family rooms available, and in cities the facilities are often every bit as good as some budget hotels. Indeed, most hostels have moved well away from the old-fashioned, institutional ambience, and many boast laundry facilities, Internet access, a sitting room, cycle stores, even cafés and bike rental.

You no longer have to be a member to use a YHA/SYHA hostel, though non-members pay a small supplement for accommodation and aren't eligible for any other hostel discounts or benefits. Otherwise, adult **membership** of the YHA costs £15.50 per year, £22 for joint/family, or from £10 for under-26s, whilst the SYHA charges just £6 per adult with children under 18 given free membership when their parent/guardian joins. Overseas visitors who belong to any **International Youth Hostel Federation** (IYHF) association in their own country have automatic membership of the YHA; if you aren't an IYHF member, you can join the YHA/SYHA in person at any affiliated hostel on your first night's stay.

Prices for members at most hostels are around £11–14 per person per night (£8–10 for under-18s), though in cities such as York, Oxford and London the overnight price is more like £17–20 (under-18s £15–17). Length of stay is normally unlimited and the hostel will provide bed linen, pillows and duvet. Hostel meals – breakfast, packed lunch or dinner – are always good value (around a fiver), while nearly all hostels also have self-catering kitchens.

It's best to book well in advance, especially as many hostels operate irregular opening days, and it's well nigh essential to do so if you want to stay at Easter, in July and August and at Christmas. You can book online, and most hostels accept payment by Master-Card or Visa. If you're tempted to turn up on spec, bear in mind that very few hostels are open year-round, many are closed at least one day a week, even in high season, and several have periods during which they take bookings from groups only. Always check – we've given the phone number and email for every hostel mentioned.

A number of independent **backpacker hostels** offer similar facilities to the YHA at much the same prices. They tend to attract a more youthful, backpacking (rather than the YHA's family/hiker) crowd, and they usually don't have membership requirements or curfews. A useful publication is the annually updated **Independent Hostel Guide** (Backpackers Press; ⓦwww.backpackerspress.com). The website ⓦwww.backpackers.co.uk also gives the lowdown on independent hostels and budget accommodation.

In the wilder parts of England and Wales – for example in the north Pennines, Snowdonia, the Lake District, Peak District, Dartmoor and Exmoor – the YHA administers some basic accommodation for walkers in **camping barns**. Housing up to twenty people, these agricultural outbuildings are often unheated and sparsely furnished, with wooden sleeping platforms – or bunks if you're lucky – a couple of tables, a toilet and cold-water supply, but they are weatherproof and extremely good value (from £5 a night); the thirteen Lake District barns have their own website, ⓦwww.lakelandcampingbarns.co.uk. The SYHA's equivalent is its chain of Rustic Hostels, often old crofters' cottages, also in isolated places and similarly frugal and inexpensive. Many parts of the UK also have privately run barns, also known as **bunkhouses** (or **bothies** in Scotland), with prices starting at around £8–10 per night.

In the UK's university towns you can often find out-of-term accommodation (Easter & Christmas holidays, plus July to Sept) in **student halls of residence**, in one-bedded rooms either with their own or shared bathrooms, or in self-contained flats with self-catering facilities. Prices start at around £15 per night, not always including breakfast. In some instances (such as Durham) where there's no youth hostel, this may be the only budget accommodation on offer in the city centre. All the useful university details are given in the Guide, but if you want a list of everything that's on offer, contact the Summer Village (℡0870/712 5002, ⓦwww .thesummervillage.com) or Venuemasters (℡0114/249 3090, ⓦwww.venuemasters .co.uk).

Camping and caravanning

There are hundreds of **campsites** in the UK, charging from £5 per tent per night in simple, family-run places to around £12 a night on large sites with laundries, shops and sports facilities. Some hostels also have small campsites on their property, charging half the indoor overnight price per person.

In addition to official sites, **farmers** may offer pitches for as little as £2 per night, but don't expect tiled bathrooms and hair dryers for that kind of money. Even farmers without a reserved camping area may let you pitch in a field if you ask first – but setting up a tent without asking will not be well received. **Camping rough** is illegal in national parks and nature reserves.

The problem with many campsites in the most popular parts of rural and coastal Britain is that tents have to share the space with **caravans**. Every summer the country's byways are clogged by migrations of these cumbersome trailers, which are still far more numerous than camper vans (RVs). The great majority of caravans, however, are permanently moored at their sites, where they are rented out for self-catering holidays.

Detailed, annually revised guides to the UK's camping and caravan sites include the official *Caravan and Camping Parks in Britain*, available in all major bookshops.

Self-catering accommodation

There are thousands of properties for rent in the UK, ranging from city penthouses to secluded cottages. **Studios and apartments** available by the night in an increas-

ing number of British cities offer an attractive alternative to hotel stays, with prices from around £100 a night, or from £140 in London. Rural self-catering **cottages and houses** work out cheaper, though the minimum rental period is usually a week. The least you can expect to pay for a small cottage sleeping four people in mid-winter would be around £200 per week, but in summer for a house near the West Country moors or in the Lake District you should budget for £500 and upwards.

We've listed some of the main **agencies** below, but every regional tourist board has details of cottage rentals in its area. Otherwise, Stilwell's (℡01305/250151, ⓦwww .stilwell.co.uk) can send you their free annual guide, *Independent Holiday Cottages*, where you select your property and then book direct with the cottage owners.

Houses and cottages

Cornish Cottage Holidays ℡01326/573808, ⓦwww.cornishcottageholidays.co.uk. Lots of thatched cottages and seaside places in the West Country.
Country Holidays ℡08700/781200, from overseas 01282/846137, ⓦwww.country-holidays .co.uk. More than 4000 properties all over the UK.
Heart of the Lakes ℡015394/33251, ⓦwww .heartofthelakes.co.uk. Excellent choice of over 300 quality properties in the Lake District.
Helpful Holidays ℡01647/433593, ⓦwww .helpfulholidays.com. Everything from cottage rentals to a castle, throughout the West Country.
Hoseasons Holidays ℡01502/502588, ⓦwww .hoseasons.co.uk. Holiday lodges and country cottages throughout England.
Landmark Trust ℡01628/825925, ⓦwww .landmarktrust.org.uk. Their handbook (£11 – refundable on first booking) lists over 180 converted historic properties, ranging from restored forts and Martello towers to a tiny radio shack used in World War II. UK-wide.
Mackay's Agency ℡ 0870/429 5359, ⓦwww .mackays-scotland.co.uk. A whole range of self-catering cottages across the whole of Scotland.
National Trust ℡0870/458 4422, ⓦwww .nationaltrustcottages.co.uk. The NT owns 320 English and Welsh cottages, houses and farmhouses, most set in their own gardens or grounds.
National Trust for Scotland ℡ 0131/243 9300, ⓦwww.nts.org.uk. The NTS lets out around fifty of its converted historic cottages and houses.

Rural Retreats ☎01386/701177, ⓦwww
.ruralretreats.co.uk. Upmarket accommodation
in restored old buildings, many of them listed.
Britain-wide.

Scottish Country Cottages ☎08700/781100,
ⓦwww.countrycottagesinscotland.co.uk. Superior
cottages with lots of character scattered across
Scotland.

Wales Cottage Holidays ☎01686/628200,
ⓦwww.wales-holidays.co.uk. A varied selection of
500 properties all over Wales.

Studios and apartments

Apartment Service ☎0208/944 1444, ⓦwww
.apartmentservice.com. Studios and apartments in
towns and cities all over England.

Holiday Serviced Apartments ☎0845/060
4477, ⓦwww.holidayapartments.co.uk. Available in
London, Brighton and Cambridge.

Serviced Stays ☎0800/093 5383, ⓦwww
.servicedstays.com. Apartments in London and
Bristol.

Eating and drinking

Though the British still tend to regard eating as a functional necessity rather
than a sociable pleasure, things are improving. Over the last decade, changing
popular tastes have transformed both supermarket shelves and café/restaurant
menus, while there's an increasing importance placed on "proper" food, whether
free-range, organic, humanely produced or locally sourced. In addition, a growing number of British chefs and restaurants are recognized as world-class, with
London now boasting more cutting-edge restaurants than New York. It's true
that visitors and holidaymakers may still encounter more than their fair share of
overpriced, over-rated or inedible meals, especially if travelling on a relentlessly
low budget, but there are, nevertheless, hundreds of good inexpensive or moderately priced restaurants to be found around the country. Moreover, for tourists
and locals alike, the pub remains the one great British social institution, and a
drink (and a meal) in a traditional "local" is still the best introduction to town or
village life.

Specialities and regional food

In many hotels and B&Bs you'll be offered an
"**English breakfast**" – or Welsh or Scottish in
the respective countries – which is basically
sausage, tomatoes, mushrooms, bacon and
eggs plus tea/coffee and toast. This used to
be the typical working-class start to the day,
but these days most British people have
adopted the cereal alternative; the majority
of places will give you this option as well.
Traditionally, a "**Scottish breakfast**" includes
oatmeal porridge eaten with salt (though
sugar is always on offer too). You may also
be served kippers or Arbroath smokies (delicately smoked haddock with butter), or a
large piece of haddock with a poached egg

on top. Oatcakes (plain savoury biscuits) and
a "buttery" – not unlike a French croissant
– will often feature; kippers and haddock are
common on English and Welsh breakfast
menus too.

For most overseas visitors the quintessential British meal is **fish and chips** (known in
Scotland as a "fish supper", even at lunchtime), a dish that can vary from the succu-
lently fresh to the indigestibly greasy: local
knowledge is the key, as most towns, cities
and resorts have at least one first-rate fish-
and-chip shop/restaurant – like Whitby's
Magpie Café (see p.628) or *Stein's Fish &
Chips* in Padstow (see p.377).

Other **traditional British dishes** are just
as ubiquitous – steak and kidney pie, liver

and onions, lamb chops, roast beef or roast chicken all figure on menu after menu in cafés, pubs and restaurants across the land. Unfortunately, though, far too many places churn out very average examples that conform to every negative stereotype about British cooking – overcooked meat, soggy veg, frozen chips and lumpy gravy. However, for every dismal meal served, there's a local café or restaurant somewhere providing excellent food at reasonable prices, from fresh soup using local, seasonal ingredients to homemade ice cream.

There's also been a revival of traditional British cuisine in the more fashionable restaurants, with some of the UK's top chefs presenting their own versions of the British working-class classics. These dishes are sometimes known as **Modern British** (or Modern English) cuisine, though this can also refer to an inventive mix of local, seasonal produce with continental, Asian or even Pacific Rim ingredients and techniques.

There's a new emphasis, too, on the importance of local growers and suppliers, and many cafés and restaurants now boast locally sourced or organic ingredients. Partly as a result, **regional specialities** are increasingly found in simple cafés and top restaurants alike, from something as basic as a proper Cornish pasty (just steak, turnip and potatoes) to Lancashire hotpot (lamb

Some traditional British dishes and foods

Bara brith – a fruit bread found in all Welsh teashops

Black pudding – blood sausage, particularly popular in the north of England

Bread and butter pudding – slices of buttered white bread layered together, covered in milk or custard, sprinkled liberally with sugar and sultanas, and baked until golden

Bubble and squeak – fried leftover potato and cabbage (and sometimes other veg)

Chip butty – a chip sandwich

Crumble – a dessert of stewed fruit topped with a crunchy cooked mix of butter, flour and sugar. Can also refer to savoury, usually vegetable, dishes (without the sugar).

Faggott – an offal meatball

Haggis – a sheep's stomach stuffed with spiced liver, offal, oatmeal and onion, traditionally eaten with bashed neeps (mashed turnips) and chappit tatties (mashed potatoes). The quintessential Scottish dish.

Laver bread (*bara lawr*) – a thoroughly tasty seaweed and oatmeal cake often included in a traditional fried breakfast in Wales

Mushy peas – soaked and boiled marrowfat peas, almost a paste, served with fish and chips

Piccalilli – a mustard pickle

Ploughman's lunch – a cheese (or sometimes ham), pickle, bread and salad plate

Shepherds' pie – savoury minced lamb topped with mashed potato (made with minced beef, it's a cottage pie)

Spotted dick – a dessert, a suet pudding with currants

Sticky toffee pudding – a national favourite, consisting of a wedge of steamed sponge drenched in a lip-smacking, caramelized hot-toffee sauce.

Stovies – a Scottish favourite, comprising a tasty mash of onion and fried potato heated up with minced beef

Toad-in-the-hole – sausages baked in Yorkshire pudding

Trifle – a wobbly, semi-solid concoction of biscuits or cake soaked in brandy with layers of fruit jelly, everything topped with custard, crystallized fruits and sugary icing bits

Yorkshire puddings – oven-baked batter cups, traditionally served with roast beef

and potato stew). The increasing interest in regional authenticity, however, can make ordering problematic – a simple bread roll, for example, is referred to as a roll, cob, bap, barmcake, teacake or bread-bun, depending on which part of Britain you're in; see above for more oddly named dishes.

Vegetarians are fairly well catered for in Britain. Away from London and the big cities, specialist vegetarian places are thin on the ground, but most restaurants and pubs have at least one vegetarian option on their menus, while Italian, Indian and Chinese restaurants usually provide a decent choice of meat-free dishes. For a list of vegetarian establishments, check the Veg Dining website (ⓦwww.vegdining.com).

Where to eat

Every town, city and resort has a selection of cheap **cafés**, characteristically unassuming places offering nonalcoholic drinks, all-day breakfasts, snacks and meals. Most are only open during the day, and tend to be cash-only establishments with few airs and graces. **Teashops** or **tearooms** tend to be more genteel, and serve a range of sandwiches, cakes, scones and light meals throughout the day, as well, of course, as tea.

Old-fashioned chrome-and-formica **coffee bars** – almost always Italian in origin – can now only be found in London and a few, mostly seaside, towns. They have been replaced by the ubiquitous American-style chain coffee shops, such as *Starbuck's, Coffee Republic* and *Caffè Nero*, which serve espresso, lattés, muffins and sandwiches.

Licensed **café-bars** on the European model are now commonplace, too – although primarily places to drink, an increasing number serve reasonably priced food. Given the challenge posed by the newcomers, **pubs** that serve food have had to raise their game and many (both rural and urban) have embraced the change in British tastes – indeed, the **gastropub** (more of an informal restaurant) is now a recognized fixture in many villages, towns and cities.

Britain's postwar immigrant communities have contributed greatly to the country's dining experience and even the smallest town boasts an **ethnic restaurant**, usually Indian (often Bangladeshi or Pakistani) or Chinese (mostly Cantonese). Most are relatively inexpensive, with the best – and most authentic – in London and the industrial cities of the Midlands (Birmingham, Leicester) and the Northwest (Manchester, Liverpool). Indeed, in many ways, the curry house is now the quintessential British restaurant, with dishes such as **chicken tikka masala** (chicken in a creamy, spicy, tomato sauce) being more popular than the traditional fish and chips. Most small towns also have the budget stand-bys, Italian restaurants and pizza places, while Spanish tapas bars, Thai restaurants and French chain bistros are well represented too.

It goes without saying that London has the best selection of **top-class restaurants**, and the widest choice of cuisines, but visitors to Manchester, Birmingham, Bristol, Leeds and other major cities hardly suffer these days. Indeed, wherever you are in the UK you're rarely more than half an hour's drive from a really good meal – and some of the very best dining experiences can be found in a suburban back street or quiet village rather than a metropolitan hot-spot. Heston Blumenthal's three-Michelin-starred *Fat Duck*, for example – often touted as the world's best restaurant – is in the small Berkshire village of Bray.

Of course, **eating out** at this level is expensive, with tasting menus at the UK's best-known Michelin-starred restaurants costing £75–100 per person. True, a great curry in London's Brick Lane, or a Cantonese feast in Manchester's Chinatown, can still be had for under £12 a head, but at even modest restaurants in the country, you can expect to pay around £20 per person for a full meal with drinks. In a decent pub, a main course

Restaurant prices

Restaurants listed in this guide have been assigned one of four price categories:

Inexpensive	under £12.50
Moderate	£12.50–20
Expensive	£20–35
Very Expensive	over £35

This is the price you can expect to pay per person for a three-course meal or equivalent, excluding drinks and service.

averages £8–9, while in a restaurant with any sort of local reputation, you'll pay £25–35 each.

Restaurants reviewed in this guide are open for **lunch** (usually noon–2/3pm) and **dinner** (7–11pm) unless otherwise stated. Pub kitchens often close in the afternoon – between about 2pm and 6pm – and on one or two evenings a week, often Sunday and Monday; few serve food after about 8.30/9pm. **Reservations** are recommended for all popular restaurants, especially at weekends – and the most famous British restaurants will require advance reservations weeks (or months) in advance. **Credit cards**, in particular American Express, are not always accepted, especially at small places, or out in the sticks.

Pubs and bars

Originating as wayfarers' hostelries and coaching inns, **pubs** have outlived the church and marketplace as the focal points of many a UK town and village. They are as varied as the country's townscapes: in larger market towns you'll find huge oak-beamed inns with open fires and polished brass fittings; in remoter upland villages there are stone-built pubs no larger than a two-bedroomed cottage. At its best, the pub can be as welcoming as the full name – "public house" – suggests. Sometimes, particularly in the more inward-looking parts of industrial Britain, you might have to dig deeper for a welcome, especially in those no-nonsense pubs where something of the old division of the sexes still holds sway – the "spit and sawdust" **public bar** is where working men can bond over a pint or two; the plusher **saloon bar**, with a separate entrance, is the preferred haunt of couples and women.

Traditional opening hours in England and Wales are Monday–Saturday 11am–11pm, Sunday noon–10.30pm, with or without an afternoon break from around 2.30pm or 3pm to 5.30pm or 6pm. "Last orders" are called five to ten minutes before closing and you then have thirty minutes to drink up before you are chucked out. However, recent changes in the legislation regarding licensing hours mean that many pubs now stay **open later**, for the most part till midnight at least on Friday and Saturday nights, even later in the big city centres. A similar state of affairs exists in Scotland, but the licensing laws were relaxed here a few years ago. The legal **drinking age** is 18 and unless there's a special family room or a beer garden, children are not always welcome.

Beer and wine

The most widespread type of English and Welsh beer is **bitter**, a dark, uncarbonated brew which should be pumped by hand from the cellar and served at room temperature. If it comes out of an electric pump, it isn't the real thing. Controversy exists over the head of foam on top: in southern England, people prefer their pint without a head, and brimming to the top of the glass; in the North and Scotland, flat beer is frowned on and drinkers prefer a short head of foam. Sweeter, darker **mild** and stronger **porter** are quite common in Welsh pubs, though virtually extinct in England. Traditional Scottish beer is a thick, dark ale known as **heavy**, graded by a shilling mark (/-) and served with a full head. Nevertheless, cold, blonde, fizzy **lager** is now more popular than bitter just about everywhere: every pub will have at least two or three brands on offer, but rarely is it a patch on bitter – as **CAMRA**, the influential Campaign for Real Ale (ⓦwww.camra.org.uk), has long been at pains to point out.

The big breweries, who own hundreds of pubs, do distribute some good bitters – Adnams, Boddingtons, John Smith and Tetley beers are, for example, fairly commonplace – but the real glory of British beer is in the local detail. Hundreds of medium-sized and small breweries still produce what are known as "**real ales**" to traditional recipes; some are widely available, others confined to one village or even just one pub.

In England's West Country, **cider**, the fermented produce of apples, is the traditional drink rather than bitter. It comes in various forms, but the most authentic is **scrumpy**, a potent and cloudy beverage that is rarely sold in pubs outside the Southwest and Shropshire, though supermarkets everywhere frequently stock it. Incidentally, scrumpy has little in common with the fizzy and very sweet cider – principally Strongbow – sold in pubs all over Britain. **Guinness**, a dark, creamy Irish stout, is popular world-wide and is on sale in hundreds of UK pubs, though purists will tell you that it doesn't compare with the stuff sold in Ireland.

The British also consume an enormous quantity of **wine**, though the wine sold in pubs is generally appalling, a strange situation in view of the excellent range of vintages available in many an off-licence and super-market.

Whisky

Scotland's national drink is **whisky** – *uisge beatha*, the "water of life" in Gaelic (and almost never referred to as "scotch") – traditionally drunk in pubs with a half-pint of beer on the side, a combination known as a "nip and a hauf". There are two types of whisky: **single malt**, made from malted barley, and **grain whisky**, which is made from maize and a little malted barley in a continuous still. **Blended whisky**, which accounts for more than ninety percent of all sales, is a mixture of the two types, with each brand's distinctive flavour coming from the malt whisky which is added to the grain in different quantities: the more expensive the blend, the higher the proportion of malts that have gone into it. Johnnie Walker, Bells, Teachers and The Famous Grouse are some of the best-known blended whiskies. All have a similar flavour, and are drunk neat or with water, sometimes with mixers such as soda or lemonade (though these additions may horrify your fellow drinkers).

Single malt whisky is infinitely superior, and, as a result, a great deal more expensive. It is best drunk neat or with a splash of water to release its distinctive flavours. Single malts vary enormously depending on the amount of peat used for drying the barley, the water used for mashing, and the type of oak cask used in the maturing process. The two most important whisky regions are **Speyside**, which produces famous varieties such as Glenlivet, Glenfiddich and Macallan, and **Islay**, which produces distinctively peaty whiskies such as Laphroaig, Lagavulin and Ardbeg.

Post, phones and the Internet

Britain has a comprehensive communications system, with post offices, post boxes and public telephone boxes liberally distributed across the country. The British have taken to the mobile phone in their millions and you can get a signal almost everywhere. Internet access is similarly commonplace. The "Listings" sections of our town and city accounts usually include service addresses and locations, but general information – about opening hours and so on – is given below.

Post and mail

The national postal system is operated by **Royal Mail** (℡08457/740740, ⓦwww.royalmail.com), whose customer service line and website provide the current cost of stamps and services and can help you find individual post offices. Virtually all **post offices** are open Monday to Friday from 9am to 5.30pm, and on Saturdays from 9am to 12.30 or 1pm. In London and other major cities main offices stay open all day Saturday. In small and rural communities you'll find sub-post offices operating out of general stores, though post office facilities are only available during the hours above even if the shop itself is open for longer. Note that you can often buy **stamps** at newsagents and other shops, as well as at post offices.

Telephones

The UK's telephone network has been privatized, though one company, British Telecom (BT), still operates the bulk of the system. Public **pay phones** are plentiful and take coins; most also accept phone- and credit cards. **Peak period** (Mon–Fri 8am–6pm) calls are more expensive than at the weekend or in the evening – and the same applies to **international calls**, though in both cases public pay-phone rates are higher than those applied to private phones. Most hotel rooms have telephones, but there is almost always an exorbitant surcharge for their use.

You can make direct-dial international phone calls from any telephone box, using coins or your credit card, though it's usually cheaper to buy a **phonecard**, available from many newsagents in denominations of £5, £10 and upwards. You dial the company's local access number, key in the pin number on the card and then dial your number. Posters detailing tariffs are displayed wherever the cards are sold. Your phone company back home may also provide a **telephone charge card**, with which, using a local access number and a PIN number, you can make calls from most hotel, public and private phones that will be charged to your own telephone account. Bear in mind, however, that rates aren't necessarily cheaper than making an ordinary call.

Every British landline number is prefixed by an **area code**, which can (but does not have to) be omitted when you are dialling a local number. However, some prefixes relate to the cost of calls rather than the location of the subscriber, including ☎0800 and ☎0808 prefixes, which are free of charge to the caller, and ☎0845 and ☎0870 numbers, where callers are charged at local rates irrespective of where they call from. Beware of **premium-rate numbers**, which are common for pre-recorded information services (including some tourist authorities), and have the prefix ☎09; these are charged at anything up to £1.50 a minute. The prefix ☎07 is for mobile phones.

For domestic and international **directory enquiries**, there are numerous competing information lines, all of them expensive. BT's domestic service, on ☎118 500, is as good as any (and it's free online at ⓦwww.bt.com); its international directory assistance number is ☎118 505. Or you can look business and service numbers up for free on the very useful ⓦwww.yell.com.

Across the UK, **mobile/cell phone** access is routine in all the major cities and in most of the countryside. There are occasional blind spots, and coverage can be patchy in rural and hill areas, but generally you should have few problems. If you want to use your mobile phone in the UK, you'll need to check cellular access with your phone provider before you set out. Also check out their **call charges** as these can be exorbitant, especially as you are likely to be charged for incoming calls that originate from back home as the people calling you will be paying the usual (local) rate. The same sometimes applies to **text messages**, though in most cases these can now be received with the greatest of ease – no fiddly codes and so forth – and at ordinary rates. In Britain, the mobile network works on GSM 900/1800. Mobiles bought in **North America** need to be **triband** to access the British network.

International calls

To call the UK from overseas: dial your international access code + ☎ 44 + area code minus initial zero + number.
To call overseas from the UK: dial your country code (**US and Canada** ☎001; **Australia** ☎0061; **Republic of Ireland** ☎00353; **New Zealand** ☎0064) + area code minus initial zero if present + number.
International operator ☎155

Internet access

There are **Internet cafés** in virtually every town and resort in Britain, while an increasing number of hotels, guest houses, hostels and tourist offices have Internet terminals for public use. Opening hours vary (count on shop hours at least), though you'll only tend to find late-night and 24-hour access in London. Charges vary wildly, but average around £2–3 an hour. Almost every **public library** in the country also offers Internet access for free, though you may be limited to 30 minutes or so.

The media

The British are fond of their daily newspapers and there are a lot to choose from, though most are drearily right-wing. As well as the nationals, most regions have their own local titles, and newsagents' shelves are stacked high with magazines of every description. As regards TV, there are five universal, terrestrial channels. Three are commercial and two are state subsidized, operated by the British Broadcasting Company (BBC). Broadcasting standards are not as high as they used to be – though they still compare favourably with most of the rest of the world – at least in part because of the rise of satellite and cable channels. The BBC also runs an extensive network of radio stations, with the excellent Radio 4 serving as its political and contemporary affairs flagship.

Newspapers and magazines

From Monday to Saturday, four **daily newspapers** occupy the quality end of the **English** newspaper market: the Rupert Murdoch–owned *Times*, the staunchly conservative *Daily Telegraph*, and the left-of-centre *Independent* and *Guardian*. Amongst the red-top **tabloids**, the most popular is the *Sun*, a pernicious, muck-raking right-wing Murdoch paper whose chief rival is the traditionally left-leaning *Daily Mirror*. The middle-brow daily tabloids – the *Daily Mail* and the *Daily Express* – are noticeably (some would say rabidly) xenophobic and right-wing. England's oldest **Sunday newspaper** is *The Observer*, a centrist publication which supplements the Sunday editions of the dailies. Meanwhile, an army of **local newspapers** – at least one in every major town and city – provides an interesting outlook on British life, with local news, events and personalities to the fore. In **Scotland**, the principal English papers are widely available, often as specific Scottish editions. The Scottish press produces two major daily papers, the liberal-left *Scotsman* and the slightly less-so *Herald*. Scotland's best-selling daily paper is the downmarket *Daily Record*. Many national Sunday newspapers include a Scottish section, but Scotland's own Sunday "quality" is *Scotland on Sunday*. Far more fun is the tabloid *Sunday Post*, read by over half the population. In **Wales**, where again English papers are widely available, the only quality Welsh daily is the *Western Mail*, a mix of local, Welsh, British and international news. There is also one quality Sunday offering, *Wales on Sunday*.

Newsagents offer a range of **specialist magazines and periodicals** covering just about every subject, with motoring, music,

---

sport, computers, gardening and home improvements leading the way. *The Economist* is essential reading in many a boardroom; the left-wing alternative is the *New Statesman*. The satirical bi-weekly *Private Eye* is a much-loved institution that prides itself on printing the stories the rest of the press won't touch, and on riding the consequent stream of libel suits.

Australians and New Zealanders in London should look out for the weekly free magazine, *TNT*, which provides a résumé of news from home as well as jobs, accommodation and events in the capital. Otherwise, the *Wall Street Journal*, *USA Today* and the *International Herald Tribune* are widely distributed, as are the magazines *Time* and *Newsweek*.

Television

There are five universal, terrestrial **television stations** in the UK. These are divided between the state-funded BBC, who operate BBC1 and BBC2, and three independent commercial channels, ITV, Channel 4 and Channel 5 (the latter still not available everywhere in the UK). Despite complaints about a slip in standards, and periodic mutterings about the licence fee (paid by all British viewers), there's still more than enough quality to keep the **BBC** in good repute both at home and abroad. Of the two BBC channels, BBC 2 is the more offbeat and heavyweight, BBC 1 more avowedly populist. Various regional companies together form the **ITV** network, and they're united by a more tabloid approach to programme making – necessarily so, because if they don't get the advertising they don't survive. **Channel 4** is similarly influenced, but is the home of hit (and hip) US comedies and serials plus a fair slice of

sleaze and cheese, while the newer **Channel 5** is slowly moving up-market following a much-mocked, tawdry start.

The UK's **satellite** and **cable** TV companies are mounting a strong challenge to the erstwhile dominance of the terrestrial channels. Live sport, in particular, is increasingly in the hands of Sky, the major satellite provider, whose 24-hour rolling **Sky News** programme rivals that of CNN. In response, both the BBC and the other commercial channels have launched their own ventures, with the BBC's digital channels, notably **News 24** (rolling news), BBC3 (young adult) and BBC4 (arts and culture), and Channel 4's subscription film channel **Film Four** and its digital entertainment channel E4.

Radio

The BBC's **radio network** (Ⓦ www.bbc.co.uk/radio) has five nationwide stations. These are **Radio 1**, which is almost exclusively devoted to new chart and urban music, and specialist DJs; **Radio 2** (Britain's most listened-to radio station), a combination of pop and specialist music, plus arts programmes, interviews and documentaries; **Radio 3**, which focuses on classical music; **Radio 4**, a high-quality blend of current affairs, arts and drama; and **Five Live**, a 24-hour rolling sports and news channel.

All have faced tough challenges for market share in recent years, the hardest hit being Radio 1, whose rivals include a plethora of local commercial stations, most notably London's **Capital Radio** (95.8 FM) and **Heart** (106.2 FM), though Radio 3 has had to struggle hard against **Classic FM** (100 to 102 FM). The BBC also operates a full roster of **local radio stations**, mostly featuring local news, chat and mainstream pop.

Opening hours and public holidays

Most businesses, shops, banks and offices remain firmly anchored to traditional daytime opening hours, though supermarkets, petrol stations and department and convenience stores are often open until late in the evening from Monday through Saturday, with limited Sunday opening too. Full opening hours for specific museums, galleries and other tourist attractions are given in the Guide.

Opening hours

General business hours for most **shops and offices** are Monday to Saturday 9am to 5.30 or 6pm, although you'll find **late-night shopping** (until 7.30pm or 8pm) commonplace in the larger towns on Wednesdays or Thursdays. The big **supermarkets** also tend to stay open until 9 or 10pm from Monday to Saturday, with larger ones staying open round the clock. Most major stores and supermarkets now **open on Sundays**, too, usually from noon to 4pm, though some small towns and villages still retain an **early-closing day** (usually Wednesday), when most shops close at 1pm.

Note that not all motorway **service stations** open for 24 hours, although you can usually get fuel any time of the day or night in larger towns and cities.

Public holidays

Britain has fewer **public holidays** than any other country in Europe, and an uneven spread at that. Banks, businesses and most shops close on public holidays (see the list below), though large supermarkets, small corner shops and many tourist attractions don't. However, nearly all museums, galleries and other attractions are **closed on Christmas Day and New Year's Day**, with many also closed on Boxing Day (Dec 26) and, in Scotland, on January 2. Confusingly, public holidays are often referred to as **bank holidays**, though it's not just the banks who have a day off.

Britain's public holidays

January 1
January 2 (Scotland only)
Good Friday
Easter Monday
First Monday in May
Last Monday in May
First Monday in August (Scotland only)
Last Monday in August
December 25
December 26

Note that if January 1, December 25 or 26 falls on a Saturday or Sunday, the following Monday is counted as the holiday.

Festivals and events

Many of the biggest occasions in the British festival calendar have indelible associations with the ruling class – from the military pageant of the Trooping of the Colour to the displays at the Royal Tournament – but these say little about the country's folk history and even less about contemporary Britain. Indeed, it's events like London's exuberant Notting Hill Carnival or a wacky village celebration that give a more accurate idea of what makes the British tick. Every major town and city has at least one annual event, some dating back centuries, others more recent concoctions, that range from medieval jousting through to contemporary performing arts.

The UK has been accumulating festivals and special events from the time of the pre-Roman Druids. For a taste of the country at its most idiosyncratic, look out for one of the numerous local celebrations that perpetuate **ancient customs**, the origins and meanings of which have often been lost or conveniently misplaced. The festival and events calendar below picks out the annual highlights, but for exhaustive lists of events contact local tourist offices. For more information on Britain's festivals, see Festive Britain insert.

Festival and events calendar

January

Celtic Connections (mid- to late Jan). A major celebration of Celtic and folk music held in venues across Glasgow.
Burns Night (Jan 25). Scots worldwide get stuck into haggis, whisky and vowel-grinding poetry to commemorate Scotland's greatest poet, Robert Burns.

February

Chinese New Year (Feb 18 2007, Feb 7 2008). Processions, fireworks and festivities in the country's two main Chinatowns in London and Manchester.
Shrove Tuesday The last day before Lent (47 days before Easter Sunday, so usually in Feb) is also known as "Pancake Day" – eating them and racing with them are traditional pastimes, nowhere more so than at the great Pancake Day Race, in Olney, Buckinghamshire. Also, the Purbeck Marblers and Stonecutters Day in Corfe Castle, Dorset, comprises a ritual football game through the streets of the village.

March

St David's Day (March 1). Celebrations all over Wales.
Whuppity Scourie (March 1). Local children race round Lanark church beating each other with home-made paper weapons in a representation (it's thought) of the chasing away of winter or the warding off of evil spirits.
Crufts Dog Show (2nd week). The culmination of the UK's four-legged-friend obsession, held each year at Birmingham's National Exhibition Centre.

Easter

British and World Marbles Championship (Good Friday). Held at Tinsley Green, near Crawley, Sussex.
Bacup Nutters Dance (Easter Saturday). Blacked-up Lancashire clog dancers mark the Bacup town boundaries.
Hare Pie Scramble and Bottle-Kicking (Easter Monday). Barmy and chaotic village bottle-kicking contest at Hallaton, Leicestershire.
Easter Parade (Easter Monday). One of Britain's largest parades (since 1885) is held in London's Battersea Park.

April

Ulverston Walking Festival (1st week). Cumbria's "Festival Town" celebrates the great outdoors with hikes and events.

May

Padstow Obby Oss (May 1). Processions, music and dancing through the streets of Padstow, Cornwall.
Helston Floral Dance (May 8). A courtly procession and dance through the Cornish town by men in top hats and women in formal dresses.
Bath International Music Festival (mid-May to 1st week June). International arts jamboree.

Glyndebourne Opera Festival (mid-May to end Aug). One of the classiest arts festivals in the country, in East Sussex.

Hay-on-Wye Festival of Literature (late May). London's literati flock to the Welsh borders for a week.

Brockworth Cheese Rolling (late May bank holiday Mon). Pursuit of a cheese wheel down a murderous Gloucestershire incline – one of the weirdest knees-ups in Britain.

Chelsea Flower Show (last week). Essential event for England's green-fingered legions at the Royal Hospital, Chelsea, in London.

June

Shinty Camanachd Cup Final (June). The climax of the season for Scotland's own stick-and-ball game, normally held in one of the main Highland towns. Also marks the beginning of the Highland Games season across the Highlands, Northeast and Argyll.

Aldeburgh Festival (June). Suffolk jamboree of classical music, established by Benjamin Britten.

Eisteddfod Genedlaethol Urdd (1st week). The largest youth festival in Europe, alternating between North and South Wales.

Cotswold Olimpicks Chipping Campden, Gloucestershire (1st Friday). Rustic sports festival and torchlight procession.

Trooping the Colour (1st/2nd Sat). Equestrian pageantry for the Queen's Official Birthday; Horse Guards' Parade, London.

Appleby Horse Fair (2nd week). The country's most important Gypsy gathering at Appleby-in-Westmorland, Cumbria.

Cardiff Singer of the World (mid-June). Huge, televised week-long music festival, with a star-studded list of international competitors.

Glastonbury Festival (last week). Top-class music and comedy line-up – the rain nearly always turns it into a mud bath, but nothing dampens the trippy-hippy vibe.

World Worm-Charming Championships (end of June). Held at Willaston, Cheshire.

July

Llangollen International Music Eisteddfod (early July). Over 12,000 participants from all over the world, including choirs, dancers, folk singers, groups and instrumentalists.

Rushbearing Festival (1st week). Symbolic procession of crosses and garlands at Ambleside in the Lake District, dating back centuries.

York Early Music Festival (2nd week). The country's premier early music festival.

Great Yorkshire Show (2nd week). England's

biggest region celebrates its heritage, culture and cuisine in a huge three-day bash at Harrogate, North Yorkshire.

Gŵyl Werin y Cnapan Ffostrasol, near Lampeter, Ceredigion (2nd weekend). The best folk and Celtic music festival in the world.

Swan Upping (3rd week). Ceremonial registering of the Thames cygnets, on the River Thames from Sunbury to Pangbourne.

Royal Tournament (last week). Precision military displays at Earls Court Exhibition Centre, London.

Cambridge Folk Festival (last week). Biggest event of its kind in England, with lots more than just folk music.

WOMAD (late July). Renowned three-day world music festival at Reading.

Urban Games (dates vary). Skater-chic comes to Clapham Common, London, for a weekend of boarding, BMXing, freestyling and other youthful arcana.

Promenade Concerts, "The Proms" (July to early Sept). Classical music concerts at the Royal Albert Hall, London, ending in the fervently patriotic Last Night of the Proms.

August

Edinburgh Festival (Aug). One of the world's great arts jamborees.

Brighton's Gay Pride (early Aug). There are Pride Days all over the UK, but Brighton holds one of the brightest and best.

Lammas Fair (early Aug). The two-day fair at St Andrews; the oldest medieval market in the country.

Royal National Eisteddfod (1st week). Wales's biggest single annual event: fun, very impressive and worth seeing if only for the pageantry.

Whitstable Oyster Festival (1st week). Oysters are washed down with champagne and Guinness, and much more, with parades and diverse musical accompaniments.

Sidmouth International Festival (1st week). Folk and roots performers from around the world, plus theatre and dance.

Whitby Regatta (2nd/3rd week). The country's oldest regatta – sea races, funfair and fireworks on the windy North Yorkshire coast.

Grasmere Lakeland Sports and Show (3rd/4th week). Wrestling, fell-running, ferret-racing and other curious Lake District pastimes.

World Bog Snorkelling Championships (bank holiday Mon). Held in Llanwrtyd Wells in Wales, the festivities include a mountain-bike bog-leaping contest.

Notting Hill Carnival (bank holiday Mon). Vivacious celebration led by London's Caribbean community but including everything from Punjabi drummers to

Brazilian salsa – music, food and floats plus hundreds of thousands of spectators.

Leeds West Indian Carnival (bank holiday Mon). England's oldest carnival, featuring processions, dancing and barbecues.

Whitby Folk Festival (bank holiday week). One of England's most traditional folk meets, a week's worth of morris and sword dancing, finger-in-your-ear singing, storytelling and more.

Reading Festival (bank holiday weekend). Berkshire's annual three-day rock and contemporary music jamboree.

September

Blackpool Illuminations (early Sept to early Nov). Five miles of extravagantly kitsch light displays on the Blackpool seafront.

Abbots Bromley Horn Dance (1st Mon after Sept 4). Vaguely pagan mass dance in mock-medieval costume – one of the most famous of Britain's ancient customs, at Abbots Bromley, Staffordshire.

October

Swansea Festival of Music and the Arts. Concerts, jazz, drama, opera, ballet and art events throughout the city.

World Conker Championship (2nd Sun). World conker-cracking at Ashton in Northamptonshire.

Glenfiddich Piping Championships (late Oct). Held at Blair Atholl for the world's top ten solo pipers.

November

London to Brighton Veteran Car Rally (1st Sunday). Ancient machines lumbering the 57 miles down the A23 to the seafront.

Guy Fawkes Night/Bonfire Night (Nov 5). Nationwide fireworks and bonfires commemorating the foiling of the Gunpowder Plot in 1605 – especially raucous celebrations at York (Fawkes' birthplace), Lancaster, Ottery St Mary in Devon, and at Lewes, East Sussex.

Lord Mayor's Procession and Show (2nd Sat). Cavalcade to mark the inauguration of the new mayor of the City of London, held since 1215.

December

Tar Barrels Parade (Dec 31). Locals in Allendale Town, Northumberland, turn up with trays of burning pitch on their heads to parade round a large communal bonfire.

Hogmanay and Ne'er Day (Dec 31 & Jan 1). Traditionally more important to the Scots than Christmas, known for the custom of "first-footing", when groups of revellers troop into neighbours' houses at midnight bearing gifts. More popular these days are huge and highly organized street parties, most notably in Edinburgh, but also in Aberdeen, Glasgow and other Scottish cities.

Sports and outdoor activities

The birthplace of football, cricket, rugby, tennis and rowing – to name just five sports – Britain boasts a series of unrivalled sporting venues and events that attract a world audience. If you prefer participating to spectating, the UK caters for just about every outdoor activity, too: we've concentrated below on walking, cycling and water sports, but there are also opportunities for anything from rock climbing to pony-trekking. The Guide highlights recommended operators in every region, or contact any local tourist office.

Spectator sports

Football (soccer) is the national game in both Scotland and England, with a wide programme of professional league matches taking place every Saturday afternoon from the middle of August to early May, and plenty of Sunday and midweek fixtures too. It's very difficult to get tickets to matches involving the most famous teams (Chelsea, Arsenal, Manchester United, Liverpool, Rangers and

Celtic), but tours of their grounds are feasible, or you can try one of the lower-league games. The two annual showpieces are the English **FA Cup Final**, the culmination of the country's biggest domestic, knock-out football competition and the **Scottish Cup Final**, played on consecutive weekends in May.

Rugby comes in two codes – 15-a-side **Rugby Union** and 13-a-side **Rugby League**, both fearsomely brutal contact sports that can make entertaining viewing even if you don't understand the rules. In England, rugby is much less popular than football, but Rugby League has a loyal and dedicated fan base in the North – especially Yorkshire and Lancashire – whilst Union has traditionally been popular with the English middle class. Rugby League has never taken off in Wales and Scotland, but Rugby Union is popular in the Scottish Borders and is effectively the **national sport in Wales**. Key Rugby Union and League games are sold out months in advance, but ordinary fixtures present few ticketing problems. The Rugby Union season runs from September to May, Rugby League February to September.

The game of **cricket** is British idiosyncrasy at its finest. Foreigners, and most Britons for that matter, marvel at a game that can last five days and still end in a draw, while few people nowadays have the faintest idea about its rules or tactics. A plethora of competitions and matches between the 18 "first-class" English counties (played April–September) means visitors can easily experience the sport, with the competitive mainstay being the (sparsely attended) four-day County Championship matches; if this seems like too much of a commitment, there are also one-day National League matches, a one-day knockout cup competition (the C&G Trophy) and the highly popular three-hour Twenty20 Cup. The most prestigious games are the five-day **Test matches** (Thurs–Mon) played between the national English and Welsh team and a touring international team, primarily the former colonies of Australia, Pakistan, India, the West Indies and South Africa. There are usually two Test Match series every summer of three or five games each. There are six main Test Match grounds – Lord's and The Oval in London,

Trent Bridge in Nottingham, Old Trafford in Manchester; Headingley in Leeds, and Edgbaston in Birmingham.

Another traditional British sporting passion that doubles as a social (and gambling) event is **horse racing**. Meetings at the country's most famous race courses have become national events and, while every big race is shown live on TV, there's no substitute for being there and tipping a winner. The grandest race in the horse-racing calendar is the **Grand National**, the "World's Greatest Steeplechase", held the last Saturday in March or the first in April and run at Liverpool's Aintree course.

Finally, if you're in England at the end of June, you won't be able to miss the country's annual fixation with tennis in the shape of the **Wimbledon Championships**. No one gives a hoot about the sport for the other fifty weeks of the year, but as long as one plucky Brit endures the early rounds of the several knockout competitions, the entire country gets caught up in tennis fever.

Sporting events calendar

Six Nations Rugby Union (Feb–March). Hotly contested tournament between Scotland, England, Wales, Ireland, France and Italy.

National Hunt Festival, Cheltenham (mid-March). The country's premier steeplechase meeting, including the Cheltenham Gold Cup. See p.290.

Grand National, Aintree (last Sat in March or the 1st Sat in April). Thrills and lots of spills in the steeplechase to end them all. See p.538.

London Marathon (April). England's biggest road race, as vicars and people dressed as teapots trail in behind the speedy pros.

FA Cup Final and the Scottish Cup Final (May). Football's two biggest domestic games.

Derby Week, Epsom (1st week June). The world's most expensive horseflesh competing in the 200-year-old Derby, the Coronation Cup and the Oaks.

Royal Ascot (mid-June). High-class horse racing attended by the wealthy and well-connected.

Wimbledon Lawn Tennis Championships (last week June & 1st week July). England's annual bout of tennis fever. See p.165.

Scottish Open Golf Championship (July). Held at a different venue each year.

Henley Royal Regatta (1st week in July). Oxfordshire rowing tournament, with tons of toffs and strawberries.

British Open Golf Championship (mid-July). The season's last Grand Slam golf tournament; variable venue.

Rugby League Challenge Cup Final (last Sat in Aug). Held since 1896, this is the culmination of the biggest knockout competition for Rugby League clubs.

Walking

Walking routes track across many of Britain's wilder areas, amid landscapes varied enough to suit any taste or predilection. We've highlighted local walks, climbs, rambles and trails throughout the Guide, but it goes without saying that even for short hikes you need to be **properly equipped**, follow local advice and listen out for local weather reports – British weather is notoriously changeable. You will also need a good **map** and the Ordnance Survey (OS) series (see p.37) hits the spot. In England and Wales you need to keep to established routes as you'll often be crossing private land, even within the national parks: all OS maps mark public rights of way. Scotland, in contrast, has a tradition of **free public access** to most of the countryside, restricted only at certain times of the year. For details of **organized walking holidays**, see p.32.

Walking in England

England's finest **walking areas** are the granite moorlands and spectacular coastlines of Devon and Cornwall in the Southwest, and the highlands of the North – notably the Peak District, the Yorkshire Dales, the North York Moors, and the Lake District. Keen hikers might want to tackle one of England's dozen or so **National Trails** (@www.nationaltrail .co.uk), which amount to some 2500 miles of waymarked path and track. Perhaps the most famous – certainly the toughest – is the **Pennine Way** (268 miles; usual walking time 16 days), stretching from the Derbyshire Peak District to the Scottish Borders, while the challenging **South West Coast Path** (630 miles; 56 days) through Cornwall, Devon, Somerset and Dorset tends to be tackled in shorter sections. Other trails are less gung-ho in character, like the **South Downs Way** (101 miles; 8 days) or the fascinating **Hadrians's Wall Path** (84 miles; 7 days).

Walking in Wales

Wales's best **walking country** is to be found within its three national parks. Almost the whole of the northwestern corner of the country is taken up by the **Snowdonia National Park**, incorporating a dozen of the country's highest peaks separated by dramatic glacial valleys and laced with hundreds of miles of ridge and moorland paths. From Snowdonia, the Cambrian Mountains stretch south to the **Brecon Beacons National Park**, with its striking sandstone scarp at the head of the South Wales coalfield, and lush, cave-riddled limestone valleys to the south. One hundred and seventy miles of Wales's southwestern peninsula make up the third park – the **Pembrokeshire Coast National Park**, best explored by the **Pembrokeshire Coast Path** that traverses the cliff tops, frequently dipping down into secluded coves. This is only one of Wales's three frequently walked **National Trails** (@www .nationaltrail.co.uk) – the other two are the 168-mile-long **Offa's Dyke Path** that traces the England–Wales border and **Glyndŵr's Way**, which weaves through mid-Wales for 120 miles. The other long-distance route of special note is the 274-mile **Cambrian Way**, cutting north–south over the Cambrian Mountains.

Walking in Scotland

The whole of **Scotland** offers good opportunities for gentle hill walking, from the smooth, grassy hills and moors of the **Southern Uplands** to the wild and rugged country of the northwest. Scotland has five main **Long Distance Footpaths (LDPs)**, each of which takes days to walk, though you can of course just cover sections of them. The **Southern Upland Way** crosses Scotland from coast to coast in the south, and is the country's longest at 212 miles; the best known is the **West Highland Way**, a 95-mile hike from Glasgow to Fort William via Loch Lomond and Glen Coe; and the gentler **Speyside Way**, in Aberdeenshire, is a mere thirty miles. The green signposts of the Scottish Rights of Way Society point to these and many other cross-country routes, while in the wilder parts the accepted freedom to roam allows extensive mountain walking, rock climbing, orienteering and allied activities.

Cycling

The **National Cycle Network** is made up of several miles of signed cycle route, a third on traffic-free paths (including disused railways and canal towpaths), the rest mainly on country roads. You're never very far from one of the numbered routes, all of which are detailed on the Sustrans website (℡0845/113 0065, ⓦwww.sustrans.org.uk), a charitable trust devoted to the development of environmentally sustainable transport.

Major routes include the well-known **C2C** (Sea-to-Sea), 140 miles between White-haven/Workington on the northwest coast and Newcastle/Sunderland on the northeast. There's also the **Cornish Way** (123 miles), from Bude to Land's End, or routes that cut through the very heart of England – like that from Derby to York (154 miles) or along the rivers Severn and Thames (128 miles, Gloucester to Reading). The classic cross-Britain route is, however, from Land's End, in the far southwest of England, to John O'Groats, on the northeast tip of Scotland – roughly a thousand miles, which can be covered in two to three weeks, depending on which of the three CTC-recommended routes you choose.

Most local tourist offices and good book-shops stock a range of **cycling guides**, with maps and detailed route descriptions. You can also get maps and guidance (some free) from Sustrans and from the Cycle Touring Club (℡0870/873 0060, ⓦwww.ctc.org. uk). For **cycling holiday operators**, see p.32.

Water sports – sailing, windsurfing and surfing

Sailing and **windsurfing** are especially popular along the south coast (particularly the Isle of Wight and Solent) and in the southwest (around Falmouth in the Carrick

Roads estuary, Cornwall, and around Salcombe and Dartmouth, both in South Devon). Here, and up in the Lake District, on Windermere, Derwent Water and Ullswa-ter, you'll be able to rent boards, dinghies and boats, either by the hour or for longer periods of instruction – say from £40 for a couple of hours' of windsurfing to £150 or so for a full day's sailing course. The **UK Sailing Academy** (℡01983/294941, ⓦwww.uk-sail.org.uk) in Cowes, on the Isle of Wight, is England's finest instruction centre for windsurfing, dinghy sailing, kayaking and kitesurfing and offers nonresidential and resi-dential courses.

Newquay in Cornwall is **England**'s undis-puted **surfing** centre, whose main break, Fistral, regularly hosts international contests. But there are quieter spots right along the north coast of Cornwall and Devon, as well a growing scene on the northeast coast from Yorkshire to Northumberland. The coastline here is often spectacular, espe-cially in Northumberland, and although the more popular breaks, such as Cayton Bay and Saltburn, are now crowded, you can find greater isolation with ease. In England's Southwest (less so in the Northeast), there are plenty of places where you can rent or buy equipment, which means that prices are kept down to reasonable levels, say around £10 per day each for board and wetsuit. Surfing in **Wales** tends to be concentrated on the south coast, around the Gower peninsula, which boasts a good variety of beach and reef breaks, but the most consistent surf beach in Wales is Freshwater West in Pembrokeshire. **Scot-land** is fast gaining a reputation for the high quality of its breaks with the number one spot being Thurso on the north coast. Many other good breaks lie within easy reach of large cities (eg Pease Bay, near Edinburgh, and Fraserburgh, near Aberdeen), while the spectacular west coast has numerous possibilities: try Sandwood Bay, the most isolated beach in Britain, or the waves of the Outer Hebrides.

Crime and personal safety

Britain is a relatively safe country and for the visitor the likelihood of being a victim of crime is low. If the worst does happen, then the British police are, on the whole, helpful, sympathetic and professional. They wear blue uniforms of various types depending on duties, but officers on the streets usually wear a distinctive domed hat with a silver tip. Most wear chest guards and carry batons, though street officers do not normally carry guns.

As far as **personal safety** goes, it's generally possible to walk around London and the larger cities without fear of harassment or assault. However, all the big conurbations have their edgy districts and at pub closing time (usually 11pm, midnight on the weekend), random **drink-related violence** is commonplace in every British city centre – be careful and err on the side of caution late at night, when badly lit streets and drunken groups should be avoided. After public transport shuts down for the night, always use official/registered cabs/taxis.

Petty crime and offences

Almost all the problems tourists encounter in the UK are to do with **petty crime** – pickpocketing and bag-snatching – rather than more serious physical confrontations. If possible, always leave your passport and valuables in a hotel or hostel safe, and exercise the usual caution on the tube,

trains and buses. If you are robbed, you need to report it to the police, not least because your insurance company will require a **crime report number** – make sure you get one.

Being caught in possession of a small quantity of "soft" **drugs** – most commonly hashish (marijuana resin) and cannabis – will probably result in a police caution. If, on the other hand, the police suspect you are dealing, you can expect to be held in custody and ultimately prosecuted. Finally, making "jokes" about bombs or **suspicious packages** in check-in lines or at security barriers is clearly foolish and will result in serious trouble and possibly prosecution.

Emergencies

For Police, Fire Brigade, Ambulance, Mountain Rescue and Coastguard, dial ☏999.

Travellers with disabilities

In the last decade, the UK has made steady progress in improving its facilities for travellers with disabilities. All new public buildings – including museums and cinemas – are now obliged to provide wheelchair access, dropped kerbs are the rule in every city and town, airports are generally fully accessible, and many buses have easy-access dropped boarding ramps. The railways have lagged behind, but are at least making moves in the right direction, and the number of accessible hotels and restaurants is increasing year on year. Reserved parking bays for blue-badge holders (ie people with disabilities) are available almost everywhere, from shopping malls to museums.

If you have specific requirements, it's always best to talk first to your travel agent, chosen hotel or tour operator. Several useful **organizations** are listed below, including RADAR, which produces an excellent annual *Holidays in Britain and Ireland* guide (available by mail order). As regards the major **car rental** firms, Hertz is the leader in offering models with hand controls.

Useful contacts

Access-Able ⓦ www.access-able.com. Online US resource for travellers with disabilities, with links to UK operators and organizations.
All Go Here ☎ 01923/840463, ⓦ www.allgohere .com. Information on accommodation and other

hospitality-related services suitable for disabled travellers throughout the UK.
Capability Scotland ☎ 0131/313 5510, ⓦ www .capability-scotland.org.uk. Well-run, well-connected organization for all disability issues and information.
Holiday Care ☎ 0845/124 9971, from overseas 44-208/760 0072, ⓦ www.holidaycare.org.uk. Holiday & travel information service – accessible accommodation, attractions & activity holidays in the UK.
RADAR (Royal Association for Disability and Rehabilitation) ☎ 020/7250 3222, ⓦ www.radar .org.uk. A good source of advice on holidays and travel in the UK. Also has a dedicated UK and Ireland accommodation website ⓦ www.radarsearch.org.
Tripscope ☎ 08457/585641, from overseas 44-117/939 7782, ⓦ www.tripscope.org.uk. Registered charity offering free advice on UK transport for those with mobility problems.

Directory

Children and babies Generally speaking, under-5s travel free on public transport and get in free to attractions; 5–16-year-olds are usually entitled to concessionary rates of up to half the adult rate/fare. Baby-changing facilities are widespread (shopping centres, train stations etc), and pharmacies and supermarkets stock every conceivable baby product, though in rural areas shops might

have less choice. Children aren't allowed in certain licensed (alcohol-serving) premises, though this doesn't apply to many restaurants, while some pubs and inns have family rooms or beer gardens where children are welcome. Some B&Bs and hotels won't accept children under a certain age (usually 12) – we've pointed out places in the Guide where this applies.

Distances, weights and measures
Distances (and speeds) on British signposts are in miles, and beer is still served in pints. Everything else – money, weights and measures – is officially metric, though you'll still hear many British people ordering "a pound of apples" and so forth.

Electricity In the UK, the current is 240V AC. North American appliances will need a transformer and adaptor; those from Europe, Australia and New Zealand only need an adaptor.

Gay and lesbian The UK offers one of the most diverse and accessible lesbian and gay scenes anywhere in Europe. Nearly every town of any size has some kind of organized gay life – from bars and clubs to community groups – with the major scenes found in London, Manchester, Brighton, Edinburgh, Glasgow, Cardiff, Swansea and Newport. Many gay and lesbian venues are listed in this book, and you'll find a free local listings sheet in virtually every one of them. Other listings and news can be found in the weekly *Pink Paper* (ⓦ www.pinkpaper .com) and the glossy monthly *Gay Times* (ⓦ www.gaytimes.co.uk), available from many newsagents and alternative bookstores. The Gay Britain Network (ⓦ www.gaybritain. co.uk) has comprehensive information and links for events, restaurants, bars, clubs and services across the UK, while ⓦ www .gaytravel.co.uk lists over 400 gay and lesbian hotels and travel establishments. Two other useful reference points are ⓦ www .scotsgay.co.uk and ⓦ www.gaywales.co.uk. The age of consent in England, Scotland and

Wales for both homosexual and heterosexual acts is 16.

Laundry Coin-operated laundries (launderettes) are commonplace in every large city and town (and often detailed in "Listings"). Most operate extended opening hours – usually about twelve hours a day – and many offer "service washes", with your laundry washed and dried for you in just a few hours. This costs around £6 for a bagful of clothes. Using a hotel laundry service is always far more expensive.

Smoking Smoking is banned from just about all public buildings and offices, and on all public transport. An increasing number of hotels and B&Bs don't allow smoking (picked out in the Guide where applicable), while many restaurants are either nonsmoking or have nonsmoking sections. Pubs – traditionally the safest haven for smokers – are beginning to follow suit and there are legislative plans afoot to ban smoking in every restaurant and pub where food is served.

Time From late October to late March, Britain is on Greenwich Mean Time (GMT), but over the summer the clocks go forward an hour for British Summer Time (BST). GMT is five hours ahead of the US Eastern Standard Time and ten hours behind Australian Eastern Standard Time.

Toilets Public loos, often in a less than pristine condition, are found at all train and bus stations and signposted on most town high streets; a fee of 10p or 20p is sometimes charged.

Guide

England

1

London

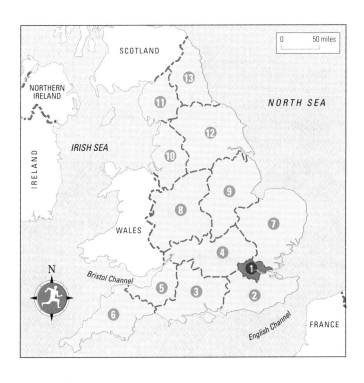

CHAPTER 1 # Highlights

* **British Museum** Quite simply one of the world's greatest museums. See p.103

* **London Eye** The universally loved observation wheel is a graceful addition to London's skyline. See p.121

* **Tate Modern** London's huge modern-art gallery is a spectacular addition to London's riverside. See p.123

* **Shakespeare's Globe Theatre** Catch a show in this amazing reconstructed Elizabethan theatre. See p.123

* **Highgate Cemetery** The steeply sloping terraces of the West Cemetery's overgrown graves are the last word in Victorian Gothic gloom. See p.137

* **Greenwich** Picturesque riverside spot, boasting a weekend market, the National Maritime Museum and old Royal Observatory. See p.138

* **Kew Gardens** Stroll amidst the exotic trees and shrubs, or head for the steamy glasshouses. See p.143

* **Hampton Court Palace** Tudor interiors, architecture by Wren and vast gardens make this a great day out. See p.145

△ London Eye

1

London

What strikes visitors more than anything about **LONDON** is the sheer size of the place. Stretching for more than thirty miles on either side of the River Thames, and with an ethnically diverse population of just under eight million, it's one of the largest cities in Europe. Londoners tend to cope with all this by compartmentalizing the city, identifying with the neighbourhoods in which they work or live, and just making occasional forays into the "centre of town" or "up West", to the West End, London's shopping and entertainment heartland.

Despite Scottish, Welsh and Northern Irish devolution, London still dominates the national horizon, too: this is where the country's news and money are made, it's where the central government resides and, as far as its inhabitants are concerned, provincial life begins beyond the circuit of the city's orbital motorway. Londoners' sense of superiority causes enormous resentment in the regions, yet it's undeniable that the capital has a unique aura of excitement and success – in most walks of British life, if you want to get on, you've got to do it in London.

For the visitor, too, London is a thrilling place – despite terrorist threats, the city is in a buoyant mood, particularly after winning the right to stage the Olympics in 2012. The facelift that the capital has undergone over the last decade or so has seen virtually every one of London's world-class **museums**, **galleries** and **institutions** reinvented, from the Royal Opera House to the British Museum. The city now boasts the world's largest modern-art gallery in Tate Modern, the tallest observation wheel in the London Eye, and two fantastic new pedestrian bridges that have helped transform the south bank of the Thames into a magnet for visitors and Londoners alike. And after years of being the only major city in the world not to have a governing body, London now has its own elected assembly, housed in an eye-catching building within sight of Tower Bridge, and a mayor who's determined to try and solve one of London's biggest problems: transport.

In the meantime, London's **traditional sights** – Big Ben, Westminster Abbey, Buckingham Palace, St Paul's Cathedral and the Tower of London – continue to draw in millions of tourists every year. Monuments from the capital's more glorious past are everywhere to be seen, from medieval banqueting halls and the great churches of Christopher Wren to the eclectic Victorian architecture of the triumphalist British Empire. There is also much enjoyment to be had from the city's quiet Georgian squares, the narrow alleyways of the City of London, the riverside walks, and the quirks of what is still identifiably a collection of villages. Even London's traffic problems are offset by surprisingly large **expanses of greenery**: Hyde Park, Green Park and St James's Park are all within a few minutes' walk of the West End, while, further afield, you can enjoy the more expansive parklands of Hampstead Heath and Richmond Park.

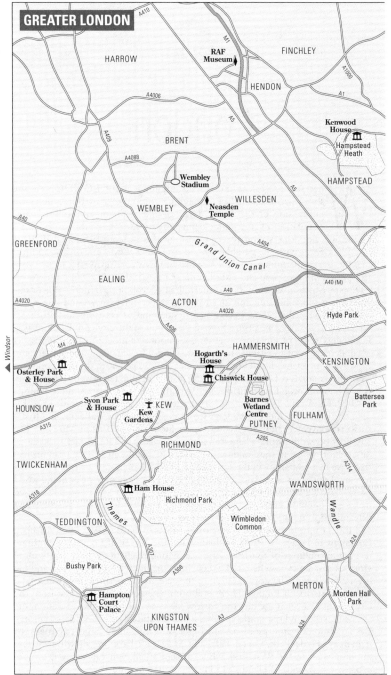

GREATER LONDON

A410

M1

RAF Museum

FINCHLEY

HARROW

HENDON

A4006

A5

A1000

A1

Kenwood House

BRENT

Hampstead Heath

A4088

A409

HAMPSTEAD

Wembley Stadium

WILLESDEN

WEMBLEY

Neasden Temple

A40

GREENFORD

A404

Grand Union Canal

A40 (M)

EALING

A40

Hyde Park

A4020

ACTON

A4020

A406

Hogarth's House

HAMMERSMITH

KENSINGTON

Osterley Park & House

Chiswick House

Battersea Park

Windsor

M4

Barnes Wetland Centre

Syon Park & House

KEW

FULHAM

HOUNSLOW

Kew Gardens

PUTNEY

A315

A205

RICHMOND

TWICKENHAM

WANDSWORTH

A316

Ham House

A214

Richmond Park

Wandle

TEDDINGTON

Wimbledon Common

A307

MERTON

Morden Hall Park

Bushy Park

A308

HAMPTON COURT PALACE

A3

A24

Hampton Court Palace

KINGSTON UPON THAMES

Thames

© Crown copyright

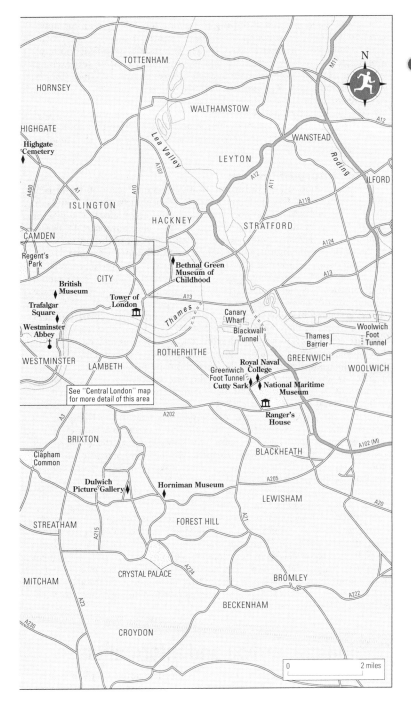

You could spend days just **shopping** in London too, mixing with the upper classes in Harrods, or sampling the offbeat weekend markets of Portobello Road, Brick Lane, Greenwich and Camden. The **music**, **clubbing** and **gay/lesbian** scenes are second to none, and mainstream arts are no less exciting, with regular opportunities to catch brilliant **theatre** companies, dance troupes, exhibitions and opera. **Restaurants** these days, are an attraction, too. London has more Michelin-starred establishments than Paris, as well as a vast range of low-cost, high-quality Chinese restaurants and Indian curry houses. Meanwhile, the city's **pubs** have heaps of atmosphere, especially away from the centre – and an exploration of the farther-flung communities is essential to get the complete picture of this dynamic metropolis.

A brief history of London

The Romans founded **Londinium** in 43 AD as a stores depot on the marshy banks of the Thames. Despite frequent attacks – not least by Queen Boudicca, who razed it in 61 AD – the port became secure in its position as capital of Roman Britain by the end of the century. London's expansion really began, however, in the eleventh century, when it became the seat of the last successful invader of Britain, the Norman duke who became **William I of England** (aka "the Conqueror"). Crowned king of England in Westminster Abbey, William built the White Tower – centrepiece of the Tower of London – to establish his dominance over the merchant population, the class that was soon to make London one of Europe's mightiest cities.

Little is left of medieval or Tudor London. Many of the finest buildings were wiped out in the course of a few days in 1666 when the **Great Fire of London** annihilated more than thirteen thousand houses and nearly ninety churches, completing a cycle of destruction begun the year before by the Great Plague, which killed as many as a hundred thousand people. Chief beneficiary of the blaze was Sir Christopher Wren, who was commissioned to redesign the city and rose to the challenge with such masterpieces as St Paul's Cathedral and the Royal Naval Hospital in Greenwich.

Much of the public architecture of London was built in the Georgian and Victorian periods covering the eighteenth and nineteenth centuries, when grand structures were raised to reflect the city's status as the financial and administrative hub of the **British Empire**. However, in comparison to many other European capitals, much of London looks bland, due partly to the German bombing raids in World War II, and partly to some postwar development that has lumbered the city with the sort of concrete-and-glass mediocrity that gives modern architecture a bad name.

Yet London's special atmosphere comes not from its buildings, but from the life on its streets. A cosmopolitan city since at least the seventeenth century, when it was a haven for Huguenot immigrants escaping persecution in Louis XIV's France, today it is truly multicultural, with over a third of its permanent population originating from overseas. The last hundred years has seen the arrival of thousands from the Caribbean, the Indian subcontinent, the Mediterranean and the Far East, all of whom play an integral part in defining a metropolis that is unmatched in its sheer diversity.

Orientation, arrival and information

Stretching for more than thirty miles at its broadest point, **London** is a big place. The majority of its sights are situated to the north of the **River Thames**, which loops through the city from west to east. However, there is no single predominant focus of interest, since London has grown not through centralized planning but by a process of agglomeration – villages and urban developments that once surrounded the core are now lost within the amorphous mass of Greater London.

Westminster, the country's royal, political and ecclesiastical power base for centuries, was once a separate city. The grand streets and squares to the north of Westminster, from **St James's** to **Covent Garden**, were built as residential suburbs after the Restoration, and are now the city's shopping and entertainment zones known collectively as the **West End**. To the east, is the original City of London – known simply as **The City** – founded by the Romans, and now one of the world's great financial centres.

Only a small slice of central London south of the Thames is worth exploring: the area stretching from the landmark observation wheel, the **London Eye** to the **Tate Modern** art gallery. In the suburbs, the **museums** of South Kensington are a must, as are literary Hampstead and Highgate, either side of half-wild **Hampstead Heath**, and **Greenwich**, with its nautical associations, royal park and observatory. Finally, there are plenty of rewarding day-trips along the Thames from **Chiswick** to **Windsor**, most notably to Hampton Court Palace and Windsor Castle.

Arrival

Flying into London, you'll arrive at one of the capital's five **international airports**: Heathrow, Gatwick, Stansted, Luton or City Airport, all of which are less than an hour from the city centre.

Heathrow (☎08700/000123, ⓦwww.baa.co.uk), fifteen miles west of the centre, has four terminals, and two train/tube stations: one for terminals 1, 2 and 3, and a separate one for terminal 4. The high-speed **Heathrow Express** trains travel nonstop to Paddington Station (every 15min; 15–20min) for £14 (less if you book online, more if you buy your ticket on board). A much cheaper alternative is to take the slow Piccadilly **Underground** line into central London (every 5–9min; 50min) for £3.80. If you plan to make several sightseeing journeys on your arrival day, buy a Travelcard (see p.79). National Express run **bus services** (☎0870/580 8080, ⓦwww.nationalexpress.com) from Heathrow to Victoria Coach Station (daily every 30min 6am–9.30pm; 1hr), which cost £10 single, £15 return. From midnight, you can take **night bus** #N9 (every 30min; 1hr) to Trafalgar Square for a bargain fare of £1.20.

The London Pass

If you're thinking of visiting a lot of fee-paying attractions in a short space of time, it's worth considering a **London Pass** (ⓦwww.londonpass.com), which gives free entry to a mixed bag of attractions including Hampton Court Palace, Kensington Palace, Kew Gardens, London Aquarium, St Paul's Cathedral, the Tower of London and Windsor Castle, plus a whole host of lesser attractions, as well as discounts at selected outlets. You can choose to buy the card with or without an All-Zone Travelcard thrown in; the saving is relatively small, but it does include free travel out to Windsor. The pass costs around £27 for one day (£18 for children), rising to £72 for six days (£48 for children); or £32 with a Travelcard (£20 for children) rising to £110 (£61 for children). The London Pass can be bought online or in person from tourist offices and London's mainline train or chief Underground stations.

Gatwick (☎08700/002468, ⓦwww.baa.co.uk), thirty miles to the south, has two terminals, North and South, connected by a monorail. The nonstop **Gatwick Express** train runs between the South Terminal and Victoria Station (every 15–30min; 30min) for £13. Other options include **Southern** services to Victoria (every 15–20min; 40min) for £9, and **Thameslink** to King's Cross (every 15–30min; 50min) for around £10.

Stansted (☎0870/000 0303, ⓦwww.baa.co.uk), London's swankiest international airport, lies roughly 35 miles northeast of the capital, and is served by the **Stansted Express** to Liverpool Street (every 15–30min; 45min), which costs £14.50 single. **Airbus #6** runs 24 hours a day to Victoria Coach Station (every 30min; 1hr 30min), and costs £10 single.

Luton airport (☎01582/405100, ⓦwww.london-luton.com) is roughly thirty miles north of the city centre, and mostly handles charter flights. A **free shuttle bus** takes five minutes to transport passengers to Luton Airport Parkway station, connected by **Thameslink** trains (every 15min; 30–40min) to King's Cross and other stations in central London; tickets cost £10 for a single fare. Alternatively, **Green Line** bus #757 runs from Luton to Victoria Station (every 30min; 1hr 15min), costing £9 single.

London's smallest airport, **City Airport** (☎020/7646 0000, ⓦwww.london cityairport.com), used primarily by business folk, is in Docklands, ten miles east of central London. The airport's **Docklands Light Railway** (**DLR**) extension runs straight into Bank in the City in around 25 minutes; tickets cost around £3.

Eurostar trains arrive at the central **Waterloo International**, south of the river. Arriving by train (☎08457/484950, ⓦwww.nationalrail.co.uk) from elsewhere in Britain, you'll come into one of London's numerous mainline stations, all of which have adjacent Underground stations linking into the city centre's tube network. Coming into London **by coach** (☎0870/580 8080, ⓦwww .nationalexpress.com), you're most likely to arrive at **Victoria Coach Station**, a couple of hundred yards south down Buckingham Palace Road from the train and Underground stations of the same name.

Information

The main tourist office in London is the **London Visitor Centre**, near Piccadilly Circus at 1 Regent St (Mon 9.30am–6.30pm, Tues–Fri 9am–6.30pm, Sat & Sun 10am–4pm; June–Sept Sat open till 5pm; ⓦwww.visitbritain.com); there's also a tiny information window in the ticket kiosk on Leicester Square (Mon–Fri 8am–11pm, Sat & Sun 11am–6pm; ⓦwww.visitlondon.com). Individual boroughs also run tourist offices; the most central is on the south side of St Paul's Cathedral (daily 9.30am–5pm; Oct–April closed Sat & Sun; ☎020/7332 1456, ⓦwww.cityoflondon.gov.uk).

Most tourist offices hand out a basic reference **map** of central London, plus plans of the public transport systems, and the maps in this chapter should be enough for most exploring; but to find your way around every nook and cranny you'll need an *A–Z Atlas* or a *Nicholson Streetfinder*, both of which have a street index covering every street in the capital; you can get them at most bookshops and newsagents for under £5. The two best, simple, foldout maps are *London: The Rough Guide Map* – which also details hotels, restaurants, attraction opening hours and so on – and *Benson's London Mini Map*.

The only comprehensive and critical weekly **listings** magazine is *Time Out*, which costs £2.50 and comes out every Tuesday afternoon. In it you'll find details of all the latest exhibitions, shows, films, music, sport, guided walks and events in and around the capital.

City transport

London's transport network is among the most complex and expensive in the world. **Transport for London** (**TfL**) provides excellent free maps and details of bus and tube services from its **travel information** offices: the main one is at Piccadilly Circus tube station (Mon–Sat 7.15am–9pm, Sun 8.15am–8pm), and there are other desks at Heathrow and various tube and train stations. There's also a 24-hour phone line for information on all bus and tube services (☎020/7222 1234) and a website (⊛www.tfl.gov.uk). If possible, avoid travelling during the **rush hour** (Mon–Fri 8–9.30am & 5–7pm), when tubes become unbearably crowded (and the lack of air conditioning doesn't help), and some buses get so full they literally won't let you on.

Except for very short journeys, the fastest way of moving around the city is by **Underground** or tube (⊛www.thetube.com), as it's known to all Londoners. The eleven different tube lines cross much of the metropolis, although south of the river is not very well covered. Each line has its own colour and name – all you need to know is which direction you're travelling in: northbound, eastbound, southbound or westbound. Services operate from around 5am Monday to Saturday, until 12.30am and from 7.30am on Sundays until 11.30pm; you rarely have to wait more than five minutes for a train from central stations. **Tickets** must be bought in advance; if you're caught without a valid ticket, you'll be charged an on-the-spot Penalty Fare of £10. A single journey in the central zone costs an unbelievable £2, so if you're intending to travel about a bit, a Travelcard is a much better bet (see box).

London's famous red **double-decker buses** are fun to ride on, but tend to get stuck in traffic jams, which prevent them running to a regular timetable. In central London, and on all the extra-long "bendy buses", you must **buy your ticket before boarding** from a machine at the bus stop. Tickets for all bus journeys cost a flat fare of £1.20. Another option is a **One-Day Bus Pass**, which costs £3 for adults and £1 for children and can be used on all buses anytime anywhere in London. Some buses run a 24-hour service, but most run between about 5am and midnight, with a network of **Night Buses** (prefixed with the letter "N") operating outside this period. Night-bus routes radiate out from Trafalgar Square at approximately twenty- to thirty-minute intervals, more frequently on some routes and on Friday and Saturday nights. Tickets are £1.20

Travelcards

To get the best value out of the transport system, buy a **Travelcard**. Available from machines and booths at all tube and train stations, and at some newsagents (look for the sign), these are valid for the bus, tube, Docklands Light Railway, Tramlink and suburban rail networks. **Day Travelcards** come in two varieties: Off-Peak – which are valid after 9.30am on weekdays and all day during the weekend – and Peak. A Day Travelcard (Off-Peak), costs £4.70 for the central zones 1 and 2, rising to £6 for zones 1–6 (including Heathrow); the Day Travelcard (Peak) starts at £5.10 for zones 1 and 2. A **3-Day Travelcard** costs £15 for zones 1 and 2, but is obviously only worth it if you need to travel during peak hours; **Weekly Travelcards** are much more economical, beginning at £18.50 for zone 1. If you're travelling with children, buy a **Family Travelcard**, which starts at £3.10 for an adult (zones 1 & 2), plus an additional 80p for each child (up to as many as four) on weekdays only; at weekends, the children go free. Despite the name, the adults and children don't have to be related, and the restrictions are the same as for Day Travelcards (Off-Peak).

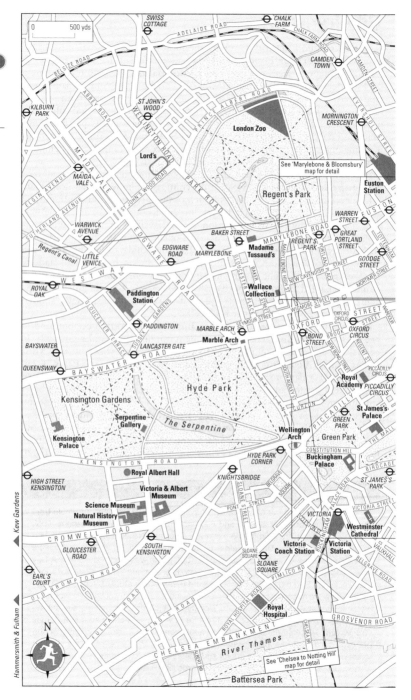

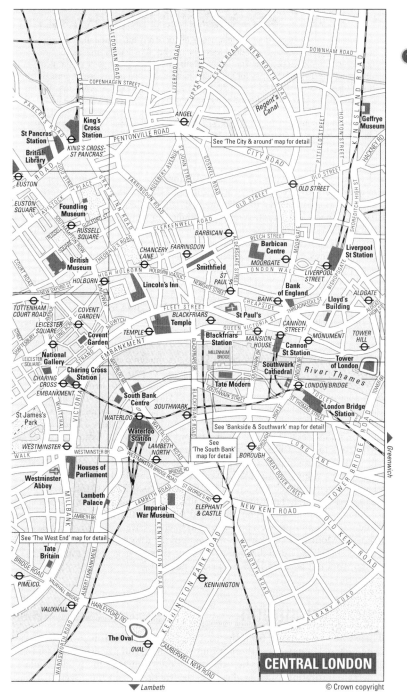

CENTRAL LONDON

81

Lambeth

© Crown copyright

Congestion charge

The latest attempt to cut down on car usage in London is the **congestion charge**, pioneered by the Mayor of London, Ken Livingstone. All vehicles entering central London on weekdays between 7am and 6.30pm are liable to a congestion charge of £8 per vehicle. Drivers can pay for the charge online, over the phone and at garages and shops, and must do so before 10pm the same day or incur a surcharge. The congestion charging zone is bounded by Marylebone and Euston roads in the north, Commercial Street and Tower Bridge in the east, Kennington Lane and Elephant & Castle in the south, and Edgware Road and Park Lane in the west – though there are plans to extend the zone westwards. For the latest, visit ⓦ www.cclondon.com.

and Travelcards (see box, p.79) are valid. All stops are treated as request stops, so you must signal to get the bus to stop, and press the bell in order to get off.

Large areas of London's suburbs are best reached by the **suburban train** network (Travelcards valid). Wherever a sight can only be reached by overground train, we've indicated the nearest train station and the central terminus from which you can depart.

Boat services on the Thames are much improved, but still do not form part of an integrated public transport system. As a result fares are quite expensive, with Travelcards currently only giving the holders a 33 percent discount. Typical **fares** are £5.50 single, £7 return Westminster to the Tower, or £7 single, £9 return Westminster to Greenwich. **Timetables** and services are complex, and there are numerous companies and small charter operators – for a full list, pick up the Thames River Services booklet from a TfL information office (☏020/7222 1234, ⓦwww.tfl.gov.uk).

Compared to many capital cities, London's metered **black cabs** are an expensive option unless there are three or more of you – a ride from Euston to Victoria, for example, costs around £12–15 (Mon–Fri 6am–8pm). After 8pm on weekdays and all day during the weekend, a higher tariff applies, and after 10pm, a much higher one. A yellow light over the windscreen tells you if the cab is available – just stick your arm out to hail it. To order a black cab in advance, phone ☏0871/871 8710, and be prepared to pay an extra £2.

Minicabs look just like regular cars and are considerably cheaper than black cabs – the best way to pick a company is to take the advice of the place you're at. If you want a woman driver, call Ladycabs (☏020/7254 3501), or a gay/lesbian-friendly driver, in which case call Freedom Cars (☏020/7734 1313).

Last, and definitely least, there are usually plenty of **bicycle taxis** available for hire in the West End. The oldest and biggest of the bunch are Bugbugs (☏020/7620 0500, ⓦwww.bugbugs.co.uk), who have over fifty rickshaws operating Monday to Saturday from 7pm until the early hours of the morning. The rickshaws take up to three passengers and fares are negotiable, though they should work out at around £5 per person per mile.

Accommodation

There's no getting away from the fact that **accommodation** in London is expensive and compared with most European cities, you pay over the odds in every category. The city's hostels are among the costliest in the world, while venerable institutions such as the *Ritz*, the *Dorchester* and the *Savoy* charge guests the very top international prices – from £300 per luxurious night.

The cheapest places to stay are the city's **campsites**, some of which also have dormitories, charging as little as £6 a night. A dorm bed in an independent **hostel** will cost you double that, while official YHA hostels charge £20 or more. Even the most basic **B&Bs** struggle to bring their tariffs down to £45 for a double with shared facilities, and you're more likely to find yourself paying £60 or more.

We've given phone numbers and websites or email addresses for all our listed accommodation, but if you fail to find a bed, try one of the various **accommodation agencies**. All London tourist offices (see p.78) operate a room-booking service, for which a small fee is levied (they also take the first night's fee in advance). The **British Hotel Reservation Centre** (BHRC; ⓦwww .bhrc.co.uk) desks at Heathrow, Gatwick and Victoria train and coach stations don't charge a fee for booking rooms, and most of their offices are open daily from 6am till midnight.

You can also book for free **online** at ⓦwww.londontown.com; payment is made directly to the hotel on checking out and they can offer discounts of up to fifty percent.

Hotels and B&Bs

With **hotels** you get less for your money in London than elsewhere in the country – generally breakfasts are more meagre and rooms more spartan than in similarly priced places in the provinces. Whatever the time of year, you should phone as far in advance as you can if you want to stay within a couple of tube stops of the West End. When choosing your **area**, bear in mind that the West End – Soho, Covent Garden, St James's, Mayfair and Marylebone – and the western districts of Knightsbridge and Kensington, are dominated by expensive, upmarket hotels, whereas Bloomsbury is both inexpensive and very central. For cheaper rooms, the widest choice is close to the main train termini of Victoria and Paddington, and the budget B&Bs of Earls Court. Where possible, we've marked the following on the maps in this chapter.

St James's, Mayfair and Marylebone

Edward Lear Hotel 28–30 Seymour St, W1 ☎020/7402 5401, ⓦwww.edlear.com; Marble Arch tube. See map, p.128. Lear's former home enjoys a great location close to Oxford Street and Hyde Park, lovely flower boxes and a plush foyer. Rooms themselves need a bit of a make-over, but the low prices reflect both this and the fact that most only have shared facilities. ➍

Lincoln House Hotel 33 Gloucester Place, W1 ☎020/7486 7630, ⓦwww.lincoln-house-hotel .co.uk; Marble Arch or Baker Street tube. See map, p.128. Dark wood panelling gives this Georgian B&B in Marylebone a ship's-cabin feel, while all the rooms are en suite and well equipped. Rates vary according to the size of the bed and length of stay. ➌

Palace Hotel 31 Great Cumberland Place, W1 ☎020/7262 5585. Marble Arch tube. See map, p.128. Small but luxurious hotel close to Marble Arch which oozes class, from the hand-painted friezes on the staircase to the four-poster beds in many of the rooms. Continental breakfast included. **⑦**

Soho, Covent Garden and The Strand

The Fielding Hotel 4 Broad Court, Bow Street, WC2 ℡ 020/7836 8305, ⓦ www .the-fielding-hotel.co.uk; Covent Garden tube. See map, p.88. Quietly and perfectly situated on a traffic-free and gas-lit court, this excellent hotel is one of Covent Garden's hidden gems. Its en-suite rooms are a firm favourite with visiting performers, since it's just a few yards from the Royal Opera House. Breakfast is extra. **⑥**

Hazlitt's 6 Frith St, W1 ℡ 020/7434 1771, ⓦ www .hazlittshotel.com; Tottenham Court Road tube. See map, p.88. Located off the south side of Soho Square, this early eighteenth-century building is a hotel of real character and charm, offering en-suite rooms decorated and furnished as close to period style as convenience and comfort allow. There's a small sitting room, but no dining room; continental breakfast (served in the rooms) is extra. **⑨**

Manzi's 1–2 Leicester St, WC2 ℡ 020/7734 0224, ⓦ www.manzis.co.uk; Leicester Square tube. See map, p.88. Set over the Italian and seafood restaurant of the same name, *Manzi's* is one of the very few West End hotels in this price range, although noise might prove to be a nuisance. Continental breakfast is included in the price. **⑤**

St Martin's Lane 45 St Martin's Lane, WC2 ℡ 020/7300 5500, ⓦ www.morganshotelgroup .com; Leicester Square tube. See map, p.88. This self-consciously chic "boutique hotel" with a bafflingly anonymous glassed facade is a big hit with the media crowd. The *Light Bar* is the most startling of the hotel's eating and drinking outlets. Rooms currently start at around £250 a double, but rates come down at the weekend. **⑨**

Seven Dials Hotel 7 Monmouth St, WC2 ℡ 020/7681 0791, ⓦ www.smoothhound.co.uk /hotels/sevendials; Covent Garden tube. See map, p.88. Pleasant family-run hotel in the heart of theatreland. All rooms are en suite and have TV, tea/coffee-making facilities and direct-dial phones. **⑤**

Bloomsbury

Hotel Cavendish 75 Gower St, WC1 ℡ 020/7636 9079, ⓦ www.hotelcavendish.com; Goodge Street tube. See map, p.105. A real bargain, with lovely owners and a walled garden. All rooms have shared facilities, and there are some good-value family rooms, too. **②**

Crescent Hotel 49–50 Cartwright Gardens, WC1 ℡ 020/7387 1515, ⓦ www.crescenthoteloflondon .com; Euston, King's Cross or Russell Square tube. See map, p.105. Comfortable and clean B&B, with pink furnishings. All doubles are en suite, but there are a few bargain singles with shared facilities. **⑥**

Ridgemount Private Hotel 65–67 Gower St, WC1 ℡ 020/7636 1141, ⓦ www.ridgemounthotel.co.uk; Goodge Street tube. See map, p.105. Old-fashioned, very friendly, family-run place, with small rooms (some with shared facilities), a garden, free hot-drinks machine and a laundry service. A reliable, basic bargain for Bloomsbury. **③**

Thanet Hotel 8 Bedford Place, WC1 ℡ 020/7636 2869, ⓦ www.thanethotel.co.uk; Russell Square tube. See map, p.105. Small, friendly, family-run B&B close to the British Museum. Rooms are clean, bright and freshly decorated, all with en-suite showers and tea- and coffee-making facilities. **⑥**

Clerkwenwell and the City

City Hotel 12 Osborn St, E1 ℡ 020/7247 3313, ⓦ www.cityhotellondon.co.uk; Aldgate East tube. See map, p.108. Spacious modern hotel on the eastern edge of the City, in the heart of the Bengali East End at the bottom of Brick Lane. The plainly decorated rooms are all en suite, and many have kitchens, too; four-person rooms are a bargain for families or small groups. **⑦**

The King's Wardrobe 6 Wardrobe Place, Carter Lane, EC4 ℡ 020/7792 2222, ⓦ www.bridgestreet.com; St Paul's tube. See map, p.108. In a quiet courtyard just behind St Paul's Cathedral, this place is part of an international chain that caters largely to a business clientele. The apartments (1- to 3-bed) offer fully equipped kitchens and workstations, a concierge service and housekeeping. Though housed in a fourteenth-century building that once contained Edward III's royal regalia, the interior is unrelentingly modern. £130–160 per night per apartment. **②**

The Rookery 12 Peter's Lane, Cowcross Street, EC1 ℡ 020/7336 0931, ⓦ www .rookeryhotel.com; Farringdon tube. See map, p.108. Rambling Georgian townhouse on the edge of the City in trendy Clerkenwell that makes a fantastically discreet little hideaway. The rooms start at £245 a double; each one has been individually designed in a deliciously camp, modern take on the Baroque period, and all have super bathrooms with lots of character. **⑨**

Zetter Hotel 86–88 Clerkenwell Rd, EC1 ℡ 020/7324 4444, ⓦ www.thezetter.com; Farringdon tube. See map, p.108. A warehouse converted with real style and a dash of Sixties glamour. Rooms are simple and minimalist, with fun touches such as lights which change colour and decorative floral panels; ask for a room at the back, overlooking quiet cobbled St John's Square. The attached restaurant serves good modern Italian food, and water for guests is supplied from the *Zetter*'s own well, beneath the building. ❼

South Bank & Southwark

London County Hall Travel Inn Belvedere Road, SE1 ☏020/7902 1619, ⓦwww.premiertravelinn .com; Waterloo or Westminster tube. See map, p.121. Don't expect river views at these prices, but the location in County Hall itself is pretty good if you're up for a bit of sightseeing. Decor and ambience are functional, but for those with kids, the flat-rate rooms are a bargain. ❺

🏃 **Southwark Rose Hotel** 43–47 Southwark Bridge Rd, SE1 ☏020/7015 1490, ⓦwww .southwarkrosehotel.co.uk; London Bridge tube. See map, p.121. The *Southwark Rose* markets itself as a budget hotel with boutique style; nice design touches raise the rooms several notches above the bland chain hotels in the area. Giant aluminium lamps hover over the lobby, which is lined with funky photographs, while the penthouse restaurant offers breakfast with a rooftop view and free Internet access. ❻

Victoria

🏃 **B&B Belgravia** 64–66 Ebury St, SW1 ☏020/7823 4928, ⓦwww.bb-belgravia .com. See map, p.88. A real rarity in this neck of the woods – a B&B with flair, very close to the train and coach station. The 17 rooms are of boutique-hotel quality, with original cornicing and large sash windows and have stylish modern touches – all have flatscreen TVs and funky bathrooms with mosaic tiling. Staff are welcoming and enthusiastic. Internet access. ❻

Morgan House 107 & 120 Ebury St, SW1 ☏020/7730 2384, ⓦwww.morganhouse.co.uk. See map, p.128. An above-average B&B, run by a vivacious couple. Great breakfasts, patio garden, and a fridge for guests to use. Most rooms are en suite. ❹

Oxford House Hotel 92–94 Cambridge St, SW1 ☏020/7834 6467, ⓕ020/7834 0225. See map, p.88. Probably the best-value rooms in the vicinity of Victoria Station, though not otherwise distinguished. Showers and toilets are shared, but kept pristine, and full English breakfast is included in the price. ❷

Paddington, Bayswater and Notting Hill

The Pavilion Hotel 34–36 Sussex Gardens, W2

☏020/7262 0905, ⓦwww.pavilion.hotel.co.uk; Paddington tube. See map, p.128. A decadent rock star's home from home, with outrageously over-the-top decor and every room individually themed, from "honky tonk Afro" to "Highland Fling". ❻

🏃 **Portobello Gold** 95–97 Portobello Rd, W1 ☏020/7460 4900, ⓦwww.portobellogold .com; Notting Hill Gate or Holland Park tube. See map, p.128. A fun and friendly option – six rooms and an apartment above a cheery modern pub. Rooms are plain and some are tiny, with miniature en-suite bathrooms, but all are fairly priced. The apartment is a brilliant option for a group – it sleeps 6 (at a bit of a pinch) and costs £150 a night; it has the feel of a cosy, down-at-heel holiday home, with a dinky Caribbean-themed bathroom and a fantastic roof terrace – the putting green and sweeping views of London make it the perfect place to relax with a bottle of wine or two. ❹

St David's Hotels 14–20 Norfolk Square, W2 ☏020/7723 3856, ⓦwww.stdavidshotels.com; Paddington tube. See map, p.128. A friendly welcome is assured at this inexpensive B&B, famed for its substantial English breakfast. Most rooms share facilities. The large rooms make it a good option for families on a budget. ❸

Vancouver Studios 30 Prince's Square, W2 ☏020/7243 1270, ⓦwww.vancouverstudios .co.uk; Bayswater tube. See map, p.128. Part of a growing trend away from standard hotel accommodation, *Vancouver Studios* offers self-contained apartments in a grand Victorian townhouse, with fully equipped kitchens and hotel-style porterage and maid service. Decor is to a high standard and mixes modern trends with traditional period touches. ❺

Knightsbridge, Kensington and Chelsea

Abbey House 11 Vicarage Gate, W8 ☏020/7721 7395, ⓦwww.abbeyhousekensington.com; High Street Kensington tube. See map, p.128. Inexpensive Victorian B&B in a quiet street just north of Kensington High Street, maintained to a very high standard by its attentive owners. Rooms are large and bright – prices are kept down by sharing facilities. Full English breakfast, with free tea and coffee available all day. Cash only. ❺

🏃 **Aster House** 3 Sumner Place, SW7 ☏020/7581 5888, ⓦwww.asterhouse.com; South Kensington tube. See map, p.128. Pleasant, nonsmoking and award winning B&B in a luxurious South Ken white-stuccoed street; there's a lovely garden at the back and a large conservatory, where breakfast is served. Singles with shared facilities start at around £90 a night. ❼

The Gore 189 Queen's Gate, SW7 ☎020/7584 6601, ⓦwww.gorehotel.com; South Kensington, Gloucester Road or High Street Kensington tube. See map, p.128. Popular, privately owned century-old hotel, awash with oriental rugs, rich mahogany, walnut panelling and other Victoriana. A pricey but excellent bistro restaurant adds to its allure, and it's only a step away from Hyde Park. Rooms, some with four-poster beds, from £190. ❽

Hotel 167 167 Old Brompton Rd, SW5 ☎020/7373 3221, ⓦwww.hotel167.com; Gloucester Road tube. See map, p.128. Small, stylishly furnished B&B with en-suite facilities, double glazing and a fridge in all rooms. Continental buffet-style breakfast is served in the attractive morning room/reception. ❻

Hampstead

🏃 **Hampstead Village Guesthouse** 2 Kemplay Rd, NW3 ☎020/7435 8679, ⓦwww.hampsteadguesthouse.com; Hampstead tube. Lovely B&B in a freestanding Victorian house on a quiet backstreet between Hampstead Village and the Heath. Rooms (most en suite, all non-smoking) are wonderfully characterful, crammed with books, pictures and handmade and antique furniture. Cute cabin-like single for £48, and a self-contained studio for £90. Meals to order. ❺

La Gaffe 107–111 Heath St, NW3 ☎020/7435 8965, ⓦwww.lagaffe.co.uk; Hampstead tube. Small, warren-like hotel situated over an Italian restaurant and bar in the heart of Hampstead Village. All rooms are en suite, if a little cramped, and there's a roof terrace for use in fine weather. ❻

Hostels and student accommodation

London's official **Youth Hostel Association (YHA) hostels** are generally the cleanest, most efficiently run hostels in the capital. However, they charge around fifty percent or more above the rates of private hostels, and tend to get booked up several months in advance. **Independent hostels** are cheaper and more relaxed, but can be less reliable in terms of facilities. A good **website** for booking independent places online is ⓦwww.hostellondon.com. Outside term time, you also have the option of staying in **student halls of residence**: the quality of the rooms varies enormously, but tends to be fairly basic and prices are slightly higher than hostels. London's **campsites** are all on the perimeter of the city, though they are without doubt the cheapest accommodation available.

Where possible we've marked the location of the following on one of the maps in this chapter.

YHA hostels

🏃 **City of London** 36 Carter Lane, EC4 ☎020/7236 4965, ⓔcity@yha.org.uk; St Paul's tube. See map, p.108. Large 200-bed hostel in a superb location opposite St Paul's Cathedral. Some twins at £50 a room, but mostly four- to eight-bed dorms for £17.20 per person. There's no kitchen, but has a café for lunch and dinner. No groups. ❷

Earls Court 38 Bolton Gardens, SW5 ☎020/7373 7083, ⓔearlscourt@yha.org.uk; Earls Court tube. See map, p.128. Better than a lot of accommodation in Earls Court, but only offering dorms of mostly ten beds – the triple bunks take some getting used to. Kitchen, café and patio garden. No groups. £19.50 per person.

Hampstead Heath 4 Wellgarth Rd, NW11 ☎020/8458 9054, ⓔhampstead@yha.org.uk; Golders Green tube. One of the biggest and best-appointed YHA hostels, with its own garden and the wilds of Hampstead Heath nearby. Rooms with 3–6 beds cost £20.40; family rooms with 2–5 beds are also available, starting at £35 for one adult and one child or £45 for two adults. ❷

Holland House Holland Walk, W8 ☎020/7937 0748, ⓦwww.hollhse.btinternet.co.uk; Holland Park or High Street Kensington tube. See map, p.128. Idyllically situated in the wooded expanse of Holland Park and fairly convenient for the centre, this extensive hostel offers a decent kitchen and an inexpensive café, but tends to be popular with school groups. Dorms only (8–20 beds), at £21.60 per person.

Oxford Street 14 Noel St, W1 ☎020/7734 1618, ⓔoxfordst@yha.org.uk; Oxford Circus or Tottenham Court Road tube. See map, p.88. The West End location and modest size (75 beds in rooms of 2, 3 and 4 beds) mean that this hostel tends to be full year-round. No children under 6, no groups, no café, but a large kitchen. From £22.60 per person. ❷

Rotherhithe 20 Salter Rd, SE16 ☎020/7232 2114, ⓔrotherhithe@yha.org.uk; Rotherhithe or Canada Water tube. London's largest purpose-built hostel can feel a little out of things, but is well connected to central London. Often has space when more central places are full. Breakfast, packed lunch and evening meals available. Rooms have 2, 4, 6 or 10 beds and cost from £24.60 per person. ❷

St Pancras 79–81 Euston Rd, NW1 ☎020/7388 9998, @stpancras@yha.org.uk; King's Cross or Euston tube. See map, p.105. Housed on six floors of a former police station, directly opposite the British Library, on the busy Euston Road. Beds cost £24.60 per person, and rooms are very clean, bright, triple-glazed and air-conditioned – some even have en-suite facilities. All doubles are en suite and family rooms are available, all with TVs, from £50.50. No groups. ❸

Private hostels

Ashlee House 261–265 Gray's Inn Rd, WC1 ☎020/7833 9400, @www.ashleehouse.co.uk; King's Cross tube. Clean and friendly hostel in a converted office block near King's Cross Station. Internet access, laundry and kitchen facilities are provided. Dorms, which vary in size from four to sixteen beds, start at £16; there are also a few private singles and twins, starting at £25 per person. Breakfast is included. ❷

Generator Compton Place, off Tavistock Place, WC1 ☎020/7388 7666, @www.the-generator .co.uk; Russell Square or Euston tube. See map, p.105. A huge, funky 800-bed hostel, tucked away down a cobbled street. The neon and UV lighting and postindustrial decor may not be to everyone's taste, but with prices starting at just £12.50 a night for a dorm bed and breakfast, it's a bargain for this part of town. Prices range from £35 for a single, £25 per person for a double and £20 per person for a triple. Dorms from £12.50 (12 beds) to £17 (4 beds). ❷

Leinster Inn 7–12 Leinster Square, W2 ☎020/7229 9641, @www.astorhostels.com; Queensway or Notting Hill Gate tube. See map, p.128. With 360 beds, this is the biggest and liveliest of the *Astor* hostels, with a party atmosphere, and two bars open until the small hours. Some rooms in all categories have their own shower. Dorm beds (4–8 per room) £14–18 per person,

singles £27.50, doubles from £45. ❷

Museum Inn 27 Montague St, W1 ☎020/7580 5360, @www.astorhostels.com; Holborn tube. See map, p.105. In a lovely Georgian house by the British Museum, this is the quietest of the *Astor* hostels. There's no bar, though it's still a sociable, laid-back place, and well situated. There are 75 beds in dorms of four to ten for £16–20, plus some twins at £50, including breakfast. Decent-sized kitchen and TV lounge, also laundry and Internet access. ❷

St Christopher's Village 161–165 Borough High St, SE1 ☎020/7407 1856, @www.st-christophers .co.uk; London Bridge tube. See map, p.124. Flagship of a chain of independent hostels, with no fewer than three properties on Borough High Street (and branches in Camden, Greenwich and Shepherd's Bush). The decor is upbeat and cheerful, the place is efficiently run and there's a party-animal ambience, fuelled by the neighbouring bar and the rooftop hot tub and sauna. Beds in dorms of 4 to 14 £13–22, twins £44. ❷

🏃 **wake up! London** 1 Queens Gardens, W2 ☎020/7262 4471, @www.wakeuplondon .co.uk; Paddington or Lancaster Gate tube. See map, p.128. New and funky hostel with single-sex four- to eight-bed dorms, singles and doubles, and great facilities, including an information desk, 24hr reception and a basement bar (with a pool table) that's open daily till 3am. A good choice if you want a party atmosphere. Dorms from £15 (8-bed). ❷

Campsites

Abbey Wood Federation Road, Abbey Wood, SE2 ☎020/8311 7708; Abbey Wood train station from Charing Cross or London Bridge. Enormous, well-equipped Caravan Club site, ten miles southeast of central London. Open all year.

Crystal Palace Crystal Palace Parade, SE19 ☎020/8778 7155; Crystal Palace train station from Victoria or London Bridge. All-year Caravan Club site; some traffic noise.

Lea Valley Leisure Centre Caravan Park Meridian Way, N9 ☎020/8803 6900; Ponders End train station from Liverpool Street. Well-equipped site, situated behind the leisure centre at Pickett's Lock, backing on to a vast reservoir.

Westminster and Whitehall

Political, religious and regal power has emanated from **Westminster** and **Whitehall** for almost a millennium. It was Edward the Confessor (1042–66) who first established Westminster as London's royal and ecclesiastical power base, some three miles west of the City of London. The embryonic English

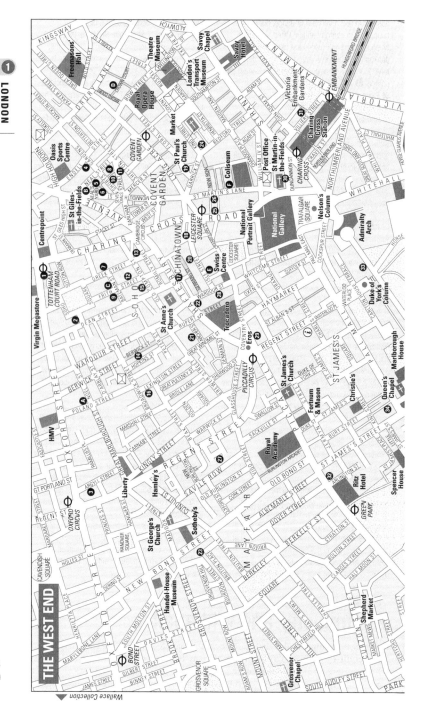

THE WEST END

Wallace Collection ▲

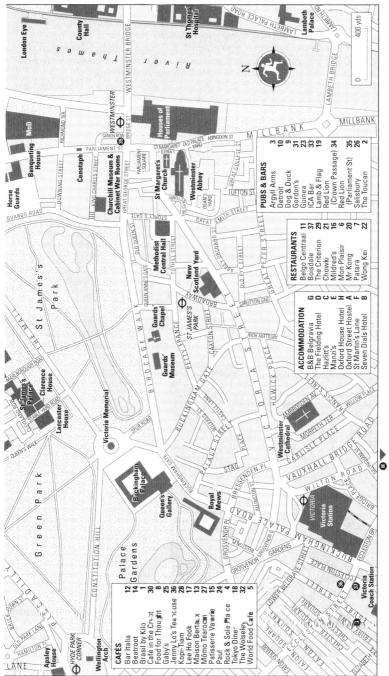

© Crown copyright

CAFÉS

Bar Italia	12
Beatroot	14
Brasil by Kilo	1
Café in the Crypt	30
Food for Thought	8
Gaby's	25
Jenny Lo's Tea House	36
Kopi-Tiam	28
Lee Ho Fook	17
Maison Bertaux	13
Mômo Tearoom	27
Patisserie Valerie	15
Paul	24
Rock & Sole Plaice	4
Tokyo Diner	18
The Wolseley	32
World Food Café	5

ACCOMMODATION

B&B Belgravia	G
The Fielding Hotel	D
Hazlitt's	C
Manzi's	E
Oxford House Hotel	H
Oxford Street Hostel	A
St Martin's Lane	F
Seven Dials Hotel	B

RESTAURANTS

Belgo Centraal	11
Boisdale	37
The Criterion	29
Chowki	16
Mildred's	6
Mon Plaisir	21
Mr Kong	20
Patara	7
Wong Kei	22

PUBS & BARS

Argyll Arms	3
Detroit	10
Dog & Duck	9
Gordon's	31
Guinea	23
ICA Bar	33
Lamb & Flag	19
Red Lion (Crown Passage)	34
Red Lion (Parliament St)	35
Salisbury	26
The Toucan	2

parliament met in the abbey in the fourteenth century and eventually took over the old royal palace of Westminster. In the nineteenth century, Whitehall became the "heart of the Empire", its ministries ruling over a quarter of the world's population. Even now, though the UK's world status has diminished, the institutions that run the country inhabit roughly the same geographical area: Westminster for the politicians, Whitehall for the civil servants.

The monuments and buildings in and around Whitehall and Westminster also span the millennium, and include some of London's most famous landmarks – **Nelson's Column**, **Big Ben** and the **Houses of Parliament**, **Westminster Abbey**, plus two of the city's finest permanent art collections, the **National Gallery** and **Tate Britain**. This is a well-trodden tourist circuit since it's also one of the easiest parts of London to walk round, with all the major sights within a mere half-mile of each other, linked by one of London's most majestic streets, **Whitehall**.

Trafalgar Square

Despite the pigeons and the traffic noise, **Trafalgar Square** is still one of London's grandest architectural set-pieces. John Nash designed the basic layout in the 1820s, but died long before the square took its present form. The Neoclassical National Gallery filled up the northern side of the square in 1838, followed five years later by the central focal point, **Nelson's Column**, topped by the famous admiral; the very large bronze lions didn't arrive until 1868, and the fountains – a real rarity in a London square – didn't take their present shape until the late 1930s.

As one of the few large public squares in London, Trafalgar Square has been both a tourist attraction and a focus for **political demonstrations** since the Chartists assembled here in 1848 before marching to Kennington Common.

On a more festive note, the square is graced each December with a giant Christmas tree, donated by Norway in thanks for liberation from the Nazis, and on **New Year's Eve**, thousands of inebriates sing in the New Year.

Stranded on a traffic island to the south of the column, and predating the entire square, is an **equestrian statue of Charles I**, erected shortly after the Restoration on the very spot where eight of those who had signed the king's death warrant were disembowelled. Charles's statue also marks the original site of the thirteenth-century **Charing Cross**, from where all distances from the capital are measured – a Victorian imitation now stands outside Charing Cross train station.

△ Nelson's Column

The northeastern corner of the square is occupied by James Gibbs's church of **St Martin-in-the-Fields** (Mon–Sat 10am–8pm, Sun noon–8pm; free; Ⓦwww.stmartin-in-the-fields.org), fronted by a magnificent Corinthian portico. Completed in 1726, the interior is purposefully simple, though the Italian plasterwork on the barrel vaulting is exceptionally rich; it's best appreciated while listening to one of the church's free lunchtime concerts. There's a licensed café in the roomy **crypt**, not to mention a shop, gallery and brass-rubbing centre (Mon–Sat 10am–6pm, Sun noon–6pm).

The National Gallery

Unlike the Louvre or the Hermitage, the **National Gallery**, on the north side of Trafalgar Square (daily 10am–6pm, Wed until 8pm; free; Ⓦwww .nationalgallery.org.uk; Leicester Square or Charing Cross tube), is not based on a royal collection, but was begun as late as 1824 by the British government. The gallery's subsequent canny acquisition policy has resulted in more than 2300 paintings, but the collection's virtue is not so much its size, but the range, depth and sheer quality of its contents.

To view the collection chronologically, begin with the **Sainsbury Wing**, the softly-softly, postmodern 1980s adjunct that playfully imitates elements of the original gallery's Neoclassicism. However, with more than a thousand paintings on permanent display in the main galleries, you'll need real stamina to see everything in one day, so if time is tight your best bet is to home in on your areas of special interest, having picked up a gallery plan at one of the information desks. **Audioguides**, with a brief audio commentary on each of the paintings on display, are available for a "voluntary contribution" of £4. Much better, however, are the gallery's **free guided tours** (daily 11.30am & 2.30pm, plus Wed 6 & 6.30pm, Sat also 12.30 & 3.30pm), which set off from the Sainsbury Wing foyer.

Among the National's **Italian** masterpieces are Leonardo's melancholic *Virgin of the Rocks*, Uccello's *Battle of San Romano*, Botticelli's *Venus and Mars* (inspired by a Dante sonnet) and Piero della Francesca's beautifully composed *Baptism of Christ*, one of his earliest works. The fine collection of Venetian works includes Titian's colourful early masterpiece *Bacchus and Ariadne*, his very late, much gloomier *Death of Acteon*, and Veronese's lustrous *Family of Darius before Alexander*. Elsewhere, Bronzino's erotic *Venus, Cupid, Folly and Time* and Raphael's trenchant *Pope Julius II* keep company with Michelangelo's unfinished *Entombment*. Later Italian works to look out for include a couple by Caravaggio, a few splendid examples of Tiepolo's airy draughtsmanship, and glittering vistas of Venice by Canaletto and Guardi.

From **Spain** there are dazzling pieces by El Greco, Goya, Murillo and Velázquez, among them the provocative *Rokeby Venus*. From the **Low Countries**, standouts include van Eyck's *Arnolfini Marriage*, Memlinc's perfectly poised *Donne Triptych*, and a couple of typically serene Vermeers. There are numerous genre paintings, such as Frans Hals' *Family Group in a Landscape*, and some superlative landscapes, most notably Hobbema's *Avenue, Middleharnis*. An array of Rembrandt paintings that features some of his most searching portraits – two of them self-portraits – is followed by abundant examples of Rubens' expansive, fleshy canvases.

Holbein's masterful *Ambassadors* and several of Van Dyck's portraits were painted for the English court; and there's home-grown **British** art, too, represented by important works such as Hogarth's satirical *Marriage à la Mode*, Gainsborough's translucent *Morning Walk*, Constable's ever-popular *Hay Wain*, and Turner's *Fighting Téméraire*. Highlights of the **French** contingent include superb works by Poussin, Claude, Fragonard, Boucher, Watteau and David.

Finally, there's a particularly strong showing of **Impressionists** and **Post-Impressionists** in rooms 43–46 of the East Wing. Among the most famous works are Manet's unfinished *Execution of Maximilian*, Renoir's *Umbrellas*, Monet's *Thames below Westminster*, Van Gogh's *Sunflowers*, Seurat's pointillist *Bathers at Asnières*, a Rousseau junglescape, Cézanne's proto-Cubist *Bathers* and Picasso's Blue-Period *Child with a Dove*.

The National Portrait Gallery

Around the east side of the National Gallery lurks the **National Portrait Gallery** (daily 10am–6pm, Thurs & Fri till 9pm; free; ⓦwww.npg.org.uk; Leicester Square or Charing Cross tube), founded in 1856 to house uplifting depictions of the good and the great. Though it has some fine works in its collection, many of the studies are of less interest than their subjects, and the overall impression is of an overstuffed shrine to famous Brits rather than a museum offering any insight into the history of portraiture. However, it's fascinating to trace who has been deemed worthy of admiration at any moment: aristocrats and artists in previous centuries, warmongers and imperialists in the early decades of the twentieth century, writers and poets in the 1930s and 1940s, and, latterly, retired footballers, and film and pop stars. The NPG's **Sound Guide** gives useful biographical background information and is available in return for a "voluntary contribution".

Whitehall

Whitehall, the broad avenue connecting Trafalgar Square to Parliament Square, is synonymous with the faceless, pinstriped bureaucracy charged with the day-to-day running of the country. Since the sixteenth century, nearly all the key governmental ministries and offices have migrated here, rehousing themselves on an ever-increasing scale. The statues dotted about Whitehall recall the days when this street stood at the centre of an empire on which the sun never set.

During the sixteenth and seventeenth centuries, however, Whitehall was the permanent residence of the kings and queens of England, and was synonymous with royalty. The original **Whitehall Palace** was the London seat of the Archbishop of York, confiscated and greatly extended by Henry VIII after a fire at Westminster forced him to find alternative accommodation. The chief section of the old palace to survive the fire of 1698 was the **Banqueting House** (Mon–Sat 10am–5pm; £4; ⓦwww.hrp.org.uk; Westminster tube), begun by Inigo Jones in 1619 and the first Palladian building to be built in England. The one room now open to the public has no original furnishings, but is well worth seeing for the superlative Rubens ceiling paintings glorifying the Stuart dynasty,

---

The Changing of the Guard

The Queen is colonel-in-chief of the seven **Household Regiments**: the Life Guards (who dress in red and white) and the Blues and Royals (who dress in blue and white) are the two Household Cavalry regiments; while the Grenadier, Coldstream, Scots, Irish and Welsh Guards make up the Foot Guards.

The **Changing of the Guard** takes place at two separate locations in London: the two Household Cavalry regiments take it in turns to stand guard at Horse Guards on Whitehall (Mon–Sat 11am, Sun 10am, with inspection daily at 4pm), while the Foot Guards take care of Buckingham Palace (April–Aug daily 11.30am; Sept–March alternate days; no ceremony if it rains). A ceremony also takes place regularly at Windsor Castle (see p.145).

commissioned by Charles I in the 1630s. Charles himself walked through the room for the last time in 1649 when he stepped onto the executioner's scaffold from one of its windows.

Across the road, two mounted sentries of the Queen's Household Cavalry and two horseless colleagues, all in ceremonial uniform, are posted daily from 10am to 4pm. Ostensibly they are protecting the **Horse Guards** building, originally built as the old palace guard house, but now guarding nothing in particular. The mounted guards are changed hourly; those standing every two hours. Try to coincide your visit with the Changing of the Guard (see box, above).

Further down this west side of Whitehall is London's most famous address, **Number 10 Downing Street** (Ⓦwww.number-10.gov.uk; Westminster tube), the seventeenth-century terraced house that has been the residence of the prime minister since it was presented to Sir Robert Walpole, Britain's first PM, by George II in 1732. Facing Downing Street's locked gates, in the middle of the road, stands Edwin Lutyens' **Cenotaph**, eschewing any kind of Christian imagery, and inscribed simply with the words "The Glorious Dead". The memorial remains the focus of the Remembrance Sunday ceremony in November.

In 1938, in anticipation of Nazi air raids, the basements of the civil service buildings on the south side of King Charles Street, south of Downing Street, were converted into the **Cabinet War Rooms** (daily 9.30am–6pm; £10; Ⓦcwr.iwm.org.uk; Westminster tube). It was here that Winston Churchill directed operations and held Cabinet meetings for the duration of World War II and the rooms have been left pretty much as they were when they finally abandoned on VJ Day 1945, making for an atmospheric underground trot through wartime London. Also in the basement is the excellent **Churchill Museum**. You can hear snippets of Churchill's most famous speeches and check out his trademark bowler, spotted bow-tie and half-chewed Havana, not to mention his wonderful burgundy zip-up "romper suit".

The Houses of Parliament

Clearly visible at the south end of Whitehall is one of London's best-known monuments, the Palace of Westminster, better known as the **Houses of Parliament** (Ⓦwww.parliament.uk). The city's finest Victorian Gothic Revival building and symbol of a nation once confident of its place at the centre of the world, it's distinguished above all by the ornate, gilded clocktower popularly known as **Big Ben**, after the thirteen-ton main bell that strikes the hour (and is broadcast across the world by the BBC).

The original medieval palace burned down in 1834, but **Westminster Hall** survived, and its huge oak hammerbeam roof makes it one of the most magnificent secular medieval halls in Europe – you get a glimpse of the hall en route to the public galleries. The **Jewel Tower** (daily: April–Oct 10am–5pm; Nov–March 10am–4pm; £2.60; EH), across the road from parliament, is another remnant of the medieval palace, now housing an excellent exhibition on the history of parliament – worth visiting before you queue up to get into the Houses of Parliament.

To watch the proceedings in either the House of Commons or the Lords, simply join the queue for the **public galleries** outside St Stephen's Gate. The public are let in slowly from about 4pm onwards on Mondays, from 1pm Tuesday to Thursday, and from 10am on Fridays. If you want to avoid the queues, turn up an hour or more later, when the crowds have usually thinned. Recesses (holiday closures) of both Houses occur at Christmas, Easter, and from August to the middle of October; phone ☎020/7219 4272 for more information or visit Ⓦwww.parliament.uk.

Question Time – when the House is at its most raucous and entertaining – takes place at 2.30pm (Mon) and 11.30am (Tues–Thurs); **Prime Minister's Question Time** is on Wednesday from noon until 12.30pm. To attend either, you need to book a **ticket** several weeks in advance from your local MP (if you're a UK citizen) or your embassy in London (if you're not). For part of the summer recess (Aug & Sept), there are public **guided tours** of the building (Mon, Fri & Sat 9.15am–4.30pm, Tues, Wed & Thurs 1.15–4.30pm; Aug also Tues 9.15am–1.15pm; £7), lasting an hour and fifteen minutes. Visitors can book in advance on ☎0870/906 3773, or simply head for the ticket office on Abingdon Green, opposite Victoria Tower. The rest of the year, your MP or embassy can organize a tour of the building, or a free guided tour up **Big Ben** (Mon–Fri 10.30am, 11.30am & 2.30pm; no under-11s).

Westminster Abbey

The Houses of Parliament dwarf their much older neighbour, **Westminster Abbey** (Mon–Fri 9.30am–4.45pm, Wed until 7pm, Sat 9.30am–1.45pm; £8; Ⓦwww.westminster-abbey.org; Westminster or St James's Park tube), yet this single building embodies much of the history of England: it has been the venue for all coronations since the time of William the Conqueror, and the site of more or less every royal burial for some five hundred years between the reigns of Henry III and George II. Scores of the nation's most famous citizens are honoured here, too (though many of the stones commemorate people buried elsewhere), and the interior is crammed with hundreds of monuments and statues.

Entry is via the north transept, cluttered with monuments to politicians and traditionally known as **Statesmen's Aisle**, shortly after which you come to the abbey's most dazzling architectural set-piece, the **Lady Chapel**, added by Henry VII in 1503 as his future resting place. With its intricately carved vaulting and fan-shaped gilded pendants, the chapel represents the final spectacular gasp of the English Perpendicular style. The public are no longer admitted to the **Shrine of Edward the Confessor**, the sacred heart of the building (except on a guided verger tour; £4) though you do get to inspect Edward I's **Coronation Chair**, a decrepit oak throne dating from around 1300 and still used for coronations.

Nowadays, the abbey's royal tombs are upstaged by **Poets' Corner**, in the south transept, though the first occupant, Geoffrey Chaucer, was in fact buried here not because he was a poet, but because he lived nearby. By the eighteenth century this zone had become an artistic pantheon, and since then, the transept has been filled with tributes to all shades of talent. From the south transept, you can view the central sanctuary, site of the coronations, and the wonderful **Cosmati floor mosaic**, constructed in the thirteenth century by Italian craftsmen, and often covered by a carpet to protect it.

Doors in the south choir aisle lead to the **Great Cloisters** (daily 8am–6pm), rebuilt after a fire in 1298 and now home to a café. At the eastern end of the cloisters lies the octagonal **Chapter House** (daily 10.30am–4pm), where the House of Commons met from 1257. The thirteenth-century decorative paving-tiles have survived intact as have the remarkable apocalyptic wall-paintings, which were executed in celebration of the eviction of the Commons. Chapter House tickets include entry to the **Abbey Museum** (daily 10.30am–4pm), filled with generations of bald royal death masks and wax effigies.

It's only after exploring the cloisters that you get to see the **nave** itself: narrow, light and, at over a hundred feet in height, by far the tallest in the country.

The most famous monument in this section is the **Tomb of the Unknown Soldier**, by the west door, which now serves as the main exit.

Tate Britain

A purpose-built gallery half a mile south of parliament, **Tate Britain** (daily 10am–5.50pm; free; ⑩www.tate.org.uk; Pimlico tube) is devoted exclusively to British art. Founded in 1897 with money from Henry Tate, inventor of the sugar cube, its collection ranges from 1500 to the present. The gallery also showcases contemporary British artists and sponsors the Turner Prize, the country's most prestigious modern-art prize.

The pictures are rehung more or less annually, but always include a fair selection of works by British artists such as Hogarth, Constable, Gainsborough, Reynolds and Blake, plus foreign artists like Van Dyck who spent much of their career over here. The ever-popular **Pre-Raphaelites** are always well represented, as are established twentieth-century greats such as Stanley Spencer and Francis Bacon alongside living artists such as David Hockney and Lucien Freud. Lastly, don't miss the Tate's outstanding **Turner collection**, displayed in the Clore Gallery.

Westminster Cathedral

Halfway down Victoria Street, which runs southwest from Westminster Abbey, you'll find one of London's most surprising churches, the stripey neo-Byzantine concoction of the Roman Catholic **Westminster Cathedral** (Mon–Fri & Sun 7am–7pm, Sat 8am–7pm; free; ⑩www.rcdow.org.uk; Victoria tube). Begun in 1895, and thus one of the last and wildest monuments to the Victorian era, it's constructed from more than twelve million terracotta-coloured bricks, decorated with hoops of Portland stone, and culminating in a magnificent tapered campanile which rises to 274 feet, served by a lift (April–Nov daily 9.30am–12.30pm & 1–5pm; Dec–March Thurs–Sun 9.30am–12.30pm & 1–5pm; £2). The **interior** is only half finished, so to get an idea of what the place will look like when it's finally completed, explore the series of **side chapels** whose rich, multicoloured decor makes use of over one hundred different marbles from around the world.

St James's

St James's, the exclusive little enclave sandwiched between St James's Park and Piccadilly, was laid out in the 1670s close to St James's Palace. Regal and aristocratic residences overlook Green Park, gentlemen's clubs cluster along Pall Mall and St James's Street, while jacket-and-tie restaurants and expense-account gentlemen's outfitters line Jermyn Street. Hardly surprising then that most Londoners rarely stray into this area. Plenty of folk, however, frequent **St James's Park**, with large numbers heading for the Queen's chief residence, **Buckingham Palace**, and the adjacent Queen's Gallery and Royal Mews.

The Mall and St James's Park

The tree-lined sweep of **The Mall** is at its best on Sundays, when it's closed to traffic. It was laid out in the first decade of the twentieth century as a memorial to Queen Victoria, and runs from Trafalgar Square to Buckingham Palace. The bombastic **Admiralty Arch** was erected to mark the entrance at the Trafalgar

The Royal Family

Tourists may still flock to see London's royal palaces, but over the last decade the British public have become more critical of the huge tax bill that goes to support the **Royal Family** (Ⓦ www.royal.gov.uk) in the style to which they are accustomed. This creeping republicanism can be traced back to 1992, which the Queen herself, in one of her few memorable Christmas Day speeches, accurately described as her *annus horribilis*. This was the year that saw the marriage break-ups of Charles and Di, and Andrew and Fergie, and the second marriage of divorcee Princess Anne.

Matters came to a head, though, over who should pay the estimated £50 million costs of repairs after the fire at Windsor Castle (p.145). Misjudging the public mood, the Conservative government offered taxpayers' money to foot the entire bill. After a furore, it was agreed that some of the cost would be raised by opening up Buckingham Palace to the public for the first time (and by cranking up the admission charges on the rest of London's royal palaces). In addition, under pressure from the media, the Queen also reduced the number of royals paid out of the Civil List, and, for the first time in her life, agreed to pay taxes on her enormous personal fortune.

Given the mounting resentment of the Royal Family, it was hardly surprising that public opinion tended to side with Princess Diana rather than Prince Charles during their various disputes. Diana's subsequent death has meant the loss of the Royal Family's most vociferous critic. Yet despite the low poll ratings, none of the political parties currently advocates abolishing the monarchy, and the public appetite for stories about the antics of the young princes (and their potential girlfriends), or the latest on Charles and Camilla, shows few signs of abating.

Square end of The Mall, while at the other end stands the ludicrous **Victoria Memorial**, Edward VII's overblown 2300-ton marble tribute to his mother, which is topped by a gilded statue of Victory, while the six outlying allegorical groups in bronze confidently proclaim the great achievements of her reign.

Flanking nearly the whole length of the Mall, **St James's Park** is the oldest of the royal parks, having been drained and enclosed for hunting purposes by Henry VIII. It was landscaped by Nash in the 1820s, and today its lake is a favourite picnic spot for the civil servants of Whitehall. Pelicans can still be seen at the eastern end of the lake, and there are ducks, swans and geese aplenty.

Buckingham Palace

The graceless colossus of **Buckingham Palace** (Aug–Sept daily 9.30am–4.15pm; £13.50; Ⓦ www.royal.gov.uk; Green Park tube), popularly known as "Buck House", has served as the monarch's permanent London residence only since the accession of Victoria. Bought by George III in 1762, the building was overhauled in the late 1820s by Nash and again in 1913, producing a palace that's as bland as it's possible to be.

For two months of the year, the hallowed portals are grudgingly nudged open; timed tickets are sold from the marquee-like box office in Green Park at the western end of The Mall – to avoid queuing, you must book in advance on Ⓣ 020/7321 2233 or online. The interior, however, is a bit of an anticlimax: of the palace's 660 rooms you're permitted to see twenty or so, and there's little sign of life, as the Queen decamps to Scotland every summer. For the other ten months of the year there's little to do here – not that this deters the crowds who mill around the railings, and gather in some force to watch the **Changing of the Guard** (see p.92), in which a detachment of the Queen's Foot Guards marches to appropriate martial music from St James's Palace (unless it rains).

The public can also pay through the nose to view a small portion of the Royal Collection, at the rebuilt **Queen's Gallery** (daily 10am–5.30pm; £7.50), on the south side of the palace. Exhibitions change regularly, drawn from a collection which is three times larger than the National Gallery, and includes masterpieces by Michelangelo, Reynolds, Gainsborough, Vermeer, Van Dyck, Rubens, Rembrandt and Canaletto, as well as the odd Fabergé egg and heaps of Sèvres china.

There's more pageantry on show at the Nash-built **Royal Mews** (March–July & Oct daily except Fri 11am–4pm; Aug & Sept Mon–Sat 10am–5pm; £6; Victoria tube), further along Buckingham Palace Road. The royal carriages, lined up under a glass canopy in the courtyard, are the main attraction, in particular the Gold Carriage, made for George III in 1762, smothered in 22-carat gilding and weighing four tons, its axles supporting four life-sized figures.

Waterloo Place to St James's Palace

St James's does, however, contain some interesting architectural set-pieces, such as **Waterloo Place**, at the centre of which stands the Guards' Crimean Memorial, fashioned from captured Russian cannon and featuring a statue of Florence Nightingale. Clearly visible, beyond, is the "Grand Old" **Duke of York's Column**, erected in 1833, ten years before Nelson's more famous one in Trafalgar Square.

Cutting across Waterloo Place, **Pall Mall** leads west to **St James's Palace**, whose main red-brick gate-tower is pretty much all that remains of the Tudor palace erected here by Henry VIII. When Whitehall Palace burned down in 1698, St James's became the principal royal residence until Queen Victoria chose to move down the road to Buckingham Palace. The rambling, crenellated complex is closed to the public, with the exception of the **Chapel Royal** (Oct to Good Friday Sun 8.30am & 11.15am; Green Park tube), situated within the palace, and the **Queen's Chapel** (Easter–July Sun 8.30am & 11.15am; Green Park tube), on the other side of Marlborough Road; both are open for services only. **Clarence House** (Aug to mid-Oct daily 9.30am–6pm; £6; ⓦ www.royal.gov.uk), connected to the palace's southwest wing, was the Queen Mother's residence and is now the official London home of Charles and Camilla; the public are allowed to view a handful of unremarkable rooms on the ground floor by guided tour only; tours are very popular so you'll need to book ahead. An even more palatial St James's residence is Princess Diana's ancestral home, **Spencer House** (Feb–July & Sept–Dec Sun 10.30am–5.45pm; £6), a superb Palladian mansion erected in the 1750s. Inside, tour guides take you through nine of the state rooms, the most outrageous of which is Lord Spencer's Room, with its astonishing gilded palm-tree columns. Note that children under 10 are not admitted.

Mayfair and Marylebone

Mayfair and **Marylebone** emerged in the late seventeenth century as London's first real suburbs, characterized by grid plan streets feeding into grand, formal squares. This expansion set the westward trend for middle-class migration, and as London's wealthier consumers moved west, so too did the city's more upmarket shops and luxury hotels, which are still a feature of the area.

Piccadilly, which forms the southern border of **Mayfair**, is no longer the fashionable promenade it once was, but a whiff of exclusivity still pervades

Bond Street and its tributaries. **Regent Street** was created as a new "Royal Mile", but, along with **Oxford Street**, it has since become London's busiest shopping district – it's here that Londoners mean when they talk of "going shopping up the West End".

Marylebone, which lies to the north of Oxford Street, is another grid-plan Georgian development, a couple of social and real-estate leagues below Mayfair, but a wealthy area nevertheless. It boasts a very fine art gallery, the **Wallace Collection**, and, in its northern fringes, one of London's biggest tourist attractions, **Madame Tussaud's**, the oldest and largest wax museum in the world.

Piccadilly Circus and Regent Street

Anonymous and congested it may be, but **Piccadilly Circus** is, for many Londoners, the nearest their city comes to having a centre. A much-altered product of Nash's grand 1812 Regent Street plan and now a major traffic interchange, it may not be a picturesque place, but thanks to its celebrated aluminium statue, popularly known as **Eros**, it's prime tourist territory. The fountain's archer is one of the city's top attractions, a status that baffles all who live here. Despite the bow and arrow, it's not the god of love at all but the *Angel of Christian Charity*, erected to commemorate the Earl of Shaftesbury, a bible-thumping social reformer who campaigned against child labour.

Regent Street, leading north off Piccadilly Circus, is reminiscent of one of Haussmann's Parisian boulevards without the trees. Drawn up by John Nash in 1812 as both a luxury shopping street and a triumphal way between George IV's Carlton House and Regent's Park, it was the city's earliest attempt at dealing with traffic congestion, slum clearance and planned social segregation, which would later be perfected by the Victorians. The increase in the purchasing power of the city's middle classes in the last century brought the tone of the street "down" and heavyweight stores catering for the masses now predominate. Among the best known are **Hamley's**, reputedly the world's largest toyshop, and **Liberty**, the department store that popularized Arts and Crafts designs in the early 1900s.

Piccadilly

Piccadilly apparently got its name from the ruffs or "pickadills" worn by the dandies who used to promenade here in the late seventeenth century. Despite its fashionable pedigree, it's no place for promenading in its current state, with traffic careering down it nose to tail most of the day and night. Infinitely more pleasant places to window-shop are the various **nineteenth-century arcades** on Piccadilly, originally built to protect shoppers from the mud and horse-dung on the streets, but now equally useful for escaping exhaust fumes.

The **Royal Academy of Arts** (daily 10am–6pm, Fri until 10pm; £5–8; ⓦ www.royalacademy.org.uk; Green Park or Piccadilly Circus tube) occupies one of the few surviving aristocratic mansions that once lined the north side of Piccadilly. The country's first-ever formal art school, the RA was founded in 1768 by a group of English painters including Thomas Gainsborough and Joshua Reynolds. The Academy hosts a wide range of art exhibitions, and an annual **Summer Exhibition** that remains a stop on the social calendar of upper-middle-class England. Anyone can enter paintings in any style, and the lucky winners get hung, in rather close proximity, and sold. RA "Academicians" are allowed to display six of their own works – no matter how awful. The result is a bewildering display, which gets panned annually by highbrow critics.

Bond Street

While Oxford Street, Regent Street and Piccadilly have all gone downmarket, **Bond Street**, which runs parallel with Regent Street, has carefully maintained its exclusivity. It is, in fact, two streets rolled into one: the southern half, laid out in the 1680s, is known as Old Bond Street; its northern extension, which followed less than fifty years later, is known as New Bond Street. They are both pretty unassuming streets architecturally, yet the shops that line them are among the flashiest in London, dominated by perfumeries, **jewellers** and designer clothing stores. In addition to fashion, Bond Street is also renowned for its fine art galleries and its **auction houses**, the oldest of which is Sotheby's, 34–35 New Bond St (Ⓦwww.sothebys.com), whose viewing galleries are open free of charge.

Handel House Museum

The German-born composer **George Friedric Handel** (1685–1759) spent the best part of his life in London, producing all the work for which he is now best known at 25 Brook Street, just west of New Bond Street, now the **Handel House Museum** (Tues–Sat 10am–6pm, Thurs till 8pm, Sun noon–6pm; £5; Ⓦwww.handelhouse.org). Although containing few original artefacts, the house has been painstakingly reconstructed and redecorated to show how it would have looked in Handel's day. Further atmosphere is provided by the harpsichord in the rehearsal room, which gets played by music students throughout the week, and with more formal performances on Thursday evenings from 6pm.

Oxford Street and around

As wealthy Londoners began to move out of the City in the eighteenth century in favour of the newly developed West End, so **Oxford Street** (Ⓦwww.oxford street.co.uk) – the old Roman road to Oxford – gradually became London's main shopping thoroughfare. Today, despite successive recessions and sky-high rents, this two-mile hotchpotch of shops is still probably England's busiest street, and is home to (often several) flagship branches of Britain's major retailers (see p.162). The street's only real landmark store is **Selfridge's**, opened in 1909 with a facade featuring the Queen of Time riding the ship of commerce and supporting an Art Deco clock.

The Wallace Collection

Immediately north of Oxford Street, on Manchester Square, stands Hertford House, a miniature eighteenth-century French chateau which holds the splendid **Wallace Collection** (daily 10am–5pm; free; Ⓦwww.wallacecollection .org), a museum-gallery best known for its eighteenth-century French paintings, Franz Hals' *Laughing Cavalier*, Titian's *Perseus and Andromeda*, Velázquez's *Lady with a Fan* and Rembrandt's affectionate portrait of his teenage son, Titus. There's a modern café in the newly glassed-over courtyard, but at heart, the Wallace Collection remains an old-fashioned place, with exhibits piled high in glass cabinets, and paintings covering every inch of wall space. The fact that these exhibits are set amidst period fittings – and a bloody great armoury – makes the place even more remarkable.

Madame Tussaud's

Madame Tussaud's (Mon–Fri 9.30am–5.30pm, Sat & Sun 9am–6pm; £24; ☎0870/400 3000, Ⓦwww.madame-tussauds.co.uk; Baker Street tube), just up

Marylebone Road from Baker Street tube, has been pulling in the crowds ever since the good lady arrived in London from Paris in 1802 bearing the sculpted heads of guillotined aristocrats (she herself only just managed to escape the same fate – her uncle, who started the family business, was less fortunate). The entrance fee might be truly extortionate, the likenesses occasionally dubious and the automated dummies inept, but you can still rely on finding London's biggest queues here. The only way to avoid joining the line is to pay extra and book a timed entry ticket in advance over the phone or on the Internet. As well as the usual parade of wax figures, the tour features live actors trained to frighten the living daylights out of visitors in the Chamber of Horrors and ends with a manic five-minute "ride" through the history of London in a miniaturized taxi.

Soho

Soho has been a favourite haunt of the capital's creative bohos and literati for many years now: Dr Johnson, Thomas de Quincey, Wagner, Marx, Rimbaud and Verlaine to name but a few. The area's reputation for tolerance also made it an obvious place of refuge from dour, postwar Britain. Jazz and skiffle venues proliferated in the 1950s, folk and rock clubs in the 1960s, and punk-rock at the end of the 1970s. The area's most recent transformation has seen it become Europe's leading gay centre, with lively bars and cafés bursting out from the Old Compton Street area.

Bounded by Regent Street to the west, Oxford Street to the north and Charing Cross Road to the east, Soho remains very much the heart of London and one of the capital's most diverse and characterful areas. Conventional sights are few and far between, yet it's a great area to wander through, with probably more streetlife than anywhere else in London – whatever hour you pass by, there's always something going on. Most folk head here to visit one of the big cinemas on **Leicester Square**, to drink in the latest hip bar or to grab a bite to eat at the innumerable cafés and restaurants, ranging from the inexpensive Chinese places that pepper the tiny enclave of **Chinatown**, to old-established Italian joints and Michelin-starred restaurants in the backstreets.

Leicester Square and Chinatown

By night, when the big cinemas and discos are doing good business, and the buskers are entertaining the crowds, **Leicester Square** is one of the most crowded places in London, particularly on a Friday or Saturday when huge numbers of tourists and half the youth of the suburbs seem to congregate here. It wasn't until the mid-nineteenth century that the square actually began to emerge as an entertainment zone; cinema moved in during the 1930s, a golden age evoked by the sleek black lines of the Odeon on the east side, and maintains its grip on the area. The Empire, on the north side, is the favourite for the big royal premieres.

Chinatown, hemmed in between Leicester Square and Shaftesbury Avenue, is a self-contained jumble of shops, cafés and restaurants that makes up one of London's most distinct and popular ethnic enclaves. **Gerrard Street**, Chinatown's main drag, has been endowed with ersatz touches – telephone kiosks rigged out as pagodas and fake oriental gates or *paifang* – though few of London's 60,000 Chinese actually live in the three small blocks of Chinatown. Nonetheless, it remains a focus for the community, a place to do business or the weekly shopping, celebrate a wedding, or just meet up for meals, particularly on Sundays, when the restaurants overflow with Chinese families tucking into *dim sum*.

Old Compton Street

If Soho has a main drag, it has to be **Old Compton Street**, which runs parallel with Shaftesbury Avenue. The corner shops, peep shows, boutiques and trendy cafés here are typical of the area and a good barometer of the latest fads. Soho has been a permanent fixture on the **gay scene** for the better part of a century, but the approach is much more upfront nowadays, with gay bars, clubs and cafés jostling for position on Old Compton Street and round the corner in Wardour Street.

The streets round here are lined with Soho institutions past and present. One of the best known is London's longest-running jazz club, *Ronnie Scott's*, on Frith Street, founded in 1958 and still capable of pulling in the big names. Opposite is *Bar Italia*, an Italian café with late-night hours popular with Soho's clubbers. It was in this building, appropriately enough for such a media-saturated area, that John Logie Baird made the world's first public television transmission in 1926.

Covent Garden and the Strand

Covent Garden's transformation from a workaday fruit and vegetable market into a fashion-conscious *quartier* is one of the most miraculous and enduring developments of the 1980s. More sanitized and brazenly commercial than neighbouring Soho, it's a far cry from the district's heyday when the piazza was the great playground (and red-light district) of eighteenth-century London. The buskers in front of St Paul's Church, the theatres round about, and the **Royal Opera House** on Bow Street are survivors in this tradition, and on a balmy summer evening, **Covent Garden Piazza** is still an undeniably lively place to be. Another positive side-effect of the market development has been the renovation of the run-down warehouses to the north of the piazza, especially around the Neal Street area, which now boasts some of the most fashionable shops in the West End, selling everything from shoes to skateboards.

As its name suggests, the **Strand**, just to the south of Covent Garden, once lay along the riverbank: it achieved its present-day form when the Victorians shored up the banks of the Thames to create the Embankment. The Strand's most intriguing sight is **Somerset House**, sole survivor of the street's grandiose river palaces, now housing several museums and galleries as well as a lovely fountain courtyard.

Covent Garden Piazza

London's oldest planned square, laid out in the 1630s by Inigo Jones, **Covent Garden Piazza** was initially a great success, its novelty value alone attracting a rich and aristocratic chentele, but over the next century the tone of the place fell as the fruit and vegetable market expanded, and theatres and coffee houses began to take over the peripheral buildings. When the market closed in 1974, the piazza narrowly survived being turned into an office development. Instead, the elegant Victorian market hall and its environs were restored to house shops, restaurants and arts-and-crafts stalls.

Of Jones's original piazza, the only remaining parts are the two rebuilt sections of north-side arcading, and **St Paul's Church**, facing the west side of the market building. The proximity of so many theatres has earned it the nickname of the "Actors' Church", and it's filled with memorials to international thespians from Boris Karloff to Gracie Fields. The space in front of the church's Tuscan portico – where Eliza Doolittle was discovered selling violets by Henry Higgins in George Bernard Shaw's *Pygmalion* – is now a legalized venue for buskers and street performers, who must audition for a slot months in advance.

The piazza's museums

A former flower-market shed on the piazza's east side is now home to **London's Transport Museum** (daily 10am–6pm, Fri opens 11am; £5.95; Ⓦ www.ltmuseum.co.uk), which is currently closed for refurbishment until 2007. It's impossible to say how the museum will be set out when it reopens, but you can be sure that there'll still be a great collection of old buses, trains and trams to clamber over and a whole lot of interactive fun to keep children amused. There's usually a good smattering of London Transport's stylish maps and posters on display, too, and you can buy reproductions, plus countless other LT paraphernalia, at the shop on the way out.

The rest of the old flower market now houses the **Theatre Museum** (Tues–Sun 10am–6pm; free; Ⓣ020/7943 4700, Ⓦ www.theatremuseum.org), an outpost of the V&A (see p.132) displaying three centuries of memorabilia from every conceivable area of the performing arts in the western world (the entrance is on Russell Street). The museum's temporary exhibitions have always been consistently engaging, as have the workshops, make-up demonstrations and occasional live performances.

The Royal Opera House

The arcading on the northeast side of the piazza was rebuilt as part of the recent redevelopment of the **Royal Opera House** (Ⓦ www.royaloperahouse.org), whose main Neoclassical facade dates from 1811 and opens onto Bow Street. Now, however, you can reach the opera house from a passageway in the corner of the arcading. The spectacular wrought-iron **Floral Hall** (daily 10am–3pm) serves as the opera house's main foyer, and is open to the public, as is the *Amphitheatre* bar/restaurant (from one and a half hours before performance to the end of the last interval), which has a glorious terrace overlooking the piazza. For backstage tours of the opera house, it's best to book in advance (Mon–Fri 10.30am, 12.30 & 2.30pm, Sat also 11.30am; £9; Ⓣ020/7304 4000).

Strand

Once famous for its riverside mansions, and later its music halls, the **Strand** – the main road connecting Westminster to the City – is a shadow of its former self. One of the few vestiges of glamour is **The Savoy**, London's grandest hotel, built in 1889 on the site of the medieval Savoy Palace on the south side of the street. César Ritz was the original manager, Guccio Gucci started out as a dishwasher here, and the list of illustrious guests is endless: Monet painted the Thames from one of the south-facing rooms, Sarah Bernhardt nearly died here, and Strauss the Younger arrived with his own orchestra.

Somerset House

Further east along the Strand, **Somerset House** (Ⓦ www.somerset-house.org .uk) is the sole survivor of the grand edifices which once lined the riverfront, its four wings enclosing a large **courtyard** (daily 10am–11pm; free) featuring a wonderful 55-jet fountain that spouts straight from the cobbles; in winter, an ice rink is set up in its place. The present building was begun in 1776 by William Chambers as a purpose-built governmental office development, but now also houses a series of museums and galleries.

The south wing, overlooking the Thames, is home to the **Hermitage Rooms** (daily 10am–6pm; £6; ⓦwww.hermitagerooms.com), featuring changing displays drawn from St Petersburg's Hermitage Museum, and the **Gilbert Collection** (daily 10am–6pm; £5; ⓦwww.gilbert-collection.org.uk), a museum of decorative arts displaying gaudy European silver and gold nick-nacks, micro-mosaics, clocks, portrait miniatures and snuffboxes. Alternatively, save yourself some money and go and admire the Royal Naval Commissioners' gilded eighteenth-century barge in the **King's Barge House**, at ground level in the south wing (daily 10am–6pm; free).

In the north wing are the **Courtauld Institute galleries** (daily 10am–6pm; £5; free Mon 10am–2pm; ⓦwww.courtauld.ac.uk), chiefly known for their dazzling collection of Impressionist and Post-Impressionist paintings. Among the most celebrated works is a small-scale version of Manet's *Déjeuner sur l'herbe*, Renoir's *La Loge*, and Degas' *Two Dancers*, plus a whole heap of Cézanne's canvases, including one of his series of *Card Players*. The Courtauld also boasts a fine selection of works by the likes of Rubens, Van Dyck, Tiepolo and Cranach the Elder. The collection has recently been augmented by the long-term loan of a hundred top-notch twentieth-century paintings and sculptures by, among others, Kandinksy, Matisse, Dufy, Derain, Rodin and Henry Moore.

Bloomsbury

Bloomsbury was built over in grid-plan style from the 1660s onwards, and the formal bourgeois Georgian squares laid out then remain the area's main distinguishing feature. In the twentieth century, it acquired a reputation as the city's most learned quarter, dominated by the dual institutions of the **British Museum** and **London University**, and home to many of London's chief book publishers, but perhaps best known for its literary inhabitants, among them T.S. Eliot and Virginia Woolf. Today, the British Museum is clearly the star attraction, but there are other sights, such as the **Dickens House Museum**, that are high on many people's itineraries. Only in its northern fringes does the character of the area change dramatically, becoming steadily seedier as you near the mainline train stations of **Euston**, **St Pancras** and **King's Cross**.

The British Museum

The **British Museum** (daily 10am–5.30pm, Thurs & Fri until 8.30pm; free; ⓦwww.british-museum.ac.uk; Russell Square, Tottenham Court Road or Holborn tube) is one of the great museums of the world. With seventy thousand exhibits ranged over two and a half miles of galleries, the museum boasts one of the largest and most comprehensive collections of antiquities, prints and drawings to be housed under one roof – seven million at the last count (a number increasing daily with the stream of new acquisitions, discoveries and bequests). Its assortment of Roman and Greek art is unparalleled, its Egyptian collection is the most significant outside Egypt and, in addition, there are fabulous treasures from Anglo-Saxon and Roman Britain, from China, Japan, India and Mesopotamia – not to mention an enormous collection of prints

△ The British Museum

and drawings, only a fraction of which can be displayed at any one time.

The building itself, begun in 1823, is the grandest of London's Greek Revival edifices, dominated by the giant Ionian colonnade and portico that forms the main entrance. At the heart of the museum is the **Great Court** (Mon–Wed, Sat & Sun 9am–6pm, Thurs & Fri 9am–11pm), with its remarkable, curving glass-and-steel roof, designed by Norman Foster. At the centre stands the copper-domed former **Round Reading Room**, built in the 1850s to house the British Library. It was here, reputedly at desk O7, beneath one of the largest domes in the world, that Karl Marx penned *Das Kapital*. The building is now a public study area, and features a multimedia guide to the museum's displays.

You'll never manage to see everything in one visit, so the best advice is to concentrate on one or two areas of interest, or else sign up with one of the museum's **guided tours**. One place you could start is the museum's collection of **Roman and Greek antiquities**, perhaps most famous for the Parthenon sculptures, better known as the **Elgin Marbles**, after the British aristocrat who walked off with the reliefs in 1801.

The **Egyptian collection** ranges from monumental sculptures, such as the colossal granite head of Amenophis III, to the ever-popular **mummies** and their ornate outer caskets. Also on display is the **Rosetta Stone**, which finally unlocked the secret of Egyptian hieroglyphs. There's a splendid series of **Assyrian reliefs** from Nineveh, depicting events such as the royal lion hunts of Ashurbanipal, in which the king slaughters one of the cats with his bare hands.

The leathery half-corpse of the 2000-year-old **Lindow Man**, discovered in a Cheshire bog, and the Anglo-Saxon treasure from the **Sutton Hoo** ship burial, are among the highlights of the prehistoric and Romano-British section. The medieval and modern collections, meanwhile, range from the twelfth-century **Lewis chessmen**, carved from walrus ivory, to twentieth-century exhibits such as a copper vase by Frank Lloyd Wright.

The dramatically lit Mexican and North American galleries, plus the African galleries in the basement, represent just a small fraction of the museum's **ethnographic collection**, while select works from the BM's enormous collection of **prints and drawings** can be seen in special exhibitions. In addition, there are fabulous **Oriental treasures** in the north wing, closest to the back entrance on Montague Place. The displays include ancient Chinese porcelain, ornate snuffboxes, miniature landscapes, and a bewildering array of Buddhist and Hindu gods.

MARYLEBONE & BLOOMSBURY

ACCOMMODATION
Ashlee House	E
Hotel Cavendish	E
Crescent Hotel	C
Generator	D
Museum Inn	F
Ridgemount	G
Private Hotel	
St Pancras Hostel	A
Thanet Hotel	B

RESTAURANTS & CAFÉS
Fairuz	9
Eat & Two Veg	3
Indian YMCA	4
Ikkyu	5
The Providores	7
Rasa Samudra	6
Wagamama	8

PUBS & BARS
Lamb	1
Museum Tavern	6
O'Conor Don	10
The Social	11

© Crown copyright

Foundling Museum

To the east of Russell Square tube is the site of the Foundling Hospital, founded in 1756 by Thomas Coram, a retired sea captain. All that remains of the original eighteenth-century buildings is the alcove where the foundlings used to be abandoned and the whitewashed loggia which now forms the border to **Coram's Fields**, a wonderful inner-city park for children, with a whole host of hens, horses, sheep, pigs and rabbits. Adults are not allowed into the grounds unless accompanied by a child. At the **Foundling Museum** (Tues–Sat 10am–6pm, Sun noon–6pm; £5; ☎020/7841 3600, Ⓦwww.foundlingmuseum .org.uk), just to the north of Coram's Fields, at 40 Brunswick Square, you can learn more about the fascinating story of the hospital. One of the hospital's founding governors – he even fostered two of the children – was the artist **William Hogarth**, and as a result the museum boasts an impressive art collection including works by Gainsborough and Reynolds, now hung in the eighteenth-century interiors carefully preserved in their entirety from the original hospital.

Dickens House

Despite the plethora of blue plaques marking the residences of local luminaries, **Dickens House** (Mon–Sat 10am–5pm, Sun 11am–5pm; £5; Ⓦwww .dickensmuseum.com), at 48 Doughty St, in Bloomsbury's eastern fringes, is the area's only literary museum. Dickens moved here in 1837 shortly after his marriage to Catherine Hogarth, and they lived here for two years, during which time he wrote *Nicholas Nickleby* and *Oliver Twist*. Although Dickens painted a gloomy Victorian world in his books, the drawing room here, in which Dickens entertained his literary friends, was decorated in a rather upbeat Regency style. Letters, manuscripts and first editions, the earliest known portrait (a miniature painted by his aunt in 1830) and the reading copies he used during extensive lecture tours in Britain and the States are the rewards for those with more than a passing interest in the novelist. You can also watch a half-hour film of his life.

The British Library

The **British Library** (Mon & Wed–Fri 9.30am–6pm, Tues 9.30am–8pm, Sat 9.30am–5pm, Sun 11am–5pm; free; Ⓦwww.bl.uk; King's Cross or Euston tube), located on the busy Euston Road on the northern fringes of Bloomsbury, opened to the public in 1998. As the country's most expensive public building it was hardly surprising that the place drew fierce criticism from all sides. Yet while it's true that the building's red-brick brutalism is horribly out of fashion, and compares unfavourably with its cathedralesque Victorian neighbour, the former *Midland Grand Hotel*, the interior of the library has met with general approval, and the high-tech exhibition galleries are superb.

With the exception of the reading rooms, the library is open to the general public. The three exhibition galleries are to the left as you enter; straight ahead is the spiritual heart of the building, a multistorey glass-walled tower housing the vast **King's Library**, collected by George III, and donated to the museum by George IV in 1823; to the side of the King's Library are the pull-out drawers of the **philatelic collection**. If you want to explore the parts of the building not normally open to the public, you must sign up for a **guided tour** (Mon, Wed & Fri 3pm, Sat 10.30am & 3pm; £6; or Sun 11.30am & 3pm if you want to see the reading rooms; £7).

The first of the three exhibition galleries to head for is the dimly lit **John Ritblat Gallery**, where a superlative selection of the BL's ancient manuscripts, maps, documents and precious books, including the richly illustrated Lindisfarne Gospels, are displayed. One of the most appealing innovations is "**Turning the Pages**", a small room off the main gallery, where you can turn the pages of selected texts "virtually" on a computer terminal. The **Workshop of Words, Sounds and Images** is a hands-on exhibition of more universal appeal, where you can design your own literary publication, while the **Pearson Gallery of Living Words** puts on excellent temporary exhibitions, for which there is sometimes an admission charge.

Holborn, Clerkenwell and Hoxton

Holborn, **Clerkenwell** and **Hoxton** lie on the periphery of the financial district of the City. **Holborn** (pronounced "Ho-bun") has long been associated with the law, and its **Inns of Court** make for an interesting stroll, their archaic, cobbled precincts exuding the rarefied atmosphere of an Oxbridge college, and sheltering one of the city's oldest churches, the twelfth-century **Temple Church**. Close by the Inns, in Lincoln's Inn Fields, is the **Sir John Soane's Museum**, one of the most memorable and enjoyable of London's small museums, packed with architectural illusions and an eclectic array of curios.

Clerkenwell, further to the northeast, is definitely off the conventional tourist trail with just a few minor sights. Since the 1990s, however, parts of the area have been transformed and, to a certain extent, gentrified, by an influx of young, loft-living designer and media types, whose arrival has had a marked effect on the choice and style of bars and restaurants on offer.

Neighbouring **Hoxton** (aka Shoreditch) to the east, has also acquired a certain caché, due to the high density of artists and architects who currently live and work here. Visually, Hoxton, a slum area badly damaged in the Blitz, remains harsher on the eye than Clerkenwell, though it, too, has more than its fair share of trendy bars and restaurants. Several of London's contemporary art dealers now have Hoxton outlets, and there's the excellent **Geffrye Museum** of furniture design to aim for too.

Temple and the Royal Courts of Justice

Temple (Temple or Blackfriars tube) is the largest and most complex of the Inns of Court, where every barrister in England must study before being called to the Bar. A few very old buildings survive here and the maze of courtyards and passageways is fun to explore. Medieval students ate, attended lectures and slept in the **Middle Temple Hall** (Mon–Fri 10am–noon & 3–4pm; free), across the courtyard, still the Inn's main dining room. The present building was constructed in the 1560s and provided the setting for many great Elizabethan masques and plays – probably including Shakespeare's *Twelfth Night*, which is believed to have been premiered here in 1602. The hall is worth a visit for its fine hammerbeam roof, wooden panelling and decorative Elizabethan screen.

The two Temple Inns share use of the complex's oldest building, **Temple Church** (Wed–Sun 11am–4pm; Ⓦwww.templechurch.com), built in 1185 by the Knights Templar. An oblong chancel was added in the thirteenth century, and the whole building was damaged in the Blitz, but the original round church – modelled on the Church of the Holy Sepulchre in Jerusalem – still stands,

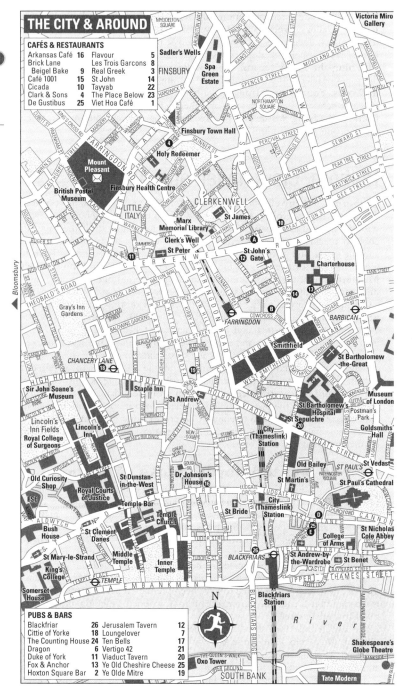

THE CITY & AROUND

CAFÉS & RESTAURANTS

Arkansas Café	16	Flavour	5
Brick Lane		Les Trois Garcons	8
Beigel Bake	9	Real Greek	3
Café 1001	15	St John	14
Cicada	10	Tayyab	22
Clark & Sons	4	The Place Below	23
De Gustibus	25	Viet Hoa Café	1

PUBS & BARS

Blackfriar	26	Jerusalem Tavern	12
Cittie of Yorke	18	Loungelover	7
The Counting House	24	Ten Bells	17
Dragon	6	Vertigo 42	21
Duke of York	11	Viaduct Tavern	20
Fox & Anchor	13	Ye Old Cheshire Cheese	25
Hoxton Square Bar	2	Ye Olde Mitre	19

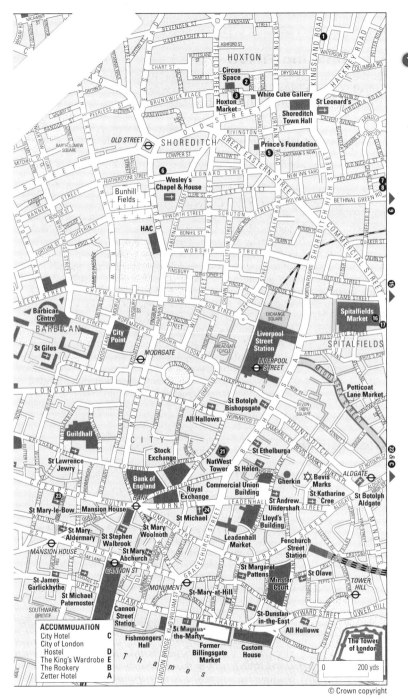

ACCOMMODATION

City Hotel	C
City of London Hostel	D
The King's Wardrobe	E
The Rookery	B
Zetter Hotel	A

0   200 yds

109

© Crown copyright

with its striking Purbeck marble piers, recumbent marble effigies of knights and tortured grotesques grimacing in the spandrels of the blind arcading.

Lincoln's Inn Fields

To the north of Temple, on the far side of the Royal Courts of Justice, lies **Lincoln's Inn Fields**, London's largest square, laid out in the early 1640s with **Lincoln's Inn** (Mon–Fri 9am–6pm; ⓦwww.lincolnsinn.org.uk; Holborn tube), the first – and in many ways the prettiest – of the Inns of Court on its east side. The Inn's fifteenth-century **Old Hall** is open by appointment only (ⓣ020/7405 1393), but you can view the early seventeenth-century **chapel** (Mon–Fri noon–2pm), with its unusual fan-vaulted open undercroft and, on the first floor, its late Gothic nave, hit by a zeppelin in World War I and much restored since.

The south side of Lincoln's Inn Fields is occupied by the gigantic Royal College of Surgeons, home to the **Hunterian Museum** (Tues–Sat 10am–5pm; free; ⓦwww.rcseng.ac.uk; Holborn tube), a fascinating collection of pickled skeletons and body pieces. Also on view is the skeleton of the "Irish giant", Charles Byrne (1761–83), who was seven feet ten inches tall, and, in the adjacent McCrae Gallery, the Sicilian midget Caroline Crachami (1815–24), who stood at only one foot ten and a half inches when she died at the age of nine.

A group of buildings on the north side of Lincoln's Inn Fields houses **Sir John Soane's Museum** (Tues–Sat 10am–5pm; first Tues of the month also 6–9pm; free; ⓦwww.soane.org; Holborn tube), one of London's best-kept secrets. The chief architect of the Bank of England, Soane (1753–1837) was an avid collector who designed this house not only as a home and office, but also as a place to stash his large collection of art and antiquities. Arranged much as it was in his lifetime, the ingeniously planned house has an informal, treasure-hunt atmosphere, with surprises in every alcove; the museum also exhibits contemporary art. At 2.30pm every Saturday, a fascinating, hour-long **guided tour** (£3) takes you round the museum and the enormous research library, next door, containing architectural drawings, books, and exquisitely detailed cork and wood models.

Clerkenwell

Poverty and overcrowding were the main features of nineteenth-century Clerkenwell, and **Clerkenwell Green** became known in the press as "the headquarters of republicanism, revolution and ultra-non-conformity". The Green's connections with **radical politics** have continued and its oldest building, built as a Welsh Charity School in 1737, is now home to the **Marx Memorial Library** (Mon–Thurs 1–2pm or by appointment; closed Aug; free; ⓦwww.marxlibrary.net), at no. 37a. One-time headquarters of the Social Democratic Federation press, this is where **Lenin** edited seventeen editions of the Bolshevik paper *Iskra* in 1902–03. The poky little back room where he worked can be viewed, preserved as it was then, as a kind of shrine.

Of Clerkenwell's three medieval religious establishments, remnants of two survive. The oldest is the priory of the Order of St John of Jerusalem; the sixteenth-century **St John's Gate** (Mon–Fri 10am–5pm, Sat 10am–4pm; free; ⓦwww.sja.org.uk), on the south side of Clerkenwell Road, is the most visible survivor of the foundation. Today, the gatehouse forms part of a **museum**, which traces the development of the order before its dissolution in this country by Henry VIII, and its re-establishment in the nineteenth century. In 1877, the St John Ambulance was founded, to provide a voluntary first-aid service to the public. It's in this field that the order is now best known in Britain – a splendid interactive gallery is devoted to the history of the service. To get to see the rest of the gatehouse, and to visit the Norman crypt of the Grand Priory Church over the road, you must take a **guided tour** (Tues, Fri & Sat 11am & 2.30pm; £5 donation requested).

Hoxton

Until recently, **Hoxton** was an unpleasant amalgam of wholesale clothes and shoe shops, striptease pubs and roaring traffic. Over the last decade, however, it has been colonized by artists, designers and architects and transformed into the city's most vibrant artistic enclave, peppered with contemporary art galleries and a whole host of very cool bars and clubs.

On City Road stands one of Hoxton's few formal sights, the Georgian ensemble of **Wesley's Chapel and House** (Mon–Sat 10am–4pm, Sun noon–1.45pm; free; Ⓦwww.wesleyschapel.org.uk). A place of pilgrimage for Methodists, the uncharacteristically ornate chapel, built in 1777, heralded the coming of age of Wesley's sect. The **Museum of Methodism** in the basement tells the story of Wesley and Methodism, and there's even a brief mention of Mrs Mary Vazeille, the 41-year-old, insanely jealous, wealthy widow he married, and who eventually left him. Wesley himself spent his last two years in the delightful Georgian house to the right of the main gates, and inside you can see his deathbed, plus an early shock-therapy machine he was particularly keen on.

The geographical focus of the area's current transformation is **Hoxton Square**, situated northeast of Old Street tube, a strange and not altogether happy mixture of light industrial units and artists' studios arranged around a leafy, formal square. Despite the lack of aesthetic charm, the area has become an increasingly fashionable place to live and work, and several leading West End **art galleries** have opened premises here, among them Jay Jopling's White Cube at the south end of the square itself.

Hoxton's one other conventional tourist sight is the **Geffrye Museum** (Tues–Sat 10am–5pm, Sun noon–5pm; free; Ⓦwww.geffrye-museum.org.uk), a museum of furniture design, set back from Kingsland Road in a peaceful little enclave of eighteenth-century ironmongers' almshouses. A series of period living rooms, ranging from the oak-panelled seventeenth century through refined Georgian and cluttered Victorian, leads to the New Gallery Extension, housing an excellent twentieth-century section and a pleasant café/restaurant. To get to the museum, take bus #149 or #242 from Liverpool Street tube.

The City

The City is where London began. Long established as the financial district, it stretches from Temple Bar in the west to the Tower of London in the east – administrative boundaries that are only slightly larger than those marked by the Roman walls and their medieval successors. However, in this Square Mile (as the City is sometimes referred to), you'll find few leftovers of London's early days, since four-fifths of the area burnt down in the Great Fire of 1666. Rebuilt in brick and stone, the City gradually lost its centrality as London swelled westwards, though it has maintained its position as Britain's financial heartland. What you see on the ground is mostly the product of three fairly recent building phases: the Victorian construction boom of the latter half of the nineteenth century; the overzealous postwar reconstruction following the Blitz; and the

The Corporation of London

The one unchanging aspect of the City is its special status, conferred on it by William the Conqueror and extended and reaffirmed by successive monarchs and governments ever since. Nowadays, with its Lord Mayor, its Beadles, Sheriffs and Aldermen, its separate police force and its select electorate of freemen and liverymen, the City is an anachronism of the worst kind. **The Corporation** (Ⓦ www .corpoflondon.gov.uk), which runs the City like a one-party mini-state, is an unreconstructed old boys' network whose medievalist pageantry camouflages the very real power and wealth it holds – the Corporation owns nearly a third of the Square Mile (and several tracts of land elsewhere in and around London). Its anomalous status is all the more baffling when you consider that the City was once the cradle of British democracy: it was the City that traditionally stood up to bullying sovereigns.

building frenzy that began in the 1980s, and which has seen nearly fifty percent of the City's office space rebuilt.

When you consider what has happened here, it's amazing that so much has survived to pay witness to the City's two-thousand-year history. Wren's spires still punctuate the skyline here and there and his masterpiece, **St Paul's Cathedral**, remains one of London's geographical pivots. At the eastern edge of the City, the **Tower of London** still stands protected by some of the best-preserved medieval fortifications in Europe. Other relics, such as the City's few surviving medieval alleyways, Wren's **Monument** to the Great Fire and London's oldest synagogue and church, are less conspicuous, and even locals have problems finding the more modern attractions of the **Museum of London** and the **Barbican** arts complex.

Perhaps the biggest change of all, though, has been in the City's population. Up until the eighteenth century the majority of Londoners lived and worked in or around the City; nowadays 300,000 commuters spend the best part of Monday to Friday here, but only 5000 people remain at night and at weekends. The result of this demographic shift is that the City is fully alive only during office hours. This means that weekdays are by far the best time to visit; many pubs, restaurants and even some tube stations and tourist sights close down at the weekend.

Fleet Street

Fleet Street's heyday was in the nineteenth century when all the major national and provincial dailies had their offices and printing presses here. From the 1980s onwards, however, the press barons relocated to Docklands and elsewhere and nowadays the street has virtually no journalistic connections at all. The best source of information about the old-style Fleet Street is the so-called "journalists' and printers' cathedral", the church of **St Bride's** (Mon–Fri 9am–5pm, Sat 11am–3pm; Ⓦ www.stbrides.com; Blackfriars tube), which boasts Wren's tallest and most exquisite spire (said to be the inspiration for the tiered wedding cake), and whose crypt contains a little museum of Fleet Street history.

The western section of Fleet Street was spared the Great Fire, which stopped just short of **Prince Henry's Room** (Mon–Sat 11am–2pm; free; Ⓦ www .cityoflondon.gov.uk/phr), a fine Jacobean house with timber-framed bay windows. The first-floor room now contains material relating to the diarist **Samuel Pepys**, who was born nearby in Salisbury Court in 1633 and baptized in St Bride's. Even if you've no interest in Pepys, the wood-panelled room is worth a look – it contains one of the finest Jacobean plasterwork ceilings in London, and a lot of original stained glass.

The City churches

The City of London boasts over forty churches (Ⓦ www.london-city-churches.org), the majority of them built or rebuilt by Wren after the Great Fire. As a general rule, weekday lunchtimes are the best time to visit these churches, many of which put on free lunchtime concerts. Below is a list of six of the most varied and interesting churches within the Square Mile:

St Bartholomew-the-Great Cloth Fair; Barbican tube. The oldest surviving church in the City and by far the most atmospheric; a fascinating building. St Paul's aside, if you visit just one church in the City, it should be this one.

St Mary Abchurch Abchurch Lane, Cannon Street; Cannon Street or Bank tube. Uniquely for Wren's City churches, the interior features a huge painted domed ceiling, plus the only authenticated Gibbons reredos.

St Mary Aldermary Queen Victoria Street; Mansion House tube. Wren's most successful stab at Gothic, with fan vaulting in the aisles and a panelled ceiling in the nave.

St Mary Woolnoth Lombard Street; Bank tube. Hawksmoor's only City church, sporting an unusually broad, bulky tower and a Baroque clerestory that floods the church with light from its semicircular windows.

St Olave Hart Street; Tower Hill tube. Built in the fifteenth century, and one of the few pre-Fire Gothic churches in the City.

St Stephen Walbrook Walbrook; Bank tube. Wren's dress rehearsal for St Paul's, with a wonderful central dome and plenty of original woodcarving.

Numerous narrow alleyways lead off the north side of Fleet Street, two of which – Bolt Court and Hind Court – eventually open out into Gough Square, on which stands **Dr Johnson's House** (May–Sept Mon–Sat 11am–5.30pm; Oct–April Mon–Sat 11am–5pm; £4.50; Ⓦ www.drjh.dircon.co.uk). The great savant, writer and lexicographer lived here from 1747 to 1759, whilst compiling the 41,000 entries for the first dictionary of the English language, two first editions of which can be seen in the grey-panelled rooms of the house. You can also view the open-plan attic, in which Johnson and his six helpers put together the dictionary.

St Paul's Cathedral

Designed by Christopher Wren and completed in 1711, **St Paul's Cathedral** (Mon–Sat 8.30am–4pm; £8; Ⓦ www.stpauls.co.uk; St Paul's tube) remains a dominating presence in the City, despite the encroaching tower blocks. Topped by an enormous lead-covered dome that's second in size only to St Peter's in Rome, its showpiece west facade is particularly magnificent. Westminster Abbey has the edge, however, when it comes to celebrity corpses, pre-Reformation sculpture, royal connections and sheer atmosphere. St Paul's, by contrast, is a soulless but perfectly calculated architectural set-piece, a burial place for captains rather than kings, though it does contain more artists than Westminster Abbey.

The best place from which to appreciate the glory of St Paul's is beneath the **dome**, decorated (against Wren's wishes) with Thornhill's trompe l'oeil frescoes. The most richly decorated section of the cathedral, however, is the Quire or **chancel**, where the mosaics of birds, fish, animals and greenery, only dating from the 1890s, are particularly spectacular. The intricately carved oak and limewood **choir stalls**, and the imposing organ case, are the work of Wren's master carver, Grinling Gibbons.

A series of stairs, beginning in the south aisle, lead to the dome's three **galleries**, the first of which is the internal **Whispering Gallery**, so called because of its acoustic properties – words whispered to the wall on one side are distinctly audible over one hundred feet away on the other, though the place is often so busy you can't hear much above the hubbub. The other two galleries are exterior: the wide **Stone Gallery**, around the balustrade at the base of the dome, and ultimately the tiny **Golden Gallery**, below the golden ball and cross which top the cathedral.

Although the nave is crammed full of overblown monuments to military types, burials in St Paul's are confined to the whitewashed **crypt**, reputedly the largest in Europe. Immediately to your right is Artists' Corner, which boasts as many painters and architects as Westminster Abbey has poets, including Christopher Wren himself, who was commissioned to build the cathedral after its Gothic predecessor, Old St Paul's, was destroyed in the Great Fire. The crypt's two other star tombs are those of **Nelson** and **Wellington**, both occupying centre stage and both with more fanciful monuments upstairs.

Museum of London and the Barbican

Despite London's long pedigree, very few of its ancient structures are now standing. However, numerous Roman, Saxon and Elizabethan remains have been discovered during the City's various rebuildings, and many of these are now displayed at the **Museum of London** (Mon–Sat 10am–5.50pm, Sun noon–5.50pm; free; Ⓦwww.museumoflondon.org.uk; St Paul's or Barbican tube), hidden above the western end of London Wall, in the southwestern corner of the Barbican complex. The museum's permanent exhibition is basically an educational trot through London's past from prehistory to the present day. This is interesting enough, but the real strength of the museum lies in the excellent temporary exhibitions, gallery tours, lectures, walks and videos it organizes throughout the year – visit the website or pick up a programme of exhibitions and events from the information desk before you set out.

The City's only large residential complex is the **Barbican**, a phenomenally ugly and expensive concrete ghetto built on the heavily bombed Cripplegate area. The zone's solitary prewar building is the heavily restored sixteenth-century church of **St Giles Cripplegate** (Mon–Fri 11am–4pm), situated across from the infamously user-repellent **Barbican Arts Centre** (Ⓦwww.barbican.org.uk), London's supposed answer to Paris's Pompidou Centre, which was formally opened in 1982. The traffic-free complex is home to the London Symphony Orchestra and holds free gigs in the foyer area.

Guildhall

Situated at the geographical centre of the City, **Guildhall** (May–Sept daily 10am–5pm; Oct–April Mon–Sat 10am–5pm; free; Ⓦwww.cityoflondon.gov.uk; St Paul's or Bank tube) has been the ancient seat of the City administration for over eight hundred years. It remains the headquarters of the Corporation of London (see p.112), and is still used for many of the City's formal civic occasions. Architecturally, however, it is not quite the beauty it once was, having been badly damaged in both the Great Fire and the Blitz, and scarred by the addition of a 1970s concrete cloister and wing.

Nonetheless, the **Great Hall**, basically a postwar reconstruction of the fifteenth-century original, is worth a brief look, as is the **Clockmakers' Museum** (Mon–Fri 9.30am–4.30pm; free; Ⓦwww.clockmakers.org), a collection of over six hundred timepieces, including one of the clocks that won John

Harrison the Longitude prize (see p.140). Also worth a visit is the purpose-built **Guildhall Art Gallery** (Mon–Sat 10am–5pm, Sun noon–4pm; £2.50, free Fri and daily after 3.30pm), which contains one or two exceptional works, such as Rossetti's *La Ghirlandata*, and Holman Hunt's *The Eve of St Agnes*, plus a massive painting depicting the 1782 Siege of Gibraltar, commissioned by the Corporation, and a marble statue of Margaret Thatcher. In the basement, you can view the remains of a **Roman amphitheatre**, dating from around 120 AD, which was discovered during the gallery's construction.

The financial centre

Bank is the finest architectural arena in the City. Heart of the finance sector and the busy meeting point of eight streets, it's overlooked by a handsome collection of Neoclassical buildings – among them, the Bank of England, the Royal Exchange and Mansion House (the Lord Mayor's official residence) – each one faced in Portland stone.

Sadly, only the **Bank of England** (ⓦ www.bankofengland.co.uk), which stores the nation's vast gold reserves in its vaults, encourages visitors. Established in 1694 by William III to raise funds for the war against France, the bank wasn't erected on its present site until 1734. All that remains of the building on which Sir John Soane spent the best part of his career from 1788 onwards is the windowless, outer curtain wall, which wraps itself round the three-and-a-half-acre island site. However, you can view a reconstruction of Soane's Bank Stock Office, with its characteristic domed skylight, in the **museum** (Mon–Fri 10am–5pm; free; Bank tube), which has its entrance on Bartholomew Lane.

East of Bank, beyond Bishopsgate, stands Richard Rogers' glitzy **Lloyd's Building**, completed in 1984. A startling array of glass and blue steel pipes – a vertical version of Rogers' own Pompidou Centre – the building is now overshadowed by Norman Foster's giant **Gherkin**, built on the site of the old Baltic Exchange which was blown up by the IRA in the early 1990s, and officially known as 30 St Mary Axe (ⓦ www.30stmaryaxe.com).

Hidden away behind a modern red-brick office

△ The Gherkin

block in a little courtyard off Bevis Marks, north up St Mary Axe from the Lloyd's building, the **Bevis Marks Synagogue** (guided tours Wed & Fri noon, Sun 11.15am; £2; Ⓦ www.sandp.org) was built in 1701 by Sephardic Jews who had fled the Inquisition in Spain and Portugal. This is the country's oldest surviving synagogue, and its roomy, rich interior gives an idea of just how wealthy the congregation was at the time. Nowadays, the Sephardic community has dispersed across London and the congregation has dwindled, though the magnificent array of chandeliers makes it popular for candle-lit Jewish weddings.

Just south of the Lloyd's building you'll find the picturesque **Leadenhall Market**, whose richly painted, graceful Victorian cast-ironwork dates from 1881. Inside, the traders cater mostly for the lunchtime City crowd, their barrows laden with exotic seafood and game, fine wines, champagne and caviar.

London Bridge and Monument

Until 1750, **London Bridge** was the only bridge across the Thames. The Romans were the first to build a permanent crossing here, but it was the medieval bridge that achieved world fame: built of stone and crowded with timber-framed houses, it became one of the great attractions of London – there's a model in the nearby church of St Magnus the Martyr (Tues–Fri 10am–4pm, Sun 10am–1pm). The houses were finally removed in the mid-eighteenth century, and a new stone bridge erected in 1831; that one now stands in the middle of the Arizona desert, having been bought for $2.4 million in the late 1960s by a gentleman who, allegedly, was under the impression he had purchased Tower Bridge. The present concrete structure, without doubt the ugliest yet, dates from 1972.

The only reason to go anywhere near London Bridge is to see the **Monument** (daily 9am–5.30pm; £2), which was designed by Wren to commemorate the Great Fire of 1666. Crowned with spiky gilded flames, this plain Doric column stands 202 feet high, making it the tallest isolated stone column in the world; if it were laid out flat it would touch the bakery where the Fire started, east of Monument. The bas-relief on the base, now in very bad shape, depicts Charles II and the Duke of York in Roman garb conducting the emergency relief operation. The 311 steps to the viewing gallery once guaranteed an incredible view; nowadays it is somewhat dwarfed by the buildings around it.

The Tower of London

One of Britain's main tourist attractions, the **Tower of London** (March–Oct Mon & Sun 10am–6pm, Tues–Sat 9am–6pm; Nov–Feb closes 5pm; £14.50; Ⓦ www.hrp.org.uk; Tower Hill tube), overlooks the river at the eastern boundary of the old city walls. Despite all the hype and heritage claptrap, it remains one of London's most remarkable buildings, site of some of the goriest events in the nation's history, and somewhere all visitors and Londoners should explore at least once. Chiefly famous as a place of imprisonment and death, it has variously been used as a royal residence, armoury, mint, menagerie, observatory and – a function it still serves – a safe-deposit box for the Crown Jewels.

Before you set off to explore the Tower complex, it's a good idea to get your bearings by taking one of the free **guided tours**, given every thirty minutes or so by one of the Tower's **Beefeaters** (officially known as Yeoman Warders). Visitors today enter the Tower along Water Lane, but in times gone by most prisoners were delivered through **Traitors' Gate**, on the waterfront. The nearby

Bloody Tower, which forms the main entrance to the Inner Ward, is where the 12-year-old Edward V and his 10-year-old brother were accommodated "for their own safety" in 1483 by their uncle, the future Richard III, and later murdered. It's also where **Walter Raleigh** was imprisoned on three separate occasions, including a thirteen-year stretch.

The **White Tower**, at the centre of the Inner Ward, is the original "Tower", begun in 1076, and now home to displays from the **Royal Armouries**. Even if you've no interest in military paraphernalia, you should at least pay a visit to the **Chapel of St John**, a beautiful Norman structure on the second floor that was completed in 1080 – making it the oldest intact church building in London. To the west of the White Tower is the execution spot on **Tower Green** where seven highly placed but unlucky individuals were beheaded, among them Anne Boleyn and her cousin Catherine Howard (Henry VIII's second and fifth wives).

The Waterloo Barracks, to the north of the White Tower, hold the **Crown Jewels**, perhaps the major reason so many people flock to the Tower; however, the moving walkways are disappointingly swift, allowing you just 28 seconds' viewing during peak periods. The oldest piece of regalia is the twelfth-century **Anointing Spoon**, but the vast majority of exhibits postdate the Commonwealth (1649–60), when many of the royal riches were melted down for coinage or sold off. Among the jewels are the three largest cut diamonds in the world, including the legendary **Koh-i-Noor**, set into the Queen Mother's Crown in 1937.

Tower Bridge

Tower Bridge ranks with Big Ben as the most famous of all London landmarks. Completed in 1894, its neo-Gothic towers are clad in Cornish granite and Portland stone, but conceal a steel frame, which, at the time, represented a considerable engineering achievement, allowing a road crossing that could be raised to give tall ships access to the upper reaches of the Thames. The raising of the bascules (from the French for "see-saw") remains an impressive sight – phone ahead to find out when the bridge is opening (☎020/7940 3984). If you buy a **ticket** (daily 9.30am–6pm; £5.50; Ⓦwww.towerbridge.org.uk), you can walk across the elevated walkways linking the summits of the towers and visit the Tower's Engine Room, on the south side of the bridge, where you can see the now-defunct giant coal-fired boilers which drove the hydraulic system until 1976, and play some interactive engineering games.

The East End and Docklands

Few places in London have engendered so many myths as the **East End** (a catch-all title which covers just about everywhere east of the City, but has its heart closest to the latter). Its name is synonymous with slums, sweatshops and crime, as epitomized by antiheroes such as Jack the Ripper and the Kray Twins, but also with the rags-to-riches careers of the likes of Harold Pinter and Vidal Sassoon, and whole generations of Jews who were born in the most notorious of London's cholera-ridden quarters and have now moved to wealthier pastures.

The area's first immigrants were French Protestant Huguenots, fleeing religious persecution in the late seventeenth century. Within three generations the Huguenots were entirely assimilated, and the Irish became the new immigrant

East End Sunday markets

Approaching from Liverpool Street, the first market you come to, on the east side of Bishopsgate, is **Petticoat Lane** (Sun 9am–2pm; Liverpool Street or Aldgate East tube), not one of London's prettiest streets, but one of its longest-running Sunday markets, specializing in cheap (and often pretty tacky) clothing. The authorities renamed the street Middlesex Street in 1830 to avoid the mention of ladies' underwear, but the original name has stuck.

Two blocks north of Middlesex Street, down Brushfield Street, lies **Old Spitalfields Market** (organic market Fri & Sun 10am–5pm; general market Mon–Fri 11am–3pm & Sun 10am–5pm; Liverpool Street tube), once the capital's premier wholesale fruit and vegetable market, now specializing in organic food, plus clothes, crafts and jewellery. Further east lies **Brick Lane** (Sun 8am–1pm; Aldgate East, Shoreditch or Liverpool Street tube), heart of the Bengali community, famous for its bric-a-brac Sunday market, wonderful curry houses and 24hr bagel bakery, and now also something of a magnet for young designers. From Brick Lane's northernmost end, it's a short walk to **Columbia Road** (Sun 8am–1pm), the city's best market for flowers and plants, though you'll need to ask the way, or head in the direction of the folk bearing plants.

population, but it was the influx of Jews escaping pogroms in eastern Europe and Russia that defined the character of the East End in the late nineteenth century. Today, the area is home to a large Bengali community, who came here from the poor rural region of Sylhet in Bangladesh in the 1960s and 1970s. Racism is still a problem in the area, directed, for the most part, against the Bengalis, and the East End remains at the bottom of the pile; even the millions poured into the neighbouring **Docklands** development have failed to make much impression on local unemployment and housing problems.

As the area is not an obvious place for sightseeing, and certainly no beauty spot – Victorian slum clearances, Hitler's bombs and postwar tower blocks have all left their mark – most visitors to the East End come for its famous **Sunday markets** (Ⓦwww.eastlondonmarkets.com). As for Docklands, most of it can be gawped at from the overhead light railway, including the vast **Canary Wharf** redevelopment, which has to be seen to be believed.

Spitalfields

Spitalfields, within sight of the sleek tower blocks of the financial sector, lies at the old heart of the East End, where the French Huguenots settled in the seventeenth century, where the Jewish community was at its strongest in the late nineteenth century, and where today's Bengali community eats, sleeps, works and prays. If you visit just one area in the East End, it should be this zone, which preserves mementos from each wave of immigration.

The easiest approach is from Liverpool Street Station, a short stroll west of **Spitalfields Market**, the red-brick and green-gabled market hall built in 1893, half of which was demolished in order to make way for yet more City offices. The dominant architectural presence in Spitalfields, however, is **Christ Church** (Tues 11am–4pm, Sun 1–4pm), built in 1714–29 to a characteristically bold design by Nicholas Hawksmoor, and now facing the market hall. Best viewed from Brushfield Street, the church's main features are its huge 225-foot-high spire and a giant Tuscan portico, raised on steps and shaped like a Venetian window (a central arched opening flanked by two smaller rectangles), a motif repeated in the tower and doors.

Against all the odds, London has won the right to stage the **Olympic Games** in 2012. Even more surprisingly, the focus of the games, the Olympic Park, is going to be in the East End, in an unpromising, run-down industrial estate by the River Lea, between Hackney Wick and Stratford. The main 80,000-seat Olympic Stadium will be built on Marshgate Lane and will become a 25,000-seat athletics stadium after the games. Close by, there'll be a 20,000-seat aquatic centre, a velodrome and BMX track (alongside the existing Eastway cycling circuit), a hockey complex and, on the site of the former Hackney greyhound stadium, a multi-sports complex for basketball, handball and volleyball. The Olympic village, housing nearly 18,000 athletes, will also be here, and will be converted to public housing after the games.

The rest of the events will take place in and around London, mostly in existing venues: Wimbledon will host the tennis and the new Wembley Stadium the football, while ExCel, the exhibition centre by Royal Victoria Dock, will be used for boxing, judo, taekwondo, weightlifting and wrestling, and Eton's new rowing centre will serve for some canoeing and kayaking events as well as for skulling. The Dome will host the artistic gymnastics, trampolining and basketball finals, along with a smaller temporary venue for rhythmic gymnastics, table tennis and badminton. Equestrian events are scheduled for Greenwich Park, while Hyde Park will host the triathlon and road cycling and Regent's Park the baseball and softball. Archery will take place at Lord's cricket ground, shooting at the Royal Artillery Barracks in Woolwich and – the one piece of planning that's really grabbed the headlines – beach volleyball will be staged on Horse Guards' Parade. Only sailing, mountain biking and the canoeing slalom will take place any great distance from the capital.

The games will certainly generate employment, and provide some badly needed housing for a deprived area, though it's difficult to judge how great the long-term benefits will really be. Despite protestations to the contrary, the environmental costs will be high, and council taxes in London – already among the highest in the country – are set to rise to pay for the privilege. On the positive side, East London's transport infrastructure looks set to improve: trains from Paris will arrive at Stratford in just over two hours from 2007, the East London Line is being extended north into Hackney and south to Crystal Palace, and further extensions are planned for the Docklands Light Railway.

The East End's most popular museum is the **Bethnal Green Museum of Childhood** (daily except Fri 10am–5.50pm; free; Ⓦ www.museumofchild hood.org.uk), situated opposite Bethnal Green tube station. The open-plan, wrought-iron hall, originally part of (and still a branch of) the V&A (see p.132), was transported here in the 1860s to bring art to the East End. The museum is currently closed for refurbishment, but when it reopens in November 2006, pride of place will, no doubt, still be reserved for its unique collection of antique dolls' houses dating back to 1673. Among the other curiosities are model trains, cars and rocking horses, dolls made from found objects and a handful of automata – Wallace the Lion gobbling up Albert is always a firm favourite.

Docklands

Built in the nineteenth century to cope with the huge volume of goods shipped along the Thames from all over the Empire, London's **Docklands** was once the largest enclosed cargo-dock system in the world. No one thought the area could be rejuvenated when the docks closed in the 1960s, but over the last twenty years, warehouses have been converted into luxury flats, waterside penthouse apartments have been built and a huge high-rise office development has sprung up around Canary Wharf.

Although Canary Wharf is on the Jubilee line, the best way to view Docklands is either from one of the boats that course up and down the Thames (see p.138), or from the driverless, overhead **Docklands Light Railway** or DLR (Ⓦwww .tfl.gov.uk/dlr), which sets off from Bank, or from Tower Gateway, close to Tower Hill tube. Tour guides give a free running commentary on DLR trains that set off on the hour from Tower Gateway (daily 10am–2pm) and Bank (Mon–Fri 11am–2pm, Sat & Sun 10am–2pm) as far as Cutty Sark.

The only really busy bit of the new Docklands, Canary Wharf is best known as the home of Britain's tallest building, Cesar Pelli's landmark tower, officially known as **One Canada Square**. The world's first skyscraper to be clad in stainless steel, it's an undeniably impressive sight, both from a distance (its flashing pinnacle is a feature of the horizon at numerous points in London) and close up. However, it no longer stands alone, having been joined by several other skyscrapers that stop just short of Pelli's stumpy pinnacle.

One of the few original warehouses left to the north of Canary Wharf has been converted into the **Museum in Docklands** (daily 10am–6pm; £5; Ⓦwww.museumindocklands.org.uk), an excellent stab at charting the history of the area from Roman times to the present day. Highlights include a great model of old London Bridge, an eight-foot-long watercolour and a soft play area for kids. Unless you're keen to visit the museum, though, there's little point in getting off the DLR at Canary Wharf. Instead, stay on the train as it cuts right through the middle of the office buildings under a parabolic steel-and-glass canopy and keep going until you reach Greenwich.

The South Bank

The **South Bank** (Ⓦwww.southbanklondon.com) – the area immediately opposite Victoria Embankment – is best known for the **London Eye**, the world's largest observation wheel and one of the capital's most popular millennium projects. The arrival of the Eye helped kick-start the renovation of the **South Bank Centre** (Ⓦwww.sbc.org.uk), London's much unloved concrete culture bunker of theatres and galleries, built, for the most part, in the 1960s. After decades in the doldrums, the centre is currently under inspired artistic direction and the whole area is enjoying something of a renaissance.

It's also worth visiting the **Imperial War Museum**, a short walk inland from the river, which contains, among other things, the most detailed exhibition on the Holocaust in Britain.

The South Bank Centre

The modern development of the South Bank dates back to the 1951 **Festival of Britain**, when the South Bank Exhibition was held on derelict land south of the Thames. The festival was an attempt to revive postwar morale by celebrating the centenary of the Great Exhibition (when Britain really did rule over half the world). The most striking features of the site were the Royal Festival Hall (which still stands), the Ferris wheel (inspiration for the current London Eye), the saucer-shaped Dome of Discovery (disastrously revisited in the guise of the Millennium Dome), and the cigar-shaped Skylon tower.

The Festival of Britain's success provided the impetus for the eventual creation of the **South Bank Centre** (Ⓦwww.sbc.org.uk), now home to artistic

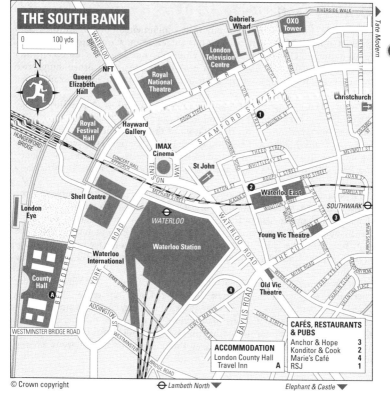

THE SOUTH BANK

0   100 yds

N

Gabriel's Wharf

OXO Tower

RIVERSIDE WALK

London Television Centre

NFT

Queen Elizabeth Hall

Royal National Theatre

Christchurch

Royal Festival Hall

Hayward Gallery

IMAX Cinema

St John

HUNGERFORD BRIDGE

Shell Centre

Waterloo East

SOUTHWARK

London Eye

WATERLOO

Young Vic Theatre

Waterloo International

Waterloo Station

County Hall

A

Old Vic Theatre

WESTMINSTER BRIDGE ROAD

CAFÉS, RESTAURANTS & PUBS	
Anchor & Hope	3
Konditor & Cook	2
Marie's Café	4
RSJ	1

ACCOMMODATION	
London County Hall Travel Inn	A

© Crown copyright   Lambeth North ▼   Elephant & Castle ▼

institutions such as the Royal Festival Hall (Ⓦwww.rfh.org.uk), the Hayward Gallery (Ⓦwww.hayward.org.uk), the National Film Theatre (NFT), the high-tech BFI London IMAX Cinema and, lastly, Denys Lasdun's National Theatre (Ⓦwww.nt-online.org). Its unprepossessing appearance is softened, too, by its riverside location, its avenue of trees, its fluttering banners, its occasional buskers and skateboarders, and the secondhand bookstalls and café outside the National Film Theatre.

The London Eye

South of the South Bank Centre proper is the **London Eye** (daily: April–Sept 9.30am–10pm; Oct–March 9am–8pm; £12.50; Ⓣ0870/500 0600, Ⓦwww .ba-londoneye.com; Waterloo or Westminster tube), the magnificently graceful millennium wheel which spins slowly and silently over the Thames. Standing 443ft high, the wheel is the largest ever built, and it's constantly in slow motion – a full-circle "flight" in one of its 32 pods takes around thirty minutes, and lifts you high above the city. It's one of the few places (apart from a plane window) from which London looks a manageable size, as you can see right out to where the suburbs slip into the countryside. Ticket prices are outrageously high, and queues can be very bad at the weekend, so book in advance over the phone or online.

County Hall

Next to the London Eye is the only truly monumental building on the South Bank, **County Hall**, with its colonnaded crescent. Completed in 1933, it housed the LCC (London County Council), and later the GLC (Greater London Council), until 1986, and is now home to, among other things, two hotels, several restaurants, a giant aquarium, a glorified amusement arcade called Namco Station and a couple of art galleries.

County Hall's most popular attraction is the **London Aquarium** (daily 10am–6pm or later; £9.75; ⓦ www.londonaquarium.co.uk; Waterloo or Westminster tube), laid out across three floors of the basement. With some super-large, multi-floor tanks, and everything from dog-face puffers to piranhas, this is somewhere that's pretty much guaranteed to please younger kids. The Touching Pool where children can actually stroke the (non-sting) rays, is particularly popular.

Three giant surrealist sculptures outside County Hall help to advertise the **Dalí Universe** (daily 10am–6pm or later; £9.75; ⓦ www.daliuniverse.com). There's no denying Dalí was an accomplished and prolific artist, but you'll be disappointed if you come expecting to see his "greatest hits" – those are scattered across the globe. The majority of the works displayed here are little-known bronze and glass sculptures, and drawings from illustrated books he published.

The imposing former council chambers on County Hall's first floor are currently occupied by the **Saatchi Gallery** (Mon–Thurs & Sun 10am–6pm, Fri & Sat 10am–10pm; £8.50; ⓦ www.saatchi-gallery.co.uk), which puts on exhibitions of contemporary art drawn from the collection of Charles Saatchi, the dealer best known for promoting the Young British Artists of the 1980s and 1990s, such as Damien Hirst and Tracey Emin. However, the gallery is moving to new premises in 2007.

Imperial War Museum

The domed building at the east end of Lambeth Road, formerly the infamous lunatic asylum "Bedlam", is now the **Imperial War Museum** (daily 10am–6pm; free; ⓦ www.iwm.org.uk; Lambeth North or Waterloo tube), by far the best military museum in the capital. The treatment of the subject is impressively wide-ranging and fairly sober, with the main hall's militaristic display offset by the lower-ground-floor array of documents and images attesting to the human damage of war. The museum also has a harrowing **Holocaust Exhibition** (not recommended for children under 14), which you enter from the third floor. The exhibition pulls few punches, and has made a valiant attempt to avoid depicting the victims of the Holocaust as nameless masses by focusing on individual cases, and interspersing the archive footage with eyewitness accounts from contemporary survivors.

Southwark

Until well into the seventeenth century, the only reason for north-bank residents to cross the Thames, to what is now **Southwark**, was to visit the infamous Bankside entertainment district around the south end of London Bridge, which lay outside the jurisdiction of the City. What started out as a red-light district under the Romans, reached its peak as the pleasure quarter of Tudor and Stuart

London, where disreputable institutions banned in the City – most notably theatres – continued to flourish until the Puritan purges of the 1640s.

Thanks to wholesale regeneration in the last few years, Southwark's riverfront is once more somewhere to head for. The area is linked to St Paul's and the City by the fabulous Norman Foster–designed **Millennium Bridge**, London's first pedestrian-only bridge. At the end of the bridge, a whole cluster of sights vie for attention, most notably the **Tate Modern** art gallery, housed in a converted power station, and next to it, a reconstruction of Shakespeare's **Globe Theatre**. The **Thames Path** connects the district with the South Bank to the west, and allows you to walk east along Clink Street and Tooley Street, home to a further rash of popular sights such as the **London Dungeon**. Further east still, Butler's Wharf is a thriving little warehouse development centred on the excellent **Design Museum**.

Tate Modern

The masterful conversion of the austere Bankside power station into the **Tate Modern** (daily 10am–6pm; Fri & Sat until 10pm; free; ⓦ www.tate.org.uk) has left plenty of the original, industrial feel, while providing wonderfully light and spacious galleries in which to show off the Tate's vast international twentieth-century art collection. The best way to enter is down the ramp from the west, so you get the full effect of the stupendously large turbine hall. It's easy enough to find your way around the galleries, with levels 3 and 5 displaying the permanent collection, level 4 used for fee-paying temporary exhibitions, and level 7 home to a café with a great view over the Thames.

Given that Tate Modern is the largest modern-art gallery in the world, you need to spend the best part of a day here to do justice to the place, or be very selective. Pick up a plan (and, for an extra £2, an audioguide), and take the escalator to level 3. The curators have eschewed the usual chronological approach through the "isms", preferring to group works together thematically: Landscape/Matter/Environment, Still Life/Object/Real Life, History/Memory/Society and Nude/Action/Body. On the whole this works very well, though the early twentieth-century canvases, in their gilded frames, do struggle when made to compete with contemporary installations.

Although the displays change every six months or so, you're still pretty much guaranteed to see at least some works by **Monet** and Bonnard, Cubist pioneers **Picasso** and Braque, Surrealists such as **Dalí**, abstract artists like **Mondrian**, Bridget Riley and Pollock, and Pop supremos **Warhol** and Lichtenstein. There are seminal works such as a replica of **Duchamp**'s urinal, entitled *Fountain* and signed "R. Mutt", and Yves Klein's totally blue paintings. And such is the space here that several artists get whole rooms to themselves, among them Joseph Beuys and his shamanistic wax and furs, and **Mark Rothko**, whose abstract "Seagram Murals", originally destined for a posh restaurant in New York, have their own shrine-like room in the heart of the collection.

From the Globe to Southwark Cathedral

Seriously dwarfed by the Tate Modern but equally spectacular is **Shakespeare's Globe Theatre** (ⓦ www.shakespeares-globe.org; Southwark or Blackfriars tube), a reconstruction of the polygonal playhouse where most of the Bard's later works were first performed, and which was originally erected on nearby Park Street in 1598. To find out more about Shakespeare and the history of Bankside, the Globe's stylish **exhibition** (daily: May–Sept 9am–noon & 12.30–5pm; Oct–April 10am–5pm; £9) is well worth a visit. It begins by detailing the

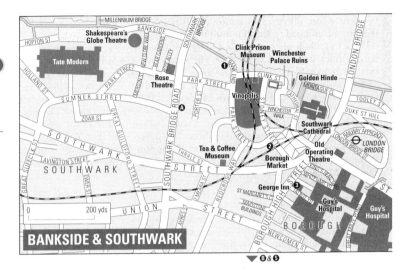

BANKSIDE & SOUTHWARK

long campaign by American actor Sam Wanamaker to have the Globe rebuilt, but it's the imaginative hands-on exhibits that really hit the spot. You can have a virtual play on medieval instruments such as the crumhorn or sackbut, prepare your own edition of Shakespeare, and feel the thatch, hazelnut-shell and daub used to build the theatre. Visitors also get taken on an informative **guided tour** round the theatre itself, except in the afternoons during the summer season, when you can only visit the exhibition (for a reduced entrance fee).

East of Bankside lies **Vinopolis** (Mon, Fri & Sat noon–9pm, Tues–Thurs & Sun noon–6pm; £11.50; Ⓦ www.vinopolis.co.uk), discreetly housed in former wine vaults under the railway arches on Clink Street. It's a strange fish: part wine bar-restaurant, part wine retailers, part museum. The focus of the complex is the "Wine Odyssey", a rather disjointed trot through the world's wine regions, for which it's pretty much essential to pay the extra £2 for an audioguide. Tickets are pricey, even if they do include five wine tastings.

Further down the suitably gloomy confines of dark and narrow Clink Street is the **Clink Prison Museum** (daily 10am–6pm or later; £4; Ⓦ www.clink .co.uk), built on the site of the former Clink Prison. The prison began as a dungeon for disobedient clerics, built under the Bishop of Winchester's Palace and later became a dumping ground for heretics, prostitutes and a motley assortment of Bankside lowlife. Given the rich history of the place, the museum is disappointing.

An exact replica of the **Golden Hinde** (daily 10am–5.30pm, but phone ahead; £3.50; ℡0870/011 8700, Ⓦ www.goldenhinde.co.uk), the galleon in which Francis Drake sailed around the world from 1577 to 1580, nestles in St Mary Overie Dock, at the eastern end of Clink Street. The ship is surprisingly small, and its original crew of eighty-plus must have been cramped to say the least. There's a lack of interpretive panels, so it's worth paying the little bit extra and getting a guided tour from one of the folk in period garb – ring ahead to check a group hasn't booked the place up.

Close by the *Golden Hinde* stands **Southwark Cathedral** (Mon–Fri 7.30am– 6pm, Sat & Sun 8.30am–6pm; free; Ⓦ www.dswark.org/cathedral), built as the medieval Augustinian priory church of St Mary Overie, and given cathedral

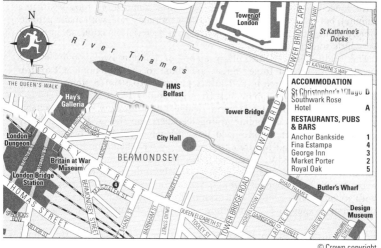

© Crown copyright

status only in 1905. Of the original thirteenth-century church, only the choir and retrochoir now remain, separated by a tall and beautiful stone Tudor screen, making them probably the oldest Gothic structures left in London. The nave was entirely rebuilt in the nineteenth century, but the cathedral contains numerous interesting monuments, from a thirteenth-century oak effigy of a knight to an early twentieth-century memorial to Shakespeare.

Borough Market (ⓦwww.boroughmarket.org.uk), squeezed underneath the railway arches by the cathedral, is one of the few wholesale fruit and vegetable markets still trading under its original Victorian wrought-iron shed. It's recently undergone a transformation from scruffy obscurity to a small foodie haven, with permanent outlets such as Neal's Yard Dairy and Konditor & Cook, joined by gourmet daytime market stalls on Fridays (noon–6pm) and, particularly, Saturdays (9am–4pm).

Endearingly ramshackle and well worth a visit, the **Bramah Tea and Coffee Museum** (daily 10am–6pm; £4; ☎020/7403 5650, ⓦwww.bramahmuseum .co.uk) is a block or so west of Borough Market at 40 Southwark St. Founded in 1992 by Edward Bramah, who began his career on an African tea garden in 1950, the museum's emphasis is firmly on tea, though the café also serves a seriously good cup of coffee. There's an impressive array of teapots from Meissen to the world's largest, plus plenty of novelty ones, and coffee machines spanning the twentieth century, from huge percolator siphons to espresso machines.

From London Bridge to Butler's Wharf

The most educative and strangest of Southwark's museums, the **Old Operating Theatre, Museum and Herb Garret** (daily 10.30am–5pm; £4; ⓦwww .thegarret.org.uk; London Bridge tube) is located to the east of the cathedral on St Thomas Street, on the other side of Borough High Street. Built in 1821 up a spiral staircase at the top of a church tower, where the hospital apothecary's herbs were stored, this women's operating theatre dates from the pre-anaesthetic era. Despite being entirely gore-free, the museum is as stomach-churning as the London Dungeon (see below). The surgeons who used this room would have concentrated on speed and accuracy (most amputations took less than a minute), but there was still a thirty percent mortality rate, with many patients simply dying of shock, and many more from bacterial infection, about which very little was known.

The vaults beneath the railway arches of London Bridge train station, on the south side of Tooley Street, are home to the ever-popular **London Dungeon** (daily: March to mid-July, Sept & Oct 10.30am–5.30pm; mid-July to Aug 9.30am–7.30pm; Nov–Feb 10.30am–5pm; £15.50; ☎020/7403 7221, ⓦwww.thedungeons.com; London Bridge tube) – to avoid the inevitable queue, buy your ticket online. Young teenagers and the credulous probably get the most out of the life-sized waxwork tableaux of folk being hanged, drawn, quartered and tortured, the general hysteria being boosted by actors dressed as top-hatted Victorian vampires, executioners and monks pouncing out of the darkness. Visitors are led into the labyrinth, an old-fashioned mirror maze, before being herded through a series of live-action scenarios, starting with an eighteenth-century courtroom, passing through the exploitative "Jack the Ripper Experience", and ending with a walk through a revolving tunnel of flames.

A little further east on Tooley Street is **Winston Churchill's Britain at War** (daily: April–Sept 10am–6pm; Oct–March 10am–5pm; £8.50; ⓦwww.britainatwar.co.uk), an illuminating insight into the stiff-upper-lip London mentality during the Blitz. The museum contains hundreds of wartime artefacts, including an Anderson shelter, where you can hear the chilling sound of the V1 "doodlebugs" and tune in to contemporary radio broadcasts. The grand finale is a walk through the chaos of a just-bombed street.

There's more World War II history at **HMS Belfast** (daily: March–Oct 10am–6pm; Nov–Feb 10am–5pm; £8; ⓦwww.iwm.org.uk), a World War II cruiser, permanently moored between London Bridge and Tower Bridge. Armed with six torpedoes, and six-inch guns with a range of over fourteen miles, the *Belfast* spent over two years of the war in the Royal Naval shipyards after being hit by a mine in the Firth of Forth at the beginning of hostilities. It later saw action in the Barents Sea during World War II and during the Korean War, before being decommissioned. The maze of cabins is fun to explore but if you want to find out more about the *Belfast*, head for the exhibition rooms in zone five.

A short stroll east of the *Belfast* is Norman Foster's startling glass-encased **City Hall** (Mon–Fri 8am–8pm; ⓦwww.london.gov.uk), the new Greater London Authority headquarters that looks like a giant car headlight. Visitors are welcome to stroll around the building and watch the London Assembly proceedings from the second floor.

In contrast to the brash offices on Tooley Street, **Butler's Wharf**, east of Tower Bridge, has retained its historical character. **Shad Thames**, the narrow street at the back of Butler's Wharf, has kept the wrought-iron overhead gangways by which the porters used to transport goods from the wharves to the warehouses further back from the river, and is one of the most atmospheric alleyways in the whole of Bermondsey. The chief attraction of Butler's Wharf is the superb riverside **Design Museum** (daily 10am–5.45pm, Fri until 9pm; £6; ⓦwww.designmuseum.org; Bermondsey or Tower Hill tube), a stylish, Bauhaus-like conversion of a 1950s warehouse at the eastern end of Shad Thames. The museum has no permanent display, but instead hosts a series of temporary exhibitions (up to four at a time) on important designers, movements or single products. The small coffee bar in the foyer is a great place to relax, and there's a pricier restaurant on the top floor.

Hyde Park, Kensington and Chelsea

Hyde Park, together with its westerly extension, Kensington Gardens, covers a distance of two miles from Oxford Street in the northeast to Kensington Palace in the southwest. At the end of your journey, you've made it to one of London's most exclusive districts, the Royal Borough of **Kensington** and **Chelsea**. Other districts go in and out of fashion, but this area has been in vogue ever since royalty moved into **Kensington Palace** in the late seventeenth century.

Aside from the shops around Harrods in Knightsbridge, however, the popular tourist attractions lie in **South Kensington**, where three of London's top (and currently free) **museums** – the Victoria and Albert, Natural History and Science museums – stand on land bought with the proceeds of the Great Exhibition of 1851. Chelsea, to the south, has a slightly more bohemian pedigree. In the 1960s, the **King's Road** carved out its reputation as London's catwalk, while in the late 1970s it was the epicentre of the punk explosion. Nothing so rebellious goes on in Chelsea now, though its residents like to think of themselves as rather more artistic and intellectual than the purely moneyed types of Kensington.

Once slummy, now swanky, **Bayswater** and **Notting Hill**, to the north of Hyde Park, are the borough's most cosmopolitan districts, with a strong Arab presence and vestiges of the African-Caribbean community who initiated and still run the city's (and Europe's) largest street **carnival**, which takes place every August Bank Holiday.

Hyde Park and Kensington Gardens

Hangings, muggings, duels and the Great Exhibition of 1851 are just some of the public events that have taken place in **Hyde Park** (Ⓦ www.royalparks.gov .uk) which remains a popular spot for political demonstrations. At the treeless northeastern corner is **Marble Arch**, erected in 1828 as a triumphal entry to Buckingham Palace, but now stranded on a busy traffic island at the west end of Oxford Street. This is a historically charged piece of land, as it marks the site of **Tyburn gallows**, the city's main public execution spot until 1783. It's also the location of **Speakers' Corner**, a peculiarly English Sunday-morning tradition, featuring an assembly of ranters and hecklers.

A more immediately appealing approach is to enter from the southeast around **Hyde Park Corner**, where the **Wellington Arch** (Wed–Sun: April–Oct 10am–5pm; Nov–March 10am–4pm; EH; £3) stands in the midst of another of London's busiest traffic interchanges. Erected in 1828, the arch was originally topped by an equestrian statue of the Duke himself, later replaced by Peace driving a four-horse chariot. Inside, you can view an exhibition on London's outdoor sculpture and take a lift to the top of the monument where the exterior balconies offer a bird's-eye view of the swirling traffic.

Close by stands **Apsley House** (Tues–Sun: April–Oct 10am–5pm; Nov–March 10am–4pm; EH; £4.95), Wellington's London residence and now a museum to the "Iron Duke". Unless you're a keen fan of the Duke, the highlight of the museum is its **art collection**, much of which used to belong to the King of Spain. Among the best pieces, displayed in the Waterloo Gallery on the first floor, are works by de Hooch, Van Dyck, Velázquez, Goya, Rubens and Murillo. The famous, more than twice life-sized, nude statue of Napoleon by Antonio Canova stands at the foot of the main staircase.

Back outside, Hyde Park is divided in two by the **Serpentine lake**, which has a popular **Lido** (mid-June to mid-Sept daily 10am–6pm; £3.50) on its south

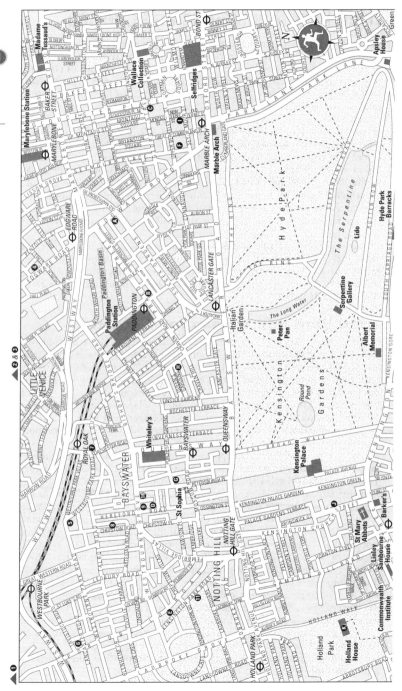

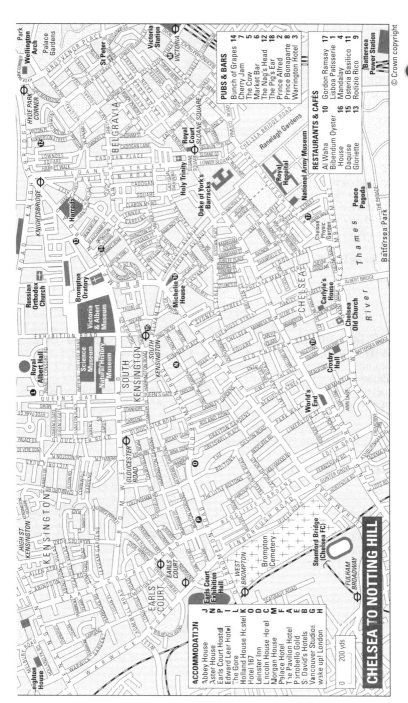

CHELSEA TO NOTTING HILL

ACCOMMODATION
Abbey House — J
Aster House — N
Earls Court Hostel — P
Edward Lear Hotel — I
The Gore — L
Holland House Hostel — K
Hotel 167 — O
Leinster Inn — D
Lincoln House Hotel — C
Morgan House — M
Palace Hotel — F
The Pavilion Hotel — A
Portobello Gold — E
St David's Hotels — B
Vancouver Studios — G
wake up! London — H

PUBS & BARS
Bunch of Grapes — 14
Cherry Jam — 7
The Cow — 5
Market Bar — 6
The Nag's Head — 12
The Pig's Ear — 18
Prince Alfred — 2
Prince Bonaparte — 8
Warrington Hotel — 3

RESTAURANTS & CAFÉS
Al Waha — 10
Bibendum Oyster House — 16
Daquise — 15
Gloriette — 13
Gordon Ramsay — 17
Lisboa Patisserie — 4
Mandalay — 11
Osteria Basilico — 1
Rodizio Rico — 9

© Crown copyright

0   200 yds

129

© Crown copyright

bank and a pretty upper section known as the **Long Water**, which narrows until it reaches a group of four fountains. The western half of the park is officially known as **Kensington Gardens**, and contains the richly decorated, High Gothic **Albert Memorial** (guided tours Sun 2 & 3pm; £4.50). Erected in 1876, the memorial is as much a hymn to the glorious achievements of Britain as to its subject, Queen Victoria's husband (who died of typhoid in 1861). Albert occupies the central canopy, gilded from head to toe and clutching a catalogue for the 1851 Great Exhibition that he helped to organize.

The Exhibition's most famous feature, the gargantuan glasshouse of the Crystal Palace, no longer exists, but the profits were used to buy a large tract of land south of the park, now home to South Kensington's remarkable cluster of museums and colleges, plus the vast **Royal Albert Hall** (ⓦ www.royalalberthall.com), a splendid iron-and-glass-domed concert hall, with an exterior of red brick, terracotta and marble that became the hallmark of South Ken architecture. The hall is the venue for Europe's most democratic music festival, the Henry Wood Promenade Concerts, better known as the **Proms**, which take place from July to September, with standing-room tickets for £4.

Kensington Palace

On the western edge of Kensington Gardens stands **Kensington Palace** (daily: March–Oct 10am–6pm; Nov–Feb 10am–5pm; £11; ⓦ www.hrp.org.uk; High Street Kensington tube), a modestly proportioned Jacobean brick mansion bought by William and Mary in 1689, and the chief royal residence for the next fifty years. KP, as it's fondly known in royal circles, is best known today as the place where **Princess Diana** lived until her death in 1997. Visitors don't get to see Diana's apartments, which were on the west side of the palace, where various minor royals still live. Instead, they can view some of Diana's frocks – and also several worn by the Queen – and then the sparsely furnished state apartments. The highlights are the trompe l'oeil ceiling paintings by William Kent, in particular the Cupola Room, and the oil paintings in the King's Gallery. En route, you'll also see the tastelessly decorated rooms in which the future Queen Victoria spent her unhappy childhood. To recover from the above, take tea in the exquisite **Orangery** (times as for palace).

Leighton House

The streets to the west of Kensington Gardens were home to an artists' colony founded by a number of wealthy Victorian artists: you can visit one of the most remarkable of these artist pads, **Leighton House**, at 12 Holland Park Rd (daily except Tues; 11am–5.30pm; guided tours Wed & Thurs 2.30pm; £3; ⓦ www .rbkc.gov.uk/leightonhousemuseum; High Street Kensington tube). "It will be opulence, it will be sincerity," Lord Leighton opined before starting work on the house in the 1860s – he later became president of the Royal Academy and was ennobled on his deathbed. The big attraction is the domed Arab Hall, decorated with Saracen tiles, gilded mosaics and woodwork drawn from all over the Islamic world. The other rooms are less spectacular but, in compensation, are hung with paintings by Lord Leighton and his Pre-Raphaelite chums.

Notting Hill

Epicentre of the country's first race riots, when busloads of whites attacked West Indian homes in the area, **Notting Hill** is now more famous for its annual **Carnival**, which began life in direct response to the riots. These days, it's one of Europe's biggest street festivals, with up to a million revellers turning up on the last weekend of August for the two-day extravaganza of parades, steel bands and deafening sound systems.

The rest of the year, Notting Hill is a lot quieter, though its cafés and restaurants are cool enough places to pull in folk from all over. On Saturdays, big crowds of Londoners and tourists alike descend on the mile-long **Portobello Road Market**, which is lined with stalls selling everything from antiques to cheap secondhand clothes, and fruit and vegetables.

△ Portobello Road shop

Within easy walking distance of Portobello Road, on the other side of the railway tracks, gasworks and canal, is **Kensal Green Cemetery** (Ⓦwww .kensalgreen.co.uk; Kensal Green tube), opened in 1833 and still a functioning burial ground. Graves of the more famous incumbents – Thackeray, Trollope and Brunel – are less interesting architecturally than those arranged on either side of the Centre Avenue, which leads from the easternmost entrance on Harrow Road. Guided tours of the cemetery take place every Sunday at 2pm (£5); on the first and third Sunday of the month, the tour includes a trip down the catacombs (bring a torch).

Knightsbridge and Harrods

South of Hyde Park lies the irredeemably snobbish **Knightsbridge**, revelling in its reputation as the swankiest shopping area in London, a status epitomized by **Harrods** (Mon–Sat 10am–7pm; Ⓦwww.harrods.com) on Brompton Road. London's most famous department store started out as a family-run grocery store in 1849, with a staff of two. The current 1905 terracotta building is owned by the Egyptian Mohammed Al Fayed and employs in excess of 3000 staff. The store even has a few sections that are architectural sights in their own right: the Food Hall, with its exquisite Arts and Crafts tiling; the Egyptian Hall, with its pseudo-hieroglyphs and sphinxes; and the fountain at the foot of the Egyptian Escalators dedicated to Di and Dodi. Note that the store has a draconian dress code: no shorts, no vest T-shirts, and backpacks must be carried in the hand.

Victoria and Albert Museum (V&A)

In terms of sheer variety and scale, the **Victoria and Albert Museum**, on Cromwell Road (daily 10am–5.45pm, Wed & last Fri of month until 10pm; free; Ⓦwww.vam.ac.uk; South Kensington tube), popularly known as the V&A, is the greatest museum of applied arts in the world. The range of exhibits on display here means that, whatever your taste, there's bound to be something to grab your attention. If you're flagging, there's a snacky café in the museum's period-piece **Poynter, Morris and Gamble** refreshment rooms.

The most celebrated of the V&A's numerous exhibits are the **Raphael Cartoons**, seven vast biblical paintings that served as designs for a set of tapestries destined for the Sistine Chapel. Close by, you can view highlights from the country's largest dress collection, and the world's largest collection of Indian art outside India. In addition, there are galleries devoted to British, Chinese, Islamic, Japanese and Korean art, as well as jewellery, glassware, metalwork and photography. Wading through the huge collection of European sculpture, you come to the surreal **Plaster Casts** gallery, filled with copies of European art's greatest hits, from Michelangelo's *David* to Trajan's Column (sawn in half to make it fit). There's even a gallery of twentieth-century objets d'art – everything from Bauhaus furniture to Swatch watches – to rival that of the Design Museum.

If you've energy left after your visit, stop by London's most flamboyant Roman Catholic church, the **Brompton Oratory**, built in neo-Baroque style in the 1880s, which lies just next door to the museum on Brompton Road.

Science Museum

Established as a technological counterpart to the V&A, the **Science Museum**, on Exhibition Road (daily 10am–6pm; free; Ⓦwww.sciencemuseum.org.uk; South Kensington tube), is undeniably impressive, filling seven floors with items drawn from every conceivable area of science, including space travel, digital technology, steam engines and carbon emissions. Keen to dispel the enduring image of museums devoted to its subject as boring and full of dusty glass cabinets, the Science Museum has updated its galleries with interactive displays, and puts on daily demonstrations to show that not all science teaching has to be deathly dry.

First stop inside should be the **information desk**, where you can pick up a museum plan and find out what events and demonstrations are taking place; you can also sign up for a free **guided tour** on a specific subject. Most people head for the **Wellcome Wing**, full of state-of-the-art interactive computers and an IMAX cinema, and geared to appeal to even the most museum-phobic teenager. To get there, you must first pass by the world's first steam engines, through the Space gallery, to the far side of the Making of the Modern World, a display of iconic inventions from Robert Stephenson's *Rocket* train of 1829 to the Ford Model T, the world's first mass-produced car.

The **Launch Pad**, one of the first hands-on displays aimed at kids, remains as popular and enjoyable as ever, as do the **Garden** and **Things** galleries, all of which are in the basement. The **Materials** gallery, on the first floor, is aimed more at adults, and is an extremely stylish exhibition covering the use of materials ranging from aluminium to zerodur (used for making laser gyroscopes), while **Energy**, on the second floor, has a great "do not touch" electric shock machine that absolutely fascinates kids.

Natural History Museum

Alfred Waterhouse's purpose-built mock-Romanesque colossus ensures the **Natural History Museum** (Mon–Sat 10am–5.50pm, Sun 11am–5.50pm; free; Ⓦ www.nhm.ac.uk; South Kensington tube) its status as London's most handsome museum. The museum has been massively redeveloped over the last decade or so, though there are still one or two sections that remain little changed since the original opening in 1881. The museum's dinosaur collection is a real hit with children, but its collections are also an important resource for serious zoologists.

The main entrance leads to the **Life Galleries**, which include the ever-popular Dinosaur gallery, with its grisly life-sized animatronic tableau of two Oviraptors roosting, while two carnivorous Velociraptors get ready to attack. Other popular sections include the Creepy-Crawlies Room, the Mammals gallery with its life-sized model of a blue whale, and the excellent **Investigate** gallery (Mon–Sat 10.30am–5pm, Sun 11.30am–5pm; term time also Mon–Fri 2.30–5pm), where children aged 7 to 14 get to play at being scientists (you need to obtain a timed ticket).

Visitors can view more of the museum's millions of zoological specimens in the collections store of the new **Darwin Centre**. To see the rest of the building, however, you need to sign up for a **guided tour** (book ahead either online or by phone ☏ 020/7942 6128; free). These set off roughly every half an hour and last about thirty minutes, allowing visitors to get a closer look at the specimens. You also get to see behind the scenes at the labs, and even talk to one of the museum's 350 scientists about their work.

If the queues for the museum are long (as they can be at weekends and during school holidays), you might be better off heading for the side entrance on Exhibition Road, which leads into the former Geology Museum, now known as the **Earth Galleries**, a visually exciting romp through the earth's evolution. The most popular sections are the slightly tasteless Kobe earthquake simulator, and the spectacular display of gems and crystals in the Earth's Treasury.

Chelsea

From the Swinging Sixties and even up to the Punk era, **Chelsea** had a slightly bohemian pedigree; these days, it's just another Wealthy West London suburb. Among the most nattily attired of all those parading down the King's Road nowadays are the scarlet or navy-blue clad Chelsea Pensioners, army veterans from the nearby **Royal Hospital** (Mon–Sat 10am–noon & 2–4pm, Sun 2–4pm; free; Sloane Square tube), founded by Charles II in 1681. The hospital's majestic red-brick wings and grassy courtyards became a blueprint for institutional and collegiate architecture all over the English-speaking world. The public are allowed to view the austere hospital chapel, and the equally grand, wood-panelled dining hall, opposite, which has a vast allegorical mural of Charles II.

The concrete bunker next door to the Royal Hospital, on Royal Hospital Road, houses the **National Army Museum** (daily 10am–5.30pm; free; Ⓦ www.national-army-museum.ac.uk). The militarily obsessed are unlikely to be disappointed by the succession of uniforms and medals, but there's little here for non-enthusiasts. The temporary exhibitions staged on the ground floor are the museum's strong point, but it's rather disappointing overall – you're better off visiting the infinitely superior Imperial War Museum (see p.122).

North London

Almost all of **North London**'s suburbs are easily accessible by tube from the centre – indeed it was the expansion of the tube which encouraged the forward march of bricks and mortar into many of these areas – though just a handful of these satellite villages, now subsumed into the general mass of the city, are worth bothering with.

First off, is one of London's finest parks, **Regent's Park**, framed by Nash-designed architecture and home of London Zoo. Close by is **Camden Town**, where the weekend market is one of the city's big attractions – a warren of stalls selling street fashion, books, records and ethnic goods.

The real highlights of north London, though, for visitors and residents alike, are **Hampstead** and **Highgate**, elegant, largely eighteenth-century developments which still reflect their village origins. They have the added advantage of proximity to one of London's wildest patches of greenery, **Hampstead Heath**, where you can enjoy stupendous views, kite flying and outdoor bathing, as well as outdoor concerts and high art in the setting of **Kenwood House**.

Regent's Park

According to John Nash's masterplan, devised in 1811 for the Prince Regent (later George IV), **Regent's Park** (Ⓦ www.royalparks.org.uk; Regent's Park, Baker Street or Great Portland Street tube) was to be girded by a continuous belt of terraces, and sprinkled with a total of 56 villas, including a magnificent pleasure palace for the Prince himself. The plan was never fully realized, due to lack of funds, but enough was built to create something of the idealized garden city that Nash and the Prince Regent envisaged. Prominent on the park's skyline is the shiny copper dome of **London Central Mosque** at 146 Park Rd (Ⓦ www.islamicculturalcentre.co.uk), an entirely appropriate addition given the Prince Regent's taste for the Orient.

The northeastern corner of the park is occupied by **London Zoo** (daily: March–Oct 10am–5.30pm; Nov–Feb 10am–4pm; £14; Ⓦwww.zsl .org/london-zoo; Camden tube). Founded in 1826 with the remnants of the royal menagerie, the zoo has had to change with the times, and now bills itself as an eco-conscious place whose prime purpose is to save species under threat of extinction. It's still not the most uplifting spot for animal-lovers, though the enclosures are as humane as any inner-city zoo could make them, and kids usually love the place. Most are particularly taken by the children's enclosure, where they can actually handle the animals, and the regular "Animals in Action" live shows. The invertebrate house, now known as BUGS, and the new monkey walk-through forest are both guaranteed winners.

Camden Town

For all the gentrification of the last twenty years, **Camden Town** retains a gritty aspect, compounded by the various railway lines that plough through the area, the canal, and the large shelter for the homeless on Arlington Street. The market, however, gives the area a positive lift on the weekends, and is now the district's best-known attraction.

For all its tourist popularity, **Camden Market** remains a genuinely offbeat place. More than 150,000 shoppers turn up here each weekend, and parts of the market now stay open week-long, alongside a similarly oriented crop of shops, cafés and bistros. The sheer variety of what's on offer, from bootleg tapes to furniture, along with a mass of street fashion and clubwear, and plenty of foodstalls, is what makes Camden so special. To avoid the crowds, which can be overpowering on a summer Sunday afternoon, you'll need to get here by 10am.

Despite having no significant Jewish associations, Camden is home to London's **Jewish Museum** (Mon–Thurs 10am–4pm, Sun 10am–5pm; £3.50; Ⓦwww.jewishmuseum.org.uk), at 129 Albert St, just off Parkway. The purpose-built premises are smartly designed, and the collection of Judaica includes treasures from London's Great Synagogue, burnt down by Nazi bombers in 1941, and a sixteenth-century Venetian Ark of the Covenant. More compelling are the temporary exhibitions, discussions and occasional concerts put on by the museum.

Hampstead and Highgate

The high points of North London, both geographically and aesthetically, the elegant, largely eighteenth-century developments of **Hampstead** and **Highgate** have managed to cling on to their village origins. Of the two,

---

Regent's Canal by boat

Three companies run **boat services** on the Regent's Canal between Camden and Little Venice, passing through the Maida Hill tunnel and stopping off at London Zoo on the way. The narrowboat *Jenny Wren* (☏020/7485 4433) starts at Camden, goes through a canal lock (the only company to do so) and heads for Little Venice, while Jason's narrowboats (☏020/7286 3428, Ⓦwww.jasons.co.uk) start at Little Venice; the London Waterbus Company (☏020/7482 2660, Ⓦwww.londonwaterbus.com) sets off from both places. Whichever you choose, you can board at either end; **tickets** cost around £5–6 one-way (and only a little more return) and journey time is 50 minutes one-way.

Highgate is slightly sleepier and more aloof, with fewer conventional sights, while Hampstead is busier and buzzier, boasting high-profile intelligentsia and discerning pop stars among its residents. Both benefit from direct access to one of London's wildest patches of greenery, **Hampstead Heath**, where you can enjoy stupendous views over London, kite flying and nude bathing, as well as outdoor concerts and high art in and around the Neoclassical country mansion of Kenwood House.

Hampstead

On the north side of Holly Bush Hill, a short walk from Hampstead tube, stands the late seventeenth-century **Fenton House** (March Sat & Sun 2–5pm; Easter–Oct Wed–Fri 2–5pm, Sat & Sun 11am–5pm; NT; £4.80; Hampstead tube). As well as housing a collection of European and Oriental ceramics, this National Trust house contains a superb collection of early musical instruments. Among the many spinets, virginals and clavichords is an early English grand piano, and an Unverdorben lute from 1580 (one of only three in the world). For an extra £1, you can hire a tape of music played on the above instruments, to listen to while you walk round.

For a fascinating insight into the modernist mindset, take a look inside **2 Willow Road** (March & Nov Sat noon–5pm; April–Oct Thurs–Sat noon–5pm; £4.60; NT; Hampstead tube), an unassuming red-brick terraced house at the far end of Flask Walk, which leads off the High Street. Built in the 1930s by the Hungarian-born architect Ernö Goldfinger, this was a state-of-the-art pad, its open-plan rooms flooded with natural light and much of the furniture designed by Goldfinger himself. An added bonus is that the rooms are packed with *objets trouvés* and works of art by the likes of Max Ernst, Marcel Duchamp, Henry Moore and Man Ray. Before 3pm, visits are by hour-long guided tour only (noon, 1 & 2pm), for which you must book in advance; after 3pm the public has unguided, unrestricted access. The house is closed during the day on the first Thursday of the month, but open in the evening instead (5–9pm).

Hampstead's most famous figure is celebrated at **Keats' House** (Tues–Sun: April–Oct noon–5pm; Nov–March noon–4pm; £3; Hampstead tube), an elegant, whitewashed Regency double villa on Keats Grove, a short walk south of Willow Road. Inspired by the peacefulness of Hampstead and by his passion for girl-next-door Fanny Brawne (whose house is also part of the museum), Keats wrote some of his most famous works here before leaving for Rome, where he died of consumption in 1821. The neat, rather staid interior contains books and letters, Fanny's engagement ring and the four-poster bed in which the poet first coughed up blood, confiding to his companion, Charles Brown, "that drop of blood is my death warrant".

The Freud Museum

One of the most poignant of London's house museums is the **Freud Museum** (Wed–Sun noon–5pm; £5; ⓦ www.freud.org.uk; Finchley Road tube), hidden away in the leafy streets of south Hampstead at 20 Maresfield Gardens. Having lived in Vienna for his entire adult life, Freud, by now semi-disabled with only a year to live, was forced to flee the Nazis, arriving in London in the summer of 1938. The ground-floor study and library look exactly as they did when Freud lived here; the collection of erotic antiquities and the famous couch, sumptuously draped in Persian carpets, were all brought here from Vienna. Upstairs, home movies of family life in Vienna are shown continually, and a small room is dedicated to his daughter, Anna, herself an influential child analyst, who lived in the house until her death in 1982.

Hampstead Heath and Kenwood

North London's "green lung", **Hampstead Heath** is the city's most enjoyable public park. It may not have much of its original heathland left, but it packs a wonderful variety of bucolic scenery into its 800 acres. At its southern end are the rolling green pastures of **Parliament Hill**, North London's premier spot for kite flying. On either side are numerous ponds, three of which – one for men, one for women and one mixed – you can swim in for free. The thickest woodland is to be found in the **West Heath**, beyond Whitestone Pond, also the site of the most formal section, **Hill Garden**, a secretive and romantic little gem with eccentric balustraded terraces and a ruined pergola. Beyond lies **Golders Hill Park**, where you can gaze at pygmy goats and fallow deer, and inspect the impeccably maintained aviaries, home to flamingos, cranes and other exotic birds.

Finally, don't miss the landscaped grounds of Kenwood, in the north of the Heath, which are focused on the whitewashed Neoclassical mansion of **Kenwood House** (daily: April–Oct 11am–5pm; Nov–March 11am–4pm; EH; free; Hampstead tube or bus #210 from Archway tube). The house is home to a collection of seventeenth- and eighteenth-century art, including a handful of real masterpieces by the likes of Vermeer, Rembrandt, Boucher, Gainsborough and Reynolds. Of the period interiors, the most spectacular is Robert Adam's sky-blue and gold library, its book-filled apses separated from the central entertaining area by paired columns. To the south of the house, a grassy amphitheatre slopes down to a lake where outdoor classical concerts are held on summer evenings.

Highgate Cemetery

Receiving far more visitors than Highgate itself, **Highgate Cemetery** (Ⓦ highgate-cemetery.org; Highgate tube), ranged on both sides of Swain's Lane, is London's best-known graveyard. The most illustrious incumbent of the **East Cemetery** (April–Oct Mon–Fri 10am–5pm, Sat & Sun 11am–5pm; Nov–March closes 4pm; £2) is **Karl Marx**. Marx himself asked for a simple grave topped by a headstone, but by 1954 the Communist movement decided to move his grave to a more prominent position and erect the vulgar bronze bust that now surmounts a granite plinth.

What the East Cemetery lacks in atmosphere is in part compensated for by the fact that you can wander at will through its maze of circuitous paths, whereas to visit the more atmospheric and overgrown **West Cemetery**, with its spooky Egyptian Avenue and sunken catacombs, you must go round with a guided tour (March–Nov Mon–Fri 2pm, Sat & Sun hourly 11am–4pm; Dec–Feb Sat & Sun hourly 11am–3pm; £3; no under-8s). Among the prominent graves usually visited are those of artist Dante Gabriel Rossetti, and lesbian novelist Radclyffe Hall.

Hendon: The RAF Museum

A world-class assembly of historic military aircraft can be seen at the **RAF Museum** (daily 10am–6pm; free; Ⓦ www.rafmuseum.org.uk; Colindale tube), located in a godforsaken part of North London beside the M1 motorway. Enthusiasts won't be disappointed, but those looking for a balanced account of modern aerial warfare will – the overall tone is unashamedly militaristic, not to say jingoistic. Those with children should head for the hands-on Aeronauts gallery; those without might prefer to explore the often overlooked display galleries, ranged around the edge of the Main Aircraft Hall, which contain an art gallery and an exhibition on the history of flight, accompanied by replicas of some of the death-traps of early aviation.

Neasden: the Shri Swaminarayan temple

Perhaps the most remarkable building in the whole of London lies just off the North Circular, in the glum suburb of **Neasden**. Here, rising majestically above the surrounding semidetached houses like a mirage, is the **Shri Swaminarayan Mandir** (daily 9am–6pm; free, ⓦ www. mandir.org; Neasden tube), a traditional Hindu temple topped with domes and shikharas, erected in 1995 in a style and scale unseen outside of India for more than a millennium. To reach the temple, you must enter through the adjacent Haveli, or cultural complex, with its carved wooden portico and balcony. After taking off your shoes, you can proceed to the Mandir (temple) itself, carved entirely out of Carrara marble, with every possible surface transformed into a honeycomb of arabesques, flowers and seated gods. Beneath the Mandir, an **exhibition** (£2) explains the basic tenets of Hinduism and details the life of Lord Swaminarayan, and includes a video about the history of the building.

South London

Now largely built up into a patchwork of Victorian terraces, **South London** nevertheless boasts one outstanding area for sightseeing, and that is **Greenwich**, with its ensemble of the Royal Naval College and the Queen's House, courtesy of Christopher Wren and Inigo Jones respectively. Most visitors, it has to be said, come to see the National Maritime Museum, the Royal Observatory, and the beautifully landscaped royal park, though Greenwich **market** (Sundays) also pulls in an ever-increasing volume of Londoners.

The only other suburban sights that stand out are the **Dulwich Picture Gallery**, a public art gallery even older than the National Gallery, and the eclectic **Horniman Museum**, in neighbouring Forest Hill.

Greenwich

Greenwich is one of London's most beguiling spots, though its town centre, laid out in the 1820s with Nash-style terraces, is nowadays plagued with heavy traffic. To escape the busy streets, head for the old covered market, now at the centre of the weekend **Greenwich Market** (Thurs–Sun 9am–5pm), a lively place full of antiques, crafts and clothes stalls that have spilled out up the High Road, Stockwell Road and Royal Hill. A short distance in from the old covered

---

Getting to Greenwich

If you're heading straight for the National Maritime Museum from central London, the quickest way to get there is to take the **train** from London Bridge (every 30min) to Maze Hill, on the eastern edge of Greenwich Park. Those wanting to start with the town or the *Cutty Sark* should alight at Greenwich station. A more scenic route is to take a **boat** from one of the piers in central London. A third option is to take the **Docklands Light Railway** (DLR) to Cutty Sark station. For the best view of the Wren buildings, though, get off the DLR at Island Gardens, admire the view across the river and then take the Greenwich Foot Tunnel under the Thames.

market, on the opposite side of Greenwich Church Street, rises Nicholas Hawksmoor's **St Alfege's Church** (Mon–Sat 10am–4pm, Sun noon–4pm; Ⓦ www.st-alfege.org), built in 1712–18, flattened in the Blitz, but now magnificently restored to its former glory.

Cutty Sark and the Old Royal Naval College

Wedged in a dry dock by the Greenwich Foot Tunnel is the majestic **Cutty Sark** (daily 10am–5pm; £4.50; Ⓦ www.cuttysark.org.uk), the world's last surviving tea clipper, built in 1869. The *Cutty Sark* spent just eight years in the China tea trade, and it was as a wool clipper that it actually made its name, making a return journey to Australia in just 72 days. Inside, there's little to see beyond the exhibition in the main hold which tells the ship's story from its inception to its arrival in Greenwich in 1954.

It's entirely appropriate that the one London building that makes the most of its riverbank location should be the **Old Royal Naval College** (daily 10am–5pm; free; Ⓦ www.greenwichfoundation.org.uk), Wren's beautifully symmetrical Baroque ensemble, initially built as a royal palace, but eventually converted into a hospital for disabled seamen. From 1873 until 1998 it was home to the Royal Naval College, but now houses the University of Greenwich and the Trinity College of Music. The two grandest rooms, situated underneath Wren's twin domes, are open to the public and well worth visiting. The **Chapel**, in the east wing, has exquisite pastel-shaded plasterwork and spectacular, decorative detailing on the ceiling, all designed by James "Athenian" Stuart after a fire in 1799 destroyed the original interior. From the chapel, you can take the underground Chalk Walk to gain access to the magnificent **Painted Hall** in the west wing, which is dominated by James Thornhill's gargantuan allegorical ceiling painting, and his trompe l'oeil fluted pilasters.

National Maritime Museum

The main entrance to the excellent **National Maritime Museum** (daily 10am–5pm; July & Aug closes 6pm; free; Ⓦ www.nmm.ac.uk), which occupies the old Naval Asylum, is on Romney Road. From here, you enter the spectacular glass-roofed central courtyard, which houses the museum's largest artefacts, among them the splendid 63-foot-long gilded **Royal Barge**, designed in Rococo style by William Kent for Prince Frederick, the much unloved eldest son of George II.

The various themed galleries are superbly designed to appeal to visitors of all ages. In **Explorers**, on Level 1, you get to view some *Titanic* relics; **Passengers** relives the glory days of transatlantic shipping, which officially came to an end in 1957 when more people went by air than by sea; **Trade & Empire**, on Level 2, is a gallery devoted to the legacy of the British Empire, warts and all, from the slave trade to the Opium Wars; **Oceans of Discovery**, on Level 3, boasts Captain Cook's sextant and K1 marine clock, Shackleton's compass, and **Captain Scott**'s overshoes, watch and funky sledging goggles.

Level 3 also boasts two hands-on galleries: **The Bridge**, where you can attempt to navigate a catamaran, a paddle steamer and a rowing boat to shore; and **All Hands**, where children can have a go at radio transmission, loading miniature cargo, firing a cannon and so forth. Finally, there's the **Nelson Gallery**, which contains the museum's vast collection of Nelson-related memorabilia, including Turner's *Battle of Trafalgar, 21st October, 1805*, his largest work and only royal commission.

Inigo Jones's **Queen's House**, originally built amidst a rambling Tudor royal palace, is now the focal point of the Greenwich ensemble, and is an integral part of the Maritime Museum. As royal residences go, it's an unassuming country house, but as the first Neoclassical building in the country, it has enormous architectural significance. The interior is currently used for temporary exhibitions. Nevertheless, one or two features survive (or have been reinstated) from Stuart times. Off the Great Hall, a perfect cube, lies the beautiful Tulip Staircase, Britain's earliest cantilevered spiral staircase – its name derives from the floral patterning in the wrought-iron balustrade.

Royal Observatory

Perched on the crest of Greenwich Park's highest hill, the **Royal Observatory** (daily 10am–5pm; July & Aug closes 6pm; free; ⓦwww.rog.nmm.ac.uk) is housed in a rather dinky Wren-built red-brick building, whose northeastern turret sports a bright-red time-ball that climbs the mast at 12.58pm and drops at 1pm GMT precisely; it was added in 1833 to allow ships to set their clocks.

Greenwich's greatest claim to fame, of course, is as the home of **Greenwich Mean Time** (GMT) and the Prime Meridian. Since 1884, Greenwich has occupied zero longitude – hence the world sets its clocks by GMT. The observatory itself was established in 1675 by Charles II to house the first Astronomer Royal, John Flamsteed, whose chief task was to study the night sky in order to discover an astronomical method of finding the longitude of a ship at sea. Astronomers continued to work here at Greenwich until the postwar smog forced them to decamp; the old observatory, meanwhile, is now a very popular museum.

The oldest part of the observatory is **Flamsteed House**, containing the Octagon Room, where the king used to show off to his guests. The Chronometer Gallery, beyond, focuses on the search for the precise measurement of longitude, and displays four of the clocks designed by **John Harrison**, including "H4", which helped win the Longitude Prize in 1763. The observatory is now in the process of redevelopment, which will eventually see the creation of a state-of-the-art **Planetarium**, housed in the South Building.

The Ranger's House and the Fan Museum

Southwest of the observatory, and backing onto Greenwich Park's rose garden, is the **Ranger's House** (Wed–Sun: April–Sept 10am–5pm; EH; £5.30), a

The Dome

The Dome (North Greenwich tube) is clearly visible from the riverside at Greenwich and from the upper parts of Greenwich Park. Designed by Richard Rogers, it cost almost £800 million of public money, and is by far the world's largest dome – over half a mile in circumference and 160ft in height – held up by a dozen, 300-foot-tall yellow steel masts. In 2000, for one year only, it housed the nation's chief millennium extravaganza: an array of high-tech themed zones set around a stage, on which a circus-style performance took place twice a day. Bad reviews and over-optimistic estimates of visitor numbers forced the government to pump in around £150 million of public money just to keep it open. Nevertheless, millions paid up to £20 each to visit, and millions went away happy.

Entertainment giants AEG have now agreed to spend yet more millions to turn the Dome into a six-floor, 23,000-seater music and sports arena, and the O2 mobile company have paid to rebrand it "the O2". The venue will reopen in 2007, host the 2009 World Gymnastics Championships and be the 2012 Olympic venue for artistic gymnastics, trampolining and basketball.

red-brick Georgian villa that houses an art collection amassed by Julius Wernher, the German-born millionaire who made his money by exploiting the diamond deposits of South Africa. His taste in art is eclectic, ranging from medieval ivory miniatures to Iznik pottery, though he was definitely a man who placed technical virtuosity above artistic merit. The high points of the collection are Memlinc's *Virgin and Child* and a pair of sixteenth-century majolica dishes decorated with mythological scenes for Isabella d'Este (located upstairs), and the Reynolds portraits and de Hooch interior (located downstairs).

Croom's Hill, running down the west side of the park, boasts some of Greenwich's finest Georgian buildings, one of which houses the **Fan Museum** at no. 12 (Tues–Sat 11am–5pm, Sun noon–5pm; £3.50; ⓦwww.fan-museum.org). It's a fascinating little place (and an extremely beautiful house), revealing the importance of the fan as a social and political document.

Dulwich Picture Gallery and the Horniman Museum

Dulwich Picture Gallery (Tues–Fri 10am–5pm, Sat & Sun 11am–5pm; £4, free on Fri; ⓦwww.dulwichpicturegallery.org.uk; West Dulwich train station from Victoria), on College Road, is the nation's oldest public art gallery, designed by John Soane and opened in 1817. Soane created a beautifully spacious building, awash with natural light and crammed with superb paintings – elegiac landscapes by Cuyp, one of the world's finest Poussin series, and splendid works by Hogarth, Gainsborough, Van Dyck, Canaletto and Rubens, plus **Rembrandt**'s tiny *Portrait of a Young Man*, a top-class portrait of poet, playwright and Royalist, the future Earl of Bristol. At the centre of the museum is a tiny mausoleum designed by Soane for the sarcophagi of the gallery's founders.

To the southeast of Dulwich Park, on the busy South Circular road, is the wacky **Horniman Museum** (daily 10.30am–5.30pm; free; ⓦwww.horniman .ac.uk; Forest Hill train station from Victoria or London Bridge), purpose-built in 1901 by Frederick Horniman, a tea trader with a passion for collecting. In addition to the museum's natural history collection of stuffed birds and animals, there's an amazingly eclectic ethnographic collection, and a musical department with more than 1500 instruments from Chinese gongs to electric guitars. Lastly, don't miss the museum's new **aquarium** in the basement, and look out for the special sessions at the **Hands on Base**, which allow you to handle and learn more about a whole range of the museum's artefacts.

Out west: Chiswick to Windsor

Most people experience **West London** en route to or from Heathrow Airport, either from the confines of the train, tube or motorway. The city and its satellites seem to continue unabated, with only fleeting glimpses of the countryside. However, in the five-mile stretch from Chiswick to Osterley there are several former country retreats, now surrounded by suburbia, which are definitely worth digging out.

The Palladian villa of **Chiswick House** is perhaps the best known of these attractions. However, it draws nothing like as many visitors as **Syon House**, most of whom come for the gardening centre rather than for the house itself, a showcase for the talents of Robert Adam, who also worked at **Osterley House**, another Elizabethan conversion, now owned by the National Trust.

Running through much of the area is the **River Thames**, once known as the "Great Highway of London" and still the most pleasant way to travel in these parts during the summer. Boats plough up the Thames all the way from central London via the **Royal Botanic Gardens** at **Kew** and the picturesque riverside at **Richmond**, as far as **Hampton Court**, home of the country's largest royal residence and the famous maze. To reach the heavily touristed royal outpost of **Windsor Castle**, however, you need to take the train.

Chiswick

Chiswick House (daily: April–Sept 10am–6pm; Oct 10am–5pm; £3.50; EH; Chiswick train station from Waterloo), is a perfect little Neoclassical villa, designed in the 1720s by the Earl of Burlington, and set in one of the most beautifully landscaped gardens in London. Like its prototype, Palladio's Villa Rotonda near Vicenza, the house was purpose-built as a "temple to the arts" where, amid his fine-art collection, Burlington could entertain artistic friends such as Swift, Handel and Pope. Entertaining took place on the **upper floor**, a series of cleverly interconnecting rooms, each enjoying a wonderful view out onto the gardens – all, that is, except the Tribunal, the domed octagonal hall at the centre of the villa, where the earl's finest paintings and sculptures would have been displayed.

If you leave Chiswick House gardens by the northernmost exit, beyond the Italian garden, it's just a short walk along the thunderous A4 road to **Hogarth's House** (Tues–Fri 1–4/5pm, Sat & Sun 1–5/6pm; closed Jan; free), where the artist spent each summer with his wife, sister and mother-in-law from 1749 until his death in 1764. Nowadays it's difficult to believe Hogarth came here for "peace and quiet", but in the eighteenth century the house was almost entirely surrounded by countryside.

Kew Bridge Steam Museum

Difficult to miss thanks to its stylish Italianate standpipe tower, **Kew Bridge Steam Museum** (daily 11am–5pm; Mon–Fri £4.25, Sat & Sun £5.75; Ⓦwww.kbsm.org; Kew Bridge train station from Waterloo; or bus #237 or #267 from Gunnersbury tube) occupies a former pumping station, on the corner of Kew Bridge Road and Green Dragon Lane, 100m west of the bridge itself. At the heart of the museum is the Steam Hall, which contains a triple expansion steam engine and four gigantic nineteenth-century Cornish beam engines. The museum also has a hands-on **Water for Life** gallery in the basement, devoted to the history of the capital's water supply. The best time to visit is at weekends, when each of the museum's industrial dinosaurs is put through its paces, and the small narrow-gauge steam railway runs back and forth round the yard (March–Nov Sun).

River transport

Westminster Passenger Services (☎020/7930 2062, Ⓦwww.wpsa.co.uk) runs four boats from Westminster Pier to Kew, and two boats to Richmond and Hampton Court daily from April to September. The full trip takes 3hr one way, and costs £13.50 single, £19.50 return. In addition, Turks (☎020/8546 2434, Ⓦwww.turks.co.uk) runs a regular service from Richmond to Hampton Court (April to mid-Sept Tues–Sun) which costs £5.50 single or £7 return.

Syon House

Across the water from Kew stands **Syon Park** (Ⓦ www.syonpark.co.uk), seat of the Duke of Northumberland since Elizabethan times, now as much a working commercial concern as a family home, embracing a garden centre, a wholefood shop, an aquatic centre stocked with tropical fish, a mini-zoo and a butterfly house, as well as the old aristocratic mansion and its gardens.

From its rather plain castellated exterior, you'd never guess that **Syon House** (April–Oct Wed, Thurs & Sun 11am–5pm; £7.50; bus #237 or #267 from Gunnersbury tube or Kew Bridge train station) contains the most opulent eighteenth-century interiors in the whole of London. The splendour of Robert Adam's refurbishment is immediately revealed, however, in the pristine **Great Hall**, an apsed double cube with a screen of Doric columns at one end and classical statuary dotted around the edges. There are several more Adam-designed rooms to admire in the house, plus a smattering of works by Van Dyck, Lely, Gainsborough and Reynolds.

While Adam beautified Syon House, Capability Brown laid out its **gardens** (daily 10.30am–5.30pm; £3.75, free with ticket to the house) around an artificial lake, surrounding it with oaks, beeches, limes and cedars. The gardens' chief focus now, however, is the crescent-shaped **Great Conservatory**, an early nineteenth-century addition which is said to have inspired Joseph Paxton, architect of the Crystal Palace. Those with young children will be compelled to make use of the **miniature steam train** (April–Oct Sun).

Another plus point for kids (and adults) is Syon's **Butterfly House** (daily: April–Sept 10am–5pm; Oct–March 10am–3.30pm; £5.25; Ⓦ www.london butterflyhouse.com), a small, mesh-covered hothouse, where you can walk amid hundreds of exotic butterflies from all over the world, as they flit about the foliage. Next door is **London Aquatic Experience** (daily 10am–5.30pm; £5; Ⓦ www.aquatic-experience.org), a purpose-built centre housing a mixed range of aquatic creatures from the mysterious basilisk, which can walk on water, to the perennially popular piranhas and crocodiles.

Osterley Park and House

Robert Adam redesigned another colossal Elizabethan mansion three miles northwest of Syon at **Osterley Park** (daily 9am–7.30pm or dusk; free), which maintains the impression of being in the middle of the countryside, despite the presence of the M4 to the north of the house. The park itself is well worth exploring, and there's a great café in the Tudor stables, but anyone with a passing interest in Adam's work should pay a visit to **Osterley House** (March Sat & Sun 1–4.30pm; Easter–Oct Wed–Sun 1–4.30pm; NT; £4.90; Osterley tube). From the outside, Osterley bears some similarity to Syon, the big difference being Adam's grand entrance portico, with its tall, Ionic colonnade. From here, you enter a characteristically cool **Entrance Hall**, followed by the so-called State Rooms of the south wing. Highlights include the **Drawing Room**, with Reynolds portraits on the damask walls and a coffered ceiling centred on a giant marigold, and the **Etruscan Dressing Room**, in which every surface is covered in delicate painted trelliswork, sphinxes and urns, a style that Adam (and Wedgwood) dubbed "Etruscan", though it is in fact derived from Greek vases found at Pompeii.

Kew Gardens

Established in 1759, the **Royal Botanic Gardens** (daily 9.30am–7.30pm or dusk; £10; Ⓦ www.kew.org; Kew Gardens tube) have grown from their original

△ Kew Gardens

eight acres into a three-hundred-acre site in which more than 33,000 species are grown in plantations and glasshouses, a display that attracts over a million visitors every year, most of them with no specialist interest at all. There's always something to see, whatever the season, but to get the most out of the place, come sometime between spring and autumn, bring a picnic and stay for the day.

Of all the glasshouses, by far the most celebrated is the **Palm House**, a curvaceous mound of glass and wrought-iron, designed by Decimus Burton in the 1840s. Its drippingly humid atmosphere nurtures most of the known palm species, while in the basement there's a small but excellent tropical aquarium. Kew's origins as an eighteenth-century royal pleasure garden are evident in the numerous follies dotted about Kew, the most conspicuous of which is the ten-storey, 163-foot-high **Pagoda**.

Richmond Park and Ham House

Richmond, upriver from Kew, basked for centuries in the glow of royal patronage, with Plantagenet kings and Tudor monarchs frequenting the river-side palace. Although most of the courtiers and aristocrats have gone, **Richmond** is still a wealthy district, with two theatres and highbrow pretensions. Richmond's greatest attraction though, is the enormous **Richmond Park** (daily: March–Sept 7am–dusk; Oct–Feb 7.30am–dusk; free; Ⓦ www.royalparks .gov.uk), at the top of Richmond Hill – 2500 acres of undulating grassland and bracken, dotted with coppiced woodland and as wild as anything in London. Eight miles across at its widest point, this is Europe's largest city park, famed for its red and fallow deer, which roam freely, and for its ancient oaks. For the most part untamed, the park does have a couple of deliberately landscaped planta-tions that feature splendid springtime azaleas and rhododendrons, in particular the Isabella Plantation.

Back down the hill, if you continue along the towpath beyond Richmond Bridge, after a mile or so, you leave the rest of London far behind and arrive at **Ham House** (April–Oct Mon–Wed, Sat & Sun 1–5pm; £7.50; NT; Richmond tube), home to the earls of Dysart for nearly three hundred years. Expensively furnished in the seventeenth century, but little altered since then, the house boasts one of the finest Stuart interiors in the country, from the stupendously ornate Great Staircase to the Long Gallery, featuring six "Court Beauties" by Peter Lely. Another bonus are the formal seventeenth-century **gardens** (Mon–Wed, Sat & Sun 11am–6pm; £3.50, free with ticket for house) especially the Cherry Garden, laid out with a pungent lavender parterre, surrounded by yew hedges and pleached hornbeam arbours.

Hampton Court

Hampton Court Palace (daily: April–Oct 10am–6pm; Nov–March 10am–4.30pm; £12; ⓦ www.hrp.org.uk; Hampton Court train station from Waterloo), a sprawling red-brick ensemble on the banks of the Thames, thirteen miles southwest of London, is the finest of England's royal abodes. Built in 1516 by the upwardly mobile **Cardinal Wolsey**, Henry VIII's Lord Chancellor, it was purloined by Henry himself after Wolsey fell from favour. In the second half of the seventeenth century, Charles II laid out the gardens, inspired by what he had seen at Versailles, while William and Mary had large sections of the palace remodelled by Wren a few years later.

The **Royal Apartments** are divided into six thematic walking tours. There's not a lot of information in any of the rooms, but guided tours, each lasting 45 minutes, are available at no extra charge for Henry VIII's and the King's apartments; all are led by period-costumed historians, who do a fine job of bringing the place to life. If your energy is lacking – and Hampton Court is huge – the most rewarding sections are: **Henry VIII's State Apartments**, which feature the glorious double hammerbeamed Great Hall; the **King's Apartments** (remodelled by William III); and the vast **Tudor Kitchens**. The last two are also served by audio tours. Part of the Royal Collection is housed in the **Renaissance Picture Gallery** and is chock-full of treasures, among them paintings by Tintoretto, Lotto, Titian, Cranach, Bruegel and Holbein.

Tickets to the Royal Apartments cover entry to the rest of the sites in the grounds. Those who don't wish to visit the apartments are free to wander around the gardens, but have to pay extra to visit the curious **Royal Tennis Courts** (50p), the palace's famously tricky yew-hedge **Maze** (£3), and the **Privy Garden** (£3), where you can view Andrea Mantegna's colourful, heroic canvases, *The Triumphs of Caesar*, housed in the Lower Orangery, and the celebrated **Great Vine**, whose grapes are sold at the palace each year in September.

Windsor and Eton

Every weekend trains from Waterloo and Paddington are packed with people heading for **WINDSOR**, the royal enclave 21 miles west of London, where they join the human conveyor-belt round **Windsor Castle** (daily: March–Oct 9.45am–5.15pm; Nov–Feb 9.45am–4.15pm; £12.50; ⓦ www.royal.gov.uk; Paddington to Windsor & Eton Central via Slough, or Waterloo to Windsor & Eton Riverside – note that you must arrive and depart from the same station, as tickets are not interchangeable). Towering above the town on a steep chalk bluff, the castle is an undeniably awesome sight, its chilly grey walls, punctuated by mighty medieval bastions, continuing as far as the eye can see. Inside, most visitors just gape in awe at the monotonous, gilded grandeur of the **State Apartments**, while the real highlights – the paintings from the Royal

Collection that line the walls – are rarely given a second glance. More impressive is **St George's Chapel** (Mon–Sat 10am–4pm), a glorious Perpendicular structure ranking with Henry VII's chapel in Westminster Abbey (see p.94), and the second most important resting place for royal corpses after the Abbey. On a fine day, it pays to put aside some time for exploring Windsor Great Park, which stretches for several miles to the south of the castle.

Crossing the bridge at the end of Thames Avenue in Windsor town brings you to **ETON**, a one-street village lined with bookshops and antique dealers, but famous all over the world for **Eton College** (Easter, July & Aug daily 10.30am–4.30pm; after Easter to June & Sept daily 2–4.30pm; £3.80; Ⓦ www .etoncollege.com), a ten-minute walk from the river. When the school was founded in 1440, its aim was to give free education to seventy poor scholars and choristers; how times have changed. The original fifteenth-century **schoolroom**, gnarled with centuries of graffiti, survives, but the real highlight is the **College Chapel**, completed in 1482, a wonderful example of English Perpendicular architecture. The self-congratulatory **Museum of Eton Life**, where you're deposited at the end of the tour, can easily be skipped unless you have a fascination with flogging, fagging and bragging about the school's facilities and alumni – Percy Bysshe Shelley is a rare rebellious figure in the roll call of Establishment greats.

Among younger children, the attractions of Windsor Castle are overshadowed by the nearby **Legoland** theme park (Easter–Oct daily 10am–5pm, later in school holidays; adults £26, under-15s £22, under-3s free; Ⓦ www.legoland .co.uk), aimed at pre-teenage children (the perfect age is around 5 to 8). Avoid visiting at the weekend or during the school holidays, however, when the queues for the various rides become grievously long and the tickets cost £4 more. On arrival, a funicular railway takes visitors down into the park, disgorging them close to Miniland, with its miniature Lego depictions of various European landmarks. The rest of the park is really just a series of rides, most of them very gentle. There are numerous places to eat, though it makes sense to take a picnic and save yourself some money.

Eating

London is an exciting (though often expensive) place in which to eat out. It's home to people from all over the globe, and you can pretty much sample any kind of cuisine here, from Georgian to Peruvian. Indeed, London now has some of Europe's best **Cantonese** restaurants, is a noted centre for **Indian** and **Bangladeshi** food, and has numerous French, Greek, Italian, Japanese, Spanish and Thai restaurants; and within all these cuisines, you can choose anything from simple meals to gourmet spreads. Traditional and modern **British** food is available all over town, and some of the best venues are reviewed below.

Cafés and snacks

There are plenty of **cafés** and small, basic restaurants all over London that can fill you up for under £10, including tea or coffee. Several of the places listed are also open in the evening, but the turnover is fast, so don't expect to linger; they're best seen as fuel stops before – or in a few cases, after – a night out. It's worth bearing in mind that most **pubs** (which are covered in the following section) serve meals, and some take their food quite seriously.

Whitehall and Westminster

Café in the Crypt St Martin-in-the-Fields, Duncannon Street, WC2; Charing Cross tube. See map, p.88. The self-service buffet food is nothing special, but there are regular veggie dishes, and the handy (and atmospheric) location makes this an ideal spot.

Jenny Lo's Teahouse 14 Eccleston St, SW1; Victoria tube. See map, p.88. Bright, bare and utilitarian yet somehow stylish and fashionable too, *Jenny Lo's* serves good Chinese food at low prices. Be sure to try the therapeutic teas. Closed Sun.

Mayfair and Marylebone

Eat & Two Veg 50 Marylebone High St, W1; Bond Street or Regent's Park tube. See map, p.105. A lively and modern veggie restaurant, with some vegan and soya protein choices. The menu is eclectic, with Thai, Greek and Italian dishes.

Mômo Tearoom 25 Heddon St, W1; Piccadilly Circus tube. See map, p.88. The ultimate Arabic pastiche, and a successful one at that. The adjacent restaurant is pricey, but the tearoom serves delicious snacks and is a great place to hang out, with tables and hookahs spilling out onto the pavement of this little Mayfair alleyway behind Regent Street.

Patisserie Valerie at Sagne 105 Marylebone High St, W1; Bond Street or Regent's Park tube. Founded as Swiss-run *Maison Sagne* in the 1920s, and preserving its wonderful decor from those days, the café is now run by Soho's fab patisserie-makers, and is without doubt Marylebone's finest.

The Wolseley 160 Piccadilly, W1; Green Park tube. See map, p.88. The lofty and stylish 1920s interior of this brasserie/restaurant (built as the showroom for Wolseley cars) is a big draw, and service is attentive and non-snooty. Given the glamour levels it's surprisingly affordable and the Viennese-inspired food delivers too. A great place for breakfast or a cream tea (£7.25).

Soho

Bar Italia 22 Frith St, W1; Leicester Square tube. See map, p.88. A tiny café that's a Soho institution, serving coffee, croissants and sandwiches more or less around the clock – as it has done since 1949.

Beatroot 92 Berwick St, W1; Piccadilly Circus tube. See map, p.88. Great little veggie café by the market, doling out hot savoury bakes, stews and salads (plus delicious cakes) in boxes of varying sizes – all under £5.

Brasil by Kilo 17 Oxford St, W1; Tottenham Court Road tube. See map, p.88. Basic and friendly refuelling stop which doles out Brazilian food at £1 per kilo. Go upstairs for the array of hot food and salads, or head for the coffee bar downstairs, which serves traditional snacks and sweets.

Gaby's 30 Charing Cross Rd, WC2; Leicester Square tube. See map, p.88. Busy café and takeaway joint that stays open till late serving a wide range of home-cooked veggie and Middle Eastern specialities. Hard to beat for value or choice and it's licensed, too.

Indian YMCA 41 Fitzroy Square, W1; Warren Street tube. See map, p.105. Don't take any notice of the signs saying the canteen is only for students – this place is open to all; just press the bell and pile in. The entire menu is portioned up into pretty little bowls; go and collect what you want and pay at the till. The food is great and the prices unbelievably low.

Maison Bertaux 28 Greek St, W1; Leicester Square tube. See map, p.88. Long-standing, old-fashioned and downbeat Soho patisserie, with tables on two floors (and one or two outside) and a loyal clientele that keeps things busy.

Patisserie Valerie 44 Old Compton St, W1; Leicester Square or Piccadilly Circus tube. See map, p.88. Popular coffee, croissant and cake emporium attracting a loud-talking, arty Soho crowd.

Chinatown

Kopi-Tiam 9 Wardour St, W1; Leicester Square tube. See map, p.88. Bright, cheap Malaysian café serving up curries, coconut rice, juices and "herbal soups" to local Malays, all for around a fiver.

Lee Ho Fook 4 Macclesfield St, W1; Leicester Square tube. See map, p.88. Difficult to find, but a genuine Chinese barbecue house – small, spartan and cheap.

Tokyo Diner 2 Newport Place, WC2; Leicester Square tube. See map, p.88. Friendly place on the edge of Chinatown that shuns elaboration for fast food, Tokyo style. Minimalist decor lets the sushi and sumo do the talking.

Covent Garden and Bloomsbury

Food for Thought 31 Neal St, WC2; Covent Garden tube. See map, p.88. Long-established but minuscule, bargain veggie restaurant and takeaway counter – the food is good, with the menu changing twice daily. Expect to queue and don't expect to linger at peak times.

Paul 29 Bedford St, WC2; Covent Garden tube. See map, p.88. Seriously French, classy *boulangerie* with a wood-panelled café at the back. Try one of the chewy *fougasses*, quiches or tarts, before launching into the exquisite patisserie.

Rock & Sole Plaice 47 Endell St, WC2; Covent Garden tube. See map, p.88. A rare survivor: a no-nonsense traditional fish-and-chip shop in central London. Takeaway, eat in or out at one of the pavement tables.

Wagamama 4 Streatham St, WC1; Tottenham Court Road tube. See map, p.105. Much copied since, *Wagamama* was the pioneer when it comes to austere, minimalist, canteen-style noodle bars. Branches around central London.

World Food Café 14 Neal's Yard, WC2; Covent Garden tube. See map, p.88. First-floor veggie café that comes into its own in summer, when the windows are flung open and you can gaze down upon trendy humanity as you tuck into pricey but tasty dishes from all corners of the globe. Closed Sun.

Clerkenwell & Hoxton

Clark & Sons 46 Exmouth Market, EC1; Angel or Farringdon tube. See map, p.108. Exmouth Market has undergone something of a transformation, so it's all the more surprising to find this genuine eel-and-pie shop still going strong. Closed Sun.

Flavour 35 Charlotte Rd, EC2; Old Street tube. See map, p.108. Tiny Shoreditch café with just four stools, serving delicious Mediterranean lunch options: big soups, grilled tuna, salads and great pastries, all freshly prepared. Closed Sun.

The City and the East End

Arkansas Café Unit 12, Old Spitalfields Market, E1; Liverpool Street tube. See map, p.108. American barbecue fuel stop, using only the very best free-range ingredients. Closed Sat.

Brick Lane Beigel Bake 159 Brick Lane, E1; Shoreditch or Whitechapel tube. See map, p.108. The bagels at this no-frills 24-hour takeaway in the heart of the East End are freshly made and unbelievably cheap, even when stuffed with smoked salmon and cream cheese.

Café 1001 1 Dray's Lane, E1; Whitechapel tube. See map, p.108. Off Brick Lane, tucked in by the Truman Brewery, this smoky café has a beaten-up studenty look, with lots of sofas to crash in, and dishes out simple sandwiches and delicious cakes.

De Gustibus 53–55 Carter Lane, EC2; St Paul's or Blackfriars tube. See map, p.108. Award-winning bakery that creates a wide variety of sandwiches, *bruschette*, *croque monsieur* and quiche to eat in or take away. Closed Sat & Sun.

The Place Below St Mary-le-Bow, Cheapside, EC2; St Paul's or Bank tube. See map, p.108. City café serving imaginative (albeit slightly pricey) vegetarian dishes in a wonderful Norman crypt. Closed Sat & Sun.

The South Bank and Southwark

Konditor & Cook 22 Cornwall Rd, SE1; Waterloo tube. See map, p.121. A cut above your average bakery, *Konditor & Cook* makes wonderful cakes and biscuits, as well as offering a choice of sandwiches and coffee and tea. There are branches elsewhere on the south side of the Thames at 10 Stoney St by Borough Market and in the Design Museum. Closed Sun.

Marie's Café 90 Lower Marsh, SE1; Waterloo tube. See map, p.121. As the name doesn't suggest, this is a Thai café – it's basic, cheap and friendly and dishes up tasty red and green curries. Bring your own booze; £1 corkage.

Kensington, Chelsea and Notting Hill

Daquise 20 Thurloe St, SW7; South Kensington tube. See map, p.128. This old-fashioned Polish café right by the tube is something of a South Ken institution, serving Polish home cooking or simple coffee, tea and cakes depending on the time of day.

Gloriette 128 Brompton Rd, SW7; South Kensington or Knightsbridge tube. See map, p.128. Long-established Viennese café that makes a perfect post-museum halt for coffee and outrageous cakes; also serves sandwiches, Wiener schnitzel, pasta dishes, goulash, and fish and chips.

Lisboa Patisserie 57 Golborne Rd, W10; Ladbroke Grove tube. See map, p.128. Authentic and friendly Portuguese *pastelaria*, with coffee and cakes, including the best custard tarts this side of Lisbon. The *Oporto* opposite, at no. 62a, is a good fallback if this place is full.

Camden and Hampstead

Café Mozart 17 Swains Lane, N6; Gospel Oak train station. Viennese café that's usefully close to the southeast side of Hampstead Heath, and also serves a few hearty Austrian dishes.

Louis Patisserie 32 Heath St, NW3; Hampstead tube. Popular central-European tearoom in Hampstead Village serving sticky cakes to a mix of Heath-bound hordes and elderly locals.

Marine Ices 8 Haverstock Hill, NW3; Chalk Farm tube. Situated halfway between Camden and Hampstead, this is a splendid and justly famous old-fashioned Italian ice-cream parlour; pizza and pasta are served in a child-friendly restaurant.

Greenwich

Goddard's 45 Greenwich Church St, SE10; Cutty Sark DLR. Established in 1890, *Goddard's* serves traditional pies (including veggie ones), eels and

Afternoon tea

The classic English **afternoon tea** – assorted sandwiches, scones and cream, cakes and tarts, and, of course, lashings of tea – is available all over London, with some of the best venues being the capital's top hotels and fashionable department stores. To avoid disappointment it's best to book ahead. Expect to spend £15–30 a head, and leave your jeans and trainers at home – most hotels will expect "smart casual attire", though only The Ritz insists on jacket and tie.

Brown's 33–34 Albemarle St, W1 ☎020/7493 6020, ⊛www.brownshotel.com; Green Park tube. Daily 2–6pm.

Claridge's Brook Street, W1 ☎020/7629 8860, ⊛www.savoy-group.co.uk; Bond Street tube. Daily 3–5.30pm.

The Dorchester 54 Park Lane, W1 ☎020/7629 8888, ⊛www.dorchesterhotel.com; Hyde Park Corner tube. Daily 3–6pm.

Fortnum & Mason 181 Piccadilly, W1 ☎020/7734 8040, ⊛www.fortnumandmason .com; Green Park or Piccadilly Circus tube. Daily 3–5.30pm.

Lanesborough Hyde Park Corner, SW1 ☎020/7259 5599, ⊛www.lanesborough .com; Hyde Park Corner tube. Mon–Sat 3.30–6pm, Sun 4–6pm.

The Ritz Piccadilly, W1 ☎020/7493 8181, ⊛www.theritzhotel.co.uk; Green Park tube. Daily 11.30am, 1.30, 3.30 & 5.30pm.

The Savoy Strand, WC2 ☎020/7836 4343, ⊛www.savoy-group.co.uk; Charing Cross tube. Mon–Fri 2–3.30pm & 4–6pm, Sat & Sun noon–1.30pm, 2–3.30pm & 4–6pm.

The Wolseley 160 Piccadilly, W1 ☎020/7499 699, ⊛www.thewolseley.com; Green Park tube. Mon–Fri 3–5.30pm, Sat & Sun 3.30–6pm.

mash in an emerald green–tiled interior, with crumble and custard for afters.

Tai Won Mein 39 Greenwich Church St, SE10; Cutty Sark DLR or Greenwich DLR and train station. Good-quality fast-food noodle bar that gets very busy at weekends. Decor is functional and minimalist; choose between rice, soup or various fried noodles, all for under a fiver.

Restaurants

Many of the restaurants we've listed will be busy on most nights of the week, particularly on Thursday, Friday and Saturday, and it's best to **reserve a table**. As for **prices**, you can pay an awful lot for a meal in London, and if you're used to North American portions, you're not going to be particularly impressed by the volume in most places. For cheaper eats, see the section above.

Marylebone and Edgware Road

Fairuz 3 Blandford St, W1 ☎020/7486 8108; Bond Street tube. See map, p.105. One of London's more accessible Middle Eastern restaurants, with an epic list of mezze, a selection of charcoal grills and one or two oven-baked dishes. Moderate.

Mandalay 444 Edgware Rd, W2 ☎020/7258 3696; Edgware Road tube. See map, p.128. Small nonsmoking restaurant that serves Burmese cuisine – a melange of Thai, Malaysian, a lot of Indian and a few things that are unique. The portions are huge, the service friendly and the prices low. Booking essential in the evening. Closed Sun. Moderate

The Providores 109 Marylebone High St, W1 ☎020/7935 6175. Bond Street or Regent's Park tube. See map, p.105. Outstanding fusion restaurant run by amiable New Zealander and split into two: snacky tapas bar downstairs and full-on restaurant upstairs. The food at both is original and wholly satisfying. Inexpensive.

Tottenham Court Road and around

Ikkyu 67a Tottenham Court Rd, W1 ☎020/7636 9280; Goodge Street tube. See map, p.105. Busy basement Japanese restaurant, good for a quick lunch or a more elaborate dinner. Either way, prices are infinitely more reasonable than elsewhere in the capital, and the food is tasty and authentic. Closed all Sat & Sun lunch. Moderate.

Rasa Samudra 5 Charlotte St, W1 ☎020/7637 0222; Goodge Street tube. See map, p.105. The food served at *Rasa Samudra* would be more at home in Mumbai than in London, consisting as it does of sophisticated Southern Indian fish dishes – a million miles from curry-house staples. Moderate.

Soho and Chinatown

Chowki 2–3 Denman St, W1 ☎020/7439 1330; Piccadilly Circus tube. See map, p.88. Large, cheap Indian restaurant serving authentic food in stylish surroundings. The menu changes every month in order to feature three different regions of India – the regional feast for around £11 is great value. Inexpensive.

The Criterion 224 Piccadilly, W1 ☎020/7930 0488; Piccadilly Circus tube. See map, p.88. The predominately French food doesn't come cheap at this Marco Pierre White restaurant (though lunch is more of a bargain), but it is one of the city's most beautiful eating places, with a sparkling gold mosaic ceiling. Closed Sun. Expensive.

Mildred's 45 Lexington St, W1 ☎020/7494 1634; Oxford Circus or Piccadilly Circus tube. See map, p.88. This has a fresher and more stylish feel than many veggie restaurants. The stir-fries, pasta dishes and burgers are wholesome, delicious and inexpensive. Inexpensive.

Mr Kong 21 Lisle St, WC2 ☎020/7437 7923; Leicester Square tube. See map, p.88. One of Chinatown's finest. To sample the restaurant's more unusual dishes order from the "Today's" and "Chef's Specials" menu, and don't miss the mussels in black-bean sauce or the fresh razor clam with garlic. Inexpensive.

Patara 15 Greek St, W1 ☎020/7437 1071; Leicester Square tube. See map, p.88. A dimly lit and glamorous place, with orchids on the tables. Wonderful fresh ingredients and fine Thai cooking. Set lunch is around £12. Moderate.

Wong Kei 41–43 Wardour St, W1 ☎020/7437 8408; Leicester Square tube. See map, p.88. A restaurant renowned for rudeness may not seem like much of a recommendation, but if you want quick, cheap Chinese then this is the place. The entire ground floor of the Art Nouveau building is given over to lone diners, so you won't feel silly if you're on your own. Inexpensive.

Covent Garden

Belgo Centraal 50 Earlham St, WC2 ☎020/7813 2233; Covent Garden tube. See map, p.88. Massive metal-minimalist cavern off Neal Street, serving excellent kilo buckets of *moules marinière*, with *frites* and mayonnaise, a bewildering array of Belgian beers to choose from, and waffles for dessert. The £6 lunchtime specials are a bargain for central London. Inexpensive.

🏃 **Mon Plaisir** 21 Monmouth St, WC2 ☎020/7836 7243; Covent Garden tube. See map, p.88. An atmospheric and formidably French restaurant with an intimate tiled and wood-panelled interior: its classic French meat and fish dishes are reliably excellent. The pre- and post-theatre menu is a bargain at £12.50 for two courses, £14.50 for three. Closed Sat eve & Sun. Moderate.

Clerkenwell & Hoxton

Cicada 132 St John St, EC1 ☎020/7608 1550; Farringdon tube. See map, p.108. Bar-restaurant set back from the street with alfresco eating and an unusual pan-Asian menu. Closed Sat lunch & Sun. Expensive.

🏃 **Real Greek** 15 Hoxton Market, N1 ☎020/7739 8212; Old Street tube. See map, p.108. Small, modern and comfortable place where the menu has authentic Greek dishes, and the service is excellent. Set lunch and early-doors dinner are a bargain. Closed Sun. Moderate.

St John 26 St John St, EC1 ☎020/7251 0848; Farringdon tube. See map, p.108. Pricey, genuinely English restaurant, specializing in all those strange and unfashionable cuts of meat that were once commonplace in rural England – brains, bone marrow etc. Closed Sat lunch & Sun. Expensive.

Viet Hoa Café 72 Kingsland Rd, E2 ☎020/7729 8293; Old Street tube. See map, p.108. Inexpensive, light and airy Vietnamese café not far from the Geffrye Museum, serving splendid "meals in a bowl" – soups and noodle dishes with everything from spring rolls to tofu. Inexpensive.

East End

Café Spice Namaste 16 Prescot St, E1 ☎020/7488 9242; Tower Hill tube. Very popular Indian on the fringe of the City that is definitely not your average curry house. Parsee delicacies rub shoulders with dishes from Goa, Hyderabad and Kashmir, and the tandoori specialities are awesome. Closed Sat lunch & Sun. Expensive.

Les Trois Garçons 1 Club Row, E1 ☎020/7613 1924; Shoreditch tube. See map, p.108. Wildly camp decor, with a bejewelled stuffed tiger to greet you at the door, handbags hanging from the ceilings, ornate tiles and glittering engraved mirrors.

The opulence is reflected in the prices and the dishes, with scallops, foie gras and oysters a regular feature. Expensive.

🏃 **Tayyab** 83–89 Fieldgate St, E1 ☎020/7247 9543; Aldgate East or Whitechapel tube. See map, p.108. Smart designer restaurant serving straightforward Pakistani fare: good, freshly cooked and served without pretension. Booking is essential and service is speedy and slick. Inexpensive.

South Bank and Southwark

🏃 **Fina Estampa** 150 Tooley St, SE1 ☎020/7403 1342; London Bridge tube. See map, p.124. One of London's few Peruvian restaurants, that also happens to be very good, bringing a little of downtown Lima to London Bridge. The menu is traditional Peruvian, with a big emphasis on seafood. Closed Sat lunch & all Sun. Moderate.

RSJ 13a Coin St, SE1 ☎020/7928 4554, ⓦwww.rsj.uk.com; Waterloo tube. See map, p.121. Regularly high standards of Anglo-French cooking make this a good spot for a meal after or before an evening at a South Bank theatre or concert hall. The set meals for around £17 are particularly popular. Closed Sat lunch & Sun. Moderate.

Kensington and Chelsea

Bibendum Oyster House Michelin House, 81 Fulham Rd, SW3 ☎020/7589 1480; South Kensington tube. See map, p.128. A glorious tiled affair built in 1911, the former garage is one of the prettiest places to eat shellfish in London – if you're really hungry, go for the "Plateau de Fruits de Mer". Moderate.

Boisdale 15 Eccleston St, SW1 ☎020/7730 6922, ⓦwww.boisdale.co.uk; Victoria tube. See map, p.88. Owned by Ranald MacDonald, son of the Chief of Clanranald, this is a very Scottish place, strong on hospitality, and fresh Scottish produce. Live jazz every evening. Closed Sun. Moderate.

🏃 **Gordon Ramsay** 68–69 Royal Hospital Rd, SW3 ☎020/7352 4441, ⓦwww.gordon ramsay.com; Sloane Square tube. See map, p.128. To order successfully here, just pick a dish or even an ingredient you like and see how it arrives; you won't be disappointed. Gordon Ramsay's Chelsea restaurant is a class act through and through, though you have to book ahead to eat here. Closed Sat & Sun. Very expensive.

Bayswater and Notting Hill

Al Waha 75 Westbourne Grove, W2 ☎020/7229 0806; Queensway or Bayswater tube. See map, p.128. Arguably London's best Lebanese restaurant; *mezze*-obsessed, but also painstaking in its preparation of the main-course dishes, where spanking fresh and accurately cooked grills predominate. Moderate.

🏃 **Osteria Basilico** 29 Kensington Park Rd, W11 ☎020/7727 9372; Ladbroke Grove tube. See map, p.128. A pretty, traditional Italian restaurant on a picturesque street just off Porto-bello Road. It's a good place for the full Italian monty – antipasto, homemade pasta and then a fish or meat dish – or just for a pizza. Moderate.

Rodizio Rico 111 Westbourne Grove, W11 ☎020/7792 4035; Notting Hill Gate or Queensway tube. See map, p.128. Eat as much as you like for around £18 a head at this Brazilian *churrascaria*. Carvers come round and lop off chunks of freshly grilled meats, while you help yourself from the salad bar and hot buffet. Closed Mon–Fri lunch. Moderate.

Camden and Hampstead

Jin Kichi 73 Heath St, NW3 ☎020/7794 6158; Hampstead tube. Eschewing the slick minimalism and sushi-led cuisine of most Japanese restaurants, *Jin Kichi* is cramped, homely and very busy (so book ahead) and specializes in grilled skewers of meat. Moderate.

Manna 4 Erskine Rd, NW3 ☎020/7722 8028, ⓦwww.manna-veg.com; Chalk Farm tube. Old-fashioned, casual vegetarian restaurant with 1970s decor, serving large portions of very good food. Closed Mon–Sat lunch. Moderate.

Trojka 101 Regent's Park Rd, NW1 ☎020/7483 3765; Chalk Farm tube. A pleasant neighbourhood restaurant with filling and tasty eastern European food: the menu has a whole section on blinis and caviar, plus there are sturdy standbys such as stroganoff, and grills served with Trojka's own tartare sauce. Moderate.

Chiswick to Richmond

Chez Lindsay 11 Hill Rise, Richmond ☎020/8948 7473; Richmond tube. Small, bright, authentic Breton *crêperie*, offering galettes, crêpes or more formal French main courses, including lots of fresh fish and shellfish, all washed down with Breton cider in traditional earthenware *bolées*. Moderate.

The Gate 51 Queen Caroline St, W4 ☎020/8748 6932; Hammersmith tube. Tucked away behind the Hammersmith Apollo, this is a vegetarian restaurant that eschews healthy, wholefood eating. It's as rich, colourful, calorific and naughty as anywhere in town, just without meat. Closed Sat lunch & Sun. Expensive.

Drinking

London's **drinking** establishments run the whole gamut from grand Victorian gin palaces to funky modern bars with resident DJs catering to a pre-club crowd. The emergence of gastropubs, where the food is as important as the drink, has had a huge impact on the rest of the pub trade.

Whitehall and Westminster

Red Lion 48 Parliament St, SW1 ☏ 020/7930 5826; Westminster tube. See map, p.88. Good old pub, convenient for Westminster Abbey and Parliament. Popular with MPs, who are called to votes by a division bell in the bar.

St James's, Mayfair and Marylebone

Guinea 30 Bruton Place, W1; Bond Street or Green Park tube. See map, p.88. Pretty, tiny, old-fashioned, flower-strewn mews pub, serving good Young's bitter and excellent steak-and-kidney pies. Closed Sun.

ICA Bar 94 The Mall, SW1; Piccadilly Circus or Charing Cross tube. See map, p.88. You have to be a member (or be visiting an exhibition or cinema/theatre/talk event) to drink at the late-opening *ICA Bar* – but anyone can join on the door (Mon–Fri £1.50; Sat & Sun £2.50). It's a cool drinking venue, with a *noir* dress code observed by the arty crowd and staff, but beware the weekend DJ nights.

O'Conor Don 88 Marylebone Lane, W1; Bond Street tube. See map, p.105. A stripped-bare, anti-theme Irish pub that's a cut above the average, with excellent Guinness, a pleasantly measured pace and Irish food on offer. Closed Sat & Sun.

Red Lion 23 Crown Passage, SW1; Green Park tube. See map, p.88. Not to be confused with the nearby pub of the same name, this is a small, local, wood-panelled place hidden away in a passageway off Pall Mall.

Soho

Argyll Arms 18 Argyll St, W1; Oxford Circus tube. A stone's throw from Oxford Circus, this is a great Victorian pub, which has preserved many of its original features and serves good real ales.

Dog & Duck 18 Bateman St, W1; Leicester Square or Tottenham Court Road tube. Tiny Soho pub that retains much of its old character, beautiful Victorian tiling and mosaics, and a loyal clientele. Closed Sat & Sun lunch.

The Social 5 Little Portland St, W1; Oxford Circus tube. See map, p.105. Industrial club-bar with great DJs playing everything from rock to rap, a truly hedonistic-cum-alcoholic crowd and the ultimate

snacks – beans on toast and fish-finger sarnies – for when you get an attack of the munchies.

The Toucan 19 Carlisle St; Tottenham Court Road tube. See map, p.88. Small bar serving excellent Guinness and a wide range of Irish whiskies, plus cheap, wholesome and filling food. So popular it can get mobbed. Closed Sun.

Covent Garden & Strand

Detroit 35 Earlham St, WC2; Covent Garden tube. See map, p.88. Cavernous underground venue with an open-plan bar area, secluded Gaudí-esque booths and a huge range of spirits. DJs take over at the weekends. Closed Sun.

Gordon's 47 Villiers St, WC2; Charing Cross or Embankment tube. See map, p.88. Cavernous, shabby, atmospheric wine bar specializing in ports, right next door to Charing Cross Station. The excellent and varied wine list, decent buffet food and genial atmosphere make this a favourite with local office workers, who spill outdoors in the summer.

Lamb & Flag 33 Rose St, WC2; Leicester Square tube. See map, p.88. Busy, tiny and highly atmospheric pub, tucked away down an alley between Garrick Street and Floral Street, where John Dryden was attacked in 1679 for writing scurrilous verses about one of Charles II's mistresses.

Salisbury 90 St Martin's Lane, WC2; Leicester Square tube. See map, p.88. Easily one of the most beautifully preserved Victorian pubs in the capital – and certainly the most central – with cut, etched and engraved windows, bronze figures, red velvet seating and a fine lincrusta ceiling.

Bloomsbury & Holborn

Cittie of Yorke 22 High Holborn, WC1; Chancery Lane tube. See map, p.108. One of London's venerable pubs, with a vaulted cellar bar, wood panelling, and grand quasi-medieval wine hall whose cosy cubicles were once the preserve of lawyers and their clients.

Lamb 94 Lamb's Conduit St, WC1; Russell Square tube. See map, p.105. Pleasant pub with a marvellously well-preserved Victorian interior of mirrors, old wood and snob screens.

Museum Tavern 49 Great Russell St, WC1; Tottenham Court Road or Russell Square tube. See map, p.105. Large and characterful old pub, right opposite the British Museum, erstwhile drinking hole of Karl Marx.

Ye Olde Mitre 1 Ely Court, off Ely Place, EC1; Farringdon tube. See map, p.108. Hidden down a tiny alleyway off Ely Place, this wonderfully atmospheric pub dates back to 1546, although it was actually rebuilt in the eighteenth century.

Clerkenwell

Duke of York 156 Clerkenwell Rd, EC1 ☏020/7837 8548; Chancery Lane tube. See map, p.108. Just the basics you need for a good pub – clear glass windows, bare boards, bold red and blue paintwork, table football, pool, TV sport, mixed clientele and groovy tunes – and a lot less posey than most of Clerkenwell. Thai food available.

Fox & Anchor 115 Charterhouse St, EC1; Farringdon or Barbican tube. See map, p.108. Handsome Smithfield market pub famous for its early opening hours (from 7am) and huge breakfasts. Closed Sat & Sun.

Jerusalem Tavern 55 Britton St, EC1; Farringdon tube. See map, p.108. Cosy converted Georgian parlour, stripped bare and slightly "distressed", serving tasty food along with an excellent range of draught beers from St Peter's Brewery in Suffolk. Closed Sat & Sun.

Hoxton

Dragon 5 Leonard St, EC2; Old Street tube. See map, p.128. Discreetly signed clubby pub with bare-brick walls and crumbling leather sofas, that attracts a mixed crowd happy to listen to whatever takes the resident DJ's fancy.

Hoxton Square Bar and Kitchen 2–4 Hoxton Square, N1; Old Street tube. See map, p.128. *Blade Runner*-esque concrete bar that attracts trendy types with its mix of modern European food, kitsch-to-club soundtracks, worn leather sofas, and temporary painting and photography exhibitions. In the summer, the drinking spills into the square in a carnival spirit.

Loungelover 1 Whitby St, E1 ☏020/7012 1234; Shoreditch tube. See map, p.128. Behind the unprepossessing facade of this former meat-packing factory lies a bizarre array of opulently camp bric-a-brac, expertly slung together to create a trendy, unique and expensive cocktail bar. Reservations recommended.

The City

Blackfriar 174 Queen Victoria St, EC4; Blackfriars tube. See map, p.128. A gorgeous, utterly original pub, with Art Nouveau marble friezes of boozy monks and a wonderful highly decorated alcove, all dating from 1905. Nonsmoking throughout.

The Counting House 50 Cornhill, EC2; Bank tube. See map, p.128. Another City bank conversion, with fantastic high ceilings, a glass dome, chandeliers and a central oval bar. Naturally enough, given the location, it's wall-to-wall suits. Closed Sat & Sun.

Vertigo 42 Tower 42, Old Broad St, EC2 ☏020/7877 7842; Bank or Liverpool St tube. See map, p.128. Rarefied drinking in this champagne bar, 590ft above the City. Each seat has an astounding view of London; drink prices are correspondingly high, and light meals are on offer. Smart jeans and trainers acceptable; booking essential.

Viaduct Tavern 126 Newgate St, EC1; St Paul's tube. See map, p.128. Glorious gin palace built in 1869 opposite what was then Newgate Prison and is now the Old Bailey. Ask to see the old cells now used for storing beer. The walls are adorned with oils of faded ladies representing Commerce, Agriculture and the Arts. Closed Sat & Sun.

Ye Old Cheshire Cheese Wine Office Court, 145 Fleet St, EC4; Blackfriars tube. See map, p.128. A famous seventeenth-century watering hole, with several snug, dark-panelled bars and real fires. Popular with tourists, but by no means exclusively so. Closed Sun eve.

East End and Docklands

Dickens Inn St Katharine's Way, E1; Tower Hill tube. Eighteenth-century timber-framed warehouse transported on wheels from its original site, with a great view over the docks, but very firmly on the tourist trail.

The Gun 27 Cold Harbour, E14; South Quay or Blackwall DLR, or Canary Wharf tube. An old dockers' pub with lots of maritime memorabilia, and – the main attraction – an unrivalled view of the Dome.

Prospect of Whitby 57 Wapping Wall, E1; Wapping tube. London's most famous riverside pub with a flagstone floor, a cobbled courtyard and great views over the Thames.

Ten Bells 84 Commercial St, E1; Liverpool Street or Shoreditch tube. See map, p.108. This plain and pleasantly ramshackle pub has Jack the Ripper associations, but the interior has some great Victorian tiling and the crowd these days is a trendy, relaxed bunch. DJs play Fri–Sun.

Town of Ramsgate 62 Wapping High St, E1; Wapping tube. Dark, narrow medieval pub where Captain Blood was discovered with the crown jewels under his cloak, and Admiral Bligh and Fletcher Christian were regular drinking partners in pre-mutiny days.

South Bank and Southwark

Anchor & Hope 36 The Cut, SE1 ☏020/7928

9898. See map, p.121. *The Anchor* is a welcoming and unfussy gastropub, dishing up truly excellent grub: soups, salads and mains such as slow-cooked pork with *choucroute*, as well as mouth-watering puds. Closed Sun.

Anchor Bankside 34 Park St, SE1; London Bridge, Southwark or Blackfriars tube. See map, p.124. While the rest of Bankside has changed almost beyond all recognition, this pub still looks much as it did when first built in 1770 (on the inside, at least). Good for alfresco drinking by the river.

George Inn 77 Borough High St, SE1; Borough or London Bridge tube. London's only surviving coaching inn – dating from the seventeenth century and now owned by the National Trust – serving a good range of real ales.

Market Porter 9 Stoney St, SE1; London Bridge tube. See map, p.124. Handsome semicircular pub with early opening hours for workers at Borough Market, and a seriously huge range of real ales.

Royal Oak 44 Tabard St, SE1; Borough or London Bridge tube. See map, p.124. Beautiful, lovingly restored Victorian pub that eschews jukeboxes and one-armed bandits and opts simply for serving real ales from Lewes in Sussex. Closed Sat & Sun.

Kensington & Chelsea

Bunch of Grapes 207 Brompton Rd, SW3; South Kensington or Knightsbridge tube. See map, p.128. This popular High-Victorian pub, complete with snob screens, is the perfect place for a post-V&A (or post-Harrods) pint, pie and chips.

The Nag's Head 53 Kinnerton St, SW1; Hyde Park Corner or Knightsbridge tube. See map, p.128. A convivial, quirky and down-to-earth little pub tucked down a posh cobbled mews, with dark wood-panelling and nineteenth-century china handpumps. The unusual sunken back-room has a flagstone floor and fires in winter.

The Pig's Ear 35 Old Church St, SW1; Sloane Square tube. See map, p.128. Deep in Chelsea village, *The Pig's Ear* is a sympathetically converted and stylish place. Enjoy a leisurely boardgame and a pint of Pig's Ear in the panelled downstairs bar, where classy pub grub is served, or head upstairs to the posh dining room.

Notting Hill

Cherry Jam 52 Porchester Rd, W2; Royal Oak tube. See map, p.128. Owned by Ben Watt (house DJ and half of pop group Everything But the Girl), this smart intimate basement place mixes a decadent cocktail bar with top-end West London DJs. Eve only.

The Cow 89 Westbourne Park Rd, W2; Westbourne Park or Royal Oak tube. See map, p.128. Vaguely Irish-themed pub that pulls in the beautiful W11

types thanks to its spectacular food, including a daily supply of fresh oysters, and excellent Guinness.

Market Bar 240a Portobello Rd, W11; Ladbroke Grove tube. See map, p.128. Self-consciously bohemian pub divided by gilded mirrors and ruched curtains and scattered with weird *objets* – all very Notting Hill.

Prince Bonaparte 80 Chepstow Rd, W2; Notting Hill Gate or Royal Oak tube. See map, p.128. Pared-down, minimalist pub, with acres of space for sitting and supping or enjoying the excellent Brit or Med food.

Maida Vale

Prince Alfred 9 Formosa St, W9; Warwick Avenue tube. See map, p.128. A fantastic period-piece Victorian pub with all its original 1862 fittings intact, right down to the glazed snob screens that divide the bar into a series of snugs, and a surprisingly young and funky clientele.

Warrington Hotel 93 Warrington Crescent, W9; Warwick Avenue or Maida Vale tube. See map, p.128. Yet another architectural gem – this time flamboyant Art Nouveau – in an area replete with them. The interior is rich and satisfying, as are the draught beers and the Thai restaurant upstairs.

Camden Town

Bar Vinyl 6 Inverness St, NW1; Camden Town tube. Small, funky glass-bricked place with a record shop downstairs (open noon–8pm) and DJs providing a breakbeat, funky house or electro vibe Thurs–Sun.

Bartok 78–79 Chalk Farm Rd, NW1; Chalk Farm or Camden Town tube. Stylish bar where punters can sink into a sofa and listen to a varied programme of classical music. Closed Mon–Fri lunch.

The Engineer 65 Gloucester Ave, NW1; Chalk Farm tube. Smart Victorian pub and restaurant for the Primrose Hill posse. The food is excellent though pricey, and it's popular, so get here early to eat in the pub, or book a table in the restaurant or lovely garden out back.

Hampstead and Highgate

The Flask 14 Flask Walk, NW3; Hampstead tube. Convivial Hampstead local that retains much of its original Victorian interior, tucked down one of Hampstead's more atmospheric lanes.

The Flask 77 Highgate West Hill, N6; Highgate tube. Ideally situated at the heart of Highgate village green – with a rambling, low-ceilinged interior and a summer terrace – and as a result, very popular.

Holly Bush 22 Holly Mount, NW3; Hampstead tube. A lovely old pub, with a real fire in winter, tucked away in the steep backstreets of Hampstead Village, which can get a bit too mobbed at weekends.

Dulwich and Greenwich

Crown & Greyhound 73 Dulwich Village, SE21; West Dulwich train station from Victoria. Grandiose Victorian pub, convenient for the Picture Gallery, with an ornate plasterwork ceiling and a nice summer beer garden.

Cutty Sark Ballast Quay, off Lassell St, SE10; Cutty Sark DLR or Maze Hill train station. This Georgian pub is the nicest place for a riverside

pint in Greenwich, and much less touristy than the *Trafalgar Tavern* (it's a couple of minutes' walk further east, following the river).

Chiswick to Richmond

Dove 19 Upper Mall, W6; Ravenscourt Park tube. Wonderful low-beamed old riverside pub with literary associations, the smallest bar in the UK (4ft by 7ft), and very popular Sunday roast dinners.

White Cross Hotel Water Lane, Richmond; Richmond tube. With a longer pedigree and more character than its rivals, the *White Cross* has a very popular, large garden.

Nightlife

On any night of the week London offers a bewildering range of things to do after dark, ranging from top-flight opera and theatre to clubs with a life span of a couple of nights. The **listings magazine** *Time Out*, which comes out every Tuesday afternoon, is essential if you want to get the most out of this city, giving full details of prices and access, plus previews and reviews.

Live music venues

Over the past five years London has established itself as the music capital of not just Europe, but the world. Rio may be sunnier, Paris prettier and Madrid madder but for sheer range and diversity there's nowhere to beat London. The **live music** scene remains extremely diverse, encompassing all variations of rock, blues, roots and world music; and although London's jazz clubs aren't on a par with those in the big American cities, there's a highly individual scene of home-based artists, supplemented by top-name visiting players.

△ Band playing at London's Astoria

General venues

Astoria 157 Charing Cross Rd, WC2 ⓦwww
.meanfiddler.com; Tottenham Court Road tube. This
central, large, balconied one-time theatre tends to
host slightly alternative bands, with club nights on
Fri & Sat.

Brixton Academy 211 Stockwell Rd, SW9
ⓦwww.brixton-academy.co.uk; Brixton tube. This
refurbished Victorian hall, complete with Neoclassical decorations, can hold 4000 but still manages to
seem small and friendly.

Cargo 83 Rivington St, EC2 ⓦwww.cargo-london
.com; Old Street tube. Small but upmarket club/
venue that hosts a wide variety of interesting live
acts, including jazz, Latin, hip-hop, indie and folk,
which are often part of their excellent line-up of
club nights.

Forum 9–17 Highgate Rd, NW5 ⓦwww
.meanfiddler.com; Kentish Town tube. The *Forum* is
North London's best medium-sized venue, and is
still a frequent stop-off point for established jazz-
funk and rock bands.

Marquee 1 Leicester Square, WC2 ⓦwww
.themarqueeclub.co.uk; Leicester Square tube. In
a labyrinthine industrial building, right on Leicester
Square, the *Marquee* boasts mainly newer acts but
also some established names.

Mean Fiddler 165 Charing Cross Rd, W1 ⓦwww
.meanfiddler.com; Tottenham Court Road tube. Next
door to the *Astoria*, the *Mean Fiddler* has a good
line-up of mainly rock and indie bands, with club
nights Fri & Sat.

Shepherd's Bush Empire Shepherd's Bush Green,
W12 ⓦwww.shepherds-bush-empire.co.uk; Shepherd's Bush tube. Grand old West London theatre
that regularly draws the cream of the crop of non-
stadium-rocking bands.

Spitz Old Spitalfields Market, 109 Commercial St,
E1; Liverpool Street tube. Friendly, small venue
in the heart of Spitalfields Market, where you
can catch a diverse range of music including
jazz, world, indie, folk, blues and electronica. The
downstairs bistro hosts free live music up to four
nights a week.

Rock, blues and indie

12 Bar Club Denmark Street, WC2
ⓦwww.12barclub.com; Tottenham Court Road

tube. Tiny, atmospheric bar, café and venue offering
blues, contemporary country and acoustic folk.

Borderline Orange Yard, off Manette Street, W1
ⓦwww. meanfiddler.com; Tottenham Court Road
tube. Small basement joint with a diverse musical
policy, making it a good place to catch new bands.

Metro 19–23 Oxford St, W1 ⓦwww.blowupmetro
.com; Tottenham Court Road tube. An intimate
venue with a forward-thinking booking policy that
tends to showcase new bands just before they get
big. Also has club nights Mon–Sat till late.

Neighbourhood 12 Acklam Rd, W10 ⓦwww
.neighbourhoodclub.net; Ladbroke Grove tube. Run
by Ben Watt of Everything But the Girl, this is a
live-music/club crossover venue in an arch under a
flyover, where the crowd is as trendy as the house-
oriented music.

Underworld 174 Camden High St, NW1 ⓦwww
.theunderworldcamden.co.uk; Camden Town tube.
Popular grungy venue under the *World's End* pub, a
great place to check out metal, hard core, ska punk
and heavy rock bands.

Jazz, world music and roots

100 Club 100 Oxford St, W1 ⓦwww.the100club
.co.uk; Tottenham Court Road tube. An unpretentious, inexpensive and fun jazz venue with an
incredible vintage.

606 Club 90 Lots Rd, SW10 ☎020/7352 5953,
ⓦwww.606club.co.uk. Fulham Broadway tube. A
rare all-jazz venue, off the end of the King's Road.
You can book a table, and if you're a non-member
you must eat if you want to drink.

Jazz Café 5 Parkway, NW1 ☎020/7916 6060,
ⓦwww.meanfiddler.com; Camden Town tube.
Excellent, chilled-out venue with an adventurous
booking policy exploring Latin, rap, funk, hip-hop
and musical fusions. Restaurant upstairs with a few
prime tables overlooking the stage (book ahead if
you want one).

Ronnie Scott's 47 Frith St, W1 ☎020/7439
0747, ⓦwww.ronniescotts.co.uk; Leicester
Square tube. The most famous jazz club in
London: small and smoky and still going strong.
Top-line names play two sets – one at around
10pm, the other after midnight. Book a table, or
you'll have to stand.

Clubs

London remains *the* place to come if you want to party after dark. The sheer
diversity of dance music has enabled the city to maintain its status as the world's
dance capital – and it's still a port of call for DJs from around the globe. Nearly
all London's **dance clubs** open their doors between 10pm and midnight. Some

are open six or seven nights a week, some keep irregular days, others just open at the weekend – and very often a venue will host a different club on each night of the week; for up-to-the-minute listings, pick up flyers from one of Soho's many record shops, or check *Time Out*.

Admission charges vary wildly, with small midweek sessions starting at around £3–5 and large weekend events charging as much as £25; around £10–15 is the average for a Friday or Saturday night, but bear in mind that profit margins at the bar are often more outrageous than at live music venues.

333 333 Old St, EC1 ⓦwww.333mother.com; Old Street tube. One of London's best clubs for new dance music; three floors of drum'n'bass, twisted disco and breakbeat madness.

93 Feet East 150 Brick Lane, E2 ⓦwww.93feeteast.co.uk; Old Street tube. An old East End brewery with four rooms across two levels, as well as an excellent rooftop balcony and outdoor space that's well worth a visit in the summer.

Bar Rumba 36 Shaftesbury Ave, W1 ⓦwww.barrumba.co.uk; Piccadilly Circus tube. Fun, small-ish West End venue with an adventurous mix of nights ranging from the future-jazz to top-notch house and R&B at weekends.

Café de Paris 3 Coventry St, W1 ⓦwww.cafedeparis.com; Leicester Square tube. Elegantly restored ballroom that plays house, garage and disco to a smartly dressed crowd of wannabes – no jeans or trainers.

Canvas Bagley's Studios, King's Cross Freight Depot, York Way, N1 ⓦwww.canvaslondon.net; King's Cross tube. Vast warehouse-style venue, making it the perfect place for enormous raves, with a different DJ in each of the three rooms, and a chill-out bar complete with sofas.

The Cross Arches 27–31, York Way, N1 ⓦwww.the-cross.co.uk; King's Cross tube. House and garage club hidden underneath railway arches, that's bigger than you imagine, but always crammed with chic clubby types.

Cuba 11–13 Kensington High St, W8; Kensington High Street tube. Grab a cocktail upstairs in the sociable bar before heading below for club nights that focus around Latin, salsa and Brazilian bossa nova.

The End 18 West Central St, WC1 ⓦwww.the-end.co.uk; Tottenham Court Rd or Holborn tube. Designed for clubbers by clubbers, *The End* is large and spacious, with chrome minimalist decor and a devastating sound system.

Fabric 77a Charterhouse St, EC1 ⓦwww.fabriclondon.com; Farringdon tube. If you're a serious dance-music fan there really isn't a better weekend venue than *Fabric*, a cavernous, underground brewery-like space with three rooms. Get there early to avoid a night of queuing.

Fridge Town Hall Parade, Brixton Hill, SW2 ⓦwww.fridge.co.uk; Brixton tube. Weekends alternate between pumping mixed/gay nights, and trance favourites with a psychedelic vibe.

Herbal 12–14 Kingsland Rd, E2 ⓦwww.herbaluk.com; Old Street tube. An intimate two-floored venue comprising a cool loft and sweaty ground-floor club – a great club to check out drum'n'bass and breaks.

Ministry of Sound 103 Gaunt St, SE1 ⓦwww.ministryofsound.co.uk; Elephant & Castle tube. A vast, state-of-the-art club, with an exceptional sound system. Corporate clubbing and full of tourists, but it still draws the top talent.

Notting Hill Arts Club 21 Notting Hill Gate, W11 ⓦwww.nottinghillartsclub.com; Notting Hill Gate tube. Basement club that's popular for everything from Latin-inspired funk, jazz and disco through to soul, house and garage, and famed for its Sunday afternoon/evening deep-house session and "concept visuals".

Scala 278 Pentonville Rd, N1 ⓦwww.scala-london.co.uk; King's Cross tube. Sprawling club that holds some unusual one-off nights as well as live bands and the long-running gay/mixed *Popstarz*.

Subterania 12 Acklam Rd, W10 ⓦwww.meanfiddler.com; Ladbroke Grove tube. Worth a visit for its diverse club nights at weekends, including the superior hip-hop and R&B-heavy *Rotation* every Friday.

Turnmills 63 Clerkenwell Rd, EC1 ⓦwww.turnmills.com; Farringdon tube. The place to come if you want to sweat to trance and house from dusk till dawn, with an alien-invasion-style bar and funky split-level dancefloor in the main room.

Gay and lesbian London

London's **lesbian and gay scene** is so huge, diverse and well established that it's easy to forget just how much – and how fast – it has grown over the last few years. **Soho** is the obvious place to start exploring, with a mix of traditional gay pubs, designer café-bars and a range of gay-run services. Details of most events appear in *Time Out*, while another excellent source of information is the London **Lesbian and Gay Switchboard** (℡020/7837 7324, Ⓦwww.queery .org.uk), which operates around the clock. The outdoor event of the year is **Pride London** (Ⓦwww.pridelondon.org) in July, a colourful, whistleblowing march through the city streets followed by a huge, ticketed party in a central London park.

Bars and clubs

Gay cafés, bars and **clubs** open up and shut down with surreal frequency – it's a good idea to check the gay press and listings mags before you set out. Bear in mind that although more and more lesbian bars admit gay men, mixed, as ever, tends to mean mostly men.

Mixed bars

The Black Cap 171 Camden High St, NW1; Camden Town tube. Venerable North London institution offering cabaret of wildly varying quality almost every night. Laugh, sing and lip-synch along, and then dance to 1980s tunes until the early hours.

The Box 32–34 Monmouth St, WC2; Covent Garden or Leicester Square tube. Popular, bright café/bar serving good food for a mixed gay/straight crowd during the day, and becoming queerer as the night draws in.

The Edge 11 Soho Square, W1; Tottenham Court Road tube. Busy, style-conscious and pricey Soho café/bar spread over several floors, and (in summer) onto the pavement. Food daily, DJs most nights.

First Out 52 St Giles High St, WC2; Tottenham Court Rd tube. The West End's original gay café/bar, and still permanently packed, serving good veggie food at reasonable prices. Girl Friday (Fri) is a busy pre-club session for grrrls; gay men are welcome as guests.

Freedom 60–66 Wardour St, W1; Piccadilly Circus tube. Hip, busy, late-opening place, popular with a straight/gay Soho crowd. The basement transforms itself at night into a funky, intimate club, complete with pink banquettes and masses of glitter balls.

Rupert Street 50 Rupert St, W1; Piccadilly Circus tube. Smart, trendy bar attracting a mixed after-work crowd with a more obviously pre-club vibe at weekends, when they remove the chairs and tables and it's packed to the rafters.

The Yard 57 Rupert St, W1; Piccadilly Circus tube. Attractive bar with courtyard, loft areas and a laid-back, sociable atmosphere – one of the best in Soho for alfresco drinking.

Lesbian bars

Candy Bar 4 Carlisle St, WC2; Tottenham Court Road tube. Now re-established at its original venue but still with the same crucial, cruisey vibe that made it the hottest girl-bar in central London.

The Glass Bar West Lodge, Euston Square Gardens, 190 Euston Rd, NW1; Euston tube. Difficult to find (and hard to forget), you knock on the door and become a member to enter this friendly and intimate late-opening women-only bar. Open from 1pm; no admission after 12.30am on Sat. Closed Sun.

Star at Night 22 Great Chapel St, W1; Tottenham Court Rd tube. Comfortable new venue open from 6pm Tues–Sat, popular with a slightly older crowd who want somewhere to sit, a good glass of wine and good conversation.

Vespa Lounge The Conservatory, Centrepoint House, 15 St Giles High St, WC1; Tottenham Court Road tube. This centrally-located girls' bar gets super busy at weekends. Pool table, video screen, cute barstaff and a predominantly young crowd. Gay men welcome as guests.

Gay men's bars

Brief Encounter 41–43 St Martins Lane, WC2; Leicester Square tube. Now back with its original name, the West End's longest-running cruise bar is a popular hangout; the upper bar offers regular cabaret, while the lower bar is very, very dark.

Central Station 37 Wharfdale Rd, N1; King's Cross tube. Award-winning, late-opening community pub on three floors, offering cabaret, cruisey club nights, and the UK's only gay sports-bar. Not strictly men-only, but mostly so.

Compton's of Soho 53 Old Compton St, W1; Leicester Square or Piccadilly tube. This large, traditional-style pub is a Soho institution, always busy with a butch crowd, but still a relaxed place to cruise or just hang out. The upstairs *Club Lounge* is more chilled and attracts a younger crowd.

Clubs

Beyond *Club Colosseum*, 1 Nine Elms Way, SW8 Ⓦ www.allthingsorange.com; Vauxhall tube. London's biggest after-hours party kicks off each Sunday morning at 4.30am and carries on until well into the morning. Two massive dancefloors, four bars, chillout areas and funky house music please an eclectic mix of up-for-it clubbers.

Crash 66 Goding St, SE11; Vauxhall tube. Four bars, two dancefloors, chill-out areas and hard bodies make this weekly Saturday-nighter busy, buzzy, sexy and mostly boyzy.

DTPM *Fabric*, 77a Charterhouse St, EC1 Ⓦ www .dtpm-online.net; Farringdon Road tube. Long-running Sunday-nighter in chic surroundings, with three dancefloors offering everything from classic DTPM shirts-off experience to mellow soulful/oldies mix.

Duckie *The Royal Vauxhall Tavern*, 372 Kennington Lane, SE11 Ⓦ www.duckie.co.uk; Vauxhall tube. Modern, rock-based hurdy gurdy provides a crea-tive and cheerfully ridiculous antidote to the dreary forces of gay house domination.

Exilio *UCL*, Houghton Street, WC2; Holborn tube. Every Saturday night, Exilio erupts in a lesbian and gay Latin frenzy, spinning salsa, cumbias and merengue, and also features live acts.

G.A.Y. *The Astoria*, 157 Charing Cross Rd, WC2; Tottenham Court Road tube. Widely considered as the launch venue for new (and ailing) boy and girl bands, this huge, unpretentious and fun-loving dance night is where the young crowd gathers.

Heaven Under the Arches, Villiers St, WC2; Charing Cross or Embankment tube. Widely regarded as the UK's most popular gay club, this legendary, 2000-capacity venue continues to reign supreme. More Muscle Mary than Diesel Doris.

Popstarz *Scala*, 27 Pentonville Rd, N1; King's Cross tube. Groundbreaking Friday-night indie club, *Popstarz* has had to enforce a gay and lesbian majority door policy as its still-winning formula of alternative toons, 70s and 80s trash, cheap beer and no attitude attracts a growing straight, studenty crowd.

Theatre

The **West End** is the heart of London's Theatreland, with Shaftesbury Avenue its most congested drag. West End theatres tend to be dominated by tour-ist-magnet musicals or similarly unchallenging shows, but others offer more intriguing productions. The government-subsidized **Royal Shakespeare Company** and the **National Theatre** often put on extremely original produc-tions of mainstream masterpieces, while some of the most exciting work is performed in what have become known as the **Off-West End** theatres. Further down the financial ladder still are the **Fringe** theatres, more often than not pub venues, where ticket prices are low, and quality variable.

Tickets under £10 are restricted to the Fringe; the box-office average is closer to £15–25, with £30–40 the usual top whack. Ticket agencies such as Ticketmaster (☎020/7344 4444, Ⓦ www.ticketmaster.co.uk) or First Call (☎020/7497 9977, Ⓦ www.firstcalltickets.com), can get seats for most West End shows, but add up to ten percent on the ticket price. The cheapest way to buy your ticket is to go to the theatre box office in person; if you book over the phone, you're likely to be charged a booking fee. Students, senior citizens and the unemployed can get **concessionary rates** on tickets for many shows, and several theatres offer reductions on standby tickets to these groups. Whatever you do, avoid the touts and the ticket agencies that abound in the West End.

The Society of London Theatre (Ⓦ www.officiallondontheatre.co.uk) runs the **Half Price Ticket Booth** in Leicester Square, now known as **tkts** (Mon–Sat 10am–7pm, Sun noon–3.30pm; Ⓦ www.tkts.co.uk), which sells on-the-day tickets for all the West End shows at discounts of up to fifty percent, though they tend to be in the top end of the price range, are limited to four per person, and carry a service charge of £2.50 per ticket.

Venues

What follows is a list of those West End theatres that offer a changing roster of good plays, along with the most consistent of the Off-West End and Fringe venues. This by no means represents the tally of London's stages, as there are scores of fringe places that present work on an intermittent basis – the weekly listings mag *Time Out* provides the most comprehensive and detailed up-to-the-minute survey.

Almeida Almeida Street, N1 ☏ 020/7359 4404, ⓦ www.almeida.co.uk; Angel or Highbury & Islington tube. Deservedly popular Off-West End venue in Islington that continues to premiere excellent new plays and excitingly reworked classics, and has attracted some big Hollywood names.

Barbican Centre Silk Street, EC2 ☏ 020/7638 8891, ⓦ www.barbican.org.uk; Barbican or Moorgate tube. The Barbican's two venues – the excellently designed Barbican Theatre and the much smaller Pit – put on a wide variety of theatrical spectacles from puppetry and musicals to new drama works, and of course Shakespeare, courtesy of the Royal Shakespeare Company who perform here (and elsewhere in London) on and off from autumn to spring each year.

Bush Shepherd's Bush Green, W12 ☏ 020/7610 4224; Goldhawk Road or Shepherd's Bush tube. This minuscule above-pub theatre is London's most reliable venue for new writing after the *Royal Court*, and it has turned out some great stuff.

Donmar Warehouse Thomas Neal's, Earlham St, WC2 ☏ 020/7369 1732, ⓦ www.donmar-warehouse.com; Covent Garden tube. A performance space that's noted for new plays and top-quality reappraisals of the classics, and whose former artistic director, Sam Mendes, managed to entice several Hollywood stars to take to the stage.

Drill Hall 16 Chenies St, WC1 ☏ 020/7307 5060, ⓦ www.drillhall.co.uk; Goodge Street tube. This studio-style venue specializes in gay, lesbian, feminist and all-round politically correct new work.

ICA Nash House, The Mall, SW1 ☏ 020/7930 3647, ⓦ www.ica.org.uk; Piccadilly Circus or Charing Cross tube. The Institute of Contemporary Arts attracts the most innovative practitioners in all areas of performance. It also attracts a fair quantity of modish junk, but the hits generally outweigh the misses.

Menier Chocolate Factory 51–53 Southwark St, SE1 ☏ 020/7907 7060, ⓦ www.menier chocolatefactory.com; London Bridge tube. Great name, great new fringe venue in an old Victorian factory; consistently good shows, and has a great bar and restaurant attached.

National Theatre South Bank Centre, South Bank, SE1 ☏ 020/7452 3000, ⓦ www.nationaltheatre .org.uk; Waterloo tube. The Royal National Theatre, as it's now officially known, consists of three separate theatres. The country's top actors and directors perform here in a programme ranging from Greek tragedies to Broadway musicals. Twenty to thirty cheap tickets go on sale on the morning of each performance – get there by 8am for the popular shows.

Open Air Theatre Regent's Park, Inner Circle, NW1 ☏ 020/7486 2431, ⓦ www.openairtheatre.org; Baker Street tube. If the weather's good, there's nothing quite like a dose of alfresco drama. This beautiful space in Regent's Park hosts a tourist-friendly summer programme of Shakespeare, musicals, plays and concerts.

Royal Court Sloane Square, SW1 ☏ 020/7565 5000, ⓦ www.royalcourttheatre.com; Sloane Square tube. The Royal Court is one of the best places in London to catch radical new writing, either in the proscenium arch Theatre Downstairs, or the smaller-scale Theatre Upstairs studio space.

Shakespeare's Globe New Globe Walk, SE1 ☏ 020/7902 1400, ⓦ www.shakespeares-globe .org; London Bridge, Blackfriars or Southwark tube. This thatch-roofed replica Elizabethan theatre uses only natural light and the minimum of scenery, and currently puts on solid, fun Shakespearean shows from mid-May to mid-September, with "groundling" tickets (standing-room only) for around a fiver.

Comedy and cabaret

The **comedy scene** continues to thrive in London, with the leading funnypersons catapulted to unlikely stardom on both stage and screen. The *Comedy Store* is the best known and most central venue on the circuit, but just about every London suburb has a pub stage giving a platform to young hopefuls (full listings appear on ⓦ www.chortle.co.uk and in *Time Out*). Note that many venues operate only on Friday and Saturday nights, and that August is a lean month, as much of London's talent heads north for the Edinburgh Festival. **Tickets** at smaller venues can be had for around £5, but in the more established places, you're looking at £10 or more.

Backyard Comedy Club 231 Cambridge Heath Rd, E2 ☏ 020/7739 3122, ⊛ www.leehurst.com; Bethnal Green tube. Purpose-built club in Bethnal Green established by comedian Lee Hurst, who has successfully managed to attract a consistently strong line-up. Thurs–Sat.

Canal Café Theatre *The Bridge House*, Delamere Terrace, W2 ☏ 020/7289 6054, ⊛ www.canal-cafetheatre.com; Warwick Avenue tube. Perched on the water's edge in Little Venice, this venue is good for improvisation acts and is home to the *Newsrevue* team of topical gagsters; there's usually something going on from Thurs–Sun.

Comedy Café 66 Rivington St, EC2 ☏ 020/7739 5706, ⊛ www.comedycafe.co.uk; Old Street tube. Long-established, purpose-built club in Shoreditch/Hoxton, often with impressive line-ups, and free admission for the new-acts slot on Wednesday nights. Wed–Sat.

Comedy Store Haymarket House, 1a Oxendon St, SW1 ☏ 020/7344 0234, ⊛ www.thecomedystore .co.uk; Piccadilly Circus tube. Widely regarded as the birthplace of alternative comedy, though no longer in its original venue, the *Comedy Store* has catapulted many a stand-up onto primetime TV. Improvisation by in-house comics on Wednesdays and Sundays, in addition to a stand-up bill; Friday and Saturday are the busiest nights, with two shows, at 8pm and midnight – book ahead.

Jongleurs Camden Lock, Dingwalls Building, 36 Camden Lock Place, Chalk Farm Road, NW1; box office ☏ 020/7564 2500, information ☏ 08707/870707, ⊛ www.jongleurs.com for branches; Camden tube. *Jongleurs* is the chain store of comedy, doling out high-quality stand-up and post-revelry disco-dancing nightly on Fridays. Book well in advance.

Cinema

There are an awful lot of **cinemas** in the West End, but very few places committed to independent films, and even fewer repertory cinemas programming serious films from the back catalogue. November's **London Film Festival** (⊛ www.lff.org.uk), which occupies half a dozen West End cinemas, is now a huge event, and so popular that many of the films sell out soon after publication of the festival's programme. Below is a selection of the cinemas that put on the most interesting programmes.

Cinemas

BFI London Imax Centre South Bank, SE1 ☏ 020/7902 1234, ⊛ www.bfi.org.uk/showing/imax; Waterloo tube. The British Film Institute's remarkable glazed drum houses Europe's largest screen. It's stunning, state-of-the-art stuff all right, showing 2D and 3D films on a massive screen, but like all IMAX cinemas, it suffers from the paucity of good material that's been shot in the format.

Electric 191 Portobello Rd, W11 ☏ 020/7299 8688, ⊛ www. the-electric.co.uk; Notting Hill Gate or Ladbroke Grove tube. One of the oldest cinemas in the country (opened 1910), the Electric has been filled out with luxury leather armchairs, footstools and sofas. Most seats cost £12.50.

Everyman Hollybush Vale, NW3 ☏ 020/7431 1777, ⊛ www.everymancinema.com; Hampstead tube. The city's oldest rep cinema, and still one of its best, with strong programmes of classics, cultish crowd-magnets and directors' seasons. Now has two screens and some very plush seating.

ICA Cinema Nash House, The Mall, SW1 ☏ 020/7930 3647, ⊛ www.ica.org.uk; Piccadilly Circus or Charing Cross tube. Vintage and underground movies shown on one of two tiny screens in the avant-garde HQ of the Institute of Contemporary Arts.

National Film Theatre South Bank, SE1 ☏ 020/7928 3232, ⊛ www.bfi.org.uk/showing/nft; Waterloo tube. Known for its attentive audiences and an exhaustive, eclectic programme that includes directors' seasons and thematic series. Around six films daily are shown in the vast NFT1 and the smaller NFT2 and 3.

Prince Charles 2–7 Leicester Place, WC2 ☏ 020/7494 3654, ⊛ www.princecharlescinema .com; Leicester Square or Piccadilly Circus tube. The bargain basement of London's cinemas (entry for most shows is just £4), with a programme of new movies, classics and cult favourites – the *Sing-Along-A-Sound-of-Music* (as well as other participatory romps) is a regular.

Classical music, opera and dance

London is spoilt for choice when it comes to **orchestras**. On most days you'll be able to catch a concert by the London Symphony Orchestra, the

London Philharmonic, the Royal Philharmonic, the Philharmonia or the BBC Symphony Orchestra, or a smaller-scale performance from the English Chamber Orchestra or the Academy of St Martin-in-the-Fields. During the week, there are also **free lunchtime concerts** by students or professionals in several London churches, particularly in the City; performances in the Royal College of Music and Royal Academy of Music are of an amazingly high standard, and the choice of work is often a lot riskier than in commercial venues.

The principal **large-scale venue** is the South Bank Centre (℡020/7960 4242, ⓦwww.sbc.org.uk), where the biggest names appear at the Royal Festival Hall (closed for refurbishment until 2007), with more specialized programmes staged in the Queen Elizabeth Hall and Purcell Room. With the outstanding London Symphony Orchestra as its resident orchestra, and top foreign orchestras and big-name soloists in regular attendance, the Barbican (℡020/7638 8891, ⓦwww.barbican.org.uk) is one of the capital's best arenas for classical music. Programming is much more adventurous than it used to be, and free music in the foyer is often very good. For **chamber music**, the intimate and elegant Wigmore Hall, 36 Wigmore St, W1 (℡020/7935 2141, ⓦwww.wigmore-hall .org.uk), is many a Londoner's favourite.

From July to September each year, **the Proms** at the Royal Albert Hall (℡020/7589 8212, ⓦwww.bbc.co.uk/proms) feature at least one concert daily, with hundreds of standing tickets sold for just £4 on the night. The acoustics aren't the world's best, but the calibre of the performers is unbeatable and the programme is a fascinating mix of standards and new or obscure works. The hall is so vast that if you turn up half an hour before the show starts there should be little risk of being turned away.

London is extremely well served for **opera**, with two opera houses, both of which have recently been refurbished. The **Royal Opera House** (℡020/7304 4000, ⓦwww.royaloperahouse.org), in Covent Garden, is the pricier and more conservative of the two, with a fairly standard repertoire performed in the original language (with surtitles), while **English National Opera** at the Coliseum on St Martin's Lane (℡020/7632 8300, ⓦwww.eno.org) puts on lively, radical productions, sung in English.

From the time-honoured showpieces of the **Royal Ballet** (℡020/7304 4000, ⓦwww.royaloperahouse.org) to the diverse and exciting range of British and international dance that goes on at Sadler's Wells (℡020/7863 8000, ⓦwww .sadlers-wells.com), and at the much smaller venue, The Place (℡020/7387 0031, ⓦwww.theplace.org.uk), there's always a **dance performance** of some kind afoot in London, and the city also has a good reputation for international dance festivals showcasing the work of a spread of ensembles. The biggest of the annual events is the **Dance Umbrella** (℡020/8741 5881, ⓦwww .danceumbrella.co.uk), a six-week season (Sept–Nov) of new work from bright young choreographers and performance artists at venues across the city.

Shopping

Whether you've got time to kill or money to burn, London is one big **shopper's playground**. Although chains and superstores predominate along the high streets, you're never too far from the kind of oddball, one-off establishment that makes shopping an adventure rather than a routine.

In the centre of town, **Oxford Street** is the city's hectic chain-store mecca, and, together with **Regent Street**, offers pretty much every mainstream clothing label you could wish for. Just off Oxford Street you can find expensive designer outlets in **St Christopher's Place** and **South Molton Street**, and even pricier designers and jewellers on the very chic **Bond Street**.

Tottenham Court Road is the place to go for stereos, computers, electrical goods and, in its northern section, furniture and design shops. **Charing Cross Road** is the centre of London's book trade, both new and secondhand. At its north end, and particularly on **Denmark Street**, you can find music shops selling everything from instruments to sound equipment and sheet music. **Soho** offers an offbeat mix of sex boutiques, specialist record shops and fabric stores, while the streets surrounding **Covent Garden** yield art and design shops, mainstream fashion chains, designer wear and camping gear; Neal Street is the place to go to indulge a shoe-shopping habit.

Just off Piccadilly, **St James's** is the natural habitat of the quintessential English gentleman, with **Jermyn Street** in particular harbouring shops dedicated to his grooming. **Knightsbridge**, further west, is home to Harrods, and the big-name fashion stores of **Sloane Street** and **Brompton Road**.

Books

The capital's biggest bookstore is Waterstones in Piccadilly (Piccadilly Circus tube), but the largest choice of bookshops is still on **Charing Cross Road**, where you'll not only find the chain stores but also the long-established and idiosyncratic Foyles at no. 113–119, and other smaller **independent shops** such as Islamic bookshop Al-hoda at no. 76–78, art specialists Zwemmer at no. 80, and numerous **secondhand stores**, including Any Amount of Books at no. 62.

Department stores

Fortnum & Mason, 181 Piccadilly (Green Park or Piccadilly Circus tube), is the place to go for fabulous, gorgeously presented and pricey food, plus upmarket clothes, furniture and stationery. **Harrods**, Knightsbridge (Knightsbridge tube), is famous for its fantastic Art Nouveau tiled food-hall, obscenely huge toy department and supremely tasteless memorial to Di and Dodi; beware the draconian dress code (see p.132). Nearby, **Harvey Nichols**, 109–125 Knightsbridge, offers all the latest designer collections and famously frivolous and pricey luxury foods. Over at Oxford Circus, several major stores are close at hand, among them: **John Lewis**, 278–306 Oxford St (Oxford Circus tube), which offers everything from buttons to stockings to furniture and household goods; **Liberty**, 210–220 Regent St (Oxford Circus tube), founded as a retail outlet for the Victorian Arts and Crafts Movement, and still the place to go for regal fabrics and decorative household goods; and **Selfridge's**, 400 Oxford St (Bond Street tube), London's first great department store, which has a wide range of clothing, food and furnishings.

Markets

Camden, running from Camden High Street to Chalk Farm Road (daily; Camden Town tube), is top of the list for market shopping on most tourist itineraries; the atmosphere is a studenty mix of clubby and grungy and the stuff on sale is mainly cheap clothes and jewellery, though the stalls around Camden Lock are generally more interesting; weekends are the best – and busiest – times to visit. **Old Spitalfields**, Commercial Street (Sun; Liverpool Street tube), is an arty-crafty market similar to Camden, but on a much smaller scale, which also offers organic fruit and veg. Nearby, **Brick Lane** (Sun; Aldgate East, Shoreditch or Liverpool Street tube) has everything from sofas and antiques to cheap junk.

Bermondsey (New Caledonian) Market, Bermondsey Square (Fri; Borough, London Bridge or Bermondsey tube), is a huge, unglamorous but highly regarded antique market that kicks off at 5am; while **Portobello**, Portobello Road (Fri–Sun; Notting Hill or Ladbroke Grove tube), is mostly boho-chic clothes and (Sat only) portable antiques. South of the river, **Greenwich**, Market Square (Sat & Sun; Cutty Sark DLR or Greenwich train station), is another small arty-crafty market, with secondhand clothing and antiques on sale too.

Music

The **megastores** are: HMV, 150 Oxford St (Oxford Circus tube); Tower Records, 1 Piccadilly Circus (Piccadilly Circus tube); Virgin Megastore, 14–16 Oxford St (Tottenham Court Road tube). For **jazz**, try Ray's on the first floor of Foyles, 113–119 Charing Cross Rd (Tottenham Court Road tube). For **indie music**, there's Sister Ray, 94 Berwick St (Oxford Circus or Piccadilly Circus tube). For **African and world music**, head to Stern's, 293 Euston Rd, NW1 (Euston Square tube). **Hip-hop** is available at Mr Bongo, 44 Poland St (Oxford Circus tube). For **house**, **techno** and **trance** go to Eukatech, 49 Endell St (Covent Garden tube).

Listings

Bike rental London Bicycle Tour Company, 1a Gabriel's Wharf, SE1 ☎020/7928 6838, ⊛www .londonbicycle.com, Waterloo or Southwark tube; On Your Bike, 52–54 Tooley St, SE1 ☎020/7378 6669, ⊛www.onyourbike.net, London Bridge tube.

Car rental For the most competitive rates, ring round a few local firms from the *Yellow Pages* (⊛www.yell.com) before you try your luck with the usual suspects.

Consulates and embassies Australia, Australia House, Strand, WC2 ☎020/7379 4334, ⊛www .australia.org.uk; Canada, Canada House, Trafalgar Square, WC2 ☎020/7528 6533, ⊛www .dfait-maeci.gc.ca; Ireland, 17 Grosvenor Place, SW1 ☎020/7235 2171, ⊛www.irlgov.ie; New Zealand, New Zealand House, 80 Haymarket, SW1 ☎020/7930 8422, ⊛www.nzembassy.com; South Africa, South Africa House, Trafalgar Square, WC2 ☎020/7451 7299, ⊛www.southafricahouse.com; USA, 24 Grosvenor Square, W1 ☎020/7499 9000, ⊛www.usembassy.org.uk.

Cricket Two Test matches are played in London each summer: one at Lord's (☎020/7432 1000, ⊛www.lords.org), the home of English cricket, in St John's Wood; the other at The Oval (☎020/7582 6660, ⊛www.surreycricket.com), in Kennington. In tandem with the full-blown five-day Tests, there's also a series of one-day internationals, two of which are usually held in London.

Football Chelsea (☎0870/300 1212, ⊛www .chelseafc.com) lifted the title for the first time in fifty years in the 2004–05 season, and with the money of Russian oil tycoon Roman Abramovich at their disposal, they look set to dominate the Premiership for some time to come. For the last decade or so, however, Arsenal (☎020/7704 4000, ⊛www.arsenal.com) have been London's most successful club; their closest rivals (geographically) are Tottenham Hotspur (☎0870/420 5000, ⊛www.spurs.co.uk). Tickets for most Premiership games start at £25–30 and are virtually impossible to get hold of on a casual basis: you need to book in advance, or try and see one of the European or knockout cup fixtures.

Hospitals For 24hr accident and emergency: St Mary's Hospital, Praed Street, W2 ☎020/7886 6666; University College London Hospital, Grafton Way, WC1 ☎020/7387 9300.

Internet cafés easyInternetcafe (⊛www.easy .everything.com) has 24hr branches at 456 Strand, off Trafalgar Square (Charing Cross tube), 9–16 Tottenham Court Rd (Tottenham Court Road tube) and 9–13 Wilton Rd (Victoria tube). Alternatively, there's the more congenial *Be the Reds!* (☎020/7209 0984; Mon–Sat 10.30am–2am) at 39 Whitfield St, just off Tottenham Court Road (Goodge Street tube) – a Korean-run place serving *kimbab* and coffee, with billiards in the basement.

Laundry Regent Dry Cleaners, 18 Embankment Place, WC2 ☎020/7839 6775, Embankment or Charing Cross tube.

Left luggage Airports: Gatwick: North Terminal ☎01293/502013 (daily 5am–9pm); South Terminal ☎01293/502014 (24hr). Heathrow: Terminal 1

⊤020/8745 5301 (daily 6am–11pm); Terminal 2 ⊤020/8745 4599 (daily 5.30am–11pm); Terminal 3 ⊤020/8759 3344 (daily 5am–11pm); Terminal 4 ⊤020/8897 6874 (daily 5.30am–11pm). London City ⊤020/7646 0000 (daily 6am–9pm). Stansted ⊤0870/000 0303 (24hr). Train stations: Charing Cross ⊤020/7402 8444 (daily 7am–11pm); Euston ⊤020/7387 1499 (daily 7am–11pm); Victoria ⊤020/7963 0957 (daily 7am–midnight); Waterloo International ⊤020/7401 8444 (daily 7am–10pm).
Lost property Airports: Gatwick ⊤01293/503162 (Mon–Sat 8am–7pm, Sun 8am–4pm); Heathrow ⊤020/8745 7727 (daily 8am–4pm); London City ⊤020/7646 0000 (Mon–Sat 5.30am–9pm, Sun 10am–9pm); Stansted ⊤0870/000 0303 (daily 6am–midnight). Buses ⊤020/7222 1234 (24hr) ⓦwww.londontransport.co.uk. Heathrow Express ⊤0845/600 1515 (daily 8am–9pm), ⓦwww .heathrowexpress.co.uk. Taxis (black cabs only) ⊤020/7833 0966 (Mon–Fri 9am–4pm). Train stations (ⓦwww.networkrail.co.uk): Euston ⊤020/7387 8699 (Mon–Fri 9am–5.30pm); King's Cross ⊤020/7278 3310 (Mon–Sat 9am–5pm); Liverpool Street ⊤020/7247 4297 (Mon–Fri 9am–5.30pm); Paddington ⊤020/7313 1514 (Mon–Fri 9am–5.30pm); Victoria ⊤020/7963 0957 (daily 7am–11pm); Waterloo ⊤020/7401 8444 (Mon–Fri 7am–11pm). Tube trains: Transport for London ⊤020/7486 2496, ⓦwww.tfl.gov.uk.
Maps Stanfords 12–14 Long Acre, WC2 ⊤020/7836 1321, ⓦwww.stanfords.co.uk.
Motorbike rental Raceways, 201–203 Lower Rd, SE16 ⊤020/7237 6494 (Surrey Quays tube) and

17 The Vale, Uxbridge Road, W3 ⊤020/8749 8181 (Shepherd's Bush tube), ⓦwww.raceways.net.
Police Central police stations include: Charing Cross, Agar Street, WC2 ⊤020/7240 1212; Holborn, 10 Lambs Conduit St, WC1 ⊤020/7704 1212; Marylebone, 1–9 Seymour St, W1 ⊤020/7486 1212; West End Central, 27 Savile Row, W1 ⊤020/7437 1212, ⓦwww.met.police .uk; City of London Police, Bishopsgate, EC2 ⊤020/7601 2222, ⓦwww.cityoflondon.police.uk.
Post offices The only (vaguely) late-opening post office is the Trafalgar Square branch at 24–28 William IV St, WC2 4DL ⊤020/7930 9580 (Mon–Sat 8am–6.30pm); it's also the city's poste restante collection point. For general postal enquiries phone ⊤0845/7740 740 (Mon–Fri 8am–7.30pm, Sat 8am–2pm), or visit the website ⓦwww.royalmail.com.
Tennis Tennis in England is synonymous with Wimbledon (⊤020/8971 2473, ⓦwww.wimbledon .com), the only Grand Slam tournament in the world to be played on grass, and for many players the ultimate goal of their careers. To buy tickets on the day, you must arrive by around 7am for tickets on Centre and No. 1 courts, or by around 9am for the outside courts (and avoid the middle Saturday of the tournament).
Train stations and information As a rough guide, Euston handles services to northwest England and Glasgow; King's Cross northeast England and Edinburgh; Liverpool Street eastern England; Paddington western England; Victoria and Waterloo southeast England. For information, contact National Rail Enquiries ⊤08457/484950, ⓦwww.nationalrail.co.uk.

Travel details

Buses

For information on all local and national bus services, contact Traveline ⊤08706/082608 (daily 7am–9pm), ⓦwww.traveline.org.uk.
London Victoria Coach Station to: Bath (every 1–2hr; 3hr 15min); Birmingham (hourly; 2hr 40min); Brighton (every 30min; 2hr); Bristol (hourly; 2hr 30min); Cambridge (every 30min; 2hr); Canterbury (hourly; 2hr); Dover (hourly; 2hr 40min–3hr 20min); Exeter (every 1–2hr; 4hr 10min); Gloucester (hourly; 3hr 15min); Liverpool (5 daily; 4hr 30min–5hr); Manchester (8 daily; 4hr 30min–5hr); Newcastle (4 daily; 6hr 30min–7hr); Oxford (every 20min, 1hr 40min); Plymouth (8 daily; 4hr 50min–5hr 15min); Stratford (3 daily; 3hr).

Trains

For information on all local and national rail services, contact National Rail Enquiries ⊤08457/484950, ⓦwww.nationalrail.co.uk.
London Charing Cross to: Canterbury West (hourly; 1hr 30min); Dover Priory (every 30min; 1hr 30min–1hr 50min).
London Euston to: Birmingham New Street (every 30min; 1hr 45min); Carlisle (every 2hr; 4hr); Lancaster (hourly; 3hr–3hr 20min), Liverpool Lime Street (hourly; 3hr); Manchester Piccadilly (hourly; 2hr 30min).
London King's Cross to: Brighton (Thameslink; every 15–30min; 1hr 15min); Cambridge (every 30min; 45min–1hr); Durham (every 1–2hr; 2hr

40min–3hr); Leeds (hourly; 2hr 20min); Newcastle (every 30min; 3hr); Peterborough (every 30min; 45min); York (every 30min; 2hr).

London Liverpool Street to: Cambridge (Mon–Sat every 30min; 1hr 20min); Norwich (every 30min–hourly; 1hr 50min); Stansted Airport (every 15–30min; 45min).

London Paddington to: Bath (every 30min–hourly; 1hr 30min); Bristol (every 30–45min; 1hr 20min); Cheltenham (every 2hr; 2hr); Exeter (every 1–2hr; 2hr 5min); Gloucester (every 2hr; 1hr 45min); Oxford (every 30min–hourly; 55min); Penzance (8–9 daily; 5hr); Plymouth (hourly; 3hr–3hr 40min); Windsor (change at Slough; Mon–Fri every 20min;

Sat & Sun every 30min; journey time 30–40min); Worcester (hourly; 2hr 20min).

London St Pancras to: Leicester (every 30min; 1hr 30min); Nottingham (hourly; 2hr 10min); Shef-field (hourly; 2hr 20min).

London Victoria to: Brighton (every 30min; 1hr); Canterbury East (hourly; 1hr 30min); Dover Priory (every 30min; 1hr 40min–1hr 55min); Gatwick (every 15min; 30min).

London Waterloo to: Portsmouth Harbour (every 30min; 1hr 30min); Southampton Central (every 30min; 1hr 15min); Winchester (every 30min; 1hr 10min); Windsor (Mon–Sat every 30min, Sun hourly; 50min).

Surrey, Kent and Sussex

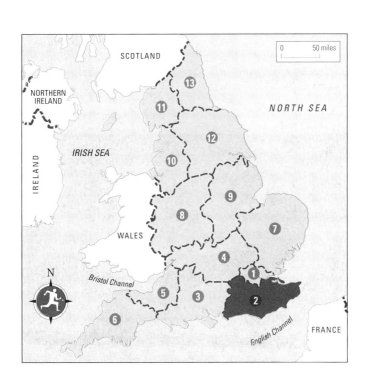

CHAPTER 2 # Highlights

* **Canterbury Cathedral**
The destination of pilgrims
in Chaucer's *Canterbury
Tales*, with a magnificent
sixteenth-century interior
that includes a shrine to
the murdered Thomas à
Becket. **See p.179**

* **The White Cliffs of Dover**
Best seen from a boat, the
famed chalky cliffs also
offer walks and vistas over
the Channel. **See p.186**

* **Rye** Superbly set hilltop
town offering some of the
best meals, accommoda-
tion and pubs in Sussex.
See p.193

* **The Royal Pavilion, Brighton** George IV's pleasure
dome, designed by Nash,
is the supreme (and only)
example of Oriental-Gothic
architecture. **See p.201**

* **Petworth House** As well
as being one of the coun-
try's most attractive stately
homes, this place is home
to a splendid art collection.
See p.209

* **Fishbourne Roman Palace**
Mosaics and a well-preserved
heating system are among
the treasures to be seen at
the country's greatest Roman
palace. **See p.211**

△ Fishbourne Roman mosaic

Surrey, Kent and Sussex

T he southeast corner of England was traditionally where London went on holiday. In the past, trainloads of Eastenders were shuttled to the hop fields and orchards of **Kent** for a working break from the city; boats ferried people down the Thames to the beaches of north Kent; while everyone from royalty to cuckolding couples enjoyed the seaside at Brighton, a blot of decadence in the otherwise sedate county of **Sussex**. The home of wealthy metropolitan commuters, **Surrey** is the least pastoral and historically significant of the three counties, though it does have a couple of places worth visiting.

The late twentieth century brought big changes to the Southeast, with many of the old seaside resorts struggling to keep their tourist custom in the face of ever more accessible foreign destinations. But the region still boasts considerable charm, its narrow country lanes and verdant meadows appearing in places almost untouched by modern life. There are even pockets of comparative wilderness, not to mention the miles of bleak and cliffy coastline.

The proximity of Kent and Sussex to the continent has dictated the history of this region, which has served as a gateway for an array of invaders. **Roman** remains dot the coastal area – most spectacularly at **Bignor** in Sussex and **Lullingstone** in Kent – and many roads, including the main A2 London to Dover road, follow the arrow-straight tracks laid by the legionaries. When **Christianity** spread through Europe, it arrived in Britain on the **Isle of Thanet** – the northeast tip of Kent, since rejoined to the mainland by silting and subsiding sea levels. In 597 AD Augustine moved inland and established a monastery at **Canterbury**, still the home of the Church of England and the county's prime historic attraction.

The last successful invasion of England took place in 1066, when the **Normans** overran King Harold's army near **Hastings**, on a site now marked by **Battle Abbey**. The Normans left their mark all over this corner of the kingdom, and Kent remains unmatched in its profusion of medieval castles, among them **Dover**'s sprawling cliff-top fortress guarding against continental invasion and **Rochester**'s huge, box-like citadel, close to the old dockyards of **Chatham**, power base of the formerly invincible British navy.

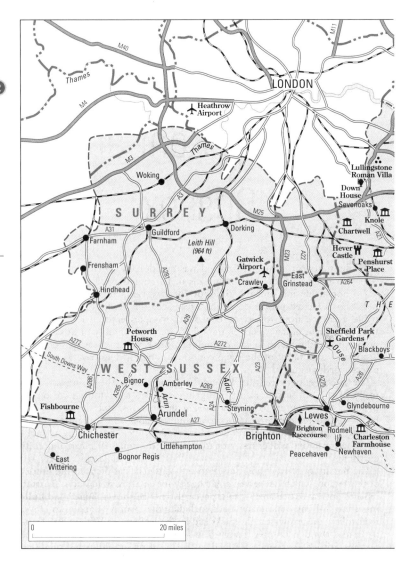

Away from the great historic sites, you can spend unhurried days in elegant old towns such as **Royal Tunbridge Wells**, **Rye** and **Lewes**, or enjoy the less elevated charms of the traditional resorts, of which **Brighton** is far and away the best, combining the buzz of a university town with a good-time atmosphere and an excellent range of eating options. Long known as "London beside the sea", the city now matches the capital for its high proportion of homeless people, though it has also seen something of a cultural renaissance in recent years, becoming the fashionable home of celebrities and refugees from the metropolis. Dramatic scenery may be in short supply hereabouts, but in places

© Crown copyright

the **South Downs Way** offers an expanse of rolling chalk uplands that, as much as anywhere in the crowded Southeast, gets you away from it all. And of course Kent, Sussex and Surrey harbour some of the country's finest **gardens**, ranging from the lush flowerbeds of **Sissinghurst** to the great landscaped estate of **Petworth House**.

Almost everywhere of interest in this corner of England is close to a **train** station. National Express services from London and other main towns are pretty good, though local **bus** services are much less impressive.

Guildford and Farnham

Thirty-five miles southwest of London, **GUILDFORD**, county town of Surrey, has little immediate appeal, though its sloping **High Street** retains plenty of architectural interest. Marked by a wonderful gilded clock projecting over the street, the **Guildhall** (guided tours Tues & Thurs 2pm & 3pm; free) has an elaborate Restoration facade disguising Tudor foundations, while further up the street, you can take a peek at the pretty courtyard of **Archbishop Abbot's Hospital**, a hospice built for the elderly in 1619 and fronted by a palatial red-brick Tudor gateway. Back down towards the river, on the left at no. 72 is the **Undercroft**, a well-preserved thirteenth-century basement of vaulted arches.

Guildford **Castle**'s Norman keep (April–Sept daily 11am–6pm; March, Oct & Nov Sat & Sun 11am–4pm; £2) sits on its motte behind the High Street. Beneath the castle, **Guildford Museum** (Tues–Sat 11am–4.45pm; free) displays mementos of the writer Lewis Carroll (aka the Reverend Charles Dodgson), author of the children's classics, *Alice's Adventures in Wonderland* and *Alice through the Looking Glass*.

Guildford's main **train station** lies just over the river to the west of the town centre, and the **bus station** is between the town centre and the train station, at the western end of North Street. The **tourist office** is at 14 Tunsgate, near the Guildhall, just off the High Street (May–Sept Mon–Sat 9am–5.30pm, Sun 10am–4.30pm; Oct–April Mon–Sat 9.30am–5pm; ☎01483/444333, ⓦwww.guildford.gov.uk).

Ten miles west of Guildford, **FARNHAM** is smaller and, in parts, more charming than Guildford. Most of the town's architecture dates from the eighteenth century, when it enjoyed a boom period based on hop farming. Farnham is also home to Surrey's only intact **castle**, built around 1138 by Henry de Blois, Bishop of Winchester, as a convenient residence halfway between his diocese and London. The castle was continuously occupied until 1927, but now houses a conference venue. The **keep** (April–Sept Fri–Sun noon–5pm; £2.60; EH), from where there are good views over the rooftops to the Downs beyond, is the only part open to the public. The **Museum of Farnham** (Tues–Sat 10am–5pm; free) at 38 West St, has material on the town's local hero, the late eighteenth-century journalist and social reformer William Cobbett, and on the highly regarded local art school.

Farnham **train station** is five minutes from the centre, over the river on the southern edge of town, while its **tourist office** occupies council offices on South Street, midway between the station and the centre (Mon–Fri 10am–4pm, Sat 9am–noon; ☎01252/715109, ⓦwww.farnham.gov.uk). Farnham makes a more attractive place to stay than Guildford: local **accommodation** choices include *Meads Guest House*, 48 West St (☎01252/715298; no credit cards; ❸), and the excellent *Stafford House Hotel*, 22 Firgrove Hill (☎01252/724336; ❸), close to the station. On Castle Street, the oak-beamed *Nelson Arms* offers reasonable bar **meals**; for Italian, the best bet is the friendly *Caffè Piccolo*, 84 West St (☎01252/723277).

The North Kent coast

Although commonly perceived as a scenic and cultural wasteland, the northern part of Kent has its fair share of attractions, all of them easily accessible from London. **Rochester** and **Chatham** boast both historic and literary interest, while the old-fashioned seaside resorts of **Whitstable** and **Broadstairs** have a growing cachet among weekenders from the capital.

Rochester and around

ROCHESTER was first settled by the Romans, who built a fortress on the site of the present **castle** (daily: April–Sept 10am–6pm; Oct–March 10am–4pm; £4), at the northwest end of the High Street; some kind of fortification has remained here ever since. In 1077, William I gave Gundulf – architect of the White Tower at the Tower of London – the See of Rochester and the job of improving the defences on the River Medway's northernmost bridge on Watling Street. The resulting castle remains one of the best-preserved examples of a Norman fortress in England, with the stark hundred-foot-high keep glowering over the town, while the interior is all the better for having lost its floors, allowing clear views up and down the dank interior. It has three square towers and a cylindrical one, the southwest tower, which was rebuilt following its collapse during the siege of 1215, when the bankrupt King John eventually wrested the castle from its archbishop. The outer walls and two of the towers retain their corridors and spiral stairwells, allowing access to the uppermost battlements.

The foundations of the adjacent **cathedral** (daily 7.30am–6pm; suggested donation £3) were also Gundulf's work, but the building has been much modified over the past nine hundred years. Plenty of Norman touches have endured, however, particularly in the cathedral's west front, with pencil-shaped towers, blind arcading and a richly carved portal and tympanum. Norman round arches, decorated with zigzags and made from lovely honey-coloured Caen stone, also line the nave. Some fine paintings survived the Dissolution, most notably the thirteenth-century depiction of the Wheel of Fortune on the walls of the choir (only half of which survives).

Rochester's most famous son, **Charles Dickens**, spent his youth here, but would seem to have been less than impressed by the place – it appears as "Mudfog" in *The Mudfog Papers*, and "Dullborough" in *The Uncommercial Traveller*. Many of the buildings feature in his novels: the *Royal Victoria and Bull Hotel*, at the top of the High Street, became the *Bull* in *Pickwick Papers* and the *Blue Boar* in *Great Expectations*, while most of his last book, the unfinished *The Mystery of Edwin Drood*, was set in the town. Dickens fans can view the outside of **Dickens' Chalet** at the southeast end of the High Street, transferred here from his former home at Gad Hill Place (now a private school). The two-storey wooden structure was the author's summer study; he was working on *The Mystery of Edwin Drood* here just before he died in 1870. Back up the High Street stands **Watts' Charity** (March–Oct Tues–Sat 2–5pm; free), a sixteenth-century almshouse featuring galleried Elizabethan bedrooms and immortalized in Dickens' short story *The Seven Poor Travellers*.

At the northwest end of the High Street, Rochester's excellent **Guildhall Museum** (daily 10am–4.30pm; free) holds a vivid model of King John's siege of the castle and a chilling exhibition on the prison ships or hulks that were used to house convicts and prisoners of war at the end of the eighteenth century.

Practicalities

Rochester **train station** is at the southeastern end of the High Street, and the **tourist office** is halfway along the High Street, opposite the cathedral at no. 95 (Mon–Sat 10am–5pm, Sun 10.30am–5pm; ☎01634/843666, Ⓦwww.medway.gov.uk). You could **spend the night** with some Dickensian ghosts at the ancient *Royal Victoria and Bull Hotel*, 16–18 High St (☎01634/846266, Ⓦwww.rvandb.co.uk; ❹), while decent B&Bs include the *Grayling House*, 54 St Margaret's St (☎01634/826593, Ⓔgraylinghouse@aol.com; no credit cards; ❷), further up the hill behind the castle. The nearest YHA **hostel** (☎0870/770 5964, Ⓔmedway@yha.org.uk; £12.50, ❶) is at Capstone Farm, Gillingham, two miles southeast of Chatham (bus #114). The best **places to eat** are all on the High Street: there are two Italian restaurants, *Giannino's*, at no. 14–16 (☎01634/828555; closed Sun), and the more expensive *Don Vincenzo* (☎01634/408373) at no. 108; or the *Cumin Club* at no. 188 (☎01634/400880) offering contemporary Indian cuisine. Alternatively, the *Coopers Arms*, on St Margaret's Street, serves good lunches in its small beer garden.

Chatham

CHATHAM, less than two miles east of Rochester, has none of the charms of its neighbour. Its chief attraction is its **Historic Dockyard** (mid-Feb to Oct daily 10am–6pm or dusk; Nov Sat & Sun 10am–dusk, last entry 2hr before closing; £10), originally founded by Henry VIII, and once the major base of the Royal Navy, many of whose vessels were built, stationed and victualled here. Well sheltered, yet close to London and the sea, and lined with tidal mud flats that helped support ships' keels during construction, the port expanded quickly and by the time of Charles II it had become England's largest naval base. This era of shipbuilding ended when the dockyards were closed in 1984, reopening soon afterwards as a tourist attraction.

The dockyard occupies a vast eighty-acre site about one mile north of the town centre along the Dock Road (ask at the tourist office in Rochester for bus times). Once there, take advantage of the free vintage-bus service to take you around the array of historically and architecturally fascinating buildings dating back to the early eighteenth century. In addition to an impressive display of fifteen historic RNLI lifeboats, there's the "**Wooden Walls**" gallery, where you can experience life as an apprentice in the eighteenth-century dockyards. Here too lies the **Ocelot Submarine**, the last warship built at Chatham, whose crew endured unbelievably cramped conditions – a major deterrent to visiting claustrophobes – and a newly restored Victorian sloop, the *Gannet*. The main part of the exhibition, however, consists of the Ropery complex, including the former rope-making room – at a quarter of a mile long, it's the longest room in the country.

Whitstable

Peculiarities of silt and salinity have made **WHITSTABLE** an oyster-friendly environment since classical times, when the Romans feasted on the region's marine delicacies. Indeed, production grew to such levels during the Middle Ages that **oysters** were exported all over Europe, but the whole industry collapsed during the twentieth century. Oysters are once more farmed in the area, but Whitstable is now more dependent on its commercial port, fishing and seaside tourism, while small-scale boat-building and a mildly bohemian ambience have made this one of the most agreeable spots along the North Kent coast to spend any time.

Follow the signs at the top of Whitstable's busy High Street to reach the seafront, a quiet shingle beach backed by some pretty weatherboard cottages. Local maritime history is illustrated in the **Whitstable Museum and Gallery** (July & Aug Mon–Sat 10am–4pm, Sun 1–4pm; Sept–June closed Sun; free), housed in the former Foresters' Hall, heralded by its eye-catching entrance on

Oxford Street, with displays on diving and some good photographs and old film footage of the town's heyday.

Whitstable's **train station** is five minutes' walk along Cromwell Road, east of Oxford Street, the southern continuation of the High Street, while the **tourist office** is next to the museum at 7 Oxford St (July & Aug Mon–Sat 10am–5pm; Sept–June Mon–Sat 10am–4pm; ☎01227/275482, ⓦwww.canterbury.co.uk). For **accommodation** along the seafront, try *Copeland House*, 4 Island Wall (☎01227/266207, ⓦwww.copelandhouse.co.uk; no credit cards, ❸), west of the High Street, with a garden that backs onto the beach, or *The Cherry Garden*, 62 Joy Lane (☎01227/266497; no credit cards; ❷), ten minutes' stroll along Seasalter Road. For **campsites**, you're best off heading to *Seaview Caravan Park* (☎01227/792246; closed Nov–March), which backs onto the beach towards Herne Bay.

Whitstable's fishing background is reflected in its **eating** places, from any number of fish-and-chip outlets along the High Street and Harbour Street to the very popular *Royal Native Oyster Stores*, The Horsebridge (☎01227/276856; closed Sun eve & Mon), one of the town's best restaurants. Opposite, *Pearson's Crab and Oyster House* (☎01227/272005) offers bar meals downstairs and has a pricier restaurant upstairs. For top-notch Italian food, head for ⅍ *Giovanni's*, 49–55 Canterbury Rd (☎01227/273034; closed Mon), while for a **drink** and excellent atmosphere check out the *Old Neptune*, standing alone in its white weatherboards on the shore.

The Thanet resorts

The **Isle of Thanet**, a featureless plain fringed by low chalk cliffs and the odd sandy bay, became part of the mainland when the navigable Wantsum Channel began silting up around the time of the first Roman invasion. In 43 AD, nearly a century after Julius Caesar's exploratory visit, the Romans got into their stride when they landed near Pegwell Bay and established Richborough port in preparation for the march inland. The Saxons followed them four hundred years later – the island is named after the "tenets", or fire beacons, which used to warn local residents of the Saxons' raids – and Augustine arrived here in 597 on a divine mission to end Anglo-Saxon paganism. The evangelist is supposed to have met King Ethelbert of Kent and preached his first sermon at a spot three miles west of Ramsgate – a cross marks the location at Ebbsfleet, next to St Augustine's Golf Club.

Over the next thousand years or so, civilization advanced to the point at which, in 1751, a local resident, one Mr Benjamin Beale, invented the bathing machine, a wheeled cubicle that enabled people to slip into the sea without undue exhibitionism. It heralded the birth of sea bathing as a recreational and recuperative activity, and by the mid-twentieth century the Isle's intermittent expanses of sand had become fully colonized as the "bucket and spade" resorts of the capital's leisure-seeking proletariat. That heyday has passed, but these earliest of resorts still cling to their traditional attractions to varying degrees.

Broadstairs

Said to have been established on the profits of shipbuilding and smuggling, today **BROADSTAIRS** is the smallest, quietest and, undoubtedly, the most pleasant of Thanet's resort towns, overlooking the pretty little Viking Bay from its cliff-top setting. Its main claim to fame is as Dickens' holiday retreat: throughout his most productive years he stayed in various hostelries here, and eventually rented an "airy nest" overlooking Viking Bay from Fort Road, since renamed **Bleak House,** where he planned the eponymous novel as well as finishing *David Copperfield*. You can get further details on the author at the **Dickens House Museum**, in the building Dickens used as a model for Betsy Trotwood's house, on the main cliff-top seafront at 2 Victoria Parade (daily 9.45am–4.30pm; £2). It also houses the town's **tourist office** (April–Sept daily 9am–5pm; Oct–March Mon–Sat 9am–4.30pm; ☏01843/861232, ⓦwww .tourism.thanet.gov.uk). The town's **Dickens Festival**, held annually since 1937, takes place in June and features lectures, dramatizations of the author's works and a nightly Victorian music hall.

It's a ten-minute walk from the **train station** to Broadstairs' seafront along the High Street. Among the ivy-covered Georgian houses in Belvedere Road, behind the High Street, *Dundonald House* at no. 43 (☏01843/862236, ⓦwww .dundonaldhousehotel.co.uk; ❸) offers good-value B&B **accommodation**, while Dickens fans should head for the pricey *Royal Albion Hotel*, 6–12 Albion St (☏01843/868071, ⓦwww.marchesi.co.uk; ❻), where part of *Nicholas Nickleby* was written. There's a YHA **hostel** housed in a Victorian villa at 3 Osborne Rd, just two minutes' walk south from the train station (☏0870/770 5730, Ⓔbroadstairs@yha.org.uk; £12.50, ❶).

For **food**, there are plenty of fish-and-chip outlets and cafés along Albion Street and Harbour Street, but for a more congenial setting, head for *Harpers Wine Bar*, also on Harbour Street (☏01843/602494; eve only), which serves moderately priced seafood dishes. Broadstairs' top restaurant is the Swiss-run *Marchesi Brothers* restaurant, 18 Albion St (☏01843/862481). As for **pubs**, the *Tartar Frigate* on Harbour Street is a solid, sociable English tavern with its own seafood restaurant upstairs, while the popular and friendly *Neptune's Hall* at the top of Harbour Street serves great beer.

Ramsgate

If Thanet had a capital, it would be **RAMSGATE**, a handsome resort, rich in robust Victorian red-brick. Most of the town is set high on a cliff linked to the seafront and harbour by broad, sweeping ramps, with the villas on the seaward side displaying wrought-iron verandas and bricked-in windows – a legacy of the tax on glazed windows. A large-scale regeneration project in the harbour and along the seafront is breathing some new life into the area.

A predictable chronicle of municipal life from Roman times onwards is presented at the **Ramsgate Maritime Museum**, in the harbour's nineteenth-century Clock House on the quayside (Easter–Sept Tues–Sun 10am–5pm; Oct Easter Thurs–Sun 11am–4.30pm; £1.50); the display is brightened by an illuminating section on the Goodwin Sands sandbanks – six miles southeast of Ramsgate – the occasional playing field of the eccentric Goodwin Sands Cricket Club.

Ramsgate's **train station** is about a mile northwest of the centre, at the end of Wilfred Road, at the top of the High Street. The **tourist office** is at 17 Albert Court, York Street (daily 9.30am–4.30pm; ☏01843/583353, ⓦwww.tourism .thanet.gov.uk). For an overnight **stay**, the *Spencer Court Hotel*, 37 Spencer Square (☏01843/594582, ⓦwww.s-h-systems.co.uk; ❶), offers comfortable accommodation in a listed Regency building, directly above the ferry terminal; or try the attractive seafront *Crescent*, 19 Wellington Crescent (☏01843/591419, ⓦwww.ramsgate-uk.com; ❸). For **food**, the reasonably priced *Surin Thai* at 30 Harbour St (☏01843/592001; closed Mon) specializes in quality Cambodian, Lao and Thai food, while the relaxed *Mariners Café Restaurant* at 42–44 Harbour Parade serves English and continental fare overlooking the harbour. Best for fish and chips is the gaudy *Peter's Fish Factory* at 96 Harbour Parade. For traditional **pubs**, try the ornately tiled *Queen's Head* on Harbour Parade, and for harbour views, real ales and live music (Sun), head for the *Churchill Tavern* on The Paragon.

Canterbury

One of England's most venerable cities, **CANTERBURY** offers a rich slice through two thousand years of history, with Roman and early Christian ruins, a Norman castle and a famous cathedral that dominates a medieval warren of time-skewed Tudor dwellings. The city began as a Belgic settlement that was overrun by the Romans and renamed **Durovernum**, which they established as a garrison and supply base. With the empire's collapse came the Saxons, who renamed the town **Cantwarabyrig**; it was a Saxon king, Ethelbert, who in 597 welcomed Augustine, despatched by the pope to convert the British Isles to

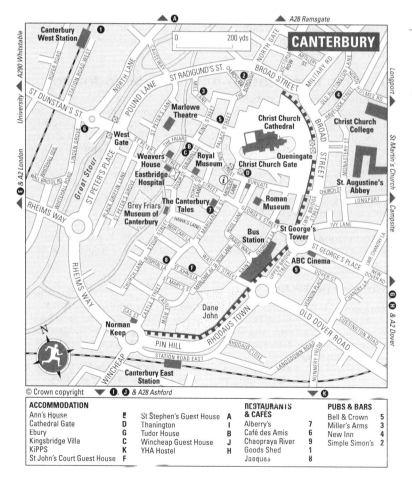

© Crown copyright

ACCOMMODATION				RESTAURANTS & CAFÉS		PUBS & BARS	
Ann's House	E	St Stephen's Guest House	A	Alberry's	7	Bell & Crown	5
Cathedral Gate	D	Thanington	I	Café des Amis	6	Miller's Arms	3
Ebury	G	Tudor House	B	Chaopraya River	9	New Inn	4
Kingsbridge Villa	C	Wincheap Guest House	J	Goods Shed	1	Simple Simon's	2
KiPPS	K	YHA Hostel	H	Jacques	8		
St John's Court Guest House	F						

②

Christianity. By the time of his death, Augustine had founded two Benedictine monasteries, one of which – Christ Church, raised on the site of the Roman basilica – was to become the first cathedral in England.

At the turn of the first millennium Canterbury suffered repeated sackings by the Danes until Canute, a recent Christian convert, restored the ruined Christ Church, only for it to be destroyed by fire a year before the Norman invasion. As Christianity became a tool of control, a struggle for power developed between the archbishops, the abbots from the nearby Benedictine abbey and King Henry II, culminating in the assassination of Archbishop Thomas à Becket in 1170, a martyrdom that effectively established the autonomy of the archbishops and made this one of Christendom's greatest shrines. Geoffrey Chaucer's *Canterbury Tales*, written towards the end of the fourteenth century, portrays the unexpectedly festive nature of pilgrimages to Becket's tomb, which was later plundered and destroyed on the orders of Henry VIII.

In 1830 a pioneering passenger railway service linked Canterbury to the sea and prosperity grew until the city suffered extensive German bombing on June 1, 1942, in one of the notorious **Baedeker Raids** – the Nazi plan to destroy Britain's most treasured historic sites as described in the eponymous German travel guides. Today the cathedral and compact town centre, enclosed on three sides by medieval walls, remain the focus for leisure-motivated pilgrims from across the globe.

Arrival, information and accommodation

Canterbury's two **train stations** – Canterbury East for services from London Victoria and Dover Priory, and Canterbury West for services from London Charing Cross and the Isle of Thanet – are south and northwest of the centre respectively, each a ten-minute walk from the cathedral. National Express services and local **buses** use the bus station just inside the city walls on St George's Lane. The busy **tourist office** is at the Butter Market at 12–13 Sun St (Jan–Easter Mon–Sat 10am–4pm; Easter–Oct Mon–Sat 9.30am–5pm, Sun 10am–4pm; Nov–Dec daily 10am–4pm; ☎01227/378100, ⓦwww .canterbury.co.uk), opposite the main entrance to the cathedral. You can access the **Internet** at Alpha Computer Systems, 10–11 Burgate Lane, Mon–Sat 9.30am–6pm).

Accommodation consists mostly of B&Bs and small hotels and can be difficult to secure in July and August – the tourist office can help, though they charge for the service.

Hotels and B&Bs

Ann's House 63 London Rd ☎01227/768767, ⓦwww.annshousecanterbury.co.uk. Traditional Victorian villa offering comfortable rooms, mostly en suite, a ten-minute walk from the centre. ❸

Cathedral Gate 36 Burgate ☎01227/464381, ⓦwww.cathgate.co.uk. Built in 1438, this venerable pilgrims' hostelry has crooked floors and exposed beams alongside more modern amenities. ❸

Ebury 65–67 New Dover Rd ☎01227/768433, ⓦwww.eburyhotel.co.uk. Very comfortable and spacious family-owned Victorian hotel, fifteen minutes' walk from the centre, with an indoor pool. ❺

Kingsbridge Villa 15 Best Lane ☎01227/766415, ⓦwww.canterburyguesthouse.com. Rooms 2 and 4 of this well-furnished Victorian house have views of the cathedral. Vegan and vegetarian breakfasts on offer too. ❶

St John's Court Guest House St John's Lane ☎01227/456425, ⓦwww.sh-systems.co.uk. Obliging and good-value guest house in a quiet but central location, just south of the old town. No credit cards. ❶

St Stephen's Guest House 100 St Stephen's Rd ☎01227/767644, ⓦwww.st-stephens.fsnet.co.uk. A mock-Tudor house on the northern side of the city, ten minutes' walk along the Stour, offering

excellent value en-suite accommodation. No credit cards. ③
Thanington 140 Wincheap ☎01227/453227, ⓦwww.thanington-hotel.co.uk. Comfortably converted Georgian building, with an indoor pool and a games room. ⑤

Tudor House 6 Best Lane ☎01227/765650. Cosy family-run B&B backing onto the River Stour, and offering canoes and boats to rent. ③
Wincheap Guest House 94 Wincheap ☎01227/762309, ⓦwww.wincheapguesthouse.co.uk. Good-value Victorian B&B, with shared facilities, close to Canterbury East station. ①

Hostels and campsites

The Caravan and Camping Club Site Bekesbourne Lane ☎01227/463216. Large year-round caravan park, one and a half miles east of the city off the A257 road to Sandwich.
KiPPS 40 Nunnery Fields ☎01227/786121, ⓦwww.kipps-hostel.com. Self-catering hostel offering single and double rooms (①) and dormitory

(£12) accommodation a few minutes' walk from Canterbury East station.
YHA Hostel 54 New Dover Rd ☎0870/770 5744, ⓔcanterbury@yha.org.uk. About a mile out of town, and 15min on foot from Canterbury East station, this friendly hostel is set in a Victorian villa. Dorm bed £16.40. Closed Jan. ①

The City

Despite the presence of a university and art and teacher-training college, England's second most visited city is a surprisingly small place with a population of just 40,000. The town centre, partly ringed by ancient walls, is virtually car free, but this doesn't stop the High Street seizing up all too frequently with tourists.

The cathedral

Mother Church of the Church of England and seat of the Primate of All England, **Canterbury Cathedral** (Mon–Sat 9am–5/6.30pm, Sun 12.30–2.30pm & 4.30–5.30pm; also closed on some days in mid-July for university graduation ceremonies; £5; ⓦwww.canterbury-cathedral.org) fills the northeast quadrant of the city with a befitting sense of authority, even if architecturally it's not the country's most impressive. A cathedral has stood here since 602, but in 1070 the first Norman archbishop, Lanfranc, levelled the original Saxon structure to build a new cathedral. Over successive centuries the masterpiece was heavily modified, and with the puritanical lines of the Perpendicular style gaining ascendancy in late medieval times, the cathedral now derives its distinctiveness from the thrust of the 235-foot-high Bell Harry Tower, completed in 1505. The precincts (daily 7am–9pm) are entered through the superbly ornate early sixteenth-century **Christ Church Gate**, where Burgate and St Margaret's Street meet. This junction, the city's medieval core, is known as the Butter Market, where religious relics were once sold to pilgrims hoping to prevent an eternity in damnation. Having paid your entrance fee, you pass through the gatehouse and get one of the finest views of the cathedral, foreshortened and crowned with soaring towers and pinnacles.

Once in the magnificent **interior**, look for the tomb of Henry IV and his wife, Joan of Navarre, and for the gilded effigy of Edward III's son, the Black Prince, all of them in the Trinity Chapel, behind the main altar. Also here, until demolished in 1538, was the shrine of Thomas à Becket; the actual spot where he died is marked by the **Altar of the Sword's Point**, in the "Martyrdom" in the northwest transept, where a jagged sculpture of the assassins' weapons is suspended on the wall. Steps from here descend to the low, Romanesque arches of the **crypt**, one of the few remaining relics of the Norman cathedral and considered

❷

△ Canterbury Cathedral

the finest such structure in the country, with some amazingly well-preserved carvings on the capitals of the columns. Particularly vivid is the medieval **stained glass**, much of which dates back to the twelfth and thirteenth centuries, notably in the Trinity Chapel, where the life and miraculous works of Thomas à Becket are depicted. Look out too for Adam delving, girt about with an animal skin, in the west window and Jonah and the whale in the Corona (beyond the Trinity Chapel). Contemporary with the windows (1220) is the white marble **St Augustine's Chair** on which all archbishops of Canterbury are enthroned; it's located in the choir at the top of the steps beyond the high altar.

On the cathedral's north flank are the fan-vaulted colonnades of the **Great Cloister**, from where you enter the **Chapter House**, with its intricate web of fourteenth-century tracery supporting the roof and a wall of stained glass. In 1935 it was a fitting venue for the inaugural performance of T.S. Eliot's *Murder in the Cathedral*.

The rest of the city

Exiting the cathedral grounds at the Queningate, you come to the vestigial remains of **St Augustine's Abbey** (daily: April–Sept 10am–6pm; Oct–March Wed–Sun 10am–4pm; £3.70; EH), occupying the site of the church founded by Augustine in 598. Built outside the city because of a Christian tradition forbidding burials within the walls, it became the final resting place of Augustine, Ethelbert and successive archbishops and kings of Kent, although no trace remains either of them or of the original Saxon church. Shortly after the Normans arrived, the church was demolished and replaced by a much larger abbey, most of which was destroyed in the Dissolution so that today only the ruins and foundations remain. Nearby, on the corner of North Holmes Road and St Martin's Lane, **St Martin's Church** (Tues & Thurs 10am–3pm, Sat 10am–1pm) is one of England's oldest churches, built on the site of a Roman villa or temple and used by the earliest Christians. Although medieval additions obscure the original Saxon structure, this is perhaps the earliest Christian site in Canterbury – it was here that Queen Bertha welcomed St Augustine in 597, and her husband King Ethelbert was baptized.

South of the Cathedral, the redevelopment of the Longmarket area between Burgate and the High Street in the early 1990s exposed Roman foundations and mosaics that are now part of the **Roman Museum** (June–Oct Mon–Sat 10am–5pm, Sun 1.30–5pm; Nov–May closed Sun; £2.90). The extant remnants of the larger building are pretty dull, and better mosaics can be seen at Lullingstone (see p.190), but the display of recovered artefacts and general design of the museum are tasteful, with Roman domestic scenes re-created, as well as a computer-generated view of Durovernum.

St Margaret's Street holds the former church that's now **The Canterbury Tales** (daily: March–June, Sept & Oct 10am–5pm; July & Aug 9.30am–5pm; Nov–Feb 10am–4.30pm; £6.95), a quasi-educational show based on Geoffrey Chaucer's book. Here, visitors equipped with headsets wander through odour-enhanced galleries where mannequins occupy idealized fourteenth-century tableaux and recount five of Chaucer's tales. Genuinely educational and better value is the **Museum of Canterbury**, round the corner in Stour Street (Mon–Sat 10.30am–5pm; also June–Oct Sun 1.30–5pm; £3.20), an interactive exhibition spanning local history from the splendour of Durovernum through to the more recent literary figures of Joseph Conrad (buried in the cemetery on London Road) and local-born Mary Tourtel, creator of the check-trousered philanthropist Rupert Bear. An excellent thirty-minute video on the Becket story details the intriguing personalities and events that led up to his assassination.

Eastbridge Hospital, standing where the High Street passes over a branch of the River Stour (Mon–Sat 10am–5pm; £1), was founded in the twelfth century to provide poor pilgrims with shelter. Downstairs is an exhibition on Chaucer's life, while storytellers in feudal garb recite parts of his book. Over the road is the wonky, half-timbered **Weavers' House**, built around 1500 – once inhabited by Huguenot textile workers, it's now a café.

Just before High Street becomes St Peter's Street, the **Royal Museum and Art Gallery** (Mon–Sat 10am–5pm; free) is housed on the first floor of an awesome mock-Tudor building. There's lots of military memorabilia in the Buffs regimental gallery, and the art gallery holds the odd Henry Moore and Gainsborough too. St Peter's Street terminates at the massive crenellated towers of the medieval **West Gate**, the only one of the town's seven city gates to have survived intact. Its prison cells and guard chambers house a small **museum** (Mon–Sat 11am–12.30pm & 1.30–3.30pm; £1.15), which displays contemporary armaments and weaponry used by the medieval city guard, as well as giving access to the battlements.

Eating, drinking and nightlife

The combination of a large student population and the tourist trade means Canterbury has a good selection of **places to eat**, many of them in old and atmospheric settings. At Canterbury West Station, ⚲ *The Goods Shed* offers everything from a bowl of soup or sandwich to a first-class full meal, with ingredients fresh from the adjacent farmers' market (☎01227/459153; closed Sun eve & all day Mon). *Alberry's*, a lively wine bar on St Margaret's Street (☎01227/452378), has snacks, pastas, fish and meat dishes, while *Café des Amis*, 93–95 St Dunstan's St (☎01227/464390), is a popular Mexican place where you can sample sizzling chicken fajitas or a delicious paella. Refined Thai cuisine at reasonable prices is served at *Chaopraya River*, 2 Dover St (☎01227/462876; closed Mon), while *Jacques*, 71 Castle St (☎01227/781000; closed Sun eve), is a homely little French bistro.

Nightlife in Canterbury keeps a low profile, though there are some good **pubs** such as the *Miller's Arms* on Mill Lane, a pleasant weir-side spot, and the *New Inn*, 19 Havelock St, one of Canterbury's tiniest pubs, popular for its real ales. At 10 Palace St, the *Bell & Crown* is another cramped medieval hostelry, while *Simple Simon's* on Church Lane attracts the university crowd and has **live music**. The university also stages gigs and hosts a good range of arty **films** at Cinema 3, and **plays** at the Gulbenkian Theatre (☎01227/769075, ⓦwww.kent.ac.uk/gulbenkian). In town, the Marlowe Theatre in The Friars (☎01227/787787, ⓦwww.marlowetheatre.com) is the main venue for drama. Finally, the **Canterbury Festival** (☎01227/452853, ⓦwww.canterburyfestival.co.uk), an international mix of music, theatre and arts, takes place over two weeks in October. For all events, see the free *What, Where and When* **listings magazine** available at the tourist office.

The Channel ports

Dover, just 21 miles from mainland Europe (Calais' low cliffs are visible on a clear day), is the Southeast's principal cross-Channel port. As a town it is not immensely appealing, even though its key position has left it with a clutch of historic attractions. To the north lie **Sandwich**, once the most important of the Cinque Ports but now no longer even on the coast, and the pleasant resort towns of **Deal** and **Walmer**, each with its own set of distinctive fortifications as well as a smattering of traditional seaside B&Bs.

Sandwich and around

SANDWICH, situated on the River Stour four miles north of Deal, is best known nowadays for giving rise to England's favourite culinary contribution when, in 1762, the Fourth Earl of Sandwich, passionately absorbed in a game

The Cinque Ports

In 1278 Edward I formalized the unofficial confederation of defensive coastal settlements – Dover, Hythe, Sandwich, New Romney and Hastings – as the **Cinque Ports** (pronounced "sink", despite its French origin). In return for providing England with maritime support, chiefly in the transportation of troops and supplies during times of war, the five ports were granted trading privileges and other liberties. Later, Rye, Winchelsea and a few other "limb" ports on the southeast coast were added to the confederation. The ports' privileges were revoked in 1685; their maritime services had become increasingly unnecessary after Henry VIII had founded a professional navy and, due to a shifting coastline, several of the ports' harbours had silted up anyway, leaving some of them several miles inland. Nowadays, only Dover is still a major working port.

of cards, ate his meat between two bits of bread for a quick snack. Aside from this incident, the town's main interest lies in its maritime connections – it was chief among the Cinque Ports (see box above) until the Stour silted up. The river still flows through town, however, its grassy willow-lined banks adding to the once great medieval port's present charm.

By the bridge over the Stour stands Sandwich's best-known feature, the sixteenth-century **Barbican**, a stone gateway where tolls were once collected. Running parallel to the river is **Strand Street**, whose crooked half-timbered facades front antique shops and private homes while, back in the town centre, another fine sixteenth-century edifice, the **Guildhall**, houses both the tourist office (see below) and a small **museum** recounting the town's history (April–Nov Tues, Wed, Fri & Sat 10.30am–12.30pm & 2–4pm, Thurs & Sun 10.30am–4pm; £1). The genteel town is separated from the sandy beaches of Sandwich Bay by the **Royal St George Golf Course** – frequent venue of the British Open tournament – and a mile of nature reserves. The reserve that most ornithologists make for is the **Gazen Salts Nature Reserve**, three miles north of town, across the Stour.

Overlooking the doleful expanse of Pegwell Bay, two miles northwest of Sandwich, is **Richborough Fort** (April–Sept daily 10am–6pm; £3.70; EH), one of the earliest coastal strongholds built by the Romans along what later became known as the Saxon Shore on account of the frequent raids by the Germanic tribe. The castle guarded the southern entrance to the Wantsum Channel, which then isolated the Isle of Thanet from the mainland. Rumour has it that Emperor Claudius, on his way to London, once rode on an elephant through a triumphal arch erected inside the castle, but all that remains within the well-preserved Roman walls are the relics of an early Saxon church. Richborough's historical significance far outshines its present appearance, especially as Pegwell Bay is now blighted by an ugly chemical works. The nicest way of reaching the fort is to take the **river bus** up the Stour from Sandwich Quay (☎07958/376183; £3.50).

Sandwich's **tourist office**, housed in the Guildhall (April–Oct daily 10am–4pm; ☎01304/613565, ⓦwww.whitecliffscountry.org.uk), can provide a list of local **hotels** and **guest houses**. Try the *Fleur de Lis*, an old coaching inn near the Guildhall at 6–8 Delf St (☎01304/611131, ⓦwww .thefleur-sandwich.co.uk; ❺), or the more modest *Le Trayas* bungalow, 10 Poulders Rd (☎01304/611056, ⓦwww.letrayas.co.uk; no credit cards; ❷), a ten-minute walk from The Quay. Your best choice for top-class **food** is the pricey *Fishermans Wharf* on the quayside (☎01304/613636), which serves excellent seafood. For something less expensive, try one of the pubs by the Barbican or *The Haven*, 20a King St, for good coffee and snacks. The twee *Little Cottage Tearooms*, on The Quay, serves the definitive Sandwich sandwich.

Deal and Walmer Castle

One of the most unusual of Henry VIII's forts is the diminutive castle at **DEAL**, six miles southeast of Sandwich and site of Julius Caesar's first successful landfall in Britain in 55 BC. The **castle** (April–Sept daily 10am–6pm; £3.70; EH) is situated off The Strand at the south end of town. Its unusual shape – viewed from the air it looks like a Tudor rose – is as much an affectation as a defensive design, though the premise was that the rounded walls would be better at deflecting missiles; inside, the comprehensive display on the other similar forts built during Henry VIII's reign is well worth a visit.

A mile south of Deal, reachable either on hourly buses or, if the weather's good, on foot along the seafront, **Walmer Castle** (April–Sept Mon–Fri & Sun 10am–6pm, Sat 10am–4pm; Oct Wed–Sun 10am–4pm; March daily 10am–4pm; £5.95; EH) is another rotund Tudor-rose-shaped affair, commissioned when the castle became the official residence of the Lord Warden of the Cinque Ports in 1730. Now it resembles a heavily fortified stately home more than a military stronghold. The best-known resident was the Duke of Wellington, who died here in 1842, and not surprisingly, the house is devoted primarily to his life and times. Busts and portraits of the Iron Duke crowd the rooms and corridors, where you'll also find the armchair in which he expired and the original Wellington boots in which he triumphed at Waterloo.

Deal's **tourist office** is situated in the Landmark Centre on the High Street (Mon–Fri 10am–4pm, Sat 10am–noon; ☎01304/369576, ⓌWwww .whitecliffscountry.org.uk). There's a whole host of places offering **accommodation** on Beach Street: try the winsome *King's Head* pub at no. 9 (☎01304/368194, Ⓦwww.kingsheaddeal.co.uk; ❸), or the nearby townhouse, *Channel View* at no. 17 (☎01304/368194; ❸), run by the same proprietor. Another option is *Dunkerley's*, next door at no. 19 (☎01304/375016, Ⓦwww .dunkerleys.co.uk; ❻), whose **restaurant** is one of Deal's finest (and priciest). For more affordable seafood there's the *Lobster Pot* (☎01304/374713), 81–83 Beach St, opposite the pier.

Dover

Badly bombed during the war, **DOVER**'s town centre and seafront just don't have what it takes to induce many travellers to linger. Although the town authorities have put a lot of effort and money into sprucing the place up, particularly the early Victorian New Bridge development along the Esplanade, Dover Castle is still by far the most interesting of the numerous attractions in the port. Entertainment of a saltier nature is offered by Dover's legendary White Cliffs, which dominate the town and have long been a source of inspiration for lovers, travellers and soldiers sailing off to war.

It was in 1168, a century after the Conquest, that the Normans constructed the keep that now presides over the bulk of **Dover Castle** (April–June & Sept daily 10am–6pm; July & Aug daily 9.30am–6.30pm; Oct daily 10am–5pm; Nov–Jan Mon & Thurs–Sun 10am–4pm; Feb & March daily 10am–4pm; £8.95; EH), a superbly positioned defensive complex that was in continuous use as some sort of military installation from then right up to the 1980s. Much earlier, the Romans had put Dover on the map when they chose the harbour as the base for their northern fleet, and erected a **lighthouse** (*pharos*)

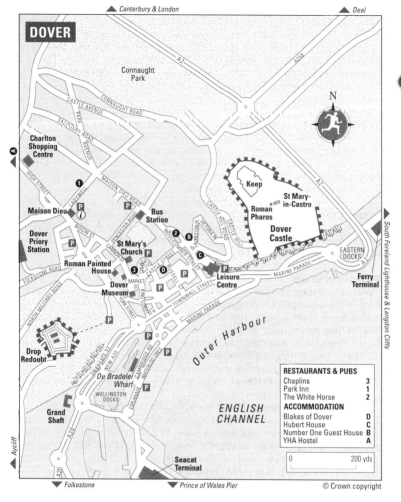

here to guide the ships into the river mouth. Beside the chunky hexagonal remains of this stands a Saxon-built church, **St Mary-in-Castro**, dating from the seventh century, with motifs graffitied by irreverent Crusaders still visible near the pulpit. Further up the hill is the impressive, well-preserved **Norman Keep**, built by Henry II as a palace. The interior has an interactive exhibition on spying, and you can climb to the lofty battlements for views over the sea to France. The castle's other main attraction is its network of **Secret Wartime Tunnels** dug during the Napoleonic Wars and extended during World War II; fifty-minute guided tours leave every twenty minutes.

Postwar rebuilding has made Dover **town centre** a rather unprepossessing place, though the **Roman Painted House** on New Street (April–Sept Tues–Sun 1–5pm; £2), once a hotel for official guests, possesses some reasonable Roman wall paintings, the remains of an underground Roman heating system and some mosaics. The nearby **Dover Museum** on the Market Square

(Mon–Sat 10am–5.30pm; £2) has three floors packed with informative displays on Dover's past, including a restored Bronze Age boat discovered in the town in 1992 – and a stuffed polar bear. In Biggin Street, the **Maison Dieu** was founded in the thirteenth century as a place for pilgrims en route to Canterbury. After the Reformation, it was turned into a naval storehouse, and in the last century became part of the town hall. The Stone Hall, with its fine timber roof, dates from 1253.

The high ground to the west of town, originally the site of a Napoleonic-era fortress, retains one interesting oddity, the **Grand Shaft** (for opening times contact Dover Museum ☎01304/201066), a 140-foot triple staircase, entered on Snargate Street, by which troops could go down at speed to defend the port in case of attack. Looming above the Grand Shaft is the formidable **Drop Redoubt** (as above for opening information), a sunken fortress built in 1808, from which guns could fire in all directions.

There are some great **walks** to be had along Dover's cliffs: to reach **Shakespeare Cliff**, catch bus #D2A from Worthington Street towards Aycliff; alternatively, there's a steep two-and-a-half-mile climb from North Military Road, off York Street, taking you by the **Western Heights**, a series of defensive battlements built into the cliff in the nineteenth century.

Practicalities

Dover Priory **train station** is situated off Folkestone Road, a ten-minute walk west of the centre; there are regular shuttle buses to the Eastern and Western docks. Buses from London run to the Eastern Docks and the town-centre **bus station** on Pencester Road. The **tourist office**, in the Old Town Gaol in Biggin Street (June–Aug daily 9am–5.30pm; Sept–May Mon–Fri 9am–5.30pm, Sat 10am–4pm; ☎01304/205108, ⍵www.whitecliffscountry.org.uk), has a free *White Cliffs Trails* pamphlet that outlines coastal and inland walks near Dover. *Café En-route* provides **Internet** access at 8 Bench St (Mon–Sat 9am–5pm), near Market Square.

Dover's best **B&Bs** include *Hubert House*, 9 Castle Hill Rd (☎01304/202253, ⍵www.huberthouse.co.uk; ❷), convenient for the Eastern Dock; the smart, good-value *Number One Guesthouse*, opposite, at 1 Castle St (☎01304/202007, ⍵www.number1guesthouse.co.uk; ❷); and *Blakes of Dover*, 52 Castle St (☎01304/202194, ⍵www.blakesofdover.co.uk; ❷), which has a very genial owner. There's a very busy YHA **hostel** in a listed Georgian house at 306 London Rd (☎0870/770 5798, ⓔdover@yha.org.uk; dorm beds £16, doubles ❶), a mile up the High Street from Dover Priory station.

Given the town's uninspiring appearance, Dover's **pubs** are surprisingly characterful: try *Park Inn*, a big revamped old boozer at 1–2 Park Place; *Ladywell*, with plenty of real ales; and *The White Horse* on St James Street, a nice old eighteenth-century pub at the foot of the castle. Dover's culinary offerings are poor, though *Blakes* (see above) has a lovely wood-panelled wine bar and restaurant, and *Chaplins*, 2 Church St, serves excellent-value **breakfasts** and **lunches**.

Hythe to Dungeness: the Romney and Denge marshes

In Roman times, the **Romney and Denge marshes** – now the southernmost part of Kent – were submerged beneath the English Channel. The lowering of the sea levels in the Middle Ages and later reclamation created a forty-square-mile area of shingle and marshland which, until the nineteenth century, was afflicted by malaria and various other malaises. Contrasting strongly with the wooded pastures of Kent's interior, the sheep-speckled marshes have an eerie, forlorn appearance, as if still unassimilated with the mainland and haunted by their maritime origins.

On the eastern edge of the reclaimed marshes, the ancient town of **HYTHE** is a sedate seaside resort bisected by the disused waterway of the **Royal Military Canal**, built as a defensive obstacle during the threat of Napoleonic invasion and linked with Rye in East Sussex (see p.193), on the marsh's western edge. Hythe's receding shoreline reduced its usefulness as a port and the nearby coast is now just a sweep of beach punctuated by **Martello Towers**, part of the chain of 74 such defensive towers built along the south and east coasts in the early nineteenth century.

West of Hythe's centre on the south bank of the canal lies the station for the fifteen-inch-gauge **Romney, Hythe and Dymchurch Railway** (April–Sept daily; March & Oct Sat & Sun; plus school holidays throughout the year; £10.50 return; ☎01797/362353, ⓦwww.rhdr.demon.co.uk), which runs fourteen miles south to **DUNGENESS**. This shingly, somewhat spooky expanse is home to a nuclear power station, as well as huge colonies of gulls, terns, smews and gadwalls: information on the birdlife can be found at the **RSPB visitor centre** (daily: March–Oct 10am–5pm; Nov–Feb 10am–4pm; £3), off the road from Dungeness to Lydd.

The Kent Weald

The Weald is usually taken to refer to the region around the spa town of **Royal Tunbridge Wells**, but in fact it stretches across a much larger area between the North and South Downs and includes parts of both Kent and Sussex, though the majority of its attractions are in Kent. During Saxon times, much of the Weald was covered in thick forest – the word itself derives from the Germanic word *Wald*, meaning forest, and the suffixes -hurst (meaning wood) and -den (meaning clearing) are commonly found in Wealden village names. Now, however, the region is epitomized by gentle hills, sunken country lanes and somnolent villages as well as some of England's most beautiful gardens – **Sissinghurst**, fifteen miles east of Tunbridge Wells, being the best known – and a scattering of highly picturesque historical sites, including **Leeds Castle**, north of Sissinghurst, and **Hever Castle**, northwest of Tunbridge Wells.

Royal Tunbridge Wells and around

Most associated in recent times with whingeing right-wing letter-writers, the prosperous spa town of **ROYAL TUNBRIDGE WELLS** – not to be confused with the more mundane Tonbridge, a few miles to the north – merits a visit, not least for its gorgeous surrounding countryside. After a bubbling spring discovered here in 1606 was claimed to have curative properties, a spa resort evolved, reaching its height of popularity during the Regency period when such restorative cures were in vogue. The distinctively well-mannered architecture of that period, generously surrounded by parklands in which the rejuvenated gentry exercised, gives the southern and western part of town its special character. In late July, the five-day **Georgian Festivities** sees the townsfolk relive the era, taking to the streets in eighteenth-century garb.

The icon of those genteel times is the **Pantiles**, an elegant colonnaded parade of shops, ten minutes' walk south of the train station, where the fashionable once gathered to promenade and take the waters. The name stems from the chunky Kent tiles made of baked clay, which were put down as paving during Queen Anne's reign. Hub of the Pantiles is the original **Chalybeate Spring** (pronounced with the emphasis on the "be") in the Bath House (Easter–Sept daily 10am–5pm), where a "Dipper" has been employed since the late eighteenth century to serve the ferrous waters. A period-dressed incumbent will fetch you a glass from the cool spring for 40p – or, with your own cup, you can help yourself for free from the adjacent source. As well as tiles, Tunbridge also produced domestic ceramics, on view with other local relics and historical artefacts in the **Museum and Art Gallery** at the top of Mount Pleasant Road (Mon–Sat 9.30am–5pm, Sun 10am–4pm; free), a fifteen-minute walk up the High Street from the Pantiles.

The Tunbridge Wells **tourist office** is housed in the Old Fish Market, in the Pantiles (May–Aug Mon–Sat 9am–5pm, Sun 10am–5pm; Sept–April Mon–Sat 10am–5pm; ℡01892/515675, Ⓦwww.visittunbridgewells.com). The **train station** is south of the town centre, where High Street becomes Mount Pleasant Road. The town has a number of plush **hotels**, such as the *Swan*, on the Pantiles itself (℡01892/543319, Ⓦwww.the-swan-hotel.com; ❺), and the chic ⚔ *Hotel du Vin* in Crescent Road (℡01892/526455, Ⓦwww.hotelduvin.com; ❻), with an excellent bistro. For cheaper lodgings, there's an attractive Regency-style **B&B** at 40 York Rd (℡01892/531342, Ⓦwww.yorkroad.co.uk; ❸).

Among the cluster of top-notch **restaurants** are *Thackeray's House*, one-time home of the writer, at 85 London Rd (℡01892/511921, Ⓦwww.thackerays restaurant.com; closed Sun eve & Mon), which offers a bargain three-course set menu at lunchtime. There are great veggie options both at the *Trinity Arts Centre Café* in a converted church on Church Road (lunch & pre-theatre deals only; closed Sun) and at *Continental Flavour*, 14 Mount Pleasant, a wholefood restaurant and shop (open daytime only; closed Sun). You're unlikely to miss the popular *Opera House* **pub**, in the town's former 1902 theatre on Mount Pleasant Road – you can sit in the foyer, the stalls or even on stage and gaze up at the balconies.

Penshurst Place and Hever Castle

Tudor timber-framed houses and shops line the high street of the attractive village of **PENSHURST**, five miles northwest of Tunbridge Wells (bus #231 or #233; not Sun). Its village church, **St John the Baptist**, is capped by an unusual four-spired tower and is entered under a beamed archway that conceals a rustic post office. However, the main reason for coming here is to visit **Penshurst Place** (daily: mid-March to Oct noon–4pm; grounds 10.30am–6pm; £7, grounds only £5.50), home to the Sidney family since 1552 and birthplace of the Elizabethan soldier and poet, Sir Philip Sidney. The fourteenth-century Barons Hall, built for Sir John de Pulteney, four times Mayor of London, is the chief glory of the interior, with its sixty-foot-high chestnut roof still in place. The ten acres of grounds include a formal Italian garden with clipped box hedges, and double herbaceous borders mixed with an abundance of yew hedges.

The moated and much altered **Hever Castle**, three miles further west (daily: March–Nov noon–5pm; £9.20, gardens only £7.30), is where Anne Boleyn, second wife of Henry VIII, grew up, and where Anne of Cleves, Henry's fourth wife, lived after their divorce. In 1903, having fallen into disrepair, the castle was bought by William Waldorf-Astor, American millionaire-owner of *The Times*, who had the house assiduously restored, panelling the rooms with worthy reproductions of Tudor woodcarvings. In the Inner Hall hangs a fine portrait of Henry VIII by Holbein; a further Holbein painting of Elizabeth I hangs on the middle floor. Upstairs, in Anne of Cleves' room, an unusually well-preserved tapestry illustrates the marriage of Henry's sister to King Louis XII of France, with Anne Boleyn as one of the ladies-in-waiting.

Outside in the grounds, next to the gift shop, is the absorbing **Guthrie Miniature Model Houses Collection**, showing the development of aristocratic seats from feudal times on. However, the best feature of the grounds is Waldorf-Astor's beautiful **Italian Garden**, built on reclaimed marshland and decorated with Roman statuary.

Sissinghurst and Leeds Castle

Sissinghurst, twelve miles east of Tunbridge Wells (late March to Oct Mon, Tues & Fri–Sun 11am–6.30pm or dusk; £7.50; NT), was described by Vita Sackville-West as "a garden crying out for rescue" when she and her husband took it over in the 1920s. Gradually, they transformed the five-acre plot into one of England's greatest and most popular modern gardens. Spread over the site of a medieval moated manor (which was rebuilt into an Elizabethan mansion of which only one wing remains today), the gardens were designed around the linear pattern of the former buildings' walls. A major part of Sissinghurst's appeal derives from the way that the flowers are allowed to spill over onto the narrow walkways, defying the classical formality of the great gardens that preceded it. The brick tower that Vita had restored and used as her study acts as a focal point and offers the best views of the walled gardens. Most impressive are the **White Garden**, composed solely of white flowers and silvery-grey foliage, and the **Cottage Garden**, featuring flora in shades of orange, yellow and red. **Bus** #297 from Royal Tunbridge Wells takes you within two miles of the gardens, while services #4 and #5 stop in Sissinghurst village on their run between Maidstone and Hastings.

Leeds Castle, fifteen miles north of Sissinghurst off the A20 (daily: April–Oct 11am–5pm; Nov–March 10.15am–3pm; grounds close 2hr later; castle, park & gardens £13, park & gardens £10.50), more closely resembles a fairy-tale palace than a defensively efficient fortress. Work on the castle began around 1120, half on an island in the middle of a lake and half on the mainland surrounded by landscaped parkland. Following centuries of regal and noble ownership (and, less glamorously, service as a prison) the castle is now run as a commercial concern, hosting conferences and sporting and cultural events. Its interior fails to match the castle's stunning external appearance and, in places, modern renovations have quashed its historical charm. The most unusual feature inside is the dog-collar museum in the gatehouse, while the grounds hold a fine aviary with some superb and colourful exotic specimens, as well as manicured gardens and a mildly challenging maze.

Sevenoaks and around

Set among the green sand ridges of west Kent, 25 miles from London, **SEVENOAKS** lost all but one of the ageing oaks from which it derives its name in a freakish storm that struck southern England in October 1987. With mere saplings having taken their place, the only real reason to visit the town is for the immense baronial estate of **Knole** (mid-March to Oct: house Wed–Sun noon–4pm; gardens Wed 11am–4pm; £6.40, gardens £2; NT), entered from the south end of Sevenoaks High Street. The house was created in 1456 by Archbishop Thomas Bourchier, who transformed the existing dwelling into a palace for himself and succeeding archbishops of Canterbury. The palace, numerically designed to match the calendar with 365 rooms, 7 courtyards and 52 staircases, was appropriated by Henry VIII, who lavished further expense on it and hunted in the thousand acres of **parkland** (free access throughout the year), still home to several hundred deer. Henry's daughter, Elizabeth I, passed the estate on to her cousin, Thomas Sackville, who remodelled the house in 1605. Part of Knole's allure is that it has preserved its Jacobean exterior and remained in the family's hands ever since. Vita Sackville-West, who in 1923 penned a definitive history of her family entitled *Knole and the Sackvilles*, was brought up here, and her one-time lover Virginia Woolf derived inspiration for her novel *Orlando* from her frequent visits to the house. The thirteen rooms open to the public feature an array of fine, if well-worn, furnishings and tapestries. Paintings by Gainsborough and Van Dyck are on display, as are Reynolds' depictions of George III and of Queen Charlotte.

Sevenoaks' **tourist office** is in the library (Mon–Sat 9.30am–5pm; Oct–March closes 4.30pm on Sat; ☎01732/450305, ⓦwww.heartofkent.org.uk), just beyond the **bus station** in Buckhurst Lane; the **train station** is north of the centre on London Road. Reasonable **accommodation** options include an attractive Edwardian B&B at 56 The Drive (☎01732/453236, ⓔslloydsks@aol .com; no smoking; ❷), close to the station, and *4 Old Timber Top Cottages*, Bethel Road (☎01732/460506, ⓦwww.timbertopcottage.co.uk; ❹), where you can have a timber-clad cottage to yourself. The nearest YHA **hostel** (☎0870/770 5890; £12.50) is an imposing Victorian vicarage in Kemsing, four miles north-east of Sevenoaks and a two-mile hike from Kemsing station; take bus #425/6 or #433 from Sevenoaks to Kemsing post office (not Sun).

For truly delicious food, go to *No. 5* (☎01732/455555), the restaurant at the *Royal Oak Hotel* at the south end of the High Street: it's pricey, but there's also a bistro in the bar, which serves decent evening meals at half the price. Alternatively, try the *Dorset Arms*, a better-than-average **pub** on Dorset Street.

Around Sevenoaks

Seven miles north of Sevenoaks and three quarters of a mile along the river west of the village of Eynsford, **Lullingstone Roman Villa** (April–Sept daily 10am–6pm; Oct, Nov, Feb & March daily 10am–4pm; Dec & Jan Wed–Sun 10am–4pm; £3.70; EH) has some of the best-preserved Roman mosaics in southeast England on show, in a pleasant location alongside the trickle of the River Darent. Believed to have been the first-century residence of a farmer, the site has yielded some fine marble busts now on display in the British Museum in London, but a superb floor remains, depicting the killing of the Chimera, a mythical fire-breathing beast with a lion's head, goat's body and a serpent's tail. Excavation in a nearby chamber has revealed early Christian iconography, which suggests that the villa may have become a Romano-Christian chapel in the third century, pre-empting the official arrival of that religion by three hundred years and making Lullingstone one of the earliest sites of clandestine Christian worship in England. From Sevenoaks there are hourly trains to Eynsford, from where it's a fifteen-minute walk.

Ten miles northwest of Sevenoaks in the village of Downe, **Down House** (Wed–Sun: April–Sept 10am–6pm; Oct 10am–5pm; Nov, Dec, Feb & March 10am–4pm; £6; EH) was home to the scientist Charles Darwin from 1842 until his death forty years later. Set in lovely grounds, overlooking the southeastern suburbs of London, the house is stuffed with Darwin memorabilia. Trains connect Sevenoaks with Orpington station, from where bus #R2 runs twice hourly (not Sun).

Six miles west of Sevenoaks, **Chartwell** (late March to June, Sept & Oct Wed–Sun 11am–5pm; July & Aug Tues–Sun 11am–5pm; £8; NT) was the residence of Winston Churchill from 1924 until his death in 1965. It's an unremarkable, heavily restored Tudor building whose main appeal is the wartime premier's memorabilia, including his paintings, which show an unexpectedly contemplative side to the famously gruff statesman. Entry to the house is by timed ticket at peak times – expect long queues. A direct bus service runs to Chartwell from Sevenoaks bus station four times daily on Sundays and public holidays.

The secluded, moated manor house of **Ightham Mote** (pronounced "I-tam"), six miles southeast of Sevenoaks just off the A227 (late March to Oct Mon, Wed–Fri, Sun & public holidays 10.30am–5.30pm; £7; NT), originates from the fourteenth century, though the original defensive appearance of this half-timbered ragstone building has been muted by Tudor alterations. A tour of the interior reveals a mixture of architectural styles ranging from the fourteenth-century Old Chapel and crypt, through a barrel-vaulted Tudor chapel with a painted ceiling to an eighteenth-century Palladian window. By bus, take the infrequent #404 from Sevenoaks (not Sun) to reach Ightham.

Hastings and around

During the twelfth and thirteenth centuries, **Hastings** flourished as an influential Cinque Port (see p.183), but in 1287 its harbour creek was silted up by the same storm that washed away nearby Winchelsea (see p.193). These days, Hastings is a curious mixture of unpretentious fishing port, traditional seaside resort and arty retreat popular with painters (there's even a street and quarter named Bohemia). In 1066, William, Duke of Normandy, landed at Pevensey Bay, a few miles west of town, and made Hastings his base, but his forces met Harold's army – exhausted after quelling a Nordic invasion near York – at **Battle**, six miles northwest of Hastings. Battle today boasts a magnificent abbey built by William in thanks for his victory. Further north, **Batemans**, once the home of Rudyard Kipling, and the classic **Bodiam Castle** are both easily reached from Hastings in a day-trip, as are the ancient Cinque Ports of **Rye** and **Winchelsea**, to the east.

Hastings

Hastings **old town**, east of the pier, holds most of the appeal of this part-tacky, part-pretty seaside resort. With the exception of the oddly neglected Regency architecture of **Pelham Crescent**, directly beneath the castle ruins, **All Saints Street** is by far the most evocative thoroughfare, punctuated with the odd, rickety, timber-framed dwelling from the fifteenth century. In the parallel High Street, the thirteenth-century **St Clement's Church** displays, at the top of its tower, a cannonball lodged by a Dutch galleon in the 1600s – its poignancy rather dispelled by a companion fitted in the eighteenth century for the sake of symmetry.

Down by the seafront, the area known as **The Stade** is characterized by its tall, black weatherboard **net shops**, most dating from the mid-nineteenth century (and still in use), but which first appeared here in Tudor times. On nearby Rock-a-Nore Road, a converted seaman's chapel houses the **Fisherman's Museum** (daily: April–Oct 10am–5pm; Nov–March 11am–4pm; free), which offers an account of the port's commercial activities and displays one of Hastings' last clinker-built luggers – a particularly hardy type of trawler. The neighbouring **Shipwreck Heritage Centre** (daily: Easter–Oct 10.30am–5pm; Nov–Easter 11am–4pm; free) details the dramas of local shipwrecks.

Castle Hill, separating the old town from the less interesting modern quarter, can be ascended by the **West Hill Cliff Railway**, from George Street, off Marine Parade. It's one of two Victorian funicular railways in Hastings, the other being the **East Cliff Railway**, on Rock-a-Nore Road (both daily: April–Oct 10.30am–5.30pm; Nov–March 11am–4.30pm; 90p). Castle Hill is where William the Conqueror erected his first **Castle** in 1066, built on the site of an existing fort, probably of Saxon origins. It was soon replaced by a more permanent stone structure, but in the thirteenth century storms caused the cliffs to subside, tipping most of the castle into the sea; the surviving ruins, however, offer an excellent prospect of the town. The castle is home to **The 1066 Story** (daily: May–Sept 11am–4pm; Oct–April 10am–3.30pm; £3.20), in which the events of the last successful invasion of the British mainland are described inside a mock-up of a siege tent.

Practicalities

Hastings' **train station** is a ten-minute walk from the seafront along Havelock Road; National Express **bus** services operate from the station at the junction of Havelock and Queen's roads. The **tourist office** is in the Town Hall on Queen's Road (Mon–Fri 8.30am–6.15pm, Sat 9am–5pm, Sun 10.30am–4.30pm; ☎01424/781111, ⓦwww.visithastings.com); there's also a smaller seafront office (Easter–Oct daily 10am–5pm; Nov–Easter Sat & Sun 11am–4pm; ☎01424/781120) near the Boating Lake on East Parade by the old town. You'll find **Internet** access at *Revolver Lounge*, 26 George St (☎01424/439899).

The best **accommodation** options are in the old town, where you'll find the cosy, timber-framed *Lavender and Lace*, 106 All Saints St (☎01424/716290, ⓦwww.lavenderlace1066.co.uk; closed Jan & Feb; no credit cards; ❸), and *Lionsdown House*, 116 High St (☎01424/420802, ⓦwww.lionsdownhouse .co.uk; no smoking; ❷), an authentic Wealden house serving organic breakfasts with homemade bread. The nearest YHA **hostel** is at *Guestling Hall* (☎0870/770 5850, ⓔhastings@yha.org.uk; £12.50), three miles east of Hastings on the road to Rye (bus #346 or #711). Hastings has a good range of affordable places for a **meal**, including *Harris*, 58 High St (☎01424/437221; closed Sun & Mon), where you can enjoy tapas in a wood-panelled setting, and *Pissarro's*, 10 South Terrace ☎01424/421363), offering a variety of bistro food with live jazz and blues accompaniment. The best fish and chips in town are served at *Mermaid*, 2 Rock-a-Nore, right by the beach.

Among the **pubs**, the local fishermen's favourite is the *Lord Nelson*, right by the front on The Bourne. On George Street, you can hear blues every Monday at *The Hastings Arms*, and jazz on Tuesdays at *The Anchor*; or check out the clubby bar, *The Street*, 53 Robertson St.

Battle

The town of **BATTLE** – a ten-minute train ride from Hastings – occupies the site of the most famous land battle in British history. Here, on October 14, 1066, the invading Normans swarmed up the hillside from Senlac Moor and overcame the Anglo-Saxon army of King Harold, who is thought to have been killed not by an arrow through the eye – a myth resulting from the misinterpretation of the Bayeux Tapestry – but by a workaday clubbing about the head. Before the battle took place, William vowed that, should he win the engagement, he would build a religious foundation on the very spot of Harold's slaying to atone for the bloodshed, and, true to his word, **Battle Abbey** (daily: April–Sept 10am–6pm; Oct–March 10am–4pm; £5.30; EH) was built four years later and subsequently occupied by a fraternity of Benedictines. The magnificent structure, though partially destroyed in the Dissolution and much rebuilt and revised over the centuries, still dominates the town, with the huge gatehouse, added in 1338, containing a good audiovisual exhibition on the battle. You can also wander through the ruins of the abbey to the spot where Harold was killed – the site of the high altar of William's abbey, now marked by a memorial stone.

Though nothing can match the resonance of the abbey, the rest of the town is worth a stroll. At the far end of High Street, the fourteenth-century **Almonry** – the present town hall – holds a **museum** (April–Oct Mon–Sat 10am–4.30pm, Sun 2–5pm; £1) that contains the only battle-axe discovered at Battle and the oldest Guy Fawkes in the country. Every year, on the Saturday nearest to November 5, this 300-year-old effigy is paraded along High Street at the head of a torch-lit procession culminating at a huge bonfire in front of the abbey gates – similar celebrations occur in Lewes (see p.197).

The **tourist office** is situated in the Gatehouse at Battle Abbey (daily: April–Sept 9.30am–5.30pm; Oct 9am–5pm; Nov–March 10am–4pm; ℡01424/773721, ⓦwww.battle-sussex.co.uk). Battle's **accommodation** tends to be expensive; less pricey B&Bs include the central and cosy *White Lodge*, 42 Hastings Rd (℡01424/772122, ⓔjanewhitelodge2@msn.com; ❷), with a heated outdoor pool in the summer, or the en-suite rooms above the *Gateway Restaurant*, 78 High St (℡01424/772856; ❷). The excellent *Food Rooms* delicatessen and **restaurant** at 53–55 High St (daytime only) serves locally sourced food, while town-centre **pubs** dishing up decent meals include the fifteenth-century *Old King's Head* on Mount Street and the *Chequers Inn* at Lower Lake, on High Street.

Rye and Winchelsea

Ten miles northeast of Hastings, perched on a hill overlooking the Romney Marshes, the ancient town of **RYE** was added as a "limb" to the original Cinque Ports (see p.183), but was subsequently marooned two miles inland by the retreat of the sea and the silting-up of the River Rother. It is now one of the most popular places in East Sussex – half-timbered, skew-roofed and quintessentially English, but also very commercialized.

From Strand Quay, head up The Deals to Rye's most picturesque street, the sloping cobbled **Mermaid Street**. At its eastern end, **Lamb House** (April–Oct Wed & Sat 2pm–6pm; £2.90; NT) was the home of the authors Henry James and (subsequently) E.F. Benson, while a blue plaque in the High Street testifies that Radclyffe Hall, author of the seminal lesbian novel, *The Well of Loneliness*, was also once a resident of the town. At the top of Mermaid Street is the peaceful oasis of Church Square, where **St Mary's Church** boasts the oldest functioning pendulum clock in the country; the ascent of the church tower offers fine views over the clay-tiled roofs. In the far corner of the square stands the **Ypres Tower** (April–Oct Mon & Thurs–Sun 10.30am–5pm; £1.90), formerly used to keep watch for cross-Channel invaders, and now a part of the **Rye Castle Museum** on nearby East Street (same times and price; combined ticket for both sites £2.90). Both places house a number of relics from Rye's past, including an eighteenth-century fire engine.

WINCHELSEA, sited on a hill two miles southwest of Rye and easily reached by train, bus, foot or bike, shares Rye's indignity of having become detached

△ Rye

from the sea, but has a very different character. Rye gets all the visitors, whereas Winchelsea feels positively deserted, an impression augmented as you pass through the medieval Strand Gate and see the ghostly ruined **Church of St Thomas à Becket**. Pillaged by the French in the fourteenth and fifteenth centuries, the church still constitutes the county's finest example of the Decorated style. Head south for a mile and a half and you get to **Winchelsea beach**, a long expanse of pebbly sand.

Practicalities

Rye's **train station** is at the bottom of Station Approach, off Cinque Ports Street, while Winchelsea's is a mile north of the town. **Bus #711** runs into the centre of both towns from Hastings. Rye's **tourist office** is on Strand Quay (March–Oct Mon–Sat 9.30am–5pm, Sun 10am–5pm; Nov–Feb daily 10am–4pm; ☎01797/226696, ⓦwww.visitrye .co.uk). The town's popularity with weekending Londoners gives it an excellent, but pricey, choice of **accommodation**. The most luxurious option is the atmospheric, fifteenth-century *Mermaid Inn* (☎01797/223065, ⓦwww .mermaidinn.com; ❼), on Mermaid Street, while the Georgian *Durrant House Hotel*, 2 Market St (☎01797/223182, ⓦwww.durranthouse.com; ❺), has a garden looking out towards Dungeness and the marshes. In Winchelsea, book in at the fourteenth-century *Strand House* (☎01797/226276, ⓦwww.thestrand-house.co.uk; ❸), at the foot of the cliff below Strand Gate. Rye's **restaurants** offer excellent seafood, for example the *Old Forge*, 24 Wish St (☎01797/223227), and the *Flushing Inn* on Market Street (☎01797/223292; closed Mon eve & all Tues). The daytime *Peacock Tearooms*, 8 Lion St (☎01797/226702), serves up snacks, cream teas and full meals in a suitably ancient setting. The fifteenth-century *Mermaid* on Mermaid Street is Rye's most atmospheric **pub**, with heavy exposed timbers throughout, though an excellent alternative is the *Ypres Castle* in Gun Gardens, down the steps behind the Ypres Tower.

Bodiam Castle

Bodiam Castle, nine miles north of Hastings (Feb–Oct daily 10am–6pm or dusk; Nov–Jan Sat & Sun 10am–4pm or dusk; £4.40; NT), is a classically stout square block with rounded corner turrets, battlements and a wide moat. When it was built in 1385 to guard what were the lower reaches of the River Rother, Bodiam was state-of-the-art military architecture, but during the Civil War, a company of Roundheads breached the fortress and removed its

Following the undulating crest of the South Downs, between the city of Winchester and the spectacular cliffs at Beachy Head, the **South Downs Way** extends over eighty miles along the chalk uplands, offering the Southeast's finest walks. If undertaken in its entirety, the bridle path is best traversed from west to east, taking advantage of the prevailing wind, Eastbourne's better transport services and accommodation, and the psychological appeal of ending at the sea. **Steyning**, the halfway-point, marks a transition between predominantly wooded sections and more exposed chalk uplands – to the east of here you'll pass the modern YHA **hostel** at Truleigh Hill (℡0870/770 6078, ℮truleigh@yha.org.uk; £12.50, ❶). Other hostels along the way are at Telscombe (℡0870/770 6062; £11.95), whose simple accommodation is in 200-year-old cottages, and Alfriston, where a southern loop can be taken which brings you to Eastbourne along the cliffs of the Seven Sisters. There's also a bunkhouse at Gumber Farm (℡01243/814484; closed Nov–Easter), near Bignor Hill.

The OS Landranger **maps** #198 and #199 cover the eastern end of the route; you'll need #185 and #197 as well to cover the lot. Half a dozen guides are available, the best being *A Guide to the South Downs Way* by Miles Jebb (Cicerone Press), and the more detailed *South Downs Way* by Paul Millmore (Aurum Press). You can also check the website ⓦwww.nationaltrails.gov.uk.

roof to reduce its effectiveness as a possible stronghold for the king. Over the next 250 years Bodiam fell into neglect until restoration in the last century by Lord Curzon. The extremely steep spiral staircases, leading to the crenellated battlements, will test all but the strongest of thighs. An absorbing fifteen-minute video portrays medieval life in a castle. You can get here from Hastings by regular bus #254.

Burwash and Bateman's

Fifteen miles northwest of Hastings on the A265, halfway to Tunbridge Wells, **BURWASH**, with its red-brick and weatherboarded cottages and Norman church tower, exemplifies the pastoral idyll of inland Sussex. Half a mile south of the village lies the main attraction, **Bateman's** (house & garden late March to Oct Mon–Wed, Sat, Sun & public holidays 11am–5pm; £5.90; garden only early March Sat & Sun 11am–4pm; Nov & Dec Wed–Sun 11am–4pm; £2.60; NT), home of the writer and journalist Rudyard Kipling from 1902 until his death in 1936. Built by a local ironmaster in the seventeenth century and set amid attractive gardens, the house features a working watermill converted by Kipling to generate electricity. Inside, the house displays Kipling's letters, early editions of his work and mementos from his travels on display. Getting to Bateman's without your own transport involves a three-mile walk from Etchingham Station, which is served by regular trains from Hastings.

Eastbourne and around

Like so many of the Southeast's seaside resorts, **EASTBOURNE** was kick-started into life in the 1840s, when the Brighton, Lewes and Hastings Rail Company built a branch line from Lewes to the sea. Past holiday-makers include George Orwell and the composer Claude Debussy, who finished writing *La Mer* here, as well as Marx and Engels. Nowadays Eastbourne has a solid reputation as a retirement town by the sea, with one of the grandest piers on the south coast jutting out from its long Promenade. The one lively exception to the prevailing sedateness is the **Towner Art Gallery and Museum** (Tues–Sat noon–5pm, Sun 2–5pm; free), a ten-minute walk northwest of the train station on High Street, Old Town. Its display of refreshingly contemporary works of art is complemented by the **"How We Lived Then" Museum of Shops**, just down from the tourist office at 20 Cornfield Terrace (daily 10am–5.30pm; £3.50), where a range of artefacts – old packages, coronation cups, toys – from the last hundred years of consumerism is crammed into mock-up shops spread over several floors.

The real reason to visit Eastbourne, however, is for expeditions onto the **South Downs**. A short walk west from Eastbourne takes you out along the most dramatic stretch of coastline in Sussex, where the chalk uplands are cut by the sea into a sequence of splendid cliffs. The most spectacular of all, **Beachy Head**, is 575ft high, with a diminutive-looking lighthouse, but no beach – the headland's name derives from the French *beau chef* meaning "beautiful head". The beauty certainly went to Friedrich Engels' head; he insisted his ashes be scattered here, and depressed individuals regularly try to join him by leaping to their doom from this well-known suicide spot. An open-top bus runs half-hourly (late May to Sept; £6.50) from Eastbourne Pier to the top of Beachy Head.

West of the headland the scenery softens into a diminishing series of chalk cliffs, a landmark known as the **Seven Sisters**. The eponymous country park provides some of the most impressive walks in the county, taking in the cliff-top path and the lower valley of the meandering River Cuckmere, into which the Seven Sisters subside.

Practicalities

Eastbourne's **train station** is a splendid Italianate terminus ten minutes' walk from the seafront up Terminus Road; the **bus station** is on Cavendish Place right by the pier. The **tourist office** is at 3 Cornfield Rd, just off Terminus Road (July to early Sept Mon–Sat 9.30am–5.30pm, Sun 10am–1pm; mid-Sept to June closed Sun; ☎01323/411400, ⊛www.eastbourne.org). The best **accommodation** options are *Sea Beach House Hotel*, 39–40 Marine Parade (☎01323/410458, ⊛www.seabeachhousehotel.com; ❹), right on the seafront, and *Sea Breeze Guest House*, 6 Marine Rd (☎01323/725440, ⊛www .seabreezeguesthouse.co.uk; no credit cards; ❷), just a hundred yards from the sea. If you'd rather stay near the South Downs Way, check in at the *Birling Gap Hotel* (☎01323/423197, ⊛www.birlinggaphotel.co.uk; ❸), a Victorian villa overlooking the dramatic cliffs between Seven Sisters and Beachy Head, or bed down at the Frog Firle YHA **hostel** (☎0870/770 5666, ⊜alfriston@yha .org.uk; £12.50) in a traditional Sussex flint building a couple of miles south of Alfriston.

The best **restaurant** is the *Café Belge* on the seafront at 11–23 Grand Parade, good for *moules et frites* and snack lunches. Otherwise head for the concentration of moderately priced places in the Terminus Road area, between the train station and the sea. If you're in need of a large ice-cream sundae, go to *Fusciardi's* opposite the Winter Gardens on Carlyle Road. The most amenable **pubs** are some distance from the seafront: the *Lamb* on the High Street and the *Hurst Arms* at 76 Willingdon Rd, a ten-minute walk inland from the station up Upperton Road.

Lewes and around

East Sussex's county town, **LEWES** straddles the River Ouse as it carves a gap through the South Downs on its final stretch to the sea. Though there's been some rebuilding, the core of Lewes remains remarkably good-looking: Georgian and crooked older dwellings still line the High Street and the narrow lanes – or "Twittens" – that lead off the High Street and its continuations, with views onto the Downs. With some of England's most appealing chalkland close by and numerous traces of its long history still visible, Lewes is a worthwhile stopover on any tour of the Southeast – and an easy one, with good rail connections with London and along the coast.

Following the Norman Conquest, William's son-in-law, William de Warenne, built a priory and castle here, the latter still dominating the High Street. In 1264 Henry III's incompetence caused a baronial revolt led by Simon de Montfort which culminated in the king's surrender at the Battle of Lewes, although de Montfort and his reduced force were annihilated within a year at the Battle of Evesham. De Montfort's name crops up all over the town, as do references to the Lewes Martyrs, the seventeen Protestants burned here in 1556, at the height of Mary Tudor's militant revival of Catholicism – an event commemorated in spectacular fashion every November 5 (see box below).

Within a few miles of Lewes lies a trio of places worth visiting: two houses associated with the Bloomsbury group – **Rodmell** and **Charleston** – and the mecca for picnicking opera-lovers, **Glyndebourne**.

The Town

The best way to begin a tour of the town from the train station is to walk up Station Road, then left down the High Street. Lewes's **Castle** (Tues–Sat 10am–5.30pm, Sun & Mon 11am–5.30pm; closed Mon in Jan; winter closes at dusk; £4.40) is hidden from view behind the houses on your right. Inside the castle complex – unusual for being built on two mottes, or mounds – the shell

---

The bonfire societies

Each November 5, while the rest of Britain lights small domestic bonfires or attends municipal firework displays to commemorate the 1605 foiling of a Catholic plot to blow up the Houses of Parliament, Lewes puts on a more dramatic show, whose origins lie in the deaths of the town's Protestant martyrs. By the end of the eighteenth century, Lewes's **Bonfire Boys** had become notorious for the boisterousness of their anti-Catholic demonstrations, in which they set off fireworks indiscriminately and dragged rolling tar barrels through the streets – a tradition still practised today, although with a little more caution. In 1845 events came to a head when the incorrigible pyromaniacs of Lewes had to be read the Riot Act, instigating a night of violence between the police and Bonfire Boys. Lewes's first **bonfire societies** were established soon afterwards to instil some discipline into the proceedings, and in the early twentieth century they were persuaded to move their street fires to the town's perimeters.

Today's tightly knit bonfire societies spend much of the year organizing the Bonfire Night shenanigans, when their members dress up in traditional costumes and parade through the town carrying flaming torches, before marching off onto the Downs for their society's big fire. At each of the fires, effigies of Guy Fawkes and the pope are burned alongside contemporary, but equally reviled, figures – chancellors of the exchequer and prime ministers are popular choices.

of the eleventh-century keep remains, and both the towers can be climbed for excellent views over the town to the surrounding Downs. Tickets for the castle include admission to the **museum** (same hours as castle), by the castle entrance, which is much better than the usual stuffy town museum.

A few minutes' walk further west along the High Street, past St Michael's Church with its unusual twin towers, one wooden and the other flint, brings you to the steep, cobbled and much photographed **Keere Street**, down which the reckless Prince Regent is alleged to have driven his carriage. Keere Street leads to **Southover Grange** (Mon–Sat 8am–dusk, Sun 9am–dusk; free), with its lovely gardens. Built in 1572 from the priory's remains, the Grange was also the childhood home of the diarist John Evelyn and now houses the local Registry Office. Past the gardens, a right turn down Southover High Street leads to the Tudor-built **Anne of Cleves House** (Tues–Sat 10am–5pm; March–Oct also Mon 11am–5pm; £3, combined ticket with the castle £6.20), given to her in settlement after her divorce from Henry VIII – though she never actually lived there. The magnificent oak-beamed Tudor bedroom is impressive, with its cumbersome "bed wagon", a bed-warming brazier which would fail the slackest of fire regulations but which the 400-year-old Flemish four-poster has managed to survive.

On the opposite side of the road and closer to the train station is the church of **St John the Baptist**, with its squat, brick tower capped by a six-foot shark for a weather vane; inside there's some superb stained glass and a tiny chapel with the lead coffins of William de Warenne and his wife Gundrada, William I's daughter. De Warenne was one of the six barons presiding over the new administrative provinces – known as the **Rapes of Sussex** – created by the Normans soon after the Conquest. Behind the church are the ruins of de Warenne's **St Pancras Priory**, once one of Europe's principal Cluniac institutions, with a church the size of Westminster Abbey. Sadly it was dismantled to build townhouses following the Dissolution and is now an evocative ruin surrounded by playing fields.

At the east end of the High Street, School Hill descends towards **Cliffe Bridge**, built in 1727 and entrance to the commercial centre of the medieval settlement. For the energetic, a path leads up onto the Downs from the end of Cliffe High Street, passing close to an obelisk commemorating the town's seventeen Protestant martyrs.

Practicalities

The **train station** lies south of High Street down Station Road, and the **bus station** is on Eastgate Street, near the foot of School Hill. The **tourist office** is at the junction of the High Street and Fisher Street (April–Sept Mon–Fri 9am–5pm, Sat 10am–5pm, Sun 10am–2pm; Oct–March Mon–Fri 9am–5pm, Sat 10am–2pm; ☏01273/483448, ⓦwww.lewes.gov.uk). For **accommodation**, try *Castle Banks Cottage*, 4 Castle Banks (☏01273/476291, ⓦwww.s-h-systems.co.uk; no smoking; no credit cards; ❸), a beamed period house with great views, tucked away off West Street, or, failing that, *The Crown Inn*, 191 High St, close to the tourist office (☏01273/480670, ⓦwww.crowninn-lewes.co.uk; ❸). The nearest YHA **hostel** is in the village of Telscombe, six miles south of Lewes (see below); there's another – a rustic wooden cabin with basic facilities – eleven miles northeast of town at Blackboys, near Uckfield (☏0870/770 5698; £11.95, ❶).

Lewes is home of the excellent Harvey's brewery and most of the **pubs** serve its wares. On the outskirts of town, the lively *Snowdrop Inn* at South Street also serves excellent **food** including vegetarian and vegan options, while *Pelham House* is a stylish brasserie on St Andrews Lane (☎01273/488600).

Around Lewes: Glyndebourne, Rodmell and Charleston

Glyndebourne, Britain's only unsubsidized opera house, is situated near the village of Glynde, three miles east of Lewes. Founded in 1934, the Glyndebourne season (mid-May to Aug) is an indispensable part of the high-society calendar, with ticket prices and a distribution system that excludes all but the most devoted opera-lovers. While the spectacle of lawns thronged with gentry and corporate bigwigs ingesting champagne and smoked salmon may put you off, the musical values at Glyndebourne are the highest in the country, using young talent rather than expensive star names, and taking the sort of risks Covent Garden wouldn't dream of. A new, award-winning theatre (seating 1200) has broadened the appeal of this exclusive venue to a wider audience, and there are tickets available at reduced prices for dress rehearsals or for standing-room-only; call ☎01273/813813 or check ⓦwww.glyndebourne.com.

Three miles south of Lewes, the main source of interest at the village of **RODMELL** is the **Monk's House** (April–Oct Wed & Sat 2–5.30pm; £2.90; NT), former home of Virginia Woolf, a leading figure of the Bloomsbury Group (see box below). She and her husband, Leonard, moved to the weatherboarded

The Bloomsbury Group

The **Bloomsbury Group** were essentially a bevy of upper-middle-class friends who took their name from the Bloomsbury area of London, where most of them lived before acquiring houses in the Sussex countryside. The Group revolved around Virginia, Vanessa, Thoby and Adrian Stephen, who lived at 46 Gordon Square, the London base of the Bloomsbury Group. Thoby's Thursday-evening gatherings and Vanessa's Friday Club for painters attracted a whole host of Cambridge-educated snobs who subscribed to Oscar Wilde's theory that "aesthetics are higher than ethics". Their diet of "human intercourse and the enjoyment of beautiful things" was hardly revolutionary, but their behaviour, particularly that of the two sisters (unmarried, unchaperoned, intellectual and artistic), succeeded in shocking London society, especially through their louche sexual practices (most of the group swung both ways).

All this, though interesting, would be forgotten were it not for their individual work. In 1922 Virginia declared, without too much exaggeration, "Everyone in Gordon Square has become famous": Lytton Strachey had been the first to make his name with *Eminent Victorians*, a series of unprecedentedly frank biographies; Vanessa, now married to the art critic Clive Bell, had become involved in Roger Fry's prolific design firm, Omega Workshop; and the economist John Maynard Keynes had become an adviser to the Treasury (he later went on to become the leading economic theorist of his day). The Group's most celebrated figure, Virginia, married Leonard Woolf and became an established novelist; she and Leonard also founded the Hogarth Press, which published T.S. Eliot's *The Waste Land* in 1922.

Eliot was just one of a number of writers, such as Aldous Huxley, Bertrand Russell and E.M. Forster, who were drawn to the interwar Bloomsbury set, but others, notably D.H. Lawrence, were repelled by the clan's narcissism and snobbish narrow-mindedness. Whatever their limitations, the Bloomsbury Group were Britain's most influential intellectual coterie of the interwar years, and their appeal shows little sign of waning today.

cottage in 1919 and Leonard stayed there until his death in 1969; both Virginia's and Leonard's remains are interred in the gardens. Nearby, you can see the River Ouse where Virginia killed herself in 1941 by walking into the water with her pockets full of stones. Inside, Bloomsbury fans can look round the study where Virginia wrote several of her novels, and her bedroom, which is laid out with period editions of her work. To get there, catch a train to Southease, from where it's a mile northwest to Rodmell village, across the river.

Six miles east of Lewes, off the A27, is another Bloomsbury Group shrine, **Charleston Farmhouse** (March–June, Sept & Oct Wed–Sun & public holidays 2–6pm; July & Aug Wed–Sat 11.30am–6pm, Sun & public holidays 2–6pm; £6; guided tours Wed–Sat; last entry 5pm), home to Virginia Woolf's sister Vanessa Bell, Vanessa's husband, Clive Bell, and her lover, Duncan Grant. As conscientious objectors, the trio moved here during World War I so that the men could work on local farms (farm labourers were exempted from military service). The farmhouse became a gathering point for other members of the Bloomsbury Group, and Duncan Grant continued to live here until his death in 1978. Almost every surface of the farmhouse interior is painted and the walls are hung with paintings by Picasso, Renoir and Augustus John, alongside the work of the markedly less talented residents. Many of the fabrics, lampshades and other artefacts bear the unmistakeable mark of the Omega Workshop, the Bloomsbury equivalent of William Morris's artistic movement.

Brighton

Recorded as the tiny fishing village of Brithelmeston in the Domesday Book, **BRIGHTON** seems to have slipped unnoticed through history until the mid-eighteenth-century sea-bathing trend established it as a resort that has never looked back since. The fad received royal approval in the 1780s when the decadent Prince of Wales (the future George IV) began patronizing the town in the company of his mistress, thus setting a precedent for the "dirty weekend", Brighton's major contribution to the English collective consciousness. Trying to shake off this blowsy reputation, Brighton now highlights its Georgian charm, its upmarket shops and classy restaurants, and its thriving conference industry. Yet, however much it tries to present itself as a comfortable middle-class town (granted city status in 2000), the essence of Brighton's appeal is its faintly bohemian vitality, a buzz that comes from a mix of English holiday-makers, thousands of young foreign students from the town's innumerable language schools, a thriving gay community and an energetic local student population from the art college and two universities.

Arrival, information and accommodation

Brighton **train station** is at the head of Queen's Road, which descends to the Clocktower and then becomes West Street, eventually leading to the seafront. The **bus station** is tucked just in from the seafront on the south side of the Old Steine. The **tourist office** is at 10 Bartholomew Square (June–Sept Mon–Fri 9am–5.30pm, Sat 10am–5pm; Oct–May Mon–Sat 9am–5pm; also March–Oct Sun 10am–4pm; ☎0906/7112255, ⊛www.visitbrighton.com), behind the town hall on the southern side of the Lanes – the maze of narrow alleyways marking Brighton's old town. There's **Internet** access at Internet Junction, 101 St George's Rd, and the Jubilee Library, Jubilee Street.

You'll find most budget **accommodation** clustered around the **Kemp Town** district, to the east of the Palace Pier, with the more elegant and expensive hotels west of the town centre around Regency Square. Brighton's official **campsite** is the *Sheepcote Valley* site (☎01273/626546), just north of Brighton Marina; take bus #1 or #7 to Wilson Avenue, or take the Volks railway and walk up Arundel Road to Wilson Avenue.

Hotels and B&Bs

Ainsley House 28 New Steine ☎01273/605310, ⓦwww.ainsleyhotel.com. Friendly, upmarket guest house in an attractive Regency terrace. **②**

Four Seasons 3 Upper Rock Gardens ☎01273/673574, ⓦwww.hotel4seasons.co.uk. Bright and light B&B in the Kemp Town area, offering good vegetarian breakfast options. No smoking. **④**

Hotel du Vin Ship Street ☎01273/718588, ⓦwww.hotelduvin.com. A Gothic Revival building in a contemporary style, luxuriously furnished in subtle seaside colours with an excellent bar and bistro. **⑦**

Hudsons 22 Devonshire Place ☎01273/683642, ⓦwww.hudsonsbrighton. co.uk. Relaxed and exclusively gay and lesbian guest house east of the centre off St James Street. **④**

Lichfield House 30 Waterloo St ☎01273/777740, ⓦwww.lichfieldhouse.freeserve.co.uk. Stylishly and colourfully furnished townhouse. **③**

New Europe 31–32 Marine Parade ☎01273/624462, ⓦwww.neweuropehotel.co.uk. Large, buzzing, gay hotel on the seafront, with late bar and regular cabaret nights. **④**

Pelirocco 10 Regency Square ☎01273/327055, ⓦwwww.hotelpelirocco .co.uk. Self-styled rock'n'roll hangout with themed rooms, a Bohemian atmosphere and a late-opening bar. **⑤**–**⑥**

Sussex Arts Club 7 Ship St ☎01273/727371, ⓦwww.sussexarts.com. Laid-back and lively hotel, though with just seven rooms, in a Regency house right in the centre of town. There's a pub on the ground floor and a club in the basement. **⑤**

The Twenty One 21 Charlotte St, off Marine Parade ☎01273/686450, ⓦwww.s-h-systems .co.uk. Classy Kemp Town B&B with very comfortable rooms in an ornate, early Victorian house. **④**

Hostels

Baggies Backpackers 33 Oriental Place ☎01273/733740. Spacious house a little west of the West Pier with large bright dorms, starting at £13 a night, and decent showers. No credit cards. **①**

Brighton Backpackers 75 Middle St ☎01273/777717, ⓦwww.brightonbackpackers .com. Established independent hostel with a lively, easy-going atmosphere. An annexe just round the

corner overlooks the seafront and offers a quieter alternative; dorm beds £11. No credit cards. **①**

YHA Hostel Patcham Place, London Road ☎0870/770 5724, ⓔbrighton@yha.org.uk. Brighton's YHA hostel is housed in a splendid Queen Anne mansion four miles north of the sea, close to the junction of the roads to Lewes and London. Bus #5, #5A, #107 or #770/1 from the town centre. Dorm beds £16.

The City

Any visit to Brighton inevitably begins with a visit to its two most famous landmarks – the exuberant **Royal Pavilion** and the wonderfully tacky **Palace Pier**, a few minutes away – followed by a stroll along the seafront promenade or the pebbly beach. Just as interesting, though, is an exploration of Brighton's car-free **Lanes**, where some of the town's diverse restaurants, bars and tiny bric-a-brac, jewellery and antique shops can be found, or a meander through the quaint, but more bohemian streets of **North Laine**.

The Royal Pavilion and Brighton Museum

In any survey to find England's most loved building, there's always a bucketful of votes for Brighton's exotic extravaganza, the **Royal Pavilion** (daily: April–Sept 9.30am–5.45pm; Oct–March 10am–5.15pm; £6.10), which flaunts

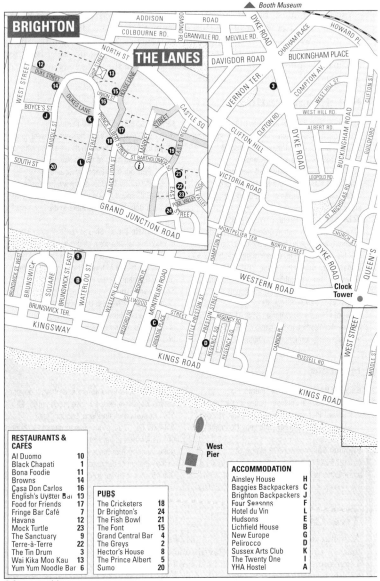

RESTAURANTS & CAFES

Al Duomo	10
Black Chapati	1
Bona Foodie	11
Browns	14
Casa Don Carlos	16
English's Oyster Bar	19
Food for Friends	17
Fringe Bar Café	7
Havana	12
Mock Turtle	23
The Sanctuary	9
Terre-à-Terre	22
The Tin Drum	3
Wai Kika Moo Kau	13
Yum Yum Noodle Bar	6

PUBS

The Cricketers	18
Dr Brighton's	24
The Fish Bowl	21
The Font	15
Grand Central Bar	4
The Greys	2
Hector's House	8
The Prince Albert	5
Sumo	20

ACCOMMODATION

Ainsley House	H
Baggies Backpackers	C
Brighton Backpackers	J
Four Seasons	F
Hotel du Vin	L
Hudsons	E
Lichfield House	B
New Europe	G
Pelirocco	D
Sussex Arts Club	K
The Twenty One	I
YHA Hostel	A

itself in the middle of the main thoroughfare of Old Steine. The building was a conventional farmhouse until 1787, when the fun-loving Prince of Wales converted it into something more regal, and for a couple of decades the prince's south-coast pied-à-terre was a Palladian villa, with mildly Oriental embellishments. Upon becoming Prince Regent, however, George commissioned John Nash, architect of London's Regent Street, to build an

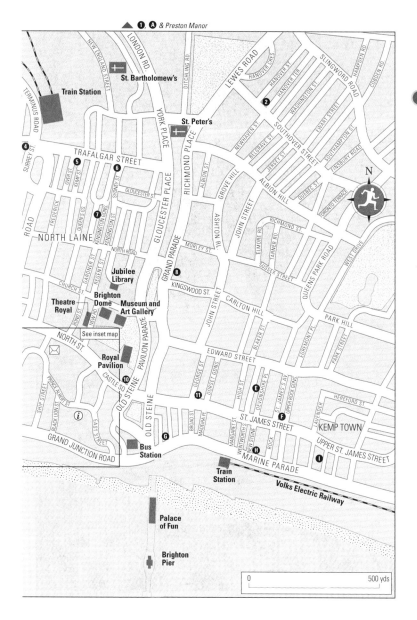

extraordinary confection of slender minarets, twirling domes, pagodas, balconies and miscellaneous motifs imported from India and China. Supported on an innovative cast-iron frame, the result defined a genre of its own – Oriental Gothic. The dour Queen Victoria was not amused by George's taste in architecture, however, and all the Pavilion's valuable fittings were carted off to her London palaces. The gutted building has now been brilliantly restored, its

△ The Royal Pavilion, Brighton

exuberant compendium of Regency exotica enhanced by the return of many of the objects that Victoria had taken away.

One of the highlights – approached via the restrained Long Gallery – is the **Banqueting Room**, which erupts with ornate splendour and is dominated by a one-ton chandelier hung from the jaws of a massive dragon cowering in a plantain tree. Next door, the huge, high-ceilinged kitchen, fitted with the most modern appliances of its time, has iron columns disguised as palm trees. The stunning **Music Room**, the first sight of which reduced George to tears of joy, has a huge dome lined with more than twenty-six thousand individually gilded scales and hung with exquisite umbrella-like glass lamps. After climbing the famous cast-iron staircase with its bamboo-look banisters, you can go into Victoria's sober and seldom-used bedroom and the North Gallery where the king's portrait hangs, along with a selection of satirical cartoons. More notable, though, is the **South Gallery**, decorated in sky blue with trompe l'oeil bamboo trellises and a carpet that appears to be strewn with flowers.

Across the gardens from the Pavilion stands the **Dome**, once the royal stables and now the town's main concert hall. Adjoining it is the refurbished **Brighton Museum and Art Gallery** (Tues 10am–7pm, Wed–Sat & public holidays 10am–5pm, Sun 2–5pm; free), which is entered just around the corner on Church Street. It houses an eclectic mix of modern fashion and design, archeology, painting and local history, including a large collection of pottery from basic Neolithic earthenware to delicate eighteenth-century porcelain figurines. The highlight of the collection of classic Art Deco and Art Nouveau furniture is Dalí's famous sofa based on Mae West's lips. The *Balcony Café* is the perfect setting for a coffee or tea.

The rest of the town

Tucked between the Pavilion and the seafront is a warren of narrow, pedestrianized thoroughfares known as **the Lanes** – the core of the old fishing village from which Brighton evolved. Long-established antiques shops, designer outlets and several bars, pubs and restaurants generate a lively and intimate atmosphere in this part of town.

North Laine, which spreads north of North Street along Kensington, Sydney, Gardner and Bond streets, is more bohemian than the Lanes, with its hub along pedestrianized Kensington Gardens. Here the eclectic shops, selling secondhand records, clothes, bric-a-brac and New Age objects, mingle with earthy coffee shops and funky cafés.

Off North Road on Jubilee Street, the **Jubilee Library** (Mon & Tues 10am–7pm, Wed & Fri 10am–2pm, Thurs 10am–8pm, Sat 10am–4pm), opened in 2005, has already become an icon of Brighton's new metropolitan image. The generous glass front complemented by blue ceramic tiling gives access to its lofty interior, in which modern sculptures mingle with state-of-the-art technology, including free **Internet** points.

Much of Brighton's **seafront** is an ugly mix of shops, entertainment complexes and hotels such as the impressively pompous *Grand Hotel* – scene of the IRA's attempted assassination of the Conservative Cabinet in October 1984. To soak up the tackier side of Brighton, take a stroll along **Brighton Pier**, completed in 1899, whose every inch is devoted to cacophonous fun and money-making (the architecturally superior West Pier, built half a mile west along the seafront in 1866, has fallen into disrepair, though is currently being restored to its former glory). From near Brighton Pier, the antiquated locomotives of **Volk's Electric Railway** (Easter to mid-Sept Mon–Fri 11am–5pm, Sat & Sun 11am–6pm; £2.40 return) – the first electric train in the country – run eastward towards the Marina and the nudist beach, usually the preserve of just a few thick-skinned souls.

In Brighton's northern suburbs, the **Booth Museum of Natural History** (Mon–Wed, Fri & Sat 10am–5pm, Sun 2–5pm; free), a mile up Dyke Road from the centre of town (bus #26 or #26A), is worth seeking out – a wonderfully fusty old Victorian museum with beetles, butterflies and animal skeletons galore, as well as some imaginative temporary exhibitions.

Eating, drinking and nightlife

Brighton has the greatest concentration of **restaurants** in the Southeast after London. Around North Laine are some great, inexpensive cafés, while for classier establishments head to the Lanes and out towards Hove. Many of the cheaper places offer discounts of around ten percent to students, so bring ID. **Nightlife** is hectic and compulsively pursued throughout the year: as well as the mainstream **theatre** and **concert** venues, there are myriad **clubs**, lots of **live music** and plenty of cinemas. Brighton has one of Britain's longest-established and most thriving **gay communities**, with a variety of lively clubs and bars drawing people from all over. It also hosts a number of gay events including the annual **Gay Pride Festival**, held over two weeks at the beginning of July – check out ⓦ www.gay.brighton.co.uk. In May, the three-week-long **Brighton Festival** (ⓣ01273/709709, ⓦ www.brighton-festival.org.uk) includes funfairs, exhibitions, street theatre and concerts from classical to jazz. For up-to-date details of **what's on**, there's an array of free listings magazines available from the tourist office, or check out the website ⓦ www.brighton.co.uk.

Cafés

Bona Foodie 21 St James's St, Kemp Town. Delicatessen with colourful, cosy café at the back, serving excellent baguettes; choose from the speciality patés and cheeses or come early for lunching in.

Fringe Bar Café 10 Kensington Gardens. Small, smart bar, with a terrace, serving good breakfasts, homemade burgers and salads. There's a restaurant below as well.

Mock Turtle 4 Pool Valley. Old-fashioned teashop crammed with bric-a-brac and inexpensive homemade cakes. Closed Sun & Mon.

The Sanctuary 51–55 Brunswick St East, Hove ⓣ01273/770002. Cool and arty vegetarian café with a relaxed ambience and cellar performance venue.

Restaurants

Al Duomo 7 Pavilion Buildings ⓣ01273/326741. Brilliant pizzeria, with a wood-burning oven. There's a more intimate sister restaurant, *Al Forno*, at 36 East St (ⓣ01273/324905). Inexpensive.

Black Chapati 12 Circus Parade ⓣ01273/699011. Innovative Asian cooking with Japanese and Thai influences as well as more conventional Indian dishes. Something of a Brighton landmark despite its out-of-the-way location, more than a mile inland, at the point where the London road enters town. Closed Mon. Moderate.

Browns 3–4 Duke St ⓣ01273/323501. A mixture of meat, seafood and pasta dishes as well as traditional favourites like Guinness-marinated

steak-and-mushroom pie, served in a continental setting. Moderate.

Casa Don Carlos 5 Union St ⓣ01273/327177. Small tapas bar in the Lanes with outdoor seating and daily specials. Also serves more substantial Spanish dishes and drinks. Inexpensive.

English's Oyster Bar 29–31 East St ⓣ01273/327980. Three fishermen's cottages knocked together to house a marble-and-brass oyster bar and a red-velvet dining room. Seafood's the speciality with a mouthwatering menu and better value than you might expect, especially the set menus. Expensive.

Food for Friends 17 Prince Albert St ⓣ01273/202310. Brighton's ever-popular wholefood veggie eatery is imaginative enough to please die-hard meat-eaters too. It's usually busy, but well worth the squeeze. Moderate.

Havana 32 Duke St ⓣ01273/773388. Very stylish continental brasserie with just a hint of tropical ambience. The menu is French influenced – the lunchtime deal is particularly good value. Expensive.

Terre-à-Terre 71 East St ⓣ01273/729051. Imaginative, global, veggie cuisine in a modern arty setting. Closed Mon lunch. Moderate–Expensive.

The Tin Drum 95–97 Dyke Rd ⓣ01273/777575. Buzzing continental-style café-bar and restaurant with a taste for Baltic-rim cooking and a blend of Eastern European influences; fresh seasonal ingredients and speciality vodkas. Moderate.

Wai Kika Moo Kau 42 Meeting House Lane ⓣ01273/323824. Funky global veggie

café/restaurant with everything from Thai curry to aubergine bake – all for around £5. Live music most evenings. Inexpensive.
Yum Yum Noodle Bar 22–23 Sydney St

☎01273/606777. Serves anything Southeast Asian – Chinese, Thai, Indonesian and Malaysian noodle dishes – situated above a Chinese supermarket. Lunch only. Inexpensive.

Pubs and bars

The Cricketers 15 Black Lion St. Just west of the Lanes, this is Brighton's oldest pub and it looks it too; very popular with good daytime pub grub served in its Courtyard Bar.
Dr Brighton's 16 King's Rd. Popular gay venue.
The Fish Bowl 74 East St. A popular pre-club choice for its range of music – sometimes better than the clubs themselves – and a good daytime menu.
The Font Union Street. Spacious converted chapel with a bar in place of the altar and occasional live music.
Grand Central Bar 29–30 Surrey St. Cool, light and comfy bar opposite the station. Exemplary, well-priced breakfasts and snacks; live jazz and funk at weekends.

The Greys 105 Southover St. Old-fashioned pub with an open fire, stone floors and wooden benches, plus good food and Belgian beers. Frequent live bands.
Hector's House 52 Grand Parade. Big bare-boards-and-sofa student pub that has nightly pre-club music (except Mon) with in-house DJs.
The Prince Albert 48 Trafalgar St. A listed build-ing, right by the train station, popular with students. Live rock upstairs, real ale downstairs; regular theme nights.
Sumo 8–12 Middle St. Designer-cool Pacific-rim bar with DJs spinning R&B and hip-hop, plus Internet access.

Nightlife

Audio 10 Marine Parade ☎01273/606906, ⓦwww.audiobrighton.co.uk. Brighton's trendiest nightclub packs them in night after night, special-izing in funk and house.
Concorde 2 Madeira Shelter, Madeira Drive ☎01273/772770, ⓦwww.concorde2.co.uk. Live music venue, with an admirably eclectic booking policy; also has club nights at the weekend.
Funky Buddha Lounge 169 King's Road Arches ☎01273/725541, ⓦwww.funkybuddha.co.uk. Tiny venue renowned for progressive house, breakbeats and soul.
Hanbury Ballroom St George's Rd, ☎01273/605789. Kemp Town's answer to main-

stream clubs – anything from Japanese manga music to jamming on laptops, plus party nights.
Honey Club 214 King's Rd Arches ☎01273/202807, ⓦwww.thehoneyclub.co.uk. Garage, trance, house, hip-hop, you name it, this club has a night for it – and big-name DJs.
Revenge 32 Old Steine ☎01273/606064, ⓦwww.revenge.co.uk. The South's largest gay club with Monday-night cabarets plus upfront dance and retro boogie on two floors.
The Zap 180–192 Kings Road Arches ☎01273/202407. Brighton's most durable club, right on the seafront spanning Seventies and Eight-ies disco and funky house; dress up.

Mid-Sussex: Sheffield Park and the Bluebell Railway

Around twenty miles northeast of Brighton, the centrepiece of the country estate of **Sheffield Park** is a Gothic mansion built for Lord Sheffield by James Wyatt. The house is closed to the public, but you can roam around the hundred-acre **gardens** (Jan to mid-Feb Sat & Sun 10.30am–4pm; mid-Feb to April & June–Sept Tues–Sun 10.30–6pm or dusk; May & Oct daily 10.30am–6pm; Nov & Dec Tues–Sun 10.30am–4pm; £5.50; combined ticket with Bluebell Railway £12.50; NT), which were laid out by Capability Brown. A mile southwest of the gardens lies the southern terminus of the **Bluebell Railway** (May–Sept daily; Oct–April Sat, Sun & school holidays; day ticket £9.50; ☎01825/722370

24hr information line, Ⓦ www.bluebell-railway.co.uk), whose vintage steam locomotives chuff nine miles north via Horsted Keynes to Kingscote. The service gets extremely crowded at weekends – especially in May, when the bluebells blossom in the woods through which the line passes.

Arundel and around

The hilltop town of **ARUNDEL**, eighteen miles west of Brighton, has for seven centuries been the seat of the dukes of Norfolk, whose fine castle looks over the valley of the River Arun. The medieval town's well-preserved appearance and picturesque setting draws in the crowds on summer weekends, but at any other time a visit reveals one of West Sussex's least spoilt old towns. North of here lie two contrasting sites: **Bignor Roman Villa**, containing some of the best Roman mosaics in the country, and the grand seventeenth-century **Petworth House**, replete with an impressive collection of paintings.

Arundel Castle, towering over the High Street (April–Oct Mon–Fri & Sun 11am–5pm; castle, keep, grounds & chapel £11; keep, grounds & chapel £6.50), is what first catches the eye in Arundel. Despite its medieval appearance, most of what you see is little more than a century old, the result of a lavish reconstruction from 1718 onwards, following the original Norman structure that was destroyed during the Civil War. From the top of the keep, you can see the current duke's spacious residence and the pristine castle grounds. Inside the castle, the renovated quarters include the impressive **Barons Hall** and the **library**, which boasts paintings by Gainsborough, Holbein and Van Dyck. On the edge of the castle grounds, the fourteenth-century **Fitzalan Chapel** houses tombs of past dukes of Norfolk including twin effigies of the seventh duke – one as he looked when he died and, underneath, one of his emaciated corpse. The Catholic chapel belongs to the Norfolk estate, but is actually physically joined to the **Church of St Nicholas**, the parish church, whose entrance is in London Road. It is separated from the altar of the main Anglican church by an iron grille and a glass screen. Although traditionally Catholics, the dukes of Norfolk have shrewdly played down their papal allegiance in sensitive times – such as during the Tudor era when two of the third duke's nieces, Anne Boleyn and Catherine Howard, became Henry VIII's wives.

West of the parish church, further along London Road, is Arundel's other major landmark, the towering Gothic bulk of **Arundel Cathedral** (daily 9am–6pm or dusk). Constructed in the 1870s by the fifteenth duke of Norfolk over the town's former Catholic church, the cathedral's spire was designed by John Hansom, inventor of the hansom cab, the earliest taxi. Inside are the enshrined remains of St Philip Howard, the fourth duke's son, who returned to the Catholic fold at a time when the Armada's defeat saw anti-Catholic feelings soar, and spent a decade in the Tower of London, where he died. The cathedral's impressive outline is more appealing than the interior, but it fits in well with the townscape of the medieval seaport. The rest of Arundel is pleasant to wander round, with the antique-shop-lined Maltravers and Arun streets being the most attractive thoroughfares.

Practicalities

Arundel is served by regular trains from London Victoria, Portsmouth, Brighton and Chichester. The **train station** is half a mile south of the town centre over the river on the A27, with **buses** arriving either on High Street or River Road. The **tourist office** is at 61 High St (Easter–Oct Mon–Sat 10am–6pm, Sun 10am–4pm; Nov–Easter daily 10am–3pm; ☎01903/882268, 🌐www.sussexbythesea.com). The best **accommodation** options are the ornate rooms of the Georgian *Town House*, 65 High St (☎01903/883847, 🌐www.thetownhouse.co.uk; ❹), and the elegant eighteenth-century *Byass House*, 59 Maltravers St (☎01903/882129, 🌐www.byasshouse.co.uk; no credit cards; ❹). Alternatively, there's the modern *Woodpeckers*, 15 Dalloway Rd (☎01903/883948; no smoking, no credit cards; ❷), on the outskirts of town. Arundel's YHA **hostel** (☎0870/770 5676, 📧arundel@yha.org.uk; £18) is in a large Georgian house by the river at Warningcamp, a mile and a half northeast of town.

If your pocket is up to it, first choice for **food** is the *Town House* (see above; closed Mon) where you dine under a spectacular Italian gilded ceiling. Otherwise try the restaurant attached to the *White Hart* pub over the river at 3 Queen St (☎01903/882374), or *Butlers Wine Bar*, 25 Tarrant St (☎01903/882222; closed Sun eve), a popular choice for steak-lovers. Further down the same road at no. 41, *The Eagle* is the best real-ale **pub** in town. During the last week in August, Arundel's **festival** (🌐www.arundelfestival.co.uk) features everything from open-air theatre to salsa bands.

Bignor and Petworth

Six miles north of Arundel, the excavated second-century ruins of the **Bignor Roman Villa** (March & April Tues–Sun 10am–5pm; May & Oct daily 10am–5pm; June–Sept daily 10am–6pm; £4.20) include some well-preserved mosaics, of which the Ganymede is the most outstanding. The site is superbly situated at the base of the South Downs and features the longest extant section of mosaic in England, as well as the remains of a hypocaust, the underfloor heating system developed by the Romans.

Adjoining the pretty little village of **PETWORTH**, eleven miles north of Arundel, **Petworth House** (mid-March to Oct Mon–Wed, Sat & Sun 11–5pm; park daily 8am–dusk; £7.50, park free; NT) is one of the Southeast's most impressive stately homes. Built in the late seventeenth century, the house contains an outstanding art collection, with paintings by Van Dyck, Titian, Gainsborough, Bosch, Reynolds, Blake and Turner – the last a frequent guest here. Highlights of the interior decor are Louis Laguerre's murals around the **Grand Staircase**, and the **Carved Room**, where work by Grinling Gibbons and Holbein's full-length portrait of Henry VIII can be seen. The extensive **Servants' Quarters**, connected by a tunnel to the main house, contain an impressive series of kitchens bearing the latest technological kitchenware of the 1870s, while the seven-hundred-acre grounds were landscaped by Capability Brown and are considered one of his finest achievements.

To get to Petworth by **public transport** from Arundel involves a train journey to Pulborough station from where you can pick up the regular Stagecoach Coastline #1 bus. Petworth's **tourist office** is on Golden Square (April–Sept Mon–Sat 10am–5pm, Sun 11am–3.30pm; March & Oct Mon–Sat 10am–4pm; Nov & Dec Fri & Sat 10am–3pm; Jan & Feb Fri & Sat 10am–2pm; ☎01798/343523, 🌐www.chichester.gov.uk). For a memorable night's **stay**, book in at the converted *Old Railway Station* (☎01798/342346, 🌐www.old-station.co.uk; ❹), two miles south of Petworth on the A285 Chichester road.

Chichester and around

The market town of **CHICHESTER** began life as a Roman settlement, and its Roman cruciform street plan is still evident in the four-quadrant symmetry of the town centre. The main streets lead off from the Gothic **Market Cross**, a bulky octagonal rotunda topped by ornate finials and a crown lantern spire, built in 1501 to provide shelter for the market traders. A short stroll down West Street brings you to Chichester's chief attraction, its Gothic **Cathedral** (daily: Easter to mid-Sept 7.15am–7pm; mid-Sept to Easter 7.15am–6pm), whose slender spire – a nineteenth-century addition – is visible out at sea. Building began in the 1070s, but the church was extensively rebuilt following a fire a century later and has been only minimally modified since about 1300, except for the spire and the unique, freestanding fifteenth-century bell tower. The **interior** is renowned for its contemporary devotional art, which includes a stained-glass window by Marc Chagall and an enormous altar-screen tapestry by John Piper. Other points of interest are the sixteenth-century painting in the north transept of the past bishops of Chichester, and the fourteenth-century Fitzalan tomb which inspired a poem by Philip Larkin, *An Arundel Tomb*. However, the highlight is a pair of reliefs in the south aisle, close to the tapestry – created around 1140, they show the raising of Lazarus and Christ at the gate of Bethany. Originally highly coloured, with semiprecious stones set in the figures' eyes, the reliefs are among the finest Romanesque stone carvings in England.

Off South Street, in the well-preserved Georgian quadrant of the city known as the Pallants, you'll find **Pallant House Gallery**, 9 North Pallant (currently closed for refurbishment; see ⓦwww.pallant.org.uk for latest information). Stone dodos stand guard over the gates of this fine mansion, which houses artefacts and furniture from the early eighteenth century, as well as more modern pieces including works by Henry Moore, Barbara Hepworth and Graham Sutherland.

Crossing East Street and heading north up Little London brings you to the **Chichester District Museum** (Tues–Sat 10am–5.30pm; free), housed in an old white weatherboarded corn store, and featuring a modest but entertaining display on local life. The **Guildhall** (June to mid-Sept Sat noon–4pm; free), a branch museum within a thirteenth-century Franciscan church in the middle of Priory Park, at the north end of Little London, has some well-preserved medieval frescoes. It was formerly a town hall and court of law, where the poet, painter and visionary William Blake was tried for sedition in 1804.

Chichester also plays host to a popular arts and cultural **festival**, which takes place over two weeks in July. It features a fairly safe programme of middlebrow plays, though the studio theatre is a bit more adventurous; for the latest details check the website ⓦwww.chifest.org.uk.

Practicalities

Chichester's **train station** lies on Stockbridge Road, with the **bus station** across the road at South Street. From either station it's a ten-minute walk north to the Market Cross, passing the **tourist office** at 29a South St (Mon 10.15am–5.15pm, Tues–Sat 9.15am–5.15pm, Sun 11am–3.30pm; Oct–March closed Sun; ☎01243/775888, ⓦwww.chichester.gov.uk). You can access the **Internet** at the *Internet Junction* café, at 2 Southdown Buildings next to the bus station.

There should be no problem finding **accommodation** except during the festival. Central B&B options include *Litten House*, with an attractive walled garden at 148 St Pancras, just off East Street (☎01243/774503, ⓦwww.littenho .demon.co.uk; no smoking; no credit cards; ❷), and the 200-year-old *Friary*

Close, Friary Lane (☎01243/527294, ⓦwww.friaryclose.co.uk; no smoking; ❸), just inside the city wall.

For something to **eat**, both the *Toad* pub, formerly a church in West Street and a lively spot for snacks and meals, and the intimate and more expensive *Café Coco*, 13 South St (☎01243/786989; closed Sun), specializing in French cuisine, are close to the cathedral. *Purchase's Wine Bar*, 31 North St (☎01243/537532; closed Sun), also serves a good selection of snacks, while *The Ship*, also on North Street, is a good place for a **drink**.

Fishbourne Roman Palace

Fishbourne, two miles west of Chichester and easily accessible by bus and train, is the largest and best-preserved Roman palace in the country (March–July, Sept & Oct daily 10am–5pm; Aug daily 10am–6pm; Nov to mid-Dec & Feb Sat & Sun 10am–4pm; £5.40). Roman relics have long been turning up hereabouts, and in 1960 a workman unearthed their source – the site of a depot used by the invading Romans in 43 AD, which is thought later to have become the vast, hundred-room palace of a Romanized Celtic aristocrat. The north wing of the remains displays floor mosaics depicting Fishbourne's famous dolphin-riding cupid as well as the more usual geometric patterns. The underfloor heating system has also been well restored, and an audiovisual programme portrays the palace as it was in Roman times. The extensive gardens attempt to re-create the appearance of the palace grounds as they would have been then.

Travel details

Buses

For information on all local and national bus services, contact Traveline ☎0870/608 2608 (daily 7am–9pm), ⓦwww.traveline.org.uk.
Arundel to: Chichester (Mon–Sat hourly; 35min); Brighton (Mon–Sat every 30min; 2hr 10min).
Battle to: Hastings (Mon–Sat hourly; 30min).
Brighton to: Chichester (Mon–Sat every 30min, Sun hourly; 2hr 30min); Eastbourne (hourly; 1hr 20min–1hr 30min); Lewes (Mon–Sat every 15min, Sun hourly; 25–30min); London Victoria (hourly; 2hr 5min); Portsmouth (Mon–Sat every 30min, Sun hourly; 3hr 30min); Tunbridge Wells (Mon–Sat hourly, Sun 7; 1hr 45min).
Broadstairs to: Dover (Mon–Sat hourly; 40min); Ramsgate (every 20–30min; 15min).
Canterbury to: Deal (Mon–Sat hourly, Sun 4; 1hr 5min); Dover (Mon–Sat hourly; 40min); London Victoria (hourly; 2hr); Ramsgate (Mon–Sat hourly; 40min); Sandwich (Mon–Sat hourly, Sun 4; 45min); Whitstable (Mon–Sat every 15min, Sun hourly, 30min).
Chatham to: Rochester (every 10min; 5min).
Chichester to: Arundel (Mon–Sat hourly; 35min), Brighton (Mon–Sat every 30min, Sun hourly; 2hr 30min); Portsmouth (Mon–Sat every 30min, Sun hourly; 45min).

Deal to: Canterbury (Mon–Sat hourly, Sun 4; 1hr 5min); Dover (Mon–Sat hourly, Sun 6; 30min); Sandwich (Mon–Sat hourly, Sun 4; 25min).
Dover to: Canterbury (Mon–Sat hourly; 40min); Deal (Mon–Sat hourly, Sun 6; 30min); Hastings (Mon–Sat hourly, Sun 6; 2hr 40min); London Victoria (hourly; 2hr 40min–3hr 20min); Sandwich (Mon–Sat 8 daily; 55min).
Eastbourne to: Brighton (hourly; 1hr 20min–1hr 30min); Hastings (Mon–Sat every 30min, Sun hourly; 1hr 10min–1hr 55min).
Guildford to: Farnham (Mon–Sat 1–2 hourly, Sun hourly; 35min); London Victoria (6 daily; 1hr).
Hastings to: Eastbourne (Mon–Sat every 30min, Sun hourly; 1hr 10min–1hr 55min); Dover (Mon–Sat hourly, Sun 6; 2hr 40min); London Victoria (2 daily; 2hr 50min–3hr 50min); Rye (Mon–Sat hourly, Sun 7; 45 min).
Hythe to: Rye (Mon–Sat hourly, Sun 7; 1hr 10min).
Lewes to: Brighton (Mon–Sat every 15min, Sun hourly; 25–30min); Tunbridge Wells (Mon–Sat every 30min, Sun 7; 1hr 10min).
Ramsgate to: Broadstairs (every 20–30min; 15min); Canterbury (Mon–Sat hourly; 40min); London Victoria (5 daily; 3hr).
Rochester to: Chatham (every 10min; 5min); Maidstone (Mon–Sat 9 daily; 45min).

Rye to: Hastings (Mon–Sat hourly, Sun 7; 45min); Hythe (Mon–Sat hourly, Sun 7; 1hr 10min).

Sandwich to: Canterbury (Mon–Sat hourly, Sun 4; 45min); Deal (Mon–Sat hourly, Sun 4; 25min); Dover (Mon–Sat 8 daily; 55min).

Sevenoaks to: Tunbridge Wells (Mon–Sat hourly; 50min).

Tunbridge Wells to: Brighton (Mon–Sat hourly, Sun 7; 1hr 45min); Lewes (Mon–Sat every 30min, Sun 7; 1hr 10min); Sevenoaks (Mon–Sat hourly; 50min).

Whitstable to: Canterbury (Mon–Sat every 15min, Sun hourly; 30min).

Trains

For information on all local and national rail services, contact National Rail Enquiries: ☎ 08457/484950, 🖥 www.nationalrail.co.uk.

Arundel to: London Victoria (Mon–Sat every 30min, Sun hourly; 1hr 20min).

Battle to: Hastings (Mon–Sat every 30min, Sun hourly; 15min); London Charing Cross (every 30min; 1hr 30min); Sevenoaks (Mon–Sat every 30min, Sun hourly; 50min); Tunbridge Wells (Mon–Sat every 30min, Sun hourly; 30min).

Brighton to: Chichester (Mon–Sat every 30min, Sun hourly; 50min); Hastings (Mon–Sat every 30min, Sun hourly; 1hr 10min); Lewes (Mon–Sat every 15min, Sun every 30min; 15min); London Victoria (every 30min; 55min); London King's Cross (Mon–Sat every 15min, Sun every 30min; 1hr 15min); London Bridge (Mon–Sat every 15min, Sun every 30min; 55min); Portsmouth Harbour (hourly; 1hr 30min).

Broadstairs to: London Victoria (Mon–Sat every 30min, Sun hourly; 1hr 50min); Ramsgate (every 15–20min; 5min).

Canterbury East to: Dover Priory (Mon–Fri every 30min, Sat & Sun hourly; 30min); London Victoria (Mon–Sat every 25min, Sun hourly; 1hr 30min).

Canterbury West to: London Charing Cross (every 30min; 1hr 30min); Ramsgate (every 30min; 20min).

Chatham to: Dover Priory (Mon–Sat every 30min, Sun hourly; 1hr); London Victoria (every 15min; 45min–1hr).

Chichester to: London Victoria (Mon–Sat every 30min, Sun hourly; 1hr 45min); Portsmouth Harbour (Mon–Sat every 30min, Sun hourly; 40min).

Dover Priory to: London Victoria (Mon–Fri every 30min, Sat & Sun hourly; 1hr 50min).

Eastbourne to: Hastings (Mon–Sat every 20min, Sun hourly; 30min); Lewes (Mon–Sat every 15min, Sun hourly; 20min); London Victoria (Mon–Sat every 30min, Sun hourly; 1hr 35min).

Farnham to: Aldershot (for connections to London Waterloo; 1–2 hourly; 5min).

Guildford to: London Waterloo (Mon–Sat every 10–20min, Sun hourly; 45min).

Hastings to: Gatwick Airport (hourly; 1hr 30min); London Victoria (hourly; 2hr); Rye (hourly; 20min).

Lewes to: Brighton (Mon–Sat every 15min, Sun every 30min; 15min); London Victoria (Mon–Sat every 30min, Sun hourly; 1hr 10min).

Ramsgate to: London Victoria (Mon–Sat every 30min, Sun hourly; 1hr 40min).

Rochester to: Dover Priory (Mon–Sat every 30min, Sun hourly; 1hr 10min); London Charing Cross (every 30min; 1hr 10min); London Victoria (Mon–Sat every 15–20min, Sun every 30min; 45min).

Rye to: Hastings (hourly; 20min).

Sandwich to: Dover Priory (every 30min; 25min); Ramsgate (hourly; 15min).

Tunbridge Wells to: London Charing Cross (Mon–Sat every 30min, Sun hourly; 55min).

Whitstable to: London Victoria (every 30min; 1hr 20min); Ramsgate (Mon–Sat every 30min, Sun hourly; 30min).

Hampshire, Dorset and Wiltshire

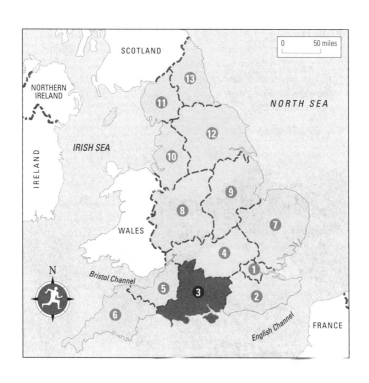

CHAPTER 3 # Highlights

✱ **Cowes Week, Isle of Wight** This yachting jamboree draws thousands, infecting even the staunchest landlubbers. **See p.227**

✱ **Wykeham Arms, Winchester** Ancient tavern serving gourmet-standard food alongside the real ales. **See p.231**

✱ **The New Forest** William the Conqueror's old hunting ground, home to wild ponies and deer, is ideal for walking, biking and riding. **See p.232**

✱ **Corfe Castle** Picturesque ruins with a weathered, romantic charm. **See p.239**

✱ **Durdle Door** This crumbling natural arch stands at the end of a splendid beach – a great place for walkers and swimmers alike. **See p.240**

✱ **Avebury** This crude stone circle has a more powerful appeal than nearby Stonehenge, not least for its great size and easy accessibility, in a peaceful village setting. **See p.255**

△ New Forest ponies

Hampshire, Dorset and Wiltshire

he distant past is perhaps more tangible in **Hampshire** (often abbreviated to "Hants"), **Dorset** and **Wiltshire** than in any other part of England. Predominantly rural, these three counties overlap substantially with the ancient kingdom of **Wessex**, whose most famous ruler, Alfred, repulsed the Danes in the ninth century and came close to establishing the first unified state in England. Before Wessex came into being, however, many earlier civilizations had left their stamp on the region. The chalky uplands of Wiltshire boast several of Europe's greatest Neolithic sites, including **Stonehenge** and **Avebury**, while in Dorset you'll find **Maiden Castle**, the most striking Iron Age hill fort in the country, and the **Cerne Abbas Giant**, source of many a legend. The Romans tramped all over these southern counties, leaving the most conspicuous signs of their occupation at the amphitheatre of **Dorchester** – though that town is more closely associated with the novels of Thomas Hardy and his distinctively gloomy vision of Wessex.

None of the landscapes of this region could be described as grand or wild, but the countryside is consistently seductive, not least the crumbling fossil-bearing cliffs around **Lyme Regis**, the managed woodlands of the **New Forest** and the gentle, open curves of **Salisbury Plain**. Its towns are also generally modest and slow-paced, with the notable exceptions of the two great maritime bases of **Portsmouth** and, to a lesser extent, **Southampton**, a fair proportion of whose visitors are simply passing through on their way to the more genteel pleasures of the **Isle of Wight**. The two great cathedral cities in these parts, **Salisbury** and **Winchester**, and the seaside resort of **Bournemouth** see most tourist traffic, and the great houses of **Wilton**, **Stourhead**, **Longleat** and **Kingston Lacy** also attract the crowds; but you don't have to wander far off the beaten track to encounter medieval churches, manor houses and unspoilt country inns a-plenty – there are few parts of England in which an aimless meander can be so rewarding.

Portsmouth

Britain's foremost naval station, **PORTSMOUTH** occupies the bulbous peninsula of Portsea Island, on the eastern flank of a huge, easily defended

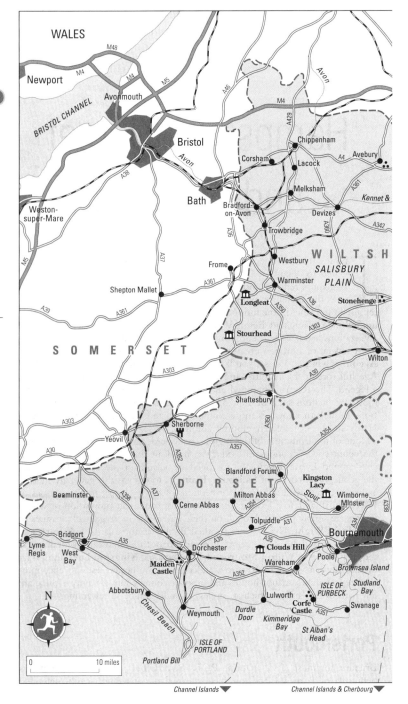

Channel Islands ▼　　　　Channel Islands & Cherbourg ▼

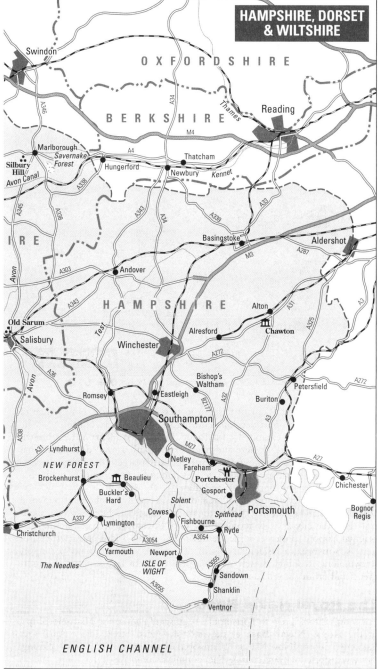

HAMPSHIRE, DORSET & WILTSHIRE

OXFORDSHIRE

Swindon

BERKSHIRE

Thames

Reading

M4

Marlborough

Savernake Forest

Silbury Hill

Avon Canal

Thatcham

A4

Hungerford

Newbury

Kennet

IRE

Avon

Basingstoke

Aldershot

A303

Andover

M3

A287

HAMPSHIRE

Alton

Old Sarum

Salisbury

Test

Alresford

Chawton

Winchester

A272

Bishop's Waltham

Petersfield

Romsey

Eastleigh

Buriton

Avon

Southampton

M27

Lyndhurst

Netley

NEW FOREST

Fareham

Chichester

Brockenhurst

Beaulieu

Portchester

Buckler's Hard

Gosport

Solent

Bognor Regis

Cowes

Spithead

Portsmouth

Christchurch

Lymington

Fishbourne

Ryde

Yarmouth

Newport

The Needles

ISLE OF WIGHT

Sandown

Shanklin

Ventnor

ENGLISH CHANNEL

Caen, St Malo, Bilbao, Cherbourg & Le Havre ▼

© Crown copyright

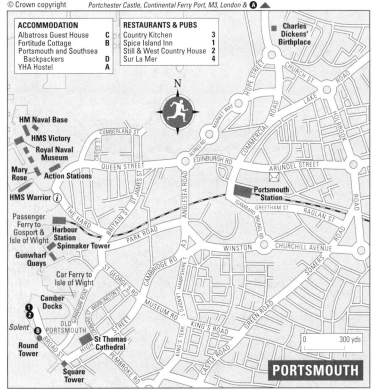

© Crown copyright   *Portchester Castle, Continental Ferry Port, M3, London &* ▲▲

ACCOMMODATION

Albatross Guest House	C
Fortitude Cottage	B
Portsmouth and Southsea Backpackers	D
YHA Hostel	A

RESTAURANTS & PUBS

Country Kitchen	3
Spice Island Inn	1
Still & West Country House	2
Sur La Mer	4

PORTSMOUTH

Southsea, IoW Hovercraft, Southsea Castle, ▼ *Royal Marines Museum, D-Day Museum,* ❸, ❹, ❸ & ❹

harbour. The ancient Romans raised a fortress on the northernmost edge of this inlet, and a small port developed during the Norman era, but this strategic location wasn't fully exploited until Tudor times, when Henry VII established the world's first dry dock here and made Portsmouth a royal dockyard. It has flourished ever since and nowadays Portsmouth is a large industrialized city, its harbour clogged with naval frigates, ferries bound for the continent or the Isle of Wight, and swarms of dredgers and tugs.

Due to its military importance, Portsmouth was heavily bombed during World War II, and bland tower blocks from the nadir of British architectural endeavour now give the city an ugly profile. Only **Old Portsmouth**, based around the original harbour, preserves some Georgian and a little Tudor character. East of here is **Southsea**, a residential suburb of terraces with a half-hearted resort strewn along its shingle beach, where a mass of B&Bs face stoic naval monuments and tawdry seaside amusements.

The Royal Naval Base

For most visitors, a trip to Portsmouth begins and ends at the **Historic Ships**, in the **Royal Naval Base** at the end of Queen Street (daily: April–Oct 9.45am–5.30pm; Nov–March 10am–5pm; last entry 1hr before closing; ⓦ www.historicdockyard.co.uk). The complex comprises three ships and as many museums, with each ship visitable separately, though most people opt for an all-inclusive ticket (£15.50), which allows for return visits. The main attractions are HMS *Victory*, HMS *Warrior* (including the Royal Naval Museum), Action Stations (an interactive simulation of life aboard a modern naval frigate), the Mary Rose Museum, and a harbour tour. Note that visits to the *Victory* are guided, with limited numbers at set times, so it's worth booking early to ensure a place, and even then you may have to wait up to two hours for your turn. Also, visitors with disabilities will have a hard time moving between decks on the two complete ships; a virtual tour by video (call ☎023/9272 2562 for details) is a good alternative.

Nearest the entrance to the complex is the youngest ship, **HMS Warrior** (£9.70), dating from 1860. It was Britain's first armoured (iron-clad) battleship, complete with sails and steam engines, and was the pride of the fleet in its day. Longer and faster than any previous naval vessel, and the first to be fitted with washing machines, the *Warrior* was described by Napoleon III as a "black snake amongst the rabbits". The ship displays a wealth of weaponry, including rifles, pistols and sabres, though the *Warrior* was never challenged nor even fired a cannon in her 22 years at sea.

HMS Victory (£9.70) was already forty years old when she set sail from Portsmouth for Trafalgar on September 14, 1805, returning in triumph three months later, but bearing the corpse of Admiral Nelson. Shot by a sniper from a French ship at the height of the battle, Nelson expired below decks three hours later, having been assured that victory was in sight. Although badly damaged during the battle, the *Victory* continued in service for a further twenty years, before being retired to the dry dock where she rests today.

Opposite the *Victory*, various buildings house the exhaustive **Royal Naval Museum** (same ticket as *Victory*). Tracing naval history from Alfred the Great's fleet to the present day, the collection includes some jolly figureheads, Nelson memorabilia and nautical models, though coverage of more recent conflicts is scantily treated.

In a shed behind the *Victory* are the remains of the **Mary Rose** (£9.70), Henry VIII's flagship, which capsized before his eyes off Spithead in 1545 while engaging French intruders, sinking swiftly with almost all her seven-hundred-strong crew. In 1982 a massive conservation project successfully raised the remains of the hull, which silt had preserved beneath the seabed. The ship itself is less absorbing than the thousands of objects retrieved near the wreck, displayed in an exhibition close to the *Warrior*. Lastly, **Action Stations** (£9.70) has interactive games, videos and graphics to simulate life aboard ship.

From the harbour

The naval theme is continued at the **Submarine Museum** on Haslar Jetty in Gosport (daily: April–Oct 10am–5.30pm; Nov–March 10am–4.30pm; last tour 1hr before closing; £4.50), reached by taking the passenger ferry from Harbour train station jetty (daily 5.30am–midnight; £1.80 return), or, from the same place, the water-bus, which gives you a half-hour tour of the harbour before dropping you in Gosport (Easter–Oct 10.30am–5pm; £5, or £1 per stop). Allow a couple of hours to explore these slightly creepy vessels – a guided tour inside HMS *Alliance* gives you an insight into life on board and the museum elaborates evocatively on the long history of submersible craft. Nearby, housed in the old armaments depot at Priddy's Hard, **Explosion! The Museum of Naval Firepower** (April–Oct daily 10am–5.30pm; Nov–March Thurs, Sat &

Sun 10am–4.30pm; £5.50) tells the story of naval warfare from the days of gunpowder to the present, much helped by computer animations.

From the pontoon beside HMS *Warrior*, ferries depart (Sun 2.45pm; £8, including entry to the fort) for the mile-long ride to **Spitbank Fort**, an offshore bastion of granite, iron and brick little altered since its construction in the 1860s. With over fifty rooms linked by passages and steps on two floors, the complex includes a 400-foot-deep well, which still draws fresh water from below the seafloor, and an inner courtyard with a café and sheltered terrace, where pub nights, parties and Sunday lunches are held – call ☎023/9250 4207 or ask at the tourist office for details.

The rest of the city

Back at the Portsmouth's Harbour train station, it's a short walk along the historic waterfront to the sleek **Gunwharf Quays** development, which hosts a myriad of stylish cafés, restaurants, nightspots and retail outlets. It's also home to Portsmouth's newest attraction, the **Spinnaker Tower** (Mon–Wed 10am–6pm, Thurs–Sat 10am–8pm, Sun 11am–5pm; £4.95). Opened in 2005, the elegant, sail-like structure rises 170m above the city, offering stunning vistas for up to twenty miles over land and sea. The two viewing decks can be reached by either a high-speed lift or a slower Panoramic glass lift (£2).

It's a well-signposted fifteen-minute walk south of the tower to what remains of **Old Portsmouth**. Along the way, you pass the simple **Cathedral of St Thomas** on the High Street, whose original twelfth-century features have been obscured by rebuilding after the Civil War and again in the twentieth century. The High Street ends at a maze of cobbled Georgian streets huddling behind a fifteenth-century wall protecting the **Camber**, or old port, where Walter Raleigh landed the first potatoes and tobacco from the New World. Nearby, the Round and Square towers, which punctuate the Tudor fortifications, are popular vantage points for observing nautical activities.

The only other point of interest in Portsmouth itself is **Charles Dickens' Birthplace** at 393 Old Commercial Rd (daily: April–Sept 10am–5.30pm; £2.50), but there are more sites of military interest a mile or so south in **Southsea**. The main attraction here is the **D-Day Museum** on Clarence Esplanade (daily: April–Sept 10am–5.30pm; Oct–March 10am–5pm; last entry 1hr before closing; £5.50), focusing on Portsmouth's role as the principle assembly point for the D-Day invasion in World War II, code-named "Operation Overlord". The museum's most striking exhibit is the 270-foot-long *Overlord Embroidery*, which illustrates the Normandy landings. Next door to the museum, the squat profile of **Southsea Castle** (April–Oct daily 10am–5pm; £2.50), built from the remains of Beaulieu Abbey (see p.233), is thought to have been the spot from where Henry VIII watched the *Mary Rose* sink in 1545. A mile further along the shoreside South Parade, just past South Parade pier, the **Royal Marines Museum** (daily: June–Aug 10am–5pm; Sept–May 10am–4.30pm; last entry 1hr before closing; £4.75) describes the origins and greatest campaigns of the navy's elite fighting force.

More compelling is **Portchester Castle** (daily: April–Sept 10am–6pm; Oct–March 10am–4pm; £3.70; EH), six miles out of the centre, just past the marina development at Port Solent. Built by the Romans in the third century this fortification boasts the finest surviving example of Roman walls in northern Europe – still over twenty feet high and incorporating some twenty bastions. The Normans felt no need to make any substantial alterations when they moved in, but a castle was later built within Portchester's precincts by Henry II, which

Richard II extended and Henry V used as his garrison when assembling the army that was to fight the Battle of Agincourt. Today its grassy enclosure makes a sheltered spot for a congenial game of cricket or a kickabout with a football.

Practicalities

Portsmouth's main **train station** is in the city centre, but the line continues to **Harbour Station**, the most convenient stop for the main sights and old town. Passenger **ferries** leave from the jetty at Harbour Station for Ryde, on the Isle of Wight (see p.223), and Gosport, on the other side of Portsmouth Harbour. Wightlink car ferries depart from the ferry port off Gunwharf Road for Fishbourne on the Isle of Wight (see p.223). There are two **tourist offices** in Portsmouth (both ☏023/9282 6722, ⓦwww.visitportsmouth.co.uk), one on The Hard, by the entrance to the dockyards (daily: April–Sept 9.30am–5.45pm; Oct–March 9.30am–5.15pm), the other on Southsea's seafront, next to the Blue Reef Aquarium (daily 9.30am–5.15pm, July–Aug closes 5.45pm).

The main concentration of **hotels and B&Bs** is south of the centre in Southsea, where you'll find the *Albatross Guest House*, 51 Waverley Rd (☏023/9282 8325, ⓦwww.albatrossguesthouse.co.uk; no smoking; no credit cards; ❷), dating from the 1860s and with nautically themed rooms. In Old Portsmouth, *Fortitude Cottage* overlooks the quayside at 51 Broad St (☏023/9282 3748, ⓦwww.fortitudecottage.co.uk; no smoking; ❸). There's a YHA **hostel** at Wymering Manor, Old Wymering Lane, Cosham (☏0870/770 6002, ⓔportsmouth@yha.org.uk; £11.95), ten minutes west of Cosham train station (or take bus #5 or #57), and an independent hostel, *Portsmouth and Southsea Backpackers*, at 4 Florence Rd, Southsea (☏023/9283 2495 or 9282 2963, ⓦwww.portsmouthbackpackers.co.uk; £12), with full facilities and some en-suite doubles (❶). Campers should head to *Southsea Leisure Park*, Melville Road, Southsea (☏023/9273 5070, ⓔinfo@southsea-caravans-ltd.co.uk) – bus #15, then walk.

Places to eat are surprisingly scarce in the old town, though you'll find a good range of hot and cold dishes at a couple of adjacent waterside hostelries in Bath Square, the *Spice Island Inn* and the *Still & West Country House*. In Southsea, try *Sur La Mer*, 69 Palmerston Rd (☏023/9287 6678; closed Sun), serving inexpensive French and seafood dishes, and ⚘ *Country Kitchen*, 59 Marmion Rd, a vegetarian and vegan restaurant with newspapers on hand and free coffee refills (daytime only; closed Sun).

Southampton

A glance at the map gives some idea of the strategic maritime importance of **SOUTHAMPTON**, which stands on a triangular peninsula formed at the place where the rivers Itchen and Test flow into Southampton Water, an eight-mile inlet from the Solent. Sure enough, Southampton has figured in numerous stirring events: it witnessed the exodus of Henry V's Agincourt-bound army, the Pilgrim Fathers' departure in the *Mayflower* in 1620 and the maiden voyages of such ships as the *Queen Mary* and the *Titanic*. Unfortunately, since its pummelling by the Luftwaffe and some disastrous postwar planning, the thousand-year-old city is now a sprawling conurbation, with little to justify more than a fleeting visit.

Core of the modern town is the **Civic Centre**, a short walk east of the train station and home to an excellent **art gallery** that's particularly strong on twentieth-century British artists such as Sutherland, Piper and Spencer (Tues–Sat 10am–5pm, Sun 1–4pm; free). The **Western Esplanade**, curving southward from the station, runs alongside the best remaining bits of the old city **walls**. Rebuilt after a French attack in 1338, they incorporate **God's House Tower**, at the southern end of the old town in Winkle Street, where there's a **Museum of Archeology** (April–Oct Tues–Fri 10am–noon & 1–5pm, Sat 10am–noon & 1–4pm, Sun 2–5pm; free). Best preserved of the city's seven gates is **Bargate**, at the opposite end of the old town, at the head of the High Street; it's an elaborate structure, cluttered with lions, classical figures and defensive apertures. In Bugle Street, the fifteenth-century, timber-framed **Tudor House Museum** (currently closed for refurbishment; call ☎023/8063 5904 for the latest details) highlights Georgian, Victorian and early twentieth-century social history, and features a grand banqueting hall and reconstructed Tudor garden. By the seafront, the **Wool House**, a fine fourteenth-century stone warehouse formerly used as a jail for Napoleonic prisoners, now holds a **Maritime Museum** (April–Oct Tues–Fri 10am–1pm & 2–5pm, Sat 10am–1pm & 2–4pm, Sun 2–5pm; Nov–March Tues–Fri 10am–4pm, Sat 10am–1pm & 2–4pm, Sun 1–4pm; free) recounting the heyday of the ocean liners.

Practicalities

Southampton's central **train station** is in Blechynden Terrace, west of the Civic Centre; the **bus** and **coach stations** are immediately south and north of the Civic Centre. The **tourist office** is at 9 Civic Centre Rd (Mon–Sat 9.30am–5pm; ☎023/8083 3333, ⓦwww.southampton.gov.uk). **Accommodation** options include two four-hundred-year-old hotels: the *Star* (☎023/8033 9939, ⓦwww.thestarhotel.com; ❺) and the *Dolphin* (☎023/8033 9955, ⓦwww.thedolphin.co.uk; ❺), both halfway down the High Street. Alternatively, there's *Linden* B&B, just north of the train station on the Polygon (☎023/8022 5653; no credit cards; ❷). Oxford Street, off Bernard Street from the High Street, has a cluster of **eating** places including *The Olive Tree* at no. 29 (☎023/8034 3333), serving moderately priced Mediterranean dishes, with pavement seating and live music on Sundays. As for **pubs**, try the tiny old *Platform Tavern* in Winkle Street, at the south end of the High Street, or the twelfth-century *Red Lion*, complete with minstrels' gallery at 55 High Street.

The Isle of Wight

In recent years the lozenge-shaped **ISLE OF WIGHT** has begun to shake off its image as a comfortable, tidy and unadventurous adjunct of rural southern England, and has started to attract a younger, livelier crowd. Despite measuring less than 23 miles at its widest point, the island packs in a surprising variety of landscapes and coastal scenery. North of the chalk ridge that runs across its centre, the terrain is low-lying woodland and pasture, deeply cut by meandering rivers, while southwards lies open chalky downland fringed by high cliffs. Its beaches have long attracted holiday-makers, and the island was a favourite of such eminent Victorians as Tennyson, Dickens, Swinburne, Julia Margaret Cameron and Queen Victoria herself, who made **Osborne House**, near Cowes, her permanent home after Albert died.

If you're dependent upon **public transport** to get around, pick up the Southern Vectis bus route map and timetable (50p) from the tourist office, ferry office or bus station at your point of arrival (call ☎01983/562264 or see the website

Sea routes to the Isle of Wight

Hovertravel ☎023/9281 1000 or 01983/811000, ⓦwww.hovertravel.co.uk. Year-round hovercraft service from **Southsea to Ryde** for foot passengers only: Mon–Fri 7.10am–8.10pm, Sat 8.15am–8.10pm, Sun 9.15am–8.10pm (late July to Aug last sailing at 8.45pm); every 30min; 10min; £12.70.

Red Funnel ☎023/8033 4010, ⓦwww.redfunnel.co.uk. Year-round ferries on two routes: **Southampton–East Cowes** hourly; 55min; £10.40 for foot passengers; £75 for car and driver plus £10.40 per passenger. **Southampton–West Cowes** high-speed foot-passenger service Mon–Fri 5.50am–10.40pm, Sat 6.20am–10.40pm, Sun 6.50am–10.40pm (last sailing at 11.40pm Thurs–Sat & daily Easter–Aug); 1–2 hourly; 22min; £15.30.

Wightlink Ferries ☎0870/582 7744, ⓦwww.wightlink.co.uk. Three routes: **Portsmouth–Ryde** year-round high-speed catamaran for foot passengers only; 1–2 hourly; 15min; £14.40. **Portsmouth–Fishbourne** year-round ferry runs once or twice hourly; 35min; £11.80 for foot passengers; about £85 for car and driver, plus £11.80 per passenger. **Lymington–Yarmouth** ferry (Easter–Dec) 4am–midnight; 2 hourly; 30min; same fares as Portsmouth–Fishbourne ferry.

All the prices quoted are for a ninety-day (Wightlink and Red Funnel) or one-year (Hovertravel) standard return ticket in high season. Wightlink and Red Funnel offer day returns as well as a range of other short-break deals for cars, with discounts of around 35 percent. Online booking is also cheaper.

ⓦwww.svoc.co.uk). The company's hourly Island Explorer **buses** (routes #7, #7A and #7C) run all round the island in about four hours. The **rail line** is a short east-coast stretch linking Ryde, Brading, Sandown and Shanklin. A Rover Ticket allows you unlimited travel on the bus and train networks (£8 for a Day Rover; £14 for a Two-Day Rover; £32 for a Weekly Rover). **Cycling** is a popular way of getting around the island, especially as bikes are carried free on all ferry services, but beware that in summer the narrow lanes can get very busy. For **bike rental** and guided rides contact Wight Offroad (☎01983/730120, ⓦwww.wightoffroad.co.uk), which delivers and collects bikes anywhere on the island. For **information** on the Isle of Wight, call ☎01983/813818, consult ⓦwww.islandbreaks.co.uk, or call in at the tourist offices detailed below.

Ryde and around

As a major ferry terminal, **RYDE** is the first landfall many visitors make on the island, but one where few choose to linger, despite some grand nine-teenth-century architecture and decent beach amusements. The **tourist office** (March–Oct Mon–Sat 9.30am–5.30pm, Sun 9am–5pm; Nov–Feb daily 9am–4.30pm; ☎01983/813818), **bus station**, **Hovercraft terminal** and **Esplanade train station** (the northern terminus of the Island Line train line) are all located near the base of the pier.

Accommodation is available right in the town centre at *Yelf's Hotel* on Union Street (☎01983/564062, ⓦwww.yelfshotel.com; ❺), one of Ryde's oldest hotels, while, just south of the Esplanade, the *Trentham Guest House*, 38 The Strand (☎01983/563418; no smoking; no credit cards; ❶), and the *Vine Guest House*, 16 Castle St (☎01983/566633; ❷; closed Nov & Dec), are both great value. The continental-style *Joe Daflo's Café Bar* at 24 Union St (☎01983/567047) is a good place for a snack or a **meal**.

As elsewhere on the island, just a couple of miles can remove you from an undistinguished urban setting into one of idyllic rusticity. Two miles west of

Ryde, outside the village of Binstead, one of the island's earliest Christian relics, **Quarr Abbey**, was founded in 1132 by Richard de Redvers for Savigny monks; its name was derived from the quarries nearby, where stone was mined for use in the construction of Winchester and Chichester cathedrals. Only stunted ruins survived the Dissolution and ensuing plunder of ready-cut stone, although an ivy-clad archway still hangs picturesquely over a farm track. In 1907 a new abbey was founded just west of the ruins, a striking rose-brick building with Byzantine overtones (daily 9am–9pm; Vespers 5pm).

Just south of the ancient village of **Brading**, on the busy Ryde-to-Sandown A3055 (bus #7, #7A or #7B), the remains of **Brading Roman Villa** lie on Morton Old Road (daily: March–Oct 9.30am–6pm; Nov–Feb 10am–4pm; £3.95). It's one of two such villas on the island (the other is in Newport; see p.227), both of which were probably sites of bacchanalian worship. The Brading site is renowned for its superbly preserved mosaics, including intact images of Medusa and depictions of Orpheus.

Nunwell House (July to early Sept Mon–Wed 1–5pm; £4.25), signposted off the A3055 less than a mile northwest of Brading, was where, in 1647, Charles I spent his last night of freedom before being taken to Carisbrooke Castle (see p.227) and thence to his eventual execution in Whitehall. The house has been in the Oglander family for nearly nine hundred years, with the present building blending Jacobean, Georgian and Victorian styles. There are guided tours of the house, and five acres of lovely gardens.

Sandown and Shanklin

The two eastern resorts of Sandown and Shanklin merge into each other across the sandy reach of Sandown Bay, representing the island's holiday-making epicentre. **SANDOWN**, a traditional 1960s bucket-and-spade resort, appropriately possesses the island's only surviving pleasure **pier**, bedecked with various traditional amusements and a large theatre with nightly entertainment in season. At the northern end of the Esplanade, the **Isle of Wight Zoo** (mid-Feb to March & Oct daily 10am–4pm; April–Sept daily 10am–6pm; Nov open weekends weather permitting; call ☎01983/403883; £5.95) contains several species of tigers, panthers and other big cats, as well as some frisky lemurs and an exhaustive selection of spiders and snakes.

SHANKLIN, with its auburn cliffs, Old Village and scenic Chine, has a marginally more sophisticated aura than its northern neighbour. The rose-clad, thatched **Old Village** may be syrupy, but the adjacent **Shanklin Chine** (daily: late March to May & mid-Sept to Oct 10am–5pm; June to mid-Sept 10am–10pm; £3.50), a twisting pathway descending a mossy ravine and decorated on summer nights with fairy lights, is undeniably picturesque; local resident John Keats once drew inspiration from the environs.

Sandown's **tourist office** is located at 8 High St, while Shanklin's is at 67 High St (both April–Oct Mon–Sat 9.30am–5.30pm, Sun 10am–4pm; Nov–Easter irregular hours; ☎01983/813818). Both towns have Island Line train stations about half a mile inland from their beachfront centres. For **accommodation in Shanklin**, try *Pink Beach*, 20 Esplanade (☎01983/862501, Ⓦwww.pink-beach-hotel.co.uk; ❸), a shocking-pink Victorian hotel, a stone's throw from the beach, or *Ryedale*, 3 Atherley Rd (☎01983/862375, Ⓦwww .ryedale-hotel.co.uk; no smoking; ❷), a family-run B&B just steps from the train station, also near the beach. In **Sandown**, try *St Catherine's*, 1 Winchester Park Rd (☎01983/402392, Ⓔstcathhotel@hotmail.com; ❹), built for the Dean of Winchester in 1860, or *Mount Brocas*, 15 Beachfield Rd (☎01983/406276,

e brocas@netguides.co.uk; no smoking; no credit cards; ❷), at the west end
of the High Street, very close to the beach. There's a YHA **hostel** right in
Sandown's centre, on Fitzroy Street (☎0870/770 6020, e sandown@yha.org
.uk; £12.50).

Sandown's *King's House Café*, 43 High St, offers **meals and refreshment**,
with great views over the sea; on Shanklin's Appley Beach, try the *Fisherman's
Cottage*, an atmospheric seafaring pub at the southern end of the Esplanade,
serving wholesome food (no credit cards; closed Nov–April).

Ventnor and around

The seaside resort of **VENTNOR** and its two village suburbs of **Bonchurch**
and **St Lawrence** sit at the foot of St Boniface Down, the island's highest
point at 787ft. The Down periodically disintegrates into landslides, creating
the jumbled terraces known locally as the **Undercliff**, whose sheltered, south-
facing aspect, mild winter temperatures and thick carpet of undergrowth have
contributed to the former fishing village becoming a fashionable health spa.
Thanks to these unique factors, the town possesses rather more character than
the island's other resorts, its Gothic Revival buildings clinging dizzily to zigzagging bends.

The floral terraces of the Cascade curve down to the slender Esplanade and
narrow beach, where former boat-builders' cottages now provide more recreational services. From the Esplanade, it's a pleasant mile-long stroll to Ventnor's
Botanical Gardens, where 22 landscaped acres of subtropical vegetation
flourish. Ventnor's **tourist office** is at 34 High St (Easter–Oct Mon–Sat
9.30am–5.30pm, Sun 10am–3pm; ☎01983/813818). For **accommodation**,
try the *Spyglass Inn* on Ventnor's Esplanade (☎01983/855338; ❸), which has a
few self-contained rooms and balconies. Some of the area's best choices are in
Bonchurch, however, where there's *Horseshoebay House*, Horseshoe Bay, right on
the beach (☎01983/856800, ⓦwww.horseshoebayhouse.co.uk; no smoking; no
credit cards; ❸), and the small Georgian *Under Rock Country House* on Shore
Road (☎01983/855274, ⓦwww.under-rock.co.uk; no smoking; no credit
cards; ❸), with a subtropical rock garden. In Ventnor town centre, *Merlin's Bistro*,
(☎01983/731173) on Blackgang Road, serves tasty and moderately priced
meals in a mellow atmosphere.

Appuldurcombe House and St Catherine's Point

Follow the B3327 for a couple of miles inland, over St Boniface Down to
Wroxall, where a track leads left for half a mile to the ruins of **Appuldurcombe House** (daily: May–Sept 10am–5pm; mid-Feb to April & Oct
10am–3pm; £2.50; EH), the island's grandest pre-Victorian house. The present
mansion was built in the late eighteenth century in the Palladian style, with
gardens landscaped by Capability Brown. Semi-abandoned in the early twentieth century, Appuldurcombe has been preserved in a picturesque state of decay,
a partially roofed but intact shell with a stately eastern facade, a spring-fed
fountain and an impressive outlook over a fold in the downs.

The western Undercliff begins to recede at the village of Niton, where a footpath continues to the most southerly tip of the island, **St Catherine's Point**,
marked by a modern lighthouse. A prominent landmark on the downs behind
is **St Catherine's Oratory**, known locally as the "Pepper Pot", and originally
a lighthouse, reputedly built in 1325. A short distance west, **Blackgang Chine**

(daily: late March to June & early Sept to Oct 10am–5pm; July to early Sept 10am–10pm; £8.50) opened as a landscaped garden in 1843 and gradually evolved into a theme park that now offers a half-dozen exhibits from Cowboy Town to Jungleland.

Yarmouth and the western tip

Linked to Lymington in the New Forest by car ferry, the pleasant town of **YARMOUTH**, on the northern coast of the Isle of Wight, makes an appealing arrival or departure point, and is also the best base for exploring the western tip of the island. Although razed by the French in 1377, the port prospered after **Yarmouth Castle** (April–Sept Mon–Thurs & Sun 11am–4pm; £2.60; EH), tucked between the quay and the pier, was commissioned by Henry VIII. The top attractions hereabouts, however, lie four miles west of Yarmouth, around the isle's western tip. From the multichrome cliffs at **Alum Bay**, a chair lift (£3.50 return) runs down to ochre-hued sands, which were used as pigments for painting local landscapes in the Victorian era. From here, it's a twenty-minute walk to the lookout on top of the three tall chalk stacks known as **The Needles**, best seen from a boat trip leaving from Alum Bay (Needles Pleasure Cruises; ☎01983/754477; £3.50).

Between the Needles and Freshwater Bay, the breezy four-mile ridge of **Tennyson Down** is one of the island's most satisfying walks, with vistas onto rolling downs and vales. There's a monument here to the poet and local resident after whom it's named. On the coastal road at Freshwater Bay, on the corner with Terrace Lane, **Dimbola Lodge** (Tues–Sun 10am–5pm, daily during school holidays; £4) was the home of pioneer photographer Julia Margaret Cameron, who settled here after visiting Tennyson in 1860. The building now houses a gallery of her work and changing exhibitions, as well as a bookshop, tearoom and vegetarian restaurant.

Yarmouth's **tourist office** is just back from the harbour (Easter–Oct Mon–Sat 9.30am–5.30pm, Sun 9.30am–4pm; Nov–Easter Mon–Fri 10am–4pm; ☎01983/813818). Affordable **accommodation** in town includes *Jireh House* in St James's Square (☎01983/760513; ❸; closed Nov–Easter), a pretty seventeenth-century stone guest house and tearoom, serving evening meals on summer Saturdays, and *Wavell's*, behind the grocer's shop on the same square (☎01983/760738; no smoking; ❸), also offering bike hire. If you're flush, you can't do better than the seventeenth–century *George*, right by the ferry dock on Quay Street (☎01983/760331; ⓦwww.thegeorge.co.uk; ❽), with elegantly furnished rooms: Charles II was once a guest here. There's a YHA **hostel** a short walk northeast from the Needles, at Totland Bay (☎0870/770 6070, ⓔtotland@yha.org.uk; closed Nov–Feb; £12.50).

The *George* is also the place **to eat**, with a pleasant panelled bar, and a separate (expensive) restaurant serving top-quality seafood meals. Alternatively, *Gossips Café*, on the main square, dishes up inexpensive snacks and light meals until 6pm.

Cowes and around

COWES, at the island's northern tip, is inextricably associated with sailing craft and boat building: Henry VIII installed a castle here to defend the Solent's expanding naval dockyards from the French and Spanish, and in the 1950s the world's first hovercraft made its test runs here. In 1820 the Prince Regent's patronage of the yacht club gave the port its cachet with the Royal Yacht Squadron, now one of the world's most exclusive sailing clubs. The first week of August sees the international yachting festival known as **Cowes Week** (Ⓦwww.cowesweek.co.uk), where serious sailors mingle with visiting royalty. There are dozens of organized events, including a spectacular fireworks display on the Friday night, and a great party atmosphere. In addition to Cowes Week, most summer weekends see some form of nautical event taking place in or around town.

The town is bisected by the River Medina, with West Cowes being the older, more interesting half, and holding most of the facilities, including the **tourist office**, at the Arcade, Fountain Quay (April–Oct Mon–Sat 9am–5pm, Sun 10am–4pm, with extended hours during Cowes Week; Nov–March Tues–Sat 9.30am–4.30pm; Ⓣ01983/813818). At the bottom of the meandering High Street, **boat trips** upriver and around the harbour leave from Thetis Wharf, near the Parade; for details contact Solent & Wight Line Cruises (Ⓣ01983/564602, Ⓦwww.solentcruises.co.uk).

The more affordable **accommodation** options include the *Union Inn* in Watch House Lane, off High Street (Ⓣ01983/293163; ❷), and *Halcyone Villa*, Grove Road, up Mill Hill Road from the east end of the High Street (Ⓣ01983/291334, Ⓔsandra@wight365.net; ❷); in East Cowes, there's the *Doghouse* (Ⓣ01983/293677; no credit cards; ❹), Crossways Road, opposite Osborne House. The town has some decent **places to eat**: the ✱ *Octopus's Garden*, 63 High St, is a café and bistro filled with Beatles memorabilia, while the harbourside *Fastnet Brasserie* (Ⓣ01983/209444) has outdoor seating, and offers pizzas and fuller meals. Bar food is available at the *Anchor* **pub** on the High Street, which also has live music, a garden and rooms (Ⓣ01983/292823; ❸).

Osborne House and Whippingham

A "floating bridge", or chain ferry (Mon–Sat 5am–midnight, Sun 6.35am–midnight; pedestrians free, cars £1.30) connects West Cowes to the more industrial East Cowes, where the only place of interest is Queen Victoria's family home, **Osborne House** (April–Sept daily 10am–6pm; Oct Mon–Thurs & Sun 10am–4pm; Nov–March Mon–Thurs & Sun pre-booked tours only; call Ⓣ01983/200022; house and grounds £8, grounds only £5.30; EH), sign-posted one mile southeast of town (bus #4 from Ryde or #5 from Newport; take either from East Cowes). The house was built in the late 1840s by Prince Albert and Thomas Cubitt as an Italianate villa, with balconies and large terraces overlooking the landscaped gardens towards the Solent. The state rooms, used for entertaining visiting dignitaries, exude an expected formality, while the private apartments feel more homely, like the affluent family holiday residence that Osborne was – far removed from the pomp and ceremony of state affairs in London. Following Albert's death, the desolate Victoria spent much of her time here, and it's where she eventually died in 1901. Since then, according to her wishes, the house has remained virtually unaltered, allowing an unexpectedly intimate glimpse into Victoria's family life.

At **WHIPPINGHAM**, a mile south of Osborne, there's another of Albert's architectural extravaganzas, the Gothic Revival **Royal Church of St Mildred** (Easter–Oct Mon–Fri 10am–5pm). The German Battenberg family, who later adopted the anglicized name Mountbatten, have a chapel here.

Newport and Carisbrooke Castle

NEWPORT, the capital of the Isle of Wight, sits at the centre of the island at a point where the River Medina's commercial navigability ends. The town isn't particularly engaging, though is worth a visit for the hilltop fortress of

Carisbrooke Castle (daily: April–Sept 10am–5pm; Oct–March 10am–4pm; £5.30; EH), on the southwest outskirts (buses #7, #7A or #7B from Newport). This austere Norman keep's most famous visitor was Charles I, detained here (and caught one night ignominiously jammed between his room's bars while attempting escape) prior to his execution in London. The **museum** in the centre of the castle features many relics from his incarceration, as well as those of the last royal resident, Princess Beatrice, Queen Victoria's youngest daughter. The castle's other notable curiosity is the sixteenth-century well-house, where donkeys still trudge inside a huge treadmill to raise a barrel 160ft up the well shaft. The remains of a **Roman villa** stand a well-signposted ten-minute walk southeast of the town centre in Cypress Road (April–Nov Mon–Sat 10am–4.30pm, July & Aug also Sun noon–4pm; £2), though it's less impressive than its sister villa in Brading (see p.224).

Winchester

Nowadays a tranquil, handsome market town, **WINCHESTER** was once one of the mightiest settlements in England. Under the Romans it was Venta Belgarum, the fifth largest town in Britain, but it was **Alfred the Great** who really put Winchester on the map when he made it the capital of his Wessex kingdom in the ninth century. For the next couple of centuries Winchester ranked alongside London, its status affirmed by William the Conqueror's coronation in both cities and by his commissioning of the local monks to prepare the **Domesday Book**. It wasn't until after the Battle of Naseby in 1645, when Cromwell took the city, that Winchester began its decline into provinciality.

Hampshire's county town now has a scholarly and slightly anachronistic air, embodied by the ancient almshouses that still provide shelter for senior citizens of "noble poverty" – the pensioners can be seen wandering round the town in medieval black or mulberry-coloured gowns with silver badges. A trip to this secluded old city is a must – not only for the magnificent **cathedral**, chief relic of Winchester's medieval glory, but for the all-round well-preserved ambience of England's one-time capital.

The City

The first minster to be built in Winchester was raised by Cenwalh, the Saxon king of Wessex in the mid-seventh century, and traces of this building have been unearthed near the present **cathedral** (daily 8.30am–6pm; £3.50 donation requested), which was begun in 1079 and completed some three hundred years later, producing a church whose elements range from early Norman to Perpendicular styles. The exterior is not its best feature – squat and massive, the cathedral crouches stumpily over the tidy lawns of the Cathedral Close. The interior is rich and complex, however, and its 556-foot **nave** makes this Europe's longest medieval church. Outstanding features include its carved Norman font of black Tournai marble, the fourteenth-century misericords (the choir stalls are the oldest complete set in the country) and some amazing monuments – **William of Wykeham's Chantry**, halfway down the nave on the right, is one of the best. Jane Austen, who died in Winchester, is commemorated close to the font by a memorial brass and slab beneath which she's interred, though she's recorded simply as the daughter of a local clergyman. Above the high altar lie the mortuary chests of pre-Conquest kings, including Canute (though the bones were mixed up after Cromwell's Roundheads

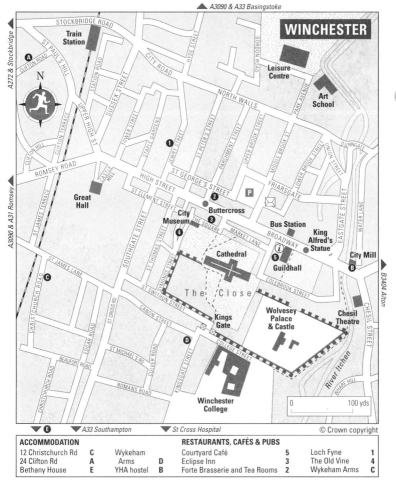

WINCHESTER

© Crown copyright

broke up the chests in 1645); William Rufus, killed while hunting in the New Forest in 1100, lies in the presbytery. Behind the impressive Victorian screen at the end of the presbytery, look out for the memorial shrine to St Swithun. Originally buried outside in the churchyard, his remains were later interred inside the cathedral where the "rain of heaven" could no longer fall on him, whereupon he took revenge and the heavens opened for forty days – hence the legend that if it rains on St Swithun's Day (July 15) it will continue for another forty. His exact burial place is unknown. Accessible from the north transept, the Norman **crypt** is only rarely open, since it's flooded for much of the time – the cathedral's original foundations were dug in marshy ground, and at the beginning of last century a steadfast diver, William Walker, spent five years replacing the rotten timber foundations with concrete. Inside are two fourteenth-century statues of William of Wykeham, and Antony Gormley's standing figure, "Sound II".

△ Winchester

Outside the cathedral, the **City Museum**, a basic local history display, sits on the Square (April–Oct Mon–Sat 10am–5pm, Sun noon–5pm; Nov–March Tues–Sat 10am–4pm, Sun noon–4pm; free). Walk west along the High Street from here to reach the **Great Hall** on Castle Street (daily: March–Oct 10am–5pm; Nov–Feb 10am–4pm; free), the vestigial remains of a thirteenth-century castle destroyed by Cromwell. Sir Walter Raleigh heard his death sentence here in 1603, though he wasn't finally dispatched until 1618, and Judge Jeffreys held one of his Bloody Assizes in the castle after Monmouth's rebellion in 1685. The main interest now, however, is a large, brightly painted disc slung on one wall like some curious antique dartboard. This is alleged to be King Arthur's Round Table, but the woodwork is probably fourteenth-century, later repainted as a PR exercise for the Tudor dynasty – the portrait of Arthur at the top of the table bears an uncanny resemblance to Henry VIII.

Head east along the High Street, past the Guildhall and the august bronze statue of King Alfred on the Broadway, to reach the River Itchen and the eighteenth-century **City Mill** (11am–5pm: March Sat & Sun; early April & July–Dec daily; mid-April to June Wed–Sun; £3; NT), where you can see restored mill machinery. Turning right before the bridge you pass what remains of the Saxon walls, which bracket the ruins of the twelfth-century **Wolvesey Castle** (April–Sept daily 10am–5pm; free; EH) and the Bishop's Palace, built by Christopher Wren. Immediately to the west up College Street stand the buildings of **Winchester College**, the oldest public school in England – established in 1382 by William of Wykeham for "poor scholars", it now educates few but the wealthy and privileged. The cloisters and chantry are open during term time and the chapel is open all year. Jane Austen moved to the house at 8 College St from Chawton in 1817, when she was already ill with Addison's Disease, dying there later the same year. The thirteenth-century **Kings Gate**, at the top of College Street, is one of the city's original medieval gateways, housing the tiny St Swithun's Church.

About a mile south of College Walk, reached by a pleasant stroll across the watermeadows of the Itchen, lies **St Cross Hospital** (April–Oct Mon–Sat 9.30am–5pm, Sun 1–5pm; Nov–March Mon–Sat 10.30am–3.30pm; £2.50). Founded in 1136 as a hostel for poor brethren, it boasts a fine church, begun in that year and completed a century or so later, where you can see a triptych by the Flemish painter Mabuse. Needy wayfarers may still apply for the "dole" at the Porter's Lodge – a tiny portion of bread and beer.

Practicalities

Winchester **train station** is about a mile northwest of the cathedral on Stockbridge Road. If you arrive by **bus**, you'll find yourself on the Broadway, conveniently opposite the **tourist office** in the imposing Guildhall (May–Sept Mon–Sat 9.30am–5.30pm, Sun 11am–4pm; Oct–April Mon–Sat 10am–5pm; ☎01962/840500, ⓦwww.visitwinchester.co.uk). Good **accommodation** options include the B&Bs at 24 Clifton Rd (☎01962/851620, ⓔjoanne .winchester@virgin.nⒺⓉ; ❷), a Victorian house in a quiet street, convenient for the train station, and at 12 Christchurch Rd (☎01962/854272; ❷), which has a conservatory and garden. Further up Christchurch Road, at no. 114, 🏠 *Bethany House* (☎01962/862188, ⓦwww.bethanyhousebandb.co.uk; ❹) was once a convent, and is now a classy guest house with modern facilities in its three spacious rooms (one with Turkish decor); close to St Cross Hospital, it's a 15-minute walk from the centre. None of the above allows smoking or takes credit cards. For character and location, however, it's hard to beat the *Wykeham Arms*, 75 Kingsgate St (☎01962/853834; ❻), a fine old hostelry with beamed, quirkily shaped rooms. Winchester's YHA **hostel** is perfectly sited in the City Mill, 1 Water Lane (☎0870/770 6092, ⓔwinchester@yha.org.uk; £11.95).

During the day, you can have **snacks** and full **meals** at the animated and central *Forte Brasserie and Tea Rooms*, 78 Parchment St (closed Sun), and at the relaxed 🏠 *Courtyard Café*, behind the Guildhall and tourist office. Opposite the cathedral, *The Old Vine*, 8 Great Minster St (☎01962/854616), has an unstuffy old-world atmosphere, ales on tap and good evening meals (book ahead). For quality seafood, head for *Loch Fyne*, 18 Jewry St (☎01962/872930), a converted jailhouse retaining its galleries and beams. The richly atmospheric 🍴 *Wykeham Arms* (☎01962/853838) also has first-class food and is the best place for a drink. Other good **pubs** include the sixteenth-century *Eclipse Inn*, 25 The Square, which has outside seating and serves pies and casseroles.

The Watercress Line and Chawton

ALRESFORD, six miles east of Winchester, is the departure-point for the **Mid-Hants Watercress Line** (March, April & Oct Sat & Sun; May–Sept & school holidays daily; ☎01962/733810, ⓦwww.watercressline.co.uk; £10), a jolly, steam-powered train, so named because it passes through the former watercress beds that once flourished here. The train chuffs ten miles to Alton, with gourmet dinners on Saturday evenings and traditional Sunday lunches served on board.

A mile southwest of Alton lies the village of **CHAWTON**, where Jane Austen lived from 1809 to 1817, during the last and most prolific years of her life, and where she wrote or revised almost all her six books, including *Sense and Sensibility* and *Pride and Prejudice*. **Jane Austen's House** (March–Nov daily 11am–4pm; Dec–Feb Sat & Sun 11am–4pm; £4.50), in the centre of the village, is a plain red-brick building, containing first editions of some of her greatest works.

The New Forest

Covering about 144 square miles, the **NEW FOREST** is England's newest National Park, and also one of southern England's main rural playgrounds, attracting about eight million visitors annually. The name itself is misleading, for much of this region's woodland was cleared for agriculture and settlement long before the Normans arrived, and its poor sandy soils support only a meagre covering of heather and gorse in many areas. The forest was requisitioned by William the Conqueror in 1079 as a game reserve, and the rights of its inhabitants soon became subservient to those of his precious deer. Fences to impede their progress were forbidden and terrible punishments were meted out to those who disturbed the animals – hands were lopped off, eyes put out. Later monarchs less passionate about hunting than the Normans gradually restored the forest-dwellers' rights, and today the New Forest enjoys a unique patchwork of ancient laws and privileges, enveloped in an arcane vocabulary dating from feudal times. The forest boundary is the "perambulation", and owner-occupiers of forest land have common rights to obscure practices such as "turbary" (peat cutting), "estover" (firewood collecting) and "mast" (letting pigs forage for acorns and beech nuts), as well as the more readily comprehensible right of pasture, permitting domestic animals to graze freely.

The **trees** of the forest are now much more varied than they were in pre-Norman times, with birch, holly, yew, Scots pine and other conifers interspersed with the ancient oaks and beeches. One of the most venerable trees is the much-visited **Knightwood Oak**, just a few hundred yards north of the A35 three miles southwest of Lyndhurst, which measures about 22ft in circumference at shoulder height. The most obvious species of New Forest **fauna** is the New Forest **pony** – you'll see them grazing nonchalantly by the roadsides and ambling through some villages. The local deer are less visible now that some of the faster roads are fenced, although several species still roam the woods, including the tiny **sika deer**, descendants of a pair that escaped from nearby Beaulieu in 1904.

To get the best from the region, you need to **walk** or **ride** through it, avoiding the places cars can reach. There are 150 miles of car-free gravel roads in the forest, making cycling an appealing prospect – pick up a book of route maps from tourist offices or bike rental shops. The Ordnance Survey Leisure Map 22 of the New Forest is best for exploring, and in Lyndhurst you'll find numerous specialist walking books and natural history guides. Lyndhurst and nearby Brockenhurst, both on train lines, have bus connections to most parts of the forest, and both have plenty of reasonably priced accommodation. There are ten **campsites** in the forest run by the Forestry Commission (T0131/314 6505, Wwww.forestholidays.co.uk), as well as several private sites. There's also a YHA **hostel** in Cottesmore House, Cott Lane, Burley, in the west of the Forest (T0870/770 5734, Eburley@yha.org.uk; closed early Oct to March, limited opening April & Sept to early Oct; £12.50), where tents and teepees can be rented.

Lyndhurst and Brockenhurst

LYNDHURST, its town centre skewered by an agonizing one-way system, isn't a particularly interesting place, though the brick **parish church** is worth a glance for its William Morris glass, a fresco by Lord Leighton and the grave of Mrs Reginald Hargreaves, better known as Alice Liddell, Lewis Carroll's model for Alice. The town is of most interest to visitors for the **New Forest Museum and Visitor Centre** in the central car park off the High Street (daily 10am–5pm; T023/8028 2269, Wwww.thenewforest.co.uk), where you can buy bus passes and maps. The **museum** (£3) focuses on the history, wildlife and industries of the forest. Nearby in Gosport Lane, AA Bike Hire (T023/8028 3349) rents **bikes**. For **accommodation** try *Forest Cottage*, at the west end of the High Street (T023/8028 3461, Wwww.forestcottage.co.uk; no credit cards; no smoking; ❷), with a well-stocked natural history library, or *Burwood Lodge*, 27 Romsey Rd (T023/8028 2445, Wwww.burwoodlodge.co.uk; no credit cards; ❸), a large old house a few minutes from the High Street. The *Parisien* café, at 64 High St, sells **snacks** that you can eat in its small garden in summer; for larger **meals**, head for the nearby *Crown Hotel*.

The forest's most visited site, the **Rufus Stone**, stands three miles northwest of Lyndhurst. Erected in 1745, it marks the putative spot where the Conqueror's son and heir, **William II** – aka William Rufus after his ruddy complexion – was killed by a crossbow bolt in 1100.

BROCKENHURST, four miles south of Lyndhurst, has **bikes for rent** at Cycle Experience, by the level-crossing (T01590/624204). Local **accommodation** choices include the *Cottage Hotel* on Sway Road (T01590/622296, Wwww.cottagehotel.org; ❼), and, a short distance further south in Sway, *Little Purley Farm*, a quiet B&B in Chapel Lane (T01590/682707; no credit cards; no smoking; ❷), with views over to the Isle of Wight. *The Snakecatcher* on Lyndhurst Road is a good **pub** that also serves terrific bar food.

Beaulieu and Buckler's Hard

The village of **BEAULIEU** (whose name originates from the French meaning "Beautiful Place", but is pronounced "Bewley"), in the southeast corner of the New Forest, was the site of one of England's most influential monasteries, a Cistercian house founded in 1204 by King John – in remorse, it is said, for ordering a group of supplicating Cistercian monks to be trampled to death. Built using stone ferried from Caen in northern France and Quarr on the Isle of Wight, the **abbey** managed a self-sufficient estate of ten thousand acres, but was dismantled soon after the Dissolution. Its refectory now forms the parish church, which, like everything else in Beaulieu, has been subsumed by the Montagu family who have owned a large chunk of the New Forest since one of Charles II's illegitimate progeny was created duke of the estate.

The estate has been transformed with a prodigious commercial vigour into **Beaulieu** (daily: May–Sept 10am–6pm; Oct–April 10am–5pm; £15.50; Ⓦ www.beaulieu.co.uk), a tourist complex comprising **Palace House**, the attractive if unexceptional family home, the abbey and the main attraction, Lord Montagu's **National Motor Museum**. An undersized monorail and an old London bus ease the ten-minute walk between the entry point and Palace House. The latter, formerly the abbey's gatehouse, contains masses of Montagu-related memorabilia while the undercroft of the adjacent abbey houses an exhibition depicting medieval monastic life. Inside, the celebrated Motor Museum, a collection of 250 cars and motorcycles, includes spindly antiques and recent classics, as well as a couple of svelte land-speed racers, including the record-breaking *Bluebird*. The entertaining "Wheels", a dizzying ride-through display, takes you on a trip through the history of motoring.

If Beaulieu amply deserves its name, **Buckler's Hard**, a couple of miles downstream on the River Beaulieu (daily: Easter–Sept 10.30am–5pm; Oct–Easter 11am–4pm; £5.25), has an even more wonderful setting. It doesn't look much like a shipyard now, but from Elizabethan times onwards dozens of men o' war were assembled here from giant New Forest oaks. Several of Nelson's ships were launched here, to be towed carefully by rowing boats past the sandbanks and across the Solent to Portsmouth. The largest house in this hamlet of shipwrights' cottages, which forms part of the Montagu estate, belonged to Henry Adams, the master builder responsible for most of the Trafalgar fleet; it's now an upmarket hotel and restaurant. At the top of the village, the **Maritime Museum** traces the history of the great ships and incorporates buildings preserved in their eighteenth-century form.

Lymington

The most pleasant point of access for the Isle of Wight (for ferry details, see p.223) is **LYMINGTON**, a sheltered haven that has become one of the busiest leisure harbours on the south coast. Rising from the quay area, the old town is full of cobbled streets and Georgian houses and has one unusual building – the partly thirteenth-century church of **St Thomas the Apostle**, with a cupola-topped tower built in 1670.

Information is available in summer from the local **visitor centre** in New Street, off the High Street (Easter–Sept Mon–Sat 10am–5pm; Oct–Easter Mon–Sat 10am–4pm; Ⓣ01590/689000). Places to **stay** in town include *The Monks Pool*, 22 Waterford Lane (Ⓣ01590/678850, Ⓦ www.camandjohn.com; ❸), a pleasant family home with a private lake, and *Durlston House*, Gosport Street (Ⓣ01590/677364, Ⓦ www.durlstonhouse.co.uk; ❹), a smart, clean town house with six guest rooms. Among Lymington's excellent **pubs**, all of which serve decent bar meals, try the *Chequers* on Ridgeway Lane, on the west side of town, the *Bosun's Chair*, on Station Road, and the harbourfront *Ship Inn*, with seats outside looking over the water.

Bournemouth and around

Renowned for its clean sandy beaches, the resort of **Bournemouth** has a single-minded holiday-making atmosphere, though neighbouring **Poole** and **Christchurch** are more interesting historically. North of this unbroken coastal sprawl, the pleasant old market town of **Wimborne** has one of the area's most striking churches, while the stately home of **Kingston Lacy** contains an outstanding collection of old masters and other paintings.

The town

BOURNEMOUTH dates only from 1811, when a local squire, Louis Tregonwell, built a summer house on the wild, unpopulated heathland that once occupied this stretch of coast, and planted the first of the pine trees that now characterize the area. The mild climate, sheltered site and glorious sandy beach encouraged the rapid growth of the resort, though today Bournemouth has acquired an unshakably genteel, elderly image. However, its geriatric nursing homes are counterbalanced by burgeoning numbers of language schools and a nightclub scene fuelled by a transient youthful population.

Apart from its pristine sandy beach (one of southern England's cleanest) Bournemouth is famed for its unusually high proportion of green space – a sixth of the town is given over to horticultural displays. Its most enthralling attraction, however, is the **Russell–Cotes Art Gallery and Museum** on East Cliff Promenade (Tues–Sun 10am–5pm; free), one of the region's best collections of Victoriana. The motley assortment of artworks and Oriental souvenirs was gathered from around the world by the Russell-Cotes family, hoteliers who grew wealthy during Bournemouth's late-Victorian tourist boom. The lavishly decorated building is jam-packed with their eclectic collections, of which the Japanese artefacts and the Pre-Raphaelite and other British art are especially striking. There's also a cliff-top landscaped garden, and a decent café.

In the centre of town, you might visit the graveyard of **St Peter's** church, just east of the Square, where Mary Shelley, author of the Gothic horror tale *Frankenstein*, is buried, together with the heart belonging to her husband, the Romantic poet Percy Bysshe Shelley. The tombs of Mary's parents – radical thinker William Godwin and early feminist Mary Wollstonecraft – are also here.

Practicalities

The **train station** and **bus station** opposite lie about a mile east of the centre, connected by frequent buses. The **tourist office** is centrally located on Westover Road (mid-July to mid-Sept Mon–Sat 9.30am–7pm, Sun 10.30am–5pm; mid-Sept to mid-July Mon–Sat 9.30am–5.30pm; ☏0906/802 0234, ⓦwww.bournemouth.co.uk). The town has **accommodation** to suit all budgets: try *Tudor Grange*, 31 Gervis Rd, East Cliff (☏01202/291472, ⓦwww .tudorgrangehotel.co.uk; ❹), with an attractive interior and gardens, or *Earlham Lodge*, 91 Alumhurst Rd, Alum Chine (☏01202/761943, ⓦwww.earlhamlodge .com; ❸), a friendly guest house near the beach. The small, friendly *Bournemouth Backpackers*, 3 Francis Rd (☏01202/299491, ⓦwww.bournemouthbackpackers.co.uk; £18), three minutes from the train and bus stations, also has some doubles (❶).

Centrally located on the Promenade by the pier, ✴*West Beach* (☏01202/587785) is a good seafood **restaurant** with great views and weekly live jazz, while *Bistro on the Beach*, right by the sea at the Southbourne end of the Esplanade

(℡01202/431473), is an ordinary café by day and a good-value restaurant in the evening (closed Sun & Mon, also Tues & Wed in winter). The *Goat and Tricycle* **pub**, 27 West Hill Rd, is worth the uphill trek for the real ales and homemade food.

The biggest and best known of Bournemouth's **nightclubs** is *Elements*, centrally located on Firvale Road, with an adjoining pre-club pub, *Circo*. The flamboyant *Opera House*, 570 Christchurch Rd, Boscombe, is worth seeking out for something a little different, while *Rubyztoo* at 29 The Triangle, at the top of Commercial Road, is Bournemouth's biggest **gay** club. On a more sedate note, the **Bournemouth International Festival** draws performers of every musical genre over a fortnight between June and July.

Christchurch

CHRISTCHURCH, five miles east of Bournemouth, is best known for its colossal parish church, **Christchurch Priory** (Mon–Sat 9.30am–5.30pm, Sun 2–5.30pm; £2 donation requested), bigger than most cathedrals. Built on the site of a Saxon minster dating from 650 AD, but exhibiting chiefly Norman and Perpendicular features, the church is the longest in England, at 311ft, and its fan-vaulted North Porch is the country's biggest. Fine views can be gained from the top of the 120-foot tower (ask at desk; £2).

The area round the old town quay has a carefully preserved charm, with the **Red House Museum and Gardens** on Quay Road (Tues–Sat 10am–5pm, Sun 2–5pm; free) containing an affectionate collection of local memorabilia. **Boat trips** (Easter to mid-Oct daily; ℡01202/429119) leave from the grassy banks of the riverside quay east to Mudeford (30min; £5 return) or upriver to the *Tuckton Tea Rooms* (20min; £2.30 return).

The **tourist office** is at 23 High St (July–Sept Mon–Fri 9.30am–5.30pm, Sat 9.30am–5pm; Oct–June Mon–Fri 9.30am–5pm, Sat 9.30am–4.30pm; ℡01202/471780, ⌾www.resort-guide.co.uk/christchurch). Christchurch's **accommodation** options can be fairly pricey, though Barrack and Stour roads, northwest of the centre, are lined with a selection of unexciting but reliable guest houses, such as *Grosvenor Lodge*, 53 Stour Rd (℡01202/499008, ⌾www.grosvenorlodge.co.uk; ❸). Alternatively, *The Three Gables*, 11 Wickfield Ave (℡01202/481166, ⌾www.3gables-christchurch.co.uk; no credit cards; ❸), is convenient for the centre and beaches. For **food**, *La Mamma*, 51 Bridge St (℡01202/471608; closed Sun lunch & Mon), serves cheap and cheerful Italian classics (including pizzas), with alfresco eating in summer, while *The Boathouse* on the Quay is rather pricey, but has good views. Recommended **pubs** include the lively *Thomas Tripp*, on Wick Lane, with outside decking and regular live music, and Christchurch's oldest pub, *Ye Olde George Inn*, with an attractive courtyard and decent food.

Poole

West of Bournemouth, **POOLE** is an ancient seaport on a huge, almost land-locked harbour. The town developed in the thirteenth century and was successively colonized by pirates, fishermen and timber traders. The old quarter by the quayside contains over a hundred historic buildings, as well as the **Waterfront Museum**, at the bottom of Old High Street (April–Oct Mon–Sat 10am–5pm, Sun noon–5pm; Nov–March Mon–Sat 10am–3pm, Sun noon–3pm; free), which traces Poole's development over the centuries, with displays of local ceramics and tiles and a rare Iron Age log boat.

From Poole's quay, you can catch one of the frequent ferries (£6.50 return) to **Brownsea Island** (daily: mid-March to late July & Sept 10am–5pm; late July to Aug 10am–6pm; Oct 10am–4pm; £4.20; NT), famed for its red squirrels, wading birds and other wildlife, which you can spot along themed trails that reveal a surprisingly diverse landscape.

One of the area's most famous gardens lies on the outskirts of Poole, **Compton Acres** (daily: March–Oct 10am–6pm; Nov–Feb 10am–4pm; £5.95), signposted off the A35 Poole Road, towards Bournemouth (buses #150 and #151). Each of the seven gardens here has a different international theme, the best of which is the elegantly understated Japanese Garden.

Poole's **tourist office** is in the Waterfront Museum (Easter–June, Sept & Oct daily 10am–5pm; July & Aug daily 9.15am–6pm; Nov–Easter Mon–Fri 10am–5pm, Sat 10am–4pm; ☎01202/253253, ⊛www.pooletourism.com). Central **accommodation** choices include the *Antelope Hotel* at 8 High Street (☎01202/672029; ❺), a handsome old hostelry. Further out, but close to the station, there's *Cranborne House*, 45 Shaftesbury Rd (☎01202/685200, ⊛www.cranborne-house.co.uk; ❹), a quality B&B fifteen minutes' walk from the Quayside.

There are several good **restaurants** on the High Street, including *Storm*, a moderately priced seafood restaurant at no. 16 (☎01202/674970; closed lunchtime, also Sun & Mon in winter), and, at the top of the street, *Alcatraz*, a relaxed Italian brasserie with outdoor tables. Good **pubs** include the *King Charles* on Thames Street, with leather armchairs.

Wimborne Minster and Kingston Lacy

An ancient town on the banks of the Stour, just a few minutes' drive north from the suburbs of Bournemouth, **WIMBORNE MINSTER**, as the name suggests, is mainly of interest for its great church, the **Minster of St Cuthberga** (Mon–Sat 9.30am–5.30pm, Sun 2.30–5.30pm). Built on the site of an eighth-century monastery, its massive twin towers of mottled grey and tawny stone dwarf the rest of the town, and at one time the church was even more imposing – its spire crashed down during morning service in 1602. What remains today is basically Norman with later features added such as the Perpendicular west tower, which bears a figure dressed as a grenadier of the Napoleonic era, who strikes every quarter-hour with a hammer. Inside, the church is crowded with memorials and eye-catching details – look out for the orrery clock inside the west tower, with the sun marking the hours and the moon marking the days of the month, and for the organ with trumpets pointing out towards the congregation instead of pipes. The **Chained Library** above the choir vestry (Easter–Oct Mon–Fri 10.30am–12.30pm & 2–4pm, Sat 10.30am–12.30pm), dating from 1686, is Wimborne's most prized possession and one of the oldest public libraries in the country.

Wimborne's older buildings stand around the main square near the minster, and are mostly from the late eighteenth or early nineteenth century. The **Priest's House** on the High Street started life as lodgings for the clergy, then became a stationer's shop. Now it is a **museum** (April–Oct 10am–4.30pm; also open two weeks after Christmas; £3), with each room furnished in the style of a different period, such as a working Victorian kitchen, a Georgian parlour and an ironmonger's shop. There's also a display of items relating to local archeology and history, while the walled garden at the rear provides an excellent spot for summer teas.

Kingston Lacy (house: mid-March to Oct Wed–Sun 11am–5pm; grounds: Feb to mid-March Sat & Sun 10.30am–4pm; mid-March to Oct daily 10.30am–6pm or dusk; Nov & Dec Fri–Sun 10.30am–4pm; house & grounds

£8, grounds only £4; NT), one of the country's finest seventeenth-century country houses, lies two miles northwest of Wimborne Minster, in 250 acres of parkland grazed by a herd of Red Devon cattle. Designed for the Bankes family, who were exiled from Corfe Castle (see p.239) after the Roundheads reduced it to rubble, the brick building was clad in grey stone during the nineteenth century by Sir Charles Barry, co-architect of the Houses of Parliament. William Bankes, then owner of the house, was a great traveller and collector, and the **Spanish Room** is a superb scrapbook of his Grand Tour souvenirs, lined with gilded leather and surmounted by a Venetian ceiling. Kingston Lacy's **picture collection** is also outstanding, featuring Titian, Rubens, Velázquez and many other old masters. Be warned, though, that this place gets so swamped with visitors that timed tickets are issued on busy weekends.

The Isle of Purbeck

Though not actually an island, the **ISLE OF PURBECK** – a promontory of low hills and heathland jutting out beyond Poole Harbour – does have an insular and distinctive feel. Reached from the east by the **ferry from Sandbanks**, at the narrow mouth of Poole harbour, or by a long and congested landward journey via the bottleneck of **Wareham**, Purbeck can be a difficult destination to reach, but its villages are immensely pretty, none more so than **Corfe Castle**, with its majestic ruins. From **Swanage**, a low-key seaside resort, the Dorset Coast Path provides access to the oily shales of Kimmeridge Bay, the spectacular cove at Lulworth and the much-photographed natural arch of **Durdle Door**. This whole coast from Purbeck to Exmouth in Devon – dubbed the **Jurassic Coast** – is a World Heritage Site on account of its geological significance and fossil remains.

Wareham and around

The grid pattern of its streets indicates the Saxon origins of **WAREHAM**, and the town is surrounded by even older earth ramparts known as the Walls. A riverside setting adds greatly to its charms, though there are horrible traffic queues in summer, and the scenic stretch along the Quay also gets fairly overrun. Nearby lies an enclave of quaint houses around **Lady St Mary's Church**, which contains the marble coffin of Edward the Martyr, murdered at Corfe Castle in 978 by his stepmother, to make way for her son Ethelred. **St Martin's Church**, at the north end of town, dates from Saxon times and holds a faded twelfth-century mural of St Martin offering his cloak to a beggar. The church's most striking feature, however, is a romantic effigy of T.E. Lawrence in Arab dress, which was originally destined for Salisbury Cathedral, but was rejected by the dean there who disapproved of Lawrence's sexual proclivities. Lawrence was killed in 1935 in a motorbike accident on the road from Bovington (6 miles west); his simply furnished cottage is at **Clouds Hill**, seven miles northwest of Wareham (mid-March to Oct Thurs–Sun noon–5pm or dusk; £3.50; NT). The small **museum** next to Wareham's town hall in East Street (Easter–Oct Mon–Sat 11am–4pm; free) displays some of Lawrence's memorabilia, as does the **Tank Museum** in Bovington Camp, five miles west of town (daily 10am–5pm; £8.50), whose main exhibits are some 150 military vehicles.

Holy Trinity Church, on South Street, contains Wareham's **tourist office** (Easter–Oct Mon–Sat 9.30am–5pm; Nov–Easter Mon–Sat 10am–3pm; ☏01929/552740, ⓦwww.purbeck.gov.uk). The best **accommodation** options are *Anglebury House*, 15 North St (℡01929/552988; no smoking; ❸), whose previous guests have included Thomas Hardy and T.E. Lawrence, and the *Old Granary* on the Quay (℡01929/552010; ❸), which also has a **restaurant** with views over the river.

Corfe Castle

The romantic ruins crowning the hill behind the village of **CORFE CASTLE** (daily. March & Oct 10am–5pm; April–Sept 10am–6pm; Nov–Feb 10am–4pm; £5; NT) are perhaps the most evocative in England. The family seat of Sir John Bankes, Attorney General to Charles I, this Royalist stronghold withstood a Cromwellian siege for six weeks, gallantly defended by Lady Bankes. One of her own men, Colonel Pitman, eventually betrayed the castle to the Round-heads, after which it was reduced to its present gap-toothed state by gunpowder.

△ Corfe Castle

Apparently the victorious Roundheads were so impressed by Lady Bankes's courage that they allowed her to take the keys to the castle with her – they can still be seen in the library at the Bankes's subsequent home, Kingston Lacy (see p.237).

The village is well stocked with tearooms and gift shops and has a couple of good **pubs** too: the *Fox* on West Street, and, below the castle ramparts, the *Greyhound*. There's comfortable **accommodation** at *The Old Curatage*, 30 East St (℡01929/481441, ⒺspudtatⒺ@supanet.com; no smoking; no credit cards; ➌), and at the *Bankes Arms Hotel* (℡01929/480206, Ⓦwww.dorset-hotel.co.uk; ➌), an old inn outside the castle entrance.

Swanage and around

Purbeck's largest town, **SWANAGE**, is a traditional seaside resort with a pleasant sandy beach and an ornate town hall. The town's station is the southern terminus of the **Swanage Steam Railway** (April–Oct daily; Nov, Dec & mid-Feb to March Sat & Sun; £7.50 all day), which runs as far as Norden, just north of Corfe Castle. For timetables, call ℡01929/425800, check at Ⓦwww .swanagerailway.co.uk or pick up a leaflet from the tourist office. On foot, you can walk north out of Swanage, past the Foreland promontory to the broad sweep of **Studland Bay**. Its most northerly stretch, **Shell Bay**, is a magnificent beach of icing-sugar sand backed by a remarkable heathland ecosystem that's home to all six British species of reptile – adders are quite common, so be careful. At the top end of the beach a chain **ferry** (daily 7am–11pm every 20min) connects the Isle of Purbeck with Sandbanks in Poole.

Swanage's **tourist office** is by the beach on Shore Road (Easter–Oct daily 10am–5pm; Nov–Easter closed Sun; ℡0870/442 0680, Ⓦwww.swanage.gov .uk), and there's a YHA **hostel**, with good views across the bay, on Cluny Crescent (℡0870/770 6058, Ⓔswanage@yha.org.uk; limited opening; £17.50). The town's numerous **accommodation** options include the spacious Victorian *Clare House*, 1 Park Rd (℡01929/422855, Ⓦwww.clare-house.com; ➍), and there's a cluster of B&Bs on King's Road near the train station. For a **meal**, head for the cosy *Trattoria*, 12 High St (℡01929/423784; closed daytime), a popular, moderately priced Italian restaurant; during the day, cappuccinos and baguettes are served next door at *Forte's Caffè Tratt*. **Bikes** can be rented from Bikeabout, 71 High St (℡01929/425050).

Durlstone Head to Durdle Door

Highlights of the coast beyond Swanage are the cliffs of **Durlstone Head** and the coastal path to **St Alban's Head**. West of this headland, **Kimmeridge Bay** shelters a remarkable marine wildlife reserve much appreciated by divers – there's a Dorset Wildlife Trust **information centre** by the slipway (Easter–Sept Tues–Sun 10am–5pm; Oct–Easter Sat & Sun noon–4pm; ℡01929/481044). The quaint thatch-and-stone villages of East and West Lulworth form a prelude to **Lulworth Cove**, a perfect shell-shaped bite formed when the sea broke through a weakness in the cliffs and then gnawed away at them from behind, forming a circular cave which eventually collapsed to leave a bay enclosed by sandstone cliffs. The mysteries of the local geology are explained at the **Lulworth Heritage Centre** (daily: March–Oct 10am–6pm; Nov–Feb 10am–4pm; free).

Immediately west of the cove, **Stair Hole** is a roofless sea cave riddled with arches that will eventually collapse to form another Lulworth. A couple of miles west, the famous limestone arch of **Durdle Door** appeals to serious geologist and casual sightseer alike. Most people take the uphill route to the arch which starts from the car park at Lulworth Cove but you can avoid the steep climb by walking from the *Durdle Door Holiday Park*, on the road to East Chaldon from West Lulworth.

WEST LULWORTH is the obvious **place to stay** or eat hereabouts. The *Castle Inn* (℡01929/400311, ⓦwww.thecastleinn-lulworthcove.co.uk; ❸), *Cromwell House Hotel* (℡01929/400253, ⓦwww.lulworthcove.co.uk; ❺), right on the coast path, and the seventeenth-century *Ivy Cottage* (℡01929/400509, ⓦwww.ivycottage.biz; no smoking; no credit cards; ❶) all make for good stopoffs. There's a YHA **hostel** at the end of School Lane West (℡0870/770 5940, ⓔlulworth@yha.org.uk; sporadic opening in winter; £11.95), a stone's throw from the Dorset Coast Path. **Campers** can find a pitch at the above-mentioned *Durdle Door Holiday Park* (℡01929/400200; closed Nov–Feb). In East Chaldon, four miles northwest of Lulworth Cove, the *Sailor's Return* has mouthwatering **pub food**.

Dorchester and around

The county town of Dorset, **DORCHESTER** still functions as the main agricultural centre for the region, and if you catch it on a Wednesday when the market is in full swing you'll find it livelier than usual. For the local tourist authorities, however, this is essentially **Thomas Hardy**'s town; he was born at Higher Bockhampton, three miles east of here, his heart is buried in Stinsford, a couple of miles northeast (the rest of him is in Westminster Abbey), and he spent much of his life in Dorchester itself, where his statue now stands on High West Street. The town appears in his novels as Casterbridge, and the countryside all around is evocatively depicted, notably the wild heathland of the east (Egdon Heath) and the eerie yew forest of Cranborne Chase. The real Dorchester has a pleasant central core of mostly seventeenth-century and Georgian buildings, though the town's origins go back to the Romans, who founded "Durnovaria" in about 70 AD. The Roman walls were replaced in the eighteenth century by tree-lined avenues called "Walks" (Bowling Alley Walk, West Walk and Colliton Walk), but some traces of the Roman period have survived. At the back of County Hall excavations have uncovered a fine Roman villa with a well-preserved mosaic floor, and on the southeast edge of town you'll find **Maumbury Rings**, where the Romans held vast gladiatorial combats in an amphitheatre adapted from a Stone Age site. The gruesome traditions continued into the Middle Ages, when gladiators were replaced by bear-baiting and public executions or "hanging fairs".

Dorchester is also associated with the notorious **Judge Jeffreys**, who, after the ill-fated rebellion of the Duke of Monmouth (another of Charles II's illegitimate offspring) against James II, held his "Bloody Assizes" in the Oak Room of the **Antelope Hotel** on Cornhill in 1685. A total of 292 men were sentenced to death, though most got away with a flogging and transportation to the West Indies, while 74 were hung, drawn and quartered, their heads stuck on pikes throughout Dorset and Somerset.

In 1834 the **Shire Hall**, further down High West Street, witnessed another *cause célèbre*, when six men from the nearby village of Tolpuddle were sentenced to transportation for banding together to form the Friendly Society of Agricultural Labourers, in order to petition for a small wage increase on the grounds that their families were starving. After a public outcry the men were pardoned, and the **Tolpuddle Martyrs** passed into history as founders of the trade union movement. The room in which they were tried is preserved as a memorial to the martyrs, and you can find out more about them in Tolpuddle itself, eight miles east on the A35, where there's a fine little **museum** (April–Oct Tues–Sat 10am–5.30pm, Sun 11am–5.30pm; Nov–March closes at 4pm; free).

The best place to find out about Dorchester's history is the engrossing **Dorset County Museum** on High West Street (July–Sept daily 10am–5pm; Oct–June Mon–Sat 10am–5pm; £5), where archeological and geological displays trace Celtic and Roman history, including a section on Maiden Castle. Pride of place goes to the re-creation of Thomas Hardy's study, where his pens are inscribed with the names of the books he wrote with them. Other museums in town include the formidably turreted **Keep Military Museum** (July & Aug Mon–Sat 9.30am–5pm, Sun 10am–4pm; Sept–June closed Sun; £3), at the top of High West Street, which traces the fortunes of the Dorset and Devonshire regiments over three hundred years and offers sweeping views over the town, and **Tutankhamun: The Exhibition**, lower down High West Street (daily 9.30am–5.30pm; £5.50), a fascinating and thorough exploration of the young pharaoh's life and afterlife through to the eventual discovery of his tomb in 1922.

Practicalities

Dorchester has two **train stations**, both of them to the south of the centre: trains from Weymouth and London arrive at Dorchester South, while Bath and Bristol trains use the Dorchester West station. Most **buses** stop around the car park on Acland Road, to the east of South Street. The **tourist office** is in Antelope Walk (April & Oct Mon–Sat 9am–5pm; May–Sept Mon–Sat 9am–5pm, Sun 10am–3pm; Nov–March Mon–Sat 9am–4pm; ℡01305/267992, ⓦwww .westdorset.com).

Dorchester's **accommodation** ranges from the superior Georgian *Casterbridge Hotel*, 49 High East St (℡01305/264043, ⓦwww.casterbridgehotel .co.uk; ❻), to budget options such as the *King's Arms*, also on High East Street (℡01305/265353; ❷), and *Maumbury Cottage*, 9 Maumbury Rd (℡01305/266726; no credit cards; ❶), near the Rings and the stations. The nearest YHA **hostel** is at Litton Cheney (℡0870/770 5922; closed Sept to mid-April; £11.95), halfway between Dorchester and Bridport.

For **food**, there are Mediterranean dishes and tasty desserts on offer at *Café Jagos*, 8 High West St (℡01305/266056); alternatively, good **pub** meals are served at the *King's Arms* (see above), and the *Royal Oak* and the *Old Ship Inn*, both on High West Street.

Maiden Castle

One of southern England's finest prehistoric sites, **Maiden Castle** (free access) stands on a hill two miles or so southwest of Dorchester. Covering about 115 acres, it was first developed around 3000 BC by a Stone Age farming community and then used during the Bronze Age as a funeral mound. Iron Age dwellers expanded it into a populous settlement and fortified it with a daunting series of ramparts and ditches, just in time for the arrival of Vespasian's Second Legion. The ancient Britons' slingstones were no match for the more sophisticated weapons of the Roman invaders, however, and Maiden Castle was stormed in a bloody massacre in 43 AD.

What you see today is a massive series of grassy concentric ridges about sixty feet high, creasing the surface of the hill. The main finds from the site are displayed in the Dorset County Museum (see opposite).

Weymouth to Bridport

Whether George III's passion for sea bathing was a symptom of his eventual madness is uncertain, but it was at the bay of **Weymouth** that in 1789 he became the first reigning monarch to follow the craze. Sycophantic gentry rushed into the waves behind him, and soon the town, formerly a workaday harbour, took on the elegant Georgian stamp which it bears today. A likeness of the monarch on horseback is even carved into the chalk downs northwest of the town, like some guardian spirit. Weymouth nowadays is a lively family holiday destination in summer, reverting to a more sedate rhythm out of season.

Just south of the town stretch the giant arms of Portland Harbour, and a long causeway links Weymouth to the odd excrescence of the **Isle of Portland**. West of the causeway, the eighteen-mile bank of pebbles known as **Chesil Beach** runs northwest towards **Bridport**.

Weymouth

WEYMOUTH had long been a port before the Georgians popularized it as a resort. It's possible that a ship unloading a cargo here in 1348 first brought the Black Death to English shores, and it was from Weymouth that John Endicott sailed in 1628 to found Salem in Massachusetts. A few buildings survive from these pre-Georgian times: the restored **Tudor House** on Trinity Street (June–Sept Tues–Fri 1pm–3.45pm; Oct–May first Sun of month 2–4pm; £2.50) and the ruins of **Sandsfoot Castle** (free access), built by Henry VIII, overlooking Portland Harbour. But Weymouth's most imposing architectural heritage stands along the Esplanade, a dignified range of bow-fronted and porticoed buildings gazing out across the graceful bay. The more intimate quayside of the Old Harbour, linked to the Esplanade by the main pedestrianized thoroughfare St Mary's Street, is lined with waterfront pubs.

Weymouth's faded gentility is now counterbalanced by a number of "all-weather" attractions, the most high-profile of which is the **Sea Life Park** in Lodmoor Country Park, east of the Esplanade (daily 10am–5pm; winter sometimes closes at 4pm; last admission 1hr before closing; £9.95), where you can get close to sharks and rays and wander among multichrome birds in the tropical house. Other attractions include the **Deep Sea Adventure** at the Old Harbour (daily 9.30am–8pm; last entry 90min before closing; £3.75), which describes the origins of modern diving and the sobering story of the *Titanic* disaster. Over the river on Hope Square, **The Timewalk**, housed in Brewer's Quay (March–Oct daily 10am–5.30pm; summer school holidays open until 9pm; last entry 1hr before closing; £4.50), contains an entertaining and educational walk-through exhibition of Weymouth's maritime and brewing past. A fifteen-minute walk southwards leads to **Nothe Fort** (May–Sept daily 10.30am–5.30pm; Oct–April hours variable; ☎01305/766626; £4.50), built 1860–72 to defend Portland Harbour. Here, you'll find displays on military themes and a museum illustrating garrison life and the castle's role in coastal defence.

Practicalities

Weymouth's **train station** is a couple of blocks west of the King's Statue on the Esplanade, which is where you'll find the town's **tourist office** (daily: April–Oct 9.30am–5pm; Nov–March 10am–4pm; ☎01305/785747, 🅦www .weymouth.gov.uk). A cluster of the town's **accommodation** options lies at the south end of the Esplanade, for instance *Chatsworth*, at no. 14 (☎01305/785012,

@www.thechatsworth.co.uk; ❺), which has a garden terrace, and the Georgian *Cavendish House*, at no. 5 (☎01305/782039; no credit cards; ❸), overlooking the bay with harbour views at the back. Nearer the train station but just a few steps from the seafront, the *Wilton Guest House* (☎01305/783317, @www .weymouthwilton-gh.co.uk; ❶), on Gloucester Street, is also good value. As for **restaurants**, you can't do better than *Perry's* for seafood, overlooking the quay-side at 4 Trinity Rd (☎01305/785799; closed Sat lunch, all day Sun & Mon lunch). For less expensive fare, try *No. 21*, an informal vegetarian restaurant at 21 East St (☎01305/767848; closed Mon–Wed eve Oct–June). Amenable **pubs** include the *Old Rooms Inn*, at the northern end of Trinity Road, an inexpensive lunch venue with a strong maritime theme, and the *Nothe Tavern*, buried among Nothe Gardens, south of the harbour on Barrack Road, which has bar meals and views from the garden.

Portland

Stark, wind-battered and treeless, the **Isle of Portland** is famed above all for its hard white limestone, which has been quarried here for centuries – Wren used it for St Paul's Cathedral, and it clads the UN headquarters in New York. It was also used for the six-thousand-foot breakwater that protects Portland Harbour – the largest artificial harbour in Britain, which was built by convicts in the mid-nineteenth century.

The causeway road by which the Isle is approached stands on the eastern-most section of the Chesil shingle. To the east you get a good view of the huge harbour, a naval base since 1872. The first settlement you come to, **FORTUNESWELL**, is surveyed by a 460-year-old Tudor fortress, **Portland Castle** (daily: Easter–June & Sept 10am–5pm; July & Aug 10am–6pm; Oct 10am–4pm; £3.60; EH), commissioned by Henry VIII. The craggy limestone of the Isle rises to 496 feet at Verne Hill, to the southeast of here.

At **Portland Bill**, the southern tip of the island, a lighthouse has guarded the promontory since the eighteenth century. You can climb the 153 steps of the present one, dating from 1906, for the views (Easter–Sept Mon–Fri & Sun 11am–5pm; £2), and it also houses Portland's **tourist office** (Easter–Sept daily 11am–5pm; ☎01305/861233). **Accommodation** options in the area include the *Pulpit Inn* on Portland Bill (☎01305/821237; ❸), and a YHA **hostel** just south of Portland Castle, on Castle Road (☎0870/770 6000, ⓔportland@yha .org.uk; limited opening Nov–Feb; £16.50).

Chesil Beach to Bridport

Chesil Beach is the strangest feature of the Dorset coast, a two-hundred-yard-wide, fifty-foot-high bank of pebbles that extends for eighteen miles, its component stones gradually decreasing in size from fist-like pebbles at Portland to "pea gravel" at Burton Bradstock in the west. This sorting is an effect of the powerful coastal currents, which make this one of the most dangerous beaches in Europe – churchyards in the local villages display plenty of evidence of wrecks and drownings. Though not a swimming beach, Chesil is popular with sea anglers, and its wild, uncommercialized atmosphere makes an appealing antidote to the south-coast resorts. Behind the beach, **The Fleet**, a brackish lagoon, was the setting for J. Meade Faulkner's classic smuggling tale, *Moonfleet*.

At the point where the shingle beach attaches itself to the shore is the pretty village of **ABBOTSBURY**, all tawny ironstone and thatch, and site of a former Benedictine abbey. The village **Swannery** (daily: mid-March to Sept 10am–6pm; Oct 10am–5pm; last admission 1hr before closing; £6.80), a wetland reserve for mute swans, dates back to medieval times, when presumably it formed part of the abbot's larder. The fifteenth-century Tithe Barn is the last remnant of the abbey, and today houses a **Children's Farm** (daily: Easter–Sept 10am–6pm; Oct 10am–5pm; last admission 1hr before closing; call for winter opening ℡01305/871817; £5.50), with goats, donkeys and Kuni Kuni pigs. Other attractions include the **Subtropical Gardens** (daily: March–Oct 10am–6pm; Nov–Feb 10am–dusk; last admission 1hr before closing; £6.80), where delicate species thrive in the microclimate created by Chesil's stones, which act as a giant radiator to keep out all but the worst frosts. Up on the downs a couple of miles inland from Abbotsbury is a monument to Thomas Hardy, not the usual one associated with Dorset, but the flag captain in whose arms Admiral Nelson expired. If you want to **stay** in Abbotsbury try *Swan Lodge*, 1 Rodden Row (℡01305/871249; ❹), or the *Ilchester Arms* in the village centre, a handsome stone inn with fine food (℡01305/871243, ⓦwww.ilchesterarms.co.uk; ❺).

BRIDPORT, just beyond the far end of Chesil Beach, is a pleasant old town of brick rather than stone, with unusually wide streets, a hangover from its rope-making days when cords made of locally grown hemp and flax were stretched between the houses. Bridport's fine buildings include a medieval church, a Georgian town hall, a fourteenth-century chantry and a Tudor building housing the local **museum** (April–Oct Mon–Sat 10am–5pm; £2).

Bridport's harbour is a mile or so south at **West Bay**, a fishing resort where majestic red cliffs rear up above the sea. Here, the renowned and expensive *Riverside Restaurant* offers fresh seafood and views over the river (book ahead; ℡01308/422011), and there's comfortable but pricey **accommodation** close to West Bay's beach at the *Bridport Arms Hotel* (℡01308/422994; ❻). Cheaper accommodation can be found further away from the harbour at *Britmead House*, 154 West Bay Rd (℡01308/422941, ⓦwww.britmeadhouse.co.uk; ❹), on the road back to Bridport. Bridport's **tourist office** is at 32 South St (April–Oct Mon–Sat 9am–5pm; Nov–March Mon–Sat 10am–3pm; ℡01308/424901, ⓦwww.bridportandwestbay.co.uk).

Lyme Regis and around

LYME REGIS, Dorset's most westerly town, shelters snugly between steep hills, just before the grey, fossil-filled cliffs lurch into Devon. Its intimate size and photogenic qualities make Lyme a popular and congested spot in high summer, though the town still lives up to the classy impression created by its regal name, which it owes to a royal charter granted by Edward I in 1284. It also has some upmarket literary associations – Jane Austen summered in a seafront cottage and set part of *Persuasion* in Lyme (and the town appears in the 1995 film adaptation), while novelist John Fowles lived here until his death in 2005, and the film adaptation of his book, *The French Lieutenant's Woman*, was shot here.

Colourwashed cottages and elegant Regency and Victorian villas line its seafront and flanking streets, but Lyme's best-known feature is a briskly practical reminder of its commercial origins: **The Cobb**, a curving harbour wall first constructed in the thirteenth century. It has suffered many alterations since, most notably in the nineteenth century, when its massive boulders were clad in neater blocks of Portland stone.

As you walk along the seafront and out towards The Cobb, look for the outlines of ammonites in the walls and paving stones. The cliffs around Lyme are made up of a complex layer of limestone, greensand and unstable clay, a perfect medium for preserving fossils, which are exposed by landslips of the water-logged clays. In 1811, after a fierce storm caused parts of the cliffs to collapse, 12-year-old Mary Anning, a keen fossil-hunter, discovered an almost complete dinosaur skeleton, a 30-foot ichthyosaurus now displayed in London's Natural History Museum.

Hammering fossils out of the cliffs is frowned on by today's conservationists, and in any case is rather hazardous. Hands-off inspection of the area's complex geology can be enjoyed on both sides of town: to the west lies the **Undercliff**, a fascinating jumble of overgrown landslips, now a nature reserve. East of Lyme, the Dorset Coast Path is closed as far as jaded **Charmouth** (Jane Austen's favourite resort), but at low tide you can walk for two miles along the beach, then, just past Charmouth, rejoin the coastal path to the headland of **Golden Cap**, whose brilliant outcrop of auburn sandstone is crowned with gorse.

Lyme's excellent **Philpot Museum** on Bridge Street (Mon–Sat 10am–5pm, Sun 11am–5pm; £2.20) provides a crash course in local history and geology, while **Dinosaurland** on Coombe Street (daily 10am–5pm, Aug until 6pm; £4) fills out the story on ammonites and other local fossils. Also worth seeing is the small **marine aquarium** on The Cobb (March–Oct 10am–5pm, with later closing in July & Aug; £3), where local fishermen bring unusual catches, and the fifteenth-century **parish church** of St Michael the Archangel, up Church Street, which contains a seventeenth-century pulpit and a massive chained Bible.

Practicalities

Lyme's nearest **train station** is in Axminster, five miles north (bus #31), and National Express runs a daily **bus** service from Exeter (see p.331). The **tourist office** is on Church Street (May–Oct Mon–Sat 10am–5am, Sun 10am–4pm; Nov–April Mon–Sat 10am–3pm; ☎01297/442138, ⓦwww.lymeregistourism.co.uk).

Central **accommodation** choices in Lyme include *Coombe House*, 41 Coombe St (☎01297/443849, ⓦwww.coombe-house.co.uk; no credit cards; ❷), a friendly B&B with large rooms and a self-catering appartment, and the *Old Monmouth Hotel*, 12 Church St (☎01297/442456, ⓦwww.lyme-regis-hotel.co.uk; no smoking; ❸). If you want to stay right next to the sea, book in at the *Cobb Arms*, Marine Parade (☎01297/443242; ❺). For a daytime snack or inexpensive **meal**, try the *Bell Cliff Restaurant* at 5–6 Broad St, also open in the evenings in summer, or ⚔ *Café Indigo*, 44–45 Coombe St (☎01297/445371; closed Wed, also Mon & Tues in winter; BYOB), a café and snack bar by day, and inexpensive pasta and pizza restaurant in the evening. The best **pubs** are the *Royal Standard* on Ozone Parade, and the *Pilot Boat* on Bridge Street, which also does excellent seafood and vegetarian meals.

Inland Dorset and southern Wiltshire

The main pleasures of inland Dorset come from unscheduled meandering through its ancient landscapes and tiny rural settlements. The rumbustious chalk-carved giant outside the village of **Cerne Abbas** is the county's most photographed site, but the major tourist honeypots are the towns of **Shaftesbury** and **Sherborne**, and, across the county boundary in Wiltshire, the landscaped garden at **Stourhead** and the brasher stately home at **Longleat**, an unlikely hybrid of safari park and historic monument.

Cerne Abbas

Seven miles north of Dorchester, just off the A352, on the #216 bus route between Dorchester and Sherborne, **CERNE ABBAS** has bags of charm, with gorgeous Tudor cottages and abbey ruins, but its main attraction is the enormously priapic **giant** carved in the chalk hillside just north of the village, standing 180 feet high and flourishing a club over his disproportionately small head. The age of the monument is disputed, some authorities believing it to be pre-Roman, others thinking it might be a Romano-British figure of Hercules. Either way, in view of his prominent feature it's probable that the giant originated as some primeval fertility symbol. Folklore has it that lying on the outsize member will induce conception, but the National Trust, who now own the site, do their best to stop people wandering over it and eroding the two-foot trenches that form the outlines.

Sherborne

Tucked away in the northwest corner of Dorset, ten miles north of Cerne Abbas, the pretty town of **SHERBORNE** was once the capital of Wessex, its church having cathedral status until Old Sarum (see p.252) usurped the bishopric in 1075. This former glory is embodied by the magnificent **Abbey Church** (daily: April–Oct 8am–6pm; Nov–March 8am–4pm), which was founded in 705, later becoming a Benedictine abbey. Most of its extant parts date from a rebuilding in the fifteenth century, and it is one of the best examples of Perpendicular architecture in Britain, particularly noted for its outstanding **fan vaulting**. The church also has a famously weighty peal of bells, led by "Great Tom", a tenor bell presented to the abbey by Cardinal Wolsey. Among the abbey church's many tombs are those of Alfred the Great's two brothers, Ethelred and Ethelbert, and the Elizabethan poet Thomas Wyatt, all located in the northeast corner. The **almshouse** on the opposite side of the Abbey Close was built in 1437 and is a rare example of a medieval hospital; another wing provides accommodation for Sherborne's well-known public school.

The town also has two "castles", both associated with Sir Walter Raleigh. Queen Elizabeth I first leased, then gave, Raleigh the twelfth-century **Old Castle** (Tues–Thurs, Sat & Sun: Easter–June & Sept 10am–5pm; July & Aug 10am–6pm; Oct 10am–4pm; £2.30; EH), but it seems that he despaired of feudal accommodation and built himself a more comfortably domesticated house, **Sherborne Castle**, in adjacent parkland (Easter–Oct Tues–Thurs & Sun 11am–4.30pm, Sat 2.30–5pm; castle & gardens £7.50, gardens only £3.50). When Sir Walter fell from the queen's favour by seducing her maid of honour, the Digby family acquired the house and have lived there ever since; portraits, furniture and books are displayed in a whimsically Gothic interior, remodelled in the nineteenth century. The Old Castle fared less happily, and was pulverized by Cromwellian cannon fire for the obstinately Royalist leanings of its occupants. The **museum** near the abbey on Church Lane (April–Oct Tues–Sat 10.30am–4.30pm, some Sundays 2.30–4.30pm; £1) includes a model of the Old Castle and photographs of parts of the fifteenth-century Sherborne Missal, a richly illuminated tome weighing nearly fifty pounds, now housed in the British Library.

The **tourist office** is at 3 Tilton Court, Digby Road (Mon–Sat: Easter–Oct 9am–5pm; Nov–Easter 10am–3pm; ☏01935/815341, ⊛www.westdorset .com). For an **overnight stay** try the *Britannia Inn*, on Westbury, just down from the abbey (☏01935/813300; ❷), or the *Half Moon*, Half Moon Street (☏01935/812017; ❹). Further down Half Moon Street, the *Church House*

Inland Dorset and southern Wiltshire

Gallery is good for teas and light lunches, as is *Oliver's*, 19 Cheap St. The *Cross Keys Hotel*, 88 Cheap St, is a cosy **pub** with a few tables outside for drinks and meals.

Shaftesbury

Fifteen miles east of Sherborne, **SHAFTESBURY** perches on a spur of lumpy hills, with severe gradients on three sides of the town. On a clear day, views from the town are terrific – one of the best vantage points is **Gold Hill**, quaint, cobbled and very steep. At its crest, the local history **museum** (April–Oct daily 10.30am–4.30pm; £1) displays a collection of locally made buttons, for which the area was once renowned.

Pilgrims used to flock to Shaftesbury to pay homage to the bones of Edward the Martyr, which were brought to the **Abbey** in 978, though now only the footings of the abbey church survive, just off the main street (April–Oct daily 10am–5pm; £2). **St Peter's Church** on the market place is one of the few reminders of Shaftesbury's medieval grandeur, when it boasted a castle, twelve churches and four market crosses.

The **tourist office** is on Bell Street (April–Sept daily 10am–5pm; Oct–March Mon–Sat 10am–3pm; ☏01747/853514, ⊛www.ruraldorset.com). **Accommodation** options include *The Chalet* on Christy's Lane, which has modern, fully equipped rooms (☏01747/853945, ⊛www.thechalet.biz; no smoking; no under-12s; no credit cards; ❸), and the *Knoll* in Bleke Street (☏01747/855243, ⊛www.pick-art.org.uk; ❸), boasting views over three counties. The *Salt Cellar* at the top of Gold Hill makes a great place for a daytime **snack** or **meal**.

Stourhead

Landscape gardening was a favoured mode of display among the grandest eighteenth-century landowners, and **Stourhead**, ten miles northwest of Shaftesbury, is one of the most accomplished examples of the genre (house Easter–Oct Mon, Tues & Fri–Sun 11am–5pm or dusk; garden daily 9am–7pm or dusk; house & garden £9.90; house £5.80; garden £5.80 or £4.30 in winter; NT). The Stourton estate was bought in 1717 by Henry Hoare, who commissioned Colen Campbell to build a new villa in the Palladian style. Hoare's heir, another Henry, returned from his Grand Tour in 1741 with his head full of the paintings of Claude and Poussin, and determined to translate their images of well-ordered, wistful classicism into real life. He dammed the Stour to create a lake, then planted the terrain with blocks of trees, domed temples, stone bridges, grottoes and statues, all mirrored vividly in the water. In 1772 the folly of **King Alfred's Tower** (April–Oct daily noon–5pm or dusk; £2.15) was added and today affords fine views across the estate and into neighbouring counties. The house, in contrast, is fairly run-of-the-mill, though it has some good Chippendale furniture.

Longleat

If Stourhead is an unexpected outcrop of Italy in Wiltshire, the African savannah intrudes even more bizarrely at **Longleat** (house April–Sept daily 10am–5.30pm; Oct–March guided tours at set times 11am–3pm; check at ☏01985/844400 or ⊛www.longleat.co.uk; safari park Easter–Oct Mon–Fri 10am–4pm, Sat, Sun & school holidays 10am–5pm; house £9, safari park £10, all attractions £18), two and a half miles south of the road from Warminster to Frome. In 1946 the sixth marquess of Bath became the first stately-home owner to open his house to the paying public on a regular basis, and in 1966 he caused even more amazement when Longleat's Capability Brown landscapes were turned into England's first drive-through **safari park**. Other attractions followed, including the world's largest hedge maze, a Doctor Who exhibition, a high-tech simulation of the world's most dangerous modes of travel, and the seventh marquess's steamy murals encapsulating his interpretation of life and the universe (children not admitted). Beyond the brazen razzmatazz, though, there's an exquisitely furnished Elizabethan house, built for Sir John Thynne, Elizabeth's High Treasurer, with the largest private library in Britain and a fine collection of pictures, including Titian's *Holy Family*.

Longleat is about four miles from the train stations of Frome and Warminster; the #53 bus (Mon–Sat) shuttles roughly every hour between Warminster and Frome train stations – though be prepared to walk the two and a half miles to the house from the entrance of the grounds.

Salisbury

SALISBURY, huddled below Wiltshire's chalky plain in the converging valleys of the Avon and Nadder, looks from a distance very much as it did when Constable painted his celebrated view of it from across the water meadows. Wiltshire's only city is designed on a pleasantly human scale, with no sprawling suburbs or high-rise buildings to challenge the supremacy of the cathedral's immense spire.

The town sprang into existence in the early thirteenth century, when the bishopric was moved from **Old Sarum**, an ancient Iron Age hillfort settled by the Romans and their successors. The deserted remnant of Salisbury's precursor now stands on the northern fringe of the town, just a bit closer in than **Wilton House** to the west, one of Wiltshire's great houses.

The City

Begun in 1220, **Salisbury Cathedral** (June–Aug Mon–Sat 7.15am–7.15pm, Sun 7.15am–6.15pm; Sept–May daily 7am–6.15pm; £4 suggested donation) was mostly completed within forty years and is thus unusually consistent in its style, with one extremely prominent exception – the **spire**, which was added a century later and at 404ft is the highest in England. Its survival is something of a miracle, for the foundations penetrate only about six feet into marshy ground, and when Christopher Wren surveyed it he found the spire to be leaning almost two and a half feet out of true. He added further tie-rods, which finally arrested the movement.

The interior is over-austere after James Wyatt's brisk eighteenth-century tidying, but there's an amazing sense of space and light in its high nave, despite the sombre pillars of grey Purbeck marble, which are visibly bowing beneath the weight they bear. Monuments and carved tombs line the walls, where they were neatly placed by Wyatt, and in the north aisle there's a fascinating clock dating from 1386, one of the oldest functioning clock mechanisms in Europe. Other features not to miss are the vaulted colonnades of the **cloisters**, and the octago nal **chapter house** (June–Aug Mon–Sat 9.30am–6.45pm, Sun noon–5.30pm; March–May, Sept & Oct Mon–Sat 9.30am–5.30pm, Sun noon–5.30pm; Nov–Feb Mon–Sat 10am–4.30pm, Sun noon–4.30pm), which displays a rare original copy of the Magna Carta, and whose walls are decorated with a frieze of scenes from the Old Testament. On most days, you can join a free 45-minute

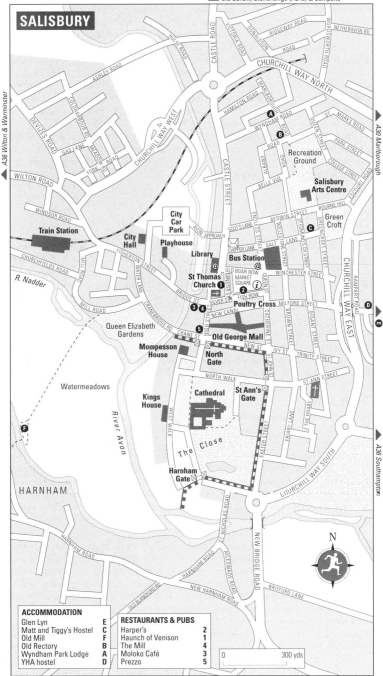

SALISBURY

▲ Old Sarum, Stonehenge (A345) & Campsite

◄ A36 Wilton & Warminster

◄ A30 Marlborough

► A30 Marlborough

► A36 Southampton

► A36 Southampton

Old Sarum, Stonehenge (A345) & Campsite

Train Station

City Hall

City Car Park

Playhouse

Library

Bus Station

St Thomas Church

Poultry Cross

Old George Mall

Mompesson House

North Gate

Queen Elizabeth Gardens

Watermeadows

Kings House

Cathedral

St Ann's Gate

The Close

Harnham Gate

HARNHAM

Recreation Ground

Salisbury Arts Centre

Green Croft

R. Nadder

River Avon

N

A36 Southampton

A338 Bournemouth ▼

© Crown copyright

ACCOMMODATION

Glen Lyn	E
Matt and Tiggy's Hostel	C
Old Mill	F
Old Rectory	B
Wyndham Park Lodge	A
YHA hostel	D

RESTAURANTS & PUBS

Harper's	2
Haunch of Venison	1
The Mill	4
Moloko Café	3
Prezzo	5

0   300 yds

tour of the church leaving two or more times a day, and there are also tours to the roof and spires (£4.50).

Surrounding the cathedral is the **Close**, the largest and most impressive in the country, a peaceful precinct of lawns and mellow old buildings. Most of the houses have seemly Georgian facades, though some, like the Bishop's Palace and the deanery, date from the thirteenth century. **Mompesson House** (Easter–Oct Mon–Wed, Sat & Sun 11am–5pm; £4.20, garden only 90p; NT), built by a wealthy merchant in 1701, contains some beautifully furnished eighteenth-century rooms and a superbly carved staircase, as displayed to great effect in the film *Sense and Sensibility*. Also in the Close is the **King's House**, home to the **Salisbury and South Wiltshire Museum** (July & Aug Mon–Sat 10am–5pm, Sun 2–5pm; Sept–June closed Sun; £4) – an absorbing account of local history. It includes a good section on Stonehenge and also focuses on the life and times of General Pitt-Rivers, the father of modern archeology, who excavated many of Wiltshire's prehistoric sites, including Avebury (see p.255).

The Close's **North Gate** opens onto the centre's older streets, where narrow pedestrianized alleyways bear names like Fish Row and Salt Lane, indicative of their trading origin. Many half-timbered houses and inns have survived all over the centre, and the last of four market crosses, **Poultry Cross**, stands on stilts in Silver Street, near the Market Square. The market, held on Tuesdays and Saturdays, still serves a large agricultural area, as it did in earlier times when the city grew wealthy on wool. Nearby, the church of **St Thomas** – named after Thomas à Becket – is worth a look inside for its carved timber roof and "Doom painting" over the chancel arch, depicting Christ presiding over the Last Judgment. Dating from 1475, it's the largest of its kind in England.

Lastly, to best appreciate the city's inspiring silhouette – the view made famous by Constable – take a twenty-minute walk through the water meadows southwest of the centre to **HARNHAM**; the *Old Mill* here serves drinks and meals.

Practicalities

Trains from London arrive half a mile west of Salisbury's centre, on South Western Road; the bus station is a short way north of the Market Place, on Endless Street. The **tourist office** is on Fish Row, just off Market Square (May Mon–Sat 9.30am–5pm, Sun 10.30am–4.30pm; June–Sept Mon–Sat 9.30am–6pm, Sun 10.30am–4.30pm; Oct–April Mon–Sat 9.30am–5pm; ☎01722/334956, ⓦwww.visitsalisbury.com) and is the starting point for informative and inexpensive **guided walks** of the city. There's free **Internet** access at the Public Library at the bottom of Castle Street, near the tourist office.

Salisbury has numerous **accommodation** possibilities to suit all pockets. One of the best is the *Old Mill*, Town Path, Harnham (☎01722/327517; ❺), a riverside inn boasting great views across the meadows to the cathedral about a mile away. There are two comfortable B&Bs near each other a short walk north of the centre: the *Old Rectory*, 75 Belle Vue Rd (☎01722/502702, ⓦwww .theoldrectory-bb.co.uk; no smoking; no credit cards; ❸), with light, airy rooms, and the Victorian ☆ *Wyndham Park Lodge*, 51 Wyndham Rd (☎01722/416517, ⓦwww.wyndhamparklodge.co.uk; no smoking; ❷), with period furnishings. A ten-minute walk east of the centre, *Glen Lyn*, 6 Bellamy Lane (☎01722/327880, ⓦwww.glenlynbandbatsalisbury.co.uk; ❸), is an elegant Victorian guest house in a quiet lane off Milford Hill, which is also home to Salisbury's **YHA hostel** (☎0870/770 6018, ⓔsalisbury@yha.org.uk; £17.50), where a separate lodge can accommodate couples or smaller groups (❶). More centrally, there's also the independent *Matt and Tiggy's Hostel*, 51 Salt Lane (☎01722/327443; £12), which is small, friendly and clean. There's a **campsite** a mile and a half north of Salisbury close to Old Sarum, *Salisbury Camping and Caravanning Club*, Hudson's Field (☎01722/320713; closed Nov to late March).

You can enjoy good-value, traditional English lunches and evening **meals** at *Harper's*, Market Square (☎01722/333118; closed Sun lunch, also Sun eve in winter), or eat Italian at *Prezzo*, close to the cathedral at 52 High St (☎01722/341333; closed Sun). **Pub** grub and drinks are dispensed at *The Mill*, Bridge Street, with riverside seating, and at the atmospheric ☘ *Haunch of Venison*, Minster Street, whose curiosities include the mummified hand of a nineteenth-century card player still clutching his cards. *Moloko Café*, 5 Bridge St, serves coffees and vodkas until late.

Old Sarum

The ruins of **Old Sarum** (daily: April–June & Sept 10am–5pm; July & Aug 9am–6pm; Oct & March 10am–4pm; Nov–Feb 11am–3pm; £2.90; EH) occupy a bleak hilltop site two miles north of the city centre – an easy walk, but there are frequent local bus connections. Possibly occupied up to five thousand years ago, then developed as an Iron Age fort whose double protective ditches remain, it was settled by Romans and Saxons before the Norman bishopric of Sherborne was moved here in the 1070s. Within a couple of decades a new cathedral had been consecrated at Old Sarum, and a large religious community was living alongside the soldiers in the central castle. Old Sarum was an uncomfortable place, parched and windswept, and in 1220 the dissatisfied clergy – additionally at loggerheads with the castle's occupants – appealed to the pope for permission to decamp to Salisbury (still known officially as New Sarum). When permission was granted, the stone from the cathedral was commandeered for Salisbury's gateways, and once the church had gone the population waned. By the nineteenth century Old Sarum was deserted, but it continued to exist as a political constituency – William Pitt was one of its representatives – and became notorious as a so-called "rotten borough", returning two MPs at a time to Westminster until the 1832 Reform Act put a stop to it. Huge earthworks, banks and ditches are the dominant features of the site today, with a broad trench encircling the rudimentary remains of the Norman palace, castle and cathedral.

Wilton

WILTON, five miles west of Salisbury, is renowned for its carpet industry and the splendid **Wilton House** (late March to Oct daily 10.30am–5.30pm; last entry 1hr before closing; £9.75, grounds only £4.50). The Tudor house, built for the First Earl of Pembroke on the site of a dissolved Benedictine abbey, was ruined by fire in 1647 and rebuilt by Inigo Jones, whose classic hallmarks can be seen in the sumptuous Single Cube and Double Cube rooms, so called because of their precise dimensions. Sir Philip Sidney, illustrious Elizabethan courtier and poet, wrote part of his magnum opus *Arcadia* here – the dado round the Single Cube room illustrates scenes from the book – and the Double Cube room was the setting for the ballroom scene in Ang Lee's film, *Sense and Sensibility*. The easel **paintings** are what makes Wilton really special, however – the collection includes paintings by Van Dyck, Rembrandt, two of the Brueghel family, Poussin, Andrea del Sarto and Tintoretto. In the grounds, the famous **Palladian Bridge** has been joined by various ancillary attractions including an adventure playground and an audiovisual show on the colourful earls of Pembroke.

Salisbury Plain and northwards

The Ministry of Defence is the landlord of much of **Salisbury Plain**, the hundred thousand acres of chalky upland to the north of Salisbury. Flags warn casual trespassers away from MoD firing ranges and tank training grounds, while rather stricter security cordons off such secretive establishments as the research centre at Porton Down, Britain's centre for chemical and biological warfare. As elsewhere, the army's presence has ironically saved much of the plain from modern agricultural chemicals, thereby inadvertently nurturing species that are all but extinct in more trampled landscapes.

Though now largely deserted except by forces families living in ugly barracks quarters, Salisbury Plain once positively throbbed with communities. Stone Age, Bronze Age and Iron Age settlements left hundreds of burial mounds scattered over the chalklands, as well as major complexes at Danebury, Badbury, Figsbury, Old Sarum, and, of course, the great circle of **Stonehenge**. North of Salisbury Plain lies the softer Vale of Pewsey, traversed by the Kennet canal, with another cluster of ancient sites to the north of the Vale, including the huge stone circle of **Avebury**, the mysterious grassy mound of **Silbury Hill** and the chamber graves of **West Kennet**.

Stonehenge

No ancient structure in England arouses more controversy than **Stonehenge** (daily: mid-March to May & Sept to mid-Oct 9.30am–6pm; June–Aug 9am–7pm; mid-Oct to mid-March 9.30am–4pm; £5.50; NT & EH; Ⓦwww .english-heritage.org.uk/stonehenge), a mysterious ring of monoliths nine miles north of Salisbury. While archeologists argue over whether it was a place of ritual sacrifice and sun-worship, an astronomical calculator or a royal palace, the guardians of the site struggle to accommodate its year-round crowds. Conservation of Stonehenge is an urgent priority, and unless you arrange for special

△ Stonehenge

access (by calling ahead on ☎01722/343834 or through the website), you must be content with walking round rather than among the stones, equipped with handsets that dispense a range of information. Plans to reroute nearby roads and build a new visitors' centre have been afoot for years, though interminable discussions to bring these about have not so far produced any result.

What exists today is only a small part of the original prehistoric complex, as many of the outlying stones were probably plundered by medieval and later farmers for building materials. The **construction** of Stonehenge is thought to have taken place in several stages. In about 3000 BC the outer circular bank and ditch were constructed, just inside which was dug a ring of 56 pits, which at a later date were filled with a mixture of earth and human ash. Around 2500 BC the first stones were raised within the earthworks, comprising approximately forty great blocks of dolerite (bluestone), whose ultimate source was Preseli in Wales. Some archeologists have suggested that these monoliths were found lying on Salisbury Plain, having been borne down from the Welsh mountains by a glacier in the last Ice Age, but the lack of any other glacial debris on the plain would seem to disprove this theory. It really does seem to be the case that the stones were cut from quarries in Preseli and dragged or floated here on rafts, a prodigious task which has defeated recent attempts to emulate it.

The crucial phase in the creation of the site came during the next six hundred years, when the incomplete bluestone circle was transformed by the construction of a circle of twenty-five **trilithons** (two uprights crossed by a lintel) and an inner horseshoe formation of five trilithons. Hewn from Marlborough Downs sandstone, these colossal stones (called sarsens), ranging from 13ft to 21ft in height and weighing up to thirty tons, were carefully dressed and worked – for example, to compensate for perspective distortion the uprights have a slight swelling in the middle, the same trick as the builders of the Parthenon were to employ hundreds of years later. More bluestones were arranged in various patterns within the outer circle over this period. The purpose of all this work remains baffling, however. The symmetry and location of the site (a slight rise in a flat valley with even views of the horizon in all directions) as well as its alignment towards the points of sunrise and sunset on the summer and winter solstices tend to support the supposition that it was some sort of observatory or time-measuring device. The site ceased to be used at around 1600 BC, and by the Middle Ages it had become a "landmark".

There's a lot less charisma about the reputedly significant Bronze Age site of **Woodhenge** (dawn–dusk; free), two miles northeast of Stonehenge. The site consists of a circular bank about 220ft in diameter enclosing a ditch and six concentric rings of post holes, which would originally have held timber uprights, possibly supporting a roofed building of some kind. The holes are now marked more durably if less romantically by concrete pillars. A child's grave was found at the centre of the rings, suggesting that it may have been a place of ritual sacrifice.

Silbury Hill, West Kennet and Avebury

The neat green mound of **Silbury Hill**, sixteen miles north of Stonehenge, is probably overlooked by the majority of drivers whizzing by on the A4. At 130ft it's no great height, but when you realize it's the largest prehistoric artificial mound in Europe, and was made by a people using nothing more than primitive spades, it commands more respect. It was probably constructed around 2600 BC, but like so many of the sites of Salisbury Plain, no one knows quite what it was for, though the likelihood is that it was a burial mound. You can't actually walk on the hill – so having admired it briefly from the car park, cross the road to the footpath that leads half a mile to the **West Kennet Long Barrow** (free access; NT & EH). Dating from about 3250 BC, this was definitely a chamber tomb – nearly fifty burials have been discovered at West Kennet.

Immediately to the west, the village of **AVEBURY** stands in the midst of a **stone circle** (free access; NT & EH) that rivals Stonehenge – the individual stones are generally smaller, but the circle itself is much wider and more complex. A massive earthwork 20ft high and 1400ft across encloses the main circle, which is approached by four causeways across the inner ditch, two of them leading into wide avenues stretching over a mile beyond the circle. The best guess is that it was built soon after 2500 BC, and presumably had a similar ritual or religious function to Stonehenge. The structure of Avebury's diffuse circle is quite difficult to grasp, but there are plans on the site, and you can get an excellent overview at the **Alexander Keiller Museum**, at the western entrance to the site (daily: April–Oct 10am–6pm or dusk; Nov–March 10am–4pm; £4.20, including Barn Gallery; NT & EH), while the nearby **Barn Gallery** holds a permanent exhibition on Avebury and the surrounding country. To the southeast of the circle, an avenue of standing stones leads half a mile beyond West Kennet towards a spot known as the Sanctuary, though there is little left to see here.

Avebury's **tourist office** (March–Oct daily 9.30am–5pm; Nov–Feb Wed–Sun 9.30am–4.30pm; ☎01672/539425, ⓦwww.visitkennet.co.uk) is in the Avebury Chapel Centre on Green Street. Next to the Barn Gallery, you can have a **snack** or cream tea at *The Circles* vegetarian restaurant, or a drink in the *Red Lion* **pub**, which also serves reasonable **meals** and has en-suite **rooms** (☎01672/539266; ❺). Alternatively, there's *The Lodge* on the High Street (☎01672/539023, ⓦwww.aveburylodge.com; no smoking; ❻), a Georgian B&B with vegetarian or vegan breakfasts and views towards the stones.

Lacock

LACOCK, twelve miles west of Avebury, is the perfect English feudal village, albeit one much gentrified by the National Trust and besieged by tourists all summer. Appropriately for so photogenic a spot, and one used as a location for several films (it features in the *Harry Potter* series), it has a fascinating museum dedicated to the founding genius of photography, Henry Fox Talbot, a member of the dynasty which has lived in the local **abbey** since it passed to Sir William Sharington on the Dissolution of the Monasteries in 1539. Sir William's descendant, William Henry Fox Talbot, was the first to produce a photographic negative, and the **Fox Talbot Museum**, in a sixteenth-century barn by the abbey gates (March–Oct daily 11am–5.30pm; £4.60, including abbey garden and cloisters, £3.20 in winter; NT), captures something of the excitement he must have experienced as the dim outline of an oriel window in the abbey imprinted itself on a piece of silver nitrate paper. The **abbey** itself (April–Oct Mon & Wed–Sun 1–5.30pm; £6; £7.40 including museum; NT) preserves a few monastic fragments amid the eighteenth-century Gothic, while the church of **St Cyriac** (free access) contains the opulent tomb of Sir William Sharington, buried beneath a splendid barrel-vaulted roof.

The village's delightfully Chaucerian-sounding hostelry, *At the Sign of the Angel*, is a good, if expensive, **hotel** and **restaurant** (☎01249/730230, ⓦwww.lacock.co.uk; ❻).

Travel details

Buses

For information on all local and national bus services, contact Traveline ☎ 0870/608 2608 (daily 7am–9pm), ⊛ www.traveline.org.uk.

Bournemouth to: Dorchester (Mon–Sat 5–6 daily; 1hr 20min); London (hourly; 2hr 35min); Salisbury (Mon–Sat every 30min, Sun 7; 1hr 15min); Southampton (10 daily; 45min–1hr 45min); Weymouth (6 daily; 1hr 20min); Winchester (5 daily; 1hr 15min–2hr).

Dorchester to: Bournemouth (Mon–Sat 5–6 daily; 1hr 20min); London (1 daily; 4hr); Weymouth (every 20–30min; 20min).

Portsmouth to: London (16 daily; 2hr 15min–3hr 30min); Salisbury (1 daily; 1hr 35min); Southampton (9 daily; 40min–1hr).

Salisbury to: Bournemouth (Mon–Sat every 30min, Sun 7; 1hr 15min); London (3 daily; 2hr 45min–3hr 50min); Portsmouth (1 daily; 1hr 30min); Southampton (hourly; 1hr).

Southampton to: Bournemouth (10 daily; 45min–1hr 45min); London (hourly; 2hr 35min); Portsmouth (10 daily; 45min–1hr); Salisbury (hourly; 1hr); Weymouth (2 daily; 2hr 25min–3hr 15min); Winchester (7 daily; 1hr 20min).

Winchester to: Bournemouth (3 daily; 1hr 15 min–1hr 35min); London (10 daily; 2hr); Southampton (6 daily; 1hr 20min).

Trains

For information on all local and national rail services, contact National Rail Enquiries ☎ 08457/484950, ⊛ www.nationalrail.co.uk.

Bournemouth to: Brockenhurst (2–3 hourly; 15–25min); Dorchester (hourly; 45min); London

(1–2 hourly; 2hr); Poole (1–4 hourly; 10–15min); Southampton (2–3 hourly; 30–45min); Weymouth (hourly; 55min); Winchester (1–3 hourly; 40min–1hr).

Dorchester to: Bournemouth (hourly; 40min); Brockenhurst (hourly; 1hr); London (hourly; 2hr 40min); Weymouth (1–2 hourly; 10–15min).

Portsmouth to: London (2–3 hourly; 1hr 35min–2hr); Salisbury (hourly; 1hr 20min); Southampton (2 hourly; 45min–1hr); Winchester (hourly; 1hr).

Ryde (Isle of Wight) to: Shanklin (every 20–40min; 20–25min).

Salisbury to: London (2 hourly; 1hr 35min); Portsmouth (hourly; 1hr 20min); Southampton (1–2 hourly; 30–40min).

Southampton to: Bournemouth (3–4 hourly; 30–50min); Brockenhurst (2–4 hourly; 10–20min); London (every 30min; 1hr 20min); Portsmouth (2 hourly; 45min–1hr); Salisbury (1–2 hourly; 30–40min); Weymouth (hourly; 1hr 40min); Winchester (3–4 hourly; 15–30min).

Winchester to: Bournemouth (1–3 hourly; 40min–1hr); London (every 15–30min; 1hr–1hr 15min); Portsmouth (hourly; 1hr); Southampton (3–4 hourly; 15–20min).

Ferries and hovercraft

Lymington to: Yarmouth, Isle of Wight (Easter–Dec 2 hourly; 30min).

Portsmouth to: Fishbourne, Isle of Wight (1–2 hourly; 35min); Ryde, Isle of Wight (1–2 hourly; 15min).

Southampton to: East Cowes, Isle of Wight (hourly; 55min); West Cowes, Isle of Wight (1–2 hourly; 22min).

Southsea to: Ryde, Isle of Wight (2 hourly; 10min).

Oxfordshire, the Cotswolds and around

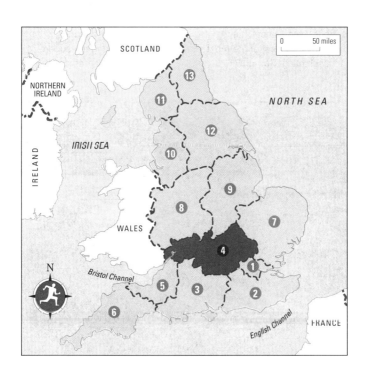

CHAPTER 4

Highlights

✳ Chiltern Hills The best base for exploring the lovely wooded scenery of the Chiltern Hills is Henley-on-Thames, site of the famous regatta. **See p.262**

✳ The Vale of White Horse Takes its name from the huge, prehistoric horse cut into the chalk of the Berkshire Downs. **See p.264**

✳ Christ Church College, Oxford Oxford boasts many beautiful old buildings, with Christ Church holding several of the most fascinating. **See p.271**

✳ Le Petit Blanc restaurant, Oxford Oxford's best restaurant, run by renowned French chef, Raymond Blanc. **See p.278**

✳ Falkland Arms, Great Tew Wonderful pub in the most charming of hamlets, deep in the heart of the Cotswolds. **See p.283**

✳ Chipping Campden, Gloucestershire Perhaps the most handsome of the Cotswolds towns, with honey-coloured stone houses flanking the superb church of St James. **See p.284**

△ The White Horse

Oxfordshire, the Cotswolds and around

Arching around the peripheries of London, the "Home Counties" are at their most appealing amidst the **Chiltern Hills**, a picturesque band of chalk uplands with wooded ridges. The hills provide an exclusive setting for many of the capital's wealthiest commuters, but for the casual visitor the obvious target is **Henley-on-Thames**, an attractive old town famous for its regatta. It's also a handy base for trips to the nearby village of **Cookham** – with its Stanley Spencer gallery – and **Reading**, known primarily as the host of two of Europe's most prestigious music festivals.

Traversing the Chilterns is the 85-mile–long **Ridgeway**, a prehistoric track – and now a national trail – that offers excellent hiking, though its finest portion is further to the west, across the Thames, on **the downs** straddling the Berkshire–Oxfordshire border. Here, the Ridgeway visits a string of prehistoric sites, the most extraordinary being the gigantic chalk horse that gives the **Vale of White Horse** its name. The Vale is dotted with pleasant little villages, and both **Woolstone** and plainer **Uffington** have places to stay, though the nearby university city of **Oxford**, with its superb architecture, museums and lively student population, is the region's star turn. It's also close to **Woodstock**, the handsome little town abutting one of England's most imposing country homes, **Blenheim Palace**.

Beyond Oxford lie the rolling hills and ridges of the **Cotswolds**, stretching northeast to southwest and covering much of **Oxfordshire** and **Gloucestershire**. Dotted with picturesque villages made from the local honey-coloured stone, the Cotswolds became rich from the medieval wool trade, whose evidence is all around in a multitude of beautiful old churches and handsome mansions. Unsurprisingly, the region attracts coachloads of visitors, though the engaging market town of Chipping Campden is still a treat, as is the region's main town, lively **Cirencester**. Ultimately, however, the Cotswolds' subtle charms only really reveal themselves when you take to the hills and valleys along its dense network of footpaths and trails, in particular the **Cotswold Way**, a

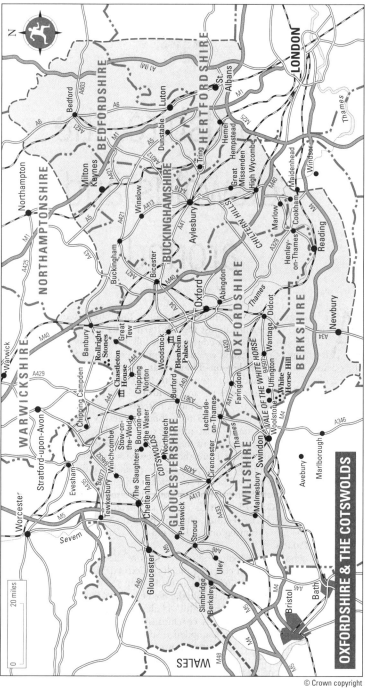

OXFORDSHIRE & THE COTSWOLDS

© Crown copyright

hundred-mile national trail that runs along the edge of the Cotswold escarpment from Chipping Campden in the northeast to Bath in the southwest.

Heading west, the land drops sharply from the Cotswold escarpment down to **Cheltenham**, an elegant Regency spa town famous for its horse racing. The town's reputation as a bastion of blue-stockinged conservatism is fairly passé now, and it has developed a more sophisticated veneer in recent years, boasting some of the best restaurants and nightlife in the region. It also makes a good base for visits to **Gloucester**, with its superb cathedral and rejuvenated harbour area, and **Stroud**, where the much-praised Museum in the Park has recently opened. The Vale of Gloucester follows the route of the **River Severn** northeast towards Worcestershire, the stone cottages of the Cotswolds giving way to the thatched, half-timbered and red-brick houses which are characteristic of **Tewkesbury**, a solidly provincial town with a magnificent abbey.

The area covered in this chapter is threaded by five **motorways**, the M25, M4, M40, M1 and A1(M). These give swift access from all directions, though drivers will need a detailed map to explore successfully its rural nooks and crannies. Long-distance **buses** mostly stick to the motorways, providing an efficient service to all the larger towns, though local services between the villages are patchy, sometimes nonexistent. **Mainline train** services leave from London's Paddington Station for Oxford, Henley-on-Thames, Reading, Cheltenham, Gloucester and Bristol, with others stopping at several Cotswold towns en route to Worcester and Hereford. In addition, there are a number of branch lines, the most useful of which links Henley-on-Thames with Cookham.

The Chiltern Hills and the Vale of White Horse

The **Chiltern Hills** extend southwest from the workaday town of Luton, beside the M1, bumping across Buckinghamshire and Oxfordshire as far as the River Thames, just to the west of Reading. At their best, the hills offer handsome countryside, comprising a band of forested chalk hills with steep ridges and deep valleys interrupted by easy, rolling farmland. The Chilterns are also one of the country's wealthiest areas, liberally sprinkled with exclusive commuter hideaways-cum-country homes – though there are unappetizing suburban blotches too. The region's most appealing town is **Henley-on-Thames**, a pleasant riverside place with a reasonable range of accommodation and within easy striking distance of the village of **Cookham**, Thameside **Reading**, and the excellent Roald Dahl Museum and Story Centre in suburban **Great Missenden**.

Crossing the Chilterns to the north and west of Henley, the **Ridgeway National Trail** offers splendid hiking, though the most diverting part of the trail is further west, amongst the more open scenery of the Berkshire and Oxfordshire downs. Here, on the edge of the **Vale of White Horse**, the trail sticks to a chalky ridge that provides magnificent views of the surrounding countryside and skirts the giant prehistoric figure after which the Vale is named. You can stay locally in the attractive YHA hostel on the ridge above **Wantage**, in the humdrum town itself, or in one of the Vale's quaint villages – tiny **Woolstone** is perhaps the most appealing.

Henley and Reading are well served from London by **train**, but for the smaller towns and villages and the Vale of White Horse you will, for the most part, be dependent on intermittent local **bus** services (℡0870/608 2608 or Ⓦwww.traveline.org.uk).

Henley-on-Thames

Three counties – Oxfordshire, Berkshire and Buckinghamshire – meet at **HENLEY-ON-THAMES**, a long-established stopping place for travellers between London and Oxford. Henley is a good-looking, affluent commuter town that is at its prettiest among the old brick and stone buildings that flank the short main drag, **Hart Street**. At one end of Hart Street is the Market Place and its large and fetching **Town Hall**, at the other stands the easy Georgian curves of **Henley Bridge**. Several operators run **boat trips** out along the Thames from the jetties just south of the bridge, including Hobbs & Sons (℡01491/572035, Ⓦwww.hobbs-of-henley.com), who offer hour-long jaunts from April to September for £5.25. There is also an imaginative **River and Rowing Museum** (daily 10am–5pm; £3), a ten-minute walk south along the river bank from the foot of Hart Street via Thames Side. This focuses on three main themes: the history of the town, the development of rowing from the Greeks onwards, and the Thames both as a wildlife habitat and as a trading link.

Henley is, however, best known for its **Royal Regatta**, the world's most important amateur rowing tournament, featuring past and potential Olympic rowers. Established in 1839, it's quintessentially English, and effectively a parade ground for the champagne-swilling antics of the rich, aristocratic and aspiring. The regatta begins on the Wednesday before the first weekend in July and runs for five days. Further information is available from the Regatta Headquarters on the east side of the Henley Bridge (℡01491/572153, Ⓦwww.hrr.co.uk).

Practicalities

Two or three times daily a direct train runs from London's Paddington Station to Henley, but mostly you have to change at Twyford. From Henley **train station**, it's a five-minute walk north to Hart Street, along Station Road and its continuation Thames Side. Henley is easy to reach by bus, too, with regular services from Oxford, Reading and London. **Buses** from Reading and points south and west mostly pull in on Hart Street, while those from the north and east – including Cookham – stop on Bell Street, immediately to the north of Hart Street. The **tourist office** (Mon–Sat 10am–4pm; ℡01491/578034, Ⓦwww.visit-henley.org.uk) is in a refurbished old barn, in a courtyard across from the Town Hall.

Henley has several first-rate **B&Bs**, including the smart and tastefully furnished *Alftrudis*, 8 Norman Ave (℡01491/573 099, Ⓦwww.alftrudis.co.uk; no credit cards; ❹), in a handsome Victorian town house in a quiet, leafy residential street. Another excellent choice is the attractive Edwardian *Lenwade*, 3 Western Rd (℡01491/573 468, Ⓦwww.w3b-ink.com/lenwade; no credit cards; ❹), with three en-suite guest rooms, comfortable furnishings and an unusual stained-glass window in the hallway. **Hotels** are thinner on the ground, but pick of the bunch is the delightful, wisteria-clad old coaching inn, the *Red Lion*, beside Henley Bridge, with over twenty well-appointed bedrooms, individually decorated in period style (℡01491/572161, Ⓦwww.redlionhenley .co.uk; ❼, breakfast extra).

The *Red Lion* has the best **restaurant** in town, but there are other more informal – and less expensive – places on Hart Street, including the *Thai Orchard* at no. 8 (℡01491/412 227), where main courses start at around £7. There are several **pubs** on Hart Street too, but the *Angel*, by the bridge, has the advantage of an outside deck overlooking the river. Even better, there are several outstanding **country pubs** within easy striking distance of Henley, probably the best of which is the one-time hideout of the highwayman Dick Turpin, the *Crooked Billet* (☎01491/681048), in **Stoke Row**, five miles west of Henley off the B481. With an open fire and low-beamed ceilings dating from the 1640s, this is the quintessential English pub, and serves superb **food** too (main courses around £13; advance booking advised).

Cookham

Heading out of Henley on the A4155, it's eight leafy miles to the bustling riverside town of **Marlow**, then three further miles to tiny **COOKHAM**, former home of **Stanley Spencer** (1891–1959). One of Britain's greatest – and most eccentric – artists, Spencer was inspired by the Bible and many of his paintings depict biblical tales transposed into his Cookham surroundings – remarkable, visionary works in which the village is turned into a sort of earthly paradise. Spencer made his artistic name in the 1920s, first as an official war artist and then for his *Resurrection: Cookham*, which attracted rave reviews when it was exhibited in London in 1927. Much of Spencer's most acclaimed work is displayed in London's Tate Britain (see p.95), but there's a fine sample here at the **Stanley Spencer Gallery** (Easter–Oct daily 10.30am–5.30pm; Nov–Easter Sat & Sun 11am–4.30pm; £1; ⓦwww.cookham.com), which occupies the old Methodist Chapel on the High Street. Three prime exhibits are *View from Cookham Bridge*, the unsettling *Sarah Tubb and the Heavenly Visitors*, and the wonderful (but unfinished) *Christ Preaching at Cookham Regatta*. The permanent collection is enhanced by regular exhibitions of Spencer paintings and the gallery also contains incidental Spencer letters, documents and memorabilia.

From **Cookham train station** (with hourly trains from Marlow on Mon–Sat, Sun), it's a fifteen-minute walk east along the High Street to the gallery. Across the street from the gallery, the *Bel & Dragon* **pub** is a good spot for a pint.

Great Missenden

About fifteen miles north of Cookham, the village of **GREAT MISSENDEN** is home to the newly opened **Roald Dahl Museum and Story Centre**, 81 High St (Tues–Sun 10am–5pm; £4.50; advance booking recommended on ☎01494/892192, ⓦwww.roalddahlmuseum.org), an unmissable treat for Dahl fans. Arguably the greatest children's story writer of all time, Dahl (1916–1990) was born in Wales, the son of Norwegian parents, but spent the later part of his life here in Buckinghamshire. Dahl had an eventful war, including a harrowing air crash in the Libyan desert, and his life after the war was no less tragic, with one of his children dying of measles, another developing hydrocephalus, and his wife, Patricia Neal, suffering three strokes when she was pregnant in 1965. Despite – perhaps partly because of these troubles – Dahl produced a series of wonderful books, tales infused with menace and comedy, malice and eccentricity, most memorably *Charlie and the Chocolate Factory*, *The Twits*, *The BFG* and *The Witches*. As well as chronicling the author's life, the museum has a replica of the hut where Dahl wrote some of his best-known books, and explores the nature of creative writing, supported by hints from contemporary writers and interactive games.

There are frequent **trains** from London Marylebone to Great Missenden and the journey takes about forty minutes; the museum is a short walk from the station.

Reading

Ten miles south of Henley, **READING** is a modern, prosperous town on the south bank of the River Thames. Guarding the western approaches to the capital, it has long been a stopping-off point for kings and queens and was once home to one of the country's richest abbeys. Henry VIII took care of the abbey, seizing its lands and hanging the abbot from the main gate; today the shattered ruins of the **abbey**, a short walk east of the pedestrianized shopping centre, are all that remains of the old town.

Reading boasts a flourishing **arts scene**, with both the Reading Film Theatre (☎0118/378 7151, ⓦwww.readingfilmtheatre.co.uk) and the Hexagon Theatre (☎0118/960 6060, ⓦwww.readingarts.com) offering a good programme of shows, though the town's cultural highlight is its two big **music festivals**. The three-day **WOMAD** (ⓦwww.womad.org; tickets ☎0118/939 0930), held each July, is a celebration of World Music, Arts and Dance, originally inspired by Peter Gabriel. Since the first WOMAD in 1982, there have been about a hundred spin-off events in twenty countries, but the Reading event remains the focus. Later in the summer, the three-day **Reading Festival** (ⓦwww.readingfestival.com) features many of the big names of contemporary music. Details of who is performing are published in the music press at least a couple of months in advance and tickets are available from record shops and ticket outlets across the country. Both festivals are held at the Rivermead Leisure Complex, Richfield Avenue, just to the north of the town centre, with the vast majority of festival-goers **camping on site**. Special buses run there from Reading train station, or you can walk – it takes about fifteen minutes.

With fast and frequent services from London Paddington and Waterloo, the **train station** is on the north side of the town centre, a short walk from the **tourist office**, in Church House, on Chain Street (Mon–Fri 10am–5pm, Sat 10am–4pm; ☎0118/956 6226, ⓦwww.readingtourism.org.uk). It runs an **accommodation**-booking service, but during the festivals you'll need to book months in advance; outside of festival-time, there's little reason to stay the night.

The Vale of White Horse

The **Vale of White Horse**, falling between Wantage, a modest market town about twenty-five miles northwest of Reading, and Faringdon, seventeen miles southwest of Oxford, is a shallow valley, whose fertile farmland is studded with tiny villages. It takes its name from the prehistoric figure cut into the chalk downs above two of its smaller hamlets – **Uffington** and **Woolstone**. Carved in the first century BC, the horse is the most conspicuous of a string of prehistoric remains that punctuates the downs and includes burial mounds and Iron Age forts. The **Ridgeway National Trail**, running along – or near – the top of the downs, links several of these sites and offers wonderful, breezy views over the vale.

Wantage

Workaday **WANTAGE** is an unassuming, somewhat care-worn town, whose crowded Market Place is overseen by a statue of its most famous son, Alfred the Great (849–99), the most distinguished of England's Saxon kings. From the south side of the Market Place – where long-distance **buses** pull in – a couple of alleys lead through to Church Street, home of the **tourist office** (Mon–Sat 10am–4.30pm, Sun 2.30–5pm; ☎01235/771447, ⓦwww.wantage.com), which sells local hiking maps, and the modest **Vale and Downland Museum** (£2.50).

Wantage is about two miles from the **Ridgeway**, and the beginning of one of its finest stretches that runs seven miles west to White Horse Hill. Several villages below White Horse Hill have B&B **accommodation** (see below), or you could head for the Ridgeway YHA **hostel** (☎0870/770 6064, ⓦwww .yha.org.uk; dorm beds £14, doubles ❶; Easter to Oct), in a prime position just off the A338 a couple of miles south of Wantage, and just a stone's throw away from the Ridgeway trail. The hostel consists of several converted timber barns set around a courtyard, with sixty beds in two- to thirteen-bedded rooms (advance reservations required with at least 48hr notice).

White Horse Hill

White Horse Hill, overlooking the B4507 six miles west of Wantage, follows close behind Stonehenge (see p.253) and Avebury (see p.255) in the hierarchy of Britain's ancient sites, though it attracts nothing like the same number of visitors. Carved into the north-facing slope of the downs above the villages of Uffington and Woolstone, the 374-foot-long **horse** looks like something created with a few swift strokes of an immense brush, and there's been no lack of weird and wonderful theories as to its origins. The first written record of the horse's existence dates from the time of Henry II, but it was cut much earlier, probably in the first century BC, making it one of the oldest chalk figures in Britain. A detailed 1994 study showed that its creators dug out the soil to a depth of a metre and then filled the hollow with clear white chalk taken from a nearby hilltop.

Just below the horse is **Dragon Hill**, a small flat-topped hillock that has its own legend. Locals long asserted that this was where St George killed and buried the dragon, a theory proved, so they argued, by the bare patch at the top and the channel down the side, where blood trickled from the creature's wounds. Here also, at the top of the hill, is the Iron Age earthwork of **Uffington Castle**, which provides wonderful views over the vale.

The Ridgeway runs alongside the horse and continues west to reach, after one-and-a-half miles, **Wayland's Smithy**, a 5000-year-old burial mound encircled by trees. It is one of the best Neolithic remains along the Ridgeway, though heavy restoration has rather detracted from its mystery. In ignorance of its original function, the invading Saxons named it after Wayland Smith, an invisible smith who, according to their legends, made invincible armour and shoed horses without ever being seen.

The B4507 passes the narrow lane that leads - after 500 yards – to the car park just below the White Horse. There are no regular buses.

Woolstone and Uffington

About three quarters of a mile below the White Horse car park, on the north side of the B4057, is the minuscule hamlet of **WOOLSTONE**. Here, the attractive *White Horse Inn* (☎01367/820726, ⓦwww.whitehorsewoolstone .co.uk; ❹) occupies a half-timbered, partly thatched old building and offers both good-quality pub food and straightforward **accommodation**, mostly in a modern annexe. A mile or so north, the much larger (and plainer) village of **UFFINGTON** has a couple of B&Bs, notably the unassuming *Norton House*, in a well-kept family home next to the post office on the main street (☎01367/820230; no credit cards; ❸). Uffington's most famous son was Thomas Hughes (1823–96), the author of *Tom Brown's School Days* – hence the pocket-sized Tom Brown's School Museum.

Oxford and around

When visitors think of **OXFORD**, they almost always think of its **university**, one of the world's great academic institutions, inhabiting honey-coloured stone buildings set around ivy-clad quadrangles. Much of this is accurate enough, but although the university dominates central Oxford both physically and mentally, the wider city has an entirely different character, its economy built on the **car plants** of Cowley to the south of the centre. It was here that Britain's first mass-produced cars were produced in the 1920s and, although there have been more downs than ups in recent years, the plants are still vitally important to the area.

The origins of the university are obscure, but it seems that the reputation of **Henry I**, the so-called "Scholar King", helped attract students in the early twelfth century, their numbers increasing with the expulsion of English students from the Sorbonne in 1167. The first **colleges**, founded mostly by rich bishops, were essentially ecclesiastical institutions and this was reflected in collegiate rules and regulations – until 1877 lecturers were not allowed to marry and women were not granted degrees until 1920. There are common architectural features, too, with the private rooms of the students arranged around quadrangles (quads), as are most of the communal rooms – the chapels, halls (dining rooms) and libraries.

Though they share a similar history, each of the university's 35 colleges has its own character and often a particular label, whether it's the richest (St John's), most left-wing (Wadham and Balliol) or most public-school-dominated (Christ Church). Collegiate rivalries are long established, usually revolving around sports, and tension between the university and the city – "Town" and "Gown" – has existed as long as the university itself. Both the colleges and the town should be high on anyone's itinerary: the university buildings include some of England's finest architecture, while the city boasts some excellent museums and numerous bars and restaurants. Getting there is easy, too: from London the journey takes just an hour by train, a little longer by bus.

Arrival

From Oxford **train station**, it's a five- to ten-minute walk east to the centre along Park End Street. Long-distance and many county-wide buses terminate at the Gloucester Green **bus station**, in the city centre adjoining George Street. The Oxford Bus Company (℡01865/785400) and Stagecoach (℡01865/772 250) operate most local and city buses, many of which terminate on the High Street and St Giles. The former also runs the **Park-and-Ride** scheme, with buses (daily Mon–Sat 6am–11pm, Sun 9am–7pm) travelling into the centre every fifteen minutes at peak times (every thirty minutes to an hour in the evening), from five large and clearly signed car parks on the main approach roads into the city. Parking costs are minimal, whereas parking in the city centre is – by municipal design – both inordinately expensive and hard to find.

Information and guided tours

The **tourist office** is plum in the centre of town at 15 Broad St (Mon–Sat 9.30am–5pm, plus late April to late Oct Sun 10am–4pm; ℡01865/726871, ⓦwww.visitoxford.org): its better booklets include the *Welcome to Oxford Visitors' Guide* (£1) and *Staying in Oxford* (£1), as well as a free **listings guide** – *This Month in Oxford*. It also offers excellent guided **walking tours**, including a two-hour gambol round the city centre and its colleges (several tours daily; book in advance; £6.50), and a once-weekly Inspector Morse tour (£7).

Further along Broad Street, the main Blackwell's bookshop also runs specialist walking tours (℡01865/333606; April to Oct; £6; advance booking recommended), including a Literary Tour of Oxford (2 weekly), a Historic Oxford Tour (1 weekly), and an Inklings Tour (1 weekly) – Inklings being the group of writers, Tolkien and C. S. Lewis included, who met regularly in Oxford in the 1930s.

Accommodation

With supply struggling to keep pace with demand, Oxford's central **hotels** are almost invariably expensive, though nowhere near as pricey as in London. There are one or two inexpensive hotels in or near the centre, but by and large they are far from inspiring and, at the budget end of the market, you're better off choosing a **guest house** or **B&B**, of which there is a healthy supply, though few are in the centre. Wherever you stay, book ahead in high season either direct or through the tourist office (see above), which operates an efficient accommodation-booking service.

Hotels

Bath Place Hotel 4 Bath Place ℡01865/791812, ⓦwww.bathplace.co.uk. This unusual, pink and blue hotel, down an old cobbled courtyard flanked by ancient buildings with higgledy-piggledy roofs, has just thirteen rooms, all of them reasonably attractive. The location is excellent – in the centre, off Holywell Street. ❻

Old Bank Hotel 92 High St ℡01865/799599, ⓦwww.oldbank-hotel.co.uk. Great location for a good, new hotel that is a slick, glistening conversion of an old bank. Over forty bedrooms decorated in smart, modern style. Some of the rooms have great views over All Souls College. ❽

Parklands Hotel 100 Banbury Rd ℡01865/554 374, ⓦwww.oxfordcity.co.uk. Pleasant fourteen-room hotel in a large Victorian house with a garden, licensed restaurant and bar. North of the centre, but connected to it by a frequent bus service. Good value. ❺

The Randolph Hotel 1 Beaumont St ℡0870/400 8200, ⓦwww.randolph-hotel.com. The most famous hotel in the city, long the favoured choice of the well-heeled, the *Randolph* occupies a large and well-proportioned brick building with a distinctive neo-Gothic interior. Now part of a chain, but with impeccable service and well-appointed bedrooms. Discounts are available at slack periods, but otherwise it's ❽

Guest houses, B&Bs and hostels

Becket Guest House 5 Becket St ℡01865/724 675. Modest bay-windowed guest house in a plain terrace close to the train station. Most rooms en suite. ❸

Brown's Guest House 281 Iffley Rd ℡01865/246 822, ⓦwww.brownsguesthouse.co.uk. Well-maintained guest house in a pleasing Victorian property with fourteen rooms, mostly en suite. ❸

Newton House 82–84 Abingdon Rd ℡01865/240 561, ⓦwww.oxfordcity.co.uk. Appealing, family-run guest house in two good-looking Victorian town houses about ten minutes' walk south of the centre – well placed for evening strolls along the Thames. The fourteen guest rooms are decorated in a smart, traditional style, and mostly en suite. ❸

Oxford Backpackers Hostel 9a Hythe Bridge St ℡01865/721761. Independent hostel with quads and dorms, holding up to eighteen people each. Fully equipped kitchen and laundry plus Internet facilities. Handy location between the train station and the centre; 24-hour access. Dorm beds £13–18.

Oxford YHA Hostel 2a Botley Rd ℡0870/770 5970, ⓦwww.yha.org.uk. Next door to the train station, this popular YHA hostel has 184 beds divided into two-, four- and six-bedded rooms. There's 24-hour access, laundry, Internet access, and an inexpensive café. Open daily all year. Dorm beds including breakfast £20.

St Michael's Guest House 26 St Michael's St ℡01865/242101. Often full, this friendly, well-kept B&B, in a cosy three-storey terrace house, has unsurprising furnishings and fittings, but a charming, central location. A real snip. ❸

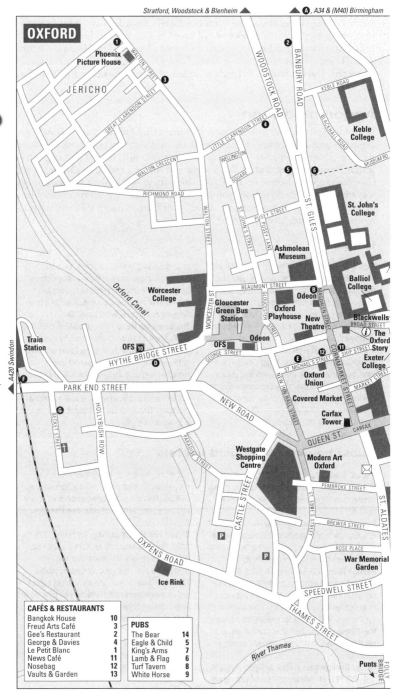

Stratford, Woodstock & Blenheim ▲   ▲ Ⓐ, A34 & (M40) Birmingham

OXFORD

❶ Phoenix Picture House

JERICHO

WOODSTOCK ROAD

BANBURY ROAD

KEBLE ROAD

Keble College

BLACKHALL ROAD

MUSEUM RD

St. John's College

ST GILES

Ashmolean Museum

Balliol College

Worcester College

BEAUMONT STREET

Ⓑ Odeon

Blackwells

Ⓘ The Oxford Story

Gloucester Green Bus Station

Oxford Playhouse

New Theatre

Exeter College

Train Station

OFS ⑩

HYTHE BRIDGE STREET

Odeon

OFS

Oxford Union

PARK END STREET

NEW ROAD

Covered Market

Carfax Tower

Westgate Shopping Centre

Modern Art Oxford

QUEEN ST.

CARFAX

PEMBROKE STREET

ST ALDATES

BREWER STREET

ROSE PLACE

War Memorial Garden

Ice Rink

SPEEDWELL STREET

THAMES STREET

River Thames

Punts

FOLLY BRIDGE

A420 Swindon

CAFÉS & RESTAURANTS

Bangkok House	10
Freud Arts Café	3
Gee's Restaurant	2
George & Davies	4
Le Petit Blanc	1
News Café	11
Nosebag	12
Vaults & Garden	13

PUBS

The Bear	14
Eagle & Child	5
King's Arms	7
Lamb & Flag	6
Turf Tavern	8
White Horse	9

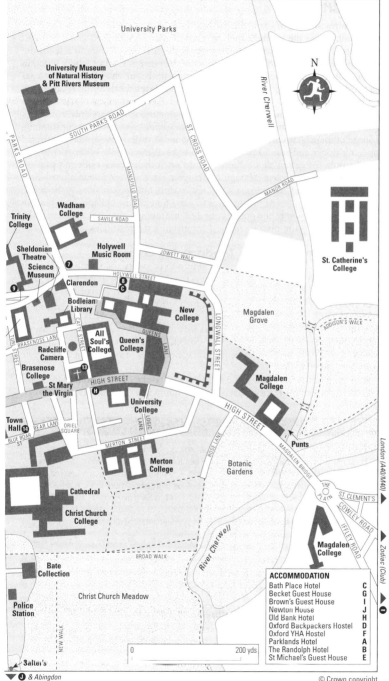

University Parks

University Museum
of Natural History
& Pitt Rivers Museum

River Cherwell

N

SOUTH PARKS ROAD

ST. CROSS ROAD

MANOR ROAD

PARKS ROAD

Wadham
College

SAVILE ROAD

St. Catherine's
College

Trinity
College

Sheldonian
Theatre
Science
Museum

Holywell
Music Room

JOWETT WALK

MANSFIELD ROAD

7

9

Clarendon

HOLYWELL STREET

8

C

Bodleian
Library

New
College

Magdalen
Grove

CATTE STREET

QUEENS LANE

ADDISON'S WALK

All
Soul's
College

Queen's
College

LONGWALL STREET

Radcliffe
Camera

TURL STREET

BRASENOSE LANE

Brasenose
College

13

Magdalen
College

St Mary
the Virgin

HIGH STREET

H

Town
Hall

14

BEAR LANE

ORIEL
SQUARE

University
College

LOGIC LANE

BLUE BOAR
ST

MERTON STREET

ROSE LANE

HIGH STREET

Punts

MAGDALEN BRIDGE

Merton
College

Botanic
Gardens

THE
PLAIN

ST. CLEMENT'S

London (A40/M40)

Cathedral

COWLEY ROAD

Zodiac (Club)

Christ Church
College

IFFLEY ROAD

Magdalen
College

BROAD WALK

River Cherwell

Bate
Collection

Christ Church Meadow

Police
Station

NEW WALK

0   200 yds

Salter's

J & Abingdon

© Crown copyright

The City

The compact centre of Oxford is wedged in between the rivers Thames and the Cherwell, just to the north of the point where they join. In theory, and on most maps, the Thames is known within the city as the "Isis", but few locals actually use the term. Central Oxford's principal point of reference is **Carfax**, a busy junction from where three of the city's main thoroughfares begin: the **High Street** runs east to Magdalen Bridge and the Cherwell; **St Aldates** south to the Thames; and **Cornmarket** north to the broad avenue of St Giles. Many of the oldest **colleges** face onto the High Street or the side streets adjoining it, their mellow stonework combining to create the most beautiful part of Oxford, though the most stunning college of them all is **Christ Church**. All the more visited colleges have restricted opening hours and some impose an admission charge, while others permit no regular public access at all. Of those that do open their doors, **college opening hours** are fairly consistent throughout the year, but there are sporadic term-time variations, especially at weekends. It's also worth noting that during the exam season, which stretches from late April to early June, all the colleges have periods when they are closed to the public entirely. For more specific information, call the relevant college – the phone numbers are given in the text below.

South from Carfax to Modern Art Oxford

Too busy to be comfortable and too modern to be pretty, the **Carfax** crossroads is not a place to hang around, though it is overlooked by an interesting remnant of the medieval town, a chunky fourteenth-century **tower**, adorned by a pair of clocktower jacks dressed in vaguely Roman attire. The tower is all that remains of St Martin's church, where legend asserts that William Shakespeare stood sponsor at the baptism of one of his friend's children. You can climb the **tower** (daily: April–Sept 10am–5.30pm; Oct–March 10am–3.30pm; £1.60) for wide views over the centre, though other vantage points – principally St Mary's (see p.272) – have the edge.

Spreading down St Aldates from the Carfax, Oxford's **Town Hall** is an ostentatious Victorian confection that reflects a municipal determination not to be

---

On the river

Punting is a favourite summer pastime among both students and visitors, but handling a punt – a flat-bottomed boat ideal for the shallow waters of the Thames and Cherwell rivers – requires some practice. The punt is propelled and steered with a long pole, which beginners inevitably get stuck in riverbed mud: if this happens, let go and paddle back, otherwise you're likely to be pulled overboard. The Cherwell, though much narrower than the Thames and therefore trickier to navigate, provides more opportunities for pulling to the side for a picnic, an essential part of the punting experience.

There are two central **boat rental** places: Magdalen Bridge boathouse (☎01865/202 643), beside the Cherwell at the east end of the High Street; and the Thames boat station at Folly Bridge (☎01865/243 421), a five- to ten-minute stroll south of the centre along St Aldates. In summer, the queues soon build up at both, so try to get there early in the morning – at around 10am. At both boathouses, expect **to pay** about £12 per hour for a boat plus a £30 deposit, and remember that sometimes ID is required. Punts can take a maximum of five passengers – four sitting and one punting. Call the boathouses for opening times – which vary – or if there are any doubts about the weather. Both boathouses also rent out **chauffeured punts** (about £25 for 30min) and **pedaloes**, which cost less, but aren't as much fun.

overwhelmed by the university. A staircase on its south side gives access to the **Museum of Oxford** (Tues–Fri 10am–4pm, Sat 10am–5pm, Sun noon–4pm; £2), which makes good use of photographs to tell the history of the city.

From the Town Hall, cross St Aldates and it's a few paces to Pembroke Street, home of the city's best contemporary art gallery, **Modern Art Oxford** (Tues–Sat 10am–5pm, Sun noon–5pm; free; ⓦ www.modernartoxford.org.uk). The gallery has an excellent programme of temporary exhibitions, featuring international contemporary art in a wide variety of media, along with lectures, films, workshops and multimedia performances (not all of which are free).

Christ Church College

Doubling back along Pembroke Street, turn right down St Aldates for the main facade of **Christ Church College** (Mon–Sat 9am–5pm, Sun 1–5pm; £4.50; ⓣ01865/276492), whose distinctive Tom Tower was added by Christopher Wren in 1681 to house the weighty "Great Tom" bell. The tower lords it over the main entrance of what is Oxford's largest and arguably most prestigious college, but visitors have to enter from the south, a signed five-minute walk away – just past the tiny War Memorial Garden and from the top of Christ Church Meadow (see below). Albert Einstein, William Gladstone and no fewer than twelve other British prime ministers studied here.

Entering the college from the south, it's a short step to the striking **Tom Quad**, the largest quad in Oxford, so large in fact that the Royalists penned up their mobile larder of cattle here during the Civil War. Guarded by the Tom Tower, the Quad's soft, honey-coloured stone makes a harmonious whole, but it was built in two main phases with the southern side dating back to Wolsey, the north finally finished in the 1660s. A wide stone staircase in the southeast corner of the Quad leads up to the **Dining Hall**, the grandest refectory in Oxford with a fanciful hammer-beam roof and a set of stern portraits of past scholars by a roll-call of well-known artists.

Just to the rear of the Tom Quad stands the **Cathedral**, which is also – in a most unusual arrangement – the college chapel. The Anglo-Saxons built a church on this site in the seventh century as part of St Frideswide Priory. The priory was suppressed in 1524, but the church survived, becoming a cathedral forty years later, though in between Wolsey knocked down the west end to make space for the Tom Quad. It's an unusually discordant church, with all sorts of bits and bobs from different periods, but it's fascinating all the same. The dominant feature is the sturdy circular columns and rounded arches of the Normans, but there are also early Gothic pointed arches and the chancel ceiling is a particularly fine example of fifteenth-century stone vaulting.

A passage at the northeast corner of the Tom Quad leads through to the **Peckwater Quad**, dominated by the whopping Neoclassical library. A few paces more and you're in the pocket-sized **Canterbury Quad**, where the **Picture Gallery** (Mon–Sat 10.30am–4.30/5pm, Sun 2–4.30/5pm; £2) is home to works by many of Italy's finest artists from the fifteenth to eighteenth centuries, including Leonardo da Vinci and Michelangelo. There's also a good showing by the Dutch – Van Dyck, Frans Hals and so forth. The Canterbury Quad abuts **Oriel Square** with Merton College (see p.272) just beyond, or you can return to the college's south entrance for Christ Church Meadow.

Christ Church Meadow and the Bate Collection

Christ Church Meadow fills in the tapering gap between the rivers Cherwell and Thames. Emerging from Christ Church, head east along Broad Walk for the Cherwell or keep straight down tree-lined (and more appealing) New Walk for the Thames. Alternatively, return to St Aldates and turn left for the **Bate Collection** (term times only, Mon–Fri 2–5pm & Sat 10am–noon; free), which contains England's most comprehensive collection of European woodwind instruments. Though only music buffs will make sense of some of the explanatory notes, you don't have to be an expert to enjoy the displays. In addition to rows of flutes and clarinets, there are all sorts of other instruments on show, from medieval crumhorns, looking like rejected walking sticks, to the country's finest example of a gamelan.

Merton College

Metres from Christ Church, on Merton Street, stands **Merton College** (Mon–Fri 2–4pm, Sat & Sun 10am–4pm; free; ☎01865/276310), historically the city's most important college. Balliol and University colleges may have been founded earlier, but it was Merton – opened in 1264 – which set the model for colleges in both Oxford and Cambridge, being the first to gather its students and tutors together in one place. Furthermore, unlike the other two, Merton retains some of its original medieval buildings, with the best of the thirteenth-century architecture clustered around **Mob Quad**, a charming courtyard with mullioned windows and Gothic doorways to the right of the Front Quad. From the Mob Quad, an archway leads through to the **Chapel**, which dates from 1290, and has never had a nave, leaving the choir as the main body of the church and the transepts as ante-chapels. In the latter is the curious funerary plaque of Thomas Bodley – founder of Oxford's most important library – his bust surrounded by ungainly, boyish-looking women in classical garb. Famous Merton alumni include T.S. Eliot, Angus Wilson, Louis MacNeice and Kris Kristofferson.

University and Queen's colleges

From Merton, narrow Logic Lane threads through to the east end of **University College** (no set opening times; ☎01865/276602), whose long, curved facade and twin gateway towers spread along the High Street. Known as "Univ", the college claims Alfred the Great as its founder, but things really got going with a formal endowment in 1249, making it Oxford's oldest college – though nothing of that period survives. The college's most famous recent alumnus was Rhodes Scholar Bill Clinton, while the former Australian premier Bob Hawke also studied here.

Across the High Street from Univ stands **Queen's College** (no set opening times; ☎01865/279120), whose handsome Baroque buildings cut an impressive dash. The only Oxford college to have been built in one period (1682–1765), Queen's benefited from the skills of several talented architects, most notably Nicholas Hawksmoor and Christopher Wren. Wren designed (or at least influenced the design of) the college's most diverting building, the **Chapel**, whose ceiling is filled with cherubs amidst dense foliage.

St Mary the Virgin

From Queen's, it's a couple of minutes' walk west along the High Street to **St Mary the Virgin** (daily 9am–5pm; free), a hotchpotch of architectural styles, but mostly dating from the fifteenth century. The church's saving graces are its elaborate, thirteenth-century pinnacled spire, its distinctive Baroque **porch** and its **tower** (£2), with wonderful views to the Radcliffe Camera (see p.274) and over **All Souls College** (Mon–Fri 2–4pm; free; ☎01865/279379), with its twin mock-Gothic towers by Hawksmoor and brightly decorated sundial by Wren. The tower can also be entered round the back of the church.

Magdalen College and the University Botanic Gardens

Heading east along the High Street, it's a short hop to **Magdalen College** (pronounced "Maudlin"; late June to Sept daily noon–6pm, Oct to late June 1–6pm or dusk; £3; ☎01865/276000), whose gaggle of stone buildings is overshadowed by its chunky medieval bell tower. Steer right from the entrance and you soon reach the **Chapel**, which has a handsome reredos, though you have to admire it through an ungainly stone screen. The adjacent **cloisters**, arguably Oxford's finest, are adorned by standing figures, some biblical and others folkloric, most notably a tribe of grotesques. Magdalen also boasts better **grounds** than most other colleges, with a bridge – at the back of the cloisters – spanning the River Cherwell to join **Addison's Walk**, which you can follow along the river and around a water meadow; rare wild fritillaries flower there in spring. Magdalen's alumni include Oscar Wilde, C.S. Lewis, John Betjeman, Julian Barnes and A.J.P. Taylor.

Across the High Street from Magdalen lie the **University of Oxford Botanic Gardens** (daily: March–April & Sept–Oct 9am–5pm; May–Aug 9am–6pm; Nov–Feb 9am–4.30pm; £2.60), whose greenery is bounded by a graceful curve of the Cherwell. First planted in 1621, the gardens comprise several different zones, from a lily pond, a bog garden and a rock garden through to borders of bearded irises and variegated plants. There are also eight large **glasshouses** featuring tropical and desert species (daily: April–Sept 10am–4.30pm; Oct–March 10–4pm).

The gardens are next to **Magdalen Bridge**, where you can rent punts (see box on p.270).

New College

Retracing your steps back along the High Street to Queen's, cut up **Queen's Lane** and you'll dog-leg your way north to **New College** (daily: Easter to early Oct 11am–5pm; £2; mid-Oct to Easter 2–4pm; free; ☎01865/279555). Founded in 1379, the college kicks off with an attractive **Front Quad**, though the splendid Perpendicular Gothic architecture of the original was spoiled by the addition of an extra storey in 1674. The adjoining **Chapel** has been mucked about, too, yet it can still lay claim to being the finest in Oxford, not so much for its design as its contents. The ante-chapel contains some superb fourteenth-century stained glass and the west window – of 1778 – holds an intriguing (if somewhat unsuccessful) Nativity scene based on a design by Sir Joshua Reynolds. Beneath it stands the wonderful *Lazarus* by Jacob Epstein; Khrushchev, after a visit to the college, claimed that the memory of this haunting sculpture kept him awake at night. The entire east wall of the main chapel is occupied by a magnificent nineteenth-century stone reredos, consisting of about fifty canopied figures, mostly saints and apostles, with Christ Crucified as the centrepiece. An archway on the east side of the Front Quad leads through to the modest **Garden Quad**, with the thick flowerbeds of the **College Garden** beckoning beyond. The north side of the garden is flanked by the largest and best-preserved section of Oxford's medieval **city wall**, though the conspicuous earthen **mound** in the middle is a later decorative addition. Notable New College alumni include the Labour Party leader Hugh Gaitskell, Tony Benn and the author John Fowles.

The Sheldonian Theatre and the Bodleian Library

The east end of Broad Street abuts some of Oxford's most monumental architecture, beginning with the **Sheldonian Theatre** (Mon–Sat 10am–noon &

2–4.30pm; winter closes 3.30pm; £1.50), ringed by a series of glum-looking, pop-eyed classical heads. The Sheldonian was Christopher Wren's first major work, a reworking of the Theatre of Marcellus in Rome, semicircular at the back and rectangular at the front. It was conceived in 1663, when the 31-year-old Wren's main job was as professor of astronomy. Designed as a stage for university ceremonies, nowadays it also functions as a concert hall, but the interior lacks any sense of drama, and even the views from the cupola are disappointing.

Wren's colleague, Nicholas Hawksmoor, designed the **Clarendon Building**, a domineering, solidly symmetrical edifice topped by allegorical figures that is set at right angles to – and lies immediately east of – the Sheldonian. The Clarendon was erected to house the University Press, but is now part of the **Bodleian Library** – the UK's largest after the British Library in London – with an estimated eighty miles of shelves distributed among various buildings. The heart of the Bodleian is located straight across from the Clarendon in the **Old Library**, which inhabits the beautifully proportioned **Old Schools Quadrangle**, built in the early seventeenth century in the ornate Jacobean Gothic style that distinguishes many of the city's finest buildings. On the quad's east side is the handsome **Tower of the Five Orders**, which gives a lesson in architectural design, with tiers of columns built according to the five Classical styles – Tuscan, Doric, Ionic, Corinthian and Composite. On the west side is the library's main entrance and, although most of the complex is out of bounds to the general public, you can pop into the **Divinity School** (Mon–Fri 9am–4.45pm, Sat 9am–12.30pm; free), one large room where, until the nineteenth century, degree candidates were questioned in detail about their subject by two interlocutors, with a professor acting as umpire. Begun in 1424, and sixty years in the making, the Divinity School boasts an extravagant vaulted ceiling, a riot of pendants and decorative bosses that comprises an exquisite example of late Gothic architecture. However, this elaborate design was never carried right through – funding was a constant problem – and parts of the school were finished off in a much plainer style with the change being especially pronounced on the south wall.

You can also sign up for an hour-long **guided tour** (mid-March to Oct Mon–Fri 10.30am, 1.30pm, 2pm & 3pm, Sat 10.30am & 11.30am; Nov to mid-March Mon–Fri 2pm & 3pm; £5) of **Convocation House**, adjacent to the Divinity School, and **Duke Humfrey's Library**, immediately above. The former is a sombre wood-panelled chamber graced by a fancy fan-vaulted ceiling, completed in 1759 but designed to look much older. The latter is distinguished by its painted beams and carved corbels, dating from the fifteenth century, but restored and remodelled by Thomas Bodley at the turn of the seventeenth century.

The Radcliffe Camera

Behind the Old Schools Quadrangle rises Oxford's most imposing – or vainglorious – building, the Bodleian's **Radcliffe Camera** (formerly the Radcliffe Library; no public access), a mighty rotunda, built between 1737 and 1748 by James Gibbs, architect of London's St Martin-in-the-Fields church. There's no false modesty here. Dr John Radcliffe was, according to a contemporary diarist, "very ambitious of glory" and when he died in 1714 he bequeathed a mountain of money for the construction of a library – the "Radcliffe Mausoleum" as one wag termed it. Gibbs was one of the few British architects of the period to have been trained in Rome and his rotunda was thoroughly Italian in style, its

△ Radcliffe Camera, Oxford

limestone columns ascending to a delicate balustrade, decorated with pin-prick urns and encircling a lead-sheathed dome.

Trinity and Exeter colleges

Back on Broad Street, the classical heads that shield the Sheldonian continue along the front of the **History of Science Museum** (Tues–Sat noon–4pm,

Sun 2–5pm; free), whose two floors display an amazing clutter of antique microscopes and astrolabes, sundials, quadrants and sextants. More obscure items include a thirteenth-century geared calendar and an "equatorium" for finding the position of the planets. The highlights are Elizabeth I's own astrolabe and Einstein's blackboard.

Across the street, **Trinity College** (daily 10.30am–noon & 2–4pm; free; ☎01865/279900) is fronted by two dinky lodge-cottages. Behind them the manicured lawn of the Front Quad stretches back to the richly decorated **Chapel**, awash with Baroque stucco work. Its high altar is flanked by an exquisite example of the work of Grinling Gibbons, with cherubs' heads peering out from delicate foliage. Behind the chapel stands **Durham Quad**, an attractive ensemble of old stone buildings begun at the end of the seventeenth century. Recent Trinity alumni include Richard Burton, Terence Rattigan and the Labour Party politician, Anthony Crosland.

From the south side of Broad Street, take Turl Street to **Exeter College** (daily 2–5pm; free; ☎01865/279600), another medieval foundation whose original buildings were chopped about in the nineteenth century. On this occasion, however, the Victorians did create something of interest in the elaborate, neo-Gothic **Chapel**, whose intricate, almost fussy detail was conceived by Gilbert Scott in the 1850s. The chapel also holds a superb Pre-Raphaelite tapestry, the *Adoration of the Magi*, a fine collaboration between William Morris and Edward Burne-Jones. Morris and Burne-Jones were both students here, as were J.R.R. Tolkien, Alan Bennett and Imogen Stubbs.

Cornmarket and the Ashmolean

Broad Street leads into the **Cornmarket**, a busy pedestrianized shopping strip lined by major stores. There's precious little here to fire the imagination, but it's only a few yards more to the **Ashmolean** (Tues–Sat 10am–5pm, Sun noon–5pm, plus late opening one evening a week in summer; free; ⓦ www.ashmol.ox.ac.uk), the university's principal museum, occupying a mammoth Neoclassical building on the corner of Beaumont Street and St Giles. The museum grew up around the collections of the magpie-like **John Tradescant**, gardener to Charles I, and an energetic traveller. During his wanderings, Tradescant built up a huge assortment of artefacts and natural specimens, which became known as Tradescant's Ark. He bequeathed all this to his friend and sponsor, the lawyer Elias Ashmole, who in turn gave it to the university. Tradescant's Ark has been added to ever since and today the Ashmolean possesses a vast and far-reaching collection covering everything from English glass and Russian icons to Egyptian mummies. The museum is currently undergoing a major expansion to create thirty new galleries, though the redevelopment will not be completed until 2011. In the meantime visitors have to take pot luck as to what is on display, though the Western Art and Egyptology sections should be largely unaffected. Pick up a **plan** at reception for the latest state of affairs.

The **Egyptian** rooms are not to be missed: in addition to well-preserved mummies and sarcophagi, there are unusual frescoes, rare textiles from the Roman and Byzantine periods and several fine examples of relief carving, such as on the shrine of Taharqa. Look out also for the **Islamic art** collection, which includes superb Islamic ceramics, and for the museum's **Chinese art**, boasting some remarkable early Chinese pottery with the simple monochrome pots of the Sung dynasty (960–1279) looking surprisingly modern. The archeologist Arthur Evans had close ties with the museum and he gifted it a stunning collection of **Minoan** finds from his years working at Knossos in Crete (1900–06): pride of place goes to the storage jars, sumptuously decorated with sea creatures and marine plants. A further highlight is the extraordinary **Alfred Jewel**, a tiny gold, enamel and rock crystal piece of uncertain purpose. The inscription reads "Alfred ordered me to be made" – almost certainly a reference to King Alfred the Great.

The museum is strong on **European art** too. Amongst the **Italian** works, keep an eye out for Piero di Cosimo's *Forest Fire* and Paolo Uccello's *Hunt in the Forest*, though Tintoretto, Veronese and Bellini feature prominently as well. There's also a strong showing of **French paintings**, with works by Pissarro, Monet, Manet and Renoir hanging alongside Cézanne and Bonnard, plus a representative selection of eighteenth- and nineteenth-century **British artists**: Samuel Palmer's visionary paintings run rings around the rest, though there are lashings of Pre-Raphaelite stuff from Rossetti and Holman Hunt to assorted cohorts.

Finally, don't miss the treasures displayed from Tradescant's Ark. Amongst the assorted curiosities, a highlight is Powhatan's mantle, a handsome garment made of deerskin and decorated with shells. Powhatan was the father of Pocahontas, and this mantle therefore dates back to the earliest contacts between English colonists and the Native Americans of modern-day Virginia. Other prime pieces include Guy Fawkes' lantern, Oliver Cromwell's death mask and the peculiar armour-plated hat that Bradshaw, the president of the board of regicides, wore when he condemned Charles I to death.

Eating and drinking

With so many students and tourists to cater for, Oxford has a wide choice of places to eat and drink. For a midday bite, one of the numerous **cafés** is ideal – some of the best are listed below and you'll find several others in the **Covered Market**, between the High Street and Cornmarket, an Oxford institution as essential to local shoppers as the Bodleian is to academics. There's also a sprinkling of first-rate **restaurants**, but the majority cater for the less expensive end of the market with varying degrees of success – again some of the better options are listed below. Reasonable food is served at most **pubs**, but those listed have been singled out for their ambience or selection of beers rather than for their menus.

Snacks and cafés

Freud Arts Café 119 Walton St. Occupying a grand building in the style of a Roman temple, this fashionable café-bar serves straightforward Italian/Mediterranean food. Live music some nights too. Main courses from as little as £4. Open daily from 11am till late. Inexpensive.

George & Davies Little Clarendon Street. Great little place offering everything from ice cream to bagels and full breakfasts. The cow mural is good fun too. Daily 8am to midnight. Inexpensive.

News Café 1 Ship St. Breakfasts, bagels and daily specials, plus beer and wine; also, as the name suggests, newspapers and TVs tuned to news broadcasts. Inexpensive.

Nosebag 6 St Michael's St. A civilized but unassuming place, with chintzy decor and background classical music. The hot and cold food attracts queues at lunchtime; less so in the evening, when it is a good place for a quick but wholesome meal. Good selection of veggie food. Daily 9.30am–10.30pm. Inexpensive.

Vaults & Garden Radcliffe Square. Attached to the church of St Mary the Virgin, this inexpensive café occupies an atmospheric stone-vaulted room and serves up good-quality coffee and cake, as well as quiche-and-salad lunches. There's a small outside area, but it's a little glum. Daily 10am–5pm. Inexpensive.

Restaurants

Bangkok House 42a Hythe Bridge St ☎01865/200705. Best Oriental restaurant in town, with superb Thai food and excellent service. The mixed starter and the coconut-milk curries are particularly good. Mains from £7–10. Inexpensive.

Gee's Restaurant 61 Banbury Rd ☎01865/553 540. Chic conservatory setting, but not as expensive as it looks. The inventive menu includes such items as chargrilled vegetables with polenta, roasted beetroot, a variety of steaks and a wide choice of breads. Strong on fish, too, with seafood main courses for around £15. Open daily for lunch and dinner plus Sunday brunch. Moderate.

Le Petit Blanc 71–72 Walton St ☎01865/510999. Renowned French chef Raymond Blanc's affordable and much praised, bistro-style restaurant offers a refreshing mix of French gourmet (corn-fed quail with lime leaf and ginger) and traditional English (pan-fried Gloucester old spot pork) cuisine. Main courses from a very reasonable £10. Moderate.

Pubs

The Bear 6 Alfred St. Tucked away down a narrow side street in the centre of town, this popular pub has a good range of beers and traditional decor.
Eagle & Child 49 St Giles. Known variously as the "Bird & Baby", "Bird & Brat" or "Bird & Bastard", this pub was once the haunt of Tolkien and C.S. Lewis. It still attracts an interesting crowd, but the modern extension at the back rather detracts from the cloistered rooms at the front.
King's Arms 40 Holywell St. Prone to student overkill on term-time weekends, but otherwise reasonably pleasant, with snug rooms at the back and a good choice of beers.

Lamb & Flag St Giles. Generations of university students have hung out in this old pub, which comes complete with low-beamed ceilings and a series of cramped but cosy rooms.
Turf Tavern Bath Place, off Holywell Street. Small, atmospheric seventeenth-century pub with a fine range of beers, and mulled wine in winter. Abundant seating outside.
White Horse 52 Broad St. A tiny, old pub with snug rooms, pictures of old university sports teams on the walls and real ales. It was used as a set for the *Inspector Morse* TV series.

Entertainment and nightlife

Oxford does not rate highly when it comes to contemporary **live music**, though devotees of **classical music** are well catered for, with the city's main concert halls and certain college chapels – primarily Christ Church, Merton and New College – offering a wide-ranging programme of concerts and recitals. As regards **theatre**, student productions dominate the repertoire, but the quality of acting varies, particularly when they tackle Shakespeare, the favourite for the open-air college productions put on for tourists during the summer.

For classical music and theatre **listings**, consult *This Month in Oxford*, available free from the tourist office. The daily *Oxford Mail* newspaper and the weekly *Oxford Times* also carry information on gigs and events. For more adventurous stuff – special club nights, etc – watch out for flyers.

Live music and clubs

OFS (Old Fire Station) 40 George St ☎01865/297170, ⊛www.ticketmaster.co.uk. Multi-purpose venue hosting musicals and theatre, plus a separate café-bar featuring one-off DJ club nights.

Zodiac 190 Cowley Rd ☎01865/420042, ⊛www.thezodiac.co.uk. Far and away Oxford's most respected indie and dance venue, with a fast-moving programme of live bands and guest DJs.

Classical music and theatre

Holywell Music Room 32 Holywell St. This small, plain, Georgian building was opened in 1748 as the first public music hall in England. It offers a varied programme, from straight classical to experimental, with occasional bouts of jazz. Programme details are posted outside and are available at the Oxford Playhouse (see below), which also sells its tickets.
New Theatre George Street ☎01865/320760, ⊛www.ticketmaster.co.uk. Popular – and populist – programme of theatre, dance, pop music,

musicals and opera, from Ross Noble to The Hollies and beyond.

Oxford Playhouse Beaumont Street ☎01865/305305, ⓦwww.oxfordplayhouse.com. Professional touring companies perform a mixture of plays, opera and concerts at what is generally regarded as the city's best theatre.

Pegasus Theatre Magdalen Road ☎01865/722851, ⓦwww.pegasustheatre.org.uk.

Low-budget, avant-garde productions dominate the programme of this adventurous theatre.

Sheldonian Theatre Broad Street ☎01865/277299. Some have criticized the acoustics here, but this is still Oxford's top concert hall and its resident symphony orchestra is the Oxford Philomusica (☎0870/6060804, ⓦwww.oxfordphil .com).

Listings

Bike rental Bikezone, 6 Lincoln House, Market Street, off Cornmarket ☎01865/728877.

Bookshops The leading university bookshop is Blackwells, with several outlets including three shops on Broad Street: Blackwells Music, Blackwells Art & Posters, and the main bookshop at 48–51 Broad St (☎01865/792792).

Buses Most local buses, including Park-and-Ride, are operated by the Oxford Bus Company (☎01865/785400), which also – amongst several companies – offers fast and frequent services to London and Gatwick and Heathrow airports. Other long-distance services are run by National Express (☎08705/808080) with most regional routes run by Stagecoach (☎01865/772250).

Cinema The Odeon cinemas on Magdalen and George streets (both ☎0871/224 4007) show the latest blockbusters, while the best arts cinema is the Ultimate Picture Palace (UPP) on Jeune Street, off Cowley Road (☎01865/245/288, ⓦwww.ulti -matepicturepalace.com). The Phoenix Picture House, 57 Walton St (☎01865/512526, ⓦwww.picture -houses.co.uk), shows mainstream and arts films, and regularly screens foreign-language films too.

Internet Free at the Central Library, Westgate Shopping Centre, at the west end of Queen Street (☎01865/815509).

Pharmacies Boots, 6 Cornmarket (☎01865/247 461).

Post office At the top of St Aldates, near the corner with High Street.

Around Oxford

As a base for exploring some of the more delightful parts of central England, Oxford is hard to beat. It's a short drive west to the Cotswolds (see pp.281–288), while nearer still – a brief bus ride north – is the charming little town of **Woodstock** and its imperious neighbour, **Blenheim Palace**, birthplace of Winston Churchill.

Woodstock

WOODSTOCK, eight miles north of Oxford, has royal associations going back to Saxon times, with a string of kings attracted by its excellent hunting. Henry I built a royal lodge here and his successor, Henry II, enlarged it to create a grand manor house-cum-palace, where the Black Prince was born in 1330. The Royalists used Woodstock as a base during the Civil War, but, after their defeat, Cromwell never got round to destroying either the town or the palace; the latter was ultimately given to (and flattened by) the Duke of Marlborough, in 1704. Long dependent on royal and then ducal patronage, Woodstock is now both a well-heeled commuter town for Oxford and a provider of food, drink and beds for visitors to Blenheim. It is also an extremely pretty little place, its handsome stone buildings gathered around the main square, at the junction of Market and High streets. It is here that you'll find the town's one sight, the **Oxfordshire Museum** (Tues–Sat 10am–5pm, Sun 2–5pm; free), a well-composed review of the archeology, social history and industry of the county. The museum shares its premises with the town's **tourist office** (Mon–Sat 9.30/10am–5/5.30pm, Sun 2–5pm, ☎01993/813 276,

Ⓦ www.oxfordshirecotswolds.org), which has a useful range of information on the nearby Cotswolds.

Woodstock has several good **pubs**, the most characterful being the *Bear*, a delightful old coaching inn across from the museum with low-beamed ceilings and antique furnishings. It also has some **rooms**, but a much better bet is the ⚐ *King's Arms*, at 19 Market St (☏01993/813636, Ⓦwww.kings-hotel-wood stock.co.uk; ➋), with fifteen chic, pastel-painted rooms, and a great **restaurant** (main courses start at about £11). Stagecoach **buses** from Oxford run to Woodstock every thirty minutes or so (hourly on Sun), with some continuing on to Chipping Norton in the Cotswolds (see p.282).

Blenheim Palace

Nowadays, successful British commanders get medals and titles, but in 1704, as a thank-you for his victory over the French at the battle of Blenheim, Queen Anne gave **John Churchill, Duke of Marlborough** (1650–1722), the royal estate of Woodstock, along with the promise of enough cash to build himself a gargantuan palace.

Work started promptly on **Blenheim Palace** (10.30am–6pm, last admission 4.45pm: mid-Feb to Oct daily; Nov to mid-Dec Wed–Sun; £13 including park, gardens & parking) with the principal architect being Sir John Vanbrugh, who was also responsible for Castle Howard in Yorkshire (see p.619). However, the duke's formidable wife, Sarah Jennings, who had wanted Christopher Wren as architect, was soon at loggerheads with Vanbrugh, while Queen Anne had second thoughts, stifling the flow of money. Construction work was halted and the house was only finished after the duke's death at the instigation of his widow, who ended up paying most of the bills and designing much of the interior herself. The end result is the country's grandest example of Baroque civic architecture, an Italianate palace of finely worked yellow stone that is more a monument than a house – just as Vanbrugh intended.

The **interior** of the main house is stuffed with paintings and tapestries, plus all manner of objets d'art, including furniture from Versailles, and stone and marble carvings by Grinling Gibbons. The Great Hall has assorted grisailles and murals that celebrate Marlborough's martial skills, though Horace Walpole, the eighteenth-century wit and social commentator, had it about right when he wrote that Blenheim resembled "the palace of an auctioneer who had been chosen King of Poland". Churchill fans may find more of interest in the **Churchill Exhibition**, which provides a brief introduction to Winston, accompanied by live recordings of some of his more famous speeches. Born here at Blenheim, Churchill (1874–1965) now lies buried alongside his wife in the graveyard of Bladon church just outside the estate.

Blenheim's formal **gardens** (same times as house, but closes at dusk in winter; £8 gardens, park & parking only) to the rear of the house, are divided into several distinct areas, including a rose garden and an arboretum, though the open **parkland** (daily 9am–6pm or dusk, last admission 1hr 15min before closing) is more enticing, leading from the front of the house down to an artificial lake, **Queen Pool**. Vanbrugh's splendid Grand Bridge crosses the lake to the **Column of Victory**, erected by Sarah Jennings and topped by a statue of her husband posing heroically in a toga. It's said that Capability Brown, who landscaped the park, laid out the trees and avenues to represent the battle of Blenheim.

There are two **entrances** to Blenheim, one just south of Woodstock on the Oxford road and another through the Triumphal Arch at the end of Park Street in Woodstock itself.

The Cotswolds

The limestone hills that make up the **Cotswolds** are preposterously photogenic, dotted with a string of picture-book villages built by wealthy cloth merchants. **Wool** was important here as far back as the Roman era, but the greatest fortunes were made between the fourteenth and sixteenth centuries, and it was at this time that many of the region's fine manors and churches were built. Largely bypassed by the Industrial Revolution, which heralded the area's commercial decline, much of the Cotswolds is technically speaking a relic, with its architecture preserved in immaculate condition. Numerous churches are decorated with beautiful carving, for which the local limestone was ideal: soft and easy to carve when first quarried, but hardening after long exposure to the sunlight. The use of this **local stone** is a strong unifying characteristic across the region, though its colour modulates as subtly as the shape of the hills, ranging from a deep golden tone in Chipping Campden to a silvery grey in Painswick.

The consequence is that the Cotswolds have become one of the country's main tourist attractions, with many towns afflicted by plagues of tearooms and souvenir and antiques shops. To see the Cotswolds at their best, you should visit off-season or perhaps avoid the most popular towns and instead escape into the hills themselves, though even in high season the charms of towns such as **Burford**, **Northleach** and **Chipping Campden** are evident. As for **walking**, this might be a tamed landscape, but there's good scope for exploring the byways, either in the gentler valleys that are most typical of the Cotswolds or along the dramatic escarpment that marks the boundary with the Severn Valley. The long-distance **Cotswold Way** runs along the top of the ridge, stretching about one hundred miles from Chipping Campden past Cheltenham, Gloucester and Stroud as far as Bath.

There are also a few larger towns in the region, the biggest true Cotswold town being **Cirencester**, a buzzing community dating back to the Romans. On the western edge, **Cheltenham** has a very different feel, predominantly Regency in tone and well supplied with bars and restaurants, while **Stroud**'s no-nonsense style is a world away from Cotswold gentility, though this old wool town is within easy reach of attractive countryside too.

Slower **trains** on the Oxford to Worcester line stop at half a dozen of the region's villages and the town of Moreton-in-Marsh, while the western edge of the Cotswolds is better served with regular trains linking Gloucester, Cheltenham, Stroud and Bristol. Otherwise, you'll be reliant on the **bus** network, which connects all the larger towns and villages, though links with the smaller, more isolated villages and Sunday services are virtually nonexistent. All the region's tourist offices have local bus **timetables**, while the larger ones can supply an excellent synopsis of train and bus services, called *Explore the Cotswolds*, produced by the Cotswolds Conservation Board (☏01451/862000, ⑱www.cotswoldsaonb.org). All Oxfordshire's tourist offices also provide the handy *Public Transport Guide*.

Burford

Some twenty miles west of Oxford you get your first real taste of the Cotswolds at **BURFORD**, where the magnificent long and wide High Street slopes down to the bridge over the River Windrush. Though sadly traffic-filled, the High Street is flanked by a remarkably homogeneous line of old buildings that feature almost every type of architectural peccadillo known to the Cotswolds: there are wonky mullioned windows and half-timbered facades with bendy beams as well as fancy bow-fronted, honey-stone houses and grand horse and carriage gateways. Down a lane off the High Street, the fascinating **church of St John** is Norman in origin, though evidence of remodelling and additions up to the seventeenth century can still be seen. Thereafter, it was pretty much left alone, its soaring spire standing high above the river, but not – by deliberate design – the town. Unusually, the chapels and chantries that clutter the **interior** were not cleared away after the Reformation, but turned into pews and **mausoleums**, the most impressive being that of Lawrence Tanfield, James I's Chancellor of the Exchequer, who lies on his canopied table-tomb with his wife. Even more unusual is the **funerary plaque** of Edmund Harman, Henry VIII's barber and surgeon, stuck to the wall of the nave and sporting four Amazonian Indians, the first representation of Native Americans in Britain.

A pleasant walk from Burford is to follow the footpath east for three miles along the River Windrush to **Widford**, a hamlet with an idyllic medieval chapel built in the middle of a field on the site of a Roman villa. Close by is **Swinbrook**, where the church of St Mary houses a monument showing six members of the Fettiplace family reclining comically on their elbows: the Tudor effigies rigid and stony-faced, their Stuart counterparts stylish and rather camp.

Practicalities

Buses to Burford pull in along the High Street, including the useful Swanbrook (ⓣ01452/712386) service from Oxford to Cheltenham via Northleach (3 or 4 daily, 1 on Sun). The **tourist office** is just off the High Street on Sheep Street (Mon–Sat: March–Oct 9.30am–5.30pm; Nov–Feb 10am–4.30pm; ⓣ01993/823 558, ⓦwww.oxfordshirecotswolds.org), where you'll also find a couple of good **hotels**. *The Bay Tree* (ⓣ01993/822791, ⓦwww.cotswold-inns-hotels.co.uk; ❽) occupies a seventeenth-century wisteria-clad stone house with twenty-odd rooms, while the *Lamb Inn* (ⓣ01993/823155, ⓦwww.lambinn-burford.co.uk; ❼), is slightly more traditional with a flagstoned bar. *The Angel Brasserie*, just off the High Street at 14 Witney St (ⓣ01993/822714, ⓦwww.theangel-uk.com; ❺), also has a handful of rooms, and its **restaurant** is the best place to eat, with a lively, creative menu written on the blackboard above the bar (mains from £12; open Thurs–Sun lunchtimes and Tues–Sat evenings).

Chipping Norton and around

The bustling market town of **CHIPPING NORTON** lies eleven miles north of Burford: its suffix 'Chipping', a common Cotswold name, derives from *ceapen*, the old English for market. Although not the prettiest of towns, it's flanked to the east by one of the least explored and most scenic corners of the Cotswolds – a region of limestone uplands latticed by long dry-stone walls and dotted with picturesque hamlets. The western approach to the town, via the A44, is dominated by the extraordinary chimneystack of the **Bliss Tweed Mill** (no public access), mounted on a domed tower, and recalling the nineteenth-century textile boom. The town was first granted a **wool fair** charter in the twelfth century, by King John, though it didn't reach its peak until three hundred years later, when it acquired many of the stalwart stone buildings that now line up along the market square. Also paid for by wealthy wool merchants, **St Mary's Parish Church**, just below the square – and beyond a row of handsome almshouses – harbours a beautiful Perpendicular Gothic nave. The vaulted porch is equally striking due to the ugly grinning devils and green men that peer down from the roof, while the east window of the south aisle is a splendid affair, spiralling out from a central tulip.

Buses to Chipping Norton pull in on West Street, a few yards from the town hall. **Accommodation** is thin on the ground, though the Georgian *Best Western Crown and Cushion* on the main square (℡01608/642533, 🌐www .thecrownandcushion.com; **5**), with a few uninspiring rooms, was once owned by Keith Moon of The Who. More distinctively, in nearby Churchill, three miles southwest of town along the B4450, *The Forge B&B* (℡01608/658173, 🌐www .cotswolds-accommodation.com; **4**) offers a handful of en-suite rooms in taste-fully renovated stone premises. Chipping Norton's most authentic **pub** is the *Chequers*, just down from the main square near St Mary's.

The Rollright Stones and Great Tew

Northwest of Chipping Norton along the A44, a small lane leads to the **Rollright Stones**, a scattering of megalithic monuments, that includes several burial chambers and barrows as well as one of the most important stone circles in the country. The **King's Men Stone Circle** is the largest of the monuments, with over seventy irregularly spaced stones forming a circle thirty metres in diameter.

From the Rollrights, a series of country roads leads east to **GREAT TEW**, one of the most beautiful Cotswold villages, its thatched cottages and honey-coloured stone houses weaving around grassy hillocks with woodland on all sides. It's also home to one of England's most idyllic pubs, the 🍺 *Falkland Arms* (℡01608/683653, 🌐www.falklandarms.org.uk; **5**), which rotates four guest beers in addition to its regular real-ale supplies, and sells a fine selection of single malts, herbal wines, snuff, and clay pipes you can fill with tobacco for a smoke in the flower-filled garden. Little has changed in the flagstone-floored **bar** since the sixteenth century, although the snug is now a small **dining room** serving delicious, homemade lunches and evening meals, with main courses from £6 (closed Sunday evenings). It also has a few well-renovated **rooms**, though booking ahead is essential.

Chastleton House

About four miles west of Chipping Norton, **Chastleton House** (April–Sept Wed–Sat 1–5pm, Oct Wed–Sat 1–4pm; £6; timed tickets, pre-bookable on ℡01494/755585; NT) is one of the region's premier country houses. Built between 1605 and 1612 by Walter Jones, a wealthy Welsh wool merchant, this ranks among the most splendid Jacobean properties in the country, set amid ornamental gardens that include England's first-ever croquet lawn (the rules of this most eccentric of games were codified here in 1865). Inside, the house looks as if it's been in a time warp for four hundred years, with unwashed upholstery, unpolished wood panelling and miscellaneous clutter clogging some of the corners. This dishevelled air partly derives from the previous owners, the Jones family, who lost their fortune in the aftermath of the Civil War – they were Royalists – and never had enough cash to modernize thereafter. It's also a credit to the National Trust, who took on the property in 1991, but wisely decided to stick to the "lived-in look". It's the general flavour of the house that is of most appeal, but there are several highlights, notably the huge barrel-vaulted long gallery, oodles of elaborate plasterwork and panelling, tapestries and exquisite glassware, and, in the beer cellar, the longest ladder (dated 1805) you're ever likely to come across. There's also a topiary garden, where the hedges are clipped into bulbous shapes reminiscent of squirrels and tortoises.

Chipping Campden

From Chipping Norton, it's about eighteen miles northwest to **CHIPPING CAMPDEN**, which gives a better idea than anywhere else in the Cotswolds as to what a prosperous wool town might have looked like in the Middle Ages. The short **High Street** is hemmed in by ancient houses, with undulating, weather-beaten roofs and the original mullioned windows, while the fifteenth-century **church of St James** (March–Oct Mon–Sat 10am–5pm, Sun 2–5pm; Nov–Feb Mon–Sat 11am–3pm, Sun 2–4pm; free), dates from the zenith of the town's wool-trading days. Inside, is the ostentatious **funerary chapel** of the Hicks family, with carved marble effigies of Lady Elizabeth and Sir Baptist Hicks, who built a huge mansion next to the church in the 1610s: sadly, it burned down shortly afterwards and only two splendid Baroque gatehouses and a pair of banqueting halls (no public access) remain. The town's seventeenth-century **Market Hall** has survived intact, however, a barn-like affair in the middle of the High Street, where farmers once gathered to sell their harvests.

A fine panoramic view rewards those who make the short but severe hike up the Cotswold Way northwest from the High Street (along West End Terrace and Hoo Lane) to **Dover's Hill**. Since 1610 this natural amphitheatre has been the stage for an Olympics of rural sports, though the event was suspended last century when games such as shin-kicking became little more than licensed thuggery. A more civilized version, the **Cotswold Olimpick Games**, has been staged each June since 1951 with hammer-throwing and tug-of-war instead.

Practicalities

Inevitably, Chipping Campden heaves with day-trippers in the summer, so try to stay overnight and explore in the evening or at dawn, when the streets are empty and the golden hues of the stone at their richest. **Buses** run here from Chipping Norton, Oxford and Stratford-upon-Avon. The town's **tourist office** is bang in the middle of town, on the High Street (daily 10am–5.30pm; ☎01386/841206, ⓦwww.chipping-campden.net), and can book accommodation – a useful service in the height of the summer when rooms are in short supply. The town's best **B&B** by a long chalk is *Badgers Hall* (☎01386/840839, ⓦwww.badgershall.com; no cards; ⑤), above its own, excellent **tearoom**, in an old stone house on the High Street; advance bookings are advised. The best **hotel** is the family-run *Cotswold House*, in an immaculately maintained Regency town house on The Square (☎01386/840330, ⓦwww.cotswoldhouse.com; ⑦), with twenty chic and modern rooms. Its **brasserie** is a good place to dine, with main courses from £12, while the *Eight Bells Inn* is a particularly cosy **pub** around the corner from the church.

Stow-on-the-Wold and around

Ambling over a steep hill some ten miles south of Chipping Campden, **STOW-ON-THE-WOLD** sucks in a disproportionate number of visitors for its size and attractions, which essentially comprise an old **marketplace** surrounded by cafés, pubs, antique and souvenir shops. The narrow walled alleyways, or "tunes", running into the square were designed for funnelling sheep into the market, which is itself dominated by an imposing Victorian hall. The town makes a good base for exploring the surrounding Cotswold villages.

Buses from Cheltenham and Cirencester pull in on the High Street, just off the main square, where the **tourist office** (April–Oct Mon–Sat 9.30am–5.30pm; Nov–March Mon–Sat 9.30am–4.30pm; ☎01451/831 082, ⓦwww.cotswold.gov.uk/tourism) sells National Express bus tickets, and can book

△ Stow-on-the -Wold

accommodation. There's a reasonable supply in Stow – try the five-roomed *Tall Trees B&B* (☎01451/831296; no credit cards; ❸), on the edge of town off the Oddington road (A436), with sweeping views and a cosy wood-burner in its modern sitting-room. Stow also has the Cotswolds' only YHA **hostel**, in a good looking Georgian town house on the main square (☎0870/7706050, ⓦwww.yha.org.uk; dorm beds £14; Easter to Oct; reservations required).

For **food**, *The Royalist Hotel*, just off the main square on the corner of Park and Digbeth streets, offers light meals in its *Eagle & Child* bar and also possesses the more formal but extremely good *947AD* **restaurant** (☎01451/830670), where a main course costs around £13. The best **teashop** in town is the *Cotswold Garden*

Tearoom, yards from the *Royalist* on Digbeth Street, which serves tasty homemade cakes and snacks.

Around Stow: Bourton-on-the-Water and the Slaughters

Some four miles south of Stow to the east of the A429, **BOURTON-ON-THE-WATER** is admittedly picturesque, with its five mini-bridges straddling the River Windrush as it courses through the centre of the village. However, this, combined with a couple of purpose-built tourist attractions such as a Model Village and Dragonfly Maze, means that it attracts more tourists than just about anywhere in the Cotswolds.

Much more enticing, though still on the day-trippers' circuit, is the tiny hamlet of **LOWER SLAUGHTER** (as in *slohtre*, old English for "marshy place"), to the west of the A429, a mile or so from Bourton. Here, the River Eye snakes through the village, overlooked by a string of immaculate and very old stone cottages. The village church blends in well, though it's largely Victorian, and there is a small museum (and souvenir shop) in a former mill. A pleasant hour's walk up the river valley brings you to **UPPER SLAUGHTER**, a pretty little village buried deep in a wooded dell. It's also home to one of the best **accommodation** options in the area, the appealing *Lords of the Manor*, a luxurious hotel in Upper Slaughter's old rectory (T01451/820243, Wwww.lordsofthemanor.com; ●).

Northleach

Nine miles south of Stow-on-the-Wold and within easy reach of Oxford, **NORTHLEACH** is one of the most appealing and least developed villages in the Cotswolds, with rows of immaculate late-medieval cottages clustered around the **Market Place** and adjoining **Green**. Its most outstanding feature, however, is the handsome Perpendicular **Church of St Peter and St Paul**, erected in the fifteenth century at the height of the wool boom, when the surrounding fields of rich limestone grasses supported a vast population of sheep. The local breed, known as the Cotswold Lion, was a descendant of flocks introduced by the Romans, and by the thirteenth century had become the largest in the country, producing heavy fleeces that were exported to the Flemish weaving towns. The income from this lucrative trade, initially controlled by the clergy but later by a handful of wealthy merchants, financed the construction of four major churches in the region, of which those at Northleach and Burford (see p.281) are the most impressive – the others are in Cirencester and Chipping Campden. The church porch is a suitably ostentatious affair with a set of finely carved corbel heads, while the floor of the nave is inlaid with an exceptional collection of **memorial brasses** marking the tombs of the merchants whose endowments paid for the church. On several, you can make out the woolsacks laid out beneath the corpse's feet – a symbol of wealth and power that features to this day in the House of Lords, where a woolsack is placed on the Lord Chancellor's seat.

Two minutes' walk along the High Street from the Market Place is Northleach's other main attraction, **Keith Harding's World of Mechanical Music** (daily 10am–6pm; £5; Wwww.mechanicalmusic.co.uk), with its antique music boxes, automata, barrel organs and mechanical instruments all stuffed into one room. The entrance fee includes an hour-long tour of the collection, of which the highlight is hearing the likes of Rachmaninov, Gershwin or Paderewski playing their own masterpieces on piano rolls.

Swanbrook **buses** (☎01452/712386) run between Oxford and Cheltenham via Burford and Northleach three or four times daily (once on Sun). There's good **accommodation** on the Market Place at the *Cotteswold House B&B* (☎01451/860493, ⓦwww.cotteswoldhouse.com; ❹), a wonderfully preserved stone cottage with exposed arches and antique oak panelling, and at the *Wheatsheaf Hotel* (☎01451/860244, ⓦwww.wheatsheafatnorthleach.com; ❹), a former coaching inn just down from the square on West End. Its excellent **restaurant** uses locally sourced ingredients: main courses, such as pan-fried chicken and slow-roasted lamb – average a very reasonable £12.

Cirencester

Ten miles from Northleach, on the southern fringes of the Cotswolds, **CIRENCESTER** makes a refreshing change from its more gentrified neighbours. Here, the "olde-worlde" image in which many Cotswold towns indulge has been exchanged for an endearingly old-fashioned atmosphere, generated partly by shops that haven't changed for decades. Under the **Romans**, the town was called Corinium and ranked second only to Londinium in size and importance. A provincial capital and a centre of trade, it flourished for three centuries and had one of the largest forums north of the Alps. However, the Saxons polished off almost all of the Roman city and the town's prosperity was only restored with the wool boom of the Middle Ages. Nowadays, Cirencester, with its handsome stone buildings, is one of the most affluent towns in the area and lays claim to be the "Capital of the Cotswolds".

Cirencester's heart is the delightful swirling **Market Place**, on Mondays and Fridays packed by traders' stalls. The eighteenth-century and Victorian facades lining the thoroughfare are dominated by the parish church of **St John the Baptist** (Mon–Sat 9.30am–5pm, Sun 2.15–5pm; £2 suggested donation), built in stages during the fifteenth century. The extraordinary flying buttresses that support the tower had to be added when it transpired that the church had been constructed upon a filled-in ditch. Its grand three-tiered south porch, the largest in England – big enough to function as the one-time town hall – leads to the nave, where slender piers and soaring arches create a superb sense of space, enhanced by clerestory windows that bathe the nave in a warm light. The church contains much of interest, including a colourful wineglass **pulpit**, carved in stone in around 1450 and one of the few pre-Reformation pulpits to have survived in Britain. North of the chancel, superb fan vaulting hangs overhead in the **chapel of St Catherine**, who appears in a still vivid fragment of a fifteenth-century wall painting. In the adjacent **Lady Chapel** are two good seventeenth-century monuments, to Humphrey Bridges and his family and to the dandified Sir William Master.

Other than the church, few medieval buildings have survived in Cirencester, with the houses along the town's most handsome streets – Park, Thomas and Coxwell – dating mostly from the seventeenth and eighteenth centuries. One of those on Park Street houses the **Corinium Museum** (Mon–Sat 10am–5pm, Sun 2–5pm; £3.70), mostly devoted to Roman and Saxon artefacts, including several wonderful **mosaic pavements**. A yew hedge the height of telegraph poles runs along Park Street, concealing **Cirencester House**, the home of the Earl of Bathurst. At no point can you see the rather plain house itself, though the attached three-thousand-acre park is open to the public, entered from Cecily Hill.

Practicalities

Despite nine roads radiating from Cirencester – five of them Roman – **bus** services to the town could be better; there are daily connections from Swindon, fourteen miles southeast, and Cheltenham, fifteen miles north. All services stop on Market Place, where the Corn Hall houses the **tourist office** (Mon–Sat 9.30am–5.30pm; Mon opens 9.45am, Dec closes 5pm; ℡01285/654180, Ⓦwww.cotswold.gov.uk); it covers the whole of the Cotswolds and has a list of local **accommodation** pinned outside. A string of **B&Bs** lines Victoria Road, a short walk east: two good options here are *The Ivy House*, in high-gabled Victorian premises at no. 2 (℡01285/656626, Ⓦwww.ivyhousecotswolds.com; no smoking; ❸), and similarly appointed *The Leauses*, at no. 101 (℡01285/653643, Ⓦwww.theleauses.co.uk; no smoking; ❸).

For **snacks** and first-class coffees, you can't do much better than *Keith's Coffee Shop* on Blackjack Street. Alternatively, the upstairs *Coffee House* in the Brewery Arts Centre off Cricklade Street serves inexpensive dishes, including vegetarian options (no credit cards; closed Sun). The best choice for a relaxing **evening meal**, however, is *Harry Hare's* at 3 Gosditch St (℡01285/652375), just behind the church, which specializes in classy versions of down-to-earth English dishes at moderate prices.

Cirencester has plenty of **pubs**, among which the *Kings Head* on Market Place and the *Waggon & Horses* at 11 London Rd stand out: the latter is also good for **bar meals**.

Malmesbury

The striking half-ruin of a Norman abbey presides over the small hill-town of **MALMESBURY**, one of the oldest boroughs in England. Lying twelve miles south of Cirencester, it's not part of the Cotswolds geologically, though the town's early wealth was based on wool. Nowadays Malmesbury is ringed by new housing estates and modern developments, but nothing can detract from the splendour of the abbey, a majestic structure boasting some of the finest Romanesque sculpture in the country.

The long High Street heads north across the river and up past a jagged row of ancient cottages on its way to the octagonal **Market Cross**, built in around 1490 to provide shelter from the rain. Nearby, the eighteenth-century **Tolsey Gate** leads through to the **Abbey** (daily: April–Oct 10am–5pm; Nov–March 10am–4pm), which was once a rich and powerful Benedictine monastery. The first abbey burnt down in about 1050, the second was roughed up during the Dissolution, but the beautiful Norman **nave** has survived, its south porch sporting a multitude of exquisite if badly worn figures. To the left of the high altar, the pulpit virtually hides the **tomb of King Athelstan**, grandson of Alfred the Great and the first Saxon to be recognized as king of England; the tomb, however, is empty, the location of the king's remains unknown. The abbey's greatest surviving treasures are housed in the parvise (room above the porch), reached via a narrow spiral staircase right of the main doorway, where pride of place is given to four Flemish **medieval Bibles**, written on parchment and sumptuously illuminated with gilt ink and exquisite miniature paintings.

Practicalities

Buses to Malmesbury – including services from Cirencester and Chippenham – pull into Market Place, a short walk from the **tourist office**, in the town hall off Cross Hayes car park (Mon–Thurs 9am–4.50pm, Fri 9am–4.20pm; Easter–Sept also Sat 10am–4pm; ℡01666/823748, Ⓦwww.wiltshiretourism .co.uk). There's no strong reason to stay the night here, but the *Old Bell* in Abbey Row (℡01666/822344, Ⓦwww.oldbellhotel.com; ❼), originally built as a guest house for the abbey, provides a great incentive, with plush rooms and lots of atmosphere. For **food**, stick to either the *Whole Hog*, a stone-walled tearoom-cum-pub overlooking Market Place, or the *Summer Café* on the High Street, which does a good line in sandwiches.

Cheltenham

Until the eighteenth century **CHELTENHAM** was like any other Cotswold town, but then the discovery of a spring in 1716 transformed it into

△ Cheltenham

Cheltenham racecourse, a ten-minute walk north of Pittville Park at the foot of Cleeve Hill, is Britain's main steeplechasing venue. The principal event of the season, the three-day **National Hunt Festival** in March, attracts forty thousand people each day. Other meetings take place in January, April, October, November and December: a list of fixtures is posted up at the tourist office. For the cheapest but arguably the best view, pay £6 (rising to £15 during the Festival, £25 on Gold Cup Day) for entry to the Best Mate Enclosure, as the pen in the middle is known. For schedules and other information, call ☏01242/513014 or check ⓦwww.cheltenham.co.uk. For the National Hunt Festival it's essential to buy tickets in advance.

Britain's most popular **spa**. During Cheltenham's prime, a century or so later, the royal, the rich and the famous descended in hordes to take the waters, which were said to cure anything from constipation to worms. These days, while a fair proportion of Cheltenham's hundred thousand-odd inhabitants are undoubtedly well-heeled, of Conservative persuasion and above retirement age, the town saves itself from too smug an image by a lively and increasingly cosmopolitan atmosphere. Its various **festivals** are established highlights of the cultural calendar – folk (Feb), jazz (April/May), literature (April and October), science (June) and classical music (July) – while Cheltenham's famous races (see box, above) and a fairly spirited nightlife complete the picture.

The focus of Cheltenham, the broad **Promenade**, sweeps majestically south from the High Street, lined with the town's grandest houses, smartest shops and most genteel public gardens. A short walk north of the High Street brings you to **Pittville**, which, planned as a spa town to rival Cheltenham, was never completed and is now mostly parkland. Here you can stroll along a few solitary Regency avenues and visit the grandest spa building, the domed **Pump Room** (Mon & Wed–Sun 11am–4pm), where you can sample England's only naturally alkaline water for free, though the building's chief function nowadays is as a concert hall. On your return route, the **Holst Birthplace Museum** is worth a glance, at 4 Clarence Rd (Tues–Sat 10am–4pm; £2.50). Once the home of the composer of *The Planets*, the intimate rooms hold plenty of Holst memorabilia – including his piano – and also give a good insight into Victorian family life. Back in the centre, the well-set-out **Art Gallery and Museum** on Clarence Street (Mon–Sat 10am–5.20pm, Thurs opens at 11am; free) marks the high point of Cheltenham. It's very good on social history, with different eras represented by table displays of personal belongings and a typical dinner of the time. There's also a fine room dedicated to the Arts and Crafts Movement, containing several pieces by Charles Voysey and Ernest Gimson, two of the period's most graceful designers. Also on display is an array of rare Chinese ceramics, and works by Cotswold artists such as Stanley Spencer and Vanessa Bell.

Practicalities

Long-distance **buses** arrive at the station in Royal Well Road, just west of the Promenade. The **train station** is on Queen's Road, southwest of the centre, a twenty-minute walk (or take buses #D or #E). The **tourist office**, at 77 Promenade (Mon–Sat 9.30am–5.15pm, Wed opens at 10am; ☏01242/522878, ⓦwww.visitcheltenham.info), can provide information on bus tours in the Cotswolds.

Accommodation is plentiful, but availability will be limited during the races and festivals. Many options are in fine Regency houses, including *Brennan*, on a quiet square at 21 St Luke's Rd (☎01242/525904; ❷), and *Crossways*, 57 Bath Rd (☎01242/527683, Ⓦwww.crosswaysguesthouse.com; no smoking; ❺), only two minutes' walk from the centre. The *Abbey Hotel*, 14–16 Bath Parade (☎01242/516053, Ⓦwww.abbeyhotel-cheltenham.com; ❸), has attractively furnished rooms and serves wholesome breakfasts overlooking the garden, while, on Bayshill Road, ⚘ *Kandinsky* (☎01242/527788, Ⓦwww.aliashotels .com; ❻) has Oriental decor and lots of funky style. Dormitory accommodation (£15) and single rooms (£21) are offered at the **YMCA**, 6 Victoria Walk (☎01242/524024, Ⓦwww.cheltenhamymca.com).

Cheltenham's **restaurants** draw in foodies from far and wide. At the top end, *Le Champignon Sauvage*, Suffolk Road (☎01242/573449; closed Sun & Mon), and *Le Petit Blanc*, The Promenade (☎01242/266800), an outpost of Raymond Blanc's famed *Manoir Aux Quat' Saisons*, both serve superlative French cuisine, with fixed-price lunches offsetting the otherwise high prices. Marginally less expensive, ⚘ *The Daffodil*, 18–20 Suffolk Parade (☎01242/700060), also offers gourmet choices in a former cinema, where the screen has been replaced by a hubbub of chefs. More affordably, you can sup on traditional English dishes at *Pie and Mash*, 10 Bennington St (☎01242/702785; closed daytime Tues & Wed, and all Sun & Mon).

Among Cheltenham's **pubs and bars**, seek out *The Beehive*, 1–3 Montpellier Villas, which has a games shed, courtyard garden and upstairs restaurant, or *Montpellier Wine Bar*, Montpellier Street, with lovely bow-fronted windows. The town's most popular **clubs** include *Subtone*, 115–117 The Promenade (☎01242/575925; closed Sun), and *Moda*, 33–35 Albion St (☎01242/570583).

Stroud and around

Five heavily populated valleys converge at **STROUD**, twelve miles west of Cirencester, creating an exhausting jumble of hills and a sense of high activity atypical of the Cotswolds. The bustle is not a new phenomenon. During the heyday of the wool trade the Frome River powered 150 mills, turning Stroud into the centre of the local cloth industry. While some of the old mills have been converted into flats, others contain factories, but only two continue to make cloth – no longer the so-called Stroudwater Scarlet used for military uniforms, but high-quality felt for tennis balls and snooker tables. In recent years, Stroud has become a thriving alternative centre, with communities of artists and New Agers in the nearby valleys, though the town itself retains a fairly dowdy image despite its scenic setting.

For visitors, the main point of interest is the excellent and family-friendly **Museum in the Park**, housed in an eighteenth-century mansion in Stratford Park, half a mile from the centre of town on the Gloucester road (April–July & Sept Tues–Fri 10am–5pm, Sat & Sun 11am–5pm; Aug also open Mon; Oct–Nov & Jan–March Tues–Fri 10am–5pm, Sat & Sun 11am–4pm; free). Beautifully laid out, the collection demonstrates the history of the town through imaginatively themed rooms such as "Clean, Fit and Tidy" and "Industry and Invention". Look out for the lovely eighteenth-century paintings showing the tentering (hanging out) of Stroud's scarlet cloth on the hillsides.

Industrial archeology is strewn the length of the Frome Valley – the so-called Golden Valley. Council offices occupy one of the valley's finest mills, **Ebley**

Mill, a twenty-minute walk west of the centre along the old Stroudwater Canal – for the best view you should then walk south across the field to the village of **Selsley**. The unused **Severn and Thames Canal** east of Stroud cuts a more picturesque route, particularly beyond Chalford, three miles east, where houses perch precariously on the hillside. Walk thirty minutes along the towpath from here and you'll end up at the mouth of the **Sapperton tunnel**, more than two miles long and a great feat of eighteenth-century engineering. It's unsafe to go inside, so seek sustenance at the nearby *Daneway Inn* instead, or head for the hilltop village of Sapperton, a world away from the hurly-burly of the Frome Valley.

Trains from London and Gloucester and **buses** from Cirencester, among other places, arrive at the station on Merrywalks. The **tourist office** is in the Subscription Rooms on George Street (Mon–Sat 10am–5pm; ☎01453/760960, ⓦwww.visitthecotswolds.co.uk), and there's an **Internet** café at 48 High St (Mon–Thurs 10am–4pm, Fri 10am–2pm). The most central place to **stay** is the *London Hotel*, 30–31 London Rd (☎01453/759992, ⓦwww.s-h-systems .co.uk; ❷), or try the *Downfield Hotel* at 134 Cainscross Rd (☎01453/764496, ⓦwww.downfieldhotel.co.uk; ❹), in a Georgian building five minutes from the High Street.

For daytime **meals**, head for *Mills Café* in Withey's Yard off High Street, which sells delicious cakes, homemade soups and other wholesome concoctions, while ✖ *Nine*, a bar/restaurant on John Street (☎01453/755447), has toasties and pastas at lunchtime, and a range of hot food in the evening; there are comfy chairs, and DJs play until late on Friday and Saturday nights.

Slimbridge

Eight miles southwest of Stroud, **SLIMBRIDGE** sits in a narrow corridor between the M5 and the Severn – a surprising location for the **Slimbridge Wildfowl and Wetlands Centre** (daily: April–Oct 9.30am–5.30pm; Nov–March 9.30am–5pm; £6.75; ⓦwww.wwt.org.uk), covering 120 acres between Sharpness Canal and the river. Since ornithologist Sir Peter Scott created it in 1946, the centre has become Britain's largest **wildfowl sanctuary**, and a breeding ground with an important conservation role. Geese, swans, ducks and a huge gathering of flamingos make up the bulk of the birdlife. While some birds are resident all year round, many are migratory: the greatest numbers congregate in the winter months, when Bewick swans, for example, migrate from Russia. There's an extensive network of trails around the sanctuary, with hides for observation.

Slimbridge has a YHA **hostel** (☎0870/770 6036, ⓔslimbridge@yha.org.uk; limited opening; £11.95), accessible from a lane opposite the *Tudor Arms* pub in the village. The only **buses** to go anywhere near Slimbridge are Stagecoach #91 to Dursley (Mon–Sat hourly) and the local Village Link Blue service, which needs booking at ☎01452/423598; both stop by the turn-off on the A38, a mile and a half east of the village. On Sunday, bus #91A goes directly to the Centre. You can reach it **by bike** on Sustrans route 41.

Berkeley

Though quite secluded within a swathe of meadows and neat gardens, **Berkeley Castle** (April–Sept Tues–Sat 11am–4pm, Sun 2–5pm; Oct Sun 2–5pm; £7.50, grounds only £4) dominates the little village of **BERKELEY**, five miles southwest of Slimbridge on the A38. The robust twelfth-century walls of the turreted fortress are softened by later accretions acquired in its gradual transformation into a family home. The interior is packed with mementos of its long history, including its grisliest moment in 1327, when Edward II was murdered here – apparently by a red-hot iron thrust into his bowels. You can view the cell where the event took place, along with dungeons, dining room, kitchen, picture gallery and the Great Hall. Outside, the grounds include an Elizabethan terraced garden and a Butterfly Farm (£2). Within easy walking distance, in the village itself, the **Jenner Museum** (April–Sept Tues–Sat 12.30–5.30pm, Sun 1–5.30pm; Oct Sun 1–5.30pm; £3.50) is dedicated to Edward Jenner, son of a local vicar and discoverer of the principle of vaccination.

For a lunchtime stop near Berkeley, follow the narrow High Street out of the centre of the village for about a mile to reach the *Salutation*, an unpretentious country **pub** with a garden. Berkeley is linked to Gloucester by a coach service (not Sun) operated by Beaumont Travel (☎01452/309770, ⓦwww .beaumont-travel.com).

Painswick

The A46 and the B4070 are equally attractive routes linking Stroud and Cheltenham, but the former has the edge because after four miles you reach the old wool town of **PAINSWICK**, where ancient buildings jostle for space on narrow streets running downhill off the busy main street. The fame of Painswick's **church** stems not so much from the building itself as from the surrounding **graveyard**, where 99 yew trees, cut into bizarre bulbous shapes resembling lollipops, surround a collection of eighteenth-century table-tombs unrivalled in the Cotswolds. However, it's the **Rococo Garden** (mid-Jan to Oct daily 11am–5pm; £4), about half a mile north up the Gloucester road and attached to Painswick House (not open to the public), that ranks as the main local attraction. Created in the early eighteenth century and later abandoned, the garden has been restored to its original form with the aid of a painting dated 1748. Although there's usually some restoration in progress, it's a beautiful example – and the country's only one – of Rococo garden design, a short-lived fashion typified by a mix of formal geometrical shapes and more naturalistic, curving lines. With a vegetable patch as an unusual centrepiece, the Painswick garden spreads across a sheltered gully – for the best vistas, walk around anticlockwise.

Painswick's **tourist office** is housed in the library on the main street (April–Oct Tues–Sat 10am–5pm, Sun 10am–1pm; ☎01452/813552). The best local **accommodation** choices include *St Anne's* on Gloucester Street (☎01452/812879; no smoking; no credit cards; ❸), an eighteenth-century town house, and *Cardynham House* on St Mary's Street (☎01452/814006, ⓦwww .cardynham.co.uk; ❺), with beautifully themed rooms, one with a lounge and private pool. Its **restaurant**, the *March Hare* (☎01452/813452; closed Sun & Mon) serves Thai food, while the nearby *Royal Oak* is Painswick's best **pub**.

Gloucester

For centuries life was good for **GLOUCESTER**. The Romans chose the spot for a garrison to guard the Severn and spy on Wales, and later for a *colonia* or home for retired soldiers – the highest status for a provincial Roman town. Commercial prestige came with trade up the River Severn, which developed into one of the busiest trade routes in Europe. The city's political importance peaked under the Normans, when William the Conqueror met here frequently with his council of nobles. The Middle Ages saw Gloucester's rise as a religious centre, and the construction of what is now the cathedral, but also witnessed its political and economic decline: navigating the Severn as far up as Gloucester was so difficult that most trade gradually shifted south to Bristol. In a brave attempt to reverse the city's fortunes, a canal was opened in 1827 to link Gloucester to Sharpness, on a broader stretch of the Severn further south. Trade picked up for a time, but it was only a temporary remedy.

Today, the canal is busy once again, though this time with pleasure boats, while the Victorian dockyards have undergone a facelift. Gloucester's most magnificent possession, however, remains its **cathedral**, whose tower is visible for miles around. Otherwise, little of the city has survived the ravages of history and the twentieth century, with the centre a mishmash of medieval ruins swallowed up by ugly new buildings, and surrounded by a web of roads.

The City

Gloucester lies on the east bank of the Severn, its centre spread around a curve in the river. **The Cross**, once the entrance to the Roman forum, marks the heart of the city and the meeting-point of Northgate, Southgate, Eastgate and Westgate streets, all Roman roads. **St Michael's Tower**, the remains of an old church, overlooks it. The **cathedral** and the **docks** lie west of the North-gate–Southgate axis.

Southgate and Westgate streets

The most interesting parish church in Gloucester is **St Mary de Crypt** on Southgate Street, mostly late medieval but with some of its original Norman features; fragments of a sixteenth-century wall painting of the *Adoration of the Magi* in the chancel show unusual detail for work of that period. The church is kept locked, but you can get the key from the tourist office across the road. Greyfriars runs alongside St Mary's, past the ruins of a Franciscan church and the Eastgate Market to the **City Museum** on Brunswick Road (Tues–Sat 10am–5pm; £2; combined ticket with Folk Museum £3), with a good archeological collection including a fragment of the Roman city wall, preserved *in situ* below ground level (viewable from the museum on summer Saturdays only, or at any time from Eastgate Street). Westgate Street, quieter and many times more pleasant than its three Roman counterparts, retains several medieval buildings. One of them, a creaking timber-framed house at the bottom of the street, contains the **Folk Museum** (Tues–Sat 10am–5pm; £2; combined ticket with City Museum £3), which illustrates the social history of the Gloucester area using an impressive collection of objects, from huge wrought-iron cheese presses to salt-filled rolling pins used to scare off witches. College Court Alley leads from Westgate Street to the haven of the cathedral, passing the Beatrix Potter shop and museum – the house sketched by the children's artist and author while she was on holiday here in 1897 and subsequently appearing in every copy of *The Tailor of Gloucester*.

The Cathedral

The superb condition of Gloucester **Cathedral** (daily 7.30am–6pm; suggested donation £3) is striking in a city that has lost so much of its past. An abbey was founded on this spot by the Saxons, but four centuries later Benedictine monks came and built their own church, begun in 1069. As a place of worship it shot to importance after the murder at Berkeley Castle of Edward II in 1327: Bristol and Malmesbury supposedly refused to take his body, but Gloucester did, and the king's shrine became a major place of pilgrimage. The money generated helped to finance the conversion of the church into the country's first and greatest example of the **Perpendicular style**: the magnificent 225-foot tower crowns the achievement. Henry VIII recognized the church's prestige by conferring on it the status of cathedral.

Beneath the reconstructions of the fourteenth and fifteenth centuries, some Norman aspects remain, best seen in the **nave**, flanked by sturdy pillars and arches adorned with immaculate zigzag mouldings. Only when you reach the choir and transepts can you see how skilfully the new church was built inside the old, the Norman masonry hidden beneath the finer lines of the Perpendicular panelling and tracery. The **choir** has extraordinary fourteenth-century misericords, and also provides the best vantage point for admiring the **east window** completed in around 1350 and – at almost 80 feet tall – the largest medieval window in Britain. Beneath it, to the left (as you're facing the east window) is the **tomb of Edward II**, immortalized in alabaster and marble and in good fettle apart from some graffiti. In the nearby **Lady Chapel**, delicate carved tracery holds a staggering patchwork of windows, virtually creating walls of stained glass. There are well-preserved monuments here, too, but the tomb of Robert II, in the **south ambulatory**, is far more unusual. Robert, eldest son of William the Conqueror, died in 1134, but the painted wooden effigy dates from around 1290. Dressed as a crusader, he lies in a curious pose, with his arms and legs crossed, his right hand gripping his sword ready to do battle with the infidel.

The innovative nature of the cathedral's design can perhaps be best appreciated in the beautiful **cloisters**, completed in 1367 and featuring the first fan vaulting in the country. The fine quality of the work is outdone perhaps only by Henry VII's Chapel in Westminster Abbey, which it inspired. The setting was used to represent the corridors of Hogwart's School of Witchcraft and Wizardry in the *Harry Potter* films. Back inside, the north transept holds the entrance to the **treasury** (Mon–Fri 10.30am–4pm, Sat 10.30am–3.30pm; free), containing flagons, chalices and other ecclesiastical bric-a-brac, and also the entrance to the **upstairs galleries** (April–Oct same days and times; £2), where an exhibition gives the lowdown on the east window and allows you to view it at close quarters, and the **Whispering Gallery** enables you to pick up the tiniest sounds from across the vaulting. Lastly, you can climb the cathedral's **tower** for the best views of Gloucester (Wed–Fri 2.30pm, Sat 1.30pm & 2.30pm; £2.50).

The Docks

The **Docks** complex was developed during the fifty years following the opening of the Sharpness canal in 1827. The import of corn represented the bulk of the port's business at that time, and huge **warehouses** were built for storing the grain. Fourteen of them have survived, mostly now converted into municipal offices and shops as well as a museum, a redevelopment at its most crudely commercial in the **Merchants' Quay** shopping centre.

The **National Waterways Museum** (daily 10am–5pm, last admission 4pm; £5.95), in the southernmost Llanthony Warehouse, completely immerses you in the canal mania that swept Britain in the eighteenth and nineteenth centuries, touching on everything from the engineering of the locks to the lives of the horses that trod the towpaths. The three floors contain plenty of atmospheric noises off, videos, accessible information and interactive displays. In the old customs house, the **Regiments of Gloucestershire Museum** (June–Sept daily 10am–5pm; Oct–May Tues–Sun 10am–5pm; £4.25) makes a potentially dull or alienating subject fascinating, with its focus on all aspects of life as a soldier, both in war and during peacetime.

Practicalities

Gloucester's **bus and train stations** are opposite one another across Bruton Way, five minutes' walk east of the Cross. The **tourist office** is at 28 Southgate St (Mon–Sat 10am–5pm; July & Aug also Sun 11am–3pm; ☎01452/396572, ⓦwww.gloucester.gov.uk/tourism). Of the few **places to stay** within easy walking distance of the train station and centre, the *Albert* at 56–60 Worcester St (☎01452/502081, ⓦwww.alberthotel.com; ❾), a listed red-brick building from the 1830s, and the Victorian *Edward* at 88–92 London Rd (☎01452/525865, ⓦwww.edwardhotel-gloucester.co.uk; ❸) offer the best value. South of the centre, there's the four-storey *Lulworth* at 12 Midland Rd (☎01452/521881; no credit cards; ❶), in a quiet location behind the park.

Gloucester's selection of **restaurants** is fairly limited, though you'll find a lively atmosphere at the café-bar in the Guildhall on Eastgate Street, open until 11pm (closed Sun & Mon). ✻ *Café René*, Greyfriars, Southgate Street (☎01452/309340), includes Desperate Dan Burgers among other dishes on its menu, and hosts popular Sunday barbeques in summer, while *Ye Olde Fish Shoppe*, in a sixteenth-century building on Hare Lane, serves excellent crispy takeaway fish until 6.30pm, though the attached restaurant stays open later (☎01452/522502; no credit cards; closed Sun). For pizzas, go to *Pizza Piazza* at Merchants' Quay (☎01452/311951) – the only reason to venture to the docks in the evening. For really tasty hot food at rock-bottom prices, however, try the *Fountain Inn*, down a narrow alley off Westgate Street, which also pulls a sublime pint of Abbot ale and has courtyard seating. The best of Gloucester's other **pubs** are all within spitting distance of the Cross, with the rambling fifteenth-century *New Inn* in Northgate Street boasting a splendid galleried courtyard and serving cheap meals.

Tewkesbury and around

The small market town of **TEWKESBURY**, ten miles north of Gloucester, stands hemmed in by the Avon and Severn rivers, which converge nearby. Pressure of space accounts for the narrow alleys and courts leading off from the main streets, of which thirty of the original ninety still survive. The comparatively unchanging face of Tewkesbury is also due to the fact that it almost completely missed out on the Industrial Revolution. Elegant Georgian houses and medieval timber-framed buildings still line several of the town's main streets – especially Church Street – and the Norman abbey has survived as one of the greatest in England.

The site of **Tewkesbury Abbey** (Mon–Sat 7.30am–6pm, closes 5.30pm in winter, Sun 7.30am–7pm; suggested donation £3) was first selected for a Benedictine monastery in the eighth century, but virtually nothing of the Saxon complex survived a sacking by the Danes, and a new abbey was founded by a Norman nobleman in 1092. The work took about sixty years to complete, with some additions made in the fourteenth century. Two hundred years later the Dissolution brought about the destruction of most of the monastic buildings, though the abbey itself survived. The sheer scale of the exterior makes a lasting impact: its colossal **tower** is the largest Norman tower in the world, while the west front's soaring recessed arch – 65 feet high – is the only exterior arch in the country to boast such impressive proportions. In the nave, fourteen stout Norman pillars steal the show, graceful despite their size, and topped by a fourteenth-century ribbed and vaulted ceiling, studded with gilded bosses (look for the musical angels). On the blue and scarlet **choir** roof, the bosses include a ring of shining suns (emblem of the Yorkist cause), said to have been put there by Edward IV after the defeat of the Lancastrians at Tewkesbury in 1471. The abbey's medieval tombs celebrate Tewkesbury's greatest patrons, with the Despensers having the best monuments, particularly Sir Edward, standard-bearer to the Black Prince, who died in 1375 and is shown as a kneeling figure on the roof of the **Trinity Chapel** to the right of the high altar: you can see it best from beside the Warwick Chantry Chapel in the north aisle. Nearby, in the ambulatory, the macabre so-called **Wakeman Cenotaph**, carved in the fifteenth century but of otherwise uncertain origin, represents a decaying corpse being consumed by snakes and other creatures.

Practicalities

Tewkesbury's **tourist office** at 64 Barton St (Mon–Sat 9.30am–5pm; April–Oct also Sun 10am–4pm; ℡01684/295027, ⓦwww.visitcotswoldsandsevern-vale.gov.uk) holds a small museum (£1) upstairs. You won't have to look far to find a **room**: almost opposite the abbey at 62 Church Street, *Abbey Antiques Guest House* (℡01684/298145; no credit cards; ❷) is colourfully furnished with antiques, while *Barton House*, 5 Barton Rd (℡01684/292049 or 07946/460601, ⓦwww.s-h-systems.co.uk; no credit cards; ❶), has an eclectic mix of furniture, and plain rooms. Tewkesbury's ancient **hotels** include the *Royal Hop Pole*, Church Street (℡01684/293236, ⓦwww.royalhoppole.co.uk; ❺), whose annexe has a loggia facing the garden.

As for **eating**, *My Great Grandfathers*, 84 Church St (closed Mon), serves excellent traditional puddings, while *Rendezvous*, 78 Church St (℡01684/290357; closed Mon), dishes up Mediterranean-style fish and meat dishes, as well as serving snacks in the cellar bar. Among the **pubs**, *Ye Olde Black Bear*, at the top of the High Street, pulls some of the best pints in town.

Travel details

Buses

For information on all local and national bus services, contact Traveline ℡0870/608 2608 (daily 7am–9pm), ⓦwww.traveline.org.uk.

Cheltenham to: Gloucester (Mon–Sat every 15min, Sun 2 hourly; 15–40min); London (11–13 daily; 2hr 35min–3hr 20min); Painswick (Mon–Sat hourly, Sun 6 daily; 30min); Stroud (Mon–Sat hourly, Sun 6 daily; 40min); Tewkesbury (Mon–Sat every 20min, Sun hourly; 30min).

Cirencester to: Cheltenham (Mon–Sat hourly; 45min); Gloucester (Mon–Sat 5 daily; 40min–1hr); Lechlade (Mon–Sat 5 daily; 1hr); Moreton-in-Marsh (Mon–Sat every 2hr; 1hr).

Gloucester to: Cheltenham (Mon–Sat every 15min, Sun 2 hourly; 15–40min); Tewkesbury (Mon–Sat hourly; 30–40min); London (12 daily; 3hr 20min–3hr 50min).

Henley to: Oxford (hourly, 50min); Reading (hourly;

20min); Wantage (hourly; 1hr 40min).

Oxford to: Buckingham (hourly; 1hr 30min); Henley (hourly; 50min); Reading (every 2hr; 1hr 30min); Wantage (hourly; 1hr).

Reading to: Henley (hourly; 20min); Oxford (every 2hr; 1hr 30min).

Stroud to: Cheltenham (Mon–Sat hourly, Sun 6 daily; 40min); Cirencester (Mon–Sat 6 daily; 35min–45min); Gloucester (Mon–Sat hourly, Sun 6 daily; 30min–1hr).

Tewkesbury to: Cheltenham (Mon–Sat every 20min, Sun hourly; 30min); Gloucester (Mon–Sat hourly; 30min–40min).

Wantage to: Henley (hourly; 1hr 40min); Oxford (hourly; 1hr).

Trains

For information on all local and national rail services, contact National Rail Enquiries ℡08457/484950, ⓦwww.nationalrail.co.uk.

Cheltenham to: Bristol (3 hourly; 45min–1hr); Gloucester (2–3 hourly; 10–15min); London (every 2hr; 2hr 10min); Stroud (every 2hr; 30min).
Gloucester to: Bristol (hourly; 50min); Cheltenham (2–3 hourly; 10–15min); London (every 2hr; 1hr 50min); Stroud (hourly; 15–20min).
Henley to: London (3 daily; 1hr).
Oxford to: Birmingham (hourly; 1hr 30min); London (1–2 hourly; 1hr); Worcester (hourly; 1hr 10min).

Bristol, Bath and Somerset

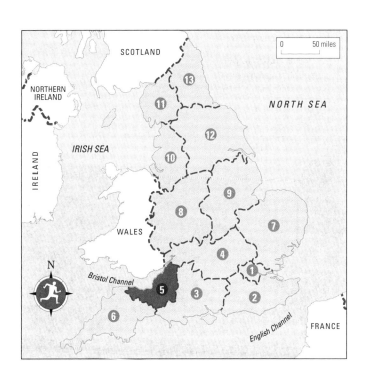

CHAPTER 5 # Highlights

* **Clifton Suspension Bridge** Brunel's iconic construction rears above the impressive Avon Gorge. **See p.307**

* **Building of Bath Museum** Get to grips with how Bath came to assume its present appearance. **See p.314**

* **Wells Cathedral** A gem of medieval masonry, not least for its richly ornamented west front. **See p.316**

* **Cheddar Gorge** Impressive rockscape, with opportunities for wild walks in the Mendips. **See p.318**

* **Glastonbury music festival** One of the |oldest, biggest and best rock festivals still retains its authentic aura. **See p.320**

* **Quantock Hills** Follow in the footsteps of Coleridge and Wordsworth on the wooded slopes of this West Somerset range. **See p.323**

△ Clifton Suspension Bridge

Bristol, Bath and Somerset

T he undulating green swards of **Somerset** encapsulate rural England at its best. Cut through by the **Mendip** and **Quantock hills**, the landscape is always varied, with tidy cricket greens and well-kept country pubs contrasting with wilder, more dramatic landscapes. A world away from this bucolic charm, the main city hereabouts is **Bristol**, one of the most dynamic and cosmopolitan centres outside London. The city's dense traffic and some hideous postwar architecture are more than compensated for by the surviving traces of its long maritime history, not to mention a great range of pubs, clubs and restaurants.

Just a few miles away, the graceful, Georgian, honey-toned terraces of **Bath** combine with the city's beautifully preserved Roman baths and a mellow café culture to make an unmissable stop on any itinerary. Within easy reach to the south lie the exquisite cathedral city of **Wells** and the ancient town of **Glastonbury**, a site steeped in Christian lore, Arthurian legend and New Age mysticism. The nearby Mendip Hills are pocked by cave systems, as at **Wookey Hole** and **Cheddar Gorge**, while to the west, **Bridgwater** and **Taunton** make useful bases for exploring the Quantocks.

The line from London's Paddington Station to Bristol, Bath and Taunton provides the **rail transport** through this region. From these centres, a network of **bus routes** connects with nearly all the places covered in this chapter – though the Mendip and Quantock hills are more easily explored with your own transport. The M4 and M5 motorways, which meet outside Bristol, are useful through-routes.

Bristol and around

On the borders of Gloucestershire and Somerset, **BRISTOL** has harmoniously blended its mercantile roots with a progressive, modern culture, fuelled in recent years by technology-based industries, a large student population, and a lively arts and media community. As well as its vibrant nightlife, the city's sights range from medieval churches to cutting-edge attractions highlighting its scientific achievements.

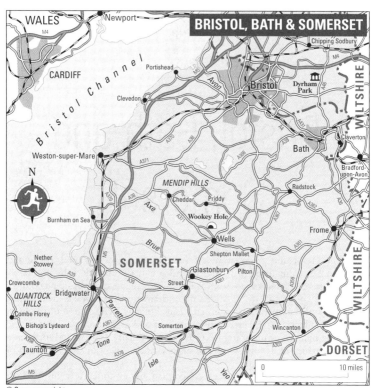

WALES
M4

Newport

BRISTOL, BATH & SOMERSET

Chipping Sodbury

M4

CARDIFF

Bristol Channel

Portishead

Avon

Bristol

Dyrham Park

WILTSHIRE

Clevedon

Claverton

Weston-super-Mare

A371

Bath

Bradford-upon-Avon

N

MENDIP HILLS

Radstock

Cheddar   Priddy

Axe

Wookey Hole

Burnham on Sea

Frome

Brue

Wells

WILTSHIRE

Nether Stowey

SOMERSET

Shepton Mallet

Crowcombe

Glastonbury   Pilton

QUANTOCK HILLS   Bridgwater

Street

Combe Florey

Parrett

Bishop's Lydeard

Somerton

Wincanton

Taunton

Tone

DORSET

M5

Isle

Yeo

| 0 | 10 miles |

© Crown copyright

Weaving through its centre, the River Avon forms part of a system of water-ways that made Bristol a great inland port, in later years booming on the transatlantic trafficking of rum, tobacco and slaves. In the nineteenth century the illustrious **Isambard Kingdom Brunel** laid the foundations of a tradi-tion of engineering, creating two of Bristol's greatest monuments – the SS *Great Britain* and the lofty Clifton Suspension Bridge. More recently, spin-offs from the aerospace industry have placed the city at the forefront of the fields of communications, computing, design and finance. Beneath the prosperous surface, Bristol has its negative aspects – high crime levels and heavy traffic, to name but two – but it remains an attractive city, predominantly hilly, and surrounded by rolling countryside.

Arrival, information and accommodation

Bristol's **bus station** is centrally located off Marlborough Street, and Temple Meads **train station** is a twenty-minute walk east of the centre, served by frequent buses #8, #8A and #9, which pass through the centre on their way to Clifton (#9 also goes to Cotham). From Bristol Parkway station, on the outskirts of town, take bus #73. The **tourist office** is in the at-Bristol complex, in the Wildwalk foyer, Harbourside (Mon–Fri 10am–5pm, Sat & Sun 10am–6pm; ☎0906/711 2191, ⓦwww.visitbristol.co.uk), and you can access the **Internet** at Bristol Life, 27 Baldwin St (Mon–Fri 10am–8pm, Sat 11am–7pm).

Most of Bristol's **accommodation** lies in the leafy areas of Cotham and Clifton, both popular student areas.

Bristol Backpackers 17 St Stephen's St ℡0117/925 7900, ⓦwww.bristolbackpackers .co.uk. Friendly independent hostel with a late bar, good showers and cheap Internet access. The area can be noisy at night. Dorm beds £14.
Hotel du Vin Narrow Lewins Mead ℡0117/925 5577, ⓦwww.hotelduvin.co.uk. Chic, warehouse conversion, centrally located, with solid comforts, contemporary decor and excellent food and wine. **❼**
Naseby House 105 Pembroke Rd ℡0117/973 7859, ⓦwww.nasebyhouse-hotel.co.uk. Plush Victorian guest house in Clifton, beautifully furnished. **❹**
St Michael's Guest House 145 St Michael's Hill ℡0117/907 7820. Simple rooms with shared

bathrooms, above one of Cotham's most popular cafés. **❷**
Sunderland Guest House 4 Sunderland Place ℡0117/973 7249 or 0797/624 9108, ⓔsunder-land.gh@blueyonder.co.uk. Basic, but quiet, clean and very near the centre, in Lower Clifton. No smoking. No credit cards. **❷**
Victoria Square Victoria Square ℡0117/973 9058, ⓦwww.vicsquare.com. Rooms are fairly plain, but the location is great, on a leafy square near Clifton Village. **❺–❻**
YHA hostel 14 Narrow Quay ℡0870/770 5726, ⓔbristol@yha.org.uk. Located in a refurbished warehouse on the quayside, with some twin rooms. Dorm beds £18–21 including breakfast. **❶**

The City

A good place to start exploring, **the Centre** was once a quay-lined dock but is now the traffic-ridden nucleus of the city, with cars swirling round the statues of Edmund Burke, MP for Bristol from 1774 to 1780, and local merchant and benefactor Edward Colston (1636–1721). The Centre is just a few steps from the cathedral and the oldest quarter of town, and is linked by water-taxi to the sights around the Floating Harbour, the waterway network that runs through the southern part of town and connects with the River Avon. Buses to all parts of the city also stop here.

From the Cathedral to the City Museum

A short walk west of the Centre, the grassy expanse of College Green is dominated by the crescent-shaped Council House and by the contrastingly medieval lines of **Bristol Cathedral** (daily 8am–6pm; suggested donation £2.50). Founded around 1140 as an abbey on the supposed spot of St Augustine's convocation with Celtic Christians in 603, it became a cathedral church with the Dissolution of the Monasteries. The two towers on the west front were erected in the nineteenth century in a faithful act of homage to Edmund Knowle, architect and abbot at the start of the fourteenth century. The cathedral's interior offers a unique example among Britain's cathedrals of a German-style hall church, in which the aisles rise to the same height as the central area. Abbot Knowle's **choir** offers one of the country's most exquisite illustrations of the early Decorated style of Gothic, while the adjoining **Elder Lady Chapel**, dating from the early thirteenth century, contains some fine tombs and eccentric carvings of animals, including a monkey playing the bagpipes accompanied by a ram on the violin. The ornate **Eastern Lady Chapel** has some of England's finest examples of heraldic glass. From the south transept, a door leads through to the **Chapter House**, a richly carved piece of late Norman architecture.

Elegant Georgian streets lead off the shop-lined **Park Street**, climbing steeply up from College Green. On Great George Street, the **Georgian House** (April–Oct Mon–Wed, Sat & Sun 10am–5pm; free) is the faithfully restored former home of a local sugar merchant. From Great George Street, or from Berkeley Square further up the hill, you can gain access to **Brandon Hill Park**, home to the 105-foot **Cabot Tower** (open daily until dusk; free), built in 1897

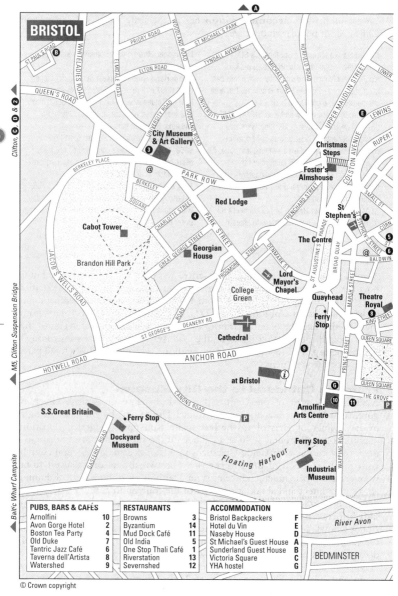

BRISTOL

PUBS, BARS & CAFÉS		RESTAURANTS		ACCOMMODATION	
Arnolfini	10	Browns	3	Bristol Backpackers	F
Avon Gorge Hotel	2	Byzantium	14	Hotel du Vin	E
Boston Tea Party	4	Mud Dock Café	11	Naseby House	D
Old Duke	7	Old India	5	St Michael's Guest House	A
Tantric Jazz Café	6	One Stop Thali Café	1	Sunderland Guest House	B
Taverna dell'Artista	8	Riverstation	13	Victoria Square	C
Watershed	9	Severnshed	12	YHA hostel	G

© Crown copyright

to commemorate the 400th anniversary of John Cabot's voyage to America, and providing the city's best panorama.

At the top of Park Street, on Queen's Road, the **City Museum and Art Gallery** (daily 10am–5pm; free) has sections on local archeology, geology and natural history, as well as an important collection of Chinese porcelain, glassware, stoneware and ivory, and some magnificent eighth-century-BC Assyrian

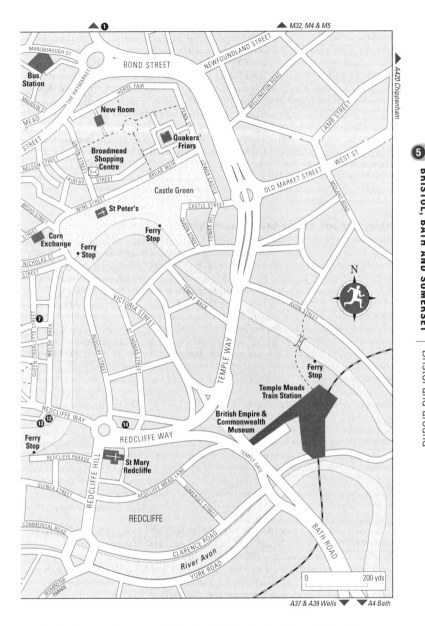

reliefs. There are also art works by English Pre-Raphaelites and French Impressionists, and a few choice older pieces, including a portrait of Martin Luther by Cranach and Giovanni Bellini's unusual *Descent into Limbo*.

From the Centre to Broadmead

One of Bristol's oldest churches, **St Stephen's**, stands just east of the Centre.

Established in the thirteenth century, rebuilt in the fifteenth and thoroughly restored with plenty of neo-Gothic trimmings in 1875, the parish church has some flamboyant tombs inside. On nearby **Corn Street**, the Georgian Corn Exchange was designed by John Wood of Bath and now holds the covered St Nicholas markets. The four engraved bronze pillars outside the entrance date from the sixteenth and seventeenth centuries and originally served as trading tables – thought to be the "nails" from which the expression "pay on the nail" is derived.

From the market, Wine Street brings you to the uninspiring **Broadmead** shopping centre, within which is hidden England's first Methodist chapel, the **New Room** (Mon–Sat 10am–4pm; free). Established by John Wesley in 1739, it looks very much as he left it, with a double-deck pulpit in the chapel, beneath a hidden upstairs window from which the evangelist could observe the progress of his trainee preachers.

King Street to St Mary Redcliffe

King Street, a short walk east from the Centre, was laid out in 1633 and still holds a cluster of historic buildings, among them the **Theatre Royal**, the oldest working theatre in the country, opened in 1766 and preserving many of its original Georgian features. Further down, and in a very different architectural style, stands the timber-framed **Llandoger Trow** pub, traditionally the haunt of seafarers, and reputed to have been the meeting place of Daniel Defoe and Alexander Selkirk, the model for Robinson Crusoe.

South of King Street, **Queen Square** is an elegant grassy area with a much-acclaimed equestrian statue of William III by Rysbrack at its centre. From the southeast corner of the square, cross Redcliffe Bridge to reach **St Mary Redcliffe** (Mon–Sat 10am–5pm, closes 4pm in winter, Sun 8am–8pm), whose spire, dating from 1872, is a distinctive feature of the city's skyline. Described by Elizabeth I as "the goodliest, fairest, and most famous parish church in England", the church was largely paid for and used by merchants and mariners who prayed here for a safe voyage. The present building was begun at the end of the thirteenth century, though it was added to in subsequent centuries. Inside, memorials and tombs recall some of the figures associated with the building, including the arms and armour of Sir William Penn, admiral and father of the founder of Pennsylvania, on the north wall of the nave, and the Handel Window in the North Choir aisle, installed in 1859 on the centenary of the death of Handel, who composed on the organ here. The whale bone above the entrance to the Chapel of St John the Baptist is thought to have been brought back from Newfoundland by John Cabot.

Above the church's north porch is the muniment room, where **Thomas Chatterton** claimed to have found a trove of medieval manuscripts; the poems, distributed as the work of a fifteenth-century monk named Thomas Rowley, were in fact dazzling fakes. The young poet committed suicide after his forgery was exposed, thereby supplying English literature with one of its most glamorous stories of self-destructive genius. The "Marvellous Boy" is remembered by a memorial stone in the south transept.

A few minutes' walk east, Bristol's **Old Station** stands outside Temple Meads Station, the original terminus of the Great Western Railway linking London and Bristol. The terminus, like the line itself, was designed by Brunel in 1840, and was the first great piece of railway architecture. Part of the building now houses the **British Empire and Commonwealth Museum** (daily 10am–5pm; £6.50), which focuses on the history of the empire and the Commonwealth that succeeded it, covering trade, slavery and culture.

Around Bristol's waterways

At the southern end of the Centre, a statue of Neptune looks out over **St Augustine's Reach**, part of the Floating Harbour. From the right-hand quay-side, you can gain access to **at-Bristol** (daily 10am–5pm; Explore £8, Wildwalk £6.50, Imax £6.50, or £17 for all three, valid for a week), a complex made up of three principal attractions: Explore, an interactive science exhibition; Wildwalk, a multimedia wildlife complex, including an indoor "tropical forest"; and an IMAX cinema (film screenings need to be booked in advance; see Ⓦ www.at-bristol.org.uk). Although chiefly aimed at families and schoolkids, there's enough here to occupy everyone for a whole day or more. The wildlife displays and scientific wizardry are most impressive, and subsidiary attractions include a shiny, spherical planetarium.

To explore further afield, a **ferry** connects the various parts of the Floating Harbour, leaving every forty minutes from St Augustine's Reach (10.30am–5.50pm; £1.30 single fare £4 forty-minute round trip £5 all-day ticket; ℡ 0117/927 3416, Ⓦ www.bristolferryboat.co.uk). It's a short ferry hop to the **Industrial Museum** (Mon–Wed, Sat & Sun 10am–5pm; free), which features a diverse collection of vehicles, mostly with Bristol connections, as well as a display of maritime models, and an exhibition on the transatlantic slave trade, including examples of West African art. West of here, you can walk or take the ferry to the **SS Great Britain** (daily: April–Oct 10am–5.30pm; Nov–March 10am–4.30pm; £7.50), the first propeller-driven, ocean-going iron ship, built in 1843 by Brunel. She initially ran between Liverpool and New York, then between Liverpool and Melbourne, circumnavigating the globe 32 times over a period of 26 years. Her ocean-going days ended in 1886 when she was caught in a storm off Cape Horn, and she was eventually recovered and returned to Bristol in 1968. Some cabins have been restored, and you can peer into the immense engine room. The same ticket allows you admission to the much smaller **Matthew**, moored close by – a replica of the vessel in which John Cabot sailed to America in 1497 – and to the adjoining **Dockyard Museum**, which gives the background of both vessels, of Cabot and his exploits, and of Bristol's long shipbuilding history.

Clifton

North and west of the City Museum (see p.304), **Clifton** was once an aloof spa resort, and is now Bristol's most elegant quarter. The select enclave of Clifton Village is centred on the Mall, close to **Royal York Crescent**, the longest Georgian crescent in the country, offering splendid views over the steep drop to the River Avon below.

A few minutes' walk from the Crescent is Bristol's most famous symbol, **Clifton Suspension Bridge**, 702ft long and poised 245ft above high water. Money was first put forward for a bridge to span the Avon Gorge by a Bristol wine merchant in 1753, though it was not until 1829 that a competition was held for a design, won by Isambard Brunel on a second round, and not until 1864 that the bridge was completed, five years after Brunel's death. Hampered by financial difficulties, the bridge never quite matched the engineer's original ambitious design, which included Egyptian-style towers topped by sphinxes at each end. You can see copies of his plans in the nearby **Visitor Centre** (currently closed for refurbishment; check at ℡ 0117/974 4664, or Ⓦ www.clifton-suspension-bridge.org.uk), alongside designs proposed by Brunel's rivals, some of them frankly bizarre.

The wide green expanse of **Clifton Downs** stretches right up to the edge of the Gorge, a popular spot for picnickers, joggers and kite-flyers. Adjacent to the

Downs, **Bristol Zoo** (daily: June–Aug 9am–5.30pm; Sept–May 9am–4.30pm; £9.70) is renowned for its animal conservation work, and also features a collection of rare trees and shrubs.

Eating, drinking and nightlife

Bristol's numerous **pubs** and **restaurants** are nearly always buzzing – especially those around King Street and Corn Street. Nightlife is equally lively: to check out the **clubs**, pick up a copy of *Venue*, the weekly listings magazine (£1.30), or consult ⓦ www.thisisbristol.com for details of what's on where.

Restaurants

Browns 38 Queen's Rd ☎ 0117/930 4777. Spacious and relaxed place for a cocktail, hamburger or fisherman's pie, housed in the Venetian-style former university refectory. Moderate.
Byzantium 2 Portwall Lane ☎ 0117/922 1883, ⓦ www.byzantium.co.uk. Once a warehouse, now a theatrical dining area, exotically themed along the lines of a 1930s Beirut hotel. The food is superb, with a good-value set-price menu. Closed Sat lunch & all Sun. Expensive.
Mud Dock Café 40 The Grove ☎ 0117/929 2171. Combined bike shop and café-bar/restaurant by the river, offering good food and balcony seating. Closed Sun eve in winter. Moderate.
Old India 34 St Nicholas St ☎ 0117/922 1136. Housed in the old Stock Exchange building, this has

classy curries to match the sumptuous surroundings. Moderate.
One Stop Thali Café 12 York Rd ☎ 0117/942 6687. Dhaba-style Asian food in the villagey Montpelier quarter (half a mile north of bus station), with live music (Sun). Closed Mon. Inexpensive.
riverstation The Grove ☎ 0117/914 4434. In a former river-police station, two great restaurants with dockside views: deli-type snacks downstairs, and a more formal upstairs area serving a range of international dishes. Inexpensive–moderate.
Severnshed The Grove ☎ 0117/925 1212. Right next to *riverstation* with a waterside terrace, this serves light, tasty dishes, and offers a good-value £7.77 two-course meal (Mon–Fri noon–7pm). Inexpensive–moderate.

Pubs, bars and cafés

Arnolfini Narrow Quay. Arts centre serving drinks and meals, with the crowd spilling onto the cobbled quayside.
Avon Gorge Hotel Sion Hill. On the edge of the Gorge in Clifton Village, this modern bar has magnificent views from its broad terrace. Meals also available.
Boston Tea Party 75 Park St. Cosy place for teas, coffees, soups and pies, with seating on two floors and a heated terrace garden.
Old Duke King Street. Trad-jazz pub with live bands most nights.

Tantric Jazz Café 39–41 St Nicholas St ☎ 0117/940 2304. Relaxed coffee stop that serves Mediterranean-style meals in the evenings, when there's live jazz and blues until late. Closed Sun.
Taverna dell'Artista King Street. A haunt of theatrical folk, this Anglo-Italian bar has pizzas and pasta, and drinks until late. Closed Sun & Mon.
Watershed St Augustine's Reach. Café-bar in an arts complex overlooking the boats, with food available until 9pm (7pm on Sun). Free Internet access.

Clubs and music venues

Academy Frogmore Street ☎ 0905/020 3999, ⓦ www.bristol-academy.co.uk. Spacious, popular place for live gigs as well as mainstream and hard-house parties. Thurs is student night.
Bierkeller All Saints St, off Broadmead ☎ 0117/926 8514, ⓦ www.bristolbierkeller.co.uk. Sweaty cellar venue playing everything from thrash metal to revival bands.

Blue Mountain Stokes Croft. Excellent non-mainstream club featuring the best funk, hip-hop and drum'n'bass in town.
Colston Hall Colston Ave ☎ 0117/922 3686, ⓦ www.colstonhall.org. Major names appear in this stalwart mainstream venue. Hosts most of the events in the classical Proms Festival in late May.

Fiddlers Willway Street, Bedminster ☎0117/987 3403, ⓦwww.fiddlers.co.uk. Mainly live folk and world music at this relaxed venue south of the river, off Bedminster Parade.
The Fleece 12 St Thomas St ☎0117/945 0996. Stone-flagged ex–wool warehouse, now a loud, sweaty pub for live rock and comedy.
St George's Great George Street ☎0845/402 4001, ⓦwww.stgeorgesbristol.co.uk. Lunchtime and evening concerts of classical, world and

jazz music are staged in this elegant Georgian church.
Thekla The Grove ☎0117/929 3301, ⓦwww .thekla.co.uk. Riverboat venue popular with students, staging regular club nights, occasional live shows, and dub every other Thurs. Food available.
Vibes 3 Frog Lane, off Frogmore Street ☎0117/934 9076, ⓦvibesbristol.co.uk. Lively gay club on two floors.

Bath and around

Though only twelve miles from Bristol, **BATH** has a very different feel from its neighbour – more harmonious, more compact and quainter. The city's elegant crescents and Georgian buildings are studded with plaques naming Bath's eminent inhabitants from its heyday as a spa resort; it was here that Jane Austen set *Persuasion* and *Northanger Abbey*, and where Gainsborough established himself as a portraitist and landscape painter. Nowadays Bath ranks as one of Britain's top tourist cities, yet the place has never lost the exclusive air those names evoke.

Bath owes its name and fame to its **hot springs** – the only ones in the country – which made it a place of reverence for the local Celtic population, though it had to wait for Roman technology to create a fully fledged bathing establishment. The baths fell into decline with the departure of the Romans, but the town later regained its importance under the Saxons, its abbey seeing the coronation of the **first king of all England**, Edgar, in 973. A new bathing complex was built in the sixteenth century, popularized by the visit of Elizabeth I in 1574, and the city reached its fashionable zenith in the eighteenth century, when **Beau Nash** ruled the town's social scene. It was at this time that Bath acquired its ranks of Palladian mansions and Regency townhouses, all of them built in the local **Bath stone**, which is still the city's leitmotif today. Three miles southeast of the centre, **Claverton** holds a museum of Americana amid gorgeous rolling countryside.

The swathes of parkland between Bath's Georgian terraces lend the city a spacious feel, but the sheer weight of traffic pouring through the central streets can be a major turn-off. Drivers are advised to use one of the **Park-and-Ride** car parks around the periphery – and if you're coming from Bristol, you can **cycle** all the way along a cycle-path that follows the route of a disused railway line and the course of the Avon.

Arrival, information and accommodation

Bath Spa **train station** and the city's **bus station** are both on Manvers Street, a short walk from the centre. The **tourist office** is right next to the abbey in Abbey Churchyard (Mon–Sat 9.30am–5/6pm, Sun 10am–4pm; ☎0906/711 2000, ⓦwww.visitbath.co.uk). Click Internet Café, 13 Manvers St (daily 10am–10pm), provides **Internet** access. Most places offering **accommodation** are small (so always phone ahead), and most demand a two-night minimum stay at weekends in high season.

Hotels and B&Bs

Belmont 7 Belmont, Lansdown Road ☎01225/423082, ⓦwww.belmontbath.co.uk. Huge doubles, some with en-suite shower, in a

centrally located B&B designed by John Wood. No credit cards. ❷

BATH

⬆ Warminster & A36

🅓 (1 mile) & American Museum (3 miles) ▲

ACCOMMODATION

Bath Backpackers Hostel	E
Bath YHA	D
Belmont	A
Cranleigh	C
Henry Guest House	G
Koryu	F
Paradise House	H
White Hart	I
YMCA	B

RESTAURANTS & CAFES

Bathtub Bistro	4
Café Retro	12
Demuths	11
Eastern Eye	6
Firehouse Rotisserie	7
Popjoy's	9
Pump Room	13
Tilley's Bistro	10
Walrus and Carpenter	8

PUBS

The Bath Tap	14
The Bell	2
The George	1
The Porter	3
The Salamander	5

Sydney Gardens

Holburne Museum

Kennet & Avon Canal

PULTENEY ROAD

Henrietta Park

Rugby Ground

Recreation Ground

Cricket Ground

Pulteney Bridge

River Avon

Victoria Art Gallery

Abbey

Roman Baths

Pump Room

Thermae Bath Spa

Building of Bath Museum

Assembly Rooms

WALCOT STREET

BROAD STREET

Jane Austen Centre

Theatre Royal

Herschel Museum

Royal Victoria Park

Green Park

River Avon

⬅ A4 Chippenham

Bus & train stations & 🅐

⬅ G & A4 Bristol

⬅ A36 Tiverton

0   200 yds

© Crown copyright

Cranleigh 159 Newbridge Hill ☎01225/310197, ⓦwww.cranleighguesthouse.com. A mile or so west of the centre, this period Victorian house has fine views from the back rooms, two four-posters and a variety of breakfast options. Frequent bus connections. No smoking. ❹

Henry Guest House 6 Henry St ☎01225/424052, ⓦwww.thehenry.com. Excellent budget choice close to the abbey, with large rooms (none en-suite) and friendly owners. No smoking. ❸

Koryu 7 Pulteney Gardens ☎01225/337642, ⓔjapanesekoryu.@aol.com. The name means "Sunshine" in Japanese – the mother-tongue of the landlady, who offers brightly painted rooms, small but clean. No shoes inside and no smoking. No credit cards. ❸

🏃 **Paradise House** 88 Holloway ☎01225/317723, ⓦwww.paradise-house .co.uk. Georgian villa an uphill trudge from the centre, but with wonderful views. Open fires in winter, four-posters in three of the rooms and two rooms opening straight onto the lush garden are further attractions. No smoking. ❻

Hostels

Bath Backpackers Hostel 13 Pierrepoint St ☎01225/446787, ⓦwww.hostels.co.uk. Aussie-run place, with no curfew, no lockout and no breakfast, but there is a kitchen, bar and Internet access. Dorm beds are £14, doubles ❶

Beau Nash and Bath's Golden Age

Richard "Beau" Nash was an ex-army officer, ex-lawyer, dandy and gambler, who became Bath's Master of Ceremonies in 1704, conducting public balls of an unprecedented splendour. Wielding dictatorial powers over dress and behaviour, Nash orchestrated the social manners of the city and even extended his influence to cover road improvements and the design of buildings. In an early example of health awareness, he banned smoking in Bath's public rooms at a time when pipe-smoking was a general pastime among men, women and children. Less philanthropically, he also encouraged gambling and even took a percentage of the bank's takings. Nonetheless, he was generally held in high esteem and succeeded in establishing rules such as the setting of specific hours and procedure for all social functions. Balls were to begin at six and end at eleven and every ball had to open with a minuet "danced by two persons of the highest distinction present". White aprons were banned, gossipers and scandalmongers were shunned, and, most radical of all, the wearing of swords in public places was forbidden, a ruling referred to in Sheridan's play *The Rivals*, in which Captain Absolute declares, "A sword seen in the streets of Bath would raise as great an alarm as a mad dog."

As for Bath's distinctive Georgian style of architecture, this was largely the work of **John Wood** ("the elder", c.1704–54) and his son, also called John Wood ("the younger", 1727–81), both champions of the Neoclassical Palladianism that originated in Renaissance Italy. Their "speculative developments", designed to cater to the seasonal floods of fashionable visitors, were constructed in the soft oolitic limestone from local quarries belonging to **Ralph Allen** (c.1694–1764), another prominent figure of the period. A deputy postmaster who made a fortune by improving England's postal routes, and later from Bath's building boom, Allen was nicknamed "the man of Bath", and is best remembered for Prior Park, the mansion he built outside the city based on the elder Wood's designs, and for his association with Pope, Fielding and other luminaries who were frequent visitors.

Lastly, the name of **William Oliver** should not be forgotten in the story of Georgian Bath. A physician and philanthropist, Oliver did more than anyone to boost the city's profile as a therapeutic centre, thanks to publications such as his *Practical Essay on the Use and Abuse of Warm Bathing in Gouty Cases* (1751), and by founding the Bath General Hospital to enable the poor to make use of the waters. He is remembered today by the Bath Oliver biscuit, which he invented.

Bath **YHA** Bathwick Hill ☎0870/770 5688,
ⓔbath@yha.org.uk. An Italianate mansion a mile
from the centre, with gardens and panoramic
views. Dorm beds (£12.50) and double rooms
available, also evening meals. Buses #18 or #418
from the station. **❶**

White Hart Widcombe Hill
☎01225/313985, ⓦwww.whitehartbath
.co.uk. The comfiest of Bath's hostels has a

kitchen, a licensed restaurant and a sunny courtyard. Dorm beds cost £14, and doubles and twins
are available. Midnight curfew. No smoking. **❶**
YMCA International House, Broad Street
☎01225/325900, ⓦwww.bathymca.co.uk. Clean,
central, with lots of room, this place charges £12–
14 for dorm beds, and singles and doubles are also
offered, with reductions for weekly stays. Prices
include breakfast (but there's no kitchen). **❶–❷**

The City

Although Bath could easily be seen on a day-trip from Bristol, it really deserves
a stay of a couple of days. The city itself is chock-full of museums, but some of
the greatest enjoyment comes simply from wandering the streets, with their pale
gold architecture and sweeping vistas.

The Baths and the Abbey

Bath's focal point is the pedestrianized Abbey Church Yard, two interlocking
squares usually busy with buskers, tourists and traders, and site of both the
Baths and the Abbey. Although ticket prices are high for the **Roman Baths**
(daily: March–June, Sept & Oct 9am–6pm; July & Aug 9am–10pm; Nov–Feb
9.30am–5.30pm; £9.50, £12.50 combined ticket with Museum of Costume),
there's two or three hours' worth of well-balanced, informative entertainment
here, with a taped commentary provided on handsets allowing you to wander
at your own pace around the temple and bathing complex, fed by water issu-

ing from a spring at a constant
46.5°C. Highlights of the remains
are the open-air (but originally
covered) Great Bath, its vapor-
ous waters surrounded by nineteenth-century pillars, terraces
and statues of famous Romans;
the Circular Bath, where bathers
cooled off; the Norman King's
Bath; and part of the temple
of Minerva. Among a quantity
of coins, jewellery and sculpture
exhibited are the gilt bronze
head of Sulis Minerva, the local
deity, and a grand, Celtic-inspired
gorgon's head from the temple's
pediment. Models of the complex
at its greatest extent give some
idea of the awe which it must
have inspired, while the graffiti
salvaged from the Roman era
– mainly curses and boasts – give
a personal slant on this antique
leisure-centre. You can get a free
glimpse into the baths from the
next-door **Pump Room**, the
social hub of the Georgian spa

△ The Roman Baths, Bath

Festivals and events

From a Scottish Highland Games gathering to the pyrotechnics of Bonfire Night, Britain's annual events and festivals illustrate the richness of the country's history and depth of its diversity. Some of course are no more than an excuse for a bizarre day out and a booze-up – the sight of the entire population of a village following a burning tar barrel or chasing a cheese downhill is not easily forgotten. May and August bank holiday weekends and the summer school holidays (July and August) are the favoured times for events to be held: contact local tourist offices for exact dates. For a full list of Britain's festivals and events, see p.59–61.

Glastonbury

When Michael Eavis held a rock festival on his Somerset farm in 1970 (audience of two thousand, ticket price a quid, headliners T-Rex), he had no idea that it would eventually turn into England's biggest summer music and arts bash. Four decades on, the annual **Glastonbury Festival of Performing Arts** (to give it its full title) sees Worthy Farm inundated by 100,000 revellers, hellbent on enjoying themselves whatever the weather – just as well, since late-June downpours are notorious for turning the three-day festival into a mudbath. Many complain that Glasto has moved away from its hippy roots, as high ticket prices, state-of-the-art security and even proper toilets have become the norm. But despite the contemporary buzz and headlining superstars, the "alternative" Glastonbury spirit is never far away – in the vast campsite village, organic cafés, circus fields, healing areas or performance tents. For more details, see p.319.

Crowds at Glastonbury

Llangollen International Music Eisteddfod

During the first week of July the town of Llangollen in the Dee valley Mid explodes in a frenzy of music, dance and poetry. The **International Music Eisteddfod** comes billed as the "world's greatest folk festival" but unlike the National Eisteddfod, which is a purely Welsh affair, the Llangollen event draws more than 12,000 amateur performers from countries around the world, all competing for prizes in their chosen disciplines. There's an irresistible *joie de vivre* as brightly costumed dancers prowl the streets and fill the fish-and-chip shops, while a burgeoning Fringe Festival offers rock and comedy gigs and performance events. For ticket details, see p.773.

Singers at Llangollen's International Music Eisteddfod

Highland Games

Competitor at the Highland Games

Despite their name, the summer **Highland Games** are held all over Scotland, not just in the Highlands. The Games probably originated in the fourteenth century as a means of recruiting the best fighting men for the clan chiefs, and were popularized in Victorian times. The most famous games take place at Braemar (p.1048) and Cowal (Dunoon; p.969), though smaller events are often more fun. The most distinctive events are known as the "**heavies**" – tossing the caber, putting the stone, and tossing the weight over the bar – all of which require prodigious strength and skill and the wearing of a kilt. Tossing the caber is the most spectacular, when the athlete must lift an entire tree trunk up, cupping it in his hands, before running with it and attempting to heave it end over end in a perfect, elegant throw. Just as important as the sporting events are the **piping** and **dancing** competitions, where you'll see girls as young as three tripping the intricate steps of the Highland Fling.

Carnival dancer

Notting Hill Carnival

Europe's greatest street party takes place over the last weekend of August (Sunday and bank holiday Monday – see p.130 for more). Born out of despair following the Notting Hill race riots of 1958, it started as little more than a few church-hall events and a carnival parade, inspired by the Caribbean roots of many of the area's residents. These days, hundreds of thousands of revellers turn out for the two-day event, following a three-mile procession around the suburb which takes up to ten hours to complete. At its heart are the truck-borne sound systems and *mas* (masquerade) bands, behind which the masqueraders dance in outrageous costumes. There are also live music stages and numerous sound systems, with the partying fuelled by cans of Red Stripe, curried goat and Jamaican patties. It's not quite Rio, but it's certainly not staid old England either.

Bonfire Night

"Remember, remember, the fifth of November", goes the old rhyme, "gunpowder, treason and plot" – and remember it the English certainly do, with night-time fireworks and fires across the country, commemorating the foiling of the 1605 Gunpowder Plot to blow up Parliament. Atop every bonfire is hoisted an effigy known as the "guy", after Guy Fawkes, one of the failed conspirators; an anonymous concoction of sticks and old clothes stuffed with newspaper suffices for most fires, but some effigies might represent resented contemporary or local figures (as, famously, at Lewes in East Sussex, which puts on the most dramatic show in the country – see p.197). Although it's November 5 that is technically Bonfire Night or Guy Fawkes' Night, many prefer to hold their bonfire on the nearest weekend, while the proximity of Halloween (October 31) has had a knock-on effect – expect ghouls and ghosts, fires and fireworks, from the end of October onwards.

Bonfire Night festivities in Lewes

Fireworks over Edinburgh at Hogmanay

Hogmanay

Hogmanay is the name Scots give to **New Year's Eve**, a celebration they have made all their own with a unique mix of tradition, hedonism and sentimentality. The roots of the Hogmanay are in pagan festivities based around the winter solstice, which in most places gradually merged with Christmas. When hardline Scottish Protestant clerics in the sixteenth century abolished Christmas for being a Catholic mass, the Scots instead put their energy into greeting the New Year. After the bells of midnight are rung, great store is still laid in "first-footing" – visiting your neighbours and bearing gifts – to welcome good luck into your house. The ideal first-foot is a tall, dark-haired male carrying a bottle of whisky; women or redheads, on the other hand, bring bad luck – though to be honest no one carrying a bottle of whisky tends to be turned away these days. All this neighbourly greeting – and the huge street parties in Edinburgh, Glasgow, Aberdeen and elsewhere – means a fair few sore heads so, while January 1 is a public holiday in the whole of the UK, only in Scotland does the holiday extend to the next day too.

The weird and wonderful

For a taste of the country at its most idiosyncratic, steer towards one of the numerous local celebrations that perpetuate **ancient customs**, the origins and meanings of which have often been lost or conveniently misplaced. The May Day frolics of the **Padstow Obby Oss**, in Cornwall, can be traced back to fertility rites in the distant past, while on March 1, to usher in the spring and ward away evil spirits, the lads and lassies of Lanark in Scotland chase each other round the local church swinging a ball of paper in an event known as the **Whuppity Scoorie**. Other events are grounded in ceremony, like **Swan Upping** (Third week in July), the traditional registering of cygnets on the River Thames, though some do nothing more than celebrate British regional eccentricity: witness Gloucestershire's **Brockworth Cheese Rolling** contest; Cheshire's annual **World Worm-Charming Championships**; the **Bog-Snorkelling Competition** every August in Llanwrtyd Wells (Mid-Wales); or Yorkshire's **World Coal-Carrying Championship**. There's a full list of Britain's weird and wonderful celebrations in our festivals and events calendar on p.59–61.

Bog-Snorkelling Competition, Wales

community and still redolent of that era, housing an excellent tearoom and restaurant.

Although there has been a church on the site since the seventh century, **Bath Abbey** (daily 9am–6pm; closes 4pm in winter; requested donation £2.50) did not take its present form until the end of the fifteenth century, when Bishop Oliver King began work on the ruins of the previous Norman building, some of which were incorporated into the new church. The bishop was said to have been inspired by a vision of angels ascending and descending a ladder to heaven, which the present facade recalls on the turrets flanking the central window. The west front also features the founder's signature in the form of carvings of olive trees surmounted by crowns, a play on his name.

The interior is in a restrained Perpendicular style, and boasts splendid fan vaulting on the ceiling, which was not properly completed until the nineteenth century. The floor and walls are crammed with elaborate monuments and memorials, and traces of the grander Norman building are visible in the Norman Chapel.

To the Circus and the Royal Crescent

Once it is finally open, visitors to Bath will be able to take the waters at **Thermae Bath Spa**, a state-of-the-art spa complex located at the bottom of the elegantly colonnaded Bath Street (daily 7am–10pm; check opening date on ☎01225/331234, ⓦwww.thermaebathspa.com). Heated by the city's thermal waters, the spa will offer everything from massages to dry flotation, and includes two open-air pools, one on the roof of its centrepiece, the New Royal Bath, Nicholas Grimshaw's sleekly futuristic "glass cube". Prices will start at £12 (for 1hr 30min), rising to £45 (full day).

North of Hot Bath Street, Westgate Street and Sawclose are presided over by the **Theatre Royal**, opened in 1805 and one of the country's finest surviving Georgian theatres. Next door, is the house where Beau Nash spent his last years (now a restaurant). Up from the Theatre Royal, off Barton Street, the gracious **Queen Square** was the first Bath venture of the architect **John Wood**, who with his son (see box p.311) was chiefly responsible for the Roman-inspired developments of the areas outside the confines of the medieval city. Wood himself lived at no. 24, giving him a vista of the northern terrace's palatial facade.

West of Queen Square, the small **Herschel Museum** (Feb to mid-Dec Mon, Tues, Thurs & Fri 1–5pm, Sat & Sun 11am–5pm; £3.50) at 19 New King St was the former home of the musician and astronomer Sir William Herschel and his sister Caroline, who together discovered the planet Uranus in 1781. Among the contemporary furnishings, musical instruments and various knick-knacks from the Herschels' life, you can see a replica of the telescope with which Uranus was identified. Just north of the square, at 40 Gay St, the **Jane Austen Centre** (daily: March–Oct 10am–5.30pm; Nov–Feb 11am–4.30pm; £5.95) provides a superficial overview of the author's connections with the city, illustrated by extracts from her writings, contemporary costumes, furnishings and household items.

At the top of Gay Street, the elder John Wood's masterpiece, **The Circus**, consists of three crescents arranged in a tight circle of three-storey houses, with a carved frieze running round the entire circle. Wood died soon after laying the foundation stone for this enterprise, and the job was finished by his son. The painter Thomas Gainsborough lived at no. 17 from 1760 to 1774.

The Circus is connected by Brock Street to the **Royal Crescent**, grandest of Bath's crescents, begun by the younger John Wood in 1767. The stately arc of thirty houses is set off by a spacious sloping lawn from which a magnificent vista extends to green hills and distant ribbons of honey-coloured stone. The interior of **No. 1 Royal Crescent**, on the corner with Brock Street, has been restored to reflect as nearly as possible its original Georgian appearance (Tues–Sun: mid-Feb to Oct 10.30am–5pm; Nov 10.30am–4pm; £4).

At the bottom of the Crescent, Royal Avenue leads onto **Royal Victoria Park**, the city's largest open space, containing an aviary and botanical gardens.

The Assembly Rooms, the Paragon and Milsom Street

The younger John Wood's **Assembly Rooms**, east of the Circus on Bennett Street, were, with the Pump Room, the centre of Bath's social scene. A fire virtually destroyed the building in 1942, but it has now been perfectly restored and houses a **Museum of Costume** (daily: March–Oct 11am–5pm; Nov–Feb 11am–4pm; £6.25, or £12.50 with Baths), an entertaining collection of clothing from the Stuart era to modern Japanese designs.

From the Assembly Rooms, Alfred Street leads to the area known as the **Paragon**. Here, accessed from the raised pavement, the Georgian-Gothic Countess of Huntingdon's Chapel houses the **Building of Bath Museum** (Tues–Sun 10.30am–5pm; £4), a fascinating exploration of the construction and architecture of Bath. At the bottom of the Paragon, off George Street, lies **Milsom Street**, a wide shopping strand designed by the elder Wood as the main thoroughfare of Georgian Bath.

The river and Great Pulteney Street

East of the abbey, Grand Parade looks down onto the formal Parade Gardens and the River Avon. The flow of the river here is interrupted by a graceful V-shaped weir just below the shop-lined **Pulteney Bridge**, an Italianate structure designed by Robert Adam. The bridge was intended to link the city centre with **Great Pulteney Street**, a handsome avenue originally planned as the nucleus of a large residential quarter on the eastern bank. The work ran into financial difficulties, however, so the roads running off it now stop short after a few yards, though there is a lengthy vista to the imposing classical facade of the **Holburne Museum** at the end of the street (Feb to mid-Dec Tues–Sat 10am–5pm, Sun 11am–5.30pm; £4.50). The three-storey building contains an impressive range of decorative and fine art, mostly furniture, silverware, porcelain and paintings, including work by Stubbs and the famous *Byam Family* by Gainsborough. When Holburne House was a bustling hotel, the pleasure gardens behind it, now **Sydney Gardens**, were the venue for concerts and fireworks, as witnessed by Jane Austen, a frequent visitor here – the family had lodgings across the street at 4 Sydney Place. Today, the slopes are cut through by the railway and the Kennet and Avon Canal. From here, it's a pleasant one-and-a-half mile saunter along the canal to the *George* pub (see opposite).

If you want to explore the river itself, rent a skiff, punt or canoe from the **Victorian Bath Boating Station** at the end of Forester Road, behind the Holburne Museum (Easter–Sept; £6 per person per hour). Organized river trips can be made from Pulteney Bridge and weir, and there are cruises on the Kennet and Avon Canal from Sydney Wharf, near Bathwick Bridge. A two-mile **nature trail** winds along the banks of the restored canal, which itself extends east as far as Reading.

Eating, drinking and nightlife

Bath has a good range of **restaurants** – though many over-exploit the twee period trappings. Coffee shops and snack bars are ubiquitous in the centre, as are pubs offering lunchtime fare.

For concerts and **events listings**, refer to the weekly *Venue* (£1.30), or the free monthly *What's On* guide, available from the tourist office. **Theatre** and ballet fans should check out what's showing at the Theatre Royal on Sawclose (☎01225/448844), which stages more experimental productions in its Ustinov Studio. There's a great range of festivals throughout the year, notably the **Bath International Music Festival** (Ⓦwww.bathmusicfest.org.uk), held between mid-May and June and featuring jazz, classical and world music; the **Bath Fringe Festival** (late May to early June; Ⓦwww.bathfringe.co.uk), with the accent on art and performance, and **Bath Literature Festival** (10 days in Feb/March; Ⓦwww.bathlitfest.org.uk). For further information on these and other festivals, call ☎01225/463362, Ⓦwww.bathfestivals.org.uk, or check out the individual websites above.

Best of Bath's **clubs** is *Moles* (☎01225/404445, Ⓦwww.moles.co.uk) on George Street, a local institution which has live music and DJs; the next-door *Porter* also has regular gigs in its Cellar Bar. Other clubs include the Moroccan-style *Fez Club*, The Paragon (☎01225/444162), and *Po Na Na*, 8 North Parade (☎01225/401115), also Moroccan-themed, with a largely student crowd – both play funk, trance, house and mainstream.

Restaurants and cafés

Bathtub Bistro 2 Grove St ☎01225/460593. Just off Pulteney Bridge, this place looks tiny from the outside but has several eating areas within. The international menu includes pure beef hamburgers and innovative vegetarian dishes. BYOB Mon & Tues. Inexpensive to moderate.

Café Retro 18 York St. A cosy place near the abbey for a cappuccino or a meal. Also open Thurs–Sat eves for inventive international dishes at moderate prices. The adjacent *Retro-to-Go* takeaway sells rolls and salads.

Demuths 2 North Parade Passage ☎01225/446059. Bath's favourite eating place for veggies and vegans, offering original and delicious dishes from around the world, as well as organic beers, wines and coffees. Decor is bright and modern. No smoking. Moderate–expensive.

Eastern Eye 8 Quiet St ☎01225/422323. Just off Milsom Street, this designer curry-house occupies a Georgian bank, with a spectacular vaulted ceiling and great food. Moderate.

Firehouse Rotisserie 2 John St ☎01225/482070. Delicious, outsized Californian pizzas and grills are the main items in this busy place with a pleasant wooden interior. Booking essential. Closed Sun. Moderate.

Popjoy's Sawclose ☎01225/460494. Once Beau Nash's house (it's named after his mistress), this somewhat twee restaurant enjoys a prime location, and serves high-quality Modern British food, with great desserts. There's a good-value pre-theatre menu. Closed Sun. Expensive.

Pump Room Abbey Church Yard ☎01225/444477. Splash out on a brunch or a Bath bun in the morning, a range of cream teas in the afternoon, or the good lunch-time menu, all accompanied by a pianist or a classical trio. It's a bit hammy, but you get a good view of the baths, and a chance to sample the waters. Open daytime only, plus evenings during the Bath Festival, Aug and Christmas. Moderate.

Tilley's Bistro 3 North Parade Passage ☎01225/484200. Informal, rather cramped French restaurant with starter-sized and -priced portions to allow more samplings, good set-price lunch-time menus and a separate vegetarian menu. Closed Sun. Moderate.

Walrus and Carpenter 28 Barton St ☎01225/314864. An extensive vegetarian menu is offered in this warren of small rooms near the Theatre Royal – though meat dishes are also available. Moderate.

Pubs

The Bath Tap 19–20 St James's Parade. Home of Bath's gay and lesbian scene, lively but relaxed, with a mixed crowd and regular cabaret and club nights.

The Bell 103 Walcot St. Excellent, easy-going tavern with a beer garden

and live music (Mon eve, Wed eve, Sun lunch-time).

The George Mill Lane, Bathampton. Popular canal-side pub twenty minutes' walk from the centre, with better than average bar food

Claverton

It's an easy excursion to **CLAVERTON**, on Bath's eastern edge, site of the **American Museum** (mid-March–Oct Tues–Sun 2–5.30pm, grounds open at noon; £6.50, grounds only £4), which occupies the early nineteenth-century Claverton Manor, where Winston Churchill made his maiden political speech in 1897. The museum shows reconstructed rooms illustrating life in the New World from the seventeenth to the nineteenth centuries, with sections devoted to textiles, whaling, the opening of the West, Native Americans and Hispano-American culture. The glorious **grounds** contain a replica of George Washington's garden, an arboretum and assorted relics. University buses #18 and #418 run throughout the year to the Avenue (the stop before the campus), from where it's a ten-minute walk to the museum.

Wells, the Mendips and Glastonbury

Wells, twenty miles south of Bristol across the Somerset border and the same distance southwest from Bath, is a miniature cathedral city that has not significantly altered in eight hundred years. You might decide to make it an accommodation stop for visiting nearby attractions in the **Mendip Hills**, such as the **Wookey Hole** caves and **Cheddar Gorge**. On the southern edge of the range, the town of **Glastonbury** has for centuries been one of the main Arthurian sites of the West Country, and is now the country's most enthusiastic centre of New Age cults.

Wells

Technically England's smallest city, **WELLS** owes its celebrity entirely to its **cathedral** (daily: April–Sept 7am–7pm; Oct–March 7am–6pm; suggested donation £5). Hidden from sight until you pass into its spacious close from the central Market Place, the building presents a majestic spectacle, the broad lawn of the former graveyard providing a perfect foreground. The west front teems with some three hundred thirteenth-century figures of saints and kings, once brightly painted and gilded, though their present honey tint has a subtle splendour of its own. Close up, the impact is slightly lessened, as most of the statuary is badly eroded and many figures were damaged by Puritans in the seventeenth century. The facade was constructed about fifty years after work on the main building was begun in 1180. The **interior** is a supreme example of early English Gothic, the long nave punctuated by a dramatic "scissor arch", one of three that were constructed in 1338 to take the extra weight of the newly built tower. Beyond the arch, there are some gnarled old tombs to be seen in the aisles of the **Quire**, at the end of which is the richly coloured stained glass of the fourteenth-century **Lady Chapel**. The **capitals and corbels** of the transepts hold some amusing narrative carvings – look out for the men with toothache and an old man caught pilfering an orchard – and, in the north transept, there's a 24-hour astronomical clock dating from 1390. From his seat high up on the right of the clock, a figure known as Jack Blandiver kicks a couple of bells every quarter-hour, heralding the appearance of a pair of jousting knights charging at each other, and on the hour he strikes the bell in front of him. Opposite the clock, a doorway leads to a graceful, much-worn flight of steps rising to the **Chapter House**, an octagonal room elaborately ribbed in the Decorated style.

The row of clerical houses on the north side of the cathedral green are mainly seventeenth- and eighteenth-century, though one, the **Old Deanery**, shows traces of its fifteenth-century origins. The chancellor's house is now a **museum** (Easter–Oct Mon–Sat 10am–5.30pm, Sun 10am–4pm; Nov–Easter Mon & Wed–Sun 11am–4pm; £3), displaying some of the cathedral's original statuary as well as a good geological section with fossils from the surrounding area.

Beyond the arch, a little further along the street, the cobbled medieval **Vicars' Close** holds more clerical dwellings, linked to the cathedral by the Chain Gate and fronted by small gardens. The cottages were built in the mid-fourteenth century – though only no. 22 has not undergone outward alterations – and have been continuously occupied by members of the cathedral clergy ever since.

On the other side of the cathedral – and accessible through the cathedral shop – are the cloisters, from which you can enter the tranquil grounds of the **Bishop's Palace** (April–July, Sept & Oct Mon–Fri 10.30am–6pm, Sun noon–6pm; Aug daily 10.30am–6pm, though occasionally closed for functions; last entry at 5pm; £4), also reachable from Market Place through the Bishop's Eye archway. The residence of the Bishop of Bath and Wells, the palace was walled and moated as a result of a rift with the borough in the fourteenth century, and the imposing gatehouse still displays the grooves of the portcullis and a chute for pouring oil and molten lead on would-be assailants. Its tranquil gardens contain the springs from which the city takes its name and the scanty but impressive remains of the **Great Hall**, built at the end of the thirteenth century and despoiled during the Reformation. Across the lawn stands the square **Bishop's Chapel** and the **Undercroft**, holding displays relating to the history of the site, state rooms and a café.

Practicalities

Wells **bus station** is off Market Street, and its **tourist office** is on Market Place (daily: April–Oct 9.30am–5.30pm; Nov–March 10am–4pm; ☎01749/672552, ⓦwww.wells.gov.uk). Good, central **accommodation** choices include *Canon Grange*, whose spacious rooms face the cathedral's west front (☎01749/671800, ⓦwww.canongrange.co.uk; ❸), and the handsome, Georgian *Richmond House*, 2 Chamberlain St (☎01749/676438, ⓦwww.richmondhouse.info; no smoking; no credit cards; ❷). Alternatively, soak up the authentically antique atmosphere in either of the old coaching inns in the centre of town: the *Crown Hotel*, Market Place (☎01749/673457, ⓦcrownatwells.co.uk; ❺), where William Penn was arrested in 1695 for illegal preaching, and the *Swan*, on Sadler Street (☎01749/836300, ⓦwww.swanhotelwells.co.uk; ❼), with limited views of the cathedral.

For **food**, a good choice is *Bekynton Brasserie*, close to the cathedral on Market Place, which serves daytime snacks and full evening meals (☎01749/675993; closed Mon–Wed eves). Round the corner on Sadler Street, there's the Italian-run *Rugantino's* (☎01749/672029), quite formal in style, and *Goodfellows*, an innovative seafood café/restaurant (☎01749/673866; closed Tues & Wed lunch and all Sun & Mon) and patisserie (open daily). Excellent wholefood is on hand at the *Good Earth* on Priory Road, near the bus station (closed eves & Sun), also with delicious takeaway items. The *City Arms* on Cuthbert Street, formerly the town gaol, is the best central **pub**, with a flower-filled courtyard and meals in an upstairs restaurant.

The Mendips

North of Wells, the **Mendip Hills** are chiefly famous for **Wookey Hole** – the most impressive of many caves in this narrow limestone chain – and for **Cheddar Gorge**, where a walk through the narrow cleft might make a starting point for more adventurous trips across the Mendips. From Wells, take buses #172 or #670 to Wookey Hole, and #126 or #826 to the gorge.

Wookey Hole

Hollowed out by the River Axe a couple of miles outside Wells, **Wookey Hole** is an impressive cave complex of deep pools and intricate rock formations, but it's folklore rather than geology that takes precedence on the guided tours (daily: April–Oct 10am–5pm; Nov–March 10am–4pm; £9.90). Highlight of the hour-long tour is the alleged petrified remains of the Witch of Wookey, a "blear-eyed hag" who was said to turn her evil eye on crops, young lovers and local farmers. At the end of the tour, there's a functioning Victorian paper mill, rooms containing speleological exhibits and a range of amusements including a collection of Edwardian fairground pieces.

The ✗ *Wookey Hole Inn* (☎01749/676776, ⓦwww.wookeyholeinn.com; ⑤), just along the street from the caves, is a good place to **stay the night**, with contemporary, fully equipped guest-rooms. The bar serves a great selection of Belgian beers, while the **restaurant** (booking essential; closed Sun eve) cooks up expensive but memorable meals; there's also regular live music.

Cheddar Gorge

Six miles west of Wookey on the A371, the rather plain village of Cheddar has given its name to Britain's best-known cheese – most of it now mass-produced far from here – and is also renowned for the **Cheddar Gorge**, lying beyond the neighbourhood of Tweentown about a mile to the north.

Cutting a jagged gash across the Mendip Hills, the limestone gorge is an impressive geological phenomenon, though its natural beauty is undermined by the minor road running through it and by the Lower Gorge's mile of shops, coach park and **tourist office** (Easter to mid-Sept daily 10am–5pm; mid-Sept to Oct daily 10.30am–4.30pm; Nov–Easter Sun 11am–4pm; ☎01934/744071, ⓦwww.somersetbythesea.co.uk). Few trippers venture further than the first few curves of the gorge, which admittedly holds its most dramatic scenery, though each turn of the two-mile length presents new, sometimes startling vistas. At its narrowest the path squeezes between cliffs towering almost five hundred feet above, and if you don't want to follow the road as far as **Priddy**, the highest Mendip village, you can reach more dramatic destinations by branching off onto marked paths to such secluded spots as **Black Rock**, just two miles from Cheddar, or **Black Down**, at 1067ft the Mendips' highest point. The tourist office can provide details of a two-and-a-half-hour circular walk and of the **West Mendip Way**, a forty-mile route extending from Uphill, near Weston-super-Mare, to Wells and Shepton Mallet.

Beneath the gorge, the **Cheddar Caves** (daily: July & Aug 10am–5.30pm; Sept–June 10.30am–5pm; £10.90) were scooped out by underground rivers in the wake of the Ice Age, and subsequently occupied by primitive communities. Today the caves are floodlit to pick out the subtle tones of the rock, and the array of tortuous rock formations that resemble organ pipes, waterfalls and giant birds. Close to Cox's Caves, the 274 steps of **Jacob's Ladder** (same ticket as caves) lead to a cliff-top viewpoint looking towards Glastonbury Tor, Exmoor and the sea. It's a muscle-wrenching climb, though you can reach the same spot more easily via the narrow lane winding up behind the cliffs. You can also survey the panorama from **Pavey's Lookout Tower** nearby.

Among Cheddar's handful of **B&Bs**, try *Chedwell Cottage*, Redcliffe Street (℡01934/743268; no credit cards; ❷), with two en-suite rooms and a garden, or on the outskirts, *Wessells House*, Upper New Rd (℡01934/744317; no credit cards; ❷), where huge breakfasts are served; both are nonsmoking. There's also a YHA **hostel**, off the Hayes (℡0870/770 5760, ✉cheddar@yha.org.uk; limited winter opening; £12.50).

Glastonbury

Six miles south of Wells, **GLASTONBURY** lies at the centre of the so-called **Isle of Avalon**, a region rich with mystical associations. At the heart of it all is the early Christian legend that the young Jesus once visited this site, a story that is not as far-fetched as it sounds. The Romans had a heavy presence in the area, mining lead in the Mendips, and one of these mines was owned by **Joseph of Arimathea**, a well-to-do merchant said to have been related to Mary. It's not completely impossible that the merchant took his kinsman on one of his many visits to his property, in a period of Christ's life of which nothing is recorded. It was this possibility to which William Blake referred in his *Glastonbury Hymn*, better known as *Jerusalem*: – "And did those feet in ancient times/Walk upon England's mountains green?"

Another legend relates how Joseph was imprisoned for twelve years after the Crucifixion, miraculously kept alive by the **Holy Grail**, the chalice of the Last Supper, in which the blood was gathered from the wound in Christ's side. The Grail, along with the spear which had caused the wound, were later taken by Joseph to Glastonbury, where he founded the abbey and commenced the conversion of Britain.

More verifiably, a Celtic monastery was founded here in the fourth or fifth century – making this the oldest Christian foundation in England. Enlarged by St Dunstan in the tenth century, **Glastonbury Abbey** (daily: Feb 10am–5pm; March 9.30am–5.30pm; April–Sept 9.30am–6pm; Oct 9.30am–5pm; Nov 9.30am–4.30pm; Dec & Jan 10am–4.30pm; £4) became the richest Benedictine abbey in the country. Three Anglo-Saxon kings (Edmund, Edgar and Edmund Ironside) were buried here, the library had a far-reaching fame, and the church had the longest known nave (580ft) of any monastic church at the time of the Dissolution. The original building was destroyed by fire in 1184 and the ruins are the rather scanty remains of what took its place, reduced to their present state at the Dissolution. Hidden behind walls at the centre of town, surrounded by grassy parkland and shaded by trees, the ruins only hint at the extent of the building, which was financed largely by a constant procession of medieval pilgrims. The most prominent and photogenic remains are the transept piers and the shell of the Lady Chapel, with its carved figures of the Annunciation, the Magi and Herod.

The abbey's **choir** introduces another strand to the Glastonbury story, for it holds what is alleged to be the tomb of **Arthur and Guinevere**. As told by William of Malmesbury and Thomas Malory, the story relates how, after being mortally wounded in battle, King Arthur sailed to Avalon where he was buried alongside his queen. The discovery of two bodies in an ancient cemetery outside the abbey in 1191 – from which they were transferred here in 1278

– was taken to confirm the popular identification of Glastonbury with Avalon. In the grounds, the fourteenth-century **abbot's kitchen** is the only monastic building to survive intact, with four huge corner fireplaces and a great central lantern above. Behind the main entrance to the grounds, look out for the thorn-tree that is supposedly from the original **Glastonbury Thorn** said to have sprouted from the staff of Joseph of Arimathea. The plant grew for centuries on a nearby hill known as Wyrral, or Weary-All, and despite being hacked down by Puritans, lived long enough to provide numerous cuttings whose descendants still bloom twice a year (Easter & Dec) – only at Glastonbury do they flourish, it is claimed.

On the edge of the abbey grounds, the fourteenth-century Abbey Barn is the centrepiece of the engaging **Somerset Rural Life Museum** (April–Oct Tues–Fri 10am–5pm, Sat & Sun 2–6pm; Nov–March Tues–Sat 10am–5pm; free), illustrating a range of local rural occupations, from cheese- and cidermaking to peat-digging, thatching and farming.

From the museum it's about a mile's hike to **Glastonbury Tor**, at 521ft a landmark for miles around. The conical hill – topped by the dilapidated **St Michael's Tower**, sole remnant of a fourteenth-century church – commands stupendous views encompassing Wells, the Quantocks, the Mendips, the once-marshy peat moors rolling out to the sea, and, on very clear days, the Welsh mountains. Pilgrims once embarked on the stiff climb here with hard peas in their shoes as penance – nowadays people come to feel the vibrations of crossing ley-lines. If you don't fancy the steep ascent, take the easier path further up Wellhouse Lane, that leads to the Tor Park from the centre of town. Alternatively, take the **Glastonbury Tor Bus** (May to mid-Sept; every 30min; £1, valid all day), from the High Street to the base of the Tor.

At the bottom of Wellhouse Lane, amid a lush garden intended for quiet contemplation, the **Chalice Well** (daily: March–Oct 10am–5.30pm; Nov–Feb 10am–4pm; £2.85) was allegedly the hiding-place of the Holy Grail. The iron-red waters were considered to have curative properties, making the town a spa for a brief period in the eighteenth century, and they are still prized – there's a tap in Wellhouse Lane.

Back in town, halfway along the High Street, the fifteenth-century church of **St John the Baptist** has one of Somerset's finest towers, while its interior has a fine oak roof and stained glass illustrating the legend of St Joseph of Arimathea. The Glastonbury thorn in the churchyard is the biggest in town.

Further down the street, the fourteenth-century **Tribunal** was where the abbots presided over legal cases; it later became a hotel for pilgrims, and now holds the small **Glastonbury Lake Village Museum** of finds from the Iron Age lake villages that once fringed the marshland below the Tor (April–Sept Mon–Thurs & Sun 10am–5pm, Fri & Sat 10am–5.30pm; Oct–March closes 1hr earlier; £2; EH).

Glastonbury Festival

Glastonbury is, of course, best known for its **music festival**, which takes place most years over three days at the end of June outside the nearby village of Pilton. Having started in the 1970s, the festival has become one of the biggest and best organized in the country, without shedding too much of its alternative feel. Bands range from huge acts such as Coldplay and Moby to up-and-coming indie groups, via old hands such as David Bowie. Though **tickets** cost around £125, they are snapped up early: for information call ☎01749/890470 or see ⓦ www.glastonburyfestivals.co.uk.

Practicalities

Buses #376 and #377 (on Sun #929 and #977) run once or twice an hour from Wells. Glastonbury's **tourist office** is housed in the Tribunal on the High Street (April–Sept Mon–Thurs & Sun 10am–5pm, Fri & Sat 10am–5.30pm; Oct–March closes 1hr earlier; ☏01458/832954, ⓦwww.glastonburytic.co.uk).

Glastonbury's **accommodation** ranges from medieval hostelries to hostels, with most places within a brief walk of the Tor and town centre.

1 Park Terrace Street Road ☏01458/835845, ⓦwww.no1parkterrace.co.uk. Large Victorian house, five minutes' walk from the centre. ❸

3 Magdalene St ☏01458/832129, ⓦwww.numberthree.co.uk. Beautifully furnished bedrooms make for a stylish stay in this Georgian house with a large walled garden, right next to the abbey. No smoking. ❻

George & Pilgrims High Street ☏01458/831146, ⓦwww.georgeandpilgrims.activehotels.com. This fifteenth-century oak-panelled inn brims with antique atmosphere. ❹

 Glastonbury Backpackers 4 Market Place ☏01458/833353, ⓦwww

.glastonburybackpackers.com. Central ex-coaching inn with café, restaurant, pool room and no curfew. Dorm beds £12, doubles ❶

Meadow Barn Middlewick Farm, Wick Lane ☏01458/832351, ⓦwww.middlewickholiday cottages.co.uk. A mile and a half north of town, this Canadian-run place offers peace and quiet in rural surroundings, with views and an indoor pool. No smoking. ❸

YHA hostel Ivythorn Hill, Street ☏0870/770 6056. The nearest YHA lies a couple of miles south of Glastonbury (bus #375 or #376; alight at Marshalls Elm crossroads and follow signs). Dorm beds are £11.95. Flexible opening in winter.

Eating, drinking and entertainment

Wedged between the esoteric shops of Glastonbury's High Street are several decent **cafés** serving inexpensive meals, including the *Blue Note Café* at no. 4, with some courtyard seating and occasional evening meals in summer, and *Hundred Monkeys* at no. 52 (☏01458/833386; closed Sun), which has seafood soup on the menu and stays open Thursday–Saturday evenings for meals and live music (currently Fri). The eclectic menu at *Hawthorns*, 8 Northload St (☏01458/831225), includes a lunchtime curry buffet, "Ethnic English" dishes and vegetarian options. Across the road at 17 Northload St, the *Who'd a Thought It* is one of the best **pubs** locally, with decent food and a garden; *Glastonbury Backpackers* (see above) is also good for ales, atmosphere and occasional live music. There are music and theatre **performances** in the abbey grounds in summer – call ☏01458/832267 or check ⓦwww.glastonburyabbey.com for details.

Bridgwater, Taunton and the Quantocks

Travelling west from Glastonbury, your route could take you through both **Bridgwater** and **Taunton**, either of which make a handy starting point for excursions into the gently undulating **Quantock Hills**, a mellow landscape of snug villages set in scenic wooded valleys or "combes". Public transport is fairly minimal round here, but you can see quite a lot on the **West Somerset Railway** between Bishops Lydeard and the coastal resort of Minehead, with stops at some of the thatched, typically English villages along the west flank of the Quantocks.

Bridgwater

Sedate **BRIDGWATER** has seen little excitement since it was embroiled in the Civil War and its aftermath, in particular the events surrounding the

Monmouth Rebellion of 1685. Having landed from his base in Holland, the Protestant Duke of Monmouth, an illegitimate son of Charles II, was enthusiastically proclaimed king at Taunton, and, having failed to take Bristol, attempted to surprise the forces of the Catholic James II on **Sedgemoor**, three miles outside Bridgwater. However, the disorganized rebel army was mown down by the royal artillery, Monmouth was captured and later beheaded, and a campaign of bloody repression was unleashed under the infamous Judge Jeffreys.

Despite some ugly outskirts, Bridgwater retains some handsome red-brick buildings in its centre, notably the thirteenth- to fourteenth-century **St Mary's Church** (limited opening; call ☎01278/422437 to check hours), identifiable by its polygonal, angled steeple soaring above the town centre. Features inside include an oak pulpit and a seventeenth-century Italian altarpiece. On Blake Street – round the corner from the red-brick Christ Church where Coleridge preached in 1797 and 1798 – Bridgwater's **Blake Museum** (Tues–Sat 10am– 4pm; free) shows relics, models and a video relating to the Battle of Sedgemoor. The sixteenth-century building is reputedly the birthplace of local hero Robert Blake, admiral under Oliver Cromwell, whose swashbuckling career is chronicled and illustrated here.

Bridgwater's **tourist office** is on King's Square (Mon–Fri 8.45am–5pm; ☎01278/436438, ⓦwww.somersetbythesea.co.uk). The best **accommodation** can be found opposite St Mary's Church at the *Old Vicarage* (☎01278/458891, ⓦwww.theoldvicaragehotel.com; no smoking; ❺), one of Bridgwater's oldest buildings. On West Quay, the *Watergate Hotel* (☎01278/423847, ⓔinfo@watergatehotel.co.uk; ❸) has fairly basic rooms, all en-suite, the best ones overlooking the river. The *Old Vicarage* serves cream teas, snacks and full **meals**, while the *Great Escape* **pub** in Angel Crescent, behind the shopping centre off the High Street, has food, outside seating and DJs at weekends. On Castle Street, the Bridgwater Arts Centre (☎01278/422700) has concerts, plays, comedy and a bar.

Taunton

Twelve miles from Bridgwater, Somerset's county town of **TAUNTON** lies in the fertile Vale of Taunton, wedged between the Quantock, Brendon and Blackdown hills. The region is famed for its production of cider and scrumpy (cider's less refined cousin), while Taunton itself is host to one of the country's biggest cattle markets.

Most of Taunton's **castle**, started in the twelfth century, was pulled down in 1662, but a part of it now houses the **County Museum** (Tues–Sat 10am–5pm; free), which includes a portrait of Judge Jeffreys among other memorabilia of local interest. Overlooking the county cricket ground are the pinnacled and battlemented towers of the town's two most important churches: **St James** and **St Mary Magdalene**, both fifteenth-century though remodelled by the Victorians. St Mary's is worth a look inside for its roof-bosses carved with medieval masks.

Otherwise Taunton should only detain you as a base to visit the Quantock villages or Exmoor. The **tourist office** is on Paul Street (Mon–Fri 9.30am–5.30pm, Sat 9.30am–5pm; ☎01823/336344, ⓦwww.heartofsomerset .com), and there are three central **B&Bs** within a few steps of each other on Wellington Road: *Brookfield* at no. 16 (☎01823/272786; ❹), *Beaufort Lodge* at no. 18 (☎01823/326420; no credit cards; ❷) – both with en-suite, nonsmoking rooms – and *Acorn Lodge* at no. 22 (☎01823/337613; no credit cards; ❷), with shared bathrooms. For a snack or **meal**, head down East Street from Fore Street to *Brettons*, a congenial wine bar and restaurant at 49 East Reach (closed lunchtime Sat & Mon, and all day Sun). Vegetarian dishes are served at the *Brewhouse Theatre and Arts Centre* on Coal Orchard, where there's usually something going on in the evening (☎01823/283244, 🌐www.thebrewhouse.net).

The Quantock Hills

The **Quantock Hills** extend just twelve miles in length, and rise to 800–900ft. Watered by clear streams and grazed by red deer, the range is enclosed by a triangle of roads leading up from Bridgwater and Taunton, within which a tangle of narrow lanes connect the secluded hamlets.

North of Taunton, the first villages you pass through on the A358 give you an immediate introduction to the flavour of the Quantocks. **BISHOPS LYDEARD**, four miles up, has a splendid church tower in the Perpendicular style; the church's interior is also worth a look for its carved bench-ends. Linked by bus #28 from Taunton's train station, the village is the terminus of the **West Somerset Railway**, with steam and diesel trains departing up to eight times daily between Easter and October (plus some dates in Nov, Dec & Jan), stopping at renovated stations on the way to Minehead, some twenty miles away (see p.357). For timetables, call ☎01643/704996, or check 🌐www.west-somerset-railway.co.uk.

A couple of miles north, **COMBE FLOREY** is almost exclusively built of the pink-red sandstone characteristic of Quantock villages. For over fifteen years (1829–45), the local rector was the unconventional cleric Sydney Smith, called "the greatest master of ridicule since Swift" by Macaulay; more recently it's been home to Evelyn Waugh. A little over three miles further or so along the A358, **CROWCOMBE** is another typical cob-and-thatch Quantock village, with a well-preserved Church House from 1515. Opposite, the parish church has some pagan-looking carved bench-ends from around the same period.

Eight miles west of Bridgwater on the A39, on the edge of the hills, the pretty village of **NETHER STOWEY** is best known for its association with **Samuel Taylor Coleridge**, who in 1796 walked here from Bristol to join his wife and child at their new home. This "miserable cottage", as Sara Coleridge called it, was visited six months later by William Wordsworth and his sister Dorothy, who soon afterwards moved into Alfoxden House, a couple of miles down the road near Holford. The year that Coleridge and Wordsworth spent as neighbours was extraordinarily productive – Coleridge composed some of his best poetry at this time, including *The Rime of the Ancient Mariner* and *Kubla Khan*, and the two poets collaborated on the *Lyrical Ballads*, the poetic manifesto of early English Romanticism. In **Coleridge Cottage** (April–Sept Thurs–Sun 2–5pm; £3.20; NT), you can see the man's parlour and reading room, and, upstairs, his bedroom and an exhibition room containing various letters and first editions.

The village has a couple of good **accommodation** choices, both on Castle Street: the handsomely furnished *Stowey Brooke House*, at no. 18 (☎01278/733356, 🌐www.stoweybrookehouse.co.uk; ❷), and the *Old Cider House* at no. 25 (☎01278/732228, 🌐www.theoldciderhouse.co.uk; ❸), which also serves evening meals. The *Rose & Crown* on St Mary Street has standard inn accommodation (☎01278/732265; ❷), and provides ales and bar meals – as does the *George* next door. There's a YHA **hostel** two miles west of Holford, itself five miles west of Nether Stowey along the A39, where you can **camp** in the grounds (☎0870/770 6006; closed early Sept to March; £11.95).

South of Nether Stowey, a minor road winds off the A39 to the highest point on the Quantocks at **Wills Neck** (1260ft); drivers can park at Triscombe Stone, on the edge of Quantock Forest, from where a footpath leads to the summit about a mile distant. Stretching between Wills Neck and the village of Aisholt, the moorland plateau of **Aisholt Common** is the heart of the Quantocks, best explored from **West Bagborough**, where a five-mile path starts at Birches Corner. Lower down the slopes, outside Aisholt, the banks of **Hawkridge Reservoir** make a lovely picnic stop.

On the Quantock seaboard, **WATCHET** is Somerset's only port of any consequence, and the place from which Coleridge's Ancient Mariner set sail. A stop away from Watchet on the West Somerset Railway is **Washford**, from where it's a ten-minute walk to **Cleeve Abbey** (daily: late March to June & Sept 10am–5pm; July & Aug 10am–6pm; Oct 10am–4pm; £3.30; EH), a Cistercian house founded in 1198. The church itself has been mostly destroyed, but the convent buildings are in excellent condition, providing the country's most complete collection of domestic buildings belonging to this austere order. An exhibition on the premises illustrates how the monks lived and how the local population pleaded in vain with Henry VIII for the abbey's survival.

Travel details

Buses

For information on all local and national bus services, contact Traveline ⓣ0870/608 2608 (daily 7am–9pm), ⓦwww.traveline.org.uk.

Bath to: Bristol (every 15–30min; 50min); London (11 daily; 3hr 20min); Salisbury (3–4 daily; 1hr 20min–2hr 30min); Wells (Mon–Sat hourly, Sun 7; 1hr 15min).

Bridgwater to: Glastonbury (Mon–Sat hourly, Sun 4 daily; 50min–1hr 10min); Taunton (Mon–Sat every 30min, Sun every 2hr; 45min); Wells (Mon–Sat hourly; 1hr 30min).

Bristol to: Bath (every 15–30min; 50min); London (hourly; 2hr 30min); Wells (hourly; 1hr).

Glastonbury to: Bridgwater (Mon–Sat hourly, Sun 4 daily; 50min–1hr 10min); Taunton (5–6 daily; 50min); Wells (1–2 hourly; 15min).

Taunton to: Bridgwater (Mon–Sat every 30min, Sun every 2hr; 45min); Glastonbury (5–6 daily; 50min).

Wells to: Bath (Mon–Sat hourly, Sun 7 daily; 1hr 15min); Bridgwater (Mon–Sat hourly, 1hr 30min); Bristol (hourly; 1hr); Glastonbury (1–2 hourly; 15min).

Trains

For information on all local and national rail services, contact National Rail Enquiries ⓣ08457/484950, ⓦwww.nationalrail.co.uk.

Bath to: Bristol (every 20min; 20min); London (1–2 hourly; 1hr 30min); Salisbury (hourly; 1hr).

Bristol to: Bath (every 20min; 20min); Birmingham (every 30min; 1hr 30min); Cheltenham (2 hourly; 45min); Exeter (1–2 hourly; 1hr 15min–1hr 45min); Gloucester (1–2 hourly; 45min–1hr 15min); London (2 hourly; 1hr 45min).

6

Devon and Cornwall

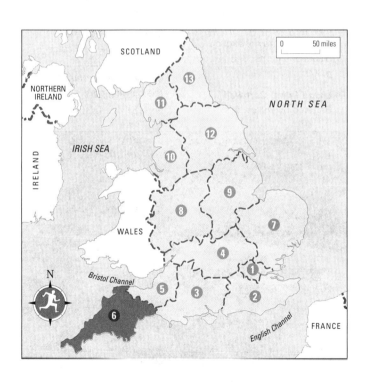

CHAPTER 6

Highlights

✳ **Sidmouth Folk Week**
Great folk and roots from around the world predominate at this annual festival. See p.336

✳ **South West Coast Path**
Ever-changing vistas ensure variety on Britain's longest waymarked path. See p.358

✳ **Eden Project, Cornwall** A disused clay pit is home to a fantastic array of exotic plants and crops. See p.363

✳ **Lizard Point, Cornwall**
Battered by waves, this unspoiled headland is the starting point for some inspiring walks. See p.368

✳ **Tate St Ives, Cornwall**
This modern gallery showcases local artists. See p.374

✳ **Surfing in Newquay**
Endless ranks of rollers draw enthusiasts from far and wide. See p.376

✳ **Seafood in Padstow, Cornwall** The local catch goes straight into the excellent restaurants of this bustling port. See p.377

△ Surfing in Newquay

Devon and Cornwall

At the western extremity of England, the counties of **Devon and Corn-wall** encompass everything from genteel, cosy villages to vast Atlantic-facing strands of golden sand and wild expanses of granite moorland. The combination of rural peace and first-class beaches has made the peninsula perennially popular with tourists, so much so that tourism has replaced the traditional occupations of fishing and farming as the main source of employment and income. Enough remains of these beleaguered communities to preserve the region's authentic character, however – even if this can be occasionally obscured during the summer season. Avoid the peak periods and you'll be seduced by the genuine appeal of this area, which beckons ever westwards into rural backwaters where increasingly exotic place-names and idiosyncratic pronunciations recall that this was once England's last bastion of Celtic culture.

Although the human history of the region has left its stamp, it's the natural landscape which exerts the strongest pull, and not just in the beauty of the long, deeply indented seaboard. Straddling the border between Devon and Somerset, **Exmoor** is one of the peninsula's three great moors, its heathery slopes much favoured by hunting parties as well as by hikers. For wilderness, however, nothing can beat the remoter tracts of **Dartmoor**, the greatest of the West Country's granite massifs, much of which retains its solitude despite its proximity to the region's only major cities. Of the two, **Exeter** is by far the more interesting, dominated by the twin towers of its medieval cathedral and offering a rich selection of restaurants and nightlife. As for **Plymouth**, much of this great naval port was destroyed by bombing during World War II, and bland postwar development has left its stamp on the rest, although enough of the city's Elizabethan core has survived to merit a visit.

The coastline on either side of Exeter and Plymouth is within easy reach. Enjoying more hours of sunshine than virtually anywhere else in England, this part of the country can sometimes come fairly close to the atmosphere of the Mediterranean, and indeed Devon's principal resort, **Torquay**, styles itself the capital of the "English Riviera". St Tropez it ain't, but there's no denying a certain glamour, alloyed with an old-fashioned charm which the seaside towns of **East Devon** and the cliff-backed resorts of the county's northern littoral also share.

Cornwall too has its pockets of concentrated tourist development – chiefly at **Falmouth** and **Newquay**, the first of these a sailing centre, the second a mecca for surfers drawn to its choice of west-facing beaches. **St Ives** is another crowd-puller, though the town has a separate identity as a magnet for the arts. Further up Cornwall's long northern coast, the rock-walled harbours of **Port Isaac** and

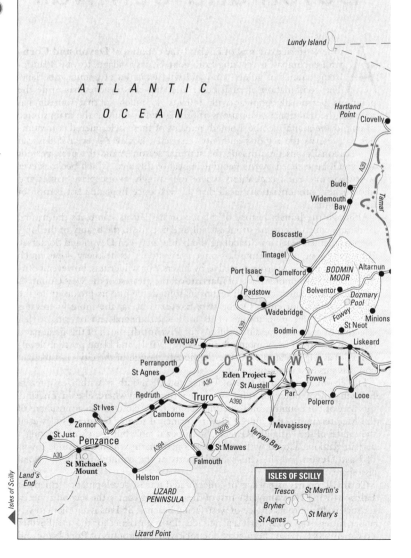

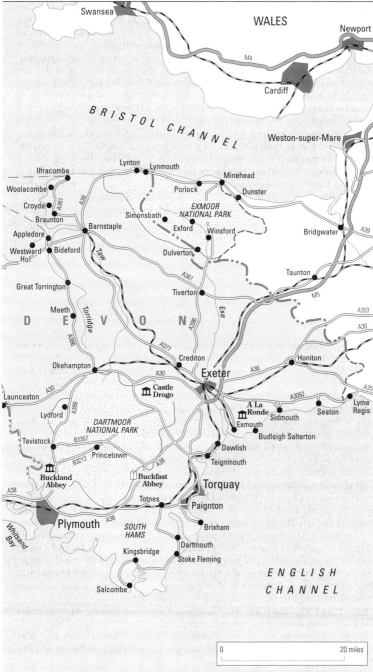

© Crown copyright

Boscastle and the fortified site of **Tintagel** have an almost embattled character in the face of the turbulent Atlantic. However, the full elemental power of the ocean can best be appreciated on the western headlands of **Lizard Point** and **Land's End**, where the cliffs resound to the constant thunder of the waves.

Unlike Devon, Cornwall preserves numerous reminders of its industrial past, not least its snowy heaps of china clay and the ubiquitous ruins of its defunct mine-works. A disused clay pit is the site of the **Eden Project**, which imaginatively highlights the diversity of the planet's plant systems with the help of science-fiction "biomes", where tropical and Mediterranean climates and conditions have been re-created.

The best way of exploring the coast of Devon and Cornwall is along the **South West Coast Path**, Britain's longest waymarked footpath, which extends for over six hundred miles from Minehead in Somerset to Poole in Dorset. Getting around by **public transport** in the West Country can be a convoluted and lengthy process, especially if you're relying on the often deficient bus network. By train, you can reach Exeter, Plymouth and Penzance, with a handful of branch lines wandering off to the major coastal resorts.

Devon

With its rolling meadows, narrow lanes and remote thatched cottages, **Devon** has long been idealized as a vision of a preindustrial, "authentic" England. But while many of its cosy, gentrified villages are inhabited largely by retired folk and urban refugees, having little in common with the county's strong agricultural, mercantile and maritime traditions, at least the stereotyped image has helped to preserve the countryside and coast in the undeveloped condition for which they are famous, and the county offers an abundance of genuine tranquillity, from moorland villages to quiet coves on the cliff-hung coastline.

Reminders of Devon's leading role in the country's **maritime history** are never far away, particularly in the two cities of **Exeter** and **Plymouth**. These days the nautical tradition is perpetuated on a domesticated scale by yachtspeople taking advantage of Devon's numerous creeks and bays, especially on its southern coast, where ports such as **Dartmouth** and **Salcombe** are awash with amateur sailors. Land-bound tourists flock to the sandy beaches and seaside resorts, of which **Torquay**, on the south coast, and **Ilfracombe**, on the north, are the busiest. The most attractive are those which have retained traces of their nineteenth-century elegance, such as **Sidmouth**, in East Devon. **Inland**, Devon is characterized by swards of lush pasture and a scattering of sheltered villages, the county's low population density dropping to almost zero on **Dartmoor**, the wildest and bleakest of the West's moors, and **Exmoor**, whose seaboard constitutes one of the West Country's most scenic littorals.

Exeter and Plymouth are on the main **rail** lines from London and the Midlands, with branch lines from Exeter linking the north coast at Barnstaple and the south-coast towns of Exmouth and Torquay. **Buses** from the chief stations fan out along the coasts and into the interior, though the service can be rudimentary for the smaller villages.

Exeter and around

EXETER's sights are richer than those of any other town in Devon or Cornwall, the legacy of an eventful history since its Celtic foundation and the establishment here of the most westerly Roman outpost. After the Roman withdrawal, Exeter was refounded by Alfred the Great and by the time of the Norman Conquest had become one of the largest towns in England, profiting from its position on the banks of the River Exe. The expansion of the wool trade in the Tudor period sustained the city until the eighteenth century, and Exeter has maintained its status as commercial centre and county town, and, despite having much of its ancient centre gutted by World War II bombing, enough has survived to justify a lengthy exploration.

Arrival, information and accommodation

Exeter has two **train stations**, Exeter Central and St David's, the latter a little further out from the centre of town, and connected by frequent city buses. South West trains from Salisbury stop at both, as do trains on the branch lines to Barnstaple and Exmouth, but most long-distance trains stop at St David's only. The **bus station** is on Paris Street, opposite the main **tourist office** at Dix's Field, off Southernhay (Mon–Sat 9am–5pm, also Sun 10am–4pm in July & Aug; ☎01392/265700, ⓦwww.exeter.gov.uk/tourism), though redevelopment of the area means that the tourist office will be moving in 2007. There's **Internet** access at the *New Horizon* café at 47 Longbrook St (☎01392/277523), which also serves Moroccan snacks.

Accommodation

Most of Exeter's cheaper **accommodation** lies north of the centre, near the two stations, though you can also find bargains more centrally.

Bendene 15 Richmond Rd ☎01392/213526, ⓦwww.bendene.co.uk. A heated outdoor swimming pool and low rates are the chief attractions of this central B&B. No credit cards. ❷
Globe Backpackers 71 Holloway St ①01392/215521, ⓦwww.exeterbackpackers.co.uk. Clean and central, with good showers and Internet access. Dorm beds £14, and a spacious double also available. ❶
Hotel Barcelona Magdalen Street ☎01392/281000, ⓦwww.aliashotels.com. Great place for a stylish splurge, in a red-brick former Victorian eye hospital. Light, spacious rooms, Gaudí-esque decor and a good bistro. ❻
Park View 8 Howell Rd ☎01392/271772, ⓦwww.parkviewhotel.freeserve.co.uk. In a quiet location overlooking a park, this Georgian B&B has smart, spacious rooms. ❸
Raffles 11 Blackall Rd ☎01392/270200, ⓦwww.raffles-exeter.co.uk. Elegant Victorian house with period furnishings and organic garden produce at breakfast. ❸
Townhouse Hotel 5 Bystock Terrace ☎01392/213079, ⓦwww.exeterhotels.com. Bright rooms, smallish but comfortable, some with views over the square. No smoking. ❹
YHA hostel 47 Countess Wear Rd ☎0870/770 5826, ⓔexeter@yha.org.uk. In a country house two miles outside the centre – take minibuses #K or #T, or buses #57 or #85, or walk along the Exe. Dorm beds £15.50.

The City

The most distinctive feature of Exeter's skyline, **St Peter's Cathedral** (daily 9.30am–5pm; £3.50 suggested donation) is a stately monument made conspicuous by the two great Norman towers flanking the nave. Close up, it's the facade's ornate Gothic screen that commands attention: its three tiers of sculpted (and very weathered) figures – including Alfred, Athelstan, Canute,

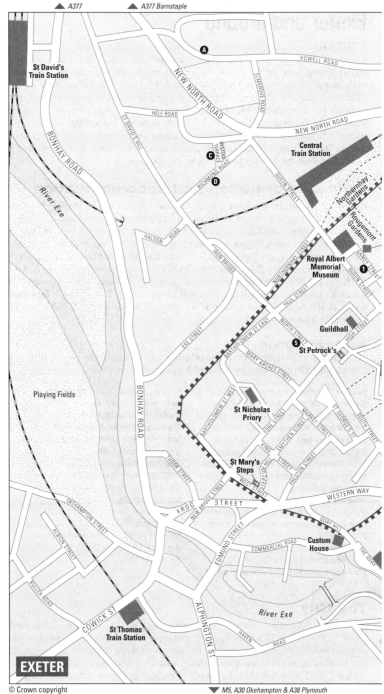

EXETER

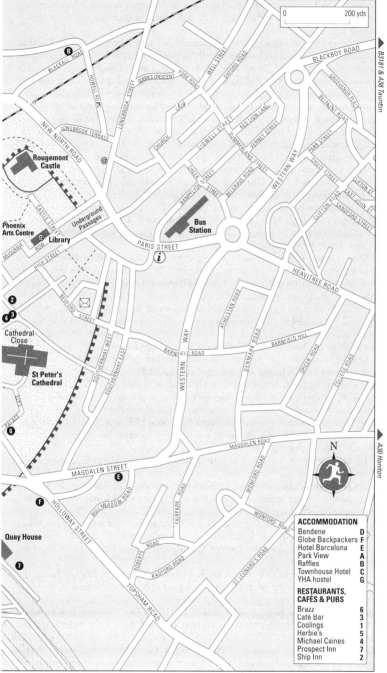

ACCOMMODATION

Bendene	D
Globe Backpackers	F
Hotel Barcelona	E
Park View	A
Raffles	B
Townhouse Hotel	C
YHA hostel	G

RESTAURANTS, CAFÉS & PUBS

Brazz	6
Café Bar	3
Coolings	1
Herbie's	5
Michael Caines	4
Prospect Inn	7
Ship Inn	2

B3181 & A38 Taunton

A30 Honiton

M5 & A376 Exmouth

William the Conqueror and Richard II – were begun around 1360, part of a rebuilding programme which left only the Norman towers from the original construction.

Entering the cathedral, you're confronted by the longest unbroken **Gothic ceiling** in the world, its **bosses** vividly painted – one, towards the west front, shows the murder of Thomas à Becket. The **Lady Chapel** and **Chapter House** – respectively at the far end of the building and off the right transept – are thirteenth-century, but the main part of the nave, including the lavish rib-vaulting, dates from the full flowering of the English Decorated style, a century later. There are many fine examples of sculpture from this period, including, in the minstrels' gallery high up on the left side, angels playing musical instruments, and, below them, figures of Edward III and Queen Philippa. Dominating the cathedral's central space are the organ pipes installed in the seventeenth century and harmonizing perfectly with the linear patterns of the roof and arches. In the **Choir** don't miss the sixty-foot **bishop's throne** or the **misericords** – decorated with mythological figures around 1260, they are thought to be the oldest in the country. Outside, a graceful statue of the theologian Richard Hooker surveys the **Cathedral Close**, a motley mixture of architectural styles from Tudor to Regency, though most display Exeter's trademark red-brickwork.

Some older buildings are still standing amid the banal concrete of the modern town centre, including, on the pedestrianized High Street, Exeter's finest civic building, the fourteenth-century **Guildhall** (Mon–Fri 10am–1pm & 2–4.30pm, Sat 10.30am–noon; sometimes closed for functions, call ☎01392/265500 to check), claimed to be England's oldest municipal building in regular use. It's fronted by an elegant Renaissance portico, and merits a glance inside for its main chamber, whose arched roof timbers rest on carved bears holding staves, symbols of the Yorkist cause during the Wars of the Roses.

On the west side of Fore Street, the continuation of the High Street, a turning leads to **St Nicholas Priory**, part of a small Benedictine foundation that became a merchant's home after the Dissolution; the interior has been restored to what it might have looked like in the Tudor era, and will house a Tudor museum when it reopens after renovation. On the other side of Fore Street, trailing down towards the river, cobbled **Stepcote Hill** was once the main road into Exeter from the west, though it is difficult to imagine this steep and narrow lane as a main thoroughfare.

Exeter's centre is bounded to the southwest by the River Exe, where the port area is now mostly devoted to leisure activities, particularly around the old **Quayside**. Pubs, shops and cafés share the space with handsomely restored nineteenth-century warehouses and the smart **Custom House**, built in 1681, its opulence reflecting the former importance of the cloth trade. The area comes into its own at night, but is worth a wander at any time, and you can **rent bikes** and **canoes** at Saddles & Paddles on the quayside (☎01392/424241, ⓦwww.sadpad.com) to explore the **Exeter Canal**, which runs five miles to Topsham and beyond.

Back at the north end of the High Street, Romansgate Passage holds the entrance to a network of **underground passages** first excavated in the thirteenth century to bring water to the cathedral precincts. The passages can be normally visited as part of a 50-minute guided **tour** – not recommended to claustrophobes – though they are currently closed due to the redevelopment of the area (call ☎01392/265206 to check the latest status). Nearby, Castle Street leads to what remains of **Rougemont Castle**, now little more than a perimeter of red-stone walls that are best appreciated from the surrounding

Rougemont and Northernhay Gardens. Following the path through this park, exit at Queen Street to drop in at the excellent **Royal Albert Memorial Museum** (Mon–Sat 10am–5pm; free), displaying everything from a menagerie of stuffed animals to mock-ups of the various building styles used at different periods in the city. The collections of silverware, watches and clocks contrast nicely with the colourful ethnography section, and the picture gallery has some good specimens of West Country art alongside work by other artists associated with Devon.

Eating, drinking and entertainment

The café inside the Royal Albert Memorial Museum serves wholesome **snacks**, while the nearby *Coolings*, in medieval Gandy Street, is a popular wine bar and bistro serving tasty lunches – it's also open until late, with DJs (currently Thurs). Opposite the cathedral, the *Café Bar* is a casually modish spot for a coffee or lunch, serving toasties, salads, burgers and pastas, and full meals in the evenings, with themed nights and live jazz on Fridays (booking advised; ☎01392/310130). It's part of the next-door *Michael Caines* (☎01392/31003; closed Sun), one of Exeter's classiest **restaurants**, where you'll find sophisticated modern European cuisine in sleek surroundings; prices are high, though there are reasonable fixed-price lunches. *Brazz*, at 10–12 Palace Gate, off South Street, is a stylish bar/bistro with a sparkly ceiling and an aquarium, while vegetarians should head for ☀ *Herbie's,* 15 North St (☎01392/258473; closed all day Sun & Mon eve), a laid-back place serving organic ice cream.

Among the **pubs**, the *Ship Inn*, in St Martin's Lane, serves reasonably priced lunches and claims to have been Francis Drake's local. The pubs and clubs on Exeter's Quay are lively: there's the seventeenth-century *Prospect Inn* with outside seating, and Exeter's two biggest **club complexes**, *Warehouse*, *Boxes* and *Boogies*, and *Volts* and *Hothouse*, all playing a mix of mainstream and retro sounds. In the town centre, *Timepiece*, Little Castle Street, occupies a former prison and has a good daytime bar with a garden, and dance music in the evening. For **live music**, especially post-punk bands, head for the *Cavern Club* (☎01392/495370, Ⓦwww.cavernclub.co.uk), with entrances in Queen and Gandy streets (also open daytime for snacks). The **Phoenix Arts Centre**, off Gandy Street (☎01392/667080, Ⓦwww.exeterphoenix.org.uk), has films, exhibitions and gigs, as well as a great café/bistro. The **Exeter Festival** (☎01392/265200, Ⓦwww.exeter.gov.uk/festival) takes place three times a year at various venues: the June/July and early November festivals feature jazz, blues and classical concerts as well as drama performances and cabaret; Vibraphonic (April/May) concentrates more on modern music.

Around Exeter

Five miles south of Exeter off the A376 (bus #57), the Gothic folly of **A La Ronde** (late March to Oct Mon–Thurs & Sun 11am–5.30pm; £4.50; NT) was the creation of two cousins, Jane and Mary Parminter, who in the 1790s were inspired by their European Grand Tour to build a sixteen-sided house possibly based on the Byzantine basilica of San Vitale in Ravenna. The end product is filled with mementos of the Parminters' tour as well as a number of their more offbeat creations, such as a frieze made of feathers culled from game birds and chickens. In the upper rooms are a gallery and staircase completely covered in shells, too fragile to be visited, though part can be glimpsed from the completely enclosed octagonal room on the first floor. From the dormer windows on the second floor, there are superb views over the Exe Estuary to Haldon Hill and Dawlish Warren.

Sidmouth

Set amidst a shelf of crumbling red sandstone, **SIDMOUTH** is the chief resort on the east Devon coast (bus #52, #52A or #52B from Exeter). The cream-and-white town boasts nearly five hundred buildings listed as having special historic or architectural interest, among them the stately Georgian homes of **York Terrace** behind the Esplanade. Both the mile-long main town beach and Jacob's Ladder, a cliff-backed shingle and sand strip to the west of town, are easily accessible and well tended. To the east, the coast path climbs steep Salcombe Hill to follow cliffs that give sanctuary to a range of birdlife including yellowhammers and green woodpeckers, as well as the rarer grasshopper warbler. Further on, the path descends to meet one of the most isolated and attractive beaches in the area, **Weston Mouth**.

The **tourist office** is on Ham Lane, off the eastern end of the Esplanade (March & April Mon–Thurs 10am–4pm, Fri & Sat 10am–5pm, Sun 10am–1pm; May–July & Sept–Oct Mon–Sat 10am–5pm, Sun 10am–4pm; Aug Mon–Sat 10am–6pm, Sun 10am–5pm; Nov–Feb Mon–Sat 10am–1.30pm; ☎01395/516441, ⓦwww.visitsidmouth.co.uk). Of the **B&Bs**, *Rock Cottage* on Peak Hill Road (☎01395/514253, ⓦwww.rockcottage.co.uk; no smoking; no credit cards; ❹) offers unrivalled sea views and access to the beach at the quieter, western end of the Esplanade. Further from the seafront, there's the atmospheric *Old Farmhouse*, on Hillside Road (☎01395/512284; no smoking; no credit cards; ❹; closed Nov–Feb). For **meals** in town, try the seafood at *Mocha Restaurant* on The Esplanade (daytime only, eves in summer), and the daily specials (including vegetarian dishes) at *Brown's Wine Bar & Bistro*, 33 Fore St (☎01395/516724; closed Sun eve). On Old Fore Street, the *Old Ship* and *Anchor* **pubs** serve excellent bar meals and suppers as well as a good range of ales.

Sidmouth hosts what many consider to be the country's best **folk festival** over eight days at the beginning of August. For details, contact the tourist office, call ☎01395/578627 or check ⓦwww.sidmouthfolkweek.co.uk.

Beer

Eight miles east along the coast, the fishing village of **BEER** lies huddled within a small sheltered cove between gleaming white headlands. A stream rushes along a deep channel dug into Beer's main street, and if you can ignore the crowds in high summer much of the village looks unchanged since the time when it was a smugglers' eyrie, its inlets used by such characters as Jack Rattenbury, who published his *Memoirs of a Smuggler* in 1837. The village is best known for its quarries, which were worked from Roman times until the nineteenth century: **Beer stone** was used in many of Devon's churches and houses, and as far afield as London. You can visit the complex of **underground quarries** (April–Sept 10am–6pm; Oct 11am–5pm; last entry 1hr before closing; £5) a mile or so west of the village on a guided tour, along with a small exhibition of pieces carved by medieval masons, among others. *Bay View* (☎01297/20489; no credit cards; ❷; closed Jan), overlooking the sea on Fore Street, is the best of the **B&Bs**, and there's a YHA **hostel** half a mile northwest, at Bovey Combe, Townsend (☎0870/770 5690, ⓔbeer@yha .org.uk; check winter opening; £11.95). For **food**, the *Barrel o' Beer* pub (☎01297/20099), on the main street, serves local delicacies such as Devon oysters and home-smoked fish.

The "English Riviera" region

The wedge of land between Dartmoor and the sea contains fertile pastures, backing onto some of Devon's most popular coastal resorts. Chief of these is **Torbay**, an amalgam of **Torquay**, **Paignton** and **Brixham**, together forming the nucleus of an area optimistically known as "**The English Riviera**". To the south, the estuary port of **Dartmouth** is linked by riverboat to historic and almost unspoiled **Totnes**. West of the River Dart, the rich agricultural district of **South Hams** extends as far as Plymouth, cleft by a web of rivers flowing off Dartmoor. The main town here is **Kingsbridge**, at the head of an estuary down which a ferry runs to the sailing resort of **Salcombe**.

Torquay

Sporting a mini-corniche and promenades landscaped with flowerbeds, **TORQUAY**, the largest of the **Torbay** resorts, comes closest to living up to the self-styled "English Riviera" sobriquet. The much-vaunted palm trees and the coloured lights that festoon the harbour by night contribute to the town's unique flavour, a blend of the mildly exotic with classic English provincialism. Torquay's transformation from a fishing village began with its establishment as a fashionable haven for invalids, among them the consumptive Elizabeth Barrett Browning, who spent three years here. In more recent years the most famous figures associated with Torquay – crimewriter Agatha Christie and traveller Freya Stark – have been joined by the fictional TV hotelier Basil Fawlty.

The town is focused on the small **harbour** and marina, separated by limestone cliffs from Torquay's main beach, **Abbey Sands**, which takes its name from **Torre Abbey**, sited in ornamental gardens behind the beachside road. The Norman church that once stood here was razed by Henry VIII, though a gatehouse, tithe barn, chapterhouse and tower escaped demolition. Just up from the marina, **Torquay Museum**, 529 Babbacombe Rd (Easter–Oct Mon–Sat 10am–5pm, also Sun 1.30–5pm in summer; Nov–Easter Mon–Sat 10am–4pm;

△ Torquay Harbour

£3), has some interesting material on Agatha Christie, who was born and raised in Torquay, as well as local history and natural history collections.

At the northern end of the harbour, **Living Coasts** (daily: March–Sept 10am–6pm; Oct 10am–5.30pm; Nov–Feb 10am–4.30pm; £6) is home to a variety of fauna and flora found on British shores, including puffins, penguins and seals. You can see the animals in their re-created habitats, and feed them at various intervals throughout the day. The rooftop café and restaurant have splendid panoramic views. Beyond here, the coast path leads round a promontory to some good sand beaches: **Meadfoot Beach**, one of the busiest, is reached by crossing Daddyhole Plain, an open greenspace named after a large chasm in the adjacent cliff caused by a landslide, but locally attributed to the devil ("Daddy"). North of the Hope's Nose promontory, the coast path leads to a string of less crowded beaches, including **Babbacombe Beach** and, beyond, **Watcombe** and **Maidencombe**.

Practicalities

Torquay's main **train station** is off Rathmore Road, southwest of Torre Abbey Gardens; most **buses** stop near the marina, close to the **tourist office** on Vaughan Parade (Easter–Sept Mon–Sat 9.30am–5.30pm, also June–Sept Sun 10am–4pm; Oct–Easter Mon–Sat 9.30am–5pm; ℡0870/707 0010, ⓦwww .englishriviera.co.uk). Most of Torquay's budget **accommodation** lies around Belgrave Road and Avenue Road, including the small, quiet *Exton*, 12 Bridge Rd (℡01803/293561, ⓦwww.extonhotel.co.uk; ❸), ten minutes from the train station. The nonsmoking *Mulberry House*, 1 Scarborough Rd (℡01803/213639; ❺), has antique pine furnishings and crisp bed linen as well as a superb restaurant (see below). For views and stately surroundings, try the *Allerdale Hotel*, Croft Road (℡01803/292667, ⓦwww.allerdalehotel.co.uk; ❹), with a long, lawned garden. The cheap, friendly *Torquay Backpackers* **hostel**, 119 Abbey Rd (℡01803/299924, ⓦwww.torquaybackpackers.co.uk; £12), has some doubles (❶), and is a ten-minute walk from the station, with a free pick-up service.

One of the best **restaurants** in Torquay is the expensive *Mulberry House Restaurant*, 1 Scarborough Rd (℡01803/213639; open lunchtime Fri–Sun, eves Wed–Sat, also Mon & Tues to residents), where the accent is on healthy and low-cholesterol dishes. Cheaper options include *Al Beb*, 64 Torwood St (℡01803/211755), for North African atmosphere and belly dancing (Fri & Sat). Also strong on atmosphere is the *Hole in the Wall* **pub** on Park Lane, which serves bar meals – it was the Irish playwright Sean O'Casey's boozer when he lived in Torquay.

Paignton and Brixham

Lacking Torquay's gloss, **PAIGNTON** is the least attractive of the Riviera's resorts, though it is home to **Paignton Zoo** (daily: summer 10am–6pm; winter 10am–4.30pm or dusk; last entry 1hr before closing; £10), a mile out on Totnes Road. Paignton's Queen's Park train station, near the harbour, is also the terminus of the **Paignton & Dartmouth Steam Railway** (June–Sept daily; March–May, Oct & Dec patchy service; ℡01803/555872, ⓦwww .paignton-steamrailway.co.uk), which connects with **Goodrington Sands** beach before following the Dart to Kingswear, seven miles south. You could make a day of it by taking the ferry from Kingswear to Dartmouth (see p.340), then taking a riverboat up the Dart to Totnes, from where you can take any bus back to Paignton – a "Round Robin" ticket (£13.50) lets you do this.

From Paignton, it's a fifteen-minute bus ride to **BRIXHAM**, a major fishing port and the prettiest of the Torbay towns. Among the trawlers on Brixham's quayside is moored a full-size reconstruction of the **Golden Hind** (March–June, Sept & Oct daily 10am–5pm; July & Aug 9am–6pm; £2.50), the surprisingly small vessel in which Francis Drake circumnavigated the world. The harbour is overlooked by an unflattering statue of William III, who landed in Brixham to claim the crown of England in 1688. Next to the statue is Brixham's **tourist office** (Easter–Sept Mon–Sat 9.30am–1pm & 2–5.30pm, Sun 10am–4pm; Oct–Easter Mon–Fri 9.30am–1pm & 2–5pm, ☎0906/680 1268). From the harbour, climb King Street and follow Berry Head Road to reach the promontory at the southern limit of Torbay, **Berry Head**, now a conservation area attracting colonies of nesting seabirds. There are fabulous views, and you can see the remains of fortifications built during the Napoleonic Wars.

For the views, the best **accommodation** is on King Street, overlooking the harbour, with the *Harbour View Hotel*, at no. 65 (☎01803/853052, Ⓦwww.s-h-systems.co.uk; ❷), and the classier *Quayside Hotel* two doors down (☎01803/855751, Ⓦwww.quaysidehotel.co.uk; ❺), which has two bars and a restaurant. Away from the harbour, the ghost-ridden *Smugglers' Haunt* on Church Hill (☎01803/853050, Ⓦwww.smugglershaunt-hotel-devon.co.uk; ❹) is creaky and cramped, but useful if everywhere else is full; all rooms are en suite. There's a YHA **hostel** four miles away outside the village of Galmpton, on the banks of the Dart (☎0870/770 5962, Ⓔriverdart@yha.org.uk; check opening; £12.50), a two-mile walk from Churston Bridge (bus #12 or #12A) – the Paignton & Dartmouth Steam Railway (see above) also passes right through the hostel's grounds.

For **food**, Brixham offers fish and more fish – from the harbourside stalls selling cockles, whelks and mussels to the moderately expensive *Yardarms* (☎01803/858266; closed Sun, Mon & eves Tues–Thurs; no kids), a semi-formal bar and bistro on Beach Approach, off the quayside. For a relaxed pint, try the *Blue Anchor* on Fore Street, with coal fires and low beams.

Totnes

Most of the Plymouth buses from Paignton and Torquay stop at **TOTNES**, on the west bank of the River Dart. The town has an ancient pedigree, its period of greatest prosperity occurring in the sixteenth century when this inland port exported cloth to France and brought back wine. Some handsome structures from that era remain, and there is still a working port down on the river, but these days Totnes has mellowed into a residential market town, popular with the alternative and New Age crowd.

The town centres on the long main street that starts off as Fore Street, site of the town's **museum** (mid-March to Oct Mon–Fri 10.30am–5pm; £1.50), occupying a four-storey Elizabethan house at no. 70. Showing how wealthy clothiers lived at the peak of Totnes's fortunes, it's packed with domestic objects and furniture, and also has a room devoted to local mathematician Charles Babbage, whose "analytical engine" was the forerunner of the computer. Fore Street becomes the **High Street** at the East Gate, a much retouched medieval arch. Beneath it, Rampart Walk trails off along the old city walls, curving round the fifteenth-century church of **St Mary**, a red sandstone building inside which you can see an exquisitely carved rood screen. Behind the church, the eleventh-century **Guildhall** (April–Sept Mon–Wed 10.30am–3.30pm; £1) was originally the refectory and kitchen of a Benedictine priory. Granted to the city corporation in 1553, the building still houses the town's Council Chamber, which you can see together with the former jail cells and courtroom.

Totnes **Castle** (daily: late March to June & Sept 10am–5pm; July & Aug 10am–6pm; Oct 10am–4pm; £2.30; EH) on Castle Street – leading off the High Street – is a classic Norman structure of the motte and bailey design, its simple crenellated keep atop a grassy mound offering wide views of the town and Dart valley. Totnes is the highest navigable point on the **River Dart** for seagoing vessels, and the starting point for **cruises to Dartmouth**, leaving from Steamer Quay (1hr 15min; £8 return; ☎01803/834488, ⓦwww.riverlink.co.uk). Riverside walks in either direction pass some congenial pubs, and near the railway bridge you can board a steam train on the **South Devon Railway**, which runs along the Dart to Buckfastleigh, adjacent to Buckfast Abbey (see p.348).

Practicalities

Totnes's **tourist office** is signposted off The Plains near the Safeway car park (Mon–Sat 9.30am–5pm; ☎01803/863168, ⓦwww.totnesinformation.co.uk). The best-value **accommodation** is at the friendly B&B, 3 Plymouth Rd, off the High Street, with simple rooms (☎01803/866917; ❷), or the *Elbow Room*, opposite the castle car park on North Street (☎01803/863480, ⓦwww.theelbowroom.totnes.co.uk; no smoking; ❸), in a 200-year-old cottage and cider press; neither place accepts credit cards. A smarter option is the atmospheric *Royal Seven Stars Hotel* on The Plains (☎01803/862125, ⓦwww.royalsevenstars.co.uk; ❺). The local YHA **hostel** (☎0870/770 5788, ⓔdartington@yha.org.uk; closed Sept to Easter; £11.95) is in a sixteenth-century cottage next to the River Bidwell, two miles from Totnes and half a mile from Shinner's Bridge (bus #X80 or #88).

The High Street has several good places to **eat** including ⚖ *Willow*, at no. 87 (☎01803/862605; closed Sun), with inexpensive vegetarian snacks, evening meals (Wed, Fri & Sat) and live music (Fri), and *Rumour*, at no. 30, serving coffees, snacks and good-value full meals such as homemade pizzas (☎01803/864682). Two of the nicest **pubs** are on the town's outskirts: the *Kingsbridge Inn* on Leechwell Street (off Kingsbridge Hill), and the *Steampacket*, by the riverside on St Peter's Quay (reached by walking west along The Plains), which is also good for evening meals.

A walkable couple of miles out of Totnes, **Dartington Hall** features a constant programme of films, performances and workshops – for details, call ☎01803/847070, or see ⓦwww.dartingtonarts.org.uk.

Dartmouth and around

South of Torbay, and eight miles downstream from Totnes, **DARTMOUTH** has thrived since the Normans recognized the trading potential of this deep-water port. Today its activities embrace fishing, freight and a booming leisure industry, as well as the education of the senior service's officer class at the Royal Naval College, built at the start of this century on a hill overlooking the port. Coming from Torbay, visitors to Dartmouth can save time and a long detour through Totnes by using the frequent ferries crossing over the Dart's estuary from Kingswear (£1; £3 for cars), the last one at around 10.45pm.

Behind the enclosed boat basin at the heart of town, the four-storey **Butterwalk**, built in the seventeenth century for a local merchant, is richly decorated with wood carvings. The timber-framed construction was restored after bombing in World War II, though still looks precarious as it overhangs the street on eleven granite columns. This arcade now holds shops and Dartmouth's small museum (Mon–Sat: April–Oct 10.30am–4.30pm; Nov–March noon–3pm; £1.50), mainly devoted to maritime curios, including old maps, prints and models of ships. Nearby **St Saviour's**, rebuilt in the 1630s from a fourteenth-century church, has long been a landmark for boats sailing upriver. The building stands at the head of Higher Street, the old town's central thoroughfare and the site of another tottering medieval structure, the *Cherub* inn. More impressive is **Agincourt House** on the parallel Lower Street, originally built by a merchant after the battle for which it is named.

Lower Street leads down to **Bayard's Cove**, a short cobbled quay lined with eighteenth-century houses, where the Pilgrim Fathers stopped en route to the New World. A twenty-minute walk from here along the river takes you to **Dart-mouth Castle** (April–June & Sept daily 10am–5pm; July & Aug daily 10am–6pm; Oct daily 10am–4pm; Nov–March Sat & Sun 10am–4pm; £3.60; EH), one of two fortifications on opposite sides of the estuary. The site includes coastal defence works from the nineteenth century and from World War II, though the main interest is in the fifteenth-century castle, the first in England to be constructed specifically to withstand artillery. If you don't relish the return walk, you can take the **ferry** back to town (Easter–Oct; every fifteen minutes; £1.50).

Continuing south along the coastal path brings you through the pretty hilltop village of **Stoke Fleming** to **Blackpool Sands**, the best and most popular beach in the area. The unspoilt cove, flanked by steep, wooded cliffs, was the site of a battle in 1404 in which Devon archers repulsed a Breton invasion force sent to punish the privateers of Dartmouth for their cross-Channel raiding.

From Dartmouth there are regular ferries across the river to **Kingswear**, terminus of the Paignton & Dartmouth Steam Railway (see p.338). Various **cruises** from Dartmouth's quay up the River Dart are the best way to see the deep creeks and the various houses overlooking the river, among them the **Royal Naval College** and **Greenway House**, birthplace of Walter Raleigh's three seafaring half-brothers, the Gilberts, and later rebuilt for Agatha Christie.

Practicalities

Dartmouth's **tourist office** is opposite the car park at Mayor's Avenue (Easter–Oct Mon–Sat 9.30am–5.30pm, Sun 10am–2pm; Nov–Easter Mon–Sat 9.30am–5pm; ☎01803/834224, ⓦwww.dartmouth-information.co.uk). The less expensive **accommodation** is either at the top of steep hills or strung along Victoria Road, a continuation of Duke Street. The hill-top choices are preferable for their views, including the spacious and elegant *Avondale* at 5 Vicarage Hill (☎01803/835831, ⓦwww.avondaledartmouth.co.uk; no credit cards; ❹), or, more centrally, *Café Caché*, 24 Duke St (☎01803/833804, ⓦwww.cafecache.co.uk; ❸), offers light and airy accommodation above a café/restaurant. The rooms above the 🎗 *Café Alf Resco* on Lower Street (☎01803/835880, ⓦwww.cafealfresco.co.uk; no credit cards; ❺) have character and charm, while the **café** itself is good for all-day break-fasts, steaming coffees and, on summer weekends, "rustic suppers", with occasional live music. Dartmouth's other **restaurants** include the ancient *Cherub Inn*, 13 Higher Street, and the *New Angel*, at 2 South Embankment (☎01803/839425; closed Sun eve & all Mon), run by celebrity chef John Burton-Race. One of the best eateries in town, it provides quality seafood at top prices, but the atmosphere is relaxed and there are harbour views.

Salcombe and around

The area between the Dart and Plym estuaries, the **South Hams**, holds some of Devon's comeliest villages and most striking coastline. The "capital" of the region, **Kingsbridge**, is a useful transport hub but lacks the appeal of **SALCOMBE**, almost at the mouth of the Kingsbridge estuary and Devon's southernmost resort, reachable on a summer ferry from Kingsbridge. Once a nondescript fishing village, Salcombe is now a full-blown sailing and holiday centre, its calm waters strewn with small pleasure-craft. Enough fishing activity and working boatyards remain to give the place a sense of purpose, while the ruined Fort Charles at the harbour entrance injects a touch of romance amid the villas and hotels. You can bone up on boating and local history at **Salcombe Maritime Museum** on Market Street, off the north end of the central Fore Street (Easter–Oct 10.30am–12.30pm & 2.30–4.30pm; £1). From a quay off Fore Street, you can take a **ferry** down to the beach at South Sands (Easter–Oct every 30min), from where it's a fifteen-minute climb to the excellent **Overbecks Museum** (mid-March to mid-July & Sept Mon–Fri & Sun 11am–5.30pm; mid-July to Aug daily 11am–5.30pm; Oct Mon–Thurs & Sun 11am–5pm; garden open daily all year 10am–6pm; £5; NT), which focuses on the area's natural history. There's great coastal walking south and west of here, eventually leading to sandy **beaches** at Thurlestone and, across the Avon estuary, Bigbury-on-Sea, while the path eastwards from **East Portlemouth** – accessible by ferry from Salcombe's quay – takes in some craggily photogenic scenery around Gammon Point and Prawle Point.

Salcombe's **tourist office** is on Market Street (Easter to mid-July, Sept & Oct daily 10am–5pm; mid-July to Aug Mon–Sat 9am–5pm, Sun 10am–5pm; Nov–March Mon–Thurs 10am–3pm, Fri & Sat 10am–5pm; ☏01548/843927, Ⓦwww.salcombeinformation.co.uk). Many of the town's **B&Bs** enjoy excellent estuary views, including *Rocarno* on Grenville Road (☏01548/842732, Ⓔrocarno@aol.com; ❷), and *Lemon Cottage*, Church Street (☏01548/842820, Ⓔsuecrabtree@yahoo.com; ❸) – both nonsmoking and neither takes credit cards. Part of Overbeck's Museum (see above) houses a YHA **hostel** (☏0870/770 6016; closed Nov to mid-April; £12.50).

For a lively **restaurant** in Salcombe, try *Captain Flint's*, 82 Fore St, which specializes in pastas and pizzas; in Kingsbridge, drop in to the boldly coloured *Pig Finca Café*, The Quay (☏01548/855777; closed Sun), which has Mediterranean dishes and weekly live music.

Plymouth and around

PLYMOUTH's predominantly bland and modern face belies its great historic role as a naval base and, in the sixteenth century, the stamping ground of such national heroes as John Hawkins and Francis Drake. It was from here that Drake sailed to defeat the Spanish Armada in 1588, and 32 years later the port was the last embarkation point for the Pilgrim Fathers, whose New Plymouth colony became the nucleus for the English settlement of North America. The importance of the city's Devonport dockyards made the city a target in World War II, when the Luftwaffe reduced most of the old centre to rubble. Subsequent reconstruction has done little to improve the place, though it would be difficult to spoil the glorious vista over **Plymouth Sound**, the basin of calm water at the mouth of the combined Plym, Tavy and Tamar estuaries, largely unchanged since Drake played his famous game of bowls on the Hoe before joining battle with the Armada.

One of the best local excursions from Plymouth is to **Mount Edgcumbe**, where woods and meadows provide a welcome antidote to the urban bustle,

Sir Francis Drake

Born around 1540 near Tavistock, **Francis Drake** worked in the domestic coastal trade from the age of 13, but was soon taking part in the first English slaving expeditions between Africa and the West Indies, led by his Plymouth kinsman John Hawkins. Later, Drake was active in the secret war against Spain, raiding and looting merchant ships in actions unofficially sanctioned by Elizabeth I. In 1572 he became the first Englishman to sight the Pacific, and soon afterwards, on board the *Golden Hind*, became the first one to circumnavigate the world, for which he received a knighthood on his return in 1580. The following year Drake was made mayor of Plymouth, settling in Buckland Abbey (see p.345), but was back in action before long – in 1587 he "singed the king of Spain's beard" by entering Cadiz harbour and destroying 33 vessels that were to have formed part of Philip II's **armada**. When the replacement invasion fleet appeared in the English Channel in 1588, Drake – along with Raleigh, Hawkins and Frobisher – played a leading role in wrecking it. The following year he set off on an unsuccessful expedition to help the Portuguese against Spain, but otherwise most of the next decade was spent in relative inactivity in Plymouth, Exeter and London. Finally, in 1596 Drake left with Hawkins for a raid on Panama, a venture that cost the lives of both captains.

and are within easy reach of some fabulous sand. East of Plymouth, the aristocratic opulence of **Saltram House** includes some fine art and furniture, while to the north you can visit Drake's old residence at **Buckland Abbey**.

The City

A good place to start a tour of the city is **Plymouth Hoe**, an immense esplanade studded with reminders of the great events in the city's history, and with glorious views over the sea. Alongside various war memorials stands a rather portly statue of Sir Francis Drake, gazing grandly out to the sea. Appropriately, there's a bowling green back from the brow. In front of the memorials, the red-and-white-striped **Smeaton's Tower** (daily: May–Oct 10am–4pm Nov–April 10am–3pm; £2.25, combined ticket with Plymouth Dome £6.50) was erected in 1759 by John Smeaton on the treacherous Eddystone Rocks, fourteen miles out to sea. When replaced by a larger lighthouse in 1882, it was reassembled here, where it gives lofty views over Plymouth Sound. Below Smeaton's Tower, **Plymouth Dome** (Easter–Sept daily 10am–5pm; Oct–Easter Tues–Sat 10am–4pm; last entry 1hr before closing; £4.75, combined ticket with Smeaton's Tower £6.50) has audiovisual exhibitions on Plymouth's history, Drake, the Mayflower Pilgrims and Captain Cook. On the seafront, Plymouth's **Royal Citadel** (May–Sept tours Tues & Thurs at 2.30pm; £3.50; EH) is an uncompromising fortress constructed in 1666, whose older sections, including the Governor's House and the Royal Chapel of St Katherine, can be seen on 75-minute tours (tickets from the Plymouth Dome and the tourist office).

At the nearby **Sutton Harbour**, the **Mayflower Steps** commemorate the sailing of the Pilgrim Fathers, with a plaque listing the names and professions of the 102 Puritans on board. Captain Cook's voyages to the South Seas, Australia and the Antarctic also started from here, as did the nineteenth-century transport ships to Australia, carrying thousands of convicts and colonists. Edging the harbour, the **Barbican** district is the heart of old Plymouth. Most of the buildings are now shops and restaurants, but off the quayside, New Street holds most of the oldest buildings, among them the **Elizabethan House** (June–Sept Tues–Sat 10am–5pm; £1.30), a captain's dwelling retaining most of the original architectural features. Cross the bridge over Sutton Harbour to reach the **National Marine Aquarium** (daily: April–Oct 10am–6pm; Nov–March 10am–5pm; last entry 1hr before closing; £8.75), a grand complex on three levels where a range of marine environments have been re-created, from moorland stream to coral reef and deep-sea ocean. The live exhibits include everything from sea horses to sharks.

Practicalities

Plymouth's **train station** is off Saltash Road (connected to the centre by bus #25 and #25a); the **bus station** is at Bretonside, just over St Andrew's Cross from Royal Parade; and the **tourist office** is off Sutton Harbour at 9 The Barbican (April–Oct Mon–Sat 9am–5pm, Sun 10am–4pm; Nov–March Mon–Fri 9am–5pm, Sat 10am–4pm; ☎0870/225 4950, ⓦwww.visitplymouth .co.uk). **Internet** access is available at the Carp Internet Café, 32 Frankfort Gate (Mon–Sat 9am–5pm).

The city's **accommodation** includes a row of B&Bs edging the Hoe on Citadel Road, including *Acorns and Lawns*, at no. 171 (☎01752/229474; no credit cards; ❶), and *The Beeches*, at no. 175 (☎01752/266475; ❶). On the west side of the Hoe, the smart *Bowling Green Hotel*, 9–10 Osborne Place, Lockyer Street (☎01752/209090, ⓦwww.bowlingreenhotel.com; no smoking; ❹), overlooks Francis Drake's fabled haunt, while *Osmond Guest House*, 42 Pier St (☎01752/229705, ⓦwww.osmondguesthouse.co.uk; no smoking; ❷), is nearer the Great Western Docks and offers a pick-up service from the bus and train stations. There's also an independent **hostel** at 172 Citadel Rd, *Globe Backpackers* (☎01752/225158, ⓔplymback@hotmail.com; £12), with double rooms (❶).

Plymouth's Barbican area has an eclectic range of **restaurants**: one of the best is *Piermaster's*, 3 Southside St (☎01752/229345; closed Sun), whose seafood is supplied straight from the harbour, while tasty Italian dishes draw the crowds at the more casual *Pasta Bar* across the road. At the top of Southside, the inexpensive *Tropical Sensation* on Notte Street serves Caribbean and African cuisine (closed daytime & all Sun). Plymouth Arts Centre, 38 Looe St, has a vegetarian restaurant (closed all Sun & Mon eve), as well as exhibitions, films and live performances (☎01752/206114, ⓦwww.plymouthac.org.uk).

The *Dolphin* **pub** on Southside Street serves simple lunchtime snacks and good ales, while *The Cooperage*, 134 Vauxhall St (☎01752/229275, ⓦwww .thecooperage.co.uk), has **live bands** and club nights.

Mount Edgcumbe, Saltram House and Buckland Abbey

Lying on the Cornish side of Plymouth Sound and visible from the Hoe, **MOUNT EDGCUMBE** features richly landscaped gardens and acres of rolling parkland and coastal paths. The **house** (April–Sept Mon–Thurs & Sun 11am–4.30pm; £4.50) is a reconstruction of the bomb-damaged Tudor original, though inside the predominant note is eighteenth-century, the rooms elegantly restored with authentic Regency furniture. Far more enticing are the impeccable **gardens** divided into French, Italian and English sections – the first two a blaze of flowerbeds adorned with classical statuary, the last an acre of sweeping lawn shaded by exotic trees – while the **park**, which is free and open all year, gives access to the coastal path. You can reach Edgcumbe by passenger **ferry** to Cremyll, leaving at least hourly from Admiral's Hard, a small mooring in Plymouth's Stonehouse district (bus #34 from Royal Parade), or, in summer, by direct motor launch from the Mayflower Steps to **Cawsand**, an old smugglers' haunt two hours' walk from the house. Cawsand itself is just a mile from the southern tip of the huge **Whitsand Bay**, the best bathing beach for miles around, though subject to dangerous shifting sands and fierce currents.

The remodelled Tudor **SALTRAM HOUSE** (daily except Fri: mid-March to Sept noon–4.30pm: Oct 11.30am–3.30pm: £7 including garden; NT), two miles east of Plymouth off the A38, is Devon's largest country house, featuring work by architect Robert Adam and fourteen portraits by **Joshua Reynolds**, who was born nearby in Plympton. The showpiece is the Saloon, a fussy but exquisitely furnished room dripping with gilt and plaster, and set off by a huge Axminster carpet especially woven for it in 1770. Saltram's landscaped **garden** (daily except Fri: mid-March to Sept 11am–5pm; Oct to mid-March 11am–4pm; Jan Sat & Sun only; Feb to mid-March closed Thurs & Fri; £3.50) provides a breather from this riot of interior design, though it's marred by the proximity of the road. You can get here on the hourly #22 bus (not Sun) from Royal Parade to Merafield Road, from where it's a fifteen-minute signposted walk.

Six miles north of Plymouth, close to the River Tavy and on the edge of Dartmoor, **BUCKLAND ABBEY** (mid-Feb to mid-March & Nov Sat & Sun 2–5pm; mid-March to Oct Mon–Wed & Fri–Sun 10.30am–5.30pm; Dec Sat & Sun 11am–5pm; £6, grounds only £3.20; NT) was once the most westerly of England's Cistercian abbeys. After its dissolution, Buckland was converted to a family home by the privateer Richard Grenville (cousin of Walter Raleigh), from whom the estate was acquired by Francis Drake in 1582, the year after he became mayor of Plymouth. It remained his home until his death, though the house reveals few traces of Drake's residence. There are, however, numerous maps, portraits and mementos of his buccaneering exploits on show, most famous of which is Drake's Drum, which was said to beat a supernatural warning of impending danger to the country. The house stands in majestic grounds which contain a fine fourteenth-century **Great Barn**, buttressed and gabled and larger than the abbey itself. To get here, take bus #83, #84 or #86 from Plymouth to Tavistock, changing at Yelverton for the hourly #55 minibus (not Sun).

Dartmoor

Occupying the main part of the county between Exeter and Plymouth, **DARTMOOR** is southern England's greatest expanse of wilderness, some 365 square miles of raw granite, barren bogland, sparse grass and heather-grown moor. It was not always so desolate, as testified by the remnants of scattered Stone Age settlements and the ruined relics of the area's nineteenth-century tin-mining industry. Today desultory flocks of sheep and groups of ponies are virtually the only living creatures to be seen wandering over the central fastnesses of the National Park, with solitary birds – buzzards, kestrels, pipits, stonechats and wagtails – wheeling and hovering high above.

The core of Dartmoor, characterized by tumbling streams and high tors chiselled by the elements, is **Dartmoor Forest**, which has belonged to the Duchy of Cornwall since 1307, though there is almost unlimited public access. Networks of signposts or painted stones exist to guide **walkers**, but map-reading abilities are a prerequisite for any but the shortest walks, and considerable

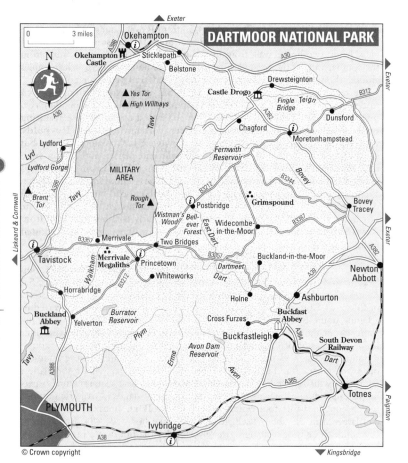

DARTMOOR NATIONAL PARK

experience is essential for longer distances. Overnight parking is only allowed in authorized places, and no vehicles are permitted beyond fifteen yards from the road; camping should be out of sight of houses and roads, and fires are strictly forbidden. Information on **guided walks** and riding facilities is available from National Park visitor centres in Dartmoor's major towns and villages, and from information points in smaller villages.

A significant portion of northern Dartmoor, containing the moor's highest tors and some of its most famous beauty spots, is run by the **Ministry of Defence**, whose firing ranges are marked by red and white posts; when firing is in progress, red flags or red lights signify that entry is prohibited. Generally, if no warning flags are flying by 9am between April and September, or by 10am from October to March, there will be no firing on that day; alternatively, check at ☎0800/458 4868 or ⓦwww.dartmoor-ranges.co.uk.

Princetown and the central moor

PRINCETOWN owes its growth to the proximity of Dartmoor Prison, a high-security jail originally constructed for POWs captured in the Napoleonic

Wars. The grim presence seeps into the village, which has a somewhat oppressed air and functional grey stone houses, some of them – like the parish church of St Michael – built by French and American prisoners. What Princetown lacks in beauty is amply compensated for by the surrounding countryside, the best of which lies immediately to the north.

Information on all of Dartmoor is given by the main **National Park information centre**, on the village's central green (daily: Easter–Oct 10am–5pm; Nov–March 10am–4pm; ☏01822/890414, ⓦ www.dartmoor-npa.gov.uk). One of the best **places to stay** locally is the nonsmoking *Duchy House* on Tavistock Road (☏01822/890552, ⓔ duchyhouse@aol.com; ❷; closed Nov). Two pubs in Princetown's central square also offer accommodation and standard bar **food**: the *Railway Inn* (☏01822/890232; ❷) and the *Plume of Feathers* (☏01822/890240; ❷), which claims to be the oldest building in town, and also offers dormitory accommodation in two bunkhouses as well as a convenient **campsite**.

Northeast of Princetown, two miles north of the crossroads at Two Bridges, the dwarfed and misshapen oaks of **Wistman's Wood** are an evocative relic of the original Dartmoor Forest, cluttered with lichen-covered boulders and a dense undergrowth of ferns. The gnarled old trees are alleged to have been the site of druidic gatherings, a story unsupported by any evidence but quite plausible in this solitary spot.

Three miles northeast of Two Bridges, the largest and best preserved of Dartmoor's **clapper bridges** crosses the East Dart river at **POSTBRIDGE**. Used by tin miners and farmers since medieval times, these simple structures consist of huge slabs of granite supported by piers of the same material; another more basic example is at Two Bridges. Postbridge has a useful **tourist office** in the car park near the bridge (Easter–Oct 10am–5pm; Nov & Dec Sat & Sun 10am–4pm; ☏01822/880272). If you're not content with strolling up and down the river here, you could venture south through **Bellever Forest** to the open moor where **Bellever Tor** (1453ft) affords outstanding views. On the edge of the forest, a mile or so south of Postbridge on the banks of the East Dart river, lies one of Dartmoor's three YHA **hostels** (☏0870/770 5692, ⓔ bellever@yha .org.uk; Nov–Feb flexible opening; £12.50) – it's on a minor road from Postbridge, accessible on Plymouth Citybus #98 from Tavistock, or else walk from Postbridge. There's also a **camping barn** close to Bellever Forest at Runnage Farm, with a bunkhouse and outdoor camping facilities as well as bikes to rent (for this and any of Dartmoor's other camping barns, it's wise to book ahead, particularly at weekends: ☏0870/770 8868, ⓔ campingbarns@yha.org.uk). You'll find more luxury in the riverside *Lydgate House Hotel*, signposted off the main road half a mile southwest of Postbridge and offering easy access to Bellever Forest and the moor (☏01822/880209, ⓦ www.lydgatehouse.co.uk; no under-12s; no smoking; ❻). Two miles northeast of Postbridge, the solitary *Warren House Inn* offers warm, firelit comfort and **meals** in an unutterably bleak tract of moorland.

To the east of the B3212, reachable on a right turn towards Widecombe-in-the-Moor, the Bronze Age village of **Grimspound** lies below Hameldown Tor, about a mile off the road. Inhabited some three thousand years ago, this is the most complete example of Dartmoor's prehistoric settlements, consisting of 24 circular huts scattered within a four-acre enclosure. The site is thought to have been the model for the Stone Age settlement in which Sherlock Holmes camped in *The Hound of the Baskervilles*; while **Hound Tor**, an outcrop three miles to the southwest, was the inspiration for Conan Doyle's tale – according to local legend, phantom hounds were sighted racing across the moor to hurl themselves on the tomb of a hated squire following his death in 1677. There's a **camping barn** here, *Great Houndtor*, with a cooking area and showers (☏0870/770 8868 or 01647/221202).

Widecombe-in-the-Moor and the southeastern moor

Four miles east of the crossroads at Two Bridges, **Dartmeet** marks the place where the East and West Dart rivers merge after tortuous journeys from their remote sources. Crowds home in on this beauty spot, but the valley is memorably lush and you don't need to walk far to leave the car park and ice-cream vans behind. From here the Dart pursues a more leisurely course, joined by the River Webburn near the pretty moorland village of **BUCKLAND-IN-THE-MOOR**, one of a cluster of moorstone-and-thatched hamlets on this southeastern side of the moor.

Four miles north, **WIDECOMBE-IN-THE-MOOR** is set in a hollow amid high granite-strewn ridges. Its church of **St Pancras** provides a famous local landmark, its pinnacled tower dwarfing the fourteenth-century main building, whose interior boasts a beautiful painted rood screen. The nearby **Church House** was built in the fifteenth century for weary churchgoers from outlying districts, and was later converted into almshouses. Widecombe's other claim to fame is the traditional song, *Widdicombe Fair*: the **fair** is still held annually on the second Tuesday of September. You could **stay** in Widecombe at the elegant *Old Rectory* (☏01364/621231, ✉rachel.belgrave@care4free.net; no smoking; no credit cards; ❷), opposite the post office and with a lovely garden, or, half a mile south, at *Higher Venton Farm* (☏01364/621235, ⓦwww.ventonfarm.com; no credit cards; ❷), a peaceful thatched longhouse where evening meals are served.

South of Buckland, the village of **HOLNE** is another rustic idyll surrounded on three sides by wooded valleys. The vicarage here was the birthplace of Charles Kingsley, author of *The Water Babies* and such Devon-based tales as *Westward Ho!*. A couple of miles east, the Dart weaves through a wooded green valley to enter the grounds of **Buckfast Abbey** (daily: May–Oct 9am–5.30pm; Nov–April 10am–4pm; free), a modern monastic complex on the site of an abbey founded in the eleventh century.

The northeastern moor

On the northeastern edge of the moor, the market town of **MORETON-HAMPSTEAD** makes an attractive entry point from Exeter. There's a Visitor **Information** Point at 10 The Square (Easter–Oct daily 9.30am–5pm; Nov–Easter Fri–Sun 10am–5pm; ☏01647/440043), and classy **accommodation** in Court Street on the western edge of the village: the *Old Post House* at no. 18 (☏01647/440900, ⓦwww.theoldposthouse.com; no credit cards; no smoking; ❷), and *Cookshayes*, at no. 33 (☏01647/440374, ⓦwww.cookshayes.co.uk; ❷; closed Nov–Feb). The village also has a first-rate **hostel**, *Sparrowhawk Backpackers*, at 45 Ford St (☏01647/440318, ⓦwww.sparrowhawkbackpackers.co.uk; £12), with some private rooms (❶), while the *Steps Bridge* YHA hostel (☏0870/770 6048, ✉bellever@yha.org.uk; closed Oct–Feb; £10) is three miles northeast, on the outskirts of **Dunsford**, on the boundary of the National Park – buses #359 (not Sun) and #82 stop nearby. Its woodland setting overlooking the Teign Gorge makes it a popular overnight stop for hikers.

Moretonhampstead has a historic rivalry with neighbouring **CHAGFORD**, a Stannary town (a chartered centre of the tin trade) that also enjoyed prosperity as a centre of the wool industry. It stands on a hillside overlooking the River Teign, with a fine fifteenth-century church and some good **accommodation** options, including the ancient *Three Crowns Hotel* (T01647/433444, Wwww .chagford-accom.co.uk; ❺), facing the church, and the sixteenth-century *Cyprian's Cot*, 47 New St (T01647/432256, Wwww.cyprianscot.co.uk. co.uk; no credit cards; no smoking; ❸). There's also a renowned and very expensive **restaurant**, the non-smoking *22 Mill Street* (T01647/432244, Wwww.22millstreet.co.uk; closed Sun and lunchtime Mon & Tues), which offers top-quality modern cuisine, and has two en-suite rooms for diners (❹).

Numerous **walks** can be made in the immediate vicinity, for instance downstream along the Teign to the twentieth-century extravaganza of **Castle Drogo** (mid-March to Oct Mon & Wed–Sun 11am–5.30pm; grounds daily 10.30am–dusk; £6.50, grounds only £4; NT), stupendously sited overlooking the Teign gorge. Having retired at the age of 33, grocery magnate Julius Drewe unearthed a link that suggested his descent from a Norman baron, and set about creating a castle befitting his pedigree. Begun in 1910, to a design by **Edwin Lutyens**, it was not completed until 1930, but the result was an unsurpassed synthesis of medieval and modern elements. Paths lead from Drogo east to **Fingle Bridge**, a noted beauty spot, where shaded green pools house trout and the occasional salmon. The *Fingle Bridge Inn* here has an adjoining **restaurant**.

The north and northwestern moor

The main centre on the northern fringes of Dartmoor, **OKEHAMPTON** grew prosperous as a market town for the medieval wool trade, and some fine old buildings survive between the two branches of the River Okement that meet here, among them the prominent fifteenth-century tower of the **Chapel of St James**. Across the road from the seventeenth-century town hall, a granite archway leads into the **Museum of Dartmoor Life** (Easter–Sept Mon–Sat

△ Dartmoor ponies

10.15am–4.30pm; £2.50), an excellent overview of habitation on the moor since the earliest times. Perched above the West Okement southwest of the centre, **Okehampton Castle** (daily: late March to June & Sept 10am–5pm; July & Aug 10am–6pm; £3; EH) is the shattered hulk of a stronghold laid waste by Henry VIII; its ruins include a gatehouse, Norman keep, and the remains of the Great Hall, buttery and kitchens.

Okehampton's station, which provides a useful Sunday **rail** connection with Exeter between late May and late September, lies a fifteen-minute walk up Station Road from Fore Street, where the **tourist office** (Mon–Sat 10am–5pm; ☎01837/53020, ⓦwww.okehamptondevon.co.uk) sits next to the museum. Nearby on Fore Street, the beamed *Fountain Hotel* (☎01837/53900; no smoking; ❹), an old coaching inn, has rooms with character, though cheaper **B&B** can be found a short walk north of here towards the station at *Meadowlea*, 65 Station Rd (☎01837/53200; no credit cards; ❷). Okehampton's YHA **hostel** (☎0870/770 5978, ⓔokehampton@yha.org.uk; closed Dec & Jan; £14) is housed in a converted goods shed at the station, and offers a range of outdoor activities.

Beyond its pubs and coffee shops, Okehampton's best **restaurant** is *The Pickled Walnut*, in a cellar hidden behind the church on Fore Street (☎01837/54242; no smoking; closed Sun, also eves Mon, Tues & Wed in winter), with a good, reasonably priced menu and a pleasant atmosphere.

Lydford

Five miles southwest of Okehampton, the village of **LYDFORD** boasts the sturdy but small-scale Lydford Castle, a Saxon outpost, then a Norman keep and later used as a prison. The chief attraction here, though, is **Lydford Gorge** (daily: April–Sept 10am–5.30pm; Oct 10am–4pm; Nov–March 10.30am–3pm; £4.50; NT), whose main entrance is a five-minute walk downhill. Two routes – one above, one along the banks – follow the ravine burrowed through by the River Lyd as far as the hundred-foot White Lady Waterfall, coming back on the opposite bank. Overgrown with thick woods, the one-and-a-half-mile gorge is alive with butterflies, spotted woodpeckers, dippers, herons and clouds of insects. The full course would take you roughly two hours at a leisurely pace, though there is a separate entrance at the south end of the gorge if you only want to visit the waterfall – the only part of the gorge open in winter.

Back in the village, the picturesque *Castle Inn*, right next to the castle, provides a beer garden and a fire-lit sixteenth-century bar for drinks and snacks, a quality **restaurant** in a curio-cluttered back room, and **accommodation** in oak-beamed rooms (☎01822/820242, ⓦwww.castleinnlydford.co.uk; ❹).

Tavistock

The main town of the western moor, **TAVISTOCK** owes its distinctive Victorian appearance to the building boom that followed the discovery of copper deposits here in 1844. Originally, however, this market and Stannary town on the River Tavy grew around what was once the West Country's most important Benedictine abbey, established in the eleventh century. Some scant remnants survive in the churchyard of **St Eustace**, a mainly fifteenth-century building with stained glass from William Morris's studio in the south aisle.

Tavistock's **tourist office** is in the town hall on Bedford Square (Easter–Oct Mon–Sat 9.30am–5pm, also Sun late July to early Sept; Nov–Easter Mon, Tues, Fri & Sat 9.30am–4.30pm; ☎01822/612938). Local **accommodation** includes *Kingfisher Cottage*, Mount Tavy Road (☎01822/613801, ⓔkingfisher .cott@btopenworld.com; no smoking; no credit cards; ❸), and, about half a mile east of Tavistock off the B3357 Princetown Road, *Mount Tavy Cottage* (T01822/614253, Wwww.mounttavy.freeserve.co.uk; ❸), set in a lush garden and offering organic breakfasts.

North of Tavistock, a four-mile lane wanders up to **Brent Tor**, 1130 feet high and dominating Dartmoor's western fringes. Access to its conical summit is easiest along a path gently ascending through gorse on its southwestern side, leading to the small church of St Michael at the top. Bleak, treeless moorland extends in every direction, wrapped in silence that's occasionally pierced by the shrill cries of stonechats and wheatears. A couple of miles eastwards, **Gibbet Hill** looms over Black Down and the ruined stack of the abandoned Wheal Betsy silver and lead mine.

6

DEVON AND CORNWALL | North Devon

North Devon

From Exeter the A377 runs alongside the scenic Tarka Line railway to **North Devon**'s major town, **Barnstaple**. Within easy reach of here, the resorts of **Ilfracombe** and **Woolacombe** draw the crowds, though the fine sandy beaches surrounding the latter give ample opportunity to find your own space. The river port of **Bideford** gives its name to a long bay that holds the precipitous village of **Clovelly**, a famous beauty spot. Away from the coast, there is plenty of scope for walking and cycling along the Tarka Trail, passing through some of the region's loveliest countryside. For a complete break, the tiny island of **Lundy** provides further opportunities for stretching the legs and clearing the lungs.

Barnstaple

BARNSTAPLE, at the head of the Taw estuary, makes an excellent North Devon base, being well connected to the resorts of Bideford Bay, Ilfracombe and

---

The Tarka Line and the Tarka Trail

North Devon makes no secret of its association with Henry Williamson's *Tarka the Otter* (1927), one of the finest pieces of nature writing in the English language. With parts of the book set in the Taw valley, it was inevitable that the Exeter to Barnstaple rail route – which follows the Taw for half of its length – should be dubbed the **Tarka Line**. Leaving almost hourly from Exeter St David's station, trains on this branch line cut through the sparsely populated heart of Devon, the biggest town en route being **Crediton**, ancient birthplace of St Boniface (patron saint of Germany and the Netherlands) and site of the bishopric before its transfer to Exeter in the eleventh century.

Barnstaple forms the centre of the figure-of-eight traced by the **Tarka Trail**, which tracks the otter's wanderings for a distance of over 180 miles. To the north, the trail penetrates Exmoor then follows the coast back, passing through Williamson's home village of **Georgeham** on its return to Barnstaple. South, the path takes in Bideford (see p.353), and continues as far as Okehampton (see p.349), before swooping up via Eggesford, the point at which the Tarka Line joins the Taw valley.

Twenty-three miles of the trail follow a former rail line that's ideally suited to **bicycles**, and there are bike rental shops at Barnstaple and Bideford. Sculptures have been placed along the route to mark its inclusion in the National Cycle Network. A good ride from Barnstaple is to **Torrington** (fifteen miles south), where you can eat at the *Puffing Billy* pub, formerly the train station.

Tourist offices sell a *Tarka Trail* booklet (£2) and give out free leaflets on individual sections of the trail.

51

Woolacombe, as well as to the western fringes of Exmoor. The town's centuries-old role as a marketplace is perpetuated in the daily bustle around the huge timber-framed **Pannier Market** off the High Street, alongside which runs **Butchers Row**, its 33 archways now converted to a variety of uses. Also off the High Street, in the pedestrianized area between it and Boutport Street, lies Barnstaple's **parish church**, itself worth a look, and the fourteenth-century **St Anne's Chapel**, converted into a grammar school in 1549 and later numbering among its pupils John Gay, author of *The Beggar's Opera*. At the end of Boutport Street, the **Museum of North Devon** (Mon–Sat 9.30am–5pm; free) is a lively miscellany that includes a collection of the eighteenth-century pottery for which the region was famous. The museum lies alongside the Taw, where footpaths make for a pleasant riverside stroll, with the colonnaded eighteenth-century **Queen Anne's Walk** – built as a merchants' exchange – providing some architectural interest and housing the **Barnstaple Heritage Centre** (April–Oct Mon–Sat 10am–5pm; Nov–March Mon–Fri 10am–4.30pm, Sat 10am–3.30pm; £2.50), which traces the town's social history by means of reconstructions and touch-screen computers.

Barnstaple's **tourist office** is at the Museum of North Devon (Mon–Sat 9.30am–5pm; ☎01271/375000, ⊛www.northdevon.com). Local **accommodation** includes the elegant but sometimes noisy *Ivy House,* Victoria Road, off Newport Road, five hundred yards south of Long Bridge (☎01271/325167; no credit cards; ❷), and, a little further out, on Landkey Road – a continuation of Newport Road – the excellent *Mount Sandford* (☎01271/342354; no credit cards; ❷), a Regency building with a beautiful garden. With your own transport, you could stay at *Broomhill Art Hotel*, Muddiford, signposted two miles north of Barnstaple off the A39, a striking combination of gallery, **restaurant** and hotel (☎01271/850262, ⊛www.broomhillart.co.uk; no credit cards; ❹).

You can pick up coffees and **snacks** at the *Old School Coffee House* (closed Sun), dating from 1659, on Church Lane, near St Anne's Chapel, while the coolly modern *PV*, 70 Boutport St (closed Sun), has a moderately priced upstairs **restaurant**; the ground floor becomes a wine bar in the evening.

Ilfracombe and around

The most popular resort on Devon's northern coast, **ILFRACOMBE** is essentially little changed since its evolution into a Victorian and Edwardian tourist centre, large-scale development having been restricted by the surrounding cliffs. In summer, if the crowds of holiday-makers become oppressive, you can escape on a coastal tour, a fishing trip or the fifteen-mile cruise to Lundy Island (see p.355), all available at the small harbour. On foot, you can explore the attractive stretch of coast running east out of Ilfracombe and beyond the grassy cliffs of Hillsborough, where a succession of undeveloped coves and inlets is surrounded by jagged slanting rocks and heather-covered hills. There are sandy **beaches** here, though many prefer those beyond **Morte Point**, five miles west of Ilfracombe, from where the view takes in Lundy. Below the promontory, the pocket-sized **Barricane Beach** is famous for the tropical shells washed up by Atlantic currents from the Caribbean. It's a popular swimming spot, though there's more space just south of here on the two miles of **Woolacombe Sands**, a broad, west-facing expanse much favoured by surfers and families alike. At the beach's more crowded northern end, a cluster of hotels, villas and retirement homes makes up the summer resort of **WOOLACOMBE**. At the quieter southern end lies the choice swimming spot of **Putsborough Sands** and the promontory of **Baggy Point**, where gannets, shags, cormorants and shearwaters gather from September to November. South of here, **Croyde Bay** is another surfers' delight, more compact than Woolacombe, with stalls on the sand renting surfboards and wet suits, while **Saunton Sands** is a magnificent long stretch of coast pummelled by endless ranks of classic breakers.

Practicalities

Ilfracombe's **tourist office** is at the Landmark on the seafront (Easter–July & Oct Mon–Sat 10am–5pm, Sun 10am–4pm; Aug & Sept daily 10am–5.30pm; Nov–Easter Mon–Fri 10am 5pm, Sat 10am 4pm; ☎01271/863001, ⓦwww .ilfracombe-tourism.co.uk), while Woolacombe's is on the Esplanade (April to late July and mid-Sept to Oct Mon–Thurs 10am–3pm, Fri & Sat 10am–5pm; late July to mid-Sept Mon–Sat 10am–5pm, Sun 10am–3pm; Nov–March Mon–Sat 10am–1pm; ☎01271/870553, ⓦwww.woolacombetourism.co.uk). Ilfracombe's numerous **accommodation** choices include *Wentworth House*, a Victorian B&B at the top of Church Hill on Belmont Road (☎01271/863048, ⓔwentworthhouse@tiscali.co.uk; no credit cards; ❷), *Sherborne Lodge Hotel*, Torrs Park (☎01271/862297, ⓦwww.smoothhound.co.uk; ❷), a roomy villa in a quiet area west of town, and *Ocean Backpackers*, an excellent independent **hostel** near the bus station and harbour at 29 St James Place (☎01271/867835, ⓦwww.oceanbackpackers.co.uk; £13), also offering double rooms (❶). In Woolacombe, *Sandunes* is one of a number of B&Bs on Beach Road (☎01271/870661, ⓦwww.sandwool.fsnet.co.uk; no smoking; no credit cards; ❷), with sea views. For **camping**, try *North Morte Farm*, near Morte Point (☎01271/870381, ⓦwww.northmortefarm.co.uk; closed Oct–Easter).

At the harbour, Ilfracombe's most famous **restaurant**, *11 The Quay* (☎01271/868091, ⓦwww.11thequay.co.uk; closed Sun eve and all Mon & Tues), is a quality seafood eaterie owned by artist Damien Hirst, with a relaxed ground-floor bar (open daily) serving tapas. In Woolacombe, surfers gather at the *Red Barn*, a popular **bar** and restaurant just behind the beach (closed Sun eve).

Bideford Bay

Like Barnstaple, nine miles to the east, the estuary town of **BIDEFORD** formed an important link in north Devon's trade network in the Middle Ages, mainly due to its **bridge**, which still straddles the River Torridge. A couple of miles downstream, the old shipbuilding port of **APPLEDORE**, lined with pastel-coloured Georgian houses, is worth a wander and a drink in one of its cosy pubs.

Bideford's **tourist office** is next to Victoria Park at the northern end of town (Easter–Sept Mon–Sat 10am–5pm, Sun 10am–1pm or 10am–4pm in July & Aug; Oct–Easter Mon, Tues, Thurs & Fri 10am–4.30pm, Wed & Sat 10am–1pm; ☎01237/477676, ⓦwww.torridge.gov.uk). **B&Bs** nearby include the *Cornerhouse*, 14 The Strand (☎01237/473722, ⓦwww.cornerhouse-guest house.co.uk; no credit cards; ❷), and the swankier *Mount* (☎01237/473748, ⓦwww.themount1.cjb.net; ❹), further out on Northdown Road, but linked to the centre by a footpath; both are nonsmoking. For a **meal** or a drink, head up Bridge Street to Market Place, where the porticoed *Old Coach Inn* provides ales and snacks.

Clovelly

West along Bideford Bay, picturesque **CLOVELLY** must have featured on more calendars, biscuit boxes and tourist posters than anywhere else in the West

Country. It was put on the map in the second half of the nineteenth century by two books: Charles Dickens' *A Message From the Sea* and *Westward Ho!* by Charles Kingsley, whose father was rector here for six years. To an extent, the character of the village has been preserved by limiting hotel accommodation and holiday homes, and restricting coach parties, though there's still a fairly regular stream of sightseers and it's best avoided altogether during school summer holidays.

Past the **visitor centre** (daily: April–Oct 9am–5pm; Nov–March 10am–4pm; £4.50) – walkers, cyclists and users of public transport have free access to the village via a separate entrance to the right – the cobbled, traffic-free main street plunges down past neat, flower-smothered cottages where sledges are tethered for transporting goods, the only way to carry supplies since the use of donkeys ended. At the bottom, Clovelly's stony beach and tiny harbour snuggle under a cleft in the cliff wall. If you can't face the return climb to the top of the village, there's a Land Rover service leaving every fifteen minutes or so from behind the *Red Lion* (Easter–Oct 9am–5.30pm; £2, or £3 return). From the visitor centre, a more level walk is possible along **Hobby Drive**, through woods of sycamore, oak, beech, rowan and holly, with grand views over the village.

Clovelly has just two **hotels**, both pricey: the *New Inn*, halfway down the High Street (℡01237/431303, @www.clovelly.co.uk; ❼), and the *Red Lion* at the harbour (℡01237/431237, @www.clovelly.co.uk; ❽). Below the *New Inn* is a small **B&B**, *Donkey Shoe Cottage* (℡01237/431601; no credit cards; ❷), and there's a greater selection of guest houses a twenty-minute walk up from the visitor centre in Higher Clovelly, including *Boat House Cottage* (℡01237/431209; ❶).

West to Hartland Point

You could drive along minor roads to **Hartland Point**, ten miles west of Clovelly, but the best approach is on foot along the coast path. The headland presents one of Devon's most dramatic sights, its jagged black rocks battered by the sea and overlooked by a solitary lighthouse 350ft up. South of Hartland Point, the saw-toothed rocks and near-vertical escarpments defiantly confront the waves, with spectacular waterfalls tumbling over the cliffs. This sheer stretch of coast has seen dozens of shipwrecks over the centuries, though many must have been prevented by the sight of the tower of fourteenth-century **St Nectan's** – a couple of miles south of the Point in the village of **STOKE** – which acted as a landmark to sailors before the construction of the lighthouse. At 128ft, it is the tallest church tower in north Devon, and inside the church boasts a finely carved rood screen and a Norman font beneath a wagon-type roof. Tea and scones are served at *Stoke Barton Farm*, just opposite (Easter–Sept Tues–Thurs, Sat & Sun).

Half a mile east of the church, gardens and lush woodland surround **Hartland Abbey** (April–June & Sept Wed, Thurs & Sun 2–5.30pm; July & Aug also Tues 2–5.30pm; gardens April–Sept daily except Sat 2–5.30pm; £6.50), an eighteenth-century country house incorporating the ruins of an abbey dissolved in 1539, and displaying fine furniture, old photographs and recently uncovered frescoes. **HARTLAND** itself, further inland, holds little appeal beyond its three pubs and café, but on the coast, **Hartland Quay** deserves a linger: once a busy port, financed in part by the mariners Raleigh, Drake and Hawkins, it was mostly destroyed by storms in the nineteenth century, and now holds a solitary pub and the excellent *Hartland Quay Hotel* (℡01237/441218; ❹), surrounded by beautiful slate cliffs. Alternatively, in Hartland itself, try the small, friendly

B&B, at 2 Harton Manor, The Square, off Fore Street (☎01237/441670; no credit cards; ❷), or, nearer Hartland Point, there's *West Titchberry Farm* (☎01237/441287; no smoking; no credit cards; ❷), for which you should follow signs for Hartland Lighthouse. Further south, at Elmscott, at the end of a three-and-a-half-mile signposted footpath from Hartland, and about half a mile from the sea, there's a YHA **hostel** in a converted Victorian schoolhouse (☎0870/770 5814; closed Oct–Easter; £11.95). The only public transport is bus #319 from Barnstaple; alight at Hartland.

Lundy Island

There are fewer than twenty full-time residents on **Lundy**, a tiny windswept island twelve miles north of Hartland Point. Now a refuge for thousands of marine birds, Lundy has no cars, just one pub and one shop – indeed little has changed since the Marisco family established itself here in the twelfth century, making use of the shingle beaches and coves to terrorize shipping along the Bristol Channel. Later, Lundy's most famous inhabitants included **William Hudson Heaven**, who bought the island in 1834 and established what became known as the "Kingdom of Heaven". His home, **Millcombe House**, an incongruous piece of Georgian architecture in the desolate surroundings, is one of many relics of former habitation scattered around the island, though a recent addition compared with the thirteenth-century **castle** standing on Lundy's southern end.

Inland, the grass, heather and bog is crossed by dry-stone walls and grazed by ponies, goats, deer and the rare soay sheep. The shores – mainly cliffy on the west, softer and undulating on the east – shelter a rich variety of **birdlife**, including kittiwakes, fulmars, shags and Manx shearwaters, which often nest in rabbit burrows. The most famous birds, though, are the **puffins** after which Lundy is named – from the Norse *Lunde* (puffin) and *ey* (island). They can only be sighted in April and May, when they come ashore to mate. Offshore, **grey seals** can be seen all the year round.

Practicalities

The MS *Oldenburg* sails to Lundy up to six times a week from Bideford or Ilfracombe between April and October, taking around two hours from both places. Day-return tickets cost around £28, period returns £47; to reserve a place, call ☎01271/863636 (day returns can also be booked from local tourist offices). Between November and March, a helicopter service from Hartland Point (see p.354) takes over, taking just seven minutes (currently Mon & Fri at midday, £77 return).

Accommodation on the island is managed by the Landmark Trust and can be booked for weekly rentals months in advance, though shorter B&B bookings can only be made within two weeks of the proposed visit. Outside the holiday season it is possible to find a double room for under £50 per night – contact the Landmark Trust to make a booking (☎01628/825925, ⓦwww.landmarktrust.org.uk). Options range from the remote *Admiralty Lookout* (lacking electricity and with only hand-pumped water), through the two-storey granite *Barn*, a hostel sleeping fourteen, to the comfortable *Old House*, where Charles Kingsley stayed in 1849, and the *Old Light*, a lighthouse built in 1820 by the architect of Dartmoor Prison. There's also a **campsite** open throughout the year, though it can get pretty rainy and windswept in winter. More information on transport and accommodation can be found on the island's website, ⓦwww.lundyisland.co.uk.

Exmoor

A high bare plateau sliced by wooded combes and splashing streams, **EXMOOR** can be one of the most forbidding landscapes in England, especially when shrouded in a sea mist. When it's clear, though, the moorland of this National Park reveals rich swathes of colour and an amazing diversity of wildlife, from buzzards to the unique **Exmoor ponies**, a species closely related to prehistoric horses. In the treeless heartland of the moor in particular, it's not difficult to spot these short and stocky animals, though fewer than twelve hundred are registered, and of these only about two hundred are free-living on the moor. Much more elusive are the **red deer**, England's largest native wild animal, of which Exmoor supports the country's only wild population, currently around two and half thousand.

Endless permutations of **walking routes** are possible along a network of some six hundred miles of footpaths and bridleways, and **horseback riding** is another option for getting the most out of Exmoor's desolate beauty – visitor centres can supply details of guided walks and local stables. Whether walking or riding, bear in mind that over seventy percent of the National Park is privately owned and that access is theoretically restricted to public rights of way; special permission should certainly be sought before camping, canoeing, fishing or similar.

Inland, there are four obvious bases for walks, all on the Somerset side of the county border: **Dulverton** in the southeast, site of the main information facilities; **Simonsbath** in the centre; **Exford**, near Exmoor's highest point of Dunkery Beacon; and the attractive village of **Winsford**, close to the A396 on the east of the moor. Exmoor's coastline offers an alluring alternative to the open moorland, all of it accessible via the **South West Coast Path**, which embarks on its long coastal journey at **Minehead**, though there is more charm to be found further west at the sister villages of **Lynmouth** and **Lynton**, just over the Devon border.

Dulverton

The village of **DULVERTON**, on the southern edge of the National Park, is the Park Authority's headquarters and so makes a good introduction to Exmoor. Information on the whole moor is available at the **visitor centre**, 7 Fore St (daily 10am–5pm; ℡01398/323841, ⓦwww.exmoor-nationalpark .gov.uk). Dulverton's best **accommodation** is *Town Mills* (℡01398/323124, ⓦwww.townmillsdulverton.co.uk; ❸), an old mill house in the centre of the village; alternatively try the *Lion Hotel* in Bank Square (℡01398/323444; ❹), or *Tongdam*, a Thai restaurant off 26 High St (℡01398/323397) with one double (❷) and a self-catering suite (❹). A mile north of Dulverton, Northcombe Farm has two **camping barns** as well as basic camping facilities (℡01398/323602). Both the *Lion* and *Tongdam* offer moderately priced **meals**.

Winsford, Exford and Dunkery Beacon

Just west of the A396 five miles north of Dulverton, **WINSFORD** lays good claim to being the moor's prettiest village. A scattering of thatched cottages ranged around a sleepy green, it is watered by a confluence of streams and rivers – one of them the Exe – giving it no fewer than seven bridges. The *Royal Oak*, a thatched and rambling old inn on the village green, offers drinks, snacks and full restaurant **meals**, though room rates are high (℡01643/851455, ⓦwww .royaloak-somerset.co.uk; ❻). On Halse Lane, *Karslake House* (℡01643/851242, www.karslakehouse.co.uk; no under-12s; ⑤) offers excellent **B&B** and serves evening meals (not Sun eve or Mon eve).

The hamlet of **EXFORD**, an ancient crossing point on the River Exe, is popular with hunting folk as well as with walkers for the four-mile hike to **Dunkery Beacon**, Exmoor's highest point at 1700ft. Local **accommodation** includes *Exmoor Lodge*, a friendly B&B on Chapel Street (☎01643/831694; no smoking; ②), and Exmoor's main YHA **hostel**, a rambling Victorian house in the centre (☎0870/770 5828, ✉exford@yha.org.uk; closed Sun Sept–June, also Mon Nov–Jan; £12.50).

Exmoor Forest and Simonsbath

6

At the heart of the National Park lies **Exmoor Forest**, the barest part of the moor, scarcely populated except by roaming sheep and a few red deer – the word "forest" denotes simply that it was a hunting reserve. In the middle of it stands the village of **SIMONSBATH** (pronounced "Simmonsbath"), home to the Knight family, who bought the forest in 1818 and, by introducing tenant farmers, building roads and importing sheep, brought systematic agriculture to an area that had never before produced any income. The Knights also built a wall round their land – parts of which can still be seen – as well as the intriguing Pinkworthy (pronounced "Pinkery") Pond, four miles to the northwest, whose exact function remains unexplained.

Simonsbath makes a good base for hikes on the moor, though **accommodation** is limited to the *Exmoor Forest Inn* (☎01643/831341, ⓦwww.exmoorforestinn.co.uk; no smoking; ⑤), studded with hunting trophies, and the *Simonsbath House Hotel* (☎01643/831259, ⓦwww.simonsbathhouse.co.uk; ⑤), former home of the Knights and now a cosy bolt-hole offering elegant rooms and a good but expensive **restaurant**. In a converted barn next to the hotel, *Boevey's* offers coffees and lunches (closed Dec & Jan), while a couple of miles outside the village on the Brayford Road, the *Poltimore Arms* at **Yarde Down** is a classic country **pub** serving excellent food.

Minehead and Dunster

The Somerset port of **MINEHEAD** quickly became a favourite Victorian watering hole with the arrival of the railway, and it has preserved an upbeat holiday-town atmosphere ever since. Steep lanes link the two quarters of **Higher Town**, on North Hill, containing some of the oldest houses, and **Quay Town**, the harbour area. It's in Quay Town that the **Hobby Horse** performs its dance in the town's three-day May Day celebrations, snaring maidens under its prancing skirt and tail in a fertility ritual resembling the more famous festivities at the Cornish port of Padstow (see p.377).

The **tourist office** is midway between Higher Town and Quay Town at 17 Friday St, off the Parade (Mon–Sat 10am–12.30pm & 1.30–4/5pm; ☎01643/702624, ⓦwww.visit-exmoor.info). **Accommodation** options include the *Old Ship Aground* right by the harbour on Quay Road (☎01643/702087; ②) and, a few minutes' walk from the tourist office, *Kildare Lodge* on Townsend Road (☎01643/702009; ⑤), a reconstructed Tudor inn designed by a pupil of Lutyens. There's a YHA **hostel** a couple of miles southeast, outside the village of Alcombe (☎0870/770 5968, ✉minehead@yha.org.uk; £11.95; limited opening Sept–March), in a secluded combe on the edge of Exmoor.

Minehead is a terminus for the **West Somerset Railway**, which curves eastwards into the Quantocks as far as Bishops Lydeard (see p.323). The area's major attraction, the old village of **DUNSTER**, is about a mile from the line's

The South West Coast Path, Britain's longest footpath, starts at Minehead and tracks the coastline along Devon's northern seaboard, round Cornwall, back into Devon, and on to Dorset, where it finishes close to the entrance to Poole Harbour. The path was conceived in the 1940s, but it was just over 25 years ago that – barring a few significant gaps – the full **630-mile route** opened, much of it on land owned by the National Trust, and all of it well signposted.

The relevant Ordnance Survey **maps** can be found at most village shops en route, while Aurum Press (ⓦwww.aurumpress.co.uk) publishes four National Trail Guides covering the route, and the **South West Coast Path Association** (ⓣ01752/896237, ⓦwww.swcp.org.uk) publishes an annual guide (£8) to the whole path, including accommodation lists, ferry timetables and transport details.

6

DEVON AND CORNWALL | Exmoor

first stop, three miles inland. Dunster's main street is dominated by the towers and turrets of its **castle** (mid-March to Oct Mon–Wed, Sat & Sun 11am–5pm; early Nov Mon–Wed, Sat & Sun 11am–4pm; grounds daily: mid-March to Oct 10am–5pm; Nov to mid-March 11am–4pm; £7.50, grounds only £4.10; NT), most of whose fortifications were demolished after the Civil War. The castle then became something of an architectural showpiece, and subject to a thorough Victorian restoration. Tours take in various portraits of the Luttrells, owners of the house for six hundred years; a bedroom once occupied by Charles I; a fine seventeenth-century carved staircase; and a richly decorated banqueting hall. The grounds include terraced gardens and riverside walks, with drama productions and other events staged here in the summer (call ⓣ0870/240 4068 for details). The nearby hilltop tower is a folly, **Conygar Tower**, dating from 1776.

Below the castle, relics of Dunster's wool-making heyday include the octagonal **Yarn Market** in the High Street, dating from 1609, while the three-hundred-year-old **water mill** at the end of Mill Lane is still used commercially for milling the various grains which go to make the flour and muesli sold in the shop (April to early Nov daily except Fri 11am–4.45pm; July–Sept also Fri; £2.50; NT) – the café, overlooking its riverside garden, is a good spot for lunch. There's a **National Park Centre** at the top of Dunster Steep by the main car park (daily 10am–5pm; ⓣ01643/821835), and **accommodation** at the traditional *Yarn Market Hotel*, 25–31 High St (ⓣ01643/821425, ⓦwww .yarnmarkethotel.co.uk; ❺), whose rooms overlook the Yarn Market.

Porlock

Six miles west of Minehead and cupped on three sides by the hogbacked hills of Exmoor, **PORLOCK** draws armies of tourists attracted to its thatch-and-cob houses and dripping charm. Many come in search of the village's literary links: according to Coleridge's own less than reliable testimony, it was a "man from Porlock" who broke the opium trance in which he was composing *Kubla Khan*, while the High Street's beamed *Ship Inn* features prominently in the Exmoor romance *Lorna Doone* and, in real life, sheltered the poet Robert Southey. Two miles west over reclaimed marshland, the tiny harbour of **PORLOCK WEIR** is a tranquil spot for a breath of sea air and a drink.

Porlock's **tourist office** is at West End, High Street (April–Oct Mon–Fri 10am–1pm & 2–5pm, Sat 10am–5pm, Sun 10am–1pm; Nov–Easter Tues–Fri 10.30am–1pm, Sat 10am–2pm; ⓣ01643/863150, ⓦwww.porlock.co.uk), where you'll also find a good choice of **accommodation**, including the Victorian *Lorna Doone Hotel* (℡01643/862404, ⓦwww.lornadoonehotel.co.uk; ❷), and *The Cottage*, a smaller and quainter B&B (℡01643/862996; ❸), as well as the *Whortleberry Tearoom* (closed Sun). All three places serve snacks, **meals** and teas.

Lynton and Lynmouth

Nine miles west of Porlock, just inside Devon, the Victorian resort of **LYNTON** perches above a lofty gorge with splendid views over the sea. Almost completely cut off from the rest of the country for most of its history, the village struck lucky during the Napoleonic Wars, when frustrated Grand Tourists – unable to visit their usual continental haunts – discovered in Lynton a domestic piece of Swiss landscape. Coleridge and Hazlitt trudged over to Lynton from the Quantocks, but the greatest spur to the village's popularity came with the publication in 1869 of R.D. Blackmore's Exmoor melodrama *Lorna Doone*, a book based on the outlaw clans who inhabited these parts in the seventeenth century.

Lynton is connected by **cliff railway** (March to mid-July & mid-Sept to Nov daily 9am–7pm; mid-July to mid-Sept daily 9am–9pm; £2.75 return) with **LYNMOUTH**, five hundred feet below at the junction and estuary of the East and West Lyn rivers. The spot was described by Gainsborough as "the most delightful place for a landscape painter this country can boast", and Shelley spent nine weeks here with his 16-year-old bride Harriet Westbrook, during which time he wrote his polemical *Queen Mab* (two different houses claim to have been the Shelleys' love nest). At the top of the village, you can explore the walks, waterfalls and an exhibition on the uses of waterpower in the wooded **Glen Lyn Gorge** (daily 10am–dusk; exhibition closed Nov–Easter; £3, gorge only £2). You can also pick up details here of various **boat trips** that depart from the harbour in summer.

Practicalities

The local **tourist office** is in Lynton's town hall on Lee Road (Mon–Sat 9.30/10am–4/5pm, Sun 10am–2/4pm; ℡0845/660 3232, ⓦwww.lynton-lynmouth-tourism.co.uk). Lynton has the better choice of budget

---

Walks from Lynton and Lynmouth

In addition to the coastal path, there are several popular walks inland in this region. The one-and-a-half-mile tramp to **Watersmeet**, for example, follows the East Lyn River to where it's joined by Hoar Oak Water, a tranquil spot transformed into a roaring torrent after a bout of rain. From the fishing lodge here – now open as a café and shop in summer – you can branch off on a range of less-trodden paths, such as the three-quarters-of-a-mile route south to **Hillsford Bridge**, the confluence of Hoar Oak and Farley Water.

North of Watersmeet, a path climbs up **Countisbury Hill** and the higher **Butter Hill** (nearly 1000ft), affording great views of Lynton, Lynmouth and the north Devon coast, and there's also a track leading to the lighthouse at **Foreland Point**, close to the coastal path. East from Lynmouth you can reach the point via a fine sheltered shingle beach at the foot of Countisbury Hill – one of a number of tiny coves that are easily accessible on either side of the estuary.

From Lynton, an undemanding expedition takes you west along the North Walk, a mile-long path leading to the **Valley of the Rocks**, where the steep heathland is dominated by rugged rock formations and grazed by herds of wild goats.

accommodation, including the friendly, Victorian B&B *The Turret*, 33 Lee Rd
(☎01598/753284, ⓦwww.turrethotel.co.uk; no smoking; no under-14s; ❷),
and the whitewashed, Georgian *St Vincent House*, Castle Hill (☎01598/752244,
ⓦwww.st-vincent-hotel.co.uk; no smoking; ❹; closed Jan & Feb), with beautifully furnished rooms. There's also a YHA **hostel** in a homely Victorian
house about one mile inland from Lynton's centre, signposted off Lynbridge
Road (☎0870/770 5942, ⒺLynton@yha.org.uk; limited opening Nov–Easter;
£11.95). In Lynmouth, central accommodation choices include *Riverside
Cottage*, above a busy teashop on Riverside Road (☎01598/752390, ⓦwww
.riversidecottage.co.uk; ❸), and the posh *Shelley's*, next to the Glen Lyn Gorge
(☎01598/753219, ⓦwww.shelleyshotel.co.uk; ❹), where you can stay in the
room supposed to have been occupied by the poet.

In Lynmouth, the **restaurant** at *St Vincent House* specializes in French and
Belgian recipes (closed Mon, also Tues & Wed in winter; expensive), while traditional English dishes and lower prices can be found at the *Kensington Tearooms*
on Castle Hill (☎01598/753591; closed Tues); both places are nonsmoking.

Cornwall

When D.H. Lawrence wrote that being in **Cornwall** was "like being at a
window and looking out of England", he wasn't just thinking of its geographical extremity. Virtually unaffected by the Roman conquest, Cornwall was for
centuries the last haven for a **Celtic culture** elsewhere eradicated by the Saxons
– a land where princes communed with Breton troubadours, where chroniclers
and scribes composed the epic tales of Arthurian heroism, and where itinerant
monks from Welsh and Irish monasteries disseminated an elemental and visionary Christianity. Primitive granite crosses and a crop of Celtic saints remain as
traces of this formative period, and though the Cornish language had ebbed
away by the eighteenth century, it is recalled in Celtic place-names that in many
cases have grown more exotic as they have mutated over time.

Another strand of Cornwall's folkloric character comes from the **smugglers**
who thrived here right up until the nineteenth century, exploiting the sheltered
creeks and hidden anchorages of the southern coasts. For many fishing villages,
contraband provided an important secondary income, as did the looting of the
ships that regularly came to grief on the reefs and rocks. Cornwall has also had
a strong **industrial economy**, based mainly on the mining of **copper** and
tin in the north, centred on the towns of Redruth and St Agnes, and in the
south on the deposits of **china clay**, which are still being mined in the area
around St Austell.

Nowadays, of course, Cornwall's most flourishing industry is tourism. The
repercussions of the holiday business have been uneven, for instance cluttering
Land's End with a tacky leisure complex but leaving Cornwall's other great
headland, **Lizard Point**, undeveloped. The thronged resorts of **Falmouth**, site
of the impressive new National Maritime Museum, and **Newquay**, the West's
chief surfing centre, have successfully adapted to the demands of mass tourism,
but its effects have been more destructive in smaller, quainter places, such as

Mevagissey, **Polperro** and **Padstow**, whose genuine charms can be hard to make out in full season. Other villages, such as **Fowey**, **Charlestown, Port Isaac** and **Boscastle**, still preserve an authentic feel, however, while you couldn't wish for anything more remote than **Bodmin Moor**, a tract of wilderness in the heart of Cornwall, or the **Isles of Scilly**, idyllically free of development. It would be hard to compromise the sense of desolation surrounding **Tintagel**, site of what is fondly known as King Arthur's Castle, or the appeal of the seaside resorts of **St Ives** and **Bude** – both with great surfing beaches – while near St Austell, the spectacular **Eden Project**, located in an abandoned clay pit, celebrates environmental diversity with visionary style.

From Looe to Veryan Bay

The southeast strip of the Cornish coast holds a string of medieval harbour towns interspersed with long stretches of magnificent coastline. The main rail stop is **St Austell**, capital of Cornwall's china clay industry, though there is a branch line connecting nearby **Par** with the north coast at Newquay. To the east of St Austell Bay, touristy **Looe** and **Polperro** are easily accessible by bus from Plymouth, and there's a rail link to Looe from Liskeard. The estuary town of **Fowey**, in a niche of Cornwall closely associated with the author Daphne Du Maurier, is most easily reached by bus from St Austell and Par, as is **Mevagissey**, to the west.

Looe and Polperro

LOOE was drawing crowds as early as 1800, when the first "bathing-machines" were wheeled out, but the arrival of the railway in 1879 was what really packed its beaches. Though the river-divided town now touts itself as something of a shark-fishing centre, most people come here for the sand, the handiest stretch being the beach in front of East Looe. Away from the rivermouth, you'll find cleaner water a mile eastwards at **Millendreath**. Most of Looe's attractions are in boating and bathing, so it's hardly surprising that the **Old Guildhall Museum** on Higher Market Street (Easter & late May to Sept Mon–Fri & Sun 11.30am–4.30pm; £1.50) includes a collection of maritime models among its exhibits; equally interesting are the fifteenth-century building's preserved prison cells and raised magistrates' benches.

East Looe's **tourist office** is at the New Guildhall, on Fore Street (Easter & May to mid-Sept daily 10am–5pm; April & mid-Sept to Oct daily 10am–2pm; ☎01503/262072). **Accommodation** in East Looe includes the three-storey *Sea Breeze* B&B, close to the beach and harbour in Lower Chapel Street (☎01503/263131, ⊛www.cornwallexplore.co.uk/seabreeze; ❷); in West Looe, there's the Victorian *St Aubyn's* on Marine Drive (☎01503/264351, ⊛www .staubyns.co.uk; no smoking; no under-7s; ❹; closed Nov–March), a mile west of the centre in the Hannafore district, with great sea views. The town abounds in inexpensive **places to eat**, including the seventeenth-century *Golden Guinea* on Fore Street, that does a brisk trade in staple seaside meals and cream teas.

Looe is linked by frequent buses with neighbouring **POLPERRO**, a smaller and quainter place, but with a similar feel. From the bus stop and car park at the top of the village, it's a five- or ten-minute walk alongside the River Pol to the pretty harbour. The surrounding cliffs and the tightly packed houses rising on each side of the stream have an undeniable charm, and the tangle of lanes is little changed since the village's heyday of pilchard fishing and smuggling, but the "discovery" of Polperro has almost ruined it, and its straggling main street – the Coombes – is now an unbroken row of tourist shops and fast-food outlets. The best places to **stay** include *The House on Props*, Talland Street (℡01503/272310; no smoking; no credit cards; ❹; closed Nov–Jan), and the central but relatively secluded *Old Mill House*, an agreeable pub on Mill Hill (℡01503/272362, ⓦwww.oldmillhouse.i12.com; ❸). There's a separate **restaurant** at the *Old Mill*, though vegetarians and seafood fans will do better at *The Kitchen* on the Coombes (℡01503/272780; eves only; closed Oct–Easter).

Fowey

The ten miles west from Polperro to Polruan are among south Cornwall's best stretches of the coastal path, giving access to some beautiful secluded sand beaches. There are frequent ferries across the River Fowey from Polruan, affording a fine prospect of the quintessential Cornish port of **FOWEY** (pronounced "Foy"), a cascade of neat, pale terraces at the mouth of one of the peninsula's greatest rivers. The major port on the county's south coast in the fourteenth century, Fowey finally became so ambitious that it provoked Edward IV to strip the town of its military capability, though it continued to thrive commercially, becoming the leading port for china clay shipments in the nineteenth century.

Fowey's steep layout centres on the distinctive fifteenth-century church of **St Fimbarrus**. Behind it stands **Place House**, an extravagance belonging to the local Treffry family, with a Victorian Gothic tower grafted onto the fifteenth- and sixteenth-century fortified building. Below the church, the **Ship Inn**, sporting some fine Elizabethan panelling and plaster ceilings, held the local Roundhead HQ during the Civil War. From here, Fore Street, Lostwithiel Street and the Esplanade fan out, the **Esplanade** leading to a footpath that gives access to some splendid coastal walks. Past the remains of a blockhouse that once supported a defensive chain hung across the river's mouth, the small beach of **Readymoney Cove** is soon reached, close to the ruins of **St Catherine's Castle**, built by Thomas Treffry on the orders of Henry VIII and offering fine views across the estuary.

Practicalities

Separated from eastern routes by its river, Fowey is most accessible by #25 and #25b **buses** from St Austell. The **tourist office**, at 5 South St (April–Oct Mon–Fri 9.30am–5.30pm, Sat 9.30am–5pm, Sun 10am–5pm; Nov–March Mon–Sat 9.30am–5pm, Sun 10.30am–4pm; ℡01726/833616, ⓦwww.fowey .co.uk), also houses the **Daphne Du Maurier Literary Centre**, a small exhibition of the author's life and work, and can provide information on the ten day Daphne Du Maurier Festival of Arts and Literature (℡01726/223535, ⓦwww .restormel.gov.uk/daphne), which takes place each May. Most of the town's pubs offer **B&B**; try the *Ship Inn* on Trafalgar Square (℡01726/832230; ❸) or the *Safe Harbour*, at the town's bus stop on Lostwithiel Street (℡01726/833379; ❸), which has less character but good views. More centrally, there's the ⚲ *Globe Posting House Hotel*, 19 Fore St (℡01726/833322, ⓦwww.globepostinghouse .co.uk; ❷), offering clean, modern accommodation in an old building, and two miles north of town near Golant, a YHA **hostel** at the Georgian mansion *Penquite House*, with views over the valley (℡0870/770 5832, ⓔgolant@yha .org.uk; closed Dec & Jan; £15.50).

Fore Street is the place for **restaurants**, with the elegant but relaxed *Q*, by the waterside at the sumptuous *Old Quay House Hotel* at no. 28 (℡01726/833302; expensive), serving top-quality seafood, and the friendly, moderately-priced restaurant at the *Globe Posting House Hotel* (see above) dishing up great food. *Sam's* at no. 20 (no credit cards; closed Mon lunch) has an eclectic menu and a fun atmosphere, with its more upmarket offshoot *Sam's The Other Place*, at no. 41 (closed Sun), serving burgers and 25 flavours of ice cream at the takeaway counter on the ground floor. The area is also well provided with good **pubs**, such as Golant's *Fisherman's Arms*, the *Old Ferry Inn* at Bodinnick and Polruan's excellent *Lugger Inn*.

St Austell and around

It was the discovery of china clay, or kaolin, in the downs to the north of **ST AUSTELL** that spurred the town's growth in the eighteenth century. An essential ingredient in the production of porcelain, kaolin had until then only been produced in northern China, where a high ridge, or *kao-lin*, was the sole known source of the raw material. Still a vital part of Cornwall's economy, the clay is now mostly exported for use in the manufacture of paper, as well as paint and medicines. The conical spoil heaps left by the mines are a feature of the local landscape, especially on Hensbarrow Downs to the north, the great green and white mounds making an eerie sight.

St Austell's nearest link to the sea is at **CHARLESTOWN**, an easy downhill walk from the centre of town. This unspoilt port is still used for china clay shipments, and provides a backdrop for the location filming that frequently takes place here. Behind the harbour, the **Shipwreck & Heritage Centre** (March–Oct daily 10am–6pm, last entry 5pm; £5.95) is entered through tunnels once used to convey the clay to the docks, and shows a good collection of photos and relics as well as tableaux of historical scenes.

On each side of the dock, the coarse sand and stone **beaches** have small rock pools, above which cliff walks lead around St Austell Bay. The bay's easternmost limit is marked by **Gribbin Head**, near which stands Menabilly House, where Daphne Du Maurier lived for 24 years – it was the model for the "Manderley" of *Rebecca*. The house is not open to the public, but you can walk down to Polridmouth Cove, where Rebecca met her watery end.

Eden Project

A disused clay pit four miles northeast of St Austell holds Cornwall's highest-profile attraction, the **Eden Project** (daily: April–Oct 10am–6pm, closes 10pm Mon–Thurs late July; Nov–March 10am–4.30pm; last entry 90min before closing; £12.50; ⓦwww.edenproject.com), reachable on bus #T9 from St Austell station, #T10 from Newquay (Easter–Oct) and #T11 from Truro and Falmouth (June–Sept). Occupying a 160-foot-deep crater whose awesome scale only reveals itself once you have passed the entrance at its lip, the project showcases the diversity of the planet's plant life in an imaginative, sometimes wacky, but refreshingly ungimmicky style. The whole site is stunningly landscaped with an array of various crops and flowerbeds, but at centre stage are the vast geodesic "biomes", or conservatories made up of ecofriendly Teflon-coated, hexagonal panels. One cluster holds groves of olive and citrus trees, cacti and other plants more usually found in the warm, temperate zones of the Mediterranean, southern Africa and southwestern USA, while the larger group contains plants from the tropics, including teak and mahogany trees, and there's a waterfall and river gushing through. Equally impressive are the external grounds, where plantations of bamboo, tea, hops, hemp and tobacco are interspersed with brilliant swathes of flowers. The whole "living theatre" presents a constantly changing spectacle, and should ideally be visited in different seasons. Allow at least half a day for a full exploration, but arrive early – or take advantage of the extended opening in summer – to avoid congestion. There are timed "story-telling" sessions, a lawn-carpeted arena where world, jazz and other music is performed, and abundant good food on hand – consult the website for events.

Note that anyone arriving at the site by bike or on foot gets a discount and can skip the queues by going straight to the fast-track ticket window. The area is well served with **bike routes** along a network of Clay Trails, including a route from St Austell station direct to Eden; see below for bike rental and accommodation in the area.

Practicalities

St Austell makes an unexciting place to stay, but there's a good **accommodation** option near the Eden Project at *Treberthan*, a farmhouse at Bodelva, halfway between Par and the site and just fifteen minutes from Eden via a footpath (℡01726/817711; no smoking; no credit cards; ❸). In Charlestown, try *T'Gallants* (℡01726/70203; ❸), a smart Georgian B&B at the back of the harbour, or *Broad Meadow House*, behind the Shipwreck Centre on Quay Road (℡01726/76636, ⓦwww.broadmeadowhouse.com; no credit cards; ❸), which, as well as B&B, offers "tent and breakfast", with family-size tents in a meadow by the sea. Behind *T'Gallants*, the *Rashleigh Arms* offers real ale and a range of **food**.

To **rent a bike**, contact Bugle Bike Hire in the village of Bugle, five miles north of St Austell on the A391 and a little less than that west of the Eden Project (Easter to mid-Oct; ℡01726/852285). Alternatively, Happy Trails (℡01726/852058, ⓦwww.happytrailsbikerides.co.uk) arranges accompanied bike rides from Bugle and other pick-up points around the network of Clay Trails that crisscross the area.

Mevagissey to Veryan Bay

MEVAGISSEY was once known for the construction of fast vessels, used for carrying contraband as well as pilchards. Today the tiny port might display a few stacks of lobster pots, but the real business is tourism, and in summer the maze of backstreets is saturated with day-trippers, converging on the inner harbour and overflowing onto the large sand beach at **Pentewan** a mile to the north. A couple of miles north of Mevagissey lie the **Lost Gardens of Heligan** (daily: April–Oct 10am–6pm, last entry 4.30pm; Nov–March 10am–5pm, last entry 3.30pm; £7.50), a fascinating Victorian garden which had fallen into neglect and was resurrected by Tim Smit, the visionary instigator of the Eden Project (see p.363). A boardwalk takes you through a jungle and under a canopy of bamboo and ferns down to the Lost Valley, where there are lakes, woods and wild-flower meadows.

Four miles south of Mevagissey juts the striking headland of **Dodman Point**, cause of many a wreck and topped by a stark granite cross built by a local parson as a seamark in 1896. The promontory holds the substantial remains of an Iron Age fort, with an earthwork bulwark cutting right across the point. Curving away to the west, the elegant parabola of **Veryan Bay** holds a string of exquisite inlets and coves, such as **Hemmick Beach**, a fine place for a dip with rocky outcrops affording a measure of privacy, and **Porthluney Cove**, a crescent of sand whose centrepiece is the battlemented **Caerhays Castle** (mid-March to May Mon–Fri 12.15–4pm; gardens mid-Feb to May daily 10am–5.30pm, last entry 4.30pm; house £5.50, garden £5.50, combined ticket £9.50), built in 1808 by John Nash and surrounded by beautiful gardens. A little further on,

△ Mevagissey

minuscule and whitewashed **Portloe** is fronted by jagged black rocks that throw up fountains of seaspray, giving it a good, end-of-the-road feel.

Practicalities

From St Austell's train station or Trinity Street, **buses** #25, #25B and #526 run to Mevagissey; Portloe is reachable on #T51 from Truro. There's an independent **tourist office** in the Sunny Corner car park (Easter–May, Sept & Oct Mon–Fri 10am–3pm; June–Aug Mon–Sat 10am–5pm, Sun 11am–4pm;

☎0870/443 2928, ⊛www.mevagissey-cornwall.co.uk), and **Internet** access at Mevagissey Telecottage, 14 Church St (Mon–Fri 9am–5pm, Sat 9am–12.30pm). In the heart of Mevagissey, the best **accommodation** option is the fifteenth-century *Fountain Inn* (☎01726/842320; ❸), on Cliff Street, off East Quay; alternatively there's the spacious Queen Anne *Lawn House*, set back from the harbour at 1 Church Lane (☎01726/842754, ⊛www.lawnhouse.co.uk; no under-16s; no smoking; no credit cards; ❹; phone ahead Nov–Easter). The nearest YHA **hostel** (☎0870/770 5712, ⓔboswinger@yha.org.uk; closed Nov–March; £12.50) is at **Boswinger**, a remote spot half a mile from Hemmick Beach and about a mile from Gorran Church Town, which is served infrequently by bus #526.

Mevagissey's **restaurants** specialize in fish: try *Roovray's*, 12 Church St (☎01726/842672), or the Portuguese *Alvorada*, 17 Church St (closed daytime except for Sun lunch in summer, also Mon & Tues Nov–Feb; ☎01726/842055). The *Fountain Inn* and the *Ship Inn* on Fore Street both offer pub grub.

Truro, Falmouth and St Mawes

Lush tranquillity collides with frantic tourist activity around **Carrick Roads**, the complex estuary basin to the south of **Truro**, the Cornish capital. At the mouth of the Carrick Roads, **Falmouth** is the major resort around here, and the site of one of Cornwall's mightiest castles, Pendennis. Its sister fort lies across the Carrick Roads in **St Mawes**, the main settlement on the **Roseland** peninsula, a luxurious backwater of woods and sheltered creeks between the River Fal and the sea.

Truro

TRURO, seat of Cornwall's law courts and other county bureaucracies, has the busy, no-nonsense feel of a provincial centre, its Georgian houses reflecting the prosperity that came with the tin-mining boom of the 1800s. Its modern shopping centre stands alongside the powerful but chronologically confused **Cathedral** (Mon–Sat 7.30am–6pm, Sun 7.30am–5pm; £3 donation requested), at the bottom of Pydar Street. Completed in 1910, it incorporates part of the fabric of the old parish church that previously occupied the site. The airy interior's best feature is its neo-Gothic baptistry, complete with emphatically pointed arches and elaborate roof vaulting. To the right of the choir, St Mary's aisle is a relic of the original Perpendicular building, other fragments of which adorn the walls, including – in the north transept – a colourful Jacobean memorial to local Parliamentarian John Robartes and his wife.

Truro's other unmissable attraction is the **Royal Cornwall Museum** (Mon–Sat 10am–5pm; free), housed in an elegant Georgian building on River Street. The exhibits include minerals, Celtic inscriptions and paintings by Cornish artists.

The town's **tourist office** is on Boscawen Street (April–Oct Mon–Fri 9am–5.30pm, Sat 9am–1pm; June–Aug Sat open till 5pm; Nov–March Mon–Fri 9am–5pm; ☎01872/274555, ⊛www.truro.gov.uk). Buses stop nearby at Lemon Quay, or near the train station on Richmond Hill. Best **accommodation** near the train station is *Gwel-Tek Lodge*, 49 Treyew Rd (☎01872/276843, ⊛www.cornwall-online/gweltek; ❸), while the Georgian *Bay Tree* lies halfway between the station and the centre at 28 Ferris Town (☎01872/240274, ⊛www.baytree-guesthouse.co.uk; ❶). At the bottom of Lemon Street, the very central *Royal Hotel* (℡01872/270345, ⓦwww.royalhotelcornwall.co.uk; ❺) has a modern, business-like feel.

Truro's **restaurants** range from *Feast*, 15 Kenwyn St (℡01872/272546; closed eves & all Sun), serving excellent vegetarian dishes as well as a choice of organic wines and Belgian beers, to *Saffron*, 5 Quay St (℡01872/263771; closed Sun), offering inexpensive brunches, seafood specials and a good-value early-evening menu. Among the **pubs**, you'll find coffee, good ale and decent bar meals at the *Wig and Pen*, on the corner of Frances and Castle streets, and at the next door *Globe Inn*.

Falmouth

The construction of Pendennis Castle on the southern point of Carrick Roads in the sixteenth century prepared the ground for the growth of **FALMOUTH**, then no more than a fishing village. Its prosperity was assured with the building of a deepwater harbour and with the port's establishment in 1689 as the base of the fast Falmouth Packets, which sped mail to the Americas. In recent years, waves of tourists have been drawn to its lush beaches, and, at the southern end of the long High Street and its continuations Market and Church streets, to its newest attraction, the **National Maritime Museum Cornwall** (daily 10am–5pm; £6.50), on the quayside off Arwenack Street. On three levels, the museum exhibits vessels from all over the world, many of them suspended in midair in the cavernous Flotilla Gallery. Smaller galleries examine specific aspects of boat-building, seafaring history, Falmouth's packet ships and Cornwall's various other links with the sea, including fishing.

A few minutes' walk west of the museum, **Pendennis Castle** stands sentinel at the tip of the promontory that separates Carrick Roads from Falmouth Bay (April–June & Sept Mon–Fri & Sun 10am–5pm, Sat 10am–4pm; July & Aug Mon–Fri & Sun 10am–6pm, Sat 10am–4pm; Oct–March daily 10am–4pm; £4.60; EH). The extensive fortification shows little evidence of its five-month siege by the Parliamentarians during the Civil War, which ended only when half its defenders had died and the rest had been starved into submission. Though this is a less-refined contemporary of the castle at St Mawes (see opposite), its site wins hands down, facing right out to sea on its own pointed peninsula, the stout ramparts offering the best all-round views of Carrick Roads and Falmouth Bay. Round Pendennis Point, south of the centre, a long sandy bay holds a succession of sheltered **beaches**: from the popular **Gyllyngvase Beach**, you can reach the more attractive **Swanpool Beach** by cliff path, or walk a couple of miles further on to **Maenporth**, from where there are some fine cliff-top walks.

Practicalities

Falmouth's **tourist office** is off the Prince of Wales Pier at 11 Market Strand (April–Sept Mon–Sat 9.30am–5.15pm; July & Aug also Sun 9.45am–1.45pm; Oct–March Mon–Fri 9.30am–5.15pm; ℡01326/312300, ⓦwww.go-cornwall.com). Most of the town's **accommodation** is near the train station and beach, including the Victorian *Melvill House Hotel*, 52 Melvill Rd (℡01326/316645, ⓦwww.melvill-house-falmouth.co.uk; no smoking; ❸), with sea or harbour views. More centrally, the *Arwenack Hotel*, 27 Arwenack St (℡01326/311185; no credit cards; ❷), offers basic, good-value accommodation, with a great view from the top room. The clean and friendly *Falmouth Lodge* backpackers' **hostel** is near the beach at 9 Gyllyngvase Terrace (℡01326/319996, ⓦwww.falmouthbackpackers.co.uk; no smoking; £14), with use of kitchen and **Internet** access.

Arwenack Street has two cool, contemporary and very busy **café/restaurants**, *Blue South* at nos. 35–37 (℡01326/212122) and *Hunky Dory* at no. 46 (℡01326/212997). On Gyllyngvase Beach, you can tuck in to grills and pizzas at the *Gylly Beach Café & Bar*, which has a lively feel and stays open in the evenings in summer (with live music on Tuesday). The *Quayside Inn*, on Arwenack Street, is the pick of the **pubs**, with outdoor tables overlooking the harbour.

St Mawes and the Roseland peninsula

At the end of a prong of land at the bottom of Carrick Roads, the secluded, unhurried town of **ST MAWES** is accessible by frequent **ferry** from Falmouth's Prince of Wales Pier. At the end of the walled seafront stands the small and pristine **St Mawes Castle** (April–June & Sept daily 10am–5pm; July & Aug daily 10am–6pm; Oct daily 10am–4pm; Nov–March Fri–Mon 10am–4pm; £3.60; EH). Built during the reign of Henry VIII to a cloverleaf design, the castle owes its excellent condition to its early surrender during the Civil War when it was besieged by Parliamentary forces in 1646. The dungeons and gun installations contain various artillery exhibits as well as some background on local social history.

Outside St Mawes, you could spend a pleasant afternoon poking around the Roseland peninsula between the Percuil River and the eastern shore of Carrick Roads. Two and a half miles north, the scattered hamlet of **ST JUST-IN-ROSELAND** holds the strikingly picturesque church of St Just standing right next to the creek, surrounded by palms and subtropical shrubbery, its gravestones tumbling down to the water's edge. In summer, there's a **ferry** from St Mawes to the southern arm of the Roseland Peninsula, which holds the equally charming twelfth- to thirteenth-century church of **St Anthony-in-Roseland**.

Practicalities

St Mawes makes an attractive – if pricey – **place to stay**. The best budget choices are a ten-minute walk up from the seafront on Newton Road, and all are run by the same family: *Newton Farm* (℡01326/270427; ❸), *Little Newton* (℡01326/270664; ❹) and *Lower Meadow* (℡01326/270036; ❹) – the latter has the best views and all are nonsmoking, with spacious rooms and friendly hosts. For location, the *St Mawes Hotel* is right on the seafront with glorious views over the estuary (℡01326/270266; ⓦwww.stmaweshotel.co.uk; ❻). The bar and brasserie here offer great views, while the *Victory Inn* is a fine old oak-beamed **pub** just off the seafront, which also serves seafood meals.

The Lizard peninsula

The **Lizard peninsula** – from the Celtic *lys ardh*, or "high point" – preserves a thankfully undeveloped appearance. If this flat and treeless expanse can be said to have a centre, it is **Helston**, a junction for buses running from Falmouth and Truro and for services to the spartan villages of the peninsula's interior and coast. The most useful **buses** are #T1, #T2 and the #T3 "Lizard Rambler", which links all the villages.

The east coast to Lizard Point

To the north of the peninsula, the snug hamlets dotted around the **River Helford** are a complete contrast to the rugged character of most of the Lizard.

Upstream, outside the village of Gweek, lies the **Gweek Seal Sanctuary** (daily: summer 10am–5pm; winter 10am–4pm; £10.50), a rehabilitation and release centre for injured seals. On the south side of the estuary, **Frenchman's Creek**, one of a splay of creeks and arcane inlets running off the river, was the inspiration for Daphne Du Maurier's novel of the same name – her evocation of it holds true: "still and soundless, surrounded by the trees, hidden from the eyes of men".

You can get over to the south bank by the seasonal ferry from Helford Passage to **Helford**, an agreeable old smugglers' haunt worth a snack stop – pub lunches are available in the *Shipwright's Arms*, whose garden overlooks the river. South of here, on the B3293, the broad, windswept plateau of Goonhilly Downs is interrupted by the futuristic saucers of Goonhilly Satellite Station and the nearby ranks of wind turbines. East, the road splits: left to **ST KEVERNE**, an inland village whose tidy square is flanked by two pubs and a church, right to **COVERACK**, a fishing port at one end of a sheltered bay. There's a handful of **places to stay** here, including the friendly *Fernleigh* (☏01326/280626; no credit cards; ❷) on Chymbloth Way, a turn-off from Harbour Road, which has wonderful bay views, and the smaller *Bakery Cottage* (☏01326/280474; no credit cards; ❶), right by the seafront. There's a YHA **hostel** just west of Coverack overlooking the bay (☏0870/770 5780, ⓔcoverack@yha.org.uk; closed Nov–March; £12.50). For **eating**, the *Lifeboat House Seafood Restaurant* (☏01326/280899; closed Mon & Oct–Easter) is pricey and often fully booked, but the fish is superb, and you can pick up first-class fish and chips from the attached takeaway.

Beyond the safe and clean swimming spot of **Kennack Sands**, the south tip of the promontory and mainland Britain's southernmost point, **Lizard Point** is marked by a plain lighthouse and a couple of low-key cafés and gift shops. Sheltered from the ceaselessly churning sea, a tiny cove holds a disused lifeboat station. From the point, a road and footpath lead a mile inland to the nondescript village called simply **THE LIZARD**, with several **accommodation** options including *Caerthillian*, a comfortable Victorian guest house (☏01326/290019; no credit cards; ❷), *Parc Brawse House* (☏01326/290466; ⓦwww.cornwall-online .co.uk/parcbrawsehouse; ❸), and *Penmenner House* (☏01326/290370; no credit cards; ❸): all are nonsmoking and in or near the village centre. Signposted from The Lizard, a Victorian villa houses a YHA **hostel** right on the coast, with majestic views (☏0870/770 6120, ⓔlizard@yha.org.uk; closed Nov–March; £15.50). In the village, the *Top House* pub provides **snacks**.

A mile west, the peninsula's best-known beach, **Kynance Cove**, has sheer hundred-foot cliffs, stacks and arches of serpentine rock and offshore outcrops. The water quality here is excellent – but take care not to be stranded by the tide.

The west coast

Four miles north of Kynance Cove, the inland village of **MULLION** has a fifteenth- to sixteenth-century church dedicated to the Breton **St Mellane** (or Malo), with a dog-door for canine churchgoers. In Mullion's centre, behind an enclosed garden at the top of Nansmellyon Road, *The Old Vicarage* (☏01326/240898, ⓦwww.s-h-systems.co.uk; no credit cards; ❹) provides elegant **accommodation**, while *Campden House*, just outside the village on The Commons (☏01326/240365; no credit cards; ❷), lies ten minutes' walk from the sea and serves snacks and evening meals. There's a small beach at **Mullion Cove**, sheltered behind a lovely harbour and more rock stacks, though the neighbouring sands at **Polurrian** and **Poldhu**, to the north, are better and attract surfers. At the cliff edge, the Marconi Monument marks the spot from which the first transatlantic radio transmission was made in 1901.

Three miles further north, strong currents make it unsafe to swim at the beautiful beach at **Loe Bar**, a strip of shingle which separates the freshwater **Loe Pool** from the sea. The elongated Pool is one of two places claiming to be where the sword Excalibur was restored to its watery source (the other is on Bodmin Moor), and the path running along its western shore as far as Helston, five miles north, makes a fine **walk**.

Another three or four miles up the coast, **PORTHLEVEN** once served to export tin ore from the inland Stannary town of **HELSTON**, the main centre on the Lizard peninsula. The town is best known for its **Furry Dance** (or Flora Dance), which dates from the seventeenth century. Held on May 8 (unless this falls on Sun or Mon, when the procession takes place on the nearest Sat), it's a stately procession of top-hatted men and summer-frocked women performing a solemn dance through the town's streets and gardens. You can learn something about it and absorb plenty of other local history in the eclectic **Helston Folk Museum** (Mon–Sat 10am–1pm, closes 4pm school holidays; £2), housed in former market buildings behind the Guildhall on Church Street. Helston has the peninsula's only **tourist office** at 79 Meneage St (Mon–Fri 10am–1pm & 2–4.30pm, Sat 10am–1pm; Aug closes 4pm on Sat; ☎01326/565431, ⓦwww .go-cornwall.com). For a drink or a **pub** snack, check out the 🥂 *Blue Anchor*, 50 Coinagehall St, a fifteenth-century monastery rest house, now a cramped pub with flagstone floors and mellow Spingo beer brewed on the premises. Across the road, the 500-year-old *Angel* hotel (☎01326/572701; ❷) offers basic **accommodation**.

The Penwith peninsula

Though more densely populated than the Lizard, the **Penwith peninsula** is a more rugged landscape, with a raw appeal that is still encapsulated by **Land's End**, despite the commercial paraphernalia superimposed on that headland. The seascapes, the quality of the light and the slow tempo of the local fishing communities made this area a hotbed of artistic activity towards the end of the nineteenth century, when the painters of Newlyn, near **Penzance**, established a distinctive school of painting. More innovative figures – among them Ben Nicholson, Barbara Hepworth and Naum Gabo – were soon afterwards to make **St Ives** one of England's liveliest cultural communities, and their enduring influence is illustrated in the St Ives branch of the Tate Gallery, showcasing the modern artists associated with the locality.

Penwith is far more easily toured than the Lizard, with a road circling its coastline and a better network of public transport from the two main towns, St Ives and Penzance, which also have most of the accommodation.

Penzance and around

Occupying a sheltered position at the northwest corner of Mount's Bay, **PENZANCE** has always been a major port, but most traces of the medieval town were obliterated at the end of the sixteenth century by a Spanish raiding party. Today the dominant style of Penzance is Georgian, particularly at the top of **Market Jew Street** (from *Marghas Jew*, meaning "Thursday Market"), which climbs from the harbour and the train and bus stations. At the top of the street is the green-domed Victorian **Market House** before which stands a statue of **Humphry Davy** (1778–1829), the local woodcarver's son who pioneered the science of electrochemistry and invented the life-saving miners' safety-lamp which his statue holds.

Turn left here into **Chapel Street**, which has some of the town's finest buildings, including the flamboyant **Egyptian House**, built in 1835 to contain a geological museum but subsequently abandoned until its restoration thirty years ago. Across the street, the **Union Hotel** dates from the seventeenth century, and originally housed the town's assembly rooms: news of Admiral Nelson's victory at Trafalgar and the death of Nelson himself was first announced from the minstrels' gallery here in 1805.

West of Chapel Street on Morrab Road, the excellent **Penlee House Gallery and Museum** (Mon–Sat: Easter–Sept 10am–5pm; Oct–Easter 10.30am–4.30pm; £2, free on Sat) features works of the Newlyn School

The Isles of Scilly

The **Isles of Scilly** are a compact archipelago of about a hundred islands, 28 miles southwest of Land's End. None is bigger than three miles across, and only five of them are inhabited – **St Mary's**, **Tresco**, **Bryher**, **St Martin's** and **St Agnes**. In the annals of folklore, the Scillies are the peaks of the submerged land of Lyonesse, a fertile plain that extended west from Penwith before the ocean broke in, drowning the land and leaving only one survivor to tell the tale. In fact they form part of the same granite mass as Land's End, Bodmin Moor and Dartmoor, and despite rarely rising above a hundred feet, they possess a remarkable variety of landscape. Points of interest include irresistible **beaches**, such as Parr Beach on St Martin's; the Southwest's greatest concentration of **prehistoric remains**; some fabulous **rock formations**; and the exuberant **Tresco Abbey Gardens** (daily 10am–4pm; £8.50). Along with tourism, the main source of income is flower-growing, for which the equable climate and the long hours of sunshine – their name means "Sun Isles" – make the islands ideal. The profusion of **wild flowers** is even more noticeable than the fields of narcissi and daffodils, and the heaths and pathways are often dense with marigolds, gorse, sea thrift, trefoil and poppies, not to mention a host of more exotic varieties introduced by visiting foreign vessels. The waters hereabouts are held to be among the country's best for **diving**, while between May and September, on a Wednesday or Friday evening, the islanders gather for **gig races**, performed by six-oared vessels – some over a hundred years old and thirty feet in length.

Free of traffic, theme parks and amusement arcades, the islands are a welcome respite from the tourist trail, the main drawbacks being the high cost of reaching the islands and the shortage of **accommodation**, most of which is on the main isle of St Mary's. All the islands except Tresco have campsites, though these usually close in the winter; camping rough is not allowed. The islands are accessible by sea or air. **Boats** to St Mary's, operated by the Isles of Scilly Steamship Group (☎0845/710 5555, ⓦwww.ios-travel.co.uk), depart from Penzance's South Pier between April and October, the crossing lasting about two and three-quarter hours. The main departure points for **flights** (also run by the Isles of Scilly Steamship Group) are Land's End, near St Just, Newquay, Exeter, Bristol and Southampton; in winter, there are departures only from Land's End and Newquay. British International (☎01736/363871, ⓦwww.scillyhelicopter.co.uk) also runs **helicopter** flights (20min) to St Mary's and Tresco from the heliport a mile east of Penzance. Launches link each of the inhabited islands, though these are sporadic in winter. The **tourist office** is in Hugh Town, St Mary's (Easter–Oct Mon–Fri 9am–6pm, Sat 9am–5pm; Nov–Easter Mon–Fri 9am–5pm; ☎01736/422536, ⓦwww.simplyscilly.co.uk).

– impressionistic harbour scenes, frequently sentimentalized but often bathed in an evocatively luminous light; there are also displays on local history.

Practicalities

Penzance's **tourist office** (May–Sept Mon–Fri 9am–5.30pm, Sat 9am–5pm, Sun 10am–1pm; Oct–April Mon–Fri 9am–5pm, Sat 10am–1pm; ☏01736/362207, Ⓦwww.go-cornwall.com) is right next to the train and bus stations on the seafront. Penzance Computers, 36b Market Jew St, provides **Internet** access. **Accommodation** choices on Chapel Street include the historic *Union Hotel* (☏01736/362319; ❸), but most of the B&Bs are west of the centre around Morrab Road, where you'll find *Kimberley House* at no. 10 (☏01736/362727, Ⓦwww.kimberleyhousepenzance.co.uk; no smoking; no credit cards; ❸). On the seafront, the nonsmoking *Camilla House Hotel* is useful for the harbour at 12 Regent Terrace, off the Promenade (☏01736/363771, Ⓦwww.camillahouse-hotel.co.uk; ❹). The tidy and friendly *Penzance Backpackers* **hostel** (☏01736/363836, Ⓦwww.pzbackpack.com; £13), which also has private rooms (❶), is on Alexandra Road, parallel to Morrab Road, and there's a YHA hostel in a Georgian mansion at Castle Horneck, Alverton (☏0870/770 5992, Ⓔpenzance@yha.org.uk; £15.50), a two-mile walk or take bus #5 or #6 from Penzance station to the *Pirate Inn*, from where it's signposted.

Coco's on Chapel Street is good for coffees, cakes, beer and tapas. Vegetarians will feel at home at *Yam Parlour*, 36 Causeway Head, a combined café/restaurant/photo gallery (☏01736/366740), and at *Brown's*, above a health shop in Bread Street, open daytime and on alternate Friday evenings for a buffet (closed Sun). On the Promenade, *The Olive Farm* sells delicious rolls and other takeaway snacks. Chapel Street has a couple of characterful **pubs**, the *Admiral Benbow*, crammed with gaudy ships' figureheads and other nautical items, and the *Turk's Head*, the town's oldest inn, reputed to date back to the thirteenth century.

St Michael's Mount

Frequent buses from Penzance leave for Marazion, five miles east, the access point to **St Michael's Mount** (late March to Oct Mon–Fri & Sun 10.30am–5.30pm; Nov to late March Mon, Wed & Fri, call to check times ☏01736/710507; £5.50; NT), a couple of hundred yards offshore. A vision of the archangel Michael led to the building of a church on this granite pile around the fifth century, and within three centuries a Celtic monastery had been founded here. The present building derives from a chapel raised in the eleventh century by Edward the Confessor, who handed over the abbey to the Benedictine monks of Brittany's Mont St Michel, whose island abbey was the model for this one. Following the Civil War, it became the residence of the St Aubyn family, who still inhabit the castle. Some of the buildings date from the twelfth century, but the later additions are more interesting, such as the battlemented **chapel** and the seventeenth-century decorations of the **Chevy Chase Room**, the former refectory. At low tide the promontory can be approached on foot via a cobbled causeway; at high tide there are boats from Marazion (£1.20).

Mousehole to Land's End

Accounts vary as to the derivation of the name of **MOUSEHOLE** (pronounced "Mowzle"), though it may be from a smugglers' cave just south of town. In any case, the name evokes perfectly this minuscule harbour, cradled in the arms of a granite breakwater three miles south of Penzance. The village attracts more visitors than it can handle, so hang around until the crowds have departed before you walk through its tight tangle of lanes to take in Mousehole's oldest house, the fourteenth-century Keigwin House (a survival of a Spanish raid in 1595, when the village was set on fire), and a drink at the *Ship Inn*, which also has **rooms** (T01736/731234; **4**). Half a mile inland, the churchyard wall at **Paul** holds a monument to Dolly Pentreath, a local resident who, at her death in 1777, was supposedly the last person to speak solely in Cornish.

Eight miles west, one of Penwith's best beaches lies at **PORTHCURNO**. Steep steps lead up from the beach of tiny white shells to the **Minack Theatre**, hewn out of the cliff in the 1930s and since enlarged to hold 750 seats, though retaining the basic Greek-inspired design. The spectacular backdrop of Porthcurno Bay makes this one of the country's most inspiring theatres – providing the weather holds. From May to September, a range of plays, operas and musicals are presented, with tickets at £6–7.50 (T01736/810181, Wwww.minack .com); bring a cushion and a rug. The attached **Exhibition Centre** (daily: April–Sept 9.30am–5.30pm; Oct–March 10am–4pm; closed during performances; £3) gives access to the theatre and explains the story of its creation.

On the shore to the east of Porthcurno, a white pyramid marks the spot where the first transatlantic cables were laid in 1880. On the headland beyond lies an Iron Age fort, **Treryn Dinas**, close to the famous rocking stone called **Logan's Rock**, a seventy-ton monster that was knocked off its perch in 1824 by a gang of sailors, among them a nephew of playwright Oliver Goldsmith. Somehow they replaced the stone, but it never rocked again.

The extreme western tip of England, **Land's End**, lies four miles west of Porthcurno. Best approached on foot along the coastal path, the 60ft turf-covered cliffs provide a platform to view the Irish Lady, the Armed Knight, Dr Syntax Head and the rest of the Land's End outcrops, beyond which you can spot the Longships lighthouse, a mile and a half out to sea, and sometimes the Wolf Rock lighthouse, nine miles southwest, or even the Isles of Scilly, 28 miles away. Although nothing can completely destroy the potency of this majestic headland, the **Land's End Experience** theme park (daily 10am–5/6pm, or earlier at quiet times; T0870/458 0099; £10), on an extensive site just behind, violates the spirit of the place, its trivializing array of lasers and unconvincing sound effects no substitute for the real open-air experience.

Whitesand Bay to Zennor

To the north of Land's End the rounded granite cliffs fall away at **Whitesand Bay** to reveal a glistening mile-long shelf of beach that offers the best swimming on the Penwith peninsula. The rollers make for good surfing and boards can be rented at **Sennen Cove**, the more popular southern end of the beach. There are a few places to **stay** around here, including *Myrtle Cottage* (T01736/871698; no credit cards; **3**), whose cosy teashop is also open to nonresidents. A few minutes' walk inland, *Whitesands Lodge* (T01736/871776, Wwww.whitesandslodge.co.uk) is a superior **hostel** with dormitory accommodation (£18), teepees (sleeping six; **5**) and B&B in a separate building (**3**).

Cape Cornwall, a highly scenic headland three miles northwards, is dominated by the chimney of the Cape Cornwall Mine, which closed in 1870. Half a mile inland the grimly grey village of **ST JUST-IN-PENWITH** was a centre of the tin and copper industry, and the rows of trim cottages radiating out from Bank Square are redolent of the close-knit community that once existed here. The tone is somewhat lightened by the grassy open-air theatre where the old Cornish miracle plays were staged; it was later used by Methodist preachers as well as Cornish wrestlers. Most of the local pubs have **accommodation**, including the traditional *Star Inn* off Bank Square (T01736/788767; no credit cards; ➊). There's also a YHA **hostel** (T0870/770 5906; closed Nov to mid-Feb; £12.50) three-quarters of a mile south (take the left fork past the post office), close to an excellent secluded **campsite**, ⚑ *Kelynack Caravan and Camping Park* (T01736/787633, W www.kelynackcaravans.co.uk; closed Nov–Easter), which also has bunks available all year (£8). In St Just, *Kegen Teg*, 12 Market Square (closed Sun), offers good coffees, lunches and ice cream.

Eight miles northeast of St Just, set in a landscape of rolling granite moorland, **ZENNOR** is where D.H. Lawrence came to live with his wife Frieda in 1916. "It is a most beautiful place," he wrote, "lovelier even than the Mediterranean." The Lawrences stayed a year and a half in the village – long enough for him to write *Women in Love* – before being given notice to quit by the local constabulary, who suspected them of unpatriotic sympathies (their Cornish experiences were later described in *Kangaroo*). Zennor's fascinating **Wayside Museum** is dedicated to Cornish life from prehistoric times (daily: March, April & Oct 11am–5pm; May–Sept 10.30am–5.30pm; £3). At the top of the lane, the church of **St Sennen** displays a sixteenth-century bench-carving of a mermaid who, according to local legend, was so entranced by the singing of a chorister that she lured him down to the sea, from where he never returned – though his singing can still occasionally be heard. Nearby, the *Tinners Arms* is a cosy place to **drink** and **eat**, while the *Old Chapel Backpackers Hostel*, next to the Wayside Museum, is a fun place **to stay** (T01736/798307, W www .backpackers.co.uk/zennor; £12): it has a family room (➋), and a café providing snacks and evening meals.

Located on a windy hillside a couple of miles inland from Zennor, off the minor road to Penzance, the Iron Age village of **Chysauster** (daily: late March to June & Sept 10am–5pm; July & Aug 10am–6pm; Oct 10am–4pm; £2.30; EH) is the best-preserved ancient settlement in the Southwest. Dating from about the first century BC, it contains two rows of four buildings, each consisting of a courtyard with small chambers leading off it, and a garden that was presumably used for growing vegetables.

St Ives

East of Zennor, the road runs four hilly miles on to the steeply built town of **ST IVES**, a place that has smoothly undergone the transition from fishing village to holiday haunt. By the time the pilchard reserves dried up around the early 1900s, the town was beginning to attract a vibrant **artists' colony**, precursors of the wave later headed by Ben Nicholson, Barbara Hepworth, Naum Gabo and the potter Bernard Leach, who in the 1960s were followed by a third wave including Terry Frost and Patrick Heron.

The place to view the best work created in St Ives is the **Tate St Ives**, overlooking Porthmeor Beach on the north side of town (March–Oct daily 10am–5.30pm; Nov–Feb Tues–Sun 10am–4.30pm; closes two or three times a year for about ten days – call T01736/796226 to check; £5.50; combined ticket with Barbara Hepworth Museum £8.50). Most of the paintings, sculptures and ceramics displayed within the airy, gleaming-white building date from 1925 to 1975, with specially commissioned contemporary works also on view as well as exhibitions. The gallery's rooftop **café** is one of the best places in town for a coffee and snack.

A short distance away on Barnoon Hill, the **Barbara Hepworth Museum** (March–Oct daily 10am–5.30pm; Nov–Feb Tues–Sun 10am–4.30pm or dusk; £4.50, combined ticket with the Tate £8.50) provides a further insight into the local arts scene. One of the foremost nonfigurative sculptors of her time, Hepworth lived in the building from 1949 until her death in a studio fire in 1975. Apart from the sculptures, which are arranged in positions chosen by Hepworth in the house and garden, the museum has background on her art, from photos and letters to catalogues and reviews.

Porthmeor Beach dominates the northern side of St Ives, its excellent water quality and surfer-friendly rollers drawing a regular crowd, while the broader **Porthminster Beach**, south of the station, is usually less busy.

Practicalities

St Ives **train station** is off Porthminster Beach, just below the **bus station** on Station Hill. The **tourist office** is in the narrow Street-an-Pol, two minutes' walk away (mid-May to Sept Mon–Fri 9am–5.30pm, Sat 9am–5pm, Sun 10am–4pm; Oct to mid-May Mon–Fri 9am–5pm, Sat 10am–1pm; ☎01736/796297, ⓦwww.go-cornwall.com).

Of the numerous **accommodation** choices near Porthminster Beach, try either of the two quiet B&Bs, *Chy-Roma*, 2 Seaview Terrace (☎01736/797539, ⓦwww.connexions.co.uk/chyroma; no credit cards. ❸), or *Starfish*, 6 Porthminster Terrace (☎01736/799575, ⓦwww.starfishbandb.co.uk; no smoking; no credit cards; ❸). More centrally, ☀ *Cornerways*, The Square ☎01736/796706, ⓦwww.cornerwaysstives.com; no credit cards; ❸), offers tasteful B&B in a modern cottage conversion. The town's swishest hotel is the small and luxurious, family-run *Garrack*, Burthallan Lane (☎01736/796199, ⓦwww.garrack .com; ❼), a fifteen-minute walk west of Porthmeor Beach, with an indoor pool, a gym and a superb restaurant. The *St Ives Backpackers* **hostel** at The Stennack (☎01736/799444, ⓦwww.backpackers.co.uk/st-ives; £16, double rooms ❶) occupies an old Wesleyan chapel school, with rates dropping outside peak season.

St Ives has a dazzling range of **restaurants**. With its sun deck and beach location, ☀ *Porthminster Beach Café*, on Porthminster Beach (☎01736/795352; closed Nov–March), makes a superb spot for coffees, lunches, cream teas and fairly expensive evening meals; under the same management, the *Porthgwidden Beach Café* in the Downalong area of town offers similar fare. *Alba*, on the harbourfront (☎01736/797222; closed Sun–Tues in winter; moderate–expensive), is a sleekly modern restaurant in a converted lifeboat house, while *Peppers*, 22 Fore St (☎01736/794014; eves only), is the place for a simple pizza or pasta in mellow surroundings. On Tregenna Place, *Isobar* is a cocktail and tapas bar with DJs on the decks and a separate club upstairs.

The north Cornish coast to Bude

Though generally harsher than the county's southern seaboard, the north Cornish coast is punctuated by some of the finest beaches in England, the most popular of which are to be found around **Newquay**, the surfers' capital, and **Padstow**, also renowned for its gourmet seafood restaurants. North of the Camel estuary, the coast is an almost unbroken line of cliffs as far as the Devon border, the gaunt, exposed terrain making a melodramatic setting for **Tintagel**, though there are more beaches at **Bude**, attracting both surfers and families. The more westerly stretches of this coast are littered with the derelict stacks and castle-like ruins of the engine-houses that once powered the region's **copper** and **tin mines**, industries that at one time led the world.

Newquay and around

It is difficult to imagine a lineage for **NEWQUAY** that extends more than a few decades, but the "new quay" was built in the fifteenth century in what was already a long-established fishing port. Up to then it had been more colourfully known as Towan Blistra, and was concentrated in the sheltered west end of the bay. The town was given a boost in the nineteenth century when a railway was constructed across the peninsula for china clay shipments. With the trains came a swelling stream of seasonal visitors, drawn to the town's superb position on a knuckle of cliffs overlooking fine golden sands and Atlantic rollers, natural advantages which have made Newquay the premier resort of north Cornwall. Try to coincide your visit to Newquay with one of the **surfing competitions** and events that run right through the summer – contact the tourist office for details.

The centre of town is a somewhat tacky parade of shops and restaurants from which lanes lead to ornamental gardens and sloping lawns on the cliff-tops. At the bottom of Beach Road, adjacent to the small harbour, the **Blue Reef Aquarium** (daily: March–Oct 10am–5pm; Nov–Feb 10am–4pm; £6.50) provides some distraction, allowing you to admire tropical fish from an underwater tunnel. Below the aquarium, in the crook of the massive Towan Head, **Towan Beach** is the most central of the seven miles of firm sandy beaches that follow in an almost unbroken succession. You can reach all of them on foot, or take bus #556 to Padstow for some of the further ones, such as **Porth Beach**, with its grassy headland, and the extensive **Watergate Bay**. The beaches can all be unbearably crowded in high season, and are popular with surfers, particularly Watergate and – west of Towan Head – **Fistral Bay**, the largest of the town beaches. On the other side of East Pentire Head from Fistral, **Crantock Beach** – reachable over the Gannel River by ferry or upstream footbridge – is usually less crowded, and has a lovely backdrop of dunes and undulating grassland. South of Crantock, **Holywell Bay** and the three-mile expanse of **Perran Beach**, enhanced by caves and natural rock arches, are also very popular with surfers.

Practicalities

Newquay's **train station** is off Cliff Road, a couple of hundred yards from the **bus station** on East Street, which itself lies opposite the **tourist office** on Marcus Hill (May–Sept Mon–Sat 9.30am–5.30pm, Sun 9.30am–1pm; Oct–April Mon–Fri 9.30am–4.30pm, Sat 9.30am–12.30pm; ☏01637/854020, ⊛www .newquay.co.uk); **Internet** access is available from here. You can rent or buy **surfing equipment** from beach stalls or from various outlets around town.

Newquay's **accommodation** is plentiful but can still be booked solid in July and August. Phone ahead for the beautifully furnished *Rockpool Cottage*, 92 Fore St (☏01637/870848, ⊛www.rockpoolcottage.co.uk; ❷; closed Jan–Easter), convenient for Fistral Beach, or the nonsmoking *Trewinda Lodge*, 17 Eliot Gardens (☏01637/877533, ⊛www.trewindalodge.co.uk; no smoking; no credit cards; ❷), a few minutes' walk from Tolcarne Beach; both B&Bs can give informed advice to surfers. For a more upmarket option in an unrivalled location, try the *Headland Hotel* (☏01637/872211, ⊛www.headlandhotel.co.uk; ❸), a huge palace standing in splendid isolation overlooking Fistral Beach; its facilities include two heated pools. Among the town's plethora of independent **hostels**, there's the modern and fully equipped ⚵ *Reef Surf Lodge*, in the centre of town at 10–12 Berry Rd (☏01637/879058, ⊛www.reefsurflodge.info; £29.50), with bunkrooms, en-suite doubles and a range of facilities; *St Christopher's*, with a great location overlooking the harbour, above *Belushi's* bar at 35 Fore St (℡01637/859111, ⓦwww.st-christophers.co.uk; £19–25), and, on Fistral Beach, *The Boarding House*, 32 Headland Rd (℡01637/873258, ⓦwww.theboardinghouse.co.uk; £22). On the cliff-top outside **Perranporth**, at the southern end of Perran Beach, there's a YHA **hostel** housed in a former coastguard station (℡0870/770 5994, ⓔperranporth@yha.org.uk; closed Oct–March; £12.50). Newquay's **campsites** include *Trevelgue* (℡01637/851851, ⓦwww.trevelgue.co.uk), a mile east of Porth Beach on Trevelgue Road.

A few stylish **eateries** lurk among Newquay's bland fast-food outlets, such as *New Harbour Restaurant*, Newquay Harbour (℡01637/874062; closed Sun eve, Mon & Tues in winter); where, in summer, you can watch the fish being cooked at the outdoor kitchen. The town also has some good **cafés**, including *The Chy*, a sleekly modern place on Beach Road, with a spacious terrace for seafood lunches, and the laid-back *Café Irie*, 38 Fore St (closed Mon–Thurs Nov–April), serving snacks, teas and, in summer, evening meals, accompanied by world music. At **Watergate Bay**, the *Beach Hut* provides surf food and fish specials all day, and is soon to be joined by *Fifteen Cornwall*, run by celebrity chef Jamie Oliver.

For a **night out**, have a drink in the Aussie-themed *Walkabout Inn* on Beachfield Avenue, with great waterside views, before hitting one of the town's **clubs**; the current hot spots are *Berties* on East Street (℡01637/872255, ⓦwww.bertiesclub.com), *Sailors* on Fore Street (℡01637/872838), *The Beach* (℡01637/872194, ⓦwww.beachclubnewquay.com) and the *Koola Club* on Beach Road (℡01637/873415, ⓦwww.thekoola.com), and *Tall Trees* on Tolcarne Road (℡01637/850313, ⓦwww.talltreesclub.co.uk).

Padstow and around

The small fishing port of **PADSTOW** is nearly as popular as Newquay, but has a very different feel. Enclosed within the estuary of the Camel – the only river outlet of any size on Cornwall's north coast – the town has long retained its position as the principal fishing port on this stretch, and can boast the best seafood restaurants. Padstow is also known for its annual **Obby Oss** festival, a May Day romp when a local in horse costume prances through the town preceded by a masked and club-wielding "teaser", in a spirited re-enactment of an old fertility rite.

On the hill overlooking Padstow, the church of **St Petroc** is dedicated to Cornwall's most important saint, a Welsh or Irish monk who landed here in the sixth century, died in the area and gave his name to the town – "Petrock's Stow". The building has a fine fifteenth-century font, an Elizabethan pulpit and some amusing carved bench-ends. The walls are lined with monuments to the local Prideaux family, who still occupy nearby **Prideaux Place**, an Elizabethan manor house with grand staircases, richly furnished rooms full of portraits, fantastically ornate ceilings and formal gardens (mid-May to early Oct Mon–Thurs & Sun 1.30–5pm, last tour at 4pm; £6.50, grounds only £2), all of which have been used as settings for various films, including *Twelfth Night* and *Oscar and Lucinda*.

The harbour is jammed with launches and boats offering cruises in Padstow Bay, while a regular **ferry** (summer daily 8am–7.30pm; winter Mon–Sat 8am–4.30pm; £3 return) carries people across the river to **ROCK** – close to the isolated church of **St Enodoc** (John Betjeman's burial place) and to the good beaches around Polzeath (see p.378). At low water, the ferry leaves from near the war memorial downstream.

The coast on the **west side** of the estuary has more beaches and some terrific walks. The rivermouth is clogged by **Doom Bar**, a sand bar that was allegedly the curse of a mermaid who had been mortally wounded by a fisherman who mistook her for a seal. Round **Stepper Point** you can reach the sandy and secluded Harlyn Bay and, turning the corner southwards, **Constantine Bay**, the area's best surfing beach. The dunes backing the beach and the rock pools skirting it make this one of the most appealing bays on this coast, though the tides can be treacherous and bathing hazardous near the rocks. Three or four miles further south, the slate outcrops of **Bedruthan Steps** were traditionally held to be the stepping-stones of a giant called Bedruthan; they can be readily viewed from the cliff-top path and the B3276, with steps descending to the broad beach below (not advised for swimming).

Padstow is also the start of an excellent **cycle-track** converted from the old rail line to Wadebridge, forming part of the **Camel Trail**, a fifteen-mile traffic-free path that follows the river up as far as Bodmin Moor. You can **rent bikes** from Trail Bike Hire (℡01841/532594) and Padstow Cycle Hire (℡01841/533533), both on South Quay, by the start of the Trail.

Practicalities

Padstow's **tourist office** is on the harbour (Easter–Oct daily 9.30am–5pm; Nov–Easter Mon–Fri 9am–4pm; ℡01841/533449, ⓦwww.padstowlive.com). Local **accommodation** includes the B&B at 4 Riverside (℡01841/532383, ⓔcullinan@freeuk.com; no credit cards; ❸), also on the harbour, and *Treverbyn House*, Treverbyn Road (℡01841/532855, ⓦwww.treverbynhouse.com; ❺), an elegant Edwardian house with great views. The nearest YHA **hostel** is well sited at Treyarnon Bay (℡0870/770 6076, ⓔtreyarnon@yha.org.uk; flexible opening Nov–March; £15.50); take the #556 Newquay bus to Constantine, then walk half a mile.

Padstow is well known for its **restaurants**, particularly those associated with star chef Rick Stein, whose *Seafood Restaurant*, at Riverside, is one of Britain's top places for fish. Its success has led to the opening of two offshoots, *St Petroc's Bistro* at 4 New St, offering a lighter version of its parent's menu, and, nearby at 10 Middle St, the cool and casual *Rick Stein's Café*. In addition, there's *Stein's Fish and Chips* on South Quay (closed Sun eve) and his **deli** next door. All three of the main places also offer classy accommodation (❻–❽); for restaurants and accommodation reservations, call ℡01841/532700 or see ⓦwww.rickstein .com. Outside the Stein empire, the *Old Custom House* and *Old Ship* **pubs** on the harbourside serve snacks, while the *London Inn* on Lanadwell Street does sandwiches, pasties and more substantial meals.

Polzeath and Port Isaac

Facing west into Padstow Bay, the beaches around **POLZEATH** are the finest in the vicinity, pelted by rollers which make this one of the best surfing sites in the West Country (tuition and gear to rent are available from stalls and shops). The *Seascape Hotel* offers about the only solid-walled **accommodation** around here (℡01208/863638, ⓦwww.seascapehotel.co.uk; ❻; closed Nov–Feb), while the popular *Tristram* **campsite** (℡01208/862215; closed Nov–Feb) is on a cliff overlooking the beach. On the seafront, the *Galleon* does various snacks and takeaways, while the *Oyster Catcher* bar is a lively evening hangout.

The next settlement of any size is **PORT ISAAC**, wedged in a gap in the precipitous cliff wall and dedicated to the crab and lobster trade. Narrow lanes lead down to the seafront, where there are a couple of pubs and a pebble beach and rock pools exposed by the low tide. The village offers a range of **accommodation**, notably the *Slipway Hotel* (℡01208/880264, 🅦www.portisaachotel.com; ❻), a sixteenth-century building right opposite the harbour, the *Old School Hotel*, higher up on Fore Street (℡01208/880721, 🅦www.cornwall-online.co.uk/old-school-hotel; ❺), and *Anchorage Guest House*, 12 The Terrace (℡01208/880629; no smoking; no credit cards; ❸) – the last two with wonderful views.

You can sample the local crab from stalls at the harbour or from either of the excellent **restaurants** at the *Slipway Hotel* and the *Old School*, which is also open for snacks and teas. The *Golden Lion* **pub** has an adjoining bistro and balcony seating overlooking the harbour.

Tintagel

East of Port Isaac, the coast is wild and unspoiled, making for some steep and strenuous walking, and providing an appropriate backdrop for the forsaken ruins of **Tintagel Castle** (daily: April–Sept 10am–6pm; Oct 10am–5pm;

△ Tintagel

Nov–March 10am–4pm; £4.10; EH). It was the twelfth-century chronicler Geoffrey of Monmouth who first popularized the notion that this was the **birthplace of King Arthur**, son of Uther Pendragon and Ygrayne. Tintagel is certainly a plausible candidate, though the **castle** ruins in fact belong to a Norman stronghold occupied by the earls of Cornwall, who after sporadic spurts of rebuilding allowed it to decay, most of it having been washed into the sea by the sixteenth century. The remains of a sixth-century **Celtic monastery** are also visible on the headland, and have provided important insights into how the country's earliest monastic houses were organized.

The easiest access to the site is from the village of **TINTAGEL**, a dreary collection of cafés and B&Bs where the only item of note is the **Old Post Office** (late March to Sept daily 11am–5.30pm; Oct daily 11am–4pm; £2.50; NT), a rickety-roofed slate-built construction dating from the fourteenth century, now restored to its appearance in the Victorian era.

Tintagel's **tourist office** is in the car park on the road from Camelford (daily: March–Oct 10am–5pm; Nov–Feb 10.30am–4pm; ℡01840/779084, ⊛ www .visittintagelandboscastle.com). Most of the **B&Bs** are a few minutes' walk along Atlantic Road, with the best being *Pendrin House* (℡01840/770560, ⊛ www .pendrinhouse.co.uk; ➋; closed Nov–Feb) and *Bosayne* (℡01840/770514, ⊛ www.bosayne.co.uk; ➍), both nonsmoking. Three-quarters of a mile west of Tintagel at Dunderhole Point, the offices of a former slate quarry now house

King Arthur in Cornwall

Did **King Arthur** really exist? If he did, it's likely that he was an amalgam of two people: a sixth-century Celtic warlord who united the local tribes in a series of successful battles against the invading Anglo-Saxons, and a local Cornish saint. Whatever his origins, his role was recounted and inflated by poets and troubadours in later centuries. There is no mention of him in the ninth- to twelfth-century *Anglo-Saxon Chronicle*, but his exploits were elaborated by the medieval chroniclers Geoffrey of Monmouth, who made Arthur the conqueror of western Europe, and William of Malmesbury, who narrated the legend that, after being mortally wounded in battle, Arthur sailed to Avalon (Glastonbury), where he was buried alongside Guinevere. The Arthurian legends were crystallized in Thomas Malory's epic, *Morte d'Arthur* (1485), further romanticized in Tennyson's *Idylls of the King* (1859) and resurrected in T.H. White's saga, *The Once and Future King* (1958).

Although there are places throughout Britain and Europe which claim some association with Arthur, it's England's West Country, and **Cornwall** in particular, that has the greatest concentration of places boasting a link. Here, the legends, fertilized by fellow Celts from Brittany and Wales, have established deep roots, so that, for example, the spirit of Arthur is said to be embodied in the Cornish chough – a bird now almost extinct. Cornwall's most famous Arthurian site is **Tintagel**, which is said to be his birthplace, and where Merlin is thought to have lived in a cave under the castle (and also on a rock near Mousehole, south of Penzance, according to some). Nearby **Bodmin Moor** is full of places with associated names such as "King Arthur's Bed" and "King Arthur's Downs", while Camlan, the battlefield where Arthur was mortally wounded fighting against his nephew Mordred, is thought to lie on the northern reaches of the moor at Slaughterbridge, near **Camelford** (which is also sometimes identified as Camelot itself). At **Dozmary Pool**, the knight Bedivere was dispatched by the dying Arthur to return the sword Excalibur to the mysterious hand emerging from the water – though Loe Pool in Mount's Bay also claims this honour. According to some, Arthur's body was transported after the battle to **Boscastle**, on Cornwall's northern coast, from where a funeral barge transported the body to Avalon.

a YHA **hostel** with great views of the coastline (℡0870/770 6068; closed Nov to mid-March; £11.95). On Fore Street, both the *Old Malt House* and the *Tintagel Arms Hotel* have **restaurants**.

Boscastle

Three miles east of Tintagel, the port of **BOSCASTLE** lies compressed within a narrow ravine drilled by the rivers Jordan and Valency, its tidy riverfront bordered by thatched and lime-washed houses. Above and behind, a collection of seventeenth- and eighteenth-century cottages can be seen on a circular walk that traces the valley of the Valency for about a mile to reach Boscastle's graceful **parish church**, tucked away in a peaceful glen. A mile and a half further up the valley, **St Juliot's** church was restored by Thomas Hardy when he was plying his trade as a young architect.

Boscastle's **tourist office** is in the car park at the bottom of the main road into the village (daily: March–Oct 10am–5pm; Nov–Feb 10.30am–4pm; ℡01840/250010, www.visittintagelandboscastle.com). *St Christopher's Hotel* (℡01840/250412, www.st-christophers-boscastle.co.uk; ❺; closed Dec–Feb) is a restored Georgian manor house at the top of the High Street with first-rate **accommodation**, but for a real Thomas Hardy experience, head for the *Old Rectory*, on the road to St Juliot (℡01840/250225, www.stjuliot.com; no smoking; no under-12s; ❸; closed Dec–March), where you can stay in the author's bedroom and roam the extensive grounds. There's also a fine old YHA **hostel** on the harbourside (℡0870/770 5710; closed mid-Oct to mid-March; £11.95). You can eat at one of the village's excellent **pubs**: in the upper part of town, the *Napoleon* has a good seafood bistro and a spacious lawned garden, while the atmospheric *Cobweb* down near the harbour serves bar food; both have live music evenings.

Bude and around

Just four miles from the Devon border, Cornwall's northernmost town of **BUDE** is built around an estuary surrounded by a fine expanse of sands. The town has sprouted a crop of hotels and holiday homes, though these have not unduly spoilt the place nor the magnificent cliffy coast surrounding it.

Of the excellent beaches hereabouts, the central **Summerleaze** is clean and wide, while the mile-long **Widemouth Bay**, south of town, is the main focus of the holiday crowds (though bathing can be dangerous near the rocks at low tide). Surfers also congregate five miles down the coast at **Crackington Haven**, wonderfully situated between 430-foot crags at the mouth of a lush valley. The cliffs on this stretch are characterized by remarkable zigzagging strata of shale, limestone and sandstone, a mixture which erodes into vividly contorted detached formations. To the **north** of Bude, acres-wide **Crooklets** is the scene of **surfing** and life-saving demonstrations and competitions. A couple of miles further on, **Sandy Mouth** holds a pristine expanse of sand with rock pools beneath the encircling cliffs. It's a short walk from here to another surfers' delight, **Duckpool**, a tiny sandy cove flanked by jagged reefs at low tide, and dominated by the three-hundred-foot **Steeple Point**.

Bude's **tourist office** is in the car park off the Crescent (April–Sept Mon–Sat 10am–5pm, Sun 10am–4pm; Oct–March Mon–Fri 10am–4pm, Sat 10am–1pm; ℡01288/354240, www.visitbude.info). The town's cheaper **accommodation** includes a cluster of B&Bs overlooking the golf course on Burn View, among them *Sunrise* at no. 6 (℡01288/353214; no credit cards; ❷), and *Palms* at no. 17 (℡01288/353962; no credit cards; ❷). Near Summerleaze Beach, the

Falcon Hotel on Breakwater Road is an old coaching inn (℡01288/352005, Ⓦwww.falconhotel.com; ❻), and there's a backpackers' **hostel** at 57 Killerton Rd (℡01288/354256, Ⓦwww.northshorebude.com; £12), with a large garden, **Internet** access and some double rooms (❶).

For style, location and cuisine, Bude's best **restaurant** is ✻ *Life's a Beach*, right on Summerleaze Beach, a café by day and a romantic (and expensive) bistro in the evening (℡01288/355222; closed winter weekday lunch and all Mon & Tues). In town, try the *Atlantic Diner*, 5–7 Belle Vue (closed all Sun & Mon eve; inexpensive–moderate), popular with shoppers and surfers alike for its burgers, steaks, curries and ice creams. **Surfing equipment** can be rented from various outlets in town.

Bodmin and Bodmin Moor

Bodmin Moor, the smallest of the West Country's great moors, has some beautiful tors, torrents and rock formations, but much of its fascination lies in the strong human imprint, particularly the wealth of relics left behind by its **Bronze Age** population. Separated from these by some three millennia, the churches in the villages of **St Neot**, **Blisland** and **Altarnun** are among the region's finest examples of fifteenth-century art and architecture.

Bodmin

BODMIN's position on the western edge of Bodmin Moor, equidistant from the north and south Cornish coasts and the Fowey and Camel rivers, encouraged its growth as a trading town. It was also an important ecclesiastical centre after the establishment of a priory by St Petroc, who moved here from Padstow in the sixth century. The priory disappeared but Bodmin retained its prestige through its church of **St Petroc**, at the end of Fore Street, built in the fifteenth century and still the largest in Cornwall (April–Sept daily 10am–3pm; at other times call ℡01208/73867). Inside, there's an extravagantly carved twelfth-century font and an ivory casket that once held the bones of the saint, while the southwest corner of the churchyard holds a sacred well. Close by, the notorious **Bodmin Jail** (daily 10am–dusk; £4.75) on Berrycombe Road is redolent of the public executions that were once guaranteed crowd-pullers here. You can visit part of the original eighteenth-century structure, including the condemned cell and some grisly exhibits chronicling the lives of the inmates.

From Bodmin Parkway, the train station three miles southeast of the centre, it's less than two miles' walk to one of Cornwall's most celebrated country houses, **Lanhydrock** (house mid-March to Sept Tues–Sun 11am–5.30pm; Oct Tues–Sun 11am–5pm: gardens daily 10am–6pm or dusk; £7.90, grounds only £4.40; NT), originally seventeenth-century but totally rebuilt after a fire in 1881. The granite exterior remains true to its original form, but the 42 rooms show a very different style, including a long picture gallery with a plaster ceiling depicting scenes from the Old Testament and servants' quarters that reveal the daily workings of a Victorian manor house. The grounds have magnificent beds of magnolias, azaleas and rhododendrons, and a huge area of wooded parkland bordering onto the River Fowey.

Practicalities

Bodmin's **tourist office** (Mon–Sat 10am–5pm; Nov–Easter closed Sat; ℡01208/76616) is in Shire Hall on Mount Folly. There's comfortable **B&B** at

Higher Windsor Cottage, 18 Castle St (☎01208/76474, ⓦwww.higherwindsor cottage.co.uk; ❷), and the beflowered, seventeenth-century *Priory Cottage*, near St Petroc's church at 34 Rhind St (☎01208/73064, ⓦwww.stayanite.com; ❷): both are nonsmoking and neither accepts credit cards. A couple of miles south of town, *Bokiddick Farm* is convenient for Lanhydrock and boasts magnificent views (☎01208/831481, ⓦwww.bokiddickfarm.co.uk; no smoking; ❹).

Off Fore Street, the *Hole in the Wall* **pub** in Crockwell Street has bar lunches, an upstairs **restaurant** and a courtyard. Wholesome snacks are served at the tiny *Providence Café*, just across from St Petroc's at 14 Honey St (closed Sun).

Blisland and the western moor

BLISLAND stands in the Camel valley on the western slopes of Bodmin Moor, three miles northeast of Bodmin. Georgian and Victorian houses cluster around a village green and a church whose well-restored interior has an Italianate altar and a startlingly painted screen. On **Pendrift Common** above the village, the gigantic **Jubilee Rock** is inscribed with various patriotic insignia commemorating the jubilee of George III's coronation in 1809. From this seven-hundred-foot vantage point you look eastward over the De Lank gorge and the boulder-crowned knoll of **Hawk's Tor**, three miles away. On the shoulder of the tor stand the Neolithic **Stripple Stones**, a circular platform once holding 28 standing stones, of which just four are still upright. The nicest **place to stay** hereabouts is *Lavethan* (☎01208/850487, ⓦwww .cornwall-online.co.uk/lavethan; no credit cards; ❺), a beautiful sixteenth-century manor set in thirty acres of park-like fields and gardens sloping to a small river; it's ten minutes' walk from the village towards St Mabyn. On Blisland's village green, you can sample good **ales and food** at the *Blisland Inn*, with outdoor tables.

Camelford and the northern tors

The northern half of Bodmin Moor is dominated by its two highest tors, both of them easily accessible from **CAMELFORD**, which offers a couple of diverting museums. The **British Cycling Museum** (Mon–Thurs & Sun 10am–5pm; phone ahead for Fri & Sat ☎01840/212811; £3), housed in the old station one mile north of town on the Boscastle Road, is a cyclophile's dream, containing some four hundred examples of bikes through the ages. More conventionally, the **North Cornwall Museum** (April–Sept Mon–Sat 10am–5pm; £2.50) in the village itself, displays domestic items and exhibits relating to the local slate industry, and also houses the **tourist office** (same hours; ☎01840/212954). Among Camelford's **accommodation**, try the *Mason's Arms* on Market Place (☎01840/213309; ❷), or the thirteenth-century, slate-hung *Darlington Inn* on Fore Street (☎01840/213314; ❷). *King's Acre* (☎01840/213561; ❸), on the B3266 between the village and the cycling museum, provides B&B and **camping** (campsite closed Nov–Easter). Both the *Mason's Arms*, which has a beer garden, and the *Darlington Inn* make good **refreshment** stops.

Rough Tor, the second highest peak on Bodmin Moor at 1311ft, is four miles' walk southeast from Camelford. The hill presents a different aspect from every angle: from the south an ungainly mass, from the west a nobly proportioned mountain. A short distance to the east stand the Little Rough Tor, where there are the remains of an Iron Age camp, and Showery Tor, capped by a prominent formation of piled rocks. Easily visible to the southeast, **Brown Willy** is, at 1375ft, the highest peak in Cornwall, as its original name signified – Bronewhella, or "highest hill". Like Rough Tor, Brown Willy shows various faces, its sugarloaf appearance from the north sharpening into a long multi-peaked crest as you approach. The tor is accessible by continuing from the summit of Rough Tor across the valley of the De Lank, or, from the south, by footpath from Bolventor.

Bolventor and Altarnun

The village of **BOLVENTOR**, lying at the centre of the moor midway between Bodmin and Launceston, is an uninspiring place close to one of the moor's chief focuses for walkers and sightseers alike – **Jamaica Inn** (℡01566/86250, ⓦwww.jamaicainn.co.uk; ❺). A staging post even before the precursor of the A30 road was laid here in 1769, the inn was described as being "alone in glory, four square to the winds" by Daphne Du Maurier, who stayed here in 1930, soaking up inspiration for her smugglers' yarn, *Jamaica Inn*. Adjacent to the rather bland hotel, the **Smuggler's Museum** (daily: Feb–Oct 10am–5pm; Nov–Jan 11am–4pm; £3.50) shows the diverse ruses used for concealing contraband.

Bolventor is not on any public transport route. If you're driving, the inn's car park is a useful place to leave your vehicle and venture forth on foot. Just a mile away, **Dozmary Pool** is another link in the West Country's Arthurian mythologies – after Arthur's death Sir Bedevere hurled Excalibur, the king's sword, into the pool, where it was seized by an arm raised from the depths. Despite its proximity to the A30, the diamond-shaped lake usually preserves an ethereal air, though it's been known to run dry in summer, dealing a bit of a blow to the legend that the pool is bottomless.

Just under four miles northeast of Bolventor, **ALTARNUN** is a pleasant, granite-grey village snugly sheltered beneath the eastern heights of the moor. Its prominent **church**, dedicated to St Nonna (mother of David, patron saint of Wales) contains a fine Norman font and 79 bench-ends carved at the beginning of the sixteenth century, depicting saints, musicians and clowns. Accessed by a private gate from St Nonna's (and also from the road), *Penhallow Manor* (℡01566/86206, ⓦwww.penhallow-manor.co.uk; no smoking; ❺), originally the vicarage, now offers tasteful **accommodation** in spacious, old-fashioned rooms. Cheaper rooms can be found 500yd towards the A30, where the *King's Head* (℡01566/86241; ❷) has beams, saggy ceilings and **meals** from around a fiver. South of Altarnun, **Withey Brook** tumbles four hundred feet in less than a mile of gushing cascades before meeting up with the River Lynher, which bounds Bodmin Moor to the east.

St Neot and the southeastern moor

The southern and eastern reaches of Bodmin Moor are far greener and more thickly wooded than the northern parts, due to the confluence of a web of rivers into the Fowey. Approached through a lush wooded valley, **ST NEOT** is one of the moor's prettiest villages. Its fifteenth-century **church** contains some of the most impressive stained-glass windows of any parish church in the country, the oldest glass being the fifteenth-century **Creation Window**, at the east end of the south aisle. A great **accommodation** option in St Neot is the seventeenth-century *Dye Cottage* (℡01579/321394, ⓦwww.cornwall-info.co.uk/dye-cottage; no credit cards; ❷), with home-grown produce for breakfast and a garden sloping down to a stream.

One of the moor's best-known beauty spots lies a couple of miles east, below Draynes Bridge, where the Fowey tumbles through the **Golitha Falls**, less a waterfall than a series of rapids. Dippers and wagtails flit through the trees, and there's a pleasant woodland walk to Siblyback Lake reservoir just over a mile away.

North and east of Siblyback Lake are some of Bodmin Moor's grandest landscapes. The quite modest elevations of Hawk's Tor (1079ft) and the lower Trewartha Tor appear enormous from the north, though they are overtopped by **Kilmar**, highest of the hills on the moor's eastern flank at 1280ft. **Stowe's Hill** is site of the moor's most famous stone pile, **The Cheesewring**, a precarious pillar of balancing granite slabs, marvellously eroded by the wind. A mile or so south down Stowe's Hill stands an artificial rock phenomenon, **The Hurlers**, a wide complex of three circles dating from about 1500 BC. The purpose of these stark upright stones is not known, though they owe their name to the legend that they were men turned to stone for playing the Celtic game of hurling on the Sabbath.

The Hurlers are easily accessible just outside **MINIONS**, Cornwall's highest village, three miles south of which stands another Stone Age survival, **Trethevy Quoit**, a chamber tomb nearly nine feet high, surmounted by a massive capstone. Originally enclosed in earth, the stones have been stripped by centuries of weathering to create Cornwall's most impressive megalithic monument.

Travel details

Buses

For information on all local and national bus services, contact Traveline ☎ 0870/608 2608 (daily 7am–9pm), 🕸 www.travelinesw.com.

Bodmin to: Newquay (3–4 daily; 30–50min); Padstow (Mon–Sat hourly, Sun 5; 55min); Plymouth (Mon–Sat every 2hr, Sun 3; 1hr 10min–1hr 30min); St Austell (Mon–Sat hourly; 50min); Truro (Mon–Sat every 2hr; 1hr 30min).

Exeter to: Newquay (2–3 daily; 3hr 15min–4hr); Penzance (3–4 daily; 4hr 30min–5hr 20min); Plymouth (hourly; 1hr 15min); Sidmouth (Mon–Sat 2 hourly, Sun hourly; 50min); Torquay (Mon–Sat hourly, Sun 3–8 daily; 1hr); Truro (2–3 daily; 3hr 30min).

Falmouth to: Helston (Mon–Sat hourly, Sun in summer 4 daily; 40min); Penzance (Mon–Sat 6 daily; 1hr 20min); St Austell (2 daily; 1hr); Truro (1–3 hourly; 35min–1hr).

Newquay to: Bodmin (4 daily; 30–50min); Exeter (2–3 daily; 3hr 15min–4hr); Padstow (Mon–Sat 5 daily, Sun 1; 1hr 25min); Plymouth (Mon–Sat every 1–2hr, Sun 4; 1hr 35min–2hr 35min); St Austell (hourly; 1hr 10min); Truro (Mon–Sat 2–4 hourly, Sun 8; 45min–1hr 30min).

Penzance to: Falmouth (Mon–Sat 6 daily; 1hr 25min); Helston (1–2 hourly; 40min–1hr); Plymouth (1–3 daily; 3hr 30min); St Austell (Mon–Sat hourly, Sun 4; 2hr); St Ives (Mon–Sat every 20–30min, Sun

hourly; 30–40min); Truro (Mon–Sat hourly, Sun 5 daily; 1hr–1hr 40min).

Plymouth to: Bodmin (Mon–Sat every 2hr, Sun 3; 1hr 10min–1hr 30min); Exeter (hourly; 1hr 15min); Falmouth (2 daily; 2hr 15min); Newquay (Mon–Sat every 1–2hr, Sun 4; 1hr 35min–2hr 35min); Penzance (1–3 daily; 3hr 20min); St Austell (5 daily; 1hr 15min); St Ives (4 daily; 3hr); Torquay (hourly; 1hr 45min); Truro (5–6 daily; 1hr 45min).

St Austell to: Bodmin (Mon–Sat hourly; 50min); Exeter (1 daily; 3hr); Falmouth (2 daily; 1hr); Newquay (hourly; 1hr 10min); Penzance (Mon–Sat hourly, Sun 4; 2hr); Plymouth (6 daily; 1hr 20min); St Ives (1–2 daily; 1hr 35min); Truro (Mon–Sat hourly, Sun every 2hr; 40min).

St Ives to: Penzance (Mon–Sat every 20–30min, Sun hourly; 30–40min); Plymouth (4 daily; 3hr); St Austell (1–2 daily; 1hr 45min); Truro (Mon–Sat hourly, Sun 2 daily; 1hr–1hr 40min).

Torquay to: Exeter (Mon–Sat hourly, Sun 3–8 daily; 1hr); Plymouth (hourly; 1hr 45min).

Truro to: Bodmin (Mon–Sat every 2hr; 1hr 30min); Exeter (2–3 daily; 3hr 35min); Falmouth (1–3 hourly; 35min–1hr); Newquay (Mon–Sat 2–4 hourly, Sun 8; 50min–1hr 30min); Penzance (Mon–Sat hourly, Sun 6 daily; 1hr 1hr 35min), Plymouth (5–6 daily; 1hr 45min); St Austell (Mon–Sat hourly, Sun every 2hr; 40min); St Mawes (Mon–Sat 7–9 daily; 1hr); St Ives (Mon–Sat hourly, Sun 2 daily; 1hr–1hr 40min).

Trains

For information on all local and national rail services, contact National Rail Enquiries ⓣ08457/484950, ⓦ www.nationalrail.co.uk.

Barnstaple to: Exeter (Mon–Sat hourly, Sun 6 daily; 1hr).

Bodmin to: Exeter (1–2 hourly; 1hr 40min); Penzance (1 hourly; 1hr 20min); Plymouth (1–2 hourly; 40min).

Exeter to: Barnstaple (Mon–Sat hourly, Sun 6 daily; 1hr); Bodmin (1–2 hourly; 1hr 45min); Bristol (1–2 hourly; 1hr 10min–1hr 25min); Exmouth (1–2 hourly; 30min); Liskeard (1–2 hourly; 1hr 30min); London (hourly; 2hr 30min); Par (hourly; 2hr); Penzance (hourly; 3hr); Plymouth (1–2 hourly; 1hr); Torquay (hourly; 45min); Totnes (1–2 hourly; 40min); Truro (hourly; 2hr 15min).

Falmouth to: Truro (10–13 daily; 25min).

Liskeard to: Exeter (1–2 hourly; 1hr 30min); Looe (hourly, not Sun in winter; 25min); Penzance (1–2 hourly; 1hr 30min); Plymouth (1–2 hourly; 25min); Truro (1–2 hourly; 50min).

Newquay to: Par (6–8 daily, not Sun in winter; 50min).

Par to: Exeter (1–2 hourly; 2hr); Newquay (6–8 daily, not Sun in winter; 50min); Penzance (hourly; 1hr 15min); Plymouth (1–2 hourly; 50min).

Penzance to: Bodmin (hourly; 1hr 20min); Exeter (hourly; 3hr); Plymouth (hourly; 2hr); St Ives (via St Erth; 1–2 hourly, not Sun in winter; 25min); Truro (1–2 hourly; 45min).

Plymouth to: Bodmin (1–2 hourly; 40min); Exeter (1–2 hourly; 1hr); Liskeard (1–2 hourly; 30min); Par (1–2 hourly; 50min); Penzance (hourly; 2hr); Truro (hourly; 1hr 15min).

St Ives to: Penzance (via St Erth; 1–2 hourly, not Sun in winter; 30min).

Torquay to: Exeter (hourly; 45min).

Truro to: Exeter (hourly; 2hr 15min); Falmouth (10–13 daily; 20min); Liskeard (1–2 hourly; 50min); Penzance (1–2 hourly; 45min); Plymouth (hourly; 1hr 20min).

7

East Anglia

CHAPTER 7

Highlights

* **Orford** Remote and peaceful hamlet making for a wonderful weekend away. **See p.400**

* **The Aldeburgh Festival** The region's prime classical music festival takes place for three weeks in June. **See p.401**

* **Southwold** A picture-perfect seaside town that is ideal for walking and bathing. **See p.402**

* **Norwich Market** This open-air market is the region's biggest and best for everything from whelks to wellies. **See p.408**

* **Holkham Bay and beach** This wide bay holds Norfolk's finest beach, acres of golden sand set against hilly dunes. **See p.415**

* **Ely** Solitary Cambridge-shire town, with a true fenland flavour and a magnificent cathedral. **See p.417**

* **Cambridge** Fine architecture, dignified old churches and manicured quadrangles jostle for position in the university city's compact centre. **See p.419**

△ Southwold beach huts

7

East Anglia

S trictly speaking, **East Anglia** is made up of just three counties – Suffolk, Norfolk and Cambridgeshire – which were settled by Angles from Holstein in the fifth century, though in more recent times it's come to be loosely applied to parts of Essex too. As a region it's renowned for its wide skies and flat landscapes, and of course such generalizations always contain more than a grain of truth – if you're looking for mountains, you've come to the wrong place. Nevertheless, East Anglia often fails to conform to its stereotype: parts of Suffolk are positively hilly, and its coastline can induce vertigo; the north Norfolk coast holds steep cliffs as well as wide sandy beaches; and even the pancake-flat fenlands are broken by wide, muddy rivers and hilly mounds, on one of which perches Ely's magnificent cathedral. Indeed, the whole region is sprinkled with fine medieval churches, the legacy of the days when this was England's most progressive and prosperous region.

Of all the region's counties, **Suffolk** is the most varied. Its undulating southern reaches, straddling the River Stour, are home to a string of picturesque, well-preserved little towns – **Lavenham** is the perfect example – which enjoyed immense prosperity during the thirteenth to sixteenth centuries, the heyday of the wool trade. Elsewhere, **Bury St Edmunds** can boast not just the ruins of its once-prestigious abbey, but also some fine Georgian architecture on its grid-plan streets, while even the much maligned county town of **Ipswich** has more to offer than it's generally given credit for. Nevertheless, for many visitors it's the north Suffolk coast that steals the local show. In **Southwold**, with its comely Georgian high street, Suffolk possesses a delightful seaside resort, elegant and relaxing in equal measure, while neighbouring **Aldeburgh** hosts one of the best music festivals in the country.

Norfolk, as everyone knows thanks to Noël Coward, is very flat. It's also one of the most sparsely populated and tranquil counties in England, a remarkable turnaround from the days when it was an economic and political powerhouse – until, that is, the Industrial Revolution simply passed it by. Its capital, **Norwich**, is still East Anglia's largest city, renowned for its Norman cathedral and castle, and for its high-tech Sainsbury Centre for Visual Arts, exhibiting a challenging collection of twentieth-century art. The most visited part of Norfolk is, however, the **Broads**, a unique landscape of reed-ridden waterways that has been intensively exploited by boat-rental companies for the last twenty years. Similarly popular, the **Norfolk coast** holds a string of busy, very English seaside resorts – **Cromer**, **Sheringham** and **Hunstanton** to name but three – but for the most part it's a charmingly unspoilt region of tiny flintstone villages with **Blakeney Point** and the surrounding marshes among the country's top nature reserves.

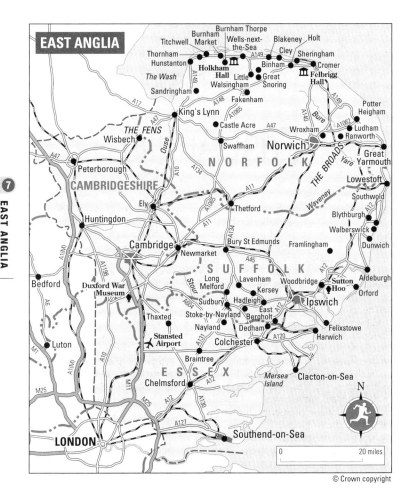

EAST ANGLIA

Burnham Thorpe
Burnham
Titchwell Market Wells-next- Blakeney Holt
the-Sea Cley
Thornham A149 Sheringham
Hunstanton Binham Cromer
Holkham Felbrigg
The Wash Hall Little Great Hall
A149 Walsingham Snoring
Sandringham Fakenham
A17 A148
A1065 Potter
King's Lynn Heigham
A47 Bure Ludham
THE FENS Ouse Castle Acre A47 Wroxham A1062 Ranworth
Wisbech Swaffham Norwich
A47 Peterborough A10 A134 N O R F O L K THE BROADS Great
Yarmouth
CAMBRIDGESHIRE Lowestoft
A11 Yare
Ely A1065 Thetford Waveney Southwold
Huntingdon A134 Blythburgh A12
A11 Walberswick
A1(M) Bury St Edmunds Framlingham Dunwich
Cambridge Newmarket A45
A11(M) S U F F O L K A12
Bedford Long Lavenham Woodbridge Sutton Aldeburgh
Duxford War Melford Kersey Hoo Orford
A6 Museum Stour Sudbury Hadleigh Ipswich
Thaxted Stoke-by-Nayland East
M1 Nayland Bergholt Felixstowe
Stansted Dedham Harwich
Luton Airport A131 Colchester A120
A10 A604
A11(M) Braintree
M25 Chelmsford A12 Mersea Clacton-on-Sea
M11 Island
M25 A130 E S S E X
N
A127
LONDON Southend-on-Sea
0 20 miles

© Crown copyright

Cambridge is the one place in East Anglia everyone visits, largely on account of its world-renowned university, whose ancient colleges boast some of the finest medieval and early modern architecture in the country. The rest of Cambridgeshire is dominated by the landscape of the **Fens**, for centuries an inhospitable marshland, which was eventually drained to provide rich alluvial farming land. The one star turn here is the cathedral town of **Ely**, settled on one of the few areas of raised ground in the fens and an easy and popular day-trip from Cambridge.

Heading into the region from the south almost inevitably takes you through **Essex**, whose proximity to London has turned much of the county into an unappetizing commuter strip with only the historic town of **Colchester** really worth a detour.

Getting around

The **train** network is at its best to and from London, with quick and frequent services from the capital to all East Anglia's major towns. One main line service links Colchester, Ipswich and Norwich, another Cambridge and Ely, which means it is relatively easy to move from one major town to another. However, once you get away from the larger towns, you have to rely on local **buses**, whose services, run by a multitude of companies, are very patchy. Indeed, in parts of north Norfolk and inland Suffolk, you may find the only way to get about is by your own transport. The largest regional bus operator is First Eastern Counties, whose **tourist tickets** provide unlimited travel on its Norfolk and Suffolk bus routes (£9 for one day; £20 for a week). These are available at major bus stations and from bus drivers. Most tourist offices carry details of local buses, while some of the more useful services are listed in the text and in "Travel details" at the end of the chapter.

Colchester

If you visit anywhere in Essex, it should be **COLCHESTER**, a busy sort of place with a castle, a university and a large army base, fifty miles or so northeast of London. Colchester prides itself on being England's oldest town and there is indeed documentary evidence of a settlement here as early as the fifth century BC. When the **Romans** invaded Britain in 43 AD they chose Colchester (Camulodunum) as their new capital, and built England's first Roman temple here. However, the town was soon eclipsed in importance by London, and became a retirement colony for legionaries instead. A millennium later, the conquering Normans built one of their mightiest strongholds in Colchester, though the conflict that most marked the town was the **Civil War**. In 1648, Colchester was subjected to a gruelling siege by the Parliamentarian army led by Lord Fairfax; after three months, during which the population ate every living creature within the walls, the town finally surrendered and the Royalist leaders were promptly executed for their pains.

Today, Colchester makes a reasonable base for further explorations of the surrounding countryside – particularly the Stour Valley towns of "Constable Country" (see pp.392–395), within easy reach a few miles to the north.

Arrival, information and accommodation

Colchester has two **train stations**, the more useful of which is Colchester North Station, for mainline services from London and Ipswich. From here it's a fifteen-minute walk south into town – follow North Station Road and its continuation North Hill until you reach the west end of the High Street. The **bus station** is off Queen Street, a couple of minutes' walk from the east end of High Street and yards from both the castle and the **tourist office**, at 1 Queen St (Mon–Sat 10am–5pm; ☏01206/282920, ⌨www.visitcolchester.com), who can supply free town maps, and book accommodation.

Colchester has its fair share of central **hotels**, including the town's oldest inn, the half-timbered *Best Western Rose & Crown*, on East Street (☏01206/866677, ⌨www.rose and crown.com; ❹), a ten minute-walk east of the tourist office, down the High Street and East Hill. The best **B&B** in town is the *Old Manse*, 15 Roman Rd (☏01206/545154, ⌨www.doveuk.com/oldmanse; ❷), with three pleasant guest rooms, set in a well-maintained, bay-windowed Victorian house on a quiet cul-de-sac; it's on the east side of the castle, a couple of minutes' walk from the tourist office.

The Town

At the heart of Colchester is its **castle**, or rather what remains of the medieval stronghold, a ruggedly imposing, honey-coloured keep, set in attractive parkland stretching down to the River Colne. Begun less than ten years after the Battle of Hastings, the keep was the largest in Europe at the time, and was built on the site of the Temple of Claudius. Inside the keep is a **museum** (Mon–Sat 10am–5pm, Sun 11–5pm; £4.70) that holds an excellent collection of Romano-British finds, including a miscellany of coins, tombstones, statues and mosaics. The museum also covers the history of the town, and has various interactive features, as well as running regular **guided tour**s (45min; £1.80) that give access to the Roman vaults, the Norman chapel and the castle roof, otherwise out of bounds. Outside, down towards the river in Castle Park, is a section of the old **Roman walls**, whose battered remains are still visible around much of the town centre.

The castle stands at the eastern end of the wide and largely pedestrianized **High Street**, which follows pretty much the same route as it did in Roman times. The most arresting building here is the flamboyant **Town Hall**, built in 1902 and topped by a statue of St Helena, mother of Constantine the Great and daughter of "Old King Cole" of nursery-rhyme fame – after whom, some say, the town was named.

Looming above the western end of the High Street is the town landmark, "**Jumbo**", a disused nineteenth-century water tower, considerably more imposing than the nearby **Balkerne Gate**, which marked the western entrance to Roman Colchester. Built in 50 AD, this is the largest surviving Roman gateway in the country, though with the remains at only a touch over six feet in height, it's far from spectacular. The gate is joined to another section of the town's **Roman Walls**, though here the effect is spoiled by the adjacent ring road.

Eating and drinking

Colchester's **oysters** have been highly prized since Roman times and the local vineyards have an equally long heritage, so it's no surprise to find the town has a good choice of first-rate **restaurants**. Note, however, that most places are closed on Sunday. Probably the best place in town is *The Hub*, 19 Head St (☎01206/564977), which offers contemporary, broadly Mediterranean dishes with main courses from around £13. Alternatively, *The Lemon Tree*, 48 St John's St (☎01206/767337; closed Sun), is moderately priced, with good lunch specials and sunny courtyard seating. For top-quality seafood, head out of town to the oyster fisheries at **West Mersea**, home of *The Company Shed*, 129 Coast Rd (☎01206/382700), where the freshest of oysters are served without any frills at rickety tables; the season runs from September to May. **Mersea Island**, home to both West and East Mersea, is located about six miles south of Colchester.

The Stour Valley and the old wool towns of south Suffolk

Five miles or so north of Colchester, the **Stour River Valley** forms the border between Essex and Suffolk, and signals the beginning of East Anglia proper. Compared with much of the region it is positively hilly, a handsome landscape of farms and woodland latticed by dense, well-kept hedges and the thick grassy banks that once kept the Stour in check. The valley is dotted with lovely little villages, where rickety, half-timbered Tudor houses and elegant Georgian dwellings cluster around medieval churches. The Stour's prettiest villages are concentrated along its lower reaches – to the east of the A134 – in Dedham Vale, with **Stoke-by-Nayland** and **Dedham** arguably the most appealing of them all. The vale is also known as "**Constable Country**", as it was the home of John Constable (1776–1837), one of England's greatest artists, and the subject of his most famous works. Inevitably, there's a Constable shrine – the much-visited complex of old buildings down by the river at **Flatford Mill**.

The villages along the River Stour and its tributaries were once busy little places at the heart of East Anglia's weaving trade, which boomed from the thirteenth to the fifteenth century. By the 1490s, the region produced more cloth than any other part of the country, but in Tudor times production shifted to Colchester, Ipswich and Norwich and, although most of the smaller settlements continued spinning cloth for the next three hundred years or so, their importance slowly dwindled. Bypassed by the Industrial Revolution, south Suffolk had, by the late nineteenth century, become a remote rural backwater, an impoverished area whose decline had one unforeseen consequence. With few exceptions, the towns and villages were never prosperous enough to modernize, and the architectural legacy of medieval and Tudor times survived. The best-preserved village is **Lavenham**, which heaves with sightseers on summer weekends, though **Sudbury** is also attractive and boasts an excellent museum devoted to the work of Thomas Gainsborough, who spent much of his time painting the local landscape.

Seeing the region by **public transport** is problematic – distances are small (Dedham Vale is only about ten miles long), but buses between the villages are infrequent and you'll find it difficult to get away from the towns. Several rail lines cross south Suffolk, the most useful being the London–Colchester–Sudbury route. More positively, **footpaths** crisscross the area, with some of the most enjoyable being in the vicinity of Dedham village. All the local tourist offices sell easy-to-use walking leaflets.

East Bergholt and Flatford Mill

"I associate my careless boyhood to all that lies on the banks of the Stour," wrote **John Constable**, who was born the son of a miller in **EAST BERGHOLT**, nine miles northeast of Colchester in 1776. The house in which he was born has long since disappeared, so it has been left to **Flatford Mill**, a mile or so to the south, to take up the painter's cause. The mill was owned by his father and was where Constable painted his most famous canvas, *The Hay Wain* (now in London's National Gallery; see p.91), which created a sensation when it was exhibited in 1824. To the chagrin of many of his contemporaries, Constable turned away from the landscape-painting conventions of the day, rendering his scenery with a realistic directness that harked back to the Dutch landscape painters of the seventeenth century. Typically, he justified this approach in unpretentious terms, observing that, after all "no two days are alike, nor even two hours; neither were there ever two leaves of a tree alike since the creation of the world." The mill itself – not the one he painted, but a Victorian replacement – is not open to the public, but the sixteenth-century thatched **Bridge Cottage** (March & April Wed–Sun 11am–5pm; May–Sept daily 10am–5.30pm; Oct daily 11am–4pm; Nov & Dec Wed–Sun 11am–3.30pm; Jan & Feb Sat & Sun 11am–3.30pm, free, except for parking; NT), which overlooks the scene,

△ Flatford Mill

has been painstakingly restored and stuffed full of Constabilia. Unfortunately, none of the artist's paintings are displayed here, but there's a pleasant riverside tearoom to take in the view. Beyond stands **Willy Lott's Cottage** (also closed to the public), which does actually feature in *The Hay Wain*.

In summer, the National Trust organizes **guided walks** around the sites of Constable's paintings (£2; call ☎01206/298260 for details), but there are many other pleasant walks to be had along this deeply rural bend in the Stour. One footpath connects the mill to the **train station** at Manningtree, two miles to the east, and another runs over to the village of Dedham, a mile and a half to the west. Alternatively, you can rent a **rowing boat** from beside the bridge and potter peacefully along the river. There's a **B&B** here too, the *Flatford Granary* (☎01206/298111; **➋**), a cottage-type affair with comfortable rooms, beamed ceilings and idyllic views.

Dedham

Constable went to school in **DEDHAM**, just upriver from Flatford Mill and one of the region's most attractive villages, with a string of ancient timber-framed houses lining its wide main street. The only sights as such are **St Mary's Church**, an early sixteenth-century structure that Constable painted on several occasions, and the **Sir Alfred Munnings Art Museum**, in Castle House (Easter–July & Sept Wed & Sun 2–5pm; Aug Wed, Thurs, Sat & Sun 2–5pm; £4; ⓦwww.siralfredmunnings.co.uk), just south of the village on the road to Ardleigh. A locally born academician, Munnings (1875–1959) is barely remembered today, but in his time he was well known for his portraits of horses. In the 1940s, Munnings became a controversial figure when, as President of the Royal Academy, he savaged almost every form of modern art there was. Few would say his paintings were inspiring, but seeing them is a pleasant way to fill a rainy afternoon. It is, however, the general flavour of Dedham which appeals most.

Monday through Saturday, a Network Colchester **bus** (☎01206/764029) runs twice daily from Colchester to Dedham, though both services depart in the late afternoon; on Sundays, First buses (☎01206/366911) run the same route every couple of hours. Dedham has one of the smartest **hotels** in the area, *Maison Talbooth* (☎01206/322367, ⓦwww.maison-talbooth.co.uk; ⓼), which occupies a good-looking Victorian country house about fifteen minutes' walk southwest of the village on the road to Stratford St Mary. All the hotel's ten large bedrooms are individually decorated in sumptuous style and dinner can be had close by at *Le Talbooth* (☎01206/323150), an expensive, but top-notch **restaurant** in an ancient timber-framed house down by the River Stour. Alternatively, there's *Dedham Hall* (☎01206/323027, ⓦwww.dedhamhall .demon.co.uk; ⓺), an old manor house set in its own grounds on the east side of the village off Brook Street – be sure to ask for a room in the house itself. The restaurant here – *The Fountain House* (closed Sun & Mon) – serves very good modern British cuisine, with a three-course set menu costing £28. You can also stay in the heart of Dedham itself at the *Marlborough Head* pub (☎01206/323250; ⓸), where a handful of very pleasant rooms are available above the bar, and excellent **food** can be had from an inventive and wide-ranging menu: main courses from about £11.

Stoke-by-Nayland

Heading northwest from Dedham, the B1029 dips beneath the A12 to reach the byroad to Higham, an unremarkable hamlet where you pick up the road to **STOKE-BY-NAYLAND**, four miles west. The most picturesque of villages, it consists of a knot of half-timbered, pastel-painted cottages and one of Constable's favourite subjects, **St Mary's church** (daily 9am–5pm; free), with its pretty brick and stone-trimmed tower. The doors of the south porch are covered by the beautifully carved figures of a medieval Jesse Tree and, although the interior is sombre and severe, it does boast a magnificent, soaring tower arch. The village also has a great old **pub**, the *Angel Inn* (☎01206/263245, ⓦwww.horizoninns .co.uk/theangel.html; ⓸), known for its adventurous food (eat in the bar or book for the restaurant) and cosy, en-suite **rooms**. There are several other good places to stay in and near the village, including the seventeenth-century *Thorington Hall* (☎01206/337329; ⓷; Easter–Sept), with four bedrooms: it's located a little over a mile east of the village back towards Higham.

Sudbury

SUDBURY, some six miles from Stoke-by-Nayland, has doubled in size in the last thirty years, to become the most important town in this part of the Stour Valley by a long chalk. A handful of timber-framed houses harks back to its days of wool-trade prosperity, but its three Perpendicular churches were underwritten by another local industry, **silk weaving**, which survives on a small scale to this day. Sudbury's most famous son, however, is **Thomas Gainsborough** (1727–1788), the leading English portraitist of the eighteenth century, whose statue, with brush and palette, stands on Market Hill, the town's predominantly Victorian market place. A superb collection of the artist's work is on display a few yards away in the house where he was born – **Gainsborough's House**, at 46 Gainsborough St (Mon–Sat 10am–5pm; £3.50). Gainsborough left Sudbury when he was just 13, moving to London where he was apprenticed to an engraver, but he was soon moonlighting and the earliest of his surviving portrait paintings – his *Boy and Girl*, a remarkably self-assured work dating from 1744 – is displayed here. In 1752, Gainsborough moved to Ipswich, where he quickly established himself as a portrait painter to the Suffolk gentry specializing in wonderful "conversation pieces", so-called because the sitters engage in polite chitchat – or genteel activity – with a landscape as the backdrop. Seven years in Ipswich was followed by a move upmarket to Bath, where he painted high-society figures, as he did when he moved back to London in 1774. During his years in Bath, Gainsborough developed a fluid, flatteringly easy style that was ideal for his aristocratic subjects, who posed in becoming postures painted in soft, evanescent colours. Examples of Gainsborough's later work exhibited here include the *Portrait of Harriet, Viscountess Tracy* (1763) and the particularly striking *Portrait of Abel Moysey, MP* (1771). Gainsborough's only assistant, his nephew **Gainsborough Dupont**, also has a room devoted to his work on the top floor of the house. There's also a pleasant **tearoom** in the garden.

Sudbury is accessible by **train** from Colchester, 14 miles away (for some services, change at Marks Tey), and is the hub of **bus** services to and from neighbouring towns and villages including Colchester and Ipswich. Once you've seen Gainsborough's house, there's little reason to spend the night, but if you decide to stay, the **tourist office** in the town hall on Market Hill (April–Sept Mon–Fri 9am–5pm & Sat 10am–4.45pm; Oct–March Mon–Fri 9am–5pm & Sat 10am–2.45pm; ☏01787/881320, ⓦwww.visit-suffolk.org.uk) can provide **accommodation** details.

Lavenham

Some eight miles northeast of Sudbury, off the A134, lies **LAVENHAM**, formerly a centre of the region's wool trade and today one of the most visited villages in Suffolk, thanks to its unrivalled ensemble of perfectly preserved half-timbered houses. The whole place has changed little since the demise of the wool industry, owing in part to a zealous local preservation society that has carefully maintained the village's antique appearance by banning from view such modern frivolities as advertising hoardings and TV aerials.

The village is at its most beguiling in the triangular **Market Place**, an airy spot flanked by pastel-painted, medieval dwellings whose beams have been bent into all sorts of wonky angles by the passing of the years. It's here you'll find Lavenham's most celebrated building, the pale-white, timber-framed **Corpus Christi Guildhall** (March & Nov Sat & Sun 11am–4pm; April Wed–Sun 11am–5pm; May–Oct daily 11am–5pm; £3.25; NT), erected in the sixteenth century as the headquarters of one of Lavenham's four guilds. In the much-altered interior (used successively as a prison and workhouse), there are exhibitions on timber-framed buildings and the wool industry, though most visitors head straight for the walled garden and the teashop. The other noteworthy building is the Perpendicular **church of St Peter and St Paul** (daily: May–Sept 8.30am–5.30pm; Oct–April 8.30am–3.30pm; free), a short walk southwest of the centre, at the top of Church Street. Local merchants endowed the church with a nave of majestic proportions and a mighty flint tower, at 141ft the highest for miles around, partly to celebrate the Tudor victory at the Battle of Bosworth in 1485, but mainly to manifest their wealth.

Practicalities

There are fairly frequent **buses** between Colchester and Bury St Edmunds that stop in Lavenham and Sudbury. Lavenham's **tourist office,** on Lady Street (April–Oct daily 10am–4.45pm; Nov–March Sat & Sun 11am–4pm; ☏01787/248207, ⓦwww.visit-suffolk.org.uk), just south off Market Place, can help with **accommodation** and sells a detailed, street-by-street walking guide. Rooms at the *Swan Hotel* (☏01787/247477, ⓦwww.theswanatlavenham .co.uk; ⓿), a splendid old inn on High Street, are some of the most comfortable in town; the building incorporates part of the Elizabethan Wool Hall and is a warren of cosy lounges and courtyard gardens. There's more luxurious accommodation at *Lavenham Priory B&B*, on Water Street (☎01787/247404, ⓦwww .lavenhampriory.co.uk; ❻), where four immaculate rooms are contained within an old Benedictine priory. Less expensive options on the Market Place include the ancient *Angel Hotel* (☎01787/247388, ⓦwww.theangelhotel-lavenham .co.uk; ❺), with eight pleasant rooms above its bar, and the dinky *Angel Gallery* (☎01787/248417, ⓦwww.lavenham.co.uk/angelgallery; ❻), with three guest rooms situated above an art shop. Cheaper B&B options can be found outside Lavenham; ask at the tourist office for details.

For **food**, the *Angel Hotel* and the *Swan* both serve excellent, moderately priced bar meals, or there's the outstanding *Great House* restaurant on Market Place (☎01787/247431; closed Sun eve & Mon): chic and smart, it specializes in classic French cuisine, with main courses around £17.

Bury St Edmunds

Appealing **BURY ST EDMUNDS** started out as a Benedictine monastery, founded to house the remains of Edmund, the last Saxon king of East Anglia, who was tortured and beheaded by the marauding Danes in 869. Almost two centuries later, England was briefly ruled by the kings of Denmark and the shrewdest of them, **King Canute**, made a gesture of reconciliation to his Saxon subjects by conferring on the monastery the status of abbey. It was a popular move and the abbey prospered, so much so that before its dissolution in 1539, it had become the richest religious house in the country. Most of the abbey disappeared long ago, and nowadays Bury is better known for its graceful Georgian streets, its flower gardens and its sugar-beet plant than for its ancient monuments. Nevertheless, it's still an amiable, eminently likeable place, one of the prettiest towns in Suffolk, and has good transport connections on to Cambridge, Colchester, Ipswich and Norwich.

The Town

The town centre has preserved much of its Norman street plan, a gridiron in which Churchgate was aligned with – and sloped up from – the abbey's high altar. It was the first planned town of Norman Britain and, for that matter, the first example of urban planning in England since the departure of the Romans. At the heart of the town, beside the abbey grounds, is **Angel Hill**, a broad, spacious square partly framed by Georgian buildings, the most distinguished being the ivy-covered **Angel Hotel**, which features in Dickens' *Pickwick Papers*. Dickens also gave readings of his work in the **Athenaeum**, the Georgian assembly rooms at the far end of the square. A twelfth-century wall runs along the east side of Angel Hill, with the bulky fourteenth-century **Abbey Gate** forming the entrance to the abbey gardens and ruins beyond.

The **abbey ruins** themselves (open access) are like nothing so much as petrified porridge, with little to remind you of the grandiose Norman complex that dominated the town. Thousands of medieval pilgrims once sought solace at St Edmund's altar and the cult was of such significance that the barons of England gathered here to swear that they would make King John sign their petition – the Magna Carta of 1215. Today, the only significant remnants are on the far side of the abbey gardens, behind the more modern cathedral (see below), and they comprise the rubbled remains of a small part of the old **abbey church** integrated into a set of unusual Georgian houses. In front, across the green, is the imposing **Norman Tower**, once the main gateway into the abbey and now a solitary monument with dragon gargoyles and fancily decorated capitals.

Incongruously, the tower is next to the front part of Bury's Anglican **Cathedral of St James** (daily: 8.30am–6pm; £2 donation requested), with chancel and transepts added as recently as the 1960s. It was a toss-up between this church and **St Mary's** (Mon–Sat 10am–4pm, 3pm in winter; free), further down Crown Street, as to which would be granted cathedral status in 1914. The presence of the tomb of the resolutely Catholic Mary Tudor in the latter was the clinching factor.

Bury's **main commercial area** is on the west side of the centre, a five-minute walk up Abbeygate Street from Angel Hill. There's been some intrusive modern planning here, but dignified Victorian buildings flank both **Cornhill** and **Buttermarket**, the two short main streets, as well as the narrower streets in between. Also between the two is **Bury St Edmunds Art Gallery** (Tues–Sat 10.30am–5pm; £1; ⓦ www.burystedmundsartgallery.org), which features a lively programme of temporary exhibitions focusing on contemporary fine and applied art.

Practicalities

From Bury St Edmunds' **train station**, it's ten minutes' walk south to Angel Hill via Northgate Street. The **bus station** is on St Andrew Street North, just north of Cornhill. The town's **tourist office**, at 6 Angel Hill (Easter–Oct Mon–Sat 9.30am–5.30pm, Sun 10am–3pm; Nov–Easter Mon–Fri 10am–4pm, Sat 10am–1pm; ⓣ 01284/764667, ⓦ www.stedmundsbury.gov.uk), provides free town maps and has a useful range of leaflets. The pick of the town's **hotels** is the immaculately maintained ⚔ *Angel*, on Angel Hill (ⓣ 01284/714000, ⓦ www .theangel.co.uk; ⓐ), a former coaching inn with wood-panelling, thick carpets and suitably smart rooms. A good alternative is the *Chantry Hotel*, 8 Sparhawk St (ⓣ 01284/767427, ⓦ www.smoothhound.co.uk/hotels/chantryh.html; ⓓ), with fifteen smart guest-rooms in two converted Georgian townhouses, located just to the south of the abbey ruins off Honey Hill.

For **restaurants**, ⚔ *Maison Bleue*, 31 Churchgate St (ⓣ 01284/760623; closed Sun & Mon), is the best option with a wide range of wonderfully fresh seafood from crab through to sardines and skate; main courses kick off at just £11. *The Vaults*, inside the medieval undercroft at the *Angel* hotel, is a good second choice with main courses from £10. Otherwise, fill up on coffee, cakes and **snacks** in either the Cathedral *Refectory* (closed Sun) or the *Scandinavia Coffee House*, 30 Abbeygate St. Of the **pubs**, don't miss the *Nutshell* (closed Sun), on The Traverse at the top of Abbeygate, which, at sixteen feet by seven and a half, claims to be Britain's smallest, and even better, serves real ales. Finally, the **Theatre Royal**, at the junction of Crown and Westgate streets (ⓣ 01284/769505, ⓦ www.theatreroyal.org), offers a year-round programme of cultural events, from Shakespeare to pantomime.

Ipswich

Situated at the head of the Orwell estuary, **IPSWICH** was a rich trading port in the Middle Ages, but its appearance today is mainly the result of a revival of fortunes in the Victorian era – give or take some clumsy postwar development. The ancient Saxon market place, **Cornhill**, is still the town's focal point, a likeable urban space flanked by a bevy of imposing Victorian edifices. From here, it's just a couple of minutes' walk to Ipswich's most famous building, the **Ancient House**, on St Stephen's Lane, whose exterior was decorated around 1670 in extravagant style, a riot of pargeting and stucco work that together make it one of the finest examples of Restoration artistry in the country. From the Ancient House, it's a short hop to the gates of **Christchurch Mansion** (Tues–Sat 10am–5pm & Sun 2.30–4.30pm; free), a handsome, if much-restored Tudor building, sporting seventeenth-century Dutch gables and set in 65 acres of parkland – an area larger than the town centre itself. The mansion's labyrinthine interior is well worth exploring, with period furnishings and a good assortment of paintings by Constable and Gainsborough, as well as more contemporary art exhibitions.

On the other side of the town centre, about half a mile southeast of Cornhill, the **Wet Dock** was the largest dock in Europe when it opened in 1845. Today, after an imaginative refurbishment, it's flanked by apartments, offices, pubs, hotels and restaurants, many converted from the old marine warehouses. Walking round the Wet Dock is a pleasant way to pass an hour or so – look out, in particular, for the proud Neoclassical **Customs House** on the Neptune Quay. In July and August, Orwell River Cruises (☎01473/836680, ⓦwww.orwellrivercruises.com) runs weekly **boat trips** from the Orwell Quay on the Wet Dock down the River Orwell to Pin Mill, a rural picnic spot on the west bank of the river; the trip lasts two and a half hours and costs £8.

Practicalities

Ipswich **train station** is on the south bank of the River Orwell, about ten minutes' walk from Cornhill along Princes Street. The **bus station** is more central, occupying part of the old cattle market, a short walk south of Cornhill and near the **tourist office**, in the converted St Stephen's church, off St Stephen's Lane (Mon–Sat 9am–5pm; ☎01473/258070, ⓦwww.visit-suffolk.org.uk).

Ipswich has one really good **hotel**, the *Salthouse Harbour*, in an imaginatively converted old warehouse, down by the Wet Dock at 1 Neptune Quay (☎01473/226789, ⓦwww.salthouseharbour.com; ➐). It has great views over the harbour from its upper floors and the rooms are decorated in modern, minimalist style. The hotel **brasserie** is good too, with a surprisingly varied menu – from liver and parsnips to daily seafood specials: main courses average around £11. For entertainment, the Ipswich Film Theatre, in the Corn Exchange beside the Cornhill (☎01473/433100, ⓦwww.ipswich-ents.co.uk), shows a mix of mainstream and art **films**.

The Suffolk coast

The **Suffolk coast** feels detached from the rest of the county: the road and rail lines from Ipswich to the seaport of Lowestoft funnel traffic five miles inland for most of the way, with patches of marsh and woodland making the separation still more complete. The coast has long been plagued by erosion and this has contributed to the virtual extinction of the local fishing industry, and, in the case of **Dunwich**, almost destroyed the whole town. What is left, however, is undoubtedly one of the most unspoilt shorelines in the country – if, that is, you set aside the Sizewell nuclear power station. Highlights include the sleepy isolation of minuscule **Orford** and several genteel resorts, most notably **Southwold**, which has evaded the lurid fate of so many English seaside towns. There are scores of delightful **walks** hereabouts, easy routes along the coast that are best followed with either OS map #156 or #0169, or the simplified *Footpath Maps* available at most tourist offices. The Suffolk coast is also host to East Anglia's most compelling cultural gathering, the three-week-long **Aldeburgh Festival**, which takes place each June.

Orford and Orford Ness

Some twenty miles from Ipswich, on the far side of Tunstall Forest, two medieval buildings dominate the tiny, appealing village of **ORFORD**. The more impressive is the twelfth-century **castle** (April–Sept daily 10am–6pm; Oct–March Thurs–Mon 10am–4pm; £4.30; EH), built on high ground by Henry II, and under siege within months of its completion from Henry's rebellious sons. Most of the castle disappeared centuries ago, but the lofty keep remains, its impressive stature hinting at the scale of the original fortifications. Orford's other medieval edifice is **St Bartholomew's Church**, where Benjamin Britten premiered his most successful children's work, *Noye's Fludde*, as part of the 1958 Aldeburgh Festival (see box, p.401).

From the top of the castle keep, there's a great view across **Orford Ness Nature Reserve**, a six-mile-long shingle spit that has all but separated Orford from the sea since Tudor times. Its mud flats and marshes harbour sea-lavender beds, which act as feeding and roosting areas for wildfowl and waders. The National Trust offers **boat trips** (April to June & Oct Sat only; July–Sept Tues–Sat; outward boats between 10am–2pm, last ferry back 5pm; £5.90, NT members £3.90; ☎01394/450057) across to the Ness from Orford Quay, four hundred yards down the road from the church, and a five-mile hiking trail threads its way along the spit. En route, the trail passes the occasional, abandoned **military building**. Some of the pioneer research on radar was carried out here, but the radar station was closed at the beginning of World War II because of the threat of German bombing – though the military stayed on until the 1980s. There are also plenty of **walks** to be had around Orford itself. One of the best is the five-mile hike north along the river wall that guards the west bank of the River Alde, returning via Ferry Road, a narrow country lane.

Orford's gentle and unhurried air is best experienced by staying overnight at the excellent ⚐ *Crown & Castle Hotel*, in a modest-looking building on the main square, Market Hill (☎01394/450205, ⓦwww .crownandcastlehotel.co.uk; ❻). Inside, the hotel is stylish with pastel-painted guest rooms and top-of-the-range beds, as well as a very good **restaurant**, where the emphasis is on local ingredients (main courses cost around £12). However, the ⚐ *Butley Orford Oysterage* (☎01394/450277, ⓦwww.butleyorfordoysterage; closed Oct–April), just a few yards away, is the real draw here. It catches its own fish and shellfish and has its own smokehouses, whose produce can be bought at the shop, ordered by email or sampled at the very reasonably priced **café/restaurant**, which is especially famous for its fresh oysters. For a **pint**, it's the *Crown & Castle* again or the *Jolly Sailor Inn*, down near the quay.

Aldeburgh and around

ALDEBURGH, just along the coast from Orford, is best known for its annual arts festival, the brainchild of composer **Benjamin Britten** (1913–76), who is buried in the village churchyard alongside the tenor Peter Pears, his lover and musical collaborator. They lived by the seafront in Crag House on Crabbe Street – named after the poet, George Crabbe, who provided Britten with his greatest inspiration (see below). Outside of June, when the festival takes place, and maybe November, when the three-day international poetry festival fills the town, Aldeburgh is the quietest of places, with just a small fishing fleet selling its daily catch from wooden shacks along the pebbled shore.

The wide **High Street** and its narrow sidestreets run close to the beach, but this was not always the case – hence their garbled appearance. The sea swallowed most of what was once an extensive medieval town long ago and today Aldeburgh's oldest remaining building, the sixteenth-century, red-brick, flint and timber **Moot Hall**, which began its days in the centre of town, now finds itself on the seashore. Several **footpaths** radiate out from Aldeburgh, with the most obvious trail leading north along the coast to Thorpeness, and others leading southwest to the winding estuary of the **River Alde**, an area rich in wildfowl.

Practicalities

Aldeburgh's festival box office (see box, below) shares its High Street premises with the village **tourist office** (daily 9am–5.30pm, till 5.15pm in winter; ☎01728/453637, ⊛www.suffolkcoastal.gov.uk/tourism), which can book **accommodation**, though during the festival you'll need to book well in advance. The town boasts several splendidly sited **hotels**, including the family-owned *Wentworth* (☎01728/452312, ⊛www.wentworth-aldeburgh .com; ❺), along the seafront from the Moot Hall: it's a good-looking Edwardian mansion with forty well-appointed guest rooms, decorated in a crisp and

---

Benjamin Britten and the Aldeburgh Festival

Born in Lowestoft in 1913, **Benjamin Britten** was closely associated with Suffolk for most of his life. The main break was during World War II when, as a conscientious objector, Britten exiled himself to the USA. Ironically enough, it was here that Britten first read the work of the nineteenth-century Suffolk poet, George Crabbe, whose *The Borough*, a grisly portrait of the life of the fishermen of Aldeburgh, was the basis of the libretto of Britten's best-known opera, *Peter Grimes*. The latter was premiered in London in 1945 to great acclaim.

In 1947 Britten founded the English Opera Group and the following year launched the **Aldeburgh Festival** as a showpiece for his own works and those of his contemporaries. He lived in the village for the next ten years and it was during this period that he completed much of his best work as a conductor and pianist. For the rest of his life he composed many works specifically for the festival, including his masterpiece for children, *Noye's Fludde*, and the last of his fifteen operas, *Death in Venice*.

By the mid-1960s, the festival had outgrown the parish churches in which it began, and moved into a collection of disused malthouses, five miles west of Aldeburgh on the River Alde, just south of the small village of **Snape** along the B1069. **Snape Maltings** was subsequently converted into one of the finest concert venues in the country. In addition to the concert hall, there's now a recording studio, a music school, various craft shops and galleries, a tearoom, and a nice pub, the *Plough & Sail*.

The Aldeburgh Festival takes place every June for two and a half weeks. Core performances are still held at the Maltings, but a string of other local venues are pressed into service too. In addition, a wide-ranging programme of musical and theatrical events runs for much of the year, with another highlight being the Proms season in August. For more information, contact Aldeburgh Productions, Snape Maltings, Concert Hall Snape, Suffolk, or the box office on Aldeburgh High Street (both ☎01728/687110, ⊛www.aldeburgh.co.uk). **Tickets** for the Aldeburgh Festival itself usually go on sale to the public towards the end of March, and sell out fast for the big-name recitals.

cheerful modern style. Of the **B&Bs**, the best is *Ocean House*, 25 Crag Path
(☎01728/452094; no cards; ❺), in an immaculately maintained Victorian dwelling right on the seafront in the centre of town; there's homemade bread for
breakfast, too. Finally, there's a YHA **hostel** in the old village school on Heath
Walk in the hamlet of **Blaxhall** (☎0870/7705702, ⓦwww.yha.org.uk; dorm
beds £11, doubles ❶): it has forty beds in two- to six-bedded rooms and is open
all year, though advance reservations are required. Blaxhall is a couple of miles
southwest of the concert facilities at Snape Maltings (see above).

There are tearooms and fish-and-chip shops on the High Street, but Aldeburgh also has a glut of terrific **café/restaurants**. *152 Aldeburgh*, 152 High St
(☎01728/454594), is one of the best, with coffee and pastries in the morning
through to stylishly prepared fresh fish dinners at night, all served in modern
surroundings; the good-value daily menu has main courses at around £10. For
drinks, head to the *White Lion Hotel*, just along the seafront from the Moot
Hall.

Dunwich

One-time seat of the kings of East Anglia, a bishopric and formerly the largest
port on the Suffolk coast, the ancient city of **DUNWICH**, about twelve miles
up the coast from Aldeburgh, reached its peak of prosperity in the twelfth
century. Over the last millennium, however, something like a mile of land has
been lost to the sea, a process that continues at the rate of about a yard a year. As
a result, the whole of the medieval city now lies underwater, including all twelve
churches, the last of which toppled over the cliffs in 1919. All that survives today
are fragments of the Greyfriars monastery, which originally lay to the west
of the city and now dangles at the sea's edge. For a potted history of the lost
city, head for the **museum** (March Sat & Sun 2.30–4.30pm; April–Sept daily
11.30am–4.30pm; Oct daily noon–4pm; free) in what's left of Dunwich – little
more than one small street of terraced houses built by the local landowner in
the nineteenth century.

A sprawling, coastline **car park** gives ready access to this part of the seashore
and is also where fishing boats still sell their catches off the shingle beach.
From the car park, it's a short stroll to the village and the remains of Greyfriars, beyond which you can hike along the coast to **Dunwich Heath**, where
the coastguard cottages house a National Trust shop and tearoom (mid-July
to mid-Sept daily 10am–5pm; mid-Sept to mid-July varies, but always open
Sat & Sun from 10am; ☎01728/648505). The heath is itself next to the
Minsmere RSPB Nature Reserve (daily 9am to dusk, or 9pm if earlier; £5),
where terns nest on the beach in summer, with avocets, marsh harriers and
bitterns circling above. In the autumn, it's a gathering place for wading birds
and waterfowl, which arrive here by the hundred. You can rent binoculars from
the RSPB **visitor centre** (for times, call ☎01728/648 281) and strike out on
the trails to the birdwatching hides.

Southwold

Perched on robust cliffs just to the north of the River Blyth, **SOUTHWOLD**
gained what Dunwich lost, and by the sixteenth century it had overtaken all
its local rivals. Its days as a busy fishing port are, however, long gone – though
a small fleet still brings in herring, sprats and cod – and today it's a genteel
seaside resort, an eminently appealing little town with none of the crassness
of many of its competitors. There are fine old buildings, a long sandy beach,
open heathland, a dinky harbour and even a little industry – in the shape of

the Adnams Brewery – but no burger bars and certainly no amusement arcades. This gentility was not to the liking of **George Orwell**, who lived for a time at his parents' house at 36 High St (a plaque marks the spot). Orwell heartily disliked the town's airs and graces, and has left no trace of his time here – apart from disguised slights in a couple of early novels.

Southwold's breezy **High Street** is framed by attractive, mainly Georgian buildings, which culminate in the pocket-sized Market Place. From here, it's a brief stroll along East Street to the curious **Sailors' Reading Room** (daily: April–Sept 9am–5pm; Oct–March 9am–3.30pm; free), decked out with model ships and nautical texts, and the bluff above the **beach**, where row upon row of candy-coloured huts march across the sands. Queen Street begins at the Market Place too, quickly leading to **South Green**, the prettiest of several greens dotted across town. In 1659, a calamitous fire razed much of Southwold and when the town was rebuilt the greens were left to act as firebreaks. Beyond South Green, both Ferry Road and the ferry footpath lead down to the **harbour**, at the mouth of the River Blyth, an idyllic spot, where fishing smacks rest against old wooden jetties and nets are spread out along the banks to dry. A harbourside footpath leads to a tiny, passenger **ferry** (Easter–May Sat & Sun 10am–12.30pm & 2–4.30pm; June–Aug daily 10am–12.30pm & 2–4.30pm; 40p), which crosses the river to Walberswick. Turn right after the *Harbour Inn* and right again to walk back into town across **Southwold Common**. The whole circular walk takes about thirty minutes.

Back on the Market Place, it's a couple of hundred yards north along Church Street to East Green, with Adnams Brewery on one side and the stumpy lighthouse on another. Close by is Southwold's architectural pride and joy, the **church of St Edmund** (daily: June–Aug 9am–6pm; Sept–May 9am–4pm; free), a handsome fifteenth-century structure whose solid symmetries are balanced by its long and elegantly carved windows. Inside, the slender, beautifully proportioned nave is distinguished by its panelled roof, embellished with praying angels, and its intricate rood screen. From the church, it's a short walk north to the **pier**, the latest (recently revamped) incarnation of a structure that dates from 1899. Built as a landing stage for passenger ferries, the pier has had a troubled history: it has been repeatedly damaged by storms, was hit by a sea-mine and then partly chopped up by the army as a protection against German invasion in World War II.

Practicalities

With frequent services from neighbouring towns, Southwold is easy to reach by **bus**. These stop on the Market Place, yards from the **tourist office**, at 69 High St (April–Sept Mon–Fri 10am–5pm, Sat 10am–5.30pm, Sun 11am–4pm; Oct–March Mon–Fri 10.30am–3.30pm, Sat 10am–4pm; ☎01502/724 729, ⓦwww.visit-southwold.co.uk), which has details of local attractions and sells walking maps. The town has two well-known **hotels** beside the Market Place, both owned and run by Adnams. The smarter of the two is ⚑ *The Swan* (☎01502/722186, ⓦwww.adnams.co.uk; ❻), which occupies a splendid Georgian building with lovely period rooms, in the main house and in a garden annexe behind, though some are a little on the small side. *The Crown*, just along the High Street (☎01502/722275, ⓦwww.adnams .co.uk; ❺), has twelve simple bedrooms, all en suite. The best **B&B** in town is the delightful ⚑ *Acton Lodge*, 18 South Green (☎01502/723217, ⓦwww .southwold.ws/actonlodge; no credit cards; ❹), which occupies a grand Victorian house complete with its own neo-Gothic tower. The interior is deco-rated in period style with three comfortable bedrooms, and the breakfasts are delicious too. Alternatively, there's a string of **guest houses** along the seafront on North Parade, including the attractive *Dunburgh*, in a good-looking Victorian house with its own mini-tower at no. 28 (☎01502/723253, ⓦwww .southwold.ws/dunburgh; ❺); the house was built in 1890 and General Booth, the founder of the Salvation Army, was a regular visitor.

Southwold has two outstanding **places to eat**. The *Crown*'s front bar serves superb informal meals, with daily fish and meat specials and an enlightened wine list where all the choices are available by the glass. Turn up, wait for a table and expect to pay £15 or so for two courses; you'll have to book if you want to eat in the adjacent restaurant, which is pricier, slightly more adventurous and just as terrific. The *Swan*'s more formal dining room is the place for a gourmet blow-out, offering a choice of set dinners at £20–30 a head. For a **drink**, sample Adnams' brews in the *Crown*'s wood-panelled back-bar or stroll along to the ⚑ *Red Lion* on South Green.

Norwich

One of the five largest cities in Norman England, **NORWICH** once served a vast hinterland of East Anglian cloth producers, whose work was brought here by river and exported to the Continent. Its isolated position beyond the Fens meant that it enjoyed closer links with the Low Countries than with the rest of England – it was, after all, quicker to cross the North Sea than to go cross-country to London. The local textile industry, based on worsted cloth (named after the nearby village of Worstead), was further enhanced by an influx of Flemish and Huguenot weavers, who made up more than a third of the population in Tudor times. By 1700, Norwich was the second-richest city in the country after London.

With the onset of the Industrial Revolution, however, Norwich lost ground to the northern manufacturing towns – the city's famous mustard company, Colman's, is one of its few industrial success stories – and this, together with its continuing geographical isolation, has helped preserve much of the ancient street plan and many of the city's older buildings, primarily the cathedral and the castle. Isolation has also meant that the population has never swelled to any great extent and today, with just 170,000 inhabitants, Norwich remains an easy and enjoyable city to negotiate. Yet the city is no provincial backwater. In the 1960s, the foundation of the University of East Anglia (UEA) made it more **cosmopolitan** and bolstered its arts scene, while in the 1980s it attracted new high-tech companies, who created something of a mini-boom, making the city again one of England's wealthiest. As East Anglia's unofficial capital, Norwich also lies at the hub of the region's **transport** network and serves as a useful base for visiting the Broads, and even as a springboard for the north Norfolk coast.

Arrival, information and accommodation

Norwich's grandiose **train station** is on the east bank of the River Wensum, ten minutes' walk from the city centre along Prince of Wales Road. Long-distance **buses** terminate at the Surrey Street Station, also little more than ten minutes' walk from the town centre, but this time to the south (though some stop in the centre on Castle Meadow too). Information on local and regional bus services is provided by the **Traveline shop**, 17–19 Castle Meadow (Mon–Sat 8.30am–5pm; ☎0870/608 2608), which sells **tourist tickets** for the largest regional bus company, First Eastern Counties: the tickets provide

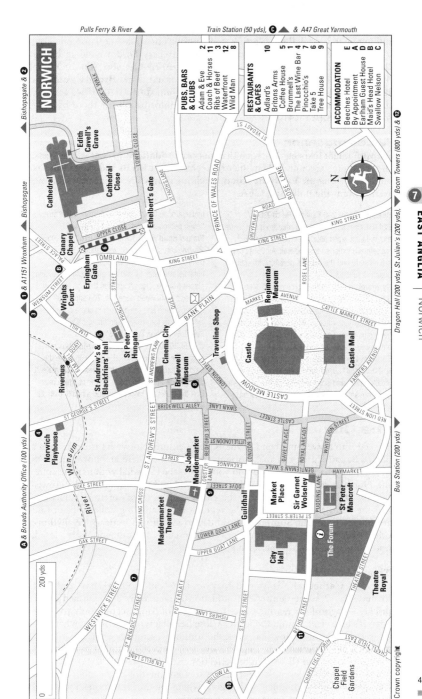

Pulls Ferry & River ▲   Train Station (50 yds), **C** ▲   & A47 Great Yarmouth

PUBS, BARS & CLUBS
Adam & Eve   2
Coach & Horses   11
Ribs of Beef   3
Waterfront   12
Wild Man   8

RESTAURANTS & CAFÉS
Adlard's   10
Britons Arms   5
Coffee House   1
Brummel's   4
The Last Wine Bar 7
Pinocchio's   6
Take 5   9

ACCOMMODATION
Beeches Hotel   E
By Appointment   A
Earlham Guest House   D
Maid's Head Hotel   B
Swallow Nelson   C

N

Edith Cavell's Grave

Cathedral

Cathedral Close

Ethelbert's Gate

Erpingham Gate

Canary Chapel

Wrights Court

St Peter Hungate

St Andrew's & Blackfriars' Hall

Cinema City

Bridewell Museum

Traveline Shop

Castle

Regimental Museum

Castle Mall

Norwich Playhouse

Riverbus

St John Maddermarket

Maddermarket Theatre

Guildhall

Market Place

Sir Garnet Wolseley

St Peter Mancroft

The Forum

City Hall

Theatre Royal

Chapel Field Gardens

Bishopsgate & ②

Bishopsgate

① & A1151 Wroxham

Dragon Hall (200 yds), St Julian's (200 yds)

Boom Towers (800 yds) & ⑫

Bus Station (200 yds)

Derham Road & A47

Earlham Road

Earlham Road & UEA

A & Broads Authority Office (100 yds)

200 yds

© Crown copyright

unlimited travel on their Norfolk and Suffolk bus routes (£9 for one day; £20 for a week). The **tourist office** is in the glassy Forum building beside the Market Place (Mon–Sat 10am–5.30/6pm; April–Oct also Sun 10.30am–4.30pm; ℡01603/727927, Ⓦwww.norwich.gov.uk). The **Broads Authority Office**, 18 Colegate (Mon–Fri 9.30am–5pm; ℡01603/610734, Ⓦwww.broads-authority.gov.uk), is a useful source of information for those heading for the Broads (see p.410).

Accommodation

As you might expect, Norwich has **accommodation** to suit all budgets, though there's precious little in the town centre. Most **B&Bs** and **guest houses** are strung along the **Earlham Road**, a tedious, mostly Victorian street running west towards the university, UEA.

EAST ANGLIA | Norwich

Beeches Hotel 2–6 Earlham Rd ℡01603/621167. Just across the ring road from the centre, this medium-sized hotel occupies three fully modernized Victorian townhouses. All 36 rooms are en suite and the place is popular with visiting business folk. ❺

By Appointment 25 St George's St ℡01603/630730. Norwich's most unusual hotel – really a restaurant with four en-suite rooms. The whole caboodle is jam–packed with antiques, and the bedrooms come complete with beamed ceilings and heavy-drape curtains. ❻

Earlham Guest House 147 Earlham Rd ℡01603/454169, Ⓦwww.earlhamguesthouse.co.uk. Spick-and-span lodgings at this family-run guest house, located in a two-storey Victorian house a good ten minutes' walk from the centre. Seven bedrooms, each with a TV. ❸

Maid's Head Hotel Tombland ℡01603/209955, Ⓦwww.corushotels.co.uk/maidshead. Bang in the centre, opposite the cathedral, this smart, chain hotel incorporates all sorts of architectural bits and pieces from Art Deco flourishes through to heavy Victorian-style wood panelling. The end result is quite pleasing and the bedrooms come complete with modern furnishings and fittings. ❻

Swallow Nelson Prince of Wales Road ℡01603/760260, Ⓦwww.swallow-hotels.com. This modern, riverside hotel, directly opposite the train station, caters to a mainly business clientele. It offers spick-and-span rooms, some of which overlook the water, an indoor pool and a health club. ❼

The City

Tucked into a sweeping bend of the River Wensum, Norwich's irregular street plan, a Saxon legacy, can make orientation difficult. There are, however, three obvious landmarks to help you find your way – the cathedral with its giant spire, the Norman castle on its commanding mound and the distinctive clocktower of City Hall. The **cathedral** and the **castle** are the town's premier attractions and the latter also holds one of the region's most satisfying collections of fine art. Finally, note that **Sunday** is a bad day to visit if you want to see anything other than the cathedral: the majority of museums and attractions are closed, not to mention most of the restaurants.

The Cathedral

Norwich **Cathedral** (daily: mid-May to mid-Sept 7.30am–7pm; mid-Sept to mid-May 7.30am–6pm; £2.50 donation requested) is distinguished by its prickly octagonal spire, which rises to a height of 315ft, second only to Salisbury. It's best viewed from the Lower Close (see below) to the south, where the thick curves of the flying buttresses, the rounded excrescences of the ambulatory chapels – unusual in an English cathedral – and the straight symmetries of the main trunk can all be seen to perfection.

The **interior** is pleasantly light thanks to a creamy tint in the stone and the clear glass windows of much of the **nave**, where the thick pillars are a powerful legacy of the Norman builders who began the cathedral in 1096. Look up to spy the nave's fan vaulting, delicate and geometrically precise carving adorned by several hundred roof **bosses** recounting – from east to west – the story of the Old and New Testaments from the Creation to the Last Judgement. Moving on down the south side of the ambulatory, you reach **St Luke's Chapel** where the cathedral's finest work of art, the *Despenser Reredos*, is a superb painted panel commissioned to celebrate the crushing of the Peasants' Revolt of 1381.

Accessible from the south aisle of the nave are the cathedral's unique **cloisters**. Built between 1297 and 1450, and the only two-storey cloisters left standing in England, they contain a remarkable set of sculpted **bosses**, similar to the ones in the main nave, but here they are close enough to be scrutinized without binoculars. The carving is fabulously intricate and the dominant theme is the **Apocalypse**, but look out also for the bosses depicting green men, pagan fertility symbols.

The cathedral precincts

Outside, beside the main entrance, stands the medieval **Canary Chapel**, the original building of Norwich School, whose blue-blazered pupils are often visible during term time – the rambling school buildings are adjacent. A statue of the school's most famous boy, Horatio Nelson, faces the chapel, standing on the green of the **Upper Close**, which is guarded by two ornate and imposing medieval gates, **Erpingham** and, a few yards to the south, **Ethelbert**. Beside the Erpingham gate is a memorial to **Edith Cavell**, a local woman who was a nurse in occupied Brussels during World War I. She was shot by the Germans in 1915 for helping Allied prisoners to escape, a fate that made her an instant folk hero; her grave is outside the cathedral ambulatory. Both gates lead onto the old Saxon market place, **Tombland**, a wide and busy thoroughfare whose name derives from the Saxon word for an open space.

Tombland is a convenient place to start an exploration of the rest of the city centre, but instead you might prefer to wander the pedestrianized **Cathedral Close**, which extends east to the river from – and including – the Upper Close. Just beyond the Upper Close is the **Lower Close**, where attractive Georgian and Victorian houses flank a scattering of wispy silver birches. Keeping straight, the footpath continues east to **Pull's Ferry**, a landing stage at the city's medieval watergate, named after the last ferryman to work this stretch of the river. It's a picturesque spot and from here you can wander along the riverbank either south to the railway station or north to Bishopgate, then back to Tombland.

From Tombland to Elm Hill and St Andrew's Hall

At the north end of Tombland, fork left into Wensum Street and cobbled **Elm Hill**, more a gentle slope than a hill, soon appears on the left. J.B. Priestley, in his *English Journey* of 1933, thought this part of Norwich to be overbearingly Dickensian, proclaiming "it difficult to believe that behind those bowed and twisted fronts there did not live an assortment of misers, mad spinsters, saintly clergymen, eccentric comic clerks, and lunatic sextons." Since then, the tourist crowds have sucked the atmosphere, but the quirky half-timbered houses still appeal. While you're here take a look at **Wright's Court**, down a passageway at no. 43, one of the few remaining enclosed courtyards which were once a feature of the city. Elm Hill quickly opens out into a triangular square centred on a plane tree, planted on the spot where the eponymous elm tree once stood. It then veers left up to **St Peter Hungate**, a good-looking, fifteenth-century flint church equipped with a solid square tower and gentle stone tracery round its windows.

Turn right at the church and it's just a few yards to **St Andrew's Hall** and **Blackfriars Hall**, two adjoining buildings that were originally the nave and chancel, respectively, of a Dominican monastery church. Imaginatively recycled, the two halls are used for a variety of public events, including concerts, weddings and antique fairs, while the crypt of the former now serves as a café (Mon–Sat 10am–4.30pm).

The Market Place

From Blackfriars Hall, it's a short walk through to the city's **Market Place**, site of one of the country's largest open-air markets (Mon–Sat), with stalls selling everything from bargain-basement clothes to local mussels and whelks. Four very different but equally distinctive buildings oversee the market's stripy awnings, the oldest of them being the fifteenth-century **Guildhall**, an attractive flint and stone structure begun in 1407. Opposite, commanding the heights of the market place, are the austere **City Hall**, a lumbering brick pile with a landmark clocktower built in the 1930s in a Scandinavian style – it bears a striking resemblance to Oslo's city hall – and **The Forum**, a flashy, glassy structure completed in 2001. The latter is home to the tourist office (see p.406) and the interactive **Origins** exhibition (Mon–Sat 10am–5.25pm, Sun 11am–4.45pm; £5.95; ⓦ www .theforumnorfolk.co.uk/visiting/origins), exploring everything to do with Norwich and Norfolk from its history to a feature on the local accent. On the south side of the Market Place is the finest of the four buildings, **St Peter Mancroft** (Mon–Fri 9.30am–4.30pm, Sat 10am–3pm; free), whose long and graceful nave leads to a mighty stone tower, an intricately carved affair surmounted by a spiky little spire. The church once delighted John Wesley, who declared "I scarcely ever remember to have seen a more beautiful parish church," a fair description of what remains an exquisite example of the Perpendicular style with the slender columns of the nave reaching up towards the delicate groining of the roof.

Back outside and just below the church is the **Sir Garnet Wolseley** pub, sole survivor of the 44 ale houses that once crowded the Market Place – and stirred the local bourgeoisie into endless discussions about the drunken fecklessness of the working class. Opposite the pub, across **Gentlemen's Walk**, the town's main promenade, which runs along the bottom of the market place, is the **Royal Arcade**, an Art Nouveau extravagance from 1899. The arcade has been beautifully restored to reveal the swirl and blob of the tiling, ironwork and stained glass, though it's actually the eastern entrance, further from Gentlemen's Walk, which is the most appealing section.

The Castle

Perched high on a grassy mound in the centre of town – and imaginatively tailored into a modern shopping-mall below – the stern walls of **Norwich Castle** date from the twelfth century. To begin with they were a reminder of Norman power and then, when the castle was turned into a prison, they served as a grim warning to potential law-breakers. Now refurbished in lavish style, the castle holds the **Castle Museum and Art Gallery** (Mon–Fri 10am–4.30pm, Sat 10am–5pm & Sun 1–5pm; £5.95 all zones), which is divided into zones. The **Art and Exhibitions** zone scores well with its temporary displays and boasts an outstanding selection of work by the **Norwich School**. Founded in 1803, and in existence for just thirty years, this school of landscape painters produced – for the most part – richly coloured, formally composed land- and seascapes in oil and watercolour, paintings whose realism harked back to the Dutch landscape painters of the seventeenth century. The leading figures were John Crome (1768–1821) – aka "Old Crome" – and John Sell Cotman (1782–1842), one of England's finest watercolourists. Both have a gallery to themselves and there's also a gallery devoted to those Dutch painters who influenced them.

The **Castle & History** zone has displays on Viking and Anglo-Saxon life as well as a gallery devoted to Boudicca.

The **castle keep** itself is no more than a shell, its gloomy walls towering above a scattering of local archeological finds and some gory examples of traditional forms of punishment. To see more of the keep, join one of the regular **guided tours** that explore the battlements and the dungeons.

Finally, a long, dark (and one-way) tunnel leads down from the Castle Museum to the **Royal Norfolk Regimental Museum** (Tues–Fri 10am–4.30pm, Sat 10am–5pm; £2.90, but included in the all-zone castle ticket), which tracks through the history of the regiment with remarkable candour – including an even-handed account of the regiment's police-keeping role in Northern Ireland. The exit leaves you below the castle on Market Avenue.

The University

The **University of East Anglia (UEA)** occupies a sprawling campus on the western outskirts of the city beside the B1108. Its buildings are resolutely modern concrete-and-glass blocks of varying designs – some quite ordinary, others like the prize-winning "ziggurat" halls of residence, designed by Denys Lasdun, eminently memorable. The main reason to visit is the high-tech **Sainsbury Centre for Visual Arts** (Tues–Sun 11am–5pm; mid-May to mid-Sept open till 8pm on Wed; £2; ⓦ www.scva.org.uk), built by Norman Foster in the 1970s. The interior houses one of the most varied collections of sculpture and painting in the country, donated by the family which founded the Sainsbury supermarket chain, in which the likes of Degas, Seurat, Picasso, Giacometti, Bacon and Henry Moore rub shoulders with Mayan and Egyptian antiquities. The centre also runs a first-rate programme of temporary exhibitions (call ☎01603/593199 for further details).

Buses #25, #26 and #27 run frequently to UEA from Castle Meadow.

Eating and drinking

There are plenty of **cafés and restaurants** in the city centre – most of them very good value. Decent pubs, though, are harder to find, maybe because previously serviceable places have been turned into ersatz "traditional" drinking dens for students.

Cafés and restaurants

Adlard's 79 Upper Giles St ☎01603/633522. Engaging modern-British restaurant with accomplished seasonal cooking from a brief but enticing menu. Closed Sun & Mon. Mains from £19 – the set menus, from around £25, may work out cheaper. Expensive.

Britons Arms Coffee House 9 Elm Hill. Homemade quiches, tarts, cakes and scones plus pies and salads in a quaint Elm Hill thatched house with a terraced garden. Mon–Sat 9.30am–5pm. Inexpensive.

Brummell's 7 Magdalen St ☎01603/625555. Serving the best seafood in town, a fish-fest in stylishly rustic surroundings. Mains from £16–20. Expensive.

The Last Wine Bar 70–76 St George's St ☎01603/626626. Converted factory building holding a smart wine bar, which serves up tasty bistro-style dishes. A couple of minutes' walk north of the river. Mains from £12. Closed Sun. Moderate.

Pinocchio's 11 St Benedict's St ☎01603/613318. Relaxed Italian restaurant in a pleasantly converted old general store, with inventive food and live music a couple of times a week. Main courses from £12. Closed Sun. Moderate.

Take 5 17 Tombland. Imaginative, budget-bistro food served in amenable surroundings. A student favourite. Mon–Sat 11am–11pm. Inexpensive.

Tree House 14 Dove St. Above the Rainbow wholefood shop, a vegetarian café-restaurant offering a daily changing menu of soups, salads and main courses, plus organic wines and beers. Main courses from £4. Open Mon–Wed 10am–5pm, Thurs–Sat 10am–9pm. Inexpensive.

Pubs, bars and clubs

Adam & Eve Bishopgate. There's been a pub on this site for seven hundred years and it's still the top spot in town for the discerning drinker, with a changing range of real ales and an eclectic wine list supplied by Adnams.

Coach & Horses Bethel Street. Pleasant city-centre pub with lived-in furnishings and fittings. Good for a quiet drink.

Ribs of Beef 24 Wensum St. Boisterous riverside drinking haunt popular with students and townies alike. Inexpensive bar food too.

Waterfront 139–41 King's St ☏01603/632717. Norwich's principal club and alternative music venue, with gigs and DJs most nights. Sponsored by UEA.

Wild Man 29 Bedford St. Long-established, city-centre watering hole – a popular student hang-out.

Entertainment

As well as its fair share of multi-screen **cinemas** showing Hollywood blockbusters, Norwich has the excellent art-house **Cinema City**, in Suckling House on St Andrew's Plain (☏01603/622047, ⊛www.cinemacity.co.uk): the premises are currently being redeveloped, however, so its films are shown at the nearby **Norwich Playhouse**, on St George's Street. The city also has several first-rate **theatres**: the Theatre Royal, on Theatre Street (☏01603/630000, ⊛www.theatre-royal-norwich.co.uk), has a wide-ranging programme of mainstream and more adventurous plays and dance, while the amateur Maddermarket, St John's Alley, off Pottergate (☏01603/620917, ⊛www.maddermarket.co.uk), offers an interesting range of modern theatre. Finally, **UEA** is a major source of entertainment for students and locals alike, hosting both gigs and classical concerts.

The Norfolk Broads

Three rivers – the Yare, Waveney and Bure – meander across the flatlands to the east of Norwich, converging on Breydon Water before flowing into the sea at Great Yarmouth. In places these rivers swell into wide expanses of water known as "**broads**", which for years were thought to be natural lakes. In fact they're

△ Boating on the Broads

the result of extensive peat cutting, several centuries of accumulated diggings made in a region where wood was scarce and peat a valuable source of energy. The pits flooded when sea levels rose in the thirteenth and fourteenth centuries to create the **Norfolk Broads**, now one of the most important wetlands in Europe – a haven for many birds such as kingfishers, grebes and warblers – and the county's major tourist attraction.

The Broads' delicate ecological balance suffered badly during the 1970s and 1980s, but the **Broads Authority** (℡01603/610734, ⓦwww.broads-authority .gov.uk) has coordinated a well-conceived clean up programme. The authority also maintains a series of information centres throughout the region and, at any of these, you can pick up a free copy of the *Broadcaster*, a useful newspaper guide to the Broads as a whole.

The region is crossed by several **train** lines, but the best – really the only – way to see the Broads themselves is **by boat**, and you could happily spend a week or so exploring the 125 miles of lock-free navigable waterways, visiting the various churches, pubs and windmills en route. Of the many **boat rental** companies, Blakes Holiday Boating (℡0870/220 2498, ⓦwww.blakes .co.uk) and Broads Tours Ltd (℡01603/782207, ⓦwww.broads.co.uk), are both well-established and operate out of Wroxham (see below). Prices for cruisers start at around £700 a week for four people in peak season, but less expensive, short-term rentals are widely available too. Houseboats are much cheaper than cruisers, but they are, of course, static.

Trying to explore the Broads by car is pretty much a waste of time, but cyclists and walkers can take advantage of the region's network of footpaths and cycle trails. There are Broads Authority **bike rental** points dotted around the region and **walkers** might consider the 56-mile Weavers' Way, a long-distance footpath that winds through the best parts of the Broads on its way from Cromer to Great Yarmouth, though there are many shorter options too.

Wroxham and Ludham

The easiest boating centre to reach from Norwich is **WROXHAM**, seven miles to the northeast and accessible by train, bus and car. Wroxham itself is short on charm, but it has a useful **Broads information centre**, on Station Road (Easter–Oct daily 9am–1pm & 2–5pm; ℡01603/782281), and plenty of places to stock up with food before heading out on a cruise.

Some six miles east of Wroxham, the village of **LUDHAM** straggles along the roadside at the tip of the Womack Water, an offshoot of the River Thurne. Just north of the village is How Hill, where the Broads Authority maintains **Toad Hole Cottage** (June–Sept daily 10am–6pm; April, May & Oct Mon–Fri 11am–1pm & 1.30–5pm; free), an old eel-catcher's cottage housing a small exhibit on the history of the trade, which was common hereabouts until the 1940s. Behind the cottage is the narrow River Ant, where you can take hour-long, wildlife-viewing **boat trips** in the *Electric Eel* from Easter to October: call ℡01692/678763 for schedule and reservations.

Potter Heigham

A couple of miles east of Ludham, **POTTER HEIGHAM** is the nominal capital of the Broads, taking its name from the pottery which once stood here on the River Thurne and from the Saxon lord of Heacham who first settled the place. Again, there's not much to keep your attention, though you can watch boaters struggling with the village's fourteenth-century bridge, regarded as one of the most difficult passages in the Broads. All the major boat-rental companies have outlets here and there's also an **information centre** (Easter–Oct daily

9am–1pm & 2–5pm; ☎01692/670779). The only public transport to Potter Heigham is by bus from Great Yarmouth.

The north Norfolk coast

The first place of any note on the **north Norfolk coast** is **Cromer**, a workaday seaside town some twenty miles north of Norwich whose bleak and blustery cliffs have drawn tourists for over a century. A few miles to the west is another well-established resort, **Sheringham**, but thereafter the shoreline becomes a ragged patchwork of salt marshes, dunes and shingle spits which form an almost unbroken series of nature reserves, supporting a fascinating range of flora and fauna. It's a lovely stretch of coast and the villages bordering it, principally **Cley**, **Blakeney** and **Wells-next-the-Sea** are prime targets for an overnight stay.

Cromer and Sheringham are the only places accessible by **train**, with an hourly service from Norwich on the Bittern Line. Local **bus** services connect all the towns and many of the villages, and there's also the **Coasthopper bus** (May–Sept Mon–Sat hourly, Sun 4 daily; Oct–March 1–2 daily), operated by Norfolk Green (☎01553/776980, ⓦwww.norfolkgreen.co.uk; timetable ☎0870/6082608), which runs the length of the coast from Cromer to Hunstanton, with some services continuing to Great Yarmouth and King's Lynn. The Coasthopper Rover ticket (£6) gives a day's unlimited travel on the route. For **walkers**, the **Norfolk Coast Path** runs from Hunstanton to Cromer (where it joins the Weavers' Way), an exhilarating route through the dunes and salt marshes; a *National Trail Guide* covers the route in detail, otherwise you'll need OS *Landranger* maps 132 and 133.

Cromer

Dramatically poised on a high bluff, **CROMER** should be the most memorable of the Norfolk coastal resorts, but its fine aspect is partly undermined by a shabbiness in its streets and shopfronts – an "atrophied charm" as Paul Theroux called it. The tower of **St Peter and St Paul**, at 160ft the tallest in Norfolk, attests to the port's medieval wealth, but it was the advent of the railway in the 1880s that heralded the most frenetic flurry of building activity. A bevy of grand Edwardian hotels was constructed along the seafront and for a moment Cromer became the most fashionable of resorts, but the gloss soon wore off and only the dishevelled **Hotel de Paris** has survived. While you're here, be sure to take a stroll out onto the **pier**, which was badly damaged in a storm in November 1993, but has since been repaired and struggles gamely on; and, of course, don't forget to grab a **crab** – J.W.H. Jonas, 7 New St, has some fine specimens.

Somewhat miraculously Cromer has managed to retain its rail link with Norwich; the **train station** is a five-minute walk west of the centre. **Buses** terminate on Cadogan Road, next to the **tourist office** (daily 10am–4pm; Nov to mid–March closed 1–2pm; ☎01263/512497), which is just 200 yards from the cliff-top promenade. An hour or two in Cromer is probably enough, though the **beach** is first-rate and the cliff-top walk exhilarating. There's no shortage of inexpensive **accommodation** – the tourist office has all the details – but it's hard to beat the enticing *Beachcomber B&B*, a cosy place with six en-suite rooms conveniently located near the centre at 17 Macdonald Rd (☎01263/513398, ⓦwww.beachcomber-guesthouse.co.uk; no cards; ❸).

Sheringham

SHERINGHAM, a popular seaside town four miles west of Cromer, has an amiable, easy-going air and makes a reasonable overnight stop, though frankly you're still only marking time until you hit the more appealing places further west. One of the distinctive features of the town is the smooth beach pebbles that face and decorate the houses, a **flinting technique** used frequently in this part of Norfolk – the best examples here are just off the High Street. The downside is that the power of the waves, which makes the pebbles smooth, has also forced the local council to spend thousands rebuilding the sea defences. The resultant mass of reinforced concrete makes for a less than pleasing seafront – one reason to head, instead, for **Sheringham Park** (daily dawn to dusk; free, but parking extra; NT), the 770-acre woodland park a couple of miles southwest of the town, laid out by Humphry Repton in the early 1800s.

Sheringham's branch-line **train station**, the terminus of the Bittern Line from Norwich, is near the **tourist office** (March–Oct Mon–Sat 10am–5pm, Sun 10am–4pm; ☏01263/824329) on Station Approach; from here, it's a five-minute walk north to the seafront, down Station Road and its continuation, the High Street. There are plenty of **B&Bs**, with one of the best being the unassuming *Two Lifeboats*, 2 High St (☏01263/822401, ⓦwww.twolifeboats .co.uk; ❺), a small, traditional hotel on the promenade; most of the bedrooms have sea views. The YHA **hostel** is a five-minute walk from the train station at 1 Cremer's Drift, just off Cromer Road (☏0870/770 6024, ⓦwww.yha.org .uk; doubles ❶, dorm beds £16), with a small self-catering kitchen and a cycle store. Set in its own grounds, it has one hundred beds, mostly in two- to four-bedded rooms, and breakfast is included in the price; ring ahead for reservations and opening days.

Dave's, 50 High St, serves the best **fish and chips** for miles around, while the *Sweet Shop*, 14 High St, dishes up Ronaldo's delicious ice creams, with flavours ranging from chocolate and ginger to cinnamon and lavender.

Cley and Blakeney Point

Travelling west from Sheringham, the **A149** meanders through a pretty rural landscape offering occasional glimpses of the sea and a shoreline protected by a giant shingle barrier erected after the catastrophic flood of 1953, a disaster which claimed over one thousand lives. After seven miles you reach **CLEY–NEXT–THE–SEA**, once a busy wool port but now little more than a row of flint cottages and Georgian mansions set beside a narrow, marshy inlet that (just) gives access to the sea. The original village was destroyed in a fire in 1612, which explains why Cley's fine medieval **church of St Margaret** is located half a mile inland at the very southern edge of the current village, overlooking the green. The Black Death brought church construction to a sudden halt here, hence the contrast between the stunted, unfinished chancel and the splendid nave, which boasts several fine medieval brasses and some folksy fifteenth-century bench-ends depicting animals and grotesques. Cley's other great draw – housed in an old forge on the main street – is the excellent **Cley Smoke House**, selling local smoked fish and other delicacies, while nearby **Picnic Fayre** has long been one of the finest delis in East Anglia.

It's about 400 yards east from the village to the mile-long byroad that leads to the shingle mounds of **Cley beach**. This is the starting point for the four-mile hike west out along the spit to **Blakeney Point**, a nature reserve famed for its colonies of terns and seals. The seal colony is made up of several hundred common and grey seals, and the old lifeboat house, at the end of the spit, is now a National Trust information centre. The shifting shingle can, however, make walking difficult, so keep to the low-water mark – which also means that you won't accidentally trample any nests. The easier alternative is to take one of the boat trips to the point from Blakeney or Morston (see below). The Norfolk Coast Path passes close to the beach too and then continues along the edge of the **Cley Marshes**, which attract a bewildering variety of waders.

As for a **place to stay**, Cley holds the outstanding ⚲ *Cley Mill B&B* (☎01263/740209, ⓦwww.cleymill.co.uk; ❺), housed in a converted windmill complete with sails and a balcony offering wonderful views over the surrounding salt marshes and seashore. Another good place is the *Three Swallows* pub (☎01263/740526; ❸), on the green by the church, which has several pleasant en-suite rooms. For **food**, *The Terroir* (☎01263/740336, ⓦwww.terroir.org.uk; closed Mon), on the High Street, is an intimate restaurant offering an innovative menu featuring the freshest of local ingredients; advance reservations are required. They also have a couple of stylish **rooms** (❼, including dinner; minimum stay two nights).

Blakeney

BLAKENEY is delightful. Once a bustling port exporting fish, corn and salt, it's now a lovely little place of pebble-covered cottages sloping up from a narrow harbour just a mile west of Cley. Crab sandwiches are sold from stalls at the quayside, the meandering high street is flanked by family-run shops, and footpaths stretch out along the sea wall to east and west, allowing long, lingering looks over the salt marshes. The only sight as such is the **church of St Nicholas**, beside the A149 at the south end of the village, whose sturdy tower and nave are made of flint rubble with stone trimmings, the traditional building materials of north Norfolk. Inside, the oak and chestnut hammer-beam roof and the delicate rood screen are the most enjoyable features of the nave, which is attached to a late thirteenth-century chancel, the only survivor from the original Carmelite friary church.

Blakeney **harbour** is linked to the sea by a narrow channel, which wriggles its way through the salt marshes. The channel is, however, only navigable for a few hours at high tide – at low tide the harbour is no more than a muddy creek (ideal for a bit of quayside crabbing and mud sliding). Depending on the tides, **boat trips** run from either Blakeney or **Morston quay**, a mile or two to the west, to both Blakeney Point (see p.413) – where passengers spend a couple of hours at the point – and to the seal colony just off the point. The main operators advertise departure times on blackboards by the quayside or you can reserve in advance with Beans Boats (☎01263/740505, ⓦwww.beansboattrips.co.uk) or Bishop's Boats (☎01263/740753). Both the seal trips and those to Blakeney Point cost £7.

For **accommodation**, the quayside ⚲ *Blakeney Hotel* (☎01263/740797, ⓦwww.blakeney-hotel.co.uk; ❽) is one of the most charming hotels in Norfolk, a rambling building with high-pitched gables and pebble-covered walls. It has a heated indoor swimming pool, a secluded garden, and cosy lounges with exquisite sea views; it also serves outstanding **lunches, afternoon teas and dinners.** The cheaper rooms can be poky and somewhat airless, so it's worth paying a little more for one with splendid views across the harbour and the marshes. Less expensive options include the *Manor Hotel* (☎01263/740376, ⓦwww.blakeneymanor.co.uk; ❺), which occupies a low-lying courtyard complex a few yards to the east of the harbour, and the *King's Arms* ⚲, just back from the quay on Westgate (☎01263/740341; ❹), a traditional pub, with low, beamed ceilings and seven modest but appealing en-suite bedrooms. The latter also serves delicious, reasonably priced **bar food**. For longer stays, *Quayside Cottages* (℡01462/768627, Ⓦwww.blakeneycottages.co.uk) rent some charming local cottages from £260 per week.

Wells-next-the-Sea

Despite its name, **WELLS–NEXT–THE–SEA**, some eight miles west of Blakeney, is situated a good mile or so from open water. In Tudor times, when it enjoyed much easier access to the North Sea, it was one of the great ports of eastern England, a major player in the trade with the Netherlands. Those heady days are long gone and although today it's the only commercially viable port on the north Norfolk coast, this is hardly a huge advantage. More importantly, Wells is also one of the county's more attractive towns, and even though there are no specific sights among its narrow lanes, it does make a very good base for exploring the surrounding coastline.

The town divides into three distinct areas, starting with **The Buttlands**, a broad rectangular green on the south side of town, lined with oak and beech trees and framed by a string of fine Georgian houses. North from here, across Station Road, lie the narrow lanes of the town centre with **Staithe Street**, the minuscule main drag, flanked by quaint old-fashioned shops. Staithe Street leads down to the **quay**, a somewhat forlorn affair inhabited by a couple of amusement arcades and fish-and-chip shops, and the mile-long byroad that scuttles north to the **beach**, a handsome sandy tract backed by pine-clad dunes. The beach road is shadowed by a high flood defence and a tiny narrow-gauge **railway**, which scoots down to the beach every twenty minutes or so from 10.30am, Easter to October (90p each way).

Buses to Wells stop on The Buttlands, a short stroll from the **tourist office** at the foot of Staithe Street (daily: mid–March to late March 10am–4pm; April to late May & mid–Sept to Oct 10am–2pm; late May to mid–Sept 10am–5pm; ℡01328/710885). Several of the best **guest houses** are along Standard Road, which runs up from the eastern end of the quayside. First choice is the elegant *Normans* (℡01328/710657; no cards; ❹), with four spacious and tastefully decorated rooms; the TV lounge has a log fire and racks of games and the first-floor look-out window provides a wide view over the marshes – binoculars are provided. Another good option is *Ilex House*, on Bases Lane (℡01328/710556, Ⓦwww.broadland.com/ilexhouse; ❸), a good-looking Georgian villa in its own grounds, just to the west of the centre, with three modern, well–appointed guest rooms. There's also a **campsite**, the sprawling and extremely popular *Pinewoods Caravan and Camping Park*, by the beach (℡01328/710439, Ⓦwww.pinewoods .co.uk; closed Nov to mid-March).

The best **pub** in town is the *Crown* on The Buttlands, which serves good food, while *Nelson's*, 21 Staithe St, is a pleasant tea and coffee shop that serves inexpensive **meals**.

Holkham Hall and Holkham Bay

One of the most popular outings from Wells is to **Holkham Hall** (June–Sept Mon & Thurs–Sun 1–5pm; £6.50; Ⓦwww.holkham.co.uk), three miles to the west and a stop on the Coasthopper bus (see p.412). This grand and self-assured stately home was designed by the eighteenth-century architect William Kent for the first earl of Leicester and is still owned by the family. The severe sandy-coloured Palladian exterior belies the warmth and richness of the interior, which retains much of its original decoration, notably the much-admired marble hall, with its fluted columns and intricate reliefs. The rich colours of the state rooms are an appropriate backdrop for a fabulous selection of **paintings**, including canvases by Van Dyck, Rubens, Gainsborough and Poussin.

The **grounds** (dawn to dusk; free) are laid out on sandy, saline land, much of it originally salt marsh. The focal point is an eighty-foot-high obelisk, atop a grassy knoll, from where you can view both the hall to the north and the triumphal arch to the south. In common with the rest of the north Norfolk coast, there's plenty of **birdlife** to observe in and around the park – Holkham's lake attracts Canada geese, heron and grebes, and several hundred deer graze the open pastures.

The footpaths latticing the estate stretch as far as the A149, from where a half-mile byroad – Lady Anne's Drive – leads north across the marshes from opposite the *Victoria Hotel* to **Holkham Bay**, which boasts one of the finest sandy beaches on this stretch of coast, golden sand flexed against pine-studded sand dunes. Warblers, flycatchers and redstarts inhabit the drier coastal reaches, while waders paddle about the mud and salt flats.

Hunstanton

The Norfolk coast pretty much ends at **HUNSTANTON**, a Victorian seaside resort that grew up to the southwest of the original fishing village – now **Old Hunstanton**. To be sure, Hunstanton has its fair share of amusement arcades, crazy golf, and entertainment complexes, as well as Britain's largest joke shop, The World of Fun on Greevegate, but the town has also hung on to its genteel origins – and its sandy beaches, backed by stripy gateau-like cliffs, are among the cleanest in the county. There's also one notable attraction within easy striking distance of the resort: **Sandringham**, one of the Queen's country residences and a major crowd pleaser.

Hunstanton **tourist office** is in the town hall (daily: April–Sept 10am–5pm; Oct–March 10.30am–4pm; ☎01485/532610) on the wide sloping green, which serves as the focal point of the resort. The nicest (and priciest) **accommodation** is among the cottages of Old Hunstanton: try *Le Strange Arms*, Golf Course Road (☎01485/534411, Ⓦwww.abacushotels.co.uk; Ⓞ), a large mansion dating from the nineteenth century, with gardens running down to the beach. There's also a YHA **hostel** in a pair of Victorian townhouses at 15 Avenue Rd (☎0870/770 5872, Ⓦwww.yha.org.uk; dorm beds £11, doubles Ⓞ; Easter to October), south of Hunstanton green. It has forty beds, in two- to eight-bedded rooms, a cycle store, garden and self-catering kitchen; advance booking required.

Sandringham House

About eight miles south of Hunstanton, off the A149, is the seven-thousand-acre estate of **Sandringham House** (April–Oct daily 11am to last entry at 4.45pm, 3pm in October; closed for two weeks late July or early Aug; £7.50; Ⓦwww.sandringhamestate.co.uk), bought in 1861 by Queen Victoria for her son, the future Edward VII. The house is billed as a private home, but few families have a drawing room crammed with Russian silver and Chinese jade. The **museum**, housed in the old coach and stable block, contains an exhibition of royal memorabilia from dolls to cars, but much more arresting are the beautifully maintained **grounds** (same dates daily 10.30am to last entry at 5pm, October 4pm), a mass of rhododendrons and azaleas in spring and early summer. The estate's sandy soil is also ideal for game birds, which was the attraction of the place for the terminally bored Edward, whose tradition of posh shooting parties is still followed by the royals.

Local **buses** #410 and #411 make the journey from Hunstanton, as does the Coasthopper service (see p.412).

Ely and around

Perched on a mound of clay above the River Great Ouse, **ELY** – literally "eel island" – was to all intents and purposes a true island until the draining of the fens in the seventeenth century. Up until then, the town was encircled by treacherous marshland, which could only be crossed with the help of the local "fen-slodgers" who knew the firm tussock paths. In 1070, **Hereward the Wake** turned this inaccessibility to military advantage, holding out against the Normans and forcing William the Conqueror to undertake a prolonged siege – and finally to build an improvised road floated on bundles of sticks. Centuries later, the Victorian writer Charles Kingsley recounted this obscure conflict in his novel *Hereward the Wake*. He presented the protagonist as the Last of the English who "never really bent their necks to the Norman yoke and … kept alive those free institutions which were the germs of our British liberty" – a heady mixture of nationalism and historical poppycock that went down a storm.

Since then, Ely has always been associated with Hereward, which is really rather ridiculous as Ely is, above all else, an ecclesiastical town and a Norman one to boot. The Normans built the **cathedral**, a towering structure visible for miles across the flat landscape and Ely's only significant sight. It's easy to see the town on a day-trip from Cambridge, but Ely does make a pleasant night's stop in its own right.

Ely Cathedral

Ely **Cathedral** (June–Sept daily 7am–7pm; Oct–May Mon–Sat 7.30am–6pm, Sun 7.30am–5pm; Mon–Sat £4.80 donation requested, free on Sun) is seen to best advantage from the south, the crenellated towers of the west side perfectly balanced by the prickly finials to the east with the distinctive timber lantern rising above them both. To approach from this direction, follow the footpath leading up the hill into the cathedral precincts from **Broad Street** – also the second turning on the right as you walk up Station Road from the train station. At the top of the footpath, pass through the medieval **Porta**, once the principal entrance to the monastery complex, and turn right to reach the main entrance on the lopsided **west front** – one of the transepts collapsed in a storm in 1701.

The first things to strike you as you enter the **nave** are the sheer length of the building and the lively nineteenth-century painted ceiling, largely the work of amateur volunteers. The nave's procession of plain late-Norman arches, built around the same time as those at Peterborough, leads to the architectural feature that makes Ely so special, the **octagon** – the only one of its kind in England – built in 1322 to replace the collapsed central tower. Its construction, employing the largest oaks available in England to support some four hundred tons of glass and lead, remains one of the wonders of the medieval world, and the effect, as you look up into this Gothic dome, is simply breathtaking. From March to October, **Octagon tours** (£4; reservations & schedule ☏01353/667 735) depart two to four times daily from the desk at the entrance, venturing up into the octagon itself.

When the central tower collapsed, it fell eastwards, onto the **choir**, the first three bays of which were rebuilt at the same time as the octagon in the Decorated style – in contrast to the plainer Early English of the choir bays beyond. Further east still is the thirteenth-century **presbytery**, which houses the relics of **St Ethelreda**, founder of the abbey in 673, who, despite being twice married, is honoured liturgically as a virgin. Also at the east end are three **chantry chapels**, the most charming of which (on the left) is an elaborate Renaissance affair dating from 1533. The other marvel at Ely is the **Lady Chapel**, a separate building accessible via the north transept. It lost its sculpture and its stained glass during the Reformation, but its fan vaulting remains, an exquisite example of English Gothic. Retracing your steps, the south triforium near the main entrance holds the **Stained Glass Museum** (Easter–Oct Mon–Sat 10.30am–5pm, Sun noon–4.30/6pm; £3.50), an Anglican money-spinner exhibiting examples of this applied art from 1240 to the present day.

The rest of the town

The rest of Ely is pretty enough, but hardly compelling after the wonders of the cathedral. To the north, the **High Street**, with its Georgian buildings and old-fashioned shops, makes for an enjoyable browse and, if you push on past the Market Place down Forehill and then Waterside, you'll come to the **Babylon Gallery** (Tues–Sat 10am–4pm, Sun 11am–5pm; free; ☎01353/669022, ⓦwww.adec.org.uk/babylon), where an imaginative programme of temporary exhibitions featuring contemporary art and craft is displayed in an attractively renovated old brewery warehouse. Alternatively, head west from the cathedral entrance across the Palace Green, to **Oliver Cromwell's House** at 29 St Mary's St (April–Oct daily 10am–5.30pm; Nov–March Mon–Fri & Sun 11am–4pm, Sat 10am–5pm; £3.85), a timber-framed former vicarage, which holds a small exhibition on the Protector's ten-year sojourn in Ely, when he was employed as a tithe collector.

Practicalities

Ely lies on a major rail intersection, receiving direct **trains** from as far afield as Liverpool, Norwich and London, as well as from Cambridge, just twenty minutes to the south. The **train station** is a ten-minute walk from the cathedral straight up Station Road and its continuation Back Hill and then The Gallery. **Buses** (from King's Lynn and Cambridge) stop on Market Street immediately north of the cathedral. The **tourist office**, in Oliver Cromwell's House (April–Oct daily 10am–5.30pm; Nov–March Mon–Fri & Sun 11am–4pm, Sat 10am–5pm; ☎01353/662062, ⓦwww.tourism.eastcambs.gov.uk), issues free town maps and will help with accommodation.

Ely has several appealing **B&Bs**, with first choice being the plush *Sycamore House*, in an attractive, detached Edwardian house near the river at 91 Cambridge Rd (☎01353/662139; no credit cards; ❹); it has four guest rooms, all decorated in a bright, modern style, and is a ten-minute walk from the train station. More central is the handy *Cathedral House*, 17 St Mary's St (☎01353/662124, ⓦwww .cathedralhouse.co.uk; no cards; ❹), an attractive Georgian townhouse with three pleasant and straightforward, en-suite bedrooms.

Of the numerous **tearooms** in town, *The Almonry* (daily 10am–5pm), in the grounds on the north side of the cathedral, has by far the best location, with garden seats granting great views of the octagon. Alternatively, there's the *Steeplegate Tea Rooms* at 16–18 High St (Mon–Sat 10am–5pm), backing onto the cathedral grounds. The pick of the town's **restaurants** is the *Old Fire Engine House*,

25 St Mary's St (☎01353/662582; closes 9pm, 5pm on Sun), a gourmet English restaurant with a good local reputation where main courses average £11.

Cambridge

On the whole, **CAMBRIDGE** is a much quieter and more secluded place than Oxford, though for the visitor what really sets it apart from its scholarly rival is "**the Backs**" – the green swathe of land that straddles the languid River Cam, providing exquisite views over the backs of the old colleges. At the front, the handsome facades of these same colleges dominate the layout of the town centre, lining up along the main streets. Most of the older colleges date back to the late thirteenth and early fourteenth centuries and are designed to a **similar plan** with the main gate leading through to a series of "courts," typically a carefully manicured slab of lawn surrounded on all four sides by college residences or offices. Many of the buildings are extraordinarily beautiful, but the most famous is **King's College**, whose magnificent **King's College Chapel** is one of the great statements of late Gothic architecture. There are 31 university colleges in total, each an independent, self-governing body, proud of its achievements and attracting – for the most part at least – a close loyalty from its students, amongst whom privately educated boys remain hopelessly over-represented.

   Cambridge is an extremely compact place, and you can **walk** round the centre, visiting the most interesting colleges, in an afternoon. A thorough exploration, covering more of the colleges, a visit to the fine art of the Fitzwilliam Museum and a leisurely afternoon on a **punt**, will however take at least a couple of days. If possible, avoid coming in high summer, when the students are replaced by hordes of sightseers. Faced with such crowds, the more popular colleges have restricted their **opening times** and several have introduced admission charges. Bear in mind, too, that during the exam period (late April to early June), most colleges close their doors to the public at least some of the time. There are **three**

△ Punting on the river

Messing about on the water

Punting is the quintessential Cambridge activity, though it's a good deal harder than it looks. First-timers find themselves zigzagging across the water and "punt jams" are very common on the stretch of the Cam beside the Backs in summer. **Punt rental** is available at several points, including the boatyard at Mill Lane (beside the Silver Street bridge), at Magdalene Bridge, and at the Garret Hostel Lane bridge at the back of Trinity College. It costs around £10 an hour (and most places charge a deposit), with up to six people in each punt. Alternatively, you can hire a **chauffeured punt** from any of the rental places for about a fiver a head.

Cambridge is also famous for its **rowing clubs**, which are clustered along the north bank of the river across from Midsummer Common. For their convenience, this stretch of water is punt-free. The most important inter-college races are the **May Bumps**, which, confusingly, take place in June.

terms – Michaelmas (Oct–Dec), Lent (Jan–March) and Easter (April–June) – and the students' biggest annual knees-up, the "May balls", are held in June.

Arrival

Cambridge **train station** is a mile or so southeast of the city centre, off Hills Road. It's an easy but tedious twenty-minute walk into the centre, or take local bus #1 or #3, which runs to downtown Emmanuel Road every ten minutes or so (less frequently on Sun and in the evening). The **bus station** is centrally located on Drummer Street, right by Christ's Pieces – and Emmanuel Road. **Stansted**, London's third airport, is just thirty miles south of Cambridge on the M11; there are hourly trains from the airport to the city, and regular bus services too. Arriving by **car**, you'll find much of the city centre closed to traffic and on-street parking well-nigh impossible – for a day-trip, at least, the best option is a **Park-and-Ride** car park; they are signposted on all major approaches.

Information and getting around

Cambridge **tourist office** is conveniently situated in the ornate former public library on Wheeler Street, off King's Parade (Mon–Fri 10am–5.30pm, Sat 10am–5pm; April–Oct also Sun 11am–4pm; information ☎0906/586 2526 premium line; ⓦ www.visitcambridge.org). It issues city maps, has lots of leaflets on local attractions and sells an in-depth guide to the city, as well as a mini-guide for 50p.

The city centre is small enough to walk round comfortably, so apart from getting to and from the train station, you shouldn't have to use the city's buses. On the other hand, cycling is an enjoyable way of getting around and has long been extremely popular with locals and students alike. **Bike rental** outlets are dotted all over town (see p.429), including a couple of places handy for the train station. When and wherever you leave your bike, padlock it to something immovable as bike theft is not infrequent. Alternatively, the tourist office runs very popular **walking tours** of the centre (1–4 daily; 2hr; £8.50; guided tours number ☎01223/457 574). Although expensive, they do include entrance to at least one college that normally charges for the privilege: book well in advance in summer.

Accommodation

Cambridge is short of central accommodation and those few **hotels** that do occupy prime locations are expensive. That said, Chesterton Lane and its

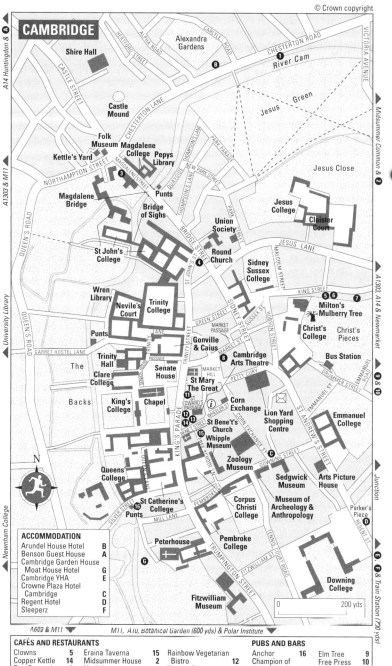

CAMBRIDGE

Shire Hall

Castle Mound

Folk Museum
Kettle's Yard
Magdalene College
Pepys Library

Punts

Magdalene Bridge

Bridge of Sighs

Union Society

St John's College

Round Church

Sidney Sussex College

Jesus College
Cloister Court

Jesus Close

Wren Library

Nevile's Court
Trinity College

Gonville & Caius

Milton's Mulberry Tree

Christ's College
Christ's Pieces

Punts

Trinity Hall
Clare College

Senate House

Cambridge Arts Theatre

Bus Station

The Backs

King's College
Chapel

St Mary The Great

Corn Exchange

St Edward's Passage

St Bene't's Church

Lion Yard Shopping Centre

Emmanuel College

Whipple Museum

Zoology Museum

Sedgwick Museum

Arts Picture House

Queens' College

St Catherine's College
Punts

Corpus Christi College

Museum of Archeology & Anthropology

Peterhouse

Pembroke College

Downing College

Fitzwilliam Museum

7

EAST ANGLIA | Cambridge

ACCOMMODATION

Arundel House Hotel	B
Benson Guest House	A
Cambridge Garden House Moat House Hotel	G
Cambridge YHA	E
Crowne Plaza Hotel Cambridge	C
Regent Hotel	D
Sleeperz	F

CAFÉS AND RESTAURANTS

Clowns	5	Eraina Taverna	15
Copper Kettle	14	Midsummer House	2
Don Pasquale	8	Nadia's	
Efes	7	Patisserie	4 & 11

Rainbow Vegetarian Bistro	12
Twenty-Two	1

PUBS AND BARS

Anchor	16
Champion of the Thames	6
Eagle	13

Elm Tree	9
Free Press	10
The Pickerel	3

© Crown copyright

continuation, Chesterton Road, the busy street running east from the top of Magdalene Street, have several reasonably priced hotels and guest houses. There are lots of **B&Bs** on the outskirts of town, with several near the train station, and it's here you'll also find the YHA **hostel**. In high season, when vacant rooms are often thin on the ground, the tourist office's efficient **accommodation booking service** can be very useful (℡01223/457581, Ⓦwww.visitcambridge.org).

Arundel House Hotel 53 Chesterton Rd ℡01223/367701, Ⓦwww.arundelhousehotels.co.uk. A converted row of late-Victorian houses overlooking the river and Jesus Green makes for one of the better mid-range hotel choices. Neat and tidy rooms with mundane modern furnishings. Breakfasts are good. ❻

Benson Guest House 24 Huntingdon Rd ℡01223/311594, Ⓔbensonhouse@btconnect.com. Pleasant, well-kept guest house in a demure brick house about five minutes' walk north from the Magdalene Bridge near New Hall College. Five rooms, three en suite. ❹

Cambridge Garden House Moat House Hotel Granta Place, Mill Lane ℡01223/259 988, Ⓦwww.moathousehotels.com. Cambridge's best central hotel, set in its own gardens with a fine riverside location: some rooms have balconies, and there's an indoor pool and health club. ❽

Cambridge YHA 97 Tenison Rd ℡0870/770 5742, Ⓦwww.yha.org.uk. This well-equipped and popular hostel has laundry and self-catering facilities, a cycle store, a games room and a small courtyard garden. There are one hundred beds in two- to

eight-bed rooms. It's close to the train station – Tenison Road is a right turn a couple of hundred yards down Station Road. Open all year. Dorm beds £16, doubles ❶

Crowne Plaza Hotel Cambridge Downing Street ℡0870/400 9180, Ⓦwww.ichotelsgroup.com. Immaculately tailored behind a dignified facade, this sleek and slick hotel is first-rate. The foyer is adventurously designed and the rooms are resolutely modern in efficient chain-hotel style. Great central location too. ❼

Regent Hotel 41 Regent St ℡01223/351470, Ⓦwww.regenthotel.co.uk. Small-scale, recently refurbished hotel in an old brick townhouse within easy walking distance of the centre, beside Parker's Piece. The thirty-odd rooms are decorated in an efficient modern style. ❻

Sleeperz Station Road ℡01223/304050, Ⓦwww.sleeperz.com. This popular hotel is in an imaginatively converted granary warehouse, right outside the train station. Most of the rooms are bunk-style affairs done out in the manner of a ship's cabin, and there are a few doubles too. All rooms are en suite, with shower and TV. ❷

The City

Cambridge's **main shopping street** is Bridge Street, which becomes Sidney Street, St Andrew's Street and finally Regent Street; the other main thoroughfare is the procession of St John's Street, Trinity Street, King's Parade and Trumpington Street. The university developed the land west of this latter route along the banks of the Cam, and now forms a continuous half-mile parade of **colleges** from Magdalene to Peterhouse, with sundry others scattered about the periphery. The **Fitzwilliam Museum**, holding the city's finest art collection, is just along Trumpington Street south of Peterhouse. The account below starts with **King's College**, whose chapel is the university's most celebrated attraction, and covers the rest of the town in a broadly clockwise direction.

King's College

Henry VI founded **King's College** (℡01223/331212) in 1441, but he was disappointed with his initial efforts, so four years later he cleared away half of medieval Cambridge to make room for a much grander foundation. His plans were ambitious, but the Wars of the Roses – and bouts of royal insanity – intervened and by the time of his death in 1471 very little had been finished. Indeed, work on what was intended to be Henry's **Great Court** hadn't even started and the site remained empty for three hundred years. The present Great Court complex – facing King's Parade from behind a long stone screen

– is largely neo-Gothic, built in the 1820s to a design by William Wilkins. However, Henry's workmen did start on the college's finest building, the much celebrated **King's College Chapel** (term time Mon–Fri 9.30am–3.30pm, Sat 9.30am–3.15pm, Sun 1.15–2.15pm; rest of year Mon–Sat 9.30am–4.30pm, Sun 10am–5pm; £4.50), on the north side of today's Great Court. Committed to canvas by Turner and Canaletto, and eulogized in no less than three sonnets by Wordsworth, it's now best known for its **boys' choir**, whose members process across the college grounds during term time in their antiquated garb to sing evensong (Tues–Sat at 5.30pm) and carols on Christmas Eve. Begun in 1446 and over sixty years in the making, the chapel is an extraordinary building. **From the outside**, it seems impossibly slender, its streamlined buttresses channelling up to a dainty balustrade and four spiky turrets, but the exterior was, in a sense at least, a happy accident – its design predicated by the carefully composed interior. Here, in the final flowering of the Gothic style, the mystery of the Christian faith was expressed by a long, uninterrupted **nave** flooded with kaleidoscopic patterns of light filtering in through copious stained-glass windows. Paid for by Henry VIII, the **stained glass** was largely the work of Flemish glaziers, with the lower windows portraying scenes from the New Testament and the Apocrypha, and the upper windows the Old Testament. Henry VIII also paid for the intricately carved wooden **choir screen**, one of the earliest examples of Italian Renaissance woodcarving in England, but the **choir stalls** beyond date from the 1670s.

Like Oxford's New College, King's enjoyed an exclusive supply of students from one of the country's public schools – in this case, Eton – and until 1851 claimed the right to award its students degrees without taking any examinations. The first non-Etonians were only accepted in 1873. Times have changed since those days, and, if anything, King's is now one of the more progressive colleges, having been one of the first to admit women in 1972. Among its most famous alumni are E.M. Forster, who described his experiences in *Maurice*, film director Derek Jarman, poet Rupert Brooke, and John Maynard Keynes, whose economic theories did much to improve the college's finances when he became the college bursar.

From King's Parade to Clare College

Originally the town's medieval High Street, **King's Parade** is dominated by King's College and Chapel, but the higgledy-piggledy shops opposite are an attractive foil to William Wilkins' architectural screen. At the northern end of King's Parade is **Great St Mary's** (daily 9am–6pm except during services; free), the university's pet church, a sturdy Gothic structure dating from the fifteenth century. Its tower (Mon–Sat 9.30am–4.30pm, Sun noon–4.30pm; £2) offers a good overall view of the colleges and a bird's-eye view of **Market Hill**, east of the church, where food and bric-a-brac stalls are set out daily. Opposite the church stands **Senate House**, an exercise in Palladian classicism by James Gibbs, and the scene of graduation ceremonies on the last Saturday in June, when champagne corks fly around the rabbit-fur collars and black gowns. It's not usually open to the public, though you can wander around the quad if the gate is open.

The northern continuation of King's Parade is Trinity Street, a short way along which, on the left, is the main entrance to **Gonville and Caius College** (☎01223/332400), known simply as Caius (pronounced "keys"), after the sixteenth-century co-founder John Keys, who latinized his name, as was then the custom with men of learning. The design of the college owes much to Keys, who placed a gate on three sides of two adjoining courts, each representing a different stage on the path to academic enlightenment: the **Gate of Humility**, through which the student entered the college, now stands in the Fellows' Garden; the **Gate of Virtue**, sporting the female figures of Fame and Wealth, marks the entrance to Caius Court; while the exquisite **Gate of Honour**, capped with sundials and decorated with classical motifs, leads to Senate House Passage and on to Senate House (see above).

Senate House Passage continues west beyond the Gate of Honour to Trinity Lane and **Trinity Hall** (☎01223/332500) – not to be confused with Trinity College – from where it's a few metres to **Clare College** (daily 10am–5pm; free, but £2 in summer; ☎01223/333200). One of seven colleges founded, rather surprisingly, by women, Clare's plain period-piece courtyards, completed in the early eighteenth century, lead to one of the most picturesque of all the bridges over the Cam, **Clare Bridge**. Beyond lies the Fellows' Garden, one of the loveliest college gardens open to the public (times as college). Back at the entrance to Clare, it's a few metres more to the North Gate of King's College, beside King's College Chapel (see above).

Trinity

Trinity College, on Trinity Street (daily 10am–5pm; £2.20; ☎01223/338 487), is the largest of the Cambridge colleges and it also has the largest courtyard. It comes as little surprise then that its list of famous alumni is probably longer than any other college: literary greats, including Dryden, Byron, Tennyson, William Thackeray and Vladimir Nabokov; the Cambridge spies Blunt, Burgess and Philby; two prime ministers, Balfour and Baldwin; Isaac Newton, Lord Rutherford, Vaughan Williams, Pandit Nehru, Bertrand Russell and Ludwig Wittgenstein, not to mention a trio of (less talented) royals, Edward VII, George VI and Prince Charles.

A statue of Henry VIII, who founded the college in 1546, sits in majesty over Trinity's **Great Gate**, his sceptre replaced with a chair leg by a student wit. Beyond lies the vast asymmetrical expanse of **Great Court**, which displays a fine range of Tudor buildings, the oldest of which is the fifteenth-century clocktower – the annual race against its midnight chimes is now common currency thanks to the film *Chariots of Fire*. The centrepiece of the court is the delicate fountain, in which, legend has it, Lord Byron used to bathe naked with his pet bear – the college forbade students from keeping dogs.

To get through to **Nevile's Court** – where Newton first calculated the speed of sound – you must pass through "the screens", a passage separating the Hall from the kitchens, a common feature of Oxbridge colleges. The west end of Nevile's Court is enclosed by one of the university's most famous buildings, the **Wren Library** (term time Mon–Fri noon–2pm, Sat 10.30am–12.30pm; rest of year Mon–Fri noon–2pm; free). Viewed from the outside, it's impossible to appreciate the scale of the interior thanks to Wren's clever device of concealing the internal floor level. In contrast to many modern libraries, natural light pours into the white stuccoed interior, which contrasts wonderfully with the dark lime-wood bookcases, also Wren-designed and housing numerous valuable manuscripts.

St John's

Next door, **St John's College**, on St John's Street (daily 10am–5pm; £2.20; ☎01223/338600), sports a grandiloquent Tudor gatehouse, distinguished by the coat of arms of the founder, Lady Margaret Beaufort, the mother of Henry VII, held aloft by two spotted, mythical beasts. Beyond, three successive courts lead to the river, but there's an excess of dull reddish brickwork here – enough for

Wordsworth, who lived above the kitchens on F staircase, to describe the place as "gloomy". The arcade on the far side of Third Court leads through to the **Bridge of Sighs**, a chunky, covered bridge built in 1831 but in most respects very unlike its Venetian namesake. The bridge is best viewed either from a punt or from the much older, more stylish Wren-designed bridge a few metres to the south. The Bridge of Sighs links the old college with the fanciful nineteenth-century **New Court**, a crenellated neo-Gothic extravaganza topped by a feast of pinnacles and a central tower – hence its nickname "the wedding cake".

From the Round Church to Magdalene

Back on St John's Street, it's a few seconds' walk to Bridge Street and the **Round Church** (June–Sept Tues–Sat 10am–5pm, Sun & Mon 1–5pm; Oct–May daily 1–4pm; free), built in the twelfth century on the model of the Holy Sepulchre in Jerusalem. It's a curious-looking structure, squat with an ill-considered late medieval extension to the rear, but the Norman pillars of the original church remain, overseen by sturdy arcading and a ring of finely carved faces.

Saving nearby Jesus College till later (see below), it only takes a minute or two to stroll up from the Round Church to **Magdalene Bridge** and **Magdalene College** (℡01223/332100) – pronounced "maudlin" – which was founded as a hostel by the Benedictines, and become a university college in 1542. Magdalene was the last of the colleges to admit women, finally succumbing in 1988. The main focus of attention, here, is the **Pepys Library** (Oct, Nov & mid-Jan to mid-March Mon–Sat 2.30–3.30pm; late April to Aug Mon–Sat 11.30am–12.30pm & 2.30–3.30pm; free), in the second of the college's ancient courtyards. Samuel Pepys, a Magdalene student, bequeathed his entire library to the college, where it has been displayed ever since in its original red-oak bookshelves – though his famous diary, which also now resides here, was only discovered in the nineteenth century.

Jesus

Back down Magdalene Street and Bridge Street, the first left after the Round Church takes you to **Jesus College** (℡01223/339339), whose intimate cloisters are reminiscent of a monastery – appropriately, as the Bishop of Ely founded the college on the grounds of a suppressed Benedictine nunnery in 1496. The main red-brick gateway is approached via a distinctive walled walkway strewn with bicycles and known as "the Chimney". Beyond, much of the ground plan of the nunnery has been preserved, especially around **Cloister Court**, the prettiest of the college's courtyards, dripping with ivy and overflowing hanging baskets. Entered from the court, the college **chapel** occupies the former priory chancel and looks like a medieval parish church; it was imaginatively restored in the nineteenth century, using ceiling designs by William Morris and Pre-Raphaelite stained glass. The poet Samuel Taylor Coleridge was the college's most famously bad student, absconding in his first year to join the Light Dragoons, and returning only to be kicked out for a combination of bad debts and unconventional opinions.

Sidney Sussex

Near Jesus, Malcolm Street cuts off Jesus Lane to reach King Street, from where it's a short stroll through to **Sidney Sussex College** (℡01223/338800), whose sombre, mostly mock-Gothic facade glowers over Sidney Street. The interior is fairly unexciting too, though the long, slender **chapel** is noteworthy for its fancy marble floor, hooped roof and Baroque wood panelling, as well as being home to former alumnus Oliver Cromwell's skull. Originally buried with full pomp and circumstance in Westminster Abbey, Cromwell's body was exhumed after the Restoration, on the orders of Charles II, and paraded through the streets of the capital, hung and decapitated. His skull was then stuck on a post, where it remained for a couple of decades. In 1960, the skull was brought to the college and buried in a secret location somewhere in the chapel.

Corpus Christi and Queens'

There are several more town-centre colleges clustered at the west end of Pembroke Street, including **Corpus Christi College** (℡01223/338000), on King's Parade, founded by two of the town's guilds in 1352. Here, the **Old Court** dates from the foundation of the college and is where Christopher Marlowe wrote *Tamburlaine* before graduating in 1587. The college library, on the south side of the court, contains a priceless collection of Anglo-Saxon manuscripts, while the north side is linked by a gallery to **St Bene't's Church**, which served as the college chapel, but is of much earlier Saxon origin. Inside, Thomas Hobson's Bible is exhibited in a glass case; Hobson was the owner of a Cambridge livery stable, where he would only allow customers to take the horse nearest the door – hence "Hobson's choice".

Nearby **Queens' College** (daily 10am–4.30pm; £1.30; ℡01223/335511), accessed through the gate on Queens' Lane, just off Silver Street, is the most popular college with university applicants, and it's not difficult to see why. In the **Old Court** and the **Cloister Court**, Queens' possesses two fairy-tale Tudor courtyards, with the first of the two the perfect illustration of the original collegiate ideal with kitchens, library, chapel, hall and rooms all set around a tiny green. Cloister Court is flanked by the Long Gallery of the President's Lodge, the last remaining half-timbered building in the university, and, in its southeast corner, by the tower where Erasmus is thought to have beavered away during his four years here, probably from 1510 to 1514. Be sure to pay a visit to the college **Hall**, off the screens passage between the two courts, which holds mantel tiles by William Morris, and portraits of Erasmus and one of the college's co-founders, Elizabeth Woodville, wife of Edward IV. Equally eye-catching is the wooden **Mathematical Bridge** over the Cam (visible for free from the Silver Street Bridge), a copy of the mid-eighteenth-century original, which – so it was claimed – would stay in place even if the nuts and bolts were removed.

The Fitzwilliam Museum

Of all the museums in Cambridge, the **Fitzwilliam Museum**, on Trumpington Street (Tues–Sat 10am–5pm, Sun noon–5pm; free; ⊛www.fitzmuseum.cam.ac.uk), stands head and shoulders above the rest. The building itself is a splendidly grandiloquent interpretation of Neoclassicism, built in the mid-nineteenth century to house the vast collection bequeathed by Viscount Fitzwilliam in 1816. Since then, the museum has been gifted a string of private collections, most of which are focused on a particular specialism. Consequently, the Fitzwilliam says much about the changing tastes of the British upper class. The **Lower Galleries,** on the ground floor, contain a wealth of antiquities including Egyptian sarcophagi and mummies, fifth-century BC black- and red-figure Greek vases, plus a bewildering display of European ceramics. Further on, there are sections dedicated to armour, glass and pewterware, medals, portrait miniatures and illuminated manuscripts, and – right at the far end – galleries devoted to Far Eastern applied arts and Korean ceramics.

The **Upper Galleries** concentrate on painting and sculpture, with an eclectic assortment of mostly nineteenth- and early twentieth-century European paintings. There are two rooms of French paintings, with works by Picasso, Matisse, Monet, Renoir, Delacroix, Cézanne and Degas, and two rooms of Italian works by the likes of Fra Filippo Lippi and Simone Martini, Titian and Veronese. Two rooms feature British paintings, with works by William Blake, Constable and Turner, Hogarth, Reynolds, Gainsborough and Stubbs, and one is devoted to Dutch art, displaying paintings by Frans Hals and Ruisdael. The post-1945 gallery is packed with a fascinating selection including pieces by the likes of Lucian Freud, David Hockney, Henry Moore, Ben Nicholson and Barbara Hepworth.

To the University Botanic Gardens

Past the Fitzwilliam Museum, turn left along busy Lensfield Road for the **Scott Polar Research Institute** (Tues–Sat 2.30–4pm; free), founded in 1920 in memory of the explorer, Captain Robert Falcon Scott (1868–1912), with displays from the expeditions of various polar adventurers, plus exhibitions on native cultures of the Arctic. There's more general interest near at hand in the shape of the **University Botanic Gardens** (daily: Feb, Mar & Oct 10am–5pm; April–Sept 10am–6pm; Nov–Jan 10am–4pm; £3), whose entrance is on Bateman Street, about five hundred yards to the south of Lensfield Road via Panton Street. Founded in 1760 and covering forty acres, the gardens are second only to Kew with glasshouses as well as bountiful outdoor displays. The outdoor beds are mostly arranged by natural order, but there's also a particularly unusual series of chronological beds, showing when different plants were introduced into Britain.

Eating and drinking

Even at Cambridge, students are not the world's greatest restaurant-goers, so although the downtown **takeaway** and **café** scene is fine, decent **restaurants** are a little thin on the ground. On any kind of budget, the myriad Italian places – courtesy of Cambridge's large Italian population – will stand you in good stead; otherwise, choose carefully, particularly in the more touristy areas, where quality isn't always all it should be. Happily, Cambridge abounds in excellent **pubs**, and our list rounds up some of the best traditional student and local drinking haunts.

Cafés and restaurants

Clowns 54 King St. Italian-style cappuccino and cakes, sandwiches and snacks, plus newspapers to browse. Off the tourist route and not part of a chain – bonuses in anyone's books. Inexpensive.

Copper Kettle 4 King's Parade. Generations of students have whiled away the hours in this resolutely old-fashioned café opposite King's College, sipping coffee, eating pastries and putting the world to rights. Inexpensive.

Don Pasquale 12 Market Hill. Great marketside location, with seats on the square for lunchtime diners. Tasty food and an especially good place for a quick pick-me-up espresso and slice of pizza. Inexpensive.

Efes 78 King St ☏01223/500005. Intimate Turkish restaurant, with chargrilled meats prepared under your nose and a decent meze selection. Main courses from £10. Moderate.

Eraina Taverna 2 Free School Lane ☏01223/368 786. Packed Greek taverna, which satisfies the hungry hordes with huge platefuls of stews and grills, as well as pizzas and curries. Try to avoid getting stuck in the basement, though at weekends (when you'll probably have to queue) you'll be lucky to get a seat anywhere. Mains from £6. Inexpensive.

Midsummer House Midsummer Common ☏01223/369299. Lovely riverside restaurant with a conservatory, specializing in top-notch French–Mediterranean cuisine. On the south side of the river, beside the footbridge just to the east of Victoria Avenue. Reservations essential. Main courses begin at about £15. Currently open Tues–Sat 7–9.30pm, Fri & Sat noon–2pm. Expensive.

Nadia's Patisserie 11 St John's St. Good sandwich and cake takeaway in the centre, opposite St John's. One of several outlets – there's another at 20 King's Parade. Inexpensive

Rainbow Vegetarian Bistro 9a King's Parade ☏01223/321551. Vegetarian restaurant with main

courses – ranging from couscous to lasagne and Indonesian *gado-gado* – all for around £7. Good-value breakfasts, and organic wines served with meals. Great location, opposite King's College. Closed Sun. Inexpensive.

Twenty-Two 22 Chesterton Rd ☏01223/351880. One of the best restaurants in Cambridge, a candlelit townhouse in which the good-value, fixed-price menu (at around £25) touches all the modern bases. Closed Sun & Mon. Expensive.

Pubs and bars

Anchor Silver St. Very popular riverside tourist haunt with views of the Backs, adjacent punt rental and an outdoor deck.

Champion of the Thames 68 King St. Gratifyingly old-fashioned central pub with decent beer and a student/academic clientele.

Eagle Bene't St. An ancient inn with a cobbled courtyard where Crick and Watson sought inspiration in the 1950s, at the time of their discovery of DNA. It's been tarted up since and gets horribly crowded, but is still worth a pint of anyone's time.

Elm Tree 42 Orchard St. Cosy local with frequent live music, mainly jazz. Just to the north of Parker's

Piece and well worth seeking out: to get there, follow Emmanuel Road north off Drummer Street, and take the third turning on the right – it's on the corner with Eden Street.

Free Press 7 Prospect Row. Classic, superbly maintained backstreet local with real ale brews and tasty bar food. It's located a few yards along the street from the *Elm Tree* – for directions, see above.

The Pickerel 30 Magdalene St. Once a brothel and one of several pubs competing for the title of the oldest pub in town, *The Pickerel* has a lively atmosphere and offers a good range of beers beneath its low beams.

Entertainment

The **performing arts** scene is at its best during term time, with numerous student **drama** productions, **classical concerts** and **gigs** culminating in the traditional whizzerama of excess following the exam season. Each college and several churches contribute to the performing arts scene, with the **King's College choir** being, of course, the most famous attraction (see p.423), though the choral scholars who perform at the chapels of St John's and Trinity are also exceptionally good. In addition, the more firmly town-based venues, such as the Corn Exchange, put on events throughout the year. For upcoming events, ask for details at the tourist office (see p.420), which issues various **listings** leaflets and also stocks the *Cambridge Agenda*, a free bi-monthly listings magazine. The Corn Exchange (see below) also sells advance tickets for most events.

Arts Picture House 38–39 St Andrew's St ☏01223/504444, ⓦwww.picturehouses.co.uk. Art-house cinema with an excellent, wide-ranging programme.

Cambridge Arts Theatre 6 St Edward's Passage, off King's Parade ☏01223/503333, ⓦwww .cambridgeartstheatre.com. The city's main repertory theatre, founded by John Maynard Keynes, and launch pad of a thousand-and-one famous careers; offers a top-notch range of cutting-edge and classic productions.

Cambridge Corn Exchange Wheeler Street

☏01223/357851, ⓦwww.cornex.co.uk. Revamped nineteenth-century trading hall, now the main city-centre venue for opera, ballet, musicals and comedy as well as regular rock and folk gigs.

Cambridge Modern Jazz Club at ☏01223/ 722811, ⓦwww.cambridgejazz.org. Phone or check out the website for details of jazz gigs and venues in Cambridge.

Junction Clifton Road ☏01223/511511, ⓦwww .junction.co.uk. Rock, indie, jazz, reggae or soul gigs, plus theatre, comedy and dance at this popular arts and entertainments venue.

Listings

Airport London Stansted airport ℡0870/000 0303, ⓦwww.stanstedairport.com.
Bike rental Station Cycles, outside the train station (℡01223/307125); Mikes Bikes, 28 Mill Rd (℡01223/312591); and H. Drake, near the train station at 56–60 Hills Rd (℡01223/363468).
Buses Most city buses pull in at – and depart from – the stops along Emmanuel Street. Close by, at the top of Emmanuel Street, the Drummer Street bus station is for long-distance services. For information on Cambridgeshire bus services, call ℡0870/608 2608.
Car rental Avis ℡0870/608 6327; Europcar ℡01223/233644; Hertz ℡0870/850 2651.

Internet Internet Exchange, 2 St Mary's Passage, opposite St Mary the Great church (Mon–Sat 10am–8pm, Sun 10am–6pm). Also free at the Central Library, 7 Lion Yard (Mon–Fri 9am–7pm, Sat 9am–5.30pm).
Pharmacies Boots, 4 St Andrews St ℡01223/350213; Lloyds, 30 Trumpington St ℡01223/359449.
Post office The main office is at 9–11 St Andrew's St (Mon–Sat 9am–5.30pm).
Taxis There are ranks at the train and bus stations. To book, call Diamond ℡01223/523523; or Panther ℡01223/715715.

Travel details

Buses

For information on all local and national bus services, contact Traveline ℡0870/608 2608, ⓦwww.traveline.org.uk.

Cambridge to: Birmingham (3 daily; 3hr 45min); Bury St Edmunds (hourly; 55min); Colchester (7 daily; 2hr 30min); Ely (every 30min; 45 min); Ipswich (daily; 2hr); King's Lynn (2 daily; 1hr 45min); London (hourly; 2hr); Manchester (2 daily; 2hr 20min); Norwich (1 daily; 2hr 50min); Peterborough (hourly; 2hr 20min); Stansted Airport (hourly; 50 min).
Colchester to: Bury St Edmunds (7 daily; 1hr 30min); Cambridge (7 daily; 2hr 30min); Ipswich (hourly, 1 hour); London (3 daily; 2hr 20min).
Ely to: Cambridge (every 30min; 45 min); King's Lynn (7 daily; 1hr); Peterborough (hourly; 1hr 40min).
Ipswich to: Aldeburgh (hourly; 1hr 30min); Bury St Edmunds (2 daily; 1hr 30min); Colchester (hourly; 1hr); London (2 daily; 3hr).
Norwich to: Bury St Edmunds (5 daily; 1hr 30min); Cambridge (1 daily; 2hr 50min); Great Yarmouth (every 15min; 30 min); London (5 daily; 3 hr); Peterborough (hourly; 2hr 50min); King's Lynn (hourly; 1hr 45min); Sheringham (every 30min; 1hr 20min).
The Norfolk **Coasthopper** bus runs from Cromer to King's Lynn – or Hunstanton – via a whole gaggle of towns and villages, including Blakeney, Sheringham and Wells. Frequencies vary on different stretches of the route and there are more buses in the summer than in the winter, but on the more

popular stretches are mostly every half-hour or hour. The operator is Norfolk Green ℡01553/776980, timetable ℡0870/608 2608.

Trains

For information on all local and national rail services, contact National Rail Enquiries ℡08457/484950, ⓦwww.nationalrail.co.uk.
Cambridge to: Bury St Edmunds (8 daily; 40min); Ely (hourly; 15min); Ipswich (6 daily; 1hr 20min); King's Lynn (hourly; 45min); London (every 30min; 1hr); Norwich (hourly; 1hr); Peterborough (hourly; 50min); Stansted Airport (10 daily; 40min).
Colchester to: Ipswich (2 hourly; 25min); London (2 hourly; 50min); Norwich (hourly; 1hr).
Ely to: King's Lynn (hourly; 30min); Manchester (hourly; 3hr 30min); Nottingham (hourly; 1hr 45min); Peterborough (hourly; 30min).
Ipswich to: Bury St Edmunds (10 daily; 30min); Ely (7 daily; 1hr); London (every 30min; 1hr 10min); Norwich (hourly; 45min); Peterborough (7 daily; 1hr 50min).
Norwich to: Cromer (every 1–2hr; 50min); Ely (hourly; 50min); Great Yarmouth (hourly; 30min); London (hourly; 2hr); Manchester (hourly; 4hr 30min); Nottingham (hourly; 2hr 30min); Peterborough (hourly; 1hr 30min); Sheringham (every 1–2hr; 1hr).
Peterborough to: Bury St Edmunds (6 daily; 1hr); Cambridge (hourly; 50min); London (2 hourly; 1hr); Manchester (hourly; 3hr); Norwich (hourly; 1hr 30min); Nottingham (hourly; 1hr 10min).

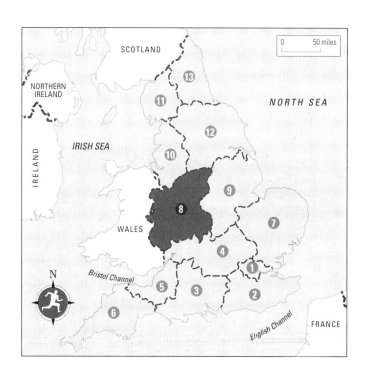

The West Midlands and the Peak District

CHAPTER 8

Highlights

✳ **The theatres, Stratford-upon-Avon** *The* place to see Shakespeare's plays. See p.438

✳ **Mappa Mundi, Hereford Cathedral** This antique map, dating to around 1000, provides a powerful insight into the medieval mind. See p.444

✳ **Hay-on-Wye** Deep in the countryside, this dinky little town has more secondhand bookshops than anywhere else in the world. See p.445

✳ **Ironbridge Gorge** The first iron bridge ever constructed arches high above the River Severn. See p.447

✳ **Ludlow** A postcard-pretty country town with half-timbered houses and a cluster of Michelin-starred restaurants. See p.452

✳ **Buxton** Good-looking former spa town and ideal base for exploring the Peak District. See p.464

△ Hay-on-Wye books

The West Midlands and the Peak District

Whilst the small country towns and untrammelled scenery of the **West Midlands** have much to recommend them, the urban epicentre of the region is **Birmingham**, Britain's second city, once the world's greatest industrial metropolis and powerhouse of the Industrial Revolution. Long saddled with a reputation as a culture-hating, car-loving backwater, Birmingham has redefined its image in recent years, initiating some ambitious architectural and environmental schemes, jazzing up its museums and industrial heritage sites and giving itself a higher profile on the nation's cultural map than it's ever had before. Admittedly, it's not an especially good-looking city, but it does hold several excellent attractions and it's certainly lively, with nightlife encompassing everything from Royal Ballet productions to all-night grooves, and a great spread of restaurants and pubs in between.

The counties to the south and west of Birmingham – Warwickshire, Worcestershire, Herefordshire and Shropshire – comprise a rural stronghold that maintains an emotional and political distance from the conurbation. The left-wing politics of the big city seem remote indeed when you're in Shrewsbury, though there's only seventy miles between them. For the most part, the four counties constitute a quiet, unassuming stretch of pastoral England whose beauty is rarely dramatic, but whose charms become more evident the longer you stay. Of the four counties, **Warwickshire** is the least obviously scenic, but draws by far the largest number of visitors, for – as the road signs declare at every entry point – this is "Shakespeare Country". The prime target is, of course, **Stratford-upon-Avon**, with its handful of Shakespeare-related sites and world-class theatre, but spare time also for the diverting town of **Warwick**, which has a superb church and a whopping castle.

Neighbouring **Worcestershire**, which stretches southwest from the urban fringes of the West Midlands, holds one principal place of interest, **Great Malvern**, a mannered inland resort spread along the rolling contours of the **Malvern Hills** – prime walking territory. From here, it's west again for **Herefordshire**, a large and sparsely populated county that's home to several charming market towns, most notably **Hay-on-Wye**, which boasts the largest concentration of secondhand bookshops in the world and **Hereford**, where the remarkable medieval Mappa Mundi map is displayed. Next door, to the north, rural **Shropshire** weighs in with **Ludlow**, one of the region's prettiest towns,

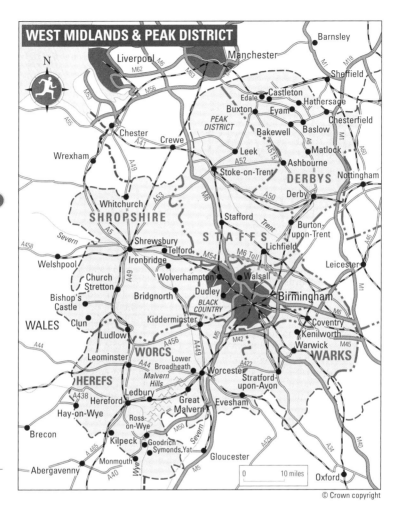

WEST MIDLANDS & PEAK DISTRICT

© Crown copyright

awash with antique half-timbered buildings, and the amiable county town of **Shrewsbury**, which is also close to the hiking trails of the Long Mynd. Shropshire has a fascinating industrial history, too, for it was here in the **Ironbridge Gorge** that British industrialists built the world's first iron bridge and pioneered the use of coal as a smelting fuel. These were two key events in the Industrial Revolution and, appropriately, the gorge's industrial heyday is recalled by a phalanx of museums.

To the north of the sprawling Birmingham conurbation is **Derbyshire**, whose northern reaches incorporate the region's finest scenery in the rough landscapes of the **Peak District National Park**. The latter offers great opportunities for moderately strenuous walks, as well as the diversions of the former spa town of **Buxton**, the limestone caverns of **Castleton** and the so-called "Plague Village" of **Eyam**. In addition, there's the grandiose stately pile of **Chatsworth House**, with its beautiful gardens.

Birmingham is the region's **public transport hub**, and is easily accessible by **train** from London Euston, Liverpool, Manchester, Leeds, York and a score of other towns. It is also well served by the National Express **bus** network, with dozens of buses leaving every hour for destinations all over Britain. Local **bus** services are excellent around the West Midlands conurbation and very good in the Peak District, but fade away badly in amongst the villages of Herefordshire and Shropshire.

Stratford-upon-Avon

Despite its worldwide fame, **STRATFORD-UPON-AVON** is at heart an unassuming market town with an unexceptional pedigree. Its first settlers forded, and later bridged, the River Avon, and developed commercial links with the farmers who tilled the surrounding flatlands. A charter for Stratford's weekly market was granted in the twelfth century, a tradition continued to this day, and the town later became an important stopping-off point for stagecoaches between London, Oxford and the north. Like all such places, Stratford had its clearly defined class system and within this typical milieu John and Mary **Shakespeare** occupied the middle rank, and would have been forgotten long ago had their first son, **William**, not turned out to be the greatest writer ever to use the English language. A consequence of their good fortune is that this ordinary little town is nowadays all but smothered by package-tourist hype and, in the summer at least, its central streets groan under the weight of thousands of tourists. Don't let that deter you: the **Royal Shakespeare Company** offers superb theatre, there are several first–rate restaurants, and you can dodge the crowds by avoiding the busiest attractions at peak times.

Arrival, information and getting around

Stratford **train station** is on the northwestern edge of town, ten minutes' walk from the centre. It receives hourly services from Birmingham (Moor Street and Snow Hill stations) and trains arrive every two hours from London Marylebone (via Warwick). Local **bus services** arrive and depart from the central Bridge Street; National Express services and most other long-distance and regional buses pull into the Riverside station on the east side of the town centre, off Bridgeway.

The **tourist office** (April–Sept Mon–Sat 9am–5.30pm, Sun 10.30am–4.30pm; Oct–March Mon–Sat 9am–5pm; ☎0870/160 7930, ⓦwww.shakespeare-country.co.uk) is located a couple of minutes' walk from the bus station by the bridge at the junction of Bridgeway and Bridgefoot. It operates an **accom-modation-booking service** (☎0870/160 7930, ⓦwww.shakespeare-country.co.uk; £3), which is very useful at the height of the summer when rooms can be in short supply. It also issues bus and train timetables, sells bus tickets and the all-in ticket for all five **Shakespeare Birthplace Trust** properties (£13), or a **Three In-Town Shakespeare Property Ticket** (£10) for the three Trust properties in the town centre; both tickets are also available from the sites themselves.

Accommodation

As one of the most popular tourist destinations in England, Stratford's **accom-modation** is pricey and often gets booked up well in advance. The town has a dozen or so **hotels**, the pick of which occupy old half-timbered buildings right

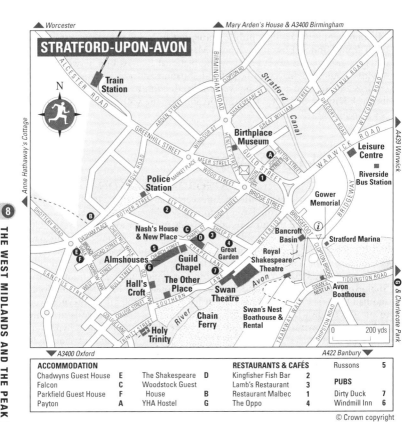

ACCOMMODATION				RESTAURANTS & CAFÉS		Russons	5
Chadwyns Guest House	E	The Shakespeare	D	Kingfisher Fish Bar	2		
Falcon	C	Woodstock Guest		Lamb's Restaurant	3	**PUBS**	
Parkfield Guest House	F	House	B	Restaurant Malbec	1	Dirty Duck	7
Payton	A	YHA Hostel	G	The Oppo	4	Windmill Inn	6

in the centre of town, but most visitors choose to stay in a **B&B**. These have sprung up in every part of Stratford, but there's a concentration to the southwest of the centre around Grove Road, Evesham Place and Broad Walk.

Hotels

Falcon Chapel Street ☎0870/6096122, ✆www.corushotels.com/thefalcon. Handily situated in the middle of town, this hotel has a half-timbered facade dating from the sixteenth century, though most of the rest is an unremarkable modern rebuild. **G**

Payton 6 John St ☎01789/266442, ✆www.payton.co.uk. On the north side of the town centre, a couple of minutes' walk from the Birthplace Museum, this comfortable hotel occupies an attractive Georgian townhouse on a quiet residential

street. Family-run, the hotel has five comfortable rooms, all en suite. A good bet and very affordable. **A**

The Shakespeare Chapel Street ☎0870/400 8182, ✆www.shakespearehotel.net. Now part of a chain, this old hotel, with its mullion windows and half-timbered facade, is one of Stratford's best known. The interior has low beams and open fires and represents a fairly successful amalgamation of the old and new. Right in the centre of town. **D**

Guest houses, B&Bs and hostels

Chadwyns Guest House 6 Broad Walk ☎01789/269077, ✆www.chadwyns.co.uk. Just

off Evesham Place, this unassuming guest house occupies a two-storey Victorian terraced house with seven en-suite rooms. Great breakfasts with vegetarian options. No cards. ❷

Parkfield Guest House 3 Broad Walk ☎01789/293313, ⓦwww.parkfieldbandb.co.uk. Very pleasant B&B in a three-storey Victorian house in a residential street off Evesham Place. There's a private car park – a useful facility in crowded Stratford – and most rooms are en suite. Under ten minutes' walk from the centre. ❸

Stratford-upon-Avon YHA Hostel Hemmingford House, Alveston ☎0870/770 6052, ⓦwww.yha .org.uk. This hostel occupies a rambling Georgian mansion on the edge of the pretty village of Alveston. There are dormitories and family rooms,

some of which are en suite, plus laundry, Internet access, car parking and self-catering facilities. Breakfasts and evening meals are on offer too. It's located two miles east of the town centre on the B4086 and served by regular bus from Stratford's Riverside bus station. Open all year. Dorm beds £16, doubles ❶

Woodstock Guest House 30 Grove Rd ☎01789/299881, ⓔwoodstockhouse @compuserve.com. A smart and neatly kept B&B five minutes' walk from the centre, by the start of the path to Anne Hathaway's Cottage (see p.439). It has five extremely comfortable bedrooms, all en suite. No credit cards. ❸

The Town

Spreading back from the River Avon, Stratford's **town centre** is flat and compact, its mostly modern buildings filling out a simple gridiron just two blocks deep and four blocks long. Running along the northern edge of the centre is Bridge Street, the main thoroughfare lined with shops and chock-a-block with local buses. At its west end **Bridge Street** divides into Henley Street, home of the **Birthplace Museum**, and Wood Street, which leads up to the market place. It also intersects with High Street. The latter, and its continuation Chapel and Church streets, cuts south to pass most of the old buildings that the town still possesses, notably **Nash's House** and, on neighbouring Old Town Street, **Hall's Croft**. From here, it's a short hop to the charming **Holy Trinity Church**, where Shakespeare lies buried, and then only a few minutes back along the river past the **theatres** to the foot of Bridge Street. In itself, this circular walk only takes about fifteen minutes, but it takes all day if you visit the attractions. In addition, there are two outlying Shakespearean properties, **Anne Hathaway's Cottage** in Shottery and **Mary Arden's House** in Wilmcote – though you have to be a really serious sightseer to want to see them all.

The Birthplace Museum

Top of everyone's itinerary is the **Birthplace Museum**, on Henley Street (June–Aug Mon–Sat 9am–5pm, Sun 9.30am–5pm; April–May & Sept–Oct Mon–Sat 10am–5pm, Sun 10.30am–5pm; Nov–March Mon–Sat 10am–4pm, Sun 10.30am–4pm; £6.70), comprising an unappetising modern visitor centre and the heavily-restored, half-timbered building where the great man was born. The visitor centre pokes into every corner of Shakespeare's life and times, making the most of what little hard evidence there is. Next door, the half-timbered birthplace dwelling is actually two buildings knocked into one. The northern, much smaller and later part was the house of Joan, Shakespeare's sister, and it adjoins the main family home, bought by John Shakespeare in 1556 and now returned to something like its original appearance.

Nash's House and New Place

Follow **High Street** south from the junction of Bridge and Henley streets, and you'll soon come to another Birthplace Trust property, **Nash's House** on Chapel Street (June–Aug Mon–Sat 9.30am–5pm, Sun 10am–5pm; April–May & Sept–Oct daily 11am–5pm; Nov–March daily 11am–4pm; £3.50). Once the property of Thomas Nash, first husband of Shakespeare's granddaughter, Elizabeth Hall, the house's ground floor is kitted out with a pleasant assortment of period furnishings. Upstairs, one display provides a potted history of Stratford, including a scattering of archeological bits and pieces, while another focuses on the house.

The adjacent gardens contain the bare foundations of **New Place** (same hours), Shakespeare's last residence, which was demolished long ago. A gate leads from here into the adjoining **Great Garden** (March–Oct Mon–Sat 9am–dusk, Sun 10am–dusk; Nov–Feb Mon–Sat 9am–4pm, Sun noon–4pm; free), a formal affair of topiary, lawns and flowerbeds; its main entrance is on Chapel Lane.

On the other side of Chapel Lane stands the **Guild Chapel**, whose chunky tower and sturdy stonework shelter a plain interior enlivened by some rather crude stained-glass windows and a faded mural above the triumphal arch. The adjoining King Edward VI **Grammar School**, where Shakespeare is thought to have been educated, incorporates a creaky line of fifteenth-century almshouses running along Church Street.

Hall's Croft

At the end of Church Street, turn left along Old Town Street for Stratford's most impressive medieval house, the Birthplace Trust's **Hall's Croft** (April–May & Sept–Oct daily 11am–5pm; June–Aug Mon–Sat 9.30am–5pm, Sun 10am–5pm; Nov–March daily 11am–4pm; £3.50). The former home of Shakespeare's elder daughter, Susanna, and her doctor husband, John Hall, the immaculately maintained Croft, with its creaking wooden floors, beamed ceilings and fine kitchen range, holds a good-looking medley of period furniture and a fascinating display on **Elizabethan medicine**. The best view of the building itself is at the back, from the neat walled garden.

Holy Trinity Church

Beyond Hall's Croft, Old Town Street steers right to reach the handsome **Holy Trinity Church** (March & Oct Mon–Sat 9am–5pm & Sun 12–5pm; April–Sept Mon–Sat 8.30am–6pm & Sun 12–5pm; Nov–Feb Mon–Sat 9am–4pm & Sun 12pm–5pm; free), whose mellow, honey-coloured stonework dates from the thirteenth century. Enhanced by its riverside setting, the church's dignified proportions are the result of several centuries of chopping and changing, culminating in the replacement of the original wooden spire with today's stone version in 1763. Inside, William Shakespeare lies buried in the **chancel** (£1), his remains overseen by a sedate and studious memorial plaque and effigy added seven years after his death.

Tickets for the RSC

As the **Royal Shakespeare Company** (information: ☎01789/403444, ⊛www.rsc .org.uk) works on a repertory system, you could stay in Stratford for a few days and see three or four different plays. Neither would they all have to be Shakespeare: the RSC does indeed focus on the great man's plays, but it offers other productions too, from new modern writing through to plays written by Shakespeare's contemporaries. The RSC performs in three venues – the **Royal Shakespeare Theatre**, where tickets start at £5 for standing room and a restricted view, rising to £40 for the best seats in the house; the **Swan** (tickets between £5 and £36); and **The Other Place** (no standing; £15 to £20). The Royal Shakespeare Theatre's foyer **box office** (Mon–Sat 9.30am–6pm, till 8pm when there is an evening performance; ☎0870/609 1110, ⊛www.rsc.org.uk) serves as the central booking agent for all three theatres. Many performances are sold out months in advance and although there's always the off-chance of a last-minute return or stand-by ticket (for unsold seats), don't bet on it.

The theatres

Doubling back from the church, turn right into the **park** just before you reach Southern Lane and you can stroll along – or at least near – the river bank, past the dinky little **chain ferry** (40p) across the Avon, to reach the town's two main Royal Shakespeare Company **theatres** – the Swan Theatre and the Royal Shakespeare Theatre. There was no theatre in Stratford in Shakespeare's day and indeed the first home-town festival in his honour was only held in 1769 at the behest of London-based David Garrick. Thereafter, the idea of building a permanent home in which to perform Shakespeare's works slowly gained momentum, and finally, in 1879, the first Memorial Theatre was opened on land donated by local beer baron Charles Flower. A fire in 1926 necessitated the construction of a new theatre, and the ensuing architectural competition, won by Elisabeth Scott, produced today's **Royal Shakespeare Theatre**. In the 1980s, the burnt-out original theatre round the back was turned into a replica "in-the-round" Elizabethan stage – the **Swan**. Even if you can't get to see a performance here, you can take a two-hour, behind-the-scenes **tour** (£5) – ask at the desk in the foyer of the Royal Shakespeare Theatre for details or call ☏01789/403405. A third RSC auditorium, **The Other Place**, close by on Southern Lane, features contemporary plays by new authors.

Anne Hathaway's Cottage

Anne Hathaway's Cottage (April–Oct Mon–Sat 9/9.30am–5pm, Sun 9.30/10am–5pm; Nov–March Mon–Sat 10am–4pm, Sun 10.30am–4pm; £5.20), also run by the Birthplace Trust, is located just over a mile west of the centre in the well-heeled suburb of Shottery. The cottage – actually an old farmhouse – is an immaculately maintained, half-timbered affair with a thatched roof and dinky little chimneys. This was the home of Anne Hathaway before she married Shakespeare in 1582, and the interior holds a comely combination of period furniture, including a superb, finely carved four-poster bed. The garden is splendid too, crowded with bursting blooms in the summertime. The adjacent orchard and **Shakespeare Tree Garden** features a scattering of modern sculptures and over forty trees, shrubs and roses mentioned in the plays, with each bearing the appropriate quotation inscribed on a plaque. The most agreeable way to get to the cottage from the town centre is on the signposted **footpath** from Evesham Place, at the south end of Rother Street.

Mary Arden's House

The Birthplace Trust also owns **Mary Arden's House** (April, May, Sept & Oct Mon–Sat 10am–5pm, Sun 10.30am–5pm; June–Aug Mon–Sat 9.30am–5pm, Sun 10am–5pm; Nov–March Mon–Sat 10am–4pm, Sun 10.30am–4pm; £5.70), three miles northwest of the town centre in the village of Wilmcote. Mary was Shakespeare's mother and the only unmarried daughter of her father, Robert, at the time of his death in 1556. Unusually for the period, Mary inherited the house and land, thus becoming one of the neighbourhood's most eligible women – John Shakespeare, eager for self-improvement, married her within a year. The house is a well-furnished example of an Elizabethan farmhouse and, though the labelling is rather scant, a platoon of guides fills in the details of family life and traditions.

Eating and drinking

Stratford is used to feeding and watering thousands of visitors, so finding refreshment is never difficult. Most places, however, are aimed firmly at the day-tripper, and standards aren't great. That said, there is a scattering of very good established **restaurants**, and a handful of **pubs** and **cafés** offering decent food, too. The best restaurants are concentrated along Sheep Street, running up from Waterside near the theatres.

Restaurants and cafés

Kingfisher Fish Bar 13 Ely St. The best fish-and-chip shop in town. Takeaway and sit-down. A five-minute walk from the theatres. Closed Sun.

Lamb's Restaurant 12 Sheep St ☎ 01789/292554. Smart and appealing restaurant serving a mouthwatering range of stylish English and Continental dishes in antique premises – beamed ceilings and so forth. Daily specials at around £7, other main courses £14–16. The best place in town. Expensive.

The Oppo 13 Sheep St ☎ 01789/269980. International cuisine in a busy but amiable atmosphere and pleasant old premises. The dishes of the day, chalked up on a board inside, are good value at around £6, otherwise mains average around £11. Moderate.

Restaurant Malbec 6 Union St ☎ 01789/269106. Smart and intimate restaurant serving top-quality seafood and meat dishes, often with a Mediterranean slant. Mains around £15. Closed Sun & Mon. Expensive.

Russons 8 Church St ☎ 01789/268822. Excellent, good-value cuisine, featuring interesting meat and vegetarian dishes on the main menu and an extensive blackboard of seafood specials. Cosy little place too. Closed Sun & Mon. Main courses around £10. Moderate.

Pubs

Dirty Duck 53 Waterside. The archetypal actors' pub, stuffed to the gunwales every night with a vocal entourage of RSC employees and hangers-on. Traditional beers in somewhat spartan premises plus a terrace for hot-weather drinking.

Windmill Inn Church Street. Popular pub with rabbit-warren rooms and low-beamed ceilings. Flowers beers, too.

Warwick

WARWICK, just eight miles northeast of Stratford and easily reached by bus and train, is famous for its massive **castle**, but it also possesses several charming streetscapes erected in the aftermath of a great fire in 1694, not to mention an especially fine church chancel. An hour or two is quite enough time to nose around the town centre, though you'll need the whole day if you decide to brave the crowds and the medieval musicians to explore the castle and its extensive grounds thoroughly.

The Castle

Towering above the River Avon at the foot of the town centre, **Warwick Castle** (daily: April–Sept 10am–6pm; Oct–March 10am–5pm; £12.95–16.95 low/high season; parking £2.50–5; Ⓦ www.warwick-castle.co.uk) is often proclaimed the "greatest medieval castle in Britain" and, if bulk equals greatness, then the claim is certainly valid, though much of the existing structure is the result of extensive nineteenth-century restoration.

The **entrance** to the castle is through the old stable block at the bottom of Castle Street. Beyond, a footpath leads round to the imposing moated and mounded **East Gate**. Over the footbridge – and beyond the protective towers – is the main **courtyard**. You can stroll along the ramparts and climb the towers, but most visitors head straight for one or other of the special displays installed inside by the present owners, Madame Tussauds. The most popular of these displays is the "Royal Weekend Party, 1898", an extravaganza of waxwork nobility hobnobbing in the private apartments which were rebuilt in the 1870s after fire damage. Rather less obviously commercial are the **Great Hall** and neighbouring **Chapel**, though both are drably Victorian, the only saving grace being the former's assorted suits of armour. The **grounds** are much more enjoyable, acres of woodland and lawn inhabited by peacocks and including a large glass **conservatory**. A footbridge leads over the River Avon to **River Island**, the site of jousting tournaments and other medieval activities.

The town centre

Outside the castle exit, **Castle Street** leads up the hill for a few yards to the High Street. Turn left and it's a brief stroll to another remarkable building, the **Lord Leycester Hospital** (Tues–Sun 10am–4/5pm; £3.20), a tangle of half-timbered buildings that lean at fairy-tale angles against the old West Gate. The complex represents one of Britain's best-preserved examples of domestic Elizabethan architecture and was established as a hostel for old soldiers by the Earl of Leicester, a favourite of Queen Elizabeth I.

Double back along the High Street, and turn left up Church Street for **St Mary's Church** (daily 10am–6pm, 4.30pm in winter; £2 donation suggested), which was rebuilt in a weird Gothic-Renaissance amalgam after the fire of 1694. One part remained untouched, however – the **chancel**, a glorious illustration of the Perpendicular style with a splendid vaulted ceiling of flying and fronded ribs. On the right-hand side of the chancel, the **Beauchamp Chapel** contains several beautiful tombs, exquisite works of art beginning with that of Richard Beauchamp, Earl of Warwick, who is depicted in an elaborate suit of armour of Italian design. The adjacent tomb of Ambrose Dudley is of finely carved alabaster, as is that of Robert Dudley, Earl of Leicester, one of Elizabeth I's most influential advisers.

Practicalities

From Warwick **train station**, on the northern edge of town, it's about ten minutes' walk to the centre via Station and Coventry Roads. More conveniently, **buses** stop on Market Street, close to the Market Square, from where it's a couple of minutes' walk east to St Mary's Church. The **tourist office** is near the castle in the old Courthouse at the corner of Castle and Jury streets (daily 9.30am–4.30pm; ☎01926/492212, ⓦwww.warwick-uk.co.uk). It has a list of local hotels and B&Bs, but with Stratford so near, there's no special reason to stay. If you do need to stay, however, *Forth House*, 44 High St (☎01926/401512, ⓦwww.forthhouseuk.co.uk; ➎), is an excellent **B&B** with two very comfortable en-suite guest rooms in a listed sixteenth-century property a short walk from the tourist office.

For a bite to **eat**, try the *Catalan*, 6 Jury St (Tues & Sun 11am–5pm, Wed–Sat 11am–10pm), a slick, modern café-restaurant, which serves tasty tapas (two for £6.25) and light lunches during the day, and Mediterranean-inspired food at night, with main courses from £12; it's located just along from the tourist office. For a **drink**, try the amiable, partly panelled *Zetland Arms*, nearby at 11 Church St.

Worcestershlre

In geographical terms, **Worcestershire** can be compared to a huge saucer, with the low-lying plains of the Severn Valley and the Vale of Evesham rising to a lip of hills, principally the Malverns in the west and the Cotswolds to the south (see pp.281–288). To the north lie the industrial and overspill towns – such as Droitwich and Redditch – that have much in common with the Birmingham conurbation, while the south is predominantly rural and holds the county's finest scenery in the **Malvern Hills**, excellent walking territory much loved by that most English of composers, **Edward Elgar**, and home to the amiable former spa town of **Great Malvern**.

The proximity of Birmingham ensures Worcestershire has a good network of **trains** and **buses**, though services are spasmodic amongst the villages in the south of the county. There's also an excellent regional public-transport **information line** covering all the West Midlands – Centro Hotline (℡0121/200 2700, ⓦwww.centro.org.uk).

Great Malvern and the Malvern Hills

One of the most exclusive and prosperous areas of the Midlands, **The Malverns** is the generic name for a string of towns and villages stretched along the eastern lower slopes of the **Malvern Hills**, which rise spectacularly out of the flat plains a few miles southwest of Worcester. About nine miles from north to south – between the A44 and the M50 – and never more than five miles wide, the hills straddle the Worcestershire–Herefordshire boundary. Of ancient granite rock, they are punctuated by over twenty summits, mostly around 1000 feet high, and in between lie innumerable dips and hollows. It's easy if energetic walking country, with great views, and there's an excellent network of hiking trails, most of which can be completed in a day or half-day.

Amongst The Malverns, it's **GREAT MALVERN** that grabs the attention, its pocket-sized centre clambering up the hillside with the crags of North Hill beckoning beyond. The Benedictines chose this hilly setting for one of their abbeys and although Henry VIII closed the place down in 1538, the **Priory Church** (daily: April–Sept 9am–6.30pm; Oct–March 9am–4.30pm; free) has survived, the crisp symmetries and elaborate decoration of its exterior witnessing the priory's former wealth.

A couple of minutes' walk away, hard by the top of Church Street, the modest **Malvern Museum** (Easter–Oct daily 10.30am–5pm; £1) is housed in the delicately proportioned Priory Gatehouse, but it concentrates on Great Malvern's days as a spa town. The spring waters hereabouts became popular at the end of the eighteenth century, but it was to be the Victorians who packed the place out – and built the grand stone houses that still line many of the town's streets. You can still sample the waters at ✸ *St Ann's Well Café* (May–June & Sept Tues–Sun 11am–3.30pm; July & Aug daily 11am–3.30pm; Oct–May Sat & Sun 11.30am–3.30pm; ℡01684/560285, ⓦwww.stannswell.co.uk), a cosy little vegetarian café which occupies an attractive Georgian building a steep fifteen-minute walk up the wooded hillside from the top of town; the signposted path begins on the far side of the main road across from the *Foley Arms Hotel*.

Back at the museum, it's a short walk down the hill to Grange Road, where **Malvern Theatres** (℡01684/892277, ⓦwww.malvern-theatres.co.uk) is the key venue for the wide range of special events the town puts on each year.

Practicalities

With its dainty ironwork and quaint chimneys, Great Malvern's rustic **train station** has fast and frequent connections with Birmingham and Worcester. It's located half a mile or so from the town centre via Avenue Road and then **Church Street**, the steeply sloping main drag. The **tourist office** is at the top of Church Street, across from the Priory Church (daily 10am–5pm; T01684/892289, Wwww.malvernhills.gov.uk).

Accommodation is plentiful, with the pick of the hotels being *The Abbey* (T01684/892332, Wwww.sarova.com; ❻), a rambling, creeper-clad Victorian hotel with mock-Tudor timbers, handsome stone doorways and plush rooms, set behind the Priory Church on Abbey Road – try and avoid the unappetizing modern wing, though. Alternatively, try the *Best Western Foley Arms Hotel*, at 14 Worcester Rd (T01684/573397, Wwww.foleyarmshotel.com; ❻), though the rooms don't match up to the attractive Georgian facade with its fancy wrought-iron balcony. The best of the B&Bs is *The Red Gate B&B*, in a large Victorian house near the train station at 32 Avenue Rd (T01684/565013; ❺) with a handful of well-appointed en-suite rooms. The nearest YHA **hostel** is a mile or two south, along the A449, in a rambling Edwardian house at 18 Peachfield Rd, Malvern Wells, (T0870/770 5948, Wwww.yha.org.uk; dorm beds £11, doubles ❶); advance reservations are required.

The **restaurant** scene in Great Malvern is not as varied as you might expect – try the smart and chic *Anupam* Asian restaurant, at 85 Church St (T01684/573814), where main courses average around £9.

Herefordshire

Over the Malvern Hills from Worcestershire, the rolling agricultural landscapes of **Herefordshire** have an easy-going charm, but the finest scenery hereabouts is along the banks of the **River Wye**, which wriggles and worms its way across the county linking most of the places of interest. Plonked in the middle is **Hereford**, a sleepy, rather old-fashioned place whose proudest possession, the cathedral's remarkable Mappa Mundi map, was almost flogged off in a round of ecclesiastical budget cuts, back in the 1980s. To the west of Hereford, hard by the Welsh border, the key attraction is **Hay-on-Wye**, which – thanks to the purposeful industry of the entrepreneurial Richard Booth – has become the world's largest repository of secondhand books, on sale in around thirty bookshops.

Herefordshire possesses one **rail line**, running north from Hereford to Shrewsbury and east to Great Malvern and Worcester. Alternatively, the county's **buses** provide a reasonable service between the villages and towns, except on Sundays when there's almost nothing at all. All the local tourist offices have bus timetables and there's **bus information** on T0870/608 2608 and Wwww .herefordshire-buses.tbctimes.co.uk.

Hereford

HEREFORD – literally "army ford" – was long a border garrison town against the Welsh, its military importance guaranteed by its strategic position beside the River Wye. Today, with the fortifications that once girdled the city all but gone, it's the **cathedral**, dating from the eleventh century, which forms the main focus of architectural interest. It lies just to the north of the River Wye at the heart of the city centre, whose compact tangle of narrow streets and squares is clumsily boxed in by the ring road. Taken as a whole, Hereford makes for a pleasant – if not exactly riveting – overnight stay.

The Cathedral and the Mappa Mundi

Hereford **Cathedral** (daily 8am–5.30pm; £2 donation suggested; Wwww .herefordcathedral.org) is a curious building, an uncomfortable amalgamation of architectural styles, with bits and pieces added to the eleventh-century original by a string of bishops and culminating in an extensive – and not especially sympathetic – Victorian refit. From the outside, the sandstone **tower** is the dominant feature, constructed in the early fourteenth century to eclipse the Norman western tower, which subsequently collapsed under its own weight in 1786. The tumbling masonry mauled the **nave** and its replacement lacks the grandeur of most other English cathedrals, though the forceful symmetries of the long rank of surviving Norman arches and piers more than hints at what went before. The **north transept** is, however, a flawless exercise in thirteenth-century taste, its soaring windows a classic example of Early English architecture.

In the 1980s, financial difficulties prompted the cathedral authorities to plan the controversial sale of one of their most treasured possessions, the **Mappa Mundi**. The government and John Paul Getty Jr rode to the rescue, with the oil tycoon stumping up a million pounds to keep the map here and install it in a brand new building. Made of sandstone, this **New Library** – located next to the cathedral at the west end of the cloisters – blends in seamlessly with the other, older buildings close by. It contains the **Mappa Mundi and Chained Library Exhibition** (Mon–Sat 10am–4/5pm, Sun 11am–4pm; Oct–March closed Sun; last admission 45min before closing; £4.50), which begins with a series of interpretative panels that lead to the Mappa, displayed in a dimly lit room. Dating from about 1300 and measuring 158cm x 133cm, this remarkable map provides an extraordinary insight into the medieval mind. It is indeed a map insofar as it suggests the general geography of the world – with Asia at the top and Europe and Africa below, to left and right respectively – but it also squeezes in history, mythology and theology.

The rest of the city

After the Mappa, Hereford's other attractions seem rather pedestrian. Nonetheless, the **Hereford Museum and Art Gallery**, in a flamboyant Victorian building opposite the cathedral on Broad Street (Tues–Sat 10am–5pm; April–Sept also Sun 10am–4pm; free), holds a mildly diverting collection of geological remains, local history and Victorian art spiced up with several interactive exhibits. From the gallery, Broad Street continues up and round into the main square, **High Town**, which is fringed by several good-looking Georgian buildings.

Practicalities

From Hereford **train station**, it's about half a mile southwest to the main square, High Town – via Station Approach, Commercial Road and its continuation Commercial Street. The long-distance **bus station** is just off Commercial Road, but most local and some regional buses stop in St Peter's Square, at the east end of High Town. The **tourist office** is directly opposite the cathedral, at 1 King St (Mon–Sat 9am–5pm, plus mid–May to mid-Sept Sun 10am–4pm; ☎01432/268430, ⓦwww.visitherefordshire.com), and issues the free *Herefordshire Visitor Guide*, with comprehensive accommodation listings.

Easily the best **hotel** in town is the *Castle House*, an immaculate refurbished Georgian mansion just a couple of minutes' walk from the cathedral on Castle Street (☎01432/356321, ⓦwww.castlehse.co.uk; ❽). It has a chic waterside terrace at the rear and each of the rooms is decorated in a plush modern version of Georgian style. Hereford also has a substantial number of B&Bs, the best of which is *Charades*, 34 Southbank Rd (☎01432/269444, ⓔcharades@btinternet.com; ❷), with six comfortable, mostly en-suite guest rooms in a large Victorian house a ten- to fifteen-minute walk northeast from the centre: take Commercial Street, then Commercial Road, cross the railway bridge, and Southbank Road is the second on the right.

There are several appealing places **to eat** just north of the cathedral on pedestrianized Church Street, with one of the best being the vegetarian café *Nutters* (Mon–Sat 9am–5pm), on Capuchin Yard. Hereford's smartest restaurant is *La Rive*, at the *Castle House* (see above), with the emphasis on local ingredients, such as Hereford beef and Gloucestershire pork; main courses start at £19.

When it comes to **drinking**, try the favourite local tipple, cider. Every pub in town serves it, with one of the most enjoyable being *The Barrels*, a traditional place five minutes' walk southeast of High Town, at 69 St Owen's St. It's also the home pub of the local Wye Valley Brewery (Ⓦwww.wyevalleybrewery .co.uk), whose trademark bitters are much acclaimed.

Hay-on-Wye

Straddling the Anglo-Welsh border some twenty miles west of Hereford, the hilly little town of **HAY-ON-WYE** is known to most people for one thing – **books**. Hay's first bookshop was opened in 1961 by the entrepreneurial Richard Booth, and the town has since become a bibliophile's paradise, with just about every spare inch of the town being given over to the trade, including the old cinema and the ramshackle stone castle. In summer, the town plays host to a succession of riverside parties and travelling fairs, the pick of which is the **Hay Festival of Literature and the Arts** (box office ☎0870/990 1299, Ⓦwww.hayfestival.co.uk), held over ten days at the end of May, when London's literary world decamps here.

Hay has an attractive setting, amidst rolling forested hills, and its narrow, bendy streets are lined with an engaging assortment of old stone houses. Before you start exploring the town, visit the tourist office (see below) to pick up its free leaflet that gives the lowdown on Hay's bookshops together with a street plan. Across the street from the tourist office, a signed footpath leads up the slope to the **castle**, a careworn Jacobean mansion built into the walls of an earlier medieval fortress. Richard Booth lives in part of the castle, but its southern extremities are given over to a pair of bookshops: **Castle Drive Books** (daily 10.30am–5pm), which has a large stock of remaindered books, and **Hay Castle Bookshop** (daily 9.30am–5.30pm; ☎01497/820503, Ⓦwww.boothbooks.co.uk), a trusty collection focused on fine art, cinema, antiquarian and photography. From here, the footpath twists its way round the western flank of the castle to meet the steps that lead down to Castle Street, home to **Bookends**, at no. 9 (April–Oct Sun–Wed 9am–5.30pm, Thurs–Sat 9am–8pm; Nov–Jan daily 9am–5pm; Feb–March Mon–Thurs 10am–4.30pm, Fri & Sun 9am–5.30pm; ☎01497/821572), where all the books cost £1.

Castle Street slopes up to the main square, High Town, from where it's straight on for Lion Street, where **Richard Booth's Bookshop**, at no. 44 (April–Oct Mon–Sat 9am–8pm, Sun 11.30am–5.30pm; Nov–March Mon–Sat 9am–5.30pm, Sun 11.30am–5.30pm; ☎01497/820322, Ⓦwww.richardbooth .demon.co.uk) is a huge, musty, bookish warehouse of a place offering almost unlimited browsing potential. At the foot of Lion Street, the town's main landmark is the ornate, rather Ruritanian, Victorian **clocktower**.

Practicalities

Buses to Hay stop in the centre of town on Oxford Road beside the main car park and the adjacent **tourist office** (daily: Easter–Oct 10am–1pm & 2–5pm;

Nov–Easter 11am–1pm & 2–4pm; ☎01497/820 144, ⓦwww.hay-on-wye.co .uk), which sells an exhaustive range of hiking books and maps, and can arrange accommodation.

Accommodation in town is plentiful, though things get booked up long in advance for the Literature Festival (see above). One of the best of the town's many B&Bs and guest houses is *The Start* (☎01497/821391, ⓦwww.the-start .net; ❸), which occupies a much modernized old house, beside the river just across the bridge from the town centre: it has three en-suite guest rooms, each decorated in a bright and breezy manner. Alternatively, try the friendly *La Fosse Guest House*, in an old three-storey cottage a brief walk east of the tourist office at the junction of Lion and Oxford roads (☎01497/820613, ⓦwww.lafosse .co.uk; ❸); all the rooms here are en suite and cheerfully furnished. A couple of miles south of Hay, just across the Welsh border in Llanigon, there's the outstanding ⚹ *Old Post Office B&B* (☎01497/820008, ⓦwww.oldpost-office .co.uk; no cards; ❸), a first-rate place in a seventeenth-century former post office, complete with wood floors and beamed ceilings: it has three rooms, two en-suite, and serves delicious vegetarian breakfasts. Back in Hay, the handiest **campsite** is *Radnors End* (☎01497/820780), in a pleasant setting five minutes' walk from the town centre across the Wye bridge on the Clyro road; washing and toilet facilities here are simple, and pitches are inexpensive (£4 per person per night).

Shepherds, 9 High Town (Mon–Sat 9.30am–5.30pm, Sun 11am–5.30pm), is an appealing **café** with a good line in snacks and mouthwatering, local ice cream. For more substantial meals, try the hard-to-beat *Granary* (daily till 9pm; ☎01497/820790), a café/bar and **restaurant** opposite the clocktower on Broad Street. It serves delicious wholefood snacks and soups as well as filling main meals (£7–9) with the emphasis on local organic produce; there's a roadside terrace, too, where hikers can kick off their boots and sink a leisurely pint.

Shropshire

One of England's largest and least populated counties, **Shropshire** stretches from its long and winding border with Wales to the very edge of the urban Black Country. It was here that the Industrial Revolution made a huge stride forward with the spanning of the River Severn by the very first **iron bridge**. The assorted industries that subsequently squeezed into the **Ironbridge Gorge** are long gone, but a series of **museums** celebrate their craftsmanship – from tiles through to iron. The River Severn also flows through the county town of **Shrewsbury**, whose antique centre holds dozens of old half-timbered buildings, though **Ludlow**, further to the south, has the edge when it comes to handsome Tudor and Jacobean architecture. In between the two lie some of the most beautiful parts of Shropshire, primarily the **Long Mynd** ridge, a prime hiking area that is readily explored from the attractive little town of **Church Stretton**.

Yet, for all its attractions, Shropshire remains well off the main tourist routes, one factor protecting the county's isolation being the paucity of its **public transport**. Shrewsbury and Telford are connected to Birmingham, whilst Ludlow and Church Stretton are connected to Shrewsbury on the Hereford rail line, but that's about the limit of the **train** services, whilst rural **buses** tend to link the county's outlying villages on just a few days of the week. There's also the **Shropshire Hills Shuttle bus** service (ⓦ www.shropshirehillsshuttles .co.uk) which runs hourly every weekend from May to October on two routes: the more useful noses round the Long Mynd and the Stiperstones and drops by Church Stretton. An adult Day Rover ticket, valid on the whole route, costs £4, and bus timetables are available at most Shropshire tourist offices and on the website.

Ironbridge Gorge

Both geographically and culturally, **Ironbridge Gorge**, the collective title for a cluster of small villages huddled in the densely wooded Severn Valley to the south of new-town Telford, looks to the West Midlands conurbation rather than rural Shropshire. Ironbridge Gorge was the crucible of the Industrial Revolution, a process encapsulated by its famous span across the Severn – the world's first **iron bridge**, engineered by Abraham Darby and opened on New Year's Day, 1781. The area's factories once churned out engines, rails, wheels and other heavy-duty iron pieces in quantities unmatched anywhere else in the world, but manufacturing has now all but vanished and the surviving monuments make the gorge the most extensive **industrial heritage site** in England – and one that has been granted World Heritage Site status by UNESCO.

The gorge itself contains several museums and an assortment of other industrial attractions spread along a five-mile stretch of the River Severn Valley. A thorough exploration takes a

△ Ironbridge

couple of days, but the **highlights** – the iron bridge itself, the Museum of Iron and the Jackfield Tile Museum – are easily manageable on a day-trip. Each museum and attraction charges its own admission fee, but if you're intending to visit several, buy a **passport ticket** (£13.25), which allows access to each of them once in any calendar year. Passport tickets are available at all the main sights and at the **Ironbridge Visitor Information Centre** (Mon–Fri 9am–5pm, Sat & Sun 10am–5pm; ☎01952/432166, ⊛www.ironbridge.org.uk), in the old toll house at the south end of the bridge in Ironbridge village. **Parking** is free at most of the sights, but not in Ironbridge village itself.

Practicalities

Every two hours or so, there is a daily (not Sun) **bus** from Shrewsbury bus station to Ironbridge village, at the heart of the gorge. At weekends from April to October, the **Gorge Connect bus** shuttles along the gorge from Coalbrookdale in the west, via Ironbridge village, to the Coalport China Museum in the east, and sometimes onto Telford bus station every half-hour (from 9am–5pm): each journey, no matter how short or long, costs 50p. There's currently no **bike** rental in the gorge (though the service may be resumed; ring the **Visitor Information Centre** to check), so when the bus isn't running, your only option for exploring the gorge is to **walk**.

Most visitors to the gorge come for the day, but there are several pleasant **B&Bs** in Ironbridge village, which is where you want to be. Two of the best are *The Library House*, which occupies a charming Georgian villa just yards from the iron bridge at 11 Severn Bank (☎01952/432299, ⊛www.library house.com; no credit cards; ➍), and *Bridge View*, whose neat and trim rooms are also a stone's throw from the bridge at 10 Tontine Hill (☎01952/432541, ⊛www.ironbridgeview.co.uk; ➋). Alternatively, *Coalbrookdale Villa* occupies an attractive neo-Gothic, Victorian ironmasters' house about half a mile up the hill from Ironbridge village in tiny Paradise, close to Coalbrookdale iron foundry (☎01952/433450, ⊛www.coalbrookdalevilla.co.uk; no credit cards; ➍). It's also yards from one of the gorge's two YHA hostels, the Victorian *Coalbrookdale*, in the old Literary and Scientific Institute building, with eighty beds parcelled up into two- to eight-bedded rooms (☎0870/770 5882, ⊛www.yha.org.uk; dorm beds £11, doubles ➊). The hostel is open during school holidays and on Fridays and Saturdays in term time, and advance reservations are required. The gorge's second hostel, *Coalport* (☎0870/770 5882, ⊛www.yha.org.uk; dorm beds £14, doubles ➊), at the east end of the gorge in the former Coalport China factory, has the same opening times but does not require advance booking.

There is one good **pub** in the gorge – the excellent *Coalbrookdale Inn*, a smashing traditional pub on the main road across from the Coalbrookdale iron foundry. It offers a tasty selection of real ales and delicious bar food.

Ironbridge village

There must have been an awful lot of nail-biting during the construction of the iron bridge over the River Severn in the late 1770s. No one was quite sure how the new material would wear and although the single-span design looked sound, many feared the bridge would simply tumble into the river. To compensate, Abraham Darby used more iron than was strictly necessary, but the end result still manages to appear stunningly graceful, arching between the steep banks with the river far below. The settlement at the north end of the span was promptly renamed **IRONBRIDGE**, and today its brown-brick houses climb prettily up the hill from the bridge. The village is also home to the **Museum**

of the Gorge (daily 10am–5pm; £2.25), located in a church-like, neo-Gothic old riverside warehouse about 500yd west of the bridge along the main road. This provides an introduction to the industrial history of the gorge and provides a few environmental pointers too.

Coalbrookdale iron foundry

At the roundabout just to the west of the Museum of the Gorge, turn right for the half-mile trip up to what was once the gorge's big industrial deal, the **Coalbrookdale iron foundry**, which boomed throughout the eighteenth and early nineteenth centuries, employing up to four thousand men and boys. The foundry has been imaginatively converted into the **Museum of Iron** (daily 10am–5pm; £5.45, including Darby Houses), with a wide range of displays on iron-making in general and the history of the company in particular. Also in the complex, across from the foundry beneath a protective canopy, are the ruins of the **furnace** where Abraham Darby pioneered the use of coke as a smelting fuel in place of charcoal.

From the foundry, it's about 100yd up to the two **Darby Houses** (mid-March to early Nov daily 10am–5pm; £3) – Dale House and Rosehill – both attractively restored, old ironmasters' homes with Georgian period rooms and a scattering of items that once belonged to the Darby family.

The Tar Tunnel and Jackfield

Heading east from the iron bridge, it's just over a mile along the river to the turning for Blists Hill (see below) and another 500yd or so to the **Tar Tunnel** (mid-March to Oct daily 10am–5pm; £1.25), built to transport coal from one part of the gorge to another, but named for the bitumen that oozes naturally from its walls.

Beside the tunnel, a **footbridge** crosses the Severn to reach **JACKFIELD**, now a sleepy little hamlet, but formerly a sooty, grimy place that hummed to the tune of two large tile factories, Maws and Craven Dunnill. Both were built in the middle of the nineteenth century to the latest industrial design, a fully integrated manufacturing system that produced literally thousands of tiles at breakneck speed. Ahead of their time, the two factories boomed from the time of their construction until the 1920s, and they have both survived in good condition. From the footbridge, it's a couple of minutes' walk west to the first of the two, which has been sympathetically converted into the **Maws Craft Centre** (ⓦ www.mawscraftcentre.co.uk), with over twenty arts, craft and specialist shops. A short walk away, in the former Craven Dunnill factory, the excellent **Jackfield Tile Museum** (daily 10am–5pm; £4.65) provides a potted history of Jackfield and its two factories. Upstairs is the superb Style Gallery, where cabinet after cabinet illustrates the different styles of tile produced here, from Art Deco through to Arts and Crafts and the Aesthetic Movement.

Coalport and Blists Hill Victorian Town

Back at the Tar Tunnel, a canal towpath leads east in a couple of minutes to **Coalport China works**, a large brick complex now housing a YHA hostel (see p.448), and the **Coalport China Museum** (daily 10am–5pm; £4.65). The museum kicks off with a couple of rooms crammed full of Coalport wares, the highlight being the gaudy and ornate pieces manufactured in the company's heyday, from around 1820 to 1890. There's also a workshop, where potters demonstrate their skills, and a Social History Gallery, which explores the hard life of the factory's workers, whose health was constantly at risk from the lead-dosed dust. The museum also includes two **bottle-kilns**, whose distinctive conical structures were long the hallmark of the pottery industry, with an explaination of how the kilns worked – though quite how the firers survived the conditions defies the imagination.

Doubling back along the river, it's a third of a mile west from Coalport to the clearly signed, mile-long side road that cuts up to the gorge's most popular attraction, the rambling **Blists Hill Victorian Town** (daily: mid-March to Oct 10am–5pm; Nov to mid-March 10am–4pm; £8.75). This encloses a substantial number of reconstructed Victorian buildings, most notably a school, a candle-makers', a doctor's surgery, a gas-lit pub and wrought-iron works. Jam-packed on most summer days, it's especially popular with school parties, who keep the period-dressed employees very busy.

Shrewsbury

SHREWSBURY, the county town of Shropshire, sits in a narrow loop of the River Severn, a three-hundred-yard spit of land being all that prevents the town centre from becoming an island. It would be difficult to design a better defensive site and the Britons were quick to erect a fort here once the Roman legions had hot-footed it out of their colony in the fifth century. In Georgian times, Shrewsbury became a fashionable staging post on the busy London to Holyhead route, and has since become an easy-going, middling market town, whose narrow lanes, courtyards and alleys fill out the hilly neck of land that comprises the centre. It's the overall feel of the place that is its main appeal, though **St Mary's Church** and its immediate environs are particularly pleasing.

Arrival, information and orientation

Shrewsbury **train station** stands at the narrow neck of the loop in the river that holds the town centre; long-distance **buses** mostly pull into the Raven Meadows bus station, off the Smithfield Road, five minutes' walk southwest from the train station, further into the centre. The **tourist office** is a five-minute walk up the hill from the train station, on The Square (May–Sept Mon–Sat 9.30am–5.30pm, Sun 10am–4pm; Oct–April Mon–Sat 10am–5pm; ☎01743/281200, ⓦwww.visitshrewsbury.com).

Accommodation

Shrewsbury has one particularly good **hotel**, the *Prince Rupert*, which occupies a cannily converted old building right in the centre of town on Butcher Row, off Pride Hill (☎01743/499955, ⓦwww.prince-rupert-hotel.co.uk; ❺); it has over seventy comfortable bedrooms, with ornate bed-head canopies that may not suit all tastes. The best of the central **B&Bs** is the *College Hill Guest House*, in a well-maintained Georgian townhouse at 11 College Hill, just south of The Square (☎01743/365744; no credit cards; ❷). Further afield, a mile east of the centre across the English Bridge, the excellent *Fieldside* B&B, at 38 London Rd (☎01743/353143; no cards; ❸), is in a large Victorian property with eight neat en-suite guest rooms; it's next to St Giles's Church, and yards from the whopping Lord Hill's Column, raised in memory of Wellington's sidekick at the Battle of Waterloo.

The Town

Poking up above the mansion-like train station, the careworn ramparts of Shrewsbury **castle** are but a pale reminder of the mighty medieval fortress that once dominated the town. **Castle Gates** winds up the hill from the station into the heart of the river loop where the medieval town took root. Here, off Pride Hill, several half-timbered buildings are dotted along **Butcher Row**, which leads into the quiet precincts of **St Alkmund's Church**, from where there's a charming view of the fine old buildings of **Fish Street**. Close by is the most interesting of the town's churches, **St Mary the Virgin** (Mon–Fri 10am–5pm, Sat 10am–4pm; free), whose sombre exterior is partly redeemed by its slender spire. Inside, the church is unusual in so far as it exhibits both the rounded arches beloved of the Normans in the nave and the pointed arches of Early English Gothic in the choir and the transepts.

From St Mary's, it's a brief stroll to the High Street, on the far side of which, in the narrow confines of The Square, is the **Old Market House**, a heavy-duty stone structure built in 1596. Continuing downhill, High Street becomes **Wyle Cop**, lined with higgledy-piggledy ancient buildings and leading to the **English Bridge**, which sweeps across the Severn in grand Georgian style. Beyond the bridge, on Abbey Foregate, is the stumpy redstone mass of the **Abbey Church** (daily: April–Oct 9.30am–5.30pm; Nov–March 10.30am–3pm; free), all that remains of the Benedictine abbey that was a major political and religious force hereabouts until the Dissolution.

Eating and drinking

For daytime **food**, try the inexpensive *Goodlife Wholefood Restaurant* (Mon–Fri 9.30am–3.30pm & Sat 9.30am–4.30pm), on Barracks Passage, just off Wyle Cop; it specializes in salads and vegetarian dishes, with main courses costing around £5. In the evening, there's a tasty tandoori at *Shalimar*, 23 Abbey Foregate by the Abbey Church, and just along the street at no. 21, sample modern British cuisine as well as light snacks and coffees at the *Peach Tree* café-restaurant. However, many locals think that the best restaurant in town is *Osteria da Paolo*, down a narrow alley off Hills Lane near the Welsh Bridge (℡01743/243 336); this homely Italian place offers mouthwatering dishes, with main courses averaging around £10.

Amongst Shrewsbury's many **pubs**, one of the most distinctive is the *Loggerheads*, at 1 Church St, an ancient place – perhaps a little too authentically so – with four small rooms and great real ales. Other recommended **pubs** include the smoke-free *Three Fishes*, in an ancient building on Fish Street, and the cosy *Coach & Horses*, on Swan Hill, just south of The Square

Church Stretton and the Long Mynd

Beginning about ten miles south of Shrewsbury, the upland heaths of the **Long Mynd**, some ten miles long and between two and four miles wide, run parallel to and just to the west of the A49. This is prime walking territory and the heathlands are latticed with footpaths, the pick of which offer sweeping views over the border to the Black Mountains of Wales. Nestled at the foot of the Mynd beside the A49 is **CHURCH STRETTON**, a tidy little village and popular day-trippers' destination that makes an ideal base for hiking the area.

Church Stretton is easy to reach from Shrewsbury and Ludlow by **train** or **bus**. Most buses stop in the centre of the village along the High Street, but some pull in beside the train station, about 600yd east of the High Street. The **tourist office** is on Church Street (April–Sept Mon–Sat 10am–1pm & 2–5pm; ℡01694/723133, ⓦwww.shropshiretourism.info/church-stretton), one block west of the High Street. It has information on off-road cycle routes and stocks an excellent range of local hiking leaflets and books, including Ian Jones's excellent *Twenty Church Stretton Walks*. The most popular local **hikes** are around the gently sloping Carding Mill Valley, from where trails lead up to the Mynd. Owned by the National Trust, the valley starts about half a mile to the north of Church Stretton; the Long Mynd **Shropshire Hills Shuttle bus service** (see p.447) begins and ends at the valley too.

There's no shortage of good-value **accommodation** in and around Church Stretton. One of the best B&Bs is the first-rate *Jinlye Guest House* (℡01694/723243, ⓦwww.jinlye.co.uk; ❺), in an attractively modernized stone cottage on Castle Hill on the edge of All Stretton, a mile north of Church Stretton. Similarly appealing is *Lawley House* (℡01694/751236, ⓦwww.virtual-shropshire .co.uk/lawley/; ❸), with two spacious and well-appointed guest rooms in a large and commanding Victorian house set in its own grounds; it's in the hamlet of Smethcott, about three miles north of Church Stretton and to the west of the A49. There are a couple of YHA **hostels** in the vicinity too, both of which make splendid bases for hiking: *Wilderhope Manor* (℡0870/770 6090, ⓦwww .yha.org.uk; open during school holidays and on Fri & Sat in term time; dorm beds £11), in a remote Elizabethan mansion in Longville-in-the-Dale, about seven miles east of Church Stretton along the B4371; and *Bridges Long Mynd* (℡01588/650656, ⓦwww.yha.org.uk; advance booking only; dorm beds £8.50), five miles west of Church Stretton near Ratlinghope.

Ludlow

Perched on a hill nearly thirty miles south of Shrewsbury, **LUDLOW** is one of the most picturesque towns in the West Midlands, if not in England – a cluster of beautifully preserved black-and-white half-timbered buildings packed around a craggy stone castle, with rural Shropshire forming a drowsy backdrop. In addition, the town is something of a gastronomic hot-spot with a clutch of outstanding, Michelin-starred restaurants.

In a spectacular setting above the rivers Teme and Corve, Ludlow's immense **Castle** (Jan Sat & Sun 10am–4pm; Feb, March & Oct–Dec daily 10am–4pm; April–July & Sept daily 10am–5pm; Aug daily 10am–7pm; £4) dates largely from Norman times. The rambling and imposing ruins that remain today include towers and turrets, gatehouses and concentric walls as well as the 110-foot **keep** and an unusual **Round Chapel** built in 1120. The castle also makes a fine open-air auditorium during the **Ludlow Festival** (℡01584/872150, ⓦwww.ludlowfestival.co.uk), three weeks of assorted musical and theatrical fun running from the end of June to early July.

The castle gates open out onto **Castle Square**, an airy rectangle, whose eastern side abuts four narrow lanes – take the one on the left, Church Street and then King Street, to reach the gracefully proportioned **Church of St Laurence** (daily 10am–5.30pm; £1 suggested donation), whose interior is distinguished by its stained-glass windows. Back outside the church, King Street leads into the **Bull Ring**, home of the *Feathers Hotel*, a fine Jacobean building with the fanciest wooden facade imaginable.

To the south of Castle Square, the gridiron of streets laid out by the Normans has survived intact, though most of the buildings date from the eighteenth century. It's the general appearance that appeals rather than any special sight, but steeply sloping **Broad Street** is particularly attractive, flanked by many of Ludlow's five hundred half-timbered Tudor and red-brick Georgian listed buildings, its north end framed by the high and mighty **Butter Cross**, a Neoclassical extravagance from 1744. At the foot of Broad Street is Ludlow's only surviving medieval **gate**, which was turned into a house in the eighteenth century.

Practicalities

From Ludlow **train station** (on the Shrewsbury–Hereford line), it's a five- to ten-minute walk southwest to the castle – just follow the signs. Most **buses** stop on Mill Street, just off Castle Square. Ludlow's **tourist office**, on Castle Square (Mon–Sat 10am–5pm, Sun 10.30am–5pm; ☎01584/875053, ⓦwww.ludlow .org.uk), has a wide range of maps and books for walkers, as well as a selection of inexpensive leaflets detailing day-hikes in the area. **Accommodation** is plentiful, though rooms can get scarce during the festival. One smashing choice is ✹ *Dinham Hall Hotel*, near the castle (☎01584/876464, ⓦwww.dinhamhall .co.uk; ❼), an attractive, bow-windowed eighteenth-century stone mansion that was previously a boarding house for Ludlow School: it has thirteen guest rooms, decorated in an appealing modern version of period style. Similarly enticing is *Mr Underhill's*, Dinham Weir (☎01584/874431, ⓦwww.mr-underhills.co.uk; ❻), in the jumble of old riverside buildings below and behind the castle walls: its six guest rooms are decorated in brisk modern style with river views. A less expensive option in the town centre is the *Wheatsheaf Inn*, a quaint little pub next to the old town gate at the foot of Broad Street (☎01584/872980; ❸).

The Ludlow area has no less than seven **restaurants** in the Michelin guide. Unsurprisingly, none are cheap, but you might treat yourself at *Mr Underhill's* (see above; reservations essential), whose skillfully crafted dishes get rave reviews again and again; set menus kick off at around £30. A second outstanding restaurant is the *Hibiscus*, 17 Corve St (☎01584/872325; reservations essential), where they serve classic French cuisine with vim and gusto, with a three-course meal costing £30–35. For something less substantial, the popular *Olive Branch*, on the Bull Ring (daily 10am–4pm), serves inexpensive light meals and salads.

Birmingham

If anywhere can be described as the first purely industrial conurbation, it has to be **BIRMINGHAM**. Unlike the more specialist industrial towns which grew up across the North and the Midlands, "Brum" – and its "Brummies" – turned its hand to every kind of manufacturing, gaining the epithet "the city of 1001 trades". It was here also that the pioneers of the Industrial Revolution – James Watt, Matthew Boulton, William Murdock, Josiah Wedgwood, Joseph Priestley and Erasmus Darwin (grandfather of Charles) – formed the **Lunar Society**, an extraordinary melting-pot of scientific and industrial ideas. They conceived the world's first purpose-built factory, invented gas lighting, and pioneered both the distillation of oxygen and the mass production of the steam engine. Thus, a modest Midlands market town mushroomed into the nation's economic dynamo with the population to match: in 1841 there were 180,000 inhabitants, a number that trebled within fifty years.

Now the second largest city in Britain, with a population of over one million, Birmingham has long outgrown the squalor and misery of its boom years and today its industrial supremacy is recalled in a crop of excellent **heritage museums** and an extensive network of **canals**. It also boasts a thoroughly multiracial population that makes it one of Britain's most cosmopolitan cities. Its shift to a post-manufacturing economy has been symbolized by an intelligent and far-reaching revamp of the city centre that included the construction of a glitzy **Convention Centre** and an extravagant refurbishment of the **Bull Ring**, while the enormous **National Exhibition Centre (NEC)** inhabits the outskirts near the international airport. Birmingham has also launched a

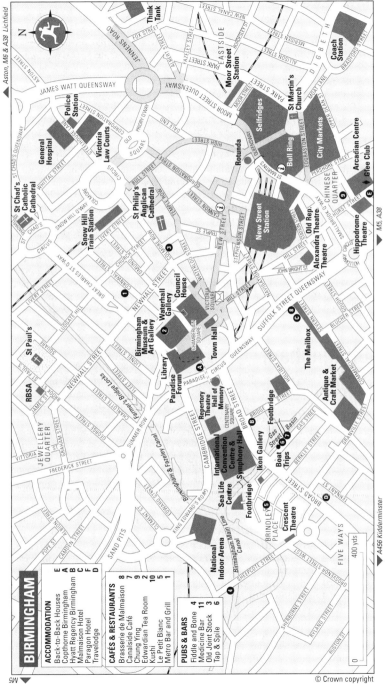

BIRMINGHAM

ACCOMMODATION

Back-to-Back Houses	E
Copthorne Birmingham	A
Hyatt Regency Birmingham	B
Malmaison Hotel	C
Paragon Hotel	F
Travelodge	D

CAFÉS & RESTAURANTS

Brasserie de Malmaison	8
Canalside Café	7
Chung Ying	9
Edwardian Tea Room	2
Kushi	10
Le Petit Blanc	5
Metro Bar and Grill	1

PUBS & BARS

Fiddle and Bone	4
Medicine Bar	11
Old Joint Stock	3
Tap & Spile	6

Aston, M6 & A38 Lichfield

M5

M5, A38

A456 Kidderminster

400 yds

© Crown copyright

veritable raft of cultural initiatives, enticing a division of the **Royal Ballet** to take up residence here, and building a fabulous new concert hall for the **City of Birmingham Symphony Orchestra**. There's no pretending that Birmingham is packed with interesting sights – it isn't – though along with its first-rate restaurant scene and nightlife, it's well worth at least a day or two.

Arrival, information and city transport

Birmingham's **international airport** is eight miles east of the city centre off the A45 and near the M42 (Junction 6); the terminal is beside Birmingham International train station, from where there are regular services into **New Street train station**, right in the heart of the city. New Street train station is where all inter-city and the vast majority of local services go, though trains on the Stratford-upon-Avon, Warwick, Worcester and Malvern lines usually use **Snow Hill** and **Moor Street stations**, both about ten minutes' walk from New Street to the north and east respectively. National Express **bus** travellers are dumped in the grim surroundings of **Digbeth coach station**, from where it's a ten-minute uphill walk to the Bull Ring.

Maps, loads of local leaflets and transport information and a free hotel-booking service are provided by all the city's **tourist offices**. The main office is at 150 New St (Mon–Sat 9.30am–5.30pm, Sun 10.30am–4.30pm; ☏0121/202 5099, ⓦwww.beinbirmingham.com), while a second, smaller office occupies a kiosk in front of New Street Station, at the junction of New Street and Corporation Street (Mon–Sat 9am–5pm, Sun 10am–4pm; same number). There is a third tourist office in the National Exhibition Centre (NEC).

Birmingham's excellent **local transport** system includes **trains**, **metro** and **buses** that delve into almost every urban nook and cranny. Various companies run these services, but they are coordinated by **Centro**, which operates a regional public-transport information hotline (☏0121/200 2700, ⓦwww.centro.org.uk). A one-day **Centrocard**, valid on all services, can be purchased from bus drivers and at train and metro stations for £5.40.

Accommodation

As you might expect, central Birmingham is liberally sprinkled with chain **hotels**, from glitzy tower blocks to more modest red-brick, with the area around Gas Street Basin and Centenary Square being the best location. Details of the city's leading hotels are published in the annual *Visitor Guide* as well as the *Birmingham Pocket Guide*, both of which are supplied free at any city tourist office (see above).

Back-to-Back Houses 50–54 Inge St
☏0870/458 4422, ⓦwww.nationaltrustcottages.co.uk. Birmingham's most original accommodation is in the National Trust's restored nineteenth-century back-to-back workers' houses (see p.460). Three of the small terraced houses have been kitted out in a sympathetic modern version of period style, with en-suite facilities, and can be rented out for a minimum of two nights. Each cottage sleeps two, with a two-night stay costing £170 in January, rising to £280 in August.
Copthorne Birmingham Paradise Circus
☏0121/200 2727, ⓦwww.millenniumhotels.com. It may look rather like a Rubik cube from the

outside, but this is a great hotel, partly because its 212 modern bedrooms are neat and trim, and partly because its location – plum in the centre beside Centenary Square – can't be bettered. It's expensive during the week, but weekends bring prices down to more reasonable levels. ⑧, ⑤ at weekends.
Hyatt Regency Birmingham 2 Bridge St
☏0121/643 1234, ⓦwww.hyatt.com. The sleek, black skyrise that towers above Centenary Square is a luxury *Hyatt* hotel. The central location is hard to beat, the city views from the guest rooms on the upper floors are superlative, and the public area has some pleasant Art Deco touches – and may

have been feng-shuied. Less positively, the rooms are decorated in uninspiring chain-hotel style and you can't open the windows. **8**, **6** at weekends.
Malmaison Hotel The Mailbox, 1 Wharfside St ☎0121/246 5000, ⓦwww.malmaison.com. An impeccably stylish, designer hotel with first-class accommodation of wit and substance – no wonder it's next door to Harvey Nichols. Every convenience and a central location. **7**
Paragon Hotel 145 Alcester St ☎0121/627 0627, ⓦwww.paragonhotel.net. Splendid conversion of

a magnificent Edwardian workhouse about fifteen minutes' walk from New Street Station out along Digbeth and its continuation, High Street. Alcester Street is on the right. Excellent-value doubles, though the surrounding area hardly inspires confidence. **4**
Travelodge 230 Broad St ☎0870/191 1564, ⓦwww.travelodge.co.uk. Workaday central chain hotel, but prices are very reasonable and it's within easy walking distance of lots of restaurants, bars and clubs. **3**

The City Centre

Many visitors get their first taste of central Birmingham at **New Street Station**, whose unreconstructed ugliness – piles of modern concrete – makes a dispiriting start, though there are plans afoot to give the place a thorough face-lift. Things soon improve with the newly developed **Bull Ring**, once itself a 1960s eyesore, but now a gleaming new shopping mall distinguished by the startling design of its leading store, **Selfridges**. A brief stroll west from here along pedestrianized **New Street** brings you to the elegantly revamped **Victoria Square**, with its tumbling water fountain, and the adjacent **Chamberlain Square**, where the city's finest museum, the **Birmingham Museum and Art Gallery**, displays a fabulous collection of Pre-Raphaelite art. Further west still, is the glossy **International Convention Centre**, from where it's another short hop to the **Gas Street Basin**, the prettiest part of the city's serpentine canal system. Close by is canalside **Brindley Place**, a smart, brick and glass complex with slick cafés and bars and the enterprising **Ikon Gallery** of contemporary art. From Brindley Place, it's a short walk southeast to **The Mailbox**, the immaculately rehabilitated former postal sorting-office with yet more chic bars and restaurants.

The Bull Ring

A few steps from New Street Station, Rotunda Square marks the intersection of New and High streets, taking its name from the **Rotunda**, a handsome and distinctive cylindrical tower that is the sole survivor of the notorious **Bull Ring** shopping centre, which fulfilled every miserable cliché of 1960s town planning until its recent demolition. The new Bull Ring shopping centre that has sprung up in its place would be a textbook example of safe yet uninspired contemporary planning were it not for two strokes of real invention. In the redevelopment, the architects split the Bull Ring shops into two separate sections and in the gap there is now an uninterrupted view of the medieval spire of St Martin's (see below), providing an effective contrast between old and new. The second coup was the design of **Selfridges**' new store, a billowing organic swell protruding from the Bull Ring's east side, and seen to good advantage from the wide stone stairway that descends from Rotunda Square to St Martin's. Reminiscent of an inside-out octopus, Selfridges shimmers with an architectural chain-mail of thousands of silver discs, altogether a bold and hugely successful attempt to create a popular city landmark.

St. Martin's Church and the City Markets

Nestling at the foot of the Bull Ring, the newly scrubbed and polished **St Martin's Church** is a fetching amalgamation of the Gothic and the

△ Selfridges, Birmingham

neo-Gothic, its mighty spire poking high into the sky. Bombed by the Luftwaffe and attacked by the Victorians, the church's interior, with its capacious three-aisled nave, is saved from mediocrity by a delightful Burne-Jones stained-glass window, a richly coloured, finely detailed affair whose panes sport angels, saints, biblical figures and scenes.

Across from the church are Birmingham's three main **markets** – two selling fresh produce, one indoor (Mon–Sat 9am–5.30pm), the other outdoor (Tues–Sat 9am–5.30pm), with the **Rag Market** (Tues, Thurs, Fri & Sat 9am–5pm) in between. At one time the Rag Market was crammed with every sort of material you could imagine and then some, but although its heyday is past it still musters up all sorts of nick-nacks, always sold at bargain-basement prices.

New Street and Victoria Square

Stretching west from the Bull Ring, **New Street** is a busy, bustling pedestrianized thoroughfare, lined with shops and stores. At its west end, it opens out into the handsomely refurbished **Victoria Square**, whose centrepiece is a large water fountain designed by Dhruva Mistry. The waterfall outdoes poor old Queen Victoria, whose **statue** is glum and uninspired, though the thrusting self-confidence of her bourgeoisie is very apparent in the flamboyant **Council House** behind her, its assorted gables and cupolas, columns and towers completed in 1879. Across the square, and very different, is the **Town Hall** of 1834, whose Classical design – by Joseph Hansom, who went on to design Hansom cabs – was based on the Roman temple in Nîmes. The building's simple, flowing lines contrast with much of its surroundings, but it's an appealing structure all the same, erected to house public meetings and musical events in a flush of municipal pride. It's undergoing a long-term refurbishment, so currently is swathed in plastic sheeting, but the plan is to turn it into a performing arts and community venue.

The Birmingham Museum and Art Gallery

Victoria Square leads into **Chamberlain Square**, where a rambling, Edwardian building is home of the **Birmingham Museum and Art Gallery** (**BM&AG**; Mon–Thurs & Sat 10am–5pm, Fri 10.30am–5pm, Sun 12.30–5pm; free). The bulk of its collection is spread over two long floors – floors 2 and 3 – with the art section, which attracts most attention, on Floor 2. Note that the museum's collection is too large for it all to be exhibited at any one time, so paintings are regularly rotated and key paintings are often moved to (and from) the Round Room, at the start of Floor 2. Furthermore, the whole show can be disturbed by temporary exhibitions, so pick up a museum plan at reception.

The BM&AG holds one of the world's most comprehensive collections of **Pre-Raphaelite** work which is concentrated on Floor 2, in rooms 14 and 17–19. Founded in 1848, the Pre-Raphaelite Brotherhood consisted of seven young artists, of whom Rossetti, Holman Hunt, Millais and Madox Brown are the best known. The name of the group was selected to express their commitment to honest observation, which they thought had been lost with the Renaissance. Many of the Brotherhood's most important paintings are (usually) displayed here, including **Dante Gabriel Rossetti**'s (1828–82) seminal, pen and ink *First Anniversary of the Death of Beatrice* (1849), inspired by Dante, and **Ford Madox Brown**'s (1821–93) powerful image of emigration, *The Last of England* (1855). The group's dedication to realism as they perceived it was unyielding and **Hunt** (1827–1910), for example, visited the Holy Land to prepare a series of religious paintings including his extravagant *The Finding of the Saviour in the Temple*. By 1853, the Brotherhood had effectively disbanded, but a second wave of artists carried on in its footsteps, with the most prominent being **Edward Burne-Jones** (1833–98), who has an entire room dedicated to his work (Room 14). The rest of the art section, though not quite as memorable, contains a first-rate collection of **eighteenth- and nineteenth-century British art**, including an extensive collection of watercolour landscapes, as well as a significant sample of European paintings.

Sharing Floor 2 is the **industrial art section**, which kicks off with the **Industrial Gallery**, set around an expansive atrium whose wrought-iron columns and balconies clamber up towards fancy skylights. The gallery holds choice selections of ceramics, metalwork and jewellery, plus a wonderful sample of locally produced stained glass retrieved from defunct churches across Birmingham. Here also is the **Edwardian Tea Room**, one of the more pleasant places in Birmingham for a cuppa (see p.461).

Moving on, Floor 1's cavernous **Gas Hall** is an impressive venue for touring art exhibitions, while the newly opened **Waterhall Gallery** (same times), just across Edmund Street from the main museum building, showcases modern and contemporary art including the likes of Francis Bacon and Bridget Riley.

Centenary Square, Gas Street Basin and The Mailbox

From the north side of Chamberlain Square, walk through the hideously kitsch **Paradise Forum** shopping and fast-food complex to get to **Centenary Square**, where a grassy lawn stretches from the city's main war memorial, the **Hall of Memory** (Mon–Sat 10am–4pm; free), to the showpiece **Symphony Hall** and **International Convention Centre (ICC)**, with the **Birmingham Repertory Theatre** on the right.

From the ICC, it's a brief stroll along Broad Street to the bridge over – and steps down to – **Gas Street Basin**, the hub of Birmingham's **canal system**. There are eight canals within the city's boundaries, covering 32 miles, though much of the canal network tunnels through the city's grimy, industrial bowels. Certain sections, however, have been immaculately restored with Gas Street Basin leading the way, inhabited by a herd of brightly painted narrow boats and edged by a delightful medley of old brick buildings. There's a good pub here too – the *Tap & Spile* (see p.461) – and regular **boat trips** leave to explore the prettier parts of the canal system. There are several operators, but Second City Canal Cruises (☎0121/236 9811; £3.50 for a one-hour cruise; advance reservations are recommended), down on the Basin, is as good as any. In summer, there's also a **water-bus** service linking several stops along the central part of the canal system (May, June & Sept Sat & Sun 10am–4pm; July & Aug daily 10am–5pm; every 45min; day pass £3.50, or 50p per stop).

Follow the towpath along the canal southeast from the Basin and you soon reach **The Mailbox**, a talented reinvention of Birmingham's old postal sorting office with restaurants, two hotels, and some of the smartest shops in the city – including Jaeger and Harvey Nichols (Mon–Wed 10am–6pm, Thurs–Sat 10am–7pm, Sun noon–6pm).

Brindley Place and the Ikon Gallery

Doubling back to the Basin, it's a short walk northwest along the canal towpath to the bars, shops and clubs of waterside **Brindley Place**. An aesthetically pleasing development, it's also home to the city's much-praised **Ikon Gallery** (Tues–Sun 11am–6pm; free; ⓦwww.ikon-gallery.co.uk), housed in a rambling Victorian building and one of the country's most imaginative venues for touring exhibitions of contemporary art.

St Philip's Cathedral

Returning to Chamberlain Square, the Council House (see p.458) marks the western end of **Colmore Row**, a busy shopping strip where pride of place goes to **St Philip's Cathedral** (mid Sept to mid-July Mon–Fri 7.30am–5/6.30pm, Sat & Sun 8.30/9am–5pm; free), a bijou example of English Baroque. Consecrated in 1715, St Philip's was initially a parish church that served as an overspill for St Martin's (see p.456). It was, however, in a more genteel location than the older church and when, in 1905, the Church of England decided to establish a new diocese in Birmingham, they made St Philip's the cathedral. The church is a handsome affair, its graceful interior adorned by four stained-glass windows that were designed by **Edward Burne-Jones**, a leading light of the Pre-Raphaelite movement (see p.458).

East of the Bull Ring: the Custard Factory

Below the Bull Ring, **Digbeth** – once the main thoroughfare through medieval Birmingham – runs southeast, jammed with traffic and jostled by decrepit industrial buildings. The only reasons to venture out here are for the bus station on the right, and – on the left off Gibb Street – the arts complex that occupies the old **Alfred Bird Custard Factory**. The factory is a homely affair set around a friendly little courtyard; the **arts complex** offers a fascinating variety of workshops and has gallery space for temporary exhibitions of modern art. There are a couple of groovy cafés and bars here too (see p.461 & p.462).

Southwest of the Bull Ring: the Back-to-Backs

The sheer scale of the industrial boom that gripped nineteenth-century Blrmingham is hard to grasp, but the statistics speak for themselves: in 1811, there were just eighty-five thousand Brummies; a century later the population was ten times greater. Inevitably, Birmingham's infrastructure could barely cope, particularly in terms of housing, with the city's newest inhabitants crowded into every conceivable nook and cranny. The concomitant demand for cheap housing spawned the back-to-back, quickly erected dwellings that were one-room deep and two, sometimes three storeys high, built in groups ("courts") around a courtyard where the privvies were located. Even by the standards of the time, this was pretty grim stuff, especially as overcrowding was commonplace. The last Birmingham courts were bulldozed in the 1970s, but one set survived and this, the **Birmingham Back-to-Backs**, 55–63 Hurst St (Tues–Sun 10am–5pm; 1hr guided tours on timed ticket; bookings on ☏0121/666 7671; £4), a short walk southwest of the Bull Ring, has now been restored by the National Trust. The NT's guided tour wends its way through three separate homes, each of which represents a different period from the early nineteenth century onwards. There is also a room devoted to a historical examination of the back-to-back and you can even stay here (see p.455).

Eating and drinking

Central Birmingham has a bevy of first-rate **restaurants** with a string of smart, new venues springing up along Broad Street, near the ICC. There's also a concentration of decent, reasonably priced restaurants in the Chinese Quarter, just south of New Street Station, on and around Hurst Street. Birmingham's gastronomic speciality is the **balti**, a delicious and inexpensive Kashmiri stew cooked and served in a small wok-like dish called a *karahi*, with naan bread instead of cutlery. Although balti houses have opened up within the city centre, the original and arguably the best are in the gritty suburb of **Balsall Heath/Moseley**, a couple of miles to the south of the centre. One or two of these are listed here – but note that many are unlicensed, so you may want to take your own booze.

The liveliest of the city-centre **pubs**, catering for a mixed bag of conference delegates and Brummies-out-on-the-ale, are liberally sprinkled along Broad Street, in the immediate vicinity of the Convention Centre, and in Brindley Place. Many are decorated in sharp, modern style, though there are more traditional places hereabouts as well – as there are in other parts of the city centre.

Cafés and restaurants

Brasserie de Malmaison The Mailbox, 1 Wharfside St ☎0121/246 5000. Delicious French cuisine with a menu that concentrates on a particular – and changing – region of France. Part of the *Malmaison Hotel* (see p.456). Mains £11–15. Moderate.

Canalside Café Gas Street ☎0121/248 7979. Cosy, distinctly New Age-ish café on the Gas Street Basin serving homemade snacks, cakes and fantastic cherry pies. A real snip, with veggie burgers, for example, costing just £3. Inexpensive.

Chung Ying 16–18 Wrottesley St ☎0121/622 5669. Arguably the best Cantonese dishes in the Chinese Quarter, and always busy. Mains £8–11. Inexpensive.

Edwardian Tea Room Birmingham Museum and Art Gallery, Chamberlain Square. This café has a great location in one of the large and fancily decorated halls of the museum's industrial section – hence all the cast-iron columns – but the food is simple and straightforward. Main meals and salads cost £3–6, but are only served between noon and 3pm. Opening hours are Mon–Sat 10.30am–4.30pm & Sun 12.30–4.30pm. Inexpensive.

Kushi 558 Moseley Rd, Moseley ☎0121/449 7678. Excellent, award-winning balti house that's unlicensed, very inexpensive, and deservedly popular. Main courses £5–8. Inexpensive.

Le Petit Blanc 9 Brindley Place ☎0121/633 7333. Directly opposite the Ikon Gallery, this swish restaurant, with its slick modern furnishings and fittings, offers first-rate French cuisine with a touch of Asia thrown in for good measure. Main courses hover around £13. Moderate.

Metro Bar and Grill 73 Cornwall St ☎0121/200 1911. Slick, modern bar-cum-restaurant with wooden floors and an unusual curved mirror on a back wall. Serves Modern British cuisine with bar plates at just £6. Open Mon–Fri noon–2.30pm & Mon–Sat 6.30–9.30pm. Moderate.

Pubs and bars

Fiddle and Bone 4 Sheepcote St ☎0121/200 2223. Canalside pub-cum-restaurant with good old-fashioned decor and regular live music, often to a very high standard.

Medicine Bar Custard Factory, Gibb Street, off Digbeth. Great bar located in a laid-back arts complex that was once a custard factory. Turns into a club late at night – see *Medicine Bar* below.

Old Joint Stock 4 Temple Row West. This delightful pub has the fanciest decor in town – with busts and a balustrade, a balcony and chandeliers, all dating from its days as a bank. A stone's throw from St Philip's Cathedral.

Tap & Spile 10 Gas St. Charming traditional pub with rickety rooms and low-beamed ceilings beside the canal on Gas Street Basin. Once the hangout of weathered canal-men, it now attracts tourists and locals in equal measure.

Nightlife and entertainment

Nightlife in Birmingham is thriving, and the **club scene** is recognized as one of Britain's best, spanning everything from word-of-mouth underground parties to meat-market mainstream clubs. **Live music** is strong in the city, too, with big-name concerts at several major venues and other, often local bands appearing at some clubs and pubs. Birmingham's showpiece **Symphony Orchestra** and **Royal Ballet** are the spearheads of the city's resurgent **classical scene**. The social calendar also gets an added fillip from a wide range of upmarket **festivals**, including the **Jazz Festival** (☎0121/454 7020, ⊛www.birminghamjazzfestival .com) for two weeks in July and the three-day **Artsfest** (⊛www.artsfest.org.uk) of film, dance, theatre and music in September.

For current information on all events, performances and exhibitions, pick up a free copy of the excellent, fortnightly *What's On*, Birmingham's definitive listings guide. It's available at all of the tourist offices and many public venues.

Clubs

Air Heath Mill Lane, off Digbeth ☎0121/766 8400, ⊛www.airbirmingham.com. Shiny, high-tech superclub attracting hundreds of house- and trance-hungry clubbers.

House of God Various venues monthly ☎07870/666856, ⊛www.hog.org.uk. Birmingham's ever-popular techno night is still going strong and loud. This is the sound of the city.

Medicine Bar Custard Factory, Gibb Square, off Digbeth ☏0121/224 7502, ⊛www.custardfactory.com. Eclectic and impeccable music policy, plus juicy live events. One of the best nights out in town. Part of the arts complex that inhabits the old Alfred Bird Custard Factory (see p.460).

The Nightingale Essex House, Kent Street ☏0121/622 1718, ⊛www.nightingaleclub.co.uk. The king of Brum's gay clubs, but popular with straights too. Five bars, three levels, two discos, a café-bar and even a garden. About ten minutes' walk south of New Street Station, along Hurst Street.

Classical music, theatre and dance

Birmingham Repertory Theatre Broad Street ☏0121/236 4455, ⊛www.birmingham-rep.co.uk. Mixed diet of classics and new work, featuring local and experimental writing.
Hippodrome Theatre Hurst Street ☏0870/730 1234, ⊛www.birmingham-hippodrome.co.uk. Lavishly refurbished, the Hippodrome is home to the Birmingham Royal Ballet. Also features touring plays and big pre– and post–West End productions, plus a splendid Christmas pantomime.
National Exhibition Centre (NEC) Bickenhill Parkway ☏0870/909 4133, ⊛www.necgroup.co.uk. The NEC's arena hosts major pop concerts.

Ten miles east of the centre beside the M42; train from New Street to Birmingham International Station.
Old Rep Theatre Station Street ☏0121/303 2323, ⊛www.oldreptheatre.org.uk. Britain's oldest repertory theatre, with regular performances from the imaginative Birmingham Stage Company.
Symphony Hall International Convention Centre, Broad Street ☏0121/780 3333, ⊛www.symphonyhall.co.uk. Acoustically one of the most advanced concert halls in Europe, home of the acclaimed City of Birmingham Symphony Orchestra (CBSO), as well as a venue for touring music and opera.

Listings

Bus enquiries Centro Hotline ☏0121/200 2700, ⊛www.centro.org.uk.
Internet Free Internet access at Birmingham Central Library, on Chamberlain Square (Mon–Fri 9am–8pm & Sat 9am–5pm; ☏0121/303 4511).

Pharmacy Boots, 67 High St ☏0121/212 1330.
Post office 1 Pinfold St at Victoria Square (Mon–Sat 9am–5.30pm).
Taxis Toa Taxis ☏0121/427 8888.

The Peak District

In 1951, the hills and dales of the **Peak District**, at the southern tip of the Pennine range, became Britain's first National Park. Wedged between **Derby**, Manchester and Sheffield, it is effectively the backyard for the fifteen million people who live within an hour's drive of its boundaries, though somehow it accommodates the huge influx with minimum fuss.

Landscapes in the Peak District come in two forms. The brooding high moorland tops of **Dark Peak**, fifteen miles east of central Manchester, take their name from the underlying gritstone, known as millstone grit for its former use – a function commemorated in the millstones demarcating the park boundary. Windswept, mist-shrouded and inhospitable, the flat tops of these peaks are nevertheless a firm favourite with walkers on the **Pennine Way**, which meanders north from the tiny village of **Edale** to the Scottish border. Altogether more forgiving, the southern limestone hills of the **White Peak** have been eroded into deep forested dales populated by small stone villages and often threaded by walking trails, some of which follow former rail routes. The limestone is riddled with complex cave systems around **Castleton** and under the region's largest centre, **Buxton**, a charming former spa-town just outside the park's boundaries and at the end of an industrialized corridor that reaches out from Manchester. The Peak District also holds one of the country's most distinctive manorial piles, **Chatsworth House**, just outside modest **Baslow**. As for a base, you're spoiled for choice, but Buxton probably wins out, with **Eyam** and Castleton coming a close second.

Public transport

There are frequent **trains** south from Manchester to end-of-the-line Buxton, while Manchester–Sheffield trains cut through Edale. The main **bus** service is the Trent Barton company's TransPeak route from Nottingham to Manchester via Derby, Matlock, Bakewell and Buxton; otherwise First's bus #272 runs regularly from Sheffield to Castleton, via Hope, and TM travel bus #65 connects Sheffield to Buxton every hour or so. If you're not planning on walking or driving between towns and villages, you'll need the essential, encyclopedic **Peak District Bus Timetable** (£1.20; or call ☎0870/608 2608), as well as the free **Derbyshire Train Times** booklet, both of which are available at local tourist and National Park information offices. Buses are more widespread than you might imagine, though there are limited winter and Sunday services, and often only sporadic links between the smaller villages. Various one-day **bus passes** allow unlimited travel to and within specified zones, with the South Yorkshire Peak Explorer (£6.75) covering the chunk of the park in Yorkshire, and the Wayfarer (£7) and the Derbyshire Wayfarer (£7.50) covering the rest.

The Peak District has a wide network of dedicated cycle lanes, tracks and old railway lines, as well as a series of **cycle rental** outlets, run by the National Park Authority (see below). The centres are located at Ashbourne (☎01335/343 156); Derwent (☎01433/651261), Hayfield (☎01663/746222), Middleton Top (☎01629/823204), and Parsley Hay, Buxton (☎01298/84493).

Information and accommodation

The main **Peak District National Park Authority office**, at Aldern House, Baslow Road, Bakewell, DE45 1AE (☎01629/816200, ⓦwww .peakdistrict.org), operates a string of **information centres** throughout the park, to supplement a host of town and village tourist offices. A variety of **maps** and **trail guides** are widely available, but for the nonspecialist it's hard to beat the *Grate Little Guides*, a series of clearly written leaflets which provide hiking suggestions and trail descriptions for a dozen or so localities. They cost £1.80 each and are on sale at almost every tourist office and information centre, though they are best used in conjunction with an OS map. For local **news and information**, pick up a copy of the official, free *Peak District* **paper** or check ⓦwww.visitpeakdistrict.com.

There's plenty of **accommodation** in and around the National Park, mostly in B&Bs, though the area also has some excellent-quality **country hotels**, with the greatest concentration of first-rate hotels and B&Bs being in the town of Buxton. The Peak District also holds numerous **campsites** and a dozen or so **hostels** as well as a network of YHA-operated **camping barns**. These are located in converted farm buildings and provide simple and inexpensive self-catering accommodation for between six and twenty-four people. For further details, contact the YHA Camping Barns Reservation Office (☎0870/770 8868, ⓦwww.yha.org.uk).

Ashbourne

Sitting pretty on the edge of the Peaks twelve miles northwest of Derby, **ASHBOURNE** is an amiable little town, whose stubby, cobbled **Market Place** is flanked by a happy ensemble of old stone buildings. Hikers tramp into town from the neighbouring dales to hang around the square's cafés and pubs, and stroll down the hill to take a peek at the suspended wooden beam spanning Church Street. Once a common feature of English towns, but now a rarity, these **gallows** were not warnings to malcontents, but advertising hoardings. Walk west along Church Street from here and you soon leave the bustling centre for a quieter part of town, all set beneath the soaring spire of **St Oswald's Church**, an imposing lime- and ironstone structure dating from the thirteenth century.

There are no trains to Ashbourne, but the town is easy to reach by bus from Derby, Buxton and Manchester. From Ashbourne **bus station**, it's a short walk to the Market Place – turn right out of the station, left at the T-junction and follow Dig Street over the river. The **tourist office**, on the Market Place (March–June, Sept & Oct Mon–Sat 9.30am–5pm; July & Aug Mon–Sat 9.30am–5pm, Sun 10am–4pm; Nov–Feb Mon–Sat 10am–4pm; ☎01335/343 666), has reams of hiking maps and guides, and can also advise on **accommodation**, though Ashbourne is best regarded as a pit-stop rather than as a base for further wanderings. For **food**, the *Patrick & Brooksbank* delicatessen, 22 Market Place, has a superb selection of takeaway delicacies, including local cheeses and hams.

Buxton

Twenty miles north of Ashbourne, **BUXTON** has had its centre imaginatively revamped, and holds a string of excellent hotels and B&Bs, making it a perfect base for exploring much of the Peaks National Park. It also boasts the outstanding **Buxton Festival** (brochure line ☎01298/70395; ⒲www.buxtonfestival .co.uk), running for two weeks in July with a full programme of classical music, opera and literary readings, as well as the first-rate **Buxton Festival Fringe** (⒲www.buxtonfringe.com), also in July, with the emphasis on contemporary music, theatre and film. The biggest festival is, however, the **Gilbert & Sullivan Festival** (⒲www.gs-festival.co.uk, ☎01422/323252), a three-week affair in August mainly featuring amateur troupes and attracting an enthusiastic audience.

Buxton has a long history as a **spa**, beginning with the Romans, who happened upon a spring from which 1500 gallons of pure water gushed every hour at a constant 28°C. Impressed by the recuperative qualities of the water, the Romans came here by the chariot-load, setting a trend that was to last hundreds of years. The spa's salad days came at the end of the eighteenth century with the **fifth Duke of Devonshire**'s grand design to create a northern answer to Bath or Cheltenham, a plan ultimately thwarted by the climate, but not before some distinguished buildings had been erected, most memorably **The Crescent**. Buxton also flourished in Victorian times, when the raft of handsome stone houses that edge the town centre today were built. The town's lean years came after 1972, when the thermal baths were closed due to lack of custom, but Buxton hung on to emerge as the most appealing town in the Peaks.

Arrival and information

There's an hourly train service from Manchester Piccadilly to Buxton, terminating two minutes' walk from The Crescent at the **train station** on Station Road. The **TransPeak bus**, running every two hours between Manchester and Nottingham, stops in Buxton's Market Place, as do the regular buses from Sheffield. The **tourist office** is in The Crescent (daily: March–Oct 9.30am–5pm; Nov–Feb 10am–4pm; ☎01298/25106, ⒲www.visitbuxton.co.uk) in what used to be the old Mineral Baths – hence the small display on Buxton's mineral water – and can book accommodation.

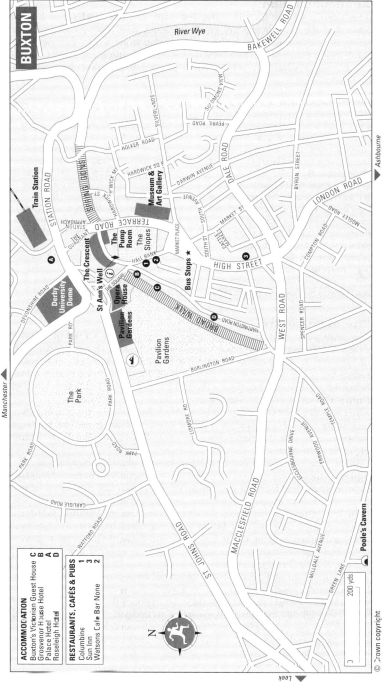

BUXTON

Bakewell ▲

Manchester ▲

Leek ▼

Ashbourne ▶

N

200 yds

© Crown copyright

ACCOMMODATION
Buxton's Victorian Guest House C
Grosvenor House Hotel B
Palace Hotel A
Roseleigh Hotel D

RESTAURANTS, CAFÉS & PUBS
Columbine 1
Sun Inn 3
Watsons Café Bar None 2

River Wye

BAKEWELL ROAD

Train Station

STATION ROAD

HOLKER ROAD

SILVER-NDS

SOLOMON'S VIEW

PEVRIL ROAD

HARDWICK SQ

Museum & Art Gallery

DARWIN AVENUE

DALE ROAD

Derby University Dome

DEVONSHIRE ROAD

The Crescent

St Ann's Well

The Pump Room

The Slopes

TERRACE ROAD

SPRING GARDENS

STATION APPROACH

THE QUADRANT

H'WICK MT

HARDWICK ST

SOUTH AVENUE

SOUTH ST

MARKET ST

MARKET PLACE

Bus Stops ★

HIGH STREET

BYRON STREET

LONDON ROAD

MOSLEY ROAD

COMPTON ROAD

Opera House

Pavilion Gardens

The Square

Hall Bank

BROAD WALK

HARTINGTON ROAD

WEST ROAD

SPENCER ROAD

PARK RD

PARK ROAD

The Park

PARK ROAD

BURLINGTON ROAD

LISMORE RD

ECCLESBOURNE DRIVE

EARNWOOD AVENUE

TEMPLE ROAD

CARLISLE ROAD

WATFORD ROAD

MACCLESFIELD ROAD

ST JOHNS ROAD

Poole's Cavern

GREEN LANE

MILLDALE AVENUE

Accommodation

The town centre is liberally sprinkled with first-rate **B&Bs** and **hotels**. Several of the best choices are on the pedestrianized Broad Walk, where a string of distinguished Edwardian and Victorian stone houses face out onto the Pavilion Gardens. Finding somewhere is rarely a problem, except during the Buxton Festival (see p.464), when advance reservations are well-nigh essential.

Buxton's Victorian Guest House 3a Broad Walk ☏01298/78759, ⓦwww.buxtonvictorian.co.uk. Cosy B&B with a handful of well-appointed rooms decorated in crossover traditional/modern style. Breakfasts feature local produce wherever feasible. Occupies one of the grand Victorian houses flanking Broad Walk. ❹

Grosvenor House Hotel 1 Broad Walk ☏01298/72439, ⓦwww.grosvenorbuxton.co.uk. There are eight en-suite guest rooms in this handsome Victorian townhouse beside the Pavilion Gardens, each decorated in a modern rendition of period style. Tasty breakfasts, plus evening meals by prior arrangement. ❹

Palace Hotel Palace Road ☏01298/22001, ⓦwww.paramount-hotels.co.uk/palace. Built to impress, the Palace was the pride of the Victorian spa, its sweeping stone facade and imposing central tower lording it over the town centre from the high ground of Palace Road. The hotel is a little careworn today, but there's no disputing the grandness of the entrance lobby and the soaring staircase beyond. The bedrooms are very comfortable and although the decor is modern, many have a quirky antique charm. Substantial discounts are commonplace – ring ahead to check. ❼

Roseleigh Hotel 19 Broad Walk ☏01298/24904, ⓦwww.roseleighhotel.co.uk. This classic three-storey gritstone Victorian townhouse, overlooking Pavilion Gardens, is an excellent place to stay; its neat and trim public rooms are decorated in attractive Victorian style, with the en-suite bedrooms similarly well appointed. Family-run and very competitively priced. ❹

The town centre

The centrepiece of Buxton's hilly, compact centre is **The Crescent**, a broad sweep of Georgian stonework commissioned by the fifth Duke of Devonshire in 1780 and modelled on the Royal Crescent in Bath. It's recently been refurbished, but remains empty while the townsfolk discuss its future, one good idea being the creation of a brand-new thermal baths. Facing The Crescent, the old **Pump Room** of 1894 provides space for art and crafts exhibitions, while the adjacent water **fountain**, supplied by St Ann's Well, is still used to fill many a local water bottle. For a better view of The Crescent, clamber up **The Slopes**, a narrow slice of park that rises behind the Pump Room, dotted with decorative urns and a war memorial.

At the west end of The Crescent, the appealing old stone buildings of **The Square** – though square it isn't – nudge up to the grandly refurbished **Buxton Opera House** (guided tours £2 donation; ring ☏0845/127 2190 for schedule), an Edwardian extravagance whose twin towers, cherubs and Tiffany glass date from 1903. Stretching back from the Opera House are the **Pavilion Gardens**, a slender string of connected buildings distinguished by their wrought-iron work and culminating in a large and glassy dome. The pavilions are actually a good deal more interesting from outside than from within, reason enough to wander off into the adjoining park, also known as the Pavilion Gardens, whose immaculate lawns and neat borders are graced by a bandstand, ponds, dinky little footbridges and fountains.

Back at the Opera House, it's impossible not to notice the enormous **dome** of what was originally the Duke of Devonshire's stables and riding school, erected in 1789. For decades, the building was used as a hospital, but the University of Derby has recently purchased it and they are in the process of turning it into a leisure and educational complex.

△ Buxton

The Market Place, and the Museum and Art Gallery

From the south end of The Square, the fetching stone terrace that comprises **Hall Bank** scuttles up to the wide and breezy but somewhat traffic-choked **Market Place**. There's nothing much here to hold the eye, but it's only a few yards back down the hill along Terrace Road to the first-rate **Buxton Museum**

and Art Gallery (Tues–Fri 9.30am–5.30pm, Sat 9.30am–5pm; Easter–Sept also Sun 10.30am–5pm; free), whose ground floor is largely devoted to temporary displays of local contemporary art. Upstairs, the "Wonders of the Peak" display tracks the history of the region from its geological construction through the Romans and on to the Victorians. Best of all, however, is the section dealing with the **petrifactioners**, who turned local semiprecious stones into ornaments and jewellery designed to tickle the fancy of the visitors who arrived here in numbers after the duke had put Buxton on the tourist map. By the 1840s, Buxton had no less than fourteen petrifactioners' shops, selling every stone trinket imaginable from plates and stone eggs to vases and obelisks.

Poole's Cavern

The Peaks are riddled with cave systems and around half a dozen have become popular tourist attractions. The nearest to Buxton – about a mile southwest of the centre, just off Green Lane – is **Poole's Cavern** (March–Oct daily 10am–5pm; £5.80), whose impressively large chambers are home to a host of orange and blue-grey stalactites and stalagmites.

Eating and drinking

Buxton has several good places to eat, but the best **restaurant** in town is the ♃ *Columbine*, a small and intimate place in the centre at 7 Hall Bank (℡01298/78752; closed Sun & Tues in winter). The menu here is short but imaginative with main courses averaging £12. An excellent second choice is the *Sun Inn*, at 33 High St, a fine old **pub** with antique beamed rooms, that serves fine ales and first-rate bar food such as beef in ale for £7.50. It's also the best place for a **pint**, or check out *Watsons Café Bar None*, on Hall Bank, a bar-cum-café with a laid-back atmosphere, inviting decor and frequent live music, especially jazz.

Castleton

The agreeable little village of **CASTLETON**, ten miles northeast of Buxton, lies on the northern edge of the White Peak, its huddle of old stone cottages ringed by hills and set beside a babbling brook. As a base for local walks, the place is hard to beat and the hikers resting up in the quiet Market Place, just off the main drag behind the church, have the choice of a healthy spread of local accommodation and services. Overseeing the whole ensemble is **Peveril Castle** (April–Oct daily 10am–5pm; Nov–March Thurs–Mon 10am–4pm; £3; EH), from which the village takes its name. William the Conqueror's illegitimate son William Peveril raised the first fortifications here to protect the king's rights to the forest that then covered the district, but most of the remains – principally the ruinous, square keep – date from the 1170s.

The limestone hills pressing in on Castleton are riddled with water-worn **cave systems,** four of which can be visited. They can all be reached by car or on foot, the latter by means of a three-and-a-half mile circular trail that begins in the village and takes two hours. The tourist office (see p.469) has a leaflet and sells maps, though most visitors settle for just one set of caves – ususally the Peak Cavern or the Speedwell Cavern.

Peak Cavern is the handiest (April–Oct daily 10am–5pm; Nov–March Sat & Sun 10am–5pm; £6, combined with Speedwell £10.50), tucked in a gully at the back of Castleton, its gaping mouth once providing shelter for a rope factory and a small village. Daniel Defoe, visiting in the eighteenth century, noted the cavern's colourful local name, the **Devil's Arse**, a reference to the fiendish fashion in which its interior contours twisted and turned.

Not too far away, 600 yards or so west from the village along the main road, is **Speedwell Cavern** (daily 9.30/10am–5/5.30pm; last entry 45min before closing; £6.50, combined with Peak £10.50). At six hundred feet below ground, this is the deepest of the four cave systems, but the main drama comes with the means of access – down a hundred dripping steps and then by boat through a quarter-mile-long claustrophobic tunnel that was blasted out in search of lead. At the end lies the Bottomless Pit, a pool where 40,000 tons of mining rubble were once dumped without raising the water level one iota.

Practicalities

Easily the most scenic approach to Castleton is from the west, either along the A625 or the A623/B6061, though the two roads merge just to the west of the village to wiggle through the dramatic Winnats Pass. However, the principal **bus** service to Castleton (First's hourly bus #272) arrives from the east – from Sheffield and Hathersage. In the opposite direction, several operators combine to link Buxton with Castleton, but buses are few and far between, one or two a day if that. The nearest **train station** is at Hope, a couple of miles or so east of Castleton along the valley. The station is on the Manchester Piccadilly, Hope Valley and Sheffield line and there are trains every hour or two; bus #272 links Hope Station with Castleton. The **Castleton Information Centre and Museum** (daily 9.30am–5pm; ☏01433/620679), a combined museum, community centre and tourist office, stands beside the car park on the west side of the village, just off the main street. It sells hiking leaflets and maps, and operates an accommodation-booking service.

 Accommodation is plentiful, but should be booked in advance at peak times. Pick of the B&Bs is the modernized *Bargate Cottage*, at the top of the Market Place (☏01433/620201, ⓦwww.bargatecottage.co.uk; no credit cards; ❷), with three well-kept en-suite rooms, kitted out in frilly modern style, and first-rate breakfasts. Alternatively, the *Cryer House* B&B, opposite the church on Castle Street (☏01433/620244; no credit cards; ❷), and also in an older

---

The Pennine Way

The 250-mile-long **Pennine Way** (ⓦwww.nationaltrail.co.uk) was the country's first long-distance footpath, officially opened in 1965. It stretches north from the boggy plateau of the Peak District's Kinder Scout, through the Yorkshire Dales and Teesdale, crossing Hadrian's Wall and the Northumberland National Park, before entering Scotland to fizzle out at the village of Kirk Yetholm. People had been using a similar route for over thirty years before the path's official opening, sticking to the crest of the Pennines where practicable, only descending to the valleys for overnight accommodation and services.

It's now one of the most popular walks in the country, either taken in sections or completed in two to three weeks, depending on your level of fitness and experience. It's a challenge in the best of weather, since it passes through some of the most remote countryside in England. You must certainly be properly equipped, able to use a map and compass, and be prepared to follow local advice about current diversions and re-routing; changes are often made to avoid erosion of the existing trail. The National Trail Guides, *Pennine Way: South* and *Pennine Way: North*, are essential, though some still prefer to stick to Wainwright's *Pennine Way Companion*. Peak National Park **information centres** along the route – like the one at Edale village – stock a selection of guides and associated trail leaflets and can offer advice. Finally, on reaching the end, you can get your certificate stamped at Edale's *Old Nag's Head* in the south or Kirk Yetholm's *Border Hotel* in the north.

building, has two guest rooms, and a pleasant conservatory. Finally, the YHA **hostel** (℡0870/770 5758, ⓦwww.yha.org.uk; advance booking required; dorm beds £11, doubles ❶) is housed in Castleton Hall, a spacious old stone mansion on the Market Place. It's well equipped with a self-catering kitchen, a café, cycle store and drying room, and its 140 beds are divided into two- to eight-bedded rooms, many of which are en-suite.

For **food**, Castleton's pubs are its gastronomic mainstay and there's nowhere better than the *Castle*, opposite the church on Castle Street, which offers tasty bar food at very affordable prices. Alternatively, *Ye Olde Nag's Head*, on the main street, offers more-than-competent bar food (6–9pm), including homemade steak-and-Guinness pies, and also holds the *Stables Tearoom* (daily 9am–5.30pm), good for snacks and light meals.

Edale village

There's almost nothing to **EDALE village**, some five miles northwest of Castleton, except for a slender, half-mile trail of stone houses, which march up the main street from the train station with a couple of pubs, an old stone church and a scattering of B&Bs on the way: indeed, it's this very somnambulant air that is the village's main appeal. Walkers arrive in droves throughout the year to set off across England's backbone on the 250-mile **Pennine Way** (see box p.469); the route's starting-point is signposted from outside the *Old Nag's Head* at the head of the village. If that sounds too daunting, there's an excellent **circular walk** (9 miles; 5hr) along the first part of the Pennine Way, leading up onto the bleak gritstone, table-top of **Kinder Scout** (2088ft), below which Edale cowers.

Hourly **trains** from Manchester, Sheffield and Hathersage stop at Edale station, providing easy access, and there is also a patchy **bus** service from Castleton. From Edale train station, it's 400 yards or so up the road to the newly revamped **Peak National Park Information Centre** (daily 9am–1pm & 2–5pm), which sells all manner of trail leaflets and hiking guides and can advise about local **accommodation**. The nearest **YHA hostel**, the *Edale YHA Activity Centre* (℡0870/770 5808, ⓦwww.yha.org.uk; dorm beds £11, doubles ❶), lies two miles east of Edale station, in an old country house at Rowland Cote, Nether Booth. It's clearly signed from the road into Edale or you can walk there across the fields from behind the information centre. It has 150 beds in two- to twelve-bedded rooms and a good range of facilities from a laundry and a café through to a self-catering kitchen. It also offers an extensive programme of outdoor pursuits, though these – and accommodation – need to be booked in advance. The hostel is popular with Pennine Way walkers – as is the YHA **camping barn** at Cotefield Farm, Ollerbrook (℡0870/770 6113), which lies on the path from the village to the hostel. There are two village **campsites**, *Fieldhead* (℡01433/670386), behind the information centre, and *Cooper's* at Newfold Farm (℡01433/670372), in the centre of Edale near the *Old Nag's Head*.

Those with more money will do better at Edale's **B&Bs**, the pick of which is *Stonecroft*, a detached Victorian house with two comfortable guest rooms near the church (℡01433/670262, ⓦwww.stonecroftguesthouse.co.uk; ❸). As for **food**, there are only two options – the *Rambler*, yards from the train station at the bottom of the village, and the *Old Nag's Head*, at the top. Both are hiker-friendly and serve bar food, though the *Rambler* has the edge.

Eyam

Within a year of September 7, 1665, the lonely lead-mining settlement of **EYAM** (pronounced "Eem"), some nine miles southeast of Castleton, had lost almost half of its population of 750 to the bubonic plague, a calamity that earned it the enduring epithet "The Plague Village". The first victim was one George Vicars, a journeyman tailor who is said to have released some infected fleas into his lodgings from a package of cloth he had brought here from London. Acutely conscious of the danger to neighbouring villages, **William Mompesson**, the village rector, speedily organized a self-imposed quarantine, arranging for food to be left at places on the parish boundary. Payment was made with coins left in pools of disinfecting vinegar in holes chiselled into the old boundary stones – and these can still be seen at **Mompesson's Well**, half a mile up the hill to the north of the village and accessible by footpath.

Long, thin and hilly, Eyam is little more than one main street – Church and then Main Street – which trails west from **The Square**, itself no more than a crossroads overlooked by a few old stone houses. First up of interest along Church Street is the comely **church of St Lawrence** (Easter–Sept Mon–Sat 9am–6pm, Sun 1–5.30pm; Oct–Easter Mon–Sat 9am–4pm, Sun 1–5.30pm; free), of medieval foundation but extensively revamped in the nineteenth century. In the church graveyard a few feet from the entrance stands a conspicuous, eighth-century carved **Celtic cross** and close by is the distinctive **table-tomb** of Mompesson's wife.

Immediately west of the church are the so-called **plague cottages**, where plaques explain who died where and when – it was here that Vicars met his maker. Another short hop brings you to **Eyam Hall** (July–Aug Mon, Wed, Thurs & Sun 11am–4pm; £4.75), which was built for Thomas Wright a few years after the plague ended, possibly in an attempt to secure his position as squire of the depleted village. Wright's heirs have lived in it ever since, building up a mildly diverting collection of furnishings, family portraits, tapestries, costumes and incidental bygones. Some of the adjacent farm buildings have been turned into a **Craft Centre** (Tues–Sun 10.30am–5pm; free) with a restaurant and gift shop.

From the hall, it's a few minutes' walk along Main Street and up Hawkhill Road to the modest Methodist chapel that now houses the **Eyam Museum** (April–Oct Tues–Sun 10am–4.30pm; £1.75). This tracks through the history of the village and has a good section on the bubonic plague – its transmission, symptoms and social aftermath.

Practicalities

Buses to Eyam all stop on The Square, and one or two also run along Main/Church Street. Easily the best of a handful of **B&Bs** is *Delf View House* (☎01433/631533, ☻www.delfviewhouse.co.uk; ❺), a beautifully kept Georgian villa set in its own grounds across the street from the church; breakfast is served in a superb old dining room with its flagstone floor, imposing fireplace and beamed ceiling. Second choice is the *Miner's Arms*, in antique premises just off The Square on Water Lane (☎01433/630853; ❹), with several perfectly adequate, en-suite rooms of a modern disposition. Finally, there's the well-equipped YHA **hostel** (☎0870/770 5830, ☻www.yha.org.uk; £11, doubles ❶), which occupies an idiosyncratic Victorian house, whose ersatz medieval towers and turrets overlook Eyam from amidst wooded grounds on Hawkhill Road, a stiff, half-mile ramble up from the museum. It has sixty beds in two- to eight-bed rooms; advance reservations are required, as opening days and dates change.

The best place **to eat** is the *Miner's Arms*, which serves filling bar meals as well as very enjoyable and moderately priced, traditional British dinners in its restaurant every evening except Sunday and Monday.

Baslow

BASLOW, some four miles southeast of Eyam, is an inconsequential little village, whose oldest stone cottages string prettily along the River Derwent. The only building of note is the **church of St Anne's**, whose stone spire pokes up above the Victorian castellations of its nave in between the river and the busy junction of the A623/A619. Baslow's main appeal is its handy location for the nearby Chatsworth estate (see below), especially if you're travelling by bus, and as home to one of the Peak's finest **hotels**, *Fischer's Baslow Hall* (℡01246/583259, Ⓦwww.fischers-baslowhall.co.uk; ❼), a mile or so out of the village back towards Eyam along the A623. In its own grounds, the hall is picture-postcard perfect, a handsome Edwardian building made of local stone with matching gables and a dinky canopy over the front door. The interior is suitably lavish and the service attentive with rooms both in the main building and in the Garden House annexe next door. The **restaurant** is superb too, and has won several awards for its imaginative cuisine – or you can pop back into Baslow for a bite at the excellent *Avant Garde Café* (daily 9am–5pm), opposite St Anne's, where they serve a delicious range of salads and light meals in bright, modern surroundings.

Chatsworth House

Fantastically popular, **Chatsworth House** (late March to late Dec daily 11am–5.30pm, last admission 4.30pm; gardens till 6pm, last admission 5pm; house & gardens £9.50, gardens only £5.75; Ⓦwww.chatsworth-house.co.uk), just south of Baslow via the A619, was built in the seventeenth century by the first duke of Devonshire and has been owned by the family ever since. The house is seen to best advantage from the **B6012**, which meanders across the estate to the west of the house, giving a full view of its vast Palladian frontage, whose clean lines are perfectly balanced by the undulating, partly wooded **parkland**, which rolls in from the south and west.

Many visitors forgo the house altogether, concentrating on the gardens instead (see below), and this is understandable given the predictability of the assorted baubles accumulated by the family. Nonetheless, amongst the maze of grandiose rooms and staircases, there are several noteworthy highlights, most memorably the ornate ceilings of the **State Apartments**, daubed with strikingly energetic cherubs. There's also the showpiece **Great Dining Room**, which has its table set as it was for the visit of George V and Queen Mary in 1933. And then there are the paintings. Amongst many, Frans Hals, Tintoretto, Veronese and Van Dyck all have works and there's even a Rembrandt – *A Portrait of an Old Man* – hanging in the chapel. The sixth duke also added a **Sculpture Gallery** to show off the pieces he had acquired on his travels, mostly large-scale Italian sculptures.

Back outside, the **gardens** are a real treat and owe much to the combined efforts of Capability Brown, who designed them in the 1750s, and Joseph Paxton (designer of London's Crystal Palace), who had a bash seventy years later. Amongst all sorts of fripperies, there are water fountains, a rock garden, an artificial waterfall, a grotto and a folly as well as a nursery and greenhouses. Afterwards, you can wend your way to the **café** in the handsomely converted former Stables.

The best way to get to Chatsworth House is **on foot** along one of the footpaths that lattice the estate. It's easy walking and the obvious departure point is Baslow on the northern edge of the estate. The *Grate Little Guide* (see p.463) to Chatsworth describes an especially pleasant four-mile loop, taking in the house and beginning and ending in Baslow. By bus, take any Bakewell–Baslow bus and ask to be put off at Edensor, from where it's about a mile east across the park to the house.

Travel details

Buses

For information on all local and national bus services, contact Traveline ☎ 0870/608 2608, ⓦ www.traveline.org.uk.

The TransPeak bus service, operated by the Trent Barton bus company, runs from Nottingham to Manchester via Derby, Matlock, Bakewell and Buxton 5 times daily. The whole journey takes 3 hours.

Birmingham to: Buxton (2 daily; 4hr); Cambridge (3 daily; 3hr 25min); Great Malvern (2 daily; 1hr 30min); Hereford (2 daily; 2hr 20min); Liverpool (6 daily; 3hr); London (hourly; 3hr); Ludlow (hourly; 2hr 10min); Manchester (hourly; 2hr 30min); Nottingham (6 daily; 1hr 30min); Oxford (5 daily; 1hr 30min); Ross-on-Wye (2 daily; 1hr 30min); Shrewsbury (2 daily; 1hr 20min); Stratford-upon-Avon (every 2 hr; 1hr); Worcester (hourly; 1hr 30min).

Buxton to: Ashbourne (4 daily; 2hr); Birmingham (2 daily; 4hr); Derby (3 daily; 1hr 30min).

Derby to: Buxton (3 daily; 1hr 30min).

Great Malvern to: Birmingham (2 daily; 1hr 30min); Hereford (1 daily; 40min); Stratford-upon-Avon (5 daily; 3hr 50min); Worcester (7 daily; 35min).

Hay-on-Wye to: Hereford (4 daily; 1hr); Ross-on-Wye (5 daily; 2hr).

Hereford to: Birmingham (2 daily; 2hr 20min); Great Malvern (1 daily; 40min); Hay-on-Wye (4 daily; 1hr); Ludlow (4 daily; 4hr); Ross-on-Wye (hourly; 40min); Shrewsbury (2 daily; 3hr 30min); Worcester (2 daily; 1hr).

Ludlow to: Birmingham (hourly; 2hr 10min); Hereford (4 daily; 4hr); Shrewsbury (6 daily; 1hr 20min); Worcester (2 daily; 2hr 15min).

Ross-on-Wye to: Birmingham (2 daily; 1hr 30min); Hay-on-Wye (5 daily; 2hr); Hereford (hourly; 40min).

Shrewsbury to: Birmingham (2 daily; 1hr 20min); Hereford (2 daily; 3hr 30min); Ludlow (6 daily; 1hr 20min); Stratford-upon-Avon (2 daily; 2hr 30min).

Stratford-upon-Avon to: Birmingham (every 2 hr; 1hr); Great Malvern (5 daily; 3hr 50min); Shrewsbury (2 daily; 2hr 30min).

Trains

For information on all local and national rail services, contact National Rail Enquiries ☎ 08457/484950, ⓦ www.nationalrail.co.uk.

Birmingham New Street to: Birmingham International (every 15–30min; 15min); Derby (every 30min; 45min); Great Malvern (every 30min; 1hr); Hereford (10 daily; 1hr 45min); Leicester (hourly; 50min); London (every 30min; 1hr 40min); Shrewsbury (hourly; 1hr 20min); Stoke-on-Trent (hourly; 1hr); Worcester (every 30min; 1hr).

Birmingham Snow Hill to: Stratford-upon-Avon (Mon–Sat hourly; 50min); Warwick (Mon–Sat hourly; 40min).

Derby to: Birmingham (every 30min; 45min); Leicester (hourly; 30min); London (hourly; 1hr 50min); Nottingham (every 20min; 35min).

Hereford to: Birmingham (hourly; 1hr 45min); Great Malvern (hourly; 30min); London (5 daily; 2hr 45min); Ludlow (hourly; 30min); Shrewsbury (hourly; 1hr); Worcester (every 1hr 30min; 40min).

Shrewsbury to: Birmingham (hourly; 1hr 20min); Church Stretton (every 30min; 15min); Hereford (hourly; 1hr); Ludlow (hourly; 30min); Telford (every 30min; 20min).

Stoke-on-Trent to: Birmingham (hourly; 1hr).

Stratford-upon-Avon to: Birmingham (Mon–Sat hourly; 1hr); London Marylebone (every 2hrs 20min); Oxford (4 daily; 1hr 10min); Warwick (Mon–Sat 8 daily; 30min).

9

The East Midlands

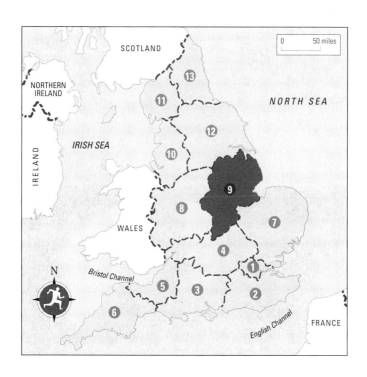

CHAPTER 9

Highlights

* **World Service Restaurant, Nottingham** Hard-to-beat Modern-British restaurant with oodles of gastronomic and decorative flair. **See p.483**

* **Rufford Country Park** Well off the usual tourist track, Rufford has a ceramic gallery, a bird sanctuary, a mill and a sculpture garden with lots of relaxed strolling in between. **See p.485**

* **Hardwick Hall** A beautifully preserved Elizabethan mansion that was the home of Bess of Hardwick. **See p.486**

* **Lincoln Cathedral** One of the finest medieval cathedrals in the land, seen at its best from a guided rooftop tour. **See p.499**

* **Stamford** Lincolnshire's prettiest town, with narrow streets framed by old limestone houses. **See p.505**

△ Lincoln Cathedral

The East Midlands

M
any tourists bypass the four major counties of the **East Midlands** – Nottinghamshire, Leicestershire, Northamptonshire and Lincolnshire – on their way to more obvious destinations, an understandable mistake given that the region is short on star attractions. The most obvious targets are **Nottingham**, **Leicester** and **Northampton** – three of the four county towns – but although they share a long and eventful history, all have been badly bruised by postwar town planning and industrial development. Nevertheless, the modern shells shelter a few historical landmarks – an especially fine church in Northampton, the castle in Nottingham, and traces of Roman baths in Leicester – and even though these are the frills rather than the substance, **Nottingham** has enough character to give it an aesthetic edge. Furthermore, if few would actually describe this trio of towns as especially good-looking, the countryside surrounding them can be delightful, with rolling farmland punctuated by wooded ridges and flowing hills, all sprinkled with prestigious country homes, pretty villages and old market towns. In Nottinghamshire, Byron's **Newstead Abbey** is intriguing, as is **Hardwick Hall**, just over the border in Derbyshire, an especially beautiful Elizabethan country home built by the redoubtable Bess of Hardwick. In addition, the eastern reaches of Nottinghamshire hold two appealing market towns – **Southwell** and **Newark**. East of Leicestershire, the easy countryside rolls over into **Rutland**, England's smallest county, where you'll find a brace of pleasant country towns, **Oakham** and **Uppingham**. South of here, the rural parts of **Northamptonshire** are studded with handsome, old stone villages and small towns – most notably **Fotheringhay** and **Oundle** – plus large country estates, the best known of which is **Althorp**, the final resting place of Princess Diana.

Lincolnshire is very different in character from the rest of the region, an agricultural backwater that remains surprisingly remote – locals sometimes call it the "forgotten" county. This was not always the case: throughout medieval times the county flourished as a centre of the wool trade with Flanders, its merchants and landowners becoming some of the wealthiest in England. Reminders of the high times are legion, beginning with the majestic cathedral that graces **Lincoln**, a dignified old city with cobbled lanes and ancient buildings. Equally enticing is the splendidly intact stone town of **Stamford**, but the county's urban attractions pretty much end there. Out in the sticks, the most distinctive feature is **The Fens**, whose pancake-flat fields, filling out much of the south of the county and extending deep into East Anglia (see Chapter 7), have been regained from the marshes and the sea. Fenland villages are generally short of charm, but the **parish churches**,

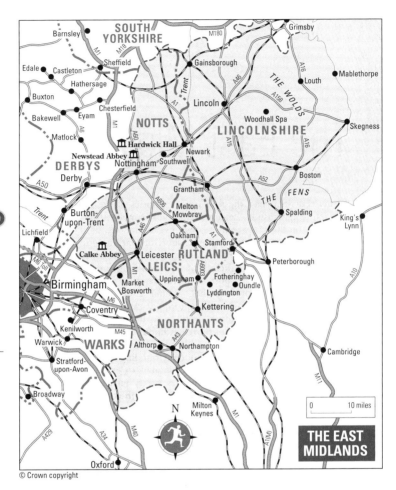

whose spires regularly interrupt the wide-skied landscape, are stunning, the most impressive of the lot being St Botolph's in the otherwise humdrum **Boston**.

In north Lincolnshire, the gentle chalky hills of the **Lincolnshire Wolds** contain the county's most diverse scenery, which is concentrated around the fetching country town of **Louth**. To the east of the Wolds is the **coast**, whose long sandy beach extends, with a few marshy interruptions, from Mablethorpe to **Skegness**, the main resort. The coast has long attracted thousands of holiday-makers from the big cities of the East Midlands and Yorkshire, hence its trail of bungalows, campsites and caravan parks – though significant chunks of the seashore are now protected as **nature reserves**.

As for public transport, travelling between the cities of the East Midlands by **train** or **bus** is simple and most of the larger towns have good regional links, too; but things are very different in the country with bus services fairly patchy.

Nottinghamshire

With a population of about 270,000, **Nottingham** is one of England's big cities, a longtime manufacturing centre for bikes, cigarettes, pharmaceuticals and lace. It is, however, more famous for Trent Bridge cricket ground and its association with **Robin Hood**, the legendary thirteenth-century outlaw. Hood's bitter enemy was, of course, the Sheriff of Nottingham, but unfortunately his home and lair – the city's imposing medieval castle – is long gone, and today Nottingham is at its most diverting in the Lace Market, whose cramped streets are crowded with the mansion-like warehouses of the Victorian lace-makers.

The county town is flanked to the south by the commuter villages of the Nottinghamshire Wolds and to the north by the gritty towns and villages of what was, until Thatcher and her cronies decimated it in the late 1980s, the Nottinghamshire coalfield. Both are unremarkable, but encrusted within the old coalfield are the thin remains of **Sherwood Forest**, the bulk of which is contained within **The Dukeries**, named after the five dukes who owned most of this area and preserved at least part of the ancient broad-leaved forest. Three of the four remaining estates – Worksop, Welbeck and Thoresby – are still in private hands, but the fourth, **Clumber Park**, is now owned by the National Trust and has some charming woodland walks. Also within the confines of the former coalfield are two fascinating country houses, **Newstead Abbey**, one-time home of Byron, and, even better, the wonderful Elizabethan extravagance of **Hardwick Hall**. Eastern Nottinghamshire is mainly agricultural, its most important town being **Newark**, an agreeable, low-key place straddling the River Trent. Newark has a castle, but the chief attraction hereabouts is the fine Norman church at nearby **Southwell**.

Fast and frequent **trains** connect Nottingham with London, Birmingham, Newark, Lincoln and Leicester, while county-wide and regional **bus** services radiate out from the city, too, making it the obvious base for exploring this part of the country.

Nottingham

Controlling a strategic crossing point over the River Trent, the Saxon town of **NOTTINGHAM** was built on one of a pair of sandstone hills whose 130-foot cliffs looked out over the river valley. In 1068, William the Conqueror built a castle on the other hill, and the Saxons and Normans traded on the low ground in between, the **Market Square**. The castle was a military stronghold and royal palace, the equal of the great castles of Windsor and Dover, and every medieval king of England paid regular visits. In August 1642, **Charles I** stayed here too, riding out of the castle to raise his standard and start the Civil War, though hardly anyone joined up, even though the king had the ceremony repeated on the next three days.

After the Civil War, the Parliamentarians slighted the castle and, in the 1670s, the ruins were cleared by the duke of Newcastle to make way for a **palace**, whose continental design he chose from a pattern book, probably by Rubens. Beneath the castle lay a market town which, according to contemporaries, was handsome and well kept. In the second half of the eighteenth century, however,

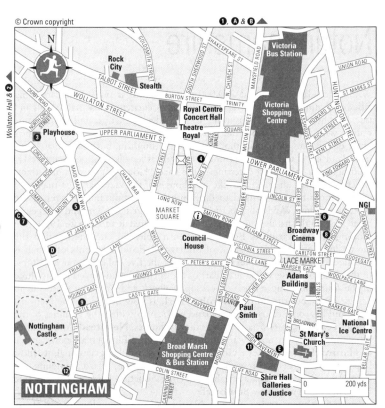

© Crown copyright

0, A & B ▲

◄ Wollaton Hall & **2**

NOTTINGHAM

0   200 yds

ACCOMMODATION		CAFÉS & RESTAURANTS		PUBS & BARS	
Best Western Westminster		French Living	4	Broadway Cinema Bar	8
Hotel	A	Harts	7	Cast	3
Greenwood City Lodge	B	Memsaab	5	Cock & Hoop	10
Harts Hotel	C	Shaw's Restaurant and		Lincolnshire Poacher	1
Lace Market Hotel	E	Café Bar	6	Pitcher & Piano	11
Rutland Square Hotel	D	World Service	9	Sir John Borlase Warren	2
				Ye Olde Trip to Jerusalem Inn	12

the city was transformed by the expansion of the lace and hosiery industries, and within the space of fifty years, Nottingham's population increased from ten thousand to fifty thousand, the resulting slum becoming a hotbed of radicalism.

The worst of Nottingham's slums were cleared in the early twentieth century, when the city centre assumed its present structure, with the main commercial area ringed by alternating industrial and residential districts. Thereafter, crass **postwar development** added tower blocks, shopping centres and a ring road, resulting in a townscape that is dishearteningly similar to many other English commercial centres.

Arrival and information

Nottingham **train station** is on the south side of the city centre, a five- to ten-minute walk from the Market Square – just follow the signs. Most long-distance **buses** arrive at the **Broad Marsh Bus Station**, down the street from the train station on the way to the centre, but some – including services from north Nottinghamshire – pull in at the **Victoria Bus Station**, a five-minute walk north of the Market Square. **Trams** link the train station with the Market Square and the city's suburbs. The **tourist office** is on the Market Square, on the ground floor of the Council House, 1 Smithy Row (Mon–Fri 9am–5.30pm, Sat 9am–5pm & Sun 10am–4pm; ☎0115/915 5330, ⓦwww .experiencenottinghamshire.com).

Accommodation

As you might expect of a big city, Nottingham has a good range of accommodation, with the more expensive **hotels** concentrated in the centre, the cheaper places and the **B&Bs** mostly located on the outskirts and beside the main approach roads.

Best Western Westminster Hotel 312 Mansfield Rd ☎0115/955 5000, ⓦwww.westminster-hotel .co.uk. Comfortable, popular mid-range hotel in a big old red-brick mansion complete with turret and high gables. On a main road about one mile north of the city centre. **❺**

Greenwood City Lodge 5 Third Ave, off Sherwood Rise ☎0115/962 1206, ⓦwww.greenwood lodgecityguesthouse.co.uk. Attractive guest house in a quiet corner of the city, down a narrow lane about a mile north of the city centre. Six bedrooms decorated in smart Victorian style. Highly recommended. **❺**

 Harts Hotel Standard Hill, Park Row ☎0115/988 1900, ⓦwww.hartshotel.co.uk.

Chic hotel, with comfort and style in equal measure: ultra-modern fixtures and fittings, Egyptian-cotton bed linen and so forth. It's quite pricey, but first rate all the same. **❼**

Lace Market Hotel 29 High Pavement ☎0115/852 3232, ⓦwww.lacemarkethotel.co.uk. Great location, footsteps from St Mary's Church, this smart hotel has thirty individually decorated rooms within a tastefully modernized Georgian house. **❼**

Rutland Square Hotel Rutland Street, off St James' Street ☎0115/941 1114, ⓦwww .forestdale.com. Enticing and tastefully furnished modern chain hotel in a good location, just by the castle. Ninety-odd rooms. **❼**

Market Square and the Castle

The **Market Square** is still the heart of the city, an airy open plaza whose shops, offices and fountains are overlooked by the grand neo-Baroque **Council House**, completed as part of a make-work scheme in 1928. From here, it's a five-minute walk west up Friar Lane to **Nottingham Castle** (daily 10am–5pm; grounds daily 9am–dusk; Sat & Sun £2, free at other times), whose heavily restored medieval gateway leads to the castle gardens, which slope up to the squat, seventeenth-century ducal **palace**. The mansion occupies the site of the medieval castle's upper bailey, and round the back, just outside the main entrance, two sets of steps lead down into the maze of ancient caves that honeycomb the cliff beneath. One set is currently open for guided tours (1–3 daily; call ☎0115/915 3700 for times; £2), and this leads into **Mortimer's Hole**, a three-hundred-foot shaft along which the young Edward III and his chums allegedly crept in October 1330 to capture the queen mother, Isabella, and her lover, Roger Mortimer. The couple had already polished off Edward III's father, the hapless Edward II, and were intent on usurping the crown, but the young Edward proved too shrewd for them and Mortimer came to a sticky end.

The interior of the ducal mansion holds the **Castle Museum and Art Gallery**, which makes a dull start on the ground floor with a series of small, piecemeal exhibitions. Much better is the "Story of Nottingham" on the lower level, a lively, well-presented and entertaining account of the city's development. In particular, look out for a small but exquisite collection of late medieval

△ Nottingham's Castle Museum and Art Gallery

alabaster carvings, an art form for which Nottingham once had an international reputation. It's worth walking up to the top floor too, for a turn round the main **picture gallery**, a handsome and spacious room, which displays a curious assortment of mostly English nineteenth-century Romantic paintings.

The Lace Market

A few minutes' walk away, on the east side of the Market Square up along Victoria Street, is the **Lace Market**, whose narrow lanes and alleys are flanked by an attractive assortment of Victorian factories and warehouses. **Stoney Street**, for one, holds the imposing **Adams Building**, whose handsome stone and brick facade combines neo-Georgian and neo-Renaissance features. The adjoining **Broadway** chips in with a line of especially homogeneous red-brick and sandstone-trimmed buildings, many featuring long attic windows designed to light what were once the mending and inspection rooms, while the space-ship–like **National Ice Centre** sits incongruously at the foot of Barker Gate. At the heart of the Lace Market is the church of **St Mary**, a good-looking, mostly fifteenth-century Gothic structure built on top of the hill that was once the Saxon town. The church abuts High Pavement, the administrative centre of Nottingham in Georgian times, and here you'll find **Shire Hall**, whose Neoclassical columns, pilasters and dome date from 1770. The Hall now accommodates the **Galleries of Justice** (April–Oct Tues–Sun 10am–4pm; Nov–March Tues–Sun 10am–3pm, plus Mon 10am–3/4pm in school holidays; £7.95; @www.galleriesofjustice.org.uk), whose child–friendly "Crime and Punishment" tour features lots of role play. Alternatively, you can wander round the building independently to see the two superbly preserved Victorian court-rooms, an Edwardian police station, some spectacularly unpleasant old cells, a women's prison with bath house and a prisoners' exercise yard.

Nearby, on Byard Lane, is the first shop of local lad **Paul Smith**, a major success story of recent British fashion.

Eating

Nottingham boasts at least a dozen top-quality **restaurants**, as well as the usual cheaper offerings – primarily French, Italian and Asian. There's also no shortage of **cafés** and **café–bars**, most with angular and ultra-modern furnishings and fittings, and serving the usual coffee and snacks.

French Living 27 King St ☏0115/958 5885. Authentic French cuisine served in an intimate basement. Daytime snacks and baguettes in the ground-floor café too. Evening main courses cost £9–15. Closed Sun & Mon. Moderate.

Harts Standard Court, Park Row ☏0115/911 0666. One of the city's most acclaimed restaurants, occupy-ing part of the old general hospital and serving an international menu of well-presented meals. Attractive pastel/modernist decor and attentive service. Reser-vations essential. Mains from about £13. Expensive.

Memsaab 12 Maid Marian Way ☏0115/957 0009. One of a new breed of Indian restau-rants, with crisp modern decor and bags of space. The food is exquisite, fusing cooking styles from different Indian regions. A large and imaginative menu with main courses starting from £9. Moderate.

Shaw's Restaurant and Café Bar 20 Broad St ☏0115/950 0009. Informal, pleasantly decorated basement restaurant, with an imaginative menu supplemented by an outstanding selection of daily specials, such as mouthwatering sardines. The ground-floor café-bar is lighter and airier, with a similar menu. Main courses average £7–9. Closed Sun. Moderate.

World Service Newdigate House, Castle Gate ☏0115/847 5587. Chic restaurant with bags of (vaguely Asiatic) flair in charming premises up near the castle. A modern British menu prepared with imagination and attention to detail. In the evening, main courses start at around £13, but there are great deals at lunchtimes with two–course set meals costing £10.50, £14 for three. Highly recommended.

Pubs and nightlife

Nottingham's **nightclub** scene is boisterous, with places moving in and out of fashion all the time. The **pubs** around Market Square have a tough edge to them, especially at the weekend, but within a few minutes' walk there's a selec-tion of lively and more enjoyable drinking-holes. For **live music**, both popular and classical, most big names play at the Royal Centre Concert Hall on Wolla-ton Street (☏0115/989 5555, @www.royalcentre-nottingham.co.uk), while nearby *Rock City* (see below) also pulls in some star turns. The Broadway, in the Lace Market at 14 Broad St (℡0115/952 6611, ⓦwww.broadway.org.uk), is the best **cinema** in town, featuring the pick of mainstream and avant-garde films.

Pubs and bars

Broadway Cinema Bar Broadway Cinema, 14 Broad St. Informal, fashionable, arty bar serving an eclectic assortment of bottled beers. Can get smoky, but there's a smaller, smoke-free café-bar upstairs, though the bar food is very average.

Cast Wellington Circus. The bar of the Nottingham Playhouse is a popular, easy-going spot with courtyard seating on summer nights, and Anish Kapoor's whopping, reflective *Sky Mirror* sculpture. There's also an attached deli (Mon–Fri 8am–7pm, Sat 9am–5pm & Sun 10am–4pm) and a pretty average restaurant.

Cock and Hoop 25 High Pavement, Lace Market. In the centre of Nottingham, this curious little split-level bar verges on the smart, with thick carpets and comfortable chairs. Real ales too.

Lincolnshire Poacher 161 Mansfield Rd. Very popular and relaxed pub a five- to ten-minute walk

from the city centre. It serves a wide selection of bottled and real ales to an older clientele.

Pitcher & Piano High Pavement. Chain-owned pub in an imaginatively converted Victorian church on the edge of the Lace Market. Good fun; very youthful.

Sir John Borlase Warren 1 Ilkeston Rd, Canning Circus. Pulling in a mixed bag of students and local residents, this rambling old pub has character and a lively, friendly atmosphere. Half a mile up the hill from the city centre along Derby Road.

Ye Olde Trip to Jerusalem Inn Below the castle in Brewhouse Yard. Carved into the castle rock, this ancient inn may well have been a meeting point for soldiers gathering for the Third Crusade. Its cave-like bars, with their rough sandstone ceilings, are delightfully secretive.

Clubs

NG1 76 Lower Parliament St ℡0115/958 8440, ⓦwww.ng1club.co.uk. Nottingham's premier gay club, but hetero-friendly too, a slick and sleek super-club with four distinct areas, multiple bars and two dance floors. Music varies enormously, but house is the core.

Rock City 8 Talbot St ℡0115/958 8484, ⓦwww.rock-city.co.uk. Giant, crowded nightclub/music

venue, with different sounds each night, from Goth to metal to indie. Regularly hosts big-name bands on UK tours.

Stealth Masonic Place, Goldsmith Street ℡0115/958 0672, ⓦwww.stealthattack.co.uk. A front-runner in the club scene with cutting-edge DJs, indie, rock and drum'n'bass. Hard to beat; great groove.

Northern Nottinghamshire

Rural **northern Nottinghamshire**, with its easy rolling landscapes and large ducal estates, was transformed in the nineteenth century by **coal** – deep, wide seams of the stuff that spawned dozens of collieries, and colliery towns, stretching north across the county and on into Yorkshire. Almost without exception, the mines have closed, their passing marked only by the old pit-head winding wheels left, bleak and solitary, to commemorate the thousands of men who laboured here. The suddenness of the pit closure programme imposed by the Conservative government in the 1980s knocked the stuffing out of the area and only now is it beginning to revive. One prop has been the tourist industry, for the countryside in between these former mining communities holds several enjoyable attractions, the best-known of which is **Sherwood Forest** – or at least the patchy remains of it – one-time haunt (allegedly) of Robin Hood. Byron is a pipsqueak in the celebrity stakes by comparison, but his family home – **Newstead Abbey** – is here too, and there are some pleasant woodland walks in the NT's **Clumber**

Park. Last but certainly not least, there's **Hardwick Hall**, a stunningly handsome Elizabethan mansion.

Reaching this quartet of attractions by **bus** from Nottingham is easy enough – with the exception of Hardwick Hall, for which you'll need your own transport.

Newstead Abbey

In 1539, **Newstead Abbey,** ten miles north of Nottingham on the A60 (house April–Sept daily noon–5pm, grounds daily 9am–6pm or dusk; £6, grounds only £3; Ⓦ www.newsteadabbey.org.uk), was granted by Henry VIII to Sir John Byron, who demolished most of the church and converted the monastic buildings into a family home. In 1798, **Lord Byron** inherited the estate, then little more than a ruin. He restored part of the complex during his six-year residence (1808–14), but most of the present structure dates from later renovations, which maintained much of the shape and feel of the medieval original while creating the warren-like mansion that exists today. **Inside**, a string of intriguing period rooms includes everything from a neo-Gothic Great Hall to the Henry VII bedroom, fitted with carved panels and painted house screens imported from Japan. Some of the rooms are pretty much as they were when Byron lived here and in the library is a small collection of the poet's possessions. The surrounding **gardens** are delightful, a secretive and subtle combination of walled garden, lake, Gothic waterfalls, yew tunnels and Japanese-style rockeries, complete with idiosyncratic pagodas.

There's a fast and frequent **bus** service leaving every twenty minutes or so from Nottingham's Victoria Bus Station to the gates of Newstead Abbey, a mile from the house; the journey takes about 25 minutes.

Rufford Country Park

Council-run country parks may be ten-a-penny, but **Rufford Country Park** (daily dawn–dusk; main facilities daily 10.30am–5pm; free) shows just how things should be done. The remains of the original twelfth-century Cistercian abbey and the country house built in its stead – but largely demolished in 1956 – are neither very substantial nor especially interesting, but the old buildings are all pleasantly maintained and the former stable block now holds a café, a better-than-average craft shop and a first-rate ceramics gallery. At the back of the stables are the gardens, both informal and formal, and an outstanding **Sculpture Garden**, which manages to be both accessible and contemporary with sculptures such as the eerily lifelike, concrete *Man and Sheep on a Bench*. Further afield is a lake and a mill, a bird sanctuary and a wetland area, all reachable via a footpath. There's a lively programme of special events and temporary art exhibitions too.

Rufford is right beside the A614 about eighteen miles north of Nottingham and reached on hourly Stagecoach **bus** #33 from Nottingham's Victoria Bus Station.

Sherwood Forest Country Park

Most of **Sherwood Forest**, once a vast royal woodland of oak, birch and bracken covering all of northern Nottinghamshire, was cleared in the eighteenth century and nowadays it's difficult to imagine the protection it provided for generations of outlaws, the most famous of whom was **Robin Hood**. There's no "true story" of Robin's life – the earliest reference to him, in Langland's *Piers*

Plowman of 1377, treats him as a fiction – but to the balladeers of fifteenth-century England, who invented most of Hood's folklore, this was hardly the point. For them, Robin was a symbol of yeoman decency, a semi-mythological opponent of corrupt clergymen and evil officers of the law; in the early tales, although Robin shows sympathy for the peasant, he has rather more respect for the decent nobleman, and he's never credited with robbing the rich to give to the poor. This and other parts of the legend, such as Maid Marion and Friar Tuck, were added later.

Robin Hood may lack historical authenticity, but it hasn't discouraged the county council from spending thousands of pounds sustaining the **Major Oak**, the creaky tree where Maid Marion and Robin are supposed to have plighted their troth. The Major Oak is on a pleasant one-mile trail that begins beside the visitor centre at the main entrance to **Sherwood Forest Country Park** (daily dawn–dusk; free), which comprises 450 acres of oak and silver birch crisscrossed with footpaths. The visitor centre is half a mile north of the village of Edwinstowe, itself just two miles northwest of Rufford Park and twenty-odd miles north of Nottingham via the A614.

Stagecoach **bus** #33 runs hourly from Nottingham's Victoria Bus Station to Edwinstowe via Rufford.

Clumber Park

North of Ollerton, Edwinstowe's immediate neighbour, the A614 trims the edge of Thoresby Park, to reach, after six miles, the main entrance of **Clumber Park** (daily dawn–dusk; free, parking for non-NT members £4), four thousand acres of park and woodland lying to the south of industrial Worksop. The estate was once the country seat of the dukes of Newcastle, and it was here in the 1770s that they constructed a grand mansion overlooking Clumber Lake. The house was dismantled in 1938, when the duke sold the estate, and today the most interesting survivor of the lakeside buildings – located about two and a half miles from the A614 – is the Gothic Revival **Chapel** (daily 10.30am–4/5.30pm; free; NT), an imposing edifice with a soaring spire and an intricately carved interior built for the seventh duke in the 1880s. Close by, the old **stable block** now houses a National Trust office, shop and **café** (same hours as chapel), and there's **bike rental** (April–Oct & winter weekends) just behind the chapel. The woods around the lake offer some delightful strolls and rides through planted woodland interspersed with the occasional patch of original forest.

From Nottingham's Victoria Bus Station, Stagecoach **bus** #33 runs hourly to Rufford and Edwinstowe, from where it travels up the west side of Clumber Park en route to Worksop; ask the driver to stop at Carburton for the 2.5-mile walk to the Clumber Park NT office. The excursion is best done as a day-trip from Nottingham, though there is a **campsite** (☎01909/482303; April–Sept) in Clumber Park's walled garden, a few minutes' walk north of the chapel.

Hardwick Hall

Born the daughter of a minor Derbyshire squire, Elizabeth, Countess of Shrewsbury (1527–1608) – aka **Bess of Hardwick** – became one of the leading figures of Elizabethan England, renowned for her political and business acumen. She also had a penchant for building and her major achievement, **Hardwick Hall** (April–Oct: house Wed, Thurs, Sat & Sun 12.30–4.30pm, gardens Wed–Sun 11am–5.30pm; house & gardens £7.20, gardens only £3.90; NT), begun when she was 62, has survived in amazingly good condition. The house was the epitome of fashionable taste, a balance of symmetry and ingenious detail in which the rectangular lines of the building are offset by line upon line of window – there's actually more glass than stone – whilst up above, her giant-sized initials (E.S.) hog every roof-line.

Inside, on the top floor, the **High Great Chamber**, where Bess received her most distinguished guests, boasts an extraordinary plaster frieze, a brightly painted, finely worked affair celebrating the goddess Diana, the virgin huntress – it was, of course, designed to please the Virgin Queen herself. Next door, the **Long Gallery** is simply breathtaking, like an indoor cricket pitch only with exquisite furnishings and fittings from the splendid chimneypieces and tapestries through to a set of portraits, including one each of the queen and Bess. The gallery was where Bess and her chums could exercise – and keep out of the sun at a time when any hint of a tan was considered plebeian.

Outside, the **garden** makes for a pleasant wander and, beyond the ha-ha (a ditch and low wall for excluding animals), rare breeds of cattle and sheep graze the surrounding **parkland** (daily 8am–6pm; free). Finally – and rather confusingly – Hardwick Hall is next to **Hardwick Old Hall** (April–Oct Wed, Thurs, Sat & Sun 10am–6pm; £3.30; EH), Bess's previous home, but now little more than a broken-down if substantial ruin.

The easiest way to reach Hardwick is along the M1; come off at Junction #29 and follow the signs from the roundabout at the top of the slip road – a three-mile trip. Note, however, that Hardwick is not signed from the motorway itself.

Eastern Nottinghamshire

Without coal, **eastern Nottinghamshire** escaped the heavy-duty industrialization that fell upon its county neighbours in the late nineteenth century. It remains a largely rural area today, its undulating farmland, punctuated by dozens of pint-sized villages, rolling seamlessly over to the River Trent, the boundary with Lincolnshire. By and large, it's a prosperous part of the county and by no means unpleasant, but for the casual visitor the attractions are distinctly low-key, being essentially confined to **Southwell** and **Newark**, both of which are easy to reach by public transport from Nottingham.

Southwell

SOUTHWELL, some fourteen miles northeast of Nottingham, is a sedate backwater distinguished by **Southwell Minster** (Mon–Sat 8am–7pm or dusk, Sun same hours, depending on services; £3 suggested donation), whose twin towers are visible for miles around, and the fine Georgian mansions facing it along Church Street. The Normans built the minster at the beginning of the twelfth century and, although some elements were added later, their design predominates, from the imposing west towers through to the dog-tooth decoration of the doorways and the bull's-eye windows of the clerestory. Inside, the proud and forceful Norman **nave** ends abruptly at the transepts with the inelegance of a fourteenth-century rood screen, beyond which lies the Early English **choir** and the extraordinary **chapter house**. The latter is embellished with naturalistic foliage dating from the late thirteenth century, some of the earliest carving of its type in England.

Snacks and light **meals** are served at the minster's café, in the modern annexe near the entrance (Mon–Sat 9.30am–5pm & Sun noon–5pm). Regular NCT buses run from outside Nottingham's post office, on Queen Street, to South-well, and onto Newark.

Newark

From Southwell, it's eight miles east to **NEWARK**, an amiable old river port and market town that was once a major staging point on the Great North Road. Fronting the town as you approach from the west are the gaunt riverside ruins of **Newark Castle** (daily dawn–dusk; free), all that's left of the mighty medieval fortress that was pounded to pieces during the Civil War by the Parliamentar-ians. From here, it's a couple of minutes walk through to the **Market Place**, an expansive square framed by attractive Georgian and Victorian facades and home to the mostly thirteenth-century church of **St Mary Magdalene** (Mon–Sat 8.30am–4.30pm, May–Sept also Sun 2–4.30pm). It's a handsome church, with a massive spire (236ft) towering over the town centre, and a well-proportioned nave cheered by some brightly restored roof paintings and a fancy reredos. Look out also for a pair of medieval *Dance of Death* **panel paintings** behind the reredos in the choir's Markham Chantry Chapel. One panel has a well-to-do man slipping his hand into his purse, the other shows a carnation-carrying skeleton pointing to the grave – an obvious reminder to the observer of his or her mortality.

Practicalities

Newark is on the Nottingham–Lincoln line with **trains** stopping at **Newark Castle train station**, on the west side of the River Trent, a five-minute walk from both the castle and the adjacent **tourist office**, on Castlegate (daily 9am–5pm; ℡01636/655765). The larger **Newark train station** is on the main London to Edinburgh line, and is located on Lincoln Road, off Northgate, a ten-minute walk from the tourist office. There is also a regular **bus** service from Nottingham to Newark via Southwell, with buses pulling into Newark **bus station**, on Lombard Street; from here it is a five-minute walk north along Castlegate to the tourist office.

For **food**, make for the excellent *Gannets*, 35 Castlegate (Mon–Fri 9am–4pm, Sat 9am–5pm & Sun 9.30am–4pm), an astoundingly good coffee bar serving daytime snacks and meals. Alternatively, the superb *Café Bleu*, opposite at 14 Castlegate (℡01636/610141; closed Sun eve), is a brilliant French restaurant dishing up top-class meals from an inventive menu (main courses average £10–14). It's one of the best restaurants in the county, with appealing decor, an outside terrace and frequent live jazz.

Leicestershire and Rutland

The compact county of **Leicestershire** is one of the more anonymous of the English shires, though **Leicester** itself is saved from mediocrity by its role as a focal point for Britain's Asian community. The county's rolling landscapes are blemished by a series of industrial settlements, though things pick up markedly at **Ashby-de-la-Zouch**, a pleasing little town graced by the substantial remains of its medieval castle. To the east of Leicestershire lies England's smallest county, **Rutland**, with two places of note – **Oakham**, the county town, and **Upping-ham**, both rural centres with some elegant Georgian architecture.

Leicester and around

At first glance, **LEICESTER** seems a resolutely modern city, but further inspection reveals traces of its medieval and Roman past, situated immediately to the west of the downtown shopping area near the River Soar. The Romans developed Leicester's precursor, Ratae Coritanorum, as a fortified town on the Fosse Way, the military road running from Lincoln to Cirencester, and the **Emperor Hadrian** kitted it out with huge public buildings. Since the late seventeenth century, Leicester has been a centre of the hosiery trade and it was this industry that attracted hundreds of Asian immigrants to settle here in the 1950s and 1960s. Today, about a third of Leicester's population is **Asian** and the city elected England's first Asian MP, Keith Vaz, in 1987. Leicester's Hindus celebrate two massive autumn **festivals**, Navrati and Diwali, while the city's sizeable Afro-Caribbean community holds England's second-biggest street festival (after London's Notting Hill Carnival), the Leicester Caribbean Carnival (Ⓦ www.lccarnival.org.uk), on the first weekend in August.

Arrival, information and accommodation

Leicester **train station**, with links to London's St Pancras Station, is on London Road, southeast of the city centre. **St Margaret's bus station** is on the north side of the centre, just off Gravel Street. The centre is signed from both, with the large Haymarket Shopping Centre an easy landmark between the two. The **tourist office** is a short walk to the south of the Haymarket at 7–9 Every St, on Town Hall Square (Mon–Wed & Fri 9am–5.30pm, Thurs 10am–5.30pm, Sat 9am–5pm; premium-rate line Ⓣ 0906/294 1113, Ⓦ www.goleicestershire.com).

With other more enticing cities nearby, there's no strong reason to overnight here, but Leicester does have a good crop of business **hotels** offering substantial discounts at weekends, such as the *Best Western Belmont House Hotel*, De Montfort Steet (Ⓣ 0116/254 4773, Ⓦ www.belmonthotel.co.uk; ⑥), a chain hotel in a modernized and extended Georgian property about 300 yards south of the train station. Alternatively, there's the *Holiday Inn*, 129 St Nicholas Circle (Ⓣ 0870/4009048, Ⓦ www.holiday-inn.com/Leicester; ⑥), a smart chain hotel, which manages to overcome its unfortunate location in the middle of the ring road by creating a relaxed and self-enclosed environment, with comfortable rooms, indoor pool and extensive fitness facilities. There's also no shortage of competitively priced **B&Bs**, though most are out of the centre; the tourist office has a substantial list, but you're unlikely to have problems finding somewhere, other than during Navrati and Diwali.

The city centre

The most conspicuous building in Leicester's crowded centre is undoubtedly the large, modern **Haymarket Shopping Centre**, but the proper landmark is the Victorian **clocktower** of 1868, standing in front of the Haymarket and marking the spot where seven streets meet. One of the seven is Cheapside, which leads in a few yards to Leicester's famous open-air produce **market** (Mon–Sat), where the young Gary Lineker, now the UK's best-known football pundit, worked on the family stall. Lineker is a much-loved figure in Leicester and has been made a Freeman of the City, giving him the right to graze his sheep in front of the town hall. Another of the seven streets is Silver Street (subsequently Guildhall Lane), which leads to **St Martin's Cathedral**, a much modified, eleventh-century structure incorporating a fine, ornately carved medieval wooden entrance porch. Next door is the **Guildhall** (Feb–Nov Mon–Wed & Sat 11am–4.30pm, Sun 1–4.30pm; free), a half-timbered building that has served, variously, as the town hall, prison and police station.

West to the Jewry Wall

From the Guildhall, it's a short walk west to St Nicholas Circle, a large roundabout that is part of the ring road: take the walkway round it to the right, and on the right behind the church is the **Jewry Wall**, a chunk of Roman masonry some 18ft high and 73ft long that was originally part of Hadrian's public baths. Hadrian's grand scheme was spoilt, however, by engineers miscalculating the line of the aqueduct that was to pipe in the water, so bathers had to rely on a hand-filled cistern replenished from the river. The adjacent **Jewry Wall Museum** (Jan–Nov Sat & Sun 11am–4.30pm; free) charts Leicester's history from prehistoric to medieval times, with the most interesting artefacts being a hotchpotch of Roman finds from Fosse Way milestones to mosaics.

South to New Walk Museum and Art Gallery

From the city centre, it's about ten minutes' walk south to Leicester's best museum, the recently refurbished **New Walk Museum and Art Gallery**, on New Walk (Mon–Sat 10am–5pm, Sun 11–5pm; free), a pedestrianized promenade that runs out from the centre to Victoria Park. The museum covers a lot of ground, from the natural world to geology and beyond, but its highlight is an extensive collection of Ancient Egyptian artefacts, featuring mummies and hieroglyphic tablets brought back to Leicester in the 1880s. Its enjoyable collection of paintings includes works by British artists such as Hogarth, Francis Bacon, Stanley Spencer and Lowry as well as a whole raft of mawkishly romantic Victorian paintings, such as Charles Green's *The Girl I Left Behind Me* (1880). Furthermore there's an outstanding collection of German Expressionist works, mostly sketches, woodcuts and lithographs by the likes of Otto Dix and George Grosz.

Belgrave

Beginning about a mile to the northeast of the centre, the cramped terraced houses of the **Belgrave** neighbourhood are the focus of Leicester's Asian community. Both Belgrave Road and its northerly continuation, Melton Road, are lined with Indian and Pakistani goldsmiths and jewellers, sari shops, Hindi music stores and curry houses. It's never dull down here, but Sunday afternoons are particularly enjoyable, when locals stroll the streets in their finest gear. Belgrave is at the heart of Leicester's celebrations during the two major Hindu festivals: **Diwali**, the Festival of Light, held in October or November, when six thousand lamps are strung out along the Belgrave Road and 20,000 people come to watch the switch-on alone; and **Navrati**, an eight-day celebration in October held in honour of the goddess Ambaji.

Eating, drinking and entertainment

People come from miles around to eat at the **Indian restaurants** along Belgrave Road. The best are clustered at the start of the road, just beyond the flyover to the northeast of the centre, and it's here you'll find the most famous, 🍴 *Bobby's*, at no. 154–156 (☎0116/266 0106). Run by Gujaratis, this bright and modern restaurant and takeaway is strictly vegetarian and uses no garlic or onions; try its delicious house speciality, the multi-flavoured Bobby's Special Chaat for just £4.50. Alternatively, the *Sayonara Thali*, at no. 49 (☎0116/266 5888), specializes in set thali meals, with several different dishes, breads and pickles served together on large steel plates; while the *Chaat House*, opposite at no. 108 (☎0116/266 0513), does wonderful masala dosas and other South Indian snacks – legendary cricket captain Kapil Dev and his Indian team ate here when they were on tour. The best restaurant in the city centre is the *Opera House*, 10 Guildhall Lane (☎0116/223 6666), in lovely old premises and with an imaginative menu featuring dishes such as ravioli with wild mushrooms (mains courses from £13–20). For a light **snack** or lunch, the *Almeida* coffee bar (Mon–Sat 8.30am–6pm) is just across Guildhall Lane from the *Opera House*.

Leicester's excellent Phoenix Arts Centre, in the city centre on Newarke Street (☎0116/255 4854, ⓦwww.phoenix.org.uk), features a first-rate mix of comedy, **music**, **theatre** and dance, whilst doubling up as an independent **cinema**.

Around Leicester

Give or take the odd industrial blip, most of **Leicestershire** is rural, its small towns and villages dotted over undulating countryside. The key attractions here, which are both best visited as day-trips, are the castle at **Ashby-de-la-Zouch**, and the hilltop church at **Breedon-on-the-Hill**.

Ashby-de-la-Zouch

ASHBY-DE-LA-ZOUCH, fourteen miles northwest of Leicester, takes its fanciful name from two sources – the town's first Norman overlord was Alain de Parrhoet la Souche and the rest means "place by the ash trees". Nowadays, Ashby is far from rustic, but it's still an amiable little place with its principal attraction, the **castle** (April–June & Sept–Oct Thurs–Mon 10am–5pm; July & Aug daily 10am–6pm; Nov–March Thurs–Mon 10am–4pm; £3.30; EH) standing just off the town's main drag, Market Street. Its rambling ruins include substantial sections of the old medieval fortifications, though the star turn is the hundred-foot-high **Hastings Tower**, a self-contained four-storey stronghold which once provided a secure inner fastness for its lord.

Regular **buses** serve Ashby from Leicester (1hr) and Nottingham (2hr), arriving on Market Street, but all are indirect, requiring a change of bus.

Breedon-on-the-Hill

It's five miles northeast from Ashby to the village of **BREEDON-ON-THE-HILL**, which sits in the shadow of the large, partly quarried hill from which it takes its name. A steep footpath and a winding, half-mile lane lead up from the village to the summit, where the fascinating church of **St Mary and St Hardulph** (daily 9.30am–6.30pm or dusk; free) occupies the site of an Iron Age hillfort and an eighth-century Anglo-Saxon monastery. Mostly dating from the thirteenth century, the church is kitted out with Georgian pulpit and pews as well as a large and distinctly rickety box pew. Much rarer are a number of **Anglo-Saxon carvings**, both individual saints and prophets and wall friezes, where a dense foliage of vines is inhabited by a tangle of animals and humans. The friezes are quite extraordinary, and the fact that the figures look Byzantine rather than Anglo-Saxon has fuelled much academic debate. The church has something else too, in the form of a set of fine alabaster tombs occupied by members of the Shirley family, who long ruled the local roost. One is an especially imposing affair with the kneeling family up above and a skeleton down below.

Rutland

Reinstated in 1997 as England's smallest county following 23 unpopular years of merger with its larger neighbour, Rutland boasts more gentle scenery and a brace of pleasant little towns – **Oakham** and **Uppingham**. Oakham is easily reached on the Leicester–Peterborough **train** line, or by regular **bus**, and there's an hourly bus service linking Oakham and Uppingham.

Oakham

Some twenty miles east of Leicester, well-heeled **OAKHAM** is Rutland's county town. It has a long history as a commercial centre, its prosperity bolstered by Oakham School, a late sixteenth-century foundation that's now one of the country's more exclusive private schools. The town's stone terraces and Georgian villas are too often interrupted by the mundanely modern to assume much grace, but Oakham does have its architectural merits – particularly in the L-shaped **Market Place**, where a brace of sturdy awnings shelter the old water pump and town stocks. A few steps from the north side of the Market Place stands **Oakham Castle** (Mon–Sat 10.30am–1pm & 1.30–5pm, Sun 2–4pm; free), comprising a banqueting hall that was originally part of a fortified house dating back to 1191. Surrounded by the grassy banks of what was once a motte and bailey castle, the hall is a good example of Norman domestic architecture, and inside the whitewashed walls are covered with horseshoes, the result of an ancient custom by which every lord or lady, king or queen, is obliged to present an ornamental horseshoe when they first set foot in the town.

Oakham School is housed in a series of impressive ironstone buildings that frame the west edge of the Market Place. On the right-hand side of the school, a narrow lane allows you to see a little more of the buildings on the way to **All Saints' church**, whose heavy tower and spire rise high above the town. Dating from the thirteenth century, the church is an architectural hybrid, but the airy interior is distinguished by the intense medieval carvings along the columns of the nave and choir, with Christian scenes and symbols set alongside dragons, grotesques, devils and demons.

Practicalities

With regular services from Leicester, Melton Mowbray and Peterborough, Oakham **train station** lies on the west side of town, five minutes' walk from the Market Place. **Buses** connect the town with Leicester, Nottingham and Melton Mowbray, and arrive on John Street, west of the Market Place. A thorough exploration of Oakham only takes an hour or so, but if you do decide to stay, the best **hotel** in town is the distinctive *Lord Nelson's House*, 11 Market Place (℡01572/723199, ⊛www.nelsons-house.com; ❺), with a handful of bedrooms decorated in Nelson–period style. The hotel's excellent and affordable **restaurant** *Nicks* (closed Sun & Mon) is also the best place to eat, with a tasty modern menu featuring local ingredients. For a drink, the *Wheatsheaf* is a traditional **pub** with a good range of beers (and a garden) across from All Saints' church at 2–4 Northgate.

Uppingham

The town of **UPPINGHAM**, seven miles south of Oakham, has the uniformity of style Oakham lacks, its narrow, meandering High Street flanked by bow-fronted shops and ironstone houses, mostly dating from the eighteenth century. It's the general appearance that pleases, rather than any individual sight, but the town is famous as the home of **Uppingham School**, a bastion of privilege whose imposing fortress-like building stands at the west end of the High Street. Founded in 1587, the school was distinctly second-rate until the middle of the nineteenth century, when a dynamic headmaster, the Reverend Edward Thring, grabbed enough land to lay out some of the biggest playing-fields in England – fitness being, of course, an essential attribute for the rulers of the British Empire.

Uppingham has one especially good **hotel**, the *Lake Isle*, in a tastefully modernized eighteenth-century town house at 16 High St East (☎01572/822951, Ⓦwww.lakeislehotel.com; ❺). The hotel **restaurant** is outstanding too, offering a superb and varied menu from guinea fowl to local venison, with main courses averaging around £15. For a **drink**, head for *The Vaults*, on the tiny Market Place.

Northamptonshire

Northamptonshire is one of the region's most diverse counties – so diverse in fact that even many Midlanders can't recall what is actually in it and what isn't. Even so, its superabundance of stately homes and historic churches has given it the tag of "County of Spires and Squires" and there's also a good scattering of charming unspoilt villages, the most picturesque of which are built of local limestone. By contrast, however, three of the county's four big towns – Wellingborough, Corby and Kettering – are primarily industrial and whatever charms they offer to their inhabitants, there's not much to attract the regular tourist. Yet the fourth town, **Northampton**, does something to bridge the gap, its busy centre possessed of several fine old buildings and an excellent museum devoted to shoe-making, the industry that long made the place tick.

Gentle hills, farmland and patchy woodland stretch right across the county, whose prime tourist attraction is **Althorp**, family home of the Spencers and the burial place of Diana, Princess of Wales. East Northamptonshire's star turn is the good-looking country town of **Oundle**, which makes the best base for visiting the delightful hamlet of **Fotheringhay**.

Getting to Northampton by **public transport** is no problem, but to reach the villages and stately homes, you'll mostly need your own vehicle – or some careful planning around patchy bus services.

Northampton

Spreading north from the banks of the River Nene, **NORTHAMPTON** is a workaday modern town whose appearance largely belies its ancient past.

Throughout the Middle Ages, this was one of central England's most important towns, a flourishing commercial centre whose now-demolished castle was a popular stopping-off point for travelling royalty. A fire in 1675 burnt most of the medieval city to a cinder, and the Georgian town that grew up in its stead was itself swamped by the industrial revolution, when Northampton swarmed with boot- and shoemakers. Their products shod almost everyone in the Empire – from Australia to Canada – as well as the British army.

Northampton's compact **centre** is at its most appealing on and around its main plaza, Market Square, which is where you'll find the town's finest buildings, notably All Saints' church and the Guildhall. Half a day is enough for a quick gambol round the sights, but if you're tempted to stay the night there's a reasonable supply of hotel accommodation and a scattering of B&Bs. The only times of the year when finding a room can be difficult are during the annual **Balloon Festival** (ⓦwww.northamptonballoonfestival.com) in August, which attracts thousands of visitors, and over the weekend of the British Grand Prix, held in July at the nearby **Silverstone** race track (ⓦwww.silverstone-circuit.co.uk).

The Town

Northampton's expansive, cobbled **Market Square** has a bustling, self-confident air, its sides flanked by a comparatively harmonious mixture of the old and the new. From here, either of a couple of narrow lanes leads through to the church of **All Saints** (Mon–Sat 9am–2pm; free), whose unusually secular appearance stems from its finely proportioned, pillared portico as well as its towered cupola. A statue of a bewigged Charles II in Roman attire surmounts the portico, a (flattering) thank-you for his donation of a thousand tons of timber after the Great Fire of 1675 had incinerated the earlier church.

Behind the church is one of Lutyens' less-inspiring monuments, a plain, blunt **war memorial** dating from 1926, and, just beyond that, in St Giles' Square, is the **Guildhall**, a flamboyant Victorian edifice constructed in the 1860s to a design by Edward Godwin. Godwin was one of the period's most inventive architects and his Gothic exterior, with its high-pointed windows and dinky turrets and towers, sports kings and queens plus scenes central to the county's history – look out for Mary, Queen of Scots' execution and the Great Fire.

The **Northampton Museum and Art Gallery** (Mon–Sat 10am–5pm, Sun 2–5pm; free), a few metres south of the Guildhall on Guildhall Road, celebrates the town's industrial heritage with a fabulous collection of **shoes**. Along with silk slippers, clogs and high-heeled nineteenth-century court shoes, there's one of the four boots worn by an elephant during the British Expedition of 1959, which retraced Hannibal's putative route over the Alps into Italy. There's celebrity footwear too, including the giant DMs Elton John wore in *Tommy*, plus whole cabinets of heavy-duty riding boots, pearl-inlaid raised wooden sandals from Ottoman Turkey, and a couple of cabinets showing just how long high heels have been in fashion.

A fine example of the work of celebrated Scottish architect **Charles Rennie Mackintosh** (1868–1928) can be seen at **78 Derngate** (late March to Nov Wed–Sun 10.30am–5pm; admission by pre-booked, timed entry only; £5.50; ℡01604/603407, ⓦwww.78derngate.org.uk), a five-minute walk southeast of the Guildhall. Mackintosh spent much of 1916–17 here in Northampton remodelling the house as the first home of two well–heeled newlyweds, Florence and Wenman Bassett-Lowke. The house bears all the Mackintosh hallmarks of strong, almost stern, right angles set against the flowing lines of floral-influenced decorative motifs, though there is some debate as to how much is actually the work of Mackintosh, and how much was down to his collaborator on the project, local architect Alexander Ellis Anderson.

Practicalities

From Northampton **train station**, which has regular services from Birmingham and London Euston, it's a ten-minute walk east to the Market Square. Buses pull into the **bus station** on Lady's Lane, behind the hideous Grosvenor Shopping Centre, immediately to the north of the Market Square; motorists aiming for the centre should park at the Grosvenor. The helpful **tourist office** is in the Guildhall, on St Giles' Square (Mon–Sat 10am–5pm; ☎01604/838800, ⓦwww.explorenorthamptonshire.co.uk).

For **accommodation**, the *Best Western Lime Trees Hotel*, 8 Langham Place, Barrack Road (☎01604/632188, ⓦwww.limetreeshotel.co.uk; ❺), occupies attractive Georgian premises a little more than half a mile north of the centre on the A508. One of the best **restaurants** in town is *Los Pintores*, almost opposite the museum at 21A Guildhall Rd (☎01604/632255; closed Sun & Mon), where they serve a wide range of Mediterranean dishes, as well as fish and chips, for about £10 in the evening (£5 at lunchtime).

The rest of Northamptonshire

The rolling countryside around **Northampton** is dotted with stately homes, of which the most diverting is **Althorp**, the last resting place of Diana, Princess of Wales. The county also boasts a string of postcard-pretty limestone villages amongst which **Oundle**, about 25 miles northeast of Northampton, is the most diverting, with historic **Fotheringhay**, a few miles further along the river, running a close second.

Althorp

Some six miles northwest of Northampton off the A428, the ritzy mansion of **Althorp** (July–Sept daily 11am–5pm, last admission 4pm; £12; ☎01604/770107,

△ Althorp

@ www.althorp.com; advance reservations advised) is the focus of the Spencer estate. The Spencers have lived here for centuries, but this was no big deal until one of the tribe, **Diana**, married Prince Charles in 1981. The disintegration of the marriage and Diana's elevation to sainthood is a story known to millions. The public outpouring of grief following Diana's death in 1997 was quite astounding, and Althorp became the focus of massive media attention as the coffin was brought up the M1 motorway from London to be buried on an island in the grounds of the family estate. Today, visitors troop round the **Diana exhibition**, in the old stable block, as well as the adjacent Althorp house, where there's a large collection of priceless paintings, including works by Gainsborough, Van Dyck and Rubens. From the house, a footpath leads round a lake in the middle of which is the islet (no access) where Diana is buried.

There are no scheduled **buses** from Northampton to Althorp, but there are sometimes special coaches; Northampton tourist office (see p.495) has details.

Oundle

Arguably Northamptonshire's prettiest town, pocket-sized **Oundle** slopes up gently from the River Nene, its congregation of old limestone houses zeroing in on the congenial **Market Place**. Preserving much of its medieval layout, Oundle boasts some of the finest seventeenth- and eighteenth-century streetscapes in the Midlands, and is a suitably exclusive setting for one of England's better-known private schools, **Oundle School**. Above all it's the general appearance of the place that appeals rather than anything in particular, the exception being the parish church of **St Peter**, whose magnificent two-hundred-foot Decorated spire soars high above the centre, though the interior – give or take the odd stained-glass window – is unremarkable.

Buses from Peterborough and Northampton stop on the Market Place, a short walk from the **tourist office**, at 14 West St (Mon–Sat 9am–5pm, Sun 1–4pm; Sept–Easter closed Sun; ☎01832/274333). The best place **to stay** in town is the seventeenth-century *Talbot Hotel*, just along from the Market Place on New Street (☎01832/273621, @ www.thetalbot-oundle.com; ❻), with 35 plush bedrooms. The hotel's oak staircase was brought here from Fotheringhay Castle (see below) and is thought to be the one that Mary, Queen of Scots, walked down on her way to her execution. Alternatively, there's the immaculate *Ashworth House*, a modest little stone guest house, five minutes' walk from the Market Place at 75 West St (☎01832/275312, @ www.ashworthhouse.co.uk; ❸). The best place for a sit-down **meal** is the *Talbot*, while takeaway baguettes and sandwiches can be bought at *Trendalls* (closed Sun), on the Market Place.

Fotheringhay

Nestling by the River Nene just four miles northeast of Oundle, the tiny hamlet of **FOTHERINGHAY** is home to the magnificent church of **St Mary and All Saints** (dawn–dusk; free), which rises mirage-like above the green riverine meadows. Begun in 1411 and a hundred and fifty years in the making, the church is a paradigm of the Perpendicular, its exterior sporting wonderful arching buttresses, its nave lit by soaring windows and the whole caboodle topped by a splendid octagonal lantern tower. The interior is a tad bare, but there are two fancily carved medieval pieces to inspect – a painted pulpit and a sturdy stone font.

Fotheringhay **castle** witnessed two key events – the birth of Richard III in 1452 and the beheading of Mary, Queen of Scots, in 1587. On the orders of Elizabeth I, Mary was executed in the castle's Great Hall with no one to stand in her defence – apart, that is, from her dog, who is said to have rushed from beneath her skirts as her head dropped off. Not long afterwards, the castle fell into disrepair and nowadays only a grassy **mound** and ditch remain to mark its position; it's signposted down a short and narrow lane on the bend of the road as you come into the village from Oundle.

Fotheringhay has an excellent **pub-restaurant**, *The Falcon* (℡01832/226254), in a neat stone building with a modern patio; its imaginative menu features delicious dishes such as lamp chump and artichoke for around £12.

Lincolnshire

The obvious place to start a visit to **Lincolnshire** is **Lincoln** itself, an old and easy-paced city whose cathedral, the third largest in England, remains the county's outstanding attraction. Northeast and east of here, the Lincolnshire **Wolds** band the county, their gentle green hills harbouring the pleasant market town of **Louth**, where conscientious objectors were sent to dig potatoes during World War II. The Wolds are flanked by the coast, so different from the rest of Lincolnshire, its brashness encapsulated by the resort of **Skegness**, though there are unspoilt stretches, too, most notably at the **Gibraltar Point Nature Reserve**.

Beguiling **Stamford**, in the southwest corner of the county, makes an alternative base: it's an attractive town whose narrow streets are flanked by a handsome ensemble of antique stone buildings, and has on its doorstep one of the great monuments of Elizabethan England, **Burghley House**. From here, it's a short hop east into **The Fens**, where you'll find some of the county's most imposing medieval **churches.** The most exquisite, however, is **St Botolph's** in the old fenland port of **Boston**, Lincolnshire's second town.

Lincoln is the hub of the county's limited **rail** network, with regular services east to Boston and Skegness and west to Newark, in Nottinghamshire. In addition, reasonable **bus** services run between Lincoln and the county's larger market towns, like Louth and Boston, but you'll struggle to get to the villages without your own transport. For **information** on all aspects of the county, check the Lincolnshire tourist board's website (Ⓦwww.visitlincolnshire.com).

Lincoln

Reaching high into the sky from the top of a steep hill, the triple towers of the mighty cathedral of **LINCOLN** are visible for miles across the flatlands. This conspicuous spot was first fortified by the Celts, who called their settlement Lindon, "hillfort by the lake", a reference to the pools formed by the River Witham in the marshy ground below. In 47 AD the Romans occupied Lindon and built a fortified town, which subsequently became, as Lindum Colonia, one of the four regional capitals of Roman Britain.

Today, only fragments of the Roman city survive, mostly pieces of the third-century town wall, and these are outdone by reminders of Lincoln's medieval heyday, which began during the reign of William the Conqueror with the

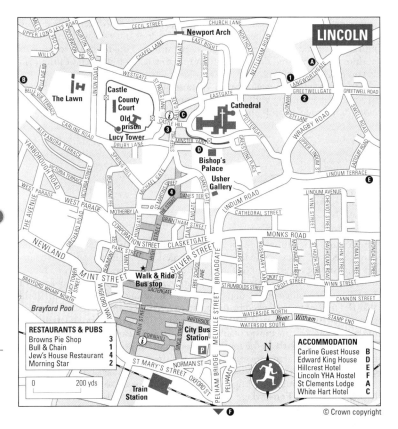

Newport Arch

LINCOLN

The Lawn
Castle
County
Court
Old
prison
Lucy Tower

Cathedral

Bishop's
Palace

Usher
Gallery

Walk & Ride
Bus stop

Brayford Pool

RESTAURANTS & PUBS
Browns Pie Shop   3
Bull & Chain   1
Jew's House Restaurant 4
Morning Star   2

City Bus
Station

River Witham

ACCOMMODATION
Carline Guest House   B
Edward King House   D
Hillcrest Hotel   E
Lincoln YHA Hostel   F
St Clements Lodge   A
White Hart Hotel   C

0   200 yds

Train
Station

© Crown copyright

construction of the **castle** and **cathedral**. Lincoln flourished, first as a Norman power-base and then as a centre of the wool trade with Flanders, until 1369, when the wool market was transferred to neighbouring Boston. It was almost five hundred years before the town revived, the recovery based upon its manufacture of agricultural machinery and drainage equipment for the surrounding fenlands. As the nineteenth-century town spread south down the hill and out along the old Roman road – the Fosse Way – so Lincoln became a place of precise class distinctions: the "**Uphill**" area, spreading north from the cathedral, became synonymous with middle-class respectability, "**Downhill**" with the proletariat. It's a distinction that remains – locals selling anything from second-hand cars to settees still put "Uphill" in brackets to signify a better quality of merchandise. For the visitor, almost everything of interest is confined to the "Uphill" part of town, and it's here you'll also find the best **pubs** and **restaurants**.

Arrival and information

Both Lincoln **train station**, on St Mary's Street, and its **bus station**, close by off Melville Street, are located "Downhill" in the city centre. From either, it's a very steep, fifteen-minute walk to the cathedral, or you can take the **Walk & Ride electric minibus** (Mon–Sat 10am–5pm & Sun noon–5pm; 3 hourly;

THE EAST MIDLANDS | Lincoln and around

498

90p each way); the nearest stop to the bus and train stations is on the High Street at the corner of Silver Street. There are two **tourist offices** (Mon–Thurs 9.30am–5.30pm, Fri 9.30am–5pm, Sat 10am–5pm; ⓦ www.lincoln .gov.uk), one on the corner of Cornhill and the High Street (☎01522/541 447), the other at 9 Castle Hill, between the cathedral and the castle (also opens Sun 10am–5pm; ☎01522/873213); both can book accommodation and guided city tours.

Accommodation

Lincoln has a good supply of competitively priced **hotels** and **B&Bs**. The best position is "Uphill", which is where all our recommendations are located, except the YHA hostel.

Carline Guest House 1–3 Carline Rd ☎01522/530422, ⓦ www.carlineguesthouse.co .uk. One of the best B&Bs in the city, *Carline* occupies a spick-and-span Edwardian house about ten minutes' walk down from the cathedral – take Drury Lane from in front of the castle and keep going. Breakfasts are first-rate, and the rooms smart and tastefully furnished. No credit cards. ❸
Edward King House The Old Palace, Minster Yard ☎01522/528778, ⓦ www.ekhs.org.uk. A distinctive B&B in a former residence of the bishops of Lincoln, immediately below the cathedral. The setting, especially the echoing entrance hall, is much grander than the rooms, where the furniture is antiquated and the beds pretty basic, but the place is cheap and some of the bedrooms have pleasing views over the medieval Bishop's Palace. ❷
Hillcrest Hotel 15 Lindum Terrace ☎01522/510182, ⓦ www.hillcrest-hotel.com. Traditional, very English hotel in a large red-brick house that was originally a Victorian rectory. Sixteen comfortable rooms with all mod cons plus a large, sloping garden. About ten minutes' walk from the cathedral, and with a helpful owner. ❺

Lincoln YHA Hostel 77 South Park ☎0870/770 5918, ⓔ lincoln@yha.org.uk. The town's YHA hostel occupies a Victorian house beside South Common park, one mile south of the train station. Beds are in two- to ten-bed rooms; there is cycle storage, laundry facilities and a self-catering kitchen. To get there from the centre, head south along Pelham Bridge and its continuation Canwick Road, and South Park is on the right nearly opposite the cemetery. Doubles ❶, dorm beds £11.
St Clements Lodge 21 Langworthgate ☎01522/521532. In a brisk, modern house a short walk from the cathedral, this comfortable and friendly B&B has three pleasant, en-suite rooms. No credit cards. ❸
White Hart Hotel Bailgate ☎01522/526222, ⓦ www.whitehart-lincoln.co.uk. Antique former coaching inn with charming public rooms, all hidden nooks and crannies. The bedrooms are not quite as distinctive, but they're comfortable enough and many overlook the cathedral. Great Uphill location. Weekend deals can slash the normal price. Breakfast not included. ❺

The Cathedral and Bishop's Palace

Not a hill at all, the charming **Castle Hill** is a wide, short and level cobbled street that links Lincoln's castle and cathedral. Its east end is marked by the arches of the medieval **Exchequergate**, beyond which soars the glorious west front of **Lincoln Cathedral** (May–Sept Mon–Sat 7.15am–8pm, Sun 7.15am–6pm; Oct–April Mon–Sat 7am–6pm, Sun 7.15am–5pm, except during services when access is restricted; £4 including guided tour – see box below), a sheer cliff-face of blind arcading mobbed by decorative carving. Most striking of all is the extraordinary band of twelfth-century carved panels that depict biblical themes with passionate intimacy, their inspiration being a similar frieze at Modena cathedral in Italy. The west front's apparent homogeneity is, however, deceptive, and further inspection reveals two phases of construction – the small stones and thick mortar of much of the facade belong to the original church, completed in 1092, whereas the longer stones and finer courses date from the early thirteenth century. These were enforced modifications, for in 1185 an earthquake shattered much of the Norman church, which was then rebuilt under the auspices of **Bishop Hugh of Avalon**, the man responsible for most of the present cathedral.

The cavernous **interior** is a fine example of Early English architecture, with the nave's pillars conforming to the same general design yet differing slightly, their varied columns and bands of dark Purbeck marble contrasting with the oolitic limestone that is the building's main material. Looking back up the nave from beneath the **central tower**, you can also see a major medieval miscalculation: Bishop Hugh's roof is out of alignment with the earlier west front, and the point where they meet has all the wrong angles. It's possible to pick out other irregularities, too – the pillars have bases of different heights, and there are ten windows in the nave's north wall and nine in the south – but these are deliberate features, reflecting a medieval aversion to the vanity of symmetry.

Beyond the rood screen lies **St Hugh's Choir**, its fourteenth-century misericords carrying an eccentric range of carvings, with scenes from the life of Alexander the Great and King Arthur mixed up with biblical characters and folkloric parables. Further on is the open and airy **Angel Choir**, completed in 1280 and dotted with stone table-tombs, its roof embellished by dozens of finely carved statuettes, including the tiny **Lincoln Imp** (see p.501). Finally, a corridor off the choir's north aisle leads to the wooden-roofed **cloisters** and the polygonal **Chapter House**, where Edward I and Edward II convened gatherings that pre-figured the creation of the English Parliament.

The Castle

From the west front of the cathedral, it's a quick stroll along Castle Hill to **Lincoln Castle** (April–Sept Mon–Sat 9.30am–5.30pm, Sun 11am–5.30pm; Oct–March Mon–Sat 9.30am–4pm, Sun 11am–4pm; £3.70). Intact and forbidding, the **castle walls** incorporate bits and pieces from the twelfth to the nineteenth centuries. and the wall walkway offers great views over town. The castle wall also encloses a large central courtyard, where the dour red-brick former prison holds one of the four surviving copies of the **Magna Carta** (see p.1143) as well as a truly remarkable **prison chapel**. Here, the prisoners were locked in high-sided cubicles, where they could see the preacher and his pulpit but not their fellow internees. Neither was this approach just applied to chapel visits: the prisoners were kept in perpetual solitary confinement, and were compelled to wear masks when they took to the exercise yard. This system was founded on the pseudo-scientific theory that defined crime as a contagious disease, but unfortunately for the theorists, their so-called Pentonville System of "Separation and Silence", which was introduced here in 1846, drove many prisoners crazy, and it had to be abandoned thirty years later; nobody ever bothered to dismantle the chapel.

The rest of the city

As for the rest of **"Uphill" Lincoln**, it's scattered with historic remains, notably several chunks of Roman wall, the most prominent of which is the second-century **Newport Arch** straddling Bailgate and once the main north gate into the city. There's also a bevy of medieval stone houses, at their best on and around the aptly named **Steep Hill** as it cuts down from the cathedral to the city centre. In particular, look out for the tidily restored twelfth-century **Jew's House**, a reminder of the Jewish community that flourished in medieval Lincoln. A rare and superb example of domestic Norman architecture, it now houses the *Jew's House Restaurant* (see below).

Set within steeply sloping gardens, below the Bishop's Palace, the **Usher Gallery** (daily 10am–5pm; free) has a diverse permanent collection, whose highlights include some fine paintings of the cathedral and its environs by William Logsdail (1859–1944), and a *Lincoln* view by Lowry. The gallery also displays an eclectic collection of coins, porcelain, and seventeenth-century watches and clocks. The timepieces were given to the gallery by James Ward Usher, a local jeweller and watchmaker who made a fortune by devising the legend of the **Lincoln Imp**. He then sold little trinkets and novelties of the imp with such success that it became the city's emblem. The legend has a couple of imps hopping around the cathedral, until one of them is turned to stone for trying to talk to the angels carved into the roof of the Angel Choir. His chum made a hasty exit on the back of a witch, but the wind is still supposed to haunt the cathedral, awaiting their return.

Eating and drinking

Lincoln has no shortage of routine **cafés** and **restaurants**, plus a couple of top-quality places that use local ingredients whenever possible: ⚲ *Browns Pie Shop*, at 33 Steep Hill (☎01522/527330), is not a pie shop at all, but an excellent and very informal restaurant with a creative menu; main courses average about £12, but save room for the puddings. Alternatively, there's the *Jew's House Restaurant*, just beyond the foot of Steep Hill, at 15 The Strait (☎01522/524851), which is smart and slightly more expensive.

As for **pubs**, there are a pair of amiable and traditional locals near the cathedral – the *Bull & Chain*, on Langworthgate, with a beer garden, and the *Morning Star*, close by on Greetwellgate, which serves real ales.

The Wolds and the coast

The rolling hills and gentle valleys of the **Lincolnshire Wolds**, a narrow band of chalky land running southeast from Caistor to just outside Skegness, stand out amidst the more mundane agricultural landscapes of north Lincolnshire. A string of particularly appealing valleys is concentrated in the vicinity of **Louth**, which, with its striking church and antique centre, is easily the most enticing of the region's towns – with the added advantage of being fairly close to the coast. A few miles to the south of Louth, the Wolds dip down to the fens, pancake-flat and creating a wide and deep arch around the intrusive stump of The Wash. In the other direction, east of the Wolds, lies the coast, whose bungalows, campsites and caravans are parked beside a sandy beach that extends, with a few marshy interruptions, north from **Skegness**, the main resort, to Mablethorpe and ulti-mately Cleethorpes. Near Skegness, the **Gibraltar Point Nature Reserve** is a welcome diversion from the bucket-and-spade/amusement-arcade commercialism.

Louth and around

Henry VIII described the county of Lincolnshire as "one of the most brutal and beestlie of the whole realm", his contempt based on the events of 1536, when thousands of northern peasants rebelled against his religious reforms. In Lincolnshire, this insurrection, the **Pilgrimage of Grace**, began in the northeast of the county at **LOUTH**, 23 miles from Lincoln, under the leadership of the local vicar, who was subsequently hung, drawn and quartered for his pains. There's a commemorative plaque in honour of the rebels beside Louth's church of **St James** (April to Christmas Mon–Sat 10.30am–4pm, Christmas to March Mon, Wed, Fri & Sat 8am–12.30pm; free), which is the town's one outstanding building, its soaring Perpendicular spire, buttresses, battlements and pinnacles set on a grassy knoll just to the west of the centre. The interior is delightful too, the sweeping symmetries of the nave illuminated by slender windows and capped by a handsome Georgian wooden roof decorated with dinky little angels. Finally, don't forget the café and its homemade cakes – locals set out early to get a slice of lemon-drizzle.

Next to the church, the well-tended gardens and Georgian houses of **Westgate** make it one of Louth's prettiest streets; you can grab a drink here at the antique *Wheatsheaf Inn*. Afterwards, it doesn't take long to explore the rest of the town centre, whose cramped lanes and alleys – focusing on the **Cornmarket** – are flanked by red-brick buildings mostly dating from the nineteenth century.

Practicalities

With regular weekday services from Boston and Lincoln, Louth's **bus station** is at the east end of Queen Street, a couple of minutes' walk from the Cornmarket: walk west along Queen Street and turn right onto the Market Place to get there. The **tourist office** is in the New Market Hall off Cornmarket (Mon–Sat 9am–4.30pm; ☎01507/609289). The best **hotel** by a long chalk is the excellent family-run *Priory*, Eastgate (☎01507/602930, Ⓦwww.theprioryhotel.com; ❺), in a Georgian villa dating from 1818 with extensive gardens; the hotel is located east of the centre, about ten minutes' walk from the Cornmarket, and its **restaurant**, which offers good-quality modern British cuisine with mains from about £11, is also the best place in town to eat.

Around Louth: the Saltfleetby-Theddlethorpe dunes

An enjoyable excursion from Louth along the **B1200** takes you east to the **coast** across about nine miles of fen farmland. This byroad is built over an old Roman road that was used to transport salt inland from the seashore salt pans, once a lucrative source of income for local traders. At the coast, turn right along the main A1031 and, after about half a mile, take the (poorly signed) gravel track on the left through the dunes of the **Saltfleetby–Theddlethorpe Dunes National Nature Reserve**. Comprising over five miles of sand dune, salt- and freshwater marsh, the reserve is at its prettiest in midsummer, when the dunes sprout buckthorn bushes and sea heather flowers, forming a carpet of violet spreading down towards the ocean. A network of trails navigates the dunes and lagoons, with the latter attracting hundreds of migratory wildfowl in spring and autumn.

Skegness

SKEGNESS, south along the coast from Saltfleetby-Theddlethorpe, has been a busy resort ever since the railways reached the Lincolnshire coast in 1875. Its heyday was pre-1960s, when the Brits began to take themselves off to sunnier climes, but it still attracts tens of thousands of city-dwellers who come for the wide, sandy beaches and for a host of attractions ranging from nightclubs to bowling greens. Every inch the traditional English seaside town, Skegness gets the edge over many of its rivals by keeping its beaches sparklingly clean and its parks spick-and-span. All that said, the seafront, with its rows of souvenir shops and amusement arcades, can be dismal, especially on rainy days, and you may well decide to sidestep the whole caboodle by heading south three miles along the coastal road to the **Gibraltar Point National Nature Reserve** (daily dawn–dusk; free). Here, a network of clearly signed footpaths patterns a narrow strip of salt- and freshwater marsh, sand dune and beach that attracts an inordinate number of birds, both resident and migratory.

Skegness's **bus** and **train stations** are next door to each other about ten minutes' walk from the seashore – cut across Lumley Square and go straight up the High Street to the landmark clocktower. The **tourist office** (April–Sept Mon–Fri 9.30am–4.30pm, Sat & Sun 10am–4.30pm; Oct–March Mon–Fri 9.30am–4pm; ☏01754/899887, ⓦwww.visitlincolnshire.com) is metres from the clocktower, opposite the Embassy Centre on Grand Parade. Skegness has scores of **hotels**, **B&Bs** and **guest houses**: one of the most appealing is the *Best Western Vine Hotel*, Vine Road (☏01754/610611, ⓦwww.bestwestern.co.uk; ❺), a rambling, ivy-clad old house set in its own grounds on a quiet residential street about three quarters of a mile from the clocktower.

The Lincolnshire Fens

The Lincolnshire section of **The Fens**, that great chunk of eastern England extending from Boston to Cambridge, encompasses some of the most productive farmland in Europe. With the exception of the occasional hillock, this flat, treeless terrain has been painstakingly reclaimed from the marshes and swamps that once drained into The Wash, a process that has taken almost two thousand years. In earlier times, outsiders were often amazed by the dreadful conditions hereabouts, but they did spawn the distinctive culture of the **fen slodgers**, who embanked small portions of marsh to create pastureland and fields, supplementing their diets by catching fish and fowl, and gathering reed and sedge for thatching and fuel. Their economy was threatened by the large-scale land reclamation schemes of the late fifteenth and sixteenth centuries, and time and again the fenlanders sabotaged progress by breaking down the banks and dams. But the odds were stacked against the saboteurs, and a succession of great landowners eventually drained huge tracts of the fenland; by the end of the eighteenth century the fen slodgers' way of life had all but disappeared. Nonetheless, the Lincolnshire Fens remain a distinctive area of introverted little villages, with just one significant settlement, the old port of **Boston**.

Boston

As it nears The Wash, the muddy River Witham weaves its way through **BOSTON**, England's second-largest seaport for much of the medieval period, when its flourishing economy was dependent on the wool trade with Flanders.

Local merchants decided to build a church that demonstrated their wealth, the result being the magnificent medieval church of **St Botolph**, whose 272-foot tower still presides over the town and surrounding fenland. The church was completed in the early sixteenth century, but by then Boston was in decline as trade drifted west towards the Atlantic and the Witham silted up. The town's fortunes only revived in the late eighteenth century when, after the nearby fens had been drained, it became a minor agricultural centre with a modest port that has, in recent times, been modernized for trade with the EU. A singular mix of fenland town and seaport, Boston is an unusual little place that is at its liveliest on **market days** – Wednesday and Saturday.

The Town

Mostly flanked by Victorian red-brick buildings, the mazy streets of Boston's cramped and compact centre, on the east side of the Witham, radiate out from the dishevelled **Market Place**. Just to the west looms the massive bulk of **St Botolph's** (daily 9am–4.30pm, Sun 8am–1pm; free), whose exterior masonry is embellished by the high-pointed windows and elaborate tracery of the Decorated style. Most of the structure dates from the fourteenth century, but the huge and distinctive **tower**, whose lack of a spire earned the church the nickname the "Boston Stump", is of later construction. The octagonal lantern is later still, added in the sixteenth century and graced by flying buttresses and pointy pinnacles. A tortuous 365-step spiral **staircase** (closed on Sun) leads to a balcony near the top, from where the panoramic views over Boston and the fens amply repay both the price of the ticket (£2.50) and the effort of the climb.

Down below, St Botolph's light and airy **nave** is an exercise in the Perpendicular, all soaring columns and high windows. The sheer purity of design is stunning, its virtuosity heightened by the narrowness of the annexe-like chancel and the elegance of the Decorated arch that partly screens it from view. Indeed, the chancel is comparatively dowdy, though it does boast some intriguing four-teenth-century **misericords**, bearing a lively mixture of vernacular scenes such as organ-playing bears and a pair of medieval jesters squeezing cats in imitation of bagpipes.

Practicalities

It's ten minutes' walk east from Boston **train station** to the town centre – head straight along Station Street and cross the bridge over the river. The **bus station** is also to the west of the centre, just five minutes' walk away from the Market Place on Lincoln Lane. The **tourist office** (Mon–Sat 9am–5pm; ☎01205/356656, ⊛www.boston.gov.uk) is in the Market Place beneath the Assembly Rooms, and has a list of **B&Bs**, including *Bramley House*, 267 Sleaford Rd (☎01205/354538; no cards; ❷), in an attractively converted eighteenth-century farmhouse, a mile west of town beyond the train station. Another good choice is the much-enlarged Victorian *Fairfield Guest House* at 101 London Rd (☎01205/362869; no cards; ❷), about two miles south of the centre: it has sixteen guest rooms (mostly en-suite), all decorated in bright and cheerful style.

Goodbarns Yard, north of the Stump on Wormgate, serves vast **pub meals** inside or out in the back garden overlooking the river. For tasty **snacks**, light meals and afternoon teas, head for the *Maud Foster Mill Tea Room* (Wed 10am–5pm, Sat 11am–5pm, Sun 1–5pm; also July & Aug Thurs & Fri 11am–5pm; ☎01205/352188), inside the eponymous windmill, on Willoughby Road. Built to grind corn in 1819, the windmill is still in full working order and at specified times you can inspect its grinding gears and sails; you can also buy the organic flour it churns out at the mill shop. From the Market Place, it's about ten minutes' walk along Strait Bargate and then Wide Bargate.

Stamford

STAMFORD is delightful, a handsome little limestone town of yellow-grey seventeenth- and eighteenth-century buildings edging narrow streets that slope up from the River Welland. The town's salad days were as a centre of the medieval wool trade and it was then that its wealthy merchants built its medley of stone houses and churches. Stamford was also the home of **William Cecil**, Elizabeth I's chief minister, who built his splendid mansion, **Burghley House**, close by. The town survived the collapse of the wool trade, prospering as an inland port after the Welland was made navigable to the sea in 1570, and, in the eighteenth century, as a staging point on the Great North Road from London. More recently, Stamford was designated the country's first Conservation Area in 1967.

The town centre

Above all, it's the harmony of Stamford's architecture that pleases, rather than any specific sight. There are, nevertheless, a handful of buildings of some special interest amongst the web of narrow streets that make up the town's compact centre, beginning with the **church of St Mary** (no regular opening hours), set beside a pristine close of proud Georgian buildings just above the main bridge on St Mary's Place. The church, with its splendid spire, has a small, airy interior, which incorporates the Corpus Christi chapel, whose intricately embossed, painted and panelled roof dates from the 1480s.

Across the street from St Mary's, several lanes thread up through to the carefully preserved **High Street**, from where Ironmonger Street leads north again to the wide and handsome Broad Street, the site of **Browne's Hospital** (June–Sept Sat & Sun 11am–4pm; £2.50), the most extensive of the town's almshouses, dating from the late fifteenth century. Not all of the complex is open to the public, but it's still worth visiting with the first room – the old dormitory – capped by a splendid wood-panelled ceiling. The adjacent chapel holds some delightfully folksy misericords, and upstairs, the audit room is illuminated by a handsome set of stained-glass windows.

From Browne's, it's a few paces more to Red Lion Square, which is overlooked by **All Saints'** (daily dawn–dusk; free). Several centuries in the making, this church is a happy amalgamation of Early English and Perpendicular features that takes full advantage of its position, perched on a small hillock. Entry is via the south porch, itself an ornate structure with a fine – if badly weathered – crocketted gable, and, although much of the interior is routinely Victorian, the carved capitals are of great delicacy. There's also an engaging folkloric carving of the Last Supper behind the high altar.

High Street St Martin's

Down the slope from St Mary's, across the reedy River Welland on **High Street St Martin's**, is the **George Hotel**, a splendid old coaching inn whose Georgian facade supports one end of the gallows that span the street – not a warning to criminals, but a traditional advertising hoarding. Along – and across

– the street, the plain and sombre, late fifteenth-century **church of St Martin** (daily 9.30am–4pm; free) shelters the magnificent tombs of the lords Burghley, with a recumbent William Cecil carved beneath twin canopies, holding his rod of office and with a lion at his feet. Just behind, the early eighteenth-century effigies of John Cecil and his wife show the couple as Roman aristocrats, propped up on their elbows, she to gaze at him, John to stare across the nave commandingly.

Burghley House

Burghley House (late March to Oct daily except Fri 11am–5pm; viewing by guided tours only every 10–20min, except self–guided on Sun; £8.20; Ⓦwww .burghley.co.uk), an extravagant Elizabethan mansion standing in parkland landscaped by Capability Brown, is located a mile and a half or so to the east of Stamford, either out along the Barnack Road or by footpath from High Street St Martin's. Completed in 1587 after 22 years' work, the house sports a mellow-yellow ragstone exterior, embellished by dainty cupolas, a pyramidal clocktower and skeletal balustrading, all to a plan by **William Cecil**, the shrewd and long-serving adviser to Elizabeth I.

With the notable exception of the Tudor kitchen, little remains of Burghley's Elizabethan interior. Instead, the house bears the heavy hand of John, fifth Lord Burghley, who toured France and Italy in the late seventeenth century, commissioning furniture, statuary and tapestries, as well as buying up old Florentine and Venetian paintings, such as Veronese's *Zebedee's Wife Petitioning Our Lord*. To provide a suitable setting for his old masters, John brought in Antonio Verrio and his assistant Louis Laguerre, who between them covered many of Burghley's walls and ceilings with frolicking gods and goddesses. These gaudy and gargantuan murals are at their most engulfing in the **Heaven Room**, an artfully painted classical temple that adjoins the **Hell Staircase**, where the entrance to the inferno is through the gaping mouth of a cat.

Practicalities

With frequent services from Peterborough and Oakham, Stamford **train station** is a five-minute walk across the river from the town centre, while the **bus station** is north of the river, on Sheepmarket, off All Saints' Street. The **tourist office** is in the Stamford Arts Centre at 27 St Mary's St (Mon–Sat 9.30am–5pm, April–Oct also Sun 10.30am–3.30pm; Ⓣ01780/755611, Ⓦwww .southwestlincs.com), and has a full list of Stamford's **B&Bs**, most of which are on the outskirts of town.

Stamford has several charming **hotels**, the most celebrated of which is the ⚒ *George Hotel*, 71 High Street St Martin's (Ⓣ01780/750750, Ⓦwww .georgehotelofstamford.com; ❼), a refurbished coaching inn with flagstone floors and antique furnishings, whose most appealing rooms overlook the cobbled courtyard. Further up the street, the attractive *Garden House Hotel* (Ⓣ01780/763359, Ⓦwww.gardenhousehotel.com; ❺) occupies a tastefully modernized eighteenth-century building with twenty smart bedrooms.

For food, it has to be the *George Hotel* – either in the formal and expensive **restaurant**, where the emphasis is on British ingredients served in imaginative ways (main courses from around £13), or in the moderately priced and infor-mal *Garden Lounge*. The *York Bar* serves inexpensive and delicious **bar food**, too, at lunchtimes.

Travel details

9

Buses

For information on all local and national bus services, contact Traveline ☏ 0870/608 2608, ⊛ www.traveline.org.uk.

Leicester to: Lincoln (hourly; 1hr 40min); Northampton (hourly; 1hr); Nottingham (every 30min; 1hr 40min); Oakham (hourly; 1hr 10min); Stamford (hourly; 2hr).

Lincoln to: Boston (hourly; 1hr 30min); Leicester (hourly; 1hr 30min); Louth (every 1–2hr; 40min); Northampton (hourly; 3hr); Nottingham (hourly; 2hr 30min); Oakham (hourly; 2hr 20min); Skegness (hourly; 1hr 45min).

Northampton to: Leicester (hourly; 1hr); Lincoln (hourly; 3hr); Nottingham (hourly; 2hr); Stamford (hourly; 2hr 30–50min).

Nottingham to: Leicester (every 30min; 1hr 40min); Lincoln (hourly; 2hr 30min); Newark (hourly; 30min); Northampton (hourly; 2hr).

Oakham to: Leicester (hourly; 1hr 10min); Lincoln (hourly; 2hr 20min); Stamford (every 30min; 20min).

Stamford to: Leicester (hourly; 2hr); Northampton (hourly; 2hr 30–50min); Oakham (every 30min; 20min).

Trains

For information on all local and national rail services, contact National Rail Enquiries ☏ 08457/484950, ⊛ www.nationalrail.co.uk.

Leicester to: Birmingham (every 30min; 1hr); Derby (hourly; 35min); Lincoln (hourly; 1hr 40min); London (every 30min; 1hr 30min); Nottingham (every 30min; 20min); Oakham (hourly; 30min); Stamford (hourly; 40–50min).

Lincoln to: Birmingham (hourly; 3hr); Boston (hourly; 1hr); Cambridge (hourly; 1hr); Leicester (hourly; 1hr 40min); London (hourly; 2hr 15min); Newark (hourly; 25min); Nottingham (hourly; 45min); Peterborough (hourly; 1hr 20min); Skegness (hourly; 1hr 40min).

Northampton to: Birmingham (every 30min; 1hr); London Euston (every 30min; 1hr 10min–1hr 40min).

Nottingham to: Leicester (every 30min; 20min); Lincoln (hourly; 45min); London (hourly; 1hr 40min); Newark (hourly; 30min).

Stamford to: Cambridge (hourly; 1hr 20min); Leicester (hourly; 40–50min); Oakham (hourly; 10min); Peterborough (hourly; 15min).

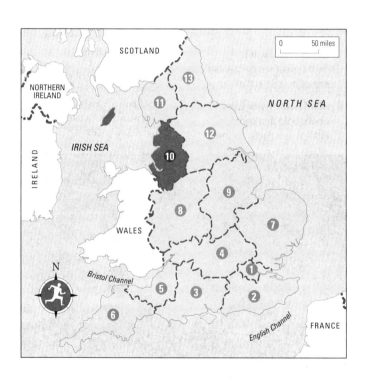

The Northwest

CHAPTER 10

Highlights

✳ **Café society, Manchester** Manchester's café-bars set the tone for this happening city. **See p.524**

✳ **City walls, Chester** The ancient walls of Chester make a fine introduction to this handsome old town. **See p.529**

✳ **World Museum Liverpool** The wonders of the world, on view at Liverpool's most family-friendly museum. **See p.536**

✳ **Blackpool Tower** Blackpool's bold answer to the Eiffel Tower lights up the skyline of the UK's favourite resort. **See p.542**

✳ **National Football Museum, Preston** For armchair fans and fanatics alike – England's national game laid bare. **See p.544**

✳ **Lancaster Castle** From the dungeons to the ornate court rooms, the castle tour is a historical tour-de-force. **See p.545**

✳ **Calf of Man** Weather permitting, don't miss a boat ride across to the Isle of Man's remote bird sanctuary. **See p.552**

△ Blackpool Tower

The Northwest

Within the **northwest** of England lie some of the ugliest and some of the most beautiful parts of the country. The least attractive zones are to be found in the sprawl connecting the country's third and sixth largest conurbations, Manchester and Liverpool, but even here the picture isn't unrelievedly bleak, as the cities themselves have an ingratiating appeal. **Manchester**, in particular, surprises many who don't expect to see beyond its dour, industrial heritage. Where once only a handful of Victorian Gothic buildings lent any grace to the cityscape, Manchester today has been completely transformed by a rebuilding programme that puts it in the vanguard of modern British urban design. Quite apart from a clutch of top-class visitor attractions – including The Lowry and the new Imperial War Museum North – where Manchester really scores is in the buzz of its thriving café and club scene, which places it at the leading edge of the country's youth culture. **Liverpool**, set on the Mersey estuary, is perhaps less appealing at first glance, though its revitalized dockside, Georgian townhouses, grand civic buildings and museums, and burgeoning café and restaurant scene soon change perceptions. Long-overdue redevelopment is also transforming the very fabric of the city, a process kick-started by the choice of Liverpool as European Capital of Culture for 2008.

The hills, which form the southern tip of the Pennine range, melt away to the west into undulating, pastoral **Cheshire**, a county of rolling green countryside and country manor houses, interspersed with dairy farms from whose churns emerge tons of crumbly white Cheshire cheese. The county town, **Chester**, with its complete circuit of town walls and partly Tudor centre, is as alluring as any of the country's northern towns.

Lancashire, which historically lay directly to the north of Cheshire, reached industrial prominence in the nineteenth century primarily due to the cotton-mill towns around Manchester and to the thriving port of Liverpool. Today, neither of those cities is part of the county, and Lancashire's oldest town, and major commercial and administrative centre, is **Preston** – home of the national museum of England's national game, football – though tourists are perhaps more inclined to linger in the charming towns and villages of the nearby **Ribble Valley**. Meanwhile, along the coast to the west and north of the major cities stretches a line of resorts which once formed the mainstay of the northern British holiday trade. Only **Blackpool** is really worth visiting for its own sake, a rip-roaring resort which has stayed at the top of its game by supplying undemanding entertainment with more panache than its neighbours. For anything more culturally invigorating you'll have to continue north to the historically important city of **Lancaster**, with its Tudor castle. Finally,

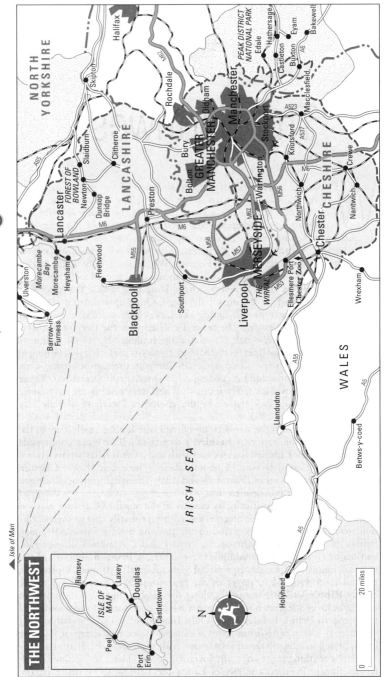

THE NORTHWEST

Isle of Man

NORTH YORKSHIRE

LANCASHIRE

GREATER MANCHESTER

CHESHIRE

MERSEYSIDE

WIRRAL

WALES

IRISH SEA

ISLE OF MAN

N

20 miles

Halifax

Skipton

Rochdale

PEAK DISTRICT NATIONAL PARK

Hathersage
Eyam
Bakewell

Edale
Castleton
Buxton

Manchester
Oldham

Stockport
Macclesfield

Knutsford
Crewe

Bury
Bolton
Warrington
Northwich
Nantwich

Forest of Bowland
Lancaster
Newton
Slaidburn
Clitheroe
Dunsop Bridge
Preston
Chester
Chester Zoo
Ellesmere Port

Ulverston
Morecambe Bay
Morecambe
Heysham
Fleetwood
Blackpool
Southport
Liverpool
Wrexham

Barrow-in-Furness

Llandudno

Betws-y-coed

Holyhead

Ramsey
Laxey
Peel
Douglas
Castletown
Port Erin

M6 M65 M55 M58 M57 M62 M56 M53 A55 A5 A6 A523 A537 A65

© Crown copyright

the semi-autonomous **Isle of Man**, only 25 miles off the coast and served by ferries from Liverpool and Heysham (or short flights from various regional airports), provides a terrain almost as rewarding as that of the Lake District but without the seasonal overcrowding.

Manchester's international **airport** picks the city out as a major UK point of arrival, and there are direct train services from the airport to Liverpool, Blackpool, Lancaster, Leeds and York, as well as to Manchester itself. Both Manchester and Liverpool are well served by **trains**, with plentiful connections to the Midlands and London, and up the west coast to Scotland. There's also a frequent rail and bus service between both cities, and from each to Chester, allowing an easy triangular loop between Greater Manchester, Merseyside and Cheshire. The major east–west rail lines in the region are the direct routes between Manchester, Leeds and York, and between Blackpool, Bradford, Leeds and York. In addition, the Morecambe/Lancaster–Leeds line slips through the Yorkshire Dales (with possible connections at Skipton for the famous Settle–Carlisle line; see p.603); further south, the Manchester–Sheffield line provides a rail approach to the Peak District. Regional **rover tickets** are available for unlimited travel between Liverpool, Manchester, the Peak District, Lancashire and Cumbria, with a variety of passes available (Freedom of the Northwest, Coast and Peaks, North Country, etc; consult ⓦwww .nationalrail.co.uk): flexi-tickets (3 days' travel in 7) start at £44.

Manchester

Few cities in the world have embraced social change so heartily as **MANCHESTER**. From engine of the Industrial Revolution to test-bed of contemporary urban design, the city has no realistic provincial English rival. Its domestic dominance expresses itself in various ways, most swaggeringly in the success of Manchester United, the richest football club in Britain, but also in a thriving music and cultural scene that has given birth to world-beaters as diverse as the Hallé Orchestra and Oasis. Moreover, the city's cutting-edge concert halls, theatres, clubs and café society are boosted by one of England's largest student populations and a blooming gay community, whose spending power has created a pioneering **Gay Village**. For inspiration, Manchester's planners look to Barcelona – another revitalized industrial powerhouse – and scoff at many of their northern rivals.

Manchester is first and foremost a Victorian manufacturing city with the imposing streets and buildings to match. Its rapid growth was the equal of any flowering of the Industrial Revolution – from little more than a village in 1750 to the world's major cotton-milling centre in only a hundred years. The spectacular rise of **Cottonopolis**, as it became known, came from the production of vast quantities of competitively priced imitations of expensive Indian calicoes, using machines evolved from Arkwright's first steam-powered cotton mill, which opened in 1783. The rapid industrialization of the area brought prosperity for a few but a life of misery for the majority. The discontent this engendered amongst the working class came to a head in 1819 when eleven people were killed at **Peterloo**, in what began as a peaceful demonstration against the oppressive Corn Laws. Things were, however, even worse when the 23-year-old Friedrich Engels came here in 1842 to work in his father's cotton plant, and the suffering he witnessed – recorded in his *Condition of the Working Class in England* – was a seminal influence on his later collaboration with Karl Marx in the *Communist Manifesto*.

◀ A664 Rochdale

◀ A56 & M62

▼ Salford Quays

MANCHESTER

N

ACCOMMODATION
Castlefield	D
Holiday Inn Express	F
Jurys Inn	H
Malmaison	B
Manchester YHA	G
The Ox	E
The Palace	I
Premier Travel Inn	A & C

Streets and locations:

ROCHDALE ROAD
OLDHAM ROAD
GEORGE LEIGH STREET
BENGAL STREET
GREAT ANCOATS STREET
NEWTON STREET
LEVER STREET
OLDHAM STREET
DALE STREET
HIGH STREET
CHURCH ST
SWAN STREET
ANGEL STREET
MILLER STREET
SHUDE HILL
THOMAS STREET
OAK STREET
TIB STREET
NORTHERN QUARTER
Craft & Design Centre ②
①
③
④
⑤
PICCADILLY
STATION APPROACH
PICCADILLY
AYTOUN STREET
HOPE S
CHINA TOWN
GAY VILLAGE
Chorlton Street Coach Station
PORTLAND STREET
CHORLTON ST
SACKVILLE STREET
CHARLOTTE STREET
MOSLEY STREET
TARIFF STREET
DUCIE STREET
STORE STREET

Piccadilly Gardens Bus Station
Piccadilly Gardens
⑨
⑪
⑫
⑬
GEORGE ST
NICHOLAS ST
PRINCESS STREET
Town Hall
ALBERT SQUARE
Central Library
PETER STREET
JACKSON'S ROW
LLOYD ST
⑩
BRAZENNOSE ST
JOHN DALTON ST
SOUTH KING ST
ST ANN'S SQUARE
ST ANN ST
ST MARY'S GATE
CROSS STREET
KING STREET
BROWN STREET
SPRING GARDENS
MARKET STREET
CORPORATION STREET
Royal Exchange
⑧
⑦
ℹ
Ⓜ
CANNON STREET
Arndale Centre
Printworks
Urbis
Victoria Station
Ⓜ
Chetham's Hospital School
Corn Exchange
Cathedral
Cathedral Visitor Centre
EXCHANGE SQUARE
WITHY GROVE
EXCHANGE STREET
DEANSGATE
NEW CATHEDRAL ST
CATHEDRAL ST
VICTORIA STREET
VICTORIA BRIDGE ST
CHEETHAM HILL ROAD
TRINITY WAY
GREAT DUCIE ST
Manchester Evening News Arena
BLACKFRIARS ROAD
CHAPEL STREET
River Irwell
footbridge
BLACKFRIARS STREET
BRIDGE STREET
Ⓐ
NEW BAILEY ST
Salford Station
People's History Museum
⑥
IRWELL STREET
TRINITY WAY
CHAPEL STREET
WATER STREET
QUAY STREET
Opera House
John Rylands Library
HARDMAN ST
Museum of Science & Industry

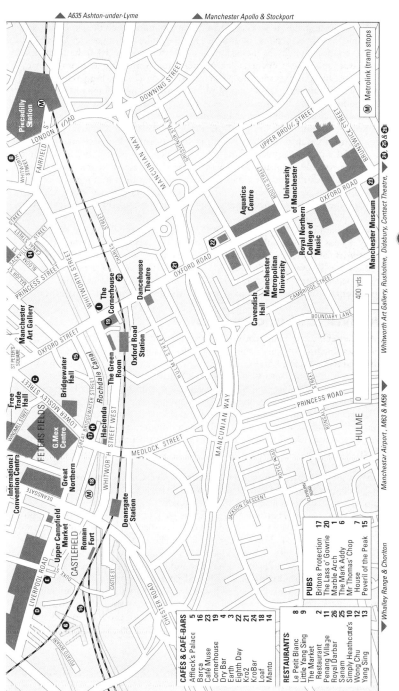

Piccadilly
Station Ⓜ

DOWNING STREET

MANCUNIAN WAY

UPPER BROOK STREET

BRUNSWICK STREET

Aquatics
Centre

University
of Manchester

Royal Northern
College of
Music

OXFORD ROAD

Manchester Museum ㉓

▼ ㉔, ㉕ & ㉖

The
Cornerhouse ❶ ㉑

Dancehouse
Theatre ㉒

Manchester
Metropolitan
University

Manchester
Art Gallery

Ⓑ

Cavendish
Hall

CAMBRIDGE STREET

BOUNDARY LANE

㉠

The Green
Room ㉑

Oxford Road
Station ㉑

⑲

Ⓒ

Bridgewater
Hall

Free
Trade
Hall

Ⓖ

Rochdale Canal

Hacienda ㉑

ST PETER'S
SQUARE

OXFORD STREET

HULME STREET

PRINCESS ROAD

International
Convention Centre

PETER'S FIELDS

G. Mex
Centre

Great
Northern

Ⓜ

Deansgate
Station

DEANSGATE

Upper Campfield
Market

Roman
Fort

CASTLEFIELD

Ⓔ

Ⓓ

Ⓕ

Ⓖ

CHESTER ROAD

DUKE STREET

LIVERPOOL ROAD

MEDLOCK STREET

MANCUNIAN WAY

0   400 yds

CAFÉS & CAFÉ-BARS	
Affleck's Palace	5
Barça	16
Café Muse	23
Cornerhouse	19
Dry Bar	4
Earth	3
Eighth Day	22
Kro2	21
KroBar	24
Loaf	18
Manto	14

RESTAURANTS	
Le Petit Blanc	8
Little Yang Sing	9
The Market Restaurant	2
Penang Village	11
Royal Darbar	26
Sanam	25
Simply Heathcote's	10
Wong Chu	12
Yang Sing	13

PUBS	
Britons Protection	17
The Lass o' Gowrie	20
Marble Arch	1
The Mark Addy	6
Mr Thomas' Chop House	7
Peveril of the Peak	15

Waterways and railway viaducts form the matrix into which the city's principal buildings have been bedded – as early as 1772 the Duke of Bridgewater had a canal cut to connect the city to the coal mines at Worsley, and in 1830 the Manchester–Liverpool railway opened. The **Manchester Ship Canal**, constructed to entice ocean-going vessels into Manchester and away from burgeoning Liverpool, was completed in 1894, and played a crucial part in sustaining Manchester's competitiveness, but within sixty years the city was in trouble, its docks, mills and canals in dangerous decline. Sporadic efforts were made to pull Manchester out of the economic doldrums of the 1960s and 1970s, but the main engine of change turned out to be the devastating **IRA bomb** which exploded in June 1996 and wiped out much of the city's commercial infrastructure. The largest explosion on the mainland since World War II, it devastated the area around the Arndale Centre and the Royal Exchange. Rather than simply patch up the buildings, however, the planning authorities embarked on an ambitious rebuilding scheme with entire new districts taking shape as once-blighted areas along the canals were reclaimed for retail and residential use.

Specific attractions are perhaps a little thin on the ground, but the city centre does possess the enjoyable **Manchester Art Gallery** as well as the extensive **Museum of Science and Industry**, next door to the canal footpaths of the creatively revamped **Castlefield** district. Further out, to the west, are the revamped **Salford Quays**, home to two prestigious museums, **The Lowry arts centre**, and the stirring and stunning **Imperial War Museum North**.

Arrival and information

Manchester's three main **train stations** form the points of a triangle that encloses much of the city centre. Most long-distance services pull into **Piccadilly Station**, facing London Road, on the east side of the centre, with some services continuing onto **Oxford Road Station** to the south of the centre. Trains from Lancashire and Yorkshire mostly terminate at **Victoria Station** on the north side of the centre. It takes about ten minutes to walk from either Victoria or Oxford Road stations to Albert Square, plumb in the middle of town; Piccadilly is further out, a dull twenty-minute hoof from Albert Square. All three stations are connected to other parts of central Manchester via the **Metroshuttle** free bus service (see opposite); Piccadilly and Victoria are also on the **Metrolink** tram line (see opposite).

Most long-distance **buses** use **Chorlton Street Coach Station**, about half way between Piccadilly train station and Albert Square, though some regional buses drop passengers in nearby Piccadilly Gardens instead.

The **Manchester Visitor Centre** is in the back of the Town Hall, bang in the centre of town on St Peter's Square (Mon–Sat 10am–5.30pm, Sun 10.30am–4.30pm; ☎0161/234 3157, ⓦwww.visitmanchester.com). It supplies a free pocket map of the city centre and a free city guide, as well as selling National Express bus tickets, holding rail timetables, and booking guided tours. It can also book accommodation and often gets good rates and knows of the best deals.

To find out **what's on** in the city, buy the weekly *City Life* listings and reviews magazine (ⓦwww.citylife.co.uk), from any newsstand or from the tourist office, and/or check out the Friday edition of the *Manchester Evening News* (ⓦwww.manchesteronline.co.uk).

City transport

About thirty minutes' walk from top to bottom, central Manchester is compact enough to cover on **foot**, though most visitors take the bus as soon as it starts raining. The **Metroshuttle** free bus service (every five to ten minutes) weaves its way across central Manchester on two routes: Service 1 runs east–west linking Piccadilly Station with Piccadilly Gardens, the Royal Exchange and Deansgate; Service 2 travels north–south between Victoria and Oxford Road train stations via Deansgate, Princess and Whitworth streets.

There is also the **Metrolink** tram network, which runs on two routes through the city centre to the suburbs: one links central Manchester with Bury in the north and Altrincham in the south; the other travels west to Eccles via Salford Quays, the location of the Imperial War Museum North (see p.522). Metrolink has **eight city-centre stops**, the most useful of which are at Piccadilly Station, Piccadilly Gardens, St Peter's Square, Market Street and Victoria Station. Metrolink trams run daily every five to fifteen minutes from 6am to midnight (Sun 7am–10.30pm). **Tickets** must be purchased from the automatic machines at Metrolink stops before the start of a journey; prices are reasonable with short hops costing about 60p and the return fare from central Manchester to Salford Quays, for example, being £1.80 at the weekend and in the evening, £2.60 at peak times.

A multitude of **local buses and trains** link the city centre with Manchester's sprawling suburbs and satellite towns. These services are coordinated by the Greater Manchester Passenger Transport Authority, **GMPTE** (enquiries on ☎0870/608 2608, Ⓦwww.gmpte.com), which operates a **Travelshop** (Mon–Sat 8am–6pm, Sun 10am–6pm) in Piccadilly Gardens, the hub of the bus network and the place to go for regional bus and train passes.

Accommodation

In the last few years, there's been a boom in the number of city-centre **hotels**, particularly among the budget chains, which means you have a good chance of finding a smart albeit formulaic, en-suite room in central Manchester for around £60–70 at almost any time of the year – though when Manchester United are playing at home hotel rooms are virtually impossible to find. Otherwise, prices tend to be higher during the week than at the weekend. Less expensive **guesthouse** and **B&B** accommodation is concentrated some way out of the centre, mainly on the southern routes into the city, whereas Manchester's YHA **hostel** occupies a prime central location in Castlefield – book well in advance.

Castlefield Liverpool Road ☎0161/832 7073, Ⓦwww.castlefield-hotel.co.uk. Medium-sized, very modern, red-brick, warehouse-style hotel handily located near the foot of Deansgate in Castlefield, opposite the Science and Industry Museum. Nicely appointed rooms, with an attached leisure club and pool (free to guests). ❺

Holiday Inn Express Waterfront Quay, Salford Quays ☎0161/868 1000 or 0870/400 9670, Ⓦwww.hiexpress.co.uk. Reasonably sized rooms in a great quay location, in a standard-issue tower block convenient for The Lowry or even Old Trafford. To get here, take the Metrolink tram to the Salford Quays tram stop. ❻

Jurys Inn 56 Great Bridgewater St ☎0161/953 8888, Ⓦwww.jurysdoyle.com. Very handy location – by Bridgewater Hall – for this large, no-fuss budget hotel. Rates are room only, but you're close

to any number of decent cafés; weekend deals can bring the price down further. ❹

🏃 **Malmaison** Piccadilly ☎0161/278 1000, Ⓦwww.malmaison.com. A couple of minutes from Piccadilly Station, the ornate Edwardian facade of this handsome hotel hides sleek interior lines and contemporary design from the *Malmaison* group. There's a gym, sauna, bar and brasserie, plus substantial weekend discounts. ❼

Manchester YHA Potato Wharf, Castlefield ☎0870/770 5950, Ⓦwww.yhamanchester.org.uk. Excellent hostel, overlooking the canal, close to the Museum of Science and Industry. The en-suite rooms sleep one to four people (you can pay more to have the room to yourself) and the bunks convert into double beds. Dorm beds £20, doubles ❶

The Ox 71 Liverpool Rd ☎0161/839 7740, Ⓦwww.theox.co.uk. Counts itself as a hotel, but is more like a guest house with nine modest, tidily furnished and en-suite rooms above a pub (see p.526); opposite the Science and Industry Museum. **❷**

The Palace Oxford Street ☎0161/288 1111, ⓦwww.principal-hotels.com. Occupying one of the city's finest Victorian buildings, a terracotta-clad extravagance designed by Alfred Waterhouse as the Refuge Assurance HQ in 1891, *The Palace* is part of a small chain of deluxe English hotels. The public rooms have all the stately grandeur you might expect, the foyer coming complete with

ersatz Roman pillars and columns. Great location too, opposite the Cornerhouse arts centre. Has 250 plush rooms and suites. **❼**

Premier Travel Inn Bishopsgate, 7–11 Lower Mosley St ☎0870/990 6444, ⓦwww .premiertravelinn.com. Good-value, chain-style hotel rooms in this handily located tower block across from the G-Mex centre. There are no less than twenty *Premier Travel Inn*s in the Manchester area with another prime location near the cathedral, just over the River Irwell in Salford, at North Tower, Victoria Bridge Street (☎0870/990 6366). Both **❸**

The City Centre

If Manchester can be said to have a centre, it's **Albert Square** and the cluster of buildings surrounding it – the Town Hall, the Central Library and the Midland Hotel, built in the railway age to host visitors to Britain's greatest industrial city. South of here, the former Central Station now functions as the **G-Mex** exhibition centre, with the Hallé Orchestra's home, **Bridgewater Hall**, opposite. **Chinatown** and the **Gay Village** are just a short walk to the east, while to the northeast, the revamped **Piccadilly Gardens** provides access to the so-called **Northern Quarter**, the funkiest of the regenerated inner-city areas. To the southwest is the **Castlefield** district, site of the **Museum of Science and Industry**. Central spine of the city is **Deansgate**, which runs from Castlefield to the cathedral and, in its northern environs, displays the most dramatic core of urban regeneration in the country, centred on the unalloyed modernity of **Exchange Square**.

Albert Square

Manchester could claim little architectural merit without its panoply of neo-Gothic buildings and monuments, most of which date from the city's salad days in the second half of the nineteenth century. One of the more fanciful is the shrine-like, canopied **monument** to Prince Albert, Queen Victoria's husband, perched prettily in the middle of the trim little square that bears his name – **Albert Square**. Overlooking the prince is Alfred Waterhouse's magnificent, neo-Gothic **Town Hall** (Mon–Fri 9am–4.30pm; free), whose mighty clocktower, completed in 1877, pokes a sturdy finger into the sky, soaring high above its complementary gables, columns and arcaded windows.

St Peter's Square and around

Just to the south of the Town Hall, facing **St Peter's Square**, the circular **Central Library** (Mon–Thurs 10am–8pm, Fri & Sat 10am–5pm) was built in 1934 as the largest municipal library in the world, a self-consciously elegant, classical construction with a domed reading room. The library is an impressive sight, though Lutyens' mournful **Cenotaph**, in the middle of St Peter's Square, now passes virtually unnoticed amid the swooshing trams.

Close by, on Peter Street, the grandiose **Midland Hotel** of 1903 is distinguished by the intricacies of its exterior tilework, all fancily fronded and fluted and incorporating a set of heraldic lions. The hotel's earlier visitors ventured out for an evening's entertainment to the **Free Trade Hall**, a few yards to the west along Peter Street and the home of the city's Hallé Orchestra for over a century, until Bridgewater Hall was completed in 1996. Amazingly, the Italianate facade survived intense wartime bombing and is now a protected part of the *Radisson Edwardian Hotel*, whose modern tower block rises up behind at a (fairly) discrete distance.

Manchester Art Gallery

Presiding over the northeast corner of St Peter's Square is Charles Barry's porticoed **Manchester Art Gallery** (Tues–Sun 10am–5pm; free; ⓦwww .manchestergalleries.org), which holds an invigorating collection of high Victorian art spread over one of the gallery's three floors – **Floor 1**. The paintings on this floor are, however, divided by theme – Face and Place, Expressing Passion and so on – rather than by artist, or indeed school of artists, which makes it difficult to appreciate the strength of the gallery's Victorian collection, especially when it comes to its forte, the Pre-Raphaelite Brotherhood. Pre-Raphaelite highlights include the highly charged eroticism of Rossetti's *Astarte Syrinca* (Room 8) and Holman Hunt's *The Light of the World* (Room 5), a painting of Jesus standing at the door (of the soul) that was familiar to generations of evangelical Protestants. There's much else – a couple of Gainsboroughs and a Stubbs, views of Victorian Manchester and a Turner or two. **Floor 2** features temporary exhibitions and a Gallery of Craft and Design, while the **Ground Floor**'s Manchester Gallery is devoted to a visual history of the city.

South to G–Mex, Bridgewater Hall and Deansgate train station

South of St Peter's Square, **Lower Mosley Street** runs past the **G–Mex** exhibition and conference centre, used as a train station until 1969, and the adjacent **International Convention Centre**. Across the street from G-Mex rises **Bridgewater Hall**, Britain's finest concert hall, balanced on shock-absorbing springs to guarantee clarity of sound. Pressing on, the apartment block at the corner of Lower Mosley Street and Whitworth Street West bears the name of the site's previous occupant, the fabulously famous – and musically seminal – **Hacienda** club, the spiritual home of Factory Records which opened in 1982 and finally closed in 1997.

Turn right along Whitworth Street West and you'll soon spot the string of café-bars and restaurants that have been shoehorned along the Rochdale canal's **Deansgate Locks**, a pattern repeated across the street in the old railway arches abutting **Deansgate Station**.

Castlefield

Best approached along Castle Street, just to the west of Deansgate Station, the remarkable tangle of railway viaducts and canals that lie sandwiched between Water Street, Liverpool Road and Deansgate make up the pocket-sized district of **Castlefield**. It was here that the country's first man-made canal, the Bridgewater Canal, brought coal and other raw materials to the city's warehouses throughout the eighteenth century, and the railways followed later, cementing Castlefield's once pre-eminent economic position, which only declined after World War II. By the early 1960s, the district was a real eyesore, but thereafter an influx of money cleaned it all up, creating Britain's first "urban heritage park" in 1982, now complete with cobbled canalside walks, an outdoor events arena, a YHA hostel (see p.517) and attractive café-bars – all set in the shadows of the sterling engineering work of the Victorian viaducts. Curiously enough, Castlefield was also where Manchester started as the **Roman fort** of Mamucium in 79 AD; the Romans abandoned their settlement in around 410 AD and the scant remains – mainly defensive ditches – are now on display in open ground between the Rochdale canal and Liverpool Road, alongside a modern reconstruction of the north gate.

The Museum of Science and Industry

From the remains of the Roman fort, it's a couple of hundred yards to the extremely popular **Museum of Science and Industry**, whose several different sections spread out along Liverpool Road (daily 10am–5pm; free, but special exhibitions extra; ℡0161/832 2244, ⓦwww.msim.org.uk). One of the most impressive museums of its type in the country, it mixes technological displays and blockbuster exhibitions with trenchant analysis of the social impact of industrialization. A free map of the museum is issued at the entrance, with key points of interest including the **Power Hall**, which trumpets the region's massive technological contribution to the Industrial Revolution by means of a hall full of steam engines, some of which are fired up daily. Pride of place here goes to a working replica of Robert Stephenson's *Planet*. Built in 1830, the *Planet* reliably attained a scorching 30mph but had no brakes; the museum's version does, and uses them at weekends (call for times), dropping passengers a couple of hundred yards away at the **Station Building**, the world's oldest passenger railway station, where the *Rocket* arrived on a rainy September 15, 1830.

North along Deansgate

Deansgate cuts through the city centre from the Rochdale canal to the cathedral, its architectural reference points ranging from Victorian industrialism to post-millennium pouting. The first major point of interest is the former **Great Northern Railway Company's Goods Warehouse**, a great sweep of brickwork dating back to the 1890s that flanks Deansgate between Great Bridgewater and Peter streets. Now incorporated into a modern retail and leisure development, the warehouse was originally an integral part of a large and extraordinarily ambitious trading depot with road and rail links up above and a canal way down below street level.

Continuing north along Deansgate you soon reach the beautifully detailed **John Rylands Library** (currently closed for refurbishment), the city's supreme example of Victorian Gothic. It was founded in 1890 by Enriqueta Ryland to house the theological works collected by her late husband, and has in the past displayed Bibles in more than three hundred languages among its million-strong general collection. Books are sure to be the main focus when the library reopens, but it's the interior detail that catches the eye – all carved and burnished wood, Art Nouveau metalwork, delicately crafted stonework and stained-glass windows.

St Ann's Square and the Royal Exchange

Tucked away off the eastern side of Deansgate, slender **St Ann's Square** is flanked by **St Ann's Church** (daily 11.30am–5pm), a trim sandstone structure whose Neoclassical symmetries date from 1709, though the stained-glass windows are firmly Victorian. The church is fronted by a **statue** of nineteenth-century Free Trader Richard Cobden, joint-leader with John Bright of the Anti-Corn-Law League, which finally forced the repeal in 1846 of the restrictive Corn Laws that had long pauperized the city's working class by keeping the price of barley, wheat, rye and oats at artificially high levels.

At the other end of the square is the **Royal Exchange**, which houses the famous **Royal Exchange Theatre** (see p.527), a theatre-in-the-round whose steel-and-glass cat's cradle sits plonked under the building's immense glass-vaulted roof. Formerly the Cotton Exchange, this building employed seven thousand people until trading finished on December 31, 1968 – the old trading board still shows the last day's prices for American and Egyptian cotton.

Exchange Square

A pedestrian high street – **New Cathedral Street** – runs north from St Ann's Square to **Exchange Square**, which, with its water features, public sculptures and massive department stores (primarily Selfridges and Harvey Nichols), has been the focus of the ambitious city-centre rebuilding programme that followed the IRA bomb of 1996. On the southeast side of the square rises the whopping **Arndale Centre**, once a real 1960s' eyesore, but now modernized and clad in glass. Opposite, across Withy Grove, the former *Mirror* newspaper building contains the futuristic **Printworks**, an adult "entertainment centre", complete with IMAX screen, cinema megaplex, and various themed bars and restaurants.

Manchester Cathedral and Chetham's School of Music

Manchester Cathedral (daily 8.30am–5pm; free), standing just across Exchange Square from the end of New Cathedral Street, dates back to the fifteenth century, though its Gothic lines have been hacked about too much to have any real architectural coherence. Its choristers are trained in **Chetham's School of Music** (ⓌWwww.chethams.org.uk), a few yards to the north of the cathedral on Long Millgate. This fifteenth-century manor house became a school and a free public library in 1653 and was subsequently turned into a music school in 1969. There are free recitals during term time and, although there's no public access to most of the complex, you can visit the oak-panelled **Library** (Mon–Fri 9am–12.30pm & 1.30–4.30pm; free) with its handsome carved eighteenth-century bookcases. Along the side corridor is the main **Reading Room**, where Marx and Engels worked on the square table that still stands in the windowed alcove.

Urbis and Victoria Train Station

Directly opposite Chetham's is the conspicuous six-storey glasswork of **Urbis** (Tues–Sun 10am–6pm; free except for special exhibitions; ⓌWwww.urbis.org.uk), a huge and distinctive sloping structure completed in 2002. Inside, the Level One Gallery is devoted to temporary exhibitions of modern culture – from punk through to graffiti and architecture – while up above, on levels Two to Four, a larger permanent exhibition explores the experience of living in the city through a whole series of interactive exhibits. Naturally enough, Manchester, as the world's first industrial city, is given due prominence.

Behind Urbis, down the slope, is **Victoria Station**, easily the most likeable of the city's several stations with its long, gently curving stone facade. Pop inside for a look at the Art Deco ticket booths and the immaculate tiled map of the Lancashire and Yorkshire Railway network as it was in the 1920s.

Piccadilly Gardens and the Northern Quarter

Piccadilly Gardens, to the east of the Arndale Centre and about ten minutes' walk from Victoria Station, is a major local transport hub and gateway to the shabby but improving **Oldham Street**, which has been adopted by "alternative" entrepreneurs who have dubbed it the **Northern Quarter**. Traditionally, this is Manchester's garment district and you'll still find shops and wholesalers selling high-street fashions, shop fittings, mannequins and hosiery, but there are also new design outlets, lots of music stores, and some funky bars and cafés. For off-beat contemporary shopping, look in Affleck's Palace (52 Church St), and the Coliseum (18–24 Church St). There are more skills and crafts on display in the excellent **Manchester Craft and Design Centre**, 17 Oak St (Mon–Sat

10am–5.30pm, plus Sun in Dec 10am–5.30pm; free; ⓦwww.craftanddesign
.com) – a great place to pick up ceramics, fabrics, earthenware, jewellery and
decorative art, or just sip a drink in the café.

Chinatown and the Gay Village

From Piccadilly Gardens, it's a short walk to **Chinatown**, whose grid of narrow
streets stretch north–south from Charlotte to Princess Street between Portland
and Lower Mosley streets, with the inevitable **Dragon Arch**, at Faulkner and
Nicolas, providing the focus for the annual Chinese New Year celebrations.
Close by, just to the southeast, the roads off Portland Street lead down to the
Rochdale canal, where Canal Street is the heart of Manchester's thriving **Gay
Village**. The pink pound has filled this part of the city with canalside cafés,
clubs, bars and businesses, thereby rescuing what had previously been a decay-
ing warehouse district.

One block west of the Gay Village, at the junction of Oxford Road and
Whitworth Street, stands the **Cornerhouse** (ⓣ0161/200 1500, ⓦwww
.cornerhouse.org), the dynamo of the Manchester arts scene. In addition to
screening art-house films (see p.527), the Cornerhouse has three floors of
gallery space (Tues–Sat 11am–6pm, Thurs till 9pm, Sun 2–6pm; free) devoted
to contemporary and local artists' work.

Salford Quays

After the Manchester Ship Canal opened in 1894, **Salford docks** played a
pivotal role in turning Manchester into one of Britain's busiest seaports. By
the 1970s, however, trade had well-nigh collapsed and the docks were forced
to close in 1982, leaving a swathe of postindustrial mess just a couple of miles
west of the city centre. Since then, an ambitious redevelopment has transformed **Salford Quays** into a hugely popular waterfront residential and leisure
complex, with gleaming new apartment blocks, shopping mall, and arts centre,
The Lowry. Also on the quays is the much-praised **Imperial War Museum
North**, with its splendidly thoughtful displays on war in general and its effects
on the individual in particular.

To get to the quays by public transport, take the **Metrolink tram** (Eccles line;
daily 6am–10.30pm; every 15min) from the city centre to the **Harbour City
tram stop**, from where it is a five-minute walk to both The Lowry and the
Imperial War Museum; for details of Metrolink tram stops in the city centre,
see p.517.

The Lowry

Perched on the water's edge, **The Lowry** (ⓣ0870/787 5780, ⓦwww.thelowry
.com) is the quays' shiny-steel arts centre, where you can do just about everything from getting married and having a meal to watching theatre or just
wandering around. A small part of The Lowry, the **Galleries** (Sun–Fri 11am–
5pm, Sat 10am–5pm; free, but £3 suggested donation), is devoted to displays of
fine art. There are some sixteen different exhibitions held here each year, but all
of them showcase a selection of the paintings of **Lawrence Stephen Lowry**
(1887–1976), Salford's most famous son. A twenty-minute **video** – *Meet Mr
Lowry* – puts flesh on the artistic bones.

Imperial War Museum North

A footbridge spans the Manchester Ship Canal to link The Lowry with the startling **Imperial War Museum North** (daily: Mar–Oct 10am–6pm; Nov–Feb

△ Imperial War Museum North

10am–5pm; free; ⓦwww.north.iwm.org.uk), designed by Daniel Libeskind. Inside, its angular lines serve as a dramatic backdrop to the displays, which kick off with the Big Picture, when the walls of the main hall are transformed into giant screens to show regularly rotated, fifteen-minute, surround-sound films. Among the hundreds of artefacts displayed in the main hall are five so-called "iconic objects", including the artillery piece that fired the first British shell in

World War I and a fire tender used when Manchester was blitzed in World War II. In addition, there are all sorts of themed displays in six separate exhibition areas – the Silos – focusing on everything from women's work in the two world wars to the build up to the attack on Iraq in 2003. It's an ambitious and carefully conceived museum with a mixture of the personal and the general that is nothing less than superb.

Old Trafford

Looming in the near distance from the Salford Quays is **Old Trafford**, the self-styled "Theatre of Dreams" and home of **Manchester United** (℡0870/442 1994, ⓦwww.manutd.com), arguably the world's most famous football team. The club's following is such that only season-ticket holders can ever attend games, though pricey **tours** of Old Trafford and its museum (daily 9.30am–4.30pm; advance booking essential) will placate fans who want to gawp at the silverware, sit in the dug-out and visit the *Red Café*. To get here, take the Metrolink tram to Old Trafford Station and walk up Warwick Road to Sir Matt Busby Way.

Eating and drinking

Second only to London in the breadth and scope of its **cafés** and **restaurants**, Manchester has something to suit everyone, from a cheap curry to a night out in a celebrity-chef hot-spot. Moreover, your money goes a lot further than it does in the capital, and even expensive places aren't usually snobby – the city is much too egalitarian for that. The bulk of Manchester's eating and drinking places are scattered around the **city centre**, but the **Rusholme** district, a couple of miles south of the centre, possesses the city's widest and best selection of Asian restaurants in a "golden mile" of curry houses that extends along the main drag, **Wilmslow Road**.

Most city-centre **pubs** dish up something filling at lunchtime, but for a trendier snack or drink, European-style **café-bars** are everywhere, especially in the city-centre developments, in the **Northern Quarter**, and in the **Gay Village** on the Rochdale Canal.

Cafés and café-bars

Affleck's Palace 52 Church St, at Oldham Street. Five floors of hip/alternative/indie boutiques, with the pick of the cafés on the top floor, where you can grab a coffee and a grilled sandwich. Closed Sun.

Barça Arch 8 & 9, Catalan Square. Trendy Castlefield bar/restaurant tucked into the old railway arches off Castle Street, a stone's throw from the Rochdale canal. Cosy lounge downstairs and a restaurant above, serving dishes with a Mediterranean slant. Restaurant closed on Sun.

Café Muse Manchester Museum, Oxford Road. Tasty, inventive snacks at this light and airy museum café that is now part of the *Kro* mini-chain (see below). Popular in equal measure with university lecturers and museum-goers. Mon–Sat 8am–5pm, Sun 10am–5pm.

Cornerhouse 70 Oxford St. The place to sip a cappuccino after viewing the galleries or catching a movie. The first-floor café (daily till 11pm) serves up mezze and pizzas, and there's also a good bar downstairs.

Dry Bar 28–30 Oldham St. The earliest of Manchester's designer café-bars, started by Factory records and the catalyst for much of what has happened since in the Northern Quarter. *Dry* is still as cool as they come.

Earth 16–20 Turner St. Gourmet vegan and organic food in a stylish Northern Quarter pit-stop with Buddhist leanings – stuffed pancakes, pies, bakes, juices and deli delights. Closed Sun.

Eighth Day 107–111 Oxford Rd. Manchester's oldest organic-vegetarian café has got spanking new premises on its old Oxford Road site – shop, takeaway and juice bar upstairs, café/restaurant downstairs. Closed Sun.

KroBar 325 Oxford Rd. Half the students in Manchester crowd into this good-natured café-bar, sited in a former men-only teetotallers' club, across from Manchester University Students' Union. Offers imaginative value-for-money food, caffeine and a vast range of on-tap beers; on a sunny day, you'll struggle to find table space outside. There's another, larger and glassier branch – *Kro2* – further up Oxford Road towards the city centre, close to the Mancunian Way overpass.

Loaf Deansgate Locks, Whitworth St West. Large queues at the weekend for this designer-industrial café-bar, though it's not nearly so crowded during the day when you can grab an outdoor table underneath the arches.

Manto 46 Canal St. Gay Village stalwart that has gone through several incarnations since it was established in 1990. *Manto* attracts a chic crowd, which laps up the cool sounds and club nights. Inexpensive fusion dishes served daily from noon till 8pm.

Restaurants

Le Petit Blanc 55 King St ☎0161/832 1000. Best place in the city for reasonably priced classic and regional French cooking, Raymond Blanc's mid-range brasserie is housed in sleek modern premises near the Royal Exchange; real food for children too. Mains average around £14.

Little Yang Sing 17 George St ☎0161/228 7722. Celebrated basement restaurant (forerunner to the larger *Yang Sing*) where the emphasis is on *dim sum*, rice or noodle dishes, and down-to-earth Cantonese cooking, with lots of choice under £8.

The Market Restaurant 104 High St ☎0161/834 3743. First-rate Northern Quarter restaurant with a regularly changing menu that serves eclectic, adventurous Modern British dishes. Also a very good wine and beer list. Reservations absolutely essential. Open Wed–Sat dinner and Wed–Fri for lunch. Main courses average around £13–16.

Penang Village 56 Faulkner St ☎0161/236 2650. You soon get the idea – Malay village scenes on the wall, a traditional fishing boat as centrepiece – but this friendly Malaysian joint backs up the decor with tasty, authentic dishes. *Ayam percik* (barbecued chicken with a mild curry sauce), beef rendang, veg curry, and the good *roti* bread are all recommended. Closed Mon. Main courses average around £8.

Royal Darbar 65–67 Wilmslow Rd, Rushholme ☎0161/224 4392. Award-winning Asian food in plain but friendly surroundings. The chef's special (he's been voted Manchester's Curry Chef of the Year twice) is *nihari*, a slow-cooked lamb dish,

while other homestyle choices appear on Sundays. Take your own booze. Main courses from as little as £7.

Sanam 145–151 Wilmslow Rd, Rusholme ☎0161/224 8824. One of Rusholme's earliest Asian arrivals, now over thirty years old, the *Sanam* serves all the usual dishes plus award-winning *gulab juman*. Drop by the takeaway sweet and snack centre, at 169 Wilmslow Rd, on the way home. No alcohol allowed. Mains from £7.

Simply Heathcote's Jackson's Row ☎0161/835 3536. This large and popular, first–floor restaurant occupies part of an old and classily revamped warehouse. Minimalist decor sets the tone and the menu; the handiwork of Lancastrian chef Paul Heathcote mixes Mediterranean and local flavours and ingredients, so expect updated working-class dishes alongside the parmesan shavings. Mains before 7pm hover around (a very reasonable) £9, £11–15 later on.

Wong Chu 63 Faulkner St ☎0161/236 2346. Simply the best of the budget Chinatown eateries, this no-frills, paper-tablecloth place serves up enormous portions of Cantonese staples. Highlights are the deep-bowl noodle soups or piled-high rice-and-meat plates, all at bargain prices.

Yang Sing 34 Princess St ☎0161/236 2200. The *Yang Sing* is one of the best Cantonese restaurants in the country, with thoroughly authentic food, from a lunchtime plate of fried noodles to the full works. Stray from the printed menu for the most interesting dishes; ask the friendly staff for advice. Main courses from £10.

Pubs

Britons Protection 50 Great Bridgewater St. Cosy, old pub with a couple of small rooms and all sorts of Victorian decorative detail – most splendidly the tiles. Also has a brickyard beer garden.

The Lass o' Gowrie 1 Charles St. Outside, glazed tiles and Victorian styling; inside, stripped floors and a microbrewery.

Marble Arch 73 Rochdale Rd. Curious real-ale house with a sloping floor, whose in-house Marble Brewery produces some fine brews – the seasonal "Ginger Marble" or the strong "Chocolate Heavy" among them.

The Mark Addy 2 Stanley St. Mainly known for its food, *The Mark Addy* – named after a local Victorian character – serves a choice of fifty cheeses and eight pâtés (including vegetarian). Eat inside, or outside by the River Irwell.

Mr Thomas' Chop House 52 Cross St. Victorian classic with a Dickensian feel to its nooks and crannies. Office workers, hardcore daytime drinkers, old goats and students all call it home. There's good-value, traditional English "chop-house" food (oysters, bubble and squeak, etc) served in the ornate dining-and-drinking room at the rear – and old-fashioned table service for anyone who can't make their own way to the bar.

The Ox 71 Liverpool Rd. Pleasant and popular old boozer that dates back to Victorian times – as does some of the tilework. Good range of cask ales along with well-above-average bar food.

Peveril of the Peak 127 Great Bridgewater St. The pub that time forgot – one of Manchester's best real-ale houses, with a youthful crowd and some superb Victorian glazed tilework outside.

Nightlife

For the last thirty years or so, Manchester has been vying with London as Britain's capital of **youth culture**, spearheaded by the success of its musical exports, from the saintly Morrissey to Badly Drawn Boy, Joy Division to Oasis. Banks of fly posters advertise what's going on in the numerous **clubs** which frequently change names and styles on different nights of the week. Manchester also has an excellent **live music** scene in pubs and clubs, with tickets for local bands usually under £5, more like £10–15 for someone you've heard of. Mega-star gigs take place either at the G-Mex Centre or one of the major stadiums, also listed below. For the broadest coverage of Manchester's musical happenings, check the weekly *City Life* magazine, which carries incisive, well-written reviews (mostly), or Friday's *Manchester Evening News*.

Smaller live-music and club venues

Band on the Wall 25 Swan St ☎0161/834 1786, ⓦwww.bandonthewall.org. Cosy Northern Quarter joint with a great reputation for its live bands – from world and folk to jazz and reggae – plus tasty club-nights to boot.

Manchester Roadhouse 8–10 Newton St, Piccadilly ☎0161/237 9789, ⓦwww.theroadhouselive .co.uk. Regular and varied gigs by local bands plus a succession of fine club-nights.

The Music Box 65 Oxford St ☎0161/273 5200, ⓦwww.themusicbox.info. The astute clubber's venue of choice with Mr Scruff keeping it unreal on many a night. Just south of the Portland Street/Oxford Street intersection. Recommended.

Sankey's Soap Beehive Mill, Jersey Street, Ancoats ☎0871/910 5200, ⓦwww.tribalgathering .co.uk. Many people's favourite night out, brought to you by the legendary Tribal Gathering crew – Friday's Tribal Sessions and Saturday's The Red Light are especially popular for their sleazy house music; other club-night specials too. Ancoats is an inner-city suburb beginning about half a mile north of Piccadilly Station.

South 4a S King St ☎0161/831 7756, ⓦwww .south-club.co.uk. Eclectic music, depending on the night, from funk, 1970s disco and house to punk or Northern Soul. Check for what's on and when. Central location near the Deansgate/John Dalton Street intersection.

Stadium venues

Carling Apollo Manchester Stockport Road, Ardwick Green ☎0161/273 6921, ⓦwww.alive .co.uk/apollo/. Huge theatre auditorium for all kinds of concerts.

G-Mex Centre Windmill Street ☎0161/834 2700, ⓦwww.g-mex.co.uk. Mid-sized city-centre indoor stadium.

Manchester Evening News Arena 21 Hunt's Bank, beside Victoria Station ☎0870/190 8000, ⓦwww.men-arena.com. Indoor stadium that seats 20,000 and hosts all the big names.

Arts and culture

Manchester is blessed with the North's most highly regarded **orchestra**, the Hallé, which is resident at Bridgewater Hall, though there are other acclaimed names here too, including the BBC Philharmonic. The Cornerhouse is the local "alternative" **arts** mainstay, while a full range of mainstream and fringe **theatres** produce a year-round programme of events. For **film**, the **Printworks** entertainment complex contains the multi-screen **Filmworks** cinema as well as an IMAX cinema, but there are plenty of other, more agreeable places to catch movies, too, including art-house screenings at the Cornerhouse.

Concerts and music

Bridgewater Hall Lower Mosley Street ☏ 0161/907 9000, ⓦ www.bridgewater-hall.co.uk. Home of the Hallé Orchestra and the Manchester Camerata; also sponsors a full programme of chamber, classical and jazz concerts.
Opera House Quay Street ☏ 0161/828 1700, ⓦ www.ticketmaster.co.uk. Major venue for touring West End musicals, drama and concerts.
Royal Northern College of Music (RNCM) 124 Oxford Rd ☏ 0161/907 5555, ⓦ www.rncm.ac.uk. Stages top-quality classical and modern-jazz concerts, including performances by Manchester Camerata.

Theatre and the arts

Cornerhouse 70 Oxford St ☏ 0161/200 1500, ⓦ www.cornerhouse.org. Engaging centre for contemporary arts, with three cinema screens, changing art exhibitions, recitals, talks, bookshop, café and bar.
Dancehouse Theatre 10 Oxford Rd ☏ 0161/237 9753, ⓦ www.thedancehouse.co.uk. Home of the Northern Ballet School, and venue for dance, drama and comedy.
Green Room 54–56 Whitworth St West ☏ 0161/615 0500, ⓦ www.greenroomarts.org. Rapidly changing fringe programme that includes theatre, dance, mime and cabaret.
Royal Exchange Theatre St Ann's Square ☏ 0161/833 9833, ⓦ www.royalexchange.co.uk. The Royal Exchange's theatre-in-the-round is the most famous stage in the city, and there's a Studio Theatre (for works by new writers) alongside the main stage.

Cinemas

Cornerhouse 70 Oxford St ☏ 0161/200 1500, ⓦ www.cornerhouse.org. The three screens at the Cornerhouse are your best bet for art-house releases, special screenings and cinema-related talks and events. Highly recommended.
The Filmworks Printworks Centre, Exchange Square ☏ 0871/224 4007, ⓦ www.thefilmworks .co.uk. State-of-the-art cinema-going with oodles of screens, IMAX movies, digital projection and comfortable seating.

Listings

Airport ⓦ www.manchesterairport.co.uk, ☏ 0161/489 3000.
Bus information For all Greater Manchester bus services, call GMPTE on ☏ 0870/608 2608, ⓦ www.gmpte.com.
Internet Free Internet at the Central Library, St Peter's Square (Mon–Thurs 10am–8pm, Fri & Sat 10am–5pm).
Pharmacy Boots, 11–13 Piccadilly Gardens

(☏ 0161/834 8244) and 20 St Ann's St (☏ 0161/839 1798).
Police 0161/872 5050.
Post office 26 Spring Gardens; 21 Brazennose St.
Taxis Mantax ☏ 0161/230 3333; Taxifone ☏ 0161/236 0074.
Train information For all Greater Manchester train services, call GMPTE on ☏ 0870/608 2608, ⓦ www.gmpte.com.

Chester

Forty miles southwest of Manchester across the Cheshire Plain, **CHESTER** has much to recommend it. A glorious two-mile ring of medieval and Roman walls encircles a kernel of Tudor and Victorian buildings, all overhanging eaves, mini-courtyards, and narrow cobbled lanes that culminate in the unique raised arcades called the "**Rows**". The town has enough in the way of sights, restaurants and atmosphere to make it an enjoyable base for a couple of days with the most obvious excursion being to its much-vaunted **zoo**.

Arrival and information

Most long-distance and regional **buses** pull in at the stops beside Vicar's Lane, a five-minute walk from the city centre. Local buses use the **Bus Exchange** right in the centre of town, between Princess and Hunter streets, off Northgate Street. From the **train station**, to the northeast of the centre, it's a good ten-minute walk down City Road and Foregate Street to the central Eastgate Clock. A shuttle bus (free with rail ticket; every 15–30min) links the train station with the Bus Exchange.

Chester has two **tourist offices**, one bang in the centre in the Town Hall on Northgate Street (April–Sept Mon–Sat 9.30am–5.30pm, Sun 10am–4pm; Oct–March Mon–Sat 10am–5pm), a second – the **Chester Visitor Centre** – on Vicar's Lane, just to the east of the town centre (April–Sept Mon–Sat 9.30am–5.30pm, Sun 10am–4pm; Oct–March Mon–Sat 9.30am–5pm, Sun 10am–4pm). They share the same telephone number and website (℡01244/402111, ⓦwww.chestertourism.com).

Accommodation

Chester is a popular tourist destination with dozens of **B&Bs** and a slew of **hotels**. For most of the year, finding a vacant room presents few problems, but at the height of the summer and on high days and holidays – like Chester Races – advance booking is strongly recommended either direct or via the tourist office.

Chester Town House B&B 23 King St ℡01244/350021, ⓦwww.chestertownhouse.co.uk. A very high-standard B&B in a comfortably furnished seventeenth-century townhouse, on a curving, cobbled central street off Northgate Street. There are five en-suite rooms and private parking. ❸

The Green Bough Hotel 60 Hoole Rd ℡01244/326241, ⓦwww.greenbough.co.uk. Hard-to-beat, award-winning, small and friendly, family-run hotel with all sorts of thoughtful details – soft carpeting, comfortable beds, and plasma TV screens in each guest room or suite. Great breakfasts too, plus three-course evening meals for £40 and a rooftop garden. One mile northeast of the city centre en route to the M53/M56. ❼

Grosvenor Place Guest House 2–4 Grosvenor Place ℡01244/324455. Pleasant townhouse B&B in a good location near the Grosvenor Museum. Rooms available with and without shower. ❷

The Mill Hotel Milton St ℡01244/350035, ⓦwww.millhotel.com. Sensitive warehouse conversion on the canal, between St Oswald's Way and Hooley Way, not far from the train station. Has its own car park and a nice waterside bar and café-bar; rooms with balcony attract a small supplement. ❺

YHA Hostel Hough Green House, 40 Hough Green ℡0870/770 5672, ⓔchester@yha.org.uk. Twenty-minutes' walk southwest of the centre, this Victorian house has a cafeteria, self-catering and laundry facilities, and a shop. Over 100 beds in two- to ten-bedded rooms; dorm beds £16 including breakfast.

The city centre

Intersecting at **The Cross**, the four main thoroughfares of central Chester are lined by **The Rows**, galleried shopping arcades that run along the first-floor of a wonderful set of half-timbered buildings with another set of shops down below at street level. This engaging tableau, which extends for the first two or three hundred yards of each of the four main streets, is a blend of genuine Tudor houses and Victorian imitations that are hard to separate out. There's no clear explanation of the origin of The Rows – they were first recorded shortly after a fire wrecked Chester in 1278 – but it seems likely that the hard bedrock that lies underneath the town centre prevented its shop keepers and merchants from constructing the cellars they required, so they built upwards instead. One of the four main streets, **Eastgate,** is intercepted by one of the old town gates, above which is perched the filigree **Eastgate Clock**, raised in honour of Queen Victoria's Diamond Jubilee.

The Town Hall and the Cathedral

North of The Cross, along **Northgate Street**, rises the neo-Gothic **Town Hall**, whose acres of red and grey sandstone look over to the **Cathedral** (Mon–Sat 9am–5pm, Sun 1–5pm; £4 including audioguide), a much modified red-sandstone structure dating back to the Normans and for most of its history a Benedictine abbey. The **nave**, with its massive medieval pillars, is suitably imposing, and on one side it sports a splendid sequence of Victorian Pre-Raphaelite mosaic panels that illustrate Old Testament stories in melodramatic style. Close by, the **north transept** is the oldest and most Norman part of the church – hence the round-headed arch and arcade – and the adjoining **choir** (or Quire) holds an intricately carved set of fourteenth-century choir stalls with some especially beastly misericords.

Around the city walls

East of the cathedral, steps provide access to the top of the two-mile girdle of the medieval and Roman **city walls** – the most complete in Britain, though in places the wall is barely above street level. You can walk past all its towers, turrets and gateways in an hour or so, and on the way round, you'll see the **Roodee**, England's oldest racecourse, laid out on a silted tidal pool where Roman ships once anchored bearing goods from the Mediterranean. Horse races are still held here throughout the year – the tourist office has the details.

The Grosvenor Museum and Chester Castle

Scores of sculpted tomb panels and engraved headstones once propped up the city wall, evidence of some nervous repair-work undertaken when the Roman Empire was in retreat. Much of this stonework was retrieved by the Victorians and is now on display at the **Grosvenor Museum**, 27 Grosvenor St (Mon–Sat 10.30am–5pm, Sun 1–4pm; free), which also has interesting background displays on the Roman Empire in general and Roman Chester in particular. The assorted centurial stones, altars and tombstones are themselves in a separate room and together they form the largest collection from a single Roman site in Britain.

Close by, on Castle Street, the **Cheshire Military Museum** (daily 10am–5pm; £2) inhabits part of the same complex as **Chester Castle** (no public access), built by William the Conqueror, though most of what you see today is resolutely Georgian and used as courts and offices. From the castle, it's an easy five- to ten-minute stroll northeast to one of the old city gates, **Newgate,** for the Roman Gardens and Amphitheatre.

The Roman Gardens and Roman Amphitheatre

Immediately to the east of Newgate, a footpath leads into the **Roman Gardens** (open access), where a miscellany of Roman stonework – odd bits of pillar and so forth – is on display amidst the surrounding greenery. Close by, along Little St John Street, is the shallow, partly excavated bowl that marks the site of the **Roman Amphitheatre** (open access); it is estimated to have held seven thousand spectators, making it the largest amphitheatre in Britain, though there's little left to see today.

Chester Zoo

Chester's most popular attraction, **Chester Zoo** (daily: April–Sept 10am–6pm; Oct–March 10am–5pm or 6pm; last admission 2hr before closing; £14.50, children 3–15 £10.50; ⓦ www.chesterzoo.org), is one of the best in Europe. It's the second-largest in Britain (after London's), spreading over 110 landscaped acres, with new attractions opening all the time. The zoo is well known for its conservation projects and has had several notable successes with endangered species. Animals are grouped by region in large paddocks viewed from a maze of pathways, from the creeping monorail or from the water-bus, with main attractions including the baby animals (elephants, giraffes and orangutans), the rainforest habitat, the bat cave and the Chimpanzee Forest with the biggest climbing frame in the country. Kids enjoy the Animal Discovery Centre, where they're encouraged to touch and learn. The zoo entrance is signposted off the A41 just to the north of Chester and reached by bus #1 (Mon–Sat only; every 30min) from the Bus Exchange.

Eating and drinking

You can't walk more than a few paces in downtown Chester without coming across somewhere to **eat and drink**, as often as not housed in a medieval or Tudor building. Given the number of day-trippers, it's not surprising that some places serve up some pretty mediocre stuff, but standards are generally high and several of the **pubs** are delightful. The cafés and restaurants listed below are open for lunch and dinner unless otherwise stated.

Cafés and restaurants

Boulevard de la Bastille Bridge St Row. One of the nicest of the arcade cafés, with tables looking over the street and doing a roaring trade in breakfasts, pastries and sandwiches. Sandwiches from as little as £1.50.
Chez Jules 69 Northgate St ☎01244/400014. Classic brasserie menu – salad Niçoise to vegetable cassoulet, Toulouse sausage to rib-eye steak – at this popular spot, housed in an attractive black-and-white, half-timbered building. In the evenings, main courses begin at about £9, but they also do a terrific–value, two-course lunch for £7.
Francs 14 Cuppin St ☎01244/317952. An excellent and very French bistro with good-value set

meals. You can also just drop in for a coffee and cake. Plat du jour £4; à la carte mains £12–14.
La Tasca 6–12 Cuppin St ☎01244/400887. Large tapas selection – Spanish cheeses to grilled prawns – and paella too. Nice spot in the summer when they throw the windows wide open. Tapas average £3–4.
Three Kings Tearoom 90 Lower Bridge St Amenable little tearoom with pleasantly fuddy-duddy decor and tasty food – a filling salad and sandwich combo costs about £4. Behind the cutest of antique shops. Open Tues–Sun 10am–4pm.

Pubs and bars

Albion Inn corner of Albion and Park streets. A true English Victorian terraced pub in the shadow of the city wall – no fruit machines or muzak. Good old-fashioned decor too, plus tasty bar food and a great range of ales. Recommended.
Mill Hotel Milton Street. Ale lovers flock to this converted Victorian corn mill to sample an excellent range of brews in a lively atmosphere.
Old Harkers Arms 1 Russell St, below the City Road bridge. Canalside real-ale pub imaginatively sited in a former warehouse. Quality bar food too.

Liverpool

Once the empire's second city, **LIVERPOOL** spent too many of the twenti-eth-century postwar years struggling against adversity. Things are looking up at last, as the successful bid to be European Capital of Culture for 2008 promises to transform the way outsiders see the city. Some may sneer at the very concept of Liverpudlian "culture", but this is already a city with a Tate Gallery of its own, as well as a series of innovative museums and a fascinating social history. Liverpool also makes great play of its musical heritage, which is reasonable enough from the city that produced The Beatles.

Liverpool gained its charter from King John in 1207 – the city will celebrate its 800th birthday with a year-long series of events during 2007. However, it remained a humble fishing village for half a millennium until the booming slave trade prompted the building of the first dock in 1715. From then until the abolition of slavery in Britain in 1807, Liverpool was the apex of the **slav-ing triangle** in which firearms, alcohol and textiles were traded for African slaves, who were then shipped to the Caribbean and America, where they were in turn exchanged for tobacco, raw cotton and sugar. After the abolition of the trade, the port continued to grow into a seven-mile chain of docks, not only for freight but also to cope with wholesale European **emigration**, which saw nine million people leave for the Americas and Australasia between 1830 and 1930. The docks had lost their pre-eminence by the middle of the twentieth century and, although the arrival of car-manufacturing plants in the 1960s stemmed the decline for a while, during the 1970s and 1980s Liverpool became a byword for British economic malaise. However, there's been a concerted effort in recent times to transform Liverpool's economy and reputation, with plans well in progress to redevelop the waterfront, rebuild parts of the city centre and refurbish its magnificent municipal and industrial buildings.

Visitors have to plan ahead if they are to get around the sights in two or three days. The **River Mersey** provides one focus, whether crossing on the famous ferry to the **Wirral** peninsula or on a tour of the attractions in the rejuvenated warehouses of **Albert Dock**. The associated **Beatles'** sights – former homes to song inspirations – can easily occupy another day. If you want a **cathedral**, they've "got one to spare" as the song goes; plus there's a multitude of exhibits in the terrific **World Museum Liverpool**, and a revitalized arts and nightlife urban quarter centred on **FACT**, Liverpool's showcase for film and the media arts.

Arrival, information, transport and tours

Trains pull in to **Lime Street Station**, while the suburban **Merseyrail** system (for trains from Chester) calls at four underground stations in the city, includ-ing Lime Street. National Express **buses** use the station on Norton Street, just northeast of Lime Street. Liverpool **airport** – officially named after John Lennon – is eight miles southeast of the city centre. From outside the main entrance, the **Airport Express #500 bus** (every 30min; 6am–1am; £2) runs into the city centre, stopping at all major bus terminals and at Lime Street; or a **taxi** to Lime Street costs around £12. Most **ferries** – from the Isle of Man, Dublin and Belfast – dock just north of Pier Head, not far from James Street Merseyrail station, though Norse Merchant arrivals are over the water on the Wirral, near Woodside ferry terminal (ferry or Merseyrail to Liverpool).

Tourist information is available from two offices (both ☎0906/680 6886, ⓦwww.visitliverpool.com): the **Queen's Square Centre** in Queen Square (Mon–Sat 9am–5.30pm, Sun & bank hols 10.30am–4.30pm) and at **Albert**

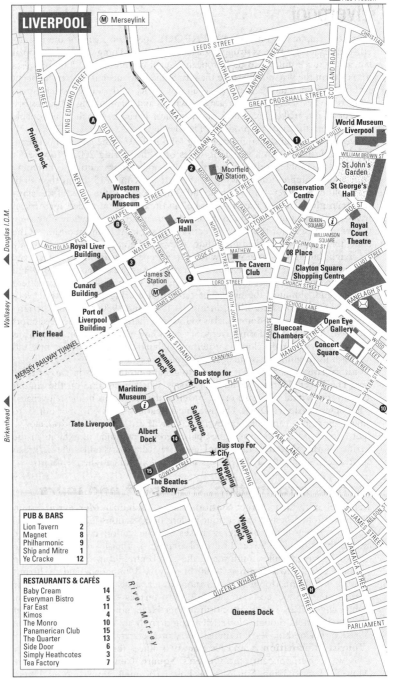

LIVERPOOL   Ⓜ Merseylink

▲ *Douglas I.O.M.*

▲ *Wallasey*

▲ *Birkenhead*

LEEDS STREET

BATH STREET

Princes Dock

KING EDWARD STREET

OLD HALL STREET

NEW QUAY

PALL MALL

VAUXHALL ROAD

MARYBONE STREET

SCOTLAND ROAD

CHRISTIAN

GREAT CROSSHALL STREET

HATTON GARDEN

TITHEBARN STREET

VERNON ST

CHAPEL STREET

MOORFIELDS

DALE STREET

CHURCHILL WAY SOUTH

DALE ST

World Museum Liverpool

WILLIAM BROWN ST

St John's Garden

STANLEY ST

VICTORIA STREET

Conservation Centre

St George's Hall

ROE ST

① Ⓜ Moorfield Station

Western Approaches Museum

NICHOLAS PLACE

CHAPEL

RUMFORD ST

COVENT GARDEN

WATER STREET

FENWICK STREET

CASTLE STREET

NORTH JOHN STREET

MATHEW

WHITECHAPEL

QUEEN SQUARE

WILLIAMSON SQUARE

RICHMOND ST

ⓘ **Royal Court Theatre**

ⓐ

Town Hall

COOK ST

The Cavern Club

08 Place

Clayton Square Shopping Centre

ELLIOT STREET

Royal Liver Building

③ ⓑ

James St Station

ⓒ

LORD STREET

CHURCH STREET

SCHOOL LANE

RANELAGH ST

Cunard Building

Ⓜ

JAMES STREET

SOUTH JOHN STREET

PARADISE STREET

Bluecoat Chambers

HANOVER STREET

Open Eye Gallery

WOOD

Port of Liverpool Building

THE STRAND

CANNING

Concert Square

SEEL STREET

FLEET

SLATER STREET

Pier Head

MERSEY RAILWAY TUNNEL

Canning Dock

Bus stop for ★ Dock

PLACE

DUKE STREET

ARGYLE ST

HENRY ST

⑩

Maritime Museum

ⓘ

Salthouse Dock

PARK LANE

FOREST S'

Tate Liverpool

Albert Dock

⑭

Bus stop For ★ City

⑮

GOWER STREET

The Beatles Story

WAPPING

Wapping Basin

ST JAMES STREET

NELSON ST

Wapping Dock

JAMAICA STREET

River Mersey

QUEENS WHARF

Queens Dock

CHALONER STREET

ⓗ

PARLIAMENT

PUB & BARS

Lion Tavern	2
Magnet	8
Philharmonic	9
Ship and Mitre	1
Ye Cracke	12

RESTAURANTS & CAFÉS

Baby Cream	14
Everyman Bistro	5
Far East	11
Kimos	4
The Monro	10
Panamerican Club	15
The Quarter	13
Side Door	6
Simply Heathcotes	3
Tea Factory	7

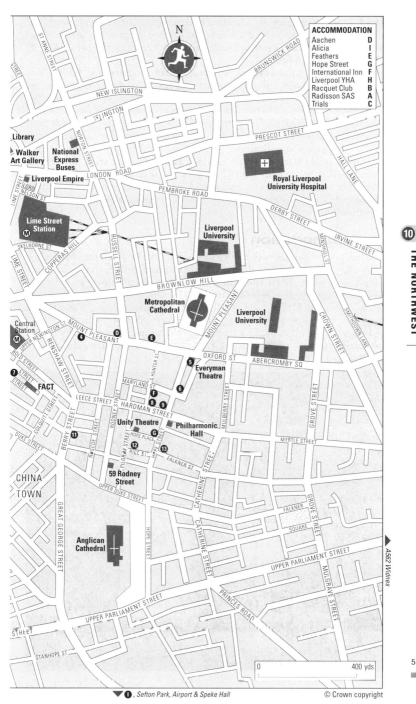

© Crown copyright

▼ ❶ , Sefton Park, Airport & Speke Hall

ACCOMMODATION

Aachen	**D**
Alicia	**I**
Feathers	**E**
Hope Street	**G**
International Inn	**F**
Liverpool YHA	**H**
Racquet Club	**B**
Radisson SAS	**A**
Trials	**C**

Dock inside the Merseyside Maritime Museum (daily 10am–5pm). Locals and visitors can find out about the Capital of Culture preparations and celebrations at the **08 Place**, 36–38 Whitechapel (daily 9am–6pm; ☎0151/233 2008, Ⓦ www.liverpool08.com).

The local transport authority is **Merseytravel** (enquiry line ☎0870/608 2608, daily 8am–8pm; Ⓦ www.merseytravel.gov.uk), which coordinates all buses, trains and ferries. Otherwise, City Sightseeing's open-top **Liverpool Bus Tour** (Ⓦ www.city-sightseeing.com) provides a hop-on-hop-off service around the city centre and Albert Dock (Easter–Oct; departures every 30–60min from 10am; 24hr ticket £5). The tourist offices have details of guided **walking tours** of the city (most Easter–Sept; from £3), or with children in tow, don't miss a trip on the amphibious half-truck-half-boat **Yellow Duckmarine** (mid-Feb to Christmas daily every hour from 11am; £11.95, cheaper off-peak; ☎0151/708 7799, Ⓦ www.theyellowduckmarine.co.uk), which departs from Gower Street, in front of Albert Dock, and trundles around the city centre before splashing down into the docks.

Accommodation

Budget hotel chains are well represented, with *Premier Travel Inn*, *Ibis*, *Express by Holiday Inn*, *Campanile* and others all with convenient city-centre locations, including down by Albert Dock. In addition, both **universities** – John Moores University (☎0151/231 3511, Ⓦ www.livjm.ac.uk/holidays) and the University of Liverpool (☎0151/794 6402, Ⓦ www.liv.ac.uk) – have hundreds of good-value single rooms available (from around £19 room only) during the Easter holidays and from late June to early September. For details of special-offer hotel weekend breaks and packages call ☎0845/601 1125 (☎0151/709 8111 from abroad).

△ Liverpool

Hotels and guest houses

Aachen 89–91 Mount Pleasant ☎0151/709 3477, ⓦwww.aachenhotel.co.uk. A range of value-for-money rooms (with and without en-suite showers) and big "eat-as-much-as-you-like" breakfasts. ❸

Alicia 3 Aigburth Drive, Sefton Park ☎0151/727 4411, ⓦwww.feathers.uk.com. Restored cotton-merchant's home with park views and a variety of inviting rooms, plus Edwardian-style bar, restaurant, conservatory and garden. ❺

Feathers 113–125 Mount Pleasant ☎0151/709 9655, ⓦwww.feathers.uk.com. A converted terrace of Georgian houses, with a variety of rooms in warm crimson tones, all en suite. Buffet breakfast included in the price. ❺

Hope Street 40 Hope St (entrance on Hope Place) ☎0151/709 3000, ⓦwww.hopestreethotel.co.uk. This former Victorian warehouse has been given a chic makeover – retaining its original brickwork and cast-iron columns but adding hardwood floors, huge beds and flat-screen TVs. Breakfast not included. ❼, deluxe rooms ❽

Racquet Club Hargreaves Building, 5 Chapel St ☎0151/236 6676, ⓦwww.racquetclub.org.uk. Boutique-style townhouse hotel, mixing good linen and traditional furniture with contemporary art and all mod cons. Breakfast not included. ❼

Radisson SAS 107 Old Hall St ☎0151/966 1500, ⓦwww.radissonsas.com. Sleek lodgings with river views and rooms with the signature *Radisson* style. It's a four-star-deluxe business hotel, but the location's good for tourists and the facilities (restaurant, bar, pool, sauna, gym, etc) are top-notch. ❼

Trials 56 Castle St ☎0151/227 1021, ⓦwww.trialshotel.com. Classy nineteenth-century building with Victorian-styled public areas and modernized "suites" with superior Jacuzzi-tub bathrooms. ❼

Hostels

International Inn 4 South Hunter St, off Hardman Street ☎0151/709 8135, ⓦwww.internationalinn.co.uk. Converted Victorian warehouse, with modern accommodation for 100 in heated, en-suite rooms sleeping two to ten people. Lounge, kitchen, laundry and baggage storage, bedding provided and no curfew. Dorm beds £15, weekends £16, twin rooms ❶

Liverpool YHA Wapping ☎0870/770 5924, ⓔliverpool@yha.org.uk. Accommodation is in smart two, three-, four- or six-bed rooms (with private bathroom and heated towel rail). Also a kitchen, café, luggage storage, laundry facilities and 24hr reception. Dorms £20.95, includes breakfast.

The City

The main sights are scattered throughout the centre of Liverpool but you can easily walk between most of them, through cityscapes ranging from revamped shopping arcades and restyled city squares to the surviving regal Georgian terraces around Rodney and Hope streets. If you're short on time, the two **cathedrals**, **Albert Dock** and the **World Museum Liverpool** are the stand-out highlights, with both the **Walker Art Gallery** and **Tate Liverpool** essential for art fans. It's worth noting that the city is undergoing a massive amount of building work in the run-up to Capital of Culture year (2008), particularly around Lime Street Station and at the huge Paradise Street retail development area (between Albert Dock and the city centre).

Around Lime Street

Emerging from **Lime Street Station** – whose cast-iron train shed was the largest in the world on its completion in 1867 – you can't miss **St George's Hall** (ⓦwww.stgeorgeshall.com), once Liverpool's crown court and one of Britain's finest Greek Revival buildings. Highly informative **tours** (daily 11.30am and 1.30pm; £4.50, EH; tickets from the tourist office or at the hall, ☎0151/225 5530) show you the highlights – the longer afternoon tour is more likely to include a trip to the imposing law courts and surviving cells.

Over the way, Liverpool's **Walker Art Gallery** on William Brown Street (daily 10am–5pm; free; ⓦwww.thewalker.org.uk) has its origins in the collection of eminent Liverpudlian William Roscoe (1753–1831), who acquired much of the early Renaissance art now on display. Liverpool's explosive economic growth in the eighteenth and nineteenth centuries is reflected in much of the Walker's collection, as British painting begins to occupy centre

The Beatles in Liverpool

Mathew Street, ten minutes' walk west of Lime Street Station, was once the womb of Merseybeat, and has now become a little enclave of Beatles nostalgia. *The Cavern* club here was where the band was first spotted by Brian Epstein; the club closed in 1966, though a latterday successor, the **Cavern Club** at 10 Mathew St, complete with souvenir shop, was rebuilt on half of the original site. The **Cavern Pub**, immediately across the way, boasts a coiffed Lennon lounging against the wall and an exterior "Wall of Fame", while the soul of Beatlemania is embodied at **The Beatles Shop**, 31 Mathew St (W www.thebeatleshop.co.uk), with the "largest range of Beatles gear in the world".

For a personal and social history of the group, head to the Albert Dock for **The Beatles Story** (daily 10am–6pm; £8.99; W www.beatlesstory.com). Then it's on to the two houses where John Lennon and Paul McCartney grew up, both now saved for the nation by the National Trust. At **20 Forthlin Rd**, home of the McCartney family from 1955–1964, visitors don headphones and tramp round the 1950s terraced house where John and Paul wrote songs and where Paul's mother Mary died. **Mendips**, the rather more genteel house where John Lennon lived between 1945 and 1963 with his Aunt Mimi and Uncle George, has been similarly preserved. The houses are only accessible on a pre-booked minibus tour (Easter–Oct Wed–Sun; booking essential; £12; NT members £6), departing at 10.30am and 11.20am from the city centre (T 0151/708 8574) and at 2.15pm and 3.55pm from Speke Hall (T 0151/427 7231). Dedicated pilgrims will also want to see all the other famous Beatles' landmarks, like Strawberry Fields (a Salvation Army home) and Penny Lane (an ordinary suburban street). This is best done on an **organized Beatles tour**, though these only show you the exteriors of the Lennon and McCartney homes.

Beatles tours

Phil Hughes T 0151/228 4565 or 07961/511223, W www.tourliverpool.co.uk. Small (8-seater) minibus tours with a guide well versed in The Beatles and Liverpool life. Three-and-a-half hour tours daily on demand, £12 per person (private tour £65); city-centre pick-ups/drop-offs, plus free refreshments.

Magical Mystery Tour T 0151/709 3285, W www.caverncitytours.com or book at tourist offices or Beatles Story. Two-hour tours (£11.95) on board a multi-coloured Mystery Bus, departing daily throughout the year from Queen Square and Albert Dock.

stage – notably works by George Stubbs, England's greatest animal painter (and native Liverpudlian), and by the Pre-Raphaelites. Impressionists and post-Impressionists drag the collection into more modern times and tastes, before the Walker embarks on its final round of galleries of contemporary British art, much of it first displayed at the gallery's biennial **John Moores Exhibition** (usually held from October of odd-numbered years to the following January).

Further along William Brown Street the **World Museum Liverpool** (daily 10am–5pm; free; W www.worldmuseumliverpool.org.uk) has emerged as the city's major family attraction. The dramatic six-storey atrium provides access to an eclectic series of themed exhibits of broad appeal – from natural history to ethnographical collections, insects to antiquities, dinosaurs to space rockets. Stand-out sections for children include the Bug House (no explanation required), plus excellent hands-on natural history and archeology discovery centres, while a Planetarium and theatre have free daily shows, with times posted at the information desk.

The cathedrals and around

On the hill behind Lime Street, off Mount Pleasant, rises the idiosyncratically shaped Catholic **Metropolitan Cathedral** of Christ the King (daily 8am–5/6pm; donation requested), denigratingly known as "Paddy's Wigwam" or the "Mersey Funnel". The spectacular 1960s Modernist design is anchored by sixteen concrete ribs which support the landmark stained-glass lantern. Ceremonial steps mark the approach from Mount Pleasant/Hope Street, with four huge bells at the top, named Matthew, Mark, Luke and John – or John, Paul, George and Ringo, as waggish tour guides insist.

At the other end of the aptly named Hope Street, the Anglican **Liverpool Cathedral** (daily 8am–6pm; donation requested) looks much more ancient but was actually completed eleven years later, in 1978, after 74 years in construction. The last of the great British neo-Gothic structures, Sir Giles Gilbert Scott's masterwork claims a smattering of superlatives: Britain's largest and the world's fifth-largest cathedral, the world's tallest Gothic arches and the highest and heaviest bells. On a clear day a trip up the 330-foot **tower** (£2.50) is rewarded by views to the Welsh hills, while the refectory café under the Gothic arches is a popular spot.

A couple of minutes' walk from the Anglican Cathedral, **59 Rodney Street** (Easter–Oct Wed–Sun, plus Nov weekends; timed tours only, call ☎0151/709 6261; £4.50, NT) was the home and studio of photographer Edward Chambre Hardman. The National Trust has restored the rooms where he lived for forty years (1948–88), and presents a wide selection of his Liverpool photographs.

The city centre

In the former warehouse and factory district between Bold Street and Duke Street (an area now known as the **Ropewalks**), apartments, urban spaces, café-bars and shops have sprouted in recent years. **FACT** at 88 Wood St (ⓦwww.fact.co.uk) – that's "Film, Art and Creative Technology" – provides a cultural anchor for the neighbourhood with its galleries for art, video and new media exhibitions (Tues–Sun 11am/noon–6/8pm; free), community projects, cinema screens, café and bar.

Nearby School Lane throws up the beautifully proportioned **Bluecoat Chambers**, originally built in 1717 as an Anglican boarding school for orphans. It's been an integral part of Liverpool's cultural life for years as the **Bluecoat Arts Centre** (ⓦwww.bluecoatartscentre.com), which is currently undergoing major refurbishment – it should reopen by 2007, though the associated **Bluecoat Display Centre** contemporary craft gallery and shop (ⓦwww.bluecoatdisplaycentre.com) remains open (access from College Lane).

Diverting towards **Queen Square**, one of the city centre's surviving Victorian warehouses, on the corner of Whitechapel and Queen Square, is occupied by the **Conservation Centre** (Mon–Sat 10am–5pm, Sun noon–5pm; free; ⓦwww.conservationcentre.org.uk). This is where Liverpool's museums and galleries undertake their restoration work and give visitors a hands-on, behind-the-scenes look.

Pier Head, Mersey Ferry and the Three Graces

Though the tumult of shipping which once fought the current here has gone, the **Pier Head** landing stage remains the embarkation point for the **Mersey Ferry** (☎0151/330 1444, ⓦwww.merseyferries.co.uk) to Woodside (for Birkenhead) and Seacombe (Wallasey). Straightforward ferry shuttles (£2.10 return) operate during the morning and evening rush hours, but at other times the boats run circular fifty-minute "river explorer" **cruises** (hourly; Mon–Fri

10am–3pm, Sat & Sun 10am–6pm; £4.80). The view back across the Mersey to the Liverpool skyline is one of the city's glories. Dominating the waterfront are the so-called **Three Graces** – namely the Port of Liverpool Building (1907), Cunard Building (1913) and, most prominently, the 322-foot-high **Royal Liver Building** (1910), topped by the "Liver Birds", a couple of cormorants which have become the symbol of the city.

Albert Dock

Albert Dock, five minutes' walk south of Pier Head, was built in 1846 when Liverpool's port was a world leader. It started to decline at the beginning of the twentieth century, as the new deep-draught ships were unable to berth here, and last saw service in 1972. A decade later the site was given a complete refit, emerging as a type of rescued urban heritage that's been copied throughout the country, but rarely as successfully as here.

The **Merseyside Maritime Museum** (daily 10am–5pm; free; Ⓦ www .merseysidemaritimemuseum.org.uk) fills one wing of the Dock. A trip through the museum can easily take two hours, with sections on the history of Liverpool's evolution as a port and shipbuilding centre, plus an illuminating display detailing Liverpool's pivotal role as a springboard for over nine million emigrants. The museum is at its best, however, in its shocking and refreshingly honest "Transatlantic Slavery" exhibit. Conditions endured on the transatlantic voyage are illustrated by a reconstruction of a slave ship, echoing with haunting voices reading from diaries of slaves and slavers.

The neighbouring **Tate Liverpool** (Tues–Sun 10am–6pm; free, special exhibitions usually £4; Ⓦ www.tate.org.uk/liverpool) is the country's national collection of modern art in the North. Popular retrospectives and an ever-changing display of individual works are its bread and butter, and there's also a full programme of events, talks and tours – the daily half-hour gallery talk at 2pm is free.

Eating, drinking and nightlife

Most of the city's **cafés and restaurants** are found at Albert Dock, around Hardman and Hope streets, or along Berry and Nelson streets, heart of Liverpool's Chinatown. Liverpool's **pubs and bars**, meanwhile, are concentrated

---

This sporting life

Liverpool's most popular recreational activity, bar none, is football. **Liverpool** football club plays at **Anfield** (ticket office ☏0151/220 2345, Ⓦ www.liverpoolfc.tv) in front of some of the nation's most loyal supporters. There are popular daily tours (not on match days) around the well-stocked museum, trophy room and dressing rooms (museum and tour £9, museum only £5; booking essential ☏0151/260 6677). **Everton**, the city's less glamorous side, command equally intense devotion at **Goodison Park** (ticket office ☏0870/442 1878; tours Mon, Wed, Fri & Sun ☏0151/330 2305, Ⓦ www.evertonfc.com; £8.50). The first Saturday in April is **Grand National Day** at **Aintree** – the "World's Greatest Steeplechase" – the race being the culmination of a meeting that starts on the previous Thursday, with tickets ranging from £7 to £65. Catch the Merseyrail to Aintree and buy a ticket on the gate or book on ☏0151/522 2929. The "Grand National Experience" (May–Oct Tues–Fri 10am–5pm; £7, booking advised on ☏0151/522 2921, Ⓦ www.aintree.co.uk) shows you the stables, weighing room and museum, plus the grave of three-times winner Red Rum, before letting you ride the National on a race simulator.

in the Ropewalks area (Concert Square, Fleet Street, Slater Street and Wood Street), though Victoria Street in the business district is another fast-developing nightlife area, with another tranche of places down at Albert Dock. The city's dance **clubs** are mainly notable for their lack of pretence, fashion playing second string to dancing and drinking. That's even true of the annual "Cream-fields" bash of clubbing superbrand Cream (Ⓦ www.cream.co.uk), held most Augusts. The evening paper, the *Liverpool Echo*, has events **listings**.

Cafés and café-bars

Baby Cream Edward Pavilion, Albert Dock ☏ 0151/702 5826. Hedonistic lounge bar that's always fun – a stylish crowd nibbles the "tear-and-share" food and sips cocktails.

Everyman Bistro 5–9 Hope St ☏ 0151/708 9545. Long-standing theatre-basement hangout with homemade quiche, pies and bakes, pizza and salad-type meals. It's also known for its beers and wines, and the bar closes at midnight, 2am at weekends. Closed Sun.

Kimos 46 Mount Pleasant ☏ 0151/709 2355. A student fave for mountainous portions of Middle Eastern/Mediterranean-style grills, kebabs, platters and salads.

The Quarter 7 Falkner St ☏ 0151/707 1965. A great lunch place, with some seats outside on the Georgian terrace. Serves an Italian bistro menu, including gourmet pizza, but you can just stop by for coffee and cake.

Tea Factory 79 Wood St ☏ 0151/708 7008. Very cool, very chic "bar and kitchen" in the Ropewalks neighbourhood.

Restaurants

Far East 1st floor, 27–35 Berry St ☏ 0151/709 6072. One of the longest-serving and most reliable of Liverpool's Cantonese eating houses: a fairly no-frills operation, but with authentic *dim sum* (noon–6pm) and other classics. Inexpensive.

London Carriage Works 40 Hope St ☏ 0151/705 2222. A see-and-be-seen Modern British restaurant in the city's coolest designer hotel. You'll need a reservation (book well in advance for weekends), or try the adjacent bar-brasserie – a tad cheaper and just as stylish. Closed Sat lunch & Sun dinner. Very expensive.

The Monro 92–94 Duke St ☏ 0151/707 9933. A gastro-pub makeover for one of the city's oldest hostelries means this is now a place for serious British eating at a reasonable price. Moderate.

Panamerican Club Britannia Pavilion, Albert Dock ☏ 0151/709 7097. Handsome warehouse conversion that brings snappy North American style and service to its cavernous bar and restaurant. Expensive.

Side Door 29a Hope St ☏ 0151/707 7888. A winning combination of Mediterranean food and reasonable prices – with a bargain pre-theatre menu of £11.95. Closed Sat lunch, Sun & Mon. Expensive.

Simply Heathcotes Beetham Plaza, 25 The Strand ☏ 0151/236 3536. Locally sourced ingredients, light lunches, grills, Sunday brunch and other delights, in one of Liverpool's favourite restaurants. Expensive.

Pubs and bars

Lion Tavern 67 Moorfields. Real ale in superbly restored Victorian surroundings, from the tiles to the stained-glass rotunda.

Magnet 45 Hardman St. Booth seating, blood-red decor, a bit of Barry White – it's groovy all right, plus there's a funky club downstairs.

Philharmonic 36 Hope St. Liverpool's finest traditional watering-hole where the main attractions are the mosaic floors, tiling, gilded wrought-iron gates and the marble decor in the gents.

Ship and Mitre 133 Dale St. For the biggest real-ale choice in Liverpool, visit this renowned Art Deco free house.

Ye Cracke 13 Rice St. Crusty backstreet pub off Hope Street, much loved by the young Lennon and with a great jukebox.

Clubs and live music

Bar Fly 90 Seel St ☏ 0870/907 0999, Ⓦ www.barflyclub.com. Great indie/rock gigs and a wide variety of club nights in the Theatre or Loft Bar – *Chibuku* and *Circus* are the big nights out.

Carling Academy 11–13 Hotham St ☏ 0151/707 3200, Ⓦ www.Liverpool-academy.co.uk. The "other" Academy is the old *Lomax* – putting on a good roster of contemporary, indie and rock gigs.

Cavern Club 10 Mathew St ☏ 0151/236 1965, Ⓦ www.cavern-liverpool.co.uk. The self-styled "most famous club in the world" has live bands Thurs to Sun; free entry except after 11pm Sat.

Liverpool Academy 160 Mount Pleasant ☏ 0151/256 5555, Ⓦ www.liverpoolacademy.co.uk. Local bands, hot touring acts and club nights (plus cheap bar) playing to a mostly student audience, though open to all.

Arts, concerts and entertainment

The **Royal Liverpool Philharmonic Orchestra**, ranked with Manchester's Hallé as the Northwest's best, dominates the city's classical music scene. **Theatre** is well entrenched in the city at a variety of venues, while FACT (see below) is the place to head for independent **cinema**.

Annual **festivals** include the Mersey Maritime Festival (June); a celebration of African arts and music in Africa Oye (June; ⓦ www.africaoye.com); the **Summer Pops** (July), when the Royal Philharmonic and top pop names perform beneath a huge marquee on the docks; the Party at the Pier (August) for big-name pop and rock; the **Liverpool International Street Festival** (July/August; ⓦ www.brouhaha.uk.com), which involves performances by a host of European theatre, music and dance groups; and **Beatles Week** and the **Mathew Street Festival** (last week August; ⓦ www.mathewstreetfestival .co.uk), with half a million visitors dancing to hundreds of local, national and tribute bands.

Bluecoat Arts Centre School Lane ⓦ www .bluecoatartscentre.com. Should reopen by 2007, for drama, dance, poetry, comedy, music and art exhibitions.
Everyman Theatre and Playhouse 5–9 Hope St ☎ 0151/709 4776, ⓦ www.everymanplayhouse .com. A launchpad of local talent, for drama, concerts, exhibitions, dance and music.
Philharmonic Hall Hope Street ☎ 0151/709 3789, ⓦ www.liverpoolphil.com. Home of the Royal

Liverpool Philharmonic Orchestra, and with a full programme of other concerts.
Picturehouse at FACT Wood Street ☎ 0151/707 44560, ⓦ www.picturehouses.co.uk. The city's only independent cinema screens. Cheaper tickets weekdays before 6pm, and cheapest all day Wed.
Royal Court Theatre Roe Street ☎ 0151/709 4321, ⓦ www.royalcourttheatre.net. Art Deco theatre and concert hall, which sees regular pop and rock gigs.

Listings

Airport ☎ 0870/750 8484, ⓦ www.liverpooljohn lennonairport.com.
Buses Merseytravel ☎ 0870/608 2608, National Express ☎ 08705/808080.
Ferries Isle of Man Steam Packet Company ☎ 08705/523523, ⓦ www.steam-packet.com; Mersey Ferries ☎ 0151/330 1444, ⓦ www .merseyferries.co.uk; Norse Merchant Ferries ☎ 0870/600 4321.
Hospital Royal Liverpool University Hospital, Prescot Street ☎ 0151/706 2000.

Internet Caffe Latte.net, 4 South Hunter St ☎ 0151/709 9683 (Mon–Fri 8am–7pm, Thurs until 3pm, Sat & Sun 9am–5.30pm).
Pharmacy Boots, Clayton Square Shopping Centre ☎ 0151/709 4711; Moss Pharmacy, 68–70 London Rd ☎ 0151/709 5271 (daily until 11pm).
Police Canning Place ☎ 0151/709 6010.
Post office City-centre office at The Lyceum, 1 Bold St.
Taxis Mersey Cabs ☎ 0151/298 2222.

Blackpool

Shamelessly brash **BLACKPOOL** is the archetypal British seaside resort, its "Golden Mile" of piers, fortune-tellers, amusement arcades, tram and donkey rides, fish-and-chip shops, candyfloss stalls, fun pubs and bingo halls making no concessions to anything but low-brow fun-seeking of the finest kind. The seven miles of wide sandy beach, backed by an unbroken chain of hotels and guest houses, attract sixteen million people each year. It was the coming of the railway in 1846 that made Blackpool what it is today: within fifty years, there were piers, promenades and theatres for the thousands who descended, plus Blackpool's own "Eiffel Tower" on the seafront. As tastes have changed, and other

British holiday resorts have suffered from the rivalry of cheap foreign packages, Blackpool has simply gone from strength to strength. Underneath the populist veneer there's a sophisticated marketing approach, which balances ever more elaborate rides and attractions with well-grounded traditional entertainment. When other resorts begin to close up for the winter, Blackpool's main season is just beginning, as over half a million light bulbs are used to create **the Illuminations** which decorate the promenade from the beginning of September to early November. Lately, Blackpool has been looking to extend its attractions further, with plans laid to build a series of entertainment complexes and leisure parks. Development is expected to take up to twenty years and cost around £1 billion, though the masterplan shies away from the inevitable comparisons with Las Vegas – laser shows, glass domes and resort-style hotels might all follow, but they will complement, not supplant, the town's Victorian heritage.

Arrival, information and accommodation

Blackpool's main train station is **Blackpool North** (direct trains from Manchester and Preston), half a dozen blocks up Talbot Road from North Pier. A few steps down Talbot Road, towards the sea, stands the **bus station**, while some trains from Preston also run to **Blackpool South**, near the Pleasure Beach. Blackpool's **airport** (Ⓦwww.blackpoolinternational.com) – which handles regular flights to and from London Stansted and the Isle of Man, plus other destinations – lies two miles south of the centre; buses run to the bus station or it's a £5 taxi ride. The main **tourist office** is at 1 Clifton St (Mon–Sat 9am–5pm; Ⓣ01253/478222, Ⓦwww.visitblackpool.com), on the corner of Talbot Road; a seasonal office sits on the promenade opposite Blackpool Tower (June–Oct Mon–Sat 9.15am–5pm, Sun 10am–4.30pm). Both offices sell **discounted admission tickets** for all major Blackpool attractions (except the Pleasure Beach), and also have Travel Cards (three-day £13, five-day £18, seven-day £20) for use on local buses and trams.

Bed-and-breakfast prices are generally low (from £15 per person, even less on a room-only basis or out of season), but rise at weekends and during the Illuminations. Anything cheap between North and Central piers is guaranteed to be noisy; for more peace and quiet (an unusual request in Blackpool, it has to be said), look for places along the more restful North Shore, beyond North Pier.

Guest houses and hotels

The Big Blue Ocean Boulevard, Blackpool Pleasure Beach Ⓣ0845/367 3333, Ⓦwww.bigbluehotel.com. Stylish family rooms with separate children's area, plus grown-up executive rooms with sofas, fireplaces and excellent bathrooms. It's next to the Pleasure Beach south entrance. ❺

Boltonia 124–126 Albert Rd Ⓣ01253/620248, Ⓦwww.boltoniahotel.co.uk. Not far from the Winter Gardens, on a corner plot which lets in lots of light – superior rooms are a bit more spacious and have large TVs. Parking available. ❷

Grosvenor View 7–9 King Edward Ave Ⓣ01253/352851. Along North Shore, a mile or so from the action. Rooms in this detached property are larger and better equipped than most. ❷

The Imperial North Promenade Ⓣ01253/623971, Ⓦwww.paramount-hotels.co.uk. The politicians'

conference favourite, a four-star hotel with sea-facing rooms, pool and gym, and the famous oak-panelled *No. 10 Bar*. It's a short tram ride away from the Tower and the rest of the sights. ❼

Number One 1 St Lukes Rd Ⓣ01253/343901, Ⓦwww.numberone-blackpool.com. An extraordinarily lavish boutique experience hosted by the ultra-amiable Mark and Claire. It's handy for the Pleasure Beach, with just three rooms, each with huge plasma-screen TV, crisp linen, thick bathrobes, DVD, games console and great bathrooms. ❼

Raffles 73–77 Hornby Rd Ⓣ01253/294713, Ⓦwww.raffleshotelblackpool.co.uk. Nice place back from Central Pier and away from the bustle, with well-kept rooms, bar, and traditional tearooms attached. ❹

The Town

With seven miles of beach and accompanying promenade, you'll want to jump on and off the electric trams if you plan to get up and down much between the piers. Most of the town-centre shops, bars and cafés lie between Central and North piers. The major event in town is **Blackpool Pleasure Beach** on the South Promenade (March–Nov daily from 10am though hours can vary; call ☎0870/444 5566, ⓦwww.blackpoolpleasurebeach.com), just south of South Pier. Entrance to the amusement park is free, but you'll have to fork out for the superb array of "white knuckle" rides including the "Big One", the world's fastest roller coaster (85mph). After this, the Pleasure Beach's wonderful array of antique wooden roller coasters – "woodies" to aficionados – seems like kids' stuff, but each is unique. The original "Big Dipper" was invented at Blackpool in 1923 and still thrills. Individual rides cost from £1 to £5, but better value is an unlimited-ride wristband (£30, usually cheaper in the off-season).

Jump a tram for the ride up to **Central Pier** with its 108-foot-high revolving Big Wheel. The **Sea-Life Centre** (July & Aug Mon–Thurs & Sun 10am–6pm; Fri & Sat 10am–10pm; Sept–June daily 10am–6pm; £8.95; ⓦwww.sealife.co.uk) nearby is one of the country's best, with eight-foot sharks looming at you as you march through a glass tunnel and a very large, lurking Giant Pacific octopus. For a taste of what Blackpool attractions used to be like, you could then hit **Louis Tussauds Waxworks**, 87–89 Central Promenade (daily 10am–10pm; £7) – these days, more Posh and Becks than Churchill and Margaret Thatcher.

Blackpool's elegant cast-iron **piers** also strike a traditional note. They're covered with arcades and amusements, while much of what passes for evening family entertainment – TV comics and variety shows – takes place in the various pier theatres. Between Central and North piers stands the 518-foot **Blackpool Tower** (daily: June–Oct 10am–11pm; Nov–May 10am–6pm; £14, £8 after 7pm; ⓦwww.theblackpooltower.co.uk), erected in 1894 when it was thought that the Northwest really ought not to be outdone by Paris. It provides the skyline's sole touch of grace, but paying the hefty entrance fee is the only way to ride up to the top for the stunning view and an unnerving walk on the see-through glass floor. The all-day ticket covers all the other tower attractions, including the stunning gilt Edwardian ballroom, plus aquarium, children's entertainers, indoor adventure playground, dinosaur ride, cafés and amusements. From the very early days, there's been a Moorish-inspired **circus** (2hr shows included in the entry ticket; two daily performances) between the tower's legs, which still functions though, in the spirit of the times, it's now animal-free.

Eating

Eating out revolves around the typical British seaside fare of fish and chips, available all over town. Given the sheer volume of customers, other restaurants don't have to try too hard: you'll have no trouble finding cheap roasts, pizzas, Chinese or Indian food, but might struggle if you're seeking a bit more sophistication. For a quieter night out, head the few miles south to genteel **St Annes** (a taxi's best), where Wood Street has a line of agreeable bars and restaurants.

Cafés and restaurants

Dress Circle Café Grand Theatre, Church Street. Dine in the ornate bar to show tunes – the food's good value, concentrating on things like a daily roast, steak, scampi and lasagne. Closes 5.30pm. Inexpensive.

Harry Ramsden's 60–63 The Promenade, corner of Church Street ☎01253/294386. The celebrated

Yorkshire chippie chain has the town's pre-eminent (and priciest) sit-down fish and chips – there's a takeaway counter too. Moderate.

September Brasserie 15–17 Queen St ☎01253/623282. The restaurant with the best reputation in town – set prices for two- and three-course meals with plenty of choice, the menu ranging from locally potted shrimps to king prawn tempura. Closed Sun, & Mon lunch. Expensive.

White Tower Ocean Blvd, Blackpool Pleasure Beach ☎01253/346710. The closest the town gets to Vegas – a lounge-style restaurant with prom views (great for the Illuminations), snappy service and Modern British food. Closed Mon, & Sat lunch. Expensive.

Yamato 28 Wood St, St Annes ☎01253/782868. A teppanyaki restaurant that's well worth the trip to watch the amiable chefs work their magic at the communal grill-tables. Good-value set menus. Moderate.

Drinking, nightlife and entertainment

If you like your nightlife late, loud and libidinous, summertime Blackpool has few English peers. In all the **pubs and clubs**, young men will be given the once-over by the hired hulks at the door, while "girls" and "ladies" can expect free drinks and entry and a lot of largely good-natured amorous jousting. *Yates' Wine Lodge* has two popular branches, in Talbot Square and between Central and South piers where you can sip an amontillado sherry or champagne on draught. There's also a plethora of Irish theme bars, while *The Wheatsheaf* on Talbot Road, opposite Blackpool North Station, features real ales from local breweries, an open fire and Beat-era memorabilia.

For **dancing**, local opinion favours *The Syndicate*, 120–140 Church St (Ⓦwww.thesyndicate.com), the UK's biggest club. *Funny Girls*, a transvestite-run bar at 5 Dickson Rd, off Talbot Road (☎0870/350 2665, Ⓦwww.itponline .co.uk), has nightly shows that attract long (gay and straight) queues. Otherwise, entertainment is based very heavily on family shows, musicals, veteran TV comedians, magicians, tribute bands, crooners and stage spectaculars put on at a variety of end-of-pier and **Pleasure Beach** (☎0870/444 5566) theatres, or at historic venues such as the **Grand Theatre** (☎01253/290190, Ⓦwww.black poolgrand.co.uk), **Winter Gardens** (☎01253/292029, Ⓦwww.blackpoollive .co.uk) and **Opera House** (☎01253/292029), all on Church Street.

Preston and around

With the siren draws of the Lakes, the Peak District and the Yorkshire Dales so close, the rest of Lancashire often gets bypassed in the rush to the surrounding national parks, and more's the pity. In **Preston**, 25 miles northwest of Manchester, the county has one of England's oldest towns, while north of the town rural Lancashire is at its most bucolic in the villages of the **Ribble Valley**.

Preston

Strategically placed on the banks of the River Ribble, **PRESTON** (possibly a contraction of "Priest's Town") was already an important market town in Anglo-Saxon times and received its royal charter in 1179 – origin of the famous Preston Guild celebrations, which since 1542 have taken place every twenty years (the next in 2012). True, there's little to show for such a long history save the nickname, "Proud Preston", but as the administrative and commercial centre of Lancashire, it's a useful shopping and service centre. Some handsome Victorian public buildings do survive, most notably the majestic Greek Revival-style **Harris Museum and Art Gallery** (Mon–Sat 10am–5pm, Sun

11am–4pm; free), in the central Market Square. Aside from exploring the "Story of Preston", the permanent collection focuses on fine art (particularly British landscape and portraiture, and contemporary photography) and decorative art. On either side of the Harris lies the modern shopping area, converging on Fishergate, the main street through town: the Victorian **Miller Arcade** (facing Fishergate) and outdoor and indoor **markets** (up Market Street; closed Sun) are the main draw.

If you needed any more incentive to stop it would be to make your way to the ground of Preston North End – one of Britain's oldest football clubs and winners of the first Football League championship – for the **National Football Museum**, Sir Tom Finney Way, Deepdale Stadium (Tues–Sat 10am–5pm, Sat matchdays until 3pm, midweek matchdays until 7.30pm, Sun 11am–5pm, also open Mon in summer school hols; free; ⓦwww.national footballmuseum.com). On one level, this is simply an unparalleled collection of football memorabilia, but you really don't have to know anything about football to enjoy the museum, since "the true story of the world's greatest game" is backed by fascinating print, film and sound material on football's origins, its social importance, the experience of fans through the ages, and other relevant themes.

For the football museum, it's a ten-minute ride on bus #19 (every 5min) from Preston **bus station**, right in the town centre. The **train station** has regular services to Lancaster, Manchester and Blackpool. The **tourist office** is in the Guild Hall, on Lancaster Road (Mon–Sat 10am–5.30pm; ☏01772/253731, ⓦwww.visitpreston.com), just round the corner from the Harris Museum.

The Ribble Valley

When the nineteenth-century Lancashire cotton weavers enjoyed a rare break from their industry they took to the bucolic retreats of the **Ribble Valley**, north of Preston, which cuts through the heart of northern Lancashire to the river's source in the Yorkshire Dales. On the banks of the Ribble, the tidy little market town of **CLITHEROE** is best seen from the terrace of its empty **Norman keep** which towers above the Ribble Valley floor. From here, the small centre is laid out before you and, if there's little else specific to see, you can at least spend an hour or two browsing around the shops and old pubs. There's been a **market** in town since the thirteenth century: it's currently held off King Street every Tuesday, Thursday and Saturday. Pendle Hill, a couple of miles to the east, was where the ten **Pendle Witches** allegedly held the diabolic rites that led to their hanging in 1612. The evidence against them came mainly from one small child, but nonetheless a considerable mythology has grown up around the witches, whose memory is perpetuated by a hilltop gathering each Halloween.

Heading northwest from Clitheroe takes you into the region known as the **Forest of Bowland** – the word "forest" is used in its traditional sense of a "royal hunting ground", and much of the land still belongs to the Crown. Small hamlets and country hotels are a feature of the district, notably the splendid *Inn at Whitewell* (☏01200/448222; various rooms ❻ or ❼), which serves fabulous food in its restaurant (reservations essential) and also has a welcoming, old-fashioned bar serving meals. At **SLAIDBURN** – the most substantial and attractive of the forest's settlements – hoary stone cottages fronted by a strip of aged cobbles set the tone. In the centre of the village, there's a truly ancient inn, the *Hark to Bounty* (☏01200/446246, ⓦwww.hark-to-bounty.co.uk; ❹), known for its good bar **food**, with a popular YHA **hostel** (☏0870/770 6034, ⓔslaidburn@yha.org.uk; £11.95; closed Nov–Easter), opposite.

Lancaster and around

LANCASTER, Lancashire's county town, dates back at least as far as the Roman occupation. However, it's the predominantly Georgian buildings built during the town's days as an important port on the slave triangle, that gives it its character today. The town makes a popular stop-off on the way to the Lakes or Dales to the north, and a good base for day-trips to the nearby resort of Morecambe and neighbouring Heysham village with its ancient churches.

Lancaster Castle (daily tours: every 30min, 10.30am–4pm; £4; @www .lancastercastle.com) has been the city's focal point since Roman times, when there was a fort on this site. It was added to throughout medieval times, becoming a crown court and prison in the thirteenth century, a role it still fulfils today – court sittings sometimes affect the schedules of the entertaining hour-long tours which visit the grandiose Shire Hall and Adrian's Tower, whose eight-foot-thick walls encircle a room hung with manacles and leg-irons. A two-minute walk down the steps between the castle and its neighbour, the **Priory Church of St Mary** (daily 10am–4.30pm; free), brings you to the seventeenth-century **Judges' Lodgings** (Easter–June & Oct Mon–Fri 1–4pm, Sat & Sun noon–4pm; July–Sept Mon–Fri 10am–4pm, Sat & Sun noon–4pm; £2), once used by visiting magistrates and now home to two local museums. Continuing down the hill and left onto Damside Street, you arrive on the banks of the **River Lune** – which lent Lancaster its name. The top floor of one of the eighteenth-century warehouses is taken up by part of the **Maritime Museum**, St George's Quay (daily: Easter–Oct 11am–5pm; Nov–Easter 12.30–4pm; £2), entered through the Old Custom House on the riverside. For a panorama of the town, Morecambe Bay and the Cumbrian fells, take a bus from the bus station (or a steep 25-minute walk up Moor Lane) to **Williamson Park** (daily 10/11am–4/5pm; park free, butterfly house £4; @www.williamsonpark.com), Lancaster's highest point. The grounds were laid out among old stone quarries by cotton workers, put out of work by the cotton famine caused by the American Civil War. Funded by local statesman and lino magnate Lord Ashton, the park's centrepiece is the 220-foot-high **Ashton Memorial**, a Baroque folly raised by his son in memory of his second wife.

Practicalities

From either the **train station** on Meeting House Lane, or the combined local **bus** and National Express station on Cable Street in town, it's a five-minute walk to the **tourist office** at 29 Castle Hill (March–Sept Mon–Sat 10am–5pm, Tues closes at 4pm; Oct–Feb Mon–Sat 10am–4pm; ℡01524/32878, @www.visitlancaster.gov.uk), in front of the castle. Annual **events and festivals** include spectacular Bonfire Night celebrations (Saturday nearest Nov 5). For anything more cultural, the main destination is **Dukes** on Moor Lane (℡01524/598500, @www.dukes-lancaster.org), the city's principal arts centre, with cinema, theatre (including open-air performances in Williamson Park in summer) and other events.

Accommodation

Old Station House 25 Meeting House Lane ℡01524/381060, @oldstationhouse@amserve .com. By the train station, providing amiable, non-smoking accommodation in two doubles and a twin, each with shower or private bathroom. No credit cards. ❸

Royal King's Arms 75 Market St ℡01524/32451, @www.swallow-hotels.com. Fifty prettily furnished rooms with smart bathrooms, plus a bar and brasserie. Ask for a castle view. ❻

Shakespeare 96 St Leonard's Gate ℡01524 /841041. Cosy rooms (en-suite, nonsmoking) in a popular townhouse hotel. No credit cards. ❸

🏃 **Sun** 63 Church St ☎01524/66006, ⊛www
.thesunhotelandbar.co.uk. Eight smart en-
suite rooms above a contemporary bar fashioned
from a 300-year-old building. Breakfast served till
11am, with full meals available in the associated
Santé café-lounge down the street. ❹, superior
rooms ❺

Cafés and restaurants

Il Bistro Morini 26 Sun St ☎01524/846252. The
best Italian in town, with a veggie-friendly Mediterranean menu. Dinner only; closed Sun. Moderate.

🏃 **Pizza Margherita** 2 Moor Lane
☎01524/36333. Friendly pizza place, with
sixteen choices on the menu (and Lancashire
cheese on a couple of them), plus a few pastas and
some salad-type starters. You can fill up for around
£12. Inexpensive.

Sun Café 25 Sun St ☎01524/845599. Stylish
café-restaurant, good for all-day breakfasts, a
sandwich and a glass of wine, or Sunday brunch
with the papers. Closed Sun at 8pm, plus Mon
evening. Moderate.

Whale Tail 78a Penny St. Veggie and wholefood
café, tucked up a yard on the first floor, serving
good breakfasts, tasty dips, salads, burgers, sandwiches and baked potatoes. Closes 4/5pm, 3pm on
Sun. Inexpensive.

Pubs

Water Witch Aldcliffe Road (across the canal
bridge). Canalside pub named after an old canal
packet boat, with posh pub food and an impressive
range of real ales and continental lagers.

Ye Olde John O'Gaunt 53 Market St. City-centre
local with home-cooked food, a large range of
whiskies and vodkas, special beers, live trad jazz
and R&B, plus a small beer garden.

Morecambe and Heysham

Although the name **MORECAMBE**, meaning "Great Bay", dates from Celtic
times, the seaside town five miles west of Lancaster only took it in the nineteenth century when it rapidly expanded from a small fishing village into a
full-blown resort. The sweep of the bay is still the major attraction, with the
lakeland fells visible beyond and the local sunsets a renowned phenomenon. The
Stone Jetty – all that remains of the former harbour – has been remodelled and
now features bird sculptures, games and motifs, recognizing Morecambe Bay as
Britain's most important wintering site for wildfowl and wading birds. A little
way along the prom stands the most popular statue of all, of one of Britain's
most treasured comedians – Eric Bartholomew, who took the stage name **Eric
Morecambe** when he met his comedy partner, Ernie Wise. Regular buses or
trains from Lancaster make the ten-minute trip to Morecambe: from the bus
or train stations, on either side of Central Drive, it's five minutes' walk to the
Stone Jetty.

The main historic interest on this side of Morecambe Bay is at **HEYSHAM**,
three miles southwest of Morecambe and best approached on foot, along the
promenade from the resort. Heysham's hidden gem is the shoreside **Heysham
Village**, centred on a group of charming seventeenth-century cottages and
barns. Settlement here can be traced back to prehistoric times, though its
proudest relic is the well-preserved Viking hog's-back tombstone in Saxon
St Peter's Church, set in a romantic churchyard below the headland. Just up
the lane, on the headland itself, the even earlier ruins of **St Patrick's Chapel**
occupy a superb vantage-point over the bay and to the lakeland hills beyond.

The Isle of Man

The **Isle of Man**, almost equidistant from Ireland, England, Wales and Scotland,
is one of the most beautiful spots in Britain, a mountainous, cliff-fringed island
just thirty-three miles by thirteen, into which are shoehorned austere moorlands and wooded glens, sandy beaches, fine castles, beguiling narrow-gauge

Ferries or the quicker **fastcraft** (ie Sea Cats), operated by the Isle of Man Steam Packet Company (℡08705/523523, 🌐www.steam-packet.com), run daily from either Heysham (near Lancaster) or Liverpool to Douglas, the capital. Departures vary according to season, and **fares** start at £15 one-way for foot passengers, £99 return for drivers, but advance-purchase tickets, short breaks and night-time sailings offer substantial savings (note that midweek travel is generally cheapest).

An increasing number of airlines offer **flights** to the island from around twenty British and Irish regional airports. Full contact details are available from the tourist office in Douglas, or on the official Isle of Man websites (see "Douglas", below). Regular prices start from £29 one-way, though special offers (down to as little as £6.99 plus tax) are sometimes available.

---

railways and scores of standing stones and Celtic crosses. It takes some effort to reach, and the weather is hardly reliable, factors that have seen tourist numbers fall since its Victorian heyday, when the island developed as rapidly as the other northwestern coastal resorts. This means, though, that the Isle of Man has been spared the worst excesses of the British tourist trade: there's peace and quiet in abundance, walks around the unspoilt hundred-mile coastline, rural villages straight out of a 1950s' picture-book, steam trains and cream teas – a yesteryear ensemble if ever there was one.

St Patrick is said to have come to the island in the fifth century AD bringing Christianity, though it was the arrival of the **Vikings** in the eleventh century which changed the face of the Isle of Man. They reigned as **Kings of Mann** – the name derived from that of the island's ancient sea-god, Manannan Mac Lir (Son of the Sea). The Scots wrested power from the Norsemen in 1275, the beginning of an ultimately unsuccessful 130-year struggle with the English for control of the island. The distinct identity of the island remained intact, however, and many true Manx inhabitants insist that the Isle of Man is not part of England, nor even of the UK. Indeed, although a Crown dependency, the island has its own government, **Tynwald**, arguably the world's oldest democratic parliament, which has run continuously since 979 AD. To further complicate matters, the island has its own sterling currency (worth the same as the mainland currency), its own laws (though they generally follow Westminster's), an independent postal service, and a Gaelic-based language which is taught in schools and seen on dual-language road signs. The island, of course, also produces its own tailless version of the domestic cat, as well as famously good kippers and queenies (scallops).

As well as the wonderful landscapes, the island's main tourist draw is the **TT (Tourist Trophy) motorcycle races** (held in the two weeks after the late-May bank holiday), a frenzy of speed and burning rubber that's shattered the island's peace annually since 1907. Tourism aside, in recent times the real money-spinner has been the **offshore finance industry**, exploiting the island's low income tax and absence of capital gains tax and death duties. The island also plays a major role in the development of e-banking and e-commerce, as well as providing incentives for the **filming** of an increasing number of movies.

Douglas

DOUGLAS, heart of the offshore finance industry, also has the vast majority of the island's hotels and best restaurants. A mere market town as late as 1850, with one pier and an undeveloped seafront, Douglas was a product of Victorian mass tourism and displays many similarities to Blackpool, just across the water. However, where once half a million people a year sported on the sands, package tourism to hotter climates has long since burst the bubble. As long as you put aside thoughts of Blackpool-style state-of-the-art entertainment, you can still have a thoroughly enjoyable time here, but it's likely to consist largely of pulling up a candy-striped deckchair and enjoying the extensive sands, with a ride on the promenade's horse-drawn tram thrown in for variety.

On Harris Promenade the lush interior of the **Gaiety Theatre** can be seen on hour-and-a-half-long tours each Saturday at 10.30am (Easter–Sept only; £6; information and box office ☏01624/694555), while further up Harris Promenade, approaching Broadway, the spruced-up **Villa Marina** gardens display more Victorian elegance. Major highlight in town, however, is the **Manx Museum**, on the corner of Kingswood Grove and Crellin's Hill (Mon–Sat 10am–5pm; free), which makes a good start for anyone wanting to get to grips with Manx culture and heritage before setting off around the island. Various rooms provide an absorbing synopsis of the island's history, packed with Neolithic standing stones, Celtic grave markers and other artefacts, while the island's natural history and environment has its own hands-on exhibition.

Practicalities

Ronaldsway Airport (flight enquiries ☏01624/821600, Ⓦwww.iom-airport .com) is around ten miles south of Douglas, close to Castletown. Buses (every 30min–1hr; 7am–11pm) connect the airport with Douglas as well as Castletown/Port St Mary. A taxi costs around £17 to Douglas. Ferries and Sea Cats dock by the **Sea Terminal** at the southern end of the Douglas waterfront. Fifty yards beyond the forecourt taxi rank, the Lord Street **bus terminal** is the hub of the island's dozen or so bus routes; there's an informative **Travel Shop** here (Mon–Thurs 8am–5.45pm, Fri 8am–12.30pm & 1.30–5.45pm, Sat 8am–12.30pm & 1.30–3.45pm; ☏01624/662525, Ⓦwww.iombusandrail.info).

The **tourist office** is in the Sea Terminal building (mid-May to Sept daily 9.15am–7pm, later in peak periods; Oct to mid-May Mon–Thurs 9.15am–5.30, Fri 9.15am–5pm, Sat & Sun restricted hours; ☏01624/686766), or check Ⓦwww.gov.im and Ⓦwww.visitisleofman.com for **information**. The island's twelve heritage sites and museums are run by Manx National Heritage (Ⓦwww.gov.im.mnh). They all have individual admission charges, though a **4 Site Ticket** (£10) can be bought from any of the attractions.

Accommodation

Admiral House Loch Promenade ☏01624/629551, Ⓦwww.admiralhouse.com. At the ferry-terminal end of the prom, this club-like retreat features comfortable rooms adorned in bold colours and with elegant bathrooms. The town's most expensive restaurant, *Ciapelli's*, is on the ground floor. ❻

Birchfield Villa York Road ☏01624/670383, Ⓔbirchfield@isleofman.uk.com. The most distinctive of Douglas's B&Bs offers three elegant rooms with a genteel atmosphere, a 5min uphill walk from the seafront (up Broadway, by the Villa Marina). ❺, 4-poster room ❻

Claremont 18–19 Loch Promenade ☏01624/673636, Ⓦwww.sleepwellhotels.com.

Sympathetically renovated promenade hotel with a good bar-brasserie. The nearby *Rutland* and *Chesterhouse* hotels are part of the same group, and similarly styled. ❺

Dreem Ard Ballanard Road, 2 miles west of the centre ☏01624/621491. Tranquil, out-of-town B&B with three en-suite rooms, including a large garden suite with its own dressing room and sitting area. No credit cards. ❸

Glen Mona 6 Mona Drive, off Central Promenade ☏01624/676755, Ⓔglenmona@manx.net. Refurbished en-suite rooms in a nice, family-run guest house just off the prom. ❹

Sefton Harris Promenade ☏01624/645500, Ⓦwww.seftonhotel.co.im. This four-star has sleek, spacious rooms offering a sea view or a balcony

over the internal water garden. Weekend rates are £10 cheaper per room; book online and you save yourself another tenner. **❼**
Welbeck Mona Drive, off Central Promenade ☏01624/675663, ⓦ www.welbeckhotel.com. Mid-sized family-run hotel 100yd up the hill off the seafront – some rooms have a sea view. Six two-person self-catering apartments also available (breakfast not included in the apartments). **❺**, apartments **❻**

Cafés and restaurants

Café Tanroagan 9 Ridgeway St ☏07624/472411. A relaxed, contemporary restaurant where fish straight off the boat is given either an assured Mediterranean twist or served simply grilled, steamed or poached. Reservations essential. Dinner only; closed Sun & Mon. Expensive.
C'est La Vie 28 Victoria St. Good-looking café-bar that's well known for its globally inspired food (until 9pm), bangers and mash to spicy Indonesian noodles. Closed Sun. Inexpensive.
Paparazzi 26 Loch Promenade ☏01624/673222. Locals like this large pizzeria-trattoria with a few more unusual specialities alongside the traditional pizzas, pastas and Italian dishes. Moderate.
Rendezvous 24 Duke St ☏01624/676833. Retro-

chic bistro with red-leather booth seating but a thoroughly contemporary menu – pan-fried scallops to fish of the day. Open from 9am for coffee, and serves a good-value lunch. Expensive.

Pubs and bars

Bar George Hill Street. A fashionable haunt housed in a converted Sunday school, opposite St George's church. Closed Sun.
Fiesta Havana 7–17 Wellington St. For drinks and cocktails, Latin American food, tapas, salsa nights and club sounds; open until 1am Fri and Sat.
Rovers Return 11 Church St. Cosy old local where you can try the local Manx beers.

Listings

Car rental Athol ☏01624/822481, ⓦ www.athol .co.im; Mylchreests ☏08000/190355, ⓦ www .mylchreests.com; Ocean Ford ☏01624/820830, ⓦ www.oceanford.com.
Hospital Noble's Hospital, Strang ☏01624/650000.
Internet *Feegan's Lounge*, 8 Victoria St (Mon–Sat 9am–6pm, Sun 1–5pm).
Police Douglas Police Station, Glencrutchery Road ☏01624/631212.
Post office Main post office is at 6 Regent St ☏01624/686141.

The rest of the island

Don't miss a trip on one of the two century-old rail services which still provide the best public transport to all the major towns and sights except for Peel. The carriages of the **Steam Railway** (Easter–Oct daily 10.15am–4.15pm; £8 return to Port Erin; ☏01624/673623) rock their fifteen-mile course from Douglas to Castletown, Port St Mary and Port Erin at a spirited pace. The rolling terrain due north of Douglas was too steep for conventional trains, but by 1893 fledgling technology was available to construct the **Manx Electric Railway** (Easter–Oct daily 9.40am–4.40pm; some later departures in summer; £7 return to Ramsey; ☏01624/663366) which runs for seventeen miles from Douglas's Derby Castle Station to Ramsey via Laxey. The "**Island Explorer**" ticket gives one (£10), three (£20), five (£30) or seven (£35) days' unlimited travel on all bus services, plus steam and electric train routes, the trip to Snaefell and horse-tram rides in Douglas. Tickets are available from the Travel Shop or the tourist office in Douglas.

Laxey

Filling a narrow valley, the straggling village of **LAXEY**, seven miles north of Douglas, spills down from its train station to a small harbour and long, pebbly beach, squeezed between two bulky headlands. The Manx Electric Railway from Douglas drops you at the station used by the Snaefell Mountain Railway (see below). Passengers disembark and then head inland and uphill to Laxey's pride, the "**Lady Isabella**" **Great Laxey Wheel** (Easter–Oct daily 10am–5pm; £3), smartly painted in red and white. With a diameter of over 72ft it's said to be the largest working waterwheel in the world. Otherwise Laxey is at its best

△ Great Laxey Wheel

down in **Old Laxey**, around the harbour, half a mile below the station, where large car parks attest to the popularity of the beach and river.

Snaefell

Every thirty minutes, the tramcars of the **Snaefell Mountain Railway** (Easter–Oct daily 10.15am–3.45pm; £7 return; ☎01624/663366) begin their thirty-minute wind from Laxey through increasingly denuded moorland to the island's highest point, the top of **Snaefell** (2036ft) – the Vikings' "Snow Mountain" – from where you can see England, Wales, Scotland and Ireland on a clear day. At the summit, most people are content to pop into the inelegant café and bar and then soak up the views for the few minutes until the return journey. But with a decent map and a clear day, you could walk back instead, following trails down the mountain to Laxey (the easiest and most direct route), Sulby Glen or the Peel–Ramsey road.

St John's

The trans-island A1 (and hourly bus #5 or #6 from Douglas) follows a deep twelve-mile-long furrow between the northern and southern ranges from Douglas to Peel. A hill at the crossroads settlement of **ST JOHN'S**, nine miles along it, is the original site of **Tynwald**, the ancient Manx government, which derives its name from the Norse *Thing Völlr*, meaning "Assembly Field". Nowadays the word refers to the Douglas-based House of Keys and Legislative Council, but acts passed in the capital only become law once they have been proclaimed here on July 5 (ancient Midsummer's Day) in an annual open-air parliament. Tynwald's four-tiered grass mound – made from soil collected from each of the island's parishes – stands at the other end of a processional path from the stone **St John's Church**, which traditionally doubled as the courthouse.

Peel and around

The main settlement on the west coast, **PEEL** is a town of some antiquity and its enduring appeal is as one of the most "Manx" of all the island's towns. Archeological evidence indicates that **St Patrick's Isle**, which guards the harbour, has had a significant population since Mesolithic times. What probably started out as a flint-working village on a naturally protected spot gained significance with the foundation of a monastery in the seventh or eighth century, parts of which remain inside the ramparts of the red-sandstone **Peel Castle** (Easter–Oct daily 10am–5pm; £3).

It's a fifteen-minute walk from the town around the river harbour and over the bridge to the castle. On the way, you'll pass the excellent harbourside House of Mannannan **heritage centre** (daily 10am–5pm; £5, combined ticket with Peel Castle £7), named after the island's ancient sea god. You should allow at least two hours to get around the museum, which concentrates strongly on participatory exhibits – whether it's listening to Celtic legends in a replica roundhouse, examining the contents and occupants of a life-sized Viking ship, walking through a kipper factory or steering a steamer.

The most regular **bus** service to Peel is the hourly #5 or #6 from Douglas. The best **accommodation** locally is five miles south of town down the A27 in **Dalby**, where *Ballacallin House Hotel* (☎01624/841100; ➎) is a traditional country inn with comfortable en-suite rooms, welcoming service, and famed sunset views. A minor road nearby runs to the little headland of **Niarbyl**, framed by clear water and fronted by a flat pebbled beach, above which sits a picture-perfect thatched cottage.

Port Erin

Plans for the southern branch of the steam railway beyond Castletown included the speculative construction of the new resort of **PORT ERIN**, at the southwestern tip of the island, an hour and a quarter's ride from Douglas. A century on, an arm of holiday apartments stretches out towards the headland, while the far side of town is marked by the breakwater and small harbour. Families relish the beach and nearby coves, and the timewarped atmosphere, which appears to have altered little in forty years.

The **train station** is on Station Road, a couple of hundred yards above and back from the beach. **Buses** #1 and #2 from Douglas/Castletown, and #8 from Peel/St John's, stop on Bridson Street, across Station Road and opposite the *Cherry Orchard* hotel. For **accommodation**, the best B&B is *Rowany Cottier* (☎01624/832287; no credit cards; ❸), a detached, nonsmoking house overlooking the bay, opposite the entrance to Bradda Glen. The nicest hotel is the *Cherry Orchard* on Bridson Street (☎01624/833811, ⓦwww.cherry-orchard .com; ❼, winter ❺), a couple of hundred yards back from the promenade, which has a range of self-catering or serviced **apartments** sleeping up to six people, available by the night.

Port St Mary

Two miles east of Port Erin, the fishing harbour still dominates little **PORT ST MARY**, with its houses strung out in a chain above the busy dockside. From here, a minor road runs out along the Meayll peninsula towards Cregneash, the oldest village on the island, part of which now forms the **Cregneash Village Folk Museum** (Easter–Oct daily 10am–5pm; £3), a picturesque cluster of nineteenth-century thatched crofts, peopled at weekends with spinners, weavers, turners and smiths dressed in period costumes. It's only a short walk south to **The Chasms**, a headland of gaping rock cliffs swarming with gulls and razorbills. The footpath then continues around **Spanish Head**, the island's southern tip, to **The Sound Visitor Centre** (daily 10am–5pm; closed Mon Nov–Easter; free), which marks the end of the road from Port St Mary. There's an excellent café, with windows looking out across The Sound to the Calf of Man (see below).

Regular **steam trains** run to Port Erin or back to Douglas from Port St Mary, with the station a ten-minute walk from the harbour. Nicest **accommodation** is at no-smoking 🌟 *Aaron House*, high up on The Promenade (☎01624/835702, ⓦwww.aaronhouse.co.uk; ❺), a lovingly re-created Victorian experience combining brass beds and clawfoot bathtubs with cake in the parlour and superb bay views. For home-cooked pub **meals**, you can't beat *The Albert* on Athol Street (no food Sun night or Mon; ☎01624/832118), by the harbour – book for evening meals at the weekend – or the family-run *Station Hotel*, by the Steam Railway stop (☎01624/832249; no credit cards; ❷), with refurbished en-suite rooms, and Thai food on Friday and Saturday nights.

Calf of Man

It really is worth making the effort to visit the **Calf of Man**, a craggy 600-acre heathland island off the southwest coast that is preserved as a bird sanctuary. Resident wardens monitor the seasonal populations of kittiwakes, puffins, choughs, razorbills, shags, guillemots and others, while grey seals can be seen all year round basking on the rocks. Bring something to eat and drink, and pack warm clothes in case the weather changes. Charter **boats** to the island operate from Port St Mary, but the most reliable scheduled service (weather permitting) is from the pier at **Port Erin** (Easter–Sept daily; £10; usually at 10.15am, 11.30am and 1.30pm; ☎01624/832339); call in advance as landing numbers are limited.

Castletown and Rushen Abbey

From the twelfth century until 1869, **CASTLETOWN** was the island's capital, but then the influx of tourists and the increase in trade required a bigger harbour and Douglas took over. So much the better for Castletown, which is a much more pleasant place than it might otherwise have been. Its sleepy harbour and low-roofed cottages are dominated by **Castle Rushen** (Easter–Oct daily 10am–5pm; £4.25), formerly home to the island's legislature and still the site of the investiture of new lieutenant-governors. Across Market Square and down Castle Street in Parliament Square you'll find the **Old House of Keys**. Built in 1821, this was the site of the Manx parliament, the Keys, until 1874 when it was moved to Douglas. The frock-coated Secretary of the House meets you at the door and shows you into the restored debating chamber, where visitors are included in a highly entertaining participatory session of the House, guided by a hologram Speaker. The visits are conducted on the hour (Easter–Oct daily 10am–noon & 2–5pm; £3) and advance tickets are available from the tourist office (Easter–Oct daily 10am–5pm) housed in the **Old Grammar School** on nearby Quay Lane.

The **steam train station** is five minutes' walk from the centre of Castletown, out along Victoria Road from the harbour, while the best place for **food** is *The Garrison*, at 5 Castle St (℡01624/824885; closes Sun at 5pm), a tapas bar with a sunny courtyard that serves coffee and snacks from 9.30am and meals from noon until 9.30pm.

The island's most important medieval religious site, **Rushen Abbey** (Easter–Oct daily 10am–5pm; £3), lies two miles north of Castletown at Ballasalla ("place of the willows"). The excavated remains themselves – low walls, grass-covered banks and a sole church tower from the fifteenth century – would hold only specialist appeal were it not for the excellent interpretation centre, which explains much about daily life in a Cistercian abbey.

Travel details

Buses

For information on all local and national bus services, contact Traveline ℡0870/608 2608, ＠www.traveline.org.uk.

Blackpool to: London (4–6 daily; 6hr); Manchester (every 2hr; 1hr 40min); Preston (every 2hr; 40min).

Chester to: Liverpool (hourly; 1hr); Manchester (3 daily; 1hr).

Lancaster to: Carlisle (4–5 daily; 1hr 10min); Kendal (hourly; 1hr); London (2–3 daily; 5hr 30min); Manchester (2 daily; 2hr).

Liverpool to: Blackpool (1 daily; 2hr); Chester (hourly; 1hr); London (5 daily; 4hr); Manchester (hourly; 40min–1hr); Preston (2 daily; 1hr).

Manchester to: Birmingham (6 daily; 3hr); Blackpool (every 2hr; 1hr 40min); Chester (3 daily; 1hr); Leeds (6 daily; 2hr); Liverpool (hourly; 40min–1hr); London (every 1–2hr; 4hr 30min–6hr 45min); Newcastle (6 daily; 5hr); Sheffield (4 daily; 2hr 40min).

Trains

For information on all local and national rail services, contact National Rail Enquiries ℡08457/484950, ＠www.nationalrail.co.uk.

Blackpool to: Manchester (hourly; 1hr 10min); Preston (hourly; 30min).

Chester to: Birmingham (5 daily; 2hr); Knutsford (hourly; 50min); Liverpool (2 hourly; 45min); London (3 daily; 3hr 30min); Manchester (2 hourly; 1hr–1hr 20min); Northwich (hourly; 30min).

Lancaster to: Carlisle (every 30–60min; 1hr); Heysham (2–3 daily; 30min); Manchester (every 30–60min; 1hr); Morecambe (every 30min–60min; 10min); Preston (every 20–30min; 20min).

Liverpool to: Chester (2 hourly; 45min); Leeds (hourly; 2hr); London (hourly; 2hr 40min); Manchester (every 30min; 50min); Preston (14 daily; 1hr 5min); York (hourly; 2hr 20min).

Manchester to: Barrow-in-Furness (Mon–Sat 7 daily, Sun 3 daily; 2hr 15min); Birmingham (hourly; 1hr 30min); Blackpool (hourly; 1hr 10min); Buxton (hourly; 50min); Carlisle (8 daily; 1hr 50min); Chester (2 hourly; 1hr–1hr 20min); Lancaster (every 30–60min; 1hr); Leeds (hourly; 1hr); Liverpool (every 30min; 50min); London (hourly; 2hr 40min); Newcastle (10 daily; 3hr); Oxenholme (4–6 daily; 40min–1hr 10min); Penrith (2–4 daily; 2hr); Preston (every 20min; 55min); Sheffield (hourly; 1hr); York (hourly; 1hr 35min).

Cumbria and the Lakes

CHAPTER 11

Highlights

✴ **Windermere** Sail a catamaran on England's largest lake. See p.561

✴ **Old Dungeon Ghyll, Langdale** A favourite inn for hikers – cosy rooms, stone-flagged floors and open fires. See p.564

✴ **Brantwood** The home of John Ruskin, beautifully sited on Coniston Water. See p.567

✴ **Keswick Launch, Derwent Water** Take a cruise around the lake, or jump off for some enjoyable local hikes. See p.570

✴ **Wordsworth House, Cockermouth** Step into the eighteenth century at the birthplace of William Wordsworth. See p.573

✴ **Helvellyn** A tough day on the fells, rewarded by scintillating views from 3000ft. See p.574

✴ **Ravenglass & Eskdale Railway.** Ride the narrow-gauge line into the heart of the Lakes. See p.576

✴ **The Rum Story, Whitehaven** West Cumbria's most intriguing museum. See p.577

△ Derwent Water

Cumbria and the Lakes

11

T he **Lake District** is England's most-hyped scenic area, and for good reasons. Within an area a mere thirty miles across, sixteen major lakes are squeezed between the steeply pitched faces of the country's highest mountains, an almost alpine landscape that's augmented by waterfalls and picturesque stone-built villages packed into the valleys. Most of what people refer to as the Lake District – or simply the Lakes – lies within the **Lake District National Park**, England's largest national park (880 square miles), established in 1951. This, in turn, falls entirely within the northwestern county of **Cumbria**, formed in 1974 from the historic counties of Cumberland and Westmorland, and the northern part of Lancashire. Consequently the region contains more than just its lakes, stretching south and west to the **Cumbrian coast**, and north to its county town of **Carlisle**, a place that bears traces of a pedigree stretching back beyond the construction of Hadrian's Wall. To the east, **Penrith** and the **Eden Valley** separate the lakes from the near wilderness of the northern Pennines.

National Express **coaches** connect London and Manchester with Windermere, Ambleside, Grasmere and Keswick, while **trains** leave the West Coast main line at **Oxenholme**, north of Lancaster, for the branch-line service to Kendal and Windermere. The only other places directly accessible by train are Penrith, further north on the West Coast line, and the towns along the Cumbrian coast. Stagecoach (Ⓦ www.stagecoachbus.com/northwest) is Cumbria's biggest **local bus** operator, and the one-day **Explorer Ticket** (£8.50) is valid on the entire network, including the two main routes – the #555 (Kendal–Windermere–Ambleside–Grasmere–Keswick) and the open-top #599 (Kendal–Windermere–Bowness–Ambleside–Grasmere). The **YHA** also operates a shuttle-bus service from Ambleside YHA to the Hawkshead, Coniston, Elterwater, Langdale and Grasmere hostels (Easter–Oct; £2.50 a journey; information on ☏ 0870/770 5672).

For more **information** about all aspects of the National Park, visit Ⓦ www .lake-district.gov.uk; while the official site of the Cumbria Tourist Board is Ⓦ www.golakes.co.uk.

CUMBRIA AND THE LAKES

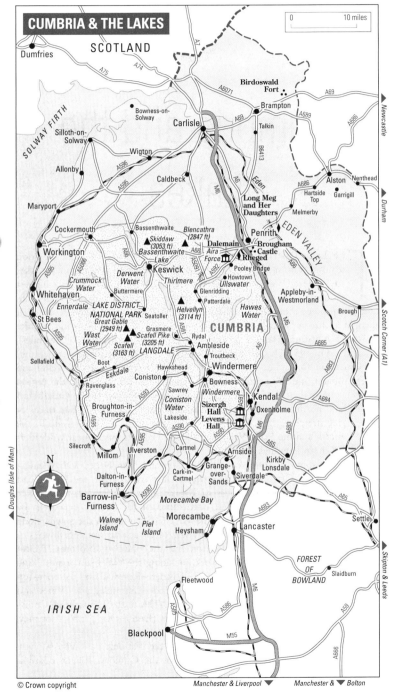

CUMBRIA & THE LAKES

0   10 miles

SCOTLAND

Dumfries

Birdoswald
Fort

SOLWAY FIRTH

Bowness-on-Solway

Silloth-on-Solway

Brampton

Carlisle

Talkin

Wigton

Allonby

Caldbeck

Alston   Nenthead

Maryport

Hartside
Top   Garrigill

Long Meg
and Her
Daughters

Melmerby

Cockermouth

Bassenthwaite

Blencathra
(2847 ft)

Penrith

EDEN VALLEY

Workington

Skiddaw
(3053 ft)

Bassenthwaite
Lake

Dalemain

Aira
Force

Brougham
Castle

Rheged

Derwent
Water

Keswick

Pooley
Bridge

Whitehaven

Crummock
Water

Buttermere

Thirlmere

Howtown

Ullswater

Appleby-in-Westmorland

St Bees

Ennerdale

LAKE DISTRICT

Glenridding

Patterdale

Brough

Great Gable
(2949 ft)

Seatoller

Helvellyn
(3114 ft)

Hawes
Water

NATIONAL PARK

Wast
Water

Scafell Pike
(3205 ft)

Grasmere

Rydal

CUMBRIA

Sellafield

Scafell
(3163 ft)

LANGDALE

Ambleside

Boot

Troutbeck

Eskdale

Hawkshead

Windermere

Ravenglass

Coniston

Bowness

Sawrey

Windermere

Kendal

Silecroft

Coniston
Water

Sizergh
Hall

Oxenholme

Levens
Hall

Millom

Ulverston

Lakeside

Cartmel

Arnside

Kirkby
Lonsdale

Dalton-in-Furness

Cark-in-Cartmel

Grange-over-Sands

Siverdale

Barrow-in-Furness

Morecambe Bay

N

*Walney
Island*

*Piel
Island*

Morecambe

Heysham

Lancaster

Settle

*FOREST
OF
BOWLAND*

Slaidburn

Fleetwood

IRISH SEA

IRISH SEA

Blackpool

© Crown copyright

Manchester & Liverpool ▼   Manchester & ▼ Bolton

The Lake District

Given a week you could see most of the famous settlements and lakes – a circuit taking in the towns of Ambleside, Windermere and Bowness, all on **Windermere**, the Wordsworth houses and sites in pretty villages such as **Hawkshead** and **Grasmere**, and the more dramatic northern scenery near **Keswick** and **Ullswater** would give you a fair sample of the whole. But it's away from the crowds that the Lakes really begin to pay dividends, so aim if you can for the dramatic valleys of **Langdale** and **Eskdale**, and the lesser-visited lakes of **Wast Water** and **Buttermere**. Four peaks exceed 3000ft – including **Scafell Pike**, the highest in England – but there are hundreds of other mountains, crags and fells to roam. Bad weather can move in quickly, even in the height of summer, so before a hike you should check the **weather forecast** – many hotels and outdoor shops post a daily forecast – or call ☎08700/550575 (recorded 24-hour line).

Kendal

The limestone-grey town of **KENDAL** might be billed as the "Gateway to the Lakes", but it's nearly ten miles from Windermere – the true start of the Lakes – and has more in common with the market towns to the east. Nonetheless, it offers rewarding rambles around the "yards" and "ginnels" which make an engaging maze on both sides of Highgate and Stricklandgate, the main streets. The **Kendal Museum**, on Station Road (Mon–Sat 10.30am–4/5pm; closed Jan to mid-Feb; £2.70; ⓦwww.kendalmuseum.org.uk), holds the district's natural history and archeological finds, bolstered by the preserved office and personal effects of **Alfred Wainwright** (1907–91), Kendal's former borough treasurer (and honorary clerk at the museum). Wainwright moved to Kendal in 1941, and by 1952, dissatisfied with the accuracy of existing maps of the fells, he embarked on what became a series of painstakingly handwritten walking guides. Many still treat them as gospel in their attempts to "bag" ascents of the 214 fells he recorded.

Kendal's other two museums are in the Georgian **Abbot Hall** (Mon–Sat 10.30am–4/5pm; closed mid-Dec to mid-Jan; gallery £4, museum £3.75, combined ticket £7.50) and its stable block, by the river to the south. The main hall houses the **Art Gallery** (ⓦwww.abbothall.org.uk), while across the way, the former stables contain the **Museum of Lakeland Life and Industry** (ⓦwww.lakelandmuseum.org.uk), filled with reconstructed seventeenth-, eighteenth- and nineteenth-century house interiors and workshops.

Kendal's **train station** is the first stop on the Windermere branch line, three minutes from the **Oxenholme** mainline station and a ten-minute walk from the centre. All buses (including National Express services) stop at the **bus station** on Blackhall Road (off Stramongate). The **tourist office** (Mon–Sat 9am–5pm, Sun 10am–4pm; Jan–Easter closed Sun; ☎01539/725758, ⓦwww .kendaltown.org) is in the Town Hall on Highgate.

The best local **B&B** is the ⚘ *Lakeland Natural Vegetarian Guesthouse* at Low Slack, Queen's Road (☎01539/733011, ⓦwww.lakelandnatural.co.uk; ❹), five minutes' walk west of the centre – breakfasts include homemade muffins, organic yoghurt and fresh fruit salad. Alternatively, along Milnthorpe Road – walk straight down Highgate and Kirkland – several places cluster together, including *The Headlands*, 53 Milnthorpe Rd (☎01539/732464; ❷). There's a YHA **hostel** at 118 Highgate (☎08/0//70 5892, ⓔkendal@yha.org.uk;

dorm beds £17.50, includes breakfast; flexible opening Nov–Easter), which is attached to The Brewery arts centre (see below).

For inexpensive veggie wholefood lunches visit the *Waterside Café* on Gulfs Road, by the river at the bottom of Lowther Street. Otherwise, the best **restaurant** is the highly regarded *New Moon*, 129 Highgate (☎01539/729254), an easy-going contemporary bistro using locally sourced ingredients. For evening entertainment, the **Brewery Arts Centre**, 118 Highgate (☎01539/725133, ⓦwww.breweryarts.co.uk), is the town's central focus. Its *Green Room Restaurant* and lively *Vats Bar* serve light lunches, pizzas, pastas and stir-fries; the centre also has a cinema, theatre, galleries and concert hall.

Windermere town and Brockhole visitor centre

WINDERMERE town is the transport hub for the southern lakes, but there's precious little else to keep you in the slate-grey streets. Instead, all the traffic pours a mile downhill to Windermere's older twin town, Bowness (see below); buses leave Windermere train station every twenty minutes in season for the ten-minute run down to the lakeside piers. It's understandable to want to rush straight to the lake, but there are a couple of nearby attractions worth the diversion, notably the **Lake District Visitor Centre at Brockhole** (Easter–Oct daily 10am–5pm; grounds & gardens open all year; free, parking fee charged), a fine mansion set in landscaped grounds on the lakeshore, three miles northwest of Windermere. It's the headquarters and main information point for the Lake District National Park, and also offers guided walks, children's activities, garden tours, special exhibitions and lectures. Buses between Windermere and Ambleside run past the visitor centre, or you can get there by Windermere Lake Cruises **launch** from Bowness (Easter–Oct; hourly service; £5.50 return).

Practicalities

All **buses** stop outside Windermere **train station**. A hundred yards away at the top of Victoria Street stands the **tourist office** (daily 9am–5/6pm, July & Aug weekends until 6.30pm; ☎015394/46499), while for **bike rental**, contact Country Lanes, The Railway Station, Windermere (☎015394/44544, ⓦwww .countrylanes.co.uk). Mountain Goat, near the tourist office on Victoria Street (☎015394/45161, ⓦwww.mountain-goat.com) offers **minibus tours** (half-day from £15, full-day £30) that take you off the beaten track, departing daily from Windermere and other lakeland towns.

Windermere doesn't have the waterside advantages of Bowness, but it does have a lot more **accommodation** – good places to look for B&Bs are on High Street and neighbouring Victoria Street at the top of town near the tourist office, with other concentrations just to the south on College Road, Oak and Broad streets.

Accommodation

Archway 13 College Rd ☎015394/45613, ⓦwww.communiken.com/archway. Nonsmoking Victorian guest house known for its breakfasts – sample pancakes, kippers, homemade yoghurt and granola. No American Express. ❸

Ashleigh 11 College Rd ☎015394/42292, ⓦwww.ashleighhouse.com. Smart, nonsmoking house whose tasteful rooms are furnished in welcoming country pine. No American Express. ❷

Boston House The Terrace ☎015394/43654, ⓦwww.bostonhouse.co.uk. Beautifully restored nonsmoking Victorian Gothic house, a minute's walk from the tourist office. No American Express. ❺

Brendan Chase 1–3 College Rd ☎015394/45638, ⓔbrendanchase@aol.com. A friendly welcome and comfortable rooms (some en-suite) – family/group rooms sleep up to five. No credit cards. ❷

Lake District Backpackers' Lodge High Street, across from the tourist office ☎015394/46374,

@ www.lakedistrictbackpackers.co.uk. Small rooms (beds £12.50) and a laid-back atmosphere, plus Internet, kitchen, satellite TV and bike storage. No credit cards.

Miller Howe Rayrigg Rd, A592 ⊕015394/42536, @ www.millerhowe.com. Gorgeous Edwardian house above the lake, featuring antique- and art-filled rooms and landscaped gardens. Rates include dinner, early-morning tea and lavish breakfast. Closed Jan. **⑨**

Mortal Man Bridge Lane, Troutbeck, 3 miles north ⊕015394/33193, @ www.themortalman.co.uk. Troutbeck's traditional inn has terrific valley views from its rooms. Closed mid-Nov to mid-Feb. **⑤**, **⑥** with dinner.

Windermere YHA High Cross, Bridge Lane, 1 mile north of Troutbeck Bridge ⊕0870/770 6094,

@ windermere@yha.org.uk. Old mansion with lake views, bike rental and kitchen. Dorm beds £13.95; open weekends-only in Dec & Jan.

Cafés and restaurants

First Floor Lakeland Ltd, behind the train station ⊕015394/88200. The daytime café inside the home furnishings/design store provides superior snacks, sandwiches and daily specials. Inexpensive.

Lamplighter Bar *Oakthorpe Hotel*, High Street ⊕015394/43547. Bistro meals (gammon, fresh fish, rack of lamb) at value-for-money prices. Closed Sun & Mon lunch. Moderate.

Lighthouse Main Rd ⊕015394/88260. Roomy café-bar with a streetside terrace, seats in the bar or first-floor dining room. Moderate.

Bowness and the lake

BOWNESS-ON-WINDERMERE – to give it its full title – spills back from its lakeside piers in a series of terraces lined with guest houses and hotels. Just back from the lake, **St Martin's Church** is notable for its stained glass, particularly that in the east window which sports the fifteenth-century arms of John Washington, an ancestor of first American president George Washington. Most tourists, though, bypass the church and everything else in Bowness, bar the lake, to visit **The World of Beatrix Potter** in the Old Laundry on Crag Brow (daily 10am–4.30/5.30pm; £6; @ www.hop-skip-jump.com). It's unfair to be judgemental – you either like Beatrix Potter or you don't – but it's safe to say that the elaborate 3D story scenes, Peter Rabbit garden, audiovisual displays, themed tearoom and gift shop here find more favour with children than the more formal Potter attractions at Hill Top and Hawkshead.

The lake itself – simply **Windermere** (from the Norse, "Vinandr's Lake", and thus never "*Lake* Windermere") – is the heavyweight of Lake District waters, at ten and a half miles long, a mile wide in parts and a shade over two hundred feet deep. Windermere Lake Cruises (see box below) operates modern cruisers and vintage steamers throughout the year, while the traditional **ferry service** is the chain-guided contraption across the water from Ferry Nab on the Bowness side to Ferry House, Sawrey (Mon–Sat 7am–10pm, Sun 9am–10pm; departures

---

Windermere cruises

Windermere Lake Cruises (⊕015394/31188, @ www.windermere-lakecruises .co.uk) operates services to Lakeside at the southern tip (£7.20 return) or to Brockhole and Waterhead (for Ambleside) at the northern end (£6.95 return). There's also a direct service from Ambleside to the Lake District Visitor Centre at Brockhole (£5.50 return), and a shuttle service across the lake between Bowness pier and Ferry House, Sawrey (£3.20 return), saving pedestrians the walk down to the car ferry. The company also operates an enjoyable 45-minute circular **cruise around the Islands** (departs several times daily from Bowness; £5.25), while a 24-hour **Freedom-of-the-Lake** ticket costs £12.50. Services on all routes are frequent between Easter and October (every 30min–1hr at peak times), and reduced during the winter – but there are sailings every day except Christmas Day.

every 20min; 40p; cars £2.50), providing access to Beatrix Potter's former home at Hill Top.

Five miles to the south of Bowness, Lakeside is the terminus of the **Lakeside and Haverthwaite Railway** (Easter–Oct 6–7 daily; £5 return; ☎015395/31594, ⓦwww.lakesiderailway.co.uk). The boat arrivals at Lakeside connect with steam train departures throughout the day, and you can buy a joint boat-and-train ticket (£11.50 return) at Bowness. Also on the quay at Lakeside is the **Aquarium of the Lakes** (daily 9am–5/6pm; £6.25; ⓦwww .aquariumofthelakes.co.uk), an entertaining natural history exhibit centred on the fish and animals found in and along a lakeland river. Again, there's a joint ticket available with the boat ride from Bowness (£12.50 return).

Practicalities

The **bus** from Windermere train station stops at the lakeside piers, also the terminus for the #517 (to Troutbeck and Ullswater). The **Cross-Lakes Shuttle** (May–Sept, Easter, bank & school hols daily; Oct weekends only) provides a useful connecting boat-and-minibus service from Bowness Pier 3 to Hill Top (£7 return), Hawkshead (£8.10) and Grizedale (£10.30).

Bowness Bay Information Centre is near the piers on Glebe Road (Easter–Oct daily 9.30am–5pm; Nov–Easter Fri–Sun 10am–4pm; ☎015394/42895). Crag Brow and then Lake Road is the main thoroughfare up from the lake towards Windermere, on and off which you'll find much of the accommodation and services; pedestrianized **Ash Street**, at the foot of Crag Brow, is where to look for restaurants and bars, from fish and chips to tapas.

Accommodation

Above The Bay 5 Brackenfield ☎015394/88658, ⓦwww.abovethebay.co.uk. Three spacious B&B rooms open onto a private terrace with stunning lake views. No credit cards. ❸

Linthwaite House Crook Rd, B5284, 1 mile south ☎015394/88600, ⓦwww.linthwaite.com. Contemporary style in an ivy-covered country house set high above Windermere. Rates include dinner. ❾

Montclare House Crag Brow ☎015394/42723, ⓦwww.montclareguesthouse.co.uk. Attractive B&B accommodation above a coffee shop – spacious family rooms have bunk beds. No credit cards. ❷

New Hall Bank Fallbarrow Rd ☎015394/43558, ⓦwww.newhallbank.com. Detached, nonsmoking Victorian house with a lake view (and just a few yards from the *Hole in't Wall* pub), whose room views get better the higher you go. ❺

Cafés, pubs and restaurants

2 Eggcups 6a Ash St ☎015394/45979. Serves the best sandwich in Bowness, plus other blackboard specials. Daytime only, closed Thurs. Inexpensive.

Hole in't Wall Fallbarrow Road ☎015394/43488. The town's oldest hostelry; cosy in winter when the fires are lit, and pleasant in summer when you can sit outside. Inexpensive.

Jackson's Bistro St Martin's Square ☎015394/46264. The local choice for a family meal or romantic night out – classic bistro dishes, including a good-value three-course *table d'hôte* menu (£13.95), available all night. Dinner only. Expensive.

Porthole 3 Ash St ☎015394/42793. Top restaurant in town, housed in a seventeenth-century cottage and specializing in regional Anglo-Italian cuisine. Closed Sat lunch, all Tues, and mid-Dec to mid-Feb. Very expensive.

Ambleside

Five miles northwest of Windermere, **AMBLESIDE** is at the heart of the southern lakes region, making it a first-class base for walkers, who are catered for by a large number of outdoors shops. The town centre consists of a cluster of grey-green stone houses, shops, pubs and B&Bs hugging a circular one-way system, which loops round just south of the narrow gully of stony Stock Ghyll. For some background on Ambleside's history, stroll a couple of minutes along

Rydal Road to the **Ambleside Museum** (daily 10am–5pm; £2.50; www
.armitt.com), whose collection catalogues the very distinct contribution to
lakeland society made by John Ruskin, Beatrix Potter and longtime Ambleside resident, writer Harriet Martineau. The rest of town lies a mile south at
Waterhead, overlooked by grass banks and the spreading trees of Borrans Park.
Two or three little cafés by Waterhead pier have outdoor seats, and you can take
drinks from the bar onto the lawns of both the *Wateredge Inn* and *Waterhead*
hotel. For a day on the lake contact the **Windermere Sailing and Adventure
School** (☎015394/43789 or 07834/855050, ⓦwww.sailadventure.co.uk), by
the YHA hostel, who can arrange windsurfing (from £25), dinghy sailing (£80)
or – best of all – a relaxing trip on their Polynesian-style catamaran (half-day
from £60).

Good walks are possible straight from the town centre, notably the short stroll
to the attractive waterfall of **Stock Ghyll Force**. The path then rises steeply to
Wansfell Pike (1581ft) and down into Troutbeck village, with the *Mortal Man*
inn a short detour to the left. The return cuts west onto the flanks of Wansfell
and around past the viewpoint at **Jenkin Crag** back to Ambleside, a total of
six miles (around 4hr).

Practicalities
Buses all stop on Kelsick Road, opposite the library. The **tourist office**
is just up the road, in Central Buildings on Market Cross (daily 9am–5pm;
☎015394/32582), or consult ⓦwww.amblesideonline.co.uk. There's **bike
rental** from Biketreks on Compston Road (☎015394/31505, ⓦwww
.biketreks.co.uk), or Ghyllside Cycles on The Slack (☎015394/33592, ⓦwww
.ghyllside.co.uk). Lake Road, running between Waterhead and Ambleside, is
lined with **B&Bs**, with other concentrations on central Church Street and
Compston Road. Zeffirelli's **cinema** (ⓦwww.zeffirellis.co.uk) has four screens
at two locations in town, while the famous annual **Ambleside Sports** gathering (traditional wrestling to fell-running) takes place on the Thursday before
the first Monday in August.

Accommodation
Ambleside Backpackers Old Lake Road
☎015394/32340, ⓦwww.englishlakesbackpackers
.co.uk. Midway between lake and town, this secluded
independent backpackers' has a decent kitchen, free
breakfasts of tea, toast and cereal, lounge and Internet. Dorm beds £14.50, weekends £15.50.
Ambleside YHA Waterhead, A591, 1 mile south
☎0870/770 5672, ⓔambleside@yha.org.uk. The
YHA's flagship regional hostel, a huge lakeside
affair with small dorms (£19.95, including breakfast), doubles (❶) and family rooms (❸), plus bike
rental, Internet and licensed café.
Brantfell Rothay Road ☎015394/32239, ⓦwww
.brantfell.co.uk. Victorian guest house with a
friendly welcome, a big choice at breakfast, and
free entry to the pool at a local leisure club. ❹
Compston House Compston Road
☎015394/32305, ⓦwww.compstonhouse.co.uk.
There's a breezy New York welcome and American-
style themed rooms in this traditional lakeland
house. No smoking. No American Express. ❹

Lakes Lodge Lake Road ☎015394/33240,
ⓦwww.lakeslodge.co.uk. A dozen spacious
rooms with upgraded bathrooms, and a good
buffet breakfast served in the informal café-style
breakfast room. Two-night minimum. No American
Express. ❺
Riverside Under Loughrigg
☎015394/32395, ⓦwww.riverside-at
-ambleside.co.uk. Charming nonsmoking guest
house on a quiet lane, half-a-mile (10min) walk
from town. No American Express. ❺
Waterhead Waterhead ☎015394/32566, ⓦwww
.elh.co.uk. Contemporary townhouse-style accommodation provides the Lakes' classiest four-star
lodgings, opposite the Waterhead piers – there's a
champagne menu in each slate-and-marble bathroom, plus garden-bar and metropolitan restaurant.
❽, including dinner ❾

Cafés and restaurants
Glass House Rydal Road ☎015394/32137. Renovated fulling mill with waterwheel, which serves

accomplished Modern British food. Closed Tues Oct–Easter. Expensive.

🏃 **Lucy's on a Plate** Church Street ☎015394/31191. Enjoyable bistro offering a daily-changing menu with tons of choice. *Lucy 4* on St Mary's Lane, just over the way,

is its moderately priced tapas-bar offshoot. Expensive.

Zeffirelli's Compston Road ☎015394/33845. Famous for its wholemeal-based pizzas, but also serving inventive pastas and veggie food. Moderate.

Great Langdale

Three miles west of Ambleside, Skelwith Bridge marks the start of **Great Langdale**, a glacial valley overlooked by the prominent rocky summits of the Langdale Pikes, the most popular of the central Lakeland fells. The #516 Langdale Rambler **bus** from Ambleside's Kelsick Road follows the minor B5343 to Elterwater (17min) and on up to the head of the valley (30min), passing all the accommodation reviewed below (except for *Langdale* YHA hostel) en route.

The pretty hamlet of **ELTERWATER** sees its fair share of Langdale-bound hikers, not least because of its old lakeland pub on the green, the *Britannia Inn* (☎015394/37210, ⓦwww.britinn.co.uk; ❻), and two local YHA **hostels**: *Elterwater*, just across the bridge from the village (☎0870/770 5816, ⓔelterwater@yha.org.uk; dorm beds £11.95; flexible opening Nov–Easter), and *Langdale*, a mile from Elterwater (☎0870/770 5908, ⓔlangdale@yha.org.uk; dorm beds £12.50; closed Nov–Feb), high on the road from Skelwith Bridge to Grasmere.

A footpath from Elterwater (signposted as the Cumbria Way) runs all the way up the valley. Three miles from Elterwater, at **Stickle Ghyll** car park, Harrison Stickle (2414ft), Pike of Stickle (2326ft) and Pavey Ark (2297ft) form a dramatic backdrop, though many walkers aim no further than **Stickle Tarn**, an hour's climb up a wide path from Stickle Ghyll. The other car park, a mile further west up the valley road by the **Old Dungeon Ghyll Hotel** (see below), is the starting-point for a series of more hardcore hikes to resonant lakeland peaks like Crinkle Crags (2816ft) or Bowfell (2960ft).

The comfortable **rooms** at the Victorian *New Dungeon Ghyll Hotel* (☎015394/37213, ⓦwww.dungeon-ghyll.com; ❻) feature dramatic fell views. You can eat here, or at the adjacent *Sticklebarn Tavern* (☎015394/37356), which has simple **bunk-barn accommodation** (£10 per night). However, the best-known accommodation in the valley is the peerless *Old Dungeon Ghyll Hotel* (☎015394/37272, ⓦwww.odg.co.uk; ❻), at the end of the B5343, seven miles northeast of Ambleside. Dinner (£20; reservations essential) is served in the dining room, but all the action is in the stone-flagged **hikers' bar**, which serves real ales and filling chips-with-everything meals.

Grasmere and around

Four miles northwest of Ambleside, the village of **GRASMERE** consists of an intimate cluster of grey-stone houses on the old packhorse road that runs beside the babbling River Rothay. It's an eminently pleasing ensemble, set back from one of the most alluring of the region's small lakes, but it loses some of its charm in summer thanks to the hordes who descend on the trail of the village's most famous former resident, **William Wordsworth** (1770–1850). Born in Cockermouth in 1770, he was sent to school in Hawkshead before a stint at Cambridge, a year in France and two in Somerset. In 1799 he returned to the Lake District, settling in the Grasmere district, where he spent the last two-thirds of his life in houses you can still visit. The poet, his wife Mary, sister

Dorothy and other members of his family are buried beneath the yews in St Oswald's churchyard, around which the river makes a sinuous curl.

Dove Cottage (daily 9.30am–5.30pm; closed mid-Jan to mid-Feb; £6; ⓦ www.wordsworth.org.uk; buses #555 and #599) – on Grasmere's south-eastern outskirts, at Town End, just off the A591 – was home to William and Dorothy from 1799 to 1808. Most of the furniture on display in the cottage

△ Dove Cottage

belonged to the Wordsworths, while in the upper rooms are various other possessions, including a pair of William's ice skates. In the adjacent museum are paintings, manuscripts (including that of *Daffodils*) and personal effects once belonging to the Wordsworths (most poignantly Mary's wedding ring), plus mementos of fellow poets **Samuel Taylor Coleridge** and **Robert Southey**, who formed a clique that became known as the "Lake Poets". A fourth member of the Cumbrian literary elite was the critic and essayist **Thomas De Quincey**, chiefly known today for his *Confessions of an English Opium-Eater*. De Quincey became a long-term guest of the Wordsworths' in 1807, taking over Dove Cottage from them in 1809.

Another mile and a half southeast along the A591 from Grasmere, **Rydal Mount** (March–Oct daily 9.30am–5pm; Nov–Feb daily except Tues 10am–4pm, closed for three weeks in Jan; £5, gardens only £2.50; ⓦ www .rydalmount.co.uk) was the home of Wordsworth from 1813 until his death in 1850. In the drawing room and library is the only known portrait of Dorothy, while memorabilia includes William's black leather sofa, his ink stand and despatch box. For many, the highlight is the garden, which has been preserved as Wordsworth designed it, complete with terraces where he used to declaim his poetry. Buses #555 and #599 pass the house on the way to Grasmere from Windermere and Ambleside.

Practicalities

Grasmere is on the main #555 and #599 **bus** routes, which both stop on the village green. The **National Park information centre** (Easter–Oct daily 9.30am–5pm; Nov–Easter Fri, Sat & Sun 10am–3.30pm; ☎015394/35245), five minutes from the green down Langdale Road, is tucked in by the main car park on Redbank Road. Bed-and-breakfast **accommodation** can be hard to come by in summer, so book well in advance.

Accommodation

Butharlyp Howe YHA Easedale Road ☎0870/770 5836, ⓔgrasmere@yha.org.uk. Closest YHA hostel to the centre, 150yd north of the green in a well-equipped lakeland house with grounds. Weekends only Nov–Jan. Dorm beds £15.50.

Grasmere Independent Hostel Broadrayne Farm, A591 ☎015394/35055, ⓦwww.grasmerehostel.co.uk. Just north of the village, past the *Travellers' Rest* pub, this stylish backpackers' is the top budget choice – 24 beds (from £15) in carpeted en-suite rooms, impressive kitchen, laundry facilities and sauna.

Harwood Red Lion Square ☎015394/35248, ⓦwww.harwoodhotel.co.uk. Genial, nonsmoking family-run hotel with eight prettily furnished rooms. Two-night minimum stay at weekends. ④

How Beck Broadgate ☎015394/35732, ⓔtrevor.eastes@btinternet.com. Two rooms available in a nonsmoking family house on the village outskirts. Full veggie breakfast provided. ③

How Foot Lodge Town End ☎015394/35366, ⓦwww.howfoot.co.uk. Spacious Victorian villa, just yards from Dove Cottage, with six nonsmoking rooms. Closed Jan. No American Express. ④

Lancrigg Vegetarian Easedale Road ☎015394/35317, ⓦwww.lancrigg.co.uk. Relaxed gourmet vegetarian country-house hotel, half a mile northwest of the village. Inventive four-course dinner included in the price. ⑧

Raise View White Bridge ☎015394/35215, ⓦwww.raiseviewhouse.co.uk. Lovely fell views from every corner of this amiable guest house. No credit cards. ⑤

Thorney How YHA ☎0870/770 5836, ⓔgrasmere@yha.org.uk. Grasmere's smaller, simpler YHA hostel, a former farmhouse, is just under a mile further along the unlit road past Butharlyp Howe. Closed Nov–Feb, and Sun & Mon March–Easter. Dorm beds £11.95.

White Moss House Rydal Water, A591, 1 mile south ☎015394/35295, ⓦwww.whitemoss.com. The ivy-clad house has antique-filled rooms in the main house and two more in a cottage suite. The food (dinner included in room rate) is wonderful. Closed Dec & Jan. ⑧

Cafés and restaurants

Jumble Room Langdale Road ☎015394/35188. Funky café-restaurant with an organic touch to its ethnically diverse menu. Closed Mon & Tues and occasional other days in winter. Moderate.

Miller Howe Café Red Lion Square ☎015394/35234. Superior café meals overlooking the green. Daytime only. Moderate.

Villa Colombina Town End ☎015394/35268. Italian café-restaurant (by Dove Cottage), serving good *antipasti* platters, pizza, pasta, steak and chicken, plus daily blackboard specials. Closed Mon in winter and all Jan. Moderate.

Coniston

Coniston Water is not one of the most immediately imposing of the lakes, yet it has a quiet beauty which sets it apart from the more popular destinations. The nineteenth-century art critic and social reformer John Ruskin made the lake his home, and today his isolated house, **Brantwood**, on the northeastern shore, provides the most obvious target for a day-trip. Some come here, too, on the *Swallows and Amazons* trail. **Arthur Ransome** was a frequent visitor, his memories and experiences providing much of the detail in his famous children's books. In the mid-1960s, the glass-like surface of Coniston Water attracted the attention of national hero **Donald Campbell**, who in 1955 had set a world water-speed record of 202mph on Ullswater, bumping it up to 276mph nine years later in Australia. On January 4, 1967, he set out to better his own mark on Coniston Water, but just as his jet-powered *Bluebird* hit an estimated 320mph, a patch of turbulence sent it into a somersault. Campbell was killed immediately and his body and boat lay undisturbed at the bottom of the lake until both were retrieved in 2001.

Coniston village

The slate-grey village of **CONISTON** (a derivation of "King's Town") hunkers below the craggy and coppermine-riddled bulk of **The Old Man of Coniston** (2628ft), which most fit walkers can climb in under two hours – from the bridge in the village, follow the path up past the *Sun Hotel* towards the *Coppermines* hostel. **Donald Campbell's grave** is found in the village cemetery behind the *Crown Hotel*, while **John Ruskin's grave** lies in St Andrew's original churchyard beneath a beautifully worked Celtic cross. Other than these, the main attraction is the excellent **Ruskin Museum** on Yewdale Road (Easter to mid-Nov daily 10am–5.30pm; mid-Nov to Easter Wed–Sun 10am–3.30pm; £3.75; ⓦwww.ruskinmuseum.com), which combines local history and geology exhibits with a fascinating look at Ruskin's life and work through his watercolours, manuscripts and personal memorabilia.

Coniston Water and Brantwood

Coniston Water is hidden out of sight, half a mile southeast of the village. From the pier, the **Steam Yacht Gondola** (Easter–Oct 11am–4pm; £6 round-trip; ☎015394/35599, ⓦwww.nationaltrust.org.uk/gondola), built in 1859, departs on hour-long circuits of the lake, though you can also stop off at Ruskin's Brantwood (see below). The other lake service is the **Coniston Launch** (Easter–Oct hourly 10.30am–4.30pm; Nov–Easter up to 4 daily depending on the weather; ☎015394/36216, ⓦwww.conistonlaunch.co.uk), which operates wooden solar-powered boats on two routes around the lake, north (£5 return, all year) or south (£7, Easter–Oct), both calling at Brantwood. Special **cruises** (call for times) include a *Swallows and Amazons* tour (£8.50), a Donald Campbell tour (£7.50), and evening trips (£9).

Nestling among trees on a hillside above the eastern shore of Coniston Water, two and a half miles by road from Coniston, **Brantwood** (mid-March to mid-Nov daily 11am–5.30pm; mid-Nov to mid-March Wed–Sun 11am–4.30pm;

£5.50, gardens only £3.75; ⓦwww.brantwood.org.uk) was home to John Ruskin from 1872 until his death in 1900. Champion of J.M.W. Turner and the Pre-Raphaelites and proponent of the supremacy of Gothic architecture, Ruskin bought Brantwood in 1871 and spent the next twenty years adding to the house and laying out its gardens. His study – hung with handmade paper that he designed himself – and dining room boast superlative lake views, bettered only by those from the Turret Room where he used to sit in later life in his bathchair, itself on display downstairs along with his mahogany desk and Blue John wine goblet.

Practicalities

Buses stop on the main road through Coniston village. A Ruskin Explorer ticket (£11.50) includes return bus travel between Bowness and Coniston, plus use of the Coniston Launch and free entry to Ruskin's house – buy the ticket on the bus. The **tourist office** (daily 9.30/10am–3.30/5.30pm; ☎015394/41533) is right in the centre on Ruskin Avenue. You can **rent bikes** from Summitreks on Yewdale Road (☎015394/41212, ⓦwww.summitreks.co.uk), which also organizes adventurous days out on water and land. Best place for a bite to eat is the *Black Bull* **pub**, right in the centre, which brews its own Bluebird beer.

Accommodation

Bank Ground Farm Coniston Water, east side ☎015394/41264, ⓦwww.bankground.com. On the lakeshore just north of Brantwood, this was the model for Holly Howe Farm in *Swallows and Amazons*. ❹

Beech Tree Guesthouse Yewdale Road ☎015394/41717. Friendly vegetarian place 150yd north of the village on the Ambleside road. Parking. No credit cards. ❸

Coniston Coppermines YHA ☎0870/770 5772, ⓔcoppermines@yha.org.uk. Peaceful, dramatic mountain setting a steep mile or so from the village. Closed Nov–March, and Sun & Mon in Sept & Oct. Dorm beds £11.95.

Coniston Holly How YHA A593, Ambleside Road ☎0870/770 5770, ⓔconistonhh@yha.org.uk. Closest hostel to the village (just a few minutes'

walk north). Limited weekend opening outside summer holiday period. Dorm beds £13.95.

Shepherds Villa Tilberthwaite Avenue ☎015394/41337, ⓦwww.shepherdsvilla.co.uk. One of the village's most popular B&Bs, with a decent sense of space, an approachable owner and nine comfortable rooms. Parking. No American Express. ❸

Sun Hotel ☎015394/41248, ⓦwww.thesun coniston.com. Fell views and family rooms, an informal restaurant and cosy real-ale bar. Minimum two-night stay at weekends. No American Express. ❻

🏃 **Yew Tree Farm** A593, 2 miles north ☎015394/41433, ⓦwww.yewtree-farm .com. Hiker-friendly accommodation in a peaceful seventeenth-century farmhouse. Three cosy oak-panelled rooms (one en-suite), plus an excellent breakfast. No credit cards. ❷

Hawkshead and around

HAWKSHEAD, midway between Coniston and Ambleside, wears its beauty well, its patchwork of cottages and cobbles backed by woods and fells and barely affected by twentieth-century intrusions. Huge car parks at the village edge take the strain, and when the crowds of day-trippers leave, Hawkshead regains its natural tranquillity. It was an important wool market at the time Words-worth was studying at **Hawkshead Grammar School** (Easter–Oct Mon–Sat 10am–12.30pm & 1.30–5pm, Sun 1–5pm; £2), founded in 1585; this is now a small museum, whose entrance lies opposite the tourist office. Wordsworth also attended the fifteenth-century **Church of St Michael** above the school, which harks back to Norman designs in its rounded pillars and patterned arches. The churchyard gives a good view over the village's twin central squares, and of Main Street, housing the **Beatrix Potter Gallery** (Easter–Oct Mon–Wed, Sat & Sun 10.30am–4.30pm; £3.50, discount available for Hill Top visitors; NT), occupying rooms once used by her solicitor husband. Fans are bustled into rooms full of Potter's original illustrations, though the less devoted might find displays on her life as keen naturalist, conservationist and early supporter of the National Trust more diverting.

It's two miles from Hawkshead, down the eastern side of Esthwaite Water to the pretty twin hamlets of Near and Far Sawrey, the first the site of Beatrix Potter's beloved **Hill Top** (Easter–Oct Mon–Wed, Sat & Sun 10.30am–4.30pm; £5, discount available for Beatrix Potter Gallery visitors; garden entry free on Thurs & Fri when house is closed; NT). A Londoner by birth, Potter bought the farmhouse here with the proceeds from her first book, *The Tale of Peter Rabbit*, and retained it as her study long after she moved out following her marriage in 1913. Its furnishings and contents have been kept as they were during her occupancy – in summer, expect to queue.

The most popular local walk from Hawkshead is to **Tarn Hows**, a body of water surrounded by spruce and pine and circled by paths and picnic spots. It's two miles from Hawkshead (or Coniston) on country lanes and paths, or can be reached by a minor road off the Hawkshead–Coniston B5285 – drivers will have to pay to use the National Trust car park.

Practicalities

The main **bus service** to Hawkshead is the #505 Coniston Rambler between Windermere, Ambleside and Coniston. This is complemented by the seasonal **Cross-Lakes Shuttle**, whose minibuses run from Hawkshead down to the Beatrix Potter house at Hill Top and on to Ferry House, Sawrey, for boat connections back to Bowness. The **National Park information centre** is at the main car park (daily 9.30/10am–3.30/5.30pm; ☎015394/36525); everything lies within five minutes' walk of here.

Accommodation and food

Ann Tyson's Cottage Wordsworth Street ☎015394/36405, ⓦwww.anntysons.co.uk. Some contend that Wordsworth briefly boarded here, and today there are B&B rooms in the barn conversion or two cottages to rent. ❸

Croft Caravan and Campsite North Lonsdale Road ☎015394/36374, ⓦwww.hawkshead-croft .com. Busy site, right by the village, with bike rental available; also caravan rental by the week. Closed Nov to mid-March.

Drunken Duck Inn Barngates crossroads, 2 miles north, off B5285 ☎015394/36347, ⓦwww.drunkenduckinn.co.uk. Superb restaurant-with-rooms in a beautifully located 400-year-old inn. The cuisine is cutting-edge (dinner around £30 excluding drinks and service;

reservations essential), the rooms eminently stylish. ❼

Esthwaite Lodge YHA Newby Bridge Rd, 1 mile south ☎0870/770 5836, ⓔhawkshead@yha.org .uk. Over 100 beds and a separate family annexe in an old Regency mansion. Closed various days Nov–Feb. Dorm beds £13.95.

King's Arms Market Square ☎015394/36372, ⓦwww.kingsarmshawkshead.co.uk. Bags of character in this old inn, with nine rooms retaining their oak beams and idiosyncratic proportions (bathrooms are up-to-date, though). Good bar meals here too. ❺

Yewfield Hawkshead Hill, 2 miles west off B5285 ☎015394/36765, ⓦwww.yewfield.co.uk. Non-smoking vegetarian guest house set amongst organic vegetable gardens. Closed mid-Nov to Jan. ❸

Keswick and Derwent Water

Standing on the shores of Derwent Water, at the junction of the main north–south and east–west routes through the Lake District, is the small market town of **KESWICK**. It's a bustling place with plenty of accommodation, and some good pubs and cafés, while several bus routes radiate from the town, getting you to the start of even the most challenging hikes. Granted its market charter by Edward I in 1276 – market day is Saturday – Keswick was an important wool and leather centre until around 1500, when these trades were supplanted by the discovery of local graphite. Northwest of the centre, up Main Street, the **Cumberland Pencil Museum** at Greta Bridge (daily 9.30am–4/5pm; £2.50; Ⓦ www.pencils.co.uk) tells the whole story. In Fitz Park on Station Road you'll find the **Keswick Museum and Art Gallery** (Easter–Oct Tues–Sat 10am–4pm; free), a quirky Victorian collection of ancient dental tools, fossils and some prized manuscripts and letters written by the Lakeland Poets. Make time, too, for **Crosthwaite Church**, a fifteen-minute walk northwest of town over Greta Bridge, resting place of the poet Robert Southey.

Keswick's most mysterious landmark is **Castlerigg Stone Circle**, set against a magnificent mountain backdrop – follow the signs from the Threlkeld rail line path (signposted by the *Keswick Country House Hotel*). Thirty-eight hunks of Borrowdale volcanic stone, the largest almost eight feet tall, form a circle a hundred feet in diameter; another ten blocks delineate a rectangular enclosure within. Back on the rail path, you can easily continue all the way to **Threlkeld** itself, three miles from town, on a delightful riverside walk with the promise of a drink in one of Threlkeld's old pubs at the end.

The shores of **Derwent Water** lie five minutes' walk south of the centre along Lake Road and through the pedestrian underpass. It's among the most attractive of the lakes, ringed by crags and studded with islets, and is most easily seen by hopping on the **Keswick Launch** (Easter–Nov daily 10am–6pm, until 8pm in July & Aug; Dec–Easter Sat & Sun 10am–6pm; £6.50 round-trip, £1.15 per stage; ☏017687/772263, Ⓦ www.keswick-launch.co.uk), which runs right around the lake calling at several points en route. There's also an enjoyable one-hour **evening cruise** (£7.50) from May Day bank holiday until mid-September. The best launch excursion is to **Cat Bells** (take the launch to Hawes End), a renowned vantage point (1481ft) above the lake's western shore – allow two and a half hours for the scramble to the top and a return to the pier along the wooded shore.

Practicalities

All **buses** use the terminal in front of the large supermarket, Lakes Foodstore, off Main Street. The **tourist office** is in the Moot Hall on Market Square (daily 9.30am–4/5.30pm; ☏017687/72645, Ⓦ www.keswick.org). For **bike rental**, there's Keswick Mountain Bikes on Southey Lane (☏017687/75202, Ⓦ www.keswickmountainbikes.co.uk). **Guided walks** – from lakeside rambles to mountain climbs – depart daily (Easter–Oct 10.15am; £6) from the Moot Hall; just turn up with a packed lunch. There's a fair amount of entertainment in Keswick throughout the year, including the **jazz festival** each May, **beer festival** in June, and the traditional **Keswick Agricultural Show** (August bank holiday). The **Theatre by the Lake** on Lake Road (☏017687/74411, Ⓦ www.theatrebythelake.com) hosts drama, concerts, exhibitions, readings and talks.

Accommodation

Acorn House Ambleside Road ☏017687/72553, Ⓦ www.acornhousehotel.co.uk. Handsome, non-smoking, eighteenth-century guest house with nine generously sized rooms. ❹

Bridgedale 101 Main St ☏017687/73914. Whether you're looking for an early breakfast, a room-only deal, en-suite room or cycle storage, you'll find it here. No credit cards. ❷

Café-Bar 26 26 Lake Rd ☏017687/80863, Ⓦ www.cafebar26.co.uk. Three stylish nonsmoking rooms above the café offer a central chintz-free base. ❷, weekends ❸

Denton House Penrith Road ☏017687/75351, Ⓦ www.vividevents.co.uk. Keswick's cheapest hostel, 10min walk from the centre (by the railway bridge, just after the ambulance/fire station). Dorm beds £12, breakfast £3 (when available, usually weekends). No credit cards.

Derwentwater YHA Barrow House, Borrowdale ☏0870/770 5792, Ⓔ derwentwater@yha.org .uk. Based in an old mansion with fifteen acres of grounds, a couple of miles south of Keswick along the B5289. Open weekends only Nov–Jan. Dorm beds £13.95.

George St John's Street ☏017687/72076, www.georgehotelkeswick.co.uk. Keswick's oldest coaching inn, with bags of character down-stairs and fully modernized rooms up. ❺

Howe Keld 5–7 The Heads ☏017687/72417, www.howekeld.co.uk. Welcoming, nonsmoking guest house with great breakfasts (vegetarian specialities included) and cosy rooms. Parking. ❹

Keswick YHA Station Road ☏0870/770 5894, ✉keswick@yha.org.uk. Good location in a converted woollen mill by the river in town. Dorm beds cost £13.95. Open all year.

Sweeney's 18–20 Lake Rd ☏017687/72990, www.sweeneysbar.co.uk. Four bright en-suite rooms above a contemporary bar-brasserie. Fell views from some windows, a good breakfast and the town's most spacious beer garden out back. ❺

Cafés, pubs and restaurants

Abraham's Tea Rooms George Fisher's, 2 Borrowdale Rd ☏017687/72178. The top-floor tearoom in the outdoor store serves homemade soups, big breakfasts and daily specials. Daytime only. Inexpensive.

Bank Tavern 47 Main St. A local reputation for good bar meals means that every table is often occupied. Inexpensive.

Lakeland Pedlar Henderson's Yard, Bell Close, off Main Street ☏017687/74492. Keswick's best café serves inventive veggie food – from breakfast burritos to veg crumble. Daytime only (till 8pm July & Aug). Moderate.

Lake Road Inn Lake Road. Intimate Jennings pub known for its good-value food, particularly the homemade pies and Borrowdale trout. Inexpensive.

Morrell's 34 Lake Rd ☏017687/72666. Modern Mediterranean styles prevail in this handsome-looking restaurant – there's a bargain Sunday *table d'hôte* menu and a decent selection of wines by the glass. Expensive.

Salsa 1 New St ☏017687/75222. Tex-Mex tapas and drinks downstairs, restaurant upstairs serving *fajitas*, tacos, ribs and wraps. Moderate.

Borrowdale

It is difficult to overstate the beauty of **Borrowdale**, with its river flats and yew trees, lying at the head of Derwent Water and overshadowed by Scafell Pike, the highest mountain in England. Climbs up the peak start from the head of the valley near Seatoller, accessible on the #77/77a (Easter–Oct 4 daily) and #79 (all year every 30min–1hr) buses from Keswick.

The minor B5289 runs south to the straggling hamlet of **ROSTHWAITE**, where *Yew Tree Farm* **B&B** (☏017687/77675, www.borrowdaleherdwick .co.uk; closed mid-Dec to Jan; no credit cards; ❸), has played host to Prince Charles on his incognito walking trips to the Lakes. There are also comfort-able rooms at the hiker-friendly *Royal Oak Hotel* (☏017687/77214, www .royaloakhotel.co.uk; ❻, includes dinner) and the smarter, neighbouring *Scafell Hotel* (☏017687/77208, www.scafell.co.uk; ❻), whose attached *Riverside Inn* is the only local **pub**. Another mile up the valley, the **Borrowdale Informa-tion Centre** at Seatoller Barn (Easter–Oct daily 10am–5pm; ☏017687/77294) marks the end of the #79 bus route from Keswick. A few slate-roofed houses cluster around the welcoming *Yew Tree* **café-restaurant-bar** (☏017687/77634; no food Mon evening; closed Jan), while virtually next door, *Seatoller House* (☏017687/77218, www.seatollerhouse.co.uk; ❹, ❻ with dinner; no dinner Tues, closed Dec–Feb) has rooms in an atmospheric seventeenth-century farm-house.

In good weather, the minor road to **SEATHWAITE** is lined with parked cars by 9am as hikers take to the paths for the rugged climbs up to some of the Lake's most famous peaks. There's a farmhouse campsite and **café** at Seathwaite, the latter open all day for fried breakfasts and other meals. For England's highest peak, **Scafell Pike** (3205ft), the approach is through the farmyard and up to Styhead Tarn via Stockley Bridge; from the tarn the classic ascent is up the thrilling Corridor Route, then descending via Esk Hause – an eight-mile (6hr) loop walk in all from Seathwaite.

Honister, Buttermere and Loweswater

Bus #77/77a from Keswick makes the steep mile-and-a-quarter grind from Borrowdale to the top of dramatic **Honister Pass**, where there's the simple *Honister Hause* YHA **hostel** (℡0870/770 5870, ⓔhonister@yha.org.uk; dorm beds £11.95; Sept–Easter flexible opening). The only other reason to stop here is for the informative guided tours of **Honister Slate Mine** (tours daily at 10.30am, 12.30pm & 3.30pm; £9.50; ℡017687/77230, ⓦwww.honister -slate-mine.co.uk), where you don a hard hat and lamp to get an idea of what slate mining entailed in the nineteenth century.

From the pass, the B5289 makes a dramatic descent into the **Buttermere Valley**, passing *Buttermere* YHA **hostel** (℡0870/770 5736, ⓔbuttermere@yha .org.uk; dorm beds £17.50, includes breakfast; Nov–Easter flexible opening), just before **BUTTERMERE** village itself (#77/77a bus from Keswick). There are no facilities in the village save a seasonal café and two hotels, of which the *Bridge* has a popular flagstoned **bar**. The four-mile, **round-lake stroll** circling Buttermere shouldn't take more than a couple of hours; you can always detour up Scarth Gap to Haystacks (1900ft) if you want more of a climb and some views.

The scenery flattens out as the road heads north from neighbouring Crummock Water and into the pastoral **Lorton Vale**, with Cockermouth just a few miles beyond. A minor road leads directly to minuscule **Loweswater**, one of the less frequented lakes, around which there's another gentle, four-mile (2hr) walk. En route, you'll pass the ⚡ *Kirkstile Inn* (℡01900/85219, ⓦwww.kirkstile.com; ❺, family suites ❼), a welcoming sixteenth-century place with contemporary rooms and excellent bistro-style meals.

Wast Water

The highest slopes in England frame the northern shores of slim, deep **Wast Water**, while on the wild southeastern banks rise the impassable screes which separate the lake from Eskdale to the south. The only road winds from the main coastal A595, via the hamlet of Nether Wasdale (two small hotels on a green), before hugging the shore of the lake, ending at **Wasdale Head**, a Shangri-la-like clearing between the mountain ranges. Here you'll find the marvellous ⚡ *Wasdale Head Inn* (℡019467/26229, ⓦwww.wasdale.com; ❻), one of the most celebrated of all lakeland inns, with legendary breakfasts, a great public bar and hearty four-course dinners (£25). Nearby, there's **B&B** at hiker-friendly *Lingmell House* (℡019467/26261, ⓦwww.lingmellhouse.com; no credit cards; ❸; closed Jan), on the track to the church, or **camping** at the National Trust's *Wasdale Head* campsite (℡019467/26220). The peaks of Pillar, Scafell or Great Gable are popular hiking targets, as is the route over the pass into Borrowdale or south over the fells to Eskdale.

Eskdale

The attractive rural ride by road or train through **Eskdale** from the west begins to peter out as you approach Dalegarth Station, terminus of the Ravenglass & Eskdale Railway (see p.576), just beyond which nestles the dead-end hamlet of **BOOT**. Three miles beyond Boot and eight hnundred feet up, the remains of granaries, bathhouses and the commandant's quarters for **Hardknott Roman**

Fort (always open; free) command a strategic and panoramic position. Beyond, over the narrow switchbacks of **Hardknott Pass**, the road drops to Cockley Beck, before making the equally alarming ascent of Wrynose Pass – this is the route back to Langdale and Ambleside.

Boot is the obvious base for extended walks in the valley, though there are B&Bs and the occasional pub in nearby hamlets such as Eskdale Green and Santon Bridge. The nearest place to Dalegarth Station is *Brook House Inn* (℡019467/23288, ⑩www.brookhouseinn.co.uk; ④), a cheery family-run hotel with a public bar and good restaurant, or in Boot itself there's the *Burnmoor Inn* (℡019467/23224, ⑩www.burnmoor.co.uk; ④). A mile east of the village on the Hardknott Pass road stands the *Woolpack Inn* (℡019467/23230, ⑩www .woolpack.co.uk; ③), another first-rate walkers' halt with a beer garden. A further 200yd beyond the pub is *Eskdale YHA* (℡0870/770 5824, ⑥eskdale@yha.org .uk; dorm beds £11.95; closed Nov–Feb).

Cockermouth

The small market town of **COCKERMOUTH**, midway between the coast and Keswick, is yet another station on the Wordsworth trail: the **Wordsworth House** on Main Street (Easter–Oct Mon–Sat 11am–4.30pm; £4.50, admission by timed ticket; ⑩www.wordsworthhouse.org.uk; NT) is where William and Dorothy were born and spent their first few years. The building has been beautifully restored, but rather than a pure period piece it's presented as a functioning eighteenth-century home – with a costumed cook willing to share recipes in the kitchen and a clerk completing the ledger with quill and ink. Various other rainy-day attractions occupy the historic buildings and yards ranged along the Main Street – including museums of printing, toys and models, and motoring – while if you follow your nose, you'll stumble upon **Jennings Brewery**, on Brewery Lane near the river. The hour-and-a-half-long Jennings Brewery Tour (£4.95; booking advisable; ℡0845/129 7190, ⑩www.jenningsbrewery .co.uk) culminates in a tasting.

All **buses** stop on Main Street, from where you follow the signs east to the **tourist office** in the Town Hall, off Market Place (Mon–Sat 9.30am–4/5pm; July–Sept also Sun 10am–2pm; Nov–March closed Sat; ℡01900/822634, ⑩www.cockermouth.org.uk). **Accommodation** is best at *Croft House*, 6–8 Challoner St (℡01900/827533, ⑩www.croft-guesthouse.com; closed Jan; ③), a stylish revamp of a Georgian townhouse or the comfortable riverside *Trout Hotel*, Crown Street (℡01900/823591, ⑩www.trouthotel.co.uk; ⑥), the town's top choice. The finest **pub** by far is *The Bitter End* on Kirkgate, home to Cumbria's smallest brewery.

Ullswater

At over seven miles long, **Ullswater** is the second-longest lake in Cumbria and much of its appeal derives from its serpentine shape. The chief lakeside settlements, Glenridding and Patterdale, are less than a mile apart at the southern tip of Ullswater, and make useful bases for one of the most popular scrambling routes in the country – up the considerable heights of Helvellyn. The #108 Patterdale Rambler **bus** service from Penrith runs via Pooley Bridge, Aira Force and Glenridding to Patterdale. The #517 Kirkstone Rambler bus from Glenridding/Patterdale continues south over the Kirkstone Pass to Bowness (Easter–early Sept daily in summer school hols, weekends & bank hols). The lake itself is traversed by the **Ullswater Steamers** (℡017684/82229, ⑩www .ullswater-steamers.co.uk), which have year-round services from Glenridding to Howtown, halfway up the lake's eastern side (£7 return; 35min), and from Howtown to Pooley Bridge, at the northern end of the lake (£6.70; 20min). Alternatively, you can buy a ticket between Glenridding and Pooley Bridge that effectively makes a two-hour, round-the-lake cruise (£10).

The former mining village of **GLENRIDDING** is probably the best base, with several inexpensive **B&Bs**, including the recommended *Beech House*, on the main road (☏017684/82037, ⓦwww.beechhouse.com; ❸). The helpful **tourist office** (Easter–Oct daily 9.30am–5.30pm; Nov–Easter Fri–Sun 9.30am–3.30pm; ☏017684/82414) is in the main car park, and there's **camping** and **bunkhouse** accommodation (from £7) half a mile away up the valley at *Gillside Caravan & Camping* (☏01768/482346; closed Nov–Feb). Hikers wanting an early start on Helvellyn stay at *Helvellyn* YHA hostel (☏0870/770 6110, ⓔhelvellyn@yha.org.uk; dorm beds £11.95; Nov–Easter flexible opening), a mile and a half up the valley road from Glenridding.

There's another **hostel** (☏0870/770 5986, ⓔpatterdale@yha.org.uk; dorm beds £13.95; Nov–March flexible opening), just south of the hamlet of **PATTERDALE**, on the A592, while Patterdale's only **pub**, the *White Lion* (☏017684/82214; ❸), also has a few rooms.

At **Gowbarrow Park**, three miles north of Glenridding, the hillside still blazes green and gold in spring, as it did when the Wordsworths visited in April 1802; it's thought that Dorothy's recollections of the visit in her diary inspired William to write his famous *Daffodils* poem. The car park here is the start of a brief walk up to **Aira Force** (40min round-trip), a bush-cloaked seventy-foot fall that's spectacular in spate. There's a tearoom (closed Nov–Easter) at the car park with an outdoor terrace.

The climb to the summit of **Helvellyn** (3114ft), the most popular of the four 3000-foot mountains in Cumbria, forms part of a day-long circuit from either Glenridding or Patterdale. The most frequently chosen approach is via the infamous **Striding Edge**, an alarming, undulating rocky ridge offering the most direct access to the summit, with **Red Tarn** – the highest Lake District tarn – a dizzying drop below. The classic return is to the northeast via the less demanding **Swirral Edge**, where a route leads down to Red Tarn, then follows the beck to the disused slate-quarry workings by *Helvellyn* hostel (see above).

The Cumbrian coast

South and west of the national park, the Cumbrian coast attracts much less attention than the spectacular scenery inland, but it would be a mistake to write it off. It splits into two distinct sections, the most accessible being the **Furness peninsulas** area (ⓦwww.lake-district-peninsulas.co.uk), just a few miles from Windermere, where varied attractions include the monastic priory at **Cartmel** and the enjoyable market town of **Ulverston**. In addition, the dramatic ruins of nearby **Furness Abbey** have been attracting visitors for almost two hundred years. The **Cumbrian coast** itself is generally judged to begin at Silecroft near Millom and stretches for more than sixty miles to the small resort of Silloth, on the shores of the Solway Firth. In between lie isolated beaches and the headland of **St Bees**, as well as the delights of the narrow-gauge **Ravenglass & Eskdale Railway** and the attractive Georgian port of **Whitehaven**. The coastal-line railway between Lancaster and Carlisle connects all points of interest.

Cartmel and Holker Hall

Sheltered several miles inland from Morecambe Bay, **CARTMEL** grew up around its twelfth-century Augustinian priory and is still dominated by the proud **Church of St Mary and St Michael** (daily 9am–3.30/5.30pm; tours Easter–Oct Wed 11am & 2pm; free), the only substantial remnant to survive the Dissolution. A diagonally crowned tower is the most distinctive feature outside, while the spacious Norman-transitional interior climaxes at a splendid chancel, illuminated by the 45-foot-high East Window. Everything else in the village is modest in scale, centred on the attractive **market square**, beyond the church, with its Elizabethan cobbles, water pump and fish slabs.

A couple of miles west of the village, on the B5278, one of Cumbria's most interesting country estates, **Holker Hall** (Easter–Oct Mon–Fri & Sun 10am–6pm; last admission 4.30pm; various combination tickets available, or all-inclusive ticket £9.25; ☎015395/58328, ⓦwww.holker-hall.co.uk) is still in use by the Cavendish family who've owned it since the late seventeenth century. The 25-acre gardens incorporate a variety of water features, with the **Lakeland Motor Museum** (Easter–Oct Mon–Fri & Sun 10.30am–4.45pm) displaying more than a hundred vehicles, from 1880s tricycles and wartime ambulances to funky 1920s bubble cars and 1980s MGs.

Trains stop at Cark-in-Cartmel, two miles southwest of the village proper; **buses** from there or from Grange-over-Sands train station (on the Cumbria coast line) run to the village. **Cartmel Races** (ⓦwww.cartmel-steeple chases.co.uk) fill the village twice a year (last weekend in May and August). Otherwise, **accommodation** should be easy to find though you will need to book in advance for Cartmel's extraordinary *L'Enclume*, Cavendish Street (☎015395/36362, ⓦwww.lenclume.co.uk; ❽; closed first 2 weeks of Jan), a highly individual Michelin-starred restaurant-with-rooms. Also on Cavendish Street is the more traditional *Cavendish Arms* (☎015395/36240, ⓦwww .thecavendisharms.co.uk; ❹), a sixteenth-century inn which retains many of its original features.

Ulverston

The railway line winds westwards to **ULVERSTON**, a close-knit market town of dappled grey limestone cottages and a jumble of cobbled alleys and traditional shops zigzagging off the central Market Place. Stalls are still set up here and in the surrounding streets every Thursday and Saturday; on Mondays, Tuesdays and Fridays, the market hall on New Market Street is the centre of commercial life. Ulverston's most famous son is Stan Laurel (born Arthur Stanley Jefferson), the whimpering, head-scratching half of the comic duo, celebrated in a mind-boggling collection of memorabilia at the **Laurel and Hardy Museum** (Feb–Dec daily 10am–4.30pm; £2.50; ⓦwww.laurel-and -hardy-museum.co.uk), up an alley at 4c Upper Brook St, near Market Place.

Ulverston **train station** is a few minutes' walk from the town centre, while **buses** arrive on Victoria Road. The **tourist office** is in Coronation Hall on County Square (Mon–Sat 9am–5pm; ☎01229/587120, ⓦwww.ulverston.net). The 70-mile **Cumbria Way** long-distance footpath from Ulverston to Carlisle starts from The Gill, at the top of Upper Brook Street – a waymarker spire marks the start. Hikers can use the *Walker's Hostel* on Oubas Hill (☎01229/585588, ⓦwww.walkershostel.freeserve.co.uk; no credit cards; £14; closed Nov & Dec), fifteen minutes' walk from the centre on the A590 near Canal Head: there are thirty beds in small rooms (you won't have to share with strangers), with vegetarian breakfasts (included) and evening meals available (£8). Otherwise, one of the nicest places to eat is the moderately priced *Farmers Arms* **pub** in Market Place, where fish is always a good choice.

Furness Abbey

Furness Abbey (Easter–Sept daily 10am–6pm; Oct–March Mon & Thurs–Sun 10am–4pm; £3.30; EH), a set of roofless sandstone arcades and pillars hidden in a wooded vale, lies a mile and a half out of Barrow-in-Furness on the Ulverston road (local buses to Dalton-in-Furness and Ulverston pass close by). Founded in 1124, it was once the most powerful abbey in the Northwest, possessing much of southern Cumbria as well as land in Ireland and the Isle of Man. It owned sheep on the local fells, controlled fishing rights, produced grain and leather, smelted iron, dug peat for fuel and manufactured salt. By the fourteenth century it had become such a prize that the Scots raided it twice, though it survived until April 1536, when Henry VIII chose it to be the first of the large abbeys to be dissolved.

Ravenglass and Muncaster

On its way from Barrow-in-Furness to Whitehaven, the Cumbrian coast railway stops at **RAVENGLASS**, which preserves a row of nineteenth-century cottages facing out across the mud flats. The station is the starting point for the **Ravenglass & Eskdale Railway** (March–Nov at least 7 trains daily; also most winter weekends, plus Christmas, New Year and Feb half-term hols; £9 return; ☎01229/717171, ⓦ www.ravenglass-railway.co.uk), known affectionately as La'al Ratty. Opened in 1875 to carry ore from the Eskdale mines to the coastal railway, the tiny train, running on a 15-inch-gauge track, winds its way through seven miles of forests and fields between the fell sides of the Eskdale Valley to Dalegarth Station near Boot.

A mile east of Ravenglass on the A595 spreads the estate of **Muncaster Castle** (Feb half-term hols to 1st week Nov; £9, £6.50 without castle entrance; ☎01229/717614, ⓦ www.muncaster.co.uk). It's one of the region's best days out – apart from the ghost-ridden rooms of the castle itself (Mon–Fri & Sun noon–5pm), there are also seventy acres of well-kept **grounds and gardens**, as well as an **owl centre** (a breeding centre for endangered species) and **meadowvole maze** (both daily 10.30am–6pm or dusk), where you'll learn about Muncaster voles, follow hiking trails, and watch entertaining bird displays (daily 2.30pm) or wild herons feeding (4.30pm, 3.30pm in winter).

St Bees

The coastal village of **ST BEES** saw a nunnery established as early as the seventh century, succeeded by St Bees Priory in the twelfth century. Long sands lie a few hundred yards west of the priory (there's a massive car park there, plus tearoom and pub), while the steep, sandstone cliffs of **St Bees Head** to the north are good for windy walks and birdwatching. The headland's lighthouse marks the start of Wainwright's 190-mile **Coast-to-Coast Walk** to Robin Hood's Bay (see p.628). St Bees is on the Cumbrian coast train line and lies just five miles south of Whitehaven, from where there's a regular bus service. There's good **accommodation** here, starting with ✠ *Fleatham House*, High House Road (☎01946/822341, ⓦ www.fleathamhouse.com; ⑤), a lovely retreat set in its own grounds just five minutes from the station (first left off Main Street). Dinner is available in the attached Italian restaurant (closed Sun

& Mon), or there's *Platform 9* at the station (✆01946/822600; dinner only), a romantic little bistro.

Whitehaven

Some fine Georgian houses mark out the centre of **WHITEHAVEN**, one of the few grid-planned towns in England. Whitehaven spent a brief period during the eighteenth century as Britain's third-busiest port (after London and Bristol), making it a prime target for an abortive raid led by Scottish-born American lieutenant John Paul Jones. Disgusted with the slave trade he witnessed while ship's mate in America, Jones returned to the port of his apprenticeship to rebel, but, let down by a drunk and potentially mutinous crew, he damaged only one of the two hundred boats in dock and his mini-crusade fell flat. All this and more is explained in **The Beacon** (Tues–Sun 10am–4.30/5.30pm; £4.40; Ⓦwww.thebeacon-whitehaven.co.uk), an enterprising heritage centre on the harbour. After seeing this, stroll up Lowther Street to the **Rum Story** (daily 10am–4/5pm; £4.95; Ⓦwww.rumstory.co.uk), housed in the eighteenth-century shop, courtyard and warehouses of the Jefferson's rum family. This is another place you could easily spend an hour or so, discovering Whitehaven's links with the Caribbean and learning all about rum, the Navy, temperance and the hideousness of the slaves' Middle Passage. Also on Lowther Street, don't miss Michael Moon's secondhand **bookshop** at no. 19 (closed Wed Jan–Easter, and closed Sun all year), a bookworm's treasure-trove.

From the **train station** you can walk around the harbour to The Beacon in less than ten minutes; the **bus station** is just across Tesco's car park from the train station. The **tourist office** is in the Market Hall on Market Place (Mon–Sat 9.30/10am–4/5pm, plus July & Aug Sun 11am–3pm; ✆01946/852939, Ⓦwww.rediscoverwhitehaven.com), just back from the harbour, and can provide details about the town's biennial **maritime festival** in June (next events 2007 and 2009). Whitehaven is the start of the 140-mile **C2C cycle route** to Sunderland/Newcastle – a metal cut-out at the harbour marks the spot. Also from the harbour, **Windrider RIB Adventures** (✆01229/582811, Ⓦwww.windrider-rib.com; £20; daily departures April–Sept) offers marine ecology tours in a high-speed powerboat around the local coastal waters.

For **accommodation**, the best central B&B is the very comfortable *Corkickle Guest House*, 1 Corkickle (✆01946/692073, Ⓔcorkickle@tinyworld.co.uk; no credit cards; ❷), five minutes' walk from the centre – keep on up Lowther Street, past Safeway and *McDonald's* to find the row of Georgian townhouses. For **meals**, *Zest Harbourside* on West Strand is a waterside café-bar doing mix-and-match tapas-style dishes. Its sister restaurant, *Zest*, on Low Road (✆01946/692848; dinner only Wed–Sat), three-quarters of a mile out of the centre (on the B5349 Whitehaven–St Bees road), is good for moderately priced Modern British cuisine.

The Eden Valley and Penrith

The Lake District might end abruptly with the market town and transport hub of **Penrith**, ten miles northeast of Ullswater, but Cumbria doesn't. To the east, the **Eden Valley** splits the Pennines from the Lake District fells, and boasts a succession of hardy market towns, prime among which is the former county town of **Appleby-in-Westmorland**. This lies on the magnificent Settle to Carlisle railway, connecting Cumbria with the Yorkshire Dales (see p.603).

Northeast of Penrith, the A686 leads you imperceptibly from Cumbria into Teesdale via the high town of **Alston** – making a superbly scenic approach to Hexham and Hadrian's Wall.

Penrith and around

Once a thriving market town on the main north–south trading route, **PENRITH** today suffers from undue comparisons with the improbably pretty settlements of the nearby Lakes. Its brisk streets, filled with no-nonsense shops and shoppers, have more in common with the towns of the North Pennines than the stone villages of south Cumbria, and even the local building materials emphasize the geographic shift. Its deep-red buildings were erected from the same rust-red sandstone used to construct **Penrith Castle** (daily 8am–dusk; free) in the fourteenth century, as a bastion against raids from the north; it's now a crumbling ruin, opposite the train station.

Three miles southwest of town, the country house of **Dalemain** (Easter–Oct Mon–Thurs & Sun, house 11am–4pm, gardens 10.30am–5pm; Nov, Dec & Feb–Easter gardens and tearoom only Mon–Thurs 11am–4pm; £6, gardens only £4; ⓦ www.dalemain.com) started life in the twelfth century as a fortified tower, but has subsequently been added to by every generation. The servants' corridors and pantries offer a glimpse of life "below stairs", while outside, the medieval courtyard and Elizabethan great barn doubled as the schoolroom and dormitory of Lowood School in the TV adaptation of Charlotte Brontë's *Jane Eyre*.

You also shouldn't miss **Rheged** (daily 10am–5.30pm; ⓦ www.rheged.com; free) at Redhills on the A66, a couple of minutes' drive from the M6 (junction 40); express buses between Penrith and Keswick stop outside. Billed as Britain's largest earth-covered building, it takes its name from the ancient kingdom of Cumbria and features a spectacular atrium-lit underground visitor centre, which fills you in on the region's culture, history and food by way of exhibitions, local art and craft displays, family activities and food bar, food hall, restaurant and terrace café. There's also a giant-format cinema screen, as well as the separate **National Mountaineering Exhibition** (same times; £5.95), presenting an entertaining history of mountain-climbers and climbing, from the Lake District to the world's highest peaks. Various discounted combination tickets are available (£9.95 to £20.55) if you want to see the movies plus the mountaineering exhibit.

Penrith **train station** is five minutes' walk south of Market Square and the main street, Middlegate. The **bus station** is on Albert Street, behind Middlegate, which is where you'll find the **tourist office** (Easter–Oct Mon–Sat 9.30am–5pm, Sun 1–4.45pm; Nov–Easter Mon–Fri 10am–4pm, Sat 10.30am–4pm; ☏01768/867466, ⓦ www.visiteden.co.uk), sharing its seventeenth-century schoolhouse premises with a small local museum. The bulk of the standard B&Bs line noisy Victoria Road (the continuation of King Street running south from Market Square). You're better off on Portland Place, behind the Town Hall, which has a more refined row of **guest houses**, including the excellent *Brooklands*, 2 Portland Place (☏01768/863395, ⓦ www.brooklands guesthouse.com; ❸).

If you're heading for Hadrian's Wall the highly scenic A686 provides an alternative trans-moor route into the North Pennines, via Alston. Travelling this way, be sure to stop at the prehistoric stone circle known as **Long Meg and her Daughters**, just outside Little Salkeld, six miles north of Penrith and just over a mile's walk from Langwathby on the Settle to Carlisle railway. Four miles further north at **Melmerby**, it's also worth calling in at the specialist *Village Bakery* (daily until 5pm; ☎01768/881811, ⓦwww.village-bakery.com), for wonderful breakfasts, lunches and teas.

Alston

Although **ALSTON** no longer has a market to back up its claim to being England's highest market town, it still has its market cross, beside the cobbled curve of the steep main road, Front Street. It's a tidily restored town, with a mix of traditional shops, tearooms and galleries, and its convenient location between Cumbria and the Northeast, and position as a hiking and biking hub, makes it a popular stopover. **Buses** link Alston with Carlisle, Hexham and Hadrian's Wall, and Newcastle. There's plenty of local **accommodation** in all price ranges, starting with Georgian country-house B&B at *Lowbyer Manor* (☎01434/381230, ⓦwww.lowbyer.com; ❹), while the best place to eat is *Alston House* (☎01434/382200, ⓦwww.alstonhouse.co.uk; ❹), at the foot of town on the main road, which has B&B rooms and an enjoyable contemporary bar-restaurant. Alston's YHA **hostel** (☎0870/770 5668, ⓔalston@yha.org.uk; dorm beds £11.95; Nov–Easter flexible opening) is five minutes' walk south of the centre (signposted off the Penrith road as you approach town).

Appleby-in-Westmorland

One-time county town of Westmorland, **APPLEBY-IN-WESTMORLAND** is protected on three sides by a lazy loop in the River Eden. The fourth was defended by the now privately owned **Appleby Castle** (closed to the public), whose Norman keep was restored by Lady Anne Clifford, who, after her father's death in 1605, spent 45 years trying to claim her rightful inheritance. The town is usually a peaceful place for a riverside stroll, but changes its character completely in June when the **Appleby Horse Fair** takes over nearby Gallows' Hill, as it has done since 1750. Britain's most important Gypsy gathering, it draws hundreds of chrome-plated caravans and more traditional horse-drawn "bow-tops", as well as the vehicles of tinkers, New Age travellers and sightseers.

The **Settle to Carlisle railway** is the best way to get to Appleby, although **bus services** from Penrith are frequent enough. The **tourist office**, in the Moot Hall on Boroughgate (April–Oct Mon–Sat 9.30am–5pm, Sun noon–4pm; Nov–March restricted hours; ☎017683/51177, ⓦwww.applebytown.org .uk), is ten minutes' walk from the station, across the river. There are a couple of **B&Bs** on Bongate, 500yd (10min walk) from town, over the river from Low Cross, then south along the Brough road. Also along here you'll find the *Royal Oak* (☎017683/51463; ❺), an aged inn with some comfortable rooms and well-regarded brasserie-style food. If the weather's fine you can't beat the café (open 10am–5pm; closed Nov–Easter) at **Rutter Falls**, an idyllic location by the tumbling waters, ford and footbridge, three miles south of town at Great Asby.

Carlisle

The county capital of Cumbria and its only city, **CARLISLE** is also the repository of much of the region's history, its strategic location having been fought over for more than two thousand years. The original Celtic settlement was superseded by a Roman town, whose first fort was raised here in 72 AD. Carlisle thrived during the construction of Hadrian's Wall and then, long after the Romans had gone, the Saxon settlement was fought over by the Danes, Normans and Scots. The struggle with the Scots defined the very nature of Carlisle as a border city: William Wallace was repelled in 1297 and Robert the Bruce eighteen years later, but Bonnie Prince Charlie's troops took Carlisle in 1745 after a six-day siege, holding it for six weeks before surrendering to the Duke of Cumberland.

The main thoroughfare of English Street is pedestrianized as far as the expansive **Green Market** square, formerly heart of the medieval city, though a huge fire in 1392 destroyed its buildings and layout. The only historic survivors are the **market cross** (1682), the Elizabethan former **Town Hall** behind it, which now houses the tourist office and, at the southern end of Fisher Street, the timber-framed **Guildhall** (1405). It's only a few steps along to **Carlisle Cathedral** (Mon–Sat 7.30am–6.15pm, Sun 7.30am–5pm; free, donation requested), founded in 1122 but embracing a considerably older heritage. Christianity was established in sixth-century Carlisle by St Kentigern (often known as St Mungo), who became the first bishop and patron saint of Glasgow. The cathedral's sandstone bulk has endured the ravages of time and siege, and there's still much to admire in the ornate fifteenth-century choir stalls and the glorious **East Window**, which features some of the finest pieces of fourteenth-century stained glass in the country.

For more on Carlisle's history, head for the **Tullie House Museum and Art Gallery** (Mon–Sat 10am–4/5pm, Sun noon–4/5pm; £5.50; ⓦwww.tulliehouse.co.uk), reached through the cathedral grounds via Abbey Street. This takes a highly imaginative approach to Carlisle's turbulent past, with special emphasis put on life on the edge of the Roman Empire – climbing a reconstruction of part of Hadrian's Wall, you learn about catapults and stone-throwers, while other sections elaborate on domestic life, work and burial practices. Nearby **Carlisle Castle** (daily 9.30/10am–4/6pm; £4; EH) was originally built by William Rufus on the site of a Celtic hillfort, though having now clocked up over nine hundred years of continuous military use, the castle has undergone considerable changes. There's a military museum located in the former armoury, but much more interesting are the excellent displays in the **Keep**, and the elegant heraldic carvings made by prisoners in a second-floor alcove. Don't leave without climbing to the battlements for a view of the Carlisle rooftops.

The local Roman highlight is **Birdoswald Fort** (March–Nov daily 10am–5.30pm; £3.60; ⓦwww.birdoswaldromanfort.org.uk; EH), signposted from the A69 fifteen miles northeast of Carlisle. One of sixteen forts along Hadrian's Wall, it has all tiers of the Roman structure intact, the defences comprising an earth ditch and a large section of masonry wall, with the trench and mound foundations behind. There's a tearoom and picnic area at the fort, as well as a residential study centre, which doubles as a YHA **hostel** from mid-July to mid-September (☎0870/770 6124, ⓔbirdoswald@yha.org.uk; dorm beds £15.50, includes entry to fort). The **Hadrian's Wall Bus** (see p.659) leaves Carlisle three times daily in summer (daily June to mid-Sept, plus Sun in April, May & Oct), calling at Birdoswald (40min), en route to the rest of the Hadrian's Wall sights.

Practicalities

From either the **train station** (just off Botchergate) or the **bus station** (off Lowther Street, parallel to English Street), it's a five-minute walk to the

tourist office in the Old Town Hall on Green Market (Mon–Sat 9.30/10am–4/5.30pm, plus May–Aug Sun 10.30am–4pm; ☏01228/625600, ⓦwww .historic-carlisle.org.uk). Most of the budget **accommodation** is east of the tourist office, concentrated in a conservation area in the streets between Victoria Place and Warwick Road.

Accommodation

Aldingham House 1 Eden Mount, Stanwix ☏01228/522554, ⓦwww.aldingham-house.co.uk. Superior B&B accommodation, a 10min walk from the centre over Eden Bridge. Three large, luxuriously appointed rooms with glorious beds, crisp linen, thick towels and superb bathrooms. ❺

Angus 14 Scotland Rd ☏01228/523546, ⓦwww .angus-hotel.co.uk. The price is right at this small family-owned hotel with moderately priced bistro (dinner only; closed Sun), a 15min walk from the centre. ❹

Number Thirty One 31 Howard Place ☏01228/597080, ⓦwww.number31.freeserv-ers.com. Grand Victorian house offering comfort in three well-appointed rooms named after their colour schemes: blue, green or yellow. ❺

Old Brewery Residences Bridge Street, Caldew-gate ☏0870/770 5752, ⓔdeec@impacthousing .org.uk. Summer-only (July & Aug) YHA accommo-dation, just past the castle, in a brewery conversion that's normally university halls of residence. Dorm beds £17.50.

The Weary Castle Carrock, Brampton, 8 miles east of Carlisle ☏01228/670230, ⓦwww.theweary .com. The inn with the "wow" factor – traditional eighteenth-century outside, utterly contemporary inside. Five sleek rooms, plus a handsome designer bar-restaurant and conservatory. No lunch Mon. ❼

Cafés and restaurants

Le Gall 7 Devonshire St ☏01228/818388. Café-bar with a brasserie-diner–style menu, popular for a late-night drink or Sunday brunch.

The Lemon Lounge 18 Fisher St ☏01228/546363. Easy-going cellar bistro with a sun-trap outdoor terrace. Closed Sun & Mon. Moderate.

Number 10 10 Eden Mount ☏01228/524183. Very agreeable townhouse restaurant that many rate as the best in the city, serving a seasonally changing Modern English menu. Dinner only; closed Sun & Mon, and Feb. Expensive.

Travel details

Buses

For information on all local and national bus serv-ices, contact Traveline ☏0870/608 2608, ⓦwww .traveline.org.uk.

Carlisle to: Appleby (1 daily; 1hr 15min); Keswick (4 daily; 1hr 30min); Lancaster (4 daily; 1hr 10min); London (3 daily; 5hr 30min); Manchester (2 daily; 2hr 30min); Newcastle (hourly; 2hr 30min); White-haven (hourly; 1hr 30min); Windermere/Bowness (3 daily; 2hr 20min).

Kendal to: Ambleside (hourly; 40min); Cartmel (7 daily; 1hr); Grasmere (hourly; 1hr); Keswick (hourly; 1hr 30min); Lancaster (hourly; 1hr); Windermere/Bowness (hourly; 30min).

Keswick to: Ambleside (hourly; 1hr); Buttermere (2 daily; 30min); Carlisle (4 daily; 1hr 30min); Cocker-mouth (7 daily; 35min); Grasmere (hourly; 40min); Kendal (hourly; 1hr 30min); Manchester (1–3 daily; 3hr); Seatoller (9 daily; 30min); Whitehaven (5 daily; 1hr 30min); Windermere (hourly; 1hr).

Windermere to: Ambleside (up to 3 hourly; 15min);

Carlisle (3 daily; 2hr 20min); Grasmere (hourly; 30min); Kendal (hourly; 30min); Keswick (hourly; 1hr); Lancaster (hourly; 1hr 45min); Manchester (3 daily; 3hr).

Trains

For information on all local and national rail services, contact National Rail Enquiries ☏08457/484950, ⓦwww.nationalrail.co.uk.

Appleby-in-Westmorland to: Carlisle (6 daily; 40min).

Carlisle to: Appleby (6 daily; 40min); Lancaster (every 30–60min; 1hr); Leeds (Mon–Sat 8 daily, 3 on Sun; 2hr 40min); London (8 daily; 4hr 20min); Manchester (2 daily; 2hr 30min); Newcastle (hourly; 1hr 20min–1hr 40min); Whitehaven (hourly; 1hr 10min).

Oxenholme (Lake District) to: Carlisle (14 daily; 40–50min); London (5 daily; 3hr 30min–5hr); Manchester (1–5 daily; 1hr 40min); Penrith (14 daily; 30min).

Windermere to: Kendal (hourly; 15min); Oxen-holme (hourly; 20min).

⑫

Yorkshire

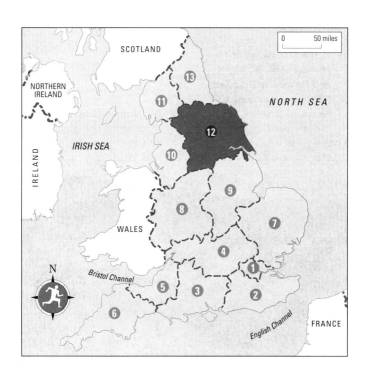

* **Millennium Galleries, Sheffield** Centrepiece of new-look Sheffield – terrific exhibitions with hothouse gardens attached. **See p.588**

* **Shopping in Leeds** Shop till you drop in the markets, malls and arcades of Yorkshire's most fashionable city. **See p.590**

* **National Museum of Photography, Film and Television, Bradford** A hands-on museum for couch potatoes and film fans of all ages. **See p.596**

* **Haworth** See the bleak moorland home of the Brontë sisters. **See p.597**

* **Malham** Make the breath-taking hike from Malham village to the glorious natural amphitheatre of Malham Cove. **See p.602**

* **Turkish Baths, Harrogate** The ultimate in personal pampering. **See p.609**

* **Jorvik, York** Travel through time to discover the sights, sounds and smells of Viking York. **See p.617**

* **The Magpie Café, Whitby** The best fish and chips in the world? **See p.631**

△ Malham Cove

Yorkshire

t's easy to be glib about **Yorkshire** – for much of the country, England's
largest county is shorthand for "up north" and all its clichéd connota-
tions, from flat caps and factories to tightfisted locals. For their part, many
Yorkshire born-and-bred are happy to play to the prejudice of southerners,
adopting an attitude roughly on a par with that of Texans or Australians in
strongly suggesting that there's really nowhere else worth considering. In its
sheer size at least, Yorkshire does have a case for primacy, while its most striking characteristics – from dialect to landscape – derive from a long history
of settlement, invention and independence that's still a source of pride today.
Yorkshire was once divided into three regions called "ridings" (North, East
and West), from the Old Norse for "third part", which correspond roughly
with the modern divisions of North, East and West Yorkshire, plus South
Yorkshire which abuts the Peak District and East Midlands. Differently named
administrative authorities confuse the issue further for locals, but for visitors
the divisions are a handy guide to the main cities and attractions – South
Yorkshire for Sheffield, West Yorkshire for Leeds, Bradford and Haworth, East
Yorkshire for Hull, and North Yorkshire for York, moors, dales and coast.

The number-one destination is history-soaked **York**, for centuries England's
second city until the Industrial Revolution created new centres of power and
influence. York's mixture of medieval, Georgian and Victorian architecture is
mirrored in miniature in the prosperous north and east of the county by towns
such as **Beverley**, centred on another soaring minster, and by the faded gentility
of the historic spa town of **Harrogate**. On the Yorkshire coast, **Bridlington**
and **Scarborough** boomed in the nineteenth century and again in the postwar
period, though these days they're living on past glories. It's in smaller resorts
with unspoiled historic centres such as **Whitby** and **Robin Hood's Bay** that
the best of the coast is to be found today. Meanwhile, a new vigour has infused
South and West Yorkshire during the last decade, and the city-centre transformations of **Leeds** and **Sheffield** in particular have been remarkable. Both are
now making open play for tourists with a series of high-profile attractions,
while **Bradford** and its National Museum of Photography, Film and Television
waylays visitors on their way to **Haworth**, home of the Brontë sisters.

During even the worst of times, broad swathes of moorland survived above
the slum and factory choked valleys, and it can come as a surprise to discover
the amount of open countryside on Leeds' and Bradford's doorsteps. The **Yorkshire Dales**, to the northwest, form a patchwork of stone-built villages, limestone hills, serene valleys and majestic heights. The county's other National Park,
the **North York Moors**, is divided into bleak upland moors and a tremendous
rugged coastline between Robin Hood's Bay and Staithes.

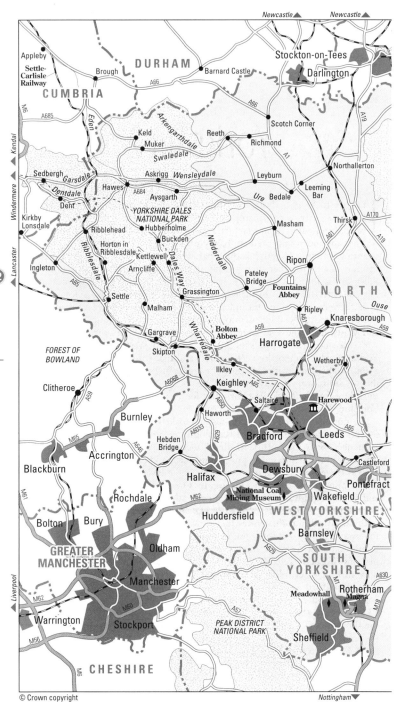

© Crown copyright

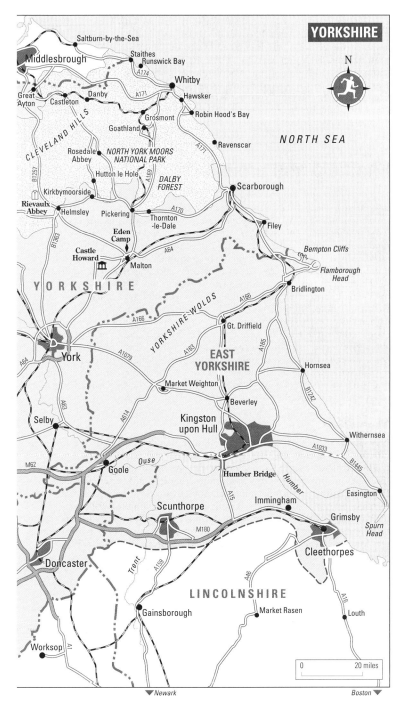

Fast **train** services on the East Coast main-line link York to London, Newcastle and Edinburgh. Leeds is also served by regular trains from London, and is at the centre of the integrated Metro bus and train system that covers most of West and South Yorkshire. There are also train services to Scarborough (from York) and Whitby (from Middlesbrough), while the famous **Settle-to-Carlisle** line, to the southern and western Yorkshire Dales, can be accessed from Leeds. The **North Country Rover** ticket (any four days in eight; £59) covers unlimited train travel north of Leeds, Bradford and Hull and south of Newcastle and Carlisle.

Sheffield and around

Yorkshire's second city, **SHEFFIELD** remains inextricably linked with its steel industry, in particular the production of high-quality cutlery. As early as the fourteenth century, the carefully fashioned, hard-wearing knives of hardworking Sheffield enjoyed national repute. Technological advances in steel production later turned Sheffield into one of the country's foremost centres of heavy and specialist engineering, which meant that the city suffered heavy bombing in World War II. However, more damaging than bombs was the steel industry's subsequent downturn, which by the 1980s had tipped parts of Sheffield into dispiriting decline. The subsequent revival has been rapid, with the centre utterly transformed by flagship architectural projects, from gardens to galleries. Steel, of course, still underpins much of what Sheffield is about – this is the city that gave the world *The Full Monty*, the black comedy about five former steel-workers carving out a new career as a striptease act. Museum collections tend to hone in on the region's industrial heritage, which is complemented by the startling science-and-adventure exhibits at **Magna** built on a disused steel works at nearby Rotherham, the former coal and iron town a few miles northeast of the city.

The City

New-look Sheffield is at its best around the landmark **Town Hall**, at the junction of Pinstone and Surrey streets. Completed in 1897, it's topped by the figure of Vulcan, the Roman god of fire and metalworking, and the facade sports a fine frieze depicting traditional Sheffield industries. The adjacent **Peace Gardens** feature monumental goblet cascades, and central water jets that whoosh up intermittently. Rising to the east, a minute's walk away, is the main symbol of the city regeneration, the stunning **Winter Gardens** (daily 8am–6pm; free), an arched steel-and-wood glasshouse almost two hundred feet long and over sixty feet high. Sheffield's **Millennium Galleries** (Mon–Sat 10am–5pm, Sun 11am–5pm; free, visiting exhibitions £4; ⓦ www.sheffield galleries.org.uk) back on to the gardens and provide pedestrian access down to Arundel Gate, the station and the Cultural Industries Quarter. In the **Metalworks Gallery** you can discover why the eighteenth-century city's natural endowments ensured the rapid development of the cutlery industry, and there's also the highly diverting **Ruskin Gallery**, based on the collection founded by John Ruskin in 1875 to improve the working people of Sheffield.

Other significant attractions are all on the city outskirts. Fifteen minutes' walk north of the cathedral, the **Kelham Island Museum** on Alma Street (Mon–Thurs 10am–4pm, Sun 11am–4.45pm; £4; ⓦ www.simt.co.uk) reveals the breadth of the city's industrial output. Many of the old machines are still working, arranged in period workshops where craftspeople demonstrate some of the finer points of cutlery production. You can then put the city's life and times into perspective a mile or so west in Weston Park, where the old Mappin Art Gallery and City Museum have been restored as the **Weston Park Museum** (consult Ⓦ www.sheffieldgalleries.org.uk for opening hours; free) – the handsome galleries here draw together the city's extensive archeology, natural history, art and social history collections. Catch bus #51 or #52 from High Street and get off at the Children's Hospital/Weston Park stop.

Magna

About six miles northeast of Sheffield, **Magna** (daily 10am–5pm; £9; Ⓦ www.visitmagna.co.uk) – the UK's first science adventure centre – is housed in a former steel-works building on Sheffield Road (A6178), Templeborough, just off the M1 (signed from junctions 33 and 34), a mile from the Meadowhall shopping complex. You can get there on bus #69 from either Sheffield or Rotherham interchanges, or it's a fifteen-minute taxi ride from Sheffield.

On entering the building, you're immediately confronted with the half-light, invasive noise and arcane hardware of a massive steel works. The vast internal space comfortably holds four gadget-packed pavilions, themed on the basic elements of earth, air, fire and water. In these you're encouraged to get your hands on a huge variety of interactive exhibits, games and machines – operating a real JCB, filling diggers and barrows, blasting a rock face, firing a water cannon, or investigating a twister. On the hour, everyone decamps to the main hall for the **Big Melt** when the original arc furnace is used in a bone-shaking light and sound show. Check the website for activities and events – and bring warm clothes for a winter visit.

Practicalities

Sheffield's **train station** is on the eastern edge of the city centre, by Sheffield Hallam University, about two hundred yards from the bus and coach station, known as **Sheffield Interchange**. Following Howard Street from the train station takes you straight up to Millennium Square in the city centre. The **tourist office** is here, inside the Winter Gardens on Surrey Street (daily 8am–6pm, staffed Mon–Sat 10am–4pm; ☎0114/221 1900, Ⓦ www.sheffieldtourism.co.uk, Ⓦ www.spinsheffield.com). Most local **buses** depart from High Street or Arundel Gate, while the **Supertram** (Ⓦ www.supertram.com) connects the city centre with Meadowhall shopping mall. For **accommodation**, *Premier Travel Inn*, *Ibis* and *Holiday Inn* all have central rooms from £50, or try the tourist office's room-booking service (☎0871/700 0121).

Sheffield has plenty of city-centre **café-bars** and good-value **restaurants**, while just south of the centre, London Road is lined with authentic Southeast Asian restaurants. Along **Division Street** and **West Street** competing theme and retro bars go in and out of fashion. Town and gown meet at the fancy retail-restaurant-and-leisure development known as **West:One** (end of Devonshire Street, at Fitzwilliam Street), while locals and students also frequent the bars and pubs of **Ecclesall Road** (the so-called "golden mile"), out of the centre to the southwest. Friday's *Sheffield Telegraph* lists the week's performances, concerts and films, or there's *Exposed*, a free monthly listings magazine, available from cafés, restaurants, shops and bars.

Hotels and guest houses

Hotel Bristol Blonk Street ☏0114/220 4000, ⓦwww.hotel-bristol.co.uk. Breezy, informal business hotel near the river, quays and markets, with good bar and restaurant. All rooms en suite, with extra fold-down sofa bed – handy for families. ❺

Houseboat Hotels Victoria Quays ☏0114/232 6556 or 07974/590264, ⓦwww.houseboathotels.com. Two moored houseboats, with en-suite bathrooms and kitchens. Continental breakfast can be arranged (£4 extra). Two people ❹, four people ❻

St Paul's 1129 Norfolk St ☏0870/122 6585, ⓦwww.macdonald-hotels.co.uk/stpauls. A contemporary city-centre four-star, right by the Winter Gardens, is Sheffield's top choice, with restaurant, bar, pool, spa and sauna. ❼

Westbourne House 25 Westbourne Rd, Broomhill ☏0114/266 0109, ⓦwww.westbournehousehotel.com. Nonsmoking Victorian townhouse, a mile out of the centre (and 10min from the bars and restaurants of Ecclesall Road). ❺

Cafés and restaurants

Blue Moon Café 2 St James St, next to the cathedral ☏0114/276 3443. Homemade vegetarian/vegan food. Closes 8pm; closed Sun. Inexpensive.

The Forum 127–129 Division St ☏0114/272 0569. Long the mainstay of the trendy Devonshire Quarter, the *Forum* has a great menu and laid-back clientele – breakfast from 10am, bar till 1am. Closed Sun. Inexpensive.

Lion's Lair 31 Burgess St ☏0114/263 4264. Gastropub that's a firm favourite with uptown types for good Modern British food. Moderate.

Nonna's 539–541 Ecclesall Rd ☏0114/268 6166. A glam see-and-be-seen Italian bar and restaurant with a great reputation. Restaurant reservations advised. Expensive.

Trippet's 89 Trippets Lane ☏0114/278 0198.

There's always a nice atmosphere in this unstuffy wine bar behind West Street, plus live jazz and blues. Moderate.

Vietnamese Noodle Bar 200–202 London Rd ☏0114/258 3608. Out of the centre, but really worth the trip for terrific Vietnamese and Chinese food. Inexpensive.

Pubs, bars and clubs

Crystal 23-32 Carver St. A former scissors factory provides stunning premises for an airy restaurant-patio, with a bar until 1.30am.

Devonshire Cat 49 Wellington St, Devonshire Green. Renowned ale-house with good, cheap food and beer matched to every selection. *The Fat Cat*, 23 Alma St (15min from the centre), is its cosier, older sister pub.

Gatecrasher One 112 Arundel St ☏0114/276 6777, ⓦwww.neverstandstill.com. The flagship of the *Gatecrasher* clubbing brand is housed in a refurbished steel and engineering works.

Leadmill 6–7 Leadmill Rd ☏0114/221 2828, ⓦwww.leadmill.co.uk. In the Cultural Industries Quarter, this place hosts live bands and DJs most nights of the week.

Takapuna 52–54 West St. Eating, greeting and drinking, with DJs and club nights – bar stays open until 2am.

Theatre and cinema

Crucible, Lyceum & Studio Tudor Square ☏0114/249 6000, ⓦwww.sheffieldtheatres.co.uk. Sheffield's theatres put on a full programme of theatre, dance, comedy and concerts. The Crucible, of course, has hosted the World Snooker Championships for thirty years.

The Showroom 7 Paternoster Row ☏0114/275 7727, ⓦwww.showroom.org.uk. The biggest independent cinema outside London. Also has a relaxed café-restaurant on one side and a great bar on the other.

Leeds and around

Yorkshire's commercial capital, and one of the fastest-growing cities in the country, **LEEDS** has undergone a radical transformation in recent years. There's still a true northern grit to its character, and in many of its dilapidated suburbs, but the grime has been removed from the impressive Victorian buildings and the city is revelling in its renaissance as a booming financial, commercial and cultural centre. The renowned shops, restaurants, bars and clubs provide one focus of a visit – it's certainly Yorkshire's top destination for a day or two of conspicuous consumption and indulgence. Museums start with the hugely impressive **Royal Armouries**, which hold the national arms and armour collection, while the **City Art Gallery** has one of the best collections of British

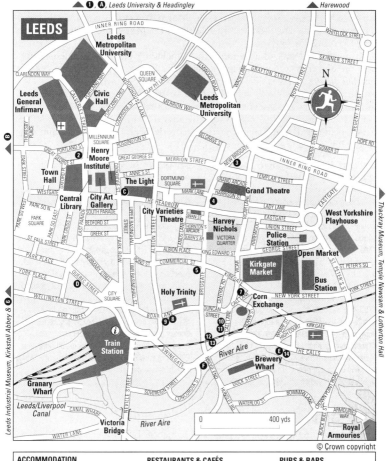

ACCOMMODATION			RESTAURANTS & CAFÉS		PUBS & BARS		
42 The Calls	E	Malmaison F	Anthony's	8	Norman	10	Bar Fibre	12	Mojo	3
Boundary	A	Quebecs D	Art's Café	11	Room	9	Elbow		North	4
Butlers	A	Radisson	Brasserie 44	14	Salvo's	1	Room	13	Victoria	2
Glengarth	B	SAS C	Harry Ramsden's	6			Milo	7	Whitelocks 5

twentieth-century art outside London. The city itself deserves the best part of two days, longer if you plan to see any of the outlying attractions, which include the fascinating **Thackray Museum** of medicine, medieval **Kirkstall Abbey** and **Harewood**, one of the country's great Georgian piles, which deserves a day's visit of its own.

Arrival, information and accommodation

Leeds Bradford airport is eight miles north of the city; there's a bus (£2) every thirty minutes to the centre, or a taxi costs £15–20. **Leeds Station** off City Square also houses the Gateway Yorkshire **tourist office** in the Arcade (Mon 10am–5.30pm, Tues–Sat 9am–5.30pm, Sun 10am–4pm; ☎0113/242 5242, ⓦwww.leeds.gov.uk). The **bus station** occupies a site to the east, behind

Kirkgate Market, on St Peter's Street. The **Metro Travel Centres** at the bus and train stations have up-to-date service details or call **Metroline** (daily 7am–8pm; ☎0113/245 7676, ⊚www.wymetro.com).

There's a good mix of accommodation, including inexpensive guest houses near the university campus, budget hotel chains (*Comfort Inn, Express by Holiday Inn, Ibis, Jury's Inn, Premier Travel Inn* and others), and a growing number of stylish designer or boutique hotels. For **short breaks** and weekends away contact the tourist office's special booking line on ☎0800/808050. Rooms are also available in self-catering **student apartments** at Clarence Dock (☎0113/343 6100), near the Royal Armouries (July to early Sept; 2-night minimum stay costs £45, £20 a night thereafter).

Guest houses and hotels

42 The Calls 42 The Calls ☎0113/244 0099, ⊚www.42thecalls.co.uk. Converted riverside grain mill, where rooms come with great beds and sharp bathrooms. Breakfast not included. Weekend rates around £99 a night. ❼

Boundary Cardigan Road, Headingley ☎0113/275 7700, ⊚www.boundaryhotel.co.uk. Good-value accommodation in a leafy suburban street, 1.5km out of the city centre. Adjacent to and associated with *Butlers* hotel (below). ❷

Butlers Cardigan Road, Headingley ☎0113/274 4755, ⊚www.butlershotel.co.uk. Cosy, smart, traditionally furnished en-suite rooms. ❸

Glengarth 162 Woodsley Rd ☎0113/245 7940, ⊚www.glengarthhotel.co.uk. Just behind the university, about a mile from the centre. Rooms are fairly basic, but prices are negotiable for multi-night stays. No credit cards. ❷ , en suite ❸

Malmaison 1 Swinegate ☎0113/398 1000, ⊚www.malmaison.com. Classy restored premises with the signature *Malmaison* style. Breakfast not included; weekend rates from £99. ❼

Quebecs 9 Quebec St ☎0113/244 8989, ⊚www.theetoncollection.com. The ultimate city boutique lodgings, in the former Leeds and County Liberal Club. The glorious Victorian oak panelling and stained glass remain, offset by chic rooms with enormous beds. Breakfast not included; weekend rates from £99. ❼

Radisson SAS No.1 The Light, The Headrow ☎0113/236 6000, ⊚www.radissonsas.com. Snazzy rooms and suites that reflect high-tech, Art Deco or modern Italian design. Weekend rates from £90 room only, £110 including breakfast, or £135 with business-class extras. ❽

The City

Opposite the train station, a prancing statue of Edward, the Black Prince, welcomes you to **City Square**, a smartened-up space that still retains its bronze nymph gas-lamps. It's a short walk to the top of East Parade where you can't miss **Leeds Town Hall**, one of the finest expressions of nineteenth-century civic pride in the country. The masterpiece of local architect Cuthbert Broderick, it's colonnaded on all sides, guarded by white lions and topped by a perky clocktower. East from the Town Hall and you're on **The Headrow**, the city's central spine, with Leeds' **City Art Gallery** (Mon–Sat 10am–5pm, Wed 10am–8pm, Sun 1–5pm; free; ⊚www.leeds.gov.uk/artgallery) the major draw. Changing selections from the permanent collection of nineteenth- and twentieth-century art and sculpture are on view, with an understandable bias towards pieces by Henry Moore and Barbara Hepworth, both former students at the Leeds School of Art; Moore's *Reclining Woman* lounges at the top of the steps outside the gallery. From the gallery, a slender bridge connects to the adjacent **Henry Moore Institute** (daily 10am–5.30pm, Wed until 9pm; free; ⊚www.henry-moore-fdn.co.uk), devoted to showcasing temporary exhibitions of sculpture from all periods and nationalities.

Most visitors then make a beeline for the brimming, shop-filled arcades on either side of pedestrianized **Briggate**. These nineteenth-century palaces of marble, mahogany, stained glass and mosaics have been magnificently restored and perhaps the most splendidly decorated of all is the light-flooded **Victoria**

Quarter, with Harvey Nichols as its designer lodestone. Across Vicar Lane, **Kirkgate Market** (closes 2pm Wed & all Sun, though farmers' market first Sun of month 9am–2pm) is the largest market in the north of England. Housed in a superb Edwardian building, it's a descendant of the medieval woollen markets that were instrumental in making Leeds the early focus of the region's textile industry. At the bottom of the street, on the corner of Vicar Lane and Duncan Street, the elliptical, domed **Corn Exchange** (open daily) was built in 1863, also by Cuthbert Broderick, whose design leaned heavily on his studies of Paris's corn exchange. This is now a hip market for jewellery, retro clothes, furnishings, music, and other bits and bobs – extra craft stores open up at weekends.

The biggest transformation in Leeds has been along the **Leeds–Liverpool Canal** and **River Aire**, formerly a stagnant relic of industrial decline. New businesses, apartments and restaurants line both sides, connected by a pleasant footpath. At **Granary Wharf**, a couple of minutes' walk from the train station, stores, restaurants and craft shops fill the extensive cobbled, vaulted arches (the "Dark Arches"), while every weekend and bank holiday a market spills out onto the canal basin. **Brewery Wharf**, on the south side (or "Left Bank" as Leeds would like it to be known), is the latest part to see redevelopment – more bars and brasseries – while further east along the river beckons the glass turret and gun-metal grey bulk of the **Royal Armouries** (daily 10am–5pm; free; Ⓦwww.armouries.org.uk). Purpose-built to house the arms and armour collection from the Tower of London, it's a hugely adventurous museum that requires a leap of faith – discard the notion that all you'll see are casefuls of weapons, and you're in for a treat. Interpretations and demonstrations take place throughout the day (you're handed a schedule on entering), so you might learn smallsword techniques from a Georgian swordsmaster or sixteenth-century javelin skills in the outdoor Tiltyard.

Out of the City

The **Thackray Museum** on Beckett Street (daily 10am–5pm, last admission 3pm; £5.50; Ⓦwww.thackraymuseum.org), next to St James' Hospital, is sited in a former workhouse a mile east of the city centre; take bus #4 from New York Street outside the bus station. Essentially a medical history museum, it has hugely entertaining displays on subjects as diverse as the history of the hearing aid and the workings of the human intestine. It's gruesome, too, with film of a Victorian limb amputation in a gallery called "Pain, pus and blood". Needless to say, children love it.

You should also see the bucolic ruins and cloisters of **Kirkstall Abbey** (dawn to dusk; free), the city's most important medieval relic. Built between 1152 and 1182 by Cistercian monks from Fountains Abbey, it was the site of four hundred years of monastic life before being surrendered to Henry VIII in 1539. The abbey lies about three miles northwest of the city centre on Abbey Road; take bus #732, #733, #734, #735 or #736.

The stately home of **Harewood**, seven miles north of Leeds (Feb–Oct daily 11am–4.30pm, grounds & bird garden 10am–6pm; Nov & Dec Sat & Sun only; £11, Sun & bank hols £13; grounds & bird garden only £8.25/£10.25; Ⓣ0113/218 1010, Ⓦwww.harewood.org), is still the home of the Earl and Countess of Harewood, who let in the great unwashed in return for nothing more than a sizeable chunk of money. To be fair, there's an enormous amount to see and do, with daily tours and talks, and current exhibitions included in the entrance fee. As well as the grand state and private rooms, the old kitchen and servants' quarters can be viewed, while outside in the magnificent **grounds** is an adventure playground and renowned **Bird Garden** – the penguins get fed at 2pm. There are frequent buses to Harewood from Leeds (including the #36, every 20min, 30min on Sun), and if you come by bus or bike, you'll get a fifty-percent discount on admission (keep your bus ticket). The house is near the junction of the A659 and the A61 Leeds to Harrogate road, and parking is free.

Eating, drinking and nightlife

Eating out in Leeds has been transformed in recent years, and Michelin stars are not unknown, but there's a down-to-earth approach to prices, with even the fanciest places offering special lunch or early-bird deals. Late-opening **café-bars** infest the centre and exploit the city's relaxed licensing laws to the full. The best of the city's **pubs** are the ornate Victorian ale-houses in which Leeds specializes, and when these close you can move on to one of the city's **DJ bars** or **clubs**, many of which have a nationwide reputation – not least because you can dance until 5 or 6am most weekends. For information about **what's on**, your best bets are the fortnightly listings magazine *The Leeds Guide* (ⓦwww .leedsguide.co.uk) or the daily *Yorkshire Evening Post*.

Café-bars and restaurants

Anthony's 19 Boar Lane ⊕0113/245 5922. The foodie's choice, where earthy flavours and ingredients dominate. It's pricey, but lunch (3 courses for under £25) is a steal. Very expensive.

Art's Café 42 Call Lane ⊕0113/243 8243. *Art's* kickstarted the Call Lane scene and it's still a relaxed hangout for drinks, dinner or a lazy Sunday brunch. Moderate.

Brasserie 44 44 The Calls ⊕0113/234 3232. Informal Modern British brasserie, serving everything from Whitby cod to duck confit. Closed Sat lunch & Sun. Expensive.

Harry Ramsden's White Cross, Otley Road, Guiseley ⊕01943/874641. If you feel like making the pilgrimage (best done in a taxi) then expect to wait in line at the original *Harry Ramsden's* fish-and-chip restaurant. Moderate.

Norman 36 Call Lane ⊕0113/234 3988. An industrial-chic interior plus Asian noodle/stir-fry/*dim sum* menu add up to one of the city's unique spots. The "Daily Norman" deal (all Mon & Tues–Fri noon–3pm) provides a meal and a beer for a fiver. Moderate.

Room Bourse Courtyard, Boar Lane ⊕0113/242 6161. Retro-chic restaurant that challenges expectations. Order prawn cocktail, and gammon and pineapple; eat tempura prawns on a tower of crushed avocado, and roast suckling pig on pineapple puree. Expensive.

Salvo's 115 Otley Rd, Headingley ⊕0113/275 5017. Pizza in Leeds to a local means *Salvo's* – as authentic as they come – though there's a classy Italian menu as well and a choice list of daily specials. Closed Sun. Expensive.

Pubs and bars

Bar Fibre 168 Lower Briggate ⊕0870/120 0888,

ⓦwww.barfibre.com. Leeds' finest gay bar comes with plenty of attitude, plus outside balcony, DJs most nights and dancing until midnight, 2am at weekends.

Elbow Room 64 Call Lane ⊕0113/245 7011, ⓦwww.theelbowroom.co.uk. Funk and food, and a very cool place to play pool.

Milo 10–12 Call Lane ⊕0113/245 7101. Unpretentious, offbeat bar, ringing the changes from old soul and reggae to indie and electronica.

Mojo 18 Merrion St ⊕0113/244 6387. A great bar, pure and simple, with fine tunes from the house i-pod and a classy drinks menu to match.

North 24 New Briggate. The city's beer specialist is more new Leeds than old – chrome tables, blond-wood bar, sharp staff – but the basics are familiar: a massive selection of guest beers, plus pie and peas or beans on toast.

Victoria Great George Street. Ornate Victorian "family and commercial hotel", restored to its former glory, with proper pub food and a period feel.

Whitelocks Turk's Head Yard, off Briggate. Leeds' oldest pub (tucked up an alley) retains its traditional decor.

Clubs and live music

Cockpit Bridge House, Swinegate ⊕0113/244 1573, ⓦwww.thecockpit.co.uk. The city's best live music venue, plus assorted indie/new wave club-nights.

Creation 55 Cookridge St ⊕0113/242 7272, ⓦwww.creation-leeds.co.uk. Hosts high-profile live bands as well as club nights, chart to cheese, in the city's largest club.

Hifi 2 Central Rd ⊕0113/242 7353, ⓦwww .thehificlub.co.uk. Über-fashionable club, playing everything from Stax and Motown to hip-hop or drum'n'bass. Also check out the indie/alternative associate club *Wire* at 2–8 Call Lane (🌐www .wireclub.co.uk).

Rehab 2 Waterloo House, Assembley Street ☎0113/244 9474. Hosts the legendary *Back to Basics* house night every Saturday and cutting-edge DJs at all times.

The Wardrobe St Peter's Square ☎0113/383 8800, 🌐www.thewardrobe.co.uk. Self-styled "café, bar, kitchen, club" with live jazz and soul acts.

The Warehouse 19–21 Somers St ☎0113/246 8287. House, garage and techno sounds bring in clubbers from all over the country.

Arts, festivals and entertainment

Opera North (🌐www.operanorth.co.uk) gives a free performance each summer at Temple Newsam, just outside the city, as does the **Northern Ballet Theatre** (🌐www.northernballettheatre.co.uk). At Kirkstall Abbey every summer there's a Shakespeare Festival (🌐www.openairshakespeare.com) with open-air productions of the Bard's works; while **Millennium Square** hosts gigs, festivals, markets and other events, including the annual **Ice Cube**, a temporary outdoor ice-rink and café (mid-Jan to end Feb). August bank-holiday weekend heralds the **West Indian Carnival** in Chapeltown, only beaten in size by Notting Hill.

City Varieties Swan St, Briggate ☎0845/644 1881, 🌐www.cityvarieties.co.uk. One of the country's last surviving music halls, though it's less music-hall fare these days and more tribute bands, comedians and cabaret.

Grand Theatre and Opera House 46 New Brig-gate ☎0113/222 6222, 🌐www.leeds.gov .uk/grandtheatre. The regular base of Opera North and Northern Ballet.

Hyde Park Picture House Brudenell Road, Head-ingley ☎0113/275 2045, 🌐www.leedscinema .com. The place to come for classic cinema with independent and art-house shows alongside more mainstream films; bus #56, #57 or #63.

West Yorkshire Playhouse Quarry Hill ☎0113/213 7700, 🌐www.wyp.org.uk. The city's most innovative theatre has two stages, plus bar, restaurant and café.

Listings

Airport Information and flight enquiries ☎0113/250 9696, 🌐www.lbia.co.uk.
Car rental Avis ☎0113/243 9771; Budget ☎0113/272 1177, Europcar ☎0113/249 0037, Hertz ☎0113/242 9548; National ☎0113/277 7997; Thrifty ☎0113/245 8111.
Hospital Leeds General Infirmary, Great George Street ☎0113/392 2512.
Internet There's free access at the Central Library, Calverley Street ☎0113/247 8274 (call for hours); also Cyber Café at West Yorkshire Playhouse,

Quarry Hill (Mon–Fri 9.30am–5.30pm; ☎0113/213 7700).
Pharmacy Boots, Leeds Station Concourse ☎0113/242 1713 (24hr).
Police Millgarth Police Station, Millgarth Street ☎0845/606 0606.
Post office Branches on New York Street, opposite Kirkgate market, and on Albion Street.
Taxis Taxis are available 24hr at the train station, outside the bus station, and on New Briggate.

Bradford

First and foremost, **BRADFORD** has always been a working town, booming in tandem with the Industrial Revolution, when it changed in decades from a rural seat of woollen manufacture to a polluted metropolis. In its Victorian heyday it was the world's biggest producer of worsted cloth, its skyline etched black with mill chimneys, and its hills clogged with some of the foulest back-to-back houses of any northern city. Contemporary Bradford is valiantly rinsing away its associations with urban decrepitude, and while it can hardly yet be compared with neighbouring Leeds as a visitor attraction it might ultimately succeed on its own distinct terms – plans are in place to restyle the entire city centre as an urban park and cultural quarter, in particular reopening the Bradford beck (stream), long buried under modern buildings, to supply a lake in front of City Hall. In the meantime, in the **National Museum of Photography, Film and Television** (Tues–Sun & public holidays 10am–6pm; free; @www.nmpft.org.uk), Bradford has one of the most visited national museums outside London, crammed with memorabilia and hardware, including the world's biggest lens and the world's first example of a moving picture. Exhibitions are devoted to every nuance of film and television, including topics like digital imaging, light and optics, and computer animation, while there are detours into the mechanics of advertising and news-gathering – even a searchable archive of classic British TV.

Three miles out of Bradford towards Keighley, along the A650 to the north, lies **Saltaire**, a model industrial village and textile mill built by the industrialist Sir Titus Salt. Trains to Saltaire Station run from Bradford's Forster Square station, or take bus #679 from the Interchange, which stops in Saltaire village. The village (still lived in today) is a perfectly preserved 25-acre realization of one man's vision of an industrial utopia. **Salt's Mill** was the biggest factory in the world when it opened in 1853, surrounded by schools, hospitals, a train station, parks, baths and wash-houses, plus 45 almshouses and around 850 homes. Further to the master's whim, the church was the first public building to be finished and was strategically placed directly outside the factory gates. Most tellingly of all, the village contained not a single pub. Salt's Mill remains the fulcrum of the village, its several floors now housing art, craft and furniture shops, and a craft centre. But its enterprising centrepiece is the **1853 Gallery** (daily 10am–6pm; free; @www.saltsmill.org.uk), an entire floor of the old spinning shed given over to the world's largest retrospective collection of the works of Bradford-born **David Hockney**.

Practicalities

Trains and buses both arrive at **Bradford Interchange** off Bridge Street, a little to the south of the city-centre grid. There's also a much smaller station at **Forster Square**, across the city, for trains to Keighley. The **tourist office** (Mon 10am–5pm, Tues–Sat 9.30am–5pm; ☎01274/433678, @www.visitbradford .com), located in Centenary Square's City Hall, is three minutes' signposted walk from the Interchange or five minutes from Forster Square.

You should hang around at least long enough to sample one of Bradford's famous **curry houses** (see below) – legacy of the city's large population with roots in the Indian subcontinent. Significant numbers of men arrived here from India, Pakistan and Bangladesh in the 1950s and 1960s. They later sent for their families, making Bradford perhaps the most multicultural centre in the UK outside London, with people of South Asian origin accounting for around 18 percent of the conurbation's total population. The major annual event is the **Bradford Festival** each June (@www.bradfordfestival.co.uk), which combines the Lord Mayor's parade and a street arts festival with Britain's biggest **Mela**, a two-day celebration of the arts, culture, food and sports of the Indian subcontinent.

Restaurants

Aakash Providence Place, Bradford Road, Cleckheaton, 10min by car from central Bradford ☎01274/878866. Transformed from an 1859 Congregational chapel, this claims to be the largest Indian restaurant in the world. Dinner only; closed Mon. Moderate.

Kashmir 27 Morley St ☎01274/726513. Two minutes up the road from the National Museum, Bradford's first curry house still sports formica tables in the basement and rock-bottom prices: it's unlicensed, though you can take your own booze. Open until 3am. Inexpensive.

Mumtaz 386–400 Great Horton Rd
☎ 01274/571861. You buy your dish by weight

here – 220g or 440g, the larger portion serves two – and the sweet lassi is legendary. Open until 1am. Inexpensive.

Haworth

Of English literary shrines, probably only Stratford sees more visitors than the quarter of a million who swarm annually into the village of **HAWORTH** to tramp the cobbles once trodden by the Brontë sisters. Indeed, during the summer the village's steep, cobbled Main Street is lost under huge crowds, herded by multilingual signs around the various stations on the Brontë trail.

Of these, the **Brontë Parsonage Museum**, at the top of the main street (daily 10/11am–5/5.30pm; £4.90; Ⓦ www.bronte.info), is the obvious focus, a modest Georgian house bought by Patrick Brontë in 1820 to bring up his family. Anne, Emily, Charlotte and their dissipated brother, Branwell, spent most of their short lives in the place, which is furnished as it was in their day, and filled with the sisters' pictures, books, manuscripts and personal treasures. You can see the sofa on which Emily is said to have died in 1848, aged just 28, for example, and the footstool on which she sat outside on fine days writing *Wuthering Heights*. The bluff **parish church** in front of the parsonage contains the family vault; Charlotte was married here in 1854. At the **Sunday School**, between the parsonage and the church, Charlotte, Anne and even Branwell did weekly teaching stints; Branwell, however, was undoubtedly more at home in the **Black Bull**, a pub within staggering distance of the parsonage near the top of Main Street.

The most popular local walk runs to **Brontë Falls** and **Bridge**, reached via West Lane

△ Haworth

and a track from the village, and to **Top Withens**, a mile beyond, a ruin fanci-
fully (but erroneously) thought to be the model for Wuthering Heights (allow
3hr for the round trip). The moorland setting, however, beautifully evokes the
flavour of the book, and to enjoy it further you could walk on another two
and a half miles to **Ponden Hall**, perhaps the Thrushcross Grange of *Wuthering Heights* (this section of path, incidentally, forms part of the Pennine Way).

Practicalities

Haworth is eight miles northwest of Bradford. To get there by **bus**, take the
#662 from Bradford Interchange to Keighley (every 10min), and change there
for the #663, #664 or #665 (every 20min), which drop off at various points
in the streets immediately below the cobbled Main Street. On Sundays, only
the #663 and #665 operate (every 30min). However, the nicest way of getting
here is on the steam trains of the **Keighley and Worth Valley Railway** (Easter
week, school hols, July & Aug daily; rest of year Sat & Sun; day rover ticket
£12; recorded information ℡01535/647777, ⓦwww.kwvr.co.uk); regular
trains from Leeds and Bradford run to Keighley for the connections. Steep
Main Street and its continuation, **West Lane**, form one long run of gift and
teashops, cafés and guest houses, with the busy Haworth **tourist office** at the
top at 2–4 West Lane (daily 9.30am–5/5.30pm; ℡01535/642329, ⓦwww
.haworth-village.org.uk).

Accommodation and food

Aitches 11 West Lane ℡01535/642501, ⓦwww
.aitches.co.uk. This place offers a few comfortable,
cottage-style en-suite rooms, and has a restaurant
for residents (set menu £15). ❸
Apothecary 86 Main St ℡01535/643642,
ⓦwww.theapothecaryguesthouse.co.uk. Traditional
guest house (nonsmoking) opposite the church,
whose rear rooms, breakfast room and attached
café have moorland views. ❷
Haworth YHA Longlands Hall ℡0870/770 5858,
ⓔhaworth@yha.org.uk. Dorm beds (£13.95) in the
mansion of a Victorian mill-owner, overlooking the
village a mile from the centre at Longlands Drive,

Lees Lane, off the Keighley road. Weekends only
Nov to mid-Dec; closed mid-Dec to Jan.
Old Registry 4 Main St ℡01535/646503,
ⓦwww.oldregistry.com. Tastefully presented
accommodation – there's a four-poster bed in
every room and coordinated furnishings throughout. Two-night minimum stay at weekends. ❺
Weaver's 15 West Lane ℡01535/643822,
ⓦwww.weaversmallhotel.co.uk. A renowned
restaurant-with-rooms housed in a converted
row of weavers' cottages. Good, modern northern
cuisine using local ingredients from around £25 a
head, plus drinks, or set lunches from £12.95. It's
essential to book ahead. ❺

The Yorkshire Dales

Protected as a National Park since 1954, the **Yorkshire Dales** form a varied
upland area of limestone hills and pastoral valleys at the heart of the Pennines.
There are over twenty main dales covering 680 square miles, crammed with
opportunities for outdoor activities, including local hikes and long-distance
footpaths, a specially designated cycle way, plus caving, pony-trekking and
other more specialist pursuits. Most approaches are from the industrial towns
to the south, via the **Settle-to-Carlisle Railway**, or along the main A65 road
from towns such as **Skipton**, **Settle** and **Ingleton**. This makes southern dales
like **Wharfedale** the most visited, while neighbouring **Malhamdale** is also
immensely popular, thanks to the fascinating scenery squeezed into its narrow
confines around **Malham**, perhaps the single most visited village in the region.
Ribblesdale, approached from Settle, is more sombre, its villages popular with

hikers intent on tackling the Dales' famous **Three Peaks** – the mountains of Pen-y-ghent, Ingleborough and Whernside. To the northwest lies the more remote **Dentdale**, while routes north lead to **Wensleydale**, known for its cheese. Finally, minor Swaledale's lower stretches encompass **Richmond**, an appealing historic town with a terrific castle.

   Public transport throughout the Dales is good, though bus services are limited in winter. However, countless special summer weekend and bank holiday services (usually between May and September, peaking in school holidays) connect almost everywhere. Pick up the invaluable, free **timetables** (Ⓦwww .dalesbus.org), available at tourist offices across the region, or consult Ⓦwww .traveldales.org.uk. Keep your bus ticket and you'll be able to claim discounts at businesses across the Dales – look for "Dales Bus Discount" window stickers. The Pennine Way cuts right through the heart of the Dales, and the region is crossed by the Coast-to-Coast Walk, but the principal local route is the **Dales Way** (Ⓦwww.dalesway.org.uk), an 84-mile footpath from Ilkley to Bowness-on-Windermere in the Lake District. Shorter **guided walks** (5–13 miles; every Sun & bank hol Mon, April–Oct) are organized by the National Park Authority and Dalesbus Ramblers (Ⓦwww.dalesbusramblers.org.uk); details are on their websites.

Skipton

SKIPTON, southernmost town of the Dales, is best visited on **market** days (Mon, Wed, Fri & Sat), when the streets and pubs are filled with what seems like half the Dales population, milling around and determined to enjoy themselves. *Sceptone*, or "Sheeptown", was a thriving agricultural settlement long before the arrival of the battling Normans. Their **Castle**, located at the top of the High Street (Mon–Sat 10am–4/6pm, Sun noon–4/6pm; £5.20; Ⓦwww .skiptoncastle.co.uk), provided the basis for the present fortress, among England's best preserved, thanks mainly to the efforts of Lady Anne Clifford, who rebuilt much of her family seat between 1650 and 1675 following the pillage of the Civil War. The alleys on the western side of the High Street emerge on to the banks of the **Leeds–Liverpool Canal**, which runs right through the centre of Skipton; a one-hour signposted heritage trail follows the towpath. Pennine Boat Trips at Waterside Court, off Coach Street, offers daily **canal cruises** (Easter–Oct & Dec; £5; ☏01756/790829, Ⓦwww.canaltrips.co.uk) that last around an hour.

   The **train station** is on Broughton Road, a ten-minute walk from the centre. The **bus station** is closer in, on Keighley Road, at the bottom of the High Street. Local services run from Skipton to Settle (not Sun) for connections on to Ingleton and Horton; Malham (not Sun); and Grassington. Drivers should follow signs for the main **car parks** behind the town hall (off High Street) or on Coach Street nearer the canal. The **tourist office**, 35 Coach St (Mon–Sat 10am–5pm, Sun 11am–3pm; ☏01756/792809, Ⓦwww.skiptononline.co.uk), offers a friendly service and details of local and seasonal events.

Accommodation

Craven Heifer Grassington Road ☏01756/792521, Ⓦwww.cravenheifer.co.uk. Stone-built Dales inn, a mile out of town (2min drive), with en-suite rooms fashioned from an old barn. Buffet continental breakfast included. ❸

Dalesgate Lodge 69 Gargrave Rd ☏01756/790672, ✉dalesgatelodge@hotmail.com.

Three en-suite doubles and one twin room available in this friendly, family-run, nonsmoking B&B. No credit cards. ❷

Woolly Sheep Inn 38 Sheep St, bottom of High Street ☏01756/700966, Ⓦwww.timothytaylor .co.uk/woollysheep. Some of the pine-furnished rooms are a bit tight on space, but comfortable nonetheless. Downstairs in the public bar there are Timothy Taylor's beers and meals served daily, lunch and dinner. Parking available. ❹

Eating and drinking

Aagrah Devonshire Place, off Keighley Road ☎01756/790807. It might be decked out like a snake-charmer's boudoir, but this Indian restaurant has a loyal local following. Dinner only. Moderate.

Bizzie Lizzies 36 Swadford St ☎01756/701131. The town's award-winning fish-and-chip shop, with a restaurant (dining over the canal) open until 9pm every night. Inexpensive.

Narrow Boat 38 Victoria St ☎01756/797922. All you want from a pub – good, inexpensive food (lunch daily, dinner until 8pm, not Fri or Sat), a no-smoking ground floor, and no piped music. Inexpensive.

Bolton Abbey

BOLTON ABBEY, five miles east of Skipton, is the name of a whole village rather than an abbey, a confusion compounded by the fact that the main monastic ruin is known as **Bolton Priory** (daily 9am to dusk; free). The priory formed part of an Augustinian community founded at nearby Embsay in 1135, and moved here in the 1150s. Turner painted the site, and Ruskin described it as the most beautiful in England, though the priory is now mostly ruined, a consequence of the Dissolution; only the nave, which was incorporated into the village church in 1170, has survived in almost its original state. The priory is the starting point for several highly popular riverside walks, including a section of the **Dales Way** footpath that follows the river's west bank to take in Bolton Woods and the **Strid** (from "stride"), an extraordinary piece of white water two miles north of the abbey, where softer rock has allowed the river to funnel into a cleft just a few feet wide.

The nicest approach to the priory is on the **Embsay and Bolton Abbey Steam Railway**, with Bolton Abbey station a mile and a half by footpath from the priory ruins. The trains (summer daily approx every hour; rest of the year Sat & Sun hourly; ☎01756/795189 or 710614, ⓦwww.embsaybolton abbeyrailway.org.uk; £6 return) start from Embsay, two miles east of Skipton, and summer buses connect Skipton and Wharfedale with the stations. Otherwise, drivers have to stump up £5 to park in one of the estate **car parks**. There's local **information** from the estate office (☎01756/718009, ⓦwww .boltonabbey.com) and an information point at **Cavendish Pavilion**, a mile north of the priory, where there's also a riverside restaurant and café. The main **hotel** is the sumptuous *Devonshire Arms* (☎01756/718111, ⓦwww .devonshirehotels.co.uk; ❾), just south of the village, owned by the duchess of Devonshire and furnished with antiques from the ancestral pile at Chatsworth; there's a good brasserie and bar too.

Wharfedale

Grassington is Wharfedale's popular main village, nine miles from Bolton Abbey. It has a good Georgian centre, albeit one tempered by dollops of fake rusticity, and the surroundings are at their best by the river, where the shallow **Linton Falls** thunder after rain. Back in the village, the cobbled Market Square is home to several inns, a few gift shops and a small local museum. Traditional rural pursuits, as well as music and arts, are celebrated in both the annual Grassington Festival (ⓦwww.grassington-festival.org.uk), held every June, and the Christmas market, held on December Saturdays in the village square.

Wharfedale's scenery above Grassington grows ever more impressive, notably a few miles north at **Littondale**, whose stunning landscape is best appreciated from **Arncliffe**, halfway up the dale, as idyllic a hamlet as you'll find, with a pub on the green that attracts walkers from far and wide. The valley-floor footpath

Coastal
Britain

With nowhere in Britain more than 75 miles from the coast, the sea – bulwark against the Spanish Armada, Napoleon and Hitler – occupies an integral part of the national psyche. Poets, painters and photographers have been inspired through the centuries by the bays and beaches, cliffs and creeks, sand dunes and shingle of the country's richly diverse coastline, which, at over 7700 miles in length (including more than a thousand islands), ranges from stark wilderness to the traditional seaside resort.

Sailing boats in Salcombe, South Devon

Beaches and water sports

Britain's beaches can compare with the best in the world in terms of sheer natural beauty. This can take many forms – from the bleak grandeur of Northumberland to the lacerated Pembrokeshire coast – while the same places can be transformed utterly according to whether it's storming or shining. For a combination of decent climate and good sand, the southwest

Britain's Top Ten beaches

Par Beach, St Martin's, Isles of Scilly. Hugely scenic and usually empty, despite the perfect sands. See p.372.

Ardudwy, Harlech, Mid-Wales. Eight miles of wide sands and dunes, including Wales's only official naturist section. See p.751.

Porthcurno, Cornwall. Surrounded by cliffs, with an open-air theatre nearby. See p.373.

Kiloran Bay, Isle of Colonsay, Argyll. Unspoiled sandy beach pounded by Atlantic breakers. See p.980.

South Harris, Western Isles, Scotland. Glorious golden sands framed by mountains and a turquoise sea. See p.1015.

Blackpool Sands, South Devon. Can get very crowded, but come out of season and you'll be seduced by this crescent of coarse white sand sheltered by pines. See p.341.

Studland Bay, Dorset. Three miles of sheltered beach on the Isle of Purbeck, accessed by a clanking chain ferry. See p.240.

Holkham, Norfolk. Beyond the pines and dunes lie miles of pancake-flat sands. See p.415.

Bamburgh, Northumberland. Sky, sea, dunes and acres of sand, with the dramatic backdrop of Bamburgh Castle. See p.669.

Rhossili, Gower peninsula, South Wales. Hike along the glorious curve of white sand and you'll soon escape the summer crowds. See p.709.

Seilebost beach, South Harris, Scotland

of England is hard to beat, especially the coasts of **Cornwall** and **Devon**. The Gulf Stream warms the northwest coast of Scotland, making the lonely beaches of the **Hebrides** a tempting proposition, while in **Wales** the best areas for sunbathing and swimming are the Gower peninsular, the Pembrokeshire coast, the Llŷn and the southwest coast of Anglesey. On the whole, England's south and east coasts are less picturesque, though the low cliffs and gravel beaches of East Anglia's shoreline give way to a string of wide sandy beaches along the **north Norfolk coast**. But it's northern Britain that can champion the finest – and wildest – strands, notably in **North Yorkshire**, in **Northumberland**, and along the coast of **northeast Scotland** from Aberdeen to Inverness.

Britain's **surf scene** is largely concentrated along the southwest coast of England, though the Welsh coast and the northeastern coast of Scotland are both increasing in popularity – see p.65 for more on Britain's best surf spots. **Windsurfers and sailors** fare best on the more sheltered English south and southwest coasts, notably Hampshire, the Isle of Wight, and Devon and Cornwall, with Devon's pretty town of Salcombe being a particular favourite for sailing. Scotland also boasts some excellent cruising grounds on the Firth of Clyde and the rugged west coast.

Most beaches are generally as **clean** as any in Europe, with the best being awarded the prestigious Blue Flag award (the Seaside award is slightly less demanding). For annually updated, detailed information on the condition of Britain's beaches, the definitive source is the annual *Good Beach Guide*, compiled by the Marine Conservation Society (ⓦwww.goodbeachguide.co.uk).

The South West Coast Path near Lizard Point, Cornwall

Coastal paths

The beaches, cliffs and gently undulating slopes of Britain's coastline invite anything from a brief leisurely stroll to a vigorous long-distance hike. In the southeast of England, invigorating excursions can be made over the lovely **Seven Sisters** cliffs around Brighton, and over the iconic **White Cliffs of Dover**. But almost every stretch of English coast is walkable, and mostly waymarked – check out the **Norfolk Coast Path** or the **Cleveland Way** along the Yorkshire coast (for both see ⓦwww.nationaltrail.co.uk). Britain's longest National Trail is the 630-mile **South West Coast Path** (ⓦwww.southwestcoastpath.com), which extends from Minehead in Somerset around the peninsula to Poole in Dorset, taking in some wild and picturesque scenery along the way. Wales's **Pembrokeshire Coast Path** (ⓦwww.pembrokeshirecoast.org.uk) is much shorter, at 186 miles, but it's arguably even more dramatic; while the 80-mile **Fife Coastal Path** in Scotland (ⓦwww.fifecoastalpath.com) takes in the golden beaches and quaint fishing villages between the Forth Rail Bridge and St Andrews' coastal golf links.

Brighton Beach

Seaside resorts

Any Brit can describe the quintessential seaside resort – the piercing screech of gulls, the ubiquitous smell of fish and chips, lobster-red flesh at every turn, rollicking fairgrounds, donkey rides, end-of-pier shows, amusement arcades, rock pools and sand castles. **Blackpool** in Lancashire is the brilliant apotheosis of the genre – utterly compelling, enormously entertaining. No other British resort comes close, though many have an equally strong independent, contemporary identity, like fashionable **Brighton** in Sussex or the lively Welsh university seaside town of **Aberystwyth**. Others hark back to Victorian and Edwardian times, when the British decamped en masse each summer to genteel resorts with fine sands and parades of elegant hotels. **Scarborough** in North Yorkshire, said to be the country's oldest resort, is a classic example, with the Welsh equivalent found at **Llandudno**. At **Southwold** in East Anglia elegance is still the keynote, and there's a faded Victorian gentility in isolated resort outposts like **Rothesay** on the Isle of Bute and **Douglas** on the Isle of Man. Meanwhile both **Bournemouth** (Dorset) and **Torquay** (Devon) combine traditional resort pursuits with an energetic club scene.

Top Ten coastal beauty spots

Esha Ness, Shetland. See p.1132. The full might of the Atlantic crashes against the sea stacks and blowholes of this dramatic headland.

Hartland Point, Devon. See p.354. Fantastic slate cliffs give this remote place an otherworldly feel.

Lulworth Cove, Dorset. See p.240. A dramatic horseshoe-shaped bay surrounded by high cliffs.

Lizard Point, Cornwall. See p.369. Raging seas surround this rocky promontory.

The Needles, Isle of Wight. See p.226. Spectacular pinnacles of rock thrust up from the sea.

St David's peninsula, Pembrokeshire, South Wales. See p.723. Dizzying sandstone cliffs punctuated by indented bays.

Robin Hood's Bay, Yorkshire. See p.628. Honeycombed cliffs and rocky reefs set the scene at this former smugglers' village.

Holy Island, Northumberland. See p.670. A castle, priory ruins and abandoned hulks of boats add to the brooding character of this ancient spot.

Calf of Man, Isle of Man. See p.552. Take the boat across to this remote bird sanctuary for its high cliffs and grassy meadows.

Dunottar Castle, Aberdeenshire, northeast Scotland. See p.1045. The country's most spectacularly sited clifftop castle.

Lindisfarne Castle on Holy Island, Northumberland

from Arncliffe on to **Litton** (2–3 miles) is a delight, where you can reward yourself with a pint in the ancient and unspoilt *Queen's Arms*.

The main centre for the upper dale is **Kettlewell** (Norse for "bubbling spring"), one of the major locations for *Calendar Girls*, the based-on-a-true-story film of doughty Yorkshire ladies who bared all for a charity calendar: it has plenty of local B&B accommodation plus a YHA hostel. Two miles away at **Starbotton**, the *Fox & Hounds* (closed Mon & all Jan) has ancient flagged floors and a huge fire in winter. There's also a great pub in **Buckden**, another couple of miles to the north, the *Buck Inn*, which has good food and beer. Finally, a mile upstream, the river flows through Langstrothdale to **Hubberholme** and the stone-flagged, whitewashed *George*, the favourite pub of archetypal Yorkshireman J.B. Priestley, who revelled in visiting a hamlet he thought "one of the smallest and pleasantest places in the world". He's buried in the churchyard of the small chapel of St Michael and All Angels, over the stone bridge from the pub.

Practicalities

Grassington's **National Park Centre** is on Hebden Road (April–Oct daily 10am–5pm; Nov–March Wed–Sun 10am–4pm; ☎0870/166 6333), across from the bus stop. Grassington also has a bank with ATM, small supermarket, post office and outdoors stores. There's a fair amount of **accommodation** in the village, but even so, at busy times you may have to look further afield – no hardship since Grassington is surrounded by tiny scenic villages, all connected by minor country roads and footpaths (both Burnsall and Appletreewick are on the Dales Way). The nearest hostels are at Malham (7 miles) or Kettlewell (8 miles).

Accommodation

Angel Barn Lodgings/Angel Inn Hetton, 4 miles southwest of Grassington ☎01756/730263, ⊛www.angelhetton.co.uk. The Dales' gastropub *par excellence* has five immaculate rooms and suites, while over the road in the inn, the Modern British food goes from strength to strength – served either in the bar-brasserie (lunch & dinner) or more formal restaurant (Mon–Sat dinner & Sun lunch). ❼, Sat night ❽

Ashfield House Summers Fold, Grassington ☎01756/752584, ⊛www.ashfieldhouse.co.uk. Lovely seventeenth-century house boasting a walled garden, good breakfasts and some special weekend deals. Closed Dec & Jan. ❺

Devonshire Fell Burnsall, 3 miles southeast of Grassington ☎01756/729000, ⊛www.devonshire hotels.co.uk. Ten bedrooms and two suites here have been given the designer treatment – although

this is a country house retreat, it's definitely not "country" in feel. Weekend two-night minimum. ❼

Grassington Lodge 8 Wood Lane, Grassington ☎01756/752518, ⊛www.grassing tonlodge.co.uk. A splash of contemporary style – coordinated fabrics, hardwood floors, DVD players, specially commissioned Dales photography – enhances this comfortable village guest-house. No credit cards. ❼

Kettlewell YHA Kettlewell, 8 miles north of Grassington ☎0870/770 5896, ✉kettlewell@yha.org .uk. The Dales' hostel is right in the village centre. Closed Dec to mid-Feb, flexible opening at other times, but daily July & Aug. Dorms £13.95.

Red Lion Burnsall, 3 miles southeast ☎01756/720204, ⊛www.redlion.co.uk. A real old country inn, with log fires, oak beams, a cosy bar, and river views from its comfortable, traditionally furnished rooms. ❼

Malhamdale

A few miles west of Wharfedale lies **Malhamdale** (⊛www.malhamdale.com), one of the National Park's most heavily visited regions, thanks to its three outstanding natural features: Malham Cove, Malham Tarn and Gordale Scar. The approach by public transport is by bus from Skipton (daily year-round service), with weekend buses from Leeds, Bradford and Keighley via Skipton. A seasonal shuttle from Settle also operates, plus a **Malham Tarn shuttle** service (weekends and bank hols Easter–Oct) which runs every 30min from the National Park Centre (see below).

Malham village itself is home to barely a couple of hundred people, who inhabit the huddled stone houses on either side of a bubbling river, but this microscopic gem attracts perhaps half a million visitors a year. Appearing in spectacular fashion a mile to the north, **Malham Cove** is a white-walled limestone amphitheatre rising three hundred feet above its surroundings. A broad track leads to the cove, passing some of England's most visible prehistoric field banks en route. From the top of the cove, a simple walk over the moors abruptly brings **Malham Tarn** into sight, a lake created by an impervious layer of glacial debris. This, too, is an area of outstanding natural interest, its numerous waterfowl protected by a nature reserve on the west bank. Meanwhile, at **Gordale Scar** (also easily approached direct from Malham village), the cliffs are, if anything, more spectacular than at Malham Cove, complemented by a deep ravine to the rear caused by the collapse of a cavern roof. There's a classic circuit which takes in cove, tarn and scar in a clockwise **walk from Malham** (8 miles; 3hr 30min).

Unless you already have maps and accommodation sorted out, your first stop should be the **National Park Centre** on the southern edge of the village (Easter–Oct daily 10am–5pm; Nov–Easter Sat & Sun 10am–4pm; ☎0870/166 6333). This is also where you'll have to park. There are several good village **B&Bs**, while the two **pubs** in Malham also have rooms. The *Buck Inn* has a popular walkers' back-bar, but the food is better at the fancier *Lister Arms* over the bridge. There's **camping** at the popular *Gordale Scar House Campsite*, Gordale Scar (☎01729/830333; closed Nov–March), just over a mile from the village – book well in advance for weekend stays.

B&Bs and hostels

Beck Hall ☎01729/830332, ⊛www.beckhallmalham.com. A varied mix of en-suite rooms – some with panelling and four-posters, others with stream and field views – plus a cosy lounge and fire, and all-year daytime café (closed Mon). Parking. ❹

Hill Top Farm ☎01729/830320. Centrally heated bunkhouse barn with kitchen, lounge and metered showers, immediately north (2min) of the National Park information centre. Beds £9, groups only at weekends.

Malham YHA ☎0870/770 5946, ⓔmalham@yha.org.uk. Purpose-built hostel that's well known as a walking and cycling centre. Dorms £13.95; Nov–Jan usually weekends only.

Miresfield Farm ☎01729/830414, ⊛www.miresfield-farm.com. A great location – first house in the village, by the river – means lovely rural views. Country-pine-style rooms vary in size, but all are en suite, and there's a small campsite with toilet and shower, and breakfast available for campers. ❸

Ribblesdale

The scenery of **Ribblesdale**, to the west of Malhamdale, is more dour and brooding than the bucolic valleys to the east. It's approached from **Settle**, starting point of the **Settle-to-Carlisle Railway**, among the most scenic rail routes in the country, with daily trains heading north through Horton to Carlisle and south to Skipton, Keighley and Leeds. Regular **buses** connect Skipton with Settle, and there's also the seasonal Sunday and bank holiday bus from Skipton to Settle, Horton and Ribblehead, continuing on to Wensleydale and Richmond.

Nestled under the wooded knoll of Castleberg, **SETTLE** has a typical seventeenth-century market square, still sporting its split-level arcaded shambles, which once housed butchers' shops. Other than on Tuesdays, when the market is in full swing, there's not much to see in the few streets behind the square and you might as well make the ten-minute climb up through the woods to the top of **Castleberg** for views over the town. A seasonal weekend and bank holiday **shuttle bus** (Easter to mid-Sept) runs over the tops to Malham in an hour, while the **train station** is less than five signposted minutes' walk from Market Place, down Station Road. While you're in town, you'll be hard pushed to resist the lure of *Ye Olde Naked Man Café* (closed Wed), serving breakfasts, proper coffee and good homemade food; a former undertakers', the café's name refers to the old adage that "you bring now't into the world and you take now't out."

The noted walking centre of **HORTON IN RIBBLESDALE** dates from Norman times but the village gained a new lease of life in the nineteenth century with the arrival of the Settle-to-Carlisle Railway. The celebrated **Pen-y-ghent Café** in the village doubles as a **tourist office** (Mon & Wed–Sun 8/9am–6pm; ☏01729/860333) and an unofficial headquarters for the famous **Three Peaks Walk**, a twenty-five-mile, twelve-hour circuit of Pen-y-ghent (2273ft), Whernside (2416ft) and Ingleborough (2373ft). As well as providing food, maps, guides and weather reports, the *Pen-y-ghent Café* operates a "safety service" for walkers, enabling anyone undertaking a long hike (including the Three Peaks) to register in and out (not Tues or Fri). Horton itself straggles along an L-shaped mile of the Settle–Ribblehead road (B6479), with the train station at the northern end and the church at the southern

△ Settle to Carlisle railway

end. The *Golden Lion* (℡01729/860206), by the church, has both **rooms** (❸) and bunk-house beds (£8; breakfast and packed lunches available), or ask at the *Pen-y-ghent Café*. There's also a grassy tents-only **campsite** at *Holme Farm* (℡01729/860281), near the church.

At the head of the valley the **Ribblehead Viaduct** cuts a superb profile, backed by some of the most uncompromising moors in the entire National Park. If it's pouring down, as it often is, take refuge in the *Station Inn* (℡01524/241274, ⓦwww.thestationinn.net), right by the station and rail bridge, which serves pub grub daily and has simple **rooms** (❸) and a **bunkhouse** with small kitchen (beds £8.50, breakfast available).

Ingleton

The straggling slate-grey village of **INGLETON** sits upon a ridge at the confluence of two streams, the Twiss and the Doe, whose beautifully wooded valleys are easily the area's best features. The four-and-a-half mile **Falls' Walk** (daily 9am–dusk; entrance fee £3.50; ℡015242/41930, ⓦwww.ingletonwater fallswalk.co.uk) is a lovely circular walk taking in both valleys, and providing viewing points over its waterfalls. Just one and a half miles out of Ingleton on the Ribblehead–Hawes road (B6255) is the entrance to the **White Scar Caves** (daily 10am–5pm; Nov–Jan Sat & Sun only, weather permitting; £6.95; ℡015242/41244, ⓦwww.whitescarcave.co.uk), the longest show cave in England. Don't be put off by the steep price – it's worth every penny for the eighty-minute tour of dank underground chambers, contorted cave formations and glistening stalactites. Tours run every hour or so, and there's a café on site.

The Inglesport **hiking store** on Main Street (℡015242/41146, ⓦwww .inglesport.com) in the village is the place for maps, equipment and weather forecasts. There's also a **tourist office** in the community centre car park, just off Main Street (April–Oct daily 10am–4.30pm; ℡015242/41049), and useful local information on the **community website** (ⓦwww.ingleton.co.uk). The main **bus stop** is outside the tourist office. The YHA **hostel** (℡0870/770 5880, ⓔingleton@yha.org.uk; £13.95; closed certain days of the week Sept–Feb) is an old stone house in its own gardens, located centrally in a lane between the market square and the swimming pool. There are a dozen local **B&Bs and guest houses**, starting with the no-smoking *Bridge End*, the handsome former mill-owner's house on Mill Lane (℡015242/41413; ❸), by the bridge and close to the Falls' Walk entrance. Most of the rest lie along Main Street, five minutes' walk south of the tourist office, where *Riverside Lodge*, 24 Main St (℡015242/41359, ⓦwww.riversideingleton.co.uk; ❸), is the pick. Ingleton has its fair share of **services** – bank, shops, bakers and grocery stores – making it a good place for hikers to stock up. The *Inglesport Café* on the first floor of the store on Main Street (daily 9am–6pm) serves hearty soups and potatoes with everything, while the tearoom at *Curlew Crafts*, back down Main Street, is a bit more refined with home-cooked blackboard specials (open daily throughout the year). None of the **pubs** in the village is up to much, though you can drive five miles up the Hawes road (B6255), beyond the hamlet of Chapel-le-Dale, to the flagstoned *Old Hill Inn* (℡015242/41256; ❹), for its cosily restored interior, good beers and posh pub food.

Dentdale

When travel writers turn out clichés like "stepping back in time", they mean to describe places like **DENT** – the main road gives way to grassy cobbles, while the huddled stone cottages sport blooming window-boxes trailing over ancient lintels, and have tiny windows to keep in the warmth. In the seventeenth and eighteenth centuries, Dentdale supported a flourishing hand-knitting industry, later ruined by mechanization. These days, the hill-farming community supplements its income through tourism and craft ventures, including the independent Dent Brewery. You can stay at either of the village's two **pubs**, the *Sun Inn* (℡01539/625208, ✉thesun@dentbrewery.co.uk; ❶) or the *George & Dragon* (℡01539/625256, ✉thedragon@dentbrewery.co.uk; ❸), which are virtually next to each other in the centre. The *Sun* is the nicer, truly welcoming to walkers and with a great traditional feel; that said, the en-suite rooms at the *George & Dragon* have been modernized and are more comfortable. There are a handful of other **B&B** possibilities, including *Stone Close Guest House* (℡01539/625231, ✉stoneclose@btinternet.com; ❷), which has a good café (noon–5pm all year; closed Mon), doubling as a National Park **information point**. Dent's **train station** (on the Settle–Carlisle line) is not in Dent at all, but four miles to the east. Dentdale **YHA hostel** (℡0870/770 5790, ✉dentdale@yha.org .uk; £13.95; flexible opening, call for details) is a couple of miles south of the station, down the Dales Way.

Wensleydale

Best known of the Dales, if only for its cheese, **Wensleydale** is the largest and most serene of the National Park's dales. Known in medieval times as Yoredale, after its river (the Ure), the dale takes its present name from an easterly village, and while there are towns to detain you, such as the market town of **Hawes**, it's Wensleydale's rural attractions that linger longest in the mind. Many will be familiar to devotees of the James Herriott books and TV series, set and filmed in the dale. Year-round **public transport** is provided by a combination of post and service buses from Hawes on varied routes, and there are also summer weekend and bank holiday services connecting Hawes to Wharfedale (#800/805), Hawes to Swaledale, Masham and Ripon (#803), Hawes to Richmond or Ribblesdale (#807), and Leyburn and Masham to Richmond or Ripon (#802).

Hawes

HAWES – from the Anglo-Saxon *haus*, a mountain pass – is head of Wensleydale in all respects: it's the chief town, main hiking centre, and home to its tourism, cheese and rope-making industries. Hawes also claims to be Yorkshire's highest market town, and received its market charter in 1699; the weekly **Tuesday market** – crammed with farmers and market traders – is still going strong. The cheese trail invariably leads to the **Wensleydale Creamery** (Mon–Sat 9.30am–5pm, Sun 10am–4pm; £2.50; ℡01969/667664, ⊛www.wensleydale .co.uk), signposted a few hundred yards south of the centre. The Creamery's tours fill you in on the history, with plenty of opportunity to see the stuff being made, and to sample and purchase in the shop – cheese isn't made every day, so call first to guarantee a viewing.

Services and accommodation in Hawes are gathered together along and just off the main A684, which runs through town. The **National Park Centre** (daily 10am–5pm; ℡0870/166 6333) shares the same building as the fascinating Dales Countryside Museum. **Accommodation** is plentiful in local B&Bs, while all the pubs on and around the market square – the *Board, Crown, Fountain, Bull's Head* and *White Hart* – have rooms, too. Pub dining is best at the *Crown* – which has a raised rear garden with valley views; otherwise, you're limited to a couple of hotel dining rooms, an Indian restaurant and a fish-and-chip café.

Accommodation and food

Hawes YHA Lancaster Terrace ☎0870/770 5854, ⒺΗawes@yah.org.uk. Modern hostel on the edge of town, at the junction of the main A684 and B6255. Some twin and family rooms available (●), otherwise dorm beds £11.95. Flexible opening Nov–March.

Herriot's Main Street ☎01969/667536, ⓌΗwww.herriotshotel.com. Small hotel just off Market Place, where a couple of the rooms have fell views. The restaurant here is the best place to eat in town, offering dishes that range from rack of Wensleydale lamb to stir-fried prawns. ●

Rookhurst Country House West End, Gayle, half-mile south (Creamery road) ☎01969/667454, Ⓦwww.rookhurst.co.uk. Rooms are either elegant Victorian (original fireplaces, stone-mullioned bay windows) or dramatically rustic (like the Attic, with its latticed oak beams and brass bed with flying cherub). There's a no-smoking, no-children policy, and a set-menu dinner (£25) is available – ask when booking. ●

Rose & Crown Bainbridge, 5 miles east of Hawes ☎01969/650225, Ⓦwww.theprideofwensleydale .com. Fifteenth-century coaching inn with restaurant and bar, overlooking an emerald village green. ●

Steppe Haugh Town Head ☎01969/667645, Ⓦwww.steppehaugh.co.uk. Plenty of pine gives a cottagey feel to this traditional B&B, at the Ingleton road turn-off at the top of town. ●

Askrigg, Aysgarth and Castle Bolton

The mantle of "Herriot country" lies heavy on **ASKRIGG**, six miles east of Hawes, as the TV series *All Creatures Great and Small* was filmed in and around the village. The *King's Arms* – a cosy old haunt with wood panelling, good beer and bar meals – displays stills from the series. For a rural retreat, you can't beat *Helm Country House* (☎01969/650443, Ⓦwww.helmyorkshire.com; ●), a seventeenth-century farmhouse a mile west with magnificent views, open fires and oak beams.

The ribbon-village of **AYSGARTH**, straggling along and off the A684, is the vortex that sucks in Wensleydale's largest number of visitors, courtesy of the **Aysgarth Falls**, half a mile below the village, where water crashes down a series of wide limestone steps. A marked nature trail runs through the surrounding woodlands and there's a car park and **National Park Centre** on the north bank (April–Oct daily 10am–5pm; Nov–March Fri–Sun 10am–4pm; ☎0870/166 6333). The **Upper Falls** and picnic grounds lie just back from here, by the bridge and church; the more spectacular **Middle** and **Lower Falls** are a ten-minute stroll to the east through shaded woodland.

There's a superb **circular walk** northeast from Aysgarth via Castle Bolton (6 miles; 4hr) – or you can simply drive to the castle in about ten minutes. The walk starts at the falls and climbs up through Thoresby, with the foursquare battlements of **Castle Bolton** (March–Nov daily 10am–5pm; restricted winter opening, call for details; ☎01969/623981, Ⓦwww.boltoncastle.co.uk; £5) a magnetic lure from miles away across the fields. The Great Hall, a few adjacent rooms, and the castle gardens have been restored, and there's also a café (free to enter).

Masham

If you're a beer fan, the handsome market town of **MASHAM** (pronounced Mass'm) is an essential place of pilgrimage. It's home to **Theakston** brewery (tours daily 11am–3pm; reservations advised; ☎01765/680000, Ⓦwww .theakstons.co.uk; £4.50), sited here since 1827, where you can learn the arcane intricacies of the brewer's art and become familiar with the legendary Old Peculier ale. The tour-price includes a free pint and there's a visitor centre and bar on site. In the early 1990s one of the Theakston-family brewing team left to set up the **Black Sheep Brewery**, also based in Masham and offering tours (daily

11am–4pm, but call for availability; £4.50; ☎01765/680100, ⊛www.black sheepbrewery.com). Both breweries are just a few minutes' signposted walk out of the centre.

There's no more agreeable **accommodation** – here, or for many miles around – than *Swinton Park* (☎01765/680900, ⊛www.swintonpark.com; ❽), a stunning stately home with elegant rooms that overlook the sweeping grounds and curving river. The hotel is only a gentle mile's stroll from Masham itself, where the *King's Head*, 42 Market Place (☎01765/689295, ⊛www.kingshead masham.com; ❹, breakfast not included), is the best place to eat in town, more restaurant than pub.

Richmond

RICHMOND is the Dales' single most tempting historical town, thanks mainly to its magnificent castle, whose extensive walls and colossal keep cling to a precipice above the River Swale. Indeed, the entire town is an absolute gem, centred on a huge cobbled market square backed onto by hidden alleys and gardens housing mainly Georgian buildings of great refinement. There's no better place to start than **Richmond Castle** (Easter–Sept daily 10am–6pm; Oct–Easter Mon & Thurs–Sun 10am–4pm; £3.60; EH). Originally built by Alan Rufus, first Norman Earl of Richmond, it retains many features from its earliest incarnation, principally the gatehouse, curtain wall and Scolland's Hall, the oldest Norman great hall in the country. There are prodigious views from the splendidly preserved fortified keep, which is over a hundred feet high, and from the Great Court, now an open lawn which ends in a sheer fall to the river below.

Most of medieval Richmond sprouted around the castle, but much of the town now radiates from the vast **Market Place**, with the Market Hall alongside (markets on Tues, Thurs, Fri & Sat). The keenest interest, perhaps, is in the town's **Theatre Royal** (1788), a fine piece of Georgian architecture that is one of England's oldest extant theatres. It's open for both **performances** (box office ☎01748/825252, ⊛www.georgiantheatreroyal.co.uk) and **tours** (mid-Feb to mid-Dec Mon–Sat 10am–4pm, on the hour; £3), while a museum at the rear gives an insight into eighteenth-century theatrical life, allowing visitors to have a go at scene-shifting, use the thunderbox prop, or try on various masks and costumes.

A signposted walk runs along the north bank of the **River Swale** out to the beautifully situated church of St Agatha and adjacent **Easby Abbey** (dawn to dusk; free; EH), the golden stone walls of which stand a mile southeast of the town centre. Founded in 1152, the abbey is now ruined, the greatest damage having been caused in 1346 when the English army was billeted here on its way to the battle of Neville's Cross.

Practicalities

Buses all stop in the Market Place; there are regular services into Wensleydale and Swaledale, and to Darlington, ten miles to the northeast, which is on the main east-coast train line. The **tourist office**, at Friary Gardens, Victoria Road (daily 9.30am–5.30pm; winter closed Sun; ☎01748/850252, ⊛www .richmond.org.uk), is helpful in finding accommodation, and also organizes **guided walking tours** around the town in summer (free, donations welcome). **Eating out** is mainly based on Richmond's **pubs** – there are half a dozen around the market square alone. However, these are nothing special, and it's far better to drive out into the gentle country to the north where prettily sited pubs like the *Shoulder of Mutton* (☎01748/822772) at Kirby Hill (3 miles) make for a decent night out.

Accommodation

Frenchgate Hotel 59–61 Frenchgate
℡01748/822087, ⓦwww.frenchgatehotel.com.
Currently being refurbished, this attractive Georgian
townhouse hotel has eight en-suite rooms and a
local reputation for its food (mains £13–16; restaurant closed Mon). **❻**

King's Head Hotel Market Place
℡01748/850220, ⓦwww.kingsheadrichmond
.com. The town's principal hotel, with traditionally
furnished rooms, lounge and log fire. Bar meals

available, or eat in the restaurant for around £25
(excluding drinks). **❻**, including dinner **❼**

Whashton Springs Near Whashton, 3
miles north of town, Ravensworth road
℡01748/822884, ⓦwww.whashtonsprings
.co.uk. This working Dales farm offers comfortable
en-suite rooms in the main house or round the
courtyard, filled with family furniture. **❸**

Willance House 24 Frenchgate ℡01748/824467.
Characterful seventeenth-century cottage in town
with three rooms. No credit cards. **❷**

Fountains Abbey

On the eastern edge of the Dales, close to the small cathedral town of Ripon,
Fountains Abbey (daily 10am–4/5pm; closed Fri Nov–Jan; £5.50; NT) is the
one Yorkshire monastic ruin you should make a point of seeing. Beautifully set in
a narrow, wooded valley, it was founded in 1133 by thirteen dissident Benedictine
monks from the wealthy abbey of St Mary's in York. Within a hundred years,
Fountains had become the wealthiest Cistercian foundation in England – several
centuries later, it's tantalizing to imagine how the landscape might have appeared
had Henry VIII not dissolved the monasteries. The estate is owned by the National
Trust, which organizes an ambitious range of activities and events – from firework displays to **free guided tours** (April–Oct daily; ℡01765/608888, ⓦwww
.fountainsabbey.org.uk). Public transport to the abbey is limited, though summer
Sunday and bank holiday bus services operate from Bradford/Leeds/Ripon (#802)
and York/Ripon/Grassington (#812) – call ℡0870/608 2608 for details.

Most immediately eye-catching is the **abbey church**, in particular the
Chapel of the Nine Altars at its eastern end, whose delicacy is in marked
contrast to the austerity of the rest of the nave. A great sixty-foot-high window
rises over the chapel, complemented by a similar window at the nave's western
doorway, over 370ft away. Equally grandiose in scale is the undercroft of the **Lay
Brothers' Dormitory** off the cloister, a stunningly vaulted space over 300ft
long that was used to store the monastery's annual harvest of fleeces. Many
other buildings are still extant – from infirmary to refectory – while outside
the abbey perimeter are the Abbey Mill and **Fountains Hall**, the latter a fine
example of early seventeenth-century domestic architecture.

A riverside walk, marked from the visitor-centre car park, takes you to a series
of ponds and ornamental gardens, harbingers of **Studley Royal** (same times
as the abbey; NT), which can also be entered via the village of Studley Roger,
where there's a separate car park. This lush medley of lawns, lake, woodland and
Deer Park (daily dawn to dusk; free) was laid out in 1720, and there are some
scintillating views of the abbey from the gardens, though it's the cascades and
water gardens which command most attention. The full circuit, from visitor
centre to abbey and gardens and then back, is a good couple of miles' walk.

Harrogate

HARROGATE – the very picture of genteel Yorkshire respectability – owes
its landscaped appearance and early prosperity to the discovery of Tewit Well in

1571. This was the first of over eighty ferrous and sulphurous springs that, by the nineteenth century, were to turn the town into one of the country's leading spas. Harrogate still manages to retain its essential Victorian and Edwardian character, and much of its appeal lies in the splendid parks and gardens – "England's floral town" keeps admirable pace with the changing seasons. The spa heritage begins with the **Royal Baths**, facing Crescent Road, now restored to their late-Victorian finery. You can experience the beautiful Moorish-style interior during a session at the **Turkish Baths and Health Spa** (separate sessions for men and women; hours vary; call ☎01423/556746; from £15). The public entrance is on Parliament Street; allow two hours for the full treatment. Just along Crescent Road from the Royal Baths stands the **Royal Pump Room**, built in 1842 over the sulphur well that feeds the baths. The **museum** here (Mon–Sat 10am–4/5pm, Sun 2–4/5pm; £2.80) re-creates something of the town's health-fixated past and also lets you sample the water; free hour-long **guided walks** leave here several times a week between April and September (information from the tourist office).

Harrogate deserves much credit for the preservation of its green spaces, most prominent of which is **The Stray**, a jealously guarded green belt that curves around the south of the town centre. To the southwest (entrance opposite the Royal Pump Room), the 120-acre **Valley Gardens** are a delight, while many visitors also make for the botanical gardens at **Harlow Carr** (daily 9am–4/6pm; £6; ⓦwww.rhs.org.uk), the northern showpiece of the Royal Horticultural Society. These lie one and a half miles out, on the town's western edge – the nicest approach is to walk (30min) through the Valley Gardens and pine woods.

Practicalities

Bus and **train** stations are on Station Parade, just a few minutes from all the central sights. Harrogate's **tourist office** (April–Sept Mon–Sat 9am–6pm, Sun 10am–1pm; Oct–March Mon–Fri 9am–5pm, Sat 9am–4pm; ☎01423/537300, ⓦwww.enjoyharrogate.com) is in the Royal Baths on Crescent Road. You shouldn't have any problem finding somewhere to stay, other than during one of Harrogate's many festivals. Of these the most famous are the **flower shows** (second weeks of April and Sept; ⓦwww.flowershow.org), but there's also the entertaining three-day **Great Yorkshire Show** (second week in July; ⓦwww.greatyorkshireshow.org).

Accommodation

Brookfield 5 Alexandra Rd ☎01423/506646, ⓦwww.brookfieldhousehotel.co.uk. Victorian B&B with period features and contemporary flourishes. Parking. **❺**

Cutlers on the Stray 19 West Park ☎01423/524471, ⓦwww.cutlers-web.co.uk. Former coaching inn, now brasserie-with-rooms (some with views across the green expanse of The Stray). **❻**

Fountains 27 King's Rd ☎01423/530483, ⓦwww.thefountainshotel.co.uk. Nonsmoking rooms have trim little bathrooms (some with bath as well as shower); it's quieter at the side, where the rooms look over a shady copse. Parking. **❹**

Hotel du Vin Prospect Place ☎01423/856800, ⓦwww.hotelduvin.com.
Beautiful boutique-style rooms overlooking The Stray (including four stunning "loft suites") featuring enormous beds and lavish bathrooms. The bistro is sensibly priced, with a three-course set dinner for under £20. **❻**, loft suites **❾**

Ruskin 1 Swan Rd ☎01423/502045, ⓦwww.ruskinhotel.co.uk. Appealing Victorian villa with seven spacious en-suite rooms, terraced bar and charming garden. **❻**

Restaurants

Betty's 1 Parliament St ☎01423/502746. Very much a Harrogate institution, with cakes and tarts to die for, and full meals also served. Closes at 9pm. Inexpensive.

Drum and Monkey 5 Montpellier Gardens ⊤01423/502650. Long-standing fish and seafood restaurant, a firm favourite with locals and out-of-towners alike. Closed Sun. Expensive.

Old Bell Tavern 6 Royal Parade ⊤01423/507930. Treat it as a pub – it's the best in town, entirely nonsmoking – or come to eat, since there are bar meals and sandwiches served daily (lunchtime and 6–7pm, Sun from noon) and a brasserie upstairs. Moderate.

Orchid 28 Swan Rd ⊤01423/560425. Wok-wielding chefs conjour up specialities from all corners of Southeast Asia, tempura to Shanghai noodles. Closed Mon & Sat lunch. Moderate.

Knaresborough

A four-mile hop east of Harrogate, **KNARESBOROUGH** rises spectacularly above the River Nidd's limestone gorge, its old townhouses, pubs, shops and gardens clustered together on the wooded northern bank, with the river itself crossed by two bridges ("High" and "Low") and an eye-opener of a rail viaduct. The rocky crag above the town is crowned by the stump of a **Castle** (Easter–Sept daily 10.30am–5pm; £2.50) dating back to Norman times, built on the site of Roman and Anglo-Saxon fortifications, but now little more than a fourteenth-century keep in landscaped grounds. The town's two novelty acts are to be found on the west side of the river. **Mother Shipton's Cave** (daily March–Oct 10am–5.30pm; £5.50; ⓦwww.mothershipton.co.uk) was home to a sixteenth-century soothsayer who predicted the defeat of the Armada, the Great Fire of London, world wars, cars, planes, iron ships – falling short, however, in the most important oracular chestnut of them all, predicting the End of the World: "The world to an end will come," she prophesied, "in eighteen hundred and eighty one." Close by is the **Petrifying Well**, where dripping, lime-soaked waters coat everyday objects – gloves, hats, coats, toys – in a brownish veneer that sets rock-hard in a few weeks.

Regular **trains** and **buses** (every 10min) from Harrogate are frequent enough to make Knaresborough an easy side-trip. A couple of miles north of town, at Ferrensby, the *General Tarleton* **gastropub** (⊤01423/340284, ⓦwww.general-tarleton.co.uk; ⓞ) is well worth the short drive for meals in either the restaurant or bar-brasserie.

York

YORK is the North's most compelling city, a place whose history, said George VI, "is the history of England". This is perhaps overstating things a little, but it reflects the significance of a metropolis that was, until the Industrial Revolution, second only to London in population and importance. The **Romans** chose a site at the confluence of two minor rivers for their military camp during campaigns against the Brigantes in 71 AD, and in time this fortress became a city – Eboracum, capital of the empire's northern European territories. Much fought over after the decline of Rome, the city later emerged as the fulcrum of Christianity in northern England. It was here, on Easter Day in 627, that Bishop Paulinus baptized King Edwin of Northumbria in a small timber chapel built for the purpose. Six years later the church became the first minster and Paulinus the first archbishop of York. In 867 the city fell to the **Danes**, who renamed it Jorvik, then made it the capital of eastern England (Danelaw). Later Viking raids culminated in the decisive **Battle of Stamford Bridge** (1066) six miles east of the city, where English King Harold defeated Norse King Harald – a pyrrhic victory in the event, for his weakened army was defeated by the Normans just a few days later at the Battle of Hastings.

Stone walls were thrown up during the thirteenth century, when the city became commercial capital of the North, its importance reflected in the new title of Duke of York, bestowed ever since on the monarch's second son. Although Henry VIII's Dissolution of the Monasteries took its toll on a city crammed with religious houses, York remained strongly wedded to the Catholic cause, and the most famous of the Gunpowder Plot conspirators, **Guy Fawkes**, was born here. During the Civil War Charles I established his court in the city, which was strongly pro-Royalist, inviting a Parliamentarian siege that was eventually lifted by Prince Rupert of the Rhine, a nephew of the King. Rupert's troops, however, were routed by Cromwell and Sir Thomas Fairfax at the **Battle of Marston Moor** in 1644, another seminal battle in England's history, which took place just six miles west of York. The city's eighteenth-century history was marked by its emergence as a social centre for Yorkshire's landed elite. Whilst the Industrial Revolution largely passed it by, the arrival of the **railways** brought renewed prosperity – it's still a key rail town – though these days, of course, it's the income from millions of tourists that largely supports the city.

Arrival, information, transport and tours

York Station lies just outside the city walls on the west side of the River Ouse, a 750-yard walk from the historic core. National Express **buses** and most other regional bus services drop off and pick up on Rougier Street, 200yd northeast of the train station, just before Lendal Bridge, though some services call at the train station, too. There's a useful **tourist office** at the train station, though the main office is over Lendal Bridge, 200yd west of the Minster in the De Grey Rooms, on Exhibition Square (Mon–Sat 9am–6pm, Sun 10am–5pm; ☎01904/621756, ⓦwww.visityork.org). A **York Pass** (1/2/3 days, £19/25/32; ⓦwww.yorkpass.com) is a good investment since admission prices soon mount up – it's available from the tourist office and gets you into thirty different attractions.

Walking is often the only way to get from A to B, given the tangled medieval layout of streets, alleys and yards, but you might consider **renting a bike**, as York is one of the country's most bicycle-friendly cities, with over forty miles of cycle lanes and paths. **Bus tours** start at around £8 per person, but much more interesting are the various **guided walks** (around £4), most famously the evening ghost walks, but also Viking- and Roman-themed walks (usually in the company of a costumed guide). One thoroughly recommended option also has the advantage of being free – the **York Association of Voluntary Guides** (☎01904/640780, ⓦwww.york.touristguides.btinternet.co.uk) offers a two-hour guided tour (daily at 10.15am), plus additional tours in summer (April–Oct at 2.15pm; June–Aug also at 6.45pm), departing from outside the Art Gallery in Exhibition Square. **YorkBoat** (☎01904/628324, ⓦwww.yorkboat.co.uk) leaves daily from King's Staith and Lendal Bridge on a one-hour "cruise on the Ouse" (Feb–Nov; cruises from £6.50, evening trips £7.50).

Accommodation

The main **B&B** concentration is in the side streets off Bootham (immediately west of Exhibition Square), with nothing much more than a ten-minute walk from the centre. Or consider the rooms at the various **budget chains** with hotels in York, like *Travelodge, Holiday Inn, Novotel, Quality Hotel*, and so on.

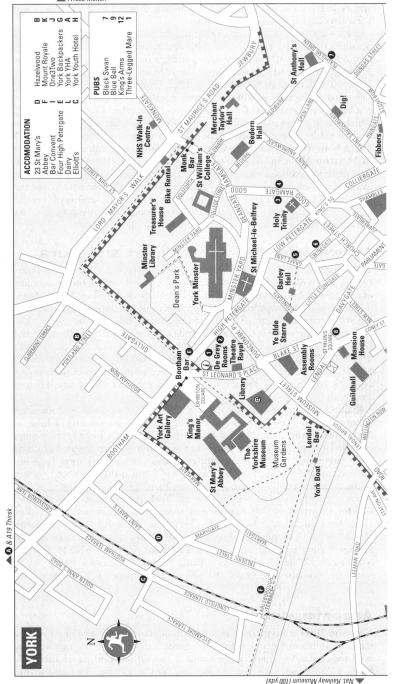

YORK

▲ A1036 Malton

ACCOMODATION

23 St Mary's	D
Abbey	F
Bar Convent	I
Four High Petergate	E
Dairy	L
Elliott's	C

Hazelwood	B
Mount Royale	K
One3Two	J
York Backpackers	G
York YHA	A
York Youth Hotel	H

PUBS

Black Swan	7
Blue Bell	9
King's Arms	12
Three-Legged Mare	1

St Anthony's Hall

Merchant Taylor's Hall

Bedern Hall

Dig!

Fibbers

NHS Walk-In Centre

Monk Bar

St William's College

Bike Rental

Treasurer's House

Minster Library

York Minster

Dean's Park

St Michael-le-Belfrey

Holy Trinity

Barley Hall

Ye Olde Starre

Bootham Bar

De Grey Rooms

Theatre Royal

Assembly Rooms

Mansion House

Guildhall

York Art Gallery

King's Manor

Library

St Mary's Abbey

The Yorkshire Museum

Museum Gardens

Lendal Bar

York Boat

▲ A & A19 Thirsk

N

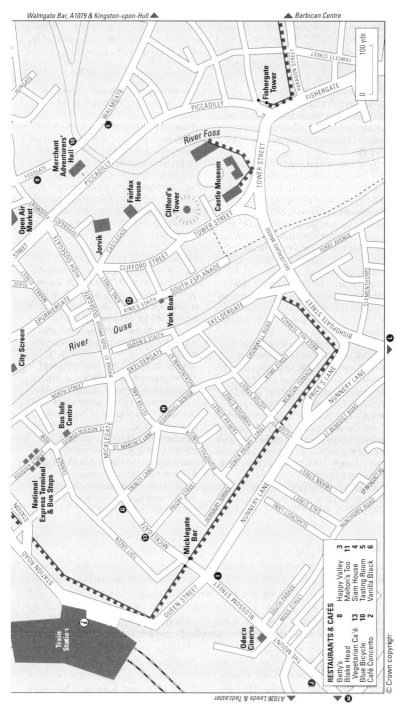

FAWCETT STREET
PARAGON STREET
FISHERGATE
Fishergate Tower
HUNGATE
WALMGATE
PICCADILLY
PICCADILLY
FOSSGATE
Merchant Adventurers' Hall
River Foss
TOWER STREET
Castle Museum
Fairfax House
Clifford's Tower
Jorvik
CASTLEGATE
TOWER STREET
Open Air Market
HIGH OUSEGATE
PAVEMENT
COPPERGATE
STREET
FEASE
MARKET STREET
CLIFFORD STREET
SPURRIERGATE
OUSEGATE
KING STREET
SOUTH ESPLANADE
York Boat
KING'S STAITH
SKELDERGATE
TERRY AVENUE
SKELDERGATE BRIDGE
CLEMENTHORPE
City Screen
Ouse
River
QUEEN'S STAITH
BRIDGE ST
OUSE BRIDGE
FETTER LANE
BUCKINGHAM ST
SKELDERGATE
BISHOPGATE STREET
CROMWELL ROAD
BAILE HILL TERRACE
NUNNERY LANE
PRICE'S LANE
KYME STREET
Bus Info Centre
NORTH STREET
MICKLEGATE
GEORGE HUDSON ST
TANNER
ST. MARTIN'S LANE
BISHOPHILL SENIOR
FAIRFAX STREET
HAMPDEN STREET
NEWTON TERRACE
VICTOR STREET
LOWER PRIORY STREET
BISHOPHILL JUNIOR
National Express Terminal & Bus Stops
MILL
ROUGIER STREET
STATION
TRINITY LANE
PRIORY STREET
CARR'S LANE
TOFT GREEN
CROSSBURY TERRACE
ST. BENEDICT ROAD
SWANN STREET
MICKLEGATE
Micklegate Bar
NUNNERY LANE
SCARCROFT LANE
DALE STREET
NORTHORPE ROAD
FOX STREET
STATION ROAD
Train Station
QUEEN STREET
BLOSSOM STREET
SOUTH PARADE
MOSS STREET
THE MOUNT
Odeon Cinema

© Crown copyright

12

YORKSHIRE

RESTAURANTS & CAFÉS	
Betty's	8
Blake Head	7
Vegetarian Café	13
Blue Bicycle	10
Café Concerto	2
Happy Valley	3
Melton's Too	11
Siam House	4
Tasting Room	5
Vanilla Black	6

Backpacker accommodation is easily found, while the **University of York** (℡01904/432222, ⓦwww.york.ac.uk) has good-value accommodation during Easter and summer holidays, either overnight B&B in well-equipped rooms or longer stays in self-contained flats/houses.

Hotels and B&Bs

23 St Mary's 23 St Mary's, Bootham ℡01904/622738, ⓦwww.23stmarys.co.uk. Very amiable family-house hotel that's peaceful (on a no-through road), but very close to centre and river. ❺

Abbey 14 Earlsborough Terrace, Marygate ℡01904/627782, ⓦwww.bedandbreakfast york.co.uk. You can't beat the location and the five rooms are styled with flair. ❸, river view ❹

Bar Convent 17 Blossom St ℡01904/643238, ⓦwww.bar-convent.org.uk. Grand Georgian building with nine single rooms (£30 each), six twins and a double; two rooms are en suite, otherwise there are separate bathrooms and access to a self-catering kitchen. ❸, en suite ❹

Dairy 3 Scarcroft Rd ℡01904/639367, ⓦwww .dairyguesthouse.co.uk. Charming Victorian house half a mile south of the station, retaining its cast-iron fireplaces, stained glass and pretty courtyard. Closed Jan. ❺

Elliott's Sycamore Place, Bootham Terrace ℡01904/623333, ⓦwww.elliottshotel.co.uk. A large detached Victorian house, with eleven spacious rooms in country pine and a friendly welcome for *Rough Guide* readers. Parking. ❺

Four High Petergate 4 High Petergate ℡01904/658516, ⓦwww.fourhighpetergateyork .co.uk. Townhouse hotel by Bootham Bar, just seconds from the Minster. Rooms have been given a classy shot-in-the-arm – teak beds, DVD players, power showers – while the adjacent bistro is one of the best in York. ❻

Hazelwood 24–25 Portland St, Gillygate ℡01904/626548, ⓦwww.thehazelwoodyork.com. A conversion of two Victorian houses offers elegant nonsmoking rooms – antique pine, rich fabrics – and there's a handsome lounge and walled garden. ❺

Mount Royale The Mount ℡01904/628856, ⓦwww.mountroyale.co.uk. Antique-filled retreat with superb garden-suites set around a private garden, together with a heated outdoor pool (open summer only) and hot tub, sauna and steam room. ❼

One3Two 132 The Mount ℡01904/600060, ⓦwww.one3two.co.uk. Indulge yourself in one of five beautifully furnished rooms in a sympathetically restored Georgian townhouse, 10min from the city centre. ❼

Hostels

York Backpackers Micklegate House, 88–90 Micklegate ℡01904/627720, ⓦwww .yorkbackpackers.co.uk. Amiable hostel with good facilities - kitchen, laundry, Internet, café and cellar bar. High-ceilinged dorms (sleeping 8 to 18) from £13, cheaper for multi-night stays, plus doubles and family rooms (❷); prices include continental breakfast.

York YHA Water End, Clifton ℡0870/770 6102, ⓔyork@yha.org.uk. Large Victorian mansion, a 20min walk from the tourist office. Beds mostly in four-bed dorms (£19.50), though private rooms (❷) also available, plus licensed café, Internet, large garden and parking.

York Youth Hotel 11–13 Bishophill Senior ℡01904/625904, ⓦwww.yorkyouthhotel.com. Good-value rooms with plenty of space, attracting a mixed international crowd. Variously priced 4-, 8- and 20-bed dorms available (£12–16), plus single and twin rooms (❶), and superior rooms (❷) with private kitchen, bathroom and TV.

The City

It's hard to get round everything in less than two days, and equally difficult to stick to any rigid itinerary. The **Minster** is the obvious place to start, and you won't want to miss a **walk around the walls**, though after that it very much depends on your interests. The medieval city is at its most evocative around the streets known as **Stonegate** and the **Shambles**, while the earlier Viking city is entertainingly presented at **Jorvik**, perhaps the city's favourite family attraction. Stand-out historic buildings include the Minster's **Treasurer's House**, Georgian **Fairfax House**, the **Merchant Adventurers' Hall**, and the stark remnants of **York Castle**. The two major museum collections are the incomparable **Castle Museum** and the **National Railway Museum** (where the appeal goes way beyond railway memorabilia), while the evocative ruins and gardens of St Mary's Abbey house the family-friendly **Yorkshire Museum**.

York Minster

York Minster (Mon–Sat 9/9.30am to last entry at 4.45pm, Sun noon–3.45pm; £5, Minster and all its attractions £7; ☎01904/557216, ⓦwww.yorkminster ,org) ranks as one of the country's most important sights. Seat of the archbishop of York, it is Britain's largest Gothic building and home to countless treasures, not least of which is the world's largest medieval stained-glass window and an estimated half of all the medieval stained glass in England. In its earliest incarnation, the Minster was probably the wooden chapel used to baptize King Edwin of Northumbria in 627. After its stone successors were destroyed by the Danes, the first significant foundations were laid around 1080 and it was from the germ of this Norman church that the present structure emerged.

Nothing else in the Minster can match the magnificence of the stained glass in the nave and transepts. The **West Window** (1338) contains distinctive heart-shaped upper tracery (the "Heart of Yorkshire"), whilst in the nave's north aisle, the second bay window (1155) contains slivers of the oldest stained glass in the country. Moving down to the crossing, the north transept's **Five Sisters Window** is named after the five fifty-foot lancets, each glazed with thirteenth-century grisaille, a distinctive frosted, silvery-grey glass. Opposite, the south transept contains a sixteenth-century, 17,000-piece **Rose Window**, commemorating the 1486 marriage of Henry VII and Elizabeth of York, an alliance which marked the end of the Wars of the Roses. The greatest of the church's 128 windows, however, is the majestic **East Window** (1405), at 78ft by 31ft the world's largest area of medieval stained glass in a single window.

The foundations, or **undercroft** (Mon–Sat 9am–5pm, Sun 12.30–5pm; £3.50), have been turned into a museum, while amongst precious church relics in the adjoining **treasury** are silver plate found in Walter de Grey's tomb and the eleventh-century *Horn of Ulf*, presented to the Minster by a relative of the tide-turning King Canute. There's also access from the undercroft to the **crypt**, the spot that transmits the most powerful sense of antiquity, as it contains portions of Archbishop Roger's choir and sections of the 1080 church, including pillars with fine Romanesque capitals. Access to the undercroft, treasury and crypt is from the south transept, also the entrance to the **central tower** (£3), which you can climb for rooftop views over the city.

Around the walls

Although much restored, the city's superb walls date mainly from the fourteenth century, though fragments of Norman work survive, particularly in the gates (known as "**bars**"), whilst the northern sections still follow the line of the Roman ramparts. **Monk Bar** at the northern end of Goodramgate is as good a point of access as any, tallest of the city's four main gates and host to a small **Richard III Museum** (daily 9/9.30am–4/5pm; £2.50; ⓦwww.richardiiimuseum.co.uk), where you're invited to decide on the guilt or innocence of England's most maligned king. For a taste of the walls' best section take the ten-minute stroll west from Monk Bar to Exhibition Square and **Bootham Bar**, the only gate on the site of a Roman gateway and marking the traditional northern entrance to the city. A stroll round the walls' entire two-and-a-half-mile length will take you past the southwestern **Micklegate Bar**, long considered the most important of the gates since it, in

△ York walls

turn, marked the start of the road to London. It was once used to exhibit the heads of executed criminals and rebels, and the engaging **Micklegate Bar Museum** (daily 9am–5pm; £2.50) tells the story by way of old lithographs, paintings and the odd gruesome skull.

Exhibition Square, Art Gallery and Yorkshire Museum

Exhibition Square, outside Bootham Bar, is the site of the refurbished **York Art Gallery** (daily 10am–5pm; free; Ⓦ www.york.art.museum), housing an extensive collection of early Italian, British and northern European paintings. The gallery puts on a year-round series of special exhibitions and events, and is noted for its collections of British studio pottery – particularly that of Bernard Leach – and twentieth-century British painters.

South of Exhibition Square on Museum Street stands the entrance to the **Yorkshire Museum** (daily 10am–5pm; £4; Ⓦ www.york.yorkshire.museum), which lies within the beautifully laid-out grounds of ruined **St Mary's Abbey**. It's one of York's better museums, with changing temporary exhibitions aimed largely at families, but otherwise strong on archeological remains which it presents in a series of rooms examining the Roman presence in the city. There are impressive displays of Viking and Anglo-Saxon artefacts, too, though chief exhibit is the fifteenth-century Middleham Jewel, found in 1985 – a diamond-shaped jewel with an oblong sapphire, acclaimed as the finest piece of Gothic jewellery in England.

Stonegate and the Shambles

The two most photographed streets in York lie south of the Minster. **Stonegate** is as ancient as the city itself. Originally the Via Praetoria of Roman York, it's now paved with thick flags of York stone, which were once carried along here to build the Minster, hence the street name. Its Tudor buildings and appurtenances retain their considerable charm – **Ye Olde Starre** at no.

40, one of York's original inns, is on every tourist itinerary (you can't miss the sign straddling the street). Look up at the shop under the inn sign for the little **red devil** – the medieval sign for a printer's premises. Step through another alley known as Coffee Yard (by the *Old Starre*) to find **Barley Hall** (Tues–Sun 10am/noon–4pm; £3.50; ⓦwww.barleyhall.org.uk), a fine restoration of a late-medieval townhouse where you can learn about fifteenth-century life by playing period games and trying on costumes.

The Shambles meanwhile, further to the south, could be taken as the epitome of medieval York. Flagstoned, almost impossibly narrow and lined with perilously leaning timber-framed houses, it was the home of York's butchers (the word "shambles" derives from the Old English for slaughterhouse), its erst-while stench and squalor now difficult to imagine, though old meat-hooks still adorn the odd house. **Newgate market** (daily 8am–5pm) lies off the Shambles, together with the core of the city's shopping streets; **Parliament Street** sees a couple of outdoor markets a year, usually in high summer and a month before Christmas.

Jorvik

The city's blockbuster historic exhibit is **Jorvik** (daily 10am–4/5pm; £7.45; ⓣ01904/543403, ⓦwww.vikingjorvik.com), located by the Coppergate shopping centre; you can avoid queuing by pre-booking your entrance ticket (though a surcharge applies). This multi-million-pound affair propels visitors in "time capsules" on a ride through the tenth-century city of York, presenting the sights, sounds and even the smells of a riverside Viking city. Most of the sites (blacksmiths' to bedrooms) and artefacts (leather shoes to wooden combs) were discovered during the 1976 excavations of Coppergate's real Viking settlement, and Jorvik shows how the artefacts were used, complete with live-action market and domestic scenes on actual Viking-age streets.

Where Jorvik shows what was unearthed at Coppergate, the associated attrac-tion that is **Dig!** (daily from 10am, last admission 3.30pm; £4.50, joint ticket with Jorvik £10.20, pre-booking advised) illustrates the science involved. Housed five minutes' walk away from Jorvik, in the medieval church of St Saviour, on St Savioursgate, a simulated dig allows you to take part in a range of excavations in the company of archeologists, using authentic tools and methods.

York Castle and the Castle Museum

Despite the rich architectural heritage elsewhere in the city, there's precious little left of **York Castle**, one of two established by William the Conqueror. Only the perilously leaning **Clifford's Tower** (daily 10am–4/6pm; £2.80; EH) remains, a stark and isolated stone keep built on one of William's mottes between 1245 and 1262. Immediately east of the tower lies the outstanding **Castle Museum** (daily 9.30am–5pm; £6.50; ⓦwww.york.castle.museum), whose extraordinary collection of early craft, folk and agricultural ephemera is complemented by costumes, toys, machinery, domestic implements and show workshops, plus exhibitions on subjects as diverse as swimming costumes through the ages and fire engines. Two entire reconstructed Victorian and Edwardian streets are highlights, though the extensive military displays and rambling dungeons are well worth seeing, too.

The National Railway Museum

The **National Railway Museum** (daily 10am–6pm; free; ⓦwww.nrm.org .uk), ten minutes' walk (600yd) from the station, is a must if you have even the slightest interest in railways, history, engineering or Victoriana – allow at least two hours, though you could spend all day. The Great Hall alone features some fifty restored locomotives dating from 1829 onwards, while the museum also has the world's most famous locomotive, the **Flying Scotsman**, which you can ride on various summer specials (days and departures vary; book at the museum or call ℡0870/421 4472; from £20). The Station Hall, a former goods station, complete with tracks and platforms, holds the major permanent exhibitions, while a separate wing, "The Works", provides access to the engineering workshop where conservation work is undertaken.

Eating and drinking

In keeping with much else in the city, many establishments are self-consciously old-fashioned, though there are some real highlights – truly historic pubs, the ultimate teashop experience that is *Betty's*, and a scattering of well-regarded restaurants.

Tearooms, cafés and café-bars

Betty's 6–8 St Helen's Square ℡01904/659142. If there are tearooms in heaven they'll be like *Betty's*. Tea, cakes and pastries are the stock in trade, with pikelets and Yorkshire fat rascals to name just a couple of specials. Open daily until 9pm.

Blake Head Vegetarian Café 104 Micklegate ℡01904/330208. Inexpensive bookstore-café for freshly baked cakes, pâtés, quiche, brunch, salads and soups. Closes at 5pm.

Café Concerto 21 High Petergate ℡01904/610478. Independent bistro with a good reputation and a relaxed atmosphere. Daily until 10pm.

Melton's Too 25 Walmgate ℡01904/629222. York's best café-bar – coffee, superior tapas, pasta, Thai green curries (a house speciality), salads, steaks and more. The food's very tasty and you're never rushed.

Restaurants

Blue Bicycle 34 Fossgate ℡01904/673990. York's favourite gourmet experience, with a seasonally changing menu that doesn't shy away from innovation. Reservations advised. Expensive.

Happy Valley 70 Goodramgate ℡01904/654745. The Asian tourists who eat here are delighted to find somewhere serving huge bowls of noodle soup, homestyle tofu dishes, pickled cabbage and more. Most dishes are £5–8, and there's a bargain set lunch. Closed Tues. Inexpensive.

Siam House 63a Goodramgate ℡01904/624677. This prettily furnished Thai restaurant rarely disappoints – the large menu caters for most tastes, and lunch is good value. Closed Sun lunch. Moderate.

Tasting Room 13 Swinegate Court East, off Grape Lane ℡01904/627879. The city's sunniest courtyard makes a great lunch destination (superior omelettes, pasta, salads etc); at dinner, the Modern British menu offers plenty of choice. Expensive.

Vanilla Black 26 Swinegate ℡01904/676750. Sophisticated vegetarian dining in a handsome restaurant. Expensive.

Pubs

Black Swan Peasholme Green. York's oldest (sixteenth-century) pub has some superb flagstones and wood panelling. It's also home of the city's folk club (℡01904/632922, ⓦ www.bsfc.org.uk).

Blue Bell Fossgate. A no-frills traditional pub – real ales, no mobile phones, non-tourist clientele – serving proper tapas (until 8.30pm, not Wed/Sat nights, not Sun) and Spanish Riojas by the glass.

King's Arms King's Staithe. Close to the Ouse Bridge, the riverside setting with outdoor tables makes it very busy in summer.

Three-Legged Mare 15 High Petergate. York Brewery's cosy outlet for its own quality beer and definitely a pub for grown-ups – no juke box, no video games and no kids.

Nightlife, culture and entertainment

For **what's on** listings see the local *Evening Press*. Useful websites include ⓦ www.thisisyork.co.uk, ⓦ www.whatsonyork.com and ⓦ www.goodeveningyork, while ⓦ www.yorkfestivals.com gives the lowdown on the annual festivals and events. Major annual events include York's **Viking Festival** (ⓦ www.viking jorvik.com) every February, and the **Early Music Festival** (℡01904/658338,

ⓦwww.ncem.co.uk), held in July, with dozens of events spread over ten days. There are also noteworthy **Roman** (September) and **Christmas** (December) festivals, while the **comedy festival** (October; ⓦwww.yorkcomedy.com) is growing in stature each year.

Venues

City Screen 13–17 Coney St ☏01904/541155, ⓦwww.picturehouses.co.uk. The city's independent cinema is the art-house choice, with three screens and a riverside café-bar.
Fibbers Stonebow House, Stonebow ☏01904/466148, ⓦwww.fibbers.co.uk. Indie, guitar-pop and tribute bands play most

nights of the week. Club nights and a café-bar too.
Grand Opera House Cumberland Street, at Clifford Street ☏01904/671818. Musicals, ballet, pop gigs and family entertainment in all its guises.
Theatre Royal St Leonard's Place ☏01904/623568, ⓦwww.yorktheatreroyal.co.uk. Musicals, pantos and mainstream theatre.

Listings

Bike rental Bob Trotter, 13–15 Lord Mayor's Walk, at Monkgate ☏01904/622868. Rates from £12 per day, £60 per week, plus a deposit. The Bus Info Centre (see below) has a free city-cycle map.
Bookshops York has almost as many secondhand/ antiquarian bookshops as tour guides. Favourites include Worm Holes, 20 Bootham, and the Minster Gate Bookshop, Minster Gate, off High Petergate.
Bus information The Bus Info Centre, 20 George Hudson St (office Mon–Fri 8.30am–5pm; telephone enquiries Mon–Sat 8am–8pm, Sun 8am–2pm; ☏01904/551400), can advise about all local and regional transport information.
Car rental Avis ☏01904/610460; Budget ☏01904/644919; Europcar ☏01904/656161; Hertz ☏01904/612586; Practical ☏01904/624277.

Hospital York District Hospital, Wigginton Road (24hr emergency number ☏01904/631313); bus #1, #2 or #3. The NHS Walk-in Centre, 31 Monkgate (daily 7am–10pm), offers care, advice and treatment without an appointment.
Internet Internet cafés come and go in York; the most reliable place is the City Library, off Museum Street (Mon–Wed & Fri 9am–8pm, Thurs 9am–5.30pm, Sat 9am–4pm).
Laundry Walmgate Bar Laundromat, 39 Huby Court ☏01904/628588.
Pharmacy Boots, Coney Street ☏01904/653657.
Police Fulford Road ☏01904/631321.
Post office 22 Lendal.
Taxis Ranks at Rougier Street, Duncombe Place, Exhibition Square, and the train station; or call Station Taxis ☏01904/623332.

Castle Howard

Immersed in the deep countryside of the Howardian Hills, fifteen miles northeast of York off the A64, **Castle Howard** (mid-Feb to Oct daily 11am–5pm; gardens open at 10am; £9.50; grounds only £6.50; ⓦwww.castlehoward .co.uk) is the seat of one of England's leading aristocratic families and among the country's grandest stately homes. It's a pricey visit, but there's no question that it's worth seeing, the grounds especially, and you could easily spend the best part of a day here. The summer Moorsbus (see p.623) comes here from Helmsley, while Yorkshire Coastliner buses run from York, Malton or Pickering – call Traveline (☏0870/608 2608) to check schedules, or take a bus tour from York.

The colossal main house was designed by **Sir John Vanbrugh** in 1699 and was almost forty years in the making – remarkable enough, even were it not for the fact that Vanbrugh was, at the start of the commission at least, best known as a playwright. He had no formal architectural training and seems to have been chosen by Charles Howard, third Earl of Carlisle, for whom the house was built, purely on the strength of his membership of the same

London gentlemen's club. Shrewdly, Vanbrugh recognized his limitations and called upon the assistance of Nicholas Hawksmoor, who had a major part in the house's structural design – the pair later worked successfully together on Blenheim Palace. If Hawksmoor's guiding hand can be seen throughout, Vanbrugh's influence is clear in the very theatricality of the building, notably in the palatial **Great Hall**. This was gutted by fire in the 1940s, but has subsequently been restored from old etchings and photographs to something approaching its original state. Vanbrugh also turned his attention to the estate's thousand-acre **grounds**, where he could indulge his playful inclinations – the formal gardens, clipped parkland, towers, obelisks and blunt sandstone follies stretch in all directions, sloping gently to two artificial lakes. The whole is a charming artifice of grand, manicured views – an example of what three centuries, skilled gardeners and pots of money can produce.

Daily outdoor **tours** (call for times; free) concentrate on aspects of the house and garden, and there's a full programme of events and childrens' activities. The annual outdoor Proms concert every August is also popular. There are **cafés** in the main house and by the larger lake, though the courtyard café at the main entrance has the nicest food.

Hull

HULL – officially Kingston upon Hull – has a maritime pre-eminence that dates back to 1299, when it was laid out as a seaport by Edward I. It quickly became England's leading harbour, and was still a vital garrison when the gates were closed against Charles I in 1642, the first serious act of rebellion of what was to become the English Civil War. Fishing and seafaring have always been important here, and today's city maintains a firm grip on its heritage while bolstering its attractions for visitors – the dramatic aquarium known as The Deep joins a superior set of free local museums that provide scope for a couple of days' worth of sightseeing. The former **High Street** has been designated an "Old Town" conservation area thanks to its crop of former merchants' houses and narrow cobbled alleys. The street now harbours a **Museums Quarter** (all attractions Mon–Sat 10am–5pm, Sun 1.30–4.30pm; free), starting at its northern end with **Wilberforce House**, the former home of William Wilberforce and containing some fascinating exhibits on slavery and its abolition. Next door is **Streetlife**, centred on a 1930s street scene of reconstructed shops, railway goods yard, and cycle and motor works. This is as much about social as transport history, with the smells of a nineteenth-century coaching yard, recorded conversations on a Hull tram, or the rules of bicycle polo vying for your attention. If this is good, then the adjoining **Hull and East Riding Museum** is even better. A life-sized mammoth and a walk-through Iron Age village set you up for the showpiece attractions, namely vivid displays of Celtic burials, medieval battles and spectacular Roman mosaics retrieved from the East Yorkshire countryside.

Protruding from a promontory overlooking the River Humber looms **The Deep** (daily 10am–6pm, last entry 5pm; £7.50; Ⓦ www.thedeep.co.uk), ten minutes' walk from the old town. Its educational displays and videos wrap around an immense thirty-foot-deep, 2.3-million-gallon viewing tank filled with sharks, rays, octopuses and any number of other deep-sea denizens. Finally, from the pier off Nelson Street, opposite the *Minerva* pub, **speed-boat trips** (Ⓣ 07815/629367, Ⓦ www.humberparascending.co.uk) whisk you along the

Humber to the docks or under the Humber Bridge on a variety of tours (£3–15 per person). Departures are every weekend, bank holiday and school holiday weekday, though it's best to call first.

Practicalities

The **train station** is on the west side of town, on the main drag of Ferensway, with the **bus station** just to the north. The main **tourist office** is on Paragon Street at Queen Victoria Square (Mon–Sat 10am–5pm, Sun 11am–3pm; ☎01482/223559, ⓦwww.hullcc.gov.uk/visithull), where you can find out about the major annual **festivals**, notably the colossal travelling funfair that is the Hull Fair (October), the Hull Literature Festival (June; ⓦwww.humbermouth.org.uk) and the Hull Jazz Festival (August). The tourist office can also help with **accommodation** and organize special weekend hotel rates (from around £25 per person per night). Hull has dozens of city-centre **pubs and café-bars**, the best of which are picked out in a "Hull Ale Trail" leaflet available from the tourist office. Meanwhile, the excellent **Hull Truck Theatre Company** (☎01482/323638, ⓦwww.hulltruck.co.uk) is where, among others, many of the plays of award-winning John Godber first see light of day.

Accommodation

Clyde House Hotel 13 John St ☎01482/214981, ⓦwww.clydehousehotel.co.uk. Cheap-and-cheerful digs offering no-frills accommodation at budget prices, plus resident parrot. **②**

Holiday Inn Hull Marina Castle Street ☎0870/400 9043, ⓦwww.holiday-inn.co.uk. The trim, pleasant rooms at the city's best central hotel overlook the marina. Good buffet breakfast served. **⑤**

Kingston Theatre Hotel 1–2 Kingston Square ☎01482/225828, ⓦwww.kingstontheatrehotel.com. Good-value hotel rooms on the city's prettiest square, across from Hull New Theatre. **④**, suites **⑤**

Cafés and restaurants

Blueberry 4 Trinity House Lane. Stylish licensed café above a sandwich shop. Daytime only, though closes 7pm Wed–Fri. Inexpensive.

Mimosa 406–408 Beverley Rd ☎01482/474748. Friendly Turkish restaurant with an open charcoal grill. Regular buses run the mile and a half up Beverley Road from the stations. Moderate.

Pave Café-Bar 16–20 Princes Ave ☎01482/333181. The best of the Pearson Park options is a contemporary watering-hole with some outdoor tables. Moderate.

Taman Ria Tropicana 45–47 Princes Ave ☎01482/345640. Sort out your *rendang* from your *laksa* at this agreeable, authentic Malaysian/Indonesian restaurant. Closed Mon. Moderate.

Pubs

George The Land of Green Ginger. Venerable pub found on Hull's most curiously named street – and featuring, if you can find it, England's smallest window.

Sailmakers' Arms Chandlers Court, High Street. The roaming landlord has filled the courtyard with statues, foliage and giant insects – not to mention a colony of scuttling chipmunks. Yes, chipmunks.

Ye Olde White Harte 25 Silver St. Has a very pleasant courtyard beer garden and a history going back to the seventeenth century.

Beverley

BEVERLEY, nine miles north of Hull, ranks as one of northern England's premier towns, its tangle of old streets, cobbled lanes and elegant Georgian and Victorian terraces the very picture of a traditional market town. Approaches are dominated by the twin towers of **Beverley Minster** (Mon–Sat 9am–4/5pm, plus Sun year-round, depending on services, but usually noon–4.30pm; donation requested; ⓦwww.beverleyminster.co.uk), visible for miles across the surrounding flatlands. Initiated as a modest chapel, the minster became a monastery under John of Beverley. Trained at Whitby and later ordained bishop of York, he was buried here in 721 and canonized in 1037 – his body lies under the crossing at the top of the nave. The collapse of the central tower in 1213 paved the way for two centuries of rebuilding, funded by bequests from pilgrims paying homage to the saint, and the result was one of the finest Gothic creations in the country. The west front, which crowned the work in 1420, is widely considered without equal, its survival due in large part to Baroque architect Nicholas Hawksmoor, who restored much of the church in the eighteenth century. Similar outstanding work awaits in the interior, most notably the fourteenth-century **Percy Tomb**, its sumptuously carved canopy one of the masterpieces of medieval European ecclesiastical art. Other incidental carving throughout the church is magnificent, particularly the 68 misericords of the oak **choir** (1520–24), one of the largest and most accomplished in England. Beverley had a renowned guild of itinerant minstrels, which provided funds in the sixteenth century for the carvings on the transept aisle capitals, where you'll be able to pick out players of lutes, bagpipes, horns and tambourines.

Beverley's **train station** is beside Station Square, just a couple of minutes' walk from the minster. The **bus station** is at the junction of Walkergate and Sow Hill Road, with the main street just a minute's walk away. The **tourist office** is at 34 Butcher Row in the main shopping area (Mon–Fri 9.30am–5.15pm, Sat 10am–4.45pm, plus Sun 11am–3pm in July & Aug; ☏01482/391672, ⓦwww.visiteastyorkshire.com); ask here about guided walks of the town. There's plenty of local **accommodation**, including *Number One*, 1 Woodlands (☏01482/862752, ⓦwww.number-one-bedandbreakfast-beverley.co.uk; no credit cards; ❷), a small B&B in a quiet Victorian house two minutes' walk from the market place. The YHA **hostel** (☏0870/770 5696, Ⓔbeverleyfriary@yha .org.uk; £11.95; closed Nov–Easter, and closed Sun & Mon) occupies one of the town's finer buildings, a restored Dominican friary that was mentioned in the *Canterbury Tales*. It's located in Friar's Lane, off Eastgate, just a hundred yards southeast of the minster.

The East Yorkshire coast

The **East Yorkshire coast** curves south in a gentle arc from the mighty cliffs of Flamborough Head to Spurn Head, a hook-shaped sand and pebble promontory formed by the constant erosion and shifting currents. Between the two points lie a handful of tranquil villages and miles of windswept beach, accessible to anyone prepared to cycle or walk the paths and lanes that fan out amidst the dunes. The main resort, Bridlington, is linked by the regular **train** service between Hull and Scarborough. There's also an hourly bus service between Bridlington and Scarborough, while the seasonal Sunday **Spurn Ranger** service (Easter–Oct; ☏01482/222222) gives access to the isolated Spurn Head coastline.

The southernmost resort on the Yorkshire coast, **BRIDLINGTON** has maintained its harbour for almost a thousand years. The seafront promenade looks down upon the town's best asset – its sweeping sandy beach. It's an out-and-out family resort, which means candy-floss, amusement arcades, boat trips and fish and chips eaten on the milling harbourfront. The historic core of town is actually a mile inland, where the **Bayle Museum**, in largely Georgian Bridlington Old Town (May–Sept Mon–Fri 10am–4pm, Sun 11am–4pm; £2), presents local history in a building that once served as the gateway to a fourteenth-century priory. The Old Town's High Street is a narrow thoroughfare of antique shops and traditional stores – the *Georgian Tea Rooms* at no. 56 has several floors of antiques and a tea garden at the rear.

Around fourteen miles of precipitous four-hundred-foot cliffs gird **Flamborough Head**, just to the northeast of Bridlington. From **Bempton**, two miles north of Bridlington, you can either follow the path all the way round to Flamborough Head or visit the RSPB sanctuary at **Bempton Cliffs**. It's the only mainland gannetry in England and you'll see gannets diving from fifty feet in the air to catch mackerel and herring. Bempton also boasts England's second-largest puffin colony, with several thousand returning to the cliffs between March and August, having spent the winter on the open seas. Late March and April is the best time to see the puffins, but the **Visitor Centre** (daily 9.30am/10am–4/5pm; ☎01262/851179, ⓦwww.rspb.org.uk) can advise on other breeds' activities.

The North York Moors

Virtually the whole of the **North York Moors** (ⓦwww.visitthemoors .co.uk) is protected by one of the country's finest national parks. On the heather-covered, flat-topped hills, the views stretch for miles, interrupted only by cultivated forests, the battered stone crosses of the first Christian inhabitants and the ruins of great monastic houses such as Rievaulx Abbey. The steam trains of the **North York Moors Railway** run between Pickering and Grosmont, where you can connect with trains on the **Esk Valley** line, running either six miles east to Whitby and the coast, or west through more remote settlements (and ultimately to Middlesbrough). The principal **bus** approaches are from Scarborough and York to the main towns of **Helmsley** and **Pickering** – pick up the free *Moors Explorer* booklet, a summary of all rail and bus routes on and around the moors, available from tourist offices and park information centres. There are also seasonal **Moorsbus** services (Easter–Oct; ☎01845/597000, ⓦwww .moors.uk.net/moorsbus), connecting Pickering and Helmsley to everywhere of interest in the National Park. Departures are several times daily in the school summer holidays, more restricted at other times (though at least every Sunday and bank holiday Monday), and get-on-get-off day tickets are £3, or £6 from certain destinations outside the park (like York, Scarborough and Hull).

Helmsley

One of the moors' most appealing towns, **HELMSLEY** makes a perfect base for visiting the western moors and Rievaulx Abbey. Local life revolves around a large cobbled market square, dominated by a monument to the second earl of Feversham, whose family was responsible for rebuilding most of the village in the nineteenth century. Signposted from the square, **Helmsley Castle** (Easter–Sept daily 10am–6pm; Oct–March Mon & Thurs–Sun 10am–4pm; £4; EH) has a visitor centre, exhibition and audio tour to fill you in on the history, while to the southwest of the town stands the Fevershams' country seat, **Duncombe Park** (May–Oct Mon–Thurs & Sun: house tours 12.30–3.30pm, garden, parkland & visitor centre 11am–5.30pm; house, gardens & parkland £6.50, gardens £3.50, parkland £2; ⓦwww.duncombepark.com), built for the Fevershams' ancestor Sir Thomas Duncombe in 1713. The lovely landscaped gardens include Britain's tallest ash and lime trees, and a brace of artfully sited temples.

The town's market cross marks the start of the 110-mile **Cleveland Way**, one of England's premier long-distance national trails, which embraces both moors and coast. The **Cleveland Way Project** (The Old Vicarage, Bondgate, Helmsley, YO6 5BP; ☏01439/770657) produces an annual accommodation guide, or consult ⓦ www.nationaltrail.co.uk. Helmsley is connected by **bus** to Pickering, Scarborough, York and Thirsk; they all stop on or near the Market Place. The **tourist office** is at the castle visitor centre (March–Oct daily 9.30am–5pm; Nov–Feb restricted hours; ☏01439/770173, ⓦ www.ryedale.gov.uk), while Helmsley's **market day** is Friday.

Accommodation and food

Crown Market Place ☏01439/770297. The best mid-range (two-star) option. Rooms are a bit worn, but comfortable, and the restaurant serves good-value lunches and evening meals. ❺

Feversham Arms 1 High St, behind the church ☏01439/770766, ⓦ www.fevershamarmshotel .com. Combines hip styling with comfort in its spacious rooms and Modern British brasserie. ❼

Helmsley YHA ☏0870/770 5860, ⓔ helmsley@yha.org.uk. East of Market Place – follow Bondgate to Carlton Road and turn left.

Open daily July & Aug, otherwise flexible opening; closed Nov–Easter. Dorm beds £13.95.

No. 54 54 Bondgate ☏01439/771533, ⓦ www.no54.co.uk. A delightful cottage-style B&B offering three superior rooms. Comfortable beds, power showers, and a sheltered terrace and garden add up to a relaxing night. ❺

Star Inn Harome, 2 miles south of the A170 ☏01439/770397, ⓦ www.thestaratharome.co.uk. A thatched pub where Michelin-rated food awaits, plus eight very nice rooms in the adjacent lodge. No food Sun eve & Mon. ❽

Rievaulx Abbey and Terrace

From Helmsley you can easily hike across country to **Rievaulx Abbey** (Easter–Sept daily 10am–6pm; Oct–March Mon & Thurs–Sun 10am–4pm; £4; EH), once one of England's greatest Cistercian abbeys. The signposted path takes around an hour and a half. Founded in 1132, the abbey became the mother church of the Cistercians in England, quickly developing to become a flourishing community with interests in fishing, mining, agriculture and the woollen industry. At its height, 140 monks and up to 500 lay brothers lived and worked at the abbey, though numbers fell dramatically once the Black Death (1348–49) had done its worst. The end came with the Dissolution, when many of the walls were razed and the roof lead stripped – the beautiful ruins, however, still suggest the abbey's former splendour.

Although they form some sort of ensemble with the abbey, there's no access between the ruins and **Rievaulx Terrace and Temples** (Easter–Oct daily 10.30am–5/6pm; £3.80; NT), a site entered from the B1257, a couple of miles northwest of Helmsley. This pleasing half-mile stretch of grass-covered terraces and woodland was laid out as part of Duncombe Park in the 1750s, and was engineered partly to enhance the views of the abbey. The resulting panorama over the ruins and the valley below is superb, and this makes a great spot for a picnic or simply for strolls along the lawns and woodland trail.

Hutton le Hole and around

Lying eight miles northeast of Helmsley, quaint **HUTTON LE HOLE** is probably the national park's biggest tourist attraction. Apart from the sheer photogenic quality of the village, the big draw is the family-oriented **Ryedale**

Folk Museum (Easter–Oct daily 10am–5.30pm; £4.50; ⓦwww.ryedalefolk museum.co.uk), an ever-expanding set of displays over a two-acre site. Special events and displays throughout the season mean there's always something going on. The museum also houses a **National Park Information Centre** (same hours as museum; ☎01751/417367), where you can buy leaflets detailing local hikes. **Accommodation** is zealously fought for – try the information centre for a list of local B&Bs, or make for *Burnley House* (☎01751/417548, ⓦwww .burnleyhouse.com; ❹), a hospitable nonsmoking Georgian house on the green with streamside garden.

A little to the northwest of Hutton le Hole the country lanes of **Farndale** are packed in spring as visitors arrive to see the area's wild daffodils – the Moorsbus runs a special "Daffodil" service every Sunday in April and over Easter. Meanwhile, trim and tidy **ROSEDALE ABBEY**, four miles northeast of Hutton le Hole, preserves only a few fragments of the Cistercian priory (1158) that gave it its name, most of them incorporated into St Lawrence's parish church. It's hard to believe now, but in the last century the village had a population of over five thousand, most employed in the ironstone workings whose remnants lie scattered all over the lonely high moors round about. The *Milburn Arms* (☎01751/417312, ⓦwww.milburnarms.co.uk; ❺; closed Jan), overlooking the small green, makes a peaceful base.

Pickering and the North Yorkshire Moors Railway

A thriving market town at the junction of the A170 and the transmoor A169 (Whitby road), **PICKERING** is visited mainly as the embarkation point of the North Yorkshire Moors Railway (NYMR; see below), though you could also make time to look round its motte and bailey **castle** on the hill north of the Market Place (Easter–Sept daily 10am–6pm; Oct Mon & Thurs–Sun 10am–4pm; £3; EH), reputedly used by every English monarch up to 1400 as a base for hunting in nearby Blandsby Park.

Buses stop outside the library and **tourist office** on The Ropery (Easter–Oct Mon–Sat 9.30am–5pm, Sun 9.30am–4pm; Nov–Easter Mon–Sat 10am–4.30pm; ☎01751/473791, ⓦwww.ryedale.gov.uk), opposite Safeway in the centre of town; the **NYMR train station** is less than five minutes' signposted walk away. The tourist office can help with **B&Bs**, though Whitby, only twenty minutes' drive away on the coast, is the better overnight destination. A couple of the **pubs** also have rooms, top choice easily being the *White Swan*, on Market Place (☎01751/472288, ⓦwww.white-swan.co.uk; ❼), with fashionably turned out bedrooms and a restaurant serving fine Modern British food at moderate prices. **Market** day in town is Monday. The nearest YHA **hostel** is a refurbished eco-hostel at the Old School, Lockton (☎0870/770 5938, ⓔlockton@yha.org.uk; £13.95; closed Oct–Easter), five miles northeast off the A169, about two miles' cross-country walk from the NYMR station at Levisham (see below); or ask to be dropped at the turn-off by the Whitby bus.

North Yorkshire Moors Railway
The **North Yorkshire Moors Railway** (talking timetables ☎01751/473535, ⓦwww.northyorkshiremoorsrailway.com) connects Pickering with the Esk Valley (Middlesbrough–Whitby) line at Grosmont, 18 miles to the north. The line was completed by George Stephenson in 1835, just ten years after the opening of the Stockton and Darlington Railway, making it one of the

earliest lines in the country. Scheduled steam **services** operate year-round (limited weekend and school hol service Nov–Feb), and a **day-return ticket** for the whole line costs £13. Steam services also run from the end of the NYMR line at Grosmont to the nearby seaside resort of Whitby during school and bank holidays, with a return fare from Pickering of £20.

Stops along the line offer a variety of walks and attractions, including **Goath-land** (the third NYMR station), a highly attractive village set in open moor-land. If it seems oddly familiar it's because it's widely known as "Aidensfield", the fictional village at the centre of the *Heartbeat* TV series, while the station doubled as "Hogsmeade" in *Harry Potter and the Philosopher's Stone*. Outside summer weekends, when it's packed to distraction, Goathland can still be a joy to wander, with signposts pointing you to the local sight, the **Mallyan Spout**, a seventy-foot-high waterfall. This lies half a mile or so from the imposing, stone *Mallyan Spout Hotel* on the common (☎01947/896486; ❺), itself the best place to stay, and certainly the best place to eat and drink. A gentle path from Goath-land runs the mile through the fields down to **Beck Hole**, an idyllic bridgeside hamlet focused on the *Birch Hall Inn*, a rural pub still doubling as a sweet shop and store, serving great slabs of sandwiches with local ham and home-baked pies. From Beck Hole it's only another two miles south to **Grosmont**, end of the line for the NYMR train.

The North Yorkshire coast

A bracing change after the flattened seascapes of East Anglia and much of East Yorkshire, the **North Yorkshire coast** (Ⓦwww.discoveryorkshirecoast .com) is the southernmost stretch of a cliff-edged shore that reaches almost unbroken to the Scottish border. **Scarborough** is the biggest resort, though it's **Robin Hood's Bay** that is the most popular of the coastal villages. However, **Whitby**, in between the two, is the best stopover, its fine sands and resort facilities tempered by its abbey ruins, cobbled streets, Georgian buildings and maritime heritage. Hourly **buses** (fewer on Sun) run along the A171 between Scarborough and Whitby, and a similarly frequent service operates to Robin Hood's Bay. The Yorkshire Coastliner service connects Leeds and York with Scarborough or Whitby. You can also reach Scarborough direct by **train** from York or Hull, and Whitby from Middlesbrough. **Walkers** should note that two of the best parts of the Cleveland Way depart from Whitby: southeast to Robin Hood's Bay (six miles) and northwest to Staithes (eleven miles), both along thrilling high-cliff sections.

Scarborough

The oldest resort in the country, **SCARBOROUGH** first attracted early seventeenth-century visitors to its newly discovered mineral springs. Fashion-able in Victorian times – when it was "the Queen of the Watering Places" – Scarborough saw its biggest transformation after World War II, when it became a holiday haven for workers from the industrial heartlands. All the traditional ingredients of a beach resort are still here in force, from superb, clean sands, kitsch amusement arcades and Kiss-Me-Quick hats to the more refined pleasures of its tight-knit old-town streets and a genteel round of quiet parks and gardens.

There's no better place to acquaint yourself with the local layout than from the walls of **Scarborough Castle** (Easter–Sept daily 10am–6pm;

Oct–March Mon & Thurs–Sun 10am–4pm; £3.30; EH), mounted on a jutting headland between two golden-sanded bays east of the town centre. Although besieged many times, the fortifications were never taken by assault, its only fall coming in the Civil War when the Parliamentarians starved the garrison into surrender. As you leave the castle, drop into the **Church of St Mary** (1180), immediately below on Castle Road, whose graveyard contains the **tomb of Anne Brontë**, who died here in 1849. Most of what passes for family entertainment takes place on the **North Bay** – massive water slides at Atlantis, the kids' amusements at Kinderland, and the miniature North Bay Railway (daily Easter–Sept), which runs up to the Sea Life Centre, with its pools of flounders, rock-pool habitats and fishy exhibits. The **South Bay** is more refined, backed by the pleasant Valley Gardens and the Italianate meanderings of the South Cliff Gardens, and topped by an esplanade from which a **hydraulic lift** (daily 10am–4pm, till 10pm July & Aug) putters down to the beach.

Practicalities

The **train station** is at the top of town facing Westborough; **buses** pull up outside or in the surrounding streets, though the National Express services (direct from London) stop in the car park behind the station. Scarborough's **tourist office** is inside the Brunswick Shopping Centre on Westborough (daily 9.30/10am–4.30/6pm; Oct–March closed Sun; ☏01723/383637). To reach the harbour and castle, walk straight down Westborough, Newborough and Eastborough, through the main shopping streets. Open-top **seafront buses** (Easter–Sept daily from 9.30am, March Sat & Sun only; £1.50) run from the *Corner Café* in North Bay to the Spa Complex in South Bay.

Scarborough is crammed with inexpensive **hotels and guest houses**. Happy hunting grounds include North Bay's Queen's Parade, where most of the guest houses have sweeping bay views and parking. Above South Bay, hotels tend to be pricier, though there's a clutch of B&Bs along and around West Street. If you're stuck, call the tourist office's **accommodation hotline**, ☏01723/383636.

Accommodation

Crown Esplanade ☏01723/357426, ⓦwww .scarboroughhotel.com. Built in 1847 in a Regency terrace above South Bay, the *Crown* makes the most of its period features, and there's a gym, pool and brasserie. ❻

Interludes 32 Princess St ☏01723/360513, ⓦwww.interludeshotel.co.uk. Quiet, non-smoking, Georgian townhouse in the old-town streets behind the harbour. It's a gay-friendly place, though all (except children) are welcome. ❸

Riviera St Nicholas Cliff ☏01723/372277, ⓦwww.rivierahotel.scarborough.co.uk. Restored Victorian hotel with bay views and comfortable en-suite rooms. ❺

Scarborough YHA Burniston Road, Scalby Mills, 2 miles north of town ☏0870/770 6022, ⓔscarborough@yha.org.uk. Occupies a converted watermill, off the A165, 10min walk from the sea. Closed Sun & Mon in Sept & Oct, and closed Nov–Easter. Dorm beds £11.95.

Whiteley 99 Queen's Parade ☏01723/373514. Formerly a Victorian merchant's house, this is a bit chintzy but with good-value en-suite rooms (a few pounds extra for a sea view). ❸

Windmill Mill Street, off Victoria Road ☏01723/372735, ⓦwww.windmill-hotel .co.uk. Eighteenth-century windmill in the town centre with country-style en-suite rooms (upper-floor ones with veranda) ranged around a cobbled courtyard. ❺

Cafés and restaurants

Café Fish 19 York Place, at Somerset Terrace ☏01723/500301. For a more sophisticated way with fish than most Scarborough restaurants – like Thai fish cakes or Cajun-style salmon. Dinner only. Expensive.

Café Italia 36 St Nicholas Cliff ☏01723/501973. Utterly charming, microscopic Italian coffee bar, where good coffee, focaccia slices and ice cream keep a battery of regulars happy. Closes 5pm. Inexpensive.

Gianni's 13 Victoria Rd ☏01723/507388. Good-natured staff bustle up and down stairs, delivering quality pizzas, pastas and quaffable wine by the carafe. Dinner only; closed Sun & Mon. Moderate.
Golden Grid 4 Sandside ☏01723/360922. The harbourside's choicest fish-and-chip establishment, "catering to the promenader since 1883". Closed Mon–Thurs dinner in winter. Moderate.

Theatre

Stephen Joseph Theatre Westborough ☏01723/370541, ⊛www.sjt.uk.com. Housed in a former Art Deco cinema, this premieres every new play of local playwright Alan Ayckbourn and promotes strong seasons of theatre and film; a good café/restaurant (seasonally changing menu: moderate prices) and bar is open daily except Sunday.

Robin Hood's Bay

Although known as Robbyn Huddes Bay as early as Tudor times, there's nothing except half-remembered myth to link **ROBIN HOOD'S BAY** with Sherwood's legendary bowman – locals anyway prefer the old name, Bay Town or simply Bay. The best-known and most heavily visited spot on the coast, the village fully lives up to its reputation, with narrow streets and pink-tiled cottages toppling down the cliff-edge site, evoking the romance of a time when this was both a hard-bitten fishing community and smugglers' den *par excellence*. From the upper village, lined with Victorian villas, now mostly B&Bs, it's a very steep walk down the hill to the harbour. Here, Bay is little more than a couple of narrow streets lined with gift shops and cafés, and a slipway that leads down to the curving, rocky shoreline. The **Old Coastguard Station** (June–Sept daily 10am–5pm; Oct–May Sat & Sun and school hols only; free; ☏01947/885900) has been turned into a visitor centre with displays relating to the area's geology and sealife. When the tide is out, the massive rock beds below are exposed, split by a geological fault line and studded with fossil remains. There's an easy circular walk (2.5 miles) to **Boggle Hole** and its YHA hostel, a mile south, returning inland via the path along the old Scarborough–Whitby railway line.

Buses from Scarborough or Whitby, seven miles north, drop you at the top of the village. Whitby has the nearest train station and tourist office; Cleveland Way walkers can make Whitby to Robin Hood's Bay in around three hours. Many people see the village as a day-trip from Whitby, and you can check on Bay accommodation in the tourist office there, or simply stroll the streets of the lower, old part of the village to see if any of the small cottage B&Bs have vacancies. There are also three good **pubs** in the lower village, two of which have rooms: the tiny *Laurel*, on Main Street (☏01947/880400; ❷; two-night minimum), whose small self-catering flat sleeps two; and the *Bay Hotel*, right on the harbour (☏01947/880278; ❸), which is the traditional start or end of the Coast-to-Coast Walk.

Boggle Hole's YHA **hostel** is one of Yorkshire's most popular, a former mill located in a wooded ravine about a mile south of Robin Hood's Bay at Mill Beck (☏0870/770 5704, ⊜bogglehole@yha.org.uk; £13.95; usually open weekends and school hols only). A couple of miles northwest of Robin Hood's Bay at Hawsker, on the A171, Trailways (☏01947/820207, ⊛www.trailways .fsnet.co.uk) is a **bike rental** outfit, with a small campsite and bunkhouse, based in the old Hawsker train station, perfectly placed for day-trips in either direction along the disused railway line. They'll deliver or pick up from local addresses, including *Boggle Hole* hostel.

Whitby

If there's one essential stop on the North Yorkshire coast it's **WHITBY**, whose historical associations, atmospheric ruins, fishing harbour and intrinsic charm make it many people's favourite northern resort. The seventh-century clifftop abbey here made Whitby one of the key foundations of the early Christian period, and a centre of great learning. Below, on the harbour banks of the River Esk, for a thousand years the local herring boats landed their catch until the great whaling boom of the eighteenth century transformed the fortunes of the town. Melville's *Moby Dick* makes much of Whitby whalers such as William Scoresby, while James Cook took his first seafaring steps from the town in 1746, on his way to becoming a national hero. All four of Captain Cook's ships of discovery – the *Endeavour, Resolution, Adventure* and *Discovery* – were built in Whitby. The town splits into two distinct halves joined by a swing bridge: the cobbled **old town** to the east, and the newer (though mostly eighteenth- and nineteenth-century) town across the bridge, generally known as **West Cliff**.

Cobbled **Church Street** is the old town's main thoroughfare, barely changed in aspect since the eighteenth century, though now lined with tearooms and gift shops. Parallel **Sandgate** has more of the same, the two streets meeting at the small marketplace where souvenirs and trinkets are sold; there's a farmer's market here every Thursday. Whitby, understandably, likes to make a fuss of Captain Cook who served an apprenticeship here from 1746–49 under John Walker, a Quaker shipowner. The **Captain Cook Memorial Museum** (March–Oct daily 9.45am–3pm; £3; ⓦwww.cookmuseumwhitby.co.uk), housed in Walker's rickety old house in Grape Lane (on the east side of the swing bridge), contains an impressive amount of memorabilia, including ships' models, letters and paintings by artists seconded to Cook's voyages.

At the end of Church Street, you climb the famous **199 steps** of the Church Stairs – now paved, but originally a wide wooden staircase built for pallbearers carrying coffins to the church of St Mary above. The cliff-top ruins of **Whitby Abbey** (Easter–Oct 10am–5/6pm; Nov–Easter Mon & Thurs–Sun 10am–4pm; £4; EH), beyond St Mary's, are some of the most evocative in England, the nave, soaring north transept and lancets of the east end giving a hint of the building's former delicacy and splendour. Its monastery was founded in 657 by St Hilda of Hartlepool, daughter of King Oswy of Northumberland, and by 664 had become important enough to host the **Synod of Whitby**, an event of seminal importance in the development of English Christianity. It settled once and for all the question of determining the date of Easter, and adopted the rites and authority of the Roman rather than the Celtic Church. **Caedmon**, one of the brothers at the abbey during its earliest years, has a twenty-foot cross to his memory which stands in front of St Mary's, at the top of the steps. His nine-line *Song of Creation* is the earliest surviving poem in English, making the abbey not only the cradle of English Christianity, but also the birthplace of English literature. You'll discover all this and more in the **Visitor Centre** (hours as above), housed in the shell of the adjacent mansion, built after the Dissolution using material from the plundered abbey.

Practicalities

Trains arrive at Station Square, a couple of hundred yards south of the bridge to the old town. Special school- and bank-holiday steam train services also stop here, departing from the NYMR station at Grosmont (see p.626). Most local buses leave from the adjacent **bus station**, though the Yorkshire Coastliner services (from Leeds, York and Pickering) and National Express buses (from London and York) sometimes stop around the corner on Langborne Road. Whitby's **tourist office** (daily: May–Sept 9.30am–6pm; Oct–April 10am–12.30pm & 1–4.30pm; ☎01723/383637) is on the corner of Langborne Road and New Quay Road.

The main **B&B** concentrations are on West Cliff, in the streets stretching back from the elegant Royal Crescent. For superior **holiday cottages** in town, contact Shoreline Cottages (☎0113/244 8410, Ⓦwww.shoreline-cottages .com). First festival of the year is the **Moor and Coast** (Ⓦwww.moorandcoast .co.uk), a weekend of traditional music, song and dance over the May bank holiday, though this is eclipsed by the annual **Whitby Folk Week** (Ⓦwww .folkwhitby.freeserve.co.uk) in August (the week immediately preceding the bank holiday). Best place to find out more is at *The Port Hole*, 16 Skinner St (☎01947/603475), a fair-trade craft shop that's also the HQ of local collective **Musicport** (Ⓦwww.musicport.fsnet.co.uk), who hosts the town's renowned annual **World Music Festival** (October).

Accommodation

Estbek House Sandsend ☎01947/893424, Ⓦwww.estbekhouse.co.uk. Georgian house, 2 miles from Whitby and just yards from the beach. Four pretty double/twin rooms, plus a relaxed fish and seafood restaurant (expensive; reservations recommended). ❺

Harbour Grange Spital Bridge, Church Street ☎01947/600817, Ⓦwww.whitbybackpackers .co.uk. Nonsmoking backpackers' hostel on the eastern side of the river with 24 beds in five small dorms (£10–11, plus £1 for bedding if required).

Number Five 5 Havelock Place ☎01947/606361. Amiable West Cliff B&B that provides a good breakfast (veggie options available). No credit cards. ❷

Shepherd's Purse 95 Church St ☎01947/820228. Popular wholefood shop and restaurant with its best rooms (with brass bedsteads and pine furniture) set around a galleried courtyard. ❸

Union Place 9 Upgang Lane ☎01947/605501, Ⓔj_d_pottas@hotmail.com. Genial B&B in an artistically restored Georgian house, with two spacious double rooms, sharing a luxurious bathroom. Breakfast is locally sourced, kedgeree to smoked salmon. No credit cards. ❷

White Horse & Griffin 87 Church St ☎01947/604857, Ⓦwww.whitehorse andgriffin.co.uk. A welcoming eighteenth-century coaching inn with stylishly decorated en-suite rooms, and a good bistro. ❹

Whitby YHA East Cliff ☎0870/770 6088, Ⓔwhitby@yha.org.uk. A stone's throw from the abbey, with superb views over the town – book well in advance. Open weekends only Nov–March. Dorm beds £11.95.

White Linen 24 Bagdale ☎01947/603635, Ⓦwww.whitelinenguesthouse.co.uk. Superior B&B, with garden at the front, courtyard out back. ❺

Café-bars and restaurants

Finley's 22 Flowergate ☎01947/606660. Easygoing café-bar with deep sofas, dishing up gourmet sandwiches, *nachos*, pasta, fish cakes and the like. Moderate.

Grapevine 2 Grape Lane 01947/820275. The tables are crammed into this funky little tapas place, and it's best to book for dinner. Moderate.

 Greens 13 Bridge St 01947/600284. Whitby's finest restaurant has a daily changing menu of local produce – fish to game. Dinner only (reservations essential), plus Fri, Sat & Sun lunch. Expensive.

 Magpie Café 14 Pier Rd 01947/602058. The traditional fish-and-chip choice in town

for over forty years. In summer you'll have to queue to get through the door. Closes 9pm. Moderate.

Pubs

Duke of York Church Street. Classic Whitby pub, at the bottom of the 199 steps, with harbour views, good-value food and occasional music.

Tap & Spile New Quay Road. The town's real-ale haunt, with a changing selection of guest beers and live music nearly every night.

Travel details

Buses

Details of minor and seasonal local bus services are frequently given in the text. It's essential to pick up either the Dales Explorer or Moors Explorer timetable booklets from a local tourist office if visiting those parts of the county. For details of the Moorsbus in the North York Moors National Park, see p.623. For information on all other local and national bus services, contact Traveline 0870/608 2608 (daily 7am–9pm), www .traveline.org.uk.

Harrogate to: Knaresborough (every 10min; 15min); Leeds (every 30–60min; 40min); York (hourly; 1hr 15min).

Helmsley to: Pickering (hourly; 40min); Scarborough (hourly; 1hr 30min); York (3 daily; 1hr 30min).

Pickering to: Helmsley (3–7 daily; 40min); Scarborough (hourly; 1hr); Whitby (5 daily; 1hr); York (hourly; 1hr 20min)

Scarborough to: Bridlington (hourly; 1hr 15min); Helmsley (hourly; 1hr 30min); Hull (1 daily; 2hr); Leeds (hourly; 3hr); Pickering (hourly; 1hr); Robin Hood's Bay (hourly; 45min); Whitby (hourly; 1hr); York (hourly; 1hr 45min).

Skipton to: Grassington (Mon–Sat hourly; 30min); Malham (4 daily; 35min); Settle (Mon–Sat hourly; 40min).

Whitby to: Robin Hood's Bay (hourly; 25min); York (4–5 daily; 2hr).

York to: Beverley (4 daily; 1hr 15min); Harrogate (hourly; 1hr 15min); Hull (5 daily; 1hr 30min); Pickering (hourly; 1hr 15min); Whitby (4–5 daily; 2hr).

Trains

Harrogate to: Knaresborough (every 30min; 15min); Leeds (every 30min; 45min); York (hourly; 30min).

Hull to: Beverley (Mon–Sat hourly, Sun 4 daily; 15min); Leeds (hourly; 1hr); London (3–4 daily; 2hr 45min); Scarborough (every 2hr; 1hr 30min); York (10 daily; 1hr 15min).

Leeds to: Bradford (every 15min; 20min); Harrogate (every 30min; 45min); Hull (hourly; 1hr); Lancaster (3 daily; 2hr); Liverpool (hourly; 2hr); London (every 30min; 2hr); Manchester (every 30min; 35min); Scarborough (every 30–60min; 1hr 15min); Settle (3–8 daily; 1hr); Sheffield (every 30min; 45min–1hr 15min); Skipton (hourly; 40min); York (every 30min; 40min).

Pickering to: Grosmont (April–Oct 5–8 daily, plus limited winter service; 1hr).

Scarborough to: Hull (every 2hr; 1hr 30min); Leeds (every 30–60min; 1hr 15min); York (every 30–60min; 45min).

Sheffield to: Leeds (every 30min; 45min–1hr 15min); London (every 45min; 2hr 30min); York (hourly; 1hr 20min).

Whitby to: Grosmont (4–5 daily; 15min); Middlesbrough (4–5 daily; 1hr 30min).

York to: Bradford (every 45min; 1hr); Durham (every 30min; 40min); Harrogate (hourly; 30min); Hull (hourly; 1hr 15min); Leeds (every 30min; 40min); London (every 30min; 2hr); Manchester (hourly; 1hr 45min); Newcastle (every 30min; 1hr); Scarborough (every 30–60min; 45min); Sheffield (hourly; 1hr 20min).

YORKSHIRE | Travel details

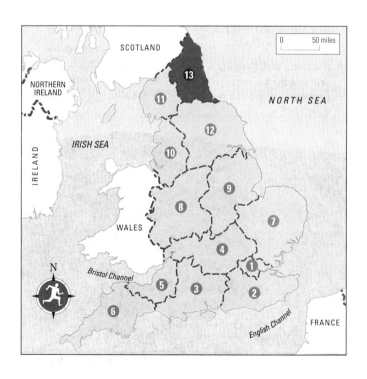

13

The Northeast

CHAPTER 13

Highlights

* **Beamish Museum** The Northeast's industrial past poignantly re-created. **See p.643**

* **Killhope Lead Mining Museum** An excellent family day out – put the kids to work down t'pit. **See p.646**

* **Newcastle nightlife** Lock up your inhibitions, leave your coat at home and hit the Toon. **See p.655**

* **Hadrian's Wall Path** Put your walking boots on to make the most of this extraordinary monument. **See p.659**

* **Chillingham Wild Cattle** Don't get too close – this herd of cows has been seeing off intruders for over 800 years. **See p.665**

* **Seabirds cruise, Farne Islands** Visit the puffins and grey seals on this windswept archipelago off the Northumberland coast. **See p.669**

* **Holy Island** Cradle of early Christianity, with a brooding, isolated atmosphere. **See p.670**

△ Hadrian's Wall

The Northeast

ngland's **northeast** (principally the counties of Durham and North-umberland) contains some of the country's biggest historic and natural attractions. In many ways a land apart from the rest of England – more remote, less affluent, its accents often impenetrable to outsiders – it also has the very stuff of English history etched across its landscapes. Romans, Vikings and Normans all left dramatic evidence of their colonization, while the Industrial Revolution exploited to the limit the Northeast's natural resources and its people. The essential sights start with one of England's most evocative ruins – Hadrian's Wall, built by the **Romans** between the North Sea and the west coast to contain the troublesome tribes of the far north. When the Romans departed, the Northeast was divided into unstable Saxon principalities until order was restored by the kings of Northumbria, who dominated the region from 600 until the 870s. It was they who nourished the region's early Christian tradition, which achieved its finest flowering with the creation of the **Lindisfarne Gospels** on what is now known as Holy Island. The monks abandoned their island at the end of the ninth century, in advance of the Vikings' destruction of the Northumbrian kingdom, and only after the Norman Conquest did the Northeast again become part of a greater England.

Long after the Northeast had ceased to be a critical military zone, its character and appearance were transformed by the **Industrial Revolution**. Towards the end of the eighteenth century two main coalfields were established – one dominating County Durham from the Pennines to the sea, the other stretching north along the Northumberland coast from the Tyne. The **world's first railway**, the Darlington and Stockton line, was opened in 1825 to move coal to the nearest port for export, while local coal and ore also fuelled the foundries that supplied the shipbuilding and heavy-engineering companies of Tyneside.

Most tourists dodge the industrial areas, bypassing the towns along the Tees Valley – Darlington, Stockton, Middlesbrough and Hartlepool – on the way to **Durham**, a handsome university-city dominated by Durham Cathedral. From Durham it's a short hop to **Newcastle upon Tyne**, distinguished by some fine Victorian buildings, the revitalized Quayside, and a vibrant cultural scene and nightlife. North, past the old colliery villages, the **Northumberland coast** boasts some superb castles – most impressively at Warkworth, Dunstanburgh and Bamburgh – as well as a string of dune-backed beaches, and a handful of offshore islands. **Holy Island** is the best known, and the only one you can stay the night on, though the **Farne Islands** nature reserve makes a great day-trip from the small resort of Seahouses. **Alnwick**, four miles inland from the sea, features another stunning castle and northern England's finest new garden, while the extravagant ramparts of **Berwick-upon-Tweed** signal the imminence of the

THE NORTHEAST

0   10 miles

N

NORTH SEA

▲ Edinburgh

Berwick-upon-Tweed

Holy Island

Waren Mill

Bamburgh

Farne Islands

Seahouses

Beadnell

Newton-by-the-Sea

Embleton

Dunstanburgh Castle

Craster

Belford

Beal

A1

B6525

Chillingham Castle

Wooler

A697

Alnmouth

Alnwick

A1

Warkworth

Amble

Ashington

A189

Blyth

Cragside

Brinkburn Priory

A697

Rothbury

Morpeth

Bellingham

A1

Belsay

NORTHUMBERLAND

Cambo

Wallington

A696

Etal Castle

Ford

Branxton

B6354

Cornhill-on-Tweed

A698

Norham Castle

Coldstream

A697

Tweed

Kirk Yetholm

The Cheviot
(2,674ft) ▲

A697

B6401

THE CHEVIOT HILLS

The Byrness

NORTHUMBERLAND NATIONAL PARK

REDESDALE

Otterburn

N. Tyne

Greenhaugh

Bellingham

KIELDER FOREST PARK

Kielder

Kielder Water

Falstone

Stannersburn

A68

SCOTLAND

Tweed

A697

▼ Edinburgh

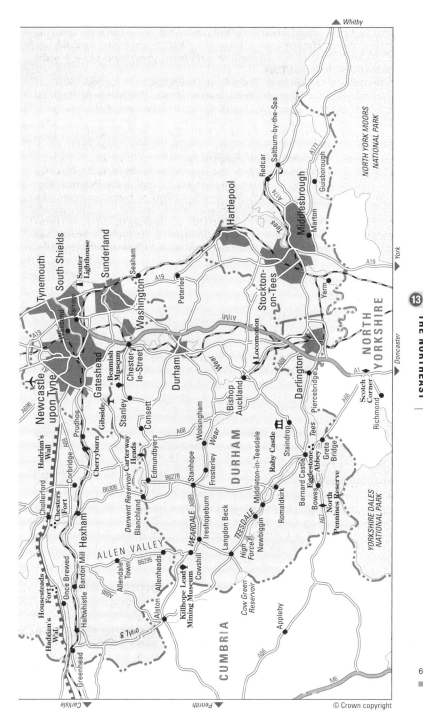

NORTH YORK MOORS NATIONAL PARK

Saltburn-by-the-Sea

Redcar

Middlesbrough

Marton

Guisborough

Hartlepool

Stockton-on-Tees

Yarm

Tees

▶ York

A19

Tynemouth

South Shields

Souter Lighthouse

Sunderland

Jarrow

Seaham

Peterlee

Washington

Newcastle upon Tyne

Gateshead

Beamish Museum

Chester-le-Street

Durham

Bishop Auckland

Wear

Darlington

Locomotion

Piercebridge

Scotch Corner

Richmond

NORTH YORKSHIRE

A1

▶ Doncaster

Prudhoe

Cherryburn

Gibside

Stanley

Consett

Carterway Heads

Edmundbyers

Wolsingham

Staindrop

Raby Castle

Middleton-in-Teesdale

Barnard Castle

Eggleston

Bowes

Greta Bridge

North Pennines Reserve

YORKSHIRE DALES NATIONAL PARK

DURHAM

Chollerford

Corbridge

Chesters Fort

Hexham

Derwent Reservoir

Blanchland

Stanhope

Frosterley

Romaldkirk

Hadrian's Wall

Housesteads Fort

Once Brewed

Bardon Mill

Haltwhistle

Greenhead

Hadrian's Wall

Allendale Town

Allenheads

Alston

Killhope Lead Mining Museum

Cowshill

ALLEN VALLEY

WEARDALE

Ireshopeburn

Langdon Beck

High Force

Newbiggin

TEESDALE

Cow Green Reservoir

Appleby

CUMBRIA

◀ Carlisle

◀ Penrith

A596

A69

A68

A66

A67

A689

B6306

B6295

B6277

B6278

A19

A1(M)

A171

A174

A66

M6

637

© Crown copyright

Scottish border. Inland, **Hadrian's Wall** can be easily visited from the appealing abbey-town of **Hexham**, while beyond the Wall are the harsh moorland, tree plantations, country towns, hiking trails and leisure opportunities of the **Northumberland National Park**.

The main East-Coast train line calls at Darlington, Durham, Newcastle and Berwick-upon-Tweed: useful **train passes** include the Northeast Regional Rover (7 days; £73) and the North Country Rover (any 4 days out of 8; £61.50), which is also valid in parts of Yorkshire and Lancashire. For **buses**, the Northeast Explorer Pass (1-day; £6.50; ⓦwww.explorernortheast.co.uk), valid after 9am on weekdays and all day at weekends, gives unlimited travel on local buses (as far south as Scarborough in North Yorkshire or west to Carlisle), plus free travel on Newcastle's Tyne and Wear metro; Hadrian's Wall has its own bus service (see p.659). The main long-distance footpath is the **Pennine Way**, which runs parallel to Hadrian's Wall from Greenhead to Housesteads, and then climaxes in a climb through the Northumberland National Park. Alternatively, the **Hadrian's Wall Path** (see p.659) provides access along the whole of Hadrian's Wall. By bike, the principal cross-region route is the 140-mile **Sea to Sea (C2C) cycle route** from Whitehaven/Workington to Sunderland/Newcastle.

Durham

The view from **DURHAM** train station is one of the finest in northern England – a panoramic prospect of Durham Cathedral, its towers dominating the skyline from the top of a steep sandstone bluff within a narrow bend of the River Wear. This dramatic site has been the resting place of St Cuthbert since 995, his hallowed remains making Durham a place of pilgrimage for both the Saxons and the Normans, who began work on the present cathedral at the end of the eleventh century. Subsequently, the bishops of Durham were granted extensive powers to control the troublesome northern marches of the kingdom, ruling as semi-independent Prince Bishops, with their own army, mint and courts of law. The bishops were at the peak of their power in the fourteenth century, yet they clung to the vestiges of their authority until 1836, when they ceded them to the Crown. They abandoned Durham Castle for their palace in Bishop Auckland and transferred their old home to the fledgling **Durham University**, England's third oldest seat of learning after Oxford and Cambridge. And so matters rest today, cathedral and university monopolizing a city centre that remains an island of privilege in what is otherwise a moderately sized, working-class town at the heart of the old Durham coalfield. It's well worth a night, or even two, and while there are attractions other than the cathedral and castle it's more the overall atmosphere that captivates, enhanced by the ever-present golden stone, slender bridges and glint of the river.

Arrival, information and accommodation

From either Durham **train station**, or the **bus station**, it's ten minutes' walk to the city centre, across the river. The "Cathedral" **bus** links train and bus stations with the Market Place and the cathedral (every 20min; 50p for all-day ticket). Drivers should park in one of the designated **car parks**, as on-street parking is difficult to find; and note that the peninsula road (to the castle and cathedral) is a toll road (Mon–Sat 10am–4pm; £2). The **tourist office** (Mon–Sat 9.30am–5.30pm, Sun 11am–4pm; ☏0191/384 3720, ⓦwww.durhamtourism.co.uk) is located at **Millennium Place**, off Claypath, a development which

DURHAM

RESTAURANTS, CAFES & PUBS
Almshouse	7
Bistro 21	1
Court Inn	8
Emilio's	6
Hide	5
Numjai	2
Swan & Three Cygnets	3
Vennel's	4

N

◄ ❶ & A691 Lanchester

Durham Light Infantry Museum & Art Gallery

FRAMWELLGATE

River Wear

SIDEGATE

Train Station

FRAMWELLGATE

FREEMANS PLACE

PROVIDENCE ROW

MILLBURNGATE

Millennium Place

Gala Theatre

Bike Rental

St Nicholas'

CLAYPATH

GILESGATE

GILESGATE

A690

A690 ►

A1(M), Sunderland, Campsite & ❹ ►

NORTH ROAD

Bus Station

◄ ❹ & A690 Penrith

MILLBURNGATE BRIDGE

SILVER ST

MARKET PLACE

NEW ELVET

LEAZES ROAD

ST HILD'S LN

St Hild & St Bede College

CROSSGATE

❸

FRAMWELLGATE BRIDGE

❹ Castle

SADDLER ST

ELVET BRIDGE

❸ ❺

❻

❷

OLD ELVET

❸

SOUTH STREET

Palace Green ❼

Durham Heritage Centre

NORTH BAILEY

NEW ELVET

COURT LANE

❽

GREEN LANE

GROVE STREET

Museum of Archeology

Cathedral

St Chad's College

Dunelm House

Durham Heritage Centre

PIMLICO

SOUTH BAILEY

River Wear

St Oswald's

CHURCH STREET

HALLGARTH STREET

WHINNEY HILL

PREBENDS BRIDGE

QUARRYHEADS LANE

STOCKTON ROAD

POTTERS BANK

St Mary's College

ELVET HILL ROAD

St Aidan's College

Trevelyan College

SOUTH ROAD

Grey College

Oriental Museum

Van Mildert College

Collingwood College

Botanic Gardens

ACCOMMODATION
Castle View	C
Farnley Tower	D
Marriott Royal County	B
Seaham Hall	A

0   200 yds

▼ A177 Darlington

© Crown copyright

◄ A1(M) & A177 Stockton

also incorporates a cinema showing a forty-minute large-format film presentation on the city's history (times vary; £4), plus theatre, public library, bar and café.

Durham's varied city-centre **accommodation** will be augmented, at the end of 2006, by a budget hotel in the Walkergate development, adjacent to Millennium Place. Meanwhile, private rooms are offered at the colleges of **Durham University** (Christmas, Easter and July–Sept), all within walking distance of the centre; the tourist office has a full list, or call the Conference and Tourism Office (☎0800/289970, ⓦwww.dur.ac.uk/conference_tourism). Prices are from £27 per person, or £37 in en-suite rooms, breakfast included. Of the dozen colleges, St Chad's, next to the cathedral, accepts **YHA bookings** in the same periods for £19.50 per person.

Guest houses and hotels

Castle View Guest House 4 Crossgate ☎0191/386 8852, ⓦwww.castle-view .co.uk. Pretty townhouse (no smoking) on a cobbled terrace next to St Margaret's Church, with six en-suite rooms and a quiet courtyard-garden. ❺

Farnley Tower The Avenue ⓦwww.farnley-tower .co.uk. A fine stone Victorian house, high on a hill, 10min walk from the centre. The best rooms have sweeping city views. ❺

Marriott Royal County Old Elvet ☎0191/386 6821, ⓦwww.marriotthotels.com. Durham's top hotel has its own riverside leisure centre with pool, while the comfortable rooms have plump beds and marble-trimmed bathrooms. ❼

Seaham Hall Lord Byron's Walk, Seaham, 10 miles northeast of Durham ☎0191/516 1400, ⓦwww .seaham-hall.com. Hip, holistic spa hotel that makes a great coastal base for city sightseeing – Durham is a 20min drive away. ❾

The City

Surrounded on three sides by the River Wear, Durham's compact centre is readily approached by two road bridges that lead from the western, modern part of town across the river to the spur containing castle and cathedral. The commercial heart of this "old town" area is the triangular **Market Place**, flanked by the Guildhall and St Nicholas' Church, both now modernized beyond distinction. The Victorian **Market Hall**, buried in the vaults of the buildings that line the west side of the square (closed Sun), hosts a lively outdoor market every Saturday, as well as farmers' markets, held on the third Thursday of the month.

Durham Cathedral

From Market Place, it's a five-minute walk up cobbled Saddler Street to **Durham Cathedral** (Mon–Sat 9.30am–6.15/8pm, Sun 12.30–5/8pm; guided tours 2–3 daily Easter week & mid-July to mid-Sept; access sometimes restricted, call ☎0191/386 4266 to check; £4 suggested donation; tours £3.50; ⓦwww.durhamcathedral.co.uk). Standing on the site of an early wooden Saxon cathedral built to house the remains of St Cuthbert, the present cathedral – a supreme example of the Norman-Romanesque style – was completed in 1133, and has survived the centuries pretty much intact. The awe-inspiring nave, completed in 1128, used pointed arches for the first time in England, raising the vaulted ceiling to new and dizzying heights. The weight of the stone is borne by massive pillars, their heaviness relieved by striking Moorish-influenced geometric patterns. A door gives access to the **tower** (Mon–Sat 10am–4pm; £2.50), from where there are fine views of the city. Cuthbert himself lies beneath a plain marble slab, his presence and **shrine** having gained a reputation over the centuries for their curative powers. The legend was given credence in 1104, when the saint's body was exhumed for reburial here, and was found to be completely uncorrupted, more than four hundred years after his death on Lindisfarne.

Almost certainly, this was the result of his fellow monks having (unintentionally) preserved the body by laying it in sand containing salt crystals – though to medieval eyes, here was testament enough to the saint's potency.

Back near the entrance, at the west end of the church, the **Galilee Chapel** was begun in the 1170s, its light and exotic decoration in imitation of the Great Mosque of Córdoba. The chapel contains the simple tombstone of the **Venerable Bede**, a Northumbrian monk credited with being England's first historian. Bede died at the monastery of Jarrow in 735, and his remains were first transferred to the cathedral in 1020. An ancient wooden doorway opposite the main entrance leads into the spacious **cloisters**, which are flanked by what remains of the monastic buildings. These include the **Treasures of St Cuthbert** exhibition (Mon–Sat 10am–4.30pm, Sun 2–4.30pm; £2.50), where you can see some striking relics of St Cuthbert, including the reassembled fragments of his delicately carved oak coffin. There's also a splendid facsimile copy of the Lindisfarne Gospels (the originals are in the British Library in London), the pages of which are turned at regular intervals.

The rest of the city

Across Palace Green from the cathedral, it's only possible to visit **Durham Castle** (Easter & July–Sept daily 10am–12.30pm & 2–4.30pm; rest of the year Mon, Wed, Sat & Sun 2–4pm; £5; ☎0191/374 3800, ⓦwww.durhamcastle .com) on a 45-minute guided tour, highlights of which include visits to the fifteenth-century kitchen, a climb up the enormous hanging staircase and the jog down to the Norman chapel, notable for its lively Romanesque carved capitals. The castle is sometimes closed for functions during its regular opening hours, so it's best to call ahead to check. Below the castle and the cathedral are the wooded banks of the **River Wear**, where a pleasant footpath runs right round the peninsula. It takes about thirty minutes to complete the circuit, passing a succession of elegant bridges with fine vantage points over town and cathedral.

The university's **Oriental Museum** (Mon–Fri 10am–5pm, Sat & Sun noon–5pm; £1.50; ⓦwww.dur.ac.uk/oriental.museum) is set among college buildings a couple of miles south of the city centre on Elvet Hill Road (take bus #5 or #6 to South Road). Highlights of its wide-ranging collection include outstanding displays of Chinese ceramics and Arabic calligraphy, a magnificent Chinese bed and Japanese wood-block prints. The nearby **Botanic Garden** (daily 10am–4/5pm; £2) has glasshouses, a café and visitor centre, all set in eighteen acres of diverse woodland, grassland and gardens near Collingwood College; buses run back to the centre from either Elvet Hill Road or South Road. North of the centre, a ten-minute walk from the train station takes you to the **Durham Light Infantry Museum and Art Gallery**, at Aykley Heads (daily: April–Oct 10am–5pm; Nov–March 10am–4pm; £3), which tells the story of World War I, in which 12,000 men from the regiment died.

Eating, drinking and entertainment

As a popular tourist and student city, Durham has plenty of inexpensive **cafés and restaurants**, dotted around the city.

Cafés and restaurants

Almshouse Palace Green. Bistro meals for around £5–6, served in a historic building in the shadow of the cathedral. In summer (May–Aug) open until 0pm. Inoxponcivo.

Bistro 21 Aykley Heads ☎0191/384 4354. Excellent Modern British cuisine in a converted farmhouse north of the centre, 10min walk from the DLI Museum and Art Gallery. Closed Sun. Expensive.

Emilio's 96 Elvet Bridge ☎0191/384 0096. The city's Italian of choice. Happy-hour pizza and pasta deals are a steal. Closed Sun lunch. Moderate.

Hide 39 Saddler St ☎0191/384 1999. The best of the café-bars with foodie pretensions, *Hide* serves a brunch-style menu during the day, with prices rising at night for a Modern British tour of world cuisine. Moderate.

Numjai 19 Millburngate Centre ☎0191/386 2020. Authentic Thai restaurant, with great views of the cathedral. Expensive.

Vennel's Saddler's Yard, Saddler Street. Self-service café dispensing sandwiches, salads, quiche and pastas in its sixteenth-century courtyard. Closes 5pm, though the upstairs bar ("Durham's bohemian retreat") opens after 7.30pm.

Pubs

Court Inn Court Lane. Best pub dining in town, a favourite with students and locals, with a classic pub menu (how can you not admire a "gourmet selection" of egg, beans and chips?), plus some intriguing blackboard specials.

Swan & Three Cygnets Elvet Bridge. Town and gown converge in this popular riverside pub with a full-to-the-brim outdoor terrace.

Live music, culture and festivals

Regular **classical concerts** are held at the cathedral, while Durham is lucky enough to have two arts-centre venues, namely the **DLI Museum and Art Gallery** (Aykley Heads ☎0191/384 2214, ⓦwww.durham.gov.uk/dli), and the **Gala Theatre** (Millennium Place ☎0191/332 4041, ⓦwww.galadurham .co.uk), which between them present music, theatre, dance, comedy and cinema. In June the **Durham Regatta** packs the riverbanks and river, while over the first weekend in July, the **Durham Summer Festival** encompasses all manner of musical entertainments and historical re-enactments; on the following Saturday, the **Miners' Gala** takes place, when the traditional lodge banners are paraded through the streets.

Listings

Bike rental Cycle Force 2000, 87 Claypath ☎0191/384 0319. Closed Thurs & Sun.

Hospital University Hospital, North Road ☎0191/333 2333.

Internet Free access at the Claypath Library, opposite the tourist office, Millennium Place.

Pharmacy Boots, 2–5 Market Place ☎0191/384 2213.

Police HQ, Aykley Heads ☎0191/386 4929; also on New Elvet ☎0191/386 4222.

Post office Silver Street.

Shopping At Fowlers Yard, Back Silver Street, behind Market Place (Wed–Sat 11am–4pm), artists and craftspeople work in a series of creative studios.

The rest of County Durham

In the 1910s, **County Durham** produced 41 million tons of coal each year, raised from three hundred pits by 170,000 miners. This was the heyday of an industry that since the 1830s had transformed the county's landscape, spawning scores of pit villages that matted the rolling hills. However, nothing could prevent the slow decline of the Durham coalfield from the 1920s: just 127 mines were left when the industry was nationalized in 1947, and today not a single pit remains. For a taste of the old days, most people visit the reconstructed colliery village (and much more) at the open-air **Beamish Museum**, north of Durham, while for the region's considerable railway heritage you shouldn't miss **Locomotion**, a fascinating outpost of the National Railway

Museum south of Durham, near Bishop Auckland. Away from the old coal-fields and railway works, the two main towns are the ecclesiastical residence of **Bishop Auckland** and the well-to-do market town of **Barnard Castle**, beyond which – to the west – lie the isolated Pennine valleys of **Teesdale** and **Weardale**.

Beamish Museum

The open-air **Beamish Museum** (Easter–Oct 10am–5pm; Nov–Easter Tues–Thurs, Sat & Sun 10am–4pm; last admission 3pm; admission £15, £6 in winter; ☎0191/370 4000, ⓦwww.beamish.org.uk) spreads out over 300 acres beside the A693, about ten miles north of Durham. It's the one County Durham attraction you really shouldn't miss, as popular with tourists as it is with local people. Buildings from all over the region have been reassembled in six main sections, linked by restored trams and buses and all painstakingly kitted out with period furnishings and fittings. Costumed shopkeepers, workers and householders can answer your questions, and you can walk through many of the buildings and workshops to find out about daily life a century or two ago. Four of the sections show life in 1913, before the upheavals brought about by World War I: a pint-sized **colliery village**, complete with drift mine (regular tours throughout the day); a **farm** inhabited by breeds of livestock that were popular in the period; a **train station** and goods shed; and a large-scale re-creation of a market **town**. Two areas date from 1825, at the beginning of the Northeast's industrial development: a **manor house**, with horse yard, formal gardens, vege-table plots and orchards; and the **Pockerley Waggonway**, where you can ride behind a replica of George Stephenson's *Locomotion*, the first passenger-carrying steam train in the world. Reckon on at least four hours to get round the lot in summer, two in winter when only the town and train station are usually open.

To **get there**, follow signs to the museum off the A1(M) Chester-le-Street exit, then follow the signs along the A693 to Stanley. Regular **buses** from Durham and Newcastle drop you close to the main entrance – get up-to-date details from Traveline on ☎0870/608 2608.

Bishop Auckland

Eleven miles southwest of Durham city, **BISHOP AUCKLAND** has been the country home of the bishops of Durham since the twelfth century and their official residence for more than a hundred years. Their palace, the gracious **Auckland Castle** (Easter–Sept Sun & Mon 2–5pm, also Wed in Aug; £4; ⓦwww.auckland-castle.co.uk), is approached through an imposing gatehouse just off the town's large Market Place. Aside from the splendid marble and limestone chapel, the rooms are rather sparse, though the long dining room is an outstanding exception, with its thirteen paintings of Jacob and his sons by Francisco de Zurbarán, commissioned in the 1640s for a monastery in South America. The town itself plays second fiddle to the castle, though don't leave until you've followed the mile-long lane from behind the Town Hall (sign-posted by the *Sportsman Inn*) to the remains of **Binchester Roman Fort** (Easter & May–Sept daily 11am–5pm; £2). Only a small portion of Roman Vinovia has been excavated, but this includes the country's best example of a hypocaust, built to warm the private bath suite of the garrison's commanding officer.

Buses from Durham drop you centrally, near Market Place, where the Town Hall, library and **tourist office** share the same premises (April–Sept Mon–Sat 9/10am–4/5pm, Sun 1–4pm; Oct–March closed Sun; ☎01388/602610).

Locomotion

The first passenger train (as opposed to freight) in the world left from the station at Shildon in 1825 – making the small County Durham town, around five miles southeast of Bishop Auckland, the world's oldest railway town. It's a heritage explored in the magnificently realised **Locomotion**, otherwise known as the **National Railway Museum at Shildon** (Easter–Oct daily 10am–5pm; Nov–Easter Wed–Sun 10am–4pm; free; ☎01388/777999, ⓦwww.locomotion .uk.com); follow the signs off the B6282 (from Bishop Auckland) or the A6072 (from the A68/A1(M)). Accompanied by an intoxicating aroma of oil and grease, this regional outpost of York's National Railway Museum traces two hundred years of railway history, spread out around a kilometre-long site. The house of the first railway works' manager, Timothy Hackworth, presents site interpretation, while depots, sidings, junctions and coal drops lead ultimately to the heart of the museum, **Collection** – a gargantuan steel hangar containing an extraordinary array of sixty locomotives, dating from the very earliest days of steam.

Barnard Castle and around

Fifteen miles southwest of Bishop Auckland, the attractive town of **BARNARD CASTLE** is overlooked by the skeletal remains of its **castle** (Easter–Oct daily 10am–4/6pm; Nov–Easter Mon & Thurs–Sun 10am–4pm; £3.30; EH), poking out from a cliff high above the River Tees. First fortified in the eleventh century, the castle was long a stronghold of the Balliols, a Norman family interminably embroiled in the struggle for the Scottish crown. Castle aside, the prime attraction is the grand French-style chateau that constitutes the **Bowes Museum** (daily 11am–5pm; £7; ⓦwww.bowesmuseum.org.uk), half a mile east of the centre, signposted along Newgate. It's a hugely rewarding collection, highlighting English period furniture, French decorative and religious art, and one of the most important Spanish collections in the UK, including El Greco's *The Tears of St Peter*. There are also tapestries, ceramics and incidental curiosities, including a late eighteenth-century mechanical silver swan in the lobby which performs daily at noon and 3pm, preening to a brief forty-second melodic burst.

From the castle in the town centre, it's a fine mile-and-a-half walk southeast (downriver) through the fields above the banks of the Tees, to the glorious shattered ruins of **Egglestone Abbey** (dawn–dusk; free), a minor foundation dating from 1195. The other local attraction lies seven miles northeast of town, up the A688, where the sprawling battlements of **Raby Castle** (Easter week, May & Sept Wed & Sun 1–5pm; June–Aug Mon–Fri & Sun 1 5pm; gardens same days 11am–5.30pm; £9, park & gardens only £4; ⓦwww.rabycastle.com) reflect the power of the Neville family, who ruled the local roost until 1569. Outside in the two-hundred-acre deer park are the walled gardens, where peaches, apricots and pineapples once flourished under the careful gaze of forty Victorian gardeners.

Buses arrive in Barnard Castle on either side of central Galgate – once the road out to the town gallows, hence the name – with the **tourist office** at its far end by the castle, on Flatts Road (daily 10am–4/6pm; Nov–March closed Sun; ☎01833/690909). Among several convenient **B&Bs** along the upper reaches of Galgate, the welcoming *Homelands*, 85 Galgate (☎01833/638757, ⓦwww.homelandsguesthouse.co.uk; no credit cards; ❸), is the best choice, offering pretty bedrooms and good breakfasts. The town has plenty of **cafés**, while the *Old Well Inn*, 21 The Bank, has a beer garden backing on to the castle walls.

Teesdale

Extending twenty-odd miles northwest from Barnard Castle, **Teesdale** begins calmly enough, though the pastoral landscapes of its lower reaches are soon replaced by wilder Pennine scenery. There's a regular bus service as far as Middleton-in-Teesdale, the valley's main settlement, but your own transport would make Teesdale an easy day's sightseeing from Barnard Castle or even Durham.

MIDDLETON-IN-TEESDALE was once the archetypal "company town", owned lock, stock and barrel by the Quaker-run London Lead Company, which began mining here in 1753. The firm built substantial stone cottages for its workforce, who in return were obliged to observe a host of regulations, such as sending their children to Sunday school and keeping off the booze. All this and more you'll learn at the town's heritage centre, known as **Meet the Middletons**, in the old Co-op at 9 Chapel Row (daily 11am–5pm; £3.60), based around the life and work of a mining family. The **tourist office** is in the central Market Place (restricted hours, though usually 10am–1pm; ☎01833/641001). The best **B&B** is nearby *Brunswick House*, 55 Market Place (☎01833/640393, ⓦwww.brunswickhouse.net; ❸), or head three miles back down the road towards Barnard Castle, to the charming village of **ROMALDKIRK**, where the ivy-clad, eighteenth-century *Rose & Crown* (☎01833/650213, ⓦwww .rose-and-crown.co.uk; ❼) has very comfortable rooms and a highly accomplished Modern British restaurant (expensive).

Past Middleton, the countryside becomes harsher and the Tees more vigorous as the B6277 travels the three miles on to **Bowlees Visitor Centre** (April–Oct daily 10.30am–5pm; Nov–March Sat & Sun 10.30am–4pm), the halt for a short walk to the rapids of **Low Force**. A mile further up the road is the altogether more compelling **High Force**, a seventy-foot cascade that rumbles over an outcrop of the Whin Sill ridge. The waterfall is on private Raby land, and visitors must pay £1 to view the falls and £1.50 to use the nearby car park, by the B6277.

Weardale

Weardale is an easy day out in a car from Durham. Seeing the dramatic highdale scenery by public transport, however, can be a frustrating business: bus #101 runs roughly hourly between Bishop Auckland and Stanhope, the main village, though to get to the fascinating lead-mining museum at Killhope, at the head of the valley, by bus, you'll have to ask the driver, or arrange it in advance with the bus company (☎01388/528235).

Weardale's main settlement, **STANHOPE**, lies about halfway up the valley. It's an elongated village that makes a useful halt for hikes on the local moors, including the enjoyable five-mile circuit from the town centre, up through the woods of **Stanhope Dene**, after which you can cool off with a splash in its open-air heated swimming pool. The village has a castle (closed to the public), built for a local MP in 1798, whose walled gardens now house the **Durham Dales Centre** – on the main road through Stanhope – in which you'll find the **tourist office** (daily 10/11am–4/5pm; ☎01388/527650, ⓦwww .durhamdalescentre.co.uk) and a café.

Nine miles upstream at Ireshopeburn, the **Weardale Museum** (Easter, May–July & Sept Wed–Sun 2–5pm; Aug daily 2–5pm; £1.50) tells the story of the dale, in particular its lead mining and Methodism (the faith of most of County Durham's lead miners). In a region dotted with Methodist chapels from the very earliest Wesleyan days, there's something of an unseemly scramble for the title of "world's oldest" – **High House Chapel** (1760), adjacent to the museum (entry included), hedges its bets with a claim to be the world's oldest Methodist chapel in continuous weekly use.

Lead and iron-ore mining flourished in and around Weardale from the 1840s to the 1880s, leaving today's landscape scarred with old workings. One of the bigger mines, situated about five miles west of Ireshopeburn, at the head of the valley and a windy 1500 feet above sea level, is now the terrific **Killhope Lead Mining Museum** (Easter–Oct daily 10.30am–5pm; plus Santa weekends in Dec; £4.50, £6 including mine visit; ⓦwww.durham.gov.uk/killhope), that presents the nineteenth-century buildings and machinery in a way that really brings home the hardships of a mining life – you can investigate the cramped mineshop, where the workers lived away from their families all week, or try your hand as a washerboy on the old washing floor. The highlight is descending **Park Level Mine** (1hr tour; call for times) with wellies, hard-hat and lamp in the company of a guide who expounds entertainingly about the realities of life underground.

Blanchland and around

The trans-moorland B6278 cuts north from Weardale at Stanhope for ten wild miles to tiny **BLANCHLAND**, a handful of stone cottages huddled round an L-shaped square that was once the outer court of a small twelfth-century abbey. The village has been preserved since 1721, when Lord Crewe, the childless bishop of Durham, bequeathed his estate to trustees on condition that they restored the old buildings. Consequently, the village bears many reminders of its monastic past, but it's the *Lord Crewe Arms Hotel* (☎01434/675251, ⓦwww .crewearms.freeserve.co.uk; ❼) that steals the show. Once the abbot's lodge, the hotel's nooks and crannies are an enticing mixture of medieval and eighteenth-century Gothic, including the dark vaulted basements, two big fireplaces left over from the canons' kitchen and a priest's hideaway stuck inside the chimney. The restaurant serves *table d'hôte* dinners for around £30, or there are cheaper meals in the public bar in the undercroft.

East of Blanchland, just past the **Derwent Reservoir**, there's a simple YHA hostel in the attractive village of **Edmundbyers** (☎0870/770 5810, ⓔedmundbyers@yha.org.uk; £11.95; Easter–Nov flexible opening, but daily in July & Aug), housed in seventeenth-century Low House. Two miles further east, at the junction with the A68, at **Carterway Heads**, the ⚹ *Manor House Inn* (☎01207/255268; ❹) has en-suite rooms overlooking the reservoir and posh pub food at around £20 a head, though there's a cheaper lunchtime menu too.

Darlington

DARLINGTON hit the big time in 1825, when George Stephenson's "Number 1 Engine", later called *Locomotion*, hurtled from here to nearby Stockton-on-Tees, with the inventor at the controls and flag-carrying horsemen riding ahead to warn of the train approaching at the terrifying speed of fifteen miles per hour. This novel form of transport soon proved popular with passengers, an unlooked-for bonus for Edward Pease, the line's instigator: he had simply wanted a fast and economical way to transport coal from the Durham pits to the docks at Stockton. Subsequently, Darlington grew into a rail-engineering centre, and didn't look back till the closure of the works in 1966.

It's little surprise, then, that all signs in town point to the **Darlington Railway Centre and Museum** (daily 10am–5pm; £2.50; ⓦ www.drcm.org.uk), housed in Darlington's North Road Station, which was completed in 1842; it's a twenty-minute walk up Northgate from the central Market Place. The museum's pride and joy is the original *Locomotion*, actually built in Newcastle, which continued in service until 1841 – other locally made engines superseded it, and some of these are on show, too, while a special events programme throughout the year offers train rides and other family diversions. The origins of the rest of Darlington lie deep in Saxon times. The monks carrying St Cuthbert's body from Ripon to Durham stopped here, the saint lending his name to the graceful riverside church of **St Cuthbert** (Easter–Sept Mon–Sat 11am–2pm; Oct–Easter Fri only 11am–1pm; free), where the needle-like spire and decorative turrets herald the delicate Early English stonework inside. One of England's largest market squares spreads beyond the church up to the restored Victorian covered **market** (Mon–Sat 8am–5pm, with a large outdoor market Mon & Sat), next to the prominent clocktower.

Darlington's **train station** is on the main line from London to Scotland (via Durham and Newcastle). From the station, walk up Victoria Road to the roundabout and turn right down Feethams for the central Market Place. You'll pass the Town Hall on Feethams, opposite which most **buses** stop, while the **tourist office** lies on the south side of Market Place at 13 Horsemarket (Mon–Fri 9am–5pm, Sat 9am–3pm, Sun 10am–2pm; ☎01325/388666, ⓦ www.visitdarlington.com). Basic **accommodation** is available at the town's Arts Centre (☎01325/348842; ➊), in Vane Terrace, less than ten minutes' walk away, where guests can also use the centre's bars and lunchtime bistro – follow Duke Street from central Skinnergate. Just round the corner from here (off Vane Terrace), the *Balmoral Guest House*, at 63 Woodland Rd (☎01325/461908, ⓦ www.balmoral-darlington.co.uk; ➌), is a spacious Victorian townhouse that retains many original features. There are several **cafés** on and around Market Place, while the traditional *Hole in the Wall* pub here serves authentic Thai meals (Mon–Sat lunch & Thurs–Sat dinner) for under a tenner. *Number Twenty 2*, 22 Coniscliffe Rd, is a self-professed "alehouse" with plenty of guest beers on tap, wine by the glass and pub lunches (not Sun). Out of town, at the eighteenth-century *George Hotel* (☎01325/374576; ➎), at **Piercebridge**, five miles west of Darlington off the A67, the en-suite rooms and restaurant look across the gentle banks of the River Tees.

Middlesbrough

MIDDLESBROUGH, Teesside's largest town, fifteen miles east of Darlington, is entirely a product of the early industrial age, with nineteenth-century iron and steel barons throwing up factories and housing almost as fast as they could ship their products out of the docks. What was a hamlet at the turn of the nineteenth century was a thriving industrial town of 100,000 people by the turn of the twentieth. When iron and steel declined in importance and the local shipbuilding industry collapsed (the last shipyard closed in 1986), Middlesbrough took to light engineering and the chemical industry, the belching plants of which still surround its outskirts. The modern centre is unremarkable in every way and the town prefers to trumpet its position as "Gateway to Captain Cook Country", fair enough given that he was born a mile and a half south of the centre in Marton in 1728. Here, the **Captain Cook Birthplace Museum** in Stewart Park (Tues–Sun 9/10am–4/5.30pm; £2.40; ⓦ www.captcook-ne.co .uk) covers the life and times of Britain's greatest seaman and explorer by way of good interpretative and interactive displays. Buses run from the bus station every fifteen minutes or so to Marton – ask the driver for the stop. For more on the captain and the local area, see ⓦ www.captaincook.org.uk, or call the local **tourist office** (ⓣ 01642/729700, ⓦ www.middlesbrough.gov.uk).

Hartlepool

If there's one Teesside town trying hard to reinvent itself it's **HARTLE-POOL**, ten miles north of Middlesbrough, England's third-largest port in the nineteenth century and once a noted shipbuilding centre. After years in the doldrums, its image has been transformed by the renaissance of its once decaying dockland area, now spruced up as **Hartlepool's Maritime Experience** (daily 10am–5pm; £6.25; ⓦ www.hartlepoolsmaritimeexperience.com). The entrance fee gets you on to the bustling eighteenth-century quayside where active attractions based around press gangs, the Royal Navy, seaport life and fighting ships stir the senses. There are also period shops, a replica eighteenth-century maritime pub, games and play area, coffee shop and market, plus a tour of **HMS Trincomalee**, a navy training ship built in 1817 and now berthed here. On the edge of the quay in the entertaining **Museum of Hartlepool** at Jackson Dock (daily 10am–5pm; free), you can climb the port's original lighthouse, board a restored paddle-steamer and trace the town's history.

Newcastle upon Tyne

At first glance **NEWCASTLE UPON TYNE** – virtual capital of the area between Yorkshire and Scotland – may appear to be just another northern industrial conurbation, but the banks of the Tyne have been settled for nearly two thousand years and the city consequently has a greater breadth of attractions than many of its rivals. The Romans were the first to bridge the river here, and the "new castle" appeared as long ago as 1080. In the seventeenth century a regional monopoly on coal export brought wealth and power to Newcastle and – as well as giving a new expression to the English language – engendered its other great industry, shipbuilding. In its nineteenth-century heyday, Newcastle's engineers and builders gave the city an elegance that has survived today in the impressive buildings of Grainger Town – indeed, only London and Bath have more listed classical buildings. Industrial decline hit Newcastle early, as highlighted by the Jarrow Crusade of 1936, but there's been an extraordinary revival over the last decade as the city has shed its dowdy provincial coat to emerge as a vibrant European arts and nightlife destination. The pre-eminent artistic symbol of this renewal is Antony Gormley's **Angel of the North**, a magnificent steel sculpture the size of a jumbo jet that welcomes anyone approaching from the south by rail or road. The city centre has been transformed, particularly along the banks of the River Tyne, where both Newcastle and Gateshead sides of the river have seen dramatic change – indeed, these days visitors are encouraged to think of the city not as Newcastle upon Tyne but as "Newcastle Gateshead". On **Gateshead Quays** are the BALTIC contemporary arts centre and Norman Foster's Sage music centre, while Newcastle's **Quayside** is scene of much of the city's contemporary nightlife. Add to these the unique Life Science Centre, the Laing art gallery, and Seven Stories, the new Centre for Children's Books, and there's a case for taking whatever time you were going to spend in the city and doubling it.

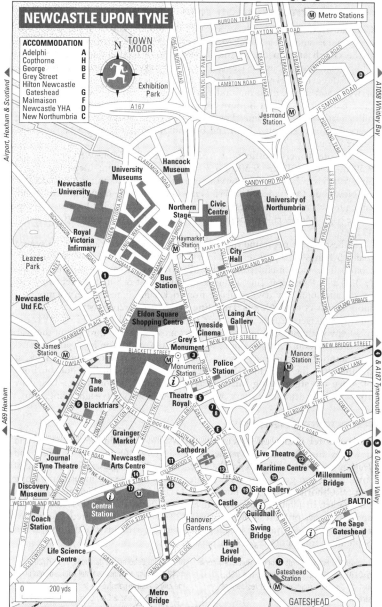

Arrival, information and transport

Central Station, on Neville Street, is a five-minute walk from the city centre or Quayside, and has a useful Metro station. National Express services arrive at the **coach station** on St James's Boulevard, not far from Central Station, while most regional bus services use the **Haymarket bus station** on the north side of the centre (Haymarket Metro). Many other city and local bus services arrive at and depart from the underground bus station a hundred yards down the same street in **Eldon Square Shopping Centre**. Newcastle's **airport**, six miles north of the city, is linked by Metro to Central Station (5.50am–11.10pm; every 7–15min; 20min; £1.80) and beyond. Alternatively, take a taxi into the centre (around £12).

There are **tourist offices** at 132 Grainger St (Mon–Wed, Fri & Sat 9.30am–5.30pm, Thurs 9.30am–7.30pm, Sun 10am–4pm; Oct–May closed Sun; ☎0191/277 8000, ⓦwww.visitnewcastlegateshead.com); in the Guildhall on Newcastle Quayside (Mon–Fri 11am–6pm, Sat 9am–6pm, Sun 9am–4pm; same phone); and on the Gateshead side in St Mary's Church, Oakwellgate, next to the Sage (Mon–Fri 9am–5pm, Sat 10am–5pm, Sun 11am–5pm; ☎0191/478 4222).

The best way to get round the conurbation is via the efficient **Metro** system (daily 5.15am–11.30pm; services every 3–15min; ⓦwww.tyneandwearmetro .co.uk). The most useful pass is the **Metro Day Saver** for unlimited rides (£3.20 after 9am Mon, Tues, Thurs & Fri, all day Sat & Sun; £2 after 9am Wed; or £2 after 6pm any day), available from ticket machines at every station; for more details contact **Nexus Traveline** (☎0870/608 2608, ⓦwww.nexus.org .uk). Tyne River Cruises' three-hour **sightseeing cruises** (£12; ☎0191/296 6740, ⓦwww.tyneleisureline.co.uk) depart most weekends throughout the year, and other days in summer, from Newcastle's Quayside. The local public transport authority also operates summer afternoon cruises from South Shields, at the mouth of the river (June–Sept; details from Nexus). Finally, a hop-on, hop-off, open-top **sightseeing bus** departs from Central Station (Easter–Dec daily 10am–4/5pm; departures every 30–60min; £6; ⓦwww.city-sightseeing.com).

Accommodation

Budget **hotel chains** offer plenty of good-value rooms in the city centre and down by the Quayside – *Premier Travel Inn, Jury's, Quality, Travel Lodge* and *Holiday Inn* all have hotels in the city centre. The biggest concentration of small hotels and **guest houses** is a mile north of the centre in Jesmond, along and off Osborne Road: take bus #30B, #31B or #80 from Central Station or Haymarket. In addition, both the University of Newcastle (☎0191/222 66318) and University of Northumbria (☎0191/227 4400) have hundreds of **student rooms** available at various locations, during Easter holidays and from July to September, from around £25 per person.

Adelphi 63 Fern Ave, off Osborne Road, Jesmond ☎0191/281 3109. Cheery family-run B&B, just off the main road, in a quiet residential street. ❸

Copthorne The Close, Quayside ☎0191/222 0333, ⓦwww.millenniumhotels.com. This stylish four-star hotel has Tyne views from most of its well-appointed rooms. Breakfast not included except for weekend packages. ❽, weekend ❼

George 88 Osborne Rd, Jesmond ☎0191/281 4442. Victorian townhouse hotel with a dozen of the city's least expensive en-suite rooms. ❸

Grey Street 2 Grey St ☎0191/230 6777, ⓦwww.greystreethotel.com. The city's sharpest designer digs retain the lofty proportions and original tiling of the Victorian bank building, but have added minimalist rooms with huge windows, flat-screen TVs and power showers. Continental breakfast included. ❼, weekend ❻

Hilton Newcastle Gateshead Bottle Bank, Gateshead Quays ☎0191/490 9700, ⓦwww.hilton
.co.uk/newcastlegateshead. The prominently sited
Hilton has a fine location near the Tyne Bridge and
Sage, though you'll want a river-facing room for the
full effect. ❼

Malmaison Quayside ☎0191/245 5000, ⓦwww
.malmaison.com. Chic lodgings in the former Co-
op building, right on the Quayside. Jazzy sounds,
crushed-velvet sofas, brasserie, bar and gym
provide the signature backdrop. Breakfast not
included. ❼

Newcastle YHA 107 Jesmond Rd, near Jesmond
Metro ☎0870/770 5972, ⓔnewcastle@yha.org
.uk. Popular townhouse hostel with sixty beds –
reserve in advance in summer. Breakfast and cheap
evening meals served, though no laundry facilities.
Closed Christmas to mid-Jan. Dorm beds £17.50.

New Northumbria 61–69 Osborne Rd, Jesmond
☎0191/281 4961, ⓦwww.newnorthumbriahotel
.co.uk. Contemporary boutique-style lodgings offering spacious rooms (some with sofa and chair) and
lovely panelled bathrooms with power showers.
Café-bar and Italian restaurant attached. ❻

The City

The city splits into several distinct areas, though it's only a matter of minutes to
walk between them. Castle and cathedral occupy the heights immediately above
the River Tyne, whose **Newcastle and Gateshead quaysides** now form the
biggest single attraction in the city. North of the cathedral lies **Grainger Town**,
the city-centre district of listed Victorian buildings that is at its most dramatic
along Grey Street. West of the centre is **Chinatown** and the two big draws of
the Discovery Museum and Life Science Centre; east is the renowned Laing
Gallery; and north the university museums and open parkland known as **Town
Moor**. Further east along the river, the old industrial **Ouseburn Valley** district
is slowly emerging as a cultural quarter, focusing on the Seven Stories children's
books centre.

Castle and Cathedral

Anyone arriving by train from the north will get a sneak preview of the **Castle**
(daily 9.30am–4.30/5.30pm; Oct–March closed Mon; £1.50), as the rail line
splits the keep from its gatehouse, the **Black Gate**, on St Nicholas' Street.
Staircases and rooms, including a bare Norman chapel, lie off a draughty Great
Hall, while down in the garrison room, prisoners were incarcerated during the
sixteenth to eighteenth centuries. There's a great view from the rooftop over the
river and city. Further along St Nicholas' Street stands the **Cathedral** (Mon–Fri
7am–6pm, Sat 8.30am–4pm, Sun 7.30am–noon & 4–7pm; free), dating mainly
from the fourteenth and fifteenth centuries and remarkable chiefly for its tower
– erected in 1470, it is topped with a crown-like structure of turrets and arches
supporting a lantern. Inside, behind the high altar, is one of the largest funerary
brasses in England; it was commissioned by Roger Thornton, the Dick Whit-
tington of Newcastle, who arrived in the city penniless and died its richest
merchant in 1430.

Along the River Tyne

On Newcastle's **Quayside** there have been fixed river crossings since Roman
times and today the Tyne is spanned by seven bridges in close proximity, the
most prominent being the looming **Tyne Bridge** of 1928, symbol of the
city. Immediately west is the hydraulic **Swing Bridge**, while modern road
and rail lines cross the river on the adjacent **High Level Bridge**, built by
Robert Stephenson in 1849 – Queen Victoria was one of the first passengers to cross, promoting the railway revolution. Beyond the Tyne Bridge, the
modern-day regeneration of the Quayside is in full swing. Riverside apartments, a landscaped promenade, public sculpture and pedestrianized squares
have paved the way for a series of fashionable bars and restaurants, centred on

the graceful **Millennium Bridge**, the world's first tilting span, which pivots to allow ships to pass.

The bridge allows pedestrians to cross the Tyne to the **Gateshead Quays**, to visit **BALTIC**, the dramatic Centre for Contemporary Art (Mon–Wed & Sat 10am–7pm, Thurs 10am–8pm, Sun 10am–5pm; free; Ⓦwww.balticmill.com), fashioned from a brick flour-mill built in the 1940s. This has been converted into a huge visual "art factory", second only in scale to London's Tate Modern. There's no permanent collection here, though the galleries display a robust series of art exhibitions, local community projects and other displays. The BALTIC is joined on the Gateshead side by **The Sage Gateshead** (Ⓦwww .thesagegateshead.org), an extraordinary billowing steel, aluminium and glass

△ The Sage Gateshead

concert hall complex that's home to the Northern Sinfonia and Folkworks, an organization promoting British and international traditional music. The public concourse provides marvellous river and city views, and there's the obligatory café-bar and bistro.

Grainger Town and the city centre

By the mid-nineteenth century, Newcastle's centre of balance had shifted away from the river, uphill to the rapidly expanding Victorian town, where classical facades of stone lined splendid new streets, most notably **Grey Street** – "that descending, subtle curve", as John Betjeman described it. The street takes its name from the Northumberland dynasty of political heavyweights whose most illustrious member was the second Earl Grey (he of the tea), prime minister from 1830 to 1834. In the middle of his term in office he carried the Reform Bill through parliament, an act commemorated by **Grey's Monument** at the top of the street. **Grainger Market** (Mon–Sat 8am–5pm) near Grey's Monument, was Europe's largest undercover market when built in the 1830s.

The Northeast's premier art collection is the **Laing Gallery** on New Bridge Street (Mon–Sat 10am–5pm, Sun 2–5pm; free; ⓦwww.twmuseums.org.uk), off John Dobson Street, behind the library. On permanent display is a sweep through British art from Reynolds to John Hoyland, with a smattering of Pre-Raphaelites, so admired by English industrial barons. The real treat here is the lashings of John Martin (1789–1854), a self-taught Northumberland painter with a penchant for massive biblical and mythical scenes inspired by the dramatic northeastern scenery. The other must-see in the gallery is the Art on Tyneside exhibition, which romps through the history of art and applied art in the region since the seventeenth century with considerable gusto. Outside the Laing's front door don't miss the notorious **Blue Carpet** – a public art installation whose tiles fold back on themselves to form unusual benches, lit from underneath.

The **Discovery Museum** in Blandford Square (Mon–Sat 10am–5pm, Sun 2–5pm; free; ⓦwww.twmuseums.org.uk) puts into context the city's history in a series of impressive displays housed in the former headquarters of the Co-operative Wholesale Society. You are confronted on arrival by the hundred-foot-long *Turbinia*, the world's first steam-turbine-powered ship, built by a brilliant local engineer, Charles Parsons. Galleries on three floors surround the *Turbinia*, with standout attractions including the "Newcastle Story", a walk through the city's past with tales from animated characters along the way, and the interactive "Science Maze" which focuses on Newcastle's pioneering inventors (including one Joseph Swan who, according to locals at least, beat Edison to the invention of the light bulb).

Heading back towards the Central Station along Westmorland Road, you can't miss the sleek, contemporary lines of the International Centre for Life. This ambitious "science village" project combines bioscience and genetics research centres with the **Life Science Centre** (Mon–Sat 10am–6pm, Sun 11am–6pm, last admission 4pm; £6.95; ☎0191/243 8210, ⓦwww.lifesciencecentre .uk), whose highlights include 3D motion-simulator rides, a sound-and-light "Big Brain" show, and a blockbuster exhibit on the history of human life. The centre is always adding new attractions, from science experiments to virtual reality experiences, while in winter an open-air **ice rink** is unveiled (mid-Nov to mid-Feb; £4.95).

The university museums

Plans for a **Great North Museum** (ⓦwww.greatnorthmuseum.org) for the region are now well established – with consequences for the university

THE NORTHEAST | Newcastle upon Tyne

museums, located just north of the centre near Haymarket Metro. The new museum (expected to open in 2009) is designed to bring together the major natural history and archeological collections currently housed in the Hancock Museum, the Museum of Antiquities, and Shefton (Greek) Museum. To this end, the Hancock will close from 2006, though the **Museum of Antiquities** (Mon–Sat 10am–5pm; free) and **Shefton Museum** (Mon–Fri 10am–4pm; free) should remain open until 2008 – the former, in particular, makes a good place to get to grips with the history of Hadrian's Wall before making a visit. The university's celebrated **Hatton Gallery** (Mon–Fri 10am–5.30pm, Sat 10am–5pm; free) will also remain open throughout – this is most famous for housing the only surviving example of German Dadaist Kurt Schwitters' *Merzbau* (a sort of architectural collage), though it also contains a permanent collection of African sculpture, and hosts a wide variety of temporary exhibitions.

Ouseburn Valley: Seven Stories

Ten minutes' walk up the River Tyne from Millennium Bridge, the old Victorian mills and warehouses in the **Ouseburn Valley** are gradually being given a new lease of life, a regeneration cemented by the 2005 opening of **Seven Stories**, 30 Lime St (Mon–Sat 10am–5pm, Thurs till 6pm, Sun 11am–5pm; £5; ℡0845/271 0777, ⓦwww.sevenstories.org.uk). This national centre for children's literature spreads across seven floors of a beautifully converted riverside mill, showcasing a unique collection of original manuscripts, documents and artwork. A couple of galleries display exhibitions exploring every facet of children's literature, though it's in the interaction between books and visitors that the centre makes its mark – whether in hands-on play and games, meet-the-writer sessions, or workshops in the Storyboat, moored outside by the Ouseburn towpath: call or check the website for a schedule of events, though weekends and school holidays see the most activity.

Eating

At the budget end of the market Italian, Indian and Chinese food dominates the scene, while at the top end of the scale the city has attracted some inventive chefs. The very cheapest places are found around Bigg Market, while in Stowell Street in Chinatown there are plenty of all-you-can-eat buffets as well as more refined Cantonese restaurants. Many city-centre restaurants offer **early bird/happy hour** deals before 7pm, while others serve **set lunches** at often ludicrously low prices.

Cafés

Café Live Live Theatre, 27 Broad Chare ℡0191/232 1331. Coffee, drinks and sandwiches downstairs in the espresso bar, and a bistro upstairs with a pricier Mediterranean/Mod Brit menu. Closed Sun.

Intermezzo 10–12 Pilgrim St ℡0191/261 2072. Good weather sees alley seating down the side of the Tyneside Cinema. Open daily until 11pm.

Pani's 61–65 High Bridge St, off Grey Street ℡0191/232 4366. This buzzy Sardinian café has a loyal clientele, who come for good-value stuffed sandwiches, *antipasti*, pasta and salads. Open until 10pm. Closed Sun.

Restaurants

Barn @ The Biscuit 16 Stoddart St ℡0191/230 3338. Superbly creative cooking in a former biscuit factory, now art gallery, east of the centre – best take a taxi. Café-style menu served at lunchtime, a la carte at dinner. Closed Sun dinner. Expensive.

Big Mussel 15 The Side ℡0191/232 1057. Mussels, chips and mayo served seven ways for a tenner. A £6 lunch and "clock saver" dinner (5.30–7pm) provide value for money. Moderate.

Café 21 21 Queen St ℡0191/222 0755. The Quayside's finest – a stylish Parisian-style bistro with a classic menu and slick service. The set lunches are a bargain for the quality. Closed Sun. Expensive.

El Coto 21 Leazes Park Rd ☎0191/261 0555. The city's best tapas place makes a good lunch stop (there's a pretty courtyard) or night out – most dishes cost around £4, though you can spend more at the upstairs grill-house. Moderate.

Mangos 43 Stowell St ☎0191/232 6522. Tradi-

tional and new-wave Cantonese dishes, from *dim sum* and country-style hotpots to sizzling-plate specials. Open until 2am. Moderate.

Secco Ristorante Salentino 86 Pilgrim St ☎0191/230 0444. Very hip, very pricey – the food mixes southern Italian dishes and Northumbrian ingredients (mains around £15). Closed Sun & Mon. Expensive.

Drinking, nightlife and entertainment

Newcastle's boisterous pubs, bars and clubs are concentrated in several distinct areas: between Grainger Street and the cathedral in the area called the **Bigg Market** (spiritual home of Sid the Sexist and the Fat Slags from *Viz* magazine); around the **Quayside**, where the bars tend to be slightly more sophisticated; and in the mainstream leisure-and-cinema complex known as **The Gate** (Newgate Street). There's really no getting away from the weekend mayhem, though the style bars around **Central Station** and **Pink Lane** at least start off the evening with more civilized intent. The grandiosely named "**Gay Quarter**" centres on the International Centre for Life. Gigs, club nights and the gay scene are reviewed exhaustively in *The Crack* (monthly; free; ⓦ www.thecrackmaga-zine.com), a **listings magazine** available in shops, pubs and bars. Top brew is, of course, **Newcastle Brown** – an ale known locally as "Dog" – produced in this city since 1927.

There's a hugely varied **theatrical and cultural life** in the city, from the offerings at the splendid Victorian Theatre Royal to those of smaller contem-porary theatre companies and local arts centres. The Sage and City Hall are the main **classical music** concert venues.

Pubs and bars

Agora 1 The Side. A *fin-de-siècle* confection of burnished wood, gilt mirrors, chandeliers and red leather, where the sounds are a soulful mix of swing, jazz and funk.

Apartment 28–32 Collingwood St. Typical of the latest wave of high-concept city bars, divided into separate rooms where you can variously drink, chat, chill or dine.

Centurion Central Station, Neville Street. The station's former first-class waiting rooms, now revived as an extraordinary bar and brasserie.

Crown Posada 31 The Side. Local beers and guest ales in a small wood-and-glass-panelled Victorian pub.

Free Trade St Lawrence Road. Walk along the Newcastle Quayside past the Millennium Bridge and look for the shabby pub on the hill, where you are invited to "drink beer, smoke tabs" with the city's pub *cognoscenti*.

Head of Steam 2 Neville St. Relaxed drinking don with good sounds, big sofas and gigs every night (except Sun) in the basement from 8pm.

Pitcher & Piano 108 Quayside. The riverfront's most spectacular bar – sinuous roof, huge plate-glass walls – by the Millennium Bridge.

Popolo 82–84 Pilgrim St. This casual American-style bar is a firm city favourite with a slightly older crowd.

Tokyo 17 Westgate Rd. The dark main bar's hand-some enough, but follow the tea-lights up the stairs for the outdoor "garden" bar, where there's at least a breath of fresh air.

Trent House 1–2 Leazes Lane. Many people's favourite pub, with a great jukebox and a surviving Space Invaders machine.

Clubs

Black Swan Newcastle Arts Centre, 69 Westgate Rd ☎0191/261 9959. Cellar bar with live music up to five nights a week – rock, folk, world and jazz – and a rollicking Friday-night salsa session.

Digital International Centre for Life, Times Square ⓦ www.dusted-design.co.uk/digital. The city's latest showpiece dance venue (currently Thurs, Fri & Sat nights) – the big draw is Saturday's *Shindig* (ⓦ www.shindiguk.com).

Foundation 57–59 Melbourne St ☎0191/261 8985, ⓦ www.foundation-club.com. Stylish venue hosting varied club nights, notably indie Thursdays and Saturday's funky house special.

Jazz Café 23 Pink Lane ☎0191/232 6505. Intimate jazz club with a late licence and live music from 8pm; salsa nights Thurs–Sat. Closed Sun.

Tuxedo Princess Hillgate Quay, Gateshead ☎0191/477 8899. A floating nightclub (aka "The Boat"), on the south side of the river, serving up scantily clad dancers and seven different styles of music in seven bars to a raucous 18–25-year-old set. Closed Sun.

World Headquarters Carliol Square ☎0191/261 7007, ⓦwww.theworldheadquarters.com. Newcastle's mellowest bar and club ("no sponsors, no corporates, no sell out"), playing funk, soul and hip-hop every Friday and Saturday, plus regular DJ slots, indie to electro.

Arts centres and concert venues

BALTIC South Shore Road, Gateshead ☎0191/478 1810, ⓦwww.balticmill.com. As well as the four contemporary art galleries, there are studio sessions and classes, films, artists' talks, community projects, dance and concerts.

City Hall Northumberland Road ☎0191/261 2606, ⓦwww.newcastle.gov.uk/cityhall. Orchestras from around the world, as well as mainstream rock, pop and comedy acts.

The Cluny 36 Lime St, Ouseburn Valley ☎0191/230 4474. The best small venue in the city (20min walk from Quayside), with gigs almost every night from 7.30pm, real ales and a nice bar.

The Sage Gateshead South Shore Road, Gateshead Quays ☎0191/443 4661, ⓦwww.thesagegateshead.org. Hosts a full programme of classical, folk, world and jazz music. Tickets from £6.

Cinema and theatre

Journal Tyne Theatre 111 Westgate Rd ☎0870/145 1200, ⓦwww.tynetheatre.co.uk. Beautifully restored Victorian theatre with a wide range of shows, comedy and gigs.

Live Theatre 27 Broad Chare ☎0191/232 1232, ⓦwww.live.org.uk. Enterprising theatre company promoting local actors and writers (Lee Hall gave his boy-ballet movie, *Billy Elliot*, its first reading here).

Northern Stage Barras Bridge ☎0871/700 0125, ⓦwww.northernstage.co.uk. The redeveloped Newcastle Playhouse (scheduled for 2006) will be home to Newcastle's own Northern Stage company.

Theatre Royal 100 Grey St ☎0870/905 5060, ⓦwww.theatreroyal.co.uk. Drama, opera, dance, musicals and comedy; also hosts the annual RSC season in Nov.

Tyneside Cinema 10 Pilgrim St ☎0191/232 8289, ⓦwww.tynecine.org. The city's premier art-house cinema. There's coffee, light meals and movie talk in the Art Deco cinema café (closes 9pm and all Sun).

Listings

Airport Newcastle International Airport ☎0870/122 1488, ⓦwww.newcastleinternational.co.uk.

Car rental Alamo/National ☎0191/214 5222; Avis ☎0191/214 0116; Budget ☎0191/261 8282; Europcar ☎0191/286 5070; Hertz ☎0191/286 6748.

Football Newcastle United play at St James's Park (ticket office ☎0191/261 1571, ⓦwww.nufc.co.uk) in front of the country's most fanatical supporters. You're unlikely to get a ticket for the big matches against major rivals, but seats go on general sale for some games.

Hospital Newcastle General Hospital, Westgate Road ☎0191/233 6161. Has 24hr A&E department, plus non-emergency NHS Walk-In Centre (daily 8am–9pm).

Internet Terminals in Virgin, Northumberland Street (shop hours), plus access at the City Library and at the Live Wires Centre in the Discovery Museum.

Pharmacies Boots, Monument Mall, Grey Street ☎0191/232 4423.

Police Corner of Market and Pilgrim streets ☎0191/214 6555.

Post office St Mary's Place, near the Civic Centre, at Haymarket.

Shopping MetroCentre, Gateshead, is the largest shopping centre in Europe (daily until 9pm; ⓦwww.metrocentre.uk.com), with over 330 shops and 50 restaurants, bars and cafés. City markets include the Sunday-morning Quayside market, under the Tyne Bridge; the covered Grainger Market (daily except Sun; plus arts and crafts market on 2nd Sat of month); and Jesmond's Armstrong Bridge market (Sun from 10am) for arts and crafts.

Taxis Ranks at Haymarket, Bigg Market, and outside Central Station. Weekend nights are the most difficult times to hail a cab; the queues at Bigg Market can be horrendous. Call Noda Taxis (☎0191/222 1888 or 232 7777) at Central Station for advance bookings.

Around Newcastle

The Metro runs east along both banks of the **River Tyne**, connecting Newcastle with several historic attractions, and with the sandy beaches at Tynemouth and Whitley Bay – the beaches are fine if you just want to see the sea, though there's no comparison with those further north up the Northumberland coast. To make a round trip of it, you can cross the river between North Shields and South Shields on the **Shields Ferry** (Mon–Sat 7am–10.50pm, Sun 10.30am–5.30pm; every 15–30min; 7min; £1 one-way); there are Metro stations on either side, a short walk from the ferry terminals.

Wallsend and Segedunum

WALLSEND, four miles east of Newcastle, was the last outpost of Hadrian's great border defence. **Segedunum**, the "strong fort", a couple of minutes' signposted walk from the Metro station (daily 9.30/10am–3.30/5.30pm; £3.50; ⓦwww.twmuseums.org.uk/segedunum), has been admirably developed as one of the prime attractions along the Wall. A range of activities takes place year-round (including summer re-enactments of Roman drill and equipment) and, besides the extensive excavations, the grounds contain a fully reconstructed bathhouse, complete with steaming pools and colourful frescoes. To complete the picture, climb the 110-foot museum tower for a spectacular overview of the remains and the adjacent ship-repair yards. The "wall's end" itself is visible at the edge of the site, close to the river and Swan Hunter shipyard, and it's from here that the **Hadrian's Wall Path** (see p.659) runs for 84 miles to Bowness on Solway in Cumbria; you can get your walk "passport" stamped inside the museum.

Jarrow

JARROW, five miles east of Newcastle, and south of the Tyne, has been ingrained on the national consciousness since the 1936 Jarrow Crusade, a march to London by unemployed protestors. However, the town made a mark much earlier, as the seventh-century St Paul's church and monastery was one of the region's early cradles of Christianity. The first Saxon church here was built in 681 AD and its monastic buildings soon attracted a reputation for scholastic learning. It was here that the **Venerable Bede** (673–735 AD) came to live as a boy, growing to become one of Europe's greatest scholars and England's first historian – his *History of the English Church and People*, describing the struggles of the island's early Christians, was completed at Jarrow in 731.

Access to the tranquil stone church of **St Paul's** (Mon–Sat 10am–4pm, Sun 2–4.30pm) and the adjacent monastery ruins is free, although they stand within the wider development that is **Bede's World** (Mon–Sat 10am–4.30/5.30pm, Sun noon–4.30/5.30pm; £4.50; ⓦwww.bedesworld.co.uk), a fascinating exploration of early medieval Northumbria. The striking multimedia museum traces the development of Northumbria and England through the use of extracts from Bede's writings, set alongside archeological finds and vivid re-creations of monastic life. After this you can take a turn through Gyrwe, the eleven-acre demonstration farm which features reconstructed timber buildings from the early Christian period. Bede's World is a signposted fifteen-minute walk through an industrial estate from **Bede Metro station**. Alternatively, buses #526 or #527 run roughly every thirty minutes from Neville Street (Central Station) in Newcastle or Jarrow Metro station.

Sunderland

SUNDERLAND, bisected by the River Wear and elevated in 1992 to the ranks of Britain's cities, shares Newcastle's long history, river setting and industrial heritage but cannot match its architectural splendour. Formed from three medieval villages flanking the Wear, it was one of the wealthiest towns in England by 1500, and later supported the Parliamentary cause in the Civil War. The twentieth century made and broke the town: from being the largest shipbuilding centre in the world, Sunderland slumped after ferocious bombing during World War II. Depression and recession did the rest. However, the city centre has seen a revival of late and now has a couple of visitor attractions to rival anything in nearby Newcastle. First stop should be the **Sunderland Museum** (Mon 10am–4pm, Tues–Sat 10am–5pm, Sun 2–5pm; free; ⓦwww .twmuseums.org.uk), which does a very good job of telling the city's history. The attached **Winter Gardens** are housed in an impressive steel and glass hothouse, while in the museum's café-brasserie you can take your drinks out on to the terrace overlooking the lake in Mowbray Park. The main interest in Sunderland lies across the River Wear, of which the landscaped **Riverside** is actually the oldest settled part of the city. Along the north bank of the river, in front of the university campus buildings, the early Christian **Church of St Peter** (Easter–Oct daily 2–4pm), built in 674 AD, is the elder sibling of St Paul's Church at Jarrow. Meanwhile, walk down from the church to the waterside to find the city's **National Glass Centre** (daily 10am–5pm; free; ⓦwww .nationalglasscentre.com), which highlights a traditional industry in Sunderland since the seventh century, when workshops turned out stained glass for the North's monastic houses. Regular tours throughout the day (£5) include a glass-making demonstration in the on-site workshop, or you can simply browse in the exhibition galleries and glass shop.

The main stop for those coming by metro from Newcastle is in the central **train station**, but get off at the previous stop, St Peter's, to walk along the north side of the river to the National Glass Centre or St Peter's Church. The **tourist office** is behind the central station on the main shopping drag, at 50 Fawcett St (Mon–Sat 9am–5pm, bank hols 10am–4pm; ☏0191/553 2000, ⓦwww .visitsunderland.com).

Hadrian's Wall and Hexham

Emperor Hadrian, who toured Roman Britain in 122 AD, wanted the empire to live at peace within stable frontiers, most of which were defined by geographical features. In northern Britain, however, there was no natural barrier, so Hadrian decided to create his own by constructing a 76-mile wall from the Tyne to the Solway Firth. It was not intended to be an impenetrable fortification, but rather a base for patrols that could push out into hostile territory and a barrier to inhibit movement. Built up to a height of fifteen feet in places, it was punctuated by "milecastles", which served as gates, depots and mini-barracks, while a chain of forts straddled the Wall at six- to nine-mile intervals. Most of Hadrian's Wall disappeared centuries ago, yet walking its length remains a popular pastime, made easier now there's an official waymarked **Hadrian's Wall Path** (see p.659). Approached from Newcastle along the valley of the Tyne, via the Roman museum and site at **Corbridge**, the prosperous-looking market town of **Hexham** makes a good base. Most visitors stick to the best-preserved portions of the Wall, which are concentrated between **Chesters**

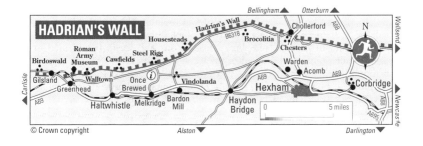

Roman Fort, four miles north of Hexham, and **Haltwhistle**, sixteen miles to the west. Scattered along this section are a variety of key archeological sites and museums, notably the remains of **Housesteads Fort** and that of **Vindolanda**, the milecastle remains at **Cawfields** and, further west, the **Roman Army Museum** near Greenhead.

A **Hadrian's Wall bus**, the #AD122, runs from Wallsend and Newcastle to Corbridge, Hexham, and all the wall sites and villages, and then on to Carlisle and Bowness-on-Solway (the end of the Hadrian's Wall Path). This operates between Easter and October, up to six times a day in each direction in high summer (Sun and bank hols only in April and October); a typical one-way ticket, from Hexham to Vindolanda, costs £2.60, though **Day Rover** tickets (1/3/7 days, £6/12/24) offer better value. There's also a year-round hourly service on the #685 bus between Newcastle and Carlisle, while a combination **rail rover** ticket with the Hadrian's Wall bus allows train travel to the minor stations between Newcastle and Carlisle. The best place to **park and ride** is at the Once Brewed Visitor Centre, where there's all-day parking and a bus stop for the Hadrian's Wall bus. You can pick up a comprehensive Hadrian's Wall **public transport timetable** from Newcastle, Hexham, Carlisle and Haltwhistle tourist offices, and the Once Brewed Visitor Centre, or contact the **Hadrian's Wall information line** on ☎01434/322002, ⊛www.hadrians-wall.org.

Corbridge

CORBRIDGE is a quiet and well-heeled commuter town overlooking the River Tyne from the top of a steep ridge. One mile west of the Market Place, accessible either by road or along the riverside footpath, lies **Corbridge Roman Site** (Easter–Oct daily 10am–4/6pm; Nov–March Sat & Sun 10am–4pm; £3.60;

The Hadrian's Wall Path

The **Hadrian's Wall Path** (⊛www.nationaltrail.co.uk/hadrianswall), an 84-mile way-marked National Trail, runs from Wallsend in the east to Bowness-on-Solway in the west, shadowing the line of the Wall. You could walk the main route in four days, but that's allowing little or no time to explore the archeological sites, remains, towns and villages on the way, so a week is a more realistic timescale. Contact the Hadrian's Wall information line (☎01434/322002) for an official free **walking and accommodation guide**; there's also the *Hadrian's Wall Path: National Trail Guide* (Aurum Press). Accommodation en route is not abundant, at least not on the Wall itself, so you should be prepared to be flexible – you may have to spend some nights a few miles from the end of your day's walk. The best time to do the walk is between May and October, as the wet winter months are not only heavier going but also contribute to erosion and archeological damage.

EH), the location of the garrison town of Corstopitum. This is the oldest fortified site in the region, first established as a supply base for the Roman advance
into Scotland in 80 AD (and thus predating the Wall itself). It remained in
regular military use until the end of the second century, after which it became
surrounded by a fast-developing town – most of the visible archeological
remains date from this period, when Corstopitum served as the nerve centre
of Hadrian's Wall. The extensive, clearly labelled remains provide an insight
into the layout of the civilian town, showing the foundations of temples, public
baths, garrison headquarters, workshops and houses as well as the best-preserved
Roman granaries in Britain.

There's plenty of **accommodation** in and around town, though nearby
Hexham makes a livelier overnight stop. The *Riverside Guest House* on Main
Street (T01434/632942, W www.theriversideguesthouse.co.uk; ❸) is a comfortable B&B with views of the Tyne, while opposite stands the town's finest choice,
the *Angel Inn* on Main Street (T01434/632119, W www.theangelofcorbridge
.co.uk; ❺), where classy lunches and dinners are served daily.

Hexham and around

In 671, on a bluff above the Tyne, four miles west of Corbridge, St Wilfrid
founded a Benedictine monastery whose church was, according to contemporary accounts, the finest to be seen north of the Alps. Unfortunately, its gold
and silver proved irresistible to the Vikings, who savaged the place in 876, but
the church was rebuilt in the eleventh century as part of an Augustinian priory,
and the town of **HEXHAM**, governed by the Archbishop of York, grew up in
its shadow. The stately exterior of **Hexham Abbey** (daily 9.30am–5/7pm; free)
still dominates the west side of the Market Place. Entry is through the south
transept, where there's a bruised but impressive first-century tombstone honouring Flavinus, a standard-bearer in the Roman cavalry, who's shown riding down
his bearded enemy. The memorial lies at the foot of the broad, well-worn steps
of the canons' **night stair**, one of the few such staircases – providing access
from the monastery to the church – to have survived the Dissolution. Beyond,
most of the high-arched nave dates from an Edwardian restoration and it's here
that you gain access to the **crypt**, a Saxon structure made out of old Roman
stones, where pilgrims once viewed the abbey's reliquaries. The nave's architect
also used Roman stonework, sticking various sculptural fragments in the walls,
many of which he had unearthed during the rebuilding.

The rest of Hexham's large **Market Place** (main market day is Tuesday) is
peppered with remains of its medieval past. The massive walls of the fourteenth-
century **Moot Hall** were built to serve as the gatehouse to "The Hall", a well-
protected enclosure that was garrisoned against the Scots. Nearby, the archbishops also built their own prison, a formidable fortified tower dating from 1330
and constructed using stones plundered from the Roman ruins at Corbridge.
Known as the **Old Gaol**, this accommodates Hexham's local history museum,
open again now after a major refit.

Four miles north of Hexham – and half a mile west of present-day Chollerford – **Chesters Roman Fort** (daily 9.30/10am–4/6pm; £3.60; EH),
otherwise known as Cilurnum, was built to guard the erstwhile Roman bridge
over the river, its six-acre plot accommodating a cavalry regiment roughly
five hundred strong. Enough remains of the original structure to pick out the
design of the fort, and each section has been clearly labelled, but the highlight is
down by the river where the vestibule, changing room and steam range of the
garrison's bathhouse are still visible, along with the furnace and the latrines.

Practicalities

Hexham's **bus station** is off Priestpopple, a few minutes' stroll east of the abbey, while the **train station** sits on the northeastern edge of the town centre, a ten-minute walk from the abbey; the **tourist office** is halfway between the two, in the main Wentworth **car park**, near Safeway (Easter–Oct Mon–Sat 9am–5/6pm, Sun 10am–5pm; Nov–Easter Mon–Sat 9am–5pm; ☎01434/652220, ⓦwww.hadrianswallcountry.org). The main focus of entertainment in town is the **Queen's Hall Arts Centre** on Beaumont Street (☎01434/652477), which puts on a year-round programme of theatre, dance, music, and art exhibitions.

There are plenty of daytime cafés, four Indian and a couple of Italian **restaurants** in town, but the only place that really stands out is *The Green Room*, Station Road (☎01434/608800; closed Sun night & Mon), an unpretentious Modern British restaurant in the old railway station waiting room. If you don't mind heading out of town, you can try one of the local **country pubs** instead: on Dipton Mill Road, two miles south of the centre (a 45min walk), *Dipton Mill Inn* (☎01434/606577) serves wholesome bar meals and own-brewed beer in a lovely streamside setting, while a similar distance to the northeast, the *Rat Inn* (☎01434/602814) at Anick (pronounced Ay-nick) has sweeping views, a pretty garden and fine food.

Accommodation

Acomb YHA Main Street, Acomb, 2 miles north of Hexham ☎01434/602864, Ⓔreservations@yha.org.uk. Simple 36-bed hostel occupying converted stable buildings in the village of Acomb – take bus #880 or #882, which pass Hexham train station. Closed Dec–Easter. Dorm beds £9.50.

Beaumont Beaumont Street ☎01434/602331, ⓦwww.beaumont-hotel.co.uk. Old-fashioned family-run hotel with spacious doubles overlooking the abbey. ❻

Hallbank Hallgate, behind the Old Gaol ☎01434/605567, ⓦwww.hallbankguesthouse.com.

A restored house in a quiet town-centre location, with eight en-suite rooms and an associated coffee shop/restaurant where you take breakfast. Parking. ❺

Kitty Frisk House Corbridge Road ☎01434/601533, ⓦwww.kittyfriskhouse.co.uk. Welcoming Edwardian retreat, half a mile from the centre (past the hospital). No credit cards. ❸

Matfen Hall Matfen, 10 miles northeast of Hexham ☎01661/886500, ⓦwww.matfenhall.com. The Northeast's ritziest golf-and-spa hotel presents a stylish take on country-house living, with modish rooms, plus pool, gym and contemporary British restaurant. ❽

Housesteads to Cawfields

Overlooking the bleak Northumbrian moors from the top of the Whin Sill, **Housesteads Roman Fort** (daily 10am–4/6pm; £3.60; EH & NT), eight miles west of Chesters, has long been the most popular site on the Wall. The fort was built in the second phase of the Hadrianic construction and is of standard design but for one enforced modification – forts were supposed to straddle the line of the Wall, but here the original stonework tracked along the very edge of the cliff, so Housesteads was built on the steeply sloping ridge to the south. Access is via the museum, from where you stroll across to the south gate, beside which lie the remains of the civilian settlement that was dependent on the one thousand infantrymen stationed within.

You don't need to pay for entrance to Housesteads to make the three-mile hike past the lovely wooded **Crag Lough** to **Steel Rigg** (car park). Leaving the Wall at Steel Rigg, it's roughly half a mile south to the main road (B6318) and the visitor centre at **Once Brewed**, where there's also a YHA hostel, pub and access road to the Vindolanda excavations. Otherwise, wall-walkers can continue another three miles west from Steel Rigg to **Cawfields** (free access). This was the site of a temporary Roman camp that again predated the Wall, and there are also the remains of another milecastle, this one perched on one of the most rugged crags on this section. There's a car park and picnic site at Cawfields, while if you make your way the mile or so south to the main B6318 you can recuperate at the *Milecastle Inn* (see below).

The **Once Brewed National Park Visitor Centre** (March–Sept daily 9.30am–5/5.30pm; reduced hours in winter, usually Sat & Sun only; ☏01434/344396) has exhibitions on both the Wall and the National Park.

Accommodation

Gibbs Hill Farm Once Brewed ☏01434/344030, ⓦwww.gibbshillfarm.co.uk. Working farm with en-suite rooms and great views of the Wall, two miles north of Steel Rigg. Also a hay-barn bunkhouse (beds £10, breakfast available for £4). ❸

Hadrian's Wall Camping and Caravan Site 2 miles north of Melkridge, just south of B6318 ☏01434/320495. Friendly, family-run site half a mile from the Wall, with showers, washing machine and dryer; breakfast available. Open all year.

Langley Castle A686, 2 miles south of Haydon Bridge ☏01434/688888, ⓦwww.langleycastle .com. The cheaper rooms are in the grounds, looking on to the castle, but all are spacious and comfortable, some with four-posters, saunas and spa baths. Also a restaurant, cocktail bar, lounge and gardens. ❼, castle rooms ❾

Once Brewed YHA Military Road, B6318, Once Brewed ☏0870/770 5980, ⓔoncebrewed@yha

.org.uk. Next to the visitor centre, providing packed lunches, three-course dinners, kitchen and lounge. Dorms (£13.95) are small (mostly four-bed). Closed Dec & Jan, and certain days Feb, March & Nov.

Twice Brewed Inn Military Road, B6318 ☏01434/344534, ⓦwww.twicebrewedinn.co.uk. Friendly community pub, 50yd up from Once Brewed visitor centre and hostel, with simple rooms, food served all day, local beers on tap and Internet access. Closed Jan. ❷, en suite ❸

Pubs

Cart's Bog Inn Langley ☏01434/684338. Just a quick drive off the Wall (and around 10min from Hexham) is this welcoming middle-of-nowhere pub with real ales and good food.

Milecastle Inn Military Road, B6318 ☏01434/320682. A cosy pub on the Wall road that specializes in great home-cooked pies.

Vindolanda

The excavated garrison fort of **Vindolanda** actually predates the Wall itself, though most of what you see today dates from the second to third century AD, when the fort was a thriving metropolis of five hundred soldiers with its own civilian settlement attached. The site (mid-Feb to mid-Nov daily 10am–5/6pm; winter reduced hours; £4.95, joint ticket with the Roman Army Museum at Greenhead £7.50; ☏01434/344277, ⓦwww.vindolanda.com) is operated by the private Vindolanda Trust, which has done an excellent job of imaginatively presenting its finds.

The ongoing **excavations** at Vindolanda are spread over a wide area, with civilian houses, an inn, administrative building, commander's house and main gates all clearly visible. Beyond lies the café, shop and museum, the latter housing the largest collection of Roman leather items ever discovered on a single site – dozens of shoes, belts, even a pair of baby boots – which were preserved in the black silt of waterlogged ditches. The most intriguing sections are concerned with the excavated hoard of **writing tablets**, now in the British Museum. The writings depict graphically the realities of military life in Northumberland, under the prefecture of Flavius Cerialis: soldiers' requests for more beer, birthday party invitations, court reports on banishments for unspecified wrongdoings, even letters from home containing gifts of underwear for freezing frontline grunts.

Roman Army Museum and Greenhead

A further four-mile trek west from Cawfields takes you past the remains of **Great Chesters Fort** before reaching a spectacular section of the Wall, known as the **Walltown Crags**, where a turret from a signal system predating the Wall still survives. The views from here are marvellous, and there's a handy nearby car park, picnic site and simple tea-and-ice-cream café. Very near the crags, at Carvoran, you can call into the Vindolanda Trust's **Roman Army Museum** (mid-Feb to mid-Nov daily 10am–5/6pm; winter reduced hours; £3.95; joint ticket with Vindolanda £7.50; ☎016977/47485, ⓦwww.vindolanda.com), which tells you everything there is to know about life in the Roman army by way of exhibits, dioramas, reconstructions and games.

Push on a mile southwest, and you're soon in minuscule **GREENHEAD**, with a tearoom, pub and YHA **hostel** (☎0870/770 5842, ⓔgreenhead@yha .org.uk; £11.95; closed Nov–Easter), the latter located in a converted Methodist chapel. ⚲ *Holmhead Guest House* (☎016977/47402, ⓦwww .holmhead.com; ➍), an old stone farmhouse sporting exposed beams, and partly built with stones taken from the Wall itself, is up a track behind the hostel. There are only four rooms, and guests should reserve in advance for the set-menu dinner (£22). There are also two **camping** spaces here, and a small bunk-barn (£10 per person), handy for Wall walkers.

Northumberland National Park

The great triangular chunk of land between Hadrian's Wall and the coastal plain is dominated by the wide-skied landscapes of the **Northumberland National Park** (ⓦwww.northumberland-national-park.org.uk), whose four hundred square miles rise to the Cheviot Hills on the Scottish border. Remote from lowland law and order, the dales were once the homelands of the **Border Reivers**, turbulent clans who ruled the local roost from the thirteenth to the sixteenth centuries The Reivers took advantage of the struggles between England and Scotland to engage in endless cross-border rustling and general brigandage, activities recalled by the ruined bastles (fortified farmhouses) and peels (defensive tower-houses) that lie dotted across the landscape. The most popular hiking trail is the **Pennine Way**, which, entering the National Park at Hadrian's Wall, cuts up through the village of Bellingham on its way to **The Cheviot**, the park's highest peak at 2674ft, finishing at Kirk Yetholm, over the border in Scotland. Bellingham is also the gateway to **Kielder Water**, a massive pine-surrounded reservoir, water-sports centre and nature reserve.

Kielder Water and Forest

The road from Bellingham skirts the forested edge of **Kielder Water** (ⓦwww .kielder.org), passing the assorted visitor centres, waterside parks, picnic areas and anchorages that fringe its southern shore. The reservoir – England's largest by volume – and surrounding forest make a good day out, particularly for cyclists and hikers; you can really get off the beaten track here and there's some reasonable local accommodation if you fancy extending your stay.

First stop is the Visitor Centre at **Tower Knowe** (daily Easter–Oct 10am–4/6pm; ☎0870/240 3549), eight miles from Bellingham, with a café and an exhibition on the history of the valley and reservoir. Another four miles west, at **Leaplish** (opening hours vary; ☎0870/240 3549), the waterside park, bar and restaurant are the focus of most of Kielder's outdoor activities and accommodation: there's also a heated indoor pool and sauna. The **Bird of Prey Centre** here (daily 10.30am–5pm; £4.50; ☎01434/250400) lays on entertaining daily flying displays, plus falconry courses and "hawk walks". Otherwise, a ninety-minute cruise on the **Osprey ferry** (Easter–Oct 5 daily; £5.50) is always a pleasure.

Five miles from Leaplish at the top of the reservoir and just three miles from the Scottish border, the forestry settlement of **Kielder Village** is dominated by Kielder Castle, built in 1775 as the hunting lodge of the Duke of Northumberland and now the **Forest Park Visitor Centre** (Easter–Oct & Dec daily 10am–5pm; Nov Sat & Sun 11am–4pm; ☎01434/250209). The castle is at the heart of **Kielder Forest Park**, Britain's largest forest, comprising several million spruce trees, crisscrossed by trails and home to red squirrels, deer, otters and countless birds, including goshawks, merlins and ospreys. Several clearly marked footpaths and bike trails lead from the castle into the forest, or you can explore some of the contemporary sculpture that Kielder is increasingly known for – like the **Minotaur Maze**, near the castle, or the **Skyspace** (1.5 miles from the castle), a light-and-space chamber best experienced at dawn or dusk.

A seasonal **Kielder Bus** (end May to mid-Oct, Sun & bank hols only) runs once daily in the morning from Newcastle to Kielder Castle, and then provides a shuttle service to Kielder attractions before returning to the city in the late afternoon. At other times, you're dependent on the local bus **from Bellingham**. You'll pass a couple of pubs on the way, while facilities in Kielder village include a general store, garage, post office, tearoom and pub (closed Mon Oct–Easter). There's **mountain-bike rental** available from Kielder Bikes (☎01434/250392; £17.50 a day) just by the castle.

As well as the **accommodation** options listed below, there are several other B&Bs in Kielder village and the surrounding area – the visitor centres can assist. The **Kielder Campsite** (☎01434/250291; closed Oct–Easter) is about half a mile north of the castle on the banks of the Tyne.

Accommodation and food

Blackcock Inn Falstone ☎01434/240200. Small inn (closed Tues) located in a pretty riverside hamlet. You can eat here, or at the tearooms opposite (summer daily, winter weekends only). ❸

Hollybush Inn Greenhaugh ☎01434/240391, ⓦwww.thehollybushinn.co.uk. Rustic old inn in a hamlet about halfway between Kielder and Bellingham. Three nice rooms available, plus bar meals and a more elaborate weekend restaurant menu. ❸

Kielder Lodges Leaplish Waterside Park ☎0870/240 3549, reservations through Hoseasons ☎01502/502588, ⓦwww.hoseasons.co.uk. A converted fishing lodge provides self-catering bunk-barn accommodation (small dorms £15) and three en-suite rooms (double £35, family £50).

Also Scandinavian-style self-catering lodges available, £260–860 per week depending on size and season.

Kielder YHA Kielder village ☎0870/770 5898, ⓔkielder@yha.org.uk. Well-equipped hostel, with some two- and three-bed rooms plus small dorms. It has a self-catering kitchen and restaurant, and is only 200 yards from the pub. Closed Nov–Easter. Dorm beds £11.95.

Pheasant Inn Stannersburn ☎01434/240382, ⓦwww.thepheasantinn .com. On the road in from Bellingham, a couple of miles before the water, this early seventeenth-century inn has eight comfortable rooms in a modern extension and decent meals served in the bar or restaurant. ❺

Rothbury and around

Straddling the River Coquet, **ROTHBURY** prospered as a late Victorian resort because it gave ready access to the forests, burns and ridges of the Simonside Hills. The small town remains a popular spot for walkers, and is also a handy base for visiting two of the Northeast's most interesting landed estates (see below). Buses stop at the bottom of Rothbury's High Street, outside the *Queen's Head*, with the useful **Tourist Information and National Park Visitor Centre** up near the cross on Church Street (April–Oct daily 10am–5/6pm;

Nov–March Sat & Sun 10am–5pm; ☎01669/620887, ⓦwww.visit-rothbury
.co.uk). There's no pressing need to stay, with Alnwick (12 miles) and the coast
so close, but the tourist office does have a folder of local B&Bs. Most of the
places to eat and drink – two or three cafés, a deli and a couple of pubs – are
strung out along the High Street, but a better move is to drive the two miles
west to **Thropton** village (Otterburn road), where the *Three Wheat Heads* and
the *Cross Keys Inn* soak up the local dining trade.

Cragside

Victorian Rothbury was dominated by Sir William, later the first **Lord
Armstrong**, the nineteenth-century arms manufacturer, shipbuilder and engineer who built his country home at **Cragside** (Easter–Sept Tues–Sun, plus
bank hols 1–5.30pm; £8.50, gardens only £5.70; NT), a mile to the east of the
village. Armstrong was an avid innovator, fascinated by hydraulic engineering
and by hydroelectric power. He dammed the stream in his property to power
several domestic appliances, such as a spit and dumb waiter in the massive
kitchen, as well as heating his personal Turkish-style plunge bath and steam
room. In 1880, he also managed to supply Cragside with electricity, making
this the first house in the world to be lit by hydroelectric power. The remains
of the original system – including the powerhouse and pumping station – are
still visible in the **grounds**, which, together with the splendid **formal gardens**,
have longer opening hours (Easter–Sept Tues–Sun 10.30am–7pm or dusk;
Nov to mid-Dec Wed–Sun 11am–4pm). Over at the visitor centre there's a
café/restaurant, and an explanatory video and other displays in the adjacent
Armstrong Energy Centre.

Wallington

Around 13 miles south of Rothbury, down the B6342 and a mile out of Cambo,
stands **Wallington** (Easter–Oct 1–4.30/5.30pm; house and gardens £7.30;
NT), an ostentatious mansion rebuilt by Sir Walter Blackett, the coal- and lead-
mine owner, in the 1740s. The house is known for its Rococo plasterwork
and William Bell Scott's Pre-Raphaelite murals of scenes from Northumbrian
history. However, it's the magnificent **gardens and grounds** (daily all year
dawn–dusk; £5.20 without house admission) that are the real delight, with
lawns, woods and lakes that are traced by easy-to-follow footpaths. A leisurely
circuit of the estate might take you a couple of hours, depending on how long
you spend in the magical **walled garden** (daily from 10am), exploring its
terracing, conservatories, arbours and water features.

Chillingham

Six miles southeast of Wooler, **Chillingham Castle** (May–Sept daily except
Sat 1–5pm, gardens and tearooms from noon; £5.50; ⓦwww.chillingham
-castle.com) was augmented at regular intervals until 1873, though it keeps the
essential structure of its mid-fourteenth-century incarnation. For fifty years
from 1933, however, Chillingham was largely left to the elements, until the
present owner set about restoring it in his own individualistic way: bedrooms,
living rooms and even a grisly torture chamber are decorated with all manner
of historical paraphernalia. In the **grounds,** you can look around a small Elizabethan topiary garden, with its intricately clipped hedges of box and yew, and
take a mile-long walk through the woods to the lake.

In 1220, the adjoining 365 acres of parkland were enclosed to protect the
local wild cattle for hunting and food. And so the **Chillingham Wild Cattle**

(Easter–Oct Mon & Wed–Sat 10am–noon & 2–5pm, Sun 2–5pm; winter by appointment; £4.50; ☎01668/215250, ⓦwww.chillingham-wildcattle.org .uk) – a fierce, primeval herd with white coats, black muzzles and black tips to their horns – have remained to this day, cut off from mixing with domesticated breeds. It's possible to visit these unique relics, who number about sixty, but only accompanied by a warden, as the animals are potentially dangerous and need to be protected from outside infection. The visit takes up to ninety minutes and involves a short country walk before viewing the cattle from a safe distance. The site is signposted from the A1 and A697; bring strong shoes or walking boots if it's wet.

The Northumberland coast

The low-lying **Northumberland coast**, stretching 64 miles north from Newcastle to the Scottish border, boasts many of the region's principal attractions, not least a succession of mighty fortresses, beginning with **Warkworth Castle** and **Alnwick Castle**, former and present strongholds of the Percys, the county's biggest landowners. Further along, there's the formidable fastness of **Bamburgh** and then, last of all, the magnificent Elizabethan ramparts surrounding **Berwick-upon-Tweed**. In between you'll find splendid sandy beaches – notably at Bamburgh – as well as the site of the Lindisfarne monastery on **Holy Island** and the seabird and nature reserve of the **Farne Islands**, reached by boat from Seahouses.

Warkworth

WARKWORTH, a coastal hamlet set in a loop of the River Coquet, is best seen from the north, from where the grey stone terraces of the long main street slope up towards the commanding remains of **Warkworth Castle** (Easter–Oct daily 10am–4/6pm; Nov–March Sat, Sun & Mon 10am–4pm; £3.30; EH). Enough remains of the outer wall to give a clear impression of the layout of the medieval bailey, but – apart from the well-preserved gatehouse through which the site is entered – nothing catches your attention as much as the keep. It was here that most of the Percy family, earls of Northumberland, chose to live throughout the fourteenth and fifteenth centuries.

From the village churchyard (or, further up, from below the castle), a delightful path heads the half-mile inland along the peaceful right bank of the Coquet to the little boat that shuttles visitors across to **Warkworth Hermitage** (Easter–Sept Wed, Sun and bank hols 11am–5pm; £2.30; EH), a series of simple rooms that were hewn out of the cliff above the river sometime in the fourteenth century.

Alnwick

The unassuming town of **ALNWICK** (pronounced "Annick"), thirty miles north of Newcastle, is renowned for its castle and gardens which overlook the River Aln immediately north of the town centre. You'll need a full day to do these justice and, as the biggest town between Hadrian's Wall and the Scottish border, Alnwick itself warrants an overnight stop anyway. It's an appealing market town of cobbled streets and Georgian houses, centred on the old cross in Market Place, site of weekly markets (Thursdays and Saturdays) since the thirteenth century (and a farmers' market on the last Friday of the month).

△ Alnwick Treehouse

Other than catching the market in full swing, the best time to visit is during the week-long **Alnwick Fair**, a medieval re-enactment which starts on the last Sunday in June.

The Percys – who were raised to the dukedom of Northumberland in 1750 – have owned **Alnwick Castle** (Easter–Oct daily 11am–5pm, grounds from 10am; £7.95, joint ticket with gardens £12; ⓦwww.alnwickcastle.com) since 1309, when Henry de Percy reinforced the original Norman keep and remodelled its curtain wall. In the eighteenth century, the castle was badly in need of a refit, so the first duke had the interior refurbished by Robert Adam in an extravagant Gothic style – which in turn was supplanted by the gaudy Italianate decoration preferred by the fourth duke in the 1850s. There's plenty to see inside, though the interior is not to everyone's taste and it can be crowded at times – not least with families on the *Harry Potter* trail, since the castle doubled as Hogwarts School in the first two films. Three of the perimeter towers contain museum collections, but the bucolic garden walks and Capability Brown–designed **grounds** are more interesting.

Signs lead you out of the grounds for the short walk to **Alnwick Garden** (daily 10am–dusk; £6, joint admission with castle £12; ⓦwww.alnwickgarden .com), which is still to be fully established but already draws crowds to marvel at its sheer scale and invention. At its heart is the computerized Grand Cascade, which shoots water jets in a regular synchronized display, while special features include a bamboo labyrinth maze and the popular Poison Garden – filled with the world's deadliest plants. Each month brings seasonal garden highlights that volunteers are happy to explain. Superior ices, teas and snacks are available from the *Garden Café*, though it's Europe's biggest **treehouse** that provides the most spectacular location for a meal – it's also open for dinner (Thurs–Sat from 6pm; ⓣ01665/511852; menus from £20).

Practicalities

Alnwick **bus station** is on Clayport Street, a couple of minutes' walk west of the Market Place, where you'll find the **tourist office**, in the arcaded Shambles (Easter–Sept Mon–Fri 9am–5/6pm, Sat 9/10am–4/5pm, Sun 10am–4pm; Oct–March closed Sun; ⓣ01665/510665, ⓦwww.alnwick.gov.uk). **Alnwick Playhouse**, just through the arch on Bondgate Without (ⓣ01665/510785, ⓦwww.alnwickplayhouse.co.uk), is a venue for theatre, music and film throughout the year.

Accommodation and food

Masons' Arms Rennington, 5 miles north-east of town on the Seahouses (B1340) road ⓣ01665/577275, ⓦwww.masonsarms.net. An old coaching inn with good food, as well as eleven bedrooms. ❹, suites ❺

Tower Restaurant & Accommodation 10 Bondgate Within ⓣ01665/603888, ⓦwww .tower-alnwick.co.uk. Stands out for its bright, tasteful, en-suite rooms and hearty breakfasts; the pine-furnished restaurant below serves meals, but closes at 8pm. ❺

White Swan Bondgate Within ⓣ01665/602109, ⓦwww.classiclodges.co.uk. Alnwick's main hotel, where you might want to pop in at least for coffee or a meal – the hotel's fine oak-panelled dining room was swiped from an old ocean liner, the *Olympic*, the twin of the *Titanic*. ❼

Craster, Dunstanburgh and Beadnell

Heading northeast out of Alnwick along the B1340, it's a six-mile hop to the region's kipper capital, the tiny fishing village of **CRASTER**, perched above a minuscule harbour. Half a dozen buses a day run here from Alnwick; the service continues to Seahouses and Bamburgh. You can buy wonderful kippers and oak-smoked salmon at Robson's factory, while the *Jolly Fisherman*, the **pub** above the harbour, features sea views from its back window and garden, and famously good crabmeat, whisky and cream soup, crab sandwiches and kipper pâté.

Most spectacularly, however, Craster provides access to **Dunstanburgh Castle** (Easter–Oct daily 10am–4/6pm; Nov–March Mon & Thurs–Sun 10am–4pm; £2.60; NT & EH), whose shattered medieval ruins occupy a magnificent promontory about thirty minutes' windy walk up the coast. Originally built in the fourteenth century, parts of the surrounding walls survive though the dominant feature is the massive keep-gatehouse, which stands out from miles around on the bare coastal spur.

A few miles north, **BEADNELL** has a pub and fine beaches, and if you had to pick just one place to stay on the coast it would be at welcoming ⊁ *Beach Court* (☎01665/720225, @www.beachcourt.com), a distinctive guest house right next to the harbour. This has glorious bay views and three lovely rooms with big bathrooms (❺, ❻ & ❼) – the most expensive of which is a "turret" suite with a canopied bed and crow's-nest observatory; breakfast is continental. You can walk from the front door along the beach to the *Ship* pub at Newton (2 miles) or even on to Dunstanburgh (7 miles).

Seahouses and the Farne Islands

From Beadnell, it's three miles north to the fishing port of **SEAHOUSES**, embarkation point for the windswept **Farne Islands**, a rocky archipelago lying a few miles offshore. Owned by the National Trust and maintained as a nature reserve, the Farnes are the summer home of hundreds of thousands of migrating seabirds, notably puffins, guillemots, terns, eider ducks and kittiwakes, and home to the only grey seal colony on the English coastline. Weather permitting, several operators run daily **boat trips** (around 2–3hr; from £10) from Seahouses quayside, usually starting at around 10am. During the bird breeding season (May–July) landings are restricted to morning trips to **Staple Island** and afternoons to **Inner Farne** – landing on either in the breeding season incurs a separate National Trust landing fee of £5. At all other times, bird-viewing trips normally land only on Inner Farne (NT fee £4), the largest of the Farne Islands where you can also visit a restored fourteenth-century chapel built in honour of St Cuthbert. Most operators also offer "sailaround" cruises, which get close to the birds and seals without landing, or you can take a trip to **Longstone Island** (not a bird sanctuary, so no landing fee) whose singular attraction is the lighthouse from where Grace Darling (see below) launched her daring rescue.

You can just wander down to the quayside and pick a departure, or contact either the **National Trust Shop**, 16 Main St (☎01665/721099), by the Seahouses traffic roundabout, or the **tourist office** (Easter–Oct daily 10am–5pm; ☎01665/720884, @www.seahouses.org), in the nearby main car park.

Bamburgh

Flanking a triangular green in the lee of its castle, three miles north of Seahouses, the tiny village of **BAMBURGH** is only a five-minute walk from two splendid sandy beaches, backed by rolling, tufted dunes. From the sands, **Bamburgh Castle** (Easter–Oct daily 11am–5pm; £6; @www.bamburghcastle .com) is a spectacular sight, its elongated battlements crowning a formidable basalt crag high above the beach. In centuries-long decline – rotted by seaspray and buffeted by winter storms – the castle was bought by Lord Armstrong in

1894, who demolished most of the structure to replace it with a cumbersome hybrid castle-mansion. The focal point of the new building was the King's Hall, a teak-ceilinged affair of colossal dimensions, whose main redeeming feature is an exquisite collection of Fabergé stone animal carvings. In the ground floor of the keep, the stone-vaulted ceiling maintains its Norman appearance, making a suitable arena for a display of fetters and man-traps.

Bamburgh is also the burial place of the celebrated heroine **Grace Darling**, who rests beneath a Gothic Revival memorial in the churchyard of thirteenth-century St Aidan's church. In September 1838, a gale dashed the steamship *Forfarshire* against the rocks of the Farne Islands. Nine passengers struggled onto a reef, where they were subsequently saved by Grace and her lighthouseman father, William. The story of Grace's brief life – she died of tuberculosis in 1842, aged 26 – is told on any Farne Islands boat trip from Seahouses, while a RNLI Grace Darling Museum opposite the church in Bamburgh (under renovation) goes into more detail.

A regular **bus** service links Alnwick and Berwick-upon-Tweed with Bamburgh, stopping by the green. At the top of the village green, the tastefully refurbished *Victoria Hotel* (☎01668/214431, ⓦwww.victoriahotel.net; ❼) has a couple of relaxing bars (meals, lunch and dinner) and a more expensive brasserie (dinner only) with a good Modern British menu. *The Greenhouse*, a few doors down at 5 Front St (☎01668/214513, ⓦwww.thegreenhouseguesthouse .co.uk; ❹), is more of a B&B, with four en-suite rooms. Other moderate B&Bs are found on Lucker Road, beyond the top of the village green. Romantics should head out to **Waren Mill**, a couple of miles to the west on the B1342 (Belford/A1 road), where the charming *Waren House Hotel* (☎01668/214581, ⓦwww.warenhousehotel.co.uk; ❼) is set in its own quiet grounds on the edge of Budle Bay.

Holy Island

There's something rather menacing about the approach to **Holy Island**, past the barnacle-encrusted marker poles that line the causeway. The danger of drowning is real enough if you ignore the safe crossing times posted at the start of the three-mile trip across the tidal flats. (The island is cut off for about five hours every day, so to avoid a tedious delay consult the **tide timetables** at one of the region's tourist offices or in the local newspapers.) Once on the island, it's easy to picture the furious Viking hordes sweeping across Holy Island, giving no quarter to the monks at this quiet outpost of early Christianity. Today's sole village is plain in the extreme, which doesn't deter summer day-trippers from clogging the car parks as soon as the causeway is open. But Holy Island has a distinctive and isolated atmosphere, especially out of season.

Once known as **Lindisfarne**, Holy Island has an illustrious history. It was here that St Aidan of Iona founded a monastery at the invitation of King Oswald of Northumbria in 634. The monks quickly evangelized the Northeast and established a reputation for scholarship and artistry, the latter exemplified by the **Lindisfarne Gospels**, the apotheosis of Celtic religious art, now kept in the British Library. The monastery had sixteen bishops in all, the most celebrated being **St Cuthbert**, who only accepted the job after Ecgfrith, another North-umbrian king, pleaded with him. But Cuthbert never settled here and, within two years, he was back in his hermit's cell on the Farne Islands, where he died in 687. His colleagues rowed the body back to Lindisfarne, which became a place of pilgrimage until 875, when the monks abandoned the island in fear of marauding Vikings, taking Cuthbert's remains with them.

The sandstone ruins of **Lindisfarne Priory** (Easter–Oct daily 9.30–4/5pm; Nov–Easter Sat, Sun & Mon 10am–2pm; £3.60; EH) are from a later Benedictine foundation, which lasted here until the Dissolution. Behind lie the scant remains of the monastic buildings while adjacent is the mostly thirteenth-century **Church of St Mary the Virgin**, whose delightful churchyard overlooks the ruins. The museum (same times as priory; entrance included in priory fee) features a collection of incised stones that constitute all that remains of the first monastery. The finest of them is a round-headed tombstone showing armed Northumbrians on one side, and kneeling figures before the Cross on the other – presumably a propagandist's view of the beneficial effects of Christianity.

Stuck on a small pyramid of rock half a mile away from the village, past the dock and along the seashore, **Lindisfarne Castle** (Easter–Oct daily except Mon, hours vary according to tide but always include noon–3pm; £5; NT; ☎01289/389244) was built in the middle of the sixteenth century to protect the island's harbour from the Scots. It was, however, merely a decaying shell when Edward Hudson, the founder of *Country Life* magazine, stumbled across it in 1901. Hudson bought the castle and turned it into a holiday home to designs by Edwin Lutyens.

The historic sites are all that most people bother with, but a walk around the island's perimeter is a fine way to spend a couple of hours. Most of the northwestern portion of the island is maintained as a **nature reserve**: from a bird hide you can spot terns and plovers, and then plod through the dunes and grasses to your heart's content.

Practicalities

The #477 **bus** from Berwick-upon-Tweed to Holy Island is dictated by the tides, but basically service is daily in August and twice weekly the rest of the year. Departure times (and sometimes days) vary with the tides, and the journey takes thirty minutes. **Information** is available from Berwick-upon-Tweed tourist office, or consult the local community website, ⓦ www.lindisfarne.org .uk. The island is short on accommodation and you should make an advance booking, whenever you visit. Straightforward **B&B** is on offer at *Castlereigh* (☎01289/389218; ❷; closed Nov–Feb), just by the green, or there are a couple of traditional **hotels**, the *Lindisfarne* (☎01289/389273; ❺) and the *Manor House* (☎01289/389207; includes dinner ❼), the latter backing on to the priory. Best pub on the island is the *Ship* on Marygate, down from the green (☎01289/389311; ❹; closed Jan).

Berwick-upon-Tweed

Before the union of the English and Scottish crowns in 1603, **BERWICK-UPON-TWEED**, twelve miles north of Holy Island, was the quintessential frontier town, changing hands no fewer than fourteen times between 1174 and 1482, when the Scots finally ceded the stronghold to the English. Interminable cross-border warfare ruined Berwick's economy, turning the prosperous Scottish port of the thirteenth century into an impoverished garrison town, which the English forcibly cut off from its natural trading hinterland up the River Tweed. By the late sixteenth century, Berwick's fortifications were in a dreadful state of repair and Elizabeth I, apprehensive of the resurgent alliance between France and Scotland, had the place rebuilt in line with the latest principles of military architecture. The ramparts are now the town's major attraction, and you'll want to stop at least long enough to take a walk around the walls. A set of interesting local museums, and the town's attractive riverside location, warrant a night's stay, especially as Berwick is a useful staging post between England and Scotland.

The Town

Berwick's **walls** – protected by ditches on three sides and the Tweed on the fourth – are strengthened by immense bastions, whose arrowhead-shape ensured that every part of the wall could be covered by fire. Today, the easy mile-long circuit along the top of the walls and ramparts offers a succession of fine views out to sea, across the Tweed and over the orange-tiled rooftops of a town that's distinguished by its elegant **Georgian mansions**. These, dating from Berwick's resurgence as a seaport between 1750 and 1820, are the town's most attractive feature, with the tapering **Lions' House**, on Windmill Hill, and the daintily decorated facades of **Quay Walls**, beside the river, of particular note.

Within the ramparts, the Berwick skyline is punctured by the stumpy spire of the eighteenth-century **Town Hall** (Easter–Oct Mon–Fri tours at 10.30am & 2pm; £1.50) at the bottom of Marygate, right at the heart of the compact centre. This retains its original jailhouse on the upper floor, now housing the **Cell Block Museum**, entertaining tours of which dwell on tales of crime and punishment in Berwick.

Opposite the church, the finely proportioned **Barracks** (Easter–Oct daily 10am–4/6pm; Nov–Easter limited hours; £3.30; EH) date from the early eighteenth century and were in use until 1964, when the King's Own Scottish Borderers regiment decamped. Inside, there's a regimental museum, as well as the "By Beat of Drum" exhibition, which in a series of picture boards and dioramas traces the life of the British infantryman from the sixteenth to the nineteenth century. These are of rather specialist interest, though most will warm to the temporary exhibitions of contemporary art in the **Gymnasium Gallery** and the superior borough museum and art gallery, sited in the **Clock Block**.

Practicalities

From Berwick **train station** it's about ten minutes' walk down Castlegate and Marygate to the town centre. Most regional **buses** stop closer in on Golden Square (where Castlegate meets Marygate), on the approach to the Royal Tweed Bridge, though some may also stop in front of the station. The **tourist office** at 106 Marygate (Easter–Sept Mon–Sat 10am–5/6pm, Sun 11am–3pm; Oct–Easter Mon–Sat 10am–4pm; ☎01289/330733, ⊛www.exploreberwick .co.uk) can book you onto informative one-hour **walking tours** of town (Easter–Oct Mon–Fri 3 daily; £3.50). For local **bike rental**, contact Tweed Cycles, 17a Bridge St (☎01289/331476), who can also give details of a scenic route to Holy Island (24 miles return). Berwick's **arts centre**, The Maltings, Eastern Lane (☎01289/330999, ⊛www.maltingsberwick.co.uk), has a year-round programme of music, theatre, comedy, film and dance, as well as river views from its licensed café.

Accommodation

 Berwick Backpackers 56–58 Bridge St ☎01289/331481, ⊛www.berwickback packers.co.uk. Not so much a backpackers' (though there's a small six-bed dorm; beds £14.95) as a self-styled "superior budget B&B". Smartly decorated en-suite rooms, including one with a gallery, another with private kitchen; prices include continental breakfast. No credit cards. ❷

Coach House Crookham, 10 miles southwest of Berwick ☎01890/820293, ⊛www.coachhouse crookham.com. Has a range of rooms in converted farm buildings sporting exposed beams. Four-course dinners available (£20). **4**

Clovelly House 58 West St ☎01289/302337, ⓦwww.clovelly53.freeserve.co.uk. A really nice B&B, centrally located on a steep cobbled street by the Arts Centre. Rooms are very smart, while breakfast is superb. No credit cards. **3**

No.1 Sallyport Bridge Street ☎01289/308827, ⓦwww.sallyport.co.uk. Berwick's most luxurious B&B, with four sensational rooms in a seventeenth-century house. Two spacious rooms and two lavish suites are elegantly furnished, retro to contemporary. Minimum 2-night weekend stays. **6**, suites **7**

Queen's Head 6 Sandgate ☎01289/307852, ⓔqueensheadhotel@berwickontweed.fsbusiness .co.uk. Old Berwick inn that's gone for the gastro-pub look – rooms are good for the price, while the daily changing blackboard menu (mains £9–18) is the best in town. **5**

Food and drink

Barrels Ale House 59–61 Bridge St ☎01289/308013, ⓦwww.thebarrelsalehouse .com. Chilled-out independent pub at the foot of the Berwick Bridge, with funky furniture, guest beers, and an interesting programme of live music and DJs.

Foxton's 26 Hide Hill ☎01289/303939. Town-centre bar-brasserie serving a varied English and Mediterranean-style menu. Closed Sun. Moderate.

Rob Roy Dock Road, Tweedmouth ☎01289/306428. The traditional choice for fish and shellfish, with a regularly changing menu. There's a cheaper bar menu too. Closed Tues & Wed lunch. Expensive.

Travel details

Buses

For more information on all local and national bus services, contact Traveline ☎0870/608 2608, ⓦwww.traveline.org.uk.
Alnwick to: Bamburgh (4–6 daily; 1hr 5min); Berwick-upon-Tweed (3 daily; 2hr).
Bamburgh to: Alnwick (4–6 daily; 1hr 5min); Craster (4–5 daily; 30–40min); Seahouses (Mon–Sat 9 daily, Sun 4; 10min).
Barnard Castle to: Bishop Auckland (Mon–Sat 9 daily, Sun 6; 50min); Darlington (hourly; 35min); Middleton-in-Teesdale (hourly; 35min); Raby Castle (9 daily; 15min).
Berwick-upon-Tweed to: Holy Island (Aug 2 daily, rest of the year 2 weekly; 30min); Newcastle (Mon–Sat 6 daily, Sun 3; 2hr 30min–3hr).
Bishop Auckland to: Barnard Castle (Mon–Sat 9 daily, Sun 6; 50min); Darlington (Mon–Sat hourly; 35min); Newcastle (hourly; 1hr 15min); Stanhope (Mon–Sat 7 daily, Sun 4; 45min); Sunderland (Mon–Sat 4 daily; 2hr).
Darlington to: Barnard Castle (hourly; 35min); Bishop Auckland (Mon–Sat hourly; 35min); Carlisle (1 daily; 3hr); Durham (every 30min; 1hr); Middleton-in-Teesdale (Mon–Sat 9 daily, Sun 3; 1hr 20min); Newcastle (every 30min; 2hr).
Durham to: Barnard Castle (1 daily; 1hr); Beamish (May–Sept 1–3 daily; 25min); Bishop Auckland (every 30min; 30min); Darlington (every 30min; 1hr); Newcastle (hourly; 1hr); Stanhope (June–Sept 1–2 weekly; 45min); Sunderland (every 15–30min; 50min).
Hexham to: Bellingham (Mon–Sat 5 daily; 40min); Haltwhistle (hourly; 40min).
Newcastle to: Alnwick (Mon–Sat 6 daily, Sun 3; 1hr 15min); Bamburgh (3 daily; 2hr 30min); Barnard Castle (1 daily; 1hr 25min); Berwick-upon-Tweed (Mon–Sat 6 daily, Sun 3; 2hr 30min–3hr); Carlisle (hourly; 2hr); Craster (3 daily; 1hr 50min); Darlington (every 30min; 2hr); Durham (hourly; 1hr); Hexham (every 30min; 1hr 15min); Rothbury (Mon–Sat 7 daily, Sun 2; 1hr 15min); Seahouses (3 daily; 2hr 10min); Warkworth (hourly; 1hr 20min).

Trains

For information on all local and national rail services, contact National Rail Enquiries ☎08457/484950, ⓦwww.nationalrail.co.uk.
Darlington to: Bishop Auckland (every 1–2hr; 30min); Durham (every 30min; 20min); Newcastle (every 30min; 35min).
Durham to: Darlington (every 30min; 20min); London (hourly; 3hr); Newcastle (every 30min; 15min); York (hourly; 50min).
Hexham to: Carlisle (hourly; 1hr); Newcastle (hourly; 40min).
Newcastle to: Berwick-upon-Tweed (hourly; 45min); Carlisle (hourly; 1hr 30min); Corbridge (hourly; 40min); Darlington (every 30min; 35min); Durham (every 30min; 15min); Haltwhistle (hourly; 1hr); Hexham (hourly; 40min); London (hourly; 2hr 45min–3hr 30min); York (hourly; 1hr).

Wales

Wales

South Wales

CHAPTER 14

Highlights

* **Blaenafon** Fascinating ironworks town plus deep-mine museum. See p.687

* **Wales Millennium Centre, Cardiff Bay** A symphony of opposites – industry and art, grand and intimate – the new WMC is a bold and brilliant addition to the capital. See p.698

* **St Fagans National History Museum** From exquisite art to rugged tales of Welsh history, all housed in Cardiff's grand civic precinct. See p.703

* **National Waterfront Museum, Swansea** A celebration of Welsh innovation and industry – the best museum in Wales. See p.707

* **Laugharne** Dylan Thomas's "heron-priested shore" evokes the spirit of the ebullient poet and playwright. See p.713

* **Carreg Cennen Castle** Fantasy fortress, great for sublime views and exploration. See p.713

* **St David's** Inspirational village with a splendid cathedral and heart-racing boat trips out to offshore islands. See p.721

△ Wales Millennium Centre

14

South Wales

The most heavily populated, and by far the most anglicized, part of Wales is the **south**. This is a region of distinct character, whether in the resurgent seaport cities of Cardiff and Swansea, the mining-scarred Valleys or the beauty of the Glamorgan, Carmarthenshire and Pembrokeshire coasts. Unlike the rest of Wales, transport connections are fast and frequent, making this region by far the easiest Welsh stop for those on a limited itinerary.

Monmouthshire, the easternmost county in Wales, abuts the English border and contains the full span of South Welsh life, from the bucolic charms of the **River Wye** and **Tintern Abbey** to **Newport**, Wales's third largest conurbation, near the remains of an extensive Roman settlement at **Caerleon**. West and north are the world-famous **Valleys**. Although all but one of the coal mines have closed, the area is still one of tight-knit towns, with a rich working-class heritage that displays itself in some excellent museums and colliery tours, such as **Big Pit** at Blaenafon and the **Rhondda Heritage Park** in Trehafod. The Valleys course down to the great ports of the coast, which once shipped Wales's products all over the world. The greatest of them all was **Cardiff**, now Wales's upbeat capital and an essential stop. Further west is Wales's second city, **Swansea** – rougher, tougher and less anglicized than the capital. It sits on an impressive arc of coast that shelves round to the delightful **Gower Peninsula**, one of the country's favourite playgrounds, that juts out into the sea like a mini-Wales of grand beaches, rocky headlands, bracken heaths and ruined castles. Too many people rush from here straight to the coastal national park of Pembrokeshire, missing out **Carmarthenshire**. Of all the routes that spoke out of the county town of **Carmarthen**, the most glorious is the winding road to **Llandeilo** along the **Tywi Valley**, past ruined hilltop forts and two of the country's finest gardens. Immediately west sits Wales's most impressively sited castle at **Carreg Cennen**, high up on the dizzy rock-plug of the Black Mountain.

The wide sands fringing Carmarthen Bay stretch towards the popular seaside resort of **Tenby**, a major stop on the 186-mile **Pembrokeshire Coast Path**. The rutted coastline of **St Bride's Bay** is the most glorious part of the coastal walk, which leads north to brush past the impeccable mini-city of **St David's**, whose exquisite cathedral shelters in its own protective hollow. Nearby are plenty of opportunities for spectacular coast and hill walks, dinghy crossings to local islands and numerous other outdoor activities.

The main road route into South Wales from England is the M4 motorway, which divides at Junction 21 near Bristol: the old **Severn Bridge** carries the M48 loop, while the M4 itself forms the Second (or **New**) **Severn Crossing** a little downstream. Both impose a **toll** on westbound traffic, payable by cash or cheque only (@www.severnbridge.co.uk): a hefty £4.90 for a car, free for

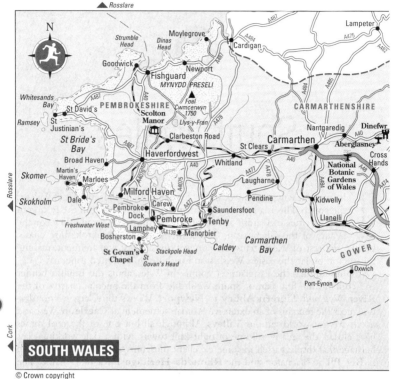

© Crown copyright

a motorbike. Cyclists and pedestrians can follow a dedicated path on the old Severn Bridge for free. The frequent **trains** along the London–Bristol–Cardiff route duck under the water courtesy of the Severn Rail Tunnel.

The Wye Valley

The **Wye Valley** (Ⓦ www.visitwyevalley.com), along with the rest of Monmouth-shire, was finally recognized as part of Wales only in the local government reorganization of 1974. Before then, the county was officially included as part of neither England nor Wales, so that maps were frequently headlined "Wales and Monmouthshire". Most of the rest of Monmouthshire is firmly and redoubt-ably Welsh, but the woodlands and hills by the meandering River Wye have more in common with the landscape over the border. The two main centres are **Chepstow**, with its massive castle, and the spruce, old-fashioned town of **Monmouth**, sixteen miles upstream. Six miles north of Chepstow lie the inspirational ruins of the Cistercian **Tintern Abbey**.

Chepstow and around

Of all the places that call themselves "the gateway to Wales", **CHEPSTOW** (Cas-Gwent) has probably the greatest claim, situated on the western bank of

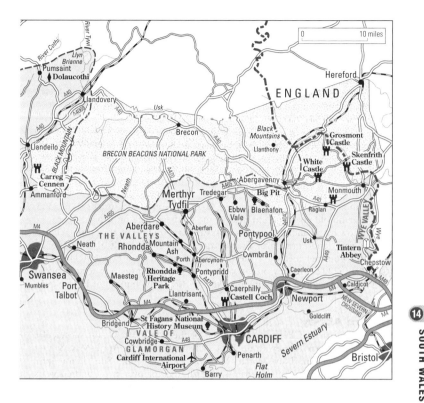

the River Wye just over a mile from where its tidal waters flow out into the muddy Severn estuary. Chepstow is a sturdy place robbed of the immediate charm of many other Welsh market towns by soulless modern developments. Nonetheless, there's an identifiably medieval street-plan hemmed in by the thirteenth-century **Port Wall**, which encases a tight loop of the River Wye and the strategically sited **Chepstow Castle** (April, May & Oct daily 9.30am–5pm; June–Sept daily 9.30am–6pm; Nov–March Mon–Sat 9.30am–4pm, Sun 11am–4pm; £3; CADW). Guarding one of the most important routes into Wales, Chepstow was the first stone castle to be built in Britain, the Great Tower keep being built in 1067 to help subdue the restless Welsh. The Lower Ward is the largest of the three enclosures and dates mainly from the thirteenth century. Here you'll find the **Great Hall**, the home of a wide-ranging exhibition on the history of the castle. Twelfth-century defences separate the Lower Ward from the Middle Ward, which is dominated by the still imposing ruins of the **Great Tower**. Beyond this is the far narrower Upper Ward, which leads up to the Barbican **watchtower** from where there are superb views looking down the cliff to the river estuary.

Opposite is the **Chepstow Museum** (July–Sept Mon–Sat 10.30am–5.30pm, Sun 2–5.30pm; Oct–June Mon–Sat 11am–5pm, Sun 2–5pm; free) containing nostalgic photographs and paintings of the trades supported in the past by the River Wye, and recording Chepstow's brief life in the early part of last century as a shipbuilding centre.

A mile north of town, **Chepstow Racecourse** (℡01291/622260, ⓦwww
.chepstow-racecourse.co.uk) is one of the country's premier racing venues, with
regular, all-year-round meets. Entrance is off the A466.

Practicalities

Chepstow's **train station** is five minutes' walk to the south of the High Street;
its **bus station** is on Thomas Street on the other side of the western Town
Gate. The **tourist office** is located in the castle car park, off Bridge Street
(daily: Nov–Easter 10am–3.30pm; Easter–Oct 10am–5.30pm; ℡01291/623772,
ⓔchepstow.tic@monmouthshire.gov.uk). There's decent B&B **accommodation** at the *First Hurdle Guesthouse*, 9 Upper Church St (℡01291/622189,
ⓦwww.firsthurdleguesthouse.co.uk; ❷), where the en-suite rooms have
firm beds and attractive decor, and, a mile east of town over the Wye, at the
wonderful *Upper Sedbury House*, Sedbury Lane (℡01291/627173, ⓦwww
.smoothhound.co.uk/hotels/uppersed; ❷). *The George Hotel* (℡01291/625363;
❺) is a grand old coaching inn next to the medieval gate on Moor Street.

Chepstow has a handful of decent **restaurants** and a host of good **pubs**. There's
a particularly good branch of *Pizza Express* at 29 High St (℡01291/630572),
while for gourmet meals, try the moderately priced *Wye Knot*, on The Back
(℡01291/622929); nearby on the same street is the *Boat Inn*, a waterside tavern
with a good veggie-friendly menu. *The Five Alls*, at the bottom of High Street,
is an earthy local pub.

Tintern Abbey

Six miles north of Chepstow, along one of the River Wye's most spectacular
stretches, **Tintern Abbey** (June–Sept daily 9.30am–6pm; April, May & Oct
daily 9.30am–5pm; Nov–March Mon–Sat 9.30am–4pm, Sun 11am–4pm;
£3.25; CADW) has inspired writers and painters for over two hundred years
– Wordsworth and Turner among them. Such is the place's popularity, however,
that it's advisable to go out of season or at either end of the day when the
hordes have thinned out. The abbey was founded in 1131 by Cistercian monks
from Normandy, though most of the remaining buildings date from the massive
rebuilding and expansion plan in the fourteenth century, when Tintern was
at its mightiest. Its survival after the depredations of the Dissolution is largely
thanks to its remoteness, as there were no nearby villages ready to use the abbey
stone for rebuilding.

The centrepiece of the complex is the magnificent Gothic **church**, whose
remarkable tracery and intricate stonework remains intact. Around the church
are the less substantial ruins of the monks' domestic quarters and cloister, mostly
reduced to one-storey rubble. The course of the abbey's waste-disposal system
can be seen in the Great Drain, an irregular channel that links kitchens, toilets
and the infirmary with the nearby Wye. The **Novices' Hall** lies handily close to
the Warming House, which together with the kitchen and infirmary would have
been the only heated parts of the abbey, suggesting that novices might have gained
a falsely favourable impression of monastic life before taking their final vows.

Monmouth and around

Enclosed on three sides by the rivers Wye and Monnow, **MONMOUTH**
(Trefynwy), fifteen miles north of Chepstow, retains some of its quiet charm as
an important border post and county town, and makes a good base for a drive
– or a long hike – around the **Three Castles** of the pastoral border-country
to the north.

The centre of the town is **Agincourt Square**, a handsome open space at the top of the wide, shop-lined Monnow Street, which descends gently to the thirteenth-century bridge over the River Monnow. The cobbled square is dominated by the arched, Georgian **Shire Hall**, in which is embedded an eighteenth-century statue of the Monmouth-born King Henry V, victor of the Battle of Agincourt in 1415. In front is the pompous statue of another local, the Honourable Charles Stewart Rolls, co-founder of Rolls-Royce and, in 1910, the first man to pilot a double flight over the English Channel. Almost opposite Shire Hall is **Castle Hill**, which you can walk up to glimpse some of the scant ruins of the **castle**, founded in 1068. A small **regimental museum** (April–Oct daily 2–5pm; Nov–March Sat & Sun 2–4pm; free) is the only part that can be visited. Priory Street leads north from Agincourt Square to the market hall, where the **Nelson Museum** (Mon–Sat 10am–1pm & 2–5pm, Sun 2–5pm; free) attempts to portray the life of one of the most successful sea-going Britons through use of the Admiral's personal artefacts, collected by Charles Rolls' mother, who was an admirer. At the bottom of Monnow Street, the road narrows to squeeze into the confines of the seven-hundred-year-old **Monnow Bridge**, crowned with its hulking stone gate of 1262, that served both as a means of defence for the town and a toll-collection point. To burn off some energy, you could **rent a canoe** for a trip up the Wye from the Monmouth Canoe & Activity Centre (☎01600/713461, ⓦwww.monmouthcanoehire.20m.com) in Castle Yard, Old Dixton Road.

The **bus station** lies at the bottom of Monnow Street and the **tourist office** is in the Shire Hall, Agincourt Square (daily: April–Oct 10am–5.30pm; Nov–March 9.30am–5pm; ☎01600/713899, ⓔmonmouth.tic@monmouthshire .gov.uk). **Accommodation** in town is thin on the ground. Try the simple but agreeable *Burton House* on St James' Square (☎01600/714958; ❷), *Tŷ Mawr* at 7 Monk St (☎01600/714261; ❷), or *Bob's* at 7 Church St (☎01600/712600, ⓦwww.bobsmonmouth.co.uk; ❸). The nearest tent-friendly **campsites** are both on Drybridge Street (over Monnow Bridge then right): the *Monnow Bridge* (☎01600/714004) is behind the *Three Horseshoes* pub, while the slightly pricier *Monmouth Caravan Park* (☎01600/714745) is a quarter of a mile beyond.

Good daytime **eating** can be had at *Cygnet's Kitchen* in White Swan Court, off Church Street, which serves substantial soups and casseroles, or at the wonderfully informal *Bob's* (see above), which offers great-value lunches and is also the best place in town for an evening blow-out. You can opt for inexpensive pub grub at the *Punch House*, in Agincourt Square, or the *Green Dragon*, in St Thomas Square, down by the Monnow Bridge.

Raglan

RAGLAN (Rhaglan), seven miles west of Monmouth, is an unassuming village worth visiting for its glorious **castle** (June–Sept daily 9.30am–6pm; April, May & Oct daily 9am–5pm; Nov–March Mon–Sat 9.30am–4pm, Sun 11am–4pm; £2.75; CADW), whose fussy and comparatively intact style makes it stand out from so many other crumbling Welsh fortresses. The last medieval fortification built in Britain, the design of which combines practical strength with ostentatious style, Raglan was begun on the site of a Norman motte in 1435 by Sir William ap Thomas. The **gatehouse**, still used as the main entrance, houses the best examples of the castle's showy decoration in its heraldic shields, intricate stonework edging and gargoyles. In the mid-fifteenth century, ap Thomas's grandson, William Herbert II, was responsible for the two inner courts, built around his grandfather's original gatehouse, hall and keep. The first is the cobbled **Pitched Stone Court**, designed to house the functional rooms like the kitchen, with its two vast, double-flued chimneys, and the servants' quarters. To the left is **Fountain Court**, a well-proportioned grassy space surrounded by opulent residences that once included grand apartments and state rooms. Separating the two are the original hall, from 1435, the buttery, the remains of the chapel and the dank, cold cellars below.

The Three Castles

The fertile, low-lying land between the Monnow and Usk rivers was important as an easy access route into the agricultural lands of South Wales, and in the eleventh century the Norman invaders built a trio of strongholds here to protect their interests. In 1201, Skenfrith, Grosmont and White castles were presented by King John to Hubert de Burgh, who employed sophisticated new ideas on castle design to replace the earlier, square-keeped castles. In 1260, the advancing army of Llywelyn ap Gruffydd began to threaten the king's supremacy in South Wales, and the three castles were refortified in readiness. Gradually, the castles were adapted as living quarters and royal administration centres, and the only return to military usage came in 1404–05, when Owain Glyndŵr's army pressed down to Grosmont, only to be defeated by the future King Henry V. The castles slipped into disrepair and were finally sold separately in 1902, the first time since 1138 that the three had fallen out of single ownership.

White Castle (Castell Gwyn; Easter–Sept Wed–Sun 10am–5pm; £2; all other times free access, generally 10am–4pm), eight miles northwest of Monmouth and six miles east of Abergavenny (see p.737), is the most awesome of the three, sited in rolling countryside with some superb views over to the hills surrounding the River Monnow. A few patches of the white rendering that gave the castle its name can be seen on the exterior walls. The grassy Outer Ward is enclosed by a curtain wall with four towers, divided by a moat from the brooding mass of the Inner Ward. A bridge leads to the dual-towered Inner Gatehouse, where you can climb the western tower for its sublime vantage point. At the back of the Inner Ward are the massive foundations of the Norman keep, demolished in about 1260.

Seven miles northeast of White Castle, in the attractive border village of Skenfrith (Ynysgynwraidd), is the thirteenth-century **Skenfrith Castle** (free access), dominated by the circular keep that replaced an earlier Norman structure. Whilst not as impressive as White Castle, Skenfrith has a pretty riverside setting, its castle walls built of a sturdy red sandstone arranged in an irregular rectangle. In the centre of the ward is a low, round keep, raised slightly on an earth mound, containing the vestiges of the private apartments of the castle's lord on the upper floors.

Five miles upstream of Skenfrith, right on the English border, the most dilapidated of the Three Castles, **Grosmont Castle** (free access), sits on a small hill above its village. Entering over the wooden bridge above the dry moat brings you into the small central courtyard, dominated on the right-hand side by the ruins of a large Great Hall dating from the first decade of the thirteenth century.

Newport and Caerleon

Dominating the once industrious valley towns of southern Monmouthshire, **Newport**, Wales's third-largest town, is a downbeat, working-class place that grew up around the docks at the mouth of the River Usk. Its rich history was largely swept away by the twentieth century, but isolated nuggets remain, most notably at Roman **Caerleon** – the "old port" on the River Usk – now a northern suburb of Newport, but predating the town by about a thousand years.

Newport

Wales's third-largest city, **Newport** (Casnewydd), fifteen miles west of Chepstow, is hardly prepossessing, its modern centre strung along the banks of the foul and muddy River Usk. Overlooking these waters stand both the pathetic remains of **Newport Castle**, and Peter Fink's giant red sculpture *Steel Wave*, a nod to one of Newport's great industries. The place does have a tremendous energy, however, and is well worth a night's stop.

The central High Street leads to Newport and Westgate squares, and the ornate, Victorian **Westgate Hotel** where, in 1839, soldiers sprayed a crowd of Chartist protesters with gunfire (see box, below) – the hotel's original pillars still show bullet marks. A hundred yards along Commercial Street, in John Frost Square, the quirky **Newport clock** shudders, shakes, spits smoke and comes near to apparent collapse every hour, usually drawing an appreciative crowd. In front of the clock is the town's library, tourist office and inspiring civic **museum** (Mon–Thurs 9.30am–5pm, Fri 9.30am–4.30pm, Sat 9.30am–4pm; free). Starting with the origins of the county of Monmouthshire, the displays examine the county's original occupations and early lifestyles, and include a section on mining, with a roll call of those killed in local pit accidents – 3508 men between 1837 and 1927. Newport's spectacular growth from a thousand townspeople in 1801 to a grimy port town of 70,000 a century later is well charted, but the two most interesting sections deal with the Chartist uprising and a fine Roman mosaic.

Dominating the Newport skyline with its comical, spidery legs is the **Transporter Bridge** (April–Sept Mon–Sat 8am–9.50pm, Sun 1–9pm; Oct–March Mon–Sat 8am–5.50pm, Sun 1–5pm; car toll 50p, free for cyclists and pedestrians), built in 1906 to enable cars and people to cross the river without disturbing the shipping channel, gliding them across the Usk on a dangling platform. A visitor centre on the west bank (April–Sept Wed–Sat & bank holidays 10am–5pm, Sun 1–5pm; Oct–March Sat 10am–5pm, Sun 1–5pm) tells its story.

Newport's **tourist office** is in the museum complex on John Frost Square (Mon–Sat 9.30am–5pm; ☎01633/842962, ✉newport.tic@newport.gov.uk), a hundred yards from Kingsway **bus station** and five minutes' walk south of the **train station**. Staying in Caerleon is a more amenable option, but there are some decent **B&Bs**, including *Craignair*, 44 Corporation Rd (☎01633/259903, ✉ruthuen-craignair@ntlworld.com; ❷), and the genteel *St Etienne*, 162 Stow

---

The Chartists

In an era when wealthy landowners bought votes from the enfranchised few, the struggles of the **Chartists** were perhaps a historical inevitability. Thousands gathered around the 1838 People's Charter that called for universal male suffrage and a secret, annual ballot for Parliament. Demonstrations in support of these principles were held all over the country, with some of the bloodiest and most vociferous taking place in the radical heartlands of industrial South Wales. On November 4, 1839, Chartists from all over Monmouthshire marched on Newport and descended Stow Hill, whereupon they were gunned down by soldiers hiding in the *Westgate Hotel*; 22 protesters were killed. The leaders of the rebellion were sentenced to death, although the self-righteous and wealthy leaders of the town subsequently commuted their punishment to transportation. Queen Victoria even knighted the mayor who ordered the shooting.

Hill (℡01633/262341, ✉etienneguesthouse@hotmail.com; ❸). If you want to be central, the *Hotel@Walkabout* (formerly the *Queen's Hotel*), 19 Bridge St (℡01633/235990, ⓦwww.walkabout.eu.com; ❸), is modern and reasonable, if pretty noisy at times. At the western end of Bridge Street, Caerau Road rises up sharply to the south, passing the relaxed, hospitable *Kepe Lodge* at no. 46a (℡01633/262351; ❸). There's a campsite at *Tredegar House* (℡01633/815600), a couple of miles west – take bus #315 or #30 from the town centre.

For **food**, *Fratelli's*, at 173 Caerleon Rd (℡01633/264602; closed Sun & Mon), is easily the finest of the city's many Italian restaurants. For coffee and a light snack, try the *Oriel* café on the top floor of the museum, or the trendy *Meze Lounge* bar, 6 Market St, which becomes a venue for live music and DJs in the evening. Newport has a buoyant **rock and dance music** scene – this is, after all, the city that produced gloriously daft hip-hop outfit Goldie Lookin' Chain. The legendary try-out pub venue, *TJ's*, over the river from the castle at 14 Clarence Place, has seen better days, but is still worth checking out. For late-night dancing try the youthful *Voodoo* on Bridge Street or *Meze Lounge* (see above).

Caerleon

Compact **CAERLEON** (Caerllion), three miles north of central Newport (bus #2; every 15min), but still within the city limits, is peppered with the remnants of the major Roman town of Isca, named after the River Usk (Wysg). The settlement was built to provide administrative and military services for the smaller, outlying camps in the rest of South Wales and grew to a size and importance on a par with the better-known York and Chester in the north of England. Although the town fell gradually into decay after the Romans had left, there were still some massive remains standing when, in 1188, episcopal envoy Giraldus Cambrensis noted with evident relish the "immense palaces, which, with the gilded gables of their roofs, once rivalled the magnificence of ancient Rome".

Although time has had an inevitably corrosive effect on the remains since Giraldus's time, there's a powerful sense of history running through the Roman **fortress baths** (Easter–Oct daily 9.30am–5pm; Nov–Easter Mon–Sat 9.30am–5pm, Sun 11am–4pm; £2.50; CADW). The bathing houses, cold hall and communal pool area are remarkably intact and beautifully presented, using audiovisual equipment, sound commentary and models. On the High Street, a Victorian Neoclassical portico is the sole survivor of the original **Legionary Museum** (Mon–Sat 10am–5pm, Sun 2–5pm; free), now housed in a modern building behind and laden with artefacts unearthed here. Opposite the Legionary Museum, Fosse Lane leads down to the hugely atmospheric Roman **amphitheatre** (free access), the only one of its kind preserved in Britain. Hidden under a grassy mound until the 1920s, the amphitheatre was built around 80 AD, at the same time as the Colosseum in Rome. Up to six thousand could watch animal baiting, military exercises or the gory combat of gladiators.

Caerleon's **tourist office** (daily: April–Oct 10am–6pm; Nov–March 10am–4pm; ℡01633/422656, ✉caerleon.tic@newport.gov.uk) lies next to the Legionary Museum, or there's more esoteric information in the delightful Ffwrrwm craft centre, down the main street. There's central B&B at *Pendragon House*, 18 Cross St (℡01633/430871; ❹), and the fractionally pricier *Great House* on Isca Road (℡01633/420216; ❹). The best place to **eat** is *Oriel*, a bistro in the courtyard of the Ffwrrwm centre.

The Valleys

No other part of Wales is as instantly recognizable as the **Valleys**, a generic name for the string of settlements packed into the narrow gashes in the mountainous terrain to the north of Newport and Cardiff. Arriving from England, the change from rolling countryside to sharp contours and a postindustrial landscape is almost instantaneous. Each of the valleys depended almost solely on coal-mining which, although nearly defunct as an industry, has left its mark on the staunchly working-class towns: row upon row of brightly painted terraced housing, tipped along the slopes at some incredible angles, are broken only by austere chapels, the occasional remaining pithead and the dignified memorials to those who died underground.

This is not traditional tourist country, but it's one of the most interesting and distinctive corners of Wales, full of sociological and human interest. Some of the former mines have reopened as gutsy and hard-hitting museums – **Big Pit** at Blaenafon and the **Rhondda Heritage Park** at Trehafod being the best – while other excellent civic museums include those at **Pontypridd**, **Aberdare** and **Merthyr Tydfil**. A few older sites, such as vast **Caerphilly Castle** and the sixteenth-century manor house of **Llancaiach Fawr**, have been attracting visitors for hundreds of years.

Blaenafon and Big Pit

Fourteen miles north of Newport, the valley of the Llwyd opens out at the airy iron and coal town of **BLAENAFON** (sometimes Blaenavon), whose

Working the black seam

The land beneath the inhospitable South Wales Valleys had some of the most abundant and accessible natural seams of **coal and iron ore** to be found, readily milked in the boom years of the nineteenth and early twentieth centuries. Wealthy, predominantly English capitalists came to Wales and ruthlessly stripped the land of its natural assets, while simultaneously exploiting those who risked life and limb underground. The mine owners were in a formidably strong position as thousands flocked to the Valleys in search of work and some sort of sustainable life. By the turn of the twentieth century, the Valleys – virtually unpopulated a century earlier – became packed with pits, chapels and immigrant workers from Ireland, Scotland, Italy and all over Wales.

In 1920, there were 256,000 men working in the 620 mines of the South Wales coalfield, providing one-third of the world's coal. Vast Miners' Institutes jostled for position with the Nonconformist chapels, whose muscular brand of Christianity was matched by the zeal of the region's politics – trade-union-led and avowedly left-wing. Great socialist orators rose to national prominence, cementing the Valleys' reputation as a world apart from the rest of Britain, let alone Wales. Even Britain's pioneering National Health Service, founded by a radical Labour government in the years following World War II, was based on a Valleys' community scheme devised by locally born politician Aneurin Bevan. Over half of the original pits closed in the harsh economic climate of the 1930s, as coal seams became exhausted and the political climate changed. In the 1900s, further closures threatened to bring the number of men employed in the South Wales coalfields down to four figures, and the miners went on strike from 1984–85. No coalfield was as solidly behind the strike as South Wales but today all of the deep pits – bar one reprieved and taken over in a workers' buyout in 1994 – have closed.

population has shrunk to five thousand, a third of its nineteenth-century size. It's a spirited and evocative place, a fact recognized by UNESCO, who granted it World Heritage Site status in 2000. The town's boom kicked off at the Blaenafon **ironworks**, just off the Brynmawr road (Easter–Oct Mon–Fri 9.30am–4.30pm, Sat 10am–5pm, Sun 10am–4.30pm; £2; group tours all year, minimum £20; CADW; ☎01495/792615, Ⓦwww.blaenavontic.com), founded in 1788. Limestone, coal and iron ore – ingredients for successful iron-smelting – were abundant locally, and the Blaenafon works was one of the largest in Britain until it closed in 1900. The line of Georgian blast furnaces, the water-balance lift and the **museum** in the workers' cottages offer a thorough picture of both the process and the lifestyle that went with it. The ironworks also contains the town's **tourist office** (same hours and contacts).

Just as it is now possible to visit the home of Blaenafon's iron industry, the town's defunct coal trade has also been transformed smoothly into the site that most clearly evokes the experience of a miner's work and life. At the **Big Pit National Mining Museum** (mid-Feb–Nov daily 9.30am–5pm; last underground tour 3.30pm; free), a mile west of the town and reached by a half-hourly shuttle bus from Blaenafon, you're kitted out with lamp, helmet and very heavy battery pack and lowered three hundred feet into the labyrinth of shafts and coal faces for a guided tour. The guides – most of whom are ex-miners – lead you through explanations and examples of the different types of coal mining, while constant streams of rust-coloured water flow by, adding to the dank and chilly atmosphere that must have terrified the small children who were once paid twopence – of which one penny was taken out for the cost of their candles – for a six-day week pulling the coal wagons along the tracks. Back on the surface, the old pithead baths, smithy, miners' canteen and winding engine house have all been preserved and filled with some fascinating displays about the local mining industry.

These days, Blaenafon is trying to reinvent itself as a **book town** to rival Hay-on-Wye on the Anglo-Welsh border (see p.445): to this end nine new bookshops opened in town on one day in June 2003. For more details, visit Ⓦwww.booktownblaenafon.com.

The Taff and Cynon valleys

The River Taff flows out into the Bristol Channel at Cardiff, after passing through a condensed couple of dozen miles of industry and population. The first town in the Taff vale is **Pontypridd**, one of the most cheerful in the Valleys, and probably the best base. Continuing north, the river splits again at **Abercynon**, where the River Cynon flows in from **Aberdare**, site of Wales's only remaining deep mine. Just outside Abercynon is the enjoyable, sixteenth-century **Llancaiach Fawr** manor house. To the north, the Taff is packed into one of the tightest of all the Valleys, passing Aberfan five miles short of the imposing valley-head town of **Merthyr Tydfil**.

Pontypridd

PONTYPRIDD, twelve miles north of Cardiff, is built up around its quirky arched **bridge**. Once the largest single-span stone bridge in Europe, it was built in 1775 by local amateur stonemason William Edwards, whose previous attempts had crumbled into the river below. Across the river is **Ynysangharad Park**, where Sir W. Goscombe John's cloying statue honours Pontypridd weaver Evan James, who composed the stirringly nationalistic song *Hen Wlad fy Nhadau* (*Land of My Fathers*), that became the Welsh national anthem. By the bridge at the end of Taff Street, a lovingly restored church houses the **Pontypridd Museum** (Mon–Sat 10am–5pm; closed bank holidays; free), one of the best museums in the Valleys. A treasure-trove of photographs, videos, models and exhibits succeeds in painting a warm picture of the town and its outlying valleys, as well as paying homage to the town's famous sons, singer Tom Jones and opera star and actor Sir Geraint Evans.

Pontypridd is well connected to bus, train and road networks. The **tourist office** (Mon–Sat 10am–5pm; ☎01443/490748) is in the museum, on Bridge Street. **Accommodation** is rather scarce: in the centre, try the bustling *Market Tavern*, on Market Street (☎01443/485331; ❷). Better bets are a few miles out, notably the well-kept and friendly *Fairmead* guest house (☎01443/411174; ❸), almost opposite Llancaiach Fawr (see below), and the floral *Llechwen Hall* (☎01443/742050, ⓦwww.llechwen.com; ❹), signposted off the A470 a couple of miles north of Pontypridd.

Llancaiach Fawr and the Welsh International Climbing Centre

Five miles north of Pontypridd, the river divides at **Abercynon**, a stark, typical valley town of punishingly steep streets lined with terraced houses that fade out into a coniferous hillside. Two miles east, just north of the village of Nelson, is the sixteenth-century **Llancaiach Fawr** (March–Oct Mon–Fri 10am–5pm, Sat & Sun 10am–6pm; Nov–Feb closed Mon; £4.95; ☎01443/412248), a Tudor house, built around 1530, that has been transformed into a living history museum set in 1645, the time of the Civil War, with all of the guides dressed as house servants, speaking the language of seventeenth-century Britain. Although potentially tacky, it is quite deftly done, with well-researched period authenticity and numerous fascinating anecdotes from the staff; visitors are even encouraged to try on the master of the household's armour. Regular **buses** from Pontypridd and Cardiff pass the entrance.

A couple of miles north of Llancaiach Fawr, just beyond the village of **Trelewis**, the old Taff Merthyr colliery has undergone stunning transformation into the **Welsh International Climbing Centre** (Mon–Fri 9am–10pm, Sat & Sun 9am–6pm; ☎01443/710749, ⓦwww.indoorclimbingwalls.co.uk). As well as vast climbing walls (£5–7.70), it offers a wide range of adventure options, including potholing and caving; instruction is available. There are also exercise

⑭

SOUTH WALES | The Valleys

Aberfan

North of Abercynon, the Taff Valley contains one sight that is hard to forget. Two neat lines of distant arches mark the graves of 144 people killed in October 1966 by an unsecured slag heap collapsing on Pantglas primary school in the village of Aberfan. Thousands of people still make the pilgrimage to the village graveyard, to stand silent and bemused by the enormity of the disaster. Among the dead were 116 children, who died huddled in panic at the beginning of their school day. A humbling and beautiful valediction can be seen on one of the gravestones, that of a 10-year-old boy, who, it simply records, "loved light, freedom and animals". Official enquiries all told the sorry tale that this disaster was almost inevitable, given the cavalier approach to safety so often displayed by the coal bosses. Gwynfor Evans, then newly elected as the first Plaid Cymru (Welsh Nationalist) MP in Westminster, spoke with well-founded bitterness when he said: "Let us suppose that such a monstrous mountain had been built above Hampstead or Eton, where the children of the men of power and wealth are at school..." But that, of course, would never have happened.

rooms, a sauna, a restaurant and bar open at weekends and evenings, and even hostel beds (£12 weekdays, £14 weekends, £16 bank holidays) in small, clean dorms. Hourly (Mon–Sat) bus #22 from Pontypridd and Nelson will drop you on the doorstep.

Aberdare

Eight miles northwest of Abercynon, towards the top of the Cynon Valley, is the spacious town of **ABERDARE** (Aberdâr), home to one of the Valleys' best museums, the **Cynon Valley Museum & Gallery** (Mon–Sat 9am–4.30pm; free), in an old tram depot next to the Tesco superstore. Exhibits portray the social history of the valley, from the appalling conditions of the mid-nineteenth century, when nearly half of all children born here died by the age of 5, to stirring memories of the 1926 General Strike and the 1984–85 Miners' Strike. Alongside are some fun videos and exhibits on Victorian lantern slides, teenage life through the ages, the miners' jazz bands and Aberdare's role as a prominent centre of early Welsh-language publishing.

Merthyr Tydfil

Downtown **MERTHYR TYDFIL** (or Tudful), ten miles north of Pontypridd, is a robust place whose main glory is its location at the top of the Taff Valley, on the cusp of the industrial coal country to the south and the grand, windy heights of the Brecon Beacons to the north. In the eighteenth century it became the largest iron-producing town in the world, as well as by far the most populous town in Wales, with four massive ironworks exploiting the local abundance of the key ingredients. A century earlier, what was then a village became a rallying point for Dissenter and Radical movements, which gained adherents as the profits from growing industrialization lined the pockets of the works owners, with little cash finding its way to the workers. Merthyr's radical-ism bubbled furiously, breaking out into occasional riots and prompting the election of Britain's first socialist MP, Keir Hardie, in 1900.

Half a mile northwest of the town centre, just off the A4102 (Bethesda Street), is **Chapel Row**, a line of skilled ironworkers' cottages built in the 1820s, one of which holds composer **Joseph Parry's Birthplace** (April–Sept Thurs–Sun 2–5pm; free). Parry wrote the national favourite, *Myfanwy*, which is now piped into the rooms, some of which are given over to a display on his life and music.

Back across the other side of the river, just beyond the Brecon Road, is a home in absolute contrast to Parry's humble and cramped birthplace. **Cyfartha Castle** (April–Sept daily 10am–5.30pm; Oct–March Tues–Fri 10am–4pm, Sat & Sun noon–4pm; free) was built in 1825 as an ostentatious mock-Gothic castle for William Crawshay II, boss of the town's original ironworks. The castle is set within vast, attractive parkland which slopes down to the river and once afforded Crawshay a view over his iron empire. The old wine cellars contain a varied and enjoyable walk through the history of Merthyr, with the political turmoil and massive exploitation of the past couple of centuries picked over in gory detail. Upstairs, the castle's grand main rooms house an **art gallery** with an impressive collection of Welsh pieces, including works by Augustus John, Cedric Morris, Vanessa Bell, Jack Yeats and Kyffin Williams.

The **train station** is a minute's walk from the High Street. North from here is Glebeland Street, with the **bus** station and, at no. 14a, the **tourist office** (April–Sept Mon–Sat 9.30am–5.30pm; Oct–March Mon–Sat 10am–5pm; ☎01685/379884, ✉tic@merthyr.gov.uk). The nearest **bike rental** is from the Garwnant visitor centre, off the A470 five miles north of town

(☎01685/723060). **Accommodation** is varied, ranging from the plush *Tregenna Hotel* in Park Terrace, next to Penydarren Park (☎01685/723627, ⓦwww.tregennahotel.co.uk; ④), to the less fussy *Chaplin's*, 30–31 High St (☎01685/387272, ⓦwww.chaplinshotel.co.uk; ③), and, cheapest of all, the *Penylan* guest house, 12 Courtland Terrace (☎01685/723179; ①). There's a **campsite** four miles north of town in the beautiful surroundings of *Grawen Farm*, Cwm Taf (☎01685/723740).

The Rhondda

Pointing northwest from Pontypridd, the **Rhondda Fawr** – sixteen miles long and never as much as a mile wide – is undoubtedly the most famous of all the Welsh valleys, as well as being the heart of the massive South Wales coal industry. For many it immediately conjures up Richard Llewellyn's 1939 book – and subsequent Oscar-winning weepie – *How Green Was My Valley*, although this was, strictly speaking, based on the author's early life in nearby Gilfach Goch, outside the valley. Between 1841 and 1924 the Rhondda's population grew from less than a thousand to 167,000, squeezed into ranks of houses grouped around sixty or so pitheads. The Rhondda, more than any other of the valleys, became a self-reliant, hard-living, chapel-going, poor and terrifically spirited breeding-ground for radical religion and firebrand politics. For decades, the Communist Party ran the town of Maerdy (nicknamed "Little Moscow" by Fleet Street in the 1930s). The last pit in the Rhondda closed in 1990, but what was left behind was not some dispiriting ragbag of depressing towns, but a range of new attractions, cleaned-up hillsides and some of the friendliest pubs and communities to be found anywhere in Britain.

Specific attractions are few, however. The only one which really stands out is the colliery museum of the **Rhondda Heritage Park** (April–Sept daily 10am–6pm, last admission 4.30pm; Oct–March closed Mon; £5.60), at **TREHAFOD**, formed by locals when the Lewis Merthyr pit closed in 1983. You can explore the engine-winding houses, lamp room and fan house, and take a simulated "trip underground", with stunning visuals and sound effects, re-creating 1950s' and late nineteenth-century life through the eyes of colliers. Although it's all looking a bit past its best these days, it's a worthwhile trip.

A **train** line from Cardiff, punctuated with stops every mile or so, runs the entire length of the Rhondda, stopping at Trehafod, a few minutes' walk from the Heritage Park. **Buses** also cover the route, continuing up into the mountains and the Brecon Beacons. **Accommodation** in the twin valleys is sparse,

Male voice choirs

Fiercely protective of its reputation as a land of song, the voice of Wales is most commonly heard amongst the ranks of **male voice choirs**. Although found all over the country, it is in the southern, industrial heartland that they are loudest and strongest. Their roots lie in the Nonconformist religious traditions of the seventeenth and eighteenth centuries, when Methodism in particular swept the country, and singing was a free and potent way of cherishing the frequently persecuted faith. Classic hymns like *Cwm Rhondda* and the Welsh national anthem, *Hen Wlad Fy Nhadau* (*Land of My Fathers*), are synonymous with the choirs, whose full-blooded interpretation of them continues to render all others insipid. Each valleys town still has its own, often depleted choir, most of whom happily accept visitors to sit in on rehearsals. Ask at the local tourist office or library, and take the chance to hear one of the world's most distinctive choral traditions in full, roof-raising splendour.

but decent places include the business-oriented *Heritage Park Hotel*, beside the Rhondda Heritage Park at Trehafod (☎01443/687057; ❻), which has its own pool, and *The Bertie* bar and B&B (☎01443/688204; ❸) at 1–3 Phillips Terrace, not far away. Nearer the top end of the Rhondda Fawr is the reasonable *Baglan Hotel* (☎01443/776111; ❷) on the main road in Treherbert.

Cardiff and around

Official capital of Wales since only 1955 (hence the ubiquitous "Europe's Youngest Capital" slogan), the buoyant city of **CARDIFF** (Caerdydd) has swiftly grown into its new status. A number of massive developments, not least the shiny new buildings housing the Welsh National Assembly and Millennium Centre for the arts on the rejuvenated Cardiff Bay waterfront, and a fabulous city-centre sports stadium, are giving the city the feel of an international capital, if not always with a very Welsh flavour – compared with Swansea, Cardiff is noticeably anglicized, though this is surely changing as more youngsters from Welsh-speaking Wales flock to the city for jobs in education, government and media.

The second marquis of Bute built Cardiff's first dock in 1839, opening others in swift succession. The Butes, who owned massive swathes of the rapidly industrializing South Wales valleys, insisted that all coal and iron exports use the family docks in Cardiff, and it became one of the busiest ports in the world. In the hundred years up to the turn of the twentieth century, Cardiff's population soared from almost nothing to 170,000, and the ambitious new civic centre in Cathays Park was well under way. The twentieth century saw varying fortunes: the dock trade slumped in the 1930s and the city suffered heavy bombing in World War II, but with the creation of Cardiff as capital in 1955, optimism and confidence in the city blossomed. Many government and media institutions have moved here from London, and the development of the dock areas around the new Assembly building in Cardiff Bay has given a largely positive boost to the cityscape.

Arrival, information and accommodation

The main **bus station** is off Wood Street, on the southwestern side of the city centre. Across the forecourt is Cardiff Central **train station**, for all intercity services as well as many suburban and Valley Line services. Queen Street station, at the eastern edge of the centre, is for local trains only. The city **tourist office**, at 16 Wood St, opposite Cardiff Central tourist office at the Old Library on The Hayes (Mon–Sat 9.30am–6pm, until 7pm July & Aug, Sun 10am–4pm; ☎ 029/2022 7281, ⊛ www.visitcardiff.info), provides good free maps of the city and plenty of information on accommodation and entertainment. You should also be able to pick up a copy of *Buzz*, a free monthly guide to arts and events in the city.

Cardiff is compact enough to walk around, as even the bay area is within thirty minutes' stroll of Central station. Once you're out of the centre, however, it's best to fall back on the extensive **bus** network, most reliably operated by the Cardiff Bus (Bws Caerdydd) company (⊛ www.cardiffbus.com). Information and passes are available from the counter next to the tourist office (Mon–Fri 8.30am–5.30pm, Sat 9am–4.30pm). A couple of useful **travel passes**, which can also be bought on-board buses, are the City Rider ticket (£3.50), which gives unlimited travel around Cardiff and Penarth for a day, and the Network Rider (£5.70), which extends the range to Caerphilly and Newport; ask about family deals. A useful **water-bus** service (hourly; £4 return; ☎ 07940/142409, ⊛ www.cardiffwaterbus.com) operates daily between Mermaid Quay, Penarth and the city centre at Taff's Mead Embankment, diagonally across from the Millennium Stadium. By 2006, it will also be running to Bute Park, by Cardiff Castle.

The main belt of guest houses and **hotels** lies along the genteel and leafy Cathedral Road, fifteen minutes' walk northwest of the city centre. You also have the option of a couple of budget **hostels** and two **campsites**.

Hotels, guest houses and B&Bs

The Big Sleep Hotel Bute Terrace ☎ 029/2063 6363, ⊛ www.thebigsleephotel.com. Opposite the Cardiff International Arena, this hotel feels exactly like the old office block it once was, but is a reasonable budget option in the city centre. ❸

Church 126 Cathedral Rd, Pontcanna ☎ 029/2034 0881. Fairly run-of-the-mill budget hotel, save for the Charlotte Church memorabilia – no surprise, as this place is run by the singer's proud parents. ❸

Courtfield 101 Cathedral Rd, Pontcanna ☎ 029/2022 7701, ⊛ www.courtfieldhotel.co.uk. Popular, comfortable and rather flouncy hotel with a largely gay clientele. ❸

Lincoln House 110 Cathedral Rd, Pontcanna ☎ 029/2039 5558, ⊛ www.lincolnhotel.co.uk. Elegant small hotel restored in a Victorian style: button-leather couches, heavy brocade and even a couple of four-poster beds. Rates include breakfast. ❺

The Old Post Office on Greenwood Lane, St Fagans ☎ 029/2056 5400, ⊛ www .old-post-office.com. Four miles from Cardiff, this old post office has been remodelled into a minimalist hotel boasting top-quality, beautifully decorated rooms and an airy conservatory restaurant. ❺

Royal Hotel St Mary St ☎ 0870/161 0807, ⊛ www .theroyalhotelcardiff.com. A central Victorian pile that's been given a modernist makeover, and very successfully too. Check website for special offers. ❻

St David's Hotel and Spa Havannah St, Cardiff Bay ☎ 029/2045 4045, ⊛ www.thestdavidshotel .com. Right on the waterfront, Cardiff's flashiest hotel, part of the Rocco Forte group, is all clean lines and elegant, understated decor. Rooms have all the expected accoutrements (including superb views from the balconies), there's a spa on site, and rates include breakfast. ❽

Town House 70 Cathedral Rd, Pontcanna ☎ 029/2023 9399, ⊛ www.thetownhousecardiff .co.uk. Hotel in a restored Victorian house with

N

▲ M4 Junction 32

▲ M4, Merthyr & Brecon

▲ Llandaff

RAILWAY STREET
CARLISLE STREET
CLIFTON STREET
CONSTELLATION ST
MOIRA PLACE

WATERLOO ROAD

R O A T H

PEN-Y-LAN ROAD

EASTERN AVENUE

Roath Park

TY-DRAW ROAD

NINIAN ROAD

MARLBOROUGH ROAD

ROATH COURT ROAD

PEN-Y-LAN RD

ALBANY ROAD

NEWPORT ROAD

BROADWAY

Royal Infirmary

College of Art

Queen Street Station

CITY ROAD

MACKINTOSH PLACE

RICHMOND ROAD

SHIRLEY ROAD

COBURN ST

SALISBURY RD

CATHAYS

STUTTGARTER STRASSE

Cathays Station

BOULEVARD DE NANTES

National Museum & Gallery

New Theatre

QUEEN STREET

FAIROAK ROAD

CRWYS ROAD

WYEVERNE RD

SENGHENNYDD RD

PARK PLACE

Sherman Theatre

MUSEUM AVE

City Hall

ALLENSBANK ROAD

CATHAYS TERRACE

Cardiff University

KING GEORGE VII AVE

County Hall

Cardiff Castle

WHITCHURCH ROAD

MAENDY ROAD

COLUM ROAD

NORTH ROAD

Welsh Institute of Sport

Bute Park

Glamorgan Cricket Ground

PONTCANNA

CATHEDRAL ROAD

River Taff

Sophia Gardens

WYNDHAM CRESCENT

BROMILLY CRESCENT

LLANDAFF ROAD

Chapter Arts Centre

CARDIFF

ACCOMMODATION

The Big Sleep Hotel	I
Cardiff Backpacker	F
Cardiff YHA Hostel	A
Church	C
Courtfield	D
Lincoln House	B
The Old Post Office	G
Royal Hotel	H
St David's Hotel & Spa	J
Town House	E

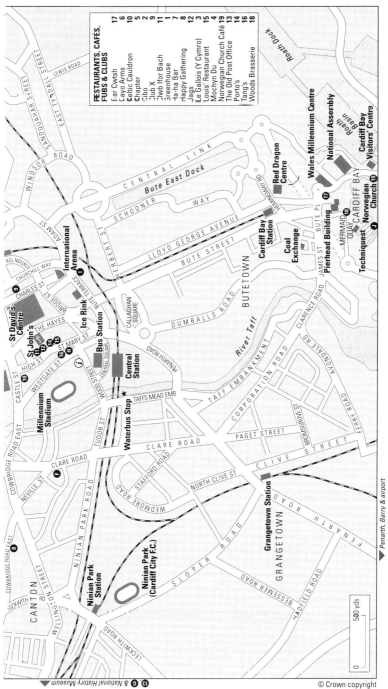

**RESTAURANTS, CAFÉS,
PUBS & CLUBS**

Bar Cwtsh	17
Cayo Arms	6
Celtic Cauldron	10
Chapter	5
Cibo	2
Club X	9
Clwb Ifor Bach	11
Greenhouse	1
Ha-ha Bar	7
Happy Gathering	8
Jags	12
Le Gallois (Y Cymro)	3
Louis' Restaurant	15
Mochyn Du	4
Norwegian Church Café	19
The Old Post Office	13
Porto's	14
Tang's	16
Woods Brasserie	18

© Crown copyright

14

SOUTH WALES

▼ *Penarth, Barry & airport*

▲ *& National History Museum*

en-suite rooms, a comfortable lounge and better-than-average facilities. ❹

Hostels

Cardiff Backpacker 96–98 Neville St, Riverside ☎029/2034 5577, ⓦwww .cardiffbackpacker.com. A fine, very friendly option, this purple-hued hostel has deservedly become something of a legend. A 10min walk from Central station, it has Internet access, pool table, on-site café and bar, and fairly cramped kitchen facilities but easy access to downtown restaurants. Bunks in single-sex and mixed dorms (max 8) for £16 and some private rooms. ❶

Cardiff YHA Hostel 2 Wedal Rd, Roath Park ☎0870/770 5750, ⓔcardiff@yha.org.uk . Large, purpose-built building just underneath the A48

Eastern Avenue flyover at the top of Roath Park, almost two miles from the city centre and reachable via buses #28 or #29 from the central bus station. No curfew. Beds are £17.50 including breakfast.

Campsites

Cardiff Caravan Park Pontcanna Fields ☎ & ⓕ029/2039 8362. Very good council-run caravan park, with limited tent pitches. Only 25min walk from the city centre. Also offers bike rental to anyone.

Lavernock Point Holiday Estate Lavernock Point, Fort Road, near Penarth ☎029/2070 7310. Back-up option if the *Cardiff Caravan Park* is full. Five miles out of the city, off the B4267; buses #P4, #P5 and #P8 pass within a mile of the site. Also with bungalows.

The City

Cardiff's sights are clustered around fairly small, distinct districts. The compact commercial centre is bounded by the **River Taff**, which flows past the tremendous **Millennium Stadium**; in this rugby-mad city, the atmosphere in the pubs and streets when Wales have a home match – particularly against the old enemy, England – is charged with good-natured, beery fervour. Just upstream, the Taff is flanked by the wall of Cardiff's extraordinary **castle**, an amalgam of Roman remains, Norman keep and Victorian fantasy. North of the castle is a series of white Edwardian buildings grouped around **Cathays Park**: the City Hall, Cardiff University and the superb **National Museum**. A mile south of the commercial centre is the area around **Cardiff Bay**, once the city's liveliest district and on the up again since the inception of the Cardiff Bay redevelopment project and the construction of the barrage to form a vast freshwater lake. The surrounding waterfront, home to some fine bars and eateries, has been spruced up considerably, the recent arrival of the stunning new **National Assembly** and **Wales Millennium Centre** buildings having helped things enormously. A couple of miles north of the city centre, **Llandaff Cathedral** warrants a visit for its strange clash of Norman and modern styles.

The city centre

Cardiff **city centre** forms a rough square bounded by the castle, Queen Street and Central stations and the Cardiff International Arena. Dominating the skyline, on the other side of Wood Street from Central Station, is the simply magnificent **Millennium Stadium** (daily tours hourly Mon–Sat 10am–5pm, Sun 10am–4pm, subject to events; ☎029/2082 2228; £5.50), which has swiftly become an iconic symbol not only of Cardiff but of Wales as a whole. Built to an incredibly tight deadline in order to be ready for the Rugby World Cup of 1999, the stadium – with its trademark retractable roof – can seat 72,500 people and has hosted sporting matches of every description, as well as an array of huge rock gigs and other spectaculars. The tours include walking the players' tunnel, visiting the dressing rooms, VIP areas and a rugby museum. They start from the **stadium shop** at Entrance Gate 3 on Westgate Street. Don't forget to stroll the walkway along the river that was specially built out on ramps to accommodate the huge swell of the stadium walls.

The districts to the east are Cardiff's main shopping areas. **Queen Street**, running from the castle to Queen Street station, is a pedestrianized thoroughfare containing a predictable clutch of big-name chain stores and covered modern malls. Far more interesting are the **Arcades**, a series of Victorian and Edwardian galleries where you'll find all of the city centre's most alluring little independent shops and cafés – great for picking up flyers and information on gigs, club nights and other such events. Particularly impressive are the **High Street and Castle arcades**, either side of the High Street near the castle. A few yards further down towards Central Station is the elegant Edwardian **indoor market** and further still the **Royal and Morgan arcades**, linking St Mary Street with the lower end of The Hayes.

Cardiff Castle

The political, geographical and historical heart of the city is **Cardiff Castle** (daily: March–Oct 9.30am–6pm, tours every 20min; Nov–Feb 9.30am–5pm, 5 tours daily; full tour £6.50, grounds only £3.30), an intriguing hotchpotch of remnants of the city's history. The fortress hides inside a vast walled yard corresponding roughly to the outline of the original fort built by the Romans. The neat Norman motte, crowned with its eleventh-century **keep**, looks down onto the turrets and towers of the domestic buildings, which date in part from the fourteenth and fifteenth centuries, but were much extended in Tudor times, when residential needs began to overtake military priorities.

In the late nineteenth century, the third marquis of Bute, one of the richest men in the world, lavished a fortune on upgrading his pile – although he only lived there for six weeks a year – commissioning architect and decorator William Burges to aid him. With their passion for the religious art and the symbolism of the Middle Ages, they systematically overhauled the buildings, adding a spire to the octagonal tower and erecting a clocktower. But it was inside that their imaginations ran free, and they radically transformed the crumbling interiors into palaces of vivid colour and intricate, high-camp design. These rooms can only be seen as part of the guided tour, making the extra cost well worthwhile. On the **Animal Wall**, visible from Castle Street, outside, stone creatures are frozen in cheeky poses.

Cathays Park and around

On the north side of the city centre is **Cathays Park**, a large rectangle of lawns and flowerbeds that forms the centrepiece for the impressive buildings of the **civic centre**. Dating from the early twentieth century, the gleaming white buildings are arranged with pompous Edwardian precision, and speak volumes about Cardiff's self-confidence, a full half-century before it was officially declared capital of Wales. The dragon-topped, domed **City Hall** is the magnificent centrepiece of the complex, an exercise in every cliché about ostentatious civic self-glory, with a roll call of statues of male Welsh heroes, including Llywelyn ap Gruffydd, St David, Giraldus Cambrensis and Owain Glyndŵr. Note the *Peace Sculpture* in the main entrance lobby: it depicts one of the women who marched from Cardiff in 1981 to establish the Greenham Common peace camp.

National Museum and Gallery

To the right stands the **National Museum and Gallery** (Tues–Sun & bank holidays 10am–5pm; free, headset tour £2.50), one of Britain's finest, attempting both to tell the story of Wales and to reflect the nation's place in the wider, international sphere. Start off at the back of the entrance lobby with the epic

"Evolution of Wales" exhibition, a fabulous mix of natural history, high-tech gizmos and hugely detailed displays. To the right of the main lobby are various temporary exhibitions and an extensive botany collection, including some stunning silk, paper and wax plant and flower models. In the first-floor archeology gallery, don't miss the Bronze Age remains and the comparatively sophisticated **Caergwrle Bowl**, a delicate, gold-leafed ornament that is 3000 years old. Nearby is the **Tregwynt Treasure Trove**, an impressive cache of gold and silver coins dating back to the Civil War, uncovered near Fishguard in 1996.

The bulk of the East Wing is given over to **fine art**, with ten galleries on the first floor containing the majority of the museum's extraordinary art collection. The oldest part of the collection starts with the fifteenth- and sixteenth-century **Italian schools**, pushing on to seventeenth-century galleries rich in **Flemish** and **Dutch** work, including Rembrandt's coolly aloof portrait of *Catrina Hooghsaet* and Jacob van Ruisdael's mesmerizing *Waterfall*. The most famous, or perhaps infamous, pieces here are the **Cardiff Cartoons**, four monumental tapestries bought at great expense in 1979 and, at the time, presumed to be the work of Rubens. The first of the great Welsh artists is shown to maximum effect in the **eighteenth-century** galleries, where landscapes by Richard Wilson include *Caernarfon Castle* and *Dolbadarn Castle*. The **nineteenth-century** galleries include a round-up of some of the century's greater painters, including J.M.W. Turner, whose *Thames Backwater, with Windsor Castle* is a characteristic wash of diffuse colour and light.

The most exciting art works are contained in galleries eleven to fifteen, kicking off with a fabulous **sculpture collection**, including many by the one-man Victorian Welsh statue industry, Goscombe John, that contrast with the more delicate Rodin pieces nearby. Gallery Thirteen is home to the National Museum's pride, the Davies collection of **Impressionist paintings**. Cézanne, Monet and Degas figure predominantly, alongside Corot's legendary *Distant view of Corbeil, morning*, Pissarro's classic views of Rouen and Paris, and Renoir's chirpy portrait of *La Parisienne*. Gallery Fourteen houses a hearty collection of Post-Impressionists, Futurists and Surrealists, while Gallery Fifteen showcases abstract work with a strong Welsh bent.

Cardiff Bay

Although you can get there by water-bus (every hour from Bute Park and Taff's Mead Embankment), train (every 20min from Queen Street station) or bus (#2, #7 or #35 from outside Central station), **Cardiff Bay** is just a half-hour stroll from the city centre along either endearingly tatty Bute Street or the new, sadly characterless "ceremonial boulevard", **Lloyd George Avenue**.

In years gone by, when the docks were some of the busiest in the world, the area was better known by its evocative name of **Tiger Bay**, immortalized by local lass Shirley Bassey. Today, Cardiff Bay is one of the world's biggest regeneration projects, the downbeat dereliction of the old docks being turned into a designer heaven. It works well in places, though it struggles at times to maintain a life beyond the shifts of the office workers who are the main users of its bars and restaurants; it's deservedly a must-see part of any Cardiff tour.

From Cardiff Bay station, turn left and head down towards the vast open space of **Roald Dahls Plass**, named after the Cardiff-born children's author. Dominating the square is the mesmerizing new **Wales Millennium Centre** (☎08700/402000, ⓦwww.wmc.org.uk), a vibrant performance space for theatre and music. Likened by critics to a copper-plated armadillo or a great snail, the WMC soars gracefully over the Bay rooftops, its exterior swathed in Welsh building materials, topped with a stainless-steel shell tinted with a bronze oxide to resist salty air. Pause before entering to mull over the inspirational bilingual inscription writ large across the frontage in seven-foot-high letter windows. Crafted by poet Gwyneth Lewis, the phrases read downwards – in English "In these stones, horizons sing" and in Welsh "Creu gwir fel gwydr, o ffwrnais awen" ("Creating truth like glass, from the furnace of inspiration") – but, ingeniously, they also read across each line, in two languages, and still make crystal-clear poetry.

The glories continue throughout the interior, fashioned from materials that hark back to Wales's mineral-extracting past. The ground floor houses the main box office, an interactive exhibition, a music shop, souvenir shop, bar and brasserie. Upstairs there's a champagne bar and entrances into the main auditorium, the acoustically sensational Donald Gordon Theatre. The best way to see all this, and other parts of the building that you won't see otherwise, is to take a **guided tour** (11 am & 2pm, advisable to pre-book on ☎029/2063 4647; £5). Daily **free performances**, of anything from poetry to hip-hop, take place in the WMC foyer, usually at lunchtime and 6pm.

At the far end of the square, down by the water's edge, is the magnificent red-brick **Pierhead Building**, a typically ornate neo-Gothic terracotta pile that now houses a surprisingly enjoyable **exhibition** (Mon–Thurs 9.30am–4.30pm, Fri 10am–4.30pm; free) about the workings of the **National Assembly for Wales**, inaugurated in 1999. At the time of writing, the new Assembly debating chamber is rising fast next door, and should be open sometime in 2006.

Harbour Drive leads down from the Assembly building towards the startling **Cardiff Bay Visitor Centre**, Harbour Drive (April–Sept Mon–Fri 9.30am–6pm, Sat & Sun 10.30am–6pm; rest of year closes 5pm; ☎029/2046 3833), a giant tubular eye peering out over the Bay. Although it's a thinly disguised PR job for the development, there are lots of good exhibits and plenty of information to pick up.

In front of the Visitor Centre is the gleaming white, stumpy-spired **Norwegian church** (daily 10am–4pm; ☎029/2045 4899 for events), an old seamen's chapel, in which Roald Dahl was christened, now converted into a nice café (see p.710) and performance and exhibition space.

Central to the whole Bay project is the kilometre-long **Cardiff Bay Barrage** (daily: April–Oct 8am–8pm; Nov–March 8am–4pm; free), built right across the Ely and Taff estuaries, transforming a vast mudflat into a freshwater lake and creating eight miles of useful waterfront. Continuing west along the waterfront brings you straight into **Mermaid Quay**, an airy jumble of shops, bars and restaurants that, on a warm day, is a fine place to hang out and watch the world amble by. The city's water-buses (see p.693) leave from here. Further west, **Techniquest**, on Stuart Street (Mon–Fri 9.30am–4.30pm, Sat & Sun 10.30am–5pm; £6.90), is a fun, hands-on science gallery – perfect for kids; while the five-star **St David's Hotel** (see p.693) acts as a stylish full-stop to the sweep of the Bay. From its car park, a path leads a couple of hundred yards to an eight-hectare **wetland reserve**, created partly to help offset the loss of wading-bird habitats when the barrage was built and the Bay flooded.

The area immediately inland from the Bay is the salty old district of **Bute-town**, whose inner-city dereliction still peeps through the rampant gentrification. James Street, behind Techniquest, is the main commercial focus, while to its north are the cleaned-up old buildings around **Mount Stuart Square**, the most impressive being the mammoth **Coal Exchange Building** built in the 1880s as Britain's central Coal Exchange. Close by, on the corner of West Bute Street, the old church of St Stephen has been converted into **The Point**, a superb venue for music and, occasionally, drama (see p.701). A block further east the **Butetown History & Arts Centre** at 5 Dock Chambers (opening times vary; ☎029/2025 6757, ⓦwww.bhac.org) records and celebrates the multicultural pedigree of the district. A few paces up the street at no. 54b, the cool, contemporary **Bay Art** gallery (Tues–Sat 10am-5pm; free) has a varied programme of exhibitions, while a block further east, in an old maritime warehouse, **Craft in the Bay** (daily 10.30am–5.30pm; free) now showcases the work of craft practitioners from all over Wales and has a cute café. Across the way, the sweeping roofline and glass-brick curtain wall of the **Red Dragon Centre** (formerly Atlantic Wharf) make a striking front for what is essentially a big box filled with a twelve-screen multiplex, bowling alley, bars and restaurants. From here it's just a short hop across the road back to Cardiff Bay train station.

Llandaff Cathedral

Two miles northwest of the city centre along Cathedral Road, the small, quiet suburb of **Llandaff** is home to a church that has now grown up into the city's **cathedral** (daily 10am–7pm; free). It's believed to have been founded in the sixth century by St Teilo, but was rebuilt in Norman style in around 1120, and worked on well into the thirteenth century. From the late fourteenth century onwards, it declined into an advanced state of disrepair, and one of the twin towers and the nave roof eventually collapsed. Restoration only began in earnest in the early 1840s, when **Pre-Raphaelite** artists such as Edward Burne-Jones, Dante Gabriel Rossetti and the firm of William Morris were commissioned to make colourful new windows and decorative panels. Their work is best seen in the south aisle.

The fusion of different styles and ages is evident from outside, especially in the mismatched western towers. Inside, the nave is dominated by Jacob Epstein's overwhelming *Christ in Majesty*, a concrete parabola topped with a soaring Christ figure. At the west end of the north aisle, the **St Illtyd Chapel** features Rossetti's cloying triptych *The Seed of David*. In the south presbytery is a tenth-century Celtic cross, the only survivor of the pre-Norman cathedral.

Eating, drinking and nightlife

Cardiff's long-standing internationalism has paid handsome dividends in the range of **restaurants**, with the influence of Italian immigrants particularly evident in the number of cafés, bistros and trattorias. There are numerous places right in the centre, most notably in the "café quarter" along Mill Lane. Most other places are within easy walking distance; there are good hunting grounds in the cheaper quarters of Cathays and Roath, particularly the curry houses along Crwys, Albany and City roads, a stone's throw from the centre beyond the university. Cardiff's **pub** life has expanded exponentially over recent years, and there are some wonderful Edwardian palaces of etched, smoky glass and deep red wood, where you'll find Cardiff's very own Brains bitter.

There's plenty of choice when it comes to **nightlife** in Cardiff, whether your tastes run to sweaty rock gigs (in English or Welsh), pumping clubs or genteel classical affairs. **Theatre** encompasses everything from the radical and alternative at The Point and Chapter to big, blowzy productions at the New Theatre or West End spectaculars at the new Wales Millennium Centre, home of the Welsh National Opera (ⓦwww.wno.org.uk). Classical **music** is best heard at the WMC or St David's Hall. Cardiff is usually on big world rock tours, thanks to the Millennium Stadium. There's no shortage of multiplex **cinemas** for the latest blockbusters, though Chapter is best for art-house movies. Cardiff also has a modest **gay and lesbian scene**, centred on Charles Street, just off Queen Street; the best information source is South Wales Friend (Tues–Thurs 7.30–9.30pm; ☎029/2034 0101).

Cafés and restaurants

Celtic Cauldron Castle Arcade. A friendly daytime café, dedicated to bringing a range of simple Welsh food – soups, stews, laver bread, cakes – to an appreciative public. Inexpensive.

Cibo 83 Pontcanna St, off Cathedral Road ☎029/2223 2226. A slice of Italy in Cardiff: a small, inexpensive and welcoming trattoria serving ciabatta sandwiches and simple, well-cooked food. No credit cards. Moderate.

Greenhouse 38 Woodville Rd, Cathays ☎029/2023 5731. Licensed vegetarian restaurant with a modern take on traditional dishes. Closed Sun & Mon. Moderate.

Happy Gathering 233 Cowbridge Rd East, Canton ☎029/2039 7531. A true Cardiff phenomenon, best and most authentic Chinese food in the city.

Jags 4 Church St. Eat-in and take-out sandwich bar serving stuffed baguettes and good coffee. Inexpensive.

Le Gallois (Y Cymro) 6–10 Romilly Crescent, Canton ☎029/2034 1264. Sophisticated and fashionable restaurant on a busy suburban road, serving delicious French cuisine with a Welsh twist. Expensive.

Louis' Restaurant 32 St Mary St. Wondrously old-fashioned restaurant, serving great dollops of well-cooked, good-value comfort food until around 7.30pm. Moderate.

Norwegian Church Café Harbour Drive. Cosy spot for Norwegian open sandwiches, salads, some scrumptious cakes and filter coffee. Inexpensive.

Porto's 40 St Mary St ☎029/2022 0060. Authentic restaurant in a dark, wood-beamed room serving massive portions of Portuguese and Madeiran favourites, including endless variations on dried cod. Moderate.

Tang's 15–23 Westgate St ☎029/2022 7771. Quite pricey, but the best all-round Chinese restaurant in the city centre, whose owners have a long pedigree in Cardiff cuisine. Expensive.

Woods Brasserie Stuart St, Cardiff Bay ☎029/2049 2400. One of Cardiff's most stylish establishments, where you'll definitely need to book in advance to sample the excellent Modern British cuisine. Moderate (lunch) expensive (evening).

Bars, pubs and clubs

Bar Cwtsh at *Jolyon's Hotel*, 5 Bute Crescent, Cardiff Bay. Cosy, smoke-free bar with a wood-burning stove and terrific atmosphere.

Cayo Arms Cathedral Rd, Pontcanna. Great pub a 5min walk up Cathedral Road from the city centre. Proudly Welsh, with Tomos Watkin beers and decent food every day until 8pm.

Chapter Market Rd, Canton. A trendy bar in the arts centre, with a good choice of real ale, imported lagers and whisky. Frequented by the Canton media and arts crowd.

Club X 39 Charles St. Stylish and popular gay club that manages to span both cheesy and cutting edge. Also has a wonderful roof garden and a great atmosphere. Open Wed till 2am, Fri 3am, Sat 4am & Sun 1am.

Clwb Ifor Bach Womanby St ☎029/2023 2199, ⓦ www.clwb.net. A sweaty and enjoyable live-music and DJ club with nightly gigs and sessions, many featuring Welsh-language bands.

Ha-ha Bar The Friary. Decent posing palace in town; an enjoyable, young and funky place that also serves great food.

Mochyn Du Sophia Close, off Cathedral Rd. Relaxed pub with tables spilling out into the greenery. Good bar menu, great beer, and popular with Welsh speakers.

Sam's Bar 63 St Mary St ☎029/2034 5189. Lively club-bar, with everything from live heavy metal through comedy and drag shows to house DJs. A good place to check the pulse of the Mill Lane "café quarter".

Theatre, cinema and classical music

Cardiff International Arena Mary Ann St ☎029/2023 4500 (enquiries), ☎029/2022 4488 (bookings). Large and imposing venue rising high over the city centre's southern streets and playing host to classical concerts, opera, and major rock and pop gigs.

Chapter Arts Centre Market Rd, Canton ☎029/2030 4400, ⓦ www.chapter.org. Multifunctional arts complex that's home to fine British and touring theatre and dance companies.

Glee Club Mermaid Quay, Cardiff Bay ☎0870/241 5093, ⓦ www.glee.co.uk. Cardiff's best comedy club, with some of the biggest names of the British stand-up circuit.

New Theatre Park Place ☎029/2087 8889, ⓦ www.newtheatrecardiff.co.uk. Splendid Edwardian city-centre theatre that plays host to big shows, musicals and pantos.

The Point West Bute St, Cardiff Bay ☎029/2049 9979, ⓦ www.thepointcardiffbay.com. This performance space converted from an old church is good for experimental theatre, music and dance, as well as more mainstream events.

Sherman Theatre Senghennydd Rd, Cathays ☎029/2064 6900, ⓦwww.shermantheatre.co.uk. An excellent two-auditorium repertory theatre hosting a mixed bag of new and translated classic Welsh-language pieces, stand-up comedy, children's entertainment, drama, music and dance. Many plays on Welsh themes in both English and Welsh.

St David's Hall The Hayes ☎029/2087 8444, ⓦwww.stdavidshallcardiff.co.uk. Part of the massive St David's shopping centre, this large venue is home to visiting orchestras and musicians from jazz to opera, and is frequently used by the excellent BBC National Orchestra of Wales.

Wales Millennium Centre Roald Dahls Plass, Cardiff Bay ☎029/2040 2000, ⓦwww.wmc.org .uk. Permanent home of the Welsh National Opera, together with a collection of other music and dance companies. Also used for touring mega-productions.

Listings

Airport Cardiff International, out at Rhoose, near Barry ☎01446/711111, ⓦwww.cial.co.uk.
Banks and exchange All major banks have branches along High St or Queen St. In addition there's American Express at 3 Queen St (Mon–Fri 9am–5.30pm, Sat 10am–1pm; ☎029/2066 5843), and Thomas Cook at 16 Queen St (Mon–Fri 9.30am–5pm, Sat 10am–1pm; ☎029/2022 4886); both cash currency and travellers' cheques.
Bike rental Taff Trail Cycle Hire at the Cardiff Caravan Park, Pontcanna Fields ☎029/2039 8362 (see p.696).
Bus enquiries Cardiff Bus ☎0870/608 2608; National Express ☎0870/580 8080.
Dentist For emergency dental work, phone Cardiff

NHS Community Dental Service on ☎029/2039 4347.
Hospital In the first instance, phone NHS Wales Direct on ☎0845/4647.
Laundries Drift Inn, 104 Salisbury Rd, Cathays Park; GP, 244 Cowbridge Rd, Canton; Launderama, 60 Lower Cathedral Rd.
Pharmacy Boots, 5 Wood St (Mon–Sat 8am–8pm, Sun 6–7pm; ☎029/2023 4043).
Police Cardiff Central Police Station, King Edward VII Ave, Cathays Park ☎029/2022 2111.
Post office The Hayes (Mon–Fri 9am–5.30pm, Sat 9am–12.30pm).
Swimming pools and spas Welsh Institute of Sport, Sophia Gardens ☎029/2030 0500.

Around Cardiff

On the edge of the northern Cardiff suburbs, the thirteenth-century fairy-tale castle of **Castell Coch** stands on a hillside in the woods, while just further north is the massive **Caerphilly Castle**. West of the city, the massively popular **National History Museum** at St Fagans tells the country's history through a collection of buildings uprooted from all over Wales.

Castell Coch

Four miles north of Llandaff, the turreted **Castell Coch** (June–Sept daily 9.30am–6pm; April, May & Oct daily 9.30am–5pm; Nov–March Mon–Sat 9.30am–4pm, Sun 11am–4pm; £3, headset tour 50p; CADW) was once a ruined thirteenth-century fortress. Like Cardiff Castle, it was rebuilt and transformed into a fantasy structure in the late 1870s by William Burges for the third marquess of Bute. With its working portcullis and drawbridge, Castell Coch is the ultimate wealthy-man's medieval fantasy, isolated on its almost alpine hillside, yet only a few hundred yards from the motorway and Cardiff suburbs. There are many similarities with Cardiff Castle, notably the lavish decor, culled from religious and moral fables, which dazzles in each room. Bus #26A from Central station drops at the castle gates, or the #132 drops in Tongwynlais, from where it's a ten-minute climb.

Caerphilly

Caerphilly (Caerffili), seven miles north of Cardiff, has smartened itself up in recent years, particularly the area around its staggering town-centre

castle (Easter–May & Oct daily 9.30am–5pm; June–Sept daily 9.30am–6pm; Nov–March Mon–Sat 9.30am–4pm, Sun 11am–4pm; £3; CADW), the first in Britain built concentrically, with an inner system of defences overlooking the outer ring. Looming out of its vast surrounding moat, the medieval fortress with its cock-eyed tower occupies over thirty acres, presenting an awesome promise not entirely fulfilled inside. The castle was begun in 1268 by Gilbert de Clare as a defence against Llywelyn the Last. For the next few hundred years Caerphilly was little more than a decaying toy, given at whim by kings to their favourites. By the turn of the twentieth century, it was in a sorry state, sitting amidst a growing industrial town that saw fit to build in the then-dry moat and castle precincts. Houses and shops were demolished in order to allow the moat to be reflooded in 1958.

You enter the castle through the much-restored **gatehouse**, where there's an exhibition on the castle's history. A platform behind the barbican wall exhibits medieval war and siege engines, overlooked on the left by the southeastern leaning tower. Of the rest of the castle, the most interesting section is the massive eastern gatehouse, which includes an impressive upper hall and oratory and, to its left, the wholly restored and re-roofed **Great Hall**.

Caerphilly is also known for its crumbly white **cheese**, made in dairies around the town, and available in a ploughman's lunch at the *Courthouse* pub, on Cardiff Road, right by the castle and a five-minute stroll from the **bus** and **train** stations.

St Fagans National History Museum and Castle

St Fagans (Sain Ffagan), four miles west of Cardiff city centre, has a rural feel that is only partially disturbed by the busloads of tourists that roll in regularly to visit the excellent **National History Museum** (daily 10am–5pm; free), built around **St Fagans Castle**, a country house erected in 1580 and furnished in early nineteenth-century style. The most impressive part of the museum is the fifty-acre outdoor collection of buildings from all corners of Wales that have been carefully dismantled and rebuilt on this site since the museum's inception in 1946. There are particular highlights, including the diminutive, whitewashed Pen-Rhiw Chapel, built in Dyfed in 1777; the pristine and evocative St Mary's Board School, built in Lampeter in Victorian times; and the stern mini-fortress of a tollhouse that once guarded the southern approach to Aberystwyth, from 1772. The superb Rhyd-y-car **ironworkers' cottages**, from Merthyr Tydfil, were originally built in around 1800. Each of the six houses, with its accompanying strip of garden, has been furnished in the style of a different period, stretching from 1805 to 1985. **Buses** #32 (hourly) and #C1 (variable times) run to the museum from Cardiff Central station.

Swansea and Gower

Dylan Thomas called **SWANSEA** (Abertawe) – his birthplace – an "ugly, lovely town", an epithet which poet Paul Durcan updated to "pretty, shitty city". Both ring true. Large, sprawling and boisterous, with around 200,000 people, Swansea may only be the second city of Wales, but it's the undoubted Welsh capital of attitude, coated in a layer of chunky bling. The city centre was massively rebuilt after devastating bomb attacks in World War II, and a jumble of tower blocks now dot the horizon. But closer inspection reveals Swansea's multifarious charms: some intact old corners of the city centre, the spacious

SWANSEA

▲ Cardiff & M4

River Tawe

Ferry Port

GRENFELL PARK ROAD

PENTRE GUINEA ROAD

FABIAN WAY

NEW CUT ROAD

QUAY PARADE

SOMERSET ST

TONTINE ST

CAMBRIAN PLACE

Dylan Thomas Centre

Environment Centre

◀ Carmarthen & M4

Train Station

STRAND

HIGH STREET

DYFATTY ST

ORCHARD ST

ALEXANDRA RD

Plantasia

Castle

St David's Square

Swansea Museum

Dylan Thomas Theatre

National Waterfront Museum

CASTLE STREET

WIND ST

CASTLE SQUARE

PRINCESS WAY

Glynn Vivian Art Gallery

Library

GROVE PLACE

MOUNT PLEASANT

CRADOCK ST

MANSEL ST

THE KINGSWAY

Market

Bus Station

Grand Theatre

Swansea Cycles

PAGE ST

ORCHARD ST

SINGLETON STREET

WEST WAY

OYSTERMOUTH ROAD

CROMWELL STREET

TERRACE ROAD

WALTER ROAD

ST HELEN'S ROAD

PAGE ST

RICHARDSON STREET

WEST WAY

ARGYLE ST

BEACH ST

ST HELEN'S

WESTERN STREET

Guildhall

DYFED AVENUE

PANT-Y-CELYN ROAD

ENLAND CRESCENT

GLAN CRESCENT

TERRACE ROAD

TON DIXON DR

EATON CRES

BRYN-Y-MOR ROAD

KING EDWARDS ROAD

ST HELEN'S AVENUE

Dylan Thomas's Birthplace

Cwmdonkin Park

UPLANDS

UPLANDS CRESCENT

BERNARD STREET

Victoria Park

Patti Pavilion

GLAMOR PARK ROAD

GLANMOR ROAD

SKETTY ROAD

GLANBR'DAN AVENUE

BRYN ROAD

BRYNMILL LANE

MUMBLES ROAD

TOWNHILL ROAD

COCKETT RD

PARC WERN ROAD

Singleton Park

Swansea University

VIVIAN ROAD

GOWER ROAD

DE LA BECHE ROAD

TY-COCH RD

▼ Mumbles

◀ Gower

N

0   500 yds

© Crown copyright

RESTAURANTS, CAFÉS, PUBS & CLUBS

Chelsea Café	4	New Capriccio	7
Didier and Stephanie	9	No Sign Bar	6
Govinda's	3	Palace	1
H2O	11	Queen's Hotel	10
Hanson's	8	Sketty Hall	12
Monkey Café	2	Street Pebble	5
Morgans	D	Café Bar	D

ACCOMMODATION

Crescent	F
Dragon	B
Grosvenor House	C
Harlton	G
Morgans	D
Oyster	H
White House Hotel	E
Windsor Lodge Hotel	A

and graceful suburb of Uplands, a wide **seafront** overlooking Swansea Bay and a bold marina development around the old docks, while spread throughout are some of the best-funded **museums** in Wales, including the stunning new National Waterfront Museum – itself reason enough to include Swansea on a tour of Wales. Situated on the edge of the **Gower peninsula**, which holds some of the country's most popular and inspirational coastal and rural scenery, Swansea makes a logical base: transport out into the surrounding areas is good, and beds tend to be less expensive in the city than in the more picturesque parts of Gower.

The city's Welsh name, Abertawe, means the settlement at the mouth of the River Tawe, a grimy ditch that is slowly being teased back to life after centuries of use as a sewer for Swansea's metal trades. The first reliable mention of Swansea dates from 1099, when a Norman castle was built here as an outpost of William the Conqueror's empire. A small settlement grew near the coalfields and the sea, developing into a mining and shipbuilding centre that, by 1700, was the largest coal port in Wales. Copper smelting became the area's dominant industry in the eighteenth century, soon attracting other metal trades to pack out the lower Tawe Valley, making it one of the world's most prolific metal-bashing centres.

Arrival, information and accommodation

Swansea is the main interchange station for trains out to the west of Wales, and for the slow line across to Shrewsbury in England. The **train station** is at the top end of the High Street, a ten-minute hike from the **bus station**, which is sandwiched between the Quadrant shopping centre and the Grand Theatre. Nearby, on Plymouth Street, is the **tourist office** (all year Mon–Sat 9.30am–5.30pm; May–Sept also Sun 10am–4pm; ☎01792/468321, ✆tourism@swansea.gov.uk), where you can pick up the comprehensive bimonthly magazine *What's On*. Most of the sights are within walking distance of each other; popular suburbs, such as Uplands and Sketty, near the university, are a bracing thirty-minute walk from the centre, though buses get you there easily. **Ferries** to Cork in Ireland leave roughly once a day from the docks, around a mile east of the town centre (☎01792/456116, ✆www.swansea-cork.ie).

There are dozens of dirt-cheap **hotels** and **B&Bs** stretched out along the seafront Oystermouth Road, whose trade is largely pitched at those catching the Swansea–Cork ferry. Better places congregate in leafy Uplands, a thirty-minute walk from town. There are no campsites or hostels in the city itself, although nearby places in Gower are easily reached.

Hotels and guest houses

Crescent 132 Eaton Crescent, Uplands ☎ & ☎01792/466814, ✆www.crescentguesthouse .co.uk. Large, pleasant, well-converted Edwardian guest house. All rooms have showers, and half have superb views over the city and the Bay. ❸
Dragon Kingsway Circle ☎01792/657100, ✆www.dragon-hotel.co.uk. The old *Holiday Inn* has been much revamped and modernized, making it a smart central option. ❺
Grosvenor House Mirador Crescent, Uplands ☎01792/461522, ✆www.grosvenor-guesthouse .co.uk. Tidy and reliable guest house with great breakfasts and hugely enthusiastic proprietors. ❹

Harlton 89 King Edward Rd, Brynmill ☎01792/466938, ✆www.harltonguesthouse .co.uk. Budget guest house that's a little yellow around the edges but perfectly adequate and very cheap. ❶
Morgans Adelaide St ☎01792/484848, ✆www.morganshotel.co.uk. Sumptuous conversion of the old Port Authority HQ into Swansea's first five-star hotel. Not at all stuffy, however, but a real worthwhile treat. ❻
Oyster 262 Oystermouth Rd ☎01792/654345. Small, friendly hotel overlooking the shore and with some en suite rooms ❷

White House Hotel 4 Nyanza Terrace, Uplands ☎01792/473856, ⓦwww.thewhitehouse hotel .co.uk. Extremely well-kept guest house with excellent rates for its well-appointed rooms, all with satellite TV. Extensive breakfasts are included in the rates, and you can get a good three-course evening meal for £10. Internet access is available. **⑤**

Windsor Lodge Hotel Mount Pleasant ☎01792/642158, ⓦwww.windsor-lodge .co.uk. Like a country hotel in the city, this two-century-old house has nicely decorated en-suite rooms, elegant but comfortable lounges and an evenings-only restaurant serving British and French cuisine. **④–⑤**

The City

Swansea's train station faces out onto the morose High Street, which heads south past the remains of the Norman **castle**, which enjoys an improved setting against the revamped Castle Square. Alexandra Road forks right off the High Street immediately south of the train station, leading down to the **Glynn Vivian Art Gallery** (Tues–Sun 10.30am–5.30pm; free), a delightful Edwardian showcase of inspiring Welsh art including the huge, frantic canvases of Ceri Richards, Wales's most respected twentieth-century painter, and works by Gwen John and her brother Augustus, whose mesmerizing portrait of Caitlin Thomas, Dylan's wife, is a real highlight. The gallery also houses a large collection of fine porcelain – of which Swansea was a noted centre in the early nineteenth century – together with contemporary works from Nantgarw, near Cardiff.

Running south from Castle Square, Wind Street (pronounced as in "whined") has been designated as the main drag of nocturnal Swansea and it is now chock-full of theme and chain bars, pubs and restaurants, with a few more unusual establishments sprinkled into the mix.

A block behind the High Street, the retail park on the Strand includes the great pyramidal glasshouse of **Plantasia** (Tues–Sun & Bank Holiday Mon 10am–5pm; £3.15), a sweaty world of wondrous tropical plants inhabited by a mini-zoo of tamarin monkeys, butterflies and numerous insects, an aquarium and a thirteen-foot Burmese python.

The main shopping streets lie to the south of town, notably underneath the Quadrant Centre where the curving-roofed **market** makes a lively sight, with traditional and long-standing stalls selling local delicacies such as laver bread (a delicious savoury made from seaweed), as well as cockles trawled from the nearby Loughor estuary, typical Welsh cakes, fish and cheeses. Hourly buses leave the Quadrant depot for **Uplands**, a twenty- to thirty-minute walk from the city centre. North of the main road, leafy avenues rise up the slopes past the sharp terraces of **Cwmdonkin Park**, at the centre of which is a memorial to Dylan Thomas inscribed with lines from *Fern Hill*, one of his best-known poems. On the eastern side of the park is Cwmdonkin Drive, a sharply rising set of solid Victorian semis, notable only for the blue plaque on no. 5, birthplace of the poet in 1914.

The spit of land between Oystermouth Road, the sea and the Tawe estuary has been christened the **Maritime Quarter** – tourist-board-speak for the old docks – built around a vast marina surrounded by legions of modern flats. The city's old South Dock, now cleaned and spruced up, features the enticingly old-fashioned **Swansea Museum** (Tues–Sun 10am–5pm; free). A small grid of nineteenth-century streets around the museum has been thoughtfully cleaned up and now houses some enjoyable cafés, pubs and restaurants.

Behind the museum, in Somerset Place, is the airy **Dylan Thomas Centre**, the national literature centre of Wales (daily 10am–4.30pm; free; ☎01792/463980), complete with theatre space, book and craft shops, a great café, and two galleries. One of these is devoted to Dylan Thomas, and includes a mock-up of the shed in which he wrote, where you can see a fascinating video on his life and work.

A hundred yards or so west, behind the *Evening Post* building, the city's **Environment Centre** (daily 10am–4pm; free) is housed in the old telephone exchange on Pier Street. As well as a resource centre for all things green and peaceful, there are regularly changing exhibitions inside.

From here, Burrows Place leads down to the marina and the sublime new **National Waterfront Museum** (daily 10am–5pm; free). Carved out of the shell of the old Industrial and Maritime Museum, the original building has been stunningly extended to accommodate a breathtakingly varied set of exhibitions dealing with Wales's history of innovation and industry. The museum is divided into fifteen zones, looking at topics such as energy, landscape, coal, genealogy, networks and money, and each section is bursting with interactive technology. Within the complex, there are shops, a café and a lovely waterfront balcony. Without doubt, this is the most impressive museum in Wales, and should not be missed.

The museum faces out onto a flotilla of yachts bobbing in the marina. Close by stands John Doubleday's statue of Dylan Thomas, dubbed "A Portrait of the Artist as Someone Else", since it looks nothing like the poet. Just behind the statue, on Gloucester Place, is the mural-splattered warehouse that has now become the **Dylan Thomas Theatre**, which intersperses productions of his work with visiting and local companies' offerings.

Eating, drinking and nightlife

Swansea is a city that knows how to have a good time, and works damn hard at it. Loads of new bars and restaurants have emerged in recent years, with Wind Street as the city's main booze artery, with a handful of late-opening club-bars that generally appeal to an older clientele than the brash younger clubs around Kingsway. For nightlife, the city is well placed, with most passing theatre, opera and music of all sorts being obliged to make a stop here. The BBC Welsh Symphony Orchestra appears at the **Brangwyn Hall** (℡01792/635489) in the Art Deco Civic Centre. Thomas's classics get a regular airing at the **Dylan Thomas Theatre** (℡01792/473238, @www.dylanthomastheatre.org.uk), by the marina, while the **Taliesin Arts Centre** (℡01792/602060, @www.taliesinartscentre.co.uk), in the university, is the city's more offbeat venue.

Cafés and restaurants

Chelsea Café Tŷ Castell House, 17 St Mary St ℡01792/464068. Local ingredients served with flair and imagination are the staples of this place, and it's all done extremely well. Moderate.

Didier and Stephanie 56 St Helen's Rd, Uplands ℡01792/655603. Small, lovely French restaurant, specializing in some fairly obscure regional Gallic surprises. Moderate.

Govinda's 8 Craddock St. Vegetarian restaurant in the Hare Krishna tradition, selling very cheap, if somewhat insipid, meals and freshly pressed juices. Inexpensive.

Hanson's Pilot House Wharf ℡01792/466200. Low-key restaurant on the far side of the marina serving tasty and well-presented dishes. Closed Sun evening. Moderate.

Morgans Adelaide St ℡01792/484848. The huge old boardroom of the Port Authority building now houses the excellent restaurant of Swansea's best hotel. Confident modern cooking with sometimes overzealous service. Expensive.

New Capriccio 89 St Helen's Rd ℡01792/648804. Popular Italian restaurant with bargain lunch menu. Closed Sun evening & Mon. Inexpensive.

Sketty Hall Singleton Park ℡01792/284011. Catering academy in beautiful surroundings, where you can sample the excellent student cuisine for reasonable prices. Booking essential. Moderate.

Street Pebble Café Bar 11 Wind St. Wicker, stones and a candlelit interior provide Wind Street's most chilled ambience: great for morning smoothies, daytime paninis or Mediterranean food in the evenings. Inexpensive–moderate.

Pubs and clubs

Celtic Pride 49 Uplands Crescent, Uplands ☎01792/645301. Good local pub with almost nightly live music, including jam sessions and Welsh music. The *Uplands Tavern*, opposite, is good for music and studenty rumpus too.

H20 Anchor Court, Victoria Quay, Swansea Marina ☎01792/648555. Fairly sterile gay club after dark; pre-club bar offering inexpensive pub food until early evening.

Monkey Café 13 Castle St ⊛www .monkeycafe.co.uk. Groovy, inexpensive, mosaic-floored café with a relaxed atmosphere and nightly DJs or live music. On a good night, the best in town.

No Sign Bar 56 Wind St. A narrow frontage leads into a long, warm pub interior, one of the oldest in town and easily the best on Wind Street. The etymology of the name is explained in depth in the window.

Palace 156 High St ☎01792/457977. Two-room club with hardcore tunes and bags of atmosphere.

Queen's Hotel Gloucester Place, near the marina. Large old hotel and pub firmly in the Swansea seafaring tradition, with good snack lunches and Sunday roasts, and bags of gritty atmosphere.

Gower

A fifteen-mile-long peninsula of undulating limestone, **Gower** (Gŵyr) is a world of its own, pointing down into the Bristol Channel to the west of Swansea. The area is fringed by sweeping yellow bays and precipitous cliffs, with caves and blowholes to the south, and wide, flat marshes and cockle beds to the north. Bracken heaths dotted with prehistoric remains and tiny villages lie between, and there are numerous castle ruins and curious churches to be found. Out of season, the winding lanes afford wonderful opportunities for exploration, but in the height of summer – July and August especially – they can be horribly congested. Buses from Swansea serve the whole peninsula, with frequent services to Mumbles, Port Eynon and even out to Rhossili.

Gower can be said to start in Swansea's western suburbs, along the coast of Swansea Bay that curves round to a point at the pleasantly old-fashioned resort of **Mumbles**. It finishes with **Rhossili Bay**, a spectacular four-mile yawn of sand backed by the village of Rhossili and occupying the entire western end of the peninsula. The southern coast is punctuated by the glorious village of **Port Eynon**, home to an excellent YHA **hostel** (☎0870/770 5998; £13 per bed; closed Nov–March) and a beautiful beach. West of Port Eynon, the coast becomes a wild, frilly series of inlets and cliffs, topped by a five-mile path that stretches all the way to the peninsula's glorious westernmost point, **Worms Head**. The northern coast merges into the tidal flats of the estuary.

Mumbles and Oystermouth

At the far westernmost end of Swansea Bay and on the cusp of Gower, **Mumbles** (Mwmbwls) is a lively and enjoyable alternative base to Swansea, with a diverse range of seaside entertainment, fine restaurants and the legendary Mumbles Mile of pubs. Derived from the French *mamelles*, or "breasts" (a reference to the twin islets off the end of Mumbles Head), Mumbles is now used to refer to the entire loose sprawl of **OYSTERMOUTH** (Ystumllwynarth) – a term used pretty much interchangeably with Mumbles. Here, the seafront is an unbroken curve of budget hotels, breezy pubs and cafés, leading down to the refurbished pier and the rocky plug of Mumbles Head. Around the headland, reached either by the longer coast road or by a short walk over the hill, is the district of **Langland Bay**, whose sandy beach is popular with surfers.

The hilltop above town is crowned by the ruins of **Oystermouth Castle** (April–Oct daily 11am–5pm; £1.20). Founded as a Norman watchtower, the castle was strengthened to withstand attacks by the Welsh before being converted for more amenable residential purposes during the fourteenth century. Today you can see the remains of a late thirteenth-century keep next to a more ornate three-storey ruin incorporating an impressive banqueting hall and state rooms.

The small **tourist office** (all year Mon–Sat 10am–5pm, Sun school holidays only noon–5pm; ☎01792/361302) is in the Methodist church on Mumbles Road, just beyond the Newton Road junction. Staff can advise on **accommodation** around Gower as well as in Mumbles. Good choices here include a number of options along the shorefront Mumbles Road: the chintzy *Coast House* at no. 708 (☎01792/368702, ⓦwww.thecoasthouse.co.uk; ❸), the elegant *Tides Reach* at no. 388 (☎01792/404877, ⓦwww.tidesreachguesthouse .co.uk; ❹), the tastefully furnished and welcoming *Alexandra House* at no. 366 (☎01792/406406, ⓦwww.alexandra-house.com; ❹) and, best of all, the lovely *Patrick's with Rooms* at no. 638 (☎01792/360199, ⓦwww.patrickswithrooms .com; ❼). Good **places to eat** cheaply include *Coffee Denn*, 34 Newton Rd, particularly good for sweet treats, and *Verdi's*, overlooking the sea at Knab Rock near the pier – a Mumbles institution for its lively Welsh–Italian atmosphere and superb pizzas and ice-cream concoctions. Moving upscale, the moderately priced *P.A.'s Wine Bar*, 95 Newton Rd (☎01792/367723), excels at fish dishes, the pricier *Knight's* at 614–616 Mumbles Rd (☎01792/363184) does fantastic fusion cuisine, and the new, truly special *2*⁄ *698* at 698 Mumbles Rd (☎01792/361616) serves beautifully prepared local beef, lamb and seafood. The scores of pubs along the seafront constitute the **Mumbles Mile**, one of Wales's most notorious pub crawls. The ones to linger in are the *Antelope*, the *Oystercatcher* and the *White Rose*.

Rhossili and Worms Head

The village of **RHOSSILI** (Rhosili), at the western end of Gower, is a centre for walkers and beach loungers alike. Dylan Thomas described the terrain to the west of the village as "rubbery, gull-limed grass, the sheep-pilled stones, the pieces of bones and feathers", and you can tread in his footsteps to **Worms Head**, an isolated string of rocks, accessible for only five hours, at low tide. Be very careful – there are deaths here every year. At the head of the road, near the village, is a well-stocked National Trust **information centre** (Easter–Oct daily 10.30am–5.30pm; Nov–Dec Wed–Sun 11am–4pm; Jan–March Sat & Sun 11am–4pm; ☎01792/390707). It posts the tide times outside for those heading for Worms Head, and holds details of local companies renting surfing and hang-gliding equipment.

Below the village, a great curve of white sand stretches away into the distance, a dazzling coastline vast enough to absorb the crowds, especially if you are prepared to head north towards **Burry Holms**, an islet that is cut off at high tide. The northern end of the beach can also be reached along the small lane that runs from Reynoldston, in the middle of the peninsula, to **Llangennith**, on the other side of the towering, 633-foot **Rhossili Down**. In the village, PJ's Surfshop (☎01792/386669, ⓦwww.pjsurfshop.co.uk) rents **surfboards** and boogie boards; a mile away at the *Hillend* campsite (see below) is another Surf School (☎01792/386426), which runs half-day (£20) and full-day (£30) **surfing courses**.

Accommodation in Rhossili village is pretty scarce: on the spot there's only really *Creek House* (☎01792/390555, ⓦwww.creekhouse.co.uk; ❸), a pleasantly understated B&B, or the *Worms Head Hotel* (☎01792/390512, ⓦwww .thewormshead.co.uk; ❹), which is OK, with spectacular views.

In Llangennith there's two lovely B&Bs in the shape of *College House* (☎01792/386214; ❸) in the middle of the village, and the very chilled

Western House (☎01792/386620, ⓦwww.llangennith.freeserve.co.uk; ❷) on the lane towards the beach. That peters out half a mile further at *Hillend* (☎01792/386204), a fabulous **campsite** behind the dunes and with direct access to the glorious beach. Back in the village, the *King's Head* is a fine pub for food and drink.

Carmarthenshire

Frequently overlooked in the stampede towards the resorts of Pembrokeshire, **Carmarthenshire** is a quiet part of the world, with few of the problems of mass tourism suffered by more popular parts of Wales. **Kidwelly**, with its dramatically sited castle, is the only reason to stop before **Carmarthen**, the unquestioned capital of its region but one which fails to live up to the promise of its status. Better to press on up the bucolic Tywi Valley, visiting the **National Botanic Garden** and the more formal grounds of **Aberglasney** on the way to **Llandeilo** and the wonderfully sited **Carreg Cennan** castle.

Keeping to the coast, the village of **Laugharne** has become a place of pilgrimage for Dylan Thomas devotees, while **Tenby** is the quintessential British seaside resort, built high on cliffs and with views across to monastic **Caldey Island**.

Kidwelly

The sleepy little town of **KIDWELLY** (Cydweli) is dominated by its imposing **castle** (June–Sept daily 9.30am–6pm; April, May & Oct daily 9.30am–5pm; Nov–March Mon–Sat 9.30am–4pm, Sun 11am–4pm; £2.50; CADW). Established around 1106 by the bishop of Salisbury as a satellite of Sherborne Abbey in Dorset, the castle is situated at a strategic point overlooking the River Gwendraeth and vast tracts of coast. On entering through the massive fourteenth-century gatehouse, you can still see portcullis slats and murder holes, through which noxious substances could be tipped onto unwelcome visitors. The gatehouse forms the centrepiece of the impressively intact outer-ward walls, which can be climbed for some great views over the grassy courtyard and rectangular inner ward to the river. A former tinplate works two miles out of town up Priory Street now operates as the small-scale and entertaining **Industrial Museum** (May–Sept Mon–Fri 10am–5pm, Sat & Sun noon–5pm; free), where many old features have been preserved, including the rolling mills where long lines of tin were rolled and spun into wafer-thin slices.

There's superb B&B **accommodation** at *Penlan Isaf Farm* (☎01554/890084, ⓦwww.penlanisaf.com; ❷), on a dairy farm overlooking the town. You can **camp** at the caravan-oriented *Carmarthen Bay Touring & Camp Site*, Tanylan Farm (☎01267/267306, ⓔtanylanfarm@aol.com; closed Oct–Easter), which perches alongside the estuary between Kidwelly and Ferryside. Good **food** and **drink** are available at the cosy *Boot & Shoe* at 2 Castle St.

Carmarthen and around

In the early eighteenth century **CARMARTHEN** (Caerfyrddin) was the largest town in the country and it remains the regional hub, a solid, if hardly thrilling place best known as the supposed birthplace of the wizard Merlin (Myrddin in Welsh gives the town its name).

The most picturesque part of town is around Nott Square where the handsome eighteenth-century **Guildhall** sits at the base of Edward I's uninspiring **castle**. From the top of Nott Square, King Street heads northeast towards the undistinguished **St Peter's Church** and the Victorian School of Art, which has now metamorphosed into **Oriel Myrddin** (Mon–Sat 10am–5pm; free), a craft centre and excellent gallery that acts as an imaginative showcase for local artists.

The severe grey Bishop's Palace at **Aborgwili**, a mile east of Carmarthen, was the seat of the Bishop of St David's between 1542 and 1974, and now houses the **Carmarthenshire County Museum** (Mon–Sat 10am–4.30pm; free). This surprisingly interesting exhibition covers the history of Welsh translations of the New Testament and Book of Common Prayer – both first translated here, in 1567. Local archeological finds, wooden dressers and a lively history of local castles compete for attention with coverage of the local coracle industry and the origins of one of Wales's first *eisteddfodau* (Welsh cultural festivals), held in Carmarthen in 1450.

Trains between Swansea and Pembrokeshire stop at the **train station**, which lies over the Carmarthen bridge on the south side of the River Tywi. All **buses** terminate at the bus station on Blue Street, north of the river, and many connect with the arrival and departure of trains. The **tourist office** is at 113 Lammas St, near the Crimea Monument (daily 9.30am–5.30pm; ☏01267/231557, Ⓦwww.carmarthenshire.gov.uk). For **accommodation** try the *Boar's Head*, 120 Lammas St (☏01267/222789; ❹), or *Y Dderwen Fach* B&B, 98 Priory St (☏01267/234193; ❶), out along the main road to Llandeilo. The *Café on the Square*, Nott Square, is perhaps the pick of the town's coffee and **snack** spots, while for full meals head for the wonderful ☕ *Quayside Brasserie*, on the Tywi quay (☏01267/223000).

The Tywi Valley

The **River Tywi** curves and darts its way east from Carmarthen through some of the most magical scenery in South Wales and a couple of budding gardens: one completely new in the form of the **National Botanic Garden of Wales**, the other a faithful reconstruction of linked walled gardens around the long-abandoned house of **Aberglasney**. The twenty-mile trip to Llandeilo is punctuated by gentle, impossibly green hills topped with ruined castles, notably the wonderful **Carreg Cennen**: it's not hard to see why the Merlin legend has taken such a hold in these parts.

The National Botanic Garden and around

Though only opened in 2000, the great glass "eye" of the **National Botanic Garden of Wales** (daily: April–Oct 10am–6pm; Nov–March 10am–4.30pm; £7, discounts for groups and those arriving by bike or public transport; Ⓦwww .gardenofwales.org.uk), seven miles east of Carmarthen, has quickly become the centrepiece of the Tywi Valley. Its central walkway leads past lakes, sculpture and geological outcrops from all over Wales, with walks down towards slate-bed plantings and different wood and wetland habitats. A double-walled garden has been teased back to life (providing vegetables for the restaurant), and enhanced with the addition of a small but exquisite Japanese garden and a bee garden that's home to a million bees.

At the top of the hill is Norman Foster's stunning oval **glasshouse**, packed with plants from regions with a Mediterranean climate including South Africa, Chile, California and the Mediterranean itself. A nearby group of buildings

△ National Botanic Garden

houses the restaurant and an excellent exhibition about the Welsh herbalists known as the Physicians of Myddfai. The entire garden has been designed around principles of sustainability: rainwater is caught and used for irrigation; the glasshouses are heated by burning wood coppiced on the grounds; and human waste is transformed into essentially pure water by means of a series of reed beds. A large tract of the surrounding land is being turned over to organic farming using Welsh breeds of cattle and sheep, and the estate's outer edges are re-creations of moorland, spring wood, prairie and native Welsh habitats.

The #166 **bus** runs twice daily from Carmarthen train station.

Aberglasney

A complementary and much older garden can be found five miles northeast at **Aberglasney** (daily: April–Sept 10am–6pm; Nov–March 10.30am–4pm; £6; Ⓦ www.aberglasney.org), half a mile south of the A40 near Broad Oak. While a partly ruined manor house is the estate's centrepiece, interest is focused on the stunning **gardens** where archeological work has peeled back half a century of neglect to reveal a set of interlinking walled gardens mostly constructed between the sixteenth and eighteenth centuries. Once massively overgrown, they have already regained much of their original formal splendour, especially the kitchen garden and what is thought to be the only secular cloister garden in Britain. A walkway leads around the top of the cloister, giving access to a set of six Victorian aviaries from where there are great views over the Jacobean pool garden. The highlight of the garden, however, is the **yew tunnel**, planted around three hundred years ago and trained over to root on the far side. The glassed-in atrium of the manor is now being populated with subtropical plants.

Llandeilo

Fifteen miles east of Carmarthen, the handsome market town of **LLAN-DEILO** is in a state of transition, with a small kernel of chi-chi cafés and shops newly opened along the main Rhosmaen Street. There's little to see in town, but a mile west is the tumbledown shell of **Dinefwr Castle** reached through the gorgeous parkland of **Dinefwr Park**. Sited on a wooded bluff above the Tywi, the castle became ill suited to the needs of the landowning Rhys family, who aspired to something a little more luxurious. The "new" castle, now named **Newton House** (mid-March to Oct Mon & Thurs–Sun 11am–5pm; house & park £3.80, park only £2.60; NT), was built in 1523, and is being progressively restored. A new interpretive centre and tearoom will open in 2006.

Behind the main street are the **tourist office** (Tues–Sat 10.30am–5pm; ☏01558/823960) in the principal car park and, a couple of blocks to the north, the **train station**. **Accommodation** is limited to the chic *Cawdor Arms*, 70 Rhosmaen St (☏01558/823500, ⓦwww.thecawdor.com; ❺), fashioned from an old coaching inn, and *Penhill* (☏01558/823060, ⓦwww.penhill.org.uk; ❷), a simple but very pleasant **B&B** a stone's throw from Carreg Cennen castle (see below). For **eating**, try the coffee and cakes at *Barita*, 139 Rhosmaen St, or head across the road for excellent semi-formal dining at the *Cawdor Arms* (three-course lunch £10, dinner £20).

Carreg Cennen

Isolated in rural hinterland, four miles southeast of Llandeilo, is one of the most magnificently sited castles in the whole of Wales, **Carreg Cennen Castle** (daily: mid-March to Oct 9.30am–6.30pm; Nov to mid-March 9.30am–dusk; £3; CADW). Urien, one of King Arthur's knights, is said to have built his fortress on the fearsome rocky outcrop, although the first known construction dates from 1248. Carreg Cennen fell to the English in 1277, during Edward I's initial invasion of Wales, and was finally abandoned after being partially destroyed in 1462 by the Earl of Pembroke, who believed it to be the base of a group of lawless rebels. The most astounding aspect of the castle is its commanding position, 300ft above a sheer drop down into the green valley of the small River Cennen. The highlights of a visit are the views down into the river valley and the long descent down into a watery, pitch-black **cave** that is said to have served as a well. Torches are essential (£1 rental from the excellent tearoom near the car park) – it's worth continuing as far as possible and then turning them off to experience absolute darkness.

Laugharne

The village of **LAUGHARNE** (Talacharn), on the western side of the Taf estuary, is a delightful spot, with its ragged castle looming over the reeds and tidal flats, and narrow lanes snuggling in behind. Catch it in high season though and you're immediately aware that Laugharne is increasingly being taken over by the legend of the poet **Dylan Thomas**.

At the end of a narrow lane is the estuaryside **Dylan Thomas Boathouse** (daily: May–Oct & Easter weekend 10am–5.30pm; Nov–April 10.30am–3.30pm; £3; ⓦwww.dylanthomasboathouse.com), the simple home of the Thomas family from 1949 until Dylan's death in 1953. It's an enchanting museum, with views of the peaceful, ever-changing water and light of the estuary and its "heron-priested shore". Inside, a period wireless set in the intact living room regales you with the rich tones of the poet reading his own work, while contemporary newspaper reports of his demise show how he was, while alive, a fairly minor literary figure. Back along the narrow lane, you can peer into the green garage where he wrote: curled photographs of literary heroes, a pen collection and scrunched-up balls of paper suggest that he is about to return at any minute. Thomas is buried in the graveyard of the parish church in the village centre, his grave marked by a simple white cross.

Dylan Thomas was the stereotypical Celt – fiery, verbose, richly talented and habitually drunk. Born in 1914 into a snugly middle-class family in Swansea's Uplands district, Dylan's first glimmers of literary greatness came when he was posted, as a young reporter, to the *South Wales Evening Post* in Swansea. Some of his most popular tales in the *Portrait of the Artist as a Young Dog* were inspired during this period.

Rejecting what he perceived as the coarse provincialism of Swansea and Welsh life, Thomas arrived in London as a broke 20-year-old in 1934, weeks before the appearance of his first volume of poetry, which was published as the first prize in a *Sunday Referee* competition. Another volume followed shortly afterwards, cementing the engaging young Welshman's reputation in the British literary establishment. He married in 1937, and the newlyweds returned to Wales, settling in the hushed, provincial backwater of Laugharne. Short stories – crackling with rich and melancholy humour – tumbled out as swiftly as poems, further widening his base of admirers, though, like so many other writers, Thomas has only gained star status posthumously. Perhaps better than anyone, he writes in an identifiably Welsh, rhythmic wallow in the language.

Thomas, especially in public, liked to adopt the persona of what he perceived to be an archetypal stage Welshman: sonorous tones, loquacious, romantic and inclined towards a stiff tipple. This role was particularly popular in the United States, where he journeyed on lucrative lecture tours. It was on one of these that he died, in 1953, poisoned by a massive whisky overdose. Just one month earlier, he had put the finishing touches to what many regard as his masterpiece: *Under Milk Wood*, a "play for voices". Describing the dreams, thoughts and lives of a straggling Welsh seaside community called Llareggub – misspelt Llaregyb by the po-faced BBC, who couldn't sanction the usage of the expression "bugger all" backwards – it is based loosely on Laugharne, New Quay in Cardiganshire, and a vast dose of Thomas's own imagination.

Laugharne plays its Thomas connections with curiously disgruntled aplomb – nowhere more so than his old boozing hole, **Brown's Hotel**, on the main street, where Thomas's cast-iron table still sits in a window alcove in the nicotine-crusted front bar. At the bottom of the main street, the gloomy hulk of **Laugharne Castle** (mid-March to Sept daily 10am–5pm; £2.75; CADW) broods over the estuary. Two of the early medieval towers survive, although most of the ruins are those of the Tudor mansion built over the original for Sir John Perrot. The views from the domed roof over the tight, huddled little town are sublime.

Tiny Laugharne has no tourist office and only limited **accommodation**, so book ahead if you want to stay. The welcoming *Swan Cottage*, 20 Gosport St (℡01994/427409; ❷), has just one room, or try *The Boat House Inn*, 1 Gosport St (℡01994/427263, ✉theboathousehotel@tiscali.co.uk; ❻). The nearest **campsite** is *Ants Hill Camping Park*, a few hundred yards north of Laugharne (℡01994/427293, ⓦwww.antshill.co.uk). For **lunches** and Welsh teas make for the *Pea Green Boat*, on the central square, and for something more substantial, go for the *Stable Door*, Market Lane (℡01994/427777; closed Mon–Wed), a relaxed conservatory restaurant and wine bar with a classy menu which might include pepper-crusted monkfish (£15). There's tasty fish and chips at the *Castle View*, while the best **drinking** hole is the cheery *New Three Mariners*.

Tenby and Caldey Island

On a natural promontory of great strategic importance, the beguilingly old-fashioned resort of **TENBY** (Dinbych-y-Pysgod) is everything a seaside resort should be. Narrow streets wind down from the medieval centre to the harbour past miniature gardens fashioned to catch the afternoon sun. Steps lead down the steeper slopes to dockside arches which still house fishmongers selling the morning's catch.

First mentioned in a ninth-century bardic poem, Tenby grew under the twelfth-century Normans, who erected a castle on the headland in their attempt to colonize South Pembrokeshire and create a "**Little England beyond Wales**" – an appellation by which the area is still known today. Three times in the twelfth and thirteenth centuries the town was ransacked by the Welsh. In response, the castle was fortified once more and the stout town walls – largely still intact – were built. Tenby prospered as a major port between the fourteenth and sixteenth centuries, and although decline followed, the arrival of the railway brought renewed wealth as the town became a fashionable resort. Lines of neat, prosperous hotels and expensive shops still stand haughtily along the seafront.

In recent years, the town's huge number of pubs and restaurants have made it one of Britain's most fashionable venues for hen and stag parties – something the authorities are keen to discourage – and in summer it can seem full to bursting point, with parking restrictions and a considerable rush on decent accommodation. Still, it is a fun place and, for those walking the Pembrokeshire Coast Path, a welcome burst of glitter and excitement.

The Town

Tenby is shaped like a triangle, with two sides formed by the coast meeting at Castle Hill. The third side is formed by the remains of the twenty-foot-high town **walls**, first built in the late thirteenth century and massively strengthened by Jasper Tudor, earl of Pembroke and uncle of Henry VII, in 1457. In the middle of the remaining stretch is the only town gate still standing, **Five Arches**, a semicircular barbican that combined practical day-to-day usage with hidden look-outs and angles acute enough to surprise invaders.

The centre's focal point is the 152-foot spire of the largely fifteenth-century **St Mary's church**, between St George's Street and Tudor Square; its pleasantly light interior shows the elaborate ceiling bosses in the chancel to good effect, and the tombs of local barons demonstrate Tenby's important mercantile tradition. Wandering the surrounding medieval streets is one of Tenby's delights. **Sun Alley** is a tiny crack between overhanging whitewashed stone houses that connects Crackwell and High streets. Due east, on the other side of the church, **Quay Hill** runs parallel, a narrow set of steps and cobbles tumbling down past some of the town's oldest houses to the top of the harbour. Wedged in a corner of Quay Hill is the fifteenth-century **Tudor Merchant's House** (April–Oct daily except Sat 11am–5pm; £2.20; NT). The compact house with its Flemish-style chimneypieces is on three floors, packed with furniture, either seventeenth- and eighteenth-century originals or Tudor repro made traditionally without glue or nails: notice the superb, inlaid 1753 marriage chest.

Practicalities

Tenby's **train station** is at the western end of the town centre, at the bottom of Warren Street. Some **buses** stop at South Parade, at the top of Trafalgar

Road, although most call at the bus shelter on Upper Park Road, just along from the **tourist office** (daily: July & Aug 10am–6pm; rest of year 10am–5pm; ☎01834/842402, ✉tenby.tic@pembrokeshire.gov.uk).

As a major resort, Tenby has dozens of **hotels** and **guest houses**, all pressed from pretty much the same mould, though paying more gets you a wider range of facilities and a sea view. The best budget place is the spotless *Boulston Cottage*, 29 Trafalgar Rd (☎01834/843289; ❷). *Glenholme*, Picton Terrace (☎01834/843909, ⓦwww.glenholmetenby.co.uk; ❷), is also agreeable and with en-suite rooms. Stepping up a little try *Lyndale House*, Warren Street (☎01834/842836; ❹), a welcoming B&B near the station that's happy to cater for vegetarians, or *Penally Abbey* (☎0871/995 8254, ⓦwww.penally-abbey .com; ❼), a luxurious country-house hotel a mile west of Tenby in Penally. Four miles west of Tenby, overlooking the cliffs, is the bright and modern *Manorbier YHA* **hostel**, at Skrinkle Haven (☎0870/770 5954, ✉manorbier@yha.org .uk; dorms £12.50; ❶; April–Oct). You can **camp** at the small and semi-official *Meadow Farm*, Northcliff, on the northern fringes of town (☎01834/844829; April–Oct).

There are dozens of **cafés** and **restaurants** around town. *Fecci and Sons*, Upper Frog Street, offers ice cream and Italian snacks, while *Café 25*, 25 High St, does good coffee and has Internet access. The wood-beamed *Coach and Horses* on Upper Frog Street serves up well-prepared bar meals and tasty Thai dishes as well as good beer. For a splurge, don't pass up ⚒ *Plantagenet House*, Quay Hill (☎01834/842350), serving delicious meals in the congenial surrounds of Tenby's oldest house, complete with massive twelfth-century Flemish chimney breast. For **pubs**, head for the *Lifeboat Tavern*, Tudor Square, or the *Normandie Hotel* on Upper Frog Street.

Caldey Island

Celtic monks first settled **Caldey Island** (Ynys Pyr), a couple of miles offshore, in the sixth century. Little is then known of the island until 1136, when it was given to the Benedictine monks who founded their priory here. They lost it with the dissolution of the monasteries in 1536, and it eventually ended up in the hands of Reformed Cistercians who have run the place for the last century.

Boats leave Tenby Harbour (or Castle Beach when the tide is out) every twenty minutes (Easter–Oct Mon–Fri 10.30am–4pm; mid-May to mid-Sept also Sat same hours; £8 return; ☎01834/844453, ⓦwww.caldey-island .co.uk) for the twenty-minute journey to the island. **Tickets** (not for any specific sailing) are sold at the kiosk in Castle Square, directly above the harbour.

The island's village is the main hub of Caldey life. As well as a tiny post office and popular tearoom, there's a **perfume shop** selling the herbal fragrances distilled by the monks from Caldey's abundant flora. The narrow road going to the left leads down to the heavily restored **chapel of St David**, whose most impressive feature is its round-arched Norman door. A lane leads south from the village to the old **priory**, and the remarkable, twelfth-century **St Illtud's church**, which houses one of the most significant pre-Norman finds in Wales, the sandstone **Ogham Cross**, found under the stained-glass window on the south side of the nave. It is carved with an inscription from the sixth century which was added to, in Latin, during the ninth. The lane continues south from the site, climbing up to the gleaming white island **lighthouse**, built in 1828, from which there are memorable views.

Southern Pembrokeshire

The southern zigzag of coast that darts west from Tenby is a strange mix of caravan parks, Ministry of Defence shooting ranges, spectacularly beautiful bays and gull-covered cliffs. From Tenby, the A4139 passes through **Penally**, with its wonderful beach, and continues past idyllic coves, the lily ponds at **Bosherston** and the remarkable and ancient **St Govan's Chapel**, squeezed into a rock cleft above the crashing waves. The ancient town of **Pembroke** really only warrants a visit to its impressive castle before pressing on to neighbouring **Lamphey**, with its fine Bishop's Palace. **Buses** to most corners of the peninsula radiate out from Haverfordwest and Pembroke.

Penally to Bosherston

The coastal path south and west of Tenby skirts the gorgeous long beach of **Penally** then hugs the cliff top for a couple of miles to **Lydstep Haven** (fee charged for the sands). A mile further west is the cove of Skrinkle Haven, and above it the excellent *Manorbier* YHA hostel (see Tenby account, p.716). A couple of miles further on, the quaint village of **MANORBIER** (Maenorbŷr), pronounced "manner-beer", was birthplace in 1146 of the Welsh-Norman historian, writer and ecclesiastical reformist Giraldus Cambrensis. Manorbier's castle (Easter–Sept daily 9.30am–5.30pm; £3.50), founded in the early twelfth century as an impressive baronial residence, sits above the village and its beach on a hill of wild gorse. The strong Norman walls surround a grass courtyard in which the extensive remains of the castle's chapel and state rooms jostle for position with the nineteenth-century domestic residence. In the walls and buildings are a warren of dark passageways to explore, occasionally opening out into little cells with lacklustre wax figures purporting to illustrate the castle's history.

The Pembrokeshire National Park and Coast Path

The **Pembrokeshire Coast** is Britain's only predominantly sea-based national park (ⓦ www.pembrokeshirecoast.org.uk), hugging the rippled coast around the entire western section of Wales. Established in 1952, the park is not one easily identifiable mass, rather a series of occasionally unconnected coastal and inland scenic patches.

Crawling around almost every wriggle of the coastline, the **Pembrokeshire Coast Path** winds 186 miles from Amroth, just east of Tenby, to its northern terminus at St Dogmael's near Cardigan. For the vast majority of the way, the path clings precariously to cliff-top routes, overlooking seal-basking rocks, craggy offshore islands, unexpected gashes of sand and shrieking clouds of sea birds. The most popular and ruggedly inspiring segments of the coast path are: the stretch along the southern coast from the castle at Manorbier to the tiny cliff chapel at Bosherston; either side of St Bride's Bay, around St David's Head and the Marloes Peninsula; and the generally quieter northern coast either side of Fishguard, past undulating contours, massive cliffs, bays and old ports.

Spring is perhaps the finest season for walking as the crowds are yet to arrive and the cliff-top flora is at its most vivid. There are numerous publications available about the coast path, of which the best is Brian John's *National Trail Guide* (£13), which includes sections of 1:25,000 maps of the route. The National Park publishes a handy *Coast Path Accommodation* guide (£2.50), detailing B&Bs and campsites along its entire length.

The rocky little harbour at **Stackpole Quay**, reached via the small lane from Freshwater East through East Trewent, is a good starting point for walks along the breathtaking cliffs to the north. Another walk leads half a mile south to one of the finest beaches in Pembrokeshire, **Barafundle Bay**, with its soft beach fringed by wooded cliffs at either end. The path continues around the coast, through the dunes of **Stackpole Warren**, to **BROAD HAVEN**, where a pleasant small beach overlooks several rocky islets, now managed by the National Trust. Road access is through the village of **BOSHERSTON** where three artificial fingers of water known as **Bosherston Lakes** (free) were beautifully landscaped in the late eighteenth century. The westernmost lake is the most scenic, especially in late spring and early summer when the lilies that form a carpet across its surface are in full bloom.

A lane from Bosherston dips south across the MoD training grounds, to a spot overlooking the cliffs where tiny **St Govan's Chapel** is wedged: it's a remarkable building, known to be at least eight hundred years old. Steps descend straight into the sandy-floored chapel, now devoid of any furnishings save for the simple stone altar.

Pembroke and around

The old county town of **PEMBROKE** (Penfro) and its fearsome castle sit on the southern side of Pembroke River, a continuation of the massive Milford Haven waterway, described by Nelson as the greatest natural harbour in the world. Despite its location, Pembroke is surprisingly dull, with one long main street of attractive Georgian and Victorian houses, some intact stretches of medieval town wall, but little else to catch the eye.

Pembroke's history is inextricably bound up with that of its impregnable **castle** (daily: April–Sept 9.30am–6pm; March & Oct 10am–5pm; Nov–Feb 10am–4pm; £3; Ⓦwww.pembrokecastle.co.uk), founded by the Normans as the strongest link in their chain of fortresses across South Wales. During the Civil War, Pembroke was a Parliamentarian stronghold until the town's military governor suddenly switched allegiance to the king, whereupon Cromwell's troops sacked the castle after a 48-day siege. Yet despite Cromwell's battering, and centuries of subsequent neglect, Pembroke Castle still inspires awe at its sheer, bloody-minded bulk. The soaring gatehouse leads into the large, grassy courtyard around the vast, round Norman **keep**, 75ft high and with walls 18ft thick. The intact towers and battlements contain many heavily restored communal rooms, now empty of furniture and, to a large extent, atmosphere too, although some of them are used to house excellent displays on the history of the castle and the Tudor empire.

Practicalities

Pembroke's **Main Street** stretches from the **train station** in the east to the walls of the castle. The **tourist office** (Easter–Oct daily 10am–5pm; ☎01646/622388), on Commons Road which runs parallel to Main Street, can provide a useful free town guide. If you decide to **stay**, head straight for *Beech House B&B*, 78 Main St (☎01646/683740; ❶), which has shared bathrooms but outdoes places charging twice as much – one room even boasts a four-poster. If it's full, try *High Noon Guesthouse*, close to the train station on Lower Lamphey Road (☎01646/683736; ❷), or stay in Lamphey (see below), a couple of miles east.

Trains continue from Pembroke to Pembroke Dock, two miles northwest, where **Irish Ferries** (☎0870/517 1717, Ⓦwww.irishferries.com) operate two daily services to Rosslare in Ireland.

For espresso and light **meals** head for *The Cornstore* (closed Sun), down by the river on Northgate Street, and for something more substantial try the nicely cooked restaurant dishes and bar meals at the *King's Arms Hotel* at 13 Main St. For **drinking** it's hard to beat a summer evening at the *Waterman's Arms*, opposite *The Cornstore*, where you can while away the hours on a veranda overlooking the Mill Pond.

Lamphey

The pleasant village of **LAMPHEY** (Llandyfai), two miles southeast of Pembroke, is best known for the ruined **Bishop's Palace** (daily 10am–5pm; £2.50; CADW), off a quiet lane to the north of the village. A country retreat for the bishops of St David's, the palace dates from around the thirteenth century, but was abandoned following the Reformation. Stout walls surround the ruins, which are scattered over a large area. Many of the palace buildings have long been lost under grassy banks. Most impressive are the remains of the Great Hall, extending across the entire eastern end of the complex. You can still see Bishop Gower's hallmark arcaded parapets running along the top, similar to those he built in the Bishop's Palace of St David's.

One of the area's swankiest **hotels** is here, in the shape of the Neoclassical *Lamphey Court Hotel* (℡01646/672273, www.lampheycourt.co.uk; ❼), opposite the Bishop's Palace. Otherwise, there's the more modest *Lamphey Hall Hotel* (℡01646/672394; ❺) by the church, or the characterful Georgian *Lower Lamphey Park* (℡01646/672906, www.lowerlampheypark.co.uk; ❸), located a few hundred yards north of the *Dial Inn*, The Ridgeway, which offers a reliable menu and good beer.

Carew

Tiny **CAREW**, four miles east of Pembroke, is a pretty place beside the River Carew. Just south of the river crossing stands the village's graceful thirteen-foot **Celtic cross**, the remarkably intact taper of the shaft covered in fine tracery of ancient Welsh designs. A small hut beyond the cross serves as the ticket office for **Carew Castle and Tidal Mill** (Easter–Oct daily 10am–5pm; £3; www.carewcastle.com). The castle, a hybrid of Elizabethan fancy and earlier defensive necessity, is a few hundred yards to the east of the **Carew French Mill**, used commercially until 1937 and now the only tide-powered mill in Wales. The impressive eighteenth-century exterior belies the rather pedestrian exhibitions and audiovisual displays inside, which describe the milling process.

Mid- and northern Pembrokeshire

The most westerly point of Wales is one of the country's most enchanting areas. The chief town of the region, **Haverfordwest**, is rather soulless but it's useful as a jumping-off point for beautiful **St Bride's Bay**. The coast here is broken into rocky outcrops, islands and broad, sweeping beaches curving between two headlands that sit like giant crab pincers facing out into the warm Gulf Stream. The southernmost headland winds around every conceivable angle, offering calm, east-facing sands at **Dale** and sunny expanses of south-facing beach at **Marloes**. At **Martin's Haven**, boats depart for the offshore islands of **Skomer**, **Skokholm** and **Grassholm**. To the north, there's spectacularly lacerated coast around **St David's peninsula**, with stunning cliffs interrupted only by occasional strips of sand. The tiny cathedral city of **St David's** is definitely a highlight. Rooks and

crows circle above the impressive ruins of the huge Bishop's Palace, sitting beneath the delicate bulk of the cathedral, the most impressive in Wales.

The north-facing coast that forms the very southern tip of Cardigan Bay is noticeably less commercialized and far more Welsh than the touristy shores of south and mid-Pembrokeshire. From the crags and cairns above St David's Head, the coast path perches precariously on the cliffs where only the thousands of sea birds have access. There are only the modest charms of small bays and desolate coves to detain you en route to the charming town of **Newport** – unless you're heading for **Fishguard** and the ferries to Ireland.

Haverfordwest

In the seventeenth and eighteenth centuries, the town of **HAVERFORD-WEST** (Hwlffordd), ten miles north of Pembroke, prospered as a port and trading centre. Despite its natural advantages, it is scarcely a place to linger, though as the main transport hub and shopping centre for western Pembrokeshire, you are likely to pass through. With your own transport, consider venturing four miles northeast along the B4329 to **Scolton Manor** (April–Oct daily 10.30am–5.30pm; £2), a modest stately home that now forms the nucleus of the diverting **Pembrokeshire County Museum**. Aside from the enchanting period rooms indoors, outhouses showcase all manner of quirky exhibits, and there's a good café and an environmentally aware visitor centre on site.

The **tourist office** (May–Sept Mon–Sat 9.30am–5pm; Oct–April Mon–Sat 10am–4pm; ☎01437/763110, ✉haverfordwes.tic@pembrokeshire.gov.uk) is next to the bus terminus, at the end of the Old Bridge. There's low-cost **accommodation** at *College Guest House*, 93 Hill St (☎01437/763710; ❷), or you could venture three miles west to the lovely *East Hook Farmhouse*, Portfield Gate (☎01437/762211, ⓦwww.easthookfarmhouse.co.uk; ❸), which serves delicious breakfasts, and dinner for under £20. There's a cheap **campsite** two miles northwest on the A487, at the *Rising Sun Inn* in Pelcomb Bridge (☎01437/765171).

For **eating**, grab a freshly filled baguette in *Dylan's*, 23 High St, or visit the inexpensive *George's*, 24 Market St (closed Sun), where you can eat in a lovely walled garden if the weather allows, or the cellar bistro if not.

Dale and around

DALE, fourteen miles west of Haverfordwest, can be unbearably crowded in peak season, but it's a pleasant enough village, whose east-facing shore makes it excellent for water sports in the lighter seas. All the activity happens around the beachside shack of West Wales Wind, Surf and Sailing (☎01646/636642, ⓦwww.surfdale.co.uk), which gives instruction in power-boating, windsurfing, surfing, sailing and kayaking (£35–75 per half-day), and rents gear. Fast boats leave from here to Skokholm and Grassholm islands (see below).

There's B&B **accommodation** on the Dale waterfront at the comfortable *Richmond House* (☎07974/925009; ❸) which also has an upscale bunkhouse with beds for £18, and at *Point Farm B&B* (☎01646/636541, ⓦwww.point farm.info; ❹; closed Dec & Jan), ten minutes' walk along the shore to the south, with cosy rooms, excellent hospitality and sea views.

Marloes

At unexciting **MARLOES**, a mile north of Dale, the broad, deserted beach is a safe place to swim, and looks out towards the island of Skokholm. From here, the coast path and a narrow road continue for two miles to the National Trust-owned swathe of **Deer Park** – which has no deer but is the name given to the grassy far tip of the southern peninsula of St Bride's Bay – and **Martin's Haven**, from where you can take a **boat** out to the islands of Skomer, Skokholm and Grassholm. The *Marloes Sands* YHA **hostel** (☎01646/636667, ⓔreservations@yha.org.uk; dorms £8.50; May to mid-Sept), consists of a series of converted farm buildings overlooking the northern end of the beach.

Skomer, Skokholm and Grassholm islands

Weather permitting, **boats** (April–Oct Tues–Sun 10am, 11am & noon; £14) run from Martin's Haven to **Skomer Island**, a 722-acre flat-topped island rich in sea birds and spectacular carpets of wild flowers, perfect for birdwatching and walking.

Though no landings are permitted, frequent, fast cruises leave from Dale to **Skokholm Island** (daily 11.30am, 4.30pm & 6.30pm; 2hr; £20), a couple of miles south of Skomer and far smaller, more rugged and remote, noted for its cliffs of warm red sandstone. Britain's first bird observatory was founded here as far back as the seventeenth century, and there are still a huge number of petrels, gulls, puffins, oystercatchers and rare Manx shearwaters. Boat trips also head out even further, to the tiny outpost of **Grassholm Island**, over five miles west of Skomer (daily 2pm; 2hr; £25). Visiting the island is an unforgettable experience, largely due to the 70,000 or so screaming gannets who call it home.

No **booking** is required for Skomer trips, but otherwise bookings are made through Dale Sailing (☎0800/0284090 or 01646/603110, ⓦwww.dale-sailing .co.uk).

St David's and around

ST DAVID'S (Tyddewi) is one of the most enchanting spots in Britain. This miniature city – really just a large village – sits back from its purple- and gold-flecked cathedral at the very westernmost point of Wales in bleak, tree-less countryside. Spiritually, it's the centre of Welsh ecclesiasticism. Traditionally founded by the Welsh patron saint himself in 550 AD, the See of St David's has drawn pilgrims for a millennium and a half – William the Conqueror included – and by 1120, Pope Calixtus II decreed that two journeys to St David's were the spiritual equivalent of one to Rome. Today, with so many historical sites, outdoor-pursuit centres, surf beaches, good cafés, superb walks, bathing and climbing, St David's and its peninsula are a must if you want to experience Wales at its wildest.

The City

From the central **Celtic cross**, the main street runs under the thirteenth-century **Tower Gate**, which forms the entrance to the serene **Cathedral Close**, backed by a windswept landscape of treeless heathland. The cathedral lies down to the right, hidden in a hollow by the River Alun. This apparent modesty is explained by reasons of defence, as a towering cathedral, visible from the sea on all sides, would have been vulnerable to attack. On the other side of the babbling Alun lie the ruins of the Bishop's Palace.

The Cathedral

From beyond the powerfully solid Tower Gate, steps lead down to the **cathedral** (donation requested; ⓦ www.stdavidscathedral.org.uk). The 125-foot tower, topped by pert golden pinnacles, has clocks on only three sides – the people of the northern part of the parish couldn't raise enough money for one to be constructed facing them. You enter through the south side of the low, twelfth-century nave in full view of its most striking feature, the intricate latticed oak **roof**. This was added to hide emergency restoration work carried out in the sixteenth century, when the nave was in danger of collapse. The nave floor still has a discernible slope and the support buttresses inserted in the northern aisle look incongruously new and temporary. At the crossing, an elaborate **rood screen** hides the organ and the choir, which sits directly under the magnificently bold and bright lantern ceiling of the tower. At the back of the south choir stalls is a unique **monarch's stall**, complete with royal crest, for, unlike any other British cathedral, the Queen is an automatic member of the St David's Cathedral Chapter.

Separating the choir and the presbytery is a finely traced, rare **parclose screen**. The back wall of the **presbytery** was once the eastern extremity of the cathedral, as can be seen from the two lines of windows. The upper row has been left intact, while the lower three were blocked up and filled with delicate gold mosaics in the nineteenth century. The colourful fifteenth-century roof, a deceptively simple repeating medieval pattern, was extensively restored by Gilbert Scott in the mid-nineteenth century. At the back of the presbytery, around the altar, the **sanctuary** has a few fragmented fifteenth-century tiles still in place. On the south side are the thirteenth-century tombs of bishops Iorwerth and Anselm de la Grace, and opposite is the disappointingly plain tomb of St David, largely destroyed in the Reformation.

The Bishop's Palace

From the cathedral, a path leads to the splendid fourteenth-century **Bishop's Palace** (mid-March to May & Oct daily 9.30am–5pm; June–Sept daily 9.30am–6pm; Nov–March Mon–Sat 9.30am–4pm, Sun 11am–4pm; £2.50; CADW). The huge central quadrangle is fringed by a neat jigsaw of ruined buildings built in extraordinarily richly tinted stone. The **arched parapets** that run along the top of most of the walls were a favourite feature of Bishop

Gower, who did more than any of his predecessors or successors to transform the palace into an architectural and political powerhouse. Two ruined but still impressive halls – the **Bishop's Hall** and the enormous **Great Hall**, with its glorious rose window – lie off the main quadrangle, above and around a myriad of rooms adorned by some eerily eroded corbels. Underneath the Great Hall are dank vaults containing an interesting exhibition about the palace and the indulgent lifestyles of its occupants. The destruction of the palace is largely due to sixteenth-century Bishop Barlow, who supposedly stripped the buildings of their lead roofs to provide dowries for his five daughters' marriages to bishops.

Practicalities

The main road from Haverfordwest enters St David's past the National Park **tourist office** (Easter–Oct daily 9.30am–5.30pm; Nov–Easter Mon–Sat 10am–4pm; ☎01437/720392, ⊛www.stdavids.co.uk), and continues for two hundred yards down High Street to the **bus station** in New Street. You can **rent bikes** from Voyages of Discovery (£10 half-day, £15 full day), tucked behind TYF, 1 High St (☎01437/721611, ⊛www.tyf.com), which runs various **outdoor courses** and pioneered **coasteering** (£40) – a half-day spent scrambling over rocks, jumping off cliffs and swimming across the narrow bays of St David's peninsula.

Good, inexpensive places to **stay** include the shared-bath *Pen Albro*, 18 Goat St (☎01437/721865; ❶); *Alandale*, 43 Nun St (☎01437/720404; ❸), with some en-suite rooms; and *Court House*, 20 Cross Square (☎01437/720811, ⊛www.courthouse.org.uk; ❶), a Quaker-run city-centre hostel with £10 beds and some twin rooms – it's often full so call ahead. Moving upscale, *Ramsey House*, Lower Moor (☎01437/720321, ⊛www.ramseyhouse.co.uk; ❺), is an excellent small hotel a quarter of a mile out on the road to Porth Clais with excellent breakfasts; or try ✴ *Crug Glas* (☎01348/831302, ⊛www.crug-glas.co.uk; ❻), four miles northeast at Abereiddy, a luxurious country house on a working farm also serving delicious four-course evening meals for around £20. The nearest **campsite** is at *Caerfai Farm*, Caerfai Bay (☎01437/720548; May–Sept), a fifteen-minute walk south of the city, and there's a YHA **hostel** in a former farmhouse two miles northwest, near Whitesands Bay (☎0870/770 6042; April–Oct).

For inexpensive **eating**, head for ✴ *The Bench*, 11 High St, a classy but relaxed restaurant, café and wine bar that's perfect for a quick espresso and panini or for lingering over pizza or fresh pasta dishes (£5–9) served inside or out; it also offers Internet access, and Italian ice cream to go. For more of a treat, *Lawton's at No. 16*, 16 Nun St (☎01437/729220), serves delicious meals (mains £14–18) in sleek modern surroundings. **Nightlife** boils down to the lively *Farmers Arms*, Goat Street, the city's only real pub, with a terrace overlooking the cathedral.

The St David's peninsula

Surrounded on three sides by inlets, coves and rocky stacks, St David's is an easy base for some excellent walking around the headland of the same name. A mile due south, the popular **Caerfai Bay** provides a sandy gash in the purple sandstone cliffs, rock which was used in the construction of the cathedral. To the immediate west is the craggy indentation of **St Non's Bay**, reached from Goat Street in St David's. St Non reputedly gave birth to St David at this spot during a tumultuous storm around 500 AD, when a spring opened up between Non's feet, and despite the crashing thunder all around, an eerily calm light filtered down onto the scene. St Non's Bay has received pilgrims for centuries, resulting in the foundation of a tiny, isolated chapel in the pre-Norman age. The ruins of the subsequent thirteenth-century chapel now lie in a field near the sadly dingy well and coy shrine where the nation's patron saint is said to have been born.

Further west, **Porth Clais** is supposedly the place at which St David was baptized. Now a boaties' haven, it was once the city's main harbour, the spruced-up remains of which can still be seen at the bottom of the turquoise river creek. Two miles west of St David's, the harbour at **St Justinian's** is little more than a lifeboat station and ticket hut for the boats over to **Ramsey Island** (ⓦwww.ramseyisland.co.uk). This dual-humped plateau, less than two miles long, has been under the able stewardship of the RSPB since 1992 and is quite enchanting. Birds of prey circle the skies above the island, but it's better known for the tens of thousands of sea birds that noisily crowd the sheer cliffs on its western side and the seals lazing sloppily about.

Boat landings are with Thousand Islands Expeditions (April–Oct daily; ☏01437/721721, ⓦwww.thousandislands.co.uk; £14) who allow up to five hours on Ramsey. During the springtime nesting season you actually see more from boats which circle the island but don't land: try Voyages of Discovery (year-round daily; ☏01437/720285 or 0800/854367; £18).

Fishguard

From St David's, the coast road runs northeast, parallel to numerous small and less-commercialized bays, to **Strumble Head**, which protects **FISH-GUARD** (Abergwaun), an attractive, hilltop town seldom seen as anything more than a brief stopoff to or from the Stena Line **ferries** and fast catamarans (☏08705/707070, ⓦwww.stenaline.com), which leave four to five times daily for Rosslare in Ireland.

In the centre of town, the **Royal Oak Inn**, where a bizarre Franco-Irish attempt to conquer Britain in 1797 at nearby Carregwastad Point is remembered. The hapless forces arrived to negotiate a cease-fire, which was turned by the assembled British into an unconditional surrender. Part of the invaders' low morale – apart from the drunken farce in which they'd become embroiled – is said to have been sparked off by the sight of a hundred local women marching towards them. The troops mistook their stovepipe hats and red flannel dresses for the outfit of a British infantry troop and instantly capitulated. Even if this is not true, it is an undisputed fact that 47-year-old cobbler Jemima Nicholas, the "Welsh Heroine", single-handedly captured fourteen French soldiers. Her grave can be seen next to the uninspiring Victorian parish church, St Mary's, behind the pub. The fabulous **Fishguard Tapestry**, which tells the story of this ramshackle invasion, should be on show in the town hall, across the street, by the end of 2006.

Buses stop in the central Market Square, right outside Fishguard's **tourist office** (July & Aug daily 10am–5pm; April–June, Sept & Oct Mon–Sat 10am–5pm; Nov–March Mon–Sat 10am–4pm; ☏01348/873484, ⓦwww.abergwaun.com). There's a subsidiary tourist office in the foyer of the Ocean Lab in Goodwick (daily: Easter–Oct 11am–5pm; Nov–Easter 10am–4pm; ☏01348/874737), around half a mile from the Rosslare ferry terminus. The **train station** is next to the ferry terminal on Quay Road. Buses usually meet ferries, though seldom the catamarans; a **taxi** (☏01348/874491) into town costs around £3.

Accommodation is plentiful and cheap, with most places well used to visitors coming and going at odd times. You'll find comfortable rooms at *Glanmoy Lodge*, on Trefwrgi Road, ten minutes' walk from the port (℡01348/874333, W www.glanmoylodge.co.uk; ❷), and up in Fishguard the peaceful *Plain Dealings* (℡01348/873655; ❷), half a mile from the centre on Tower Hill. The understated elegance of *Cefn-y-Dre* farmhouse (℡01348/875663, W www .cefnydre.co.uk; ❺) can be experienced a mile out of Fishguard following Hamilton Street. There are central **dorms** at *Hamilton Backpackers Lodge*, 21–23 Hamilton St (℡01348/874797; dorms from £13; ❶), and well-appointed **camping** at *Gwaun Vale Caravan Park* (℡01348/874698) on the B4313, a mile and a half southeast of town.

Head to *Three Main Street* for good coffee and **snacks**, then along the street to the *Royal Oak*, Main Square, for a pub meal and good beer.

Newport

NEWPORT (Trefdraeth) is an ancient and proud little town set on a gentle slope that courses down to the estuary of the Afon Nyfer. There's little to do except stroll around, but you'd be hard pressed to find a better place to do it. Just short of the Nevern estuary bridge, on the town side, **Carreg Coetan Arthur**, a well-preserved, capped Neolithic burial chamber, can be seen behind the holiday bungalows. The footpath that runs along the river either side of the bridge is marked as the Pilgrims' Way; follow it eastwards for a delightful riverbank stroll to Nevern, a couple of miles away. Another popular local walk is up to the craggy and magical peak of **Carn Ingli**, the Hill of Angels, behind the town. On Lower St Mary Street, the old school has metamorphosed into the excellent **West Wales Eco Centre** (Mon–Fri 9.30am–4.30pm; variable extended hours in summer; free), a venue for exhibitions, advice and resources on various aspects of sustainable living.

Newport's nearest beach, the **Parrog**, is complete with sandy stretches at low tide. On the other side of the estuary is the vast dune-backed **Traethmawr beach**, reached over the town bridge down Feidr Pen-y-Bont. Newport also makes a good jumping-off point for **Pentre Ifan**, a couple of miles south of Newport, with its massive, four-thousand-year-old capstone.

The **tourist office** (April–Oct Mon–Sat 10am–5.30pm; ℡01239/820912) is on Long Street, just off the main road. There's plenty of **accommodation** tucked in behind the Eco Centre on Lower St Mary Street, the *Trefdraeth* YHA **hostel** (℡01239/820080 or 0870/421 2314, E reservations@yha.org.uk; ❶) is a classy conversion of an old school with £12.50 bunks and a couple of private rooms; otherwise, *The Globe* B&B (℡01239/820296; ❷) is about the cheapest around and serves continental breakfast. If your budget is a bit bigger, try *Tree Tops B&B*, West Street (℡01239/820048, W www.bandbtreetops.co.uk; £30pp; ❹), or the superb *Cnapan Country House* on East Street (℡01239/820575, W www.online-holidays.net/cnapan; ❼; closed Jan & Feb). The nearest **campsite** is the *Morawelon* (℡01239/820565), just west of town, at the Parrog, with nice gardens and its own café.

For **food**, the *Cnapan Country House* (closed Mon & Tues) serves exquisite meals, or there are solid pub classics, including good curries, at the *Royal Oak*, on Bridge Street. *Café Fleur* on Market Street does fantastic sweet and savoury crêpes, panini, smoothies and good coffee.

Travel details

Buses

For information on all local and national bus services, contact Traveline ☎ 0870/608 2608, ⓦ www .traveline.org.uk.

Cardiff to: Abergavenny (hourly; 1hr 20min); Aberystwyth (2 daily; 4hr); Blaenafon (hourly, 1 change; 1hr 40min); Brecon (5 daily; 1hr 25min); Caerphilly (every 30min; 40min); Cardiff International Airport (every 30min; 30min); Chepstow (hourly; 1hr 20min); London (6 daily; 3hr 10min); Merthyr Tydfil (every 30min; 45min); Newport, Monmouthshire (every 30min; 45min); Swansea (every 30min; 1hr).

Carmarthen to: Aberystwyth (hourly; 2hr 15min); Haverfordwest (3 daily; 1hr); Kidwelly (8 daily; 25min); Laugharne (10 daily; 25min); Llandeilo (12 daily; 30–40min); Swansea (every 30min; 1hr 20min); Tenby (2 daily; 45min).

Chepstow to: Cardiff (hourly; 1hr 20min); Monmouth (at least hourly; 50min); Newport, Monmouthshire (hourly; 50min); Tintern (8 daily; 20min).

Fishguard to: Cardigan (hourly; 50min); Haverfordwest (hourly; 40min); Newport, Pembrokeshire (hourly; 20min); St David's (7 daily; 50min).

Haverfordwest to: Carmarthen (3 daily; 1hr); Fishguard (hourly; 40min); Manorbier (hourly; 1hr 10min); Newport, Pembrokeshire (hourly; 1hr); Pembroke (hourly; 45min); St David's (hourly; 45min); Tenby (9 daily; 1hr).

Llandovery to: Brecon (5 daily; 45min); Llandeilo (8 daily; 50min).

Merthyr Tydfil to: Abergavenny (every 30min; 1hr 30min); Brecon (9 daily; 40min); Cardiff (every 30min; 45min); Swansea (hourly; 1hr).

Monmouth to: Abergavenny (6 daily; 40min); Chepstow (at least hourly; 50min); Raglan (hourly; Tintern (7 daily; 30min).

Newport (Monmouthshire) to: Abergavenny (hourly; 1hr); Blaenafon (every 15min; 1hr); Brecon (every 2hr; 2hr 20min); Caerphilly (every 30min; 40min); Cardiff (every 30min; 40min); Chepstow (hourly; 50min).

Newport (Pembrokeshire) to: Fishguard (hourly; 20min); Haverfordwest (hourly; 1hr 10min).

Pembroke to: Bosherston (2 daily; 1hr); Haverfordwest (hourly; 45min); Manorbier (every 30min; 20min); Pembroke Dock (every 10min; 10min); Stackpole (2 daily; 20min); Tenby (hourly; 40min).

St David's to: Broad Haven (2 daily; 40min); Fishguard (7 daily; 50min); Haverfordwest (hourly; 45min).

Swansea to: Brecon (3 daily; 1hr 30min); Cardiff (every 30min; 1hr); Carmarthen (every 30min; 1hr 20min); Dan-yr-ogof (4 daily; 1hr); Merthyr Tydfil (hourly; 1hr); Mumbles (every 10min; 15min); Oxwich (8 daily; 1hr); Port Eynon (8 daily; 50min); Rhossili (Mon–Sat 10 daily; 1hr).

Tenby to: Carmarthen (1 daily; 1hr); Haverfordwest (9 daily; 1hr); Manorbier (hourly; 20min); Pembroke (hourly; 40min).

Trains

For information on all local and national rail services, contact National Rail Enquiries ☎ 08457/484950, ⓦ www.nationalrail.co.uk.

Cardiff to: Abergavenny (hourly; 40min); Bristol (every 30min; 50min); Caerphilly (every 30min; 20min); Carmarthen (6 daily; 1hr 45min); Chepstow (hourly; 40min); Haverfordwest (10 daily; 2hr 40min); London (hourly; 2hr); Merthyr Tydfil (hourly; 1hr); Newport, Monmouthshire (every 15–20min; 10min); Pontypool (hourly; 30min); Swansea (every 30min; 50min).

Carmarthen to: Cardiff (3 daily; 1hr 30min–2hr); Fishguard (2 daily; 1hr); Haverfordwest (11 daily; 45min); Pembroke (7 daily; 1hr 10min); Swansea (hourly; 45min); Tenby (7 daily; 50min).

Haverfordwest to: Cardiff (2 daily; 2hr 40min); Carmarthen (11 daily; 45min); Swansea (7 daily; 1hr 30min).

Newport (Monmouthshire) to: Abergavenny (hourly; 30min); Cardiff (every 15–20min; 10min); Chepstow (hourly; 20min); London (hourly; 1hr 50min); Swansea (hourly; 1hr 20min).

Pembroke to: Lamphey (7 daily; 3min); Manorbier (7 daily; 10min); Pembroke Dock (7 daily; 10min); Tenby (7 daily; 20min).

Swansea to: Cardiff (at least hourly; 50min); Carmarthen (hourly; 50min); Haverfordwest (7 daily; 1hr 30min); Llandrindod Wells (4 daily; 2hr 20min); London (2 daily; 3hr); Newport, Monmouthshire (hourly; 1hr 20min); Pembroke (6 daily; 2hr); Tenby (7 daily; 1hr 40min).

Tenby to: Carmarthen (7 daily; 50min); Pembroke (7 daily; 20min); Swansea (7 daily; 1hr 40min).

Mid-Wales

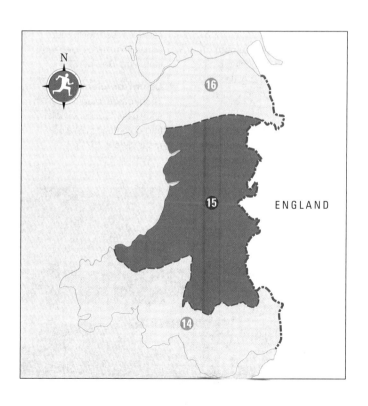

Highlights

✻ **Sgwd yr Eira waterfall**
A waterfall you can dive through, in the midst of the Brecon Beacons National Park. **See p.735**

✻ **Abergavenny Food Festival**
If food is the new religion, then this lovely town in the Black Mountains is fast becoming a new Jerusalem. **See p.737**

✻ **Andrew Logan Museum of Sculpture** A surprising blast of high camp and glitter in bucolic Montgomeryshire. **See p.747**

✻ **Harlech** A perfect castle and beautiful town wedged between the mountains and the sea. **See p.750**

✻ **Mawddach Estuary**
Sublime estuary crossed by the rickety rail bridge to Barmouth. **See p.750**

✻ **Ardudwy Beach** Eight miles of one of the best beaches in Wales, with wide sands and a warm sea. **See p.751**

✻ **Aberystwyth** Lively, seaside resort town rooted firmly in Welsh culture and language. **See p.757**

✻ **Centre for Alternative Technology** Imaginative showcase for sustainable and community develop-ment. **See p.757**

△ Aberystwyth from Constitution Hill

15

Mid-Wales

M id-Wales is a huge, beautiful region, crisscrossed by breathtaking mountain passes, dotted with characterful little towns and never far from water – whether sparkling rivers, great lakes or the sea of the Cambrian coast. This is certainly the least-known part of Wales, and that is, perhaps, to its advantage, for it's here that you'll find Welsh culture at its most beguiling and most natural, folded into the contours of the land as it has been for centuries.

A quarter of the area of Wales is occupied by the inland county of **Powys**, whose name harks back to a fifth-century Welsh kingdom. By far the most popular attraction is **Brecon Beacons National Park**, stretching from the dramatic limestone country of Fforest Fawr in the west through to the English border beyond the Black Mountains. The best bases are the tiny city of **Brecon** or the market town of **Abergavenny**.

North of the Beacons lie the old spa towns of Radnorshire, among them twee **Llandrindod Wells**. The quiet countryside to the north, crossed by spectacular mountain roads such as the **Abergwesyn Pass** from Llanwrtyd, is barely populated, dotted with ancient churches and introspective villages. In the east, the border town of **Knighton** is the home of the flourishing **Offa's Dyke Path** industry. **Montgomeryshire** is the northern portion of Powys, similarly underpopulated and remote. Like many country towns in Mid-Wales, beautiful **Llanidloes** has a healthy stock of old hippies amongst its population, contributing to a thriving arts and crafts community and a relaxed atmosphere. It's also a great base for the mountains, forests and boggy heathland that surround it.

The enduringly popular **Cambrian coast** stretches from **Harlech** down to **Cardigan**, with some great beaches, backed by burbling rivers and stunning mountains, most notably the massif of **Cadair Idris**. South of the great mountain is **Machynlleth**, a great base for beaches, mountains, shopping and the **Centre for Alternative Technology**, a showpiece for community living and renewable energy resources. Back on the coast, the beguiling "capital" of Mid-Wales, **Aberystwyth**, is a great mix of seaside resort, university city and market town. From here, wide sands and beaches give way to cliff-top paths and small sandy coves, as the coast heads towards Pembrokeshire. The region's interior here is best seen around two river valleys: the lush and quiet **Teifi**, running through old-fashioned market towns like **Lampeter**, and the dramatic ravines around the **Rheidol**.

MID WALES

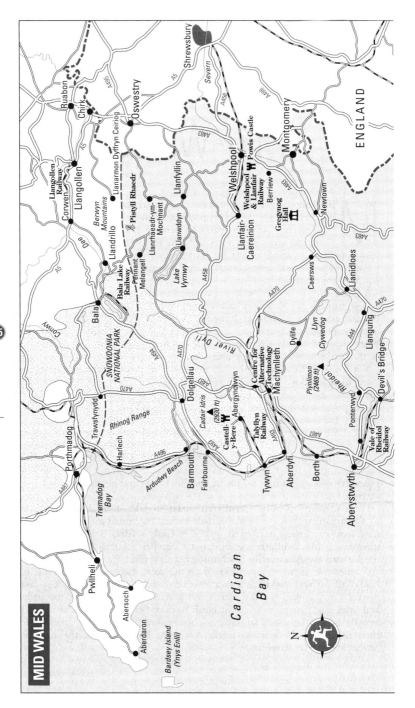

Shrewsbury

ENGLAND

Montgomery

Welshpool

Powis Castle

Welshpool & Llanfair Railway

Berriew

Gregynog Hall

Llanfair-Caereinion

Newtown

Oswestry

Llanfyllin

Llanwddyn

Llanrhaeadr-ym-Mochnant

Pistyll Rhaedr

Llanarmon Dyffryn Ceiriog

Chirk

Ruabon

Llangollen Railway

Corwen

Llangollen

Berwyn Mountains

Llandrillo

Dee

Lake Vyrnwy

Melangell

Pennant

Bala Lake Railway

Bala

Conwy

Caersws

Llanidloes

A470

Dylife

Llyn Clywedog

Llangurig

A44

SNOWDONIA NATIONAL PARK

A470

River Dyfi

Centre for Alternative Technology

Machynlleth

Pumlumon (2469 ft)

Rheidol

Devil's Bridge

Trawsfynydd

Dolgellau

Abergynolwyn

Cadair Idris (2930 ft)

Castell-y-Bere

Talyllyn Railway

Ponterwyd

Rhinog Range

Harlech

Barmouth

Fairbourne

Arddwy Beach

Tywyn

Aberdyfi

Borth

Vale of Rheidol Railway

Aberystwyth

Porthmadog

Tremadog Bay

Pwllheli

Abersoch

Aberdaron

Bardsey Island (Ynys Enlli)

Cardigan Bay

N

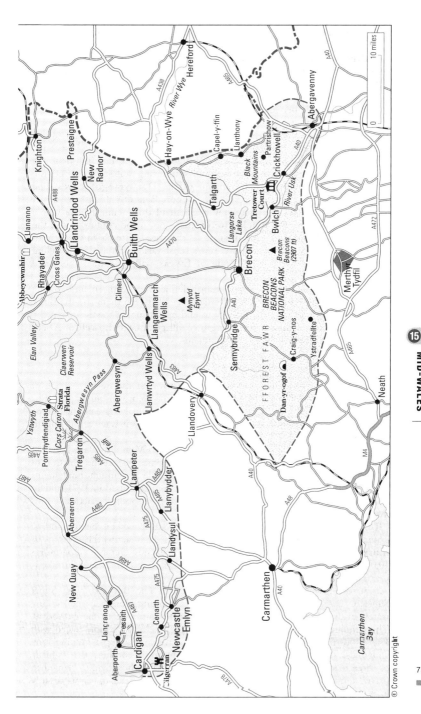

© Crown copyright

The Brecon Beacons National Park

The **Brecon Beacons National Park** has the lowest profile of Wales's three national parks, but it is nonetheless the destination of thousands of urban walkers, largely from the industrial areas of South Wales and the English West Midlands. Rounded, spongy hills of grass and rock tumble and climb around river valleys that lie between sandstone and limestone uplands, peppered with glass-like lakes and villages that seem to have been hewn from one rock. The national park straddles Powys from west to east, covering 520 square miles. Most remote is the area at the far western side, where the vast, open terrain of **Fforest Fawr** forms miles of tufted moorland tumbling down to a rocky terrain of rivers, deep caves and spluttering waterfalls around the village of **Ystradfellte** and the chasms of the **Dan-yr-ogof caves**. The heart of the national park comprises the **Brecon Beacons** themselves, a pair of 2900-foot hills and their satellites which lend their name to the whole park. East of Brecon, the **Black Mountains** – not to be confused with the singular Black Mountain some distance to the west – stretch all the way to the English border, and offer the region's most varied scenery, from rolling upland wilderness to the gentler **Vale of Ewyas**, with its ruined abbey and isolated churches.

The Monmouthshire and Brecon Canal defines the northern limit of the Beacons and forges a passage along the Usk Valley between them and the Black Mountains. This is where you're likely to end up staying, in towns such as the sturdy county seat of **Brecon**, the overgrown village of **Crickhowell**, or **Abergavenny**, nestled below the Black Mountains.

Brecon

BRECON (Aberhonddu) is a sturdy county town at the northern edge of the central Beacons. The proliferation of handsome Georgian buildings and its proximity to the hills and lakes of the national park make it a popular stopping-off place and a good base for day-walks in the well-waymarked hills to the south.

The town's highlight is the **Brecknock Museum** (Mon–Fri 10am–5pm, Sat 10am–1pm & 2–5pm; April–Sept also Sun noon–5pm; £1), at the junction of The Bulwark and Glamorgan Street. Displays include agricultural implements unique to the area, a nineteenth-century assize court last used in 1971, and an antique collection of painstakingly carved Welsh "love spoons" – betrothal gifts for courting Welsh lovers.

Running east, The Bulwark becomes The Watton, where the foreboding frontage of the South Wales Borderers' **barracks** glares across the street to its **museum** (April–Sept daily 10am–5pm, 4pm weekends; Oct–March Mon–Fri 10am–5pm; £3), packed with mementos from the regiment's three-hundred-year existence.

From the town-centre crossroads, northwest of The Bulwark, High Street Superior goes north, becoming The Struet, running alongside the rushing waters of the Honddu. Off to the left, a footpath climbs up to the **cathedral**. The building's dumpy external appearance belies its lofty interior, graced with a few Norman features from the eleventh century, including a hulking font. The mid-sixteenth-century **Games Monument**, in the southern aisle, is made of three oak beds and depicts an unknown woman whose hands, clasped in prayer, remain intact, but whose arms and nose have been unceremoniously hacked off.

BRECON BEACONS NATIONAL PARK

N

▲ Monmouth

Hereford
Hay-on-Wye
Hay Bluff
✝ Llanthony Priory
Llanthony
Cwmyoy
Llanfihangel Crucorney
Skirrid Fawr
Abergavenny
Blorenge
Blaenafon
Pontypool

Honddu River
Capel-y-ffin
Mynydd Ddu Forest
Black Mountains
Partrishow
Craig Mawr
Llanbedr
Crickhowell
Sugar Loaf
Big Pit
Nantyglo
A4043

Twmpa
Waun Fach
Pen y Gader-Fawr
Cwmdu
Tretower Court
Usk
Clydach Gorge
A467
A4046
Ebbw Vale

Three Cocks
Talgarth
A479
Bwlch
Llangynidr
Monmouth & Brecon Canal
Brynmawr
Tredegar
A4048

Glasbury
Bronllys
Pengenffordd
Mynydd Troed
Llangorse
Llangorse Lake
Talybont
Talybont Reservoir
Pentwyn Reservoir
Pontsticill
Brecon Mountain Railway
Butetown
A469

Llyswen
Buith Wells
Upper Chapel

A470
Pencelli
Llanfrynach
Cribyn
Pen y Fan
Neuadd Reservoir
Brecon Beacons
Taf Fechan Forest
Merthyr Tydfil
A470
Cardiff
Aberdare

Mynydd Epynt
Sennybridge
Mountain Centre ℹ
Libanus
Corn Du
Brecons Reservoir
Fan Frynych
Storey Arms
Fan Fawr
Ystradfellte Reservoir
Llwyn-onn Reservoir
Cefn Coed
A4059
Penderyn
Hirwaun
A4061

Llanwrtyd Wells
Cynghordy
Llanddeusant
Bannau Sir Gaer
Llyn y Fan Fawr
Fan
Brycheiniog
Dan-yr-ogof
Craig-y-nos
G-hirych
Fforest Fawr
Fan Nedd
Penwyllt
Henrhyd Waterfall
Coed y Rhaladr
Ystradfellte
Portneddfechan
A465
Neath

Myddfai
Glastynydd Forest
Llyn y Fan Fach
Black Mountain
Cray Reservoir
A4067
Ystradgynlais
A4109
Pontardawe

Llandovery
Llangadog
Bethlehem
Llandeilo
A40
Brynaman
A4069
A4068
Ammanford
A474
Swansea

Llanwrda
A482
Carreg Cennen
Trapp
A483
A474
A482

5 miles
0

© Crown copyright

▼ Pumsaint   ▼ Carmarthen

Popular for walking and pony trekking, the central **Brecon Beacons**, grouped around the two highest peaks in the national park, are easily accessible from Brecon, which lies just six miles to the north. This is classic old red-sandstone country, sweeping peaks rising up out of glacial scoops of land. Although the peaks never quite reach 3000ft, the terrain is unmistakeably, and dramatically, mountainous. The panorama fans out from the **Brecon Beacons Mountain Centre** (daily: March–June & Sept–Oct 9.30am–5pm; July & Aug 9.30am–6pm; Nov–Feb 10.30am–4.30pm; ☎01874/623366), on a windy ridge just off the A470 turn-off at Libanus, six miles southwest of Brecon. As well as a fantastic café that specializes in local ingredients, there are interesting displays on the flora, fauna, geology and history of the area, together with a well-stocked shop of maps, books and guides.

Pen y Fan (2907ft) is the highest peak in the Beacons. Together with **Corn Du** (2863ft), half a mile to the west, they form the two most popular ascents in the park, particularly along the well-trampled muddy red path that starts from Pont ar Daf, half a mile south of Storey Arms, on the A470, midway between Brecon and Merthyr Tydfil. This is the most direct route from a road, where a comparatively easy five-mile round trip gradually climbs up the southern flank of the two peaks. A longer and generally quieter ascent leads up to the two peaks along the "Gap" route, the ancient road that winds its way north from the Neuadd reservoirs, immediately south of Brecon. This passes through the only natural break in the sandstone ridge of the central Beacons, heading to the bottom of the lane that eventually joins the main street in Llanfaes, Brecon, as Bailihelig Road. Although the old road is no longer accessible for cars, car parks at either end open out onto the track for an eight-mile round-trip ascent up Pen y Fan and Corn Du from the east.

⑮

Practicalities

The **tourist office** (daily: Easter–Oct 9.30am–5.30pm; Nov–Easter 9.30am–5pm; ☎01874/622485, ✆brectic@powys.gov.uk) is in the Lion Yard car park off Lion Street. For details of the town's annual **jazz festival**, held over a long weekend in mid-August, call ☎01874/611622 or visit ⓦwww.breconjazz .co.uk. There is free **Internet access** at the town library on Ship Street (Mon & Wed–Fri 9.30am–5pm, Tues 9.30am–7pm, Sat 9.30am–1pm). **Bike rental** is available at the Brecon Cycle Centre, 9 Ship St (☎01874/622651), and Bikes & Hikes, 10 The Struet (☎01874/610071).

Brecon and adjacent Llanfaes bulge with **accommodation** to suit all pockets, except during the August jazz festival. Best bets are the warm and welcoming *Pickwick House*, St John's Road (☎01874/624322, ⓦwww.pickwick-house .brecon.co.uk; ❸), with excellent, predominantly organic breakfasts and evening meals; and the nonsmoking *Cantre Selyf*, 5 Lion St (☎01874/622904, ⓦwww .cantreselyf.co.uk; ❺), an imposing seventeenth-century townhouse, all creaking floors and moulded plaster ceilings. The YHA **hostel** *Ty'n-y-Caeau*, Groesford (☎0870/770 5718, ✆tynycaeau@yha.org.uk; ❶), is two miles east of the town. It can be reached via Slwch Lane, a path from Cerrigcochion Road in Brecon, or it's a one-mile walk from the bus stops at either Cefn Brynich lock (Brecon–Abergavenny buses) or Troedyrharn Farm (Brecon–Hereford buses). *Brynich Caravan and Camping Park*, Brynich (☎01874/623325), is situated a mile east of town, just off the A470, overlooking the town and the river.

For daytime **eating**, *The Café*, 39 High St, offers a warm, relaxed atmosphere and a good range of Free Trade coffees and hearty soups and sandwiches, while *Llanfaes Dairy*, just across the river at 19 Bridge St, is a wonderful home-made ice-cream dairy. For superb modern Welsh cuisine, head three miles northwest of town to ⚔ *Felin Fach Griffin*, a smart gastropub just off the A470 in Felinfach (☎01874/620111; ●) which also has airy, classic rooms. The *Bull's Head*, 86 The Struet, is the pick of the town's **pubs**.

The Fforest Fawr

Covering a vast expanse of hilly landscape west of the central Brecon Beacons, the **Fforest Fawr** (Great Forest) seems something of a misnomer for an area of largely unforested sandstone hills dropping down to a porous limestone belt in the south. The name, however, refers to its former status as a hunting area. The hills rise up to the south of the A40, west of Brecon, with the dramatic A4067 piercing the western side of the range and the A470 defining the Fforest's eastern limit. Between the two, a twisting mountain road crosses a bleak plateau and descends into one of Britain's classic limestone landscapes, around the hamlet of **YSTRADFELLTE**. With a dazzling countryside of lush, deep ravines on its doorstep, Ystradfellte has become a phenomenally popular centre for its walks over great pavements of bone-white rock next to cradling potholes, disappearing rivers and crashing waterfalls.

A mile to the south, the River Mellte tumbles into the dark mouth of the **Porth-yr-ogof** (White Horse Cave), emerging into daylight a few hundred yards further south. A signposted path heads south from the Porth-yr-ogof car park and into the green gorge of the River Mellte. After little more than a mile, the first of three waterfalls is reached at **Sgwd Clun Gwyn** (White Meadow Fall), where the river crashes fifty feet over two huge, angular steps of rock before hurtling down the course for a few hundred yards to the other two falls – the impressive **Sgwd Isaf Clun Gwyn** (Lower White Meadow Fall) and, around the wooded corner, the **Sgwd y Pannwr** (Fall of the Fuller). The path continues to the confluence of the rivers Mellte and Hepste, half a mile further on. A quarter of a mile along the Hepste is the most popular of the area's falls, the **Sgwd yr**

△ Porth-yr-ogof cave

Eira (Fall of Snow), whose rock below the main tumble has eroded back six feet, allowing you to walk directly behind a dramatic twenty-foot curtain of water. A shorter two-mile walk to Sgwd yr Eira leads from **PENDERYN** village, off the A4059, three miles north of Hirwaun, reached by regular buses from Aberdare. You might want to stop off on the main road through Penderyn at the **Welsh Whisky Distillery** (☎01685/813300, ⓦwww.welsh-whisky.co.uk), where it is hoped a visitor centre will be operational by the beginning of 2007.

In the middle of Ystradfellte, you'll find the popular *New Inn*, which serves basic meals, a few yards from *Tŷ-y-Berllan* (☎01639/722242; ❷), an unfussy **B&B**. Half a mile south is a decent **campsite** at *Penllwyn-Einion Farm* (☎01639/720542).

Dan-yr-ogof Showcaves

Six miles of upland forest and squelchy moor lie between Ystradfellte and the **Dan-yr-ogof Showcaves** (April–Oct daily 10am–4pm; Nov–March call for details; ☎01639/730284, ⓦwww.showcaves.co.uk; £9.50), off the A4067 to the west. Only discovered in 1912, they are claimed to form the largest system of subterranean caverns in northern Europe, and, although new attractions and relentless marketing have turned them into something of an overdone theme park, the caverns are truly awesome in their size. In a self-guided tour, the path first leads you into the **Dan-yr-ogof** cave, the longest showcave in Britain, and a warren of caverns framed by stalactites and frothy limestone deposits. Although the whole cave is known to be around ten miles long, you'll be steered around a circular route of about a mile and a half. Back outside, you pass a downbeat re-created Iron Age "village", and walk through a hideous park of fibreglass dinosaurs to get to the **Cathedral Cave**, a succession of spookily lit caverns that lead into the "cathedral", a hugely impressive 150-foot-long, 70-foot-high cave, where a cheesy *son et lumière* performance provides unnecessary diversion. Reachable via a precarious path behind the dinosaur park is **Bone Cave**, the third and final cavern, known to have been inhabited by prehistoric tribes, with some 42 human (and many animal) skeletons found here. Elsewhere on site there's also a short **dry ski slope** and a **pony trekking centre**.

There's little reason to **stay** at the site, though it offers self-catering units (from £250 per week for a double) and **camping**. There's another, very basic camping option half a mile north at *Maes-yr-eglwys Farm* (☎01639/730849), by the *Tafarn-y-Garreg* pub. Between there and the showcaves, the *Gwyn Arms* serves decent meals.

The Black Mountains

The northeasternmost section of the national park centres on the **Black Mountains**, far quieter than the central belt of the Brecon Beacons and skirted by the wide valley of the River Usk. The only exception to the Black Mountains' unremitting sandstone is an isolated outcrop of limestone, long divorced from the southern belt, that peaks due north of Crickhowell at Pen Cerrigcalch (2302ft). The Black Mountains have the feel of a landscape only partly tamed by human habitation: tiny villages, isolated churches and delightful lanes are folded into an undulating green landscape which levels out to the south around the pretty villages of **Tretower** and **Crickhowell**.

Tretower

Rising out of the valley floor, dominating the view from both the A40 and the A479 mountain road, the solid round tower of the **castle and court** (daily: Easter–Sept 10am–5pm; Oct–Easter 10am–4pm; £2.50; CADW) at **TRETOWER** (Tre-twˆr), ten miles southeast of Brecon, was built to guard the pass. The bleak, thirteenth-century round tower replaced an earlier Norman fortification, and in the late fourteenth century was supplemented by a comparatively luxurious manor house, itself being gradually expanded over the ensuing years. An enjoyable audioguide tour takes you around an open-air gallery and wall walk, and explains late medieval building methods using the exposed plaster and beams where work is still under way.

Crickhowell

Compact **CRICKHOWELL** (Crucywel), four miles southeast of Tretower, on the northern bank of the wide and shallow Usk, makes for a lively base from which to explore the surrounding area. There isn't much to see in town, however, apart from a grand seventeenth-century **bridge**, with thirteen arches visible from the eastern end and only twelve from the west, spawning many a local myth. **Table Mountain** (1481ft) provides a spectacular northern backdrop, topped by the remains of the 2500-year-old hill fort (*crug*) of Hywel, accessed on a path past The Wern, off Llanbedr Road. Many walkers follow a route north from Table Mountain, climbing two miles up to the plateau-topped limestone hump of **Pen Cerrig-calch** (2302ft).

The **tourist office** (April–Oct daily 9am–1pm & 2–4.30pm; ☎01837/812105) is in Beaufort Chambers, on Beaufort Street. **Accommodation** is abundant, with a grandiose coaching inn, the *Bear Hotel*, on Beaufort Street (☎01873/810408, ⓦwww.bearhotel.co.uk; ❺), and the cheerfully relaxed *Dragon* on the High Street (☎01873/810362, ⓦwww.dragonhotel.co.uk; ❹); for cheaper B&B, try *Greenhill Villas* on Beaufort Street (☎01873/811177; ❷). The town-centre *Riverside Park* **campsite** lies on New Road (☎01873/810397).

There's no shortage of places to **eat** and **drink** in and around Crickhowell. Try the slightly twee *Cheese Press*, 18 High St, for daytime snacks – the quiches are great. There's heartier fare, including good curries, at the *Corn Exchange* bar opposite. Evening food is almost universally available in the town's pubs: the *Bear Hotel* (see above) wins legions of awards for its heavenly, pricier-than-average bar and restaurant food. Down by the town bridge, the *Bridge End* pub, part of which is an old tollhouse, is a very fine bet for food, including some impressive vegetarian selections. A mile along the A40 towards Brecon is the fabulous *Nantyffin Cider Mill Inn* (☎01873/810775), great for real ales and ciders as well as tasty food.

Abergavenny and around

Flanking the Brecon Beacons National Park, the lively market town of **ABERGAVENNY** (Y Fenni), seven miles southeast of Crickhowell, is a slick and confident town with an ever-growing reputation for its fine cuisine, which reaches something of a zenith during the town's September **Food Festival**. It also makes a great base, with a fine range of places to eat, drink and sleep, and the town is a magnet to walkers bound for the local mountains: **Sugar Loaf** and the legend-infused **Holy Mountain** (Skirrid Fawr). Stretching north from town, the **Vale of Ewyas** runs along the foot of the Black Mountains, where the astounding churches at Partrishow and Cwmyoy are lost in rural isolation. Abergavenny also makes a good base for visiting Monmouthshire's "Three Castles" (see p.684), set in the pastoral border country to the east.

Although only a couple of miles and a few hills away from the iron and coal towns of the Valleys (see p.687), Abergavenny grew on the basis of its weaving and tanning trades, giving it an entirely different feel. These industries prospered alongside a flourishing market, which is still the focal point for a wide area, drawing many people up from the Valleys every Tuesday. In World War II, Hitler's deputy, Rudolf Hess, was kept in the town's mental asylum as a prisoner, after his plane crash-landed in Scotland in 1941. He was allowed a weekly walk in the nearby hills, growing, it is said, to love the Welsh countryside.

From the train station, Monmouth Road rises gently, eventually becoming High Street, off which you'll find the fragmented remains of the medieval **castle**, whose ugly Victorian keep houses the **town museum** (Easter–Sept daily 11am–5pm though closed 1–2pm outside school summer hols; Oct–Easter Mon–Sat 11am–1pm & 2–4pm; free), which displays ephemera from the town's history and a reconstruction of Basil Jones' grocery shop, once on Main Street. After the death of Jones' son in 1989, the contents of the shop were transported to the museum lock, stock and biscuit barrel. Some goods are of recent origin, but much dates from the 1930s and 1940s – some even from the nineteenth century. Abergavenny's parish church of **St Mary**, on Monk Street, contains some superb tombs that span the entire medieval period. There are effigies of members of the notorious de Braose family, along with the tomb and figure of Sir William ap Thomas, founder of Raglan Castle (see p.683). Look out for the **Jesse Tree**, a recumbent, twice-life-sized statue of King David's father that would once have formed part of an altarpiece tracing the family lineage from Jesse to Jesus.

Practicalities

Abergavenny's **train station** lies on the well-used line between Newport and Hereford. Buses depart from Swan Meadow **bus station**, right by the joint **tourist office** (daily: April–Oct 10am–5.30pm; Nov–March 10am–4pm; ☎01873/857588, Ⓔabergavenny.tic@monmouthshire.gov.uk) and **Brecon Beacons National Park office** (Easter–Sept daily 9.30am–5.30pm; ☎01873/853254, Ⓦwww.breconbeacons.org). You can **rent bikes** from Gateway Cycles, 32 Frogmore St (☎01873/858519), or, if they have any left, from the *Black Sheep* bunkhouse right by the train station (see below).

Accommodation comes mainly in the form of B&Bs, many on the Monmouth Road between the town centre and the train station: *Maes Glas*, Raglan Terrace, Monmouth Road (☎01873/854494, Ⓔmaesglasbb@amserve .com; ❷), is the best. Nearby, the Georgian *Park Guest House*, 36 Hereford Rd (☎01873/853715, Ⓔparkguesthouse@hotmail.com; ❷), is also very good, while the central *King's Head* pub on Cross Street (☎01873/853575, Ⓦwww.kingshead.20fr.com; ❸) has inexpensive, well-appointed rooms. Right by the station, *Black Sheep Backpackers, Great Western Hotel*, 24 Station Rd (☎01873/859125, Ⓦwww.blacksheepbackpackers.com; ❶), is a welcoming bunkhouse-cum-pub, with accommodation in twin, quad and dorm rooms and continental breakfast included. The nearest place to pitch a **tent** is *Pyscodlyn Farm Caravan and Camping Site* (☎01873/853271), two miles west of town off the A40 – any Brecon or Crickhowell bus will pass by.

In the last fifteen years, **food** has become Abergavenny's main claim to fame – the town's annual **Food Festival** (☎01873/851643, Ⓦwww .abergavennyfoodfestival.co.uk), in mid-September, is now one of the most prestigious in Britain. Not surprisingly, there are plenty of **places to eat**, among them the moderately priced *Greyhound Vaults*, Market Street, great for a wide range of tasty Welsh and English specialities, including the best vegetarian dishes in town. ⌖*Trading Post*, 14 Neville St, is a trendy coffee house and bistro, while the very expensive *Walnut Tree Inn* (☎01873/852797), on the B4521 at

Llanddewi Sgyrrid, two miles north of town, is a legendary foodies' paradise for superb Italian and Mediterranean cuisine. Of Abergavenny's **pubs**, the best is the staunchly traditional *Hen & Chickens*, Flannel Street, just off the High Street, with a separate dining room for inexpensive food.

The Vale of Ewyas

In total contrast to the urban Valleys, just a few miles to the south, the northern finger of Monmouthshire, stretching along the English border, is one of the most enchanting and reclusive parts of Wales. The main A465 Hereford road leads six miles north out of Abergavenny to Llanfihangel Crucorney, where the B4423 diverges off to the north into the beautiful **Vale of Ewyas**, along the banks of the Honddu River.

After a mile, a lane heads west towards the enchanting valley of Gwyrne Fawr, and the delightful church and well of St Issui in the hamlet of **Partrishow**. First founded in the eleventh century, the tiny church was refashioned in the thirteenth and fourteenth centuries. In the 1500s it acquired a lacy rood screen, carved out of solid Irish oak and adorned with crude symbols of good and evil – most notably in the corner, where an evil dragon consumes a vine, a symbol of hope and wellbeing. The rest of the whitewashed church breathes simplicity by comparison. Of special note are the wall texts painted over the picture of a skeleton and scythe. Before the Reformation, such pictures were widely used to teach an illiterate population about the scriptures, until King James I ordered that such "popish devices" be whitewashed over and repainted with scripture texts.

Back on the main B4423, the road winds its way up the valley's western side, past the fork at the *Queen's Head* pub (☎01873/890241), a great place to **camp**. In the adjacent village of **Cwmyoy**, the parish church of St Martin has substantially subsided due to geological twists in the underlying rock. Nothing squares up: the tower leans at a severe angle from the bulging body of the church, and the view inside from the back of the nave towards the sloping altar, askew roof and straining windows is unforgettable.

Llanthony and around

Four miles further up this most remote of valleys is the hamlet of **LLAN-THONY**, little more than a small cluster of houses, an inn and a few outlying farms around the wide-open ruins of **Llanthony Priory** – a grander setting, and certainly a quieter one, than Tintern, though the buildings are far more modest in scale. It was founded in around 1100 by the Norman knight William de Lacy, who, it is said, was so captivated by the spiritual beauty of the site that he renounced worldly living and founded a hermitage, attracting like-minded recluses and forming Wales's first Augustinian priory. The roofless church, with its pointed transitional arches and squat tower, was constructed in the latter half of the twelfth century and retains a real sense of spirituality and peace. There are two good places to **stay**: the *Abbey Hotel* (☎01873/890487, ⓦwww .llanthonypriory.supanet.com; ❸; Nov–March weekends only), fashioned out of part of the tumbledown priory, was built in the eighteenth century as a hunting lodge; while along the road is the *Half Moon Inn* (☎01873/890611; ❷), serving superb beer and good-value meals.

From Llanthony, the road slowly climbs four miles alongside the narrowing Honddu River to the isolated hamlet of **CAPEL-Y-FFIN**, from where it's a further mile to the YHA **hostel** (☎0870/770 5748; closed Dec & Jan; Nov & Feb weekends only; £10.50), which also has pony trekking and **camping**. The road then weaves a tortuous route up over **Gospel Pass** and onto the howling, windy moor of **Hay Bluff**, on the glorious roof of the Black Mountains, before descending five miles to the border town of Hay-on-Wye (see p.445).

The Wells towns

The **spa towns** of mid-Wales, strung out along the Heart of Wales rail line between Swansea and Shrewsbury, were once all obscure villages, but with the arrival of the great craze for spas in the early eighteenth century, anywhere with a decent supply of apparently healing water joined in on the act. Royalty and nobility spearheaded the fashion, but the arrival of the railways opened them to all.

Today, best of the bunch is undoubtedly the westernmost spa of **Llanwrtyd Wells**, hunkered down beneath stunning mountain scenery and with a real pulse to the place. The most famous of the four – **Llandrindod Wells** – attracted the international elite in its Victorian heyday, but it's been a steady slide downhill since then, and the place is struggling these days. In between, the larger town of Builth Wells was very much the spa of the Welsh working classes and there's no reason to stop, except in mid-July when it hosts the massive and utterly absorbing **Royal Welsh Show**, Britain's biggest rural jamboree. The fourth spa town, Llangammarch Wells, warrants even less attention.

Llanwrtyd Wells and around

Of the four spa towns, **LLANWRTYD WELLS**, twenty miles northwest of Brecon, is the most appealing, especially for visitors. This was the spa to which the Welsh – farmers of Dyfed alongside the Nonconformist middle classes from Glamorgan – came to the great *eisteddfodau* (festivals of Welsh music, dance and poetry) in the valley of the River Irfon. Nowadays, it's the Welsh capital of wacky events – from the world bog-snorkelling championships to a Man versus Horse race and numerous biking/walking/beer-drinking combination weekends. Call the tourist office for more information or see Ⓦwww.green-events.co.uk.

Main Street runs through the centre of town, crossing the Irfon River just below the main square, Y Sgwar, dominated by a stunning sculpture of a red kite. On the opposite side of Main Street, Dolecoed Road winds for half a mile along the river to the *Dolecoed Hotel*, built near the original sulphurous spring. Although the distinctive aroma had been noted in the area for centuries, it was truly "discovered" in 1732 by the local priest, Theophilus Evans, who drank from an evil-smelling spring after seeing a rudely healthy frog pop out of it. The spring, named **Ffynnon Drewllyd** (Stinking Well), bubbles up amongst the dilapidated spa buildings a hundred yards behind the hotel.

Llanwrtyd's **tourist office** is in Tŷ Barcud just off the main square (daily 10am–5pm; ☎01591/610666, Ⓦwww.llanwrtyd-wells.powys.org.uk). **Accommodation** includes the lively *Neuadd Arms* in the main square (☎01591/610236, Ⓦwww.neuaddarmshotel.co.uk; ❸), which also does good bar **food**, with some great curries; the lovely *Carlton House* (☎01591/610248, Ⓦwww.carltonrestaurant.co.uk; ❹), yards away on Dolecoed Road, which also has cheaper rooms (including two bargain singles) across the street at its brasserie; and the fairly grand *Lasswade* on Station Road (☎01591/610515, Ⓦwww.lasswadehotel.co.uk; ❺). The marvellous *Drover's Rest* **restaurant** by the river bridge (☎01591/610264, Ⓦwww.food-food-food.co.uk; ❸) serves wholesome, traditional Welsh dishes and snacks, and has some classy, cosy B&B accommodation. Finally, the ♣ *Stonecroft Inn* on Dolecoed Road (☎01591/610332) is a superb pub with great food and regular live folk, R&B and rock music as well as beds (£13.50) in a small, self-catering **hostel** annexe. There's very basic tent-only **camping** on the Dolwen Fields, 200m off the main road south from the town square, although 48 hours' notice is required (☎01591/610626, ✉g.jones@virgin.net).

Bike rental is available at *Cycles Irfon* (☎01591/610710, or 610668 out of hours) on the Maesydre industrial estate off the Beulah Road to the north of town.

The Abergwesyn Pass

A lane from Llanwrtyd meets up with another road from Beulah at the riverside hamlet of **ABERGWESYN**, five miles north of Llanwrtyd. From here, you can drive the quite magnificent winding thread of an ancient cattle-drovers' road – the **Abergwesyn Pass** – up the perilous **Devil's Staircase** and through dense conifer forests to miles of wide, desolate valleys where sheep graze unhurriedly. At the little bridge over the tiny Tywi River, a track heads south past an isolated, gas-lit YHA **hostel** at **DOLGOCH** (☎0870/770 5796; closed Oct–April). Remote paths lead from the hostel through the forests and hillsides to the exquisitely isolated chapel at **Soar-y-Mynydd** and over the mountains to the next YHA **hostel** at **TYNCORNEL**, *Tŷ'n-y-cornel* (☎0870/770 8868; closed Oct to late March), five miles from Dolgoch. Although the Abergwesyn Pass, which ends in the market square of Tregaron in Ceredigion, is less than twenty miles long, it takes a good hour in a car to negotiate the twisting, narrow road safely. The old drovers, driving their cattle to Shrewsbury or Hereford, would have taken a day or two to cover the same stretch.

Llandrindod Wells

Once the most chichi spa resort in Wales, **LLANDRINDOD WELLS** (Llandrindod) is a pale imitation of its former self. Although many of the fine Victorian buildings still stand, the hotels do business and the flower boxes bristle with colour, there's something empty at the town's heart, and it will take more than a lick of paint to sort it out.

It was the railway that made Llandrindod, arriving in 1864 and bringing carriages full of well-to-do Victorians to the fledgling spa. Llandrindod blossomed, new hotels were built, neat parks were laid out and the town came to rival many of the more fashionable spas and resorts over the border. Like so many coastal resorts, however, Llandrindod has been on the slide for years. The hotels have come to rely on ever-ageing visitors, the grand old spa – the reason for the town's existence in the first place – is a mess, and nothing radical or new seems to have been tried in the town for decades. That all said, there is plenty of accommodation here, the surrounding countryside is lovely and transport links are good.

Llandrindod's Victorian opulence is still very much in evidence in the town's grandiose public buildings, even if many are in a sorry state these days. Plans are afoot to restore the lavish **spa pump room** in **Rock Park**, but little has come of this yet and the place continues to crumble. A free chalybeate fountain, in a glade to the front of the pump room, lets you sample more than enough of the town's metallic, salty spa water. The architecture around the park entrance is Llandrindod at its most confidently Victorian, with elaborately carved terracotta frontages and expansive gabling.

The High Street, running from here to the centre, contains antique, junk and book shops. The tourist office, on Temple Street behind, houses the small **Radnorshire Museum** (Tues–Thurs 10am–1pm & 2–5pm, Fri 10am–1pm & 2–4.30pm, Sat 10am–1pm; free), closed at the time of writing but due to be reopened by mid-2006. The **National Cycle Exhibition**, on the corner of Temple Street and Spa Road (March–Oct daily 10am–4pm; call ☎01597/825531 for winter hours; £2.50), is a nostalgic collection of over 250 bikes, from a reproduction 1818 Hobbyhorse to relatively modern folding bikes and choppers, including styles that look far too uncomfortable to have been a success.

Practicalities

Buses pull in by the **train station** in the heart of town, between High Street and Station Crescent. The **tourist office** is on Temple Street (April–Sept Mon–Fri 9.30am–5.30pm, Sat & Sun 9.30am–5pm; Oct–March Mon–Fri 10am–1pm & 2–5pm; ☎01597/822600, ✉llandtic@powys.gov.uk). **Bikes** can be rented from Greenstiles Cyles (☎01597/824594), in Imperial Buildings, Temple Street, if arranged in advance.

As Mid-Wales's major tourist centre for the past 130 years, Llandrindod is well served for **accommodation**. For something smart and reasonably close to the station, try *Greylands*, High Street (☎01597/822253; ❷), or nearby *Rhydithon*, Dyffryn Road (☎01597/822624; ❷). The *Kincoed Hotel*, Temple Street (☎01597/822656; ❷), is well appointed but not a patch on the Edwardian elegance of the *Metropole Hotel*, on the same street (☎01597/822881, ⓦwww.bw-metropole.co.uk; ❺), an old spa hotel with a pool, the centrepiece of the town. Its *Radnor* **restaurant**, open to nonresidents, is stuffy and pricey but offers the best local cuisine in town. For reasonably priced food, head for the *Aspidistra*, on Station Crescent, a decent daytime café serving cheap and wholesome sandwiches, snacks and meals, or the *Llanerch Inn*, Llanerch Lane, central Llandrindod's only **pub**, and an excellent one at that – a cosy sixteenth-century inn that predates most of the surrounding town, serving a solid menu of good-value, well-cooked classics.

North and East Radnorshire

Radnorshire has long been one of the most sparsely populated counties in England and Wales, its north and east still being especially remote. In the northwest, Rhayader is the only settlement of any size, a gateway to the four interlocking reservoirs of the **Elan Valley** and the surrounding wild, spartan countryside of waterfalls, bogland and bare peaks. The countryside to the northeast of Rhayader is tamer, and lanes and bridle paths delve in and around the woods and farms, occasionally brushing through minute settlements like the village of **Abbeycwmhir**, whose name is taken from its deserted Cistercian abbey. The hills roll eastwards towards the handsome town of **Knighton**, perched right on the English border, beside some of the most intact parts of **Offa's Dyke**.

Elan Valley and around

The poet Shelley spent his honeymoon in buildings now submerged by the waters of the **Elan Valley** reservoirs, a nine-mile-long string of four lakes built between 1892 and 1903 to supply water to the rapidly growing industrial city of Birmingham, 75 miles east. Although the lakes enhance an already beautiful and idyllic part of the world, the way in which Welsh valleys, villages and farmsteads were seized and flooded to provide water for English cities is something that Welsh nationalists have long protested. The tourist board prefers to advertise the profusion of rare plants and birds that resulted, notably the red kites.

From the workaday market town of **RHAYADER**, ten miles west of Llandrindod Wells, the B4518 heads southwest four miles to **ELAN** village, a curious collection of stone houses built in 1909 to replace the reservoir constructors' village that had grown up on the site. Just below the Caban Coch, the **Elan Valley Visitor Centre** (mid-March to Oct daily 10am–5.30pm; ☎01597/810898) incorporates a tourist office and a permanent exhibition about the history and ecology of the area. Frequent guided **walks** and even **Land Rover safaris** head off from the centre, and a road tucks in along the bank of Caban Coch to the **Garreg Ddu** viaduct, where it winds along for four spectacular miles to the vast, rather chilling 1952 dam on **Claerwen Reservoir**. More remote and less popular than the Elan lakes, Claerwen is a good base for a serious **walk** from the far end of the dam across eight or so harsh but beautiful miles to the monastery of Strata Florida (see p.765). Alternatively, you can follow the path that skirts around the northern shore of Claerwen to the lonely **Teifi Pools**, glacial lakes from which the River Teifi springs.

Back at the Garreg Ddu viaduct, a more popular road continues north along the long, glassy finger of Garreg Ddu reservoir, before doubling back on itself just below the awesome **Pen-y-garreg** dam and reservoir; if the dam is overflowing, the vast wall of foaming water is mesmerizing. At the top of Pen-y-garreg lake, it's possible to drive over the final dam on the system, at **Craig Goch**. Thanks to its gracious curve, elegant Edwardian arches and neat little green cupola, this is the most photographed of all the dams.

ABBEYCWMHIR (Abaty Cwm Hir), seven miles northeast of Rhayader, takes its name from the **abbey** whose sombre ruins (free access) lie beneath the village. Cistercian monks founded the site in 1146, planning one of the largest churches in Britain. Destruction by Henry III's troops in 1231 scuppered

△ Elan Valley reservoir

plans to continue building, but the sparse ruins – a rocky outline of the floor plan – lie in a conifer-carpeted valley alongside a gloomy green lake, lending weight to the site's melancholic associations. Llywelyn ap Gruffydd's body was rumoured to have been buried here, and a new granite slab carved with a Celtic sword lies on the altar to commemorate this last native prince of Wales.

Practicalities

Bus #103 runs to the Elan Valley Visitor Centre from Llandrindod and Rhayader (Mon–Fri). The main **accommodation** base in the area is the *Elan Valley Hotel* (☏01597/810448, ⓦwww.elanvalleyhotel.co.uk; ❸), an imposing, neocolonial pile on the Rhayader side of Elan village. It's also very good for eating, drinking and entertainment. Otherwise, you may want to make use of Rhayader, where buses stop opposite the **tourist office** (April–Oct daily 9.30am–12.30pm & 1.30–5.30pm; Nov–March Mon, Tues, Thurs–Sat 10am–4pm; ☏01597/810591, ⓦwww.rhayader.co.uk), housed in the leisure centre. Eighteenth-century coaching inns still line Rhayader's main streets, with more modern **accommodation** at the *Elan Hotel*, West Street (☏01597/810109, ⓦwww.elanhotel.co.uk; ❸), and the cheerful *Brynteg* B&B on East Street (☏01597/810052; ❷). The cheapest place in town is *Greenfields* on South Street (☏01597/811101; ❶), which offers B&B and hostel beds (£13.50). There's a **campsite** (☏01597/810183) at *Wyeside*, off the A44 north of Rhayader. **Bikes** can be rented from Clive Powell Mountain Bikes (☏01597/811343, ⓦwww.clivepowell-mtb.co.uk) on West Street.

Knighton

A town that straddles King Offa's eighth-century border as well as the modern Wales–England divide, **KNIGHTON** (Tref-y-clawdd, the "Town on the Dyke"), twenty miles northeast of Llandrindod, has come into its own as the most obvious centre for those walking the **Offa's Dyke Path**. Located almost exactly halfway along the route, it's a lively, attractive place that easily warrants a visit, although it has few specific sights. The town is so close to the border that its **train station** is actually in England. From here, Station Road crosses the River Teme into Wales and climbs a couple of hundred yards to Brookside Square. Further up the hill is the town's alpine-looking Victorian clocktower, at the point where Broad Street becomes West Street and the steep High Street soars off up to the left, past rickety Tudor buildings and up to the mound of the old **castle**.

Offa's Dyke

Offa's Dyke has provided a potent symbol of Welsh–English antipathy ever since it was created in the eighth century as a demarcation line by King Offa of Mercia, ruler of central England. George Borrow, in his classic *Wild Wales*, notes that, once, "It was customary for the English to cut off the ears of every Welshman who was found to the east of the dyke, and for the Welsh to hang every Englishman whom they found to the west of it."

The earthwork – up to 20ft high and 60ft wide – made use of natural boundaries like rivers in its run north to south, and is best seen in the sections near **Knighton**. Today's England–Wales border crosses the dyke many times, although the basic boundary has changed little since Offa's day. A glorious, 177-mile **long-distance footpath**, opened in 1971, runs the length of the dyke from Prestatyn in the north to Chepstow, and is one of the most rewarding walks in Britain.

In West Street, the excellent **Offa's Dyke Centre** (Easter–Oct daily 9am–5.30pm; Nov–Easter Mon–Fri 9am–5pm, Sat & Sun 11am–3pm; ☎01547/528753, ⓦwww.offasdyke.demon.co.uk) also houses the **tourist office** (same hours; ☎01547/529424). **Accommodation** in Knighton is plentiful and generally good value: there's the revamped *Knighton Hotel* right in the middle on Broad Street (☎01547/520530; ❸), *Fleece House* B&B, at the top of High Street (☎01547/520168, ⓦwww.fleecehouse.co.uk; ❷), and the bargain *Jenny Stothert's*, behind the imposing parish church at 15 Mill Green (☎01547/520075; ❶), where you can also **camp**. For **eating** and drinking, it's hard to beat the comfortable 🕈 *Horse & Jockey*, at the town end of Station Road.

Montgomeryshire

The northern part of Powys is made up of the old county of **Montgomeryshire** (Maldwyn), an area of enormously varying landscapes and few inhabitants. The solid little town of **Llanidloes** is a base for ageing hippies on the River Severn (Afon Hafren). To the east, the muted old county town of **Montgomery**, with its fine Georgian architecture, perches amid gentle, green hills above the border and Offa's Dyke. Further north, **Welshpool**, the only major settlement, is packed in above the wide flood plain of the Severn; an excellent local museum, toy rail line, good pubs and reasonable hotels make it a fair stop. On the southern side of Welshpool is Montgomeryshire's one unmissable sight, the sumptuous **Powis Castle** and its exquisite terraced gardens.

Llanidloes and around

Thriving when so many other small market towns seem in danger of atrophying, the secret of success for **LLANIDLOES**, twelve miles north of Rhayader, seems to be in its adaptability. It has developed from a rural village to a weaving town, and has latterly become a centre for artists, craftspeople and assorted alternative lifestylers. One of Mid-Wales's prettiest towns, the four main streets meet at the black and white **market hall**, built on timber stilts in 1600 to allow the market – which has long since moved – to take place on the cobbles beneath. Running parallel with the length of the market hall are China Street and Long Bridge Street, the latter good for some interesting little shops. Off Long Bridge Street is Church Street, which opens out into a yard surrounding the dumpy parish church of **St Idloes** (daily 10.30am–3.30pm; free), the impressive fifteenth-century hammerbeam roof of which is said to have been poached from Abbeycwmhir. The fantastic **Millennium Window** in the church was designed and built by two local stained-glass artists.

From the market hall, the broad Great Oak Street heads west to the **town hall**, originally built as a temperance hotel to challenge the boozy *Trewython Arms* opposite. A plaque on the closed hotel commemorates Llanidloes as an unlikely-seeming place of industrial and political unrest, when, in April 1839, Chartists stormed the hotel, dragging out and beating up special constables who had been despatched to the town in a futile attempt to suppress political activism amongst the town's flannel weavers. In the town hall, you'll also find the wonderfully eclectic **museum** (Easter–Sept daily except Wed 11am–1pm & 2–5pm; Oct–Easter Mon, Tues, Thurs & Fri 11am–1pm & 2–5pm, Sat 10am–1pm; £1), where the diverting collection of old local prints and mementos pales beside the stuffed two-headed lamb, born locally in 1914.

China Street curves down to the car park, from where all **bus** services operate. The **tourist office** (April–Sept daily 9.30am–5pm; Oct–March Mon–Sat 9.30am–5pm; ☎01686/412605, ✉llantic@powys.gov.uk) is at 54 Long Bridge St, near the market hall. **Accommodation** spans the delightful *Red Lion Hotel* (☎01686/412270; ❷) and the more modest *Unicorn* (☎01686/413167, ☏413516; ❶), both on Long Bridge Street. The nicest option is ⚑ *Lloyds Hotel* (☎01686/412284, ⓦwww.lloydshotel.co.uk; ❸), on Cambrian Place, which is also a superb restaurant – booking is essential. You can **camp** at *Dol-llys Farm* (☎01686/412694), on the northern fringe of town. Among the many options for **food**, there's wholesome veggie fare in the laid-back *Great Oak Café* on Great Oak Street, or a few doors down, a great example of that Welsh daytime caff institution, the *National Milk Bar*. For a bit of a treat, go to *Lloyds* (see above). Most of the **pubs** here serve food – the *Unicorn* (see above) and the olde-worlde *Mount Inn* on China Street are the best options. One event worth investigating is the annual **Fancy Dress Night**, held on the first Friday of July, when the pubs open late, the streets are cordoned off and virtually the whole town gets kitted out.

Montgomery and around

Tiny **MONTGOMERY** (Trefaldwyn), around twenty miles northeast of Llanidloes, is Montgomeryshire at its most anglicized. From the mound of its **castle**, situated just on the Welsh side of Offa's Dyke, there are wonderful views over the lofty church tower and the handsome Georgian streets, notably the impressively symmetrical main street – well-named Broad Street – which swoops up to the perfect little red-brick **town hall**, crowned by a pert clocktower. The rebuilt tower of Montgomery's parish **Church of St Nicholas** dominates the snug proportions of the buildings around it. Largely thirteenth-century, the highlights of its spacious interior include a 1600 monument to local landowner Sir Richard Herbert and his wife. Their eight children – who included prominent Elizabethan poet George – have been carved in beatific kneeling positions behind them. Call in too at the engaging **Old Bell Museum**, just by the town hall (April–July & Sept Wed–Fri & Sun 1.30–5pm, Sat 10.30am–5pm; Aug Mon–Fri & Sun 1.30–5pm, Sat 10.30am–5pm; £1), an enjoyable collection of excavated artefacts, scale models of local castles, and mementos from Montgomery civic life.

Montgomery is within striking distance of one of the best-preserved sections of **Offa's Dyke**, traced by the long-distance footpath (see box on p.744), which runs on either side of the B4386. Ditches almost twenty feet high give one of the best indications of the dyke's original appearance. To the south of the main road, the England–Wales border still runs along the line of the dyke, twelve hundred years after it was built. If you want to **stay** here, the best options are *Brynwylfa* (☎01686/668555; ❷), a beautiful townhouse at 4 Bishops Castle St, or *Little Brompton Farm* (☎01686/668371, ⓦwww.littlebromptonfarm.co.uk; ❷), two miles south of town and handy for the Offa's Dyke Path – you can also **camp** there. For **food** and **drink** head for the *Checkers* pub on Broad Street.

Berriew

Three miles northwest of Montgomery, the neat village of **BERRIEW** (Aberrhiw) is more redolent of the Tudor settlements over the English border than anywhere in Wales. Its black-and-white houses are grouped picturesquely around a small church, the shallow waters of the River Rhiw and the posh, half-timbered *Lion Hotel* (☎01686/640452; ❺), which does excellent food. Just over the river bridge, the **Andrew Logan Museum of Sculpture** (Easter weekend noon–6pm; May–Oct Wed–Sun noon–6pm; Nov–Christmas Sat & Sun noon–4pm; Ⓦwww.andrewlogan.com; £2) seems an improbably camp addition to the tidy Berriew landscape. In the 1970s, British sculptor Logan inaugurated the great drag-and-grunge ball known as the Alternative Miss World Contest, launchpad of the late Divine's career. A "Divine Shrine" and some dazzling outfits from the contests form a large chunk of the museum's exhibits, sharing space with Logan's oversized horticultural sculptures, gaudy model goddesses and a twelve-foot-high encrusted glass "cosmic egg".

A mile further down the lane from the museum, where it meets the main A493, you'll find **Glansevern Hall Gardens** (May–Sept Thurs–Sat & bank holidays noon–6pm; £3.50), a beautifully cool collection of plants, trees and follies gathered around a gorgeous Georgian mansion.

Welshpool and around

Eastern Montgomeryshire's chief town of **WELSHPOOL** (Y Trallwng), seven miles north of Montgomery, was formerly known as just Pool, its prefix added in 1835 to distinguish it from the English seaside town of Poole in Dorset. It lies in the valley of the River Severn, just three miles from the English border, and is an attractive place to visit, with a number of fine Tudor, Georgian and Victorian buildings in the centre, and the sumptuous Powis Castle nearby.

Along Severn Street from the **train station**, a humpback bridge over the much-restored **Montgomery Canal** hides the canal wharf and a wharfside warehouse that has been carefully restored as the **Powysland Museum** (all year Mon, Tues, Thurs & Fri 11am–1pm & 2–5pm; May–Sept also Sat & Sun 10am–1pm & 2–5pm; Oct–April also Sat 11am–2pm; £1). The impressive local history collection includes archeological nuggets such as those from an old local woodhenge, and displays medieval remains from the now-obliterated local Cistercian abbey of Strata Marcella.

From the *Royal Oak Hotel*, at the centre of town, follow Broad Street – which changes name five times as it rises up the hill – towards the tiny Raven Square terminus station of the **Welshpool and Llanfair Light Railway** (April to late May, Sept & Oct weekends only; Easter & late May–Aug daily; generally 2–3 trains a day; £9.90 return; ☎01938/810441). The eight-mile narrow-gauge rail line was open to passengers for less than thirty years prior to its closure in 1931. Now, scaled-down engines once more chuff their way along to the peaceful little village of **Llanfair Caereinion**, a good base for daytime walks, with good pub food at the *Goat Hotel*. The post office, opposite the church, stocks free leaflets on some good local circular walks.

Practicalities

The pompous neo-Gothic turrets of Welshpool's old Victorian **train station** (its modern replacement is directly behind) sit at the top of Severn Street, which leads down into the town centre – the intersection of Severn, Berriew, Broad and Church streets. The **tourist office** (daily 9.30am–5.30pm; ☎01938/552043, Ⓔweltic@powys.gov.uk) is fifty yards up Church Street in the Vicarage Gardens car park. There's plenty of **accommodation** in town, including the central *Royal Oak* (☎01938/552217; ❺), a traditional coaching inn at the main crossroads. Dozens of **B&Bs** line Salop Road; *Montgomery House* (☎01938/552693; ❷) is the surest bet. Further from the centre are a couple of options: the splendid Georgian luxury of *Trefnant Hall Farm* (☎01686/640262;

❷), a couple of miles further up the lane to Powis Castle, and, two miles to the north of town, the beautiful *Lower Trelydan Farm* (☎01938/553105, Ⓦwww .lowertrelydan.com; ❸). **Camping** is good at the *Green Dragon Inn*, a mile along the Shrewsbury road at Buttington (☎01938/553076). The best **eating** in town is at the *Royal Oak* pub, which has managed to retain its old-world grandiosity while including a superb all-day café-bar. Cheap and filling breakfasts, lunches and teas are served in the *Buttery*, opposite the town hall on the High Street. Many of the town's **pubs** do lunchtime food, with some, notably the *Talbot* in the High Street and the *Raven* up by the narrow-gauge train station, serving decent evening meals as well.

Powis Castle

In a land of ruined castles, the sheer scale and beauty of **Powis Castle** (April–Oct Mon & Thurs–Sun castle 1–5pm, gardens 11am–6pm; July & Aug Tues–Sun, same times; castle £8.80, gardens and museum only £6.20; NT), a mile from Welshpool up Park Lane, is quite staggering. On the site of an earlier Norman fort, the castle was started in the reign of Edward I by the Gwenwynwyn family; to qualify for the site and the barony of De la Pole, they had to renounce all claims to Welsh princedom. In 1587, Sir Edward Herbert bought the castle and began to transform it into the Elizabethan palace that survives today. Inside, the **Clive Museum** – named after Edward Clive, son of Clive of India, who married into the family in 1784 – forms a lively account of the British in India, through diaries, letters, paintings, tapestries, weapons and jewels. But it is the sumptuous period rooms that impress most, from the vast, kitsch frescoes by Lanscroon above the balustraded staircase, to the mahogany bed, brass and enamel toilets and decorative wall hangings of the state bedroom. The elegant **Long Gallery** has a rich sixteenth-century plasterwork ceiling overlooking winsome busts and marble statuettes of the four elements, placed between the glowering family portraits. The **gardens**, designed by Welsh architect William Winde, are spectacular. Dropping down from the castle in four huge, stepped terraces, the design has barely changed since the seventeenth century, with a charmingly precise orangery and topiary that looks as if it is shaved daily. In summer, outdoor **concerts**, frequently with firework finales, take place in the gardens.

Llanfyllin and around

The hills and plains of northern Montgomeryshire conceal a maze of deserted lanes and farm outposts along the contours that swell up towards the north and the foothills of the Berwyn Mountains. The only real settlement of any size is **Llanfyllin**, ten miles northwest of Welshpool, a handsome and friendly hillside town with a Thursday market. There is really nothing to do though, and you'd do better continuing on to the hiking and nature-communing around **Lake Vyrnwy**, or pressing north to **Pistyll Rhaeadr**, Wales's highest waterfall.

The Rhaeadr Valley

For a place so near the English border, **LLANRHAEADR-YM-MOCH-NANT**, six miles north of Llanfyllin, is surprisingly Welsh in its language and appearance. The small, low-roofed village is remembered as the serving parish of Bishop William Morgan, who translated the Bible into Welsh in 1588, but it's mostly visited as a base for **Pistyll Rhaeadr**, Wales's highest waterfall, at 240ft. The river tumbles down the crags in two stages, flowing under a natural stone arch known as the Fairy Bridge. Don't miss out on walking to the top of the fall, for vertiginous views down the valley, and paths up into the moody Berwyns. Pistyll Rhaeadr is a place rich in legend, which you can gen up on in the cute riverside 🏛 *Tan-y-Pistyll* licensed café. The owners also offer B&B (☎01691/780392; ❸) and **camping**, and operate various retreats and spiritually inclined groups.

The village itself has three great **pubs** – the *Three Tuns*, *Hand Inn* and *Wynnstay Arms* – and excellent-value **B&Bs**: next to the post office on the central square is *Powys House* (☎01691/780201, ⓦwww.llanrhaeadrym.co.uk; ❷); alternatively, try the plusher *Bron Heulog* on Waterfall Street (☎01691/780521, ⓦwww.kraines.enta.net; ❸).

Lake Vyrnwy

A monument to the self-aggrandizement of the Victorian age, **Lake Vyrnwy** (Llyn Efyrnwy) combines its functional role as a water supply for Liverpool with a touch of architectural genius in the shape of the huge nineteenth-century dam at its southern end and the Disneyesque turreted straining-tower that edges out into the icy waters. It's a magnificent spot, and a popular centre for walking and birdwatching, with nature trails. The village of **LLANWDDYN** was flattened and rebuilt at the eastern end, the inhabitants receiving compensation of just £5 for losing their homes. The story is told, somewhat apologetically, in the RSPB **Vyrnwy Visitor Centre** (April–Oct daily 10.30am–5.30pm; Nov–March Sat & Sun only; free), which is located on the western side of the dam and coexists with an **RSPB Visitor Centre** (same hours). A few yards down the road, there's a **tourist office** (Easter–Oct daily 10am–5pm; Nov–Easter daily except Wed 10am–3pm; ☎01691/870346) and *Artisans Coffee Shop* (☎01691/870377), from where you can **rent bikes**.

Lake Vyrnwy's immediate surroundings have some of the best **accommodation** in the region, notably the grand *Lake Vyrnwy Hotel* (☎01691/870692, ⓦwww.lakevyrnwy.com; ❼), overlooking the waters above the southeastern shore. If you just want a look, the hotel serves a full afternoon tea in a chintzy lounge overlooking the lake. There's a great **B&B** just beyond the visitor centre at *The Oaks* (☎01691/870250, ⓦwww.vyrnwyaccommodation .co.uk; ❸), and daytime snacks and full evening meals are available at *Lake View* (☎01691/870286), on the lakeside road beyond the *Lake Vyrnwy Hotel*. If you're **camping**, there are five tent pitches at *Fronheulog* (☎01691/870662), at the top of the hairpin bends on the road to Llanfyllin, or in Llanwddyn itself at *Bryn Fedwen* (☎01691/870288).

The Cambrian coast

Cardigan Bay (Bae Ceredigion) takes a huge bite out of the west Wales coast, leaving behind the Pembrokeshire peninsula in the south and the Llŷn in the north. Between them lies the **Cambrian coast**, a loosely defined mountain-backed strip periodically split by tumbling rivers, which stretches from Harlech down to Cardigan. Before the railway and improved roads were built during the nineteenth century, the awkward barrier of the Cambrian Mountains served to isolate this stretch of coast from the rest of Wales. Today, large sand-fringed sections are peppered with low-key coastal resorts, peopled in the summer by families from the English Midlands. The presence of English-dominated resorts and the influx of rat race refugees to this staunchly nationalistic part of the country has, on occasion, fuelled local antipathy, although visitors are unlikely to see anything more controversial than the odd piece of graffiti or flyposting.

Coastal highlights include the hilltop fortress of **Harlech**, the bucket-and-spade resort of **Barmouth** and the fabulous stretch of **Ardudwy beach** between them. Barmouth sits at the head of the beautiful **Mawddach estuary**, which snakes its way inland to the old county town of **Dolgellau**, sheltering beneath the northern flank of **Cadair Idris** (2930ft), one of Wales's most inspirational mountains.

To the south, the flat river plain and rolling hills of the **Dyfi Valley** lay justifiable claim to being one of the greenest corners of Europe, an area replete with B&Bs and other businesses started up by idealistic New Agers who have flocked to this corner of Wales since the late 1960s. The focal point is the genial town of **Machynlleth**, a candidate for the Welsh capital in the 1950s and site of Owain Glyndŵr's embryonic fifteenth-century Welsh parliament. In the hills to the north, the self-contained **Centre for Alternative Technology** runs on cooperative lines and makes for an interesting day out.

South of Machynlleth is the county of **Ceredigion**, formerly known as Cardiganshire. Lying as it does between the two national parks of the Pembrokeshire Coast and Snowdonia, Ceredigion is often overlooked by visitors, but it shouldn't be. In many ways, it combines the best of both national parks – the stunning mountain scenery of southern Snowdonia with the little ports and sandy coves of Pembrokeshire, and all soaked in a relaxed, upbeat and firmly Welsh culture. The county's main town is ebullient **Aberystwyth**, a top spot for everything from serious study and exhibitions in the National Library to student-oriented raves and bar culture. It's also a great base for the luscious countryside inland, especially the waterfalls and woods of the **Vale of Rheidol** out towards mythical **Devil's Bridge**.

The southern Ceredigion coast is broken by some spirited little ports: most notably Georgian **Aberaeron**, higgledy-piggledy **New Quay** and the old county town of **Cardigan**, where the **River Teifi** flows into the sea. Towns and sights inland along the Teifi are worth exploring, especially the mighty castle at **Cilgerran** and the charming little university town of **Lampeter**. Near the source of the Teifi is the atmospheric **Strata Florida Abbey**.

Harlech

One of the undoubted highlights of the Cambrian coast is charming **HARLECH**, 25 miles due west of Bala, with its time-worn castle dramatically clinging to its rocky outcrop, and the town cloaking the ridge behind, commanding one of Wales's finest views over Cardigan Bay to the Llŷn. There are good beaches nearby, and the town's twisting, narrow streets harbour places where you can eat and sleep surprisingly well for such a small place.

Harlech's substantially complete **castle** (June–Sept daily 9.30am–6pm; April, May & Oct daily 9.30am–5pm; Nov–March Mon–Sat 9.30am–4pm, Sun 11am–4pm; £3; CADW) sits on its 200-foot-high bluff, a site chosen by Edward I for one more link in his magnificent chain of fortresses. Begun in 1285, it was built of a hard Cambrian rock, known as Harlech grit, hewn from the moat. The sea, which originally protected one side of the fortress, has now receded, leaving the castle dominating a stretch of duned coastline. Harlech withstood a siege in 1295, but was taken by Owain Glyndŵr in 1404. The young Henry VII withstood a seven-year siege at the hands of the Yorkists until 1468, when the castle was again taken. It fell into ruin, but was put back into service for Charles I during the Civil War; in March 1647, it was the last Royalist castle to fall. The first defensive line comprised the three successive pairs of gates and portcullises built between the two massive half-round towers of the **gatehouse**, where an **exhibition** now outlines the castle's history. Much of the castle's outermost ring has been destroyed, leaving only the twelve-foot-thick curtain walls rising up 40ft to the exposed **battlements**. Only the towering gatehouse prevents you from walking the full circuit.

Harlech's **train station** is below the castle on the main A496. Most **buses** call both here and on High Street, a few yards from the **tourist office** (Easter–Oct daily 10am–5pm; (℡01766/780658, ℰticharlech@hotmail.com). The pick of the local places to **stay** is the cosy, informal *Castle Cottage*, on Pen Llech near the castle (℡01766/780479, ⓌWww.castlecottageharlech.co.uk), a "restaurant with rooms" that's often booked well ahead. Other possibilities include the *Plas Newydd* **hostel** (℡0870/770 5926, ℰllanbedr@yha.org.uk; dorm beds £10.50; open April–Oct), three miles south in Llanbedr, where the lane also heads west to the sprawling **camping** resort at Shell Island (℡01341/241453, ⓌWww .shellisland.co.uk), great for camp fires in the dunes and walks on the splendid **Ardudwy Beach** (part of which, near the village of Dyffryn Ardudwy, is officially naturist). If you want to camp in Harlech itself, head for the summer-only *Min y Don* campsite, Beach Road (℡01766/780286), three minutes' walk from the beach; take the first right out of the station. There are some wonderful places to **eat** on High Street, including *Cemlyn* (℡01766/780637), by day an upscale café and by night a quality restaurant; the inexpensive but licensed *Plas Café* (℡01766/780204), with a good range of food and fabulous views from the garden and conservatory; the bistro-style *Yr Ogof* (℡01766/780888), where you'll find a good-value range of inventive vegetarian and meat dishes; and the classy, modern *Castle Cottage*.

Barmouth and around

Continuing along the coast, the best approach to **BARMOUTH** (Abermaw) is from the south, where the Cambrian coast rail line sweeps across the Mawddach River from tiny **Fairbourne**, over 113 rickety-looking wooden spans. It's still the haunt of English holiday-makers from the Midlands, who fashioned Barmouth as a sea-bathing resort in the nineteenth century, but also warrants some attention for breezy rambles on the cliffs of **Dinas Oleu**, above the town, and a great walk around the mouth of the estuary (see box, below). Central attractions don't extend beyond the **Tŷ Gwyn Museum** (July–Sept daily 10.30am–5pm; free), a medieval tower house – now a Tudor museum – where Henry VII's uncle, Jasper Tudor, is thought to have plotted Richard III's

---

Walking the Barmouth–Fairbourne Loop

The best lowland walk in the Cambrian Coast region, the **Barmouth–Fairbourne Loop** (5 miles; 300ft ascent; 2–3hr) is a fine way to spend an afternoon with impressive mountain scenery, and estuarine and coastal views all the way. The walking component can be virtually eradicated by using both the mainline and Fairbourne railways. The route first crosses the estuary rail bridge (50p) to Morfa Mawddach mainline station, then follows the lane to the main road, crossing it onto a footpath that loops behind a small wooded hill to Pant Einion Hall, then follows another lane back to the main road near Fairbourne. In Fairbourne, turn north, either walking along the beach to the quay at the end of the spit or catching the **Fairbourne Railway** (Easter–Oct; 3–6 daily) to the **passenger ferry** (Easter–Oct; hourly) across the estuary mouth back to Barmouth.

⑮

MID-WALES | The Cambrian coast

751

downfall; and the **Tŷ Crwn Roundhouse**, on the hill behind (same times) which once acted as a lockup for drunken sailors.

Buses from Harlech and Dolgellau stop on Jubilee Road, near the **train station** and just a few yards from the **tourist office**, Station Road (Easter–Oct daily 10am–6pm; ⓣ01341/280787, ⓦwww.barmouth-wales.co.uk). **Accommodation** is plentiful, and best at the *Bae Abermaw Hotel*, Panorama Hill (ⓣ01341/280550, ⓦwww.baeabermaw.com; ❼), a former Victorian hotel that has gone all contemporary, or the seafront *Wavecrest Hotel*, 8 Marine Parade (ⓣ01341/280330, ⓦwww.lokalink.co.uk/wavecrest; ❸). Two miles north of Barmouth, *Llwyndû Farmhouse* in Llanaber (ⓣ01341/280144, ⓦwww.llwyndu-farmhouse.co.uk; ❺) is one of the finest farmhouse B&Bs in Wales.

The closest of a long string of **campsites** is *Hendre Mynach*, Llanaber Road (ⓣ01341/280262; closed Jan & Feb), a mile north of town and just off the beach. Basic **cafés** are plentiful, though for just a little more money you can get mammoth French sticks, good pizzas and decent veggie meals at *Isis* on The Quay. Nearby, in Church Street, *The Last Inn*, in a former cobbler's shop, serves good **pub** meals, while its outside tables catch the afternoon sun.

Dolgellau

A former county town, **DOLGELLAU** still maintains an air of unhurried importance, never more so than when all the area's farmers pile into town for market. It's a handsome place indeed, though its dark buildings, seemingly hewn from the one rock, can appear foreboding when gleaming in the frequent downpours. In fine weather, with the lofty crags of **Cadair Idris** framing the grey squares and streets, Dolgellau feels as Welsh and exotic as is possible.

Other than its proximity to Cadair Idris and the Mawddach Estuary, the town has little to offer beyond the **Quaker Interpretive Centre**, above the tourist office (Easter–Oct daily 9.30am–5.30pm; Nov–Easter Mon & Thurs–Sun

△ Dolgellau with Cadair Idris in background

Dolgellau is a good base for **walks**, whether fairly easy rambles, like the first two described here, or more strenuous mountain hiking. The OS Explorer 1:25,000 map #OL23, Cadair Idris & Llyn Tegid, is recommended, particularly for the ascent of Cadair Idris.

Torrent Walk

The attractive lowland **Torrent Walk** (2 miles; 1hr; 100ft ascent), follows the course of the Clywedog River as it carves its way through the bedrock. Stroll downstream past the cascades and through some gnarled old woodland that drips with antiquity. Bus #32/X32 can take you the 2.5 miles east along the A470, from where it's a couple of hundred yards or so down the B4416 (signposted to Brithdir) to a sign on the left-hand side marking the beginning of the walk.

Precipice Walk and New Precipice Walk

Though the path is narrow in places and there are some steep banks, the **Precipice Walk** (3–4 miles; 2hr; negligible ascent) can hardly be called precipitous. In fact it is very easy going, simple to follow, and has great views to the 1000-foot ramparts of Cadair Idris and along the Mawddach Estuary – best in late afternoon or early morning sun. The path makes a circuit around Foel Cynwch, starting three miles north of Dolgellau from a public car park on the road to Llanfachreth. For those without a vehicle, there's access from a path beside Cymer Abbey. Even less precipitous, the **New Precipice Walk** (4 miles; 2hr; 700ft ascent) combines luscious views of the estuary with a ramble along the old tramways of the Foel Ispri gold mine. Access is easiest from the signed path at the very western end of Llanelltyd village, two miles northwest of Dolgellau.

Cadair Idris ascents

More ambitious Victorians climbed **Cadair Idris** on the since-eroded Fox's Path, now widely ignored in favour of the straightforward, classic **Pony Path** (6–7 miles; 2500ft ascent; 4–5hr), starting three miles up Cadair Road in the car park at Tŷ Nant. As you begin by the sign near the telephone box, the view to the craggy flanks of the massif are tremendous, but they disappear as you climb steeply to the col, where a left turn leads to the summit shelter on **Penygadair** (2930ft). The most impressive ascent of Cadair Idris, however, is up the **Minffordd Path** (6 miles; 2900ft ascent; 5hr), which leads up to and then around the glacial lake of Cwm Cau before reaching the summit. The path starts just west of the *Minffordd Hotel* where the A487 meets the B4405.

9.30am–4.30pm). This details the lives of Quakers forced by persecution to seek a better life in Pennsylvania, where some towns still bear Welsh names: Bangor, Bryn Mawr and others.

Dolgellau has no train station but is well served by **buses**, all of which pull into the central Eldon Square, close to the **tourist office** (hours as Quaker Interpretive Centre; ℡01341/422888, ℮ticdolgellau@hotmail.com. Central **accommodation** is best found at the *Clifton House Hotel*, Smithfield Square (℡01341/422554, ⓦwww.clifton-house-hotel.co.uk; ❸/❹), a good-value hotel built in an ex–police station and jail – the basement cells are used as a restaurant. Outside town, the eighteenth-century *Tyddyn Mawr Farmhouse*, Islawrdref (℡01341/422331, ⓦwww.lokalink.co.uk/dolgellau/tyddynmawr; ❹), stands on the slopes of Cadair Idris at the foot of the Pony Path, while the superb seventeenth-century *George III Hotel*, Penmaenpool (℡01341/422525, ⓦwww.landmark-inns.co.uk; ❻), overlooks the Mawddach Estuary, two miles west of Dolgellau. There's a **hostel**, *Kings*

YHA, at Penmaenpool, four miles west of Dolgellau (☎01341/422392 or 0870/770 5900, ✉kings@yha.org.uk; open April–Aug), with six-bed rooms at £9.50 per person. The tent-only *Bryn-y-Gwyn* **campsite**, Cader Road (☎01341/422733), is less than a mile southeast of town. The best **restaurant** in town is the creative, affordable ✈ *Dylanwad Da*, 2 Smithfield St (☎01341/422870; closed Feb), while *Y Sospan* (☎01341/423174), on Queen Square behind the tourist office, is a dependable central bistro for good lunches and bookable dinners. The *Stag Inn* on Bridge Street is a straightforward town-centre pub with good beer and a garden.

Dolgellau's mid-July festival of folk and rock, **Sesiwn Fawr** (literally "Big Session"; booking hotline ☎08712/301314, ⓦwww.sesiwnfawr.co.uk), is undoubtedly the town's finest hour.

Tywyn and around

TYWYN is primarily of interest as a base for the Talyllyn and Dysynni valleys, although the town does have miles of sandy beach and the five-foot-high **Ynysmaengwyn**, or St Cadfan's Stone, within the Norman nave of the **Church of St Cadfan** (daily 9am–5pm, later in summer), which bears the earliest example of written Welsh, dating back to around 650 AD.

Tywyn's three main roads meet at the joint **train station** and main **bus stop**, a short walk from the **tourist office**, opposite the entrance to the leisure centre on High Street (Easter–Oct daily 9.30am–1pm & 2–5pm; ☎01654/710070, ✉tywyn.tic@gwynedd.co.uk), and, two hundred yards to the south, the Talyllyn narrow-gauge train station (Tywyn Wharf). The Talyllyn Valley is served by the #30 **bus**, running from Tywyn to Abergynolwyn, continuing to Minffordd (where you can catch #32 to Dolgellau or Machynlleth). The cheapest **accommodation** is the basic *Llys Maldwyn* B&B, opposite the tourist office on High Street (☎01654/711058; ❷), while the *Monfa*, 4 Pier Rd (☎01654/710858; ❸), between the seafront and the High Street, is a more comfortable alternative. For something smarter, there's the *Corbett Arms Hotel* on Corbett Square, just a little further up the main street from the parish church (☎01654/710264; ❻). The handiest **campsite**, ten minutes' walk from town on the Aberdyfi road, is the *Vaenol Camping Park* (☎01654/710232). The best **eating** in town is upstairs at the moderately priced *Proper Gander* on High Street (☎01654/711270).

The Talyllyn and Dysynni valleys

The **Talyllyn narrow-gauge railway** (April–Oct & late Dec daily plus some winter weekends; ☎01654/710472, ⓦwww.talyllyn.co.uk; £10 unlimited one-day travel) belches seven miles inland through the delightful wooded Talyllyn Valley to Nant Gwernol. From 1866 to 1946, the rail line was used to haul slate to Tywyn Wharf station. Just four years after its closure, enthusiasts restarted services, making this the world's first volunteer-run railway. At a leisurely 15mph, the round trip takes two hours, longer if you get off to take in some fine broadleaf-forest walks. The best of these starts at Dolgoch Falls station, where three well-marked trails (maximum 1hr; leaflet 30p) lead off to the lower, mid- and upper falls. At the end of the line, more woodland walks take you around the site of the old slate quarries. The new **Narrow-Gauge Museum** (open when trains are running; free) at Tywyn Wharf station contains displays about Tywyn's railway, other narrow-gauge lines in Britain, and much about Thomas the Tank Engine, loosely inspired by the Talyllyn line.

From Tywyn, the road runs parallel to the Talyllyn Railway, meeting it at **Dolgoch Falls**, a couple of miles short of the valleys' largest settlement,

Abergynolwyn, comprising a few dozen quarry-workers' houses, a shop and a pub, the excellent *Railway Inn*. The Dysynni Valley branches north-west here, but Talyllyn Valley continues northeast to **Tal-y-llyn Lake** (Llyn Mwyngil) and the fifteenth-century **St Mary's**, a fine example of a small Welsh parish church, unusual because of its chancel arch painted with an alternating grid of red and white roses, separated by grotesque bosses.

The **Dysynni Valley** has more to offer in the way of sights, though the lack of public transport makes it difficult to get to. A mile and a half northwest of Abergynolwyn, a side road cuts northeast to the hamlet of **Llanfihangel-y-Pennant** and the scant, but impressive, ruins of **Castell-y-Bere** (free access; CADW), a fortress built by Llywelyn the Great in 1221 to protect the mountain passes. One of the most massive of the Welsh castles, it was besieged twice before being consigned to seven centuries of obscurity and decay. There's still plenty to poke around, with large slabs of the main towers still standing, but it's primarily a great place just to sit gazing at Cadair Idris, or three miles seaward to **Craig yr Aderyn** (Birds' Rock), a 760ft-high cliff where thirty breeding pairs of cormorants have remained loyal to the spot as, over the centuries, the sea has receded. Also worth seeing is the fabulous three-dimensional patchwork map of the Dysynni Valley that can be found just up the road in the vestry of Llanfihangel-y-Pennant church.

Good places to **stay** include *Tan-y-Coed-Isaf* (☎01654/782639; ❸; March–Oct), a superb farmhouse B&B close to Dolgoch Falls, and the *Riverside Guest-house* in Abergynolwyn (☎01654/782235; ❷), which has a limited number of bargain **tent sites**.

Machynlleth and around

Eighteen miles northeast of Aberystwyth, the town that might have been the nation's capital, **MACHYNLLETH** (pronounced "ma-hun-thleth"), consists essentially of just two streets. The wide main street, **Heol Maengwyn**, is busiest on Wednesdays, when a lively market springs up out of nowhere; **Heol Penrallt** intersects at the fussy clocktower. Glyndŵr's partly fifteenth-century **Parliament House** (Easter–Sept Mon–Sat 10am–5pm; other times by arrangement on ☎01654/702827; free) sits halfway along Heol Maengwyn, a modest-looking black-and-white-fronted building, concealing a large interior. Displays chart the course of Glyndŵr's life, his military campaign, his downfall, and the 1404 parliament, when he controlled almost all of what we now know as Wales. The sorriest tales are from 1405 onwards when tactical errors and the sheer brute might of the English forced a swift retreat and an ignominious end to the greatest Welsh uprising.

Opposite the Parliament House, a path leads into the landscaped grounds of **Plas Machynlleth**, the elegant seventeenth-century mansion of the Marquess of Londonderry. Its solitude is entirely intentional: in the 1840s the Marquess bought up all the surrounding buildings and had them demolished, and rerouted the main road away from his grounds. For the last decade, the Plas has been home to the **Celtica** museum, a resource for all matters Celtic, though this is scheduled to close in 2006 and plans for the building's future are currently unclear.

On the other side of the central clocktower, housed in the beautifully serene old chapel Y Tabernacl on Heol Pen'rallt, is the **Museum of Modern Art Wales** (MOMA Cymru: Mon–Sat 10am–4pm; free; ☎01654/703355, ⓦwww .momawales.org.uk), which hosts an ongoing programme of temporary exhibitions. It is also the place to go for films, theatre, comedy, concerts and the August

Owain Glyndŵr

No name is so frequently invoked in Wales as that of **Owain Glyndŵr**, a potent figurehead of Welsh nationalism since he rose up against the occupying English in the early fifteenth century. Little is known about the real Glyndŵr, although he is described in Shakespeare's *Henry IV, Part I* as "not in the roll of common men". There's little doubt that the charismatic Owain fulfilled many of the mystical medieval prophecies about the rising up of the red dragon. Born in the late fourteenth century to an aristocratic family, he had a conventional upbringing, part of it studying English in London, where he became a loyal and distinguished soldier of the English king. He returned to Wales to take up his claim as Prince of Wales, being directly descended from the princes of Powys and Cyfeiliog, but became the focus of a rebellion born of discontent simmering since Edward I's stringent policies of subordinating Wales.

Goaded by a parochial land dispute in North Wales in which the courts failed to back him, Glyndŵr garnered four thousand supporters and declared anew that he was Prince of Wales. He attacked Ruthin, and then Denbigh, Rhuddlan, Flint, Hawarden and Oswestry, before encountering English resistance at Welshpool, but whole swathes of North Wales were his for the taking. The English king, Henry IV, dispatched troops and rapidly drew up a range of severely punitive laws against the Welsh, even outlawing Welsh-language bards and singers. Battles continued to rage until, by the end of 1403, Glyndŵr controlled most of Wales.

In 1404, Glyndŵr assembled a parliament at Machynlleth, drawing up mutual recognition treaties with France and Spain, and being crowned king of a free Wales. A second parliament in Harlech took place a year later, with Glyndŵr making plans to carve up England and Wales into three as part of an alliance against the English king. The English army, however, attacked the Welsh uprising with increased vigour, and the Tripartite Indenture was never realized. From then on, Glyndŵr lost battles, ground and castles, and was forced into hiding, dying, it is thought, in Herefordshire. The draconian anti-Welsh laws stayed in place until the accession to the English throne of Henry VII, who had Welsh origins, in 1485. Wales became subsumed into English custom and law, and Glyndŵr uprising became an increasingly powerful symbol of frustrated Welsh independence. Even in the 1980s, a shadowy organization that razed several English holiday-homes took the name Meibion Glyndŵr – the Sons of Glyndŵr.

Gŵyl Machynlleth festival, which combines classical and some folk music with theatre and debate.

Practicalities

The **train station** is a five-minute walk up Heol Pen'rallt from the town's central clocktower, which is the main **bus stop**, though many also call at the train station. The **tourist office** (daily: Easter–Sept 9.30am–6pm; Oct–Easter 10am–5pm; ☏01654/702401, ✉mactic@powys.gov.uk) is next to the Glyndŵr Parliament House on Heol Maengwyn. **Bike rental** is available from The Holey Trail at 31 Heol Maengwyn (☏01654/700411).

B&B **accommodation** includes the *Maenllwyd*, on Newtown Road, the eastern extension of Heol Maengwyn (☏01654/702928; ❸), and *Gwelfryn*, at 6 Greenfields, Bank Street (☏01654/702532; ❷). Hotels include the grand *Wynnstay Arms* on Heol Maengwyn (☏01654/702941; ❻), though if money's no object, the Michelin-starred luxury of *Ynyshir Hall*, near the Ynys-hir Nature Reserve at Eglwysfach, six miles southwest on the A487 (☏01654/781209, ⓦwww.ynyshir-hall.co.uk; ❾/❾) is wonderful. There's a shiny new *Reditreks* **bunkhouse** off Heol Powys in central Machynlleth (☏01654/702184, ⓦwww.reditreks.com), with beds for £15 and basic **camping**; otherwise, the nearest site is three miles north near the Centre for Alternative Technology (CAT) at *Llwyngwern Farm* (℡01654/702492). Six miles north, in the slate village of Corris, the holistically minded *Canolfan Corris* **hostel** occupies the former village school (℡01654/761686, ⓦwww.canolfancorris.com; dorms £12.50, £15 with breakfast; mid-Feb to Oct & weekends Nov–Feb), easily reached by bus.

There are plenty of **cafés**, **restaurants** and **pubs** in town, including a popular veggie wholefood café, the CAT-run *Quarry Café*, near the clocktower on Heol Maengwyn. Lunch and dinner are great at the *Wynnstay Arms*, which also has a superb pizzeria in its courtyard bar. The *Skinners Arms* on Heol Pen'rallt is cheaper but cosy and good for food or beer. Liveliest pub is either the *Skinners* or the *White Lion*, by the clocktower.

Centre for Alternative Technology

Since its foundation in the middle of the oil crisis of 1974, the **Centre for Alternative Technology**, or Canolfan y Dechnoleg Amgen (daily: Easter–Sept 10am–5.30pm; Oct–Easter 10am–dusk; £8 summer, £6 winter, £1 discount to those arriving by bike or public transport; ℡01654/705950, ⓦwww.cat.org.uk) – three miles north of Machynlleth off the A487 – has become one of the biggest attractions in Wales. Over almost three decades, seven acres of a once-derelict slate quarry have been turned into an almost entirely sustainable community, generating eighty percent of its own power from wind, sun and water. But this is no back-to-the-land hippie commune. Right from the start, the idea was to embrace technology – much of the on-site equipment was developed and built here, reflecting the centre's achievements in this field – and, most importantly, to promote its application in urban situations.

CAT's earnest education is leavened with flashes of pizazz, particularly in the water-balanced **cliff railway** (Easter–Oct only), which whisks the visitor 200ft up to the main site from the car park. It is also a beautiful site, sensitively land-scaped using local slate and wood, and you can easily spend half a day sauntering around. There's plenty for kids to do, including a children's theatre (mainly mid-July to Aug), the wholefood restaurant turns out delicious food, and the excellent bookshop stocks a wide range of alternative literature along with crafts and intriguing toys.

Primarily, though, this is a working community which exists more to educate by example than entertain, partly facilitated by the new environmental information centre housed in a rammed-earth building. Residential courses are offered, the most popular being a guide to building your own energy-efficient home, and for £5.50 per night to cover bed and board, you can get a week-long taster of life and work at the centre between March and September – see the website for details.

Aberystwyth and around

The liveliest seaside resort in Wales, **ABERYSTWYTH** is an essential stop. Being rooted in all aspects of Welsh culture, it is possibly the most enjoyable and relaxed place to gain an insight into the national psyche. As the capital of sparsely populated Mid-Wales, and with one of the most prestigious colleges of the University of Wales in the town, there are plenty of cultural and entertainment diversions, as well as an array of Victorian and Edwardian seaside trappings. In 1907, the National Library was inaugurated here, and Cymdeithas yr Iaith (the Welsh Language Society) was founded here in 1963. Aberystwyth's politics

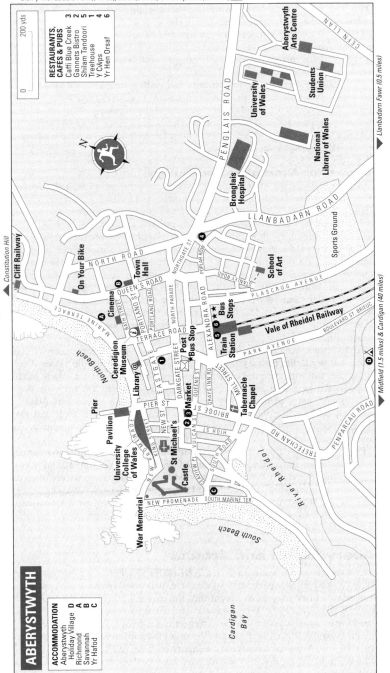

Glan-y-Mor Leisure Park (3 miles), Borth (5 miles) & Machynlleth (20 miles) ▲

ABERYSTWYTH

ACCOMMODATION
Aberystwyth Holiday Village **D**
Richmond **A**
Savannah **B**
Yr Hafod **C**

RESTAURANTS, CAFES & PUBS
Caffi Blue Creek **3**
Gannets Bistro **2**
Shilam Tandoori **5**
Treehouse **1**
Y Cwps **4**
Yr Hen Orsaf **6**

0 — 200 yds

Constitution Hill ▲

Llanbadarn Fawr (0.5 miles) ▶

Midfield (1.5 miles) & Cardigan (40 miles) ▶

Cardigan Bay

© Crown copyright

are firmly radical Welsh, and in a country that still struggles with its inherent conservatism, the town is a blast of fresh air.

The Town

With two long, gentle bays curving around between rocky heads, Aberystwyth's position is hard to beat. **Constitution Hill** (430ft), at the north end of the long Promenade, rises sharply away from the rocky beach. It's a favourite jaunt, crowned with a tatty jumble of amenities – café, picnic area, millennium beacon, telescopes and an octagonal **camera obscura** (Easter–Oct daily 10am–5.30pm; free) – reached on foot or by the clanking 1896 **cliff railway** (daily: July & Aug 10am–6pm, mid-March to June, Sept & Oct 10am–5pm; £2.50 return) from the grand terminus building at the top of Queen's Road, behind the Promenade. South along the Promenade – officially called Marine Terrace – and off to the left on Terrace Road, the **Ceredigion Museum** (Mon–Sat 10am–5pm; free) houses cosy reconstructed cottages, a dairy and a nineteenth-century pharmacy in the atmospherically ornate Edwardian music hall, the Coliseum.

Marine Terrace continues past the spindly **pier** to the dazzling **Old College**, all turrets, friezes and mosaics. Originally a John Nash–designed villa, it was later converted to a hotel to soak up the anticipated masses arriving on the new railway line. When the venture failed, the building was sold to the fledgling university. The Promenade cuts around the front of the building to the ruins of Edward I's thirteenth-century **castle** (free access), a fine place for a picnic, but notable more for its breezy position than for the buildings themselves.

To the east of town, Penglais Road climbs the hill northwards towards the **university**'s main campus and the **National Library of Wales** (Mon–Sat 9.30am–5pm; free; Ⓦ www.llgc.org.uk), which has excellent temporary exhibitions and the **World of the Book**, a well-rounded introduction to the history of the written word and printing in Wales, shown in an absorbing range of old texts, maps, photos, and the Morgan's 1588 Welsh Bible. Above the National Library is the university campus, which includes the superb **Aberystwyth Arts Centre**, always a sure bet for a couple of decent exhibitions.

Practicalities

Aberystwyth's main line and Vale of Rheidol **train stations** are adjacent on Alexandra Road, a ten-minute walk from the seafront on the southern side of the town centre. Local **buses** stop outside the station, with long-distance ones using the depot immediately next door, by the entrance to the park. The busy **tourist office** (July & Aug daily 10am–6pm; Sept–June Mon–Sat 10am–5pm; ☎01970/612125, Ⓔ aberystwythtic@ceredigion.gov.uk) is a ten-minute stroll from the station, straight down Terrace Road towards the seafront. On Your Bike, in the Old Police Yard, Queens Road (☎01970/626996), does **bike rental**.

There are hundreds of places to **stay**, mostly in the streets around the station and along South Marine Terrace, where you'll find *Yr Hafod*, at no. 1 (☎01970/617579, Ⓔ johnyrhafod@aol.com; ❸). The well-priced *Savannah* guest house, 27 Queens Rd ☎01970/615131, Ⓦ www.savannahguesthouse .co uk; ❸), is another good choice, as is the *Richmond Hotel* at 44–45 Marine Terrace (☎01970/612201, Ⓦ www.richmondhotel.uk.com; ❻) Outside termtime, B&B is also available on the Penglais and seafront sites of the University College of Wales (☎01970/621960, Ⓦ www.aber.ac.uk/visitors; £17.50 a night). The nearest place to pitch a **tent** is the *Aberystwyth Holiday Village* (①01970/624211), off the main Penparcau Road to the south of town, a twenty-minute walk from the station.

Aberystwyth's cultural and gastronomic life is an ebullient, year-round affair, thriving on students in term-time and visitors in the summer. Just behind the market, on St James Square, *Gannets Bistro*, at 7 (℡01970/617164; Wed–Sat), creates imaginative, inexpensive dishes from local farm and sea produce, while *Caffi Blue Creek*, is a relaxed small daytime café with comfy sofas and cheerful vibe. 🍴 *Shilam Tandoori*, Station Building, Alexandra Road (℡01970/615015), is a superb modern Indian restaurant with unusual specialities and good vegetarian choices, or there's the organic, mostly vegetarian *Treehouse* at 14 Baker St (℡01970/615791; closed Sun). For decent and very reasonable **pub food**, you're best off at *Yr Hen Orsaf*, which, as its name implies, is in the old station buildings on Alexandra Road – you can even have a pint or a meal under a stunning glass canopy on the platform. For no-nonsense **drinking**, Aberystwyth has scores of options: try the *Castle Hotel* on South Road, a harbourside pub that's built in the style of an ornate Victorian gin palace, and which has regular gigs. *Y Cŵps* (Coopers Arms), Llanbadarn Road, is fun and friendly, with regular Welsh folk and jazz nights. For a slice of Edwardian gentility, take afternoon tea in any of the seafront hotels along the Promenade. The Aberystwyth Arts Centre, at the university's Penglais site (℡01970/623232, ⊛www.aber .ac.uk/artscentre), has art-house **cinema** and touring **theatre**, while the Drwm, at the National Library, Penglais (℡01970/632548), is a funky new centre for film, lectures and concerts.

The Vale of Rheidol

Inland from Aberystwyth, the River Rheidol winds its way up to a secluded, wooded valley, where occasional old industrial workings have moulded themselves into the contours, rising up past waterfalls and hamlets to Devil's Bridge. It's a glorious route, and by far the best way to see it is on board one of the trains of the **Vale of Rheidol railway** (2–4 services daily April–Oct; £12.50 return; ℡01970/625819, ⊛www.rheidolrailway.co.uk;), a narrow-gauge steam train that wheezes its way along sheer rock faces from the terminus in Aberystwyth to Devil's Bridge. It was built in 1902, ostensibly for the valley's lead mines but with a canny eye on its tourist potential as well, and has run ever since. Partway along, a punishing path on the north side of the river from the Rhiwfron halt scrambles up over the mines for a mile to the sombre little village of Ystumtuen, a former lead-mining community. From here it's a couple of miles' walk to Devil's Bridge.

Folk legend, perfect Picturesque scenery and travellers' lore combine at **DEVIL'S BRIDGE** (Pontarfynach), twelve miles east of Aberystwyth, a tiny settlement built solely for the growing visitor trade of the last few hundred years. Be warned, however, that Devil's Bridge is a seriously popular day-excursion: in order to escape some of the inevitable congestion, it's wisest to come here at the beginning or end of the day, or out of season.

The main attraction here is the **bridge** itself, which is actually three stacked bridges spanning the chasm of the churning River Mynach, yards upstream from its confluence with the Rheidol. The road bridge in front of the Alpine *Hafod Arms* **hotel** (℡01970/890232, ⊛www.hafodarms.co.uk; ❹/❻) is the most modern of the three, dating from 1901. Immediately below it, wedged between the rock faces, are the stone bridge from 1753 and, at the bottom, the original bridge, dating from the eleventh century and reputedly built by the monks of Strata Florida Abbey (see p.765). For a remarkable view of the bridges, you have to enter the turnstile (£1) downstream of the bridge and head down slippery steps to the deep cleft of the **Punch Bowl**, where the water pounds and hurtles through the gap crowned by the bridges. More dramatic still, the gate on the other side (Easter–Oct daily 9.30am–5.30pm; £2.50; at other times access through turnstiles; £2) leads west to a path that tumbles down into the valley below the bridges, descending ultimately to the crashing **Mynach Falls**. The scenery here is magnificent: sharp, wooded slopes rise away from the frothing river and distant mountain peaks surface on the horizon. Platforms overlook the series of falls, from where a set of steep steps takes you further down to a footbridge dramatically spanning the river at the bottom of the falls.

There's a **campsite** – *Woodlands Caravan Park* (☎01970/890233) – by the petrol station, just beyond the bridges.

Aberaeron

ABERAERON, sixteen miles along the coast from Aberystwyth, comes as something of a surprise. It's a sea town that's turned away from the ocean, its colourful Georgian houses preferring to look in on themselves and the town's internal harbour. Aberaeron's unusual look comes from its odd pedigree, being built in one fell swoop during the early nineteenth century by the Reverend Alban Gwynne. He spent his way through his wife's inheritance by dredging the Aeron Estuary and constructing a formally planned town around it as a new port for Mid-Wales.

Georgian planning is most evident around the central **Alban Square**, with graceful terraces of quoin-edged buildings and the odd pedimented porch, all writ small in keeping with the Ceredigion coast. From there, the grid of narrow streets stretches away to the sea at **Quay Parade**, the neat line of ordered, colourful houses on the seafront.

Sadly, despite its architectural attractiveness, Aberaeron is almost unique amongst the Ceredigion resorts for its unappealing **beach**. Consequently, the most agreeable activity in Aberaeron is just to amble around the streets and waterfront and graze in its cafés and pubs. Aberaeron's one essential sight lies three miles east along the A482 at **Llanerchaeron** (house and gardens late March to Oct Wed–Sun 11am–5pm; £5.20; parkland all year dawn–dusk; free; NT), make for a good excursion. Once an integrated smallholding typical of this region, the estate is currently undergoing restoration and boasts exquisite kitchen gardens and a pristine, Nash-designed main house.

Aberaeron's **tourist office** is on Quay Parade, the seafront road (July & Aug daily 10am–6pm; Easter–June & Sept daily 10am–5pm; Oct–Easter Mon–Sat 10am–5pm; ☎01545/570602, @aberaeron@ceredigion.gov.uk). Overlooking the harbour on Cadwgan Place are the *Coedmor*, at no. 2 (☎01545/571615, ⓦwww.coedmorbandb.co.uk; ❸), and, better still, the *Arosfa*, at no. 8 (☎01545/570120, ⓦwww.arosfaguesthouse.co.uk; ❹). The best place in town, though, is the central *Harbourmaster Hotel*, Pen Cei (☎01545/570755, ⓦwww.harbour-master.com; ❻), with ultra-modern rooms, great breakfasts, endless creature comforts and a relaxed, informal atmosphere. The nearest local **campsite** is the *Aeron Coast*, on the A487 just north of town (☎01545/570349). For **food**, the best place to eat is the relaxed café/bistro at the *Harbourmaster Hotel* on Pen Cei. Daytime alternatives include the *Hive on the Quay*, Cadwgan Place (April to mid-Sept), which serves fine local seafood in its conservatory, and has scrumptious **honey ice cream** to eat in or take away.

New Quay and around

Along with Laugharne in Carmarthenshire (see p.713), **NEW QUAY** (Cei Newydd), seven miles from Aberaeron, lays claim to being the original Llareggub in Dylan Thomas's *Under Milk Wood*. Certainly, it has the little tumbling streets, prim Victorian terraces, cobbled stone harbour and air of dreamy isolation that Thomas evoked in his play but, in the height of summer, the quiet isolation can be hard to find. Although there is a singular lack of excitement in New Quay, it's a truly pleasant base for good beaches, walking, surfing, eating and drinking.

The pretty **harbour** and small, curving beach are backed by a higgledy-piggledy line of multicoloured shops and houses. The beachfront streets comprise the **lower town** – the more traditionally "seaside" part of New Quay, full of cafés, pubs and beach shops. Tucked away down the slipway above the beach is the interesting **Marine Wildlife Centre** (April–Oct daily 10am–5pm; donation requested), with some good displays on the dolphins, seals and sea birds of Cardigan Bay. Sharply inclined streets lead to the residential **upper town**, with some delightful views over the sweeping shoreline below. The northern beach soon gives way to a rocky headland, **New Quay Head**, where an invigorating path steers along the top of aptly named **Bird Rock**.

Buses stop on Park Street, from where it's a walk down any of the steep streets to the seafront, where you'll find the **tourist office**, centrally located at the junction of Church Street and Wellington Place (April–Sept daily 10am–6pm; ☎01545/560865, ✉newquay@ceredigion.gov.uk). **Accommodation** includes the *Hungry Trout* on Glanmor Terrace (☎01545/560680; ❸), with two pleasant rooms, and the nicely refurbished *Hotel Penwig* (☎01545/560910; ❸). The nearest **campsite** is the *Neuadd Neuadd* (☎01545/560709), fifteen minutes' walk away, behind the *Penrhiwllan Inn*, at the top of the hill on the way to Synod Inn. New Quay contains innumerable cheap **cafés**, amongst which the *Mariner's Café*, by the harbour wall, is a sure bet. Most of the **pubs** serve food, the best being the *Seahorse* on Margaret Street.

Tresaith and Llangranog

The most popular stopping-off point on the stretch of coast south of New Quay is Aberporth, an elderly resort built around two less than appealing bays, easily shown up by the neighbouring hamlet of **TRESAITH**, a mile to the east, which staggers down the tiny valley to a delightful beach. There are **dinghy races** from the beach every Sunday in summer. Around the rocks to the right of the beach, the River Saith plummets over the mossy black rocks in a waterfall. For **accommodation**, there's the superb Georgian *Glandr* (☎01239/811442, ⓦwww.glandwrtresaith.co.uk; ❺) at the top of the village on the road to Aberporth, and a little further along, a wonderful tent-only cliff-top **campsite** at the far end of the *Llety Caravan Park* (☎01239/810354), from where a pretty footpath descends straight to the beach.

Three miles north of the A487, **LLANGRANOG** is the most attractive village on the Ceredigion coast, wedged in between bracken and gorse-beaten hills, the main streets winding to the tiny seafront. The beach can become horribly congested in midsummer, when it's better to follow the cliff path to **Cilborth Beach**, and on to the glorious NT-owned headland, **Ynys Lochtyn**. In Llangranog, you can **stay** on the seafront either at the excellent *Ship Inn* (☎01239/654423; ❹) or the earthier *Pentre Arms* (☎01239/654345; ❷); both do good **food**. Between Penbryn and Llangranog is the *Maesglas* caravan park (☎01239/654268), which takes **tents**.

Cardigan

An ancient borough and fomer port at the lowest bridging point of the Teifi Estuary, **CARDIGAN** (Aberteifi) was founded by the Norman lord

Roger de Montgomery around a castle in 1093. From the castle mound by the bridge, Bridge Street sweeps through High Street to the turreted oddity of the **Guildhall**. Through the Guildhall courtyard is the town's superb **covered market**, a typically eclectic mix of fresh food, local crafts and secondhand stalls. Across the bridge from the town centre, the **Cardigan Heritage Centre** (Canolfan Hanes Aberteifi; March–Oct daily 10am–5pm; £2), housed in an old granary, tells the story of the port's rise and fall.

The helpful **tourist office** (Easter–Aug daily 10am–6pm; Sept–Easter Mon–Sat 10am–5pm; ☎01239/613230, ⓔcardigantic@ceredigion.gov.uk) is in the foyer of Theatr Mwldan, Bath House Road. **Accommodation** includes the old-fashioned *Black Lion* pub on High Street (Llew Du; ☎01239/612532; ❸), which also does food, or the basic but decent *Highbury House*, the old county gaol, on Pendre (☎01239/613403; ❶). A mile and a half east of town, the sixteenth-century *Rosehill Farm* in Llangoedmor (☎01239/612019, ⓦwww.rosehillfarm.co.uk; closed Nov–March; ❸) offers a gorgeous riverside setting and excellent evening meals. There's a YHA **hostel** four miles away at Poppit Sands, at the end of the Pembrokeshire Coast Path (☎0870/770 5996, ⓔpoppit@yha.org.uk; closed Nov–Feb; dorms £10.50); buses connect in July and August, but otherwise terminate half a mile short. For **food**, try the inexpensive Theatr Mwldan café or *Food For Thought*, 13 Pendre, which offers a good range of hearty snacks and coffees.

The Teifi Valley

The Teifi is one of Wales's most eulogized rivers, for its rich spawn of fresh fish, its meandering rural charm and the coracles that were a regular feature from pre-Roman times. On the way to its estuary at Cardigan, it flows through some gloriously green and undulating countryside, winding its way over the falls at **Cenarth** and passing the massive ramparts of **Cilgerran Castle**. Further upstream, the river also takes in the proudly Welsh university town of **Lampeter**, and the river's infancy can be seen near the ruins of **Strata Florida Abbey**, beyond which the river emerges from the dark and remote **Teifi Pools**.

Cilgerran Castle

Just a couple of miles up the Teifi River from Cardigan, the attractive village of **CILGERRAN** clusters around its wide main street. Behind is the bulk of the **castle** (daily: April–Oct 9.30am–6.30pm; Nov–March 9.30am–dusk; £2.50; CADW), founded in 1100 at a commanding vantage point on a high wooded bluff above the river, then still navigable for sea-going ships. This is the legendary site of the 1109 abduction of Nest (the "Welsh Helen of Troy") by a love-struck Prince Owain of Powys. Her husband, Gerald of Pembroke, escaped by slithering down a toilet waste chute through the castle walls. The two massive drum towers still dominate the castle, and the outer walls, some four feet thicker than those facing the inner courtyard, are traced by vertiginously high walkways. The outer ward, over which a modern path now runs from the entrance, is a good example of the keepless castle that evolved throughout the thirteenth century.

A footpath runs down from the castle to the river's edge; an exhibition at the quay about local industries – coracles included – also covers the story of America-bound emigrants leaving from Cardigan. Guided two-hour **canoe trips** leave from the quay in summer.

Cenarth and around

A tourist magnet since it was swooped on by nineteenth-century Romantics and artists, **CENARTH**, five miles east of Cilgerran, is a pleasant spot but hardly merits the mass interest that it receives. The village's main asset, its **waterfalls**, are close to the main road, connected by a path from opposite the *White Hart* pub. This runs past the **National Coracle Centre** (Easter–Oct daily except Sat 10am–5.30pm; other times by arrangement ☎01239/710980; £3), a small museum with displays of these curiously designed boats from all over the world, before continuing to a restored seventeenth-century flour mill by the falls' edge.

The area's prolific past as a weaving centre is best seen at the National Museum's customarily excellent **Museum of the Welsh Woollen Industry** (daily: April–Sept 10am–5pm; Oct–March Tues–Sat 10am–5pm; free), in the village of **Dre-Fach Felindre**, eight miles southeast of Cenarth, which once had over forty working mills.

Lampeter

Twenty miles east of Cenarth, **LAMPETER** (Llanbedr Pont Steffan or, popularly, Llambed) is best known as a remote outpost of the British university system. St David's University College was Wales's first university college, founded in 1822 by the bishop of St David's to aid Welsh theological students who couldn't afford to travel to England for their education; it only became part of the University of Wales in the 1970s. With a healthy student population and large numbers of resident hippies, the small town is well geared up for young people and visitors.

There's not a great deal to see, and what you are able to visit is fairly low-key. A decent heritage trail, with plaques marking out historical places of interest, is accompanied by a leaflet that you can pick up at the library (see below). **Harford Square** forms the hub of the town. The main buildings of the **University College** lie off College Street, and include a quadrangle modelled on an Oxbridge college and the motte of Lampeter's long-vanished castle – a strange sight amidst such order. The High Street is the most architecturally distinguished part of town, its eighteenth-century coaching inn, the *Black Lion*, dominating the streetscape; you can see its old stables and coach house through an archway.

Leaflets in the town library – through the archway of the old town hall and past the supermarket – and the noticeboards in the Mulberry Bush health-food shop at 2 Bridge St are the closest Lampeter get to a tourist office. *Haulfan*, 6 Station Terrace, behind University College (☎01570/422718, ⓦwww .haulfanguesthouse.co.uk; ❷), is the best **B&B**, or you could try the *Black Lion*, High Street (☎01570/422490; ❹). Just off the B4343 is one of the area's best farmhouse B&Bs, at *Pentre Farm*, near Llanfair Clydogau, five miles from Lampeter (☎01570/493313; ❸). The nearest **campsite** is five miles northeast, at Moorlands, near Llangybi (☎01570/493543).

Lampter's restaurant scene can be fairly lacklustre, though there's decent daytime **eating** at the *Sosban Fach*, 1 Bridge St, opposite the classy chippy *Lloyds*, which stays open until 9pm. In the evenings, *Shapla* on College Street does the best curries for miles around. Stick your head into *Conti's Café*, on Harford Square – the food is cheap and not that great, but the decor is wonderfully time-warped, plastered with ageing accolades for the café's homemade ice cream. Just south of town, where the A485 joins the A482, the *Cwmann Tavern* is the best bet for catching the beery local **music** scene.

Strata Florida Abbey and the Teifi Pools

Twenty miles northeast of Lampeter, the mighty **Strata Florida Abbey** (May–Sept daily 10am–5pm; £2; Oct–April unrestricted entry) dominates the bucolic Ystrad Fflur, the Valley of the Flowers. This Cistercian abbey was founded in 1164, swiftly growing into a centre for milling, farming and weaving, and becoming an important political centre for Wales. In 1238, Llywelyn the Great, whose conquering exploits throughout the rest of Wales had brought him to the peak of the Welsh feudal pyramid, summoned the lesser Welsh princes here. He was near death, and worried that his work of unifying Wales under one ruler would disintegrate, so he commanded the assembled princes to pay homage not just to him but also to his son, Dafydd, so sealing the succession. The church here was vast – larger than the cathedral at St David's – and, although very little survived Henry VIII's dissolution of the monasteries, the huge Norman west doorway gives some idea of its dimensions. Fragments of one-time side chapels include beautifully tiled medieval floors, and there's also a serene cemetery, but it's really the abbey's position that impresses most, in glorious rural solitude amongst wide-open skies and fringed with a scoop of sheep-flecked hills. A yew tree in the neighbouring graveyard shades the spot where Dafydd ap Gwilym, fourteenth-century bard and contemporary of Chaucer, is said to be buried.

The narrow lane running due east from Strata Florida leads to Tyncwm, a farm with bridleways to the drenched grass and craggy outcrops around the **Teifi Pools**, a series of sombre lakes where the Teifi River rises, set in stern, but rewarding, walking country.

Travel details

Buses

For information on all local and national bus services, contact Traveline ☏0870/608 2608, Ⓦ www.traveline.org.uk.

Aberaeron to: Aberystwyth (every 30min; 40min); Cardigan (8 daily; 50min); Carmarthen (10 daily; 1hr 40min); Lampeter (10 daily; 40min); New Quay (hourly; 20min).

Abergavenny to: Brecon (7 daily Mon–Sat; 1hr); Cardiff (hourly; 1hr 20min); Clydach (hourly; 30min); Crickhowell (7 daily Mon–Sat; 20min); Llanfihangel Crucorney (6 daily; 15min); Merthyr Tydfil (hourly; 1hr 30min); Monmouth (6 daily; 40min); Newport (hourly; 1hr 10min); Pontypool (hourly; 25min); Raglan (6 daily; 20min).

Aberystwyth to: Aberaeron (every 30min; 40min); Borth (hourly; 20min); Caernarfon (4 daily; 3hr); Cardigan (9 daily; 1hr 30min–2hr); Carmarthen (mostly hourly; 2hr 20min); Devil's Bridge (2 daily Mon–Sat; 50min); Lampeter (Mon–Sat hourly; 1hr 15min); Machynlleth (hourly; 45min); New Quay (hourly; 1hr); Ponterwyd (7 daily Mon–Sat; 30min); Pontrhydfendigaid (3 daily Mon–Sat; 45min); Tregaron (7 daily; 45min); Ynyslas (hourly; 30min).

Barmouth to: Bala (mostly hourly; 1hr); Blaenau Ffestiniog (5 daily; 1hr); Dolgellau (hourly; 30min); Harlech (hourly; 30min); Llangollen (mostly hourly; 2hr); Wrexham (mostly hourly; 2hr 30min).

Brecon to: Abergavenny (Mon–Sat 7 daily, none on Sun; 1hr); Cardiff (1 daily; 1hr 20min); Craig-y-nos/Dan-yr-ogof (2 daily; 30min); Crickhowell (Mon–Sat 7 daily, none on Sun; 25min); Hay-on-Wye (6 daily; 50min); Libanus (9 daily; 10min); Llandrindod Wells (Mon–Sat 2 daily, none on Sun; 1hr); Merthyr Tydfil (10 daily; 40min); Swansea (2–3 daily; 1hr 30min).

Cardigan to: Aberaeron (8 daily; 50min); Aberporth (hourly; 25min); Aberystwyth (9 daily; 1hr 30min–2hr); Carmarthen (hourly; 1hr 30min); Cenarth (10 daily; 25min); Cilgerran (8 daily; 10min); Drefach Felindre (hourly; 30min); Newcastle Emlyn (10 daily; 25min); New Quay (hourly; 1hr).

Dolgellau to: Bala (10 daily; 35min); Barmouth (hourly; 30min); Llangollen (mostly hourly; 1hr 30min); Machynlleth (mostly hourly; 30min); Porthmadog (6 daily, 40min); Tywyn (8 daily; 55min).

Harlech to: Barmouth (hourly; 30min); Blaenau Ffestiniog (4 daily; 35min); Dyffryn Ardudwy (mostly hourly; 15min).

Knighton to: Ludlow (3 daily; 1hr 10min); Presteigne (7 daily; 30min).

Lampeter to: Aberaeron (10 daily; 40min); Aberystwyth (Mon–Sat hourly; 1hr 15min); Carmarthen (mostly hourly; 1hr); Llanddewi Brefi (6 daily Mon–Sat; 25min); Tregaron (Mon–Sat 8 daily; 20–35min).

Llandrindod Wells to: Abbeycwmhir (1 postbus daily Mon–Fri; 2hr); Aberystwyth (1 daily; 2hr); Brecon (3 daily Mon–Sat; 1hr); Builth Wells (hourly; 20min); Disserth (2 daily; 15min); Elan Village (1 postbus daily Mon–Fri; 40min); Hay-on-Wye (1 daily Wed & Sat; 1hr); New Radnor (2 daily Mon–Sat; 30min); Newtown (3 daily; 1hr 10min); Rhayader (3 daily; 30min).

Llanfyllin to: Llanwddyn for Lake Vyrnwy (Mon–Sat 3–4 daily; 30min); Welshpool (Mon–Sat 1 daily; 40min).

Llanidloes to: Aberystwyth (5 daily; 1hr); Dylife (1 postbus daily; 30min); Newtown (9 daily; 30min); Ponterwyd (1 daily; 40min); Shrewsbury (4 daily; 2hr); Welshpool (5 daily; 1hr 10min).

Llanwrtyd Wells to: Abergwesyn (1 daily postbus; 20min); Builth Wells (3 daily; 45min).

Machynlleth to: Aberdyfi (8 daily; 20min); Aberystwyth (hourly; 45min); Corris (hourly; 15min); Dolgellau (mostly hourly; 30min); Tywyn (8 daily; 35min).

New Quay to: Aberaeron (hourly; 20min); Aberporth (hourly; 40min); Aberystwyth (hourly; 1hr); Cardigan (hourly; 1hr).

Tywyn to: Aberdyfi (8 daily; 10min); Abergynolwyn (3 daily; 18min); Corris (3 daily; 30min); Dolgellau (8 daily; 55min); Fairbourne (8 daily; 35min); Machynlleth (8 daily; 35min).

Welshpool to: Berriew (6 daily Mon–Sat; 20min); Llanidloes (5 daily; 1hr 10min); Llanfyllin (1 daily Mon–Sat; 40min); Llanymynech (5 daily; 30min);

Montgomery (4 daily Mon–Sat; 25min); Newtown (7 daily; 40min); Oswestry (5 daily; 1hr); Shrewsbury (7 daily; 50min).

Trains

For information on all local and national rail services, contact National Rail Enquiries ⓣ 08457/484950, ⓦ www.nationalrail.co.uk.

Abergavenny to: Cardiff (hourly; 40min); Hereford (hourly; 20min); Newport (hourly; 30min); Pontypool (hourly; 10min).

Aberystwyth to: Birmingham (8 daily; 3hr); Machynlleth (9 daily; 30min); Shrewsbury (8 daily; 2hr); Welshpool (8 daily; 1hr 30min).

Barmouth to: Aberdyfi (10 daily; 30min); Harlech (7 daily; 25min); Machynlleth (8–10 daily; 50min); Porthmadog (7 daily; 45min).

Harlech to: Barmouth (6 daily; 30min); Birmingham (5 daily; 4hr 15min); Machynlleth (6 daily; 1hr 20min); Porthmadog (7 daily; 20min).

Knighton to: Llandrindod Wells (4 daily; 40min); Llanwrtyd Wells (4 daily; 1hr 10min); Shrewsbury (4 daily; 1hr); Swansea (4 daily; 3hr 10min).

Llandrindod Wells to: Knighton (4 daily; 40min); Llanwrtyd Wells (4 daily; 30min); Shrewsbury (4 daily; 1hr 40min); Swansea (4 daily; 2hr 20min).

Machynlleth to: Aberdyfi (8–10 daily; 20min); Aberystwyth (9 daily; 30min); Barmouth (10 daily; 50min); Birmingham (7 daily; 2hr 15min); Harlech (7 daily; 1hr 20min); Porthmadog (7 daily; 1hr 45min); Shrewsbury (7 daily; 1hr 20min).

Tywyn to: Aberdyfi (10 daily; 5min); Barmouth (7 daily; 25min); Harlech (7 daily; 1hr); Machynlleth (7 daily; 30min); Porthmadog (7 daily; 1hr 10min).

Welshpool to: Aberystwyth (6 daily; 1hr 30min); Birmingham (6 daily; 1hr 30min); Machynlleth (6 daily; 1hr); Newtown (6 daily; 20min); Pwllheli (4 daily; 3hr); Shrewsbury (6 daily; 20min).

16

North Wales

Highlights

* **Llangollen** Robust and enjoyable riverside town, with an internationally famous eisteddfod. See p.772

* **Snowdon** Wales's highest mountain is a stunning hike, or a gentle ascent by rack-and-pinion railway. See p.782

* **Beddgelert** Fabulously atmospheric slate-mining town amid rugged mountains, best reached by a wonderful narrow-gauge railway. See p.783

* **Portmeirion** Pretty, quirky fantasy village, the "home for fallen buildings". See p.788

* **Caernarfon Castle** The mightiest link in Edward I's chain of Norman castles. See p.791

* **Beaumaris** A good base for Anglesey's beaches and Neolithic remains. See p.794

* **Conwy** Compact town, with a fantastic castle and an intact ring of walls. See p.798

* **Llandudno** The town's classy gentility is nicely offset by the ruggedness of the neighbouring Great Orme peak. See p.802

△ Snowdonia National Park sign

North Wales

The fast A55 dual carriageway has made the **North Wales** coast considerably more accessible in recent times, but this hasn't tamed the wilder aspects of this stunningly beautiful area. Wales's north coast and its natural offshoot, the isle of Anglesey, not only encompass the geographical extremities of the country, but comprise an area exhibiting the extremes of Welsh life. As you walk around most of the brash seaside towns along the eastern section of the coast, only the street signs give any indication that you are in Wales at all; further west, there are places where English is seldom spoken other than to visitors.

Without doubt, **Snowdonia** is the crowning glory of North Wales. This tightly packed bundle of soaring cliff faces, jagged peaks and plunging waterfalls measures little more than ten miles by ten, but packs enough mountain paths to keep even the most jaded walking enthusiast happy for weeks. Even if lakeside ambles and rides on antiquated steam trains are more your style, you can't fail to appreciate the natural grandeur of the scenery, occasionally revealing an atmospheric Welsh castle ruin or decaying piece of quarrying equipment.

Snowdonia is the heart of the massive **Snowdonia National Park** (Parc Cenedlaethol Eryri), which extends north and south, beyond the bounds of Snowdonia itself (and this chapter), to encompass the Rhinogs, Cadair Idris (see p.753) and 23 miles of superb coastal scenery.

One of the best approaches to Snowdonia is along the **Dee Valley**, a fertile landscape much fought over between the English and the Welsh. North Wales's largest town, **Wrexham**, makes the best of its industrial heritage, but there's a more tangibly Welsh feel to fabulous **Llangollen**, a great base for a variety of ruins, rides and rambles, as well as the venue each summer for the colourful International Eisteddfod festival.

Pressing on along the A5 – the region's second, inland main road – you hit the fringes of Snowdonia at **Betws-y-Coed**, great for easy walks but slightly twee. Heading deeper into the park, old mining and quarry towns such as **Beddgelert**, **Llanberis** and **Blaenau Ffestiniog** make arguably better bases – with great hiking on their doorstep and plenty of intrinsic interest. On the eastern fringes of Snowdonia, **Bala** tempts with water sports: either lake sailing or whitewater rafting down the Tryweryn.

To the west of Snowdonia is the former slate port of **Porthmadog**, home to the wonderful **Ffestiniog Railway** and the quirky pretend village of **Portmeirion**. Beyond lies the gentle rockiness of the **Llŷn peninsula** where Wales ends in a flourish of small coves and seafaring villages. Roads loop back along the Llŷn to **Caernarfon** which is overshadowed by its stupendous castle, the mightiest link in Edward I's Iron Ring of thirteenth-century fortresses across North Wales.

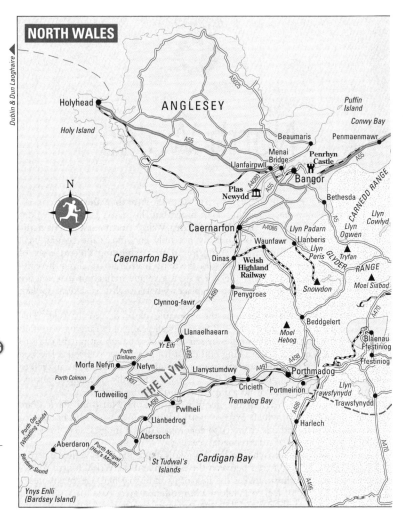

Across the Menai Strait lies the island of **Anglesey**, a gentle patchwork of beautiful beaches and sites of ancient heritage, well worth exploration. Edward's final castle, a masterpiece of design, is sited in **Beaumaris**, and catamarans and ferries from Anglesey's main town, **Holyhead**, provide the fastest route to Dublin.

Back on the mainland, the university and cathedral city of **Bangor** is the area's most cosmopolitan haunt, while remaining solidly Welsh in outlook and language. The same could certainly not be said for the string of seaside resorts along the North Wales coast, among which **Conwy** – another walled bastide town built by Edward I – and genteel **Llandudno**, always a cut above the rest, are the highlights. Further east towards England, faded Victorian resorts are the mainstay. However, a few surprises come embedded into this matrix of bingo

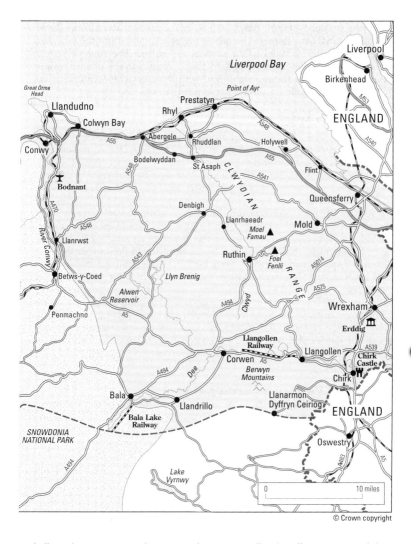

© Crown copyright

halls and caravan sites: the National Portrait Gallery's collection at **Bodelw-yddan**, Britain's smallest cathedral at **St Asaph**, and the allegedly miraculous waters at **Holywell**.

Wrexham and the Dee Valley

Wrexham (Wrecsam) is the largest town in North Wales but, save for its proximity to the **Clywedog Valley** and **Erddig Hall** stately home, offers little reason to linger. If you have your own transport you are better off exploring the local attractions from **Llangollen**, which grew up partly as a market centre but also served the needs of cattle drovers who used the passage carved by the **River Dee** (Afon Dyfrdwy) through the hills – the easiest route from the fattening grounds of northwest Wales to the markets in England. The ruins of both a Welsh castle and a Cistercian abbey drew the Romantics to this dramatic gorge naturally blessed with surging rapids, and with the nineteenth-century arrival of the railway, Llangollen became a firm tourist favourite.

Wrexham and around

Despite some fine older buildings amidst the identikit chainstores, time in **WREXHAM** is best spent at **St Giles' Church** (daily 11am–3pm; free), its 1520s five-tier Gothic tower rising gracefully above the kernel of small lanes at the end of Hope Street. The same design was used at Yale University, in homage to the ancestral home of the college's benefactor, Elihu Yale, whose tomb lies at the tower's base.

Wrexham has two **train stations**, half a mile apart, all services stopping at Wrexham General on Mold Road, ten minutes' walk northwest of the centre. Walking into town from here, Mold Street becomes Regent Street and then Hope Street, from which King Street branches off left to the **bus station**, for National Express coaches (tickets from Key Travel, King Street) and frequent local buses serving Chester and Llangollen. The **tourist office**, Lambpit Street (Mon–Sat: April to mid-Oct 10am–5pm; mid-Oct to March 10am–4pm; ℡01978/292015, ⓦwww.borderlands.co.uk), is reached by turning left where Hope Street turns to the right. Good, central places to **stay** include *Hampson Guest House*, 6 Chester Rd (℡01978/357665, ⓦwww.wrexhamhotels.com; ❷), or the fancier ⚘ *Lemon Tree*, 29 Rhosddu Rd (℡01978/261211, ⓦwww.lemon-tree.net; ❹), tastefully converted from an old priory, which also serves good meals.

Clywedog Valley and Erddig Hall

The **Clywedog Valley**, which forms an arc around the western and southern suburbs of Wrexham, was the crucible of lead mining and iron smelting in the northern Welsh borders during the eighteenth century. The seven-mile-long **Clywedog Trail** now links a series of former industrial sites: fascinating, if a bit heavy on packaged heritage.

Coal continued to be extracted in the valley until 1986, with some mines tunnelling under the nearby stately home of **Erddig Hall** (daily except Thurs & Fri: house April–Sept noon–5pm, Oct & Nov noon–4pm; garden March–June & Sept 11am–6pm, July & Aug 10am–6pm, Oct & Nov 11am–5pm; £7.40, outbuildings & gardens only £3.80; NT), two miles south of Wrexham, adding subsidence to the troubles of an already decaying seventeenth-century building. The ancestral home of the Yorke family, the house is now managed by the National Trust and has been restored to its 1922 appearance. While the family's State Rooms upstairs have their share of fine furniture and portraits, the real interest lies in the quarters of the servants, whose lives were fully documented by their unusually benevolent masters. Eighteenth- and early nineteenth-century portraits of staff are still on display in the Servants' Hall, and each has a verse written by one of the Yorkes. You can also see the blacksmith's shop, lime yard, stables, laundry, kitchen and still-used bakehouse.

Llangollen and around

LLANGOLLEN, twelve miles southwest of Wrexham, is the embodiment of a Welsh town in both setting and character, clasped tightly in the narrow Dee

Valley between the shoulders of the Berwyn and Eglwyseg mountains. Along the valley's floor, the waters of the River Dee run down to the town, licking the angled buttresses of the weighty Gothic bridge, which has spanned the river since the fourteenth century. On its south bank, half a dozen streets form the core of the scattered settlement flung out across the low hills. Every July, the town comes alive for the **International Music Eisteddfod**.

As the only river crossing point for miles, Llangollen was an important town long before the early Romantics arrived at the end of the eighteenth century, when they were cut off from their European Grand Tours by the Napoleonic Wars. Turner came to paint the swollen river and the Cistercian ruin of **Valle Crucis**, a couple of miles up the valley; John Ruskin found the town "entirely lovely in its gentle wildness"; and writer George Borrow made Llangollen his base for the early part of his 1854 tour detailed in *Wild Wales*. The rich and famous came not just for the scenery, but to visit the "Ladies of Llangollen", an eccentric couple who became the toast of society from their house, Plas Newydd. But by this stage some of the town's rural charm had been eaten up by the works of one of the century's finest engineers, Thomas Telford, who squeezed both his London–Holyhead trunk road and the **Llangollen Canal** alongside the river.

The Town

Standing in twelve acres of formal gardens, half a mile up Hill Street from the southern end of Castle Street, the two-storeyed mock-Tudor **Plas Newydd** (Easter–Oct daily 10am–5pm; £3) was, for almost fifty years, home to the **Ladies of Llangollen**. Lady Eleanor Butler and Sarah Ponsonby were a lesbian couple from Anglo-Irish aristocratic backgrounds, who tried to elope together at the end of the eighteenth century. After two botched attempts dressed in men's clothes, they were grudgingly allowed to leave their family seats in 1778 with an annual allowance of £280, enough to settle in Llangollen, where they became celebrated hosts and legendary local characters. Despite their desire for a "life of sweet and delicious retirement", they didn't seem to mind the constant stream of gentry who called on them. Walter Scott was well received, though he found them "a couple of hazy or crazy old sailors" in manner, and like "two respectable superannuated clergymen" in their mode of dress. Visitors' gifts of sculpted **wood panelling** formed the basis of the riotous friezes of woodwork that cover the walls of their modest house, visited on a self-guided audio tour (free). It is a wonderful if slightly oppressive effect set off by a mixed bag of furniture in a style similar to that owned by the ladies. Llangollen takes its name from the **Church of St Collen**, on Bridge Street (May–Sept daily 1.30–6pm; free), outside which is a triangular railed-off monument to the ladies and their devoted maid.

The hills around Llangollen echo to the shrill cry of steam engines easing along the **Llangollen Railway** (April–Oct 3–7 services most days; call ahead at other times; £8 return; ☎01978/860979, ⓦwww.llangollen-railway.co.uk), shoehorned into the north side of the valley. From Llangollen's time-warped station it runs along eight miles of the old Ruabon–Barmouth line to Carrog, the belching steam engines creeping west along the riverbank, hauling ancient carriages which proudly sport the liveries of their erstwhile owners.

Across the street is the Llangollen Canal, one of the finest feats of British canal building. Its architect, Thomas Telford, succeeded in building a canal without locks through fourteen miles of hilly terrain, most spectacularly by means of the thousand-foot-long **Pontcysyllte Aqueduct**, passing 127ft over the River Dee at Froncysyllte, four miles east. **Canal trips** (Easter–Oct daily; £8.50; ☎01978/860702, ⓦwww.horsedrawnboats.co.uk) across the aqueduct leave from Llangollen Wharf, almost opposite the train station.

Practicalities

Buses stop on Market Street, while the nearest **train station** is five miles away at Ruabon, passed by frequent buses on the Llangollen–Wrexham run. The **tourist office** on Castle Street (daily: Easter–Oct 9.30am–5.30pm; Nov–Easter 9.30am–5pm; ☎01978/860828, ⓔllangollen@nwtic.com) is fifty yards from the bridge and less than a hundred yards from the bus stop on Market Street. There's **bike rental** from ProAdventure on Parade Street (☎01978/861912, ⓦwww.proadventure.co.uk).

Finding **rooms** in Llangollen can be a chore in summer, especially during the eisteddfod in July. Low-cost, central B&Bs worth checking out include the non-smoking *Hafren*, on Berwyn Street (☎01978/860939; ❷), with shared bathroom and minimal single supplement, and *Hillcrest*, on Hill Street (☎01978/860208, ⓦwww.hillcrest-guesthouse.com; ❸), an appealing licensed Victorian guesthouse up towards Plas Newydd with excellent breakfasts. Moving upmarket, go for ⚥ *Gales*, 18 Bridge St (☎01978/860089, ⓦwww.galesofllangollen.co.uk; ❸), a comfortable guest house above a wine bar; or *Bryn Howel* two miles east off the A539 (☎01978/860331, ⓦwww.brynhowel.com; ❻), set in beautiful grounds and with good facilities including sauna, solarium, free trout fishing and a top-class restaurant.

The YHA **hostel**, on Tyndwr Road, a mile and a half east of town (☎0870/770 5932, ⓔllangollen@yha.org.uk; dorms £11), requires reservations at least two days in advance and is often booked solid with groups. Camp at *Wern Isaf Farm* (☎01978/860632; £4 per person), a simple farmhouse campsite just under a mile up Wern Road: turn right over the canal on Wharf Hill.

Though not extensive by city standards, Llangollen boasts a fairly good selection of **restaurants** and no shortage of cafés around town. *The Gallery*, 15 Chapel St (☎01978/860076; closed Sun & Mon), is a good start for moderately priced pizza and pasta dishes. *Gales Wine Bar* (see above) has great old church pews and an extensive cellar, and serves tasty bistro-style food. The *Hand Hotel*, 26 Bridge St, is a straightforward local **pub** where you can listen to a male voice choir in full song (Mon & Fri 7.30pm) or sink a pint in the gorgeous riverside garden. Top no-nonsense boozing haunt is the youthful *Bull Hotel* on Castle Street.

The panoramic view, especially at sunset, justifies the 45-minute slog up to **Castell Dinas Brân** (Crow's Fortress Castle), a few evocative stumps of masonry perched on a hill 800ft above the town, and reached by a path beginning near Llangollen Wharf. This was once the district's largest and most important Welsh fortress, built in the 1230s by the ruler of northern Powys, Prince Madog ap Gruffydd Maelor. Edward I soon captured it as part of his first campaign against Llywelyn ap Gruffydd, but the castle was left to decay.

The gaunt ruin of **Valle Crucis Abbey** (Easter–Sept daily 10am–5pm, £2; all other times free access; CADW), a mile or so west of Llangollen, greets you with its largely intact west wall, pierced by the frame of a rose window. Though one of the last Cistercian foundations in Wales, and the first Gothic abbey in Britain, it is no match for Tintern Abbey (see p.682), but nevertheless stands majestically in a pastoral – and much less-visited – setting. After the Dissolution, in 1535, the church fell into disrepair with the monastic buildings employed as farm buildings. Now they hold displays on monastic life, reached by a detour through the mostly ruined cloister and past the weighty vaulting of the chapterhouse.

Snowdonia

What the coal valleys are to the south of the country, the mountains of **Snowdonia** (Yr Eryri) are to the north – the defining feature, not just in their physical form, but in the way they have shaped the communities within them. To Henry VIII's antiquarian John Leland, the region seemed "horrible with the sight of bare stones"; now it is widely acclaimed as the most dramatic and alluring of all Welsh scenery, a compact, barren land of tortured ridges dividing glacial valleys, whose sheer faces belie the fact that the tallest peaks only just top three thousand feet. It was to this mountain fastness that Llywelyn ap Gruffydd, the last true prince of Wales, retreated in 1277 after his first war with Edward I; it was also here that Owain Glyndŵr held on most tenaciously to his dream of regaining for the Welsh the title of Prince of Wales. Centuries later, the English came to remove the mountains: slate barons built huge fortunes from Welsh toil and reshaped the patterns of Snowdonian life forever, as men looking for steady work in the quarries left the hills and became town dwellers. By the mid-nineteenth century, those with the means began flocking here to marvel at the plunging waterfalls and walk the ever-widening paths to the mountaintops. Numbers have increased rapidly since then and thousands of hikers arrive every weekend for some of the country's best walks over steep, exacting and constantly varying terrain.

Not surprisingly, the **Snowdon** massif (Eryri) is the focus of the Snowdonia National Park. Several of the ascent routes are superb, and you can always take the cog railway up to the summit café from **Llanberis**. But the other mountains are as good or better, often far less busy and giving unsurpassed views of Snowdon. The **Glyders** and **Tryfan** – best tackled from the **Ogwen Valley** – are particular favourites.

If you are serious about doing some **walking** – and some of the walks described here are serious, especially in bad weather (Snowdon gets 200 inches of rain a year) – you need a good map such as the 1:50,000 OS *Landranger* #115 or the 1:25,000 OS *Outdoor Leisure* #17; bear in mind that conditions, especially on higher ground, are notoriously changeable. Weather reports and walking conditions are often posted on the doors or noticeboards of outdoor shops and tourist offices.

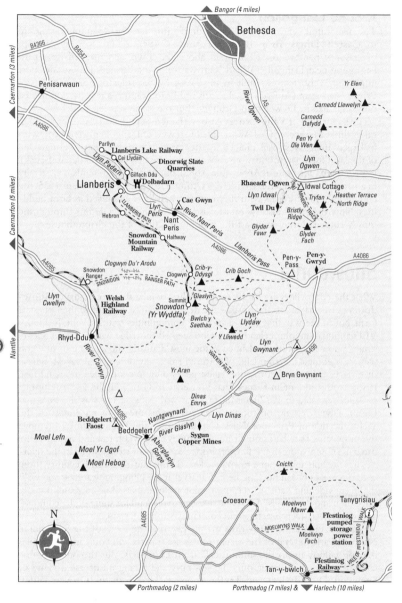

But Snowdonia isn't all about walking. Small settlements are dotted in the valleys, usually coinciding with some enormous mine or quarry. Foremost among these are **Blaenau Ffestiniog**, the "Slate Capital of North Wales", where a mine opens its caverns for underground tours, and **Beddgelert** whose former copper mines are also open to the public. The only place of any size not associated with slate mining is **Betws-y-Coed**, a largely Victorian resort away

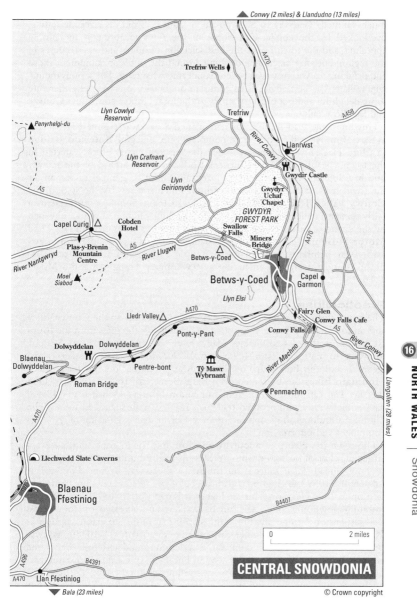

Conwy (2 miles) & Llandudno (13 miles)

Trefriw Wells

Llyn Cowlyd
Reservoir

Penyrhelgi-du

Trefriw

River Conwy

Llanrwst

A458

A470

Llyn Crafnant
Reservoir

Llyn
Geirionydd

Gwydir Castle

Gwydyr
Uchaf
Chapel

GWYDYR
FOREST PARK

A5

Swallow
Falls

Miners'
Bridge

Capel Curig

Cobden
Hotel

A5

River Llugwy

Betws-y-Coed

A470

Plas-y-Brenin
Mountain
Centre

River Nantgwryd

Moel
Siabod

Betws-y-Coed

Capel
Garmon

Llyn Elsi

Lledr Valley

A470

Pont-y-Pant

Fairy Glen
Conwy Falls Cafe

Conwy Falls

A5

River Conwy

Dolwyddelan

Dolwyddelan

River Machno

Blaenau
Dolwyddelan

Pentre-bont

Tŷ Mawr
Wybrnant

Roman Bridge

Penmachno

A470

Llangollen (28 miles)

16

NORTH WALES | Snowdonia

Llechwedd Slate Caverns

Blaenau
Ffestiniog

B4407

0   2 miles

A496

B4391

CENTRAL SNOWDONIA

A470   Llan Ffestiniog

Bala (23 miles)

© Crown copyright

from the higher peaks, and a springboard for the walkers' hamlets of **Capel Curig** and **Pen-y-Pass**.

Betws-y-Coed and around

Sprawled out across a flat plain at the confluence of the Conwy, Llugwy and Lledr valleys, **BETWS-Y-COED** (pronounced "betoos-ei-coyd"), the much-vaunted "Gateway to Snowdonia", is hard to avoid. Its riverside setting, overlooked by the conifer-clad slopes of the Gwydyr forest, is undeniably appealing, and the town boasts the best selection of hotels and guest houses in the region, but after an hour mooching around the outdoor equipment shops and drinking tea you may well be left wondering what to do. For serious mountain walkers, the best advice is to continue on, but for everyone else there are some delightful and popular easy strolls to the local beauty spots of the **Conwy** and **Swallow** falls.

This one-time lead-mining town remained a backwater until 1815 when, as part of his A5 toll road, Telford completed the graceful **Waterloo Bridge** (Y Bont Haearn), speeding access for the leisured classes already alerted to the town's beauty by J.M.W. Turner's landscapes. The arrival of the railway line in 1868 lifted its status from coaching station to genteel resort, an air the town tries to maintain, albeit without much success. By the station, the **Conwy Valley Railway Museum** (daily 10.15am–5pm; £1.50) presents a fairly standard collection of memorabilia and shiny engines, slightly enlivened by the chance of a short ride on a miniature train (£1.50) or tram (£1). The **Motor Museum** (Easter–Oct daily 10am–6pm; £1.50), a couple of hundred yards away behind the tourist office, is little better, with a half-dozen classic bikes and fifteen cars, including a 1934 Bugatti Straight 8 and a Model T Ford.

Practicalities

The **train station**, for services from Llandudno Junction up the Conwy Valley and on to Blaenau Ffestiniog, is just a few paces across the grass from the **tourist office**, at Royal Oak Stables (daily: Easter to mid-Oct 9.30am–5.30pm; mid-Oct to Easter 9.30am–4.30pm; ☎01690/710426, ✉tic.byc@eryri-npa .gov.uk), and the **bus stop**, outside St Mary's church, on the main street. **Mountain bikes** can be rented from Beics Betws (☎01690/710829), behind the *Tan Lan* café on the A5: front-suspension bikes (£14 half-day, £18 full day) come with a photocopied trail map marked with suggested routes. The Ultimate Outdoors shop, opposite Pont-y-Pair bridge, is good for all kinds of equipment and information.

The town has plenty of **accommodation**, but has to cope with an ever-larger number of visitors pushing prices up in the summer, when you need to book ahead. *Glan Llugwy*, on the A5, a short way beyond Pont-y-Pair (☎01690/710592; ❷), is good and cheap, but if you need an en-suite bathroom step up to *Rose Hill*, Lôn Muriau, Llanrwst Road (☎01690/710455, ⓦwww .rosehill-snowdonia.co.uk, ❸), run by walkers and accessed on foot across the suspension bridge by the train station. A more luxurious option is ⚐ *Pengwern*, Allt Dinas, a mile east on the A5 (☎01690/710480, ⓦwww .snowdoniaaccommodation.com; ❺), a welcoming and tastefully decorated country house set in two acres of woods. The *Betws-y-Coed YHA* **hostel**, two miles west (☎01690/710796, ⓦwww.swallowfallshotel.co.uk; ❶), has £13 dorms, rooms, camping, and meals at the adjacent *Swallow Falls Hotel*. The closest **campsite** is *Riverside* (☎01690/710310; Easter–Oct), right behind the station.

For a town so geared to tourism, there are surprisingly few places to **eat**. For coffee and snacks visit *Café Active*, Holyhead Road, above the Cotswold Outdoor Rock Bottom shop, which also has the town's only Internet access. Best bets for full meals are *The Stables* in the *Royal Oak Hotel* on High Street, and the ⚐ *Tŷ Gwyn*, on the A5, a wood-beamed pub that's a great place to tuck into good bar or restaurant meals over a pint or two.

The Conwy and Swallow Falls

Nothing in Betws-y-Coed can compete with getting out to the gorges and waterfalls in the vicinity, and **walking** is the ideal way to see them. In the final gorge section of the River Conwy, a couple of miles above Betws-y-Coed, the river plunges fifty feet over the **Conwy Falls** into a deep pool. The *Conwy Falls Café*, reached by bus #64 (8 daily), collects a small fee entitling you to view the falls and a series of rock steps that once formed part of a primitive fish ladder. A mile or so downstream, the churning waters of the River Conwy negotiate a staircase of drops and enter **Fairy Glen** (50p) a cleft in a small wood which takes its name from the Welsh fairies, the Tylwyth Teg, who are said to be seen hereabouts. The two sights are linked by a mile-long path following a cool green lane giving glimpses of the river through the woods. **Swallow Falls**, two miles west along the A5 towards Capel Curig, is the region's most visited sight, where £1 entitles you to see this pretty cascade. Better still, leave the car park on the north side of Pont-y-Pair, in town, and follow the **Llugwy Valley Walk** (3 miles; 400ft ascent; 1hr 30min), a forested path following the twisting and plunging river upstream towards Capel Curig. Less than a mile from Pont-y-Pair you reach the steeply sloping **Miners' Bridge**, which linked miners' homes at Pentre Du, on the south side of the river, to the lead mines in Llanrwst. Just beneath the bridge are a series of idyllic plunge pools, perfect for swimming. The path follows the river on your left for another mile to a slightly obscured view of Swallow Falls. Detailed maps are available from the tourist office showing numerous routes back through the Gwydyr Forest, or you can continue half a mile to the road bridge from where you can wait for the bus back to Betws-y-Coed.

Capel Curig

Tantalizing flashes of Wales's highest mountains are glimpsed through the forested banks of the Llugwy as you climb west from Betws-y-Coed on the A5, but Snowdon eludes you until the final bend before **CAPEL CURIG**. The tiny, scattered village, six miles west of Betws-y-Coed, is the site of a major centre for outdoor enthusiasts. A quarter of a mile along the A4086 to Llanberis from the main road junction, **Plas-y-Brenin: the National Mountaineering Centre** (℡01690/720214, ⓦwww.pyb.co.uk) runs renowned residential courses and offers indoor climbing, lake canoeing and dry-slope skiing sessions (daily 10am–9pm; £10 for 2hr), during July and August. There is also a climbing wall (daily 10am–11pm; £3), and the opportunity to hear talks or watch slide shows of expeditions (usually Mon, Tues & Sat 8pm; free).

There are plenty of places to **stay**, though none is especially luxurious. The best is either the *Bron Eryri* (℡01690/720240, ⓦwww.eryriguesthouse.fsnet.co.uk; ❸), a comfortable and welcoming B&B half a mile outside the village towards Betws-y-Coed, or the wonderful ⚔ *Bryn Tyrch Hotel* (℡01690/720223; ❸), also on the A5, but closer to the main road junction. The cheapest option in the village is the YHA **hostel** (℡0870/770 5746, ⓔcapelcurig@yha.org.uk; ❶, dorms £16; mid-Feb to mid-Dec), five hundred yards along the A5 towards Betws-y-Coed. Two and a half miles west down the Ogwen Valley you can stay for a good deal less in the *Gwern Gof Uchaf* bunkhouse and **campsite** (see p.781).

During the day, walkers patronize the *Snowdonia Café*, next to the YHA. In the evening they retire to the warm and lively **bar** of the *Bryn Tyrch Hotel* (see above), which serves great **food**, much of it vegan and vegetarian, or head for the sociable bar at the Plas-y-Brenin centre.

The Ogwen Valley

Northwest of Capel Curig, the A5 forges through the **Ogwen Valley** which separates the frequently mist-shrouded Carneddau range from the **Glyders** range and its triple-peaked **Tryfan**, perhaps Snowdonia's most demanding mountain. West of Tryfan, the road follows the shores of **Llyn Ogwen**, past the YHA hostel and down **Nant Ffrancon**, a perfect example of a U-shaped valley, carved and smoothed by rocks frozen into the undersides of a glacier ten thousand years ago.

The hostel is the start of some of Wales's most demanding and rewarding hikes (see box), and the easier half-hour walk to the still Llyn Idwal. It nestles in the

---

Walks from Ogwen: Tryfan and the Glyders

Tourists hike up Snowdon, but mountain connoisseurs invariably prefer the sharply angled peaks of **Tryfan and the Glyders**, with their challenging terrain, cantilevered rocks and views back to Snowdon. The sheer number of good walking paths on the Glyders make it almost impossible to choose one definitive circular route. The individual sections of the walk have therefore been defined separately in order to allow the greatest flexibility. All times given are for the ascents: expect to take approximately half the time to get back down. **Maps** are essential for all these walks: the OS *Outdoor Leisure* 1:25,000 *Snowdonia* #17 is by far the best bet.

The main route up Tryfan (3002ft) follows the so-called **Miners' Track** (2 miles; 1350ft ascent; 2hr) from Idwal Cottage, taking the path to Cwm Idwal, then, as it bears sharply to the right, keeping straight ahead and making for the gap on the horizon. This is **Bwlch Tryfan**, the col between Tryfan and Glyder Fach, from where the **South Ridge** of Tryfan (800yd; 650ft ascent; 30min) climbs past the Far South Peak to the summit. This last section is an easy scramble which finishes at the twin monoliths of **Adam and Eve** on the summit. The courageous, or foolhardy, make the jump between them as a point of honour at the end of every ascent. In theory, the leap is trivial, but the consequences of overshooting would be disastrous.

If you've got the head for it, go for the **North Ridge of Tryfan** (1 mile; 2000ft ascent; 1hr–1hr 30min), one of the most rewarding scrambles in the country. It's never as precarious as Snowdon's Crib Goch, but you get a genuine mountaineering feel as the valley floor drops rapidly. The route starts in the lay-by at the head of Idwal Lake and goes left across rising ground, until you strike a vague path heading straight up, following the crest of the ridge to the summit.

The assault on **Glyder Fach** (3260ft) begins at Bwlch Tryfan, reached either by the Miners' Track from Idwal Cottage or by the south ridge from Tryfan's summit. The trickier route follows **Bristly Ridge** (1000yd; 900ft ascent; 40min) which isn't marked on OS maps but runs steeply south from the col up past some daunting-looking towers of rock. It isn't that difficult in dry conditions, and saves a long hike southeast along a second section of the Miners' Track (1.5 miles; 900ft ascent; 1hr 30min). The summit lies to the west of the ridge, a chaotic jumble of huge grey slabs that many people don't bother climbing up, preferring to be photographed on a massive cantilevered rock a few yards away.

From Glyder Fach, it's an easy enough stroll to **Glyder Fawr** (3280ft), reached by skirting round the tortured rock formations of **Castell y Gwynt** (Castle of the Winds), then following a cairn-marked path to the dramatic summit of frost-shattered slabs angled like ancient headstones (1 mile; 200ft ascent; 40min). Glyder Fawr is normally approached from Idwal Cottage, following the **Devil's Kitchen Route** (2.5 miles; 2300ft ascent; 3hr) past Idwal Lake, then to the left of the Devil's Kitchen, zigzagging up to a lake-filled plateau. Follow the path to the right of the lake and turn left for the summit where two paths cross.

magnificent cirque, **Cwm Idwal**, where early botanists found rare arctic-alpine plants, the main reason for designating Cwm Idwal as Wales's first nature reserve in 1954. An easy path leads up to the reserve from the car park, where the café (daily 8.30am–5pm; later on summer weekends) will give you a nature-trail booklet.

Six daily **buses** along the valley provide access to the limited supply of **accommodation**. The most sophisticated is the *Idwal Cottage* YHA **hostel** (℡0870/770 5874, ⓔidwal@yha.org.uk; dorms £12.50; Feb–Oct), at the western end of Llŷn Ogwen, five miles from Capel Curig. Residents can get meals at the hostel; the valley is otherwise self-catering. The best **camping** is at *Gwern Gof Uchaf*, at the foot of Tryfan (℡01690/720294, ⓦwww.tryfanwales .co.uk), which also has a good bunkhouse (£6 per person).

Llanberis and Snowdon

Mention **LLANBERIS**, ten miles west of Capel Curig, to any mountain enthusiast and they will think of **Snowdon**. The two seem inseparable, not least because of the Llanberis Path to the summit (see p.784) and the five-mile-long umbilical of the **Snowdon Mountain Railway**, Britain's only rack-and-pinion railway, which runs alongside. This is the nearest you'll get to an alpine climbing village in Wales, its single main street thronged with weatherbeaten walkers and climbers. At the same time, Llanberis is very much a Welsh rural community, albeit a depleted one now that slate is no longer being torn from the flanks of Elidir Fawr, the mountain across the town's twin lakes. The quarries, which for the best part of two centuries employed up to three thousand men, closed in 1969, making way for the construction of the Dinorwig Pumped Storage Power Station.

Three of the routes up Snowdon start five miles east of Llanberis at the top of the Llanberis Pass, one of the deepest, narrowest and craggiest in Snowdonia. At the summit, a hostel, café and car park comprise the settlement of **PEN-Y-PASS**. Frequent Sherpa #S1 **buses** travel up daily to Pen-y-Pass, the recommended approach even if you have a car, since the Pen-y-Pass car park is expensive and almost always full. Use the "Park and Ride" car park at the bottom of the pass, near the *Vaynol Arms*.

The Town

Scattered remains are all that is left of thirteenth-century **Dolbadarn Castle** (free access; CADW), on the road to **Parc Padarn**, where lakeside oak woods are gradually recolonizing the discarded workings of the defunct Dinorwig Slate Quarries. Here, the **Welsh Slate Museum** (Easter–Oct daily 10am–5pm; Nov–Easter daily except Sat 10am–4pm; free; ⓦwww.nmgw.ac.uk) occupies the former maintenance workshops of what was once one of the largest slate quarries in the world. The line shafts and flapping belts driven by a fifty-foot-diameter waterwheel provide a backdrop to workbenches where former quarry workers demonstrate their skills at turning an inch-thick slab of slate into six, or even eight, perfectly smooth slivers. The craftsmen here operate an ageing foundry, producing pieces for the scattered branches of the National Museum of Wales, as well as repairing the rolling stock belonging to the nearby **Llanberis Lake Railway** (July & Aug 4–8 daily; March–June & Sept to early Oct 3–5 daily; £6 return; ⓦwww.lake-railway.co.uk), which formerly transported slate and workers between the Dinorwig quarries and Port Dinorwig on the Menai Strait. It's a tame forty-minute round trip with little to do at the end except come back and explore the old slate workings.

In 1974, five years after the quarry closed, work began on hollowing out the vast underground chambers of the **Dinorwig Pumped Storage Power Station**, designed to provide power on demand. If you can bear the thinly disguised electricity industry advertisement that precedes it, you can take an hour-long minibus tour around the enormous pipework in the depths. For this, you need to call at **Electric Mountain** (June–Aug daily 9.30am–5.30pm; April, May, Sept & Oct daily 10.30am–4.30pm; Feb, March, Nov & Dec Wed–Sun 10.30am–4.30pm; £6.50; ⓦwww.electricmountain.co.uk), by the lake beside the A4086, the town-centre bypass.

Practicalities

All **buses** to Llanberis stop near the **tourist office**, 41b High St (Easter–Oct daily 9.30am–5pm; Nov–Easter Mon & Fri–Sun 11am–4pm; ⓣ01286/870765, ⓔllanberis.tic@gwynedd.gov.uk). For guided hiking, rock climbing and kayaking contact High Trek Snowdonia, Tal y Waen, Deiniolen (ⓣ01286/871232, ⓦwww.climbing-wales.co.uk), or Bryn Du Mountain Centre, Ty Du Road (ⓣ01286/870556, ⓦwww.boulderadventures.co.uk). The Llanberis Path (see box, p.784), Snowdon Ranger Path and Pitt's Head Track to Rhyd-Ddu are open to **cyclists**, although a voluntary agreement exists restricting cycle access to and from the summit between 10am and 5pm (May–Sept).

There's plenty of low-cost **accommodation** in or close to town: *The Heights*, 74 High St (ⓣ01286/871179, ⓦwww.heightshotel.co.uk; ❸, dorms £14), caters to the walking and climbing set, offering B&B, dorms, a good restaurant and a lively bar. Two other options on High Street are the lovely *Plas Coch* (ⓣ01286/872122, ⓦwww.plas-coch.co.uk; ❹), which has one cheaper attic room; and *Erw Fair* (ⓣ01286/872400, ⓦwww.erwfair.com; ❷), which also has more expensive en-suites.

Llanberis YHA **hostel**, Llwyn Celyn (ⓣ0870/770 5928, ⓔllanberis@yha.org.uk; dorms £12.50), is half a mile uphill along Capel Goch Road, signposted off High Street; and there's simple **camping** at *Cae Gwyn* (ⓣ01286/870718; £3.50 per person, bunkhouse £7) in Nant Peris, 2 miles southeast of Llanberis.

Out of town, head three miles northwest to *Graianfryn* (ⓣ01286/871007, ⓦwww.fastasleep.me.uk; ❷), an exclusively vegetarian and vegan farmhouse in Penisarwaun. Four miles east of town is the *Pen-y-Pass YHA* hostel (ⓣ0870/770 5990, ⓔpenypass@yha.org.uk; ❶, dorms £12.50), with the *Pen-y-Gwryd Hotel* (ⓣ01286/870211, ⓦwww.pyg.co.uk; ❺; March–Oct), where you'll find plenty of muddy boots in the bar, a mile further east.

For **food** of gut-splitting proportions, climbers and walkers flock to *Pete's Eats*, 40 High St, while *Y Bistro*, 43–45 High St (ⓣ01286/871278; closed Sun & Mon), is the best restaurant for miles around. The *Vaynol Arms*, two miles east of Llanberis and the only pub before Pen-y-Gwryd, serves good beer and very tasty food in a convivial atmosphere; it's usually full of campers from across the road.

Snowdon and the Snowdon Mountain Railway

The highest British mountain outside Scotland, the **Snowdon massif** (3560ft) forms a star of shattered ridges with four major peaks: Crib Goch, Crib-y-ddysgl, Y Lliwedd and the main summit, **Yr Wyddfa**. Snowdon sports some of the finest walking and scrambling in the park. Hardened outdoor enthusiasts dismiss it as overused, and it can certainly be crowded in summer when a thousand visitors a day can be pressed into the postbox-red carriages of the Snowdon Mountain Railway, while another 1500 pound the well-maintained paths.

Opprobrium is chiefly levelled at the **Snowdon Mountain Railway** (mid-March to Oct 6–25 trains daily; £20 return; ☎ 01286/870223, Ⓦ www.snowdonrailway.co.uk), completed in 1896, purely for the fact that it exists. Seventy-year-old carriages pushed by equally old steam locos still climb, in just under an hour, from the eastern end of Llanberis opposite the *Royal Victoria Hotel* to the summit café and bar (open when the trains are running to the top). A "Railway Stamp" (13p) affixed to your letter – along with the usual Royal Mail one – entitles you to use the highest postbox in the UK and enchant your friends with a "Summit of Snowdon – Copa'r Wyddfa" postmark. Times, type of locomotive and final destination vary with demand and

△ Snowdon Mountain Railway

ice conditions at the top: to avoid disappointment, buy your tickets early on clear summer days. If you walk up by one of the routes detailed in the "Walks on Snowdon" box, you can take the train down, if there is space (£14).

Beddgelert

Almost all the rain that falls on Snowdon spills down either the Glaslyn or Colwyn rivers which meet at the huddle of grey houses, prodigiously brightened with floral displays in summer, that make up **BEDDGELERT**. A sentimental tale fabricated by a wily local publican to lure punters tells how the town got its name. **Gelert's Grave** (*bedd* means burial place), an enclosure just south of town, is supposedly the final resting place of Prince Llywelyn ap Iorwerth's faithful dog, Gelert, who was left in charge of the prince's infant son while he went hunting. On his return, the child was gone and the hound's muzzle was soaked in blood. Jumping to conclusions, the impetuous Llywelyn slew the dog, only to find the child safely asleep beneath its cot and a dead wolf beside him. Llywelyn hurried to his dog, which licked his hand as it died.

Beyond the "grave", the river crashes down the bony and picturesque **Aberglaslyn Gorge** towards Porthmadog. You can walk past Gelert's Grave, then cross over the bridge onto a path which hugs the left bank for a mile affording a closer look at the river's course through chutes and channels in sculpted rocks. Return the same way.

A mile in the opposite direction up Nantgwynant, the **Sygun Copper Mine** (daily: Easter–Oct 10am–5pm; Nov–Easter 10.30am–4pm; Ⓦ www.syguncoppermine.co.uk; £8) is the dilapidated remnant of what, until a century ago,

Walks up Snowdon

The following are justifiably the most popular of the seven accepted **walking** routes up **Snowdon**. All are easy to follow in good weather but you should still carry the 1:25,000 *OS Explorer #OL17* map.

Llanberis Path

The easiest, longest and most derided route up Snowdon, the **Llanberis Path** (5 miles to summit; 3200ft ascent; 3hr) follows the rail line which gets gradually steeper to the "Finger Stone" at **Bwlch Glas** (Green Pass). This marks the arrival of the Snowdon Ranger Path, and three routes coming up from Pen-y-Pass to join the Llanberis Path for the final ascent to **Yr Wyddfa**, the summit.

The Miners' and Pig tracks

The **Miners' Track** (4 miles to summit; 2400ft ascent; 2hr 30min) is the easiest of the three routes up from Pen-y-Pass, a broad track leading south then west to the dilapidated remains of the former copper mines in Cwm Dyli. Skirting around the right of a lake, the path climbs more steeply to the lake-filled Cwm Glaslyn, then again to Upper Glaslyn, from where the measured steps of those ahead warn of the impending switchback ascent to the junction with the Llanberis Path.

The stonier **Pig Track** (3.5 miles to summit; 2400ft ascent; 2hr 30min) is really just a variation on the Miners' Track, leaving from the western end of the Pen-y-Pass car park and climbing up to **Bwlch y Moch** (the Pass of the Pigs) before meeting the Miners' Track prior to the zigzag up to the Llanberis Path.

Snowdon Horseshoe

Some claim that the **Snowdon Horseshoe** (8 miles round; 3200ft ascent; 5–7hr) is one of the finest ridge walks in Europe. The route makes a full anticlockwise circuit around the three glacier-carved cwms of Upper Glaslyn, Glaslyn and Llydaw. Not to be taken lightly, it includes the knife-edge traverse of **Crib Goch**, which requires a head for heights at any time, and a minimum of an ice axe and crampons in winter. The path follows the Pig Track to Bwlch y Moch, then pitches right for the moderate scramble up to Crib Goch. If you balk at any of this, turn back; if not, pick your way along the sensational ridge to **Crib-y-ddysgl** (3494ft) and, on easier ground, to the summit. The return to Llyn Llydaw and the Miners' Track is via **Bwlch-y-Saethau** (Pass of the Arrows) and **Y Lliwedd** (2930ft).

NORTH WALES | Snowdonia

had been the valley's prime source of income from Roman times. The multiple levels of tunnels and galleries can now be visited on a 45-minute self-guided tour, accompanied by the disembodied voice of a miner describing his life in the mine.

Buses all stop by the Tŷ Isaf National Trust shop (Easter–Oct Wed, Sat & Sun 1–4pm), by the village bridge and just a few yards from the **tourist office** (Easter–Oct daily 9.30am–5.30pm; Nov–Easter Fri, Sat & Sun 9.30am–4.30pm; ℡01766/890615, ⓦwww.beddgelerttourism.com). The best places to **stay** are *Beddgelert Bistro & Antiques*, Waterloo House, directly opposite the bridge (℡01766/890543; ❷), with three attractive en-suite rooms above the restaurant; *Plas Tan-y-Graig* (℡01766/890310, ⓦwww.plastanygraig.co.uk; ❷), also near the bridge, a decent budget B&B aimed at walkers and cyclists; and *Sygun Fawr Country House*, three quarters of a mile away off the A498 (℡01766/890258, ⓦwww.sygunfawr.co.uk; ❺), a sixteenth-century house in its own grounds with a sauna and great four-course evening meals (£20). The excellent *Beddgelert Forest Campsite* (℡01766/890288) is a mile out on the Caernarfon road, four miles before the highly rated *Snowdon Ranger YHA* **hostel** (℡0870/770 6038,

@snowdon@yha.org.uk; dorms £11; mid-Feb to Dec). The *Bryn Gwynant YHA* hostel (T0870/770 5732, @bryngwynant@yha.org.uk; Jan–Oct; dorms £11) is beautifully sited in Nantgwynant, four miles northeast of Beddgelert on the A498, and has a **campsite** where you can use the hostel's facilities for half the adult rate.

Blaenau Ffestiniog and around

BLAENAU FFESTINIOG sits at the head of the bucolic Vale of Ffestiniog, a dramatic contrast to the forbidding town, hemmed in by stark slopes strewn with heaps of splintered slate. When clouds hunker low in this great cwm and rain sheets the grey roofs, grey walls and grey paving slabs, it can be a terrifically gloomy place. Thousands of tons of slate were once hewn from the labyrinth of underground caverns here each year, but these days the town is only kept alive by its extant slate-cavern tour, and by tourists who change from the Lledr Valley train line onto the wonderful, narrow-gauge **Ffestiniog Railway** (see p.787), which winds up from Porthmadog.

It's difficult to get a real feeling of what slate means to the town without a visit to the **Llechwedd Slate Caverns** (daily: March–Sept 10am–6pm; Oct–Feb 10am–5pm last tour 45min before closing; single tour £8.75, both tours £13.25;

The Welsh slate industry

Slate derives its name from the Old French word *esclater*, meaning to split – an apt reflection of its most highly valued quality. The Romans recognized the potential of the substance, roofing the houses of Segontium with it (see p.792), and Edward I used it extensively in his Iron Ring of castles around Snowdonia, but it wasn't until around 1780 that Britain's Industrial Revolution kicked in, leading to greater urbanization and boosting the demand for Welsh roofing slates. Cities grew: Hamburg was reroofed with Welsh slate after its fire of 1842, and it is the same material which still gives that rainy-day sheen to interminable rows of English mill-town houses.

For the 1862 London Exhibition, one skilled craftsman produced a sheet of slate ten feet long, a foot wide and a sixteenth of an inch thick – so thin it could be flexed – firmly establishing Welsh slate as the finest in the world. By 1898, Welsh quarries – largely run, like the coal and steel industries of the south, by the English – were producing half a million tons of dressed slate a year, almost all of it from Snowdonia. At Penrhyn and Dinorwig, mountains were hacked away in terraces, sometimes rising 2000ft above sea level, with the teams of workers negotiating with the foreman for the choicest piece of rock and the selling price for what they produced. They often slept through the week in damp dormitories on the mountain, and tuberculosis was common, exacerbated by the slate dust. At Blaenau Ffestiniog, the seams required mining underground rather than quarrying, but conditions were no better, with miners even having to buy their own candles, the only light they had. In spite of this, thousands left their hillside smallholdings for the burgeoning quarry towns. Few workers were allowed to join Undeb Chwarelwyr Gogledd Cymru (the North Wales Quarrymen's Union), and in 1900 the workers in Lord Penrhyn's quarry at Bethesda went out on strike. They stayed out for three years, but failed to win any concessions. Those who got their jobs back were forced to work for even less money as a recession took hold, and although the two world wars heralded mini-booms as bombed houses were replaced, the industry never recovered its nineteenth-century prosperity, and most quarries and mines closed in the 1950s.

Sadly, what little slate is produced today mostly goes for things besides roofing: floor tiles, road aggregate, and an astonishing array of nasty ashtrays and coasters etched with mountainscapes.

ⓦ www.llechwedd-slate-caverns.co.uk), on the edge of town on the road to Betws-y-Coed. There are two tours available. On the **Miners' Tramway Tour**, you are plied with facts about slate mining as a small train takes you a third of a mile along one of the oldest levels to the enormous Cathedral Cave and the open-air Chough's Cavern. The awe-inspiring scale of the place justifies the trip, even without the tableaux of Victorian miners at work. On the more dramatic **Deep Mine Tour**, a steeply inclined railway takes you down to a labyrinth of tunnels through which you are guided by an irksome taped spiel of a Victorian miner. The long caverns angling back into the gloom are increasingly impressive, culminating in one filled by a beautiful opalescent pool.

Practicalities

The **train station** on the High Street serves both the Ffestiniog line to Porthmadog and mainline train services from Betws-y-Coed, and is a short walk up the main drag from the **tourist office** (Easter–Oct daily 9.30am–12.30pm & 1.30–5.30pm; ⓣ01766/830360), opposite the *Queen's Hotel*. **Buses** stop either in the station car park or along High Street. Most visitors ride the train up from Porthmadog, visit the slate mine and leave, so **accommodation** is limited, but excellent value. In town, *Isallt Guest House* on Church Street (ⓣ01766/832488; ❷) is good, or step up to the *Queen's Hotel*, 1 High St (ⓣ01766/830055, ⓦ www.queens-snowdonia.co.uk; ❹), handily sited by the station. Two miles south on the A470 (Manod Road) is *Cae Du* (ⓣ01766/830847, ⓦ www.caedu .co.uk; ❷), in a sixteenth-century farmhouse, while one of the best choices in the area is *Bryn Elltyd* (ⓣ01766/831356, ⓦ www.accommodation-snowdonia .com; ❷), a fine B&B about a mile from town in Tanygrysiau, which overlooks Llyn Ystradau and is run by a qualified mountain leader.

All-day breakfasts and simple lunches are served at *Isallt Café*, near the train station, and the *Lakeside Café* by the information centre at Tanygrisiau. For more substantial **meals**, the *Queen's Hotel* offers tasty, moderately priced dishes, and there's good pub food at *The Commercial* on Commercial Square half a mile north. The chippy across the road from *The Commercial* is the best in town.

Bala

The little water-sports town of **BALA** (Y Bala), twenty miles east of Blaenau Ffestiniog, is set at the northern end of Wales's largest natural lake, **Llyn Tegid**. The lake is perfect for windsurfing due to the winds buffeting up the Talyllyn Valley, which slices thirty miles northeast from the coast, along the Bala geological fault. Bala Adventure and Watersports Centre (ⓣ01678/521059, ⓦ www .balawatersports.com) runs courses and rents equipment for **windsurfing**, **kayaking** and **sailing**.

Around two hundred days a year dam-released water crashes down the white-water course of **Canolfan Tryweryn**, four miles west up the A4212, facilitating commercial **whitewater rafting** trips (ⓣ01678/521083, ⓦ www .ukrafting.co.uk), down a mile-and-a-half course. Either go for two runs down (40–60min; £25) or two-hour session (4–7 people for £195 midweek and £280 at weekends). Stepping up a notch, try the Orca, a two-person inflatable in which you tackle the rapids unguided (half-day £65 per person).

The only public transport access is on **bus** #X94, which runs from Llangollen to Dolgellau, stopping on Bala's High Street. The **tourist office** (April–Oct daily 10am–5.30pm; Nov–March Mon & Fri–Sun 10am–4pm; ⓣ01678/521021, ⓔ bala.tic@gwynedd.gov.uk) is on Pensarn Road on the lakeside, five minutes' walk away.

Bala has plenty of good **places to stay**, including the welcoming *Traian*, 95 Tegid St (☎01678/520059; ②), with shared bathrooms, and *Abercelyn*, a fine country house half a mile south of Bala on the A494 (☎01678/521109, ⓦwww.abercelyn.co.uk; ④).

The central *Bala Backpackers*, 32 Tegid St (☎01678/521700, ⓦwww .bala-backpackers.co.uk; dorms £10–12), is also handy, and there's **camping** at *Pen-y-Bont*, just by the lakeside steam-railway station off the B4391 Llandrillo backroad (☎01678/520549; April–Oct).

The Llŷn

The Llŷn takes its name from an Irish word for peninsula – aptly for this most westerly part of North Wales, which, until the fifth century, had a significant Irish population. The cliff- and cove-lined finger of land juts out south and west, separating Cardigan and Caernarfon bays, its hills tapering away along the ancient route to Aberdaron, where pilgrims sailed for Ynys Enlli (Bardsey Island). Today, it's the beaches that lure people to the south-coast family resorts of **Cricieth**, **Pwllheli** and **Abersoch**, and unless you want to rent windsurfers or canoes, it's preferable to press on along the narrow roads that dawdle down towards **Aberdaron**. Not even Snowdonia can match the remoteness of the tip of the Llŷn, and nowhere in Wales is more staunchly Welsh: road signs are still bilingual but the English is frequently obliterated; Stryd Fawr is used instead of High Street, and in most local shops you'll only hear Welsh spoken.

The Llŷn is reached through one of the two gateway towns: **Porthmadog**, home to the private "dream village" of **Portmeirion** and terminus of the **Ffestiniog Railway**; or **Caernarfon**, where a magnificent fortress guards the mouth of the Menai Strait.

Porthmadog and around

Located right at the point where the Llŷn peninsula meets the Cambrian coast, **PORTHMADOG** was once the busiest slate port in North Wales. Nowadays, it's a pleasant enough town to spend a night or two, although it sadly makes little of its situation on the north bank of the vast, mountain-backed estuary. Two things it does make a fuss about are the Italianate folly of Portmeirion, almost three miles east of town, and the Ffestiniog Railway that originally carried slate down from Blaenau Ffestiniog through verdant mountain scenery. Porthmadog would never have existed at all without the entrepreneurial ventures of a Lincolnshire MP named William Alexander Madocks, who named the town after both himself and the Welsh prince Madog, who some say sailed from the nearby Ynys Fadog (Madog's Island) to North America in 1170. Between 1808 and 1812, Madocks fought tides and currents to build the mile-long embankment of The Cob, southeast of present-day Porthmadog, enclosing seven thousand acres of the estuary. A wharf was built and, with the completion of the Ffestiniog Railway in 1836, the town spread along a waterfront thick with orderly heaps of slate and the masts of merchant ships.

Without a doubt, the **Ffestiniog Railway** (Easter–Oct 4–8 trains daily; Nov–Easter mainly weekends; return to Blaenau Ffestiniog £16, to Tan-y-Bwlch £9.50, discounts on first and last trains of the day; ☎01766/516000, ⓦwww.festrail.co.uk) ranks as Wales's finest narrow-gauge rail line, twisting and looping up 650ft from the wharf at Porthmadog to the slate mines at Blaenau Ffestiniog, thirteen miles away. It once carried slate from the mines down to the port with the help of gravity, horses riding with the goods then hauling the empty carriages back up again. Steam had to be introduced to cope with the 100,000 tons of slate a year that Blaenau Ffestiniog was churning out by the late nineteenth century, but the slate roofing market collapsed between the wars and the line was abandoned in 1946. Most of the tracks and sleepers had disappeared by 1954, when a bunch of dedicated volunteers began reconstruction, only completing the entire route in 1982. Leaving Porthmadog, trains cross The Cob and then stop at **Minffordd**, a mile from Portmeirion.

Portmeirion

The area's main lure is the unique, Italianate private village of **PORTMEIRION** (daily 9.30am–5.30pm; Ⓦwww.portmeirion-village.com; £6), set on a small rocky peninsula in Tremadog Bay, three miles east near Minffordd. You can walk there in an hour from Porthmadog, or catch the Express #98 bus which goes right to the gate. By train, take either the main line or Ffestiniog trains to Minffordd, from where it's a signposted 25-minute walk to Portmeirion.

Perhaps best known as "The Village" in the 1960s cult British TV series *The Prisoner*, Portmeirion was the brainchild of eccentric architect Clough Williams-Ellis, and his dream to build an ideal village using a "gay, light-opera sort of approach". The result is certainly theatrical: a stage set with a lucky dip of buildings arranged to distort perspectives and reveal tantalizing glimpses of the seascape behind.

In the 1920s, Williams-Ellis bought the site and turned an existing house into a hotel, the income from this providing funds for his "Home for Fallen Buildings". Endangered structures in every conceivable style from all over Britain and abroad were brought here and arranged around a Mediterranean piazza: a Neoclassical colonnade from Bristol, Siamese figures, a Jacobean town hall, a campanile and a pantheon. Painted in pastel shades of turquoise, ochre and buff yellows, it is continually surprising, with hidden entrances and cherubs popping out of crevices – eclectic yet never quite inappropriate.

More than three thousand visitors a day come to ogle in summer, when it can be a delight; fewer in winter, when it seems just bizarre. Other than buying *Prisoner* memorabilia there's little to actually do, so bring a picnic and spend the afternoon exploring the delightful grounds. In the evening, when the village is closed to the public, patrons at the opulent, waterside *Portmeirion Hotel* (Ⓣ01766/770000, Ⓦwww.portmeirion-village.com; ❽) and the chic Victorian "castle" *Castell Deudraeth* (same contacts; ❽) get to see the place at its best – peaceful, even ghostly.

Practicalities

Porthmadog's High Street runs between the mainline **train station**, at the north end, and the **Ffestiniog station**, by the harbour about half a mile to the south. In between the two, National Express **coaches** stop outside the *Royal Sportsman* while local **bus** services stop outside the *Australia Inn*. The helpful **tourist office** (Easter–Oct daily 9.30am–5.30pm; Nov–Easter daily except Wed 10am–5pm; Ⓣ01766/512981, Ⓦwww.porthmadog.co.uk) is by the harbour on High Street

While limited budgets are well catered for, there's not much really decent **accommodation**, unless you're prepared to splash out for a night at the swanky *Portmeirion Hotel* in Portmeirion (see above). For **B&B** try *Treforris*, Garth Road (Ⓣ01766/512853; ❶), in a large house overlooking the harbour a fifteen-minute walk west, or *Yr Hen Fecws*, 15 Lombard St (Ⓣ01766/514625; ❸), with comfy, uncluttered rooms, beside a popular restaurant of the same name (see below).

Several good options are dotted around the village of Tremadog, a mile north, including the *Snowdon Lodge* on Church Street (℡01766/515354, ⓦwww .snowdonlodge.co.uk; dorms £14 including breakfast, ❶/❷), a well-organized and welcoming backpackers' **hostel** in the house where T.E. Lawrence was born. Best of all is *Plas Tan-yr-Allt* (℡01766/514545, ⓦwww.tanyrallt.co.uk; ❺), a gorgeous luxury B&B in a house once owned by Shelley, a few hundred yards from Tremadog on the road to Beddgelert. For camping, head for the pleasant, family-oriented *Tyddyn Llwyn* (℡01766/512205), fifteen minutes' walk west along the A497 which spurs off High Street.

For **food** in Porthmadog, there's *Yr Hen Fecws*, at 16 Lombard St (℡01766/514625), a lively bistro with some good veggie options, or *Caffi y Morwr Madog*, Pencei, a small modern café with some pavement tables overlooking the harbour, serving decent espresso coffee and a range of bagels, snacks, "catch of the day" meals and desserts.

If you've got transport or want to walk up an appetite, there's fantastic pub food to be had in nearby Tremadog, less than a mile north, at the *Golden Fleece*. For **drinking**, make for *Y Llong* (The Ship) at 14 Lombard St, a busy pub (one room nonsmoking) that sells real ales including those from Porthmadog's new Purple Moose microbrewery.

Cricieth and around

When sea-bathing became the Victorian fashion, English families descended on the sweeping sand and shingle beach at **CRICIETH** (sometimes Criccieth), five miles west of Porthmadog, a quiet, amiable resort dominated by the battle-worn remains of **Cricieth Castle** (daily: mid-March to May & Oct 10am–5pm, June–Sept 10am–6pm, £2.90; Nov to mid-March 10am–4pm, free; CADW), with its twin-towered gatehouse. Started by Llywelyn ap Iorwerth in 1230, it was strengthened by Edward I around 1283, and razed by Owain Glyndŵr in 1404, leaving little besides a plan of broken walls. It's a great spot to sit and look over Cardigan Bay to Harlech, but leave time for the ticket office, where there's a workaday exhibition on Welsh castles and a wonderful animated cartoon based on the twelfth-century Cambrian travels of Giraldus Cambrensis as he gathered support for the Third Crusade.

Buses and **trains** along the Cambrian coastline stop a couple of hundred yards west of Y Maes, the open square at the centre of Cricieth. **Accommodation** is plentiful, with the *Moelwyn*, 27–29 Mona Terrace (℡01766/522500, ⓔmoelwyn@aol.com; ❹; March–Nov), a smart choice with great sea views. For something cheaper head for *Craig-y-Môr*, West Parade (℡01766/522830; ❷; March–Oct), a guest house with well-appointed rooms and some with fine sea views; or *Tyddyn Morthwyl Farm and Caravan Park*, a mile and a half north on Caernarfon Road (the B4411) (℡01766/522115), which has good camping (£7 per tent) and a bunkhouse (£6 per person). *Mynydd Ednyfed* (℡01766/523269, ⓦwww.cricieth.net; ❺) is a classy country hotel a mile north on Caernarfon Road.

For such a small town, good **restaurants** are surprisingly abundant. In town, make for *Moelwyn* (see above), which has a superb sea-facing restaurant; or head out to *Mynydd Ednyfed* (see above). The *Prince of Wales*, on Stryd Fawr, offers a great **pub** atmosphere and decent bar meals.

Llanystumdwy

A mile west of Cricieth, the village of **LLANYSTUMDWY** celebrates its most famous son, the Welsh patriot, social reformer and British prime minister David

Lloyd George. He grew up in Highgate House, now part of the **Lloyd George Museum** (Easter–May Mon–Fri and bank holiday weekends 10.30am–5pm; June Mon–Sat 10.30am–5pm; July–Sept daily 10.30am–5pm; Oct Mon–Fri 11am–4pm; £3), comprising a fairly dull collection of gifts, awards and caskets honouring the statesman, displays full of anecdotes and little-known facts, and a couple of short films giving a broad sweep of his life. Lloyd George is buried under a memorial by the River Dwyfor – a boulder and two simple plaques by Portmeirion designer Clough Williams-Ellis. **Bus** #3 from Porthmadog and Cricieth passes through the village on its way to Pwllheli.

Pwllheli and Abersoch

PWLLHELI (pronounced "poolth-heli") is the market town for the peninsula, a role it has maintained since 1355 when it gained its charter, though there's little sign of its history nowadays. Primarily useful as the final stop for Cambrian coast **trains** and the terminus for National Express **coaches** (which stop on Y Maes, the main square), it's a thoroughly Welsh place: even in the tourist season you'll hear far more Welsh spoken here than English. The **tourist office** is on Station Square (April–Oct daily 9am–5pm; Nov–March Mon–Wed, Fri & Sat 10.30am–4.30pm; ☎01758/613000, ⓔpwllheli.tic@gwynedd.gov.uk). During the summer you can rent **mountain bikes** at Llŷn Cycle Hire, 2 Ala Rd (☎01758/612414). If you decide to **stay**, try *Bank Place* on Stryd Fawr (☎01758/612103; ❶) or, four hundred yards away, *Llys Gwyrfai*, 14 West End Parade (☎01758/614877; ❷), a comfortable guest-house with sea views and home-cooked meals.

It is generally better to push seven miles beyond Pwllheli to **ABERSOCH**, a former fishing village pitched in the middle of two golden bays. Over the last century it has become a thoroughly anglicized resort, with a distinctly haughty opinion of itself. Such high self-esteem isn't really justified, but at high tide the harbour is attractive, and the long swathe of the beach-hut-backed Town Beach is a fine spot. A short walk along the beach shakes off most of the crowds, but a better bet is to make for three-mile-long **Porth Neigwl** (Hell's Mouth), two miles to the southwest, which ranks as one of the country's best **surf beaches**; you'll need your own gear, and beware of the undertow if you're swimming. Back in Abersoch, you can get instruction and **rent windsurfers**, surfboards and wetsuits from West Coast Surf Shop, Lôn Pen Cei (☎01758/713067, ⓦwww.westcoastsurf.co.uk), by the harbour. **Buses** from Pwllheli make a loop through the middle of Abersoch, stopping on Lôn Pen Cei by the **tourist office** (April–Sept daily 10.30am–4.30pm; Oct–March Sat & Sun 11am–1pm; ☎01758/712929, ⓦwww.abersochtouristinfo.co.uk). For **accommodation**, try the modest and comfortable *Llwyn Du*, Lôn Sarn Bach (☎01758/712186; ❶); *Angorfa Guest House*, Lôn Sarn Bach (☎01758/712967; ❸); and the welcoming *Goslings at the Carisbrooke*, Lôn Sarn Bach (☎01758/712526, ⓦwww.abersoch-carisbrookehotel.co.uk; ❺), which is particularly well set up for families.

There are some decent **places to eat**: *Mañana*, on Lôn Pen Cei, serves Mexican and Italian food, while just up the road is *Angelina's* (☎01758/712353), with a broad menu (plus yummy desserts). *The Ship*, out of town in Llanbedrog, near Pwllheli, is excellent.

Aberdaron and Bardsey Island

The small, lime-washed fishing village of **ABERDARON** backs a pebble beach two miles short of the tip of the Llŷn. For a thousand years, from the sixth century onwards, it was the last stop for pilgrims to **Bardsey Island**

(Ynys Enlli: the Island of the Currents), just offshore, where three visits were proclaimed equivalent to one pilgrimage to Rome. Many pilgrims came to die here, earning the place its epithet "The Isle of Twenty Thousand Saints". Bardsey is heart-stoppingly beautiful and well worth a visit – there are self-catering cottages available on the island, or you could just go for a day-trip. For details of both, contact the Bardsey Island Trust (☎01758/112233, ⓦwww.enlli.org). In olden days, the final gathering place before the treacherous crossing was the fourteenth-century Y Gegin Fawr (Great Kitchen), a stone building which still operates as a **café** in the middle of Aberdaron. Today, pilgrims are more likely to be attracted by poetry, as, until 1978, **R.S. Thomas** (1913–2000) was the minister at Aberdaron's seafront church of St Hywyn.

Without your own transport, the only way to get to Aberdaron is to catch bus #17 from Pwllheli (Mon–Sat). **Accommodation** is fairly limited; the least expensive option is *Brynmor* (☎01758/760344; ❷), overlooking the bay, just up the road to Porth Oer. The *Tŷ Newydd* hotel (☎01758/760207; ❺) is a good bet too; make time for a pint or meal on their beach terrace as the sun sets. The best and quietest **campsite** around is *Mur Melyn* (no phone), just over a mile out from Aberdaron, midway to Porth Oer; take the B4413 west, fork right, then turn left at Pen-y-Bont house.

Caernarfon

It was in **CAERNARFON**, in 1969, that Charles, the current heir to the throne, was invested as Prince of Wales, a ceremony which reaffirmed English sovereignty over Wales in this, one of the most nationalist of Welsh-speaking regions. Since 1282, when the English defeated Llywelyn ap Gruffydd, the last Welsh prince of Wales, the title has been bestowed on heirs to the English (and then British) throne, but it wasn't until 1911 that the machinations of David Lloyd George – MP for Caernarfon and future prime minister – brought a theatrical investiture ceremony to the centre of his constituency: an odd move for a proto-nationalist, considering the symbolic implications. Caernarfon's location on the Menai Strait with views across to Anglesey makes it an appealing place, but apart from the vastly imposing **castle** there isn't too much to see. You can't walk along the near-complete rectangle of town walls and the rest of the town has been ripped through by a main road and boxed in by modern buildings. That said, it's a spirited and lively town, is well situated on the Menai Strait, between the mainland and Anglesey, and has good bus connections to Llanberis and Snowdonia.

The Town

In 1283, Edward I started work on **Caernarfon Castle** (June–Sept daily 9.30am–6pm; Easter–May & Oct daily 9.30am–5pm; Nov–Easter Mon–Sat 9.30am–4pm, Sun 11am–4pm; £4.75; CADW), the strongest link in his Iron Ring, a decisive hammer-blow to any Welsh aspirations to autonomy and the ultimate symbol of Anglo-Norman military might. Edward attempted to appease the Welsh by paying tribute to aspects of local legend. The Welsh had long associated their town with the eastern capital of the Roman Empire: Caernarfon's old name, Caer Cystennin, was also the name used for Constantinople, and Constantine himself was believed to have been born at Segontium (see below). Edward's architect, James of St George, exploited this connection in the distinctive limestone and sandstone banding and the polygonal towers, both reminiscent of the Theodosian walls in present-day Istanbul.

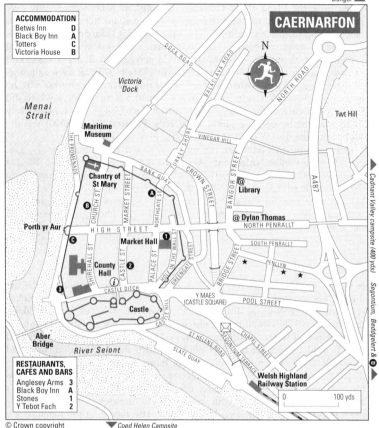

CAERNARFON

N

ACCOMMODATION
Betws Inn   **D**
Black Boy Inn   **A**
Totters   **C**
Victoria House   **B**

Menai
Strait

Victoria
Dock

Twt Hill

**Maritime
Museum**

**Chantry of
St Mary**

BANK QUAY

CROWN STREET

BANGOR STREET

VINEGAR HILL

BALACLAVA ROAD

DOCK ROAD

NORTH ROAD

TURKEY SHORE

A487

@ **Library**

@ **Dylan Thomas**
NORTH PENRALLT

SOUTH PENRALLT

THE PROMENADE

CHURCH ST

MARKET STREET

NORTHGATE ST

HIGH STREET

Porth yr Aur

Market Hall

**County
Hall**

SHIREHALL ST

CASTLE ST

PALACE ST

HOLE IN THE WALL ST

GREENGATE STREET

BRIDGE STREET

PENLLYN

★

★ ★ ★

CASTLE DITCH

Y MAES
(CASTLE SQUARE)

POOL STREET

Castle

CASTLE HILL

**Aber
Bridge**

River Seiont

ST HELEN'S ROAD

SLATE QUAY

SEGONTIUM TERRACE

CHAPEL STREET

**Welsh Highland
Railway Station**

0   100 yds

**RESTAURANTS,
CAFES AND BARS**
Anglesey Arms   **3**
Black Boy Inn   **A**
Stones   **1**
Y Tebot Fach   **2**

© Crown copyright   ▼ *Coed Helen Campsite*

► *Cadnant Valley campsite (400 yds)*

Segontium, Beddgelert & ● D ►

16

   In military terms, the castle is supreme. It was taken once, before building was complete, but then withstood two sieges by Owain Glyndŵr with a garrison of only 28 men-at-arms. Entering through the **King's Gate**, the castle's strength is immediately apparent. Embrasures and murder holes between the octagonal towers face in on no fewer than five gates and six portcullises, and that's once you have crossed the moat. Inside, the huge lawn gives a misleading impression since both the wall dividing the two original wards and all the buildings that filled them crumbled away long ago. The towers are in a much better state, and linked by an exhausting honeycomb of wall-walks and tunnels. The tallest is the **King's Tower** whose three slender turrets are adorned with eagle sculptures and give the best views of the town. To the south, the Queen's Tower is entirely taken up by the numbingly thorough **Museum of the Royal Welch Fusiliers**, while the Northeast Tower houses the **Prince of Wales Exhibition**, just outside which is the Dinorwig slate dais used for Charles's investiture.
   A ten-minute walk along the A4085 Beddgelert road brings you to **Segontium Roman Fort** (fort daily 10.30am–4.30pm; museum daily except Mon 12.30–4.30pm; free; CADW), the western end of the Roman road from Chester. The Romans occupied this five-acre site for three centuries from around

78 AD, though most of the remains are from the final rebuilding after 364. The ground plan is seldom more than shin-high and somewhat baffling, making the museum and displays in the ticket office pretty much essential.

The narrow-gauge **Welsh Highland Railway** (mid-March to Oct 2–6 trains most days; ☎01766/516000, ⓦwww.festrail.co.uk) starts in Caernarfon, just near the harbour on St Helen's Road. Ultimately, it will run 25 miles to Porthmadog via Beddgelert, but currently runs to Rhyd-Ddu, starting point for southerly ascents of Snowdon (unlimited one-day travel £16), with a stop outside the *Snowdon Ranger YHA* hostel. Joint tickets with the Ffestiniog Railway are available.

Practicalities

With no mainline train station, the hub of Caernarfon's public transport system is Penllyn, where **buses** stop. The **tourist office** is close by on Castle Street (Easter–Oct daily 9.30am–5pm; Nov–Easter Mon–Sat 10am–5pm; ☎01286/672232, ⓔcaernarfon.tic@gwynedd.gov.uk). There are a number of **accommodation** options close to the centre such as *Victoria House*, 13 Church St (☎01286/678263; ❸), a good-value B&B within the town walls, and the characterful *Black Boy Inn* (☎01286/673604; ❸/❹), in one of the town's oldest buildings on Northgate Street. Five miles southeast of Caernarfon, the excellent *Betws Inn*, A4085 in Betws Garmon (☎01286/650324, ⓦwww.betws-inn .co.uk; ❸), occupies a stylishly restored former drovers' inn where wonderful three-course dinners (£15) are served by arrangement. *Totters*, 2 High St (☎01286/672963, ⓦwww.applemaps.co.uk/totters; dorms £12), is a superb and very friendly independent **hostel**. The nearest **campsite** is *Cadnant Valley* (☎01286/673196; £9–12 per tent; closed Nov–Feb), ten minutes' walk east of town near the start of the A4086 to Llanberis.

Caernarfon boasts a number of low-key and likeable **restaurants**: try the bistro-style fare at *Stones*, 4 Hole in the Wall St (closed Sun & Mon), or a cream tea at ⚔ *Y Tebot Bach*, 13 Castle St (closed Sun & Mon), which serves modern food with old-fashioned attention to detail in a smoke- and chip-free tearoom. The cheapest option is the excellent **bar meals** at the aforementioned *Black Boy Inn*. For **drinking**, start with a pint on the sea wall outside the *Anglesey Arms*.

The island of Anglesey

Across the Menai Strait from Caernarfon, **Anglesey** (Ynys Môn) welcomes visitors to "Mam Cymru", the Mother of Wales, attesting to the island's former importance as the national breadbasket. In the twelfth century Giraldus Cambrensis noted that "when crops have failed in other regions, this island, from its soil and its abundant produce, has been able to supply all Wales," and the land remains predominantly pastoral, with small fields, stone walls and white houses reminiscent of parts of Ireland or England. Linguistically and politically, though, Anglesey is intensely Welsh, with seventy percent of the islanders being first-language Welsh-speakers. The island was the crucible of pre-Roman druidic activity in Britain, and there are still numerous Neolithic remains at which to soak up the atmosphere of a pagan past. Especially since the advent of the A55 main road, many people charge straight through to **Holyhead** and the Irish ferries, missing out on Anglesey's many charms. There's the ancient town of **Beaumaris**, with its fine castle, the Whistler mural at **Plas Newydd** (not to be confused with Plas Newydd in Llangollen; see p.773) and some superb coastal scenery: a necklace of fine sandy coves and rocky headlands that's a match for anywhere in the country.

Beaumaris

The original inhabitants of **BEAUMARIS** (Biwmares) were evicted by Edward I to make way for the construction of his new castle and bastide town, dubbed "beautiful marsh" in an attempt to attract English settlers. Today the place can still seem like the small English outpost Edward intended, with its elegant Georgian terrace along the front (designed by Joseph Hansom, of cab fame) and more plummy English accents than you'll have heard for a while. While Beaumaris repays an afternoon mooching around and enjoying the views across the Strait, it also boasts more sights than the rest of the island put together, inevitably drawing the crowds in summer.

Beaumaris Castle (June–Sept daily 9.30am–6pm; mid-March to May & Oct daily 9.30am–5pm; Nov to mid-March Mon–Sat 9.30am–4pm, Sun 11am–4pm; £3; CADW) might never have been built had Madog ap Llywelyn not captured Caernarfon in 1294. When asked to build the new castle, James of St George abandoned the Caernarfon design in favour of a concentric plan, developing it into a highly evolved symmetrical octagon. Sited on flat land at the edge of town, the castle is denied the domineering majesty of Caernarfon or Harlech, its low outer walls appearing almost welcoming until you begin to appreciate the concentric layout of the defences protected by massive towers, a moat linked to the sea and the Arab-influenced staggered entries through the two gatehouses. Despite more than thirty years' work, the project was never quite finished, leaving most of the inner ward empty and the corbels and fireplaces built into the walls unused. You can explore the internal passages in the walls but the low-parapet wall-walk, from where you get the best idea of the castle's defensive capability, remains off limits. Impressive as they are, none of these defences was able to prevent siege by Owain Glyndŵr, who held the castle for two years from 1403, although they did withhold a Parliamentarian siege during the Civil War.

Almost opposite the castle stands the Jacobean **Beaumaris Court** (Easter–Sept daily 10.30am–5pm; £2.50, joint ticket with gaol £4), built in 1614 and the oldest active court in Britain. It is now used only for the twice-monthly Magistrates Court, but until 1971 the quarterly Assize Courts were held here. These were traditionally held in English, giving the jury little chance to follow the proceedings and Welsh-speaking defendants no defence against prosecutors renowned for slapping heavy penalties on minor offences. On session days you can watch the trials, but won't be able to take the recorded tour or inspect *The Lawsuit*, a plaque in the magistrates' room depicting two farmers pulling the horns and tail of a cow while a lawyer milks it.

Many citizens were transported from the court to the colonies for their misdemeanours; others only made it a couple of blocks to the 1829 **Beaumaris Gaol**, Steeple Lane (same hours; £2.50, joint ticket with court £4), which was considered a model prison, with running water and toilets in each cell, and an infirmary. Advanced perhaps, but nonetheless a gloomy place: witness the windowless punishment-cell, the yard for stone breaking and the treadmill water-pump operated by the prisoners. The least fortunate inmates were publicly hanged – the fate of a certain Richard Rowlands, whose disembodied voice leads the recorded tour of the building and various displays on prison life.

After all this gloom, a good way to lift the spirits is aboard one of the **pleasure cruises** (☎01248/810251; £5) out to (but not landing on) Puffin Island. The booking kiosk is at the foot of the pier.

Practicalities

With no trains or tourist office, Beaumaris seems poorly served, but it does have a regular **bus** service to Bangor (#53, #57 & #58). The best of the very limited range of **places to stay** are *Mountfield* B&B, immediately east of the castle (☎01248/810380; ❹), and the ancient and luxurious ✠ *Ye Olde Bull's Head Inn*, 18 Castle St (☎01248/810329, ⓦwww.bullsheadinn.co.uk; ❻), used as General Mytton's headquarters during the Civil War. *Kingsbridge* is the nearest **campsite**, two miles north in Llanfaes (☎01248/490636). *Pier House Café*, Bron Menai, is the best of the daytime **eating** options, while for something more substantial you can't miss *Ye Olde Bull's Head Inn* (see above), with a chic, modern brasserie, a fine formal restaurant and a great bar. For something simpler visit the wonderfully cosy *Sailor's Return* pub on Church Street.

Llanfairpwllgwyngyllgogerychwyrndrobwllll andysiliogogogoch

In the 1880s a local tailor invented the longest place-name in Britain in a successful attempt to draw tourists. However, it is an utter disappointment to arrive at **Llanfairpwllgwyngyllgogerychwyrndrobwllllandysiliogogogoch**, which translates as "St Mary's Church in the hollow of white hazel near a rapid whirlpool and the Church of St Tysilio near the red cave" – commonly shortened to **LLANFAIRPWLL**. All you'll find here is a train station, a tacky wool shop and a **tourist office** (Mon–Sat 9.30am–5.30pm, Sun 10am–5pm; closes 5pm Oct–Easter; ☎01248/713177, ⓔllanfairpwll@nwtic. com), the only one worth its salt on the island.

The marquises of Anglesey still live at **Plas Newydd** (April–Oct daily except Thurs & Fri noon–5pm; gardens open an hour earlier; £5, garden only £3; NT), a mile and a half south of Llanfairpwll, a modest three-storey mansion with incongruous Tudor caps on slender octagonal turrets. Inside, architect James Wyatt was given free stylistic rein, producing a Gothic music room followed by a Neoclassical staircase hall with a cantilevered staircase and deceptively solid-looking Doric columns – actually just painted wood. Corridors of oils and period rooms lead to the highlight, a 58-foot-long wall consumed by a trompe l'oeil painting by **Rex Whistler**, who spent a couple of years here in the 1930s. Walking along his imaginary seascape, your position appears to shift by over a mile as the mountains of Snowdonia and a whimsical composite of elements, culled from Italy as well as Britain, change perspective. Portmeirion (see p.788) is there, as are the Round Tower from Windsor Castle and the steeple from St Martin-in-the-Fields in London. Whistler himself appears as a gondolier, and again as a gardener in one of the two right-angled panels at either end, which appear to extend the room further. The prize exhibit in the **Cavalry Museum**, a few rooms further on, is the world's first articulated false leg, all wood, leather and springs, designed for the first marquis, who lost his leg at Waterloo.

Holyhead and around

Holy Island (Ynys Gybi) is blessed with Anglesey's best scenery and cursed with its most unattractive town. The spectacular sea cliffs around South Stack, and the Stone Age and Roman remains on Holyhead Mountain are just a couple of miles from workaday Holyhead, whose ferry routes to Ireland and good transport links mean you'll probably find your way there at some stage.

The local council's valiant attempts to brighten up **HOLYHEAD** (Caergybi; pronounced in English as "holly-head") somehow make this town of dilapidated shopfronts and high unemployment even more depressing. In 1727, Swift found it "scurvy, ill provided and comfortless", and little seems to have changed. The town is linked by ferries and catamarans run by Stena Line (℡08705/707070, ⓦwww.stenaline.com) and Irish Ferries (℡08705/171717, ⓦwww.irishferries.com) to both Dublin Port and Dun Laoghaire, six miles south of Dublin. Fortunately, train and ferry timings are reasonably well integrated, so you shouldn't need to spend much time here. The **tourist office** (daily 8.30am–6pm; ℡01407/762622, Ⓔholyhead@nwtic.com), in the ferry terminal, can point you to the recently upgraded **Holyhead Maritime Museum**, Newry Beach (Easter–Oct hours yet to be decided; £2; ℡01407/769745), with some interesting displays in the old lifeboat station.

Shun the bunch of poor **B&Bs** along the A5 into the town in favour of those around Walthew Avenue, most easily reached by turning left just before the tourist office onto the beachfront Prince of Wales Road, then left again into Walthew Avenue. While *Orotavia*, at no. 66 (℡01407/760259; ❷), is simple and cosy, the best of the bunch is *Yr Hendre* (℡01407/762929; ❸), round the corner on Porth-y-Felin Road. Fast **food** is the staple diet in Holyhead, but you can still eat well: the *Castle Bakery*, 83 Market St, is about the best café, and *Raja's*, 8 Newry St, serves the tastiest Bengal curries around.

Holyhead Mountain and South Stack

The northern half of Holy Island is ranged around the skirts of the 700-foot **Holyhead Mountain** (Mynydd Twr), its summit ringed by the seventeen-acre **Caer y Twr** (free access; CADW), one of the largest Iron Age sites in North Wales. The best approach is by car or bus #22 to the car park at **South Stack** (Ynys Lawd), two miles west of Holyhead, from where a path (30min) leads to the top of Holyhead Mountain. Most visitors only walk the few yards to the cliff-top **Ellin's Tower Seabird Centre** (Easter–Sept daily 10am–5pm; free) where, from April until the end of July, binoculars and closed-circuit TV give an unparalleled opportunity to watch up to three thousand birds – razorbills, guillemots and the odd puffin – nesting on the nearby sea cliffs while ravens and peregrines wheel outside the tower's windows. A twisting path leads down from the tower to a suspension bridge over the surging waves, leading over to the now fully automated pepper-pot **lighthouse** (Easter–Sept daily 10.30am–5.30pm; £3). Tickets are issued at the *South Stack Kitchen*, a café-cum-interpretative centre a hundred yards back down the lane. Nearby, nineteen low stone circles make up the **Cytiau'r Gwyddelod** or the "Huts of the Irish", a common name for any ancient settlement – in this case late Neolithic or early Bronze Age.

The north coast

Anglesey connects with the mainland at the university town of **Bangor**, a lively enough place, though best used as base for visiting **Penrhyn Castle** or as a springboard for Snowdonia. Heading east you leave the Menai Strait behind and are onto the **north coast** proper, where the castle town of **Conwy** and elegant **Llandudno** are essential stops. Beyond Llandudno the resorts get tackier, though there's reason enough to stop for the National Portrait Gallery at **Bodelwyddan**, the tiny cathedral at **St Asaph** and the ancient shrine at **Holywell**.

Bangor

BANGOR, across the bridge from Anglesey, is not big, but as the largest town in Gwynedd and home to Bangor University, it passes in these parts for cosmopolitan. The students decamp for the summer, leaving only a trickle of visitors to replace them. Bangor is a hotbed of passionate Welsh nationalism, hardly surprising in such a staunchly Welsh-speaking area, and it's a dramatic contrast from the largely English-speaking north-coast resorts.

Bangor's thirteenth- to fifteenth-century **cathedral**, on Deiniol Road (daily 11am–5pm; free), boasts the longest continuous use of any cathedral in Britain, easily predating the town. Pop in if only to see the sixteenth-century wooden **Mostyn Christ**, depicted bound and seated on a rock.

Just over the road, the **Bangor Museum and Art Gallery**, Ffordd Gwynedd (Tues–Fri 12.30–4.30pm, Sat 10.30am–4.30pm; free), offers snippets of local history enlivened by a traditional costume section and an archeology room, containing the most complete Roman sword found in Wales. The art gallery concentrates on predominantly Welsh contemporary works. For a good look down the Menai Strait to Telford's graceful bridge (the world's first large iron suspension bridge, completed in 1826), walk along Garth Road to Bangor's rejuvenated and pristine **Victorian Pier** (25p), which reaches halfway across to Anglesey.

Penrhyn Castle

There can hardly be a more vulgar testament to the Anglo-Welsh landowning gentry's oppression of the rural Welsh than the nonetheless compelling **Penrhyn Castle** (late March to June, Sept & Oct daily except Tues noon–5pm; July & Aug daily except Tues 11am–5pm; £7, £5 grounds, kitchens & railway museum only; NT), two miles east of Bangor. This monstrous, nineteenth-century neo-Norman fancy, with over three hundred rooms dripping with luxurious fittings, was funded by the quarry's huge profits. The sugar and slate fortune built by anti-abolitionist Richard Pennant, first Baron Penrhyn, provided the means for his self-aggrandizing great-great-nephew George Dawkins to hire architect Thomas Hopper, who spent thirteen years from 1827 encasing the neo-Gothic hall in a Norman fortress complete with monumental five-storey keep.

Everything is on a massive scale. Three-foot-thick oak doors separate the rooms, ebony is used to dramatic effect and a slate bed was built for the visit of Queen Victoria. The decoration is glorious, and fairly true to the Romanesque style, with its deeply cut chevrons, billets and double-cone ornamentation. The family amassed Wales's largest private painting collection, including numerous family likenesses, a Gainsborough landscape, Canaletto's *The Thames at Westminster* and a Rembrandt portrait. Also worth a visit are the Victorian kitchen and servants' quarters, something of an antidote to the opulence "above stairs".

Buses #5, #6 and #7 run frequently from Bangor to the gates, from where it is a mile-long walk to the house.

Practicalities

All north-coast trains stop at Bangor **train station**, Station Road, half a mile along Deiniol Road from the **tourist office** (April–Sept Mon, Wed & Fri

9.30am–4pm, Tues, Thurs & Sat 9.30am–5pm; ☏01248/352786, Ⓔbangor
.tic@gwynedd.gov.uk). Bangor doesn't have a huge choice of places to **stay**.
Most of the cheaper **accommodation** is at the northern end of Garth Road
(the continuation of Deiniol Road), about twenty minutes' walk from the
train station: try *Dilfan* (☏01248/353030; ➋). *Eryl Môr*, 2 Upper Garth Rd
(☏01248/353789, Ⓦwww.erylmorhotel.co.uk; ➌), is a quiet and comfortable hotel with views over Bangor's pier and the Menai Strait. Five miles
southwest of town on the B4366 is *Tŷ Mawr Farm* (☏01286/670147, Ⓦwww
.tymawrfarm.co.uk; ➌), a working farm with good food and a cosy welcome.

Bangor's YHA **hostel**, *Tan-y-Bryn* (☏0870/770 5686, Ⓔbangor@yha.org.uk;
dorms £21.50), is signposted off the A56, ten minutes' walk east of the centre
(bus #6 or #7 along Garth Road). The nearest **campsite** is the very laid-back
Treborth Hall Farm (☏01248/364104), fifteen minutes' walk (or bus #5) from
Upper Bangor, on the road out towards the Menai Bridge.

With the possible exception of Llandudno, Bangor offers the widest selection
of **eating** possibilities in North Wales. *Fat Cat Café Bar*, 161 High St, serves
huge burgers, salmon-and-broccoli pasta quills and the like at modest prices,
while *Herbs*, 307 High St (closed Sun), is a great veggie daytime café with a
salad bar, serving two-course specials for £8. Put your Welsh language skills to
good use at *Tafarn Y Glôb*, a traditional **pub** on Albert Street, where ordering
in Welsh is pretty much a house rule. For "a pint of beer, please" try *un peint
o gwrw, os gwelwch chi'n dda* (pronounced "een paint o gooroo, os gweloch un
tha"). *Y Castell*, on Glanrafon, a street opposite the cathedral, is a very popular
student pub.

Conwy and around

CONWY, twenty miles east of Bangor, is one of the highlights of the north
coast. Backed by a forested fold of Snowdonia, the town boasts a fine castle, a
nearly complete belt of town walls and a wonderful setting on the Conwy Estuary. Nowhere in the core of medieval and Victorian buildings is more than two
hundred yards from the irregular triangle of protective masonry formed by the
town walls. This makes it wonderfully easy to potter around and though you'll
get to see everything you want to in a day, you may well want to stay longer.

Conwy Castle

Conwy Castle (mid-March to May & Oct daily 9.30am–5pm; June–Sept
daily 9.30am–6pm; Nov–March Mon–Sat 9.30am–4pm, Sun 11am–4pm;
£4, joint ticket with Plas Mawr £6.50; CADW) is the toughest-looking link
in Edward I's Iron Ring of fortresses. After advancing west of the Conwy River
in 1283, Edward decided to maintain a bridgehead by establishing another of
his bastide towns. He chose a strategic knoll at the mouth of the river and set
James of St George to fashion a castle to fit its contours. With the labour of
1500 men it took only five years.

Richard II stayed at the castle on his return from an ill-timed trip to Ireland
in 1399, until lured from safety by Bolingbroke's vassal, the earl of Northumberland. Northumberland swore in the castle's chapel to grant the king safe passage,
but Richard was taken and Bolingbroke became Henry IV. Just two years later,
on Good Friday, when the fifteen-strong castle guard were at church, two cousins of Owain Glyndŵr took the castle and razed the town for Glyndŵr's cause.
The castle then fell into disuse, and was bought in 1627 for £100 by Charles I's
secretary of state, Lord Conway of Ragley, who then had the task of refortifying
it for the Civil War. At the restoration of the monarchy, the castle was stripped
of all its iron, wood and lead, and was left substantially as it is today.

△ Conwy Castle

Being overlooked by a low hill, the castle appears less easily defended than others along the coast, but James constructed eight massive **towers** in a rectangle around the two wards, the inner one separated from the outer by a **drawbridge** and **portcullis**, and further protected by turrets atop the four eastern towers, now the preserve of crows. Strolling along the wall-top gallery, you can look down onto something unique in the Iron Ring fortresses, a roofless but largely intact interior. The outer ward's 130 foot-long **Great Hall** and the **King's Apartments** are both well preserved, but the only part of the castle to have kept its roof is the **Chapel Tower**, named for the small room built into the wall whose semicircular apse still shows some heavily worn carving. On the floor below, there's a small exhibition on religious life in medieval castles which won't detain you long from exploring the passages.

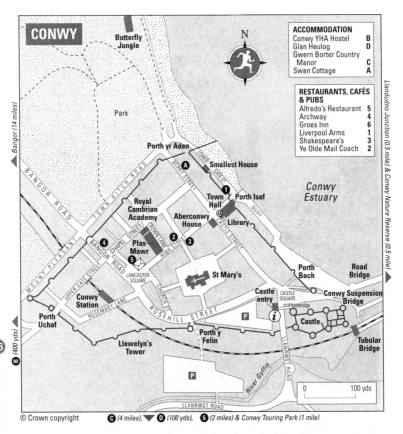

ACCOMMODATION

Conwy YHA Hostel   B
Glan Heulog   D
Gwern Borter Country
   Manor   C
Swan Cottage   A

RESTAURANTS, CAFÉS & PUBS

Alfredo's Restaurant   5
Archway   4
Groes Inn   6
Liverpool Arms   1
Shakespeare's   3
Ye Olde Mail Coach   2

Butterfly Jungle

Park

Porth yr Aden

Smallest House

Royal Cambrian Academy

Town Hall

Porth Isaf

Aberconwy House

Library

Conwy Estuary

Plas Mawr

LANCASTER SQUARE

St Mary's

Porth Bach

Road Bridge

Conwy Suspension Bridge

Conwy Station

Porth Uchaf

Castle entry

CASTLE SQUARE

footbridge

Castle

Llewelyn's Tower

Porth y Felin

Tubular Bridge

River Gyffin

LLANRWST ROAD

© Crown copyright   **C** *(4 miles),* ▼ **D** *(100 yds),* **G** *(2 miles) & Conwy Touring Park (1 mile)*

Bangor (14 miles)

BANGOR ROAD

TOWN DITCH ROAD

BERRY STREET

LOWER GATE ST

QUAY

CASTLE STREET

CROWN LANE

HIGH STREET

CHAPEL STREET

BANGOR ROAD

MOUNT PLEASANT

UPPER GATE STREET

ROSEMARY LANE

CHURCH STREET

ROSEHILL STREET

LLANRWST ROAD

Llandudno Junction (0.5 mile) & Conwy Nature Reserve (0.5 mile)

B *(400 yds)*

The rest of the town

Anchored to the castle walls as though a drawbridge, Telford's narrow **Conwy Suspension Bridge** (mid-March to Oct daily 11am–5pm; £1, joint ticket with Aberconwy House £3.50; NT) was part of the 1826 road improvement scheme, prompted by the need for better communications to Ireland after the Act of Union, and contemporary with his far greater effort spanning the Menai Strait. Restored to its original state, without tarmac, signs or street lighting, it now operates as a footbridge.

The approach to the modern replacement bridge has created the only breach in the thirty-foot-high **town walls**, which branch out from the castle into a three-quarter-mile-long circuit, enclosing Conwy's ancient quarter. Inaccessible from the castle they were designed to protect, the walls are punctuated by 21 evenly spaced horseshoe towers, seven of which can be visited on the **wall-walk**, starting from Porth Uchaf on Upper Gate Street and running down to a spur into the estuary. Here, you come down off the walls beside brightly rigged trawlers, mussel boats, and the self-proclaimed **smallest house in Britain** (Easter to mid-Oct daily 10am–5pm and often later in good weather; 75p), only 9ft by 5ft in total. Porth Isaf, the nearby gate in the town walls, leads up Lower High Street to the fourteenth-century timber-and-stone **Aberconwy**

House, Castle Street (mid-March to Oct daily except Tues 11am–5pm; £3, joint ticket with suspension bridge £3.50; NT), a former merchant's house, its rooms decked out in styles that recall its past. Continue along the High Street to the Dutch-style **Plas Mawr** at no. 20 (June–Aug Tues–Sun 9.30am–6pm; mid-March to May & Sept Tues–Sun 9.30am–5pm; Oct Tues–Sun 9.30am–4pm; £4.50, joint ticket with castle £6.50; CADW), a beautifully restored Elizabethan townhouse, built in 1576 for Robert Wynn, one of the first Welsh people to live in the town. Much of the dressed stonework was replaced during renovations in the 1940s and 1950s, but the interior sports more original features, in particular the friezes and superb moulded plaster ceilings depicting fleurs-de-lis, griffons, owls and rams. The tour concludes with a wonderfully scatological exhibition on sixteenth- and seventeenth-century ideas about disease and cleanliness.

Light relief from all the worthy history is on hand at the quay, where regular **river cruises** (30min £4; 45min £5.50) operate on the Conwy Estuary.

Practicalities

Llandudno Junction, less than a mile across the river to the east, serves as the main **train station**; only slow, regional services stop in Conwy itself. National Express **coaches** pull up outside the town walls on Town Ditch Road, while local **buses** use the stops in the centre, mostly on Lancaster Square or Castle Street. The **tourist office** (☎01492/592248) shares the same building and hours as the castle ticket office.

Accommodation in the centre of town is a bit thin, so booking ahead is advisable in summer. ⚡ *Swan Cottage*, 18 Berry St (☎01492/596840, ⓦwww .swancottage.btinternet.co.uk; ❶), is the least expensive central B&B with small but attractive rooms, one with en-suite facilities, and two with great estuary views. *Glan Heulog*, Llanrwst Road, on the outskirts of town half a mile towards Llanrwst on the B5106 (☎01492/593845, ⓦwww.snowdoniabandb.co.uk; ❸), is about the best B&B within easy walking distance of Conwy. Further afield, there's *Gwern Borter Country Manor*, Barker's Lane (☎01492/650360, ⓦwww .snowdoniaholidays.co.uk; ❹), a comfortable manor on a Conwy Valley farm just north of Rowen (bus #19), with sauna, gym and pony trekking available and easy access to walks into the nearby Carneddau range.

Bus #19 also goes past the nearest **campsite**, the family-oriented *Conwy Touring Park*, a mile or so south along the B5106 (☎01492/592856; April–Oct). The YHA **hostel** (☎0870/770 5774, Ⓔconwy@yha.org.uk; ❶, dorms £14) is on Lark Hill, a ten-minute hike from town up the road to Sychnant Pass, where people staying can also hire bikes.

Conwy has relatively few **restaurants**, and on a fine evening you could do worse than fish and chips from *Archway*, 12 Bangor Rd, eaten on The Quay with a pint from the *Liverpool Arms*. Alternatively, eat straightforward Italian at *Alfredo's*, Lancaster Square (☎01492/592381), or something classy from *Shakespeare's* in the Castle Hotel on High Street, easily the finest restaurant in town where linen and crystal set the tone for dishes such as beef fillet with oxtail ragout or roasted halibut (both £18).

Good **pubs** are easier to find: try *Ye Olde Mail Coach*, 16 High St, for decent beer, food and occasional music, or head two miles south on the B5106 to Llanrwst to the fifteenth-century *Groes Inn*, the best pub in the area, which serves excellent bar meals and good cask ales.

Bodnant Garden

Thousands come to Conwy specifically to see **Bodnant Garden** (mid-March to Oct daily 10am–5pm; £5.50; NT), beside the lower reaches of the Conwy, eight miles to the south. During May and June, the Laburnum Arch flourishes and banks of rhododendrons are in full and glorious bloom all over what ranks as one of the finest formal gardens in Britain. Laid out in 1875 around Bodnant Hall (no public access) by its then owner, English industrialist Henry Pochin, the garden spreads out over eighty acres of the eastern Conwy Valley. Facing southwest, the bulk of the gardens – divided into an upper terraced garden and lower pinetum and wild garden – catch the late afternoon sun as it sets over the Carneddau range. Though it's arranged so that shrubs and plants provide a blaze of colour throughout the opening season, autumn is a perfect time to be here, with hydrangeas still in bloom and fruit trees shedding their leaves. Bus #25 runs here from Llandudno (every 2hr), calling at Llandudno Junction, or it's a two-mile walk from the Tal-y-Cafn train station (request stop) on the Conwy Valley line.

Llandudno

The twin limestone hummocks of the 680-foot **Great Orme** and its southern cousin the Little Orme provide a dramatic frame for the gently curving Victorian frontage of **LLANDUDNO**, four miles north of Conwy, Wales's most enduring archetype of the genteel British seaside resort. Despite the arrival of more rumbustious fun-seekers, Llandudno retains an undeniably dignified air but steers clear of retirement-home stagnation.

Llandudno's early history revolves around the Great Orme, where St Tudno, who brought Christianity to the region in the sixth century, built the monastic cell that gives the town its name. When the early Victorian copper mines looked about to be worked out, in the mid-nineteenth century, local landowner Edward Mostyn exploited the growing craze for sea-bathing and set about a speculative venture to create a seaside resort for the upper middle classes. Work got under way around 1854 and the town rapidly gained popularity over the next fifty years, becoming synonymous with the Victorian ideal of a respectable resort.

The Town and around

First-time visitors are inevitably drawn to Llandudno's nineteenth-century **pier** (open all year; free), one of the few remaining in Wales. It juts out 2220 feet into Llandudno Bay, a leisurely ten-minute stroll along The Promenade from Vaughan Street and the region's premier contemporary art gallery, the **Oriel Mostyn**, 12 Vaughan St (Mon–Sat 10.30am–5.30pm; free; ⓦ www.mostyn .org), which hosts temporary shows featuring works by artists of international renown, with a particular leaning towards the current Welsh arts scene. Kids are better entertained at the **Alice in Wonderland Visitor Centre**, 3–4 Trinity Square (April–Oct daily 10am–5pm; Nov–March closed Sun; £2.95; ⓦ www .wonderland.co.uk), where they are guided through the "Rabbit Hole", full of fibreglass Mad Hatters and March Hares, while a headset treats them to readings of *Jabberwocky* and the like. The Alice books were inspired by Lewis Carroll's meeting with one Alice Liddell, the daughter of friends, here in Llandudno.

The view from the top of the **Great Orme** (Pen y Gogarth) ranks with those from the far loftier summits in Snowdonia, combining the seascapes east towards Rhyl and west over the sands of the Conwy Estuary with the brooding, quarry-chewed northern limit of the Carneddau range where Snowdonia crashes into the sea. This huge lump of carboniferous limestone was subject to some of the same stresses that folded Snowdonia, producing fissures filled by molten mineral-bearing rock. A Bronze Age settlement developed around what are now the **Great Orme Copper Mines** (Feb–Oct daily 10am–5pm; £5; ☎01492/87047, ⊛www.greatormemines.co.uk), accessed via the tramway (see below). Hard hats and miners' lamps are provided for the **guided tour** through just a small portion of the tunnels, enough to get a feel for the cramped working conditions and the dangers of falling rock.

The base of the Great Orme is traditionally circumnavigated on **Marine Drive**, a five-mile anticlockwise circuit from just near Llandudno's pier. The best way to get to the copper mines and the grasslands on top of the Orme is by the San Francisco–style **Great Orme Tramway** (Easter–Oct 10am–6pm; £4.50 return, £3.40 single; ⊛www.greatormetramway.com), which creaks up from the bottom of Old Road, much as it has done since 1902.

Practicalities

Llandudno's central **train station** (not to be confused with the main-line Llandudno Junction, three miles south), is at the corner of Augusta and Vaughan streets, five minutes' walk southeast from the **tourist office**, 1–2 Chapel St (Easter–Sept daily 9am–5.30pm; Oct–Easter Mon–Sat 9am–5pm; ☎01492/876413, ⊛www.llandudno-tourism.co.uk). Chapel Street runs parallel to Mostyn Street, where local **buses** stop. Less than ten minutes' walk south, National Express **coaches** pull in to the coach park on Mostyn Broadway. **Bike rental** is available from Snowdonia Cycle Hire (☎01492/878771, ⊛www.snowdoniacyclehire.co.uk) which will deliver and collect bikes within a six-mile radius of Llandudno.

Finding a **place to stay** is not usually a problem, though in high summer and especially on bank holidays, booking ahead is wise. The cheapest place is the central *Llandudno Hostel*, 14 Charlton St (☎01492/877430; ❶), which has £13 beds and a family room. The greatest concentration of budget places is along St David's Road, just west of the station, where you'll find the excellent-value, nonsmoking *Cliffbury Hotel*, 34 St David's Rd (☎01492/877224, ⊛www.cliffburyhotel.co.uk; ❷). *No. 9*, 9 Chapel St (☎01492/877251; ❶), is one of the least expensive and best equipped of a string of low-cost hotels just along from the tourist office, while *Plas Madoc*, 60 Church Walks (☎01492/876514, ⊛www.vegetarianguesthouse.com; ❸), is an exclusively vegetarian guest house with great food, near the base of the Great Orme. The chic, boutique ✻ *Escape B&B*, 48 Church Walks (☎01492/877776, ⊛www.escapebandb.co.uk; ❺), is very classy; and there's **camping** at *Dinarth Hall Farm*, Dinarth Hall Road, Rhos-on-Sea (☎01492/548203), three miles east of Llandudno, accessible on buses #14 and #15.

Llandudno has plenty of excellent **restaurants**. *Badgers*, in the Victoria Centre on Mostyn Street, is a cut above the average lunch spot, while the basement bistro at ✻ *Richards*, 7 Church Walks, dishes up delicious meals, many based on local seafood. For substantial, tasty bar food, try the *Cottage Loaf*, Market Street, a flag-floored **pub** built from old ships' timbers on top of an old bakehouse, or the *King's Head*, on Old Road, the oldest pub in town, where Edward Mostyn and his surveyor mapped out the town. For sheer raucous drinking, the bars along Upper Mostyn Street are generally full and extremely lively.

Bodelwyddan to Holywell

Visitors in a hurry might be tempted to hurtle along the A55 between Llandudno and the English border without stopping. Certainly it is one of the least appealing stretches of Welsh coastline, with its mile upon mile of caravan

NORTH WALES | The north coast

parks and amusement arcades, but a handful of sights just inland each warrant breaking the journey briefly.

Aficionados of nineteenth-century portraiture won't want to miss the works on display at **Bodelwyddan**, which is just a short hop from **St Asaph**, home to Britain's smallest cathedral. Castle buffs should then head north to **Rhuddlan**, while those of an ecclesiastical bent will be happier at **Holywell**, a site of pilgrimage since the seventh century.

Bodelwyddan Castle: the National Portrait Gallery

The finest art showcase in North Wales is **Bodelwyddan Castle** (late July–early Sept daily 10.30am–5pm; late March–late July & early Sept–Oct daily except Fri 10.30am–5pm; Nov–March Thurs 9.30am–6pm, Sat & Sun 10.30am–4pm; £4.50, gardens £2; ⓦ www.bodelwyddan-castle.co.uk), an outpost of the National Portrait Gallery some eighteen miles east of Conwy. The opulent Victorian interiors of what is essentially a nineteenth-century mansion provide a suitable setting for hundreds of paintings by the likes of Millais, Rossetti, Browning, John Singer Sargent and Landseer. Look out for two sensitive portraits highlighting the Pre-Raphaelite movement's support for social reform: William Holman Hunt's portrayal of the vociferous opponent of slavery and capital punishment, Stephen Lushington; and Ford Madox Brown's double portrait of Henry Farell, prime mover in the passing of the 1867 Reform Bill, and suffragette Millicent Garrett.

St Asaph

The tiny city of **ST ASAPH** (Llanelwy), two miles east of Bodelwyddan, is centred on Britain's smallest **cathedral** (daily 8am–dusk; free), no bigger than many village churches. It was founded around 570 by St Kentigern, the patron saint of Glasgow, and takes its name from the succeeding bishop, St Asaph. Both are commemorated in the easternmost window in the north aisle. From 1601 until his death in 1604, the bishopric was held by **William Morgan**, who was responsible for the translation of the first Welsh-language Bible in 1588. This version replaced the English ones used up until that time and was so successful that the Privy Council decreed that a copy of Y Beibl should be allocated to every Welsh church, thereby setting a standard for prose and codifying the language. Without his efforts, many claim, Welsh would have died out. A thousand Morgan Bibles were printed, of which only nineteen remain, one of them displayed in the south aisle along with notable prayer books and psalters.

The cathedral is perfect for a quick visit between **buses**, which stop outside.

Rhuddlan Castle

Rhuddlan Castle (Easter–Sept daily 10am–5pm; £2.75; CADW) lies two miles north of St Asaph in what is effectively an insignificant suburb of the coastal resort of Rhyl. Built between 1277 and 1282 as a garrison and royal residence for Edward I, the impressive castle commands a canalized section of the river protected by **Gillot's Tower**. Behind, the castle's massive towers were the work of James of St George, who was responsible for the concentric plan that allowed archers on both outer and inner walls to fire simultaneously. Important though the castle was, Rhuddlan earns its position in history as the place where Edward I signed the **Statute of Rhuddlan** on March 19, 1284, consigning Wales to centuries of subjugation by the English. An unintentionally ironic plaque in Rhuddlan's main street details the terms of the statute.

Holywell

A place of pilgrimage for thirteen hundred years, **HOLYWELL** (Treffynnon), just off the A55 ten miles east of St Asaph, comes billed as "The Lourdes of Wales" – but without the tacky souvenir stalls. The cause of all the fuss is **St Winefride's Well** (daily: April–Sept 9am–5.30pm; Oct–March 10am–4pm; 60p), a calm pool capacious enough to accommodate the dozens of the faithful who dutifully wade through the waters three times in the hope of curing their ailments, a relic of the Celtic baptism by triple immersion. The existence of the spring was first noted by the Romans, who used the waters to relieve rheumatism and gout. The traditional legend, however, states that in around 660, the virtuous Winefride (Gwenfrewi in Welsh) was decapitated here after resisting the amorous advances of Prince Caradoc; the well is said to have sprung up at the spot where her head fell. Richard I and Henry V provided regal patronage, ensuring a steady flow of believers to what became one of the great shrines of Christendom, and James II came here to pray for a son and heir. Pilgrims spent the night praying in the Perpendicular **St Winefride's Chapel** (key from the ticket office; CADW), built around 1500 to enclose three sides of the well. Pilgrimages still take place on St Winefride's Day (the nearest Sunday to June 22), when a couple of thousand pilgrims are led through the streets behind a relic, part of Winefride's thumb-bone.

Frequent **buses** between Rhyl and Chester stop at the bus station, from where it is a ten-minute walk along High Street to the well.

Travel details

Buses

For information on all local and national bus services, contact Traveline ⓣ 0870/608 2608, ⓦ www.traveline.org.uk.

Aberdaron to: Pwllheli (9 daily; 40min).
Abersoch to: Pwllheli (10 daily; 15min).
Bala to: Dolgellau (13 daily; 40min); Llangollen (13 daily; 1hr).
Bangor to: Beaumaris (every 30min; 30min); Betws-y-Coed (3 daily; 1hr 15min); Caernarfon (every 20min; 30min); Conwy (every 30min; 45min); Holyhead (every 30min; 1hr 15min); Llanberis (hourly; 30–50min); Llandudno (every 30min; 1hr).
Beaumaris to: Bangor (every 30min; 30min).
Beddgelert to: Caernarfon (10 daily; 30min); Pen-y-Pass (9 daily; 20min); Porthmadog (7 daily; 25min).
Betws-y-Coed to: Bangor (3 daily; 1hr 15min); Capel Curig (every 30min; 10min); Idwal Cottage (6 daily; 20min); Llanrwst (roughly hourly; 10min); Penmachno (8 daily; 10min); Pen-y-Pass (every 30min; 20min).
Blaenau Ffestiniog to: Caernarfon (roughly hourly; 1hr 30min); Harlech (4 daily; 40min); Porthmadog (hourly; 30min).

Caernarfon to: Bangor (every 20min; 30min); Beddgelert (10 daily; 30min); Blaenau Ffestiniog (roughly hourly; 1hr 30min); Criccieth (at least hourly; 45min); Llanberis (hourly; 25min); Porthmadog (at least hourly; 50min); Pwllheli (at least hourly; 45min).
Capel Curig to: Bethesda (5 daily; 20min); Betws-y-Coed (every 30min; 10min); Idwal Cottage (6 daily; 10min); Pen-y-Pass (every 30min; 10min).
Conwy to: Bangor (every 30min; 45min); Llandudno (every 30min; 20min); Llanrwst (every 30min; 30min).
Criccieth to: Caernarfon (at least hourly; 45min); Llanystumdwy (every 30min; 5min); Porthmadog (every 30min; 15min); Pwllheli (every 30min; 25min).
Holyhead to: Bangor (every 30min; 1hr 15min); Llanfairpwll (every 30min; 1hr).
Llanberis to: Bangor (hourly; 30–50min); Caernarfon (hourly; 25min); Pen-y-Pass (every 30min; 15min).
Llandudno to: Bangor (every 30min; 1hr); Conwy (every 30min; 20min); Llanrwst (every 30min; 1hr); Rhyl (every 15min; 1hr).
Llanfairpwll to: Bangor (every 30min; 15min); Holyhead (every 30min; 1hr).

Llangollen to: Bala (13 daily; 1hr); Chirk (7 daily; 20min); Wrexham (at least hourly; 40min).
Pen-y-Pass to: Beddgelert (9 daily; 20min); Betws-y-Coed (every 30min; 20min); Capel Curig (every 30min; 10min); Llanberis (every 30min; 15min).
Porthmadog to: Beddgelert (7 daily; 25min); Blaenau Ffestiniog (hourly; 30min); Caernarfon (at least hourly; 50min); Criccieth (every 30min; 15min); Dolgellau (5 daily; 50min); Pwllheli (every 30min; 40min).
Pwllheli to: Aberdaron (9 daily; 40min); Abersoch (10 daily; 15min); Caernarfon (at least hourly; 45min); Chester (1 daily; 4hr); Criccieth (every 30min; 25min); Manchester (1 daily; 7hr); Nefyn (roughly hourly; 15min); Porthmadog (every 30min; 40min).
Wrexham to: Chester (every 15min; 40min); Chirk (hourly; 40min); Llangollen (at least hourly; 40min).

Trains

For information on all local and national rail services, contact National Rail Enquiries ℡08457/484950, ⓦ www.nationalrail.co.uk.
Bangor to: Chester (25 daily; 1hr); Colwyn Bay (21 daily; 25min); Conwy (11 daily; 20min); Holyhead (20 daily; 30–40min); Llandudno Junction (27 daily; 20min); Llanfairpwll (7-daily; 10min).
Betws-y-Coed to: Blaenau Ffestiniog (6 daily; 30min); Llandudno Junction (6 daily; 30min).

Blaenau Ffestiniog to: Betws-y-Coed (6 daily 30min); Llandudno Junction (6 daily; 1hr); Porthmadog by Ffestiniog Railway (April–Oct 4–8-daily; 1hr).
Conwy to: Bangor (11 daily; 20min); Holyhead (6 daily; 1hr); Llandudno Junction (10 daily; 3min).
Criccieth to: Barmouth (7 daily; 55min); Machynlleth (7 daily; 1hr 45min); Porthmadog (7 daily; 10min); Pwllheli (7 daily; 15min).
Holyhead to: Bangor (20 daily; 30–40min); Chester (20 daily; 1hr 40min); Llandudno Junction (20 daily; 50min); Llanfairpwll (7 daily; 30min).
Llandudno to: Betws-y-Coed (6 daily; 40min); Blaenau Ffestiniog (6 daily; 1hr 10min); Llandudno Junction (6 daily; 10min).
Llandudno Junction to: Bangor (27 daily; 20min); Betws-y-Coed (6 daily; 30min); Holyhead (20 daily; 1hr).
Llanfairpwll to: Bangor (7 daily; 10min); Holyhead (7 daily; 30min).
Porthmadog to: Barmouth (7 daily; 45min); Blaenau Ffestiniog by Ffestiniog Railway (Easter–Oct 4–8 daily; 1hr); Harlech (7 daily; 20min); Machynlleth (7 daily; 1hr 40min); Pwllheli (7 daily; 25min).
Pwllheli to: Criccieth (7 daily; 15min); Machynlleth (7 daily; 2hr); Porthmadog (7 daily; 25min).
Wrexham to: Liverpool (change at Bidston; hourly; 1hr 15min).

Scotland

Scotland

Edinburgh and the Lothians

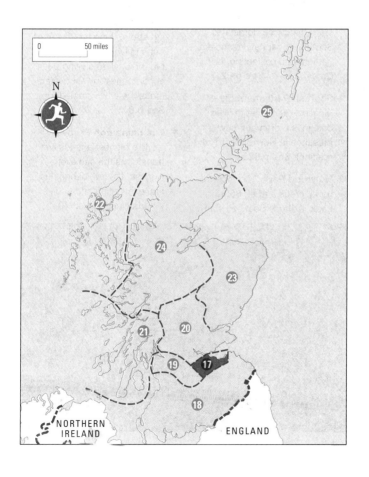

CHAPTER 17 # Highlights

* **The Old Town** The evocative heart of the historic city, with its tenements, closes, courtyards, ghosts and catacombs cheek-by-jowl with many of Scotland's most important buildings. **See p.820**

* **Edinburgh Castle** Perched on an imposing volcanic crag, the castle dominates Scotland's capital, its ancient battlements protecting the Crown Jewels. **See p.821**

* **Scottish Parliament** Enric Miralles' quirky yet thrilling design is a dramatic new presence in Holyrood's royal precinct. **See p.828**

* **Holyrood Park** Wild moors, rocky crags and an 800-foot peak (Arthur's Seat), all slap in the middle of the city. **See p.830**

* **Museum of Scotland** The treasures of Scotland's past housed in a dynamic and superbly conceived building. **See p.831**

* **Café Royal Circle Bar** In a city filled with excellent drinking spots, there are few finer pubs in which to sample a pint of local 80 shilling beer, accompanied by six oysters (once the city's staple food). **See p.845**

* **The Edinburgh Festival** The world's biggest arts festival transforms the city every August: it's bewildering, inspiring, exhausting and endlessly entertaining. **See p.848**

△ Edinburgh Castle

Edinburgh and the Lothians

V enerable, dramatic **EDINBURGH**, the showcase capital of Scotland, is a historic, cosmopolitan and cultured city. The setting is wonderfully striking: perched on a series of extinct volcanoes and rocky crags which rise from the generally flat landscape of the Lothians, with the sheltered shoreline of the Firth of Forth to the north. "My own Romantic town", Sir Walter Scott called it, although it was another native author, Robert Louis Stevenson, who perhaps best captured the feel of his "precipitous city", declaring that "No situation could be more commanding for the head of a kingdom; none better chosen for noble prospects."

The centre has two distinct parts, divided by **Princes Street Gardens**, which run roughly east–west under the shadow of **Edinburgh Castle**, in the very heart of the city. To the north, the dignified, Grecian-style **New Town** was immaculately laid out in the eighteenth century, after the announcement of a plan to improve conditions in the city. The **Old Town**, on the other hand, with its tortuous alleys and tightly packed closes, is unrelentingly medieval, associated in popular imagination with the underworld lore of body snatchers Burke and Hare, and the schizophrenic Deacon Brodie, inspiration for Stevenson's *Dr Jekyll and Mr Hyde*. Indeed, Edinburgh's ability to capture the literary imagination has recently seen it dubbed a World City of Literature by **UNESCO**, on top of the World Heritage Site status already enjoyed by a large section of the centre including both Old and New towns.

Set on the hill which sweeps down from the fairy-tale Castle to the royal **Palace of Holyroodhouse**, the Old Town preserves all the key reminders of its role as a historic capital, augmented now by the dramatic new **Scottish Parliament building**, opposite the palace. Immediately beyond, a tantalizing glimpse of the wild beauty of Scotland's scenery can be had in **Holyrood Park**, an extensive area of open countryside dominated by **Arthur's Seat**, the largest and most impressive of the volcanoes.

In August and early September, around a million visitors flock to the city for the **Edinburgh Festival**, which is in fact a series of separate festivals that make up the largest arts extravaganza in the world. Among Edinburgh's many museums, the exciting **National Museum of Scotland** houses ten thousand of Scotland's most precious artefacts, while the **National Gallery of Scotland**

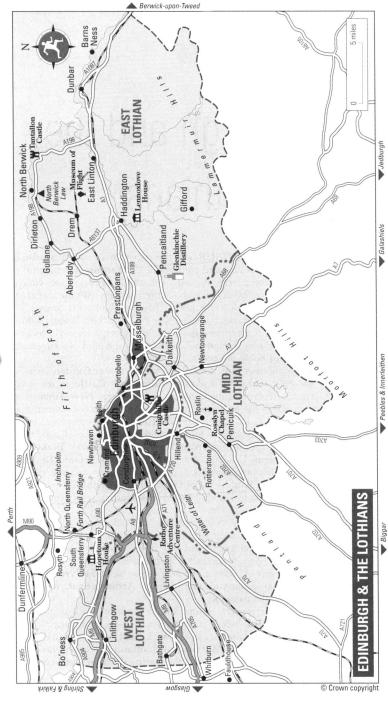

EDINBURGH & THE LOTHIANS

© Crown copyright

and its offshoot, the **Scottish National Gallery of Modern Art**, house two of Britain's finest collections of paintings.

Beyond the centre, Edinburgh's liveliest area is **Leith**, the city's medieval port, whose seedy edge is softened by a series of great bars and upmarket seafood restaurants, along with the presence of the former royal yacht **Britannia**, now open to visitors. The wider rural hinterland of Edinburgh, known as the **Lothians**, mixes rolling countryside and attractive country towns with some impressive historic ruins.

Some history

It was during the **Dark Ages** that the name Edinburgh – at least in its early forms of Dunedin or Din Eidyn ("fort of Eidyn") – first appeared. A strategic fort atop the Castle Rock volcano served as the nation's **southernmost border post** until 1018, when King Malcolm I established the River Tweed as the permanent frontier. During the reign of Malcolm Canmore in the late eleventh century, the Castle became one of the main seats of the court, and the town, which was given privileged status as a **royal burgh**, began to grow. In 1128 King David established Holyrood Abbey at the foot of the slope, later allowing its monks to found a separate burgh, known as **Canongate**.

Under King James IV, the city enjoyed a short but brilliant **Renaissance era**, which saw not only the construction of a new palace alongside Holyrood Abbey, but also the granting of a **royal charter** to the College of Surgeons, the earliest in the city's long line of academic and professional bodies. This period came to an abrupt end in 1513 with the calamitous defeat by the English at the Battle of Flodden leading to several decades of political instability. In the 1540s, King Henry VIII's attempt to force a royal union with Scotland led to the sack of Edinburgh, prompting the Scots to turn to France: French troops arrived to defend the city, while the young queen Mary was dispatched to Paris as the promised bride of the Dauphin, later Francois II of France. While the French occupiers succeeded in removing the English threat, they themselves antagonized the locals, who had become increasingly sympathetic to the ideals of the **Reformation**. When the radical preacher John Knox returned from exile in 1555, he quickly won over the city to his Calvinist message.

James VI's rule saw the foundation of the University of Edinburgh in 1582, but following the **Union of the Crowns** in 1603 the city was totally upstaged by London: although James promised to visit every three years, it was not until 1617 that he made his only return trip. The **Union of the Parliaments** of 1707 dealt a further blow to Edinburgh's political prestige, though the guaranteed preservation of the national church and the legal and educational systems ensured that it was never relegated to a purely provincial role. On the contrary, it was in the second half of the eighteenth century that Edinburgh achieved the height of its intellectual influence, led by an outstanding group, including David Hume and Adam Smith. Around the same time, the city began to expand beyond its medieval boundaries, laying out the **New Town**, a masterpiece of the Neoclassical style.

Industrialization affected Edinburgh less than any other major city in the nation, and it never lost its white-collar character. Nevertheless, the city underwent an enormous **urban expansion** in the course of the nineteenth century, annexing, among many other small burghs, the large port of Leith. In 1947 Edinburgh was chosen to host the great **International Festival** which served as a symbol of the new peaceful European order; despite some hiccups, it has flourished ever since, with tourism now being a mainstay of the local economy.

⑰

In 1997 the Scottish people voted resoundingly in favour of re-establishing their own **parliament**. Inevitably, the early years of the parliament have seen petty squabbling mixed with dizzying constitutional manoeuvring, but with debates, decisions and demonstrations about crucial aspects of the government of Scotland now taking place in Edinburgh, there has been a notable upturn in the city's sense of importance. It has continued to assert itself as a significant centre for finance, research and arts not just in Britain, but also throughout Europe, although what many had hoped to be the crowning achievement of the age, the inspiring new parliament building which opened its doors in 2004, is for the moment tarnished by its spectacularly overblown budget and ongoing rows about design and management.

Arrival, information and transport

Although Edinburgh occupies a large area relative to its population – less than half a million people – most places worth visiting lie within the compact city centre, which is easily explored on foot. This is divided clearly and unequivocally between the maze-like **Old Town**, which lies on and around the crag linking the Castle and the Palace, and the **New Town**, laid out in a symmetrical pattern on the undulating ground to the north.

    Edinburgh International Airport (☎0870/040 0007, ⓦwww.baa.com) is at Turnhouse, seven miles west of the city centre, close to the start of the M8 motorway to Glasgow. Airlink shuttle bus #100 runs to Waverley Station in the centre of town every ten or twenty minutes between 5am and midnight, and at least hourly through the night (journey time 30min; £3). **Taxis** charge around £15–20 for the same journey.

    At the eastern end of Princes Street right in the heart of the city, **Waverley Station** (timetable and fare enquiries ☎0845/748 4950, ⓦwww.nationalrail .co.uk) is the arrival point for all mainline trains. There's a second mainline train stop, **Haymarket Station**, just under two miles west on the lines from Waverley to Glasgow, Fife and the Highlands, although this is only really of use if you're staying nearby. The **bus and coach** terminal for local and intercity services is located on the east side of St Andrew Square, two minutes' walk from Waverley Station.

Information

Edinburgh's main **tourist office** is found on top of Princes Mall near the northern entrance to the train station (April & Oct Mon–Sat 9am–6pm, Sun 10am–6pm; May, June & Sept Mon–Sat 9am–7pm, Sun 10am–7pm; July & Aug Mon–Sat 9am–8pm, Sun 10am–8pm; Nov–March Mon–Wed 9am–5pm, Thurs–Sat 9am–5pm; ☎0845/2255121, ⓦwww.edinburgh .org). The much smaller **airport branch** is in the main concourse, directly opposite Gate 5 (daily: April–Oct 6.30am–10.30pm; Nov–March 7.30am–9.30pm).

    Open-top **bus tours** are big business in Edinburgh, with three rival companies taking largely similar routes around the main sights. All three cost much the same, depart from Waverley Bridge and allow you to get on and off at leisure: the most entertaining is MacTours (☎0131/556 2244, ⓦwww.mactours .co.uk; £8.50). Several companies offer **walking tours**, including Auld Reekie Tours (☎0131/557 4700, ⓦwww.auldreekietours.co.uk) and Mercat Tours (☎0131/557 6464, ⓦwww.mercat-tours.co.uk). These two also offer

night-time ghost tours, as does the entertaining Witchery Tours (☏01.
6745, ⓦwww.witcherytours.com) and the spine-tingling City of the
graveyard tour (☏0131/225 9044, ⓦwww.blackhart.uk.com).

City transport

Most of Edinburgh's **public transport** services terminate on or near Princes
Street. The city is generally well served by **buses**; the white and maroon
Lothian Buses provide the most frequent and comprehensive coverage of the
city (timetables and passes from offices on Waverley Bridge, Shandwick Place
or Hanover Street; enquiry line ☏0131/555 6363, ⓦwww.lothianbuses.co.uk),
and all buses referred to in the text are run by Lothian unless otherwise stated.
Usefully, every bus stop displays diagrams indicating which services pass by and
the routes they take; some also have digital displays indicating when buses are
next due.

It is emphatically not a good idea to take a **car** into central Edinburgh; despite
the presence of several expensive multistorey car parks, finding somewhere to
park involves long and often fruitless searches. In addition, Edinburgh's street
parking restrictions are famously draconian: illegally parked cars are very likely
to be fined £60 by one of the swarms of inspectors who patrol day and night.

Accommodation

As befits its status as a busy tourist city and important commercial centre, Edinburgh has a greater choice of **accommodation** than anywhere else in Britain
outside London. **Hotels** (and large backpacker **hostels**) are essentially the only
options you'll find right in the heart of the city, but within relatively easy reach
of the centre, the selection of **guest houses**, **B&Bs**, **campus accommodation** and even **campsites** broadens considerably.

Prices are significantly higher than elsewhere in Scotland, with double rooms
starting at £60 per night. Budget hotel chains offer the best value for basic
accommodation right in the centre. It's worth making advance **reservations** at
any time of year, though it's strongly recommended for stays during the Festival
and around Hogmanay when places often get booked out months ahead. The
tourist board operates an accommodation booking service (☏0845/2255 121,
ⓦwww.visitscotland.com): the £3 fee is waived if you book online.

Hotels and guest houses

The abundance of hotels in the city centre mean that you can often find good
deals in quieter periods, and it's always worth looking out for special offers
advertised by all the chains. Generally offering much better value for money
and a far more homely experience are Edinburgh's vast range of **guest houses**,
small hotels and **bed & breakfast** establishments, many located on the edges
of the New Town and the inner suburbs of Bruntsfield and the Grange.

Old Town

Bank Hotel 1 South Bridge ☏0131/622 6800,
ⓦwww.festival-inns.co.uk. Notable location in a
1920s bank at the crossroads of the Royal Mile and
South Bridge, with *Logie Baird's Bar* downstairs
and nine unusually decorated but comfortable
rooms upstairs on the theme of famous Scots. ❺

Ibis Edinburgh Centre 6 Hunter Square
☏0131/240 7000, ⓦwww.accorhotels.com.
Probably the best-located chain hotel cheapie in
the Old Town, within sight of the Royal
Mile; rooms are modern and inexpensive, but
there are few facilities other than a rather plain
bar. ❺

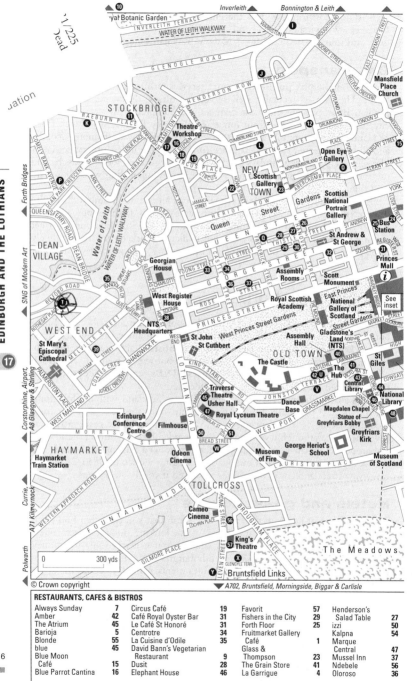

© Crown copyright

▼ A702, Bruntsfield, Morningside, Biggar & Carlisle

RESTAURANTS, CAFES & BISTROS

Always Sunday	7	Circus Café	19	Favorit	57	Henderson's
Amber	42	Café Royal Oyster Bar	31	Fishers in the City	29	Salad Table	27
The Atrium	45	Le Café St Honoré	31	Forth Floor	25	izzi	50
Barioja	5	Centrotre	34	Fruitmarket Gallery		Kalpna	54
Blonde	55	La Cuisine d'Odile	35	Café	1	Marque
blue	45	David Bann's Vegetarian		Glass &		Central	47
Blue Moon		Restaurant	9	Thompson	23	Mussel Inn	37
Café	15	Dusit	28	The Grain Store	41	Ndebele	56
Blue Parrot Cantina	16	Elephant House	46	La Garrigue	4	Oloroso	36

CENTRAL EDINBURGH

▲ A1 Berwick-upon-Tweed

Arthur's Seat (823ft)

Salisbury Crags

ACCOMMODATION

Ardenlee Guest House	J	Gerald's Place	O
Balmoral	R	High Street Hostel	F
Bank Hotel	E	Holyrood Aparthotel	S
Bonham Hotel	T	Ibis Edinburgh Centre	G
Brodies 1	D	Point Hotel	W
Bruntsfield SYHA Hostel	Y	Regent House Hotel	N
Canon Court Apartments	I	Rick's Restaurant with	
Castle Rock	V	rooms	Q
Davenport House	L	St Christopher's Inns	A
Edinburgh Backpackers		The Scotsman Hotel	B
Hostel	C	Six Mary's Place	X
Edinburgh City Centre		The Stuarts B&B	H
Express by Holiday Inn	M	Travelodge Edinburgh Central	U
Galloway Guest House	P	The Witchery Apartments	

Original Khushi's	52	Urban Angel	26	The Barony Bar	14	Human Be-In	54
Plaisir du Chocolat	3	Valvona & Crolla	13	The Basement	21	Jolly Judge	40
Prego	8	Valvona & Crolla		Bennets Bar	57	Opal Lounge	30
A Room in the Town	22	VinCaffè	24	Bert's Bar	11 & 39	Oxford Bar	27
The Snug	17	The Witchery by		Blue Blazer	51	Peartree House	53
Suruchi	49	the Castle	42	Bow Bar	43	Traverse Bar Café	45
Thai Me Up in				Café Royal Circle Bar	31	Villager	44
Edinburgh	20	**PUBS & BARS**		Cumberland Bar	12	Whighams Wine Cellars	38
Terrace Café	10	Albanach	6	The Dome	32		
Tower	48	Baillie	18	Doric Tavern	2		

Point Hotel 34–59 Bread St ☎0131/221 5555, ⓦwww.point-hotel.co.uk. Having been treated to a radical contemporary makeover, this former department store is now one of Edinburgh's most stylish and individual modern hotels. There's a popular cocktail bar and a decent restaurant at street level. ❻

The Scotsman Hotel 20 North Bridge ☎0131/556 5565, ⓦwww.thescotsmanhotel .co.uk. The plush but non-stuffy new occupant of the grand old offices of the *Scotsman* newspaper is one of Edinburgh's headline hotels. It's five-star stuff with modern gadgets and fittings, but the marble staircase and walnut-panelled lobby have been retained, and you can sleep in the editor's old office. Rooms from £260. ❾

Travelodge Edinburgh Central 33 St Mary's St ☎0870/191 1637, ⓦwww.travelodge.co.uk. There's more than a hint of concrete brutalism about the look of this chain hotel, but it's well priced, and centrally located, 100 yards from the Royal Mile opposite a clutch of decent restaurants. ❺

The Witchery Apartments Castlehill, Royal Mile ☎0131/225 5613, ⓦwww.thewitchery.com. Seven riotously indulgent suites grouped around this famously spooky restaurant just downhill from the castle; expect antique furniture, big leather armchairs, tapestry-draped beds, oak panelling and huge roll-top baths, as well as ultra-modern sound systems and complimentary bottles of champagne. Top of the range, unique and memorable. ❾

New Town

Ardenlee Guest House 9 Eyre Place, New Town ☎0131/556 2838, ⓦwww.ardenleeguesthouse .com. Welcoming nonsmoking guest house at the foot of the New Town, with original Victorian features and nine reasonably spacious rooms, seven of which are en suite, and some suitable for families. ❺

Balmoral Hotel 1 Princes St ☎0131/556 2414, ⓦwww.roccofortehotels.com. This elegant Edinburgh landmark is the finest grand hotel in the city, with nearly two hundred plush rooms (many with good views), full business facilities, a swimming pool and gym and two highly rated restaurants. ❼

Bonham Hotel 35 Drumsheugh Gardens ☎0131/623 9301, ⓦwww.thebonham.com. One of Edinburgh's most stylish boutique hotels, cheekily hiding behind a grand West End Victorian facade and offering an interesting mix of fine period and chic contemporary design throughout. ❽

Davenport House 58 Great King St, New Town ☎0131/558 8495, ⓦwww.davenport-house.com. A grand, regally decorated guest house in an attractive Georgian townhouse; a well-priced

and intimate alternative to some of the nearby hotels. ❺

Edinburgh City Centre Express by Holiday Inn Picardy Place, Broughton ☎0131/558 2300, ⓦwww.hieedinburgh.co.uk. A great location in an elegant old Georgian tenement near the top of Broughton Street, with 160 rooms featuring neat but predictable chain-hotel decor and facilities. ❻

Galloway Guest House 22 Dean Park Crescent, Stockbridge ☎0131/332 3672, Ⓔgalloway_ theclarks@hotmail.com. Friendly, family-run option with ten rooms in elegant Stockbridge, within walking distance of the centre. Traditional in style but neat and well priced. ❸

Gerald's Place 21b Abercromby Place, New Town ☎0131/558 7017, ⓦwww.geraldsplace.com. A real taste of homely New Town life at an upmarket but wonderfully hospitable and comfy basement B&B. ❻

Regent House Hotel 3 Forth St, Broughton ☎0131/556 1616, ⓦwww.regenthousehotel.co.uk. A small four-floor hotel that makes up for its lack of glamour with a great location: right in the heart of Broughton on a quiet side-street. Some rooms are big enough to accommodate 3–5 people. Large rooms from £30 per person. Doubles ❺

Rick's Restaurant with rooms 55a Frederick St, New Town ☎0131/622 7800, ⓦwww .ricksedinburgh.co.uk. Ten sought-after rooms at the back of a popular New Town bar and restaurant. The rooms are beautifully styled with beds fitted with walnut headboards and plush fabrics, plus DVD player, and look out onto a cobbled lane behind. ❻

Six Mary's Place Raeburn Place, Stockbridge ☎0131/332 8965, ⓦwww.sixmarysplace.co.uk. A collectively run alternative-style guest house with eight smart, fresh-looking rooms, a no-smoking policy, and excellent home-cooked vegetarian breakfasts served in a sunny conservatory. ❺

Leith and North Edinburgh

Ardmor House 74 Pilrig St, Pilrig ☎0131/554 4944, ⓦwww.ardmorhouse. com. Victorian townhouse with some lovely original features combined with smart contemporary decor. Gay-owned, straight-friendly, and located halfway between town and Leith. ❺

Botanic House Hotel 27 Inverleith Row, Inverleith ☎0131/552 2563, ⓦwww.botanichousehotel .com. A small but smart family-run hotel with fresh and bright decor that echoes the Botanic Gardens, which can be seen over the garden wall. There's a cosy but stylish bar in the basement that also serves food. Buses #23 & #27 go into town. ❺

⑰

Edinburgh Waterfront Express by Holiday Inn
Britannia Way, Ocean Drive ☏ 0870/744 2163,
ⓦ www.hiex-edinburgh.com. Purpose-built budget
hotel that's a good mid-price option in the Leith
area. Within walking distance of Leith's best local
restaurants and the Ocean Terminal shopping centre,
and an easy bus ride (#1, 11, 22 or 35) into town. ❻

Fraoch House 66 Pilrig St, Pilrig ☏ 0131/554
1353, ⓦ www.fraochhouse.com. A relaxing six-
bedroom guest house with a slick, modern look
created by its young owners. It's a ten- to fifteen-
minute walk from both Broughton Street and the
heart of Leith. ❺

Inverleith Hotel 5 Inverleith Terrace, Inverleith
☏ 0131/556 2745, ⓦ www.inverleithhotel.co.uk.
Pleasant option near the Botanic Gardens, with
twelve rooms of various sizes in a Victorian terraced
house; all are en suite and tastefully decorated with
wooden floors, antiques and tapestries. ❺

Malmaison 1 Tower Place ☏ 0131/468 5000,
ⓦ www.malmaison.com. Chic, modern hotel set in
the grand old Seamen's Hostel just back from the
wharf-side. Bright, bold original designs in each
room, as well as CD players and cable TV. Also has
a gym, room service, Parisian brasserie and café-
bar serving lighter meals. ❻

South of the centre

Ashdene House 23 Fountainhall Rd, Grange
☏ 0131/667 6026, ⓦ www.ashdenehouse.com.
Well-run, environmentally friendly, nonsmoking
guest house, furnished in traditional Victorian style
and located in the quiet southern suburbs. Bus #42
stops a few minutes' walk away. ❺

Cluaran House 47 Leamington Terrace, Viewforth
☏ 0131/221 0047, ⓦ www.cluaran-house
-edinburgh.co.uk. Tasteful and welcoming B&B
with lots of original features and paintings. Serves
good traditional and vegetarian breakfasts. Close
to Meadows with bus links (including #11 & #23)
from nearby Bruntsfield Place. ❻

The Greenhouse 14 Hartington Gardens, Viewforth
☏ 0131/622 7634, ⓦ www.greenhouse-edinburgh
.com. A fully vegetarian/vegan guest house, right

down to the soaps and duvets, with a relaxed
rather than right-on atmosphere. The rooms are
neat and tastefully furnished, with fresh fruit and
flowers in each. Minimum stay two nights. Buses
#11 & #23 from Bruntsfield Place. ❺

MW Guest House 94 Dalkeith Rd, Newington
☏ 0131/662 9265, ⓦ www.mwguesthouse.co.uk.
One of only a few guest houses in town with
a fresh, contemporary design – think muted
tones and blonde wood. As it's set in a Victorian
villa, every room is a bit different; those at the
back are a bit quieter. For drivers the public
parking here is easier than at other Southside choices. The linked *MW Townhouse* (11
Spence St) just round the corner is equally well
presented. ❹

Prestonfield Priestfield Road, Bruntsfield
☏ 0131/225 7800, ⓦ www.prestonfield.com. This
seventeenth-century mansion set in its own park
below Arthur's Seat was recently taken over by
the *Witchery* team (see p.818), and its extravagant
Baroque makeover has helped make it one of
Edinburgh's most lavish and over-the-top places
to stay. ❾

The Stuarts B&B 17 Glengyle Terrace, Bruntsfield
☏ 0131/229 9559, ⓦ www.the-stuarts.com. A
five-star bed and breakfast, with three comfortable
and well-equipped rooms in a basement beside
Bruntsfield Links. ❻

Out of the centre

Joppa Turrets Guest House 1 Lower Joppa,
Joppa ☏ 0131/669 5806, ⓦ www.joppaturrets
.demon.co.uk. The place to come if you want an
Edinburgh holiday by the sea: a quiet establishment
on the beachfront in Joppa, five miles east of the
city centre (buses #15 & #26). ❹

The Original Raj Hotel 6 West Coates
☏ 0131/346 1333, ⓦ www.rajempire.com.
Imaginatively conceived and pleasantly
executed, this townhouse hotel has seventeen
rooms themed on India and the splendour of the
Raj. Jump on buses #12, 26 or 31 (journey time
10–15min). ❺

Hostel, self-catering apartments and campus accommodation

Edinburgh is one of the UK's most popular backpacker destinations, and there are
a large number of hostels in and around the city centre, ranging in size, atmosphere and quality. Custom-built **self-catering serviced apartments** with no
minimum let are popular with business travellers, and make a viable alternative
to guest houses. They're also well worth considering for longer stays, for example
during the Festival. **Campus accommodation** is available in the city during the
summer months, though it's neither as useful or cheap as might be expected.

Argyle Backpackers Hotel 14 Argyle Place, Marchmont ☎0131/667 9991, ⓦwww.argyle -backpackers.co.uk. Quiet, less intense version of a typical backpackers' hostel, pleasantly located in three adjoining townhouses near the Meadows in studenty Marchmont. It's walking distance to town, or you can get bus #41 from the door. The small dorms have single beds (from £12), and there's a dozen or so double/twin rooms (❶), as well as a pleasant communal conservatory and garden at the back.

Brodies 1 12 High St, Old Town ☎0131/556 6770, ⓦwww.brodieshostels.co.uk. Tucked down a typical Old Town close, with four fairly straightforward dorms (from £15) sleeping up to a dozen, and limited communal areas. It's smaller than many hostels, and a little bit more homely as a result.

Bruntsfield SYHA Hostel 7 Bruntsfield Crescent, Bruntsfield ☎0870/004 1114, ⓦwww.syha.org.uk. Overlooking the leafy Bruntsfield Links a mile south of Princes Street, with accommodation mostly in dorms sleeping six to ten – some of these are partially screened-off "pod rooms" which offer a bit more privacy and security than standard dorms. Nonsmoking, and Internet access available. Dorm beds from £14.50.

Canon Court Apartments 20 Canonmills ☎0131/474 7000, ⓦwww.canoncourt.co.uk. A block of smart, comfortable self-catering one- and two-bedroom apartments not far from Canonmills Bridge over the Water of Leith at the northern edge of the New Town. Studio apartments from £74 per night.

Castle Rock Hostel 15 Johnston Terrace, Old Town ☎0131/225 9666, ⓦwww.scotlands-top -hostels.com. Tucked below the castle ramparts, with 200 or so beds arranged in large, bright dorms (£12.50), as well as triple and quad rooms and some doubles (❷). The communal areas include a games room with pool and table tennis.

Edinburgh Backpackers Hostel 65 Cockburn St, Old Town ☎0131/220 2200, ⓦwww.hoppo.com. Very central, with large but bright dorms (£14) and a decent number of doubles (❷) in a tall Old Town building. The communal areas are pretty standard, though there is a bar and café at street level.

Globetrotter Inn 46 Marine Drive, Cramond ☎0131/336 1030, ⓦwww.globetrotterinns.com. A big departure from the buzzy city-centre hostels, in a sylvan parkland setting four miles from the centre with lovely views of the Firth of Forth. The 350-plus beds are mostly bunks (from £15) with privacy curtains and individual reading lights, but there are also doubles (❷). There's access to a gym and sauna, lots of parking and an hourly shuttle service into town, as well as regular buses (#42). Families and kids are not encouraged.

High Street Hostel 8 Blackfriars St, Old Town ☎0131/557 3984, ⓦwww.scotlands-top-hostels .com. Lively and popular hostel in an attractive sixteenth-century building just off the Royal Mile. Dorms only, from £12.50, but good communal facilities.

Holyrood Aparthotel Nether Bakehouse Close, Holyrood ☎0131/524 3200, ⓦwww .holyroodaparthotel.com. A block of two-bedroom self-catering apartments near the Scottish Parliament. The location has lots of Old Town atmosphere, and the accommodation is slick and modern with most mod-cons. Apartments from £120 (two people sharing).

St Christopher's Inns 9–13 Market St, Old Town ☎0131/226 1446, ⓦwww.st-christophers.co.uk. Huge and a little corporate but very much in the modern hostel style – dorms (from £16) are of varying size, and have en-suite bathrooms, some with TVs, and there are a few double rooms (❸). There's a small communal area but no kitchen; the ground-floor bar serves food, though it's known more for its noisy party atmosphere and screenings of antipodean rugby games. Slightly more expensive than most other hostels.

University of Edinburgh Pollock Halls of Residence 18 Holyrood Park Rd, Newington ☎0131/651 2007, ⓦwww.edinburghfirst.com. Unquestionably the best setting of any of the city's university accommodation, right beside the Royal Commonwealth Pool and Holyrood Park, and with a range of accommodation from single rooms (£28), twins (£56) and en-suite doubles (£72) to self-catering flats (from £350 per week). Available Easter and June to mid-Sept only.

The Old Town

The **OLD TOWN**, although only about a mile long and 300 yards wide, represents the total extent of the twin burghs of Edinburgh and Canongate for the first 650 years of their existence, and its general appearance and character remain indubitably medieval. Containing as it does the majority of the city's most famous tourist sights, it makes by far the best starting point for your explorations. The Old Town is compact enough to see the highlights in a single day, though a thorough visit requires several days. No matter how pressed you are, make sure you spare time for the wonderfully varied scenery and breathtaking vantage points of **Holyrood Park**, an extensive tract of open countryside on the eastern edge of the Old Town that includes Arthur's Seat, the peak of which rises so distinctively in the midst of the city.

The Castle

The history of Edinburgh, and indeed of Scotland, is indissolubly bound up with its **Castle** (daily: April–Oct 9.30am–6pm; Nov–March 9.30am–5pm, last entry 45 min before closing; £9.80; ⓦ www.historic-scotland.gov.uk), which dominates the city from its lofty seat atop an extinct volcanic rock. The disparate styles of the fortifications reflect the change in its role from defensive citadel to national monument, and today, as well as attracting more visitors than anywhere else in the country, the castle is still a military barracks and a home to Scotland's crown jewels. The oldest surviving part of the complex is from the twelfth century, while the most recent additions date back to the 1920s.

Though you can easily take in the views and wander round the castle yourself, you might like to join a **guided tour** (every 15min in high season; 25min; free), for much talk of war, boiling oil and cannon roar. Alternatively, **audio guides** (£3) are available from a booth just inside the gatehouse.

The Esplanade

The castle is entered via the **Esplanade**, a parade ground laid out in the eighteenth century and enclosed a hundred years later by ornamental walls. For most of the year it acts as a coach park, though huge grandstands are erected for the Edinburgh Military Tattoo (see p.852), which takes place every night during August, coinciding with the Edinburgh Festival. A shameless and spectacular pageant of swinging kilts and massed pipe bands, the tattoo makes full use of its dramatic setting.

Entry to the Esplanade is free, and if you don't want to pay the castle's pricey entry fee, it offers a taste of the precipitous location and eye-stretching views.

The lower defences

The **gatehouse** is a Romantic-style addition to the castle from the 1880s, complete with the last drawbridge ever built in Scotland. Standing guard by the drawbridge are real-life soldiers, members of the regiment in residence at the castle; while their presence in full dress uniform is always a hit with camera-toting tourists, it's also a reminder that the castle is still a working military garrison. Rearing up behind is the most distinctive and impressive feature of the castle's silhouette, the sixteenth-century **Half Moon Battery**, which marks the outer limit of the actual defences. Once through the gatehouse, continue uphill along Lower Ward, passing through the **Portcullis Gate**, a handsome Renaissance gateway.

Beyond this, the wide main path is known as Middle Ward, with the six-gun **Argyle Battery** to the right. Further west on **Mill's Mount Battery**, a well-known Edinburgh ritual takes place – the daily firing of the one o'clock gun. Originally designed for the benefit of ships in the Firth of Forth, these days it's an enjoyable ceremony for visitors and a useful time signal for city-centre office workers. There's an interesting little exhibition about the history of the firing of the gun in a room immediately below Mill's Mount Battery. Both batteries offer wonderful panoramic views over Princes Street and the New Town to the coastal towns and hills of Fife across the Forth.

National War Museum of Scotland

Located in the old hospital buildings, down a ramp between the café/restaurant immediately behind the one o'clock gun and the Governor's House, the **National War Museum of Scotland** covers the last four hundred years of Scottish military history. Scots have been fighting for much longer than that, of course, but the slant of the museum is very definitely towards the soldiers who fought *for* the Union, rather than against it (or against themselves).

St Margaret's Chapel

Near the highest point of the castle, **St Margaret's Chapel** is the oldest surviving building in the castle, and probably also in Edinburgh itself. Built by King David I as a memorial to his mother, and used as a powder magazine for three hundred years, this tiny Norman church was rediscovered in 1845 and eventually rededicated in 1934, after sympathetic restoration.

The battlements in front of the chapel offer the best of all the castle's panoramic views. Here you'll see the famous fifteenth-century siege gun, **Mons Meg**, which could fire a 500-pound stone nearly two miles. Just below the battlements there's a small, immaculately-kept **cemetery**, the last resting place of the **soldiers' pets**. Continuing eastwards, you skirt the top of the Forewall and Half Moon batteries, passing the 110-foot **Castle Well** en route to **Crown Square**, the highest, most important and secure section of the entire complex.

The Palace

The eastern side of Crown Square is occupied by the **Palace**, a surprisingly unassuming edifice built round an octagonal stair turret heightened in the

The Stone of Destiny

Legend has it that the **Stone of Destiny** (also called the Stone of Scone) was "Jacob's Pillow", on which he dreamed of the ladder of angels from earth to heaven. Its real history is obscure, but it is known to have been moved from Ireland to Dunadd by missionaries, and thence to Dunstaffnage, from where Kenneth MacAlpine, king of the Dalriada Scots, brought it to the abbey at Scone, near Perth, in 838. There it remained for almost five hundred years, used as a coronation throne on which all kings of Scotland were crowned.

In 1296, an over-eager Edward I stole what he believed to be the Stone and installed it at Westminster Abbey, where, apart from a brief interlude in 1950 when it was removed by Scottish nationalists and hidden in Arbroath for several months, it remained for seven hundred years. All this changed in December 1996 when, after an elaborate ceremony-laden journey from London, the Stone returned to Scotland, in one of the doomed attempts by the Conservative government to convince the Scottish people that the Union was a good thing. Much to the annoyance of the people of Perth and the curators of Scone Palace (see p.955), and to the general indifference of the people of Scotland, the Stone was placed in Edinburgh Castle.

However, speculation surrounds the authenticity of the Stone, for the original is said to have been intricately carved, while the one seen today is a plain block of sandstone. Many believe that the canny monks at Scone palmed this off onto the English king (some say that it's nothing more sacred than the cover for a medieval septic tank), and that the real Stone of Destiny lies hidden in an underground chamber, its whereabouts a mystery to all but the chosen few.

nineteenth century to bear the castle's main flagpole. Begun in the 1430s, the palace owes its Renaissance appearance to King James IV, though it was remodelled for Mary, Queen of Scots, and her consort Henry, Lord Darnley, whose entwined initials (MAH), together with the date 1566, can be seen above one of the doorways.

Another section of the palace has recently been refurbished with a detailed audiovisual presentation on the nation's crown jewels, properly known as the **Honours of Scotland**, the originals of which are housed in the Crown Room at the end of the display. Despite the slow-moving, claustrophobic queues that shuffle past the displays, the jewels are still impressive, serving as one of the most potent images of Scotland's nationhood. They were last used for the Scottish-only coronation of Charles II in 1651, before being locked away in a chest following the Union of 1707. For over a century they were out of sight and presumed lost, before being rediscovered in 1818 as a result of a search initiated by Sir Walter Scott. The glass case containing the Honours also holds the **Stone of Destiny** (see box, above), a remarkably plain object lying incongruously next to the opulent crown jewels.

The Royal Mile

The **Royal Mile**, the name given to the ridge linking the castle with Holyrood, was described by Daniel Defoe, in 1724, as "the largest, longest and finest street for Buildings and Number of Inhabitants, not in Bretain only, but in the World". Almost exactly a mile in length, it is divided into four separate streets – Castlehill, Lawnmarket, High Street and Canongate. From these, branching out in a herringbone pattern, are a series of tightly packed closes and steep lanes entered via archways known as "pends". After the construction of the New Town, in the eighteenth and nineteenth century much of the housing along the Royal Mile degenerated into a notorious slum, but has since become once again a highly desirable place to live. Although marred somewhat by rather too many tacky tourist shops and the odd misjudged new development, it is still among the most evocative parts of the city, and one that particularly rewards detailed exploration.

Castlehill

The narrow uppermost stretch of the Royal Mile is known as **Castlehill**. Rising up to the north, on the edge of the Castle Esplanade, is **Ramsay Gardens**, some of the most picturesque city-centre flats in the world. The oldest part is the octagonal Goose Pie House, home of the eighteenth-century poet Allan Ramsay, author of *The Gentle Shepherd* and father of the better-known portrait painter of the same name. The rest of Ramsay Gardens dates from the 1890s and was the brainchild of Patrick Geddes, a pioneer of the modern town-planning movement, who created these desirable apartments in an attempt to regenerate the Old Town.

Opposite the Weaving Centre, the **Scotch Whisky Heritage Centre** (daily: June–Sept 9.30am–7pm; Oct–May 10am–6pm; last tour 90min before closing; £8.50; ⓦwww.whisky-heritage.co.uk) mimics the kind of tours offered at distilleries in the Highlands, and while it can't match the authenticity of the real thing, the centre does offer a thorough introduction to the "water of life" (*uisge beatha* in Gaelic). On the ground floor, a well-stocked shop gives an idea of the sheer range and diversity of the drink, while downstairs there's a pleasant whisky bar and restaurant, *Amber* (see p.840).

The imposing black church at the foot of Castlehill is **The Hub** (Tues–Sat 9.30am–11pm, Sun & Mon 9.30am–6pm; ⓣ0131/473 2010, ⓦwww.eif .co.uk/thehub), also known as "Edinburgh's Festival Centre". Although the

Festival only takes place for three weeks every August and early September, The Hub is open year-round, providing performance, rehearsal and exhibition space, a ticket centre and a café. The building itself was constructed in 1845 to designs by James Gillespie Graham and Augustus Pugin, one of the co-architects of the Houses of Parliament in London. Permanent works of art have been incorporated into the centre, including over two-hundred delightful foot-high sculptures by Scottish sculptor Jill Watson, depicting Festival performers and audiences.

Lawnmarket

Below the Hub, the Royal Mile opens out into the broader expanse of **Lawn-market**, where you'll find **Gladstone's Land** (daily: April–Oct 10am–5pm; July & Aug 10am–7pm; £5; NTS), the Royal Mile's best surviving example of a typical seventeenth-century tenement. The tall, narrow building – not unlike a canalside house in Amsterdam – would have been home to various families living in cramped conditions. The building is owned by the National Trust for Scotland, who have carefully restored the warren of tight little staircases, tiny rooms, creaking floorboards and peek-hole windows. The upper floors contain apartments which are rented to visitors.

A few paces further on, steps lead down to Lady Stair's Close and the **Writers' Museum** (Mon–Sat 10am–5pm; also Sun noon–5pm during the Festival; free;

Robert Louis Stevenson

Born in Edinburgh into a distinguished family of lighthouse engineers, **Robert Louis Stevenson** (1850–94) was a sickly child, with a solitary childhood dominated by his governess, Alison "Cummie" Cunningham, who regaled him with tales drawn from Calvinist folklore. Sent to the University to study engineering, Stevenson rebelled against his upbringing by spending much of his time in the lowlife howffs and brothels of the city. A set of topographical pieces about his native city was later collected together as *Edinburgh: Picturesque Notes*, which conjure up nicely its atmosphere, character and appearance – warts and all.

Stevenson's other early successes were two **travelogues**, *An Inland Voyage* and *Travels with a Donkey in the Cevennes*, kaleidoscopic jottings based on his journeys in France, where he went to escape Scotland's weather, which was damaging his health. It was there that he met Fanny Osbourne, an American ten years his senior.

Having married the now-divorced Fanny, Stevenson began an elusive search for an agreeable climate that led to Switzerland, the French Riviera and the Scottish Highlands. He belatedly turned to the novel, achieving immediate acclaim in 1881 for **Treasure Island**, a highly moralistic adventure yarn that began as an entertainment for his stepson and future collaborator, Lloyd Osbourne. In 1886, his most famous short story, **Dr Jekyll and Mr Hyde**, despite its nominal London setting, offered a vivid evocation of Edinburgh's Old Town: an allegory of its dual personality of prosperity and squalor, and an analysis of its Calvinistic preoccupations with guilt and damnation. The same year saw the publication of the historical romance **Kidnapped**, an adventure novel which exemplified Stevenson's view that literature should seek above all to entertain.

In 1887 Stevenson left Britain for good, travelling first to the United States. A year later, he set sail for the South Seas, and eventually settled in **Samoa**. However, Scotland continued to be his main inspiration: he wrote *Catriona* as a sequel to *Kidnapped*, and was at work on two more novels with Scottish settings, *St Ives* and *Weir of Hermiston*, a dark story of father and son confrontation, at the time of his sudden death from a brain haemorrhage in 1894. He was buried on the top of Mount Vaea overlooking the Pacific Ocean.

ⓦ www.cac.org.uk), housed in Lady Stair's House – a Victorian embellishment of a seventeenth-century residence set to one side of an open courtyard. Dedicated to Scotland's three greatest literary lions, Sir Walter Scott, Robert Louis Stevenson and Robert Burns, the museum has a slightly lacklustre collection of portraits, manuscripts and showcases filled with odd knick-knacks and relics associated with the writers – Scott's walking stick and a plastercast of Burns' skull among them. The house itself holds as much interest as the exhibits, its tight, winding stairs and pokey, wood-panelled rooms offering a flavour of the medieval Old Town. Continuing the literary theme, the courtyard outside, known as the Makars' Court after the Scots word for the "maker" of poetry or prose, has a series of paving stones inscribed with quotations from Scotland's most famous writers and poets.

High Street and the High Kirk of St Giles

Across the junction with George IV Bridge is the third section of the Royal Mile, known as the **High Street**, which occupies two blocks either side of the intersection between North Bridge and South Bridge. The dominant building of the southern side of the street is the **Kirk of St Giles** (May–Sept Mon–Fri 9am–7pm, Sat 9am–5pm, Sun 1–5pm; Oct–April Mon–Sat 9am–5pm, Sun 1–5pm; ⓦ www.stgilescathedral.org.uk; free), the original sole parish church of medieval Edinburgh, from where John Knox launched and directed the Scottish Reformation. St Giles is often referred to as a cathedral, although it has only been the seat of a bishop on two brief and unhappy occasions in the seventeenth century. According to one of the city's best-known legends, the attempt in 1637 to introduce the English prayer book, and thus Episcopal government, so incensed a humble stallholder named Jenny Geddes that she hurled her stool at the preacher, prompting the rest of the congregation to chase the offending clergy out of the building. A tablet in the north aisle marks the spot from where she let rip.

⓱

The resplendent **crown spire** of the kirk is formed from eight flying buttresses and dates back to 1485, while inside, the four massive piers supporting the tower were part of a Norman church built here around 1120. In the nineteenth century, St Giles was adorned with a whole series of funerary monuments on the model of London's Westminster Abbey; around the same time it acquired several attractive Pre-Raphaelite stained-glass windows designed by Edward Burne-Jones and William Morris.

At the southeastern corner of St Giles, the **Thistle Chapel** was built by Sir Robert Lorimer in 1911 as the private chapel of the sixteen knights of the Most Noble Order of the Thistle, the highest chivalric order in Scotland. Self-consciously derivative of St George's Chapel in Windsor, it's an exquisite piece of craftsmanship, with an elaborate ribbed vault, huge drooping bosses, and extravagantly ornate stalls showing off Lorimer's bold Arts and Crafts styling.

Parliament Square

St Giles is surrounded on three sides by **Parliament Square**, which itself is dominated by the continuous Neoclassical facades of the **Law Courts**, originally planned by Robert Adam (1728–92), one of four brothers in a family of architects whose work helped imbue the New Town with much of its grace and elegance. Because of a shortage of funds and consequent delays, the present exteriors were built to designs by Robert Reid (1776–1856), who faithfully quoted from Adam's architectural vocabulary without matching his flair.

17

Upper High Street

On the opposite side of the Royal Mile from Parliament Square, the U-shaped **City Chambers** were designed by John Adam, brother of Robert, as the Royal Exchange. Local traders never warmed to the exchange, however, so the town council established its headquarters there instead. Beneath the City Chambers lies **Mary King's Close**, one of Edinburgh's most unusual attractions. When work on the chambers began in 1753, the tops of the existing houses on the site were simply sliced through at the level of the High Street and the new building constructed on top of them. Because the tenements had been built on a steep hillside, this process left parts of the houses together with the old streets (or closes) which ran alongside them intact but entirely enclosed among the basement and cellars of the City Chambers. You can visit this rather spooky subterranean "lost city" on **tours** led by costumed actors (daily every 20min: April–Oct 10am–9pm; Nov–March 10am–4pm; 1hr; £7.25; ⓦwww .realmarykingsclose.com), who take you round the old, cold stone shells of the houses where various scenes from the Close's history have been re-created.

Lower High Street

Beyond the intersection of North Bridge and South Bridge and just a little way downhill, jutting out into the street from the main line of buildings, is the fifteenth-century **John Knox's House** (Mon–Sat 10am–6pm, Sun noon–6pm; £3; ⓦwww.scottishstorytellingcentre.co.uk). With its distinctive external staircase, clustered high chimneys and timber projections, the building is a classic representation of the Royal Mile in its medieval heyday. Inside the house is a museum about the building and John Knox, the minister who led the Reformation in Scotland and established Calvinist Presbyterianism as the dominant religious force in the country. John Knox's House is linked to the Scottish Storytelling Centre, which is due to reopen in 2006 after a major redevelopment. The complex will include a theatre, café, story-telling garden and indoor storytelling court, with regular performances and events.

Canongate

For over seven hundred years, the district through which the eastern section of the Royal Mile, the Canongate, runs, was a burgh in its own right, officially separate from the capital. A notorious slum area even into the 1960s, it has been the subject of some of the most ambitious **restoration** programmes in the Old Town, though the lack of harmony between the buildings renovated in different decades can be seen fairly clearly. For such a central district, it's interesting to note that most of the buildings here are residential, and by no means are they all bijou apartments. As you wander down the Canongate, look out for the eclectic range of shops, which include a gallery of historic maps and sea charts, an old-fashioned whisky bottler and a genuine bagpipe-maker.

Next door to the turreted steeple and odd external box-clock of the late sixteenth-century **Canongate Tolbooth** is **Canongate Kirk**. It was built in the 1680s to house the congregation expelled from Holyrood Abbey when the latter was commandeered by James VII (James II in England) to serve as the chapel for the Order of the Thistle. The kirk has a modesty rarely seen in churches built in later centuries, with a graceful curved facade, a mixture of arched and round windows, and a bow-shaped gable to the rear. The surrounding churchyard provides an attractive and tranquil stretch of green in the heart of the Old Town, and affords fine views of Calton Hill; it's also one of the city's most exclusive cemeteries, home to the bodies of political economist Adam Smith, Mrs Agnes McLehose (better known as Robert Burns' "Clarinda") and

Robert Fergusson, regarded by some as Edinburgh's greatest poet, despite his death at the age of 24.

Opposite the church, the **Museum of Edinburgh** in Huntly House (Mon–Sat 10am–5pm; also Sun noon–5pm during Aug; free; ⓦ www.cac.org.uk) is the city's principal collection devoted to local history, though the museum is as interesting for the network of wood-panelled rooms within as for its rather quirky array of artefacts. These do, however, include a number of items of real historical significance, in particular the National Convention, the petition for religious freedom drawn up on a deerskin parchment in 1638, and the original plans for the layout of the New Town drawn by James Craig, chosen by the city council after a competition in 1767.

Among the intriguing series of closes and entries on this stretch of Canongate, look out for **Dunbar's Close**, on the north side of the street, which has a beautiful seventeenth-century walled garden tucked in behind the tenements. Opposite this is the entry to Crichton's Close, through which you'll find the **Scottish Poetry Library** (Mon–Fri 11am–6pm, Sat 1pm–5pm; free; ⓦ www.spl.org.uk), a small island of modern architectural eloquence amid a cacophony of large-scale developments.

Holyrood

At the foot of Canongate lies **Holyrood**, for centuries known as Edinburgh's royal quarter, with its ruined thirteenth-century **abbey** and the **Palace of Holyroodhouse**. In recent years, however, the area has been transformed by Enric Miralles' dazzling but highly controversial **Scottish Parliament**, which was deliberately landscaped to blend in with the cliffs and ridges of Edinburgh's most dramatic natural feature, the nearby **Holyrood Park** and its slumbering peak, Arthur's Seat.

The Palace of Holyroodhouse

In its present form, the **Palace of Holyroodhouse** (daily: April–Oct 9.30am–6pm; Nov–March 9.30am–4.30pm; last admission 1hr before closing; £8.50; ⓦ www.royal.gov.uk) is largely a seventeenth-century creation, planned for Charles II. Tours of the palace move through a series of royal **reception rooms** featuring some outstanding encrusted plasterwork, each more impressive than the last – an idea Charles II had picked up from his cousin Louis XIV's Versailles – while on the northern side of the internal quadrangle, the **Great Gallery** extends almost the full length of the palace and is dominated by portraits of 96 Scottish kings, painted by Jacob de Wet in 1684 to illustrate the lineage of Stewart royalty: the result is unintentionally hilarious, as it is clear that the artist's imagination was taxed to bursting point by the need to paint so many different facial types without having an inkling as to what the subjects actually looked like. Leading from this into the oldest part of the palace, known as James V's tower, the formal, ceremonial tone gives way to dark medieval history, with a tight spiral staircase leading to the chambers used by Mary, Queen of Scots. These contain various relics, including jewellery, associated with the queen, though the most compelling room is a tiny supper room, from where in 1566 Mary's Italian secretary, David Rizzio, was dragged by conspirators, who included her jealous husband Lord Darnley, to the outer chamber and stabbed 56 times.

Holyrood Abbey

Immediately adjacent to the palace are the evocative ruins of **Holyrood Abbey** (free access as part of Holyroodhouse tour), some of which date from the thirteenth century. The roof tumbled down in 1768, but the melancholy scene has inspired artists down the years, among them Felix Mendelssohn, who in 1829 wrote "Everything is in ruins and mouldering . . . I believe I have found the beginning of my Scottish Symphony there today." Adjacent to the abbey are the formal palace gardens, open to visitors during the summer months and offering some pleasant strolls.

The Queen's Gallery

Essentially an adjunct to Holyrood palace, the **Queen's Gallery** (April–Oct 9.30am–6pm; Nov–March 9.30am–4.30pm; last admission 1hr before closing; £5 or £11 joint ticket with Holyroodhouse; ⓦ www.royal.gov.uk) is located in the shell of a former church directly between the palace and the parliament. It's used to display changing exhibitions from the Royal Collection, a vast array of art treasures held by the Queen on behalf of the British nation. Because the pieces are otherwise exhibited only during the limited openings of Buckingham and Windsor palaces, the exhibitions here tend to draw quite a lot of interest.

The Scottish Parliament

For all its grandeur and size, Holyrood Palace is in danger of being upstaged by the striking buildings which make up the new **Scottish Parliament** (for visiting details, see box, p.829). By far the most controversial public building to be erected in Scotland since World War II, it houses the country's directly elected assembly, which was reintroduced in 1999 – Scotland had had no parliament of its own since 1707, when it joined the English assembly at Westminster as part of the Union of the two nations.

Made up of various linked elements rather than one single building, the complex was designed by Catalan architect **Enric Miralles**, whose death in 2000, halfway through the building process, caused ripples of uncertainty as to whether he had in fact set down his final draft. Initial estimates for the building's cost were tentatively put at £40 million; by the time the Queen cut the ribbon

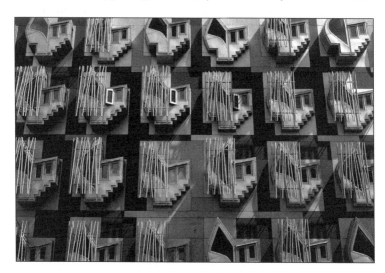

△ The Scottish Parliament building (exterior)

Visiting the Scottish Parliament

There's free access into the entrance lobby of the Parliament, entered from Horse Wynd, opposite the palace, where you'll find a small exhibition providing some historical, political and architectural background. If parliament is in session, it's normally possible to watch proceedings in the debating chamber from the public gallery – again, access is free, though you have to get a pass from the front desk in the lobby. For a more detailed appreciation of the quality and features of the rest of the interior, join one of the regular **guided tours** (45min; £3.50; ⊕0131/348 5200).

There's action in the debating chamber only on "Business days" (Tues–Thurs 9am–7pm when parliament is sitting), when the tours aren't as extensive. On "Non-business days" (Mon & Fri when Parliament is sitting, or Mon–Fri if Parliament is in recess), the doors are open April–Oct 10am–6pm, Nov–March 10am–4pm, as well as Sat & Sun 10am–4pm throughout the year. For further details see ⓦ www.scottish .parliament.uk.

in October 2004, the final bill was in the region of £450 million. A major public inquiry into the overspend blamed costing failures early in the project and criticised the spendthrift attitude of politicians and civil servants alike, yet the building is still an impressive – if imperfect – testament to the ambition of Miralles. Indeed, it has won over the majority of the architectural community, scooping numerous prizes including in 2005, Britain's prestigious Royal Institute of British Architects (RIBA) Stirling Prize.

One of the most memorable features of the building are the fanciful motifs and odd architectural signatures running through the design, including the anvil-shaped cladding, and the extraordinary windows of the offices for MSPs (Members of the Scottish Parliament), said to have been inspired by a monk's contemplative cell. The stark concrete of the new building's interior may not be to all tastes, though several of the staircases and passageways remain evocative of the country's medieval castles.

The main **debating chamber** itself is grand yet intimate, with light flooding in through high windows and a complex network of thick oak beams, lights and microphone wires. The European-style layout is a deliberate move away from the confrontational Westminster model, though detractors of the parliament have been quick to point out that while the traditional inter-party insults still fly, the quality of the parliamentarians' rhetoric rarely matches that of the soaring new arena.

Our Dynamic Earth

The Scottish Parliament building is by no means the only newcomer to this historic area. On the Holyrood Road, beneath a miniature version of London's Millennium Dome, **Our Dynamic Earth** (April–Oct daily 10am–5pm; July–Aug daily 10am–6pm; Nov–March Wed–Sun 10am–5pm; last admission 1hr 10min before closing; £8.95; ⓦ www.dynamicearth.co.uk), is a high-tech attraction based on the theme of the wonders of the natural world and aimed at children between 5 and 15. Galleries cover the formation of the earth and continents with crashing sound effects and a shaking floor, while the calmer grandeur of glaciers and oceans are explored through magnificent large-screen landscape footage; further on, the polar regions – complete with a real iceberg – and tropical jungles are imaginatively re-created, with interactive computer screens and special effects at every turn. Outside, the dramatic **amphitheatre** which incorporates the steps leading up to the main entrance serves as a great venue for outdoor theatre and music performances, most notably during the Festival.

Holyrood Park, Arthur's Seat and Duddingston

Holyrood Park – or Queen's Park – a natural wilderness in the very heart of the modern city, is unquestionably one of Edinburgh's greatest assets. Packed into an area no more than five miles in diameter is an amazing variety of landscapes – hills, crags, moorland, marshes, glens, lochs and fields – representing something of a microcosm of Scotland's scenery.

Two of the most rewarding walks begin from just outside the palace grounds: one, along a pathway nicknamed the "Radical Road", traverses the ridge immediately below the **Salisbury Crags**, one of the main features of the Edinburgh skyline. This is arguably a finer walk than the sharper climb to the top of Arthur's Seat. A better looped walk of about an hour's duration from Holyrood is to follow the "Volunteer's Walk" up the glen behind the Crags, then return along the Radical Road.

The usual starting point for the ascent of **Arthur's Seat**, which at 823ft above sea level easily towers over all of Edinburgh's numerous high points, is Dunsapie Loch, reached by following the tarred Queen's Drive in a clockwise direction from the palace gates. Part of a volcano which last saw action 350 million years ago, its connections to the legendary Celtic king are fairly sketchy: the name is likely to be a corruption of the Gaelic *Ard-na-said*, or "height of arrows". From Dunsapie Loch it's a twenty-minute climb up grassy slopes to the rocky summit. On a clear day, the views might just stretch to the English border and the Atlantic Ocean; more realistically, the landmarks which dominate are Fife, a few Highland peaks and, of course, Edinburgh laid out on all sides.

⑰ Cowgate and the Grassmarket

At the bottom of the valley immediately south of the Royal Mile, and following a roughly parallel course from the Lawnmarket to St Mary's Street, is the **Cowgate**. One of Edinburgh's oldest surviving streets, it was also formerly one of the city's most prestigious addresses. However, the construction of the great **viaducts** of George IV Bridge and South Bridge entombed it below street level, condemning it to decay and neglect. In the last decade or so the Cowgate has experienced something of a revival, with various nightclubs and Festival venues establishing themselves, though few tourists venture here and the contrast with the neighbouring Royal Mile remains stark.

The Grassmarket

At the western end of the Cowgate is an open, partly cobbled area girdled by tall tenements known as the **Grassmarket**, which was used as the city's cattle market from 1477 to 1911. Despite the height of many of the surrounding buildings, it offers an unexpected view up to the precipitous walls of the castle and, come springtime, it's sunny enough for cafés to put tables and chairs along the pavement. However, the Grassmarket is best remembered as the location of Edinburgh's public gallows – the spot is marked by a tiny garden. The notorious body-snatching duo of William Burke and William Hare had their lair in a now-vanished close just off the western end of the Grassmarket, and for a long time before its recent gentrification it had a seamy edge, with brothels, drinking dens and shelters for down-and-outs. Tucked away in the northwest corner is the award-winning modern architecture of **Dance Base** (☎0131/225 5525, ⓦwww.dancebase.co.uk), Scotland's National Centre for Dance, which holds classes, workshops and shows. Elsewhere, the Grassmarket's row of pubs has become a focus for stag and hen parties, and there's also a series of interesting shops, in particular the offbeat, independent boutiques on the unusual, two-tier **Victoria Street**, with arcaded shops below and a pedestrian terrace above.

Greyfriars and around

The **statue of Greyfriars Bobby** at the southwestern corner of **George IV Bridge** must rank as Edinburgh's most sentimental tourist attraction. Bobby was a Skye terrier acquired as a working dog by a police constable named John Gray. When Gray died in 1858, Bobby was found a few days later sitting on his grave, a vigil he maintained until his death fourteen years later. Bobby's legendary dedication was picked up by Disney, whose 1960 feature film of the story ensured that streams of tourists have paid their respects ever since.

The grave Bobby mourned over is in the **Greyfriars Kirkyard**, which has a fine collection of seventeenth-century gravestones and mausoleums, including one to the Adam family of architects. The kirkyard is visited regularly by ghost tours (see p.814) and was known for grave robbing long before Burke and Hare became the city's most notorious exponents of the crime. Greyfriars Kirk itself was built in 1620 on land which had belonged to a Franciscan convent, though little of the original late-Gothic-style building remains. A fire in the mid-nineteenth century led to significant rebuilding and the installation of the first organ in a Presbyterian church in Scotland; today's magnificent instrument, by Peter Collins, arrived in 1990.

National Museum of Scotland

Immediately opposite *Greyfriars Bobby*, on the south side of Chambers Street, stands the striking honey-coloured sandstone **National Museum of Scotland** (Mon–Sat 10am–5pm, Tues 10am–8pm, Sun noon–5pm; free; ⓦwww .nms.ac.uk). Custom-built in the 1990s, Scotland's premier museum displays many of the nation's most important historical artefacts as a means of telling the country's history from earliest man to the present day. The collection is generally, though not strictly, laid out in chronological order over seven different levels. The labyrinthine feel of the rooms and stairways is a little disorienting at first, though the unexpected views of different parts of the museum above and below are a deliberate effect to emphasize the interconnected layers of Scotland's history.

The main entrance is at the base of the tower (although it is also possible to enter through the neighbouring Royal Museum; see p.832). The information desk is located just before you get to **Hawthornden Court**, the central atrium of the museum and a useful orientation point; on this level you'll also find the shop and access to the Royal Museum café. Free **guided tours** on different themes take place throughout the day, and **audio headsets** (free) give detailed information on the displays.

The first sections, **Beginnings** and **Early People**, are on Level 0. Here, Scotland's story before the arrival of man is presented with audiovisual displays, artistic re-creations, and a selection of rocks and fossils. Alongside, the period from the arrival of the first people to the end of the first millennium AD is the most engrossing section of the entire museum, an eloquent testament to the remarkable craftsmanship, artistry and practicality of Scotland's early people. Among the artefacts on display, highlights are the **Trappain treasure** hoard, 20kg of silver plates, cutlery and goblets found buried in East Lothian; the **Cramond Lioness**, a sculpture from a Roman tombstone found recently in the Firth of Forth; and the beautifully detailed gold, silver and amber **Hunterston brooch**, dating from around 700 AD.

The **Kingdom of the Scots** on Level 1 covers the period between Scotland's development as a single independent nation and the Union with England in 1707. Many famous Scots are represented here, including Robert the Bruce, Mary, Queen of Scots, and her son James VI. Star exhibits include the **Monymusk reliquary**, an intricately decorated box said to have carried the remains of St Columba, and the **Lewis chessmen**, exquisitely idiosyncratic twelfth-century pieces carved from walrus ivory.

Level 3 shows exhibits under the theme **Scotland Transformed**, covering the century or so following the Union of Parliaments in 1707. This was the period which saw the last of the Highland uprisings under Bonnie Prince Charlie (whose silver travelling-canteen is on display), yet also witnessed the expansion of trade links with the Americas and developments in industries such as weaving, and iron and steel production.

Scotland went on to pioneer many aspects of heavy engineering, with ship and locomotive production to the fore. Largest of the exhibits in **Industry and Empire** on Level 4 is the steam locomotive *Ellesmere*. As well as industrial progress, other fields are covered too, including the influence of Scots around the world, both as a result of emigration, and through such luminaries as James Watt, Charles Rennie Mackintosh and Robert Louis Stevenson.

Royal Museum of Scotland

Interlinked with the National Museum, though also with its own entrance, is the Royal Museum of Scotland (same hours; free), a dignified Venetian-style palace with a cast-iron interior modelled on that of the former Crystal Palace in London. The Royal Museum has been an Edinburgh institution for over one hundred years and is a wonderful example of Victorian Britain's fascination with antiquities and natural history. The wonderfully airy **Great Hall**, framed in cast iron, displays sculpture from Classical Greece and Rome alongside Buddhas from Japan, and the bizarre Millennium Clock, a ten-metre tall, Heath Robinson–style contraption which clicks and whirls into motion at 11am, noon, 2pm and 4pm. Rooms leading off from here hold collections of stuffed animals and birds, including the full skeleton of a blue whale.

The University of Edinburgh and around

Immediately alongside the Royal Museum is the earliest surviving part of the **University of Edinburgh**, variously referred to as Old College or Old Quad, although nowadays it houses only a few university departments; the main campus colonizes the streets and squares to the south. The small **Talbot Rice Art Gallery** (Tues–Sat 10am–5pm, also Mon 10am–5pm & Sun 2–5pm during the Festival; free; ⓦwww.trg.ed.ac.uk) occupies the southwest corner of the Old College, and hosts some excellent touring and temporary avant-garde exhibitions – the show held during the Festival is normally of a high standard.

A little further up Nicolson Street is the stately facade of **Surgeons' Hall**, a handsome Ionic temple built by Playfair as the headquarters of the Royal College of Surgeons. Inside is one of the city's most unusual and morbidly compelling **museums** (Mon–Fri noon–4pm; free; ⓦwww.rcsed.ac.uk). In the eighteenth and nineteenth centuries Edinburgh developed as a leading centre for medical and anatomical research, nurturing world-famous pioneers such as James Young Simpson, founder of anaesthesia, and Joseph Lister, the father of modern surgery. The museum's intriguing exhibits range from early surgical tools to a pocketbook covered with the leathered skin of body snatcher

William Burke. The elegant **Playfair Hall** contains an array of specimens and jars from the college's anatomical and pathological collections dating back to the eighteenth century.

The New Town

The **NEW TOWN**, itself well over two hundred years old, stands in total contrast to the Old Town: the layout is symmetrical, the streets are broad and straight, and most of the buildings are Neoclassical. Originally intended to be residential, today the New Town is the bustling hub of the city's professional, commercial and business life, dominated by shops, banks and offices.

The existence of the New Town is chiefly due to the vision of **George Drummond**, who made schemes for the expansion of the city soon after becoming Lord Provost in 1725. Work began on the draining of the Nor' Loch below the Castle in 1759, a job that took some sixty years. The North Bridge, linking the Old Town with the main road leading to the port of Leith, was built between 1763 and 1772 and, in 1766, following a public competition, a plan for the New Town by 22-year-old architect **James Craig** was chosen. Its gridiron pattern was perfectly matched to the site: central **George Street**, flanked by showpiece squares, was laid out along the main ridge, with parallel **Princes Street** and **Queen Street** on either side, built up on one side only, so as not to block the spectacular views of the Old Town and Fife.

In many ways, the layout of the greater New Town is its own most remarkable sight, an extraordinary grouping of squares, circuses, terraces, crescents and parks with a few set pieces such as **Charlotte Square** and the assemblage of curiosities on and around **Calton Hill**. However, it also contains assorted Victorian additions, notably the **Scott Monument** on Princes Street, the **Royal Botanic Garden** on its northern fringe, as well as two of the city's most important public collections – the **National Gallery of Scotland** and, further afield, the **Scottish National Gallery of Modern Art**.

Princes Street

Although only allocated a subsidiary role in the original plan of the New Town, **Princes Street** had developed into Edinburgh's principal thoroughfare by the middle of the nineteenth century, a role it has retained ever since. Its unobstructed views across to the Castle and the Old Town are undeniably magnificent. Indeed, without the views, Princes Street would lose much of its appeal; its northern side, dominated by ugly department stores, is almost always crowded with shoppers, and few of the original eighteenth-century buildings remain.

Princes Street Gardens

It's hard to imagine that the **gardens** (dawn to dusk; free) which flank nearly the entire length of Princes Street were once the stagnant, foul-smelling Nor' Loch, into which the effluent of the Old Town flowed for centuries. The railway has since replaced the water and today a sunken cutting carries the main lines out of Waverley Station to the west and north. The gardens, split into East and West sections, were originally the private domain of Princes Street residents and their well-placed acquaintances, only becoming a public park in 1876. These days, the swarhes of green lawn, colourful flower beds and mature trees are a green lung for the city centre: on sunny days local office workers appear in their droves at lunchtime, while around Christmas (late Nov to early Jan daily

10am–10pm) the gardens' eastern section is home to an ice rink (£6.50) and a towering Ferris wheel (£2). The larger and more verdant western section has a floral clock and the Ross Bandstand, a popular Festival venue.

The Scott Monument

Facing the Victorian shopping emporium Jenners, and set within East Princes Street Gardens, the 200-foot-high **Scott Monument** (April–Sept Mon–Sat 9am–6pm, Sun 10am–6pm; Oct–March Mon–Sat 9am–3pm, Sun 10am–3pm; £3) was erected in memory of prolific author and patriot Sir Walter Scott within a few years of his death. The architecture is closely modelled on Scott's beloved Melrose Abbey (see p.864), while the rich sculptural decoration shows 16 Scottish writers and 64 characters from Scott's famous *Waverley* novels. On the central plinth at the base of the monument is a **statue** of Scott with his deerhound Maida, carved from a thirty-ton block of Carrara marble. Inside the memorial, a tightly winding spiral staircase climbs to a narrow platform near the top: from here, you can enjoy some inspiring – if vertiginous – vistas of the city below, and hills and firths beyond.

The National Gallery of Scotland

Princes Street Gardens are bisected by the **Mound**, one of only two direct road links between the Old and New towns (the other is North Bridge). Its name is an accurate description: it was formed in the 1780s by dumping piles of earth and other waste brought from the New Town's building plots. At the foot of the mound on the Princes Street level are two grand Neoclassical buildings: the **National Gallery of Scotland** and the **Royal Scottish Academy** (daily 10am–5pm, Thurs till 7pm; free, entrance charge for some temporary exhibitions; Ⓦwww.natgalscot.ac.uk). Both were designed by William Henry Playfair (1790–1857), though the exterior of the National Gallery is considerably more austere than the Athenian-style Academy. The recently completed **Weston Link** established a new entrance to both galleries with an underground passageway joining the two buildings. Built as a "temple to the fine arts" in 1850, the National Gallery houses Scotland's finest array of European and Scottish art from the early 1300s to the late 1800s, with an outstanding clutch of works ranging from High Renaissance to Post-Impressionism. Its modest size makes it a manageable place to visit in a couple of hours and affords a pleasantly unrushed atmosphere.

One of the gallery's most recent acquisitions is a superb painting by **Botticelli**, *The Virgin Adoring the Sleeping Christ Child*, which has undergone careful restoration to reveal its striking luminosity and depth of colour. Of four mythological scenes by **Titian**, the sensuous *Three Ages of Man* is one of his most accomplished early compositions, while *Diana and Acteon* and its pendant *Diana and Calisto*, painted for Philip II of Spain, illustrate the highly impressionistic freedom of his late style. **El Greco**'s *A Fable* was painted during his early years in Italy, this being the best of the three versions of the composition, though his subject matter remains tantalizingly ambiguous.

Poussin's *Seven Sacraments* are proudly displayed in their own room, the floor and central octagonal bench of which repeat some of the motifs in the series. **Rubens**' *The Feast of Herod* is an archetypal example of his sumptuously grand manner, and was recently enlivened by meticulous restoration: its gory subject matter is overshadowed by the gaudy depiction of the delights of the table. Among the four canvases by **Rembrandt** is a poignant *Self-Portrait Aged 51*, and the ripely suggestive *Woman in Bed*, which is thought to represent the biblical figure of Sarah on her wedding night.

17

Contemporary art in Edinburgh

In addition to the contemporary art collections in the city's National Galleries there are a number of smaller, independent galleries around the city that are well worth exploring.

Edinburgh Printmakers 23 Union St ☎0131/557 2479, ⓦwww.edinburgh -printmakers.co.uk. A highly respected studio and gallery dedicated to contemporary printmaking.

Fruitmarket Gallery 45 Market St ☎0131/225 2383, ⓦwww.fruitmarket.co.uk. The stylish modern design of this dynamic and much-admired art space is the capital's first port of call for top-grade international artists – recent years have seen shows by the likes of Jeff Koons and Bill Viola.

Open Eye Gallery 34 Abercromby Place ☎0131/557 1020, ⓦwww.openeyegallery .co.uk. One of the city's best commercial galleries features a number of Scotland's top contemporary artists.

Scottish Gallery 16 Dundas St ☎0131/558 1200, ⓦwww.scottish-gallery.co.uk. One of a number of small galleries on this New Town street; some of the most striking works here are in the basement area dedicated to applied art.

One of the gallery's most recent major purchases is **Canova**'s 1817 statue *The Three Graces* – saved at the last minute from California's Getty Museum. There's also a superb group of early Impressionist works such as **Camille Pissarro**'s *Kitchen Garden L'Hermitage*. Impressionist masters have a strong showing, including a collection of **Degas**' sketches, paintings and bronzes, as well as **Monet**'s *Haystacks (Snow)* and **Renoir**'s *Woman Nursing Child*. Representing the Post-Impressionists are three exceptional examples of **Gauguin**'s work, including *Vision After the Sermon*, set in Brittany, **Van Gogh**'s *Olive Trees*, and **Cézanne**'s *The Big Trees* – a clear forerunner of modern abstraction.

The gallery's Scottish and English works include some of **Sir Henry Raeburn**'s large portraits – the swaggering masculinity of *Sir John Sinclair in Highland Dress* shows Raeburn's technical mastery, though he was equally confident when working on a smaller scale for one of the gallery's most popular pictures, *The Rev Robert Walker Skating on Duddingston Loch*. The gallery also owns a brilliant array of watercolours by **Turner**, faithfully displayed each January when damaging sunlight is at its weakest.

Charlotte Square

At the western end of George Street, **Charlotte Square** was designed by Robert Adam in 1791, a year before his death. Generally regarded as the epitome of the New Town's elegant simplicity, the square was once the most exclusive residential address in Edinburgh, and though much of it is now occupied by offices, the imperious dignity of the architecture is still evident. Indeed, the north side, the finest of Adam's designs, is once again the city's premier address, with the official residence of the First Minister of the Scottish Executive at no. 6 (Bute House), the Edinburgh equivalent of 10 Downing Street.

The lower floors of neighbouring no. 7 are open to the public under the name of the **Georgian House** (daily: March & Nov 11am–3pm; April–Oct 10am–5pm; July & Aug 10am–7pm; last entry 30min before closing, £5; ⓦwww.nts.org.uk). Restored by the NTS, its interior provides a revealing sense of well-to-do New Town living in the early nineteenth century. The buildings on the south side of the square have also been superbly restored by the NTS to something approaching their Georgian grandeur, and now house the NTS main **headquarters** in Scotland. It's well worth paying a visit to no. 28 to peer at the sumptuous interior. One floor up, a small **gallery** (Mon–Fri 11am–3pm; free) shows a collection of twentieth-century Scottish art, including a number of attractive examples of the work of the Scottish Colourists. In August each year, the gardens in the centre of the square are colonized by the temporary tents of the Edinburgh Book Festival (see p.851).

Queen Street

At the eastern end of Queen Street, just to the north of St Andrew Square, is the **Scottish National Portrait Gallery** (daily 10am–5pm, Thurs open till 7pm; free, entrance charge for some temporary exhibitions). A fantastic medieval Gothic palace in red sandstone, the Portrait Gallery makes an extravagant contrast to the New Town's prevailing Neoclassicism. The exterior of the building is encrusted with statues of famous national heroes, a theme reiterated by William Hole's tapestry-like frieze depicting notable figures from Scotland's past, in the stunning two-storey entrance hall. Unlike the more global outlook of its sister National Gallery (see p.834), the Portrait Gallery devotes itself to images of famous Scots – a definition stretched to include anyone with the slightest connection to the country. Taken as a whole, it's an engaging procession through Scottish history, with familiar faces from Bonnie Prince Charlie and Mary, Queen of Scots, to Alex Ferguson and Sean Connery appearing along the way.

Calton Hill

Edinburgh's tag as the "Athens of the North" is nowhere better earned than on **Calton Hill**, the volcanic peak which rises up above the eastern end of Princes Street. Numerous architects homed in on it as a showcase for their most ambitious and grandiose buildings and monuments, whose presence emphasize Calton's aloof air and sense of detachment today. But the hill and its odd collection of buildings aren't just for looking *at*: this is also one of the best viewpoints from which to appreciate the city as a whole, with its tightly knitted suburbs, landmark Old and New Town buildings and, the sea beyond – much closer to Edinburgh than many visitors expect.

Set majestically on the slopes of Calton Hill looking towards Arthur's Seat, sits one of Edinburgh's greatest buildings, the **Old Royal High School**. With its bold central portico of Doric columns and graceful symmetrical colonnaded wings, Thomas Hamilton's elegant building of 1829 is regarded by many as the epitome of Edinburgh's Athenian aspirations. The capital's high school was based here between 1829 and 1968, at which point the building was converted to house a debating chamber and became Scotland's parliament-in-waiting. However, soon after the re-establishment of a Scottish parliament had been confirmed in 1997 the building was controversially rejected as too small for the intended assembly, with a brand-new building at Holyrood favoured instead. Currently used as offices by the city council, the latest plan is to convert it into a museum of the history of photography.

Robert Louis Stevenson reckoned that Calton Hill was the best place to view Edinburgh, "since you can see the Castle, which you lose from the Castle, and Arthur's Seat, which you cannot see from Arthur's Seat." Though the panoramas from ground level are spectacular enough, those from the top of the **Nelson Monument** (April–Sept Mon 1–6pm, Tues–Sat 10am–6pm; Oct–March Mon–Sat 10am–3pm; £3), perched near the summit of Calton

Hill, are even better. Alongside, the **National Monument** is often referred to as "Edinburgh's Disgrace", yet many locals admire this unfinished and somewhat ungainly attempt to replicate the Parthenon atop Calton Hill. Begun as a memorial to the dead of the Napoleonic Wars, the project's shortage of funds led architect William Playfair to ensure that even with just twelve of the massive columns completed, the folly would still serve as a striking landmark. It's one of those constructions which is purposeless yet still magnetic; with a bit of effort and care you can climb up and around the monument, sit and contemplate from one of the huge steps or meander around the base of the mighty pillars.

Designed by Playfair in 1818, the **City Observatory** is the largest of the buildings at the summit of Calton Hill. Because of pollution and the advent of street lighting, which impaired views of the stars, the observatory proper had to be relocated to Blackford Hill before the end of the nineteenth century. The complex isn't open to the public, but a stroll around its perimeter offers a broad perspective over the city, with views out to the Forth Bridges and Fife.

Mansfield Place Church

The highlight of the Broughton Street area, northwest of Calton, is the neo-Norman **Mansfield Place Church**, on the corner of Broughton and East London streets. It contains a cycle of **murals** by the Dublin-born **Phoebe Anna Traquair**, a leading light in the Scottish Arts and Crafts movement. Covering vast areas of the walls and ceilings of the main nave and side chapels, the wonderfully luminous paintings depict Biblical parables and texts, with rows of angels, cherubs flecked with gold and worshipping figures painted in delicate pastel colours. Viewing of the murals is restricted to one Sunday afternoon each month, although more regular opening is normally arranged during the Festival: for details see ⓦ www.mansfieldtraquair.org.uk.

The Royal Botanic Garden

Just beyond the northern boundaries of the New Town, with entrances on Inverleith Row and Arboretum Place, is the seventy-acre site of the **Royal Botanic Garden** (daily: March & Oct 10am–6pm; April–Sept 10am–7pm; Nov–Feb 10am–4pm; free; ⓦ www.rbge.org.uk). Filled with mature trees and a huge variety of native and exotic plants and flowers, the "botanics" (as they're commonly called) are most popular simply as a place to stroll and lounge around on the grass. Towards the eastern side of the gardens, a series of ten glasshouses (entry £3.50), including the elegant 1850s Palm House, show off a steamy array of palms, ferns, orchids, cycads and aquatic plants. Art is also a strong theme within the botanics, with a gallery showing changing contemporary exhibitions in the attractive eighteenth-century Inverleith House at the centre of the gardens, while scattered all around are a number of outdoor sculptures, including a giant pine cone by landscape artist Andy Goldsworthy. Parts of the garden are also notable for some great vistas: the busy *Terrace Café* (see p.843) beside Inverleith House offers one of the city's best views of the Castle and of Old Town's steeples and monuments. **Guided tours** (£4) leave from the West Gate on Arboretum Place at 11am and 2pm (April–Sept).

The West End

The western extension to the New Town was the last part to be built, deviating from the area's overriding Neoclassicism with a number of Victorian additions.

17

Just over the Water of Leith are two compelling collections of contemporary art, the well-established **Scottish National Gallery of Modern Art** and its newer neighbour, the **Dean Gallery**, both of which regularly host worthwhile seasonal and touring exhibitions.

The most pleasant way of getting to the galleries is on foot along the **Water of Leith walkway**, which can be joined at Stockbridge or the Dean Village. Alternatively, a free **bus** runs there on the hour (Mon–Sat 11am–5pm, Sun noon–5pm) from outside the National Gallery on the Mound, via the National Portrait Gallery. Alternatively, bus #13 runs along Belford Road, from the western end of George Street.

The Scottish National Gallery of Modern Art

Set in spacious wooded grounds at the far northwestern fringe of the New Town, the **Scottish National Gallery of Modern Art** on Belford Road (daily 10am–5pm, Thurs open till 7pm; free, entrance charge for some temporary exhibitions; ⓦ www.natgalscot.ac.uk) was Britain's first collection devoted solely to twentieth-century painting and sculpture. It operates in tandem with Dean Gallery across the road (see p.838); the extensive wooded grounds of the galleries serve as a sculpture park, featuring works by Jacob Epstein, Henry Moore, Barbara Hepworth and, most strikingly, Charles Jencks, whose prize-winning *Landform*, a swirling mix of ponds and grassy mounds, dominates the area in front of the Gallery of Modern Art. Inside, the display space is divided between temporary exhibitions and selections from the gallery's own holdings including early twentieth-century Post-Impressionists, the Fauves, German Expressionism, Cubism and Pop Art. There's a strong section on living British artists, while modern Scottish art ranges from the Colourists – whose works are attracting ever-growing posthumous critical acclaim – to the distinctive styles of contemporary Scots including portraitist John Bellany, and the poet-artist-gardener Ian Hamilton Finlay.

The Dean Gallery

Opposite the Modern Art Gallery on the other side of Belford Road is the latest addition to the National Galleries of Scotland, the **Dean Gallery** (same hours; free; ⓦ www.natgalscot.ac.uk), housed in an equally impressive Neoclassical building completed in 1833. The interior of the gallery, built as an orphanage, has been dramatically refurbished specifically to make room for the work of Edinburgh-born sculptor **Sir Eduardo Paolozzi**, described by some as the father of Pop Art. The collection includes some three thousand sculptures, two thousand prints and drawings and three thousand books.

There's an awesome introduction to Paolozzi's work in the form of the huge *Vulcan*, a half-man, half-machine which squeezes into the Great Hall immediately opposite the main entrance – view it both from ground level and the head-height balcony to appreciate the sheer scale of the piece. No less persuasive of Paolozzi's dynamic creative talents are the rooms to the right of the main entrance, where his London studio has been expertly re-created, right down to the clutter of half-finished casts, toys and empty pots of glue.

The ground floor also holds a world-renowned collection of **Dada** and **Surrealist** art; Marcel Duchamp, Max Ernst and Man Ray are all represented. Look out also for Dalí's *The Signal of Anguish* and Magritte's *Magic Mirror* along with work by Miró and Giacometti – all hung on crowded walls with an assortment of artefacts and ethnic souvenirs.

Out from the centre

Just over a mile northeast of the city centre is **Leith**, a fascinating mix of cobbled streets and new developments, run-down housing and an excellent eating and drinking scene, which majors on seafood but also includes some of the city's top restaurants side by side with well-worn, friendly pubs. Elsewhere, Edinburgh's **zoo** is a perennial favourite with children, who will also enjoy the quiet ruins of **Craigmillar Castle** to the south of the city.

Leith

Although **LEITH** is generally known as the port of Edinburgh, it developed independently of the city up the hill, its history bound up in the hard graft of fishing, shipbuilding and trade. The presence of sailors, merchants and continental traders also gave the place a cosmopolitan – if slightly rough – edge, which is still obvious today in Leith's fascinating mix of cobbled streets and flash new housing, container ships and historic buildings, ugly council flats and trendy waterside bistros.

The best way to absorb Leith's history and seafaring connections is to take a stroll along **The Shore**, a tenement-lined road running alongside the Water of Leith. Until the mid-nineteenth century this was a bustling and cosmopolitan harbour, visited by ships from all over the world, but as vessels became increasingly large, they moored up instead at custom-built docks built beyond the original quays. Instead, the focus is on the numerous **pubs and restaurants** that line the street, many of which spill tables and chairs out onto the cobbled pavement on sunny days.

A little to the west of The Shore, moored alongside **Ocean Terminal**, a huge shopping and entertainment centre designed by Terence Conran, is one of the world's most famous ships, **Britannia** (daily: April–Sept 9.30am–6pm; Oct–March 10am–5pm; last entry 90min before closing; £9; Ⓦwww.royaly achtbritannia.co.uk). Launched in 1953, *Britannia* was used by the royal family for 44 years for state visits, diplomatic functions and royal holidays. Visits to *Britannia* begin in the **visitor centre**, within Ocean Terminal, where royal holiday snaps and video clips of the ship's most famous moments are shown. An audio handset is then handed out and you can roam around the yacht, which has been largely kept as she was when in service, with a well-preserved 1950s dowdiness. Certainly the atmosphere is a far cry from the opulent splendour which many expect.

To get to Ocean Terminal from the city, jump on one of the tour **buses** that leave from Waverley Bridge; otherwise, take buses #11, #22 or #34 from Princes Street, or #35 from the Royal Mile.

Edinburgh Zoo

A couple of miles due west of the city centre, **Edinburgh Zoo** (daily: April–Sept 9am–6pm; March & Oct 9am–5pm; Nov–Feb 9am–4.30pm; £9, family ticket from £28; Ⓦwww.edinburghzoo.org.uk) is set on an eighty-acre site on the slopes of Corstorphine Hill (buses #12, #26, #31 & #100 from town). Established in 1913, the zoo has a reputation for preserving rare and endangered species, with the emphasis moving away from bored animals in cages to imaginatively designed habitats and viewing areas. The place is permanently packed with kids, and the zoo's most famous attraction is its **penguin parade** (April–Sept daily at 2.15pm, and in sunny days in March & Oct), when rangers encourage a bunch of the flightless birds to leave their pen and waddle around a short circuit of pathways.

Craigmillar Castle

Situated around five miles southeast of Edinburgh's centre, amidst green belt, **Craigmillar Castle** (April–Sept daily 9.30am–6.30pm; Oct–March Sat–Wed 9.30am–4.30pm; last entry 30min before closing; £3; HS), is one of the best-preserved ruined medieval fortresses in Scotland. Though it's located next to the ugly council housing scheme of Craigmillar, one of Edinburgh's most deprived districts, the immediate setting feels very rural and Craigmillar Castle enjoys splendid views back to Arthur's Seat and Edinburgh Castle. The oldest part of the complex dates from the early 1400s; surrounded in the 1500s by a quadrangular wall with cylindrical corner towers, it was used on occasion by Mary, Queen of Scots. It was abandoned to picturesque decay in the mid-eighteenth century, and today the peaceful ruins and their adjoining grassy lawns make a great place to explore, with children in particular loving the run of their very own castle.

Take **bus** #30, #33 or #82, from North Bridge to Little France, from where the castle is a ten-minute walk along Craigmillar Castle Road.

Eating

The last decade has seen a marked upsurge in the quality of Edinburgh's **cafés** and restaurants: there's now a clutch of original, upmarket and stylish **restaurants**, serving **contemporary** or **modern Scottish** cuisine and championing top-quality local meat, game and fish. As with most large cities in Britain, there's a good selection of mid-market chains and long-established Chinese, Indian and Mexican places, as well as more interesting outposts of Thai, North African and Spanish cuisine.

Royal Mile and around

Cafés and bistros

Always Sunday 170 High St ☎0131/622 0667. Proof that there's room for a bit of real food even on the tourist-thronged Royal Mile, this pleasant independent café serves healthy lunches, home-made cakes, fresh smoothies and Fairtrade coffee. Open daily till 6pm. Inexpensive.

Elephant House 21 George IV Bridge ☎0131/220 5355. Extolled as one of the places where hard-up single mum J.K. Rowling nursed her cups of coffee while penning the first Harry Potter novel, this is a decent daytime and evening café with a terrific room at the back full of philos-ophizing students and visitors peering dreamily at the views of the Castle. Daily 8am–11pm. Inexpensive.

Fruitmarket Gallery Café 45 Market St ☎0131/226 1843. This attractive café feels like an extension of the gallery space, its airy, reflective ambience enhanced by the wall of glass onto the street. Stop in for soups, coffees or a Caesar salad. Mon–Sat 11am–5.30pm, Sun noon–4.30pm. Inexpensive.

Plaisir du Chocolat 251–253 Canongate ☎0131/556 9524. Classy Parisian tearoom and chocolatier serving delicious, if pricey, lunches, luxurious patisserie treats, an array of gourmet teas and real hot-chocolates. Open daily 10am–6pm. Moderate.

Restaurants

Amber Scotch Whisky Heritage Centre, 354 Castle-hill ☎0131/477 8477, ⊛www.amber-restaurant .co.uk. Neat, contemporary-styled place serving a good choice of light Scottish food such as potted shrimp at lunchtime, and more substantial and expensive dishes in the evenings (Fri & Sat only), when there's a "whisky sommelier" on hand to suggest the best drams to accompany your honey-roast rack of Highland lamb or saddle of Balmoral venison. Expensive.

Barioja 19 Jeffrey St ☎0131/557 3622. Open throughout the day and good for a lunchtime *boca-dillo* sandwich or late-afternoon drink and snack, this Spanish-owned bar makes a decent stab at tapas in a metropolitan setting. Inexpensive. The more upmarket *Igg's*, a Spanish–Scottish hybrid, is next door.

David Bann's Vegetarian Restaurant 56–58 St Mary's St ☎0131/556 5888, ⓦwww.davidbann.com. Thoroughly modern vegetarian restaurant, open long hours and offering a wide choice of interesting, unconventional dishes such as courgette and sweetcorn fritters or celeriac and sweet potato roulade. The prices are very reasonable and the overall design is stylish and classy – not an open-toed sandal in sight. Moderate.

The Grain Store 30 Victoria St ☎0131/225 7635, ⓦwww.grainstore-restaurant.co.uk. Often missed by passers-by, this unpretentious restaurant is a relaxing haven amongst the bustle of the Old Town, serving fairly uncomplicated but top-quality modern Scottish food such as saddle of venison with beetroot fondant or toasted goat's cheese with caramelized walnuts. Reasonable lunchtime and set-price options. Expensive.

La Garrigue 31 Jeffrey St ☎0131/557 3032, ⓦwww.lagarrigue.co.uk. A place of genuine charm and quality, with a menu and wine list dedicated to the produce and traditions of France's Languedoc region – the care and honesty of the cooking shines through in dishes such as cassoulet or bream with chard. Moderate.

Prego 38 St Mary's St ☎0131/557 5754, ⓦwww.prego-restaurant.com. Classy but not overpriced Italian place with a short, confident seasonal menu (no pizza) and knowledgeable service. It's a bit like eating in Italy, which is a rare find in Britain. Closed Sun. Moderate.

Suruchi 14a Nicolson St ☎0131/556 6583, ⓦwww.suruchirestaurant.co.uk. Popular establishment serving genuine South Indian dishes – bizarrely, the menu is written in broad Scots. Look out for cross-cultural specials such as tandoori trout. Moderate.

Tower Museum of Scotland, Chambers Street ☎0131/225 3003, ⓦwww.tower-restaurant.com. Unique setting on Level 5 of the new Museum of Scotland; at night you are escorted along the empty corridors to the restaurant, where spectacular views to the floodlit Castle are revealed. Excellent modern Scottish food such as shellfish and expensive chargrilled Aberdeen Angus steaks in a self-consciously chic setting. Expensive.

The Witchery by the Castle 352 Castlehill ☎0131/225 5613, ⓦwww.thewitchery.com. A fine-dining Scottish restaurant that only Edinburgh could create, set in magnificently over-the-top medieval surroundings full of Gothic panelling, tapestries and heavy stonework, all a mere broomstick-hop from the Castle. The rich fish and game dishes are pricey, but you can steal a sense of it all with a lunch or pre- or post-theatre set menu (£12.50). Expensive.

New Town and the West End

Cafés and bistros

Glass & Thompson 2 Dundas St ☎0131/557 0909. Tasteful, upmarket café deli with huge bowls of olives and an irresistible glass counter filled with delicious food; scattered tables and chairs mean you can linger over a made-to-order sandwich or top-notch cake and coffee. Closed evenings. Inexpensive.

Urban Angel 121 Hanover St ☎0131/225 6215. Right-on but easy-going subterranean bistro with a diverse and flexible blackboard menu using lots of organic and Fairtrade produce. Closed Sun eve. Moderate.

Valvona & Crolla Vin Caffè 11 Multrees Walk ☎0131/557 0088, ⓦwww.valvonacrolla.com. Suave sister venue to the famous Leith Walk deli, with an espresso bar and takeaway downstairs, and classy Italian snacks, meals and wine by the glass upstairs. Moderate–expensive.

Restaurants

Café Royal Oyster Bar 17a W Register St ☎0131/556 4124. An Edinburgh classic, with its splendidly ornate Victorian interior (featured in *Chariots of Fire*), stained-glass windows, marble floor and Doulton tiling. Time-honoured seafood dishes, including freshly caught oysters, served in a civilized, chatty setting. Very expensive.

Centotre 103 George St ☎0131/225 1550, ⓦwww.centotre.com. Slick but welcoming bar, café and restaurant in an ornate former bank, offering unfussy, top-quality Italian food from fresh pastries and coffee to interesting pizzas or a simple but blissful plate of gorgonzola served with a ripe pear. All accompanied by a seriously impressive drinks list. Moderate.

Dusit 49a Thistle St, West End ☎0131/220 6846, ⓦwww.dusit.co.uk. The bold but effective blend of Thai flavours and well-sourced Scottish ingredients here brings a bit of originality and refinement to the often-predictable Thai dining scene – specialities include guinea fowl with red curry sauce and vegetables stir-fried with a dash of whisky. Moderate.

Fishers in the City 58 Thistle St ☎0131/225 5109, ⓦwww.fishersbistro.co.uk. New Town incarnation of Leith's best-loved seafood bistro. This one has a sleek modern interior, great service and some stunning seafood. Expensive.

Forth Floor Harvey Nichols, 30–34 St Andrew Square ☏ 0131/524 8350, ⓦ www.harveynichols .com. While the rooftop views don't quite match its rivals *Oloroso* and the *Tower*, Harvey Nics is a real contender among the city's fine modern Scottish options, with dishes such as seared scallops with fig salsa, or pot-roast pork. The restaurant gets the glass frontage, while the brasserie with its simpler risottos and grills is less pricey but less memorable. Closed Sun & Mon evening. Moderate–expensive.

Henderson's Salad Table 94 Hanover St ☏ 0131/225 2131, ⓦ www .hendersonsofedinburgh.co.uk. A much-loved Edinburgh institution, this self-service basement vegetarian restaurant offers freshly prepared hot dishes plus a decent choice of salads, soups and cakes. The slightly antiquated cafeteria feel can be off-putting, but the food is honest, reliable and always tasty. Light live jazz every evening. Open Mon–Sat 8am–10.30pm. Inexpensive–moderate.

La Cuisine d'Odile 13 Randolph Crescent, West End ☏ 0131/225 5685. Genuine lunch-only French home cooking in a basement under the French Institute. There's a really authentic feel to the food, with lots of inexpensive terrines, flans, game dishes and some superb desserts, including a signature "Choc'Odile" chocolate tart. Closed Sun, Mon & July. Inexpensive.

Le Café St Honoré 34 Thistle St Lane ☏ 0131/226 2211, ⓦ www.cafesthonore.com. A little piece of Paris discreetly tucked away in a New Town back lane. Fairly traditional top-quality French fare

– grilled oysters, warm duck salad and tarte tatin. Closed Sun. Moderate.

Mussel Inn 61–65 Rose St ☏ 0131/225 5979, ⓦ www.mussel-inn.com. After feasting on a kilo of mussels and a basket of chips for under £10 you'll realize why there's a demand to get in here. Owned by two west-coast shellfish farmers, which ensures that the time from sea to stomach is minimal. Closed Sun. Moderate.

Number One 1 Princes St ☏ 0131/557 6727, ⓦ www.thebalmoralhotel.com/restaurant1.html. Chef Jeff Bland is one of only two Michelin-star holders in Edinburgh; what's on offer is Scottish haute cuisine served in an overtly upmarket subterranean dining space within the five-star *Balmoral Hotel*. Lunches are (just about) affordable for a taste of the artistry; or for a bravura performance there's a six-course tasting menu, with dishes such as foie gras poached in port, for £60. Very expensive.

Oloroso 33 Castle St ☏ 0131/226 7614, ⓦ www.oloroso.co.uk. Edinburgh's most glamorous upmarket dining space, with a rooftop location giving views to the Castle and the Forth. The Scottish menu features strong flavours such as chump of lamb or roast salmon, followed by playful puddings – try the deep-fried jam sandwich with ice cream. Eating (or drinking) at the more convivial bar is a cost-effective way to enjoy the setting, but the best views are from the balcony. Expensive.

A Room in the Town 18 Howe St ☏ 0131/225 8204, ⓦ www.aroomin.co.uk/thetown. Manages to combine a friendly, relaxed atmosphere with decent, Scottish-slanted seasonal food. BYOB keeps the bills down. Sister restaurant *A Room in the West End* is below ground at 26 William St. Moderate.

Broughton and Leith Walk

Cafés and bistros

Blue Moon Café 1 Barony St ☏ 0131/557 0911. One of the best-known beacons of Edinburgh's gay scene, this easy-going, straight-friendly café-bar serves decent coffee, hearty breakfasts and light meals right through to 11pm. Moderate.

Valvona & Crolla 19 Elm Row, Leith Walk ☏ 0131/556 6066, ⓦ www.valvonacrolla.com. The café at the back of this Italian deli – arguably Britain's finest – serves authentic and delicious breakfasts, lunches and snacks. The best advert for the café is the walk through the shop – which has food stacked from floor to ceiling, with display

cabinets full of sublime olives, meats and cheeses. Open Mon–Sat 8am–5pm. Moderate.

Restaurants

Thai Me Up in Edinburgh 4 Picardy Place ☏ 0131/558 9234, ⓦ www.tmeup.com. Not the most convincing of names, but the Thai cooking is fresh, dynamic and colourful. The menu is short and to the point, with specialities including steamed fish and beef in red curry sauce, and the "authentic" Thai artefacts are subtle enough to allow the food to take centre stage. Moderate.

Stockbridge and around

Cafés and bistros

Circus Café 15 North West Circus Place, Stockbridge ☏0131/220 0333. An ultra-chic bank conversion with impeccable foodie credentials: a deli and wine shop in the basement, and an upstairs café that's open until 11pm and makes use of the best of the produce with platters, salads and reasonably priced main dishes. Moderate.

The Gallery Café Scottish National Gallery of Modern Art, Belford Road, Dean Village ☏0131/332 8600. Far more than a standard refreshment stop for gallery visitors, the cultured setting (which includes a lovely outside eating area) and appealing menu of hearty soups, healthy salads and filled croissants pulls in reassuring numbers of locals. Open daily 10am–4.30pm. Moderate.

Terrace Café Royal Botanic Garden, Inverleith ☏0131/552 0616. A great location in the middle of the garden, with outside tables offering stunning views of the city skyline, but the food isn't that memorable and it can be busy (and noisy) with families. Inexpensive.

Restaurants

Blue Parrot Cantina 49 St Stephen's St, Stockbridge ☏0131/225 2941. Cosy, quirky, basement Mexican restaurant, with a frequently changing evening menu that makes a decent effort to deviate from the predictable clichés; house specialties include *pescado baja* (haddock with a creamy lime sauce). Evenings only. Moderate.

The Snug 33a St Stephen's St, Stockbridge ☏0131/225 9397. Friendly wee Scottish restaurant tucked into a basement room, where the dishes involve reasonably imaginative combos of classic local produce such as salmon and beef. Moderate.

Lothian Road and Tollcross

Cafés and bistros

blue 10 Cambridge St ☏0131/221 1222. With minimalist modern decor, this impressive café/bistro hits the spot in terms of standards of food and service. It's handy for a quality pre- or post-theatre bite, with tasty modern dishes such as sea bass and baby onion tatin or confit duck leg with black pudding mash for under £10, and is one of the city's more sophisticated child-friendly options. Closed Sun. Moderate.

Ndebele 57 Home St ☏0131/221 1141. Colourful African café offering sandwiches with lots of alternative fillings, salads and *biltong* for homesick South Africans. Open daily till 10pm. Inexpensive.

Restaurants

The Atrium 10 Cambridge St ☏0131/228 8882, ⓦ www.atriumrestaurant.co.uk. One of the most consistently impressive of Edinburgh's top-end restaurants. Quirky, arty design including features such as railway-sleeper tables, while the food focuses on high-quality Scottish produce including Buccleuch beef *carpaccio*, or warm berries served with mascarpone sorbet. Closed Sunday. Very expensive.

izzi 119 Lothian Rd ☏0131/466 9888 ⓦ www.izzi-restaurant.co.uk. Set among the bright lights and late-night revelry of Lothian Road, this is a slick, contemporary restaurant offering both Chinese and Japanese cuisine, including some of the better sushi around. Moderate.

Marque Central 30b Grindlay St ☏0131/229 9859, ⓦ www.marquecentral.co.uk. Right next door to the Lyceum Theatre and Usher Hall, it's a good spot for pre- and post-theatre deals. At any time a place for imaginative modern Scottish food. Closed Sun & Mon. Moderate to expensive.

Southside

Cafés and bistros

Blonde 75 St Leonards St ☏0131/668 2917. Pleasant neighbourhood bistro, serving intriguing global combos such as salmon with black-olive noodles and venison with cardamom and bitter chocolate. Closed Mon lunch. Moderate.

Favorit 30–32 Leven St, Bruntsfield ☏0131/221 1800. Thoroughly modern café-diner dishing up coffees, fruit shakes, cakes and big sandwiches, as well as drinks, right through to 12.30am. The branch at 19–20 Teviot Place is open even later.

Restaurants

Fenwicks 15 Salisbury Place, Newington ☎0131/667 4265, ⓦwww.fenwicks-restaurant .co.uk. One of the better places to eat in this part of town, this is a pleasant chef-owned operation serving dishes based around good Scottish produce. Moderate.

Hanedan 41 W Preston St, Newington ☎0131/667 4242. A small and relatively simple Turkish BYOB restaurant. There's an authenticity to the kebabs, *moussaka* and *dolmates* which makes this place an interesting alternative to cheaper Italian or bistro fare. Closed Mon. Moderate.

Kalpna 2–3 St Patrick's Square, Newington ☎0131/667 9890. Outstanding vegetarian Indian restaurant serving authentic Gujarati dishes. Four

set meals, including a vegan option, stand alongside the main menu. Moderate.

Original Khushi's 26–30 Potterrow, Newington ☎0131/667 0888, ⓦwww.khushis.com. The latest incarnation of Edinburgh's (and one of Britain's) oldest curry houses; now it's a slick, friendly, modern curry café serving some excellent food and lip-smacking *lassis*. No corkage on BYOB. Moderate.

Sweet Melinda's 11 Roseneath St, Marchmont ☎0131/229 7953. A smart seafood restaurant in a single, timber-panelled room with a friendly neighbourhood feel. It's edging towards the expensive side, but it's worth shelling out for dishes such as mackerel served with chorizo, or exquisitely fried squid. Closed Sun & lunchtime Mon. Moderate–expensive.

Leith

Cafés and bistros

Daniel's 88 Commercial St ☎0131/553 5933. Likeable, well-run bistro in an attractive setting on the ground floor of a converted warehouse. Food is heartily French, with many dishes from the Alsace; the *tarte flambée*, one of the house specialities, is a simple but delicious onion and bacon pizza. Open daily 10am–10pm. Moderate.

Restaurants

Fishers 1 The Shore ☎0131/554 5666, ⓦwww.fishersbistros.co.uk. One of the first wave of seafood bistros which put Leith's dining scene on the map, the menu here has an appealing range of expensive and fancy fish dishes, but there are also impressive bar-style snacks such as fishcakes and chowder. Reservations recommended. Moderate.

Restaurant Martin Wishart 52 The Shore ☎0131/553 3557, ⓦwww.martin-wishart.co.uk. One of only two Michelin-starred restaurants in Edinburgh, this place wows the gourmets with highly accomplished, French-influenced Scottish

food (three-course lunch for around £20, five-course evening tasting-menu at £55). The food is incredible, though the decor is rather beige. Reservations recommended. Closed Sat lunch, Sun & Mon. Very expensive.

The Shore 3–4 The Shore ☎0131/553 5080. A well-lived-in bar/restaurant with huge mirrors, wood panelling and aproned waiters who serve up good fish dishes and decent wines. Live jazz, folk and hubbub floats through from the adjoining bar. Moderate.

The Vintner's Rooms 87 Giles St ☎0131/554 6767, ⓦwww.thevintnersrooms.com. Splendid French restaurant in a seventeenth-century warehouse; the small but ornate Rococo dining room is a marvel and the food – from seafood to game – isn't bad either. Closed Sun eve & Mon. Expensive.

The Waterfront 1c Dock Place ☎0131/554 7427 ⓦwww.waterfrontwinebar.co.uk. This former lock-keeper's cottage has a wonderfully characterful wine-bar and a waterside conservatory, with fish dishes dominating. Moderate.

Pubs and bars

Many of Edinburgh's **pubs**, especially in the Old Town, have histories that stretch back centuries, while others, particularly in the New Town, are unaltered Victorian or Edwardian period pieces. Add a plentiful supply of trendy modern **bars**, and there's enough to cater for all tastes. The standard licensing hours are 11am–11pm (12.30–11pm on Sundays), but many honest howffs stay open later and, during the Festival especially, it's no problem to find bars open till at least 1am. Edinburgh has a long history of brewing beer, though only one working **brewery** remains in the city itself, the small Caledonian Brewery in the western reaches of town: tours cost £7.50 (☎0131/337 1286 or ⓦ www.Caledonian-brewery.co.uk for details).

A fun way to explore Edinburgh's pubs is to take the **Edinburgh Literary Pub Tour**, a pub crawl with culture around Old and New Town watering holes. Starting from the *Beehive Inn*, 18–20 Grassmarket (☎0131/226 6665, ⓦ www.edinburghliterarypubtour.co.uk), and led by professional actors, the tour introduces you to the scenes, characters and words of the major figures of Scottish literature, including Burns, Scott and MacDiarmid.

The Royal Mile and around

Albanach 197 High St. A contemporary take on the Scottish theme bar: traditional elements such as bare stone and wood mix with hints of the Highlands colouring, but there's nothing old-fashioned about the place. Young trendies mingle with tourists chuffed they've found somewhere without looped bagpipe music. Standard bar food served.

Bow Bar 80 West Bow. Wonderful old wood-panelled bar that won an award as Britain's best drinkers' pub a few years back. Choose from among nearly 150 whiskies or a changing selection of first-rate Scottish and English cask beers.

Doric Tavern 15 Market St. Long-established upstairs wine bar (open till 1am) is a favoured watering hole of journalists and artists. The brasserie beside the wine bar serves reliable, good-quality Scottish food.

Jolly Judge 7a James Court. Atmospheric, low-ceilinged bar in a close just down from the Castle. Cosy in winter and pleasant outside in summer.

North Bridge 20 North Bridge. Plush cocktail bar and brasserie of *The Scotsman* hotel (see p.818), with its slick, glass island bar contrasting with ornate pillars and original panelling. Decent food is served at intimate tables for two on the encircling balcony.

Villager 49–50 George IV Bridge. The bar of the moment in this part of town, so expect the local glitterati and lots of designer clothing in amongst the chocolate brown sofas and teetering bar stools.

New Town and West End

Café Royal Circle Bar 17 W Register St. As notable as the *Oyster Bar* restaurant next door, the *Café Royal* is worth a visit just for its Victorian decor, notably the huge, elliptical island bar and the tiled portraits of renowned inventors. More than that, the beer and food are good, too.

Cumberland Bar 1 Cumberland St. One of the few pubs in this part of the New Town, this mellow, cultured, old-fashioned place full of wood panelling and cosy nooks is a delightful find, and serves excellent cask-conditioned ales.

The Dome 14 George St. Opulent conversion of a massive New Town bank, thronging with well-dressed locals. Probably the most impressive bar interior in Edinburgh, though the ultra-chic atmosphere can be a bit intense. Sun–Thurs open till 11.30pm, Fri & Sat till 1am.

Opal Lounge 51 George St. A much talked-about, low-ceilinged bar with a faintly Oriental theme, loud music and a long cocktail list. Over-dressed twentysomethings flock here for a glimpse of local celebrities, but usually have to stand in a queue and squeeze past the bouncers to get in.

Oxford Bar 8 Young St. An unpretentious, unspoilt, no-nonsense city bar – which is why local crime-writer Ian Rankin and his Inspector Rebus like it so much. Fans duly make the pilgrimage, but fortunately not all the regulars have been scared off. Open until 1am.

Whighams Wine Cellars 13 Hope St, Charlotte Square. One of the more sophisticated venues in the city centre, with an impressive wine list and some gloomy subterranean cubby holes. Recent expansion has added a stylish edge, and there's good seafood available, too.

Broughton and Leith Walk

The Barony Bar 81–85 Broughton St. A fine old-fashioned bar which manages to be big and lively without being spoilt. Being taken over by a chain has blunted its appeal a bit, but there's still real ale and a blazing fire.

The Basement 10a Broughton St. This dimly lit, grungy drinking hole has long been a favourite of the bohemian Broughton-Street crowd, with odd furniture made from old JCBs and filling food served by Hawaiian-shirted staff. Open till 1am.

Stockbridge

Baillie Bar 2 St Stephen St. The best of the district's traditional pubs, with English and Scottish ales as well as reasonable pub grub. Open Sun–Thurs till midnight, Fri & Sat till 1am.

Bert's Bar 2–4 Raeburn Place, Stockbridge (also 29 William St, West End). Popular locals' pubs with a lived-in feel, despite their relatively recent arrival.

Both serve excellent beer and tasty pies, and strive to be authentic, non-theme-orientated venues, though the telly rarely misses any sporting action.

Lothian Road and Toll-cross

Bennets Bar 8 Leven St, Tollcross. Edwardian pub with mahogany-framed mirrors and Art Nouveau stained glass; gets packed in the evening, particularly when there's a show at the King's Theatre next door. Mon–Sat serves lunch and opens till midnight.

Blue Blazer 2 Spittal St. This traditional Edinburgh howff with an oak-clad bar and church pews serves as good a selection of real ales as you'll find anywhere in the city. Open till 1am.

Traverse Bar Café Traverse Theatre, 10 Cambridge St. Much more than just a theatre bar, attracting a lively, sophisticated crowd who dispel any notion of a quiet interval drink. Good food available. One of *the* places to be during the Festival.

Southside

Human Be-In 2–8 West Crosscauseway, Newington. One of the trendiest student bars around, with huge plate-glass windows to admire the beautiful people and tables outside for summer posing. Good food too. Open till 1am.

Peartree House 36 W Nicolson St, Newington. Fine bar in an eighteenth-century house with old sofas and a large courtyard – one of central Edinburgh's very few beer gardens. Serves budget bar lunches. Open Mon–Wed & Sun until midnight, Thurs–Sat until 1am.

Leith

Cameo Bar 23 Commercial St. Relaxed place with nooks and crannies, odd art, and an astro-turf putting green out the back.

Kings Wark 36 The Shore. Real ale in an atmospheric restored eighteenth-century pub right in the heart of Leith, with bar meals chalked up on the rafters. Open till midnight Fri & Sat.

The Shore 3–4 The Shore. Atmospheric traditional bar with an adjacent restaurant (see p.844). There's regular live jazz or folk music as well as real ales and good bar snacks.

Elsewhere in the city

Athletic Arms (The Diggers) 1–3 Angle Park Terrace, Polwarth. Known to all as *Diggers* after the spade-wielding employees of the cemetery across the road, this is a place of pilgrimage if you're into sport (Murrayfield and Hearts' Tyncastle ground are just along the road) and real ale, with the Caledonian Brewery's beers well represented. Open Mon–Thurs till midnight, Fri & Sat till 1am, Sun till 6pm.

Canny Man's (Volunteer Arms) 237 Morningside Rd, Morningside. Atmospheric and idiosyncratic pub-cum-museum adorned with anything that can be hung on the walls or from the ceiling. Local ales and over 200 whiskies on offer, as well as snacks.

Sheep Heid Inn 43 The Causeway, Duddingston. One of Edinburgh's best-known historic pubs, the building has barely survived various predictable makeovers, but despite this, remains an attractive spot. Decent meals are available at the bar, and there's an old-fashioned skittle alley out the back.

Nightlife and entertainment

Inevitably, Edinburgh's **nightlife** is at its best during the Festival (see p.848), which can make the other 49 weeks of the year seem like an anticlimax. However, at any time the city has plenty to offer, especially in the realm of **theatre** and **music**.

The **nightclub** scene is lively, with some excellent venues hosting a changing selection of one-nighters. You can normally hear **live jazz**, **folk** and **rock** every evening in one or other of the city's pubs, and there are also permanent venues large enough to host large touring **orchestras** and **ballet** companies. The city boasts a couple of excellent art-house **cinemas**, and its top **comedy** club, The Stand, 5 York Place (℡0131/558 7272, ⓦwww.thestand.co.uk), has a different act every night with some of the UK's top comics headlining at the weekends: the bar is worth a visit in itself. Edinburgh also has a dynamic **gay** culture, for years centred round the top of Leith Walk and Broughton Street, where the first gay and lesbian centre appeared in the 1970s. Since the start of the 1990s, more and more gay enterprises, especially cafés and nightclubs, have moved into this area, now dubbed the "Pink Triangle".

Hogmanay

Edinburgh hosts Europe's largest **New Year's Eve street party**, with around 100,000 people on the streets of the city enjoying the culmination of a week-long series of events. On the night itself, stages are set up in different parts of the city centre, with big-name rock groups and local ceilidh bands playing to the increasingly inebriated masses. The high point of the evening is, of course, midnight, when hundreds of tons of fireworks are let off into the night sky above the Castle, and Edinburgh joins the rest of the world singing "**Auld Lang Syne**", an old Scottish tune with lyrics by Robert Burns, Scotland's national poet. For information about celebrations in Edinburgh, and how to get hold of tickets for the street party, go to ⓦ www.edinburghshogmanay.org.

Out of the capital, the best way to celebrate **Hogmanay** is to join one of the street parties which are held in the middle of towns and cities, often centred around a prominent clockface which rings out "the bells" at midnight. For more details about the background to Hogmanay, see *Festivals* colour section.

The best way to find out **what's on** is to pick up a copy of *The List*, a fortnightly listings magazine covering both Edinburgh and Glasgow (£2.20).

Nightclubs

Cabaret Voltaire 36–38 Blair St ⓣ 0131/220 6176. A nightclub in the atmospheric setting of the Old Town's underground vaults. Head here for some fine R&B and hip-hop at weekends, as well as live acoustic sets in the week.

Ego 14 Picardy Place ⓣ 0131/478 7434. A former casino, this big venue hosts *Wiggle*, which plays to a gay and mixed crowd monthly on Saturdays, and the epic party-night *Vegas*.

Honeycomb 15–17 Niddrie St ⓣ 0131/530 5540, ⓦ www.the-honeycomb.com. In amongst the vaults and hidden passageways beneath the Old Town, hosting big drum'n'bass night *Manga* and the free *Motherfunk* on Tuesdays.

The Liquid Room 9c Victoria St ⓣ 0131/225 2564, ⓦ www.liquidroom.com. One of the best of the larger venues, with nights including cabaret-cum-disco *Snatch* (Thurs), gay-friendly *Taste* (Sun), and *Colours* (Sat), a monthly house/techno club drawing big-name DJs.

Gay clubs and bars

CC Bloom's 23–24 Greenside Place ⓣ 0131/556 9331. Edinburgh's only uniquely gay club, with a big dance floor, stonking rhythms and a young, friendly crowd.

Sala 60 Broughton St ⓣ 0131/478 7069. Fresh food, light Spanish snacks and drinks in a relaxed atmosphere at the Edinburgh Gay, Lesbian and Bisexual Centre. Open 11am–11pm. Closed Mon.

The Street 2 Picardy Place ⓣ 0131/556 4272. Located at the top of Broughton Street, at the "gateway" to the Pink Triangle, this mainstream,

gay-friendly bar is a sociable spot and good for watching the world (and talent) pass by.

Live music venues

Corn Exchange 11 Newmarket Rd, Slateford ⓣ 0131/477 3500, ⓦ www.ece.uk.com. Once a slaughterhouse, now a 3000-capacity venue for big-name contemporary pop and rock acts, though the location, three miles west of the centre, is a bit off-putting.

Henry's Jazz Cellar 8 Morrison St, off Lothian Road ⓣ 0131/467 5200. Edinburgh's premier jazz and hip-hop venue, with live music every night and regular top performers.

The Liquid Room 9c Victoria St ⓣ 0131/225 2564, ⓦ www.liquidroom.com. Good-sized venue frequented by visiting indie and local R&B bands.

Queen's Hall 89 Clerk St ⓣ 0131/668 2019, ⓦ www.queenshalledinburgh.co.uk. Converted Georgian church which now operates as a concert hall; it's used principally by the Scottish Chamber Orchestra and Scottish Ensemble, and much favoured by jazz, blues and folk groups.

Sandy Bell's 25 Forrest Rd ⓣ 0131/225 2751. A friendly bar and a good bet for folk music most nights of the week.

Usher Hall Corner of Lothian Road and Grindlay Street ⓣ 0131/228 1155, ⓦ www.usherhall.co.uk. Edinburgh's main civic concert hall, seating over 2500. Excellent for choral and symphony concerts, but less suitable for solo vocalists. The upper-circle seats are cheapest and have the best acoustics, but the sound quality is overall much improved after a recent refurbishment.

Theatre and dance

Dance Base 14–16 Grassmarket ☎ 0131/225 5255, ⓦ www.dancebase.co.uk. Scotland's sparkling new National Centre for Dance is used mostly for modern-dance workshops and classes, but also hosts occasional performances.

Festival Theatre Nicolson Street ☎ 0131/529 6000, ⓦ www.eft.co.uk. The largest stage in Britain, principally used for Scottish Opera and Scottish Ballet's appearances in the capital, but also for everything from the children's show *Singing Kettle* to Engelbert Humperdinck.

King's Theatre 2 Leven St ☎ 0131/529 6000. Stately Edwardian civic theatre that majors in pantomime, touring West End plays and the occasional major drama or opera performance.

Playhouse Theatre 18–22 Greenside Place ☎ 0870/606 3424, ⓦ www.eft.co.uk. The most capacious theatre in Britain, formerly a cinema. Recently refurbished, and used largely for extended runs of popular musicals and occasional rock concerts.

Royal Lyceum Theatre 30 Grindlay St ☎ 0131/248 4848, ⓦ www.lyceum.org.uk. Fine Victorian civic theatre with a compact auditorium. The leading year-round venue for mainstream drama.

Traverse Theatre 10 Cambridge St ☎ 0131/228 1404, ⓦ www.traverse.co.uk. Unquestionably one of Britain's premier venues for new plays and avant-garde drama from around the world. Going from strength to strength in its new custom-built home beside the Usher Hall, with a great bar downstairs and the popular *blue* café-bar upstairs.

Art-house cinemas

Cameo 38 Home St, Tollcross ☎ 0131/228 2800, ⓦ www.picturehouses.co.uk; bookings ☎ 0131/228 4141. A treasure of an art-house cinema; screens more challenging mainstream releases and cult late-nighters. Tarantino's been here and thinks it's great.

Filmhouse 88 Lothian Rd ☎ 0131/228 2688, ⓦ www.filmhousecinema.com. Three screens showing an eclectic programme of independent, art-house and classic films. The café is a hangout for the city's dedicated film-buffs.

Shopping

Despite the relentless advance of the big chains, it's still possible to track down some characterful and unusual shops in central Edinburgh. **Princes Street**, one of Britain's most famous shopping streets, is all but dominated by standard chain outlets, though no serious shopper should miss out on a visit to Edinburgh's venerable department store, Jenners, at 48 Princes St, opposite the Scott Monument. More fashionable upmarket shops and boutiques are to be found on and around parallel **George Street**, including a newly created shopping area on the east side of St Andrew Square. There's nothing compelling about central Edinburgh's two big shopping malls, **Princes Mall** and the **St James Centre**, which are dominated by the big names.

For more original outlets, head for **Cockburn Street**, south of Waverley Station, a hub for trendy clothes and record shops, while on **Victoria Street** and in and around the **Grassmarket** you'll find an eclectic range of antique, crafts, food and book shops. Along and around the **Royal Mile** there are several distinctly offbeat places among the tacky-souvenir sellers.

The Edinburgh Festival

The **Edinburgh Festival** is an umbrella term which encompasses different festivals taking place at around the same time in the city. The principal events are the **Edinburgh International Festival** and the much larger **Edinburgh Festival Fringe**, but there are also **Film**, **Book**, **Jazz and Blues** and **Television** festivals, the **Military Tattoo** on the Castle Esplanade and the **Edinburgh Mela**, an Asian festival held over a weekend in late August/early September.

△ The Festival

For the visitor, the sheer volume of the Festival's output can be bewildering: virtually every branch of arts and entertainment is represented somewhere, and world-famous stars mix with pub singers in the daily line-up. It can be a struggle to find **accommodation**, get hold of the tickets you want, book a table in a restaurant or simply get from one side of town to another; you can end up seeing something truly dire, or something mind-blowing; you'll inevitably try to do too much, stay out too late or spend too much money – but then again, most Festival veterans will tell you that if you don't experience these things then you haven't really done the Festival. Dates, venues, names, star acts, happening bars and burning issues change from one year to the next. This unpredictability is one of the Festival's greatest charms, so while the following information will help you get to grips with it, be prepared for – indeed, enjoy – the unexpected.

For up-to-the-minute **information** at any time of year, ⓦ www.edinburgh festivals.co.uk has links to the home pages of most of Edinburgh's main festivals. In addition to each festival's own programme, various publications give information about what's on day by day during the Festival. Every day the Fringe Office publishes *The Guide*, giving a chronological listing of virtually every show scheduled for that day. It's available free from the Office (see below) and hundreds of other spots around Edinburgh, as well as with *The Guardian* newspaper's Scottish edition. Of the local newspapers, the best coverage is in *The Scotsman*, which issues a dedicated daily Festival supplement.

The Edinburgh International Festival

The **Edinburgh International Festival** (sometimes called the "Official Festival") is very much a highbrow event, and forays into populist territory remain rare. It attracts truly international stars, along with some of the world's finest orchestras and opera, theatre and ballet companies. Performances take place at the city's larger venues such as the Usher Hall and the Festival Theatre and, while ticket prices run to over £40, it is possible to see shows for £10 or less if you're prepared to queue for the handful of tickets kept back until the day.

The most popular single event in the Festival is the dramatic **Fireworks Concert**, held late at night on the final Saturday of the International Festival: the Scottish Chamber Orchestra belts out pop classics from the Ross Bandstand in Princes Street Gardens, accompanied by a spectacular fireworks display high up above the ramparts of the Castle. Unless you want a seat right by the orchestra you don't need a ticket for this event: hundreds of thousands of people view the display from various vantage points throughout the city.

The International Festival's year-round headquarters are located at **The Hub** (see p.823); you can contact them for further **information**, including the annual programme, which is released in April.

The Edinburgh Festival Fringe

Even standing alone from its sister festivals, the **Edinburgh Festival Fringe** is easily the world's largest arts gathering. Each year sees around 15,000 performances from over 700 companies, with more than 12,000 participants from all over the world. There are something in the region of 1500 shows every day, round the clock, in 200 venues around the city. While the headlining names at the International Festival reinforce the Festival's cultural credibility, it is the dynamism, spontaneity and sheer exuberance of the Fringe which dominates Edinburgh every August, giving the city its unique atmosphere.

Crucially, no artistic control is imposed on those who want to produce a show, a defining element of the Fringe. This means that the shows range from the inspired to the diabolical, and ensures a highly competitive atmosphere, in which one bad review in a prominent publication means box-office disaster. Many unknowns rely on self-publicity, taking to the streets to perform highlights from their show, or pressing leaflets into the hands of every passer-by.

17

Fringe venues

In addition to the many tiny and unexpected auditoriums, the four **main Fringe venues** are The Assembly Rooms, The Pleasance, The Gilded Balloon and a relative newcomer known as "C" – they're all safe bets for decent shows and a bit of starspotting. Venue complexes rather than single spaces, the last three colonize clusters of different-sized spaces for the duration of the Festival.

The atmosphere at the **Pleasance**, 60 The Pleasance (℡0131/556 6550, ⊛www .pleasance.co.uk), is usually less frenetic than at the other venues, with classy drama and whimsical appearances by panellists on Radio 4 game shows. The **Assembly Rooms**, 50 George St (℡0131/226 2428, ⊛www.assemblyrooms.com), provide a slick, grand setting for top-of-the-range drama and big-name music and comedy acts. The Fringe's premier comedy venue, **The Gilded Balloon**, Teviot Row House, Bristo Square (℡0131/668 1633, ⊛www.gildedballoon.co.uk), lost its long-standing home in a fire in early 2003, but was up and running in various new venues around town by the time the Festival came along. The disparate locations of **C** (℡0870/701 5105, ⊛www.cthefestival.com) have the most varied programme of the big four, and in recent years have been known to stage controversial productions that other venues might be too wary to promote.

While it's nothing like as large as the venues above, you shouldn't ignore the programme put on at the **Traverse Theatre**'s (see p.848) three stages. Long a champion of new drama, the "Trav" combines the avant-garde with professional presentation and its plays are generally among the Fringe's most acclaimed.

Performances go on round the clock: if so inclined, you could sit through twenty shows in a day.

The full Fringe **programme** is usually available in June from the Festival Fringe Office, 180 High St (℡0131/226 0000, ⊛www.edfringe.com). During the Festival, tickets are sold at the Fringe box office, at the back of the Fringe Office (daily 10am–9pm), the venue itself, or through the website. **Ticket** prices for most Fringe shows start at £5, and average from £8 to £14 at the main venues, with the better-known acts going for even more.

The International Festival and the Fringe don't quite coincide: the former tends to run over the last two weeks of **August** and the first week of **September**, whereas the latter starts a week earlier, culminating on the last weekend in August.

The smaller festivals

The **Edinburgh International Film Festival** (℡0131/228 2688, ⊛www .edfilmfest.org.uk) runs for the last two weeks of August and is a chance to see some of the year's big cinema hits before they go on general release, along with a varied and exciting bill of reissued movies. The **Edinburgh International Book Festival** (℡0131/624 5050, ⊛www.edbookfest.co.uk) also takes place in the last two weeks of August, and is the largest celebration of the written word worldwide. It's held in a tented village in Charlotte Square, with talks, readings and signings by a star-studded line-up of visiting authors, as well as panel discussions and workshops. The **Edinburgh International Jazz and Blues Festival** (⊛www.jazzmusic.co.uk) runs immediately prior to the Fringe in the first week in August, easing the city into the festival spirit. Highlights include **Jazz On A Summer's Day**, a musical extravaganza in Princes Street Gardens, and a colourful New Orleans–style **street parade**.

Staged in the spectacular stadium of the Edinburgh Castle Esplanade throughout August, the **Military Tattoo** (℡0131/225 1188, ⓦwww.edintattoo.co.uk) is an unashamed display of pomp and military pride. The programme of choreographed drills, massed pipe bands, historical tableaux, energetic battle re-enactments, national dancing and pyrotechnics has been a feature of the Festival for fifty years, the emotional climax provided by a lone piper on the Castle battlements.

Listings

Bike rental Biketrax, 11 Lochrin Place ℡0131/228 6633, ⓦ www.biketrax.co.uk; Edinburgh Cycle Hire, 29 Blackfriars St ℡0131/556 5560, ⓦ www.cyclescotland.co.uk.

Car rental Arnold Clark, Lochrin Place ℡0131/228 4747 or 0845/607 4500; Avis, 5 West Park Place ℡0870/153 9103; Budget, Edinburgh Airport ℡0131/333 1926; Europcar, Waverley Station ℡0870/607 5000; Hertz, 10 Picardy Place ℡0870/8460013; Thrifty Car Rental, 42 Haymarket Terrace ℡0131/337 1319.

Genealogical research General Register Office for Scotland ℡0131/334 0380, ⓦ www .scotlandspeople.gov.uk; Scottish Genealogy Society, 15 Victoria Terrace ℡0131/220 3677; Scottish Roots, 22 Forth St ℡0131/477 8214.

Hospital Royal Infirmary, Little France (℡0131/536 1000), has a 24hr casualty department.

Internet Terminals where you can access the Internet for free are increasingly common around town, as are Wi-Fi hot-spots. Dedicated Internet cafés include Bytes & Slices, 3 Waverley Steps (Mon–Fri 8am–9.30pm, Sat & Sun 10am–8pm;

℡0131/557 8887); Double Dutch, 27–29 Marshall St (Mon–Fri 8am–8pm, Sat & Sun 10am–8pm; ℡0131/667 9997); and Internet Café, 98 West Bow (daily 10am–11pm; ℡0131/226 5400).

Left luggage Counter by platform 1 at Waverley Station; £5 per item (daily 7am–11pm; ℡0131/550 2333).

Lost property Edinburgh Airport ℡0131/333 1000; Edinburgh Police HQ ℡0131/311 3141 (lost property found in taxis is sent here); Lothian Buses ℡0131/554 4494; Network Rail ℡0131/550 2333.

Pharmacy Boots, 48 Shandwick Place (Mon–Fri 7.30am–8pm, Sat 7.30am–6pm, Sun 10am–5pm; ℡0131/225 6757) has the longest opening hours.

Police In an emergency call ℡999. Otherwise contact Lothian and Borders Police HQ, Fettes Avenue ℡0131/311 3131.

Post office 8–10 St James Centre (Mon & Wed–Sat 9am–5.30pm, Tues 9.30am–5.30pm; ℡0845/722 3344).

Taxis Central Radio Taxis ℡0131/229 2468; City Cabs ℡0131/228 1211.

East Lothian

East Lothian consists of the coastal strip and hinterland immediately east of Edinburgh, bounded by the Firth of Forth to the north and the Lammermuir Hills to the south. All of it is within easy day-trip range from the capital, though there are places you can stay overnight if you're keen to explore it properly. Often mocked as the "home counties" of Edinburgh, there's no denying its well-ordered feel, with prosperous farms and large estate houses dominating the scenery. There's something for most tastes here, including the wide sandy beaches by **Aberlady**, famous golf courses of **Gullane**, the enjoyable Seabird Centre at **North Berwick**, dramatic cliff-top ruins at **Tantallon** and the supersonic draw of **Concorde** at the Museum of Flight.

North Berwick and around

NORTH BERWICK has a great deal of charm and a somewhat faded, old-fashioned air, its guest houses and hotels extending along the shore in all their

Victorian and Edwardian sobriety. Two nearby volcanic heaps, the **Bass Rock** and **North Berwick Law**, are the town's defining physical features. The former can be observed closely from North Berwick's principal attraction, the **Scottish Seabird Centre** (April–Oct daily 10am–6pm; Nov–March Mon–Fri 10am–4/5pm, Sat & Sun 10am–5.30pm; £6.95; ⓦwww.seabird.org), by the harbour. It offers an introduction to all the sea birds found around the Scottish coast, particularly the 100,000-plus gannets and puffins which nest on the Bass Rock every summer. Among the interactive exhibits and child-oriented displays there's a live link to cameras mounted on the volcanic island, showing close-up pictures of the birds in their nesting grounds. Weather permitting, **boat trips** to the Bass Rock leave from North Berwick harbour: Jewels of the Forth (ⓣ01620/890202, ⓦwww.jewelsoftheforth.co.uk) has exclusive landing rights on the rock, while Aquatrek (ⓣ01620/893952, ⓦwww.aquatrek.co.uk) runs cruises around the rock and past some of the other nearby islands.

North Berwick is served by a regular **train** from Edinburgh Waverley (30min), with discount deals for those heading for the Seabird Centre (ask at Waverley ticket office or call ⓣ08457/550033). From the station it's a ten-minute walk east to the town centre, and the **tourist office** (April–Sept Mon–Sat 9am–6/8pm, Sun 11am–4/6pm, April & May closed Tues; Oct Mon–Sat 9am–5pm; ⓣ01620/892197) on Quality Street. One of the best **cafés** in town is at the Seabird Centre, with panoramic views over the beach. For a daytime snack or coffee in town, try *Zanzibar* at 81 High St, or the *Bass Rock Bistro*, at 37–39 Quality St (ⓣ01620/890875, ⓦwww.bassrockcafe.co.uk), which also does evening meals on Friday and Saturday nights.

Tantallon Castle

The melodramatic ruins of **Tantallon Castle** (April–Sept daily 9.30am–6.30pm; Oct–March Mon–Wed, Sat & Sun 9.30am–4.30pm; £3.30; HS), three miles east of North Berwick on the A198, stand on precipitous cliffs facing the Bass Rock. With a sheer drop down to the sea on three sides and a sequence of moats and ditches on the fourth, the castle's desolate invincibility is daunting, especially when the wind howls over the remaining battlements and the surf crashes on the rocks far below. You can reach Tantallon Castle from North Berwick by the Dunbar **bus** (#120; Mon–Sat 6 daily, Sun 2 daily), which takes fifteen minutes, or you can walk there from town along the cliffs in around an hour.

Museum of Flight

A few miles southwest of North Berwick, on an old military airfield by East Fortune, the **Museum of Flight** (April–Oct daily 10am–5pm; Nov–March Sat & Sun 10am–4pm; £5, Concorde boarding pass £3 extra, pre-booking essential; ⓣ0870/421 4299, ⓦwww.nms.ac.uk/flight) is now home to *Alpha Alpha*, British Airways' first **Concorde**. The supersonic passenger jet, one of only twenty such planes built, has been reassembled to show how she looked when decommissioned in 2003. A visit onboard is restricted to a slightly stooped wander through the forward half of the aircraft, with the chance to look at the cockpit through a perspex partition; elsewhere, a short film tells the story of *Alpha Alpha*, while information boards and display cabinets allow you to follow the Concorde project as a whole, from the early days of Anglo-French bickering to the tragic Paris crash of 2000. In and around the older hangars on the site, you can see over fifty vintage aircraft including a Vulcan bomber, a Comet airliner, a Spitfire and a Tigermoth. To get to the museum by public transport,

⑰

catch First **Bus** #131 from North Berwick and Drem, both of which have train connections from Edinburgh.

Dunbar

Twelve miles along the coast from North Berwick lies **DUNBAR** and the **John Muir Birthplace** at 126 High St (April–Oct Mon–Sat 10am–5pm, Sun 1–5pm; Nov–March closed Mon & Tues; free; ⓦwww.jmbt.org.uk). Birthplace of the explorer and naturalist who created the United States national-park system, it's an engaging interpretative and education centre about the pioneer's life and legacy. Dunbar's delightfully intricate double **harbour** also merits a stroll, with its narrow channels, cobbled quays and roughened rocks, set beside the shattered remains of the castle.

The town's **tourist office** is at 143a High St (April, May, Sept & Oct Mon–Sat 9am–5pm; June–Aug Mon–Sat 9am–6/8pm, Sun 11am–4/6pm; ⓣ01368/863353). For **food**, the best place is *The Rocks* on Marine Road (ⓣ01368/862287; ❹), or try the *Creel*, near the old harbour (ⓣ01368/863279, ⓦwww.creelrestaurant.co.uk), for bistro-style meals.

Haddington

Inland, East Lothian's main town, **HADDINGTON**, preserves an intriguing ensemble of seventeenth- to nineteenth-century architectural styles with everything of any interest labelled and plaqued. Heading east from the town centre along High Street, it's a brief walk down Church Street – past the hooped arches of **Nungate Bridge** – to the hulking mass of **St Mary's Church** (Easter–Sept Mon–Sat 11am–4pm, Sun 2–4.30pm; free), Scotland's largest parish church. Built close to the reedy River Tyne, the church dates from the fourteenth century, but it's a real hotchpotch of styles, the squat grey tower uneasy above clumsy buttressing and pinkish-ochre stone walls. Inside, on the **Lauderdale Aisle**, a munificent tomb features the best of Elizabethan alabaster carving, moustached knights and their ruffed ladies lying beneath a finely ornamented canopy.

Fast and frequent **buses** connect Haddington with Edinburgh, fifteen miles to the west, and with North Berwick on the east coast, with all services stopping on High Street. There's no **tourist office**, but orientation is easy and *A Walk Around Haddington* (£1), detailing every building of any conceivable consequence, is available from local newsagents. For daytime **snacks** the place to seek out is *Jaques & Lawrence* at 37 Court St, opposite the post office. For an evening **meal**, try the *Waterside Bistro*, at 1–5 Waterside, across the river from St Mary's (ⓣ01620/825674), or *Bonars Brasserie*, Tyne House, Poldrate, on the edge of town (ⓣ01620/822100).

Glenkinchie Distillery

Six miles west of Haddington along the A6093, the village of Pencaitland is the closest place to Edinburgh where malt whisky is made. Set in a peaceful dip in the rolling countryside about two miles outside Pencaitland, the **Glenkinchie Distillery** (Easter–Oct Mon–Sat 10am–5pm, Sun noon–5pm; Nov daily noon–4pm; Dec–Easter Mon–Fri noon–4pm; last tour 1hr before closing; £5) is one of only a handful found in the Lowlands of Scotland. Here, of course, they emphasize the qualities which set Glenkinchie, a lighter, drier malt, apart from the peaty, smoky whiskies of the north and west. Also in the tour there's an impressive scale model of a distillery, allowing you to place all the different processes in context, and a room where the art of blending is explained.

Midlothian

Immediately south of Edinburgh lies the old county of **MIDLOTHIAN**, once called Edinburghshire. It's one of the hilliest parts of the Central Lowlands, with the Pentland chain running down its western side, and the Moorfoots defining its boundary with the Borders to the south. Midlothian's main town is **Dalkeith**, eight miles southeast of central Edinburgh.

Newtongrange and Roslin

A mile or so south of Dalkeith, the Lady Victoria Colliery at **NEWTON-GRANGE** is now open to the public as the **Scottish Mining Museum** (daily: Feb–Oct 10am–5pm; Nov–Jan 11am–3pm; £4.45; ⓦwww.scottishminingmuseum.com). Staffed in large part by former miners, the museum mixes coal-mining heritage and artefacts with hands-on exhibits for children and the chance to see some of the key working parts of the colliery.

The tranquil village of **ROSLIN** lies seven miles south of the centre of Edinburgh, from where it can be reached by bus #15A (Mon–Fri) or First Bus #141 (Sat) from St Andrew Square. An otherwise nondescript place, the village has two unusual claims to fame: it was near here, at the Roslin Institute, that the world's first cloned sheep, Dolly, was created in 1997, and it's also home to the mysterious, richly decorated late-Gothic **Rosslyn Chapel** (Mon–Sat 9am–6pm, Sun noon–4.45pm; £6; ⓦwww.rosslynchapel.org.uk). Construction of the chapel halted soon after its founder's death in 1484, and the vestry built onto the facade nearly four hundred years later is the sole subsequent addition. After a long period of neglect, the chapel is currently undergoing a massive restoration, though it's still open to the public.

Rosslyn's exterior bristles with pinnacles, gargoyles, flying buttresses and canopies, while inside the stonework is even more intricate. The foliage carving is particularly outstanding, with botanically accurate depictions of over a dozen different leaves and plants. The rich and subtle figurative sculptures have given Rosslyn the nickname of "a Bible in stone", though they're more allegorical than literal. The greatest and most original carving of all is the extraordinary knotted **Apprentice Pillar**. According to local legend, the pillar was made by an apprentice during the absence of the master mason, who killed him in a fit of jealousy on seeing the finished work. A tiny head of a man with a slashed forehead, set at the apex of the ceiling at the far northwestern corner of the building, is popularly supposed to represent the apprentice, his murderer the corresponding head at the opposite side.

The imagery of carvings such as the floriated cross and five-pointed star, together with the history of the family, the St Clairs of Rosslyn, which owns the chapel, leave little doubt about its links to the Knights Templar and free-masonry. More intriguing still are claims that, because of such connections, Rosslyn Chapel has been the repository for items such as the lost Scrolls of Solomon's Temple in Jerusalem, the true Stone of Scone and, most famously, the Holy Grail. This particular conspiracy theory led to the chapel appearing in the climax of Dan Brown's best-selling book *The Da Vinci Code*, and its subsequent film starring Tom Hanks, which has ensured a flood of visitors to the chapel in recent years.

⑰

West Lothian

To many, West Lothian is a poor relative to the rolling, rich farmland of East and Midlothian, with a landscape dominated by motorways, industrial estates and giant hillocks of ochre-coloured mine waste called "bings". However, in the royal palace at **Linlithgow**, the area boasts one of Scotland's more magnificent ruins. Nearby, the village of **South Queensferry** lies under the considerable shadow of the **Forth rail and road bridges**, though it's an interesting enough place in its own right, with a historic high street and the notable stately home of **Hopetoun** nearby.

Linlithgow

Roughly equidistant (fifteen miles) from Falkirk, to the west, and Edinburgh is the ancient royal burgh of **LINLITHGOW**. The town itself has largely kept its medieval layout, but development since the 1960s has sadly stripped it of some fine buildings, notably around the **Town Hall** and **Cross** – the former marketplace – on the long High Street.

Though hidden from the main road, **Linlithgow Palace** (daily: April–Sept 9.30am–6.30pm; Oct–March 9.30am–4.30pm; last admission 45min before closing; £4) is a splendid fifteenth-century ruin romantically set on the edge of Linlithgow Loch and associated with some of Scotland's best-known historical figures – including Mary, Queen of Scots, who was born here in on 8 December 1542 and became queen six days later. From the top of the northwest tower, Queen Margaret looked out in vain for the return of James IV from the field of Flodden in 1513 – indeed, the views from her bower, six storeys up from the ground, are exceptional. The ornate octagonal **fountain** in the inner courtyard, with its wonderfully intricate figures and medallion heads, flowed with wine for the wedding of James V and Mary of Guise.

This is a great place to take children: the elegant, bare rooms echo with footsteps and there's a labyrinthine network of spiral staircases and endless nooks and crannies. The galleried **Great Hall** is magnificent, as is the adjoining kitchen, which has a truly cavernous fireplace.

There are a few decent places to **eat** in Linlithgow: for good pub food try *The Four Marys*, opposite the Cross on High Street, which also has real ales, while *Marynka*, also on High Street at no. 57 (℡01506/840123, ⓦwww.marynka .com), is a brighter, more modern bistro-style place.

Ratho Adventure Centre

One of Scotland's most exciting modern developments, the **Ratho Adventure Centre** (Mon–Fri 8am–10.30pm, Sat & Sun 9.30am–8pm; free, times and charges for activities vary; ℡0131/333 6333, ⓦwww.adventurescotland .com) incorporates the world's largest indoor climbing arena, with a remarkable 2400 square metres of artificial climbing wall. Opened in 2003 at a cost of over £24 million, the spectacular vision of its architect founders was to enclose (and roof) a disused quarry, creating a giant area that's now used for international climbing competitions as well as classes (from £20 for a one-hour session) for climbers of all levels, including beginners and children. Above the centre, just under the glass roof, the SkyRide (£8) is a stomach-churning aerial obstacle course 100ft off the ground, which you take on secured into a sliding harness.

17

South Queensferry and around

Eight miles northwest of Edinburgh city centre is the small town of **SOUTH QUEENSFERRY**, best known for its location at the southern end of the two mighty Forth Bridges. It's an attractive old settlement, with a narrow, cobbled High Street lined with tightly packed buildings, most of which date from the seventeenth and eighteenth centuries. The town's small **museum**, 53 High St (Mon & Thurs–Sat 10am–1pm & 2.15–5pm, Sun noon–5pm; free), contains historical relics and information on the building of the two bridges which loom overhead.

South Queensferry has a couple of excellent spots to **eat**, including ⚓ *The Boathouse* (☎0131/5429; closed Mon) at 19b High St – it's actually down a flight of stairs leading to the beach – which serves moderately expensive but classy local seafood and has great views out to the bridges. A few doors away at no. 17, *Orocco Pier* (☎0131/331 1298, ⊛www.oroccopier.co.uk) is more ostentatiously slick and contemporary, but is a good spot for a drink with a view, some pleasant bistro food, or a comfy bed for the night (➏).

Hopetoun House

Sitting in its own extensive estate on the south shore of the Forth, just to the west of South Queensferry, **Hopetoun House** (April–Sept daily 10am–5.30pm, last admission 1hr before closing; £7 house and grounds, £3.50 grounds only; ⊛www.hopetounhouse.com) ranks as one of the most impressive stately homes in Scotland. The original house was built at the turn of the eighteenth century for the first Earl of Hopetoun by Sir William Bruce, the architect of Holyroodhouse. A couple of decades later, William Adam carried out an enormous extension, engulfing the structure with a curvaceous main facade and two projecting wings – superb examples of Roman Baroque pomp and swagger. Hopetoun's architecture is undoubtedly its most compelling feature, but the furnishings aren't completely overwhelmed, with some impressive seventeenth-century tapestries, Meissen porcelain, and a distinguished collection of paintings. The house's grounds include a long, regal driveway and lovely walks along woodland trails and the banks of the Forth, as well as plenty of places for a picnic.

Inchcolm

From South Queensferry's Hawes Pier, just west of the rail bridge, the *Maid of the Forth* (April & Oct Sat & Sun; May, June & Sept Sat, Sun & some weekdays; July & Aug daily; £13; confirm sailing times in advance on ☎0131/331 5000, ⊛www.maidoftheforth.co.uk) heads out in the direction of the island of **Inchcolm**, located about five miles northeast of South Queensferry near the Fife shore. The island is home to the best-preserved medieval **abbey** in Scotland: although the abbey itself is half-ruined, the tower, octagonal chapterhouse and echoing cloisters are intact and well worth exploring. The hour and a half you're given ashore by the boat timetables also allows time for a picnic on the abbey's lawns or the chance to explore Inchcolm's old military fortifications and its extensive bird-nesting grounds.

17

Travel details

Buses

For information on all local and national bus services, contact Traveline ☎0870/608 2608 (daily 7am–10pm), ⓦwww.travelinescotland.com.
Edinburgh (St Andrew Square) to: Aberdeen (hourly; 3hr 50min); Dundee (hourly; 1hr 45min–2hr); Fort William (4 daily direct; 4hr); Glasgow (every 15min; 1hr 10min); Inverness (hourly; 3–4hr); London (6 daily; 7hr 50min); Newcastle-upon-Tyne (2 daily; 3hr 15min); Perth (hourly; 1hr 20min).

Trains

For information on all local and national rail services, contact National Rail Enquiries ☎08457/484950, ⓦwww.nationalrail.co.uk or ⓦwww.firstscotrail.com.
Edinburgh to: Aberdeen (hourly; 2hr 20min); Dunbar (8 daily; 30min); Dundee (hourly; 1hr 45min); Glasgow (2–4 hourly; 50min); Inverness (5 daily direct; 3hr 50min); London (hourly; 4hr 30min); Newcastle-upon-Tyne (hourly; 1hr 30min); North Berwick (hourly; 30 min); Perth (6 daily; 1hr 15min); Stirling (every 30min; 45min).

Flights

Edinburgh to: Belfast (Mon–Fri 8 daily; Sat & Sun 4 daily; 55min); Cardiff (2 daily; 1hr 10min); Dublin (Mon–Fri 4 daily, Sat & Sun 3 daily; 1hr); Kirkwall (Mon–Fri 2 daily, Sat & Sun 1 daily; 1hr 55min); Lerwick (1 daily; 1hr 30min); London City (Mon–Fri 12 daily, Sat 1, Sun 4 daily; 1hr 15min); London Gatwick (Mon–Fri 14 daily, Sat & Sun 6 daily; 1hr 15min); London Heathrow (Mon–Fri 18 daily, Sat & Sun 11–15 daily; 1hr); London Luton (Mon–Fri 6, Sat & Sun 4 daily; 1hr 20min); London Stansted (Mon–Fri 6 daily, Sat & Sun 4–6 daily; 1hr 10min); Stornoway (Mon–Fri 3 daily, Sat 2, Sun 1; 1hr 10 min); Wick (Mon–Fri 1 daily; 1hr 10min).

Southern Scotland

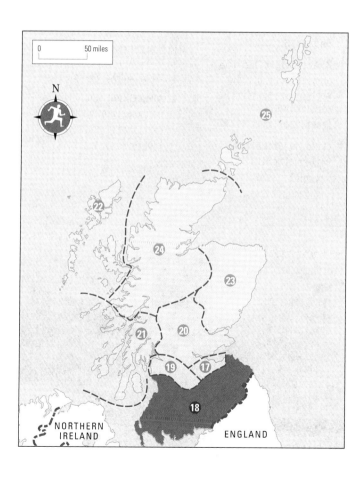

CHAPTER 18 **Highlights**

* **Melrose Abbey** Border abbey with the best-preserved sculptural detail, set in a charming town. See p.864

* **Caerlaverock** One of Scotland's most photogenic moated castles. See p.875

* **Kirkcudbright** One-time artists' colony, and the best-looking town in the "Scottish Riviera". See p.878

* **Galloway Forest Park** Go mountain biking along remote forest tracks, or hiking on the Southern Upland Way. See p.880

* **Alloway** The village where poet Robert Burns was born, and the best of many Burns pilgrimage spots in the region. See p.886

* **Culzean Castle** Stately home with a fabulous cliff-edge setting. See p.886

* **Ailsa Craig** Watch baby gannets learn the art of flying and diving for fish. See p.887

△ Culzean Castle

18

Southern Scotland

S outhern Scotland divides neatly into three distinct regions: the Borders, Dumfries and Galloway, and Ayrshire. Although none of the regions has the highest of tourist profiles, those visitors who whizz past on their way to Edinburgh, Glasgow or the Highlands are missing out on a huge swathe of Scotland that is in many ways the very heart of the country. Its inhabitants, particularly in the Borders, bore the brunt of long wars with the English, its farms have fed Scotland's cities since industrialization, and two of the country's literary icons, Sir Walter Scott and Robbie Burns, lived and died here.

Geographically, the region is dominated by the **Southern Uplands**, a chain of bulging round-topped hills and weather-beaten moorland, punctuated by narrow glens, fast-flowing rivers and blue-black lochs. This region is at its most dramatic in the **Galloway Forest Park** to the southwest, with peaks reaching to over 2000ft, crisscrossed by numerous popular walking trails. Back in the valleys, and down by the coast, the landscape is fairly lush – farming country for the most part, with tourism an important, but secondary, industry. On the coast, you'll find enormous variety: the east coast is fairly bleak, with dramatic cliffs interspersed with tiny fishing villages; the **Solway coast**, in the southwest, is much gentler, indented by sandy coves and estuaries; while the Ayrshire coast, by contrast, is much more heavily populated, and in parts an almost continuous stretch of seaside resorts and industrial centres.

Lying north of the inhospitable Cheviot Hills, which separate Scotland from England, the **Borders** region is dominated by the meanderings of the **River Tweed**. None of the towns along the Tweed is of any great size, yet they have provided inspiration for countless folkloric ballads telling of bloody battles with the English and clashes between the notorious warring families, the Border Reivers. The small but delightful town of **Melrose**, in the heart of the Borders, is the most obvious base for exploring the region, and has the most impressive of the four **Border abbeys** founded by the medieval Canmore kings, all of which are now reduced to romantic ruins.

Dumfries and Galloway, occupying the southwestern corner of Scotland, gets even more overlooked than the Borders, though the region remains popular with Lowland Scots and folk from the north of England. If you do make the effort to get off the main north–south highway to Glasgow, you'll find several more ruined abbeys, medieval castles, forested hills and dramatic tidal flats and seacliffs ideal for birdwatching. The key resort is the modest, but charming town of **Kirkcudbright**, halfway along the marshy Solway coast, well placed for exploring the rest of the county.

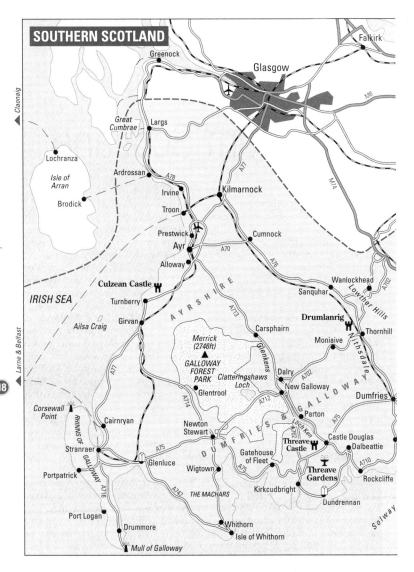

Ayrshire is rich farming country, and not an obvious destination for first-time visitors to Scotland. It has fewer sights than its neighbours, with almost everything of interest confined to the coast. However, the **golf courses** along its gentle coastline are among the finest links courses in the country, and golfers can buy three- and five-day passes from tourist offices allowing free or reduced-fee access to many of the region's golf courses. Fans of **Robert Burns** could happily spend several days exploring the author's old haunts, especially at **Ayr**, the county town, and the nearby village of Alloway, the poet's birthplace.

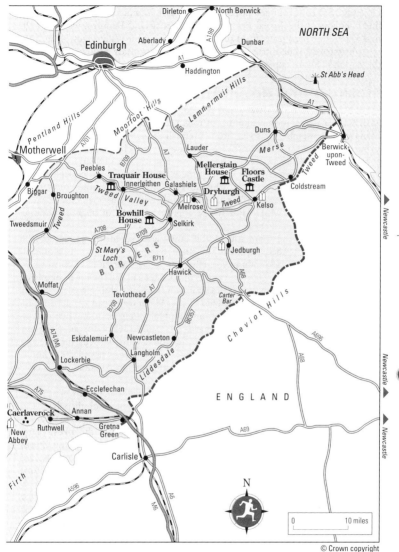

© Crown copyright

The Borders

Sandwiched between the Cheviot Hills on the English border and the Pentland and Moorfoot ranges to the south of Edinburgh, is the **Borders** region (Ⓦ www.scot-borders.co.uk). If you've travelled from the south across the bleak moorland of neighbouring Northumberland, you'll be struck by the green lushness of the **Tweed valley**, the pivotal feature of the region's geography. Yet the Borders also incorporates some of the wildest stretches of the Southern

Uplands, with bare, rounded peaks and heathery hills punctuated by valleys. The finest section of the Tweed lies between **Melrose** and **Peebles**, where you'll find a string of attractions, from the eccentricities of Sir Walter Scott's mansion at **Abbotsford** to the intriguing Jacobite past of **Traquair House**, along with the region's famous abbeys, founded in the reign of King David I (1124–53).

Melrose and around

Tucked in between the Tweed and the gorse-backed Eildon Hills, minuscule **MELROSE** is the most beguiling of towns, its narrow streets trimmed by a harmonious ensemble of styles, from pretty little cottages and tweedy shops to high-standing Georgian and Victorian facades. Its chief draw is its ruined abbey, by far the best of the Border abbeys, but it's also perfectly positioned for exploring the Tweed valley. Most of the year it's a sleepy little place, but as the birthplace in 1883 of the **Rugby Sevens** (seven-a-side games), it swarms during Sevens Week (second week in April), and again in early September when it hosts the **Melrose Music Festival**, a popular weekend of traditional music attracting folkies from afar.

To the north of the town square, the pink- and red-tinted stone ruins of **Melrose Abbey** (April–Sept daily 9.30am–6.30pm; Oct–March Mon–Sat 9.30am–4.30pm, Sun 2–4.30pm; £4; HS) soar above their riverside surroundings. Founded in 1136, Melrose was the first Cistercian settlement in Scotland and grew rich selling wool and hides to Flanders. The English repeatedly razed Melrose, most viciously under Richard II in 1385 and the earl of Hertford in 1545, and most of the remains date from the intervening period, when extensive rebuilding abandoned the original Cistercian austerity for an elaborate Gothic style inspired by the abbeys of northern England. The sculptural detailing at Melrose is of the highest quality, but it's easy to miss if you don't know where to look, so taking advantage of the free audioguide, or buying yourself a guidebook, is a good idea.

The site is dominated by the **Abbey Church**, which has lost its west front, and whose nave is reduced to the elegant window arches and chapels of the south aisle. Amazingly, however, the stone **pulpitum** (screen), separating the choir monks from their lay brothers, is preserved. Beyond, the **presbytery** has its magnificent perpendicular window, lierne vaulting and ceiling bosses intact, with the capitals of the surrounding columns sporting the most intricate of curly kale carving. In the **south transept**, another fine fifteenth-century window sprouts yet more delicate, foliate tracery and the adjacent cornice is enlivened by weathered angels playing musical instruments. Look out, too, for the statue of the Virgin and Child, high on the south side of the westernmost surviving buttress, the Coronation of the Virgin on the east end gable, and the numerous mischievous **gargoyles**, such as the pig playing the bagpipes on the roof on the south side of the nave.

Practicalities

Buses to Melrose stop in Market Square, from where it's a brief walk north to the abbey ruins and the **tourist office** opposite (Mon–Sat 10am–5pm, Sun 10am–2pm). Melrose has a clutch of **hotels**, with prices generally higher than you might expect. The best of the bunch is ⚿ *Burt's*, a smartly converted old inn on Market Square (☎01896/822285, ⓦwww.burtshotel.co.uk; ⑥), with small but comfortable rooms. Across the street is the ten-bedroom *Townhouse* (☎01896/822645, ⓦwww.thetownhousemelrose.co.uk; ⑤), owned by the same family as *Burt's*. It's among Melrose's simple **B&Bs**, however, that you'll get the real flavour of the place, most notably at the easy-going and comfortable *Braidwood*, on Buccleuch Street (℡01896/822488, Ⓦwww .braidwoodmelrose.co.uk; ❷), a stone's throw from the abbey, and the equally agreeable *Dunfermline House* (℡01896/822411, Ⓦwww.dunmel.freeserve.co.uk; ❷) opposite – advance booking is recommended at both in summer. The town also has an SYHA **hostel** (℡0870/004 1141, Ⓦwww.syha.org.uk; March–Oct) in a sprawling Georgian villa overlooking the abbey from beside the access road into the bypass. The *Gibson Caravan Park* **campsite** (℡01896/822969) is in the town centre, just off the High Street, opposite the Greenyards rugby grounds.

Melrose has a good choice of **eating** options. *Marmion's Brasserie* (℡01896/822245), on Buccleuch Street, serves well-prepared imaginative meals, as does the award-winning restaurant in the *Station Hotel* on Market Square. *Burt's* does excellent bar meals, and if you're feeling energetic, walk 500 yards past the abbey and across the old suspension bridge to Gattonside, where the *Hoebridge Inn* (℡01896/823082; closed Mon), once a bobbin mill and now one of the Borders' best restaurants, serves homemade Scottish food in relaxed, low-key surroundings. For a light lunch or snack, head to *Russell's* (closed Thurs), a traditional tearoom on Market Square, or *Haldane's Fish & Chip Shop* (closed Wed) next door. For **pubs**, try the friendly *King's Arms* on the High Street, or the *Ship Inn*, on East Port at the top of the square: it's the liveliest in town, especially during the Folk Festival and on Saturday afternoons when the Melrose rugby team have played at home. Melrose also has its very own pint-sized **theatre**, *The Wynd* (℡01896/823854, Ⓦwww.thewynd.com), which shows films and puts on gigs as well as live drama; it's tucked away down the alleyway, north off the main square.

Abbotsford

The stately home of **Abbotsford** (mid-March to May & Oct Mon–Sat 9.30am–5pm, Sun 2–5pm; June-Sept Mon–Sat 9.30am–5pm, Sun 9.30am–5pm; £4.75), three miles up the Tweed from Melrose, was designed to satisfy the Romantic inclinations of **Sir Walter Scott**, who lived here from 1812 until his death. Abbotsford (as Scott chose to call it) took twelve years to evolve, with the fanciful turrets and castellations of the Scots Baronial exterior incorporating copies of medieval originals. Despite all the exterior pomp, the interior is surprisingly small and poky, with just six rooms open for viewing on the upper floor. Visitors start in the wood-panelled study, with its small writing desk made of salvage from the Spanish Armada, at which Scott banged out the Waverley novels at a furious rate. The heavy wood-panelled library boasts Scott's collection of more than nine thousand rare books and an extraordinary assortment of memorabilia, the centrepiece of which is Napoleon's pen case and blotting book, but which also includes Rob Roy's purse and *skene dhu* (knife), and the inlaid pearl crucifix that accompanied Mary, Queen of Scots, to the scaffold. You can also see Henry Raeburn's famous portrait of Scott hanging in the drawing room, and all sorts of weapons – notably Rob Roy's sword, dagger and gun – in the armoury.

The fast and frequent Melrose–Galashiels **bus** provides easy access to Abbotsford: ask for the Tweedbank island on the A6091, from where the house is a ten-minute walk up the road.

Dryburgh Abbey

Hidden away in a U-bend in the Tweed, three or four miles east of Melrose, the remains of **Dryburgh Abbey** (April–Sept daily 9.30am–6.30pm; Oct–March Mon–Sat 9.30am–4.30pm, Sun 2–4.30pm; £3.30; HS) occupy an idyllic position against a hilly backdrop, with ancient cedars, redwoods, beech and lime trees and wide lawns flattering the pinkish-red hues of the stonework. The Premonstratensians founded the abbey in the twelfth century, but they were never as successful as their Cistercian neighbours in Melrose. The ruins of the **Abbey Church** are less substantial than Melrose or Jedburgh, and virtually nothing survives of the nave, though the transepts have fared better, their chapels now serving as private burial grounds for, among others, Sir Walter Scott and Field Marshal Haig, the World War I commander whose ineptitude cost thousands of soldiers' lives. The night stairs, down which the monks stumbled in the early hours of the morning, survive in the south transept, and lead even today to the monks' dormitory. Leaving the church via the east processional door in the south aisle, with its dog-tooth decoration, you enter the cloisters, the highlight of which is the barrel-vaulted **Chapter House**, complete with low stone benches and blind interlaced arcading.

Next door to the abbey is the sprawling red-sandstone *Dryburgh Abbey Hotel* (℡01835/822261, ⓦwww.dryburgh.co.uk; ❼), a hunting, shooting, fishing kind of place. Dryburgh is not easy to get to by **public transport**, though it's only a mile's walk north of St Boswell's on the A68, and a pleasant three or four miles from Melrose. Drivers and cyclists should approach the abbey via the much-visited **Scott's View**, to the north on the B6356, overlooking the Tweed valley, where the writer and his friends often picnicked and where Scott's horse stopped out of habit during the writer's own funeral procession. The scene

---

Sir Walter Scott

Walter Scott (1771–1832) was born in Edinburgh to a solidly bourgeois family whose roots were in Selkirkshire. As a child he was left disabled by polio and his anxious parents sent him to recuperate at his grandfather's farm in Smailholm, where the boy's imagination was fired by his relatives' tales of derring-do, the violent history of the Borders retold amidst the rugged landscape that he spent long summer days exploring. Scott returned to Edinburgh to resume his education and take up a career in law, but his real interests remained elsewhere. Throughout the 1790s he transcribed hundreds of old Border ballads, publishing a three-volume collection entitled *Minstrelsy of the Scottish Borders* in 1802. An instant success, *Minstrelsy* was followed by Scott's own *Lay of the Last Minstrel*, a narrative poem whose strong story and rose-tinted regionalism proved very popular.

More poetry was to come, most successfully *Marmion* (1808) and *The Lady of the Lake* (1810), not to mention an eighteen-volume edition of the works of John Dryden and nineteen volumes of Jonathan Swift. However, despite having two paid jobs, one as the sheriff-depute of Selkirkshire, the other as clerk to the Court of Session in Edinburgh, his finances remained shaky. He had become a partner in a printing firm, which put him deeply into debt, not helped by the enormous sums he spent on his mansion, Abbotsford. From 1813, Scott was writing to pay the bills and thumped out a veritable flood of historical novels using his extensive knowledge of Scottish history and folklore. He produced his best work within the space of ten years: *Waverley* (1814), *The Antiquary* (1816), *Rob Roy* and *The Heart of Midlothian* (both 1818), as well as two notable novels set in England, *Ivanhoe* (1819) and *Kenilworth* (1821). In 1824 he returned to Scottish tales with *Redgauntlet*, the last of his quality work.

A year later Scott's money problems reached crisis proportions after an economic crash bankrupted his printing business. Attempting to pay his creditors in full, he found the quality of his writing deteriorating with its increased speed and the effort broke his health. His last years were plagued by illness, and in 1832 he died at Abbotsford and was buried within the ruins of Dryburgh Abbey.

inspired Joseph Turner's *Melrose 1831*, now on display in the National Gallery of Scotland (see p.834).

Kelso and around

KELSO, ten miles or so downstream from Melrose, at the confluence of the Tweed and Teviot, grew up in the shadow of its now-ruined Benedictine **abbey** (April–Dec daily; free), once the richest and most powerful of the Border abbeys. Unfortunately, the English savaged Kelso three times in the first half of the sixteenth century. Such was the extent of the devastation – compounded by the Reformation – that less survives of Kelso than any of the Border abbeys. Nevertheless, at first sight, it looks pretty impressive, with the heavy Norman west end of the abbey church almost entirely intact. Beyond, little remains, though it is possible to make out the two transepts and towers which gave the abbey the shape of a double cross, unique in Scotland.

Kelso town managed to rebuild itself and is now centred on **The Square**, an unusually large cobbled expanse presided over by the honey-hued Ionic columns, pediment and oversized clock belltower of the elegant **Town Hall**. To one side stands the imposing *Cross Keys Hotel*, with its distinctive rooftop balustrade, and a supporting chorus of three-storey eighteenth- and nineteenth-century pastel buildings on every side. Leaving the Square along Roxburgh Street, take the alley down to the **Cobby Riverside Walk**, where a brief stroll leads to Floors Castle (see below). En route, but hidden from view by the islet in the middle of the river, is the spot where the Teviot meets the Tweed. This bit of river, known as The Junction, has long been famous for its **salmon fishing**, with permits – costing thousands – booked years in advance. Permits for fishing other, less expensive reaches of the Tweed and Teviot are available from Tweedside Tackle, 36 Bridge St (℡01573/225306).

Practicalities

Kelso **bus station** on Roxburgh Street is a brief walk from The Square, where you'll find the **tourist office** in the Town Hall (Mon–Sat 10am–5pm, Sun 10am–2pm). **Accommodation** is rarely a problem: one of the best B&Bs in town is *Abbey Bank*, near Kelso Pottery on The Knowes (℡01573/226550, ⓔdiah@abbeybank.freeserve.co.uk; ❸), a Georgian house with large double beds and a lovely south-facing garden. Another good choice is the *Ednam House Hotel* (℡01573/224168, ⓦwww.ednamhouse.com; ❻), a splendid Georgian mansion set back off Bridge Street, with antique furnishings and gardens that abut the Tweed; make sure you're not put in the modern extension. Lastly, there's the *Roxburghe Hotel* (℡01573/450331, ⓦwww.roxburghe.net; ❼), a luxury hotel two miles south of Kelso on the A698 at Heiton, owned by the duke and duchess of Roxburghe, which also boasts an eighteen-hole championship golf course.

Most **eating** places are just off The Square: the *Cobbles Inn* restaurant is housed in a former pub just up Bowmont Street – check the specials menu for the best dishes – while the *Cross Keys* in the square specializes in local produce. *Oscar's Wine Bar* in Horsemarket is popular in the evenings (open daily) or try the excellent ✦ *Queen's Bistro* in the *Queen's Head Hotel* in Bridge Street for more gourmet fare. For a snack, there's *Le Jardin*, next to Kelso Pottery (closed Mon).

Floors Castle

If you stand on Kelso's handsome bridge over the Tweed, you can easily make out the pepperpot turrets and castellations of **Floors Castle** (Easter–Oct daily 10am–4.30pm; £6; Ⓦ www.floorscastle.com), a vast, pompous mansion a mile or so northwest of the town. The bulk of the building was designed by William Adam in the 1720s, and, picking through the Victorian modifications, the interior still demonstrates his uncluttered style. However, you won't see much of it, as Floors is still privately owned and just ten rooms and a basement are open to the public. Highlights include paintings by Matisse, Augustus John and Odilon Redon, and some fine Brussels and Gobelin tapestries.

Mellerstain House

Six miles northwest of Kelso off the A6089, **Mellerstain House** (Easter & May–Sept daily except Tues 12.30–5pm; Oct Sat & Sun only; £5.50; Ⓦ www .mellerstain.com) represents the very best of the Adam brothers' work – William designed the wings in 1725, and his son Robert the castellated centre fifty years later. Robert's love of columns, roundels and friezes culminates in a stunning sequence of plaster-moulded, pastel-shaded ceilings: the **library** is the highpoint of the tour for Adam lovers, with four unusual long panels in plaster relief of classical scenes that relegate the books to second place. The art collection, which includes works by Constable, Gainsborough, Ramsay and Veronese, is also noteworthy. After a visit you can wander the formal Edwardian gardens, which slope down to the lake.

Smailholm Tower

In marked contrast to Mellerstain is the craggy **Smailholm Tower** (April–Sept daily 9.30am–6.30pm; Oct–March Sat 9.30am–4.30pm, Sun 2–4.30pm; £2.50; HS), perched on a rocky outcrop a few miles to the south. Its rough rubble walls average six feet in thickness and both the entrance – once guarded by a heavy door plus an iron yett (gate) – and the windows are disproportionately small. These were necessary precautions: on both sides of the border, clans were engaged in endless feuds, a violent history that stirred the imagination of Sir Walter Scott, who was but a "wee, sick laddie" when he was brought here to live in 1773. Inside, press on up to the roof, where two narrow **wall-walks**, jammed against the barrel-vaulted roof and the crow-stepped gables, provide panoramic views. On the north side the watchman's seat has also survived, stuck against the chimney stack for warmth and with a recess for a lantern.

Jedburgh

Ten miles south of Melrose, **JEDBURGH** nestles in the lush valley of the Jed Water near its confluence with the Teviot, out on the edge of the wild Cheviot Hills. During the interminable Anglo-Scottish Wars, Jedburgh was the quintessential frontier town, a heavily garrisoned royal burgh incorporating a mighty castle and abbey. Though the castle was destroyed by the Scots in 1409 to keep it out of the hands of the English, the abbey survived, albeit in ruins. Today, Jedburgh is the first place of any size that you come to on the A68, having crossed over Carter Bar from England, and as such gets quite a bit of passing tourist trade.

Founded in the twelfth century as an Augustinian priory, **Jedburgh Abbey** (May–Sept daily 9.30am–6.30pm; Oct–April Mon–Sat 9.30am–4.30pm, Sun 2–4.30pm; £4; HS) is the best-preserved of all the Border abbeys, its vast church towering over a sloping site right in the centre of town, beside the Jed Water. Entry is through the bright **visitor centre** at the bottom of the hill, where you can view Jedburgh's most treasured archeological find, the **Jedburgh Comb**, carved around 1100 from walrus ivory and decorated

18

Jedburgh festivals

Jedburgh is at its busiest during the town's two main **festivals**. The **Common Riding**, or Callants' Festival, takes place in late June or early July, when the young people of the town – especially the lads – mount up and ride out to check the burgh boundaries, a reminder of more troubled days when Jedburgh was subject to English raids. In similar spirit, early February sees the day-long **Jedburgh Hand Ba'** game, an all-male affair between the "uppies" (those born above Market Place) and "downies" (those born below). In theory the aim of the game is to get hay-stuffed leather balls – originally representing the heads of English men – from one end of town to the other, but there's more at stake than that: macho reputations are made and lost during the two two-hour games.

with a griffin and a dragon. Enter the **Abbey Church** itself via the west door to appreciate fully the three-storey nave's perfectly proportioned parade of columns and arches, a fine example of the transition from Romanesque to Gothic design, with pointed window arches surmounted by the round-headed arches of the triforium, which, in turn, support the lancet windows of the clerestory. Be sure you climb up the narrow staircase in the west front to the balcony overlooking the nave, where you can contemplate how the place must have looked all decked out for the marriage of Alexander III to Yolande de Dreux in 1285.

It's a couple of minutes' walk from the abbey to the small, square **Market Place**, up the hill from which, at the top of Castlegate, stands **Jedburgh Castle Jail** (Easter–Oct Mon–Sat 10am–4.30pm, Sun 1–4pm; £2), an impressive castellated nineteenth-century pile built on the site of the old royal castle, with displays on prison life throughout the ages. Back down near the Market Place, signs will guide you to **Mary, Queen of Scots' House** (March–Nov Mon–Sat 10am–4.30pm, Sun 11am–4.30pm; £3). Despite the name, it seems unlikely that Mary ever actually stayed in this particular sixteenth-century house. The house's highlights are a copy of Mary's death mask and one of the few surviving portraits of the Earl of Bothwell.

Practicalities

Buses pick up and drop off at Canongate near the town centre. Yards away on Murray's Green is the **tourist office** (Mon–Sat 9.30am–5pm, Sun 10am–5pm). For **accommodation**, try *Meadhon House*, 48 Castlegate (℡01835/862504; ❷), with a conservatory round the back overlooking a lovely garden, or the Georgian *Glenbank House Hotel* in Castlegate (℡01835/862258, ⊛www.glenbankhotel.co.uk; ❸). Another great choice is *Hundalee House* (℡01835/863011, ⊛www.accommodation-scotland.org; March–Oct; ❷), a seventeenth-century mansion house in open grounds, a mile south of town on the A68. Three miles south of Jedburgh on the A68, there's also the comfortable *Jedforest Hotel* (℡01835/840222, ⊛www.jedforesthotel.com; ❻), whose restaurant has an excellent reputation. Of the two **campsites** nearby, the *Jedwater Caravan Park* (℡01835/840219; March–Oct) is cheaper and more secluded, in a pleasant riverside site four miles south of town on the A68.

There's a shortage of good **eating** places, but probably the best place is *Simply Scottish*, 6–8 High St (℡01835/864696), a smart but relaxed bistro-style café/restaurant serving inexpensive Scottish meals, as well as pasta dishes and the usual snacks. You should also try the local speciality Jethart Snails, sticky boiled sweets invented by a French POW in the 1700s and on sale everywhere.

Selkirk and around

Just south of the River Tweed, some five miles southwest of Melrose, lies the royal burgh of **SELKIRK**. The old town sits high up above Ettrick Water; down in the valley by the riverside, the town's imposing grey-stone woollen mills are mostly boarded up now, an eerie reminder of a once prosperous era. There's precious little reason to linger in Selkirk itself, though the town sits on the edge of some lovely countryside, and serves as the gateway to the picturesque, sparsely populated valleys of Yarrow Water and Ettrick Water, to the west.

At the centre of Selkirk, at one end of the High Street, you'll find the tiny **Market Square**, overlooked by a statue of Sir Walter Scott, behind which stands the former Town House, now dubbed **Sir Walter Scott's Courtroom** (April–Sept Mon–Sat 10am–4pm; July & Aug also Sun 2–4pm; Oct–March Mon–Sat 1–4pm; free), where he served as sheriff for 33 years. At the other end of the High Street is a rather more unusual statue of **Mungo Park**, the renowned explorer and anti-slavery advocate, born in the county in 1771. Just off Market Square to the south is **Halliwell's House Museum** (April–Sept Mon–Sat 10am–5pm, Sun 10am–noon; July & Aug Mon–Sat 10am–5.30pm, Sun 10am–1pm; Oct Mon–Sat 10am–4pm; free), an old-style hardware shop with an informative exhibit on the industrialization of the Tweed valley. Down by the river at the junction of the A7 with the B7014, **Selkirk Glass** (Mon–Sat 9am–5pm, Sun 11am–5pm; free) is a thriving craft industry that stands in stark contrast to the neighbouring mills. Visitors arrive by the coachload to sit in the café and watch glass-blowers making intricate paperweights and the like.

The **tourist office** is in Halliwell's House (same hours) off Market Square, and can help with **accommodation**. First choice for those with an unlimited budget is the upmarket ⚑ *Philipburn House Hotel* (☎01750/720747, ⓦwww .philipburnhousehotel.co.uk; ❻), an unusual eighteenth-century house set in its own grounds a mile west of the town centre; the hotel offers expensive, but excellent Scottish cuisine. Slightly more modest in price, but still full of character is the *Heatherlie House Hotel* (☎01750/721200, ⓦwww.heatherlie .freeserve.co.uk; ❺), a Victorian mansion a sharp left turn up from the road to Ettrick at Heatherlie Park.

Bowhill House

Three miles west of Selkirk off the A708, **Bowhill House** (July daily 1–5pm; £6) is the property of the duke of Buccleuch and Queensberry, a seriously wealthy man. Beyond the grandiose mid-nineteenth-century mansion's facade of dark whinstone is an outstanding collection of French antiques and European **paintings**: in the dining room, there are portraits by Reynolds and Gainsborough and a Canaletto cityscape, while the drawing room boasts Boulle furniture, Meissen tableware, paintings by Ruysdael and Lorrain, as well as two more family portraits by Reynolds. Look out also for the Scott Room, which features another splendid Raeburn portrait of Sir Walter, and the Monmouth Room, commemorating the illegitimate son of Charles II, who married Anne of the Buccleuchs; among other items, his execution shirt is on display.

The wooded hills of **Bowhill Country Park** adjoining the house (Easter–June & Aug daily except Fri 11am–5pm; July daily noon–5pm; £2) are crisscrossed by scenic footpaths and cycle trails: you can rent **mountain bikes** from the visitor centre. Getting to Bowhill by **public transport** is difficult: the Peebles bus, leaving

Selkirk daily at 2pm, will drop you at General's Bridge (takes 10min), from where it's a mile or so walk through the grounds to the house.

Peebles and around

Fast, wide, tree-lined and fringed with grassy banks, the Tweed looks at its best at **PEEBLES**, a handsome royal burgh that sits on the north bank, about fifteen miles northwest of Selkirk. The town itself has a genteel, relaxed air, its wide, handsome High Street bordered by houses in a medley of architectural styles, mostly dating from Victorian times, and ending in the soaring crown spire of the **Old Parish Church** (daily 10am–4pm) at the western end.

Halfway down the High Street is the **Tweedale Museum & Gallery** (Mon–Fri 10am–noon & 2–5pm, April–Oct also Sat 10am–1pm, 2–4pm; free), housed in the Chambers Institute, named after a local worthy who presented the building to the town in 1859, complete with an art gallery dedicated to the enlightenment of his neighbours. He stuffed the place with casts of the world's most famous sculptures and, although most were lost long ago, today's "Secret Room", once the Museum Room, boasts two handsome friezes: one a copy of the Elgin marbles taken from the Parthenon; the other of the **Triumph of Alexander**, originally cast in 1812 to honour Napoleon.

Of the various walks through the hills surrounding Peebles, the five-mile **Sware Trail** is one of the easiest and most scenic, weaving west along the north bank of the river and looping back to the south. On the way, it passes **Neidpath Castle** (mid-June to Aug Mon–Sat 10.30am–4.30pm, Sun 12.30–4.30pm; £3), a gaunt medieval tower-house perched high above the river on a rocky bluff. It's a superb setting, and the interior possesses a pit prison and a great hall bedecked with stunning batik wall hangings depicting the life of Mary, Queen of Scots.

Practicalities

Buses stop outside Peebles' post office, a few doors down from the well-stocked **tourist office** on the High Street (Mon–Sat 9am–5pm, Sun 11am–4pm). Peebles boasts a vast number of **B&Bs**: try *Rowanbrae,* a trim, pint-sized Victorian place on a quiet cul-de-sac on Northgate, off the east end of High Street (☎01721/721630, ✉john@rowanbrae.freeserve.co.uk; ❶), or *Viewfield,* 1 Rosetta Rd (☎01721/721232, ✉mmitchell38@yahoo.com, ❶), an attractive detached Victorian house a ten-minute walk west of the bridge, with rooms overlooking a lovely garden. For upmarket **hotels** you have to head out of town: *Castle Venlaw Hotel* (☎01721/720384, ⓦwww.venlaw.co.uk; ❻) is a Scots baronial house set in its own grounds on the edge of town up the Edinburgh Road, while the *Cringletie House Hotel* (☎01721/730233, ⓦwww.cringletie .com; ❽) is a still more splendid baronial pile a couple of miles further up the Edinburgh Road. Of the two **campsites** on the edge of town, the *Rosetta Caravan Park* (☎01721/720770; April–Oct) is the quieter, set in fields surrounded by mature woods, a fifteen-minute walk north of the High Street.

The best place to **eat** is the *Sunflower* (☎017221/722420), a tiny, brightly coloured restaurant at 4 Bridgegate, just off Northgate, which does sandwiches at lunch time, and more adventurous (and slightly pricier) evening meals. *The Halcyon Restaurant* in Eastgate (above Villleneuve's Wines) serves upmarket designer meals in formal, elegant surroundings at quite a moderate price. You can also munch on a baguette and get a good coffee at the **café** in the Eastgate Theatre, a state-of-the-art church conversion (ⓦwww.eastgatearts.com). As for **pubs**, the *Crown Hotel* on the High Street is a cosy place to hunker down; the

⑱

Tontine Hotel, opposite, is a grander place with views south over the Tweed, and a standard hotel menu. For really good pub food, try one of the bar meals at the *Castle Venlaw Hotel*.

Traquair House

Six miles east of Peebles, a mile or so south of the A72, **Traquair House** (daily: April, May & Sept noon–5pm; June–Aug 10.30am–5pm; Oct 11am–4pm; £5.80, grounds only £2.50; ⓦwww.traquair.co.uk) is the oldest continuously inhabited house in Scotland, with the present owners – the Maxwell Stuarts – having lived here since 1491. Persistently Catholic, the family paid for its principles: the fifth earl got two years in the Tower of London for his support of Bonnie Prince Charlie, Protestant millworkers repeatedly attacked their property, and by 1800 little remained of the family's once enormous estates – certainly not enough to fund any major rebuilding.

Consequently, Traquair's main appeal is its ancient shape and structure. The whitewashed facade is strikingly handsome, with narrow windows and trim turrets surrounding the tiniest of front doors – an organic, homogeneous edifice that's a welcome change from other grandiose stately homes. Inside, the house has kept many of its oldest features. You can see original vaulted cellars, where locals once hid their cattle from raiders; the twisting main staircase as well as the earlier medieval version, later a secret escape route for persecuted Catholics; a carefully camouflaged priest's hole; and even a **priest's room** where a string of resident chaplains lived in hiding. In the **museum room** there is a wealth of treasures, including a fine example of a Jacobite Amen glass, a rosary and crucifix owned by Mary, Queen of Scots, and the cloak worn by the earl of Nithsdale during his dramatic escape from the Tower of London.

It's worth sparing time for the surrounding **gardens**, where you'll find a **hedge maze**, several craft workshops and the **Traquair House Brewery** dating back to 1566, which was revived in 1965, and claims to be the only British brewery that still ferments totally in oak. You can learn about the brewery and taste the ales in the Brewery Shop, as well as buy them. There's an attractive café serving snacks in an estate cottage on the redundant avenue which leads to the locked **Bear Gates**; Bonnie Prince Charlie departed the house through the gates, and the then owner promised to keep them locked till a Stuart should ascend the throne.

If you're really taken by the place, you can stay in one of its three guest **rooms** (☏01896/830323; ❾), decked out with antiques and four-posters, on a bed-and-breakfast basis only.

Dumfries and Galloway

The southwest corner of Scotland, now known as **Dumfries and Galloway** (ⓦwww.dumfriesandgalloway.co.uk), has stately homes, deserted hills and ruined abbeys to compete with the best of the Borders. It also has something the Borders don't have, and that's the **Solway coast**, a long, indented coastline of sheltered sandy coves that's been dubbed the "Scottish Riviera" – an exaggeration perhaps, but it's certainly Scotland's warmest, southernmost stretch of coastline.

Dumfries is the obvious gateway to the region, a pleasant enough town that's only really a must for those on the trail of **Robert Burns**, who spent the last part of his life here. Further west, and more attractive is

Kirkcudbright, once a bustling port thronged with sailing ships, later an artists' retreat, and now a tranquil, well-preserved little eighteenth- and early nineteenth-century town. Contrasting with the essentially gentle landscape of the Solway coast, is the brooding presence of the **Galloway Hills** to the north, their beautiful moors, mountains, lakes and rivers centred on the 150,000-acre **Galloway Forest Park**, a seriously underused hill-walking and mountain-biking paradise.

Dumfries and around

Situated on the wide banks of the River Nith a short distance inland from the Solway Firth, **DUMFRIES** is by far the largest town in southwest Scotland, with a population of more than thirty thousand. Long known as the "Queen of the South" (as is its football club), the town flourished as a medieval seaport and trading centre. Its success attracted the attention of many English armies, but Dumfries survived to prosper and enough remains of the warm red-sandstone buildings that distinguish it from other towns in the southwest to make Dumfries worth at least a brief stop. It also acts as a convenient base for exploring the Solway coast, to the east and west, and is second only to Ayr for its associations with Robbie Burns.

The Town

Dumfries' pedestrianized **High Street** runs roughly parallel to the Nith; at its northern end, presiding over a floral roundabout, is the **Burns Statue**, a sentimental piece of Victorian frippery in white Carrara marble, featuring the great man holding a posy in one hand while the other clutches at his heart. His faithful hound, Luath, lies curled around his feet – though it doesn't look much

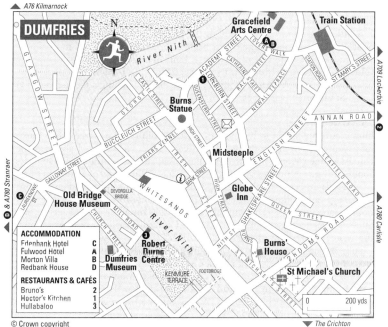

© Crown copyright

like a Scots collie (as Luath was). Further down the High Street, Burns' body lay in state at the town's most singular building, the **Midsteeple**, an appealingly wonky hotchpotch of a place, built in 1707 to fulfil the multiple functions of town prison, clocktower, courthouse and arsenal.

If you're on Burns' trail, make sure you duck down the alleyway to the whitewashed **Globe Inn**, a little further down the High Street, which was Burns' most famous *howff* (pub). Southeast of the High Street, in Burns Street, stands **Burns' House** (April–Sept Mon–Sat 10am–5pm, Sun 2–5pm; Oct–March Tues–Sat 10am–1pm & 2–5pm; free), a simple sandstone building where the poet died of rheumatic heart disease in 1796, a few days before the birth of his last son, Maxwell. Inside, along with the usual collection of Burns memorabilia, one of the bedroom windows bears his signature, scratched with his diamond ring. As a member of the Dumfries Volunteers, Burns was given a military funeral, before being buried nearby in a simple grave by **St Michael's Church** (Mon–Fri 10am–4pm; free), a large red-sandstone church, built in 1745. In 1815, Burns was dug up and moved across the graveyard to a purpose-built **Mausoleum**, a bright white Neoclassical eyesore, which houses a slightly ludicrous statue of Burns being accosted by the Poetic Muse.

From the church, head down to the shallow and fast-running Nith, and cross over to the old water mill which houses the **Robert Burns Centre**, or RBC (April–Sept Mon–Sat 10am–8pm, Sun 2–5pm; Oct–March Tues–Sat 10am–1pm & 2–5pm; free), with a simple exhibition on the poet's years in Dumfries and an optional twenty-minute slide show (£1.55). On the hill above the RBC stands the **Dumfries Museum** (April–Sept Mon–Sat 10am–5pm, Sun 2–5pm; Oct–March Tues–Sat 10am–1pm & 2–5pm; free), from which there are great views over the town. The museum is housed partly in an eighteenth-century windmill, which was converted into the town's observatory in the 1830s, and features a **camera obscura** on its top floor (April–Sept; £1.80), well worth a visit on a clear day.

A little upstream from the RBC is the pedestrian-only **Devorgilla Bridge**, built in 1431 and one of the oldest bridges in Scotland. Attached to its south-western end is the town's oldest house, built in 1660, now home to the tiny **Old Bridge House Museum** (April–Sept Mon–Sat 10am–5pm, Sun 2–5pm; free), stuffed full of Victorian domestic bric-a-brac, including a teeth-chattering range of Victorian dental gear.

Practicalities

Dumfries **train** station is five minutes' walk east of the town centre, while **buses** drop you off at Whitesands beside the River Nith, where you'll also find the **tourist office** (Mon–Sat 10am–5pm; June–Sept also Sun noon–5pm). Dumfries abounds in **guest houses** and **B&Bs**: for value and convenience, you can't beat *Morton Villa*, 28 Lovers Walk (☏01387/255825; ❷), a large Victorian house with a pleasant garden, or the very welcoming *Fulwood Hotel* (☏01387/252262; ❷), next door at no. 30. If you're looking for a bona fide **hotel**, head for Laurieknowe Street, a five- to ten-minute walk west of Devorgilla Bridge, where you'll find the welcoming, family-run *Edenbank* (☏01387/252759, ⓦwww.edenbankhotel .co.uk; ❹), or there's *Redbank House* (☏01387/247034, ⓦwww.redbankhouse .co.uk; ❸), a pristine red-brick mansion set within its own wooded garden at the edge of town on the A710, boasting a sauna, snooker room and gym.

By far the best option for **food** is ⌘ *Hullabaloo* (☏01387/259679, ⓦwww .hullabaloorestaurant.co.uk; closed Mon & Sun eve), a stylish restaurant in the RBC, with a riverside summer terrace. Another good choice is *Hector's Kitchen*, a much smaller place at 20 Academy St (closed Sun), which offers toasties, baguettes, nachos and crêpes for lunch, and more substantial fare in the evening. *Bruno's* (℡01387/255757; closed Tues) is a family-friendly Italian restaurant on Balmoral Road that's become a Dumfries institution, with the equally popular *Balmoral* chippie round the side which justifiably claims to sell the best chips in the southwest.

Two of Burns' favourite drinking places are still in operation: the *Hole i' the Wa'* **pub**, down an alley opposite Woolworth's on High Street, serves the usual bar food; but for somewhere with a bit more atmosphere, make for the smoky, oak-panelled *Globe Inn* on the High Street, which is crammed with memorabilia connected with the poet but is otherwise little changed since his time. The *Robert the Bruce* pub, with its Neoclassical portico at the top of Buccleuch Street, is a very popular church conversion. **Films** are regularly shown at the RBC (℡01387/264808, ⓦwww.rbcft.co.uk; Tues–Sat). Grierson and Graham, 10 Academy St (℡01387/259483), offer **bike rental**, useful for reaching the nearby Solway coast.

Drumlanrig Castle

Seventeen miles north of Dumfries, **Drumlanrig Castle** (May–Aug daily noon–4pm; May & June closed Fri; ⓦwww.buccleuch.com; £7) is not a castle at all, but the grandiose stately home of the Duke of Buccleuch and Queensberry, one of the country's wealthiest men. The highlights of the richly furnished interior are the **paintings**, in particular, Rembrandt's *Old Woman Reading*, and Hans Holbein's formal portrait of Sir Nicholas Carew, Master of the Horse to Henry VIII. Also be sure to check out the striking 1950s portrait of the present duchess, all debutante coiffure and high-society décolletage, by John Merton in the morning room, and, in the serving room, John Ainslie's *Joseph Florence, Chef*, a sharply observed and dynamic portrait much admired by Walter Scott. As well as the house, Drumlanrig offers a host of other attractions, including formal **gardens** and a forested **country park** (mid-April to Sept daily 11am–5pm; £3). The old stableyard beside the castle contains a visitor centre, a few shops, the inevitable tearoom, and also a useful **bike rental** outlet, as the park is crisscrossed by footpaths and cycle routes; elsewhere in the grounds, there's an adventure playground. If you're heading here by bus from Dumfries or Ayr, bear in mind it's a one-and-a-half-mile walk from the road to the house.

Caerlaverock

Caerlaverock Castle (daily: April–Sept 9.30am–6.30pm; Oct–March 9.30am–4.30pm; £4; HS), eight miles southeast of Dumfries, is a picture-perfect ruined castle. Not only is it moated, it's built from the rich local red sandstone, is triangular in shape and has preserved its mighty double-towered gatehouse. The most surprising addition, however, lies inside, where you're confronted by the ornate Renaissance facade of the **Nithsdale Lodging**, erected in the 1630s by the first earl of Nithsdale. The decorated tympana above the windows feature lively mythological and heraldic scenes in what was clearly the latest style. Sadly, Nithsdale didn't get much value for money: just six years later he and his royal garrison were forced to surrender after a thirteen-week siege and bombardment by the Covenanters, who proceeded to wreck the place. It was never inhabited again.

Three miles further east, at Eastpark, is the **Caerlaverock Wildfowl and Wetlands Trust (WWT) Centre** (daily 10am–5pm; ⓦwww.wwt.org.uk /visit/caerlaverock; £4.40), more than a thousand acres of protected salt marsh and mud flat edging the Solway Firth. The centre is equipped with screened approaches that link the main observatory to a score of well-situated bird-watchers' hides. It's famous for the 25,000 or so barnacle geese that winter here between September and April. The rest of the year, when the geese are away nesting in Svalbard, there's plenty of other flora and fauna to look out for, as well as the natterjack toad. Throughout the year the wild whooper swans have a daily feeding time and the wardens run free wildlife safaris; call ☎01387/770200 for up-to-date details. You can **camp** or stay in one of the **rooms** in the centre's converted farmhouse (ℇ.info.caerlaverock@wwt.org.uk; ❸), which has its own observation tower, plus a kitchen and washing machine for guests' use. Both the castle and the centre are reached along the B725; this is the route the bus takes, mostly terminating at the castle but sometimes continuing to the start of the two-mile lane leading off the B725 to the centre.

Ruthwell

From Caerlaverock, it's another seven miles along the B725 to **RUTHWELL**, whose modest country church houses the remarkable eighteen-foot **Ruth-well Cross** (the keys are kept at one of the houses at the foot of the lane). An extraordinary early Christian monument from the eighth century when Galloway was ruled by the Northumbrians, the cross was considered idolatrous during the Reformation, smashed to pieces and buried. Only in the nineteenth century was the cross finally reassembled and given its own purpose-built semicircular apse. The decoration reveals a strikingly sophisticated style and iconography, probably derived from the eastern Mediterranean. The main inscriptions are in Latin, but running round the edge is a poem written in the Northumbrian dialect in runic figures. However, it's the biblical carvings on the main face that really catch the eye, notably Mary Magdalene washing the feet of Jesus.

New Abbey and Sweetheart Abbey

NEW ABBEY is a tidy little one-street village, eight miles south of Dumfries, that evolved in order to service its giant neighbour, **Sweet-heart Abbey** (April–Sept daily 9.30am–6.30pm; Oct–March Mon–Wed, Sat & Sun 9.30am–4.30pm; £2; HS), which lies romantically ruined to the east. The abbey takes its unusual name from its founder, Devor-gilla de Balliol, lady of Gallo-way, who carried the embalmed heart of her husband, John Balliol (of Oxford college fame) around with her for the last 22 years of her life – she is buried with the casket, in the pres-bytery. The last of the Cister-cian abbeys to be founded in

△ Sweetheart Abbey

Scotland – in 1273 – Sweetheart is dominated by the red-sandstone abbey church, which remains intact, albeit minus its roof. Its grassy nave is flanked by giant compound piers supporting early Gothic arches, and above them a triforium. The other great survivor is the precinct wall, to the north and east of the abbey, a massive structure – up to ten feet high and four feet wide in places – made from rough granite boulders.

The *Abbey Cottage* **tearoom** is renowned for its good coffee, teas and home-made cakes, and enjoys an unrivalled view over the abbey. At the centre of the village, two **pubs** face one another across a cobbled square: the *Abbey Arms* (☎01387/850489, ✉enquiries@abbeyarms.netlineuk.net; ❸) and the *Criffel Inn* (☎01387/850244, ⓦwww.criffelinn.com; ❸); both have seats outside, serve pub food and do B&B.

The Colvend coast

The **Colvend coast**, twenty miles or so southwest of Dumfries, is probably one of the finest stretches of coastline along the so-called "Scottish Riviera". The best approach is via the A710, which heads south through New Abbey, before cutting across a handsome landscape of rolling farmland to the aptly named Sandyhills, and, beyond, to **ROCKCLIFFE**, a beguiling little place of comfortable villas sheltered beneath wooded hills and nestled around a beautiful, rocky sand and shell bay. Excellent B&B **accommodation** is available at *Millbrae House* (☎01556/630217; March–Oct; ❷), a whitewashed cottage a short stroll from the bay. For **camping**, the *Castle Point Caravan Site* (☎01556/630248; March–Oct) is in a secluded spot, just south of the village, a stone's throw from the seashore. The *Garden House* tearoom (closed Mon & Tues), at the entrance to the village, provides simple sustenance and has a garden at the back.

For vehicles, Rockcliffe is a dead end, but it's the start of a pleasant half-hour's walk along the Jubilee Path to neighbouring **KIPPFORD**, a tiny, lively yachting centre strung out along the east bank of the Urr estuary. En route, the path passes the Celtic hillfort of the **Mote of Mark**, a useful craggy viewpoint. At low tide you can walk over the Rough Firth causeway from the shore below across the mud flats to **Rough Island**, a humpy twenty-acre bird sanctuary owned by the National Trust for Scotland – it's out of bounds in May and June during the nesting season. The reward for your gentle stroll is a drink and a bite to eat at the ever-popular *Anchor Hotel* (☎01556/620205; ❹), on Kippford's waterfront, which serves tasty **bar meals**. If you need to stay the night, head for the *Rosemount* (☎01556/620214, ⓦwww.rosemountguesthouse.com; Feb–Nov; ❷), an excellent **guest house** close by on the seafront.

Castle Douglas and around

Most folk come to **CASTLE DOUGLAS** (ⓦwww.castledouglas.net), eighteen miles southwest of Dumfries, simply in order to visit the nearby attractions of Threave Garden and Castle. **Threave Garden** (daily 9.30am to sunset; £5; NTS) is a pleasant mile or so's walk south of Castle Douglas, along the shores of Loch Carlingwark. The garden features a magnificent spread of flowers and woodland, sixty acres subdivided into more than a dozen areas, from the bright, old-fashioned blooms of the Rose Garden to the brilliant banks of rhododendrons in the Woodland Garden and the ranks of primula, astilbe and gentian in the Peat Garden. In springtime, thousands of visitors turn up for the flowering of more than two hundred types of daffodil and, from late May onwards, the herbaceous beds are the main attraction, with most of them arranged like islets in a sea of lawn (so that they can be viewed from all sides).

The nicest way of reaching **Threave Castle** (April–Sept daily 9.30am–6.30pm; £3; HS), a mile or so north of the gardens, is to walk through the estate. However you decide to get there, you should follow the signs to the Open Farm, from where it's a lovely fifteen-minute walk down to the River Dee. Here you ring a brass bell for the boat to take you over to the flat and grassy island on which the stern-looking tower house stands. Built for one of the Black Douglases, Archibald the Grim, the sturdy, rectangular fortress was completed shortly after the War of Independence, in around 1370. The rickety curtain-wall to the south and east is all that remains of the artillery fortifications, hurriedly constructed in the 1450s in a desperate – and unsuccessful – attempt to defend the castle against James II's new-fangled cannon. The Covenanters wrecked the place in 1640 after a thirteen-week siege, but enough remains of the interior to make it worth exploring.

Practicalities

Castle Douglas **tourist office** (April–June, Sept & Oct Mon–Sat 10am–4.30pm, Sun 11am–4pm; July & Aug Mon–Sat 10am–6pm, Sun 11am–5pm) is at the top end of King Street. All the old coaching inns on King Street offer **accommodation**, but you're better off trying one of the well-built Victorian guest houses out on Ernespie Road, such as *Albion House* (☎01556/502360; March–Oct; ❷), at no. 49. Alternatively, just south of Castle Douglas, the *Smithy House* (☎01556/503841, ⊛www.smithyhouse.co.uk; ❸) is a nicely converted *smiddy* overlooking Loch Carlinwerk. Campers should make for the *Lochside* **campsite** (☎01556/502949; Easter–Oct), beside Loch Carlingwark, a short walk from the bottom of King Street down Marle Street. The best place to grab a bite **to eat** is *Designs* (⊛www.designsgallery.co.uk; closed Sun), a café at the back of an arts and crafts shop at 179 King St, with a lovely conservatory and garden, serving great ciabattas and decent coffee. **Bike rental** – useful for getting out to Threave – is available from the Castle Douglas Cycle Centre on Church Street (☎01556/504542; closed Thurs & Sun).

Kirkcudbright and around

KIRKCUDBRIGHT – pronounced "kir-coo-bree" – hugging the muddy banks of the River Dee ten miles southwest of Castle Douglas, is the only major town along the Solway coast to have retained a working harbour. In addition, it has a ruined castle and the most attractive of town centres, a charming medley of simple two-storey cottages with medieval pends, Georgian villas and Victorian townhouses, all built in a mixture of sandstone, granite and brick, and attractively painted up, with their windows and quoins picked out. It comes as little surprise, then, to find that Kirkcudbright became something of a magnet for Scottish artists from the late nineteenth century onwards. It may no longer live up to the tourist board's "artists' town" label, but it does have a rich artistic heritage that's easy and enjoyable to explore.

The most surprising sight in Kirkcudbright is **MacLellan's Castle** (April–Sept daily 9.30am–6pm; £2.50; HS), a pink-flecked sixteenth-century tower house that sits at one end of the High Street by the harbourside. Part fortified keep and part spacious mansion, the castle was built in the 1570s for the then Provost of Kirkcudbright, Sir Thomas MacLellan of Bombie. Its interior is well preserved, from the kitchen (complete with bread oven) to the spyhole known as the "**laird's lug**", behind the fireplace of the Great Hall. Sir Thomas MacLellan is buried in the neighbouring **Greyfriars Kirk** (currently closed for major refurbishment), where his tomb is an eccentrically crude attempt at Neoclassicism; it even incorporates parts of someone else's gravestone.

Near the castle, on the L-shaped High Street, is **Broughton House** (daily: Easter, July & Aug 10am–5pm; April–June, Sept & Oct noon–5pm; Feb & March garden only daily 11am–4pm; £8; NTS), a smart Georgian townhouse and former home of the artist **Edward Hornel** (1863–1933). Hornel was an important member of the late nineteenth-century Scottish art scene, who spent his childhood a few doors down the street, and returned in 1900 to establish an artists' colony in Kirkcudbright with some of the "Glasgow Boys" (see p.908). At the back of the house Hornel added a studio and a vast, glass-roofed, mahogany-panelled gallery, now filled with the mannered, vibrantly coloured paintings of girls at play, which he churned out in the latter part of his career. Hornel's trip to Japan in 1893 imbued him with a lifelong affection for the country, and his surprisingly large, densely packed, wonderful, rambling **gardens** have a strong Japanese influence.

For background information on Kirkcudbright, visit the imposing, church-like **Tolbooth**, with its stone-built clocktower and spire. Built in the 1620s, the building now houses the **Tolbooth Art Centre** (May–Sept Mon–Sat 10am–6pm, Sun 2–5pm; Oct–April Mon–Sat 11am–4pm; £1.50), which has, on the upper floor, a small permanent display of works by some of Kirkcudbright's erstwhile resident artists, including Hornel's striking *Japanese Girl*, and S.J. Peploe's Colourist view of the Tolbooth. The ten-minute video gives you a good, succinct overview of Kirkcudbright's artistic heritage. Don't miss the **Stewartry Museum** (May–Sept Mon–Sat 10am–6pm, Sun 2–5pm; Oct–April Mon–Sat 11am–4pm; free), an extraordinary collection of local exhibits packed into a purpose-built Victorian building on St Mary Street.

Practicalities

Buses to Kirkcudbright stop by the harbour car park, next to the **tourist office** (April–June, Sept & Oct Mon–Sat 10am–5pm, Sun noon–4pm; July & Aug Mon–Sat 9.30am–6pm, Sun 10am–5pm), where you can get help finding **accommodation**. One of the best options is *14 High St* (☎01557/330766, Ⓔ14highstreet@kirkcudbright.co.uk; April–Sept; ❸), next door to Broughton House, with a garden overlooking the river, followed by *Baytree House*, at no. 110 (☎01557/330824, Ⓦwww. baytreekirkcudbright.co.uk; ❹), another Georgian house with comfortable rooms, good cooking, and a beautiful garden with sundeck. Cheaper B&B can be found at 1 Gordon Place (☎01557/330472; ❷), at the castle end of the High Street. The *Silvercraigs* caravan and **campsite** (☎01557/330123; Easter to late Oct) is five or ten minutes' walk from the centre down St Mary's Street and Place, on a bluff overlooking town.

Kirkcudbright is strangely limited when it comes to **restaurants**. Top choice is the *Auld Alliance*, 5 Castle St (☎01557/330569), a superior, if pricey, restaurant offering an old-fashioned fusion of French and Scottish cuisine, where you need to book ahead. Otherwise, there's the usual bar food at the *Best Western*–run *Selkirk Arms Hotel* on the High Street, which boasts a large garden out the back. There are also several decent daytime **cafés**: try *Mulberries*, on St Cuthbert Street, or, for more substantial fare, *Harbour Lights*, further up the street (open Fri & Sat eve in season). For a **drink**, the busy *Masonic Arms*, on Castle Street, pulls a reasonable pint of real ale.

Gatehouse of Fleet

Like Castle Douglas, **GATEHOUSE OF FLEET** (Ⓦwww.gatehouse-of-fleet .co.uk), ten miles west of Kirkcudbright, has a distinctive long, dead-straight

18

main street. However, the quiet streets of Gatehouse have none of the life and bustle of Castle Douglas. It's the country setting that sets Gatehouse apart, rather than any particular sight. Ann Street is the most picturesque, at the end of which you can gain access to the wooded grounds of **Cally House Gardens** (Easter–Sept Tues–Fri 2–5.30pm, Sat & Sun 10am–5.30pm; ⓦwww .callygardens.co.uk; £1.50). A palatial Neoclassical country mansion (now the *Cally Palace Hotel*), Cally House was built in the 1760s, and is proof positive of the fortune already owned by the Murray family, even before James Murray began his cotton enterprise. Back in town, the **Mill on the Fleet** (April–Oct daily 10.30am–5pm; £1.50), opposite the car park by the river at the bottom of the High Street, traces the economic and social history of Gatehouse and Galloway from inside a restored grey-granite bobbin mill. Perched on a hill a mile southwest of Gatehouse stands **Cardoness Castle** (April–Sept daily 9.30am–6.30pm; Oct Mon–Wed & Sat & Sun 9.30am–4.30pm; Nov–March Sat & Sun 9.30am–4.30pm; £2.50; HS), a classic late fifteenth-century fortified tower house, which boasts some fashionably decorated fireplaces and plenty of en-suite latrines, plus excellent views out to Fleet Bay in the distance.

Practicalities

The **tourist office** (mid-March to June, Sept & Oct Mon–Sat 10am–4.30pm, Sun 11am–4pm; July & Aug Mon–Sat 10am–5.30pm, Sun 10.30am–4.30pm)

Galloway Forest Park

Galloway Forest Park (ⓦwww.forestry.gov.uk/gallowayforestpark) is Britain's largest forest park, stretching all the way from the southern part of Ayrshire right down to Gatehouse of Fleet, laid out on land owned by the Forestry Commission. Many hikers aim for the park's **Glen Trool** by following the A714 north for about ten miles to Bargrennan, where a narrow lane twists the five miles over to the glen's Loch Trool. There are just a few **accommodation** choices around Glentrool: the small *House O'Hill Hotel* (☎01671/840243; ❷), shortly after you turn off the A714, provides basic accommodation, beer, food and, occasionally, great music, or there's the *Glentrool campsite* (☎01671/840280, ⓦwww.glentroolholidaypark.co.uk; March–Oct) a little further up the road before you get to Glentrool village. From here, there's a choice of magnificent **hiking** and **cycling** trails, as well as lesser tracks. Several longer routes curve round the grassy peaks and icy lochs of the Awful Hand and Dungeon ranges, whilst another includes part of the Southern Upland Way, which threads through the Minnigaff Hills to Clatteringshaws Loch.

A twenty-mile stretch of the A712 from Newton Stewart east to New Galloway, known as the **Queen's Way**, cuts through the southern periphery of Galloway Forest Park, a landscape of glassy lochs, wooded hills and bare, rounded peaks. You'll pass all sorts of **hiking trails**, some the gentlest of strolls, others long-distance treks. For a short walk, stop at the **Grey Mare's Tail Bridge**, about seven miles east of Newton Stewart, where the Forestry Commission has laid out various trails, all delving into the pine forests beside the road, crossing gorges, waterfalls and burns. A few miles further on is **Clatteringshaws Loch**, a reservoir surrounded by pine forest, with a fourteen-mile footpath running right round.

There are three **visitor centres** (April–Oct daily 10.30am–5pm; ☎01671/402420, ⓦwww.forestry.gov.uk) in the forest park: at Clatteringshaws by the loch; Glentrool; and Kirroughtree, off the A75 east of Newton Stewart. The visitor centres each have a tearoom, several waymarked walks and lots of information on activities and events; you can also pick up a leaflet about the various works of art strewn about the forest park.

is situated by the car park by the river. The place to stay is the sumptuous *Cally Palace* **hotel** (℡01557/814341, Ⓦwww.callypalace.co.uk; ❼; closed Jan), though make sure you're placed in the old house rather than the ugly modern extension, and dress smartly if you're going to eat there. **B&B** in Gatehouse itself is available at the terraced *Bobbin Guest House*, 36 High St (℡01557/814229; ❷), or at the *Murray Arms Hotel* (℡01557/814207, Ⓦwww.murrayarms.com; ❺), the old coaching inn next to the clocktower, where Robbie Burns wrote *Scots wha hae*. For good **pub food**, head for the bar or the conservatory of the welcoming *Masonic Arms*, just up Ann Street. For the ultimate array of whiskies, try the *Anwoth Hotel*, at the bottom of the High Street. The *Gatehouse* **café**, inside the original "Gatehouse", the oldest (and once the only) house in town, serves takeaways and snacks all day, washed down with Sulwath ales from Castle Douglas.

Wigtown

West of Gatehouse of Fleet, and seven miles south of Newton Stewart, **WIGTOWN** (Ⓦwww.wigtown-booktown.co.uk) is a tiny place, considering it was once the county town of Wigtownshire. Despite its modest size, it has a remarkable main square, a vast, triangular-shaped affair, its layout unchanged since medieval times. Overlooking and dominating the square and its central bowling green are the gargantuan, rather exotic-looking **County Buildings**, built in French Gothic style, and now home to the town's library. Wigtown styles itself as "Scotland's National Book Town" (Ⓦwww.wigtown-booktown .co.uk), with a highly rated **literary festival** in late September and ten to fifteen **bookshops** occupying some of the modest houses which line the square, and more elsewhere in the vicinity; for a map of their locations, head for the **information centre** (Mon–Fri 9am–noon & 1–5pm), on the main square. Most are closed on Sundays, the one notable exception being *Readinglasses*, which also has a small **café**.

Whithorn and around

Fifteen miles south of Wigtown is **WHITHORN** (Ⓦwww.whithorn.com), a one-street town which nevertheless occupies an important place in Scottish history, for it is here in 397 that **St Ninian** is thought to have founded the first Christian church north of Hadrian's Wall. According to the Venerable Bede, Ninian built a church in "a manner to which the Britons were not accustomed", and it became known as Candida Casa, "a bright and shining place", translated by the southern Picts he had come to convert as "Hwiterne" (White House) – hence Whithorn. No one can be sure where the Candida Casa actually stood, and very little is known about Ninian's life, but his tomb at Whithorn soon became a popular place of pilgrimage and, in the twelfth century, a Premonstratensian priory was established to service the shrine. For generations the rich and the royal made the trek here, the last being Mary, Queen of Scots, in 1563, but then came the Reformation and the prohibition of pilgrimages in 1581.

These days, it takes a serious leap of the imagination to envisage Whithorn as a medieval pilgrimage centre. For this reason, it's a good idea to start by watching the audiovisual show at the **Whithorn Dig** (Whithorn Story; Easter–Oct daily 10.30am–5pm; £2.70; HS members £1.90) on the main street. Heading outside, the dig site is pretty uninspiring, as are the nearby ruins of the nave of **Whithorn Priory**, though the latter does have a couple of finely carved thirteenth-century south-facing doorways. The most compelling early Christian relics found in the vicinity – a series of standing crosses and headstones – are housed in the onsite **Whithorn Museum**.

The pilgrims who crossed the Solway to visit St Ninian's shrine landed at the **ISLE OF WHITHORN**, four miles south of Whithorn, no longer an island, but an antique and picturesque little seaport. If you continue to the end of the harbour, you'll pick up signs to the minuscule remains of the thirteenth-century **St Ninian's Chapel**, which some believe was the site of the original Candida Casa. If you want to **stay**, try the unassuming *Steam Packet Inn* (☎01988/500334, @www.steampacketinn.com; ❸), right on the quay in Isle of Whithorn; it does pub food that's above-average in quality and price, and has a moderately expensive **restaurant**.

Stranraer

No one could say that **STRANRAER** (@www.stranraer.org) was beautiful, and if you're heading to (or coming from) Northern Ireland, there's really no reason to linger longer than you have to. If you find yourself with time to kill, head for the town's only real attraction, the **Castle of St John** (Easter to mid-Sept Mon–Sat 10am–1pm & 2–5pm; free), a ruined four-storey tower house built around 1500, which stands on the main street, one block inland from the harbour front.

The **train station** is right by the Stena Line **ferry** terminal (☎0870/570 7070, @www.stenaline.co.uk) on the East Pier, from where boats depart for Belfast. A couple of minutes' walk away, on Port Rodie, is the **bus station**. Stena Line's fast HSS **catamarans** depart for Belfast from the West Pier on the other side of the harbour. P&O Irish Sea ferries (☎0870/2424 777, @www.poirishsea.com) to and from Larne, arrive not in Stranraer, but at the port of **CAIRNRYAN**, some five miles north; note, though, that bus services to Cairnryan are infrequent and aren't integrated with the ferry times.

Stranraer's **tourist office** is at 28 Harbour St (April–Oct 9.30am–5.30pm, Sun 10.30am–4.30pm; Nov–March Mon–Sat 10am–4pm) between the two piers. Should you need **accommodation**, head for the *Harbour Guest House* (☎01776/704626, @www.harbourguesthouse.com; ❸), a decent **B&B** on the seafront on Market Street, just a short stroll from either pier. You'll have few problems **eating out** if you're after fish and chips, pizzas or pub grub. *L'Aperitif* on London Road (☎01776/702991) is a friendly Italian restaurant or there's the moderately expensive restaurant of the *North West Castle Hotel* (☎01776/704413, @www.northwestcastle.co.uk; ❻), the vast, whitewashed crenellated pile next to the police station on Port Rodie.

A better bet, if you want to splash out on a posh hotel with a wonderful view, is to head out to **Corsewall Point**, eleven miles north of Stranraer, at the northern tip of the Rhinns of Galloway, where the (still functioning) 1815 **lighthouse** has been incorporated into the luxury ⚓ *Corsewall Lighthouse Hotel* (☎01776/853220, @www.lighthousehotel.co.uk; ❻). If you don't have your own transport, the owners will collect you from Stranraer, as long as you book in advance.

Portpatrick to the Mull of Galloway

Situated roughly halfway along the west shore of the Rhinns of Galloway, the hilly, hammer-shaped peninsula at the end of the Solway coast, **PORTPATRICK** has an attractive pastel-painted seafront that wraps itself round a small rocky bay, sheltered by equally rocky cliffs. Until the mid-nineteenth century, when sailing ships were replaced by steamboats, Portpatrick was a thriving seaport, serving as the main embarkation point for Northern Ireland, with coal, cotton and British troops heading in one direction, Ulster cattle and linen in the other.

Portpatrick has several good **hotels** and **guest houses**, the best of which is the lilac-painted *Waterfront Hotel* (☎01776/810800, @www.waterfront hotel.co.uk; ❹), with a contemporary interior. Cheaper choices include the comfortable Victorian *Carlton Guest House*, also on the harbour at 21 South Crescent (☎01776/810253; ❷), or the *Knowe Guest House* (☎01776/810441, @www.theknowe.co.uk; ❶), a bright, white B&B overlooking the harbour, with a tearoom in its conservatory. There are several caravan and **campsites** in a row on the hill overlooking Portpatrick and Dunskey Castle, quite a distance from town (and the sea), but accessed by a pleasant walk along the disused railway and clifftop trail; *Sunnymeade* (☎01776/810293; March–Oct) has the better facilities, but *Castle Bay* (☎01776/810462; March–Oct) has the more informal atmosphere.

For **pubs** and **grub**, *The Crown* on the seafront is probably the cosiest, though the adjacent *Harbour Inn* has real ale. For something more formal and slightly pricier, head to the *Waterfront Bistro* next door.

It's twenty miles south from Portpatrick to the **Mull of Galloway** (@www.mull-of-galloway.co.uk), but it's well worth the ride. This precipitous headland, crowned by a classic whitewashed Stevenson lighthouse, from which you can see the Isle of Man, as well as the coasts of Ireland and England, really feels like the end of the road. It is, in fact, the southernmost point in Scotland, and a favourite nesting spot for guillemots, razorbills and kittiwakes. The headland has a **visitor centre** (Easter–Sept daily 10.30am–5pm) in a building near the **lighthouse**, which can be climbed on summer weekends (April–Sept Sat & Sun 10am–3.30pm; £2). Just below the car park, perched on the cliff edge, is an excellent ⚜ **café**, serving hot meals and snacks (Nov–March closed Wed & Thurs), with a terrace that provides armchair birdwatching.

Ayrshire

The rolling hills and rich soil of **Ayrshire** (@www.ayrshire-arran.com) make for prime farming country, and as such are not really top of most visitors' Scottish itinerary. **Ayr**, the county town and birthplace of Robert Burns, is handsome enough, but won't distract you for long. Most folk wisely stick to the coastline, attracted by the wide, flat sandy **beaches** and the region's vast number of **golf** courses. South of Ayr, the most obvious points of interest are **Culzean Castle**, with its Robert Adam interior and extensive wooded grounds, and the off-shore islands of **Ailsa Craig**, home to the world's second largest gannetry. North of Ayr, where the towns benefited from the industrialization of Glasgow, there are even fewer places to detain you, with the exception of **Irvine**, home to the Scottish Maritime Museum.

Ayr and around

With a population of around fifty thousand, **AYR** is by far the largest town on the Firth of Clyde coast. It was an important seaport and trading centre for many centuries, and rivalled Glasgow in size and significance right up until the late seventeenth century. Nowadays, the town won't keep you long, though it pulls in the crowds for the Scottish Grand National and the Scottish Derby (@www.ayr-racecourse.co.uk), and the local tourist industry continues to do

Robert Burns

The first of seven children, **Robert Burns** (ⓦ www.robertburns.org), the national poet of Scotland, was born in Alloway on January 25, 1759. His father, William, was employed as a gardener until 1766 when he became a tenant farmer at Mount Oliphant, near Alloway, moving to Lochlie farm, Tarbolton, eleven years later. A series of bad harvests and the demands of the landlord's estate manager bankrupted the family, and William died almost penniless in 1784. These events had a profound effect on Robert, leaving him with an antipathy towards political authority and a hatred of the land-owning classes.

With the death of his father, Robert became head of the family and they moved again, this time to a farm at Mossgiel, near Mauchline. Burns had already begun writing **poetry** and **prose** at Lochlie, recording incidental thoughts in his *First Commonplace Book*, but it was here at Mossgiel that he began to write in earnest, and his first volume, *Poems Chiefly in the Scottish Dialect*, was published in Kilmarnock in 1786. The book proved immensely popular, celebrated by ordinary Scots and Edinburgh literati alike, with the satirical trilogy *Holy Willie's Prayer*, *The Holy Fair* and *Address to the Devil* attracting particular attention. The object of Burns' poetic scorn was the kirk, whose ministers had obliged him to appear in church to be publicly condemned for fornication – a commonplace punishment in those days.

Burns spent the winter of 1786–87 in the capital, lionized by the literary establishment. Despite his success, however, he felt trapped, unable to make enough money from writing to leave farming. He was also in a political snare, fraternizing with the elite, but with radical views and pseudo-Jacobite nationalism that constantly landed him in trouble. His frequent recourse was to play the part of the unlettered ploughman-poet, the noble savage who might be excused his impetuous outbursts and hectic womanizing.

He had, however, made useful contacts in Edinburgh and as a consequence was recruited to collect, write and rearrange two volumes of songs set to traditional Scottish tunes. These volumes, James Johnson's *Scots Musical Museum* and George Thomson's *Select Scottish Airs*, contain the bulk of his **songwriting**, and it's on them that Burns' international reputation rests, with works like *Auld Lang Syne*, *Scots Wha Hae*, *Coming Through the Rye* and *Green Grow the Rushes, O*. At this time, too, though poetry now took second place, he produced two excellent poems: *Tam o' Shanter* and a republican tract, *A Man's a Man for a' That*.

Burns often boasted of his sexual conquests, and he fathered several illegitimate children; but in 1788, he eventually married **Jean Armour**, a stonemason's daughter from Mauchline, with whom he already had two children, and moved to Ellisland Farm, near Dumfries. The following year he was appointed excise officer and could at last leave farming, moving to Dumfries in 1791. Burns' years of comfort were short-lived, however. His years of labour on the farm, allied to a rheumatic fever, damaged his heart, and he died in Dumfries on July 21, 1796, aged 37.

Burns' work, inspired by a romantic nationalism and tinged with a wry wit, has made him a potent symbol of "Scottishness". Ignoring the anglophile preferences of the Edinburgh elite, he wrote in Scots vernacular about the country he loved, an exuberant celebration that filled a need in a nation culturally colonized by England. Today, Burns Clubs all over the world mark every anniversary of the poet's birthday with the Burns' Supper, complete with Scottish totems – haggis, piper, and whisky bottle – and a ritual recital of Burns' *Ode to a Haggis*.

steady business out of the fact that Robbie Burns was born in the neighbouring village of **Alloway** (see p.886).

Ayr's town centre, wedged between Sandgate and the south bank of the treacly River Ayr, is busy most days with shoppers from all over the county. The town's most venerable sight is the medieval **Auld Brig**, east off the High Street. It survived the threat of demolition in the early twentieth century thanks largely to its featuring in a Burns poem, and is now one of the oldest stone bridges in Scotland, having been built during the reign of James IV (1488–1513). A short stroll upstream from the bridge stands the much-restored **Auld Kirk**, the church funded by Cromwell as recompense for the one he incorporated into the town's fortress. The church's dark and gloomy interior retains the original pulpit (call ☎01292/262580 for access).

All you can see of Cromwell's zigzag **Citadel**, built to the west of the town centre in the 1650s, is a small section of the old walls – the area is still known locally as "the Fort". To the south of the citadel are the wide, gridiron streets of Ayr's main Georgian and Regency residential development. **Wellington Square** is the area's showpiece, its trim gardens and terraces overlooked by the **County Buildings**, a vast, imposing Palladian pile from 1820. The opening of the Glasgow-to-Ayr train line in 1840 brought the first major influx of holiday-makers to the town, but today, only a few hardy visitors and local dog-walkers take a stroll along Ayr's bleak, long **Esplanade** and beach, which look out to the Isle of Arran. The one building of note is the distinctive whitewashed **Ayr Pavilion**, built in 1911 with four tall corner towers – it now houses the suitably tacky Pirate Pete's indoor adventure playground.

Practicalities

Ayr is the nearest large town to **Glasgow Prestwick airport** (☎01292/511000, ⓦwww.gpia.co.uk), which lies three miles north and has regular trains to Ayr and Glasgow. Ayr **train** station is ten minutes' walk southeast of the town centre; the **bus** station is in the centre at the foot of Sandgate, near the **tourist office**, at 22 Sandgate (July & Aug Mon–Sat 9am–6pm, Sun 10am–5pm; Oct–June Mon–Sat 9am–1pm & 2–5pm), which can help with **accommodation**. Of the numerous choices on Queen's Terrace, head for *Craggallan* (☎01292/264998, ⓦwww.craggallan.com; ❷), a friendly little guest house with a dining table that converts into a billiards table, or try the purpose-built, modern *Horizon Hotel* on the seafront (☎01292/264384, ⓦwww.horizonhotel .com; ❺). In the leafy streets to the south of the town centre, *The Crescent* is a lovely spacious Victorian house with a four-poster suite, at 26 Bellevue Crescent (☎01292/287329, ⓦwww.26crescent.freeserve.co.uk; ❸). Campers should head for the *Heads of Ayr* caravan and **campsite** (☎01292/442269; March–Oct), three miles south of town along the coastal A719, beside the popular **Heads of Ayr Farm Park** (Easter–Oct daily 10am–5pm; ⓦwww .headsofayrfarmpark.co.uk).

Arguably the town's best **restaurant** is *Fouters*, 2a Academy St, a cellar bistro off Sandgate (☎01292/261391, ⓦwww.fouters.co.uk; closed Mon & Sun), or try one of the town's good Italian places, such as the long-established *Bonfanti* (☎01292/266577), at the top of Sandgate, or *Cecchini* (☎01292/263607, ⓦwww.cecchinis.com; closed Sun), an inexpensive family-run pizza and pasta joint on the eastern side of Wellington Square. A few doors up is the *Rupee Room* (☎01292/283002), a popular Indian restaurant, decked out with modern minimalist furnishings. You can have eat-in or takeaway fish and chips from *Wellington*, a long-established chippie at the corner of Sandgate and Fort Street, while *Renaldo's* next door is renowned for its authentic Italian ice cream and Ayr rock. A mixed crowd packs out the *West Kirk*, a **pub** in a converted church on Sandgate; but the most historic drinking den in town is the thatched *Tam o' Shanter*, on the High Street, though it's no museum piece.

Alloway

ALLOWAY, formerly a small village but now on the outskirts of Ayr, is the birthplace of Robert Burns (1759–96), Scotland's national poet. The first port of call is the **Burns Cottage and Museum** (daily: April–Sept 9.30am–5.30pm; Oct–March 10am–5pm; £3), the poet's birthplace, a low, whitewashed, thatched cottage where animals and people lived under the same roof. Much altered over the years, it nevertheless gives a good impression of what the place must have been like when Burns, the first of seven children, was born in the box bed in the only room in the house. The nearby two-room museum boasts all sorts of Burnsiana.

Ten minutes' walk down the road from the cottage are the plain, roofless ruins of **Alloway Kirk**, where Robert's father William is buried, and where Burns set much of *Tam o' Shanter*. Down the road from the church, the **Brig o' Doon**, the picturesque thirteenth-century humpback bridge over which Tam is forced to flee for his life, still stands, curving gracefully over the river. High above the river and bridge, towers the **Burns Monument** (daily: April–Sept 9am–5pm; Oct–March 10am–4pm; free), a striking Neoclassical temple in a small, carefully manicured garden. To enter the garden, you need to approach via the nearby **Tam o' Shanter Experience** (daily: April–Sept 10am–5.30pm; Oct–March 10am–5pm; £1.50), on the opposite side of the road from Alloway Kirk. Don't bother with the "Experience" itself, however, as its low-budget audiovisual presentation of *Tam o' Shanter* fails to do justice to Burns' poem.

True Burns junkies might want to eat, drink and stay at the *Brig o' Doon* **hotel** on the banks of the River Doon (☎01292/442466, ⊛www.brigadoon.com; ➐), reputed to be another of Burns' drinking haunts. To reach Alloway from Ayr town centre, **bus** #1 and #57 set off from Sandgate (Mon–Sat hourly) and go right to the Tam o' Shanter Experience; otherwise, catch bus #58 or #60 from the bus station to Alloway.

Culzean Castle

Sitting on the edge of a sheer cliff, looking out over the Firth of Clyde to Arran, **Culzean Castle** (pronounced "Cullane"; daily April–Oct 11am–4.30pm; £7; NTS), ten miles south of Ayr, couldn't want for a more impressive situation. The current castle is actually a grand, late eighteenth-century stately home, designed by highly successful Scottish Neoclassical architect **Robert Adam**, for the tenth earl of Cassillis (pronounced "cassles"). The most brilliantly conceived work by Adam is the Oval Staircase, where tiers of classical columns lead up to a huge glazed cupola. Other highlights include a portrait of Napoleon by Lefèvre, a superb Chippendale four-poster bed, a great book-shaped tin bath and a boat-shaped cradle. Many folk come here purely to stroll and picnic in the castle's 560-acre **country park** (daily 9.30am to dusk; park £8), mess about by the beach, or simply have tea and cakes.

You can **stay** at Culzean (☎01655/884455, ⊛www.culzeancastle.net; April–Oct; ➒), on the top floor, where six double bedrooms have been done out in a comfortably genteel style. A less grand option is the nearby *Culzean Castle* **campsite** (☎01655/760627; March–Oct), in the woods by the castle entrance, with great views across to Arran.

Irvine

IRVINE, twelve miles north of Ayr, was once the principal port for trade between Glasgow and Ireland, and later for coal from Kilmarnock, its halcyon

If the weather's half decent, it's impossible to miss the views of the island of **Ailsa Craig**, which lies ten miles off the south Ayrshire coast in the middle of the Firth of Clyde. The island's name means "Fairy Rock" in Gaelic, though the island looks more like an enormous muffin than a place of enchantment. It would certainly have been less than enchanting for the persecuted Catholics who escaped to the island during the Reformation. The island's granite has long been used for making what many consider to be the finest curling stones, and in the late nineteenth century, 29 people lived on the island, either working in the quarry or at the Stevenson lighthouse. With its volcanic, columnar cliffs and 1114ft summit, Ailsa Craig is now a **bird sanctuary** that's home to some 40,000 gannets. The best time to make the trip is at the end of May and in June when the fledglings are trying to fly. Several companies set off from Girvan, nearly twenty miles south of Ayr, and **cruise** round the island, but only Mark McCrindle is licensed to land (May to late Sept 1–2 daily; exact timings and prices depend on the length of trip and the tides; ℡01465/713219, ⓦwww.ailsacraig.org .uk). It takes about an hour to reach the island, so you've enough time to walk up to the summit of the rock and watch the birds, weather permitting.

⑱

days recalled in the enjoyable **Scottish Maritime Museum** (April–Oct daily 10am–5pm; ⓦwww.scottishmaritimemuseum.org; £3), which is spread across several locations around the town's beautifully restored old harbour. The best place to start is in the late nineteenth-century **Linthouse Engine Shop**, on Harbour Road, a hangar-like building housing everything from old sailing dinghies and canoes to giant ship's turbines. Free guided tours set off regularly for the nearby **Shipyard Worker's Tenement Flat**, which has been restored to something like its appearance in 1910, when a family of six to eight would have occupied its two rooms and scullery (and rented one of them out to a lodger). Moored at the **pontoons** on Harbour Street is an assortment of craft, which you can board, including a tug, a trawler, a "puffer" boat and the oldest seagoing steam yacht in the country.

Arriving at Irvine's adjacent **train** or **bus stations**, you'll find yourself exactly halfway between the harbour, to the west, and the Riverfront shopping complex and old town, to the east. Kilwinning Road, heading north out of Irvine, has several inexpensive **B&Bs** such as *Laurelbank Guest House*, at no. 3 (℡01294/277153, ⓔlaurelbankguesthouse@hotmail.com; ❷); should you wish to pamper yourself a bit more, head for *Annfield House*, 6 Castle St (℡01294/278903, ⓦwww.annfieldhousehotel.co.uk; ❺), a big Victorian mansion overlooking the river at the end of Sandgate, that has spacious bedrooms and its own bar and **restaurant**.

Travel details

Buses

For information on all local and national bus services, contact Traveline ℡0870/608 2608 (daily 7am–10pm), ⓦwww.travelinescotland.com.

Ayr to: Ardrossan (Mon–Sat every 30min, Sun every 2hr; 55min); Culzean Castle (Mon–Sat hourly, Sun every 2hr; 30min); Dumfries (Mon–Sat every 2hr; 2hr 10min); Glasgow (hourly; 55min); Portpatrick (Mon–Sat 6 daily; 2hr 25min); Stranraer (4–6 daily; 2hr).

Castle Douglas to: Dumfries (Mon–Sat hourly, 4 on Sun; 45min); Kirkcudbright (Mon–Sat hourly, 6 on Sun; 20min).

Dumfries to: Ayr (Mon–Sat every 2hr; 2hr 10min); Caerlaverock (Mon–Sat every 2hr, 2 on Sun; 30min); Carlisle (Mon–Sat hourly, Sun every 2hr; 1hr 25min); Castle Douglas (Mon–Sat hourly, 4 on Sun; 45min); Gatehouse of Fleet (Mon–Sat 8 daily, 3 on Sun; 55min–1hr 25min); Kirkcudbright (Mon–Sat hourly, 6 on Sun; 1hr 10min); New Abbey (Mon–Sat hourly, 4 on Sun; 15min); Newton Stewart (Mon–Sat 8 daily, 2 on Sun; 1hr 30min); Rockcliffe (5 daily; 1hr); Stranraer (Mon–Sat 8 daily, 2 on Sun; 2hr 10min).

Edinburgh to: Dumfries (Mon–Sat 4 daily, 2 on Sun; 2hr 40min); Jedburgh (3–4 daily; 1hr 50min); Kelso (4–6 daily; 2hr); Melrose (hourly; 2hr 15min); Peebles (hourly; 1hr); Selkirk (hourly; 1hr 40min).

Gatehouse of Fleet to: Kirkcudbright (Mon–Sat 8–10 daily, 5 on Sun; 20min); Newton Stewart (Mon–Sat 10–12 daily, 3 on Sun; 25min); Stranraer (Mon–Sat every 2hr, 3 on Sun; 1hr 20min).

Jedburgh to: Kelso (Mon–Sat 5–7 daily; 25min); Melrose (Mon–Sat 1–2 hourly, 7 on Sun; 30min).

Kelso to: Melrose (Mon–Sat 7–9 daily, 5 on Sun; 30–40min).

Melrose to: Jedburgh (Mon–Sat 1–2 hourly, 7 on Sun; 30min); Kelso (Mon–Sat 7–9 daily, 5 on Sun; 30–40min); Peebles (Mon–Sat hourly, 6 on Sun; 1hr 10min); Selkirk (Mon–Sat hourly, 2 on Sun; 20min).

Newton Stewart to: Glentrool (Mon–Sat 7 daily, 4 on Sun; 20min); Stranraer (Mon–Sat 15 daily, 5 on Sun; 45min); Whithorn (Mon–Sat hourly, 4 on Sun; 50min); Isle of Whithorn (Mon–Sat hourly, 4 on Sun; 1hr).

Trains

For information on all local and national rail services, contact National Rail Enquiries ℡ 08457/484950, Ⓦ www.nationalrail.co.uk.
Ayr to: Glasgow Central (every 30min; 50min); Irvine (every 30min; 15min); Prestwick Airport (every 30min; 7min); Stranraer (Mon–Sat 7 daily, 2 on Sun; 1hr 20min).

Dumfries to: Carlisle (Mon–Sat 14 daily, 5 on Sun; 40min); Glasgow Central (Mon–Sat 8 daily, 2 on Sun; 1hr 50min); Stranraer (Mon–Sat 2 daily; 3hr).

Glasgow Central to: Ayr (every 30min; 55min); Dumfries (Mon–Sat 8 daily, 2 on Sun; 1hr 50min); Irvine (every 30min; 35min); Kilmarnock (hourly; 40min); Prestwick Airport (every 30min; 45min); Stranraer (Mon–Sat 4 daily, Sun 2 daily; 2hr).

Stranraer to: Ayr (Mon–Sat 7 daily, 2 on Sun; 1hr 20min); Dumfries (Mon–Sat 2 daily; 3hr); Glasgow Central (Mon–Sat 4 daily, Sun 2 daily; 2hr).

Ferries (summer timetable)

Ardrossan to: Brodick, Isle of Arran (4–6 daily; 55min).
Cairnryan to: Larne (7–9 daily; 1hr–1hr 45min).
Stranraer to: Belfast (7–8 daily; 1hr 45min–3hr 15min).
Troon to: Larne (2 daily; 1hr 50min).

19

Glasgow and the Clyde

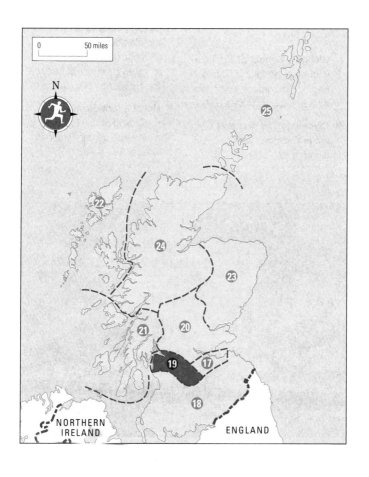

CHAPTER 19 # Highlights

* **Gallery of Modern Art**
  Idiosyncratic but populist
  collection of contemporary
  artworks, bang in the heart of
  the city. **See p.900**

* **Necropolis** Elegantly crumbling graveyard on a city-
  centre hill behind the ancient
  cathedral, with great views.
  See p.903

* **Glasgow School of Art** Take
  a student-led tour of Charles
  Rennie Mackintosh's architectural masterpiece. **See p.903**

* **Clydeside** The river that
  made Glasgow: walk or cycle
  along it, take a boat on it,

cross a bridge over it, or get
a view of it from the futuristic
Science Centre. **See p.909**

* **Burrell Collection** An inspired
  and eclectic art collection
  displayed in a purpose-built
  museum in Pollok Park. **See
  p.911**

* **"Glaesga nightlife"** Sample
  the glamour and the grit
  with cocktails at the *Rogano*
  followed by a pint of heavy at
  the *Horseshoe Bar*. **See p.915**

* **New Lanark** Stay for next-
  to-nothing at this fascinating
  nineteenth-century planned
  village. **See p.922**

△ The Armadillo, on Glasgow's River Clyde

Glasgow and the Clyde

R ejuvenated, upbeat **Glasgow**, Scotland's largest city, has not tradition-
ally enjoyed the best of reputations. Set on the banks of the mighty
River Clyde, this former industrial giant can still initially seem a grey
and depressing place, with the M8 motorway screeching through the
centre and dilapidated housing estates on its outskirts. However, the effects of
Glasgow's remarkable overhaul, set in motion in the 1980s by the "Glasgow's
Miles Better" campaign and crowned by the awarding of the title of European
City of Culture in 1990, are still much in evidence, even if the momentum has
slowed. Glasgow's image of itself has changed irrevocably and few visitors will
be left in any doubt that the city is, in its own idiosyncratic way, a cultured and
dynamic place well worth getting to know.

The city has much to offer, including some of the best-financed and most
imaginative museums and galleries in Britain – among them the showcase
Burrell Collection of art and antiquities – nearly all of which are free. Glasgow's **architecture** is some of the most striking in the UK, from the restored
eighteenth-century warehouses of the **Merchant City** to the hulking Victorian
prosperity of George Square. Most distinctive of all is the work of local lumi-
nary Charles Rennie Mackintosh, whose elegantly streamlined Art Nouveau
designs appear all over the city, reaching their apotheosis in the stunning
School of Art. Recent development of the old shipyards of the Clyde, notably
in the space-age shapes of the **Glasgow Science Centre**, hint at yet another
string to the city's bow: combining design with innovation. The metropolis
boasts thriving live-music venues, distinctive places to eat and drink, busy theatres, concert halls and an opera house. Above all, the feature that best defines the
individualism and peculiar attraction of the city is its **people**, whether rough-
edged comedians on the football terraces or bright young things dressed to the
nines in the trendiest of bars.

Despite all the upbeat hype, Glasgow's gentrification has passed by deprived
inner city areas such as the **East End**, historically the breeding ground for the
city's much-lauded **socialism**, celebrated in the wonderful **People's Palace**
social-history museum. Indeed, even in the more stylish quarters of Glasgow
there's a gritty edge that's never far away, reinforcing a peculiar mix of grime
and glitz which the city seems to have patented.

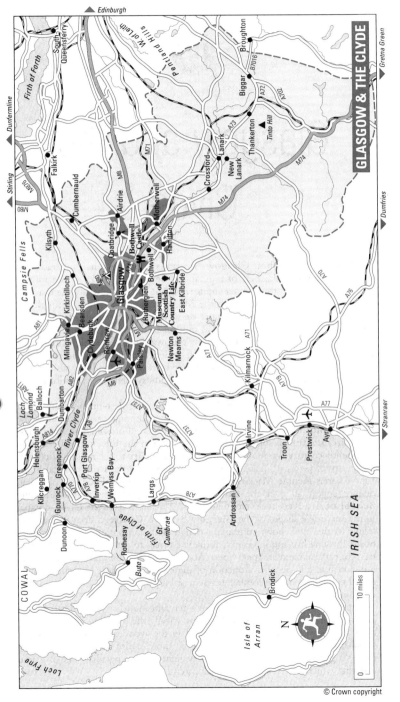

GLASGOW & THE CLYDE

© Crown copyright

Quite apart from its own attractions, Glasgow makes an excellent base from which to explore the **Clyde valley and coast**, made easily accessible by a reliable train service. Chief among the draws is the remarkable eighteenth-century **New Lanark** mills and workers' village, a World Heritage Site, while other day-trips might take you towards the scenic Argyll sea lochs, past the old shipbuilding centres on the Clyde estuary.

Glasgow

GLASGOW's earliest history, like so much else in this surprisingly romantic city, is obscured in a swirl of myth. Its name is said to derive from the Celtic *Glas-cu*, which loosely translates as "the dear, green place" – a tag that the tourist board is keen to exploit as an antidote to the sooty images of popular imagination. It is generally agreed that the first settlers arrived in the sixth century to join Christian missionary **Kentigern** – later to become St Mungo – in his newly founded monastery on the banks of the tiny Molendinar Burn.

William the Lionheart granted the town an official charter in 1175, after which it continued to grow in importance, peaking in the mid-fifteenth century when the **university** was founded on Kentigern's site – the second in Scotland after St Andrews. This led to the establishment of an archbishopric, and hence city status, in 1492, and, due to its situation on a large, navigable river, Glasgow soon expanded into a major industrial **port**. The first cargo of tobacco from Virginia offloaded in Glasgow in 1674, and the 1707 Act of Union between Scotland and England – despite demonstrations against it in Glasgow – led to a boom in trade with the colonies. Following the **Industrial Revolution** and James Watt's innovations in steam power, coal from the abundant seams of Lanarkshire fuelled the ironworks all around the Clyde, worked by the cheap hands of the Highlanders and, later, those fleeing the Irish potato famine of the 1840s.

The **Victorian** age transformed Glasgow beyond recognition. The population boomed from 77,000 in 1801 to nearly 800,000 at the end of the century, and new tenement blocks swept into the suburbs in an attempt to cope with the choking influxes of people. By the turn of the twentieth century, Glasgow's industries had been honed into one massive **shipbuilding** culture. Everything from tugboats to transatlantic liners were fashioned out of sheet metal in the yards that straddled the Clyde. In the harsh economic climate of the 1930s, however, unemployment spiralled, and Glasgow could do little to counter its popular image as a city dominated by inebriate violence and (having absorbed vast numbers of Irish emigrants) sectarian tensions. The **Gorbals** area in particular became notorious as one of the worst slums in Europe. The city's image has never been helped by the depth of animosity between its two great rival football teams, Catholic **Celtic** and Protestant **Rangers**.

Shipbuilding, and many associated industries, died away almost completely in the 1960s and 1970s, leaving the city depressed, jobless and directionless. Then,

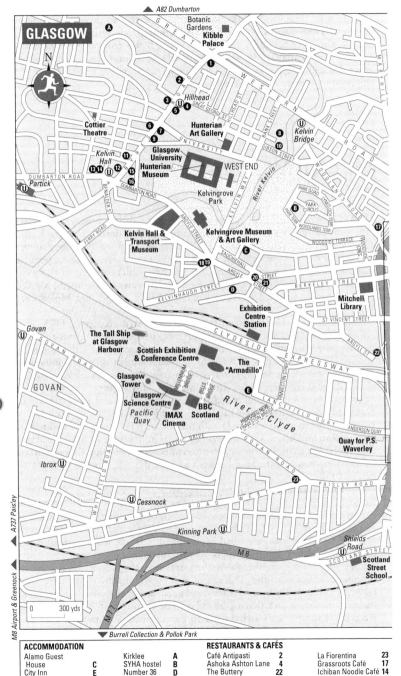

▲ A82 Dumbarton

GLASGOW

N

Botanic
Gardens
**Kibble
Palace**

Hillhead

**Cottier
Theatre**

*Kelvin
Hall*

Partick

DUMBARTON ROAD

DUMBARTON ROAD

**Hunterian
Art Gallery**

**Glasgow
University
Hunterian
Museum**

WEST END

*Kelvin
Bridge*

*Kelvingrove
Park*

**PARK
CIRCUS**

**Kelvin Hall &
Transport
Museum**

**Kelvingrove Museum
& Art Gallery**

**Mitchell
Library**

**Exhibition
Centre
Station**

CLYDESIDE

Govan

**The Tall Ship
at Glasgow
Harbour**

**Scottish Exhibition
& Conference Centre**

**The
"Armadillo"**

**Glasgow
Tower**

GOVAN

**Glasgow
Science Centre**

*Pacific
Quay*

**IMAX
Cinema**

**BBC
Scotland**

*River
Clyde*

Ibrox

Cessnock

**Quay for P.S.
Waverley**

Kinning Park

M 8

*Shields
Road*

**Scotland
Street
School**

0   300 yds

▼ Burrell Collection & Pollok Park

M8 Airport & Greenock   A737 Paisley

ACCOMMODATION		RESTAURANTS & CAFÉS			
Alamo Guest		Kirklee	**A**	Café Antipasti	**2**	La Fiorentina	**23**
House	**C**	SYHA hostel	**B**	Ashoka Ashton Lane	**4**	Grassroots Café	**17**
City Inn	**E**	Number 36	**D**	The Buttery	**22**	Ichiban Noodle Café	**14**
				Chow	**9**	Kember & Jones	**7**

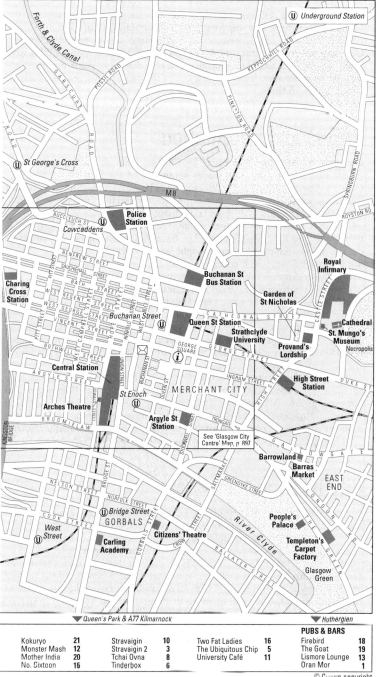

U Underground Station

Forth & Clyde Canal

U St George's Cross

M8

U Cowcaddens

Police Station

RENFREW STREET

SAUCHIEHALL STREET

Charing Cross Station

BATH STREET

WEST REGENT STREET

WEST GEORGE STREET

VINCENT STREET

Buchanan Street

U

Buchanan St Bus Station

Queen St Station

CATHEDRAL STREET

Garden of St Nicholas

Royal Infirmary

CASTLE STREET

Strathclyde University

GEORGE SQUARE

GEORGE STREET

Provand's Lordship

Cathedral

St. Mungo's Museum

Necropolis

BOTHWELL STREET

i

Central Station

INGRAM STREET

HIGH STREET

High Street Station

ARGYLE STREET

St Enoch

U

M E R C H A N T   C I T Y

DUKE ST

Arches Theatre

BROOMIELAW

KINGSTON BRIDGE

Argyle St Station

TRONGATE

STOCKWELL STREET

See 'Glasgow City Centre' Map, p 897

GALLOWGATE

Barrowland

Barras Market

EAST END

NELSON STREET

NORFOLK STREET

BRIDGE ST

U Bridge Street

GORBALS

COOK STREET

West Street

U

Citizens' Theatre

GREENDYKE STREET

SALTMARKET

River Clyde

LONDON RD

THE GREEN

People's Palace

Carling Academy

GORBALS STREET

CROWN ST

BALLATER STREET

Templeton's Carpet Factory

Glasgow Green

▼ Queen's Park & A77 Kilmarnock

▼ Rutherglen

					PUBS & BARS	
Kokuryo	21	Stravaigin	10	Two Fat Ladies	16	Firebird	18
Monster Mash	12	Stravaigin 2	3	The Ubiquitous Chip	5	The Goat	19
Mother India	20	Tchai Ovna	8	University Café	11	Lismore Lounge	13
No. Sixteen	16	Tinderbox	6			Oran Mor	1

895

© Crown copyright

in the 1980s, the self-promotion campaign began, snowballing towards the 1988 Garden Festival and year-long party as European City of Culture in 1990. Glasgow then beat off competition from Edinburgh and Liverpool to become **UK City of Architecture and Design** in 1999. These various titles have helped to reinforce the impression that Glasgow, despite its many problems, has successfully broken the industrial shackles of the past and evolved into a city of stature and confidence.

Arrival and information

Glasgow International airport (☎0870/040 0008, ⊛www.glasgowairport .com) is at Abbotsinch, eight miles southwest of the city. From here, the Glasgow Airport Link bus (£3.30) runs from bus stops 1 or 2 into the central Buchanan Street bus station every ten to fifteen minutes during the day; the journey takes 25 minutes. Airport taxis charge around £17.

Glasgow Prestwick airport (☎0871/223 0700, ⊛www.gpia.co.uk) is thirty miles south of Glasgow, near Ayr. From here the simplest way to get to the city is by train: there's a station right by the terminal (alight at the airport not Prestwick Town), with trains taking 45 minutes to reach Glasgow Central station (Mon–Sat every 30min, Sun hourly).

Nearly all **trains** from England come into **Central station**, which sits over Argyle Street, one of the city's main shopping thoroughfares. Bus #398 from the front entrance on Gordon Street shuttles every ten minutes to **Queen Street station**, at the corner of George Square, terminus for trains serving Edinburgh and the north. The walk between the two takes about ten minutes. Bus #398 also stops at **Buchanan Street bus station**, arrival point for regional and intercity **coaches**.

The city's efficient **tourist office** is at 11 George Square (April & May Mon–Sat 9am–6pm, Sun 10am–6pm; June & Sept Mon–Sat 10am–7pm, Sun 10am–6pm; July & Aug Mon–Sat 9am–8pm, Sun 10am–6pm; Oct–March Mon–Sat 9am–6pm; ☎0141/204 4400, ⊛www.seeglasgow.com). There's also a tourist office in Glasgow **airport's** international arrivals hall (daily 7.30am– 5pm, except Oct–April Sun 8am–3.30pm; ☎0141/848 4440).

City transport

Although it can be tough negotiating Glasgow's steep hills, **walking** is the best way of exploring any one part of the city. However, as the main sights are scattered – the West End, for example, is a good thirty-minute walk from the centre – you'll probably need to use the comprehensive **public transport** system.

The best way to get between the city centre and the West End is to use the **Underground** (Mon–Sat 6.30am–11pm, Sun 11am–5.30pm), whose stations are marked with a large orange U. If you're travelling beyond the city centre or the West End, or to the main sights on the Southside, you may need to use the bus and train networks. The array of different **bus** companies and the various routes they take is perplexing even to locals, and there's no easy guide to using them other than picking up individual timetables at the Travel Centre on St Enoch's Square.

The suburban **train** network is swift and convenient. Suburbs south of the Clyde are connected to Central station, either at the mainline station or the subterranean low-level station. The trains are an excellent way to link to points west and northwest of Glasgow, including Milngavie (for the start of the West Highland Way), Dumbarton and Helensburgh.

City tours

An alternative way to get round the sights of the city is to take a **city tour**: City Sightseeing (April–Oct daily 9.20am–4.40pm; £8.50) runs **open-top bus** tours, which leave every thirty minutes from George Square on a continuous circuit of all the major attractions in the city centre and West End, allowing you to get on and off as you please. You can combine this with a **river taxi** trip on the Clyde (£5.50 extra), or take one of the fast **powerboats** run by Seaforce (from £6 for 30min; ☎0141/221 1070, ⊛www.seaforce.co.uk), based at Glasgow Harbour near the SECC.

Back on dry land, Journeyman Tours (☎0800/093 9984, ⊛www.journeymantours.co.uk; Oct–April advance booking only) can guide you **on foot** round the Merchant City (Sun–Thurs 7.30pm) or on a **pub and ceilidh** tour (Fri & Sat 7pm). Mercat Tours also offers a guided **ghost tour** round some of

© Crown copyright

ACCOMMODATION		CAFÉS AND RESTAURANTS					PUBS AND BARS	
Bowley's	C	Brian Maule at		Ichiban Japanese		Café Cosmo	26	The Arches	21
The Brunswick	E	Le Chardon d'Ur	6	Noodle Cafe	19	Tron Theatre	25	Babbity Bowster	20
Euro Hostel	G	City Merchant	17	Mao	22	Wee Curry Shop	1	Bar 10	13
Langs	A	The Dhabba	23	Mono	28	Where the		Blackfriars	24
Malmaison	D	Dragon-i	2	Oko	14	Monkey Sleeps	5	Corinthian	15
Radisson SAS	F	Fratelli Sarti	4	Café Ostra	12	Willow Tea Rooms	3	Horseshoe Bar	9
Saint Judes	B	Gamba	8	Rogano	11	The 13th Note Café	27	Pot Still	7
		Café Gandolfi and		Smith's of Glasgow	16			Republic Bier Halle	10
		Bar Gandolfi	18						

the spookier parts of the city (☎0141/586 5378 or 07761 092948, ⓦwww
.mercat-glasgow.co.uk).

Accommodation

There's a good range of **accommodation** in Glasgow, from a large,
well-run SYHA hostel through to some highly fashionable (and not
over-priced) designer hotels in the centre. In general, prices are significantly lower than in Edinburgh, and given that many hotels are business-oriented, you can often negotiate good deals at weekends. If you're
prepared to sacrifice character and ambience, you'll often find the
cheapest rooms at the **budget chain hotels** dotted throughout the
city centre. Big players include *Ibis* (☎0141/225 6000, ⓦwww.ibishotel
.com), *Travel Inn* (☎0870/238 3320, ⓦwww.travelinn.co.uk), and *Express by
Holiday Inn* (☎0141/548 5000, ⓦwww.hiexpressglasgow.co.uk) – the latter
two also have hotels in a handy position near Glasgow Airport.

City centre

Bewley's 110 Bath St ☎0141/353 0800,
ⓦwww.bewleyshotels.com. Angular, glass-fronted
new central hotel, part of the famous Irish chain,
with rooftop views from the upper floors and
double, triple and family rooms at a year-round
flat rate. ❹

🏃 **The Brunswick** 106 Brunswick St
☎0141/552 0001, ⓦwww.brunswickhotel
.co.uk. A small, independent and individual
designer hotel in the heart of the Merchant City;
fashionable but good value, with minimalist furniture and a smart bar and restaurant. ❸
Langs 2 Port Dundas Place ☎0141/333 1500,
ⓦwww.langshotels.co.uk. Big, sassy, classy but
refreshingly independent modern hotel with a spa,
trendy restaurants and lots of mod cons. ❻
Malmaison 278 West George St ☎0141/572
1000, ⓦwww.malmaison.com. Glasgow's version
of the sleek, chic mini-chain, an austere Grecian-
tomple frontage masking a superbly comfortable
designer hotel. ❼
Radisson SAS 301 Argyle St ☎0141/204 3333,
ⓦwww.radisson.com. Huge place by Central
station with 250 rooms, a health centre and
a decent brasserie – it's also one of the more
dramatic pieces of modernist architecture in the
city centre. ❻
Saint Judes 190 Bath St ☎0141/352 8800,
ⓦwww.saintjudes.com. Elegant contemporary
boutique hotel with six rooms and some exquisite
designer touches. ❻

West End and Clydeside

Alamo Guest House 46 Gray St ☎0141/339
2395, ⓦwww.alamoguesthouse.com. Good-value,
family-run boarding house next to Kelvingrove
Park. Small but comfortable rooms. ❷
City Inn Finnieston Quay ☎0141/240 1002,
ⓦwww.cityinn.com. One of the better of the chain
hotels made interesting by its riverside location
right under the Finnieston crane; stylish rooms and
decent rates. ❻
Kirklee 11 Kensington Gate ☎0141/334 5555,
ⓦwww.kirkleehotel.co.uk. Characterful West End
B&B in an Edwardian townhouse, with antique
furniture, and walls crammed with paintings and
etchings. ❺
Number 36 36 St Vincent Crescent ☎0141/248
2086, ⓦwww.no36.co.uk. Neat, comfortable
guest house in a lovely crescent, well located for
Kelvingrove, the SECC and transport links to the
city centre. ❹
One Devonshire Gardens 1 Devonshire Gardens,
Great Western Road ☎0141/339 2001, ⓦwww
.onedevonshiregardens.com. Glasgow's most
exclusive and exquisite small hotel, a ten-minute
walk up the Great Western Road from the Botanic
Gardens. It's the top choice for visiting pop and
film stars. ❼

Southside

Best Western Ewington 132 Queen's Drive
☎0141/423 1152, ⓦwww.ewingtonhotel
.co.uk. A grand, upmarket hotel with a nice
outlook onto Queen's Park and a subterranean
restaurant. Prices can drop dramatically at
weekends. ❺
Boswell Hotel 27 Mansionhouse Rd ☎0141/632
9812. Informal, relaxing hotel in an old Queen's
Park villa with a popular locals' bar and conservatory restaurant. ❹

Hostels and self-catering

Glasgow doesn't have nearly as many **hostels** as Edinburgh, though it isn't short of bed space, thanks to the bright-pink liveried, seven-storey *Euro Hostel* smack in the centre of the city at 318 Clyde St (℡0141/222 2828, ⓦwww .euro-hostels.com), which tries to bridge the gap between backpacker hostel and budget hotel. Its 360 beds are all bunks but they're in smart en-suite rooms sleeping two, four, six or more – some of which have great views. Bed and continental breakfast is from £13.75.

The popular and recently upgraded SYHA hostel, 7–8 Park Terrace (℡0870/004 1119, ⓦwww.syha.org.uk), is located in a large townhouse in one of the West End's grandest terraces: dorm beds cost £15. It's a ten-minute walk south of Kelvinbridge underground station; bus #11 or #44 from the city centre leaves you with a short stroll west up Woodlands Road.

Low-priced **self-catering** rooms and flats are available at the University of Glasgow (℡0141/330 4116, ⓦwww.cvso.co.uk) from June to mid-September, mostly located in the West End, with prices starting at around £15 per person per night. The University of Strathclyde (℡0141/553 4148, ⓦwww.rescat .strath.ac.uk) has various sites available during the same period, most of which are around the cathedral: B&B in single rooms is available near the main campus in Cathedral Street starting at £25 per person per night, though you can pick up four-bed rooms for as little as £60.

The city centre

Glasgow's large **city centre** is ranged across the north bank of the River Clyde. At its geographical heart is **George Square**, a nineteenth-century municipal showpiece crowned by the enormous **City Chambers** at its eastern end. Behind this lies one of the greatest marketing successes of the 1980s, the **Merchant City**, an area which blends magnificent Victorian architecture with yuppie conversions. The grand buildings and trendy cafés cling to the borders of the run-down **East End**, a strongly working-class district that chooses to ignore its rather showy neighbour. The oldest part of Glasgow, around the **Cathedral**, lies immediately north of the East End.

George Square and around

Now hemmed in by the city's grinding traffic, the imposing architecture of **George Square** reflects the confidence of Glasgow's Victorian age. The wide-open plaza almost has a continental airiness about it, although there isn't much subtlety about the eighty-foot column rising up at its centre. It's topped by a statue of Sir Walter Scott, even though his links with Glasgow are, at best, sketchy. Haphazardly dotted around the great-writer's plinth are a number of dignified statues of assorted luminaries, ranging from Queen Victoria to Scots heroes such as James Watt and wee Robbie Burns. The florid splendour of the **City Chambers**, opened by Queen Victoria in 1888, occupies the entire eastern end of the square. Built from wealth gained by colonial trade and heavy industry, it epitomizes the aspirations and optimism of late-Victorian city elders. You can head inside and wander around the ground floor, where you'll see domed mosaic ceilings and two mighty Italian marble stairwells; but to get any further join in one of the free **guided tours** of the labyrinthine interior (Mon–Fri 10.30am & 2.30pm).

⑲

The Gallery of Modern Art

Queen Street leads south from George Square to **Royal Exchange Square**, whose focal point is a graceful mansion built in 1775 for tobacco lord William Cunninghame. The most ostentatious of the Glasgow merchants' homes, it now houses the **Gallery of Modern Art** (**GOMA**; Mon–Wed & Sat 10am–5pm, Thurs 10am–8pm, Fri & Sun 11am–5pm; free). With a down-to-earth, populist feel lacking in many of the country's grander art collections, the gallery has found favour with the public since its opening in 1996, though critics have been less impressed.

The spacious ground-floor gallery is principally used for temporary exhibitions, though large-scale socially committed works by the "New Glasgow Boys" – Peter Howson, Adrian Wiszniewski, Ken Currie and Steven Campbell – are often included. Look out too for the kinetic sculpture *Titanic* by Russian émigré Eduard Bersudsky, made of scrap metal and old junk, but symbolizing freedom of movement and expression.

Glasgow's architecture

Founded on religion, built on trade and now well established as a cultural centre, Glasgow is known for its architectural riches, from its medieval cathedral to the modern glass-lined galleries of the Burrell Collection. Most dominant is the legacy of the **Victorian age**, when booming trade and industry allowed merchants to commission the finest architects of the day. The celebrated work of **Charles Rennie Mackintosh** (see box on p.906) took Glasgow's architecture to the forefront of early twentieth-century design, with a last flowering of homespun genius before economic conditions effectively stopped the architectural trade in its tracks, its revival only really taking hold in the 1980s and 1990s.

The city's expansion: 1750–1850

Glasgow's great expansion was initiated in the eighteenth century by wealthy tobacco merchants who built the grand edifices of public and municipal importance that still make up much of the **Merchant City**. One of the finest Merchant City views is down Garth Street, which frames the Venetian windows and Ionic columns of the **Trades Hall**, designed by Robert Adam in 1791, while nearby **Hutcheson Hall** boasts an elegant tower that moves from a square through octagonals to a drum – an early nineteenth-century architectural nod to the Renaissance by the architect David Hamilton.

Further west, **Royal Exchange Square** is one of the best examples of a typical Glasgow square: treeless, bare and centred around a building of importance, the 1829 **Royal Exchange**, now housing the Gallery of Modern Art. As workers piled into the centre of Glasgow in the early nineteenth century, filling up the already crowded tenements, wealthy residents began moving west to the gridded streets that line **Blythswood Hill** (mostly developed after 1820) with two- or three-storey terraces, their porches and heavy cornices providing textural relief to the endless sandstone monotony. The dignified proportions and design of **Blythswood Square** are a highlight of this area; at no. 5 the later Art Nouveau doorway designed by Charles Rennie Mackintosh sits incongruously amongst the Georgian solidity. Above all, the long streets provide a beautiful selection of open-ended views, one moment leading into the heart of the city, the next filled with distant hills and sky.

"Greek" Thomson and the Victorians

Long since overshadowed by Charles Rennie Mackintosh, the design of **Alexander "Greek" Thomson**, in the latter half of the nineteenth century, though well respected

Down in the basement there's an art library and café, while the smaller galleries on the two upper floors are either linked together for larger exhibitions or used to show smaller themed shows by contemporary artists from around the world.

Along Buchanan Street

Buchanan Street runs north–south one block west of George Square, defining Glasgow's main shopping district. At the southern end of the street is **Princes Square**, one of the most stylish and imaginative shopping centres in the country, hollowed out of the innards of a soft sandstone building. The interior, all recherché Art Deco and ornate ironwork, has lots of pricey, highly fashionable shops.

At 11 Mitchell Lane, an otherwise nondescript alleyway between Buchanan Street and Union Street, is **The Lighthouse** (Mon & Wed–Sat 10.30am–5pm, Tues 11am–5pm, Sun noon–5pm; £3; ⓦ www.thelighthouse.co.uk), a

in its time, has been sadly neglected. As his nickname suggests, his work took the principles of Greek architecture, but reprocessed them in a highly unique manner. Energetic and talented, he designed buildings from lowly tenements to grand suburban villas. The 1857 **St Vincent Street Church**, his best work, has a massive simplicity and serenity lightened by the use of exotic Egyptian and Hindu motifs, particularly in the tower with its decorated egg-shaped dome. Thomson's buildings are beginning to receive the recognition they deserve: most recently, the National Trust has opened his finest domestic dwelling, **Holmwood House**, on the Southside, to the public.

West from Park Circus lies **Glasgow University** (1866–86), its Gothic Revivalism – the work of Sir George Gilbert Scott – representing everything that Greek Thomson despised; he called it "sixteenth-century Scottish architecture clothed in fourteenth-century French details". Scottish features abound, such as crow-stepped gables, round turrets with conical caps and the top-heavy central tower. Inside, cloisters and quadrants sum up a suitably scholastic severity.

Originally conceived as a convenient way to house the influx of workers in the late 1800s, the Glasgow **tenement** design became more refined as the wealthy middle-classes began to realize its potential. Mainly constructed between 1860 and 1910, tenements have three to five storeys with two or three apartments per floor. Important rooms are picked out with bay windows, middle storeys are emphasized by architraves or decorated panels below sill or above lintel, and street junctions are given importance by swelling bay windows, turrets and domes. A fascinating example of the style of these buildings, as well as the typical life inside them, can be seen at the **Tenement House** (see p.904). Further grand tenement buildings can be found west of the university in the streets off **Byres Road**, in particular the Baronial red sandstone of Great George Street.

The present

The 1980s onwards have seen the return of the grand public building as inheritor of architectural innovation. Beginning with the imaginative **Burrell Collection**, the theme has been taken up by the titanium-clad behemoths of Clydeside: the unmistakeable Clyde Auditorium, better known as the "**Armadillo**", the curvaceous **Science Centre** and its new neighbour, the glass shoe-box of BBC Scotland's new HQ. This is not to ignore the poverty of artistry which went into great works such as the Kingston Bridge and Royal Concert Hall, but few could argue that Glasgow has failed to open itself to innovation and ideas.

spectacularly converted Charles Rennie Mackintosh building which has found new life as Scotland's Centre for Architecture, Design and the City. The 1895 building was Mackintosh's first public commission, and housed the offices of the *Glasgow Herald* newspaper; it mounts temporary exhibitions on design and architecture alongside the permanent **Mackintosh Interpretation Centre**, a great place to learn more about the man and his work.

The Merchant City

The grid of streets that lies immediately east of the City Chambers is known as the **Merchant City** (ⓦwww.glasgowmerchantcity.net), an area of eighteenth-century warehouses and homes which in the last two decades has been sandblasted and swabbed clean with greater enthusiasm and municipal money than any other part of Glasgow in an attempt to bring residents back into the city centre. The expected flood of yuppies, however, was more like a trickle, yet the expensive designer shops, style bars and bijou cafés continue to flock here, giving the area a pervasive air of sophistication and chic. A Merchant City Trail leaflet, which guides you around a dozen of the most interesting buildings in the area, is available at the tourist office.

The East End

East of Glasgow Cross, down Gallowgate beyond the train lines, lies the **East End**, the district that perhaps most closely corresponds to the old perception of Glasgow. Hemmed in by Glasgow Green to the south and the old university to the west, this densely packed industrial area essentially created the city's wealth. Today isolated pubs, tatty shops and cafés sit amidst this dereliction, in sharp contrast to the gloss of the Merchant City only a few blocks west. Walking around here you definitely get the sense that you're off the tourist trail, and there's no doubt that the area offers a rich flavour of working-class Glasgow, though unless you're here after dark it's not as threatening as it may feel.

Between London Road and the River Clyde are the wide and tree-lined spaces of **Glasgow Green**. Reputedly Britain's oldest public park, the Green has been common land since at least 1178, and has been a popular spot for Sunday-afternoon strolls for centuries. It's also home to the **People's Palace** (Mon–Thurs & Sat 10am–5pm, Fri & Sun 11am–5pm; free), a wonderfully haphazard evocation of the city's history. This squat, red-sandstone Victorian building was purpose-built as a museum back in 1898 – almost a century before the rest of the country caught on to the fashion for social-history collections. Many of the displays are designed to instill a warm glow in the memories of older locals: the museum is refreshingly unpretentious, with visitors almost always outnumbered by Glaswegian families.

Glasgow Cathedral and around

Built in 1136, destroyed in 1192 and rebuilt soon after, stumpy-spired **Glasgow Cathedral** (April–Sept Mon–Sat 9.30am–6pm, Sun 2–5pm; Oct–March Mon–Sat 9.30am–4pm, Sun 2–4pm; free; ⓦwww.glasgowcathedral.org.uk) was not completed until the late fifteenth century. Dedicated to the city's patron saint and reputed founder, St Mungo, the cathedral is effectively on two levels, the crypt being part of the lower church. On entering, you arrive in the impressively lofty nave of the **upper church**, with the lower church entirely hidden from view. Beyond the nave, the **choir** is hidden by the curtained stone pulpit, making the interior feel a great deal smaller than might be expected from outside. In the choir's northeastern corner, a small door leads into the gloomy **sacristy**, in which Glasgow University was first founded over five hundred years ago. Two sets of steps from the nave lead down into the **lower church**, where you'll find the dark and musty **chapel** surrounding the tomb of St Mungo. The saint's relics were removed in the late Middle Ages, although the tomb still forms the centrepiece. The chapel itself is one of the most glorious examples of medieval architecture in Scotland, best seen in the delicate fan vaulting rising up from the thicket of cool stone columns.

Cathedral Square

Opposite the cathedral on Cathedral Square, the **St Mungo Museum of Religious Life and Art** (Mon–Thurs & Sat 10am–5pm, Fri & Sun 11am–5pm; free), housed in a late twentieth-century pastiche of a Scots medieval townhouse, focuses on objects, beliefs and art from Christianity, Buddhism, Judaism, Islam, Hinduism and Sikhism. Outside is Britain's only permanent "dry stone" Zen Buddhist garden, with slabs of rock, white gravel and moss arranged to suggest the forms of land and sea.

The Necropolis

Rising up behind the Cathedral and inspired by the Père Lachaise cemetery in Paris, the atmospheric **Necropolis** is a grassy mound covered in a fantastic assortment of crumbling and tumbling gravestones, ornate urns, gloomy catacombs and Neoclassical temples. Various paths lead through the rows of eroding, neglected graves, and from the summit, next to the column topped with an indignant John Knox, there are superb **views** of the city and its trademark mix of grit and grace – the steaming chimneys of the Tennants brewery, the traffic on the M8 motorway, the crowded city-centre offices, the serene cathedral itself, and a wide cityscape of spires and high-rise blocks to the south and east. Free one-hour **tours** of the cemetery are run by Glasgow City Council (phone ☎0141/552 1142 for details).

Sauchiehall Street and around

Glasgow's most famous street, **Sauchiehall Street**, runs in a straight line west from the northern end of Buchanan Street, past some unexciting shopping malls to a few of the city's most interesting sights. Charles Rennie Mackintosh fans should head for the **Willow Tea Rooms** (Ⓦwww.willowtearooms .co.uk), above Henderson the Jeweller at 217 Sauchiehall St. This is a faithful reconstruction (opened in 1980 after more than fifty years of closure) on the site of the 1904 original, which was created for Kate Cranston, one of Rennie Mackintosh's few contemporary supporters in the city. Taking inspiration from the word *Sauchiehall*, which means "avenue of willow", he chose the willow leaf as a theme to unify the whole structure from the tables to the mirrors and the ironwork.

The Glasgow School of Art

Rising above Sauchiehall Street to the north is one of the city centre's steepest hills, with Dalhousie and Scott streets veering up to Renfrew Street, where you'll find Charles Rennie Mackintosh's **Glasgow School of Art** at no. 167 (guided tours April–Sept daily 10.30, 11am, 11.30am, 1.30pm, 2pm & 2.30pm; Oct–March Mon–Sat 11am & 2pm; booking advised; £6;

△ Glasgow School of Art

Ⓣ0141/353 4526, Ⓦwww.gsa.ac.uk). Widely considered to be the pinnacle of Mackintosh's work, the school is a characteristically angular building of warm sandstone which, due to financial constraints, had to be constructed in two sections (1897–99 and 1907–09). There's a clear change in the architect's style from the earlier severity of the mock-Baronial east wing to the softer lines of the western half.

The only way to see the school is to take one of the student-led **guided tours** (dependent on curricular activities), which show off key examples of Mackintosh's dynamic and inspired touch and a handful of the most impressive rooms. All over the school, from the roof to the stairwells, Mackintosh's unique touches recur – light Oriental reliefs, tall-backed chairs and stylized Celtic illuminations.

The Tenement House

Just a few hundred yards north of the School of Art – on the other side of a sheer hill – is the **Tenement House**, 145 Buccleuch St (March–Oct daily 1–5pm; £5; NTS). In a typical tenement block still lived in on most floors, the first floor holds the perfectly preserved home of Agnes Toward, who moved here with her mother in 1911, changing nothing and throwing very little out until she was hospitalized in 1965. The flat gives every impression of still being inhabited, with a cluttered hearth and range, kitchen utensils, recess beds, framed religious tracts and sewing machine all untouched. Tenement flats were home to the vast majority of Glaswegians for much of the twentieth century, and as such developed a culture and vocabulary all of their own: the "hurley", for example, was the bed on castors which was kept below the box bed in an alcove off the kitchen.

The West End

The urbane **West End** seems a world away from Glasgow's industrial image and the hustle and bustle of the city centre. In the 1800s, the city's wealthy merchants established huge estates away from the soot and grime of city life, and in 1870 the ancient university was moved from its cramped home near the cathedral to a spacious new site overlooking the River Kelvin. Elegant housing swiftly followed, the Kelvingrove Museum and Art Gallery was built to house the 1888 International Exhibition and, in 1896, the Glasgow District Subway – today's Underground – started its circuitous shuffle from here to the city centre.

The hub of life in this part of Glasgow is **Byres Road**, running between Great Western Road and Dumbarton Road past Hillhead underground station. Shops, restaurants, cafés, some enticing pubs and hordes of students give the area a sense of style and vitality. Glowing red-sandstone tenements and graceful terraces provide a suitably upmarket backdrop to this cosmopolitan district.

The main sights straddle the banks of the cleaned-up River Kelvin, which meanders through the gracious acres of the **Botanic Gardens** and the slopes, trees and statues of **Kelvingrove Park**. Overlooked by the Gothic towers and turrets of **Glasgow University**, Kelvingrove Park is home to the pride of Glasgow's civic collection of art and artefacts, **Kelvingrove Museum and Art Gallery**, off Argyle Street.

Kelvingrove Art Gallery and Museum

Founded on donations from the city's Victorian industrialists, the huge, red-sandstone fantasy castle of **Kelvingrove Museum and Art Gallery** is a brash statement of Glasgow's nineteenth-century self-confidence. Opened at an international fair held in 1901, Kelvingrove (as it's popularly known) is intricate and ambitious both in its riotous outside detailing and within, where a superb galleried main hall running the depth of the building gives way to attractive upper balconies and small, interlinked display galleries.

Following a massive, three-year refurbishment, the art gallery and museum is due to reopen in the summer of 2006. There's little doubt that Kelvingrove will very quickly re-establish itself as one of Glasgow's – and indeed Scotland's – most popular attractions. As with many of the city's collections of art and artefacts, the affection of, and use by, local residents is as important as tourist numbers.

Although the displays are set to include a World War II Spitfire suspended from the roof of the West Court, the most compelling aspect of the museum is likely to remain the paintings, which include Salvador Dalí's stunning *St John of the Cross*. The focus of huge controversy when it was purchased by the city in 1952 for what was regarded as the vast sum of £9200, it has returned to Kelvingrove following a prolonged period at the St Mungo Museum of Religious Life and Art. Other favourites include Rembrandt's calm *A Man in Armour*, Constable's *Hampstead Heath* and some notable paintings by Pissarro, Monet and Renoir. You can also acquaint yourself with significant Scottish art by Charles Rennie Mackintosh, the Glasgow Boys and the Scottish Colourists (see box, p.906).

The **opening hours** for the reopened museum and art gallery are likely to be similar to other Glasgow City Council Museums, namely Monday–Thursday and Saturday 10am–5pm, Friday and Sunday 11am–5pm, with free admission. Updates are available at ⓦwww.glasgowmuseums.com.

The work of the architect **Charles Rennie Mackintosh** (1868–1928) is synonymous with the image of Glasgow. Historians may disagree over whether his work was a forerunner of the Modernist movement or merely the sunset of Victorianism, but he undoubtedly created buildings of great beauty, idiosyncratically fusing Scots Baronial with Gothic, Art Nouveau and modern design. Though the bulk of his work was conceived at the turn of the twentieth century, since the postwar years Mackintosh's ideas have become particularly fashionable, giving rise to a certain amount of ersatz **"Mockintosh"** in his home city, with his distinctive lettering and small design features used time and again by shops, pubs and businesses. Fortunately, there are also plenty of examples of the genuine article, making the city something of a pilgrimage centre for art and design students from all over the world. A one-day **Mackintosh Trail Ticket** (£12) includes entry to twelve principal Mackintosh buildings as well as unlimited Underground and bus travel. They can be bought from the tourist office, from any of the attractions on the trail or from ⓦ www.crmsociety.com.

Although his family did little to encourage his artistic ambitions, as a young child Mackintosh began to cultivate his interest in drawing from nature during walks in the countryside, taken to improve his health. This talent was to flourish when he joined the Glasgow School of Art in 1884, whose vibrant new director, Francis Newberry, encouraged his pupils to create original and individual work. Here he met Herbert MacNair and the sisters Margaret and Frances MacDonald, whose work seemed to be sympathetic with his, fusing the organic forms of nature with a linear, symbolic Art Nouveau style. Nicknamed **"The Spook School"**, the four created a new artistic language, using extended vertical design, stylized abstract organic forms and muted colours, reflecting their interest in Japanese design and the work of Whistler and Beardsley. However, it was architecture that truly challenged Mackintosh, allowing him to use his creative artistic impulse in a three-dimensional and cohesive manner.

His big break came in 1896, when he won the competition to design a new home for the **Glasgow School of Art** (see p.903). This is his most famous work, but a number of smaller buildings created during his tenure with the architects Honeyman and Keppie, which began in 1889, document the development of his style. One of his earliest commissions was for a new building to house the *Glasgow Herald* on Mitchell Lane, off Argyle Street. A massive tower rises up from the corner, giving the building its popular name of **The Lighthouse**; it now houses the Mackintosh Interpretation Centre (see p.901).

In the 1890s Glasgow went wild for tearooms, where the middle classes could play billiards and chess, read in the library or merely chat. The imposing Miss Cranston, who dominated the Glasgow teashop scene and ran the most elegant establishments, gave Mackintosh great freedom of design, and in 1896 he started to plan the interiors for her growing business. Over the next twenty years he designed articles

Glasgow University and the Hunterian bequests

Dominating the West End skyline, the gloomy turreted tower of **Glasgow University** (ⓦ www.gla.ac.uk), designed by Sir George Gilbert Scott in the mid-nineteenth century, overlooks the glades edging the River Kelvin. In the dark neo-Gothic pile under the tower you'll find the **University Visitor Centre and Shop** (Mon–Sat 9.30am–5pm); from May to September **historical tours** of the campus are run from here (phone ☎0141/330 5511 for details).

from teaspoons to furniture and, finally, as in the case of the **Willow Tea Rooms** (see p.913), the structure itself.

Mackintosh designed few **religious buildings**: Queens Cross Church of 1896, at the junction of Garscube and Maryhill roads in the northwest of the city, is the only completed example standing. Hallmarks include a sturdy box-shaped tower and asymmetrical exterior with complex heart-shaped floral motifs in the large chancel window. To give height to the small and peaceful interior, Mackintosh used an open-arched timber ceiling, enhanced by carved detail and an oak pulpit decorated with tulip-form relief. It isn't the most unified of structures, but shows the flexibility of his distinctive style. It is now home to the **Charles Rennie Mackintosh Society** (Mon–Fri 10am–5pm; March–Oct also Sun 2–5pm; £2; ☏0141/946 6600, ⊕www.crmsociety.com).

The spectre of limited budgets was to haunt Mackintosh throughout his career, and he never had the chance to design and construct with complete freedom. However, these constraints didn't manage to dull his creativity, as demonstrated by the **Scotland Street School** of 1904, just south of the river opposite Shields Road underground station (Mon–Thurs & Sat 10am–5pm, Fri & Sun 11am–5pm; free). Here, the two main stairways that frame the entrance are lit by glass-filled bays that protrude from the building. It is his most symmetrical work, with a whimsical nod to history in the Scots Baronial conical tower roofs and sandstone building material. Mackintosh's forceful personality and originality did not endear him to construction workers: he would frequently change his mind or add details at the last minute, often overstretching budgets. This lost him the support of local builders and architects, despite his being admired on the continent, and prompted him to move to Suffolk in 1914 to escape the "philistines" of Glasgow and to re-evaluate his achievements. Indeed, the building which arguably displays Mackintosh at his most flamboyant was one he never saw built, the **House for an Art Lover** (April–Sept Mon–Wed 10am–4pm, Thurs–Sun 10am–1pm; Oct–March Sat & Sun 10am–1pm but closed occasionally for functions; £3.50; ☏0141/353 4770, ⊕www.houseforanartlover.co.uk), constructed in Bellahouston Park in 1996, 95 years after plans for it were submitted to a German architectural competition.

Having moved away from Glasgow, Mackintosh made use of his natural ability to draw flora and fauna, often in botanical detail and coloured with delicate watercolour washes. While living in 1923–27 in Port Vendres, on the Mediterranean coast of southwestern France, he produced a series of still lifes and landscape works which express something of his architectural style: houses and rocks are painted in precise detail with a massive solidity and geometric form, and bold colours unite the patterned texture of the landscape, within an eerie stillness unbroken by human activity. These are a final flowering of his creative talent, a delicate contrast to the massive legacy of stonework left behind in the city that he loved.

Beside the Visitor Centre is the **Hunterian Museum** (Mon–Sat 9.30am–5pm; free), Scotland's oldest public museum, dating back to 1807. The collection was donated to the university by ex-student William Hunter, a pathologist and anatomist whose eclectic tastes form the basis of a fairly diverting zoological and archeological jaunt.

Opposite, across University Avenue, is Hunter's more frequently visited bequest, the **Hunterian Art Gallery** (Mon–Sat 9.30am–5pm; free), best known for its wonderful works by James Abbott McNeill Whistler: only Washington, DC, has a larger collection. The gallery's other major collection is of nineteenth- and twentieth-century Scottish art, including the

In the 1870s a group of Glasgow-based painters formed a loose association that was to imbue Scottish art with a contemporary European flavour far ahead of the rest of Britain. Dominated by five men – Guthrie, Lavery, Henry, Hornel and Crawhall – "**The Glasgow Boys**" came from very different backgrounds, but all rejected the eighteenth-century conservatism which spawned little other than sentimental, anecdotal renditions of Scottish history peopled by "poor but happy" families. They dubbed these paintings "**gluepots**" for their use of megilp, an oily substance that gave the work the brown patina of age, and instead began to experiment with colour, liberally splashing paint across the canvas. The content and concerns of the paintings, often showing peasant life and work, were as offensive to the art establishment as their style: until then most of Glasgow's public art collections had been accrued by wealthy tobacco lords and merchants, who had a taste for Classical style and noble subjects.

Sir James Guthrie, taking inspiration from the *plein air* painting of the Impressionists, spent his summers in the countryside, observing and painting everyday life. Instead of happy peasants, his work shows individuals staring out of the canvas, detached and unrepentant, painted with rich tones but without undue attention to detail or the play of light. Typical of his finest work during the 1880s, *A Highland Funeral* was hugely influential for the rest of the group, who found inspiration in its restrained emotional content, colour and unaffected realism. Seeing it persuaded **Sir John Lavery**, then studying in France, to return to Glasgow. Lavery was eventually to become an internationally popular society portraitist, his subtle use of paint revealing his debt to Whistler, but his earlier work, depicting the middle class at play, is filled with fresh colour and figures in motion.

Rather than a realistic aesthetic, an interest in colour and decoration united the work of friends **George Henry** and **E.A. Hornel**. The predominance of colour, pattern and design in Henry's *Galloway Landscape*, for example, is remarkable, while their joint work *The Druids* (both part of the Kelvingrove collection; see p.905), in thickly applied impasto, is full of Celtic symbolism. In 1893 both artists set off for Japan, funded by Alexander Reid and later William Burrell, where their work used vibrant tone and texture for expressive effect and took Scottish painting to the forefront of European trends.

Newcastle-born **Joseph Crawhall** was a reserved and quiet individual who combined superb draughtsmanship and simplicity of line with a photographic memory to create watercolours of an outstanding naturalism and freshness. Again William Burrell was an important patron, and a number of Crawhall's works reside at the Burrell Collection (see p.911).

The Glasgow Boys school reached its height by 1900 and did not outlast World War I, but the influence of their work cannot be underestimated, shaking the foundations of the artistic elite and inspiring the next generation of Edinburgh painters, who became known as the "**Colourists**". Samuel John Peploe, John Duncan Fergusson, George Leslie Hunter and Francis Cadell shared an understanding that the manipulation of colour was the heart and soul of a good painting. All experienced and took inspiration from the avant-garde of late nineteenth-century Paris as well as the landscapes of southern France. **J.D. Fergusson**, in particular, immersed himself in the bohemian, progressive Parisian scene, rubbing shoulders with writers and artists including Picasso. Some of his most dynamic work, such as *Rhythm* (1911), displays elements of Cubism, yet is still clearly in touch with the Celtic imagery of Henry, Hornel and, indeed, Charles Rennie Mackintosh. The influence of post-Impressionists such as Matisse and Cézanne is obvious in the work of all four, with their seascapes, society portraits and still lifes bursting with fluidity, unconventionality and, above all, manipulation of colour and shape. The work of the Scottish Colourists has become highly fashionable and valuable over the last couple of decades, with galleries and civic collections throughout the country featuring their work prominently.

quasi-Impressionist Scottish landscapes of William McTaggart, a forerunner of the Glasgow Boys movement, itself represented here by Guthrie and Hornel. Taking the aims of this group one step further, the monumental dancing figures of J.D. Fergusson's *Les Eus* preside over a small collection of work by the Scottish Colourists, including Peploe, Hunter and Cadell. A small selection of French Impressionism includes works by Boudin and Pissarro, with Corot's soothing *Distant View of Corbeil* being a highlight from the Barbizon school.

A side gallery leads to the **Mackintosh House** (£2.50, free after 2pm Wed), a re-creation of the interior of the now-demolished Glasgow home of Margaret MacDonald and Charles Rennie Mackintosh. Its exquisitely cool interior contains over sixty pieces of Mackintosh furniture on three floors. In addition, a permanent Mackintosh exhibition gallery shows a selection of his two-dimensional work, from watercolours to architectural drawings.

The Botanic Gardens

At the northern, top end of Byres Road, where it meets the Great Western Road, is the main entrance to the **Botanic Gardens** (daily 7am–dusk; free). The best-known glasshouse here, the hulking, domed **Kibble Palace** (closed for refurbishment until 2006), houses a damp, musty collection of swaying palms from around the world. Nearby, the **Main Range Glasshouse** is home to lurid flowers and plants luxuriating in the humidity, including stunning orchids, cacti, ferns and tropical fruit. Between the two in the old curator's house is a small **visitor centre** (daily 11am–4pm; free), with art exhibitions and computer games aimed at younger visitors.

In addition to the area around the main glasshouses, there are some beautifully remote paths in the gardens that weave along the closely wooded banks of the deep-set River Kelvin, linking up with the walkway which runs alongside the river all the way down to Dumbarton Road, near its confluence with the Clyde.

Clydeside

"The **Clyde** made Glasgow and Glasgow made the Clyde" runs an old saying, full of sentimentality for the days when the river was the world's premier shipbuilding centre, and when its industry lent an innovation and confidence which made Glasgow the second city of the British Empire. Despite the hardships heavy industry brought, every Glaswegian would follow the progress of the skeleton ships under construction in the riverside yards, cheering them on their way down the Clyde as they were launched. The last

---

The Waverley

One of Glasgow's best-loved treasures is the **Waverley**, the last seagoing paddle steamer in the world, which spends the summer cruising "doon the watter" to various ports on the Firth of Clyde and the Ayrshire coast from its base at Anderson Quay between Finnieston and the Kingston Bridge. Built on Clydeside as recently as 1947, she's an elegant vessel to look at, not least when she's thrashing away at full steam with the hills of Argyll or Arran in the background. Contact ☎0845/130 4647 or ⊛www.waverleyexcursions.co.uk for sailing times and itinerary.

of the great liners to be built on **Clydeside** was the *QE2* in 1967, yet such events are hard to visualize today, with the banks of the river all but devoid of any industry: shipbuilding is now restricted to a couple of barely viable yards, as derelict warehouses, crumbling docks and overgrown wastelands crowd the river's flanks.

Glasgow is often accused of failing to capitalize on its river, and it's only in the last few years, with a flurry of construction, that it's once again becoming a focus of attention. Striking riverside buildings including the titanium-clad **Armadillo** concert hall and **Glasgow Science Centre** have become icons of the city's forward-thinking image.

The Glasgow Science Centre

On the south bank of the river, linked to the SECC by pedestrian Bell's Bridge, are the three space-age, titanium-clad constructions which make up the **Glasgow Science Centre** (Science Mall or IMAX £6.95, both £9.95; Ⓦ www.gsc.org.uk). Of the three buildings, the largest is the curvaceous, wedge-shaped **Science Mall** (daily 10am–6pm). Behind the vast glass wall which faces the river are four floors of interactive exhibits ranging from lift-your-own-weight pulleys to high-tech thermograms. The centre covers almost every aspect of science, from simple optical illusions to cutting-edge computer technology, including a section on moral and environmental issues – lots of good fun, although weekends and school holidays are busy and noisy.

Alongside the Science Mall is the bubble-like **IMAX theatre**, which shows a range of mostly science- and nature-based documentaries on its giant screen. Also on the site is the 127-metre **Glasgow Tower**, built with an aerofoil-like construction to allow it to rotate to face into the prevailing wind. Glass lifts ascend to the viewing cabin at the top, offering suitably panoramic views, but it has been dogged with technical difficulties since it opened, preventing visitor access on a reliable schedule.

The Southside

The section of Glasgow south of the Clyde is generally described as the **Southside**, though within this area there are a number of districts with recognizable names, including the notoriously deprived Gorbals and Govan, which are sprinkled with new developments but still derelict and tatty in many parts. There's little reason to venture here unless you're making your way to the Science Centre (see above), or the famously innovative Citizens' Theatre (see p.917). Further south, inner-city decay fades into altogether gentler and more salubrious suburbs, including Queen's Park, home to Scotland's national football stadium, **Hampden Park**, Pollokshaws and the rural landscape of Pollok Park, which contains one of Glasgow's major museums, the **Burrell Collection**.

Southside attractions are fairly widely spread. A **train** from Central station is best for Hampden Park (Mount Florida station), and for Pollok Park either take the train to Pollokshaws West station (not to be confused with Pollokshields West), or **bus** #45, #47 or #57 to Pollokshaws Road, or a **taxi** (£8-10 from the centre). From the park gates a **free minibus** runs every half-hour between 10am and 4.30pm to the Burrell Collection.

Hampden Park and the Scottish Football Museum

Two and a half miles due south of the city centre, just to the west of the tree-filled Queen's Park, the floodlights and giant stands of Scotland's national football stadium, **Hampden Park**, loom over the surrounding suburban tenements and terraces. It's home to the engaging **Scottish Football Museum** (Mon–Sat 10am–5pm, Sun 11am–5pm; £5), with extensive collections of memorabilia, video clips and displays covering almost every aspect of the game. On view is the Scottish Cup, the world's oldest football trophy and a re-creation of the old changing room at Hampden, as well as a bizarre life-sized reconstruction of the most famous goal in Scottish footballing history, scored during the 1978 World Cup in Argentina.

The Burrell Collection

Located in Pollok Park some six miles southwest of the city centre, the outstanding **Burrell Collection** (Mon–Thurs & Sat 10am–5pm, Fri & Sun 11am–5pm; free), the lifetime collection of shipping magnate Sir William Burrell (1861–1958), is, for some, the principal reason for visiting Glasgow.

Football in Glasgow

Football, or *fitba'* as it's pronounced locally, is one of Glasgow's great passions – and one of its great blights. While the city can claim to be one of Europe's premier footballing centres, it's known above all for one of the most bitter rivalries in any sport, that between **Celtic** and **Rangers**. Two of the largest clubs in Britain, with weekly crowds regularly topping 60,000, the Old Firm, as they're collectively known, have dominated Scottish football for a century, most notably in the last fifteen years as they have lavished vast sums of money on foreign talent in an often frantic effort both to outdo each other and to stay in touch with the standards of the top English and European teams.

The roots of Celtic, who play at Celtic Park in the eastern district of Parkhead (☎0141/551 8653, ⓦwww.celticfc.co.uk), lie in the city's immigrant Irish and **Catholic** population, while Rangers, based at Ibrox Park in Govan on the Southside (☎0870/600 1993, ⓦwww.rangers.co.uk), have traditionally drawn support from local **Protestants**. As a result, sporting rivalries have been enmeshed in a sectarian divide which many argue would not have remained so long, nor so deep, had it been divorced from the footballing scene. Although Catholics do play for Rangers, and Protestants for Celtic, sections of supporters of both clubs seem intent on perpetuating the feud. While large-scale violence on the terraces and streets has not been seen for some time – thanks in large measure to canny policing – Old Firm matches often seethe with bitter passions, and sectarian-related assaults do still occur in parts of the city.

However, there is a less intense side to the game, found not just in the fun-loving "Tartan Army" which follows the (often rollercoaster) fortunes of the Scottish national team, but also in Glasgow's smaller clubs, who actively distance themselves from the distasteful aspects of the Old Firm and plod along with homegrown talent in the lower reaches of the Scottish league. **Queen's Park**, residents of Hampden (☎0141/632 1275, ⓦwww.queensparkfc.co.uk), **St Mirren**, the Paisley team (☎0141/889 2558, ⓦwww.stmirrenfc.co.uk), and the much-maligned **Partick Thistle**, who play at Firhill Stadium in the West End (☎0141/579 1971, ⓦwww.ptfc.co.uk), offer the best chances of experiencing the more down-to-earth side of Glaswegian football – along with all-important reminders that it is, in the end, only a game.

Unlike many other art collectors, Sir William's only real criterion for buying a piece was whether he liked it or not, enabling him to buy many "unfashionable" works, which cost comparatively little but subsequently proved their worth.

The simplicity and clean lines of the Burrell building are its greatest assets, with large picture windows giving sweeping views over woodland and serving as a tranquil backdrop to the objects inside. An airy covered **courtyard** includes the **Warwick Vase**, a huge bowl containing fragments of a second-century AD vase from Emperor Hadrian's villa in Tivoli. On three sides of the courtyard, a trio of dark and sombre panelled rooms have been re-erected in faithful detail from the Burrells' Hutton Castle home, their heavy tapestries, antique furniture and fireplaces displaying the same eclectic taste as the rest of the museum.

Elsewhere on the ground floor are Greek, Roman and earlier artefacts, including an exquisite mosaic Roman cockerel from the first century BC and a 4000-year-old Mesopotamian lion's head. Nearby, also illuminated by enormous windows, the **Oriental Art** collection forms nearly a quarter of the whole display, ranging from Neolithic jades through bronze vessels and Tang funerary horses to cloisonné. Burrell considered his **medieval and post–medieval European art**, which encompasses silverware, glass, textiles and sculpture, to be the most valuable part of his collection: these are ranged across a maze of small galleries.

Upstairs, the cramped and comparatively gloomy **mezzanine** is probably the least satisfactory section of the gallery, not the best setting for its sparkling array of paintings by the likes of Degas, Pissarro, Manet, Cézanne and Boudin.

Eating

Glaswegians have always enjoyed socializing, and while this has traditionally implied an evening of drinking and dancing, dining out now fits comfortably into the social agenda. **Contemporary Scottish** cuisine featuring fresh West-Coast seafood or locally reared meat, often cooked with French and other international influences, is a particular strength in Glasgow, and in recent years the positive attitude to Scottish, seasonal and wholesome food has filtered down to more affordable bistros, diners and cafés. The sheer number of **Italian** eating options betrays the continuing popularity of the pizza–pasta option, though among imported cuisine it's **Indian** food which is most commonly associated with Glasgow, long established as one of Britain's curry capitals.

City centre and the Merchant City

All the cafés and restaurants in this section are marked on the Glasgow City Centre map on p.897, unless otherwise stated.

Cafés, diners and café-bars

Café Gandolfi and Bar Gandolfi 64 Albion St ☎0141/552 6813, ⌨www.cafegandolfi.com. This bona fide landmark was one of the first to test the waters in the Merchant City. Designed with distinctive wooden furniture that its creator, the late Tim Stead, called "sculpture in disguise", *Gandolfi* serves up Scottish staples (including great black pudding), soups, salads, fish dishes and Continental cuisine. The bar upstairs is more contemporary but the food's still good. Moderate.

Café Ostra 15 John St ☎0141/552 4433, ⌨www.cafeostra.com. More casual sister to *Gamba* (see p.913), this seafood café is not the cheapest option on this list, but it serves good fresh food right through the day, has excellent wines, and the added lure of outdoors seating. Moderate.

Café Source 1 St Andrews Square ☎0141/548 6020, ⌨www.cafesource.co.uk. In the basement of an eighteenth-century church, this café serves up Scottish favourites with mostly local produce. The church is a folk music and Scottish dance centre, and the café has frequent live jam sessions. Inexpensive.

Tron Theatre Chisholm Street off the Trongate ☎0141/552 8587, ⓦwww.tron.co.uk. Arty hangout (see p.917) for writers and theatrical types, with a contemporary street-side café bar and a Victorian pub/restaurant inside. Moderate.

Where the Monkey Sleeps 182 West Regent St ☎0141/226 3406, ⓦwww.wherethemonkey sleeps.com. Owned by gregarious art-school graduates who acquired their barista skills between classes, this hip home-grown café doubles as a gallery. Food options focus on soups and sandwiches and the espresso is superb. Usually closes at 7pm. Inexpensive.

Willow Tea Rooms 217 Sauchiehall St ☎0141/332 0521, ⓦwww.willowtearooms .co.uk. An authentic landmark on the Charles Rennie Mackintosh trail, the first-floor dining room here offers tea with scones and midday meals. A similarly themed branch is at 97 Buchanan St (☎0141/204 5242). Closes before 5pm. Moderate.

Restaurants

Brian Maule at Le Chardon d'Or 176 West Regent St ☎0141/248 3801, ⓦwww.lechardon dor.com. Owner/chef Maule once worked with the Roux brothers at London's *Le Gavroche*. Fancy but not pretentious French-influenced food. Closed Sun (& Mon bank holidays). Expensive.

The Buttery 652 Argyle St ☎0141/221 8188; see map on p.894. Located near the shadow of the M8 flyover, this atmospheric, Victorian-era fine-dining restaurant offers complex but deftly handled Scottish dishes. Book ahead. Closed Sun & Mon. Expensive.

City Merchant 97 Candleriggs ☎0141/553 1577, ⓦwww.citymerchant.co.uk. Popular brasserie that blazed the Merchant City trail that plenty of others have followed. Fresh Scottish produce from Ayrshire lamb to the house speciality, West-Coast seafood. Closed Sun. Expensive.

The Dhabba 44 Candleriggs ☎0141/553 1249, ⓦwww.thedhabba.com. This is not your typical Glasgow curry house: prices are higher, and portions are smaller but the menu has some truly interesting options and fresh ingredients which put it a few steps above others. Moderate–expensive.

Dragon-i 311–313 Hope St ☎0141/332 7728, ⓦwww.dragon-i.co.uk. Intriguing mix of Chinese and Far East influences in the dishes at this restaurant across from the Theatre Royal; good pre-theatre menu. Moderate.

Fratelli Sarti 133 Wellington St or 121 Bath St ☎0141/204 0440, ⓦwww.fratellisarti.com. The Sarti brothers' flagship Italian café and restaurant: authentic and popular. The formal dining space is accessed from the Bath Street entrance; the more atmospheric café round the corner opens in the mornings Mon–Sat. Moderate.

 Gamba 225a West George St ☎0141/572 0899, ⓦwww.gamba.co.uk. This modern basement restaurant offers probably the best meal in Glasgow. Continental contemporary sophistication prevails, with dishes such as sashimi of fresh fish or roast halibut served with lobster. If you love fish, come here. Closed Sun. Expensive.

Ichiban Japanese Noodle Café 50 Queen St ☎0141/204 4200, ⓦwww.ichiban.co.uk. Japanese-style informal eating, with long benches and tables shared by diners. Bowls (or plates) of noodles and sushi are specialities here; service is efficient. There's a second branch at 184 Dumbarton Rd, in the West End (☎0141/334 9222). Inexpensive.

Mao 84 Brunswick St ☎0141/564 5161, ⓦwww .cafemao.com. Bright café-bar in the Merchant City serving a range of Asian cuisine, including spicy Korean and Indonesian dishes. Moderate.

Mono 12 King's Court ☎0141/553 2400, ⓦwww .gomono.com. This places combines a fully vegan restaurant, Fairtrade food shop, bar and indie CD shop. Lots of space and home-made organic drinks. Inexpensive.

Oko 68 Ingram St ☎0141/572 1500, ⓦwww .okorestaurants.com. Locally owned restaurant bringing freshly prepared sushi on colour-coded plates and a *Yo!Sushi*-style conveyor belt to the Merchant City. Not open for lunch Sun & Mon. Moderate.

Rogano 11 Exchange Place ☎0141/248 4055, ⓦwww.rogano.co.uk. An Art Deco fish restaurant and Glasgow institution, decked out in 1935 in the style of the *Queen Mary* ocean liner. *Café Rogano*, in the basement, is cheaper, or just have some oysters at the bar. Expensive.

Smith's of Glasgow 109 Candleriggs ☎0141/552 6539. Owner/chef Michael Smith re-creates Parisian brasserie style in the Merchant City, with seasonally changing menus and complimentary apéritifs. Closed Sun. Moderate.

The 13th Note Café 50–60 King St ☎0141/553 1638, ⓦwww.13thnote.co.uk. Vegetarian and vegan fare with Greek and other Mediterranean influences in one of Glasgow's hipper drinking and indie/experimental music haunts on arty King Street. Inexpensive.

Wee Curry Shop 7 Buccleuch St ☎0141/353 0777. Tiny place near the Glasgow Film Theatre and Sauchiehall Street shops, serving homemade Indian bargain meals to compete with the best in town. BYOB. Closed Sun. Inexpensive.

West End

All the cafés and restaurants in this section are marked on the Glasgow map on p.894–895.

Cafés, diners and café-bars

Kember & Jones 134 Byres Rd ℡0141/337 3851, ⓦwww.kemberandjones.co.uk. Opened in 2004, this café and deli quickly became a popular spot in an already competitive market. No hot food, but good freshly made salads and sandwiches using ingredients sold at the deli counter. Inexpensive.

Monster Mash 41 Byres Rd ℡0141/339 3666, ⓦwww.monstermashcafe.co.uk. Fancy some classic bangers and mash? This is the place for you, with a range of top-quality sausages (including meat-free options) and selection of mash potatoes, plus hearty portions of chicken pie or macaroni cheese. Inexpensive.

Stravaigin 2 8 Ruthven Lane ℡0141/334 7165, ⓦwww.stravaigin.com. A popular diner/bistro that serves excellent burgers alongside an innovative menu similar to the award-wining modern Scottish *Stravaigin* restaurant (see below). Moderate.

Tchai Ovna 42 Otago Lane ℡0141/357 4524, ⓦwww.tchaiovna.com. A low-key bohemian hangout near the Kelvin River with cakes, snacks and a selection of teas from around the world. Tobacco is forbidden but the house water-pipe with dried fruit serves as a substitute. Inexpensive.

Tinderbox 189 Byres Rd ℡0141/339 3108. A modern espresso café-bar offering an array of lattes, cappuccinos and the like as well as designer looks. Even in trendy Glasgow, it remains amazingly successful. Inexpensive.

University Café 87 Byres Rd ℡0141/339 5217. A bona fide institution adored by at least three generations of students and West End residents. Formica tables in snug booths, glass counters and original Art Deco features, where the favourites are fish'n'chips or mince'n'tatties rounded off with an ice-cream cone. Sometimes closes in afternoon. Inexpensive.

West End restaurants

Ashoka Ashton Lane 19 Ashton Lane ℡0141/337 1115, ⓦwww.harlequingroup.net. Lively curry house in the Harlequin chain which has franchises across the west of Scotland; all have consistent quality. Other *Ashoka* restaurants are at 1284 Argyle St (℡0141/339 3371), and on the Southside at 268 Clarkston Rd (℡0141/637 0711). Moderate.

Café Antipasti 337 Byres Rd ℡0141/337 2737. A busy Italian bistro serving tasty and well-priced pastas and salads. No bookings are taken, so expect a queue on busy nights. Second outlet in town at 305 Sauchiehall St (℡0141/332 9002). Inexpensive.

Chow 98 Byres Rd ℡0141/334 9818. Proof that Chinese restaurants can be modern and non-kitsch. This bijou diner with extra tables upstairs offers excellent value-for-money meals. Moderate. A second outlet trades at 52 Bank St (℡0141/357 6682).

Grassroots Café 93 St Georges Rd ℡0141/333 0534, ⓦwww.grassroots.co.uk. Although the competition is not especially stiff, this vegetarian outlet (just cross the M8 motorway from the city centre) has the best reputation for meat-free fare in Glasgow. Fresh, creative cooking and a relaxed atmosphere. Inexpensive–moderate.

Kokuryo 1138 Argyle St ℡0141/334 5566. Opened in late 2004, a Korean restaurant in a tiny space but with lots of big flavours on your plate, whether spiced *kimchi* or sizzling pork and beef. Inexpensive–moderate.

Mother India 28 Westminster Terrace, off Sauchiehall Street ℡0141/221 1663. This is one of the best Indian restaurants in Glasgow. Home cooking with some original specials as well as the old favourites at affordable prices in laid-back surroundings. Moderate. Also worth trying if you're on a budget is the nearby spin-off: *Mother India's Café* at 1355 Argyle St (℡0141/339 9145). Inexpensive.

No. Sixteen 16 Byres Rd ℡0141/339 2544. A local favourite, with daily menus of Scottish produce, from pigeon to fillet of sea bream. Moderate.

Stravaigin 28–30 Gibson St ℡0141/334 2665, ⓦwww.stravaigin.com. Scottish meat and fish are given an international make-over using a host of unexpected ingredients, offering unusual flavour combinations. Adventurous fine-dining in the basement restaurant and an exceptional-value menu in the street-level bar-café. Restaurant closed Mon. Moderate upstairs, expensive downstairs.

Two Fat Ladies 88 Dumbarton Rd ☎0141/339 1944. Perhaps the second-best fish restaurant in Glasgow, after *Gamba* (see p.913). Intimate space with the kitchen right up front. Moderate–expensive. A new outlet has recently opened at 118a Blythswood St (☎0141/847 0088) in the city centre.

The Ubiquitous Chip 12 Ashton Lane ☎0141/334 5007, ⊛www.ubiquitouschip.co.uk. Opened in 1971, *The Chip* led the way in headlining Scotland's quality fresh produce at the heart of a contemporary, upmarket dining experience. Some say it's living on its reputation, but it's still up there. Expensive but less pricey options upstairs in the bistro.

Southside

Cafés, diners and café-bars

1901 1534 Pollokshaws Rd ☎0141/632 0161. Once known as the *Stoat & Ferret*, this French-influenced bistro/pub near Pollok Country Park is a lesser-known gem serving hearty Mediterranean food. Moderate.

Koshkemeer 271 Pollokshaws Dr ☎0141/423 9494. New in 2004, this welcoming and unpretentious place offers Kurdish cuisine – the only we know of in Scotland. Especially good is the mixed grill and the flat breads served with most every meal. Unlicensed, but okay to BYOB. Inexpensive.

Restaurants

Art Lovers' Café In House for an Art Lover (see p.907), Bellahouston Park, 10 Dumbreck Rd

☎0141/353 4779. The dining room, looking onto a charming garden in this showcase house based on unfinished Mackintosh designs, offers sublime Scottish cooking at lunch. Closed evenings. Moderate.

La Fiorentina 2 Paisley Rd West ☎0141/420 1585, ⊛www.la-fiorentina.com; see map on p.894. A critical favourite that also tops popular surveys, this Tuscan-oriented restaurant has become an institution. Not far from the Glasgow Science Centre in Govan. Moderate.

Mitchell's 107 Waterside Rd, Carmunock ☎0141/644 2255. This restaurant began near the Mitchell library in the city centre, but now runs on the southern, nearly rural, city fringes, serving good-value Scottish and Continental cooking. Closed Mon & Tues. Moderate–expensive.

Drinking

Glasgow's mythical tough-guy image has been linked with its **pubs**, mistakenly believed by a few to be no-go areas for visitors. Today, however, the city is much changed and many of the once windowless, nicotine-stained working-men's taverns have been converted into airy modern bars. Most drinking dens in the **city centre**, the adjoining **Merchant City** and the fashionable **West End** are places to experience real Glaswegian bonhomie.

As for **opening hours**, from Sunday to Thursday, many pubs and bars will serve until midnight, although some outside the centre close at 11pm during the week. On Friday and Saturday, you'll often find bars open until 1am – and occasionally later. After closing time, your option is to head to a nightclub (see p.917), some of which don't close until 5am.

Pubs and bars

City centre and Merchant City

All the pubs and bars in this section are marked on the Glasgow City Centre map on p.897.

The Arches 253 Argyle St. The basement bar is a focal point in this contemporary arts centre under Central station. Decent pub grub and an arty clientele.

Babbity Bowster 16–18 Blackfriars St, off the High Street. Lively place with an unforced and kitsch-free Scottish feel that features spontaneous folk sessions at the weekend. Good beer and wine, tasty food and some outdoor seating.

Bar 10 10 Mitchell St. Across from the Lighthouse architecture centre, and considered the granddaddy of Glasgow style bars. Still popular and suitably chic.

Blackfriars 36 Bell St. Excellent beer selection (both imported and hand-pulled UK ales) in suitably worn environment. There are often jazz or comedy performances in the basement space.

Corinthian 191 Ingram St. A remarkable renovation of a florid, early Victorian Italianate bank. Three distinct bars, one restaurant and a private club: dress smartly.

Horseshoe Bar 17 Drury St. A must for pub aficionados. An original "Gin Palace" with the longest continuous bar in the UK, this is reputedly Glasgow's busiest drinking hole; karaoke upstairs.

Pot Still 154 Hope St. Whisky galore! At least 500 different single malts are found in this traditional pub, which has a decent ale selection as well.

Republic Bier Halle 9 Gordon St. Chunky modern industrial design using shuttered concrete and blocks of stone in subterranean setting. Serves 130 different beers.

West End

All the pubs and bars in this section are marked on the Glasgow map on p.894–895.

Firebird 1321 Argyle St. Airy modern drinking spot near the Kelvingrove Art Gallery, with a wood-stoked pizza oven producing some tasty snacks, plus DJs to keep the pre-clubbing crowd entertained.

The Goat 1287 Argyle St. Occupying a large corner location, this two-floor pub has modern sensibilities

and is geared to a slightly more grown-up bunch of West End cool cats.

Lismore Lounge 206 Dumbarton Rd. Decorated with specially commissioned stained-glass panels depicting the Highland Clearances, this bar is a meeting point for the local Gaels, who come here to chat, relax and listen to the impromptu music sessions.

Oran Mor Byres Road at corner of Great Western Road ☎0141/357 6200. Arguably the most impressive addition in many years to Glasgow's nightlife scene, with a big bar, club venue and performance space/auditorium (plus two different dining rooms) all within a tastefully – and expensively – restored Kelvinside parish church.

Southside

Heraghty's Free House 708 Pollokshaws Rd. Authentic Irish pub that prides itself on pouring the perfect pint of Guinness. Still living down its history of not having a women's loo: one's been installed for several years now.

The Taverna 778 Pollokshaws Rd. A favourite of many who stay in this neck of the Southside, in a bright, light corner location with potted palms and a selection of real ales.

Tusk 18 Moss Side Rd. Operated by the company behind the *Corinthian* (see above), *Tusk* is almost as flamboyant, with a giant Buddha as its focal point.

(19)

Nightlife and entertainment

Glasgow offers a thriving **contemporary music** scene, with loads of new bands emerging every year, Franz Ferdinand being the best-known recently. There's a clutch of venues, from the famous *Barrowlands* to *King Tut's Wah Wah Hut*, where you've a good chance of catching a live act, while the city's **clubbing scene** has long been rated among the best in the UK. Opening hours hover between 11pm to 3am, though some stay open until 5am. Cover charges are variable: expect to pay around £5 during the week and up to £20 at the weekend. Drinks are usually about thirty percent more expensive than in the pubs.

On the **performing arts** scene, Glasgow is no slouch either: it's home to Scottish Opera, Scottish Ballet and the Royal Scottish National Orchestra. Most of the larger theatres, cinema multiplexes and concert halls are in the city centre; the West End is home to just one or two venues while the Southside can boast two theatres noted for cutting-edge drama, the Citizens' and Tramway.

For detailed **listings** on what's on, pick up the comprehensive fortnightly magazine *The List* (£2.20), which also covers Edinburgh, or consult Glasgow's *Herald* or *Evening Times* newspapers.

Clubs

The Arches 30 Midland St, off Jamaica Steet ☎0141/221 4001, ⓦwww.thearches.co.uk. In converted railway arches under Central station, the club portion of this arts venue offers an eclectic array of music: hard house, trance, techno and funk.

Fury Murry's 96 Maxwell St, behind the St Enoch Centre ☎0141/221 6511, ⓦwww.furyslive.co.uk. Student-oriented and lively, with music spanning the 1960s to recent indie and chart favourites.

Sub Club 22 Jamaica St ☎0141/248 4600, ⓦwww.subclub.co.uk. Near legendary venue and base to the noteworthy *Subculture* and *Optimo* clubs, the home of house and techno in Scotland.

The Tunnel 84 Mitchell St ☎0141/204 1000. Contemporary and progressive house music club with arty decor (dig the gents' cascading waterfall walls) and fairly strict dress codes.

Gay clubs and bars

Bennett's 90 Glassford St, Merchant City ☎0141/552 5761. Glasgow's longest-running gay club (recently reopened after a fire): predominantly male, fairly traditional and with commercially oriented music.

Delmonica's 68 Virginia St ☎0141/552 4803. One of Glasgow's liveliest gay bars, in a popular area, with a mixed, hedonistic crowd and some kind of entertainment or event nightly.

LGBT Centre 11 Dixon St ☎0141/221 7203, ⓦwww.glgbt.org.uk. Licensed café in addition to more institutional support such as information and reading rooms.

Polo Lounge 84 Wilson St, off Glassford Street ☎0141/553 1221. Original Victorian decor – marble tiles and open fires – and gentleman's-club atmosphere upstairs, with dark, pounding nightclub underneath; attracts a gay and gay-friendly crowd.

Revolver 6a John St ☎0141/553 2456. Geared more towards the art of conversation than dance, although the jukebox is tops; welcomes men and women.

Live-music venues

Barrowland 244 Gallowgate ☎0141/552 4601, ⓦwww.glasgow-barrowland.com. Legendary East-End ballroom that hosts some of the sweatiest and best gigs you may ever encounter. With room for a couple of thousand, it mostly books bands securely on the rise but still hosts some big-time acts who return to it as their favourite venue in Scotland.

Carling Academy 121 Eglington St ☎0870/771 2000, ⓦwww.glasgow-academy.co.uk. Owned by the same people behind London's *Brixton Academy*, this renovated theatre south of the River Clyde has stolen a bit of the *Barrowland*'s thunder since opening in 2002.

King Tut's Wah Wah Hut 272a St Vincent St ☎0141/221 5279, ⓦwww.kingtuts.co.uk. Famous as the place where Oasis were discovered, and still presenting one of the city's best live-music programmes. Also has a good bar, with an excellent jukebox.

Theatres and comedy venues

Arches Theatre 253 Argyle St ☎0141/565 1023, ⓦwww.thearches.co.uk. Hip subterranean venue with its own avant-garde theatre company, that revives old classics and introduces new talent.

Citizens' Theatre 119 Gorbals St ☎0141/429 0022, ⓦwww.citz.co.uk. The "Citz" has evolved from its 1960s working-class roots into one of Britain's most respected and innovative contemporary theatres. Three stages, concession rates for students and free preview nights.

King's Theatre 297 Bath St ☎0141/240 1111, ⓦwww.kings-glasgow.co.uk. Gorgeous interiors within an imposing red-sandstone Victorian building; the programme is good quality, if mainstream.

The Stand 333 Woodlands Rd ☎0870/600 6055, ⓦwww.thestand.co.uk. Sister to the first-rate comedy club in Edinburgh, booking local, national and international acts.

Theatre Royal 282 Hope St ☎0141/332 9000, ⓦwww.theatreroyalglasgow.com. This late nineteenth-century playhouse was revived in the mid-1970s as the opulent home of Scottish Opera, whose recent productions include an acclaimed *Ring* cycle. It also plays regular host to visiting theatre groups, including the Royal Shakespeare Company, as well as orchestras

Tramway 25 Albert Drive, off Pollokshaws Road ☎0141/330 3501, ⓦwww.tramway.org. Based in a converted tram terminus, whose lofty proportions qualified it as the only suitable UK venue for Peter Brooks' famous production of the *Mahabharata* in 1998. Premier avant-garde venue for experimental theatre, dance and music, as well as art exhibitions.

Tron Theatre 63 Trongate ☎0141/552 4267, ⓦwww.tron.co.uk. Varied repertoire of some mainstream and, more importantly, challenging productions from itinerant companies, such as Glasgow's Vanishing Point. Folk music performances in theatre bar.

Concert halls

Glasgow Royal Concert Hall 2 Sauchiehall St ☎0141/353 8000, ⓦwww.grch.com. One of Glasgow's less memorable modern buildings, this is the venue for big-name touring orchestras and the home of the Royal Scottish National Orchestra. Also features major rock and R & B stars, and middle-of-the-road music-hall acts.

Scottish Exhibition and Conference Centre, and Clyde Auditorium Finnieston Quay ☎ 0870/040 4000, ⓦ www.secc.co.uk. The SECC is a gigantic airplane-hangar-like space with dreadful acoustics that, unfortunately, is Scotland's only indoor venue for world-touring megastars from Bob Dylan to 50 Cent. The adjacent Clyde Auditorium – better known as the Armadillo – is smaller but more melodic.

Cinemas

Cineworld 7 Renfrew St ☎ 0870/907 0789.

Formerly the UGC, this gigantic multistorey cinema shows first-run Hollywood and a few art films.
Glasgow Film Theatre 12 Rose St ☎ 0141/332 8128, ⓦ www.gft.org.uk. Dedicated art, independent and repertory cinema house. Its in-house *Café Cosmo* is an excellent place for pre-show drinks.
Odeon City Centre 56 Renfield St ☎ 0871/224 4007, ⓦ www.odeon.co.uk. Multiscreen cinema showing the latest releases. Another Odeon complex is across the river at Springfield Quay, Paisley Road.
Grosvenor Ashton Lane ☎ 0141/339 8444, ⓦ www.grosvenorcinema.co.uk. Renovated two-screen neighbourhood film house with bar and sofas you can reserve for screenings of mostly mainstream films.

Shopping

Glasgow's **shopping** is reckoned to be the second best in the UK – after London, of course. The main area for spending in the city centre is formed by the Z-shaped and mostly pedestrianized route of **Argyle, Buchanan and Sauchiehall streets**. Along the way you'll find Princes Square, the city's poshest malls, plus major department stores such as M&S, Debenhams and John Lewis and branches of high-street chains including Hugo Boss, Gap, Karen Millen and Urban Outfitters. The Buchanan Galleries, a bland complex built around John Lewis, features some high-fashion budget stores.

Otherwise, make for the **West End** – or the **Merchant City**, with its chichi and pricey Italian Centre for some imported glamour or home-grown Cruise for designerwear on Ingram Street. In general the Merchant City and West End have more eccentric and individual offerings – the latter being the place to head for secondhand and antiquarian **book shops**.

△ Princes Square

Listings

Bike rental and routes A good selection can be found at West End Cycles, 16 Chancellor St (☎0141/357 1344), which is located close to the start of the Glasgow to Loch Lomond route, one of a number of cycle routes which radiate out from the city. For further details, check ⊛www.sustrans.co.uk.

Car rental Arnold Clark, multiple branches (☎0845/607 4500); Avis, 70 Lancefield St (☎0141/221 2827); Budget, 101 Waterloo St (☎0141/243 2047). Car hire at the airport includes Budget (☎0141/889 1479) and Hertz (☎0870/846 0007).

Gay and lesbian contacts Strathclyde Lesbian and Gay Switchboard (☎0141/847 0447); Glasgow Lesbian, Gay, Bisexual and Transgender (LGBT) Centre, 11 Dixon St (☎0141/221 7203, ⊛www .glgbt.org.uk).

Hospital 24hr casualty department at the Royal Infirmary, 84 Castle St near Glasgow Cathedral (☎0141/211 4000).

Internet EasyEverything is at 57–61 St Vincent St (☎0141/222 2365). Most libraries also offer Internet access.

Left luggage Buchanan Street bus station and lockers at Central train station.

Police Strathclyde Police HQ, Pitt Street (☎0141/532 2000). For emergencies, dial 999.

Post office General information (☎0845/722 3344). Main office at 47 St Vincent St (Mon–Fri 8.30am–5.45pm, Sat 9am–5.30pm); other city-centre offices at 87–91 Bothwell St and 228 Hope St.

Taxis Glasgow Wide TOA (☎0141/429 7070); Glasgow Private Hire (☎0141/774 3000).

The Clyde

The **River Clyde** is the dominant physical feature of Glasgow and its environs, an area which comprises the largest urban concentration in Scotland, with almost two million people living in the city and satellite towns. Little of this immediate hinterland can be described as beautiful, with crisscrossing motorways and relentlessly grim housing estates dominating much of the landscape. Beyond the urban sprawl, rolling green hills, open expanses of water and attractive countryside eventually begin to dominate, not always captivating initially, but holding promises of wilder country beyond.

West of the city, regular trains and the M8 motorway dip down from the southern bank of the Clyde to **Paisley**, where the distinctive cloth pattern gained its name, before heading back up to the edge of the river again as it broadens into the **Firth of Clyde**. North of Glasgow trains terminate at tiny Milngavie (pronounced "Mill-guy"), which acts as the start of Scotland's best-known long-distance footpath, the **West Highland Way** (see p.938).

Southeast of Glasgow, the industrial landscape of the **Clyde valley** eventually gives way to a far more attractive scenery of gorges and towering castles. Here lie the stoic town of **Lanark**, where eighteenth-century philanthropists built their model workers' community around the mills of **New Lanark**, and the spectacular **Falls of Clyde**, a mile upstream.

The Firth of Clyde – south bank

The swift journey from Glasgow along the M8, coupled with the proximity of the international airport, can belie the fact that **Paisley** is not a suburb of Glasgow but a town in its own right, with a long and distinctive history, particularly in the textile trade. Further west, the former shipbuilding centres of Port Glasgow and **Greenock** crowd the riverbank, followed by the old-fashioned resort of **Gourock**, and eventually Wemyss Bay, where thousands of Glaswegians used to alight for their steamer trip "doon the watter", but today of note only for its CalMac **ferry** connection to Rothesay on Bute (see p.969).

Paisley

Founded in the twelfth century as a monastic settlement around an abbey, **PAISLEY** expanded rapidly after the eighteenth century as a linen-manufacturing town, specializing in the production of highly fashionable imitation Kashmiri shawls. It quickly eclipsed other British centres producing the cloth, eventually lending its name to the swirling pine-cone design.

Opposite the town hall, Paisley's **Abbey** (Mon–Sat 10am–3.30pm; free) was built on the site of the town's original settlement and was massively overhauled in the Victorian age. The unattractive, fat grey facade of the church does little justice to its renovated interior, which is tall, spacious and elaborately decorated; the elongated choir, rebuilt extensively throughout the last two centuries, is illuminated by jewel-coloured stained glass from a variety of ages and styles.

Paisley's bland pedestrianized **High Street** leads westwards from the town hall towards the **Museum and Art Gallery** (Tues–Sat 10am–5pm, Sun 2–5pm; free), sheltering behind pompous Ionic columns that face the grim buildings of Paisley University. The main reason for coming here is to see the Shawl Gallery, which deals with the growth and development of the Paisley pattern and shawls, showing the familiar pine-cone (or teardrop) pattern from its simple beginnings to elaborate later incarnations. Paisley's identity as a centre for craftsmanship is also celebrated in displays of the work of contemporary local artisans, as well as a number of working looms looked after by a weaver-in-residence. The Upper Gallery houses a small art collection including works by Glasgow Boys Hornel, Guthrie and Lavery (see box on p.908), as well as one or two paintings by local boy John Byrne, artist and playwright best known for his plays *The Slab Boys* and *Tutti Frutti*.

Practicalities

Regular **trains** from Glasgow Central connect with Paisley's Gilmour Street station in the centre of town. Buses leave its forecourt every ten minutes for Glasgow International airport, two miles north of the town. The **tourist office** is right in the centre at 9a Gilmour St (April–Sept Mon–Sat 9.30am–5.30pm, Sun noon–5pm; Oct–March Mon–Sat 10am–5pm; ☎0141/889 0711).

For **food** the Paisley Arts Centre has a small bar, daytime café and outside seating, while *Aroma Room* is a more modern spot right opposite the Museum and Art Gallery, which serves coffees, snacks and lunches. Both *Cardosi's* on Storie Street and *Raeburn's Bistro and Grill* on New Street have decent evening menus.

Greenock and Gourock

GREENOCK, west of Glasgow, was the site of the first dock on the Clyde, founded in 1711, and the community has grown on the back of shipping ever since. From Greenock's Central train station (also served by hourly Citylink buses from Glasgow's Buchanan Street station), it's a short walk to the dockside, where the Neoclassical **Custom House** is Greenock's finest building, splendidly located looking out over the river. Now the principal office for

HM Customs & Excise in Scotland, it has an informative **museum** inside (Mon–Fri 10am–4pm; free), which covers the work of the Customs and Excise departments, with displays on illicit whisky distilleries as well as more modern contraband.

Greenock's town centre has been disfigured by astonishingly unsympathetic developments. More attractive, and indicative of the town's wealthy past, is the western side of town, with its mock-Baronial houses, graceful churches and quiet, tree-lined avenues. Here the **McLean Museum and Art Gallery** in Union Street (Mon–Sat 10am–5pm; free) contains pictures and contemporary records of the life and achievements of Greenock-born James Watt, prominent eighteenth-century industrialist and pioneer of steam power, as well as featuring a small art gallery with work by Glasgow Boys Hornel and Guthrie plus Colourists Fergusson, Cadell and Peploe.

On the train line west of Greenock, Fort Matilda station perches below **Lyle Hill**, an invigorating 450-foot climb that is well worth the effort for the astounding views over the purple mountains of Argyll and the creeks and lochs spilling off the Firth of Clyde. West of here lies the dowdy old resort of **GOUROCK**, once a holiday destination for generations of Glaswegians, but today only of significance as a **ferry** terminal: both CalMac (enquiries ☎01475/650100, sales ☎0870/565 0000, ◐www.calmac.co.uk) and the more frequent Western Ferries (☎01369/704452, ◐www.western-ferries.co.uk) ply the twenty-minute route across the Firth of Clyde to Dunoon on the Cowal peninsula (see p.968). There's also a year-round passenger ferry to Kilcreggan and Helensburgh on the north bank of the Clyde (check ◐www.spt.co.uk for details).

The Firth of Clyde – north bank

Heading west out of Glasgow, the A82 road and the train tracks both follow the north bank of the river, passing through Clydebank, another ex-shipbuilding centre, and Bowling, the western entry point of the newly reopened Forth & Clyde canal. Three miles beyond Bowling, they reach the town of **DUMBARTON**, founded in the fifth century, but today for the most part a brutal concrete sprawl. Only **Dumbarton Castle** (April–Sept daily 9.30am–6.30pm; Oct–March Sat–Wed 9.30am–4.30pm; £3), which sits atop a twin outcrop of volcanic rock surrounded by water on three sides, is worth stopping to see. First founded as a Roman fort, the castle became a royal seat, from which Mary, Queen of Scots, sailed for France to marry Henri II's son in 1548. Since the 1600s, the castle has been used as a garrison and artillery fortress to guard the approaches to Glasgow; most of the current buildings date from this period.

Helensburgh

HELENSBURGH, twenty miles or so northwest of Glasgow, is a smart, Georgian grid-plan settlement overlooking the Clyde estuary. The inventor of TV, John Logie Baird, was born here, as was Charles Rennie Mackintosh, who in 1902 was commissioned by the Glaswegian publisher Walter Blackie to design **Hill House** on Upper Colquhoun Street (April–Oct daily 1.30–5.30pm; NTS; £8). Without doubt the best surviving example of Mackintosh's domestic architecture, the house is stamped with his very personal, elegant interpretation of Art Nouveau – right down to the light fittings and fire irons – characterized by his sparing use of colour and stylized floral patterns. Various upstairs rooms are given over to interpretative displays on the architect's use of light, colour, form and texture, while changing exhibitions on contemporary domestic design from around Britain are a testament to Mackintosh's ongoing influence and inspiration. After exploring the house, head for the **tearoom** in the kitchen quarters, or wander round the beautifully laid-out **gardens**.

The Clyde valley

Mostly following the course of the Clyde upstream, the journey southeast of Glasgow into Lanarkshire is dominated by endless suburbs, industrial parks and wide strips of concrete highway. The principal road here is the M74, though you'll have to get off the motorway to find the main points of interest, which tend to lie on or near the banks of the river. On the outskirts of the new town of East Kilbride, the **National Museum of Scottish Country Life**, set on a historic farm, offers an in-depth look at the history of agriculture in Scotland. Further south, **New Lanark** is a remarkable eighteenth-century planned village.

National Museum of Scottish Country Life

On the edge of **EAST KILBRIDE** new town, seven miles southeast of Glasgow centre, the **National Museum of Scottish Country Life** (daily 10am–5pm; £4; NTS) is an unexpected union of historic farm and modern museum. The site of the museum, **Kittochside**, is a 170-acre farm which avoided the intensive farming that came to dominate agriculture in Britain after World War II, and it has been retained as a working model farm showcasing traditional methods of farming.

The custom-built, £6million museum building on the edge of the farm uses space and light creatively to show displays about Scots' relationship with the land over centuries and the farm equipment they have used, from early ploughs to the combine harvester. A tractor and trailer shuttles visitors the half-mile up to the eighteenth-century **farmhouse**, which is furnished much as it would have been in the 1950s, the crucial decade just before traditional methods using horses and hand-tools were replaced by tractors and mechanization. There are **paths** leading from the farmhouse around the surrounding fields, and you're encouraged to wander along these, not just to get a sense of the wider farm, but also to see and experience the farm in use.

Transport isn't straightforward if you don't have your own vehicle. **Bus** #31 from Glasgow's St Enoch Centre to East Kilbride takes you past the museum (Stewartfield Way), or you can get the **train** from Glasgow Central, and then take a taxi for the final three miles to the museum.

Lanark and New Lanark

The neat little market town of **LANARK** is an old and distinguished burgh, sitting in the purple hills high above the River Clyde, its rooftops and spires visible for miles around. There's little to see in town unless you are around during the lively **Lanimer** celebrations in early June, one of Scotland's oldest ceremonies of riding the marches or boundaries, which goes back to 1140. Most people head straight on to the village of **NEW LANARK** (ⓦ www.newlanark.org), a mile below the main town on Braxfield Road, whose importance as a centre of social and industrial innovation has recently been recognized by UNESCO, who include it on their list of World Heritage Sites.

The first sight of the village, hidden away down in the gorge, is unforgettable: large, broken, curving walls of honeyed warehouses and tenements, built in Palladian style, are lined up along the turbulent river's edge. The community was founded by David Dale and Richard Arkwright in 1785 to harness the power of the Clyde waterfalls in their cotton-spinning industry, but it was Dale's son-in-law, Robert Owen, who revolutionized the social side of the experiment in 1798, creating a "village of unity". Believing the welfare of the workers to be crucial to industrial success, Owen built adult educational facilities, the world's first day nursery and playground, and schools in which dancing and music were obligatory and there was no punishment or reward.

While you're free to wander around the village, which rather unexpectedly for such a historic site is still partially residential, to get into any of the **exhibitions** (all daily 11am–5pm) you need to buy a passport ticket (£5.95; various discount tickets are available, including an all-in ticket covering admission and the return train and bus trip from Glasgow). The Neoclassical building which now houses the visitor reception was opened by Owen in 1816 under the utopian title of **The Institute for the Formation of Character**. These days, it houses the **New Millennium Experience**, which whisks visitors on a chairlift through a social history of the village, conveying Robert Owen's vision not just for the idealized life at New Lanark, but also what he predicted for the year 2000.

Other parts of New Lanark village prove just as fascinating: everything, from the co-operative store to the workers' tenements and workshops, was built in an attempt to prove that industrialism need not be unaesthetic. Situated in the Old Dyeworks, the **Scottish Wildlife Trust Visitor Centre** (daily Jan & Feb noon–4pm; March–Dec 11am–5pm; free) provides information about the history and wildlife of the area. Beyond the visitor centre, a riverside path leads you the mile or so to the major **Falls of the Clyde**, where at the stunning tree-fringed Cora Linn, the river plunges 90ft in three tumultuous stages.

Practicalities

Lanark is the terminus of **trains** from Glasgow Central. The town's **tourist office** (May–Sept daily 10am–5pm; Oct–April Mon–Sat 10am–5pm, ☎01555/661661) is housed in the Horsemarket, next to Somerfields supermarket, one hundred yards west of the station.

By far the most original **accommodation** options in the area, at both ends of the market, make use of reconstructed mill buildings in New Lanark: the SYHA **hostel** (☎0870/004 1143, @www.syha.org.uk) has two-, four- and five-bed rooms in the cutely named Wee Row on Rosedale Street, while the *New Lanark Mill* (☎01555/667200, @www.newlanark.org; ❻) is a four-star **hotel** with good views and lots of character.

Travel details

Buses

For information on all local and national bus services, contact Traveline ☎0870/608 2608 (daily 7am–10pm), @www.travelinescotland.com.

Glasgow Buchanan Street to: Aberdeen (every 2hr; 3hr 20min); Campbeltown (3 daily; 4hr 20min); Dundee (hourly; 1hr 45min); Edinburgh (every 15min; 1hr 10min); Fort William (3 daily; 3hr); Glen Coe (3 daily; 2hr 30min); Inverness (every 2hr,

4–5hr); Kyle of Lochalsh (3 daily; 5hr); Loch Lomond (hourly; 45min); London (5 daily; 8hr); Oban (3 daily; 3hr); Perth (hourly; 1hr 35min); Portree (3 daily; 6hr); Stirling (hourly; 45min).

Trains

For information on all local and national rail services, contact National Rail Enquiries ☎08457/484950, ⓦwww.nationalrail.co.uk or ⓦwww.firstscotrail.com.

Glasgow Central to: Ardrossan for Arran ferry (every 30min; 45min); Ayr (every 30min; 50min); East Kilbride (every 30min; 30min); Gourock (every 30min; 50min); Greenock (every 30min; 40min); Lanark (every 30min; 50min); London (every 1–2hr; 5–6hr); Paisley (every 10min; 10min); Queen's Park (every 15min; 6min); Stranraer (5 daily; 2hr 10min); Wemyss Bay (hourly; 50min).

Glasgow Queen Street to: Aberdeen (hourly; 2hr 35min); Balloch (every 30min; 45min); Dumbarton (every 20min; 35min); Dundee (hourly; 1hr 20min); Edinburgh (every 15min; 50min); Fort William (Mon–Sat 3 daily, Sun 1–2 daily; 3hr 40min); Helensburgh (every 30min; 40min); Inverness (3 daily; 3hr 25min); Milngavie (every

30min; 25min); Oban (Mon–Fri 3 daily, Sat 4 daily, Sun 1–3 daily; 3hr); Perth (hourly; 1hr); Stirling (hourly; 30min).

Flights

Glasgow International to: Barra (2 daily; 1hr 5min); Belfast (Mon–Fri 8 daily; Sat & Sun 3 daily; 45min); Benbecula (Mon–Sat 2 daily; Sun 1 daily; 1hr); Campbeltown (Mon–Fri 2 daily; 40min); Dublin (4 daily; 1hr); Islay (Mon–Fri 2 daily, Sat 1 daily; 45min); Kirkwall (1 daily; 2hr); Lerwick (Mon–Fri 2 daily, Sat & Sun 1 daily; 1hr 30min–3hr); London City (Mon–Fri 3 daily, Sun 1 daily; 1hr 30min); London Gatwick (Mon–Fri 6 daily, Sat & Sun 4 daily; 1hr 30min); London Heathrow (Mon–Fri 20 daily, Sat & Sun 12 daily; 1hr 30min); London Luton (Mon–Fri 7 daily, Sat 3 daily, Sun 4 daily; 1hr 15min); London Stansted (Mon–Fri 5 daily, Sat 3 daily, Sun 4 daily; 1hr 30min); Stornoway (Mon–Fri 4 daily, Sat 2 daily, Sun 1 daily; 1hr 10min); Tiree (Mon–Sat 1 daily; 50min).

Glasgow Prestwick to: Cardiff (Mon–Fri 2 daily, Sat & Sun 1 daily; 1hr 10min); Dublin (Mon–Fri 3 daily, Sat & Sun 2 daily; 45min); London Stansted (5 daily; 1hr 10min).

20

Central Scotland

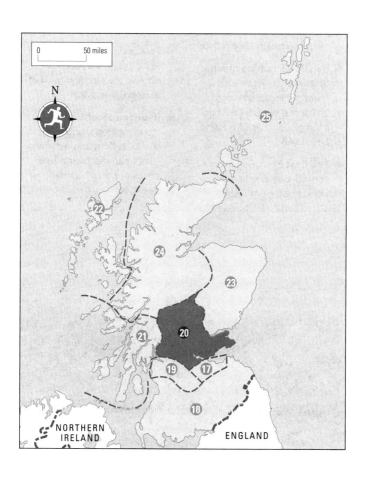

CHAPTER 20 Highlights

✳ **Stirling Castle** Impregnable, impressive and resonant with history. If you see only one castle in Scotland, make it this one. **See p.932**

✳ **The Trossachs** Pocket Highlands with shining lochs, wooded glens and noble peaks. Great for hiking and mountain biking. **See p.940**

✳ **Himalayas putting green, St Andrews** The world's finest putting course right beside the world's finest golf course; a snip at £1 a round. **See p.946**

✳ **The East Neuk** Buy freshly cooked lobster from the wooden shack at Crail's historic stone harbour or dine in style at *The Cellar* restaurant in the fishing town of Anstruther. **See p.949**

✳ **Forth Rail Bridge** An icon of Victorian engineering spanning the Firth of Forth, floodlit to stunning effect at night. **See p.952**

✳ **Folk music** Join in a session at the bar of the *Taybank Hotel* in the dignified town of Dunkeld. **See p.956**

✳ **Rannoch Moor** One of the most inaccessible places in Scotland, where hikers can discover a true sense of remote emptiness. **See p.960**

△ Rannoch Moor

20

Central Scotland

entral Scotland, the strip of mainland north of the densely populated Glasgow–Edinburgh axis and south of the main swathe of Highlands, is an accessible, popular and richly varied region. The Highland Boundary Fault, running southwest to northeast across the region, has rendered central Scotland the main stage for some of the most important events in Scottish history. Today the landscape is not only littered with remnants of the past – well-preserved medieval towns and castles, royal residences and battle sites – but also coloured by the many romantic myths and legends that have grown up around it.

Stirling, its imposing castle perched high above the town, was historically the most important bridging point across the River Forth, and from the castle battlements you can see the site of two of Scotland's most famous battlefield victories. Beyond Stirling are the fabled mountains, glens, lochs and forests of the **Trossachs**, with its archetypal Scottish scenery. Popular for walking and, in particular, cycling, much of the Trossachs, together with the attractive islands and "bonnie banks" of **Loch Lomond**, form part of Scotland's first national park, established in 2002.

In the eastern part of this central region, between the firths of Forth and Tay, lies the county of **Fife**, a Pictish kingdom which boasts a fascinating coastline sprinkled with historic fishing villages and sandy beaches, while on the North Sea fringe lies the historic university town of **St Andrews**, famous worldwide for its venerable golf courses and as the home of the game's governing body.

Occupying the same strategic position at the mouth of the River Tay as Stirling holds on the Forth, the ancient town of **Perth** has as much claim as anywhere to be the gateway to the Highlands. North and west of Perth, **Highland Perthshire** begins to show its charms, where mighty woodlands blend with gorgeously rich scenery.

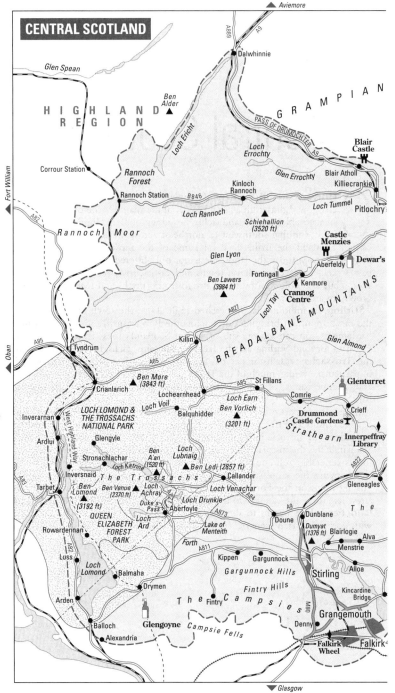

CENTRAL SCOTLAND

CENTRAL SCOTLAND

20

928

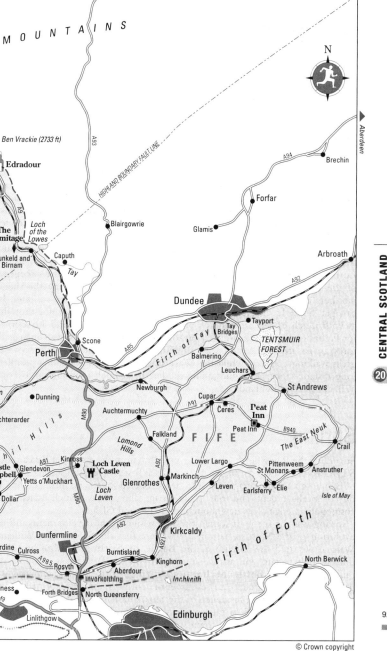

Braemar

0   10 miles

MOUNTAINS

N

Aberdeen

▲ Ben Vrackie (2733 ft)

Edradour

HIGHLAND BOUNDARY FAULT LINE

A93

A9

Brechin

A94

The
Hermitage

Loch
of the
Lowes

Blairgowrie

Forfar

Glamis

Arbroath

Dunkeld and
Birnam

Caputh

Tay

A92

Dundee

Tay
Bridges

Tayport

TENTSMUIR
FOREST

Scone

Firth of Tay

A85

Perth

A85

Balmerino

Leuchars

Earn

A85

Newburgh

St Andrews

Dunning

A91

Cupar

Peat
Inn

A9

Auchtermuchty

Ceres

Peat Inn

Auchterarder

Ochil Hills

Falkland

FIFE

B940

The East Neuk

Crail

A823

Lomond
Hills

A92

Lower Largo

Pittenweem

A91

Castle
Campbell

Kinross

Loch Leven
Castle

Markinch

St Monans

Anstruther

Glendevon

Glenrothes

Leven

Earlsferry

Elie

Yetts o'Muckhart

Loch
Leven

Isle of May

A91

Dollar

M90

A92

Dunfermline

Kirkcaldy

Firth of Forth

Kincardine

Culross

A985

Burntisland

North Berwick

Rosyth

Kinghorn

A921

Bo'ness

Inverkeithing

Inchkeith

M9

Forth Bridges

North Queensferry

Linlithgow

Edinburgh

© Crown copyright

Stirling, Loch Lomond and the Trossachs

The central lowlands of Scotland were, for several centuries, the most strategically important area in Scotland. In 1250, a map of Britain was compiled by Matthew Paris, a monk of St Albans, which depicted Scotland as two separate land masses connected only by the thin band of Stirling Bridge; although this was a figurative interpretation, Stirling was once the only **gateway** from the fertile central belt to the rugged, mountainous north.

As a result, **Stirling** and its fine castle, from where you can see both snow-capped Highland peaks and Edinburgh, is unmissable for anyone wanting to grasp the complexities of Scottish history. To the south of the city on the road to Edinburgh lies **Falkirk**, its industrial heritage now enlivened by the extraordinary Falkirk Wheel, while to the north and west lie the fabled mountains, glens, lochs and forests of the **Trossachs**, stretching west from **Callander** to Loch Lomond.

To the west of the region, **Loch Lomond** – the largest and most romanticized stretch of fresh water in Scotland – is at the heart of the **Loch Lomond and the Trossachs National Park**, though the peerless scenery of the loch and its famously "bonnie banks" can be tainted by the sheer numbers of tourists and day-trippers who stream towards it in summer. It can get similarly clogged in the neighbouring Trossachs region, although, as with much of this area, there's plenty in the way of trips and attractions for families, as well as for those keen on **outdoor activities**: well-managed forest tracks are ideal for mountain biking; the hills of the Trossachs provide great walking country; while the **West Highland Way**, Scotland's premier long-distance footpath, winds along the length of Loch Lomond up to Fort William in the Highlands.

Stirling

Straddling the River Forth a few miles upstream from the estuary at Kincardine, **STIRLING** (ⓦ www.stirling.co.uk) appears at first glance like a smaller version of Edinburgh. With its crag-top castle, steep, cobbled streets and mixed community of locals, students and tourists, it's an appealing place, though it lacks the cosmopolitan edge of its neighbours Edinburgh and Glasgow.

Stirling was the scene of some of the most significant developments in the evolution of the Scottish nation. It was here that the Scots under William Wallace defeated the English at the **Battle of Stirling Bridge** in 1297, only to fight – and win again – under Robert the Bruce just a couple of miles away at the **Battle of Bannockburn** in 1314. Stirling enjoyed its golden age in the fifteenth to seventeenth centuries, most notably when its castle was the favoured residence of the Stuart monarchy and the setting for the coronation in 1543 of the young Mary, future Queen of Scots. By the early eighteenth century the town was again besieged, its location being of strategic importance during the Jacobite rebellions of 1715 and 1745. Today

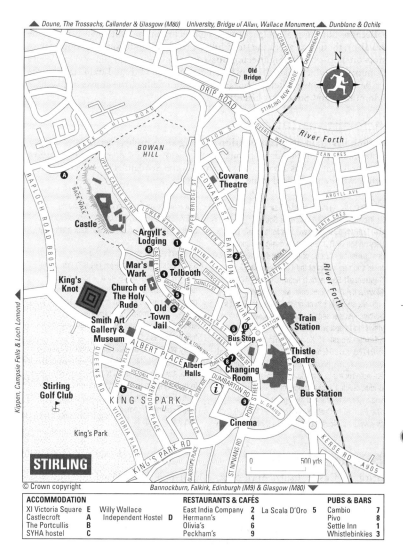

Doune, The Trossachs, Callander & Glasgow (M80)   University, Bridge of Allan, Wallace Monument,   Dunblane & Ochils

N

Old Bridge

DRIP ROAD

STIRLING NEW BRIDGE

River Forth

GOWAN HILL

Cowane Theatre

ARGYLL AVE

Castle

Argyll's Lodging

Mar's Wark

Tolbooth

King's Knot

Church of The Holy Rude

Old Town Jail

Smith Art Gallery & Museum

River Forth

Train Station

Bus Stop

Thistle Centre

ALBERT PLACE

Albert Halls

Changing Room

Stirling Golf Club

KING'S PARK

Bus Station

King's Park

Cinema

STIRLING

0   500 yds

© Crown copyright   Bannockburn, Falkirk, Edinburgh (M9) & Glasgow (M80) ▼

Kippen, Campsie Fells & Loch Lomond ◄

CENTRAL SCOTLAND | Stirling

20

ACCOMMODATION		RESTAURANTS & CAFÉS		PUBS & BARS	
XI Victoria Square	E	East India Company	2	Cambio	7
Castlecroft	A	Hermann's	4	Pivo	8
The Portcullis	B	Olivia's	6	Settle Inn	1
SYHA hostel	C	Peckham's	9	Whistlebinkies	3
Willy Wallace Independent Hostel	D	La Scala D'Oro	5		

Stirling is known for its **castle** and the lofty **Wallace Monument**, a mammoth Victorian monolith high on Abbey Craig to the northeast.

Information and getting around

The main **tourist office** is near the town centre at 41 Dumbarton Rd (April & May Mon–Sat 9am–5pm; June & Sept Mon–Sat 9am–6pm, Sun 10am–4pm; July & Aug Mon–Sat 9am–7pm, Sun 9.30am–6pm; Oct Mon–Sat 9.30am–5pm; Nov–March Mon–Fri 10am–5pm, Sat 10am–4pm; ℡01786/475019); there's a second tourist centre outside the main castle entrance (daily 9.30am–5/6pm; ℡01786/479901).

Because Stirling is a compact town, sightseeing in the Old Town is best done **on foot**, though to avoid the steep hills or reach more distant attractions, take a hop-on/hop-off City Sightseeing **bus tour** (April–Oct 9.30am–4.30pm every 30min; £7) which takes a circular route around the bus and train stations, the castle, the attractive satellite village of Bridge of Allan, the university, Wallace Monument and Smith Art Gallery.

Accommodation

Stirling has good **accommodation** ranging from backpacker hostels to large hotels, and is understandably popular both as a lower-key alternative to Glasgow or Edinburgh, and as a base for exploring central Scotland. For a fee, the tourist office will help you find somewhere to stay.

Hotels and B&Bs

XI Victoria Square 11 Victoria Square ☎01786/475545, ⓦwww.xivictoriasquare.com. Very stylish B&B in town with designer rooms, complimentary drams of malt whisky, great breakfasts and fine views of the Old Town. ⑥

Castlecroft Ballengeich Road ☎01786/474933, ⓦwww.castlecroft.uk.com. Modern guest house with six en-suite rooms on the site of the King's Stables just beneath the castle rock, with terrific views north and west. ❸

Kilronan House 15 Kenilworth Rd, Bridge of Allan ☎01786/831054, ⓦwww.kilronan.co.uk. A grand Victorian family house built in 1853 with spacious en-suite rooms in the fine Victorian spa town of Bridge of Allan, just a couple of miles north of Stirling and easily reached by regular buses. ❷

The Portcullis Castle Wynd ☎01786/472290, ⓦwww.theportcullishotel.com. Traditional hotel with four en-suite rooms in an imposing building built in 1787. Dramatic Old-Town location adjacent to the castle. Cosy bar, open log fire and beer garden. ⑤

Hostels

SYHA hostel St John Street ☎0870/004 1149, ⓦwww.syha.org.uk. Located at the top of the town, a strenuous trek with a backpack, in a converted church with an impressive 1824 Palladian facade. All rooms have showers and toilets en suite, and facilities include a games room and Internet access. Dorms £15.

Willy Wallace Independent Hostel 77 Murray Place ☎01786/446773, ⓦwww.willywallacehostel .com. A welcoming, friendly place, a hundred yards from the station in an old Victorian building, this is the liveliest budget option in town, with a big, bright common room, six dorms (£14), a double and a twin (both 1).

Stirling Castle

Stirling Castle (daily: April–Sept 9.30am–6pm; Oct–March 9.30am–5pm; £8.50, includes entry to Argyll's Lodging) must have presented would-be invaders with a formidable challenge. Its impregnability is most daunting when you approach the town from the west, from where the sheer 250ft drop down the side of the crag is most obvious. The rock was first fortified during the Iron Age, though what you see now dates largely from the fifteenth and sixteenth centuries. Built on many levels, the main buildings are interspersed with delightful gardens and patches of lawn, while endless battlements, cannon ports, hidden staircases and other nooks and crannies make it thoroughly explorable and inspiring. Free **guided tours** begin at the well in the lower square (July–Sept every 30min; Oct–June at varying times; ☎01786/431316); a comprehensive audio guide in six languages is also available for £2.

From the esplanade, cross a bridge over the grassy moat to Guardroom Square. From here, you can head up through the much modified but still imposing **Forework**, designed by James IV with classic round towers, arrow slits and battlements to underline his romantic view of royal authority. Through the archway is the **Outer Close**, the first of two main courtyard areas. Looming over, the magnificently restored **Great Hall** dates from

1501–03 and was used as a barracks by the British army until 1964. The building stands out across Stirling for its controversially bright, creamy yellow cladding, added after the discovery during renovations of a stretch of the original sixteenth-century limewash. Inside, the hall has been restored to its original state as the finest medieval secular building in Scotland, complete with five gaping fireplaces and an impressive hammer-beam ceiling of rough-hewn wood. To one side of the Great Hall, displays in the restored castle **kitchens** make a lively attempt to re-create the preparations for the spectacular Renaissance banquet given by Mary, Queen of Scots, for the baptism of the future James VI.

On the sloping upper courtyard of the castle, the **Chapel Royal** was built in 1594 by James VI for the baptism of his son, to replace an earlier chapel that was deemed insufficiently impressive. The interior is charming, with a seventeenth-century fresco of elaborate scrolls and patterns. Alongside, the **King's Old Building**, at the highest point in the castle, now houses the museum of the Argyll and Sutherland Highlanders regiment, with its collection of well-polished silver and memorabilia. Go through a narrow passageway between the King's Old Building and the Chapel Royal to get to the **Douglas Gardens**, reputedly the place where the eighth Earl of Douglas, suspected of treachery, was thrown to his death by James II in 1452. It's a lovely, quiet corner of the castle, with mature trees and battlements over which there are splendid views of the rising Highlands beyond, as well as a bird's-eye view down to the **King's Knot**, a series of grassed octagonal mounds which, in the seventeenth century, were planted with box trees and ornamental hedges.

The Old Town

Stirling evolved from the top down, starting with its castle and gradually spreading south and east onto the low-lying flood plain. In the eighteenth and nineteenth centuries, as the threat of attack decreased, the centre of commercial life crept down towards the River Forth, with the modern town growing on the edge of the plain over which the castle has traditionally stood guard.

Leaving the castle, head downhill into the old centre of Stirling, fortified behind the massive, whinstone boulders of the **town walls**, built in the mid-sixteenth century and intended to ward off the advances of Henry VIII, who had set his sights on the young Mary, Queen of Scots, as a wife for his son, Edward. The walls now constitute some of the best-preserved town defences in Scotland, and can be traced by following the path known as **Back Walk**, which leads right under the castle, taut along the edge of the crag. Though a little overgrown in places, it's a great way to take in the castle's setting, and in various places you'll catch panoramic views of the surrounding countryside.

A short walk down St John Street, a sweeping driveway leads up to the impressive **Old Town Jail** (daily 10am–5pm; ☏01786/450050, ⊛www.oldtownjail .com). Built by Victorian prison reformers, it was rescued from dereliction in 1994, with part of the building turned into offices and a substantial section used to create an entertaining visitor attraction. Telling the history of the building and prisons in general, tours are either self-led using an audio handset (£4.50) or taken by actors (April–Sept daily; Oct–March Sat & Sun; £5.75), who enthusiastically change costumes and character a number of times. Take the glass lift up to the prison roof for spectacular views across Stirling and the Forth Valley.

Directly opposite the Old Town Jail, between St John Street and Broad Street, is the original medieval prison, the **Tolbooth**, now the city's most inspirational music and arts centre (daily from 9am; ☏01786/274000, ⊛www.stirling.gov .uk/tolbooth).

The Lower Town and around

The further downhill you go in Stirling's Lower Town, the more recent the buildings become. The main **shopping** area is down here, along Port Street and Murray Place. The only other sight of note is the **Smith Art Gallery and Museum** on Dumbarton Road, near the King's Knot (Tues–Sat 10.30am–5pm, Sun 2–5pm; ⊛www.smithartgallery.demon.co.uk; free). Founded in 1874 with a legacy from local painter and collector Thomas Stuart Smith, it houses "The Stirling Story", a reasonably entertaining whirl through the history of the town, balancing out the stories of kings and queens with more social and domestic history.

The National Wallace Monument

A mile and a half north of the Old Town over the new bridge, the prominent **National Wallace Monument** (daily: March–May & Oct 10am–5pm; June 10am–6pm; July & Aug 9.30am–6pm; Sept 9.30am–5pm; Nov–Feb 10.30am–4pm; £6, including a free audio tour handset; ☏01786/472140) is a freestanding, five-storey tower built in the 1860s as a tribute to Sir William Wallace, the freedom fighter who led Scottish resistance to Edward I, the "Hammer of the Scots", in the late thirteenth century. A hero to generations of Scots, Wallace was shot to international fame by Mel Gibson in the epic movie *Braveheart*. The crag on which the monument is set was the scene of Wallace's greatest victory, when he sent his troops charging down the hillside onto the plain to defeat the English at the Battle of Stirling Bridge in 1297. Exhibits inside the tower include Wallace's long steel sword and the Hall of (Scottish) Heroes, a row of stern white marble busts featuring John Knox and Adam Smith, as well as a life-sized "talking" model of Wallace, who tells visitors about his preparations for the battle. If you can manage the climb – up 246 spiral steps – to the top of the 220ft tower, you'll be rewarded with superb views across to Fife and Ben Lomond. Bus #62 or the City Sightseeing bus (see above) will get you here.

Bannockburn

A couple of miles south of Stirling centre, on the A872, all but surrounded by suburban housing, the **Bannockburn Heritage Centre** (daily: April–Oct 10am–5.30pm; Nov, Dec, Feb & March 10.30am–4pm; £5; NTS) commemorates the most famous battle in Scottish history, when King Robert the Bruce won his mighty victory over the English at the **Battle of Bannockburn** on June 24, 1314. It was this battle, the climax of the Wars of Independence, which united the Scots under Bruce and led to independence from England.

Inside the centre there's an audiovisual presentation on the battle, highlighting the brilliantly innovative tactics Bruce employed in mustering his army to defeat a much larger English force. Pondering the scene is a stirring equestrian **statue** of Bruce, set against the skyline of Stirling Castle, the English army's approach to which he was intentionally blocking. The actual site of the main battle is still a matter of debate: most agree that it didn't take place near the present visitor centre, but on a boggy carse a mile or so to the west. Bus #56 leaves for Bannockburn from Murray Place every hour.

Restaurants and cafés

Stirling doesn't have a strong reputation for its **restaurants**, though a few places serve quality contemporary Scottish cuisine and lighter bistro-style food, and inevitably there's a range of tearooms, cafés and pubs. In **Bridge of Allan**, foodies head straight for *Clive Ramsay*'s delicatessen at 28 Henderson St (the main street), one of the best delis in Scotland which also has a great **café**-restaurant (daily 8am–late; ☎01786/833903, ⓦwww.cliveramsay.com) serving everything from breakfast through to table d'hôte dinners at night.

East India Company 7 Viewfield Place ☎01786/471330. Good Indian food, Raj-style decor, and the friendliest service in town. Moderate.
Hermann's 58 Broad St ☎01786/450632. Set in the historic Mar Place House towards the top of the Old Town, with a downstairs brasserie open at lunchtime and upmarket Austrian-Scottish dining such as jager schnitzel (veal) or Scottish lamb with cheese potatoes in the evening. Expensive.
Olivia's 5 Baker St ☎01786/446277. Modern Scottish cooking in a reasonably smart but informal, small restaurant. Mon–Fri evenings only. Moderate.
Peckham's 52 Port St ☎01786/463222. Plain decor but tasty international modern dishes within the same building as a popular deli. Moderate.
La Scala D'Oro Tolbooth, Jail Wynd, ☎01786/274010. Contemporary dishes based on a fusion of Scottish and Italian cuisine. Open for lunch & dinner including a pre-theatre menu. Moderate to expensive.

Nightlife and entertainment

Nightlife in Stirling revolves around **pubs** and **bars** and is dominated by the student population. The *Settle Inn*, 91 St Mary's Wynd, Stirling's oldest alehouse (est. 1733), serves a wide range of Scottish real ales to an eclectic crowd. Nearby at no. 73, *Whistlebinkies* has regular folk music sessions and reasonable bar meals. The hipper modern bars in town include *Cambio*, located in an old bank at 1 Corn Exchange, and its next-door neighbour *Pivo*, a popular hangout with DJs playing regularly.

For **live music**, head for the Tolbooth (see p.934), where you can see local and touring folk, rock and jazz acts. The main venue for **theatre** and **film** is the excellent MacRobert Arts Centre (☎01786/466666, ⓦwww.macrobert .org) on the university campus, which shows a good selection of mainstream and art-house films, as well as occasional jazz and dance performances.

Around Stirling

Stirling's strategic position between the Highlands and Lowlands was not only important in medieval times, but as the Industrial Revolution grew across Scotland's central belt so the town's proximity to the Forth gave it renewed significance. To the north and west of Stirling, the historic aspect of the region is reflected in the cathedral at **Dunblane** and the imposing castle at **Doune**, while to the south, the area around **Falkirk** tells of a rich industrial heritage. An undoubted highlight of this hinterland is the massive **Falkirk Wheel**, a spectacular feat of modern engineering at the interchange of the newly restored Forth & Clyde and Union canals.

Dunblane and Doune

Five miles north of Stirling, **DUNBLANE** is a small, attractive place which has been an important ecclesiastical centre since the seventh century, when the Celts founded the Church of St Blane here. **Dunblane Cathedral**

(April–Sept Mon–Sat 9.30am–6pm, Sun 1.30pm–6pm; Oct–March Mon–Sat 9.30am–4pm, Sun 2–4pm; free; ☎01786/823388; HS) dates mainly from the thirteenth century, and restoration work carried out a century ago has returned it to its Gothic splendour. Various memorials within the cathedral include a tenth-century Celtic cross-slab standing stone and a modern, four-sided standing stone by Richard Kindersley commemorating the tragic shooting in 1996 of sixteen Dunblane schoolchildren and their teacher by local man, Thomas Hamilton.

Three miles west of Dunblane, **DOUNE** is a sleepy village surrounding a stern-looking, fourteenth-century **castle** (April–Sept daily 9.30am–6.30pm; Oct–March Mon–Wed & Sat 9.30am–4.30pm, Sun 2pm–4.30pm; £3; HS). A marvellous semi-ruin standing on a small hill in a bend of the River Teith, the castle's greatest claim to fame is as the setting for the 1970s movie *Monty Python and the Holy Grail*; the shop by the gatehouse keeps a scrapbook of stills from the film, as well as a small selection of souvenirs including bottles of the locally brewed Holy Grail Ale. Close to the castle, **accommodation** is available at the excellent *Glenardoch House*, Castle Road (☎01786/841489; May–Sept; ❸), an eighteenth-century country-house B&B with two comfortable en-suite rooms and a beautiful riverside garden.

The Falkirk Wheel

Ten miles southeast of Stirling on the M9 to Edinburgh, **FALKIRK** has a good deal of visible history, going right back to the remains of the Roman Antonine Wall. The town was transformed in the eighteenth century, however, by the construction of first the Forth & Clyde Canal, allowing easy access to Glasgow and the west coast, and then the Union Canal, which continued the route through to Edinburgh. Just twenty years later, the trains arrived, and the canals gradually fell into disuse.

While Falkirk's two canals were a very visible sign of the area's industrial heritage, it was only in recent years that their leisure potential was realized, thanks to British Waterway's £84.5 million **Millennium Link** project to restore the canals and re-establish a navigable link between east and west coasts. The icon of this project is the remarkable **Falkirk Wheel** (❿www .thefalkirkwheel.co.uk), two miles west of Falkirk town centre. Opened in 2002, the giant grey wheel, the world's first rotating boat-lift, scoops boats in two giant buckets, or caissons, the 115 feet between the levels of the two canals.

Beneath the wheel, a **visitor centre** (daily: April–Oct 9am–6pm; Nov–March 9.30am–5pm; free) provides information and sells tickets for a one-hour **boat trip** from the lower basin into the wheel, along the Union Canal, and back again (daily: April–Oct 9.30am–5pm, every 30min; Nov–March 10am–3pm, hourly; £8). If you want to simply see the wheel in action, this is best done by walking around the basin and adjoining towpaths.

Loch Lomond

The largest stretch of fresh water in Britain (23 miles long and up to five miles wide), **Loch Lomond** is the epitome of Scottish scenic splendour, thanks in large part to the ballad which fondly recalls its "bonnie, bonnie banks". The song was said to have been written by a Jacobite prisoner captured by the English, who, sure of his fate, wrote that his spirit would

Literary Britain

Britain offers the unique experience of following in the footsteps of some of the world's most famous writers. In many cases, this means a visit to a birth- or burial place, or to a dedicated museum, but it's often far more rewarding to immerse yourself in the natural fabric of British literature – tramping the lakeland fells in the company of Wordsworth, say, or exploring the streets of Dickens' Rochester. And for the works themselves, Britain has one essential stop, Hay-on-Wye (p.445), the town on the Anglo-Welsh border entirely devoted to books – its annual literary festival (every May; ⓦwww.hayfestival.co.uk) is the nation's biggest book-related jamboree.

Shakespeare country

Warwickshire in the West Midlands is – as the road signs attest – "Shakespeare Country", though to all intents and purposes it's a county with just one destination – the small market town of Stratford-upon-Avon (p.435–440), birthplace of England's greatest writer. So few facts about Shakespeare's life are known that Stratford can be a disappointment for the serious literary pilgrim, its buildings and sights hedged with "reputedlys" and "maybes". Real Shakespeare country could just as easily be London, where his plays were written and performed (there was no theatre in Stratford in Shakespeare's day). But, from the house where he was born to the church in which he's buried, Stratford at least provides a coherent centre for England's Shakespeare industry – and it's certainly the most atmospheric place to see a production by the Royal Shakespeare Company.

Wordsworth's Lake District

William Wordsworth and the Lake District are inextricably linked, and in the streets of Grasmere, Hawkshead and Cockermouth, and the fells surrounding Ullswater and Borrowdale you're never very far from a house or sight associated with the poet and his circle. Wordsworth's views on nature and the natural world stood at the very heart of all his poetry, and it's still a jolt to encounter the very views that inspired him – from his carefully tended garden at Rydal Mount (p.566) to the dancing and reeling daffodils of Gowbarrow Park (p.574). His telling eye provided local snapshots that resonate today with observant visitors – like Grasmere church's "naked rafters intricately crossed" – while in his own *Guide to the Lakes* (published in 1810 "for the minds of persons of taste") he did much to advertise the charms of the region he loved.

A host of golden daffodils at Wordsworth Point, Ullswater

Haworth and the Brontës

The Brontës Parsonage Museum, Haworth

Quite why the sheltered life of the Brontë sisters, Charlotte, Emily and Ann, should exert such a powerful fascination is a puzzle, though the contrast of their pinched provincial existence in the Yorkshire village of Haworth (p.597) with the brooding moors and tumultuous passions of their novels may well form part of the answer. The mementos, possessions and manuscripts in their old home, the village parsonage, and the family vault in the parish church only tell half the story. It's out on the bleak moors above Haworth that inspiration struck, and where works like *Wuthering Heights* and *The Tenant of Wildfell Hall* progressed from mere parlour entertainments to melodramatic studies of emotion and obsession.

Ten literary diversions

Brantwood, Cumbria. There's not a more finely sited writer's house in Britain than John Ruskin's Victorian home set high above Coniston Water in the Lake District. See p.567.

Chawton, Hampshire. Visit the modest house where Jane Austen lived and wrote her most celebrated works. See p.232

Dumfries, southwest Scotland. Robbie Burns spent the last five years of his life in the town known as the "Queen of the South". See p.874.

Dundee, northeast Scotland. The spiritual home of the *Dandy* and *Beano*, comics that

have entertained generations of British kids. See p.1030.

Hill Top, Cumbria. Join the crowds at Beatrix Potter's beloved lakeland farmhouse. See p.569.

Jamaica Inn, Cornwall. The inspiration for Daphne Du Maurier's swashbuckling smuggling tale. See p.384.

Laugherne, South Wales. There's a powerful atmosphere at the simple home of Dylan Thomas. See p.713.

Monk's House, East Sussex. Once the home of Virginia Woolf – she and her husband Leonard were buried in the gardens. See p.199.

Rochester, Kent. Although born in Portsmouth, and much associated with London, it's here that Charles Dickens spent his youth (and set most of his last book, *The Mystery of Edwin Drood*). See p.173.

Writers' Museum, Edinburgh. Explore the works and personal effects of Robert Burns, Sir Walter Scott and Robert Louis Stevenson. See p.824.

Hardy's Wessex

Hardy's Birthplace, Lower Bockhampton, Dorset

Thomas Hardy resurrected the old name of Wessex to describe the region in which he set most of his fiction. In his books, the area stretched from Devon and Somerset to Berkshire and Oxfordshire, though its central core was Dorset, the county where Hardy spent most of his life. His books richly depict the life and appearance of the towns and countryside, often thinly disguised – thus Salisbury as "Melchester", Weymouth as "Budmouth Regis", and Bournemouth as "Sandbourne". But it is Dorchester (p.241), county town of Dorset and the "Casterbridge" of his novels, which is portrayed in most detail, to the extent that many of the buildings and landmarks that still remain can be identified, especially in *The Mayor of Casterbridge* and *Far From the Madding Crowd*.

Watching the detectives

Many British contemporary crime writers have moved beyond the enclosed country-house mysteries of Agatha Christie to serve up realistic, recognizable depictions of life – and death – in the country's towns, cities and rural areas. Colin Dexter's morose Inspector Morse flits between town and gown in university Oxford in a cerebral series of whodunnits, while in the elegantly crafted novels of PD James it's the remote coast and isolated villages of East Anglia that often provide the backdrop. The other "Queen of Crime", Ruth Rendell (also writing as Barbara Vine), is at home with the misfits and drop-outs of suburban London, though it's in "Kingsmarkham" – inspired by Midhurst in West Sussex – that her Inspector Wexford series is set. London, of course – its corruption, gangs, villains and violence – occupies many writers, but Britain's other cities also have their chroniclers. Val McDermid, and her sassy private eye, Kate Brannigan, nail contemporary Manchester, while in the dysfunctional character of John Rebus, Scottish writer Ian Rankin has found a way to get to the heart of Edinburgh and its contradictions. Britain's rural areas don't escape the escalating body count either. Peter Robinson's Inspector Banks series is set in the Yorkshire Dales, and for Stephen Booth and his Derbyshire detective Ben Cooper it's the Peak District. But for sheer chutzpah, it's hard to beat Malcolm Pryce's madcap reworking of American noir for Welsh Aberystwyth and its druid-run clubs, 24-hour whelk stalls and toffee-apple dens.

See the "Books" section on p.1167 for reviews of some of Britain's best contemporary crime fiction.

Oxford's dreaming spires, setting for Colin Dexter's Morse mysteries

△ Loch Lomond
△ Loch Lomond

return to Scotland on the low road much faster than those of his living compatriots on the high road.

Designated Scotland's first national park in 2002, the **Loch Lomond and the Trossachs National Park** (Ⓦwww.lochlomond-trossachs.org) covers a large stretch of scenic territory from the lochs of the Clyde Estuary to Loch Earn and Loch Tay, on the southwest fringes of Perthshire, with the centre-piece being Loch Lomond. The most popular gateway into the park is the town of **Balloch**, just 19 miles from Glasgow city centre. Both Balloch and the western side of the loch around **Luss** are often packed with day-trippers and tour coaches, though the loch's eastern side, abutting the Trossachs, is very different in tone, with wooden ferryboats puttering out to a scattering of tree-covered islands off the village of **Balmaha**.

Balloch

The main settlement on Loch Lomond–side is **BALLOCH**, at the southwest-ern corner of the loch, where the water channels into the River Leven for its short journey south to the Firth of Clyde. Surrounded by housing estates and stuffed with undistinguished guest-houses, Balloch has few redeeming features, and is little more than a suburb of the much larger factory-town of Alexandria, to the south. However, Balloch's accessibility from Glasgow by both car and train ensured that it was chosen as the focal point of the national park with the siting of the huge **Loch Lomond Shores** complex (Ⓦwww.lochlomondshores.com). Signposted from miles around, it contains the **National Park Gateway Centre** (daily 9.30am–6pm, extended hours in the summer; Ⓣ01389/722199 or 0845/3454978), which has background on the park, **tourist information** and a leaflet outlining all transport links within the park, as well as Internet access and a "retail crescent" including a branch of Jenners. Alongside, **Drumkinnon Tower** is a striking, stone-built, cylindrical building which houses a giant-screen auditorium showing films about the natural and cultural history of the area, while its top-floor

The West Highland Way

Opened in 1980, the spectacular **West Highland Way** was Scotland's first long-distance footpath, stretching some 95 miles from Milngavie (pronounced "mill-guy"; six miles north of central Glasgow, to Fort William, where it reaches the foot of Ben Nevis, Britain's highest mountain. Today, it is by far the most popular such footpath in Scotland, and while for many the range of scenery, relative ease of walking and nearby facilities make it a classic route, others find it a little too busy in high season, particularly in comparison with the relative isolation which can be found in many other parts of the Highlands.

Passing through the lowlands north of Glasgow, the route runs along the eastern shores of Loch Lomond, over the Highland Boundary Fault Line, then round Crianlarich, crossing open heather moorland across the **Rannoch Moor** wilderness area. It passes close to **Glen Coe**, notorious for the massacre of the MacDonald clan, before reaching **Fort William**. Apart from a stretch between Loch Lomond and Bridge of Orchy, when the path is within earshot of the main road, this is wild, remote country: north of Rowardennan on Loch Lomond, the landscape is increasingly exposed, and you should be well prepared for sudden and extreme weather changes.

Though this is emphatically not the most strenuous of Britain's long-distance walks – it passes between lofty mountain peaks, rather than over them – a moderate degree of fitness is required as there are some steep ascents. If you're looking for an added challenge, you could work a climb of Ben Lomond or Ben Nevis into your schedule. You might choose to walk individual sections of the Way (the eight-mile climb from Glen Coe up the Devil's Staircase is particularly spectacular), but to tackle the whole thing you need to set aside at least seven days; avoid a Saturday start from Milngavie and you'll be less likely to be walking with hordes of people, and there'll be less pressure on accommodation. Most walkers tackle the route from south to north, and manage between ten and fourteen miles a day, staying at hotels, B&Bs and bunkhouses en route. Camping is permitted at recognized sites.

Although the path is clearly waymarked, you may want to check one of the many maps or guidebooks published: the **official guide**, published by Mercat Press (£14.99), includes a foldout map as well as descriptions of the route, with detailed cultural, historical, archeological and wildlife information. Further details about the Way, including a comprehensive accommodation list, can be found at Ⓦwww .west-highland-way.co.uk, which also has links to tour companies and transport providers, who can take your luggage from one stopping point to the next.

lookout post and small café afford excellent views over the loch towards Ben Lomond.

Beside Drumkinnon Tower, Can You Experience (Ⓣ01389/602576, Ⓦwww .canyouexperience.com) organizes a number of **activities**, including nature walks, canoe, bike and pedalo rental. Loch **cruises** (including a 2–3hr trip to Luss) leave from the nearby slipway with Sweeney's Cruises (Ⓣ01389/752376, Ⓦwww.sweeney.uk.com).

Opposite the Balloch **train station** – with connections to Glasgow Queen Street – is a small **tourist office** (daily: May 10am–5pm; June & Sept 10am–5.30pm; July & Aug 9.30am–6pm; Ⓣ01389/753533). There's little point staying in Balloch: instead, head two miles northwest of the train station, to one of Scotland's most impressive SYHA **hostels** (Ⓣ0870/004 1136, Ⓦwww.syha.org .uk; April–Oct), just off the A82. A grand country house with turrets, stained-glass windows and walled gardens, it has dorms sleeping 5–10 for £15.50 a person.

The eastern shore of Loch Lomond and the islands

The tranquil **eastern shore** is far better for walking and appreciating the loch's natural beauty than the overcrowded western side. The dead-end B837 from Drymen will take you halfway up the east bank, as far as you can get by car or bus (#309 from Balloch and Drymen runs to Balmaha every 2hr), while the West Highland Way sticks close to the shores for the entire length of the loch, beginning at the tiny lochside settlement of **BALMAHA**, which stands on the Highland Boundary Fault, the geological fault that separates the Highlands from the Lowlands. If you stand on the viewpoint above the pier, you can see the fault line clearly marked by a series of woody islands that form giant stepping stones across the loch. Many of the loch's 37 **islands** are privately owned, and, rather quaintly, an old wooden mail-boat still delivers post to four of them. It's possible to join the **mail-boat cruise**, which is run by MacFarlane & Son from the jetty at Balmaha (May, June & Sept Mon, Thurs & Sat 11.30am returns 2pm; July & Aug Mon–Sat 11.30am returns 2pm; Oct–April Mon & Thurs 10.50am returns 12.50pm; £8; ☎01360/870214, ⓦwww .balmahaboatyard.co.uk). In summer the timetable allows a one-hour stop on Inchmurrin Island, the largest and most southerly of the islands inhabited by just ten permanent residents; if you're looking for an island to explore, however, a better bet is **Inchailloch**, the closest to Balmaha. Owned by Scottish Natural Heritage, it has a two-mile, signposted nature trail round the island. It's possible to row here yourself using a boat hired from MacFarlane & Son (from £10/hr), or you can use their on-demand ferry service (£4 return).

Balmaha gets very busy in summer, not least with day-trippers on the West Highland Way. Beside the large car park is a **National Park Centre** (April–Sept daily 10am–6pm) for information on local forest walks, and you can **stay** at the well-run *Oak Tree Inn*, set back from the boatyard (☎01360/870357, ⓦwww.oak-tree-inn.co.uk), with en-suite double rooms (❹) and bunk-bed quads (❸). It's also a convivial pub that serves **food** all day. A cheaper option is the *Balmaha Bunkhouse Lodge* (☎01360/870084) across the road, with a couple of twin rooms (❶) as well as dorms (£14.50). **Camping** is available two miles north, on the lochside at Milarrochy Bay (☎01360/870236; March–Oct), or, a couple of miles or so further up the road, at *Cashel*, a lovely secluded Forestry Commission campsite (☎01360/870234, ⓦwww.forestholidays.co.uk; mid-March to Oct).

The western shore of Loch Lomond

Despite the roar of traffic hurtling along the upgraded A82, the **west bank** of Loch Lomond is an undeniably beautiful stretch of water and gives better views of the loch's islands and surrounding peaks than the heavily wooded east side. **LUSS** is without doubt the prettiest village in the region, with prim, identical sandstone and slate cottages garlanded in rambling roses, and a narrow sandy, pebbly strand. However, its charms are no secret, and its streets and beach can become unbearably crowded in summer.

Seventeen miles north at **TARBET**, at the point where the A83 heads off west into Argyll, the A82 continues north along the banks of the loch towards Crianlarich. There's one more **train station** on Loch Lomond at **ARDLUI**, while a couple of miles further north at **Inverarnan**, there's a bridge over the river behind the ⚔ *Drover's Inn* (☎01301/704234, ⓦwww .droversinn.co.uk; ❸), one of Scotland's most idiosyncratic **hotels**. The bar has a roaring fire, barmen dressed in kilts, weary hill-walkers sipping pints and bearded musicians banging out folk songs. Down the creaking corridors, past moth-eaten stuffed animals, are a number of supposedly haunted and resolutely old-fashioned rooms.

The Trossachs

Often described as the Highlands in miniature, the **Trossachs** area boasts a magnificent diversity of scenery, with dramatic peaks and mysterious, forest-covered slopes that live up to all the images ever produced of Scotland's wild land. It is country ripe for stirring tales of brave kilted clansmen, a role fulfilled by Rob Roy Macgregor, the seventeenth-century outlaw whose name seems to attach to every second waterfall, cave and barely discernible path. The Trossachs' high tourist profile was largely attributable in the early days to Sir Walter Scott, whose novels *Lady of the Lake* and *Rob Roy* were set in and around the area. Since then, neither the popularity nor beauty of the region have waned, and in high season the place is jam-packed with coaches full of tourists as well as walkers and mountain-bikers taking advantage of the easily accessed scenery. Autumn is a better time to come, when the hills are blanketed in rich, rusty colours and the crowds are thinner.

If you don't have your own transport, take the **Trossachs Trundler**, a useful minibus service which loops round Callander, Loch Katrine and Aberfoyle four times a day (10am–4pm) from late May to early October; helpfully for walkers, it stops on demand and can also cope with two bikes and wheelchairs. The bus is timed to connect with sailings of the SS *Sir Walter Scott* on Loch Katrine (see p.941), and costs £5 for a day pass or £12 for two adults and four children (for further details call ☎01786/451200).

20

Rob Roy

A member of the outlawed Macgregor clan, **Rob Roy** (meaning "Red Robert" in Gaelic) was born in 1671 in Glengyle, just north of Loch Katrine, and lived for some time as a respectable cattle-farmer and trader, supported by the powerful Duke of Montrose. In 1712, finding himself in a tight spot when a cattle deal fell through, Rob Roy absconded with £1000, some of it belonging to the duke. He took to the hills to live as a brigand, his feud with Montrose escalating after the duke repossessed Rob Roy's land and drove his wife from their house. He was present at the Battle of Sheriffmuir during the earlier Jacobite uprising of 1715, ostensibly supporting the Jacobites but probably as an opportunist: the chaos would have made cattle-raiding easier. Eventually captured and sentenced to transportation, Rob Roy was pardoned and returned to **Balquhidder**, northeast of Glengyle, where he remained until his death in 1734.

Rob Roy's status as a local hero in the mould of Robin Hood should be tempered with the fact that he was without doubt a notorious bandit and blackmailer. His life has been much romanticized, from Sir Walter Scott's 1818 novel *Rob Roy* to the 1995 film starring Liam Neeson, although the tale does serve well to dramatize the clash between the doomed clan culture of the Gaelic-speaking Highlanders and the organized feudal culture of lowland Scots, which effectively ended with the defeat of the Jacobites at Culloden in 1746. His **grave** in Balquhidder, a simple affair behind the ruined church, is one of the principal sights on the unofficial Rob Roy trail, though the peaceful graveyard is mercifully underdeveloped and free of the tartan trappings which has seen the Trossachs dubbed "Rob Roy Country".

Hiking and biking in the Trossachs

Despite the steady flow of coach tours taking in the scenic highlights of the area, the Trossachs is ideal for exploring **on foot** or on a **mountain bike**. This is partly because the terrain is slightly more benign than the Highlands proper, but much is due to the excellent management of the **Queen Elizabeth Forest Park**, a huge chunk of the national park between Loch Lomond and Loch Lubnaig. The main visitor centre for the area, David Marshall Lodge, is just outside Aberfoyle (see below).

For **hill-walkers**, the prize peak is Ben Lomond (3192ft), best accessed from Rowardennan on Loch Lomond's east shore. Other highlights include Ben Venue (2370ft) and Ben A'an (1520ft) on the shores of Loch Katrine, as well as Ben Ledi (2857ft), just northwest of Callander, which all offer relatively straightforward but very rewarding climbs and, on clear days, stunning views. Walkers can also choose from any number of waymarked routes through the forests and along lochsides; pick up a map of these at the visitor centre.

The area is also a popular spot for **mountain biking**, with a number of useful rental shops, a network of forest paths and one of the more impressive stretches of the National Cycle Network cutting through the region from Loch Lomond to Killin. If you don't have your own bike, you can **rent** one from Wheels Cycling Centre (℡01877/331100), next to *Trossachs Backpackers* (see p.942) a mile and a half southwest of Callander, the best rental place in the area, with front- or full-suspension models available, as well as baby seats and children's cycles. Also well set up is Trossachs Cycles (℡01877/382614), at the *Trossachs Holiday Park* on the A81 two miles south of Aberfoyle, while more centrally located is Mounter Bikes (℡01877/331052), beside the visitor centre in Callander (see p.942).

The Central Trossachs

Each summer the sleepy little town of **ABERFOYLE**, twenty miles west of Stirling, dusts itself down for its annual influx of tourists. Though of little appeal itself, Aberfoyle's position in the heart of the Trossachs is ideal, with **Loch Ard Forest** and **Queen Elizabeth Forest Park** stretching across to Ben Lomond and Loch Lomond in the west, the long curve of Loch Katrine and Ben Venue to the northwest, and Ben Ledi to the northeast. North of Aberfoyle, the A821 road to Loch Katrine winds its way into the Queen Elizabeth Forest, snaking up **Duke's Pass** (so called because it once belonged to the Duke of Montrose). You can walk or drive the short distance to the park's excellent **visitor centre** at David Marshall Lodge (Jan Sat & Sun 10am–4pm; Feb Thurs–Sun 10am–4pm; March–Dec daily 10am–4/6pm; car park £1; ℡01877/382258), where you can pick up maps of the walks and cycle routes in the forest, get background information on the flora and fauna of the area, which includes roe deer and birds of prey, or settle into the café with its splendid views over the tree tops. Adjacent to the centre, there's an excellent adventure park for children, while various marked paths wind through the forest, giving glimpses of the lowlands and surrounding hills.

Loch Katrine

Heading down the northern side of the Duke's Pass you come first to **Loch Achray**, tucked under Ben A'an. At the head of the loch, a road leads the short distance through to the southern end of **Loch Katrine** at the foot of Ben Venue (2370ft). Here, an elegant Victorian passenger **steamer**, the SS *Sir Walter Scott*, has been plying the waters since 1900, chugging up to the wild country of Glengyle. It does two daily runs from the pier (April–Oct; ℡01877/376316), the first departing at 11am and stopping off at Stronachlachar before returning almost two hours later (£7.25); the one-hour afternoon cruise leaves at 1.45pm but doesn't make any stops (£6.25). A popular combination is to **rent a bike** from the Katrinewheels (℡01877/376316) hut by the pier, take the steamer up to Stronachlachar, then cycle back along the road around the north side of the loch.

From Loch Katrine the A821 heads due east past the tiny village of **Brig o'Turk**, where it's worth looking in on the *Byre Inn*, a tiny pub and restaurant set in an old stone barn with wooden pews and a welcoming open fire. If you fancy staying here, the historic *Burnt Inn House* (℡01877/376212, ⓦwww .burntinnhouse.co.uk; ❸) offers simple, farmhouse-style B&B.

Callander

CALLANDER, on the eastern edge of the Trossachs, sits on the banks of the River Teith at the southern end of the **Pass of Leny**, one of the key routes into the Highlands. Significantly larger than Aberfoyle, eleven miles west, it is a popular summer holiday base and suffers in high season for being on the main tourist trail from Stirling through to the west Highlands. The chief attraction in town is the **Rob Roy and Trossachs Visitor Centre** in a converted church at Ancaster Square on the main street (daily: March–May & Oct 10am–5pm; June–Sept 10am–6pm; Nov–Feb 11am–4pm; ℡01877/330342). Downstairs holds Callander's **tourist office**, while upstairs a hammed-up audiovisual display (£3.60) offers an entertaining and partisan account of the life and times of Rob Roy and those who have portrayed him in film and fiction.

Callander's best central **accommodation** is at *Callander Meadows*, 24 Main St (℡01877/330181, ⓦwww.callandermeadows.co.uk; ❸), an attractive townhouse with three comfortable en-suite rooms and an excellent restaurant. Alternatively, head two miles southeast along the Doune road to *The Conservatory* in Ballachallan (℡01877/339190, ⓦwww.ballachallan.co.uk; ❹), an eighteenth-century farmhouse with three pleasant, well-presented en-suite rooms. A mile southwest of town down a turn-off from the A81 to Port of Menteith, ⚐ *Trossachs Backpackers*, Invertrossachs Road (℡01877/331200, ⓦwww .scottish-hostel.co.uk), is a friendly, well-equipped and comfortable 32-bed hostel and activity centre, with self-catering dorms (£13.50) and family rooms. **Bike rental** and advice on the best local cycle routes is available here too, at Wheels Cycling Centre (℡01877/331100, ⓦwww.scottish-cycling.co.uk).

Callander has few **restaurants** worth recommending: *Callander Meadows* (see above; restaurant closed Tues & Wed) dishes up delicious, freshly cooked lunches and dinners, while *The Conservatory* fish restaurant (see above; closed Mon & Tues) serves great Scottish seafood dishes at reasonable prices in a pleasant conservatory dining room. For good **pub food** try the convivial *Lade Inn* in Kilmahog, a mile west of Callander. For unbeatable fresh sandwiches, great coffee and a fine selection of breads, cheeses and other deli items head for *Deli Ecosse* adjacent to the visitor centre.

Fife

The ancient Kingdom of **Fife**, designated as such by the Picts in the fourth century, is a small area barely fifty miles at its widest point, but one which has a definite identity, inextricably linked with the waters which surround it on three sides – the Tay to the north, the Forth to the south, and the cold North Sea to the east. Despite its small size, Fife encompasses several different regions, with a marked difference between the rural north and the semi-industrial south. Fishing still has a role, but ultimately it is to **St Andrews**, Scotland's oldest university town and the home of the world-famous Royal and Ancient Golf Club, that most visitors are drawn. Development here has been cautious, and both the town itself and the surrounding area retain an appealing and old-fashioned feel. South of St Andrews, the tiny stone harbours of the fishing villages of the **East Neuk** are an appealing extension to any visit to this part of Fife.

Inland from St Andrews is the absorbing village of **Falkland** with its impressive ruined palace. To the **south**, the perfectly preserved town of **Culross** is the most obvious draw with its cobbled streets and collection of historic buildings. Otherwise, southern Fife is dominated by the town of **Dunfermline**, a former capital of Scotland, and industrialized **Kirkcaldy**, with the **Forth Rail Bridge** and Road Bridge the most memorable sights of this stretch of coastline.

St Andrews and the East Neuk

Confident, poised and well groomed, if a little snooty, **ST ANDREWS**, Scotland's oldest **university town** and a pilgrimage centre for **golfers** from all over the world, is situated on a wide bay on the northeastern coast of Fife. Of all Scotland's universities, St Andrews is the most often compared to Oxford or Cambridge both for the dominance of gown over town, and for the intimate, collegiate feel of the place. In fact, the university attracts a significant proportion of English undergraduates, among them, famously, Prince William, who spent four years studying here.

According to legend, the town was founded, pretty much by accident, in the fourth century. **St Rule** – or Regulus – a custodian of the bones of St Andrew in Patras in southern Greece, had a vision in which an angel ordered him to carry five of the saint's bones to the western edge of the world, where he was to build a city in his honour. The conscientious courier set off, but was shipwrecked on the rocks close to the present harbour. Struggling ashore with his precious burden, he built a shrine to the saint on what subsequently became the site of the **cathedral**; St Andrew became Scotland's patron saint and the town its ecclesiastical capital.

From St Andrews, the attractive beaches and little fishing villages of the **East Neuk** (*neuk* is Scots for "corner") are within easy reach, although the area can also be approached from the Kirkcaldy side. Though golf and coastal walks are a shared characteristic, the East Neuk villages have few of the grand buildings and important bustle of St Andrews, with old cottages and merchants' houses huddling round stone-built harbours in scenes fallen upon with joy by artists and photographers.

Arrival, information and getting around

St Andrews' nearest **train station** (on the Edinburgh–Dundee line) is five miles northwest at Leuchars, across the River Eden, from where regular buses make the fifteen-minute trip into town. When you buy your rail ticket to Leuchars, ask for a St Andrews rail-bus ticket which includes the bus fare. The **tourist office**, 70 Market St (April–June Mon–Sat 9.30am–5.30pm, Sun 11am–4pm; July & Aug Mon–Sat 9.30am–7pm, Sun 10am–5pm; Sept & Oct Mon–Sat 9.30am–6pm,

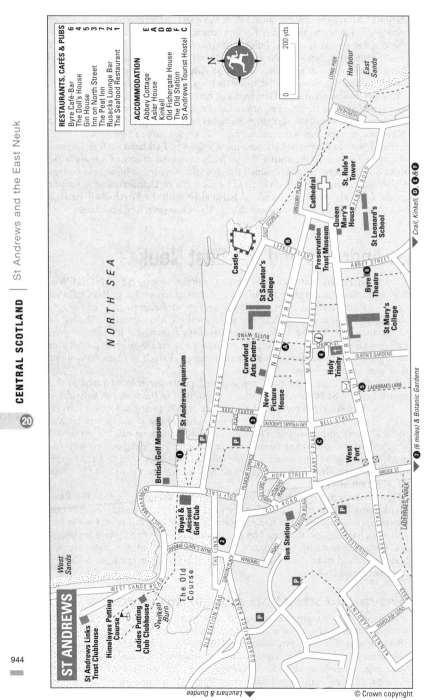

ST ANDREWS

St Andrews Links
Trust Clubhouse

West Sands

The Old Course

NORTH SEA

British Golf Museum

St Andrews Aquarium

Himalayas Putting Course

Ladies Putting Club Clubhouse

Swilken Burn

Royal & Ancient Golf Club

Castle

St Salvator's College

Preservation Trust Museum

Cathedral

St. Rule's Tower

Queen Mary's House

St Leonard's School

Crawford Arts Centre

New Picture House

Holy Trinity

St Mary's College

Byre Theatre

Church St

West Port

Bus Station

RESTAURANTS, CAFÉS & PUBS

Byre Café-Bar	6
The Doll's House	4
Gin House	5
Inn on North Street	3
The Peat Inn	7
Rusacks Lounge Bar	2
The Seafood Restaurant	1

ACCOMMODATION

Abbey Cottage	E
Aslar House	A
Kinkell	D
Old Fishergate House	B
The Old Station	F
St Andrews Tourist Hostel	C

N

0   200 yds

◀ Leuchars & Dundee

▶ 7 (6 miles) & Botanic Gardens

▶ Crail, Kinkell, D, E & F

© Crown copyright

Sun 11am–4pm; Nov–March Mon–Sat 9.30am–5pm; ☎01334/472021), holds comprehensive information about St Andrews and northeast Fife.

An open-top hop-on/hop off **bus tour** (July & Aug daily 11am–3pm; £6) takes a one-hour spin around the main sights, although the town is compact enough to explore thoroughly on foot. Guided **walking tours** around the university buildings (mid-June to Aug Mon–Fri 11am & 2.30pm; ☎01334/462245; £4) leave from Butt's Wynd, beside the chapel by St Salvator's College, while the St Andrews Links Trust runs walking tours of the Old Course, starting from the Golf Shop just behind the 18th green (May & June Sat & Sun 11am–4pm; July & Aug daily 11am–4pm; ☎01334/466666, @www.standrews.org.uk; £2).

The town's fiendish **parking** system requires vouchers (Mon–Sat 9am–5pm; 60p/hr) which you can get from the tourist office and some local shops – you may find it easier leaving your car in one of the free car parks fringing the centre. Spokes, at 37 South St (☎01334/477835), offers **bike rental**.

Accommodation

With St Andrews' wide-ranging appeal to visitors, there's no shortage of **accommodation** both in town and around, although average prices in all categories vie with Edinburgh's as the highest in Scotland. There are plenty of **guest houses**, though rooms often get booked up in the summer, when you should definitely book in advance.

Abbey Cottage Abbey Walk ☎01334/473727, @www.abbeycottage.co.uk. Inexpensive B&B in a cottage with a pretty garden, south of the cathedral, near the harbour. ❸

Aslar House 120 North St ☎01334/473460, @www.aslar.com. A smart guest-house in a three-storey townhouse with an unusual round tower at the back. ❺

Kinkell By Brownhills ☎01334/472003, @www.kinkell.com. Countryside B&B in a lovely family farmhouse near the beach, about two miles south of town off the A917. ❺

Old Fishergate House North Castle Street ☎01334/470874, @www.oldfishergatehouse .co.uk. Seventeenth-century townhouse in the oldest part of St Andrews, with two spacious twin rooms full of period features. ❺

The Old Station Stravithie Bridge ☎01334/880505, @www.theoldstation.co.uk. A couple of miles south

of town on the B9131 to Anstruther, with tasteful rooms in the main house (based around a former station waiting-room). Alternatively, you can stay in the imaginatively designed suite in an old railway carriage parked alongside. Main house ❺, carriage ❼

St Andrews Tourist Hostel St Mary's Place ☎01334/479911, @www.hostelsaccommodation .com. Superbly located backpacker hostel in a pleasant converted townhouse above *The Grill House* restaurant, with plenty of dorm beds (£16), but no doubles.

University of St Andrews ☎01334/462000, @www.escapetotranquillity.com. Rents out rooms in various student residences between June and September, all on a B&B basis. Self-catering houses also available. Single rooms from £27.50, twin ❸

The Town

The centre of St Andrews still follows its medieval layout. On the three main thoroughfares, **North Street**, **Market Street** and **South Street**, which run west to east towards the ruined Gothic cathedral, are several of the original university buildings from the fifteenth century. Narrow alleys connect the cobbled streets, attic windows and gable ends shape the rooftops, and here and there you'll see the old wooden doors with heavy knockers and black iron hinges.

St Andrews Cathedral and Castle

The ruin of the great **cathedral** (visitor centre April–Sept daily 9.30am–6.30pm; Oct–March 9.30am–4.30pm; £3, joint ticket with castle £5;

Golf in St Andrews

St Andrews **Royal and Ancient Golf Club** (or "R&A") has been the international governing body for golf since 1754, when a meeting of 22 of the local gentry founded the Society of St Andrews Golfers, being "admirers of the ancient and healthful exercise of golf". The game itself has been played here since the fifteenth century. Those early days were instrumental in establishing Scotland as the home of golf, for the rules were distinguished from those of the French game by the fact that participants had to manoeuvre the ball into a hole, rather than hit an above-ground target. It was not without its opponents, however – particularly James II who, in 1457, banned his subjects from playing since it was distracting them from archery practice.

The approach to St Andrews from the west runs adjacent to the famous **Old Course**, one of seven courses in the immediate vicinity of the town. The R&A's strictly private **clubhouse**, a stolid, square building dating from 1854, is at the eastern end of the Old Course overlooking both the 18th green and the long strand of the West Sands. The British Open Championship was first held here in 1873, having been inaugurated in 1860 at Prestwick in Ayrshire, and since then it has been held at St Andrews regularly, pulling in enormous crowds. Pictures of golfing greats from Tom Morris to Tiger Woods, along with clubs and a variety of memorabilia donated by famous players, are displayed in the admirable **British Golf Museum** on Bruce Embankment, along the waterfront below the clubhouse (April–Oct Mon–Sat 9.30am–5.30pm, Sun 10am–5pm; Nov–March Mon–Sat 10am–4.30pm; £5).

Where to play

It is possible to **play** any of the town's courses, ranging from the nine-hole Balgove course (£10 per round) to the venerated Old Course itself – though for the latter you'll need a valid handicap certificate and must enter a daily ballot for tee times; if you're successful the green fees are £115 in summer. All this and more is explained at the clubhouse of the **St Andrews Links Trust** (ⓦ www.standrews.org.uk), the organization which looks after all the courses in town, located alongside the fairway of the first hole of the Old Course. Arguably the best golfing experience in St Andrews, even if you can't tell a birdie from a bogey, is the **Himalayas** (April–Sept Mon–Sat 10.30am–6.30pm, Sun noon–6.30pm; £1), a fantastically lumpy eighteen-hole putting course in an ideal setting next to the Old Course and the sea. Officially the Ladies Putting Club, founded in 1867, with its own clubhouse, it has grass as perfectly manicured as the championship course, and you can have all the thrill of sinking a six-footer in golf's most famous location, at a bargain price.

grounds year-round 9am–6.30pm; free; HS), at the east end of town, gives only an idea of the importance of what was once Scotland's largest cathedral. Founded in 1160, the cathedral was plundered and left to ruin during the Reformation by supporters of John Knox, fresh from a rousing meeting.

The cathedral site, above the harbour where the land drops to the sea, can be a blustery place, with the wind whistling through the great east window and along the stretch of turf that was once the central aisle. In front of the window a slab is all that remains of the high altar, where the relics of St Andrew were once enshrined. Previously, it is believed that they were kept in **St Rule's Tower**, the austere Romanesque monolith next to the cathedral, which was built as part of an abbey in 1130. From the top of the tower (a climb of 157 steps), there's a good view of the town and surroundings, and of the remains of the monastic buildings which made up the priory. Around the entire complex is a sturdy wall dating from the sixteenth century, over half a mile long and with three gateways.

△ Golf in St Andrews

Not far north of the cathedral, the rocky coastline curves inland to the ruined **castle** (same hours as cathedral; £3, joint ticket with cathedral £5; HS), with a drop to the sea on two sides and a moat on its inland side. Founded around 1200 and extended over the centuries, it was built as part of the Palace of the Bishops and Archbishops of St Andrews and was consequently the scene of some fairly grim incidents at the time of the Reformation. There's not a great deal left of the castle, since it fell into ruin in the seventeenth century, and most of what can be seen dates from the sixteenth century, apart from the fourteenth-century Fore Tower.

Around the university

A little way down North Street from the cathedral, housed in a picturesque sixteenth-century cottage with a low wooden door, the **St Andrews Preservation Trust Museum and Garden** (June–Sept daily 2–5pm; occasionally open by appointment at other times of year; free; W www.standrewspreservationtrusts .co.uk) presents an intimate picture of the town's history and glamorous golf connections. Further along North Street, the enclosed quadrangle of **St Salvator's College** is the oldest part of the scattered campus of the town's famous university. Guided tours of the university buildings start from here (see p.945), or you can wander freely around the buildings at your own pace. Almost all the oldest and most attractive university buildings are found along North and South streets, with more recent parts of the campus dotted around the centre of town and further out.

The beaches

St Andrews has two great **beaches**, the West Sands which stretch for two miles from just below the R&A Clubhouse, and the shorter, more compact, East Sands which curve round from the harbour beyond the cathedral. The West Sands are best known from the opening sequences of the Oscar-winning film *Chariots of Fire*; while it's still used by budding athletes, less energetic activities include sandcastle competitions, dips in the North Sea and birdwatching at the lonely north end. The blustery winds, which are the scourge of golfers and walkers alike, do at least make the beach a great place to **fly kites**: Wind and Water (T 07890/647227, W www.wind-and-water.co.uk) offers a range of introductory tuition sessions.

Eating, drinking and entertainment

St Andrews has no shortage of **restaurants** and **cafés**. There are a number of blow-out options, but given the local student population, there's also plenty of choice at the cheaper end of the market, as well as lots of good **pubs**. As you'd expect of a university town, there's also a healthy cultural scene: the **Byre Theatre** (T 01334/475000, W www.byretheatre.com), which began life in an old cowshed in 1933, now occupies a stylish modern building on Abbey Street, with a pleasant café/bistro (see below). There's also a small **cinema**, the New Picture House (T 01334/473509, W www.nphcinema.co.uk).

Restaurants and cafés

Byre Café-Bar Abbey Street W www .byretheatre.com. One of the nicer spots in town for a leisurely coffee or light meal; interesting contemporary dishes include red snapper and venison steak. Moderate.

The Doll's House 3 Church Square T 01334/477422, W www.dolls-house.co.uk. Stylish modern dishes based around top Scottish produce, with a continental feel to the outdoor tables and occasional jazz evenings. Moderate–expensive.

The Peat Inn Cupar, six miles southwest of town T 01334/840206, W www.thepeatinn.co.uk. The first Scottish restaurant to receive a Michelin star, when founding chef David Wilson established a great reputation based on local specialities with French influences. The dining area is intimate

without being cramped, and a three-course meal – perhaps featuring lobster broth, venison or roast monkfish – will set you back at least £40 per head. Also has eight plush if pricey suites attached (8). Closed Sun & Mon. Expensive.

The Seafood Restaurant The Scores T 01334/479475, W www.theseafoodrestaurant.com. Sister to its acclaimed namesake in St Monans, this restaurant has an amazing location in a custom-built glass building on the beach between the Aquarium and the Old Course. The venue has as much wow-factor as its fish-dominated menu. Expensive.

Pubs and bars

Gin House 116 South St. Raucous spot and a current student favourite. Full of chrome and wood, with regular DJs playing and food served all day.

Inn on North Street 127 North St. Tends to attract slightly older students, but houses the popular *Lizard* basement nightclub on Friday & Saturday.

Rusacks Lounge Bar 16 Pilmour Links. Hotel bar with the best views of the Old Course; settle into one of their comfy chairs and watch golfers through huge windows as you sip pricey drinks.

The East Neuk

Extending south of St Andrews as far as Largo Bay, the **East Neuk** is famous for its series of quaint fishing villages, all crow-stepped gables and red pan-tiled roofs, the Flemish influence in the architecture indicating a history of strong trading links with the Low Countries. Not surprisingly the area is dotted with windy **golf courses**, and there are also plenty of bracing coastal paths, including the waymarked **Fife Coastal Path**: tracing the shoreline between St Andrews and the Forth Rail Bridge, it's at its most scenic in the East Neuk stretch. **Bus** #95 runs from Leven around the coast to St Andrews.

Crail

CRAIL is the archetypally charming East Neuk fishing village, its maze of rough cobbled streets leading steeply down to a tiny stone-built harbour surrounded by piles of lobster creels, and with fishermen's cottages tucked into every nook and cranny in the cliff. Though often populated by artists at their easels and camera-toting tourists, it is still a working harbour, and if the boats have been out you can buy fresh lobster and crab cooked to order from a small wooden shack on the harbour edge (see below). The **tourist office** is at the **Crail Museum and Heritage Centre**, 62 Marketgate (Easter–Sept daily 10am–1pm & 2–5pm, Sun 2–5pm; free), where you can trace the history of the town. The **Crail Pottery**, 75 Nethergate (Mon–Fri 9am–5pm, Sat & Sun 10am–5pm), is worth a visit for its wide range of locally made pottery, while the **Jerdan Gallery**, 42 Marketgate South (daily 11am–5pm, closed Tues), displays contemporary paintings, sculptures and ceramics by top Scottish artists.

The best places to sit down and **eat** are at ⚓ *Mrs Riley's* lobster and crab shack at the harbour (mid-April to early Oct Tues–Sun noon–4pm), or at *Crail Harbour Gallery and Tearoom* (daily 10.30am–5pm, closed Mon & Tues in winter), tucked into a wee cottage on the way down to the harbour: it serves fresh coffee and toasted panini and has a terrace overlooking the Isle of May. The various hotels in the village serve **bar meals**, and you can get fish and chips from *Borellas* on the High Street.

Anstruther and around

ANSTRUTHER is the largest of the East Neuk fishing harbours, but it too has an attractively old-fashioned air and no shortage of character in its houses and narrow streets. It's also home to the wonderfully unpretentious **Scottish Fisheries Museum** (April–Oct Mon–Sat 10am–5.30pm, Sun 11am–5pm; Nov–March Mon–Sat 10am–4.30pm, Sun noon–4.30pm; £4.50). Set in an atmospheric complex of sixteenth- to nineteenth-century buildings with timber ceilings and wooden floors, it chronicles the history of the Scottish fishing and whaling industries with ingenious displays, including a whole series of exquisite ships' models built on site by a resident model-maker. Anstruther's helpful **tourist office** (Easter–Sept Mon–Sat 10am–5pm, Sun 11am–4pm; Oct Mon–Sat 10am–4pm, Sun 11am–4pm; ☎01333/311073) is next to the museum.

Located on the rugged **Isle of May**, several miles offshore from Anstruther, is a lighthouse erected in 1816 by Robert Louis Stevenson's grandfather, as well

20

as the remains of Scotland's first lighthouse, built in 1636. The island is now a nature reserve and bird sanctuary, and can be reached by boat from Anstruther (May–Sept 1 daily; May & June no sailing on Tues; £15; ☎01333/310103, ⓦwww.isleofmayferry.com). Check in advance for departure times, as crossings vary according to weather and tide, and allow between four and five hours for a round trip.

Tucked in beside the museum in one of the village's oldest buildings, once a cooperage and smokehouse, is the East Neuk's most impressive fish **restaurant**, 🍴 *The Cellar*, at 24 East Green (☎01333/310378; booking recommended). For decent fish and chips, head for the *Anstruther Fish Bar*, at 44 The Shore, a regular award-winner.

Central Fife

The main A92 road cuts right through **Central Fife**, ultimately connecting the Forth Road Bridge on the southern coast of Fife with the Tay Road Bridge on the northern coast. The main settlement of this inland region is **Glenrothes**, a new town created after World War II in old coal-mining territory. Generally the scenery in this part of the county is pleasant rather than startling, though it is worth making a detour to **Falkland** and its magnificent ruined palace.

Falkland

The **Howe of Fife**, north of Glenrothes, is a low-lying stretch of ground (or "howe") at the foot of the twin peaks of the heather-swathed **Lomond Hills** – West Lomond (1696ft) and East Lomond (1378ft). Nestling in the lower slopes of East Lomond, the narrow streets of **FALKLAND** are lined with fine and well-preserved seventeenth- and eighteenth-century buildings. The village grew up around **Falkland Palace** (March–Oct Mon–Sat 10am–6pm, Sun 1–5.30pm; £10, gardens only £5; NTS), which stands on the site of an earlier castle, home to the Macduffs, the Earls of Fife. James IV began the construction of the present palace in 1500; it was completed and embellished by James V, and became a favoured country retreat for the royal court. The palace was completely restored by the third Marquess of Bute, and today it is a stunning example of Early Renaissance architecture, complete with corbelled parapet, mullioned windows, round towers and massive walls. Free audio guides lead you round a cross section of public and private rooms in the south and east wings. Outside, the **gardens** are also worth a look, their well-stocked herbaceous borders lining a pristine lawn. Don't miss the high walls of the oldest real (or Royal) tennis court in Britain – built in 1539 for James V and still used.

The concentration of charming old cottages and historic buildings in the heart of Falkland also make it a particularly pleasant place to wander around. Both the *Hunting Lodge Hotel*, on High Street, opposite the palace (☎01337/857226; ❷), and the *Covenanter Hotel* (☎01337/857224, ⓦwww.covenanterhotel.com; ❷ in separate cottage, ❸ in hotel), just up the road, are comfortable traditional **inns**, with great pubs as well as a couple of rooms upstairs. Also on the High Street, *The Greenhouse* (☎01337/858400; closed Mon & Tues) is a small modern **restaurant** serving local organic food. Not far out of the village on the A912, there's a good little farm shop and **café** (daily 10am–6pm) at Pillars of Hercules Organic Farm.

Southern Fife

Although the coast of **southern Fife** is predominantly industrial – with everything from cottage industries to the refitting of nuclear submarines – thankfully only a small part has been blighted by insensitive development. Thanks to its proximity to the early coal mines, the charming village of **Culross** was once a lively port which enjoyed a thriving trade with Holland, the Dutch influence obvious in its lovely gabled houses. It was from nearby **Dunfermline** that Queen Margaret ousted the Celtic Church from Scotland in the eleventh century; her son, David I, founded an abbey here in the twelfth century. Southern Fife is linked to Edinburgh by the two **Forth bridges**, the red-painted girders of the Rail Bridge representing one of Britain's great engineering spectacles.

Culross

CULROSS (pronounced "Coorus") is one of Scotland's most picturesque settlements, all cobbled streets and squat cottages with crow-stepped gables, thanks in large part to the work of the National Trust for Scotland, which has been renovating its whitewashed, pan-tiled buildings since 1932. For an excellent introduction to the burgh's history, head to the **National Trust Visitor Centre** (Easter–Sept daily noon–5pm; joint ticket for Town House, Palace and Study £8; NTS), located in the **Town House** facing Sandhaven, where goods were once unloaded from ships. The most impressive building in the village is the nearby ochre-coloured **Culross Palace** (same hours), built by wealthy coal merchant George Bruce in the late sixteenth century; it's not a palace at all – its name comes from the Latin *palatium*, or "hall" – but a grand and impressive house, with lots of small rooms and connecting passageways. Inside, well-informed staff point out the wonderful painted ceilings, pine panelling, antique furniture and curios; outside, dormer windows and crow-stepped gables dominate the walled court in which the house stands.

The charm of Culross is evident simply by wandering through its narrow streets looking for old inscriptions above windows or investigating crooked passageways with names such as "Wee Causeway" and "Stinking Wynd". Leading uphill from the Town House, a cobbled alleyway known as **Back Causeway**, leads up to the **Study** (same hours as visitor centre), a restored house that takes its name from the small room at the top of the corbelled projecting tower, reached by a turnpike stair. Further up the hill from the Study lie the remains of **Culross Abbey**, founded by Cistercian monks on land given to the church in 1217 by the Earl of Fife. The nave of the original building is a ruin, a lawn studded with great stumps of columns. This adjoins the fine seventeenth-century **manse** and the choir of the abbey, which became the **Parish Church** in 1633. Inside, alabaster figures of Sir George Bruce, his lady, three sons and five daughters decorate a splendid family tomb.

Dunfermline

Scotland's capital until the Union of the Crowns in 1603, **DUNFERMLINE** lies inland seven miles east of Culross, north of the Forth bridges. The oldest part of **Dunfermline Abbey** (April–Sept daily 9.30am–6.30pm; Oct–March Mon–Wed & Sat 9.30am–4.30pm, Thurs 9.30am–12.30pm, Sun 2–4.30pm, closed Fri; ⓦ www.dunfermlineabbey.co.uk; £2.50; HS) is attributable to Queen Margaret, who began building a Benedictine priory in 1072, the remains of which can still be seen beneath the nave of the present church; her son, **David I**, raised the priory to the rank of abbey in the following century. In 1303, during the first of the **Wars of Independence**, the English king Edward I occupied the palace and ordered the destruction of most of the monastery buildings. **Robert the Bruce** helped rebuild the abbey, and when he died of leprosy 25 years later he was buried here, although his body went undiscovered until building began on a new parish church in 1821. Inside, the stained glass is impressive, and the columns are artfully carved into chevrons, spirals and arrowheads.

The guest house of Margaret's Benedictine monastery, south of the abbey, became the **palace** in the sixteenth century under James VI, who gave both it and the abbey to his consort, Queen Anne of Denmark. Charles I, the last monarch to be born in Scotland, entered the world here in 1600. Today, all that is left of it is a long, sandstone facade, especially impressive when silhouetted against the evening sky.

The Forth Bridges

The highlight of Fife's **south coast** is one of Scotland's largest man-made structures, the impressive Forth Rail Bridge, which joins Fife at **NORTH QUEENSFERRY**. Until the opening of the road bridge, this small fishing village was the northern landing point of the ferry from South Queensferry (see p.857), but today everything in the village is quite literally overshadowed by the two great bridges, each about a mile and a half in length, which traverse the Firth of Forth at its narrowest point.

The cantilevered **Forth Rail Bridge**, built from 1883 to 1890 by Sir John Fowler and Benjamin Baker, ranks among the supreme achievements of Victorian engineering, with some 50,000 tons of steel used in the construction of a design that manages to express grace as well as might. The only way to cross the rail bridge is aboard a train heading to or from Edinburgh, though inevitably this doesn't allow much of a perspective of the spectacle itself. For the best **panorama** of it, make use of the pedestrian and cycle lane on the east side of the road bridge.

Derived from American models, the suspension format chosen for the **Forth Road Bridge** alongside makes an interesting modern complement to the older structure. Erected between 1958 and 1964, it finally killed off the 900-year-old ferry, and now attracts such a heavy volume of traffic that a second road crossing is being considered.

For some background to the construction of both structures, head to the **Forth Bridges Exhibition** (daily 9am–9pm; free), occupying a couple of rooms tacked onto the modern *Corus Hotel* (previously the *Queensferry Lodge Hotel*), accessed off the B981 road that leads from the A90 to North Queensferry, which has a series of storyboards, photographs, models and displays.

Tucked beneath the mighty rail bridge is **Deep-Sea World** (daily: April–Oct 10am–6pm; Nov–March 11am–5pm; £8.55; ☏01383/411880, ⓦwww .deepseaworld.com), one of Scotland's most popular family attractions. Full of weird and wonderful creatures from sea horses to piranhas, the highlight is a huge aquarium that boasts the world's largest underwater viewing tunnel, through which you glide on a moving walkway while sharks, conger eels and all manner of fish from the deep swim nonchalantly past.

Perthshire

Genteel, attractive **Perthshire** is, in many ways, the epitome of well-groomed rural Scotland. An area of gentle glens, mature woodland, rushing rivers and peaceful lochs, it's the long-established domain of Scotland's well-to-do country set. First settled over eight thousand years ago, it was ruled by the Romans and then the Picts before Celtic missionaries established themselves, enjoying the amenable climate, fertile soil, and ideal defensive and trading location.

Occupying a strategic position at the mouth of the River Tay, the ancient town of **Perth** has as much claim as anywhere to be the gateway to the Highlands. Salmon, wool and, by the sixteenth century, whisky – Bell's, Dewar's and the Famous Grouse brands all hail from this area – were exported, while a major import was Bordeaux claret. At nearby **Scone**, Kenneth MacAlpine established the capital of the kingdom of the Scots and the Picts in 846. When this settlement was washed away by floods in 1210, William the Lion founded Perth as a royal burgh and it stood as Scotland's capital until the mid-fifteenth century.

North and west of Perth, **Highland Perthshire** begins to weave its charms: mighty woodlands blend with gorgeously rich scenery, particularly along the banks of the River Tay. The area is dotted with neat, confident towns and villages like **Dunkeld** and **Birnam**, with its mature trees and lovely ruined cathedral, and **Aberfeldy** set deep amongst farmland east of Loch Tay. Further north, the countryside becomes more sparsely populated and spectacular, with some wonderful walking country, especially around **Pitlochry**, **Blair Atholl** and the wild expanses of **Rannoch Moor** to the west.

Perth and around

Surrounded by fertile agricultural land and beautiful scenery, the bustling market town of **PERTH** was Scotland's capital for several centuries. During

---

Outdoor activities in Perthshire

To many, Perthshire is a celebration of the great outdoors, with **activities** ranging from gentle strolls through ancient oak forests to white-knuckle rides down frothing waterfalls. The variety of landscapes and relative accessibility from the central belt has led to a significant number of **outdoor operators** being based in the area: the tourist board's **Activity Line** (℡01577/861186, ⑩www.adventureperthshire .co.uk) can give advice and contacts for over thirty companies who comply with the Adventure Perthshire Operators' Charter. For canyoning, cliff-jumping and sphereing (which involves tumbling down a hillside inside a giant plastic ball), contact adrenalin junkies Nae Limits (℡01350/727242, ⑩www.naelimits.co.uk), based in Dunkeld; while for rafting through the best rapids on the Tay at Grandtully, try Splash (℡01887/829706, ⑩www.rafting.co.uk) or Freespirits (℡01887/829280, ⑩www .freespirits-online.co.uk), both based in or near Aberfeldy. Also in Aberfeldy is the National Kayak School (⑩www.nationalkayakschool.com), and the rather more sedate Highland Adventure Safaris (℡01887/820071, ⑩www.highlandadventuresa faris.co.uk), who take four-wheel-drive tours to search for golden eagle eyries, stags and pine martens,

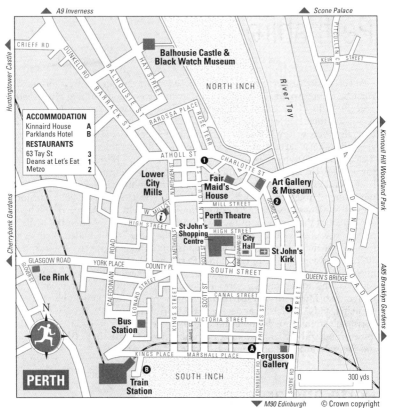

ACCOMMODATION
Kinnaird House   A
Parklands Hotel   B
RESTAURANTS
63 Tay St   3
Deans at Let's Eat 1
Metzo   2

© Crown copyright

M90 Edinburgh

20

the reign of James I, Parliament met here on several occasions, but its glory was short-lived: the king was murdered in the town's Dominican priory in 1437 by the treacherous Sir Robert Graham. Despite decline in the seventeenth century, the community expanded in the eighteenth and has prospered ever since; today the whisky and insurance trades employ significant numbers, and Perth remains an important town.

The Town

Perth's compact **centre** occupies a small patch on the west bank of the Tay. Two large areas of green parkland, known as the North and South Inch, flank the centre. The city's main shopping areas are **High Street** and **South Street**, as well as St John's shopping centre on King Edward Street. Perth is at its most attractive along **Tay Street**, with a succession of grander buildings along one side and the attractively landscaped riverside embankment on the other.

On the corner of Tay Street and Marshall Place, Perth's highlight is the **Fergusson Gallery** (Mon–Sat 10am–5pm; free), located in a striking round Victorian sandstone water tower, and home to an extensive collection of work by J.D. Fergusson, foremost artist of the Scottish Colourist movement (see p.908). He was greatly influenced by Impressionist and Post-Impressionist artists, creating a distinctive approach which marries both movements' freedom of style with bold use of colour and lighting – shown, for example, in his portrait of Elizabeth Dryden entitled *The Hat with the Pink Scarf*. As well as oils, the collection includes sketches, notebooks and sculpture: among the latter, look out for *Eastre: Hymn to the Sun*, an exotic, radiant, and almost sexy, brass head dating from 1924.

Scone Palace

Just a couple of miles north of Perth on the A93, **Scone Palace** (pronounced "skoon"; April–Oct daily 9.30am–5.30pm; £6.95, grounds only £3.50, Ⓦ www.scone-palace.co.uk) is one of Scotland's finest historical country homes. Owned and occupied by the Earl and Countess of Mansfield, the two-storey building on the eastern side of the Tay is stately but not overpowering, far more a home than an untouchable monument. The rooms, although full of priceless antiques and lavish furnishings, feel lived-in and used.

The abbey that stood here in the sixteenth century was where all Scottish kings until James IV were crowned. Long before that, Scone was the capital of Pictavia, and it was here that Kenneth MacAlpine brought the famous Coronation **Stone of Destiny**, or Stone of Scone, now to be found in Edinburgh Castle and ruled as the first king of a united Scotland. A replica of the (surprisingly small) stone can be found on Moot Hill, immediately opposite the palace.

In the **grounds** you'll also find a beech-hedge maze in the pattern of the heraldic family crest and avenues of venerable trees. Scone was the birthplace of botanist and plant collector **David Douglas**, and following the trail named after him you'll encounter a fragrant pinetum planted in 1848 with many of the exotics he discovered in California and elsewhere. To get to Scone from Perth, catch the open-topped tour bus, or bus #3 or #58.

Practicalities

Perth's **tourist office** is on West Mill Street (April–June, Sept & Oct Mon–Sat 9am–5pm, Sun 11am–4pm; July & Aug Mon–Sat 9am–6.30pm, Sun 10am–5pm; Nov–March Mon–Fri 9am–5pm, Sat 10am–4pm; ☎01738/450600, Ⓦ www.perthshire.co.uk). While it's easy to walk to all the main attractions in the centre of Perth, there's also an open-topped **tour bus** (July & Aug) that loops around town and stops at the sights on the outskirts, including Scone Palace (see above).

Of the numerous central **hotels**, aim for the fourteen-bedroom *Parklands Hotel*, close to the railway station at 2 St Leonards Bank (☎01738/622451, Ⓦ www.theparklandshotel.com; ❻), which has a touch of contemporary styling about it. There are **B&Bs** and guest houses on most of the approach roads into town; while Marshall Place, overlooking the South Inch, is a good central spot: *Kinnaird House*, at no. 5 (☎01738/628021, Ⓦ www.kinnaird-guesthouse.co.uk; ❸), offers a warm welcome in a lovely townhouse with well-equipped en-suite rooms.

Perth has some excellent **restaurants**. At the top end of the market is *63 Tay Street* (☎01738/441451, Ⓦ www.63taystreet.co.uk; closed Sun & Mon), serving classy and expensive modern Scottish fare in a designer setting. *Deans at Let's Eat*, 77 Kinnoull St (☎01738/643377, Ⓦ www.letseatperth.co.uk; closed Sun & Mon), is run by one of Scotland's better chefs using top quality local produce to create innovate dishes in a pleasantly homely environment. For more moderately priced fare try *Metzo* at 33 George St (☎01738/626016, Ⓦ www.metzorestaurant.co.uk), a relaxed bistro serving decent if familiar dishes with international influences.

Strath Tay to Loch Tay

Due north of Perth, both the railway and main A9 trunk road speed through some of Perthshire's most attractive countryside, before heading into the bleaker Highlands. Perthshire has been dubbed **"Big Tree Country"** in recognition of its magnificent woodland, much of which is found around the valley – or "strath" – of the River Tay, as it heads towards the sea from attractive **Loch Tay**. On the eastern side of the loch the Tay calmly glides past the attractive country town of **Aberfeldy**. The loch itself, meanwhile, is set up among the high Breadalbane mountains, which include the striking peak of **Ben Lawers**, Perthshire's highest, and the hills which enclose the long, enchanting **Glen Lyon**.

Dunkeld and Birnam

Twelve miles north of Perth on the A9, **DUNKELD** was proclaimed Scotland's ecclesiastical capital by Kenneth MacAlpine in 850. The town is one of the area's most pleasant communities, with handsome whitewashed houses, appealing arts and crafts shops and a charming cathedral. The **tourist office** is at The Cross in the town centre (April–June, Sept & Oct Mon–Sat 10am–5pm, Sun 11am–4pm; July & Aug Mon–Sat 9.30am–6.30pm, Sun 10am–5pm; Nov–March Mon, Tues, Fri–Sun 10am–4pm; ☏01350/727688). Dunkeld's partly ruined **cathedral** (daily: May–Sept 9.30am–6.30pm; Oct–April 9.30am–4pm; ⓦwww.dunkeldcathedral.org.uk; free) is on the northern side of town, in an idyllic setting amid lawns and trees on the east bank of the Tay. The present structure consists of the fourteenth-century choir and the fifteenth-century nave; the choir, restored in 1600 (and several times since), now serves as the parish church, while the nave remains roofless apart from the clocktower.

Dunkeld is linked to its sister community, **BIRNAM**, by Thomas Telford's seven-arched bridge of 1809. This little village has a place in history thanks to Shakespeare, for it was on Dunsinane Hill, to the southeast of the village, that Macbeth declared: "I will not be afraid of death and bane/Till Birnam Forest come to Dunsinane," only to be told later by a messenger "I look'd toward Birnam, and anon me thought/The Wood began to move. . ."

The **Birnam Oak**, a gnarly old character propped up by crutches which can be seen on the waymarked riverside walk, is inevitably claimed to be a survivor of the infamous mobile forest. Several centuries after Shakespeare, another literary personality, Beatrix Potter, drew inspiration from the area: a Potter-themed exhibition and garden, aimed at both children and adults, can be found on the main road in the impressive barrel-fronted **Birnam Institute** (daily 10am–5pm; ⓦwww.birnaminstitute.com; free), a busy, modern theatre, arts and community centre.

Practicalities

There are several large **hotels** in Dunkeld and Birnam, including the *Dunkeld House Hilton* (☏01350/727771, ⓦwww.hilton.co.uk/dunkeld; ❼ including dinner), a vast country-estate house on the banks of the Tay to the north of Dunkeld, which incorporates a spa, swimming pool and excellent outdoor-pursuits facilities. Much less grand, but full of personality, is the central *Taybank Hotel*, Tay Terrace (☏01350/727340, ⓦwww.taybank.com; ❷), a real beacon for music fans who come for the regular live sessions in the convivial bar; the rooms are simple and inexpensive, and the rate includes a continental breakfast. Alternatively, there's the pleasant *Waterbury Guest House* (☏01350/727324,

ⓦwww.waterbury-guesthouse.co.uk; ❸) on Murthly Terrace in Birnam. For **food**, try the decent bar meals at the *Taybank* (the stovies are particularly filling); during the day the *Foyer Café* in the Birnam Institute (see above) serves coffee, cakes and light meals, or you can pick up some delicious snacks and sandwiches at the Robert Menzies deli in Dunkeld.

Around Dunkeld

Dunkeld and Birnam are surrounded by some lovely countryside: a mile and a half from Birnam is **The Hermitage**, set in a grandly wooded gorge of the plunging River Braan. Here you'll find a pretty eighteenth-century folly, also known as Ossian's Hall, which neatly frames a dramatic waterfall. Nearby, you can see a Douglas fir which is claimed to be the tallest tree in Britain. Two miles east of Dunkeld, the **Loch of the Lowes** is a nature reserve that offers a rare chance to see breeding ospreys, among other wildfowl; its **visitor centre** (April–Sept 10am–5pm; ☎01350/727337; £2) has video relay screens and will point you in the direction of the best vantage points.

Aberfeldy and around

From Dunkeld the A9 runs north alongside the Tay for eight miles to Ballinluig, and the turn-off along the A827 to **ABERFELDY**. A generally prosperous settlement of large stone houses and 4WDs, Aberfeldy acts as a service centre for the wider Loch Tay area, with an enthusiastic **tourist office** at The Square (April–June, Sept & Oct Mon–Sat 9.30am–5pm, Sun 11am–3pm; July & Aug Mon–Sat 9.30am–6.30pm, Sun 10am–4pm; Nov–March Mon–Sat 10am–4pm; ☎01887/820276) providing advice on local accommodation and details of nearby walking trails.

The town's main attraction is **Dewar's World of Whisky** at the Aberfeldy Distillery (April–Oct Mon–Sat 10am–6pm, Sun noon–4pm; Nov–March Mon–Sat 10am–4pm; ⓦwww.dewarswow.com; £5), which puts on an impressive show of describing the making of whisky. The rest of the small town centre is a busy mixture of craft and tourist shops, the most interesting being **The Watermill** on Mill Street (Mon–Sat 9am–5pm, Sun noon–5pm; ⓦwww.aberfeldywatermill.com), an inspiring book shop, art gallery and café located in a superbly restored, early nineteenth-century mill.

Accommodation in and around Aberfeldy includes *Guinach House*, by The Birks (☎01887/820251, ⓦwww.guinachhouse.co.uk; ❻), a tastefully decorated guest house in well-tended grounds, and *Balnearn Guest House* on Crieff Road (☎01887/820431, ⓦwww.balnearnhouse.com; ❷). Two miles out of town, just beyond Castle Menzies, *Farleyer* (☎01887/820332, ⓦwww.farleyer.com; ❻) is a smart, contemporary restaurant with nine tasteful rooms. Alternatively, the settlement of Weem, half a mile from Aberfeldy on the north side of the Tay, has a couple of **bunkhouses**: *Glassie Farm* (☎01887/820265, ⓦwww.thebunkhouse.co.uk) and *Adventurer's Escape* (☎01887/820498, ⓦwww.adventurers-escape.co.uk).

Your best bet for a good cup of coffee or a lunchtime **snack** is the relaxed café in *The Watermill*. Decent **bar meals** can be found at the *Ailean Chraggan Inn* in Weem, or for something more upmarket, *Farleyer Restaurant* (see above) serves both bistro-style and more formal modern Scottish dining.

Loch Tay

Aberfeldy grew up around a crossing point on the River Tay, which leaves it oddly six miles adrift of **Loch Tay**, a fourteen-mile-long stretch of fresh water which all but hooks together the western and eastern Highlands. Guarding the northern end of the loch is **KENMORE**, a cluster of whitewashed estate houses and well-tended gardens. The main attraction here is the **Scottish Crannog Centre** (mid-March to Oct daily 10am–5.30pm; Nov Sat & Sun 10am–4pm; £4.75; Ⓦwww.crannog.co.uk), one of the best heritage museums in the country. Crannogs are Iron-Age loch dwellings built on stilts over the water, with a gangway to the shore which could be lifted up to defy a hostile intruder, whether animal or human. Here, visitors can walk out over the loch to a superbly reconstructed, thatched, wooden crannog, complete with sheepskin rugs, wooden bowls and other evidence of the way life was lived 2500 years ago.

Dominating the northern side of Loch Tay is moody **Ben Lawers** (3984ft), Perthshire's highest mountain; from the top there are incredible views towards both the Atlantic and the North Sea. The ascent – which should not be tackled unless you're properly equipped for Scottish hill-walking – takes around three hours from the NTS visitor centre (May–Sept daily 10.30am–5pm; ☏01567/820397), located at 1300ft and reached by a winding hill road off the A827.

Glen Lyon

North of Breadalbane, the mountains tumble down into **Glen Lyon** – at 34 miles long, the longest enclosed glen in Scotland – where, legend has it, the Celtic warrior Fingal built twelve castles. The narrow single-track road through the glen starts at **Keltneyburn**, near Kenmore at the northern end of the loch; a few miles on, the village of **FORTINGALL** is little more than a handful of pretty thatched cottages, although locals make much of their 5000-year-old yew tree, believed (by them at least) to be the oldest living thing in Europe. The venerable tree can be found in the churchyard, showing its age a little but well looked after, with a timeline nearby listing some of the events the yew has lived through. One of these, bizarrely, is the birth of Pontius Pilate, reputedly the son of a Roman officer stationed near Fortingall in the last years BC.

Highland Perthshire

North of the Tay valley, Perthshire doesn't discard its lush richness immediately, but there are clear indications of the more rugged, barren influences of the Highlands proper. The principal settlements of **Pitlochry** and **Blair Atholl**, both just off the A9, are separated by the narrow gorge of Killiecrankie, a crucial strategic spot in times past for anyone seeking to control movement of cattle or armies from the Highlands to the Lowlands. Greater rewards, however, are to be found further from the main drag, most notably in the winding westward road along the shores of **Loch Tummel** and **Loch Rannoch** past the distinctive peak of **Schiehallion**, which eventually leads to the remote wilderness of **Rannoch Moor**.

Pitlochry

PITLOCHRY has, on the face of it, a lot going for it, not least the backdrop of Ben Vrackie and the River Tummel slipping by. However, there's little charm to be found on the main street, filled with crawling traffic and endless shops selling cut-price woollens, knobbly walking sticks and glass baubles. Its one nearby attraction is Scotland's smallest distillery, the **Edradour Distillery** (March–Dec Mon–Sat 9.30am–5/6pm, Sun 11.30am–5pm; Jan & Feb Mon–Sat 10am–4pm, Sun noon–4pm; free; Ⓦwww.edradour.co.uk), set in an idyllic position tucked into the hills a couple of miles east of Pitlochry on the A924.

On the western edge of Pitlochry, just across the river, lies Scotland's renowned "Theatre in the Hills", the **Pitlochry Festival Theatre** (Ⓣ01796/484626, Ⓦwww.pitlochry.org.uk). A variety of productions – mostly mainstream theatre from the resident repertoire company, along with regular music events – are staged in the summer (May–Oct) and on winter weekends (Nov–April). By day it's worth coming here to wander around **Explorers: the Scottish Plant Hunters' Garden** (daily: April–June, Sept & Oct 10am–5pm; July & Aug 10am–7.30pm; £3; tours June–Sept Wed 10.30am & Sun 11.30am & 2.30pm; Ⓦwww.explorersgarden.com), an extended garden and forest area which pays tribute to Scottish botanists and collectors who roamed the world in the eighteenth and nineteenth centuries in search of new plant species. This is very much a modern rather than traditional garden, with carefully constructed, sinuous trails taking you past some attractive landscapes and features such as an open-air amphitheatre (sometimes used for outdoor performances), sculptures and the David Douglas pavilion, a soaring chamber beautifully constructed from Douglas fir.

Pitlochry's **tourist office** is at 22 Atholl Rd (April–June & Oct Mon–Sat 9am–6pm, Sun 10am–5pm; July–Sept Mon–Sat 9am–7pm, Sun 9.30am–6pm; Nov–March Mon–Fri 10am–5pm, Sat 10am–4pm; Ⓣ01796/472215). For **bike rental**, advice on local cycling routes, as well as general outdoor gear, try Escape Route at 3 Atholl Rd (Ⓣ01796/473859, Ⓦwww.escape-route.biz).

As a well-established holiday town, Pitlochry is packed with grand houses converted into large- and medium-sized **hotels**. The *Moulin Hotel* (Ⓣ01796/472196, Ⓦwww.moulinhotel.co.uk; ❹), at Moulin on the outskirts of Pitlochry along the A924, is a pleasant and popular old travellers' inn with a great bar and its own brewery, while *Craigatin House and Courtyard* (Ⓣ01796/472478, Ⓦwww.craigatinhouse.co.uk; ❹) on the northern stretch of the main road through town, is an attractive, contemporary **B&B** with large beds, soothing decor and a pleasant garden. Right in the centre at 134 Atholl Rd, *Pitlochry Backpackers Hotel*, (Ⓣ01796/470044, Ⓦwww.scotlands-top-hostels.com) is a **hostel** based in a former hotel with dorms (£13) as well as ten twin and double rooms (❶).

Pitlochry is the domain of the tearoom and you have to hunt to find decent places for a full **meal**: *The Old Armoury* (Ⓣ01796/474281, Ⓦwww.theold armouryrestaurant.com), on a back road between the train station and dam, is a civilized restaurant, while the best bet for traditional pub grub is the *Moulin Inn*, handily placed at the foot of Ben Vrackie.

Loch Tummel and Loch Rannoch

West of Pitlochry, the B8019/B846 makes a memorably scenic, if tortuous, traverse of the shores of **Loch Tummel** and then **Loch Rannoch**. Celebrated by Harry Lauder in his famous song *The Road to the Isles*, these two lochs and their adjoining rivers were much changed by massive hydroelectric schemes built in the 1940s and 1950s, yet this is still a spectacular stretch of countryside and one which deserves leisurely exploration. **Queen's View** at the eastern end of Loch Tummel is an obvious vantage point, looking down the loch to the misty peak of **Schiehallion** (3520ft), whose name comes from the Gaelic meaning "Fairy Mountain". One of Scotland's few

Rannoch Moor

Rannoch Moor occupies roughly 150 square miles of uninhabited and uninhabitable peat bogs, lochs, heather hillocks, strewn lumps of granite and a few gnarled Caledonian pine, all of it over 1000ft above sea level. Perhaps the most striking thing about the moor is its inaccessibility: one road, between Crianlarich and Glen Coe, skirts its western side, while another struggles west from Pitlochry to reach its eastern edge at Rannoch Station. The only regular form of transport is the West Highland railway, which stops at Rannoch and, a little to the north, Corrour Station, which has no road access at all. Corrour stole an unlikely scene in *Trainspotting* when the four heroes headed here for a taste of the great outdoors; there's a SYHA **hostel** a mile away on the shores of Loch Ossian (☎0870/004 1139, ⓦwww.syha.org.uk; April–Oct), making the area a great place for hikers seeking somewhere genuinely off the beaten track. From Rannoch Station it's possible to catch the train to Corrour and walk the nine miles back; it's a longer slog west to the eastern end of Glen Coe (see p.1078), the dramatic peaks of which poke up above the moor's western horizon. Determined hill-walkers will find a clutch of Munros around Corrour, including remote Ben Alder (3765ft), high above the forbidding shores of Loch Ericht.

freestanding hills, it's a popular, fairly easy and inspiring climb, with views on a good day to both sides of the country and north to the massed ranks of Highland peaks. The path up starts at Braes of Foss, just off the B846 which links Aberfeldy with Kinloch Rannoch: allow 3–4 hours to the top and back.

Beyond Loch Tummel, at the eastern end of Loch Rannoch, the small community of **KINLOCH RANNOCH** doesn't see a lot of passing trade – fishermen and hill-walkers are the most common visitors. Otherwise, the only real destination here is **Rannoch Station**, a lonely outpost on the Glasgow–Fort William West Highland train line, sixteen miles further on at the end of the road. There is a simple tearoom in the station building, as well as a pleasant small hotel, the *Moor of Rannoch* (☎01882/633238, ⓦwww.moorofrannoch.co.uk; ❺), but even these struggle to diminish the feeling of isolation. Here you can contemplate the bleakness of Rannoch Moor, a wide expanse of bog, heather and wind-blown pine tree which stretches right across to the imposing entrance to Glen Coe (see p.1078). A local **bus** (#85) from Kinloch Rannoch and a postbus from Pitlochry (#223; departs 8am) provide connections to the railway station.

North of Pitlochry

Four miles north of Pitlochry, the A9 cuts through the **Pass of Killiecrankie**, a breathtaking wooded gorge which falls away to the River Garry below. This dramatic setting was the site of the **Battle of Killiecrankie** in 1689, when the Jacobites quashed the forces of General Mackay. Legend has it that one soldier of the Crown, fleeing for his life, made a miraculous jump across the 18ft **Soldier's Leap**, an impossibly wide chasm halfway up the gorge. Exhibits at the slick NTS **visitor centre** (April–Oct daily 10am–5.30pm; ☎01796/473233; parking £2) recall the battle and examine the gorge in detail.

Blair Atholl

Three miles north of Killiecrankie, the village of **BLAIR ATHOLL** makes for a much quieter and more idiosyncratic stop than Pitlochry. The **Atholl Estates**

Information Centre (April–Oct daily 9am–4.45pm; ☎01796/481646, ⓦwww
.athollestatesrangerservice.co.uk) provides details of the extensive network of
local walks and bike rides as well as interesting information on surrounding
flora and fauna. Nearby, you can wander round the **Water Mill** on Ford Road
(April–Oct daily 10.30am–5.30pm; £1.50), which dates from 1613, and witness
flour being milled; better still, you can enjoy home-baked scones and light
lunches in its pleasant timber-beamed tearoom.

By far the most important and eye-catching building in these parts, however,
is **Blair Castle** (April–Oct daily 9.30am–last admission 4.30pm; Nov–March
Tues & Sat 9.30am–12.30pm; £6.90, grounds only £2.20; ⓦwww.blair-castle
.co.uk), seat of the Atholl dukedom. This whitewashed, turreted castle presents
an impressive sight as you approach up the driveway leading from the centre
of Blair Atholl village, especially if a piper is playing. The pipers belong to the
Atholl Highlanders, a select group retained by the duke as his private army – a
unique privilege afforded to him by Queen Victoria, who stayed here in 1844.
Highlights are the soaring **entrance hall**, with every spare inch of wood panelling covered in weapons of some description, and the vast **ballroom**, with its
timber roof, antlers, and mixture of portraits.

Travel details

Buses

For information on all local and national bus services, contact Traveline ☎0870/608 2608 (daily
7am–10pm), ⓦwww.travelinescotland.com.
Aberfeldy to: Pitlochry (3 daily; 30min); Killin (5
daily; 1hr).
Aberfoyle to: Callander (June–Sept Thurs–Tues
4 daily; 25min); Port of Menteith (June–Sept
Thurs–Tues 4 daily; 10min).
Balloch to: Balmaha (every 2hr; 25min); Luss (8–9
daily; 15min).
Callander to Loch Katrine (June–Sept 4 daily;
55min).
Dunfermline to: Culross (hourly; 20min); Edinburgh (every 30min; 1hr 20min); Glasgow (hourly;
1hr 15min); Kirkcaldy (every 30min; 30min); Stirling (hourly; 1hr 15min).
Kinloch Rannoch to: Pitlochry (4 daily; 1hr);
Rannoch Station (3 daily; 40min).
Perth to: Aberfeldy (10 daily; 1hr 15min); Crieff
(hourly; 45min); Dundee (hourly; 45min); Dunkeld
(hourly; 30min); Edinburgh (hourly; 1hr 20min);
Glasgow (hourly; 1hr 35min); Gleneagles (hourly;
25min); Inverness (hourly; 2hr 45min); Oban
(2 daily, 3hr); Pitlochry (hourly; 45min); Stirling
(hourly; 40–50min).
St Andrews to: Dundee (every 20min; 40min);
Dunfermline (hourly; 1hr 30min); Edinburgh (every
30min; 2hr 10min); Glasgow (hourly; 2hr 30min);
Glenrothes (hourly; 45min); Kirkcaldy (every 30min;
1hr); Stirling (every 2hr; 2hr).

Stirling to: Aberfoyle (4 daily; 45min); Callander
(hourly; 45min); Dollar (6 daily; 35min); Doune
(hourly; 25min); Dunblane (hourly; 25min); Dundee
(hourly; 1hr 30min); Edinburgh (hourly; 1hr 10min);
Falkirk (every 40–50min; 30min); Glasgow (hourly;
50min); Inverness (every 2hr; 3hr 20min); Killin
(3–4 daily; 1hr 30); Perth (hourly; 40min); St
Andrews (3 daily; 2hr).

Trains

For information on all local and national rail
services, contact National Rail Enquiries
☎08457/404950, ⓦwww.nationalrail.co.uk or
ⓦwww.firstscotrail.com.
Balloch to: Glasgow (every 30min; 40min).
Crianlarich to: Fort William (2–4 daily; 1hr 50min);
Glasgow Queen Street (2–4 daily; 1hr 50min); Oban
(3–6 daily; 1hr 10min).
Dunfermline to: Edinburgh (every 30min; 30min);
Kirkcaldy (hourly; 40min).
Falkirk to: Edinburgh (every 30min; 35min); Glas-
gow Queen Street (every 30min; 25min); Stirling
(every 30min; 15min).
Leuchars (for St Andrews) to: Aberdeen (1–2
hourly; 1hr 30min); Dundee (1–2 hourly; 15min);
Edinburgh (1–2 hourly; 1hr).
Perth to: Aberdeen (hourly; 1hr 40min); Blair
Atholl (3–7 daily; 40min); Dundee (hourly; 25min);
Dunkeld (3–7 daily; 20min); Edinburgh (9 daily; 1hr
25min); Glasgow Queen Street (hourly; 1hr 5min);
Inverness (4–9 daily; 2hr); Pitlochry (4–9 daily;
30min), Stirling (hourly; 30min).

Rannoch to: Corrour (2–4 daily; 12min); Fort William (2–4 daily; 1hr); Glasgow Queen Street (2–4 daily; 2hr 45min); London Euston (sleeper service; Sun–Fri daily; 11hr).

Stirling to: Aberdeen (hourly; 2hr 15min); Dundee (hourly; 1hr); Edinburgh (hourly; 1hr); Falkirk Grahamston (hourly; 30min); Glasgow Queen Street (hourly; 30min); Inverness (3–5 daily; 2hr 30min); Perth (hourly; 30min).

Ferries

Rosyth to: Zeebrugge (3–7 weekly; 18hr).

Argyll

CHAPTER 21

Highlights

* **Mount Stuart, Bute** Overblown aristocratic mansion, set in beautiful grounds. **See p.969**

* **Loch Fyne Oyster Bar, Cairndow** Scotland's finest smokehouse and seafood outlet. **See p.970**

* **Tobermory, Mull** Picturesque fishing village, with colourful houses along a sheltered harbour. **See p.973**

* **Golden beaches** Kiloran Bay on the Isle of Colonsay is a perfect sandy beach, but there are plenty more on Islay, Coll and Tiree. **See p.980**

* **Isle of Gigha** The perfect island escape: sandy beaches, friendly folk, decent hotel and lovely gardens. **See p.982**

* **Goat Fell, Arran** Spectacular views over north Arran's craggy mountain range and the Firth of Clyde. **See p.986**

* **Wintering geese on Islay** Thousands of barnacle and white-fronted geese winter here before flying off each summer to Greenland. **See p.988**

* **Port Charlotte, Islay** Idyllic village of pretty whitewashed houses, looking out over a sandy beach. **See p.989**

△ Loch Fyne seafood

21

Argyll

Cut off for centuries from the rest of Scotland by the mountains and sea lochs that characterize the region, **Argyll** remains remote, its scatter of offshore islands forming part of the Inner Hebridean archipelago (the remaining Hebrides are dealt with in the next chapter). Geographically as well as culturally, this is a transitional area between Highland and Lowland, boasting a rich variety of scenery, from lush, subtropical gardens warmed by the Gulf Stream to flat and treeless islands on the edge of the Atlantic. It's in the folds and twists of the countryside, the interplay of land and water and the views out to the islands that the strengths and beauties of mainland Argyll lie. The one area of man-made sights you shouldn't miss, however, is the cluster of **Celtic** and **prehistoric sites** near Kilmartin. Overall, the population is tiny; even **Oban**, Argyll's chief ferry port, has just seven thousand inhabitants, while the prettiest town, **Inveraray**, boasts less than eight hundred.

The eastern duo of **Bute** and **Arran** are the most popular of Scotland's more southerly islands, the latter – now, strictly speaking, part of Ayrshire – justifiably so, with spectacular scenery ranging from the granite peaks of the north to the Lowland pasture of the south. Of the Hebridean islands covered in this chapter, mountainous **Mull** is the most visited, though it is large enough to absorb the crowds, many of whom are only passing through en route to the tiny isle of **Iona**, a centre of Christian culture since the sixth century. **Islay**, best known for its distinctive malt whiskies, is fairly quiet even in the height of summer, as is neighbouring **Jura**, which offers excellent walking opportunities. And, for those seeking further solitude, there are the more remote islands of **Tiree** and **Coll**, which, although swept with fierce winds, boast more sunny days than anywhere else in Scotland.

The region's name derives from *Aragaidheal*, which translates as "Boundary of the Gaels", the Irish Celts who settled here in the fifth century AD, and whose **kingdom of Dalriada** embraced much of what is now Argyll. Known to the Romans as *Scotti* – hence "Scotland" – it was the Irish Celts who promoted Celtic Christianity, and whose Gaelic language eventually became the national tongue. In the twelfth century, the immensely powerful Somerled became king of the Hebrides and lord of Argyll. His successors, the MacDonalds, established Islay as their headquarters in the 1200s, but were in turn dislodged by Robert the Bruce, whose allies, the **Campbells**, eventually gained control of the entire area as the dukes of Argyll; even today, they remain one of the largest landowners in the region.

In the aftermath of the Jacobite uprisings, Argyll, like the rest of the Highlands, was devastated by the **Clearances**, with thousands of crofters evicted to make room for profitable sheep farming – "the white plague" – and cattle rearing.

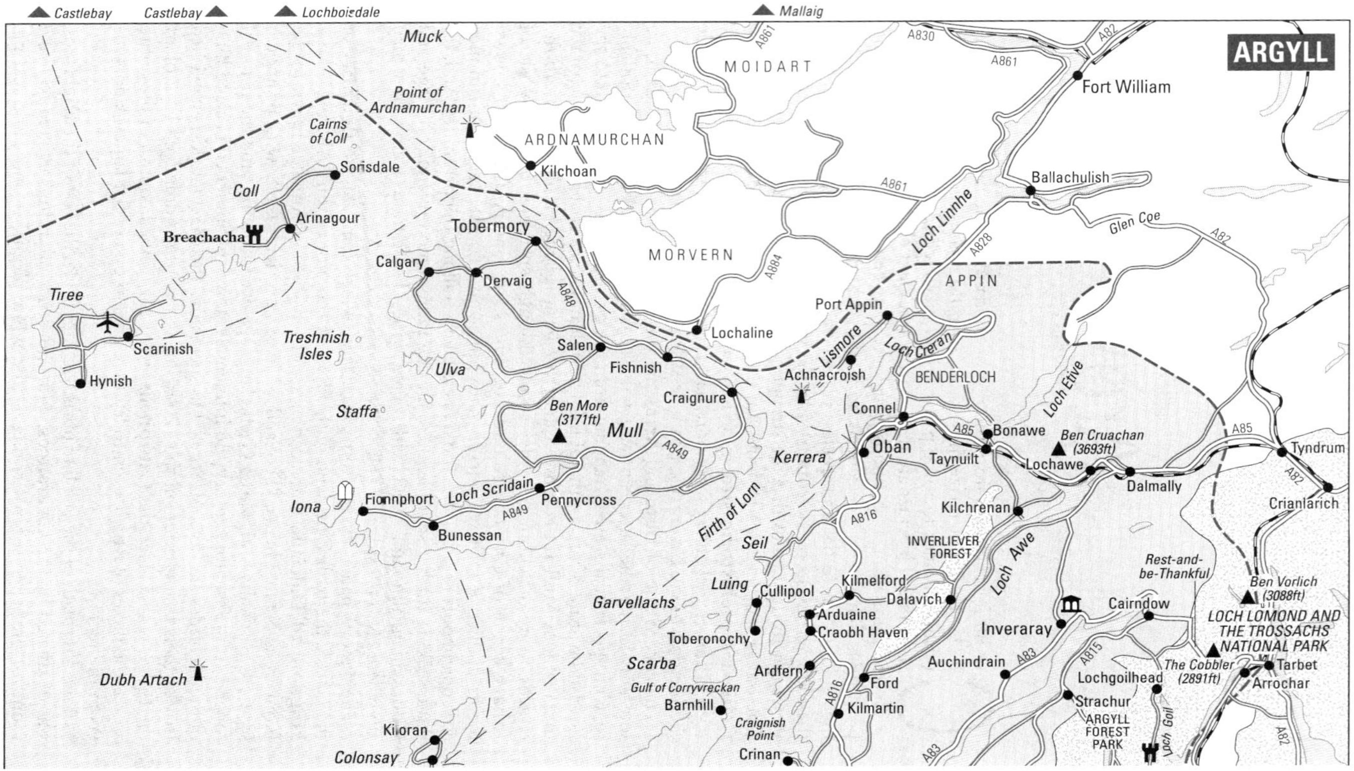
ARGYLL
Castlebay
Castlebay
Lochboisdale
Mallaig
Muck
Point of Ardnamurchan
Cairns of Coll
ARDNAMURCHAN
Kilchoan
MOIDART
Fort William
Ballachulish
Glen Coe
Loch Linnhe
MORVERN
APPIN
Sorisdale
Coll
Arinagour
Breachacha
Tobermory
Calgary
Dervaig
Tiree
Scarinish
Hynish
Treshnish Isles
Ulva
Staffa
Salen
Fishnish
Lochaline
Port Appin
Lismore
Loch Creran
Achnacroish
BENDERLOCH
Craignure
Ben More (3171ft)
Mull
Connel
Oban
Bonawe
Ben Cruachan (3693ft)
Loch Etive
Taynuilt
Lochawe
Dalmally
Tyndrum
Crianlarich
Kerrera
Iona
Fionnphort
Loch Scridain
Pennycross
Bunessan
Firth of Lorn
Seil
Kilchrenan
INVERLIEVER FOREST
Loch Awe
Rest-and-be-Thankful
Ben Vorlich (3088ft)
LOCH LOMOND AND THE TROSSACHS NATIONAL PARK
Luing
Cullipool
Kilmelford
Dalavich
Garvellachs
Arduaine
Craobh Haven
Inveraray
Cairndow
Toberonochy
Scarba
Ardfern
Auchindrain
The Cobbler (2891ft)
Tarbet
Arrochar
Lochgoilhead
Loch Goil
Gulf of Corryvreckan
Ford
Strachur
Barnhill
Kilmartin
ARGYLL FOREST PARK
Dubh Artach
Kiloran
Colonsay
Craignish Point
Crinan
A830
A861
A82
A828
A884
A848
A849
A85
A816
A83
A815

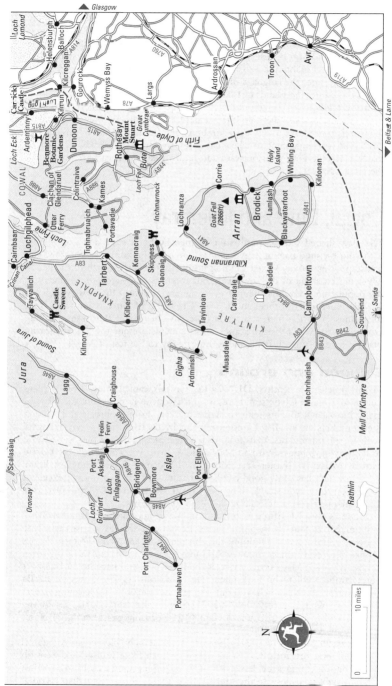

© Crown copyright

More recently forestry plantations have dramatically altered the landscape, while purpose-built marinas have sprouted all around the heavily indented coastline. Today the traditional industries of fishing and farming are in deep crisis, as is the modern industry of fish farming, leaving the region ever more dependent on tourism, EU grants and a steady influx of new settlers to keep things going, while Gaelic, once the language of the majority in Argyll, retains only a tenuous hold on the outlying islands of Islay and Tiree.

Public transport throughout Argyll is minimal, though buses do serve most major settlements, and the train line reaches Oban. In the remoter parts and on the islands, you'll have to rely on a combination of walking, shared taxis and the postbus. If you're planning to take a **car** across to one of the islands, it's essential that you reserve both your outward and return journeys as early as possible, as the ferries get very booked up.

Cowal, Bute and Inveraray

The claw-shaped **Cowal peninsula**, formed by Loch Fyne and Loch Long, is the most-visited part of Argyll, largely due to its proximity to Glasgow. The landscape is extremely varied, ranging from Munros in the north to the gentle low-lying coastline of the southwest, but most visitors – and the majority of the population – confine themselves to the area around **Dunoon** (which has Cowal's chief tourist office) in the east. The island of **Bute** is separated from the peninsula by the merest sliver of water, its chief town **Rothesay** rivalling Dunoon as the Clyde's major seaside resort. The picturesque town of **Inveraray** sits at the head of Loch Fyne, and is the gateway to the rest of Argyll.

Dunoon and around

In the nineteenth century, **DUNOON**, Cowal's capital, grew from a mere village to a major Clyde seaside resort and favourite holiday spot for Glaswegians. Nowadays, tourists tend to arrive by ferry from Gourock and, though their numbers are smaller, Dunoon remains by far the largest town in Argyll, with 13,000 inhabitants. Apart from its practical uses and a fine pier, there's little to tempt you to linger. With an hour or so to spare, you could visit the **Castle House Museum** (Easter–Oct Mon–Sat 10.30am–4.30pm, Sun 2–4.30pm; £1.50), which has some good hands-on nature stuff for kids, and an excellent section on the Clyde steamers, or the **Cowal Bird Garden** (April–Oct daily 10.30am–6pm; £4), a mile along the A885 to Sandbank.

Dunoon's **tourist office** is located on Alexandra Parade (Mon–Fri 9am–5.30pm, Sat & Sun 10am–5pm). There are two car **ferries** across the Clyde between Gourock and Dunoon; the shorter, more frequent Western Ferries service runs every thirty minutes to Hunter's Quay, a mile north of the town centre; while CalMac's boats arrive at the main pier, and have better transport connections if you're on foot. There's an enormous choice of average **B&Bs** – the tourist office can help you out – or try the pricier but welcoming *Abbot's Brae* above West Bay (℡01369/705021, ⓦwww.abbotsbrae.co.uk; ❺) or the smart *Dhailling Lodge* (℡01369/701253, ⓦwww.dhaillinglodge.com; ❹), closer to town on Alexandra Parade.

Chatters, 58 John St (℡01369/706402; Wed–Sat only; closed Jan & Feb), is Dunoon's best **restaurant**, offering delicious Loch Fyne seafood and Scottish beef. For something a bit less pricey, try the simple **café** run by the Baptist Church right next door to the tourist office; there's also a vast Italian menu at

La Cantina in Argyll Street (closed Mon). Dunoon boasts a two-screen **cinema** (a rarity in Argyll) on John Street, but the town's most famous entertainment is the **Cowal Highland Gathering** (www.cowalgathering.com), the largest of its kind in the world, held here on the last weekend in August.

Around Dunoon

Five miles north of Dunoon, at the southern tip of the exceptionally narrow freshwater **Loch Eck**, are the beautifully laid-out **Benmore Botanic Gardens** (daily: March & Oct 10am–5pm; April–Sept 10am–6pm; £3.50). An offshoot of Edinburgh's Royal Botanic Gardens, they are famed for their rhododendrons and especially striking for their avenue of Great Redwoods, planted in 1863 and now over 100ft high. There's also an excellent, inexpensive **café** by the entrance, with an imaginative menu.

The Isle of Bute

The island of **BUTE** is in many ways simply an extension of the Cowal peninsula, from which it is separated by the narrow Kyles of Bute. Thanks to its consistently mild climate and a ferry link with Wemyss Bay, Bute has been a popular holiday and convalescence spot for Clydesiders – particularly the elderly – for over a century.

Bute's only town, **ROTHESAY** (www.isle-of-bute.com) is a handsome Victorian resort set in a wide sweeping bay, backed by green hills, with a classic palm-tree promenade and 1920s pagoda-style Winter Gardens. It creates a better general impression than Dunoon, with its period architecture and the occasional flourishes of wrought-ironwork. Even if you're just passing through, you should pay a visit to the ornate **Victorian toilets** (daily: Easter–Sept 8am–9pm; Oct–Easter 9am–5pm; 15p) on the pier, which were built by Twyfords in 1899 and have since been declared a national treasure. Men have the best time, since the porcelain urinals steal the show, but women can ask for a guided tour.

Rothesay also boasts the militarily useless, but architecturally impressive, moated ruins of **Rothesay Castle** (April–Sept daily 9.30am–6.30pm; Oct–March Sat–Wed 9.30am–4.30pm; £3; HS), hidden amid the town's backstreets but signposted from the pier. Built around the twelfth century, it was twice captured by the Vikings in the 1200s; such vulnerability was the reasoning behind the unusual, almost circular curtain-wall, with its four big drum towers, only one of which remains fully intact.

A very good reason for coming to Bute is to visit **Mount Stuart** (May–Sept Sun–Fri 11am–5pm, Sat 10am–1.30pm; £7; www.mountstuart.com), three miles south of Rothesay. Seat of the fantastically wealthy seventh marquis of Bute (aka former racing driver Johnny Dumfries), the mansion was built for the third marquis between 1879 and World War II, as an incredible High Gothic fancy, drawing architectural inspiration from all over Europe. The sumptuous interior was decked out by craftsmen who worked with William Burges on the marquis's earlier medieval concoctions at Cardiff Castle. The gardens (£3.50), established in the eighteenth century by the third earl of Bute, are equally impressive.

Practicalities

Rothesay's **tourist office** is opposite the pier at 15 Victoria St (daily 10am–5pm; longer hours in peak season). There's no shortage of modest places to **stay** along the seafront, but one of the most attractive is *Cannon House* (01700/502819,

@www.cannonhousehotel.co.uk; ❹), a Georgian house close to the pier on Battery Place, while the nearby *Commodore* guest house (☎01700/502178, @www.commodorebute.com; ❶) is more modest, but equally accommodating. Further out in Ascog, the B&B at *Ascog Farm* (☎01700/503372; ❷) is exceptionally good value. The best **food** options are *The Bistro* in the Winter Garden, with a superb view of the bay, or the highly original and engaging *Port Royal Hotel* in Port Bannatyne, which describes itself as a "Waterfront Russian Tavern". For Rothesay's finest fish and chips, head for the *West End Café* on Gallowgate.

Arrochar to Cairndow

Approaching from Glasgow along the A82, followed by the A83, you enter Argyll at **ARROCHAR**, at the head of Loch Long. The village itself is ordinary enough, but the setting is dramatic. There's a **train station** a mile or so east, just off the A83 to Tarbert (see p.982), and numerous **hotels** and **B&Bs**; try the very friendly *Lochside Guest House* on the main road (☎01301/702467, @www.stayatlochlomond.comLochside; ❸), or *Fascadail* (☎01301/702344, @www.fascadail.com; ❷), a guest house with a glorious garden, situated a little to the south on the quieter A814 to Garelochhead.

Approaching Cowal from the east, you're forced to climb Glen Croe, a strategic hill pass whose saddle is called **Rest-and-be-Thankful**, for obvious reasons. From here, continue along the A83 down the grand Highland sweep of **Glen Kinglas** to **CAIRNDOW**, at the head of Loch Fyne. A mile or so around the head of the loch on the main road is famous **⚓ Loch Fyne Oyster Bar** (☎01499/600236, @www.loch-fyne.com), which sells more oysters than anywhere else in the country, plus lots of other fish and seafood treats. You can stock up on provisions or eat at the moderately expensive restaurant.

Inveraray

A classic example of an eighteenth-century planned town, **INVERARAY** was built on the site of a ruined fishing village in 1745 by the third duke of Argyll, head of the powerful Campbell clan, in order to distance his newly rebuilt castle from the hoi polloi in the town and to establish a commercial and legal centre for the region. A set piece of Scottish Georgian architecture, Inveraray has a truly memorable setting, the brilliant white arches of Front Street reflected in the still waters of **Loch Fyne**, which separate it from the Cowal peninsula.

Squeezed onto a promontory some distance from the duke's new castle, Inveraray's "New Town" has a distinctive **Main Street** (set at a right angle to Front Street), flanked by whitewashed terraces, whose window casements are picked out in black. At the top of the street, the road divides to circumnavigate the town's Neoclassical church, originally built in two parts: the southern half served the Gaelic-speaking community, while the northern half served those who spoke English.

East of the church is **Inveraray Jail** (daily: April–Oct 9.30am–6pm; Nov–March 10am–5pm; £5.95), whose attractive Georgian courthouse and grim prison blocks ceased to function in the 1930s. The jail is now an imaginative and thoroughly enjoyable museum, which graphically recounts prison conditions from medieval times. You can also sit in the beautiful semicircular courthouse and listen to the trial of a farmer accused of fraud.

A ten-minute walk north of the New Town, the neo-Gothic **Inveraray Castle** (April, May & Oct Mon–Thurs & Sat 10am–1pm & 2–5.45pm, Sun 1–5.45pm; June–Sept Mon–Sat 10am–5.45pm, Sun 1–5.45pm; £5.90) remains the family home of the Duke of Argyll. Built in 1745, its most startling feature is the armoury hall, whose displays of weaponry – supplied to the Campbells by the British government to put down the Jacobites – rise through several storeys; look out for Rob Roy's rather sad-looking sporran and dirk handle (a "dirk" being a dagger, traditionally worn in Highland dress).

Practicalities

Inveraray's **tourist office** is on Front Street (April–Oct Mon–Sat 9am–5pm, Sun noon–5pm; Nov–March Mon–Fri 10am–3pm, Sat & Sun 11am–3pm), as is the town's chief **hotel**, the historic *Argyll* (℡01499/302466, ✆www .the-argyll-hotel.co.uk; ❺), now part of the *Best Western* chain. A cheaper, but equally well-appointed alternative is the Georgian *Fernpoint Hotel* (℡01499/302170; ❸), by the pier, which has a nice pub garden. The SYHA **hostel** (℡0870/004 1125, ✆www.syha.org.uk; mid-March to Sept) is in a modern building a short distance north on the A819 Dalmally road. The **bar** of the central *George Hotel* is the town's liveliest spot, while the best place to sample Loch Fyne's delicious fresh fish and seafood is the *Loch Fyne Oyster Bar* (see p.970), six miles up the A83.

Oban

The solidly Victorian resort of **OBAN** (✆www.oban.org.uk) enjoys a superb setting distinguished by a bizarre granite amphitheatre, dramatically lit at night, on the hilltop above the town. Despite a population of just eight thousand, it's by far the largest port in northwest Scotland, and the main departure point for ferries to the Hebrides. If you arrive late, or are catching an early boat, you may have to spend the night here; if you're staying elsewhere, it's a useful base for wet-weather activities and shopping.

The only truly remarkable sight in Oban is the town's landmark, **McCaig's Tower**, a stiff ten-minute climb from the quayside. Built in imitation of Rome's Colosseum, it was the brainchild of a local businessman a century ago, who had the twin aims of alleviating off-season unemployment among the local stonemasons and creating a museum, art gallery and chapel. In his will, McCaig gave instructions for the lancet windows to be filled with bronze statues of the family, though no such work was ever undertaken. Instead, the folly has been turned into a sort of walled garden, and provides a wonderful seaward panorama, particularly at sunset.

Practicalities

The CalMac **ferry terminal** (℡01631/566688, ✆www.calmac.co.uk) for the islands is on Railway Pier, a stone's throw from the **train station**, which is itself adjacent to the **bus station** on Station Square. The **tourist office** (April–Oct Mon–Fri 9am–5pm, Sat & Sun 10am–5pm; longer hours in peak season; Nov–March Mon–Fri 9.30am–5pm, Sat 10am–4pm, Sun noon–4pm) is housed in a converted church on Argyll Square.

Oban is positively heaving with **hotels** and **B&B**s. Top choices include the hospitable *Kilchrenan House* (℡01631/562663, ✆www.kilchrenanhouse .co.uk; ❹), a tasteful place on the Corran Esplanade; and the *Caledonian Hotel*, on Station Square (℡0871/222 3415, ✆www.go2oban.co.uk; ❸), the best of Oban's big central hotels. There are also three **hostels**, the friendliest, cheapest and most central of which is the *Oban Backpackers*, on Breadalbane Street (℡01631/562107, ✆www.scotlands-top-hostels.com; March–Oct).

Campers should head for *Oban Divers Caravan Park* on Glenshellach Road (℡01631/562425, ⓦwww.obandivers.co.uk; April–Oct), a mile and a half from Oban up a pretty glen.

Oban has two top fish **restaurants**: on the North Pier, the swanky designer *Ee-usk* (℡01631/565666) serves glistening seafood platters and fresh fish dishes; while the less glamorous *Waterfront* (℡01631/563110), on the CalMac pier, rustles up impressive dishes using the best of the daily catch. Alternatively, head for George Street, where you'll find *Coast* (℡01631/569 9900), a Scottish contemporary bistro; the cheap, cheerful and more youthful *Mondo*; *Oban Fish & Chip Shop & Restaurant*, at no. 116; and a **café** on the mezzanine above the impressive *Kitchen Garden* deli, for sit-down snacks. Oban's only half-decent **pub** is the *Oban Inn* opposite the North Pier, with a classic dark-wood-flagstone-and-brass bar downstairs and lounge bar with stained glass upstairs. Oban is also one of the few places in Argyll with a **cinema**, confusingly known as the Highland Theatre (℡01631/562444), at the north end of George Street.

The Isle of Mull

Mull (ⓦwww.holidaymull.org.uk) is by far the most accessible of the Hebrides: just forty minutes from Oban by ferry. As so often, first impressions largely depend on the weather – it's the wettest of the Hebrides (and that's saying something) – as without the sun the large tracts of moorland, particularly around the island's highest peak, Ben More (3196ft), can appear bleak and unwelcoming.

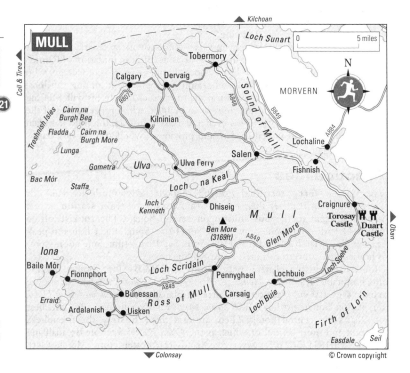

There are, however, areas of more gentle pastoral scenery around **Dervaig** in the north and the indented west coast varies from the sandy beaches around **Calgary** to the cliffs of Loch na Keal. The most common mistake is to try and "do" the island in a day or two: flogging up the main road to the picturesque capital of **Tobermory**, then covering the fifty-odd miles between there and Fionnphort, in order to visit **Iona**. Mull is a place that will grow on you only if you have the time and patience to explore.

Craignure and around

CRAIGNURE is the main arrival point, linked by frequent daily **car ferry** to Oban (booking advised). It's little more than a scattering of cottages with a small shop, a bar, some toilets and a CalMac and **tourist office** situated opposite the pier (April–Sept Mon–Fri 8.30am–5pm, Sat 9am–5pm, Sun 10am–5pm; Oct–March Mon–Sat 9am–5pm, Sun 11am–5pm). The *Craignure Inn* (☎01680/812305, ⊛www.craignure-inn.co.uk; ❺), just a minute's stroll up the road towards Fionnphort, is a snug **pub** to hole up in. There's also a well-equipped **campsite** (☎01680/812496, ⊛www.shielingholidays.co.uk; April–Oct) on the south side of Craignure Bay, behind the new village hall.

Two castles lie immediately southeast of Craignure. **Torosay Castle** (April to mid-Oct daily 10.30am–5.30pm; £5.50), a full-blown Scots baronial creation, is linked to Craignure by the narrow-gauge **Mull Rail** (Easter to mid-Oct; £4 return). Its magnificent **gardens** (daily: summer months 9am–7pm, winter dawn–dusk; £4.50) include an avenue of eighteenth-century Venetian statues, a Japanese section and views over to neighbouring Duart. The house itself, in the mid-nineteenth-century style, is stuffed with junk relating to the present owners, the little-known Guthries.

Lacking the gardens, but perched on a picturesque spit of rock a couple of miles east of Torosay, **Duart Castle** (April Sun–Thurs 11am–4pm; May–Oct daily 10.30am–5.30pm; £4.50) is clearly visible from the Oban–Craignure ferry. Headquarters of the once-powerful MacLean clan from the thirteenth century, it was burnt down by the Campbells and confiscated after the 1745 rebellion. Finally in 1911, the 26th clan chief, Fitzroy MacLean (1835–1936), managed to buy it back and restore it. You can peek at the dungeons, climb up to the ramparts, study the family photos, and learn about the world scout movement – the 27th clan chief became chief scout in 1959. After your visit, you can enjoy homemade cakes and tea at the castle's excellent tearoom (May–Sept).

Tobermory

Mull's chief town, **TOBERMORY** (⊛www.tobermory.co.uk), at the northern tip of the island, is easily the most attractive fishing port on the west coast of Scotland, its clusters of brightly coloured houses and boats sheltering in a bay backed by a steep bluff. Founded in 1788 by the British Society for Encouraging Fisheries, it never really took off as a fishing port and only survived due to the steady influx of crofters evicted from other parts of the island during the Clearances.

Apart from the beauty of the setting, the harbour's shops are good for browsing, and you could pay a visit to the **Hebridean Whale and Dolphin Trust** (April–Oct daily 10am–5pm; Nov–March Mon–Fri 11am–5pm; free; ⊛www.whaledolphintrust.co.uk), run by a welcoming bunch of enthusiasts. To book whale-watching trips, contact Mull & Iona Trips and Tours (Easter–Oct daily 9am–6pm; ☎01688/302808), beside *MacGochan's* pub (near the distillery).

△ Tobermory harbour

The **Mull Museum,** further along Main Street (Easter to mid-Oct Mon–Fri 10am–4pm, Sat 10am–1pm; £1), is a good wet-weather retreat which packs a great deal of information and artefacts – including a few objects salvaged from the sixteenth-century wreck of the *San Juan*, a Spanish Armada ship that sank in the bay. A stiff climb up Back Brae will bring you to the island's main arts centre, **An Tobar** (March–Dec Mon–Sat 10am–5pm; June–Aug also Sun 1–4pm; free; Ⓦwww.antobar.co.uk), which hosts exhibitions, a variety of live events, and contains a café with comfy sofas set before a real fire.

Practicalities

The **tourist office** (April–Oct Mon–Fri 10am–5pm, Sat & Sun noon–5pm; longer hours in peak season) is at the far end of Main Street. There are several **accommodation** options on Main Street: try the excellent *Fàilte* (Ⓣ01688/302495; ❹), or the small, friendly SYHA **hostel** (Ⓣ0870/004 1151, Ⓦwww.syha.org.uk; March–Oct). *Ach-na-Craiboh* (Ⓣ01688/302301, Ⓦwww.tobermoryholidays.co.uk; ❸) is a lovely house up the hill near the golf course with guest rooms in a garden "bothy". The nearest **campsite** is *Newdale* (Ⓣ01688/302624, Ⓦwww.tobermory-campsite.co.uk; April–Oct), nicely situated one and a half miles outside Tobermory on the B8073 to Dervaig.

Main Street is heaving with **places to eat,** including a highly rated fish-and-chip van on the old pier which also serves scallops. The best of Main Street's **restaurants** is probably *The Water's Edge* in the *Tobermory Hotel,* or for something more exotic, *Javier's Restaurant* (Ⓣ01688/302350) above *MacGocha's* (on the opposite side of the harbour near the distillery) serves hearty Argentinian-Hispanic cuisine. The *Mishnish,* on Main Street, has been the most popular local **pub** for many years, and features live music at the weekend.

Dervaig and Calgary

The gently undulating countryside west of Tobermory, beyond the freshwater Mishnish lochs, provides some of the most beguiling scenery on the island. The only village of any size is **DERVAIG**, which nestles beside narrow Loch

Chumhainn, just eight miles southwest of Tobermory. Distinguished by its unusual pencil-shaped church spire and single street of dinky whitewashed cottages and old corrugated-iron shacks, Dervaig has a wide choice of **places to stay**. On the outskirts of Dervaig, the Victorian *Druimard Country House* (℡01688/400345, ⓦwww.druimard.co.uk; ❻) is a pleasant, comfy place serving good dinners. There are also several pleasant B&Bs, including the vegetarian-friendly *Glenview* (℡01688/400239; April–Oct; ❷), a lovely 1890s house on the edge of the village, and the excellent *Cuin Lodge* (℡01688/400346, ⓦwww.cuin-lodge.mull.com; ❷), an old shooting lodge overlooking the loch, to the northwest of the village. There's also a **bunkhouse** (℡01688/400492) right in the centre of the village, with bedding provided, as well as disabled facilities.

The road continues cross-country to **CALGARY**, once a thriving crofting community, now an idyllic holiday spot boasting Mull's finest sandy bay, backed by low-lying dunes and machair, with wonderful views over to Coll and Tiree. There's just one hotel, the delightful *Calgary Farmhouse* (℡01688/400256, ⓦwww.calgary.co.uk; March–Nov; ❺), whose excellent, moderately priced *Dovecote* restaurant (closed Mon) is (unsurprisingly) housed in a converted dovecote. The south side of the beach is a favourite spot for **camping** rough, though the only facilities are the public toilets.

The Isle of Staffa

Seven miles off the west coast of Mull, **Staffa** is the most romantic and dramatic of Scotland's many uninhabited islands. On its south side, the perpendicular rock-face features an imposing series of black basalt columns, known as the Colonnade, which have been cut by the sea into cathedralesque caverns, most notably **Fingal's Cave**. The Vikings knew about the island – the name derives from their word for "Island of Pillars" – but it wasn't until 1772 that it was "discovered" by the world. Turner painted it, Wordsworth explored it, but Mendelssohn's *Die Fingalshöhle*, inspired by the sounds of the sea-wracked caves he heard on a visit here in 1829, did most to popularize the place – after which Queen Victoria gave her blessing, too. The geological explanation for these polygonal basalt organ-pipes is that they were created by a massive subterranean explosion some sixty million years ago. A huge mass of molten basalt burst forth onto land and, as it cooled, solidified into what are, essentially, crystals. To **get to Staffa**, you can join one of the many boat trips from Fionnphort, Iona, Ulva Ferry, Dervaig or Oban. From Fionnphort and Iona, trips run twice daily from April to October and cost £18 per person on the *Iolaire* (℡01681/700358, ⓦwww.staffatrips.f9.co.uk), while *Turus Mara* (℡0800/085 8786, ⓦwww.turusmara.com), which operates out of Ulva Ferry, on Mull's west coast, costs a bit more.

Ben More and the Ross of Mull

From the southern shores of Loch na Keal, which almost splits Mull in two, rise the terraced slopes of **Ben More** (3169ft) – literally "big mountain" – a mighty extinct volcano, and the only Munro in the Hebrides outside of Skye. Stretching for twenty miles west of Ben More as far as Iona is Mull's rocky southernmost peninsula, the **Ross of Mull**, which, like much of Scotland, appears blissfully tranquil in good weather, and desolate and bleak in bad.

The road ends at **FIONNPHORT**, facing Iona, probably the least attractive place to stay on the Ross, though it has a nice sandy bay backed by pink granite rocks to the north of the ferry slipway. Partly to ease congestion on Iona, and to give their neighbours a slice of the tourist pound, Fionnphort was chosen as the site for the **St Columba Centre** (Easter–Sept daily

10.30am–1pm & 2–5.30pm; free); inside, a small exhibition outlines Iona's history, tells a little of Columba's life, and has a few facsimiles of the illuminated manuscripts produced by the island's monks.

The Isle of Iona

Less than a mile off the southwest tip of Mull, **IONA** – just three miles long and not much more than a mile wide – has been a place of pilgrimage for several centuries, and a place of Christian worship for more than 1400 years. It was to this flat Hebridean island that **St Columba** fled from Ireland in 563 and established a monastery which was responsible for the conversion of more or less all of pagan Scotland as well as much of northern England. This history and the island's splendid isolation have lent it a peculiar religiosity; in the much-quoted words of Dr Johnson, who visited in 1773, "That man is little to be envied . . . whose piety would not grow warmer among the ruins of Iona." Today, however, the island can barely cope with the constant flood of day-trippers, and charges visitors entry to its abbey, so to appreciate the special atmosphere and to have time to see the whole island, including the often-overlooked west coast, you should plan on staying at least one night.

The passenger ferry from Fionnphort drops you off at the island's main village, **BAILE MÓR** (literally "large village"), which is in fact little more than a single terrace of cottages facing the sea. Just inland lie the extensive pink-granite ruins of the **Augustinian nunnery**, built around 1200 but disused since the Reformation – if nothing else, it gives you an idea of the state of the present-day abbey before it was restored. Across the road to the north is the **Iona Heritage Centre** (Easter–Oct Mon–Sat 10.30am–4.30pm; £2), with displays on the social history of the island over the last two hundred years, including the Clearances, which nearly halved the island's population of five hundred in the mid-nineteenth century. At a bend in the road, just south of the manse and church, stands the fifteenth-century **MacLean's Cross**, a fine, late medieval example of the distinctive, flowing, three-leaved foliage of the Iona school.

No buildings remain from Columba's time: the present **abbey** (daily: April–Sept 9.30am–6.30pm; Oct–March 9.30am–4.30pm; £3.30; HS) dates from the arrival of the Benedictines in around 1200, was extensively rebuilt in the fifteenth and sixteenth centuries, and was restored virtually wholesale early last century. Adjoining the facade is a small steep-roofed chamber, believed to be St Columba's grave, now a small chapel. The three high crosses in front of the abbey date from the eighth to tenth centuries, and are decorated with the Pictish serpent and boss and Celtic spirals for which Iona's early Christian masons were renowned. For reasons of sanitation, the cloisters were placed, contrary to the norm, on the north side of the church (where running water was available); entirely reconstructed in the late 1950s, they now shelter a useful historical account of the abbey's development.

Iona's oldest building, the plain-looking **St Oran's Chapel**, lies south of the abbey, and boasts an eleventh-century door. Oran's Chapel stands at the centre of Iona's sacred burial ground, **Reilig Odhráin** (Oran's Cemetery), which is said to contain the graves of sixty kings of Norway, Ireland, France and Scotland, including Duncan and Macbeth. The best of the early Christian gravestones and medieval effigies that once lay in the Reilig Odhráin have unfortunately been removed to the Infirmary Museum, behind the abbey.

A brief history of Iona

Legend has it that **St Columba** (Colum Cille), born in Donegal in northwestern Ireland some time around 521, was a direct descendant of the semi-legendary Irish king, Niall of the Nine Hostages. A scholar and soldier priest, who founded numerous monasteries in Ireland, he is thought to have become involved in a bloody dispute with the king when he refused to hand over a copy of St Jerome's Psalter, copied illegally from the original owned by St Finian of Moville. This, in turn, provoked the Battle of Cúl Drebene (Cooldrumman) – also known as the **Battle of the Book** – at which Columba's forces won, though with the loss of over 3000 lives. The story goes that, repenting this bloodshed, Columba went into exile with twelve other monks, eventually settling on Iona in 563. The bottom line, however, is that we know very little about Columba, though he undoubtedly became something of a cult figure after his death in 597. He was posthumously credited with miraculous feats such as defeating the Loch Ness monster and banishing snakes (and, some say, frogs) from the island.

Whatever the truth about Columba's life, in the sixth and seventh centuries, Iona enjoyed a great deal of autonomy from Rome, establishing a specifically **Celtic Christian** tradition. Missionaries were sent out to the rest of Scotland and parts of England, and Iona quickly became a respected seat of learning and artistry; the monks compiled a vast library of intricately **illuminated manuscripts** – most famously the Book of Kells (now on display in Trinity College, Dublin) – while the masons excelled in carving peculiarly intricate crosses. Two factors were instrumental in the demise of the Celtic tradition: a series of Viking raids, the worst of which was the massacre of 68 monks on the sands of Martyrs' Bay in 806; and relentless pressure from the established Church, beginning with the Synod of Whitby in 664, which chose Rome over the Celtic Church, and culminated in the suppression of the Celtic Church by King David I in 1144.

In 1203, Iona became part of the mainstream Church with the establishment of an **Augustinian nunnery** and a **Benedictine monastery** by Reginald, son of Somerled, lord of the Isles. During the Reformation, the entire complex was ransacked, the contents of the library burnt and all but three of the island's 360 crosses destroyed. Although plans were drawn up at various times to turn the abbey into a Cathedral of the Isles, nothing came of them until 1899, when the then owner, the eighth duke of Argyll, donated the abbey buildings to the **Church of Scotland**, which restored the abbey church for worship over the course of the next decade. Iona's modern resurgence began in 1938, when **George MacLeod**, a minister from Glasgow, established a group of ministers, students and artisans to begin rebuilding the remainder of the monastic buildings. What began as a mostly male, Gaelic-speaking, Presbyterian community is today a lay, mixed and ecumenical retreat. The entire abbey complex has been successfully restored, and is now looked after by Historic Scotland, while the island, apart from the church land and a few crofts, is in the care of the National Trust for Scotland.

Practicalities

There's no **tourist office** on Iona, and as demand far exceeds supply you should organize **accommodation** well in advance. Of the island's two **hotels**, the stone-built *Argyll* (☎01681/700334, ⊛www.argyllhoteliona.co.uk; ❻), in the terrace of cottages overlooking the Sound of Iona, is by far the nicer, although the larger alternative, the *St Columba Hotel* (☎01681/700304, ⊛www.stcolumba-hotel.co.uk; ❻), is pretty good too. As for **B&Bs**, try *Iona Cottage* (☎01681/700579, ✉ck@ionacottage.freeserve.co.uk; ❷), which overlooks the jetty or *Shore Cottage* (☎01681/700744, ⊛www.shorecottage.co.uk; Jan–Oct; ❷), a short walk south. **Camping** is not permitted on Iona, but there is a terrific ⚐ **hostel** (☎01681/700781, ⊛www.ionahostel.co.uk) in the north of the island looking out to the Treshnish Islands. If you want to stay with the **Iona Community**, contact the MacLeod Centre (℡01681/700404, Ⓦwww .iona.org.uk), popularly known as the "Mac". The **restaurant** at the *Argyll* isn't bad, and the grub at the *Martyrs' Bay Restaurant* by the jetty is reasonable too; for even more convivial surroundings you can eat from the same menu in the adjoining bar. For something lighter during the day, there's a **tearoom** beside the Heritage Centre.

Coll, Tiree and Colonsay

Coll and **Tiree** are among the most isolated of the Inner Hebrides, and if anything have more in common with the outlying Western Isles than with their closest neighbour, Mull. Each is roughly twelve miles long and three miles wide, both are low-lying, treeless and exceptionally windy, with white sandy beaches and the highest sunshine records in Scotland. Isolated between Mull and Islay, **Colonsay** – eight miles by three at its widest – is nothing like as bleak and windswept as Coll or Tiree. All three islands are served by CalMac ferries from Oban.

The Isle of Coll

The fish-shaped rocky island of **Coll** (Ⓦwww.isleofcoll.org), with a population of around a hundred, lies less than seven miles off the coast of Mull. The CalMac ferry drops off at Coll's only real village, **ARINAGOUR**, whose whitewashed cottages dot the western shore of Loch Eatharna. Half the island's population lives in the village, and it's here you'll find the hotel and pub, post office, churches and a couple of shops.

On the southwest coast there are two edifices, both confusingly known as **Breachacha Castle**, and both built by the MacLeans. The older is a fifteenth-century tower house recently restored, and now a training centre for Project Trust overseas aid volunteers. The less attractive "new castle", to the northwest, is made up of a central block built around 1750 and two side pavilions added a century later, and is currently being restored. Much of the area around the castles is now owned by the RSPB, with the aim of protecting the island's small corncrake population. A vast area of **giant sand dunes** lies to the west of the castles, with two glorious golden sandy bays stretching for over a mile on either side. At the far western end is *Caolas*, where you can get a cup of tea and home-baked goodies, or stay the night (℡01879/230438, Ⓦwww.caolas.net; full board ❺); it also has a compact **self-catering** bothy (❸) and bikes and boats available for guests.

In Arinagour, the small, family-run *Coll Hotel* (℡01879/230334, Ⓦwww .collhotel.com; ❸) can also provide **accommodation**. Otherwise, there are a couple of B&Bs: *Tigh-na-Mara* (℡01879/230354; ❷), a purpose-built guest house near the pier, and *Achamore* (℡01879/230430; ❶), a traditional nineteenth-century farmhouse B&B, just north of Arinagour. *Garden House* (℡01879/230374), down a track on the left before the turn-off for the castles, runs a **campsite** in the shelter of an old walled garden. The *Coll Hotel* doubles as the island's social centre, and does excellent **meals.**

The Isle of Tiree

Tiree (Ⓦwww.isleoftiree.com), as its Gaelic name *tir-iodh* ("land of corn") suggests, was once known as the breadbasket of the Inner Hebrides, thanks to its acres of rich machair (sandy, grassy, lime-rich land). Nowadays crofting and tourism are the main sources of income for the resident population of around 750. One of the most distinctive features of Tiree is its architecture, in particular the large numbers of "pudding" or "spotty" houses, where only the mortar is painted white. Tiree's sandy beaches also attract large numbers of windsurfers for the Tiree Wave Classic (Ⓦwww.tireewaveclassic.com) every October.

The ferry calls at Gott Bay Pier, now best known for **An Turas** (The Journey), Tiree's award-winning artistic "shelter". Just up the road from the pier is the village of **SCARINISH**, home to a post office, some public toilets, a supermarket, a butcher's and a bank, with a petrol pump back at the pier. Also in Scarinish you'll find **An Iodhlann** (June–Sept Tues–Fri noon–5pm; Oct–May Mon–Fri 10.30am–3.30pm; £3) – meaning "haystack" in Gaelic – the island's two-roomed archive which puts on occasional exhibitions.

The most intriguing sights lie in the bulging western half of the island, where Tiree's two landmark hills rise up. Below the higher of the two is **HYNISH**, with its restored **harbour**, designed by Alan Stevenson in the 1830s to transport building materials for the magnificent 140-foot-tall **Skerryvore Lighthouse**, which lies on a sea-swept reef some twelve miles southwest of Tiree. Up on the hill behind the harbour, a stumpy granite signal tower, whose signals used to be the only contact the lighthouse keepers had with civilization, now houses a **museum** telling the history of the Herculean effort required to erect the lighthouse; weather permitting, you can see the lighthouse from the tower's viewing platform.

As well as a daily **ferry** connection from Oban, Tiree has **flights** (Mon–Sat) to and from Glasgow. The best way to get around is on the Ring'n'Ride **minibus** service (Mon–Sat 7am–6pm, Tues until 10pm; ☏01879/220419), which will take you anywhere on the island. There are two **hotels**: the newly refurbished *Scarinish* (☏01879/220308, Ⓦwww.tireescarinishhotel.com; ❹), overlooking the old harbour, and the *Tiree Lodge* (☏01879/220368; ❷), a mile or so east of Scarinish along Gott Bay. Better still is *Kirkapol House* (☏01879/220729, Ⓦwww.kirkapoltiree.co.uk; ❸), just beyond *Skerryvore House*, a great B&B in a converted kirk. Good **hostel** accommodation is available at the *Millhouse* (☏01879/220435, Ⓦwww.tireemillhouse.co.uk), near Loch Bhasapol, in the northwest of the island, either in bunks or twins (❶). There's no official campsite, but **camping** is allowed with the local crofter's permission. As for **eating**, the bar meals at both the *Scarinish* and *Tiree Lodge* are good, and there are unpretentious snacks and meals available at the pine-clad *Rural Centre* café by the airport.

The Isle of Colonsay

Isolated between Mull and Islay, **Colonsay** (Ⓦwww.colonsay.org.uk) is not as bleak and windswept as Coll or Tiree. Its craggy, heather-backed hills even support the occasional patch of woodland, plus a bewildering array of plant and bird life, wild goats and rabbits, and one of the finest quasi-tropical gardens in Scotland. The population is currently around a hundred, down from a pre-Clearance peak of just under a thousand. CalMac **ferries** call daily except Tuesday and Saturday from Oban (2hr 15min), and once a week from Kennacraig via Islay (Wed; 3hr 35min), when a day-trip is possible, giving you around six hours on the island.

The ferry docks at **SCALASAIG**, on the east coast, where there's a post office/shop, a petrol pump, a restaurant and the island's hotel. Right by the pier,

㉑

the old waiting room now serves as the island's heritage centre and is usually open when the ferry docks. Two miles north of Scalasaig is **Colonsay House**, built in 1722 by Malcolm MacNeil. In 1904, the island and house were bought by Lord Strathcona, who made his fortune building the Canadian Pacific Railway and who was responsible for the house's lovely woodland **gardens** (April–Sept Wed & Fri), which are slowly being restored to their former glory. To the north of Colonsay House, where the road ends, you'll find the island's finest sandy beach, the breathtaking **Kiloran Bay**, where the breakers roll in from the Atlantic.

The **Isle of Oronsay**, half a mile to the south, is only an island when the tide is in, and, as you can't stay overnight, it can only be visited as a day-trip from Colonsay. The two are separated by "The Strand", a mile of tidal mud flats which act as a causeway for two hours either side of low tide; check locally for current timings. The ruins of the **Oronsay Priory** date back to the fourteenth century, and it still has the original church and cloisters. The highlight, however, is the Oronsay Cross, a superb example of late medieval artistry from Iona, and the numerous finely carved grave slabs that lie within the Prior's House.

Colonsay's only **hotel**, the *Isle of Colonsay* (℡ 01951/200316, ⓔ reception@thecolonsay.com; ❻), is within easy walking distance of the pier in Scalasaig and serves very decent bar snacks. Alternatively there's the superb 🗶 *Seaview* **B&B** (℡ 01951/200315; April–Oct; ❸), or the budget *Keepers' Lodge*, in Kiloran (℡ 01951/200312), a very comfortable **hostel** with a real fire. An alternative to **eating out** at the hotel bar is the *Pantry*, above the pier in Scalasaig, which offers simple home-cooking as well as teas and cakes (ring ahead for evening meals; ℡ 01951/200325).

Mid-Argyll

Mid-Argyll is a vague term that loosely describes the central wedge of land south of Oban and north of Kintyre. The highlights of this gently undulating scenery lie along the sharply indented west coast, in particular the rich Bronze Age and Neolithic remains in the **Kilmartin** valley, one of the most important prehistoric sites in Scotland.

LOCHGILPHEAD, on the shores of Loch Fyne, is the chief town in the area, though it has little to offer beyond its practical use: it has a supermarket, several banks and a **tourist office** at 27 Lochnell St (April–Oct Mon–Sat 10am–5pm, Sun noon–5pm; longer hours in summer). It also has an excellent modern veggie **restaurant** called *Pinto's* (℡ 01546/602547; Tues–Sat), on the main street.

Kilmartin Glen

The **Kilmartin Glen** is the most important prehistoric site on the Scottish mainland. The most remarkable relic is the **linear cemetery**, where several cairns are aligned for more than two miles, to the south of the village of Kilmartin. These are thought to represent the successive burials of a ruling family or chieftains, but nobody can be sure. The best view of the cemetery's configuration is from the Bronze Age **Mid-Cairn**, but the Neolithic **South Cairn**, dating from around 3000 BC, is by far the oldest and the most impressive, with its large chambered tomb roofed by giant slabs. Close to the Mid-Cairn, the two **Temple Wood stone circles** appear to have been the architectural focus of burials in the area from Neolithic times to the Bronze Age. Visible to the south

21

are the impressively cup-marked **Nether Largie standing stones** (no public access), the largest of which looms over 10ft high.

Situated on high ground to the north of the cairns is the tiny village of **KILMARTIN**, where the old manse adjacent to the village church now houses a **Museum of Ancient Culture** (daily 10am–5.30pm; ⓦwww.kilmartin.org; £4.50), which is both enlightening and entertaining. The **café** is equally enticing, with local home-baked produce on offer, which you can wash down with heather beer (also open early evening Thurs–Sat). The nearby church is worth a brief reconnoitre, as it shelters the badly damaged and weathered **Kilmartin crosses**, while a separate enclosure in the graveyard houses a large collection of medieval grave slabs of the Malcolms of Poltalloch.

To the south of Kilmartin, beyond the linear cemetery, lies the raised peat bog of Mòine Mhór (Great Moss), best known as home to the Iron Age fort of **Dunadd**, one of Scotland's most important Celtic sites, occupying a distinctive 176-foot-high rocky knoll once surrounded by the sea but currently stranded beside the winding River Add. It was here that Fergus, the first king of Dalriada, established his royal seat, having arrived from Ireland in around 500 AD. Its strategic position, the craggy defences and the view from the top are all impressive, but it's the **stone carvings** between the twin summits which make Dunadd so remarkable: several lines of inscription in ogam (an ancient alphabet of Irish origin), the faint outline of a boar, a hollowed-out footprint and a small basin. The boar and the inscriptions are probably Pictish, since the fort was clearly occupied long before Fergus got there, but the footprint and basin have been interpreted as being part of the royal coronation rituals of the kings of Dalriada. It's thought that the Stone of Destiny was used at Dunadd before being moved to Scone Palace (see p.955), then to Westminster Abbey in London, where it languished until it was returned to Edinburgh in 1996.

The nearest **B&B** is at *Dunchraigaig House* (☎01546/605209, ⓔdunchraigaig@aol .com; ❸), a large detached Victorian house situated opposite the Ballymeanoch standing stones. For **food**, your best options are the museum café (see above), and the vegetarian *Pinto's* in Lochgilphead (see p.980).

Crinan Canal

In 1801 the nine-mile-long **Crinan Canal** opened, linking Loch Fyne, at Ardrishaig south of Lochgilphead, with the Sound of Jura, thus cutting out the long and treacherous journey around the Mull of Kintyre. The canal runs parallel to the sea for quite some way before hitting a flight of locks either side of **CAIRNBAAN** (there are fifteen in total); a walk along the towpath is both picturesque and pleasantly unstrenuous. A useful pit stop can be made at the *Cairnbaan Hotel* (☎01546/603668; ❻), an eighteenth-century coaching inn overlooking the canal, with a decent restaurant and bar meals featuring locally caught seafood.

There are usually one or two yachts passing through the locks, but the most relaxing place from which to view the canal in action is **CRINAN**, a pretty little fishing port at its western end. Crinan's tiny harbour is, for the moment at least, still home to a small fishing fleet. Every room in the *Crinan Hotel* (☎01546/830261, ⓦwww.crinanhotel.com; ❾) looks across Loch Crinan to the Sound of Jura. If the *Crinan* is beyond your means, try the secluded **B&B** *Tigh-na-Glaic* (☎01546/830245; ❸), perched above the harbour, also with views out to sea, or the superb *Bellanoch House* (☎01546/830149, ⓦwww .bellanochhouse.co.uk; ❻), a grand, old schoolhouse right on the canal, a mile or so before Crinan. Bar **meals** at the *Crinan* are moderately expensive, but utterly delicious. Down on the lockside there's a cheaper, cheerful **café** called the *Coffee Shop* (Easter–Oct), serving mouthwatering homemade cakes and wonderful clootie dumplings.

Kintyre

But for the mile-long isthmus between West Loch Tarbert and the much smaller East Loch Tarbert, the little-visited peninsula of **KINTYRE** (Ⓦ www .kintyre.org) – from the Gaelic *Ceann Tire*, "land's end" – would be an island. Indeed, in the eleventh century, when the Scottish king, Malcolm Canmore, allowed Magnus Barefoot, king of Norway, to lay claim to any island he could circumnavigate by boat, Magnus succeeded in dragging his boat across the Tarbert isthmus and added the peninsula to his Hebridean kingdom. During the Wars of the Covenant, the vast majority of the population and property were wiped out by a combination of the 1646 potato blight and the destructive attentions of the earl of Argyll. Kintyre remained a virtual desert until the earl began his policy of transplanting Gaelic-speaking Lowlanders to the region. They probably felt quite at home here, as the southern half of the peninsula lies on the Lowland side of the Highland Boundary Fault.

Tarbert

A distinctive rocket-like church steeple heralds the fishing village of **TARBERT** (in Gaelic *An Tàirbeart*, meaning "isthmus"), sheltering an attractive little bay backed by rugged hills. Tarbert's harbourfront is pretty, and is best appreciated from the rubble of Robert the Bruce's fourteenth-century **castle** above the town to the south.

Tarbert's **tourist office** (April–Oct Mon–Sat 10am–5pm, Sun noon–5pm; longer hours in summer) is on the harbour. There's no shortage of **B&Bs**, though none are outstanding – try *Springside* on Pier Road (☎01880/820413, Ⓔ marshall.springside@virgin.net; ❷), which overlooks the harbour. The best **food** is to be had courtesy of the French chef at the evening-only 🎗 *Corner House Bistro* (☎01880/820263), just by the side of the *Corner House* pub, or at the more expensive, but equally excellent *Anchorage* (☎01880/820881; Oct–March eves only), on the south side of the harbour.

The Isle of Gigha

Gigha (Ⓦ www.isle-of-gigha.co.uk) – pronounced "gheeya" – is a low-lying, fertile island three miles off the west coast of Kintyre, reputedly occupied for five thousand years. Like many of the smaller Hebrides, Gigha was bought and sold numerous times after its original lairds, the MacNeils, sold up, and was finally bought by the 140 or so inhabitants themselves in 2001.

The ferry from Tayinloan, 23 miles south of Tarbert, deposits you at the island's only village, **ARDMINISH**, where you'll find the post office and shop. The main attraction on the island is the **Achamore Gardens** (daily 9am–dusk; £4), a mile and a half south of Ardminish. Established by the first postwar owner, Sir James Horlick of hot drink fame, their spectacularly colourful display of azaleas is best seen in early summer. The real draw of Gigha, however, apart from the peace and quiet, is the white sandy beaches – including one at Ardminish itself – that dot the coastline.

Gigha is so small – six miles by one mile – that most visitors come here just for the day. It is, however, possible **to stay** either at the *Post Office House* (℡01583/505251, Ⓦwww.gighastores.co.uk; ❷) or at the beautiful *Achamore House* (℡01583/505400, Ⓦwww.achamorehouse.com; ❺), in the midst of Achamore Gardens. The licensed *Boathouse*, by the pier, is the place to go for delicious **food**, while the shop offers **bike rental**.

Campbeltown

CAMPBELTOWN's best feature is its setting, in a deep bay sheltered by Davaar Island and the surrounding hills. With a population of around five thousand, it's also one of the largest towns in Argyll and, if you're staying in the southern half of Kintyre, its shops are by far the best place to stock up on supplies. Campbeltown's heyday was the Victorian era, when shipbuilding was going strong, coal was shipped by canal from Drumlemble, the fishing fleet was vast and Campbeltown had no fewer than 34 whisky distilleries – today only three remain. The deeply traditional, family-owned **Springbank distillery**, off Longrow, is the only distillery in Scotland that does absolutely everything from malting to bottling, on its own premises. There are regular no-nonsense guided tours (Easter–Sept Mon–Thurs by appointment; £3; ℡01586/552085, Ⓦwww.springbankdistillers.com). At the end, you get a voucher to exchange for a miniature at Eaglesomes, on Longrow South, whose range of whiskies is awesome.

On the town's palm-tree-dotted waterfront you'll find the **Wee Pictures**, a little Art Deco cinema on Hall Street, built in 1913 and still going strong (daily except Fri; ℡01586/533657, Ⓦwww.weepictures.co.uk). Next door is the equally delightful **Campbeltown Museum and Library** (Tues–Sat 10am–1pm & 2–5pm, Tues & Thurs also 5.30–7.30pm; free), built in 1897 in the local sandstone. The library also hides the **Linda McCartney Memorial Garden**, which features a slightly ludicrous bronze statue of Linda holding a lamb, commissioned by the ex-Beatle, who owns a farm nearby. Campbeltown's newest attraction is the **Scottish Owl Centre** (April to early Oct daily except Tues 1.30–4.30pm; Ⓦwww.scottishowlcentre.tk; £5), signposted off the B842 to Machrihanish, five minutes' walk out of town. The centre has a huge collection of owls spread out in terraced aviaries, ranging from the tiny Scops Owl to the world's largest, the Eurasian Eagle Owl. Try and time your visit with the daily flight display at 2.30pm.

Campbeltown's **tourist office** is on the Old Quay (April–Oct Mon–Fri 10am–5pm, Sun noon–4pm; Nov–March Mon–Fri 9am–4pm), and will happily hand out a free map of the town. The best centrally located **accommodation** is the delightful family-run *Ardshiel Hotel*, on Kilkerran Road (℡01586/552133, Ⓦwww.ardshiel.co.uk; ❺), situated on a lovely leafy square, just a block or so back from the ferry terminal. On the north side of the bay, *Craigard House* (℡01586/554242, Ⓦwww.craigard-house.co.uk; ❻), a former whisky-distiller's sandstone mansion, is even more palatial. For an inexpensive, central B&B, head for *Westbank Guest House*, on Dell Road (℡01586/553660; ❷), off the B842 to Southend. The best bar **food** is to be found at the *Ardshiel Hotel*.

The Mull of Kintyre

The bulbous, hilly end of Kintyre, to the south of Campbeltown, features some of the most spectacular scenery on the whole peninsula, mixed with large swathes of Lowland-style farmland. Most people venture west of Campbeltown to make a pilgrimage to the **Mull of Kintyre** – the nearest Britain gets to Ireland, whose coastline, just twelve miles away, appears remarkably close on fine days. Although the Mull was made famous by the mawkish number-one hit by Paul McCartney, with the help of the Campbeltown Pipe Band, there's nothing specifically to see in this godforsaken storm-racked spot but the view and a memorial to the 29 military personnel who died in 1994 when an RAF helicopter crashed into the hillside. The roads up to the "**Gap**" (1150ft) – where you must leave your car – and particularly down to the lighthouse, itself 300ft above the ocean waves, are terrifyingly tortuous.

The Isle of Arran

Shaped like a kidney bean and occupying centre stage in the Firth of Clyde, **Arran** (Ⓦ www.visitarran.net) is the most southerly (and therefore the most accessible) of all the Scottish islands. The Highland–Lowland dividing line passes right through its centre – hence the cliché about it being like "Scotland in miniature" – leaving the northern half sparsely populated, mountainous and bleak, while the lush southern half enjoys a much milder climate. Despite its immense popularity, the tourists, like the population of around five thousand – many of whom are incomers – tend to stick to the southeastern quarter of the island, leaving the west and the north relatively undisturbed.

Transport on Arran itself is pretty good: daily **buses** circle the island (Brodick tourist office has timetables and an Arran Rural Rover day-ticket costs just £4).

Brodick

Although the resort of **BRODICK** (from the Norse *breidr vik*, "broad bay") is a place of only moderate charm, it does at least have a grand setting in a wide, sandy bay set against a backdrop of granite mountains. As the island's capital and main communication hub, Brodick is by far the busiest town on Arran.

The local dukes of Hamilton used to rule over the town from **Brodick Castle** (daily: April–Sept 11am–4.30pm; Oct 11am–3.30pm; £10; NTS), on a steep bank on the north side of the bay. The interior is comfortable if undistinguished, but the walled **gardens** (daily 9.30am–dusk; gardens and country park only £5) and extensive grounds contain a treasury of exotic plants and trees and command a superb view across the bay. Hidden in the grounds is a bizarre Bavarian-style summerhouse lined entirely with pine cones, one of three built by the eleventh duke to make his wife, Princess Marie of Baden, feel at home.

Brodick's **tourist office** (May–Sept Mon–Thurs & Sat 9am–5pm, Fri 9am–7.30pm, Sun 10am–5pm; Oct–April Mon–Sat 9am–5pm) is by the CalMac pier, and has reams of information on every activity from pony trekking to paragliding. Unless you've got to catch an early-morning ferry, however, there's little reason to stay in Brodick, though should you need to, the best **rooms** close to the ferry terminal are at the excellent *Dunvegan Guest House*, on Shore Road (℡01770/302811, Ⓔ dunveganhouse1@hotmail.com; ❹), or *Carrick Lodge* (℡01770/302550; March to mid-Nov; ❸), a spacious sandstone manse south of the pier on the Lamlash road. The nearest **campsite** is *Glenrosa* (℡01770/302380), a lovely, but very basic farm site (cold water only and no showers), two miles from town off the B880 to Blackwaterfoot. For **food**, the only place that really stands out is the expensive seafood restaurant *Creelers* (℡01770/302797; Easter–Oct), on the road to the castle.

㉑

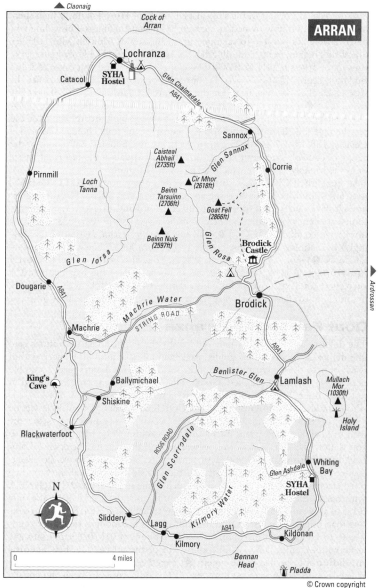

© Crown copyright

Lamlash and Holy Island

The southern half of Arran is less spectacular and less forbidding than the north; it's more heavily forested and the land is more fertile, and for that reason the vast majority of the population lives here. With its distinctive Edwardian architecture and mild climate, **LAMLASH** epitomizes the sedate charm of southeast Arran.

You can take a boat out to the slug-shaped hump of **Holy Island**, which shelters the bay, and is now owned by a group of Tibetan Buddhists – providing you don't dawdle, it's possible to scramble up to the top of Mullach Mór (1030ft), the island's highest point, and still catch the last ferry back. The Holy Island ferry runs more or less hourly (℡01770/600998; £8 return), and you can stay at the Buddhist centre (℡01387/373232, ⓦwww.holyisland.org; full board ❹). To **stay** in Lamlash in style, head for the comfortable *Lilybank* (℡01770/600230; Easter–Oct; ❸), which does good homemade food. Another option is the *Aldersyde Bunkhouse* (℡01770/600959), a basic, purpose-built **hostel** south of the pier behind the *Aldersyde Hotel*. You can **camp** at the fully equipped *Middleton Camping Park* (℡01770/600255; April–Oct), just five minutes' walk south of the centre of Lamlash. The best food option is the **bar meals** at the *Pier Head Tavern*, or at the friendly *Drift Inn*, which has tables by the shore.

An established Clydeside resort for over a century now, **WHITING BAY**, four miles south of Lamlash, is spread out along a very pleasant bay, though it doesn't have quite the distinctive architecture of Lamlash. However, there are some excellent places to **stay**, including the *Royal* (℡01770/700286, ⓦwww.royalarran.co.uk; March–Oct; ❸) and the *Argentine House Hotel*, run (confusingly) by a multilingual Swiss couple (℡01770/700662, ⓦwww.argentinearran.co.uk; ❷), both on Shore Road. Whiting Bay also boasts an SYHA **hostel** (℡0870/004 1158; April–Oct), at the southern end of the bay. The **food** is very good (and expensive) at both hotels; otherwise, it's snacks at the *Coffee Pot*, or simple bistro fare at the *Pantry* (closed Sun eve) opposite the post office.

Goat Fell and Lochranza

The desolate north half of Arran – effectively the Highland part – features bare granite peaks, the occasional golden eagle and miles of unspoilt scenery, within reach only to those prepared to do some serious hiking. Arran's most accessible peak is also the island's highest, **Goat Fell** (2866ft), which can be ascended in just three hours from Brodick, though it's a strenuous hike.

You can also hike up Goat Fell from **CORRIE**, Arran's prettiest little seaside village, six miles north of Brodick, where a procession of pristine cottages lines the road to Lochranza and wraps itself around an exquisite little harbour and pier. If you want to use Corrie as a base for hiking, book ahead at the *North High Corrie Croft* **bunkhouse** (℡01770/302310), ten minutes' steep climb above the village.

The ruined castle which occupies the mud flats of the bay, and the brooding north-facing slopes of the mountains which frame it provide **LOCHRANZA** with one of the most spectacular settings on the island. Despite being the only place of any size in this sparsely populated area, Lochranza attracts far fewer visitors than other Arran resorts, and its main sight is the modern **distillery** (mid-March to Oct daily 10am–6pm; Nov & Dec phone ℡01770/830264, ⓦwww.arranwhisky.com; £3.50), at the south end of the village. The best **accommodation** is to be had at the superb ❦ *Apple Lodge* (℡01770/830229; ❹), the old village manse where you'll get excellent home-cooking, or at the equally welcoming *Lochranza Hotel* (℡01770/830223, ⓦwww.lochranza.co.uk; ❷), whose bar is the centre of the local social scene. Lochranza also has an SYHA **hostel** (℡0870/004 1140; March–Oct), situated halfway between the distillery and the castle, and a well-equipped **campsite** (℡01770/830273, ⓦwww.arran.netLochranza; April-Oct), beautifully placed by the golf course on the Brodick road, where deer come to graze in the early evening. The distillery **café** offers salads, pasta dishes, baguettes and Scottish specialities during the day; in the evening, your only option is bar meals at the *Lochranza*.

Islay and Jura

The fertile, largely treeless island of **ISLAY** (@www.isle-of-islay.com) is famous for one thing – single malt **whisky**. The smoky, peaty, pungent quality of Islay whisky is unique, recognizable even to the untutored palate, and all the island's distilleries will happily take visitors on a guided tour, ending

Islay whisky

Islay has woken up to the fact that its whisky distilleries are a major tourist attraction. Nowadays, each distillery offers guided tours, traditionally ending with a generous dram, and a refund of your entrance fee if you buy a bottle in the shop – be warned, however, that a bottle of single malt is no cheaper at source, so expect to pay over £20 for the privilege. Phone ahead to make sure there's a tour running, as times do change frequently.

Ardbeg ☎01496/302244, @www.ardbeg.com. The 10-year-old Ardbeg is traditionally considered the saltiest, peatiest malt on Islay (and that's saying something). Bought by Glenmorangie in 1997, the distillery has been thoroughly overhauled and restored, yet it still has bags of character inside. The *Old Kiln Café* is excellent (Mon–Fri 10am–4pm; June–Aug daily 10am–5pm). Guided tours regularly 11.30am–2.30pm; £2.

Bowmore ☎01496/810671, @www.morrisonbowmore.com. Bowmore is the most touristy of the Islay distilleries, too much so for some. However, it is by far the most central distillery (with unrivalled disabled access), and also one of the few still doing its own malting and kilning. Guided tours Mon–Fri 10am, 11am, 2pm & 3pm, Sat by appointment; £2.

Bruichladdich ☎01496/850190. Bruichladdich was rescued in 2001 by a group of whisky fanatics and is the only independent distillery left on Islay. Guided tours Easter–Oct Mon–Fri 10.30am, 11.30am & 2.30pm, Sat 10.30am & 2.30pm; Nov–Easter Mon–Fri 11.30am & 2.30pm, Sat 10.30am; £3.

Bunnahabhain ☎01496/840646, @www.bunnahabhain.com. A visit to Bunnahabhain (pronounced "Bunna-have-in") is really only for whisky obsessives. The road from Port Askaig is windy, the whisky is the least characteristically Islay, and the distillery itself is only in production for a few months each year. Guided tours April–Oct Mon–Fri 10.30am, 12.45pm, 2pm & 3.15pm; free.

Caol Ila ☎01496/302760, @www.discovering-distilleries.com. Caol Ila (pronounced "Cul-eela"), just north of Port Askaig, is a modern distillery, the majority of whose lightly peaty malt goes into blended whiskies. No-frills guided tours are by appointment (April–Oct Mon–Thurs 9.30am, 10.45am & 1.45pm, Fri 9.30am & 10.45am; £3).

Kilchoman ☎01496/850011, @www.kilchomandistillery.com. The first new distillery on the island for over a century, Kilchoman is farm-based and aims to grow the barley, malt, distil, mature and even bottle its whisky on-site. The distillery welcomes visitors (10am–5.30pm: May, June & Sept Mon–Sat; July & Aug daily; Oct–Dec Mon–Fri) and there are regular guided tours (11am & 3pm; £3).

Lagavulin ☎01496/302730. Lagavulin probably is the classic, all-round Islay malt, with lots of smoke and peat. The distillery enjoys a fabulous setting and is extremely busy all year round. Phone ahead for details of the guided tours (Mon–Fri 9.30am, 11.15am & 2.30pm; £3), at the end of which you'll get a taste of the best-selling 10-year-old malt.

Laphroaig ☎01496/302418, @www.laphroaig.com. Another classic smoky, peaty Islay malt, and another great setting. One bonus at Laphroaig is that you get to see the malting and see and smell the peat kilns. Phone ahead to book the regular guided tours (Mon–Fri 10.15am & 2.15pm; free).

with the customary complimentary tipple. In medieval times, Islay was the political centre of the Hebrides, with **Finlaggan**, near Port Askaig, the seat of the MacDonalds, lords of the Isles. The picturesque, whitewashed villages you see on Islay today, however, date from the planned settlements founded by the Campbells in the late eighteenth and early nineteenth centuries. Apart from whisky and solitude, the other great draw is the **bird life** – there's a real possibility of spotting a golden eagle, or the rare crow-like chough, and no possibility at all of missing the scores of white-fronted and barnacle geese who winter here in their thousands. The long, whale-shaped neighbouring island of **Jura** is one of the wildest and most mountainous of the Inner Hebrides, its entire west coast uninhabited and inaccessible except to the dedicated walker.

Port Ellen and around

Laid out as a planned village in 1821 by Walter Frederick Campbell, and named after his wife, **PORT ELLEN** is the chief port on Islay, with the island's largest fishing fleet, and main CalMac ferry terminal. The neat whitewashed terraces of Frederick Crescent, which overlook the town's bay of golden sand, are pretty enough, but the strand to the north, up Charlotte Street, is dominated by the modern maltings, on the Bowmore road, whose powerful odours waft across the town. For **accommodation** in Port Ellen itself, the best place is *Caladh Sona* (℡01496/302694, ⓔhamish.scott@lineone.net; March–Oct; ❷), a detached house at 53 Frederick Crescent, followed by the artistic *Carraig Fhada* B&B by the lighthouse (℡01496/302114; ❶). Another option is to head out of Port Ellen up the A846 towards the airport, to the excellent *Glenmachrie Farmhouse* (℡01496/302560, ⓦwww.glenmachrie.com; ❺), a whitewashed, family-run guest house, which does superb home-cooking, and fantastic breakfasts. Alternatively, there's an independent **campsite** at the stone-built *Kintra Farm* B&B (℡01496/302051, ⓦwww.kintrafarm.co.uk; April–Sept; ❷), three miles northwest of Port Ellen, at the southern tip of Laggan Bay.

From Port Ellen, a dead-end road heads off east along the coastline, passing three **distilleries** in as many miles: Laphroaig, Lagavulin and lastly Ardbeg, whose *Old Kiln Café* is the best place to grab a bite to eat in the area. Six miles beyond Ardbeg, slightly off the road, the simple thirteenth-century **Kildalton Chapel** boasts a wonderful eighth-century Celtic ringed cross made from the local "bluestone", which is a rich blue-grey. The quality of the scenes matches any to be found on the crosses carved by the monks in Iona.

Bowmore

At the northern end of the seven-mile-long Laggan Bay, across the monotonous peat bog of Duich Moss, lies **BOWMORE**, Islay's administrative capital, with a population of around 800. It's a striking place, laid out in a grid plan rather like Inveraray, with the whitewashed terraces of Main Street climbing up the hill in a straight line from the pier on Loch Indaal to the town's crowning landmark, the **Round Church**, whose central tower looks uncannily like a lighthouse. Built in the round, so that the devil would have no corners in which to hide, it has a plain, wood-panelled interior, with a lovely tiered balcony and a big central mushroom pillar. A little to the west of Main Street is **Bowmore distillery** (see box, p.987), the first of the legal Islay distilleries, founded in 1779, and still occupying its original whitewashed buildings by the loch.

Islay's only official **tourist office** is in Bowmore (April–Oct Mon–Sat 10am–5pm; May–Aug also Sun 2–5pm; Nov–March Mon–Fri noon–4pm); it can help find **accommodation** anywhere on Islay or Jura. Bowmore itself is

㉑

not necessarily the best place to stay on the island, but if you choose to, head for Main Street where you'll find the town's cosiest and most central pub, the *Harbour Inn* (☎01496/810330, ⓦwww.harbour-inn.com; ❻). Alternatively, *Lambeth House* is one of the town's better B&Bs (☎01496/810597; ❷), centrally located on Jamieson Street.

If you're visiting Islay between mid-September and the third week of April, it's impossible to miss the island's staggeringly large wintering population of **barnacle and white-fronted geese**. During this period, the geese dominate the landscape, feeding incessantly off the rich pasture, strolling by the shores, and flying in formation across the winter skies. You can see the geese just about anywhere on the island – there are an estimated 15,000 white-fronted and 40,000 barnacles here (and rising) – though in the evening, they tend to congregate in the tidal mud flats and fields around **Loch Gruinart**, which is now an **RSPB nature reserve**.

Port Charlotte

PORT CHARLOTTE, named after the founder's mother, is generally agreed to be Islay's prettiest village, its immaculate whitewashed cottages clustered around a sandy cove overlooking Loch Indaal. On the northern fringe of the village, in a whitewashed former chapel, the imaginative **Museum of Islay Life** (Easter–Oct Mon–Sat 10am–5pm, Sun 2–5pm; Nov–Easter Mon–Sat; £2), has a children's corner, quizzes, a good library of books about the island, and tantalizing snippets about eighteenth-century illegal whisky distillers. The **Wildlife Information Centre** (Easter–Oct daily except Sat 10am–3pm; July & Aug daily 10am–5pm; £2.50), housed in the former distillery warehouse, is also worth a visit for anyone interested in the island's fauna and flora.

Port Charlotte is the perfect place to stay on Islay. The welcoming *Port Charlotte Hotel* (☎01496/850360, ⓦwww.portcharlottehotel.co.uk; ❻) has the best **accommodation** – the seafood lunches served in the bar are very popular, and there's a good (though expensive) restaurant. For B&B, you're better off at *Octofad Farm* (☎01496/850594, ⓦwww.octofadfarm.com; April–Oct; ❶), a few miles down the road beyond Nerabus. Port Charlotte is also home to Islay's SYHA **hostel** (☎0870/004 1128, ⓦwww.syha.org.uk; April–Sept), housed in an old bonded warehouse next door to the Wildlife Information Centre. The *Croft Kitchen* (☎01496/850230; April–Oct), opposite the museum, serves simple **food**, such as sandwiches and cakes, as well as inexpensive seafood during the day and more adventurous fare in the evenings (except Wed). The **bar** of the *Port Charlotte* is very easy-going, while the local craic (and occasional live music) goes on at the *Lochindaal Inn*, down the road, where you can also tuck into a very good, locally bred steak.

Finlaggan and Port Askaig

Just beyond Ballygrant, on the road to Port Askaig, a narrow road leads off north to **Loch Finlaggan**, site of a number of prehistoric crannogs (artificial islands) and, for four hundred years from the twelfth century, headquarters of the lords of the Isles, semi-autonomous rulers over the Hebrides and Kintyre. Unless you need shelter from the rain, or are desperate to see the head of the commemorative medieval cross found here, you can happily skip the **information centre** (Easter & Oct Tues, Thurs & Sun 2–4pm; May–Sept daily except Sat 2.30–5pm; £2), to the northeast of the loch, and simply head on down to the site itself (access at any time), which is dotted with interpretive panels. Duckboards allow

②

you to walk out across the reed beds of the loch and explore the main crannog, **Eilean Mor**, where several carved gravestones are displayed under cover in the chapel, which seem to support the theory that the lords of the Isles buried their wives and children here, while having themselves interred on Iona.

Islay's other **ferry** connection with the mainland, and its sole link with Colonsay and Jura, is from **PORT ASKAIG**, a scattering of buildings that tumble down a little cove by the narrowest section of the Sound of Islay (*Caol Ila*). Easily the most comfortable **place to stay** nearby is the lovely whitewashed *Kilmeny Farmhouse* (℡01496/840668, Ⓦwww.kilmeny.com; ❻), southwest of Ballygrant, a place that richly deserves all the superlatives it regularly receives, its rooms furnished with antiques, its dinners (Mon–Fri only) worth the extra £25 a head. The *Ballygrant Inn* is a good **pub** in which to grab a pint, as is the bar of the *Port Askaig Hotel*, which enjoys a wonderful position by the pier at Port Askaig, with views over to the Paps of Jura.

The Isle of Jura

Jura's distinctive Paps – so called because of their smooth breast-like shape, though there are in fact three of them – seem to dominate every view off the west coast of Argyll, their glacial rounded tops covered in a light dusting of quartzite scree. The island's name is commonly thought to derive from the Norse *dyr-oe* (deer island) and, appropriately enough, the current deer population of six thousand far outnumbers the 180 humans. With just one road, which sticks to the more sheltered eastern coast of the island, and only one hotel and a smattering of B&Bs, Jura is an ideal place to go for peace and quiet and some great walking.

If you're just coming over for the day from Islay, and don't fancy climbing the Paps, you could happily spend the day in the lovely wooded grounds of **Jura House** (daily 9am–5pm; £2), five miles up the road from Feolin Ferry, where the car ferry from Port Askaig arrives. Pick up a booklet at the entrance to the grounds, and follow the path down to the sandy shore, a perfect picnic spot in fine weather. Closer to the house itself, there's an idyllic **walled garden**, divided in two by a natural rushing burn that tumbles down in steps. The garden specializes in antipodean plants, which flourish in the frost-free climate; in season, you can buy some of the garden's organic produce or take tea in the tea tent.

Anything that happens on Jura happens in the island's only real village, **CRAIGHOUSE**, eight miles up the road from Feolin Ferry. The village enjoys a sheltered setting, overlooking Knapdale on the mainland – so sheltered, in fact, that there are even a few palm trees thriving on the seafront. There's a shop, a post office, the island hotel and a tearoom, plus the tiny **Isle of Jura distillery** (℡01496/820240, Ⓦwww.isleofjura.com), which is very welcoming to visitors.

The family-run *Jura Hotel* in Craighouse is the island's only **hotel** (℡01496/820243, Ⓦwww.jurahotel.co.uk; ❺): it's not much to look at from the outside, but warm and friendly within, and centre of the island's social scene. The hotel does moderately expensive bar meals, and has a shower block and laundry facilities for those who wish to **camp** in the hotel gardens. For **B&B**, look no further than Mrs Boardman at 7 Woodside (℡01496/820379; ❹; April–Sept). Very occasionally a **minibus** (℡01496/820314) meets the **car ferry** (℡01496/840681) from Port Askaig – phone ahead to check times.

In April 1946, Eric Blair (better known by his pen name of **George Orwell**), suffering badly from TB and intending to give himself "six months' quiet" in which to write his novel *1984*, moved to a remote farmhouse called Barnhill, on the northern tip of Jura. He lived out a spartan existence there for two years but was forced to return to London shortly before his death. The house, 23 miles north of Craighouse up an increasingly poor road, is as remote today as it was in Orwell's day, and sadly there is no access to the interior.

Travel details

Trains

Glasgow (Queen Street) to: Arrochar and Tarbert (Mon–Sat 3–4 daily, Sun 1–3 daily; 1hr 20min); Oban (Mon–Sat 3–4 daily, Sun 1–3 daily; 3hr).

Mainland buses (excluding postbuses)

Arrochar to: Inveraray (3 daily, Sun 2 daily; 35min); Lochgilphead (3 daily; 1hr 30min).
Campbeltown to: Glasgow (2–3 daily; 4hr 25min).
Dunoon to: Inveraray (Mon–Sat 3 daily, Sun 0–3 daily; 1hr 10min).
Glasgow to: Arrochar (3–5 daily; 1hr 10min); Campbeltown (2–3 daily; 4hr 25min); Inveraray (4–6 daily; 1hr 45min); Kennacraig (Mon–Sat 2 daily, Sun 1 daily; 3hr 30min); Lochgilphead (2–3 daily; 2hr 40min); Oban (Mon–Sat 4 daily, Sun 2 daily; 3hr); Tarbert (2–3 daily; 3hr 15min).
Inveraray to: Dunoon (Mon–Sat 3 daily, Sun 0–3 daily; 1hr 10min); Lochgilphead (2–3 daily; 40min); Oban (Mon–Sat 3 daily, Sun 2 daily; 1hr 5min); Tarbert (2–3 daily; 1hr 30min).
Kennacraig to: Claonaig (Mon–Sat 3 daily; 15min).
Lochgilphead to: Campbeltown (3–5 daily; 1hr 45min); Crinan (Mon–Sat 3–4 daily; 20min); Oban (Mon–Sat 2–4 daily; 1hr 30min); Tarbert (3–4 daily; 30min).
Oban to: Lochgilphead (Mon–Sat 2–4 daily; 1hr 30min); Mallaig (1 daily; 2hr 30min).
Tarbert to: Campbeltown (Mon–Sat 4 daily, Sun 2 daily; 1hr 15min); Claonaig (Mon–Sat 3 daily; 30min); Kennacraig (3–6 daily; 15min).

Island buses

Arran

Brodick to: Blackwaterfoot (Mon–Sat 12 daily, Sun 6 daily; 30min); Corrie (4–6 daily; 20min); Lamlash (Mon–Sat 14–16 daily, Sun 4 daily; 10–15min); Lochranza (Mon–Sat 6 daily, Sun 3 daily; 45min).

Bute

Rothesay to: Kilchattan Bay (Mon–Sat 4 daily, Sun 3 daily; 30min); Mount Stuart (every 45min; 15min); Rhubodach (Mon–Fri 1–2 daily; 20min).

Colonsay

Scalasaig to: Kilchattan (Mon–Fri 2–4 daily; 30min); Kiloran Bay (Mon–Fri 2–3 daily; 12min); The Strand (Mon–Fri 1 daily; 15min).

Islay

Bowmore to: Port Askaig (Mon–Sat 8–10 daily, Sun 1 daily; 30–40min); Port Charlotte (Mon–Sat 5–6 daily; 25min); Port Ellen (Mon–Sat 9–12 daily, Sun 1 daily; 20–30min); Portnahaven (Mon–Sat 5–7 daily; 50min).

Mull

Craignure to: Fionnphort (Mon–Sat 3–4 daily, Sun 1 daily; 1hr 10min); Fishnish (3 daily; 10min); Tobermory (4–6 daily; 45min).
Tobermory to: Calgary (Mon–Sat 2 daily; 45min); Dervaig (Mon–Fri 3 daily, Sat 2 daily; 30min); Fishnish (2–4 daily; 40min).

Car ferries (summer timetable)

To Arran: Ardrossan–Brodick (4–6 daily; 55min); Claonaig–Lochranza (8–9 daily; 30min).
To Bute: Colintraive–Rhubodach (frequently; 5min); Wemyss Bay–Rothesay (every 45min; 30min).
To Coll: Oban–Coll (daily except Thurs & Fri; 2hr 40min).
To Colonsay: Kennacraig–Colonsay (Wed 1 daily; 3hr 35min); Oban–Colonsay (daily except Tues & Sat; 2hr 15min); Port Askaig–Colonsay (Wed 2 daily; 1hr 15min).
To Dunoon: Gourock–Dunoon (hourly; 20min); McInroy's Point–Hunter's Quay (every 30min; 20min).
To Gigha: Tayinloan–Gigha (hourly; 20min).
To Islay: Colonsay–Port Askaig (Wed 2 daily; 1hr 15min); Kennacraig–Port Askaig (1–3 daily; 2hr); Kennacraig–Port Ellen (1–3 daily; 2hr 10min).
To Jura: Port Askaig–Feolin Ferry (Mon–Sat hourly, Sun 3 daily; 10min).
To Kintyre: Portavadie–Tarbert (hourly; 25min)
To Mull: Kilchoan–Tobermory (Mon–Sat 7 daily; June–Aug also Sun 5 daily; 35min); Lochaline–Fishnish (Mon–Sat every 50min, Sun hourly; 15min); Oban–Craignure (Mon–Sat 6–7 daily, Sun 4–5 daily; 45min).

To Tiree: Barra–Tiree (Wed 1 daily; 3hr 5min); Oban–Tiree (daily; 3hr 40min).

Passenger-only ferries (summer timetable)

To Iona: Fionnphort–Iona (Mon–Sat frequently, Sun hourly; 5min).

Flights

Glasgow to: Campbeltown (Mon–Fri 2 daily; 35min); Islay (Mon–Fri 2 daily, Sat 1 daily; 40min); Tiree (Mon–Sat 1 daily; 45min).

ARGYLL | Travel details

Skye and the Western Isles

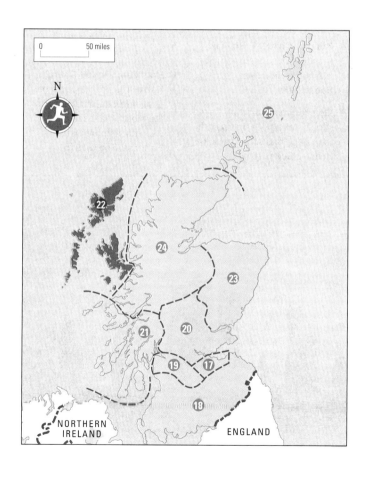

CHAPTER 22

Highlights

✳ **Loch Coruisk boat trip, Skye**
Take the boat from Elgol to
the beautiful, remote, glacial
Loch Coruisk in the midst of
the Skye Cuillin, and walk
back. **See p.1000**

✳ **Skye Cuillin** These jagged
peaks make Skye a great
place to visit. **See p.1000**

✳ **Kinloch Castle, Rùm** The
most outrageous Edwardian
pile in the Hebrides.
See p.1006

✳ **Gearrannan (Garenin), Lewis**
A painstakingly restored crofting village of thatched blackhouses. **See p.1012**

✳ **Calanais (Callanish),
Lewis** Scotland's finest
standing stones are set in
a serene lochside setting.
See p.1012

✳ **Golden sandy beaches**
Harris and the Uists have
some stunning, mostly
deserted, golden beaches,
backed by flower-strewn
machair. **See p.1015**

✳ **Roghadal (Rodel) Church,
Harris** The pre-Reformation
St Clement's Church boasts
the most ornate sculptural
decoration in the Outer
Hebrides. **See p.1015**

△ Calanais standing stones

Skye and the Western Isles

A procession of Hebridean islands, islets and reefs off the northwest shore of Scotland, **Skye and the Western Isles** between them boast some of the country's most alluring scenery. It's here that the turbulent seas of the Atlantic smash up against an extravagant shoreline hundreds of miles long, a geologically complex terrain whose rough rocks and mighty sea cliffs are interrupted by a thousand sheltered bays and, in the far west, a long line of sweeping sandy beaches. The islands' interiors are equally dramatic, a series of formidable mountain ranges soaring high above great chunks of boggy peat moor, a barren wilderness enclosing a host of lochans, or tiny lakes.

Each island has its own distinct character, though the grouping splits quite neatly into two. **Skye** and the **Small Isles** – the improbably named **Rùm**, **Eigg**, **Muck** and **Canna** – are part of the Inner Hebrides, which also include the islands of Argyll (see p.965). Beyond Skye, across the unpredictable waters of the Minch, lie the Outer Hebrides or Outer Isles, nowadays known as the **Western Isles**, a 130-mile-long archipelago stretching from **Lewis** and **Harris** in the north to **Barra** in the south. The region has four obvious areas of outstanding natural beauty to aim for: on Skye, the harsh peaks of the **Cuillin** and the bizarre rock formations of the **Trotternish** peninsula; on the Western Isles, the mountains of **North Harris** and the splendid sandy beaches that string along the Atlantic seaboard of **South Harris** and the **Uists**.

Skye and the Western Isles were first settled by Neolithic farming peoples in around 4000 BC. They lived along the coast, where they are remembered by scores of remains, from passage graves through to stone circles, most famously at **Calanais** (Callanish) on Lewis. Viking colonization gathered pace from 700 AD onwards – on Lewis four out of every five place-names is of Norse origin – and it was only in 1266 that the islands were returned to the Scottish crown. James VI (James I of England), a Stuart and a Scot, though no Gaelic-speaker, was the first to put forward the idea of clearing the Hebrides. However, it wasn't until after the Jacobite uprisings, in which many Highland clans disastrously backed the wrong side, that the **Clearances** began in earnest.

The isolation of the Hebrides exposed them to the whims and fancies of the various merchants and aristocrats who bought them up. Time and again, from the mid-eighteenth century to the present day, both the land and its people were sold to the highest bidder. Some proprietors were well-meaning, but

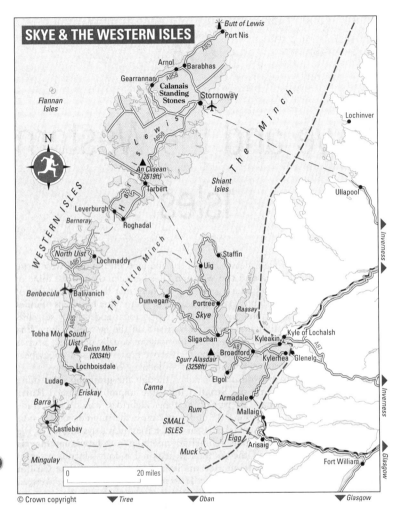

© Crown copyright ▼ Tiree   ▼ Oban   ▼ Glasgow

others simply forced the inhabitants onto ships bound for North America at gunpoint. Always the islanders were powerless and almost everywhere they were driven from their ancestral homes. However, their language survived, ensuring a degree of cultural continuity, especially in the Western Isles, where even today the first language of the vast majority is **Gaelic** (pronounced "gallic").

Skye

Jutting out from the mainland like a giant butterfly, the bare and bony promontories of **Skye** (Ⓦwww.skye.co.uk) fringe a deeply indented coastline. Despite the unpredictability of the weather, **tourism** has been an important part of the island's economy for a hundred years, since the train line pushed through to **Kyle of Lochalsh** in the western Highlands in 1897. From Kyle, it was the briefest of boat trips across to Skye, and the Edwardian bourgeoisie was soon swarming over to walk its mountains, whose beauty had been proclaimed by an earlier generation of Victorian climbers.

Though some estimate that today only half the island's population are indigenous *Sgiathanachs* (pronounced "Ski-anaks"), Skye remains the most important centre for **Gaelic culture** and language outside the Western Isles. For a taste of Gaelic culture, don't miss the Skye and Lochalsh Festival, *Feis an Eilein* (Ⓦwww .feisaneilein.com), which takes place over two weeks in mid-July.

Skye's most popular destination is the **Cuillin** ridge, whose jagged peaks dominate the island during clear weather. More easily accessible and equally dramatic in their own way are the rock formations of the **Trotternish** peninsula, in the north, from where there are inspirational views across to the Western Isles. If you want to escape the summer crush, head for **Duirinish** or the **Isle of Raasay**, off Skye's east coast. Of the island's two main settlements, **Portree** is the only one with any charm, and a useful base for exploring the Trotternish.

Most visitors still reach Skye via Kyle of Lochalsh, which is linked to Inverness by **train** and to Kyleakin, on the eastern tip of the island, by the **Skye Bridge**. The more scenic approach is by **ferry** from Mallaig, further south, crossing to Armadale. A third option is the privately operated summer-only car ferry that leaves the mainland at Glenelg, south of Kyle of Lochalsh, to arrive at Kylerhea. **Bus** services, while adequate between the villages, virtually close down on Sundays.

Sleat

Ferry services (Mon–Sat 7–8 daily; mid-May to mid-Sept also Sun; 30min) from Mallaig connect with the **Sleat** (pronounced "Slate") **peninsula**, Skye's southern tip, an uncharacteristically fertile area that has earned it the sobriquet "The Garden of Skye". The CalMac ferry terminal is at **ARMADALE** (Armadal), an elongated hamlet stretching along the wooded shoreline. If you're leaving Skye on the early-morning ferry or you arrive late and need to stay near Armadale, your best bet is *Armadale SYHA* **hostel** (☎0870/004 1103, Ⓦwww .syha.org.uk; April–Sept), a convenient ten-minute walk up the A851 towards Broadford with a good position overlooking the bay; dorm beds around £12. Alternatively, the *Flora MacDonald Hostel* (☎0783/447 6378, Ⓦwww.isle-of -skye-tour-guide.co.uk), two miles further up the same road, is a converted barn with bunkbeds (£9 per person), family rooms and even B&B (❸), and will fetch you from the ferry. **Bike rental** is available from the SYHA hostel or the local petrol station (☎01471/844249), close to the pier.

On the A851, past the SYHA hostel, you'll find the handsome forty-acre **Armadale Castle Gardens** (April–Oct daily 9.30am–5.30pm; £4.80; Ⓦwww.clandonald.com). Within the gardens lies the shell of the MacDonalds' neo-Gothic castle, a café and a library for those who want to chase up their ancestral Donald connections. The gardens' slick, purpose-built **Clan Donald Museum** has a good section on the Jacobite period and its aftermath and one or two top-notch works of art by Angelika Kaufmann, and Raeburn.

Continuing northeast, it's another eight miles to **ISLEORNSAY** (Eilean Iarmain), a secluded little village of whitewashed cottages that was once Skye's main fishing port. You can **stay** at the mid-nineteenth-century *Isleornsay Hotel* – also known by its Gaelic name *Hotel Eilean Iarmain* – a pricey place with excellent service, whose **restaurant** serves great seafood (☎01471/833332, Ⓦwww .eilean-iarmain.com; ❼), but where you can also just have a good bar meal by

22

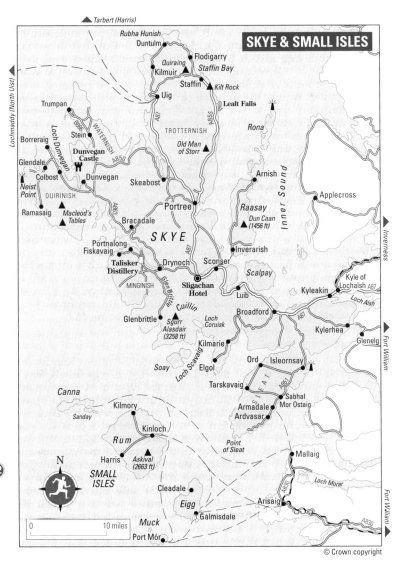

© Crown copyright

an open fire. Another couple of miles brings you to the turning for *Kinloch Lodge Hotel* (☎01471/833333, ⓦwww.claire-macdonald.com; ❽ including dinner), an old hunting lodge owned by Lord Macdonald of Macdonald, and serving excellent food guaranteed by his wife Claire, whose cookery books are internationally famous.

Kyleakin and Broadford

The **Skye Bridge** links the tidy hamlet of **KYLEAKIN** (Caol Acain – pronounced "Ka*la*kin") with the Kyle of Lochalsh on the mainland. Strictly speaking there are two bridges which rest on an island in the middle, **Eilean Bàn**, whose lighthouse cottages were once the home of author and naturalist Gavin Maxwell. The house has been turned into a museum, but can only be visited on a guided tour; numbers are limited and tours must be booked in advance through the **Bright Water Visitor Centre** in Kyleakin (April–Oct Mon–Fri 10am–5pm; free; ℡01599/530040, ⊛www.eileanban.org). The centre itself is well worth a visit, as it's full of hands-on things for children of all ages.

With its ferry now defunct, Kyleakin has reinvented itself as something of a backpackers' hangout – to the consternation of some villagers (in summer, the population more than doubles). If you're looking for a party atmosphere, then head for *Saucy Mary's* **pub and hostel** (℡01599/534845, ⊛www.saucymarys .com; dorm beds £12.50), where there's often live music until the early hours, or snuggle down at the cosy *Dun Caan Hostel* (℡01599/534087, ⊛www .skyerover.co.uk; dorm beds £12). **Bike rental** is available from *Dun Caan* and Skye Bikes (℡01599/534795) on the pier.

Skye's second-largest village is the charmless **BROADFORD** (An t-Ath Leathann), where you'll find a **tourist office** (Easter–Oct Mon–Fri 9.30am–5pm; June–Aug also Sat & Sun 9.30am–4pm; ℡01471/822713) by the 24-hour garage on the main road, as well as a laundry, small shop and bureau de change. Two **B&Bs** which stand out are the delightful old croft-house *Lime Stone Cottage*, 4 Lime Park (℡01471/822142, ⊛www.limestonecottage .co.uk; ❸), near the Serpentarium, and the modern, comfortable *Ptarmigan* (℡01471/822744, ⊛www.ptarmigan-cottage.com; ❸), on the main road, with views over the bay. If you want a bite **to eat**, try the justifiably popular *Creelers Seafood Restaurant* (℡01471/822281, ⊛www.skye-seafood-restaurant .co.uk) at the south end of the bay, which also does takeaway. For top-notch French seafood, head for the award-winning *Rendezvous* (booking advisable, on ℡01471/822001) a mile or so east of Broadford.

Isle of Raasay

Travelling west from Broadford, with the Skye Cuillin to your left and the sea to your right, it's thirteen miles to Sconsor, where a CalMac car ferry leaves for the lovely **Isle of Raasay** (Mon–Sat 8–10 daily; 15min), which, with its bleak and barren hills, remains well off the tourist trail. Raasay's population stands around two hundred, and the Free Presbyterian Church has a strong following here – the island keeps a strict observance of the Sabbath, with no work or play on Sundays.

The ferry docks at the southern tip of the island, an easy fifteen-minute walk from **INVERARISH**, a tiny village set within thick woods on the island's southwest coast. The grand Georgian mansion of **Raasay House**, built by the MacLeods in the late 1740s, is now an outdoor centre offering comfortable **accommodation** in pleasantly casual rooms (℡01478/660266, ⊛www .raasay-house.co.uk; ❶). You can also **camp** in the grounds or stay in the bunkhouse, and they'll happily collect you from the ferry terminal. In addition, you can join the centre's **activity programme** (£12–65), which includes anything from sailing, windsurfing and canoeing, to climbing and hill-walking for all ages. Close by is the welcoming *Isle of Raasay Hotel* (℡01478/660222, ⊛www .isleofraasayhotel.co.uk; ❹), which serves traditional Scottish food and has views of the Cuillin that surpass any other.

A rough track cuts up the steep hillside from the village to Raasay's isolated but beautifully placed SYHA **hostel** (℡0870/004 1146, ⊛www.syha.org.uk;

May–Sept; dorm beds £12). Most of the rest of Raasay is starkly barren, a rugged and rocky terrain of sandstone in the south and gneiss in the north, with the most obvious feature being the curiously truncated basalt cap on top of **Dun Caan** (1456ft), where Boswell "danced a Highland dance" on his visit to the island with Dr Johnson in 1773.

The Cuillin and the Red Hills

For many people, the **Cuillin**, whose sharp snowcapped peaks rise mirage-like from the flatness of the surrounding terrain, are the *raison d'être* for a visit to Skye. When the clouds finally disperse, they are the dominating feature of the island, visible from every other peninsula. There are basically three approaches to the Cuillin: from the south, by foot or by boat from Elgol; from the *Sligachan Hotel* to the north; or from Glen Brittle to the west of the mountains. Glen Sligachan is one of the most popular routes, dividing as it does the granite of the round-topped **Red Hills** (sometimes known as the Red Cuillin) to the east from the dark, coarse-grained jagged-edged gabbro of the real Cuillin (also known as the Black Cuillin) to the west. With some twenty Munros between them, these are mountains to be taken seriously, and many routes through the Cuillin are for experienced climbers only.

Elgol and Loch Coruisk

The road to **ELGOL** (Ealaghol), fourteen miles southwest of Broadford at the tip of the Strathaird peninsula, is one of the most dramatic on the island, leading right into the heart of the Red Hills and then down a precipitous slope, with a stunning view from the top down to Elgol pier. The chief reason for visiting Elgol is, weather permitting, to take a **boat** across Loch Scavaig (March–Sept 2 daily; £20–30 return), past a seal colony, to a jetty near the entrance of **Loch Coruisk** (from *coire uish*, "cauldron of water"). An isolated, glacial loch, this needle-like shaft of water, nearly two miles long but only a couple of hundred yards wide, lies in the shadow of the highest peaks of the Black Cuillin, a wonderfully overpowering landscape. The journey by sea takes 45 minutes and passengers spend about one and a half (or six and a half) hours ashore. It's essential to book ahead (between 7.30am to 10am on ☎0800/731 3089; ⓦwww.bellajane.co.uk); rigid-inflatable boat trips are also offered to the Small Isles.

Walkers can use the boat on a one-way trip (£15) to get to Loch Coruisk, from where there are numerous possibilities for hiking amidst the Red Hills, the most popular (and gentle) of which is the eight-mile trek north over the pass into **Glen Sligachan**. Alternatively, you could walk round the coast to the sandy bay of **Camasunary**, over two miles to the east – a difficult walk that involves a tricky river crossing and negotiating "The Bad Step", an overhanging rock with a thirty-foot drop to the sea – and either head north to Glen Sligachan or return south three miles along the coast to Elgol.

The only public transport is the morning **postbus** from Broadford (Mon–Fri 2 daily, Sat 1 daily; 2hr; check in Broadford post office). If you want a bite to eat, Elgol has a coffee shop, and the excellent seafood **restaurant** at *Coruisk House* (☎01471/866330, ⓦwww.seafood-skye.co.uk; April–Oct; ⑥), which also offers **B&B** in its bright and cheerful rooms. Alternatively, try *Rowan Cottage* (☎01471/866287, ⓦwww.rowancottage-skye.co.uk; March–Oct; ④), a lovely **B&B** a mile or so east in Glasnakille. By far the most popular place to stay, though, is the **campsite** (April–Oct) by the *Sligachan Hotel* (☎01478/650204, ⓦwww.sligachan.co.uk; ⑤) on the A87, at the northern end of Glen Sligachan;

22

the hotel also has a **bunkhouse**. Its huge *Seamus Bar* serves food for weary walkers until 11pm, with its own real ales, and often live bands; there's also a more formal restaurant serving splendid food.

Glen Brittle

Six miles along the A863 to Dunvegan from the *Sligachan Hotel*, a turning signed "Carbost and Portnalong" quickly leads to the entrance to stony **Glen Brittle**, edging the most spectacular peaks of the Cuillin; at the end of the glen, idyllically situated by the sea, is the village of **GLENBRITTLE**. Climbers and serious walkers tend to congregate at the SYHA **hostel** (℡0870/004 1121, Ⓦwww.syha.org.uk; April–Sept; dorm beds £13) or the beautifully situated **campsite** (℡01478/640404; April–Oct), a mile or so further south behind the wide sandy beach at the foot of the glen. From mid-May to September two buses a day (Mon–Sat only) from Portree make it to Glenbrittle; both the hostel and the campsite have grocery stores, the only ones for miles.

From the valley a score of difficult and strenuous trails lead east into the **Black Cuillin**, a rough semicircle of peaks rising to about 3000ft, which surround Loch Coruisk. One of the easiest walks is the five-mile round-trip from the campsite up **Coire Lagan**, to a crystal-cold lochan squeezed in among the sternest of rock faces. Above the lochan is Skye's highest peak, **Sgurr Alasdair** (3258ft), one of the more difficult Munros, while Sgurr na Banachdich (3166ft), to the northwest, is considered the most easily accessible Munro in the Cuillin. The Mountain Rescue Service has produced a book of walks for those who are not climbers, available locally.

Dunvegan and Duirinish

After the Portnalong and Glen Brittle turning, the A863 slips north across bare rounded hills to skirt the bony sea cliffs and stacks of the west coast. After twenty miles or so, it reaches **DUNVEGAN** (Dùn Bheagain), an unimpressive place, but a good base for exploring the interesting Duirinish peninsula. The main tourist trap in the village is **Dunvegan Castle** (daily: mid-March to Oct 10am–5pm; Nov to mid-March 11am–4pm; £7, gardens only £5; Ⓦwww .dunvegancastle.com) which sprawls on top of a rocky outcrop, sandwiched between the sea and several acres of beautifully maintained gardens. Seat of the Clan MacLeod since the thirteenth century, the present greying, rectangular fortress dates from the 1840s. Inside, you don't get a lot of castle for your money and the contents are far from stunning, the most intriguing being the battered remnants of the **Fairy Flag** which was allegedly carried back to Skye by Norwegian king Harald Hardrada's Gaelic boatmen after the Battle of Stamford Bridge in 1066.

The hammerhead **Duirinish peninsula** lies to the west of Dunvegan, much of it inaccessible to all except walkers prepared to scale or skirt the area's twin flat-topped basalt peaks: Healabhal Bheag (1600ft) and Healabhal Mhor (1538ft), better known as **MacLeod's Tables**, for legend has it that the MacLeod chief held an open-air royal feast on the lower of the two for James V. The area's turbulent history, and a great deal about nineteenth-century crofting, is told through fascinating contemporary news cuttings at **Colbost Folk Museum** (Easter–Oct daily 9am–6pm; £1.50), situated in a restored blackhouse, four miles up the road from Dunvegan. A guide is usually on hand to answer questions, the peat fire smokes all day, and there's a restored illegal whisky-still round the back.

22

Practicalities

Dunvegan has a **tourist office** (Mon–Sat 9am–5.30pm) and several good **hotels** and **B&Bs** dotted along the main road: try the converted traditional croft *Roskhill House* (☎01470/521317, ⓦwww.roskhillhouse.co.uk; March–Nov; ❹), or the beautifully situated *Silverdale Guesthouse* (☎01470/521251, ⓦwww.silverdaleskye.com; ❸), just before you get to Colbost. There are also a couple of excellent lochside **campsites**: one at Loch Greshornish, a mile north of Edinbane on the A850 (☎01470/582230, ⓦwww.skyecamp.com; April–Sept; bike and canoe rental available), and another on Loch Dunvegan (☎01470/521531, ⓦwww.kinloch-campsite.co.uk; April–Nov), on the road to Colbost.

The area's culinary Mecca is the expensive *Three Chimneys* **restaurant** (☎01470/511258, ⓦwww.threechimneys.co.uk; closed Sun lunch), beside Colbost Folk Museum, which serves sublime three-course meals at £45 a head; there are also six fabulous rooms at the restaurant's adjacent *House Over-By* (❾), which cost £240 for bed and breakfast. Much more reasonable is the sixteenth-century 🍴 *Stein Inn* (☎01470/592362, ⓦwww.steininn.co.uk; ❸), in Stein, with welcoming fires and good **pub food**. Next door is the pricier *Lochbay Seafood Restaurant* (☎01470/592235; Easter–Oct closed Sat & Sun; Aug closed Sun), where you'll need to book ahead. Without doubt, the best place to eat in Dunvegan is *The Old School* (☎01470/521421), whose excellent food belies its appearance from outside.

Portree

Although referred to by the locals as "the village", **PORTREE** is Skye's only real town. It's also one of the most attractive fishing ports in northwest Scotland, its deep, cliff-edged harbour filled with fishing boats and circled by multicoloured restaurants and guest houses. Up above the harbour is the spick-and-span town centre, spreading out from **Somerled Square**, built in the late eighteenth century as the island's administrative and commercial centre, and now housing the bus station and car park. The **Royal Hotel** on Bank Street occupies the site

△ Portree fishing harbour

of *McNab's Inn* where Bonnie Prince Charlie took leave of Flora MacDonald (see p.1005), and where, 27 years later, Boswell and Johnson had "a very good dinner, porter, port and punch".

A mile or so out of town on the Sligachan road is the **Aros Centre** (daily 9am–6pm; open later in summer; ⓦwww.aros.co.uk), one of Skye's most successful tourist attractions despite the fact that it's little more than an enormous souvenir shop. If it's wet, you can watch a live RSPB webcam centred on sea eagles' nests and an audiovisual roam around the island (£4). Aros also hosts gigs and contains a **cinema**, an exhibition space, a licensed bar and a popular café, and there's a play area for small kids. For a view of the contemporary visual arts scene, **An Tuireann Arts Centre**, housed in a converted fever hospital on the Struan road (Mon–Sat 10am–5pm; free; ⓦwww.antuireann .org.uk), puts on exhibitions, stages concerts, and has an excellent small licensed café where even the counter is a work of art, with an imaginative range of food on offer.

Practicalities

Hours vary enormously at Portree's **tourist office**, just off Bridge Street, so the ones here are just a guideline (April–Oct Mon–Sat 9am–8pm, Sun 10am–4pm; Nov–March Mon–Sat 9am–5.30pm); the office will, for a small fee, book **accommodation**. Probably the best hotel is the comfortable *Cuillin Hills* (ⓣ01478/612003, ⓦwww. cuillinhills-hotel-skye.co.uk; ❽), ten minutes' walk out of town along the northern shore of the bay, though ⚑ *Viewfield House Hotel* (ⓣ01478/612217, ⓦwww.viewfieldhouse.com; mid-April to mid-Oct), on the southern outskirts of town, is also worth investigating for its Victorian atmosphere, stuffed polecats and antiques. Portree is also stuffed with B&Bs, although they may all be full in high season: try *Medina* (ⓣ01478/612821; ❶; Easter–Sept), a well-run B&B in a quiet spot by the *Cuillin Hills Hotel*, or *Balloch* in Viewfield Road (ⓣ01478/612093; ❷; Easter–Oct). Portree's only **hostel** is the clean and smart *Portree Independent Hostel* (ⓣ01478/613737, ⓦwww .portreehostel.f9.co.uk) housed in the Old Post Office on the Green. *Torvaig* **campsite** (ⓣ01478/612209; April–Oct) is clean, well-kept, with a friendly owner, and lies a mile and a half north of town off the A855 Staffin road.

For Portree's best **food**, head to Bosville Terrace: here, the *Bosville Hotel*'s outstanding but pricey *Chandlery* restaurant (eves only) offers set menus from £28 a head, although the adjacent *Bosville Bistro* is much cheaper. Also on Bosville Terrace is *Harbour View* (ⓣ01478/612069, ⓦwww.harbourviewskye .co.uk; closed Wed), a seafood restaurant, with candlelit ambience and very fresh fish on the menu. For somewhere more relaxed, try *Café Arriba*, at the top of road down to the harbour, which offers an array of reasonably priced Mediterranean dishes, or for good **fish and chips**, there's an excellent chippy on the harbour. The bar of the *Pier Hotel* on the quayside is the favourite fishermen's **pub**, while the *Tongadale* on Wentworth Street is a lively spot. Currently the most popular evening venue is the *Isles Inn* on Somerled Square, with excellent bar meals as well as live music.

Trotternish

Protruding twenty miles north from Portree, the **Trotternish peninsula** boasts some of the island's most bizarre scenery, particularly on the east coast, where volcanic basalt has pressed down on the softer sandstone and limestone underneath, causing massive landslides. These, in turn, have created pinnacles and pillars that are at their most eccentric in the Quiraing, above Staffin Bay, on the east coast. An occasional bus service (Mon–Sat 2–4 daily) along the road encircling the peninsula gives access to almost all the peninsula.

The east coast

The first geological eccentricity on the **Trotternish** peninsula, six miles north of Portree along the A855, is the **Old Man of Storr**, a distinctive 165ft column of rock, shaped like a willow leaf, which, along with its neighbours, is part of a massive land-slip. Huge blocks of stone still occasionally break off the cliff face of the Storr (2358ft) above and slide downhill. It's a half-hour trek up a footpath to the foot of the column from the woods beside the car park. Further north, **Staffin Bay** is spread out before you, dotted with whitewashed and "spotty" houses. A single-track road cuts across the peninsula from the north end of the bay, allowing access to the **Quiraing**, a spectacular forest of mighty pinnacles and savage rock formations. There are two car parks: from the first, beside a cemetery, it's a steep half-hour climb to the rocks; from the second, on the saddle, it's a longer but more gentle traverse.

Most **accommodation** choices on the east coast enjoy fantastic views out over the sea. Just beyond Lealt Falls there's the very welcoming and comfortable *Glenview Inn* (℡01470/562248, ⓦwww.glenview-skye.co.uk; ❹), with an excellent restaurant, and a **campsite** (℡01470/562213; April–Sept) south of Staffin Bay. In fine weather, you can enjoy good bar snacks on the castellated terrace of the stylish *Flodigarry Country House Hotel* (℡01470/552203, ⓦwww .flodigarry.co.uk; ❻), three miles up the coast from Staffin. Behind the hotel (and now part of it) is the cottage where local heroine Flora MacDonald lived, and had six of her seven children, from 1751 to 1759. If the hotel's rooms are beyond your means, you can **camp** or stay at the neat and attractive *Dun Flodigarry* **hostel** (℡01470/552212), a couple of minutes' walk away.

The west coast

Heading down the west shore of the Trotternish, two miles beyond Duntulm is the **Skye Museum of Island Life** (Easter–Oct Mon–Sat 9.30am–5.30pm; £1.75), an impressive cluster of thatched blackhouses on an exposed hill overlooking Harris. The museum, run by locals, gives a fascinating insight into a way of life that was commonplace on Skye a hundred years ago. The blackhouse, now home to the ticket office, is much as it was when it was last inhabited in 1957, while the two houses to the east contain interesting snippets of local history. Behind the museum in the cemetery up the hill are the graves of **Flora MacDonald** and her husband. Thousands turned out for her funeral in 1790, creating a funeral procession a mile long – indeed, so widespread was her fame that the original family mausoleum fell victim to souvenir hunters and had to be replaced. The Celtic cross headstone is inscribed with a simple tribute by Dr Johnson, who visited her in 1773: "Her name will be mentioned in history, if courage and fidelity be virtues, mentioned with honour."

A further five miles south is the ferry port of **UIG** (Uige), which curves its way round a dramatic, horseshoe-shaped bay, and is the arrival point for CalMac ferries from Tarbert (Harris) and Lochmaddy (North Uist). Most folk come to Uig to take the ferry to the Western Isles, so if you need to stay near the ferry terminal, try the inexpensive **B&B**, *Orasay*, 14 Idrigill (℡01470/542316, ⓦwww.orasay.freeserve.co.uk; ❶), or the **campsite** just behind (℡01470/542714, ⓦwww.uig-camping-skye.co.uk), which also offers **bike rental**. By contrast, the SYHA **hostel** (℡0870/004 1155; April–Oct) is high up on the south side of the village, with exhilarating views over the bay; dorm beds cost £13. The *Pub at the Pier* offers basic meals, and serves local beers,

Prince Charles Edward Stewart – better known as **Bonnie Prince Charlie** or "The Young Pretender" – was born in Rome in 1720, where his father, "The Old Pretender", claimant to the British throne, was living in exile. At the age of 25, having little military experience, no knowledge of Gaelic, an imperfect grasp of English and a strong attachment to the Catholic faith, the prince set out for Scotland on a French ship, disguised as a seminarist from the Scots College in Paris. He arrived on the Outer Hebridean island of Eriskay on July 23, 1745, and was immediately implored to return to France by the clan chiefs, who were singularly unimpressed by his lack of army. Charles was unmoved and went on to raise the royal standard at Glenfinnan, gather together a Highland army, win the Battle of Prestonpans, march south into England and reach Derby before finally (and foolishly) agreeing to retreat. Back in Scotland, he won one last victory, at Falkirk, before the final disaster at Culloden in April 1746.

The prince spent the following five months in hiding, with a price of £30,000 on his head, and literally thousands of government troops searching for him. He certainly endured his fair share of cold and hunger whilst on the run, but the real price was paid by the Highlanders themselves, who risked and sometimes lost their lives by aiding and abetting the prince. The most famous of these was, of course, 23-year-old **Flora MacDonald**, whom Charles met on South Uist in June 1746. Flora was persuaded – either by his beauty or her relatives, depending on which account you believe – to convey Charles "over the sea to Skye", disguised as an Irish servant girl by the name of Betty Burke. She was arrested just seven days after parting with the prince in Portree, and held in the Tower of London until July 1747. She went on to marry a local man, had seven children, and in 1774 emigrated to America, where her husband was taken prisoner during the American War of Independence. Flora returned to Scotland and was reunited with her husband on his release; they resettled in Skye and she died at the age of 68.

Charles eventually boarded a ship back to France in September 1746, but, despite his promises – "for all that has happened, Madam, I hope we shall meet in St James's yet" – never returned to Scotland, nor did he ever see Flora again. After mistreating a string of mistresses, he eventually got married at the age of 52 to the 19-year-old princess of Stolberg, in an effort to produce a Stewart heir. They had no children, and she eventually fled from his violent drunkenness; in 1788, a none-too-"bonnie" Prince Charles died in the arms of his illegitimate daughter in Rome. Bonnie Prince Charlie became a legend in his own lifetime, but it was the Victorians who really milked the myth for all its sentimentality, conveniently overlooking the fact that the real consequence of 1745 was the virtual annihilation of the Highland way of life.

including those made by the nearby brewery (Mon–Fri tours by appointment; ☎01470/542477, ⊛www.skyebrewery.co.uk).

The Small Isles

The history of the **Small Isles**, which lie to the south of Skye, is typical of the Hebrides: early Christianization, followed by a period of Norwegian rule that ended in 1266 when the islands fell into Scottish hands. Their support for the Jacobite cause resulted in hard times after the failed rebellion of 1745, but the biggest problems came with the introduction of the **potato** in the mid-eighteenth century. The consequences were as dramatic as they were unforeseen: the success of the crop and its nutritional value – when grown in conjunction with traditional cereals – eliminated famine at a stroke, prompting a population explosion. In 1750, there were just a thousand islanders, but by 1800 their numbers had almost doubled. At first, the problem of overcrowding was camouflaged by the **kelp** boom, in which the islanders were employed. But the economic bubble burst with the end of the Napoleonic Wars and most owners eventually resorted to forced Clearances.

Since then, each of the islands has been bought and sold several times, though only **Muck** is now privately owned by the benevolent laird, Lawrence Mac-Ewen. **Eigg** hit the headlines in 1997, when the islanders bought the island themselves. The other islands were bequeathed to national agencies: **Rùm**, by far the largest and most-visited of the group, possessing a cluster of formidable volcanic peaks and the architecturally remarkable Kinloch Castle, passed to the Nature Conservancy Council (now Scottish Natural Heritage) in 1957; while **Canna**, in many ways the prettiest of the isles with its high basalt cliffs, is owned by the National Trust for Scotland.

Accommodation on the Small Isles is limited and requires **forward planning** at all times of year; formal public transport is nonexistent, but the locals will usually oblige if you have heavy baggage to shift.

Getting to the Small Isles

CalMac ferries run to the Small Isles every day except Sunday from Mallaig (☏01687/462403, ⓦwww.calmac.co.uk). Day-trips are possible to each of the islands on certain days, and to all four islands on Saturdays, if you catch the 7.30am ferry. From May to September, the **Sheerwater**, run by Arisaig Marine (☏01687/450224, ⓦwww.arisaig.co.uk), operates a daily service from Arisaig to Rùm, Eigg or Muck. This is a much more pleasant route, not least because if any marine mammals are spotted en route, the boat will pause for a bit of whale watching. Day-trips are possible to Eigg on most days, allowing four to five hours ashore, and to Rùm and Muck on a few days, allowing two to three hours ashore – advance booking is advisable.

Rùm

Like Skye, **Rùm** is dominated by its Cuillin, which, though only reaching a height of 2663ft at the summit of Askival, rises up with comparable drama straight up from the sea in the south of the island. Rùm's chief formal attraction is **Kinloch Castle** (guided tours most days at around 2pm; £5), a squat red sandstone edifice fronted by colonnades and topped by crenellations and turrets, that dominates the village of Kinloch. Completed at enormous expense in 1900 – the red sandstone was shipped in from Arran and the soil for the gardens from Ayrshire – its interior is a perfectly preserved example of Edwardian decadence, "a living memorial of the stalking, the fishing and the sailing, the tenantry and plenty of the days before 1914". From the galleried hall, with its tiger rugs, stags' heads and giant Japanese incense-burners, to the "Extra Low Fast Cushion" of the Soho snooker table in the Billiard Room, the interior is packed with knick-knacks and technical gizmos accumulated by **Sir George Bullough** (1870–1939), the spendthrift son of self-made millionaire Sir John Bullough, who bought the island as a sporting estate in 1888. As such, it was only really used for a few weeks each autumn, during "the season", yet employed an island workforce of one hundred all year round. Bullough's guests were woken at eight each morning by a piper; later on, an orchestrion, an electrically driven barrel organ (originally destined for Balmoral) crammed in under the stairs, would grind out an eccentric mixture of pre-dinner tunes – *The Ride of the Valkyries* and *Ma Blushin' Rosie* among others; a demo is included in the tour.

The ballroom has a sprung floor, the library features a gruesome photographic collection from the Bulloughs' world tours, but the *pièce de résistance* has to be Bullough's **Edwardian bathrooms**, whose baths have hooded walnut shower cabinets, fitted with two taps and four dials, which allow the bather to fire high-pressure water at their body from every angle.

Two gentle waymarked **heritage trails** start from Kinloch, both taking around two hours. For longer walks, you must fill in route cards and pop them into the White House (Mon–Fri 9am–12.30pm), where the reserve manager can give useful advice. The island's best beach is at **KILMORY**, to the north (5hr return), though this part of the island is only open to the public at the weekend as it's given over to the study of red deer; it's also closed completely in June, during calving, and October, during rutting. When the island's human head count peaked at 450 in 1791, the hamlet of **HARRIS** on the southwest coast (6hr return) housed a large crofting community; all that remains now are several ruined blackhouses and the extravagant **Bullough Mausoleum**, built by Sir George to house the remains of his father in the style of a Greek Doric temple, overlooking the sea.

You need to book **accommodation** in advance. Kinloch Castle lets a few of its four-poster rooms (**⑤**), but it's basically run as an independent **hostel** (℡01687/462037), with dormitories in the old servants' quarters; dorm beds cost £12. There are also two simple mountain **bothies** (maximum stay three nights), in Dibidil and Guirdil, and basic **camping** near the old pier – book ahead for both with the White House (℡01687/462026). Wherever you're staying, you can either do self-catering – hostellers can use the hostel kitchen – or eat the unpretentious **food** offered in the hostel's licensed bistro, which serves full breakfasts, offers packed lunches and charges just over £10 a head for a three-course evening meal. B&B is sometimes available on the island – ask at the hostel for the latest. There is also a small shop/off-licence/post office in Kinloch. Bear in mind that Rùm is the wettest of the Small Isles, and is known for having some of the worst **midges** in Scotland – come prepared for both.

Eigg

Eigg (🌐 www.isleofeigg.org) is without doubt the most easily distinguishable of the Small Isles from a distance, since the island is mostly made up of a basalt plateau 1000ft above sea level, and a great stump of columnar pitchstone lava, known as An Sgurr, rising out of the plateau another 290ft. It's also by far the most vibrant, populous and welcoming of the Small Isles, with a strong sense of community.

Ferries now arrive at the new causeway, which juts out into **Galmisdale Bay** at the southeast corner of the island where **An Laimhrig** (The Anchorage), the island's community centre, stands, housing a shop, post office, tearoom and information centre. Davie's minibus meets incoming ferries, and will take you to wherever you need to go on the island (℡01687/482494; £2). If time is limited, you could simply head for the nearby **Lodge**, the former laird's house and gardens which the islanders plan to renovate in the future. With the island's great landmark, **An Sgurr** (1292ft), watching over you wherever you go, many folk feel duty-bound to climb it, and enjoy the wonderful views over to Muck and Rùm (3–4hr return).

The nicest place **to stay** on Eigg is ⚡ *Kildonan House* (℡01687/482446; full board **④**), an eighteenth-century wood-panelled house beautifully situated on the north side of Galmisdale Bay, with good home-cooking. The island boasts a very comfortable **bunkhouse**, *Glebe Barn* (℡01687/482417), where you must book ahead, while basic **camping** is possible at Galmisdale Bay and with Sue Hollands in Cleadale (℡01687/482480, ⓔsuehollands@talk21.com). **Bike rental** is available from Eigg Bikes (℡01687/482432) by the pier.

Muck

Smallest and most southerly of the Small Isles, **Muck** (ⓦwww.islemuck.com) is low-lying, mostly treeless and extremely fertile, and as such shares more characteristics with the likes of Coll and Tiree than its nearest neighbours. **PORT MÓR**, the village on the southeast corner of the island, is where visitors arrive. A road, just over a mile in length, connects Port Mór with the island's main farm, **GALLANACH**, which overlooks the rocky seal-strewn skerries on the north side of the island. The nicest sandy beach is Camas na Cairidh, to the east of Gallanach. Despite being only 452ft above sea level, it really is worth climbing **Beinn Airein**, in the southwest corner of the island, for the 360-degree panoramic view; the return journey from Port Mór takes around two hours.

You can **stay** with one of the MacEwen family at *Port Mór House* (℡01687/462365; full board ❹); the rooms are pine-clad and enjoy great views, and the food is delicious. Alternatively, there's the island's **bunkhouse** (℡01687/462362), a characterful, wood-panelled bothy. You can also hire the island **yurt** or **tipi** (℡01687/462362, ⓔjenny@isleofmuck.fsnet.co.uk), or **camp rough** for free; ask at the craft shop in Port Mór and bring supplies with you, as there is no shop. The craft shop springs into life when day-trippers arrive, and doubles as a licensed **restaurant**.

Canna

Measuring five miles by one, and with a population of less than twenty, **Canna** is run as a single farm and bird sanctuary by the National Trust for Scotland. For visitors, the chief pastime is walking: from the dock it's about a mile across a grassy basalt plateau to the bony sea cliffs of the north shore, which rise to a peak around **Compass Hill** (458ft) – so called because its high metal content distorts compasses – in the northeastern corner of the island, from where you get great views across to Rùm and Skye. The cliffs of the buffeted western half of the island are a breeding ground for both Manx shearwater and puffin, though both have suffered from the island's rat infestation. Some seven miles offshore stands the **Heiskeir of Canna**, a curious mass of stone columns sticking up thirty feet above the water.

Accommodation is extremely limited, but with permission from the NTS you may **camp rough**. The NTS rep on Canna is Wendy MacKinnon, who can help answer most queries (℡01687/462465, ⓦwww.harbourview-canna .co.uk). Remember, however, that there are no shops on Canna (bar the post office), so you must bring your own supplies, or order them to be delivered from Mallaig.

The Western Isles

Beyond Skye, across the unpredictable waters of the Minch, lie the wild and windy Outer Hebrides or Outer Isles, also known as the **Western Isles** (ⓦwww.visithebrides.com), a 130-mile-long archipelago stretching from Lewis and Harris in the north to the Uists and Barra in the south. An elemental beauty pervades each of the more than two hundred islands that make up the Long Isle,

Gaelic in the Western Isles

Except in Stornoway, and Balivanich on North Uist, **road signs** in the Western Isles are almost exclusively in **Gaelic**, a difficult language to the English-speaker's eye, with complex pronunciation, though the English names can often provide a rough pronunciation guide. Particularly if you're driving, it's a good idea to buy the bilingual Western Isles **map**, *Bord Turasachd nan Eilean*, available at most tourist offices. To reflect the signposting, we've put the Gaelic first in the text, with the English equivalent in brackets. Thereafter we've stuck to the Gaelic names, to try to familiarize readers with their (albeit variable) spellings – the only exceptions are in the names of islands and ferry terminals, where we've stuck to the English names (with the Gaelic in brackets) partly to reflect the ferry company CalMac's own policy.

as it's sometimes known, though only a handful are inhabited, by a total population of just under 27,000 people. This is truly a land on the edge, where the turbulent seas of the Atlantic smash up against a geologically complex terrain whose rough rocks and mighty sea cliffs are interrupted by a thousand sheltered bays and, in the far west, a long line of sweeping sandy beaches. The islands' interiors are equally dramatic, a series of formidable mountain ranges soaring high above great chunks of boggy peat moor, a barren wilderness enclosing a host of tiny lakes, or lochans.

The Outer Hebrides remain the heartland of **Gaelic** culture, with the language spoken by the vast majority of islanders, though its everyday usage remains under constant threat from the national dominance of English. Its survival is, in no small part, due to the efforts of the Western Islands Council and the Scottish Executive, and down to the influence of the church in the region: the Free Church and its various Presbyterian offshoots in Lewis, Harris and North Uist, and the Roman Catholic Church in South Uist and Barra.

The interior of the northernmost island, **Lewis**, is mostly peat moor, a barren and marshy tract that gives way abruptly to the bare peaks of **North Harris**. Across a narrow isthmus lies **South Harris**, presenting some of the finest scenery in Scotland, with wide beaches of golden sand trimming the Atlantic in full view of a rough boulder-strewn interior. Across the Sound of Harris, to the south, a string of tiny, flatter isles – **North Uist**, **Benbecula**, **South Uist** – linked by causeways, offer breezy beaches, whose fine sands front a narrow band of boggy farmland, which, in turn, is mostly bordered by a lower range of hills to the east. Finally, tiny **Barra** contains all these landscapes in one small Hebridean package, and is a great introduction to the region.

In direct contrast to their wonderful landscapes, villages in the Western Isles are rarely very picturesque in themselves, and are usually made up of scattered, relatively modern croft houses dotted about the elementary road system. **Stornoway**, the only real town in the Outer Hebrides, is eminently unappealing. Many visitors, walkers and nature watchers forsake the settlements altogether and retreat to secluded cottages and B&Bs.

Transport practicalities

Several airlines operate fast and frequent daily **flights** from Glasgow, Edinburgh and Inverness to Stornoway on Lewis, and from Glasgow to Barra and Benbecula (Mon–Sat only). CalMac **car ferries** run from Ullapool in the Highlands to Stornoway (Mon–Sat only); from Uig, on Skye, to Tarbert (Mon–Sat) and Lochmaddy (daily); and from Oban to South Uist and Barra (daily), via Tiree (Thurs only). There's also an **inter-island ferry** from Leverburgh, on Harris, to Berneray (Mon–Sat only), and thence to the Uists, and between Eriskay, at the foot of the Uists, and Barra. For more on ferry services, see "Travel details" on p.1021.

Lewis (Leodhas)

Lewis is the largest and most populous of the Western Isles and the northernmost island in the Hebridean archipelago. Most of its 20,000 inhabitants live in the crofting and fishing villages strung out along the northwest coast, between **Calanais** and **Port Nis**, in one of Scotland's most densely populated rural areas. On this coast you'll also find the islands' best-preserved **prehistoric remains** – Dùn Charlabhaigh broch and Calanais standing stones – as well as a smattering of ancient crofters' houses in various stages of abandonment. The landscape is mostly flat peat bog – hence the island's name, derived from the Gaelic *leogach* (marshy) – but the shoreline is more dramatic especially around Rubha Robhanais (Butt of Lewis), a group of rough rocks on the island's northernmost tip, near Port Nis. To the south, where Lewis is physically joined with Harris, the land rises to just over 1800ft, providing a more exhilarating backdrop for the excellent beaches that pepper the isolated west coast. **Stornoway**, on the east coast, is the only substantial town in the Western Isles, but it's really only useful for stocking up on provisions or catching the bus: there are regular services to all parts of the island, most usefully to Port Nis and Tarbert, and along the 45-mile round trip from Stornoway to Calanais, Carlabhagh, Arnol and back.

Stornoway (Steornabhagh)

In these parts, **STORNOWAY** is a buzzing metropolis, with over six thouand inhabitants. It's the social hub of the island and, perhaps most importantly of all, home to the Western Isles Council or **Comhairle nan Eilean Siar** (www .cne-siar.gov.uk), which has done so much to promote Gaelic language and culture, and stem the tide of anglicization. For the visitor, however, the town is unlikely to win any great praise – aesthetics are not its strong point, and the urban pleasures on offer are limited.

Stornoway's best-looking building is the old **Town Hall** on South Beach, a splendid Scots Baronial building, its rooftop peppered with conical towers, above which a central clocktower rises. One block east along South Beach, you'll find **An Lanntair**, Gaelic for "lantern", Stornoway's long-awaited new arts centre (Mon–Sat 10am–10pm; free; www.lanntair.com), which houses a 250-seat auditorium and cinema, and gallery space for temporary exhibitions, plus a very pleasant café-bar. Anyone remotely interested in Harris Tweed should head for the **Lewis Loom Centre** (Mon–Sat 9am–6pm; £1; www .lewisloomcentre.co.uk), run by an eccentric and engaging man and located at the far end of Cromwell Street, in the Old Grainstore off Bayhead. Continuing up the pedestrian precinct into Francis Street, you'll eventually reach the **Museum nan Eilean** (April–Sept Mon–Sat 10am–5.30pm; Oct–March Tues–Fri 10am–5pm, Sat 10am–1pm; free; www.cne-siar.gov .uk), with lots of information about the island's history and its herring and weaving industries.

To the northwest of the town centre stands **Lews Castle** (www.lews-castle .com), a nineteenth-century Gothic pomposity built by Sir James Matheson in 1863 after resettling the crofters who used to live here. As the former laird's pad, it's seen as a symbol of old oppression by many. Its chief attraction is its mature wooded grounds, a unique sight on the Western Isles, and its **Woodland**

Centre (Mon–Sat 10am–5pm; free; ⓦ www.lewscastlegrounds.org.uk), which has a straightforward exhibition on the history of the castle and the island upstairs, with a live CCTV link to a nearby nest box, and a decent **café** serving soup, salads and cakes downstairs.

Practicalities

The best thing about Stornoway is the convenience of its services. The island's **airport** (ⓣ 01851/707400, ⓦ www.hial.co.uk) is four miles east of the town centre: the hourly bus takes fifteen minutes, or else it's £5 by taxi. The CalMac **ferry terminal** is on South Beach, close to the **bus station**, and the **tourist office** is near North Beach at 26 Cromwell St (April to mid-Oct Mon–Fri 9am–6pm, Sat 9am–5pm, plus open to meet the evening ferry; mid-Oct to March Mon–Fri 9am–5pm).

Of the **hotels**, the *Royal Hotel* on Cromwell Street (ⓣ 01851/702109, ⓦ www.calahotels.com; ❺) is your best bet. Alternatively, there's the *Park Guest House* on James Street (ⓣ 01851/702485; ❷), whose public areas have bags of lugubrious late-Victorian character, the bedrooms significantly less, or the *Hebridean Guest House*, 61 Bayhead St (ⓣ 01851/702268, ⓦ www .hebrideanguesthouse.co.uk; ❹), with rooms newly furnished in pine. Of the **B&Bs**, try *Fernlea*, a listed Victorian house, along leafy Matheson Road, at no. 9 (ⓣ 01851/702125, ⓔ maureenmacmillan@amserve.com; ❸), or *Fair Haven*, 28 Francis St (ⓣ 01851/705862, ⓦ www.hebrideansurf.co.uk; ❶), primarily a centre for surfers, but welcoming all; accommodation includes bunk, family and single rooms (dorm beds from £10) and there's a good **restaurant** too.

Food options have improved in Stornoway over the last couple of years, with first choice being the ✈ *Thai Café*, 27 Church St (ⓣ 01851/701811; closed Sun), which serves inexpensive authentic Thai food. The *Royal Hotel*'s café-bar *HS-1*, is a stylish, modern place offering everything from simple fare like baked potatoes to stir-fries and curry. *MacNeills* on Cromwell Street is the liveliest central **pub**, or there's the tiny *Criterion*, on Point Street. An Lanntair runs a regular programme of **gigs and films**.

The road to Port Nis (Port of Ness)

Northwest of Stornoway, the A857 crosses the vast, barren **peat bog** of the interior, an empty undulating wilderness riddled with stretchmarks formed by peat cuttings and pockmarked with freshwater lochans. For the people of Lewis the peat continues to serve as a valuable energy resource, its pungent smoke one of the most characteristic smells of the Western Isles. Plans are afoot to build Europe's largest **wind farm** (ⓦ www.lewiswind.com) here, with over two hundred wind turbines, each standing 400ft high, harnessing a renewable resource that the Western Isles has in vast quantities.

Twelve miles across the peat bog the road approaches the west coast of Lewis near Barabhas and divides, heading southwest towards Calanais (see p.1012), or northeast through a string of scattered settlements to the fishing village of **PORT NIS** (Port of Ness). Shortly before Port Nis, a minor road heads two miles northwest to the hamlet of **EOROPAIDH** (Europie) – pronounced "yor-erpee". Here, by the road junction that leads to the Butt of Lewis, stands the simple stone structure of **Teampull Mholuaidh** (St Moluag's Church), thought to date from the twelfth century. From Eoropaidh, a narrow road twists to the bleak and blustery northern tip of the island, Rubha Robhanais – known to devotees of the BBC shipping forecast as the **Butt of Lewis** – where a lighthouse sticks up above a series of sheer cliffs and stacks, alive with sea birds and a great place for marine mammal-spotting.

Four to six buses a day run from Stornoway to Port Nis (Mon–Sat). The best **accommodation** in the area is at *Galson Farm Guest House* (☎01851/850492, Ⓦwww.galsonfarm.freeserve.co.uk; ❹), an eighteenth-century farmhouse in Gabhsann Bho Dheas (South Galson), halfway between Barabhas and Port Nis, with a **bunkhouse** close by (phone number as above). The only tearoom is *Harbour View* in Port Nis, the only **pub** the *Cross Inn* in Cros, and there are only a few shops (supplemented by mobile ones) in these parts, so it's as well to stock up in Stornoway before you set out.

Arnol and around

Heading southwest from the crossroads near Barabhas brings you to several villages that meander down towards the sea. In **ARNOL**, the remains of numerous blackhouses lie abandoned by the roadside; at the north end of the village, no. 42 has been preserved as the **Arnol Blackhouse** (Mon–Sat: May–Sept 9.30am–6.30pm; Oct–March 9.30am–4.30pm; £4; HS) to show exactly how a true blackhouse or *taigh dubh* would have been. The dark interior is lit and heated by a small peat fire, which is kept alight in the central hearth of bare earth, and is usually fairly smoky as there's no chimney; instead, smoke drifts through the thatch, helping to kill any creepy-crawlies, keep out the midges and turn the heathery sods and oat-straw thatch itself into next year's fertilizer. There's a great **B&B** two miles away in Siabost Bho Deas (South Shawbost) at *Airigh* (☎01851/710478, Ⓦwww.airighbandb.co.uk; ❷), while behind Siabost's church is the *Eilean Fraoich* **campsite** (☎01851/710504; April–Oct). You can grab a bite to **eat** at the *Shawbost Inn*.

Five miles on at Carlabhagh (Carloway), a mile-long road leads off north to the beautifully remote coastal settlement of **GEARRANNAN** (Garenin), where nine thatched crofters' houses – the last of which was abandoned in 1974 – have been restored to give a great impression of what a **Baile Tughaidh** or blackhouse village (Mon–Sat 9.30am–5.30pm; £2.50) was like. The first house you come to is the ticket office and **café**; the second has been restored to its condition at the time of abandonment; while the third house tells the history of the village and the folk who lived there. Opposite, another house has been renovated to contain a basic GHHT **hostel** (Ⓦwww.gatliff.org.uk), and several others have been converted into **self-catering** houses (Ⓦwww.gearrannan.com).

Just beyond Carlabhagh, about 400 yards from the road, the two-thousand-year-old **Dùn Charlabhaigh Broch** perches on top of a conspicuous rocky outcrop overlooking the sea. This is one of Scotland's best preserved brochs (a circular, prehistoric stone fort), its dry-stone circular walls reaching a height of more than 30ft on one side. Dùn Charlabhaigh also has its very own **Doune Broch Centre** (June–Sept Mon–Sat 10am–6pm; free), situated at a discreet distance, stone-built and sporting a turf roof. It's a good wet-weather retreat, and fun for kids, who can walk through a hay-strewn mock-up of the broch. A mile or so beyond the broch, beside a lochan, is the *Doune Braes Hotel* (☎01851/643252, Ⓦwww.doune-braes.co.uk; ❺), a friendly, unpretentious former schoolhouse, whose bar serves tasty seafood dishes.

Calanais (Callanish)

Five miles south of Carlabhagh lies the village of **CALANAIS** (Callanish), site of the islands' most dramatic prehistoric ruins, the **Calanais Standing Stones**, whose monoliths – nearly fifty of them – occupy a serene lochside setting. There have been years of heated debate about the origin and function of the stones – slabs of gnarled and finely grained gneiss up to 15ft high – though almost everyone agrees that they were lugged here by Neolithic peoples between 3000 and 1500 BC. Such an endeavour could, it's been argued, only be prompted by the desire to predict the seasonal cycle upon which these early farmers were entirely dependent, and indeed many of the stones are aligned with the position of the sun and the stars. This rational explanation, based on clear evidence that this part of Lewis was once a fertile farming area, dismisses as coincidence the ground plan of the site, which resembles a colossal Celtic cross, and explains away the central burial chamber as a later addition of no special significance. These two features have, however, fuelled all sorts of theories ranging from alien intervention to human sacrifice.

A blackhouse adjacent to the main stone circle has been refurbished as a **tearoom** – it has limited snacks, but bags more atmosphere than the **Calanais Visitor Centre** (Mon–Sat: April–Sept 10am–6pm; Oct–March 10am–4pm; museum £1.75) on the other side of the stones, to which all the signs direct you from the road. The centre runs a decent restaurant and a small museum, but with so much information on the panels beside the stones there's little reason to visit it.

There are several good **places to stay** in Calanais: try the modern *Eshcol Guest House* (℡01851/621357, ⓦwww.eshcol.com; ❹), no beauty from the outside, but very well-run and comfortable within, or the newly built *Leumadair Guest House* (℡01851/612706, ⓦwww.leumadair.co.uk; ❹). For **food**, you should head to *Tigh Mealros* (℡01851/621333; closed Sun), in Gearraidh na h-Aibhne, which serves good, inexpensive lunches and evening meals, featuring local seafood.

Harris (Na Hearadh)

Harris, to the south of Lewis, is much hillier, more dramatic and much more appealing than its neighbour, its boulder-strewn slopes descending to aquamarine bays of dazzling, white sand. The shift from Lewis to Harris is almost imperceptible, though Harris itself is clearly divided by a minuscule isthmus, into the wild, inhospitable mountains of **North Harris** and the gentler landscape and sandy shores of **South Harris**. Crofting continues on Harris on a small scale, supplemented by the tweed industry, and shellfish fishing continues on Scalpay, while the rest of the population gets by on whatever employment is available: roadworks, crafts and, of course, tourism. There's a regular **bus** connection between Stornoway and **Tarbert**, and an occasional service that circumnavigates South Harris.

Tarbert (An Tairbeart)

The largest place on Harris is the ferry port of **TARBERT**, sheltered in a green valley on the narrow isthmus that marks the border between North and South Harris. Its mountainous backdrop is impressive, and the town is attractively laid out on steep terraces sloping up from the dock. It boasts Harris's only **tourist office** (April–Oct Mon–Fri 9am–5pm, Sat 9am–1pm & 2–5pm, also open to greet the evening ferry; winter hours variable), close to the ferry terminal.

Close to Tarbert's ferry terminal, there's a very good **B&B**, *Tigh na Mara* (℡01859/502270, ⓦwww.tigh-na-mara.co.uk; ❷), while *Ardhasaig House* (℡01859/502066, ⓦwww.ardhasaig.co.uk; ❻) is a small, newly modernized and TV-free **hotel** up the Stornoway road, looking out over North Harris. You'll need to book ahead to stay in the popular *Leachin House* (℡01859/502157, ⓦwww.leachin-house.com; ❻), which looks out west to the sea, just off the road to Stornoway. There's an excellent **hostel** called the *Rockview Bunkhouse*

22

Harris Tweed

Far from being a picturesque cottage industry, as it's sometimes presented, the production of **Harris Tweed** is vital to the local economy, with a well-organized and unionized workforce. Traditionally, the tweed was made by women from the wool of their own sheep, to provide clothing for their families, using a 2500-year-old process. Each woman was responsible for plucking the wool by hand, washing and scouring it, dyeing it with lichen, heather flowers or ragwort, carding (smoothing and straightening the wool, often adding butter to grease it), spinning and weaving. Finally the cloth was dipped in urine and "waulked" by a group of women, who beat the cloth on a table to soften and shrink it whilst singing Gaelic waulking songs. Harris Tweed was originally made all over the islands, and was known simply as *clò mór* (big cloth).

In the mid-nineteenth century, the Countess of Dunmore, who owned a large part of Harris, started to sell surplus cloth to her aristocratic friends; she then sent two sisters from Srannda (Strond) to Paisley to learn the trade. On their return, they formed the genesis of the modern industry, which serves as a vital source of employment, though demand (and therefore employment levels) can fluctuate wildly as fashions change. To earn the official Harris Tweed Association trademark of the Orb and the Maltese Cross – taken from the Countess of Dunmore's coat of arms – the fabric has to be hand-woven on the Outer Hebrides from 100 percent pure new Scottish wool, with other parts of the manufacturing process taking place only in local mills.

The main centre of production is now Lewis, where the wool is dyed, carded and spun; you can see all these processes by visiting the **Lewis Loom Centre** in Stornoway (see p.1010). In the last few decades there has been a revival of traditional tweed-making techniques, with several small producers following old methods. One such place is **Soay Studio** at the western end of Tarbert (May–Sept Tues–Thurs 9am–12.30pm & 1.30–4pm; ℡01859/502361), which uses indigenous plants and bushes to dye the cloth: yellow comes from rocket and broom; green from heather; grey and black from iris and oak; and, most popular of all, reddish brown from crotal, a flat grey lichen scraped off rocks.

(℡01859/502626; dorm beds £10), on Main Street, which also offers **bike rental**. The lounge and **bar** of Tarbert's *Harris Hotel* act as the local social centre, but the best **fish and chips** are dispensed by ⚜ *Ad's Take-Away* (April–Oct; closed Sun), next to the *Rockview Bunkhouse*. Otherwise, you're best off heading for the very pleasant *First Fruits* **tearoom** (April–Sept; closed Sun), behind the tourist office, serving real coffee, home-made cakes, toasties and so forth, plus evening meals (Tues–Fri).

North Harris (Ceann a Tuath na Hearadh)

The A859 north to Stornoway takes you over a boulder-strewn saddle between mighty **Sgaoth Aird** (1829ft) and An Cliseam or the **Clisham** (2619ft), the highest peak in the Western Isles. This bitter terrain, littered with debris left behind by retreating glaciers, offers but the barest of vegetation, with an occasional cluster of crofters' houses sitting in the shadow of a host of pointed peaks, anywhere between 1000ft and 2500ft high. These bulging, pyramidal mountains reach their climax around the dramatic shores of the fjord-like **Loch Seaforth**. The only place to stay in this area is the GHHT **hostel** (ⓦ www.gatliff.org.uk; £8) in the lonely coastal hamlet of **REINIGE-ADAL** (Rhenigdale). To reach the hostel on foot from Tarbert (3hr one way), take the path from Caolas Scalpaigh (Kyles Scalpay), which threads its way through the peaks of the craggy promontory that lies trapped between Loch Shìphoirt and Loch an Tairbeart.

South Harris (Ceann a Deas na Hearadh)

The mountains of **South Harris** are less dramatic than in the north, but the scenery is equally breathtaking. There's a choice of routes from Tarbert to the ferry port of **Leverburgh**, which connects with North Uist: the east coast, known as Na Baigh (The Bays), is rugged and seemingly inhospitable, while the **west coast** is endowed with some of the finest stretches of golden sand in the whole of the archipelago, buffeted by the Atlantic winds. Paradoxically, most people on South Harris live along the harsh eastern coastline of **Bays** rather than the more fertile west side. But not by choice – they were evicted from their original crofts to make way for sheep-grazing.

The main road from Tarbert into South Harris snakes its way west for ten miles across the boulder-strewn interior to reach the coast. Once there, you get a view of the most stunning **beach**, the vast golden strand of **Tràigh Losgaintir**. The road continues to ride above a chain of sweeping sands, backed by rich **machair** that stretches for nine miles along the Atlantic coast. In good weather, the scenery is particularly impressive, with foaming breakers rolling along the golden sands set against the rounded peaks of the mountains to the north and the islet-studded turquoise sea to the west – and even on the dullest day the sand manages to glow beneath the waves. *Beul-na-Mara* (℡01859/550205, ⓦwww.beulnamara.co.uk; ❸) is a very good, modern **B&B** in Seilebost, overlooking the sands of Tràigh Losgaintir; but the most luxurious **guest house** in the area is five miles further south in Sgarasta (Scarista), where the beautifully furnished rooms of the Georgian former manse of *Scarista House* (℡01859/550238, ⓦwww.scaristahouse.com; ❾) overlook yet more golden sands; the **restaurant's** meat and seafood is among the freshest and finest on the Western Isles, and some of the most expensive, at nearly £40 a head.

From Taobh Tuath the road veers to the southeast to trim the island's south shore, eventually reaching the sprawling settlement of **LEVERBURGH** (An t-Ob), named after Lord Leverhulme, who planned to turn the place into the largest fishing port on the west coast of Scotland. It's a place that has languished for quite some time, but has picked up quite a bit since the establishment of the CalMac **car ferry** service to Berneray and the Uists. There's a good choice of **accommodation** in Leverburgh: try *Caberfeidh House* (℡01859/520276; ❷), a lovely stone-built Victorian building by the turn-off to the ferry, or *Sorrel Cottage*, a mile and a half from the ferry (℡01859/520319, ⓦwww.sorrelcottage.co.uk; ❷), which specializes in vegetarian and seafood cooking and offers **bike rental**. A cheaper alternative is the quirky, timber-clad ⚑ *Am Bothan* (℡01859/520251, ⓦwww.ambothan.com), a luxurious **bunkhouse** that's very welcoming, has great facilities, and is only a few minutes' walk from the ferry; dorm beds £13. On the north side of the bay, the *An Clachan* co-op store houses a small **information office**. For local langoustines, homemade cakes and the usual comfort **food**, head for *The Anchorage*, by the ferry slipway, and look out for the occasional live-music night.

Three miles southeast of Leverburgh and a mile or so from Renish Point, the southern tip of Harris, is the old port of **ROGHADAL** (Rodel), where a smattering of ancient stone houses lies among the hillocks surrounding the dilapidated harbour where the ferry from Skye used to arrive. On top of these grassy humps is **St Clement's Church** (Tur Chliamainn), burial place of the MacLeods of Harris and Dunvegan in Skye. Dating from the 1520s, the church's bare interior is distinguished by its wall tombs, notably that of the founder, Alasdair Crotach (also known as Alexander MacLeod), whose heavily weathered effigy lies beneath an intriguing backdrop and canopy of sculpted reliefs depicting vernacular and religious scenes – elemental representations of, among others, a stag hunt, the Holy Trinity, St Michael, and the devil and an angel weighing the souls of the dead. Look out, too, for the *sheila-na-gig* (a naked pre-Christian fertility goddess) halfway up the south side of the church tower; unusually, she has a brother displaying his genitalia too, below a carving of St Clement on the west face. Beyond the church, tucked away by a quiet harbour, the *Rodel* **hotel** (T01859/520210, Wwww.rodelhotel.co.uk; ⑥) has been totally refurbished inside and serves decent bar **meals.**

North Uist (Uibhist a Tuath)

Compared to the mountainous scenery of Harris, **North Uist** – seventeen miles long and thirteen miles wide – is much flatter and for some comes as something of an anticlimax. Over half the surface area is covered by water, creating a distinctive peaty-brown lochan-studded "drowned landscape". Most visitors come here for the trout and salmon fishing and the deerstalking, both of which (along with poaching) are critical to the survival of the island's economy. Others come for the smattering of prehistoric sites, the birds, or the sheer peace of this windy isle, and the solitude of North Uist's vast sandy beaches, which extend – almost without interruption – along the north and west coasts.

Despite being situated on the east coast, some distance away from any beach, the ferry port of **LOCHMADDY** (Loch nam Madadh, or "Loch of the Dogs") makes a good base for exploring the island. The village itself, occupying a narrow, bumpy promontory, is nothing special, but it does have a **tourist office** (April to mid-Oct Mon–Sat 9am–5pm; also open to greet the evening ferry), and the nearby **Taigh Chearsabhagh** (Mon–Sat 10am–5pm; Wwww .taigh-chearsabhagh.org), a converted eighteenth-century merchant's house. Now home to a community arts centre, with a simple airy café, post office and shop, it also has an excellent museum which puts on some seriously innovative exhibitions. Taigh Chearsabhagh was one of the prime movers behind the Uist Sculpture Trail that starts outside the arts centre on the shore, and takes visitors to some remote corners of the Uists. The first and most popular of the sculptures, **Both nam Faileas** ("Hut of the Shadow"), is a short walk past the Uist Outdoor Centre, across a footbridge.

Lochmaddy's **accommodation** options include the long-established and recently refurbished *Lochmaddy Hotel* (T01876/500331, Wwww .lochmaddyhotel.co.uk; ⑤); the Georgian *Old Courthouse* (T01876/500358, Emjohnson@oldcourthouse.fsnet.co.uk; ③), the Uists' former jail; and the islands' newest hotel, *Tigh Dearg* (T01876/500700, Wwww.tighdearghotel .co.uk; ⑦), whose stylish modernity comes as something of a culture shock in these parts: guests get free use of the hotel's gym, sauna and steam room. Beyond lies the *Uist Outdoor Centre* (T01876/500480, Wwww.uistoutdoorcentre .co.uk), which has **hostel** accommodation (dorm beds £10) and offers a wide range of outdoor activities, from canoeing to "rubber tubing".

Several prehistoric sights lie within easy cycling distance of Lochmaddy, the most significant being the **Barpa Langass**, a large, mostly intact, chambered cairn seven barren miles to the southwest along the A867. North Uist's other main draw is the **Balranald RSPB Reserve**, on the western tip of the island and best known for its population of corncrakes: there are usually one or two making a loud noise right outside the RSPB **visitor centre**, from which you can pick up a leaflet outlining a two-hour walk along the headland, marked by posts. A wonderful carpet of flowers covers the machair in summer, and there are usually corn buntings and arctic terns inland, and gannets, Manx shearwater

St Kilda

Britain's westernmost island chain is the NTS-owned **St Kilda** archipelago (⊛www .kilda.org.uk), roughly a hundred miles west southwest of the Butt of Lewis and over forty miles from its nearest landfall, Griminish Point on North Uist. Dominated by the highest cliffs and sea stacks in Britain, Hirta, St Kilda's main island, was occupied on and off for some two thousand years, with the last 36 Gaelic-speaking inhabitants evacuated at their own request in 1930. Immediately after evacuation, the island was bought by the Marquess of Bute, who was keen to protect the island's population of somewhere between one and two million puffins, gannets, petrels and other sea birds. In 1957, having agreed to allow the army to build a missile-tracking radar station here linked to South Uist, the Marquess bequeathed the island to the NTS (☎01463/232034, ⊛www.nts.org.uk). Despite its inaccessibility, several thousand visitors make it out to St Kilda each year; the resident NTS ranger usually gives a little talk, you get to see the museum, send a postcard and enjoy a drink at the army's pub, the *Puff Inn*. If you have your own yacht, you need permission in order to land; several boat companies also offer **day-trips** from Uig and Leverburgh to St Kilda for around £125 per person – ask at the tourist office for details. Between mid-May and mid-August, the NTS organizes volunteer **work parties**, which either restore and maintain the old buildings or take part in archeological digs. Volunteers are expected to work 24–36 hours a week for two weeks, for which they must pay around £500 per person, though, with only twelve people on each party and more applications than there are places, there's no guarantee you'll get on one. Volunteers meet at Oban, and should be prepared for a rough, fifteen-hour overnight crossing. For the armchair traveller, the best general book on St Kilda is Tom Steel's *The Life and Death of St Kilda*.

and skuas out to sea. On a clear day you can see the unmistakeable shape of St Kilda, looking miraculously near. There's a very welcoming, family-run **hostel** *Taigh mo Sheanair* (☎01876/580246, ⓔcarnach@amserve.net; dorm beds £11), where you can also **camp**; it's a clearly signposted fifteen-minute walk from the main road, south of the crossroads at Clachan, a couple of miles south of Barpa Langass.

Bhearnaraigh (Berneray)

The ferry to Harris leaves from the very southeastern point of **Berneray**, a low-lying island immediately to the north of North Uist and connected to the latter via a causeway. Two miles by three, with a population of just over a hundred, the island has a superb three-mile-long sandy beach on the west and north coasts, backed by rabbit-free dunes and machair. Its other great draw is the wonderful GHHT **hostel** (⊛www.gatliff.org.uk; dorm beds £8), which occupies a pair of thatched blackhouses in a lovely spot by a beach, beyond Loch a Bhàigh and the main village. Alternatively you can stay at "Splash" MacKillop's *Burnside Croft* **B&B** (☎01876/540235, ⊛www.burnsidecroft .fsnet.co.uk; Feb–Nov; ❷) in Borgh (Borve), overlooking the machair and dunes, and enjoy storytelling evenings; **bike rental** is also available. There's a **tearoom** called *The Lobster Pot* in the shop on the main road, near the junction, and a **bus** connection with Lochmaddy, on North Uist.

Benbecula (Beinn na Faoghla)

Blink and you could miss the pancake-flat island of **Benbecula** (put the stress on the second syllable), sandwiched between Protestant North Uist and Catholic

South Uist. Most visitors simply trundle along the main road that cuts across the middle of the island in less than five miles – not such a bad idea, since the island is scarred from the postwar presence of the Royal Artillery who until recently made up half the local population.

The legacy of Benbecula's military past is only too evident in barracks-like **BALIVANICH** (Baile a Mhanaich), the grim, grey island capital in the northwest. The only reason to come here is if you're flying into or out of **Benbecula airport** (direct flights to Glasgow, Barra and Stornoway), need to take money out of the Bank of Scotland ATM (the only one on Benbecula and South Uist), do some laundry (the laundrette is behind the bank). There's no tourist office and no need to stay here, but if you need a bite to eat, you can stop by the *Stepping Stone* (closed Mon eve), a purpose-built **café/restaurant** divided into the *Food Base* café which serves up cheap filled rolls, hot meals, and chips with everything, and the underwhelming £20-a-head *Sinteag* restaurant (eves only), up the steps.

South Uist (Uibhist a Deas)

To the south of Benbecula, the island of **South Uist** is arguably the most appealing of the southern chain of islands. The west coast boasts some of the region's finest machair and beaches – a necklace of gold and grey sand strung twenty miles from one end to the other – while the east coast features a ridge of high mountains rising to 2034ft at the summit of Beinn Mhor.

One of the best places to gain access to the sandy shoreline is at **TOBHA MÒR** (Howmore), a pretty little crofting settlement with a fair number of restored houses, many still thatched, including one distinctively roofed in brown heather. A GHHT **hostel** (Ⓦ www.gatliff.org.uk; dorm beds £8) occupies one such house near the village church, from where it's an easy walk across the flower-infested machair to the gorgeous beach. Close by the hostel are the shattered, lichen-encrusted remains of no fewer than four medieval churches and chapels, and a burial ground now harbouring just a few scattered graves.

Five miles south of Tobha Mòr, on the main road, the Kildonan Museum or **Taigh-tasgaidh Chill Donnain** (April & May Mon–Sat 11am–4pm; June–Sept Mon–Sat 10am–5pm, Sun 2–5pm; £1.50) includes mock-ups of Hebridean kitchens through the ages, two lovely box beds and an impressive selection of old photos, accompanied by a firmly unsentimental yet poetic written text on crofting life in the last two centuries. Pride of place goes to the sixteenth-century **Clanranald Stone**, carved with the arms of the clan who ruled over South Uist from 1370 to 1839, which used to lie in the church at Tobha Mòr. The museum also runs a café serving sandwiches and homemade cakes.

The *Orasay Inn* (☎01870/610298, Ⓔ orasayinn@btinternet.com; ❸) is a good **hotel** in a peaceful spot off the road to Loch a Charnain (Lochcarnan), in the northeastern corner of the island; the bar meals are good value and the breakfasts are great. South Uist's chief settlement and ferry port, **LOCH-BOISDALE**, occupying a narrow, bumpy promontory on the east coast, has much less to offer than Lochmaddy. There's a **tourist office** (Easter to mid-Oct Mon–Sat 9am–5pm; open to meet the ferry) and the refurbished *Lochboisdale Hotel* (☎01878/700332, Ⓦ www.lochboisdale.com; ❹) which does decent bar meals, including succulent local cockles. There are also several small, perfectly friendly **B&Bs** within comfortable walking distance of the dock, one of the best (and nearest) being *Brae Lea House* (☎01878/700497, Ⓔ braelea@supanet.com; ❸).

Eriskay (Eiriosgaigh)

Connected to the south of South Uist by a causeway is the barren, hilly island of **Eriskay**, famous for its patterned jerseys (on sale at the community centre), and a peculiar breed of pony, originally used for carrying peat and seaweed. The island, which measures just over two miles by one, and shelters a small fishing community of about 150, makes a great day-trip from South Uist. The walk up to the island's highest point, **Beinn Sciathan** (607ft; 2hr return from the village), is well worth the effort on a clear day, as you can see the whole island, plus Barra, South Uist, and across the sea to Skye, Rùm, Coll and Tiree. On the way up or down, look out for the diminutive Eriskay ponies, who roam free on the hills but tend to graze around Loch Crakavaig, the island's freshwater source. CalMac runs a **car ferry to Barra** (4–5 daily; 40min) from a new harbour on the southwest coast of Eriskay.

For a small island, Eriskay has had more than its fair share of historical headlines. The island's main beach on the west coast, Coilleag a Phrionnsa (Prince's Cockle Strand), was where **Bonnie Prince Charlie** landed on Scottish soil on July 23, 1745 – the sea bindweed that grows there to this day is said to have sprung from the seeds Charles brought with him from France. Eriskay's other claim to fame came in 1941 when the 8000-ton **SS Politician** or *Polly* as it's fondly known, sank on its way from Liverpool to Jamaica, along with its cargo of bicycle parts, £3 million in Jamaican currency and 264,000 bottles of whisky, inspiring Compton MacKenzie's book – and the Ealing comedy (filmed here in 1948) – *Whisky Galore!* (released in the US as *Tight Little Island*). The ship's stern can still be seen to the northwest of the Isle of Calvey at low tide, and one of the original bottles (and lots of other related memorabilia) is on show in the island's purpose-built pub, *Am Politician*, on the west coast.

Barra (Barraigh)

Just four miles wide and eight miles long, **Barra** (Ⓦ www.isleofbarra.com) has a well-deserved reputation for being the Western Isles in miniature. It has sandy beaches, backed by machair, glacial mountains, prehistoric ruins, Gaelic culture, and a welcoming Catholic population of just over 1300. The only settlement of any size is **CASTLEBAY** (Bàgh a Chaisteil), which curves around the barren rocky hills of a wide bay on the south side of the island. It's difficult to imagine it now, but Castlebay was a herring port of some significance back in the nineteenth century, with up to four hundred boats in the harbour, and curing and packing factories ashore. Barra's religious allegiance is immediately announced by the large Catholic church, Our Lady, Star of the Sea, which overlooks the bay; to underline the point, there's a Madonna and Child on the slopes of **Sheabhal** (1260ft), the largest peak on Barra, and a fairly easy hike from the bay.

As its name suggests, Castlebay has a castle in its bay, the medieval islet-fortress of Caisteal Chiosmuil or **Kisimul Castle** (April–Sept daily 9.30am–6.30pm; £3.30; HS), ancestral home of the MacNeil clan. The castle burnt down in the eighteenth century, but in 1937 the 45th MacNeil chief bought the island back and set about restoring Kisimul. There's nothing much to see inside, but the whole experience is fun – head down to the slipway at the bottom of Main Street, where the ferryman will take you over (weather permitting; Ⓣ 01871/810313). To learn more about the history of the island, and about the postal system of the Western Isles, it's worth paying a visit to Barra Heritage Centre, known as **Dualchas** (March, April & Sept Mon, Wed & Fri 11am–4pm; May–Aug Mon–Sat 11am–4pm; £2; Ⓦ www.barraheritage.com), on the road

22

that leads west out of town; the museum also has a handy **café** serving soup, toasties and cakes.

One of Barra's most fascinating sights is its **airport**, on the north side of the island, where planes land and take off from the crunchy shell sands of Tràigh Mhór, better known as **Cockle Strand**; the exact timing of the flights depends on the tides, since at high tide the beach (and therefore the runway) is covered in water. The popular airport **café**, *Cafaidh Fosgailte* (closed Sun) serves home-made soup, sandwiches and cakes.

There are two **ferry terminals** on Barra: from Eriskay, you arrive at an unin-habited spot on the northeast of the island; from Oban, Lochboisdale or Tiree, you arrive at the main terminal in Castlebay itself. Barra Car Hire (℡01871/810243) will deliver **cars** to either terminal, and Barra Cycle Hire (℡01871/810438) will do the same with **bikes**. Barra's **tourist office** (April–Oct Mon–Sat 9am–1pm & 2–5pm; also open to greet the Oban ferry) is on Main Street in Castlebay just round from the pier. In Castlebay itself, the *Castlebay Hotel* (℡01871/810223, Ⓦwww.castlebay-hotel.co.uk; ❺) is the more welcoming of the town's two **hotels**, followed by *Tigh-na-Mara* (℡01871/810304, Ⓔighnamara@aol.com; ❷), a Victorian guest house a couple of minutes' walk from the pier, overlook-ing the sea. Alternatively, there's *Dunard Hostel* (℡01871/810443, Ⓦwww .dunardhostel.co.uk; dorm beds £11), a relaxed, family-run place 200 yards west of the ferry terminal. The best option outside Castlebay is *Northbay House* (℡01871/890255, Ⓦwww.barraholidays.co.uk; April–Oct; ❸), a converted school in Buaile nam Bodach (Balnabodach). Places to **eat** in Castlebay include the *Kisimul* **café** (closed Sun) that specializes in cheap-and-cheerful Scottish fry-ups, or, for fancier fare, the *Castlebay Hotel*'s cosy **bar**, which regularly has cockles, crabs and scallops on its menu, and good views out over the bay.

Travel details

Trains

Aberdeen to: Kyle of Lochalsh (Mon–Sat 3 daily, 1 on Sun; 5hr).
Fort William to: Mallaig (4–5 daily; 1hr 25min).
Glasgow Queen Street to: Mallaig (Mon–Sat 4 daily, 2 on Sun; 5hr 20min).
Inverness to: Kyle of Lochalsh (Mon–Sat 3–4 daily, 1–2 on Sun; 2hr 30min).

Buses

Mainland

Glasgow to: Broadford (3–4 daily; 5hr 25min); Portree (3–4 daily; 6hr–6hr 30min); Uig (Mon–Sat 3–4 daily; 7hr 40min).
Inverness to: Broadford (2 daily; 2hr 50min); Portree (2 daily; 3hr 15min).
Kyle of Lochalsh to: Kyleakin (every 30min; 10min).

Skye

Armadale to: Broadford (Mon–Sat 3–10 daily; 45min); Portree (Mon–Sat 3–10 daily; 1hr 20min); Sligachan (Mon–Sat 3–10 daily; 1hr 10min).

Broadford to: Portree (Mon–Sat 5–10 daily; 40min).
Dunvegan to: Glendale (Mon–Sat 1–2 daily; 30min).
Kyleakin to: Broadford (Mon–Sat 4–10 daily, 3–5 on Sun; 15min); Portree (Mon–Sat 4 daily, 3–5 on Sun; 1hr); Sligachan (Mon–Sat 7–8 daily, 5 on Sun; 45min); Uig (Mon–Sat 2 daily; 1hr 20min).
Portree to: Carbost (Mon–Fri 4–5 daily, 1 on Sat; 35min); Duntulm (Mon–Sat 2–4 daily; 1hr); Dunvegan (Mon–Sat 2–4 daily; 50min); Glenbrittle (April–Sept Mon–Sat 2 daily; 1hr); Staffin (Mon–Sat 2–4 daily; 40min); Uig (Mon–Sat 4–5 daily; 30min).

Lewis/Harris

Stornoway to: Arnol (Mon–Sat 4–6 daily; 35min); Barabhas (Mon–Sat 8–12 daily; 25min); Calanais (Mon–Sat 4–6 daily; 40min); Carlabhagh (Mon–Sat 4–6 daily; 1hr); Leverburgh (Mon–Sat 4–5 daily; 1hr 55min); Port Nis (Mon–Sat 4–6 daily; 1hr); Siabost (Mon–Sat 4–6 daily; 45min); Tarbert (Mon–Sat 4–5 daily; 1hr 5min).
Tarbert to: Leverburgh (Mon–Sat 9–11 daily; 55min–1hr).

The Uists and Benbecula

Berneray to: Lochmaddy (Mon–Sat 6–7 daily;
20–50min).

Lochboisdale to: Eriskay (Mon–Sat 6–7 daily;
35min).

Lochmaddy to: Balivanich (Mon–Sat 5–6 daily;
45min–2hr); Balranald (Mon–Sat 3 daily; 50min);
Lochboisdale (Mon–Sat 5–6 daily; 2hr).

Barra

Castlebay to: Airport/Ferry for Eriskay (Mon–Sat
6–7 daily; 35–45min).

CalMac ferries (summer timetable)

To Barra: Eriskay–Barra (5 daily; 40min); Lochboisdale–Castlebay (Mon & Tues; 1hr 30min);
Oban–Castlebay (1 daily; 4hr 50min); Tiree–Castlebay (Thurs; 3hr).

To Canna: Eigg–Canna (Mon & Sat; 2hr 15min);
Mallaig–Canna (Mon, Wed, Fri & Sat; 2hr
40min–3hr 50min); Muck–Canna (Sat; 1hr 35min);
Rùm–Canna (Mon, Wed, Fri & Sat; 55min).

To Eigg: Canna–Eigg (Mon & Sat; 2hr 15min);
Mallaig–Eigg (Mon, Tues & Thurs–Sat; 1hr 15min–
2hr 25min); Muck–Eigg (Tues & Thurs–Sat; 30min);
Rùm–Eigg (Mon & Sat; 1hr–3hr 30min).

To Harris: Berneray–Leverburgh (Mon–Sat 3–4
daily; 1hr); Uig–Tarbert (Mon–Sat 2 daily; 1hr
45min).

To Lewis: Ullapool–Stornoway (Mon–Sat 2–3 daily;
2hr 45min).

To Muck: Canna–Muck (Sat; 1hr 35min); Eigg–
Muck (Tues, Thurs & Sat; 30min); Mallaig–Muck
(Tues, Thurs, Fri & Sat; 1hr 40min–4hr 20min);
Rùm–Muck (Sat; 2hr 45min).

To North Uist: Leverburgh–Berneray (Mon–Sat
3–4 daily; 1hr); Uig–Lochmaddy (1–2 daily; 1hr
45min).

To Raasay: Sconser–Raasay (Mon–Sat 9–11 daily,
Sun 2 daily; 15min).

To Rùm: Canna–Rùm (Mon, Wed, Fri & Sat; 55min);
Eigg–Rùm (Mon & Sat; 1hr–3hr 30min); Mallaig–
Rùm (Mon, Wed, Fri & Sat; 1hr 20min–2hr 30min);
Muck–Rùm (Sat; 1hr 10min).

To Skye: Glenelg–Kylerhea (daily frequently;
15min); Mallaig–Armadale (Mon–Sat 8–9 daily;
mid-May to mid-Sept also Sun; 30min).

To South Uist: Castlebay–Lochboisdale (Mon, Tues
& Fri–Sun; 1hr 40min); Oban–Lochboisdale (daily
except Wed; 4hr 50min–6hr 40min).

Flights

Benbecula to: Barra (Mon–Fri 1 daily; 20min);
Stornoway (Mon–Fri 2 daily; 30min).

Edinburgh to: Stornoway (Mon–Fri 3 daily, Sat &
Sun 1–2 daily; 1hr).

Glasgow to: Barra (Mon–Sat 1 daily; 1hr 5min);
Benbecula (Mon–Fri 2 daily, Sat & Sun 1 daily; 1hr);
Stornoway (daily; 1hr 10min).

Inverness to: Stornoway (Mon–Fri 4 daily, Sat &
Sun 1–2 daily; 35–40min).

Travel details

SKYE AND THE WESTERN ISLES

Northeast Scotland

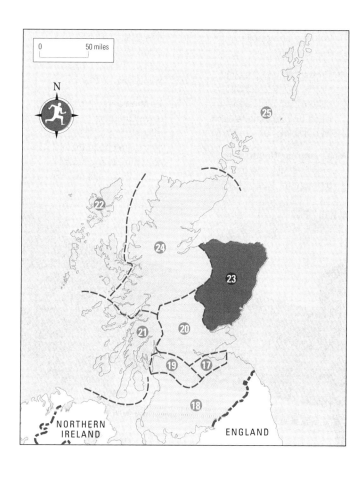

CHAPTER 23

Highlights

* **DCA** Arts centre/cinema/café at the hip new heart of Dundee's up-and-coming cultural scene. See p.1031

* **Arbroath smokie** A true Scottish delicacy: succulent haddock still warm from the oak smoker. See p.1033

* **Pictish stones** Fascinating carved relics of a lost culture, standing alone in fields or in museums such as at Meigle. See p.1036

* **Dunnottar Castle** The moodiest cliff-top ruin in the country. See p.1045

* **Speyside Way** Walking route taking in Glenfiddich, Glenlivet and Glen Grant, with the chance to drop in and taste their whiskies too. See p.1049

* **Museum of Scottish Lighthouses** Lights, lenses and legends at one of the best small museums in the country, in Fraserburgh. See p.1051

* **Pennan and Gardenstown** One-street fishing villages on the Aberdeenshire coast: there's no room for any more between the cliff and the sea. See p.1052

△ Speyside Way

Northeast Scotland

A large triangle of land thrusting into the North Sea, **northeast Scot-land** comprises the area east of a line drawn roughly from Perth north to the fringe of the Moray Firth at Forres. The area takes in the county of Angus and the city of Dundee to the south and, beyond the Grampian mountains, the counties of Aberdeenshire and Moray and the city of Aberdeen. Geographically diverse, the landscape in the south of the region is made up predominantly of undulating farmland, but, as you get further north of the Firth of Tay, this gives way to wooded glens, mountains and increasingly harsh land fringed by a dramatic coast of cliffs and long sandy beaches.

The northeast was the southern kingdom of the **Picts**, reminders of whom are scattered throughout the region in the form of numerous symbolic and beautifully carved stones found in fields, churchyards and museums. Remote, self-contained and cut off from the centres of major power in the south, the area never grew particularly prosperous, and a handful of feuding and intermarrying families, such as the Gordons, the Keiths and the Irvines, grew to wield disproportionate influence, building many of the region's **castles** and religious buildings, and developing and planning its towns.

Many of the most appealing settlements are along the coast, but while the fishing industry is but a fondly held memory in many parts, a number of the northeast's ports have been transformed by the discovery of **oil** in the North Sea in the 1960s – particularly **Aberdeen**, Scotland's third-largest city. Despite its relative isolation in the Scottish context, Aberdeen remains a sophisticated city which, for the time being, still rides a diminishing wave of oil-based prosperity. At the same time, **Dundee**, the northeast's next-largest metropolis, is fast losing its depressed postindustrial image with a reinvigorated cultural scene and some heavily marketed tourist attractions, including *Discovery*, the ship of Captain Scott ("of the Antarctic"). A little way up the Angus coast lies the historically important town of **Arbroath** while, inland, the picturesque **Angus glens** cut into the Grampian mountains, offering a readily accessible taste of wild Highland scenery to both hikers and skiers.

North of the glens and west of Aberdeen, **Deeside** is a fertile yet ruggedly attractive area made famous by the Royal Family, who have favoured the estate at **Balmoral** as a summer holiday retreat ever since Queen Victoria fell in love with it back in the 1840s. Beyond Deeside are the eastern sections of the **Cairngorm National Park**; while tranquil **Speyside**, a little way northwest, is best known as Scotland's premier whisky-producing region, where **malt whisky trails**, both official and unofficial, can be followed. The northeast coast offers yet another aspect of a diverse region, with rugged cliffs, empty beaches and historic fishing villages tucked into coves and bays.

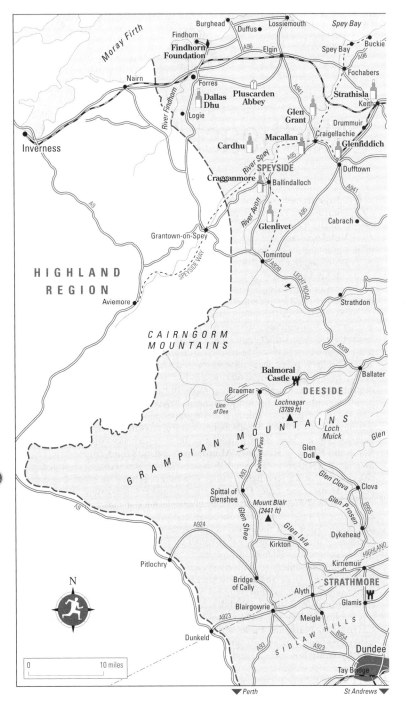

Moray Firth

Burghead
Duffus
Lossiemouth
Spey Bay

Findhorn
**Findhorn
Foundation**

Elgin

Spey Bay
Buckie

A96

A98
Fochabers

Nairn

Forres

River Findhorn

**Dallas
Dhu**

**Pluscarden
Abbey**

A941

Strathisla
Keith

Logie

**Glen
Grant**

Drummuir
Craigellachie

Cardhu

Macallan

Glenfiddich

Inverness

River Spey

SPEYSIDE

Dufftown

Cragganmore
Ballindalloch

A9

A95

A941

River Avon

Cabrach

Glenlivet

Grantown-on-Spey

Tomintoul

**HIGHLAND
REGION**

SPEYSIDE WAY

LECHT ROAD

Strathdon

Aviemore

A939

*CAIRNGORM
MOUNTAINS*

A939

**Balmoral
Castle**

Braemar

*Lochnagar
(3789 ft)*
▲

DEESIDE

Ballater

*Linn
of Dee*

*Loch
Muick*

Glen

G R A M P I A N   M O U N T A I N S

Cairnwell Pass

Glen
Doll

Glen Clova
Clova

Spittal of
Glenshee

*Mount Blair
(2441 ft)*
▲

Glen Prosen

B955

Glen Shee

Glen Isla

Dykehead

Kirkton

HIGHLAND

Pitlochry

A924

Kirriemuir

STRATHMORE

N

Bridge
of Cally

Alyth

Glamis

Blairgowrie

Meigle

A926

S I D L A W   H I L L S

B954

A923

Dunkeld

A93

A923

Dundee

0   10 miles

Tay Bridge

▼ *Perth*   *St Andrews* ▼

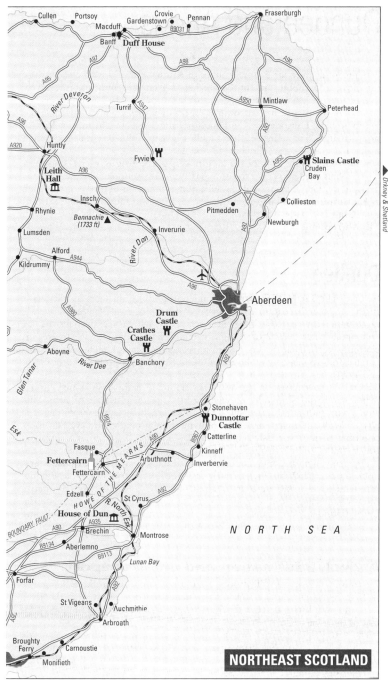

NORTHEAST SCOTLAND

Dundee and Angus

The predominantly agricultural county of **Angus**, east of the A9 and north of the Firth of Tay, holds some of the northeast's greatest scenery and is relatively free of tourists, who tend to head further west for the Highlands proper. The coast from **Montrose** to **Arbroath** is especially inviting, with scarlet cliffs and sweeping bays: **Dundee** itself, although not the most obvious tourist destination, has in recent years become a rather dynamic and progressive city, and makes for a less snooty alternative to Aberdeen.

In the north of the county, the long fingers of the **Angus glens** – heather-covered hills tumbling down to rushing rivers – are overlooked by the southern peaks of the Grampian mountains. Handsome if uneventful market towns such as **Kirriemuir** and **Blairgowrie** make good bases in the area, while extravagant **Glamis Castle** is well worth a visit, and Angus is liberally dotted with **Pictish remains**.

Dundee

At first sight, **DUNDEE** (Ⓦwww.dundeecity.gov.uk) can seem a grim place. In the nineteenth century it was Britain's main processor of jute, the world's most important vegetable fibre after cotton, which earned the city the tag "Juteopolis". The decline of manufacturing wasn't kind to Dundee, but regeneration is very much the buzz word today, with some commentators drawing comparisons to Glasgow's reinvention of itself as a city of culture in the 1980s and 1990s.

Dundee's heyday was in the 1800s, its train and harbour links making it a major centre for shipbuilding, whaling and the manufacture of **jute**. This, along with jam and journalism – the three Js which famously defined the city – has all but disappeared, with only local publishing giant D.C. Thomson, publisher of the timelessly popular *Beano* and *Dandy*, as well as a spread of other comics and newspapers, still playing a meaningful role in the city.

The major sight is Captain Scott's Antarctic explorer ship, **RRS Discovery**, docked underneath the Tay Road Bridge. **Verdant Works** is a re-created jute mill which has picked up tourism awards for its take on the city's distinctive industrial heritage. You should also try to spend some time at the upbeat **DCA** (Dundee Contemporary Arts), the totemic building of the developing cultural quarter around which most of the city's lively artistic and social life revolves.

Arrival, information and city transport

By **train**, you'll arrive at Taybridge Station on South Union Street (enquiries ℡0845/748 4950), about 300 yards south of the city centre near the river. Long-distance **buses** arrive at the Seagate bus station, a couple of hundred yards east of the centre.

The very helpful **tourist office** is right in the centre of things at 21 Castle St (June–Sept Mon–Sat 9am–6pm, Sun noon–4pm; Oct–May Mon–Sat 9am–5pm; ℡01382/527527, Ⓦwww.angusanddundee.co.uk). Dundee's centre is reasonably compact and you can walk to most sights; **local buses** leave from

DUNDEE

RESTAURANTS, CAFES & PUBS

Agacan	2
Andre's	6
Jute	7
Laing's	1
Rama Thai	5
Ship Inn	3
Trades House Bar	4

ACCOMMODATION

Apex City Quay Hotel	D
Discovery Quay Travel Inn	E
Dundee Student Villages	C
Fisherman's Tavern	B
Nelson Guest House	A
West Park Conference Centre	C

▲ Broughty Ferry

▲ **B**, **3** & Broughty Ferry

Leuchars

Victoria Dock

Unicorn

City Quay Shopping Centre

PEEP O'DAY LANE

EAST DOCK STREET

VICTORIA ST

PRINCES STREET

BLACKSCROFT

FOUNDRY LANE

KING STREET

ALLAN STREET

WEST VICTORIA DOCK RD

SOUTH VICTORIA DOCK RD

Tay Road Bridge (Toll)

NELSON ST

VICTORIA ROAD

QUEEN'S ST

COWGATE

Bus Station

TRADER LANE

SEAGATE

MARKETGAIT

MURRAYGATE

PANMURE ST

Wellgate Shopping Centre

ALBERT SQUARE

COMMERCIAL ST

St Paul's Cathedral **5**

Olympia Leisure Centre

EARL GREY PLACE

McManus Art Galleries & Museum

BELL STREET

Travel Dundee

REFORM STREET

CASTLE STREET

i

CITY SQUARE

HIGH STREET

Caird Hall

SOUTH

DISCOVERY QUAY

BARRACK ST

Howff Burial Ground

Overgate Shopping Centre **4**

St Mary's Church

UNION ST

RRS Discovery

Discovery Point

CONSTITUTION ROAD

WARD ROAD

WEST BELL STREET

WEST MARBET ST

SOUTH WARD ROAD

NORTH LINDSAY STREET

OVERGATE LANE

Train Station **E**

RIVERSIDE DRIVE

NORTH MARKETGAIT

WEST MARKETGAIT

SOUTH MARKETGAIT

BROWN STREET

SESSION STREET

TEMPLES LANE

DOUGLAS STREET

MAIN HILL

GUTHRIE STREET

WEST HENDERSON WYND

Verdant Works

HAWKHILL

WEST PORT

PARK PLACE

HAWK HILL

Dundee Repertory Theatre

NETHERGATE

SOUTH TAY ST

DCA **7**

Sensation

GREENMARKET

SMALLS WYND

University of Dundee

PERTH ROAD

▲ Ninewells Hospital & Balgay Hill

2, **1** & Airport ▲

▲ Cullaig

▲ Dundee Law

A ▲

N

0   200 yds

© Crown copyright

23 NORTHEAST SCOTLAND | Dundee

1029

the High Street or from Albert Square, one block to the north; for bus information, call ☎01382/201121, check Ⓦwww.traveldundee.co.uk or go to Travel Dundee, in the Forum Centre at 92 Commercial St.

Accommodation

Dundee has no recommended hostel or backpacker accommodation – the cheaper **B&B**s on the fringes of the city centre are the most reasonable alternative. You'll find plenty of rooms out by the suburb of Broughty Ferry, connected to the city by a twenty-minute bus ride.

Apex City Quay Hotel West Victoria Dock Road ☎01382/202404, Ⓦwww.apexhotels.co.uk. Large, sleek and modern hotel in the redeveloping dockland area, incorporating a spa, pool and restaurant. ❼

Cullaig Rosemount Terrace, Upper Constitution St ☎01382/322154, Ⓦwww.cullaig.co.uk. Victorian terraced guest house, within walking distance of town on the lower slopes of Dundee Law. ❷

Discovery Quay Premier Travel Inn Riverside Drive ☎01382/203240, Ⓦwww.premiertravelinn .com. Bland, modern chain hotel well positioned right beside Discovery Point and the railway station. ❸

Dundee Student Villages ☎01382/573111, Ⓦwww.Scotland2000.com/seabraes. En-suite single or double rooms (❶) or exclusive use of flats sleeping up to 8, located at Seabraes, just west of the city centre. Also B&B accommodation is available in the West Park Conference Centre on Perth Road (☎01382/647171, Ⓦwww .westparkcentre.com; ❸). Both July & Aug only.

Fisherman's Tavern 12 Fort St, Broughty Ferry ☎01382/775941, Ⓦwww.fishermans-tavern -hotel.co.uk. Refurbished en-suite rooms above a cosy traditional pub with decent food, great real ales and malt whiskies. ❹

Nelson Guest House 8 Nelson Terrace ☎01382/225354. Inexpensive B&B with three twin rooms, located up the hill from the downtown area. ❶

The City and around

The best approach to Dundee is across the mile-and-a-half-long **Tay Road Bridge** from Fife. While the Tay bridges aren't nearly as spectacular as the bridges over the Forth near Edinburgh, they do offer a magnificent panorama of the city on the northern bank of the firth. The road bridge, opened in 1966, has a central walkway for pedestrians. Running parallel half a mile upstream is the **Tay Rail Bridge**, opened in 1887 to replace the spindly structure which collapsed in a storm in December 1879 only eighteen months after it was built, killing the crew and 75 passengers on a train passing over the bridge at the time.

Dundee's city centre, dominated by large shopping malls filled with mundane chain stores, is focused on **City Square**, a couple of hundred yards north of the Tay. The attractive square, set in front of the city's imposing Caird Hall, has been much spruced up in recent years, with fountains, benches and extensive pedestrianization making for a relaxing environment. Where Reform Street meets City Square, look out for a couple of other statues to Dundee heroes: **Desperate Dan** and **Minnie the Minx**, both from the *Dandy* comic, which is produced a few hundred yards away in the D.C. Thomson building on Albert Square. Also on Albert Square, the **McManus Art Galleries and Museum** (Ⓦwww.mcmanus.co.uk) is Dundee's most impressive Victorian structure and the city's largest civic exhibition space; it is closed for renovation until 2008.

Ten minutes' walk west of here, on West Henderson Wynd in Blackness, an award-winning museum, **Verdant Works**, tells the story of jute from its harvesting in India to its arrival in Dundee on clipper ships (April–Oct Mon–Sat 10am–6pm, Sun 11am–6pm; Nov–March Wed–Sat 10.30am–4.30pm, Sun 11am–4.30pm; £5.95, joint ticket with Discovery Point £10.95; Ⓦwww .verdant-works.co.uk). The museum, set in an old jute mill, makes a lively attempt to re-create the turn-of-the-century factory floor, the highlight

❷₃

being the chance to watch jute being processed on fully operational quarter-size machines originally used for training workers.

The Cultural Quarter

Immediately west of the city centre, High Street becomes Nethergate and passes into Dundee's "**Cultural Quarter**". As well as the university and the highly respected Rep theatre, the area is also home to the best concentration of pubs and cafés in the city. Principal among the many arts venues is the hip and exciting **DCA**, or Dundee Contemporary Arts, at 152 Nethergate (Mon–Sat 10.30am–midnight, Sun noon–midnight; galleries Tues–Sun 10.30am–5.30pm, until 8.30pm Thurs, Sun noon–5.30pm; ☎01382/909252, ⓦwww.dca.org .uk), a stunningly designed complex which incorporates galleries, a print studio and an airy café-bar (see p.1032). The centre, opened in 1999, was designed by Richard Murphy, who converted an old, brick garage and car showroom into an inspiring new space, with a bright, sleek interior and distinctive ship-like exterior. It's worth visiting for the stimulating temporary and touring exhibitions of contemporary art, and an eclectic programme of art-house films and cult classics.

The waterfront

Just south of the city centre, at the water's edge alongside the Tay Road Bridge, the domed **Discovery Point** is an impressive development centring on the Royal Research Ship *Discovery* (April–Oct Mon–Sat 10am–6pm, Sun 11am–5pm; Nov–March Mon–Sat 10am–5pm, Sun 11am–5pm; £6.45, joint ticket with Verdant Works £10.95; ⓦwww.rrs-discovery.co.uk). Something of an icon for Dundee's renaissance, *Discovery* is a three-mast steam-assisted vessel built in Dundee in 1901 to take Captain Robert Falcon Scott on his polar expeditions. A combination of brute strength and elegance, she has been beautifully restored, with polished wood panels and brass trimmings giving scant indication of the privations suffered by the crew: temperatures on board would plummet to -28°C in the Antarctic, and turns at having a bath came round every 47 days. Before stepping aboard you're led through a series of displays about the construction of the ship and Scott's journeys, including the chill-inducing "Polarama" about life in Antarctica.

Out from the centre

Two miles west of the centre is the sprawling Ninewells Hospital, not an obvious draw for fans of modern architecture. In the grounds of the hospital, however, is **Maggie's Centre**, designed by US architect Frank Gehry, best known for Bilbao's Guggenheim Museum. Gehry's first public commission in the UK, the building is one of a series of cancer-support centres that offer a calm, inspiring environment for patients and their families. It features a distinctively freeform style with a wavy roof constructed from timber clad with stainless steel. The building is not open to the general public, and is operational through the week, but for anyone interested in seeing one of Gehry's visionary constructions up close it is possible to walk around it at weekends. Buses #22 and #9x go to the hospital; if you're travelling by car use the main hospital car park.

Eating, drinking and nightlife

The west end of Dundee, around the main university campus and Perth Road, is the best area for **eating and drinking**; the city centre has a few good pubs and one or two decent restaurants tucked away. Broughty Ferry is a pleasant alternative, with a good selection of pubs and restaurants which get particularly busy on summer evenings.

Restaurants and cafés

Agacan 113 Perth Rd ☎01382/644227. Tiny Turkish restaurant with an unmistakeable colourful exterior, and rough-hewn walls inside; they serve up decent kebabs and stuffed pittas, and also do take-aways. Moderate. Closed lunchtimes & all day Mon.

Andre's 134a Nethergate ☎01382/224455. A cosy, endearing bastion of traditional French dining – expect *coq au vin* or *moules marinière* done just the way they should be. Moderate. Closed Mon.

Jute Dundee Contemporary Arts (DCA), 152 Nethergate. Trendy spot occupying a large open-plan space on the lower level of this arts centre which works equally well for a coffee, lunch or pre-cinema snack. There's table service for the decent range of sandwiches and light meals, served until 9.30pm. Inexpensive.

Rama Thai 32–34 Dock St ☎01382/223366.

Grand Thai restaurant with chunky carved furniture and a tasty, well-executed menu. Moderate.

Ship Inn 121 Fisher St, Broughty Ferry. A narrow pub with a warm atmosphere right on the water-front. The bistro upstairs has views over the Tay and serves big platefuls of great seafood. Moderate.

Pubs

Fisherman's Tavern 12 Fort St, Broughty Ferry. Best real-ale pub around, and plenty of seafood on the menu. Not quite on the sea, but tucked away in a low-ceilinged cottage.

Laing's 8 Roseangle, off Perth Rd. Usually packed on warm summer nights, thanks to its beer garden and great river views.

Trades House Bar 40 Nethergate. Probably the best pub in the centre of town, with nice wood fittings, stained-glass windows and some decent ales.

Nightlife

Right at the heart of the Cultural Quarter on Tay Square, north of Nethergate, is the prodigious Dundee Repertory Theatre (☎01382/223530, ⓦwww.dundeereptheatre.co.uk), an excellent place for indigenously produced contemporary **theatre** and home of the only permanent repertory company in Scotland. For **movies**, DCA (☎01382/909900, ⓦwww.dca.org.uk) has two comfy auditoriums showing an appealing range of foreign and art-house movies alongside the more challenging mainstream releases.

Listings

Bike rental Easy Ride Cycles, off Wm Fitzgerald Way, Barns of Claverhouse ☎01382/505683.

Books Ottakars, 80 High St; Waterstone's, 34 Commercial St.

Bus information Scottish Citylink ☎0870/550 5050; Strathtay Scottish for regional buses ☎01302/220345; Traveline Scotland ☎0870/608 2608.

Car rental Arnold Clark, East Dock St ☎01382/225382; Alamo, 45–53 Gellatly St ☎01382/224037; Hertz, 18 West Marketgate ☎01382/223711.

Hospital Ninewells Hospital in the west of the city has an Accident and Emergency department (☎01382/660111).

Internet Central Library, Wellgate Shopping Centre (Mon–Fri 9.30am–8.30pm, Sat 9.30am–4.30pm). The tourist office also has Internet access.

Pharmacy Boots is at 49–53 High St (Mon–Sat 8.30am–6pm, Tues opens 9am, Thurs closes 7pm, Sun 12.30–5pm).

Police Tayside Police HQ, West Bell St ☎01382/223200.

Post office 4 Meadowside (Mon–Fri 9am–5.30pm, Sat 9am–12.30pm).

Taxis There are taxi ranks on Nethergate, or call City Cabs ☎01382/203020; Handy Taxis ☎01382/225825; or, in Broughty Ferry, Discovery Taxis ☎01382/732111.

The Angus coast

Two roads link Dundee to Aberdeen and the northeast coast of Scotland. By far the more pleasant option is the slightly longer A92 coast road, which joins the inland A90 at Stonehaven, just south of Aberdeen. Intercity **buses** follow both roads, while the coast-hugging train line from Dundee is one of the most picturesque in Scotland, passing attractive beaches and impressive cliffs, and stopping in the old seaports of **Arbroath** and **Montrose**.

Arbroath

Since it was settled in the twelfth century, local fishermen have been landing their catches at **ARBROATH**, about fifteen miles northeast of Dundee. The town's most famous product is the **Arbroath smokie** – line-caught haddock, smoke-cured over smouldering oak chips, and still made here in a number of family-run smokehouses tucked in around the harbour. One of the most approachable and atmospheric is M&M Spink's tiny whitewashed premises at 10 Marketgate; chef and cookery writer Rick Stein described the fish here, warm from the smoke, as "a world-class delicacy". By the late eighteenth century, chiefly due to its harbour, Arbroath had become a trading and manu-facturing centre, famed for boot-making and sail-making (the *Cutty Sark*'s sails were made here).

The town's real glory days, however, came much earlier in the thirteenth century with the completion in 1233 of **Arbroath Abbey** (daily: April–Sept 9.30am–6.30pm; Oct–March 9.30am–4.30pm; £3.30; HS), whose rose-pink sandstone ruins, described by Dr Johnson as "fragments of magnificence", stand on Abbey Street. Founded in 1178 but not granted abbey status until 1285, it was the scene of one of the most significant events in Scotland's history when, on April 6, 1320, a group of Scottish barons drew up the **Declaration of Arbroath**, asking the Pope to reverse his excommunication of Robert the Bruce and recognize him as king of a Scottish nation independent from England. The wonderfully resonant language of the document still makes for a stirring expression of Scottish nationhood: "For so long as one hundred of us remain alive, we will never in any degree be subject to the dominion of the English, since it is not for glory, riches or honour that we do fight, but for freedom alone, which no honest man loses but with his life." It was duly dispatched to Pope John XXII in Avignon, who in 1324 agreed to Robert's claim. A radically designed **visitor centre** at the Abbey Street entrance offers some in-depth background on these events and other aspects of the history of the building.

Arbroath's helpful **tourist office** is at Market Place right in the middle of town (April, May & Sept Mon–Fri 9am–5pm, Sat 10am–5pm; June–Aug Mon–Sat 9.30am–5.30pm, Sun 10am–3pm; Oct–March Mon–Fri 9am–5pm, Sat 10am–3pm; ☎01241/872609). For somewhere **to stay**, try the appealing *Harbour Nights Guest House* (☎01241/434343, ⓦwww.harbournights-scotland .com; ❸), down by the harbour at 4 The Shore, which is also where you'll find the best **restaurants** and **pubs**. A little north of town in the village of Auchmithie, the *But'n'Ben* restaurant (☎01241/877223; closed Tues) specializes in delicious, moderately priced Scottish dishes and seafood.

Montrose and around

A seaport and market town since the thirteenth century, **MONTROSE** is posi-tioned on the edge of a virtually landlocked two-mile-square lagoon of mud known as the Basin. On the south side of the Basin, a mile out of Montrose along the A92, the **Montrose Basin Wildlife Centre** (mid-March to mid-Nov daily 10.30am–5pm; mid-Nov to mid-March Fri–Sun 10.30am–4pm; £3; ⓦwww.montrosebasin.org.uk) has binoculars, high-powered telescopes, bird hides and remote-control video cameras. In addition, the centre's resident ranger leads regular guided walks around the reserve.

In the centre of town, two blocks behind the soaring kirk steeple at the lower end of High Street, the **Montrose Museum and Art Gallery** (Mon–Sat 10am–5pm; free), on Panmure Place on the western side of Mid Links park, is one of Scotland's oldest museums, dating from 1842. For a small-town museum, it has some particularly unusual exhibits, among them the so-called Samson Stone, a Pictish relic dating from 900 AD bearing a carving of Samson slaying the Philistines. Outside the museum entrance stands a winsome study of a boy by local sculptor William Lamb (1893–1951). More of his work can be seen in the moving **William Lamb Memorial Studio** on Market Street (July to mid-Sept daily 2–5pm; at other times, ask at the museum; free), including bronze heads of the Queen, Princess Margaret and the Queen Mother. Finally, don't ignore the town's fabulous golden **seashore**. The beach road, Marine Avenue, across from the town museum, heads down through sand dunes and golf links to car parks fringing the fine, wide beach overlooked by a slender white lighthouse.

Montrose **tourist office** is squeezed into a former public toilet next to the library, at the point where Bridge Street merges into the lower end of High Street (April–June & Sept Mon–Sat 10am–5pm; July & Aug Mon–Sat 9.30am–5.30pm; ℡01674/672000). For B&B **accommodation**, try *36 The Mall*, in the northern section of the town (℡01674/673464, ⓦwww.36themall .co.uk; ❸) or, a couple of miles north of town, make for *Woodston Fishing Station* (℡01674/850226, ⓦwww.woodstonfishingstation.co.uk; ❸), a neat, antique-filled house on the clifftop at St Cyrus. The best place to **eat** is *Roo's Leap*, a lively sports bar and restaurant by the golf club off the northern end of Traill Drive, with an unusual mix of moderately priced Scottish, American and Australian cuisine.

The House of Dun

Across the Basin, four miles west of Montrose, is the Palladian **House of Dun** (April–June & Sept Wed–Sun 11.30am–5.30pm; July & Aug daily 11.30am–5.30pm; £8; NTS), accessible on the hourly Montrose–Brechin bus #30; ask the driver to let you off outside. Built in 1730 for David Erskine, Laird of Dun, to designs by William Adam, the house opened to the public in 1989 after extensive restoration, and is crammed full of period furniture and objets d'art. Inside, the ornate relief plasterwork is the most impressive feature, extravagantly emblazoned with Jacobite symbolism. The buildings in the courtyard – a hen house, gamekeeper's workshop and potting shed – have been renovated, and include a tearoom and a craft shop.

Strathmore and the Angus glens

Immediately north of Dundee, the low-lying Sidlaw Hills divide the city from the rich agricultural region of **Strathmore**, whose string of tidy market towns lies on a fertile strip along the southernmost edge of the heather-covered lower slopes of the Grampian mountains. These towns act as gateways to the **Angus glens** (ⓦwww.angusglens.co.uk), a series of tranquil valleys penetrated by single-track roads and offering some of the most rugged and majestic land-scapes in northeast Scotland. It's a rain-swept, wind-blown, sparsely populated area, whose roads become impassable with the first snows, sometimes as early

㉓

as October, and where the summers see clouds of ferocious midges. The most useful road through the glens is the A93, which cuts through **Glen Shee**, linking Blairgowrie to Braemar on Deeside (see p.1048). It's pretty dramatic stuff, threading its way over Britain's highest main-road pass, the **Cairnwell Pass** (2199ft).

Blairgowrie and Glen Shee

The upper reaches of **Glen Shee**, the most dramatic and best known of the Angus glens, are dominated by its **ski fields**, ranged over four mountains above the Cairnwell mountain pass. To get to Glen Shee from the south you'll pass through the well-heeled little town of **BLAIRGOWRIE**, set among raspberry fields and a good place to pick up information and plan your activities. Blairgowrie **tourist office** (July & Aug Mon–Sat 9.30am–6.30pm, Sun 11am–4pm; April–June, Sept & Oct Mon–Sat 9.30am–5pm, Sun 11am–3pm; Nov–March Mon–Sat 10am–4pm; ℡01250/872960, ⓦwww.perthshire.co.uk) is on the high side of the Wellmeadow. A number of Blairgowrie's grand houses offer **B&B**, among them the attractive *Duncraggan* (℡01250/872082; ❷) on Perth Road and *Heathpark House* (℡01250/870700, ⓦwww.heathparkhouse.com; ❸) on the Coupar Angus Road. **Camping** is available at the year-round *Blairgowrie Holiday Park* on Rattray's Hatton Road (℡01250/876666), walking distance from the Wellmeadow.

Blairgowrie boasts plenty of places to **eat**: *Cargills* by the river on Lower Mill Street (℡01250/876735; closed Tues) is the best bet for a moderately priced formal meal or civilized coffee and cakes; for a good local **pub** try the *Ericht Alehouse* on Wellmeadow or head six miles north of town on the A93 to the welcoming *Bridge of Cally Hotel* (℡01250/886231, ⓦwww.bridgeofcallyhotel.com; ❺), which serves food all day, plus real ales by an open fire. Back in Blairgowrie you can rent **bikes** from Crichton's Cycle Hire, 87 Perth St (℡01250/876100).

Nearly twenty miles north of Blairgowrie, the small settlement of **SPITTAL OF GLENSHEE** (the names derives from the same root as "hospital", indicating a refuge), though ideally situated for skiing, has little to commend it other than the busy *Gulabin Bunkhouse* on the A93, run by Cairnwell Mountain Sports (℡01250/885255, ⓦwww.cairnwellmountainsports.co.uk), which rents out skis and bikes and offers instruction in activities such as kayaking and mountaineering.

23

Skiing at Glen Shee

Glen Shee is the most extensive and accessible of Scotland's ski areas, just over two hours from both Glasgow and Edinburgh. At the base station, Ski Glenshee (℡013397/41320, ⓦwww.ski-glenshee.co.uk) offers information, ski rental and lessons, while Cairnwell Mountain Sports at the Spittal of Glenshee (℡01250/885255, ⓦwww.cairnwellmountainsports.co.uk), also offers lessons, skis and boards. **Ski rental** starts at around £15 a day, with lessons around £15 per half-day. **Lift passes** cost £22 per day or £88 for a five-day (Mon–Fri) ticket. For the latest snow and **weather conditions**, phone Ski Glenshee or check out the Ski Scotland website (ⓦhttp://ski.visitscotland.com). Should you be more interested in **cross-country** skiing, there are some good touring areas in the vicinity; contact Cairnwell Mountain Sports (see above) or Braemar Mountain Sports (℡013397/41242, ⓦwww.braemarmountainsports.com) for information and equipment rental.

Meigle and Glen Isla

Fifteen miles north of Dundee on the B954 lies the tiny settlement of **MEIGLE**, home to Scotland's most important collection of early Christian and Pictish inscribed stones. Housed in a modest former schoolhouse, the **Meigle Museum** (April–Sept daily 9.30am–6.30pm; £2.20; HS) displays some thirty pieces dating from the seventh to the tenth centuries, all found in and around the nearby churchyard. The majority are either gravestones that would have lain flat, or cross slabs inscribed with the sign of the cross, usually standing. Most impressive is the 7ft-tall great cross slab, said to be the gravestone of Guinevere, wife of King Arthur, carved on one side with a portrayal of Daniel surrounded by lions, a beautifully executed equestrian group, and mythological creatures including a dragon and a centaur.

Three miles north of Meigle is **Alyth**, near which, legend has it, Guinevere was held captive by Mordred. The sleepy village lies at the south end of **Glen Isla**, which runs parallel to Glen Shee and is linked to it by the A926. Ten miles or so up the glen is the tiny hamlet of **KIRKTON OF GLENISLA**, where you'll find the cosy ⚶ *Glenisla Hotel* (☎01575/582223, ⓦ www.glenisla-hotel.com; ❸), which is great for classy homemade bar food and convivial drinking.

Glamis Castle

The wondrously over-the-top, pink-sandstone **Glamis Castle** (mid-March to Oct daily 10am–6pm, last tour 4.30pm; Nov & Dec noon–4pm; £7, grounds only £3.50; ⓦ www.glamis-castle.co.uk), set in an extensive land-scaped park complete with deer and pheasants beside the picturesque village of **GLAMIS** (pronounced "glahms"), is one of Scotland's most famous castles. Shakespeare chose it as a central location in *Macbeth*, and its **royal connections** (as the childhood home of the late Queen Mother) make it an essential stop on every coach tour of Scotland.

Obligatory guided tours take visitors through various rooms within the castle, including the fifteenth-century **Crypt**, with its 12ft-thick walls enclosing a haunted "lost" room; the arch-roofed **Drawing Room**, with delightful wedding-cake plasterwork (dated 1621); and **King Malcolm's Room**, so called because it is believed he died nearby in 1034. Glamis' **grounds** are worth a few hours in their own right, holding lead statues of James VI and Charles I at the top of the main drive, a seventeenth-century Baroque sundial, a formal Italian garden, and verdant walks out to Earl John's Bridge and through the woodland.

Kirriemuir and glens Clova and Doll

The sandstone town of **KIRRIEMUIR**, known locally as Kirrie, is set on a hill six miles northwest of Forfar on the cusp of glens Clova and Prosen. The main cluster of streets have all the appeal of an old film set, with their old-fashioned bars, tiled butcher's shop, tartan outlets and haberdasheries somehow managing to avoid being contrived and quaint – although the recent recobbling of the town centre around a twee statue of Peter Pan undermines this somewhat. Peter Pan's presence is justified, however, since Kirrie was the birthplace of his creator, **J.M. Barrie**. A local handloom-weaver's son, Barrie first came to notice with his series of novels about "Thrums", a village based on his hometown. The story of Peter Pan, the little boy who never grew up, was penned by Barrie in 1904 – some say as a response to a strange upbringing dominated by the memory of his older brother, who died as a child. **Barrie's birthplace**, a plain little whitewashed cottage at 9 Brechin Rd (April–June & Sept Sat–Wed noon–5pm; July & Aug Mon–Sat 11am–5pm, Sun 1–5pm; £5; NTS), is open to visitors, with a series of small rooms decorated as they would have been during Barrie's childhood, as well as displays about his life and works.

Kirriemuir's helpful **tourist office** is in Cumberland Close (July & Aug Mon–Sat 9.30am–5.30pm; April–June & Sept Mon–Sat 10am–5pm; ☎01575/574097), in the new development behind *Visocchi's* in the main square. **Accommodation** is available at the attractively upgraded *Airlie Arms*, St Malcolm's Wynd (☎01575/572847, ⓦwww.airliearms-hotel.co.uk; ❹), or at the working *Muirhouses Farm* (☎01575/573128, ⓦwww.muirhousesfarm.co.uk; ❸), on the edge of town, which offers a taste of the rolling countryside.

Glen Clova and Glen Doll

With its stunning cliffs, heather slopes and valley meadows, **Glen Clova** – which in the north becomes **Glen Doll** – is one of the loveliest of the Angus glens. Although it can get unpleasantly congested in peak season, the area is still remote enough to enable you to leave the crowds with little effort. Wildlife is abundant, with deer on the mountains, wild hares and even grouse and the occasional buzzard. The meadow flowers on the valley floor and arctic plants (including great splashes of white and purple saxifrage) on the rocks also make it something of a botanist's paradise. The hamlet of **CLOVA** has little more than the hearty *Glen Clova Hotel* (☎01575/550350, ⓦwww.clova.com; ❺), which also has a refurbished bunkhouse (£11 per night) and a private fishing loch. **Meals** and real ale are available in the lively *Climbers' Bar* at the side of the hotel.

Aberdeenshire and Moray

Aberdeenshire and Moray cover some 3500 square miles of open and varied country dotted with historic and archeological sights, from neat NTS properties and eerie prehistoric rings of standing stones to quiet kirkyards and a rash of dramatic castles. Geographically, the counties break down into two distinct areas: the **hinterland**, once barren and now a patchwork of fertile farms, rising towards high mountains, sparkling rivers and gentle valleys; and the **coast**, a classic stretch of rocky cliffs, remote fishing villages and long, sandy beaches.

For visitors, the large city of **Aberdeen** is the obvious focal point of the region, and while it's not a place to keep you engrossed for long, it does boast some intriguing architecture, attractive museums and a lively social scene. From here, it's a short hop west to **Deeside**, where the trim villages of **Ballater** and **Braemar** act as a gateway to the spectacular mountain scenery of the Cairngorms National Park, which covers much of the upland areas in the west of this region. Further north, the "Malt Whisky Country" of Speyside has less impressive scenery but no shortage of diversions in its numerous whisky distilleries, while the dramatic **coast** beyond is punctuated by picturesque fishing villages left almost unchanged by the centuries.

Aberdeen

Scotland's third-largest city, **ABERDEEN** (Ⓦ www.aberdeen-grampian.com), commonly known as the Granite City, lies 120 miles northeast of Edinburgh on the banks of the rivers Dee and Don, smack in the middle of the northeast coast. Based around a working harbour, it's a place that people either love or hate. Certainly, while some extol the many tones and colours of Aberdeen's **granite** buildings, others see only uniform grey and find the city grim, cold and unwelcoming. The weather doesn't help: Aberdeen lies on a latitude north of Moscow and the cutting wind and driving rain (even if it does transform the buildings into sparkling silver) can be tiresome.

In the twelfth century, Alexander I noted "Aberdon" as one of his principal towns, and by the thirteenth century it had become a centre for **trade and fishing**. A century or so later Bishop Elphinstone founded the Catholic university in the area north of town known today as **Old Aberdeen**, while the rest of the city developed as a mercantile centre and important port. By the mid-twentieth century, Aberdeen's traditional industries were in decline, but the discovery of **oil** in the North Sea transformed the place from a depressed port into a boom town. Since the 1970s, oil has made Aberdeen a hugely wealthy and self-confident place. Despite (or perhaps because of) this, it can seem a soulless city; there's a feeling of corporate sterility and sometimes Aberdeen seems to exist only as a departure point for the transient population of some ten to fifteen thousand who live on the 130 oil platforms out to sea.

Staying in such a prosperous place has its advantages. There are some reasonable restaurants and hotels while certain sights, including Aberdeen's splendid **Art Gallery** and the excellent **Maritime Museum**, are free. Furthermore, the fact that the city is the bright light in a wide hinterland helps it to sustain a lively **nightlife**, with some decent pubs and a colourful arts and cultural scene.

㉓

Oil and Aberdeen

When **oil** was discovered in BP's Forties Field in 1970, Aberdonians rightly viewed it as a massive financial opportunity, and – despite fierce competition from other British ports, Scandinavia and Germany – the city succeeded in persuading the oil companies to base their headquarters here. The city's **population** swelled by sixty thousand, and earnings escalated from fifteen percent below the national average to a figure well above it. At the peak of production in the **mid-1980s**, 2.6 million barrels a day were being turned out, and the price had reached $80 a barrel. The effect of the 1986 slump – when oil prices dropped to $10 a barrel – was devastating: jobs vanished at the rate of a thousand a month, house prices dropped and Aberdeen soon discovered just how dependent on oil it was. The moment oil prices began to rise, crisis struck again with the loss of 167 lives when the **Piper Alpha oil rig** exploded, precipitating an array of much-needed but very expensive safety measures.

Oil remains the cornerstone of Aberdeen's economy, keeping unemployment down to one of the lowest levels in Britain and driving up house prices in the city itself and an increasingly wide area of its rural hinterland. Predictions of the imminent decline in oil reserves and the end of Aberdeen's economic boom are heard frequently, but reliable indicators suggest that the black gold will be flowing well into the next decade. Even so, business leaders are already looking to refocus existing expertise and make Aberdeen just as famous for the new game in town – renewable energy.

ABERDEEN

N

© Crown copyright

PUBS & BARS

Old Blackfriars	3
Prince of Wales	5
Revolution	6
St Machar Bar	2
Under the Hammer	7

RESTAURANTS & CAFÉS

Ashvale	12
Café 52	8
Foyer	11
Howies	10
Lemon Tree	1
Nargile	4
Silver Darling	9

ACCOMMODATION

Aberdeen Youth Hostel	F
Allan Guest House	I
Campbell's Guest House	B
Crombie Johnston Halls	A
Ferryhill House	J
Globe Inn	D
Marcliffe at Pitfodels	H
Simpson's	G
Skene House Rosemount	C
Travelodge	E

200 yds

Old Aberdeen, **1 & 2**

Episcopal Cathedral

Mercat Cross

KING ST

Tolbooth

Marischal College

Provost Skene's House

St Nicholas Kirk

Aberdeen Art Gallery

Academy Shopping Centre

Belmont Picture House

His Majesty's Theatre

Union Terrace Gdns.

Maritime Museum & Old Provost Ross's House

Bus Station

Train Station

St Mary's Catholic Cathedral

Music Hall

Ferry Terminal

Harbour

Fish Market

BLAIKIES QUAY

REGENT QUAY

TRINITY QUAY

MARISCHAL STREET

VIRGINIA STREET

CASTLE STREET

THE GREEN

GUILD STREET

MARKET STREET

JAMIESONS QUAY

PALMERSTONE RD

ESPLANADE RD

COLLEGE STREET

CROWN STREET

DEE STREET

BON ACCORD STREET

SPRINGBANK TERRACE

BON ACCORD CRESCENT

BON ACCORD TERRACE

SUMMER STREET

SKENE STREET

ROSEMOUNT VIADUCT

SCHOOLHILL

BELMONT ST

UNION TERRACE

UNION STREET

BRIDGE STREET

BON ACCORD SQUARE

GOLDEN SQUARE

NORTH SILVER STREET

HUNTLY STREET

CHAPEL STREET

ROSE STREET

WEST END

THISTLE STREET

A. BYN PL

GT WESTERN RD

HOLBURN STREET

JUSTICE MILL LANE

CROWN TERRACE

DENBURN ROAD

CORRECTION WYND

THE BROW

BLACKFRIARS

▲ Beach

▲ Footdee & **9**

▶ Duthie Park & Winter Gardens

▶ Old Aberdeen, **1 & 2**

▶ Ringroad & Airport

Arrival, information and city transport

Aberdeen's Dyce **airport**, seven miles northwest of town, is served by flights from most parts of the UK and a few European cities. The main **train station** is on Guild Street, in the centre of the city (℡0845/748 4950), with the **bus** terminal right beside it. Aberdeen is also linked to Lerwick in Shetland and Stromness in Orkney by **ferry**, with regular crossings from Jamieson's Quay in the harbour; see p.1054 for details.

From the train and bus station it's a five-minute uphill walk to Union Street, Aberdeen's main thoroughfare. The **tourist office**, 23 Union St, is at the east end (April–June, Sept & Oct Mon–Sat 9am–5.30pm; July & Aug Mon–Sat 9am–6.30pm, Sun 10am–4pm; Nov–March Mon–Sat 9am–4.30pm; ℡01224/288828).

Aberdeen's centre is best explored on foot, but you might need to use **buses**, most of which pass along Union Street, to reach some sights. For information on city bus services, call the Busline (℡01224/650065).

Accommodation

As befits a high-flying business city, Aberdeen has a large choice of **accommodation** – much of it is characterless and expensive. Cheapest of all are the **hostel** and **student halls** left vacant for visitors in the summer. The emphasis on business trade in hotels and guest houses means weekday rates are often considerably more expensive than weekends.

Aberdeen Youth Hostel 8 Queens Rd ℡0870/004 1100, ⓦwww.syha.org.uk. Rather soulless hostel with dorms for four to sixteen (£14.75). Doors close at 2am but you can arrange to get in later. Bus #14 or #15 from Union St.

Allan Guest House 56 Polmuir Rd ℡01224/584484, ⓦwww.theallan.co.uk. Tasteful and enthusiastically run guest house not far from Duthie Park. Filling meals or a light supper available if arranged in advance. ❹

Campbell's Guest House 444 King St ℡01224/625444, ⓦwww.campbellsguesthouse .com. Standard rooms but highly recommended breakfasts. One mile from the city centre and handy for the beach and Old Aberdeen. ❷

Crombie Johnston Halls College Bounds, Old Aberdeen ℡01224/273444, ⓦwww.abdn .ac.uk/hospitality. Private rooms in the best student halls, in one of the most interesting parts of the city. Available from early July to Sept, though some year-round accommodation also available. ❶

Ferryhill House 169 Bon Accord St ℡01224/590867, ⓦwww.ferryhillhousehotel .co.uk. A mansion set apart in its own grounds within walking distance of Union Street. Its historic pub has real ale, a beer garden and decent food. ❸

Globe Inn 13–15 North Silver St ℡01224/624258. Easy-going city-centre inn with seven en-suite rooms above a bar that hosts live jazz, blues and traditional music. Rate includes continental breakfast. ❷

Marcliffe at Pitfodels North Deeside Rd, Pitfodels ℡01224/861000, ⓦwww.marcliffe .com. Four miles west of the city centre, this forty-room hotel in its own grounds is by far the most luxurious and tasteful option in the area. There's a fine restaurant with a suitably upmarket ambience. ❼

Simpson's 59–63 Queens Rd ℡01224/327777, ⓦwww.simpsonshotel.co.uk. Style-conscious boutique hotel in a granite terraced house, with an excellent brasserie and good weekend rates. ❻

Skene House Rosemount 96 Rosemount Viaduct ℡01224/645971, ⓦwww.skene-house.co.uk. Serviced apartments with 1–3 rooms, all with TVs. Good central location. ❹

Travelodge 9 Bridge St ℡01224/584555, ⓦwww.travelodge.co.uk. Typically bland budget option – but you can't beat the convenient location, right next to Union Street and minutes from the stations. ❹

The City

The centre of Aberdeen is dominated by mile-long **Union Street**, still the grandest and most ambitious single thoroughfare in Scotland – although these days its impressive architecture is sometimes lost among the shoppers and chain stores. The key to the early nineteenth-century city planners who conceived the street was the building of the ambitious **Union Street Bridge**, spanning two hills and the Denburn gorge. The first attempt, a triple-span design by Glasgow architect David Hamilton, bankrupted the city and collapsed during construction. The famous Thomas Telford then proposed the single-arch structure that became an engineering wonder of its age.

Any exploration of the **city centre** should begin at the open, cobbled **Castlegate**, where Aberdeen's long-gone castle once stood. At its centre is the late seventeenth-century **Mercat Cross**, carved with a unique gallery of Stewart sovereigns alongside some fierce gargoyles. Castlegate was once the focus of city life but nowadays seems rather lifeless unless you dart along the easily missed lane to **Peacock Visual Arts**, 21 Castle St (℡01224/639539, Ⓦwww.peacockvisualarts.co.uk), a hub for issue-based exhibitions often featuring rising international stars. The view from here up gently rising Union Street – a jumble of grey spires, turrets and jostling double-decker buses – is quintessential Aberdeen.

Heading west, Union Street brings you to Broad Street where, at 45 Guestrow, **Provost Skene's House** (Mon–Sat 10am–5pm, Sun 1–4pm; free) is Aberdeen's oldest surviving private house, dating from 1545; it's now a museum, with a costume gallery, archeological exhibits, period rooms and a café-bar. Don't miss the Painted Gallery, where a cycle of beautiful religious tempera paintings from the mid-seventeenth century show scenes from the life of Christ.

Marischal College and museum

On Broad Street stands Aberdeen's most imposing edifice, and the world's second-largest granite building after the Escorial in Madrid – exuberant **Marischal College**, whose tall, steely-grey pinnacled neo-Gothic facade is in absolute contrast to the hideously utilitarian concrete office blocks opposite. This spectacular building, with all its soaring, surging lines, is not to everyone's taste – it was once described by a minor art historian as "a wedding cake covered in indigestible grey icing". The college was founded in 1593 by the fourth Earl Marischal, and coexisted as a separate Protestant university from Catholic King's, just up the road, for over two centuries. It was long Aberdeen's boast to have as many universities as the whole of England, and it wasn't until 1860 that the two were united as the University of Aberdeen.

These days, the university has all but moved from the college and the building is largely closed to the public. What you can see is the **Marischal Museum** (Mon–Fri 10am–5pm, Sun 2–5pm; free) with its wealth of weird exhibits, many gathered by Victorian anthropologists and other collectors who roamed the world filling their luggage with objects. Sensitive to the cultural crassness this represents to modern tastes, the museum concentrates as much on the phenomenon of these collectors as what they brought back.

The Aberdeen Art Gallery and around

A little further west up Schoolhill, Aberdeen's engrossing **Art Gallery** (Mon–Sat 10am–5pm, Sun 2–5pm; free) was purpose-built in 1884 to a Neoclassical design by Mackenzie. You enter via the airy **Centre Court**, dominated by Barbara Hepworth's central fountain; the walls highlight the gallery's policy of acquiring contemporary art, with British work to the fore, including one of Francis Bacon's Pope paintings. The **Side Court** contains *Jungled*, a garish, erotic spin on stained-glass windows by Gilbert and George, and works by YBAs (Young British Artists) gifted by the Saatchi Collection, including Jordan Baseman's extraordinary *I Love You Still*, made from tree limbs and human hair.

The **upstairs** rooms house the main body of the gallery's painting collection. The permanent collection is occasionally moved around, and some rooms are given over to temporary exhibitions. The sheer number of landscapes crowding the walls of **Room One** can be disconcerting, but closer inspection reveals a superb collection of Victorian narrative art including Pre-Raphaelite canvases by Rossetti and Waterhouse. **Room Two** steps back in history, concentrating on eighteenth-century painters such as landscape artist Alexander Nasmyth and Scotland's famous portraitists, Henry Raeburn and Alan Ramsay. **Room Three** and **Room Four** feature changing displays from the gallery's permanent collections, while **Room Six** and the adjoining balcony concentrate on British twentieth-century painting. Predictably popular is the Impressionist collection, including works by Boudin, Courbet, Sisley, Monet, Pissarro and a deliciously bright Renoir, *La Roche Guyon*. The strong connections between the French schools and the development of modernism in Scottish painting saw the emergence of the "Glasgow Boys" in the 1880s (see p.908), exemplified here by John Lavery's *The Tennis Party*. The Scottish Colourists are also in evidence: Peploe's *Landscape, Cassis* shows off his instinct for colour, with daringly angled foreground tree trunks in rich blue, chocolate and purple shadows. You'll also find a good selection of modern Scottish artists, including Peter Howson and Joan Eardley, who captured the landscape around Catterline, a coastal village just south of Aberdeen, so memorably.

Opposite the gallery is a designer shopping arcade called **The Academy**, a gateway to Aberdeen's more Bohemian quarter: cobbled Belmont and Little Belmont streets feature a number of the city's more interesting bars, shops and restaurants, with farmers' markets on the last Saturday of each month. West of Belmont Street, across the Denburn gorge, spanned by the Union Bridge and Schoolhill viaduct, the sunken **Union Terrace Gardens** are a welcome relief from the hubbub of Union Street.

The harbour

Old, cobbled Shiprow winds down from Castlegate at the east end of Union Street to the north side of the **harbour**. Just off this steep road, peering towards the harbour through a striking glass facade, is the **Maritime Museum** (Mon–Sat 10am–5pm, Sun noon–3pm; free), which combines a modern, airy museum with the aged labyrinthine corridors of **Provost Ross's House**. The museum is a thoroughly engrossing, imaginative tribute to Aberdeen's maritime traditions.

Just inside the front entrance are blackboards, computer readouts and barometers showing everything from the time of high tide to the up-to-the-minute price of a barrel of crude oil. Suspended above the foyer and visible from five different levels is a spectacular 27ft-high model of an oil rig, which, along with terrific views over the bustling harbour, serves as a constant reminder that Aberdeen's maritime links remain very much alive. While large sections of the museum are devoted to North Sea oil and gas, the older industries of herring-fishing, whaling, shipbuilding and lighthouses also have their place. Passages lead into Provost Ross's House, where intricate ship's models and a variety of nautical paintings and drawings are on display.

At the bottom of Shiprow the cobbles meet Market Street, which runs the length of the **harbour**. Brightly painted oil-supply ships, sleek cruise ships and peeling fishing boats jostle amid an ever-constant clatter and the screech of well-fed seagulls. With high fences, rushing traffic and a series of drab office blocks, it's not the most attractive part of the city, although you can encounter plenty

23

of life and colour if you follow your nose to the **fish market**, off Market Street, best visited early (Mon–Fri opens 7.30am) when the place is in full swing. Be warned, however, that it's not set up for visitors and entry is not guaranteed.

At the north end of Market Street, Trinity Quay runs past industrial yards and down York Street towards **Footdee**, or Fittie (an easy walk or bus #14 or #15 from Union Street), a quaint nineteenth-century fishermen's village of higgledy-piggledy cottages backing onto the sea.

Old Aberdeen

An independent burgh until 1891, tranquil **Old Aberdeen**, a ten-minute ride north of the city centre on bus #20 from Marischal College at Littlejohn Street, has maintained a village-like identity. Dominated by King's College and St Machar's Cathedral, its medieval cobbled streets, wynds and little lanes are beautifully preserved. The southern half of cobbled High Street is overlooked by **King's College Chapel** (Mon–Fri 8am–4pm; free), the first and finest of the college buildings, completed in 1495, with a chunky Renaissance spire. The highlight of the interior, which unusually has no central aisle, are the ribbed arched wooden ceiling and the rare and beautiful examples of medieval Scottish woodcarving in the screen and the stalls. From the college, High Street leads a short way north to **St Machar's Cathedral** on the leafy Chanonry (daily 9am–5pm, except during services; free; ☎01224/485988), overlooking Seaton Park and the River Don. The site was reputedly founded in 580 by Machar, a follower of Columba, and the cathedral, a huge fifteenth-century fortified building, is one of the city's first great granite edifices.

The beach

Aberdeen can surely claim to have the best sandy **beach** of all Britain's large cities. Less than a mile east of Union Street is a great two-mile sweep of clean sand, broken by groynes and lined all along with an esplanade, where most of the city's population seems to gather on sunny days. Towards the south is a concrete expanse of chain restaurants, a fairly tatty amusement park, a multiplex cinema and a vast leisure centre. Further north, most of the beach's hinterland is devoted to golf links.

Eating, drinking and nightlife

Aberdeen is not short of good **cafés** and **restaurants**, mostly around Union Street. Like most ports Aberdeen caters for a transient population with a lot of disposable income and a desire to get drunk as quickly as possible. Although you'll find no shortage of loud, flashy **bars** catering to such needs, there are still a number of more traditional **pubs** which, though usually packed, are well worth a visit.

Cafés and restaurants

Ashvale 44–48 Great Western Rd ☎01224/575842, ⓦwww.theashvale.co.uk. One of Scotland's finest, and biggest, fish-and-chip shops. Restaurant open daily until 11pm; takeaway until 1am. Inexpensive.

Café 52 52 The Green ☎01224/590094, ⓦwww.cafe52.net. Cosy, bohemian hangout by day that turns into a crowded restaurant by night, with an imaginative take on popular dishes. Closed Sun evening and Mon daytime. Moderate.

Foyer 82a Crown St ☎01224/582277, ⓦwww.foyerrestaurant.com. Top-notch contemporary bistro in a tastefully converted church, acting as the commercial arm of a charity for disadvantaged young people and the homeless. Moderate.

Howies 50 Chapel St ☎01224/639500. Aberdeen outpost of an Edinburgh institution, serving modern Scottish cooking in a welcoming environment. Well-priced set meals and house wine. Moderate.

Lemon Tree 5 West North St ☎01224/621610, Ⓦwww.lemontree.org. Easy-going daytime café inside an arts venue, serving snacks and meals – including good vegetarian and vegan options – to live music. Open Thurs–Sun. Inexpensive.

Nargile 77–79 Skene St ☎01224/636093. Much-loved family-run Turkish restaurant. Closed Sun, although the newer West End sister restaurant in Forest Avenue, *Rendezvous at Nargile*, and the informal *Nargile Meze Bar* on Rose Street, are open seven days. Moderate.

Silver Darling Pocra Quay, North Pier ☎01224/576229. Attractively located at the harbour in Footdee, this impressive restaurant majors in sophisticated French seafood dishes. Closed Sat lunch & Sun. Expensive.

Pubs and bars

Old Blackfriars 52 Castle St. A genuinely tradi-tional pub that puts ersatz copyists to shame: cosy interior, great selection of beers and pub grub, and a constant buzz of conversation.

Prince of Wales 7 St Nicholas Lane. The quintes-sential Aberdeen pub with a long bar and flagstone floor. With fine pub grub, renowned real ales and a Sunday-evening folk session, it's little wonder that it's often crowded.

Revolution 25 Belmont St. Stylish bar with explo-sive cocktails and a perfect understanding of the vagaries of Scottish weather – there's a fire and comfy sofas as you go in, and rooftop alfresco drinking out back.

St Machar Bar 97 High St, Old Aberdeen. The medieval quarter's only pub, a pokey, old-fashioned bar attracting an intriguing mix of King's College students and workers.

Under the Hammer 11 North Silver St. This snug little basement wine bar with a continental vibe is a popular refuge when icy winter winds hit the city.

Clubs, live-music venues and concert halls

Drummonds 1 Belmont St. Unapologetically murky bar with the emphasis on live music, providing a welcome contrast to glossier neighbours; the intimate stage attracts upcoming talent and the occasional big name.

The Globe Inn 13–15 North Silver St ☎01224/624258. Pleasant city-centre inn with jamming sessions on Tuesdays and live jazz, blues and covers bands Thurs–Sun.

Lemon Tree 5 West North St ☎01224/642230, Ⓦwww.lemontree.org. The fulcrum of the city's arts scene, with a great buzz and regular live music, club nights and comedy.

Snafu 5 Union St ☎01224/622660, Ⓦwww .clubsnafu.com. Aberdeen's best dance club, attracting frequent visits from the hottest DJs around.

The Tunnels Carnegies Brae ☎01224/211121. Thriving live-music venue, with an intriguing mix of rising young bands, open-mic sessions and club nights with reggae, hip-hop, ska and Northern Soul to the fore. There's also a record shop drawing on the manager's vinyl collection – possibly the biggest in Scotland.

Theatres and cinemas

Belmont Picture House 9 Belmont St ☎01224/343536, Ⓦwww.picturehouses.co.uk. Art-house cinema showing the more cerebral new releases alongside classic, cult and foreign-language films. There's a comfortable café inside and some good places nearby for a bite before or after.

His Majesty's Rosemount Viaduct ☎0845/270 8200, Ⓦwww.aberdeenperformingarts.com. Aberdeen's main theatre, in a beautiful Edward-ian building, with a programme ranging from highbrow drama and opera to pantomime. A new extension, including a café and restaurant, aims to keep the cultural buzz going throughout the day.

Lemon Tree 5 West North St ☎01224/642230, Ⓦwww.lemontree.org. Avant-garde events with off-the-wall comedians and plays, many coming hotfoot from the Edinburgh festivals.

Listings

Airport ☎08700/400006.

Bike rental Alpine Bikes, 66–70 Holburn St ☎01224/211455; Anderson's Cycles ☎01224/ 641520.

Book shops The largest are Waterstone's, 269–271 Union St, and Ottakar's, in the Mall Trinity, Union Street. Winram's, 32–36 Rosemount Place, and The Old Aberdeen Bookshop, 140 Spittal, are best for secondhand, while Books and Beans, 22 Belmont St, offers a more populist selection.

Bus information First Aberdeen Busline ☎01224/650065.

Car rental Arnold Clark, Girdleness Road ☎01224/249159, Lang Stracht (airport pick-ups) ☎01224/663723; Budget, Wellheads Drive (airport pick-ups) ☎01224/793333; National, 16 Broomhill

Rd ☎01224/595366 and airport ☎0870/400 4502.

Ferry information ☎0845/600 0449, ⓦwww .northlinkferries.co.uk.

Hospital The Royal Infirmary, on Foresterhill, northeast of the town centre, has a 24hr casualty department (☎01224/681818).

Internet Free access in the Central Library on Rosemount Viaduct (Mon–Thurs 9am–8pm, Fri & Sat 9am–5pm). Otherwise, try the tourist office, *Costa Coffee* on Loch Street, next to the Bon Accord Centre, or the Family History Society at 158–164 King St.

Pharmacies Boots is at 161 Union St (Mon–Wed & Fri 7.45am–6pm, Thurs 7.45am–8pm, Sat 8.30am–6pm, Sun noon–5pm; ☎01224/211592). For late-night pharmacies phone ☎0845/456 6000.

Police Main station is on Queen Street ☎0845/600 5700, including the lost property office.

Post office The central office is in the St Nicholas Centre, between Union Street and Upperkirkgate (Mon, Wed–Fri 9am–5.30pm, Tues & Sat 9.30am–5.30pm), with another branch at 489 Union St (Mon, Wed–Fri 9am–5.30pm, Tues 9.30am–5.30pm, Sat 9.30am–12.30pm).

Taxis ComCab ☎01224/353535.

Stonehaven and the Mearns

South of Aberdeen, the A92 and the main train line follow the coast to the busy, pebble-dashed town of **STONEHAVEN**. On one side of the harbour, Stonehaven's oldest building, the **Tolbooth** (June–Sept Mon & Wed–Sun 1.30–4.30pm; free), built as a storehouse during the construction of Dunnottar Castle (see p.1045), is now a museum of local history and fishing. The old High Street, lined with some fine townhouses and civic buildings, connects the harbour and its surrounding old town with the late eighteenth-century planned centre on the other side of the River Carron. On New Year's Eve, High Street is the location for the ancient ceremony of **Fireballs**, when locals parade its length swinging metal cages full of burning debris around their heads to ward off evil spirits for the year ahead. The **new town** focuses on the market square, with Stonehaven's wonderful open-air Art Deco **swimming pool** a little north (June & early Sept Mon–Fri 1–7.30pm, Sat & Sun 10am–6pm; July & Aug Mon–Fri 10am–7.30pm, Sat & Sun 10am–6pm; £3; ⓦwww.stonehavenopenairpool .co.uk): opened in 1934, it's always packed with locals on a sunny day.

The **tourist office** is at 66 Allardice St, the main street past the square (April–June, Sept & Oct Mon–Sat 10am–1pm & 2–5pm; July & Aug Mon–Sat 10am–7pm, Sun 1–5.30pm; ☎01569/762806). For **B&B**, try *Arduthie House* on Ann Street (☎01569/762381, ⓦwww.arduthieguesthouse.com; ❸) or, a few miles south of town on the A92, *Dunnottar Mains Farm* (☎01569/762621, ⓦwww.dunnottarmains.co.uk; ❷). A good choice for **food** is the smart Art Deco *Carron Restaurant* at 20 Cameron St (☎01569/760460, ⓦwww.carron -restaurant.co.uk), or the moderately expensive *Tolbooth Seafood Restaurant* (☎01569/762287, ⓦwww.tolbooth-restaurant.co.uk; closed Mon), above the museum on the harbour. For cheaper **pub** food or just a drink, try the entertaining *Marine Hotel* or the attractive *Ship Inn*, both on the harbour.

Two miles south of Stonehaven (the tourist office sells a walking guide for the scenic amble), **Dunnottar Castle** (Easter–Oct Mon–Sat 9am–6pm, Sun 2–5pm; Nov–Easter Fri–Mon 9.30am–4pm, Dec & Jan closes 3pm; £4) is one of the finest of Scotland's ruined castles, a huge ninth-century fortress set on a three-sided sheer cliff jutting into the sea – a setting striking enough to be chosen as the backdrop for Zeffirelli's movie version of *Hamlet*. Once the principal fortress of the northeast, its ruins are worth a good root around, and there are any number of dramatic views out to the crashing sea. Siege and bloodstained drama splatter the castle's past: in 1297 the whole English Plantagenet garrison were burnt alive here by William Wallace, while one of the more

23

△ Dunnottar Castle

gruesome tales from the castle's history tells of the imprisonment and torture of 122 men and 45 women Covenanters in 1685 – an event, as it says on the Covenanters' Stone in the churchyard, "whose dark shadow is for evermore flung athwart the Castled Rock".

Inland from here, the straggling village of **ARBUTHNOTT** was the home of prolific local author, **Lewis Grassic Gibbon** (1901–35), whose romanticized realism perfectly encapsulates the spirit of the surrounding agricultural Mearns area. *Sunset Song*, his most famous work, is an essential read for those travelling in this area. The community-run **Grassic Gibbon Centre** (April–Oct daily 10am–4.30pm; £2.50), on the B967 through the village, is a great introduction to this fascinating and self-assured man who died so young.

㉓ Deeside

More commonly known as **Royal Deeside**, the land stretching west from Aberdeen along the River Dee revels in its connections with the Royal Family, who have regularly holidayed here, at **Balmoral**, since Queen Victoria bought the estate. Eighty thousand Scots turned out to welcome her on her first visit in 1848, but some weren't so charmed: one local journalist remarked that the area was about to be "desolated by cockneys and other horrible reptiles". Today, most locals are fiercely protective of the royal connection.

Deeside is undoubtedly handsome in a fierce, craggy, Scottish way, and the royal presence has helped keep a lid on any unattractive mass development. The villages strung along the A93, the main route through the area, are well heeled and have something of an old-fashioned air. Facilities for visitors hereabouts are first-class, with a number of bunkhouses and hostels, some decent hotels, and plenty of castles and grounds to snoop around. It's also an excellent area for **outdoor activities**, with hiking routes into both the Grampian and Cairngorm mountains, and good mountain biking, horse riding and skiing.

West of Aberdeen

Ten miles west of Aberdeen on the A93, **Drum Castle** (daily: April, May & Sept 12.30–5.30pm; June–Aug 10am–5.30pm; grounds 9.30am–sunset all year; £8, NTS grounds only £3) stands in a clearing in the ancient **woods of Drum**, made up of the splendid pines and oaks that covered this whole area before the shipbuilding industry precipitated mass forest clearance. The castle itself combines a 1619 Jacobean mansion with Victorian extensions and the original, huge thirteenth-century keep, which has been restored and reopened.

Further along the A93, four miles west of Drum Castle, **Crathes Castle** (daily: April–Sept 10am–5.30pm; Oct 10am–4.30pm; £10; NTS) is a splendid sixteenth-century granite tower house adorned with flourishes such as overhanging turrets, gargoyles and conical roofs. Its thick walls, narrow windows and tiny rooms loaded with heavy old furniture make Crathes rather claustrophobic, but it is still worth visiting for some wonderful painted ceilings, either still in their original form or sensitively restored; the earliest dates from 1602. The grounds include an impressive walled garden complete with yew hedges clipped into various shapes.

Twelve miles further west on the A93, **ABOYNE** is a typically well-mannered Deeside village at the mouth of **Glen Tanar**, which runs southwest from here for ten miles or so deep into the Grampian hills. The glen, with few steep gradients and some glorious stands of mature Caledonian pine, is ideal for walking, mountain biking or horse riding; the ranger information point two miles into the glen off the B976 has details of suitable routes, while the Glen Tanar Equestrian Centre (☎01339/886448) offers one- and two-hour horse rides.

Ballater and Balmoral

Ten miles west of Aboyne is the neat and ordered town of **BALLATER**, attractively hemmed in by the river and fir-covered mountains. It was in Ballater that Queen Victoria first arrived in Deeside by train from Aberdeen back in 1848; she wouldn't allow a station to be built any closer to Balmoral, eight miles further west. The local shops, having provided Balmoral with groceries and household basics, flaunt their royal connections with oversized "By Appointment" crests sported above the doorways of most businesses from the butcher to the newsagent. To take advantage of the fresh air and natural beauty that Victoria loved so much, Ballater makes an excellent base for local **walks and outdoor activities**. There are numerous hikes from Loch Muik (pronounced "mick"), including the well-worn but strenuous all-day trek up and around Lochnagar (3789ft), the mountain much painted and written about by the current Prince of Wales. Good-quality **bikes** can be rented from Cabin Fever (☎013397/54004), beside the station on Station Square, or Cycle Highlands (☎013397/55864) at 16 Bridge St.

Ballater's **tourist office** is in the former train station on Station Square (daily: July & Aug 9am–6pm; Sept–June 10am–5pm; ☎013397/55306). Good-quality bunkhouse **accommodation** is available at the *Schoolhouse*, Anderson Road (☎013397/56333, ⓦwww.theschool-house.com), which also provides inexpensive evening meals, and there are plenty of reasonable B&Bs in town, including nonsmoking *Inverdeen House* on Bridge Square (☎013397/55759, ⓦwww.inverdeen.com; ❸). For **camping**, head for *Anderson Road Caravan Park* (☎013397/55727; Easter–Oct) down towards the river. There are numerous **places to eat**: the *Green Inn Restaurant*, 9 Victoria Rd (☎013397/55701, ⓦwww.green-inn.com, ❹), is pricey but excellent, with its French influenced menu, while *La Mangiatoia* (☎013397/55999), on Bridge Square opposite the *Monaltrie Hotel*, is a cheaper, cheerful family pizza/pasta place.

Balmoral Estate

Originally a sixteenth-century tower house built for the powerful Gordon family, **Balmoral Castle** (April–July daily 10am–5pm; also weekly guided tours Nov & Dec; £6; ☎013397/42534, ⊛www.balmoralcastle.com) has been a royal residence since 1852, when it was converted to the Scottish Baronial mansion that stands today. The Royal Family traditionally spend their summer holidays here each August, but even dedicated royalists may find the castle something of a disappointment. The public are permitted to view only the ballroom, an exhibition room and the grounds; with so little of the castle on view, it's worth making the most of the grounds and larger estate.

Braemar

Continuing westwards for another few miles, the road rises to 1100ft above sea level in the upper part of Deeside and the village of **BRAEMAR**, situated where three passes meet. It's an invigorating, outdoor kind of place, well patronized by committed hikers, but probably best known for its Highland Games, the annual **Braemar Gathering**, on the first Saturday of September (⊛www.braemargathering.org). Since Queen Victoria's day, successive generations of royals have attended, and the world's most famous Highland Games have become rather an overcrowded, overblown event. You're not guaranteed to get in if you just turn up; the website has details of how to book tickets in advance.

Braemar's **tourist office** is in the modern building known as the Mews, in the middle of the village on Mar Road (June & Sept daily 9am–5pm; July & Aug daily 9am–6pm; Oct Mon–Sat 9am–5pm, Sun 1–5pm; Nov–May Mon–Sat 10.30am–1.30pm & 2–5pm, Sun 1–4pm; ☎013397/41600). *Clunie Lodge Guest House*, Clunie Bank Road (☎013397/41330, ⊛www.clunielodge.com; ❷), is a good **B&B** with lovely views up Clunie Glen, while *Rucksacks* is an easy-going **bunkhouse** well equipped for walkers and backpackers. For **food**, avoid the large hotels and try either *Taste*, a coffee shop and moderately priced contemporary restaurant on the road out to the Linn of Dee, or *The Gathering Place*, a pleasant bistro at the heart of the village.

Speyside

Strictly speaking, the term **Speyside** refers to the entire region surrounding the River Spey, but to most people the name is synonymous with the **whisky triangle**, stretching from just north of Craigellachie, down towards Tomintoul in the south and east to Huntly. Indeed, there are more whisky distilleries and famous brands concentrated in this small area (including Glenfiddich and Glenlivet) than in any other part of the country. Running through the heart of the region is the River Spey, whose clean, clear, fast-running waters not only play such a vital part in the whisky industry, but also make it one of Scotland's finest angling locations. At the centre of Speyside is the quiet market town of **Dufftown**, full of solid, stone-built workers' houses and dotted with no fewer than nine whisky distilleries. Along with the well-kept nearby villages of **Craigellachie** and **Aberlour**, it makes the best base for a tour of whisky country, whether on the official Malt Whisky Trail or more independent explorations.

The **Speyside Way**, with its beguiling blend of mountain, river, wildlife and whisky, is fast establishing itself as an appealing and less-taxing alternative to the popular West Highland and Southern Upland long-distance footpaths. Starting at **Buckie** on the Moray Firth coast (see p.1066), it follows the fast-flowing River Spey from its mouth at Spey Bay south to **Aviemore** (see p.1067), with branches linking it to **Dufftown**, Scotland's malt whisky capital, and **Tomintoul** on the remote edge of the Cairngorm mountains. Some 65 miles long without taking on the branch routes, the whole thing is a five- to seven-day expedition, but its proximity to main roads and small villages means that it is excellent for shorter walks or even bicycle trips, especially in the heart of **distillery** country between Craigellachie and Glenlivet: Glenfiddich, Glenlivet, Macallan and Cardhu distilleries, as well as the Speyside Cooperage, lie directly on or a short distance off the route. Other highlights include the chance to encounter an array of **wildlife**, from dolphins at Spey Bay to ospreys at Loch Garten, as well as the restored **railway** trips on offer at Dufftown and Aviemore. The path uses disused railway lines for much of its length, and there are simple campsites and good B&Bs at strategic points along the route. For more details contact the Speyside Way Visitor Centre in the old railway station at Aberlour, just back from the main square (May–Oct daily 10am–5pm; Nov–April open when ranger in office; ☎01340/881266, ⓦwww.speysideway.org).

Dufftown

The cheery community of **DUFFTOWN**, founded in 1817 by James Duff, the fourth Earl of Fife, proudly proclaims itself "Malt Whisky Capital of the World" with good reason – it produces more of the stuff than any other town in Britain. There are nine distilleries around Dufftown (not all of them still working), as well as a cooperage and a coppersmith, and an extended stroll around the outskirts of the town gives a good idea of the density of whisky distilling going on, with glimpses of giant warehouses filled with barrels of the stuff, and whiffs of fermenting barley or peat smoke lingering on the breeze.

There isn't a great deal to do in town, but it's a useful starting point for orienting yourself towards the whisky trail. On the edge of town along the A941 is the town's largest working distillery, **Glenfiddich** (see p.1050), as well as the old Dufftown train station, which has been restored by enthusiasts in recent years and is now the departure point for the **Keith & Dufftown Railway** (April–Sept Sat & Sun 3 trips daily, June–Aug also runs Fri; 40min; ☎01340/821181, ⓦwww.keith-dufftown.org.uk for journey times), which uses restored diesel locomotives to chug through whisky country to Keith, home of the Strathisla distillery (see p.1051).

Dufftown's official **tourist office** is located inside the handsome clocktower at the centre of the square (July & Aug Mon–Sat 10am–6pm, Sun 11am–3pm; April–June, Sept & Oct Mon–Sat 10am–1pm & 2–5pm, Sun 11am–3pm; ☎01340/820501), though an informal information and accommodation booking service has developed at The Whisky Shop (☎01340/821097) across the road.

There's a handful of places to stay in Dufftown itself, although you may prefer to stay elsewhere on Speyside, closer to the attractive countryside. For **B&B**, *Tannochbrae*, 22 Fife St (☎01340/820541, ⓦwww.tannochbrae.co.uk; ❸), is a pleasant, enthusiastically run place with a small restaurant, *Scott's*, on the ground floor. You can also rent **bikes** from here.

Touring Malt Whisky Country

Speyside is the heart of Scotland's **whisky** industry, with over fifty distilleries testimony to a unique combination of clear, clean water, benign climate and gentle upland terrain. Yet it's worth keeping in mind that in these parts whisky is a hard-edged, multimillion-pound business dominated by huge corporations, and it sometimes comes as a surprise to visitors that a lot of distilleries are unglamorous industrial units, and by no means all are open to the public. Having said that, there are plenty located in attractive historic buildings which now go to some lengths to provide an engaging experience for visitors. Mostly this involves a tour around the essential stages in the whisky-making process, though for real enthusiasts a number of distilleries now offer pricier connoisseur tours.

There are eight distilleries on the official **Malt Whisky Trail** (ⓦwww.maltwhiskytrail .com). Unless you're seriously interested in whisky, it's best to just pick out a couple that appeal: we've chosen some of the highlights below. All offer a guided tour (some are free, others charge but then give you a voucher which is redeemable against a bottle of whisky from the distillery shop), with a tasting to round it off. Most people travel the route by car, though you could cycle parts of it, or even walk using the Speyside Way (see box on p.1049).

Glen Grant, Rothes (April–Oct Mon–Sat 10am–4pm, Sun 12.30–4pm; free). A well-known, floral whisky aggressively marketed to a younger market. A regular, well-informed tour, but the highlight here is the attractive Victorian gardens, a mix of well-tended lawns and mixed, mature trees which include a tumbling waterfall and a hidden whisky-safe.

Glenfiddich, on the A941 just north of Dufftown (April to mid-Oct Mon–Sat 9.30am–4.30pm, Sun noon–4.30pm; mid-Oct to March Mon–Fri 9.30am–4.30pm; free). The biggest and slickest of all the Speyside distilleries, and the first to offer regular tours to visitors, despite the fact that it's still owned by the same Grant family who founded it in 1887. It's a light, sweet whisky packaged in triangular-shaped bottles – unusually,

Craigellachie

Four miles north of Dufftown, the small settlement of **CRAIGELLACHIE** (pronounced "Craig-*ell*-ach-ee") sits above the confluence of the sparkling waters of the Fiddich and the Spey. From the village, you can look down on a beautiful iron bridge over the Spey built by Thomas Telford in 1815. For an unusual alternative to a distillery tour, the **Speyside Cooperage** (Mon–Fri 9.30am–4pm; £3.10) is worth a visit: after the exhibition explaining the ancient and skilled art of cooperage, you're shown onto a balcony overlooking the workshop where the oak casks for whisky are made and repaired by fast-working, highly skilled coopers.

For somewhere **to stay** in the village there's an extremely welcoming and tasteful B&B attached to the ⚘ *Green Hall Gallery* on Victoria Street (☎01340/871010, ⓦwww.aboutscotland.comGreenhall; ❸); in Archiestown, a few miles west of Craigellachie, the pleasant, traditional *Archiestown Hotel* (☎01340/810218, ⓦwww.archiestownhotel.co.uk; ❻) caters for fishermen and outdoor types, and serves good evening **meals**.

The coast

The **coast** of northeast Scotland from Aberdeen to Inverness has a rugged, sometimes bleak fringe, with pleasant if undramatic farmland rolling inland.

the bottling is still done on the premises and is part of the tour (offered in various languages). A Connoisseurs' Tour is available (£12), as well as an even more specialized tour of the linked Balvenie distillery (£20). Glenfiddich also has its own café-bar and an artists-in-residence programme each summer.

Glenlivet, on the B9008 to Tomintoul (April–Oct Mon–Sat 10am–4pm, Sun 12.30–4pm; free). A famous name in a lonely hillside setting. This was the first licensed distillery in the Highlands, following the 1823 Act of Parliament which aimed to reduce illicit distilling and smuggling. The Glenlivet 12-year-old malt is a floral, fragrant medium-bodied whisky. A stretch of the Speyside Way passes through the distillery grounds.

Strathisla, Keith (April–Oct Mon–Sat 10am–4pm, Sun 12.30–4pm; £5). A small, old-fashioned distillery claiming to be Scotland's oldest (1786); it's certainly one of the most attractive, with classic pagoda-shaped buildings and the River Isla rushing by. Inside are some impressive and interesting bits of equipment such as an old-fashioned mashtun and brass-bound spirit safes. The malt itself has a rich almost fruity taste and is pretty rare, but is used as the heart of the better-known Chivas Regal blend. You can arrive here on board one of the restored trains of the Keith & Dufftown Railway (see p.1049).

A number of other distilleries, not on the official trail, can also be visited:

Macallan, near Craigellachie (April–Oct Mon–Sat 9.30am–5pm, Nov–March Mon–Fri 11am–3pm; ☎01340/872280), can only take ten people on its tours, and therefore doesn't attract coach parties. Three different tours leave the small, modern visitor centre: the half-hour "Macallan experience" (free), a one-hour, in-depth "Spirit of Macallan" tour (£8), and the "Macallan Precious Whisky Tour" (£15).

Aberlour, on the outskirts of the village (April–Oct Mon–Sat 10.30am & 2pm, Sun 11.30am & 3pm; £7.50; booking essential ☎01340/881249). The twice-daily tours are quite specialized, with a tutored nosing and the chance to buy and fill your own bottle of cask-strength single malt.

Still, if the weather is good, it's worth spending a couple of days meandering through the various little fishing villages and along the miles of deserted, unspoilt beaches.

The largest coastal towns are Peterhead and **Fraserburgh**, both dominated by sizeable fishing fleets; while neither has much to offer the visitor, the latter is home to one of Scotland's most attractive small museums, the Museum of Scottish Lighthouses. More appealing to most visitors are the quieter spots along the Moray coast, including the charming villages of **Pennan**, **Gardenstown**, **Portsoy** and nearby **Cullen**. The other main attractions are **Duff House** in Banff, a branch of the National Gallery of Scotland; the working abbey at **Pluscarden** by Elgin; and the **Findhorn Foundation**, near Forres.

Fraserburgh and the north coast

The large and fairly severe-looking **FRASERBURGH** (ⓦ www .visitfraserburgh.com) is home of the excellent **Museum of Scottish Lighthouses** (April–Oct Mon–Sat 10am–5pm, Sun noon–5pm, July & Aug open till 6pm; Nov–March Mon–Sat 11am–4pm, Sun noon–4pm; £4.75), where you can see a collection of huge lenses and prisms gathered from decommissioned lighthouses. It also has a display on various members of the famous "Lighthouse" Stevenson family (including the father and grandfather of author Robert Louis Stevenson), who designed many of them. Highlight of the museum is the tour of Kinnaird Head lighthouse, preserved as it was when the last keeper left in 1991, with its century-old equipment still in perfect working order.

Fraserbugh's **tourist office**, in Saltoun Square (April–Oct Mon–Sat 10am–1pm & 2–5pm; ℡01346/518315), gives out information about the surrounding area. The rest of the town centre isn't particularly inspiring; for a bite to eat, *Zanres* opposite the tourist office does decent **fish and chips**.

West of Fraserburgh

PENNAN, twelve miles west of Fraserburgh, is a tiny fishing hamlet consisting of little more than a single row of whitewashed stone cottages tucked between a cliff and the sea. The movie *Local Hero* was filmed here in 1982 and you can stay at one of the landmarks from the film, the recently upgraded *Pennan Inn* (℡01346/561201, ✉thepennaninn@btinternet.com; ➍), whose restaurant specializes in local seafood and game.

The tiny village of **CROVIE** (pronounced "crivie"), on the other side of Troup Head from Pennan, is equally appealing. Tucked against the steep cliffs, it's so narrow that its residents have to park their cars at one end of the village and continue to their houses on foot. Similar but a little larger, **GARDENS-TOWN**, a short way west, boasts a hotel, the *Garden Arms* (℡01261/851260, ⓦwww.gardenarms.co.uk; ➋), as well as a couple of art galleries and the small but excellent *Harbour Restaurant and Café* (℡01261/851690; booking recommended), which overlooks the collection of small local boats tied up to the quayside.

Banff

Heading west along the coast from Pennan brings you, after ten miles, to Macduff and its neighbour **BANFF**, separated by little more than a beautiful seven-arch bridge over the River Deveron. Banff has a mix of characterful old buildings and boarded-up shops, which give little clue to the extravagance of **Duff House** (generally April–Oct daily 11am–5pm; Nov–March Thurs–Sun 11am–4pm; ⓦwww.duffhouse.org.uk; £5.50; HS), the town's main attraction. Built to William Adam's design in 1730, the house has been painstakingly restored and reopened as an outpost of the **National Gallery of Scotland**'s extensive collection, with the emphasis on period artwork, and temporary exhibitions of work from the collections are mounted regularly. Beyond the house there are extensive **grounds** with an adventure playground, some pleasant parkland and riverside walks, and various odd buildings including a fishing "temple" and the Duff dynasty's mausoleum. Banff's **tourist office** (April–June & Sept Mon–Sat 10am–1pm & 2–4pm; July & Aug Mon–Sat 10am–1pm & 2–5pm; ℡01261/812419) is housed in the old gatehouse of Duff House in St Mary Square.

Cullen to Spey Bay

Twelve miles west of Banff is **CULLEN**, strikingly situated beneath a superb series of arched viaducts. The town is made up of two sections: Seatown, by the harbour, and the new town on the hillside. The local delicacy, **Cullen skink** – soup made from milk (or cream), potato and smoked haddock – is available at local hotels and bars.

West of Cullen, the scruffy, working fishing town of **BUCKIE** marks the northern end of the **Speyside Way** long-distance footpath (see p.1049). This follows the coast west for five miles to windy **Spey Bay**, at the mouth of the River Spey. It's a remote spot bounded by sea and river and sky; interpretation is offered by a small but dedicated **wildlife centre** (April–Oct daily 10.30am–5pm; Nov–March Sat & Sun 10.30am–5pm; ⓦwww.wdcs .org/wildlifecentre; free), whose main mission is research of the Moray Firth dolphin population (for more on which, see p.1066).

Elgin and around

The lively market town of **ELGIN**, just inland about fifteen miles west of Cullen, grew up in the thirteenth century around the River Lossie. On North College Street, a few blocks from the tourist office and clearly signposted, is the lovely ruin of **Elgin Cathedral** (April–Sept daily 9.30am–6.30pm; Oct–March Sat–Wed 9.30am–4.30pm; £3.30; HS). Once considered Scotland's most beautiful cathedral, rivalling St Andrews in importance, it's little more than a shell today, though it does retain its original facade. Founded in 1224, the three-towered building was extensively rebuilt after a fire in 1270, and stood as the region's highest religious house until 1390 when the inimical Wolf of Badenoch (Alexander Stewart, Earl of Buchan and illegitimate son of Robert II) burned the place down, along with the rest of the town, in retaliation for having been excommunicated by the Bishop of Moray when he left his wife.

Seven miles southwest of Elgin, **Pluscarden Abbey** (daily 9am–5pm; free; ⓦwww.pluscardenabbey.org) is one of only two abbeys in Scotland with a permanent community of monks. It was founded in 1230, though the small group of Benedictine monks who established the present community arrived in 1948. They are an active bunch, running stained-glass workshops, making honey and even recording Gregorian chants on CDs. The abbey itself is airy and tranquil, with the monks' singing often eerily floating through from the connecting chapel.

Elgin's **tourist office** is at 17 High St (April–June & Sept Mon–Sat 10am–5pm, Sun 11am–3pm; July & Aug Mon–Sat 9am–6pm, Sun 11am–4pm; Oct–March Mon–Sat 10am–4pm; ⓣ01343/542666). *The Lodge*, 20 Duff Ave (ⓣ01343/549981, ⓦwww.thelodge-elgin.com; ❸), is a good-quality **B&B**, while five miles east of town, the *Old Church of Urquhart* (ⓣ01343/843063, ⓦwww.oldkirk.co.uk; ❷) is an unusual and comfortable B&B in an imaginatively converted church on Meft Road.

Findhorn

On the coast northwest of Elgin is **FINDHORN**, a tidy village with some neat fishermens' cottages and a delightful harbour dotted with moored yachts. It also has a small **Heritage Centre** (May & Sept Sat & Sun 2–5pm; June–Aug Wed–Mon 2–5pm; free) in the village's former salmon-net sheds and grass-roofed ice house, as well as a couple of good pubs: on a sunny day, a pint or some seafood on the terrace of the *Kimberbey Inn* is hard to beat. For **B&B** here, try *Yellow Sands* (ⓣ01309/691351, ⓦwww.yellowsands.com; ❸).

Findhorn is best known, however, for the controversial **Findhorn Foundation** (see box, below), based beside the town's caravan park about a mile before the village itself. Visitors are generally free to stroll around the community – you can pick up a guide booklet (£3) from the shop or visitor centre – or take a **guided tour** (April–Sept Mon, Wed, Fri–Sun 2pm; £2) for a more informed look at the Foundation's different activities and projects.

The Findhorn Foundation

In 1962, with little money and no employment, Eileen and Peter Caddy, their three children, and friend Dorothy Maclean, settled on a caravan site at Findhorn. Dorothy believed she had a special relationship with what she called the "devas... the archetypal formative forces of light or energy that underlie all forms in nature – plants, trees, rivers", and from the uncompromising sandy soil they built a remarkable garden filled with plants and vegetables, far larger than had ever been seen in the area.

A few of those who came to see the phenomenon stayed to help out and tune into the spiritual aspect of the daily life of the nascent community. With its emphasis on inner discovery and development, but unattached to any particular doctrine or creed, the **Findhorn Foundation** has today blossomed into a permanent community of a couple of hundred people, with a well-developed series of courses and retreats on subjects ranging from astroshamanic healing to organic gardening, drawing another 8000 or so visitors each year. The original caravan still stands, surrounded by a whole host of newer timber buildings and other caravans employing solar power, earth roofs and other green initiatives.

The foundation is not without its detractors: Findhorn is accused of being overly well-heeled, and a glance into the shop or a tally of the smart cars parked outside the well-appointed eco-houses does give some substance to such ideas. However, there's little doubt that the community appeals to large numbers of people, and the reputation of the place is such that it attracts visitors both sympathetic and cynical – and both find something to feed their impressions.

Travel details

Buses

For information on all local and national bus services, contact Traveline ☎0870/608 2608 (daily 7am–10pm), ⓦwww.travelinescotland.com.
Aberdeen to: Ballater (hourly; 1hr 45min); Banff (hourly; 1hr 55min); Braemar (hourly; 2hr 10min); Crathie for Balmoral (hourly; 1hr 55min); Cullen (hourly; 2hr 30min); Dundee (hourly; 2hr); Elgin (hourly; 2hr 35min); Fraserburgh (hourly; 1hr 20min); Stonehaven (every 30min; 25min).
Dufftown to: Aberlour (Mon–Sat hourly; 15min); Elgin (Mon–Sat hourly; 50min).
Dundee to: Aberdeen (hourly; 2hr); Arbroath (hourly; 50min); Blairgowrie (hourly; 1hr); Glamis (2 daily; 40min); Kirriemuir (hourly; 1hr 10min); Meigle (hourly; 40min); Montrose (hourly; 1hr 10min).
Elgin to: Aberdeen (hourly; 2hr 35min); Findhorn (hourly; 25min); Pluscarden (1 daily schooldays only; 20min).
Fraserburgh to: Banff (2 daily; 55min).

Trains

For information on all local and national rail services, contact National Rail Enquiries

☎08457/484950, ⓦwww.nationalrail.co.uk or ⓦwww.firstscotrail.com.
Aberdeen to: Arbroath (every 30min; 1hr); Dundee (every 30min; 1hr 15min); Edinburgh (1–2 hourly; 2hr 35min); Elgin (Mon–Sat 10 daily, Sun 5 daily; 1hr 30min); Glasgow (hourly; 2hr 35min); London (5 daily direct; 7hr); Montrose (every 30min; 45min); Stonehaven (every 30min; 15min).
Dundee to: Aberdeen (every 30min; 1hr 15min); Arbroath (hourly; 20min); Edinburgh (1–2 hourly; 1hr 15min); Glasgow (hourly; 1hr 15min); Montrose (hourly; 15min).

Ferries

Aberdeen to: Kirkwall, Orkney (Thurs, Sat & Sun plus Tues in summer; 6hr); Lerwick, Shetland (daily; 10–12hr overnight).

Flights

Aberdeen to: Kirkwall, Orkney (2 daily; 55min); Sumburgh, Shetland (Mon–Fri 3 daily, Sat & Sun 2 daily; 1hr).

The Highland region

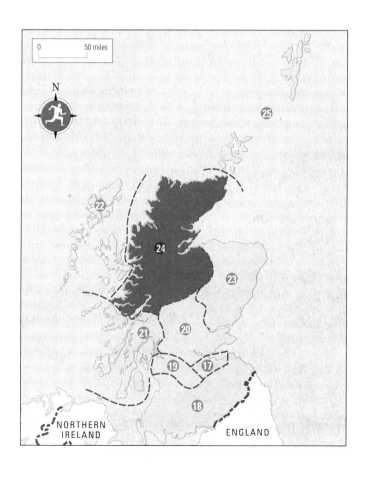

* **West Highland Railway** From Glasgow to Mallaig via Fort William: the further north you travel, the more spectacular it gets. See p.1060

* **The Cairngorms** Scotland's grandest mountain massif, a place of rare plants, wild animals, inspiring vistas and challenging outdoor activities. See p.1067

* **Glen Coe** Spectacular, moody, poignant and full of history – a glorious place for hiking or simple admiration. See p.1078

* **Loch Shiel** This romantic, unspoilt loch is where Bonnie Prince Charlie first raised an army. See p.1081

* **Knoydart** Only reached by boat or a two-day hike over the mountains, this peninsula also boasts mainland Britain's most isolated pub, the welcoming *Old Forge*. See p.1083

* **Wester Ross** Scotland's finest scenery – a heady mix of dramatic mountains, rugged sea lochs, sweeping bays and scattered islands. See p.1085

* **Ceilidh Place, Ullapool** The best venue for modern Highland culture, with evenings of music, song and dance. See p.1089

* **Cromarty** Set on the fertile Black Isle, this charming small town boasts beautiful vernacular architecture and dramatic east-coast scenery. See p.1099

△ The Cairngorms

The Highland region

The **Highland region** of Scotland, covering the northern two-thirds of the country, holds much of the mainland's most spectacular scenery: a classic combination of mountains, glens, lochs and rivers surrounded on three sides by a magnificently pitted and rugged coastline. The inspiring landscape and the tranquillity and space which it offers are without doubt the main attractions of the region. You may be surprised at just how remote much of it still is: the vast peat bogs in the north, for example, are among the most extensive and unspoilt wilderness areas in Europe, while a handful of the west coast's isolated crofting villages can still be reached only by boat.

Capital of the Highlands and the only major urban centre in the region, **Inverness** is an obvious springboard for more remote areas, with its good transport links and facilities, and while there are some engaging historic sites nearby, the city itself is of limited appeal. South of Inverness, the **Strathspey** region, with a string of villages lying along the River Spey, is dominated by the dramatic **Cairngorm mountains**, an area brimming with attractive scenery and opportunities for outdoor activity.

The Monadhliath mountains lie between Strathspey and **Loch Ness**, the largest and most famous of the necklace of lochs which make up the **Great Glen**, an ancient geological fault-line which cuts southwest across the region from Inverness to the town of **Fort William**. From Fort William, located beneath Scotland's highest peak, Ben Nevis, it's possible to branch out to some fine scenery – most conveniently the beautiful expanses of **Glen Coe**, but also in the direction of the appealing **west coast**, notably the remote and tranquil **Ardnamurchan peninsula**, the "Road to the Isles" to **Mallaig**, and the lochs and glens that lead to **Kyle of Lochalsh** on the most direct route to Skye. Between Kyle of Lochalsh and **Ullapool**, the main settlement in the northwest, lies **Wester Ross**, home to quintessentially west-coast scenes of sparkling sea lochs, rocky headlands and sandy beaches set against some of Scotland's most dramatic mountains, with Skye and the Western Isles on the horizon.

The little-visited **north coast** stretching from wind-lashed **Cape Wrath**, at the very northwest tip of the mainland, east to **John O'Groats** is even more rugged, with sheer cliffs and sand-filled bays bearing the brunt of frequently fierce Atlantic storms. The main settlement on this coast is **Thurso**, jumping-off point for the main ferry service to Orkney.

On the fertile **east coast**, stretching north from Inverness to the old herring port of **Wick**, green fields and woodland run down to the sweeping sandy beaches of the **Black Isle** and the **Cromarty** and **Dornoch firths**. This region is rich with historical sites, including the **Sutherland Monument** by Golspie, **Dornoch**'s fourteenth-century sandstone cathedral, and a number of places

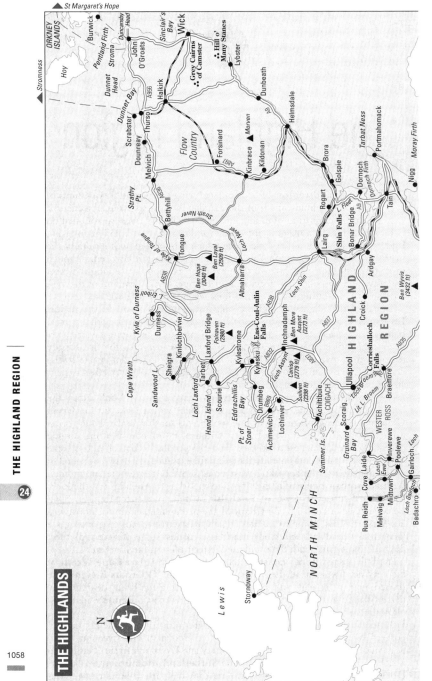

THE HIGHLANDS

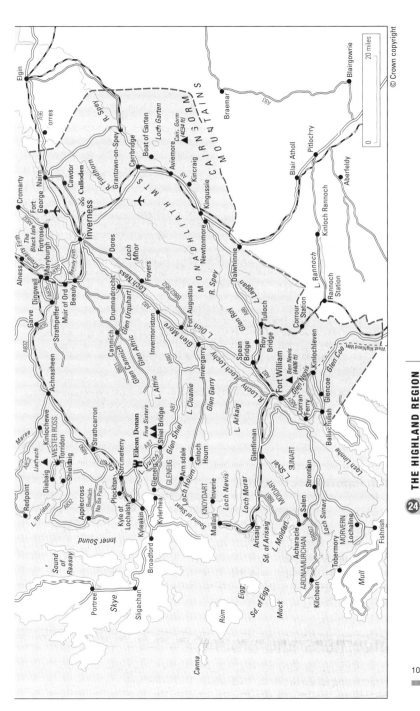

THE HIGHLAND REGION

24

The West Highland Railway

Scotland's most famous railway line, and a train journey counted by many as among the world's most scenic, is the brilliantly engineered **West Highland Railway**, running from Glasgow to Mallaig via Fort William. The line is in two sections: the southern part travels from **Glasgow** Queen Street station along the Clyde estuary and up Loch Long before switching to the banks of Loch Lomond on its way to **Crianlarich**, where the train divides with one section heading for Oban. After climbing around Beinn Odhar on a unique horseshoe-shaped loop of viaducts, the line traverses desolate **Rannoch Moor**, where the track had to be laid on a mattress of tree roots, brushwood and thousands of tons of earth and ashes. By this point the line has diverged from the road, and travels through country which can otherwise be reached only by long-distance footpaths. The train then swings into Glen Roy, passing through the dramatic **Monessie Gorge** and entering **Fort William** from the northeast.

The second leg of the journey, from Fort William to Mallaig, is arguably even more spectacular, and from June to mid-October one of the scheduled services is pulled by the **Jacobite Steam Train** (Mon–Fri, late July & Aug also Sun; departs Fort William 10.20am, departs Mallaig 2.10pm; day-return £26; book on ☎01463/239026; ⓦwww .steamtrain.info). Shortly after leaving Fort William the railway crosses the Caledonian Canal beside Neptune's Staircase by way of a swing bridge at **Benavie**, before travelling along the shores of Locheil and crossing the magnificent 21-arch viaduct at **Glenfinnan**, where the steam train, in its "Hogwarts Express" livery, was filmed for the *Harry Potter* movies. At Glenfinnan station there's a small **museum** dedicated to the history of the West Highland line, as well as two old railway carriages which have been converted into a restaurant and a bunkhouse (see p.1082). Not long afterwards the line reaches the coast, where there are unforgettable views of the Small Isles and Skye as it runs past the famous silver sands of **Morar** and up to **Mallaig**, where there are connections to the ferry which crosses to Armadale on Skye.

If you're planning on travelling the West Highland line, and in particular linking it to other train journeys (such as the similarly attractive route between Inverness and Kyle of Lochalsh), it's worth considering one of ScotRail's multiday **rover tickets**.

linked to the Clearances, a poignantly remembered chapter in the Highland story.

Transport practicalities

Unless you're prepared to spend weeks on the road, the Highlands are simply too vast to see in a single trip. Most visitors, therefore, base themselves in one or two areas, exploring the coast or hills on foot, and making longer hops across the interior by car or public transport. With a little forward planning you can see a surprising amount using **buses** and **trains**, especially if you fill in with **postbuses** (for which you can get timetables at most post offices, or see ⓦwww.postbus.royalmail.com). It's worth remembering, however, that on Sundays bus services are sporadic at best, and you may well find most shops and restaurants closed.

Inverness and around

Over one hundred miles from any other principal Scottish settlement and with a population of around 80,000, **Inverness** is the only city in the Highlands. A good base for day-trips and a jumping-off point for many of the more remote parts of the region, it is not a compelling place to stay for long and inevitably you are drawn to the attractions of sea and mountains beyond. The approach to the city on the A9 over the barren Monadhliath mountains from Perth and Aviemore provides a spectacular introduction to the district, with the **Great Glen** to the left, stretching southwestwards towards Fort William. To the north is the huge, rounded form of Ben Wyvis, whilst to the east lies the **Moray Firth**, whose lovely coastline boasts some of the region's best castles and historic sites, including the whimsical **Cawdor Castle**, featured in Shakespeare's *Macbeth*, and **Culloden**, site of the infamous battle and ensuing massacre that ended Bonnie Prince Charlie's uprising in 1746.

Inverness

Straddling a nexus of road and rail routes, **INVERNESS** is the busy and prosperous hub of the Highlands, and an inevitable port of call if you're exploring the region by public transport: **buses** and **trains** leave for communities right across the far north of Scotland. Though boasting few conventional sights, the city's setting on the banks of the River Ness is appealing.

Tours and cruises from Inverness

Inverness is the departure point for a range of day **tours** and **cruises** to nearby attractions, including Loch Ness and the Moray Firth.

City Sightseeing runs an open-topped double-decker **city tour** of **Inverness** (May–Sept daily every 45min; £5.50), which you can hop on and off all day. You can buy tickets on board, at the tourist office or at the office in the train station (May–Sept daily 9am–6pm).

For **Loch Ness cruises**, which typically incorporate a visit to a monster exhibition at Drumnadrochit and Urquhart Castle, try Jacobite Cruises (T01463/233999, W www.jacobite.co.uk): it runs a courtesy bus from the tourist office to its dock at Tomnahurich Canal Bridge on Glenurquhart Road, a mile and a half south of Inverness town centre. Alternatively, Discover Loch Ness tours (T01456/450168 or 0800/731 5565, W www.discoverlochness.com) combines an insightful introduction to the monster-hype with visits to places of geological or historical interest; while Loch Ness Express (T0800/328 6426) provides a daily ferry service from Dochgarroch at the eastern end of Loch Ness down to Fort Augustus (2hr 30min; £13 one way, £25 return): a free shuttle bus runs to Dochgarroch from Inverness tourist office.

Inverness is about the one place where transport connections allow you to embark on a major **grand tour** of the Highlands. It is possible to catch the early train to Kyle of Lochalsh, a bus onto Skye and across the island to catch the ferry to Mallaig, which meets the train to Fort William, from where you can take a bus back to Inverness, all in less than twelve hours.

For trips to the northwest, Dearman Coaches has a daily service (bikes accepted) to **Ullapool**, **Lochinver**, **Durness**, **Smoo Cave** and back, stopping at several hostels en route (April–Sept Mon–Sat, £21, six-day rover ticket £36).

Puffin Express (T01463/717181, W www.puffinexpress.co.uk) runs enjoyable day-trips to **John O'Groats**, with the chance to see puffins and visit prehistoric sites; it also offers a package which includes an overnight stop on **Orkney**. You can get to the islands and back on a gruelling full-day whistle-stop tour on the Orkney Bus, which leaves Inverness bus station every day during the summer (£46; advance bookings at the tourist office or on T01955/611353, W www.jogferry.co.uk).

See p.1066 for details of **dolphin-spotting** cruises on the Moray Firth.

24

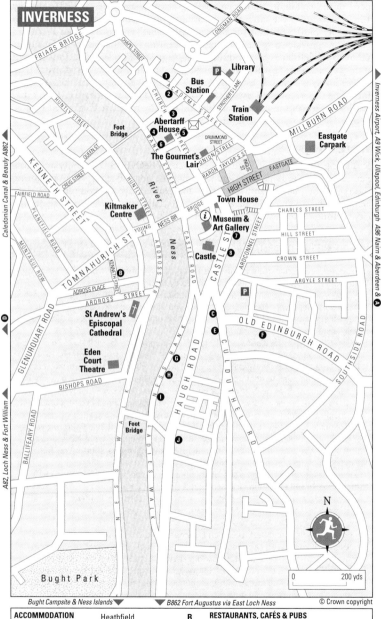

INVERNESS

A9 Wick, Ullapool & Edinburgh

FRIARS BRIDGE

LONGMAN ROAD

CHARLES STREET

ACADEMY STREET

Bus Station

Library

CHURCH STREET

STROTHER'S LANE

Train Station

Abertarff House

Foot Bridge

HUNTLY STREET

QUEEN ST.

CREIG STREET

FAIRFIELD ROAD

KENNETH STREET

DRUMMOND STREET

UNION STREET

BARON TAYLOR'S ST.

The Gourmet's Lair

MILLBURN ROAD

Eastgate Carpark

HIGH STREET

EASTGATE

INGLIS ST.

Kiltmaker Centre

BRIDGE STREET

Town House

Museum & Art Gallery

CHARLES STREET

HILL STREET

Castle

CASTLE STREET

CROWN STREET

ARDCONNEL STREET

ARGYLE STREET

PLANTEFIELD ROAD

MONTAGUE ROW

TOMNAHURICH ST.

YOUNG ST.

NESS BR.

ARDROSS TER.

Ness

River Ness

CASTLE ROAD

ADROSS PLACE

ARDROSS STREET

GLENURQUHART ROAD

St Andrew's Episcopal Cathedral

Eden Court Theatre

BISHOPS ROAD

BALLIFEARY ROAD

NESS BANK

NESS WALK

Foot Bridge

HAUGH ROAD

LADIES WALK

OLD EDINBURGH ROAD

SOUTHSIDE ROAD

CULDUTHEL RD.

N

Bught Park

0   200 yds

© Crown copyright

Caledonian Canal & Beauly A862

Inverness Airport, A9 Wick, Ullapool, Edinburgh, A96 Nairn & Aberdeen & A

A82, Loch Ness & Fort William

Bught Campsite & Ness Islands

B862 Fort Augustus via East Loch Ness

24

1062

Arrival, information and accommodation

Inverness **airport** (☎01667/464000) is at Dalcross, seven miles east of the city. The **bus station** (☎01463/233371) and **train station** (☎0845/748 4950) both lie just off Academy Street to the northeast of the centre. The **tourist office** (March–May Mon–Sat 9am–5pm; June–Aug Mon–Sat 9am–6pm, Sun 10am–4pm; Sept & Oct 9am–5pm, Sun 10am–4pm) is in an unsightly 1960s block on Castle Wynd, just five minutes' walk from the station. Inverness is one of the few places in the Highlands where you're unlikely to have problems finding **accommodation**, although in July and August you'll have to book ahead. Good places to look include both banks of the river south of the Ness Bridge, and Kenneth Street and its offshoots on the west side of the river.

Hotels and B&Bs

Brae Ness 17 Ness Bank ☎01463/712266, ⓦwww.braenesshotel.co.uk. A homely Georgian hotel with only ten rooms (all nonsmoking) overlooking the river and St Andrews Cathedral. May–Sept. ❺

Edenview 26 Ness Bank ☎01463/234397, ⓔedenview@clara.co.uk. Very pleasant B&B in a riverside location as good as that of the more expensive hotels, five minutes' walk from the centre. Nonsmoking. March–Oct. ❸

🏃 **Glenmoriston Town House Hotel** 20 Ness Bank ☎01463/223777, ⓦwww .glenmoriston.com. Classy and stylishly modern hotel harbouring a high-quality French restaurant, *Abstract*. ❼

The truth about tartan

To much of the world, **tartan** is synonymous with Scotland. It's the natural choice of packaging for Scottish exports from shortbread to Sean Connery, and when the Scottish football team travels abroad to play a fixture, the high-spirited "Tartan Army" of fans is never far behind.

Originally called **Helande**, the first form of tartan was a fine, hard and almost showerproof cloth spun in Highland villages from the wool of the native sheep, dyed with preparations of local plants and with patterns woven by artist-weavers. It was worn as a huge single piece of cloth, or **plaid**, which was belted around the waist and draped over the upper body, rather like a knee-length toga. The natural colours of old tartans were clear but soft, and the broken pattern gave superb camouflage, unlike modern versions, where garish, clashing colours are often used to create impact.

The myth-makers were about four centuries ahead of themselves in dressing up the warriors of the film *Braveheart* in plaid: in fact tartan did not become popular in the Lowlands until the beginning of the eighteenth century, when it was adopted as the anti-Union badge of the **Jacobites**. After Culloden, a ban on the wearing of tartan in the Highlands lasted some 25 years; in that time it became a fondly held emblem for emigrant Highlanders in the colonies and was incorporated into the uniforms of the new Highland regiments in the British Army. Then Sir Walter Scott set to work glamorizing the clans, dressing George IV in a kilt (and, just as controversially, flesh-coloured tights) for his visit to Edinburgh in 1822. By the time Queen Victoria set the royal seal of approval on both the Highlands and tartan with her extended annual holidays at Balmoral, the concept of tartan as formal dress rather than rough Highland wear was assured.

Scotsmen today will commonly wear the **kilt** for weddings and other formal occasions; properly made kilts, however – comprising some four yards of 100 percent wool – are likely to set you back £300 or more, with the rest of the regalia at least doubling that figure. If the contents of your sporran don't stretch that far, most places selling kilts will rent outfits on a daily basis. The best place to find better-quality material is a recognized Highland outfitter rather than a souvenir shop: in Inverness, try the Scottish Kiltmaker Centre at the Highland House of Fraser shop (see p.1064).

Inverness and around | THE HIGHLAND REGION

❷❹

1063

Heathfield 2 Kenneth St ☎01463/230547. A very comfortable and friendly place at the quiet end of a street packed with B&Bs. All rooms centrally heated and some are en suite. Nonsmoking. No credit cards. ❷

Ivybank Guest House 28 Old Edinburgh Rd ☎01463/232796, ⓦwww.ivybankguesthouse .com. A grand Georgian home just up the hill from the castle, with open fires and a lovely wooden interior. ❷

Moyness House 6 Bruce Gardens ☎01463/233836, ⓦwww.moyness.co.uk. Warm, welcoming, upmarket B&B on west side of Inverness, with original Victorian features and a nice walled garden. ❺

Riverview House 2 Moray Park, Island Bank Rd ☎01463/235557. A welcoming B&B in a characterful old house a little further down the river than some pricier guest houses, but still an easy stroll from the centre. ❸

Hostels

Bazpackers Top of Castle Street ☎01463/717663. The most cosy and relaxed of the city's hostels, with thirty beds including two double rooms and a twin (❶); some dorms are mixed (£12 per person). Has good views and a garden, which is used for barbecues, as well as the usual cooking facilities. Nonsmoking.

Inverness Student Hotel 8 Culduthel Rd ☎01463/236556, ⓦwww.scotlands-top-hostels .com. A busy 50-bed hostel (£13 per person) with the usual facilities and fine views over the river. Part of the MacBackpackers group, so expect minibus tours to pull in most days.

SYHA hostel Victoria Drive, off Millburn Road, about three-quarters of a mile east of the centre ☎0870/004 1127, ⓦwww.syha.org.uk. One of SYHA's flagship hostels, though hardly central: it's fully equipped with large kitchens and communal areas, eco-friendly facilities and ten four-bed family rooms among the 166-bed total (dorm beds £15).

The Town

The logical place to begin a tour of Inverness is the central **Town House** on the High Street. Built in 1878, this Gothic pile hosted Prime Minister Lloyd George's emergency meeting to discuss the Irish crisis in September 1921, and now houses council offices. Looming above the Town House and dominating the horizon is **Inverness Castle**, a predominantly nineteenth-century red-sandstone edifice perched picturesquely above the river. It houses the Sheriff Court and, in the summer and autumn months, the **Castle Garrison Encounter** (March–Oct Mon–Sat 10am–5pm; £6), an entertaining and noisy interactive exhibition in which the visitor plays the role of a new recruit in the eighteenth-century Hanoverian army. Around 7pm during the summer, a lone piper clad in full Highland garb performs for tourists on the castle esplanade.

Below the castle, the **Inverness Museum and Art Gallery** on Castle Wynd (Mon–Sat 9am–5pm; free; ⓦwww.invernessmuseum.com) gives a good general overview of the development of the Highlands. Informative sections on geology, geography and history occupy the ground floor, while upstairs you'll find a muddled selection of silver, taxidermy, weapons and bagpipes, alongside an art gallery that occasionally attracts worthwhile touring exhibitions.

Just across Ness Bridge from Bridge Street is the **Kiltmaker Centre** in the Highland House of Fraser shop (June–Sept Mon–Sat 9am–9pm, Sun 10am–5pm; Oct–May Mon–Sat 9am–5.30pm; £2). Entered through the factory shop, a small but imaginative visitor centre, complete with the outfits worn by actors for the *Braveheart* and *Rob Roy* blockbuster films, sets out everything you ever wanted to know about tartan.

Rising from the west bank directly opposite the castle, **St Andrews Episcopal Cathedral** was intended by its architects to be one of the grandest buildings in Scotland. However, funds ran out before the giant twin spires of the original design could be completed. The interior is pretty ordinary, too, though it does claim an unusual octagonal chapterhouse. Alongside the cathedral, **Eden Court Theatre** (ⓦwww.eden-court.co.uk) is currently closed for refurbishment, but is due to reopen in spring 2007 as Scotland's multi-arts centre. From here, you can wander a mile or so upriver to the peaceful **Ness Islands**, an attractive, informal public park linked by footbridges.

Eating, drinking and nightlife

Inverness has lots of eating places, including a few excellent-quality gourmet options. The best place for **picnic food** is The Gourmet's Lair, a well-stocked deli at 8 Union St. The liveliest **nightlife** revolves around the pubs and, on Friday and Saturday nights, the city's main nightclub, *Bakoo* on High Street. The far end of Academy Street has a cluster of good **pubs**; the public bar of the *Phoenix* is the most original town-centre place, though *Blackfriars* across the street has a better atmosphere with entertainment five nights a week, including ceilidhs. *Hootenanny's*, on Church Street, is a popular and lively pub, hosting lots of live gigs and ceilidhs.

Cafés and restaurants

Abstract *Glenmoriston Town House Hotel* 20 Ness Bank ☎01463/223777, ⊛www.abstractrestaurant .com. Best known for its appearance on the TV show *Ramsay's Kitchen Nightmares*, this award-winning French restaurant positively oozes style and chic. Closed Mon. Expensive.

Café 1 75 Castle St ☎01463/226200. Impressive contemporary Scottish cooking using good local ingredients in a bistro-style setting. Closed Sun. Moderate–expensive.

The Mustard Seed 16 Fraser St ☎01463/220220. The most stylish place in town for an informal meal – an airy converted church with stone walls, smart table settings and an upbeat approach, serving Scottish and European-influenced cuisine and a range of light,

bistro-style dishes. Mouthwatering daily specials. Despite the wow factor, it's reasonably priced. Moderate.

The Red Pepper 74 Church St. Linked to *The Mustard Seed*, this is the city's hip coffee-bar hangout with lots of freshly made sandwiches. Takeaway available. Inexpensive.

River Café and Restaurant 10 Bank St ☎01463/714884. Healthy wholefood lunches, great high-tea with freshly baked cakes, and tasty evening meals. Inexpensive–moderate.

La Tortilla Asesina 99 Castle St ☎01463/709809. Simple but lively tapas restaurant, serving all the old favourites as well as some "tartan tapas" using mostly local ingredients. Moderate.

Listings

Bike rental Highland Cycles, 16a Telford St ☎01463/234789 (8.30am–5.30pm).

Book shops Leakey's is located in a former church on Church Street and filled with almost 100,000 secondhand books and a cosy café. Great spot to browse with a warming wood stove in winter (Mon–Sat 10am–4.30pm). There's also Waterstones at 50–52 High St.

Car rental Budget is on Railway Terrace, behind the train station ☎01463/713333; Europcar has an office on Telfer Street ☎01463/235337; Focus Vehicle Rental is at Shore Street ☎01463/709517; Aberdeen 4x4 Self-Drive is at 15b Harbour Rd ☎01463/871083; and Sharps Reliable Wrecks is based at Inverness train station, Academy Street ☎01463/236684, as well as the airport.

Cinemas With the Eden Court Theatre undergoing refurbishment, head for the seven-screen Warner Village complex (☎0870/240 6020), on the A96 Nairn road about two miles from town centre.

Hospital Raigmore Hospital (☎01463/704000) on the southeastern outskirts of town close to the A9.

Internet Highland libraries provide 30min free Internet access. There are also terminals in the tourist office and at Mailbox Etc outside the railway station.

Post office 14–16 Queensgate (Mon–Sat 9am–5.30pm; ☎0845/722 3344); also noon–5pm at Tesco's.

Taxis Inverness Taxis ☎01463/220222; Tartan Taxis ☎01463/233033.

Culloden

Five miles east of Inverness, the windswept moorland of **CULLODEN** (site open all year, free), witnessed the last ever battle on British soil when, on April

16, 1746, the Jacobite cause was finally subdued – a turning point in the history of the Scottish nation.

The second Jacobite rebellion had begun on August 19, 1745, with the raising of the Stuarts' standard at **Glenfinnan** on the west coast (see p.1082). Shortly after, Edinburgh fell into Jacobite hands, and Bonnie Prince Charlie began his march on London. The English had appointed the ambitious young Duke of Cumberland to command their forces, and his pursuit, together with bad weather and lack of funds, eventually forced the Jacobites to retreat north. They ended up at Culloden, where, ill-fed and exhausted, they were hopelessly outnumbered by the English. The open, flat ground of Culloden Moor was totally unsuitable for the Highlanders' style of courageous but undisciplined fighting, which needed steep hills and lots of cover to provide the element of surprise, and they were routed. After the battle, in which 1500 Highlanders were slaughtered (many of them as they lay wounded on the battlefield), Bonnie Prince Charlie fled west to the hills and islands. He eventually escaped to France, leaving his erstwhile supporters to their fate – the clans were disarmed, the wearing of tartan and playing of bagpipes forbidden, and the chiefs became landlords greedy for higher and higher rents. Within a century, the Highland way of life had changed out of all recognition.

Today you can walk freely around the battle site; flags show the positions of the two armies, and **clan graves** are marked by simple headstones. The **visitor centre** (daily: Feb, March, Nov & Dec 11am–4pm; April & May 9am–5.30pm; June–Aug 9am–6pm; Sept & Oct 9am–5.30pm; £5; NTS) provides background information through detailed displays and a film show, as well as a short play set on the day of the battle presented by local actors (June–Sept only; included in

24

The dolphins of the Moray Firth

The **Moray Firth**, a great wedge-shaped bay forming the eastern coastline of the Highlands, is one of only three areas of UK waters that supports a resident population of **dolphins**. Over a hundred of these beautiful, intelligent marine mammals live in the estuary, the most northerly breeding ground for this particular species – the bottle-nosed dolphin (*Tursiops truncatus*) – in Europe, and you stand a good chance of spotting a few, either from the shore or a boat.

One of the best places to look for them is **Chanonry Point**, on the Black Isle (see p.1099) – a spit of sand protruding into a narrow, deep channel, where converging currents bring fish close to the surface, and thus the dolphins close to shore; a rising tide is the most likely time to see them. **Kessock Bridge**, one mile north of Inverness, is another prime dolphin-spotting location. You can go all the way down to the beach at the small village of North Kessock, underneath the road bridge, where there's a decent place to have a drink at the pub in the *North Kessock Hotel*, or you can stop above the village in a car park just off the A9 at the Dolphin Visitor Centre and listening post (June–Oct 9.30am–4.30pm; free). Set up by a team of zoologists from Aberdeen University, the centre has hydrophones that allow you to eavesdrop on the clicks and whistles of the dolphins' underwater conversations.

Several companies run dolphin-spotting **boat trips** around the Moray Firth from £10 for one hour. Operators currently accredited by the Dolphin Space Programme (see ⓦwww.morayfirth-partnership.org and ⓦwww.wdcs.org) include Phoenix, based in Nairn (℗01667/456078), Moray Firth Cruises, Inverness (℗01463/717900), and the WDCS Wildlife Centre, Spey Bay (℗01343/820339). Also, on the Black Isle, on the northern side of the Firth, try Dolphin Trips Avoch (℗01381/622383, ⓦwww .dolphintripsavoch.co.uk) or Ecoventures, Cromarty (℗01381/600323, ⓦwww .ecoventures.co.uk).

admission fee), or you can take the evocative hour-long guided **walking tour** (June–Sept 4 daily 10.30am–3pm; £4).

Fort George

Eight miles or so of undulating coastal farmland separate Culloden from **Fort George** (daily: April–Sept 9.30am–6.30pm; Oct–March 9.30am–4.30pm; £6; HS), an old Hanoverian bastion with walls a mile long, considered by military architectural historians to be one of the finest fortifications in Europe. Crowning a sandy spit that juts into the middle of the Moray Firth, it was built between 1747 and 1769 as a base for George II's army, in case the Highlanders should attempt to rekindle the Jacobite flame. By the time of its completion, however, the uprising had been firmly quashed and the fort has been used ever since as a barracks.

Apart from the sweeping panoramic views across the Firth from its ramparts, the main incentive to visit Fort George is the **Regimental Museum** of the Queen's Own Highlanders. Displayed in polished glass cases is a predictable array of regimental silver, coins, moth-eaten uniforms and medals, along with some macabre war trophies, ranging from blood-stained nineteenth-century Sudanese battle robes to Iraqi gas masks gleaned in the First Gulf War. Walking on the northern, grass-covered casemates, which look out into the estuary, you may be lucky enough to see the school of bottle-nosed **dolphins** (see above) swimming in with the tide.

The Cairngorms and Strathspey

Rising high in the heather-clad hills above remote Loch Laggan, forty miles due south of Inverness, the **River Spey**, Scotland's second longest river, drains northeast towards the Moray Firth through one of the Highlands' most spellbinding valleys. Famous for its ancient forests, salmon fishing and ospreys, the area around the upper section of the river, known as **Strathspey**, is dominated by the sculpted **Cairngorms**, Britain's most extensive mountain massif, unique in supporting subarctic tundra on its high plateau. Though the area has been admired and treasured for many years as one of Scotland's prime natural assets, the Cairngorms National Park was declared only in 2004, and even then with grumblings from conservationists about inadequate planning regulations and unnatural boundaries. Outdoor enthusiasts flock to the area to take advantage of the superb hiking, water sports and winter snows, aided by the fact that the area is easily accessible by road and rail from both the Central Belt and Inverness. A string of villages along the river provide useful bases for setting out into the wilder country, principal among them **Aviemore**, a rather ugly straggle of housing and hotel developments which nevertheless has a lively, youthful feel to it. Rather unusually for Scotland, the area boasts a wide choice of good-quality accommodation, particularly in the budget market, with various easy-going hostels run by and for outdoor enthusiasts.

Note that Strathspey is distinct from Speyside, located further downstream to the north and famous for its whiskies, which is described on p.1048.

Aviemore and around

The once-sleepy village of **AVIEMORE** was first developed as a ski and tourism resort in the mid-1960s and, over the years, it fell victim to profiteering

Cairngorms National Park

Britain's biggest national park, the **Cairngorms National Park** (Ⓦ www.cairngorms
.co.uk) covers some 1500 square miles and incorporates the **Cairngorms massif**,
the UK's largest mountainscape and only sizeable plateau over 2500ft. While Aviemore and the surrounding area is the main point of entry, particularly for those planning outdoor activities, it's also possible to access the eastern side of the park from
both Deeside and Donside in Aberdeenshire (see p.1046).

The name Cairngorm comes from the Gaelic *An Carm Gorm*, meaning "the blue
hill" after the blueish-tinged stones found in the area, and within the park there are
52 summits over 2953ft, as well as a quarter of Scotland's native woodland, and a
quarter of the UK's threatened wildlife species. The conservation of the landscape's
unique flora and fauna is, of course, one of the principal reasons national-park status
was conferred. However, an important role for the park is to incorporate the communities living within it and integrate the array of outdoor activities enjoyed by visitors.

Vegetation in the area ranges from one of the largest tracts of ancient **Caledonian
pine and birch forest** remaining in Scotland, at Rothiemurchus, to subarctic tundra
on the high plateau, where **alpine flora** such as starry saxifrage and the star-shaped
pink flowers of moss campion peek out of the pink granite in the few months of
summer that the ground is free of snow. **Birds of prey** you're most likely to see are
the **osprey**, best seen at Loch Garten's osprey observation centre (see p.1070), or
fishing on the lochs around Aviemore, though golden eagles and peregrine falcons
can occasionally be seen higher up.

---

developers with scant regard for the needs of the local community. Although a
large-scale face-lift has removed some of the architectural eyesores of that era,
the settlement remains dominated by a string of soulless shopping centres and
sprawling housing estates surrounding a Victorian railway station. That said,
Aviemore is well-equipped with services and facilities for visitors, and is the
most convenient base for the Cairngorms, benefits which for most folk far
outweigh its lack of aesthetic appeal.

Summer activities

In summer, the main activities around Aviemore are **walking** (see box on
p.1069) and **water sports**. Two centres offer sailing, windsurfing and canoeing including equipment rental and tuition: the Loch Morlich Watersports
Centre (☎01479/861221, Ⓦ www.lochmorlich.com) is five miles or so east
of Aviemore on the way to Cairn Gorm mountain, in a lovely setting with a
sandy beach; while the Loch Insh Watersports Centre is six miles up-valley near
Kincraig, in equally beautiful surroundings.

The area is also great for **mountain biking**, with both Rothiemurchus and
Glenmore estates providing waymarked routes. The Rothiemurchus Visitor
Centre at Inverdruie has route maps, and you can also rent bikes here from
Bothy Bikes (☎01479/810111, Ⓦ www.bothybikes.co.uk), who have another
shop in the Aviemore Shopping Centre beside the train station on Grampian
Road.

Winter activities

Scottish **skiing** on a commercial level first really took off in Aviemore. By
continental European and North American standards it's all on a tiny scale, but
occasionally snow, sun and lack of crowds coincide and you can have a great day.
February and March are usually the best times, but there's a chance of decent
snow at any time between mid-November and April. Lots of places – not just

Ordnance Survey Explorer Maps nos. 402 & 403 or OS Outdoor Leisure Map no. 3.

Walking of all grades is a highlight of the Aviemore area, though before setting out you should heed the usual safety guidelines. These are particularly important if you want to climb to the high tops, which include a number of Scotland's loftiest peaks. However, as well as the high mountain trails, there are some lovely and well-signposted **low-level walks** in the area. It takes an hour or so to complete the gentle circular walk around pretty **Loch an Eilean** (with its ruined castle) in the Rothiemurchus Estate, beginning at the end of the back road that turns east off the B970 two miles south of Aviemore. The helpful estate **visitor centres** at the lochside and by the roadside at Inverdruie provide more information on the many woodland trails that crisscross this area. A longer 2–3hr walk through this estate, famous for its atmospheric native woodland of gnarled Caledonian pines and shimmering birch trees, starts at the near end of **Loch Morlich**.

Another good shortish (half-day) walk leads along a well-surfaced forestry track from Glenmore Lodge up towards the **Ryvoan Pass**, taking in An Lochan Uaine, known as the "Green Loch" because of its amazing colours that range from turquoise to slate grey depending on the weather. The **Glenmore Forest Park Visitor Centre** by the roadside at the turn-off to Glenmore Lodge is the starting point for the three-hour round-trip climb of Meall a' Bhuachaillie (2654ft), which offers excellent views and is usually accessible year-round. The centre has information on other trails in this section of the forest.

The **Speyside Way** (see p.1049), the long-distance footpath which begins on the Moray Firth coast at Buckie and follows the course of the Spey through the heart of whisky country, now extends to Aviemore, with plans for further links down to Kingussie and Newtonmore. A pleasant day-trip involves walking the way from Aviemore to Boat of Garten, on to the RSPB osprey sanctuary at Loch Garten, and then returning on the **Strathspey Steam Railway** (June–Sept 5 daily; less regular service at other times; ☎01479/810725, ⒲www.strathspeyrailway.co.uk for details).

in Aviemore itself – sell or rent equipment; for a rundown of ski schools and rental facilities in the area, check out the tourist office's *Ski Scotland* brochure or visit ⒲ski.visitscotland.com.

The **Cairngorm Ski Area**, about eight miles southeast of Aviemore, above Loch Morlich in Glenmore Forest Park, is well served in winter by buses from Aviemore. You can rent skis, boards and other equipment from the Day Lodge at the foot of the ski area (☎01479/861261, ⒲www .cairngormmountain.com), which also has a shop, a bar and restaurant, as well as the base station for the **funicular railway**, the principal means of getting to the top of the ski slopes. The facilities include a ski school, cafés at three different levels and a separate terrain park for skiers and boarders. If there's lots of snow, the area around **Loch Morlich** and into the **Rothiemurchus Estate** provides enjoyable cross-country skiing through lovely woods, beside rushing burns and even over frozen lochs.

Practicalities

Aviemore's businesslike **tourist office** is in the heart of things at 7 The Parade, Grampian Road (April–Oct Mon–Sat 9am–5pm, Sun 10am–4pm; Nov–March Mon–Fri 9am–5pm, Sat 10am–4pm). There's no shortage of **accommodation** locally. *Ravenscraig Guest House* (☎01479/810278, ⒲www.aviemoreonline.com; ❸), on the Grampian Road, has twelve rooms and is welcoming and family-friendly, while *Ardlogie Guest House* on Dalfaber Road (☎01479/810747,

ⓦwww.ardlogie.co.uk; ❸) is smaller and slightly cheaper. Alternatively, try the secluded and upmarket *Corrour House Hotel* at Inverdruie, two miles southeast of Aviemore (☎01479/810220, ⓦwww.corrourhousehotel.co.uk; ❺). Aviemore's large SYHA **hostel** (☎0870/004 1104, ⓦwww.syha.org.uk; dorm beds £11) is well placed within walking distance of the centre of the village, while the *Aviemore Bunkhouse* (☎01479/811181, ⓦwww.aviemore-bunkhouse.com; dorm beds £14) is a large, modern place beside the *Old Bridge Inn* on Dalfaber Road, again within walking distance from the station. Towards the Cairngorms, there's another SYHA hostel at Loch Morlich (Christmas–Oct; ☎0870/004 1137), as well as excellent accommodation in twin rooms (with shared facilities) just up the road at *Glenmore Lodge* (☎01479/861256, ⓦwww.glenmorelodge.org.uk; ❷) – full use of their superb facilities, which include a pool, weights room and indoor climbing-wall, is included.

All along Aviemore's main drag are bistros, hotels and takeaways serving fairly predictable, run-of-the-mill **food**. One exception is the 🍴 *Mountain Café* (☎01479/812473), above Cairngorm Mountain Sports, which serves an all-day menu of wholesome snacks and freshly prepared meals, often using local produce. Alternatively, *The Old Bridge Inn* on the east side of the railway on Dalfaber Road, dishes up decent pub grub and real ales in a mellow, cosy setting, while *Café Mambo*, in Aviemore Shopping Centre on Grampian Road, matches its bright, funky decor with a cheerful burger'n'chips-style menu.

Cairn Gorm mountain

From Aviemore, a road leads past Rothiemurchus and Loch Morlich and winds its way up into the Cairngorms, reaching the Coire Cas car park at a height of 2150ft. Here is the base station for the ski area with a **ranger office** (daily: April–Oct 9am–5pm; Nov–March 8.30am–4.30pm) where you can find out about the area's various trails. It's also the departure point for the **Cairn Gorm Mountain Railway** (daily 10am–5.15pm; last train up 4.30pm; trains run every 15min; £8.50; ⓦwww.cairngormmountain.com), a two-car funicular railway that whisks skiers in winter, and tourists at any time of year, along a mile and a half of track to the top station at an altitude of 3600ft, not far from the summit of Cairn Gorm mountain.

Loch Garten and around

The **Abernethy Forest RSPB Reserve** on the shore of **LOCH GARTEN**, seven miles northeast of Aviemore and eight miles south of Grantown-on-Spey, is famous as the nesting site of one of Britain's rarest birds. A little over fifty years ago, the **osprey**, known in North America as the fish hawk, had completely disappeared from the British Isles. Then, in 1954, a single pair of these exquisite white-and-brown raptors mysteriously reappeared and built a nest in a tree half a mile or so from the loch. Thereafter the area became the centre of an effective high-security operation, though now the birds are well established not only here but elsewhere across the Highlands. The best time to visit is between April and August, when the RSPB opens an **observation centre** (daily 10am–6pm; £3.50; ☎01479/821409), complete with powerful telescopes and CCTV monitoring of the nest. This is the place to get a glimpse of osprey chicks in their nest; you'll be luckier to see the birds perform their trademark swoop over water to pluck a fish out with their talons. The reserve is also home to several other species of rare birds and animals, including the Scottish crossbill, capercaillie, whooper swan and red squirrel; once-weekly **guided walks** leave from the observation centre (Wed 9.30am).

Loch Garten is about a mile and a half west of **BOAT OF GARTEN** village, which has a number of good **accommodation** options: *Fraoch Lodge*, 15 Deshar Rd (T01479/831331, Wwww.scotmountain.co.uk; ❶), is an excellent hostel with four twin rooms and a family room that sleeps four, while the ✱ *Old Ferryman's House* (T01479/831370; ❷), just across the Spey, is a wonderfully homely, hospitable B&B, with no TV, lots of books, and delicious evening meals and breakfasts.

Newtonmore and Kingussie

Twelve miles southwest of Aviemore, close neighbours **NEWTONMORE** and **KINGUSSIE** (pronounced "king-*yoos*-ee") are pleasant villages at the head of the Strathspey valley separated by a couple of miles of farmland. On the **shinty** field, however, their peaceful coexistence is forgotten and the two become bitter rivals; in recent years Kingussie has been the dominant force in the game, a fierce, home-grown relative of hockey (Wwww .shinty.com). The chief attraction hereabouts is the excellent **Highland Folk Museum** (T01540/661307, Wwww.highlandfolk.com), split between complementary sites in the two towns. The Kingussie section (April–Sept Mon–Sat 9.30am–5pm; Oct Mon–Fri 9.30am–4pm; Nov–March by appointment; guided tours on the hour; £2.50) contains an absorbing collection of artefacts typical of the traditional Highland ways of life. The larger outdoor site at Newtonmore (April–Aug daily 10.30am–5.30pm; Sept daily 11am–4.30pm; Oct Mon–Fri 11am–4.30pm; £5, or £6 for both sites), tries to create more of a living history museum, with a vintage bus offering a jump-on/jump-off tour round reconstructions of a working croft, a water-powered sawmill, a church where recitals on traditional Highland instruments are given, and a small village of blackhouses constructed using only authentic tools and materials.

Kingussie is also notable for the ruins of **Ruthven Barracks** (free access), standing east across the river on a hillock. The best-preserved garrison built to pacify the Highlands after the 1715 rebellion, it makes for great exploring by day and is impressively floodlit at night.

The Great Glen

The **Great Glen**, a major geological fault line cutting diagonally across the Highlands from Fort William to Inverness, is the defining geographic feature of the north of Scotland. A huge rift valley was formed when the northwestern and southeastern sides of the fault slid in opposite directions for more than sixty miles, while the present landscape was shaped by glaciers that retreated only around 8000 BC. The glen is impressive more for its sheer scale than its beauty, but the imposing barrier of loch and mountain means that no one can travel into the northern Highlands without passing through it. With the two major service centres of the Highlands at either end it makes an obvious and rewarding route between the west and east coasts.

Of the Great Glen's four elongated lochs, the most famous is **Loch Ness**, home to the mythical monster; lochs **Oich**, **Lochy** and **Linnhe** (the last of these a sea loch) are less renowned though no less attractive. All four are linked by the Caledonian Canal. The southwestern end of the Great Glen is dominated by **Fort William**, the second-largest town in the Highland region. Situated at the heart of the Lochaber area, it's a useful base with plenty of places to stay and eat, and an excellent hub for accessing a host of outdoor activities. Dominating the scene to the south is **Ben Nevis**, Britain's highest peak, best approached from scenic Glen Nevis. The most famous glen of all, **Glen Coe**, lies on the main A82 road half an hour's drive south of Fort William. Nowadays the whole area is unashamedly given over to tourism, and Fort William is swamped by bus tours throughout the summer, but, as ever in the Highlands, within a thirty-minute drive you can be totally alone.

Loch Ness and around

Twenty-three miles long, unfathomably deep, cold and often moody, **Loch Ness** is bounded by rugged heather-clad mountains rising steeply from a wooded shoreline with attractive glens opening up on either side. Its fame, however, is based overwhelmingly on its legendary inhabitant Nessie, the "Loch Ness monster", who ensures a steady flow of hopeful visitors to the settlements dotted along the loch, in particular **Drumnadrochit**. Nearby, the impressive ruins of **Castle Urquhart** – a favourite monster-spotting location – perch atop a rock on the lochside and attract a deluge of bus parties during the summer. Almost as busy in high season is the village of **Fort Augustus**, at the more scenic south-west tip of Loch Ness, where you can watch queues of boats tackling one of the Caledonian Canal's longest flights of locks.

Nessie

The world-famous **Loch Ness monster**, affectionately known as **Nessie** (and by serious aficionados as *Nessiteras rhombopteryx*), has been a local celebrity for some time. The first mention of a mystery creature crops up in St Adamnan's seventh-century biography of **St Columba**, who allegedly calmed an aquatic animal which had attacked one of his monks. Present-day interest, however, is probably greater outside Scotland than within the country, and dates from the building of the road along the loch's western shore in the early 1930s. In 1934, the *Daily Mail* published London surgeon R.K. Wilson's sensational photograph of the head and neck of the monster peering up out of the loch, and the hype has hardly diminished since. Recent encounters range from glimpses of ripples by anglers to the famous occasion in 1961 when thirty hotel guests saw a pair of humps break the water's surface and cruise for about half a mile before submerging.

Photographic evidence is showcased in the two "Monster Exhibitions" at Drumnadrochit, but the most impressive of these exhibits – including the renowned black-and-white movie footage of Nessie's humps moving across the water, and Wilson's original head and shoulders shot – have now been exposed as fakes. Indeed, in few other places on earth has watching a rather lifeless and often grey expanse of water seemed so compelling, or have floating logs, otters and boat wakes been photographed so often and with such excitement. Yet while even high-tech sonar surveys carried out over the past two decades have failed to come up with conclusive evidence, it's hard to dismiss Nessie as pure myth. After all, no one yet knows where the unknown layers of silt and mud at the bottom of the loch begin and end: best estimates say the loch is over 750 feet deep, deeper than much of the North Sea, while others point to the possibilities of underwater caves and undiscovered channels connected to the sea. With the possibility of a definitive answer sending shivers through the local tourist industry, monster-hunters are these days recruited over the web: Ⓦwww.lochness.co.uk offers round-the-clock **webcams** for views across the loch, while Ⓦwww.lochnessinvestigation.org is packed with research information.

Drumnadrochit

Situated above a verdant, sheltered bay of Loch Ness fifteen miles southwest of Inverness, **DRUMNADROCHIT** is the southern gateway to remote Glen Affric and the epicentre of Nessie-hype complete with a rash of tacky souvenir shops and two rival monster exhibitions. Of the pair, the **Loch Ness 2000 Exhibition** (daily: Easter–May 9.30am–5pm; June & Sept 9am–6pm; July & Aug 9am–8pm; Oct–Easter 10am–3.30pm; £5.95), though more expensive, is the better bet, offering an in-depth rundown of eyewitness accounts and information on various research projects that have attempted to shed further light on the mysteries of the loch. The **Original Loch Ness Monster Visitor Centre and Lodge Hotel** (daily: July & Aug 9am–9pm; Sept–June 9am–4/5pm; £5) has a less impressive exhibition, though it's worth stopping for the delicious array of home-baking offered at the adjacent comfortable **hotel** (☎01456/450429, ⓦwww.lochness-hotel.com; ❺), and to go in search of the resident ghost within its tartan interior.

Both centres run **cruises** on the loch: Deep Scan Cruises is at the Loch Ness 2000 Exhibition (Easter to mid-Oct hourly; 1hr; £10; ☎01456/450218), while the *Nessie Hunter* (hourly: Easter–Sept 9am–6pm; Oct–Dec 10am–3pm; 50min; £10; ☎01456/450395) can be booked at the Original Loch Ness Monster Visitor Centre. A more relaxing alternative is to head out **fishing** with a local gillie – the boat costs around £20 each (flexible) based on a group of four for two hours: contact Bruce (Easter–Sept; ☎01456/450279).

Most photographs allegedly showing the monster have been taken a couple of miles east of Drumnadrochit, around the thirteenth-century ruined lochside **Castle Urquhart** (daily: April–Sept 9.30am–6.30pm; Oct–March 9.30am–4.30pm; £6; HS). It's one of Scotland's classic picture-postcard ruins, crawling with tourists by day but particularly splendid floodlit at night when all the crowds have gone.

Drumnadrochit's **tourist office** (April–June & Oct Mon–Sat 9am–5pm; July & Aug Mon–Sat 9am–6pm, Sun 10am–4pm; Sept Mon–Sat 9am–5pm, Sun 10am–4pm; Nov–March Mon–Fri 10am–1.30pm; ☎01456/459076) is in the middle of the main car park in the village. Between here and Urquhart Castle, *Gillyflowers* (☎01456/450641, ⓦwww.cali.co.ukFreewayGillyflowers; ❷) is a very welcoming **B&B** in a renovated 1780s farmhouse, while **hotels** include the friendly and secluded *Benleva* in the Lewiston area of the village (☎01456/450080, ⓦwww.benleva.co.uk; ❹), and the relaxed country-house hotel, *Polmaily House*, three miles up the Glen Urquhart road (☎01456/450343, ⓦwww.polmaily.co.uk; ❼). For **hostel** beds (£12.50 per person), there's the immaculate and friendly *Loch Ness Backpackers Lodge* in Lewiston (☎01456/450807, ⓦwww.lochness-backpackers.com).

Most of the hotels in the area – the *Benleva* in particular – serve good bar **food**; in Drumnadrochit the *Glen Café* on the village green has a short and simple menu with basic grills, while the slightly more upmarket *Fiddlers' Café Bar* next door offers local steaks, salmon and hearty lunches

Glen Affric

Due west of Drumnadrochit is a vast area of high peaks, remote glens and few roads which includes **Glen Affric**, generally held as one of Scotland's most beautiful landscapes and heaven for walkers, climbers and mountain-bikers. The approach to the glen is through the small settlement of **CANNICH**, fourteen miles west of Drumnadrochit on the A831. A quiet, uninspiring village, Cannich has an excellent **campsite** (☎01456/415364) where mountain bikes can be rented, as well as the friendly *Glen Affric Backpackers Hostel* (☎01456/415263,

@www.glenaffric.org; all beds £10) which offers inexpensive twin or four-bed rooms.

Hemmed in by a string of Munros, Glen Affric is great for picnics and pottering, particularly on a calm and sunny day, when the still water reflects the islands and surrounding hills. From the car park at the head of the single-track road along the glen, ten miles southwest of Cannich, there's a selection of **walks**: the trip around Loch Affric will take you a good five hours but captures the glen, its wildlife and Caledonian pine and birch woods in all their remote splendour.

Fort Augustus

FORT AUGUSTUS, a tiny, busy village at the scenic southwestern tip of Loch Ness, was named after George II's son, the chubby lad who later became the "Butcher" Duke of Cumberland of Culloden fame; today, the village is dominated by comings and goings along the Caledonian Canal, which leaves Loch Ness here. In the small **Caledonian Canal Heritage Centre** (July–Sept daily 10am–5pm; free), in Ardchattan House on the northern bank of the canal, you can view old photos and records about the history of the canal and watch a black-and-white film of the days when paddle boats and large barges passed through the locks every day. **Boat trips** leave from the swing bridge, with the new *Loch Ness Express* (Easter–Oct daily; one way 80min, £13; return 2hr 30min, £25; ☏0800/3286426, @www.lochnessexpress.com) which runs up the length of Loch Ness and carries bikes for free, or with *Cruise Loch Ness* (March–Nov daily; 1hr; £8; ☏01320/366277, @www.cruiselochness.com).

Fort Augustus's helpful **tourist office** (daily: April–May 10am–5pm; June & Sept 9am–5pm; July & Aug 9am–6pm; Oct 10am–4.30pm; ☏01320/366779) hands out useful free walking leaflets. There's **hostel** accommodation at *Morag's Lodge* to the east of the village (☏01320/366289; dorm beds £13.50) and at the well-equipped, thirty-bed *Stravaigers Lodge* (☏01320/366257; dorm beds £15) on Glendoe Road. The *Old Pier* (☏01320/366418, ✉jenny@oldpierhouse.com; ❹) is a particularly appealing **B&B** right on the loch at the north side of the village, with two roaring log fires and the option of renting two-person Canadian canoes (£10 per day) and horse riding (min £50 for two people) in the mountains. The best place to **rent bikes** or **water–sports** equipment, including boats and canoes, is from Monster Activities (☏01809/501340, @www.monsteractivities.com) at South Laggan, eight miles southwest at the head of Loch Lochy.

Fort William

With its stunning position on Loch Linnhe, tucked in below the snow-streaked bulk of Ben Nevis, **FORT WILLIAM** (known by the many walkers and climbers that come here as "Fort Bill"), should be a gem. Sadly, the same lack of taste that nearly saw the town renamed "Abernevis" in the 1950s is evident in the ribbon bungalow development and ill-advised dual carriageway – complete with grubby pedestrian underpass – which have wrecked the waterfront. The main street and the little squares off it are more appealing, though occupied by some decidedly tacky tourist gift shops. Ultimately, however, Fort William is an important regional centre, with facilities including a cinema, swimming pool and a large supermarket.

Practicalities

The busy **tourist office** is on Cameron Square, just off High Street (April, May & Sept Mon–Sat 9am–5pm, Sun 10am–4pm; June–Aug Mon–Sat 9am–6pm,

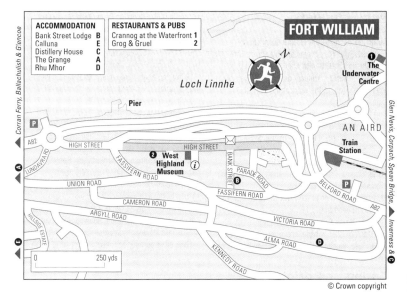

ACCOMMODATION
Bank Street Lodge **B**
Calluna **E**
Distillery House **C**
The Grange **A**
Rhu Mhor **D**

RESTAURANTS & PUBS
Crannog at the Waterfront **1**
Grog & Gruel **2**

FORT WILLIAM

Loch Linnhe

The Underwater Centre

Pier

AN AIRD

HIGH STREET

HIGH STREET

Train Station

West Highland Museum

PARADE ROAD

BANK STREET

BELFORD ROAD

UNION ROAD

FASSIFERN ROAD

FASSIFERN ROAD

CAMERON ROAD

ARGYLL ROAD

VICTORIA ROAD

ALMA ROAD

KENNEDY ROAD

HILLSIDE ESTATE

A82

LUNDAVRA RD

0   250 yds

© Crown copyright

Corran Ferry, Ballachulish & Glencoe

Glen Nevis, Corpach, Spean Bridge

Inverness &

Sun 10am–4pm; Oct Mon–Fri 10am–5pm, Sat 10am–4pm, Sun 10am–2pm; Nov–March Mon–Fri 10am–5pm, Sat 10am–4pm; ☎01397/703781, ⓦwww.visithighlands.com). High-spec **mountain bikes** are available for rent at Off Beat Bikes, 117 High St (☎01397/704008, ⓦwww.offbeatbikes.co.uk); they know the best routes, issue free maps and also have a branch at the Nevis Range gondola base station (June–Sept; ☎01397/705825), with forest rides and an annual World Cup downhill mountain-bike event in September. The Underwater Centre (☎01397/703786, ⓦwww.theunderwatercentre.co.uk), at the water's edge beyond the train station and Morrison's supermarket, runs PADI courses and offers guided **dives**. Local **mountain guides** include Alan Kimber of *Calluna* (see below), or contact the Snowgoose Mountain Centre (☎01397/772467, ⓦwww.highland-mountain-guides.co.uk), at the *Smiddy Bunkhouse and Blacksmiths Lodge* (see p.1076), which also offers instruction and residential courses on activities such as hill-walking, mountaineering and canoeing.

Accommodation in town

Bank Street Lodge Bank Street ☎01397/700070, ⓦwww.bankstreetlodge.co.uk. A 43-bed centrally located lodge-cum-hostel that's handy for transport and the town centre; dorm beds from £11.
Calluna Heathercroft, Connachie Road ☎01397/700451, ⓦwww.fortwilliamholiday.co.uk or westcoast-mountainguides.co.uk. Well-run self-catering and hostel accommodation for individual, family and group stays. Free pick-up from town is available. Owner is one of the area's top mountain guides, so there's plenty of outdoor advice available; dorm beds from £11.
Distillery House North Road ☎01397/700103, ⓦwww.visit-fortwilliam.co.uk. Very comfortable,

well-equipped upper-range guest house situated ten minutes' walk north of the town centre near the Glen Nevis turn-off. ❺
The Grange Grange Road ☎01397/705516, ⓦwww.thegrange-scotland.co.uk. Top-grade accommodation in a striking old stone house, with four luxurious en-suite doubles and a spacious garden. Vegetarian breakfasts on request. Non-smoking. April–Oct. ❻
Rhu Mhor Alma Road ☎01397/702213, ⓦwww.rhumhor.co.uk. Congenial and characterful B&B, ten minutes' walk from the town centre, offering good breakfasts; vegetarians and vegans are catered for by arrangement. ❷

1075

Accommodation out of town

Achintee Farm Guest House Glen Nevis
℡01397/702240, 🖰www.achinteefarm.com.
Friendly, smart B&B with adjoining hostel
(the *Ben Nevis Bunkhouse*) right by the *Ben Nevis Inn* (see below), at the start of the Ben Nevis footpath. ❹

Ben Nevis Bunkhouse Achintee Farm, Glen Nevis
℡01397/702240, 🖰www.achinteefarm.com. A
more civilized option than the nearby SYHA place,
with hot showers and a self-catering kitchen.
Located just over the river from the Ben Nevis
Visitor Centre – reach it by following the Ben Nevis
path across the river or by taking Achintee Road
along the north side of the River Nevis from Clag-gan. Dorm beds from £11.

The Ben Nevis Inn Achintee, Glen Nevis
℡01397/701227. A basic and cosy 20-bed
bunkhouse housed within the rustic and lively pub

just north of the *Achintee Farm Guest House* (see
above). Dorm beds from £11.

Farr Cottage Lodge Corpach, on the main A830
℡01397/772315, 🖰www.farrcottage.co.uk.
Well-equipped, lively hostel with range of dorms
(£12.50) and double/twin rooms ❶. Offers a multi-tude of outdoor activities with evening entertain-ment including whisky tastings.

Rhiw Goch Banavie ℡01397/772373, 🖰www2
.prestel.co.uk/rhiwgoch. Comfortable and welcom-ing B&B overlooking Neptune's Staircase with great
views to Ben Nevis. Good breakfasts. ❸

Smiddy Bunkhouse & Blacksmiths Back-packer Lodge Corpach ℡01397/772467,
🖰www.highland-mountain-guides.co.uk. A cosy
14-bed hostel and simpler 12-bed bunkhouse,
next to Corpach train station at the entrance to the
Caledonian Canal. Part of the Snowgoose Mountain
Centre, offering year-round mountaineering, kayak-ing and other outdoor activities; dorm beds £12.50.

Eating and drinking

Fort William has a reasonable range of places to **eat** and **drink**. The pick of
the bunch is the moderately priced *Crannog at the Waterfront* (℡01397/705589,
🖰www.oceanandoak.co.uk), next to the Underwater Centre beyond the
railway station. On the High Street, the *Grog and Gruel* is the place to go for
Scottish real ales, entertainment and traditional pub grub. There are also a
number of places out of town that serve good food: for a smart meal, *An Crann*
(℡01397/773114; closed Sun), just outside Banavie on the B8004 (Highland
Country bus #40), offers tasty Scottish dishes in a delightful, cosy setting; while
the most convivial atmosphere is in the 🍴 *Ben Nevis Inn* (see above) up Glen
Nevis, where you'll get excellent, moderately priced food.

Glen Nevis

A ten-minute drive south of Fort William, **GLEN NEVIS** is indisputably
among the Highlands' most impressive glens: a classic U-shaped glacial valley
hemmed in by steep bracken-covered slopes and swaths of blue-grey scree.
Herds of shaggy Highland cattle graze the valley floor, where a sparkling river
gushes through glades of trees. Highland Country **bus** #42 (every 1hr 20min)
runs from Fort William bus station to the SYHA hostel, two and a half miles
up the Glen Nevis road; some buses carry on another two and a half miles (late
May to Oct only) up the glen to the car park by the Lower Falls.

A great **low-level walk** (six miles round-trip) runs from the end of the
road at the top of Glen Nevis. The good but very rocky path leads through a
dramatic gorge with impressive falls and rapids, then opens out into a secret
hanging valley, carpeted with wild flowers, with a high waterfall at the far end.
Of all the walks in and around Glen Nevis, however, the **ascent of Ben
Nevis** (4406ft), Britain's highest summit, inevitably attracts the most atten-tion. Despite the fact that it's quite a slog up to the summit, and it's by no
means the most attractive mountain in Scotland, in high summer the trail is
teeming with hikers, whatever the weather. It can snow round the summit
any day of the year, so take the necessary precautions; in winter, of course,
the mountain should be left to the experts. The most obvious **route** to the

△ Ben Nevis

summit, a Victorian pony path up the whaleback south side of the mountain, built to service the observatory that once stood on the top, starts from the helpful **Glen Nevis visitor centre**, a mile and a half along the Glen Nevis road (daily: Easter to mid-May & Oct 9am–5pm; mid-May to end Sept 9am–6pm): allow a full day for the climb (8hr).

The Nevis Range

Seven miles northeast of Fort William by the A82, on the slopes of **Aonach Mhor**, one of the high mountains abutting Ben Nevis, the **Nevis Range** (☎01397/705825, ⓦwww.nevis-range.co.uk) is Scotland's highest winter ski area. Highland Country bus #42 runs from Fort William (year-round; Mon–Sat 5 daily, 3 on Sun) to the base station of the country's only **gondola** system (daily: 10am–5pm; July & Aug 9.30am–6pm; closed mid-Nov to mid-Dec for maintenance; £8 return). The one-and-a-half mile gondola trip (15min), rising 2000ft, gives an easy approach to some high-level walking as well as spectacular views from the terrace of the self-service restaurant at the top station. From the top of the gondola station, you can experience Britain's only World Cup standard **downhill mountain-bike course** (mid-May to mid-Sept 11am–3pm; £10 includes gondola one way), a hair-raising 3km route, that's not for the faint-hearted. There's also 25 miles of waymarked off-road bike routes, known as the Witch's Trails, on the mountainside and in the Leanachan Forest, ranging from gentle paths to cross-country scrambles. Off Beat Bikes (☎01397/704008, ⓦwww.offbeatbikes.co.uk) rents general mountain bikes as well as full-suspension bikes for the downhill course from their shops in Fort William and at the gondola base station (mid-May to mid-Sept).

The Great Glen | **THE HIGHLAND REGION** | ㉔

Glen Coe

Sixteen miles south of Fort William on the A82, breathtakingly beautiful **Glen Coe** (literally "Valley of Weeping") is justifiably the best known of the Highland glens: a spectacular mountain valley between velvety-green conical peaks, their tops often wreathed in cloud, their flanks streaked by cascades of rock and scree. In 1692 it was the site of a notorious massacre, in which the MacDonalds were victims of a long-standing government desire to suppress the clans. When clan chief **Alastair MacDonald** missed the deadline of January 1, 1692, to sign an oath of allegiance to William III, a plot was hatched to make an example of "that damnable sept". **Campbell of Glenlyon** was ordered to billet his soldiers in the homes of the MacDonalds, who for ten days entertained them with traditional Highland hospitality. In the early morning of February 13, the soldiers turned on their hosts, slaying between 38 and 45, and causing more than three hundred to flee in a blizzard.

Beyond the small village of **GLENCOE** at the western end of the glen, the glen itself (a property of the National Trust for Scotland since the 1930s) is virtually uninhabited, and provides outstanding climbing and walking. A mile south of the village, the NTS **visitor centre** (April–Aug daily 9.30am–5.30pm; Sept & Oct daily 10am–5pm; Nov–Feb Fri–Mon 10am–4pm; March daily 10am–4pm; £5; NTS) is an interesting eco-friendly building, where you'll find a good exhibition with a balanced account of the massacre alongside some entertaining material on rock and hill-climbing down the years. Informative ranger-led **guided walks** (Easter & June–Sept) leave from the centre, while a

Walks around Glen Coe

Ordnance Survey Explorer Map no. 384.

A good introduction to the splendours of Glen Coe is a half-day hike over the **Devil's Staircase**, which follows part of the old military road that once ran between Fort William and Stirling. Part of the West Highland Way and marked by thistle signs, the trail starts at the village of **Kinlochleven** and leads uphill to the 1804ft pass, then down the other side into Glen Coe, where it affords stunning views of Loch Eilde and Buachaille Etive Mhor. In fine settled weather, the trail is safe and a good option for families and less-experienced hikers.

Set right in the heart of the glen, the half-day **Allt Coire Gabhail** hike starts at the car park opposite the distinctive Three Sisters massif on the main A82. From the road, drop down to the floor of the glen and cross the River Coe via the wooden bridge, where the path heads straight up the Allt Coire Gabhail for a couple of miles to a false summit directly ahead – actually the rim of the so-called "Lost Valley" which the Clan MacDonald used to flee to and hide their cattle in when attacked.

Undoubtedly one of the finest walks in the Glen Coe area not entailing the ascent of a Munro is the **Buachaille Etive Beag** circuit, which follows the textbook glacial valleys of Lairig Eilde and Lairig Gartain, ascending 1968ft in only nine miles of rough trail. Park near the waterfall at **The Study** – the gorge part of the A82 through Glen Coe – and walk up the road until you see a sign pointing south to "Loch Etiveside". The path angles up from here to the top of the pass, a rise of 787ft from the road. From here, follow the burn until you can pick up the trail heading up the eastern side of Stob Dubh (the "Black Peak"), which leads to the col of the Lairig Gartain, and onwards to the top of the pass. Drop down the other side to the main road, where the roughly parallel route of the old military road offers a gentler and safer return to the Study with superb views of the Three Sisters – finer than those ever seen by drivers.

cabin area provides information on the local weather and wildlife, and a café sells good cakes.

There's a good selection of **accommodation** in Glen Coe and the surrounding area, with the lively ⚔ *Clachaig Inn* (☎01855/811252, ⓦwww.clachaig .com; ❺) being a great place to swap stories with fellow climbers and to reward your exertions with cask-conditioned ales and heaped platefuls of food; it's three miles south of Glencoe village on the minor road off the A82. More basic options include an SYHA **hostel** (☎0870/004 1122, ⓦwww.syha.org .uk; dorm beds £14) on a backroad halfway between Glencoe village and the *Clachaig Inn*; the year-round *Red Squirrel* **campsite** (☎01855/811256) nearby; and a grassier NTS campsite (☎01855/811397; April–Oct) on the main road.

Kinlochleven

At the easternmost end of Loch Leven, the settlement of **KINLOCHLEVEN** was best known for many years as the site of a huge, unsightly aluminium smelter built in 1904. The disused smelter is now home to an innovative new indoor mountaineering centre called **The Ice Factor** (☎01855/831100, ⓦwww.ice-factor.co.uk). Built at a cost of over £2.5 million, this impressive facility includes the world's largest artificial ice-climbing wall (13.5m) as well as a range of more traditional climbing walls and other facilities such as steam room, sauna and an inexpensive café. Alongside, another part of the aluminium smelter has been transformed into the **Atlas Brewery**, which you can tour on summer evenings (Easter–Sept Mon–Sat tour starts at 5.30pm; ☎01855/831111). Kinlochleven stands at the foot of the spectacular Mamore hills, popular with Munro-baggers, and is a day's walk from Fort William on the **West Highland Way**.

The west coast

For many people, the Highlands' starkly beautiful **west coast** – stretching from the **Morvern peninsula** (opposite Mull) in the south to wind-lashed **Cape Wrath** in the far north – is the finest part of Scotland. Serrated by fjord-like sea lochs, the long coastline is scattered with windswept white-sand beaches, cliff-girt headlands, and rugged mountains sweeping up from the shoreline. The fast-changing weather rolling off the North Atlantic can be harsh, but it can also often create memorable plays of light, mood and landscape. When the sun shines, the sparkle of the sea, the richness of colour and the clarity of the views out to the scattered Hebrides are simply irresistible. This is the least populated part of Britain, with just two small towns, and yawning tracts of moorland and desolate peat bog between crofting settlements.

The **Vikings**, who ruled the region in the ninth century, called it the "South Land", from which the modern district of Sutherland takes its name. After Culloden, the Clearances emptied most of the inland glens of the far north, however, and left the population clinging to the coastline, where a herring fishing industry developed. Today, tourism, crofting, fishing and salmon farming are the mainstay of the local economy, supplemented by EU construction grants and subsidies to farm the sheep you'll encounter everywhere.

For visitors, **cycling** and **walking** are the obvious ways to make the most of the superb scenery, and countless lochans and crystal-clear rivers offer superlative trout and salmon **fishing**. The shattered cliffs of the far northwest are an ornithologist's dream, harbouring some of Europe's largest and most diverse

sea-bird colonies, while the area's craggy mountaintops are the haunt of the elusive golden eagle.

The most visited part of the west coast is the stretch between Kyle of Lochalsh and Ullapool. Lying within easy reach of Inverness, this sector boasts the region's more obvious highlights: the awesome mountainscape of **Torridon**, **Gairloch**'s sandy beaches, the famous botanic gardens at **Inverewe**, and **Ullapool** itself, a picturesque and bustling fishing town from where ferries leave for the Outer Hebrides. However, press on further north, or south, and you'll get a truer sense of the isolation that makes the west coast so special. Traversed by few roads, the remote northwest corner of Scotland is wild and bleak, receiving the full force of the North Atlantic's frequently ferocious weather. The scattered settlements of the far southwest, meanwhile, tend to be more sheltered, but they are separated by some of the most extensive wilderness areas in Britain – lonely peninsulas with evocative Gaelic names like **Ardnamurchan**, **Knoydart** and **Glenelg**.

Without your own vehicle, **transport** can be a problem. There's a reasonable **train** service from Inverness to Kyle of Lochalsh and from Fort William to Mallaig, and a useful **summer bus** service connects Inverness to Ullapool, Lochinver, Scourie and Durness. **Driving** is a much simpler option: the roads aren't busy, though they are frequently single-track and scattered with sheep.

Morvern to Knoydart: the "Rough Bounds"

The remote and sparsely populated southwest corner of the Highlands, from the empty district of **Morvern** to the isolated peninsula of **Knoydart**, is a dramatic, lonely region of mountain and moorland fringed by a rocky, indented coast whose stunning white beaches enjoy wonderful views to Mull, Skye and other islands. Its Gaelic name, *Garbh-chiochan*, translates as the "**Rough Bounds**", implying a region geographically and spiritually apart. Even if you have a car, you should spend some time here exploring on foot; there are so few roads that some determined hiking is almost inevitable.

The Ardnamurchan peninsula

A nine-mile drive south of Fort William down Loch Linnhe, the five-minute ferry crossing at **Corran Ferry** (daily every 15min: summer 7am–9pm; winter 7am–8pm; car and passengers £5.20, foot passengers and bicycles go free) provides the most direct point of entry for Morvern and the rugged **Ardnamurchan peninsula**. The most westerly point on the British mainland, the peninsula lost most of its inhabitants during the infamous Clearances (see p.1103) and is now sparsely populated with only a handful of tiny crofting settlements clinging to its jagged coastline. Ardnamurchan, however, can be an inspiring place for its pristine, empty beaches, wonderful vistas of sea and island, and the sense of nature all around. A variety of **walking** routes, from hill climbs to coastal scrambles, are detailed in a guide produced annually by the local community (available from tourist offices and most shops on the peninsula, priced around £4).

The coastal hamlet of **SALEN** marks the turn-off for Ardnamurchan Point: from here it's a further 25 miles of scenic but slow driving along the single-track road which follows the northern shore of Loch Sunart. Along this road, just west of the hamlet of **GLENBORRODALE**, look out for the engaging **Glenmore Natural History Centre** (April–Oct Mon–Sat 10.30am–5.30pm, Sun noon–5.30pm; ⓦwww.ardnamurchannaturalhistory centre.co.uk; £2.50), which provides an inspiring introduction to the diverse flora, fauna and geology of Ardnamurchan. The centre is housed in a sensi-tively designed timber building, complete with turf roof and wildlife ponds. CCTV cameras relay live pictures of the surrounding wildlife, catching the comings and goings of a pine marten's nest, underwater pools in the nearby river and a heronry.

Nine miles west of the Glenmore Centre, **KILCHOAN** is Ardnamurchan's main village – a straggling but appealing crofting township overlooking the Sound of Mull. A **car ferry** runs from here to Tobermory (Mon–Sat 8am–6.45pm 7 daily; June–Aug also Sun 10.15am–4.45pm 5 daily; 35min). The community centre in the village houses a **tourist office** (Easter–Oct daily 9am–5pm; ☎01972/510222, @www.ardnamurchan.com), who can book accommodation; the community centre (and its simple tearoom) are open year-round and can provide informal local advice. **Accommodation** isn't plenti-ful in Kilchoan, and in summer you're advised to book well ahead. You can normally **camp** in the gardens of the *Kilchoan House Hotel* (☎01972/510200); for B&B, try *Doirlinn House* (☎01972/510209, @dorlinnhouse@yahoo .co.uk; ❷; March–Oct), or *Tigh a'Ghobhainn* (☎01972/510771, @mairihunter .kilchoan@virgin.net; ❷; March–Oct), both with lovely views over the Sound of Mull.

The road continues beyond Kilchoan to the rocky, windy **Ardnamur-chan Point** and its famous **lighthouse**. The lighthouse buildings house a small café and an absorbing **exhibition** (April–Oct daily 10am–5pm; £5; ☎01972/510210), with well-assembled displays about lighthouses in general, their construction and the people who lived in them. Best of all is the chance to climb up the inside of the Egyptian-style lighthouse tower; at the top, a guide is on hand to tell some of the tall tales relating to the lighthouse and show you around the lighting mechanism.

Also worth exploring around the peninsula are the myriad coves, beaches and headlands along the long coastline. The finest of the sandy beaches is about three miles north of the lighthouse at **Sanna Bay**, a shell-strewn strand and series of dunes which offers truly unforgettable vistas of the Small Isles to the north, circled by gulls, terns and guillemots.

Acharacle and Castle Tioram

At the eastern end of Ardnamurchan, just north of Salen where the A861 heads north towards the district of Moidart, the main settlement is **ACHARACLE**, an ancient crofting village set back a few hundred yards from the seaward end of freshwater **Loch Shiel**. A mile north of Acharacle, a side road running north off the A861 winds for three miles or so to **Loch Moidart**, a calm and shel-tered sea loch. Perched atop a rocky promontory protruding out into the loch is **Castle Tioram** (pronounced "cheerum"), one of Scotland's most atmospheric historic monuments. Reached via a sandy causeway that's only just above the high tide, the thirteenth-century fortress, whose Gaelic name means "dry land", was the seat of the MacDonalds of Clanranald until it was destroyed by their chief in 1715 to prevent it from falling into Hanoverian hands while he was away fighting for the Jacobites. Today, a certain amount of controversy surrounds the upkeep of the place: while the setting and approach are undoubtedly stunning, large notices and fences keep you from getting too close to the castle due to the danger of falling masonry.

The Road to the Isles

The "**Road to the Isles**" (@www.road-to-the-isles.org.uk) from Fort William to Mallaig, followed by the West Highland Railway and the narrow, winding

A830, traverses the mountains and glens of the Rough Bounds before break-ing out onto a spectacularly scenic coast of sheltered inlets, stunning white beaches and wonderful views to the islands of Rùm, Eigg, Muck and Skye. This is country commonly associated with **Bonnie Prince Charlie**, whose adven-tures of 1745–46 began and ended on this stretch of coast, with his first, defiant gathering of the clans at **GLENFINNAN**, nineteen miles west of Fort William at the head of lovely Loch Shiel. The spot is marked by a column (now a little lop-sided, Pisa-like), crowned with a clansman in full battle dress, erected as a tribute by Alexander MacDonald of Glenaladale in 1815.

Glenfinnan is a poignant place, a beautiful stage for the opening scene in a brutal drama which was to change the Highlands for ever. The **visitor centre** and café (daily: April, May, Sept & Oct 10am–5pm; June–Aug 9.30am–5.30pm; Nov Sat & Sun 10am–4pm; £3; NTS), opposite the monument, gives an account of the '45 uprising through to the rout at **Culloden** eight months later (see p.1065). A **boat trip** on the loch with Loch Shiel Cruises (℡01687/470322, 🌐www.highlandcruises.co.uk) offers a chance to view some very remote scen-ery and occasionally a golden eagle, and is highly recommended.

Glenfinnan is one of the most spectacular parts of the **West Highland Rail-way** line (see box on p.938), not only for the glimpse it offers of the monu-ment and graceful Loch Shiel, but also the mighty 21-arched Loch nan Uamh **viaduct** built in 1901 and one of the first-ever large constructions made out of concrete. You can learn more about the history of this section of the railway at the **Glenfinnan Station Museum** (June–Sept daily 9.30am–4.30pm; 50p), set in the old booking office of the station. Next door, two old railway carriages have been converted into a highly original **restaurant** and **bunkhouse**: the *Dining Car* (June–Sept daily 10am–5pm; ℡01397/722300) is open for light lunches, home-baking, and evening meals if you book ahead, while the *Sleeping Car* (℡01397/722295; year-round), a converted 1958 camping coach, sleeps ten in bunkbeds.

West of Glenfinnan, the A830 runs alongside captivating Loch Eilt and onto a coast marked by acres of white sands, turquoise seas and rocky islets draped with orange seaweed. **ARISAIG**, scattered round a sandy bay at the west end of the Morar peninsula, makes a good base for exploring this area. A recently constructed **bypass** now whizzes cars (and, more importantly, fish lorries) on their way to Mallaig, but you shouldn't miss the slower coast road, which enjoys the best of the scenery.

Stretching for eight miles or so north of Arisaig is a string of stunning white-sand **beaches** backed by flowery machair, with barren granite hills and moorland rising up behind, and wonderful seaward views of Eigg and Rùm. The next settlement of any significance is **MORAR**, where the beach scenes from *Local Hero* were shot. Of the string of **campsites** along the coast road *Camusdarach* (℡01687/450221, 🌐www.road-to-the-isles.org.uk) isn't quite on the beach but is quieter and less officious than others nearby. **B&B** is also available in the converted billiard room of its attractive main house (❶).

Mallaig

A cluttered, noisy port whose pebble-dashed houses struggle for space with great lumps of granite tumbling down to the sea, **MALLAIG**, 47 miles west of Fort William, is not pretty. As the main ferry stop for Skye, the Small Isles and Knoydart, it's always full of visitors, though the continuing source of the village's wealth is its **fishing** industry: on the quayside, piles of nets, tackle and ice crates lie scattered around a bustling modern market. When the fleet is in, trawlers encircled by flocks of raucous gulls choke the harbour, and the pubs, among the liveliest on the west coast, host bouts of serious drinking.

Apart from the daily bustle of Mallaig's harbour, the main attraction in town is **Mallaig Marine World**, north of the train station near the harbour (March–Oct daily 9.30am–5.30pm; Nov–Feb Mon–Sat 11am–5.30pm; £3), where tanks of local sea creatures and informative exhibits about the port provide an unpretentious introduction to the local waters.

The **tourist office** (April–Oct Mon–Sat 10am–5pm; Nov–March Mon, Tues & Fri 11am–3pm) is by the harbour, with the CalMac ticket office (☎01687/462403), serving passengers for Skye and the Small Isles, nearby. For transport to Knoydart, Bruce Watt Cruises (☎01687/462320, ⍟www .knoydart-ferry.co.uk) sails to Inverie, on the Knoydart peninsula, every morning and afternoon (mid-May to mid-Sept Mon–Fri; mid-Sept to mid-May Mon, Wed & Fri); the loch is sheltered, so crossings are rarely cancelled.

For **B&B**, head around the harbour to East Bay, where you'll find the cheery *Western Isles Guest House* (☎01687/462320, ⍟www.road-to-the-isles.org.uk /western-isles.html; ❸), or there's *Sheena's Backpackers' Lodge* (☎01687/462764), a refreshingly laid-back independent **hostel** overlooking the harbour, with mixed dorms (£13), self-catering facilities and a sitting room: its *Tea Garden* is a great place to watch the world go by while tucking into a bowl of cullen skink (soup made from smoked haddock), a pint of prawns or homemade scones. Alternatively, the *Fishmarket Restaurant*, facing *Sheena's*, features lots of fresh seafood, while the *Cornerstone*, across the road from the tourist office, serves the freshest of fish and chips – or a portion of scallops and chips if you're feeling decadent.

The Knoydart peninsula

Many people regard the **Knoydart peninsula** as mainland Britain's most dramatic and unspoilt wilderness area. Flanked by **Loch Nevis** ("Loch of Heaven") in the south and the fjord-like inlet of **Loch Hourn** ("Loch of Hell") to the north, Knoydart's knobbly green peaks – three of them Munros – sweep straight out of the sea, shrouded for much of the time in a pall of grey mist. To get to the heart of the peninsula, you must catch a **boat** from Mallaig or Glenelg, or else **hike** for a couple of days across rugged moorland and mountains and sleep rough in old stone bothies (most of which are marked on Ordnance Survey maps).

At the end of the eighteenth century, around a thousand people eked out a living from this inhospitable terrain through crofting and fishing. These days the peninsula supports around seventy people, most of whom live in the hamlet of **INVERIE**. Nestled beside a sheltered bay on the south side of the peninsula, it has a pint-sized post office, a shop, and mainland Britain's most remote pub, the *Old Forge*.

Three-quarters of a mile east of the village on the side of the mountain, there's an upmarket independent **hostel**, *Torrie Shieling* (☎01687/462669, ⍟torrie@knoydart.org; £16 per person), which is popular with hikers and families, while the Knoydart Foundation runs a simple **bunkhouse** (☎01687/462242, ⍟www.knoydart-foundation.com) nearby in some old steadings. In Inverie itself there's just one guest house, the *Pier House* (☎01687/462347, ⍟www.thepierhouseknoydart.co.uk; ❶ for dinner, B&B), a great place to stay. It has its own **restaurant** serving à la carte evening meals, including some good veggie options: dinner is available to non-residents (three courses from around £15). The ✹ *Old Forge* is one of Scotland's finer pubs, with a convivial atmosphere where visitors and locals mix, generous bar meals often featuring freshly caught seafood, real ales, an open fire, and a good chance of live music of an evening. You can rent **mountain bikes** from *Pier House*; they've established various mountain-bike trails in the area, and also run mountain walks for groups of four or more.

Kyle of Lochalsh and around

As the main gateway to Skye, **Kyle of Lochalsh** used to be an important transit point for tourists, locals and services. However, with the building of the Skye Bridge in 1995, Kyle was left as merely the terminus for the train route from Inverness, with little else to offer. Of much more interest to most visitors is nearby **Eilean Donan Castle**, one of Scotland's most famous and popular sights, perched at the end of a stone causeway on the shores of **Loch Duich**. A few miles north of Kyle of Lochalsh, the delightful village of **Plockton** is a refreshing alternative to its utilitarian neighbour, with cottages grouped around a yacht-filled bay and Highland cattle wandering the streets.

Kyle of Lochalsh

KYLE OF LOCHALSH is not particularly attractive and is ideally somewhere to pass through rather than linger. With the building of the **Skye road bridge**, traffic has little reason to stop before rumbling over the channel a mile to the west. **Buses** run to Kyle of Lochalsh from Glasgow via Fort William and Invergarry (3 daily; 5hr 10min–6hr) and from Inverness via Invermoriston (3 daily; 2hr–2hr 30min), and all continue at least as far as Portree on Skye: book in advance for all of them (℡0870/550 5050, ⊛www.citylink.co.uk). Buses also shuttle across the bridge to Kyleakin on Skye every thirty minutes or so. **Trains** run to Kyle of Lochalsh from Inverness (Mon–Sat 3 daily, 1 on Sun; 2hr 30min); the train line is a rail enthusiast's dream, even if scenically it doesn't quite match the West Highland line to Mallaig.

Kyle's **tourist office** (April–June, Sept & Oct Mon–Sat 9.30am–5pm; July & Aug Mon–Sat 9.30am–6pm, Sun 10am–4pm), on top of the small hill near the old ferry jetty, can book **accommodation** – a useful service as there are surprisingly few options. One of the most pleasant B&Bs in the area is the *Old Schoolhouse* at Erbusaig, built in the 1820s and located two miles north of Kyle towards Plockton (℡01599/534369, ⊛www.oldschoolhouse87.co.uk; ❹). There's a simple bunkhouse in town, *Cúchulainn's* (℡01599/534492), above a pub across the main street from the tourist office. To **eat**, sample the steak and homemade puddings at the *Waverley Restaurant* (5.30–9.30pm, closed Thurs; ℡01599/534337), or for a snack visit *Sheila's Café* opposite the tourist office.

Eilean Donan Castle

After Edinburgh's hilltop fortress, **Eilean Donan Castle** (March & Nov 10am–4pm; April–Oct daily 10am–5.30pm; £4.75), ten miles north of Shiel Bridge on the A87, has to be Scotland's most photographed monument. Presiding over the once strategically important confluence of lochs Alsh, Long and Duich, the forbidding crenellated tower rises from the water's edge, joined to the shore by a narrow stone bridge and with sheer mountains as a backdrop. The original castle was established in 1230 by Alexander II to protect the area from the Vikings. Later, during a Jacobite uprising in 1719, the castle was blown up and it lay in ruins until John Macrae-Gilstrap had it rebuilt between 1912 and 1932. Eilean Donan has since featured in several major **films**, including *Highlander*, *Entrapment*, and the James Bond adventure *The World is Not Enough*. Three floors, including the banqueting hall, the bedrooms and the troops' quarters are open to the public, with various Jacobite and clan relics also on display, though like many of the region's most popular castles, the large numbers of people passing through make it hard to appreciate the real charm of the place.

Plockton

A fifteen-minute train ride north of Kyle at the seaward end of islet-studded Loch Carron lies the unbelievably picturesque village of **PLOCKTON**: a chocolate-box row of neatly painted cottages ranged around the curve of a tiny harbour and backed by a craggy landscape of heather and pine. The unique brilliance of Plockton's light has also made it something of an artists' hangout, and during the summer the waterfront, with its row of shaggy palm trees, even shaggier Highland cattle, flower gardens and pleasure boats, is invariably dotted with painters dabbing at their easels.

The friendly, cosy *Haven Hotel*, on Innes Street (☏01599/544223; ❼), has king-sized beds and is renowned for its excellent food, whilst the family-run *Plockton Inn*, also on Innes Street (☏01599/544222, ⓦwww.plocktoninn.co.uk; ❺), is an equally friendly and informal alternative. Of the fifteen or so **B&Bs**, *The Shieling* (☏01599/544282; ❷) has a great location on a tiny headland at the top of the harbour, while at the cosy, main-street retreat *An Caladh*, "the resting place on the shore" (☏01599/544356; ❷), guests have free use of two wooden sailing dinghies and can watch the owner sail in with the morning catch of prawns. On the outskirts of Plockton, there's the attractive *Station Bunkhouse* (☏01599/544235).

Plockton boasts a wealth of good places to **eat**: *The Haven*, the *Plockton Inn* and *The Plockton Hotel* all have excellent seafood **restaurants**, while *Off the Rails Restaurant and Tearoom* (ⓦwww.off-the-rails.co.uk), in the train station, serves evening fare that includes local shellfish and game.

Wester Ross

Wester Ross, the western seaboard of the old county of Ross-shire, is widely regarded as the most glamorous stretch of this coast. Here all the classic elements of Scotland's **coastal scenery** – dramatic mountains, sandy beaches, whitewashed crofting cottages and shimmering island views – come together in spectacular fashion. Though popular with generations of adventurous Scottish holidaymakers, only one or two places feel blighted by tourist numbers, with places such as **Applecross** and the peninsulas north and south of **Gairloch** maintaining an endearing simplicity and sense of isolation. There is some tough but wonderful **hiking** to be had in the mountains around **Torridon** and **Coigach**, while **boat trips** out among the islands and the prolific sea- and birdlife of the coast are another draw. The main settlement is the attractive fishing town of **Ullapool**, port for ferry services to Stornoway in the Western Isles, but a pleasant enough place to use as a base, not least for its active social and cultural scene.

The Applecross peninsula

The most dramatic approach to the **Applecross peninsula** (the English-sounding name is a corruption of the Gaelic *Apor Crosan*, meaning "estuary") is from the south, up a classic, glacial U-shaped valley and over the infamous **Bealach na Bà** (literally "Pass of the Cattle"). Crossing the forbidding hills behind Kishorn and rising to 2053ft, with a gradient and switchback bends worthy of the Alps, this route – a popular cycling piste – is hair-raising in places, but the panoramic views across the Minch to Raasay and Skye more than compensate.

The sheltered, fertile coast around **APPLECROSS** village (Ⓦwww
.applecross.info), where the Irish missionary monk Maelrhuba founded a
monastery in 673 AD, comes as a surprise after the bleakness of the moorland
approach. Maybe it's the journey, but Applecross feels like an idyllic place: you
can wander along lanes banked with wild iris and orchids, and explore beaches
and rock pools on the shore. There's a small **Heritage Centre** (April–Oct
Mon–Sat noon–4pm; Ⓦwww.applecrossheritage.org.uk) overlooking Clachan
church and graveyard, and a number of short **waymarked trails** along the
shore – great for walking off a pub lunch.

The old, tastefully refurbished and family-run ⚑*Applecross Inn* (Ⓣ01520/744262,
Ⓦwww.applecross.net; ❹), right beside the sea, is the focal point of the community, with **rooms** upstairs, and a lively bar that serves delicious, freshly prepared
local seafood and produce (noon–9pm). There's **camping** as you come into the
village from the pass at the *Applecross Campsite* (Ⓣ01520/744268), also home to
the *Flower Tunnel* café-bar (daily 11am–9.30pm).

Loch Torridon

Loch Torridon marks the northern boundary of the Applecross peninsula, its
awe-inspiring setting backed by the appealingly rugged mountains of **Liathach**
and **Beinn Eighe**, tipped by streaks of white quartzite. The greater part of this
area is composed of the reddish 750-million-year-old Torridonian sandstone,
and some 15,000 acres of the massif are under the protection of the National
Trust for Scotland, which runs a **Countryside Centre**, by Torridon Village by
the head of the loch (Easter to Sept Mon–Sat 10am–6pm; £3), where you can
learn about the local geology, flora and fauna. On the south side of the loch
stands one of the area's grandest **hotels**, the smart, rambling Victorian *Loch Torridon Hotel* (Ⓣ01445/791242, Ⓦwww.lochtorridonhotel.com; ❾), set amid well-
tended lochside grounds. The hotel also runs the adjacent *Ben Damph Lodge*
(March–Oct; ❺), a cyclist- and walker-friendly conversion of an old farmstead, with neat twins and doubles and a bistro-bar. Close to the Countryside
Centre is a rather unsightly SYHA **hostel** (Ⓣ0870/004 1154, Ⓦwww.syha.org
.uk; March–Oct; dorm beds £13) and a council-run **campsite**.

Walks around Torridon

Ordnance Survey Explorer Map no. 433.

There can be difficult conditions on virtually all hiking routes around Torridon, and
the weather can change very rapidly. If you're relatively inexperienced but want to
do the magnificent ridge walk along the **Liathach** (pronounced "lee-ach") massif,
or the strenuous traverse of **Beinn Eighe** (pronounced "ben ay"), you can join a
National Trust Ranger Service guided hike (July & Aug; Torridon Countryside Centre;
Ⓣ01445/791221).

For those confident to go it alone, one of many possible routes takes you behind
Liathach and down the pass, **Coire Dubh**, to the main road in Glen Torridon. This is
a great, straightforward, full-day walk, covering thirteen miles and taking in superb
landscapes. A rewarding walk even in rough weather is the seven-mile hike up the
coast from **Lower Diabaig**, ten miles northwest of Torridon village, to **Redpoint**. On
a clear day, the views across to Raasay and Applecross from this gentle undulating
path are superlative, but you'll have to return along the same trail, or else make your
way back via Loch Maree on the A832. If you're staying in Shieldaig, the track that
winds up the peninsula running north from the village makes a pleasant ninety-minute
round walk.

△ Loch Maree

Loch Maree

About eight miles north of Loch Torridon, **Loch Maree**, dotted with Caledonian pine-covered islands, is one of the west's scenic highlights, best viewed from the A832 road that skirts the loch's southern shore, passing the **Beinn Eighe Nature Reserve**, the UK's oldest wildlife sanctuary. Parts of the reserve are forested with Caledonian pinewood, which once covered the whole of the country, and it is home to wildlife including pine marten, wildcat, buzzards and golden eagles.

A mile north of Kinlochewe, the well-run **Beinn Eighe Visitor Centre** (Easter & May–Oct daily 10am–5pm) on the A832, uses excellent audiovisual presentations and child-friendly displays to inform visitors about the area's rare species. Outside, the "talking trails" provide an easy walk through the vicinity, while several longer **walks** start from the car park, a mile north of the visitor centre.

Gairloch and around

GAIRLOCH spreads itself around the northeastern corner of the wide sheltered bay of Loch Gairloch, with its sometimes sandy, sometimes rocky shores. During the summer, Gairloch thrives as a low-key holiday resort with several tempting sandy beaches and some excellent coastal walks within easy reach. The main supermarket and **tourist office** (June–Sept daily 9am–5.30pm; Oct Mon–Sat 9am–5.30pm; Nov–May Mon–Sat 10am–4pm) are in Achtercairn, right by the **Gairloch Heritage Museum** (March–Sept Mon–Sat 10am–5pm; Oct Mon–Fri 10am–1pm); £3), which has eclectic, appealing displays covering geology, archeology, fishing and farming that range from a mock-up of a croft house to an early knitting machine. Probably the most interesting section is the archive made by elderly locals – an array of photographs, maps, genealogies, lists of place names and taped recollections, mostly in Gaelic.

There's a good choice of **accommodation** around Gairloch: opposite the post office, the *Mountain Lodge* (℡01445/712316; March–Dec; ❷) has rooms, and you can get good coffee and fresh scones at the laid-back *Mountain Café*

next door, with views over the bay. There are also some very good **B&Bs** in the section of the village known as Strath, including Gaelic-speaking Miss Macken-zie's *Duisary* (☎01445/712252, ⓦwww.duisary.freeserve.co.uk; April–Oct; ➋). Alternatively, try *Heatherdale* (☎01445/712388, ⓔBrochod1@aol.com; March to end Oct; ➌) to the south of the village near the pier, or, further south again, just before the turn-off to Badachro, the atmospheric and tastefully furnished *Kerrysdale House* (☎01445/712292, ⓦwww.kerrysdalehouse.co.uk; ➋), set in lovely gardens.

For **food**, head for the pier, where the *Old Inn* (ⓦwww.theoldinn.co.uk) offers seafood on its bar menu and a very good range of Scottish real ales, while the nearby *Creel Restaurant* serves delicious fare. The *Steading Restaurant*, tucked beside the Gairloch Museum, is also a popular eatery, as are the nearby *Mountain Lodge* and the bistro-style *Café Blueprint* across the road, where you'll also find the chip shop.

The Gairloch coast

The area's real attraction, however, is its beautiful coastline, easily explored on a wildlife-spotting **cruise**: several operators, including Gairloch Marine Life Centre & Cruises (Easter–Oct; ☎01445/712636), run informative and enjoyable boat trips across the bay in search of dolphins, seals and even the odd whale. One of the most impressive stretches of **coastline** is around the north side of the bay, along the single-track B8021, at **BIG SAND**, which has a cleaner and quieter beach than Gairloch, with an excellent **campsite** above it (☎01445/712152). Just before Big Sand, there's an SYHA **hostel** at Carn Dearg (☎0870/004 1110, ⓦwww.syha.org.uk; April–Sept; dorm beds £12.50), spectacularly set on the edge of a cliff with views to Skye. Three miles beyond at **Rubha Reidh** (pronounced "roo-a-ray"), you can stay at the headland's still operational Stevenson-designed *Rua Reidh Lighthouse* (☎01445/771263, ⓦwww.ruareidh.co.uk; ➊), which looks out to the Outer Hebrides. Comfort-able accommodation includes a bunkhouse (£9.50), double and family rooms (meals extra; book ahead in high season), with slap-up **afternoon teas** and homemade cakes (Tues & Thurs 11am–5pm).

Three miles south of Gairloch, a narrow single-track lane winds west to **BADACHRO**, a sleepy former fishing village in a very attractive setting with a wonderful pub, the ⚓ *Badachro Inn* (ⓦwww.badachroinn.com), right by the water's edge, where you can sit in the beer garden watching the boats come and go and tuck into deliciously fresh seafood with a real ale. Some 300m away, seek out the former Victorian shooting lodge, *Shieldaig Lodge Hotel* (☎01445/741250, ⓦwww.shieldaiglodge.com ➌), for comfortable and secluded accommodation. Beyond Badachro, the road winds for five more miles along the shore to **REDPOINT**, a straggling hamlet with beautiful beaches of peach-coloured sand and great views to Raasay, Skye and the Western Isles.

Poolewe and around

It's a fifteen-minute hop by bus over the headland from Gairloch to the trim little village of **POOLEWE** which sits by a small bay at the sheltered south-ern end of Loch Ewe. Half a mile across the bay from Poolewe on the A832, **Inverewe Gardens** (daily: April–Oct 9.30am–9pm or dusk; Nov–March 9.30am–4pm; £8; NTS), a verdant oasis of foliage and riotously colourful flower collections, forms a vivid contrast to the wild, heathery crags of the adjoining coast. The gardens were the brainchild of **Osgood MacKenzie**, who inherited the surrounding 12,000-acre estate from his stepfather, the laird of Gairloch, in 1862. Taking advantage of the area's famously temperate climate (a consequence of the Gulf Stream, which draws a warm sea current from Mexico to within a stone's throw of these shores), MacKenzie collected plants from all over the world for his walled garden, which still forms the nucleus of the complex. Protected from Loch Ewe's corrosive salt breezes by a dense brake of Scots pine, rowan, oak, beech and birch trees, the fragile plants flourished on rich soil brought here as ballast on Irish ships to overlay the previously infertile beach gravel and sea grass.

Thousands of visitors pour through here annually, but the place rarely feels overcrowded. Strolling around the lotus ponds, palm trees and borders ablaze with exotic blooms, it's amazing to think you're at the same latitude as Hudson's Bay. Mid-May to mid-June is the best time to see the rhododendrons and azaleas, while the herbaceous garden reaches its peak in July and August, as does the wonderful Victorian vegetable and flower garden beside the sea. The **visitor centre** (April–Sept daily 9.30am–5pm) houses an informative display on the history of the garden and is the starting point for **guided walks** (May–Sept).

Ullapool

ULLAPOOL (ⓦ www.ullapool.co.uk), the northwest's principal centre of population, was founded at the height of the herring boom in 1788 by the British Fisheries Society, on a sheltered arm of land jutting into Loch Broom. The grid-plan town is still an important fishing centre, though the **ferry** link to Stornoway on Lewis (see p.1106) means that in high season it's swamped by visitors. Though busy, Ullapool remains a hugely appealing place and a good base for exploring the northwest Highlands. Regular **buses** run from here to Inverness and Durness, as well as an early-morning run through to the remote train station at Lairg. **Day-trips to Lewis** by ferry and bus can be organized through Caledonian MacBrayne (ⓣ 0870/565 0000; £26.25). Accommodation is plentiful and Ullapool is an obvious hideaway if the weather is bad, with cosy pubs, a swimming pool and a lively **arts centre**, the *Ceilidh Place*.

Information and accommodation

The well-run **tourist office** (April, May & Sept Mon–Sat 9.30am–5pm; June–Aug Mon–Sat 9am–5pm, Sun 10am–4pm; Oct Mon–Fri 10am–5pm; Nov & Dec Mon–Fri 2–5.30pm) is on Argyle Street.

Accommodation

The Ceilidh Place West Argyle Street ⓣ 01854/612103, ⓦ www.theceilidhplace .com. Tasteful and popular hotel, with the west coast's best bookshop, a relaxing first-floor lounge, a great bar-restaurant, sea views and a laid-back atmosphere. Also has a good-value bunkhouse for £15 per person. ❻

Dromnan Garve Road ⓣ 01854/612333, ⓦ www.dromnan.co.uk. Excellent B&B run by very friendly hosts, who serve up a hearty breakfast. ❸

The Shieling Garve Road ⓣ 01854/612947. Another very friendly, comfortable guest house overlooking the loch, with immaculate, spacious rooms (nos. 4 and 5 have the best views), superb breakfasts (try their homemade venison and leek sausages) and a sauna. ❸

SYHA hostel Shore Street ⓣ 0870/004 1156, ⓦ www.syha.org.uk. Busy hostel on the front, with Internet access, laundry, and lots of good information about local walks. March–Oct. Dorm beds £13.50.

Waterside House 6 West Shore St ⓣ 01854/612140, ⓦ www.waterside.uk.net. Three tastefully furnished en-suite rooms in a very pleasant, sea-front B&B. ❸

West House West Argyle Street ⓣ 01854/613126, ⓦ www.scotpackers-hostels.co.uk. Lively, welcoming hostel with four- to six-bed dorms; some en-suite. Internet access (£1). Bike rental available (£10 per day). Dorm beds £12.

The Town

Day or night, most of the action in Ullapool centres on the **harbour**, which has an authentic and salty air, especially when the boats are in. By day, attention focuses on the comings and goings of the ferry, fishing boats and smaller craft, while in the evening, yachts swing on the current, the shops stay open late, and customers from the *Ferry Boat Inn* line the sea wall. During summer, booths advertise trips to the **Summer Isles** – a cluster of uninhabited islets two to three miles offshore – to view sea-bird colonies, dolphins and porpoises.

The only conventional attraction in town is the award-winning **museum**, in the old parish church on West Argyle Street (April–Oct Mon–Sat 10am–5pm; Nov–March Sat 10am–4pm; £4), where photographs, audiovisual and touch-screen displays provide an insight into life in a Highland community, including crofting, fishing, local religion and emigration. During the Clearances, Ullapool was one of the ports through which evicted crofters left to start new lives abroad.

Eating, drinking and entertainment

The two best **pubs** in Ullapool are the *Arch Inn*, home of the Ullapool football team, and the *Ferry Boat Inn* (known as the "FBI"), where you can enjoy a pint of real ale at the lochside – midges permitting. **Live Scottish folk music** is a special feature at *The Ceilidh Place* or on Thursday nights at the *FBI*. For those in search of fine dining, the *Point Restaurant* (March–Oct Tues–Sat) above the *Arch Inn* on the shore, serves delicious, fresh, homemade dishes, while the *Caley Inn* on Quay Street combines Scottish fusion cuisine with the chance to sample several real ales.

Assynt

If you've come as far as Ullapool it really is worth continuing further north into the ever more dramatic, remote and highly distinctive hills of **Assynt** (Ⓦwww .assynt.co.uk), which marks the transition from Wester Ross into Sutherland. One of the least populated areas in Europe, this is a landscape not of mountain ranges but of extraordinary peaks rising individually from the moorland. It's an area of peaceful, slow backroads, which, after twisting through idyllic crofts, invariably end up at a deserted beach or windswept headland with superb views west to the Outer Hebrides.

Coigach

Coigach (Ⓦwww.coigach.com) is the peninsula immediately to the north of Loch Broom, accessible via a slow, winding single-track road that leaves the A835 ten miles north of Ullapool. Coigach's main settlement is **ACHIL-TIBUIE**, an old crofting village scattered across the hillside above a series of white-sand coves and rocks tapering into the Atlantic, from where a fleet of small fishing boats carries sheep, and tourists to the enticing pastures of the **Summer Isles** which lie a little way offshore. For **boat** trips round the isles, including some time ashore on the largest, Tanera Mor, Ian Macleod's boat *Hectoria* (Ⓣ01854/622200) usually runs twice a day from the pier (Easter–Oct). The village attracts gardening enthusiasts, thanks to the unlikely presence of the **Hydroponicum** (April–Sept daily 10am–6pm; Oct Mon–Fri 11.30am–3.30pm; Ⓦwww.thehydroponicum.com; £4.95), a cross between a giant green-house and a futuristic scientific research station, and, it has to be said, something of an eyesore. Dubbed "The Garden of the Future", all kinds of flowers, fruits and vegetables are grown without using soil. Bumper crops of strawberries, salad leaves, figs and even bananas result – guided tours (on the hour) explain how it's all done. Five miles northwest of the Hydroponicum at Altandhu, the **Achiltibuie Smokehouse** (☎01854/622353; April–Sept Mon–Sat 9.30am–5pm; free) is also worth a visit, to see meat, fish and game being cured in the traditional way and to buy some afterwards.

For **accommodation**, the wonderfully understated *Summer Isles Hotel* (☎01854/622282, ✉info@summerisleshotel.co.uk; Easter–Oct; ❼), just up the road from the Hydroponicum, enjoys a perfect setting with views over the islands. The hotel buys in Hydroponicum fruit and vegetables and has its own chicken run. Of Achiltibuie's several **B&Bs**, *Dornie House* (☎01854/622271, ✉dorniehousebandb@aol.com; Easter–Nov; ❶), halfway to Altandhu, is welcoming and provides huge breakfasts. There's also a beautifully situated twenty-bed SYHA **hostel** (☎0870/004 1101, ⓦwww.syha.org.uk; May–Sept), three miles southeast of Achiltibuie down the coast at Achininver.

Lochinver and around

The potholed and narrow road north from Achiltibuie through Inverkirkaig is unremittingly spectacular, threading its way through a tumultuous landscape of secret valleys, moorland and bare rock, past the distinctive sugar-loaf **Suilven** (2398ft). Sixteen miles due north of Ullapool (although more than thirty by road), **LOCHINVER** is one of the busiest fishing harbours in Scotland, from where large trucks head off for the continent. The **tourist office** (April–Oct Mon–Sat 10am–5pm, June–Sept also Sun 10am–4pm), within the excellent **Assynt Visitor Centre**, gives an interesting rundown on the area's geology, wildlife and history and has a CCTV link to a nearby heronry; a countryside ranger is available for advice, and there is a whole series of guided walks and activities put on from May to September. The area is also popular with **fishing** enthusiasts: you can get information on permits at the tourist office or post office and at The Cottage, Culag Square (☎01571/844076), where boats can be rented.

Heading **north** from Lochinver, there are two possible routes: the fast A837, which runs eastwards along the shore of Loch Assynt to join the northbound A894, or the narrow, more scenic B869 **coast road** that locals dub "The Breakdown Zone", because its ups and downs claim so many victims during summer. Hugging the indented shoreline, this route offers superb views of the Summer Isles, as well as a number of rewarding side-trips to beaches and dramatic cliffs.

The first village worthy of a detour on the road north is **ACHMELVICH**, three miles northwest of Lochinver, where a tiny bay cradles a stunning white-sand beach lapped by startlingly turquoise water. There's a **campsite** and a basic 36-bed SYHA **hostel** (☎0870/004 1102, ⓦwww.syha.org.uk; April–Sept) just behind the largest beach. However, for total peace and quiet, head to other, equally seductive beaches beyond the headlands.

A wilderness of mountains, moorland, mist and scree, the area east of Lochinver, traversed by the A837, is centred on **Loch Assynt** and bounded by the gnarled peaks of the Ben More Assynt massif. At the southeastern tip of Loch Assynt, **INCHNADAMPH** is home to the *Inchnadamph Hotel* (☎01571/822202, ⓦwww.inchnadamphhotel.co.uk; ❺), a seventeenth-century coaching inn which makes a wonderful Highland retreat. Just along the road, the Assynt Field Centre or *Inchnadamph Lodge* (☎01571/822218, ⓦwww.inch-lodge.co.uk; ❶) has basic, comfortable bunk rooms and spacious B&B accommodation.

Kylesku and around

KYLESKU, 33 miles north of Ullapool on the main A894 road, is the point where a curvaceous road bridge sweeps over the mouth of lochs Glencoul and

Glendhu. Here, the congenial *Kylesku Hotel* (☎01971/502231; March–Oct; ❺) by the water's edge above the old ferry slipway, has a welcoming bar popular with locals, and serves **fresh seafood** including lobster, langoustines, mussels and local salmon. Statesman Cruises runs entertaining **boat trips** (March–Oct twice daily except Sat; round trip 2hr; £12.50; ☎01571/844446 or 01971/502345) from the jetty below the *Kylesku Hotel* to the 650ft **Eas-Coul-Aulin**, Britain's highest waterfall, located at the head of Loch Glencoul; otters, seals, porpoises and minke whales can occasionally be spotted along the way. The boat also makes regular trips out to **Kerracher Gardens** (mid-May to mid-Sept Tues, Thurs & Sun at 1pm; £12.50), which are only accessible from the sea; this remarkable west-coast garden harnesses the Gulf Stream weather to create a riot of colour and exotic vegetation in the rugged Highland scenery.

The far northwest coast

The Sutherland coastline north of Kylesku is a bridge too far for some, yet for others the stark, elemental beauty of the Highlands is to be found on the **far northwest coast** as nowhere else. Here, the peaks become more widely spaced and settlements smaller and fewer, linked by twisting single-track roads and shoreside footpaths that make excellent hiking trails. Places to stay and eat can be thin on the ground, particularly out of season, but the lack of infrastructure is testimony to the isolation which this corner of Scotland delivers in such sweeping style.

Scourie and Handa Island

Ten miles north of Kylesku, the widely scattered crofting community of **SCOURIE**, on a bluff above the main road, surrounds a beautiful sandy beach. Scourie has some good **accommodation** including the charming *Scourie Lodge* (☎01971/502248; March–Oct; ❻), an old shooting retreat surrounded by trees on the north side of the sandy bay. Visible just offshore to the north of Scourie is **HANDA ISLAND**, a huge chunk of red Torridon sandstone surrounded by sheer cliffs, carpeted with machair and purple-tinged moorland, and teeming with sea birds. A **wildlife reserve** administered by the Scottish Wildlife Trust (🕸www.swt.org.uk), Handa Island supports one of the largest sea-bird colonies in northwest Europe. It's a real treat for ornithologists, with razorbills and guillemots breeding on its guano-splashed cliffs during summer. From late May to mid-July, large numbers of puffins waddle comically over the turf-covered clifftops where they dig their burrows. You'll need about three hours to follow the **footpath** around the island. Camping is not allowed, but the SWT is currently revamping a popular **bothy** for bird-watchers (reservations essential on ☎01463/714746). Weather permitting, **boats** (☎01971/502347) leave for Handa throughout the day (Easter to Sept Mon–Sat; £8) from the tiny cove of **TARBET**, three miles northwest of the main road and accessible by postbus from Scourie.

Kinlochbervie and Sandwood Bay

North of Scourie, the road sweeps inland through the starkest part of the Highlands, where rocks piled on rocks, bog and water create an almost alien landscape. The B801 side road branches off to **KINLOCHBERVIE**, which for all the world seems to be a typical, straggling West Highland crofting community with a **hotel** (☎01971/521275; ❺) until you turn a corner and encounter an incongruously huge fish market and modern concrete harbour, where trucks from all over Europe pick up cod and shellfish. There's a mobile bank and petrol pump and, if you're in need of sustenance, try the **fish and chips** at the *Fishermen's Mission* (closed Sat & Sun); otherwise Kinlochbervie is not a place to linger.

A single-track road continues northwest of Kinlochbervie through isolated **OLDSHOREMORE**, a working crofters' village with a small store selling provisions, above a stunning white-sand beach. Beyond, at **BLAIRMORE**, an enlarged car-park is testament to the growing number of visitors making the four-mile walk across peaty moorland to **Sandwood Bay**. The shell-white sandy **beach** at the end of the rough track is a breathtaking sight and one of the most beautiful in Scotland. Flanked by rolling dunes and lashed by fierce gales for much of the year, the dramatic leaning rock-stack to the south is said to be haunted by a bearded mariner – one of many sailors to have perished on this notoriously dangerous stretch of coast since the Vikings first navigated it over a millennium ago. Around the turn of the twentieth century, the beach, whose treacherous undercurrents make it unsuitable for swimming, also witnessed Britain's most recent recorded sighting of a mermaid. Turning back and past Blairmore at **SHEIGRA**, where the road ends, you can **camp** behind the beach.

The north coast

Though a constant stream of sponsored walkers, caravans and tour groups makes it to the dull town of **John O'Groats**, surprisingly few visitors travel the whole length of the Highlands' wild **north coast**. Those that do, however, rarely return disappointed. Pounded by one of the world's most ferocious seaways, Scotland's rugged northern shore is backed by barren mountains in the west, and in the east by lochs and open rolling grasslands. Between its far ends, mile upon mile of crumbling cliffs and sheer rocky headlands shelter bays whose perfect white beaches are nearly always deserted, even in the height of summer – though, somewhat incongruously, they're also home to Scotland's best surfing waves.

Though only a wee place, **Durness** is a good jumping-off point for nearby Balnakiel beach, one of the area's most beautiful sandy strands, and for rugged **Cape Wrath**, the windswept promontory at Scotland's northwest tip, which has retained an end-of-the-world mystique lost long ago by John O'Groats. **Thurso**, the largest town on the north coast, is really only visited by those en route to Orkney. More enticing are the huge sea-bird colonies clustered in clefts and on remote stacks at **Dunnet Head** and **Duncansby Head**, to the east of Thurso.

Durness and around

Scattered around a string of sheltered sandy coves and grassy cliff-tops, **DURNESS** (W www.durness.org) is the most northwesterly village on the British mainland. It straddles the turning point on the main A838 road as it swings east from the inland peat bogs of the interior to the north coast's fertile strip of limestone machair. Durness village sits above its own sandy bay, Sango Sands, while half a mile to the east is **SMOO**, which used to be an RAF station. In between Durness and Smoo is the millennial village hall, whose windblown and rather forlorn community garden harbours a memorial commemorating the Beatle **John Lennon**, who used to come to Durness on family holidays as a kid (and even revisited the place in the 1960s with Yoko). It's worth pausing at Smoo to see the 200ft-long **Smoo Cave**, a gaping hole in a sheer limestone cliff formed partly by the action of the sea and partly by the small burn that flows through it.

A narrow road winds a mile or so northwest of Durness to **BALNAKIEL**, passing **Balnakiel Craft Village** en route. The craft village is housed in a grim 1940s military base, transformed in the 1960s into a sort of industrial estate for arts and crafts, thanks to the carrot of cheap rents for studio and living quarters. A dozen or so workshops continue to function including a woodwind-instrument maker, a picture framer, painters, potters and leather workers. There's also the friendly *Loch Croispol* book shop, which runs an excellent daytime **café** (daily 10am–5pm, but restricted winter opening) and serves Sunday lunch (℡01971/511777, Ⓦwww.scottish-books.org).

Practicalities

Public transport to Durness is sparse; the key service is the Dearman Coaches link (May–Sept Mon–Sat 1 daily) from Inverness via Ullapool and Lochin-ver. Postbuses provide a more complicated year-round alternative and meet trains at Lairg; check schedules at the post office or tourist office. The helpful Durness **tourist office** (March–Oct Mon–Sat 10am–5pm; July & Aug also Sun 10am–4pm; Nov–Feb Mon–Fri 10am–1.30pm) has a small **visitor centre** that features excellent interpretive panels detailing the area's history, geology, flora and fauna, with insights into the daily life of the community.

In terms of **accommodation**, ⚹ *Mackays Room and Restaurant*, at the western edge of the village, stands out for its welcome, tasteful Highland decor and emphasis on freshly prepared cooking with the personal touch (℡01971/511202, Ⓦwww.visitmackays.com ❺). The proprietor also runs the clean and popular *Lazy Crofter Bunkhouse* (℡01971/511202, Ⓦwww .durnesshostel.com) next door. Alternatively, *Puffin Cottage* (℡01971/511208, Ⓦwww.puffincottage.com; April–Sept; ❶) is a very pleasant B&B, and there's also a basic SYHA **hostel** (℡0870/004 1113, Ⓦwww.syha.org.uk; March–Oct; dorm beds £12), beside the Smoo Cave car park half a mile east of the village. The *Seafood Platter* on the outskirts of the village towards Tongue is great value, serving the freshest of seafood and succulent steaks in a small, cosy **restaurant**.

Cape Wrath

An excellent day-trip begins two miles southwest of Durness at **KEOLDALE**, where (tides permitting) a foot-passenger **ferry** (daily: May & Sept 11am & 1.30pm; June–Aug 9.30am, 11am & 1.30pm; ℡01971/511376; £7 return) crosses the spectacular Kyle of Durness estuary to link with a **minibus** (℡01971/511343; May–Sept) that runs the eleven miles out to **Cape Wrath**, mainland Britain's most northwesterly point. Note that Garvie Island (An Garbh-eilean) is an air bombing range, and the military regularly close the road to Cape Wrath, so check first with Durness tourist office or the MOD advisory line (℡0800/833300). The headland takes its name not from the stormy seas that crash against it for most of the year, but from the Norse word *hvarf*, meaning "turning place" – a throwback to the days when Viking warships used it as a navigation point during raids on the Scottish coast.

Tongue to Thurso

There's great drama in the landscape between Tongue and Thurso, as the A836 – still single-track for much of the way – wends its way over bleak and often totally uninhabited rocky moorland, intercut with sandy sea lochs. Tiny little

24

Tongue is pleasant enough, as is the equally small settlement of **Bettyhill**, to the east, but the real reason to venture this far is to explore the countryside: **Ben Hope** (3040ft), the most northerly Munro, and the fascinating blanket bog of the **Flow Country** even further inland.

Tongue and around

The road takes a wonderfully slow and circuitous route around Loch Eriboll and east over the top of A' Mhoine moor to the pretty crofting township of **TONGUE**. Dominated by the ruins of **Castle Varrich** (Caisteal Bharraich), a medieval stronghold of the Mackays (three-mile return walk), the village is strewn above the east shore of the **Kyle of Tongue**, which you can either cross via a new causeway, or by following the longer and more scenic single-track road around its southern side. When the tide recedes, this shallow estuary becomes a mass of golden sand flats, superb on sunny days, with the sharp profiles of **Ben Hope** (3040ft) and **Ben Loyal** (2509ft) looming like twin sentinels to the south.

The best **accommodation** in Tongue is the *Tongue Hotel* (☏01847/611206, ⓦwww.tonguehotel.co.uk; April–Oct; ❻), the plush, former hunting lodge of the Duke of Sutherland, which serves delicious food, and has a cosy downstairs bar. The SYHA **hostel** (☏0870/155 3255, ⓦwww.syha.org.uk; dorm beds £12) is right beside the causeway a mile north of the village centre on the Kyle's east shore. Over on the western side of the Kyle, five miles away at **Talmine**, a converted nineteenth-century church with great views towards the Orkney Islands is home to the popular *Cloisters* B&B (☏01847/601286, ⓦwww.cloistertal.demon.co.uk; ❷). There is also a very basic **campsite** opposite the sandy beach.

Bettyhill and around

Twelve miles east of Tongue, **BETTYHILL** is a major crofting village, set among rocky green hills. In Gaelic, it was known as *Am Blàran Odhar* (Little Dun-coloured Field), but the origins of the English name are unknown; however, it was definitely not named after Elizabeth, Countess of Sutherland, who presided over the Strathnaver Clearances. The story of those terrible times is told by local schoolchildren at the delightful and loyally maintained **Strathnaver Museum** (April–Oct Mon–Sat 10am–1pm & 2–5pm; £1.90), housed in the old Farr church, set apart from the main village. A short stroll north of the church is the splendid sheltered **Farr beach**, which forms an unbroken arc of pure white sand between the Naver and Borgie rivers. Even more visually impressive is the River Naver's narrow tidal estuary, to the west of Bettyhill, and **Torrisdale beach**, which ends in a smooth white spit that forms part of the **Invernaver Nature Reserve**.

As you move east from Bettyhill, the north coast changes dramatically as the hills on the horizon recede to be replaced by fields fringed with flagstone walls. At the hamlet of **MELVICH**, twelve miles east of Bettyhill, the A897 cuts south through Strath Halladale, the Flow Country and the Strath of Kildonan to Helmsdale on the east coast (see p.1104). Five miles east of Melvich, **Dounreay Nuclear Power Station** (ⓦwww.ukaea.org.ukDounreay), is a surreal collection of chimney stacks and box like buildings, including the famous golf-ball-shaped DLR (Dounreay Fast Reactor). Established back in 1955, Dounreay pioneered the development of fast reactor technology and was the first reactor in the world to provide mains electricity. The reactors themselves have long since closed, though Dounreay remains by far the biggest employer on the north coast, with decommissioning estimated to take another thirty years at a cost of £2.7 billion.

The helpful **visitor centre** (Easter to end Oct daily 10am–4pm; free) details the processes (and, unsurprisingly, the benefits) of nuclear power, and seeks to offer explanations for a range of issues such as the area's "leukaemia cluster" and the radioactive particles that continue to be found on the nearby beaches.

The Flow Country

From Melvich, you can head forty miles or so south towards Helmsdale on the A897, through the **Flow Country**, whose name comes from *flói*, an Old Norse word meaning "marshy ground". This huge expanse of blanket bog is a valuable "carbon sink" and home to a wide variety of wildlife. At the train station at **FORSINARD**, fourteen miles south of Melvich and easily accessible from Thurso, Wick and the south, there is an RSPB **visitor centre** (April–Oct daily 9am–6pm; ☎01641/571225), with CCTV coverage of hen harriers nesting, as well as a **Peatland Centre**, which explains the wonders of peat. To get to grips with the whole concept of blanket bog, take a leaflet and follow the short **Dubh Lochan Trail** that's been laid out over the flagstones, through peat banks to some nearby black lochans.

Thurso

Approached from the isolation of the west, **THURSO** feels like a metropolis. In reality, it's a relatively small service centre visited mostly by people passing through to the adjoining port of **Scrabster** to catch the ferry to Orkney, or by increasing numbers of surfers attracted to the waves on the north coast. The town's name derives from the Norse word *Thorsa*, literally "River of the God Thor", and in Viking times it was a major gateway to the mainland. Thurso's grid-plan streets boast some rather handsome Victorian architecture in the local, greyish sandstone, though there's nothing really specific to detain you. **Traill Street** is the main drag, turning into the pedestrianized Rotterdam Street and High Street precinct at its northern end. On the High Street, by the side of the old Victorian town hall, is **Thurso Heritage Museum** (June–Sept Mon–Sat 10am–1pm & 2–5pm; £1) whose most intriguing exhibits are the Ulbster Stone in the entrance, which features elephants, fish and other beasts; the Skinnet Stone, intricately carved with enigmatic symbols; and a runic cross.

The **Scrabster ferry terminal** is a mile or so northwest of town, with regular buses from the train station in the morning, and from Olrig Street in the afternoon. There's a helpful riverside **tourist office** (April–Oct Mon–Sat 10am–5pm; June–Sept also Sun 10am–4pm), and a good supply of **accommodation**. Of the B&Bs, *Murray House*, 1 Campbell St (☎01847/895759, ⓦwww.murrayhousebb.com; ❷), is central, comfortable and friendly, or try *Tigh na Abhainn*, an old house by the river (☎01847/893443; ❷). There are several **hostels**, the best of which is *Sandra's*, 24/26 Princes St (☎01847/894575, ⓦwww.sandras-backpackers.ukf.net; dorm beds £11.50), a refurbished, clean and well-run place owned by the popular chippie downstairs; it also offers **bike rental** (£14) and **Internet** access. By far the best place **to eat** in Thurso is the popular *Le Bistro*, 2 Traill St (☎01847/893737; Tues–Sat); for fresh seafood, head for *The Captain's Galley* in Scrabster. If you're coming to **surf**, Andy Bain of Thurso Surf offers surf lessons and advice (April–Sept; ☎01847/831866, ⓦwww.thursosurf.com), or try Tempest Surf (☎01847/892500) on Riverside Road.

Dunnet Head and the Castle of Mey

Thurso doesn't have much of a beach, so if you want to sink your toes into sand, head five miles east along the A836 to **Dunnet Bay**, a vast golden beach

△ The Castle of Mey

backed by huge dunes. The bay is popular with surfers, and even in the winter you can usually spot intrepid figures far out in the Pentland Firth's breakers. At the northeast end of the bay, there's a **Ranger Centre** (April–Sept Tues–Fri & Sun 2–5pm) beside the excellent campsite, where you can pick up information on good local history and nature walks.

Despite the publicity that John O'Groats customarily receives, mainland Britain's most northerly point is in fact **Dunnet Head**, north of Dunnet along the B855, which runs for four miles over bleak heather and bog to the tip of the headland, crowned with a Stevenson lighthouse, at 105m above sea-level. On a clear day you can see the whole northern coastline from Cape Wrath to Duncansby Head, and across the treacherous Pentland Firth to Orkney.

Roughly fifteen miles east of Thurso, just off the A836, lies the Queen Mum's former Scottish home and the most northerly castle on the UK mainland, the **Castle of Mey** (May–July & mid-Aug to Sept Sat–Thurs 10.30am–4pm; Ⓦ www.castleofmey.org.uk; £7). It's a modest little place, hidden behind high flagstone walls, with great views north to Orkney, and a herd of the Queen Mother's beloved Aberdeen Angus grazing out front. The Queen Mum used to spend every August here, and unusually for a royal palace, it's remarkably unstuffy inside, the walls hung with works by local amateur artists (and watercolours by Prince Charles), the sideboards cluttered with tacky joke ornaments and the video library well stocked with copies of *Fawlty Towers* and *Dad's Army*.

John O'Groats and around

Romantics expecting to find a magical meeting of land and water at **JOHN O'GROATS** (Ⓦ www.visitjohnogroats.com) are invariably disappointed – sadly it remains an uninspiring tourist trap. The views north to Orkney are fine enough, but the village offers little more than a string of souvenir and craft shops, and cafés thronged with coach parties. The village gets its name from the Dutchman, Jan de Groot, who obtained the ferry contract for the hazardous crossing to Orkney in 1496. The eight-sided house he built for his eight quarrelling sons (so that each one could enter by his own door) is echoed in the octagonal tower of the much-photographed but neglected *John O'Groats Hotel*. Aside from regular **buses** to Wick and Thurso, there are frequent if irregular links with Land's End (the far southwest tip of England; see p.373), maintained by a succession of walkers, cyclists, vintage-car drivers and pushers of baths.

There are several **boat trips** to be had: John O'Groats Ferries (℡01955/611353, ⓦwww.jogferry.co.uk) offers a leisurely afternoon cruise round the sea-bird colonies and stacks of Duncansby Head or the seal colonies of Stroma (mid-June to Aug daily at 2.30pm; 1hr 30min; £14). North Coast Marine Adventures (Easter to Oct daily; ℡01955/611797, ⓦwww.northcoast-marine-adventures .co.uk) offers rather more high-adrenalin 30min trips in a rigid inflatable (£13), and a 1hr scenic wildlife tour (£16).

If you're disappointed by John O'Groats, press on a couple of miles further east to **Duncansby Head**, which, with its lighthouse, dramatic cliffs and well-worn coastal path, has a lot more to offer. The birdlife here is prolific, and south of the headland lie some spectacular 200ft cliffs, cut by sheer-sided clefts known locally as *geos*, and several impressive sea-stacks, including a very photogenic triangular one.

The east coast

The **east coast** of the Highlands, between Inverness and Wick, is nowhere near as spectacular as the west, with gently undulating moors, grassland and low cliffs where you might otherwise expect to find sea lochs and mountains. While many visitors speed up the main A9 road through this region in a headlong rush to the Orkneys' prehistoric sites, those who choose to dally will find a wealth of brochs, cairns and standing stones, many in remarkable condition. The area around the Black Isle and the Tain was a Pictish heartland, and has yielded many important finds. Further north, from around the ninth century AD onwards, the **Norse** influence was more keenly felt than in any other part of mainland Britain, and dozens of Scandinavian-sounding names recall the era when this was a Viking kingdom.

The nineteenth-century **Clearances** hit the region hard, as countless ruined cottages and empty glens show. To make way for sheep, hundreds of thousands of crofters were evicted and forced to emigrate to New Zealand, Canada and Australia, or else take up fishing in one of the numerous herring ports established on the coast. The fishing heritage is a recurring theme along this coast, though there are only a handful of working boats scattered around the harbours today, and while the oil boom has brought a transient prosperity to one or two places over the past few decades, the area remains one of the country's poorest, reliant on relatively thin pickings from sheep farming, fishing and tourism.

The one stretch of the east coast that's always been relatively rich is the **Black Isle** just over the Kessock Bridge heading north out of Inverness, whose main village, **Cromarty**, is the region's undisputed highlight, with a crop of elegant mansions and appealing fishermen's cottages clustered near the entrance to the Cromarty Firth. Beyond **Dornoch**, a golfing resort recently famous as the site of Madonna's wedding, the ersatz–Loire château **Dunrobin Castle** is the main tourist attraction, a monument as much to the iniquities of the Clearances as to the eccentricities of Victorian taste. **Wick**, the largest town on this section

24

of coast, has an interesting past inevitably entwined with the fishing industry, whose story is told in a good heritage centre, but is otherwise uninspiring. The relatively flat landscapes of this northeast corner – windswept peat bog and farmland dotted with lochans and grey-and-white crofts – are a surprising contrast to the more rugged country south and west of here.

The Black Isle and around

Sandwiched between the Cromarty Firth to the north and, to the south, the Moray and Beauly firths which separate it from Inverness, the **Black Isle** is not an island at all, but a fertile peninsula whose rolling hills, prosperous farms and stands of deciduous woodland make it more reminiscent of Dorset or Sussex than the Highlands. It probably gained its name because of its mild climate: there's rarely frost, which leaves the fields "black" all winter; another explanation is that the name derives from the Gaelic word for black, *dubh* – a possible corruption of St Duthus.

Fortrose and Rosemarkie

FORTROSE, six miles east of Munlochy, is a quietly elegant village dominated by the beautiful ruins of an early thirteenth-century **cathedral** (daily 9am–8pm; free access). Founded by King David I, it now languishes on a lovely green bordered by red-sandstone and colour-washed houses. Nearby **Chanonry Point**, reached by a backroad from the north end of Fortrose, juts into a narrow channel in the Moray Firth; the point, fringed on one side by a beach of golden sand and shingle, is an excellent place to look for **dolphins** (see p.1066). Come here when the tide is rising and you stand the best chance of spotting a couple leaping through the surf in search of fish. **ROSEMARKIE**, a lovely one-street village a mile north of Fortrose at the northwest end of the beach, is thought to have been evangelized by St Boniface in the early eighth century. The cosy **Groam House Museum** (May–Sept Mon–Sat 10am–5pm, Sun 2–4.30pm; Oct–April Sat & Sun 2–4pm; free), at the bottom of the village, displays a bumper crop of intricately carved Pictish standing stones (among them the famous Rosemarkie Cross Slab), and shows an informative video highlighting Pictish sites in the region. A lovely mile-and-a-half **woodland walk**, along the banks of a sparkling burn to Fairy Glen, begins at the car park just beyond the village on the road to Cromarty. Good **bar food** in this area is available at the *Plough Inn*, just down the main street from the museum in Rosemarkie, or at *The Anderson* (☎01381/620236, ⓦwww.theanderson.co.uk), a pleasantly individual hotel around the corner from the cathedral in Fortrose.

Cromarty

An ancient legend recalls that the twin headlands flanking the entrance to the **Cromarty Firth**, known as The Sutors (from the Gaelic word for shoemaker), were once a pair of giant cobblers who used to protect the Black Isle from pirates. Nowadays, however, the only giants in the area are Nigg and Invergordon's colossal oil rigs, marooned in the estuary like metal monsters marching out to sea, and forming a surreal counterpoint to the web of tiny streets and chocolate box workers' cottages of **CROMARTY**. The Black Isle's main settlement, Cromarty was an ancient ferry crossing-point on the pilgrimage trail to St Duthus's shrine in Tain, but lost much of its trade during the nineteenth century to places served by the railway; a branch line to the town was begun but never completed. Cromarty didn't became a prominent port until 1772 when the entrepreneurial local landlord, George Ross, founded a hemp mill here, fuelling a period of prosperity during which Cromarty acquired some of Scotland's finest Georgian houses: these, together with the terraced fishers' cottages of the nineteenth-century herring boom, have left the town with a wonderfully well-preserved concentration of Scottish domestic architecture.

To get a sense of Cromarty's past, wander through the town's pretty streets to the **museum** housed in the old **Courthouse** on Church Street (daily: April–Oct 10am–5pm; Nov–Dec noon–4pm; £3.50), which tells the history of the town using audiovisuals and animated figures. Dolphin- and other wildlife-spotting trips are offered locally by Ecoventures (℡01381/600323, ⓦwww .ecoventures.co.uk), who blast out through the Soutars to the Moray Firth. The tiny two-car Nigg–Cromarty **ferry** (June–Oct daily 8am–6.15pm), Scotland's smallest, also doubles as a cruiser on Wednesday evenings in summer; you can catch it from the jetty near the lighthouse.

For **B&B**, try one of the attractive old houses on Church Street, such as Mrs Robinson's at no. 7 (℡01381/600488; ❶), where you can also **rent bikes**. A little way out of town in the direction of Dingwall, *Newfield B&B* (℡01381/610325, ⓦwww.newfield-bb.co.uk; ❷) is also a pleasant option. For something **to eat**, there are few more down-to-earth but satisfying restaurants in the Highlands than ⚜ *Sutor Creek* at 21 Bank St (℡01381/600855, ⓦwww .sutorcreek.co.uk; closed Mon–Wed in winter). A small, friendly place run as a local co-operative, it serves delicious fresh pizza cooked in a wood-fired oven, though the imaginative toppings (and the daily blackboard specials) are local and seasonal rather than conventionally Italian.

Dingwall and Strathpeffer

Most traffic nowadays takes the upgraded A9 north from Inverness, bypassing the small market town of **DINGWALL** (from the Norse *thing*, "parliament", and *vollr*, "field"), a royal burgh since 1226 and former port that was left high and dry when the river receded during the nineteenth century. Today, it has succumbed to the curse of British provincial towns and acquired an ugly business park and characterless pedestrian shopping street. Dingwall's only real claim to fame is that it was the birthplace of Macbeth, whose family occupied the now ruined castle on Castle Street. You're unlikely to want to hang around here for long – for somewhere pleasant to stay move onto Strathpeffer or push on north.

STRATHPEFFER, a mannered and leafy Victorian spa town surrounded by wooded hills four miles west of Dingwall, is pleasant enough but suffers from a high density of coach parties. During its heyday, this was a renowned European **health resort** reached by the tongue-twisting Strathpeffer Spa Express train from Aviemore. A recent face-lift has seen the town's attractive grand pavilion transformed into a performing arts centre, the Strathpeffer Pavilion (ⓦwww .strathpefferpavilion.org) and the nearby **Pump Room** (March–Oct Mon–Sat 10am–6pm, Sun 2–5pm; £2) converted into a visitors' centre, where displays and videos relate the history of the resort. You can also sample water here from five local wells which were supposed to treat all manner of ailments – most of today's visitors, however, find the sulphurous-smelling liquid more masochistic than medicinal.

Tourist information is available in the front section of the Pump Room (see above for opening hours). The large **hotels** in the village are very popular with bus tours, so try one of the smaller places such as *Brunstane Lodge* (℡01997/421261, ⓦwww.brunstanelodge.com; ❺). There's also **B&B** at the upmarket *Craigvar* (℡01997/421622, ⓦwww.craigvar.com; ❹), which overlooks the main square, or the hospitable and spacious *Dunraven Lodge* on Golf

24

Course Road (℡01997/421210, ⓦwww.dunravenlodge.co.uk; ❸). Also on the square, the excellent **bike** shop, Square Wheels (℡01997/421000, ⓦwww .squarewheels.biz; closed Tues), rents out bikes and offers good advice on some enjoyable local routes.

Strathpeffer is within striking distance of the bleak **Ben Wyvis**, and so is also a popular base for walkers. One of the best hikes in the area is up the hill of Cnoc Mor, where the vitrified Iron-Age hillfort of **Knock Farrel** affords superb panoramic views to the Cromarty Firth and the surrounding mountains.

The Dornoch Firth and around

North of the Cromarty Firth, the hammer-shaped **Fearn peninsula** can still be approached from the south by the ancient ferry-crossing from Cromarty to Nigg, though to the north the link is a more recent causeway over the **Dornoch Firth**, the inlet which marks the northern boundary of the peninsula. On the southern edge of the Dornoch Firth the A9 bypasses the quiet town of **TAIN**, an attractive, old-fashioned small town of grand whisky-coloured sandstone buildings that was the birthplace of **St Duthus**, an eleventh-century missionary who inspired great devotion in the Middle Ages. Tain's main attraction is the **Glenmorangie whisky distillery** where the highly rated malt is produced (℡01862/892477; shop Mon–Fri 9am–5pm, April–Oct also Sat 10am–4pm, June–Aug also Sun noon–4pm; tours Mon–Fri 10.30am–3.30pm, Sat 10.30am–2.30pm, Sun 12.30–2.30pm; £2.50 including discount voucher); it lies beside the A9 on the north side of town. Booking is recommended for the tours.

Bonar Bridge and Carbisdale Castle

Before the causeway was built across the Dornoch Firth, traffic heading along the coast used to skirt west around the estuary, crossing the Kyle of Sutherland at the village of **BONAR BRIDGE**. There's little of note here other than the **bridge** itself, which has had three incarnations before the present steel construction of 1973, all recalled on a stone plinth on the north side.

Towering high above the River Shin, three miles northwest of Bonar Bridge, the daunting neo-Gothic profile of **Carbisdale Castle** overlooks the Kyle of Sutherland. The castle was erected between 1906 and 1917 for the dowager Duchess of Sutherland, following a protracted family feud. Designed in three distinct styles (to give the impression it was added to over a long period of time), Carbisdale was eventually acquired by a Norwegian shipping magnate in 1933, and finally gifted, along with its entire contents and estate, to the Scottish Youth Hostels Association, which has turned it into what must be one of the most opulent **hostels** in the world, full of white Italian marble sculptures, huge gilt-framed portraits, sweeping staircases and magnificent drawing rooms. It also has standard hostel facilities such as self-catering kitchens, games rooms, TV rooms and dorms (£15), as well as four-bed family rooms (℡0870/004 1109, ⓦwww.carbisdale.org; March–Oct). The best way to get here by public transport is to take a **train** to nearby Culrain station, which lies within easy walking distance of the castle. **Buses** from Inverness (3 daily; 1hr 30min) and Tain (4 daily; 25min) only stop at **Ardgay**, three miles south.

Dornoch

DORNOCH, a genteel and appealing town eight miles north of Tain, lies on a flattish headland overlooking the **Dornoch Firth**. It's something of a middle-class holiday resort, with solid Edwardian hotels, trees and flowers in profusion, and miles of sandy beaches giving good views across the estuary to the Fearn

㉔

peninsula. The town is also renowned for its championship **golf course**, Scotland's most northerly first-class course. Dornoch was the scene for Scotland's most prestigious rock'n'roll wedding of recent times, when Madonna married Guy Ritchie at nearby Skibo Castle and had her son baptized in Dornoch **cathedral**, which was founded in 1224 and built of local sandstone. The vaulted roof is particularly appealing, while the stained-glass windows in the north wall were later additions, endowed by the expat Andrew Carnegie. Opposite, the castellated **Old Town Jail** is home to a series of upmarket craft shops under the banner Jail Dornoch, while tucked in behind the *Castle Hotel* is the local **Historylinks Museum** (10am–4pm: April & May Mon–Fri; June–Sept daily; £2), which tells the story of Dornoch, from local saints to the Madonna herself.

Local **tourist information** can be found beside the *Coffee Shop* in the cluster of buildings near the cathedral (April–Sept daily 9.30am–5.30pm; Oct–March Mon–Sat 10am–5pm, Sun 11am–5pm), where there's also **bike rental** available. There's no shortage of **accommodation**: both in great locations opposite the cathedral, try *Tordarroch B&B* (T01862/810855; March–Oct; ❷), or *Trevose* (T01862/810269; March–Sept; ❷), which is swathed in roses. The characterful *Dornoch Castle Hotel* (T01862/810216, Wwww.dornochcastlehotel.com; ❺), in the Bishop's Palace on the Square, has a cosy old-style bar and relaxing tea garden. The *Caravan Park* (T01862/810423, Wwww.dornochcaravans .co.uk; April–Oct) is attractively set between the manicured golf course and the uncombed vegetation of the sand dunes which fringe the beach; it offers **camping** but gets busy with caravans in July and August.

Expensive gourmet meals are available at *2 Quail* **restaurant** (T01862/811811; May–Sept Tues–Sat; Oct–April Thurs–Sat) on Castle Street, which also has tasteful rooms (❺). Alternatively, *Luigi's*, also on Castle Street, serves familiar but decent Italian-style snacks and meals: it's open during the day and, in summer, on weekend evenings.

North to Wick

North of Dornoch, the A9 hugs the coastline for most of the sixty or so miles to **Wick**, the principal settlement in the far north of the mainland. Perhaps the most important landmark in the whole stretch is the **Sutherland Monument** near Golspie, erected in memory of the first Duke of Sutherland, the landowner who oversaw the eviction of thousands of his tenants in a process known as the Clearances. The bitter memory of those times resonates through most of the small towns and villages on this stretch, including **Badbea**, the gold-prospecting village of **Helmsdale**, **Dunbeath** and **Lybster**.

Dunrobin Castle and the Sutherland Monument

Ten miles north of Dornoch on the A9 lies the straggling red-sandstone town of **GOLSPIE**, whose status as an administrative centre does little to relieve its dullness. The main reason to stop here is to look around **Dunrobin Castle** (April–May & early Oct Mon–Sat 10.30am–4.30pm, Sun noon–4.30pm; June–Sept daily 10.30am–5.30pm; £6.70), overlooking the sea a mile north of town. Approached via a long tree-lined drive, this fairy-tale confection of turrets and pointed roofs – modelled by the architect Sir Charles Barry (designer of the Houses of Parliament) on a Loire château – is the seat of the infamous Sutherland family, at one time Europe's biggest landowners, with a staggering 1.3 million acres, and the principal driving force behind the Clearances in this area. The castle is on a correspondingly vast scale, boasting 189 furnished rooms, of which the tour takes in only seventeen. Staring up at the pile from the midst of its elaborate **formal gardens**, it's worth remembering that such extravagance was paid for by uprooting literally thousands of crofters from the surrounding glens.

Immediately behind Golspie, you can't miss the 100ft **monument** to the first Duke of Sutherland, which peers proprietorially down from the summit of the 1293ft **Beinn a'Bhragaidh** (Ben Bhraggie). An inscription cut into its base recalls that the statue was erected in 1834 by "a mourning and grateful tenantry [to] a judicious, kind and liberal landlord [who would] open his hands to the distress of the widow, the sick and the traveller". Unsurprisingly, there's no reference to the fact that the duke, widely regarded as Scotland's own Josef Stalin, forcibly evicted 15,000 crofters from his million-acre estate. It's worth the stiff **climb** to the top of the hill (round trip 1hr 30min) for the wonderful views south along the coast past Dornoch to the Moray Firth and west towards Lairg and Loch Shin. The path is steep and strenuous in places, however, and there's no view until you're out of the trees, about twenty minutes from the top. Head up Fountain Road about halfway along Golspie's main street; after crossing the railway line and passing through Rhives farm steading, follow the Beinn a'Bhragaidh footpath (BBFP) signs along the path into the woods.

The Highland Clearances

Once the clan chiefs had been forbidden their own armies after the defeat at Culloden, they had no need of the large tenantry that had previously been a vital military asset – and yet the second half of the eighteenth century saw the Highland population double after the introduction of the easy-to-grow and nutritious potato. The clan chiefs adopted different policies to deal with the new situation. Some encouraged emigration, and as many as six thousand Highlanders left for the Americas between 1800 and 1803 alone. Other landowners developed alternative forms of employment for their tenants, mainly fishing and the gathering of kelp. This brown seaweed was burnt to produce soda ash, which was used in the manufacture of soap, glass and explosives. Other landowners developed sheep runs on the Highland pastures, introducing hardy breeds like the black-faced Linton and the Cheviot. But extensive sheep farming proved incompatible with a high peasant population, and many landowners decided to clear their estates of tenants, some of whom were forcibly moved to tiny plots of marginal land, where they were to farm as crofters.

The pace of these **Highland Clearances** accelerated after the end of the Napoleonic Wars in 1815, when the market price for kelp, fish and cattle declined, leaving sheep as the only profitable Highland product. As the dispossessed Highlanders scratched a living from the acid soils of some tiny croft, they learnt through bitter experience the limitations of the clan. Famine followed, forcing large-scale emigration and leaving the huge uninhabited areas found in the region today. The crofters eked out a precarious existence, but they hung on throughout the nineteenth century, often by taking seasonal employment away from home.

In the 1880s, however, a sharp downturn in agricultural prices made it difficult for many crofters to pay their rent. This time, inspired by the example of the Irish Land League, they resisted eviction, forming the **Highland Land Reform Association** and the **Crofters' Party**. In 1886, in response to the social unrest, Gladstone's Liberal government passed the **Crofters' Holdings Act**, which conceded three of the crofters' demands: security of tenure, fair rents to be decided independently, and the right to pass on crofts by inheritance. But Gladstone did not attempt to increase the amount of land available for crofting and shortage of land remained a major problem until the **Land Settlement Act** of 1919 made provision for the creation of new crofts. Nevertheless, the population of the Highlands continued to decline during the twentieth century, with many of the region's young people finding city life more appealing.

Helmsdale, Dunbeath and Lybster

Eleven scenic miles north along the A9 from Golspie, **HELMSDALE** is an old herring port, founded in the nineteenth century to house the evicted inhabitants of Strath Kildonan, which lies behind it. The Strath was the unlikely location of a gold rush in the 1860s, and a few determined prospectors still pan the Kildonan Burn. The full story of the area's gold hunters is told in the attractively designed **Timespan Heritage Centre**, beside the river (April–Oct Mon–Sat 10am–5pm, Sun noon–5pm; £4), along with tales of Viking raids, witch-burning, Clearances and fishing. The centre also has an art gallery and a plain café.

Just north of Helmsdale, the A9 begins its long haul up the **Ord of Caithness**. Once over the pass, the landscape changes dramatically as heather-clad moors give way to miles of treeless green grazing lands, peppered with derelict crofts and latticed by long drystone walls. As you come over the pass, look out for signs to the ruined village of **Badbea**, reached via a ten-minute walk from the car park at the side of the A9. Built by tenants cleared from nearby Ousdale, the settlement now lies deserted, although its ruined hovels show what hardship the crofters had to endure: the cottages stood so near the windy cliff edge that children had to be tethered to prevent them from being blown into the sea.

DUNBEATH, hidden at the mouth of a small strath twelve miles north of Ord of Caithness, was another village founded to provide work in the wake of the Clearances. The local landlord built a harbour here in 1800, at the start of the herring boom, and the settlement briefly flourished. Today it's a sleepy place, with lobster pots stacked at the quayside and views of windswept Dunbeath Castle (no public access) on the opposite side of the bay. The novelist Neil Gunn was born here in one of the terraced houses under the flyover that now swoops above the village; you can find out more about him at the **Dunbeath Heritage Centre** (April–Oct daily 10am–5pm; Nov–March Mon–Fri 11am–3pm; £2), signposted from the road.

Seven miles north of Dunbeath, the planned village of **LYBSTER** (pronounced "libe-ster") was established at the height of the nineteenth-century herring boom, when 200-odd boats worked out of its harbour; now there are just one or two. The **Water Lines** heritage centre by the harbour (May–Sept daily 11am–5pm; £2.50) is an attractive modern display about the "silver darlings" and the fishermen that pursued them; there's a snug café downstairs. There's not much else to see here apart from the harbour area: the upper town is a grim collection of grey pebble-dashed bungalows centred on a broad main street.

Wick

Originally a Viking settlement named *Vik* (meaning "bay"), **WICK** has been a royal burgh since 1589. It's actually two towns: Wick proper, and **Pultneytown**, immediately south across the river, a messy, rather run-down community planned by Thomas Telford in 1806 for the British Fisheries Society to encourage evicted crofters to take up fishing. Wick's heyday was in the mid-nineteenth century, when it was the busiest herring port in Europe, with a fleet of over 1100 boats, exporting tons of fish to Russia, Scandinavia and the West Indian slave plantations. Robert Louis Stevenson described it as "the meanest of man's towns, situated on the baldest of God's bays", and something of that down-at-heel atmosphere is apparent today. It's not somewhere you're likely to linger; if you're here for a few hours, the area around the harbour in Pultneytown, lined with rows of fishermen's cottages, is most worth a wander, with acres of largely derelict net-mending sheds, stores and cooperages around the harbour giving some idea of the former scale of the fishing trade. The town's story is told in the loyally maintained, but far from slick **Wick Heritage Centre** in Bank Row, Pultneytown (Easter–Oct Mon–Sat 10am–5pm; £2), and the only other visitor attraction is the fairly simple **Pulteney Distillery** (Mon–Fri 10am–1pm & 2–4pm; tours at 11am & 2pm or by arrangement ☎01955/602371; £3.50 includes discount voucher) on nearby Huddart Street, a few blocks back from the sea.

The best of the **hotels** is *Mackay's*, on the south side of the river in the town centre (☎01955/602323, ⓦwww.mackayshotel.co.uk; ❺), while reasonable **B&B** options include *Quayside*, 25 Harbour Quay (☎01955/603229, ⓦwww .quaysidewick.co.uk; ❷), and lovely *Bilbster House* (☎01955/621212, ⓦwww .accommodationbilbster.com; April–Oct, in winter by arrangement; ❷), five miles towards Thurso.

There's a poor choice of **eating** options, though the moderately priced *Bord de l'Eau* (☎01955/604400; closed Mon) on Market Street, which runs along the north side of the river, offers a reasonable menu of classic French standards. Among the local **pubs**, try the *Alexander Bain* (named after the inventor of the fax machine, who lived locally) in Market Place, or the bar in *Mackay's Hotel*.

Travel details

Buses

For information on all local and national bus services, contact Traveline ☎0870/608 2608 (daily 7am–10pm), ⓦwww.travelinescotland.com.

Aviemore to: Edinburgh (5 daily; 2hr 30min–3hr 30min); Glasgow (7 daily; 3hr 30min); Grantown-on-Spey (Mon–Sat 6–8 daily; 40min); Inverness (hourly; 45min).

Fort William to: Acharacle (Mon–Sat 2–3 daily; 1hr 30min); Drumnadrochit (6 daily; 1hr 30min); Edinburgh (1 direct daily; 4hr); Fort Augustus (6 daily; 1hr); Glasgow (4 daily; 3hr); Inverness (6 daily; 2hr); Kilchoan (1 daily; 3hr 35); Mallaig (1 daily; 1hr 30min); Oban (Mon–Sat 4 daily; 1hr 30min); Portree, Skye (1 daily; 3hr).

Gairloch to: Inverness (Mon–Sat 1 daily; 2hr 45min); Redpoint (Mon–Fri 1–2 daily during school term only; 1hr 35min).

Inverness to: Aberdeen (hourly; 3hr 40min); Aviemore (hourly; 45min); Drumnadrochit (8 daily; 25min); Durness (Mon–Sat 1 daily, May–Sept only; 5hr); Fort Augustus (6 daily; 1hr); Fort William (6 daily; 2hr); Glasgow (6 daily direct; 3hr 35min–4hr 25min); Kyle of Lochalsh (3 daily; 2hr); Perth (10 daily; 2hr 35min); Portree, Skye (3 daily; 3hr); Thurso (4–5 daily; 3hr 30min); Ullapool (Mon–Sat 2–3 daily; 1hr 30min); Wick (4–5 daily; 3hr).

Kyle of Lochalsh to: Fort William (3 daily; 1hr 50min); Glasgow (3 daily; 5hr); Inverness (2 daily; 2hr).

Lochinver to: Inverness (Easter–Sept 1 daily; 3hr 10min); Ullapool (Mon–Sat 2 daily; 1hr).

Thurso to: Inverness (4–5 daily; 3hr 30min); John O'Groats (Mon–Fri 5 daily, 2 on Sat; 1hr); Wick (Mon–Fri hourly, Sat & Sun 6 daily; 35min).

Ullapool to: Durness (Mon–Sat 1 daily, Easter–Sept only; 3hr); Inverness (Mon–Sat 2–3 daily; 1hr 30min).

Wick to: John O'Groats (4 daily Mon–Sat; 50min).

Trains

For information on all local and national rail services, contact National Rail Enquiries ☎08457/484950, ⓦwww.nationalrail.co.uk or ⓦwww.firstscotrail.com.

Aviemore to: Cairngorm ski area (hourly; 30min); Edinburgh (Mon–Sat 6 daily, 3 on Sun; 2hr 30min); Glasgow (2–3 daily; 2hr 30min); Inverness (Mon–Sat 9 daily, 3 on Sun; 1hr).

Fort William to: Arisaig (Mon–Sat 4 daily, 2 on Sun; 1hr 10min); Crianlarich (3–4 daily; 1hr 50min); Glasgow (2–3 daily; 3hr 45min); Glenfinnan (Mon–Sat 4 daily, 2 on Sun; 35min); London (Sun–Fri 1 nightly; 12hr); Mallaig (Mon–Sat 4 daily, 2 on Sun; 1hr 25min).

Inverness to: Aberdeen (Mon–Sat 10 daily, 5 on Sun; 2hr 15min); Aviemore (Mon–Sat 9 daily, 5 on Sun; 40min); Dingwall (Mon–Sat 7–8 daily, 2–4 on Sun; 25min); Edinburgh (Mon–Sat 6 daily, 3 on Sun; 3hr 30min); Helmsdale (Mon–Sat 3 daily, 1 on Sun; 2hr 20min); Kyle of Lochalsh (Mon–Sat 3–4

24

daily, 1–2 on Sun; 2hr 40min); London (Mon–Fri & Sun 1 nightly; 11hr); Plockton (Mon–Sat 3–4 daily, 1–2 on Sun; 2hr 15min); Thurso (Mon–Sat 3 daily, 1–2 on Sun; 3hr 25min); Wick (Mon–Sat 3 daily, 1–2 on Sun; 4hr).

Kyle of Lochalsh to: Dingwall (Mon–Sat 3–4 daily, 1–2 on Sun; 2hr); Inverness (Mon–Sat 3–4 daily, 1–2 on Sun; 2hr 40min); Plockton (Mon–Sat 3–4 daily, 1–2 on Sun; 15min).

Thurso to: Dingwall (Mon–Sat 3 daily, 1–2 on Sun; 3hr); Inverness (Mon–Sat 3 daily, 1–2 on Sun; 3hr 20min); Wick (Mon–Sat 3 daily, 1–2 on Sun; 35min).

Wick to: Dingwall (Mon–Sat 3 daily, 1–2 on Sun; 3hr 30min); Inverness (Mon–Sat 3 daily, 1–2 on Sun; 4hr).

Ferries

To Lewis: Ullapool–Stornoway (Mon–Sat 2 daily; 2hr 45min).

To Mull: Kilchoan–Tobermory (Mon–Sat 7 daily; June–Aug also Sun 5 daily; 35min); Lochaline–Fishnish (Mon–Sat every 50min, Sun hourly; 15min).

To Orkney: Gill's Bay–St Margaret's Hope (3 daily; 1hr); John O'Groats–Burwick (passengers only; 2–4 daily; 40min); Scrabster–Stromness (2–3 daily; 2hr).

To Skye: Glenelg–Kylerhea (daily frequently; 15min); Mallaig–Armadale (Mon–Sat 8–9 daily, mid-May to mid-Sept also Sun; 30min).

To the Small Isles: Mallaig to Eigg, Rùm, Muck and Canna; see p.1021.

Flights

Inverness to: Edinburgh (Mon–Fri 4 daily, Sat & Sun 1 daily; 45min); Glasgow (Mon–Fri 1 daily; 50min); Kirkwall (2 Mon–Fri, 1 Sun; 45min); London (Gatwick 3 daily; Luton Mon–Fri 1 daily; 1hr 30min); Shetland (Mon–Fri 2 daily; 1hr 40min); Stornoway (Mon–Fri 4 daily; 40min).

Wick to: Edinburgh (Mon–Sat 1 daily; 1hr 10min); Inverness (Mon–Fri 2 daily; 35min); Kirkwall (Mon–Sat 1 daily; 25min).

Orkney and Shetland

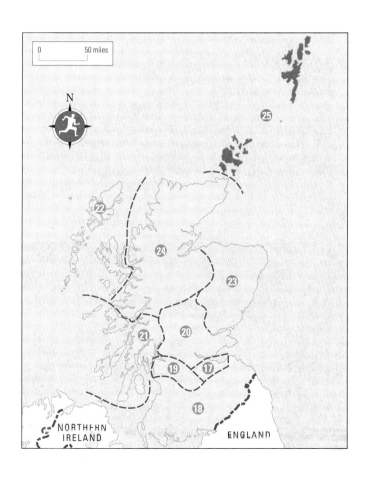

CHAPTER 25

Highlights

* **Skara Brae** Neolithic village giving a fascinating insight into prehistoric life. See p.1113

* **St Magnus Cathedral, Kirkwall** Beautiful red-stone cathedral built by the Vikings. See p.1115

* **Tomb of the Eagles** Fascinating Neolithic site on South Ronaldsay. See p.1116

* **Balfour Castle** Eat, sleep and live like a king in Orkney's most sumptuous castle hotel. See p.1119

* **Westray** Thriving Orkney island with sea-bird colonies, sandy beaches and a ruined castle. See p.1120

* **Isle of Noss** Guaranteed seals, puffins and dive-bombing "bonxies". See p.1129

* **Mousa** Remote Shetland islet with a two-thou-sand-year-old broch. See p.1129

* **Jarlshof** Site mingling Iron Age, Bronze Age, Pictish, Viking and medieval settlements. See p.1130

△ St Magnus Cathedral, Kirkwall

Orkney and Shetland

R eaching up towards the Arctic Circle, and totally exposed to turbulent Atlantic weather systems, the **Orkney** and **Shetland** islands gather neatly into two distinct and very different clusters. Often referring to themselves first as Orcadians or Shetlanders, and with unofficial but widely displayed flags, their inhabitants regard Scotland as a separate entity; the mainland to them is the one in their own archipelago, not the Scottish mainland. This feeling of detachment arises from their distinctive geography, history and culture, in which they differ not only from Scotland but also from each other.

The seventy or so **Orkney Islands** lie just a short step north of the Scottish mainland. With the major exception of **Hoy**, which is high and rugged, these islands are mostly low-lying, gently sloping and richly fertile, and for centuries have provided a reasonably secure living for their inhabitants from farming and, to a much lesser extent, fishing. There's a peaceful continuity to Orcadian life reflected not only in the well-preserved treasury of Stone Age settlements, such as **Skara Brae**, and standing stones, most notably the **Stones of Stenness**, but also in the rather conservative nature of society here today.

Sixty miles further north, the **Shetland Islands** are in nearly all respects a complete contrast. Ice-sculpted sea inlets cut deep into the land which rises straight out of the water to rugged, heather-coated hills. With little fertile ground, Shetlanders have traditionally been crofters rather than farmers, often looking to the sea for an uncertain living in fishing and whaling or the naval and merchant services. The Norse heritage is clear in every road sign and there are many well-preserved prehistoric sites, such as **Mousa Broch** and **Jarlshof**.

It's impossible to underestimate the influence of the **weather** up here. More often than not, it will be windy and rainy, though you can have all four seasons in one day. The wind-chill factor is not to be taken lightly, and there's frequently a dampness or drizzle in the air, even when it's not actually raining. Even in late spring and summer, when there can be dry spells and long days with lots of sunshine, you still need to come prepared for wind, rain and, most frustrating of all, the occasional sea fog. The one good thing is that midges are less of a problem, except on Hoy.

Orkney

Just a short step from John O'Groats, the **Orkney Islands** are a unique and fiercely independent archipelago. For an Orcadian, the "Mainland" invariably

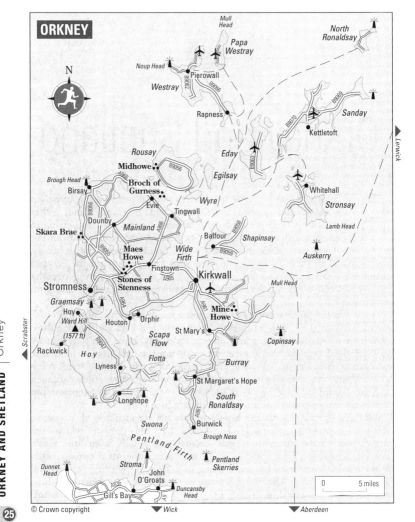

means the largest island in Orkney rather than the rest of Scotland, and throughout their history they've been linked to lands much further afield, principally Scandinavia.

Orkney Mainland has two chief settlements: the old port of **Stromness**, an attractive old fishing town on the far southwestern shore, and the central capital of **Kirkwall**, which stands at the dividing point between East and West Mainland. The whole of Mainland is relatively heavily populated and farmed throughout, and is joined by causeways to a string of southern islands, the largest of which is **South Ronaldsay**. The island of **Hoy**, the second-largest in the archipelago, to the south of Mainland, presents a superbly dramatic landscape, with some of the highest sea-cliffs in the country. Hoy, however, is atypical: Orkney's smaller, much quieter **northern islands** are low-lying, elemental but fertile outcrops of rock and sand, scattered across the ocean.

Small communities began to settle in the islands around 4000 BC, and the village at **Skara Brae** on the Mainland is one of the best-preserved Stone Age settlements in Europe, and just one of numerous archeological sites in Orkney. From the ninth century, the islands became a **Norse earldom** and although the last of the Norse earls was killed in 1231, the Vikings had a lasting cultural and linguistic impact on the islands. With the end of Norse rule, the islands became the preserve of **Scottish earls**, who exploited and abused the islanders, although a steady increase in sea trade did offer some chance of escape. The **Hudson Bay Company** recruited hundreds of Orcadians to work in the Canadian fur trade and the islands remained an important staging post in the **whaling industry** and the herring boom until the early twentieth century. More recently, the choice of **Scapa Flow**, Orkney's natural harbour, as the Royal Navy's main base brought plenty of money and activity during both world wars, and left the seabed scattered with wrecks – which these days make for wonderful diving opportunities. Since the mid-1970s the large **oil terminal** on the island of

Getting to and around Orkney

Orkney is connected to the Scottish mainland by several **ferry** routes. Pentland Ferries (℡01856/831226, ⑩www.pentlandferries.co.uk) operates the shortest car ferry crossing, from **Gill's Bay**, on the north coast near John O'Groats (and linked by bus to Wick and Thurso) to **St Margaret's Hope** on South Ronaldsay (3–4 daily; 1hr). Services to **Stromness** from **Scrabster** (2–3 daily; 1hr 30min), which is connected to nearby Thurso by a shuttle bus, are run by Northlink Ferries (℡0845/600 0449, ⑩www.northlinkferries.co.uk), who also operate ferries to **Kirkwall** from **Aberdeen** (4 weekly; 6hr) and from **Lerwick** in Shetland (3 weekly; 5hr 30min). John O'Groats Ferries (℡01955/611353, ⑩www.jogferry.co.uk) runs a passenger ferry from **John O'Groats** to **Burwick** on South Ronaldsay (May & Sept 2 daily; June–Aug 4 daily; 40min), its departure timed to connect with the arrival of the Orkney Bus from Inverness; there's also a free taxi service from Thurso train station. Direct **flights** serve Kirkwall airport from Sumburgh in Shetland, Wick, Inverness and Aberdeen, and there are good connections from Edinburgh, Glasgow, Manchester, Birmingham and London. All can be booked through British Airways (℡0870/850 9850, ⑩www.ba.com).

Bus services on the Orkney Mainland are infrequent, and skeletal on Sundays, making a Day Rover (£6) or Three-Day Rover (£15) of limited value (see ⑩www.rapsons.co.uk for more). On the smaller islands, a minibus usually meets the ferry and will take you to your destination; in addition, folk are very friendly and it's easy enough to hitch a lift. **Cycling** is not a bad option, though the wind can make it hard going. Instead of bringing your car, **renting a car** locally will save you the steep ferry fares. If time is limited, you may want to consider one of the informative bus or minibus **tours** on offer: Wildabout Orkney Tours (℡01856/851011, ⑩www.orknet.co.uk/wildabout) has good-value tours of the chief sights on the Mainland and Hoy. Getting to the other islands from the Mainland isn't difficult, though it is expensive: Orkney Ferries (℡01856/872044, ⑩www.orkneyferries.co.uk) operates daily **ferries** to all the islands except North Ronaldsay, which has a weekly boat on Fridays. If you're taking a car on any of the ferries, it's essential to book your ticket well in advance. There are also **flights** from Kirkwall to some of the islands, operated by Loganair (℡01856/072494, ⑩www.loganair.co.uk), using a tiny eight-seater plane. Loganair also offers **sightseeing flights** over Orkney, which are spectacular in fine weather (but cancelled in bad), as well as a discounted **Orkney Adventure** ticket, which allows you return tickets to three islands for around £70, and a special £12 offer on return flights to North Ronaldsay or Papa Westray if you stay over.

Flotta, combined with EU development grants, have brought surprise windfalls, stemming the exodus of young people.

Stromness

STROMNESS has to be one of the most enchanting ports at which to arrive by boat, its picturesque waterfront a procession of tiny sandstone jetties and slate roofs. As one of Orkney's main points of arrival, Stromness is a great introduction, and one that's well worth spending a day exploring, or using as a base in preference to Kirkwall. Its natural sheltered harbour must have been used in Viking times, but the town itself only really took off in the eighteenth century when the Hudson's Bay Company made Stromness its main base from which to make the long journey across the North Atlantic: crews from Stromness were also hired for herring and whaling expeditions – and, of course, press-ganged into the Royal Navy. Today Stromness remains an important harbour town and fishing port and is the focus of the popular four-day **Orkney Folk Festival** (⦿www .orkneyfolkfestival.com), held in May.

The Town

Unlike Kirkwall, the old town of Stromness still hugs the shoreline, its one and only street a narrow, winding affair still paved with great flagstones and fed by a tight network of alleyways or closes. The central section, which begins at the *Stromness Hotel*, is known as **Victoria Street**, though it has several other names as it heads southwards. On the east side the houses are gable-end-on to the waterfront, and originally each would have had its own pier, from which merchants would trade with passing ships.

The first of the old jetties, south of the modern harbour, houses the **Pier Arts Centre** (Tues–Sat 10.30am–12.30pm & 1.30–5pm; free). The art gallery hosts temporary exhibitions, often featuring painting and sculpture by local artists, as well as having a remarkable permanent display of twentieth-century British art. Ten minutes' walk further down the main street is the **Stromness Museum** (April–Sept daily 10am–5pm; Oct–March Mon–Sat 11am–3.30pm; £2.50), which boasts a Halkett cloth boat, an early inflatable like the one used by John Rae, the Stromness-born Arctic explorer, whose fiddle, octant and shotgun are also on display. There are also numerous salty artefacts gathered from shipwrecks, including some barnacle-encrusted crockery from the German High Seas Fleet that sank in Scapa Flow.

Practicalities

Arriving by ferry, you disembark at the modern ferry terminal, which also houses the **tourist office** (April–Oct Mon–Fri 8am–5pm, Sat 9am–4pm, Sun 10am–3pm; Nov–March Mon–Fri 9am–5pm). As far as **hotels** go, the venerable Victorian *Stromness Hotel* (☏01856/850298, ⦿www.stromnesshotel .com; ❻) – the town's first – is probably your best bet. For something with more character, head for *Miller's House and Harbourside Guest House*, at 7 & 13 John St (☏01856/851969, ⦿www.orkneyisles.co.uk/millershouse; ❷), in the town's oldest property. *Brown's Hostel* is a laid-back family-run **hostel** at 45–47 Victoria St (☏01856/850661); there's also a well-equipped **campsite** (☏01856/873535; May to mid-Sept) in a superb (but exposed) setting a mile south of the ferry terminal at Point of Ness. **Bike rental** is available from Stromness Cycle Hire, opposite the ferry terminal (☏01856/850750), and from Orkney Cycle Hire, near the museum (☏01856/850255).

Stromness has a couple of decent **places to eat**, starting with *Julia's Café and Bistro* (summer also Fri–Sun eve), opposite the ferry terminal. The moderately expensive evening-only *Hamnavoe Restaurant* at 35 Graham Place (☎01856/850606; April–Sept; closed Mon) offers the town's most ambitious cooking in a very pleasant setting. *Bistro 76*, part of the *Orca Hotel* on Victoria Street, serves imaginative food in snug surroundings (booking advisable; ☎01856/851803; closed Sun). The downstairs *Flattie Bar* of the *Stromness Hotel* is a congenial place to warm yourself by a real fire (or depending on the season, sit outside) with a **drink**; the most popular pub is, however, the *Ferry Inn*, opposite.

West Mainland

The great bulk of the **West Mainland** is fertile, productive farmland, fenced off into a patchwork of fields used either to produce crops or for cattle grazing. It is, however, fringed by some spectacular coastline, particularly in the west, and littered with some of the island's most impressive prehistoric sites, such as the village of **Skara Brae**, the standing **Stones of Stenness** and the chambered tomb of **Maes Howe**.

The Stones of Stenness and Maes Howe

The parish of **Stenness** lies along the main road from Stromness to Kirkwall, south of the twin lochs of Stenness and Harray, which are separated by a couple of promontories, that once stood at the heart of Orkney's most important Neolithic ceremonial complex. The most visible part of the complex are the **Stones of Stenness**, originally a circle of twelve rock slabs, now just four, the tallest of which is over 16ft and remarkable for its incredible thinness. A broken table-top lies within the circle, which is surrounded by a much-diminished henge (a circular bank of earth and a ditch) with a couple of entrance causeways. Less than a mile to the northwest, you reach another stone circle, the **Ring of Brodgar**, a much wider circle dramatically sited on raised ground. Here there were originally sixty stones, 27 of which now stand; of the henge, only the ditch survives.

There are several quite large burial mounds visible to the south of the Ring of Brodgar, but these are entirely eclipsed by one of the most impressive Neolithic burial chambers in the whole of Europe, **Maes Howe** (April–Sept guided tours daily every 45min 9.45am–5.15pm; Oct–March Mon–Sat 9.45am–3.45pm, Sun 2–4.30pm; ☎01856/761606; £4; HS), which lies less than a mile northeast of the Stones of Stenness. Dating from around 3000 BC, Maes Howe is in an excellent state of preservation, partly due to the massive slabs of sandstone it was constructed from, the largest of which weighs over thirty tons. Perhaps its most remarkable aspect is that the tomb is aligned so that the rays of the winter solstice sun reach right down the passage to the ledge of one of the three cells built into the walls of the tomb. When Maes Howe was opened in 1861, it was found to be virtually empty, thanks to the work of generations of grave-robbers who had left behind only a handful of human bones. The Vikings entered in the twelfth century, leaving large amounts of runic graffiti, cut into the walls of the main chamber and still clearly visible today. In summer, to visit the tomb, you must buy a **timed ticket** for a specific guided tour, either over the phone or direct from the nearby converted nineteenth-century Tormiston Mill, by the main road, which houses the ticket office; in winter, you can wander around the site freely.

Skara Brae

Around seven miles north of Stromness, the beautiful white curve of the Bay of Skaill is home to **Skara Brae** (April–Sept daily 9.30am–6.30pm; Oct–March

Mon–Sat 9.30am–4.30pm, Sun 2–4.30pm; £6; HS), where the extensive remains of a small Neolithic fishing and farming village, dating back to 3000 BC, were discovered in 1850 after a fierce storm. The village is very well preserved, its houses huddled together and connected by narrow passages which would originally have been covered over with turf. The houses themselves consist of a single, spacious living room, filled with domestic detail, including fireplaces, cupboards, beds and boxes, all ingeniously constructed from slabs of stone.

Unfortunately, the sheer numbers now visiting Skara Brae mean that you can no longer explore the site itself properly, but only look down from the outer walls. Before you reach the site you must buy a ticket from the **visitor centre**, which houses an excellent **café-restaurant**. After a short video, you pass through a small introductory **exhibition**, with a few replica finds, before proceeding to a full-scale replica of House 7 (the best-preserved house); it's all a tad neat and tidy, but it'll give you the general idea.

Birsay and Evie

Occupying the northwest corner of the Mainland, the parish of **BIRSAY** was the centre of Norse power in Orkney for several centuries before the earls moved to Kirkwall. Today a tiny cluster of homes is gathered around the sandstone ruins of the **Earl's Palace**, which was built in the second half of the sixteenth century by Robert Stewart, Earl of Orkney, using the forced labour of the islanders. The palace appears to have lasted barely a century before falling into rack and ruin, though the crumbling walls and turrets retain much of their grandeur.

Just over half a mile northwest of the palace is the **Brough of Birsay**, a substantial Pictish settlement on a small tidal island only accessible during the two hours each side of low tide. The focus of the village was – and still is – the sandstone-built twelfth-century **St Peter's Church**. Close by is a large complex of Viking-era buildings, including several houses, a sauna and some sophisticated stone drains.

On the north coast, the village and parish of **EVIE** looks out across the turbulent waters of Eynhallow Sound towards the island of Rousay. Its chief draw is the **Broch of Gurness** (April–Sept daily 9.30am–6.30pm; £3; HS), the best-preserved broch on an archipelago replete with them, and one which is still surrounded by a remarkable complex of later buildings. As at Birsay, the sea has eaten away half the site, but the broch itself, dating from around 100 BC, still stands, its walls reaching a height of 12ft in places, its inner cells still intact. The compact group of homes clustered around the broch have also survived amazingly well, with much of their original and ingenious stone shelving and fireplaces still in place.

Practicalities

The best **B&B** in the West Mainland is the carefully converted *Mill of Eyrland* (☎01856/850136, ⊛www.millofeyrland.com; ❸), in a delightful setting on the A964 to Orphir. Also worth recommending is *Woodwick House* (☎01856/751330, ⊛www.woodwickhouse.co.uk; ❹), situated in a beautiful, secluded position southeast of Evie. The simple *Eviedale* **campsite**, run by Dale Farm (☎01856/751270, ⊛www.creviedale.orknet.co.uk; April–Oct) in Evie, also rents out cottages.

Kirkwall

Initial impressions of **KIRKWALL**, Orkney's capital, are not always favourable. However, it does have one great redeeming feature – its sandstone **cathedral**, without doubt the finest medieval building in the north of Scotland. Nowadays, the town is very much divided into two main focal points: the old **harbour**, at the north end of the town, where inter-island ferries come and go all year round, and the flagstoned **main street**, which changes its name four times as it twists its way south from the harbour past the cathedral.

The Town

Standing at the very heart of Kirkwall, **St Magnus Cathedral** (Mon–Sat 9am–6pm, Sun 2–6pm) is the town's most compelling sight. This beautiful red-sandstone building was begun in 1137 by the Orkney Earl Rognvald, who built the cathedral in honour of his uncle Magnus, killed on the orders of his cousin Haakon in 1117. The first version of the cathedral was somewhat smaller than today's structure, which has been added to over the centuries, with a new east window in the thirteenth century, an extension to the nave in the fifteenth century and a new west window to mark the building's 850th anniversary in 1987. Today much of the detail in the soft sandstone has worn away – the capitals around the main doors are reduced to gnarled stumps – but it's still an immensely impressive building, its shape and style echoing the great cathedrals of Europe. Inside, the atmosphere is surprisingly intimate, the bulky sandstone columns drawing your eye up to the exposed brickwork arches, while around the walls is a series of mostly seventeenth-century tombstones, many carved with a skull and crossbones and other emblems of mortality.

To the south of the cathedral are the ruined remains of the **Bishop's Palace** (April–Sept daily 9.30am–6.30pm; Oct & Nov Mon–Sat 9.30am–4.30pm, Sun 2–4.30pm; £2.50; HS), residence of the Bishop of Orkney since the twelfth century. Most of what you see now, however, dates from the time of Bishop Robert Reid, sixteenth-century founder of Edinburgh University. A narrow spiral staircase takes you to the top of the palace for a good view over the cathedral and Kirkwall's rooftops. The ticket for the Bishop's Palace also covers entry to the neighbouring **Earl's Palace**, built by the infamous Earl Patrick Stewart around 1600 using forced labour. With its grand entrance, fancy oriel windows, dank dungeons, massive fireplaces and magnificent central hall, it is reckoned to be one of the finest examples of Renaissance architecture in Scotland. The roof may be missing, but many domestic details remain, including a set of toilets and the stone shelves used by the clerk to do his filing.

Opposite the cathedral stands the sixteenth-century Tankerness House, now home to the **Orkney Museum** (Mon–Sat 10.30am–5pm; May–Sept also Sun 2–5pm; free). Among the more unusual artefacts to look out for are a witch's spell box, and a lovely whalebone plaque from a Viking boat grave discovered on Sanday.

Practicalities

Northlink **ferries** from Shetland and Aberdeen (and all cruise ships) dock at the new Hatston terminal, a mile or so northwest of town; the buses waiting at Hatston will take you to Stromness, or into the centre of Kirkwall. Kirkwall **airport** is about three miles southeast of town on the A960; a bus (Mon–Sat 7–8 daily; 15min) will take you to the **bus station,** a few minutes' walk west of the centre. For **bike rental** head for Cycle Orkney, Tankerness Lane (⊕01856/875777). The helpful **tourist office** is on Broad Street beside the cathedral graveyard (April–Sept daily 8.30am–8pm; Oct–March Mon–Sat 9.30am–5pm). Most events are advertised in *The Orcadian*, which comes out on Thursdays (⊛www.orcadian.co.uk), or tune into the news programme *About Orkney* on BBC Radio Orkney (93.7 FM; Mon–Fri 7.30–8am).

The waterfront *Ayre Hotel* on Ayre Road (☎01856/873001, ⓦwww .ayrehotel.co.uk; ❻) offers the smartest **accommodation** in town; equally central is the more pubby *Albert* on Mounthoolie Lane (☎01856/876000, ⓦwww.alberthotel.co.uk; ❸). The *Eastbank House* (☎01856/870179, ⓦwww .eastbankhouse.co.uk; ❸) is a recently converted former hospital on East Road, with kitchen facilities for guests, or try the *Peter & Naomi* B&B (☎01856/872249; ❸) at 13 Palace Rd, right by the cathedral. The SYHA **hostel** (☎0870/004 1133; April–Sept; dorm beds £13) is ten minutes' walk out of the centre on the road to Orphir. More central is the small, privately run *Peedie Hostel* (☎01856/875477) on the waterfront beside the *Ayre Hotel*. There's also a **campsite** (☎01856/879900; mid-May to mid-Sept) behind the Pickaquoy Leisure Centre, five minutes' walk west of the bus station.

The best **café** in town is the venerable *Trenabies* on Albert Street, which does high teas, and more adventurous bistro fare in the evening. Another good café for lunch is the *Mustard Seed* (closed Wed & Sun), in the small Christian book-shop at 86 Victoria St. Otherwise, you'll have to head for one of the town's hotels: the *Kirkwall*, on Harbour Street, is probably the best option, as it offers both **bar meals** and reasonable à la carte.

The liveliest **pub** is the *Torvhaug Inn* at the harbour end of Bridge Street; another good place to try is the *Bothy Bar* in the *Albert Hotel*, which sometimes has live music. Kirkwall has its very own state-of-the-art **nightclub**, *Fusion* (Thurs–Sat; ⓦwww.fusionclub.co.uk), which occasionally attracts top-name DJs and also stages live gigs. The Pickaquoy Leisure Centre (ⓦwww.pickaquoy .com) – known locally as the "Picky" – contains the New Phoenix **cinema** (☎01856/879900). Kirkwall's chief cultural bash is the week-long **St Magnus Festival** (ⓦwww.stmagnusfestival.com), a superb arts festival based in Kirkwall.

East Mainland and South Ronaldsay

Southeast from Kirkwall, the narrow spur of the **East Mainland** juts out into the North Sea and is joined, thanks to the remarkable Churchill Barriers (see box, p.1117), to several smaller islands, the largest of which are Burray and South Ronaldsay. One sight you should pay a quick visit to is the Iron Age mound of **Mine Howe** (May Wed & Sun 11am–3pm; June to early Sept daily 11am–5pm; rest of Sept Wed & Sun 11am–2pm; £2.50), just off the A960 beyond the airport. Originally Mine Howe would have been a large mound surrounded by a deep ditch, but only a small section has been excavated. At the top of the mound a series of steps leads steeply down to a half-landing, and then plunges even deeper to a small chamber some twenty feet below the surface. The whole layout is unique and has left archeologists totally baffled, though, naturally, numerous theories as to its purpose abound, from execution by ritual drowning to a temple to the god of the underground.

At the southern end of the Churchill Barriers is low-lying **South Ronald-say**, the largest of the islands linked to the Mainland. Its main settlement is **ST MARGARET'S HOPE** – or "The Hope", as it's known locally – a pleasing little gathering of stone-built houses overlooking a sheltered bay. The Hope was once a thriving port, but nowadays, despite the presence of the Pentland Ferries terminal, it remains a very peaceful place.

One of the most enjoyable archeological sights on Orkney is the ancient chambered burial cairn at the southeastern corner of South Ronaldsay, known as the **Tomb of the Eagles** (daily: March 10am–noon; April–Oct 9.30am–6pm; Nov–March by appointment; £5; ☎01856/831339, www.tombodtheeagles.co.uk). Discovered, excavated and still owned by local farmer Ronald Simpson, the tomb makes a refreshing change from the usual interpretative centre. First off, you get to look round the family's private museum of prehistoric artefacts; then, you get a brief guided tour of a nearby Bronze Age **burnt mound**, which is basically a Neolithic rubbish dump; and finally you get to walk out to the **chambered cairn**, by the cliff's edge, where human remains were found alongside talons and carcasses of sea eagles. To enter the cairn, you must lie on a trolley and pull yourself in using an overhead rope.

If you want **to stay** in St Margaret's Hope itself you should head for *The Creel* (☎01856/831311, www.thecreel.co.uk; ⑥) on the harbourfront, with a view over the bay and one of Scotland's best, award-winning **restaurants**. More modest bar meals are available from the *Murray Arms Hotel* (☎01856/831205, www.murrayarmshotel.com; ④), on Back Road, which has rooms above the pub and a backpackers' **hostel** round the side (dorm beds £10). Elsewhere, you're spoilt for choice with *Shoreside* (☎01856/831560, www.orkneyholiday.com; ③), a **B&B** back down the road to Kirkwall, where you're guaranteed fresh fish and shellfish, and *Roeberry House* (☎01856/831228, www.roeberry.co.uk; ③), an imposing country house two miles west of The Hope along the B9043. For a **hostel** and **campsite** with some character, head for *Wheems* (☎01856/831537; April–Oct; dorm beds £10), on the eastern side of South Ronaldsay, a mile and a half from the war memorial on the main road outside The Hope.

Hoy

Hoy, Orkney's second-largest island, rises sharply out of the sea to the southwest of the Mainland. The least typical of the islands, but certainly the most dramatic, its north and west sides are made up of great glacial valleys and mountainous moorland rising to over 1500ft, dropping into the sea off the red-sandstone cliffs of St John's Head.

Walkers arriving by passenger ferry from Stromness at Moaness Pier, near the tiny village of **HOY**, and heading for Rackwick (four miles southwest), can either take the well-marked footpath that passes Sandy Loch or catch the minibus via the single-track road. From the road, duckboards head across the heather to the **Dwarfie Stane**, Orkney's most unusual chambered tomb, cut from a solid block of sandstone and dating back to 3000 BC.

RACKWICK is an old crofting and fishing village squeezed between towering sandstone cliffs on the west coast. A small farm building beside the hostel (see below) serves as a tiny **museum** (open any time; free), with a few old photos and a brief rundown of Rackwick's rough history. Despite its isolation, Rackwick has a steady stream of walkers and climbers passing through it en route to the **Old Man of Hoy**, a great sandstone column some 450ft high, perched on an old lava flow which protects it from the erosive power of the sea. The well-trodden footpath from Rackwick is an easy three-mile walk (3hr return).

Lyness

Along the sheltered eastern shore of Hoy, high moorland gives way to a gentler environment similar to that on the rest of Orkney. Hoy defines the western boundary of Scapa Flow, and **LYNESS** played a major role for the Royal Navy during both world wars. Many of the old wartime buildings have been cleared away over the last few decades, but the harbour and hills around Lyness are still scarred with the scattered remains of concrete structures which once served as hangars and storehouses during World War II, and are now used as barns and cowsheds. The old oil pump-house, which still stands opposite the new Lyness ferry terminal, has been turned into the **Scapa Flow Visitor Centre & Museum** (April–Oct Mon–Sat 9am–4.30pm, Sun 10.30am–4pm; July–Sept Sun until 6.15pm; Nov–March Mon–Fri only; free), a fascinating insight into wartime Orkney. The pump house itself retains much of its old equipment – you can even ask for a working demo of one of the oil-fired boilers – used to pump oil off tankers moored at Lyness into sixteen tanks, and from there into underground reservoirs cut into the neighbouring hillside. On request, an audiovisual show on the history of Scapa Flow is screened in the sole surviving tank, which has incredible acoustics. Even the café has an old NAAFI feel about it.

Practicalities

Two **ferry services** run to Hoy: a passenger ferry from Stromness to Moaness pier, by Hoy village (Mon–Fri 4–5 daily, Sat & Sun 2 daily; 25min; ☎01856/850624), which also serves the small island of Graemsay; and the roll-on/roll-off car ferry from Houton on the Mainland to Lyness (Mon–Fri 6 daily, Sat & Sun 2–4 daily; 45min–1hr 25min; ☎01856/811397), which sometimes calls in at the oil terminal island of Flotta, and begins and ends its daily schedule at Longhope. There's no bus service on Hoy, but those arriving on the passenger ferry from Stromness should find a **minibus** waiting to take them to Rackwick. **Bike rental** is available from Moaness Pier (☎01856/791225).

There are only a few places **to stay** in North Hoy. Luckily one of them is *The Glen* (☎01856/792162; ❷), in Rackwick, run by a friendly local couple; they also offer dinner and will collect guests from Hoy. In addition, there are two SYHA-affiliated **hostels**; to book ahead, you must contact the local education

25

department (☎01856/873535 ext 2415). The *North Hoy Hostel* (May to mid-Sept; dorm beds £13) in Hoy village is the larger of the two, but the *Rackwick Hostel* (mid-March to mid-Sept), with just eight beds (£13), enjoys a better location. You can **camp** in Rackwick, either behind the hostel or beside *Burnside Cottage* (☎01856/791316), a heather-thatched **bothy**. There's no shop in Rackwick, so take all your supplies with you; the post-office shop in Hoy only sells chocolate, but the *Hoy Inn*, near the post office, serves very good **bar meals** in season. South Hoy has a handful of good accommodation options, including *St John's Manse* (☎01856/791240; ❸), south of Lyness, overlooking Longhope; in Longhope itself is the welcoming *Stromabank Hotel*, a nicely converted old schoolhouse (☎01856/701494, ⓦwww.stromabank.co.uk; ❸), which also does good bar **food** (closed Thurs).

Shapinsay

Just a few miles northeast of Kirkwall, **Shapinsay** is the most accessible of Orkney's northern isles. A gently undulating grid-plan patchwork of rich farmland, it's a bit like an island suburb of Kirkwall, which is clearly visible across the bay. Its chief attraction for visitors is **Balfour Castle** (May–Sept guided tours Sun 3pm; see below for details of the all-inclusive ticket), the imposing baronial pile designed by David Bryce and completed in 1848 by the Balfour family of Westray, who had made a small fortune in India the previous century. The Balfours died out in 1960 and the castle was bought by a Polish cavalry officer, Captain Tadeusz Zawadski, whose family now run the place as a hotel. The guided tours are great fun, finishing off with complimentary tea and cakes in the servants' quarters.

Less than thirty minutes from Kirkwall by **ferry** (Mon–Fri 5 daily, Sat & Sun 4 daily), Shapinsay is an easy day-trip. If you want to visit the castle, you should phone ahead and book an **all-inclusive ticket** from Balfour Castle (£18), which includes a return ferry ticket. The ferry for the guided tour leaves at 2.15pm, but you can catch an earlier ferry if you want to have some time to explore the rest of the island. It's also possible **to stay** for dinner, bed and breakfast in lord-of-the-manor style at the 🏠 *Balfour Castle Hotel* (☎01856/711282, ⓦwww.balfourcastle.co.uk; ❾); the rooms are vast and beautifully furnished, and you also get to use the library and the other public rooms. More modest **B&B** is available at *Girnigoe* (☎01856/711256, ⓦwww.girnigoe.net; ❷), a comfortable Orcadian croft close to the north shore of Veantro Bay. Even if you're just coming for the day, it's worth popping into *The Smithy* (May–Sept; ☎01856/711722, ⓦwww.shapinsaysmithy.com), the wonderfully cosy licensed **café** below the island's heritage centre, which serves delicious food (daily lunchtime plus Fri & Sat eve) and also offers **bike rental**.

Rousay

Just over half a mile from the Mainland's northern shore, the hilly island of **Rousay** is home to a number of intriguing prehistoric sites. The first trio of sights is spread out over a couple of miles, on and off the road that leads west from the ferry terminal. **Taversoe Tuick**, the nearest chambered cairn, is unusual in that it exploits its sloping site by having two storeys, one entered from the upper side and one from the lower. A little further west is the **Blackhammar Cairn**, which is divided into "stalls" by large flagstones, rather like the more famous cairn at Midhowe (see below). Finally, there's the **Knowe of Yarso**, another stalled cairn dating from the same period that's a stiff climb up the hill from the road, worth it if only for the magnificent view.

The mile-long **Westness Walk** heritage trail begins at Westness Farm, four miles west of the ferry terminal, and passes several archeological sites. **Midhowe Cairn**, about a mile on from the farm, comes as something of a surprise, both for its immense size – it's known as "the great ship of death", and measures nearly 100ft in length – and for the fact that it's now entirely surrounded by a stone-walled barn with a corrugated roof. Unfortunately, you can't actually explore the roofless communal burial chamber, dating back to 3500 BC, but only look down from the overhead walkway. A couple of hundred yards beyond Midhowe Cairn is **Midhowe Broch**, built as a sort of fortified family house, surrounded by a complex series of ditches and ramparts. The interior of the broch is divided into two separate rooms, each with their own hearth, water tank and quernstone, all of which date from the final phase of occupation around the second century AD.

Practicalities

Rousay makes a good day-trip from the Mainland, with regular **car ferry** sailings from Tingwall (30min), linked to Kirkwall by buses. In season, you can join one of the very informative **minibus tours** run by Rousay Traveller (June–Aug Tues–Fri; £16; ☎01856/821234). **Accommodation** on Rousay is limited: try the hostel at *Trumland Farm* (☎01856/821252), half a mile or so west of the terminal, with a couple of dorms (£10), camping and **bike rental**. The *Taversoe Inn*, further along the road, offers unpretentious accommodation (☎01856/821325, ✉TaversoeHotel@aol.com; ❶) and good bar **meals**. The *Pier* **pub**, right beside the terminal, serves bar meals at lunchtime and will make up fresh crab sandwiches if you phone in advance (☎01856/821359).

Westray and Papa Westray

Although exposed to the full force of the Atlantic weather in the far northwest of Orkney, **Westray** shelters one of the most tightly knit and prosperous island communities with a fairly stable population of six hundred or so. Old Orcadian families still dominate every aspect of life, giving the island a strong individual character.

The main village and harbour is **PIEROWALL** in the north, a good eight miles from the Rapness ferry terminal on the southernmost tip of the island. The island's most impressive ruin is the colossal sandstone hulk of **Noltland Castle**, which stands above the village half a mile west up the road to Noup Head. This Z-plan castle, which is pockmarked with over seventy gun loops, was begun around 1560 by Gilbert Balfour, a shady character from Fife, who was Master of the Household to Mary, Queen of Scots, and was implicated in the murder of her husband Lord Darnley.

The northwestern tip of Westray rises up sharply, culminating in the dramatic sea cliffs of **Noup Head**. During the summer months the guano-covered rock ledges are packed with over 100,000 nesting sea birds, primarily guillemots, razorbills, kittiwakes and fulmars, with puffins as well – a truly awesome sight, sound and smell. For a close view of puffins, head for **Castle o'Burrian**, a sea stack in the southeast of the island.

Practicalities

Westray is served by car **ferry** from Kirkwall (2–3 daily; 1hr 25min; ☎01856/872044), or you can **fly** from Kirkwall (Mon–Sat 2 daily; 12min). **Guided tours** of the island by minibus or bike can also be arranged with Westraak (☎01857/677777, ⓦwww.westraak.co.uk). J&M Harcus of Pierowall

(☎01857/677450) runs a **bus service** which will take you from Rapness to Pierowall, though you should phone ahead to check it's running. For **bike rental**, contact either of the hostels (see below).

Westray's finest **accommodation** is at the ☆ *Cleaton House Hotel* (☎01857/677508, ⓦwww.cleatonhouse.com; ❺), a whitewashed Victorian manse about two miles southeast of Pierowall, with great views. This is also the best place on the island to sample Westray's organic salmon, either in the expensive **restaurant** or the congenial **bar**. The *Pierowall Hotel* (☎01857/677472, ⓦwww.orknet.co.ukPierowall; ❷), in Pierowall itself, is less stylish and less expensive, but equally welcoming, with a popular bar and a well-justified reputation for excellent fish and chips, fresh off the boats. **B&B** is available at *No. 1 Broughton* (☎01857/677726, ⓦwww.no1broughton.co.uk; ❸), a recently renovated mid-nineteenth-century house on the edge of Pierowall. Westray is positively spoilt for **hostels**: ☆ *Bis Geos* (☎01857/677420, ⓦwww.bisgeos.co.uk), on the road to Noup Head, has unbeatable views along the cliffs and out to sea, while the luxurious ☆ *Barn* (☎01857/677214, ⓦwww.thebarnwestray.co.uk) is situated in an old farm at the southern edge of Pierowall; it's easier to get to, has a small **campsite** adjacent to it, and genuinely friendly hosts.

Papa Westray

Across the short Papa Sound from Westray is the island of **Papa Westray**, known locally as "Papay" (ⓦwww.papawestray.co.uk). With a population hovering precariously around seventy, Papay has had to fight hard to keep itself viable over the last couple of decades, helped by a hefty influx of outsiders. To get an idea how life used to be when the Traill family ruled over the island, visit the small **museum** (free access) in an old bothy opposite Holland House, at the centre of the island.

A road leads down from Holland House to the western shore, where the **Knap of Howar** stands. Dating from around 3500 BC, this Neolithic farm building makes a fair claim to being the oldest standing house in Europe. Half a mile north along the coast is **St Boniface Kirk**, a restored pre-Reformation church, with a bare flagstone floor, dry-stone walls, a little wooden gallery and just a couple of surviving box pews.

Papay is an easy day-trip from Westray, with a regular **passenger ferry** service from Pierowall (2–5 daily, 25min). On Tuesdays and Fridays, the **car ferry** from Kirkwall to Westray continues on to Papa Westray; at other times, a bus (which accepts a limited number of bicycles) from Rapness connects with the Pierowall passenger ferry. Papay is also connected to Westray by the **world's shortest scheduled flight** – two minutes in duration, or less with a following wind. You can also fly direct from Kirkwall to Papa Westray (Mon–Sat 2–3 daily, 1 on Sun) for a special return fare of £12 if you stay overnight. Papay's Community Co-operative has a **minibus**, which will take you from the pier to wherever you want on the island, and can arrange a Papay Peedie Tour (mid-May to mid-Sept Tues, Thurs & Sat; £30; ☎01857/644321). It also runs a shop, a sixteen-bed SYHA-affiliated **hostel** (ⓦwww.syha.org.uk; dorm beds £12) and the *Beltane House* **B&B** (☎01857/644267, ⓔpapaybeltane2@hotmail .com; ❸), all housed within the old estate-workers' cottages at Beltane, east of Holland House.

Eday

A long, thin island at the centre of Orkney's northern isles, **Eday** is dominated by a great block of heather-covered upland, with farmland confined to a narrow strip of coastal ground. The chief points of interest are all in the northern half of the island, beyond the community shop on the main road. This marks the beginning of the signposted **Eday Heritage Walk**, which covers all the main sights (about 3hr). The walk initially follows the road heading northwest, past the hide overlooking **Mill Loch**, where several pairs of red-throated divers regularly breed. Clearly visible to the north of the road is the fifteen-foot **Stone of Setter**, weathered into three thick, lichen-encrusted fingers. From here, you can climb the hill to reach the **Vinquoy Chambered Cairn**, which has a similar structure to that of Maes Howe. You can crawl into the tomb through the narrow entrance: a skylight inside lets light into the main, beehive chamber, but not into the four side-cells.

Eday's terminal for **ferries** (1–2 daily; 1hr 15min–2hr) is at Backaland pier in the south. Car rental and taxis can be organized through Mr A. Stewart by the pier (℡01857/622206), who also runs **minibus tours** (May–Aug Mon, Wed, Fri & Sun). It's also possible to do a day-trip **flight** on Wednesdays from Kirkwall to Eday (℡01856/872494 or 873457). Friendly **B&B** with full board is available at *Skaill Farm*, a traditional farmhouse just south of the airport (℡01857/622271; ❸). The basic SYHA-affiliated **hostel** occupies an exposed spot just north of the airport; it's run by Eday Community Association (℡01857/622206; April–Sept; dorm beds £11), who will also advise on **camping**.

Stronsay

A beguiling combination of green pastures, white sands and clear turquoise bays, **Stronsay** was one of the main Scottish centres for the curing of herring until the 1930s. **WHITEHALL** is the island's only real village, made up of rows of stone-built fishermen's cottages set between two large piers. Wandering along the tranquil, rather forlorn harbourfront today, you'll find it hard to believe that the village once supported five thousand people in the fishing industry during the summer season, as well as a small army of coopers, coal merchants, butchers, bakers, several Italian ice-cream parlours and a cinema. It was said that, on a Sunday, you could walk across the decks of the boats all the way to **Papa Stronsay**, the tiny island that shelters Whitehall from the north, on which a new monastery has been built by the Order of Transalpine Redemptorists. The old fish market by the pier houses a **museum**, with a few photos and artefacts from the herring days; ask at the adjacent café.

Stronsay is linked to Kirkwall by a regular car **ferry** service (2 daily; 1hr 40min–2hr), and weekday **flights** (Mon–Sat 2 daily; 25min). There's no bus service, but D.S. Peace (℡01857/616335) operates taxis and **rents cars**. Of the few **accommodation** options, the *Stronsay Fish Mart* **hostel** (℡01857/616346; dorm beds £10) in the old fish market by the pier, and the refurbished *Stronsay Hotel* (℡01857/616213, ⓦwww. stronsay.co.uk/stronsayhotel; ❸) opposite, are both good choices. A cheaper alternative is the *Stronsay Bird Reserve* (℡01857/616363; ❷), a nicely positioned **B&B** in a lovely old crofthouse, which also tolerates camping on the shores of Mill Bay. The *Stronsay Hotel* does good pub **food**.

Sanday

Sanday (ⓦwww.sanday.co.uk), though the largest of the northern isles, is also the least substantial, a great low-lying, drifting dune strung out between several rocky points. The island's sweeping aquamarine bays and vast stretches of clean white sand are the finest in Orkney, and in dry, clear weather it's a superb place to spend a day or two. The entire coastline presents the opportunity for superb walks, with particularly spectacular sand dunes to the south of Cata Sand. The most impressive archeological sight is **Quoyness Chambered Cairn**, on the fertile farmland of Els Ness peninsula, dating from before 2000 BC, and partially reconstructed to a height of around 13ft. Also worth a visit is the **Sanday Light Railway** (T 01857/600700, W www.sandaylightrailway.co.uk), a passenger-carrying seven-and-a-quarter-inch-gauge railway that winds its way round the farmhouse of Strangquoy (phone to confirm when it's running).

Ferries arrive at the southern tip of the island and are met by a **minibus** (book on T 01857/600284). The airfield is in the centre of the island, with regular **flights** to Kirkwall (Mon–Sat 1–2 daily; 10min). The fishing port of **Kettletoft**, where the ferry used to dock, is where you'll find the island's two **hotels**: of the two, *The Belsair* (T 01857/600206, E laura@belsair.fsnet .co.uk; ❶) has the slightly more adventurous restaurant menu, while the *Kettletoft* has a lively bar that's popular with the locals. Of the numerous **B&Bs**, try the *Marygarth Manse* (T 01857/600467; ❶), in Broughtown, who can also organize car and **bike rental**. If you're on a budget, head for nearby *Ayre's Rock* (T 01857/600410, E diane@ayresrock.fsnet.co.uk; dorm beds £12), a well-equipped **hostel** and **campsite** by the Bay of Brough with washing and laundry facilities, a chip shop (Sat only), and bike rental.

North Ronaldsay

North Ronaldsay has a unique outpost atmosphere, brought about by its extreme isolation. Measuring just three miles by one and rising only 66ft above sea level, the island is almost overwhelmed by the enormity of the sky, the strength of wind and the ferocity of the sea – so much so that its very existence seems an act of tenacious defiance. Despite these adverse conditions, North Ronaldsay has been inhabited for centuries, and continues to be heavily farmed, from old-style crofts whose roofs are made from huge local flagstones.

The island's **sheep** are a unique, tough, goat-like breed, who feed mostly on seaweed, giving their flesh a dark tone and a rich, gamey taste, and making their thick wool highly prized. A high **drystone dyke**, completed in the mid-nineteenth century and running the thirteen miles around the edge of the island, keeps them off the farmland, except during lambing season. The most frequent visitors are ornithologists, who come to catch a glimpse of the rare migrants who land here briefly on their spring and autumn migrations. The only features to interrupt the island's flat horizon are two lighthouses: the attractive, stone-built **Old Beacon**, first lit in 1789, but topped by a huge bauble of masonry since 1809; and the **New Lighthouse** (May–Sept Sun 12.30–5.30pm; at other times by appointment; £3; T 01857/633257), built in 1854 half a mile to the north and rising to a height of over 100ft.

The **ferry** from Kirkwall runs only once a week (usually Fri; 2hr 40min–3hr), though day-trips are possible on occasional summer Sundays (phone T 01856/872044 for details). Your best bet is to catch a **flight** from Kirkwall (2–3 daily; 15min): if you stay the night on the island, you're eligible for a £12 return fare. A **minibus** usually meets the ferries and planes (phone T 01857/633244) and will take you to the lighthouse. You can **stay** at the eco-friendly *Bird Observatory* (T 01857/633200, W www.nrbo.f2s.com), which offers full board either in private guestrooms (❸) or in a **bunkhouse**; the observatory's *Obscafé* is a sort of pub-restaurant and serves decent meals. Full-board accommodation is also available at *Garso*, in the northeast (T 01857/633244, E christine@garso.fsnet.co.uk; ❸). The *Burrian Inn*, to the southeast of the war memorial, is the island's small **pub**, and does hot food.

Shetland

In nearly all respects **Shetland** is a complete contrast with Orkney. Orkney lies within sight of the Scottish mainland, whereas Shetland lies beyond the horizon. Many maps plonk the islands in a box somewhere off Aberdeen, but in

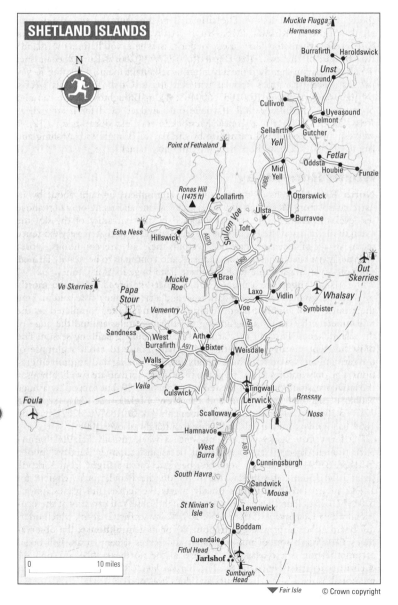

SHETLAND ISLANDS

N

Muckle Flugga
Hermaness

Burrafirth   Haroldswick

Unst

Baltasound

Cullivoe

Uyeasound
Belmont

Sellafirth   Gutcher

Yell

Point of Fethaland

Fetlar

Oddsta
Mid   Houbie   Funzie
Yell

Ronas Hill
(1475 ft)   Collafirth

Otterswick

Esha Ness   Hillswick

Ulsta
Toft

Burravoe

Ve Skerries

Out
Skerries

Papa   Muckle
Stour   Roe   Brae

Laxo   Vidlin   *Whalsay*

Vementry   Voe   Symbister

Sandness   West   Aith
Burrafirth   Bixter
Walls   Weisdale

Vaila
Culswick   Tingwall

Foula   *Bressay*

Lerwick

Scalloway   *Noss*

Hamnavoe

West
Burra
Cunningsburgh

South Havra

Sandwick
Mousa

St Ninian's
Isle   Levenwick

Boddam

Quendale
Fitful Head   **Jarlshof**

1124

0   10 miles

Sumburgh
Head

Fair Isle   © Crown copyright

fact they're a lot closer to Bergen in Norway than Edinburgh. Shetland endures the most violent weather experienced in the British Isles. In winter, gales are routine and Shetlanders take even the occasional hurricane in their stride, marking a calm fine day as "a day atween weathers". There are some good spells of dry, sunny weather from May to September, but it's the "**simmer dim**", the twilight which lingers through the small hours at this latitude, that makes Shetland summers so memorable.

The islands' capital, **Lerwick**, is a busy little port and the only town of any size. Many parts of Shetland can be reached from here on a day-trip. **South Mainland**, south of Lerwick, is a narrow finger of land that runs some 25 miles to **Sumburgh Head**; this area is particularly rich in archeological remains, including the Iron Age **Mousa Broch** and the ancient settlement of **Jarlshof**. A further 25 miles south of Sumburgh Head is the remote but thriving **Fair Isle**, synonymous with knitwear and exceptional birdlife. Even more remote are the distinctive peaks and precipitous cliffs of the island of **Foula**, 14 miles west of Mainland. Shetland's three **North Isles** bring Britain to a dramatic, windswept end: **Yell** has the largest population of otters in Shetland; **Fetlar** is home to the rare red-necked phalarope; north of **Unst**, there's nothing until you reach the North Pole.

People have lived in Shetland since **prehistoric times**, certainly from about 3500 BC, and the islands display spectacular remains. For six centuries they were part of the **Norse empire** which brought together Sweden, Denmark and Norway. The Scottish king annexed Shetland in 1472 and Scottish **mainland lairds** set about grabbing what land and power they could, controlling the fish trade and the tenants who supplied it through a system of truck, or forced barter. During the two world wars, Shetland's role as gatekeeper between the North Sea and North Atlantic meant that the defence of the islands and control of the seas around them were critical. Careful negotiation in the 1970s, backed up by pioneering local legislation, produced a substantial income from North Sea **oil** which has been reinvested in the community. However, it's clear that the boom days are over, and the islanders are having to think afresh how to carve out a living in the new millennium.

Lerwick

Very much the focus of Shetland's commercial life, **LERWICK** is home to about 6600 people, just less than a third of the islands' population. All year, its sheltered **harbour** at the heart of the town is busy with ferries, fishing boats, oil-rig supply vessels and in summer, the quaysides come alive with local pleasure craft, visiting yachts and cruise liners. Behind the old harbour is the

△ Lerwick

compact town centre, made up of one long main street, Commercial Street; from here, narrow lanes, known as "**closses**", rise westwards to the late-Victorian new town.

Arrival, information and accommodation

The **ferry terminal** is situated in the unprepossessing north harbour, about a mile from the town centre. **Flying** into Sumburgh Airport, you can take one of the regular buses to Lerwick; taxis (around £25) and car rental are also available. Buses stop on the Esplanade, very close to the old harbour and Market Cross, or at the Viking bus station on Commercial Road a little to the north of the town centre. The **tourist office** (May–Sept Mon–Sat 8am–6pm, Sun 10am–1pm; Oct–April Mon–Fri 9am–5pm; ⓦwww.visitshetland.com) is at the Market Cross on Commercial Street.

The *Kvelsdro House Hotel*, Greenfield Place (☎01595/692195, ⓦwww .kgqhotels.co.uk; ⓪), is Lerwick's luxury **accommodation** option, followed by the venerable *Queen's Hotel* right on the waterfront on Commercial Street (℡01595/692826, Ⓦwww.kgqhotels.co.uk; ❻). *Alder Lodge Guest House*, 6 Clairmont Place (℡01595/695705; ❸), is the best middle-range choice, followed by *Carradale Guest House*, 36 King Harald St (℡01595/692251, Ⓦwww.carradale.shetland.co.uk; ❷), situated in a large, comfortable Victorian family home. The SYHA **hostel** (℡01595/692114, Ⓔreservations@syha.org .uk; April–Sept; dorm beds £13) at Islesburgh House on King Harald Street, offers unusually comfortable surroundings, with useful laundry facilities. The *Clickimin* **campsite** (℡01595/741000, Ⓔmail@srt.org.uk; May–Sept) enjoys the excellent facilities of the neighbouring Clickimin leisure centre.

The Town

Lerwick's attractive, flagstone-clad **Commercial Street** is still very much the core of the town. Its narrow, winding form, set back one block from the Esplanade, provides shelter from the elements even on the worst days. The street's northern end is marked by the towering walls of **Fort Charlotte** (daily: June–Sept 9am–10pm; Oct–May 9am–4pm; free), begun for Charles II in 1665 during the wars with the Dutch, burnt down by the Dutch fleet in August 1673, and repaired and named in honour of George III's queen in the 1780s.

Although the **closses** that connect the Street to Hillhead are now a desirable place to live, it's not so long ago that they were regarded as slum-like dens of iniquity. Hillhead, up in the Victorian new town, is dominated by the splendid **Town Hall** (Mon–Thurs 9am–5pm, Fri 9am–4pm; free), a Scottish Baronial monument to civic pride, built by public subscription. Lerwick's chief tourist sight, however, is the **Shetland Museum** (Wed–Sat 10am–5pm; Ⓦwww .shetland-museum.org.uk; free), which has recently moved to new purpose-built waterfront premises at Hay's Dock, off Commercial Road, and houses a wonderful collection of nauticalia. Its more unusual exhibits include Shetland's oldest telephone, fitted with a ceramic mouthpiece, and a carved head of Goliath by Adam Christie (1869–1950), a Shetlander who spent much of his life in Montrose Asylum.

A mile or so southwest of the town centre on the road leading to Sumburgh, the much-restored **Clickimin Broch** stands on what was once a small island in Loch Clickimin. The settlement here began as a small farmstead around 700 BC and was later enclosed by a defensive wall. The main tower served as a castle and probably rose to around 40ft, as at Mousa (see p.1129), though the remains are now not much more than 10ft high.

In earlier times the seasonal nature of the Shetland fishing industry led to the establishment of small stores, known as **böds** (see box, above), often incorporating

Up Helly-Aa

On the last Tuesday in January, whatever the weather, Lerwick's new town is the setting for the most spectacular part of the **Up Helly-Aa**, a huge fire festival, the largest of several held in Shetland from January to March. Around nine hundred torchbearing participants, all male and all in extraordinary costumes, march in procession behind a grand Viking longship. The annually appointed Guizer Jarl and his "squad" appear as Vikings with shields and silver axes; each of the forty or so other squads is dressed for their part in the subsequent entertainment, perhaps as giant insects, space invaders or ballet dancers. Their circuitous route leads to the King George V Playing Field where, after due ceremony, all the torches are thrown into the longship, creating an enormous bonfire. A firework display follows, then the participants, known as "guizers", set off in their squads to do the rounds of more than a dozen "halls" (which usually include at least one hotel and the Town Hall) from around 8.30pm in the evening until 8am the next morning, performing some kind of act – usually a comedy routine – at each.

Up Helly-Aa itself is not that ancient, dating only from Victorian times, when it was introduced to replace the much older Christmas tradition of rolling burning tar barrels through the streets, which was banned in 1874. Seven years later a torchlight procession took place, which eventually developed into a full-blown Viking celebration, known as "Up Helly-Aa". Although this is essentially a community event with entry to halls by invitation only, visitors are welcome at the Town Hall, for which tickets are sold in early January; contact the tourist office well in advance. To catch some of the atmosphere of the event, check out the annual Up Helly-Aa exhibition in the **Galley Shed** on St Sunniva Street (mid-May to mid-Sept Tues 2–4pm & 7–9pm, Fri 7–9pm, Sat 2–4pm; £3), where you can see a full-size longship, costumes, shields and photographs.

sleeping accommodation, beside the beaches where fish were landed and dried. Just beyond Lerwick's main ferry terminal, a mile and a half north of the town centre, stands the **Böd of Gremista** (May to mid-Sept Wed–Sun 10am–1pm & 2–5pm; free; ⓦwww.shetland-museum.org.uk), the birthplace of **Arthur Anderson** (1792–1868). The displays explore Anderson's life as beach boy (helping to cure and dry fish), naval seaman, businessman, philanthropist, Shetland's first native MP and founder of Shetland's first newspaper, the *Shetland Journal*.

Eating, drinking and entertainment

Lerwick's best **restaurant** is *Monty's Bistro* on Mounthooly Street (ⓣ01595/696555; closed Mon & Sun), serving inexpensive and delicious meals and snacks at lunchtimes, and accomplished contemporary cooking in the evening. Other places to try include the very good Indian *Raba*, 26 Commercial Rd, and the Chinese Thai *Great Wall*, located above the Viking Bus Station. The *Peerie Café* (closed Sun), on the Esplanade, is a great café, with imaginative cakes, soup and sandwiches. The *Fort Café* (closed Sun lunch), situated below Fort Charlotte at 2 Commercial St, is Lerwick's best fish-and-chip shop.

The friendliest **pub** in town is the upstairs bar in the *Lounge*, up Mounthooly Street, where local musicians often play sessions. The Garrison Theatre (ⓣ01595/692114, ⓦwww.islesburgh.org.uk), by the Town Hall, shows occasional **films** as well as putting on theatre productions, comedy acts and live gigs. The *Islesburgh Community Centre* has introduced regular **crafts and culture evenings** (late May to early Sept Mon & Wed 7–9.30pm), where you can buy local knitwear, chat to locals and listen to traditional music.

In late April or early May, musicians from all over the world converge on Shetland for the excellent four-day **Shetland Folk Festival** (℡01595/694757, Ⓦwww.shetlandfolkfestival.com), which embraces a wider range of musical styles than the title might suggest, and involves concerts and dances in every corner of the islands. Further musical gatherings take place in mid-June with the three-day **Blues Festival** (Ⓦwww.lerwick.plus.com/sbf/frameset .html), and in mid-October at the **Accordion and Fiddle Festival** (Ⓦwww .shetlandaccordionandfiddle.com). For details of **what's on**, listen in to *Good Evening Shetland* on BBC Radio Shetland, 92.7 FM (Mon–Fri 5.30pm), or buy the *Shetland Times* on Fridays (Ⓦwww.shetlandtoday.co.uk). Some events are also advertised on Shetland's independent radio station SIBC, 96.2 FM.

Bressay and Noss

Shielding Lerwick from the full force of the North Sea is the island of **Bressay**, dominated at its southern end by the conical Ward Hill (744ft) – "da Wart" – and accessible on an hourly car and passenger ferry from Lerwick (takes 5min). The chief reason most visitors pass through Bressay is in order to visit the tiny but spectacular island of **Noss** – the name means "a point of rock" – just off Bressay's eastern shore. The island was inhabited until World War II but is now given over to sheep farming and is also a National Nature Reserve. Scottish Natural Heritage operates an inflatable as a ferry from the landing stage below the car park on the east side of Bressay (May–Aug Tues, Wed & Fri–Sun; £3 return; phone ℡0800/107 7818). On the island, the old farmhouse of Gungstie contains a small **visitor centre** where the warden will give you a free map and guide. Behind the house is an old stud farm for **Shetland ponies**, which were sent to work in the mines of County Durham in northeast England. The most memorable feature of Noss is its cliffed coastline rising to a peak at the massive 500-foot **Noup**, home to vast colonies of cliff-nesting gannets, puffins, guillemots, shags, razorbills and fulmars. Be warned: if you stray off the marked path, the great skuas will do their best to intimidate with dive-bombing raids that may hit you hard.

South Mainland

Shetland's **South Mainland** is a long, thin finger of land, only three or four miles wide, but 25 miles long, ending in the cliffs of Sumburgh Head and Fitful Head. It's a beautiful area with wild landscapes but also good farmland, and has yielded some of Shetland's most impressive archeological treasures – in particular, Jarlshof.

From Leebitton, in the district of Sandwick, halfway to Sumburgh Head, you can take a small passenger **ferry** (mid-April to mid-Sept 2 daily; 15min; £8 return; ℡01950/431367, Ⓦwww.mousaboattrips.co.uk) to the small **Isle of Mousa**, on which stands Scotland's best-preserved broch. Rising to more than 40ft, and looking rather like a Stone Age cooling tower, **Mousa Broch** has a remarkable presence, and features in both *Egil's Saga* and the *Orkneyinga Saga*, contemporary chronicles of Norse exploration and settlement. The low entrance passage leads through two concentric walls to a central courtyard, divided into separate beehive chambers. Between the walls, a rough (very dark) staircase leads to the top parapet (torch provided). From late May to late July, a large colony of around six thousand **storm petrels** breeds in and around the broch walls, fishing out at sea during the day, and only returning to the nests after dark. The ferry also runs late-night trips (Wed & Sat weather permitting), setting off in the "simmer dim" twilight around 11pm.

The main road leads eventually to Sumburgh airport, to the west of which is **Old Scatness Broch & Iron Age Village** (May–Oct Sun–Thurs 10am– 5.30pm; £2), where a vast Iron Age settlement is currently being excavated. First off, you get a guided tour of the site from a viewing platform, followed by a taste of Norse and Pictish life in a restored wheelhouse, and a weaving demonstration. South of the airport lies **Jarlshof** (April–Sept daily 9.30am– 6.30pm; HS; £3.30; Oct–March open access to grounds; free), the largest and most impressive of Shetland's archeological sites. The best-preserved buildings are the Pictish wheelhouses surrounding a Neolithic broch, and also the Norse longhouses. Towering over the whole complex is the laird's house, originally built by Robert Stewart, Earl of Orkney, in the late sixteenth century.

The Mainland comes to a dramatic end at **Sumburgh Head**, about two miles from Jarlshof. The lighthouse, designed by Robert Stevenson, was built in 1821; although not open to the public, its grounds offer great views to Noss in the north and Fair Isle to the south. This is also the easiest place in Shetland to get close to **puffins**. During the nesting season, you simply need to look over the western wall by the lighthouse gate to see them arriving at their burrows with beakfuls of fish or giving flying lessons to their offspring; on no account should you try to climb over the wall.

The best **accommodation** in the South Mainland is at *Setterbrae* (℡01950/440468, ⓦwww.setterbrae.co.uk; ❸), a comfortable B&B a stone's throw from the *Spiggie Hotel* (℡01950/460563, ⓦwww.thespiggiehotel.co.uk; ❺), which has a lively bar serving real ales, and a **restaurant** with great views over the Loch of Spiggie. There's also a **camping böd** in *Betty Mouat's Cottage* (℡01595/694688, ⓦwww.camping-bods.com; April–Sept), in Scatness, at the tip of the peninsula, close to the airport. At Levenwick, around eighteen miles south of Lerwick, there's a small, terraced **campsite** (℡01950/422207, ⓦwww .levenwick.shetland.co.uk; May–Sept), with hot showers, a tennis court and a superb view over the east coast.

Fair Isle

Tiny **Fair Isle** (ⓦwww.fairisle.org.uk) is marooned in the sea halfway between Shetland and Orkney. At one time Fair Isle's population was not far short of four hundred, but by the 1950s, the population had shrunk to just 44, a point at which evacuation and abandonment of the island was seriously considered. George Waterston, who'd bought the island and set up a bird observatory in 1948, passed it into the care of the National Trust for Scotland in 1954 and rejuvenation began.

The croft land and the island's scattered houses are concentrated in the south, but the focus for many visitors is the **Bird Observatory**, built just above the sandy bay of North Haven where the ferry from Shetland Mainland arrives. It's one of Europe's major centres for ornithology and its work in watching, trapping, recording and ringing resident and migrant birds goes on all year. Fair Isle is, of course, even better known for its **knitting** patterns, still produced with great skill by the local knitwear co-operative. There are a few samples on display at the island's **museum** (Mon 2–5pm, Wed 10am–noon, Fri 2–4.30pm; free; ℡01595/760244), situated next door to the Methodist chapel.

The passenger **ferry** (℡01595/760222) connects Fair Isle with either Lerwick (on alternate Thurs; 4hr 30min) or Grutness in Sumburgh (Tues, Sat & alternate Thurs; 3hr). **Flights** go from Tingwall (Mon, Wed, Fri & Sat) or Sumburgh (Sat); a one-way ticket costs £28, and day-trips are possible (Mon, Wed & Fri). Camping is not permitted, but there is full-board **accommodation** at the *Fair*

Isle Lodge & Bird Observatory (☎01595/760258, ⓦwww.fairislebirdobs.co.uk; full board ➎) in twins and singles or hostel-style dorms. A good **B&B** option is *Upper Leogh* in the south of the island (☎01595/760248; ➋).

Scalloway

Once the capital of Shetland, **SCALLOWAY**'s importance waned throughout the eighteenth century as Lerwick grew in trading success and status. Nowadays, Scalloway is fairly sleepy, its prosperity still closely linked to the fluctuations of the fishing industry. In spite of modern developments nearby, the town is dominated by the imposing shell of **Scalloway Castle**, a classic fortified tower house built with forced labour in 1600 by the infamous Earl Patrick Stewart, who held court in the castle and gained a reputation for enhancing his own power and wealth through the calculated use of harsh justice. He was eventually arrested and imprisoned in 1609 for aggressive behaviour towards his fellow landowners; his son, Robert, attempted an insurrection and both were executed in Edinburgh in 1615. On Main Street, the small **Scalloway Museum** (May–Sept Mon 9.30–11.30am & 2–4.30pm, Tues–Fri 10am–noon & 2–4.30pm, Sat 10am–12.30pm & 2–4.30pm; free) attempts to tell the story of the Shetland Bus, the link between Shetland and Norway which helped to sustain the Norwegian resistance in World War II.

Scalloway has very little **accommodation** apart from the *Scalloway Hotel* (☎01595/880444; ➎), on the harbourfront, whose bar acts as the local pub. For **food**, head for *Da Haaf* (☎01595/880747; closed Sat & Sun), the unpretentious licensed restaurant in the North Atlantic Fisheries College, which serves a wide range of fresh fish, simply prepared, and has broad harbour views.

The Westside

The western Mainland of Shetland – known as the **Westside** (ⓦwww.walls .shetland.co.uk) – boasts outstanding **coastal scenery**, with dramatic cliffs, intimate coves and some fine beaches. The crossroads for the area is effectively Bixter, southwest of which lies the finest Neolithic structure in the Westside, dubbed the **Staneydale Temple** by the archeologist who excavated it because it resembled one on Malta. Whatever its true function, it was twice as large as the surrounding oval-shaped houses (now in ruins) and was certainly of great importance, perhaps as some kind of community centre. The foundations measure more than 40ft by 20ft internally with immensely thick walls, still around 4ft high, whose roof would have been supported by spruce posts (two postholes can still be clearly seen).

The best **accommodation** and **eating** options on the Westside are in and around Walls, 24 miles northwest of Lerwick. In Walls itself, *Voe House* (☎01595/694688, ⓦwww.camping-bods.com; April–Sept) is the largest **camping böd** on Shetland, with its own peat fire, while the wonderfully welcoming *Skeoverick* (☎01595/809349; ➋) is a lovely modern crofthouse B&B a mile or so north of Walls. The only guest house in the area is *Burrastow House* (☎01595/809307, ⓦwww.users.zetnet.co.ukBurrastow-house-hotel; April– Oct; ➎), beautifully situated three miles southwest of Walls; with fresh Shetland ingredients and a French chef, the cooking is superb, though dinner is available to non-residents only at the weekend.

Foula

Southwest of Walls, at "the edge of the world", **Foula** is without a doubt the most isolated inhabited island in the British Isles, separated from the nearest

25

point on Mainland Shetland by about fourteen miles of often turbulent ocean. Its western **cliffs**, the second highest in Britain after those of St Kilda, rise at **The Kame** to some 1220ft above sea level; a clear day at The Kame offers a magnificent panorama stretching from Unst to Fair Isle. On a bad day, the exposure is complete and the cliffs generate turbulent blasts of wind known as "flans", which rip through the hills with tremendous force. In addition to its forty human inhabitants, the island is home for a quarter of a million **birds**, including a colony of **great skuas** or "bonxies" which you can't fail to notice in the breeding season.

It's essential to book and reconfirm the summer passenger **ferry** from Walls (Tues, Thurs & Sat; 2hr; ☎01595/753254) to Ham, in the middle of Foula's east coast. There are also regular **flights** from Tingwall (Mon–Wed & Fri; ☎01595/753226); tickets cost around £25 one way and day-trips are possible on Wednesdays (mid-Feb to mid-Oct) and Fridays all year. Foula's only **B&B** is *Leraback* (☎01595/753226, ⓦwww.originart.com; ❸), near Ham, which does full board only.

North Mainland

The **North Mainland**, stretching more than thirty miles north from the central belt around Lerwick, is wilder than much of Shetland, with almost relentlessly bleak moorland and some rugged and dramatic coastal scenery. You're bound to pass by **VOE**, as it sits at the main crossroads of the area, but it's easy to miss the picturesque old village, a tight huddle of homes and workshops down below the road around the pier (and signposted Lower Voe). Set at the head of a deep, sheltered sea loch, Voe has a Scandinavian appearance, helped by the presence of the **Sail Loft**, now a large **camping böd** (☎01595/694688, ⓦwww.camping-bods .com; April–Sept). Across the road, the old butcher's is now the *Pierhead Restaurant & Bar*: the cosy wood-panelled **pub** has a real fire, occasional live music and offers a good bar menu, a longer version of which is on offer in the upstairs restaurant, featuring local mussels and the odd catch from the fishing boats.

Eight miles northeast of Voe down the B9071, *Lunna House* (☎01806/577311, ⓦwww.lunnahouse.co.uk; ❷), originally built in 1660, is best known as the initial headquarters from which the Shetland Bus resistance operation was conducted during World War II. It's now a wonderful **place to stay**, with spacious bedrooms, lovely views and a top-class breakfast. North of Voe the main road divides: the northern leg leads to Toft, the ferry terminal for the island of Yell (see p.1133), while the other branch cuts northwest to **BRAE**, a sprawling settlement expanded in some haste in the 1970s to accommodate the workforce for the huge **Sullom Voe Oil Terminal** nearby. Brae boasts one of Shetland's finest **hotels**, *Busta House* (☎01806/522506, ⓦwww.bustahouse .com; ❻), a lovely laird's house which sits across the bay of Busta Voe from modern Brae. It's worth coming here for a drink or an excellent meal in the hotel's pub-like bar.

Northmavine, the northwest peninsula of North Mainland, begins a mile west of Brae at **Mavis Grind**, a narrow isthmus at which it's said you can throw a stone from the Atlantic to the North Sea, or at least to Sullom Voe. **HILLSWICK**, the main settlement, boasts **Da Böd**, once the oldest pub in Shetland, said to have been founded by a German merchant in 1684, now an alternative veggie café and wildlife sanctuary called *The Booth* (☎01806/503348; June–Sept; closed Mon).

Just outside Hillswick, a side road leads west to the exposed headland of **Esha Ness** (pronounced "*Ay*sha Ness"), celebrated for its splendid coastline views. A mile or so south off the main road is the **Tangwick Haa Museum** (May–Sept Mon–Fri 1–5pm, Sat & Sun 11am–7pm; free), which tells the often moving story of this remote corner of Shetland and its role in the dangerous trade of deep-sea fishing and whaling. To the north the road ends at the **Esha Ness Lighthouse**, a great place to view the cliffs, stacks and, in rough weather, blow-holes of this stretch of coast, and the starting point for an excellent three-hour walk. One of the few places to stay in Esha Ness is *Johnnie Notions* **camping böd** (☎01595/694688, ⓦwww.camping-bods.com; April–Sept; no electricity), up a turning north off the main road, in Hamnavoe.

The North Isles

Many visitors never make it out to Shetland's trio of remote **North Isles**, which is a shame, as the ferry links are frequent and inexpensive, and the roads fast. Certainly, there is no dramatic shift in scenery: much of what awaits you is familiar undulating peat moorland, dramatic coastal cliffs and silent glacial voes. However, with Lerwick that much further away, the spirit of independence and self-sufficiency in the North Isles is much more keenly felt. **Yell**, the largest of the three, is best known for its vast otter population. **Fetlar**, the smallest, is home to the rare red-necked phalarope. **Unst**, though, probably has the widest appeal, partly as the most northerly land mass in the British Isles, but also for its nesting sea-bird population.

Yell

The interior of **Yell** (ⓦwww.yell-tourism.shetland.co.uk) features a lot of peat moorland, but the coastline is gentler and greener and provides an ideal habitat for a large population of **otters**. At **BURRAVOE**, in the southeast corner, there's also a lovely whitewashed laird's house that now houses the **Old Haa Museum** (late April to Sept Tues–Thurs & Sat 10am–4pm, Sun 2–5pm; free), which is stuffed with artefacts, and has lots of material on the history of the local herring and whaling industries; there's a very pleasant wood-panelled café on the ground floor. In the north, the area around **CULLIVOE** has relatively gentle, but attractive, coastal scenery. The **Sands of Brekken** are made from crushed shells, and are beautifully sheltered in a cove a mile or two north of Cullivoe.

  Ferries from Toft on the Mainland are frequent and inexpensive, and taking a car over is easy, too (1–2 hourly; 20min). One of the best **B&Bs** is *Hillhead* in Hamnavoe (☎01957/722274, ⓔrita.leask@btopenworld.com; ❶), a comfort-able modern house, offering great home-cooking; you can also stay with the very welcoming, story-telling Tullochs at *Gutcher Post Office* (☎01957/744201, ⓔmargaret.tulloch@btopenworld.com; ❷) by the Unst ferry terminal. A cheaper alternative is to stay in the **camping böd** at *Windhouse Lodge* (☎01595/694688, ⓦwww.camping-bods.com; April–Sept), the gatehouse on the main road near Mid Yell. With very little competition, the best **eating** out option is the funky, camp *Wind Dog Café* (ⓦwww.winddogcafe.co.uk) at Gutcher, which offers evening meals (if you book ahead) and provides Internet access, as well as hosting story-telling from the inimitable Tullochs and other events.

Fetlar

Fetlar is the most fertile of the North Isles, much of it grassy moorland and lush green meadows with masses of summer flowers. At the main settlement, **HOUBIE**, you can learn more about the island from the nearby welcoming **Fetlar Interpretive**

Centre (May–Sept Mon–Fri 1–5pm, Sat & Sun 2–5pm; £2; ⓦ www.fetlar.com). Fetlar is also one of the very few places in the UK where you'll see graceful **red-necked phalarope** (late May to early Aug): the island boasts ninety percent of the British phalarope population, and a hide has been provided overlooking the marshes (or mires) to the east of the **Loch of Funzie** (pronounced "finny"). **Ferries** (5–6 daily; 25–40min) depart from both Gutcher on Yell and Belmont on Unst, docking at Hamar's Ness, three miles northwest of Houbie. The only public transport is an infrequent and small postcar (Mon, Wed & Fri 2 daily). **Accommodation** boils down to *Gord* (ⓣ01957/733227, ⓔlynboxall @zetnet.co.uk; ❸), a comfortable modern house attached to the island shop in Houbie, and the **camping böd** in Aithbank (ⓣ01595/694688, ⓦwww.camping-bods.com; April–Sept), a cosy wood-panelled cottage, a mile east of Houbie. There's also *Garths* **campsite** (ⓣ01957/733227; May–Sept), a simple field just to the west of Houbie, with toilets, showers and drying facilities.

Unst

Much of **Unst** (ⓦwww.unst.org) is rolling grassland but the coast is more dramatic: a fringe of cliffs relieved by some beautiful sandy beaches. As Britain's most northerly inhabited island, there is a surfeit of "most northerly" sights, which is fair enough, given that many visitors only come here in order to head straight for Hermaness, to see the sea birds and look out over Muckle Flugga and the northernmost tip of Britain, to the North Pole beyond. The island has been badly affected by the recent closure of the local RAF radar base at Saxa Vord: it used to employ a third of the island's population, which has now fallen to around six hundred.

On the south coast, not far from the ferry terminal, is **UYEASOUND**, east of which lie the ruins of **Muness Castle**, a diminutive defensive structure, built in 1598 with matching bulging bastions and corbelled turrets at opposite corners (keys and torch from the house nearby). Unst's main settlement is **BALTASOUND**, an old herring port, where the excellent **Unst Heritage Centre** (May–Sept daily 2–5pm; free) occupies the old school building by the main crossroads. From Baltasound, the main road crosses a giant boulder field of serpentine, a greyish green, occasionally turquoise rock that weathers to a rusty orange. The **Keen of Hamar**, east of Baltasound, and clearly signposted from the main road, is one of the largest expanses of serpentine debris in Europe, and is home to an extraordinary array of plantlife.

Beyond the Keen of Hamar, the road drops down into **HAROLDSWICK**, where near the shore you'll find the **Unst Boat Haven** (May–Sept daily 2–5pm; otherwise a key is available from the adjacent shop, free), displaying a beautifully presented collection of historic boats with many tools of the trade and information on fishing. The road that heads off northwest leads to the bleak headland of **Hermaness**, home to more than 100,000 nesting sea birds. There's an excellent **visitor centre** in the former lighthouse-keepers' shore station, where you can pick up a leaflet showing the marked routes across the heather to the view over to **Muckle Flugga** lighthouse and **Out Stack**, the most northerly bit of Britain. The views from here are inevitably marvellous, as is the birdlife; there's a huge gannetry on one of the stacks, and puffins burrow all along the cliff-tops.

Book in advance for the regular **ferries** that shuttle from Gutcher on Yell over to **BELMONT** on Unst (1–2 hourly; 10min; ⓣ01957/722259). The best and most unusual **accommodation** is the family-owned *Buness House* (ⓣ01957/711315, ⓦwww.users.zetnet.co.ukBuness-house; ❻), a seventeenth-century Haa in Baltasound. Another very good bet is *Prestagaard*

(℡01957/755234, ⓦwww.prestegaard.shetland.co.uk; ❷), a modest Victorian B&B in Uyeasound, where you'll also find the clean and modern *Gardiesfauld Hostel* (℡01957/755240, ⓦwww.gardiesfauld.shetland.co.uk; April–Sept; dorm beds £11), near the pier, which allows **camping** and offers **bike rental**.

Travel details

Orkney

Ferries to Orkney (summer only)

Aberdeen to: Kirkwall (4 weekly; 6hr).
Gill's Bay to: St Margaret's Hope (3–4 daily; 1hr).
John O'Groats to: Burwick (passengers only; 2–4 daily; 40min).
Lerwick to: Kirkwall (3 weekly; 5hr 30min).
Scrabster to: Stromness (2–3 daily; 1hr 30min).

Inter-island ferries (summer only)

To Eday: Kirkwall–Eday (1–2 daily; 1hr 15min–2hr).
To Hoy: Houton–Lyness (Mon–Fri 6 daily, Sat & Sun 2–4 daily; 45min–1hr 25min); Stromness–Hoy (passengers only; Mon–Fri 4–5 daily, Sat & Sun 2 daily; 25min).
To North Ronaldsay: Kirkwall–North Ronaldsay (1 weekly, usually Fri; 2hr 40min–3hr).
To Papa Westray: Kirkwall–Papa Westray (Tues & Fri; 2hr 15min); Pierowall (Westray)–Papa Westray (passengers only; 2–5 daily; 25min).
To Rousay: Tingwall–Rousay (5–6 daily; 30min).
To Sanday: Kirkwall–Sanday (2 daily; 1hr 25min).
To Shapinsay: Kirkwall–Shapinsay (Mon–Fri 5 daily, Sat & Sun 4 daily; 45min).
To Stronsay: Kirkwall–Whitehall (2 daily; 1hr 40min–2hr).
To Westray: Kirkwall–Westray (2–3 daily; 1hr 25min).

Inter-island flights (Mon–Sat only)

Kirkwall to: Eday (Wed; 8–26min); North Ronaldsay (2–3 daily; 15min); Papa Westray (Mon–Sat 2–3 daily, 1 on Sun; 12–19min); Sanday (Mon–Sat 1–2 daily; 10min); Stronsay (Mon–Sat 2 daily; 25min); Westray (Mon–Sat 2 daily; 12min).

Buses on Orkney Mainland

Kirkwall to: Burwick (3–4 daily; 50min); Birsay (Mon–Fri 2 daily; 45min); Evie (Mon–Sat 4 daily; 30min); Houton (Mon–Fri 5 daily, 3 on Sat; 30min); St Margaret's Hope (Mon–Fri 4 daily, 2 on Sat; 40min); Skara Brae (June–Aug Mon–Fri 2 daily; 1hr 15min); Stromness (Mon–Fri hourly, 8 on Sat, 4 on Sun; 30min); Tingwall (Mon–Fri 4 daily, Sat & Sun 2–3 daily; 35min).
Stromness to: Skara Brae (3–4 daily; 20min); Tingwall (Wed & Fri 2 daily; 1hr).

Shetland

Ferries to Shetland (summer only)

Aberdeen to: Lerwick (daily; 12hr).
Kirkwall (Orkney) to: Lerwick (3–4 weekly; 6hr).

Inter-island ferries (summer only)

To Bressay: Lerwick–Bressay (hourly; 7min).
To Fair Isle: Lerwick–Fair Isle (alternate Thurs; 4hr 30min); Grutness–Fair Isle (Tues, Sat & alternate Thurs; 3hr).
To Fetlar: Belmont (Unst) and Gutcher (Yell)–Hamar's Ness (5–6 daily; 25–40min).
To Foula: Scalloway–Foula (alternate Thurs; 3hr 30min); Walls–Foula (Tues, Sat & alternate Thurs; 2hr).
To Unst: Gutcher (Yell)–Belmont (1–2 hourly; 10min).
To Yell: Toft–Ulsta (1–2 hourly; 20min).

Inter-island flights (summer only)

Sumburgh to: Fair Isle (Sat; 15min).
Tingwall to: Fair Isle (Mon, Wed & Fri 2 daily, 1 on Sat; 25min); Foula (Mon & Tues 1 daily, Wed & Fri 2 daily; 15min); Out Skerries, calling at Whalsay on request (Mon & Wed 1 daily, Thurs 2 daily; 20min); Papa Stour (Tues 2 daily; 10min).

Buses on Shetland Mainland

Lerwick to: Brae (Mon–Sat 4–6 daily, 1 on Sun in school term; 45min); Hamnavoe (Mon–Sat 2 daily; 30min); Hillswick (Mon–Sat 1 daily; 1hr 40min); Scalloway (Mon–Sat hourly; 15min); Sumburgh (Mon–Sat 5 daily, 3 on Sun; 45min); Toft (Mon–Sat 4–5 daily; 50min); Vidlin (Mon–Sat 2 daily; 45min);

Voe (Mon–Sat 5–6 daily, Sun school term 1 daily; 30min); Walls (Mon–Sat 1–3 daily; 45min).

Buses on Unst

Baltasound to: Haroldswick (Mon–Sat 3–4 daily; 10min).
Belmont to: Baltasound (Mon–Sat 2–3 daily; 20min); Uyeasound (Mon–Sat 2–3 daily; 5min).

Buses on Yell

Mid Yell to: Gutcher (Mon–Sat 1–5 daily, Sun 1 daily in school term; 20min).
Ulsta to: Burravoe (Mon–Sat 1 daily; 15min); Gutcher (Mon–Sat 1–3 daily, 1 on Sun in school term; 30min).

25

Contexts

Contexts

History

Off and on, **Britain** has been inhabited for the best part of half a million years, though the earliest archeological evidence of human life dates from about **250,000 BC**. These meagre remains, found near Swanscombe, east of London across the Thames from Tilbury, belong to one of the migrant communities whose comings and goings depended on the fluctuations of the Ice Ages. Renewed glaciation then made the area uninhabitable once more, and the next traces – mainly roughly worked flint implements – were left around 40,000 BC by cave-dwellers at Creswell Crags in Derbyshire, Kent's Cavern near Torquay and Cheddar Cave in Somerset. The last spell of intense cold began about 17,000 years ago, and it was the final thawing of this last **Ice Age** around 5000 BC that caused the British Isles to separate from the European mainland.

The sea barrier did nothing to stop further migrations of nomadic hunting communities, drawn by the rich forests that covered ancient Britain. In about 3500 BC a new wave of colonists arrived from the continent, probably via Ireland, bringing with them a **Neolithic** culture based on farming and the rearing of livestock. These tribes were the first to make some impact on the British environment, clearing forests, enclosing fields, constructing defensive ditches around their villages and digging mines to obtain flint used for tools and weapons. Fragments of Neolithic pottery have been found near Peterborough and at Windmill Hill, near Avebury in Wiltshire; other settlements – like the well-preserved village of Skara Brae in Orkney – were near the sea, enabling them to supplement their diet by fishing and to develop their skills as boat builders. The most profuse relics of this culture are their graves, usually stone-chambered, turf-covered mounds (called long barrows, cairns or cromlechs), which are scattered throughout the country; the most impressive ones are at Belas Knap in Gloucestershire, Barclodiad y Gawres in Anglesey, and Maes Howe on Orkney.

The transition from the Neolithic to the Bronze Age began around 2000 BC, with the immigration from northern Europe of the so-called **Beaker Folk** – named from the distinctive cups found at their burial sites. Originating in the Iberian peninsula and bringing with them bronze-workers from the Rhineland, these newcomers had a well-organized social structure with an established aristocracy, and quickly intermixed with the native tribes. Many of Britain's **stone circles** were completed at this time, including Stonehenge in Wiltshire, and Calanais on the Isle of Lewis, while many others belong entirely to the Bronze Age – for example, the Hurlers and the Nine Maidens on Cornwall's Bodmin Moor. Large numbers of earthwork forts were also built in this period, suggesting a high level of tribal warfare, but none were able to withstand the waves of Celtic invaders who, spreading from a homeland in central Europe, began settling in Britain around 600 BC.

The Celts

Highly skilled in battle, the **Celts** soon displaced the local inhabitants from one end of Britain to the other, establishing a sophisticated farming economy and a social hierarchy that was headed by **Druids**, a priesthood with attendant poets, seers and warriors. Through a deep knowledge of ritual, legend and the mechanics of the heavens, the Druids maintained their position between the people and a pantheon of over four thousand gods. Familiar with Mediterranean artefacts through their far-flung trade routes, they introduced a superior method of metalworking that favoured iron rather than bronze, from which they forged not just weapons but also coins. Gold was used for ornamental works – the first recognizable British art – heavily influenced by the symbolic, patterned **La Tène** style still thought of as quintessentially Celtic.

The principal Celtic contribution to the landscape was a network of hillforts or brochs, and other defensive works stretching over the entire country, the greatest of them at **Maiden Castle** in Dorset, a site first fortified almost 3000 years earlier, and **Mousa** in the Shetland Islands. The original Celtic tongue – the basis of modern Welsh and Scottish Gaelic – was spoken over a wide area, gradually dividing into Goidelic (or Q-Celtic) now spoken in Ireland and Scotland, and Brythonic (P-Celtic) spoken in Wales and Cornwall, and later exported to Brittany in France. Great though the Celtic technological and artistic achievements were, the people and their pan-European cousins were unable to maintain an organized civic society to match that of their successors, the Romans.

The Romans

The **Roman** invasion began hesitantly, with small cross-Channel incursions by **Julius Caesar** in 55 and 54 BC. Britain's rumoured mineral wealth was a primary motive behind these raids, but the immediate spur to the eventual conquest nearly a century later was the dangerous collaboration between British Celts and the fiercely anti-Roman tribesmen in France, and the need of the emperor **Claudius**, who owed his power to the army, for a great military triumph. The death of the British king Cunobelin, who ruled all southeast England and was the original of Shakespeare's Cymbeline, offered the opportunity Claudius required, and in August 43 AD, a substantial force landed in Kent, from where it fanned out, soon establishing a base along the estuary of the Thames. Joined by Claudius and a menagerie of elephants and camels for the major battles of the campaign, the Romans soon reached Camulodunum (Colchester), and within four years were dug in on the frontier of south Wales, though Wales itself and the north of England were not subdued for another thirty years.

By 80 AD the Roman governor, **Agricola**, felt secure enough in the south of Britain to begin an invasion of the north, building a string of forts across the Clyde–Forth line and defeating a large force of Scottish tribes at Mons Graupius. The long-term effect of his campaign, however, was slight. In 123 AD the emperor Hadrian decided to seal the frontier against the northern tribes and built **Hadrian's Wall**, which stretched from the Solway Firth to the Tyne and was the first formal division of the island of Britain. Twenty years later, the Romans again ventured north and built the **Antonine Wall** between the Clyde and the Forth. This was occupied for about forty years, but thereafter the Romans, frustrated by the inhospitable terrain of the Highlands, largely gave up their attempt to subjugate the north, and instead adopted a policy of containment.

The written history of Britain begins with the Romans, whose rule lasted nearly four centuries. For the first time most of England was absorbed into a unified and peaceful political structure, in which commerce flourished and cities prospered, particularly **Londinium**, which immediately assumed a pivotal role in the commercial and administrative life of the province. Although Latin became the language of the Romano-British ruling elite, local traditions were allowed to coexist alongside Roman customs, so that Celtic gods were often worshipped at the same time as Rome's, and sometimes indeed merged with them. Perhaps the most important legacy of the Roman occupation, however, was the introduction of **Christianity** from the third century on, becoming firmly entrenched after its official recognition across the empire by Constantine in 313.

The Anglo-Saxons

As early as the reign of Constantine, Roman England was being raided by Germanic Saxon pirates. As economic life declined and rural areas became depopulated, so individual military leaders began to usurp local authority and by the start of the fifth century England had become irrevocably detached from what remained of the Roman Empire. Within fifty years the **Saxons** were settling on the island, the start of a gradual conquest that – despite bitter resistance led by such semi-mythical figures as King Arthur, who is alleged to have held court at Caerleon in Wales – culminated in the defeat of the native Britons in 577 at the **Battle of Dyrham** (near Bath). Driving the recalcitrant Celtic tribes west, the invaders eliminated the Romano-British culture and by the end of the sixth century the bulk of England was divided into the Anglo-Saxon kingdoms of Northumbria, Mercia, East Anglia, Kent and Wessex, and only in Scotland, Wales and the far southwest of England did the ancient Celtic traditions survive. In the fifth century, Irish-Celtic invaders formed distinct colonies in parts of Wales and in the northwest of Scotland, and between the fifth and the eighth centuries ascetic evangelical missionaries from Celtic Ireland spread the gospel around western Britain, promoting the eremitical tradition of living a reclusive life. In south Wales, **St David** was the most popular (and subsequently Wales's patron saint), while in northwest Scotland, **St Columba** founded several Christian outposts, the most famous of which was on the island of Iona.

Elsewhere, the revival of Christianity in England was driven mainly by the arrival of **St Augustine**, who was dispatched by Pope Gregory I and landed on the Kent coast in 597, accompanied by forty monks. The missionaries were received by Ethelbert, who gave Augustine permission to found a monastery at **Canterbury**, where the king himself was then baptized, followed by ten thousand of his subjects at a grand Christmas ceremony. Despite some reversals in the years that followed, the Christianization of England proceeded quickly, so that by the middle of the seventh century all the Anglo-Saxon kings had at least nominally adopted the faith. Tensions and clashes between the Augustinian missionaries and the more freebooting Celtic monks inevitably arose, to be resolved by the **Synod of Whitby** in 663, when it was settled that the English church should follow the rule of Rome, thereby ensuring a realignment with the European cultural mainstream.

The central English region of **Mercia** became the dominant Anglo-Saxon kingdom in the eighth century under kings Ethelbald and Offa, the latter being responsible for the greatest public work of the Anglo-Saxon period, **Offa's Dyke**, an earthwork stretching from the River Dee to the Severn, marking the border with Wales. After Offa's death **Wessex** gained the upper hand, and by 825 King Egbert had conquered or taken allegiance from all the other English kingdoms. The supremacy of Wessex coincided with the first large-scale Norse or **Viking** invasions, which began with coastal pirate raids, such as the one that destroyed the great monastery of Lindisfarne in 793, but gradually grew into a migration, initially concentrated in the Scottish islands of Orkney, Shetland and the Hebrides.

In 865, a substantial Danish army landed in East Anglia, and within six years they had conquered Northumbria, Mercia and East Anglia. The Danes then set their sights on Wessex, whose new king was the formidable and talented **Alfred** the **Great** (871–899). Despite the odds, Alfred successfully resisted the Danes and eventually the two warring parties signed a truce, which fixed an uneasy border between Wessex and Danish territory – the **Danelaw** – to the north. Ensconced in northern England and what is today the East Midlands, the Danes soon succumbed to Christianity and internal warfare, while Alfred modernized his kingdom and strengthened its defences.

Alfred's successor, **Edward the Elder** (899–925), capitalized on his efforts, establishing Saxon supremacy over the Danelaw to become the de facto over-lord of all England. The relative calm continued under Edward's son, **Athelstan** (925–40), who extended his overlordship over much of Scotland and Wales, and his son, **Edgar** (959–75), who became the first ruler to be crowned **king of England** in 973. However, this was but a lull in the Viking storm. Returning in force, the Vikings milked Edgar's son **Ethelred the Unready** ("lacking coun-sel"; 978–1016) for all the money they could, but the ransom (the Danegeld) paid brought only temporary relief and Ethelred hot-footed it to Normandy, leaving the Danes in command.

The first Danish king of England was **Canute** (1016–35), a shrewd and gifted ruler, but his two disreputable sons quickly dismantled his carefully constructed Anglo-Scandinavian empire. Thereafter, the Saxons regained the initiative, restoring Ethelred's son, **Edward the Confessor** (1042–66), to the throne in 1042. It was a poor choice. Edward was more suited to be a priest than a king and he allowed power to drift into the hands of his most powerful subject, Godwin, Earl of Wessex, and his son Harold. On Edward's death, the Witan – a sort of council of elders – confirmed **Harold** (1066) as king, ignoring several rival claims including that of William, Duke of Normandy. William's claim was a curious affair, but he always insisted – however improbable it may seem – that the childless Edward the Confessor had promised him his crown. Unluckily for Harold, his two main rivals struck at the same time. First up was his alienated brother **Tostig** and his ally King Harald of Norway, a giant of a man reliably reckoned to be seven feet tall. They landed with a Viking army in Yorkshire and Harold hurriedly marched north to meet them. Harold won a crushing victory at the battle of Stamford Bridge, but then he heard that William of Normandy had invaded the south. Rashly, Harold did not pause to muster more men, but dashed south, where William famously routed the Saxons – and killed Harold – at the **Battle of Hastings** in 1066. On Christmas Day, William the Conqueror was installed as king in Westminster Abbey.

England: Normans and Plantagenets (1066–1399)

Making little attempt to reach any understanding with his new subjects, **William I** (1066–87) imposed a Norman aristocracy, reinforcing his rule with a series of strongholds, the grandest of which was the Tower of London. Initially, there was some resistance, but William crushed these sporadic rebellions with great brutality. But perhaps the single most effective controlling measure was the compilation of the **Domesday Book** between 1085 and 1086. Recording land ownership, type of cultivation, the number of inhabitants and their social status, it afforded William an unprecedented body of information about his subjects, providing the framework for the administration of taxation, the judi-cial structure and feudal obligations.

William was succeeded by his son **William Rufus (**1087–1100), an ineffec-tual ruler who died in mysterious circumstances – killed by an unknown assail-ant's arrow while hunting in the New Forest – and the throne passed to **Henry I (**1100–35), William I's youngest son. Henry spent much of his time struggling with his unruly barons, but at least he proved to be more conciliatory in his dealings with the Saxons, even marrying into one of their leading families. On his death in 1135, William I's grandson Stephen of Blois (1135–54) contested the accession of Henry's daughter Mathilda and the result was a long-winded civil war. Matters were eventually resolved when both factions accepted Mathilda's son as **Henry II** (1154–1189), the first of the **Plantagenets**, so-called after this branch of the family. Energetic and far-sighted, Henry kept his barons firmly in check and instigated profound administrative reforms, including the introduction of trial by jury. England was not Henry's only concern, as his inheritance had bequeathed him great chunks of France, though his downfall was his attempt to subordinate Church to Crown. This went terribly awry in 1170, when Henry sanctioned the murder in Canterbury Cathedral of his erstwhile drinking companion **Thomas à Becket**, whose canonization just three years later created an enduring Europe-wide cult.

The last years of Henry's reign were riven by quarrels with his sons, the eldest of whom, **Richard I** (or Lionheart; 1189–99), spent most of his ten-year reign crusading in the Holy Land. Neglected, England fell prey to the scheming of Richard's brother **John** (1199–1216), the villain of the Robin Hood tales, who became king in his own right after Richard died of a battle wound in France in 1199. But John's inability to hold on to his French possessions and his rumbling dispute with the Vatican alienated the English barons, who eventually forced him to consent to a charter guaranteeing their rights and privileges, the **Magna Carta**, which was signed in 1215 at Runnymede, on the Thames.

The power struggle with the barons continued into the reign of **Henry III** (1216–72), but Henry's successor, **Edward I** (1272–1307), was much more in control of his kingdom than his predecessor. Edward was also a great law-maker, but he became obsessed by military matters, spending years subduing Wales and imposing English jurisdiction over Scotland. Fortunately for the Scots – it was too late for Wales – the next king of England, **Edward II** (1307–27), proved to be completely hopeless and in 1314 Robert the Bruce inflicted a huge defeat on his guileless army at the battle of Bannockburn (see below). This spelt the beginning of the end for Edward, who was subsequently murdered by his wife Isabella and her lover Roger Mortimer in 1327.

Edward III (1327–77) began by sorting out the Scottish imbroglio before getting stuck into his main preoccupation – his (essentially specious) claim to the throne of France. Starting in 1337, the resultant **Hundred Years' War** kicked off with several famous English victories, principally Crécy in 1346 and Poitiers in 1356, but was interrupted by the outbreak of the **Black Death** in 1349. The plague claimed about one and a half million English souls – some one-third of the population – and the scarcity of labour that followed gave the peasantry more economic clout than they had ever had before. Predictably, the landowners attempted to restrict the concomitant rise in wages, but thereby provoked the widespread rioting that culminated in the **Peasants' Revolt** of 1381. The rebels marched on London under the delusion that they could appeal to the king – now **Richard II** (1377–99) – for fair treatment, but they soon learnt otherwise. The king did indeed meet a rebel deputation in person, but his aristocratic bodyguards took the opportunity to kill the peasants' leader, **Wat Tyler**, the prelude to the enforced dispersal of the crowds and mass slaughter.

The conquest of Wales (1272–1415)

William the Conqueror did not attempt to conquer Wales, but instead he installed a huge retinue of barons, the **Lords Marcher**, along the border both to keep an eye on the Welsh and secure his frontier. This remained the position until **Edward I** decided to conquer Wales at the end of the thirteenth century, prompted by the actions of a Welsh chief, **Llywelyn the Last**, who had failed to attend Edward's coronation and refused to pay him homage. With effective use of sea power, Edward had little trouble in forcing Llywelyn into Snowdonia and when peace was restored with the **Treaty of Aberconwy**, Llywelyn was deprived of almost all his land but left with the hollow title of "Prince of Wales". Shortly afterwards, Llywelyn's brother **Dafydd** rose against Edward, dragging Llywelyn along with him. Edward crushed the revolt, captured Llywelyn, and executed him. The **Treaty of Rhuddlan** in 1284 set down the terms by which the English monarch was to rule Wales: much of it was given to the Lords Marcher, the rest was divided into administrative and legal districts similar to those in England. Though the treaty is often seen as a symbol of English subjugation, it respected much of Welsh law and provided a basis for civil rights and privileges. Many Welsh were content to accept Edward's rule, but in 1294 a rebellion led by **Madog ap Llywelyn** spread across Wales and was only halted by Edward's swift and brutal response. Most of the privileges enshrined in the Treaty of Rhuddlan were now rescinded and the Welsh were brought firmly under the English heel.

Defeated but not broken, the Welsh were ultimately rallied by the charismatic Welsh hero **Owain Glyndŵr**, who declared himself "Prince of Wales" in 1400, and with a posse of local supporters attacked the English. The English king **Henry IV** misjudged the situation and imposed restrictions on Welsh landownership, thereby swelling the ranks of Glyndŵr's supporters, who captured the key fortress of Conwy Castle (while the garrison was at church) in 1401. In 1404, Glyndŵr summoned a parliament in Machynlleth, and had himself crowned Prince of Wales, with envoys of France, Scotland and Castile in attendance. He then demanded independence for the Welsh Church from Canterbury and set about securing alliances with those English noblemen who had grievances with Henry IV. However, a succession of defeats soon prompted Glyndŵr's allies to desert him and the rebellion fizzled out, though Glyndŵr was never captured and, ignoring English offers of a royal pardon, disappeared into the mountains, where he died in 1415 or 1416.

Scotland in the Middle Ages (1057–1320)

In the post-Roman period, the petty chieftains of the **Picts** and **Scotti** – followed later by the Vikings – battled for control of Scotland, but by the ninth century **Kenneth MacAlpine**, king of the Scotti and son of a Pictish princess, was able to create a united kingdom known as Alba, later as Scotia. His successors extended MacAlpine's frontiers by marriage and conquest until, by 1034, almost all of modern Scotland was under their rule.

In 1040, **Macbeth** famously killed King Duncan and usurped the Scottish throne, but in 1057 Duncan's son, **Malcolm III**, returned to Scotland, where he defeated Macbeth and began a long reign which was to transform Scottish society. Malcolm, known as Canmore ("Bighead"), had spent the seventeen years of Macbeth's rule in exile at the English court and he now sought to apply to Scotland the range of ideas he had absorbed south of the border. Malcolm and his heirs established a secure dynasty based on succession through the male line and replaced the old Gaelic system of blood ties with **feudalism**: the followers of a Gaelic king were his kindred, whereas the followers of a feudal king were his vassals. The Canmores successfully feudalized much of southern and eastern Scotland by making grants to their Norman, Breton and Flemish followers, but beyond that, traditional clan-based forms of social relations persisted, a division which was to define much of Scotland's later history.

The Canmores also began to reform the **Church**. Malcolm III's English wife **Margaret** brought Scottish religious practices into line with those of the rest of Europe – and was eventually canonized – while **David I** (1124–53) imported monks to found a series of monasteries, principally in the Borders at Kelso, Melrose, Jedburgh and Dryburgh. By 1200 the country was covered by a network of eleven bishoprics, although church organization remained weak within the Highlands. Similarly, the dynasty founded a series of **royal burghs**, towns such as Edinburgh, Stirling and Berwick, and bestowed upon them charters recognizing them as centres of trade. The charters usually granted a measure of self-government, vested in the town corporation or guild, and the monarchy hoped this arrangement would both encourage loyalty and increase the prosperity of the kingdom. Scotland's Gaelic-speaking clans had little influence within the burghs, and by 1550 Scots – a northern version of Anglo-Saxon – had become the main language throughout the Lowlands.

Progress as an independent nation, however, was threatened after 1286, when **Alexander III** died, leaving a hotly disputed succession, which gave Edward I, the king of England, an opportunity to intervene. In 1291 Edward presided over a conference where the rival claimants to the Scottish throne presented their cases. Edward chose John Balliol, in preference to **Robert the Bruce**, and obliged John to pay him homage, thus turning Scotland into a vassal kingdom. Bruce refused to accept the decision, thereby continuing the conflict, and in 1295 Balliol renounced his allegiance to Edward and formed an alliance with **France** – the beginning of what is known as the "Auld Alliance". In the conflict that followed, Balliol was defeated and imprisoned, and Edward seized control of almost all of Scotland.

Edward had shown little mercy during his conquest of Scotland and his cruelty seems to have provoked a truly national resistance. This focused on **William Wallace**, a man of relatively lowly origins who forged an army of peasants, lesser knights and townsmen that was fundamentally different from the armies raised by the nobility. Figures like Balliol, holding lands in England, France and Scotland, were part of an international aristocracy for whom warfare was merely the means by which they struggled for power. Wallace, by contrast, led proto-nationalist forces determined to expel the English from their country. Probably for that very reason Wallace never received the support of the nobility, and, after a bitter ten-year campaign, he was betrayed, captured and then executed in London in 1305.

With Wallace out of the way, feudal intrigue resumed. In 1306 **Robert the Bruce**, the erstwhile ally of the English, defied Edward and had himself crowned king of Scotland. Edward died the following year, but the turbulence dragged on until 1314, when Bruce decisively defeated a huge English army under Edward II at the battle of **Bannockburn**. At last Bruce was firmly in control of his kingdom, and in 1320 the Scots asserted their right to independence in a successful petition to the pope, now known as the **Arbroath Declaration**.

England: the houses of Lancaster and York

In 1399, **Henry IV** (1399–1413), the first of the **Lancastrian** kings, supplanted the weak and indecisive Richard II, and was then succeeded by his own son, the bellicose **Henry V** (1413–22), who promptly renewed the Hundred Years' War with vigour. Henry famously defeated the French at the battle of **Agincourt**, a comprehensive victory that forced the French king to acknowledge Henry as his heir in the Treaty of Troyes of 1420. However, Henry died just two years later and his son, **Henry VI** (1422–61 & 1470–1471) – or rather his regents – all too easily succumbed to a French counter attack inspired by **Joan of Arc** (1412–1431); by 1454, only Calais was left in English hands.

It was soon obvious that Henry VI was mentally unstable, and consequently two aristocratic factions attempted to wrest control. These were the Yorkists, whose emblem was the white rose, and the Lancastrians, represented by the red rose – hence the **Wars of the Roses**. At first, the Lancastrians had the better of things, but the Yorkist **Edward IV** seized the crown in 1461. Imprudently, Edward then attempted to shrug off his most powerful backer, Richard Neville, Earl of Warwick – aka "Warwick the Kingmaker" – and Warwick returned the favour by switching sides. Edward was driven into exile and Henry VI returned for a second term as king – but not for long. In 1471, Edward IV returned, Warwick was killed and Henry captured – and subsequently dispatched – when the Yorkists crushed the Lancastrians at the battle of Tewkesbury.

Edward IV (1461–70 & 1471–83) proved to be a precursor of the great Tudor princes – licentious, cruel and despotic, but also a patron of Renaissance learning. In 1483, his 12-year-old son succeeded as **Edward V** (1483), but his reign was cut short after only two months, when he and his younger brother were murdered in the Tower of London – probably by their uncle, the Duke of Gloucester, who was crowned **Richard III** (1483–85). Richard was famously toppled at Bosworth Field in 1485 by Henry Tudor, Earl of Richmond, who took the throne as **Henry VII** (1485–1509).

England: the Tudors (1485–1603)

The opening of the **Tudor** period brought radical transformations. A Lancastrian through his mother's line, **Henry VII** promptly reconciled the Yorkists by marrying Edward IV's daughter Elizabeth, thereby ending the Wars of the Roses at a stroke. It was a shrewd gambit and others followed. Henry married his daughter off to James IV of Scotland and his son to Catherine, the daughter of Ferdinand and Isabella of Spain – and by these means England began to assume the status of a major European power. There were economic stirrings too, with the burgeoning wool and cloth trades spawning an increasingly prosperous merchant class.

Henry's son, **Henry VIII** (1509–47) is best remembered for his separation of the English Church from Rome and his establishment of an independent Protestant church – the **Church of England**. However, Henry was not a Protestant himself and such was his early orthodoxy that the pope even gave him the title "Defender of the Faith" for a pamphlet he wrote attacking Luther's treatises. In fact, the schism between Henry and the pope was triggered not by doctrinal issues but by the failure of his wife **Catherine of Aragon** – widow of his elder brother – to provide Henry with male offspring. Since Pope Clement VII refused to grant him a decree of nullity, Henry dismissed his longtime chancellor Thomas Wolsey and turned instead to Thomas Cromwell, who helped make the English Church recognize Henry as its head. One of the consequences was the **Dissolution of the Monasteries**, which conveniently gave both king and nobles the chance to get their hands on valuable monastic property. The Dissolution was completed in two stages in the late 1530s, though Henry was temporarily delayed by the **Pilgrimage of Grace**, a widespread rebellion that began in Louth, in Lincolnshire, and spread across the north buoyed by pro-Catholic sentiment.

In his later years Henry became a corpulent, syphilitic wreck, six times married but at last furnished with an heir, **Edward VI** (1547–53), who was only nine years old when he ascended the throne. His short reign saw Protestantism established on a firm footing, with churches stripped of their images and Catholic services banned, yet on Edward's death most of the country readily accepted his half-sister **Mary** (1553–58), daughter of Catherine of Aragon and a fervent Catholic, as queen. She returned England to the papacy and married the future Philip II of Spain, forging an alliance whose immediate consequence was war with France and the loss of Calais, the last of England's French possessions. The marriage was unpopular and so was Mary's decision to begin persecuting Protestants, executing the leading lights of the English Reformation, Hugh Latimer, Nicholas Ridley and Thomas Cranmer, the archbishop of Canterbury who was largely responsible for the first **English prayer book**, published in 1549.

When she came to the throne in 1558 on the death of her half-sister, **Elizabeth I** (1558–1603) looked very vulnerable. The country was divided by religion – Catholic against Protestant – and threatened from abroad by Philip II of Spain, the most powerful man in Europe. Famously, Elizabeth eschewed marriage and, although a Protestant herself, steered a delicate course between the two religious groupings. Her prudence rested well with the English merchant class, who were becoming the greatest power in the land, its members mostly opposed to foreign military entanglements. An exception was, however, made for the piratical activities of the great English seafarers of the day, sea captains like Walter Raleigh, Martin Frobisher, John Hawkins and Francis Drake, who made a fortune raiding Spain's American colonies. Inevitably, Philip II's irritation took a warlike turn, but the **Spanish Armada** he sent in 1588 was defeated, thereby establishing England as a major European sea power. Elizabeth's reign also saw the efflorescence of a specifically English Renaissance, especially in the field of literature with such major talents as **William Shakespeare** (1564–1616).

Wales under the Tudors (1485–1603)

Welsh allegiance during the Wars of the Roses lay broadly with the Lancastrians, who had the support of the ascendant north Welsh Tewdwr (or Tudor) family. Welsh expectations of the first Tudor monarch, Henry VII, were high and though Henry lived up to some of them – removing many of the restrictions on land ownership imposed at the start of Glyndŵr's uprising, and promoting many Welshmen to high office – administration remained piecemeal. Control was still shared between the Crown and largely independent Marcher lords until a uniform administrative structure was achieved under Henry VIII.

Wales had been largely controlled by the English monarch since the Treaty of Rhuddlan in 1284, but the **Acts of Union** in 1536 and 1543 formalised English sovereignty over the country. At the same time the Marches were replaced by shires (the equivalent of modern counties), the Welsh laws codified by Hywel Dda were made void and partible inheritance gave way to primogeniture, the eldest son becoming the sole heir. For the first time the Welsh and English enjoyed legal equality, but the break with native traditions wasn't well received. Most of the people remained poor, the gentry became increasingly anglicized, the use of Welsh was proscribed, and legal proceedings were held in English (a language few peasants understood).

As for the **church**, Christianity had always been a ritual way of life rather than a philosophical code in Wales and consequently Protestantism soon supplanted Catholicism during the religious upheavals of Henry VIII's reign. What the

Reformation did promote was a more studied approach to religion and learning in general. Under the reign of Elizabeth I, Jesus College was founded in Oxford for Welsh scholars, and the Bible was translated into Welsh for the first time by a team led by Bishop **William Morgan**.

With new landownership laws enshrined in the Acts of Union, the stimulus provided by the Dissolution hastened the emergence of the Anglo-Welsh gentry, a group eager to claim a Welsh pedigree while promoting the English language and the legal system, which helped to perpetuate their hegemony. Meanwhile, landless peasants remained poor, only gaining slightly from the increase in cattle trade with England and the slow development of mining and ore smelting.

The Stewarts in Scotland (1371–1603)

In the decades following the death of Bruce in 1329, the Scottish monarchy gradually declined. The last of the Bruce dynasty died in 1371, to be succeeded by the "Stewards", hence **Stewarts** (known as Stuarts in England). However, a series of them came to the throne while still children, so the power vacuum was filled by the nobility, whose key members exercised control as Scotland's regents while carving out territories that they ruled with the power, if not the title, of kings. **James IV** (1488–1513), the most talented of the early Stewarts, might have restored the authority of the Crown, but his invasion of England ended in a terrible defeat for the Scots – and his own death – at the **Battle of Flodden Field**.

The reign of **Mary, Queen of Scots** (1542–87), typified the problems of the Scottish monarchy. Mary came to the throne when just one week old, and immediately caught the attention of the English king, Henry VIII, who sought, first by persuasion and then by military might, to secure her hand in marriage for his 5-year-old son, Edward. Beginning in 1544, the English launched a series of devastating attacks on Scotland, an episode Sir Walter Scott later called the "Rough Wooing", until, in the face of another English invasion in 1548, the Scots – or at least those not supporting Henry – turned to the "Auld Alliance". The French king proposed marriage between Mary and the Dauphin Francis, promising in return military assistance against the English. The 6-year-old queen sailed for France in 1548, leaving her loyal nobles and their French allies in control, and her husband succeeded to the French throne in 1559. When she returned thirteen years later, following the death of Francis, she had to pick her way through the rival ambitions of her nobility and deal with something entirely new – the religious Reformation.

The **Reformation** in Scotland was a complex social process, whose threads are hard to unravel. Nevertheless, it's quite clear that by the middle of the sixteenth century the established Church was held in general contempt. Protestantism became associated with anti-French feeling brought on, in no small measure, by Mary of Guise, the French mother of the absent Queen Mary, who had become regent of Scotland in 1554: Mary of Guise appointed Frenchmen to high office rather than Scots, thereby alienating the Scottish nobility. In 1557, a group of Scottish nobles banded together to form the **Lords of the Congregation**, whose dual purpose was to oppose French influence and promote the reformed religion. With English military backing, the Protestant lords succeeded in deposing Mary of Guise in 1559, and, when the Scottish Parliament assembled shortly afterwards, it asserted the primacy of Protestantism by prohibiting Mass and abolishing the authority of the pope. The nobility proceeded to confiscate two thirds of Church lands, a huge prize that did much to bolster their new beliefs.

Even without the economic incentives, Protestantism was a highly charged political doctrine. As the Protestant reformer **John Knox** told Queen Mary at their first meeting in 1561, subjects are not bound to obey an ungodly monarch. Mary tried to avoid an open breach with her Protestant subjects, but her difficulties were exacerbated by a disastrous second marriage to **Lord Darnley**. A cruel and politically inept character, his jealousy led to his involvement in the murder of Mary's favourite, **David Rizzio**, who was dragged from the queen's chambers at Holyrood and stabbed 56 times. The incident caused Scottish Protestants more than a little unease, though they were even more horrified when, in 1567, Darnley himself was murdered and Mary promptly married the **Earl of Bothwell**, widely believed to be the murderer. This was too much to bear, and the Scots rose in rebellion, driving Mary into exile in England at the age of just 25. The queen's illegitimate half-brother, the Earl of Moray, became regent and her son, the infant James, was left behind to be raised a Protestant prince. Mary, meanwhile, was seen as such a threat to the English throne that Queen Elizabeth I had little choice but to imprison and ultimately execute her in 1587.

With Mary gone, Knox could concentrate on the organization of the reformed Church, or **Kirk**, which he envisaged as a body empowered to intervene in the daily lives of the people. Andrew Melville, another leading reformer, proposed the abolition of all traces of episcopacy – the rule of the bishops in the Church – and suggested instead a **presbyterian** structure, administered by a hierarchy of assemblies, part elected and part appointed. At the bottom of the chain, beneath the General Assembly, Synod and Presbytery, would be the Kirk session, responsible for church affairs, the performance of the minister and the morals of the parish. In 1592, the Melvillian party achieved a measure of success when presbyteries and synods were accepted as legal church courts and the office of bishop was suspended.

United Kingdom:1603–1660

The son of Mary, Queen of Scots, **James VI of Scotland** succeeded Elizabeth as **James I of England** (1603–1625), thereby **uniting the English and Scottish crowns**. Thereafter, James quickly moved to end hostilities with Spain and adopted a policy of toleration to the country's Catholics. Inevitably, both initiatives offended many Protestants, whose worst fears were confirmed in 1605 when **Guy Fawkes** and a group of Catholic conspirators were discovered preparing to blow up the king and Houses of Parliament in London in the foiled **Gunpowder Plot**: Fawkes himself was hung, drawn and quartered. **Puritan** fundamentalism and commercial interests converged with the founding of the first permanent **colony in North America** in Virginia in 1608. Twelve years later, the Pilgrim Fathers landed in New England, establishing a colony that would absorb about a hundred thousand Puritan immigrants by the middle of the century.

Meanwhile, James restored the Scottish bishops, much to the fury of the Presbyterians and assorted Protestants, and in England succeeded in alienating his landed gentry. He clung to an absolutist vision of the monarchy – the divine right of kings – that was totally out of step with the Protestant leanings of the majority of his subjects and he also relied heavily on court favourites, especially the much reviled George Villiers, Duke of Buckingham. It was a recipe for disaster, but it was to be his successor, **Charles I** (1625–49), who reaped the whirlwind. Charles inherited James's dislike of the Protestants and approval of absolutism, ruling without Parliament from 1629 to 1640. However, he overreached himself when he tried to impose a new Anglican prayer book on the Kirk. Scottish reformers denounced these changes as "popery" and organized the **National Covenant**, a religious pledge that committed the signatories to "Labour by all means lawful to recover the purity and liberty of the Gospel as it was established and professed." Charles declared all the "**Covenanters**" to be rebels, a proclamation endorsed by his Scottish bishops. Consequently, when the king backed down from military action and called a General Assembly of the Kirk, the assembly promptly abolished the episcopacy. Charles pronounced the proceedings illegal, but lack of finance stopped him from mounting an effective military campaign – whereas the Covenanters, well financed by the Kirk, assembled a proficient army under Alexander Leslie. In desperation, Charles summoned the English Parliament hoping it would pay for an army, but – like the calling of the General Assembly in Scotland – the decision was a disaster and Parliament refused to support Charles. Indeed, the **Long Parliament**, as it became known, impeached several of Charles's allies – most notably Archbishop Laud, who was ultimately executed – and compiled its grievances in the Grand Remonstrance of 1641.

Facing the concerted hostility of the Long Parliament, the king withdrew to Nottingham where he raised his standard, the opening act of the **Civil War**. The Royalist forces ("Cavaliers") were initially successful, winning the battle of Edgehill. In response, **Oliver Cromwell** overhauled the Parliamentarian army ("Roundheads"), to create the formidable **New Model Army**, which won the battles of Naseby and Marston. Charles surrendered to the Scots, who handed him over to the English Parliament, by whom he was ultimately executed in January 1649. The following year, at the invitation of the Earl of Argyll, Charles's son, the future Charles II, returned from exile to Scotland. In order to secure his royal inheritance, Charles was obliged to renounce his father and sign the Covenant, two bitter pills taken to impress the Scots. In the event, however, the "Presbyterian Restoration" was short-lived: Cromwell invaded, defeated the Scots at Dunbar and forced Charles into exile.

For the next eleven years the whole of Britain was a **Commonwealth** – at first a true republic, then, after 1653, a **Protectorate** with Cromwell as Lord Protector and commander-in-chief. He reformed the government, secured commercial treaties with foreign nations and used his New Model Army to put the fear of God into his various enemies. The turmoil of the Civil War and the pre-eminence of the army spawned a host of leftist sects, the most notable of whom were the **Levellers**, who demanded wholesale constitutional reform, and the more radical **Diggers**, who proposed common ownership of all land. **Nonconformist** religious groups also flourished, prominent among them the pacifist **Quakers**, led by George Fox (1624–91), and the **Dissenters**, to whom the most famous writers of the day, John Milton (1608–74) and John Bunyan (1628–88), both belonged. Cromwell died in 1658 to be succeeded by his son **Richard**, who ruled briefly and ineffectually, and in May 1660, Parliament voted to restore the monarchy and **Charles II** (1660–85), the exiled son of the previous king, was crowned.

The Restoration and the later Stuarts (1660–1714)

The terms of the **Restoration** included a general amnesty for all those who had fought against the Stuarts, except those who had signed Charles I's death warrant. With the re-establishment of a royal court came a new exuberance in art, literature and theatre, and the foundation of the **Royal Society**, whose scientific endeavours were furthered by Isaac Newton (1642–1727). However this period also saw the **Great Plague** of 1665 and the **Great Fire of London** (1666), though the London that rose from the ashes was an architectural show-case for Christopher Wren (1632–1723) and his fellow classicists. Politically, there were still underlying tensions between the monarchy and Parliament, though the latter was more concerned with the struggle between the **Whigs** and **Tories**, political factions representing, respectively, the low-church gentry

△ Monument to the Great Fire of London

and the high-church aristocracy. There was a degree of religious toleration too, but its brittleness was all too apparent in the anti-Catholic riots of 1678.

The succession of the Catholic **James II (**1685–88), brother of Charles II, provoked much opposition, though there was still an indifferent response when the Protestant **Duke of Monmouth**, the favourite among Charles II's illegitimate sons, raised a rebellion in the West Country. Monmouth was defeated at Sedgemoor, in Somerset, in July 1685; nine days later he was beheaded at Tower Hill, and in the subsequent **Bloody Assizes** of Judge Jeffreys, hundreds of rebels and suspected sympathizers were executed or deported. James's unpopularity increased with his **Declaration of Indulgence**, that removed anti-Catholic restrictions, and further when the birth of his son secured a Catholic succession. In alarm, the country's most powerful Protestants sent for **William of Orange**, the Dutch husband of Mary, the Protestant daughter of James II, to save them from Catholic tyranny. William landed in Devon and, as James's forces simply melted away, he speedily took control of London in the **Glorious Revolution** of 1688. This was the final postscript to the Civil War – although it was another three years before James and his Jacobite forces were finally defeated in Ireland.

William and Mary (1688–94) were made joint sovereigns after they agreed to a **Bill of Rights** defining the limitations of the monarchy's power and the rights of its subjects, thereby making Britain a **constitutional monarchy**, in which the roles of legislature and executive were separate and interdependent. The model was broadly consistent with that outlined by the philosopher and political thinker **John Locke** (1632–1704), whose essentially Whig doctrines of toleration and social contract were gradually embraced as the new orthodoxy.

After Mary's death, William (1694–1702) ruled alone; during his reign the **Act of Settlement of 1701** was passed, barring Catholics, or anyone married to one, from succession to the English throne. This Act did not, however, apply in Scotland, and the English feared that the Scots would invite James II's son, James Edward Stuart, back from France to be their king. These fears were allayed when Scotland passed the **Act of Union** uniting the English and Scottish parliaments in 1707, though neither the Scottish legal system nor the Presbyterian Kirk were merged with their English equivalents.

After William's death the crown passed to Mary's sister **Anne** (1702–14), whose reign saw British armies winning a string of remarkable victories on the continent, beginning with the Duke of Marlborough's triumph at Blenheim in 1704, followed the next year by the capture of Gibraltar, establishing a British presence in the Mediterranean. These military escapades were part of the Europe-wide **War of the Spanish Succession**, which rumbled on until the Treaty of Utrecht in 1713 – a treaty which all but settled the European balance of power for the rest of the eighteenth century.

The Hanoverians (1714–1815)

On Anne's death, the succession passed – in accordance with the terms of the Act of Settlement – to the Protestant Elector of Hanover, who became **George I** (1714–27) of England. This prompted the first major **Jacobite uprising** in support of James Edward Stuart, the "Old Pretender" (Pretender in the sense of having pretensions to the throne, Old to distinguish him from his son Charles, the "Young Pretender"). Its timing appeared perfect: Scottish opinion was moving against the Union, which had failed to bring Scotland any tangible economic benefits and neither were Jacobite sentiments confined to Scotland – there were many in England who toasted the "king across the water". In 1715, the Earl of Mar raised the Stuart standard at Braemar Castle in Scotland

and just eight days later he captured Perth, where he gathered an army of over 10,000 men, drawn mostly from the Episcopalians of northeast Scotland and from the Highlands. Mar's rebellion took the government by surprise. They had only 4000 soldiers in Scotland, under the command of the Duke of Argyll, but Mar dithered until he lost the military advantage. There was an indecisive battle at Sheriffmuir, but by the time the Old Pretender landed in Scotland in December 1715, 6000 veteran Dutch troops had reinforced Argyll. The rebellion disintegrated rapidly and James slunk back to exile in France.

Back in London, power slowly leaked away from the monarchy into the hands of the Whig oligarchy and the king ceased to attend Cabinet meetings, his place being taken by his chief minister. Most prominent of these ministers was **Robert Walpole** (1676–1745), regarded as the UK's **first prime minister**. To all intents and purposes, Walpole governed the country from 1721 to 1742, a tranquil period militarily, with the country standing aloof from foreign affrays, though the Jacobites were always just over the horizon.

Peace ended in the reign of **George II** (1727–60), when England declared war on Spain in 1739 at the start of yet another dynastic squabble, the eight-year War of the Austrian Succession. Then, in 1745, came the second and most dangerous of the Jacobite rebellions, with the **Young Pretender**, **Charles Stuart** (aka Bonnie Prince Charlie) and his Highland army reaching as far south as Derby, just 120 miles from London, and creating pandemonium in the capital. However, their lines of supply were over-extended, and they failed to rally the Lowland Scots – never mind the English – to their cause, so were obliged to retreat north. A Hanoverian army under the brutal Duke of Cumberland caught up with them at Culloden Moor near Inverness, in April 1746, and hacked them to pieces. Jacobite hopes died at Culloden and the prince lived out the rest of his life in drunken exile. In the aftermath of the uprising, the wearing of tartan, the bearing of arms and the playing of bagpipes were all banned. Rebel chiefs lost their land and the Highlands were placed under military occupation. Most significantly, the government prohibited the private armies of the chiefs, thereby effectively destroying the clan system.

Meanwhile, the **Seven Years' War** (1756–1763) harvested England yet more overseas territory in India and Canada at the expense of France and, in 1768, **Captain James Cook** sailed to New Zealand and Australia, thereby netting another chunk of the globe. In 1760, **George III** (1760–1820) succeeded his father. The early years of his sixty-year reign saw a revived political struggle between king and Parliament, enlivened by the intervention of John Wilkes, first of a long and increasingly vociferous line of parliamentary radicals. The contest was exacerbated by the deteriorating relationship with the thirteen colonies of North America, a situation brought to a head by the **American Declaration of Independence** and Britain's subsequent defeat in the Revolutionary War. Chastened by this disaster, Britain chose not to interfere in the momentous events taking place across the Channel, where France, long its most consistent foe, was convulsed by revolution. Out of the turmoil emerged the most daunting of enemies, **Napoleon** (1769–1821), whose stunning military progress was interrupted by Nelson at **Trafalgar** in 1805 and finally stopped ten years later by the Duke of Wellington at **Waterloo**.

The Industrial Revolution

Britain's triumph over Napoleon was largely due to the country's financial strength, born of the **Industrial Revolution**. This switch from an agricultural to a manufacturing economy completely changed Britain in the space of a hundred years. The earliest mechanized production lines were in the Lancashire **cotton mills**, where cotton spinning was transformed from a cottage industry into a highly productive factory-based system. Initially, river water powered the mills, but the technology changed after James Watt patented his **steam engine** in 1781. Watt's engines needed **coal**, which made it convenient to locate mills and factories near coal mines, a tendency that was accelerated as **ironworks** took up coal as a smelting fuel, vastly increasing the output from their furnaces. Accordingly, there was a shift of population towards the Midlands, central Scotland and the north of England, where the great coal reserves were located, and as the industrial economy boomed and diversified, so these regions' towns mushroomed at an extraordinary rate. Steel towns like Sheffield grew up, huge cotton warehouses were built in Manchester and vast dock facilities in Liverpool, where raw materials from India and the Americas came in and manufactured goods went out. Commerce and industry were also served by improving transport facilities, such as the building of a network of **canals**, but the great leap forward came with the arrival of the **railway**, heralded by the Stockton–Darlington line in 1825, followed five years later by the Liverpool–Manchester railway, where George Stephenson's *Rocket* made its first outing.

Boosted by a vast influx of Jewish, Irish, French and Dutch workers, the country's population rose from about eight and a half million at the beginning of George III's reign to more than fifteen million at its end. But while the factories and their attendant towns expanded, so the rural settlements of England declined, inspiring the elegiac pastoral yearnings of Samuel Taylor Coleridge and William Wordsworth, the first great names of the **Romantic** movement, though later Romantic poets such as Percy Bysshe Shelley and Lord Byron took a more socially engaged position. Meanwhile discontent was rising among the nation's factory workers when machines put thousands of them out of work, and the **Chartist** movement was born to demand parliamentary reform – the most important of the industrial boom towns were still unrepresented in Parliament – and the repeal of the **Corn Laws**, which kept the price of bread artificially high. In 1819, during a mass demonstration in support of parliamentary reform in Manchester, protestors were hacked down by troops in what became known as the **Peterloo Massacre**.

The following year, a weak, blind and insane George III died to be succeeded, in fairly rapid succession, by two of his sons, **George IV** (1820–30) and then **William IV** (1830–37). Tensions continued to run high throughout the 1820s, until a series of judicious parliamentary acts were passed: the **Reform Act** of 1832 established the principle (if not always the practice) of popular representation; the **Poor Law** of 1834 improved the condition of the most destitute; and the repeal of the Corn Laws in 1846 reduced the price of bread. Significant sections of the middle classes supported progressive reform, as evidenced by the immense popularity of **Charles Dickens** (1812–70), whose novels railed against poverty and injustice. Dickens' social concerns had been anticipated in the previous century by John Wesley (1703–91) and his **Methodists**, who – along with other Nonconformist Christians – led the anti-slavery campaign. As a result of their efforts, slavery was banned in Britain in 1772 and throughout the British Empire in 1833, ending a trade that had been a major factor in the prosperity of several seaports, including Bristol and Liverpool.

Victorian Britain

William IV was succeeded by his niece, **Victoria** (1837–1901), whose long reign witnessed the zenith of British power. For much of the period, the economy boomed, and the British trading fleet was easily the mightiest in the world, with Victoria becoming the symbol of both the nation's success and the imperial ideal. There were extraordinary intellectual achievements too – as typified by the publication of Charles Darwin's *On the Origin of Species* in 1859. Britain's industrial and commercial prowess was best embodied by the great engineering feats of **Isambard Kingdom Brunel** (1806–1859) and by the **Great Exhibition** of 1851, a display of manufacturing achievements without compare.

With trade at the forefront of the agenda, much of the era's political debate crystallized into a conflict between the **Free Traders** – led by the Whigs, who formed the Liberal Party – and the **Protectionists** under Bentinck and **Disraeli**, guiding light of the Tories, or Conservatives. During the last third of the century, Parliament was dominated by the duel between Disraeli and the Liberal leader **Gladstone**. It was Disraeli who eventually passed the Second Reform Bill in 1867, further extending the electoral franchise, but it was Gladstone's first ministry of 1868–74 that passed some of the century's most far-reaching legislation, including compulsory education, and the full legalization of trade unions.

There were foreign entanglements, too. In 1854 troops were sent to protect the Ottoman empire against the Russians in the **Crimea**, an inglorious debacle whose horrors were relayed to the public by the first-ever press coverage of a military campaign and by the revelations of **Florence Nightingale** (1820–1910), who was appalled by the lack of medical care for soldiers. The fragility of Britain's hold over the Asian subcontinent was exposed during the **Indian Mutiny** of 1857, though the imperial status quo was eventually restored and Victoria took the title Empress of India after 1876. Thereafter, the British army fought a series of minor wars against poorly armed Asian and African opponents, but promptly came unstuck when it faced the Dutch settlers of South Africa in the **Boer War** (1899–1902). The British ultimately fought their way to a sort of victory, but the discreditable conduct of the war prompted a military shake-up at home that was to be of significance in the coming European war.

The two World Wars (1914–1945)

On Victoria's death, she was succeeded by her son, **Edward VII** (1901–10), whose leisurely life could be seen as the epitome of the complacent era to which he gave his name. This complacency came to an end with the accession of **George V** (1910–36) and more specifically on August 4, 1914, when the Liberal government, honouring the Entente Cordiale signed with France in 1904, declared war on Germany. Hundreds of thousands volunteered for the army, but their enthusiastic nationalism was not enough to ensure a quick victory and **World War I** dragged on for four miserable years. Britain and her allies eventually prevailed, but the number of dead beggared belief, undermining the British people's respect for their ruling class, whose generals had displayed a startling combination of incompetence and indifference to the plight of their men. Many looked admiringly towards the Soviet Union, where communists had rid themselves of the Tsar and seized control in 1917.

At the war's end in 1918 the political fabric of Britain was changed dramatically when the sheer weight of public opinion pushed Parliament into extending the **vote** to all men over 21 and to women over 30. This tardy liberalization of women's rights owed much to the efforts of the radical **Suffragettes**, led by Emmeline Pankhurst and her daughters Sylvia and Christabel, but the process was only completed in 1929 when women were at last granted the vote at 21, on equal terms with men.

During this period, the **Labour Party** supplanted the Liberals as the main force on the left wing of British politics, its strength built on an alliance between the working-class trade unions and middle-class radicals. Labour formed its first government in 1923 under **Ramsay MacDonald** (1866–1937), but the publication of the **Zinoviev Letter**, a forged document that purported to be a letter from the Soviets urging British leftists to promote revolution, undermined MacDonald's position and the Conservatives were returned with a large parliamentary majority in 1924. Two years later, a bitter dispute between the nation's colliers and the owners of the coal mines escalated into a **General Strike**, which quickly spread from the coal mines to the railways, the newspapers and the iron and steel industries. The strike lasted nine days and involved half a million workers, provoking the government into draconian action – the army was called in, and the strike was broken. The economic situation deteriorated further after the crash of the New York Stock Exchange in 1929, precipitating a worldwide depression. Unemployment reached over 2.8 million in 1931, generating a series of mass demonstrations, which peaked with the **Jarrow March** from the Northeast to London in 1936. The same year, economist John Maynard Keynes argued in his *General Theory of Employment, Interest and Money* for a greater degree of state intervention in the management of the economy, though the whole question soon became overshadowed by international events.

Abroad, the structure of the **British Empire** had undergone profound changes since World War I. The status of **Ireland** had been partly resolved following the electoral gains of the nationalist Sinn Féin in 1918. Their success led to the establishment of the Irish Free State in 1922, though (and this was to cause endless problems thereafter) the six counties of the mainly Protestant North (Ulster) chose to stay part of the United Kingdom. Four years later, the **Imperial Conference** recognized the autonomy of the British dominions, comprising all the major countries that had previously been part of the Empire. This agreement was formalized in the 1931 Statute of Westminster, whereby each dominion was given an equal footing in a **Commonwealth of Nations**, though each still recognized the British monarch. The royal family itself was shaken in 1936 by the **abdication of Edward VIII** (1936), following his decision to marry a twice-divorced American, Wallis Simpson. In the event, the succession passed smoothly to his brother **George VI** (1936–52), though the royals had a hard job regaining their popularity among the population as a whole.

Non-intervention in both the Spanish Civil War and the Sino-Japanese War was paralleled by a policy of appeasement towards **Adolf Hitler**, who began to rearm Germany in earnest in the mid-1930s. This policy was epitomized by the antics of Prime Minister Neville Chamberlain, who returned from meeting Hitler and Mussolini at Munich in 1938 with an assurance of good intentions that he took at face value. Consequently, when **World War II** broke out in September 1939, Britain was seriously unprepared. In May 1940 the discredited Chamberlain stepped down in favour of a national coalition government headed by the charismatic **Winston Churchill** (1874–1965), whose bulldog persistence and heroic speeches provided the inspiration needed in the backs-against-the-wall mood of the time. Partly through Churchill's manoeuvrings, the United States became a supplier of foodstuffs and munitions to Britain, then broke trade links with Japan in June in protest at their attacks on China. In response to the Japanese bombing of Pearl Harbour on December 7, 1941, the US joined the war, declaring against both Japan and Germany, and its intervention, combined with the stirring efforts of the Soviet Red Army, swung the military balance. In terms of the number of casualties, World War II was not as calamitous as World War I, but its impact upon the civilian population of Britain was much greater. In its first wave of **bombing** on the UK, the Luftwaffe caused massive damage to industrial and supply centres such as London, Glasgow, Swansea, Coventry, Manchester, Liverpool, Southampton and Plymouth. In later raids, intended to shatter morale rather than factories and docks, the cathedral cities of Canterbury, Exeter, Bath, Norwich and York all took a battering too. At the end of the fighting, almost a third of all the houses in the nation had been destroyed or damaged, nearly a quarter of the million-strong members of the British armed forces had lost their lives, and over 58,000 civilians were dead.

Postwar Britain: from Attlee to Thatcher: 1945–1990

The end of the war in 1945 was quickly followed by a general election. Hungry for change (and demobilization), the electorate replaced Churchill with the Labour Party under **Clement Attlee** (1883–1967), who, with a large parliamentary majority, set about a radical programme to **nationalize** the coal, gas, electricity, iron and steel industries, as well as the inland transport services. Building on the plans for a social security system presented in Sir William Beveridge's report of 1943, the **National Insurance Act** and the **National Health Service Act** were both passed early in the Labour administration, giving birth to what became known as the **welfare state**. But despite substantial American aid, the huge problems of rebuilding the economy made austerity the keynote, with the rationing of food and fuel remaining in force long after 1945.

In April 1949, Britain, the United States, Canada, France and the Benelux countries signed the **North Atlantic Treaty** as a counterbalance to Soviet power in Eastern Europe, thereby defining the country's postwar international commitments. Yet confusion regarding Britain's post-imperial role was shown up by the **Suez Crisis** of 1956, when Anglo-French and Israeli forces invaded Egypt to secure control of the Suez Canal, only to be hastily recalled following international (American) condemnation. Revealing severe limitations on the country's capacity for independent action, the Suez incident resulted in the resignation of the Conservative prime minister Anthony Eden, who was replaced by the more pragmatic **Harold Macmillan** (1894–1986). Nonetheless, Macmillan maintained a nuclear policy that suggested a continued desire for an international role, and nuclear testing went on against a background of widespread marches under the auspices of the Campaign for Nuclear Disarmament.

The 1960s, dominated by the Labour premiership of **Harold Wilson** (1916–1995), saw a boom in consumer spending, some pioneering social legislation (primarily on the legalization of homosexuality and abortion), and a corresponding cultural upswing, with London becoming the hippest city on the planet. The good times lasted barely a decade. Though Tory prime minister Edward Heath led Britain into the brave new world of the **European Economic Community** (ECC), the 1970s were a decade of recession and industrial strife. A succession of public-sector strikes and mistimed decisions by James Callaghan's Labour government handed the 1979 general election to the Conservatives, led by **Margaret Thatcher** (b.1925), Britain's first female prime minister.

Thatcher went on to win three general elections, steering the UK into a period of sharp social polarization. While taxation policies and easy credit fuelled a consumer boom for the professional classes, the erosion of manufacturing industry and the weakening of the welfare state impoverished a great swathe of the population. However, Thatcher won an increased majority in the 1983 election, largely thanks to the successful recapture of the **Falkland Islands**, a remote British dependency in the south Atlantic, retrieved from the occupying Argentine army in 1982. Her electoral domination was also assisted by the fragmentation of the Labour opposition, from which the short-lived Social Democratic Party had split in panic at what it perceived as the leftward radicalization of the party.

Social and political tensions surfaced in sporadic urban rioting and the year-long **miners' strike** (1984–85) against colliery closures, a bitter industrial dispute in which the police were given unprecedented powers to restrict the movement of citizens. The violence in Northern Ireland also intensified, and in 1984 the bombing campaign of the IRA came close to killing the entire Cabinet when they blew up the Brighton hotel where the Conservatives were staying during their annual conference.

The 1990s to today

The divisive politics of Thatcherism reached their apogee with the introduction of the **Poll Tax**, a desperately unpopular tax that led ultimately to Thatcher's overthrow by Conservative colleagues who feared defeat should she lead them into another general election. The uninspiring new leader was **John Major** (b.1943), who nonetheless managed to win the Conservatives a fourth term of office in 1992, albeit with a much reduced Parliamentary majority. While his government presided over steady economic growth, they gained little credit amid allegations of mismanagement, incompetence, corruption and feckless leadership. The Conservatives were also divided over Europe, with the pro–European Union (formerly EEC) faction pitted against the vocal right-wing Eurosceptics, who were vehemently against the EU in general and the proposed common currency – the euro – in particular.

The early 1990s saw further difficulties for the **Royal Family**, with the messy break-up of the marriage of Prince Charles and Diana. Revelations about the cruel treatment of Diana by both the prince and his family badly damaged the royals' reputation, including that of **Queen Elizabeth II** (1952–present). By contrast with her in-laws, **Diana**, who was formally divorced from Charles in 1994, appeared warm-hearted and glamorous, so much so that her death in a car accident in Paris in 1997 had a profound impact on the British, leading to unprecedented public grieving.

Meanwhile, the **Labour Party**, which had been wracked by factionalism in the 1980s, regrouped under Neil Kinnock and then John Smith, though neither reaped the political rewards. These dropped into the lap of a new and dynamic young leader, **Tony Blair** (b.1953), who soon began to move the party away from traditional left-wing socialism. Blair's mantle of idealistic, media-friendly populism worked to devastating effect, sweeping the Labour Party to power in the **general election of May 1997** on a wave of genuine popular optimism. There were immediate rewards in enhanced relations with Europe and progress in the Irish peace talks, and Blair's electoral touch was soon repeated in Labour-sponsored **devolution referenda**, whose results semi-detached Scotland and Wales from their larger neighbour. The Scots got a Parliament, the Welsh an Assembly, reflecting different levels of devolution – the first has more powers than the second. There was also much Labourite tub-thumping about the need to improve **public services**, but Blair only set about the task in earnest after the **general election of June 2001**, which Labour won with another parliamentary landslide. This second victory, however, reflected little of the optimism of before and voter turnout was lower than any time since World War II. Few voters fully trusted Blair and his administration, who developed a reputation for laundering events to present the government in the best possible light, known as "spin".

In Blair's second term, despite massive and much-needed investment in public services, with education and health being the prime beneficiaries, and a concerted attempt to lift (many of) the country's poorer citizens out of poverty, the government was dogged by further accusations of spin – and with every justification. Nonetheless, the ailing Conservative Party failed to capitalize on the situation, leaving Blair streets ahead of his political rivals in the opinion polls when two hijacked planes hit New York's World Trade Centre on **September 11, 2001**. Blair rushed to support President Bush, joining in the attack on Afghanistan and then, much to the horror of millions of Brits, sending British forces into **Iraq** alongside the Americans in 2003. Saddam Hussein was deposed with relative ease, but neither Bush nor Blair seemed to have a coherent exit strategy, and back home Blair was widely seen as having spun Britain into the war by exaggerating the danger Hussein presented with his alleged Weapons of Mass Destruction. No weapons were ever found leaving Blair looking vulnerable, though his political opponents failed to deliver the *coup de grâce* and Blair managed to win a **third general election in May 2005**, having promised to step down before the end of the term. It remains to be seen whether his arch rival and putative successor in the Labour Party, **Gordon Brown**, can fight off the challenge from the other parties, and, indeed, from members of his own party.

Books

M ost of the books listed below are paperbacks in print – those that are out of print (o/p) should be easy to track down either in second-hand book shops or through Amazon's used and secondhand book service (ⓦwww.amazon.co.uk, ⓦwww.amazon.com). Note also that while we recommend all the books we've listed below, we do have our favourites, however partial and partisan – and these have been marked with a 🏃.

Travel and journals

🏃 **Bill Bryson** *Notes from a Small Island*. Bryson's best-selling and highly amusing account of an extended journey round Britain.

William Cobbett *Rural Rides.* First published in 1830, Cobbett's account of his various fact-finding tours bemoaned the death of the old rural England and its customs, while decrying both the growth of cities and the iniquities suffered by the exploited urban poor.

David Craig *On the Crofter's Trail.* Using anecdotes and interviews with descendants, Craig conveys the hardship and tragedy of the Highland Clearances without being mawkish.

Daniel Defoe *Tour through the Whole Island of Great Britain*. Defoe, the son of a London butcher, was a novelist, pamphleteer, journalist and sometime spy. This classic travelogue opens a fascinating window onto 1720s Britain.

Charles Jennings *Up North*. A provocative, but very readable account of a mid-1990s journey round the north of England, by a self-confessed southerner.

Jan Morris *The Matter of Wales.* Prolific half-Welsh travel writer Jan Morris immerses herself in the country that she evidently loves. Highly partisan and fiercely nationalistic, the book combs over the origins of the Welsh character, and describes the people and places of Wales with precision and affection.

Samuel Pepys *The Diary of Samuel Pepys.* Pepys kept a voluminous diary from 1660 until 1669, recording the fall of the Commonwealth, the Restoration, the Great Plague and the Great Fire, as well as describing the daily life of the nation's capital. The unabridged version is published in eleven weighty tomes; there's also an abridged version.

J.B. Priestley *English Journey*. Quirky account of Bradford-born author's travels around England in the 1930s.

Paul Theroux *The Kingdom by the Sea*. Thoroughly bad-tempered critique of a depressed and drizzly nation.

Dorothy Wordsworth *Journals*. The engaging diaries of William's sister, with whom he shared Dove Cottage in the Lake District, provide a vivid account of walks and visits, and reflect Dorothy's fascination with the natural world.

History, society and politics

🏃 **David Boyle** *Blondel's Song: the capture, imprisonment and ransom of Richard the Lionheart*. The imprisonment of King Richard I on his way back from the Crusades is a curious tale of medieval deceit, which this book tells in splendid style. It also provides a superb insight into the medieval Christian mind.

Asa Briggs *Social History of England.* Immensely accessible overview of English life from Roman times to the 1980s.

Beatrix Campbell *Diana, Princess of Wales: How sexual politics shook the monarchy* (o/p). A little hastily written perhaps, but still the most penetrating insight into the life and times of Diana – and the appalling callousness of her in-laws. Read this and you'll never want Charles to be king. Also her *Goliath: Britain's Dangerous Places* explores the decline of traditional working-class culture and the rise of the English yob – the young, violent male.

Alan Clark *Diaries: In Power.* Candid, conceited and often cutting account of the inner sanctum of Thatcher's government by this controversial former minister. Easily the most interesting of the barrow-loads of political memoirs churned out in the 1980s and 1990s.

Linda Colley *Britons: Forging the Nation 1707–1837.* Successful and immaculately researched book that offers all sorts of fresh insights into eighteenth-century Britain and the evolution of a national identity.

David Daiches (ed) *The New Companion to Scottish Culture.* More than 300 articles interpreting Scottish culture in its widest sense, from eating to marriage customs, the Scottish Enlightenment to children's street games.

Friedrich Engels *The Conditions of the Working Class in England.* Portrait of life in England's hellish industrial towns, written in 1844 when Engels was only 24.

Mark Girouard *Life in the English Country House.* Fascinating documentation of the day-to-day existence of the landed gentry; packed with the sort of facts that get left out by tour guides.

Christopher Hill *The English Revolution* and *The World Turned Upside-Down.* Britain's foremost Marxist historian, Hill is without doubt the most interesting writer on the Civil War and Commonwealth period.

Eric Hobsbawm *Industry and Empire.* Ostensibly an economic history of Britain from 1750 to the late 1960s charting Britain's decline and fall as a world power, this book's great skill lies in its detailed analysis of the effects on ordinary people. By the same author, *Captain Swing* focuses on the labourers' uprisings of nineteenth-century England, while his magnificent trilogy, *The Age of Revolution 1789–1848*, *The Age of Capital 1848–1875* and *The Age of Extremes 1914–1991* can't be beaten.

Philip Jenkins *A History of Modern Wales 1536–1990.* Magnificently thorough book, placing Welsh history in its British and European contexts. Unbiased and rational appraisal of events and the struggle to preserve Welsh consciousness.

Michael Lynch (ed) *The Oxford Companion to Scottish History.* A copious collection, covering two thousand years and subjects as varied as climate, archeology, folklore and national identity.

George Orwell *The Road to Wigan Pier*; *Down and Out in Paris and London*; *1984*; and *Animal Farm. Wigan Pier* depicts the effects of the Great Depression on the industrial communities of Lancashire and Yorkshire, while *Down and Out* is Orwell's harrowing tramp's-eye view of the world, written with first-hand experience. Orwell's most famous books are, of course, *1984* and *Animal Farm*, both cautionary political tales set to an imaginary but notably British backdrop.

A.J.P. Taylor *The First World War: An Illustrated History*. Penetrating analysis of how the war started and why it went on for so long; first published in 1963, but still unsurpassed. Similarly unrivalled is *The Origins of the Second World War*, also published in the 1960s.

E.P. Thompson *The Making of the English Working Class*. A seminal text – essential reading for anyone who wants to understand the fabric of English society.

Wynford Vaughan-Thomas *Wales – a History* (o/p). One of the country's most missed broadcasters and writers, Vaughan-Thomas's masterpiece is this warm and spirited history of Wales. Working chronologically from the pre-Celtic dawn to the aftermath of the 1979 devolution vote, the book offers perhaps the clearest explanation of the evolution of Welsh culture.

Regional guides

Paul Bailey (ed) *Oxford Book of London*. Authoritative anthology of writings, observations and opinions about the capital. Published in 1995.

Joe Fisher *The Glasgow Encyclopedia* (o/p). The essential Glasgow reference book, covering nearly every facet of this complex urban society.

Christopher Hibbert (ed) *Pimlico County History Guides*. An informative series giving a detailed history of selected English counties. Those covered – and still in print – include Bedfordshire, Cambridgeshire, Dorset, Lincolnshire, Norfolk, Oxfordshire, Somerset (with Bath and Bristol), Suffolk and Sussex.

Simon Jenkins *England's Thousand Best Churches* and *England's Thousand Best Houses*. Jenkins is a well-known UK journalist and these two superb books describe the pick of England's churches and houses in lucid detail. Wittily written, the books are divided into counties with a star system to indicate the best. For the houses book, Jenkins adopts a wide brief, including all sorts of curiosities from caves in Nottingham to prefabs in Buckinghamshire.

Jan Morris *Oxford*. Adulatory but inspiring collection on Oxford by the famous travel writer.

Pathfinder Walks Series of practical guides with maps and route descriptions to popular outdoor spots such as the Yorkshire Dales, Chilterns, Cornwall and Cotswolds. Produced by the Ordnance Survey.

A. Wainwright *A Coast to Coast Walk*. Beautiful palm-sized guide by acclaimed English hiker and Lake District expert. Printed from his handwritten notes and sketched maps. Also in the series are seven authoritative books covering a variety of walks and climbs in the Lake District.

Ben Weinreb and Christopher Hibbert *The London Encyclopaedia*. More than a thousand pages of concisely presented and well-illustrated information on London past and present – the most fascinating single book on the capital.

Art, architecture and archeology

John Betjeman *Ghastly Good Taste, Or, A Depressing Story of the Rise and Fall of English Architecture*. Classy – and classic – one-hundred page account of England's architecture written by one of the country's shrewdest poet-commentators. First published in 1970.

William Gaunt *English Painting.* This succinct and excellently illustrated book provides a useful introduction to its subject, covering the Middle Ages to the twentieth century in just 260 pages.

Samantha Hardingham *London: A guide to recent architecture.* A handy pocket-sized book detailing the best of the capital's modern buildings.

Andrew Hayes *Archaeology of the British Isles.* Useful introduction to the subject from Stone Age caves to early medieval settlements.

🏃 **Duncan MacMillan** *Scottish Art 1460–2000* and *Scottish Art in the Twentieth Century.* The former is a lavish overview of Scottish painting with good sections on landscape, portraiture and the Glasgow Boys, while the latter covers the last hundred years in splendid detail.

🏃 **Thomas Pakenham** *Meetings With Remarkable Trees.* Unusual but intriguing large-format picture book about the author's favourite sixty trees, delving into their character as much as the botany.

Nikolaus Pevsner *The Englishness of English Art.* Wide-ranging romp through English art concentrating on Hogarth, Reynolds, Blake and Constable, including a section on the Perpendicular style and landscape gardening.

Pevsner and others *The Buildings of England, Scotland and Wales.* Magisterial series, at least one volume per county, covering just about every inhabitable structure in the country. This project was initially a one-man show, but later authors have revised Pevsner's text, inserting newer buildings but generally respecting the founder's personal tone.

Fiction before 1900

🏃 **Jane Austen** *Pride and Prejudice*; *Sense and Sensibility*; *Emma*; *Persuasion.* All-time classics on manners, society and the pursuit of the happy ever after; all laced with bathos and subtly ironic plot twists.

R.D. Blackmore *Lorna Doone.* Blackmore's swashbuckling, melodramatic romance, set on Exmoor, has done more for West Country tourism than anything else since.

James Boswell *The Life of Samuel Johnson.* England's most famous man of letters and pioneer dictionary-maker has his engagingly low-life Scottish biographer to thank for the longevity of his reputation.

Charlotte Brontë *Jane Eyre.* Deep, harrowing and quietly feminist story of a much put-upon governess.

🏃 **Emily Brontë** *Wuthering Heights.* The ultimate bodice-ripper, complete with volcanic passions, craggy landscapes, ghostly presences and gloomy villagers.

John Bunyan *Pilgrim's Progress.* Simple, allegorical tale of hero Christian's struggle to achieve salvation.

Geoffrey Chaucer *Canterbury Tales.* Fourteenth-century collection of bawdy tales told in verse during a pilgrimage to Canterbury. If you don't fancy struggling with the Old English of the original, there are lots of translations – into blank verse, prose and even rhyming couplets.

Daniel Defoe *Journal of a Plague Year.* An account of the Great Plague seen through the eyes of an East End saddler and written some sixty years after the event.

Thomas De Quincey *Confessions of an English Opium Eater.* Tripping out with the most famous literary drug-taker after Coleridge – *Fear and Loathing in Las Vegas* it isn't, but neither is this a simple cautionary tale.

🏃 **Charles Dickens** *Bleak House*; *David Copperfield*; *Little Dorritt*; *Oliver Twist*; *Hard Times.* Many of Dickens' novels are set in London, including *Bleak House*, *Oliver Twist* and *Little Dorritt*, and these contain some of his most trenchant pieces of social analysis; *Hard Times*, however, is set in a Lancashire mill town, while *David Copperfield* draws on Dickens' own unhappy experiences as a boy, with much of the action taking place in Kent and Norfolk.

George Eliot *Scenes of Clerical Life*; *Middlemarch*; *Mill on the Floss.* Eliot (real name Mary Ann Evans) wrote mostly about the county of her birth, Warwickshire, the setting for the three depressing tales that comprise her fictional debut, *Scenes of Clerical Life. Middlemarch* is a gargantuan portrayal of English provincial life prior to the Reform Act of 1832, while *Mill on the Floss*

△ Charles Dickens

is based on her own childhood experiences.

Henry Fielding *Tom Jones*. Mock-epic comic novel detailing the exploits of its lusty orphan-hero; set in Somerset and London.

Thomas Hardy *Far from the Madding Crowd; The Mayor of Casterbridge; Tess of the D'Urbervilles; Jude the Obscure.* Hardy's novels contain some famously evocative descriptions of his native Dorset, but at the time of their publication it was Hardy's defiance of conventional pieties that attracted most attention: *Tess*, in which the heroine has a baby out of wedlock and commits murder, shocked his contemporaries, while his bleakest novel, the Oxford-set *Jude the Obscure*, provoked such a violent response that Hardy gave up novel-writing altogether.

Sir Walter Scott *Waverley*. The first of the books that did much to create the romanticized version of Scottish life and history. Others include *Rob Roy*, a rich and ripping yarn that transformed the diminutive brigand into a national hero.

William Shakespeare *Complete Works*. The entire output at a bargain price. For individual plays, you can't beat the Arden Shakespeare series, each volume containing illuminating notes and good introductory essays.

Lawrence Sterne *Tristram Shandy*. Anarchic, picaresque eighteenth-century ramblings based on life in a small English village; full of bizarre textual devices – like an all-black page in mourning for one of the characters.

Robert Louis Stevenson *Dr Jekyll and Mr Hyde; Kidnapped; The Master of Ballantrae; Treasure Island; Weir of Hermiston*. Superbly imagined and pacily written nineteenth-century tales of intrigue and adventure.

William Makepeace Thackeray *Vanity Fair*. A sceptical but compassionate overview of English capitalist society by one of the leading realists of the mid-nineteenth century.

Anthony Trollope *Barchester Towers*. Trollope was an astonishingly prolific novelist who also, in his capacity as a postal surveyor, found time to invent the letter box. The "Barsetshire" novels, of which Barchester Towers is the best known, are set in and around a fictional version of Salisbury.

Izaak Walton *Compleat Angler*. Light-hearted, seventeenth-century fishing guide set on London's River Lea. Sprinkled with poems and songs, it has gone through more reprints than any other comparable book in the English language.

Contemporary fiction

Peter Ackroyd *English Music*. A typical Ackroyd novel, constructing parallels between interwar London and distant epochs to conjure a kaleidoscopic vision of English culture. His other novels, such as *Chatterton*, *Hawksmoor* and *The House of Doctor Dee*, are variations on his preoccupation with the English psyche's darker depths.

Julian Barnes *England, England; Metroland*. One of the UK's most versatile writers, Barnes seems to be

able to turn his hand to just about anything. His controversial *England, England* is a satire on the role of tourism in England with the country being re-created as a theme park on the Isle of Wight, while *Metroland* tells the story of two boys growing up in London's suburbs.

George Mackay Brown *Beside the Ocean of Time*. A child's journey through the history of an Orkney island, and an adult's effort to make sense of the place's secrets in the late twentieth century.

John Buchan *The Complete Richard Hannay*. This one volume includes *The 39 Steps*, *Greenmantle*, *Mr Standfast*, *The Three Hostages* and *The Island of Sheep*. Good gung-ho stories with a great feel for Scottish landscape.

Joseph Conrad *The Secret Agent*. Spy story based on the 1906 anarchist bombing of Greenwich Observatory, exposing the hypocrisies of both the police and anarchists.

Daphne Du Maurier *Frenchman's Creek*; *Jamaica Inn*; *Rebecca*. Nail-biting, swashbuckling romantic novels set in the author's adopted home of Cornwall.

Helen Fielding *Bridget Jones's Diary*. Originating as a newspaper column, Fielding's fictional account of contemporary female "neuroses" proved to be the literary phenomenon of the late 1990s, spawning a host of lesser imitators.

E.M. Forster *Howards End*. Bourgeois angst in Hertfordshire and Shropshire, by one of the country's best-loved modern novelists.

John Fowles *The Collector*; *The French Lieutenant's Woman*; *Daniel Martin*. *The Collector*, Fowles' first novel, is a psychological thriller in which the heroine is kidnapped by a psychotic pools-winner, the story being told once by each protagonist. *The French Lieutenant's Woman*, set in Lyme Regis on the Dorset coast, is a tricksy neo-Victorian novel with a famous DIY ending, while *Daniel Martin* is a dense, realistic novel set in postwar Britain.

Lewis Grassic Gibbon *A Scots Quair*. A landmark trilogy, set in northeast Scotland during and after World War I, the events are seen through the eyes of Chris Guthrie, "torn between her love for the land

and her desire to escape a peasant culture". Strong, seminal work.

William Golding *The Spire*; *Rites of Passage*. Atmospheric novel centred on the building of a cathedral spire, taking place in a thinly disguised medieval Salisbury. Also, if you ever wondered what it was like to be at sea in an early nineteenth-century British ship, try the splendid *Rites of Passage* trilogy.

Robert Graves *Goodbye to All That*. Horrific and humorous memoirs of public school and World War I trenches, followed by postwar trauma and life in Wales, Oxford and Egypt.

Graham Greene *Brighton Rock*; *The Human Factor*; *The Heart of the Matter*. Three of the best from the prolific Greene: *Brighton Rock* is a melancholic thriller with heavy Catholic overtones, set in the criminal underworld of a seaside resort; *The Human Factor*, written some forty years later, probes the underworld of London's spies; while *The Heart of the Matter* is a searching and very English novel exploring the Anglo-Catholic mindset.

James Kelman *The Busconductor Hines*; *How Late It Was*. The first is a wildly funny story of a young Glasgow bus conductor with an intensely boring job and a limitless imagination. *How Late It Was* is Kelman's award-winning and controversial look at life from the perspective of a blind Glaswegian drunk. A disturbing study of personal and political violence, with language to match.

D.H. Lawrence *Sons and Lovers*; *Lady Chatterley's Lover*; *Selected Short Stories*. Lawrence's magnificent prose on working-class life in Nottinghamshire's pit villages never went down well with the locals. His early short stories contain some of his finest writing, as does *Sons and Lovers*, a fraught, autobiographical novel, and the infamous *Lady Chatterley's Lover*.

Laurie Lee *Cider with Rosie.* Reminiscences of adolescent frolics in the rural Cotswolds of the 1920s.

Richard Llewellyn *How Green Was My Valley; Up into the Singing Mountain* (o/p); *Down Where the Moon is Small* (o/p); *Green, Green My Valley Now* (o/p). Vital tetralogy in eloquent and passionate prose, following the life of Huw Morgan from his youth in a South Wales mining valley through emigration to the Welsh community in Patagonia and back to 1970s Wales. A bestseller during World War II and still the best introduction to the vast canon of "valleys novels", *How Green Was My Valley* captured a longing for a simple if tough life, steering clear of cloying sentimentality.

Ian McEwan *Atonement; Enduring Love; Saturday.* Many reckon McEwan to be England's finest contemporary novelist, his dark and brooding works punctuated by the unforeseen and the accidental. *Atonement* was possibly his most masterful book, tracing the course of three lives from a sweltering country garden in 1935 to absolution in the new century. *Enduring Love* – with its gripping beginning – is a close rival, while *Saturday* provides an evocative insight into contemporary London.

Alan Sillitoe *Saturday Night and Sunday Morning.* Gritty account of factory life and sexual shenanigans in Nottingham in the late 1950s.

Dylan Thomas *Under Milk Wood; Collected Stories; Collected Poems: 1934–1953. Under Milk Wood* is Thomas's most popular play, telling the story of a microcosmic Welsh seaside town over a 24-hour period. *Collected Stories* contains all of Thomas's classic prose pieces: *Quite Early One Morning*, which metamorphosed into *Under Milk Wood*, the magical *A Child's Christmas in Wales* and the compulsive, crackling autobiography, *Portrait of the Artist as a Young Dog.* Thomas's beautifully wrought and inventive poems carry a deep, pained concern with mortality and the nature of humanity.

Evelyn Waugh The *Sword of Honour Trilogy* is a brilliant satire of the World War I officer class laced with some of Waugh's funniest set-pieces. The best-selling *Brideshead Revisited* is possibly his worst book, rank with snobbery, nostalgia and money-worship.

Irvine Welsh *Trainspotting.* A contemporary trawl through the horrors of drug addiction, sexual fantasy, urban decay and hopeless youth. Still Welsh's most famous book, though (thankfully) his unflinching attention is not without humour.

PG Wodehouse *Thank You, Jeeves; A Damsel in Distress.* For many, Wodehouse (1881-1975) is the quintessential English humourist and his deftly crafted tales – with their familiar cast of characters, primarily Bertie Wooster and Jeeves – have remained popular for decades.

Virginia Woolf *Orlando; Mrs Dalloway.* Woolf's lover, Vita Sackville-West, is the model for *Orlando*, whose life spans four centuries and both genders. *Mrs Dalloway*, which relates the thoughts of a London society hostess and a shell-shocked war veteran, sees Woolf's "stream of consciousness" style in full flow.

Contemporary crime fiction

Stephen Booth *Black Dog; Scared to Live.* The Derbyshire Peak District, its locations and traditions are the backdrop for Booth's effective thrillers, in which detective Ben Cooper pursues the truth

P.D. James *A Mind to Murder*. Prolific crime writer, famous for her whodunits starring detective Adam Dalgleish. This one is as good as any.

Ian Rankin *Knots and Crosses*; *The Falls*. Britain's best-selling crime author introduced John Rebus in 1987 and since then the hard-drinking, anti-authoritarian, emotionally scarred detective has featured in almost twenty novels. He inhabits the mean streets of Edinburgh that the tourists rarely see, though in cherished locations like the *Oxford Bar* pub visitors can rub shoulders with Rebus.

Ruth Rendell/Barbara Vine *From Doon With Death*; *Gallowglass*; *King Solomon's Carpet*; *Grasshopper*. Rendell writes brilliantly and disturbingly of contemporary dysfunction in all its guises. Her longstanding Inspector Wexford series is set in the fictional West Sussex town of Kingsmarkham, but it's writing as Barbara Vine that Rendell excels in a sense of place, namely London, creating serious, memorable fictions from unsung locales like Kilburn and Cricklewood, the London tube, and the streets and rooftops of Maida Vale.

Peter Robinson *Gallows View*; *A Piece of My Heart*. Robinson's lauded Inspector Banks series has used the bleak corners and beauty spots of the Yorkshire Dales to dramatic effect. His gritty novels featuring the troubled, music-loving detective show a sophistication gleaned from studying creative writing under Joyce Carol Oates.

Poetry before 1900

William Blake *The Complete Poems*. Blake ranges from the limpid wisdom of *Songs of Innocence and Experience* to the mystical complexities of the prophetic books. He is unique among major poets in illustrating his own work, most of which is set in, or has a significant relationship to, London.

Robert Burns *Selected Poems*. Comprises the best-known work of Scotland's most famous bard, who employed vigorous vernacular language. Immensely popular all over the world, his famous early poems include *Auld Lang Syne* and *My Love Is Like A Red, Red Rose*.

Lord Byron *Selected Poems*. Byron was a best-seller in his day celebrated for his exotic poems of adventure such as *The Corsair*, and he is also a master of the Romantic lyric; but the core of his achievement lies in his unfailingly inventive satire on all aspects of early nineteenth-century life, *Don Juan*.

Samuel Taylor Coleridge Coleridge wrote little, but to the highest quality. *Kubla Khan* and *The Rime of the Ancient Mariner* are amongst the strangest products of the Romantic period, but equally noteworthy are the quieter "conversation" poems such as *Frost at Midnight*.

John Donne *The Complete English Poems*. Donne (1572–1631), the greatest of the "metaphysical poets", brought passionate physicality and brilliant intellectual rigour to both his love poetry and religious verse.

John Keats *Selected Poems*. Keats was potentially one of the greatest writers who ever lived. Even given his early death – he was only 25 – his achievements in poems such as the *Ode to Autumn* are extraordinary.

Percy Bysshe Shelley *Selected Poems*. Shelley's poetry moves from swooning romantic intensity to a vigorously expressed hatred of the establishment of his day. He is a seminal figure in the pantheon of English radical dissent.

Alfred Tennyson *Selected Poems.* Tennyson's is perhaps the most purely musical poetry in English, filled with sensuous detail and dreamy evocations of natural beauty and the past. *In Memoriam* shows him to be the great poet of Victorian doubt and faith.

William Wordworth *Selected Poetry.* It's impossible to exaggerate Wordsworth's originality and his influence on the future direction of English culture; his presence is clearly felt in the novels of Dickens and George Eliot as well as in the work of later poets. His understanding of what it means to be human can only be described as profound.

Contemporary poetry

W.H. Auden *Collected Poems.* Auden combines the themes of history, politics and love in poems that are definitive expressions of his times. The politically committed work of the 1930s gives way to a later religious commitment, but all his work is marked by stylistic virtuosity.

John Betjeman *Collected Poems.* Betjeman was the English poet laureate; his humorous and often nostalgic work was profoundly concerned with England and the English.

T.S. Eliot *The Waste Land.* Published in 1922, this is considered one of the cornerstones of Modernist writing, offering a revolutionary vision of Western civilization imbued with resonant images of contemporary and ancient London.

Ted Hughes Just before his death in 1998, Hughes published *Birthday Letters*, a moving account of his relationship with the poet Sylvia Plath, and his response to her suicide. *New Selected Poems 1957–1994* is the most comprehensive collection of his work available.

Philip Larkin *Collected Poems.* Larkin used plain language in his work, the subject of which is often the insignificance of human life. Many of the poems achieve an apparently unstudied beauty, though in fact Larkin published very little, preferring to refine his verse to its basic elements.

Hugh MacDiarmid *Selected Poems.* A poet and nationalist who sought, through his fine lyrical verse, to reinvigorate the use of Scottish literary language.

Roger McGough *Blazing Fruit: Selected Poems.* A contemporary Liverpool poet, whose witty rhetorical verse is instantly recognizable. Some of McGough's earlier work, alongside Adrien Henri and Brian Patten, can be found in the influential collection *The Mersey Sound*.

Wilfred Owen *The Poems of Wilfred Owen.* As with Keats, Owen's early death was a tragedy for English literature. His war poetry is at its best in the likes of *Strange Meeting*, with its strikingly original use of half-rhymes.

Film

For much of its history the British **film industry** has largely been an English affair, with its major studios (Ealing, Pinewood and Shepperton) not far from central London and its stars drawn from the ranks of the capital's stage. However, unlike the Hollywood star system, the English film industry tended – and still significantly relies on – strong ensemble playing. While **Ealing's** films were a byword for social comedy, other significant elements have included the **Hammer horror series** (usually featuring either or both Christopher Lee and Peter Cushing), costume dramas typified by the **Gainsborough** company's productions and the **James Bond** films, while the **Carry On** series kept a generation of comedy actors in work long past their sell-by dates. In the 1960s, English films developed a justifiable reputation for social realism, which has been maintained in more recent times by directors such as **Ken Loach** and **Mike Leigh**.

Today's British film industry is in a healthier state now than perhaps at any point since the 1930s, with a diversity and vitality that reflects the dominance of independent productions. Some film fans might argue that the influence of television means that many such productions are essentially small-screen ventures, but within the last ten years a string of pictures have enjoyed great success internationally.

The films listed below are all set in the UK. They are not exclusively greats – though some rank amongst the best movies ever made – but all depict a particular aspect of British life, whether reflecting the experience of immigrant communities, exploring the country's history, or depicting its richly varied landscapes.

The 1930s and 1940s

Brief Encounter (David Lean, 1945). Wonderful weepie as Trevor Howard and Celia Johnson teeter on the edge of adultery at a commuter railway station. Noël Coward was responsible for the clipped dialogue, Rachmaninov for the flushed, dreamy score.

Brighton Rock (John Boulting, 1947). A fine adaptation of Graham Greene's novel, featuring a young, genuinely scary Richard Attenborough as the psychopathic hood Pinkie, who marries a witness to one of his crimes to ensure her silence. Beautiful cinematography and good performances, with a real sense of *film noir* menace.

A Canterbury Tale (Michael Powell and Emeric Pressburger, 1944). Set in a wartime Kent village, where a plucky land girl, a small-town GI and a sardonic English sergeant are billeted. Overseen by a mysterious local magistrate, they make their own pilgrimage to Canterbury, the cathedral glowing high over bomb-damaged streets. A mystical vision of English history is fused with bucolic images of rural life, a restrained exploration of the characters' personal suffering underlying a truly magical masterpiece.

Fires Were Started (Humphrey Jennings, 1943). One of the best films to come out of the British documentary tradition, this is the story of the experiences of a group of firemen through one night of bombing during the Blitz. The use of real firemen as performers rather than professional actors, and the avoidance of formulaic heroics, gives the film great power as an account of the courage of ordinary people who fought, often uncelebrated, on the home front.

Great Expectations (David Lean, 1946). Early film by one of England's finest directors – *Lawrence of Arabia*, *Bridge on the River Kwai* – this superb rendition of the Dickens novel features magnificent performances by John Mills (as Pip) and Finlay Currie (as Abel Magwitch). The scene in the graveyard is nothing short of wonderful.

Henry V (Laurence Olivier, 1944). Featuring glowing Technicolor backdrops, this wonderful piece of wartime propaganda is emphatically "theatrical", the action spiralling out from the Globe Theatre itself. Olivier is a brilliantly charismatic king, the pre-battle scene where he goes disguised amongst his men being delicately muted and atmospheric.

Jane Eyre (Robert Stevenson, 1943). Joan Fontaine does a fine job of portraying Jane, and Orson Welles is a suavely sardonic Rochester – the scene where he is thrown from his horse in the mist hits the perfect melodramatic pitch. With the unlikely tagline "A Love Story Every Woman Would Die a Thousand Deaths to Live!", it briefly features a young Elizabeth Taylor as a dying Helen Burns.

Kind Hearts and Coronets (Robert Hamer, 1949). As with the best of the Ealing movies, this is a savage comedy on the cruel absurdities of the British class system. With increasing ingenuity, Dennis Price's suave and ruthless anti-hero murders his way through the d'Ascoyne clan (all brilliantly played by Alec Guinness) to claim the family title.

The Life and Death of Colonel Blimp (Michael Powell and Emeric Pressburger, 1943). An epic celebration of the oft-ridiculed romantic spirit of the English, personified by the wonderful Roger Livesey. We follow him through the actual and emotional duels of his youth, against his equally dashing German foe, to crusty old age in World War II. A daring and visually stunning story of love and friendship, it was hated by Churchill for supposedly being unpatriotic, which is surely recommendation enough.

The Private Life of Henry VIII (Alexander Korda, 1933). The catalyst for a boom in British film-making – thanks to the success of the gargantuan Charles Laughton in the title role – this film has little now to commend it other than some superb cinematography and Laughton's own sometimes grotesque performance.

Rebecca (Alfred Hitchcock, 1940). Hitchcock does Du Maurier: Laurence Olivier is wonderfully enigmatic as Maxim de Winter, and Joan Fontaine glows as his meek second wife, living in the shadow of her mysterious predecessor. Perfectly paced and beautifully shot, Hitch's first Hollywood picture is a true classic.

The Thirty-Nine Steps (Alfred Hitchcock, 1935). Hitchcock's best-loved British movie, full of wit and bold acts of derring-do. Robert Donat stars as innocent Richard Hannay, inadvertently caught up in a mysterious spy ring and forced to flee both the spies and the agents of Scotland Yard. In a typically perverse Hitchcock touch, he spends a generous amount of time handcuffed to Madeleine Carroll, fleeing across the Scottish countryside, before the action returns to London for the film's great music-hall conclusion.

Whisky Galore! (Alexander Mackendrick, 1949). When a shipwrecked stock of the water of life is washed ashore on a remote Scottish island, the locals contrive all manner of cunning ruses to conceal its presence from the pursuing authorities. A beautiful Ealing comedy, with real sympathy for its eccentric little community as they battle the forces of dull authority in the entirely laudable ambition of having a good time at no expense.

The Wicked Lady (Leslie Arliss, 1945). One of the best of Gainsborough Studios' series of escapist romances, this features a magnificently amoral and headstrong Margaret Lockwood, wooed into a criminal double life by James Mason's quintessentially dashing highwayman. Its opulent re-creation of eighteenth-century England is terribly appealing, as are the tempestuous entanglements of its two wayward stars.

1950 to 1970

Billy Liar! (John Schlesinger, 1963). Tom Courtenay is stuck in a dire job as an undertaker's clerk in a northern town, and spends his time creating extravagant fantasies. His life is lit up by the appearance of Julie Christie, who holds out the glamour and promise of swinging London. Touching and amusing.

Carry On Screaming (Gerald Thomas, 1966). One of the better efforts from the Carry On crew, with most of the usual suspects (Kenneth Williams, Charles Hawtrey, Joan Sims) hamming it up in a Hammer Horror spoof and serving up a few scares along with the usual single-entendre jokes.

Dracula (Terence Fisher, 1958). Classic Hammer Horror flick, loosely based on Bram Stoker's original book and pairing Christopher Lee as the blood-sucking count with Peter Cushing's vampire-staking Van Helsing.

Far From the Madding Crowd (John Schlesinger, 1967). A largely successful and imaginative adaptation of Hardy's doom-laden tale of the desires and ambitions of wilful Bathsheba Everdene. Julie Christie is a radiant and spirited Bathsheba, Terence Stamp flashes his blade to dynamic effect, Alan Bates is quietly charismatic as dependable Gabriel Oak, and the West Country setting is sparsely beautiful.

Kes (Kenneth Loach, 1969). This is the unforgettable story of a neglected Yorkshire schoolboy who finds solace and liberation in training his kestrel. As a still-pertinent commentary on poverty and an impoverished school system, it's bleak but idealistic. Pale and pinched David Bradley, who plays Billy Casper, is hugely affecting.

The Ladykillers (Alexander Mackendrick, 1955). Alec Guinness is fabulously toothy and malevolent as "Professor Marcus", a murderous conman who lodges with a sweet little old lady, Mrs Wilberforce. The professor and his ragbag of criminal accomplices – their sinister intent a hilarious counterpoint to Mrs Wilberforce's genteel tea parties – try to pass themselves off as musicians, while, thanks to her innocent interventions, the body count inexorably mounts.

A Man for All Seasons (Fred Zinnemann, 1966). Sir Thomas More versus Henry VIII: one of British history's great moral confrontations made skilfully tedious by this film's stage-bound, talky origins in Robert Bolt's play. Despite muted, atmospheric visuals and a heavenly host of theatrical talent (including a cheering appearance by Orson Welles as Cardinal Wolsey), nothing can save this from paralysing dullness.

Night and the City (Jules Dassin, 1950). Great *film noir*, with Richard

Widmark as an anxious nightclub hustler on the run. Gripping and convincingly sleazy, the London streetscapes have an expressionist edge of horror.

Performance (Nicolas Roeg/Donald Cammell, 1970). Credited with precipitating James Fox's breakdown and subsequent retirement from the movies, this shape-shifting tale of gangsters and pop culture is the best account of the hedonistic end to Britain's psychedelic 1960s. Well known for its strange drug-hazed second half, the film is also brilliantly funny in parts and should be cherished for its hilarious destruction of the myth of Kray-style criminals.

Saturday Night and Sunday Morning (Karel Reisz, 1960). Reisz's monochrome captures all the grit and dead-end grind of Albert Finney's life working in a Nottingham bicycle factory and his attempts to find excitement and romance in the city.

The 1970s and 1980s

Akenfield (Peter Hall, 1974). A powerfully involving evocation of English rural life whose ingredients include glowing cinematography and Michael Tippett's wonderful music. Past and present are skilfully contrasted, but the heart of the film lies in its sometimes ecstatic, but also harsh, rendering of the past.

Babylon (Franco Rosso, 1980). A moving account of black working-class London life. We follow the experiences of young Blue through a series of encounters that reveal the insidious forces of racism at work in Britain. Good performances and a great reggae soundtrack: an all too rare example of Black Britain taking centre stage in British movies.

A Clockwork Orange (Stanley Kubrick, 1971). Famously banned in

This Sporting Life (Lindsay Anderson, 1963). One of the key British films of the 1960s, *This Sporting Life* tells the story of a northern miner turned star player for his local rugby team. The young Richard Harris gives a great performance as the inarticulate anti-hero, able only to express himself through physical violence, and the film is one of the best examples of the gritty "kitchen sink" genre it helped to usher in.

The War Game (Peter Watkins, 1965). Watkins' astonishing documentary approach to the effects of a Russian nuclear attack on southeast England, using both local people and various official "talking heads", shocked its commissioner, the BBC, into refusing to show it; hardly surprising, since its overall effect was to question our trust in authority. Much dated in comparison to modern computer-driven special effects, it still retains the power to alarm.

the UK by director Kubrick, this is a genuinely disturbing if now slightly dated depiction of violence and society's reaction to it, in which young droog Alex – played with charm and menace by Malcolm McDowell – finds himself first the perpetrator and then the victim, to a rousing soundtrack of Beethoven classics.

Comrades (Bill Douglas, 1986). In 1830s England, a group of farm workers decide to stand up to the exploitative tactics of the local landowner, and find themselves prosecuted and transported to Australia. Based on the true story of the Tolpuddle Martyrs, this combines political education (the founding of the modern union movement) with a moving and visually stunning celebration of working lives.

Distant Voices, Still Lives (Terence Davies, 1988). Beautifully realized autobiographical tale of growing up in Forties and Fifties Liverpool. The mesmeric pace is punctuated by astonishing moments of drama, and the whole is a very moving account of how a family survives and triumphs, in small ways, against the odds.

Frenzy (Alfred Hitchcock, 1972). Hitchcock comes back to Blighty in top form, with the story of a man on the run, under suspicion for the vicious "necktie" murders carried out in Covent Garden. Trademark sly black humour combines with a disturbing exploration of sexual immaturity.

Get Carter (Mike Hodges, 1971). Although not the masterpiece some claim, this is still one of the most vivid and interesting British gangster

△ Michael Caine in *Get Carter*

movies, featuring a monumentally evil outing for Michael Caine as the eponymous villain, returning to his native Newcastle to avenge his brother's death. Great use of its northeast locations and a fine turn by playwright John Osborne as the local godfather don't quite, however, compensate for its now faintly ridiculous misogyny.

Gregory's Girl (Bill Forsyth, 1981). John Gordon Sinclair is engaging and gangly as Gregory, whose adolescent dreams are filled with football-playing schoolgirl siren Dorothy. Gregory's gauche attempts to woo her keep the gentle plot tripping along nicely, his teachers making sardonic asides and his little sister proffering grave advice.

Hope and Glory (John Boorman, 1987). A glorious autobiographical feature about the Blitz seen through the eyes of 9-year-old Bill, who revels in the liberating chaos of bomb-site playgrounds, tumbling barrage balloons and shrapnel collections. His older sister's unfettered romps with a Canadian soldier and the adults' privation and occasional despair are an additional source of amusement for Bill and his tiny sister.

The Last of England (Derek Jarman, 1987). Derek Jarman was a genuine maverick presence in Eighties Britain; this is his most abstract account of the state of the nation. Composed of apparently unrelated shots of decaying London landscapes, rent boys, and references to emblematic national events such as the Falklands War, this may not be to all tastes, but it is a fitting testament to a unique talent in British film-making.

The Madness of King George (Nicholas Hytner, 1994). Adapted from an Alan Bennett play, this eighteenth-century royal romp has an irritating staginess, with the king's loopy antics played against a cartoon-like court and an England apparently devoid of real people.

Mona Lisa (Neil Jordan, 1986). This fine London-based thriller has powerful performances from Bob Hoskins, Michael Caine and then-newcomer Cathy Tyson, the latter playing a high-class prostitute who recruits Hoskins to help find her lost friend. This takes him, and us, on a nightmarish exploration of the dark side of Eighties London, lightened only slightly by an utterly convincing, poignant love story, as Bob begins to fall for his beautiful employer.

My Beautiful Laundrette (Stephen Frears, 1985). A slice of Thatcher's Britain, with a young Asian, Omar, on the make, opening a ritzy laundrette. His lover, Johnny (Daniel Day-Lewis), is an ex–National Front glamour boy, angry and inarticulate when forced by the acquisitive Omar into a menial role in the laundrette. The racial, sexual and class dynamics of their relationship are closely observed, and mirror the tensions engendered by the Asian presence in a hostile London.

On the Black Hill (Andrew Grieve, 1987). A visually absorbing adaptation of Bruce Chatwin's rather slight novel of Welsh farming folk. Hardyesque characterization and a similar predilection for doom, with a strong performance by Bob Peck as stubborn Amos Jones, trapped in an unhappy marriage to a middle-class woman.

The Wicker Man (Robin Hardy, 1973). A classic more by virtue of its unutterable weirdness than any great achievements of film-making. Edward Woodward plays a detective investigating the mysterious disappearance of a local girl on an isolated Scottish island, and finds himself drawn into a strange world of maypole dancing and inadvertently hilarious pagan rites. Christopher Lee manages to keep a straight face throughout.

Withnail and I (Bruce Robinson, 1986). Richard E. Grant is superb as the raddled, drunken Withnail, an out-of-work actor with a penchant for drinking lighter fluid. Paul McGann is the "I" of the title – a bemused and beautiful spectator of Withnail's wild excesses, as they abandon an astonishingly grotty London flat for the wilds of a remote cottage, and the attentions of With-nail's randy Uncle Monty. A rare look at the 1960s that avoids nostalgia, and opts instead for emotional truth.

The 1990s to the present

Bend It Like Beckham (Gurinder Chadha, 2003). Immensely success-ful film focusing on the coming of age of a football-loving Punjabi girl in a suburb of London. Both socially acute and comic.

Bhaji on the Beach (Gurinder Chadha, 1993). An Asian women's group takes a day-trip to Blackpool in this issue-laden but enjoyable picture. A lot of fun is had contrast-ing the seamier side of British life with the mores of the Asian aunt-ies, though the male characters are cartoon villains all.

Billy Elliot (Stephen Daldry, 2000). Set against the depressing backdrop of the turbulent miners' strike of 1984, this ultimately feel-good film tells the story of a young boy (Jamie Bell), torn between his unexpected love of dance and the disintegration of his family.

Brassed Off (Mark Herman, 1996). A pacy film about British working-class life that eschews pathos, opting instead for uncompromising anger, underscored by robust black humour. With the imminent demise of the town's coal pit, the future for the Grimley Colliery Brass Band looks hopeless. Danny (Pete Postlethwaite) valiantly attempts to keep the band alive as the emotional lives of the musicians collapse.

Braveheart (Mel Gibson, 1995). Cod-Highland high camp, with a shaggy-haired Mel Gibson wielding his claymore as thirteenth-century Independence hero William Wallace. The English are thieving effete scum, the Scots all warm-blooded noble savages, and history takes a firm back seat. Filmed largely in Ireland.

Breaking the Waves (Lars von Trier, 1996). A lyrical, moving drama set in a devout community in the north of Scotland. An innocent young woman, Bess (Emily Watson), falls in love with Danish oil-rig worker Jan (Stellan Skarsgaard). Blaming herself for the injury which cripples him, she embarks on a masochistic sexual odyssey, which rapidly takes her into dark and uncharted waters.

Bridget Jones's Diary (Sharon Maguire, 2001). American Renée Zellweger put on a plummy English accent and several pounds to play the lead in this *Pride and Prejudice* for the new millennium. Ably assisted by deliciously nasty love-interest Hugh Grant, the film stands out as one of the better British romantic comedies of the last few years.

Dirty Pretty Things (Stephen Frears, 2003). A tumbling mix of melodrama, social criticism and black comedy, this forceful, thought-provoking film explores the world of Britain's illegal migrants.

East Is East (Damien O'Donnell, 1999). Seventies Salford is the setting for this lively comedy, with a Paki-stani chip-shop owner struggling to keep control of his seven children as they rail against the strictures of Islam and arranged marriages. Inven-tively made, and with some pleasing performances.

Elizabeth (Shekhar Kapur, 1998). Charismatic Cate Blanchett is, thankfully, the still heart of this history-lite and madly over-blown production, where all political and emotional nuance is lost in an orgy of decapitations, swirling cloaks and stagy thunderstorms.

Enigma (Michael Apted, 2001). This blockbuster, scripted by playwright Tom Stoppard, is a fictional tale depicting Britain's wartime efforts to crack the Germans' Enigma encrypting machine, with Kate Winslet excelling amongst a generally fine cast.

Four Weddings and a Funeral (Mike Newell, 1994). Standard rom-com that used an American actress and gags based on English eccentricities to pull in big audiences worldwide. Unrepresentative of contemporary England with its Hugh Grant-led cast of middle-class whites, it still manages some very funny – and quite moving – set-pieces.

The Full Monty (Peter Cattaneo, 1997). Six Sheffield ex–steel workers throw caution to the wind and become male strippers, their boast being that all will be revealed: the "full monty". Unpromising physical specimens all, they score an unlikely hit with the local lasses. The film was itself an unlikely hit worldwide: the theme of manhood in crisis is sensitively explored, and the long-awaited striptease is a joy to behold.

Gosford Park (Robert Altman, 2001). Astutely observed upstairs-downstairs murder mystery set in class-ridden 1930s England. The multi-layered plot is typical of the director while the who's who of great British actors is led by the superb Maggie Smith – and only let down by Stephen Fry's bumbling police inspector who looks like he's wandered in from an entirely different film.

Harry Potter and the Philosopher's Stone (Chris Colombus, 2001). The first film in a series about hero Harry Potter's life at wizard school did wonders for the English tourist industry with its use of places such as Alnwick Castle as locations. The subsequent films are also darkly enjoyable, with excellent ensemble casts – Spall, Gambon, Rickman, Thompson et al.

Howards End (James Ivory, 1991). E.M. Forster's tale of the forward-thinking Schlegel sisters, and their relationship with the conventional, domineering Wilcoxes. One of many immaculate British costume dramas, with precise performances from Vanessa Redgrave, Helena Bonham Carter and, most notably, Emma Thompson as Margaret Schlegel.

Little Voice (Mark Herman, 1998). Entertaining screen adaptation of Jim Cartwright's hit play about reclusive "Little Voice" (Jane Horrocks), who comes miraculously to life only on stage, brilliantly impersonating Fifties stars such as Marilyn Monroe. It features a great performance from Michael Caine as the impossibly seedy agent who seeks to exploit her bizarre talent, and offers a great glimpse of seaside England, with all its eccentric charm.

Lock, Stock and Two Smoking Barrels (Guy Ritchie, 1998). Four lads attempt to pay off gambling debts by making a drug deal in this over-stylized and rather shallow picture, which, though it has a modern setting, pays dubious homage to the London of the Kray twins. However, the suits are sharp, the production is slick and football's hardman-turned-actor Vinnie Jones turns in a surprisingly solid debut performance.

Nil by Mouth (Gary Oldman, 1997). With strong performances by Ray Winstone (Ray) as a boorish

South Londoner and Kathy Burke (Valery) as his battered wife, this brave and bleak realist picture depicts Ray as a victim of his own violence, as well as the devastatingly vulnerable Valery. Brace yourself.

Notting Hill (Roger Michell, 1999). After their huge hit with *Four Weddings*, writer Richard Curtis and actor Hugh Grant returned with more middle-class jollity. Grant reprises his bumbling floppy-haired Englishman role and falls for a glamorous American (Julia Roberts) – again. Spanning a year in the life of Notting Hill, it perversely fails to feature the event for which this part of London is best known: the biggest and best street carnival in Europe.

Orlando (Sally Potter, 1992). Although modest in budget terms, this is a vivid and visually beautiful adaptation of Virginia Woolf's novel, following its hero/heroine through 400 years of British history. Tilda Swinton is perfectly cast as the androgynous immortal, and choice moments spanning Elizabethan England to the present day (through the Civil War and Victoria's reign, for example) are perfectly and mysteriously realized.

Ratcatcher (Lynne Ramsay, 1999). Set in 1970s Glasgow during a refuse-workers' strike, Ramsay's striking first feature follows 12-year-old James, who accidentally drowns his friend as the rubbish around the tenement blocks mounts. Weaving rich humour into the gloomy narrative, Ramsay layers poetic images of the city, rejecting realism for a lyrical, symbolic approach.

The Remains of the Day (James Ivory, 1993). Kazuo Ishiguro's masterly study of social and personal repression translates beautifully to the big screen. Anthony Hopkins is the overly decorous butler who gradually becomes aware of his master's fascist connections, Emma Thompson the

housekeeper who struggles to bring his real, deeply suppressed feelings to the surface.

Richard III (Richard Loncraine, 1995). A splendid film version of a renowned National Theatre production, which brilliantly transposed the action to a fascist state in the 1930s. The infernal political machinations of a snarling Ian McKellan as Richard are heightened by Nazi associations, and the style of the period imbues the film with the requisite glamour, as does languorously drugged Kristin Scott-Thomas as Lady Anne.

Secrets and Lies (Mike Leigh, 1995). Much-loved Mike Leigh slice-of-life drama, with wonderful Timothy Spall at the head of a spectacularly dysfunctional London family. His sister Cynthia (Brenda Blethyn), her heart of gold buried in boozy, cloying unhappiness, is reunited with the black daughter she gave up for adoption at birth. Over-long improvised sequences, and a depiction of suburban vulgarity which comes close to parody, are lifted by stunning ensemble performances and sustained by the simple strength of its central tenet: that secrets and lies in a family will only cause unnecessary pain.

Sense and Sensibility (Ang Lee, 1995). Jane Austen's sprightly essay on the merits of well-modified behaviour is nicely realized by Lee, and neatly scripted by Emma Thompson. Thompson and Kate Winslet are charming as the downtrodden Dashwood sisters: Winslet is a brilliantly over-wrought, romantic Marianne, while Thompson turns in a perfect performance as prudent Elinor.

Small Faces (Gillies MacKinnon, 1995). A moving little saga about the lives of three brothers growing up in 1960s Glasgow amid feuding gangs of local teenagers. We follow

CONTEXTS | Film

C

the rough education of young Lex, torn between the excitement and real danger of a life of fighting, and the alternative artistic ambitions of his older brother. A convincing and occasionally very funny re-creation of the period.

Trainspotting (Danny Boyle, 1996). High-octane dip into the heroin world of a group of young Scotsmen with key scenes played out in London. Best cinematic representation of a heroin fix ever.

24 hour Party People (Michael Winterbottom, 2002). Steve Coogan plays the entrepreneurial and inspirational Tony Wilson in this fast-moving re-creation of the early days of Manchester's Factory Records. Stunning soundtrack too.

Glossary of architectural terms

Aisle Clear space parallel to the nave, usually with lower ceiling than the nave.

Altar Table at which the Eucharist is celebrated, at the east end of the church. (When church is not aligned to the geographical east, the altar end is still referred to as the "east" end.)

Ambulatory Passage behind the chancel.

Apse The curved or polygonal east end of a church.

Arcade Row of arches on top of columns or piers, supporting a wall.

Ashlar Dressed building stone worked to a smooth finish.

Bailey Area enclosed by castle walls.

Barbican Defensive structure built in front of main gate.

Barrel vault Continuous rounded vault, like a semi-cylinder.

Boss A decorative carving at the meeting point of the lines of a vault.

Box pew Form of church seating in which each row is enclosed by high, thin wooden panels.

Broach spire Octagonal spire rising straight out of a square tower.

Broch A Scottish, circular, dry-stone fort, dating from the Iron Age.

Buttress Stone support for a wall; some buttresses are wholly attached to the wall, others take the form of an outer support with a connecting half-arch, known as a "flying buttress".

Capital Upper section of a column, usually carved.

Chancel Section of the church where the altar is located.

Chantry Small chapel in which mass was said for the soul of the person who financed its construction; none built after the Reformation.

Choir Area in which the church service is conducted; next to or same as chancel.

Clerestory Upper storey of nave, containing a line of windows.

Coffering Regular recessed spaces set into a ceiling.

Crenellations Battlements with square indentations.

Crossing (church) The intersection of the nave, choir and transepts.

Decorated Middle Gothic style; about 1280–1380.

Dogtooth Form of early Gothic decorative stonework, looking like raised "X"s.

Dormer Window raised out of the main roof.

Early English First phase of Gothic architecture in England, about 1150–1280.

Fan vault Late Gothic form of vaulting, in which the area between walls and ceiling is covered with stone ribs in the shape of an open fan.

Finial Any decorated tip of an architectural feature.

Flushwork Kind of surface decoration in which tablets of white stone alternate with pieces of flint; very common in East Anglia.

Gargoyle Grotesque exterior carving, usually a decorative form of water spout.

Hammer beam Type of ceiling in which horizontal brackets support vertical struts that connect to the roof timbers.

Jesse Tree Christian legend asserts that Jesse, the father of King David, was the ancestor of Jesus, and Jesse windows trace the genealogical tree by means of their stained-glass pictures.

Keep Main structure of a castle.

Lady Chapel Chapel dedicated to the Virgin, often found at the east end of major churches.

Lancet Tall, narrow and plain window.

Lantern Upper part of a dome or tower, often glazed.

Misericord Carved ledge below a tip-up seat, usually in choir stalls, as support when occupant stands.

Motte Mound on which a castle keep stands.

Mullion Vertical post between the panes of a window.

Nave The main part of the church usually to the west of the central crossing.

Ogee Double curve; distinctive feature of Decorated style.

Oriel Projecting window.

Palladian Seventeenth- and eighteenth-century classical style adhering to the principles of Andrea Palladio.

Pediment Triangular space above a window or doorway.

Perpendicular Late Gothic style, about 1380–1550.

Pier A massive column, often consisting of several fused smaller columns.

Pilaster Flat column set against a wall.

Reredos Painted or carved panel behind an altar.

Rood screen Wooden screen supporting a crucifix (or rood), separating the choir from the nave; few survived the Reformation.

Rose window Large circular window, divided into vaguely petal-shaped sections.

Sedilia Seats for the participants in the church service, usually on the south side of the choir.

Stalls Seating for clergy in the choir area of a church.

Tracery Pattern formed by narrow bands of stone in a window or on a wall surface.

Transept Section of the main body of the church at right angles to the choir and nave.

Triforium Arcade above the nave or transept in a church.

Tympanum Panel over a doorway, often carved in medieval churches.

Vault Arched ceiling.

Travel store

TRAVEL

& MORE

Visit us online
www.roughguides.com
Information on over 25,000 destinations around the world

- **Read** Rough Guides' trusted travel info

- **Share** journals, photos and travel advice with other readers

- Get exclusive Rough Guide **discounts** and travel deals

- Earn membership points every time you contribute to the

  Rough Guide community and get free books, flights and trips

- Browse thousands of **CD reviews** and artists in our music area

ONLINE

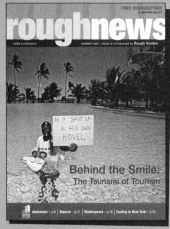

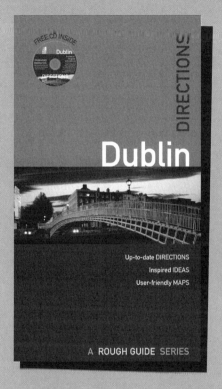

NOTES

NOTES

NOTES

NOTES

NOTES

NOTES

Small print and
Index

A Rough Guide to Rough Guides

Published in 1982, the first Rough Guide – to Greece – was a student scheme that became a publishing phenomenon. Mark Ellingham, a recent graduate in English from Bristol University, had been travelling in Greece the previous summer and couldn't find the right guidebook. With a small group of friends he wrote his own guide, combining a highly contemporary, journalistic style with a thoroughly practical approach to travellers' needs.

The immediate success of the book spawned a series that rapidly covered dozens of destinations. And, in addition to impecunious backpackers, Rough Guides soon acquired a much broader and older readership that relished the guides' wit and inquisitiveness as much as their enthusiastic, critical approach and value-for-money ethos.

These days, Rough Guides include recommendations from shoestring to luxury and cover more than 200 destinations around the globe, including almost every country in the Americas and Europe, more than half of Africa and most of Asia and Australasia. Our ever-growing team of authors and photographers is spread all over the world, particularly in Europe, the USA and Australia.

In the early 1990s, Rough Guides branched out of travel, with the publication of Rough Guides to World Music, Classical Music and the Internet. All three have become benchmark titles in their fields, spearheading the publication of a wide range of books under the Rough Guide name.

Including the travel series, Rough Guides now number more than 350 titles, covering: phrasebooks, waterproof maps, music guides from Opera to Heavy Metal, reference works as diverse as Conspiracy Theories and Shakespeare, and popular culture books from iPods to Poker. Rough Guides also produce a series of more than 120 World Music CDs in partnership with World Music Network.

Visit www.roughguides.com to see our latest publications.

Rough Guide travel images are available for commercial licensing at www.roughguidespictures.com.

Rough Guide credits

Text editors: Amanda Tomlin and Ann-Marie Shaw
Layout: Ajay Verma
Cartography: Jasbir Sandhu
Picture editor: Mark Thomas
Production: Aimee Hampson
Proofreader: Diane Margolis
Cover design: Chloë Roberts
Photographers: Mark Thomas (London &
England), Helena Smith (Scotland), Tim Draper
(England), Paul Whitfield (Wales)
Editorial: London Kate Berens, Claire Saunders,
Geoff Howard, Ruth Blackmore, Polly Thomas,
Richard Lim, Clifton Wilkinson, Alison Murchie,
Karoline Densley, Andy Turner, Keith Drew,
Edward Aves, Nikki Birrell, Helen Marsden, Alice
Park, Sarah Eno, Joe Staines, Duncan Clark,
Peter Buckley, Matthew Milton, Tracy Hopkins,
David Paul, Lucy White, Ruth Tidball; **New York**
Andrew Rosenberg, Richard Koss, Steven Horak,
AnneLise Sorensen, Amy Hegarty, Hunter Slaton,
April Isaacs, Sean Mahoney
Design & Pictures: London Simon Bracken, Dan
May, Diana Jarvis, Jj Luck, Harriet Mills; **Delhi**
Madhulita Mohapatra, Umesh Aggarwal, Jessica
Subramanian, Amit Verma, Ankur Guha, Pradeep
Thapliyal

Production: Sophie Hewat, Katherine Owers
Cartography: London Maxine Repath, Ed Wright,
Katie Lloyd-Jones; **Delhi** Manish Chandra,
Rajesh Chhibber, Ashutosh Bharti, Rajesh Mishra,
Animesh Pathak, Jasbir Sandhu, Karobi Gogoi,
Amod Singh
Online: New York Jennifer Gold, Suzanne Welles,
Kristin Mingrone; **Delhi** Manik Chauhan,
Narender Kumar, Manish Shekhar Jha, Lalit
Kumar Sharma, Rakesh Kumar, Chhandita
Chakravarty
Marketing & Publicity: London Richard Trillo,
Niki Hanmer, David Wearn, Demelza Dallow,
Louise Maher; **New York** Geoff Colquitt, Megan
Kennedy, Katy Ball; **Delhi** Reem Khokhar
Custom publishing and foreign rights: Philippa
Hopkins
Manager India: Punita Singh
Series editor: Mark Ellingham
Reference director: Andrew Lockett
PA to managing and publishing directors:
Megan McIntyre
Publishing director: Martin Dunford
Managing director: Kevin Fitzgerald

Publishing information

This 6th edition published June 2006 by **Rough
Guides Ltd**
80 Strand, London WC2R 0RL
345 Hudson St, 4th Floor,
New York, NY 10014, USA
14 Local Shopping Centre, Panchsheel Park,
New Delhi 110017, India
Distributed by the Penguin Group
Penguin Books Ltd
80 Strand, London WC2R 0RL
Penguin Putnam, Inc.
375 Hudson Street, NY 10014, USA
Penguin Group (Australia)
250 Camberwell Road, Camberwell,
Victoria 3124, Australia
Penguin Books Canada Ltd,
10 Alcorn Avenue, Toronto, Ontario
M4V 1E4 Canada
Penguin Group (New Zealand)
Cnr Rosedale and Airborne Roads
Albany, Auckland, New Zealand
Cover design by Peter Dyer.

Typeset in Bembo and Helvetica to an original
design by Henry Iles.
Printed in Italy by LegoPrint.
© Rough Guides, 2006

1224pp includes index.
A catalogue record for this book is available from
the British Library.
ISBN 13: 978-1-84353-686-4
ISBN 10: 1-84353-686-2

The publishers and authors have done their best
to ensure the accuracy and currency of all the
information in **The Rough Guide to Britain**;
however, they can accept no responsibility for
any loss, injury, or inconvenience sustained by
any traveller as a result of information or advice
contained in the guide.

1   3   5   7   9   8   6   4   2

Help us update

We've gone to a lot of effort to ensure that the
sixth edition of **The Rough Guide to Britain**
is accurate and up to date. However, things
change – places get "discovered", opening
hours are notoriously fickle, restaurants and
rooms raise prices or lower standards. If you
feel we've got it wrong or left something out,
we'd like to know, and if you can remember the
address, the price, the time, the phone number,
so much the better.
We'll credit all contributions, and send a copy of
the next edition (or any other Rough Guide if you

prefer) for the best letters. Everyone who writes
to us and isn't already a subscriber will receive
a copy of our full-colour thrice-yearly newsletter.
Please mark letters: "**Rough Guide Britain
Update**" and send to: Rough Guides, 80 Strand,
London WC2R 0RL, or Rough Guides, 4th Floor,
345 Hudson St, New York, NY 10014. Or send an
email to **mail@roughguides.com**.
Have your questions answered and tell others
about your trip at
www.roughguides.atinfopop.com.

Acknowledgements

The authors and editors would like to thank English Heritage, the National Trust, the National Trust for Scotland, Historic Scotland and VisitScotland for their assistance.

Rob Andrews would like to thank all the knowledgeable, helpful and enthusiastic staff of Britain's museums and galleries, and Bea Uhart for her invaluable tips in Southeast England.

Phil Lee would like to thank his editor, Amanda Tomlin, for all her hard work on this new edition of Britain.

Donald Reid would like to thank Colin Hutchison, Barry Shelby, Henry Hepburn, Robin Lee and Isla Leavery-Yap for their contributions to the Scotland chapters.

Paul Whitfield would like to thank Glenda Lloyd Davies at the Wales Tourist Board and all those who shared thoughts, experiences and Welsh mountain paths including Jo Farrington, Neil Woods, Brett McGill and Carl Pulley. Also to Liz Porter for guiding me around the Wind Street nightlife, and to Irene for putting up with half-done DIY projects abandoned during lengthy bouts of research and writing.

Readers' letters

Thanks to all the readers who took the trouble to write in with their comments and suggestions. In particular, our thanks to:

Sarah Anslow; Gaele Amiot-Cadey; Dave and Sonja Attwood-Vlaming; Heather Barback; Julie Barrie; Mark Bigley; Helen Bennell; Anders Berglund; Ian and John Besch; Anthony Bradbury; Katy Broadhead; J Burkitt; Darren Burling; Adam Butler; Mary Byrne; Robert Carding; Michaela Carlowe; Richard Chandler; David Clarke; Michael Clegg; Kim Coates; Guy and Varry Cocker; Alina Congreve; Joe Cowley; Barry Cox; Jim Craig; Olga Crawford; Peter Daly; Carolyn Datta; Matthew Davies; Linda Davis; Mike Dean; Andy Dennis; N V & P Dixon; Noric Dorn; James Dress; Roman Dubowski; Carol Farrington; Ann Feltham; Norinda Fennema; Kathy Field; Kevin Fitzgerald; Chris Fort; Paul Gaskell; Andrew Godley; Colin Good; Sean Gostage; Fiona Green; Phillip Greenstein; Matthew Hall; Alastair Hamilton; Andy Hamnett; Bart Hansen; David Hanson; Aybike Hatemi; Chris Heaps; Timothy Heavisides; Gerard Heelan; Danny Heijl; Andrea Hemingway; Catherine Henderson; Ian and Mayumi Hepburn; Les and Faye Hinzman; R Holland; Jerry Holmes; Peter Hopkins; David Hopkinson; David Hoult; Linda Howe; Marian Hoyle; Margaret Hughes; P Hughes; Stephen Hughes; Neil Humphreys; A R Hundleby; David James and Dawn Gameson; Manya Johnson; Peter Johnson; David & Catriona Jones; Jody Joseph; Cindy Kasfikis; Paul Kegan; Lyndsey Kelly; JC Kershaw; John F. King; Sheelagh Knapp; Reto Kromer; Johan Labbert; Carl Lauren; Mike Lawton; Jan Leech; Chris Leighton & Barbara Stevenson; Tom Lewis; The Libermanns; Eric Lien; Tim Lloyd; Jeff Lyons; Richard Lysons; Frank Maas; Doug MacDougall; Barbara MacGregor; Lynden Mack; Karin Mackinnon Hugh & Inge Madewell; Brent Marshall; Pam Martin; Matt and Carrie; Ben McCallum; Stephanie McCarthy; Karen McCaughtrie; Myfanwy McLaren; Kalba Meadows; Christopher Mills; Helen Misur; Jim Murchison; Steve Murray; Melanie Neal; Irene Nichols; Steven & Judith Niechcial; Nick Palmer; Tom Paton; Alex Pattison-Appleton; Mike Pavasovic; Trevor Pollard; Hugh Raven; Jennifer Roche; Dyana & Mel Rodriquez; Margaret Rollason; Grace Rose-Miller; Sheila Rowell; Mary Ellen Ryan; Ed Schlenk; Jackie Scott; Michael Scott; Millicent Scott; Karen See; Claudia Senecal; Alberto Saz Serraro; Helen Shaw; Odette Smith; Elliot Sparks; Annette Spencer; Chris Stocks; Nic Stubbs; Rachel and Kerry Sutton-Spence; Mark Tami; Geoff Taylor; Sue Taylor; R. Thomas; Dominic Thompson; Andrea Todd; Stuart Todd; Marten van Eldert; Annelies van 't Hof; Liz Wadsworth; Jim Ward; Eva Weber; David White; Brenda Williams; Adrian Wood; Helen Woods; Janet Young; Liesi Ziegelwanger; and Olivia Zurkinden.

Photo credits

All photography © Rough Guides except the following:

Cover
Main front picture: Wasdale and Illgill Head, Cumbria © National Trust
Back picture: Grassmarket, Edinburgh © Alamy
Inside picture: The London Eye, photography by Mark Thomas © Rough Guides

Introduction
Deckchairs on Brighton Pier, England © Anthony Webb/Axiom
Eilean Donan Castle in winter, Scotland © Pearl Bucknall/Getty Images
St Michael's Mount, Cornwall, England © Peter Adams/Getty Images
Lobster pots and house, Stromness, Scotland © Ian Cumming/Axiom
Otters, Derbyshire, England © Getty Images

Things not to miss
01 New Year celebrations, Newcastle, England © Graeme Peacock/Alamy
03 Radcliffe Camera, Oxford, England © Paul Quayle/Axiom
05 Minke whale off the coast of Scotland © Visual & Written SL/Alamy
07 Kinloch Castle, Isle of Rum, Scotland © Michael Jenner/Alamy
10 Coasteering in Wales © Buzz Pictures/Alamy
13 Iona Abbey cloisters, Scotland © David Robertson/Alamy
15 Drinkers outside the Coach and Horses pub, London, England © Ian Cumming/Axiom
18 Portmerion, Wales © Peter Raven/Mark Custance/Alamy
20 Man playing at the Whitby Music Festival © Allan Ivy/Alamy
21 Victoria Quarter, Leeds © Doug Houghton/Alamy
23 The Cairngorms, Scotland © David Gowans/Alamy
24 Walker and dog, Dorset, England © Sue Carpenter/Axiom
25 The National Museum of Wales © eye35.com/Alamy
27 Boat on Ullswater, Lake District, England © Chris Coe/Axiom
31 Glenfinnan Monument, Scotland © BL Images/Alamy
32 Tobermory, Isle of Mull, Scoland © Charles Bowman/Axiom

Black-and-whites
p.155 Band at the Astoria, London © Mark Thomas
p.432 Book stall at Hay-on-Wye © Chloe Roberts
p.550 The Great Laxey Wheel, Isle of Man © Chris Coe/British Tourist Authority
p.876 Sweetheart Abbey © David Crundby/Alamy
p.1126 Lerwick Harbour © David Robertson/Alamy
p.1150 Monument to the Great Fire of London © PCL/Alamy
p.1164 Engraving of Charles Dickens © Chris Hellier/Corbis
p.1174 Michael Caine in Get Carter © Movie Store

Festivals and events
Arts troupe from China at the Llangollen Festival, Wales © Photolibrary Wales/Alamy
Glastonbury Festival, England © Toby Adamson/Axiom
Singers performing at the Llangollen Festival, Wales © Photolibrary Wales
Competitor at the World Bog Snorkelling Championships, Llanwrtyd, Wales © Jeff Morgan/Alamy

Coastal Britain
View over Seilebost Beach, Harris, Scotland © Ellen Rooney/Axiom
Lindisfarne Castle on Holy Island, Northumberland, England © Gary Cook/Alamy

Literary Britain
Shakespeare's first folio © Graeme Robertson/Getty Images
Tourist sign at Shakespeare's birthplace in Stratford-on-Avon © Altrendo Travel/Getty Images
Daffodils at Wordsworth Point, Ullswater © David Noble Photography/Alamy
Portrait of Charlotte Brontë © David Lyons/Alamy
Child reading the Beano © Photofusion Picture Library/Alamy
Thomas Hardy's birthplace, Dorset, England © Neil McAllister/Alamy
Spires of Oxford, England © Dorling Kindersley

Index

Map entries are in colour.

INDEX

E

F

INDEX

I

M

Map symbols

maps are listed in the full index using coloured text

▪▪▪▪▪	National border	⚔	Battle site
▪▪▪▪	County border	▪	Tower
▪▪▪	Chapter division boundary	♀	Museum
M4	Motorway	⊤	Public gardens
●●●●●	Toll Motorway	⩙	Mountain range
═══	Main road	▲	Mountain peak
═══	Minor road	☀	Hill
▬▬▬	Pedestrianized street	⚲	Waterfall
⫿⫿⫿	Steps	⩘	Marshland
▪▪▪▪▪	Path	⚑	Lighthouse
▬▪▬	Railway	⚡	Ski area
— —	Ferry route	⚐	Golf course
———	Waterway	⊠–⊠	Gate
▪▪▪▪	Wall	⌣	Bridge
♦	General point of interest	♟	Whisky distillery
✈	Airport	⚊	Campsite
⊖	London Underground station	△	Youth hostel
Ⓤ	Glasgow Underground station	⬤	Hostel
Ⓜ	Metro station	⊞	Hospital
★	Bus stop	ⓘ	Tourist office
🅿	Parking	⊠	Post office
🏛	Stately home	@	Internet access
♜	Castle	⚓	Swimming pool
🏛	Abbey	▪	Building
⸸	Church/chapel (regional maps)	✚	Church (town maps)
✡	Synagogue	✝	Cemetery
⸫	Ruins	▪	Park
◠	Cave	▪	Forest
⚘	Standing stones	▪	Beach

Swashball.qdtech.co.uk

(INDGO)

REFLECTIONS WMV

Rainforest/we beleive

Give me Sunshine

Set Plosor Free

Richard Poster

To Jeff Thanks for

♂Julie Your me 16.45 29/06/2008

Richard Vere-Compton